The Oxford Companion to

Edited by **Alison Latham**

OXFORD
UNIVERSITY PRESS

OXFORD
UNIVERSITY PRESS

Great Clarendon Street, Oxford OX2 6DP

Oxford University Press is a department of the University of Oxford.
It furthers the University's objective of excellence in research, scholarship,
and education by publishing worldwide in

Oxford New York

Auckland Bangkok Buenos Aires Cape Town Chennai
Dar es Salaam Delhi Hong Kong Istanbul Karachi Kolkata
Kuala Lumpur Madrid Melbourne Mexico City Mumbai Nairobi
São Paulo Shanghai Taipei Tokyo Toronto

Oxford is a registered trade mark of Oxford University Press
in the UK and in certain other countries

Published in the United States
by Oxford University Press Inc., New York

© Oxford University Press 2002

Database right Oxford University Press (maker)

First published 2002
Reprinted 2002

British Library Cataloguing in Publication Data
Data available

Library of Congress Cataloging in Publication Data
Data available
ISBN 0-19-866212-2

3 5 7 9 10 8 6 4 2

Typeset in Pondicherry, India, by Alliance Phototypesetters
Printed in Great Britain by
Biddles Ltd
www.Biddles.co.uk

Preface

This *Oxford Companion to Music* is a new edition of two quite different earlier *Companions*, and has been conceived to draw on the strengths of both. Percy A. Scholes published the first *Oxford Companion to Music* in 1938. It was quickly recognized as a unique reference book, ranging well beyond the confines of a conventional dictionary. Scholes intended it for a wide variety of readers; a leading figure in the music-appreciation movement, he was able to approach the subject from many different angles, writing in an informed and accessible way. For several generations his *Companion* was the standard one-volume music reference book, for the amateur, the professional and, particularly, the student (and aspiring student); it came out in several new impressions and after Scholes's death in 1958 was revised and edited by John Owen Ward. The fact that it survived into the 21st century is testimony to its breadth, comprehensiveness and, indeed, its distinctive character.

By the early 1970s musical life was undergoing rapid change. The development of new recording techniques and the growth of specialist music broadcasting made available a vast, hitherto inaccessible repertory of Western music, ranging from medieval polyphony to the avant-garde. Equally important was a growing musical internationalism. A listener's experience of 'exotic' music was no longer confined to passages of *couleur locale* in Western compositions: concerts of non-Western music, especially from the Indian subcontinent and Indonesia, became a regular part of musical life. At the same time, musical knowledge was expanding. When Scholes's *Companion* was published, *Grove's Dictionary of Music and Musicians* (the standard encyclopedia in the English-speaking world) was in five volumes; in 1980 the new edition was in 20 volumes (the revised edition of 2001 is in 29).

It became clear that a new kind of *Oxford Companion to Music* was required. It was also clear that one person could not now be expected to command the breadth of knowledge and interest that allowed music historians of an earlier generation to cover the topic as comprehensively as had Scholes. Moreover, the discipline of musicology was both expanding and becoming more specialized. Denis Arnold, editor of *The New Oxford Companion to Music*, engaged a team of contributors; his two-volume edition, published in 1983, thus spoke with many voices—but it was none the less indebted to Scholes in several respects, not least in following his principles of comprehensiveness and orientation towards the general reader. Although Arnold retained some material from Scholes, and wrote a substantial number of entries himself (demonstrating his wide-ranging interests), he also reflected the increasing diversity of scholarship by including some long and distinguished essays by others. Notably, he greatly increased the coverage of non-Western music and provided a wealth of illustrative material.

Now, at the beginning of the 21st century, conventional musical distinctions—between 'art' music and 'popular' music, 'popular' music and 'world' music, even between 'sacred' and 'secular' music—are becoming blurred. The subject of 'music' itself is vast and rapidly expanding. It is written about and studied in a quite different way, too. What one might call the Darwinian view of music history—simple musical forms gradually evolving to reach a highpoint (generally considered to be manifested in either late 18th- or late 19th-century Germany)—has been repeatedly called into question as historians increasingly wish to address music from within its social-historical and cultural context. Ideas and techniques from other disciplines, from anthropology, literary criticism, iconography, linguistics, and so on, have come into play. The ways in which music has been disseminated and received offer further insights, as does research into performance practices of the past. Music education is now much more broadly based than it was in the mid-20th century, with music technology, world musics, composition, and performance studied alongside conventional Western music history and 'theory'.

Where does this leave the editor of a new *Oxford Companion to Music*? In determining its content and structure, there was one overriding factor: this book is a successor to Scholes and Arnold (to both of whom I am immeasurably indebted), and although it is comprehensively updated, it retains their basic principles: to be wide-ranging, to be complete in itself, and to be intended for a broad spectrum of readers, from the professional who wants ready access to facts, to the music student at school or university, to the keen amateur who needs a book, which, in Scholes's words, 'will not embarrass ... by a manner of expression so technical as to add new puzzles to the puzzle which sent [him or her] to the book'.

Because this edition is now in one volume, a format for which *Companion* devotees have long been petitioning, issues of space and scope were crucial from the outset. It was decided that the focus should be broadly the same as that of its predecessors, with the effect that this new edition should perhaps now more properly be entitled 'The Oxford Companion to Western Music'. Non-Western and popular musics are included, but mostly in so far as they have had an impact on the Western classical tradition. This should not be perceived as a retrograde step: world and popular musics are now huge subjects in their own right, with their particular specialists and literature, and should be recognized as such rather than given brief token coverage here. Similarly, because there is now much readily available writing on dance and pop music, those chunks of music history are surveyed only generally.

Although a few of the articles in this *Companion* have been reprinted from Arnold, and others are revised and updated, there is a wealth of original material to bring this edition firmly into the 21st century. Readers will now find many articles on music in relation to other subjects—politics, religion, sociology, psychology, semiotics, computers, technology, for example. The role of women in music is surveyed and there are new entries on women composers and performers. Historical musicology (and its specialist branches), analysis, theory, ethnomusicology, notation, terminology, and music education are discussed at some length. Other topics covered include acoustics, aesthetics, broadcasting and recording, and copyright.

'Life and works' entries on composers have always been at the heart of the *Companion*. The contexts of composers' creative lives, however, are vital to an understanding of their music, so this *Companion* offers major new surveys of historical periods as well as musical histories of countries and regions. Essays on such subjects as exoticism, nationalism, and artistic movements add a further dimension. Also new are articles on performers; space limitations have restricted these to artists who are no longer alive and who had significant influence on composition or performance. The number of entries on individual works has been increased. A new feature of this edition is an index of people to whom reference is made but who have no entry of their own. (It goes without saying that *The New Grove Dictionary of Music and Musicians* and its associated specialist dictionaries provide an abundance of articles beyond the scope of a one-volume reference book, as well as work-lists and bibliographies.)

This edition of the *Companion*, like Arnold's, has benefited from the expertise of a large group of specialist contributors from several countries, who have both written new entries and undertaken revisions. Any unsigned article is either by me or has been taken over from earlier editions and is therefore my responsibility. My aim has been to preserve the character of Scholes's edition, to combine it with the wider-ranging approach of Arnold's, and to reinvigorate and update this much-loved *Companion* for the 21st century. Most of all I hope this edition continues to contribute to people's understanding and enjoyment of music—that, in short, readers of many persuasions do indeed find it companionable.

Acknowledgements

In the early planning stages of the *Companion*, I benefited from the advice of several consultants who trawled through headword lists and made constructive suggestions about content and balance: Elsie Arnold, Tim Ashley, Clive Brown, John Caldwell, Iain Fenlon, Nigel Fortune, Peter Manning, Arnold Myers, Roger Parker, Nick Sandon, Marian Smith, John Wagstaff, John Warrack, Arnold Whittall, and Carl Woideck. I am also grateful to Paul Griffiths, who became consultant and principal contributor on all North American topics, and to Bruce Phillips, who was instrumental in the inception of this new edition and who has been a source of useful advice on commissioning.

Some of these people joined my large team of contributors, to whom I am extremely indebted, not only for what they have written but for their much-appreciated loyalty to the project generally. Many allowed themselves to be persuaded into writing a great deal more than they had originally intended, and many were generous with help and advice beyond their own particular areas. I owe a special debt of gratitude to Stanley Sadie and Nicholas Temperley; and Richard Langham Smith and Roger Parker were constant supports.

Other colleagues and friends offered useful advice on content and commissioning: Mike Ashman, John Baily,

Stephen Banfield, John Casken, John Deathridge, David Fanning, Peter Franklin, Sally Groves, Tess Knighton, Geoffrey Norris, Annette Richards, John Tyrrell, and Michael Wood.

Mick Card, Jeffrey Dean, Richard Partridge, and Jenny Wilson helped with the preparation and editing of a few self-contained subject areas, as did Lalage Cochrane, who compiled the index.

Several members of Oxford University Press have been involved with this *Companion*: Michael Cox, Pam Coote, Alison Jones, Joanna Harris, Wendy Tuckey, John Mackrell, and Wendy Maule. It presented them with some unprecedented challenges and I am most grateful for their continued faith in it.

It is hard to express adequately my gratitude to Polly Fallows. She has been an indefatigable editorial assistant, whose commitment, hard work, and good humour have been a constant source of strength. The book has benefited immeasurably from her ability to unravel lexicographical tangles and her meticulous copy-editing and proof-reading.

Finally, I thank my family, for whom the *Companion* became somewhat like a sixth, shadowy (but demanding) member. Thomas was an indispensable IT consultant; Nicholas and Peter keyed and scanned entries and undertook numerous essential administrative chores; my husband Richard gave me unstinting encouragement and wise advice. I am deeply indebted to them all.

ALISON LATHAM

Pinkneys Green, Berkshire
November 2001

Contributors

Authors

The names in bold type are those of contributors to the present edition; their biographies follow on pages vii–xi.

AA	**Andrew Ashbee**	DJ	David Johnson	JN	Judith Nagley
AB	Anthony Baines†	**DL**	**Dorothea Link**	**JR**	**Julian Rushton**
ABo	Ann Bond	DM	David Mason	JRe	John Reed†
ABu	**Ann Buckley**	**DMi**	**David Milsom**	JRo	Jerome Roche†
ABul	**Alison Bullock**	**DN**	**David Nice**	JS	**Jim Samson**
ABur	**Anthony Burton**	DW	Derek Watson	**JSm**	**Jan Smaczny**
AJ	**Alan Jefferson**	**DY**	**David Yearsley**	**JSn**	**John Snelson**
AL	**Alison Latham**	**ER**	**Elizabeth Roche**	JT	**Jon Tolansky**
ALa	**Andrew Lamb**	**EW**	**Emma Wakelin**	JW	**John Warrack**
ALi	**Alex Lingas**	**FD**	**Frank Dobbins**	**JWa**	**John Wagstaff**
AP	**Anthony Pryer**	**FL**	**Fiona Little**	**JWal**	**Jonathan Walker**
APa	Andrew Parrott	**GGS**	**Gian Giacomo Stiffoni**	**KC**	**Kenneth Chalmers**
APo	**Anthony Pople**	**GH**	**George Hall**	**KG**	**Kenneth Gloag**
AS	**Adrienne Simpson**	**GMcB**	**Gerard McBurney**	**KH**	**Kenneth Hamilton**
AT	**Andrew Thomson**	GMT	G. M. Tucker	KS	Keith Swanwick
ATh	**Adrian Thomas**	GN	Geoffrey Norris	**LB**	**Leslie Bunt**
AVJ	**Andrew V. Jones**	GP	George A. Proctor	**LC**	**Lalage Cochrane**
AW	**Arnold Whittall**	**HA**	**Helen Anderson**	**LD**	**Lucy Davies**
BB	**Bojan Bujić**	HAv	Hanoch Avenary	**LF**	**Lewis Foreman**
BC	**Barry Cooper**	HM	Helen Myers	**LH**	**Laughton Harris**
BJ	Burnett James	**HMacd**	**Hugh Macdonald**	LO	Leslie Orrey
BN	**Brian Newbould**	HR	**Henry Roche**	**MA**	**Martin Anderson**
BR	Bernarr Rainbow†	**HRe**	**Helmut Reichenbächer**	**MAM**	**Miguel Ángel Marín**
BS	**Basil Smallman**	**IF**	**Iain Fenlon**	**MAS**	**Mary Ann Smart**
BW	**Bryan White**	**IR**	**Ian Rumbold**	MB	Malcolm Boyd†
BWa	**Benjamin Walton**	**JAS**	**Julie Anne Sadie**	**ME**	**Mark Everist**
CB	**Clive Brown**	**JB**	Julian Budden	**MF-W**	**Marina Frolova-Walker**
CBa	**Christina Bashford**	**JBe**	**Jane Bellingham**	MG	Miron Grindea†
CC	**Caryl Clark**	**JBo**	**John Borwick**	MH	Michael Hurd
CF	**Christopher Fifield**	**JC**	**Jonathan Carr**	**MHe**	**Monika Hennemann**
CFr	Christopher Fry	**JCa**	**John Caldwell**	**MK**	**Michael Kennedy**
CH	**Crawford Howie**	JD	Jonathan Dunsby	**MP**	**Megan Prictor**
CM	Christopher Moore	**JDi**	**Jeremy Dibble**	**MPa**	**Max Paddison**
CP	**Carole Pegg**	**JG**	**James Grier**	MT	Mark Tucker†
CRW	**Christopher Wilson**	**JH**	**Janet Halfyard**	NC	Nym Cooke
CW	**Christopher Webber**	**JJD**	**Jeffrey Dean**	**ND**	**Nicola Dibben**
CWi	**Charles Wilson**	**JK**	**Judith Kuhn**	NG	Noël Goodwin
DA	Denis Arnold†	**JM**	**John Milsom**	**NPDC**	**Neal Peres Da Costa**
DF	**David Fallows**	**JMo**	**Jeremy Montagu**	**NT**	**Nicholas Temperley**
DH	**David Hiley**	JMT	J. M. Thomson†	**OR**	**Owen Rees**

PA	Peter Allsop	RBu	Roger Bullivant	SF	Sophie Fuller
PD	Peter Davies	RC	Richard Crawford	SFa	Sarah Faulder
PF	Pauline Fairclough	RCh	Rupert Christiansen	SH	Sarah Hibberd
PFa	Polly Fallows	RCM	Roderick Conway Morris	SJ	Stephen Johnson
PG	Paul Griffiths	RL	Robin Langley	SM	Stephen Muir
PGa	Peter Gammond	RLa	Robert Layton	SMcV	Simon McVeigh
PH	Peter Holman	RLS	Richard Langham Smith	SS	Stanley Sadie
PL	Peter Lynan	RN	Roger Nichols	TA	Tim Ashley
P-LR	Pablo-L. Rodríguez	RO	Robert Orledge	TC	Tim Carter
PM	Peter Manning	RP	Roger Parker	TM	Thomas Mathiesen
PS	Percy Scholes†	RPa	Richard Partridge	TRJ	Timothy Rhys Jones
PSp	Piers Spencer	RS	Robert Samuels	TS	Tom Sutcliffe
PW	Peter Wilton	RSt	Robert Stevenson	WGJ	W. Glyn Jenkins
RA	Richard Andrewes	RW	Richard Wigmore	WT	Wendy Thompson
RB	Roger Bowers	SA	Styra Avins		

Contributors to the present edition

PETER ALLSOP is Reader in Musicology at the University of Exeter; he is author of *The Italian 'Trio' Sonata* (1992) and *Arcangelo Corelli: New Orpheus of our Times* (1999) and has published numerous editions of that repertory.

HELEN ANDERSON is an arts consultant and administrator.

MARTIN ANDERSON is a writer and publisher; he specializes in the music of the Nordic and Baltic countries.

RICHARD ANDREWES is Head of Music in the University of Cambridge Library; he has been involved with the International Association of Music Libraries, RISM, RILM, and RIPM.

ANDREW ASHBEE is a lecturer, writer, and editor; he specializes in English 16th- and 17th-century music.

TIM ASHLEY is a music critic for *The Guardian* and a translator; he specializes in German music, art, and literature and is author of *Richard Strauss* (1999).

STYRA AVINS is Adjunct Professor of Music History at Drew University, NJ, and a cellist; she is author of *Johannes Brahms: Life and Letters* (1997).

CHRISTINA BASHFORD is Senior Lecturer in Music at Oxford Brookes University; she is editor (with Leanne Langley) of *Music and British Culture, 1785–1914: Essays in Honour of Cyril Ehrlich* (2000).

JANE BELLINGHAM was an editor for the revised edition of *The New Grove Dictionary of Music and Musicians* (2001).

JOHN BORWICK is a writer and broadcaster; he worked for the BBC, was a founder and senior lecturer on the B.Mus. (Tonmeister) course at Surrey University, and has written and edited several books on audio engineering.

ROGER BOWERS is Reader in Medieval and Renaissance Music at the University of Cambridge; he is author of *English Church Polyphony: Singers and Sources from the 14th to the 17th Century* (1999).

CLIVE BROWN is Professor of Applied Musicology at the University of Leeds; he is author of *Louis Spohr: A Critical Biography* (1984) and *Classical and Romantic Performing Practice* (1999).

ANN BUCKLEY is a research associate of the Centre for Medieval and Renaissance Studies, Trinity College, Dublin, and coordinator of RIdIM UK.

BOJAN BUJIĆ is Reader in Musicology at Magdalen College, Oxford; he specializes in 16th- and early 17th-century music in Italy and the Adriatic area of Croatia and on the aesthetics of music in the 19th and early 20th centuries.

ALISON BULLOCK was an editor for the revised edition of *The New Grove Dictionary of Music and Musicians* (2001).

LESLIE BUNT is Professor in Music Therapy at the University of the West of England; he is also director of postgraduate music-therapy training at the University of Bristol and of the Music Space Trust.

ANTHONY BURTON is a broadcaster and writer; for 15 years he was a producer and manager for BBC Radio 3.

JOHN CALDWELL is Professor of Music at the University of Oxford; he is author of *English Keyboard Music Before the 19th Century* (1973), *Editing Early Music* (1985), and two volumes of *The Oxford History of English Music* (1991, 1999), and has made several editions of early English music.

JONATHAN CARR is a foreign correspondent for *The Financial Times* and *The Economist*; his books include biographies of the former German chancellor Helmut Schmidt and of

Mahler and he is working on a history of the Wagner family.

TIM CARTER is Distinguished Professor (David G. Frey Professor in Music) at the University of North Carolina at Chapel Hill; his books include *Music in Late Renaissance and Early Baroque Italy* (1992), *Music, Patronage and Printing in Late Renaissance Florence* (2000), and a forthcoming volume on Monteverdi's dramatic music.

KENNETH CHALMERS is a translator and writer; he is author of *Béla Bartók* (1995).

RUPERT CHRISTIANSEN is opera critic of *The Daily Telegraph*; he is author of several studies of 19th-century cultural history.

CARYL CLARK teaches music at the University of Toronto; she has written on the operas of Haydn and Mozart.

LALAGE COCHRANE was an editor for the revised edition of *The New Grove Dictionary of Music and Musicians* (2001).

BARRY COOPER is Reader in Music at the University of Manchester; he is author of *Beethoven and the Creative Process* (1990), *Beethoven's Folksong Settings* (1994), and *Beethoven* (2000), and editor and co-author of *The Beethoven Compendium* (1991).

LUCY DAVIES worked on the revised edition of *The New Grove Dictionary of Music and Musicians* (2001).

JEFFREY DEAN is an editor, book designer, and typesetter; he was a senior editor for the revised edition of *The New Grove Dictionary of Music and Musicians* (2001) and has written on late 15th- and early 16th-century continental sacred music.

NICOLA DIBBEN is a lecturer in music at the University of Sheffield; she specializes in music perception, gender and identity in popular music, and music theory and analysis.

JEREMY DIBBLE is Reader in Music at the University of Durham; a specialist in 19th- and early 20th-century British music, he has written on Parry, Stanford, and Elgar.

FRANK DOBBINS is Reader in Musicology at Goldsmiths College, University of London; he is author of *Music in Renaissance Lyons* (1992) and editor of *The Oxford Book of French Chansons* (1987) and has edited numerous chansons and madrigals.

JONATHAN DUNSBY is Professor of Music at the University of Reading; his books include *Schoenberg: Pierrot lunaire* (1992) and *Performing Music: Shared Concerns* (1996).

MARK EVERIST is Professor of Music at the University of Southampton; he is author of *French Motets in the Thirteenth Century: Music, Poetry and Genre* (1994) and *Music Drama at the Paris Odéon, 1824–1828* (2002) and has edited three volumes of the *Magnus liber organi*.

PAULINE FAIRCLOUGH is a postgraduate student at the University of Manchester; she is writing a doctoral thesis on Shostakovich.

DAVID FALLOWS is Professor of Musicology at the University of Manchester; his books include *Dufay* (1982), *Songs and Musicians in the Fifteenth Century* (1996), and *A Catalogue of Polyphonic Songs, 1415–1480* (1999).

POLLY FALLOWS is a copy-editor and proof-reader; she was a senior editor for the revised edition of *The New Grove Dictionary of Music and Musicians* (2001) and editorial assistant for this *Companion*.

SARAH FAULDER is Chief Executive of the Music Publishers' Association and a solicitor.

IAIN FENLON is Reader in Music at the University of Cambridge and Fellow and Director of Studies at King's College; his books include *Music and Patronage in Sixteenth-Century Mantua* (1980–2) and a forthcoming volume on music and culture in the Italian Renaissance, and he is editor of *The Renaissance* (Man and Music/Music in Society, 1989).

CHRISTOPHER FIFIELD is a conductor, broadcaster, and writer; among his

books are biographies of Bruch (1988) and Hans Richter (1993).

LEWIS FOREMAN is a writer; his books include a biography of Bax (1983) and *From Parry to Britten: British Music in Letters 1900–1945* (1987).

MARINA FROLOVA-WALKER is a lecturer in music at the University of Cambridge and a Fellow of Clare College; she specializes in Russian music.

SOPHIE FULLER is a lecturer in music at the University of Reading; she is author of *The Pandora Guide to Women Composers: Britain and the United States, 1629–Present* (1994).

PETER GAMMOND is a writer and editor; his many publications include *The Oxford Companion to Popular Music* (1991) and books on jazz, ragtime, music hall, Offenbach, Ellington, and music on record.

KENNETH GLOAG is a lecturer in music at Cardiff University; he specializes in 20th-century British music and critical and cultural theory, including popular music, and is author of a book on Tippett's *A Child of our Time* (1999).

JAMES GRIER is Professor of Music History at the University of Western Ontario; he is author of *The Critical Editing of Music* (1996) and studies of music and liturgy in medieval Aquitaine.

PAUL GRIFFITHS is a writer and critic based in New York; his books include *A Concise History of Modern Music* (1978), studies of Boulez, Cage, Messiaen, Ligeti, Davies, Bartók, Stravinsky, and the string quartet, the novels *Myself and Marco Polo* (1989) and *The Lay of Sir Tristram* (1991), and the librettos of *The Jewel Box* (Mozart, 1991), *Marco Polo* (Tan Dun, 1996), and *What Next?* (Elliott Carter, 1999).

JANET HALFYARD is a lecturer at the Birmingham Conservatoire; she specializes in music and theatre, extended vocal technique, and film music.

GEORGE HALL is a writer and editor; he has published (with Christopher

Palmer) a new English edition of Milhaud's autobiography (1992).

KENNETH HAMILTON is a concert pianist and Senior Lecturer in Music at the University of Birmingham; he specializes in 19th-century music, particularly (as both performer and writer) the Romantic virtuoso repertory.

MONIKA HENNEMANN teaches music at Cincinnati University; she specializes in the music of Mendelssohn.

SARAH HIBBERD is a research fellow at Royal Holloway, University of London; she specializes in opera in 19th-century France.

DAVID HILEY is Professor of Musicology at the University of Regensburg; he is author of *Western Plainchant: A Handbook* (1993), is co-editor (with Richard L. Crocker) of *The Early Middle Ages to 1300* (The New Oxford History of Music, ii, 2/1990), and has made many editions of plainchant and medieval music.

PETER HOLMAN is Reader in Historical Musicology at the University of Leeds; he is author of *Four and Twenty Fiddlers: The Violin at the English Court, 1540–1690* (1993), and of studies of Purcell and Dowland, and is director of the Parley of Instruments and musical director of Opera Restor'd.

CRAWFORD HOWIE is a lecturer in music at the University of Manchester; he specializes in Schubert and Bruckner, of whom he is writing a documentary biography.

ALAN JEFFERSON is a writer; his books include several on Richard Strauss and centenary studies of Beecham (1979) and Lotte Lehmann (1988).

STEPHEN JOHNSON is a critic and broadcaster; he specializes in Scandinavian music and is author of *Bruckner Remembered* (1998).

ANDREW V. JONES is Senior Lecturer in Music at the University of Cambridge and Director of Studies at Selwyn College; he specializes in Carissimi and Handel (whose *Rodelinda* he has edited) and in 1985

he founded the Cambridge Handel Opera Group.

MICHAEL KENNEDY is music critic of *The Sunday Telegraph*; his books include studies of Vaughan Williams, Elgar, Mahler, Britten, Walton, and two of Strauss, biographies of Barbirolli (1971) and Boult (1987), and *The Oxford Dictionary of Music* (1985, 2/1994).

JUDITH KUHN is a postgraduate student at the University of Manchester; she is writing a doctoral thesis on Shostakovich.

ANDREW LAMB is a writer and broadcaster; he specializes in light music and musical theatre and his writings include books on Kern, Offenbach, and Waldteufel.

RICHARD LANGHAM SMITH is Reader in Music at the University of Exeter; co-author (with Roger Nichols) of a book on *Pelléas et Mélisande* (1989), he reconstructed Debussy's *Rodrigue et Chimène* and is preparing a new edition of *Carmen*.

ROBERT LAYTON is a writer and editor; formerly a BBC radio producer and editor of the BBC Music Guides, he is author of studies of Berwald, Grieg, Dvořák, and Sibelius, and is co-author of *The Penguin Guide to Compact Discs*.

ALEXANDER LINGAS is Assistant Professor of Music History at Arizona State University and Visiting Fellow at the European Humanities Research Centre, University of Oxford; he is director of the vocal ensemble Cappella Romana.

DOROTHEA LINK teaches music at the University of Georgia; she was a senior editor for the revised edition of *The New Grove Dictionary of Music and Musicians* (2001) and is author of *The National Court Theatre in Mozart's Vienna* (1998).

FIONA LITTLE was an editor for *The New Grove Dictionary of Opera* and the revised edition of *The New Grove Dictionary of Music and Musicians* (2001).

PETER LYNAN is a writer and editor; a specialist in 18th-century British

music, he has made an edition of Maurice Greene's *Jephtha*.

GERARD McBURNEY is a composer, writer, broadcaster, and a teacher at the RAM; he specializes in Russian music.

HUGH MACDONALD is Avis Blewett Professor of Music at Washington University, St Louis; he is author of *Skryabin* (1978), *Berlioz* (1982), and *Selected Letters of Berlioz* (1995), and is general editor of the New Berlioz Edition and of Berlioz's *Correspondance générale*, vols.v–viii.

PETER MANNING is Professor of Music at the University of Durham, where he founded and now directs the university's electronic music studio; his writings include *Electronic and Computer Music* (1993).

MIGUEL ÁNGEL MARÍN is a lecturer and Vice-Principal of New Technologies at the University of La Rioja; he is author of *Music on the Margin: Urban Musical Life in Eighteenth-Century Jaca (Spain)* (2002) and co-author of *Pliegos de Villancicos en la British Library (Londres) y la University Library (Cambridge)* (2000).

THOMAS J. MATHIESEN is Distinguished Professor (David H. Jacobs Chair in Music) at Indiana University (Bloomington), where he is also Director of the Center for the History of Music Theory and Literature; he is author of *Aristides Quintilianus on Music in Three Books* (1983), *Apollo's Lyre: Greek Music and Music Theory in Antiquity and the Middle Ages* (1999), and *Greek Views of Music* (1998).

DAVID MILSOM is a writer, lecturer, and performer; he specializes in 19th-century performance practice, particularly violin playing.

JOHN MILSOM is a musicologist and writer; a specialist in Renaissance music, he has published widely on Josquin des Prez, Tudor England, music printing, and compositional process, has taught in Oxford and the USA, and has edited *Early Music*.

JEREMY MONTAGU is an instrument collector; formerly curator of the Bate Collection of Musical Instruments at the University of Oxford, he is author of many books on instruments.

STEPHEN MUIR is a lecturer in music at the University of Leeds; he specializes in 19th- and early 20th-century Russian music, and 19th-century vocal performance practice.

BRIAN NEWBOULD is Professor of Music at the University of Hull; he has written studies of Schubert, of whose unfinished works he has made performing versions.

DAVID NICE is a writer, broadcaster, and lecturer; he specializes in Russian music and his books include a forthcoming biography of Prokofiev.

ROGER NICHOLS is a writer, broadcaster, and pianist; his books include studies of Debussy, Ravel, and Messiaen, a forthcoming history of music in Paris, 1917–29, and *Mendelssohn Remembered* (1997).

ROBERT ORLEDGE is Professor of Music at the University of Liverpool; he is author of books on Fauré (1979), Debussy (1982), Koechlin (1989), and Satie (1990 and 1995).

MAX PADDISON is Professor of Music at the University of Durham; he has written widely on aesthetics, the philosophy and sociology of music, and critical theory, and his books include *Adorno's Aesthetics of Music* (1993) and *Adorno, Modernism and Mass Culture* (1996).

ROGER PARKER is Professor of Music at the University of Cambridge; he was founding co-editor of the *Cambridge Opera Journal*, is general editor (with Gabriele Dotto) of the Donizetti Critical Edition, and is author of *Leonora's Last Act* (1997), among other books.

RICHARD PARTRIDGE is an editor and a viol and fiddle player; he was an editor for the revised edition of *The New Grove Dictionary of Music and Musicians* (2001) and is editor of *The Consort*.

CAROLE PEGG is an ethnomusicologist and social anthropologist; she was founding co-editor of the *British Journal of Ethnomusicology*, was a senior editor for the revised edition of *The New Grove Dictionary of Music and Musicians* (2001), and is author of *Mongolian Music, Dance, and Oral Narrative: Performing Diverse Identities* (2001).

NEAL PERES DA COSTA is a historical keyboard specialist and co-founder of the ensemble Florilegium.

ANTHONY POPLE is Professor of Music at the University of Nottingham; he was editor of the journal *Music Analysis* from 1995 to 2000 and has published widely on 20th-century music.

ANTHONY PRYER is a lecturer in music at Goldsmiths College, University of London; he specializes in medieval music, aesthetics, and the music of Monteverdi.

MEGAN PRICTOR has written on music appreciation and the media in England in the early 20th century.

OWEN REES is Fellow in Music at Queen's College, Oxford, and lecturer in music at Somerville College; he has written on Portuguese, Spanish, and English music of the 16th and 17th centuries and directs the ensembles A Capella Portuguesa and the Cambridge Taverner Choir.

HELMUT REICHENBÄCHER is an associate producer in Radio Music for the CBC.

TIMOTHY RHYS JONES is a lecturer in music at the University of Exeter; he specializes in Viennese Classical music and is author of a book on Beethoven's 'Moonlight' and other sonatas (1999).

ELIZABETH ROCHE is a writer and critic; she specializes in musical life in Britain in the late 19th and 20th centuries and is co-author (with Jerome Roche) of *A Dictionary of Early Music from the Troubadours to Monteverdi* (1981).

HENRY ROCHE is head of the music staff of the Royal Ballet, Covent Garden, and a concert pianist;

he is the great-great-grandson of Moscheles.

PABLO-L. RODRÍGUEZ is Associate Professsor of Music at the University of La Rioja; he has written on the music, musicians, and ceremonies at the 17th-century Spanish Habsburg court.

IAN RUMBOLD is an editor and research associate to the New Berlioz Edition; he specializes in early 15th-century continental polyphony and 19th-century French music.

JULIAN RUSHTON is West Riding Professor of Music at Leeds University; he is author of two opera handbooks on Mozart, *Classical Music: A Concise History* (1988), three studies of Berlioz, and a book on Elgar's 'Enigma' Variations, and he has published editions of music by Elgar and Potter.

JULIE ANNE SADIE is a writer and editor; she is author of the *Companion to Baroque Music* (1991) and studies of French music, and co-editor (with Rhian Samuel) of *The New Grove Dictionary of Women Composers* (1994).

STANLEY SADIE is a writer and editor; he was formerly a music critic for *The Times*, was editor of *The Musical Times*, *The New Grove Dictionary of Music and Musicians* (1980, revised 2001), and *The New Grove Dictionary of Opera* (1992), and is author of studies of Handel, Mozart, and opera.

JIM SAMSON is Professor of Music at Royal Holloway, University of London; his many books have centred on the music of Chopin but have also ranged widely over 19th- and 20th-century music, analysis, and aesthetics.

ROBERT SAMUELS is a lecturer in music at the Open University; he specializes in the analysis of 19th- and 20th-century music and has written on Schubert, Schumann, and Mahler.

ADRIENNE SIMPSON is the author of several books on New Zealand music and music theatre.

Jan Smaczny is Professor of Music at Queen's University, Belfast; he specializes in Czech music, particularly Dvořák, and his books include studies of the Prague Provisional Theatre repertory and of Dvořák's Cello Concerto (1999).

Basil Smallman is Emeritus Professor of Music at the University of Liverpool; he is a conductor and composer and author of books on Passion music, Schütz, and chamber music.

Mary Ann Smart is Associate Professor of Music at the University of California, Berkeley; she has written widely on Bellini and Donizetti, has edited Donizetti's *Dom Sébastien*, and is author of *Resonant Bodies* (2002).

John Snelson is a writer and editor; he specializes in musical theatre and was a senior editor for the revised edition of *The New Grove Dictionary of Music and Musicians* (2001).

Piers Spencer is a music educationist and consultant in pedagogy; he is co-editor of the *British Journal of Music Education*.

Gian Giacomo Stiffoni is Professor of Musicology at the University of La Rioja; he specializes in 18th-century opera and is author of *Non son cattivo comico: Caratteri di riforma nei drammi giocosi di Da Ponte per Vienna* (1998).

Tom Sutcliffe is opera critic of the London *Evening Standard*; he is author of *Believing in Opera* (1996), editor of *The Faber Book of Opera* (2000), and a member of the Church of England General Synod.

Nicholas Temperley is a musicologist and writer; he is editor of *Music in Britain: The Romantic Age, 1800–1914* (1981) and of *The Lost Chord: Essays on Victorian Music* (1989), author of *The Music of the English Parish Church* (1979), and he

edited the *Symphonie fantastique* for the New Berlioz Edition.

Andrew Thomson is a writer; he is author of *The Life and Times of Charles-Marie Widor* (1987) and *Vincent d'Indy and his World* (1997).

Adrian Thomas is Professor of Music at Cardiff University, where he runs the Central European Music Research Centre; he specializes in 20th-century Polish music and has written and broadcast on Górecki, Lutosławski, and Panufnik.

Jon Tolansky is a writer, broadcaster, and musical archivist; a former member of several leading orchestras, he was also co-founder of the Music Performance Research Centre.

John Wagstaff is librarian of the music faculty at the University of Oxford; he has written on aspects of music publishing in 19th-century England.

Emma Wakelin was an editor for the revised edition of *The New Grove Dictionary of Music and Musicians* (2001).

Jonathan Walker is a musicologist; he specializes in ancient Greek music theory, 14th-century polyphony, early Soviet music, jazz, and hip-hop.

Benjamin Walton is a research fellow at St Anne's College, Oxford; he has written on Rossini.

John Warrack is a writer; formerly music critic of *The Sunday Telegraph* and lecturer in music at the University of Oxford, he is co-author (with Ewan West) of *The Oxford Dictionary of Opera* and his other books include studies of Weber and Tchaikovsky and a history, *German Opera* (2001).

Christopher Webber is an actor, writer, and stage director; he has a special interest in Spanish music, has translated a number of zarzuelas for production, and his plays (sev-

eral on musical subjects) include *Dr Sullivan and Mr Gilbert*.

Bryan White is a lecturer in music at the University of Leeds; he specializes in 17th- and 18th-century English music, of which he has made editions, and he is a singer and conductor.

Arnold Whittall is Professor Emeritus of Music Theory and Analysis at King's College London; his books include *Music Analysis in Theory and Practice* (with Jonathan Dunsby, 1988), *Romantic Music* (1987), studies of Britten and Tippett, and *Music Since the First World War* (1977), enlarged as *Musical Composition in the Twentieth Century* (2000).

Richard Wigmore is a writer and broadcaster; he was a senior editor for the revised edition of *The New Grove Dictionary of Music and Musicians* (2001), and is author of *Schubert: The Complete Song Texts* (1988).

Charles Wilson is a lecturer in music at Cardiff University; he specializes in 20th-century music and was a senior editor for the revised edition of *The New Grove Dictionary of Music and Musicians* (2001).

Christopher R. Wilson is Senior Lecturer in Music at the University of Reading; a specialist in music and literature, particularly of the English Renaissance and Victorian and early 20th-century Britain, he is working on musical imagery in Shakespeare.

Peter Wilton is Director of Music of the Gregorian Association and a singer; he has made many editions of chant.

David Yearsley teaches music at Cornell University; he has made several recordings of 17th- and 18th-century organ music and is author of *Bach and the Meanings of Counterpoint* (2002).

Abbreviations

AB	Alberta	Dec.	December	IRCAM	Institut de Recherche et de Coordination Acoustique/Musique
AD	Anno Domini (year of Our Lord)	Derbys.	Derbyshire		
		dim.	diminutive		
AK	Alaska	DJ	disc jockey	ISCM	International Society for Contemporary Music
AL	Alabama	D.Mus.	Doctor of Music		
Amer.	American	D.Phil.	Doctor of Philosophy	It.	Italian
AR	Arkansas	DVD	digital versatile disc	ITV	Independent Television
Aug.	August	EBU	European Broadcasting Union	Jan.	January
AZ	Arizona			Jap.	Japanese
b	born	ed(s).	editor(s)	K	Köchel (Mozart's works)
BA	Bachelor of Arts	edn	edition	KS	Kansas
bapt.	baptized	EMI	Electrical and Musical Industries	KY	Kentucky
BBC	British Broadcasting Corporation			LA	Louisiana
		ENO	English National Opera	Lancs.	Lancashire
BC	British Columbia	esp.	especially	Lat.	Latin
BC	before Christ	Ex.	(music) example	Leics.	Leicestershire
Berks.	Berkshire	facs.	facsimile	Lincs.	Lincolnshire
B.Mus.	Bachelor of Music	Feb.	February	LP	long-playing record
Bucks.	Buckinghamshire	Fig.	Figure	LPO	London Philharmonic Orchestra
bur.	buried	FL	Florida		
BWV	Bach-Werke-Verzeichnis	*fl*	*floruit* (flourished)	LSO	London Symphony Orchestra
c.	*circa* (approximately)	FM	frequency modulation		
CA	California	Fr.	French	MA	Massachusetts; Master of Arts
Cambs.	Cambridgeshire	GA	Georgia		
CBC	Canadian Broadcasting Corporation	Ger.	German	MB	Manitoba
		Gk.	Greek	MD	Maryland
CBS	Columbia Broadcasting Systems	Glam.	Glamorgan	ME	Maine
		Glos.	Gloucestershire	MGM	Metro-Goldwyn-Mayer
CD	compact disc	Hants.	Hampshire	MI	Michigan
ch.	chapter	Herts.	Hertfordshire	MIDI	musical instrument digital interface
Ches.	Cheshire	HI	Hawaii		
Chin.	Chinese	HMV	His Master's Voice	Middx.	Middlesex
CO	Colorado	Hob.	Hoboken	MN	Minnesota
Co.	Company; County	Hung.	Hungarian	MO	Missouri
CT	Connecticut	Hz	Hertz	MS	Mississippi
Cz.	Czech	IA	Iowa	MT	Montana
D	Deutsch	ID	Idaho	Mus.B.	Bachelor of Music
d	died	IL	Illinois	Mus.D.	Doctor of Music
Dan.	Danish	IN	Indiana	NB	New Brunswick
DAT	digital audio tape	incl.	including	NBC	National Broadcasting Company
DC	District of Columbia	IPEM	Instituut voor Psychoakustiek en Muziek		
DE	Delaware			NC	North Carolina

ND	North Dakota	PQ	Quebec province	Sp.	Spanish
NE	Nebraska	*R*	photographic (facsimile)	Ss.	Santissimo, Santissima
NF	Newfoundland and		reprint		(Most Holy)
	Labrador	RAF	Royal Air Force	St	Saint
NH	New Hampshire	RAM	Royal Academy of Music	Staffs.	Staffordshire
NJ	New Jersey	RCA	Radio Corporation of	Swed.	Swedish
NM	New Mexico		America	swv	Schütz-Werke-Verzeichnis
no(s).	number(s)	RCM	Royal College of Music	TN	Tennessee
Nor.	Norwegian	repr.	reprint(ed)	trans.	translation, translated by
Northumb.	Northumberland	rev.	revised	TX	Texas
Notts.	Nottinghamshire	RI	Rhode Island	UK	United Kingdom of Great
Nov.	November	RILM	Répertoire International		Britain and Northern
nr	near		de Littérature		Ireland
NS	Nova Scotia		Musicale	UCLA	University of California at
NT	North West Territories	RISM	Répertoire International		Los Angeles
NV	Nevada		des Sources Musicales	USA	United States of
NY	New York state	RMCM	Royal Manchester College		America
Oct.	October		of Music	USSR	Union of Soviet Socialist
OH	Ohio	RNCM	Royal Northern College		Republics
OK	Oklahoma		of Music	UT	Utah
ON	Ontario	Rom.	Romanian	VA	Virginia
op., opp.	opus, opera	rpm	revolutions per minute	VHF	very high frequency
OR	Oregon	RSAMD	Royal Scottish Academy	vol(s).	volume(s)
ORTF	Office de Radiodiffusion-		of Music and Drama	VT	Vermont
	Télévision Française	rv	Ryom-Verzeichnis	WA	Washington
Oxon	Oxfordshire		(Vivaldi's works)	Warwicks.	Warwickshire
p(p).	page(s)	S. (pl. SS)	San, Sant', Santa, Santo,	WI	Wisconsin
PA	Pennsylvania		São (Saint)	Wilts.	Wiltshire
PE	Prince Edward Island	SC	South Carolina	WNO	Welsh National Opera
Ph.D.	Doctor of	SD	South Dakota	Worcs.	Worcestershire
	Philosophy	Sept.	September	WV	West Virginia
pl.	plural	sing.	singular	WY	Wyoming
Pol.	Polish	SK	Saskatchewan	Yorks.	Yorkshire
Port.	Portuguese	Som.	Somerset	YT	Yukon Territories

Note to the Reader

Cross-references are indicated by an *asterisk or by a direction to see ANOTHER ARTICLE. To avoid cluttering the text, however, 'obvious' cross-references, for example from works to their composers, are used only in exceptional cases.

Contributors' initials are given at the end of entries; where an entry has been revised from an earlier edition, the original author's initials (or a dash if the entry was anonymous) are separated from the present contributor's by an oblique stroke. A key to these initials is on pp. vi–vii, and information about contributors to this edition is on pp. vii–xi.

Further reading suggestions are supplied for many articles. These are not comprehensive but are intended as guides; items are arranged chronologically, those separated by semicolons being by the same author.

An index of people who are referred to in the *Companion* but who do not have their own entries begins on p. 1399.

a

A. 1. The sixth degree (submediant) of the scale of C major (see SCALE, 3). It is commonly used as a standard in the tuning of instruments, and orchestras tune to 'concert A'. See PITCH, 1.

2. Abbreviation for *alto or *altus.

3. Abbreviation for *antiphon.

a (It.), **à** (Fr.). 'With', 'for', 'to', 'at'. Terms beginning with this preposition or its compounds are normally given under the word or first noun immediately following, e.g. *a *battuta, a bene *placito, a *cappella, à la *pointe d'archet*. In early music, the Italian form refers to the number of voices in a polyphonic work ('*a 2*' means in two voices); in music after *c.*1700 it indicates that two instruments should play the same line.

Aaron [Aron], Pietro (*b* Florence, *c.*1480; *d* after 1545). Italian theorist. He claimed to have been associated with Josquin, Obrecht, Isaac, and Agricola while in Florence. From about 1516 he was a priest at Imola, where he remained until 1522. He then served as *maestro da casa* in the household of Sebastiano Michiel in Venice before entering the monastery of S. Leonardo at Bergamo in 1536. Although his writings on music were largely influenced by earlier theorists such as Tinctoris, he made a valuable contribution to modal theory and was the first to apply the system of eight modes to polyphonic music in his *Trattato* (Venice, 1525). His explanations of counterpoint are considered to be the best of those in the generation before Zarlino.   LC

ab (Ger., 'off'). A term indicating the removal of a mute or an organ stop.

ABA, ABACA. Symbolization for, respectively, *ternary and *rondo form, in which the different letters represent the various thematic or structural sections.

Abaco, Evaristo Felice dall'. See DALL'ABACO, EVARISTO FELICE.

abandonné (Fr.), **abbandonatamente, con abbandono** (It.). 'Free', 'relaxed'.

abbassare (It., 'to lower'). A specific type of *scordatura in which the string of an instrument of the violin family is tuned to a lower pitch than usual in order that a note outside its normal compass may be obtained.   DM1

Abbatini, Antonio Maria (*b* Città di Castello, 26 Jan. 1595; *d* Città di Castello, ?after 15 March 1679). Italian composer. He may have studied with the Nanino brothers in Rome and he held a number of positions in the city, including *maestro di cappella* of S. Maria Maggiore (1649–57) and S. Luigi dei Francesi (1657–67). However, he is best known for two comic operas to librettos by Giulio Rospigliosi (later Pope Clement IX): *Dal male il bene* (in collaboration with Marazzoli; performed at the Barberini Palace in Rome in 1654) and *La comica del cielo* (1668).   TC

abbellimenti (It.). 'Embellishments'; see ORNAMENTS AND ORNAMENTATION.

abdämpfen (Ger.). 'To damp down', 'to muffle'—i.e. to mute, especially in connection with timpani.

Abduction from the Seraglio, The. See ENTFÜHRUNG AUS DEM SERAIL, DIE.

Abegg Variations. Schumann's op. 1 (1829–30), for piano; it is dedicated to his friend Meta Abegg, whose name is represented by the notes A–B♭–E–G–G (German B = English B♭) at the beginning of the theme.

Abel, Carl Friedrich (*b* Cöthen, 22 Dec. 1723; *d* London, 20 June 1787). German composer and viol player. In his early years he was probably taught by his father, who also played the viol. C. F. Abel had joined the court orchestra at Dresden, then under Hasse, by 1743; he remained there until 1758, when he set out on the travels that were to take him to London the following year. There he gave a number of recitals and became known as a concert director. In 1765 he and J. C. Bach began a successful and renowned series of subscription concerts, known as the Bach–Abel concerts, which ran until 1781, latterly at the Hanover Square Rooms.

Abel was one of the principal early exponents of the Italianate *galant* style in London, and his symphonies and concertos had some influence on the early symphonic style of Mozart. He also composed pieces for viol and much other chamber music. His death was hastened by overindulgence in alcohol. DA/PL

Abendmusik [Abendlied] (Ger., 'evening music', 'evening song'). The series of concerts held at the Marienkirche in Lübeck, Germany, during the 17th and 18th centuries.

Abgesang (Ger.). The final, contrasting strophe of *Bar* form.

abgestossen (Ger., 'separated'). An 18th-century violin *staccato.

Abingdon, Henry. See ABYNGDON, HENRY.

abnehmend (Ger., 'decreasing', 'subsiding'). *Diminuendo*.

Abraham and Isaac. 1. Britten's Canticle II (1952) for alto, tenor, and piano, a setting of a text from the Chester miracle play.

2. Sacred ballad by Stravinsky (1962–3), for baritone and chamber orchestra; to a Hebrew text, it is dedicated to the people of Israel.

abridged sonata form. A musical form closely related to *sonata form. Its 'abridgment' lies in the fact that, in the development section, new thematic material is presented rather than a development of the themes of the exposition.

Abschiedsymphonie. See 'FAREWELL' SYMPHONY.

absetzen (Ger.). 1. 'Remove', 'take off'.

2. In 16th-century music *absetzen in die Tabulatur* means 'to transcribe into tablature'.

Absil, Jean (*b* Bon-Secours, Hainaut, 23 Oct. 1893; *d* Uccle, Brussels, 2 Feb. 1974). Belgian composer and teacher. After studying the organ at the Brussels Conservatory, he took composition lessons from Paul Gilson. His conservative training was supplemented by his absorption of more modern trends, especially the polytonality of Milhaud. He was an important advocate of contemporary music in Belgium, and an influential teacher at the Brussels Conservatory and his own school in Etterbeek. Absil wrote prolifically for orchestra, bands, chorus, piano, and many different ensembles; his works for saxophone, solo and quartet, are an important contribution to the instrument's repertory. ABUR

absolute music. Instrumental music that exists, and is to be appreciated, simply as such, in contradistinction to *programme music.

absolute pitch. See EAR AND HEARING, 3.

abstract music. 1. Another term for *absolute music.

2. A term used by some German writers (*abstrakte Musik*) to mean music lacking in sensitivity, 'dry' or 'academic' in style.

Abstrich (Ger.). In string playing, 'down-bow'.

abwechseln (Ger.). 'To exchange', i.e. to alternate instruments in the hands of the same player.

Abyngdon [Abingdon], **Henry** (*b* c.1420; *d* 1497). English singer, organist, and probably composer. He sang with the chapel choirs of Eton College and the Chapel Royal. No music by him survives, but the fact that he was awarded the Mus.B. by Cambridge University— the first person to receive that degree—suggests that his skills extended beyond performing. JM

Abzug. 1 (Ger., 'a drawing down'). A term used in the 16th and 17th centuries in connection with a lute tuning where the lowest string is lowered a whole tone (*im Abzug*) or, by extension, for an extra, open string, added below the stopped courses (*mit Abzügen*).

2 (Ger., 'departure', 'withdrawal'). An *appoggiatura that makes a decrescendo on to the principal note, or a trill with only one repercussion, i.e. the equivalent of the inverted *mordent.

Academic Festival Overture (*Akademische Festouvertüre*). Brahms's op. 80 (1880), dedicated to Breslau University in slightly ironic acknowledgment of an honorary doctorate conferred on the composer; it incorporates German student songs, notably *Gaudeamus igitur*.

academy. A term used to denote a number of more or less formal gatherings of individuals.

Plato's favourite place to teach was out of doors in a grove named Academe, and since antiquity 'the Academy' has been a metonymy for the Platonic school of philosophy. In 1470 the Florentine humanist Marsilio Ficino, who translated Plato's writings into Latin, proclaimed the re-foundation of Plato's Academy in Florence. It is doubtful whether Ficino's academy was an actual institution rather than simply an ideal, but the concept proved an attractive and fruitful one in late 15th- and 16th-century Italy. Groups of intellectually minded men (and occasionally women), which were springing up spontaneously and informally in many Italian cities, soon adopted a more formal organization (much like later gentlemen's clubs) and the title of 'Accademia'.

On the whole these academies were literary and philosophical in focus, though musical issues were often debated and musical accompaniment to poetry and drama was widespread; for instance, the famous Teatro Olimpico in Vicenza, designed by Palladio for the Accademia Olimpica, was inaugurated in 1585 by a performance of Sophocles' *Oedipus rex* in Italian with choruses by Andrea Gabrieli. The earliest academy devoted to music was the Accademia Filarmonica of Verona (1543), which survives and possesses an important collection of musical instruments. Academies were ubiquitous in Italy by 1570, when Jean-Antoine de Baïf helped found the Académie de Poésie et Musique in Paris under royal sponsorship. Although this academy was short-lived, its idea of *musique mesurée à l'antique* profoundly influenced the chansons of Claude Le Jeune and the later *air de cour*. Other, less formal groups of intellectuals like Giovanni de' Bardi's *camerata in Florence, which helped give birth to monody, are sometimes loosely described as academies.

The Accademia Filarmonica of Bologna (1666), founded on the model of Adriano Banchieri's Accademia dei Floridi (1614) and still in existence, became one of the great concert *societies of early modern times. Its members have included many well-known musicians, among them Corelli, Mozart, Puccini, and Ravel. The Académie Royale de Musique (1669) was formed for the purpose of naturalizing opera in France; it was led in 1672–87 by Lully, and after many reorganizations the Académie Nationale de Musique remains the institution behind the Paris Opéra. The Accademia degli Arcadi was founded in Rome in 1690. Music was only one of its preoccupations, but Corelli and Alessandro Scarlatti were among its members, and it is especially important for having given rise in the early 18th century to the new type of opera libretto associated with the names of Apostolo Zeno and Pietro Metastasio.

Since 1700 the name 'academy' has been given to a variety of different types of institution that have little in common with the distinctive earlier sort. Some are national organizations on the pattern of the French royal academies; others, like the Royal Academy of Music in London (1822) or the Accademia di S. Cecilia in Rome (1876), are schools of music, or conservatories. Following a usage that goes back to 16th-century Italy, 'academy' has also signified a concert society or (especially in 18th- and early 19th-century Germany and Austria) a concert itself.   JJD

📖 F. YATES, *The French Academies in the Sixteenth Century* (London, 1947) · D. CHAMBERS and F. QUIVIGER (eds.), *Italian Academies of the Sixteenth Century* (London, 1995)

Academy of Ancient Music. A society of aristocratic amateur musicians, founded in London in 1726 to foster 'ancient' church music (it may have originated as early as 1710). Pepusch was one of its directors, and Handel played at its meetings. It disbanded in 1792.

a cappella (It.). 'In the church style'; see CAPPELLA.

accelerando, accelerato (It.). 'Becoming faster'; it is usually abbreviated to *accel.*

accent. 1. Emphasis given to a particular musical event by a sudden increase (or, occasionally, decrease) in volume (dynamic accent), a lengthening of duration (expressive lengthening), a slight anticipatory silence (articulation), or a combination of these. The dynamic accent is the most common type and may be indicated by any one of a number of signs or markings, for example >, ‒, *fz*, *sf*, *sfz*, *fp*, or the short slur. Expressive lengthening, which Hugo Riemann termed *agogic' (*Musikalische Dynamik und Agogik*, Leipzig, 1884), may also be indicated by the sign '‒'. Instruments unable to produce dynamic accent through changes of volume (e.g. harpsichords and organs) can achieve the effect either by a lengthening or by the use of a preceding silence, or both.

Certain notes may be 'self-accenting' because of their relatively high or low position. 'Metrical accentuation' can be used to give extra emphasis to strong beats in a bar, or deliberately to throw the listener off balance by emphasizing weak beats (see BEAT, 1; SYNCOPATION). Accentuation can also be a subtle expressive device, the effect being attributable to the performer rather than being notated by the composer.

See also DYNAMIC MARKS; PERFORMANCE PRACTICE, 8.   —/NPDC

2 (Fr.). The *springer.

3 (Fr.). An *appoggiatura that inserts a grace note between two notes a 3rd apart, or that repeats the first of two notes a 2nd apart.

accentus (Lat.). A term used from the 16th century to describe the parts of the Roman Catholic liturgy that are sung by the priest, i.e. the simple plainchant recitations. The term used for the parts sung by trained singers (soloists and choir)—the more developed forms of plainchant such as antiphons, responsories, and hymns—is *concentus*.

acciaccatura (It., 'crushed note'; Fr.: *pincé étouffé*; Ger.: *Zusammenschlag*). A late Baroque keyboard *ornament. It consists in the simultaneous striking of the main note with a dissonant auxiliary note (usually one step below), the latter being released immediately 'as if it was Fire' (Geminiani, *A Treatise of Good Taste in the Art of Musick*, 1749). The acciaccatura was used to particular effect for emphasis in arpeggiated chord-playing. Usually unnotated, it was characteristic of improvisatory Italian continuo playing. Certain of Domenico

Scarlatti's sonatas include dense chords containing many dissonant notes, possibly intended as acciaccaturas.

The term 'acciaccatura' has commonly but incorrectly been used for the short *appoggiatura, represented by the sign ♪.   SMcV/NPDC

accidental. A sign used in musical notation either for a note outside the given key of a piece of music or to cancel such a note. The sharp raises the note before which it is placed by one semitone; the flat lowers it by one semitone; the double sharp and double flat respectively raise and lower it by a whole tone; the natural cancels any other accidental. These signs and their names in English, French, German, and Italian are shown in Table 1 (their early shapes are given in parentheses where applicable).

The origins of such signs can be traced to the *Aliae regulae* (*c*.1030) of Guido of Arezzo. Guido suggested that two different forms of the letter b be used to describe the pitches B♭ and B♮, stipulating ♭ *rotundum* (Lat., 'round') for the former, and ♭ *quadratum* (Lat., 'square') for the latter. They are the earliest known accidentals in Western music, and they developed into the modern flat (♭→♭) and natural (♭→h→♮) signs, and thence to the sharp (♮→♯) sign.

In modern usage a sign is valid for the note that it precedes (but not for the same note in octaves above or below) throughout the rest of the bar, unless expressly contradicted by another sign. Some composers frequently add bracketed accidentals in order to clarify complicated passages or chords. However, in music before 1700 (and some even later) an accidental is not valid for the entire bar but only for the note before which it occurs and for immediate repetitions of the same note (a practice observed by Bach). Where an accidental affects a note which is tied over a bar-line, it remains valid for the tied note in the following bar. It was in the 17th century that the modern forms of the double sharp and the double flat became accepted—the former makes an appearance as early as 1615 in Trabaci's *Il secondo libro de ricercare*.

In medieval and Renaissance music (up to *c*.1600), there is some doubt as to the extent to which accidentals were left unspecified, but it is generally agreed that, with the exception of tablatures, the sources of this period do not supply all the necessary accidentals, leaving some to the performers' discretion. There is, however, a great deal of controversy about the principles according to which implied accidentals should be supplied. In modern scholarly editions, accidentals recommended by the editor are usually placed in small type above the relevant notes, to distinguish them from those that appear in the original sources. For further discussion of this problem, see MUSICA FICTA; see also HEXACHORD.   —/AP

accompagnato (It.). 'Accompanied': hence *recitativo accompagnato*, a *recitative accompanied by instrumental ensemble rather than by continuo alone; early examples are found in Monteverdi, Schütz, and Handel. The gerund *accompagnando* designates a subsidiary part.

accord (Fr.; It.: *accordo*). 1. 'Chord'.
2. The 'tuning' of an instrument. See ACCORDATURA.

accordatura (It., 'tuning'). A term used both generally and for the normal tuning of stringed instruments in contrast with special tunings (e.g. *scordatura).

accorder (Fr.). 'To tune'; *accordé*, *accordée*, 'tuned'.

accordion (Fr.: *accordéon*; Ger.: *Ziehharmonika*, *Akkordeon*; It.: *fisarmonica*). Generic term for a family of portable free-reed organs, each consisting of ranks of *free reeds set in two casings (one held in each hand) and connected by bellows. The player causes air from the bellows to activate particular reeds by pressing keys or buttons set in the side of the casings. The accordion has many forms, the chief distinction being between 'single action' or diatonic instruments and 'double action' or chromatic instruments. With single action each key sounds a different note on the press and on the draw of the bellows. With double action each key gives the same note on both the press and the draw. Double action requires two reeds for each note, one arranged to speak when air is expelled from the bellows, the other when air is drawn in. All varieties of accordion (including the *concertina and the *bandoneon) have been made in both double- and single-action models.

TABLE 1	♯	♭	𝄪 (✳, ▦)	♭♭	♮
English	sharp	flat	double sharp	double flat	natural
French	dièse	bémol	double dièse	double bémol	bécarre
German	Kreuz	Be	Doppelkreuz	Doppel-Be	Auflösungszeichen, Quadrat
Italian	diesis	bemolle	doppio diesis	doppio bemolle	bequadro

The melodeon or German accordion is a single-action button accordion, very popular for folk music. In its simplest form it has a single row of ten melody buttons in the right-hand manual giving a diatonic scale (the most common keys being C, D, G, or A), and two bass buttons in the left giving the tonic root and triad on the press and the dominant root and triad on the draw. More complex instruments have two, three, or even four rows of melody buttons, each giving a different diatonic scale, and additional bass buttons. Common two-row key combinations include C/F, Bb/C, and D/G. The push-and-pull of the bellows helps to impart a strong rhythmic drive to a performance.

The two main types of double-action, chromatic accordion are the piano accordion, with a piano-style keyboard in the right-hand manual, and the 'continental chromatic' accordion. The latter has from three to five rows of buttons; the interval between two adjacent buttons in a row is a minor 3rd, and between rows, a semitone. With this system, fingering patterns are the same in every key. Several varieties of continental chromatic are popular throughout Europe and in North America; this is the type characteristic of the French 'musette' school, and is the one known in Russia as the *bayan*.

The full-size bass keyboard of continental chromatics and piano accordions has 120 buttons; known as the Stradella or 'fixed' bass, it comprises two rows of bass notes arranged in 5ths, and four rows containing major, minor, dominant 7th, and diminished chords respectively. Some instruments have an extra 'free-bass' manual of buttons arranged chromatically with a range of five octaves. 'Combi' accordions have a single manual of bass buttons which can be switched from fixed- to free-bass. On some accordions separate banks of reeds with a variety of timbres may be brought into play by pressing tabs set above the manuals.

The accordion was the result of the era of experimentation with the free reed (introduced to Europe from China in the late 18th century) that also produced the *reed organ and the *harmonica. Prototype accordions were invented in the 1820s by C. F. L. Buschmann in Berlin and Cyrillus Demian in Vienna. French and Belgian makers including Charles Buffet, J.-B.-N. Fourneaux, and M. Busson developed the instrument further, while in England Charles Wheatstone invented the concertina. Commercial production began to take off in the 1850s, when the Hohner company was established in Trossingen, Germany. Castelfidardo and Stradella in Italy have also been centres of accordion production since the 1870s, though the old European businesses have faced strong competition from East Asian manufacturers in recent years. MIDI electronics

were applied to accordions during the last decades of the 20th century.   RPa

📖 T. Charuhas, *The Accordion* (New York, 1955) · A. Baines (ed.), *Musical Instruments through the Ages* (Harmondsworth, 1961, 2/1966) · R. Flynn, E. Davison, and E. Chavez, *The Golden Age of the Accordion* (Schertz, TX, 1990)

accoupler (Fr.; It.: *accoppiare*). 'To couple'. The term is used in connection with organ stops, hence *accouplé* (Fr.), *accoppiato* (It.), 'coupled'; *accouplement* (Fr.), *accoppiamento* (It.), 'coupling', 'coupler'; *accouplez* (Fr.), an instruction to couple.

accusé, accusée (Fr.). 'With emphasis'.

acht (Ger.). 'Eight'; *Achtel, Achtelnote*, 'eighth', 'eighth-note', i.e. the *quaver; *Achtelpause*, 'quaver rest'; *achtstimmig*, in eight voices or parts; *Achtfuss*, an 8′ organ stop.

acid rock. See PSYCHEDELIC ROCK.

Acis and Galatea. Masque, or serenata, in one, later two, acts by Handel to a libretto by John Gay and others after Ovid (Cannons, 1718); it was revived in London in 1732 incorporating new material, principally from Handel's cantata *Aci, Galatea e Polifemo* (Naples, 1708).

acoustic. 1. A term sometimes applied to instruments relying on an air-filled resonator or soundbox to transmit their sound, to distinguish them from those that are amplified electronically, for example the acoustic guitar as opposed to the electric guitar; many instruments have an electronic form as well as an acoustic one.   JMo

2. Related to the sense of hearing or the science of sound.

acoustic bass. 1. An organ stop (also known as Quint) dependent on the acoustic phenomenon of resultant tones. If two pipes a 5th apart are exactly in tune, a third note (the 'subjective fundamental'; see ACOUSTICS, 8) will be heard an octave below the lower. This saves the cost and space of large bass pipes, though the sound may be louder than desired and tuning complications are inevitable (see TEMPERAMENT).

2. A term used to distinguish between electric bass guitars and acoustic instruments such as the double bass.   JMo

acoustics 1. Introduction; 2. Sources of musical sounds; 3. Music and noise; 4. Pitch of sound; 5. Harmonics; 6. Timbre; 7. Resonance; 8. Combination tones and beats; 9. Transmission of sound; 10. Radiation and reflection of sound, 11. Intensity of sound

1. Introduction

Acoustics is the science of sound and hearing. Sound is a form of energy and involves vibratory motion. When a piano is played in a concert hall, for example, the energy exerted by the player causes the hammers to strike the strings and set them into vibration. This vibration is taken up by the soundboard and radiated as a 'pressure wave' through successive layers of air particles. The members of the audience hear the sounds when the air sets their eardrums in motion to produce signals that are communicated to the brain via nerve-fibres. This simple description, of course, takes no account of the subtleties introduced by the player, the instrument itself, and the acoustic properties of the hall.

2. Sources of musical sounds

In the present context we think first of the various families of musical instruments, but there are many other sources of sound to which human ears can respond. The characteristics of human hearing, evolved in prehistoric times, naturally set limits to the ranges of loudness and pitch over which musical instruments and voices may usefully extend.

It seems likely that the first musical instruments were simple percussive devices such as blocks of wood or hollowed-out tree-trunks, the precursors of the present-day percussion family. The introduction of stretched skins and metals would have added variety and produced notes of definite pitch. The first wind instruments would have been reedless, ancestors of the recorder and flute, their air columns being set into vibration by the player blowing across the opening at one end of a bamboo or other pipe. Cutting out fingerholes to alter the effective length of the air column would greatly have extended the scope by producing a choice of notes of different pitch. Blowing edgewise on to blades of grass could have led to the development of reed instruments in which the vibrating reed, activated by the player's breath, became the source of the sound, and the air column acted as a tuned resonator to determine the pitch of the note emitted.

In brass instruments, such as the trumpet and horn, air is forced between the player's lips, placed more or less tightly against the mouthpiece. The lip vibrations act as the source and, again, it is the effective length of the air column that sets the pitch. The human voice works similarly by forcing air through a gap in the vocal cords, with the chest, mouth, and throat cavities acting as resonators.

3. Music and noise

The traditional distinction between music and noise, defining one as 'pleasant' and the other as 'unwanted', has become blurred as composers have increasingly used sounds from a wide variety of sources in their works. A better working definition of music might be 'organized sound', which implies some human agency creating patterns of sound that will entertain or intrigue the listener. These may include dissonant as well as tuneful or consonant sounds, random or aleatory elements as well as strict measures, and editing together of tape or digitally produced fragments of speech and other sounds (e.g. steam-engines or traffic noise).

While music has pushed out its boundaries in this way, becoming louder at live pop concerts and a public nuisance in its 'background' or 'portable stereo' manifestations, noise has also increased. The sound of mechanized transport, on the roads and in the air, has adversely affected the quality of many people's lives. However, in spite of these overlaps between 'music' and 'noise', Western music remains the province of the traditional instruments of the orchestra and the singing voice. And the primary characteristics of all such music are rhythm and a regular scale of pitch intervals.

4. Pitch of sound

It is well known that the pitch of a note on the musical scale is directly related to the rate of vibration. If a circular saw is speeded up, the number of vibrations or sound impulses per second (caused by the individual teeth striking the wood) goes up and so does the pitch. The lowest vibration rate that produces a musical note, rather than a succession of separate pulses of sound, is about 20 per second. At the high-pitched end the limit is about 20,000 vibrations per second, though people vary in their ability to hear such sounds.

A complete vibration is called a 'cycle'; it consists of a full excursion of the vibrating element from its rest position out to one side, back through the centre, out in the opposite direction, and then to the centre again. This is illustrated in Fig. 1, where the motion of the tip of a tuning-fork fitted with a small pen is traced on a moving roll of paper. The amplitude of the vibration,

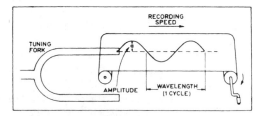

Fig. 1. Diagram showing how the vibrations of a tuning-fork may be traced on a moving roll of paper; the amplitude (a) and frequency can be measured on the resulting recorded wave-form.

corresponding to the loudness of the sound heard, is not uniform in practice; the naturally occurring variation is known as the 'envelope' of the sound wave. The number of cycles per second is called the 'frequency', given in Hertz (Hz), one Hertz being one cycle per second. For many years there was no agreed standard for the true pitch of written scores, but in 1939 International Standard Pitch was set at 440 Hz for a' (the note A above middle C; see PITCH, 2). The precise pitch of one note on the staff having been set, the rest follow a simple arithmetic sequence (but see SCALE; TEMPERAMENT). It can easily be demonstrated, for example, that the basic musical interval of an octave corresponds to a doubling or halving of the frequency. Thus the octaves of A on a piano keyboard have frequencies and musical notation as shown in Fig. 2.

The natural or 'fundamental' frequency of vibration of a stretched string is determined by three factors: its length, tension, and mass (or weight) per unit length. The piano has separate strings for each of its 88 notes, graduated in length and thickness to give reasonably equal values of tension. The instruments of the violin family make do with only four strings of equal length, which the player fine-tunes by adjusting the tension before playing. The effective length of the strings is then varied by pressure (stopping) from the fingers. Tension is also used to tune the skins of timpani, for example, whereas the fundamental pitch of wind instruments is essentially fixed by the length of the contained column of air. The player can alter this by means of fingerholes, keys, valves, or a slide (on the trombone) and also, on brass instruments, by changing the lip pressure against the mouthpiece.

5. Harmonics

Few sound sources perform such simple vibrations as to emit a single frequency. The pure tone of a tuning-fork and some notes from a flute come close, and electrical oscillators can generate a single frequency. The richer sounds heard from most musical instruments result from the simultaneous setting up of several modes of vibration whenever the instrument is played. A vibrating string, for example, can oscillate as a whole to produce the fundamental note which establishes the pitch of the note we hear. At the same time, the string will break up into partial modes of vibration, with each half, third, or quarter behaving like a separate string (see Fig. 3). This will generate a series of overtones having two, three, and four (etc.) times the frequency of the fundamental (see Fig. 4). These are called 'harmonics' (see HARMONIC SERIES) and contribute much to the richness of individual instruments (see below, 6). It will be seen that the octaves above the fundamental (or 'first harmonic') correspond to the second, fourth, eighth (etc.) harmonics, having two, four, and eight times the fundamental frequency. The seventh and higher odd-numbered harmonics do not fall precisely on notes of the scale; thus they introduce dissonance, so it is fortunate that the upper harmonics tend to weaken progressively.

In wind instruments, an 'open pipe' is equivalent to a stretched string, except that the two open ends are points of maximum rather than minimum amplitude (antinodes; see Fig. 5). The centre point, for the lowest (fundamental) vibration mode, is one of zero amplitude (node) and the full series of harmonics is possible. In a 'closed pipe', however, one end becomes a point of zero

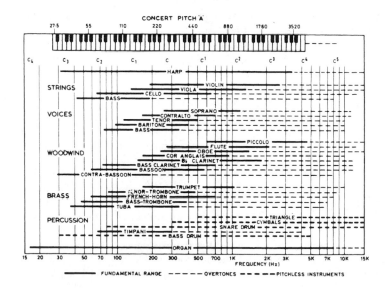

Fig. 2. Frequencies of the octaves of A, based on $a' = 440$ Hz; also shown are the fundamental notes on different instruments, and the extent of the overtones or harmonics.

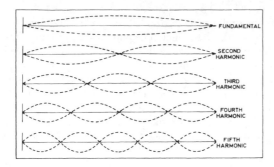

Fig. 3. Series of harmonic modes on a vibrating string, generating overtones at 2, 3, 4, 5, etc., times the fundamental frequency.

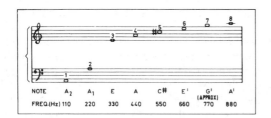

Fig. 4. The harmonic series up to the eighth harmonic of A.

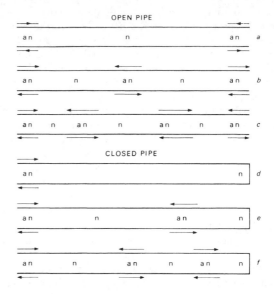

Fig. 5. Diagram showing nodes (*n*) and antinodes (*an*) in open and closed pipes.

amplitude, and the fundamental frequency is an octave below that for an open pipe of equal length. Only odd-numbered harmonics are formed, and a different timbre is produced (see below, 6). Tapered or conical pipes set up acoustic conditions of other kinds. A closed conical pipe produces the full harmonic series and generally behaves like an open cylindrical (straight-sided) pipe of the same length.

String players are accustomed to playing 'harmonics', which the composer will indicate by placing an '°' over the notes in question. The technique used is to touch the string very lightly at its centre, or at a third of its length. This inhibits the formation of the fundamental, and the note heard is respectively an octave, or an octave plus a 5th, higher, with a thin, silvery quality.

Note production in *brass instruments is based firmly on the harmonic series. The player can select any one of the first dozen or so harmonics by altering lip pressure and technique. Naturally the pitch intervals are wide apart at the lower end of the range for the given tube length. The ability to play only notes of the harmonic series is the characteristic feature of such simple instruments as the bugle or posthorn. Further notes became available when added lengths of tube, known as crooks or shanks, could be fitted. This gave a new (lower) fundamental and its associated series of harmonics. The later introduction of *valves extended the

versatility of brass instruments to cover the full chromatic scale, the player merely pressing on piston keys to select fixed crooks of different lengths. The trombone already had this facility, as well as gliding, portamento, and vibrato effects, since one tube slides into another to give continuous control of overall tube length.

6. Timbre

As a rule, then, each note from a musical instrument consists of a fundamental tone, which usually sets the pitch of the note, together with a number of harmonics (overtones at frequencies which are simple multiples of the fundamental). The tone-colour or special 'timbre' of each instrument is largely a function of the numbers and strengths of the harmonics present. Trained listeners can not only distinguish between the different families of instruments but even recognize individual violins, flutes, clarinets, etc.

In common with most percussion instruments, the piano is incapable of producing continuous notes. The notes begin to decay from the instant of striking, with the higher harmonics tending to die out first so that the timbre smooths out as the loudness diminishes. The ability to recognize different instruments is also helped by the 'attack' or 'transient' with which each note begins. The transient can contain very high frequencies up to and beyond the limit of human hearing. This explains one difficulty experienced by the makers of electronic musical instruments: they may successfully generate and mix a family of overtones to simulate the sound of a flute or oboe, for example, yet the sound may disappoint because the 'attack' is missing (see ELECTRONIC MUSICAL INSTRUMENTS). Transients are also difficult to record and reproduce faithfully since they require extended 'bandwidth' and fast-reacting circuitry and loudspeakers.

7. Resonance

For a sound source to radiate sound waves effectively it must be capable of setting a substantial volume of air into vibration. Tuning-forks and violin strings, for example, are inefficient since their motion cuts through the air without imparting much energy to it. Much louder sounds can be produced, however, if the stem of a tuning-fork or the ends of a stretched string are touched on to a table top, or better still a hollow wooden box. Then the initial vibrations are transmitted into the table or box and the resultant sympathetic vibrations are able to produce a greater amount of air movement.

As musical instruments evolved, ways were found of increasing this reinforcement of sound volume using the fundamental principle of resonance: that any structure having both mass and elasticity will exhibit one or more 'natural' frequencies of vibration which are relatively easy to stimulate. To take the simple example of a garden swing, children soon find that applying even a tiny push in time with each 'cycle' of the swing's natural motion can build up much higher amplitudes. The swing is behaving like a tuned resonator which responds strongly to a driving force at its own natural frequency but is less responsive at other frequencies. Musical equivalents include the resonating tubes mounted under each bar of a marimba or vibraphone.

However, when constructing the soundboard (or body) of a piano or violin, it is necessary to produce a broadly tuned resonator capable of reinforcing the string tones over a wide range of fundamental and harmonic frequencies. In practice, instruments of the violin family do not resonate with equal efficiency at all frequencies. They remain to some extent frequency-selective, in spite of the special shaping, tensioning, and varnishing techniques evolved to achieve the most pleasing tonal quality, responsiveness, and sonority. Each instrument will therefore 'colour' the sound to some extent, and small differences will always exist.

Many instruments tend to reinforce harmonics in a particular band of frequencies, no matter which fundamental is being sounded. This pitch region is known as a 'formant', and it may be necessary for the player consciously or subconsciously to keep it under control. The human voice is a prime example of physical differences contributing individual colorations—and

indeed each vowel sound is characterized by two fixed formant regions.

The important effects of resonance on musical sounds are also found in any room where music is being performed. Every room has natural resonant frequencies, referred to as 'eigentones' and related to the dimensions of length, breadth, and height. The room is not unlike a complex organ pipe in which standing waves are set up between parallel wall, floor, and ceiling surfaces. Selective resonance at these eigentone frequencies will inevitably colour the sound, especially in small rectangular rooms where the resonant frequencies are high enough to fall within the musical range. Some control can be introduced using soft furnishings to damp out the resonances or irregular wall shapes to increase diffusion of the sound energy. See ARCHITECTURAL ACOUSTICS.

8. Combination tones and beats

When more than one note is sounding it is often possible to distinguish each one by ear, but side effects occur depending on how close the notes are in pitch. Imagine that one instrument plays the note d' constantly (440 Hz) while another plays a note that can be varied in pitch. If the second instrument also plays 440 Hz, there is perfect unison and the note simply sounds louder. But if the second note is sharpened slightly, say to 445 Hz, a note of some intermediate pitch is heard that pulsates in loudness as the peaks and troughs of the two waves drift in and out of step. These pulsations are called 'beats', and in this example (known also as a 'difference tone') there will be five beats per second. Piano tuners and others listen for, and work to eliminate, beats as a means of accurate adjustment of correct pitch.

Raising the pitch of the second instrument produces a degree of unpleasant dissonance which varies with the frequency difference and falls effectively to zero at the familiar consonant intervals of a major 3rd (4:3), perfect 5th (3:2), and octave (2:1). In the special case where the octave is sounded, and for all adjacent numbered harmonics, the difference frequency is in fact the fundamental. This accounts for the effect known as the 'subjective fundamental', heard when a small radio set, for example, appears to reproduce bass notes which its small dimensions would normally be unable to radiate effectively. The beating between adjacent harmonics causes the brain to 'hear' the non-existent fundamental (see ACOUSTIC BASS, 1).

9. Transmission of sound

The invisible nature of sound waves has encouraged those engaged in research to improvise models or analogies both to aid their own understanding and to explain the nature of sound to the world at large. In 1660, for example, Robert Boyle proved by suspending a watch inside a glass jar that sound needs a physical medium for its transmission. The alarm bell of the watch could initially be heard quite clearly, but when the air was gradually pumped out the ringing became fainter and eventually inaudible. Returning air to the jar restored the ringing sound. Similar experiments with sound sources immersed in water prove that sound travels as easily through liquids as through gases. Solids too make an efficient medium for the transmission of sound, as witness the stories of Amerindians pressing their ears to a railway track to listen for trains several miles distant.

Clearly the medium itself does not travel from the source to the observer; it merely hands on the vibratory motion in the same way as a chain of firefighters might pass buckets of water from a tank to the place of a fire. In a sound wave, each particle of the medium passes on the energy as imitative vibration about its normal position. The speed of transmission is greater when the vibrating particles are closer together, which suggests that the speed of sound is greater in liquids than in gases, and greater still in solids. Typical values are as shown in Table 1.

TABLE I

Speed of sound in various media at 15°C

medium	metres per second	feet per second
air	340	1120
water	1420	4600
wood (oak)	4400	14,500
aluminium	5100	16,700

The speed of sound in air increases by about 0.61 metres per second for each 1°C rise in temperature. It should be noted that the nominal speed is only about 1200 km per hour. Comparison of this with the speed of light and radio waves (297,600 km per second) explains why the sound of distant wood-chopping, for example, is heard some little time after the axe is seen to strike the wood. It also makes clear the need to group musicians reasonably close together if time lags caused by distance are to be kept to a minimum.

A popular analogy for the transmission of sound is dropping a stone into a still pond, causing ripples to spread outwards in the form of ever-widening circles. The stone drags down some water particles, these drag adjoining particles, and the motion is progressively imitated by successive layers of particles. The original particles then swing upwards again, and so on. This single shock wave is analogous to a handclap, but it would be possible to produce the equivalent of a sustained musical note by vibrating a plunger up and down to generate continuously radiating waves. It should be noted first that the advancing wave is a perfect circle, showing that the speed of transmission is equal in all directions; second, increasing the vibration rate does not alter the speed of the travelling waves but merely causes the wave crests to move closer together; third, increasing the amplitude of plunger motion (more energy) again leaves the speed of the waves unchanged but it does increase their magnitude and the distance they will travel before the energy is dissipated.

As has been stated, sound is vibration, and one way of demonstrating the motion of the tip of a tuning-fork was illustrated in Fig. 1. A more versatile method for showing—and even recording—the vibratory nature of sound waves was the Phonautograph, devised by Leon Scott in 1857. This consisted of a large horn, to collect the incident sound energy, with a thin membrane at the narrow end. A bristle was attached to the membrane and rested against the lampblacked surface of a revolving cylinder. If a flute was played near the horn, the bristle vibrated in sympathy and inscribed a wavy line on the cylinder. Counting the number of wave cycles traced per second gave the frequency of the note, and the distance occupied by one cycle was defined as the 'wavelength'. Given that the velocity of a wave is the distance travelled per second, we arrive at the universal formula which holds for wave transmissions and recording media of all kinds: 'velocity = frequency × wavelength'.

The nominal velocity of sound in air having already been noted as 340 metres per second, it follows that the wavelength of a note at 340 Hz is 1 metre, that at 34 Hz it is 10 metres, and so on. For the generally accepted range of audible frequencies, 20–20,000 Hz, wavelengths in air range from 17 metres to a mere 17 mm.

10. Radiation and reflection of sound

The concept of wavelength has a direct bearing on how sound waves travel out from various sound sources, are reflected by obstacles in their path, and build up or decay in rooms or concert halls.

When a sound source is small compared with the wavelength of the note it is radiating, the waves travel outwards with equal strength in all directions in a three-dimensional version of the pond waves discussed above, the wavefront being an expanding sphere. Since the original amount of energy is being spread over a larger area, the intensity of the sound (i.e. the energy passing through a given area of the wavefront; see below, section 11) diminishes progressively. Given that the area of the surface of a sphere is proportional to the square of the radius, the intensity will fall as the square of the distance travelled, the well-known 'inverse square law'.

By contrast, a source that is larger than the wavelength generates a plane (or flat) wavefront whose intensity falls off only slightly with distance. Since sound wavelengths range from several metres down to a few millimetres, it can be seen that most musical instruments and loudspeakers are intermediate in size. They therefore tend to radiate bass notes (long wavelengths) rather inefficiently in all directions and higher notes (short wavelengths) strongly in specific directions, generally along a major axis.

Like other waves, sound waves are bounced or reflected when they meet a wall or obstacle. Again the wavelength is important, and an obstacle must be relatively large for reflection to take place. Longer wavelength sounds effectively bend round the obstacle and continue outwards (the process known as 'diffraction'). When a wave meets a large surface at right angles, it is reflected back along its original path. This sets up an interference pattern called a 'standing wave' with peaks and troughs of sound energy at multiples of a quarter-wavelength from the reflecting surface. This explains the appearance of 'dead spots' in auditoria and unwanted resonance in small rooms (see ARCHITECTURAL ACOUSTICS). Reflection is most efficient from a hard surface like marble, of course, whereas soft or porous surfaces absorb some of the incident sound energy. Similarly, an irregular or indented surface tends to scatter or diffuse the sound.

When a reflected sound reaches an observer after the direct wave by an interval of more than about ¹⁄₂₀ of a second, it appears as an 'echo' and two distinct sounds are heard. This implies a distance of about 17 metres, so that echoes can become audible in large halls, churches, and city streets, for example. Another common experience is the change in pitch that occurs when there is relative movement between source and listener. This is known as the Doppler effect; good examples are the sudden lowering of pitch of a passing train siren, or the similar effect heard when one is on a train passing a stationary bell, perhaps at a level crossing. The actual frequency heard in such cases depends on the sum of the velocities of sound and the train. Thus more cycles per second reach an observer moving towards a source (higher pitch) and fewer when moving away (lower pitch).

11. Intensity of sound

The sensation of 'loudness' is evidently related to the magnitude of the air vibrations close to the ears, and will therefore depend on the power of the source (measured in watts) and the distance between source and observer. Only about 1 per cent of the energy expended by a musician emerges as sound, the rest being lost as heat in overcoming friction, etc. Table 2 shows the wide range of total powers radiated by typical sources.

TABLE 2

Typical power levels

musical source	power (watts)
75-piece orchestra (*fff*)	70
bass drum	25
pipe organ	13
cymbals	10
trombone	0.6
piano	0.4
75-piece orchestra (*mf*)	0.09
flute	0.06
normal speech	0.000024
violin (*ppp*)	0.0000038

In practice, only a small fraction of the sound radiated by a source reaches the ears of any one listener; the intensity (the power passing through a given area; see above, section 10) is therefore very small indeed. The human ear can respond to an astonishing range of intensities over a ratio of about 10 million million to one. The relationship between intensity and subjective loudness is not strict, but a tenfold increase in intensity roughly equals a doubling in loudness. There are 12 such steps between the quietest and loudest sound thresholds (see EAR AND HEARING). Each step is called a Bel, and a smaller, more convenient unit—the decibel (dB)—is commonly used. Table 3 gives some examples of intensity levels. Note that the decibel is a unit of relative rather than absolute level and the figures listed are with respect to the standard 'threshold of hearing' intensity, one million-millionth of a watt per square centimetre. This is the weakest sound audible to normal ears and corresponds to an eardrum amplitude of less than the diameter of an atom.

TABLE 3

Typical sound levels

source or situation	sound level (dB)
threshold of pain	130
symphony orchestra (*fff*)	110
underground-train interior	94
average street traffic	74
conversational speech	60
suburban sitting-room	45
broadcasting studio	20
threshold of hearing	0

The ear is not equally sensitive at all frequencies, but reaches a peak in acuity in the 1000–2000 Hz region. The standard frequency for acoustic measurements is 1000 Hz (kiloHertz, abbreviated to kHz) and the 'loudness unit' or 'phon' is used to describe the loudness level of any sound by reference to the intensity level in dB of an equally loud tone at 1000 Hz. Coincidentally, one phon is approximately the smallest detectable difference in loudness.　　　　　　　　　　　JBo

📕 A. WOOD, *The Physics of Music* (London, 7/1975) · C. A. TAYLOR, *Sounds of Music* (London, 1976) · M. CAMPBELL and C. GREATED, *The Musician's Guide to Acoustics* (London, 1987)

action. 1. On keyboard instruments, the mechanism which transmits finger motion on a key to the tangents (*clavichord), jacks (*harpsichord), hammers (*pianoforte), or pallets (which admit air to *organ pipes or *accordion reeds). On the *harp the action is the pedal-operated mechanism for changing the tuning of the strings.

2. The way in which an instrument speaks, and the fine adjustment of its 'set-up'. The action on a guitar or violin (or other stringed instrument, plucked or bowed) is the height of the strings off the fingerboard towards the bridge, which affects ease of playing and tuning in the higher registers. Keyboard instruments may be said to have a 'light' or 'heavy' action (or *touch) depending on how hard and how far the keys must be depressed to produce a sound.　　　　　　　　　　　JMo, RPA

act tune. In the English theatre of the late 16th and early 17th centuries, instrumental music played between the acts of a play or *semi-opera. Composers were expected to write new music for each production, providing the four act tunes to be performed between each of the five acts, the First and Second Music (played for the entertainment of the waiting audience), and the overture (usually in the French style), which preceded the rise of the curtain. Purcell composed such suites for 13 plays and semi-operas; these were published posthumously as *Ayres for the Theatre* in 1697.

See also INCIDENTAL MUSIC.　　　　　　JBe

actus musicus (Lat., 'musical action'). In German Protestant music of the 17th and 18th centuries, a semi-dramatic vocal composition based on a biblical story. It is similar in form and function to the contemporary Lutheran *historia*, but more elaborate, and was a forerunner of the German *oratorio.

The *actus musicus* was a through-composed work that set both biblical and non-biblical texts and was generally performed at the end of a liturgical service. The earliest known piece designated 'actus musicus' is Andreas Fromm's *De divite et Lazaro* (1649), which contains instrumental symphonias, solo arias, recitatives, choruses, a dialogue, and a Protestant chorale tune.　　　　　　　　　　　JBe

Actus tragicus. The name by which Bach's church cantata *Gottes Zeit ist die allerbeste Zeit* ('God's time is the best time') BWV106 is known; it was written for a funeral, probably in 1708.

adagietto (It., dim. of *adagio*). Slow, but less so than *adagio; it is also used as a movement title, most famously for the fourth movement of Mahler's Fifth Symphony.

adagio (It.). A tempo indication which, when it first appeared in the early 17th century, and from the 19th century onwards, generally means 'very slow', the equivalent of *lento* or *largo*; in the 18th century it sometimes implied that ornamentation was necessary. In some earlier music, for example by Frescobaldi (where it appears as *adasio*), it probably meant 'leisurely' (between *largo* and *andante*). It has occasionally been qualified as *adagissimo* (still slower). The term 'adagio' is often also used for the slow movement of a multi-movement work, irrespective of whether it is so marked.

Adam, Adolphe (Charles) (*b* Paris, 24 July 1803; *d* Paris, 3 May 1856). French composer. After studying at the Paris Conservatoire with Reicha and Boieldieu he began to write songs for the vaudeville theatres; having helped Boieldieu to orchestrate the overture for his opera *La Dame blanche* (1825), he had his first one-act opera *Pierre et Catherine* (1829) produced at the Opéra-Comique. Following the July Revolution he went to London, where his brother-in-law, Pierre François Laporte, was director at Covent Garden; through him two of Adam's works were produced in 1832. With *Le Chalet* (1834) he wrote what is considered to be the first true French operetta—light and frivolous, with music nearer to the popular vaudeville idiom. The opera that established his reputation throughout Europe was *Le Postillon de Longjumeau* (1836), from which the aria 'Mes amis, écoutez l'histoire' has remained a favourite of tenors.

On his return from a visit to St Petersburg, Adam wrote the work by which he is best remembered today, the ballet *Giselle* (1841), which is notable for its use of recurring leitmotivic themes. In 1847, following a disagreement with the director of the Opéra-Comique, he bought a theatre, the Opéra-National, where he staged his own works and those of lesser-known French composers. But the 1848 Revolution put an end to the project; Adam was financially ruined and turned to journalism to supplement his income. In 1850 he was appointed professor of composition at the Paris

Conservatoire. However, he continued to write *opéras comiques*, including *Giralda* (1850), acknowledged as one of his finest pieces, and *Si j'étais roi* (1852).

The composer of some 70 operas, Adam is remembered as a pioneer and writer of graceful, fluent music in an Italianate idiom with dramatic power. He was also a prolific composer of potpourris, piano arrangements, and songs, including the *Cantique de Noël* (1850). His two volumes of reminiscences, *Souvenirs d'un musicien* (Paris, 1857) and *Derniers souvenirs d'un musicien* (Paris, 1859), were published posthumously.   SH

Adam de la Halle [Adan le Bossu] (*b* Arras, 1245–50; *d* Naples, ?1285–8). French poet and composer. He lived and worked at Arras in northern France but studied in Paris and is often described by contemporary sources as 'maistre'. In the late 1270s he was in the service of Robert II, Count of Artois, with whom he travelled in Italy. There he entered the service of Charles of Anjou, who died in 1285. Adam's career and whereabouts after that date are uncertain, but in 1288 his nephew wrote of his departure from Arras and of his death. An 'Adam le Boscu' was among the minstrels engaged for the coronation of Edward II in 1307, but he may have been a younger member of the family.

As a composer Adam followed the courtly tradition of the *trouvères in his monophonic songs and lively music dramas (of which *Le Jeu de Robin et de Marion*, written while he was in the service of Charles of Anjou in Italy, is the best known), as well as writing chansons and motets in a more complex polyphonic style.
                                                                                             JM

Adams, John (Coolidge) (*b* Worcester, MA, 15 Feb. 1947). American composer. At Harvard he studied the clarinet as well as composition, with Leon Kirchner among others, after which he took a post teaching and conducting at the San Francisco Conservatory (1971–81). He was then composer-in-residence with the San Francisco Symphony (1979–85), who introduced his first big works: *Harmonium* (1980), with chorus, and *Harmonielehre* (1984–5). These and other early pieces, especially *Phrygian Gates* for piano (1977), *Shaker Loops* for strings (1978), and *Grand Pianola Music* for ensemble (1981–2), established his reputation as a composer who could use minimalist-style repetition with flair, polish, and sometimes humour, unafraid to show his roots in American popular music, and who could emulate the grand tonal unfolding of Wagner and Bruckner.

The style is the same in his first opera, *Nixon in China* (Houston, 1987), where world leaders—Nixon, Mao and his wife, Kissinger, Chou En-lai—are seen at a historic moment engaging only in small talk and nostalgia. *The Death of Klinghoffer* (Brussels, 1991), a second opera with the same librettist (Alice Goodman) and director (Peter Sellars), showed a darker response to recent world events, this time the hijacking of a cruise ship by Palestinian freedom fighters. Since then his major works have all been orchestral pieces, including the Chamber Symphony (1992), concertos for violin (1993), clarinet (*Gnarly Buttons*, 1996), and piano (*Century Rolls*, 1997), and the symphony-length *Naive and Sentimental Music* (1998). These are sometimes more chromatic and more intricately textured than his earlier music, parts of the Chamber Symphony and the Violin Concerto being especially lively with cross-rhythms, but the harmonic sweep and the repetitive detail are the same, as is the joyous mix of classical and popular affiliations.   PG

Adan Le Bossu. See ADAM DE LA HALLE.

added sixth chord. A triad, usually the subdominant, with an extra note, the 6th (in the key of C major: F–A–C–D); this chord can be thought of as the supertonic 7th chord in first inversion. In strict harmony, the chord should resolve on to the dominant or tonic chord, but many composers have used it purely for effect. It is a popular final chord in jazz.

Addinsell, Richard (Stewart) (*b* London, 13 Jan. 1904; *d* London, 14 Nov. 1977). English composer. He studied at the RCM and at Oxford. A composer of light music, he scored his first notable success with the *Warsaw Concerto*, a sub-Rakhmaninov fragment for piano and orchestra written for the film *Dangerous Moonlight* (1941). He also composed many other film scores, music for revues, and songs for Joyce Grenfell, whose regular accompanist he was.   PG

Addison, John (Mervin) (*b* West Chobham, Surrey, 16 March 1920; *d* Bennington, VT, 7 Dec. 1998). English composer. He studied composition with Gordon Jacob at the RCM, the oboe with Leon Goossens, and the clarinet with Frederick Thurston. His practical experience as a wind player was reflected in his first major work, the Woodwind Sextet of 1949. He also produced a ballet *Carte blanche* in 1952 and the same year made a realization of the Gay–Pepusch ballad opera *Polly*, given at the Aldeburgh Festival. Later he wrote incidental music for plays and film scores including *Reach for the Sky* (1956), *Tom Jones* (1963), *The Charge of the Light Brigade* (1968), *Sleuth* (1973), and *A Bridge Too Far* (1977).   PG/JD1

addolorato (It., 'pained'). Sadly.

Adelaide. Song for voice and piano, op. 46 (1794–5), by Beethoven, a setting of a poem by Friedrich von Matthisson.

Adélaïde Concerto. A violin concerto falsely ascribed to Mozart, who was said to have written it when he was ten and to have dedicated it to the Princess Adélaïde, daughter of King Louis XV of France; it was first performed in Paris in 1931 by Marius Casadesus, who in 1977 admitted he had written it himself.

Adès, Thomas (*b* London, 31 March 1971). English composer. After early success as a performer he studied at Cambridge with Alexander Goehr and Robin Holloway and rapidly came to the fore as a composer with an exceptional assurance of style and technique, his music blending vividness of detail with a clear sense of overall design. His most substantial scores, including a chamber opera, *Powder her Face* (Cheltenham, 1995), *Arcadiana* for string quartet (1994), and the symphonic orchestral work *Asyla* (1997), show few signs of sympathy with the rigours of 20th-century constructivism, avoiding the consistent textural fragmentation and formal disjunction of an expressionistic aesthetic. Affinities with composers as diverse as Ives and Janáček, Ligeti and Nancarrow do nothing to undermine the individual and subtly crafted quality of his compositions, whose remarkable variety of mood ranges from the laid-back acknowledgment of pop music to an intense and tender romanticism.   AW

Adeste fideles ('O come, all ye faithful'). Hymn on the prose for Christmas Day, now ascribed to John Francis Wade (1711–86), a Latin teacher and music copyist of Douai. The words first appeared in *Evening Offices of the Church* (1760 edition) and the tune was first printed in *An Essay on the Church in Plain Chant* (1782) by Samuel Webbe.

à deux (Fr.), **a due** (It.), **a 2.** A term with two opposite meanings, depending on the context. Applied to two orchestral instruments notated on the same staff (e.g. flutes 1 and 2), it indicates that they should play in unison. However, applied to a group of instruments that usually play in unison (e.g. first or second violins), it means that they are to divide into two bodies, each taking one of the two lines notated on the staff (see DIVISI). Similarly, in vocal or instrumental music *a 2, a 3,* and so on, indicate division into that number of parts.

A deux mains (Fr.) and *a due mani* (It.) mean 'for two hands'; *à deux voix* (*choeurs*) (Fr.) and *a due voci* (*cori*) (It.), 'for two voices (choirs)'. The terms *à deux cordes* (Fr.) and *a due corde* (It.), 'on two strings', are used in string music to indicate that the same note should be played on two strings together, in order to increase the tone power.

adiastematic neumes. Neumes (see NOTATION, 1) that give an idea of melodic movement without recording exact pitch, and that give less information on relative pitch than *heighted neumes or *diastematic neumes.

Adieux, Les. The French title (in full 'Les Adieux, l'absence et le retour') given by the publisher to Beethoven's Piano Sonata no.26 in E♭ op. 81a (1809–10), which Beethoven called *Das Lebewohl (Abwesenheit und Wiedersehn)*; he dedicated it to his patron Archduke Rudolph on his departure from Vienna for nine months.

adjunct. A term applied to notes inessential to the harmony, such as accented or unaccented *passing notes.

Adler, Guido (*b* Eibenschütz [now Ivančice], 1 Nov. 1855; *d* Vienna, 15 Feb. 1941). Austrian musicologist. He studied at the Vienna Conservatory with Bruckner, and became a fervent Wagnerian, giving lectures on the *Ring* at Bayreuth in 1875–6. He then took to music history, on which he was one of the most distinguished writers. Professor at Prague (1885) and then at Vienna (where he was Hanslick's successor in 1898), he taught virtually the whole of the next generation of German musicologists, including Egon Wellesz, Knud Jeppesen, and Hans Gál.   DA

Adler, Samuel (*b* Mannheim, 4 March 1928). American composer and teacher of German origin. He arrived in the USA in 1939 and studied at Harvard with Walter Piston, Randall Thompson, and Hindemith. After military service, conducting the Seventh Army Symphony, he taught at North Texas State University and then from 1966 at the Eastman School, where in 1973 he became chairman of the composition department. An influential teacher, he has also been prolific as a composer, in a midstream modernist style, producing operas, symphonies, synagogue music, and much else.   PG

adoración (Sp.). A Latin American religious folksong, synonymous with *aguinaldo* and *villancico.

Adorno, Theodor W(iesengrund) (*b* Frankfurt, 11 Sept. 1903; *d* Visp, Switzerland, 6 Aug. 1969). German philosopher, sociologist, and musicologist. He studied philosophy, worked as a music critic, and had composition lessons with Berg. In 1934 he was forced to emigrate, moving first to Oxford, then in 1938 to New York; he spent time in Los Angeles before returning to Frankfurt, where he became a prominent member of the 'Frankfurt School'. He was a leader of left-wing social thinking, his ideology profoundly influenced by the rise of Fascism and the failure of Marxism, and by existentialism. Thus he was a fierce supporter of avant-garde music, which he insisted should be 'difficult' and remain outside the 'cultural industry' (his term) designed for social repression; his many writings embody polemics against popular music and musical amateurism.

　　See also SOCIOLOGY OF MUSIC.　　　　　　　AL

📖 L. ZUIDERVAART, *Adorno's Aesthetic Theory: The Redemption of Illusion* (Cambridge, MA, 1991) · M. PADDISON, *Adorno's Aesthetics of Music* (Cambridge, 1993); *Adorno, Modernism and Mass Culture: Essays on Critical Theory and Music* (London, 1996)

Adriana Lecouvreur. Opera in four acts by Cilea to a libretto by Arturo Colautti after Eugène Scribe and Ernest Legouvé's play (Milan, 1902).

Adson, John (*d* London, 29 June 1640). English recorder and cornett player, arranger, and composer. In 1614 he became one of the London waits, a post he held until his death. From 1633 he was also employed as a court musician. His publication *Courtly Masquing Ayres* (1621), a collection of lively dances for instrumental consort, includes arrangements of works by unidentified court composers, and original works by Adson himself.　　　　　　　　　　　　　　　　　　JM

a due (It.). See À DEUX, A DUE, A 2.

Adventures of Mr Brouček, The. See EXCURSIONS OF MR BROUČEK, THE.

Adventures of the Vixen Bystrouška, The. See CUNNING LITTLE VIXEN, THE.

aeolian harp. A stringed instrument sounded by the wind. It goes back to ancient times: it is mentioned in Psalm 137 and in legends of the origins of stringed instruments in many cultures, including the Homeric tradition. The modern aeolian harp is usually a form of *zither, with strings—all tuned to the same pitch—running across a soundbox; it is placed in a window or wherever the wind will blow across it. As the strings vibrate, their different thicknesses make them sound different harmonics, thus producing soft, ethereal chords.　　　　　　　　　　　　　　　　　　JMo

Aeolian mode. The name given by Heinrich Glarean (in his treatise *Dodecachordon*) to the authentic mode on A. See MODE, 2.

Aeolian-Skinner Organ Co. American firm of organ builders founded in South Boston, MA, in 1901 by Ernest M. Skinner (1866–1961). He developed stops imitating orchestral instruments. His firm merged with the Aeolian Co. in 1931 and closed in 1973. Among its organs are those at Grace Cathedral, San Francisco (1934), and the Kennedy Center, Washington, DC (1969).　　　　　　　　　　　　　　　　　　AL

aeoliphone. See WIND MACHINE.

aerophone. A term used in *organology for wind instruments, whether the air is outside the instrument (e.g. *bullroarer) or inside (*wind instruments proper). It does not cover instruments that fit better into other categories, such as those with strings (e.g. *aeolian harp) or wind-blown percussion (e.g. wind chimes). See INSTRUMENTS, CLASSIFICATION OF.　　　　JMo

aesthetics of music. Succinctly, 'aesthetics of music' could be defined as 'speculation on the nature of music excluding the purely physical attributes of sound'. The term 'aesthetics' has been variously defined as a theory of sensuous perception, a study of taste, and a theory of beauty in nature and art; in time it became widely accepted as a concept denoting the philosophical investigation of the theory of art.

　　Questions such as 'What is music?', 'Does music express emotions?', and 'How does music communicate?' traditionally determined the field of the aesthetics of music. Historical, psychological, and sociological considerations, however legitimate in their own right, are not normally understood as forming a part of aesthetic investigation. Yet a question such as 'What is music?' contains a historical and even an anthropological element, and the question 'Does music express emotions?' cannot do without a reference to psychology. It is, however, possible to narrow the field of aesthetics applied to music by asking, 'What is specifically musical in music?', although even this is not entirely free from historical, geographical, and psychological considerations. In addition, the intellectual tools likely to be applied in the argument are those developed in the Western tradition from classical Greek thought to the present day. In many non-Western cultures these issues would be considered largely irrelevant.

　　It is philosophically challenging to explain music's power to evoke a definite reaction in listeners through the material which is unique to the art and has otherwise little or no relevance in real life. Some have seen in the organization of that material a powerful representation of human feelings, others a play of forms in sound.

1. Historical sketch; 2. Conclusion

1. Historical sketch

The earliest recorded ideas on the nature of music came from the disciples of Pythagoras (6th century BC). The discovery that relationships between musical pitches could be represented numerically formed an important link between music on the one hand and arithmetic and astronomy on the other. Music was seen as an earthly reflection of a higher cosmic order, and a link was established between it and morality through the theory of *ethos* ('nature', 'disposition').

Plato maintains (in *Republic*, iii. 12) that music, when properly applied, is an ethical force in education and for this purpose has to be closely controlled against innovations. At the root of his thinking lies the belief that music has a definite content which can be transmitted to the listeners. Aristotle is less critical of music and recognizes its various uses, from a pleasurable activity to a force 'producing a certain effect on the moral character of the soul' (*Politics*, viii. 5). On the other hand, Aristoxenus of Tarentum (4th–3rd century BC) voiced doubt about the theory of *ethos*, while Philodemus of Gadara (1st century BC) maintained that meaning contained in the words sung is erroneously attributed to the music itself. Thus the conflict between 'emotionalism' (or heteronomous aesthetics) and 'formalism' (or autonomous aesthetics) appears to be an old dilemma in European civilization.

The attitude of the early Christian Church towards music rested on an ambivalence: music was indispensable in liturgy, yet was based on sensuous experience; indulgence in long vocal jubilations suggests an acceptance of a pleasurable, hence sinful, activity, yet, because of its non-conceptual nature, music brings humankind into a closer communion with God.

The Aristotelian idea of music as an embodiment of passion played a decisive role in the theoretical foundations of the new genre of opera and in much of the 17th- and 18th-century thought on music. Music was seen as a form of discourse and a means of conveying and evoking emotions, although in order to overcome its abstract nature the principles of musical communication had to be based on borrowings from rhetoric.

In the late 18th and early 19th centuries the increased participation of the bourgeoisie as listeners and amateur music-makers meant that music had to be explained to the new consumers, while the establishment of systematic philosophies in the German cultural tradition guaranteed the importance of general aesthetic theories and encouraged speculation on the nature of music.

Stressing the cognitive nature of art, Immanuel Kant (1724–1804) assigned a lowly position to music in his system of the arts since the absence of clearly conveyed information makes music a mere pleasurable arabesque. Georg Friedrich Wilhelm Hegel (1770–1831), following the Romantic enthusiasm for music, affirmed its importance, placing it among the arts as second only to poetry. Arthur Schopenhauer (1788–1860) built a system of philosophy by contrasting the world of phenomena, or 'representations', with an essence, or the 'will', of which music was a close copy. This is the kernel of the Romantic notion that music is the carrier of hidden meanings and deeply felt emotions ('the universal imageless language of the heart'). An opposite view was held by Eduard Hanslick (1825–1904), who in his *Vom Musikalisch-Schönen* ('On the Musically Beautiful'; 1854) advocated supremacy of instrumental music and of formal principles which cannot mirror the emotions. He is often accused of 'formalism', although he states that forms in music are not rigid or imposed from the outside but adapt themselves to the nature of the musical substance ('the champagne in music has the property of growing with the bottle'). In England, Edmund Gurney (*The Power of Sound*, 1880) came close to Hanslick's stand.

In the early 20th century, as the Romantic aesthetics declined, the autonomist stance found some prominent adherents. Among the composers, Schoenberg negated the importance of subjective feelings, and Stravinsky implicitly classed them as a peripheral quality which wears off in time, leaving the untarnished musical substance to be found in the music of a past era. A belief in a specific, 'ahistorical', quality of music inspired by the school of phenomenological aesthetics shaped the thought of Hans Mersmann, August Halm, Roman Ingarden, and Nicolai Hartmann. This became better known only in a disguised form in the analytical studies of Heinrich Schenker (see ANALYSIS, 3). In the 1940s Susanne Langer (1895–1985) set out an aesthetic theory in which she tried to reconcile Hanslick's notion of musical form with the heteronomist aesthetics by claiming that the emotions do exist in music, but in a symbolized form.

Later, the links with general linguistics and the theory of signs led towards the formation of the *semiotics of music, which attempts to explain the means and the possibilities of musical communication, viewing a musical work as a system of signs. By attaching importance to the link between the work of art and the recipient it reverses the line of investigation characteristic of earlier German aesthetics which tended to lead from the work of art into the metaphysical presuppositions of its existence (see also ANALYSIS, 6).

2. Conclusion

Although the basic issues raised by the aestheticians lead into philosophy of mind, logic, and moral philosophy, the reaction against grandiose complete systems of philosophy of the past means that aesthetics has found itself in a crisis. There is a belief that aesthetics of music, dependent as it is on historical knowledge, can concern itself only with what music once was and not with what it is or what it should be, and that a proliferation of quickly changing systems in experimental music discourages any aesthetic theory. This would be true only if aesthetics were discussing the actualities of musical existence. Since it is within the scope of aesthetics to ask questions about musical potentialities—modes of existence, relationship of composition and performance, degree of fixed and unpredictable elements, and the specific nature of musical time—the discipline has every chance of remaining a live one. Such relatively recent innovations as recorded sound and electronic and computer music, far from limiting the scope of aesthetics, open broad possibilities for speculation on the theme of what music is.   BB

Aevia [Aeuia]. A 'word' confected from the vowels of 'Alleluia'. It was used as an abbreviation in much the same way as was *Evovae*.

affabile (It.). 'Affable', i.e. in a gentle, pleasing manner.

affannato, affannoso (It.). 'Breathless', 'agitated'.

affections, doctrine of (Ger.: *Affektenlehre*). A term formulated in the early 20th century by German musicologists (Hermann Kretzschmar, Arnold Schering) to describe an aesthetic theory of the Baroque period relating to musical expression. Following Ancient Greek and Latin orators who believed that the use of certain modes of *rhetoric influenced the emotions, or affections, of their listeners, the theorist-musicians of the late 17th and early 18th centuries argued that the 'affection' of a text should be reflected in its musical setting through an appropriate choice of key and judiciously crafted qualities of melody, thus arousing the appropriate affection in the listener.

This difficult concept was in its own time the subject of many theoretical treatises, few of which agree in detail. As early as 1602 Caccini had referred to 'moving the affections of the spirit', but the theory's most vocal exponents—Heinichen, Mattheson, F. W. Marpurg, and Quantz—wrote in the first half of the 18th century. They advocated a unity of the affections, claiming that any single piece or movement, whether vocal or instrumental, should encompass only one affection—joy, sorrow, love, hate, anger, etc.—and they enumerated and described different categories of affection, exemplifying ways of setting each to music.

Such a theory was a natural product of an age of rationalism—a desire to impose system and order on human emotional response. Mattheson (*Der vollkommene Capellmeister*, 1739) maintained that 'Everything occurring without praiseworthy affections is nothing, does nothing and means nothing'. The 19th century, with its very different views on creative impulse and spontaneous emotional response, had no place for so formalized and rationalist a theory. Interestingly, the

theory has been partly rehabilitated by the recent interest in the process of narrativity in music.

See also FIGURES, DOCTRINE OF.   JN/BB

Affekt (Ger.). 'Fervour'; *affektvoll*, 'full of fervour'; *mit Affekt*, 'with warmth', 'with passion'. In Germany in the Baroque era the term was used to describe the expressive character of a piece. See also AFFECTIONS, DOCTRINE OF.

Affektenlehre (Ger.). See AFFECTIONS, DOCTRINE OF.

affetto, affetti (It., 'affection', 'affections'). 1. A term that appears in the title of various late 16th- and early 17th-century publications, probably to emphasize the 'affective', 'emotional', character of the music. See AFFECTIONS, DOCTRINE OF.

2. In early violin sonatas, a type of ornament (*tremolo or *arpeggio).

affettuoso, affettuosa (It.). 'Affectionate', 'tender'; *con affetto* (It.), *affectueusement* (Fr.), 'with affection', i.e. warmly. The term was used in the early 17th century by Caccini, Monteverdi, and Frescobaldi, among others, and extensively in the 18th century by Couperin and Leclair, for slow movements; as an independent tempo indication, it falls between *adagio* and *andante*.

affrettando (It.). 'Hurrying'.

Africa, South. See SOUTH AFRICA.

Africaine, L' ('The African Woman'). Opera in five acts by Meyerbeer to a libretto by Eugène Scribe (Paris, 1865); it was begun in 1837 but Meyerbeer was constantly interrupted by changes to the libretto and died the year before it was staged. Subsequent alterations were made to both libretto and score, notably by François-Joseph Fétis, who made cuts to reduce its six-hour duration.

African Sanctus. Work by David Fanshawe for two sopranos, piano, organ, chorus, percussion, amplified lead and rhythm guitars, and tape-recordings made in Africa (London, 1972; revised Toronto, 1978).

Afro-Cuban jazz. A modern style that used a blend of *bebop and Latin American characteristics of Cuban origin. The trumpeter Dizzy Gillespie was one of the first major jazz figures to exploit the style, producing several classic recordings in the 1940s (e.g. *Afro-Cuban Suite*, 1948) while Stan Kenton was popularizing the music in the big-band field with such recordings as *Peanut Vendor* and *Machito* (1947). Tadd Dameron, Charlie Parker, and Bud Powell were others who dabbled in the style.   PGA

Afternoon of a Faun. See Après-midi d'un faune', Prélude à 'L'.

Agende (Ger., from Lat. *agenda*, 'to be done'). 'Liturgy', 'ritual'. The German Protestant Church ritual of service.

Age of Gold, The (*Zolotoy vek*). Ballet in three acts by Shostakovich to a scenario by Aleksandr Ivanovsky; it was choreographed by Semyon Kaplan and Vasily Vainonen (Leningrad, 1930). Shostakovich arranged an orchestral suite from it (op. 22*a*).

Age of Steel, The (*Stal'noy skok*). Ballet in two scenes by Prokofiev; it was choreographed by Leonid Massine (Paris, 1927). Prokofiev arranged a four-movement orchestral suite from it (op. 44*bis*).

agevole (It., 'comfortable'). Lightly and freely.

aggregate. A term used in the analysis of atonal music, usually in the form '12-note aggregate', to denote a brief passage in which each note of the chromatic scale is present once.

agiatamente (It., 'comfortable'). Freely; not to be confused with *agitatamente* (see AGITATO).

agile, agilement (Fr.). 'Agile', 'with agility'.

Agincourt Song. An English song commemorating the country's victory at Agincourt in 1415, when it was probably written; it is for two voices and three-part chorus. The tune has been included in some modern hymnbooks and Walton used it in his film music for *Henry V* (1944).

agitato (It.). 'Agitated', 'restless'; *agitatamente*, 'in an agitated manner'.

Agnus Dei (Lat., 'Lamb of God'). Part of the Ordinary of the *Mass, sung during the Breaking of the Bread. Omitted from Anglican Holy Communion from 1552, it was officially reinstated in the 1960s (see COMMON PRAYER, BOOK OF).

agogic (from Gk. *agōgē*, 'leading'). **1.** A term introduced by Hugo Riemann (*Musikalische Dynamik und Agogik*, Leipzig, 1884) to describe accentuation demanded by the nature of a particular musical phrase rather than by the regular metric pulse of the music (metrical accentuation). For instance, any of the following may be given prominence by a slight expressive lingering conferring the effect of an *accent: the first note, highest note, or final cadence of a phrase; a note significantly higher or lower than the preceding notes and reached by a leap; or a pungent discord about to resolve to a concord.

2. In a wider sense, 'agogic' refers to aspects of expression in performance created by rhythmic modification, e.g. *rallentando*, *accelerando*, rubato, or pause.

Agon. Ballet by Stravinsky, choreographed by George Balanchine (New York, 1957).

Agrell, Johan Joachim (*b* Loth, Ostergotland, 1 Feb. 1701; *d* Nuremberg, 19 Jan. 1765). Swedish composer, violinist, and harpsichordist. The son of a priest, he studied at Uppsala University, where he played in the university orchestra. He worked at Kassel, 1734–46, before obtaining the post of Kapellmeister at Nuremberg. There his responsibilities included directing the music in many of the town's churches, and composing vocal works (now lost) for special occasions. His instrumental music shows a tendency towards the *galant* style, and in his own day he achieved fame as a composer of the newly emerging symphony. He also wrote a number of harpsichord concertos.   LC

agréments (Fr.). A generic term for the 'small ornaments' found in 17th- and 18th-century French music. See ORNAMENTS AND ORNAMENTATION, 3*b*.

Agricola, Alexander (*b c.*1446; *d* Valladolid, Aug. 1506). Franco-Flemish composer. Like many of his contemporaries, he spent much of his career in Italy—at Milan, Florence, and, with the Aragonese court, Naples—though he also worked briefly at Cambrai and on several occasions for the French royal chapel. He joined the household of Philip the Handsome, Duke of Burgundy and King of Castile, in 1500, and it was during a visit to Spain with the court that he died, apparently of the plague. In terms both of quantity and of quality, Agricola's compositions rank on a level with those of Compère and Brumel, being less numerous and on the whole less innovatory than those of Josquin. His secular works—chansons and instrumental pieces—were particularly widely known, although he also wrote masses (Petrucci published a collection of them in 1504), motets, and miscellaneous liturgical items. Much of his output displays a fondness for lively, syncopated, and decorative melodic lines, in contrast to the plainer declamatory style which Josquin was developing at this time.   JM

Agricola, Johann Friedrich (*b* Döbitschen, Saxe-Altenburg, 4 Jan. 1720; *d* Berlin, 2 Dec. 1774). German musicographer, composer, singing teacher, and organist. The son of a government official, he learnt music from an early age. He studied law at Leipzig University, taking lessons at the same time from J. S. Bach, before moving to Berlin in 1741. Writing under the pseudonym Flavio Anicio Olibrio he published pamphlets in 1749 and 1751 on the French and Italian styles, favouring Italian music in opposition to F. W. Marpurg, who advocated the French style. He wrote many other articles, and assisted Jakob Adlung with the publication of his *Musica mechanica organoedi* (Berlin, 1768).

As a composer Agricola found an outlet for his Italianate operas at the court of Frederick the Great; however, he often had difficulty complying with the tastes of his patron. He enjoyed greater success as a singing instructor: his translation of Tosi's *Opinioni de' cantori antichi e moderni* (as *Anleitung zur Singekunst*, 1757) was considered to be of great importance, and Burney reported that he was regarded as the 'best singing master in Germany'. He was also a renowned organist, directed a concert series at his home, and wrote many songs, keyboard pieces, and sacred works.
                                                                                    LC

Agrippina. Opera in three acts by Handel to a libretto by Vincenzo Grimani (Venice, 1709).

Aguilera de Heredia, Sebastián (*b* ?Zaragoza, *c.*1565; *d* Zaragoza, 16 Dec. 1627). Spanish priest and composer. He was organist at the cathedrals of Huesca and Zaragoza. His works include organ pieces, psalms for four voices, and the *Canticum Beatissimae Virginis* (Zaragoza, 1618), 36 settings of the *Magnificat* for from four to eight voices.   WT

aguinaldo (Sp.). See ADORACIÓN.

Ägyptische Helena, Die ('The Egyptian Helen'). Opera in two acts by Richard Strauss to a libretto by Hugo von Hofmannsthal (Dresden, 1928; revised Salzburg, 1933).

ähnlich (Ger.). 'Similar', 'like'.

Aho, Kalevi (*b* Forssa, 9 March 1949). Finnish composer, writer, and teacher. He studied composition with Rautavaara at the Sibelius Academy in Helsinki, writing his First Symphony (1969) while he was still a student; he graduated in 1971. Aho is a prolific and assured composer, with 11 symphonies to his credit. The early ones exhibit a traditionalist concern with counterpoint, of which he is a master; with the Fifth (1975–76) he entered what he called a 'maximalist' phase characterized by orchestral density and urgency of expression; the later symphonies (up to no. 11, 1998–9) show a postmodern openness, subsuming an initial stylistic diversity in a symphonic manner inherited from Bruckner, Sibelius, and Shostakovich. His operas include the monodrama *Avain* ('The Key', 1979) and *Hyönteiselämää* ('Insect Life', 1987), and he has also written a considerable quantity of chamber and vocal music.   MA

Aichinger, Gregor (*b* Regensburg, 1564; *d* Augsburg, 21 Jan. 1628). German composer. In 1578, while at Ingolstadt University, he met Jacob Fugger (of the international banking family), who in 1584 appointed him his household organist at Augsburg. While travelling abroad he became a pupil of Giovanni Gabrieli in Venice. Following conversion to Roman Catholicism, he returned to Germany a priest and held various church posts in Augsburg. His sacred works are mainly in the classic polyphonic style of Lassus; but Venetian influence is evident in his *Cantiones ecclesiasticae* (1607), one of the earliest German publications to include a continuo part, together with instructions about its use in performance.   BS

Aida. Opera in four acts by Verdi to a libretto by Antonio Ghislanzoni after a scenario by Auguste Mariette (Cairo, 1871; Milan, 1872); it was not, as is often supposed, written for the opening of the Suez Canal in 1869, nor commissioned by the Khedive of Egypt to open the new Cairo Opera House, which was inaugurated in 1869 with *Rigoletto*.

air. 1. A term used in England from the 16th century to the 19th to mean a song or melody, for example the *Londonderry Air*. See also AYRE.

2. In France, *air* denoted a solo song with lute accompaniment, again from the 16th century. There were several types, including the *air de cour and the *air à boire. The term could be applied to instrumental as well as vocal music in 17th- and 18th-century stage works, the *airs* providing interludes between passages of accompanied recitative. There were four main types of operatic *air*: the 'dialogue' *air*, with continuo accompaniment, used as an alternative to recitative; the 'monologue' *air*, usually an extended piece on the scale of the Italian aria, reserved for moments of emotional crisis or reflection; the 'maxim' *air*, a lighthearted reflection on the trials of life, often sung by secondary characters; and dance-songs.

3. As in France, in England in the early 17th century the instrumental air formed part of stage entertainments such as *masques (e.g. Adson's *Courtly Masquing Ayres*, 1621).

4. The air found its way into the Baroque and Classical *suite as an optional movement, generally lyrical rather than dance-like. The second movement of Bach's Orchestral Suite no. 3—known today as 'Air on the G String'—is one example.

air à boire (Fr.). 'Drinking song'. A simple type of *air* (see AIR, 2) which enjoyed great popularity in the late 17th and 18th centuries. From 1694 public demand was so great that collections were issued monthly for 30 years. Composers of *airs à boire* included Campra, Charpentier, Couperin, Lully, and Rameau.

air and variations. See VARIATION FORM.

air column. The body of air contained within the *bore of a tubular wind instrument. Sounding a note causes the air column to vibrate; the frequency of the vibrations determines the pitch of the note heard. The acoustic properties of the air column are affected by the shape of the bore (which may be conical or cylindrical) and its length, which may be altered by the use of valves to increase or decrease tubing on brass instruments, or by the opening and closing of side holes in woodwind instruments.   LC

air de cour (Fr., 'court *air*'). A type of short strophic song cultivated in France during the late 16th century and the first half of the 17th. It was usually for four or five unaccompanied voices or for solo voice with lute or keyboard. *Airs de cour* were generally published in collections containing works by several composers. Adrian Le Roy's *Livre d'airs de cour* (1571) was the earliest publication to carry the title. Among the most important composers of the genre were Gabriel Bataille, Michel Lambert, Pierre Guédron, Antoine Boësset, and Étienne Moulinié.

The *air de cour* grew out of the popular homophonic vaudeville (see VAUDEVILLE, 1) and was influenced by the declamatory style of *musique mesurée*. The rhythmic freedom and fluid word-setting characteristic of the genre proved to be of vital importance in the subsequent development of French music. Lully in particular absorbed these elements into his own works, where they played a large part in the establishment of an idiomatic French recitative style.   —/JBE

Air on the G String. The title given to an arrangement (1871) for violin and piano (or strings) by *Wilhemj of the second movement (Air) of Bach's Orchestral Suite no. 3 in D; in the arrangement the melody is transposed to C major so that it can be played exclusively on the lowest (G) string of the violin.

Ais (Ger.). The note A♯; *Aisis*, the note A𝄪.

aisé (Fr.). 'With ease', i.e. unhurried.

Akademie (Ger.). 'Academy'. In the 18th century the term also denoted a concert or recital.

A Kempis, Nicolaes (*b* c.1600; *d* Brussels, *bur.* 11 Aug. 1676). Flemish composer and organist. He was the organist at Ste Gudule, Brussels, taking over from Anthoen van den Kerckhoven in 1626 and being named as his successor on 25 November 1627. He composed four books of *Symphoniae*, which contain the earliest known sonatas written in the Low Countries. The

pieces are scored mostly for strings (though they occasionally call for bassoon, cornett, and trombone) and range from solo sonatas with continuo accompaniment to six-part works. They were probably intended for domestic use. Two of Nicolaes's sons, Thomas [Petrus] and Joannes Florentius, were also organists.   LC

Akhmatova: Requiem. Work (1979–80) by Tavener for solo soprano and baritone and orchestra, to a text combining poems of Anna Akhmatova and prayers for the dead from the Orthodox liturgy.

Akhnaten. Opera in three acts by Glass to a libretto by the composer, Shalom Goldman, Robert Israel, and Richard Riddell (Stuttgart, 1984).

Akkord (Ger.). 'Chord'.

Akzent (Ger.). 'Accent', 'stress'; *akzentuieren*, 'to accentuate', 'to stress'.

Alain, Jehan (Ariste) (*b* Saint Germain-en-Laye, 3 Feb. 1911; *d* Petit-Puy, nr Saumur, 20 June 1940). French composer and organist. His sister is the distinguished organist Marie-Claire Alain (*b* 1926). He studied the organ with Marcel Dupré and composition with Paul Dukas and Jean Roger-Ducasse at the Paris Conservatoire (1927–39). Tragically, he was killed in action early in World War II. His very individual, modally based organ works include the Orient-inspired *Deux Danses à Yavishta* (1934), *Le Jardin suspendu* (1934), and *Variations sur un thème de Clément Jannequin* (1937). The two superb *Fantaisies* (1934 and 1936) are characterized by Skryabinesque mystical harmonies and flickering ostinato patterns. Best known is *Litanies* (1937), in which liturgical-style thematic repetitions culminate in an incandescent climax.   PG/AT

Alaleona, Domenico (*b* Montegiorgio, Ascoli Piceno, 16 Nov. 1881; *d* Montegiorgio, 28 Dec. 1928). Italian composer, conductor, musicologist, and teacher. As a historian and a choral conductor, he led the revival of interest in early Italian choral music. His research into equal divisions of the octave led to the construction of a 'pentaphonic harmonium', which he used in his only opera, *Mirra* (Rome, 1920). He also wrote a Requiem for chorus, and many songs.   ABur

alba (Provençal). A 'dawn song' that describes lovers parting, usually including a dialogue with a watchman who warns them of approaching danger. It was absorbed into the Minnesinger repertory as the *Tagelied*.

Albéniz, Isaac (Manuel Francisco) (*b* Camprodón, Catalunya, 29 May 1860; *d* Cambô-les-Bains, 18 May 1909). Spanish pianist and composer. He made his first public appearance as a pianist in Barcelona at the age of four. Three years later he was refused admission to the

Paris Conservatoire because he was too young, and in 1872 he stowed away on a ship bound for the Americas. After a tour of the USA, where he supported himself by playing the piano, further European travels, and periods of study at the Leipzig and Brussels conservatories, he returned to Barcelona. There he met Felipe Pedrell, who introduced the previously salon-bound pianist to the folk music of his own country. Later, he refined his playing technique with Liszt in Budapest.

An English tour in 1889 earned him enough money to undertake a period of study in Paris with d'Indy and Dukas. In 1890 he returned to London, where he was befriended by the banker Francis Burdett Money-Coutts (Lord Latymer), who paid Albéniz a large stipend to set his English historical and legendary opera librettos. The single success of this collaboration was *Pepita Jiménez* (Barcelona, 1896), a Spanish subject far better suited to the composer's temperament. In 1893 he settled in Paris, where his compositions began to attract attention and respect, though ill health forced him to live in the south of France for most of the last decade of his life.

Albéniz drew his materials from the European salon and Spanish folk music, but—like his friends Debussy and Ravel—he revelled in the enlarged harmonic palette of the Impressionist style, of which he was an early master. His most important works are for his own instrument, and the two *Suites españolas* (1886–9), together with the 12 pieces in four books making up *Iberia* (1906–8), vividly evoke the sights and sounds of his native country while taxing the player's technique to the full. *Iberia*, in particular, with its brilliant instrumental effects, remains a dazzling compendium of rhythmic vigour, harmonic subtlety, and sheer pianistic virtuosity.   WT/CW

📖 W. A. CLARK, *Isaac Albéniz: Portrait of a Romantic* (London, 1999)

Albert, Eugen (Francis Charles) **d'** (*b* Glasgow, 10 April 1864; *d* Riga, 3 March 1932). German pianist and composer, of mixed parentage. He won a scholarship to the National Training School of Music, where he studied the piano with Ernst Pauer. At 17 he also won the Mendelssohn Scholarship, which enabled him to study abroad in Vienna, and in Weimar with Liszt. He was befriended and supported by Brahms and Hanslick, but his increasingly pro-German affiliations lost him the affection of the British public during World War I. His six marriages included a stormy three-year relationship with the pianist Teresa Carreño.

D'Albert's concert works show the influence of Brahms; they include piano music, songs, chamber music, a symphony (1886), two piano concertos (1884, 1893), and a cello concerto (1899). In the 20 operas that increasingly absorbed him the influences are more eclectic. *Die Abreise* (1898) is a charming one-act sentimental comedy reflecting the lighter side of Cornelius, whereas *Tiefland* (1903), his greatest success, skilfully imported the manner of verismo to Germany. Both of these retain some hold on the repertory. *Die toten Augen* (1916) is a post-Wagnerian piece much influenced by Strauss.   WT/JW

Albert, Heinrich (*b* Lobenstein, Thuringia, 8 July 1604; *d* Königsberg [now Kaliningrad], 6 Oct. 1651). German composer. He was a cousin and pupil of Schütz. Initially he studied law at Leipzig, but from 1630 he settled in Königsberg, as cathedral organist. He is important for his contribution to German song, most notably with his *Arien oder Melodien* (1638–50), a large collection of sacred and secular songs with instrumental accompaniment, designed to provide a spiritual resource for family events such as weddings, anniversaries, and funerals. Many of his texts are by Simon Dach, the leader, after Opitz, of the Königsberg poets' circle.

WT/BS

Albert, Prince (Consort) [Franz Karl August Albert Emanuel, Prince of Saxe-Coburg-Gotha] (*b* Rosenau, Coburg, 26 Aug. 1819; *d* London, 14 Dec. 1861). German organist and composer. He married Queen Victoria in 1840. An enthusiastic music lover, composer, and performer in his youth, he tried to mould British musical taste by promoting the German and Viennese Classics and, in particular, the music of Mendelssohn. He did much to expand the court band into a full-size orchestra capable of performing Bach, Schubert, and Mendelssohn at Buckingham Palace and Windsor Castle. He was also director of the Concert of Ancient Music (1846) and was responsible for planting the idea of a national college of music, which eventually materialized in the National Training School (later the RCM).

Prince Albert left about 40 completed songs, with others in draft, along with some church music and the cantata *Invocazione all'armonia*, given several times during the year of the Great Exhibition (1851). His musical style was heavily influenced by Mendelssohn. An edition of his compositions was issued about 1882.

WT/JD1

Albert Herring. Chamber opera in three acts by Britten to a libretto by Eric Crozier adapted from Guy de Maupassant's short story *Le Rosier de Madame Husson* (1888) (Glyndebourne, 1947).

Alberti, Giuseppe Matteo (*b* Bologna, 20 Sept. 1685; *d* Bologna, 1751). Italian violinist and composer (not to be confused with Domenico Alberti, originator of the 'Alberti bass'). He spent his whole career in Bologna, as a violinist at S. Petronio, and from 1734 as acting *maestro*

di cappella at S. Domenico; he was a member of the Accademia Filarmonica and served as its president in various years from 1721. He composed pleasingly tuneful violin concertos and sonatas which were especially popular in England and elsewhere in northern Europe. The concertos, though not posing great technical difficulties, were among the first to show Vivaldi's influence, while the sonatas are more Corellian in style. Alberti also contributed to the development of the Bolognese trumpet sonata repertory.

DA/ER

Alberti bass. A type of accompaniment to a melody, most commonly found in keyboard music, which consists of a series of 'broken chords' treated as shown in Ex. 1. It takes its name from the 18th-century Italian composer Domenico Alberti, in whose harpsichord sonatas it occurs frequently. Although such composers as C. P. E. Bach, Haydn, and Mozart made effective use of the formula, in the hands of the numerous composers of rococo and *galant* keyboard music it soon became stereotyped and commonplace.

Ex. 1

etc.

Albicastro, Henricus [Weissenburg, Johann Heinrich von] (*b* before 1670; *d* after 1738). Composer and violinist, possibly of Swiss origin, resident in the Netherlands. He served as a cavalry officer in the War of the Spanish Succession and registered as a student of music at Leiden University in 1681. He later lived in Amsterdam, where his nine publications of instrumental music appeared. His solo violin sonatas follow the Corellian *sonata da chiesa* pattern and are technically advanced, including German-style double stopping as well as Italianate figurations. Both they and his concertos, which in some ways resemble those of Torelli, are notable for their contrapuntal textures and their use of rich and daring chromatic harmony. Albicastro was acknowledged as an influence by J. J. Quantz, who studied his works along with those of Biber.

DA/ER

Albinoni, Tomaso Giovanni (*b* Venice, 14 June 1671; *d* Venice, 17 Jan. 1751). Italian composer. The son of a prosperous stationer, he initially entered the business himself and held a licence to make and sell playing-cards; by the time of his father's death in 1709, however, he was no longer effectively involved with it, styling himself 'musico veneto'. Nothing is known of his musical education, but he may have been a pupil of Legrenzi. He never held a paid professional position as

a musician in Venice, preferring to remain a dilettante, though he lacked the social status and wider artistic and cultural interests normally associated with the term. His contacts with other Venetian musicians were therefore limited, and his own reputation as a musician depended entirely on his activities as a composer (although, his wife being a well-known singer, he is said to have run a successful singing school).

Judging by the dedicatees of his publications and the opera commissions he received, however, Albinoni enjoyed the patronage of European aristocrats and princes of the church, including Cardinal Ottoboni, the Duke of Mantua, Grand Prince Ferdinand III of Tuscany, Emperor Charles VI, and the Elector of Bavaria. In 1722 the last named invited him to Munich to produce an opera for a royal wedding. He composed nearly 50 operas, most of them for Venice (and now lost), and published ten collections of instrumental music; the last of these appeared in 1735. In 1741 he seems to have given up composition altogether—indeed, nothing is known of the final ten years of his life, except that he was bedridden for the last two.

In his own time Albinoni was famous throughout Europe, especially for his sonatas and concertos, which were particularly popular with amateurs and regarded as on a par with those of Corelli and Vivaldi; his solo cantatas also had a considerable following but are less well known today. Perhaps because of his relative professional isolation he developed a distinctive musical language, which combines a pronounced melodic gift with an individual approach to chromatic harmony and a greater fondness for contrapuntal textures than displayed by many of his contemporaries, for example Vivaldi. His violin writing, however, is more conservative than Vivaldi's, especially in its use of higher positions. The much-performed and recorded G minor Adagio ascribed to Albinoni is a modern composition by Remo Giazotto based on a fragment of one of his works.

DA/ER

📖 M. TALBOT, *Tomaso Albinoni: The Venetian Composer and his World* (Oxford, 1990)

alborada (Sp.). 'Morning song'. The word has come to be applied to a type of instrumental music, sometimes played on bagpipes and small drum, in which rhythmic freedom is a striking characteristic. Rimsky-Korsakov (*Spanish Capriccio*) and Ravel (*Alborada del gracioso*, the fourth of the *Miroirs* for piano) have made use of the genre. See also ALBA; AUBADE.

Alborado del gracioso ('The Fool's Morning Song'). Piano piece by Ravel, the fourth of his *Miroirs* (1905); he orchestrated it in 1918.

Albrechtsberger, Johann Georg (*b* Klosterneuburg, 3 Feb. 1736; *d* Vienna, 7 March 1809). Austrian organist, composer, theorist, and teacher. After studies in his home town, he went to the school at Melk Abbey and subsequently studied philosophy at the Jesuit seminary in Vienna. About 1775 he became organist at Raab (now Győr) in Hungary, later holding similar posts in Lower Austria and at Melk. He was made second court organist in Vienna in 1772 and was promoted to first organist in 1792. A year later he was appointed Kapellmeister at St Stephen's Cathedral, remaining there until his death. Albrechtsberger was a follower of the 'old style': he was a master of counterpoint, with an understanding of Bach's techniques as well as Palestrina's. He was a prolific composer, of church music and instrumental works, and author of an influential treatise on composition. He taught a whole generation of Viennese musicians, including Beethoven (who, like Mozart, thought highly of him) and Hummel.

DA

Albright, William (*b* Gary, IN, 20 Oct. 1944; *d* Ann Arbor, MI, 17 Sept. 1998). American composer, organist, and pianist. He studied with Ross Lee Finney and George Rochberg at the University of Michigan, then with Messiaen in Paris (1968–9) before he returned to Michigan to complete his graduate studies and, in 1970, join the faculty. His discovery, during his student years, of ragtime and stride piano music was a revelation. He performed and recorded a great deal of this repertory, and it influenced his composing. In the field of organ music—sometimes allied to ragtime in his exuberant style—he expanded the repertory not only with his own works but through commissioning other composers.

PG

Album für die Jugend ('Album for the Young'). Schumann's op. 68 (1848), for piano, a collection of pieces for young players.

album-leaf (Fr.: *feuille d'album*; Ger.: *Albumblatt*, pl. *Albumblätter*). A 19th-century title for a short instrumental piece, usually of an intimate character and dedicated to a friend or patron. Album-leaves were generally written for piano, e.g. Schumann's *Albumblätter* op. 124 or his *Bunte Blätter* op. 99.

Alceste. Opera in three acts by Gluck to an Italian libretto by Ranieri Calzabigi after Euripides (Vienna, 1767); Gluck made a revised French version with a libretto translated by Marie François Louis Gand Leblanc Roullet (Paris, 1776). In the preface to the score of the Italian version, Gluck outlined his ideas for operatic reform. Euripides' story was also used for operas by

Lully (1674), Handel (1727), Anton Schweitzer (1773), and Wellesz (1924).

Alcina. Opera in three acts by Handel to an anonymous libretto after Ariosto's *Orlando furioso* (1516) (London, 1735).

Aldeburgh Festival. English music festival established in 1948. See FESTIVALS, 2.

aleatory music. Music in which chance or indeterminacy are compositional elements. The term gained currency during the second half of the 20th century to define the kind of music referred to by Pierre *Boulez in his article 'Alea' (*Nouvelle revue française*, 59, 1957). In Latin, 'alea' is a die or dice, and Boulez described 'a preoccupation, not to say obsession, with chance' among composers of his generation. What was implied was a reaction against the impossibly precise and strict notational conventions of postwar avant-garde composition, in favour of allowing an element of freedom of choice for interpreters of compositional texts. This might involve varying the order of precisely notated events, or, more radically, determining the contents of events themselves in the light of new notational practices which avoided specifying every detail of pitch, rhythm, and dynamic (see Boulez, Piano Sonata no. 3, 1955–7; *Stockhausen, *Klavierstück XI*, 1956).

In these terms, aleatory music is part of that experimental impulse which flourished after 1945. Inspired in particular by John *Cage, it explored ways of renewing progressive initiatives in the belief that earlier 20th-century radicalism, centring on Schoenbergian atonality and 12-note technique, had failed to maintain its initial momentum, lapsing into neo-classical decadence (see INDETERMINATE MUSIC). AW

Aleko. Opera in one act by Rakhmaninov to a libretto by Vladimir Ivanovich Nemirovich-Danchenko after Pushkin's *The Gypsies* (1824) (Moscow, 1893).

Alessandro. Opera in three acts by Handel to a libretto by Paolo Antonio Rolli adapted from Ortensio Mauro's *La superbia d'Alessandro* (1690) (London, 1726); it was revived as *Rossane* (London, 1743).

Alexander Balus. Oratorio (1748) by Handel to a text compiled by Thomas Morell.

Alexander Nevsky. Cantata (1939) by Prokofiev, for mezzo-soprano, chorus, and orchestra, a setting of a text by the composer and Vladimir Lugorsky; it is a reworking of the music Prokofiev wrote for Sergey Eisenstein's film of the same name (1938).

Alexander's Feast. Handel's setting (1736) of Dryden's *Ode for St Cecilia's Day* (1697) with additions from

Newburgh Hamilton's *The Power of Music*; Mozart later reorchestrated it.

Alfano, Franco (*b* Posillipo, nr Naples, 8 March 1875; *d* San Remo, 27 Oct. 1954). Italian composer. He studied at the Naples and Leipzig conservatories. His first great success came with the opera *Risurrezione* (Turin, 1904, after Tolstoy), which betrays the influence of earlier verismo composers. *La leggenda di Sakùntala* (Bologna, 1921, rev. 1952) is an exotic opera owing much to *fin de siècle* French models. He also wrote ballets, orchestral works, and chamber music. Alfano is now chiefly remembered for having completed Puccini's *Turandot* from the composer's sketches.   PG/RP

Alfonso und Estrella. Opera in three acts by Schubert to a libretto by Franz von Schober (Weimar, 1854). Its overture was also used for *Rosamunde* but is not the piece known as *Rosamunde* overture (which was composed for *Die Zauberharfe*).

Alfred. Masque by Arne to a libretto by James Thomson and David Mallett (Cliveden, now in Berkshire, 1740); it contains the song 'Rule, Britannia!'. Arne expanded it from two to three acts and revised it; it was performed as an oratorio and several times during the 1950s on the London stage.

Alfvén, Hugo (Emil) (*b* Stockholm, 1 May 1872; *d* Falun, 8 May 1960). Swedish composer, conductor, and violinist. He studied at the Royal Conservatory in Stockholm (1887–91), then had private composition lessons with Johan Lindegren. After continuing his studies abroad, he worked as a choral conductor and as musical director of the Uppsala University orchestra. Alfvén's choral output is extensive, but apart from the oratorio *Herrans bön* ('The Lord's Prayer', 1901) he is best known today for his five symphonies and programmatic orchestral pieces, for example *Midsommarvaka* ('Midsummer Vigil', 1903), in which an essentially late Romantic style is freshened by his imaginative use of Swedish folk tunes.   PG/SJ

Alison, Richard. See ALLISON, RICHARD.

Ali-Zadeh, Franghiz (Ali Aga Kïzï) (*b* Baku, 28 May 1947). Azerbaijani composer and pianist. She studied composition with Kara Karayev and the piano with Khalilov at the Azerbaijan State Conservatory and later taught there, becoming professor in 1996. As a pianist she has promoted new music by Russian and other European composers. In 1992 she moved to Turkey. Her works incorporate European and traditional Azerbaijani stylistic elements, and include *Gabil Sajahy* for cello and piano (1979), a ballet *Empty Cradle* (1993), film scores, and vocal and instrumental chamber pieces.   JK

Alkan [Morhange], (Charles-)**Valentin** (*b* Paris, 30 Nov. 1813; *d* Paris, 29 March 1888). French pianist and composer, of Jewish descent. He was one of the most fascinating and puzzling figures of Romantic music. A child prodigy, he won the first prize for *solfège* at the Paris Conservatoire when he was seven. A prominent streak of misanthropy and shyness in his nature resulted in his concert career being sporadic. He rarely played outside Paris, and retired from the concert platform for long periods. He was a virtuoso of astonishing technical ability with a very wide repertory. Like that of Chopin, with whom he enjoyed a good friendship, Alkan's musical output was centred almost exclusively on the piano (a Symphony in B minor from 1844 is lost, two cantatas entered for the Prix de Rome at the Paris Conservatoire remain unpublished, but one of the few other works not to feature the piano—the *Marcia funebre sulla morte d'un papagallo*, 'Funeral March on the Death of a Parrot'—at least evinces a sense of the ridiculous). His early music is almost entirely in the brilliant but vapid style of Kalkbrenner and Herz, but from the *Trois morceaux dans le genre pathétique* (1837) his compositions display more individuality and imagination.

Alkan's most significant works include the *Grande sonate: Les quatre âges* (1848), a novel four-movement work in progressive tonality (B minor/major, D♯ minor/F♯ major, G major, G♯ minor) which follows a man's life from the age of 20 (a dashing scherzo) to a worryingly premature decrepitude at the age of 50 (the fourth movement, entitled 'Prométhée enchaîné' and directed to be performed 'extrèmement lent'). In between is a cinematic second movement (30 years—'Quasi Faust'), an adapted sonata form, the themes of which bear a passing resemblance to those in Liszt's sonata of a few years later, and at the climax of which two hands have to cope with the demands of a seven-voice fugue. The 'heureux ménage' of the third movement portrays a happy family man of 40, cleansed of his Faustian angst and surrounded by 'les enfants' in semiquavers, with whom he says a prayer before packing them off to bed. The whole is rarely performed, but the second movement has been played on its own as an occasional *tour de force*. The much later *Sonatine* (1861), more concise than the *Grande sonate*, lacks programmatic references but still represents a daunting technical challenge, as do the *12 études* in all the major keys op. 35 (1847).

Alkan's greatest work, however, is the companion set to op. 35—the *12 études* in all the minor keys op. 39 (1857). This vast collection is more comparable to Bach's *Clavier-Übung* than a conventional set of studies, comprising an overture, a symphony (in four movements), and a concerto (in three movements), along with a 'Scherzo diabolico' and two additional pieces—'Comme le vent' and 'En rythme molossique'. As the movements of the symphony and concerto are individual studies, the key sequence of both pieces is unconventional, as is the sheer scale of the music (the first movement of the concerto lasts nearly half an hour). All the hallmarks of Alkan's mature style are here. Although his harmony is mainly diatonic, the music abounds with acerbic dissonances caused by the inflexibility of the part-writing. Alkan rarely compromises the logic of his counterpoint, and a similar inflexibility was noted in his playing, which avoided the indulgent rubato of many of his contemporaries. His use of rhythm and metre was also individual; his music is full of repetitive ostinato rhythms, but an interest in the Basque *zorcico*—a dance with five beats in the bar— stimulated two impromptus with this time signature and an isolated example with a seven-beat metre.

Melodically, Alkan was powerfully influenced by Mendelssohn, Schumann, and especially Chopin, but his music rarely shows the lyrical gifts of these composers. This may be the most important reason why it has remained on the periphery of the repertory, in spite of the intellectual command of his finest works. His music was greatly admired by Liszt and Busoni. The short, more accessible lyric pieces, in spite of a few intriguing examples (such as 'Heraclitus and Democritus'), rarely show Alkan at his best; but the punishing difficulty and epic length of his great works ensure that they will be rarely performed, except by pianists with the requisite technique, stamina and—not least—spare time. KH

📖 R. Smith, *Alkan*, 2 vols. (London, 1976–87) · B. François-Sappey and J. Arnould (eds.), *Charles Valentin Alkan* (Paris, 1991)

all', alla (It.). 'To the', 'at the', i.e. in the manner of, e.g. *alla zingarese*.

alla breve (It.). An indication meaning 'double the speed', so that, for example, 4/4 is given the effect of 2/2 (i.e. the basic time unit becomes the minim, rather than the crotchet shown in the time signature).

alla mente (It.). An improvised passage.

allant (Fr.). 1. 'Going', i.e. *andante*; *un peu plus allant*, 'a little more quickly'.

2. 'Continuing', e.g. *allant grandissant*, 'continuing to grow', i.e. getting louder.

alla Palestrina (It.). 'In the style of Palestrina'. By the 17th century this had come to be termed the *stile antico* or *stile osservato*. It was revived in the 19th century by the *Cecilian Movement. The Danish scholar Knud Jeppesen was the first to make a detailed analysis of Palestrina's polyphony (*The Style of Palestrina and the*

Dissonance, Eng. trans. 1927, 2/1946), which had a far-reaching influence on the teaching of counterpoint.

allargando (It.). 'Broadening', i.e. becoming slower, often with an accompanying crescendo.

alla turca (It., 'in the Turkish style'). A term applied to music of the Classical period composed in a supposedly Turkish style, often involving percussion instruments, derived from the traditions of *janissary music. Notable examples are Mozart's Rondo alla turca (Piano Sonata in A k331/300i) and *Die Entführung aus dem Serail*. SS

alla zingarese (It.). 'In the Gypsy style'.

alla zoppa (It., 'lame', 'limping'). 1. A term used in the 17th century to describe dance movements in syncopated rhythm.

2. A term used more specifically to describe a rhythm where the second quaver of a 2/4 bar is accentuated (Ex. 1).

Ex. 1

alle (Ger.). 'All', i.e. tutti (see TUTTO).

allegramente (It.), **allégrement** (Fr.). 'Brightly'; see ALLEGRO.

allegretto (It., dim. of *allegro*). A tempo faster than *andante* but slower than *allegro* and in a lighter style. The term is also used for a short piece or movement with the tempo marked *allegretto* or *allegro*.

Allegri, Gregorio (*b* 1582; *d* Rome, 7 Feb. 1652). Italian composer and singer. After spending his early years as a choirboy and then as a tenor at the Roman church of S. Luigi dei Francesi, he became a pupil of G. M. Nanino in 1600. Various posts as singer and composer followed, culminating in his appointment as a tenor in the papal choir. He wrote a great deal of church music in both concertato and contrapuntal styles, but his fame rests on a setting of the *Miserere* which was sung in the Sistine Chapel each year during Holy Week. Ironically, the setting is in an unremarkable *falsobordone* style, its interest resting almost entirely on the ornaments traditionally added by the singers, and therefore presumably not by Allegri. These passages were kept a papal secret until 1840, but Mozart copied them down from memory after two hearings (or maybe only one) when he was 14, a considerable feat. DA/TC

allegro (It.). 'Bright', 'lively'. The term was originally used as an expression mark rather than a tempo indication, e.g. *allegro e presto*, *andante allegro*, but it now simply means 'quick'. It is also used for a fast piece or movement, particularly the first movement, in sonata form, of a sonata, symphony, or similar multi-movement work.

Allegro, il Penseroso ed il Moderato, L'. Choral work (1740) by Handel to a text by Charles Jennens partly after Milton.

allein (Ger.). 'Alone'; e.g. *eine Violine allein*, 'one solo violin'.

alleluia. The Latin form of the Hebrew exclamation 'hallelujah' ('Praise the Lord'). It appears in the Hebrew Bible as a superscription to 20 psalms, indicating its probable use as their refrain in the Temple of Jerusalem. Subsequently, it was used widely in the worship of the early Christian Church as an acclamation and a response. In the Latin West 'alleluia' came to be associated especially with the Paschal season, but in the Greek East it was sung throughout the liturgical year in joyful and penitential contexts. At the Byzantine service of Orthros, for example, it both adorns the psalms of the Polyeleos on feasts and replaces the opening responsory 'The Lord is God' during solemn fasts. With the single exception of Holy Saturday, an alleluiarion, i.e. an alleluia (originally melismatic) with verses, is sung at every Eastern Orthodox Divine Liturgy between the Apostolic reading and the Gospel. The Byzantine repertory of alleluiaria appears to have been borrowed by the Roman Church in the later 7th or early 8th century. In addition to its specialized use during Old Roman Paschal Vespers, it became traditional as a part of the Proper of the Roman Mass, sung between the gradual and the Gospel. In penitential seasons and in Requiem Masses it is replaced by the *tract; on the eves of Easter and Pentecost both the alleluia and the tract are sung; and in the period after the Saturday in Easter Week two alleluias are sung, rather than a gradual and an alleluia.   —/ALi

Alleluiasymphonie. Haydn's Symphony no. 30 in C major (1765), so called because part of an Easter plainchant alleluia is quoted in the first movement.

allemande (Fr., 'German'; It.: *alemana, allemanda*) [alman, almaine]. A couple dance popular from the early 16th century to the late 18th; as an instrumental form it was one of the four standard movements of the Baroque *suite. Music for the allemande first appears in books of dances (e.g. those published by Phalèse and Susato); it was in moderate duple time and was frequently followed by a more lively afterdance in triple time (the 'tripla').

The instrumental form of the allemande (as opposed to the dance) developed from the 17th century onwards; there are examples for ensembles and solo instruments such as the lute, guitar, and keyboard (the Fitzwilliam Virginal Book contains over 20). As part of the Baroque suite, it was often followed by a courante using the same thematic material (e.g. Handel's keyboard Suite in D minor), and was generally in quadruple time with a flowing, imitative character.

By the beginning of the 19th century, 'à l'allemande' meant simply any dance 'in the German style', for example the ländler (as in Beethoven's Bagatelles op. 119).   —/JBe

Allen, Sir Hugh (Percy) (*b* Reading, 23 Dec. 1869; *d* Oxford, 17 Feb. 1946). English conductor, organist, and educationist. After leaving Reading School he became assistant organist at Chichester Cathedral. An organ scholarship at Christ's College, Cambridge, in 1892 prepared him for posts at St Asaph (1897–8), Ely (1898–1900), and New College, Oxford (1901–18). On Parry's death in 1918 he was appointed director of the RCM; the same year he also succeeded Walter Parratt as professor of music at Oxford. He retired from the RCM in 1937 but retained his position at Oxford until his death in a road accident. An able choral conductor, he worked with both the London and Oxford Bach Choirs. Along with Elgar and Nikisch, he directed the Leeds Festival of 1913.   DA/JDi

📖 C. BAILEY, *Hugh Percy Allen* (London, 1948)

allentando, allentamente (It.). 'Slowing down'; see also RALLENTANDO.

Allison [Alison], **Richard** (*fl* 1588–1608). English composer. He appears to have been a private musician to the nobility and aristocracy; his patrons included Ambrose Dudley, Earl of Warwick, and Sir John Scudamore. Allison composed imaginative works for mixed consorts of instruments, and more sober settings of metrical psalms, some of which (published in 1599) unusually have accompanying parts for lute, orpharion, cittern, and bass viol.   JM

allmählich (Ger.). 'Gradually'.

All-Night Vigil. A composite service of monastic origin celebrated in the Byzantine rite before a Sunday or festal Eucharist. Originally featuring the entire psalter, it now encompasses the Palestinian offices of Vespers, Matins, and Prime. Choral settings of the resurrectional vigil of Saturday evening include those by Tchaikovsky, Rakhmaninov, and Tavener.   ALi

allo. Abbreviation of *allegro.

all'ongarese (It., 'in Hungarian style'). Music in the 'Hungarian' style, i.e. based on Gypsy dances, became very popular in the early 19th century, and composers including Beethoven and Schubert wrote piano pieces 'all'ongarese'. Later in the century the Hungarian dances of Liszt, Joachim, and Brahms gave new impetus to the popularity of the Hungarian style.

alman [almain]. See ALLEMANDE.

Alma Redemptoris mater. See ANTIPHONS OF THE BLESSED VIRGIN MARY.

Almira. Opera in three acts by Handel to a libretto by Friedrich Christian Feustking after an Italian text by Giulio Pancieri (Hamburg, 1705).

Alpensinfonie, Eine ('An Alpine Symphony'). Tone-poem, op. 64 (1911–15), by Richard Strauss; in 22 sections, it describes a day in the mountains and is scored for an orchestra of over 150, including wind and thunder machines.

alphorn. A long wooden trumpet of the Swiss and Austrian Alps. It is made by splitting a young tree in half, hollowing the two halves, and reuniting them, usually with an airtight covering of bark wound round them. Similar instruments are played in Scandinavia, the Balkans, South America, and West Africa. The instrument is normally associated with herdsmen in the high mountains, but lowland versions exist in the marshes of the Netherlands and on the Russian–Polish borders. The Swiss calls have been copied by many composers, including Beethoven, Brahms, Rossini, and Wagner.

al segno (It., 'to the sign'). An indication to go to the sign (𝄋), meaning either 'return to the sign' (i.e. the same as *dal segno*), or 'continue until you reach the sign'. See also DA CAPO.

Also sprach Zarathustra ('Thus Spake Zoroaster'). Tone-poem, op. 30 (1895–6), by Richard Strauss, based on Friedrich Nietzsche's poem of the same name. Delius set 11 sections of the poem in *A *Mass of Life*.

alt. 1 (It.). 'High'; term for the notes of the octave in the range g' to f'', which are said to be *in alt* (those in the octave above are said to be *in altissimo*). It is usually used with reference to the voice.

2 (Ger.). 'Alto' (contralto) voice. As a prefix to the names of instruments, it signifies the alto voice of a family.

alta (It.). 1. 'High'.

2. A 15th-century dance form, the equivalent of the *saltarello.

3. A standard loud music (*alta musica*) ensemble in the 15th century, consisting of two (sometimes three) shawms and a slide trumpet or, later, a sackbut. See also HAUT, BAS.

Altenberglieder (*Fünf Orchesterlieder nach Ansichts-kartentexten von Peter Altenberg*). Five songs for voice and orchestra, op. 4 (1912), by Berg to picture-postcard texts by Peter Altenberg (pseudonym of Richard Englander, 1862–1919). Schoenberg conducted the first performance of two of them in Vienna in 1913 but they caused such a hostile disturbance that the rest of the programme had to be abandoned; they were not performed complete until 1952, in Vienna.

Altenburg, Johann Ernst (*b* Weissenfels, 15 June 1734; *d* Bitterfeld, 14 May 1801). German trumpeter, organist, and theorist. The son of a military trumpeter, Johann Caspar Altenburg (1689–1761), Johann Ernst was taught to play in the high clarino register of the trumpet as an apprentice in 1752. He became a freeman of the Guild of Trumpeters, only to find that he had little prospect of employment. He therefore studied the organ but had the chance to practise his old instrument again during the Seven Years War, being employed as a field trumpeter in the French army. At the end of the war he reverted to playing the organ but was unable to find any position more important than that of organist in various small village churches. He is best known for his treatise (Halle, 1795) on the 'heroic and musical trumpeter's and kettledrummer's art', which provides valuable information on trumpet technique in the late Baroque period.   DA/LC

altered chord. A chord which has one or more of its notes chromatically altered by accidentals foreign to the key. The most common altered chords are the *Neapolitan 6th and the three kinds of *augmented 6th.

alternatim (Lat., 'alternately'). The term used to describe performance by two (occasionally more) performers or groups of performers in alternation. It is most commonly found in church worship in the singing of psalms and canticles, where alternate groups of singers have performed alternate verses since the late 4th century, a manner of performance that survives in Christian liturgy to this day. This is known as antiphonal psalmody.

Another type of alternation, even more ancient, contrasted a soloist with congregation or choir. The soloist sang the verses of the psalm and the others responded with a refrain. Uses of this format, known as responsorial psalmody, include the prokeimenon and alleluiarion of the Byzantine Divine Liturgy, and the gradual, tract, and alleluia of the Roman Mass.

From the 10th century onwards, it was customary in the West to compose polyphonic settings of the soloists' portions of responsorial psalmody (as in the remarkable collections of polyphony from Winchester, late 10th century, and Notre Dame of Paris, late 12th century). When choirs became capable of singing part-music, it was their sections which were set polyphonically (as in compositions by Taverner, Tallis, and Sheppard).

Stanzaic genres such as hymns have very often been performed *alternatim*. Again, polyphonic might alternate with plainsong verses (as in the hymns and sequences by Dufay).

From the 15th century, the organ was increasingly used as a substitute for vocal polyphony (see VERSET). The most notable repertory of *alternatim* organ music is from 17th- and 18th-century France (by such composers as François Couperin and Grigny). DH/ALi

alternativo (It.), **alternativement** (Fr.). A term often used in 18th-century dance music (e.g. in the bourrées of Bach's suites) for a contrasting middle section, later known as 'Trio'. Sometimes the term is applied to the entire piece, in which case it apparently implies that the two contrasting sections may be 'alternated' at the performer's discretion.

Althorn (Ger.). The E♭ *tenor horn.

altiste (Fr.). 1. 'Viola player'.
2. Alto (contralto) singer.

alto (It., 'high'). 1. For the male alto, see ALTO VOICE.
2. A low-register female voice, properly referred to as *contralto. (In the standard choir grouping SATB, the A usually refers to the contralto part but can also denote the male-voice part.)
3. The middle-pitched member of a family of instruments, with a range lower than treble or soprano and higher than tenor.
(Fr.). 4. 'Viola'.

alto clef. See CLEF.

alto horn. The American name for the English E♭ *tenor horn.

Alto Rhapsody. The name by which Brahms's Rhapsody op. 53 (1869), for alto voice, male chorus, and orchestra, is known; the text is from Johann Wolfgang von Goethe's *Harzreise im Winter* ('Winter Journey through the Harz Mountains').

alto voice. The male alto has a range of some two octaves, from about F below middle C to the soprano *e″* or even *f″*, although it is rare to find a singer who can sing throughout this range with ease, some concen-

trating on the upper registers, others on the lower. The male alto is sometimes distinguished from the *countertenor on the grounds that the former is a 'natural' high tenor, using the head voice (see VOICE, 4) with a powerful, even heroic, sound, while the latter is produced as a *falsetto, tending towards the lower part of the range and having a comparatively weak sound; but usually the two terms are interchangeable.

The revival of the male alto in the 20th century was due largely to the talents of Alfred Deller (1912–79), for whom the part of Oberon in Britten's *A Midsummer Night's Dream* was conceived. Outstanding among Deller's British successors have been James Bowman, Paul Esswood, and Michael Chance. Prominent male altos from Europe and the USA have included Russell Oberlin, Jochen Kowalski, Andreas Scholl, and David Daniels. In the latter part of the 20th century the male alto voice became closely associated with the revival of Baroque opera, especially the works of Handel.

—/RW

altus (Lat., 'high'). In early vocal music, the abbreviated form of *contratenor altus* ('high [part] against the tenor'), the voice part immediately above the tenor in a vocal ensemble. See CONTRATENOR.

Alwyn, William (*b* Northampton, 7 Nov. 1905; *d* Southwold, 11 Sept. 1985). English composer, flautist, and teacher. He studied under J. B. McEwen at the RAM (1920–3), where he later taught composition (1926–55). In 1926 he joined the LSO as a flautist. He drew a veil over the works he wrote before 1939 (which included concertos, several string quartets, and a large-scale oratorio, *The Marriage of Heaven and Hell*, of 1936), considering them technically inferior. After 1939 his creative output was dominated by five symphonies, together with operas, songs, and chamber pieces. He also produced scores for over 120 documentary films and 69 feature films, the most important of which were *Desert Victory* (1943), *Odd Man Out* (1946), and *The Fallen Idol* (1948). His artistic apologia is enshrined in the essay-poem *Daphne, or The Pursuit of Beauty*, written in retirement at Southwold in 1972. JDi

📖 F. ROUTH, 'William Alwyn', *Contemporary British Music* (London, 1970), 55–69 · S. CRAGGS and A. POULTON, *William Alwyn: A Catalogue of his Music* (Hindhead, 1985) [incl. brief biography]

Alyab'yev, Aleksandr Aleksandrovich (*b* Tobolsk, Western Siberia, 4/15 Aug. 1787; d Moscow, 22 Feb./6 March 1851). Russian composer. He led a colourful life, seeing active military service during the war against Napoleon and marching with the Russian army on Dresden and Paris in 1812. But in 1825 he was found guilty of manslaughter (having apparently struck an opponent during a card game) and after a three-year imprisonment was exiled to his native Siberia. In the early 1830s he was allowed to travel to the Caucasus for health reasons, but he later moved further north to Orenburg and finally settled in Moscow.

A prolific and enterprising composer, Alyab'yev is known chiefly for his gentle, folk-tinged song *Solovey* ('The Nightingale', 1826), which several singers—among them Adelina Patti and Pauline Viardot—later performed in the Singing Lesson scene of Rossini's *Il barbiere di Siviglia*; it was also transcribed for piano by Liszt (1842), formed the basis of a set of piano variations by Glinka (1833), and was reused by Alyab'yev himself in the slow movement of his Third String Quartet (1825). His chamber works largely conform to the idioms of the day, but some (like the Third Quartet) distinguish themselves by their use of fresh rhythms and bold harmony. Of his stage music, only the vaudevilles were performed during his lifetime, while his operas remained in manuscript.   GN/MF-W

alzato [alzati] (It., from *alzare*, 'to raise', 'to lift off'). A direction to remove, for example, a mute in instrumental playing.

Alzira. Opera in a prologue and two acts by Verdi to a libretto by Salvadore Cammarano after Voltaire's play *Alzire, ou Les Américains* (1736) (Naples, 1845).

amabile (It.). 'Amiable', 'lovable'.

Amadei, Filippo (*fl* 1690–1730). Italian composer and cellist. He was active in Rome as an instrumentalist under the patronage of Cardinal Ottoboni from 1690 to about 1711, and also composed cantatas and oratorios. By 1719 he was giving concerts in London, where he became known as 'Sigr Pippo'. In 1720 he joined the orchestra of the Royal Academy of Music under Handel's direction. The opera *Muzio Scevola*, performed in 1721, was composed jointly by Amadei, Giovanni Bononcini, and Handel, and Amadei also wrote arias for other Academy productions. He probably returned to Rome about 1723, and may have served Cardinal Ottoboni until 1729.   DA/ER

Amadigi di Gaula ('Amadis of Gaul'). Opera in three acts by Handel to an anonymous libretto adapted from Antoine Houdar de Lamotte's libretto *Amadis de Grèce* (1699) (London, 1715).

Amahl and the Night Visitors. Opera in one act by Gian Carlo Menotti to his own libretto; it was the first television opera (NBC, New York, 1951; staged Bloomington, IN, 1952).

amarevole, amarezza (It.). 'Bitterly', 'bitterness'.

Amati. Italian family of violin makers who worked in Cremona. Andrea (*b* before 1511; *d* 1577) originated and perfected the violin, viola, and cello. His sons Antonio (*c*.1540–1607) and Girolamo (*c*.1561–1630) experimented with shape. Girolamo's son Nicola (1596–1684) was the finest craftsman, whose best instruments (the 'Grand Amatis') were slightly wider and extremely responsive; his pupils included Andrea *Guarneri and Antonio *Stradivari.   AL

ambitus (Lat., 'circuit'). The range of a melody in Gregorian chant.

Ambros, August Wilhelm (*b* Mauth [now Vysoké Mýto, nr Prague], 17 Nov. 1816; *d* Vienna, 26 June 1876). Austrian writer on music. He was a distinguished lawyer and civil servant in Prague and subsequently Vienna. He had a passion for music and wrote a great deal of music journalism culminating in an outstanding history of music in three volumes (Leipzig, 1862–8); two more volumes were added posthumously from his notes and transcriptions. He lectured extensively and was involved with numerous projects, including the Central Commission for the Study and Preservation of Artistic and Historical Monuments, and the St Cecilia Association. He was among the first to recognize the greatness of many Renaissance composers.
          DA/LC

Ambrosian chant. See Beneventan chant.

âme (Fr., 'soul'). Soundpost.

Amen (Heb., 'so be it'). The terminal word of prayer in Jewish, Christian, and Muslim worship. It has been extended many times by composers into a lengthy composition, for example the 'Amen Chorus' of Handel's *Messiah*. Shorter settings have been made for liturgical use. The so-called *Dresden Amen was composed by J. G. Naumann for use in the royal chapel at Dresden (and was also used throughout Saxony); Wagner introduced it into *Parsifal*, and Mendelssohn into his 'Reformation' Symphony.

Amen cadence. See cadence.

amener (Fr., 'to lead'). A 17th-century dance in triple time, found in the instrumental suites of Heinrich Biber and J. C. F. Fischer. The term *amener* probably derives from the *branle, in which one couple led the rest of the dancers.

American in Paris, An. Tone-poem (1928) by Gershwin.

American Musicological Society (AMS). Founded in 1934 for 'the advancement of research in the various fields of music as a branch of learning', the AMS holds an annual conference and also arranges meetings within its 15 regional chapters. Publications include the quarterly *Journal of the American Musicological Society* (*JAMS*) and a biannual *Newsletter*.   JBo

American organ. A variety of *reed organ, distinguished from the *harmonium by having suction bellows rather than pressure bellows.

'American' Quartet. The nickname of Dvořák's String Quartet in F op. 96 (1893), so called because he composed it in America incorporating African-American tunes.

Amériques. Orchestral work (1921) by Varèse; it includes parts for cyclone whistle, fire siren, crow-call, etc.

Amfiparnaso, L'. Madrigal comedy in a prologue and 13 scenes by Orazio Vecchi to his own texts (possibly in collaboration with Giulio Cesare Croce); for five voices, it was not intended to be staged and was first performed in Modena in 1594 (published 1597).

Amico Fritz, L'. Opera in three acts by Mascagni to a libretto by P. Suardon (pseudonym of Nicola Daspuro) after Erckmann-Chatrian (Rome, 1891).

Ammerbach, Elias Nikolaus (*b* Naumburg, nr Leipzig, *c*.1530; *d* Leipzig, *bur.* 29 Jan. 1597). German organist and arranger. He studied at Leipzig University, and from 1561 to 1595 was organist at St Thomas's, Leipzig. He published some attractive keyboard music, including dances and hymn arrangements. His first book, *Orgel oder Instrument Tablatur* (Leipzig, 1571), represents the earliest printed German organ music; letters are used to express pitches, with rhythm signs added above them. His instructions for ornamentation and fingering are valuable sources of information about the German school of organ playing.   DA/LC

Amner, John (*b* Ely, 1579; *d* Ely, 1641). English church musician, organist, and composer. His entire adult career was spent at Ely Cathedral, where he was appointed Master of the Choristers in 1610 and served as organist; he was also a minor canon there. In 1613 he received the degree of B.Mus. from Oxford University; Cambridge awarded him an equivalent degree the year before his death. Amner is best known for his anthems and church music, which follow in the polyphonic tradition of Byrd and Gibbons. In 1615 he published *Sacred Hymns*, a collection of pieces for domestic use, which includes the delightful Christmas anthem *O ye little flock*.   JM

Amor brujo, El ('Love, the Magician'). Ballet in one act by Falla to a scenario by Gregorio Martínez Sierra after an Andalusian Gypsy tale (Madrid, 1915); it includes songs, originally intended to be sung by the ballerina, and the famous *Ritual Fire Dance*. Falla arranged an orchestral suite from it (1916).

amore (It., 'love'; Fr.: *amour*). 1. A term found in expression marks, e.g. *amorevole*, *amoroso* (It.), 'loving'; *amorevolmente*, *amorosamente* (It.), 'lovingly', 'tenderly'.
    2. When attached to instrument names (e.g. viola d'amore, flûte d'amour), the term implies a richer and rounder tone than that of the normal instrument and probably a lower pitch. Woodwind 'd'amore' instruments usually have a bulbous bell, and stringed instruments have sympathetic strings.   JMo

amoroso (It.). 'Loving', 'affectionate'. The fourth movement of Mahler's Symphony no. 7 is Andante amoroso. See also AMORE, 1.

Amy, Gilbert (*b* Paris, 29 Aug. 1936). French composer. He studied with Messiaen and Milhaud at the Paris Conservatoire (1955–60), also receiving instruction from Boulez. Since 1962 he has appeared widely as a conductor specializing in contemporary music; he was Boulez's successor as director of the Domaine Musical concerts (1967–73). His early works are very close to those of Boulez in style, but in the 1970s and 80s he gradually moved towards a more continuous, relaxed, and even Romantic manner.   PG

Anacreontic Society. A London society founded in 1766 for aristocratic amateur musicians, who admitted a few professionals as honorary members. They met in a tavern in the Strand, where songs, catches, and glees were sung before and after supper. The society had a fine reputation (membership was highly prized), and Haydn visited it in 1791. Its constitutional song, performed at every meeting, was John Stafford Smith's *To Anacreon in Heaven*, the tune of which was later adopted by the Americans for their national anthem *The Star-Spangled Banner*. The society was dissolved in 1794.
    The same name was used by a concert society in Belfast (1814–66), founded to encourage orchestral music.

anacrusis (from Gk. *anakrousis*, 'a striking up'). An unstressed note or group of notes at the beginning of a phrase of music, forming an *upbeat. The term is also used of poetic metre.

analysis 1. Introduction; 2. History; 3. Schenker and deep structure; 4. Schoenberg and the musical surface; 5. Set theory; 6. Conclusion

1. Introduction

Analysis is interpretation—even a kind of performance, in the sense that analysts explore the materials and meanings of compositions and attempt to communicate their findings, through speaking or writing. At one extreme, such communication counts as criticism, the analyst offering opinions about works derived in the main from attitudes and predispositions which, however well informed, are instinctive rather than consciously and deliberately worked out. At the other extreme, analysis can call on an extensive range of theories about music, and techniques for analysing musical materials and compositional procedures, which are worthy of study in their own right. Historically, these extremes have been categorized as hermeneutic and formalist respectively.

With *hermeneutics, the emphasis is on interpretative strategies which value the composition's historical, social and aesthetic context as much as its inherently musical materials, and which do not shrink from comment about the expressive content and generic context of all kinds of music, not merely those with texts or verbal programmes. By contrast, a formalist approach focuses on the melodic, harmonic, contrapuntal, and rhythmic functions present in the composition, as well as its small- and large-scale structural elements. In exploring their evolving understanding of a musical work over extended periods of time, analysts depend principally on the most reliable edition of the score. But the generative process whereby that edition was arrived at, by way of what can be reconstructed from drafts, sketches, and other documents, may not be brought into the analysis, if only on the grounds that a very different set of scholarly skills and aptitudes is required for the adequate interpretation of such materials.

This underlines the sense of analysis as an ongoing activity in which an interpretation of the work in question is put together from a variety of processes and procedures. Although analysts present the results of their inquiries as not only relevant and important, but also true (to their own experience and understanding of the work), they will usually accept that any such 'truths', while not necessarily provisional, are certainly partial, capable of being complemented by other approaches taken from different positions on the continuum between the extremes of the hermeneutic and the formalist defined above. Those extremes are, needless to say, far from mutually exclusive, and it would be a poor analysis which did not intensify, or even transform, the aural experience of the music for those able to respond to the analysis itself. The ultimate purpose of analysis is to construct interpretations which make it possible for the musical work to be aesthetically as well as intellectually appreciated to a greater extent—or at least in different ways—than had been the case before the analysis was considered.

2. History

While there was little in the way of systematic theorizing about techniques of analysis before the 19th century, there was much theorizing about music itself. From the time of Plato, Aristotle, Aristoxenus, and other Ancient Greeks, through medieval philosophers like *Boethius and on to writers of the early Renaissance, speculation about the effects of music as a spiritual and psychological force brought with it a consistent concern to explore the nature of sound itself, as an acoustical phenomenon of nature which could be adapted and creatively manipulated by human beings. Once it had become possible, by the end of the 15th century, to think of the composer as someone who wrote music for others to perform, rather than primarily as a performer (see COMPOSITION), there was an increasing tendency for theorists to discuss specific compositions and their creators.

It was therefore a relatively small step from the kind of critical and technical comments on composers in the treatises of *Tinctoris, *Glarean, and *Zarlino, before the end of the 16th century, to such early examples of genuine analysis as Burmeister's study of the rhetorical character of Lassus's motet *In me transierunt* (1606). It was not until much later that analysis changed from being primarily a tool for teaching good compositional practice, as found in Kirnberger and Koch in the late 18th century, to technically based inquiry motivated essentially by admiration for the achievements of the work in question. Indeed, as early as E. T. A. Hoffmann's essay on Beethoven's Fifth Symphony (1809–10), or Schumann's study of Berlioz's *Symphonie fantastique* (1835), the intention was not to provide students with models to be imitated, but rather to marvel at the mysteries and challenges thrown down by creative genius at its most uncompromising and imaginative.

From the early 19th century onwards, critical and technical writing tended to be closely bound together, while academic instruction made increasing reference to procedures in masterworks which could be codified and imitated by students, few of whom could aspire to comparable mastery. Around the end of the 19th century and the beginning of the 20th, Arnold *Schoenberg and Heinrich Schenker, both based in Vienna, began to produce a series of theoretical works in which their understanding of the role of analysis in composition teaching and critical appreciation was strongly contrasted. Between them, they set the agenda for the central topics of debate concerning musical analysis which have been relevant ever since.

3. Schenker and deep structure

As far as tonal music is concerned—or at any rate that music from the late 17th century to the early 20th which can be unambiguously described as tonal—the theoretical and analytical principles of Heinrich Schenker (1868–1935) have provided the most comprehensive and sophisticated means of defining the relative significance of all the contrapuntal, harmonic, and melodic elements in a composition, with reference to both vertical and horizontal relationships. As will be clear from Ex. 1, there is an enormous difference between Schenker's approach to tonal structure and that of a theorist (like Schoenberg) who labels chords in ways that stress their vertical constitution and relation to the main tonality (e.g. I 6-3), but shows less concern for their relative significance or function in the structure as a whole. No less radical—and different from Schoenberg—were Schenker's avoidance of emphasis on the surface manipulations of thematic ideas and his downplaying of the significance of general formal categories (ternary, rondo, sonata, etc.) on the grounds that these were relatively superficial frameworks for the composing out of true tonal structures.

Schenker's various treatises contain a wealth of analytical illustrations but no straightforward statement of analytical method. The difficulty of clarifying and codifying his procedures arises from the fact that they evolved over at least three decades, while his most important writings, notably *Das Meisterwerk in der Musik* and *Der freie Satz*, are not only an explanation—often oblique and densely argued—of tonal structure as he understood it but also a polemic directed against those composers, from Wagner and on to Schoenberg and Stravinsky, who seemed to be set on destroying what he valued most. It says much for the force of his technical perceptions that later analysts and theorists have been convinced by them, despite the often distasteful, even racist language in which they are expressed. Schenker's vision was of an art deriving from nature (the *harmonic series expressed through the triad) which had been brought to fulfilment by a handful of great German masters who had 'experienced even their most extended works ... as entities which could be heard and perceived as a whole'. Moreover, it was a rather special kind of whole, in which 'the goal is everything'. Unity and goal are enshrined in his concept of the *Ursatz*, the fundamental two-voice structure that generates all true tonal compositions, in which an upper

line descends by step from one of the notes of the tonic triad to the tonic itself.

Ex. 1a is an adaptation of Schenker's analysis of Brahms's Waltz op. 39 no. 1, showing the *Ursatz* at the top, and two subsequent levels, representing the 'background' and 'middleground' of the structure. Schenker's 'foreground' sketch for the first eight bars is shown as Ex. 1b; and it will be clear from this that the essential technique is one of reduction and abstraction: not only are the many repetitions and doublings in the actual music not represented even at foreground level, but the registral location of the bass line is changed, so that the example will fit on to one staff.

Even so, it would be wrong to argue that the Schenkerian analytical process consists of progressively discarding all the various decorative, motivic, and other less vital structural elements until the music is reduced to its abstract, unrhythmic *Ursatz*—at which point any one of many hundreds of compositions with the same fundamental structure might be in question. A more accurate description is that the analytical process consists of the demonstration of several separate yet interacting structural levels of three basic types (foreground, middleground, background), all of which express the goal-directedness and coherence of the music—the ways in which its unifying tonic triad is projected and elaborated. This elaboration, or prolongation, according to linear processes of voice-leading, Schenker saw as deriving from the procedures of strict counterpoint ('voice-leading' translates the German term *Stimmführung*; 'part-writing' is not an adequate translation since it does not imply goal-directedness). In the analysis, clear distinctions are made between structural and decorative (prolongational) elements, and the function of everything is presented systematically, in ways that enable the analyst to demonstrate the most far-reaching relationships between what is unique about the work and what it shares with other examples of tonal composition.

It is Schenker's concern with the organic integration generated from a deep structure which made him the supreme advocate of a classic style of composition, in which contrast and diversity are not merely subordinate to unifying forces but are generated by the spatial and temporal evolution of those forces. This was the ultimate fulfilment of one aspect of 19th-century aesthetic philosophy. No less obviously, it sets aside certain complementary concepts, without which much Romantic and all modernist art is unthinkable. There is certainly a place for local, temporary ambiguities and even discontinuities in Schenker's concept of music, but they can never be given the fundamental role and decisive importance that non-classical musical expression makes possible.

Ex. 1 (*a*)

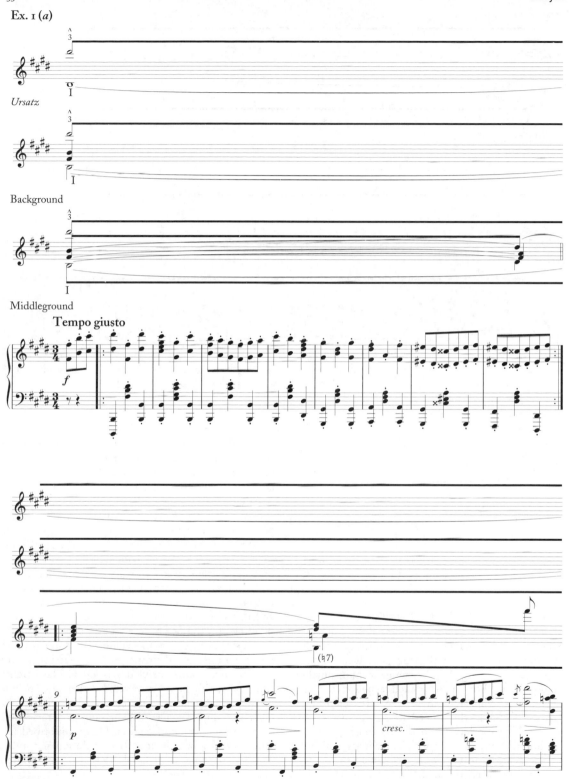

Ursatz

Background

Middleground

Ex. 1 (*a*) (*cont.*)

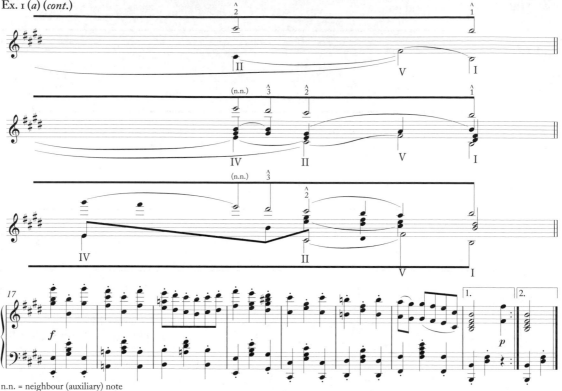

n.n. = neighbour (auxiliary) note

Analysis adapted from Schenker, *Der freie Satz*, Fig. 49, 2.

(*b*)

Foreground

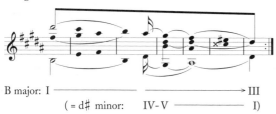

B major: I ——————— ——————→ III

(= d♯ minor: IV-V ——————→ I)

4. Schoenberg and the musical surface

Something of this alternative, less deeply organicist view of music emerges in Schoenberg's theoretical writings. While far from thoroughgoingly modernist—apart from anything else, they rarely mention anything to do with total chromaticism and 12-note technique—these often emphasize the surface characteristics of particular chords, the immediate significance of generative thematic ideas, and the different qualities of traditional formal frameworks. These ideas, which had a long pedigree in 19th-century German theory, were greatly influential on analytical practice after 1900,

despite the fact that—like Schenker's notions of tonal structure—they are hard to confine in a straightforward set of principles and procedures of the kind useful in academic analysis courses.

After Schoenberg himself, Rudolph Réti (1885–1957) and Alan Walker (*b* 1930) were among those who explored the extent to which a basic shape (sometimes equated with the German term *Gestalt* or *Grundgestalt*) may function as a generative thematic cell, transformed into multifarious guises across the surface of the music, and connecting all the themes, however apparently contrasted. Such explorations are inevitably open-ended, and are vulnerable to objections about special pleading and the failure to establish sufficiently comprehensive principles of procedure. (Ex. 2 shows Réti's interpretation of thematic interconnectedness in Schumann's *Kinderszenen*.) It was left to Hans Keller (1919–85) to lift the entire process of thematic analysis on to another plane with his 'composed' or 'functional' analyses, which are played alongside, or interspersed with, the original work and enable the informed listener to *hear* a process of motivic evolution and interconnection, rather than simply view it on the printed page.

Ex. 2

From Rudolph Réti, *The Thematic Process in Music* (1962).

Appropriately, however, the analytical explication of the multiple tendencies and implications of the compositional surface became even more diverse in the later decades of the 20th century. On the one hand, the new science of cognitive psychology was invoked by a group of important writers, from Leonard B. Meyer and Eugene Narmour to John Sloboda and Fred Lerdahl, to promote their attempts to define how, and how far, transformational processes and patterns can be perceived by listeners. On the other hand, there have been attempts to develop analytical procedures for musical compositions which apply techniques derived from the systematic study of linguistics. Semiology, or *semiotics, is essentially concerned with sign-systems, and, like

cognitive psychology, its musical applications, by Jean-Jacques Nattiez and Raymond Monelle among others, have been valuable in helping to counter the bias favouring deep or abstract structures found not only in Schenker but also in much post-tonal theory; see below, 5. Cognitive psychologists and semiologists alike recognize that the actual surface of a composition deserves to be studied closely and methodically in ways which involve the clear definition of degrees of similarity and difference in every dimension, not just pitch.

5. Set theory

The Schenkerian emphasis on goal-directedness, unity, and the elaboration of elements from a tonal triad can scarcely be transferred without adaptation to music written before the tonal system and triadic harmony were fully established, even though the hierarchies particular to modal composition from before 1600 and after 1900 make it possible to demonstrate various levels of structure within the voice-leading. With post-tonal, or atonal, music, too, the application of voice-leading analysis has made only limited headway—understandably so, when textures are often so fragmented that linear connections, and any sense of progress towards a goal, are difficult to detect. Yet much atonal music is also apparently athematic, and the detection of basic cells and shapes becomes an equally haphazard affair in the absence of the kind of general principles by means of which a large repertory of works could be considered as a coherent whole.

One solution to this problem has been to develop a means of describing all possible collections of pitch and interval *classes without reference to triadic or tonal functions. This process reduces the total number of such collections, or *sets, to manageable proportions, arguing that it is possible to relate certain apparently different collections to the same basic collection, or 'prime form'. Thus, if C–D♭–E♭ is a prime form (because the smallest of the two interval classes is placed first), then E♭–D♭–C and C–E♭–D♭ can be regarded as permutations of this same initial collection, rather than as different collections. As a result, the total number of prime form sets that contain between three and nine pitch classes is a mere 220.

This procedure derives from the mathematical principles of set theory. The decisive figure in its development as an analytical tool was an American composer who, although he never studied with Schoenberg, learnt much from the analysis of his music—Milton Babbitt (b 1916). However, it was not until the early 1970s that another American, Allen Forte, published the first extended account of the analytical possibilities offered by set theory (*The Structure of Atonal Music*, 1973). Ex. 3 shows the graphic component of Forte's analysis of Webern's piece for violin and piano, op. 7 no. 3, with sets of different sizes identified by the number of pitch classes in them (ranging here from 3 to 8): thus, 3–1 is the first of the sets comprising three pcs, 3–9 the ninth. (The letter 'Z' is used to identify a particular constraining property of the system.) Since the 1970s many other writers, notably Joseph Straus, have built on the foundations of Forte's work, benefiting from the clearly codified analytical procedures he outlines.

Set-theoretic analysis is undoubtedly most illuminating when brought to bear on large-scale works like Berg's *Wozzeck*, in which the kind of relationships it reveals are far less obvious, yet of greater aesthetic interest, than those found in such miniatures as Schoenberg's op. 19 Piano Pieces. To facilitate such ambitious projects, computer programs are available to identify sets and define relationships, although this 'mechanical' activity often creates suspicion in those conscious of the difficulties of deciding how to divide up—segment—a composition in order to compute its constituent sets. Nevertheless, set-theoretic analysis is well established and frequently used, whether on its own or as part of a wider exercise in the hermeneutic as well as 'formalist' study of complex post-tonal works. Apart from the special case of 12-note composition, where the analysis can proceed from knowledge about the identity of the set forms chosen by the composer, the resistance of post-tonal music to the kind of systematization or common practice found in modal or tonal composition makes it particularly challenging as material for analytical interpretation.

6. Conclusion

No brief account of what the analytical process involves can possibly serve to justify analysis, still less to explain why the activity can be so satisfying. The object of analysis is not to glorify (or even refine) a particular analytical technique but to show that the expressive and formal content of a major masterwork can be valuably illuminated through the conventions and procedures of that technique. Schenker's magnificent study of Beethoven's 'Eroica' Symphony, with its foreground, middleground, and background graphs for the entire four-movement composition, may have little or nothing to say about how the work was conceived and created, and still less about the nature and significance of its connection with concepts of the heroic. And while analysis of a 12-note composition by Webern is likely to come closer to the composer's own thinking about matters of technique and procedure, there will still be many aspects of that composition about which analysts can only speculate—in a well-informed manner, of course—rather than offer certainty.

An analysis, whether primarily verbal or primarily graphic, will always be a kind of 'alter ego' to the composition itself. But the sense of the analysis as, in essence, a performed interpretation, a reading of a text—in the way that a performance of the score reads the text with the aim of persuading those who attend that a convincingly personal interpretation is taking place—serves to reinforce the character of the analyst as someone who seeks to blend subjectivity with authority, to communicate conviction. It is therefore appropriate that the analysis of musical performance itself should

Ex. 3

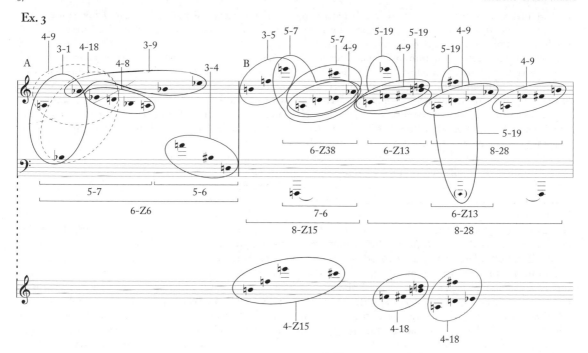

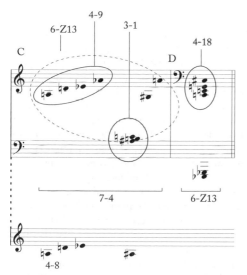

From Allen Forte, *The Structure of Atonal Music* (1973).

have become an increasingly prominent activity since 1980, within a musicological climate that acknowledges the idea of interpretation as something as multivalent and diverse as composition itself, and as multivalent and diverse as the theoretical principles and analytical techniques that can be brought to bear on its interpretation.   AW

📖 I. BENT, with W. DRABKIN, *Analysis*, The New Grove Handbooks in Music (London, 1987) · J. DUNSBY and A. WHITTALL, *Music Analysis in Theory and Practice* (London, 1988) · J. N. STRAUS, *Introduction to Post-Tonal Theory* (Englewood Cliffs, NJ, 1990) · M. EVERIST (ed.), *Models of Musical Analysis: Music before 1600* (Oxford, 1992) · J. DUNSBY (ed.), *Models of Musical Analysis: Early Twentieth-Century Music* (Oxford, 1993) · I. BENT (ed.), *Music Analysis in the Nineteenth Century*, i: *Fugue, Form, and Style*; ii: *Hermeneutic Approaches* (Cambridge, 1994) · N. COOK, *Analysis through Composition: Principles of the Classical Style* (Oxford, 1996) · A. CADWALLADER and D. GAGNÉ, *Analysis of Tonal Music: A Schenkerian Approach* (Oxford, 1998)

anapaest. A poetic foot of three syllables, weak–weak–strong. The adjective is 'anapaestic'. For its equivalent in the rhythmic modes, see NOTATION, 2.

anche (Fr.). 'Reed'.

ancient Greek music. The Greek *mousikē* refers to any art over which the Muses preside, but, in the Hellenic and Hellenistic periods, particularly to music. Music played a central role in the civic and religious life of the people as well as providing relaxation and entertainment; it was also the object of scientific and philosophical inquiry.

    1. History and function; 2. Instruments; 3. Music theory; 4. Extant melos

1. History and function

The pure phenomena of music attracted the interest of various early philosophical schools, especially the

Pythagoreans, who primarily viewed it as a paradigm for important truths found in its harmonious reflection of number—for them, the ultimate reality. The use of a harmonious structure in actual individual pieces was of secondary interest, though they were concerned with its mimetic characteristics, which gave music its power in human life. Plato followed the Pythagorean tradition in using music as a cosmological paradigm in his *Timaeus*, but he was also aware of its influence on behaviour and concerned himself in the *Republic* and *Laws* with such practical issues as the types of music to be allowed in an enlightened civilization.

Aristotle, too, was interested in the educational function of music and its role in the development of character, though his positions, which are most fully developed in book 8 of the *Politics*, differed somewhat from those of Plato. Within Aristotle's scientific tradition, his disciple Aristoxenus developed a highly sophisticated system for analysing musical phenomena in a treatise transmitted under the title *Harmonic Elements*. By the 2nd century BC, the practical, scientific, and philosophical traditions of music were waning. Nevertheless, authors in the Roman, Byzantine, and Islamic empires continued to write treatments of the subject in Latin, Greek, and Arabic. In the West, however, the music and its theory began to be forgotten after the time of Boethius and Cassiodorus, leaving only imperfect traces in later treatises.

The music of the ancient Greeks cannot be reconstructed in full, but a broad range of source material exists from which a reasonably clear picture can be formed. Four principal types of source pertain to the subject: literature, works of graphic or plastic art, archaeological remains, and notated pieces of music. None of these alone presents a complete picture, but as a complex they begin to reveal the richness of *mousikē*.

In the modern sense, a history of ancient Greek music cannot be written. Citation or paraphrase in Pseudo-Plutarch's *On Music* of works with historical or biographical titles by such authors as Alexander, Aristoxenus, Glaucus of Rhegium, and Heraclides Ponticus are tantalizing, but as the treatises themselves do not survive, it is impossible to know whether they would have addressed precisely matters of chronology, biography, attribution, and factual detail necessary for a modern historical treatment. Other literary sources, while providing information about musical matters, tend to be technical, antiquarian, or museographic rather than historical. Thus, the picture of ancient Greek music and musical life reconstructed from the surviving sources remains chronologically and historically ambiguous.

The Greeks used specific musical forms for a wide range of occasions. The settings for these compositions are lost (with the exception of the musical fragments), but the texts themselves provide evidence about form, structure, and rhythm, and in some cases describe music-making itself. Forms were typified by subject matter, rhythm and metre, large-scale structure, and so on. Plato (*Laws* 3.700A8–E4) observes that the types were once distinct: a hymn would not be confused with a dirge, dithyramb, or paean—implying that this distinction was beginning to be lost in his day. Fuller typologies are found in Athenaeus' *Sophists at Dinner* and Photius' *Bibliotheca*, which preserves a summary of Proclus' *Useful Knowledge*. Proclus sets up three classifications and lists the types associated with each: (1) for the gods—hymn, prosodion, paean, dithyramb, nomos, adonidia, iobakchos, and hyporcheme; (2) for humans—encomion, epinikion, skolion, erotica, epithalamia, hymenaios, sillos, threnos, and epikedeion; (3) for the gods and humans—partheneion, daphnephorika, tripodephorika, oschophorika, and eutika. Whether or not this typology would have been shared by earlier Greek writers such as Plato, it is clear that the Greeks were conscious of specific musical types and their distinctions.

Such pieces of music were called *melos*, which in its perfect form (*teleion melos*) comprised not only the melody and the text (including its elements of rhythm and diction) but also stylized dance movement. Melic and rhythmic composition (respectively, *melopoiïa* and *rhuthmopoiïa*) were the processes of selecting and applying the various components of melos and rhythm to create a complete work. The compositions of the first classification played important roles in religious and civic life, with the nomos becoming the particular vehicle for musical innovation and the development of the virtuoso. The epinikion provided a form in which important personal and human victories could be memorialized to inspire future generations. In the dithyramb, partheneion, and hyporcheme, the relationship of dance and music was especially prominent; but the most complete union of music, text, movement, and costume was developed in the drama which formed a centrepiece of the civic and religious festivals of the Greeks. Similarly, everyday social life was supported by compositions of the third classification: wedding and funeral music, love songs, work songs, banquet songs, and so on. In each piece, musicians drew on a wealth of tradition, an innately sonorous language, and virtually limitless combinations of rhythms, metres, *tonoi*, inflections of melodic scale, gesture, and dance, some of which are described in the technical treatises.

Music-making already plays an important role in the *Iliad* and the *Odyssey*, whether or not they were sung or recited, and beginning at least as early as the 7th century, extended solo and choral musical forms existed, with and without instrumental accompaniment, as did pure instrumental music. Virtuosity and innovation became prominent in 6th-century instrumental music, which encouraged complexity in the other musical forms, in spite of the objection of conservative poets and philosophers. In Plato's *Republic* (4.424B5–c6), for example, Socrates deplores innovations in music because they threaten the fundamental structure of the state: 'One must be cautious about changing to a new type of music as this risks a change in the whole. The modes (*tropoi*) of music are never moved without movement of the greatest constitutional laws'. This passage emphasizes the larger Greek concept of *mousikē*: music occupied a prominent place in everyday life not only because it was amusing and socially valuable but also because it embodied larger universal principles and was a vehicle for higher understanding.

2. Instruments

Although fundamentally vocal and literary in character, ancient Greek music also used a considerable array of musical instruments from the four traditional Hornbostel–Sachs classifications: idiophones, membranophones, aerophones, and chordophones. The authors of various lexicographic works provide detailed classifications of musical instruments, many of which are also portrayed on red- and black-figure vases, in terracotta statuary, and on gemstones and bas-reliefs. A number of instruments survive as archaeological artefacts, and reconstructions of individual instruments have led to various conclusions about timbre, pitch, tuning, and performance practice.

The primary idiophones and membranophones are the *krotala*, *kroupezai* or *kroupala*, *kumbala* or *krembala*, sistrum (*seistron*), *rhombos*, *tumpana*, and bells (*kōdōn*), all of which were associated to some extent with the cults of Dionysus and Cybele. Each instrument had certain specific uses, but any might be used to articulate rhythmic and metric patterns. In at least some cases, they must have coordinated performers by marking time.

The primary aerophones of the Greeks were the aulos, syrinx (panpipes), hydraulis, salpinx, and horn (*keras*); they, too, were associated with the cults of Dionysus and Cybele. The aulos was the most important, and literary sources contain substantial detail about its origin, history, and construction; archaeological remains and iconographic representations provide specific examples, allowing almost complete reconstructions to be made. The aulos is a reed instrument (not a flute, as the term is still quite frequently translated) and, as such, consists of two distinct parts: a mouthpiece and a resonator, both of which are extensively described in Greek technical treatises. Auloi came in various shapes and sizes and were normally played in pairs; whether the pipes played in unison or in some other manner is uncertain. The aulete commonly made use of the *phorbeia*, a kind of mouth-band, to provide a tight seal round both mouthpieces. With its unique sound and flexibility of pitch and dynamics, the aulos was capable of playing the subtly inflected scales described in the treatises, in low or high registers, outdoors in the theatre or processions, or indoors at symposia or private occasions.

The chordophones can be separated into two major classes: lyres and psalteria. Instruments of the first class have freely resonating strings strummed with a plectrum; those of the second were plucked by the fingers. *Phorminx* and *kitharis* are early terms associated with instruments of the first class, joined later by *lyra*, *chelys* or *chelus*, *barbiton* (or *barbitos*), and *kithara*. Iconography suggests that the *chelys* lyre was the small instrument constructed on a tortoise (*chelys*) shell used in music lessons and for private music-making; the *phorminx*, an instrument of moderate size with a rounded bottom and perhaps a fuller tone; the *barbiton*, associated with Dionysian ceremonies, a *chelys* lyre with long arms and probably a low and resonant tone; and the *kithara*, commonly associated with Apollo, the large concert instrument used in contests, the theatre, and festivals. The second class includes the *psaltērion* itself; the *epigoneion* and *simikion*, instruments of as many as 40 strings, perhaps rather like the modern zither; the *magadis*, *pēktis*, and *phoenix*, instruments with strings tuned in pairs, not unlike the modern dulcimer; and the *sambukē* and the *trigōnon*, which were held aloft, like the modern Irish harp, and—especially in the case of the *trigōnon*—played primarily by women in the home.

3. Music theory

A significant body of Greek literature can properly be considered music theory. Like other literary sources, these extend over a wide period from the 4th century BC to the 4th century AD, or even later, if works written in late antiquity and the Middle Ages in Latin, Greek, and Arabic are included. Of the earlier treatises, some are technical manuals that provide valuable detail about the Greeks' musical system, including notation, the function and placement of notes in a scale, characteristics of consonance and dissonance, rhythm, and types of musical composition. This group includes the *Division of a Canon* (sometimes erroneously attributed to Euclid); Cleonides, *Harmonic Introduction*; Nicomachus of Gerasa, *Manual of Harmonics*; Theon of Smyrna, *On Mathematics Useful for the Understanding of Plato*; Gaudentius, *Harmonic Introduction*; Alypius, *Introduction to Music*; Bacchius, *Introduction to the Art of Music*; and others. By contrast, the *Harmonic Elements* of Aristoxenus, *On Music* by Aristides Quintilianus, and the *Harmonics* by Claudius Ptolemy are elaborate books showing the way in which *mousikē*, by revealing universal patterns of order, leads to the highest levels of knowledge and understanding. Beyond the evidence it supplies about the Greeks' own music, the theory is also significant as an intellectual monument that exerted a profound influence on later Latin, Byzantine, and Arabic musical writings.

Three traditions emerge in the corpus of ancient Greek music theory: a Pythagorean tradition (including manifestations in Platonism and Neoplatonism) concerned with number theory, the relationships between music and the cosmos, and the influence of music on behaviour; a scientific tradition of harmonics associated with a group known as 'Harmonicists'; and an Aristoxenian tradition based on Aristotelian principles. Although the characteristics of each tradition can be generalized, no single treatise provides a comprehensive treatment of any of the traditions.

The side of Pythagoreanism concerned with musical science is primarily known through the *Division of a Canon* and the writings of Plato, Aristotle, Plutarch (including the treatise *On Music* attributed to Pseudo-Plutarch), Nicomachus of Gerasa, Theon of Smyrna, Claudius Ptolemy, and (as later merged with Neoplatonism) Porphyry, Aristides Quintilianus, Iamblichus, and subsequent writers. Plato's *Timaeus*, for example, presents a model for the creation of the universe embodying characteristic Pythagorean ratios and means and producing a kind of musical shape (Fig. 1). As a series of ratios, the numbers on the left represent such musical intervals as the octave (2:1), double octave (4:1), and triple octave (8:1), while the numbers on the right represent the octave and a 5th (3:1), the triple octave and a tone (9:1), and the quadruple octave and a major 6th (27:1).

Fig. 1.

Following an introduction defining the physical basis of sound as a series of motions, the *Division of a Canon* uses some of these same ratios and applies them to such musical topics as consonance, the magnitudes of certain consonant intervals, the location of movable notes in an enharmonic tetrachord, and the location of the notes of the Immutable System on a monochord. Since pitches of notes can be related to the number of motions of a string and therefore consist of certain numbers of parts, they can be described and compared in numerical terms and ratios, such as multiple, superparticular, and superpartient. Consonant notes (i.e. those spanning the 4th, 5th, octave, 12th, and 15th) are found in a multiple or a superparticular ratio (i.e. 4:3, 3:2, 2:1, 3:1, and 4:1) formed only of the numbers of the *tetraktus* of the decad (i.e. 1, 2, 3, 4, the sum of which is 10).

Pythagoreans were also concerned with intervals smaller than the 4th, which they identified through mathematical processes. The tone, for instance, was shown to be the difference (9:8) between the 5th and the 4th, and various sizes of 'semitones' were identified, such as 256:243 (the 'leimma'), 2187:2048 (the 'apotome'), and 'semitones' that could be created by proportioning the ratio 9:8 to create any number of small subdivisions (e.g. 18:17:16 or 36:35:34:33:32 and so on). The size of the semitone and the addition of tones and semitones to create 4ths, 5ths, and octaves became a subject of controversy between the Pythagoreans, who insisted on a fundamentally arithmetic approach, and the Aristoxenians, who adopted a geometric approach to the measurement of musical space.

The Harmonicists, known primarily through Aristoxenus' negative assessment of them, based their theory on the sequence of pitches in the range of an octave, which they represented in a series of diagrams; they were also preoccupied with the characteristics of the aulos and musical notation, both of which Aristoxenus dismisses as useless for scientific investigation. Although the precise nature of their diagrams cannot be determined, they may have been something like those that form the final two sections of the *Division of a Canon* or the monochord division of Thrasyllus preserved in Theon of Smyrna's *On Mathematics Useful for the Understanding of Plato*. According to Aristoxenus, the Harmonicist Eratocles (*fl* 5th century BC) was primarily interested in the seven possible cyclic orderings of the intervals in an octave. Aristoxenus derides this apparently typical Harmonicist approach because it fails to take into account the various musical syntheses (including possible species of the 5th and 4th) that would produce many more than seven species. Aristoxenus further objected that the Harmonicists' identification of a series of *tonoi* separated by some small interval resulted simply in a closely packed diagram rather than in any useful understanding of musical phenomena.

The most systematic discussion of musical phenomena is found in the fragmentary *Harmonic Elements* of Aristoxenus and later treatises based on its principles (especially the Aristoxenian epitome by Cleonides and parts of the treatises of Gaudentius, Bacchius, Ptolemy, and Aristides Quintilianus). Aristoxenus was concerned with the philosophical definitions and categories necessary to establish a complete and correct view of the musical reality of scales and *tonoi*, two primary elements of musical composition, and in the first part of his treatise he introduces and discusses such subjects as motion of the voice, pitch, compass, intervals, consonance and dissonance, scales, melos, continuity and consecution, genera, synthesis, mixing of genera, notes, and position of the voice. From these, he develops a set of seven categories (genera, intervals, notes, scales, *tonoi*, modulation, and melic composition), framed by two additional categories: first, hearing and intellect, and last, comprehension. As the later authors did not share Aristoxenus' broader philosophical interests, the framing categories and much of the subtlety of language and argument largely disappeared, while the seven 'technical' categories (especially the first three) were rearranged and expanded to include additional technical details—such as the names of the individual notes—that Aristoxenus took for granted.

4. Extant melos

Music notated with symbols from the tables of Alypius has been preserved on stone, on papyrus, and in manuscripts. Egert Pöhlmann identified 40 pieces (including five he regarded as forgeries) in his edition, which is still the only reasonably comprehensive study of the music itself; current scholarship recognizes about 45 pieces, the approximation arising from differences of opinion about the proper characterization of a 'piece'. The most important of these are (on stone) the Delphic hymns (*c*.127 BC), originally installed on the walls of the Athenian Treasury at Delphi, one of which (perhaps by a certain Athenaeus) is notated in vocal notation, the other (by Limenius) in instrumental notation; the Epitaph of Seikilos (1st century AD), inscribed on a tombstone and consisting of a brief heading (including the name of Seikilos) and a complete epigram meticulously notated in vocal and rhythmic notation; two fragments (on papyrus) from tragedies by Euripides, *Iphigenia in Aulis*, 1499–1509 and 784–92, and *Orestes*, 338–44; and a group of hymns (in manuscript) addressed to the Muses, the sun, and Nemesis, commonly attributed to Mesomedes.

TM

📖 E. Pöhlmann, *Denkmäler altgriechischer Musik* (Nuremberg, 1970) · T. J. Mathiesen, *Apollo's Lyre: Greek Music and Music Theory in Antiquity and the Middle Ages* (Lincoln, NE, 1999)

ancient Mesopotamian and Egyptian music. The two earliest civilizations at the foundation of the modern West, Mesopotamia and Egypt had arrived at a settled political order by the end of the 4th millennium BC and entered into the historical record during the 3rd with the rise of writing. Throughout the ancient period, Egypt was a centralized monarchy, while Mesopotamia was at first characterized by a number of independent city-states. The original Sumerians were conquered about 2350 BC by the Semitic Akkadians, who established a united empire; this was eventually superseded by the Babylonian (*c*.1800–1100) and Assyrian (*c*.1200–500) empires. The conquests of Alexander the Great hybridized both ancient civilizations with a profound and lasting infusion of Greek culture, though distinctive elements remained until both regions became part of Arabic culture after the Muslim conquest (7th century AD). Music was of great importance throughout the histories of both civilizations.

The accidents of archaeological preservation have biased our knowledge of Mesopotamian and Egyptian music in different ways. The more extreme desert conditions of Egypt have permitted the survival of more instruments, whereas the more durable writing medium used in Mesopotamia (clay tablets rather than papyrus) has preserved more written texts, especially those of a technical nature. But a great deal of pictorial evidence remains from both regions, along with much information in literary and religious texts about the place and function of music.

Music had an important role in all aspects of Mesopotamian and Egyptian culture. We are informed about nursery songs, pastoral, agricultural, and industrial work songs, the piping of shepherds and string-playing in taverns, singing and dancing at weddings and lamenting at funerals, the military use of trumpets and other wind and string instruments. Music formed an important element of courtly life, and of course was of crucial significance in the religious ritual. Upper-class women took a major role in the last two activities: the earliest known composer was Enheduanna (*fl c*.2300 BC), daughter of Sargon I of Akkad, high priestess and sponsor of the cult of the goddess Inanna (the words of some of her hymns survive), while the tomb of Mereruka, a 6th-Dynasty (*c*.2323–2150 BC) king of Egypt, shows his wife Seshseshet accompanying her own song on a harp. Women also took part in the more popular kinds of music-making. Much instrumental music at Mesopotamian and Egyptian courts was performed by male or female slaves. Pictures and carvings from both regions show musical accompaniment to explicit sexual scenes.

Although more instruments survive from Egypt, our knowledge of Mesopotamian instruments extends deeper into the past. A complete bone wind instrument with fingerholes, and two further fragments, are known from the 5th millennium BC; a fragment of a similar clay instrument comes from late 4th-millennium Uruk, and silver pipes were found in the Royal Tombs of Ur (*c.*2600 BC). Both flutes and single- and double-reed instruments are well attested from Mesopotamia and Egypt later in the historical record, but it is not clear to which category these earliest ones belong. The round harp is the classic string instrument of the earliest period in both regions; indeed, the earliest examples of Mesopotamian writing show a pictogram of a round harp. The lyre, in both symmetrical and asymmetrical forms, was also important in Mesopotamia from a very early date, and a large symmetrical lyre with its soundbox in the form of a bull was especially prestigious. The lyre was introduced into Egypt from Mesopotamia during the New Kingdom (1550–1070 BC), as was the long-necked lute, itself new in Mesopotamia in the late 2nd millennium. About the end of the 2nd millennium the bull lyre and the round harp died out in Mesopotamia, the place of the latter being taken by the angular harp, which was also later adopted in Egypt where it did not supplant the round form.

Twinned double-reed pipes appeared in Mesopotamia during the 2nd millennium BC and were later introduced to Egypt. Horns and trumpets are known from both regions, but do not appear to have been as common as the other types of instrument. Percussion, however, took a large place in both cultures. Clappers of various materials and designs were common from the earliest times. Drums, sometimes very large, were important in Mesopotamian ritual, while the characteristic instrument of Egyptian ceremony was the sistrum or rattle. A rectangular frame drum, always played by women, was prominent at banquets during the Egyptian New Kingdom; 1st-millennium Mesopotamia seems to have possessed tuned metal gong drums. The ritual importance of percussion instruments is shown by the naming of hymn genres after them in Sumerian times, while Virgil portrayed Cleopatra as rattling a sistrum to rally her forces at the Battle of Actium.

There is little to indicate what the music of ancient Egypt sounded like, but we are better informed about Mesopotamia. Nearly 100 cuneiform tablets provide information about tuning systems, and scholars have reached consensus that, at least from the early 2nd millennium BC onwards, Mesopotamian music was characterized by the following: it was based on a seven-note diatonic scale with octave equivalence; it used a system of *modes corresponding closely to the later (and better-known) Greek *harmoniai*; it knew the circle of 5ths, which was used in the practical tuning of instruments.

The names of individual pitches were of less importance than the names of intervals, which were conceived as between pairs of strings rather than pitches and consequently might vary depending on the tuning: for instance the 3rd, called 'bridge of the middle', signified the equivalent of F–A in the 'normal' tuning, F♯–A in 'open', or F♯–A♯ in 'middle'. The interval names (and the governing tuning) are used as a musical 'notation' in the handful of surviving tablets with performance instructions, all from ancient Ugarit (now Ras Shamra, Syria) about 1400 BC; only one of these is complete, and no consensus has been reached as to how it should be transcribed. The interval names comprise 3rds, 4ths, 5ths, and 6ths; the surviving hymns are all in the same tuning, and the 4th corresponding to the tritone in that tuning is avoided in all; a Sumerian–Akkadian vocabulary includes a term for 'unison' contrasted with another meaning 'their singing/playing is balanced'. These facts have led some scholars (to the horror of others) to conclude that Mesopotamian music may well have included not only monophony but also polyphony.   JJD

Ancient Voices of Children. Work (1970) by Crumb for soprano and treble with instrumental ensemble, to words by Federico García Lorca.

ancora (It.). 1. 'Again', an indication to repeat a section. 2. 'Still', 'yet', e.g. *ancora più forte*, 'still louder'.

andamento (It., 'walking'). An 18th-century term for sequence (see SEQUENCE, 1), or for a fugal subject which is longer than usual.

andante (It., 'walking'). Moderately slow; since the late 18th century it is taken to indicate a speed between *adagio* and *allegro*. *Più andante* or *molto andante* generally means slower than *andante*. The term is also used for a piece or movement in a moderately slow tempo and of a less solemn nature than an *adagio*.

Andante favori. A piano piece by Beethoven, originally written as the slow movement of his Piano Sonata in C op. 53 (1803), 'Waldstein', but detached and published as a separate work.

Andante spianato. The title of Chopin's op. 22 for piano (1834), composed as an introduction to his Grand Polonaise in E♭ (1830–1) for piano and orchestra.

43

andantino (It.). The diminutive of *andante*, now taken to indicate a tempo slightly less slow than *andante*, though in the 18th century it implied a tempo slower than *andante*. The term is also used for a piece or movement at such a tempo.

An der schönen, blauen Donau ('By the Beautiful Blue Danube'). Waltz, op. 314 (1867), by Johann Strauss (ii). It is known in English simply as *The Blue Danube*.

Anderson, Julian (David) (*b* London, 6 April 1967). English composer. He studied with John Lambert and Alexander Goehr, and with Tristan Murail in Paris. Oliver Knussen was another significant mentor, and Anderson's characteristic blend of timbral refinement and free-flowing, well-ventilated textures owes something to Knussen's example. Anderson won the Royal Philharmonic Society's prize for young composers in 1992, and had his first major success with *Khovorod*, commissioned by the London Sinfonietta, in 1994. He has combined work as a composition teacher at the RCM with the production of a steady stream of new works, including two substantial orchestral scores commissioned by the BBC, *The Crazed Moon* (1996) and *Stations of the Sun* (1998).   AW

Anderson, Laurie (*b* Chicago, 5 June 1947). American composer and performer. She studied art history at Barnard College and sculpture at Columbia University, and in the mid-1970s began giving performances dependent on her voice (and her idiosyncratic poetic language), advanced electronic technology, and her position midway between experimental musician and rock star. With *Big Science* (1982) and later albums she moved into the rock world, but she has maintained her individuality and her career as a performer in avant-garde venues, as with her opera *Songs and Stories from Moby Dick* (1999).   PG

Anderson, Leroy (*b* Cambridge, MA, 29 June 1908; *d* Woodbury, CT, 18 May 1975). American composer, of Swedish descent. He studied music and languages at the New England Conservatory and Harvard and from 1929 to 1935 worked as an organist, choirmaster, conductor, and teacher. In 1935 he became a freelance composer and arranger, working mainly for the Boston Pops Orchestra, which he occasionally conducted. After serving in the army (1942–6) he returned to the Boston Pops, which recorded his works, winning him an international reputation. His often humorous light music, with its novel orchestral effects, includes *Jazz Pizzicato* (1938), *Fiddle-Faddle* (1947), *Sleigh Ride* (1948), and *The Typewriter* (1950).   PGA

An die ferne Geliebte ('To the Distant Beloved'). Song cycle, op. 98 (1815–16), by Beethoven; the six songs, for voice and piano, are settings of poems by Alois Jeitteles. The cycle is not to be confused with Beethoven's songs *Lied aus der Ferne* and *Der Liebende* (both 1809), to words by Christian Ludwig Reissig, and *An die Geliebte* (1811, revised ?1814), to words by J. L. Stoll.

André. German family of composers and music publishers, of French extraction. Johann [Jean] André (1741–99) had lessons in thoroughbass while training for a role in his family's silk-manufacturing business. In Frankfurt he began translating *opéras comiques*. His first original stage work, *Die Töpfer* (1773), was admired by Goethe, who commissioned him to set his libretto *Erwin und Elmire* (1775). He went on to write about 20 *Singspiele*, other stage works, and songs. In 1774 André left the family silk firm to set up a music-publishing house in Offenbach. He established relations with Pleyel, Haydn, and Gyrowetz, and by 1797 his firm had published a thousand items.

His son Johann Anton (1775–1842) studied in Mannheim. On his father's death he took over the publishing firm and introduced the lithographic process, opening branches in Paris and London. In 1800 in Vienna he bought the 'Mozart-Nachlass' from the composer's widow, thereafter devoting himself to cataloguing and preparing editions of Mozart's works; he paved the way not only for Otto Jahn and Ludwig Köchel but for all subsequent Mozart scholarship. He held several court appointments and composed two operas and vocal and instrumental music in most of the Classical genres; of his *Lehrbuch der Tonsetzkunst* only two of the projected six volumes were completed. He had several musical sons, Carl August (1806–87), Julius (1808–80), and Jean Baptiste (1823–82); it was August (1817–87) who continued the publishing firm, which passed to his descendants. It is now best known for its rich archives.   AL

Andrea Chénier. Opera in four acts by Giordano to a libretto by Luigi Illica (Milan, 1896).

Andricu, Mihail (Gheorghe) (*b* Bucharest, 3 Jan. 1895; *d* Bucharest, 4 Feb. 1974). Romanian composer, pianist, and teacher. He studied at the Bucharest Conservatory (1903–9), where he later taught (1926–59), and travelled widely as Enescu's accompanist. He was a prolific composer, of elegantly neo-classical music, consummately crafted and with a Haydnesque spring; his output includes three ballets, 11 symphonies (1944–70), 13 sinfoniettas (1945–72), eight suites for orchestra (1924–67), three chamber symphonies (1927, 1961, 1965), and concertos for violin (1960) and cello (1961), as well as chamber and piano music, songs, and choral pieces.   MA

Andriessen, Hendrik (Franciscus) (*b* Haarlem, 17 Sept. 1892; *d* Heemstede, 12 April 1981). Dutch composer, organist, and teacher. He was the brother of the composer, pianist, and teacher Willem Andriessen and father of the composers Louis and Jurriaan (1925–96) Andriessen. He had lessons in piano and organ with Louis Robert and J. B. de Pauw and in composition with Bernhard Zweers at the Amsterdam Conservatory (1914–16), where he later taught harmony (1926–34). Highly regarded as an organist, he held positions at St Joseph's, Haarlem, succeeding his father (1913–34), and Utrecht Cathedral (1934–49), where his improvisations, frequently using Gregorian chant, attracted attention. He was also an esteemed educationist, serving as director of the Royal Conservatory in The Hague (1949–57) and as professor at the Catholic University at Nijmegen.

Andriessen's style, which shows a taste for the monumental, is grounded in his contrapuntal training, inspired by his love of Bach; it is combined with harmonies that embrace both the diatonic and the chromatic, allowing him to use dissonance freely in a strongly tonal (often modally inflected) framework. He composed prolifically for the organ, producing one of the largest and most important bodies of work of the 20th century, including *Fête-Dieu* (1916), *Sonata da chiesa* (1927), Passacaglia (1929), Sinfonia (1940), and a Theme and Variations (1949). He wrote four fine symphonies (1930, 1937, 1946, 1954), much church music, including two masses and two *Te Deum* settings, and chamber music and songs. Andriessen's stature has yet to be recognized. His voice, rooted in the past and reaching into the future, is entirely individual; his music is unfailingly noble and often exquisitely beautiful.   MA

Andriessen, Louis (Joseph) (*b* Utrecht, 6 June 1939). Dutch composer and teacher, son of Hendrik Andriessen. Studies with his father (from 1953) were followed by composition lessons from Kees van Baaren at the Royal Conservatory in The Hague (1957–62), then (1962–5) with Berio in Milan and Berlin. His politically aware avant-garde music made a considerable impact in the Netherlands of the late 1960s, and in 1972 he set up the wind ensemble De Volharding ('Perseverance') to popularize new music; another experimental group, Hoketus, followed in 1976 (it survived until 1978). Andriessen began teaching at his alma mater in 1974, taking a composition class from 1978.

His breakthrough as a composer came in 1976 with *De Staat* ('The Republic', after Plato), for four women's voices and ensemble. He is a prolific composer, writing for an extraordinarily wide range of instrumental and vocal combinations: *The Garden of Ryoan-gi* (1967) is

for three electric organs, *Hoe het is* ('How it is', 1969) for live electronics and 52 strings, *The Nine Symphonies of Beethoven* (1970) for orchestra and ice-cream seller's bell, *Workers Union* (1975) for 'any loud group of instruments', and *De Stijl* ('The Style', the third part of the trilogy *De Materie*, 'Matter'; 1984–5) for four female voices, woman speaker, eight voices, and large ensemble. There is also a considerable amount of music for more conventional forces—though the music itself is far from conventional. Andriessen, who discovered his own brand of minimalism independently of the West Coast Americans, is open to a wide variety of influences, ranging from medieval music via Bach, Ives, and Stravinsky to Charlie Parker and Miles Davis, all digested to varying degrees in a style which can blend a high-voltage electrical surge with an ironic sense of the macabre, as in his *Trilogy of the Last Day* (1996–7).

MA

   📖 E. Restagno (ed.), *Andriessen* (Turin, 1996)

Andrieu, Jean-François d'. See Dandrieu, Jean-François.

Anerio, Felice (*b* Rome, *c*.1560; *d* Rome, 26 or 27 Sept. 1614). Italian composer. He was a choirboy at S. Maria Maggiore and a soprano at the Cappella Giulia, and held various other positions as a singer before becoming *maestro di cappella* at the Collegio Inglese. He was much in demand as a musician in Rome, and in 1594 he succeeded Palestrina as composer to the papal chapel; he was later commissioned, with Soriano, to reform the Roman Gradual (see plainchant, 3). His church music was very much in the style of Palestrina, but he also wrote lighter music, and some of his canzonettas inspired (to put it no more strongly) Morley's well-known book of *Canzonets to Two Voyces*.   DA

Anerio, Giovanni Francesco (*b* Rome, *c*.1567; *d* Graz, June 1630). Italian composer, brother of Felice Anerio. His career in Rome was similar to that of his brother, but he also spent some years as *maestro di cappella* at Verona Cathedral and in the 1620s went to Poland, where he directed the music of King Sigismund III. Also a follower of Palestrina, he composed some solo motets in a more modern style, as well as some dialogue pieces which are important in the early history of the oratorio (see oratorio, 1).   DA

Anfang (Ger.). 'Beginning'; *vom Anfang*, 'from the beginning', is thus equivalent to **da capo*.

Anfossi, Pasquale (*b* Taggia, 25 April 1727; *d* Rome, ? Feb. 1797). Italian opera composer. Having begun his career in Naples as a theatre orchestra violinist, he turned to composition, taking lessons from Sacchini and Piccinni. Throughout the 1770s he worked mainly in Rome and Venice. In late 1782 he travelled to London, where his *Il trionfo della constanza* was performed at the King's Theatre on 19 December; he subsequently served as music director there before returning to Italy in 1786. In July 1792 he was appointed *maestro di cappella* at St John Lateran, Rome, where he remained until his death. He wrote over 60—possibly over 70—operas, both heroic and comic; many are spectacular and based on exotic themes. He also wrote sacred music including about 20 oratorios.

LC

angelica (It., 'angel lute'; Fr.: *angélique*; Ger.: *Angelika*). An extended lute of the late Baroque period resembling a small theorbo, but with 16 or 17 strings tuned to a diatonic scale; thus it is effectively a harp on the body of a lute.

JMo

anglaise (Fr.). 1. A 17th- and 18th-century country dance, usually in quick duple time (e.g. in Bach's French Suite no. 3).

2. Any dance thought to be connected with England (e.g. the hornpipe; see HORNPIPE, 2).

Anglebert, Jean-Henry d'. See D'ANGLEBERT, JEAN-HENRY.

Anglican chant. A simple harmonized melody for singing the unmetrical texts, principally the psalms and the canticles, of Anglican services. The main principle of 'single' chants is that of the Gregorian tones (Ex. 1): a short two-part melody is repeated to each verse of the text, the varying numbers of syllables in the different lines being accommodated by the flexible device of a reciting note at the opening of each line, while the succeeding notes are sung in time and (normally) take one syllable each. Chants accommodating two verses are called double chants. Triple chants have been composed and a few quadruple chants also exist, but in use these become tiresome.

Early Anglican chants, such as those published in Morley's *A Plaine and Easie Introduction to Practicall Musicke* (1597), were adapted directly from Gregorian tones and resemble continental *falsobordone*. The number of chants sung in cathedrals and colleges proliferated after 1660, at which time the melody was moved from the tenor to the soprano. With the Oxford Movement of the 19th century, the desire for a 'fully choral' service was extended, until (after much opposition, and sometimes even grave disorder) it gradually reached almost every village church. In order to facilitate the coordination of text and melody by non-professional choirs and congregations, various methods of 'pointing' texts with signs marking changes of melodic direction were developed.

Ex. 1

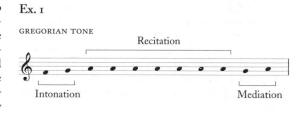

GREGORIAN TONE

ANGLICAN CHANT

With recent liturgical reforms, opportunities for psalmody and for the chanting of canticles have diminished. In some churches Anglican chant has been superseded by responsorial psalms or 'Gelineau' chanting with refrains or antiphons.

PS/CM/ALi

Anglican parish church music. At the time of the *Reformation, a surprising number (though probably far from a majority) of English parish churches possessed organs. These were usually small instruments which can have had little function beyond helping the performance of the plainchant. Following the suppression of chantries in 1548, the standard of musical performance in a good many parish churches declined precipitously as choirs were disbanded and organs allowed to decay. The 'clerks' (lay or in minor orders) who formerly assisted the priest became reduced to one 'parish clerk', on whom the leading of congregational psalms and responses devolved.

Congregational performances of metrical psalms, inspired by continental precedents and encouraged by the Calvinist wing of the Church of England, soon became the primary form of music in parish services and remained so for approximately two centuries. The main source of metrical psalmody during this period was *The Whole Booke of Psalmes* (1562), which came to be known as the 'Old Version' (see HYMN, 3). Ever slower tempos accompanied by increasing amounts of ornamentation gave rise to a heterophonic style of singing known as the 'Old Way'.

After the Restoration, organs were installed in some town parishes, where the singing was most often led by the 'charity children' of the parish. These were either the children of the various free (weekday) schools for the poor or the Sunday-school children, who once a week received free instruction in reading, writing, the Catechism, and the Bible. During the 18th century a custom arose in rural churches of employing small orchestras in the west galleries. Together with a small choir they led the metrical psalms or hymns and performed occasional simple anthems. The disappearance of the church orchestra is due in the first instance to the introduction of the barrel organ in the late 18th century and then to that of the harmonium, introduced from France in the 1840s.

The Oxford Movement of the 19th century introduced a fashion for male choirs (surpliced and sitting in the chancel) and for the chanting of the responses and psalms. In fact it was an attempt to transplant what had previously been considered the cathedral and college chapel type of service to the town and village parish church. The old type of service lingered, however, in a good many churches until nearly the end of the 19th century.

Many changes have occurred since World War II. Parish church congregations have dwindled, and mixed choirs have replaced choirs of men and boys in some churches. Liturgical reforms, in particular the publication of the *Alternative Service Book* (1980) and *Common Worship* (2001), have placed greater emphasis on the Sunday Eucharist and congregational participation. Congregational (generally unison) settings are often used for parts of the service such as the Kyrie and Gloria, while the choir may contribute a motet at the offertory or during the communion. Music in popular styles, involving the use of guitars, piano, and percussion, 'folk' groups, and recorded music, is now commonplace. PS/CM/AL1

📖 N. TEMPERLEY, *The Music of the English Parish Church* (Cambridge, 1979) · J. ROSENTHAL (ed.), *The Essential Guide to the Anglican Communion* (London, 1998)

angosciosamente (It.). 'With anguish'.

ängstlich (Ger.). 'Anxiously', 'uneasily'.

anhalten, anhaltend (Ger.). 'To hold on', 'continuing'.

Anhang (Ger.). 'Appendix', 'supplement'. A term used in scholarly editions of music to denote the appendices which may contain, for instance, alternative readings or variants of certain portions of the music or text. It can also be used for appendices to catalogues, listing additional works.

anhemitonic scale [tonal scale]. A *scale with no semitones, i.e. one of the four pentatonic scales or a whole-tone scale.

anima (It., 'soul'). Soundpost.

animando (It.). 'Animating'; *animandosi*, 'becoming animated'; *animato* (It.), 'animated'. Often used to qualify *allegro*, it implies (increasingly) rapid tempo.

animé (Fr.). 'Animated', i.e. at a moderately quick tempo.

animo, animoso (It.). 'Spirit', 'spirited'.

Animuccia, Giovanni (*b* Florence, *c.*1500; *d* Rome, March 1571). Italian composer. Little is known of his life, except that he was in charge of the singers at the Cappella Giulia, Rome, from 1555, when he succeeded Palestrina. He was a friend of Filippo Neri and the first *maestro di cappella* to the famous Oratory at S. Girolamo (see ORATORIO, 1), writing some *laudi* for its use. He also experimented with a simpler choral style, to meet the demands of the *Council of Trent that the words should be clearly heard. A prolific and eminent composer, he was the first in Florence to write extended madrigal cycles. DA/TC

anmutig (Ger.). 'Graceful'.

Anna Amalia, Duchess of Saxe-Weimar (*b* Wolfenbüttel, 24 Oct. 1739; *d* Weimar, 10 April 1807). German composer and patron. A niece of Frederick the Great, she married Duke Ernst of Saxe-Weimar at 16, taking up the regency on his death two years later until her eldest son succeeded in 1775. She studied with Ernst Wolf, and was responsible for gathering round herself a group of writers, artists, musicians, and intellectuals who included Wieland, Herder, and Goethe. Weimar classicism was not only literary: J. A. Hiller's *Die Jagd* and Anton Schweitzer's *Alceste* were both first performed in Weimar, and Anna Amalia wrote the music for Goethe's Singspiel *Erwin und Elmire* and for his play *Das Jahrmarktsfest zu Plundersweilen*. Her music is skilful and well turned, no less professional than much of its time, though her real achievement was as a patron who created an artistic centre that was unique in its day and an example for many years to come. WT/JW

Anna Amalia of Prussia (*b* Berlin, 9 Nov. 1723; *d* Berlin, 30 March 1787). German music patron and composer, the youngest sister of Frederick the Great. She was taught music by the cathedral organist, Gottlieb Heyne (1684–1758), and became a competent player of stringed keyboard instruments as well as the organ; she may also have played the violin, lute, and flute. She studied composition with J. P. Kirnberger and wrote a Passion oratorio, *Der Tod Jesu*, to a libretto by the poet K. W. Ramler. Her musical soirées attracted illustrious artists from all over Europe, though she increasingly disliked the more modern styles of her time. She left an extensive music library, now in the Königliche Bibliothek, Berlin.   LC

Anna Bolena. Opera in two acts by Donizetti to a libretto by Felice Romani after Ippolito Pindemonte's *Enrico VIII ossia Anna Bolena* and Alessandro Pepoli's *Anna Bolena* (Milan, 1830).

Anna Magdalena Books. Two collections of keyboard music by Bach (from his *Clavier-Büchlein*), presented to his second wife, Anna Magdalena, in 1722 and 1725.

Années de pèlerinage ('Years of Pilgrimage'). Three volumes of piano pieces by Liszt, composed between 1835 and 1877. Book 1 (published 1855), on Swiss subjects, includes many pieces composed in 1835–8, published as *Album d'un voyageur* and later revised; book 2 (1858) is on Italian subjects; book 3 (completed in 1877) is a more heterogeneous collection and several of the pieces have titles relating to Liszt's stay at the Villa d'Este, near Tivoli.

Anonymous. A term that has been used to designate unknown writers of medieval treatises, e.g. Anonymous IV (*fl* 13th century).

anreissen (Ger., 'to tear at'). In string playing, an exceptionally forceful pizzicato.

Ansatz (Ger.). 1. On wind instruments, 'embouchure'.
  2. On string instruments, 'attack'.
  3. In singing, the arrangement of the vocal apparatus.
  4. In piano playing, 'touch'.

Anschlag (Ger.). 1. In keyboard playing, 'touch'.
  2. A double *appoggiatura, in the second sense of that term.
  3. 'Attack'.

anschwellend (Ger.). 'Swelling', i.e. getting louder.

Ansermet, Ernest (*b* Vevey, 11 Nov. 1883; *d* Geneva, 20 Feb. 1969). Swiss conductor. After beginning his career as a mathematician, he studied music in Paris and Geneva and taught himself conducting. He first came to prominence as the conductor in 1915 of Diaghilev's Ballets Russes, with which he toured widely. In 1918 he founded the Suisse Romande Orchestra; he was its

music director for nearly half a century. Fastidious in matters of detail and clarity, he was a champion of contemporary music, giving premieres of works by Stravinsky, Ravel, Falla, Satie, and others, and developing new techniques for conducting complex avant-garde works. He was particularly highly regarded as an interpreter of French music.   JT

answer. A term used, particularly in fugal writing, to denote the second (and fourth) statements of the subject, or theme, usually at the interval of a perfect 4th or 5th. See FUGUE.

antecedent and consequent. Terms applied to a common principle for constructing musical phrases. According to Schoenberg (*Fundamentals of Musical Composition*, 1967), the simplest form of *period involves the balancing of an initial, antecedent statement or phrase by a consequent statement or phrase, often of the same length (see Ex. 1). Far from being an antithesis of the antecedent, the consequent will commonly begin in the same, or a similar, way. Balance is achieved harmonically. If the antecedent outlines a tonic-to-dominant progression, the consequent will tend to close on the tonic: as Schoenberg notes, this will happen 'if the period is a complete piece (e.g. children's songs)'. In more substantial structures, where the antecedent focuses primarily on tonic harmony, the consequent is as likely to move to the dominant, or some other chord, as to return to the tonic.   AW

Ex. 1

Beethoven, 'Archduke' Trio, 2nd movement, bars 1–8.

Ante-Communion. The first part of the Anglican Holy Communion Service.

Antheil, George [Georg] (Johann Carl) (*b* Trenton, NJ, 8 July 1900; *d* New York, 12 Feb. 1959). American composer of German descent. After studies with Ernest Bloch he moved to Europe, where he quickly inserted himself into the avant-garde milieu, gaining the acquaintance of James Joyce and the admiration of Ezra Pound. His most notorious work, the *Ballet mécanique*, was originally conceived in 1923 as accompaniment for an abstract film by Fernand Léger but was soon revised as a concert piece for eight pianos, pianola, eight xylophones, two electric doorbells, and aeroplane propeller. Representing what Antheil called 'musical engineering', the work asserts the primacy of rhythmic structure, showing the influence of Stravinsky in its changing metres, its ostinatos, and its development of small rhythmic units. It also exemplifies, like the *Airplane Sonata* for piano (1922), that 'machine age' art heralded by the Italian *Futurists.

In 1933 Antheil returned to the USA, and his music became much more conservative, neo-classical in its vigorous counterpoint and its thematic construction. This later period saw the composition of various orchestral and dramatic works, including ballet scores for George Balanchine (*Dreams*, 1935) and Martha Graham (*Course*, 1936).   PG

    E. Pound, *Antheil and the Treatise on Harmony* (Chicago, 1927/R1968) · G. Antheil, *Bad Boy of Music* (Garden City, NY, 1945/R1990)

anthem. An English-language choral piece of moderate length for use in worship, typically on a prose text selected from the Bible or the liturgy. The term is not used for settings of unvarying liturgical texts, such as the *canticles (see also SERVICE). Some anthems have texts in verse—for example psalm paraphrases or hymns, or even original poems—though none of these were termed 'anthem' until well into the 19th century. The word has been extended beyond church use in the term *'national anthem'.

Anthems have been sung in the Church of England since the Reformation. They have been one of the most characteristic of English forms, evolving in relative independence of continental idioms. At several points in their long history they have risen to heights of beauty and creativity. More recently they have been adopted by other Protestant denominations.

Anthems are capable of a wide range of expression and meaning. Some are suitable for daily worship, some for grand occasions; some are public and extroverted in character, others express the most intimate feeling. An anthem can be in a single, homogeneous movement, or on a large time-scale, with room for contrasts of forces, key, and mood between sections. What they all have in common is the idea of a choir leading, guiding, and intensifying, by means of music, the unspoken religious feelings of a listening congregation.

    1. The cathedral anthem to 1714; 2. The cathedral anthem since 1714; 3. The parochial and non-Anglican anthem

1. The cathedral anthem to 1714

The word 'anthem' is older than the Reformation. It was an Anglicization of *antiphon, and meant a short Latin plainchant used before a psalm, or a longer one at the end of the daily offices of Lauds, Compline, and Vespers, especially sung in praise of the Virgin Mary, or other saint. The texts of such antiphons could also be set polyphonically. The first English-language anthems date from just before the official introduction of English services under the Act of Uniformity (1549); some were adapted from Latin antiphons or motets, others may have originated as private devotional pieces. Elizabeth I's *Injunctions* of 1559 set the place and character of the anthem for the next four centuries:

> In the beginning, or in the end of common prayers, either at morning or evening, there may be sung an hymn, or such-like song, to the praise of Almighty God, in the best sort of melody and music that may be conveniently devised, having respect that the sentence of the hymn may be understood and perceived.

So the reformed anthem was something outside the daily liturgy, and wide scope was allowed in the choice of both text and music. Indeed, for parish churches, the same injunction was held to authorize the congregational singing of metrical psalms. In cathedrals and other choral foundations anthems could be, and often were, sung four times a day, before and after Morning and Evening Prayer (also known as Matins and Evensong). In the 1662 revision of the *Book of Common Prayer*, new prayers were added at the end of the service. To confirm the long-established singing of an anthem after the third collect, which was now no longer the final prayer, a clarification was added which has since become famous: 'In quires and places where they sing, here followeth the anthem'. This placed the anthem within the service for the first time; but it did not end the practice of singing one before the service as well.

Early Elizabethan anthems were modelled on the Latin antiphon or motet, but they cautiously followed the queen's injunction by being largely syllabic, with a minimum of counterpoint. Beautifully simple four-part settings in this vein were written by Tye, Tallis, Sheppard, and Mundy, often for small choirs of men without boys, and hence reaching only a high alto ('meane') register. They were accompanied on an organ.

The golden age of the anthem was from about 1590 to 1640, when several cathedrals, and more especially the Chapel Royal, acquired sufficient resources, including competent boys' choirs, to permit a more ambitious musical programme. Byrd, Gibbons, and Tomkins led a large group of composers in the production of a magnificent repertory. In addition to the quietly devotional tone of earlier anthems, they could now vividly depict the widely contrasting emotions demanded by texts expressing praise, love, penitence, grief, or fear, and could even use word-painting in the fashion of the madrigal. Five voice parts were the norm; six to eight were not unusual. Solo voices were contrasted with full choirs in the *verse anthem, sometimes with the accompaniment of viols. In contrast to the Italian *seconda pratica*, however, anthem composers never went to extremes of verbal expression. Imitative counterpoint was maintained, usually alternating with sections of homophony. Gibbons, for instance, remained a recognizably Anglican composer by preserving a balance between expression and sobriety, and by his exquisite attention to English stress patterns.

A second highpoint occurred during the Restoration (1660–1714) following the Puritan interregnum. Again the Chapel Royal monopolized the best singers and composers, and in addition Charles II demanded the French styles he had come to know during his exile. Anthems written for the Chapel Royal at this time make much use of jaunty dotted rhythms in triple time, with accompaniments, ritornellos, and overtures for violins. In keeping with the king's personal taste, gloom, profundity, and learned counterpoint were avoided. A few singers with spectacular voices were exploited, and the verse anthem became unbalanced in its preference for the solo voice, even spawning a new variety, the 'solo anthem', that was essentially a solo cantata closing with a brief Alleluia or Amen for the chorus.

The leading composers of the day, Locke, Humfrey, Blow, and Purcell, were extraordinarily gifted, and when they were not writing for the king they followed more interesting paths. They cultivated Baroque techniques of expressive intensity, perhaps a late derivative of the Monteverdi school, often shown in extreme dissonance and chromaticism. At the same time there was a distinct revival of Elizabethan contrapuntal traditions, especially in provincial cathedrals, and most completely in 'full' (as opposed to verse) anthems. Queen Anne (1702–14) was the last sovereign to take a personal interest in the Chapel Royal, and in her time standards were maintained (but without conditions attached) by such composers as Croft, Clarke, and Weldon.

2. The cathedral anthem since 1714

In the 18th century, with religious and dynastic wars largely ended, the Church of England settled down to a time of peace, self-confidence, and occasional splendour. Under a new wave of Italian influence the anthem tended to be broken into separate sections of recitative, aria, ensemble, and chorus, with the arias increasingly elaborate and the choruses emphasizing grandeur rather than intensity. Handel's splendid anthems for George II's coronation (1727) and Queen Caroline's funeral (1737) exemplify the newer ideal. His leading English-born contemporary, Greene, was at his best in the pathetic vein. Later Georgian composers such as

Boyce, Crotch, and Attwood continued to write and publish anthems, sometimes highly polished but rarely showing pronounced originality. Their length, formality, and emphasis on the solo voice have tended to keep them out of the modern repertory. Anthems were still classified as full, verse, and solo, but full anthems were less often performed, and even they frequently had verses for soloists between the full choral sections. However, a new type of short full anthem, often a setting of one of the seasonal collects (prayers), gained in popularity after about 1800.

In Victorian times, this more intimate and touching style of anthem developed at the hands of composers like Goss, Walmisley, and Stainer. It clearly owed much to the Classical masters, more especially Mozart; later influences were Spohr, Mendelssohn, and Gounod. A solitary genius, Samuel Sebastian Wesley, transformed the large-scale anthem, in the face of worsening conditions in the cathedral choirs, with his inspired settings of texts chosen for their dramatic force and his individual treatment of dissonance. The reform and retrenchment of cathedral choirs, especially after 1870, accompanied by the growth of disciplined choirs in many parish churches, gave a new incentive to both publishers and composers. Unprecedented quantities of anthems began to appear in cheap octavo editions, and the best were often the work of composers like Parry, Stanford, and Vaughan Williams, who were not professionally connected to the church. Not surprisingly, a secular, often symphonic character began to prevail in the anthem, which enjoyed another brief flowering in the early 20th century. The hymn-anthem, incorporating a popular hymn tune or carol, was one product of the expansion of anthem singing beyond the cloistered cathedral setting; another was the occasional choice of poetic rather than scriptural texts.

Some later composers such as Herbert Howells, and including the American Leo Sowerby and the Canadian Healey Willan, continued to treat the anthem as a serious part of their output. At the same time the early 20th century saw a notable revival of the glories of past cathedral music, especially of the Elizabethan and Jacobean periods, and this has been maintained. On the other hand the Victorian innovation of replacing the anthem with hymn settings, excerpts from oratorios and cantatas, mass movements, motets, and adaptations has never entirely gone away, so that the continuous and distinctive anthem tradition has turned into something much more eclectic.

Liturgical changes since the 1960s have removed Morning and Evening Prayer, the normal contexts for anthems, from their central position in worship, and have shifted the emphasis from choral to congregational singing. The new service book, *Common Worship*

(2001), makes no provision for anthems, beyond mentioning 'hymns or anthems' as one of three options to end the service of 'Morning/Evening Prayer from *The Book of Common Prayer*', the others being a sermon or further prayers. With declining attendance and choir membership, only a few cathedrals and college choirs have the capacity to do justice to the great anthems of the past, or to tackle new ones of any difficulty. These few often command astonishingly high standards of performance, and there are vigorous continuing efforts to defend and preserve the great cathedral tradition. But inevitably, like mass settings and sacred cantatas before them, anthems are moving from the church service to the choral concert and the sound recording, and are now most often enjoyed purely as music, not as an integral part of a religious experience.

3. The parochial and non-Anglican anthem

Anglican parish churches, still largely organless, began to develop voluntary choirs in the late 17th century and were soon urged 'as much as may be, to imitate their mother churches the *cathedrals*'. From 1701 (in Henry Playford's *Divine Companion*) leading composers were commissioned to provide simplified anthems for parish choirs. They were soon imitated by self-appointed country singing teachers, who developed a type of anthem that was far from the canons of art music but was a legitimate form of expression for rural singers, often accompanied by church bands after 1760. This tradition is now undergoing revival and re-evaluation as 'west gallery music'. But in Victorian times it suffered a slow demise, as barrel organs and harmoniums replaced the bands, and a surpliced choir in the chancel tended to supersede the old gallery singers, bringing a return to conventional art music. Professional composers, for example Goss and Stainer, again began to write simple parochial anthems.

The country anthem of the Georgian period gave rise to an astonishing flowering of anthems in primarily Congregational or Unitarian communities in America (1770–1810), led by Billings, but this too was eventually defeated by the onward march of urban prosperity. In both Britain and North America, many non-Anglican Protestant churches took up anthem singing, often encouraging the whole congregation to join in. The *Tonic Sol-fa system in Britain and the *shape-note system in America brought professionally composed anthems within the reach of untrained groups of singers. Today many urban Protestant churches in the USA boast a large choir and a staff of musicians. The 'anthem' slot in their choral services is filled sometimes by actual anthems of British or American composition, sometimes by other sacred music of various origins.   NT

📖 E. A. WIENANDT and R. H. YOUNG, *The Anthem in England and America* (New York, 1970) · P. le HURAY, *Music and the Reformation in England, 1549–1660* (Cambridge, 2/1978) · N. TEMPERLEY, *The Music of the English Parish Church* (Cambridge, 1979) · W. J. GATENS, *Victorian Cathedral Music in Theory and Practice* (Cambridge, 1986) · I. SPINK, *Restoration Cathedral Music, 1660–1714* (Oxford, 1995)

anthems, national. See NATIONAL ANTHEMS.

anticipation. A note that occurs immediately before the chord to which it belongs; in Ex. 1, the quaver E is part of the following C major chord, and 'anticipates' it.

Ex. 1

Antico, Andrea (*b* Montona, Istria, *c.*1480; *d* after 1538). Italian music publisher and composer. He was active in Rome and Venice, where he was the main business competitor of Ottaviano *Petrucci. Whereas Petrucci printed music using multiple impressions, however, Antico printed in one impression from woodblocks cut by himself. He mainly published secular music, including several books of frottolas, and madrigals by such composers as Arcadelt and Verdelot. His few sacred publications include motets by Willaert.

JWA

Antigone. Plays by Sophocles and Euripides that have been used as the subject of several operas, notably by Hasse (1743), Gluck (1756), Zingarelli (1790), Honegger (1927), and Orff (1949); Mendelssohn (1841) and Saint-Saëns (1894) wrote incidental music to Sophocles' play.

antimasque. One of the entries in a *masque.

antiphon. A liturgical chant sung as the refrain to the verses of a psalm. The word *antiphonon* is Greek, used by some ancient Greek writers to mean 'octave'. Its meaning of an independent chant performed with psalms in Christian worship dates from the 4th century, known for instance from the practice of the churches of Antioch and Jerusalem.

Antiphons sung as propaganda by crowds of Arians and Orthodox in the streets of Constantinople during the archiepiscopacy of St *John Chrysostom (398–404) established patterns of psalmody that later dominated the offices and processional liturgy of the mature Byzantine cathedral rite. The term *antiphonon* thereby came to mean the complex of intonations, verses, and refrains constituting each antiphonated psalm. In the modern Eastern Orthodox Church, the term generally refers to (1) antiphonated psalms taken from stational rites of Constantinople and prefixed in sets of three to the Divine Liturgy; (2) by extension, Psalm 103, Psalm 145, and the Beatitudes (the *Typika*), prefixed to the Divine Liturgy on many days in Palestinian monastic use; (3) the *anavathmoi*, poetic chants from the *oktoechos* originally sung as refrains to the Psalms of Ascents (Psalms 120–33) at Sunday and Festal Orthros; and (4) the 15 antiphons of the Passion, sung today without their verses at Orthros on Holy Friday.

Decomposition of early psalmodic forms may also be seen in the Latin West, where the repetition of an antiphon after each verse of a psalm became increasingly rare after the 9th century. Instead, antiphons often came to be sung only before and after the performance of a psalm. The earliest sources with music (which appear from the 10th century) reflect the very large number of psalms sung during a day's services in the Middle Ages in often containing over 1200, sometimes over 2000 antiphons. Most are simple in style and many are set to 'prototype' melodies—popular tunes expanded or contracted in accordance with the number of syllables in the new text. The mode of the antiphon determines the choice of psalm tone to which the succeeding psalm will be sung. Consequently there are many collections of antiphons arranged tonally (all the D-mode antiphons first, then the E-mode, etc.), in books known as 'tonaries'. But the chief music book containing antiphons was the *antiphoner.

Antiphons were most often used in the Roman rite for the psalms of the Office (the largest groups being for Matins, Lauds, and Vespers). But they were also used at Mass, for the introit, offertory, and communion chants. There are two special categories of antiphons, not connected to a psalm and not usually simple in style: the *antiphons of the Blessed Virgin Mary, sung daily at Compline from the 13th century; and processional antiphons, sung during religious processions, or at a place where a procession paused (a 'station').

DH/ALi

📖 O. STRUNK, *Essays on Music in the Byzantine World* (New York, 1977) · D. HILEY, *Western Plainchant: A Handbook* (Oxford, 1993) · E. NOWACKI, 'Antiphonal psalmody in Christian antiquity and early Middle Ages', *Essays on Medieval Music in Honor of David G. Hughes*, ed. G. Boone (Cambridge, MA, and London, 1995), 287–316

antiphonal psalmody. In its strictest and original sense, the chanting of psalmodic texts by alternating choirs or soloists with the addition of one or more refrains (*antiphona*) after each verse. Following the disappearance of the refrains in the Roman rite, the term also came to be applied to the *alternatim* performance of psalms and canticles. ALi

antiphoner [antiphonal, antiphonale, antiphonary]. A liturgical book of the Roman rite containing the chants of the *Office hours (i.e. Matins, Lauds, Prime, Terce, Sext, None, Vespers, and Compline). Secular and monastic classes of antiphoners are distinguished by the number and ordering of their chants. Modern editions antedating the Second Vatican Council (1962–5) include the *Antiphonale monasticum* (1934) produced by the Benedictines of Solesmes and the Vatican edition provided for secular churches in 1912 (rev. 1949). The *Psalterium monasticum* (1981) and the *Liber hymnarius* (1982) reflect the liturgical changes brought about by the promulgation of the Liturgy of the Hours (Liturgia Horarum) in 1971.

See also LIBER USUALIS. AP/ALi

antiphons of the Blessed Virgin Mary [Marian antiphons]. Antiphons of the Roman rite sung in honour of the Virgin Mary without connection to a psalm. Although some are very ancient, the best known and most elaborate date from the 11th century onwards. It became the custom to sing one daily at Compline from the 13th century. The most famous are *Alma Redemptoris mater*, sung from the beginning of Advent until 2 February; *Ave regina coelorum*, sung from 2 February until Wednesday in Holy Week; *Regina coeli laetare*, sung from Easter Sunday until the Friday after Pentecost; and *Salve regina*, sung from Trinity Sunday to the Saturday before the first Sunday of Advent.

—/ALi

antiphony. A term, derived from Christian chant, that refers to the singing of sections of a chant by two choirs in alternation. 'Antiphony' is also used of alternation between forces in polyphonic choral music (see CORI SPEZZATI) or instrumental music, and is often encountered in ethnomusicological descriptions of similar practices ('call and response') in non-Western music.

PW

antique cymbals. Chromatic sets of small, thick *cymbals played either with a metal beater or clashed together in pairs. They are occasionally called 'finger cymbals'.

Antony and Cleopatra. Opera in three acts by Barber to a libretto by Franco Zeffirelli after Shakespeare (New York, 1966).

Antwort (Ger.). 'Answer', in *fugues.

anvil (Fr.: *enclume*; Ger.: *Amboss*; It.: *incudine*). A percussion *idiophone, usually consisting of one or two thick metal bars of indefinite pitch, mounted on a frame and struck with hammers to imitate the blacksmith's anvil. Occasionally a real anvil will be used, but these are usually too large and heavy to be practical. Some composers specify a pitch, for instance Wagner in *Das Rheingold* (F in three octaves).   JMo

Aperghis, Georges (*b* Athens, 23 Dec. 1945). Greek composer. He went to live in France in 1963. His early works were influenced by Xenakis, but the composer with whom he has the closest affinity is Mauricio Kagel. He summarizes his approach as 'faire musique de tout'—'to make music from everything'. Most of his works, even those for instruments, have a theatrical element; in 1976 he formed his own Atelier Théâtre et Musique to perform them. Aperghis has composed six operas, including *Tristes tropiques* (after Lévi-Strauss, 1996). His frequently performed *Récitations* for soprano (1982) are based on ideas about language and narrative.   ABur

aperto (It., 'open'). 1. 'Clear', 'distinct'.

2. A term used in horn playing to indicate unstopped notes.

3. An indication in 14th-century music of alternative endings to sections (see also OUVERT AND CLOS).

4. A term used by Mozart in some of his early works as a qualification to *allegro*, its precise meaning now unclear.

Apollo. See APOLLON MUSAGÈTE.

Apollon musagète (*Apollo musagetes*; 'Apollo, Leader of the Muses'). Ballet in two scenes by Stravinsky, scored for strings; it was choreographed by Adolph Bolm (Washington, DC, 1928) and later the same year by George Balanchine (Paris). Stravinsky revised the work in 1947 and it is now known as *Apollo*.

Apostel, Hans Erich (*b* Karlsruhe, 22 Jan. 1901; *d* Vienna, 30 Nov. 1972). German-born Austrian composer. After beginning his career at the Karlsruhe Opera, he moved to Vienna in 1921, supporting himself by private teaching and later as a reader for a music publisher. He studied with Schoenberg and Berg, and used their 12-note methods in all his later compositions, allied to clear formal structures. Apostel's music was banned during the Nazi period, but later received frequent performances and several awards. It includes works for orchestra and many different solo instruments and ensembles, as well as several song cycles.   ABur

Apostles, The. Oratorio, op. 49 (1903), by Elgar, for six soloists, chorus, and orchestra, to a biblical text compiled by the composer; Elgar composed a sequel, *The *Kingdom*.

apothéose (Fr.). A work written in honour of a dead person, e.g. François Couperin's two *apothéoses*, for Corelli (1724) and Lully (1725). See also TOMBEAU.

Appalachia. 'Variations on an Old Slave Song' (1903) by Delius, for baritone, chorus, and orchestra, a reworking of his *American Rhapsody* for orchestra (1896).

Appalachian dulcimer. A zither, originally from the south-eastern USA, now widely used by folk musicians. A raised fingerboard above a gently curved soundbox carries three (or more) strings, two of them drones. The melody string is tuned to the dominant.   JMo

Appalachian Spring. Ballet in one act by Copland, choreographed by Martha Graham (Washington, DC, 1944); it is scored for 13 instruments. Copland arranged a suite (1944), then orchestrated it (1945). The whole ballet was also orchestrated (1945).

'Appassionata' Sonata. The publisher's apt title given to Beethoven's Piano Sonata no. 23 in F minor op. 57 (1804–5) when it was published in an arrangement for piano duet (1838).

appassionato, appassionata (It.). 'Impassioned'.

appena (It.). 'Scarcely', 'slightly'; see PEINE, À.

Appenzeller, Benedictus (*b* c.1480–8; *d* after 1558). Flemish composer. He was associated with the chapel of Mary of Hungary in Brussels from 1536 until at least 1551, when he travelled with her to Germany. His best-known work, a lament on the death of Josquin, suggests that he may have been Josquin's pupil. His other works include masses, motets, *Magnificat* settings, chansons, and dances.   JM

applause. The custom of showing one's pleasure at music by immediately following it with a noise, usually by clapping but sometimes also by the drumming of feet, is perhaps as old as the art of music itself. It springs partly from the desire of an audience to express excitement immediately. The volume of sound in the last quarter-minute of a performance largely governs the volume of applause that follows, a loud ending usually 'bringing the house down' whatever the merits or demerits of the composition or performance as a whole (a high note at the end of a vocal piece sometimes has the same effect).

Audiences frequently applaud at the end of the singer's part in an operatic aria (often also with random shouts of 'Bravo/Brava'), thereby drowning what may be a beautiful orchestral postlude; the same has been known to happen at the end of a cadenza in a concerto, though since audiences at orchestral concerts are usually more knowledgeable than those at the opera this is rarer. Similarly, in the opera house applause often begins before the curtain falls, and spectacular scenic effects are often greeted with loud clapping regardless of what the conductor is coaxing from the musicians in the pit; audiences may applaud or laugh at jokes they read in the *surtitles before the point at which the singer utters the words in question. Ballet audiences traditionally applaud not only every solo and many *pas de deux*, but often the very appearance on stage of a star performer.

Audiences sometimes respond, whether in the theatre or concert hall, by rising to their feet: a 'standing ovation'. But on the whole we are more restrained than our forebears. It is not deemed proper to applaud at the end of an individual movement of a symphony, concerto, or sonata, however exciting it may have been. It is also considered disruptive to clap individual songs or short instrumental pieces rather than at the end of each group at lieder recitals or early music concerts.

The question has often been raised whether an audience should not also have the right to express disappointment. In some countries hissing is not unknown, but elsewhere the understanding is that complaints destroy the social atmosphere. In Britain booing is rare, but it has attracted media attention since the late 1980s. It is not uncommon, at a curtain call, for the cast and conductor of an opera to be greeted with a warm reception but the director and designer to be booed. Slow hand-clapping (which in Britain signifies disapproval) and uncoordinated clapping represent different responses in different places.

Audiences occasionally pass beyond mere noisy protest. The throwing of oranges seems to have been a widely recognized means of expressing disappointment. After Marinetti's Futurist programmes in Italy in the early 1920s, crockery and a variety of fruit and vegetables were thrown at the performers, and when Weill's *Aufstieg und Fall der Stadt Mahagonny* was performed at Frankfurt in 1930, stink-bombs were thrown and a man was killed by a beer-mug during the 'discussion' that followed. According to Grétry, opera audiences in mid-18th-century Rome made a practice of signalling their recognition of plagiarisms by calling out the name of the original composer; thus one might hear cries of 'Bravo Sacchini! Bravo Cimarosa! Bravo Paisiello!'

In the 1770s Burney wrote that at musical performances in Italian churches, since clapping was prohibited, 'they cough, hem and blow their noses to express admiration'. This recalls the 'humming' common among 17th-century English church congregations who wished to express approval of some passage in a sermon. While applause during a service is unknown today, when churches are used as concert halls the secular conventions apply. However, in concert performances of church music, particularly Bach's Passions, applause is out of place, at least until the end of the whole work (and even then, the greatest compliment the audience can pay the performers is a

moment of silence). Handel's oratorios, on the other hand, intended for concert rooms and theatres, should be received in the same way as secular works of the period.

Applause may be bought. The 'claque', or group of hired applauders, has been a part of musical and theatrical life in many countries and was common in London in the mid-19th century, particularly at the Royal Italian Opera, and in the early 20th century at the Metropolitan Opera House, New York.

See also ENCORE.   PS/DA/AL

applied music. The American term for a course in performance studies, as opposed to theory.

appoggiando (It., 'leaning'). A style of playing in which succeeding notes are closely connected and stressed.

appoggiatura (It., from *appoggiare*, 'to lean'; Fr.: *appoggiature*; Ger.: *Vorschlag*). A dissonant note that 'leans' on a harmony note, taking part of its time value. Typically the dissonance is a step above or below the main note. Today the term has two applications: generally, it denotes a harmonic resource where a note in one chord is held over as a momentary, discordant part of the combination which follows; more specifically, it is an *ornament. The ornament has gone by a variety of different names (forefall, backfall; Fr.: *appuyé, coulé, port de voix*) and has been indicated and performed in many ways over several centuries. One Baroque sign was the hook (Ex. 1). The most common representation has been by a small note, but its notated value need not correspond to the length it has when played.

Ex. 1

Shortly after 1750 German writers codified appoggiatura performance with two main categories: the first type, the (normal) long appoggiatura, takes half the value of the main note, or, if placed before a dotted note, two thirds of its value (in compound time, an appoggiatura on to a dotted note tied to another note takes the full length of the dotted note). The second type is the short appoggiatura (Ex. 2a); in certain circumstances (for example when the main note is one of a series of reiterated notes, or when the main note is a short one and is followed by others of the same value) the appoggiatura should be played much shorter (but still on the beat), as in Ex. 2b and c. In either case the two notes will typically be slurred and played with a

Ex. 2

diminuendo. There was also a 'passing appoggiatura', used only to fill in gaps between notes a 3rd apart and (exceptionally for an appoggiatura) taken before the beat instead of on it.

The standard long and occasional short appoggiaturas are the norm for the Classical period, but the notation and performance of the appoggiatura before 1750 is a more complex and controversial subject. There are cases in Bach's music, for example, where the long appoggiatura is inappropriate, and the performer must be alert to the possibility of shortening the ornament to a third or a quarter of the value of the main note, in response to the melodic and harmonic context. The extempore addition of the appoggiatura as an expressive device was common in the Baroque period. As with other ornaments (e.g. the trill, to which it is often allied), the absence of an ornament mark did not preclude its use or even its necessity. A particular convention applies to vocal recitative of the late 18th century. It was expected that appoggiaturas would be added in such circumstances as Ex. 3, where the vocal line ends on two repeated notes.

Ex. 3

During the 19th century, composers began to write long appoggiaturas in full notation. The short appoggiatura was then notated by the new sign ♪. Disagreement among 20th-century scholars about the placing of the short appoggiatura either before or on the beat mirrors the opposing views of theorists of the previous century. 19th-century treatises and ornament tables suggest that both interpretations were common; in practice the speed with which such grace notes are played, combined with the subtle rhythmic nuances of good performance, often make it difficult for the ear to perceive clearly whether the note occurs on or before the beat.

The expression 'double appoggiatura' has been used for three different effects: two simultaneous appog-

giaturas, the figure shown in Ex. 4, and the slide (see SLIDE, 2).   SMcV/BW

Ex. 4

appreciation of music. A term used frequently in the early to mid-20th century, particularly in the UK and the USA, to describe the process of learning how to listen to serious music. It implies not only enjoyment of music, but also the knowledge that can help those without previous training to go beyond enjoyment to 'understanding'. 'Music(al) appreciation' was fashionable both in schools and with the general public, and its principles and methods still underpin much music teaching, particularly in the USA.

1. History; 2. Techniques

1. History

Instruction in music appreciation has focused on the canonic works of the west European repertory from the 18th century onwards. It does not necessarily treat the subject chronologically or historically. In the early to mid-20th century, proponents of music appreciation were convinced of the morally, spiritually, and socially elevating properties of art music. Books that aimed to explain and promote serious works in non-technical language became widely available. These decades also saw the birth of radio broadcasts and the increasing impact of older technologies such as the gramophone and player-piano: musical experience thus moved from the public arena to the home.

With these developments, individuals and groups saw new opportunities to encourage the appreciation of music, particularly among those less privileged materially. In this context, listening to music was held up as a valuable activity in its own right, gaining ground on musical participation, which had long been a beacon of self-improvement. In England, Percy Scholes and Walford Davies both achieved popularity with their BBC radio broadcasts; Antony Hopkins's weekly programmes *Talking about Music*, each dedicated to a discussion of a single work, ran for over 20 years.

Modern examples of initiatives to enhance music appreciation include the television series *Howard Goodall's Big Bangs* (2000), the radio series *Discovering Music*, and innumerable CD-ROMs and websites.

2. Techniques

In learning to appreciate music, it is necessary to distinguish between the arts of composing, performing, and listening, each requiring unique skills and training. The ability to listen intelligently is enhanced only minimally, for instance, by learning to write four-part harmony or by improving instrumental technique. Rather, music appreciation is developed by educating the listener in three main areas. First, a historical overview is necessary to place individual works in context; attention is therefore usually given to the lives and works of the 'great' composers and the circumstances in which key works were composed. Second, a knowledge of musical form is required, to enable the listener to distinguish the statement and transformation of important melodic themes, harmonic patterns, and the overall shape of a work. Third, it is important for the listener to understand basic musical terminology—to know what is implied by such formal types as sonata or rondo, directions in tempo and expression, and harmonic references (for example to tonic and dominant).

The overarching requirement is that of repeated, attentive listening (which is why the appreciation movement coincided with the advent of recorded sound): repetition provides the listener with understanding through recognition of thematic material and musical idiom. After familiarity with a musical work is acquired, some kind of analytical engagement—examining thematic development, methods of modulation and orchestration, and patterns of tension and release—can enhance understanding, enjoyment, and discrimination.

See also EDUCATION. MP

Apprenti sorcier, L' ('The Sorcerer's Apprentice'). Symphonic scherzo (1897) by Dukas based on Johann Wolfgang von Goethe's ballad *Der Zauberlehrling*, which, in turn, is based on a dialogue in Lucian (2nd century AD). In the Disney film *Fantasia* the apprentice was represented by Mickey Mouse.

appuyé (Fr., 'leant on'). Emphasized; see APPOGGIATURA.

Après-midi d'un faune', Prélude à 'L' ('Prelude to "The Afternoon of a Faun" '). Orchestral work by Debussy (1894), an 'impression' of a poem by Stéphane Mallarmé; it was choreographed and danced by Vaslav Nijinsky for Diaghilev's Ballets Russes (Paris,

1912). Debussy intended to compose a *Prélude*, *Interlude*, and *Paraphrase finale*, but completed only the *Prélude*.

aptitude tests. See TESTS.

aquarelle (Fr., 'water-colour'). A title sometimes given to a piece of music of delicate texture.

Aquin, Louis-Claude d'. See DAQUIN, LOUIS-CLAUDE.

Arabella. Opera in three acts by Richard Strauss to a libretto by Hugo von Hofmannsthal after his novel *Lucidor* (Dresden, 1933).

arabesque (Fr.; Ger.: *Arabeske*). A term originally used to describe the ornamental style of Arabic art and architecture, used in music in two ways. 1. In ballet, an arabesque is a posture in which the body is supported on one leg, with the other leg extended horizontally backwards; the arms can be held in various positions. The term in this sense dates from at least the 18th century.

2. A florid, delicate composition, for example Debussy's *Deux arabesques* for piano.

Araia, Francesco (*b* Naples, 25 June 1709; *d* after 1761). Italian composer. He made his debut as a composer at the age of 14 and had written operas for various Italian cities before 1735, when he became *maestro di cappella* to the Russian imperial court at St Petersburg. He remained there, composing operas and cantatas, until 1759, when he retired to Italy; in 1762 he was recalled to provide music for the coronation of Emperor Peter III, but he returned to Italy again after the latter's assassination, and settled in Bologna. When or where he died is not known.   ER

Arban, (Joseph) Jean-Baptiste (Laurent) (*b* Lyons, 28 Feb. 1825; *d* Paris, 9 April 1889). French cornet player and conductor. Although he was primarily a conductor (from salon orchestras to the Paris Opéra), his work as a pedagogue at the Paris Conservatoire became hugely significant in the field of cornet and trumpet playing; his instruction manual, *Grande méthode complète pour cornet à pistons et de saxhorn* (Paris, 1864), remains so to this day.   CF

Arbre des songes, L' ('The Tree of Dreams'). Violin Concerto (1979–85) by Dutilleux.

Arcadelt, Jacques (*b* ?1505; *d* Paris, 1568). ?French composer. He spent much of his time in Italy. He seems to have had early connections with the Medici and Florence, and from about 1537 he may have been working in Venice, but in 1551 he went to France, where he served Charles of Lorraine and perhaps also Henri II. He was one of the earliest madrigal composers (he wrote over 200), and his first book of four-voice madrigals (1539) was among the first major successes of the printing trade, enjoying 33 editions in a century. Most of his 126 chansons were composed in France; the later ones are nearly all homophonic.   DA/TC

arcata (It.). In string playing, the 'bowstroke'; often followed by *in giù* (down-bow), or *in su* (up-bow); *arcato*, 'bowed', indicates a return to use of the bow after a pizzicato passage.

'Archduke' Trio. Nickname of Beethoven's Piano Trio in B♭ op. 97 (1810–11), dedicated to his patron the Archduke Rudolph of Austria.

Archer, Violet (Balestreri) (*b* Montreal, 24 April 1913; *d* Ottawa, 21 Feb. 2000). Canadian composer, pianist, and teacher. She studied at the McGill Conservatorium, Montreal, and in the USA with Bartók and Hindemith. She taught at McGill, North Texas State College, and the University of Oklahoma, and from 1962 to 1978 at the University of Alberta. Her music, influenced by Canadian landscape and folklore, includes an opera and many orchestral, choral, chamber, and piano works.   ABUR

    📖 K. MacMillan and J. Beckwith (eds.), *Contemporary Canadian Composers* (Toronto, 1975)

archet (Fr.). 'Bow'.

arch form. At its simplest, arch form is synonymous with *ternary form, comprising three sections, ABA, where the first is repeated after a contrasting middle section. The form may be extended, however, to create a larger 'arch', for example ABCBA, where the first two sections are repeated in reverse order after the contrasting middle section, thereby creating a mirror symmetry. Bartók in particular favoured this form, a notable example being the *Music for Strings, Percussion, and Celesta*.

architectural acoustics. Music performed in an enclosed space sounds different from the way it does when heard in the open air. With practice, we can deduce with surprising accuracy the size, shape, and richness of furnishing of our surroundings from the way the sounds of musical instruments or voices have been modified and added to on their way to our ears. For the basic behaviour of sound waves, see ACOUSTICS. The following article considers how sounds are affected by the room or auditorium acoustics.

1. Reflection; 2. Directional effects; 3. Reverberation; 4. Designing for good acoustics; 5. Problems of small rooms; 6. Sound reinforcement; 7. Assisted resonance; 8. Sound insulation

1. Reflection

In completely free space, sounds travel outwards from their source with diminishing intensity until all the energy has been dissipated in the ever-widening wavefront or lost as heat in the air itself. By contrast, sound waves in a concert hall are repeatedly turned back on themselves and bounced in criss-cross patterns throughout the enclosed space. The audience therefore hears not only the direct sound but also a mixture of later—and weaker—sounds. These multiple reflections are delayed in accordance with the extra distance travelled; and they diminish in intensity through normal dissipation and absorption at each boundary reflection.

A near-perfect reflector such as a polished wood floor will reflect almost 100 per cent of the incident energy, but soft furnishings, porous fibre-tiles, or pliant panels will absorb part of that energy. In practice, the different kinds of absorber are frequency-selective, and good acoustic design depends on careful disposition of various absorbers to control reflections evenly at bass, middle, and treble frequencies.

2. Directional effects

Sound sources are described as directional or nondirectional depending on whether they are physically large or small compared with the wavelength of the musical notes being radiated (see ACOUSTICS, 10). For similar reasons, reflectors of different sizes and shapes may modify the distribution, i.e. diffusion, of sounds throughout a room not only by frequency-selective reflection but also by re-radiating some bands of frequencies uniformly and others in a directional manner. If curved surfaces are essential, a convex shape is generally preferred because it tends to scatter sounds and help produce uniform listening conditions. Concave surfaces focus sounds back along their axis and give rise to local echoes or dead spots.

A domed ceiling is a classic example of the concave shape to be avoided. The Royal Albert Hall in London is perhaps specially unfortunate in having both an oval plan and a high domed ceiling focusing sounds on to parts of the audience area. The effects of marked echoes were complained of for many years until arrays of 'flying saucers' were suspended beneath the huge dome. The underside of the saucers is convex, to scatter the upward-travelling sound waves, and their tops carry absorbent material to capture any sounds that missed the saucers on the way up and rebounded from the ceiling. In the same way, recesses or coffering should be of generous proportions so that their scattering effect will be felt through most of the frequency spectrum.

3. Reverberation

Although members of an audience receive the direct sound followed by a wedge or 'tail' of countless reflected waves, they are not normally conscious of these as separate entities or echoes. The hearing mechanism (see EAR AND HEARING) works in such a way that sound repetitions arriving within about ½₀ of a second of each other are run together and heard as one. Note, however, that 'flutter echoes' can arise between parallel walls.

The prolongation effect is known as 'reverberation'. A smooth decay is to be preferred, secured by careful acoustic design to produce evenly diffused sounds. The time taken for sounds to fall to inaudibility is called the 'reverberation time' (strictly the time to fall to a millionth of its original value, or to −60 dB). Reverberation time increases in direct proportion to the volume (size) of the enclosure—the greater distances stretching the decay period—but is reduced by the introduction of absorbent materials. An audience also mops up sound energy quite effectively, so rehearsals in an empty hall sound much more reverberant than the actual concert. To reduce this difference, modern concert-hall seating can be designed so that each seat absorbs about the same amount of sound whether occupied or not.

4. Designing for good acoustics

For speech, the principal criteria for design are adequate loudness and a high degree of intelligibility. This suggests a short reverberation time; yet too dry an acoustic will lack the reflected energy needed to carry adequate sound levels to listeners at greater distances from the platform. Attention to room shape and seating layout is necessary, and a sloping or raked floor will help to give listeners in the back row a clear view of the speakers and a better chance of hearing properly.

For music, there are additional acoustic requirements, making acoustic design as much art as science. From an examination of existing halls generally rated as having 'good acoustics', Leo L. Beranek, for example, listed 18 criteria of quality in his book *Music, Acoustics and Architecture*. Historically, increasingly large halls have been built, with correspondingly greater reverberation times, as the size of orchestras has grown. Thus Baroque and chamber music are suited to a reverberation time of less than 1.5 seconds, Classical music about 1.7, and Romantic music about 2.2 seconds. A longer decay at low frequencies makes for fullness of tone or warmth, whereas good definition or clarity demands a rise at high frequencies.

Modern concert halls often incorporate some means of varying the reverberation characteristics to suit different musical or non-musical events. A good example is Symphony Hall in Birmingham (opened in 1991) where a movable circular canopy over the platform area directs sound towards specific regions of the auditorium, and reverberation chambers round the periphery can be opened to increase reverberation time.

Performing musicians naturally demand a sense of ease and power in producing adequate tone without fatigue. This is helped by strategic placing near the players of reflecting surfaces which also enable them to hear each other clearly. There seems no doubt that composers of all periods consciously or unconsciously wrote in such a way as to suit the environment in which their music would be performed.

5. Problems of small rooms

In the reverberant sound field of a large hall, the random streams of reflected sound waves produce a reasonably consistent diffusion of sound. In small rooms, however, distinct interference patterns are set up by multiple reflections between parallel walls, floor, and ceiling. These 'standing wave' resonances, which form a kind of three-dimensional organ-pipe effect, occur at frequencies of which the distances between the parallel surfaces are multiples of a half-wavelength. A harmonic series of these room resonances, or 'eigentones', exists for each room dimension, and the uneven boosting of certain frequencies causes coloration of the sound. Selective bass absorption is needed, or a special design using non-parallel walls.

6. Sound reinforcement

It is economically impossible to limit the use of most halls to musical forces of optimum size and acoustic power. The question of amplification then arises for quiet instruments or voices. In many churches and lecture theatres, the building shape or shortcomings in the acoustic distribution call for augmentation of the natural sounds, either overall or selectively in particular areas. The basic components for sound reinforcement or 'public address' are a microphone, amplifier, and loudspeaker. The arrangement is inherently unstable, however, as most users can testify, since any amplified sound from the loudspeaker that falls on the microphone is again amplified and sent to the loudspeaker with the possibility of uncontrolled feedback. Directional microphones can ease the problem since their less sensitive side(s) can be directed towards the loudspeaker(s) and so reduce unwanted pickup of the amplified sound. Directional loudspeaker arrays can also beam the sound waves into specific areas to give more efficient reinforcement without feedback.

7. Assisted resonance

A special kind of sound reinforcement, called assisted resonance, is used in some halls to increase the reverberation time within certain frequency bands. A classic example is the Royal Festival Hall in London, where the original 1948 design had called for a reverberation period of 1.7 seconds, rising to 2.5 seconds at low frequencies. When the hall was built, however, the low-frequency reverberation time measured only 1.4 seconds and, while this gave excellent definition, the hall was criticized as lacking fullness of tone. In 1964 matters were improved by assisted resonance using 172 microphones at roof level, amplifiers tuned to narrow frequency bands in the range 58–700 Hz, and arrays of loudspeakers.

8. Sound insulation

A requirement in every type of auditorium is for the lowest practical level of extraneous noise, whether airborne or transmitted through the structure of the building. A first step in planning is to choose a quiet site—not very practicable in a large city—and to design the building with as many layers or shells as possible on the side nearest to railway lines or other identifiable sources of noise. Aircraft noise is an increasing problem requiring the use of massive roofs on insulating supports, with suspended ceilings, floating floors, and multi-layered exterior walls. The Bridgewater Hall in Manchester (opened in 1996) has achieved almost total exclusion of external noise. Its massive 22,500-tonne weight is suspended on some 300 isolation spring bearings, and its three-layer roof has an outer sheet of steel lined with acoustic panels.

See also CONCERT HALLS. JBo

  📖 L. L. BERANEK, *Music, Acoustics and Architecture* (New York, 1962) · C. GILFORD, *Acoustics for Studios and Auditoria* (London, 1972)

archlute. A *lute with long, unstopped, diatonically tuned diapasons (bass strings) running beside the normal stopped strings, and attached to a second pegbox at the end of a long extension to the neck. It differs from the *theorbo in that its body is smaller and the stopped string length is shorter; the stopped strings are tuned to normal Renaissance lute tuning and always consist of double *courses, whereas the theorbo has a *re-entrant tuning and is sometimes strung with single courses.

arcicembalo. A term used in mid-16th-century Italy by Nicola Vicentino for a harpsichord with 35 keys to the octave, capable of producing microtones. See KEYBOARD.

arco (It.). 'Bow'; *coll'arco* ('with the bow'), an instruction to stop playing pizzicato.

Arditi, Luigi (*b* Crescentino, 22 July 1822; *d* Hove, 1 May 1903). Italian composer and conductor. He studied at the Milan Conservatory and began his musical career as a violinist. By the age of 20 he had had his opera *I briganti* (composed 1841) staged in Milan, and by 1843 he was directing opera in Vercelli. He left Italy that year and went to Havana, where he wrote and produced his opera *Il corsaro*. He toured the principal North American cities as a conductor, went to Constantinople in 1856, and in 1858 settled in London, where he was appointed musical director of Her Majesty's Theatre. He conducted at Covent Garden and other theatres, giving the first English performances of Boito's *Mefistofele* and Mascagni's *Cavalleria rusticana*. He also conducted the Promenade Concerts at Covent Garden (1874–7). Although he wrote many operas and numerous songs and dances, he is mainly remembered for two waltz-songs, the hugely successful *Il bacio* ('The Kiss', 1860) and *Parla* (1870). He published *My Reminiscences* (London, 1896). PGA/RP

ardito (It.). 'Bold'; *arditamente*, 'boldly'.

Arensky, Anton Stepanovich (*b* Novgorod, 30 June/12 July 1861; *d* nr Terioki, Finland [now Zelenogorsk, Russia], 12/25 Feb. 1906). Russian composer. He studied with Rimsky-Korsakov at the St Petersburg Conservatory, then taught harmony and counterpoint at the Moscow Conservatory (among his pupils were Medtner, Rakhmaninov, and Skryabin). Later he returned to St Petersburg as director of the imperial court chapel (1895), resigning in 1901 with a substantial pension which allowed him the freedom to compose.

 Rimsky-Korsakov's assertion (*Chronicle of my Musical Life*) that Arensky 'would soon be forgotten' has largely been vindicated, though his First Piano Trio (1894) and *Variations on a Theme of Tchaikovsky* (1894) are occasionally performed. He also composed three operas, piano music, songs, chamber music, and several orchestral works, including two symphonies (no. 1, 1883; no. 2, 1889), a Piano Concerto (1882), and a Violin Concerto (1901). Rimsky-Korsakov likened Arensky's musical temperament to that of Anton Rubinstein, probably having in mind the ready absorption of influences which his music seems to reveal: Chopin, Mendelssohn, Tchaikovsky, and Rimsky-Korsakov himself had a noticeable influence on his eclectic style. Arensky died of consumption, having for years led a life of drinking and gambling which undermined his health and finances. GN/MF-W

Arezzo, Guido of. See GUIDO OF AREZZO.

Argentina. See LATIN AMERICA, 3.

Argento, Dominick (*b* York, PA, 27 Oct. 1927). American composer. He studied at the Peabody Conservatory, at the Eastman School, and privately with Weisgall, who encouraged his inclination towards opera. He was professor of composition at the University of Minnesota (1959–97) and in 1964 was a joint founder of Minnesota Opera. His operas, which place a high value on theatrical effectiveness and Italian-style lyricism, include *Christopher Sly* (Minneapolis, 1963), *Postcard from Morocco* (Minneapolis, 1971), *A Water Bird Talk* (Brooklyn, 1975), *The Voyage of Edgar Allan Poe* (St Paul, 1976), *Casa Nova's Homecoming* (St Paul, 1985), and *The Dream of Valentino* (Washington, 1995). Among his other works are choral settings and songs.

PG

aria (It., 'air'; Fr.: *air*; Ger.: *Arie*). A self-contained song for solo voice, often forming part of an opera or other large work.

1. Origins and meanings; 2. The aria in Italian opera; 3. The aria and *air* in other contexts

1. Origins and meanings

The closed, self-contained song is universal and immemorial, but it did not become associated with the word 'aria' until the 16th century, when a phrase such a 'l'aere veneziano' ('the Venetian manner') gradually came to refer to a song in that manner. In Caccini's printed collection of solo songs called *Le nuove musiche* (1602) an 'aria' was distinguished from a 'madrigal' in having a strophic text, with the same music, or a variation of it, set to each strophe. The term soon came to refer to those portions of operas, oratorios, or cantatas that were formal, lyrical songs, as opposed to those in speech-imitating *recitative, but the distinction was loose until 1650 or so. In course of time that became its primary meaning (see below, section 2), while a song written as a separate piece was more likely to be termed 'canzona', 'canzonetta' or 'arietta', 'Lied' or 'Gesang', or 'chanson'. In the Classical period the concert aria with orchestral accompaniment developed in imitation of the opera aria, as a vehicle for solo singers in public concerts, but the other terms remained the normal ones for songs with keyboard, harp, or guitar accompaniment.

The term 'aria', or its French equivalent *air*, was also used as the name of a tuneful binary movement in a dance suite, or, for example, in the *Aria mit verschiedenen Veränderungen* ('Aria with Diverse Variations')—the title under which Bach's 'Goldberg' Variations were published. In English 18th-century usage the word 'air' was the normal one for 'song', for 'tune' (as when it was printed above one part in a hymn-tune setting), or for 'tunefulness' (as when a reviewer complained that one of Haydn's symphonies was 'wanting in air').

2. The aria in Italian opera

The earliest type of opera aria was a strophic song, with or without variations; one of the most elaborate is 'Possente spirto' from Monteverdi's *L'Orfeo* (1607). Extended melismas and embellishments were always a feature of the more prominent arias. The normal number of strophes had declined from four or five to two by 1650, and the musical form of each strophe, at first quite variable, became standardized as ABB', ABA', or ABA: each section consisted of a single phrase, or two complementary phrases, so there was room for as many as 40 to 50 arias in an opera. The most common accompaniment throughout the 17th century was for continuo alone, with *ritornellos for three to five instrumental parts between the strophes; but after about 1640 the *aria concertata* began to appear, with melodic instruments intervening between vocal phrases or even accompanying the voice.

The ABA, or *da capo form (so called because the repetition of the A section could be indicated by writing the words *da capo* after the B section), prevailed after 1670. The A section was usually a simple antecedent–consequent melody with a half-cadence in the middle, its second half sometimes extended by repetition. Innovations included the motto opening (a brief word or phrase declaimed, interrupted, then repeated with continuation), the 'tag' ending (an analogous procedure at the end), and imitative interplay between voice and bass. Such features were much used by Legrenzi and Alessandro Scarlatti, for instance in Scarlatti's *Eraclea* (1700). (See OPERA, 3 and 5.)

Between 1700 and 1760 the *da capo* form became longer, more standardized, and more universal, at least in *opera seria*. The text was normally in two stanzas of equal or unequal length. The first was heard twice over in the A section, which became a full binary form, with a middle cadence and ritornello in the dominant key (or, in a minor-key aria, the relative major) repeated in the tonic at the end, with many word repetitions, melismas, and a final trill inviting a *cadenza, leading into the concluding ritornello in the tonic key. The B section, based on the second stanza, was usually shorter and less stable, moving through several related keys. The first stanza was then heard twice more as the A section was repeated. The accompaniment was generally for strings alone, relying on the singer to provide colour.

Metastasio, who in the 1720s became the pre-eminent librettist of *opera seria*, provided similes lending themselves to musical illustration (birds, breezes, wars, arrows, and the like). Often his two stanzas expressed contrasting or complementary sentiments, especially where the character's situation was one of indecision; composers took the opportunity to write a B section in a different mood, sometimes with a change of key, mode, metre, or tempo. The restatement of A, though still not written out, could be greatly varied in performance by embellishments and a more spectacular cadenza. In some cases the opening ritornello was not repeated, so the words *dal segno* ('from the sign') replaced *da capo*. In the hands of Vinci or Hasse an aria could last as long as 12 to 15 minutes and made a complete break in the dramatic action, the singer standing at centre stage facing the audience and ignoring any other characters, even the one to whom the words were nominally addressed.

Criticism of the *da capo* aria was mounting towards the mid-18th century, and various ways of shortening it were found, generally by telescoping the second A to a shortened version that stayed in the tonic key. More drastic was the reduction to a single statement of the binary A section encompassing both stanzas of the text. This form, called 'cavatina' at the time, predominated in Graun's *Montezuma* (1755). A later modification of the *da capo* form approached *sonata form by having the first A section end with material in the dominant key, which was recapitulated in the tonic at the end of the second A: for instance 'Zeffiretti lusinghieri' in Mozart's *Idomeneo* (1781). Other forms originated in *opera buffa* (see OPERA, 6), such as a simple binary ABA′B′. Generally the serious characters in *opera buffa* were given similar music to those in *opera seria*, but comic characters like Figaro could be more freely treated, with various through-composed forms, patter songs, and interruptions for stage business.

From the 1770s a new type began to evolve as a showpiece for the prima donna or other principal character: the *rondò* (not to be confused with the instrumental rondo: see RONDO FORM), in which the return of the opening melody of what sounded like a *da capo* form was interrupted by a change to a faster tempo, with new melodic material ('Dove sono' in Mozart's *Le nozze di Figaro* is a familiar example). Sometimes a still faster 'stretta' was added to provide a brilliant conclusion and exit. From this double form evolved the cantabile–cabaletta, which became the standard vehicle of virtuosity for the great 19th-century opera stars. By Rossini's time it had replaced most of the other types, and was equally adapted to serious and comic operas (see, for instance, 'Io sono docile' in *Il barbiere di Siviglia*, 1816). It was often extended by introductory recitatives and arioso passages, termed a 'scena', and by interpolations between the two main sections that might include stage business, entrances of other characters, and even a chorus, as in 'Casta diva' from Bellini's *Norma* (1831). The cantabile portion of this aria has a famous introduction in which a flute anticipates the vocal line; by this time, many arias had rich orchestral colouring, sometimes including an obbligato, such as the trumpet in 'Cercherò lontana terra' from Donizetti's *Don Pasquale* (1845).

In the later 19th century the aria as a separate entity began to disintegrate. Forms became more varied; the traditional and highly predictable cabaletta and stretta went out of favour, and Verdi in his later years sought to modify the 'number' opera into a fluid medium that could more realistically express an unfolding drama without artificial interruptions. The set-piece song now tended to revert to a single movement, such as a 'romanza' maintaining a single mood, or a through-composed piece that followed the changing emotions of the character, as in 'Ritorna vincitor' in *Aida* (1871). With the coming of *verismo and the works of Puccini, the aria lost all expectations of any particular form, and could rarely be separated from surrounding music, so that the term itself lost its meaning.

3. The aria and *air* in other contexts

The French equivalent of the *da capo* aria was, confusingly, termed 'ariette' in the 18th-century *tragédie lyrique*, where each of the five acts would generally begin with a specimen; the term *air* was reserved for short arioso sections embedded in recitative. Ternary form remained in vogue for large-scale songs in French operas through most of the 19th century: an example is 'Je dis que rien ne m'épouvante' in Bizet's *Carmen* (1875). The *couplet*, a song in two strophes with a refrain, was another popular type typical of *opéra comique, and lent itself to character songs such as 'Votre toast' in *Carmen*. Vernacular operas in other countries had tended to favour simple strophic songs or rondo forms that hardly rose to the dignity of 'arias', but Mozart's *Singspiel imported Italianate aria types: *Die Zauberflöte* has strophic songs for Papageno, but modified (sonata-form type) arias for Pamina ('Ach, ich fühl's') and the Queen of Night ('Der Hölle Rache'). Beethoven, Weber, and Wagner (in his early operas) maintained this double tradition, but the aria finds no place in Wagner's later music dramas.

It played a full part in oratorio, following much the same course as in serious opera. Handel in his English oratorios structured arias with more freedom than in his Italian operas, often departing from *da capo* form and combining aria, recitative, and chorus in ways designed to suit the dramatic situation. Italian solo cantatas of the late 17th and early 18th centuries contained arias on the operatic model. Bach in his church cantatas and passions also frequently used the *da capo* form, but greatly extended the range of instrumental colour in his accompaniments. Most 19th-century oratorios were conservative in their aria types, avoiding the cabaletta and other display pieces; by the time of Elgar's *The Dream of Gerontius* (1900) no recognizable 'arias' remained.   NT

Ariadne auf Naxos ('Ariadne on Naxos'). Opera in one act by Richard Strauss to a libretto by Hugo von Hofmannsthal; the first version (Stuttgart, 1912) was performed with a condensed version of Molière's *Le Bourgeois gentilhomme* (1670), for which Strauss had written incidental music, but it was subsequently staged as an independent work, with a new prologue (Vienna, 1916).

Ariane et Barbe-bleue. Opera in three acts by Dukas to a libretto by Maurice Maeterlinck after Charles Perrault (Paris, 1907).

Arianna, L'. Opera (*tragedia*) in a prologue and eight scenes by Monteverdi to a libretto by Ottavio Rinuccini (Mantua, 1608); the score is thought to be lost, the only surviving section being *Lamento d'Arianna*. Alexander Goehr composed an opera to the same Rinuccini libretto (London, 1995).

arietta (It., dim. of *aria*). An operatic song, but shorter and less developed than an *aria. The term was first used in the mid-17th century.

ariette (Fr.). In 18th-century French opera, a *da capo* aria in the Italian style; in *opéra comique* it was a short, simple song.

Ariettes oubliées ('Forgotten Ariettas'). Six songs (1885–7) by Debussy for voice and piano, settings of poems by Paul Verlaine.

Ariodante. Opera in three acts by Handel to a libretto adapted from Antonio Salvi's *Ginevra, principessa di Scozia* (1708) after Ludovico Ariosto's *Orlando furioso* (London, 1735). Méhul wrote a three-act opera on the subject, to a libretto by François-Benoît Hoffman (Paris, 1799).

arioso (It.). 1. In vocal music, a term indicating a lyrical, as opposed to declamatory, manner of performance.

2. By extension, a short passage of accompanied *recitative that has a regular metre and a melodic character.

3. A short aria in the operas of, for example, Handel.

4. Rarely, an instrumental piece or passage of a lyrical character (e.g. Beethoven's Piano Sonata op. 110).

Ariosti, Attilio (Malachia [Clemente]) (*b* Bologna, 5 Nov. 1666; *d* England, ?1729). Italian composer. An illegitimate scion of the noble Ariosti family, he entered the Servite monastery in Bologna (as Frate Ottavio) in 1688. In 1697, after a short period at the Mantua court, he went to Berlin as Kapellmeister to the Electress Sophia Charlotte, but in 1703, in view of his controversial position as a Catholic cleric at a Protestant court, he was recalled to Italy. Instead, however, he attached himself to the Austrian court, becoming Joseph I's diplomatic agent in Italy and enjoying a luxurious way of life which in 1711 led to demands that he be unfrocked. From 1716 he built up a successful career in London—he was associated with Handel in the Royal Academy of Music—but all traces of him disappear after 1728. As well as operas he composed many attractive works for viola d'amore which were extremely popular in his own time; some have been arranged for the modern viola or cello.   DA/ER

arlecchinesco (It.). Music in the spirit of a harlequinade.

Arlecchino ('Harlequin'). Opera in one act by Busoni to his own libretto (Zürich, 1917).

Arlen, Harold [Arluck, Hyman] (*b* Buffalo, NY, 15 Feb. 1905; *d* New York, 23 April 1986). American composer. Among his songs are 'Get Happy', 'Stormy Weather', 'It's Only a Paper Moon', 'That Old Black Magic', and 'Over the Rainbow' (*The Wizard of Oz*, 1939). His theatre scores include *St Louis Woman* (1946).

PGA/ALA

Arlésienne, L' ('The Woman of Arles'). Incidental music by Bizet for Alphonse Daudet's play (Paris, 1872); it consists of 27 items, some of which Bizet incorporated into the ballet of *Carmen*. There are two orchestral suites, one arranged by Bizet (1872), the other posthumously by Ernest Guiraud (1879).

Armenian chant. The plainchant of the Armenian rite. Armenian Christianity possesses distinct forms of the Divine Office and Eucharist that were influenced in their development by the rites of Jerusalem, Alexandria, Constantinople, and Rome. Between the 7th and 12th centuries, many hymns were written to accompany the cathedral psalmody of the Armenian morning and evening offices, which to a certain extent they eventually displaced.

The melodies of Armenian chant are organized according to a system of eight modes (*oktoechos*) distinguished by characteristic melodic formulas and scales. Musical notation survives from the 9th century in two forms, neither of which shows exact pitches: (1) an 'ecphonetic' notation governing the recitation of scriptural lessons, and (2) the *khaz* melodic notation, which flourished until the 16th century. A diastematic form of *khaz* notation was introduced during the 19th century, which later saw the first transcriptions of Armenian chant into Western staff notation, some of which were also set to polyphony.　　　ALı

Armide. Opera in five acts by Gluck to a libretto by Philippe Quinault after Torquato Tasso's poem *Gerusalemme liberata* (1581) (Paris, 1777). There are nearly 50 operas based on Tasso's story, notably those by Lully (1686), Handel (*Rinaldo*, 1711), Jommelli (1770), Salieri (1771), Haydn (1784), Rossini (1817), and Dvořák (1904).

armonia (It.). 1. 'Harmony'.
　2. 'Chord'.

armonica. See GLASS HARMONICA.

armonioso, armoniosamente (It.). 'Harmonious', 'harmoniously'.

Arne, Michael (*b* London, *c*.1740; *d* Lambeth, 14 Jan. 1786). English composer. The son of Thomas Arne, he was brought up by his aunt, the actress Mrs Cibber, who introduced him to the stage. His father wanted him to be a singer, but according to Burney he instead 'acquired a powerful hand on the harpsichord'. He played and composed for the London pleasure gardens and theatres, writing *Edgar and Emmeline* for Drury Lane in 1761 and later enjoying success with his music for Garrick's *Cymon* (1767). His interest in alchemy led to financial difficulties and a stint in a debtors' prison. In 1766 he married the singer Elizabeth Wright, but she died only three years later; he married a second time in 1773, having toured Germany with his future wife, one of his pupils, in 1771–2. In Hamburg he directed the first public performance in Germany of Handel's *Messiah*.　　　DA/PL

Arne, Thomas Augustine (*b* London, *bapt.* 28 May 1710; *d* London, 5 March 1778). English composer. The son of an upholsterer, he was educated at Eton College, and although his father intended that he should pursue a legal apprenticeship it was clear from the start that his interests lay in music. He learnt the violin with Michael Festing. Having performed in a pirated version of Handel's *Acis and Galatea* at the Haymarket Theatre in 1732, with his brother and sister (later the actress Mrs Cibber), Arne became involved in an enterprise to establish opera in English in London in direct competition with the Italian opera companies that were then dominant. He set Addison's libretto *Rosamond*, which was performed in 1733, but soon afterwards the company split up.

Thereafter Arne devoted himself to the theatre. The ups and downs of his career were those of most theatre musicians, but he seems to have been something of a scoundrel, pushing his favourite singers on to theatre managers. For some years he was house composer at Drury Lane, where his setting of Milton's pastoral *Comus*, one of his most successful theatre works, was first performed in 1738. For Drury Lane he also wrote songs for productions of Shakespeare's plays in the 1740s. In 1742 he followed Handel to Dublin, where he performed not only his own but also Handel's music. Back in London he continued to compose for Drury Lane, and his music—including his many songs and his keyboard concertos—became very popular at the pleasure gardens. His oratorio *Judith* was written for the Lenten season in 1761. His greatest achievement came the following year when *Artaxerxes*, a full-scale English opera, was staged at Covent Garden; it was still being performed in the 19th century. No less popular was the pasticcio *Love in a Village*.

Yet competition between the theatres was intense, and from the late 1760s Arne's productions suffered. Although he found some consolation in giving concerts of catches and glees, his finances were precarious. Among his last theatre works were the masque *The Fairy Prince* (1771) and the afterpiece *May Day* (1775). Arne was a talented composer with a particular melodic gift ('Rule, Britannia!', in the masque *Alfred*, 1740, is by far his best-known melody), and he also wrote much fine instrumental music. He was the most important English theatre composer of his day, and his musical style effectively integrates both late Baroque and early Classical characteristics.　　　DA/PL

　📖 R. FISKE, *English Theatre Music in the Eighteenth Century* (Oxford, 2/1986)

Arnell, Richard (Anthony Sayer) (*b* London, 15 Sept. 1917). English composer. He studied with John Ireland at the RCM (1935–8) and spent most of the next decade in the USA, where his ballet *Punch and the Child* was produced in 1947. His other works include five symphonies, the 'symphonic portrait' *Lord Byron*, and various chamber pieces, all displaying a talent for fluent, graceful music in a conservative but cosmopolitan style.　　　PG

Arnold, Malcolm (Henry) (*b* Northampton, 21 Oct. 1921). English composer. He studied composition at the RCM (1938–40), then played the trumpet in London orchestras until 1948, when he became an independent composer, earning his living by writing film scores (including that for *The Bridge on the River Kwai*, 1957). His substantial output includes symphonies, concertos, and a variety of chamber pieces. His style owes something to Sibelius, Bartók, and Shostakovich but is nevertheless distinctly personal in its expressiveness and exuberance.　　　PG/AW

📖 H. COLE, *Malcolm Arnold: An Introduction to his Music* (London, 1989)

Arnold, Samuel (*b* London, 10 Aug. 1740; *d* London, 2 Oct. 1802). English organist, composer, and editor. He was educated in the Chapel Royal and in 1764 went as harpsichordist and composer to Covent Garden; there he compiled pasticcios, including *The Maid of the Mill* (1765). He subsequently enjoyed a successful career as an opera composer and director, producing nearly 100 operas and other stage works (mostly for the Little Theatre in the Haymarket) as well as several oratorios. He owned Marylebone Gardens for a short period, and became organist and composer to the Chapel Royal. Among his most important projects were the revision of Boyce's *Cathedral Music* and a collected edition of Handel's works, which was not completed. In 1787 Arnold and J. W. Callcott founded the Glee Club. Two years later Arnold became conductor of the Academy of Ancient Music, and in 1793 he was appointed organist of Westminster Abbey. DA/PL

Aroldo. Opera in four acts by Verdi to a libretto by Francesco Maria Piave after his libretto **Stiffelio* (Rimini, 1857).

Aron, Pietro. See AARON, PIETRO.

arpa (It.). 'Harp'.

arpa doppia (It., 'double harp'). An early form of chromatic harp, dating from about 1600, with one rank of diatonic strings and a second rank for accidentals. See HARP, 2*b*.

arpège (Fr.). 'Arpeggio'; *arpéger*, to spread a chord; *arpègement*, the spreading of a chord.

arpeggiando, arpeggiato (It.). Terms used in string playing to denote a bouncing bowstroke played on broken chords, so that each bounce is on a different string. A famous example occurs in the cadenza of Mendelssohn's Violin Concerto.

arpeggiare (It., 'to play the harp'). An instruction to spread the notes of a chord, usually from the bottom upwards, in harp-like fashion. See ARPEGGIO, 1.

arpeggio (It.; Fr.: *arpège*). 1. The notes of a chord 'spread', i.e. played one after the other from the bottom upwards, or from the top downwards. The effect is chiefly used in keyboard and harp music (chords of three or four notes may be spread on a string instrument, but not in quite the same way). In modern notation, an arpeggio appears as shown in Ex. 1. It generally begins on the beat, though sometimes the last note of the chord should coincide with the beat. In

piano music, some arpeggios are played simultaneously in both hands, or as a long continuous arpeggio in which one hand takes over from the other (indicated by a long wavy line connecting the two staves).

Ex. 1

The execution of arpeggios varied in the 17th and 18th centuries and was often left to the performer's discretion. In some 18th-century music the word 'arpeggio' is found written before a chordal sequence, indicating that the player may extemporize arpeggios in either direction at will. The performance of keyboard continuo, especially in recitative passages, requires the frequent arpeggiation of chords.

2. In exercises to develop the technique, instrumentalists (especially pianists) practise arpeggios formed out of triads; and proficiency in scales and arpeggios is a basic requirement for most practical examinations.

arpeggione. A bowed, six-string instrument with guitar tuning (*E–A–d–g–b–e'*) and frets, played like a cello. It was invented by J. G. Staufer in Vienna in 1823, and Schubert wrote a sonata for it in 1824 (D821).

JMo

arraché (Fr.). 'Torn': a forceful pizzicato.

arrangement (Ger.: *Bearbeitung*). The adaptation of music for a medium different from that for which it was originally composed, for example the recasting of a song as a piano piece, or of an orchestral overture as an organ piece. This was a common practice before the gramophone made reproduction of the original readily available. Such a process, if undertaken seriously, involves much more than simply transferring a score from one medium to the other, since many passages that are effective in the original would sound much less so in another medium. The arranger should always aim to consider how the composer would have written the music had that medium been the original one.

Before the early 17th century, motets, madrigals, and other vocal pieces were frequently played by string or wind instruments, with or without voices, and the phrase 'apt for viols or voices' (in various languages) often appears on the title pages of publications from the mid-16th century. The resulting 'arrangements' differed little from the original, any added ornamentation being improvisatory in nature. Similarly, the arrangements of such pieces for lute or keyboard were basically no more than intabulations, with florid embellishments incorporated to enhance the sustained notes—a process anticipating the long-standing practice, still widespread, of virtuoso performers producing elaborate transcriptions of already difficult pieces in order to dazzle their audiences.

In the early Baroque era, instrumental music also became subject to arrangement, and the degree of freedom in the process of adaptation increased greatly, as in Bach's versions for harpsichord or organ of violin concertos by Vivaldi. In later periods Bach himself became a favourite subject for arrangers, with the great Chaconne for solo violin a prominent example. Schumann went so far as to write a whole 'piano accompaniment' to the violin part, while Brahms and Busoni arranged it for piano, the former for left hand alone, the latter in ways that make it virtually a new piece. Since Bach himself radically rewrote the Prelude from the E major Partita for solo violin as an organ work, he could hardly have complained at Busoni's licence.

Brahms and Busoni were continuing a tradition whereby the great 19th-century pianists often made arrangements of works for less accessible forces. Well-played orchestral concerts were rare in many towns, while the more ambitious operas were unperformable in many provincial opera houses. Liszt transcribed Beethoven's symphonies, as well as a myriad other vocal and instrumental works, for piano. Some of his arrangements are relatively simple and do not over-inflate the original, but many demand a virtuoso technique and could have been played by few people other than the arranger himself. It is therefore often the case that the most effective 19th-century arrangements are those, like the versions by Schumann and Liszt of Paganini's *Caprices* for solo violin, that are already virtuoso works in their original medium.

Equally significant, in a different way, were the piano-duet arrangements made in the later 19th century which covered virtually the whole range of classical orchestral and chamber music. These allowed competent domestic pianists to come to know intimately works they could hear only rarely, if at all, and the tradition—popular with music publishers, for obvious reasons—of making works accessible in this way continued well into the 20th century. In addition, the 19th century saw an increasing tendency to provide sentimental salon arrangements of classical pieces, for example Gounod's notorious *Ave Maria* (1859), based on the first Prelude from Bach's '48'; and in the earlier 20th century many popular compositions by classical composers were cannibalized by jazz composers and arrangers.

Relatively few arrangements have survived as regular concert items since the mid-20th century, although various versions of Bach D minor organ toccata can still be heard. Musorgsky's *Pictures at an Exhibition*, usually in Ravel's orchestration but sometimes in others, remains popular, as are some of the arrangements Stravinsky made of his own larger pieces, often to enhance their value as sources of copyright revenue. Such treatments as the Musorgsky–Ravel are usually justified on the grounds that the music benefits from transference to a different, even more appropriate medium—although it is not agreed by every authority that Musorgsky's piano writing is incompetent or implicitly 'orchestral'. In the case of his arrangement of Brahms's Piano Quartet op. 25 for large orchestra, Schoenberg claimed that not only was the original rarely played but it was always badly played, as if his orchestration was certain to become a regular repertory item. In the age of electronic reproduction, arrangement can still satisfy the desire of composers to work occasionally with material which is not their own, as a way of linking on to the great tradition and thereby pleasing audiences in ways in which their own music might not always succeed.   AW

Arrau, Claudio (*b* Chillán, 6 Feb. 1903; *d* Vienna, 9 June 1991). Chilean pianist. He studied with Martin Krause in Berlin, made his recital debut in 1914, and in 1915 appeared as a soloist under Nikisch. He was famed for cycles of Mozart, Beethoven, and Schubert, but he also played Chopin, Liszt, Debussy, and Schoenberg. A thoughtful artist, equally at home in the recording studio and on the concert platform, he was also renowned for giving absorbing master classes.   CF

📖 J. Horowitz, *Conversations with Arrau* (New York, 1982, 2/1992)

Arriaga (y Balzola), Juan Crisóstomo (Jacobo Antonio) (*b* Bilbao, 27 Jan. 1806; *d* Paris, 17 Jan. 1826). Spanish violinist and composer. His first opera, *Los esclavos felices*, was written and produced in Bilbao when he was only 13. In 1821 he entered the Paris Conservatoire, and before his untimely death he completed three string quartets, two sacred works, a second opera and some incidental music, a handful of piano studies, two overtures, and an attractive Symphony in D, which is still performed. With the rise of Spanish nationalism in the 1850s, Arriaga became a cult figure, and the elegant substance of the symphony and quartets in particular go far towards justifying his fame.   WT/CW

Ars Antiqua (Lat., 'ancient art'). A term used in French theoretical writings of the early 14th century to describe earlier notational systems that had been superseded by the technical advances of the *Ars Nova. Some historians have used the term to embrace all polyphonic music of the late 12th and the 13th centuries, in particular the contents of the *Magnus liber organi* (a collection of music for the entire church year attributed to Léonin and said to have been revised by Pérotin, used in many parts of Europe), but including also the large 13th-century repertory of motets, most of which survive anonymously in manuscript collections. For the notational devices associated with the Ars Antiqua period, see NOTATION, 1 and 2.

arsis and thesis (from Gk.). Terms that originally referred to the 'raising' and 'lowering', respectively, of the foot in ancient Greek dance. When applied to music they generally refer to the *upbeat and *downbeat.

In the 16th and 17th centuries, the phrase 'per arsin et thesin' meant 'inversion' (see INVERSION, 3); however, the same phrase was used in the 18th century to describe a fugue in which the answer is in inverted rhythm, i.e. with strong beats in the subject becoming weak beats in the answer, and vice versa.

Ars Nova. The title (meaning 'new art') of a treatise (c.1322) transmitting the teachings of Philippe de Vitry, which has come to be used to describe a period of musical composition (and the music written during that period), beginning in about 1315 and ending about 1375. Vitry and some of his contemporaries set the music of their time apart from earlier music (which they termed Ars Antiqua) because of a change in musical technique. The new techniques, as described in Vitry's treatise, essentially consist in a more advanced method of notation that allowed for a far greater range of measured rhythmic note divisions than had been possible before. Vitry's notation was based on a system advocated by Franco of Cologne (c.1280), but further developed so that three levels of notational division were made possible: from long to breve, breve to semibreve, and semibreve to minim (a newly defined note-value). In each division the upper value could be worth two or three of the lower value, so that a wide range of subdivisions was possible. The significance of the new notation system was that rhythmically complex music could be notated in a much clearer way than had previously been possible.

Vitry was the key figure in a conjectural line of composers and theorists, working in the wake of Franco, who seemed to be striving towards ever more elaborate musical expression. The first (surviving) works that show the hallmarks of his teaching were copied into the extended version of the poem *Le Roman de Fauvel* (MS Paris, Bibliothèque Nationale, fonds français 146) in about 1316–18. However, some slightly earlier motets show structural features that characterize the classic 'Vitriacan' motet, even if their composers did not have the ability to notate such a wide range of note-values as Vitry's changes permitted. The Ars Nova motet is characterized, in general terms, by the use of *isorhythm, with one (or two) slow-moving lower voice(s) notated in longs (and duplex longs) and breves, supporting two faster-moving upper voices notated predominantly in semibreves and minims.

None of Vitry's songs is known to survive, but his notational theory, exemplified in the *Ars nova* writings by numerous citations of motets, was also used for the secular repertory. Machaut was the most prolific song composer of the 14th century, and he adopted (and occasionally overshot) Vitry's notational rules. Indeed, because of the lack of music securely attributable to any other composer from the first three quarters of the 14th century, we take our characterization of French Ars Nova music almost entirely from the work of these two outstanding figures.

It is clear that the developments that Vitry set out arose from a desire to break new musical boundaries, and the term 'Ars Nova' necessarily implies this heightened awareness of the musical art along with the purely technical feat. It is interesting that the concept of a 'new art' arose at a time when the polyphonic art song was beginning to emerge as an important compositional genre; the three most important song forms of the next century and beyond—*ballade*, *rondeau*, and *virelai*—reached their classic forms in the works of Machaut, via a process that it may be impossible to unravel owing to the lack of surviving precedents. But it is certain that the newly complex sacred and secular music shared many features, a fact that was most disturbing to the religious establishment, as shown by Pope John XXII's famous bull *Docta sanctorum* of 1325, in which he railed against the 'novellae scholae discipuli' (disciples of the new school); in this case 'new' was certainly not meant as a compliment. The theorist Jacobus of Liège was another who apparently preferred the ways of the old school, comparing their 'musica modesta' to the 'musica lasciva' of the moderns.

The end of the 'Ars Nova' period has been difficult to delineate, mainly because, unlike for the Ars Antiqua–Ars Nova transition, there was no comparable reference to new thought in the written theory, even though it is clear that far-reaching changes took place in the late 14th century. Thus the concept of a period of 'Ars Nova' is a modern one, introduced early in the 20th century, and its boundaries have been movable in scholarly discussion. It was most frequently taken to comprise French music of the 14th century; however, more recently the term *ars subtilior* has been coined to denote, broadly, the music of French composers in the late 14th century (after Machaut).

There has, furthermore, been some debate as to whether 'Ars Nova' should be applied to Italian 14th-century music. It is certainly true that there were changes in Italy, allowing for more precise rhythmic notation, at about the same period as Vitry was working (indeed, he was well known in some Italian circles). Unlike those in France, however, these notational modifications do not seem to have gone hand in hand with a new way of perceiving and conceiving music, and thus it may be more appropriate to confine the term to the description of French music alone.

ABUL

> 📖 D. LEECH-WILKINSON, 'Ars Antiqua—Ars Nova—Ars Subtilior', *Antiquity and the Middle Ages*, ed. J. McKinnon, Man and Music/Music and Society (London, 1990), 218–40 · D. F. WILSON, *Music of the Middle Ages* (New York, 1990) · D. LEECH-WILKINSON, 'The emergence of *ars nova*', *Journal of Musicology*, 13 (1995), 285–317

ars subtilior (Lat., 'the more subtle art'). A term used to describe French vocal music of the late 14th century. Composers after Machaut developed a sophisticated and complex musical style using the new note-values introduced in the *Ars Nova period and developing their potential for complex rhythmic schemes. See NOTATION, 3.

Artaria. Austrian firm of music publishers. Founded in 1765 at Mainz, it moved to Vienna soon afterwards. Already renowned as art and map publishers, Artaria also rapidly achieved a dominant position in Viennese musical life. In 1780 they issued six of Haydn's piano sonatas (Hob. XVI: 20, 35–9), the first of over 300 Haydn editions to appear under their imprint. Artaria eventually became Mozart's principal publisher, starting with a set of piano and violin sonatas in 1781 and then issuing over 100 early editions of his music. They also took over publications from Mozart's former publisher F. A. Hoffmeister.

Artaria produced Beethoven's first published work, a set of piano variations, in 1793, but their relationship had its stormy side, reflected in the letters of publisher and composer. Nevertheless, by 1858 Artaria had over 100 of Beethoven's works in their catalogue, which also included Gluck, Boccherini, and Clementi. They remained active until the second half of the 19th century, when the quality of their publications declined. Following closure of their music-publishing business in 1858, their assets were eventually taken over by Josef Weinberger, and their unique and valuable collection of composer autographs passed to the Preussische Staatsbibliothek in Berlin.

JMT/JWA

Artaxerxes. Opera in three acts by Arne probably to his own libretto after Pietro Metastasio (London, 1762). There are many operas on the subject, for example by Hasse (1730), Gluck (1741), Piccinni (1762), Paisiello (1771), and Cimarosa (1784).

Art de toucher le clavecin, L' ('The Art of Playing the Harpsichord'). Treatise by François Couperin, published in Paris in 1716 and revised in 1717. An influential harpsichord method, known to have been used by J. S. Bach, it covers many aspects of technique and performance and includes eight pieces as teaching material.

articulation. A term denoting the degree to which each of a succession of notes is separated in performance; it may lie at either of the extremes of *staccato and *legato, or anywhere between the two. Articulation may be expressive or structural; if the latter, it is analogous to the use of punctuation in language. The shaping of phrases is largely dependent on articulation, particularly on keyboard instruments, where finely controlled attack and decay on individual notes is prescribed. The composer's intentions may be notated as dots, dashes, accents, and slurs. Articulation marks were rare in the Baroque period and earlier, when composers expected a knowledge of current practices to inform the performer's approach to articulation.

On stringed instruments, articulation relies on the type of bowing, and in wind playing largely on tonguing, while in keyboard playing it depends on touch. Articulation in singing is produced by such techniques as *portamento or the taking of breaths, and by the treatment of vowels and consonants. A performance venue may influence articulation: a church or reverberant concert hall will require extremely pointed articulation, otherwise the individual notes will merge into an indistinguishable mass, whereas a 'drier', less reverberant acoustic requires a more subtle approach.

See also PERFORMANCE PRACTICE, 8. —/BW

artificial harmonics. See ACOUSTICS, 5.

art music, art song. Terms used to describe music that is written down and that takes a more or less established form to transmit some sort of artistic expression. The term is often used in contradistinction to *folk and *popular music, as well as some forms of liturgical music (especially plainchant) and dance music, but, particularly since the 20th century, the distinctions have become blurred. JBE

Art of Fugue, The (*Die Kunst der Fuge*). A collection of *fugues and *canons by Bach, BWV1080, composed in the 1740s to display a wide variety of contrapuntal techniques using the same simple subject; the medium is unspecified but almost all the movements are playable on a solo keyboard instrument. It has survived unfinished and the intended order of the numbers is uncertain but it consists of 14 fugues ('contrapuncti') for different voices, four canons, a pair of mirror fugues, and an incomplete quadruple fugue. Completions of the final fugue have been made by Donald Tovey, and by Busoni in his *Fantasia contrappuntistica*.   AL

art rock. An ambiguous term, meaning either the *glam rock of David Bowie or Roxy Music, or the tendency among some *progressive rock musicians (e.g. Emerson, Lake and Palmer and Yes) to be influenced by 'art music', by composing multi-movement works with thematic development, or by playing arrangements for rock band of classical pieces. The term is also applied to experimental bands and artists, for example Laurie Anderson.   KG

Artusi, Giovanni Maria (*b* c.1540; *d* Bologna, 18 Aug. 1613). Italian theorist and composer. He was a canon at S. Salvatore, Bologna, and studied in Venice with Zarlino. His earlier writings are largely concerned with rules of counterpoint and the use of dissonances. His criticisms of some of Monteverdi's madrigals initiated a famous controversy that highlighted the distinctions between the old *prima pratica* and the more modern *seconda pratica*. Artusi objected to what he perceived as the liberties taken by Monteverdi with regard to certain harmonic, melodic, and rhythmic aspects of the music in order to express the text more fully.

See also PRIMA PRATICA, SECONDA PRATICA.
                                                                        LC

Artyomov, Vyacheslav Petrovich (*b* Moscow, 29 June 1940). Russian composer. He studied composition with Nikolay Sidel'nikov at the Moscow Conservatory, inheriting from his teacher an interest in folk music, evident in his *Poteshki* ('Funny Songs', 1964) and *Severnïye pesni* ('Northern Songs', 1966). Under the influence of Stravinsky he developed the ritualistic aspect of his folk prototypes, as in the primitivist *Totem* for percussion (1976). Most of the later works reflect his mystical spirituality and draw inspiration from different religions, but a special emphasis on meditation emerges, for example in the Requiem (1988), and the symphonies *Put' k Olimpu* ('The Way to Olympus', 1984) and *Na poroge svetlogo mira* ('On the Threshold of a Bright World', 1990).   JWAL

As (Ger.). The note A♭.

a.s. Abbreviation for *al *segno*.

Asaf'yev, Boris Vladimirovich (*b* St Petersburg, 17/29 July 1884; *d* Moscow, 27 Jan. 1949). Russian music critic, composer, and musicologist. He studied composition at the St Petersburg Conservatory under Rimsky-Korsakov and Lyadov (1904–10), concurrently reading history and philology at the university, from which he

graduated in 1908. He was appointed professor at the conservatory in 1925.

Asaf'yev's career as a critic and music journalist dates from 1914, when he began contributing numerous articles to papers and journals, often under the pseudonym Igor' Glebov. In 1926 he co-founded the Leningrad branch of the Association of Contemporary Music and established the Circle for New Music. He published *Kniga o Stravinskom* ('A Book about Stravinsky') in 1929 (Eng. trans. 1982) and began the first part of his two-volume theoretical work *Muzïkal'naya forma kak protsess* ('Musical Form as a Process') in 1930. It was published, with the second volume *Intonatsiya* ('Intonation'), in 1947 (Eng. trans. 1976).

As a composer Asaf'yev is best known for his ballets, in particular *Plamya Parizha* ('The Flames of Paris', 1932). As a theorist he continues to be influential in Russia, but dissemination of his work in the West has been slow.   PF

Ascanio in Alba. Serenata in two acts by Mozart to a libretto by Giuseppe Parini (Milan, 1771).

Ascension, L' ('The Ascension'). Orchestral work (1933) by Messiaen, arranged for organ (1934).

Ashley, Robert (Reynolds) (*b* Ann Arbor, MI, 28 March 1930). American composer. He studied at the University of Michigan and the Manhattan School, but was more influenced by Cage. With Gordon Mumma he was co-founder of the Cooperative Studio for Electronic Music at Ann Arbor (1958–66); the two then joined with David Behrman and Alvin Lucier in the Sonic Arts Union (1966–73), giving concerts of live electronic music which might include *The Wolfman* (1964), which Ashley wrote for his own amplified voice and tape. His interest in vocal expression and marginal personalities led him in the 1970s into opera, generally involving his own continuously murmuring voice. *Perfect Lives* (1983) is a video opera in seven half-hour episodes.   PG

Ashton, Hugh. See ASTON, HUGH.

Asola, Giovanni Matteo (*b* Verona, ?1532 or earlier; *d* Venice, 1 Oct. 1609). Italian composer. He was active in Verona, where he may have studied with Ruffo, before holding appointments at the cathedrals of Treviso (1577) and Vicenza (1578); in 1582 he became chaplain at S. Severo, Venice. Much of his church music is for two or more choirs, and he adopted several of the traits of the Venetian school of Andrea Gabrieli and his contemporaries; however, he also shows the strong influence of Palestrina, whom he admired greatly, preparing and editing a book of Vesper psalms dedicated to him in 1592. One book of madrigals for two voices was composed, astonishingly, in strict canon throughout.   DA

assai (It.). 'Very', e.g. *allegro assai*, 'very fast'. It was sometimes used in the 18th century to mean 'rather', like the French *assez*.

Assedio di Corinto, L'. See Siège de Corinthe, Le.

assez (Fr.). 'Rather', e.g. *assez vite*, 'rather fast'.

Associated Board of the Royal Schools of Music. A British joint examining body, established in 1889 to conduct local examinations in music. In 1947 the *Royal Academy of Music and the *Royal College of Music were joined by the *Royal Scottish Academy of Music and Drama and the *Royal Manchester College of Music; on the amalgamation (1973) of the RMCM with the Northern School of Music the resulting *Royal Northern College of Music became the fourth member of the constitution. The Board conducts graded examinations in performance (voice, piano, string, and wind instruments) and a parallel series in the theory of music. These examinations take place both in the UK and overseas, especially in Commonwealth countries. The Board publishes its own examination material and respected editions of standard works, such as Bach's '48' and sonatas by Haydn, Mozart, and Beethoven. In the 1990s it invited composers to contribute to *Spectrum*, an anthology of piano pieces in a range of contemporary styles.

Latterly, the Board has extended its range of examining activities, pioneering graded examinations in jazz performance and choral singing. It has become more closely involved in the professional advancement of instrumental teachers, developing the Certificate in Teaching of the Associated Board of the Royal Schools of Music (CTABRSM) and other diplomas (LRSM and FRSM). It has also carried out useful research into the provision of instrumental teaching in the UK.

PSp

Association Européenne des Festivals de Musique. Association based in Geneva to which many organizers of European *festivals are affiliated.

Association of Professional Music Therapists. See British Society for Music Therapy.

Aston [Ashton], **Hugh** [Hugo] (*b* c.1485; *d* Nov. 1558). English church musician and composer. Nothing is known about his early career before 1510, the year in which he supplicated for the degree of B.Mus. from Oxford University. In 1525 he was Master of the Choristers at the collegiate church of St Mary in Leicester, and soon afterwards turned down the offer of an equivalent position at Wolsey's newly founded Cardinal College (now Christ Church), Oxford. He remained at St Mary's until its dissolution in 1548. Aston wrote both sacred and secular music; a small number of his liturgical compositions survive, together with a celebrated 'Hornepype' for keyboard.   JM

Asyla. Orchestral work (1997) by Adès in four movements played continuously.

Atempause (Ger., 'breathing pause'). A tiny pause on a weak beat, often indicated by an apostrophe, to emphasize the following strong beat, a guide to phrasing rather than an indication that a wind player or singer should take a breath; it is used effectively in Viennese waltzes.

Athalia. Oratorio (1733) by Handel to a text by Samuel Humphreys after Jean Racine.

Atlántida (*Atlantis*). 'Scenic cantata' in a prologue and three parts by Falla to a text based on Jacint Verdaguer's Catalan poem; it was completed by Ernesto Halffter (Milan, 1962).

Atmosphères. Orchestral work (1961) by Ligeti.

atonality. The antonym of *tonality; atonal music (the term 'post-tonal' is preferred by some theorists) is that which does not adhere to any system of key or mode. Some writers reserve the terms for music that is also not serial, for example Schoenberg's *Pierrot lunaire*, Berg's *Wozzeck*, and works by Webern, Varèse, Ives, and others. See also serialism; twelve-note music.

attacca (It.). 'Attack'; often given as *attacca subito* ('attack quickly'), it is used at the end of a movement to indicate that the next should follow immediately without a break.

attacco (It., 'attack'). A very short fugue subject of perhaps three or four notes, used as material for imitation.

attack (Fr.: *attaque*). The prompt and decisive beginning of a note or passage by either vocal or instrumental performers. Good 'attack' is a vital element in rhythm. The principal first violin in an orchestra (leader; Amer.: concertmaster) is in French called the *chef d'attaque*, 'leader of the attack'.

Attaingnant, Pierre (*b* probably Douai, c.1494; *d* Paris, 1551 or 1552). French music printer, publisher, and bookseller. As a bookseller in Paris in the reign of

François I he experimented for several years with music types, and in 1527–8 produced his *Chansons nouvelles*, embodying the results. His clear, handsome, diamond-shaped notation, with staff-segments attached, required only one impression (that is, he was able to print notes and staves in one operation), thus halving setting and printing times and paving the way for cheap printed music. From 1537 until his death he was official printer of the king's music. Attaingnant was the first music publisher to distribute on a European scale; he was responsible for the wide diffusion of the French 16th-century chanson and demonstrated how influential the printing press could be as a catalyst in humanistic culture.

See also PRINTING AND PUBLISHING OF MUSIC, 4.

JMT/JWA

📖 D. HEARTZ, *Pierre Attaingnant, Royal Printer of Music: A Historical Study and Bibliographical Catalogue* (Berkeley, CA, 1969)

Attey, John (*fl* 1622). English composer. He served as private musician to the Earl of Bridgewater, whose daughters he instructed in music. In 1622 he published a collection of songs for voice (or consort of voices), lute, and bass viol, late examples of the genre first made famous by Dowland.   JM

Attila. Opera in a prologue and three acts by Verdi to a libretto by Temistocle Solera and Francesco Maria Piave after Zacharias Werner's play *Attila, König der Hunnen* (1808) (Venice, 1846).

Attwood, Thomas (*bapt.* London, 23 Nov. 1765; *d* London, 24 March 1838). English organist and composer. He was educated in the Chapel Royal, then became a page to the Prince of Wales (later George IV), who sent him to study in Italy. After tuition in Naples (1783–5) with Felipe Cinque and Gaetano Latilla he moved to Vienna (1785–7), where he was a favourite pupil of Mozart. Returning to the English court in 1787, he was music instructor to members of the royal family. In 1796 he was appointed organist at St Paul's Cathedral and composer to the Chapel Royal. He was a founder member of the Philharmonic Society (1813) and one of the first professors at the RAM (1823). Mendelssohn, a close friend, dedicated his op. 37 preludes and fugues to Attwood and stayed with him at his home in Norwood.

A composer of over 30 stage works, Attwood published instrumental music, songs, and glees as well as the sacred music for which he is now chiefly remembered—notably the exquisite anthems *Turn thee again, O Lord* (1817), *Come, Holy Ghost* (1831), and *Turn thy face from my sins* (1835), which reflect his indebtedness to Mozart.   WT/JD1

aubade (Fr., from *aube*, 'dawn'; Ger.: *Morgenlied*). Early morning music. The repertory of the troubadours included the *alba, and in 17th- and 18th-century courts aubades were played in honour of royalty. Composers who have used the term as a title for instrumental music include Lalo (two *Aubades* for wind and string ensemble or small orchestra). The Spanish equivalent is the *alborada.

aube (Fr.). See ALBA.

Auber, Daniel François Esprit (*b* Caen, 29 Jan. 1782; *d* Paris, 12 May 1871). French composer. In 1802 his father sent him to London, where he found success as a performer and as a composer of *romances*, but he returned the next year after the outbreak of war between England and France. He attracted Cherubini's attention with a one-act opera, and from him received his first real composition lessons in 1805. His earliest attempts at writing operas were unsuccessful, but his father's bankruptcy spurred him on to more determined efforts, and the *opéras comiques La Bergère châtelaine* ('The Lady Shepherdess', 1820) and *Emma* (1821) won considerable popularity. Thereafter Auber produced a stream of operas until 1869.

Many of his works resulted from his lifelong collaboration with the librettist Eugène Scribe. They were known for their *opéras comiques* (though they also wrote a number of ballets), and *La Muette de Portici* (1828), for the Opéra, was acknowledged as the first *grand opéra*. In this work the visual element was integrated convincingly into the drama with a dancing, miming heroine and spectacular tableaux at the end of each act. Furthermore, the symbolic significance of its revolutionary hero, Masaniello, was seized on during the July Revolution, the Belgian revolt of 1830, and later uprisings. *La Muette de Portici* enjoyed enormous success throughout 19th-century Europe, was famously praised by Wagner, and exerted a significant influence on the development of European opera. Auber and Scribe continued to collaborate on *opéras comiques*, including *Fra Diavolo* (1830) and *Le Domino noir* ('The Black Domino', 1837), and on several more *grands opéras*. In *Gustave III* (1833) a masked ball is presented, with some 300 people on stage (the story is more familiar to present-day audiences from Verdi's *Un ballo in maschera*, 1859).

Auber had a facility for simple, popular melodies and clear harmony, and for sparkling orchestration and dramatic ensembles; like many of his contemporaries he was influenced by Rossini's vocal writing. His arias became more expressive in the 1840s, but he also continued to use popular song types such as barcarolles, ballades, and chansons. Though best known for his operas, Auber wrote a body of sacred music (mostly in the 1850s and 60s), as well as songs, cantatas, and orchestral and chamber pieces. He was much honoured, becoming director of the Paris Conservatoire in 1842 and *maitre de chapelle* to Napoleon III in 1852.   SH

Aubert, Jacques [*le vieux, le père*] (*b* Paris, 30 Sept. 1689; *d* Belleville, nr Paris, 17 or 18 May 1753). French violinist and composer. In 1719 he joined the household of the Prince of Condé, providing music for the prince's divertissements at Chantilly. In 1727 he became a member of the Vingt-Quatre Violons, and a year later was a first violin in the Opéra orchestra. He made his first appearance at the Concert Spirituel in 1729, and wrote most of his subsequent compositions for that concert series.

Aubert's six Italianate violin concertos (1734) were the first such works to be printed in France; his other instrumental music includes five books of violin sonatas, duets for two violins or flutes, and orchestral suites; they are fluent, graceful, and technically accomplished.   WT

audition. 1. The faculty of hearing. See EAR AND HEARING.

2. A hearing given to a performer, usually for the purpose of determining his or her level of ability and admissibility to, for instance, some school, music college, professional group of musicians, or cast. Professional orchestras select their players by audition, often attended by a panel of orchestra members and administrators. The word is also used as a verb, meaning to perform or, conversely, to hear someone performing for such a purpose.

Auer, Leopold (von) (*b* Veszprém, 7 June 1845; *d* Loschwitz, nr Dresden, 15 July 1930). Hungarian violinist. His virtuosity was restricted by physical limitations to his hands and he is largely remembered for refusing the dedication and premiere of Tchaikovsky's concerto. He was, however, a significant teacher, in London, Dresden, Philadelphia, and St Petersburg (1868–1917), where he was also court violinist, playing solos at the Imperial Ballet; Mischa Elman, Efrem Zimbalist, and Heifetz were among his pupils. He made important editions of the standard violin repertory as well as writing teaching and interpretation manuals.   CF

📖 L. AUER, *My Long Life in Music* (New York, 1923)

auf (Ger.). 'On'; e.g. *auf der G*, 'on the G (string)'.

Aufforderung zum Tanz ('Invitation to the Dance'). Weber's *Rondo brillant* in D♭ for piano (1819), which consists of an introduction (the 'invitation'), a waltz, and an epilogue; it was orchestrated by Berlioz (1841) and, much altered, by Weingartner, and used by

Diaghilev's Ballets Russes as music for *Le Spectre de la rose*.

Auflage (Ger.). 'Edition'.

auflösen (Ger., 'to loosen', 'to untie'). In harp playing, to lower again a string which has been raised in pitch.

Auflösung (Ger.). 1. The resolution of a discord.

2. The cancellation of an accidental; *Auflösungszeichen*, the natural sign (♮).

Aufstieg und Fall der Stadt Mahagonny ('Rise and Fall of the City of Mahagonny'). Opera in three acts by Weill to a libretto by Bertolt Brecht (Leipzig, 1930).

Aufstrich (Ger.). 'Up-bow' in string playing; 'down-bow' is *Niederstrich*.

Auftritt (Ger.). 'Scene' (of an opera or other stage work).

Aufzug (Ger., 'pulling up'). The raising of a curtain; hence an 'act' of an opera, etc.

Augener. English firm of music publishers, originally established in 1853 as music importers. As publishers, Augener used the lithographic process soon after its introduction to England, and from 1867 onwards produced cheap editions of the classics, as well as modern works, in their familiar Augener Edition. They also became known for educational music, and for their journal *The Monthly Musical Record* (1871–1960), edited successively by J. S. Shedlock, Richard Capell, J. A. Westrup, and Gerald Abraham.   JMT/JWA

Augenmusik (Ger.). *'Eye music'.

augmentation. A compositional procedure in which the note-values of a musical statement are lengthened (usually doubled), as in the climactic presentation of certain fugue subjects (e.g. Bach's C major Fugue for organ BWV547).   AW

augmented fourth. See TRITONE.

augmented interval. A major or perfect *interval increased by a semitone.

augmented sixth chord. The chords of the augmented 6th are *altered chords, built on the flattened submediant. The three common forms, with typical resolutions in the key of C, are given in Ex. 1. The so-called 'Italian' and 'French' 6ths usually resolve on to the dominant chord, and the 'German' 6th on to the dominant or the second inversion of the tonic; the 'German' 6th may also, by an enharmonic change, be transformed into a *dominant 7th of the flattened supertonic (in C major, D♭ major or minor; Ex. 2).

Ex. 1

'Italian' 6th   'French' 6th   'German' 6th

Ex. 2

augmented triad. See TRIAD.

Auld Lang Syne. A ritual song of parting used in England and Scotland. The tune first appeared in the overture to William Shield's opera *Rosina* (1782), played by bassoons in imitation of the bagpipe, and acquired Robert Burns's words in 1794. This origin has been disputed by some Scottish authorities, who argue that the tune can be found in Scottish publications of the period and that Shield, who lived not far from the Scottish border, may well have heard it and copied it.

Auletta, Pietro (*b* San Angelo, Avellino, *c*.1698; *d* Naples, Sept. 1771). Italian composer. He was a student at the conservatory of S. Onofrio, Naples, and worked as *maestro di cappella* at S. Maria la Nova while composing operas for production at theatres in Naples. In 1752 a pasticcio derived from his comic opera *Orazio* (1737) was given in Paris as *Il maestro di musica*, forming one of a series of Italian operas which provoked the Querelle des *Bouffons. Auletta continued as a popular and successful opera composer in Naples until 1740, when there was a sudden drop in his output.

aulos. 1. The *reedpipe (not a flute, as often translated) of the Ancient Greeks, one of the two main wind instruments (with the Roman *tibia*) of the classical world. As frequently illustrated, its two pipes were held divergently, one in each hand. The bore was cylindrical and held a double reed, though single reeds are sometimes shown. Both pipes were usually the same length. See also ANCIENT GREEK MUSIC, 2.

Similar instruments were used throughout ancient Western Asia and the Middle East. The Sardinian *launeddas* is a modern derivative, though the melody pipes differ in length and it has acquired a third pipe as a drone. There are clear connections with such single cylindrical pipes as the Turkish *ney*, the Iranian and Caucasian *bālabān*, the Chinese *guan*, and the Japanese *hichiriki*.

2. A generic term denoting a pipe of any sort; it is still used in that sense in Greece.   JMo

aural training. See EAR-TRAINING.

Auric, Georges (*b* Lodève, Hérault, 15 Feb. 1899; *d* Paris, 23 July 1983). French composer. He studied at the Paris Conservatoire and the Schola Cantorum, but his career was determined much more by his association with Cocteau, Poulenc, and others as a member of Les *Six. His early works exude the carefree spirit of the group, and he always shared Poulenc's delight in incongruity, remaining at the same time open to new ideas, even to those of the French avant-garde of the 1950s and 60s. His large output included an opera, ballets, scores for films by René Clair and Cocteau and for several Ealing comedies, chamber music, songs, and piano pieces. He also served as a music critic, and was director of the Paris opera houses (1962–8).

PG/ABur

Ausdruck (Ger.). 'Expression'; *mit Ausdruck, ausdrucksvoll*, 'expressively'.

Ausfüllgeiger (Ger., 'filling-out-fiddler'). A *ripieno part.

Ausgabe (Ger.). 'Edition'.

aushalten (Ger.). 'To sustain'; *ausgehalten*, 'sustained'.

Aus Italien ('From Italy'). Symphonic fantasy, op. 16 (1886), by Richard Strauss, inspired by his visit to Italy.

Aus meinem Leben. See FROM MY LIFE.

äusserst (Ger.). 'Extremely', e.g. *äusserst schnell*, 'extremely fast'.

Australia 1. Indigenous music; 2. European-derived folk music; 3. Art music to 1900; 4. 1900–50; 5. Since 1950

1. Indigenous music

Although the Aborigines have inhabited Australia continuously for at least 40,000 years, the country was physically isolated for much of this time following the submersion beneath the ocean of the land-link to southern Asia. Such evolutionary development in music as is found in other countries was inhibited by the nomadic existence, the inhospitable terrain, and the absence both of musical instruments capable of generating any kind of scale and of any form of writing or notation.

The earliest settlers from Britain and other parts of the world, beginning with the establishment of a penal settlement in the Sydney Cove Colony in 1788, therefore found a relatively undeveloped musical tradition that relied entirely on the human voice accompanied by rhythmic beating or rattling together of sticks, hand-clapping, and other percussive devices.

This music was nevertheless complex, reflecting highly ordered rituals and religious beliefs, and may be the oldest still-performed music in the world. An important element in the subtle and intricate Aboriginal rhythms is the *didjeridu, an instrument first played in the northern part of the country, consisting of a slightly conical tube, usually made from a eucalyptus or gum-tree branch with its centre eaten out by termites. An aural kaleidoscope of timbres, birdcalls, and animal cries can be produced by a skilled player, ensuring that Australian Aborigine music is clearly distinguishable from that of any other race.

2. European-derived folk music

Australia's folk music is mainly derivative and foursquare with only elementary tonal harmonization. It includes sea shanties, work songs, and street ballads based on, or parodying, Irish or English originals, as well as songs from other ethnic minorities from Greece, Italy, and Asian countries. Several hundred Australian folksongs have been collated, the most popular today including *The Wild Colonial Boy* and the ubiquitous *Waltzing Matilda*.

Since the end of World War II, however, a richer and more pluralistic society has evolved, as immigrants from many different countries have brought with them their own folk traditions. In spite of this progressive loss of individuality, Australia's folk music, whether urban, rural, or Aboriginal, looks certain to resist any cultural domination from Britain, the USA, or elsewhere.

3. Art music to 1900

Art music in Australia, from small beginnings at the end of the 18th century, remained wholly dependent on European—mainly British—culture for more than a century. The country's geographical isolation limited the numbers of musicians (composers, performers, and teachers) to a few immigrants and visitors. As Australian-born musicians appeared, they tended to leave the country in search of wider opportunities. The earliest music of European origin included quadrilles played by regimental bands in the penal settlements. After 1830, free settlers began to arrive and the musical public grew in numbers, establishing chamber music concerts, visits by virtuoso soloists, and private music academies. Notable itinerant musicians involved in this activity included Vincent Wallace and Isaac Nathan (1790–1864).

The gold rushes of the 1850s generated a middle-class culture and a growing demand for commercial theatre, choral societies, and the drawing-room piano. The Royal Philharmonic Society of Melbourne was founded as early as 1853 and a sheet-music industry began to flourish. Successful opera seasons were held in Melbourne, Adelaide, Sydney, and Brisbane in the closing decades of the 19th century, and the popularity of opera has been a feature of music in Australia to the present day. Chairs of music were established at the universities of Melbourne (1891) and Adelaide (1884), with independent conservatories soon added in Melbourne (1895), Adelaide (1898), and Sydney (1916). A symphony orchestra was assembled in Melbourne for a centenary celebration (1888) and concerts enjoyed increasing popularity. Composers of this time included Marshall Hall (1867–1915), Fritz Hart (1874–1949), and most notably Alfred Hill, whose use of Aboriginal and Maori mythology reflected his desire to achieve a regional identity, in contrast to the prevailing dependence on the tradition of German Romanticism.

4. 1900–50

The opening decades of the 20th century saw the emergence of a strong national awareness in Australia. The writer and amateur musician Henry Tate (1873–1926) proposed that composers should use the melodic and rhythmic patterns of Australian birdcalls and so 'lead in the direction of a distinctly Australian work'. Percy Grainger was more subtle and prophetic in suggesting that Australian composers should get to know the music of Asia and the South Pacific. Indeed such later composers as Sculthorpe, Meale, Conyngham, Boyd, and Wesley-Smith have all incorporated elements of Indonesian, Japanese, or Vietnamese music in their work.

Developments in radio broadcasting from 1924 made a considerable breakthrough in Australia's cultural development, overcoming the restrictions of the continent's isolation and the pattern of urban concentrations separated by vast distances. The Australian Broadcasting Commission, established in 1932, has been described by Roger Covell as 'the most important single factor in professional music making in Australia'. Orchestral ensembles were soon set up, later to become permanent symphony orchestras in Sydney (1945), Brisbane (1947), Hobart (1948), Adelaide (1948), Melbourne (1949), and Perth (1950).

Composers of the second generation, active during the period between the wars and after, include Roy Agnew, John Antill, Clive Douglas, George English, Felix Gethen, Raymond Hanson, Robert Hughes, Frank Hutchens, Miriam Hyde, Dorian LeGallienne, James Penberthy, Margaret Sutherland, and Arthur Benjamin. At first there was something of a time-lag before the new paths being explored by Stravinsky, Schoenberg, and Varèse were followed in Australia, but modern communications soon enabled Australian composers to be aware of what was happening elsewhere.

5. Since 1950

The postwar period witnessed a succession of important developments affecting the performing arts in Australia. The Australian Musica Viva Chamber Music Society (founded in 1945) promoted tours by many front-rank ensembles. The Australian Opera was created by the Elizabethan Theatre Trust (1956) and its activities were complemented by the Victoria State Opera and opera companies in the other states. An Australian branch of the ISCM was launched in 1956 and has continued to play a key role in fostering new music. This upsurge in the performing arts is also demonstrated by the building of concert halls in all states and several opera houses. The Sydney Opera House (1973) with its spectacular exterior and harbour location has become a readily recognized symbol of Australian cultural development. The opera house in Adelaide has been called 'Richard Wagner's home in Australia' following a successful production of the *Ring* cycle and the Australian premiere (in 2001) of *Parsifal*. The Australian Ballet company has built up a strong reputation with about 200 performances annually at home and on tour.

Musical education has been considerably expanded at all levels, with new conservatories and music departments at the universities of Sydney (1948), Western Australia (1958), Monash, Melbourne (1965), Queensland (1965), New South Wales (1966), Flinders, Adelaide (1966), New England (1966), and La Trobe, Melbourne (1974).

A wide range of musical activities has benefited from the sponsorship of such organizations as the Australian Council for the Arts and the Commonwealth Assistance to Australian Composers (both established in 1967), the Music Board of the Australian Council (from 1973), and the Guild of Australian Composers (with branches in every state). These have supported composition and performing projects, seminars, workshops, and periods of study abroad for composers, performers, and instrument makers. The Australian Broadcasting Commission (since 1982, Corporation), already mentioned, has become the chief patron of Australian composers, commissioning and performing numerous new works.

Instead of lagging behind the developments in other parts of the world, Australian composers now play a leading part in such avant-garde techniques as electronic music, computer-based composition, and music theatre. Key names include Keith Humble and Don Banks, who returned to Australia after being involved in new music activities in Paris and London respectively, Nigel Butterley, Peter Sculthorpe, and Larry Sitsky; immigrant composers like Tristram Cary, John Exton, Elena Kats-Chernin, Bozidar Kos, and Roger Smalley; and new-generation Australian-born composers, among them Alison Bauld, Anne Boyd, Barry Conyngham, Richard Meale, and Martin Wesley-Smith. The list of Australian performers who have achieved international recognition includes Florence Austral (soprano), Valda Aveling (piano), Richard Bonynge (conductor), Peter Dawson (bass-baritone), Robert Helpmann (choreographer), Leslie Howard (piano), Nellie Melba (soprano), Yvonne Minton (mezzo-soprano), Elsie Morison (soprano), Geoffrey Parsons (piano), Joan Sutherland (soprano), and Barry Tuckwell (horn).   LH/JBo

R. Covell, *Australia's Music: Themes of a New Society* (Melbourne, 1967) · A. McCredie, *Musical Composition in Australia* (Canberra, 1969) · J. Murdoch, *Australia's Contemporary Composers* (Melbourne, 1972) · F. Callaway and D. Tunley (eds.), *Australian Composition in the Twentieth Century* (Melbourne, 1978) · J. Murdoch, *A Handbook of Australian Music* (Melbourne, 1983) · B. Broadstock (ed.), *Sound Ideas: Australian Composers Born since 1950* (Sydney, 1995) · N. Saintilan, A. Schultz, and P. Stanhope, *Biographical Directory of Australian Composers* (Rocks, NSW, 1996) · W. Bebbington (ed.), *The Oxford Companion to Australian Music* (Melbourne, 1998)

Austria. The musical history of the German-speaking parts of Europe was inextricably linked until comparatively recently; that of Austria is therefore discussed together with that of *Germany.

Auszug (Ger.). 1. An arrangement, usually for piano (*Klavier-Auszug*), of an opera, orchestral work, etc.
2. 'Extract'.

authentic. 1. A description of a work that can be positively attributed, in all its essential details, to a given composer.
2. In the context of ethnomusicology, the term refers to an uninterrupted folk tradition, unaffected by outside influences, and not the revival of that tradition.
3. Authentic performance (now a somewhat discredited term) implies the use of instruments (or replicas of them), and of performance practices, that are believed to have been familiar to the composer. See AUTHENTICITY.

authentic cadence. See CADENCE.

authenticity. A term sometimes applied to the performance of music of the past in a historical context; as such it is both contentious and ill-defined. It is open to more than one interpretation, including the objective of performing a work in accordance with the composer's believed intentions, or as other musicians performed it during his or her lifetime, or using the instruments and practices known to the composer. The divergence of practice that may result from the pursuit of these differing aims presents great difficulty in defining the boundaries of authenticity. Furthermore, the available evidence regarding the nature of performance in a given historical period is often patchy and contradictory. In consequence, many aspects of performance inevitably rely on intuition and so can never be verified empirically as 'authentic'. The gap that exists between a strict dictionary definition of authenticity, with its connotations of 'genuine' and 'original', and the difficulties of realizing this ideal, have led many scholars and performers to reject the term in favour of 'historically informed', 'historically aware', or *'period' performance.

One of the most important developments surrounding the issue of authenticity has been the rediscovery of obsolete instruments and the use of familiar instruments (e.g. the violin) in their historical states. This revival was spurred in the first instance by Arnold *Dolmetsch's experimentation with old instruments in the first decades of the 20th century, though only after World War II did a wider group of musicians perform, and later record, using early instruments. Today the music of Bach, Mozart, and even Brahms is regularly performed on instruments (or replicas of instruments) from their respective periods and several ensembles and orchestras have been formed specifically for this repertory. For some, this use of 'authentic' or 'original' instruments has become synonymous with authenticity. Other elements of performance that have been re-evaluated in the interest of authenticity include the forces involved, for example using one or two voices to a part in Baroque music rather than a large choir, and using a smaller orchestra for Classical and early Romantic symphonies than had become fashionable by the 20th century.

The sounds of these instruments, and the recovery of practices associated with them, have had a profound effect on what might, until recently, have been called the conventional performance of historical music. Present-day performers commonly adopt practices of earlier periods whether or not they use historically accurate instruments. Nevertheless, the inconsistency with which ideas of historical performance are applied, combined with the gaps in our knowledge of historical practice, make a literal interpretation of the term 'authenticity' impracticable.

See also PERFORMANCE PRACTICE.   BW

📖 H. HASKELL, *The Early Music Revival* (London, 1988) · N. KENYON (ed.), *Authenticity and Early Music* (Oxford, 1988) · P. KIVY, *Authenticities: Philosophical Reflections on Musical Performance* (Ithaca, NY, and London,

1995) · R. TARUSKIN, *Text and Act: Essays on Music and Performance* (New York, 1995)

auto (Sp.). A dramatic street-play, normally religious or allegorical (*auto sacramental*), which originated in medieval times. It was interspersed with songs or incidental music, and later became increasingly secular. Early examples were by Lope de Vega, Calderón, and others.

autograph. A manuscript written in the hand of its author or composer. The term 'holograph' is now frequently used to mean a manuscript wholly in the hand of its composer or author, as opposed to a copy (written by somebody else) with 'autograph' annotations made by the composer.

Manuscripts copied or annotated by the composer can show light on all aspects of composition, from the initial planning stages (in sketch manuscripts) to revisions of the completed work and details of performance practice. In particular, autograph material can be used to 'correct' changes or errors made by copyists in cases where such changes have been passed down into more recent published versions—though musicologists must be aware that in some cases the copyist may have had access to information or knowledge that is not obvious to the modern scholar.

The rate of survival of autograph material is in approximately inverse proportion to the age of the music. So, whereas autograph material for more recent composers is relatively common, and there are important collections of manuscripts of Beethoven and J. S. Bach, there is no demonstrable instance of the survival of musical autograph material before the 16th century. Some early collections may contain works copied by their composers, but the lack of supporting evidence makes such possibilities very difficult to prove.

See also SOURCES.   —/ABul

autoharp (Ger.: *Akkordzither*). A form of *zither invented in Germany in the 1880s to enable melodies to be accompanied easily by ready-made chords. Transverse bars above the strings are each marked with a chord name; pressing down the C major bar silences, with felt pads, all notes foreign to a C major chord, and the other bars have the same function in other keys.   JMo

automatic musical instruments. Instruments on which sound is produced without human intervention (in this they differ from other *mechanical musical instruments). Some, for example the *aeolian harp, are sounded by the wind; in many areas bamboos or other tubes are arranged so that the wind can blow across their open ends, and wind chimes are known worldwide.

Others are sounded by water in a number of ways: dripping into tuned vessels, tipping a balance, or turning a wheel. Water-operated singing birds are said to have been invented in the 3rd century BC, and elaborate water organs (fed from natural streams, with music pinned on barrels turned by waterfalls) and displays of automata were a popular conceit for gardens and grottoes in the 16th and 17th centuries. A number of Arabic treatises in about the 9th century describe similar, if somewhat simpler, instruments.   JMo

auxiliary note. A variety of *passing note which, instead of proceeding to another note, returns to the one it has just left. Such a note may be either diatonic or chromatic. Shakes, mordents, and turns provide examples of the auxiliary note applied as ornamentation.

avant-garde (Fr.). Originally a military designation for an advance party of soldiers, the term has come to signify a group of composers or other artists who assume the role of pioneers on behalf of their generation, rejecting established practice in their striving to pave the way for the future. In the polemics of Schumann, Wagner, and the New German School, certain defining avant-garde traits can already be discerned, among them a refusal to capitulate either to tradition (perceived as moribund) or to mass culture (perceived as regressive), and the positive expectation of hostile and uncomprehending reactions from contemporaries. Many avant-garde figures, notably Schoenberg in the 20th century, remained hopeful of the ultimate acceptance and wider adoption of their innovations—even though such recognition would, paradoxically, entail the reintegration of the avant-garde into the dominant artistic establishment. Such was widely perceived as the fate of the European avant-garde after World War II, its composers (including Boulez and Stockhausen) rapidly absorbed into the institutions of the radio station and international music festival, and its techniques (such as serialism and open form) acquiring the status of new orthodoxies. The notion of an avant-garde, enshrining as it does the characteristically modernist belief in the inevitability of progress within a single, authentic historical tradition, came to be viewed by many as no longer credible in the pluralistic, post-modern climate of the late 20th century.

See also TWENTIETH CENTURY, THE.   CWi

Ave Maria (Lat., 'Hail, Mary'). The salutation of the Virgin Mary by the Archangel Gabriel (Luke 1: 28) used liturgically by the Eastern and Western churches, usually together with that of Elizabeth (Luke 1: 42). In the Roman rite, a petition was added to the biblical texts in the 15th century to create a prayer that has often been set by composers, occasionally with textual vari-

ants. The Eastern Orthodox text sung at the dismissal of Vespers and set in Slavonic by Rakhmaninov and Stravinsky is shorter, introducing the two salutations with 'Virgin Mother of God' and following them with 'for you have borne the Saviour of our souls'.

—/ALi

Ave maris stella ('Hail, star of the sea'). A hymn of the Roman Catholic Church, sung to several different melodies; these, but one in particular, were often used as the basis of Renaissance polyphonic settings of the text (including by Dufay), for masses (Josquin, Victoria, etc.), and for keyboard works (e.g. Cabezón, Titelouze).

Aventures, Nouvelles Aventures. Works by Ligeti to his own texts for three solo voices and seven instruments; they were composed in 1962 and 1962–5 and arranged for performance in 1966; later that year they were expanded and combined for the stage as *Aventures & Nouvelles Aventures* (Württemberg, 1966).

Ave regina coelorum. See ANTIPHONS OF THE BLESSED VIRGIN MARY.

Ave verum corpus (Lat., 'Hail, true body'). A paraliturgical Latin hymn of late medieval origin, expressing devotion to the Host as the body of Christ. A popular affirmation of the Catholic doctrine of the Eucharist, it was often set to music after the Reformation, most famously by Byrd and Mozart.   ALi

Avison, Charles (*b* Newcastle upon Tyne, *bapt.* 16 Feb. 1709; *d* Newcastle upon Tyne, 9 or 10 May 1770). English composer and writer on music. According to Burney he received instruction from Geminiani in London. In 1736 he was appointed organist at St Nicholas's, the principal church in Newcastle, and in 1738 he became musical director of an annual series of subscription concerts in the city; later he organized a similar series in Durham. Among the musicians he attracted to the north-east were Felice Giardini and William Shield.

As well as composing many concerti grossi essentially in the 'ancient' style of Geminiani, some of which were published in full score, Avison arranged 12 of Domenico Scarlatti's harpsichord sonatas for string orchestra. He was also a notable composer of accompanied keyboard sonatas. His *Essay on Musical Expression* (1752) is an important contribution to music criticism and aesthetics of the period. It falls into three parts: a consideration of the effect of music on the emotions; an analysis of individual composers and their styles (controversially concluding that Handel was a lesser composer than Geminiani or Benedetto

Marcello); and a discussion of instrumental performance practice, particularly in concertos.   DA/PL

Avni, Tzvi (*b* Saarbrücken, 2 Sept. 1927). German-born Israeli composer. He studied composition with Mordecai Seter and Paul Ben Haim in Israel, and with Copland and Lukas Foss in the USA. Having also studied electronic techniques with Vladimir Ussachevsky and R. Murray Schafer, he became director of the electronic music studio at the Rubin Academy, Jerusalem, in 1971. Avni began his career with folk-inspired nationalist works, but later became more radical in technique and language, often using tape, though still concentrating on Jewish subjects.
                                                    ABur

awards. See COMPETITIONS IN MUSIC.

ayre. The old English spelling of *air. Morley used the word to embrace all forms of secular vocal music except the serious madrigal, but it came to denote the *lute-song of the period 1597–1622.

Ayrton, Edmund (*b* Ripon, *bapt.* 19 Nov. 1734; *d* Westminster, 22 May 1808). English organist and composer. The brother of William Ayrton, organist at Ripon, he became organist and *rector chori* at Southwell Minster in 1755. The following year he studied for a short time with James Nares. He subsequently took up posts in London as Gentleman of the Chapel Royal, vicar choral at St Paul's Cathedral, and lay vicar at Westminster Abbey, and he was Master of the Children at the Chapel Royal from 1780 to 1805. He composed mainly church music, notably the anthem *Begin unto my God*, sung to mark the end of the American War of Independence.
                                                    PL

azione sacra (It., 'sacred action'). A term used to describe the Italian *sepolcro* (a musical enactment of the Passion set at the holy sepulchre, usually presented within a single act) as cultivated by the Habsburg court in Vienna during the second half of the 17th century. As the term spread from Vienna to Italy it became synonymous with 'oratorio' in general, as it did also in Vienna during the 18th century (see ORATORIO, 4). Apostolo Zeno and Pietro Metastasio used the term for their oratorio texts.
                                                    JBe

azione teatrale (It., 'theatrical action'). A genre of music theatre popular in the 18th century, especially at the courts of Vienna. Similar to the *festa teatrale*, but usually on a smaller scale, the *azione teatrale* generally had a plot with a mythological or allegorical theme and was presented in a single act with up to five characters and a small orchestra. Pietro Metastasio wrote the librettos for 12 such works between 1721 and 1765, collaborating with several composers, including Gluck (e.g. *La contesa de' numi*, 1749). See also SERENATA.
                                                    JBe

Azzaiolo, Filippo (*fl* Bologna, 1550s–60s). Italian composer and singer. He is known for three books of villottas, which contain some attractive songs using popular tunes and texts.

B. 1. The seventh degree (leading note) of the scale of C major (see SCALE, 3).

2. In German, the note B♭ (B♮ is called H).

3. Abbreviation for *bass (e.g. SATB: soprano, alto, tenor, bass) or for *bassus.

Babbitt, Milton (Byron) (*b* Philadelphia, 10 May 1916). American composer. He studied music and mathematics at the University of North Carolina, the University of Pennsylvania, and New York University, his composition teachers including Philip James and Marion Bauer. His graduate studies took him to Princeton University, where he had lessons from Roger Sessions and joined the teaching staff. During World War II he worked in mathematics in Washington and Princeton. He then wrote a Broadway musical (he is an expert on the genre) before returning to the Princeton music department in 1948. Latterly he also taught at Juilliard.

Babbitt had a strong influence as a teacher and as a theorist, developing the principles of *serialism to embrace rhythm and dynamics in a cogent manner with the aid of terms derived from mathematics (*combinatoriality, *set). His music grows out of such concerns and is always marked by a supreme elegance, even when, as in some works of the 1970s, its surface is complex. Earlier pieces tend to be more lucid, and later ones, from his lively 70s and 80s, more playful. His output includes five quartets and much other chamber music, a long series of major piano compositions, rather few orchestral pieces, songs, and works composed with electronically synthesized sounds (*Ensembles for Synthesizer*, 1962–4; *Philomel*, with soprano, 1964). PG

📖 M. BABBITT, *Words about Music* (Madison, WI, 1987) · A. W. MEAD, *An Introduction to the Music of Milton Babbitt* (Princeton, NJ, 1994)

Babiy-Yar. The subtitle of Shostakovich's Symphony no. 13 in B♭ minor op. 113 (1962), a setting of five poems by Yevgeny Yevtushenko for bass, male chorus, and orchestra; Babiy-Yar was the site of the grave of thousands of Russian Jews murdered by the Germans during World War II.

Bacchanalia (Fr.: *bacchanale*). An orgy of riotous dancing or singing in honour of Bacchus, the Greek and Roman god of wine. Glazunov included one in his ballet *The Seasons*, and there are bacchanalian episodes in Wagner's *Tannhäuser* (the Venusberg scene) and Saint-Saëns's *Samson et Dalila*.

bacchetta (It., 'stick'). A drumstick or beater.

Bacchus et Ariane. Ballet in two acts by Roussel to a scenario by Abel Hernant, choreographed by Serge Lifar (Paris, 1931).

Bacewicz, Grażyna (*b* Łódź, 5 Feb. 1909; *d* Warsaw, 17 Jan. 1969). Polish composer, violinist, and pianist. Her instrumental and compositional studies in Paris with Boulanger, André Touret, and Carl Flesch (1932–4) provided the technical and aesthetic foundation for her subsequent careers, although she made concert tours widely only until the mid-1950s. She is especially noted for her extensive and idiomatic writing for string instruments (several sonatas, seven quartets, two piano quintets, ten concertos). The postwar decade, in spite of its political constrictions, was her heyday. Her Third Quartet (1947) and Concerto for String Orchestra (1948) epitomize the elegance and resilience of her particular brand of neo-classicism. Some works incorporate folk elements (Fourth String Quartet, 1951), others refer back to Szymanowski (Second Piano Sonata, 1952). In the more liberal climate after 1956, she began to experiment with 12-note techniques, which proved most successful in those works that moved furthest beyond her neo-classical leanings (Sixth String Quartet, 1960; *Pensieri notturni*, 1961). ATh

📖 J. ROSEN, *Grażyna Bacewicz: Her Life and Works* (Los Angeles, 1984) · A. THOMAS, *Grażyna Bacewicz: Chamber and Orchestral Music* (Los Angeles, 1985)

Bach. German family of musicians. Providing the most remarkable array of musical talent ever chronicled within a single family group, the Bachs, over 70 of whom served at some time as professional musicians, lived and worked in central Germany, mainly in Thuringia, from the early 16th century to the 18th. All apart from the earliest were Protestants and originated from three ancestral lines—of Meiningen, Arnstadt, and Franconia. Some were town musicians (fiddlers or pipers), others organists, Kantors, or Kapellmeister, and not a few were composers of at least local distinction. The order of descent is shown in the accompanying skeletal family tree. An account of the life and work of Johann Sebastian Bach is given separately below.

Among the sons of Heinrich Bach (1615–92), a town musician in Schweinfurt, Erfurt, and Arnstadt, two achieved special regard as composers: **Johann Christoph Bach** (i) (*b* Arnstadt, Dec. 1642; *bur.* Eisenach, 2 April 1703), who was an organist at Eisenach from 1665 and the composer of motets, organ music, and cantatas, a fine example of which is *Es erhub sich ein Streit* ('There was war'), for two five-part choruses, two violins, four violas, and continuo, together with four trumpets and timpani; and **Johann Michael Bach** (*b* Arnstadt, 9 Aug. 1648; *d* Gehren, 17 May 1694), who served as organist, town clerk, and instrument maker in Gehren. He is remembered for his elegantly fashioned motets and cantatas, most notably his Lenten dialogue *Liebster Jesu, hör mein Flehen*

('Dearest Jesus, hear my entreaties'), the participants in which are supported by continuo and various obbligato instruments: Christ (two violins), the Canaanite woman (two violas), and the three disciples (a double bass). In October 1707 his daughter, Maria Barbara, became J. S. Bach's first wife.

Later descendants include **Johann Nicolaus Bach** (*b* Eisenach, 10 Oct. 1669; *d* Jena, 4 Nov. 1753), the eldest son of Johann Christoph (i), who served as university and town organist at Jena, and is chiefly remembered for his *Missa sopra 'Allein Gott in der Höhe'* for chorus, strings, and continuo (*c.*1716) and his student burlesque, *Der jenaischer Wein- und Bierrufer*; from the Meiningen line, **Johann Ludwig Bach** (*b* Thal, nr Eisenach, 10 Sept. 1677; *d* Meiningen, *bur.* 1 May 1731), a distant cousin of J. S. Bach whose output includes motets, funeral music, and cantatas, including the vividly dramatic *Gott ist unser Zuversicht* ('God is our hope and strength'), some copies of which, in the hand of Johann Sebastian, survive; and, from the Franconian line, **Johann Lorenz Bach** (*b* Schweinfurt, 10 Sept. 1695; *d* Lahm im Itzgrund, nr Coburg, 14 Dec. 1773), who studied at Weimar with J. S. Bach, his first cousin, and

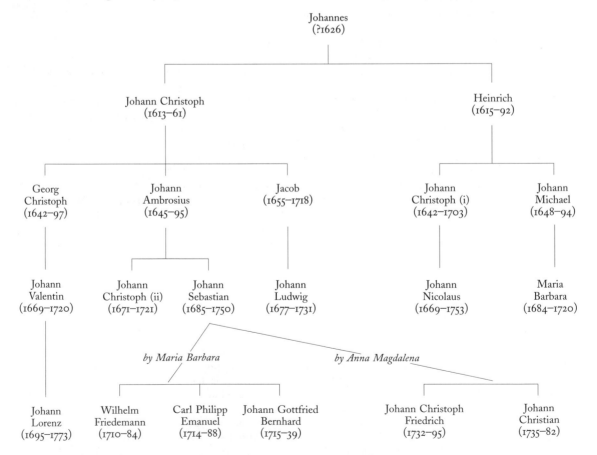

from 1718 served as Kantor at Lahm, where he remained for the rest of his long career. Although none of the above can be described as a major figure in the history of German music, collectively they help, by the consistent patterns of their lives, to explain the dedication and professionalism of the greatest member of the family, whose career was cast in much the same mould as theirs.

Johann Sebastian Bach was the youngest of the eight children of **Johann Ambrosius Bach** (*b* Erfurt, 22 Feb. 1645; *d* Eisenach, 20 Feb. 1695), a town musician in Eisenach, and his first wife Maria Elisabeth (née Lämmerhirt). After the death of his parents Sebastian was sent, with his brother Johann Jacob, to live with their eldest brother, **Johann Christoph Bach** (ii) (*b* Erfurt, 16 June 1671; *d* Ohrdruf, 22 Feb. 1721), who was organist at Ohrdruf, near Arnstadt, and a one-time pupil of Pachelbel.

Of the 20 children of J. S. Bach's two marriages, five of the six sons to survive infancy became musicians and three gained particular renown as composers. His eldest son, **Wilhelm Friedemann Bach** (*b* Weimar, 22 Nov. 1710; *d* Berlin, 1 July 1784), began his musical studies with his father, who composed the well-known *Clavier-Büchlein* ('Little Keyboard Book') for him, and received his formal education in Cöthen at the Lateinschule and in Leipzig at the Thomasschule and university. In 1733, already recognized as a virtuoso performer, he was appointed organist at the Sophienkirche in Dresden, with part-time duties which left him considerable time for composition. Notable works from this period are his delightful concerto for two unaccompanied harpsichords (*c.*1740)—of which Sebastian Bach made a copy (*c.*1742) and Brahms published an edition (in 1864)—and his suite-like Sinfonia in F, the first of a set of five (*c.*1733–46). In 1746 he went to Halle as director of music at the Liebfrauenkirche and two other churches (St Ulrich and St Moritz) and, with excellent vocal and instrumental resources at his disposal, was able to present a number of elaborate cantatas, both of his father's and his own composition. However, in 1764, after becoming unsettled at Halle, he resigned his post and thereafter earned his living, mainly in Brunswick and Berlin, as a recitalist and private teacher. One of his pupils was Sarah Levy, great-aunt of Felix Mendelssohn. Despite his undoubted gifts, and the engaging character of several of his works, he appears to have been largely overshadowed as a composer by his father, whose style he never fully outgrew.

Carl Philipp Emanuel Bach (*b* Weimar, 8 March 1714; *d* Hamburg, 14 Dec. 1788) was the second surviving son of J. S. and Maria Barbara Bach. After studying composition and keyboard playing at the Leipzig Thomasschule with his father, he went on to study law at the University of Frankfurt an der Oder. In 1740 he became harpsichordist at the court of Frederick the Great at Potsdam, with the main duty of accompanying his employer's performances on the flute, a post that proved increasingly unrewarding because of Frederick's ultra-conservative musical tastes and his view that his accompanist should be prepared to accommodate, dutifully, all his errors and anomalies. However, despite his attempts to secure another post (at Zittau in 1753, and possibly at Leipzig, after his father's death in 1750), Emanuel was unable to obtain release and remained in Berlin for 28 years. During that time he published his 'Prussian' and 'Württemberg' sonatas, numerous keyboard concertos, and his renowned textbook, the *Versuch über die wahre Art das Clavier zu spielen* (1753; Eng. trans. by W. J. Mitchell, *Essay on the True Art of Playing Keyboard Instruments*, New York, 1949), which has remained (with Quantz's *Versuch* of 1752), a standard source on 18th-century performance practice.

In 1768 he moved to Hamburg, where he succeeded Telemann as Kantor of the Johanneum and director of music at the five principal churches. In the wake of Telemann he found himself committed to a huge workload, involving some 200 performances each year, both in the churches and in the city. From this period date his oratorios *Die Israeliten in der Wüste* ('The Israelites in the Wilderness', 1769) and *Auferstehen und Himmelfahrt Jesu* ('Resurrection and Ascension of Jesus', 1787), 21 Passion settings (not all of which have survived), and numerous cantatas and other choral works. In the vast array of his keyboard works he was the leading exponent of the *empfindsamer Stil* ('sensitive style'; see EMPFINDSAMKEIT), in which delicate forms of musical expression are designed in such a way as to 'move the affections'. In 1750 he inherited his share of his father's manuscripts, which he carefully preserved, ensuring that they would be passed on after his death for safe keeping to a group of his friends, including Marpurg and Agricola.

The third surviving son of J. S. Bach's second marriage, **Johann Christoph Friedrich Bach** (*b* Leipzig, 21 June 1732; *d* Bückeburg, nr Hanover, 26 Jan. 1795), commonly known as the 'Bückeburg Bach', received early musical training from his father and studied law, from 1749, at Leipzig University. In 1750 he was appointed chamber musician (later Konzertmeister) to the court of Count Wilhelm of Schaumburg-Lippe in Bückeburg, where he remained for the rest of his career. In these congenial cultural surroundings, where Italian music was eagerly cultivated, Friedrich composed chamber works, keyboard sonatas, concertos, and symphonies, in which a gradual move is evident towards a Classical style. For six years, from 1771, he enjoyed close friendship with the celebrated poet Gottfried Herder (temporarily pastor and counsellor to the court), who provided him with librettos for his cantatas and oratorios. In 1778 he travelled, with Wilhelm Friedrich Ernst, the first son of his marriage with Lucia Elisabeth Münchhausen, to London to visit his brother Johann Christian and to attend the renowned Bach–Abel concerts. On his return to Bückeburg he mounted performances at court of *Iphigénie en Tauride* and *Die Entführung aus dem Serail* to express his new-found regard for the work of Gluck and Mozart.

Though relatively short-lived, the youngest son of J. S. Bach and his second wife, Anna Magdalena, **Johann Christian Bach** (*b* Leipzig, 5 Sept. 1735; *d* London, 1 Jan. 1782), travelled more extensively and was more widely acclaimed than any of his brothers. After his father's death he studied for some years with Carl Philipp Emanuel Bach in Berlin, and in 1754 moved to Bologna, where he received instruction (particularly in strict counterpoint) from Padre Martini. In 1757 he became a Roman Catholic, and three years later was appointed organist at Milan Cathedral, for which he composed a number of sacred works. Soon, however, to the neglect of his cathedral duties, he turned towards the theatre, and in 1760 composed for Turin his first *opera seria*, *Artaserse*, to a text by Metastasio; during the next two years he provided for the Teatro S. Carlo in Naples his highly successful *Catone in Utica* and *Alessandro nell'Indie*. In May 1762 he was appointed composer to the King's Theatre in London, and after initial success with *Orione* (1762) went on to furnish his new public with four further operas and the oratorio *Gioas, re di Giuda* (1770). In prosperous circumstances he made London his home, enjoying royal patronage (from 1764 as music instructor to Queen Charlotte) and composing prolifically in all the principal instrumental genres of the time: keyboard sonatas, chamber works, overtures, symphonies, and concertos.

During 1764 Bach met Leopold Mozart and his children, who were visiting London, and made a deep impression on the eight-year-old Wolfgang, who in homage arranged some of the older composer's sonatas as concertos, and in later years often acknowledged the artistic debt he owed him. Also in 1764, Bach began his association with Carl Friedrich Abel (1723–87) and in the following year founded with him the major series of London concerts with which their names were to become firmly linked. In 1772 he visited Mannheim for the production of his opera *Temistocle*, the success of which brought an invitation to return in 1775 with a further opera, *Lucio Silla*, based on an adaptation of the libretto set by Mozart in Milan in 1772. In 1773 he married the Italian opera singer Cecilia Grassi, and three years later, at the request of Padre Martini, had

his portrait painted by Thomas Gainsborough. In 1779 he went to Paris for the premiere of his last opera, *Amadis de Gaule*, based on a French libretto previously used by Gluck. On his final return to London, however, he found his former repute in decline and his concert venture facing severe problems. Under heavy financial pressures (with debts of some £4000) his health soon began to deteriorate, and on New Year's Day 1782 he died. His funeral expenses were paid by Queen Charlotte, and a sufficient sum was granted to his widow to enable her to return to her native Italy.

DA/BS

📖 C. S. TERRY, *John Christian Bach* (London, 1929; new edn, rev. H. C. R. Landon, 1967) · K. and I. GEIRINGER, *The Bach Family* (London, 1954, 2/1976) · S. L. CLARK (ed.), *C. P. E. Bach Studies* (Oxford, 1988) · H. G. OTTENBERG, *Carl Philipp Emanuel Bach*, trans. P. J. Whitmore (Oxford, 1991) · D. R. MELAMED (ed.), *Bach Studies 2* (Cambridge, 1995)

Bach, Johann Sebastian (*see opposite page*)

B–A–C–H. The letters of Bach's surname, which in German pitch nomenclature read B♭–A–C–B♮ (B denotes B♭ and H denotes B♮); these notes were used as a musical motif by Bach himself in *The Art of Fugue*. Many composers have adopted it, principally for fugal compositions and notably in the 19th century after the *Bach Revival. Among those who used it are J. C. Bach, Schumann (Six Fugues op. 60), Liszt, Rimsky-Korsakov, Reger, Busoni (*Fantasia contrappuntistica*), Karg-Elert, Casella, Schoenberg, Webern, Dessau, Pärt, and Louis Andriessen.

Bacheler, Daniel (*b* ?*c*.1574; *d* after 1610). English composer. He was one of the leading composers of instrumental music in Elizabethan and Jacobean England: his works for lute were especially popular during his lifetime, and rank second only to Dowland's in quality. He also wrote consort music. Little is known of his life except that he lived in Aston Clinton in Buckinghamshire and was a groom of the Queen's Privy Chamber.

JM

Bachianas brasileiras. Nine works (1930–45) by Villa-Lobos, for various combinations of voices and instruments, exploring affinities between the spirit of Bach's counterpoint and Brazilian folk music; each is a suite with two titles, one reflecting the Baroque influence, the other referring to a Brazilian popular form. The best known is no. 5, for soprano and at least eight cellos.

Bach Revival. J. S. Bach was the first major composer whose music was rediscovered after a period of obscurity. The revival of his music, beginning about 50 years after his death, was the seminal event that led

(*cont. on p. 84*)

Johann Sebastian Bach
(1685–1750)

The German composer Johann Sebastian Bach was born in Eisenach on 21 March 1685 and died in Leipzig on 28 July 1750.

Early years, Arnstadt, and Mühlhausen

Bach—the supreme musical genius of the late Baroque period—occupies a central position in the most gifted family in musical history (see BACH); he was the youngest of the eight children of Johann Ambrosius Bach (1645–95) and his first wife Maria Elisabeth, née Lämmerhirt (1644–94). Within ten years of his birth he lost both his parents—his mother in May 1694 and his father less than a year later—and was sent with his brother Johann Jacob to live with their eldest brother, Johann Christoph Bach (ii) (1671–1721), who was organist at Ohrdruf, near Arnstadt. Under Christoph's care Sebastian received sound instruction in musical technique and taught himself composition mainly by copying out the works of other composers. In 1700 he gained a scholarship at the Michaelisschule in Lüneburg, where he sang in the choir and probably made contact with the organist and composer Georg Böhm. In July 1702 he was offered the post of organist at Sangerhausen but was thwarted by the reigning duke, who preferred a candidate of his own choice; for several months thereafter he occupied his time as a lackey and violinist at Weimar.

On 9 August 1703 Bach was appointed organist and choirmaster at the church of St Boniface in Arnstadt, with a good salary and relatively light duties. However, he came frequently into conflict with the church authorities, partly because of the confusion he was alleged to have created among the congregation with his 'curious embellishments' of the chorales, partly through his unwillingness to rehearse fractious students in concerted music, and, most particularly, through his unauthorized extension, by some three months, of the leave granted him to visit Lübeck and attend Buxtehude's *Abendmusiken* concerts. Dismayed by these rebukes, and eager to find wider scope for his ambitions than Arnstadt could offer, Bach transferred in June 1707 to Mühlhausen as organist at the Blasiuskirche where, despite theological quarrels between J. A. Frohne, the church's Pietist superintendent, and C. G. Eilmar, an Orthodox Lutheran pastor at the Marienkirche nearby, he found fruitful outlets for his energies, initiating a major renovation of the church's organ and composing his first important church cantatas, including *Aus der Tiefen rufe ich* ('Out of the deep have I called') BWV131 in 1707 or 1708 and *Gott ist mein König* ('God is my King') BWV71 for the installation of the city council in 1708. In October 1707, in the village church at Dornheim, he married Maria Barbara Bach, his second cousin, who bore him seven children, including Wilhelm Friedemann and Carl Philipp Emanuel.

Weimar and Cöthen

In June 1708 Bach was appointed organist and court musician to Duke Wilhelm Ernst of Weimar. From this period there date many of his best-known organ works—the Prelude and Fugue in D major BWV532, the Fantasia and Fugue in G minor BWV542, the Toccata, Adagio, and Fugue in C major BWV564, and many of the chorale preludes in the *Orgel-Büchlein* ('Little Organ Book') BWV599–644—together with keyboard arrangements of works by Vivaldi and others, which involved him in a study of the Italian concerto style of crucial importance to his expanding creative armoury. Promotion to Konzertmeister in 1714 brought with it the duty of providing a new church cantata each month, the earliest of which—*Himmelskönig, sei willkommen* ('King of Heaven, be thou welcome') BWV182, for Palm Sunday 1714—he may well have intended as the first in a complete year cycle. However, with the death in December 1716 of Samuel Drese, the Weimar Kapellmeister, and the subsequent frustration of his hopes of succeeding to the vacant post, Bach's provision of cantatas soon ceased. His search for new employment was rewarded in August 1717, when the post of Kapellmeister to the court of Prince Leopold of Anhalt-Cöthen was offered to him. However, release from his existing employment was not readily secured, and there ensued a battle of wills with Duke Wilhelm which ended, in December, only after Bach had suffered a month's imprisonment and been discharged in disgrace.

At Cöthen Bach at first found congenial employment with a generous ruler who was keenly interested in music and was an able player of the violin, bass viol, and harpsichord. The strict Calvinism embraced by the prince and his court precluded involvement with elaborate church music, but the existence of a lively *collegium musicum* provided the opportunity for Bach to complete and perform several instrumental works, including his keyboard suites and inventions, the first book of *The Well-Tempered Clavier*, various violin and cello sonatas, suites, and partitas, and the six Brandenburg Concertos. However, his agreeable mode of life at Cöthen was sadly disrupted in July 1720, while he was away in Carlsbad, by the death of Maria Barbara, which left him with four young children to raise. On 3 December 1721, following a normal custom of the time, he took a second wife, Anna Magdalena Wilcken, the 20-year-old daughter of a court trumpeter; she was to bear him a further 13 children, of whom ten died in infancy. A week later Prince Leopold married Friederica Henrietta of Anhalt-Bernburg, who turned out to be no lover of music (nor indeed of any form of culture) and resented her husband's preoccupation with the art. The change in his circumstances that this brought about prompted Bach—though not without misgivings about losing his status as a court Kapellmeister—to apply in 1722 for the post of Thomaskantor at Leipzig, which had fallen vacant on the death of Johann Kuhnau. After submitting himself to the customary *Probe* (a test of competence in organ playing and composition), and after both Telemann and Graupner had declined the position (the latter because he was unable to secure release from his current employment), Bach was finally appointed in April 1723.

Leipzig

At Leipzig, Bach and his pupils from the Thomasschule were required to provide the music for the city's four main churches. At two of them (St Thomas and St Nicholas) a cantata was performed by the school's first choir, at each church in turn on most Sundays, and at both on major feast-days. The duties in the other two churches were normally delegated. On Sunday afternoons it was customary for the cantata given at the morning service in one of the main churches to be repeated at the other during Vespers, and on Good Friday for an oratorio-style Passion to be performed annually, again at Vespers and at each church venue in turn. In order to meet these demands Bach completed, during the first five years of his tenure, no fewer than three annual cycles of cantatas (some 150 works), together with his two great Passions, the *St John* (1724) and *St Matthew* (1727), his *Magnificat* (the

first version, in E♭, 1723), and numerous motets and other sacred pieces. The regular performing resources available to him comprised, for each church service, up to 16 first-choir singers and some 18 instrumentalists. On Sundays the cantata was sung from about 7.30 a.m., and it is not unlikely that some of the performances were poor. It remains, indeed, a sublime mystery that Bach's exalted creative ideals appear to have been so little constrained by the limited means at his disposal.

In September 1723 Bach sought to regain his traditional right, as Thomaskantor, to direct the music for the 'old service' at the university church in Leipzig—a right which had been transferred temporarily on Kuhnau's death to J. G. Görner, organist of the Nikolaikirche. But after petitioning the Elector of Saxony without response, Bach was forced to accept a compromise whereby he shared the work, and the salary, with Görner. In 1730, increasingly disenchanted with the conditions at St Thomas's, Bach submitted a memorandum to the church authorities setting out his minimum requirements for a well-regulated church music—and received in response only a threat to reduce his salary. At this point he seems to have considered seeking a new post, possibly at Danzig, as is suggested by a letter he wrote in October 1730 to his former colleague, Georg Erdmann, who was Russian representative there; but nothing came of the idea. Meanwhile, in September 1730, the appointment as rector at the Thomasschule of Johann Matthias Gesner, who was deeply interested in music and had sound plans for reforms at the school, for a time brought welcome relief to Bach's situation. However, Gesner moved to Göttingen four years later, and his successor, J. A. Ernesti, though a fine scholar, showed little appreciation of the educational importance of music. With him Bach was soon in conflict, openly over the appointment of choir prefects, but more fundamentally over their divergent views about the true nature of a liberal education.

From 1729, for some 13 years (with a two-year interregnum from 1737), Bach acted as director of the *collegium musicum* that Telemann had founded in Leipzig in 1702 and, with the support of university students and semi-professional musicians, was able to provide regular weekly concerts. No details have survived of the music performed by the society, but it is likely to have included Bach's concertos for one or more harpsichords (transcriptions mainly from earlier violin concertos), the second and third of his Orchestral Suites, and the secular cantatas *Der Streit zwischen Phoebus und Pan* ('The Dispute between Phoebus and Pan') and the Coffee Cantata ('Schweigt stille, plaudert nicht'—'Be silent, don't chatter'). Other instrumental compositions whose revision or creation occupied him at this time were the four sets of *Clavier-Übung* ('Keyboard Practice', 1731–42), which embrace his harpsichord partitas, so-called Organ Mass, Italian Concerto, and Goldberg Variations, and the second volume of *The Well-Tempered Clavier* (*c*.1742). Although his output of church cantatas decreased quite sharply after 1729, there have survived some fine examples from the early 1730s, notably *Wachet auf, ruft uns die Stimme* ('Awake, the voice is calling us') BWV140 and *Der Herr ist mein getreuer Hirt* ('The Lord is my faithful shepherd') BWV112 (both from 1731) and *Wär Gott nicht mit uns diese Zeit* ('Were God not with us at this time') BWV14 (1735).

On 27 July 1733 Bach sought to advance his status at Leipzig by petitioning Friedrich August II, the new Elector of Saxony, for a court title, submitting as 'trifling proof of his skill' the Kyrie and Gloria of a Lutheran Mass, later to become the first sections of the B minor Mass. After much delay the title of Royal Court Composer was conferred on him in November 1736, and in gratitude, on 1 December, he gave a two-hour recital on the new Silbermann organ at the Sophienkirche, Dresden, where his son Wilhelm Friedemann was organist. During his last years Bach was concerned chiefly to revise and order many of his earlier compositions and to create substantial new works of an abstract, highly technical nature. The B minor Mass was completed by 1748 with the addition of the residual sections of the Roman rite—Credo, Sanctus–Osanna–Benedictus, Agnus Dei–Dona nobis pacem—largely with music 'parodied' with great skill from earlier cantata movements. There exists no certain evidence that the Mass was performed in Bach's lifetime, and it is not unlikely that he regarded it mainly as an exemplar for later generations of the mastery he had attained in all the main sacred genres of his time.

On 7 May 1747 Bach visited Potsdam at the invitation of Frederick the Great, and was given a 'royal theme' on which to improvise. Subsequently, this theme served as the basis of his *Musical Offering* (September 1747), a collection of ricercars and canons of a diverse and searching character, together with a trio sonata in the *galant* style, as a concession to Frederick's more modern tastes. Canonic writing, which he had already explored methodically in the 'Goldberg' Variations (1741), features again, majestically treated, in the Canonic Variations for organ on *Vom Himmel hoch da komm ich her* ('From highest heaven I come') BWV769 (*c*.1746–7), in which the canonic lines are combined with, or derived from, the Lutheran Christmas hymn. In 1747 this work and the *Canon triplex* BWV1076 were submitted by the composer as the 'scientific communication' required of him on joining the Corresponding Society of Musical Sciences, founded at Leipzig in 1738 by Christoph Mizler, a one-time pupil of Bach. Since the scientific nature of the society's work accorded well with Bach's compositional aims at this period, he provided the *Musical Offering* as his annual 'communication' in 1748, and probably intended to submit in the following year *The Art of Fugue*, his vast compendium of contrapuntal techniques (both fugal and canonic), had it not apparently remained unfinished at his death. Towards the end of his life he went blind, a condition that two enervating operations by the English surgeon John Taylor did nothing to alleviate; and it is thought likely that he may have suffered from a severe form of diabetes. He died in Leipzig on 28 July 1750 and was buried with honour three days later in the graveyard of the Johanniskirche, near the south wall of the church. Anna Magdalena received, on his death, only a pittance from his estate, and died in considerable poverty on 27 February 1760.   BS

📖 H. T. DAVID and A. MENDEL (eds.), *The Bach Reader: A Life of Johann Sebastian Bach in Letters and Documents* (New York, 1945, 2/1966) · M. BOYD, *Bach* (London, 1983, 3/2000); R. L. MARSHALL, *The Music of Johann Sebastian Bach: The Sources, the Style, the Significance* (New York, 1989) · L. DREYFUS, *Bach and the Patterns of Invention* (Cambridge, MA, 1996) · J. BUTT (ed.), *The Cambridge Companion to Bach* (Cambridge, 1997) · M. BOYD (ed.), *J. S. Bach* (Oxford, 1999) · C. WOLFF, *Johann Sebastian Bach: The Learned Musician* (New York, 2000) ultimately to the comprehensive historicism now prevailing in the world of classical music.

The mid-18th century witnessed a rejection of Bach's styles and ideals in favour of the *style *galant*, though there was always a small group of devotees, centred in Berlin and including his son C. P. E. Bach. Gottfried van Swieten carried the tradition to Vienna, where in the 1780s he organized meetings for the performance and discussion of the master's works. Three separate editions of *The Well-Tempered Clavier* appeared in 1801. J. N. Forkel's pioneering biography (1802) led the way in a nationalistic cult of Bach; other prominent figures in the early stages were C. F. Zelter and Friedrich Rochlitz. Zelter drew on his extensive collection of Bach manuscripts for early revivals of the sacred works, culminating in the famous performance of the *St Matthew Passion* by the Berlin Singakademie in 1829, directed by Zelter's pupil Mendelssohn. Meanwhile in England, where the revival of old music had begun much earlier than in Germany, there was a parallel movement. Early proponents of Bach in England were Clementi, C. F. Horn, and A. F. C. Kollmann, and their most ardent follower was Samuel Wesley.

However, by the mid-19th century only a few of the vocal works had been published. The revival was completed by the formation of the Bach-Gesellschaft, which methodically proceeded to publish all the known works of Bach in full score over the next 50 years. This monumental work not only completed the Bach Revival, securing Bach a permanent place among the greatest composers of all time: it also established the basic principles for scholarly musical editions that have been followed ever since. For the 20th century, the chief remaining task was the study of performance practice of Bach's time, which allowed the scores to be interpreted in a manner more faithful to the composer's intentions. NT

Bach trumpet. A valved piccolo D trumpet used in modern orchestras for playing Baroque music.

Bach-Werke-Verzeichnis. See BWV.

Bäck, Sven-Erik (*b* Stockholm, 16 Sept. 1919; *d* Stockholm, 10 Jan. 1994). Swedish composer. He studied the violin at the Musikhögskola (1938–43) and composition with Rosenberg (1940–5) in Stockholm before investigating early music at the Schola Cantorum, Basle, and further studying composition with Petrassi in Rome (1951–2). He initially made his living as a violinist, playing in the Kindel (1940–4) and Barkel (1944–53) Quartets, as well as an orchestral musician. He was one of Sweden's first modernist composers, adopting serial procedures early in his career and later incorporating electronics into his music. His

generous output includes music for stage, orchestra, various chamber combinations, and chorus. MA

backbeat. In rock music, the accentuation of the second and fourth beat of a 4/4 bar.

backfall. A 17th-century English term for a descending *appoggiatura, notated and performed as in Ex. 1. See also FOREFALL.

Ex. 1

or

badinage, badinerie (Fr., 'playfulness', 'trifling'; Ger.: *Tändelei*). An optional movement occasionally found in the 18th-century *suite; it is in a frivolous style but of no particular form. Bach included a Badinerie in his Orchestral Suite in B minor (BWV1067) and Telemann wrote a Badinage for his *Musique de table*, book 3 (1733).

Badings, Henk [Hendrik Herman] (*b* Bandung, Java, 17 Jan. 1907; *d* Maarheeze, 26 June 1987). Dutch composer and teacher. He studied mine engineering and geology at the Technical University in Delft (1924–30) and was self-taught in composition. He held teaching appointments in the Netherlands and Germany, notably that of director of the Hague Conservatory (1941–4). His earlier works, thickly scored and with long melodic lines, were influenced by Hindemith, Honegger, and Milhaud, but the 1950s brought a lightening of texture. At the same time Badings began an occasional involvement with electronic music, sometimes using new tuning systems. His works include much orchestral music, cantatas, and chamber compositions. His collaboration with the occupying Germans in World War II was not readily forgiven: although he was allowed to resume his professional activities in 1947, his involvement with the Nazis cast a shadow over his music from which it has yet to emerge. PG/MA

📖 P. T. KLEMME, *Henk Badings, 1907–87: Catalog of Works* (Pinewood, MI, 1993)

bagatelle (Fr., Ger.). A short and unpretentious instrumental piece, usually for keyboard. François Couperin gave the title *Les Bagatelles* to pieces in his *Pièces de clavecin* (ordre 10); Beethoven wrote 26 piano bagatelles, of which *Für Elise* is one.

bagpipe (Fr.: *cornemuse, musette, biniou*, etc.; Ger.: *Dudelsack, Sackpfeife*, etc.; It.: *cornamusa, piva, zampogna*, etc.; Sp.: *cornamusa, gaita, zampoña*). A wind instrument consisting, in its simplest form, of a reedpipe with fingerholes (the chanter) inserted into an air reservoir usually made from skin or bladder (the bag), into which air is driven from a blowpipe that is a tube terminating in a non-return valve. The air may be supplied from the player's lungs or by bellows pumped with the elbow. The player compresses the bag with the arm to build up the pressure required to make the reed vibrate. Most bagpipes are also provided with one or more drone pipes.

The pipes are inserted into the bag through wooden stocks tied into the openings which, in the case of bags made from whole sheep- or goatskins, occur naturally at such points as the neck and legs. Modern bags are often made from tanned sheepskin cut to shape, rubber, or rubberized cloth. Many west European bagpipes, including the Scottish Highland bagpipe, the Irish *uilleann* pipes, the Galician *gaita*, the Italian *zampogna*, the Breton *biniou*, and the French *cornemuse*, have chanters with a conical bore and a double reed like a *shawm. Others, for example the Czech and Polish *dudy*, the Dalmatian *diple*, and the North African *zukra*, have cylindrical chanters with single reeds like that of a clarinet (though the cylindrical chanter of the Northumbrian small-pipes has a double reed). Drones usually have a cylindrical bore with one or more sliding joints for tuning, and single reeds. Exceptions are the *zampogna*, the musette, and the *uilleann* pipes, which have double reeds throughout. The *zukra* is an example of a bagpipe with a double chanter of two parallel canes held side by side and terminating in a cowhorn bell. Bagpipes of many different types are found all over Europe, and elsewhere from Tunisia to India.

Examples of bellows-blown bagpipes include the Northumbrian small-pipes, the Scottish Lowland or Border bagpipe, the Irish *uilleann* bagpipe, the musette, and the *dudy*. The *uilleann* pipes are unique in two respects: the chanter can be made to sound a complete upper octave as well as the lower (most bagpipes have a compass of only a 9th), and accompanying chords can be played on three additional pipes called 'regulators', provided with brass keys that are opened with the lower edge of the right hand without interrupting the music of the chanter.

The origins of the bagpipe are unknown. A reference by Aristophanes may indicate its presence in ancient Greece, and it was certainly known in Rome, where Nero is said to have played the *aulos with his arm. Although the Highland pipe became universally known as it accompanied British armies round the world, most other forms of bagpipe experienced a wide revival during the 20th century. This encompassed the re-invention of some bagpipes that died out long ago and for which only iconographical evidence remains; these include various English types, and certain bagpipes that are reappearing in northern Spain.

Most bagpipes are solo instruments, though some are also associated with marching bands, notably the Highland pipe and the Galician *gaita*. The latter is often played in groups of two or three, with melodies characteristically in 3rds. The *biniou* is usually heard in duet with a rustic shawm (the *bombarde*). The musette, a refined instrument and the first with keys on the chanter to provide semitones, became fashionable among the French aristocracy during the 17th century. Some bagpipes are played in ensemble with other instruments.

See also BLADDER PIPE.   RPA

📖 A. BAINES, *Bagpipes* (Oxford, 1960, 3/1995) · R. D. CANNON, 'The bagpipe in northern England', *Folk Music Journal*, 2/2 (1971), 127–47 · F. COLLINSON, *The Bagpipe* (London, 1975) · A. RICCI and R. TUCCI, 'Folk musical instruments in Calabria', *Galpin Society Journal*, 41 (1988), 36–58 · D. CAMPBELL, 'Eastern bagpipes: Origins, construction and playing techniques', *Chanter* (1995–6), 8–20 · J. MAY, 'The *uilleann* pipes', *Songlines*, 4 (1999), 40–8

baguette (Fr., 'stick'). A drumstick or beater; *baguette d'éponge*, a sponge-headed timpani stick frequently required by Berlioz instead of the wooden type.

baile [bayle] (Sp.). An entertainment of dance, poetry, and music between acts of a 17th- or 18th-century play. The term can also refer simply to dancing, to particular dance forms, or to ballet. See also BALLO.

Bainbridge, Simon (Jeremy) (*b* London, 30 Aug. 1952). English composer. He studied with John Lambert in London and with Gunther Schuller in the USA. His early successes were with instrumental and orchestral compositions, notably the Viola Concerto (1978) written for the American virtuoso Walter Trampler and the BBC-commissioned *Fantasia for Double Orchestra* (1984). Bainbridge's ability to build substantial forms from a combination of lyrically refined details and more highly charged, dramatic musical gestures found memorable expression in *Ad ora incerta*, four orchestral songs from Primo Levi for mezzo-soprano with bassoon obbligato (1993), a work whose imaginative intensity is a worthy match for Levi's poetic meditations on the horrors of the Holocaust; it won the Grawemeyer Award for composition in 1997. Bainbridge followed *Ad ora incerta* with *Four Primo Levi Settings* for mezzo-soprano, clarinet, viola, and piano in 1996.

AW

Baird, Tadeusz (*b* Grodzisk Mazowiecki, 26 July 1928; *d* Warsaw, 2 Sept. 1981). Polish composer. In his early 20s he formed Group 49 with Jan Krenz and Kazimierz Serocki to promote *socialist realism in music, and his music up to the mid-1950s is a mixture of simple neoclassicism and elegiac lyricism (Symphony no. 2, 1952). With Serocki he initiated the Warsaw Autumn festival in 1956, and his music of that time quickly accumulated experience of serial techniques. His orchestral *Four Essays* (1958) is characteristic of his blend of Mahler, Berg, and newer compositional idioms. His subsequent music—often cast as orchestral song cycles (*Listy Goethego*, 'Goethe Letters', 1970)—maintained its dark-hued lyricism. Sometimes his soul-searching became deeply troubled, as in his one-act opera after Joseph Conrad, *Jutro* ('Tomorrow', 1966), or his intensely dramatic orchestral 'tone-poem', *Psychodrama* (1972). He remains one of the most individual and underrated of postwar Polish composers.   ATh

 📖 *Muzyka*, 29/1–2 (Warsaw, 1984) [Baird issue]

Baiser de la fée, Le ('The Fairy's Kiss'). Ballet in four scenes by Stravinsky with a scenario after Hans Christian Andersen's *The Ice Maiden*, based on piano pieces and songs by Tchaikovsky linked by passages Stravinsky composed in a similar style; it was choreographed by Bronislava Nijinska (Paris, 1928).

Bakfark, Valentin [Bálint] (*b* Brassó, Transylvania [now Brașov, Romania], ?1526–30; *d* Padua, 22 Aug. 1576). Hungarian lutenist and composer. He spent his youth at the Hungarian court and subsequently travelled widely, serving both the Polish king, Sigismund Augustus II, and Emperor Maximilian II. In his time he was renowned throughout Europe as a virtuoso performer. His works are mainly transcriptions of madrigals, chansons, and motets by other composers, but he wrote a number of fantasias, which represent a peak in the old, strictly polyphonic style of writing for the lute.   DA/LC

Balada, Leonardo (*b* Barcelona, 22 Sept. 1933). Catalan-born American composer. His early modernist experiments yielded in the mid-1960s to hard-textured rhythmic structures influenced by geometric art. His later music is mellowed by reminiscences of Catalan songs and ballads. He collaborated with Dali in the surrealistic film *Chaos and Creation* (1960) and has written in all major forms, notably *María Sabina* (1969) for narrator, chorus, and orchestra, three operas including *Death of Columbus* (1994), and *Steel Symphony* (1972). He took American nationality in 1981.   CW

Balakirev, Mily Alekseyevich (*b* Nizhniy Novgorod, 21 Dec. 1836/2 Jan. 1837; *d* St Petersburg, 16/29 May 1910). Russian composer, pianist, and conductor. He had piano tuition, largely from his mother, and informal musical discussions with his mentor, Aleksandr Ulïbïshev (1794–1858)—the most distinguished musical figure in his home town (and the author of an early Mozart biography)—at whose musical soirées Balakirev appeared as a pianist and conductor. At the age of 18 he moved to St Petersburg and soon made a public debut playing his own Piano Concerto. His brief encounter with the ailing Glinka made a lasting impression: he later fashioned himself as Glinka's heir in the cause of Russian national music. Perhaps more important was his friendship with Vladimir Stasov, whose aspirations for Russian music were already well developed. Gradually a circle of young composers formed round Balakirev and Stasov, among them Musorgsky, Borodin, Rimsky-Korsakov, and Cui. Stasov was later to give them a nickname: 'the Mighty Handful' (more often known, in Anglophone countries, as 'The *Five').

Thanks to his greater experience in composition, his superb pianistic skills and his broad knowledge of the repertory, Balakirev acted as mentor for the young amateurs, supervising, correcting, and often rewriting their early works: Rimsky-Korsakov's and Borodin's First Symphonies were both effectively collaborations with Balakirev, though he did not seek acknowledgment. His role in shaping the musical style of The Five was enormous and remains underestimated. His *Overture on Three Russian Songs* (1858) and *Czech Overture* (1867) led the younger composers to produce a body of similar works on Russian and foreign themes, and his collection of 40 Russian folksongs with piano accompaniment (1866) laid the foundations of a new style of folksong harmonization and ultimately shaped many features of The Five's harmonic style in all genres.

Balakirev's three visits to the Caucasus in the mid-1860s, from which he returned with a treasury of folk tunes and new oriental idioms, also proved to be of great musical importance. The striking originality of *Gruzinskaya pesnya* ('The Georgian Song', 1864), the piano fantasy *Islamey* (1869), and other works inspired by these visits immediately caught the attention of his younger colleagues, thus establishing the orientalist strain in Russian music which led in time to such repertory favourites as Rimsky-Korsakov's *Sheherazade* and Borodin's Polovtsian Dances. The young Tchaikovsky also briefly fell under Balakirev's spell and sought his advice during the composition of *Romeo and Juliet*, which even featured Balakirev's most characteristic keys, B minor and D♭ major.

Balakirev was also able to assist his younger colleagues by conducting their works in the concerts of the Free Music School and those of the Russian Music Society (he was chief conductor from 1867 to 1869, succeeding Anton Rubinstein). The Free Music School, which opened in 1862, was his personal project, developed in opposition to the Germanic tendencies of the St Petersburg Conservatory; unlike that institution, it offered instruction to students who could afford to pay little or nothing. The near-failure of the school, and a deterioration in his finances in the late 1860s, caused Balakirev to withdraw from even his close friends and to abandon his musical activities. Having been a convinced atheist, he now became a fervent Orthodox believer and took minor clerical orders.

Balakirev reappeared in Russian musical life only in the 1880s; in 1882 he completed a major work, the symphonic poem *Tamara* (1882), which he had originally drafted in the 1860s. In spite of its age it made a strong impression on both the public and critics, thanks to its brilliant orchestration and fiery oriental themes. By 1897, however, when he introduced his First Symphony, another recently completed work of the 1860s, the judgment was much less favourable, Rimsky-Korsakov sharply criticizing its outmoded style. Balakirev had failed to complete these works of the 1860s partly because he expended much of his creative energy in helping his younger colleagues; his withdrawal from musical life in the 1870s had brought his own development to a halt, but in the mean time the other members of The Five had grown into mature artists who now easily outshone their former mentor. Understandably, Balakirev resented this and his relations with them never returned to their old footing.

Again he participated in the running of the Free Music School, which had survived its earlier difficulties. He now began to collect a new generation of followers, the most eminent being Sergey Lyapunov, who shared Balakirev's fondness for a virtuoso Lisztian style of piano composition and combined it with Balakirev's own Russian–oriental style. From 1883 to 1894 Balakirev also held the directorship of the Court Cappella Choir, one of the most important musical posts in Russia. Nevertheless his enthusiasm for these tasks was muted and he was a difficult colleague: at the school he delegated much of his work to Lyapunov and others, while at the Cappella he relied heavily on Rimsky-Korsakov, now his deputy. As a pianist he still performed his beloved Liszt and Chopin, but now only privately, for small groups. Although his last large-scale works, the Second Symphony and the B minor Piano Sonata, were composed in the first years of the

20th century, they sound like products of the 1860s, the decade Balakirev the composer never left.

MF-W

M. O. ZEITLIN, *The Five* (New York, 1959) · E. GARDEN, *Balakirev: A Critical Study of his Life and Music* (London, 1967); 'The influence of Balakirev on Tchaikovsky', *Proceedings of the Royal Musical Association*, 107 (1980–1), 86–100; 'Balakirev's influence on Musorgsky', *Musorgsky in memoriam, 1881–1981*, ed. M. H. Brown (Ann Arbor, MI, 1982), 11–27; 'Balakirev: The years of crisis (1867–1876)', *Russian and Soviet Music: Essays for Boris Schwarz*, ed. M. H. Brown (Ann Arbor, MI, 1984), 147–55

balalaika. A Russian long-necked lute with a triangular body and three strings, the two lowest usually tuned in unison and the *chanterelle a 4th higher. Originally a folk instrument, it is made today in sizes from descant to double bass for balalaika orchestras. The *dombra* is a similar instrument, but with a round body. JMo

balancement (Fr., 'wavering'). An 18th-century term for tremolo, used mainly to denote the *Bebung in clavichord music or a *vibrato in vocal and string music.

Balassa, Sándor (*b* Budapest, 20 Jan. 1935). Hungarian composer. A late starter as a musician, he studied at the Budapest Conservatory, and later at the Liszt Academy of Music with Endre Szervánszky; from 1964 to 1980 he worked as a producer at Hungarian Radio. His works, freely atonal until a partial return to tonality later in his career, and always imaginatively varied in texture and lyrical in manner, include three operas—*Az ajtón kívül* ('The Man Outside', 1978), *A harmadik bolygó* ('The Third Planet', 1989), and *Karl és Anna* (1995), all performed in Budapest—as well as choral, orchestral, and chamber music. ABur

Balbastre, Claude-Bénigne (*b* Dijon, 22 Jan. 1727; *d* Paris, 9 May 1799). French organist and composer. He was taught the organ by his father and, after moving to Paris in 1750, studied composition with Rameau. He frequently played at the Concert Spirituel, and in 1760 he was appointed one of the organists at Notre Dame, gaining an international reputation. In 1776 he became organist to the future Louis XVIII; his royal connections brought about his downfall at the Revolution, and he died in poverty.

Balbastre's early keyboard pieces have descriptive titles in the manner of Couperin and Rameau, but he gradually turned to writing sonatas in the *galant* style. His *noëls*, which he performed every year at midnight Mass at St Roch, were extremely popular. He is credited with the invention of the 'fortepiano organisé', a combination of piano and organ with a single keyboard. DA/LC

Balfe, Michael William (*b* Dublin, 15 May 1808; *d* Rowney Abbey, Herts., 20 Oct. 1870). Irish composer and baritone. He moved to England after the death of his father in 1823 and earned his living as a violinist at Drury Lane. Under the patronage of Count Mazzara he studied in Rome and Milan; he also visited Paris, where he was introduced to Rossini by Cherubini and made his singing debut in Rossini's *Il barbiere di Siviglia*. He then travelled widely in Italy. After his third opera, *Enrico Quarto*, had been performed at the Teatro Carcano, Milan (1833), he returned to London, where he achieved great success with *The Siege of Rochelles* (1835) and *The Maid of Artois* (1836) at Drury Lane. An attempt in 1841 to establish a national English Opera at the Lyceum Theatre (backed by Queen Victoria and the Prince Consort) foundered after only a year, but shortly after the success of *Le Puits d'amour* in Paris Balfe triumphed at Drury Lane in 1843 with *The Bohemian Girl*, which ran for over 100 nights. (It was also produced in Italian as *La zingara* in London in 1858.) In 1846 he took over from Costa as conductor of Her Majesty's Theatre until its closure in 1852.

After visits to St Petersburg, Vienna, and Trieste, Balfe continued to compose English opera, this time for the Pyne–Harrison company at Covent Garden, which produced six works (1857–63), among them *The Rose of Castille* (1857) and *Satanella* (1858). In 1864 he retired to Hertfordshire, where he wrote his last (unfinished) opera, *The Knight of the Leopard*. The year before his death *The Bohemian Girl* was produced in Paris (as *La Bohémienne*), its success earning him national honours from both France and Spain. In addition to his operas, Balfe is well known for his songs *Come into the garden, Maud* and *Excelsior*.   JDı

ballabile (It.). 'Suitable for dancing', i.e. in a dance style. A movement in 19th-century opera intended for dancing. Verdi included examples in *Ernani*, *Macbeth*, and *Aida*.

ballad (from Lat. *ballare*, 'to dance'). Although the origin of the term 'ballad' is in medieval dance-song, the word had lost this connotation by the late Middle Ages. By the 14th century it referred to a strophic solo song with a narrative text. Ballads are ubiquitous in Europe, particularly in the British Isles, Denmark, Spain, and east European countries. They are primarily products of oral tradition, but from the 16th century onwards they were also published in 'broadsides' (broadsheets). A ballad is not to be confused with a *ballade*.

Some of the subject matter of ballad texts may be much older than the form itself: it has been suggested that long epics were the music of tribes, whereas the shorter metrical, strophic, solo song is the music of

peasants, which developed in feudal society; thus, the stories told in ballads, which tend to concentrate on a single event, are probably often vignettes from originally much longer epic tales. F. J. Child (*English and Scottish Popular Ballads*, 1882–98) often traced affiliations between the narratives of songs across Europe, suggesting great antiquity of subject matter. Subjects include apocryphal Christian legends (*The Cherry-Tree Carol*), miracles (*Sir Hugh*), outlaws (*Robin Hood*), historical themes, the truth often embellished (*Queen Eleanor's Confession*), maritime events (*Henry Martin*), and marital strife (*The Farmer's Curst Wife*); in Scotland, common themes are the feuding between clans (*The Bonny Earl of Moray*) and border raids into England (*Dick o' the Cow*).

In the typical 'common' or 'ballad' metre a stanza has four lines, though many other structures are also found. The melodies have been more recently recorded than the texts, but there is evidence that some tune types are of considerable antiquity. In England, the Ionian (major) mode is the most popular for ballad tunes; however, others are commonly found: the Mixolydian (G), the Dorian (D), and the Aeolian (A). Tunes with gapped scales, especially hexatonic and pentatonic, seem more common in Scotland and the USA. Germany stands out as a place where major and minor tonality largely supplanted modality.

Ballads printed on broadsides were not generally provided with melodies; these would be supplied from oral tradition. Sometimes their texts were topical, a way of passing on news and gossip. In America, the circulation of stories in this way could lead to ballads in blues form (*Frankie and Johnny*). Ballad studies have been much more vigorously pursued in the USA than in Britain; the existence of detractors should, however, be noted: it has been suggested that workers' songs from oral tradition have been so 'mediated' by centuries of literary editors that the very concept of a ballad might be considered fake (see also FOLK MUSIC).

The ballad is also found as German art song (see LIED); some of its texts are adaptations of traditional English ballads. Poets who wrote in this genre include Bürger, Goethe, and Herder. Perhaps the most influential ballad composer was Zumsteeg, who provided models for Schubert, on whom later lieder composers drew.

*Ballad opera was a popular theatrical entertainment whose airs were taken from the repertory of popular ballad tunes. Towards the end of the 18th century, there developed the English 'sentimental' ballad, found in English opera for a hundred years or so; it was also commercially successful from the mid-19th century until the early 20th, when 'ballad concerts' were common; hence, perhaps, the postwar phenomenon of the pop or rock ballad, a song usually with a narrative text and in a slow tempo.   PW

📖 C. M. SIMPSON, *The British Broadside Ballad and its Music* (New Brunswick, NJ, 1966) · B. H. BRONSON, *The Ballad as Song* (Berkeley, CA, 1969) · H. SHIELDS, *Narrative Singing in Ireland* (Dublin, 1993) · W. B. McCARTHY, *The Ballad Matrix: Personality, Milieu, and the Oral Tradition* (Bloomington, IN, 1995) · D. DUGAW (ed.), *The Anglo–American Ballad: A Folklore Casebook* (New York, 1995) · T. CHEESMAN and S. RIEUWERTS (eds.), *Ballads into Books: The Legacies of Francis James Child* (Berne, 1997)

ballade (Fr.). 1. One of three standard poetic forms used for 14th- and 15th-century chansons (see also RONDEAU; VIRELAI). Similar forms can be found in 12th- and 13th-century monophonic songs; in many of these cases the *ballade* and *virelai* forms are not clearly distinct from each other. The distinction became more pronounced in the early 14th century in the songs of Jehan de L'Escurel, while the *ballade* achieved definitive expression in the works of Guillaume de Machaut, with three structurally identical stanzas each concluding with the same refrain line (shown in italics) and each sung to the same music, in the form aab:

> Gais et jolis, liez, chantans et joieus
> Sui, ce m'est vis, en gracieus retour   } a
>
> Pleins de desir et en cuer familleus
> De reveoir me dame de valour,   } a
>
> Si qu'il n'est mauls, tristesse ne dolour
> Qui de mon cuer peüst Joie mouvoir: } b
> *Tout pour l'espoir que j'ay de li veoir.*

Within each stanza the rhyme used for the first couplet will be repeated for the second; both will be sung to the first section of the music (a), with first-time (*ouvert*) and second-time (*clos*) endings, while the second section of music (b) will carry the remaining lines.

The *ballade* remained the dominant poetic form for late 14th-century composers, who often set texts in which the standard theme of courtly love is combined with classical or mythological allusions. Some *ballades* record important events, while others contain extravagant praise of leading political figures; here the form could be used to advantage by repeating a name or motto as the final refrain line of each stanza. In Trebor's *Se July Cesar*, for example, the dedicatee, Gaston Count of Foix (known as 'Phebus'), is compared to some great names of the past:

> Se July Cesar, Rolant et roy Artus
> Furent pour conqueste renoumez ou monde, } a
>
> Et Yvain, Lancelot, Tristain ne Porus
> Eurent pour ardesse los, pris et faconde, } a

> Au jor d'uy luist et en armez tous ceuronde
> Cyl qui por renon et noble sorte   } b
> 'Febus avant' en s'enseigne porte

In the 15th century the *ballade* lost popularity, except in England, as a medium for courtly love songs, but it was retained in pieces written for specific occasions, for example Dufay's *Resvelliés vous*, composed for the wedding of Carlo Malatesta in 1423, or Ockeghem's *Mort tu as navré de ton dart*, a lament for the death in 1460 of the great chanson composer Binchois.

PD/ABUL

📖 L. SCHRADE (ed.), *The Works of Guillaume de Machaut*, ii, Polyphonic Music of the Fourteenth Century, 3 (Monaco, 1956) · L. EARP, 'Lyrics for reading and lyrics for singing in late medieval France: The development of the dance lyric from Adam de la Halle to Guillaume de Machaut', *The Union of Words and Music in Medieval Poetry*, ed. R. A. Baltzer, T. Cable, and J. Wimsatt (Austin, TX, 1991) · W. FROBENIUS, 'Ballade (Mittelalter)', *Handwörterbuch der musikalischen Terminologie*, ed. H. H. Eggebrecht (Stuttgart, 1998) · D. FALLOWS, *A Catalogue of Polyphonic Songs, 1415–1480* (Oxford, 1999)

2. Name given by Chopin to a long, dramatic type of piano piece, the musical equivalent of a poetic *ballad of the heroic type. He wrote four: op. 23 in G minor, op. 38 in F, op. 47 in A♭, and op. 52 in F minor. Brahms, Liszt, Grieg, and Fauré were among other composers to use the title for instrumental works.

ballad horn. A late 19th-century valved brass instrument at concert pitch and circular in shape, built for amateurs.

Ballad of Baby Doe, The. Opera in two acts by Douglas Moore to a libretto by John Latouche (Central City, CO, 1956).

ballad opera. A peculiarly English form of theatrical entertainment, though related to the French *vaudeville of the end of the 17th century and beginning of the 18th, and to the German *Singspiel, on which it had an influence. It consists of a spoken play with interpolated songs, and in this respect resembles the 'dramatic opera' of Purcell's time; but the songs were shorter and far more frequent (as many as 70 in some cases), and their music was borrowed from popular songs of the day.

The inventor of ballad opera was the poet John Gay, who launched *The Beggar's Opera* in 1728. It was a pungent satire on the vices of high society and government (especially Walpole, the Prime Minister): these included the fashions of Italian opera, always strongly criticized in London for being an 'unnatural' dramatic entertainment in a foreign tongue which the audience could not understand. Gay set his story firmly in London's low life, and brilliantly adapted popular music of all kinds, from street songs to pieces from operas by Purcell, Bononcini, and Handel, writing fresh lyrics that frequently alluded to the existing texts of the songs. There are no true ensembles, and the few choruses are sung in unison. The accompaniment was played by a small group of string instruments and a harpsichord. A French *overture was composed for the work by Pepusch, using one of the songs as the basis of the fast section.

The Beggar's Opera spoke directly to an audience with a strong dramatic tradition in which music had played a secondary role. Its success was unparalleled, and it was widely imitated during the succeeding decade, during which time about 90 ballad operas were written. Its low-life settings were copied in such pieces as *The Cobbler's Opera*, set in Billingsgate; but Charles Johnson's *The Village Opera* (1729) started a trend for more sentimental, pastoral subjects, with little in the way of satire or wit. None came near the success of *The Beggar's Opera*, partly because Gay had skimmed off many of the best songs in the public domain. The fashion soon died down.

The popularity of ballad opera caused serious difficulties for the Italian opera houses and their composers, including Handel; and even after the craze had died, shorter works in the same style (sometimes misleadingly called 'farces') became popular as afterpieces to spoken plays. A derivative of ballad opera appeared in the 1760s, with Arne's *Thomas and Sally* (1760) and *Love in a Village* (1762), establishing a line that continued all the way through Shield, Bishop, and Balfe to Gilbert and Sullivan's operettas, and beyond into musical comedy. But these followers are better termed comic operas. They are not true ballad operas; their music, even if it makes use of existing songs, is fashioned by a professional composer.

The peculiar Englishness of the ballad-opera genre lies in the greater importance of the words than the music; in the true specimens, most of the tunes have a distinctive English flavour. Only *The Beggar's Opera* had sustained success in the 20th century; another masterpiece, Brecht and Weill's *Die Dreigroschenoper* ('The Threepenny Opera', 1928), was inspired by it in its social message, using some of the same characters and even one of the songs. In America, ballad opera began with the importation of an English work, *Flora, or Hob in the Well*, which was given at Charleston, South Carolina, in 1735. The first American performance of *The Beggar's Opera* itself took place in New York in 1750. Thereafter all the most popular English comic operas were quickly imported, and, indeed, for long they formed the sole operatic entertainment in the English colonies and successor states, since Italian and French opera did not reach that part of America until

the 1790s, and no serious attempt to promote Italian opera was made until 1825.   PS/NT

📖 R. FISKE, *English Theatre Music in the Eighteenth Century* (London, 1973, 2/1986) · Y. NOBLE (ed.), *Twentieth Century Interpretations of The Beggar's Opera* (Englewood Cliffs, NJ, 1975)

Ballard. French family of music printers and composers. See LE ROY & BALLARD.

ballata (It.). One of the three poetic forms used in Italian secular songs from the late 13th century to the early 15th (the other two being the *madrigal and the *caccia); the form may be illustrated by this poem, set to music by Matteo da Perugia:

> Gia da rete d'amor libera et sciolta
> Era questa alma et hor e in pianti volta } *ripresa*
>
> Che tue eterna bellezze al mondo sole
> Qual non ebbe Dyana in fonte o in riva } *piede 1*
>
> Con sembianti leggiadri et con parole
> Han d'ogni alto parlar la mente priva } *piede 2*
>
> Pero nympha celeste tanto diva
> Ne me sia dal bel viso merze tua } *volta*
>
> Gia da rete d'amor libera et sciolta
> Era questa alma et hor e in pianti volta. } *ripresa*

To set such a poem the composer would provide two sections of music (referred to below as a and b). The *ripresa* (or refrain) would be sung to the first section, and the two *piedi*, presenting a different rhyme, to the second; for the *volta* and final statement of the *ripresa* the first section would again be used. The resulting musical form is AbbaA (with the *ripresa* indicated by the capital A).

The *piedi* and *volta* together form a stanza. Some *ballate* have several stanzas, but it is not clear whether the *ripresa* was repeated between each one (Ab¹b¹a¹Ab²b²a²A, etc.) or merely stated at the beginning and end of the poem (Ab¹b¹a¹b²b²a² . . . A). The *ballata* resembles the *virelai* in form; its connection to the French *ballade* is therefore bound up with the linked development of the French forms. Early *ballate* are monophonic, and polyphonic works were first written down in about 1360, after which date the form attained a popularity among Italian composers equivalent to that enjoyed by the *ballade* north of the Alps. Of the 154 secular works of Francesco Landini, for example, 141 are *ballate*. This preference is indicated on a more modest scale by other leading composers including Bartolino da Padova, Andrea da Firenze, and Paolo Tenorista.

Later Italian composers became increasingly preoccupied with the fashionable French musical style and the forms associated with it, and, paradoxically, the *ballata* makes its final significant appearance among the works of Frenchmen working in Italy during the 1420s and 30s, for example Guillaume Dufay and Hugo de Lantins.   PD/ABul

📖 N. Pirrotta (ed.), *The Music of Fourteenth-Century Italy*, Corpus mensurabilis musicae, 8 (Rome, 1954–64) · F. A. Gallo, 'Ballata (Trecento)', *Handwörterbuch der musikalischen Terminologie*, ed. H. H. Eggebrecht (Wiesbaden, 1980); 'The musical and literary tradition of fourteenth-century poetry set to music', *Musik und Text in der Mehrstimmigkeit des 14. und 15. Jahrhunderts*, ed. U. Günther and L. Finscher (Kassel, 1984) · A. Ziino, 'Rime per musica e per danza', *Storia della letteratura italiana: Il Trecento*, ed. E. Malato (Rome, 1995)

ballet and theatrical dance. 1. Origins to 1830; 2. Romantic and Classical ballet: 1830–1900; 3. Diaghilev and the West: 1900–40; 4. Ballet in the USSR: 1917–91; 5. Modern dance in the USA and Europe; 6. Dance and composition after 1960

1. Origins to 1830

Ballet as an element of theatrical performance originates directly in the court entertainments of Renaissance Italy, where princely and ducal houses rivalled each other in the splendour of their diversions. These entertainments combined dance, poetry, music, and pageantry, brought to France when Catherine de' Medici married Henry II in 1533. She appointed an Italian violinist and arranger of dances, Balthazar de Beaujoyeux, who supervised the *Ballet des Polonais* (1573), the first important court ballet, with music by Lassus. He made his name with *Circé, ou Le Balet comique de la Royne* (1581), launching the genre known as **ballet de cour*.

In 1652 Lully entered the service of Louis XIV. Lully famously collaborated with Molière in a series of *comédies-ballets*, of which *Le Bourgeois gentilhomme* (1676) is probably the best known. The first purely danced production was *Le Triomphe de l'Amour* (1681), choreographed by Pierre Beauchamp (1636–1705) to Lully's music.

Professional ballet dates from 1672 and the creation by Louis XIV of the Académie Royale de Musique et de Danse (later the Paris Opéra); this academy included a school of dancing for training artists, initially for Lully's *tragédies lyriques* and later for the *opéras-ballets* devised by Campra and popularized by Rameau, most famously in *Les Indes galantes* (1735). Like its forerunners, the *opéra-ballet* combined dance and vocal music, but its themes were more lighthearted than those of the *tragédie lyrique*.

The 18th century saw the creation of the *ballet d'action*, in which the narrative was relayed entirely in music and movement. The earliest such work dates from 1702 and is attributed to the English choreographer John Weaver. He later staged the first serious *ballet d'action*, *The Loves of Mars and Venus* (1717), at Drury Lane

Theatre in London. The genre was not widely imitated in France at the time, but in Vienna Franz Hilverding (1710–68) began to create dramatic *ballets d'action* in the 1740s. It was for one of his assistants, Gasparo Angiolini (1731–1803), that Gluck composed *Don Juan* in 1761. This work (on the same plot as Mozart's *Don Giovanni*) was unusual not only for having a contemporary rather than a mythological story but a vividly descriptive score which made the music an important dramatic element in the ballet rather than merely a background accompaniment to virtuoso dancing.

The outstanding choreographer of the *ballet d'action* was Jean-Georges Noverre (1727–1810), who replaced artificial convention and virtuoso display with more realistically and dramatically expressive dancing and music; one of his best-received works, however, was the relatively lightweight *Les Petits Riens* (1778), to a score by Mozart. Other important figures were two of Noverre's pupils: Jean Bercher Dauberval (1742–1816), who first brought everyday figures into ballet with *La Fille mal gardée* (1789); and Charles Didelot (1767–1837), who went to Russia.

In Italy, Salvatore Viganò (1769–1821) collaborated with Beethoven for *The Creatures of Prometheus*, performed in Vienna in 1801. Beethoven's music for *Prometheus* is unusual for its time in being wholly composed specifically for a ballet (Frederick Ashton choreographed a new version in 1970, celebrating the Beethoven bicentenary); until then, ballets were danced to scores partly composed by a musician working at the theatre and partly made up of melodies from well-known songs, often from operas. Any original music was usually written to fit the set dances, corresponding to the rhythm, structure, and number of bars prescribed by the choreographer. Original scores started to become common only after 1820: a notable contributor was Hérold, whose music for *La Fille mal gardée* (1828) remains the basis of present-day productions. Halévy, Hérold's successor at the Paris Opéra, composed a score for Jean Aumer's ballet *Manon Lescaut* (1830), which may have been the first to use a form of leitmotif to identify characters; Meyerbeer is known to have admired it on that account.

2. Romantic and Classical ballet: 1830–1900

The terms 'Romantic' and 'Classical' in ballet apply in the opposite chronological sequence to their musical usage, Romantic ballet preceding Classical. During the 19th century, ballet gained many of its more familiar features, such as dancing on pointe-shoes, the multilayered tutu diaphanous skirt, and the use of steps to create an illusion of weightless and effortless grace, all of which emphasized the ballerina as the central figure, rather than her male partner. Ballet became an art of illusion and required composers to provide music comparable of lightness and elegance. The Romantic ballet in Paris was dominated by such dancers as Marie Taglioni (1804–84) and Carlotta Grisi (1819–99), who respectively created the title roles in two of the most important Romantic ballets, *La Sylphide* (1832) and *Giselle* (1841). *Giselle* is distinguished for being the only Romantic ballet that has been continuously in the repertory. Its composer was Adolphe Adam, who extended the early use of leitmotif to reinforce emotional and dramatic effect. From the first performance, however, a *pas de deux* by Friedrich Burgmüller was interpolated, and other unattributed additions were made in its later Russian productions. It has also been continuously reorchestrated, Adam's original orchestration having long since been lost.

In 1845 Perrot created a historic *pas de quatre* at Her Majesty's Theatre, London, featuring four leading ballerinas of the day: Taglioni, Grisi, Fanny Cerrito (1817–1909), and Lucile Grahn (1819–1907). Grahn represented the Danish school of Romantic ballet established by August Bournonville (1805–79), who directed the Danish court ballet (now the Royal Danish Ballet) for almost half a century. He created more than 50 ballets including in 1836 his own version of *La Sylphide* for Grahn, based on Taglioni's but with new music by Herman Lövenskjold. It is this version which has survived largely intact to the present day.

Ballet remained associated with opera throughout the 19th century. Weber's opera *Silvana* (1810) centres on a mostly mute woodland spirit who dances; Glinka incorporated dances into the narrative of his operas *Ivan Susanin* and *Ruslan and Lyudmila*. Similarly, Rossini included two dance scenes in *Guillaume Tell* (1829). Taglioni performed in the premiere and also appeared in Meyerbeer's *Robert le diable* (1831), in which, again, the ballet serves a narrative rather than purely decorative function.

Although none of the great 19th-century composers showed any interest in writing music specifically for ballet, it rapidly became a required element in all opera productions in Paris, regardless of the dramatic context. Verdi therefore added ballet sequences to several of his operas, including *I Lombardi*, *Il trovatore*, *Macbeth*, *Don Carlos*, and *Otello*, although he declined to insert a ballet into *Rigoletto* for the Paris audience.

Wagner added a ballet for the Paris production of *Tannhäuser* (1861) though he placed it at the beginning of the opera, causing a minor riot at the first performance. Some French composers, including Berlioz, Gounod, and Massenet, wrote *opéras-ballets*; others wrote both operas and ballets, among them Adam, Auber, and Adam's pupil Delibes, whose music for *Coppélia* (1870) and *Sylvia* (1876) began to improve the quality of ballet music at a time when ballet itself was falling into decline in Europe. During the first half of the 19th century, many of ballet's luminaries, including Taglioni, Grisi, and Grahn, had taken productions to St Petersburg and Moscow, inspiring what was soon to become Russia's dominance of ballet. By the end of the century, Russia had became a leader rather than an imitator, almost entirely as a result of the work of one choreographer, Marius Petipa (1818–1910).

Petipa created 46 original ballets from which crystallized the Classical ballet style. Among his most enduring are his choreographies of two scores by Tchaikovsky: *Swan Lake* and *The Sleeping Beauty*. His 1895 choreography of *Swan Lake* was staged after Tchaikovsky's death and almost 20 years after the original Moscow production. However, *The Sleeping Beauty* (1890) was a true collaboration between composer and choreographer, with Petipa giving a detailed sequence of dances with musical requirements, providing much practical help to Tchaikovsky.

Tchaikovsky and Petipa were brought together again for *Nutcracker* (1892), but illness compelled Petipa to devolve most of the choreography to his assistant, Lev Ivanov (1834–1901). Ivanov's memorial production of the first Lakeside scene from *Swan Lake* after Tchaikovsky's death in 1893 led to the 1895 production of the full ballet by Ivanov and Petipa together, from which most later versions have derived.

3. Diaghilev and the West: 1900–40

The Ballets Russes, founded by the impresario Serge Diaghilev, was a collaboration between dancers, artists, and composers reacting against the relative conservatism of the Petipa repertory that had come to dominate Russian theatres. The company's style was an eclectic mix of the Wagnerian idea of the *Gesamtkunstwerk*, Russian folk art, Classical ballet, and the influence of the American Isadora Duncan (1878–1927). Duncan visited Russia in 1904, demonstrating her unique freestyle dancing, inspired by images from ancient Greek vases. She in turn influenced the young Mikhail Fokine (1880–1924), as well as the designer Léon Bakst (1866–1924). These varied influences resulted in the distinctive style and repertory of the Ballets Russes.

In 1909 'Les Ballets Russes de Serge Diaghilev' performed for the first time at the Théâtre du Châtelet in Paris. This season included Fokine's *Le Pavillon d'Armide*, *Les Sylphides*, and *Cleopatra*, with Act II of Borodin's opera *Prince Igor* (for which Fokine had choreographed the scene of the Polovtsian Dances) and Glinka's *Ruslan and Lyudmila*. The success of this first tour resulted in annual seasons of the Russian Ballet in London and Paris until the outbreak of war in 1914; they included the premieres of Stravinsky's first three historic ballets, *The Firebird* (1910), *Petrushka* (1911), and *The Rite of Spring* (1913). The impact of the Russian stage designers, notably Bakst and Benois, changed a generation's taste in theatre design

Fokine's ballets initiated a seminal new policy: he often created choreography to exciting music not composed for dancing, for example a collection of Chopin's pieces for *Les Sylphides*. However, Diaghilev commissioned original music for ballet, now from leading and innovatory composers, thus reversing the 19th-century practice by which ballet was not generally considered a genre for the serious composer. The company's most famous collaboration was that with Stravinsky, whose early reputation was built on Diaghilev's commissions. Stravinsky wrote a dozen ballet scores over the course of his career and many other of his works have been set by choreographers. Music was also commissioned from Debussy (*Masques et bergamasques* and *Jeux*), Ravel (*Daphnis et Chloé*), and Richard Strauss (*Josephslegende*), all before 1914. 1917 saw Satie, Picasso, Jean Cocteau, and Leonid Massine (1895–1979) collaborating on *Parade*, followed over the next decade by works from Falla, Poulenc, Auric, Milhaud, Prokofiev, and Lambert. Diaghilev demonstrated that music could and should have an organic function in ballet, not merely serve a decorative purpose.

Marie Rambert (1888–1982) and Ninette de Valois (1898–2001), both members of the Ballets Russes, brought Classical ballet to Britain. Rambert formed Ballet Rambert in 1926; from 1987 it continued as Rambert Dance Company. De Valois founded the Vic-Wells Ballet in 1931; it was the resident company at Covent Garden after World War II and became the Royal Ballet in 1956. De Valois staged ballets from the existing Russian tradition as well as works of her own in collaboration with British composers; these included *Job* (1931) with Vaughan Williams, *The Rake's Progress* (1935) with Gavin Gordon, and *Checkmate* (1937) with Bliss. Rambert's protégé Frederick Ashton (1904–88), who worked with the Royal Ballet, similarly choreographed to a wide range of music; he created Walton's *Façade* in 1931, and commissioned *Ondine* (1958) from Henze, a composer who had written much for ballet. An important aspect of Rambert's policy was a commitment to contemporary music, the repertory before 1939 including works by Poulenc, Honegger, and Prokofiev.

Ballet also reached the USA through the Ballets Russes. Their production of *Apollon musagète* (1928), later renamed *Apollo*, began an enduring partnership between Stravinsky and George Balanchine (1904–83). Balanchine, like Stravinsky (with whose music he had a special affinity), settled in the USA, where he founded the School of American Ballet in 1934 and the New York City Ballet in 1948, now one of the world's great companies. Balanchine was a highly influential figure, whose preference was for non-literary or plotless ballets, exploiting solo or multiple movement in patterns closely related to the score. His impact helped to interest American composers in the genre. Among the early resulting works were Aaron Copland's *Billy the Kid* (1938) for Eugene Loring and *Rodeo* (1942) for Agnes de Mille.

4. Ballet in the USSR: 1917–91

Throughout Russia's Communist period, ballet was dominated by two companies, the Bol'shoy, based in Moscow, and the Kirov (formerly the Mariinsky, home of the original Ballets Russes dancers) in Leningrad. As a mainstay of the Imperial Theatres, ballet was nearly rejected entirely by the Soviets, but was reprieved by the first Soviet Commissar for Education, Anatoly Lunacharsky, as a national asset; this produced a permanent Classical or folk-dance company, or both, in each of the constituent republics.

The Soviet adoption of *socialist realism in art applied as much to ballet as any other genre, and although not adopted as an official policy until 1932, its influence can already be seen in Nijinska's choreography for Stravinsky's *Les Noces* (1923); in this, the first 'folk art' ballet in the Ballets Russes repertory, the typically elaborate and often impractical costumes of earlier times were replaced with plain, uniform costumes similar to those being worn by contemporary 'blue blouse' theatre companies in the new Soviet state. Some of the most successful Soviet ballets were written by composers who were later condemned for *'formalism' in 1948, including Shostakovich and Prokofiev. Shostakovich, who genuinely supported Socialism, wrote film, opera, and ballet scores as a means of serving the cause; these included *The Age of Gold* (1930), which helped establish his reputation, and *The Bolt* (1931).

While still focusing on a Classical technique, Soviet ballet largely gave way to neo-Romantic dance dramas which set emotional human narratives against a revolutionary political background. Like Shostakovich, when Prokofiev went back to the USSR in 1933 he turned to film and ballet scores to place his music in the service of the Soviet people; this resulted in three ballets, *Romeo and Juliet* (1935), *Cinderella* (1944), and *The Stone Flower* (1950). *Romeo and Juliet* was choreographed at the Kirov (the new name for the Mariinsky) in 1940 by Leonid Lavrovsky (1905–57), who also choreographed the first version of *The Stone Flower* in 1954 after Prokofiev's death. Rostislav Zakharov (1907–84) took charge of the Bol'shoy Ballet in Moscow, where he choreographed the first production of

Cinderella in 1945. During World War II the Kirov escaped the siege of Leningrad by being evacuated to Perm.

At its height the USSR developed a wealth of talent, with 34 companies in 32 cities (Moscow and Leningrad each having two). It was thus accepted that different choreographers would make their own versions of the same score. *Spartacus*, for which Khachaturian composed the original music, was one of the most successful Soviet ballets; its first choreography dates from 1956, but the best known version is Yuri Grigorovich's (1968) for the Bol′shoy ballet, which remains in the repertory to the present day.

The influence of Soviet ballet in the West became significant when the Bol′shoy and Kirov Ballets began touring, in 1956 and 1962 respectively. This inspired a new focus on Classical style, particularly in the work of such choreographers as Kenneth MacMillan, who made his own version of *Romeo and Juliet* in 1965. Nevertheless the general lack of innovation in Soviet ballet is a prime reason why leading dancers like Rudolf Nureyev (1938–93), Natalya Makarova (*b* 1940), and Mikhail Baryshnikov (*b* 1948) took these tours as an opportunity to pursue their careers by defecting to the West, where they in turn have exercised a major influence on choreographers and dancers alike. After the fall of the USSR in 1991, many of the star performers of the Bol′shoy and Kirov departed for the West; and Russian dancers and companies regularly toured there throughout the 1990s, presenting late 19th- and early 20th-century classics in gala-style events often without orchestra and to mixed acclaim. The loss of heavily state-subsidized funding had a significant impact on Russian ballet companies, but after a decade of disruption, the Kirov and Bol′shoy in particular seem to be flourishing, using tours of the West to raise money.

5. Modern dance in the USA and Europe

'Modern dance' as a separate genre began to appear early in the 20th century as a reaction to the formal conventions and stylized technique of Classical ballet. There is now considerable cross-over between ballet and modern dance and most dancers have some training in both. American women had a profound influence on the evolution of modern dance. Isadora Duncan, already mentioned as an influence on Fokine in Russia, wore loose tunics based on Greek vase paintings and danced barefoot to such composers as Beethoven and Brahms at a time when dance was considered too trivial for the classics of the musical canon. Another pioneer was Ruth St Denis (1877–1969) who, with her husband Ted Shawn (1891–1972), established a company and a school under the name

Denishawn at Los Angeles in 1915. St Denis was a pioneer of truly abstract dance with 'music visualisations', plotless dances which attempted to translate the musical structure of a composition into movement. One of these works, *Soaring* (1920), to Schubert's *Aufschwung*, is still performed.

During the 1920s several Denishawn dancers left to pursue their own paths, among them Martha Graham (1894–1991), the most influential figure in modern dance in the mid-20th century. Graham created more than 150 works, among them *Appalachian Spring* (1944) written for her by Copland. Other composers with whom she collaborated include Barber, Chávez, Menotti, Schuman, and Surinach. Graham's company produced many of the West's leading contemporary choreographers, including Glen Tetley (*b* 1926), Paul Taylor (*b* 1930), Robert Cohan (*b* 1925), and Merce Cunningham (*b* 1919). Cunningham established an original and controversial collaboration with John Cage: they generally worked separately, agreeing only on the work's duration, relationships between movement and music subsequently arising by chance.

European modern dance was greatly influenced by the work of Rudolf Laban (1879–1978), who developed a system of dance teaching and notation that is still widely taught. His followers included Mary Wigman (1886–1973) and Kurt Jooss (1901–79). Jooss's reputation derives chiefly from *The Green Table* (1932), and he was the choreographer for the first production of Stravinsky's *Persephone* by the Ida Rubinstein company (Paris, 1934). Jooss in turn nurtured the talent of Pina Bausch (*b* 1940), one of Europe's most influential contemporary choreographers. Bausch typifies much of modern dance's approach to music: her works range from a new version of *The Rite of Spring* (1975), to those set to assemblages of existing music from Bach to popular songs, and to works with no score in a traditional sense, such as *Bluebeard* (1977) which uses a repeated fragment of Bartók's opera played on stage on a tape recorder.

The younger generation of American choreographers is led by Mark Morris (*b* 1956) who demonstrates a similar eclecticism, his creations ranging from an 'opera-ballet' version of Purcell's *Dido and Aeneas* (1989) to new commissions such as Lou Harrison's *Rhymes with Silver* (1997). It is a feature of contemporary dance that the music tends to be drawn either from the modern repertory or from the Baroque era: 19th-century music, which makes up much of the classical ballet repertory, is the least often heard in this context.

6. Dance and composition after 1960

During the latter half of the 20th century, the relationship between choreographers and composers altered on a number of levels and for a number of reasons. Choreographers created some works to be danced without continuous musical accompaniment, for example Bausch's *Café Müller* (1978); others used not music but text, either recorded or spoken by the dancers, as in the work of the American choreographer Bill T. Jones (*b* 1952). Conversely, some composers in Europe and the USA used compositional ideas and techniques to 'compose' movement and dance. In this repertory there is a dance sequence using serial procedures in Zimmermann's opera *Die Soldaten* (1965), Kagel's *Pas de cinq* (1965) and *Kontra-danse* from *Staatstheater* (1969–70), Stockhausen's dancing clarinettist in *Harlequin* (1975), and the trombonist in *Donnerstag aus Licht* (1978–80); and Hoyland's *Dumb-Show* (1983).

More conventionally, Maxwell Davies is notable for having written two full-length ballet scores, *Salome* (1978) and *Caroline Mathilde* (1990), as well as *Vesalii icones* (1969) for dancer, cello, and ensemble. The American Philip Glass has collaborated with the eminent choreographers Twyla Tharp (*b* 1942) and Jerome Robbins (*b* 1918). Birtwistle included dance sequences in some of his operas including *The Mask of Orpheus* (1984) and *Gawain* (1991). Several of these works have doubled singers with dancers, including *Die Soldaten*, Stockhausen's *Licht* cycle (in which each character is played by an instrumentalist, singer, and dancer), and *The Mask of Orpheus*.

By the end of the 20th century, fewer leading composers wrote orchestral scores specifically for ballet partly because of the financial constraints on the companies commissioning them: they require large resources for performance and expensive rehearsal time. None the less choreographers turn regularly to contemporary music, be it orchestral or chamber, instrumental or electroacoustic, popular or art music. The diversity of the music selected by modern choreographers in part derives from the quality of modern recording and reproduction technology, which has made a wide range available electronically at a standard suitable for professional performance. The general shift of focus away from large ballet companies towards small dance ensembles has further eroded the convention of using or commissioning large orchestral scores played live; only the largest ballet companies still do so. See also CHOREOGRAPHY. NG/JH

📖 M. CLARKE and C. CRISP, *The History of Dance* (London, 1981) · B. HASTINGS, *Choreographer and Composer* (Boston, 1983) · S. AU, *Ballet and Modern Dance* (London, 1988) · L. GARAFOLA, *Diaghilev's Ballets Russes* (Oxford, 1989) · J. ANDERSON, *Art without Boundaries* (London, 1997) · S. J. COHEN (ed.), *International Encyclopedia of Dance* (Oxford, 1998)

ballet de cour (Fr., 'court ballet'). A French courtly entertainment of the late 16th and 17th centuries. It borrowed elements from the French *entremets* and the Italian *intermedio* and was the ancestor of both modern ballet and French opera.

A *ballet de cour* normally consisted of up to five *entrées* (dances and choruses) with corresponding *vers* (librettos distributed to the spectators), each introduced by spoken or sung *récits*; it opened with an *ouverture* and concluded with a *grand ballet* in which at least once a year the king danced. The first *ballet de cour*, *Circé, ou Le Balet comique de la Royne* (1581), was created by the Italian violinist Balthazar de Beaujoyeux at the court of Catherine de' Medici; it combined music, dance, pageantry, and poetry, similar to the 17th-century English masque, in a spectacle of dramatic unity, perhaps inspired by the humanistic philosophy of Baïf's Académie de Poésie et de Musique.

The *ballet de cour* continued at the French court, notably under Louis XIV, who created the Académie Royale de Danse in 1661, led by his dancing-master Pierre Beauchamp (1636–1705), and the Académie Royale de Musique in 1669 under Pierre Perrin (*c*.1620–75). The former was concerned with social and courtly dancing; the latter aimed to develop a distinctively French opera through the combination of poetry and music. After this enterprise failed, the two institutions merged in 1672 as the Académie Royale de Musique et de Danse (which eventually became the Opéra) under Beauchamp and Lully. Lully's contemporaneous reputation was as much as a dancer in the *ballet de cour* as for his music. In collaboration with Beauchamp and the librettist Philippe Quinault (1635–88), he transformed the ballet by combining elements of *ballet de cour* with Italian opera in such works as *Alcidiane* (1658) and the *Ballets des Muses* (1666); ultimately he created a new genre, *tragédie lyrique*, with works including *Cadmus et Hermione* (1673) and *Le Triomphe de l'Amour* (1681). JH

📖 J. R. ANTHONY, *French Baroque Music from Beaujoyeulx to Rameau* (London, 1973, 3/1997) · R. M. ISHERWOOD, *Music in the Service of the King* (Ithaca, NY, and London, 1973)

Ballet mécanique ('Mechanical Ballet'). Work by Antheil, conceived as a film score, originally for 16 player pianos and percussion; synchronizing it with the film was impossible, so Antheil arranged it for two pianos, one player piano with amplifier, three xylophones, electric bells, three propellers, tam-tam, four bass drums, and siren, and it was performed in Paris in 1926.

balletto (It.; Fr.: *ballet*) [ballett]. 1. An Italian dance popular in the 16th and 17th centuries.

2. An Italian dance-song, 'invented' by G. G. Gastoldi in his *Balletti a cinque voci* (1591) and deriving from the original dance and from the canzonetta (especially in its form: two repeated sections, each ending with a refrain of such nonsense syllables as 'fa-la' or 'lirum-lirum'). Gastoldi designed his pieces for dancing ('per cantare, sonare, e ballare'), using strong, regular rhythms, homophonic textures, and simple melodies and harmonies. Their strophic structure allowed few opportunities for detailed depiction of the text. Such composers as Adriano Banchieri and Orazio Vecchi included balletti in their madrigal comedies, while Sigismondo d'India wrote a set for the Duke of Savoy's wedding celebrations in 1621.

Gastoldi's balletti were extremely popular outside Italy, and the style was taken up by composers in Germany and, particularly, in England. Morley and other English composers used more irregular rhythms and more word-painting, transforming their 'balletts' into something less suitable for dancing and more like a miniature madrigal than their Italian models. Morley's *Balletts to Five Voyces* (1591) include English versions of balletti, canzonettas, and villanellas by Gastoldi, Vecchi, Marenzio, and other Italian composers.

—/EW

ballo (It.; Fr.: *bal*; Ger.: *Ball*; Sp.: *baile*). **1.** A ball, i.e. a social dance; *tempo di ballo*, 'at dancing speed'.

2. A formal court dance of the 15th to the 17th centuries. Unlike simpler social dances, the *ballo* could have up to four changes of metre and was choreographed by a dancing master. Several contemporary treatises include descriptions of both steps and music for the *ballo*. JH

3. The music for a ball. The term *ballo* occurs in this context mainly in the 16th century, when it denoted a collection of dances of the period, such as branles, pavans and galliards, and saltarellos. Sometimes the complete sequence of dances used at a court ball would subsequently be published. The term was also used in connection with stage music—thus Monteverdi's *Ballo delle ingrate* ('Dance of the Ungrateful Women') is a sequence of dance-type movements.

Ballo in maschera, Un ('A Masked Ball'). Opera in three acts by Verdi to a libretto by Antonio Somma after Eugène Scribe's libretto (for Auber) *Gustave III, ou Le Bal masqué* (Rome, 1859).

bamboula. A small drum used in Latin American and West Indian music.

Banchieri, Adriano (*b* Bologna, 3 Sept. 1568; *d* Bologna, 1634). Italian composer and monk. For most of his life he was organist at the monastery of S. Michele in Bosco, Bologna. He wrote several important treatises, including *L'organo suonarino* (Venice, 1605), which contains valuable information on how to perform organ music. He composed much church and instrumental music, but his fame rests on his spirited and diverting madrigal comedies, especially *Il festino nella sera del giovedì grasso avanti cena* (Venice, 1608), a splendid entertainment for the last Thursday of Carnival. DA

band. A group of instruments. The term was originally used for any group, but today there is a somewhat snobbish distinction between orchestras and bands. *Brass bands use only cup-mouthpiece instruments (as well as percussion). Concert or wind bands, often now called wind orchestras, include all the winds and percussion and are derived from *military bands. Jazz bands originated in the late 19th and early 20th centuries and grew into the swing orchestras of the 1930s. Dance bands have varied from the medieval one-man band of pipe and tabor to the small symphony orchestras of Johann Strauss (i); as always, financial considerations dictate the size. Opera orchestras are usually identical with contemporary symphony orchestras, though new instruments are often heard in the pit before they reach the concert platform. Pit bands for stage musicals vary in size and constituents according to musical fashion and the requirements of the score. On-stage bands (*banda*, pl. *bande*, in Italian opera scores) are most commonly wind and percussion. JMo

Bandar-log, Les. Orchestral work (1946) by *Koechlin after Rudyard Kipling.

bandola. See BANDURRIA.

bandoneon. A square-built button accordion or *concertina, invented in the 1840s by Heinrich Band of Krefeld. It has been popular since the early 1900s in the tango orchestras of Argentina, Uruguay, and Brazil.

bandora. A form of bass *cittern invented by John Rose in 1562 and widely used at the time. It was wire-strung with six double *courses, which were played with the fingers. The tuning was similar to that of the modern guitar (with the intervals 4th–4th–4th–3rd–4th). Its body was flat-backed and had a festooned outline. No original specimens survive, but several conjectural reconstructions have been made. JMo

bandura. A zither with the body of a lute, popular in Ukraine. A short, unfretted neck, carrying up to a dozen bass strings tuned from the peg-head, is set to one side of a broad circular body with 30 or more diatonically tuned wire strings attached to wrest pins set in its rim. Originally a solo minstrel's instrument, it is now made in sizes from treble to bass for playing in orchestras. JMo

bandurria [bandola]. A plucked string instrument, the Spanish equivalent of the *mandolin. Known in Latin America as the *bandola*, it has six double courses of wire strings tuned in 4ths. It is small and high-pitched, though its deep, flat-backed body gives it a strong sound. It usually plays the melody, accompanied by guitars. JMo

Banister, John (i) (*b* London, *c*.1625; *d* London, 3 Oct. 1679). English instrumentalist, composer, and impresario. The son of a London wait, he joined the King's Musick as a violinist in 1660, and two years later he became leader of the royal band of 24 Violins. He was demoted for insolence and financial irregularities in 1667 but continued to play in the band while extending his outside engagements. He wrote incidental music for a number of plays performed in London in the 1660s and 70s, but is chiefly remembered as the promoter of the first regular series of public concerts to be held in England (1672–9). He was buried in Westminster Abbey. WT/AA

Banister, John (ii) (*b* London, *bapt.* 11 Sept. 1662; *d* London, 9 Jan. 1736). English violinist and recorder player, son of John Banister (i). He succeeded his father in the 24 Violins in 1679. He remained in court service until his death, but early in the 18th century played at the Drury Lane, Queen's, and Lincoln's Inn theatres. He also made frequent solo appearances. His works include *The Compleat Tutor to the Violin* (1698). WT/AA

banjo. A plucked string instrument with a shallow body consisting of a hoop or rim covered with a tautly stretched membrane (the 'head') of parchment, skin, or plastic (like a *frame drum). The body used to be carried on an extension of the neck, which passed diametrically through the rim below the head. This is now replaced by a steel rod by which the neck is attached to the body, and which strengthens the rim and stops it from pulling forward under the tension of the strings. Early banjos were fretless, frets being first added to the fingerboard in the 1870s. A wooden back (the 'resonator') was added during the same period, to reflect the sound waves back to the head and forward through holes in the flange, thus increasing the resonance and sustain.

The traditional five-string banjo has a short fifth string (the 'thumb string') with a tuning-peg about a third of the way down the neck, behind the fifth fret. (On some models the thumb string travels down a tunnel under the fingerboard from the fifth fret to the main peg-head.) This string is normally played open, as

a kind of intermittent drone (i.e. it is not stopped with fingers of the left hand). There is a variety of tunings. The strings, which pass over a low bridge resting on the head, are usually plucked with the fingers; there are a number of different finger-picking techniques.

The banjo was developed by slaves on West Indian and American plantations, and is reminiscent of some West African instruments. It was popularized in the 19th century by 'minstrels' and, later, by jazz bands. In late 19th-century USA, and also in Britain, the banjo became a popular parlour instrument, and 'classic' concert styles were also developed by soloists. The five-string banjo is still common among traditional musicians in the south-eastern USA, and is characteristic of *bluegrass music.

Because the drumskin belly gives a loud and strident sound, versions of other instruments were made with banjo bodies but tuned like the parent instrument, before the days of electronic amplification. Thus the guitar-banjo has six strings tuned like a *guitar; the banjulele or ukulele-banjo is tuned like the *ukulele; the mandolin-banjo is tuned like a *mandolin, and so on. The tenor banjo, with four strings tuned $c–g–d'–a'$ and played with a plectrum, was designed for use in jazz and dance orchestras, and is much used in Irish traditional music. JMo

Banks, Don (*b* South Melbourne, 25 Oct. 1923; *d* Melbourne, 12 Sept. 1980). Australian composer. He studied at the Melbourne University Conservatorium (1947–9) and privately with Seiber (1950–2) and Dallapiccola (1952–3); discussions with Babbitt also proved influential. Banks lived in London throughout most of the 1950s and 60s, working as a composer for films and television, and also taking an active part in societies for promoting contemporary music. In 1972 he was appointed to a university post in Canberra. His music shows a feeling for vivid musical gesture, forcefully developed within a sound-world reminiscent of Schoenberg or Varèse (or, more rarely, of jazz). Among his works are concertos for horn (1965) and violin (1968), other orchestral pieces, and diverse chamber compositions. PG

📖 J. MURDOCH, *Australia's Contemporary Composers* (Melbourne, 1972), 16–21

Bantock, Sir Granville (Ransome) (*b* London, 7 Aug. 1868; *d* London, 16 Oct. 1946). English composer. The son of a successful gynaecologist, he was prepared for the Indian Civil Service, then trained as a chemical engineer. Determined to pursue music as a profession, in 1889 he entered the RAM, where he studied with Frederick Corder. As a student he had several large-scale works performed including his one-act opera

Caedmar (1892). On leaving the RAM in 1893 he edited the *New Quarterly Musical Review* (until 1896) and gained experience as a conductor with a world tour of Sidney Jones's *The Gaiety Girl* (1894–5) and a national tour of Stanford's *Shamus O'Brien* (1896–7). As musical director of the New Brighton Tower Pleasure Gardens (1897–1900) he promoted the music of Parry, Stanford, Elgar, and Sibelius. He held the posts of principal at the Birmingham and Midland Institute of Music (1900–34) and Peyton Professor of Music at Birmingham University (1908–34) in succession to Elgar, later teaching at Trinity College, London. He was knighted in 1930.

Stylistically influenced by the late German Romantics, Bantock's many works (often huge in scale and received by audiences at the time as 'ultra-modern') were inspired by heroic, legendary, or exotic themes. This is true of his operas (including *The Seal Woman*, 1924) and much of his incidental music, and also of the six tone-poems written between 1900 and 1902 (notably *Dante and Beatrice* and *Fifine at the Fair*, a favourite of Beecham) and the symphonies: the 'Hebridean' (1913), 'Pagan' (1923–8), 'The Cyprian Goddess' (1938–9), and the 'Celtic' (1940). In similar vein is the massive setting of Edward FitzGerald's translation of *The Rubáiyát of Omar Khayyám* as a trilogy of oratorios (1906), not to mention the four song cycles written between 1898 and 1905 and culminating in the magnificent *Sappho*. There were also two highly challenging symphonies for unaccompanied choir, *Atalanta in Corydon* (1911) and *Vanity of Vanities* (1913).

After World War I changing tastes largely eclipsed Bantock's music, yet, though he wrote many works on a more modest scale for practical reasons, the BBC still performed his gargantuan setting of *The Song of Songs* (1922) and the shorter *The Pilgrim's Progress* (1928).

DA/JDı

📖 M. Bantock, *Granville Bantock: A Personal Portrait* (London, 1972)

bar. A line drawn vertically through a staff or staves of musical notation, normally indicating division into metrical units (of two, three, four beats, etc.); now also the name for the metrical unit itself, the line being commonly called a 'bar-line'. American usage, however, normally reserves the term 'bar' for the line itself, describing the metrical unit as a 'measure'.

See also DOUBLE BAR; NOTATION, 3; RHYTHM, 2 and 3.

Barbe-bleue ('Bluebeard'). Operetta in three acts by Offenbach to a libretto by Henri Meilhac and Ludovic Halévy (Paris, 1866).

Barber, Samuel (*b* West Chester, PA, 9 March 1910; *d* New York, 23 Jan. 1981). American composer. At the age of 14 he entered the Curtis Institute in Philadelphia, where he studied composition with Rosario Scalero, and where from 1931 to 1933 he taught the piano. From then he earned his living from his music. The opulent, openly Romantic style of his early works is well shown in the String Quartet in B minor (1936), whose slow movement, orchestrated as the Adagio for Strings, quickly gained wide popularity. In the Violin Concerto (1939–40) he began to extend his harmonic range, but his music remained firmly tonal and warmly expressive. The vein of American neo-classicism that entered his music in the 1940s, in such works as the Piano Sonata (1949), refined his style without changing it fundamentally.

Much of Barber's best music is to be found in his vocal works, which include two operas introduced at the Metropolitan in New York, *Vanessa* (1958, libretto by Gian Carlo Menotti) and *Antony and Cleopatra* (1966). His songs, including the cycle *Hermit Songs* (1952–3) and *Dover Beach* with string quartet accompaniment (1931), show a relaxed sensitivity to verbal rhythm, while the soprano scena *Knoxville: Summer of 1915* (1948) is deeply characteristic in its nostalgia and its rich but elegant orchestral writing.   PG

📖 N. Broder, *Samuel Barber* (New York, 1954) · B. B. Heyman, *Samuel Barber: The Composer and his Music* (Oxford, 1994)

barber-shop singing. A style of singing, usually for male-voice quartet, characterized by close harmony, with prominent use of 7th chords, and chromatic melody; its present form developed in the USA in the late 19th century. Its ancestry is in the madrigal, the round, the glee (which fostered numerous glee clubs), and the partsong. The barber-shop connection goes back to Shakespeare's time, when a lute was kept handy so that customers could amuse themselves with a little music. Such singing enjoyed a huge revival in the American West during the gold rush. It was taken up by professionals with the minstrel shows of the 1840s and gospel singing groups.

The close-harmony quartet vogue arrived in the early days of recording with the Comedy Harmonists, the Golden Gate Quartet, the Mills Brothers, and numerous successors, male and female. It also became popular as an amateur activity. The Society for the Preservation and Encouragement of Barber Shop Quartet Singing in America was formed in 1938, and worldwide competitions are regularly held. The repertory inevitably includes such favourites as *Nelly Dean* and *Sweet Adeline*.   PGA

Barbiere di Siviglia, Il ('The Barber of Seville'). Opera in two acts by Rossini to a libretto by Cesare Sterbini after both Beaumarchais's play (1775) and the libretto often attributed to Giuseppe Petrosellini for Paisiello's opera of the same name (Rome, 1816); it was originally called *Almaviva, ossia L'inutile precauzione*, presumably to differentiate it from Paisiello's opera (St Petersburg, 1782), which was the most successful of the several other operatic versions of the play.

Barbieri, Francisco Asenjo (*b* Madrid, 3 Aug. 1823; *d* Madrid, 17 Feb. 1894). Spanish composer and musicologist. He entered the Madrid Conservatory in 1837, studying the piano and composition. After his father's death in the Civil War he supported himself by playing in a military band and theatre orchestras, as a café pianist, and through his activities as a copyist, composer, chorus master, and singer. He began to concentrate on dramatic works, and from 1850 onwards gave new life to the zarzuela. His many successes in the genre included *Jugar con fuego* (1851), *Los diamantes de la corona* (1854, a Spanish translation of the Scribe libretto used by Auber), *Pan y toros* (1854), and above all the classic and richly tuneful *El barberillo de Lavapiés* (1874). The focus of his work was to create a national style less dependent on Italian influences. As a musicologist, Barbieri was substantially responsible for the revival of interest in the treasures of early Spanish music. He transcribed and edited the priceless collection of Spanish secular music in the Royal Palace library as *Cancionero musical de los siglos XV y XVI*. He also founded the journal *La España musical* and wrote numerous articles.   WT/ALa

Barbirolli, Sir **John** (*b* London, 2 Dec. 1899; *d* London, 29 July 1970). English conductor. Born into a family of musicians of Italian origin, he began his career as a distinguished cellist. Teaching himself conducting, he formed his own string orchestra in 1924 and within three years was established as a demanding and imaginative orchestral and opera conductor. He conducted the Covent Garden Touring Company (1929–33). In 1936 he succeeded Toscanini as music director of the New York Philharmonic Orchestra, and in 1943 returned to England to rebuild the depleted Hallé Orchestra in Manchester.

In great demand by international orchestras and opera houses, with which he appeared as guest conductor, Barbirolli nevertheless devoted much of the rest of his life to the Hallé, rehearsing meticulously and bringing it world fame for its character and flexibility. At Covent Garden (1951–4), he conducted Kathleen Ferrier in her last public appearance (*Orfeo ed Euridice*, 1953). He was a romantic and spontaneously volatile interpreter of a wide repertory, and one of the early advocates of Mahler when his music was little performed. His interpretations of Elgar, Vaughan Williams, Verdi, Puccini, and Sibelius were renowned, and he introduced many works to English audiences. He arranged much music and in 1949 was knighted.

                                                                JT

📖 M. KENNEDY, *John Barbirolli, Conductor Laureate* (London, 1971)

barcarolle (Fr.; It.: *barcarola*) [barcarole]. A song in 6/8 or 12/8 time sung by Venetian gondoliers, with an accompaniment suggesting the rocking of a boat. Operatic barcarolles are found in Weber's *Oberon* (1826), Auber's *Fra Diavolo* (1830), Verdi's *Otello* (1887), and Offenbach's *Les Contes d'Hoffmann* (1881). The genre was also transferred to instrumental media: examples for piano were written by Mendelssohn (*Lieder ohne Worte* op. 19 no. 6), Chopin (op. 60), and Fauré, who wrote 13.

Bärenreiter. German firm of music publishers. Founded in Augsburg in 1923 by Karl Vötterle (1903–75), it has been based in Kassel since 1927. In its early years it was identified with the German youth movement (*Wandervogel*), through such contemporary composers as Hugo Distler, and with the associated rediscovery of early music.

First editions of music by Schütz and the launch of the periodical *Musik und Kirche* marked a decade of expansion in its educational and early-music activities, but it was Votterle's pioneering of the production of *Urtext* scores that laid the foundations for the company's development as a leading international publisher after World War II. Since 1951 it has produced a distinguished series of scholarly editions, including the complete works of Gluck, Bach, Mozart, Schütz, Lassus, Bizet, Berwald, Berlioz, Schubert, and Janáček; a new critical edition of Beethoven's symphonies was published in the late 1990s.

Bärenreiter's parallel commitment to new music can be seen in its contemporary catalogue, which includes works by Manfred Trojahn, Charlotte Seither, and Matthias Pintscher, alongside those of more established figures such as Barraqué, Huber, and Krenek.

Bärenreiter continues to publish books and periodicals, including the multi-volume encyclopedia *Die Musik in Geschichte und Gegenwart* (*MGG*), a revised edition of which was initiated in 1994. The Bärenreiter Group has branches in the UK, USA, Switzerland, and the Czech Republic.   HA

Bar form. A musical design originally associated with the poetic forms of the German *Minnesinger and *Meistersinger. The name is taken from the medieval German term for 'strophe'—*Bar*. The form can be represented by the letter scheme AAB, where the first strophe, or more correctly *Stollen*, is repeated, and the last strophe, or *Abgesang*, provides a contrast. Wagner used *Bar* form in his opera *Die Meistersinger von Nürnberg* in a deliberate attempt to imitate the medieval design. Alfred Lorenz in his book *Das Geheimnis der Form bei Richard Wagner* (Berlin, 1924–33) saw this form as one of the principal organizing elements in all Wagner's music dramas, not only *Die Meistersinger*.

GMT

Bargiel, Woldemar (*b* Berlin, 3 Oct. 1828; *d* Berlin, 23 Feb. 1897). German composer and pianist. The child of his mother's second marriage, he was the half-brother of Clara Schumann, who, with her husband, provided Woldemar with much support in his early career. After lessons with the theorist Siegfried Wilhelm Dehn, in 1846 he entered the Leipzig Conservatory, where he was taught by Gade, Hauptmann, Moscheles, and Rietz. From 1850 he himself taught privately in Leipzig to make ends meet. In 1859 Ferdinand Hiller appointed him teacher of piano and theory at the Cologne Conservatory, from where he went on to a position in Rotterdam. Joachim brought him to the Berlin Music Academy in 1874; his students there included Leopold Godowsky and Paul Juon.

Bargiel's style lies halfway between that of his brother-in-law and Brahms (with whom he worked on the complete editions of Chopin and Schumann) and he enjoyed the esteem of both men. His output includes a symphony, three overtures, an octet for strings, four string quartets, three piano trios, works for chorus and orchestra, and a considerable quantity of music for piano.

MA

bariolage (Fr.). In string playing, a special effect used to produce a contrast in tone-colour. It is achieved by playing the same note alternately on two different strings, one stopped and the other open; the term is also used for a repeated passage played on different strings.

baritone. 1. A male voice with a range between those of the bass and the tenor: roughly *A* to *g'*, going up to *ab'* or even *a'* in Italian and French opera. Until the early 19th century the term was little used, and there was no formal distinction between the baritone and bass voices. The quality of a baritone voice may vary from dramatic, as required for Verdi and Wagner roles, to light and almost tenor-like, sometimes called 'baryton Martin' after the French opera singer Jean-Blaise Martin (1767–1837). For the bass-baritone, see BASS, 1.

2. A valved brass instrument in 9' Bb. In Britain baritones are narrower in bore than *euphoniums, but in American usage the names are synonymous.

baritone clef. See CLEF.

bar-line. See BAR.

Barnard, John (*b* ?1591; *fl c*.1641). English composer. He was a minor canon of St Paul's Cathedral in the early 17th century, and compiled *The First Book of Selected Church Musick* (1641). This was the only printed collection of services and anthems for English cathedral use to appear between 1565 and the Civil War; it draws upon the Elizabethan as well as the Jacobean repertory. Between about 1625 and 1638 Barnard also collected a large body of English liturgical music in manuscript, and was himself the composer of two of the pieces.

JM

Barnett, John (*b* Bedford, 15 July 1802; *d* Leckhampton, Glos., 16 April 1890). English composer of Prussian-Jewish and Hungarian parentage. His early works included songs, piano sonatas, and choral pieces, but from 1826 to 1833 he wrote music for burlesques, farces, and melodramas. From 1832 he was musical director of the Olympic Theatre. His opera *The Mountain Sylph*, produced at the Lyceum shortly after it reopened as the English Opera House in 1834, broke new ground in England by using recitative instead of the conventional spoken dialogue. A well-constructed musical drama strongly inspired by Weber, it was a great success, running for 100 nights and remaining in the repertory to the end of the century. After further, unsuccessful attempts to promote English opera Barnett abandoned the London stage and moved to Cheltenham, where he became well known as a singing teacher.

His nephew, **John Francis Barnett** (*b* London, 16 Oct. 1837; *d* London, 24 Nov. 1916), was a composer and conductor. His cantata *The Ancient Mariner* was performed at the 1867 Birmingham Festival and his completion (from the autograph sketches) of Schubert's Symphony in E at the Crystal Palace in 1884.

JD1

Baroque era, the (*see opposite page*)

Barraqué, Jean (*b* Puteaux, 17 Jan. 1928; *d* Paris, 17 Aug. 1973). French composer. He studied at the Paris Conservatoire with Jean Langlais and Messiaen (1948–51), during which period he began to work on two compositions, the Piano Sonata (1950–2) and *Séquence* (1950–5), that show an uncommon willingness to tackle large-scale forms with the disintegrated means of advanced *serialism. Both works display also his Romantic temperament, evident in the Beethovenian breadth of the sonata and in the lyrical ecstasy of *Séquence*, which is scored for soprano, piano, and instruments.

Barraqué spent his life in obscurity, teaching a little, writing articles (and also a book on Debussy; Paris, (*cont. on p. 105*)

The Baroque era

The Baroque era is usually defined as the period from about 1600 to the middle of the 18th century. Its music is widely considered to have certain common features that justify its being regarded as a 'style period'. In criticism of the fine arts, the term 'Baroque'—a French word, derived from the Portuguese *barroco*, meaning a misshapen pearl—was first applied to the music of Rameau's opera *Hippolyte et Aricie* (1733), to signify boldness, harshness, and incoherence. It was soon adopted into criticism of the art and architecture of the preceding era, to indicate irregularity and extravagance. J.-J. Rousseau (1768) defined Baroque music as that in which 'the harmony is confused, charged with modulations and dissonances, the melody is harsh and unnatural, the intonation awkward, the movement constrained'. In art criticism it came during the 19th century to stand for the 'decadent' final stages of Renaissance art; it was only in the early 20th that it began to be used for a musical style period and to lose its negative connotations.

With Manfred Bukofzer's *Music of the Baroque Era* (1947) the idea of a definable style period in music was made more specific, involving the analysis of technical musical features that could be regarded as belonging to the era and the drawing of parallels or analogies with other aspects of cultural history. While the century and a half from 1600 to 1750 is regarded as a convenient division, it is widely understood that many characteristics of Baroque style can be discerned in some music (especially Italian) of the second half of the 16th century, and that others persisted in some (mostly peripheral) parts of Europe well into the latter part of the 18th although elsewhere the signs of a new stylistic era are perceptible as early as the 1720s. Some writers subdivide the Baroque era into three parts: early, up to the mid-17th century; middle, up to the late 17th century; and late, up to the deaths of Bach and Handel.

The central aesthetic principle of the Baroque was that music should express affective states and should move the listener's passions; these were dictated by the words to be set (or the composer's interpretation of them) in vocal music, but applied too to instrumental works. This development had its roots in the rise of humanism and the consequent study of classical rhetorical principles during the 16th century, and by the philosophy of the Counter-Reformation. During the 17th century, theorists, in Germany in particular, developed a complex series of parallels between *rhetoric and music, analysing musical figures analogous to the orator's figures of speech. These were to be used for affective purposes, to arouse idealized emotional states in the listener (see AFFECTIONS, DOCTRINE OF; FIGURES, DOCTRINE OF).

Stylistically speaking, several features can be specified as characteristic of the early Baroque, distinguishing it from the preceding era. While Renaissance music, broadly speaking, is seen as characterized by smooth polyphony, flowing lines, and homogeneous textures, in the Baroque era composers sought contrast, on several different planes: between loud and soft (seen for example in the *Sonata pian e forte* of Giovanni Gabrieli, 1597); between solo and tutti or otherwise contrasting groups (the concertato style), as in the various kinds of concerto, including the vocal motet as well as the instrumental type, that came into existence during the era, and affected many other genres of music; between different instrumental and vocal colours; between fast and slow, both in alternating sections of a multi-section piece, and even between different voices or instruments (a fast-moving voice combining with a slow-moving one). The late Renaissance Venetian tradition of writing for multiple choirs (vocal or instrumental) and using spatial effects, and the later development of that tradition on a more massive scale associated with Roman church music of the 17th century, is a central outcome of Counter-Reformation thinking: overwhelming the listener's emotions with the grandeur and magnificence of the music, just as the great cathedrals of the time did with their massive architecture (many in Italy, but also beyond—for example Salzburg and St Paul's, London).

A fundamental feature of Baroque music, as compared with music of previous eras, is the role of the bass, instrumental or vocal, as the controlling voice of the harmony. In Renaissance polyphony the bass voice normally has the same musical texture as the upper voices; in early Baroque music, the new feeling for harmony, and especially the growing sense of tonality, determined that the bass line should move in certain set progressions that helped establish the music's key structure and the harmonic shape of its phrases (the standard rhythmic patterns of dance music, with their need for regular cadences, played a considerable part in this development). It was often static or slow-moving, especially in monody, to accommodate and support an expressive vocal line. The concept of 'melody and bass' dates, essentially, from the beginning of the Baroque period. From this time comes the rise of the song with accompaniment, and also the instrumental line with accompaniment, as in the new sonata. Vocally, this began with Florentine monody, the vocal line of melody based on heightened speech inflections and rhythms (supposedly following the patterns of declamation in classical Greek tragedy), which in due course was to lead to the development of recitative and aria (the essential components of opera, oratorio, cantata, and many other genres). The same applies in, for example, the French *air de cour* and the English lute-song. This was the era when variations above a ground bass, in which the progressions of the bass governed the structure, became a standard mode of composition.

This polarity of melodic line and bass—or often of a pair of equal upper lines and bass—is a distinguishing feature of Baroque music. So too is the form of accompaniment that developed to accommodate this new style and its harmonic background: the continuo. The word 'accompaniment' has no application in Renaissance polyphony and this is one of the most significant developments in the early Baroque: the rise of the concept of accompanying from a bass line, with added chords. The continuo player, typically at the harpsichord, organ, occasionally the viol, or a plucked instrument such as lute or theorbo, played from a bass line, adding supporting harmony, sometimes (and increasingly as time went on) with figures to indicate what chords should be played, providing the essential harmonic underpinning of the music. Often the chordal continuo player was himself supported by a player of a sustaining line, such as a bass viol, cello,

violone, or bassoon, for the essential parts, melody and bass, and their interdependence were then clearer to the listener. The continuo is present in virtually all the music of the Baroque era, and its use ran on into the Classical era; even in the late 19th century figured-bass accompaniments were still being written (for example by Bruckner) and played.

The newness of this style was recognized at the time, and deplored by some, more conservative, musicians: dispute arose in the first years of the 17th century between the theorist Artusi, and Monteverdi, who described the older practice as *prima pratica' (which he acknowledged as suitable for certain types of music, principally sacred) and the newer as 'seconda pratica'. Monteverdi's brother, the theorist Giulio Cesare Monteverdi, referred to the precedence given to 'harmony' (meaning the fluent progression of the part-writing) in the *prima pratica* and to the expression of the text through melody in the *seconda*. Other leading figures, notably Giulio Caccini, referred to the new style simply as the 'nuove musiche' (using the term for the title of his publication of a book of monodies). Caccini's monodies involve elaborate musical ornamentation, designed to enhance their expressiveness and at the same time to show the singer's virtuosity, with trills and many other kinds of decorative writing: ornamentation and variation are often regarded as distinguishing features of the Baroque, in music as in the visual arts, though that view is in some respects an oversimplification.

These musical developments were not isolated from the other changes taking place in the 16th and 17th centuries, in religious, intellectual, social, economic, and political spheres as well as the arts. The Counter-Reformation, with its dictates about priorities in church music—that words should not be obscured by the interweaving of polyphonic lines—and its promotion of religious fervour, encouraging the strong expression of affects, led to the rise of the oratorio, vernacular as well as Latin. Its secular counterpart was opera, whose history begins with the Baroque.

All these developments were Italian, and until its final decades the Baroque was an era of Italian musical hegemony. Monody arose out of the thinking of the Florentine academicians and humanists. It was in Florence that the first operas were produced, in 1598 (Peri's *Euridice*) and 1600, in Rome that the first oratorio was given, in 1600 (Cavalieri's *Rappresentatione di Anima, et di Corpo*), and in Venice that the first public opera house was opened, in 1637. Dramatic music continued to flourish, especially in Venice (where Cavalli and Stradella worked), Rome (the oratorios of Carissimi and Stradella), and Naples (Alessandro Scarlatti was a leading figure for 40 years in both the last two, in oratorio as well as opera). The earliest ensemble and violin sonatas are by such men as Giovanni Gabrieli, Merula, Salamone Rossi, Castello, and Marini, and it was in the works of Corelli that the trio sonata arrived at its classical shape. The instrumental concerto developed initially in Bologna, with such composers and Cazzati and Torelli, and at Rome, with Corelli, but its final Baroque fruition was at Venice in the music of Albinoni, the Marcellos, and above all Vivaldi. The leading early makers of violins, whose potential for rhythmic vitality distinguished them in the Baroque era from the viols preferred in the Renaissance, worked in Verona, Brescia, Venice, and Cremona.

This central role of Italy in European musical development was widely recognized north of the Alps. Italian musicians travelled to work at courts across Europe, and northern musicians regularly went to Italy for training and to enable them to absorb the most recent musical thinking. Italian opera was the standard courtly entertainment across Europe, not only in the German-speaking countries, Bohemia, and Poland but in England, Scandinavia, and Russia; only France stood apart, and that gave rise to much local controversy. Richelieu had attempted, unsuccessfully, to introduce Italian opera with a performance of Luigi Rossi's *Orfeo* in 1647, and Cavalli provided a festive opera, *Ercole amante*, in 1662. But the man who chiefly created a distinctive French operatic style was the Florentine-born Lully, who forged a French-language opera drawing on the traditions of French theatrical declamation and incorporating lavish spectacle and dance: he established a monopolistic position and eliminated competition.

After his death in 1687 the traditions were continued, although fierce pamphlet wars raged between advocates of Italian opera and those of French, and later between the Lullistes and the supporters of Rameau, whose richly inventive operas had considerable impact in the second quarter of the 18th century. A new form, *opéra-ballet*—essentially a collection of divertissements—came into being in reaction to the Lullian *tragédie* and flourished particularly during the Regency; and *opéra comique*, with spoken dialogue, later arose from the popular, parodistic musical theatre at the Paris fairs. In instrumental music, the French came very late to the abstract sonata (the earliest true examples, so called, are Couperin's trio sonatas of the 1690s), preferring the dance suite or the *pièce de viole* as cultivated by Marais; their keyboard composers favoured the dance suite and the character piece. The principal ecclesiastical form was the *grand motet*, extended psalm settings designed for the royal chapels, of which the finest examples are those of Lalande and Charpentier; the latter, one of the few Italian-trained French composers, also wrote oratorios and other dramatic works.

Austria, with strong political and dynastic ties with Italy, was particularly italophile. Ferdinand II brought Italian musicians to his court in 1619. Monodies and concertato motets were current in Austria in the early decades of the century, and opera was given in Salzburg as early as 1614 and in Vienna in 1630. Italians occupied many of the main positions at the imperial court in Vienna for many years. The hugely grandiose performance in 1668 of Cesti's *Il pomo d'oro* for Leopold I's marriage was a landmark in Austrian operatic history. The main contributions of native Austrians were in instrumental music: important composers include Schmelzer, the first native court Kapellmeister (1679–80); Biber, a violin virtuoso who composed virtuoso sonatas (some of them programmatic) for his own instrument and for ensemble, as well as (probably) the 53-part Mass in the Roman style given in Salzburg Cathedral in 1682; Georg Muffat, who worked there and at Passau, studied and composed in both Italian and French styles, and discussed performance issues in print. At the end of the period J. J. Fux, court Kapellmeister in Vienna (1715–41), was the leading theorist of his time and established teaching methods that were used throughout the Classical era and long beyond.

German musical culture was damaged by the ravages of the Thirty Years War during the first half of the 17th century, but the multiplicity of princelings thereafter and the existence of free, mercantile cities (such as Frankfurt, Hamburg, Leipzig, Lübeck, and Nuremberg), as well as the divide between the two confessions, ensured a wide diversity in music in the latter part of the Baroque. Italian influence was strong here too. Schütz went to Venice to study with Gabrieli and Monteverdi and was much affected by their example in his *Psalmen Davids* and his *Kleine geistliche Concerte* as well as his madrigals and his other church music. The

Italianate motet developed into the sacred German cantata, in German or in Latin; from the time of Praetorius onwards the cantata based on the chorale, an essential element in Protestant worship, became increasingly important, as the work of such composers as Schein, Scheidt, and Buxtehude shows, and it reached its apogee in the music of J. S. Bach. Similarly, the Protestant Passion setting flourished in central and northern Germany, with Schütz, Theile, and others, and ultimately Keiser, Telemann, Handel, and Bach. Small-scale sacred song—hymns and devotional song for domestic use—also flourished.

Operatic activity was more sporadic: opera houses were established at some of the larger, more Italianate courts (notably Munich and Dresden); German- or mixed-language opera was naturally favoured at the municipal opera houses, in the free cities, of which the one in Hamburg was the first (1678) and attracted such composers as Keiser, Mattheson, and Handel. Germany was slow to develop the Italian-style sonata, and ensemble and orchestral music drew on the French dance suite at least as much as Italian models; German composers often showed a propensity for elaborate counterpoint. Organ and harpsichord music, influenced by Sweelinck in the north and Italian models in the south—Froberger, who contributed to the formation of the keyboard suite, had been a pupil of Frescobaldi in Rome—flourished particularly; leading organ composers include Buxtehude and Reincken in the north, Pachelbel in the south. The climax to the German Baroque came in the work of Telemann, who contributed generously in all genres, Handel, and J. S. Bach.

Outside the three central musical cultures of Europe, the Baroque had local but generally Italian-influenced dialects. Spanish music was conservative; the principal development was in the villancico, a vernacular genre which in the Counter-Reformation became increasingly popular and important in worship as well as in secular contexts. Opera was slow to gain a foothold: *La púrpura de la rosa*, attributed to Hidalgo, was given at the Madrid court in 1660, but the zarzuela, a lighter pastoral opera, had considerable currency from the late 17th century. Much Spanish music was sent to settlements in the New World. In England, local genres included the court masque, popular in the early 17th century; the 'semi-opera', essentially a play with several inserted masques, cultivated especially by Purcell; and the verse anthem, an Anglican counterpart to the concertato motet. Opera, some desultory earlier efforts apart, began only in the first decade of the 18th century and was established with the attempts of Handel, his colleagues, and his patrons to set up properly supported opera companies (attempts that have still to succeed).

It is in the work of Handel and Bach—along with a select group of their contemporaries, among them Domenico Scarlatti, Vivaldi, Rameau, and Telemann in particular—that the Baroque era reached its climax. Bach worked in a local, ecclesiastically based, German Protestant tradition, centred on Thuringia and Saxony; his music is more learned and more richly worked, and profounder in its expressive implications, than that of any of his contemporaries, and he carried contrapuntal techniques to new levels. Handel, born in Saxony, trained in central Germany, Hamburg, and Italy, and domiciled in London, composed in a fully cosmopolitan musical language, writing the finest Italian operas of his day, creating the English oratorio and the organ concerto, and investing traditional forms with new meanings through the richness and variety of his invention. These two men, born a few kilometres and a few days apart, and at opposite poles of temperament, crown the musical achievements of the Baroque era.

SS

J. A. SADIE (ed.), *Companion to Baroque Music* (London, 1990) · C. V. PALISCA, *Baroque Music* (Englewood Cliffs, NJ, 3/1991) · J. H. BARON, *Baroque Music: A Research and Information Guide* (New York, 1993) · N. ANDERSON, *Baroque Music: From Monteverdi to Handel* (London, 1994)

1962), and pursuing research in musical aesthetics for the Centre National de la Recherche Scientifique (from 1961). His creative attention had turned, since 1956, to making a vast system of musical glosses on Hermann Broch's novel *The Death of Virgil*, but only three parts were completed: . . . *au delà du hasard* in 1959, *Chant après chant* in 1966, and *Le Temps restitué* in 1968. These, together with the Concerto for clarinet, vibraphone, and six instrumental trios (1968), testify to the grandeur, the beauty, and the honesty of his vision, concerned above all with the mortality of man and the uselessness of artistic endeavour.   PG

Barraud, Henry (*b* Bordeaux, 23 April 1900; *d* Paris, 28 Dec. 1997). French composer and administrator. After an apprenticeship in the wine trade, he studied at the Paris Conservatoire with Dukas and Louis Aubert, but was expelled for excessive modernism. From 1944 to 1965 he was on the staff of French Radio as head of music, and then director of the network later called France-Culture; he himself became a well-known broadcaster. His music, eclectic in its stylistic and literary inspiration and always finely crafted, includes operas, oratorios and other choral works, three symphonies and much else for orchestra, and chamber music.   ABur

barré (Fr.). A term used in lute and guitar playing for the simultaneous shortening of the length of all or several strings by placing the forefinger across them at some particular fret. The same effect may be produced artificially by use of the **capo tasto*.

barrelhouse. A style of loud, earthy piano-playing designed to overcome the noise of the 'barrelhouse', a low-class American establishment serving drink from the barrel. The style led to the development of **boogie-woogie*.   PGA

barrel organ. See MECHANICAL MUSICAL INSTRUMENTS; ORGAN, 10.

Barrett, Richard (*b* Swansea, 7 Nov. 1959). Welsh composer. After obtaining a degree in genetics he studied composition with Peter Wiegold; he has spent much time teaching and composing abroad—in Germany, Australia, and the Netherlands. As a performer he has been active in the spheres of live electronics and improvisation. His compositions have the ultra-expressionistic intensity and elaborate notation that usually earn the label 'complex' and link him with Brian Ferneyhough and Michael Finnissy. Barrett's works are certainly challenging to performers and first-time listeners alike, but they always have a strong poetic quality. Such pieces as the set of five *Negatives* for nine players (1988–93) and *Vanity* for orchestra (1990–4),

with its final, brief allusion to Schubert's song *Der Tod und das Mädchen*, testify to his ability to create large-scale and gripping musical structures.   AW

Barry, Gerald (*b* Clare Hill, Co. Clare, 28 April 1952). Irish composer. After studies in Dublin he worked with Stockhausen and Mauricio Kagel in Germany, as well as with Peter Schat in the Netherlands and Friedrich Cerha in Austria. The influence of Kagel's surrealist music-theatre pieces was decisive in forming an idiom that can bring an individual accent to minimalist repetitiveness (often with its roots in Irish folk music) and can alternate between driving energy (*Chevaux-de-frise*, 1988, and *Hard D*, 1992, both for orchestra) and the more songlike lyricism to be found in the operas. Of these, *The Triumph of Beauty and Deceit* (Channel 4 Television, 1993) is especially successful in its constructive reworking of operatic conventions.   AW

Barsanti, Francesco (*b* Lucca, 1690; *d* London, late 1772). Italian flautist, oboist, and composer. After studying science at Padua University, in 1714 he travelled to London with Francesco Geminiani and played in the orchestra of the Italian Opera. By 1735 he was living in Edinburgh; he remained there until 1743, when he and his Scottish wife returned to London. During his time in Scotland he was the most accomplished composer to have lived there; his compositions include concerti grossi (which are unusual in their use of oboes, trumpets, and drums), some fine recorder sonatas, and arrangements of Scottish songs.   DA/ER

Bartered Bride, The (*Prodaná nevěsta*). Opera in three acts by Smetana to a libretto by Karel Sabina (Prague, 1866); Smetana made five versions of it, expanding it from two acts to three, the fifth and commonly performed version having its premiere in 1870.

Barthélemon, François-Hippolyte (*b* Bordeaux, 27 July 1741; *d* Christ Church, Surrey, 20 July 1808). French violinist and composer. After studying in Paris, in 1764 he went to London, where he became a prominent musical figure, performing at the King's Theatre, Marylebone and Vauxhall pleasure gardens, the Academy of Ancient Music, and elsewhere. In 1766 he married the English singer Polly (also known as Mary or Maria) Young, with whom he often performed. He was acquainted with Haydn, and his reputation as a violinist was such that when he died Salomon is said to have lamented, 'We have lost our Corelli'. His many stage compositions included a collaboration with Charles Dibdin for the Shakespeare jubilee of 1769. He also wrote instruction books for the violin, harpsichord or piano, and harp, and a manual on the use of figured bass.   LC

Bartók, Béla (Viktor János) (*b* Nagyszentmiklós, Hungary [now Sinnicolau Mare, Romania], 25 March 1881; *d* New York, 26 Sept. 1945). Hungarian composer. The greatest musician ever produced by Hungary, Bartók was not only a composer but also an excellent pianist and a thorough student of folk music. His folksong research had a penetrating influence on his music, yet so too did his reverence for composers of the past, especially Beethoven and Bach, and his awareness of the musical present. All this gave rise to a very original and perfectly homogeneous style, Hungarian in tone but universal in its expressive power.

1. The early years; 2. The years of maturity

1. The early years

Bartók was brought up by his mother after his father's early death, and it was she who encouraged the musicality he showed from infancy, both in composing and in playing the piano. In 1898 he gained a free scholarship to the academy in Vienna, the capital of the Austro-Hungarian Empire, but he chose instead to follow his older friend Dohnányi in studying in Budapest, where he was a composition pupil of Hans Koessler. This was a decisive move, for it brought him into contact with the Hungarian nationalist movement: in 1902 he wrote his first songs with Hungarian texts, and the next year he produced the symphonic poem *Kossuth*, celebrating in Straussian terms the life of the national hero. Then, in 1904, he made the discovery that opened the way to a specifically Hungarian musical style: he heard for the first time a real Hungarian folksong, not one of the Gypsy tunes used by Liszt and Brahms.

During the next few years he produced a steady stream of musical arrangements and scholarly articles based on the folksongs he was collecting, often in collaboration with his friend Zoltán Kodály. In 1907 the two men took appointments at the Budapest Academy, and, in the face of opposition, they set about bringing a new vitality and national pride into Hungarian musical life. Bartók's First Quartet (1909) is typical of this period in combining features from Hungarian folk music with others taken from contemporaries in the West (Strauss's influence now wanes in favour of Debussy's), and in doing so within the most testing of classical genres.

His next major effort was a Hungarian opera, *Bluebeard's Castle* (1911; Budapest, 1918), in which he follows Debussy and Musorgsky in finding a vocal style to suit the particular qualities of his language. The brilliant orchestration still leans in the direction of Strauss, and also Debussy, whose influence is predominant in the fairy ballet *The Wooden Prince* (1917).

Here the most distinctively Bartókian element is a grotesque dance led by the xylophone, comparable to the once notorious *Allegro barbaro* for piano (1911). A successful production of the ballet in 1917 led to the staging of the opera in the following year, and Bartók now began to receive wider attention. The Viennese publishing house of Universal Edition (who handled the music of Schoenberg, Berg, and Webern) took over his scores, among the first works to benefit being the Second Quartet (1915–17), which shows Bartók beginning to build a coherent style on the basis of folksong. New influences now began to enter his music. The Three Studies for piano (1918) and the two sonatas for violin and piano (1921 and 1922) stand on the brink of atonality and show an acquaintance with Schoenberg in the contrapuntal freedom of their wide-ranging lines, while the ballet *The Miraculous Mandarin* (1918–19; Cologne, 1926) recalls in part *The Rite of Spring*. Before long, however, these influences had been fully absorbed; the orchestral *Dance Suite* (1923) was both Bartók's first great popular success and the first work in a 'middle period' of supreme confidence and maturity.

2. The years of maturity

Bartók was now an international figure. Between the wars he toured Europe and America as a concert pianist, writing for himself the Sonata and the suite *Out of Doors* (both 1926) as well as the first two piano concertos (1926 and 1930–1). Both of these had their first performances at festivals of the International Society for Contemporary Music, in which Bartók took a leading part from its foundation in 1922. However, he retained his teaching post in Budapest, and he continued his studies of folk music, though he made no more collecting expeditions. One of his main tasks as an ethnomusicologist was the classifying of variants of a melody, and his intensive work on that may well have contributed to the far-reaching variation technique he developed. This is shown, for example, in the Third Quartet (1927), a single movement in which the first part is densely worked from a small motif, the second is a set of canonic variations, and the third and fourth recapitulate the first and second respectively. From this Bartók proceeded to the symmetrical five-part forms (ABCBA) of the Fourth and Fifth Quartets (1928 and 1934) and the Second Piano Concerto, all of which show how he could find the essence of folk melodies and rhythms without actual quotation.

The works of this period also show a continuing interest in new sound resources. Bartók's piano writing in the First Piano Concerto and the Sonata is often stridently percussive, though there are also examples here, as in *Out of Doors*, of atmospheric 'night music'. In the Concerto, too, he scrupulously indicates how the percussion players are to obtain novel effects, looking forward to the Sonata for two pianos and percussion (1937). And in writing for strings, whether in the quartets or the *Music for Strings, Percussion, and Celesta* (1936), he calls for a wide variety of textures and playing techniques. The *Music for Strings*, which characteristically ends by converting a twisting chromatic theme into an open diatonic one, mirrors a development that was taking place in Bartók's style. Partly influenced by the elegant counterpoint of Bach (see the opening movement of the Second Piano Concerto), his music became clearer in harmony and more luminous in spirit. The change is already well advanced in the Second Violin Concerto (1937–8) and the Sixth Quartet (1939), for all the expressive intensity of both works, but it is even more marked in the works written after Bartók had emigrated to the USA in 1940.

Cut off from his friends, depressed by the progress of the war, lacking concert engagements, Bartók spent his last years in quiet neglect. He completed only two new works, the ebullient Concerto for Orchestra (1943) and the post-Bachian Sonata for unaccompanied violin (1944), leaving Tibor Serly to complete the last few bars of the Third Piano Concerto (1945) and to compose the Viola Concerto (1945) from sketches.   PG

📖 H. Stevens, *The Life and Music of Béla Bartók* (New York, 1953, 3/1993) · E. Lendvai, *Béla Bartók: An Analysis of his Music* (London, 1971) · J. Ujfalussy, *Béla Bartók* (Budapest, 1971) [in Eng.] · T. Crow (ed.), *Bartók Studies* (Detroit, 1976) · B. Suchoff (ed.), *Béla Bartók: Essays* (London, 1976) · P. Griffiths, *Bartók* (London, 1984) · M. Gillies, *The Bartók Companion* (London, 1994)

Bartolozzi, Bruno (*b* Florence, 8 June 1911; *d* Fiesole, 12 Dec. 1980). Italian composer and theorist. He studied the violin at the Florence Conservatory (1926–30), then worked as a performer before returning to the conservatory for composition studies under Paolo Fragapane (1946–9). His works, cast in a Dallapiccola-like serial style, have excited less interest than his development of new playing techniques on woodwind instruments, making it possible for musicians to sound chords. He wrote the book *New Sounds for Woodwind* (London, 1967, 2/1982).   PG

baryton. A special form of bass *viol used mainly in Austria and Germany in the Baroque and Classical periods. As well as the six bowed strings it had up to 20 wire strings, which sounded sympathetically and could be plucked by the left thumb through the open back of the neck. The baryton seems to have originated in the early 17th century, probably in England as a development of the *lyra viol with sympathetic strings. It remained in use for about 200 years. The most famous baryton player, in the late 18th century, was Prince

Nicolaus Esterházy, whose court composer, Joseph Haydn, wrote many pieces for him. Probably because the instrument was played mainly by such exalted amateurs as Prince Nicolaus, a number of highly decorated examples survive in museums.   JMo

barzelletta (It., 'little jest'). An Italian poetic form used around 1500, especially for the *frottola.

bas (Fr.). See HAUT, BAS.

bass. 1. The lowest male voice, with a range of roughly *E* to *f'*. The quality of a bass voice can vary widely, from the *Bass-buffo*, or *komischer Bass*, of Osmin in Mozart's *Die Entführung aus dem Serail* to the majestic tones of Sarastro in *Die Zauberflöte*. In the 19th century the bass voice was used either for villains (Caspar in Weber's *Der Freischütz*, Gounod's Méphistophélès) or for kings and other figures of authority. Slavonic basses are able to achieve great depth, sometimes reaching *G'*. The 'bass-baritone' has a range that extends higher, but it retains the bass quality on the lower notes; in Wagner's *Ring* cycle, the part of Wotan is sung by a bass-baritone (Wagner called the voice 'hoher Bass').   —/RW

2. The lowest note in a chord. For the distinction between 'root' and 'bass', see ROOT, ROOT POSITION.

3. The lowest regions of musical pitch.

4. A low-pitched member of a family of instruments, with a range lower than tenor and higher than contrabass or double bass.

5. Colloquial name for the *double bass or electric bass guitar; also the name for the bass tuba or bombardon in *military bands and *brass bands.

bassadanza (It.). See BASSE DANSE.

Bassani, Giovanni Battista (*b* Padua, *c.*1657; *d* Bergamo, 1 Oct. 1716). Italian composer and organist. By 1672 he was organist to the illustrious Accademia della Morte in Ferrara. In 1677 he was admitted to the Accademia Filarmonica of Bologna—far too late to lend credibility to the unlikely notion that he was Corelli's teacher. He moved to Modena in 1680, but returned to Bologna in 1682 as *principe* of the academy. Within a year or so he was again in Ferrara, now as *maestro* to the Accademia della Morte, and in 1686 he became *maestro di cappella* at Ferrara Cathedral. He spent the last four years of his life at the important church of S. Maria Maggiore in Bergamo. Bassani was a prolific composer in many genres both vocal and instrumental, but his fame lay largely on his op. 5 trio sonatas (1683), which were especially popular in England before the success of Corelli's works carried all before them.   DA/PA

Bassano. Italian family of Venetian origin. They settled in England in the 1530s, and over the next 130 years or so played an important part in the musical life of the

English court. The Bassanos were particularly associated with the royal wind music, as players of recorders, sackbuts, and other wind instruments. The first generation of the family in England settled at the court of Henry VIII in about 1535: **Lewis** [Aluisio] (*d c.*1550), **John** [Giovanni] (*d c.*1570), **Anthony** (i) [Giovanni Antonio] (*d c.*1574), **Jasper** [Giovanni Gasparo] (*d* 1577), and **Baptista** [Giovanni Baptista] (*d* 1576). They all played in the Royal Music until their deaths. Two other Bassano brothers, **Augustine** [Agostino] (*d* 1604) and **Lodovico** (*d* 1593), came to London from Venice at a later date and were appointed to the Royal Music in the 1550s. They may have been younger brothers of the first five, and both were composers as well as performers.

By 1581 a second generation of Bassanos had joined the court musicians. They were all sons of Anthony (i): **Mark Anthony** (*d c.*1599), **Arthur** (*d* 1624), **Edward** (i) (*d c.*1607), **Andrea** (*d c.*1628), and **Jerome** [Jeronimo] (*d c.*1631), who composed consort music. By the early 17th century a third generation had succeeded their fathers, including **Anthony** (ii) (*d* before 1660), **Edward** (ii) (*d c.*1638), and **Henry** (*d* 1665).

Perhaps the most celebrated member of the family was **Emilia Lanier** (1569–1645), the daughter of Baptista Bassano. At the time of her marriage to the recorder player Alfonso Lanier she was pregnant by the queen's cousin, Lord Hunsdon, but it was her supposed relationship with another famous Elizabethan that ensures her fame today, since some scholars believe she was William Shakespeare's mistress and the mysterious 'Dark Lady' of the sonnets.   WT

Bassano, Giovanni (*b c.*1558; *d* Venice, 1617). Italian composer and cornett player. He was employed among the instrumentalists of St Mark's, Venice, from 1576 until his death. His teaching pieces and his manual on ornamentation, *Ricercate, passaggi et cadentie* (1585), remain a valuable source of information on the virtuoso performance of madrigals and motets. Some of his canzonettas were published by Morley with English translations in 1597; they were perhaps transmitted to London by the English branch of the *Bassano family.   DA

Bassarids, The. Opera with intermezzo in one act (four movements) by Henze to a libretto by W. H. Auden and Chester Kallman after Euripides' *Bacchae* (Salzburg, 1966).

bass-bar. The wooden girder glued inside the belly of a bowed string instrument under the line of the lowest string to support the left foot of the bridge. It is sometimes carved integrally from the wood of the belly, in which case it is usually positioned centrally under the bridge.   JMo

bass clef. See CLEF.

bass drum (Fr.: *grosse caisse*; Ger.: *grosse Trommel*; It.: *gran cassa, tamburo grande*). The largest orchestral drum. Normally it has two heads, though single-headed drums, called 'gong drums', were popular in the 19th century. Mounted on a stand, the bass drum can usually be tilted for ease of playing. In a marching band it is strapped to the drummer's body. The old practice of fixing a cymbal to the shell to clash another against it with one hand while striking the bass drum with a stick in the other has long been abandoned save for special effects.

The bass drum was introduced from Turkey in the late 18th century for the military band. Then greater in length than in diameter, it was called 'long drum' in English. It came into the orchestra from the band and from opera but was not generally adopted until the end of the 19th century. The military bass drum, which acquired its modern shape during the 19th century, maintains an important role in the marching band both for the basic rhythm and to signal changes in the march pattern and in the music being played.

As a part of the drum kit, the bass drum has shrunk over the years with changes in the sound desired and in its auxiliary functions, and with the introduction of synthetic materials for the drum-head. By the 1950s the bass drum, on which a tom-tom (later two) was mounted, was usually about 60 cm in diameter, and some jazz drummers used one as small as 41 cm. The kit bass drum is played with a hard-cored pedal. The orchestral instrument uses softer beaters, like giant timpani sticks, often double-ended so that a roll may be played one-handed by twisting the wrist. Military beaters are similar but harder.   JMo

basse (Fr.). 'Bass', i.e. the lowest male voice.

basse chantante (Fr.), **basso cantante** (It.). 'Singing bass'; a lyric bass voice, sometimes of baritone quality.

basse chiffrée (Fr.). 'Figured bass'; see CONTINUO.

basse continue (Fr.). 'Continuo bass'.

basse danse (Fr., 'low dance' [i.e. close to the ground]; It.: *bassadanza*). The principal court dance of the 15th and early 16th centuries. It was performed by couples with a stately and dignified gliding motion; the afterdance (e.g. the *tordion* or *recoupe*) was characterized by livelier movements and leaps. The earliest known music for the basse danse dates from the 15th century, a particularly important source being the repertory and choreographies contained in three Burgundian manuscripts of the late 15th century. The melodic material is centred on a kind of cantus firmus, round which the other parts improvised. Each note of this tenor corresponded to one step of the dance and the melody was frequently derived from a pre-existing source; in the 16th century this was often the upper part of a French chanson, for example Willaert's *Jouyssance vous donneray.*   —/JBe

basse de violon (Fr.). 'Bass violin'.

basse fondamentale (Fr.). 'Fundamental bass'.

Basset [Bassett] (Ger., 'small bass'). 1. A small *double bass used as a chamber bass and also by folk musicians and dance bands, especially travelling ones. 'Basset' was the common name for the cello in Austria and southern Germany during the 18th century.   JMo

2. A wind instrument (e.g. recorder or shawm) in tenor or baritone range, but pitched low enough to function as a bass if required.

basset horn (Fr.: *cor de basset*; Ger.: *Bassetthorn*; It.: *corno di bassetto*). An alto clarinet with its range extended downwards (hence 'basset') to written *C*, instead of *E*. It was invented in about 1765, probably by Anton and Michael Mayrhofer in Passau. Originally it had a curved body (hence the name 'horn'), later replaced by two straight sections linked by an angled knee joint; a wooden block at the lower end contained the basset extension, which ran down, up, and down again to a downward-projecting bell. Modern instruments are straight, with an upturned metal bell. 18th-century basset horns had two basset keys, for D and C, but by the end of the century the instrument was fully chromatic. The bore is no wider than that of a clarinet, but the greater length produces an attractive reedy sound. Today the usual size is F, a 4th below the normal clarinet. Because Mozart wrote for the basset horn in some 20 works, makers kept it available, and it was also used by Beethoven, Spohr, Mendelssohn, and Richard Strauss.   JMo

bass horn. An early 19th-century upright, V-shaped brass instrument with fingerholes and keys.

basso (It.). 'Low', 'bass'.

basso buffo (It., 'comic bass'). A term used to describe a bass who specializes in comic roles. Such parts, usually resourceful servants or elderly, gullible men, became important in Italian *opera buffa* from the mid-18th century. Famous examples of *basso buffo* roles are Mozart's Leporello (*Don Giovanni*) and Figaro, Rossini's Don Basilio (*Il barbiere di Siviglia*), and Donizetti's Don Pasquale.   RW

basso continuo (It., 'continuous bass'). Another name for the *figured bass, one of the principal features of Baroque compositional and performance practice style. Certain contemporary writers, for example Pepusch

(1724), noted that the basso continuo 'is the Thorough Bass, or Continual Bass, and is commonly distinguished from the other Basses by Figures over the Notes', which are to be 'realized' on a keyboard instrument or theorbo.

See also CONTINUO.   CRW

bassoon (Fr.: *basson*; Ger.: *Fagott*; It.: *fagotto*). A conical-bore woodwind instrument played with a double reed. The lowest of the four orchestral woodwinds, it was developed from the Renaissance curtal or *dulcian in the mid-17th century as part of the general reconstruction of all woodwind instruments that took place in France. Because of its tube length (254 cm in the modern bassoon) the bore is doubled back on itself, making an instrument of *c.*134 cm in length.

Early dulcians were often carved from a single piece of wood; the modern bassoon has four wooden joints together with a curved metal crook or 'bocal' and double reed (see Fig. 1a). The crook (1) fits into the tenor or wing joint (2), so called because it has a wing-shaped protuberance on one side, obliquely drilled with the three left-hand fingerholes. The double or butt (boot) joint (3) is oval in section to contain two parallel tubes connected at the bottom by a metal U-tube concealed under a protecting cap. The long or bass joint

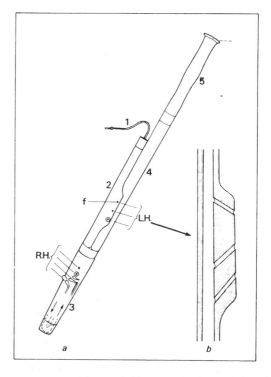

Fig. 1. Bassoon: (a) view as held, omitting hand rest and most of the keys; (b) section of wing joint.

(4) lies parallel with the wing joint and leads up to the bell joint (5) which is tipped with an ornamental ring of ivory, wood, or plastic. The fingerholes on the wing and butt are drilled obliquely so that they spread out along the bore (Fig. 1*b*) while not exceeding finger-span on the outside. The weight is taken by a sling round the neck, a seat strap hooked to the bottom of the cap, or a cello-like spike. This leaves both thumbs free to control 12 or more keys on the back of the instrument.

The three middle fingers on each hand control the six fingerholes, and the thumbs and little fingers control keys that extend the bass range down to *B*♭′. The modern bassoon has a range of *B*♭′–*f*′. Minor variations in bore profile can affect intonation, and all bassoonists have to experiment to some extent to find fingerings that suit their own instrument.

Early bassoons had three or four keys. By the beginning of the 19th century eight were normal, but during that century, as with all woodwind, two distinct systems—French and German—developed, with quite different keywork and bore profiles. Today the German system, developed by Carl Almenraeder and the firm of Heckel in Biebrich, is almost ubiquitous on account of its uniformity of tone and the general safety of its upper range. The French system, developed principally by the firm of Savary in Paris, had a livelier range of tone-quality but was more difficult to play well, so that today the Heckel system is the more common, even in France.

While one of the bassoon's initial functions was to provide a bass to the oboes in the Baroque orchestra, as a soloist it has been a tenor instrument more than a bass. Although a number of composers have written concertos for it, it shines best in the orchestra, with many effective solos, and as a chamber-music instrument in wind quintets, sextets, and octets and other ensembles.

Of other sizes, the commonest is the *contrabassoon. A treble or *fagottino*, sounding an octave above the bassoon, is known to have existed, for some 18th-century examples survive, though nothing is known of its use. It may have been, as 19th- and early 20th-century examples certainly were, built by makers as a showpiece. The tenoroon, on which the lowest note was *F*, was used in some places to teach children before the existence of modern systems that bring fingerholes within the reach of small hands; it seems also to have been used occasionally in English church bands, but again nothing else is known of its use. Unlike all other woodwinds, the range and versatility of the bassoon seem to have been such that composers were content with the normal instrument and saw no advantages in using the equivalent of piccolos, altos, and tenors.

JMo

📖 A. BAINES, *Woodwind Instruments and their History* (London, 1957, 3/1967) · L. G. LANGWILL, *The Bassoon and Contrabassoon* (London, 1967) · W. JANSEN, *The Bassoon: Its History, Construction, Makers, Players and Music* (Buren, 1978–81)

basso ostinato (It., 'obstinate bass'). A form of *ground bass in which a short bass pattern is repeated many times unchanged and above which melodic variations occur.

basso profondo (It., 'deep bass'). A bass voice of exceptionally low range.

basso ripieno (It.). A bass part for only the tutti sections of 18th-century orchestral works. See RIPIENO, 1.

basso seguente. See CONTINUO.

bassus (Lat.). In early vocal music, the abbreviated form of *contratenor bassus* ('low [part] against the tenor'), the voice part immediately below the tenor and the lowest in the ensemble. See CONTRATENOR.

bass violin (Fr.: *basse de violon*). The bass instrument of the violin family in the 16th and 17th centuries. It is thought to have been used mainly for continuo playing. In its earliest form it had three strings, tuned *F–c–g*, but as larger versions with longer string lengths began to be built a fourth string, *B*♭′, was added. In this form the instrument was the precursor of the *violoncello. Smaller bass violins, tuned in 5ths probably from *F* or *G*, were also made; these could be played standing or even walking.

Bastien und Bastienne. Opera in one act by Mozart to a libretto by Friedrich Wilhelm Weiskern and Johann Müller revised by Johann Andreas Schachtner, after Marie-Justine-Benoîte Favart and Henry de Guerville's opera *Les Amours de Bastien et Bastienne*; it was first performed at Friedrich Anton Mesmer's house (Vienna, 1768).

Bat, The. See FLEDERMAUS, DIE.

bataille (Fr., 'battle'). See BATTLE PIECE.

Bataille, Gabriel (*b* c.1575; *d* Paris, 17 Dec. 1630). French composer and lutenist. He was music master to Maria de' Medici and Anne of Austria in the early 17th century. His published anthologies of *airs de cour* include arrangements of works by other composers and some of his own fine psalm settings.   DA

Bateson, Thomas (*b* c.1570; *d* Dublin, March 1630). English church musician and composer. Nothing is known about his career until 1599, when he was appointed organist of Chester Cathedral. Ten years later he moved to a similar position at Christ Church Cathedral, Dublin, which he held until his death.

During his years in Ireland he was awarded the degrees of B.Mus. and MA by Trinity College, Dublin. Bateson's music for the church is largely lost, and he is remembered today for his two books of madrigals, published in London in 1604 and 1618.   JM

baton. The rod with which a conductor directs an orchestra. The skilled conductor can convey all manner of nuances by movement of the stick, especially of its point. 19th-century batons were thick and clumsy and were often gripped centrally by the whole hand. Today they are delicately balanced and are usually controlled by finger and thumb. Many patterns are available to suit different hands and styles. See also CONDUCTING.

JMo

battaglia (It., 'battle'). See BATTLE PIECE.

Battaglia di Legnano, La ('The Battle of Legnano'). Opera in four acts by Verdi to a libretto by Salvadore Cammarano after Joseph Méry's play *La Bataille de Toulouse* (1828) (Rome, 1849).

battement (Fr., 'beating'). 1. A 17th-century term for any ornament consisting of two adjacent notes, such as a *mordent or *trill.

2. In modern usage (in the plural, *battements*), acoustical 'beats'. See ACOUSTICS, 8.

Batten, Adrian (*b* Salisbury, 1591; *d* London, 1637). English church musician and composer. He probably began his career at Winchester Cathedral as a boy chorister. In 1614 he moved to Westminster Abbey, where he remained as a singing-man and occasional music-copyist for the next 12 years. His last appointment was at St Paul's Cathedral in the City of London. Batten was a prolific composer of anthems and service music in the manner of Byrd and Gibbons, some of which remain in the modern cathedral repertory.

JM

batterie (Fr.). 1. Percussion instruments in general.

2. A drumroll.

3. An 18th-century term for arpeggio, broken-chord figuration, etc.

4. *Rasgueado*.

Battishill, Jonathan (*b* London, May 1738; *d* Islington, 10 Dec. 1801). English composer. He began his career as a chorister at St Paul's Cathedral. In the 1750s he appeared as a singer in Handel's *Alexander's Feast* at the Little Haymarket Theatre and was appointed conductor at Covent Garden, where he met a singer and actress whom he later married. He wrote music for a pantomime, *The Rites of Hecate*, for Drury Lane in 1763 and collaborated with Michael Arne on an opera, *Almena* (1764): its production was not a success. In the 1760s Battishill became organist at various London churches and began to compose sacred music; his anthems *Call to remembrance* and *O Lord, look down from heaven* are particularly fine and unusually expressive. He wrote little music after 1777, when his wife eloped with an actor and he found consolation in drink.

WT/PL

Battistelli, Giorgio (*b* Albano Laziale, 25 April 1953). Italian composer. He studied composition with Giancarlo Bizzi and in the 1970s founded two groups for performing experimental music. In 1993 he was appointed director of the Cantiere Internazionale d'Arte in Montepulciano and in 1996 artistic director of the Orchestra Regionale Toscana. He has written many stage works, from 1987 to his own librettos, often inspired by subjects from history or film and adopting innovatory forms; they include *Jules Verne* (1987), *Le Combat d'Hector et d'Achille* (1989), *Keplers Traum* (1990), *Frau Frankenstein* (1993), and *The Cenci* (1997).

AL

📖 M. GAMBA, *Conversazione con Giorgio Battistelli* (Milan, 1992)

Battistini, Mattia (*b* Rome, 27 Feb. 1856; *d* Colle Baccaro, nr Rieti, 7 Nov. 1928). Italian baritone. He studied with Venceslao Persichini and Eugenio Terziana and made his debut as Alfonso XI in *La favorita* in Rome (1878). He soon became famous for his vocal strength, nobility, and characterization, his mastery of bel canto phrasing, and his virtuoso agility. With a repertory of over 80 roles, he was particularly acclaimed in parts as varied as Rigoletto, Boccanegra, Iago, Renato, Eugene Onegin, Don Giovanni, Tonio, Scarpia, and Wolfram. Between 1903 and 1924 he recorded prolifically.   JT

Battle of the Huns. See HUNNENSCHLACHT.

battle piece (Fr.: *bataille*; It.: *battaglia*). A composition in which the sounds of battle are realistically imitated, a type of 'programme music' especially popular from the 16th century to the 18th. One of the most celebrated early examples is Janequin's chanson *La Bataille*, inspired by the Battle of Marignano (1515); early instrumental examples were written by Lassus (*A la bataglia*) and Byrd (*The Battell* from *My Ladye Nevells Booke*). The vocal *battaglie* of Monteverdi (*Canti guerrieri*, from his *Madrigali guerrieri et amorosi*) have never been surpassed.

The Napoleonic Wars inspired two well-known instrumental battle pieces: Beethoven's *Wellingtons Sieg, oder Die Schlacht bei Vitoria* and Tchaikovsky's *1812* overture, while both Prokofiev ('Battle on the Ice', from *Alexander Nevsky*) and Walton (music for the Battle of Agincourt in Shakespeare's *Henry V*) made significant contributions to battle music in film scores. Notable operatic battles occur in Lully's *Alceste* and Verdi's *Macbeth*.

Battle Symphony. See WELLINGTONS SIEG.

battre (Fr.: 'to beat'). A term applied both to conducting and to playing percussion instruments.

battuta (It.). 'Beat', 'bar', 'measure'; *a battuta* indicates a return to strict time after, for example, a passage *ad libitum* or *a piacere* or an *accelerando* or *rallentando*. It can also mean the strong beat at the beginning of each bar; Beethoven's direction 'Ritmo di tre [quattro] battute' in the Scherzo of his Ninth Symphony indicates that three (or four) bars, each of a single beat, are to be grouped together.

Baude Cordier. See CORDIER, BAUDE.

Bauerncantate. See PEASANT CANTATA.

Bauld, Alison (*b* Sydney, 7 May 1944). Australian composer. She studied at Sydney University, then, after moving to England in 1969, in London with Elisabeth Lutyens and Hans Keller, and at the University of York. Having worked early in her career as an actor, mime, singer, and dancer, she has introduced speech and other theatrical elements into nearly all her works. She wrote her own texts for the choral drama *Van Diemen's Land* (1976) and the chamber opera *Nell* (London, 1988).

ABur

Bauldeweyn [Bauldewijn], Noel (*b* c.1480; *d* after 1512). Franco-Flemish church musician and composer. Virtually nothing is known about his life, other than that he was Master of the Choristers at St Rombouts, Mechelen, in 1509–13. Seven masses by him survive, the best known of which is modelled on his own chanson *En douleur et tristesse*. Like many other composers of his generation, he is credited with several pieces that also have ascriptions to Josquin des Prez.

JM

Bax, Sir Arnold (Edward Trevor) (*b* Streatham, 8 Nov. 1883; *d* Cork, 3 Oct. 1953). English composer. He studied at the Hampstead Conservatoire (1898–1900) and with Frederick Corder at the RAM (1900–5). The eldest son of a wealthy Nonconformist family, he enjoyed independent means and was able to devote himself entirely to composition and writing; the only major appointment he accepted was that of Master of the King's Music, in 1942. His earlier works, which include the tone-poems *In the Faery Hills* (1909), *The Garden of Fand* (1913–16), and *Tintagel* (1917–19), are imbued with the spirit of Celtic legend, an interest ignited by his reading W. B. Yeats's *The Wanderings of Usheen* in 1902. Others, for example *November Woods* (1917), *The Happy Forest* (1914–21), and *The Tale the Pine-Trees Knew* (1931), evince an affinity with nature, landscape, and legend.

Bax later turned his attention to abstract forms, producing important cycles of string quartets, piano sonatas, concertos, and symphonies. The latter, spanning the years 1923–39, form a substantial corpus of works, ranging from the angry tones of the First Symphony of 1923 (inspired by the tragedy of the Easter Rising of 1916 and the death of several Irish friends), through the epic Second Symphony (1926) and the Third (1929), which established the hallmark of a closing, serene epilogue, to the more classical Seventh (1939) with its variation finale. In addition to the string quartets he produced many other colourful chamber works including the fine *Elegiac Trio* (1916) for flute, viola, and harp, an *Irish Elegy* for cor anglais, harp, and string quartet (also written in the aftermath of the 1916 uprising), the striking Harp Quintet (1919), and three works for larger forces: a nonet (1928–30), an octet (1934), and a septet (1936).

A composer with great facility, Bax developed a vivid orchestral palette drawn eclectically from Wagner, Richard Strauss, Debussy, Elgar, and the Russians, all of whom he admired. He wrote plays, novels, and poetry under an Irish pseudonym, Dermot O'Byrne, and in 1943 he published his autobiography, *Farewell my Youth*. He was knighted in 1937.

PG/JDi

C. SCOTT-SUTHERLAND, *Arnold Bax* (London, 1973) · L. FOREMAN, *Arnold Bax: A Composer and his Times* (Aldershot, 2/1988)

Bayadère, La (*Bayaderka*; 'The Temple Dancer'). Ballet in four acts by Minkus to a scenario by Sergei Khudekov and Marius Petipa, who choreographed it (St Petersburg, 1877).

bayan. See ACCORDION.

Bayle, François (*b* Tamatave, Madagascar, 27 April 1932). French composer. After studies with Stockhausen and Messiaen he specialized in electronic music, becoming director of the Groupe de Recherches Musicales in 1966. Most of his compositions are for tape, using natural or synthesized sounds or both, usually alone but sometimes with live performers.

ABur

Bay Psalm Book. See PSALMODY.

Bayreuth. A town in northern Bavaria, home of the Festspielhaus designed by Wagner and site of the annual festival, established in 1876, devoted to his operas. See FESTIVALS, 4; OPERA HOUSES.

Bazin, François (Emmanuel Joseph) (*b* Marseilles, 4 Sept. 1816; *d* Paris, 2 July 1878). French composer, teacher, and conductor. At the Paris Conservatoire (1834–40) he won first prizes for harmony, counterpoint, and organ, and also the Prix de Rome. He went on to pursue a career divided between theatre composition, teaching at the Conservatoire, and conducting. His successes at the Opéra-Comique included *Maître Pathelin* (1856) and, above all, *Le Voyage en Chine* (1865). He also composed a Mass and other choral works. He published a harmony tutor in 1858 and succeeded Ambroise Thomas as professor of composition at the Conservatoire in 1871.   ALa

Bazzini, Antonio (*b* Brescia, 11 March 1818; *d* Milan, 10 Feb. 1897). Italian violinist and composer. He spent his early life on concert tours throughout Europe. After some years in Paris he returned to Italy, where he became professor of composition (1873), then director (1882), of the Milan Conservatory. He wrote an opera and some orchestral works but was best known for his chamber music; he also wrote the famous showpiece for violin *La Ronde des lutins*. His many pupils included Puccini.   DA/RP

BBC. See BROADCASTING.

Be (Ger.). The flat sign (see FLAT, 1).

Beach, Amy (Marcy) [née Cheney] (*b* Henniker, NH, 5 Sept. 1867; *d* New York, 27 Dec. 1944). American composer and pianist. She made her debut as a pianist in 1885 with the Boston Symphony, but on her marriage later that year she retired from the concert platform and concentrated on composition—though she re-emerged to introduce her Piano Concerto in 1900, again with the Boston Symphony. Other works of this period include a large-scale Mass (1890), a 'Gaelic' Symphony (1896), a Violin Sonata (1896), and a Piano Quintet (1907). She was widowed in 1910 and resumed her performing career in Europe, where the fine quality and traditional correctness of her music caused astonishment—whether more for her sex or her nationality it is hard to say. In 1914 she returned to the USA, where she produced, among other works, a String Quartet (1929), the opera *Cabildo* (Athens, GA, 1932), and a Piano Trio (1938). She published her music under her married name of Mrs H. H. A. Beach. In the 1980s there was a revival of her work by feminist historians and performers.   PG

□ A. F. BLOCK, *Amy Beach, Passionate Victorian: The Life and Work of an American Composer, 1867–1944* (New York, 1998)

Beamish, Sally (*b* London, 26 Aug. 1956). English composer. She began her career as a viola player but concentrated on composition after moving to Scotland in 1989. There is a distinctly Scottish flavour to several of her works, including the piano trio *Piobaireachd*

(1991) and the oboe concerto *Tam Lin* (1992), but her music calls on a wide range of literary and religious sources, for example in the Violin Concerto (1994), which alludes to Erich Maria Remarque's *All Quiet on the Western Front*, and the Viola Concerto (1995), which evokes Peter's denial of Christ.   AW

bearbeiten (Ger.). 'To work over', 'to arrange'; *bearbeitet*, 'arranged'; *Bearbeitung*, 'arrangement'.

Bear, The. See OURS, L'.

Beard, John (*b* c.1717; *d* Hampton, 5 Feb. 1791). English tenor. He studied with Bernard Gates at the Chapel Royal and made his solo debut as the Israelite Priest in Handel's *Esther* in 1732. Handel was so impressed with his voice that he engaged him for his Covent Garden company, with which he made his debut as Silvio in the third version of *Il pastor fido* (1734). His musicianship and his undemonstrative strength as a singer and actor inspired Handel to write many heroic parts for him; these had a vital influence in the rise of the tenor as a performer of the male roles that had hitherto been taken by castratos and women. From 1761 to 1767 Beard was the manager of the Covent Garden Theatre; his refusal to lower prices for afterpieces led to the notorious riot there during a performance of Arne's *Artaxerxes* in 1762, and he had to make a public apology.   JT

beat (Fr.: *temps*; Ger.: *Zahlzeit, Schlag*; It.: *battuta*). **1.** The basic unit of time in mensural music, i.e. that chosen by the conductor when he 'beats' time. The beats are usually categorized according to where they fall in the bar: as 'weak' beats (the second and fourth in a four-beat bar, the second and third in a three-beat bar, or the second in a two-beat bar), or 'strong' beats (the first and, to a lesser degree, the third in a four-beat bar, and the first in a three-beat or a two-beat bar). For other terms used to describe different kinds of beat, see ANACRUSIS; DOWNBEAT; UPBEAT.

2. A 17th-century English term for an ornament, describing either an ascending *appoggiatura, or an ascending appoggiatura repeated several times, so that it is virtually an inverted *trill. In the 18th century, 'beat' denoted a *mordent.

beater [drumstick, mallet] (Fr.: *baguette*; Ger.: *Schlägel*; It.: *bacchetta*). The stick with which a percussion instrument is made to sound. The main essentials for drumsticks are that they be matched pairs and of weight suited to the drum. Thus, dance-band side-drum sticks are lighter than orchestral ones, and military sticks will be heavier still. Side-drum sticks are usually of plain wood (e.g. hickory). *Brushes may also be used, and are a common alternative to drumsticks on the drum kit.

Timpani sticks usually have felt heads, sometimes with a balsawood core, on wooden, cane, or aluminium shafts. Timpanists carry a range of sticks of different size and hardness to produce different tone-colours. Bass-drum beaters (Fr.: *mailloche*) are similar in appearance to timpani sticks but are bigger and heavier. Gong beaters are heavier still.

Cymbal beaters usually have hard felt heads. Xylophone and glockenspiel mallet-heads, once wooden, are now more often made of plastic (sometimes brass for the glockenspiel). Marimba and vibraphone mallets have wound-wool covers. Tubular-bell hammers are usually of coiled rawhide.   JMo

beating reed. See REED.

Béatitudes, Les ('The Beatitudes'). Oratorio, op. 53 (1869–79), by Franck, for soloists, chorus, and orchestra, to a text based on the Sermon on the Mount (Matthew 5: 3–12).

Beatrice di Tenda. Opera in two acts by Bellini to a libretto by Felice Romani after Carlo Tedaldi-Fores's play *Beatrice di Tenda* (Venice, 1833).

Béatrice et Bénédict ('Beatrice and Benedick'). Opera in two acts by Berlioz to his own libretto after Shakespeare's *Much Ado about Nothing* (Baden-Baden, 1862).

Beatrix [Beatriz] de Dia. Possibly the name of the *trobairitz* Comtessa de *Dia.

beats (Fr.: *battements*; Ger.: *Schwebungen*; It.: *battimenti*). An acoustical phenomenon produced, for example, by two instruments playing in near unison. See ACOUSTICS, 8.

Beauharnais, Hortense Eugénie de (*b* Paris, 10 April 1783; *d* Arenenberg, 5 Oct. 1837). French composer. The stepdaughter of Napoleon Bonaparte, she later married Louis Bonaparte, her third son becoming Napoleon III. She sang, studied the piano, harp, and lyre, and composed *romances* on medievally inspired texts, which she performed (with songs by her contemporaries) at gatherings at her home. *Partant pour la Syrie* was adopted by the Bonapartists during the Restoration and became a national hymn under Napoleon III; many, however, have disputed her authorship. Her songs were first published in 1813 in a lavish edition.   SH

Beautiful Maid of the Mill, The. See SCHÖNE MÜLLERIN, DIE.

bebop [be-bop, bop]. A new style of jazz developed in the 1940s, emphasizing more sophisticated harmonies and rhythms than earlier jazz. It was pioneered by Charlie Parker, Dizzy Gillespie, and Thelonious Monk. See JAZZ, 3.   PGA

Bebung (Ger., from *beben*, 'to tremble'; Fr.: *balancement*; It.: *tremolo*). A *vibrato effect unique to the clavichord. After a key is depressed the tangent remains in contact with the string, and subsequent gentle variation of finger pressure causes an undulation of pitch similar to violin vibrato, helping to 'reinforce the tone' (D. G. Türk, *Clavierschule*, 1789). An important expressive device in 18th-century clavichord-playing, *Bebung* was nevertheless used sparingly and was only exceptionally notated, for example by C. P. E. Bach (*Versuch*, 1753) and Türk (see Ex. 1). It was deployed to good effect 'only on long notes, and in pieces of a melancholy character' according to Türk, who warned of 'the distressing exaggeration caused by using too much pressure'. Some sources link *Bebung* with the similarly notated *Tragen der Töne* ('sustaining of the tone'), but the latter was probably more akin to a reiteration or emphasis than a vibrato.

Although the term is occasionally used in connection with tied repeated notes in piano music (e.g. in Beethoven's Sonata op. 110), *Bebung* is impossible on the piano and this usage is therefore inappropriate.
                                          SMcV/NPDC

Ex. 1

C. P. E. Bach

Türk

(*a*) written   (*b*) sounding

bécarre (Fr., 'square b'). 1. The natural sign (see NATURAL, 2). The term derives from one of the two forms of the letter 'b' used in medieval notation; see DURUM AND MOLLIS.

2. In 17th-century usage, 'major', e.g. *fa bécarre*, F major.

Bechstein. German firm of piano makers founded in Berlin in 1853 by Wilhelm Carl Bechstein (1826–1900). His first grand piano was inaugurated in 1856 by Bülow; he went on to make thousands of fine concert grands, model B grands, and uprights, the favourites of generations of pianists. In 1901 the firm opened a concert room in London, later renamed the Wigmore Hall.
                                                AL

Becker, John (Joseph) (*b* Henderson, KY, 22 Jan. 1886; *d* Wilmette, IL, 21 Jan. 1961). American composer. He studied at the Cincinnati Conservatory and spent most of his professional life teaching at Catholic colleges in the Midwest. His *Symphonia brevis* (1929), the third of seven symphonies, marked a change from a Romantic style to dissonant counterpoint, and his name began to be cited alongside those of Ives, Ruggles, and Wallingford Riegger. Other works include the ballets *Abongo* (1933), for large percussion ensemble, and *A Marriage with Space* (1935), for speaking chorus and orchestra, and also pieces making a vehement social protest. He produced little after World War II.
PG

Beckwith, John (*b* Victoria, BC, 9 March 1927). Canadian composer, critic, and teacher. He studied in Toronto, and later in Paris with Nadia Boulanger. He taught at Toronto University for many years, becoming dean of the music faculty from 1970 to 1977, as well as working as a writer, critic, and broadcaster. His compositions include three operas, choral music, songs, orchestral and instrumental pieces, and several collages for radio—the techniques of which influenced his later concert music.
ABUR

 📖 T. McGEE (ed.), *Taking a Stand: Essays in Honour of John Beckwith* (Toronto, 1995)

bedächtig (Ger.). 'Cautious', 'deliberate', i.e. slow.

Bedford, David (Vickerman) (*b* London, 4 Aug. 1937). English composer. He studied with Lennox Berkeley at the RAM and with Luigi Nono in Venice (1960). His early works reflected the freer attitudes to musical form and notation that became fashionable during the 1960s as antidotes to the ultra-complex avant-garde initiatives of the immediate postwar years. Bedford's liking for sustained, radiant harmonies, often tonal in character, led him to work a good deal in the crossover territory between art music and rock music. He also taught in various schools and colleges, composing pieces with the specific needs of young people and non-specialist performers in mind.
PG/AW

Bedyngham [Bedingham], **John** (*b* ?Oxford, ?1422; *d* Westminster, 1459–60). English composer. For some time he was verger at the collegiate chapel of St Stephen, Westminster. His surviving works include two masses, individual mass movements, and some eight songs, several of which bear conflicting attributions to Dunstaple (including the popular and widely circulated *O rosa bella*), Dufay, or Frye. Bedyngham's music, like that of many of his English contemporaries, was popular and influential on the Continent, and survives largely in foreign sources.
JM

Beecham, Sir Thomas (*b* St Helens, 29 April 1879; *d* London, 8 March 1961). English conductor and impresario. He studied composition with Charles Wood in London but as a conductor was largely self-taught. At the age of 20 he deputized for Hans Richter with the Hallé Orchestra. In 1907 he was engaged by Delius for a concert, beginning his lifelong devotion to the composer. In 1909, with the fortune he inherited from the family pill company, he founded the Beecham Symphony Orchestra. He gave opera seasons from 1910 in London, including at Covent Garden, where he gave many premieres. He sponsored Diaghilev's Ballets Russes there and at Drury Lane (1913–14). Throughout World War I, Beecham conducted the Hallé, Royal Philharmonic Society, and LSO. In 1915 he founded the Beecham (later British National) Opera Company and that year was knighted.

 Bankrupted in 1920 at his father's death, Beecham withdrew from musical life. On his return, he began to focus on the orchestral repertory. Dissatisfied with playing standards, in 1932 he founded the London Philharmonic Orchestra. That year he became artistic director at Covent Garden until it closed at the outbreak of war in 1939; during his tenure he conducted several *Ring* cycles. He then went to the USA, where he appeared at the Metropolitan Opera, New York, and with many American orchestras. Returning to London, in 1946 he formed his last orchestra, the Royal Philharmonic, with which he toured internationally. He made many records of his specialities—Delius, Mozart, Haydn, French music—and wrote an autobiography *A Mingled Chime* (1944). A key figure in 20th-century British musical life (sometimes controversially), he was renowned for his ability to communicate with audiences and players, his stylish phrasing, and his acerbic wit.
JT

 📖 A. JEFFERSON, *Sir Thomas Beecham: A Centenary Tribute* (London, 1979) · A. BLACKWOOD, *Sir Thomas Beecham: The Man and the Music* (London, 1994)

Beeson, Jack (Hamilton) (*b* Muncie, IN, 15 July 1921). American composer and teacher. He studied at the Eastman School and privately with Bartók in New York in 1944–5. At that time he was associated with Columbia University, to which he returned as MacDowell Professor of Composition (1965–88). His operas, following those of Douglas Moore in Americanism of style and subject, include *Lizzie Borden* (New York, 1965). Other works include choral settings and songs.
PG

Bees' Wedding, The. Nickname of Mendelssohn's *Lieder ohne Worte* no. 34 (op. 67 no. 4) in C major (book 6, 1845) for piano, also entitled 'Spinnerlied'.

Beethoven, Ludwig van (*see page 116*)

(*cont. on p. 119*)

Ludwig van Beethoven
(1770–1827)

The German composer Ludwig van Beethoven was born in Bonn on 16 December 1770 and died in Vienna on 26 March 1827.

Beethoven's output includes nine symphonies, six piano concertos, 35 piano sonatas, 16 string quartets, ten violin sonatas, and much else. His career and music are often divided into three periods. In the first, up to about 1802, when the influence of Haydn and Mozart was most conspicuous, he composed large amounts of piano and chamber music, as well as several concertos and two symphonies. The second period continues up to about 1815 (or 1812 in some accounts), beginning with Beethoven's full realization that he was to face increasing deafness, and exhibits expansion of forms and other innovations. The third period, in which each major work is extremely distinctive and original, continued until his death, and was marked by a conspicuous decline in output, coupled with a greater profundity of thought and complexity of working methods.

While this division into three periods is extremely helpful in giving an overview of Beethoven's development, it has been criticized by some as too simplistic: it ignores changes within periods, and disguises the fact that features associated primarily with one period often appear in others. Certain of his early works, such as the Cantata on the Death of Joseph II (1790) and the Righini Variations (1791), have much in common with works of the early 1800s, while the 16 sets of Variations on National Airs (1818–19) mostly lack the formal, motivic, and textural complexity typical of his late period. Thus the present essay will observe this tripartite division only in part.

Early years
Beethoven came from a musical family, though none of his forebears was a composer. His grandfather Ludwig or Louis (1712–73), of Flemish birth, was Kapellmeister to the court of the Elector of Cologne at Bonn. His father Johann (c.1740–1792) was a professional tenor there, and also taught singing and piano. Beethoven's mother, Maria Magdalena (1746–87), the daughter of a kitchen overseer, had recently been widowed when she met Johann. Three of their children survived infancy: Ludwig and two brothers, Caspar Carl (1774–1815) and

Nikolaus Johann (1776–1848). Ludwig knew and admired his grandfather, but his relationship with his father was less happy. Johann gave him much instruction in music, but was evidently too strict at times, and was prone to bouts of heavy drinking.

Beethoven's instruction in piano and theory was passed from his father to Christian Neefe after the latter's arrival in Bonn in 1779, and the pupil made excellent progress. When Neefe was appointed court organist in 1782, Beethoven proved an able deputy, and that same year he published his first composition—the Dressler Variations. Shortly afterwards Neefe announced prophetically that Beethoven 'would surely become a second Wolfgang Amadeus Mozart were he to continue as he has begun'. Beethoven composed several more works during 1783–4, most of them showing marked originality, and he soon became court organist himself alongside Neefe. By 1787 he was ready to travel to Vienna to seek lessons from Mozart. After only two weeks there, however, he heard that his mother, of whom he was very fond, had fallen ill; he returned home promptly, arriving shortly before her death. Within two years his father was an alcoholic, and Beethoven was placed at the head of the family.

In 1790, after a period in which he composed few known works, he wrote the above-mentioned Cantata on the Death of Joseph II, who had been a most enlightened ruler. Much of the cantata is in a style instantly recognizable as Beethoven's, but it was not performed at Bonn, partly because it was so difficult, with highly irregular figuration and awkward melodic lines. Two years later, when Haydn was passing through Bonn on the way back to Vienna from his first London visit, Beethoven showed him some compositions (the cantata was probably one of them), and arrangements were made for Beethoven to go to Vienna to study with Haydn. He left Bonn in November 1792, presumably expecting to return in due course (as had other musicians who had gone away to study), and his salary continued to be paid until 1794. In fact, he never went back, and lived in Vienna for the rest of his life.

The first decade in Vienna

Beethoven's ties with Bonn were quickly loosened by the death of his father in December 1792. Meanwhile Vienna held great attractions, being effectively the musical capital of the German-speaking countries. Mozart had died in 1791, and several patrons looked to Beethoven to fill the void, which in some ways he did, in spite of his different temperament—blunt, irascible, and ambitious, though good-natured, noble-minded, and idealistic. Virtuoso pianists were much in demand, especially at the private houses of the nobility, and he soon proved that his pianistic ability was a match for anyone. His improvisations were particularly outstanding, and frequently moved his audiences to tears.

Beethoven's lessons with Haydn continued until 1794, when the latter left for his second visit to London. Beethoven then studied with J. G. Albrechtsberger, who seems to have been much more systematic, taking Beethoven through a rigorous course of contrapuntal study. Haydn had evidently been more easygoing, but there is no indication that Beethoven's relationship with him was strained, as is sometimes stated. They clearly had a warm mutual admiration, and in 1796 Beethoven dedicated his Sonatas op. 2 to Haydn as a mark of respect and gratitude. By this time Beethoven had made his first public appearance in Vienna as a pianist, in March 1795, playing a recently completed piano concerto (probably the so-called no. 1 in C major, though he had written at least two earlier piano concertos). In 1796 he undertook an extensive tour of Prague, Dresden, Leipzig, Berlin, and, later in the year, Pressburg (Bratislava). His compositions were by now proving extremely popular with those who preferred the more earnest, serious type of music. Members of the nobility frequently commissioned new works or paid for dedications, and further income came from publication. Thus Beethoven was able to support himself without any salary from Bonn.

The piano sonatas of this period contain the essence of his style. They are often closer to Clementi's than to Haydn's, with a tendency towards heavier textures and pianistic effects; but their high level of originality and complexity must not be overlooked. The chamber music, for example the Three Piano Trios op. 1 (1795), is more reminiscent of Haydn, containing material more finely chiselled, and concentrating more on motivic development. Meanwhile his wind music and concertos owe most to Mozart, though again they display much originality. His finest chamber works of these years are the Six String Quartets op. 18, composed in 1798–1800 and published in 1801. In 1800 he also completed his First Symphony, after much preparation and several false starts. Haydn was again the chief model, but Beethoven introduced many daring innovations, including beginning the symphony with an out-of-key discord.

By the time he was 30 Beethoven was a highly successful composer and pianist. Though not particularly shrewd as a businessman (his brothers showed greater commercial skills when they negotiated with publishers on his behalf), he was able to make a reasonable living through performance and composition for several years. Then disaster struck. Some kind of infection contracted about 1797 led to progressive loss of his hearing. By 1800 he was seeking medical advice, and by 1802 he was becoming desperate at the lack of any sign of a cure. The effects were not completely incapacitating: it was over ten years before he had to give up performing completely. Yet the emotional shock was enormous, and he felt obliged to withdraw from society, wishing to conceal his deafness. In October 1802, after a six-month spell in the quiet village of Heiligenstadt as a final attempt at a cure, he wrote a document addressed to his brothers and designed to be read after his death, in which he tells of his thoughts of suicide, of his devotion to art, and of his readiness to allow fate to take its course.

The second decade in Vienna

This 'Heiligenstadt Testament' (as it has become known), written almost exactly ten years after Beethoven's arrival in Vienna in 1792, can be seen as a turning-point in his deafness crisis. On returning from Heiligenstadt he plunged into composition with renewed energy. An oratorio, *Christus am Ölberge* (1803), quickly followed, in which he explores the whole question of suffering, using ideas strikingly similar to some in the Heiligenstadt Testament—heroic triumph over adversity by a lone individual, through love of humanity. The idea of heroism also filled his next orchestral work, the celebrated 'Eroica' Symphony (1803–4). This was inspired by and originally dedicated to Napoleon, the heroic embodiment of the French Revolution. When Napoleon declared himself emperor, however, Beethoven's deep loathing of tyranny made him angry enough to substitute the dedication, 'Composed to celebrate the memory of a great man'. The 'Eroica' was far longer than any previous symphony, while its expansion of Haydn's method of thematic development ensures that the vast first movement is continuously absorbing. This work, more than any other, enabled his subsequent music to be worked out on an unprecedentedly large scale.

Beethoven's great opera *Fidelio* followed, though its two early versions of 1805 and 1806 proved unsatisfactory and it did not reach its final form until 1814. Other notable works in the remarkably fertile period immediately after the 'Eroica' include the Fourth, Fifth, and Sixth Symphonies (1806–8), four concertos (the Triple Concerto of 1804, the Violin Concerto of 1806, and two piano concertos of 1806–9), the famous 'Waldstein' and 'Appassionata' Sonatas (1804–5), and the 'Razumovsky' Quartets (1806). Many of these works are also heroic in mood, although some are much more gentle and lyrical, for instance the Violin Concerto and especially the 'Pastoral' Symphony (no. 6), which expresses a Romantic love of nature, though more as feelings than portrayal of actual scenes. The slow movements of the works of this period often have a hymn-like profundity and calm, while the scherzos are deliberately rough and boisterous in mood, with sudden changes in dynamics and off-beat accents. The finales are frequently expansive, lighthearted and seemingly straightforward, but they embody considerable complexity and innovation in their manipulation of standard formal principles. The sense of 'journey's end' that they invariably exude may be one of triumph, as in the Fifth Symphony, or peace, as in the Sixth, or limitless vitality, as in the third 'Razumovsky' Quartet.

Several of Beethoven's latest compositions received their premiere at a grand four-hour concert in December 1808. By this time he had been offered the post of Kapellmeister at Kassel. It was a tempting offer, since he still had no regular income, but three Viennese noblemen (Prince Lobkowitz, Archduke Rudolph, and Prince Kinsky) decided to fund an annuity for him on condition that he remain in Vienna, and he accepted this. The French invasion of Vienna in May 1809 left him drained of energy for several months; he soon renewed his intensity of composition, but many of the works in the next three years are less well known, leading some to assume that his output dwindled long before it actually did. These works include the incidental music to Goethe's *Egmont* (1810), for which the overture is still popular; a series of folksong settings, including 53 completed in 1810; and two substantial one-act *Singspiele* of 1811, written for the opening of a theatre in Budapest.

1812–24

Although Beethoven had fallen in love several times since arriving in Vienna, he had still not married. One reason, his financial insecurity, had been overcome with the establishment of his annuity in 1809, and he began actively planning marriage, but the plans fell through. By 1812 he had fallen in love again, and on 6–7 July that year he wrote a passionate letter to an unnamed woman referred to as his 'Immortal Beloved'. Her identity has remained a mystery, though she is believed by most to

be Antonie Brentano; Antonie was already married with several children, so there was no chance of a happy outcome to their relationship. Indeed the Brentanos left Vienna that year, and Beethoven remained a bachelor.

Around this time he composed his Seventh and Eighth Symphonies (1811–12) and, in complete contrast, the programmatic *Wellingtons Sieg* (known as the 'Battle Symphony'), celebrating the defeat of the French at the Battle of Vitoria in 1813. If the Seventh Symphony, energetic in rhythm, splendid in orchestration, and magnificent in thematic integration, seems the apotheosis of Beethoven's post-'Eroica' years, the Eighth is correspondingly witty and clever. The year 1814 saw the Congress of Vienna, during which Beethoven's popularity was at its height, with the new symphonies, the revised *Fidelio*, and a number of little-known patriotic works receiving successful public performances.

By the end of the decade the situation had changed. Rossini's music had ousted Beethoven's in popularity in Vienna, though he was still recognized as a great composer. Many of his friends and patrons had either died or left Austria; his hearing had deteriorated so far that he had to rely on notebooks for conversations; and on the death of his brother Carl in 1815, he embarked on a legal struggle to gain custody of his nephew Karl, whose mother was by all accounts a worthless woman. He eventually succeeded, but only after making great sacrifices for Karl and expending enormous amounts of energy that could otherwise have been devoted to composition. His output was also affected by periods of ill health, especially during 1817 and 1821, when he wrote very little. Regarded by many as eccentric if not mad, as he wandered the streets of Vienna with musical sketchbook in hand, jotting down any ideas that came to him, he was actually in the process of creating a series of masterpieces of even greater stature, size, and originality than his earlier works.

The first works providing clear signs of his late style are the two Cello Sonatas op. 102, written as early as 1815. The thematic material is fragmentary; fugal writing and polyphonic textures are given increased prominence; and no. 1 upsets traditional formal patterns, altering the standard number and order of movements. In mood they show Beethoven isolated spiritually as well as musically, but in place of the sense of triumph and heroism comes an other-worldly calm. The new style persisted in the 'Hammerklavier' Sonata of 1818 and a series of three more sonatas (opp. 109–11) of 1820–2. Meanwhile the 'Hammerklavier' was the first of a series of mighty works in which Beethoven expanded his scale of thought just as he had done with the 'Eroica'. The enormous set of 33 Diabelli Variations

(1819–23) overlapped with the magnificent *Missa solemnis*, intended for the installation of Archduke Rudolph as Archbishop of Olmütz (Olomouc) in 1820, but not completed in its final version until nearly three years later. This is the last in a long line of 'symphonic' masses by various Viennese composers, though Beethoven's could be used liturgically only on the grandest of ceremonial occasions. Written 'from the heart', it reflects his deep personal faith. The Ninth ('Choral') Symphony was completed in 1824. It is formed on an altogether more expansive scale than his earlier symphonies, and its moods range from the despair of the opening theme to the utter jubilation of the song of joy in the finale. The introduction of solo and choral voices in this finale is only the most obvious of many innovations in the work as a whole.

The last years

By 1824 Beethoven was suffering from several ailments, which were sometimes exacerbated rather than relieved by his doctors. Relations with his nephew reached their nadir in summer 1826. Karl was by now 19 and feeling increasingly an adolescent desire for greater freedom, which Beethoven rigorously denied him, and he eventually attempted suicide, though he narrowly escaped death. Beethoven meanwhile was engaged principally, during these last years, on a series of string quartets (opp. 127, 130, 131, 132, and 135) in which the originality of previous works is taken still further: each one shows extraordinary innovations of form, character, texture, rhythm, or key structure, and they possess a visionary quality that makes them seem ever new and transcendent.

They were completed by October 1826, after which Beethoven embarked on a string quintet. Little of this was composed, however, before his final illness set in and he became unable to work. He continued to be held in much honour, and received many visitors, but his illness grew steadily worse and he died on 26 March 1827, as a thunderstorm raged outside. His funeral was an impressive affair: the poet Franz Grillparzer wrote a moving oration, and a huge crowd followed the procession to the cemetery.

Beethoven's influence

For many, Beethoven is not only a great composer, but the greatest of all, though this is not a very meaningful concept since different composers have different methods and objectives. His music ranges over the gamut of human emotions, each of them portrayed with unprecedented intensity, and it also exhibits an extraordinary command over the basic elements—chords, rests, motifs, registers, keys, and instrumental timbres. And it possesses a nobility of purpose that elevates the human spirit. Beethoven's goal was to write music of immeasurable quality and lasting worth, and to achieve it he made thousands of pages of rough drafts or sketches, in an effort to reach the perfection that he knew was impossible. Never has a composer had such an influence on his successors—though Wagner may run him close. Many composers followed specific innovations of his, by introducing a chorus into a symphony, basing a symphony on a programme, linking movements thematically, opening a concerto without an orchestral ritornello, expanding the possibilities of key structure within a movement or a work, introducing new instruments into the symphony orchestra, and so on.

Acknowledged in his lifetime as a musical Titan, a hero who rose from humble origins and conquered extreme adversity with his genius, he lifted music from its role as sheer entertainment and made it the object of hushed reverence—music written for its own sake as an elevating power. Great composers today are appreciated as worthy of enormous respect, and this is due in no small part to the changed perceptions of music's function that Beethoven brought about.   DA/BC

📖 E. ANDERSON (ed. and trans.), *The Letters of Beethoven* (London, 1961) · D. ARNOLD and N. FORTUNE (eds.), *The Beethoven Companion* (London, 1971) · W. KINDERMAN, *Beethoven* (Oxford, 1995) · B. COOPER (ed.), *The Beethoven Compendium* (London, 2/1996) · B. COOPER, *Beethoven* (Oxford, 2000)

Beggar's Opera, The. *Ballad opera in three acts arranged and partly composed by Pepusch to a libretto by John *Gay (London, 1728). It was reworked several times in the 20th century, notably by Frederic Austin (1920), Edward Dent (1944), Britten—who virtually created a new work (1948), Bliss (1953), and Muldowney (1982). Kurt Weill's Die *Dreigroschenoper sets the libretto to new music.

Begleitung (Ger.). 'Accompaniment'; *begleitend*, 'accompanying'.

behend [behende] (Ger.). 'Agile', 'nimble'; *behendig*, 'nimbly'.

Beisser (Ger., 'biter'). An 18th-century name for the *mordent.

beklemmt (Ger.). 'Anguished', 'oppressed'.

Bel. A unit for measuring change in the intensity of sound. See ACOUSTICS, 11.

Belaieff, Mitrofan Petrovich. See BELYAYEV, MITROFAN PETROVICH.

bel canto (It., 'beautiful singing'). A term usually applied to one of two types of singing. 1. In arias in mid-17th-century operas and cantatas (e.g. by Cesti or Carissimi) the recitative style developed by the early opera composers was abandoned in favour of a smooth, expressive melody, in which the qualities of the voice could be shown to the full.

2. The arias in Italian operas of the late 18th and early 19th centuries (notably those by Bellini) were similarly lyrical and fluid, unlike those of later in the century (e.g. in the works of Verdi), which exploited the dramatic force of the voice. In bel canto singing the emphasis was on evenness of tone and also on the singer's skill in executing highly ornate and florid passages with ease.   —/JBE

belebend, belebt (Ger.). 'Lively', 'animated'; *belebter*, 'more animated'.

Belgium. See LOW COUNTRIES.

Belisario. Opera in three acts by Donizetti to a libretto by Salvatore Cammarano after Luigi Marchionni's adaptation of Eduard von Schenk's *Belisarius* (1820) (Venice, 1836).

bell. 1. (Fr.: *cloche*; Ger.: *Glocke*; It.: *campana*). An *idiophone consisting of a vessel in which the zone of maximum vibration is at the rim (unlike a *gong, which vibrates most strongly at the centre). It therefore either hangs from or rests on its apex (the point furthest from the rim); 'resting bells' lie in the hand or on a cushion. Bells can be hollowed from wood (e.g. some types of cowbell) or made from glass or ceramics, but most are cast or forged from metal. They come in many varieties of two basic forms: the cup or 'open' bell, and the hollow sphere or crotal. Both types are universal and of ancient origin. All bells have a device at the apex for attachment (e.g. a lug, loop, or bolt-hole).

Open bells are sounded either by a clapper suspended inside the bell from the apex or from the outside by a hammer (as in automatic clock-chiming) or a suspended ramrod (used in Buddhist temples against large bells). If a clapper is used, either the bell is swung by pulling on a rope to bring the sides against the clapper (the most common method in west European tower bells) or the clapper is pulled by a rope or wire attached to it (common in east European tower bells and in carillons). Crotals usually contain one or more loose pellets, which bounce freely against the inside as the crotal is agitated. Sets of tuned, non-swinging bells are known as chimes (see CHIME, 1). However, not all chimes are bells: some are other kinds of idiophone with a bell-like timbre (e.g. *tubular bells) or *metallophones (e.g. the *glockenspiel). The term 'chiming' is used of a tower bell swinging at an angle generally under 180°; when the angle is wider the bell is 'tolling'; in 'ringing' it is swung through a full circle.

Animal bells (*cowbells) are used worldwide as instruments. They are forged from sheet iron, folded and welded or riveted into shape in characteristic patterns that vary widely according to area. In West and Central Africa two or three conical iron bells are forged together at their apex to form a two- or three-note instrument. This is held in the left hand and struck with a hammer in the right, and may be made to 'talk' by manipulating the bells against the body to produce changes in sound.

The casting (founding) of small bells was known in South-East Asia by 3000 BC, spreading to India and Egypt by 2000 BC and to China probably by the 11th century BC. By about 1000 BC the Chinese were making bells that were too large to carry. In Europe small open bells, mostly forged, were in use by the 5th century AD, in the Christian Church for signalling and outside it for secular purposes. Bellfounding began in 6th-century Italy among the Benedictines, but it was not until the 10th century that bells large enough to need being hung in a tower were developed. Modern European tower bells are cast from bell-metal, a bronze of about 78% copper to 22% tin. Only gradually did makers learn how to tune the bells by grinding carefully chosen spots in the interior, so bringing the overtones (which are naturally inharmonic and, if uncorrected, produce an unpleasant-sounding vibration) into consonance with the nominal pitch of the bell.

Most west European tower bells are chimed at their natural pendular speed; small bells, therefore, sound in faster succession than large bells. A large peal of bells chimed in this way produces a random sequence of pitches. In English *change-ringing the bell may be balanced upside down and swung through a full circle, the moment of its sounding being controlled by the ringer. This is made possible, and with least effort, by passing the rope round the flanged circumference of a large wheel, a method first introduced in the 16th century.

Besides being widely used for signalling—for alarms, summons, or national or local rejoicing—bells have associated powers in many cultures. In some their sound is believed to protect the souls of the dying from evil spirits, in others to avert pestilence or even thunderstorms.

Many composers have demanded the sound of bells too large and heavy to be accommodated on the concert platform. In such cases tubular bells, bell plates, or electronic simulation may be substituted. Bells and bell-ringing have often been imitated by composers for symbolic purposes, from Byrd's fantasia for virginals *The Bells* to Ravel's piano piece *La Vallée des cloches*.

See also HANDBELL.

2. (Fr.: *pavillon*; Ger.: *Schalltricht*; It.: *campana*). The distal end of an open-ended wind instrument, especially the flared end of brass instruments and some woodwinds (e.g. the *shawm). The term is also used of the bass extension of many woodwind instruments which do not have a flared bell but may have a globular (*cor anglais) or only slightly out-curved shape (*bassoon). The profile of the bell has a considerable influence on the tone-quality.   JMo

  📖 W. WESTCOTT, *Bells and their Music* (New York, 1970) · P. PRICE, *Bells and Man* (Oxford, 1983) · T. D. ROSSING (ed.), *Acoustics of Bells* (Strondsburg, PA, 1984)

'Bell' Anthem. Purcell's verse anthem *Rejoice in the Lord alway* (*c*.1682–5); its name, which dates from the composer's lifetime, alludes to the pealing scale passages of the instrumental introduction.

Belle Hélène, La ('The Fair Helen'). Opera in three acts by Offenbach to a libretto by Henri Meilhac and Ludovic Halévy after classical mythology (Paris, 1864).

Bellini, Vincenzo (*b* Catania, Sicily, 3 Nov. 1801; *d* Puteaux, nr Paris, 23 Sept. 1835). Italian composer. Born into the profession, he was taught composition by his grandfather; but although he showed precocious talent it was not until 1819 that the city council raised the money to send him to the Naples Conservatory. There he remained for six years, his teachers including Giovanni Furno, Giacomo Tritto, and eventually the director Zingarelli. Among his fellow students was his lifelong friend and biographer Francesco Florimo; both narrowly escaped expulsion for their sympathy with the Carbonari uprising of 1820.

Bellini's chief student compositions were the romanza *Dolente immagine di Fille mia* (his first work to be published), a Mass in A minor, and the Concertino for oboe and strings, in which a genuine melodic talent is discernible. His passing-out piece was *Adelson e Salvini* (Naples, 1825), an *opera semiseria*, which was given in the students' theatre with such success that its author was invited to compose an opera for the Teatro S. Carlo. The heroic opera *Bianca e Fernando* (Naples, 1826)—the second name changed to Gernando out of respect for royalty—repeated the triumph of its predecessor. Much impressed, the impresario Domenico Barbaia engaged Bellini to write an opera for La Scala,

Milan. *Il pirata* (1827), a romantic tragedy, was the first of his many collaborations with the poet Felice Romani, to whose elegant verses and feeling for words Bellini responded immediately. Critics drew attention to the expressiveness of the melodies, the absence of conventional vocal pyrotechnics, and the importance given to the recitatives.

Il pirata was the first opera to carry Bellini's name abroad. Such was his fame that the commission given to Vaccai for an opera with which to open the Teatro Carlo Felice in Genoa was revoked in Bellini's favour. As there was insufficient time to compose a new work he adapted and, with Romani's help, improved *Bianca e Fernando* (Genoa, 1828), which now reverted to its original title. In *La straniera* (Milan, 1829), another romantic tragedy, Bellini carried lyrical plainness to its limit, so giving rise to a controversy in the press for and against this new 'canto declamato'. From then on he admitted more fioritura into his style. *Zaira* (Parma, 1829), based on Voltaire, failed largely because Bellini had aroused local feeling against himself. However, he was able to reclaim much of the music in *I Capuleti e i Montecchi* (Venice, 1830), especially as both operas had a hero *en travesti*.

With *La sonnambula* (Milan, 1831), a sentimental *opera semiseria*, Bellini consolidated his success; however, the tragic *Norma*, produced at La Scala in the same year, is generally accounted his masterpiece, though it failed at its premiere. (Both operas had the great Giuditta Pasta in the title role.) A pause of over a year followed, during which time the composer paid a visit to Naples and Sicily amounting to a triumphal progress. His next assignment, the historical tragedy *Beatrice di Tenda* (Venice, 1833), was delayed by difficulties with Romani which eventually led to a breach between them, each blaming the other for the opera's poor reception.

Bellini took refuge in a visit to London, where he was feted by fashionable society. A performance of *La sonnambula* in English (which he hated) brought to his attention Maria Malibran, whom he recognized as an ideal interpreter of his music. He then travelled to Paris where he was engaged, together with Donizetti, to write for the Théâtre Italien. He chose the romantic historical subject of *I Puritani* (Paris, 1835), with the exiled Count Pepoli as his librettist. Performed with the constellation of Giulia Grisi, Giovanni Battista Rubini, Antonio Tamburini, and Luigi Lablache (later to be known as the 'Puritani quartet') in the principal roles, the opera was an immediate and lasting success, with the advance in thematic cohesion and in richness of harmony and scoring matched by an innovatory design which partly avoids the violent conflicts that usually fuel Italian serious opera. Future plans included a work for the Opéra, a version of *I Puritani* for Naples reworked for Malibran, and more operas with Romani (with whom he was now reconciled). Bellini's death of an intestinal complaint took the musical world completely by surprise.

Although he embodied the Italian operatic tradition at its most restricted, not to say provincial, Bellini made a greater impact outside his country than any of his compatriots, with the possible exception of Rossini. Wagner, Schumann, Berlioz, and Tchaikovsky all paid him tribute; and his influence on Chopin is patent. He was admired not so much for his operas considered in their entirety as for his melodies, to which one might aptly apply Milton's lines 'notes of many a winding bout of linked sweetness long drawn out'. Equally personal is Bellini's use of simple appoggiatura discords on strong beats, which combine with a 'soft' orchestration to give a movingly poignant effect. Together with the tenor Rubini he helped to give a new direction to the bel canto tradition, towards greater naturalism of expression.

With his romantic good looks and ingenuous manner Bellini charmed all who met him, including those whom he disliked. The surviving letters, however, reveal a less sympathetic personality—self-absorbed, envious of possible rivals (especially Pacini and Donizetti), ungallant in his treatment of women—yet a man whose deep loyalty to a few friends, above all Florimo, commands a certain respect.   JB/RP

📖 F. FLORIMO, *Bellini: Memorie e lettere* (Florence, 1882) · L. CAMBI, *Vincenzo Bellini: Epistolario* (Milan, 1943) · F. PASTURA, *Bellini secondo la storia* (Parma, 1959) · L. ORREY, *Bellini* (London, 1969) · H. WEINSTOCK, *Vincenzo Bellini: His Life and Operas* (New York, 1971; London, 1972) · M. R. ADAMO and F. LIPPMANN, *Vincenzo Bellini* (Turin, 1982) · S. MAGUIRE, *Vincenzo Bellini and the Aesthetics of Early Nineteenth-Century Italian Opera* (New York and London, 1989) · J. ROSSELLI, *The Life of Bellini* (Cambridge, 1996)

bell lyra [lyre]. A form of *glockenspiel used for marching. A lyre-shaped metal frame at the top of a pole supports a couple of octaves of steel bars arranged vertically, the lowest at the bottom, like a glockenspiel placed on edge. The pole is carried in a socket like that of a flag-bearer and since one hand is used to hold it upright, there is only one free to play the instrument. Parts therefore need to be simpler than those for the orchestral instrument. The bell lyra was introduced in Germany to replace the *Turkish crescent and retains that instrument's pair of dangling horsehair plumes.
                    JMo

bell plates. Orchestral substitutes for bells, often more satisfactory than *tubular bells.

bell-ringing. See CHANGE-RINGING.

'Bell' Rondo. See CAMPANELLA, LA.

Bells, The. Choral symphony, op. 35 (1913), by Rakhmaninov, for soprano, tenor, and baritone soloists, chorus, and orchestra, a setting of a text by Konstantin Balmont adapted from Edgar Allan Poe's poem.

bell tree. A chromatic set of small cup bells mounted concentrically one above the other on a handle, often played glissando. The 19th-century *Turkish crescent was also sometimes called a bell tree.

belly [sound-table, table]. The upper surface or *soundboard of the body or *resonator of stringed instruments, including keyboards, over which the strings pass. The belly is usually made of a softwood such as spruce.   JMo

Belshazzar. Oratorio (1745) by Handel to a biblical text by Charles Jennens.

Belshazzar's Feast. Cantata by Walton for baritone, chorus, and orchestra, to a text compiled from biblical sources by Osbert Sitwell (Leeds, 1931).

Belyayev [Belaieff], **Mitrofan Petrovich** (*b* St Petersburg, 10/22 Feb. 1836; *d* St Petersburg, 28 Dec. 1903/10 Jan. 1904). Russian music publisher and impresario. Though always a keen amateur musician, it was only in the 1880s that he began to use his riches from the timber industry for the benefit of Russian music. On hearing Glazunov's First Symphony in 1882 he first offered to arrange for its publication but was then fired with the idea of creating his own publishing house. He set up the business in Leipzig in order to secure international copyright, soon attracting a large group of Russian composers which became known as the Belyayev Circle (Belyayevskïy Kruzhok). As well as Glazunov he published works by The Five, Lyadov, Nikolay Tcherepnin, and many others, and later was among the first to promote Skryabin's music. As an impresario and patron he financed the Russian Symphony Concerts (from 1885) and the Russian Quartet Nights (from 1891), and in 1884 established the annual Glinka Award for new Russian music, which continued up to the Revolution.   GN/MF-W

bémol (Fr., 'soft [i.e. rounded] b'; It.: *bemolle*). 1. The flat sign (see FLAT, 1). The term derives from one of the two forms of the letter 'b' used in medieval notation; see DURUM AND MOLLIS.

2. In 17th-century usage, 'minor', e.g. *mi bémol*, E minor.

ben, bene (It.). 'Well', 'much'; e.g. *ben marcato*, 'well marked'; *ben bene*, 'really well'.

Benda. Bohemian family of musicians that flourished in the 18th century. **Franz [František] Benda** (*b* Staré Benátky, *bapt.* 24 Nov. 1709; *d* Nowawes, nr Potsdam, 7 March 1786) was a chorister at St Nicholas, Prague. He went to Vienna in 1786, then to Warsaw in 1729. In 1733 he became a violinist in the orchestra of Crown Prince Frederick (later Frederick the Great), in whose service he remained until his death. He is better known as a performer than a composer; nevertheless his works include 17 symphonies and 17 violin concertos.

His brother **Georg** (Anton) [Jiří Antonín] **Benda** (*b* Staré Benátky, *bapt.* 30 June 1722; *d* Köstritz, 6 Nov. 1795), also a violinist, was best known as a composer. In 1750 he became Kapellmeister to the court at Saxe-Gotha; the success there of his only Italian opera, *Xindo riconosciuto* (1765), led to a period of study in Italy. The arrival in Gotha of the Seyler company resulted in the melodrama *Ariadne auf Naxos*, for the lyrical actress Charlotte Brandes, then *Medea* (both 1775) for the more dramatic Sophie Seyler. These highly effective works, in which spoken dialogue alternates with or is accompanied by music, encouraged many other composers, including Reichardt, Vogler, Danzi, and Winter, to follow Benda's example at a time when the problem of German recitative was greatly exercising musicians. Mozart, influenced by Benda especially in *Zaide*, once intended to be among them. Benda's operas include *Walder* (1776), an effective pastoral *Singspiel* with a serious plot and some through-composed scenes, and a setting of *Romeo und Julie* (1776), which dispenses with many of Shakespeare's characters and concentrates chiefly on the role of Juliet. Benda also wrote much church music. A number of other members of the family became musicians.

DA/JW

Bendl, Karel (*b* Prague, 16 April 1838; *d* Prague, 20 Sept. 1897). Czech composer and conductor. He studied at the Prague Organ School (where his firm friendship with Dvořák began), graduating in 1858. After conducting in Brussels and Amsterdam during 1864 and spending two years (1878–80) in France and Italy as choirmaster for Baron von Dervies, he spent the rest of his working life in Prague. As a conductor he made significant contributions to the Czech music revival, as a deputy in the Prague Provisional Theatre (1874–5) and as musical director of the choral society Hlahol, succeeding Smetana (1865–77). Many of his 300 choruses remain stalwarts of the partsong repertory in the Czech Republic. He later became organist of the church of St Nicholas (1877–8, 1886–90), and in 1894 deputized for Dvořák, teaching composition at the Prague Conservatory.

Bendl composed chiefly vocal music. Besides numerous choruses and songs, and such works as the popular cantata *Švanda dudák* ('Švanda the Bagpiper', 1880; revised as an opera-ballet, 1896), his reputation rests largely on his 12 surviving operas, ten of which were performed during his lifetime. These range widely in style, from grand opera (*Lejla*, 1867, and *Břetislav*, 1870, in which he collaborated with Smetana's librettist, Eliška Krásnohorská) to comedy (*Stary ženich*, 'The Old Bridegroom', 1874, and *Karel Skřeta*, 1883), and verismo in *Máti Míla* ('Mother Míla', 1895). While Bendl's melody reflects Czech folk influences, his style looks more to the early German Romantics, in particular Mendelssohn. His earlier operas were important in conditioning taste among audiences in Prague—*Lejla* was the first opera of the Czech revival to be published in vocal score—and his idiomatic approach to word-setting was influential. JSM

📖 J. TYRRELL, *Czech Opera* (Cambridge, 1988)

Benedicamus Domino (Lat., 'Let us bless the Lord'). A versicle, with the response 'Deo gratias' ('Thanks be to God'), in the liturgy of the Roman rite. It occurs at the end of nearly all medieval *Offices (the exceptions being certain forms of Matins), and replaces the *Ite missa est* in Masses that do not have a Gloria.

—/ALı

Benedicite (Lat., 'Bless [the Lord]'). The song of the three Hebrew children Shadrach, Meshach, and Abednego (Gk. and Lat.: Ananias, Mishael, and Azarias) in the fiery furnace from the Septuagint (Greek) version of Daniel 3. Used in Christian worship from early times, it was part of the medieval Latin rites of Benevento, Gaul, Milan, Spain, and Rome, as well as in Byzantine and Russian liturgical dramas. Today it is one of the canticles appointed for the morning *Offices of the Armenian, Byzantine, Syrian, Ethiopian, Roman, and Anglican traditions.

—/ALı

Benedict, Sir Julius (*b* Stuttgart, 27 Nov. 1804; *d* London, 5 June 1885). German-born British composer and conductor. He studied with Hummel and Weber in Germany before moving to Naples as conductor of the S. Carlo and Fondo theatres. In 1835 he moved to London and soon became musical director at Drury Lane (1838–48) during a fertile period of English Romantic opera. He was also conductor at Her Majesty's Theatre (from 1852), the Norwich Festival (1848–78), and the Liverpool Philharmonic Society (1876–80). In spite of his German roots, Benedict was influenced most in his operas—even those for the English stage—by the Italians. At first unable to rival the popularity of either Balfe or Wallace, he later equalled their success with *The Lily of Killarney* (Covent Garden, 1862), produced by the Pyne–Harrison company. He wrote a number of cantatas for Norwich, including *The Legend of St Cecilia* (1866), and the oratorio *St Peter* for Birmingham (1870). He also produced two piano concertos, overtures, a symphony, and many solo fantasias for piano on operatic themes. He was knighted in 1871 after becoming a naturalized British citizen.   JD1

Benediction [Benediction of the Blessed Sacrament] (from Lat. *benedictio*, 'blessing'). A rite of the Roman Catholic Church in which the Host is presented for veneration in a monstrance, which is then used to bless the congregation. Arising in the later Middle Ages, the rite remained extra-liturgical until it was finally recognized by the Church in 1958. Music for this service includes not only the prescribed chant *Tantum ergo sacramentum* (taken from the Corpus Christi hymn *Pange lingua*), but also settings of many other Latin and vernacular texts.   —/AL1

Benedictus (Lat., 'Blessed'). **1.** 'Benedictus qui venit in nomine Domini' ('Blessed is he that comes in the Name of the Lord'), a paraphrase of Matthew 21: 9 traditionally incorporated into the Sanctus of Christian Eucharistic Prayers. Often set separately by Western composers since the Middle Ages, it was omitted in the 1552 Book of *Common Prayer.

2. The song of Zacharias, 'Benedictus Dominus Deus Israel' ('Blessed is the Lord God of Israel'), Luke 1: 68–79. The canticle of Lauds in most medieval Latin rites, it is sung today at the morning offices of the Anglican, Armenian, Byzantine, and Roman rites, as well as during the Night Office of the Ethiopian Horologion (Book of Hours) of the Copts.   —/AL1

beneplacito, a. See PLACITO.

Benet [Bennet], **John** (*fl* 2nd quarter of the 15th century). English composer. He was a contemporary of Dunstaple and helped define the character of mid-15th-century English church music. He has not been positively identified, but may have been a singing-man or choirmaster working in the City of London. Benet composed masses, mass movements, and motets, and is important as an early innovator in the genre of the *cyclic mass.   JM

Beneventan chant. A repertory of Latin plainchant for the rite celebrated in the Lombard duchy of Benevento between the 7th and 11th centuries. Called 'Ambrosian' chant by its medieval practitioners, Beneventan chant is distantly related to the Milanese repertory of the same name. During the 11th century the liturgy of Benevento was suppressed and replaced by its Roman counterpart. Among the small number of chants to have survived are

propers for Holy Week, notably including *Otin to stauron/O quando in Cruce*, a hymn for Good Friday borrowed from the Byzantine rite, as well as several other bilingual Greek–Latin settings.   AL1

Ben Haim, Paul (*b* Munich, 1 Oct. 1897; *d* Tel Aviv, 14 Jan. 1984). Israeli composer. He studied at the music academy and at the university in Munich (1915–20), then worked as assistant to Bruno Walter and Hans Knappertsbusch at the Munich Staatsoper. His career as a conductor in Germany was cut short by Hitler's rise to power, and in 1933 he emigrated to Palestine. Thereafter he produced a large body of works in all concert genres, including two symphonies, and concertos for violin, cello, and piano. Many of his compositions incorporate themes derived from the folk music of the Holy Land, and his success in achieving a fusion between solid German Romanticism and Middle Eastern modality was emulated by many younger Israeli composers.   PG

Benjamin, Arthur (Leslie) (*b* Sydney, 18 Sept. 1893; *d* London, 10 April 1960). Australian-English composer and pianist. He studied at the RCM with Stanford (1911–14), then served in World War I. After a brief return to Australia as a piano professor at the New South Wales Conservatorium (1919–21) he settled permanently in London. In 1926 he was appointed to the staff of the RCM, where Britten was among his pupils. An able concert pianist, he appeared as soloist in his own Piano Concertino (1926) and in the first performance of Lambert's Piano Concerto (1931). The dry and neo-classical style of his earlier works is well shown in the Violin Concerto (1932) and in two comic operas, *The Devil Take Her* (1931) and *Prima donna* (1933, performed 1949). In later compositions, including the Symphony (1944–5), the *Concerto quasi una fantasia* (1949) for piano and orchestra, and the opera *The Tale of Two Cities* (1949–50; Sadler's Wells, 1957), his stylistic process is more profound. However, he is probably best known for one of his light pieces, *Jamaican Rumba* (1938).   PG/JD1

📖 R. M. SCHAFER, *British Composers in Interview* (London, 1963), 47–52

Benjamin, George (*b* London, 31 Jan. 1960). English composer. He studied in Paris with Messiaen before working at Cambridge with Alexander Goehr and Robin Holloway. His compositions began to be widely known while he was still a student, with the orchestral work *Ringed by the Flat Horizon* played at the Proms in 1980. This was followed rapidly by major works for the Aldeburgh Festival (*A Mind of Winter*, 1981) and the London Sinfonietta (*At First Light*, 1982), which revealed a distinctive idiom not excessively beholden to any of Benjamin's eminent teachers. A period at IRCAM led to *Antara* for 16 players and electronics (1987, revised 1988–9), but Benjamin's continued closeness to the French musical scene, not least as a conductor specializing in such composers as Gérard Grisey and Boulez, has not compromised the independence of his own compositional voice. During the 1990s he completed relatively little, but *Sudden Time* for orchestra (1993), *Three Inventions* for chamber orchestra (1995), and *Palimpsest* (2000), a short orchestral work conducted by Boulez during the celebrations of his 75th birthday, testify to Benjamin's continuing significance.

AW

 📖 R. Nieminen and R. Machart, *George Benjamin* (London, 1997)

Bennet, John (i). See Benet, John.

Bennet, John (ii) (*b* ?1575–80; *d* after 1614). English composer. Virtually nothing is known about his life; some link with the north-west of England is implied by the dedication of his principal publication, *Madrigalls to Foure Voyces* (London, 1599). His best-known madrigal, *All creatures now are merry-minded*, was commissioned by Thomas Morley for his anthology *The Triumphes of Oriana* (1601). A few psalm settings and partsongs by him also survive. JM

Bennett, Sir Richard Rodney (*b* Broadstairs, 29 March 1936). English composer. He studied with Lennox Berkeley and Howard Ferguson at the RAM, and with Boulez in Paris during the late 1950s. Always a prolific composer, he acquired an early reputation through his substantial vocal and instrumental scores, notably operas (for example *The Ledge*, 1961, and *The Mines of Sulphur*, 1963, both given at Sadler's Wells), which made effective use of a progressive, expressionistic style deriving more from Berg than from Boulez. Bennett is also an accomplished jazz pianist, and his facility in this area, as also in the composition of large-scale, often lush film scores (*Far from the Madding Crowd*, *Nicholas and Alexandra*, and a host of others), led him to concentrate increasingly on these more commercial aspects of music-making, without wholly abandoning 'serious' composition. A long-term resident of the USA, he was knighted in 1999. PG/AW

Bennett, William Sterndale. See Sterndale Bennett, William.

Bentzon, Niels Viggo (*b* Copenhagen, 24 Aug. 1919; *d* Frederiksberg, 25 April 2000). Danish composer and pianist. He studied with Knud Jeppesen and others at the Royal Danish Conservatory (1939–43), where from 1950 to 1988 he taught theory and composition. He was also active as a pianist, painter, poet, and critic and

wrote several books. His enormous output, amounting to well over 600 works, shows the steady development of a vigorous, dissonant, diatonic style, influenced by Hindemith, Schoenberg, and Stravinsky. His works consist principally of orchestral and chamber music, much of it for piano, and he also wrote operas and ballets. PG

Benvenuto Cellini. Opera in two acts by Berlioz to a libretto by Léon de Wailly and Auguste Barbier, assisted by Alfred de Vigny, loosely based on Cellini's memoirs (Paris, 1838); Berlioz revised it twice in 1852, the second time into three acts, but withdrew it because of its failure. He used some of the music from it in the overture *Le Carnaval romain*.

bequadro (It., 'square b'). The natural sign (see NATURAL, 2).

Berberian, Cathy [Catherine] (*b* Attleboro, MA, 4 July 1925; *d* Rome, 6 March 1983). American soprano. As well as studying singing with Giorgina del Vigo she learnt mime, Hindu and Spanish dancing, writing, and opera composition, the last at Columbia and New York universities. After her debut in 1957 in Naples she was chosen by Cage and then Berio to perform experimental works demanding extreme tessitura and flamboyant, virtuoso displays. She developed a new vocabulary of declamatory and theatrical sounds and effects in all kinds of register, which she performed in improvisations with brilliant articulation and dramatic physical gestures. This inspired a number of composers to write for her, notably Berio (whom she married), Stravinsky, and Henze. Among her own works was the *Stripsody* soliloquy (1966). She was also a cultivated and dramatic performer of 17th-century opera, notably Monteverdi. JT

berceuse (Fr.; Ger.: *Wiegenlied*, *Schlummerlied*). A lullaby, or cradle-song, usually in 6/8 time with a rocking accompaniment. It was taken over into art music from the folk repertory not only as a song but also as a short instrumental piece, often for piano. Among well-known examples are those by Schumann (in *Kinderszenen*), Grieg (*Lyric Pieces* op. 38), Fauré (*Dolly* suite), Debussy (*Children's Corner*, *Berceuse héroïque*), Chopin (op. 57), and Liszt. Busoni wrote a *Berceuse élégiaque* for orchestra.

Berchem, Jacquet [Giachetto] **de** [Jachet] (*b* Berchem-lez-Anvers, nr Antwerp, *c*.1505; *d* Monópoli, nr Bari, before March 1567). Franco-Flemish composer. He was based in Italy, and is frequently confused with his contemporary Jachet of Mantua. Following a period of residence in Venice in the 1530s, in 1546 he was appointed *maestro di cappella* at nearby Verona Cathedral.

Later he moved south to Monópoli, where in 1553 he married into a local noble family. Berchem is important for his many madrigal settings. These include a cycle called *Capriccio* (published in 1561, but composed earlier), which sets no fewer than 91 stanzas of Ariosto's epic poem *Orlando furioso*.   JM

Berenice (*Berenice, regina d'Egitto*; 'Berenice, Queen of Egypt'). Opera in three acts by Handel to a libretto anonymously adapted from Antonio Salvi's *Berenice, regina d'Egitto* (1709) (London, 1737); the well-known minuet is from the overture.

Berg, Alban (Maria Johannes) (*b* Vienna, 9 Feb. 1885; *d* Vienna, 24 Dec. 1935). Austrian composer. Born into a Viennese bourgeois family, and into an ambience where literature and music were common concerns, he began to compose songs, without instruction, when he was 15. In 1904 one of his older brothers showed some of his efforts to Schoenberg, who thereupon accepted him as a pupil. Poetic settings continued to flow from his pen—the *Seven Early Songs*, collected for publication in 1928, date from 1905–8—but under Schoenberg's guidance he learnt the rigours of sustained instrumental composition. His formal studies with Schoenberg came to an end in 1910, yet for the rest of his life he revered his teacher as a musical father, and dedicated to him four of his small output of 12 major works.

Berg began studying with Schoenberg at a propitious time. Not only did he find a sympathetic companion in Anton Webern, he was also able to witness Schoenberg's development towards atonality. Though Schoenberg did not encourage his pupils to imitate him, it was natural that the young Berg should wish to emulate his master. Thus his op. 1, the single-movement Piano Sonata (1907–8), reflects the crisis of the time, overreaching its tonal foundations in a manner that shows Berg's personal enthusiasms for Mahler and Debussy. It was intended as only a first movement, but Berg took Schoenberg's advice to let it stand alone: it certainly says enough, and probably could not have been continued at a time when the composer's style was developing rapidly. The last of his Four Songs op. 2 (1909–10) is atonal, though with the tonal leanings which were always to remain in his music.

His 'graduation exercise' was the tightly developed and challenging String Quartet (1910), an extreme point in his journey away from tonality in the wake of Schoenberg. This work shows how completely he had attained artistic maturity under Schoenberg, but equally astonishing are his *Altenberglieder* (1912), a set of five songs for soprano and orchestra. Never having written for the orchestra before, and not himself a performer of any great aptitude, he produced a score rich in complex, subtle, and evocative textures that are completely original, going beyond what is borrowed from, again, Mahler and Debussy. In 1913 Schoenberg placed the work on the programme of a concert he was giving in Vienna, but the reaction of the audience to these exquisite but (in textural terms) lavish miniatures brought about the abandonment of the performance. The influence of Mahler, especially his Sixth Symphony, is again prominent in the Three Orchestral Pieces (1914–15), comprising a prelude (in which melodic-harmonic music arises from the noise of percussion and subsides back), a waltz-rondeau, and an immense, fateful march. Berg's use of these archetypes was Mahlerian, and was to continue—notably in his first opera, *Wozzeck*. Mahlerian, too, is the weight of the music and its dramatic force, especially in the finale, which is also remarkable for its dense layerings of contrary voices.

Berg began *Wozzeck* while serving in the Austrian army during World War II, and it is tempting to suppose that his experience as a soldier gave him some clues in composing music for the humble batman anti-hero, the proud drum major, and the neurotically obsessed superior officers of Georg Büchner's fragmentary drama. *Wozzeck*, however, creates its own world of sinister symbols and of sharply defined characters at the mercy of system, fate, and self-delusion. Its two central characters, Wozzeck and his partner Marie, are victims who cannot communicate even with each other, and who are pushed by circumstances to their double tragedy. Marie's murder at Wozzeck's hands is followed by the ripest, grandest music of the score: a tragic interlude in D minor. Wozzeck's suicide leaves their luckless child abandoned on the stage. Completed in 1921, the opera was first staged in Berlin in 1925 and immediately established Berg's reputation. It was soon being performed across the world, and thereby gave him financial security.

His next work was the Chamber Concerto for piano, violin, and 13 wind instruments (1923–5), written for Schoenberg's 50th birthday and designed to celebrate the fellowship of Schoenberg, Berg, and Webern. It is filled with triple ideas: there are three movements and three main motifs (based on translating the composers' names into notes)—the number symbolism extends even to the bar-counts of sections within movements. And yet the work sounds like a free, Romantic outflowing, even when the central Adagio doubles back on its tail halfway through. Such a strictly composed piece might suggest that Berg was ready to adopt the technique of *serialism which Schoenberg had recently elaborated, but in fact his approach to the new method was tentative. He began with an isolated song, *Schliesse mir die Augen beide* (1925), and then, in the *Lyric Suite* for string quartet (1925–6), interleaved serial with non-serial movements. Aptly described by Adorno as a 'latent opera', this work was shown, after the death of Berg's widow in 1976, to have a detailed programme concerning a long-standing love affair the composer had with Hanna Fuchs-Robettin: his initials and hers, AB (A–B♭) and HF (B♮–F), are written into the music.

In 1928 Berg began work on his second opera, *Lulu*, constructing his own libretto from two plays by Frank Wedekind. Progress was twice interrupted, for the sensuous concert aria *Der Wein* (1929), based on Baudelaire's paean to alcohol, and the valedictory Violin Concerto (1935), in which Berg turned to consider the death of Manon Gropius, the teenage daughter of Mahler's widow by her second husband: the score is dedicated 'in memory of an angel' and portrays Manon's fragility and grace—the fragility and grace, perhaps, of all human life—in its four linked sections, of which the last finds a measure of appeasement in quoting a Bach chorale. Here again, as in the *Lyric Suite*, serialism is combined with tonality, strict abstract form with programme music.

Berg died before the first performance of the concerto, leaving the final act of *Lulu* unfinished (it was completed by Friedrich Cerha for the first performance of the whole opera in 1979). *Lulu* is about the classic operatic subjects—love, death, and sexual power—treated in a manner that is typically at once sumptuous and sardonic. The central character is a force of nature, whose chief features are a violent attractiveness to men and an equally violent independence. Through the first half of the work she rises through society; then, with numerous correspondences in the dramatic and musical substance, she falls, to reach her nadir as a prostitute, murdered at the hands of Jack the Ripper. As in *Wozzeck*, the death of the main female character brings forth the most glorious music. But if magnificent valediction was one of Berg's strongest suits, his work also shows an extraordinary ability to integrate the most diverse moods, styles, and techniques in portraits of early modern life.   PG

> 📖 H. REDLICH, *Alban Berg* (London, 1957) · W. REICH, *Alban Berg* (London, 1965) · H. BERG (ed.), *Alban Berg: Letters to his Wife* (London, 1971) · M. CARNER, *Alban Berg* (London, 1975) · G. PERLE, *The Operas of Alban Berg* (London, 1980–5) · A. POPLE (ed.), *The Cambridge Companion to Berg* (Cambridge, 1997)

bergamasca (It.; Fr.: *bergamasque*). A term originally used to describe peasant dances and songs from the district around Bergamo in northern Italy. Early examples date from the mid-16th century. In the late 16th century the dance had a fixed harmonic scheme for the accompanying guitar: I–IV–V–I. Many 17th-century guitar pieces were written on this pattern.

Bergamo is also associated with the *commedia dell'arte*, and any age that has seen a resurgence of interest in the Harlequin figure has seen a crop of instrumental pieces bearing the title 'bergamasca'. This is particularly evident in France in the 18th and late 19th centuries. Paul Verlaine's famous lines in *Clair de lune*:

> que vont charmant masques et bergamasques
> Jouant de luth et dansant et quasi
> Tristes sous leurs déguisements fantasques

inspired an orchestral suite, *Masques et bergamasques*, by Fauré, and a *Suite bergamasque* for piano by Debussy.

Berger, Arthur (Victor) (*b* New York, 15 May 1912). American composer and critic. He studied with Walter Piston at Harvard and with Milhaud at Mills College. After some years as a critic, notably under Virgil Thomson on the *New York Herald Tribune*, he began teaching at Brandeis University. In 1957 he adopted serialism, but without essential change to his spare, motivically based style, to his careful productivity or to his preference for small-scale instrumental media.
                                                                   PG

bergerette (Fr., 'shepherd maid'). 1. In the 15th century, a French poetic and musical form, identical in structure with the *virelai, but with only one stanza.

2. A title occasionally used for 16th-century instrumental dances in quick triple time, similar to the *saltarello.

3. An 18th-century *air*, setting pastoral or amorous verse, very similar to the *brunette.

Bergman, Erik (Valdemar) (*b* Nykarleby, 24 Nov. 1911). Finnish composer, conductor, critic, and teacher. He studied composition with Erik Furuhjelm in Helsinki, graduating in 1938, then with Heinz Tiessen in Berlin and Wladimir Vogel in Switzerland. Back in Helsinki, he became a choral conductor (from 1943) and critic (from 1945), and was later (1963–76) professor of composition at the Sibelius Academy. Throughout the second half of the 20th century Bergman was Finland's leading modernist composer, his music embracing serial technique and showing an acute awareness of colour and timbre. His substantial worklist includes an opera, *Det sjungande tardet* ('The Singing Tree'; Helsinki, 1995), written in his late 70s, orchestral scores, concertos (including for piano and violin), many chamber works, often for unusual combinations of colour, and an enormous quantity of vocal music.   MA

Berio, Luciano (*b* Oneglia, 24 Oct. 1925). Italian composer. Born into a family of composers, he had his first lessons from his father, then went to the Milan Music Academy, where his teachers were Giorgio

Ghedini and Giulio Paribeni. In 1951, after leaving the academy, he studied serial methods with Luigi Dallapiccola at Tanglewood. The Stravinsky-like neo-classicism of his early works, for instance the *Magnificat* for two sopranos, choir, and instruments (1949), was now replaced by a graceful serial manner, well shown in *Chamber Music* for soprano and instrumental trio (1952). The further development of his style was influenced by his contacts with Stockhausen, Boulez, and others. In the orchestral *Allelujah II* (1956–8), for example, he offered a response to Stockhausen's *Gruppen*, and in *Tempi concertati* for four solo instruments and ensemble (1958–9) he made a further contribution to the music of complex, superposed serial structures.

All Berio's works of the 1950s, however, show two individual characteristics which have remained prominent: a liking for supple, almost physical gestures and a view of music informed by contemporary linguistic studies. The former is well demonstrated in his *Sequenza* series for solo instruments, which includes a virtuoso aria for flute (*Sequenza I*, 1958), a comic study for trombone (*Sequenza V*, 1966), an obsessive oboe piece (*Sequenza VII*, 1969), and a 20-minute stretch of continuous bassoon sound achieved by circular breathing (*Sequenza XII*, 1994). Some of these have, in a typical manner, spawned larger works: *Sequenza VI* for viola (1967), for instance, is enveloped by music for nine instruments in *Chemins II* (1967) and for large orchestra in *Chemins III* (1968), while *Sequenza X* for trumpet (1984) gave rise to *Kol-Od* for trumpet and ensemble (1996).

Berio's merging of music into language is naturally most evident in his vocal works, where he creates a fluid reciprocity between verbal sound and instrumental sound, linguistic sense and musical meaning. Notable examples include *Circles* for soprano, harp, and two percussionists (1960), *Epifanie* for soprano and orchestra (1959–61), *Laborintus II* for voices, instruments, and tape (1965), *Sinfonia* for eight voices and orchestra (1968–9), *Coro* for chorus and orchestra (1974–6), and *Ofanim* for solo singer, children's voices, instruments, and electronics (1988–97). The central movement of the *Sinfonia*, which weaves a tapestry of textual and musical quotations around the scherzo from Mahler's Second Symphony, is only an extreme example of widely allusive, dreamlike streams to be found in much of Berio's music with voices; and such purely orchestral works as *Formazioni* (1985–7) are almost comparable in their fluidity, expressive warmth, and richness of reference. While embracing all the innovations of the 1950s, he has consistently refused to lose contact with the traditions and challenges of earlier music, even if that contact has to be maintained across a distance.

All Berio's concerns meet in opera, and though his approach to the genre was cautious—by way of the eponymously titled *Opera* (1967–70, rev. 1977) and various smaller theatre pieces—his later output revolves round four full-length operas: *La vera storia* (1982), *Un re in ascolto* (1984), *Outis* (1996), and *Cronaca del luogo* (1999). In none of these works is there a conventional story. Instead Berio prefers his drama, like his music, to be polyphonic, allusive, ambiguous, and even self-contradictory. *La vera storia*, for example, begins as a dismantling of elements in the story of *Il trovatore*, elements which it then reassembles, and *Outis* takes the figure of Ulysses on new journeys, reaching forward to the 20th century. Berio has composed electronic works, arrangements of folksongs, and versions of music by composers from Monteverdi to Lennon and McCartney by way of Schubert, Verdi, Brahms, Mahler, and Falla, as well as a few rare examples of avant-garde light music, for instance *Opus Number Zoo* for wind quintet (1950–1), in which he openly displays the good humour that is often below the surface of his more serious works.   PG

📖 D. OSMOND-SMITH, *Berio* (Oxford, 1991)

Bériot, Charles-Auguste de (*b* Leuven, 20 Feb. 1802; *d* Brussels, 8 April 1870). Belgian violinist and composer. A pupil of Pierre Baillot, he toured Europe from 1829, at first with the singer Maria Malibran, whom he married in 1836. He directed the violin faculty of the Brussels Conservatory from 1843, but later became blind. His technique combined brilliant virtuosity with the classical Parisian style established by Viotti to create a new, Romantic Franco-Belgian school. Among his compositions are ten violin concertos and many *Duos brillants* for violin and piano, while his methods as a teacher are documented in several instruction books.

IR

Berkeley, Sir **Lennox** (Randall Francis) (*b* Oxford, 12 May 1903; *d* London, 26 Dec. 1989). He studied at Oxford, then with Nadia Boulanger in Paris (1927–33). This experience gave him a facility for writing music of melodic elegance, clear texture, and rhythmic wit, often with suggestions of the neo-classical Stravinsky or Poulenc; the style is well shown in the Serenade for strings (1939) and the First Symphony (1940).

After World War II, during which Berkeley worked for the BBC, his music began to develop, sometimes gaining a darker and more enigmatic character, while retaining the conciseness and control of earlier works. This new depth of feeling is apparent in the *Four Poems of St Teresa* for contralto and strings (1947), one of several works expressing Berkeley's Roman Catholic faith. By contrast with the First Symphony, the Second

(1954–8), and still more the single-movement Third (1969), show an urgency in the musical development. Berkeley nevertheless continued to write music of a charming, ingratiating kind, ranging from divertimento-like chamber and instrumental pieces to a comedy of manners, *A Dinner Engagement* (Aldeburgh, 1954), the first of three one-act operas. His more substantial three-act opera *Nelson* (Sadler's Wells, 1954) was less successful. Berkeley taught composition at the RAM (1946–68) and was knighted in 1974.

PG/AW

   📖 P. DICKINSON, *The Music of Lennox Berkeley* (London, 1988)

Berkeley, Michael (Fitzhardinge) (*b* London, 29 May 1948). English composer. The son of Lennox Berkeley, he studied with his father and Richard Rodney Bennett. He played in rock groups and worked in broadcasting while establishing an early reputation as an effective composer in a relatively conservative style. Berkeley's *Fantasia concertante* for small orchestra (1978) and Chamber Symphony (1980) gave evidence of richer and more progressive musical thinking, and his ability to explore important topics on a large canvas with no loss of dramatic intensity has been especially striking in *Or Shall We Die?*, an oratorio with an explicit anti-war message on a text by Ian McEwan (1983), and the operas *Baa Baa Black Sheep* (Cheltenham, 1993) and *Jane Eyre* (Cheltenham, 2000).   AW

Berlin, Irving [Baline, Israel] (*b* Mogilev, Belorussia, 29 April/11 May 1888; *d* New York, 22 Sept. 1989). Russian-born American songwriter. His family emigrated to the USA when he was four. At 16 he became a singing waiter and began writing songs, among them *Alexander's Ragtime Band* and *Everybody's Doing It* (both 1911). He showed his true capacity as a songwriter in the musical comedies *Annie Get your Gun* (1946) and *Call me Madam* (1950) and the films *Top Hat* (1935), *Follow the Fleet* (1936), and *Carefree* (1938). His most enduring hit is 'White Christmas', from the film *Holiday Inn* (1942).   PGA/ALA

Berlioz, Hector (*see page 130*)

Bernac [Bertin]**, Pierre** (*b* Paris, 12 Jan. 1899; *d* Villeneuve-les-Avignon, 17 Oct. 1979). French baritone. He gave his first recital in 1925, making a strong impression with his vocal refinement, sensitive phrasing, and imaginative projection of the words. From the mid-1930s he was a leading interpreter of French song. He began a close partnership with Poulenc, who wrote many works for him, and from the early 1940s his light, high baritone inspired works by a number of composers including Jolivet, Sauguet, Françaix, Hindemith,

Berkeley, and Barber. He became a world authority on the teaching of French *mélodie* and in 1970 published *The Interpretation of French Song*.   JT

   📖 M. CHIMÈNES, *Pierre Bernac* (Paris and London, 1999)

Bernacchi, Antonio Maria (*b* Bologna, 23 June 1685; *d* Bologna, 13 March 1756). Italian alto castrato. He studied with Francesco Pistocchi and Giovanni Ricieri in Bologna and in 1703 made his opera debut at Genoa, showing prodigious technical talent and command in florid writing. He became greatly in demand in Italy, Germany (singing in Munich, 1720–7), and England, where Handel engaged him for the 1729–30 season. He sang in the premieres of Handel's *Lotario* and *Partenope*. As a teacher he exerted a great influence; in 1736 he founded a celebrated singing school in Bologna.   JT

Bernardi, Stefano (*b* Verona, *c*.1585; *d* ?Salzburg, 1636). Italian composer and theorist. He was a priest and eventually *maestro di cappella* at Verona Cathedral from 1611 to 1622. In 1624 he moved to Salzburg, where he was responsible for the music (his own contribution, a *Te Deum* for 12 choirs, is now lost) at the celebrated and magnificent consecration of the new cathedral in 1628. He wrote madrigals in the older polyphonic style as well as some with continuo parts, and his church music includes masses in a style based on that of Palestrina alongside others in the more modern concertato manner.   DA

Bernart de Ventadorn (*b* Ventadorn, nr Limoges, ?*c*.1130–40; *d* Dalon, Périgueux, *c*.1190–1200). Troubadour poet and composer. In spite of his humble birth—his father is thought to have been a baker at Ventadorn castle—Bernart became one of the most famous of the troubadours. He worked first at the court of Eleanor of Aquitaine, whose marriage to Henry Plantagenet took him on a short visit to England some time after 1150, and later in the service of Raymond V, Count of Toulouse. His last years may have been spent in a monastery in Périgueux. Of more than 40 poems thought to be by him, 18—an unusually large number for the period—survive with their melodies intact. This is partly due to the popularity and wide circulation of his songs in the north of France, where they appear to have influenced the developing art of the trouvères.

JM

Berners, (Gerald Hugh Tyrwhitt-Wilson, Baronet) **Lord** (*b* Apley Park, Bridgnorth, 18 Sept. 1883; *d* Faringdon, 19 April 1950). English composer. Educated at Eton, he was largely self-taught as a musician. He was encouraged by Stravinsky and Casella, and was friendly with Walton and Lambert. His neo-classical, anti-German,

(*cont. on p. 132*)

Hector Berlioz
(1803–69)

The French composer Louis-Hector Berlioz was born in La Côte-St-André, Isère, on 11 December 1803 and died in Paris on 8 March 1869.

The early years

Berlioz's father was a doctor and a prominent citizen of La Côte-St-André. The young Hector was taught the flute and guitar and was beginning to compose by the age of 14. Even as a child his mind responded vividly to Romantic literature, both French and Latin, and he felt the impulse always to express that response in musical form. At the age of 17 he went to Paris to pursue a medical career, remaining there for the rest of his life.

In Paris his encounter with music, especially opera, weakened his already slight interest in medicine and he soon abandoned those studies in favour of a career as a composer, taking lessons with Le Sueur and later attending the Conservatoire (1826–30). He became an habitué of the Opéra and a profound admirer of the French tradition, especially Gluck and Spontini. In the face of parental displeasure he earned his living at first by singing in a theatre chorus and by giving guitar lessons, though later he became best known as a critic and a conductor. The occupation of journalism sustained him throughout his working life, and though he declared a profound distaste for it, he was one of the most perceptive and vital writers of his time.

Several strong passions determined the development of Berlioz's music. After Gluck he discovered Weber and later Beethoven; he greatly disliked Rossini and Italian music. In 1827 he was introduced to Shakespeare's plays, followed soon after by Goethe's *Faust*. Other favourite writers, admired also by the leading figures of French Romanticism, were Chateaubriand, Thomas Moore, Byron, Scott, Fenimore Cooper, and E. T. A. Hoffmann, as well as the younger French writers themselves—Victor Hugo, Alfred de Vigny, Auguste Barbier, and others.

Berlioz's first substantial composition was a Mass (1824), which he later disowned. It was rediscovered in Belgium in 1992 and found to foreshadow a number of passages in his mature works. The Mass was followed by an opera, *Les Francs-juges* (1826), which is mostly lost. From 1826 to 1830 he competed annually for the *Prix de Rome, but won it only on his fifth attempt. An overpowering passion for the Irish Shakespearean actress Harriet Smithson, whom he first saw in 1827, led to the composition in 1830 of the *Symphonie fantastique*, his first masterpiece, a five-movement programme symphony in which the tale of unrequited love is recounted.

After the Prix de Rome

The Prix de Rome gave Berlioz a scholarship for five years, the first two of which were spent away from Paris, mostly in Rome. He returned in 1832 with *Lélio*, a sequel to the *Symphonie fantastique*, which includes parts for solo singers, a chorus, and an actor. He was introduced to Harriet Smithson, declared his love, and married her in 1833, settling down to nine years of unremitting labour as composer, critic, and conductor. A series of works came in close succession: *Harold en Italie*, a symphony with viola solo, in 1834; the opera *Benvenuto Cellini* in 1836, played at the Opéra in 1838 and rudely rejected by the Parisian public; the Requiem (*Grande Messe des morts*) in 1837; *Roméo et Juliette*, a large choral symphony, in 1839; the *Grande symphonie funèbre et triomphale*, for military band, in 1840; the song cycle *Les Nuits d'été* in 1841. He also wrote many smaller songs and choruses in this period and gave several concerts every season. He received two government commissions but secured no permanent position in Paris.

In 1842 Berlioz began a series of concert tours to Belgium, Germany, and Austria, and for the next 20 years was frequently abroad, travelling many times to Germany, five times to London, and twice to Russia. *La Damnation de Faust* was composed during one such tour in 1845–6. The gradual failure of his marriage and the awareness of more appreciative audiences abroad kept him almost constantly on the move. He became disillusioned and embittered about Paris, especially after the failure of *La Damnation de Faust*, and he watched with sadness the general decline in taste and artistic fervour in the later part of his life. He became gradually less and less inclined to undertake new compositions.

The *Te Deum* was composed in 1849 and a brief choral work, *La Fuite en Égypte* ('The Flight into Egypt'), in 1850. Thereafter Berlioz wrote no music for three years and was persuaded only with difficulty to enlarge this work into the choral trilogy *L'Enfance du Christ*, whose great and unexpected success in 1854 in part encouraged him to embark on the largest and grandest work of his whole output, *Les Troyens*, a five-act opera based on Virgil. He had contemplated this ambitious project for many years and finally set it down from 1856 to 1858. He never succeeded in getting it performed complete, a truncated version of the last three acts being staged in Paris only in 1863. A comic opera, *Béatrice et Bénédict*, based on Shakespeare's *Much Ado about Nothing*, was staged at Baden-Baden in 1862.

The last dozen years of Berlioz's life were chronically affected by Crohn's disease, and after 1863 he sank into a deepening despair, especially after the death of his only son, Louis, in 1867. He died in 1869. His *Memoirs*, compiled over a long period, were published in 1870.

Berlioz's music and aesthetic views

Berlioz was no pianist and he wrote no solo music for the instrument; nor is there any chamber music. His works use voices and instruments in many combinations and in many genres. He made a special study of orchestral technique and instrumentation and published a treatise on the subject, the *Grand traité d'instrumentation et d'orchestration modernes* (Paris, 1843; Eng. trans. 1855). He also wrote a handbook on conducting, *Le Chef d'orchestre*, in 1855 (Paris, 1856; Eng. trans. 1917). His orchestral style is distinctive and brilliant, and it greatly influenced future developments through Liszt, Wagner, and the Russians. Liszt was for a long period one of his closest friends; he never established the same rapport with Wagner, although their encounters were usually fraternal and friendly.

Berlioz wrote many songs with piano accompaniment, and the better ones, such as *La Captive* (1832) and *Les Nuits d'été* (1840–1), were later orchestrated. None of his music is abstract or purely formal; each work has a poetic or evocative title, or a sung text or a programme, and this literary or pictorial content determines its style, its instrumentation, its mood, and its form. His pieces thus often fall between established genres, such as concerto and symphony, or opera and cantata, or scena and song. Much of it relates to his favourite literature or to personal experience: the *Symphonie fantastique* and *Lélio* sprang from two love affairs; Shakespeare inspired the *Tempest* overture in 1830, the *King Lear* overture in 1831, a group of Hamlet pieces in 1844, *Roméo et Juliette* in 1839, and *Béatrice et Bénédict* in

1862; Goethe's *Faust* generated the *Huit scènes de Faust* in 1829 and its fuller working as *La Damnation de Faust* in 1846; from Scott came the overtures *Waverley* (1827) and *Rob Roy* (1831); Byron and his own travels inspired *Harold en Italie* (1834).

The *Grande symphonie funèbre et triomphale* is a ceremonial work for military band, deriving in style from the stirring outdoor music of the French Revolution. The *Grande Messe des morts* is related to the same tradition, with its four groups of brass added to the huge orchestral and choral forces. Berlioz called the *Te Deum* the 'brother' of the Requiem, it being also conceived for large forces, including a chorus of 600 children, in a large building. He always insisted on the proper relationship of music to its spatial surroundings, hating noisy music in small theatres but exploiting the extraordinary effects of well-distributed masses in great architectural spaces.

L'Enfance du Christ is a different kind of sacred work, being intimate in scale and devotional in style, though Berlioz was not himself an orthodox believer. Its hints of operatic stage action are found similarly in *La Damnation de Faust*, a dramatic concert work with many suggestions of movement and action but none the less conceived for the theatre of the imagination.

Berlioz always liked to amplify the seen with the unseen. Thus the nightmarish devilry of the *Symphonie fantastique* is purely to be imagined, not seen; so too are the will-o'-the-wisps and the inhabitants of pandemonium in *La Damnation de Faust*. In his operas there are many offstage scenes. In *Roméo et Juliette* the love scene is evoked by the orchestra alone: we are left to imagine the lovers' exchange of words. This dependence on the imagination must be coupled with his intrinsic faith in expression as the cornerstone of his aesthetic outlook. He held firm to his belief in the capacity of music to embody images, ideas, and feelings, ranging from the literalness of programme music to the less easily defined area where the music reflects its text or subject with as much veracity as possible. The composer's personal identification with a subject and his integrity in presenting it in musical form were paramount.

These ideas were shared by many Romantic artists, and in his early works Berlioz seems to conform to the popular image of the inspired creative artist, cutting new paths and discarding outworn forms. But after the innovations of his first works, revolutionary though they were, he preferred to consolidate his style and technique and he returned more and more to the outlook and classical serenity of Gluck. *Les Troyens* can be described as a deeply Classical work imbued throughout with Romantic passion. Although Berlioz admired such contemporary composers as Liszt and Mendelssohn, he took little interest in imitating their music and remained stylistically aloof and independent. He thus had relatively few direct imitators and no pupils. His music was always strikingly individual and cannot be simply categorized.

Berlioz's views on all aspects of music were repeatedly and cogently expressed in his feuilletons for the daily and weekly press, so the misunderstanding from which he suffered in his lifetime and for many years thereafter is hard to comprehend. He published three collections of articles which reveal his reverent attitude to the composers he most admired (Gluck, Spontini, Beethoven), his scorn for the pettiness of Parisian music, his longing for a society where the arts might be fostered free of commercialization and self-interest, and his mordant sense of humour. His profound passion for great art, his belief in its exclusive nature, and the powerful sense of commitment against no matter what odds are striking aspects of his personal credo.

HMacD

📖 J. Barzun, *Berlioz and the Romantic Century* (Boston, MA, 1950, 2/1969) · D. Cairns (trans.), *The Memoirs of Hector Berlioz* (London, 1969, 2/1970) · B. Primmer, *The Berlioz Style* (London, 1973) · H. Macdonald, *Berlioz* (London, 1982) · D. K. Holoman, *Berlioz* (Cambridge, MA, and London, 1989) · D. Cairns, *Berlioz*, 2 vols. (London, 1989–99) · P. Bloom, *The Life of Berlioz* (Cambridge, 1998)

anti-Romantic inclinations produced the *Valses bourgeoises* for piano duet (1919), the parodistic *Trois petites marches funèbres* (for a statesman, a canary, and a rich aunt) of 1920 for piano solo, and numerous satirical songs. His later works include a one-act opera *Le Carosse du Saint Sacrement* (Paris, 1924), five ballet scores including *The Triumph of Neptune*, staged by Diaghilev in 1926, and *A Wedding Bouquet* (1936), commissioned by Lambert for Sadler's Wells with a nonsense text by Gertrude Stein and decor by Berners himself. He also produced film scores for *Halfway House*, *Champagne Charlie* (both 1944), and *Nicholas Nickleby* (1947). Besides composing he painted (exhibiting his work at the Lefèvre Gallery in London), wrote novels, and produced an autobiography in two volumes, *First Childhood* (1934) and *A Distant Prospect* (1954).

PG/JDi

📖 M. Amory, *Lord Berners: The Last Eccentric* (London, 1998)

Bernhard, Christoph (*b* Kolberg, Pomerania [now Kolobrzeg, Poland], 1 Jan. 1628; *d* Dresden, 14 Nov. 1692). German composer and theorist. In 1649 he became a singer in the court chapel of Dresden under Schütz. Although disappointed at his lack of promotion, because of a strong prejudice in favour of Italians, he stayed in Dresden for most of his life, eventually (when the Italian vogue had passed) becoming Kapellmeister. Schütz asked that Bernhard should compose a funeral motet for him, and this was performed at the ceremony in 1672. Bernhard is most important for his musical treatises, and especially for his classification of the styles of Baroque music according to purpose—church (*stylus gravis*, the 'Palestrina style'), chamber (*stylus luxurians communis*, naming Monteverdi as the founder), and theatre (*stylus luxurians theatralis*, where language is master of the music).

DA

Bernier, Nicolas (*b* Mantes-la-Jolie, 5 or 6 June 1665; *d* Paris, 6 July 1734). French composer. He was a boy chorister in the collegiate church of his native town. After studies in Rome, possibly with Caldara, he settled in Paris in 1692, becoming a celebrated harpsichord teacher. From 1694 to 1698 he was *maître de chapelle* at Chartres Cathedral, returning to Paris as director of music at St Germain-l'Auxerrois. He later succeeded Charpentier as director of music at the Sainte Chapelle (1704) and Lalande as *sous-maître* of the royal chapel (1723).

In addition to sacred compositions, Bernier published secular cantatas (he was among the first in France to do so); four of eight books appeared in 1703 along with his first collection of *petits motets*. He contributed a divertissement to the Duchess of Maine's celebrated Grandes Nuits de Sceaux (1715) and published a treatise on counterpoint, *Principes de composition* (n.d.). Louis-Claude Daquin was among his pupils.

WT/JAS

Bernstein, Leonard (*b* Lawrence, MA, 25 Aug. 1918; *d* New York, 14 Oct. 1990). American composer and conductor. He studied with Walter Piston and Edward Burlingame Hill at Harvard University (1935–9) and with Fritz Reiner (conducting), Randall Thompson (orchestration), and Isabelle Vengerova (piano) at the Curtis Institute, Philadelphia (1939–41). He also studied conducting under Koussevitzky at the Tanglewood summer schools (1940–3). In 1943 he made a highly successful debut, substituting for Bruno Walter at a New York Philharmonic concert; this launched him on his international career as a conductor and eventually led to his appointment as music director of the orchestra (1958–68). He also taught at Tanglewood (1948–55), Brandeis University (1951–5), and the Massachusetts Institute of Technology.

While pursuing an active career as a conductor and lecturer Bernstein enjoyed success as a composer for both Broadway and the serious concert platform. With *West Side Story* (1957) he scored one of the greatest hits of the postwar American musical stage, and his three symphonies (no. 1 'Jeremiah', 1941–4; no. 2 'Age of Anxiety' with solo piano, 1947–9; no. 3 'Kaddish' with soloists and choirs, 1961–3) won admiration for their bold confrontation of contemporary moral and religious issues. His multifarious output also included a jazz-style ballet (*Fancy Free*, 1944), a theatrical presentation of the liturgy for faithless times (*Mass*, 1971), a contrastingly confident set of psalm settings (*Chichester Psalms*, 1965), a high-spirited operetta (*Candide*, 1956), and a satirical opera to his own libretto (*Trouble in Tahiti*, Waltham, MA, 1952).

Though eclectic in style and varied in genre, Bernstein's works are united by his wholehearted involvement and by his deep American roots. Like that of Copland, his music draws on Stravinsky and on traditional and popular sources, especially the song styles of American musicals, while his attempts to deal with 20th-century angst sometimes led him close also to Mahler, Berg, or Shostakovich.   PG

📖 L. BERNSTEIN, *The Joy of Music* (New York, 1959); *The Infinite Variety of Music* (New York, 1969); *The Unanswered Question* (Cambridge, MA, 1981) · M. SECREST, *Leonard Bernstein: A Life* (New York, 1995).

Berti, Giovanni Pietro (*d* Venice, 1638). Italian singer and organist. He served in both capacities at St Mark's, Venice. His two volumes of pleasing *Cantade et arie* were published in Venice in the 1620s. He was one of the first composers to use the term 'cantata' for extended songs using the principle of *strophic variation, and some of these pieces show the beginnings of a clear division into recitative and aria.   DA

Bertin, Louise(-Angélique) (*b* Bièvres, 15 Jan. 1805; *d* Paris, 26 April 1877). French composer. She studied with Reicha and Fétis, and became an original composer whose operas show harmonic and orchestral daring and dramatic intensity. She suffered from discrimination for being female, from partial paralysis, and from the political unpopularity of her family. She published a few songs and composed instrumental music and cantatas. Her last two operas, though neither was successful, are substantial documents of French Romantic music. *Fausto* (Paris, Théâtre Italien, 1831), to an Italian libretto, was the first French opera on this theme; *Esmeralda* (Paris Opéra, 1836), to a problematic libretto by Victor Hugo himself, concentrates on elaborate concerted numbers at the expense of solo music.   JR

Berton, Henri-Montan (*b* Paris, 17 Sept. 1767; *d* Paris, 22 April 1844). French composer. He was a professor at the Paris Conservatoire and was also appointed musical director at the Théâtre de l'Impératrice (Opera Buffa) and chorus master at the Opéra. Known principally as an opera composer, he had a facility for ensemble writing and for Italianate melodies. His anti-clerical *Les Rigueurs du cloître* (1790) was an early example of a *rescue opera, and *Aline, reine de Golconde* (1803) achieved great international success. In later works Berton collaborated with Boieldieu, Cherubini, and Kreutzer.   SH

Bertoni, Ferdinando (Gasparo) (*b* Salò, 15 Aug. 1725; *d* Desenzano del Garda, 1 Dec. 1813). Italian composer. He wrote mainly operas and sacred music, and may have been the first to introduce the *cavatina to opera. He spent much of his working life in Venice, composing many cantatas and serenatas for state occasions; he also wrote some instrumental music. He travelled twice to London, where he worked at the King's Theatre (1778–80 and 1781–3). In 1785 he was appointed *maestro di cappella* at St Mark's, Venice; he retired in 1808.   LC

Bertrand, Antoine de (*b* Fontanges, Auvergne, 1530–40; *d* Toulouse, *c*.1581). French composer. He was a member of a group of humanists in Toulouse around 1560. His 84 chansons, many to poems by Ronsard, show Italian influence, being written in an almost madrigalian style and using chromaticism in the manner of Cipriano de Rore and Nicola Vicentino. Some of the effects are extraordinary, as is his use of microtones.   DA

beruhigend (Ger.). 'Becoming calmer'.

Berwald, Franz (Adolf) (*b* Stockholm, 23 July 1796; *d* Stockholm, 3 April 1868). Swedish composer. He was the most original Scandinavian symphonist before Sibelius. His career encompassed those of Chopin, Schumann, Mendelssohn, and, save for one year, Berlioz. The family was of German stock, and the name is possibly derived from Bärwalde in north Germany. In 1772 Berwald's father settled in Stockholm, where he joined the orchestra of the Royal Opera. In his youth Berwald also served the Royal Opera, as a violinist and viola player, but his gifts were many-faceted and he possessed a fertile and resourceful intelligence. His early works, including a Septet, a Violin Concerto, and two string quartets made little impression in his native Sweden.

In 1829 he went to Berlin in the hope of furthering his musical career but met with little success. He spent many vital years on non-musical projects, founding a successful orthopaedic enterprise in Berlin (1835–41) based on the most highly developed techniques. In 1841 he moved to Vienna where success, albeit short-lived, released a burst of creative energy: all four symphonies come from the same productive years (1842–5). By the 1850s Berwald had given up hope of advancement in the Swedish musical establishment. He had been passed over for two posts to which he felt his talents entitled him and he turned to other non-musical activities, this time in the north of Sweden as manager of a sawmill and a glass works. The late 1840s and the 1850s saw the composition of much of his chamber music: two string quartets (1849), two piano quintets (1853, 1857), five piano trios, and a piano concerto (1855). Only late in life did he gain acceptance: his opera *Estrella di Soria* was successfully mounted by the Royal Opera in 1862, and he was elected professor of composition at the Swedish Royal Academy of Music a year before his death.

Only one of Berwald's mature symphonies, the *Sinfonie sérieuse* (1842), was performed in his lifetime; his masterpiece, the *Sinfonie singulière* (1845), had to wait 60 years for its premiere. The *Sinfonie capricieuse* was the last to reach the public: a performing edition prepared by Ernst Ellberg was given in Stockholm in 1914 under Sibelius's brother-in-law, Armas Järnefelt. An early Symphony in A (1820), which survives only in fragmentary form (recently completed by Duncan Druce), shows his Beethovenian sympathies; but in his music what seem at first to be resonances of earlier composers are often prophecies of later masters. Much of it, however, such as the opening of the *Sinfonie singulière*, is quite unlike all other music of its time—or indeed of any time. In the *Singulière* he enfolds the scherzo into the body of the slow movement, a formal experiment that he first tried in the Septet (1828) and developed still further in the E♭ String Quartet (1849), in which both the slow movement and the scherzo are embedded in the body of the first movement. There is a freshness of vision and an expressive vitality in all four symphonies and in the tone-poems, such as *Elfenlek* ('Play of the Elves', 1841) and *Wettlauf* ('Racing', 1842), that betoken a fresh and novel sensibility and earn him a special place in 19th-century music.   RLa

📖 R. Layton, *Berwald: A Critical Study* (London, 1959) · I. Bengtsson and E. Lömnäs (eds.), *Franz Berwald: Die Dokumente seines Lebens* (Stockholm, 1970; in Swed. and Ger.)

Bes (Ger.). B♭♭.

Besard, Jean-Baptiste (*b* Besançon, *c*.1567; *d* after 1616). Burgundian lutenist and composer. The son of a merchant, he graduated from Dôle University in 1587 and went to study the lute with Lorenzini in Rome. From there he wandered round Europe, visiting, and possibly settling in, Augsburg. His massive *Thesaurus harmonicus* (Cologne, 1603/*R*), containing 403 works, is the most important early 17th-century collection of lute music. His own compositions are among the first to show a real flair for the sound of the instrument.   DA

beschleunigend (Ger.). 'Getting faster', i.e. *accelerando.

bestimmt (Ger.). 'Decisively'; it is sometimes used for a line in a score which is to be given prominence.

Besuch der alten Dame, Der ('The Visit of the Old Lady'). Opera in three acts by Einem to a libretto by Friedrich Dürrenmatt after his tragicomedy (Vienna, 1971).

Béthune, Conon de. See Conon de Béthune.

betont (Ger.). 'Stressed', 'emphasized'.

Betrothal in a Monastery (*Obrucheniye v monastïre; Duen'ya*). Opera in four acts by Prokofiev to a libretto by the composer and Mira Aleksandrovna Mendelson (Prokof'yeva) after Richard Brinsley Sheridan's opera libretto *The Duenna, or The Double Elopement* (1775) (Prague, 1946).

Bettelstudent, Der ('The Beggar Student'). Operetta in three acts by Millöcker to a libretto by F. Zell and Richard Genée after Edward Bulwer-Lytton's *The Lady of Lyons* and Victorien Sardou's *Les Noces de Fernande* (Vienna, 1882).

Bevin, Elway (*b c*.1554; *d* Bristol, 1638). Welsh organist, theorist, and composer. He worked first at Wells, then, from 1585 until 1638, as Master of the Choristers at Bristol Cathedral. Many of his works use canonic writing, a technique which also features prominently in his treatise, *A Briefe and Short Instruction in the Art of Musicke* (1631).   JM

beweglich (Ger.). 'Agile', 'sprightly'.

bewegt (Ger.). 'Agitated', 'moved' (in the sense of both motion and emotion); *bewegter*, 'quicker'.

bezifferter Bass (Ger.). 'Figured bass'.

Bg. (Ger.). Abbreviation for *Bogen*, 'bow'; *Bogenstrich*, 'bowstroke'.

Bianchi, (Giuseppe) Francesco (*b* Cremona, *c*.1752; *d* Hammersmith, 27 Nov. 1810). Italian composer. He studied with Pasquale Cafaro and Jommelli in Naples and achieved his first success with his opera *Giulio Sabino*, performed in Cremona in 1772. From 1775 to 1778 he worked in Paris as a harpsichordist and composer of comic operas at the Théâtre Italien. Subsequent appointments included that of *vicemaestro* at the

Metropolitana, Milan, and second organist at St Mark's, Venice. Bianchi enjoyed a successful collaboration with the librettist Gaetano Sertor and was the first composer to work with Giuseppe Maria Foppa. Notable features of his operas include the use of programmatic battle music, action-ensemble finales, and some highly innovatory instrumentation, especially for the woodwind. He also wrote some sacred music.

LC

Biber, Heinrich Ignaz Franz von (*b* Wartenberg, nr Reichenberg [now Liberec], Bohemia, Aug. 1644; *d* Salzburg, 3 May 1704). Bohemian composer and violinist. After early service to the Prince-Bishop of Olomouc, he transferred in 1670 to the Archbishop's Kapelle at Salzburg, where he remained for the rest of his life, becoming Kapellmeister in 1684. In 1690 he was knighted by Emperor Leopold I.

The most renowned virtuoso violinist of his time, Biber is remembered mainly for his contributions to the solo violin repertory. These include his 16 Mystery (or Rosary) Sonatas (*c*.1676, for special October services at Salzburg Cathedral), designed to evoke the spirit of various biblical scenes depicted in the manuscript, and his eight Sonatas for solo violin with continuo (1681), which demand exceptional technical skill of the performer. A particular feature in some of his violin compositions is the use of unorthodox (*scordatura) tunings—for example the tuning of the E string a tone lower—by which easier fingerings for double and triple stops, arpeggios, and octave doublings can be achieved.

Biber also composed two operas, *Chi la dura, la vince* (1687) and *Alessandro in pietra* (1689), of which only the former has survived complete, instrumental ensemble music, including a *Sonata Sancti Polycarpi* for eight trumpets and timpani, and a large quantity of sacred music in both *a cappella* and concertato styles. Important among the latter is his Requiem in F minor (*c*.1695) for SSATB soloists and chorus, strings, trombones, and organ continuo, which is noted for its idiomatic writing for both solo voices and strings, its splendidly varied scoring patterns between solo and choral sections, and its colourful musical responses, melodic and harmonic, to nuances of meaning in the text.

DA/BS

📖 W. S. NEWMAN, *The Sonata in the Baroque Era* (New York, 3/1972)

bibliography. 1. Introduction; 2. Reference bibliography; 3. Descriptive bibliography

1. Introduction

'Bibliography' has two distinct meanings. The definition perhaps more generally recognized by the non-specialist is of a listing of documentary sources relating to a particular topic, for example a composer, musical genre, or epoch; but bibliography can also refer to the close study of printed and manuscript documents themselves, and covers such matters as printing techniques, collation (that is, the study of how the pages within a printed book, score, or manuscript are assembled), binding, watermarks, printers' and publishers' marks, and so on. There is no consensus about the terminology used to distinguish the two types of bibliographical endeavour, and in this article the assembly of lists of materials on a particular topic will be referred to as 'reference' bibliography, and the practice of studying prints and manuscripts as 'descriptive' bibliography, following the example of the millennial edition of *The New Grove Dictionary of Music and Musicians*. Each type is examined separately below. While bibliographies in many subjects confine themselves to the printed word, those dealing with music may, of course, include the listing of musical scores as well.

As with bibliography, the study of sound recordings, or *discography'*, likewise covers both the study of manufacture and issue of recordings, and the construction of lists of the same. More modern terms such as 'filmography' and 'videography', on the other hand, are used only in the sense of reference bibliography

2. Reference bibliography

Reference bibliography involves the bringing together of material on a particular topic, to facilitate a survey of previous writing on it and, consequently, to provide a useful starting-point for newcomers to the topic as well as a systematically organized list for all types of user. The material gathered is customarily organized either alphabetically by author, which facilitates identification of the chief scholars in the field (because in most cases they are likely to have been the most prolific writers on the topic), or chronologically by date of publication. Other methods of organization are possible, for example by language or, in the case of figures on whom much has been written, by dividing material on a musician's life from writings on his or her musical works.

A typical reference in a bibliography will record the author(s) of a work, its title, its place and date of publication and, in most cases, its publisher as well (*Grove* is a notable exception in this last regard). Other information might follow, for example comments by the compiler of the bibliography on the value or otherwise of a particular source. Such comments can be quite extensive and make up what is then called an 'annotated' bibliography. In the case of manuscripts, the compiler will note the current location of the manuscript in question, often using a standardized system of abbreviations. In the case of music these usually follow a system of sigla developed by the Répertoire International des Sources Musicales (RISM) and consisting of an initial letter representing a country, followed by further letters that uniquely identify a specific repository. Thus for example *GB-Lbl* designates the British Library in London; *A-Wn*, the Österreichische Nationalbibliothek (National Library of Austria) in Vienna.

In former times the assembly of a reference bibliography typically involved a search through printed reference works and catalogues for relevant material, and bibliographies mainly listed printed sources—books, journal articles, music scores. Today, bibliographic lists may also include citations of sites on the World Wide Web, while the gathering together of appropriate material of all kinds is facilitated by the availability of vast computer-based databanks whose contents are accessible via the Web or CD-ROM. Compilers of bibliographies on musical topics can call on online versions of the *Music Index*, which started life in the USA in 1949 as a print publication, and the *International Index of Music Periodicals*, one of a new generation of reference tools that have never existed on the printed page. Each of these sources confines itself to periodical literature. Citations—and, indeed, annotations in the form of abstracts—for books on music, dissertations, journal articles, and reviews are to be found in the RILM (Répertoire International de Littérature Musicale) database, produced in New York.

By 2001, details of some 40 million items (including music ones) could be gathered via the American OCLC company's ever-growing 'Worldcat' online database; and the music catalogues (of books, scores, and, occasionally, recordings) of some of the world's great libraries are accessible in electronic form. But although such resources bring benefits—not the least being that the bibliographer can find citations of a large body of material without having to leave his or her desk—a problem has been created in that compilers can track down references to vast numbers of print and manuscript resources, but with little hope of ever having the opportunity to check on the availability and usefulness of all the items themselves. The compilation of a comprehensive bibliography on any but the smallest of subjects has become increasingly difficult, and selective bibliographies such as those in *Grove*, whose compilers attempt to list only the most significant writings on a topic, take on added value. Annotated bibliographies are valuable for the same reason, in that they allow users, especially newcomers to a topic, to be discriminating in what they read.

3. Descriptive bibliography

While reference bibliography at its best may both list and assess the contents of particular items, descriptive bibliography is concerned rather with the physical object that carries those contents: in the case of music this will typically be a book or score, printed or in manuscript. It is not, therefore, primarily an evaluative discipline except in so far as it may establish an order of excellence for particular printers, scribes or engravers, papermakers, or binders. Bibliographers are frequently interested in the history or economics of publishing (the development of printing technology, the foundation and disappearance of particular publishers, etc.), in book production and, particularly in the case of older items, in establishing the uniqueness or otherwise of a specific copy of an item. Consequently, various conventions for descriptive bibliography have grown up, invented primarily to enable the accurate description of an item to be made as briefly as possible, and to allow comparison between apparently identical copies of a specific work.

The descriptive bibliographer will, typically, describe the title page of a book or a musical edition, including such elements as printed borders and other decorative devices, typography, and content. He or she will note its size, and such details as whether its height exceeds its width, and whether it is in small or large format. Such words as 'folio', 'quarto', and 'octavo' are often used as shorthand for this purpose, although they in fact describe the number of times a standard-sized paper sheet has been folded to make the item in question, rather than giving precise dimensions. The number of pages in a sewn gathering may indicate how the item has been assembled. Information such as a watermark in the paper may help identify a place and date of production. A printer's device, or 'colophon', consisting either of plain text, a unique illustration, or both, may appear at the beginning or end; and even such details as endpapers (the pieces of stiff paper, often decorated, that are attached directly on to the front and back boards of an item) may be worth noting. Binding, especially if original, can be tremendously significant, particularly where a specific buyer has purchased an item in loose pages and had it bound to his or her own specification. These bindings may include the buyer's coat of arms or other unique device: such books or musical editions are termed 'association' copies, a term also used where, for example, an owner has signed the title page of a book, or has inserted his or her bookplate into it.

Assigning a date to a particular manuscript is an issue that affects all academic disciplines equally, but for printed music a lack of publication dates on scores, particularly from the 18th century onwards, raises special problems. Descriptive bibliographers of music spend much time attempting to date one edition of a work in relation to another. The process may be helped by the custom of many publishers, from the 18th century to the 20th, of using plate numbers, by which a specific composition was printed from engraved or lithographic plates that bore a number (or a combination of numbers and letters) to enable the publisher to identify that composition, storing the plates by number in a warehouse against the day when they might be required for a reprint edition. Estienne *Roger of Amsterdam was probably the first to use this system, from about 1712–13.

But plate numbers are only one of a number of pieces of bibliographical evidence that may help establish the date of issue of an item. The use of particular decorative fonts of type, or the appearance on a title page of a price in currency that is known to have become obsolete after a specific date, are two other examples. The description on a title page of an author or composer as 'deceased' will provide a *terminus ante quem*, or date before which publication cannot have taken place. Publishers' names and addresses also change over time—partnerships are created and dissolved, new premises procured—and music bibliographers have expended much effort tracking such changes, as they also help in the bibliographical process. Thus Anik Devriès and François Lesure have issued a three-volume *Dictionnaire des éditeurs de musique français*, while for the British Isles there are works by Frank Kidson (*British Music Publishers, Printers and Engravers*), Charles Humphries and William C. Smith (*Music Publishing in the British Isles from the Beginning until the Middle of the Nineteenth Century*), and John Parkinson (*Victorian Music Publishers: An Annotated List*).

Music bibliography as a discipline abounds in studies of individual publishers, right back to the first efforts of Ottaviano *Petrucci in 1501, and even beyond. Comparative lists of English music publishers' plate numbers for the first half of the 19th century have been compiled by Alan Tyson and Oliver Neighbour; Otto Erich Deutsch has published on the same topic, taking a broader chronological and geographical sample. Tyson is also known for his brilliant bibliographical studies of watermarks in paper used by Mozart.

Some might argue with the descriptive bibliographer's obsession with dates, and it is true that, while they help chart the history of a specific narrative or musical composition, they can lead bibliographers and bibliophiles into the conceit of, for example, collecting only first editions. But the comparison of different editions, maybe from different publishers, is a matter of

great moment to music bibliographers, musicologists, and performers, since changes in text will be reflected in performance. It is partly for this reason that editors of *Gesamtausgaben*, or scholarly collected editions of composers' works, so painstakingly document textual differences between the sources used in the preparation of their editions; and why publishers such as Henle of Munich have set so much store by publication of an 'original', unadulterated text (or *Urtext*) that they believe best represents a composer's intentions.   JWa

Biches, Les ('The Hinds'; 'The Little Darlings'). Ballet in one act by Poulenc to his own scenario, incorporating choral settings of 17th-century texts; it was choreographed by Bronislava Nijinska (Monte Carlo, 1924). Poulenc arranged a suite from the score (1939–40).

bichord. Two strings tuned in unison. See COURSE.

bicinium (Lat.). An unaccompanied composition for two voices or instruments. The term was also used more specifically for the teaching pieces composed by 16th-century Germans, as in Rhau's *Bicinia gallica, latina et germanica* (1545). In the 17th century, Scheidt used the term for two-part versets or variations in organ music.

big band. A style of jazz, equivalent to *swing, that arose in the 1930s. It was characterized by a larger band than had prevailed earlier, made up of sections of the various wind instruments rather than individual musicians, and consequently relied more heavily on written arrangements while still highlighting improvised solos.   PGa

Bilitis, Chansons de. See CHANSONS DE BILITIS.

Billings, William (*b* Boston, 7 Oct. 1746; *d* Boston, 29 Sept. 1800). American composer, singing teacher, and author. He came from a poor background and was largely self-taught. He began teaching in 1769. In 1770 he published *The New-England Psalm-Singer*, which contained about 120 compositions together with detailed instructions to singers; this was the first publication consisting entirely of American music, as well as the first containing music by a single American composer. Billings's most popular collection was *The Singing Master's Assistant* (1778), which went to four editions. His didactic writing was greatly influenced by the English west gallery composer William Tans'ur, and sometimes betrays a robustly independent view of the role of the composer, and a disdain for compositional 'rules'. Billings also produced other literary work, including some of the texts he set to music; in 1783 he became editor of the new *Boston Magazine*, his musical fortunes having declined. Hostility from the Boston gentry soon removed him from this post, and increasingly he had to work outside music.

Billings's publications, intended for church performance, were all for four-part choir. He developed an expanded musical language in America: homophonic metrical psalm and hymn tunes with the melody in the tenor, a few *fuging tunes, and anthems of similar form to the verse anthem; he also composed canons. Of his anthems, *Peace* contains instrumental 'symphonies' for gallery instruments, and the lost *I was glad when they said unto me* was provided with organ accompaniment, at a time when there was still considerable hostility to its use.   PW

📖 D. P. McKay and R. Crawford, *William Billings of Boston, Eighteenth-Century Composer* (Princeton, NJ, 1975)

Billington, Elizabeth [née Weichsel] (*b* London, 27 Dec. 1765; *d* nr Venice, 25 Aug. 1818). English soprano. She first appeared in public as a pianist when she was six. She was taught singing by J. C. Bach and after his death continued her vocal studies with James Billington, whom she married in 1783. She made her debut in Dublin in Gluck's *Orfeo ed Euridice*, but it was in her performance at Covent Garden in 1786 in Arne's *Love in a Village* that she quickly rose to fame. After several successful years in England she went to Naples, where she sang at S. Carlo. Bianchi's *Inez de Castro* was written for her debut there (1794), and further operas were composed for her by Paisiello and Paër. In 1801 she returned to England, where she was so sought after that she appeared on alternate nights at the Drury Lane and Covent Garden theatres. She was renowned for her musicianship and technical brilliance.   JT

Billy Budd. Opera by Britten to a libretto by E. M. Forster and Eric Crozier after Herman Melville's unfinished story (1891); it was originally in four acts (London, 1951) but Britten made a two-act version (broadcast 1961; staged London, 1964).

Billy the Kid. Ballet in one act by Copland to a scenario by Lincoln Kirstein; it was choreographed by Eugene Loring (Chicago, 1938).

binary form. A musical structure consisting of two parts or sections. The first modulates from the tonic key and concludes with a cadence in a related key, usually the dominant for pieces in the major, the relative major for pieces in the minor. The second section starts in the new key and works back to the tonic. For example, if the piece is in C major the first section will end with a cadence on G major; the second will then begin in G major but modulate back to C major, the key in which the piece will end. It is usual to repeat each of the two sections of the structure. Sometimes the second section of a binary piece is considerably longer than the first

because other related keys are often explored on the way back to the tonic key, to give the piece more interest.

Although many late Renaissance dances comprised three strains, binary form came to be used in nearly all dance movements (allemandes, courantes, sarabandes, gigues, etc.) in 17th- and 18th-century dance suites. Whereas early Baroque dances often remained in one key throughout, by the mid-Baroque period the tonal scheme as described above had become the norm. However, there were exceptions; Domenico Scarlatti, for example, sometimes chose to modulate to the mediant at the end of the first section. Some of the finest examples of binary form are found in Bach's music, for instance in the Bourrée no. 2 from his second English Suite (Ex. 1). The piece divides into two main sections. The first, eight bars in length, opens in the tonic key of A major and modulates to the dominant, E major, in which there is a firm cadence in bars 7–8. Section 2 is 16 bars long and opens in the dominant key. But instead of returning directly to the home key the music proceeds through F♯ minor, the relative minor of the tonic (bar 16), and passes again through the dominant (bar 18) in a harmonic sequence leading to the subdominant key of D major (bar 20), before closing in the home key.

During the mid- and late Baroque periods, various characteristics became apparent in binary-form movements. One such feature was the use of 'rhyming cadences', whereby the cadence at the end of the first section was heard again in the tonic key at the end of the second. In its simplest form, this was a repetition of the cadential chords. Some composers, especially Bach and Domenico Scarlatti, took this principle further by repeating whole passages. Another device was to repeat the last few bars of the piece; in France this became known as the *petite reprise*. The expansion of binary form and its combination with *ternary form led eventually to the development of Classical *sonata form.

Binary-form pieces continued to be written in the 19th century, usually cast as a 'theme and variations'; one example is the Andante of Beethoven's 'Appassionata' Sonata. The form is also found in some of Schumann's piano music. In the 20th century, binary form was used as the basis for complex structural devices.

See also FORM, 5.   GMT/LC

Binchois [Gilles de Bins] (*b* ?Mons, *c*.1400; *d* Soignies, 20 Sept. 1460). Burgundian composer. He is first heard of as an organist at the church of Ste Waudru, Mons, in 1419. In 1423 he moved to Lille, and shortly after this entered the service of William de la Pole, First Duke of

binary form, Ex. 1

Suffolk (the English occupied northern France at this time); they returned to the vicinity of Mons (Hainaut) in 1425. There is no evidence that Binchois ever visited England, but some of his works are settings of the Sarum Use, at least one song is found in an English manuscript, and his ballade *Dueil angoisseus* was used as the basis of a mass setting by the English composer Bedyngham.

In about 1426 Binchois joined the Burgundian court of Philip the Good, and one of his few datable works is the motet *Nove cantum melodie* for the baptism of the Burgundian Prince Anthoine in January 1431. There was some contact between Binchois and Dufay—their first meeting seems to have been in 1434, when the Burgundian and Savoy courts were at Chambéry, and in 1449 Dufay stayed with Binchois in Mons. Binchois retired to Soignies in 1452 and there became provost of the collegiate church of St Vincent. It is possible that he had some connection with the famous Feast of the Pheasant in Lille (1454), where the chanson *Je ne vis oncques la pareille*, ascribed to Binchois in one source and to Dufay in another, was performed.

Binchois was one of the most able and yet thoroughly traditional composers of the 15th century. His surviving works include 28 mass movements, 32 psalms, motets, and small sacred works, and 54 chansons, 47 in *rondeau* form and seven in *ballade* form. Some of his sacred output is severely practical, with simple note-against-note harmonizations of the chant, which appears in the top voice as was usually the case in continental music of that period. Although he wrote pairs of mass movements, they are linked rather loosely (by overall range, the sequence of time signatures, etc.), and no pair shares the same tenor. He avoided large-scale works, writing no cyclic masses and only one isorhythmic motet (*Nove cantum melodie*).

Binchois's songs are his most attractive compositions: typical features include the use of under-3rd cadences, rather short-breathed phrases, triple rhythm (the only song in duple time is *Seule esgaree*), and the apparent repetition of material. In fact these superficial repetitions serve to demonstrate Binchois's flexibility, since it is rare for two phrases to have exactly the same rhythmic or melodic contour, and consecutive phrases rarely end on the same pitch or note-value. The song *Je me recommande* is a fine example of his style and illustrates many of the features that make Binchois a supreme miniaturist.

Binchois's death was lamented in Ockeghem's *Mort, tu as navré de ton dart*, which tells us that Binchois was a soldier in his youth (perhaps with the Duke of Suffolk), and which opens with what seems to be a quotation from an otherwise unknown Binchois chanson. AP

📖 A. Kirkman and D. Slavin (eds.), *Binchois Studies* (Oxford, 2000)

bind. Another name for the *tie.

Bingham, Judith (Caroline) (*b* Nottingham, 21 June 1952). English composer. She studied singing, as well as composition with Alan Bush, Eric Fenby, and Hans Keller. She sang professionally with the BBC Singers, 1983–96, and many of her works are vocal, like the large-scale *Irish Tenebrae* (1990) and *Salt in the Blood* for chorus and brass, commissioned for the 1995 BBC Proms. She has also written several vividly imagined orchestral works, including *Chartres* (1988) and *The Temple at Karnak* (1996). AW

'Bird' Quartet. Nickname of Haydn's String Quartet in C major op. 33 no. 3 (1781), so called because the grace notes in the main subject of the first movement and the violin duet in the trio of the Scherzando suggest birdsong.

Birds, The. See UCCELLI, GLI.

Birtwistle, Sir Harrison (Paul) (*b* Accrington, 15 July 1934). English composer. He studied composition with Richard Hall at the RMCM, where his fellow students included Peter Maxwell Davies and Alexander Goehr. His early works, such as *Monody for Corpus Christi* (1959) for soprano and three instruments, were influenced by aspects of medieval and early Renaissance music, and reflect the intricate textures and expressionistic lyric intensity characteristic of the 'Manchester School'. However, the shrill sonorities and severe, sharply juxtaposed forms of *Tragoedia* (1965) for wind quintet, harp, and string quartet owe more to Stravinsky, Varèse, and Messiaen than to Schoenberg or Webern, and with this work, and the ensuing opera, *Punch and Judy* (Aldeburgh, 1968), which incorporated it, Birtwistle found the personal voice that he exploited and developed thereafter.

Birtwistle co-founded the Pierrot Players (later the Fires of London) with Maxwell Davies in 1968, but *Verses for Ensembles*, his first substantial work after *Punch and Judy*, was written for the London Sinfonietta, with which he has continued a particularly fruitful relationship. During the 1970s and early 80s a sequence of major vocal and instrumental compositions, including *The Triumph of Time* for orchestra, and a second opera *The Mask of Orpheus*, first performed to great acclaim in 1986 (ENO), helped to consolidate Birtwistle's position as a leading figure on the European scene; *The Mask of Orpheus* won the 1986 Grawemeyer Award. From 1975 to 1981 Birtwistle was director of music at the National Theatre, and though in later years he has taught at universities and colleges he has concentrated primarily on composition.

Between 1990 and 2000 Birtwistle completed three more operas, *Gawain* (Covent Garden, 1991), *The Second Mrs Kong* (Glyndebourne, 1994), and *The Last Supper* (Berlin and Glyndebourne, 2000), and such notable instrumental and orchestral scores as *Pulse Shadows* and *Exody*. His commitment to the kind of mainstream modernism which is essentially expressionistic in character, communicating through the forceful rhythmic projection of what are often very simple pitch structures in various modal and symmetrical formations, has ensured that his work remains in high regard, and his influence on many younger composers has been considerable. He was knighted in 1988.   PG/AW

   📖 M. HALL, *Harrison Birtwistle* (London, 1984); *Harrison Birtwistle in Recent Years* (London, 1998) · R. ADLINGTON, *The Music of Harrison Birtwistle* (Cambridge, 2000) · J. CROSS, *Harrison Birtwistle: Man, Mind, Music* (London, 2000)

bis (Fr.). 'Twice', i.e. again, a second time. 1. An instruction that a passage so marked should be repeated.

   2. A term used by French and Italian audiences to demand an *encore.

bisbigliando (It., 'whispering'). In harp playing, a special effect resembling a tremolo, obtained by moving the finger quickly against the string.

Bishop, Sir **Henry R**(owley) (*b* London, 18 Nov. 1786; *d* London, 30 April 1855). English composer and conductor. He studied with Francesco Bianchi. In 1810 he was appointed composer and musical director at Covent Garden, and in 1814 he began to 'adapt' other composers' operas (including Mozart's *Le nozze di Figaro* and *Don Giovanni* and Rossini's *Il barbiere di Siviglia* and *Guillaume Tell*) for the English stage, in the manner of pasticcios. As well as composing operas, he wrote songs for mangled versions of Shakespeare's plays and found time to travel abroad. He was a founder member in 1813 of the Philharmonic Society, for which he conducted several concerts, directed performances of the Lenten Oratorio Concerts from 1819, and was a professor of harmony at the RAM (though he did little teaching there).

Bishop resigned from Covent Garden in 1824 and moved to Drury Lane, where in 1826 he staged *Aladdin* as a rival to Weber's *Oberon*—in vain. In 1830 he became director at Vauxhall Gardens, continuing to write prolifically for the stage until 1840; his last opera, *The Fortunate Isles* (an allegorical and national masque), was produced that year at Covent Garden during Queen Victoria's wedding celebrations.

After failing to secure the posts of organist at St George's Chapel, Windsor (1835), and Gresham Professor of Music (1837), Bishop was appointed Reid Professor of Music at Edinburgh University in 1841 but was asked to resign two years later, having refused to give lectures. He nevertheless succeeded Crotch as professor at Oxford in 1848 and obtained the D.Mus. with his installation ode for the chancellor, Lord Derby, in 1853. He was principal conductor of the Ancient Concerts (1840–8) and was knighted in 1842.

Bishop is best known today for his glees and songs (including *Home, Sweet Home*). He was married twice: his second wife, Ann Riviere, sang by the name of Madame Anna Bishop, but she disgraced herself by eloping to the Continent with the French harpist Nicolas Bochsa in 1839.   WT/JDI

   📖 R. NORTHCOTT, *The Life of Sir Henry R. Bishop* (London, 1920)

bitonality. The combination of two keys simultaneously. An early example is Charles Ives's *Psalm 67* (1898), in which two choral groups sing opposed triads—for example, of C major and G minor. The harmonic clashes of bitonality, which may be mysterious (as in the Ives), plangent, or acerbic, are especially associated with the music of Darius Milhaud.   PG

biwa. Generic term for Japanese shallow-bodied short-necked lutes deriving from the Chinese *pipa*.

Bizet, Georges (Alexandre César Léopold) (*b* Paris, 25 Oct 1838; *d* Bougival, nr Paris, 3 June 1875). French composer. His father was a singing teacher and modest composer (formerly a hairdresser-cum-wigmaker) and his mother was an excellent pianist and the sister of a much more distinguished singing teacher, François Delsarte. Bizet was brought up in a musical atmosphere and soon showed such gifts that he was admitted to the Paris Conservatoire at the age of nine. There he won a long list of prizes, including first prize for solfège in 1849, second prize for piano in 1851, and first prize for organ and fugue in 1855. He studied the piano with Marmontel and composition with Halévy, and while still a student he composed the brilliant Symphony in C, which follows Classical models but displays a distinct individuality. In 1856 he won the second prize in the Prix de Rome with his cantata *David*, and in a competition promoted by Offenbach he shared first prize, with Lecocq, for an operetta. The two winners had their settings of *Le Docteur Miracle* performed on consecutive nights in 1857.

In 1857 Bizet won the Prix de Rome with the cantata *Clovis et Clotilde*, which gave him a bursary for five years. He spent the first three in Italy, a period he greatly enjoyed. The main products of his Italian stay were a choral *Te Deum*, an *opera buffa*, *Don Procopio*, in the manner of Donizetti, and an *ode-symphonie* based on the life of Vasco da Gama. He also made a start on a four-movement symphony that appeared many years later with the title *Roma*.

On his return to Paris in 1860, Bizet settled into the life that he was to pursue for his remaining 15 years: courting librettists, singers, and opera managers for commissions, playing the piano for rehearsals (his gifts as a sight-reader were legendary), composing smaller works such as piano pieces and songs for publication, and writing piano arrangements of operas. Gounod's supporting interest in the young Bizet had given him his first commission of this kind, arranging *La Nonne sanglante* in 1855, but it was an occupation that was to drain much of his precious time in later years. He never showed much interest in teaching.

In 1863 the Théâtre Lyrique commissioned *Les Pêcheurs de perles*; though it was indifferently received by the press (with the honourable exception of Berlioz), it displays a fresh talent and a lively theatricality that has won it a place in the modern repertory. Bizet's next opera, *Ivan IV*, was conceived on a grand scale, but it was not completed and it remained unstaged for nearly 100 years. *La Jolie Fille de Perth* appeared at the Théâtre Lyrique in 1867; its libretto is an unhappy distortion of Scott, and the music, though brilliant at its best, is uneven. A number of other operatic ventures came to nothing at this time.

In 1869 Bizet married Geneviève, the daughter of his teacher Halévy (who had died in 1862), but their ménage was soon interrupted by the outbreak of the Franco-Prussian War and the turmoil of the Commune. Bizet served in the National Guard and managed to escape from Paris during a part of the upheaval. When normal life resumed, he produced two small masterpieces, the one-act *opéra comique Djamileh*, which was staged in 1872, and the delicate suite of pieces for piano duet, *Jeux d'enfants*, five of which were orchestrated. There followed his affecting and colourful incidental music for Daudet's play *L'Arlésienne*, scored for a small orchestra. Arranged as a suite for larger orchestra, it was one of Bizet's first works to win popularity.

Another operatic project, *Don Rodrigue*, was abandoned in 1873 when the Opéra, for which it was intended, burnt down. But Bizet was already at work on his opera *Carmen*, commissioned by the Opéra-Comique. It immediately caused controversy, its subject being considered too risqué for such a venue, and the tragic implications of Carmen's death on stage being

unusually realistic for the lighter genre of *opéra comique*. After many delays and difficulties it was produced in March 1875, and though it created a scandal in the press, it was successful with the public. Bizet was by this time ill with a heart complaint accentuated by rheumatism, and although he was planning an oratorio, *Geneviève de Paris*, he made no progress and died quite suddenly within three months of the opening of *Carmen*.

This masterpiece found fame abroad long before it was revived in Paris. With the spoken dialogues set as recitative by Bizet's friend Ernest Guiraud, it was played in Vienna at the end of 1875 and quickly taken up all over the world; it is now one of the most popular of all operas. Whether Bizet would have built on this achievement is impossible to guess, but he was still only 36 when he died, and the promise of great works still to come is unmistakable. The sharpness of its characterization and the forceful realism of its action—not to mention its abundance of great tunes—reveal a composer of exceptional dramatic gifts.   DA/HMacd

📖 M. Curtiss, *Bizet and his World* (London, 1959) · W. Dean, *Bizet* (London, 1948, 3/1975) · S. McClary, *Carmen* (Cambridge, 1992)

Björling, Jussi [Johan Jonaton] (*b* Stora Tuna, 5 Feb. 1911; *d* Stockholm, 9 Sept. 1960). Swedish tenor. He had singing lessons with his father, a professional singer, and in 1928 entered the Stockholm Conservatory. He made his official debut at the Royal Opera in Stockholm as Don Ottavio in *Don Giovanni*. In 1936 he appeared as Manrico in *Il trovatore* at the Vienna State Opera, where he was acclaimed for his *legato* line, remarkable breath control, and perfect intonation. For the next 24 years he was in demand worldwide, particularly for lyrical roles, to which his ringing yet highly refined voice was ideally suited. He was not an imaginative actor, but his performances had a romantic ardour as well as a gentle intimacy that captivated his audiences.   JT

📖 A.-L. Björling and A. Farkas, *Jussi* (Portland, OR, 1996)

Blacher, Boris (*b* Niu-chang, China, 19 Jan. 1903; *d* Berlin, 30 Jan. 1975). German composer. Of German–Russian parentage, he attended schools in Niu-chang, Irkutsk, and Charbin. In 1922 he moved to Berlin to study at the Technische Hochschule, also taking composition lessons with Friedrich Ernst Koch. He remained in Berlin for the rest of his life. At first he earned his living from routine musical work copying and arranging, but in 1945 he was appointed professor of composition at the Hochschule, where he stayed until his retirement in 1970; his pupils included Gottfried von Einem.

Blacher's music shows a cool, ironic use of tonality, comparable more to Stravinsky than to any other German composer. His forms are brittle and mosaic-like, often employing the technique of 'variable metres' which he invented to systematize rapid metrical change. Another prominent characteristic in some works is the use of jazz and popular styles. Blacher's output includes several ballets and operas, among the latter an objective treatment of Shakespeare in *Romeo und Julia* (1943, broadcast 1947, staged Salzburg, 1950), and the rather less austere *Abstrakte Oper no. 1* (Mannheim, 1953). The Paganini Variations (1947) show the colourful dexterity of his orchestral writing.

PG

📖 H. H. STUCKENSCHMIDT, *Boris Blacher* (Berlin, 1963)

Black Angels (Thirteen Images from the Dark Land). Work (1970) by Crumb for amplified string quartet; conceived as a response to the Vietnam War, it depicts a 'voyage of the soul' in three stages—Departure, Absence, Return—and makes much use of diabolic imagery and number symbolism.

black bottom. A black jazz dance, made up of slides, twists, and hops together with a slap to the backside, which appeared in various forms from the end of the 19th century. It became widely popular when it was introduced in *George White's Scandals of 1926* danced to the Henderson, DeSylva, and Brown song. Its more swinging rhythms replaced the ragtime-based *charleston for a short time. PGA

'Black Key' Étude. Nickname of Chopin's *Étude* in G♭ major op. 10 no. 5 (1830) for piano, so called because the right hand confines itself to the black keys.

bladder and string. See BUMBASS.

bladder pipe. A *wind-cap instrument in which the reed is enclosed by an animal bladder that serves, like the bag of a *bagpipe, as an air reservoir. It is depicted in European works of art and mentioned in literature from the 13th century but seems to have died out by the 17th century, except as a children's instrument or one occasionally played by shepherds. RPA

Blake, David (Leonard) (*b* London, 2 Sept. 1936). English composer. He studied at Cambridge and in East Berlin with Hanns Eisler, who influenced not only his musical style but also his views on the social functions of art. On his return to England he took up a teaching post at the University of York, remaining there until his retirement. His earlier works reflect the language of Eisler's teacher Schoenberg in their thematic serialism, but they also display a mordant economy closer to Eisler himself, and even to Weill. Later

compositions, including the operas *Toussaint* (ENO, 1977) and *The Plumber's Gift* (ENO, 1989), are more eclectic and reintroduce rich tonal harmony. AW

Blake, Howard (*b* London, 28 Oct. 1938). English pianist and composer. After studying at the RAM with Harold Craxton (piano) and Howard Ferguson (composition) he worked as a pianist, arranger, and composer for radio, films, and television. His greatest success was with his score for the animated film *The Snowman* (1982), later reworked as a ballet and a stage show (both 1993). His melodic gift has also been demonstrated in the ballet *Eva* (1996), vocal and choral music including the 'dramatic oratorio' *Benedictus* (1980, rev. 1986), and orchestral works including concertos for clarinet (1985), piano (1991), and violin (1993).

ABur

Blasinstrumente (Ger.). 'Wind instruments'.

Blasmusik (Ger.). 'Wind music', i.e. music for wind instruments.

Blavet, Michel (*b* Besançon, *bapt.* 13 March 1700; *d* Paris, 28 Oct. 1768). French flautist and composer. He taught himself to play various wind instruments and in 1723 moved to Paris in the service of Duke Charles-Eugène Lévis. In 1725 he helped to inaugurate the Concert Spirituel, appearing there regularly as a soloist. He benefited from the patronage of the Prince of Carignan (to whom he dedicated his op. 1 sonatas for two flutes) and the Count of Clermont, but he declined a post at the court of Frederick, Prince of Prussia. In about 1736 he became a member of the Musique du Roi and in 1740 he joined the Opéra orchestra. Blavet's chamber sonatas, like those of his colleague the violinist Leclair *l'aîné*, unite French and Italian styles, taking particular inspiration from the works of Corelli and Vivaldi. Blavet also composed several stage works for Clermont's private theatre at Berny, and his divertissement with *secco* recitatives, *Le Jaloux corrigé* (1752), was performed in a double bill with Rousseau's *Le Devin du village* (1752) at the Paris Opéra.

DA/JAS

Blechmusik (Ger.). 'Brass-band music'.

Blest Pair of Sirens. Cantata (1887) by Parry to words from Milton's *At a Solemn Music*.

blind octaves [interrupted octaves]. A device found in virtuoso piano writing in which the rapid alternation between each hand of octaves, or of octaves with single notes, produces an effect approximating to continuous triple octaves.

Bliss, Sir Arthur (Drummond) (*b* London, 2 Aug. 1891; *d* London, 27 March 1975). English composer. He studied at Cambridge University (1910–13) and briefly with Stanford at the RCM (1913–14) before serving in the army during World War I. He was wounded in the Battle of the Somme, during which he also lost his gifted brother, Kennard Bliss. The catharsis of this traumatic experience was later expressed in *Morning Heroes*, a choral symphony written in 1930. After the war he fell under the spell of Stravinsky and Diaghilev, and his first experimental compositions—*Madame Noy* (1918), the Rhapsody (1919), and *Rout* (1920)—show an attraction towards neo-classicism. A return to the English mainstream was marked by *A Colour Symphony* (1921–2), a study of heraldic symbolism which established many of his stylistic characteristics.

Between 1923 and 1925 Bliss lived in the USA. On his return to England he resumed composition with alacrity, notably with such works as the *Introduction and Allegro* and *Hymn to Apollo* (both 1926). One of his most virtuoso works for orchestra was the brilliant *Music for Strings* (1935), but he also produced three substantial concertos—for two pianos (1924, rev. 1968), violin (1955), and cello (1970)—and some fine chamber pieces including the Oboe Quintet (1927) and the Clarinet Quintet (1931). Much of Bliss's best later music was written for the theatre or films. The ballets *Checkmate* (1937), *Miracle in the Gorbals* (1944), and *Adam Zero* (1946) show his gift for vivid illustrative writing. As an opera composer he was less successful, but in film he scored a triumph with *Things to Come* (1934–5). Bliss was knighted in 1950 and appointed Master of the Queen's Music in 1953. He published an autobiography, *As I Remember* (London, 1970, 2/1989).

PG/JD1

📖 L. FOREMAN, *Arthur Bliss: A Catalogue of the Complete Works* (London, 1979; suppl. 1988) · S. CRAGGS, *Arthur Bliss: A Bio-Bibliography* (Westport, CT, 1988); *Arthur Bliss: A Source Book* (Brookfield, VT, 1996)

Blitheman [Blytheman], **John** (*b* c.1525; *d* London, 23 May 1591). English composer and organist. He was Master of the Choristers at Christ Church, Oxford, in 1564, and succeeded Tallis as organist to the Chapel Royal in 1585. Some of his keyboard music has survived in the *Mulliner Book.   JM

Blitzstein, Marc (*b* Philadelphia, 2 March 1905; *d* Fort-de-France, Martinique, 22 Jan. 1964). American composer. Born into a wealthy family, he studied at the Curtis Institute with Alexander Ziloti (piano) and Rosario Scalero (composition). In 1926 he went to Paris to study with Nadia Boulanger, and the next year he had lessons with Schoenberg in Berlin. His early compositions were typical of the Boulanger school, strongly influenced by Stravinsky's neo-classicism. The direction of his music changed when he returned to the

USA in 1931 at the height of the economic depression. He allied himself with the left, looked to the working classes for his audience, and began to write mainly for the theatre, films, and broadcasting. *The Cradle will Rock* (Venice, 1937), much the most successful of his stage works, was a political piece dealing with the rise of organized labour in the steel industry. Somewhat in the manner of Weill, his mature music combines tunes of popular type with complex harmonies, occasionally worked out in strict forms.   PG

Bloch, Ernest (*b* Geneva, 24 July 1880; *d* Portland, OR, 15 July 1959). Swiss-born American composer. His violin and composition studies included periods in Geneva (with Jaques-Dalcroze), Brussels (Ysaÿe), Frankfurt (Knorr), and Munich (Thuille). In 1904 he returned to work for his father in Geneva, where he composed his opera *Macbeth* (Paris, Opéra-Comique, 1910), a bold music drama combining influences from Debussy, Wagner, and Musorgsky. He then concentrated on specifically Jewish pieces, of which the 'Hebraic rhapsody' *Schelomo* for cello and orchestra (1915–16) is his best-known work. Although it uses no Jewish material, the music has a flowing rhythmic impulse suggestive of Hebrew chant.

In 1916 Bloch emigrated to the USA, where he taught at the Mannes School in New York (1917–20), the Cleveland Institute of Music (1920–5), and the San Francisco Conservatory (1925–30); his pupils included Roger Sessions and Quincy Porter. He continued to compose steadily, influenced by neo-classicism in such works as the Concerto Grosso no. 1 (1924–5) but retaining the melodic warmth that had characterized his earlier Jewish music. He returned to Switzerland in 1930 and began to write large-scale works including the Jewish liturgical setting *Avodath an Hakodesh* (1930–3) and the Violin Concerto (1937–8). In 1939 he went back to the USA, settled in Oregon, and taught summer courses at the University of California at Berkeley. During this final period he concentrated on larger abstract forms; such works as the Second and Third Quartets (1945, 1952), the *Concerto symphonique* for piano and orchestra (1947–8), and the two solo violin suites (1958) show the full flowering of his generous Romanticism.   PG

📖 S. BLOCH and I. HESKES, *Ernest Bloch, Creative Spirit* (New York, 1976) · R. STRASSBURG, *Ernest Bloch: Voice in the Wilderness* (Los Angeles, 1977) · D. Z. KUSHNER, *Ernest Bloch: A Guide to Research* (New York, 1988)

block harmony. A succession of similar or identical chords.

Blodek, Vilém (*b* Prague, 3 Oct. 1834; *d* Prague, 1 May 1874). Czech composer, teacher, flautist, and pianist. A musically talented child, he studied the flute, piano, and composition at the Prague Conservatory. After some years of independent teaching and performing (1853–60) he was appointed professor of flute at the Prague Conservatory. He then divided his time between teaching at the conservatory, for which he wrote a flute tutor (1861), and composing music for plays at the Czech Provisional Theatre and the German Estates Theatre. The stress of these activities proved too much and Blodek's last three years were spent in a mental home. His early death was regretted since his music shows unfulfilled promise. The orchestral works—a Symphony (1859), a Flute Concerto (1862), some overtures—beyond their debt to Mendelssohn and Weber display a talent and originality second only, among his contemporaries, to Smetana's; his unfinished opera *Zítek* (1869) makes interesting use of arioso and open forms. His comic opera *V studni* ('In the Well', 1867) proved the most popular one-act Czech opera of the 19th century. Though clearly influenced by *The Bartered Bride*, the work was assured of lasting success by its melodic inventiveness.   JSM

Blomdahl, Karl-Birger (*b* Växjö, 19 Oct. 1916; *d* Kungsängen, nr Stockholm, 14 June 1968). Swedish composer. He studied with Hilding Rosenberg in the late 1930s and early 40s, and began to compose in a Hindemithian manner; the Concerto Grosso (1944) is typical. In his Third Symphony (1950) he began to introduce Schoenbergian serial methods, though here the influence of Bartók is stronger. Then, while promoting contemporary music in his position as chairman of the Fylkingen concert society (1950–4), he began to adopt avant-garde procedures. His later orchestral works, which include the ballet *Sisyphos* (1954) and *Forma ferritonans* (1961), show this development, though there is still a Hindemith-like weight and vigour. Blomdahl was professor of composition at the Royal Academy of Music in Stockholm (1960–4) and director of the Swedish radio music department (1964–8), where he helped found an electronic music studio.
                                                                PG

Blond Eckbert. Opera in two acts by Weir to her own libretto after Ludwig Tieck's *Der blonde Eckbert* (London, 1994).

Blondel de Nesle (*fl* 1180–1200). Trouvère. Beyond the likelihood that he came from Picardy, his identity is disputed. According to one theory he was a commoner, or the younger son of a minor nobleman; another theory identifies him as the magnate Jehan II de Nesle. His songs appear to have circulated widely, to judge from the large number of manuscripts in which they survive. As is typical of trouvère song, they sometimes allude to other works in the repertory, and are themselves cited in the songs of his contemporaries.
                                                                JM

Blow, John (*b* Newark, Feb. 1649; *d* London, 1 Oct. 1708). English composer. His earliest musical education was probably at the Magnus Song School in Newark; he became a chorister at the Chapel Royal on the Restoration of Charles II and was precocious enough to have some compositions published when he was only 14. He was appointed organist of Westminster Abbey in 1668 and royal 'musician for the virginals' the following year. His memorial states that he was 'scholar to the excellent musician Dr Christopher Gibbons'. In 1674 he became a Gentleman of the Chapel Royal, then succeeded Pelham Humfrey as Master of the Children there and as Composer, posts he held until his death.

In 1679 he gave up his Westminster Abbey place in favour of Henry Purcell, his pupil, taking it up again after the latter's death, together with Purcell's job as tuner of keyboard instruments at court. He also shared with Nicholas Staggins the court post of Composer for the Violins from 1682 to 1685, but this was abolished when the court establishment was revised by James II. From 1687 to 1703 he was also Almoner and Master of the Choristers at St Paul's Cathedral, and from 1700 was given a new post of Composer to the Chapel Royal. He may have been the first Doctor of Music to be awarded the degree by the Archbishop of Canterbury (in 1677).

With his busy life in various churches, it was natural for Blow to become a fluent composer of anthems and services. He was a master of the verse anthem with strings, favoured at the court of Charles II, and his contrapuntal style, using English false relations and 'old-fashioned' harmonies, is frequently extremely expressive: some of his best works are those setting highly emotional words. As a composer of secular music he was generally less successful, but if his attempts at the lighter song style do not match the melodiousness of some of his contemporaries, his odes contain powerful music, especially the masterly *Ode on the Death of Mr Henry Purcell* (published 1696) for countertenor duet, two recorders, and continuo, a threnody worthy of its subject. His short opera *Venus and Adonis* (produced London, c.1684) was intended for court circles; although uneven in quality it has fine moments. Blow also made a major contribution to the English organ and harpsichord repertory of his day.   DA/AA

📖 I. SPINK, *Restoration Cathedral Music, 1660–1714* (Oxford, 1995)

Bluebeard's Castle (*A Kékszakállú herceg vára*; 'Duke Bluebeard's Castle'). Opera in one act by Bartók to a libretto by Béla Balázs after a fairy tale by Charles Perrault (Budapest, 1918).

bluebeat. See SKA.

Blue Danube, By the Beautiful. See AN DER SCHÖNEN, BLAUEN DONAU.

bluegrass. Part of the American *country music tradition, with its heyday in the 1940s. Its characteristics are a quick tempo, with fiddle, banjo, and mandolin prominent. The greatest exponent is generally thought to be Bill Monroe, whose *Blue Moon of Kentucky* is definitive.   KG

blue note. One of the degrees of the scale perceived as departing in blues or jazz performance from the standard diatonic scale. The flattened 3rd and 7th (sometimes the flattened 5th) often appear in major-key contexts, and microtonal variants are common. Blue notes are best thought of as variations within a single flexible pitch area (as in many non-Western traditions) rather than as substitute notes, though interpreted in the latter way they offered an element of *exoticism to mid-20th-century art music.   JJD

blues. A black American folksong tradition that influenced deeply the evolution of *jazz and other popular musics of the 20th century. In origin, 'the blues' refers to a state of melancholy or depression; it came during the second half of the 19th century to be seen by black Americans as their characteristic emotion, and was later applied to the kind of singing that expressed it. The archetypal 'downhome' or country blues is an improvised solo song, with the (male) singer accompanying himself on guitar or banjo. The verbal form is typically a three-line stanza, the first line of which is immediately repeated while the singer extemporizes the third, rhyming line, and this is supported by a conventional 12-bar harmonic scheme: four bars on the tonic (two accompanying the first line), often with a flattened 7th in the fourth bar; two on the subdominant (accompanying the second line); two more on the tonic; two on the dominant 7th (accompanying the rhyming line); and a final two on the tonic. *Blue notes take their name from their idiomatic use in the style. Some of the earliest downhome blues singers to be recorded were Charley Patton (1929–34), the founder of a Mississippi blues tradition, and the Texan Blind Lemon Jefferson (from 1926). Many were recorded both in studios and in the field during the 1920s and 30s; among those who later acquired a large white audience were Robert Johnson (*d* 1938), Leadbelly, and Lightnin' Hopkins.

Beginning in about 1910 a popularizing type of blues had been pioneered by the Memphis bandleader W. C. Handy and was diffused by Mamie Smith (*Crazy Blues*, 1920) and other female singers, who performed on stage with the accompaniment of a New Orleans-style jazz band. This so-called 'classic' blues was immensely popular throughout the 1920s, and did much to sell what were then called 'race' records, aimed at the black audience. Classic blues exploited other musical resources drawn from the *ragtime and early jazz traditions; the 12-bar, three-line song form was often loosened or abandoned, and extended instrumental solos were common. Two of the foremost singers in this style were Ma Rainey and the extraordinary Bessie Smith; their heirs include Nina Simone and Odetta.

During the Depression of the 1930s Big Bill Broonzy helped make Chicago the centre of an approach to blues performance that drew on qualities of both the downhome and classic traditions. After World War II, as the music of black Americans became more appreciated by white audiences, an important school of Chicago blues arose, whose most notable exponents were Muddy Waters, Howlin' Wolf, and B. B. King. Their music used electronic amplification, and was more closely allied to the emerging styles of *rhythm and blues and *rock and roll. It acquired huge popularity and was extremely influential on white musicians. From the 1960s onwards, the blues became a central ingredient of the universal world of commercial popular music; at present it is cultivated by non-black musicians throughout Europe and in parts of Asia as well as North America. But it has ceased to be a central ingredient of black American musical expression, which has adopted in its place first *soul and *gospel, more recently *rap and *hip-hop.

The title of 'blues' is sometimes given to music that expresses the characteristic emotional state without drawing on the distinctive resources of the core tradition.   JJD

📖 P. OLIVER, *The Story of the Blues* (London, 1969, 2/1996) · J. TODD TITON, *Early Downhome Blues: A Musical and Cultural Analysis* (Urbana, IL, 1977, 2/1994) · G. KUBIK, *Africa and the Blues: Connections and Reconnections* (Jackson, MI, 1999)

Blüthner. German firm of piano makers founded in Leipzig in 1853 by Julius Blüthner (1824–1910). In 1873 he patented aliquot scaling (the addition of a fourth, sympathetic string to each trichord group in the treble) to enrich the upper register. His largely hand-made pianos, with their round tone, are highly prized.   AL

Blytheman, John. See BLITHEMAN, JOHN.

B minor Mass. A Latin Mass by Bach, BWV232, for soloists, chorus, and orchestra, assembled between 1747 and 1749.

bocca chiusa (It.). '[With the] mouth closed', i.e. humming. See also BOUCHE FERMÉE.

Boccherini, (Ridolfo) **Luigi** (*b* Lucca, 19 Feb. 1743; *d* Madrid, 28 May 1805). Italian composer and cellist. His father, a double-bass player, sent him to study in Rome at an early age, then went with him to Vienna, where they played in the orchestra of the imperial court theatre for several seasons. In 1764 Luigi was appointed a cellist in a leading musical establishment in Lucca, the Cappella Palatina, but in 1766 he set off on a concert tour with a friend, Filippo Manfredi, arriving in Paris in 1767; there he published some string quartets and trios and a set of sonatas for keyboard with violin accompaniment. Boccherini and Manfredi next went to Spain, where they played in opera performances and concerts. From 1770 Boccherini was composer and performer to the infante, Don Luis, at Aranjuez and later at Avila, a position he held until Don Luis died in 1785. During those years he composed many string quintets requiring two cellos.

His next appointment (1786) was as chamber composer to Prince Friedrich Wilhelm of Prussia, shortly afterwards crowned King Friedrich Wilhelm II (*d* 1797), who was an enthusiastic cellist. Although Boccherini probably never went to Prussia, he regularly sent music to his patron. For a number of years he was also employed by the Benavente-Osuna family, and his opera *La Clementina* was performed at the Countess of Benavente's palace in Madrid in 1786. His later years were clouded by ill health, but he continued to compose and from 1800 was employed by Lucien Bonaparte to organize and compose for his concerts.

Boccherini's works include about 30 symphonies, some concertos (most for cello), and, most important, over 300 chamber works. One of his contemporaries described him as 'Haydn's wife'—quite aptly, for whereas Haydn's strength lay chiefly in vigorous Allegro movements and tightly constructed development sections, Boccherini was at his most characteristic in sweet, cantabile melodies. More obviously *galant* in style than Haydn, he was by no means lacking in imagination. In the Symphony in D minor op. 12 no. 4 (1771), for example, the slow introduction returns at the opening of the finale, where it leads to a chaconne based on 'Enfer' ('Hell') from Gluck's ballet *Don Juan*; and in some of his quartets he indulged in a mild form of programme music, with imitations of birds and other country sounds. His quintets are his most successful music: in them the first violin and the 'alto violoncello' (a high cello part) are given the more elaborate melodies, while the other instruments are used for little more than filling in.   DA/FL

📖 G. DE ROTHSCHILD, *Luigi Boccherini: His Life and Work*, trans. A. Mayor (London, 1965)

boceto (Sp.). 'Sketch'; the word was used as a title by Granados and some other Spanish composers.

Bochsa, (Robert) **Nicolas Charles** (*b* Montmédy, Lorraine, 9 Aug. 1789; *d* Sydney, 6 Jan. 1856). French harpist and composer. He was official harpist to Napoleon, then to Louis XVIII, in whose service he composed seven operas. In 1817 he left France to avoid imprisonment for forgery and took up residence in London, where he was successful as a harpist and a concert impresario. He was declared bankrupt and revealed as a bigamist but through the king's influence was engaged as music director at the King's Theatre (1826–30). In 1839 he eloped with Henry Bishop's wife, Anna, and toured in Europe, America, and Australia as a harp virtuoso. He contributed to the development of modern harp technique, his compositions including many works for the instrument; he also wrote a much-admired harp method.   PS/DA/SH

Bockstriller (Ger.). *'Goat's trill'.

bodhrán (Erse). A *frame drum of Ireland, usually played with a short stick.

Bodley, Seóirse (*b* Dublin, 4 April 1933). Irish composer and teacher. He studied at the Royal Irish Academy of Music, the Stuttgart Musikhochschule, and University College, Dublin, where he became associate professor of music. His compositions, which include five symphonies and many other orchestral and choral works, incorporate some Irish folk music, of which he has made a special study; but he has also used serial and aleatory techniques, electronics, and computers.   PG/ABUR

Boehm, Theobald (*b* Munich, 9 April 1794; *d* Munich, 25 Nov. 1881). German flautist, goldsmith, and ironmaster. A virtuoso flautist in the Munich court orchestra, he opened a flute factory in Munich in 1828. In 1832 he introduced his new 'ring key' mechanism for simplifying fingering (the Boehm System) and in 1847 he brought out an improved metal flute, the design of which has remained essentially unchanged. He also wrote two flute manuals. From 1833 to 1846 he was in charge of reorganizing the Bavarian steel industry.
                                                                                          AL

Boehm system. The name belongs both to Theobald Boehm's acoustically correct system for the bore and fingerholes of *flutes and to the mechanism of keys, rods, and axles that made it possible to cover those holes. The two flute systems of 1832 (the 'conical Boehm') and 1847 (essentially the modern flute) improved both tone and tuning. The mechanisms were applied to all woodwinds with varying success, most notably to the clarinet.   JMo

Boëllmann, Léon (*b* Ensisheim, Alsace, 25 Sept. 1862; *d* Paris, 11 Oct. 1897). French composer and organist. He studied with Gigout at the École Niedermeyer in Paris, becoming organist at St Vincent-de-Paul; his early death, however, ended a composing career of considerable promise. Of his organ works, best known is the tuneful *Suite gothique* (1895) with its distinctive Toccata finale; there is also a *Deuxième suite*. His orchestral music includes the *Variations symphoniques* for cello and orchestra. Among his elegant, inventive chamber works, the Piano Quartet in F minor and cyclic Piano Trio in G major stand out.   WT/AT

Boëly, Alexandre (Pierre François) (*b* Versailles, 19 April 1785; *d* Paris, 27 Dec. 1858). French organist and composer. Father figure to the 19th-century French organ school, he was organist at St Germain-l'Auxerrois in Paris, where he had the organ fitted with a German pedalboard. His command of that instrument earned him a considerable reputation, and he was one of the first French organists to play the music of Bach. He left a striking legacy of compositions which combine fantasy and control, his music developing alongside improvements to the instrument. He thus founded a more serious school of French composer-organists whose tradition was continued by Franck and Saint-Saëns. His 24 pieces op. 12 (1843) and 12 pieces op. 18 (1856) are typical of his style.   RLS

Boesmans, Philippe (*b* Tongeren, 17 May 1936). Belgian composer. He studied at the Liège Conservatoire and with Henri Pousseur, with whom he later collaborated at the Liège electronic music studio. He was appointed composer-in-residence to the Théâtre de La Monnaie, Brussels, in 1986; his works include three operas, among them *Wintermärchen* (after Shakespeare's *A Winter's Tale*, 1999). He has also written pieces for orchestra and large ensembles (some with electronics), string quartets, and other chamber music.   ABur

Boësset, Antoine (de) (*b* Blois, 1586; *d* Paris, 8 Dec. 1643). French composer. He married Pierre Guédron's daughter and succeeded to his father-in-law's post of *Maître des enfants de la musique de la chambre du roy*. On Guédron's death in 1623 he became *surintendant* of the Royal Music. A favourite of Louis XIII, who showered honours on him, he composed pleasant *airs de cour* and ballet music.

Antoine's son, **Jean-Baptiste** (de) **Boësset** (*b* Paris, 1614; *d* Paris, 1685), inherited some of his father's posts and was also a composer, although it is possible that most of the surviving works ascribed to him are in fact by his father.   DA

Boeuf sur le toit, Le ('The Ox on the Roof'). Ballet by Milhaud to a scenario by Jean Cocteau (Paris, 1920); it was first performed as a music-hall spectacle, then as a ballet.

Bogen (Ger.). 'Bow'.

Bohème, La ('Bohemian Life'). 1. Opera in four acts by Puccini to a libretto by Giuseppe Giacosa and Luigi Illica after Henry Murger's novel *Scènes de la vie de Bohème* (1849) (Turin, 1896).

2. Opera in four acts by Leoncavallo to his own libretto after Murger's novel (Venice, 1897); it was revised as *Mimì Pinson* (Palermo, 1913).

Bohemia. See Czech Republic, 1–3.

Bohemian Girl, The. Opera in three acts by Balfe to a libretto by Alfred Bunn after Joseph Mazilier's and Jules-Henri Vernoy de Saint-Georges's ballet-pantomime *La Gypsy*, based on Miguel de Cervantes's story *La gitanilla* (London, 1843); it was given in Italian (London, 1858) as *La zingara* and in Paris (1869) as *La Bohémienne*.

Bohemia's Meadows and Forests. See From Bohemia's Woods and Fields.

Böhm, Georg (*b* Hohenkirchen, Thuringia, 2 Sept. 1661; *d* Lüneburg, 18 May 1733). German organist and composer. In the early 1690s, after study in Gotha and at Jena University, he went to Hamburg, where he met Reincken and Buxtehude, and absorbed into his keyboard writing significant French and Italian influences. From 1698 he served until his death as organist at the Johanniskirche in Lüneburg, where he may well have given encouragement to the young J. S. Bach. He is chiefly remembered for his organ works, but he also composed cantatas, songs, and a *St John Passion* (1704) formerly attributed to Handel.   WT/BS

Böhm, Karl (*b* Graz, 28 Aug. 1894; *d* Salzburg, 14 Aug. 1981). Austrian conductor. He studied at the Vienna Conservatory and with Guido Adler. After three years as a répétiteur at the Graz Opera, in 1921 he went to Munich to assist Bruno Walter, who strongly influenced him, as did Karl Muck. From the mid-1920s he made a reputation and held a succession of posts in German opera houses. In 1934 he began his important reign at the Dresden Opera, where he gave the premieres of several of Richard Strauss's operas. He became admired for his deep knowledge of the German and Austrian operatic and symphonic repertory as well as contemporary works. He conducted regularly at the Salzburg Festival and in Bayreuth.   JT

Boieldieu, (François-)Adrien (*b* Rouen, 16 Dec. 1775; *d* Jarcy, 8 Oct. 1834). French composer. He studied music with the organist of Rouen Cathedral and was himself appointed organist of St André, Rouen, in 1791. He wrote many *romances*, and two *opéras comiques* that were produced at the Théâtre des Arts; their success encouraged him to move to Paris in 1796. Four years later *Le Calife de Bagdad* set the seal on his reputation. He enrolled as a pupil with Cherubini, who had criticized his lack of technique, and his next work revealed greater skill and originality. Boieldieu, a formidable pianist, was made a professor at the Paris Conservatoire in 1798. In 1802 he married a beautiful dancer; but she was unfaithful to him and, in spite of his successful career in Paris, two years later he entered the service of Tsar Alexander I in St Petersburg, remaining there as director of the French Opera until 1811. During that time he wrote nine *opéras comiques* and incidental music to Racine's tragedy *Athalie*.

On his return to Paris, Boieldieu met with renewed success as an opera composer with *Jean de Paris* (1812), in which his lyricism and colourful orchestration came together. He continued to write *opéras comiques*, alone or in collaboration with other composers, and was granted several official marks of recognition, including the post of court composer in 1815. The climax of his career came with the production of *La Dame blanche* ('The White Lady', 1825), with a libretto based on novels by Walter Scott. Supporters of French *opéra comique* were delighted to have such a successful opera with which to combat the current vogue for Rossini, although in fact Boieldieu was influenced by the Italian composer, notably in his pacing and use of cumulative rhythms and in his construction of ensembles. Perhaps in part because of its popular Rossinian idiom *La Dame blanche* went on to become one of the most successful operas in 19th-century Europe. The failure of his next work, *Les Deux Nuits* ('The Two Nights', 1829), was followed by a gradual worsening of the tuberculosis he had contracted in Russia.   SH

bois (Fr., 'wood'). *Avec le bois*, 'with the wood' (of the bow, i.e. *col legno*); *les bois*, 'the woodwind'; *baguette de bois*, 'wooden-headed drumstick'.

Boismortier, Joseph Bodin de (*b* Thionville, 23 Dec. 1689; *d* Roissy-en-Brie, 28 Oct. 1755). French composer. He spent his early years in Metz and Perpignan, settling in Paris in 1723. He was an immensely prolific and technically polished composer whose opus numbers run to over 100, mostly sets of six sonatas (many are for amateurs, calling for a modest level of skill, and some

are for the fashionable instruments of the day as well as violin, flute, etc.). In style his music shows marked Italian influence. His sacred works include a Christmas motet that incorporated well-known *noëls* and was popular at the Concert Spirituel. Boismortier held positions leading the orchestra at the fair theatres, St Germain and St Laurent. His highly successful career left him a rich man.   DA/JAS

Boito, Arrigo [Enrico] (*b* Padua, 24 Feb. 1842; *d* Milan, 10 June 1918). Italian composer, librettist, and man of letters. His parents, an Italian painter and a Polish countess, separated when he and his brother were children. He studied at the Milan Conservatory but was from the beginning an intellectual with an interest in literature and foreign languages. With his friend Franco Faccio (subsequently famous as a conductor) he was granted a government subsidy for having written a patriotic cantata *Le sorelle d'Italia* (1861) and went to Paris for a time, travelling also in Poland, Germany, and England.

On his return to Milan (1862) Boito earned a living (with financial help from his brother, who became a well-known architect and restored some Venetian public buildings) by journalism and achieved a reputation as a leading figure in Italy's nascent bohemian movement, the *scapigliatura*: he offended Verdi by a particularly nasty remark concerning the current state of Italian opera. It was this reputation, rather than the music, which caused an uproar at the premiere of his opera *Mefistofele* (1868), an ambitious and somewhat diffuse distillation of Goethe's *Faust*; the orchestration was so dense that the opera was immediately accused of imitating Meyerbeer and other 'foreign' composers.

The initial failure of *Mefistofele* depressed Boito to the extent of deflecting him from composition, even though he was already thinking about another opera, *Nerone*. But the publisher Ricordi had noted his gifts and encouraged him to translate opera librettos, including *Der Freischütz* and *Tristan und Isolde*; this led in turn to the writing of several original librettos, including that of Ponchielli's *La Gioconda*. The successful revival of *Mefistofele* in a revised version at Bologna in 1875 finally established his reputation as a composer and assured his prosperity; but Ricordi, wishing to inspire Verdi to return to composition, saw Boito as the ideal librettist and reintroduced them in 1879. The result (after much suspicion on Verdi's part) was *Otello*, a masterpiece that owed a great deal to Boito's skill and taste.

In the early 1890s he again worked with Verdi, writing a libretto for *Falstaff*, a work that owes almost as much to Boito's subtle pointing of character and situation as to Verdi's music. Verdi, now a great friend, entrusted Boito with the preparations of the first performance (Paris, 1898) of his *Quattro pezzi sacri*, and encouraged him to finish *Nerone*, but this Boito never did. (Completed by Toscanini and Tommasini, it was produced in 1920 to public acclaim; but it had limited success and remains little known, critical opinion being that Boito was attempting something too complex for his musical gifts.) He became a senator in the Italian parliament in 1912; he had been awarded an honorary D.Mus. by Cambridge University in 1893, and was highly honoured and liked in Italy. He died after suffering from heart disease for some years.

DA/RP

📖 T. G. KAUFMAN, 'Arrigo Boito', *Verdi and his Major Contemporaries* (New York, 1990), 13–25

Bolcom, William (Elden) (*b* Seattle, 26 May 1938). American composer and pianist. He studied at the University of Washington, in Paris with Milhaud and Messiaen, and at Stanford with Leland Smith. In 1973 he began teaching at the University of Michigan. His large output shows an openness to music of all kinds, including American popular music, of which he is a noted performer, especially as accompanist to his wife, the singer Joan Morris. Among his works are two large-scale operas (*McTeague*, 1992, *A View from the Bridge*, 1999; both given in Chicago), symphonies and concertos, chamber music, and the concert-length *Songs of Innocence and Experience* for soloists, choirs, and orchestra (1956–82).

PG

Boléro. Ballet in one act by Ravel, choreographed by Bronislava Nijinska (Paris, 1928); it consists of the repetition of a theme, in C major almost throughout, in an unvarying rhythm and with a gradual crescendo. It has subsequently been choreographed by Serge Lifar (1941), Maurice Béjart (1961), and Leonid Lavrovsky among others.

Bologna, Jacopo da. See JACOPO DA BOLOGNA.

Bomarzo. Opera ('gothic melodrama of sex and violence') in two acts (15 scenes with instrumental interludes) by Ginastera to a libretto by Manuel Mujica Láinez after his own novel *Bomarzo* (Washington, DC, 1967).

bombarde. The English and French name (Ger.: *Pommer*) for the late medieval tenor *shawm, often with a bell in a shape perhaps reminiscent of the artillery mortar of the same name. In Brittany and parts of Italy the name survives today for the treble shawm used with the *bagpipe. In 19th-century Germany the name was revived as *Bombardon* for bass brass instruments, ini-

tially the keyed *bass horn and *ophicleide, and later for valved tubas.

AB/JMo

bombardon. In Britain, the E♭ bass tuba, and sometimes bass brass instruments in general, in military and especially brass bands. In Germany, *Bombardon* was a generic name for bass brass instruments in the 19th century. In Italy, *bombardino* means the *euphonium.

JMo

Bond, Capel (*b* Gloucester, *bapt.* 14 Dec. 1730; *d* Coventry, 14 Feb. 1790). English composer. He was apprenticed in 1742 to the organist of Gloucester Cathedral and acted for a time as sub-organist. From 1749 until his death he lived in Coventry, where he was organist at the churches of St Michael and All Angels and Holy Trinity. He conducted the first Birmingham Festival in 1768 and introduced Handel's oratorios to the Midlands. His own works include anthems and six concertos, four of them concerti grossi for strings and continuo and one each for trumpet and bassoon.

WT/PL

bones. *Clappers made from beef ribs or hardwood. They are played in pairs, each about 15 cm long, one held between the first and second fingers and the other between the second and third. They are clacked together with flicks of the wrist, and are capable of great rhythmic complexity. Pairs of *spoons produce a similar sound, but are played using a slightly different technique.

JMo

bongos [bongo drums]. A pair of small single-headed drums of different sizes, created in Cuba in about 1900 and originally used in Latin American dance bands. They are always played with the fingers, unlike the slightly larger but otherwise similar *timbales which are played with light sticks. Like *congas, bongos are highly tensioned, and a wide variety of sounds and pitches can be produced, using hand pressure and differing types and placement of strokes.

JMo

Bonini, Severo (*b* Florence, 23 Dec. 1582; *d* Florence, 5 Dec. 1663). Italian composer and writer on music. A Vallombrosan monk, he did various tours of duty in abbeys in and around Florence and in Forlì, ending up as *maestro di cappella* at Santa Trinità in Florence from 1640. Earlier, he had studied with Caccini and had published both secular and sacred music in the new styles of solo song and duet. His *Discorsi e regole sovra la musica* in manuscript (1649–50) contains an important, if biased, survey of the music of his time.

TC

Bonne Chanson, La ('The Good Song'). Song cycle, op. 61 (1892–4), by Fauré, settings of nine poems by Paul Verlaine.

Bononcini. Italian family of composers and instrumentalists. **Giovanni Maria Bononcini** (*b* Montecorone, nr Modena, *bapt.* 23 Sept. 1624; *d* Modena, 18 Nov. 1678) was a member of the 17th-century Modena school of violinist-composers and had published several volumes of trio sonatas by 1671, when he became a member of the court orchestra at Modena; in 1673 he was appointed *maestro di cappella* at the cathedral. He was an important precursor of Corelli in the development of the trio sonata and the evolution of violin technique. His sonatas also demonstrate the contrapuntal skills to be expected of the author of an influential treatise on counterpoint; they were popular in England and may have influenced Purcell.

   Giovanni Bononcini (*b* Modena, 18 July 1670; *d* Vienna, 9 July 1747) was the eldest son of Giovanni Maria, after whose death he went to Bologna; there he studied with Colonna and at the age of 15 became a member of the Accademia Filarmonica. By 18 he had become both *maestro di cappella* at S. Giovanni in Monte and a musician at S. Petronio, and had produced a large quantity of instrumental and sacred music. In 1692 he went to Rome, where he composed the opera *Il trionfo di Camilla*, which enjoyed unprecedented success in Italy and elsewhere. In 1697 he entered the service of Leopold I in Vienna at an enormous salary.

   By the time he returned to Italy in 1713 Bononcini was one of the most celebrated composers in Europe; his recruitment by the Earl of Burlington as composer to the Royal Academy of Music in London must have been a considerable coup for that organization. He arrived in London in 1720, and his first two seasons were triumphantly successful, but his association with aristocratic Jacobite sympathizers, one of whom was imprisoned for treason, brought him many influential enemies and seriously damaged his career. Nevertheless he remained in England until 1731, when the discovery that a piece performed under his name was actually by Lotti effectively forced him to leave for France. He returned to Vienna after a short visit to Lisbon.

   With Handel and Alessandro Scarlatti, Bononcini was one of the most famous composers of his time. In London he was regarded as virtually Handel's equal; both had their fervent supporters, giving rise to a contemporary jingle with the final couplet:

> Strange! That such high dispute should be
> Twixt Tweedledum and Tweedledee.

Bononcini, however, seems to have been best at simple, tuneful arias; Handel easily excelled him in more extended ones expressing strong emotions and delineating character.

   Antonio Maria Bononcini (*b* Modena, 18 June 1677; *d* Modena, 8 July 1726), the younger brother of Giovanni, also studied in Bologna. He then worked in Vienna until 1713, when he returned to Italy, becoming *maestro di cappella* at Modena in 1721. Padre Martini praised the skilful counterpoint and bold use of harmony in his small output of opera, cantatas, and church music, but these factors may have militated against his achieving a popular success comparable to that of his brother.   DA/ER

Bonporti, Francesco Antonio (*b* Trent, *bapt.* 11 June 1672; *d* Padua, 19 Dec. 1749). Italian composer. He studied music while training for the priesthood in Rome in 1691–5, and may have been a pupil of Corelli. In 1697 he returned to Trent as a minor cleric at the cathedral. Between 1696 and 1745 he published 11 volumes of instrumental music, including a collection of 100 minuets for violin and continuo, and a book of solo motets. He described himself as an amateur musician, and it appears that his principal motive in publishing was to secure the influence of a patron who would advance his ecclesiastical career, but the only appointments he obtained were purely titular. In 1740 he moved to Padua. His music does not deserve its present neglect; some of it was known to Bach (to whom a number of Veracini's pieces were once attributed, and who may have taken the title 'Invention' from him), and Veracini's repertory included one of Bach's sonatas.

                                                                                ER

boobams. Small tunable drums introduced in the USA in the 1950s. A set consists of resonating tubes of different lengths, originally of bamboo (hence the name) but now more commonly of synthetic material. The plastic drum-head at one end is struck with fingers or soft beaters. Pitch depends on the length of the air column, not the tension or diameter of the head. Sets of boobams cover two octaves or so and are arranged in the same pattern as a keyboard.   JMo

boogie-woogie [boogie]. A percussive and propulsive jazz piano style, supposed to have been developed in the *barrelhouses of the USA on the basis of earlier guitar blues from the lower Mississippi region; hence its early designation as the 'fast Western' style. Boogie-woogie is characterized by forceful, repeated bass figuration, almost always using the 12-bar format of the blues, with independent right-hand improvisation. Its moods range from the gentle blues of Jimmy Yancey to the stomping duets of Albert Ammons and Pete Johnson. 'Pine Top' Smith is generally credited as the first to use the title in *Pine Top's Boogie Woogie* (1928), though the style is earlier, and it remains an enduring accompaniment style in blues, rock and roll, and rhythm and blues.   PGᴀ

Book of Common Prayer. See COMMON PRAYER, BOOK OF.

Boosey & Hawkes. English firm of music publishers and instrument manufacturers. Thomas Boosey founded Boosey & Company in 1816 as an extension of his father's book trade. Initially importing foreign music, the company expanded rapidly, acquiring the rights to publish works by Rossini, Bellini, Donizetti, and Verdi. Later they turned to publishing ballads, made popular through the Boosey Ballad Concerts, launched in 1867. In the mid-19th century the company branched out as manufacturers of wind and brass instruments.

In 1930 Boosey amalgamated with the firm of Hawkes & Son. Founded in 1865 by William Henry Hawkes, this company had followed a rival course to Boosey & Co, specializing in music for brass and military bands and in instrument manufacture. In the decade following the merger, Boosey & Hawkes strengthened their publishing position with the acquisition of such composers as Bartók, Mahler, Kodály, and Delius. In 1935 they signed up the then unknown Benjamin Britten, remaining his principal publishers until 1963. Expansion continued in the 1940s with works by Richard Strauss, Stravinsky, Prokofiev, Rakhmaninov, Copland, and Martinů joining the catalogue. The company pursued its policy of promoting contemporary music throughout the latter half of the 20th century, its major composers including Adams, Louis Andriessen, Bernstein, Birtwistle, Carter, Górecki, MacMillan, Maxwell Davies, and Reich. The list was further enhanced in 1996 with the acquisition of the German publishing house Bote & Bock. In 1992 a Media Music division was launched to provide music for film, television, and commercials. Boosey & Hawkes has subsidiary companies in Australia, France, Germany, Japan, and the USA. HA

bop. See BEBOP.

Border pipes. See LOWLAND PIPE.

Bordes, Charles (Marie Anne) (*b* La Roche-Corbon, 12 May 1863; *d* Toulon, 8 Nov. 1909). French conductor, musicologist, and composer. He was a pupil of Franck and in 1892 founded the Association des Chanteurs de Saint-Gervais to perform the then almost unknown choral masterpieces of Palestrina, Lassus, Victoria, and others in the church of St Gervais in central Paris. Debussy became an ardent supporter. In 1894 Bordes, with d'Indy and Guilmant, founded the Schola Cantorum, which was likewise designed to promote the music of the 16th and 17th centuries. Bordes's 20 or so songs include some of the earliest settings of Verlaine. One contemporary described him as 'possessed by the

demon of enterprise, and filled with apostolic fury'. He died in poverty. RN

Bordoni [Hasse], Faustina (*b* Venice, 30 March 1697; *d* Venice, 4 Nov. 1781). Italian mezzo-soprano. Her singing teacher was Michelangelo Gasparini. In 1716 she made her debut in Venice in Pollarolo's *Ariodante*. For the following nine years she sang regularly there in operas by, among others, Albinoni, Lotti, and Orlandini, winning great admiration for her virtuosity, dramatic incisiveness, imaginative embellishments, and colourful acting. After her German debut in 1723 in Munich, she was in demand in Germany as well as in Austria and England. She created five new roles in Handel's works, including *Alessandro* and *Admeto*. In London she also sang in a notorious performance of Bononcini's *Astianatte* in which a fight broke out between her and her rival Francesca Cuzzoni. She was acclaimed in Milan and Rome, and in 1731 she and her husband, Johann Adolf Hasse, were engaged by the court in Dresden. There they achieved outstanding success, Bordoni singing in over 15 of Hasse's operas. JT

bore. The cavity of a tube. In a wind instrument, the bore profile determines the proportions of the *air column, while its length determines the lowest note of the instrument. The fundamental frequency may be unobtainable on an instrument with a narrow bore, and higher harmonics may be harder to sound with a wide bore. Reed instruments with conical bores (e.g. oboes) *overblow at the octave, and the clarinet, which has a cylindrical bore, overblows at the 12th. Tone-quality and intonation can be affected by minute irregularities in the bore. JMo

borea (It.). See BOURRÉE.

Boréades, Les (*Abaris*; 'The Descendants of Boreas'). Opera in five acts by Rameau to a libretto attributed to Louis de Cahusac; it is not known to have been performed complete during the composer's lifetime but was probably given in concert at Lille in the 1770s.

Borghi, Giovanni Battista (*b* Camerino, Macerata, 25 Aug. 1738; *d* Loreto, 25 Feb. 1796). Italian composer. He studied at the Naples Conservatory before taking up a position as *maestro di cappella* at Orvieto Cathedral in 1759. From 1778 until his death he served at the Santa Casa in Loreto, taking frequent breaks from his ecclesiastical duties to work on his operas, both serious and comic, which were performed mainly in Venice, Florence, and Rome. His most successful opera was *La morte di Semiramide* (Milan, 1791). The fact that his sacred music survives in many manuscript sources suggests that it was widely used. LC

Boris Godunov. Opera in seven scenes, or a prologue and four acts, by *Musorgsky to his own libretto adapted from Aleksandr Pushkin's play *The Comedy of the Distress of the Muscovite State, of Tsar Boris, and of Grishka Otrepyev* (1826), supplemented in the revised version with extracts from Nikolay Karamzin's *History of the Russian Empire* (1829). The original version was rejected by St Petersburg Opera in 1870, so Musorgsky revised it (St Petersburg, 1874). Rimsky-Korsakov's first revision was given in St Petersburg in 1896 and his second revision (the version that has most often been performed) in Paris in 1908.

Bořkovec, Pavel (*b* Prague, 10 June 1894; *d* Prague, 22 July 1972). Czech composer and teacher. He studied composition with Foerster and Suk. His early affinity with late Romanticism was superseded by an adherence to neo-classicism exemplified in such works as the Partita (1936), Concerto Grosso (1941), and the opera *Paleček* ('Tom Thumb', 1947). As professor of composition at the Prague Academy of Musical Arts he proved a major influence on the postwar generation of Czech composers.   JSM

Borodin, Aleksandr Porfir'yevich (*b* St Petersburg, 31 Oct./12 Nov. 1833; *d* St Petersburg, 15/27 Feb. 1887). Russian composer and chemist. An illegitimate son of a Georgian prince, he received a well-rounded home education; he spoke several languages fluently, played the flute and the cello, and showed an aptitude for the natural sciences. In 1856 he graduated from the Medico-Surgical Academy, two years later completing his doctoral dissertation in medicine. From 1864 he was a professor of chemistry at the Academy, and in 1872 also took part in the foundation of the Women's Medical Courses, teaching there until 1885. He was a scientist of international importance (there is even a chemical reaction that bears his name). Throughout his life, music remained an amateur pursuit to which he could devote himself only when on holiday or sick leave: his musical friends jokingly wished him sickness rather than good health. His output is therefore small (though he composed with great facility) and he completed few large-scale works.

As a student Borodin participated in amateur music-making and wrote several chamber ensembles, among them a Piano Quintet (1862), which provides evidence of his technical proficiency but also a debt to Mendelssohn and Schumann. He began to take composition more seriously and to create an individual voice after meeting Balakirev in 1862; he joined the Balakirev circle of young composers (Musorgsky, Rimsky-Korsakov, Cui), which later became known as The Five. Under Balakirev's guidance he undertook a larger project, and in 1867 completed his First

Symphony. The songs of this decade often showed still greater originality, for example the free use of major 2nds in *Spyashchaya knyazhna* ('The Sleeping Princess').

Encouraged by the public success of the First Symphony (performed in 1869 under Balakirev), Borodin was sufficiently confident to undertake a more ambitious task: an opera on a Russian epic tale. *Prince Igor*, as the opera was to be called, was eagerly awaited by The Five and their supporters, but progress was slow, in spite of much friendly prodding; some numbers, including the celebrated Polovtsian Dances, even had to be orchestrated and copied collectively for concert performance because of the many other demands on Borodin's time.

The music that did materialize shows Borodin at the height of his compositional powers, as did the Second Symphony (1877), which his friends considered a companion-piece to the opera, hence the symphony's nickname 'Bogatïrskaya' (from *bogatïri*, the mighty warriors found in Russian epics). Both symphonies were written in a monumental, heroic style, but Borodin's two quartets (no. 1, 1879; no. 2, 1881) show that he was no less capable of producing long, flowing melodies, often with an oriental tinge. Between the two he completed his 'symphonic sketch' *In the Steppes of Central Asia*. Unlike the other members of The Five, Borodin never quoted Russian folksongs, but artfully incorporated their features into his own music; he was therefore considered no less 'Russian' than his colleagues.

In spite of his dwindling productivity during the late 1870s and the 1880s, Borodin grew in fame as a composer and began to receive attention from abroad. Liszt was one of his first Western admirers, to whom Borodin paid several visits during his European trips, finding him an agreeable host. Borodin also won the enthusiastic patronage of the Comtesse de Mercy-Argenteau, who organized concerts of his music in Brussels and Liège in 1885. In 1887, at the peak of his double career in music and chemistry, Borodin had a fatal heart attack while attending a ball. His friends mourned a kind and generous man as well as a great talent. Glazunov and Rimsky-Korsakov attended to his unfinished works: Acts III and IV of *Prince Igor* required further compositional work, and Rimsky-Korsakov orchestrated the results; Glazunov, possessor of an exceptional musical memory, was able to provide the Overture, which he had once heard the composer play at the piano. Glazunov also succeeded in recovering from his memory two movements of Borodin's projected Third Symphony.   PS/MF-W

📖 G. ABRAHAM, *Borodin: The Composer and his Music* (London, 1927/R); *Studies in Russian Music* (London, 1935,

2/1969), 102–18, 119–41; *On Russian Music* (London, 1939/*R*), 90–112, 147–68, 169–78

borre, borree. Old English spellings of *bourrée.

Bortnyansky, Dmitry Stepanovich (*b* Hlukhiv, Ukraine, 1751; *d* St Petersburg, 28 Sept./10 Oct. 1825). Russian composer of Ukrainian extraction. As a child he was a member of the imperial court chapel choir in St Petersburg, where he studied with Galuppi, director of the chapel at the time. He then won a scholarship to study in Italy, where he wrote three operas, *Creonte* (1776), *Alcide* (1778), and *Quinto Fabio* (1779). Returning to Russia in 1779, he became Kapellmeister to the court chapel choir and was appointed director in 1796. He is best remembered as a composer of sacred music, and especially for his elegant choral concertos (about 50), which combine contrapuntal development with Classical forms. Among his secular works are several *opéras comiques*—notably *Le Faucon* (1786) and *Le Fils rival, ou La Moderne Stratonice* (1787), produced at the Russian court by amateur forces under Bortnyansky himself—as well as keyboard sonatas, chamber ensembles, and a *Symphonie concertante* (1790). GN/MF-W

Bose, Hans-Jürgen von (*b* Munich, 24 Dec. 1953). German composer. He was, by his own account, 'brought up in a typical German tradition', studying composition and piano at the Frankfurt Musikhochschule. He had early success at home and abroad, receiving premieres from both the London Sinfonietta and the Ensemble InterContemporain in 1978. In 1992 he was appointed professor of composition at the Staatliche Hochschule für Musik in Munich. Bose is best known for his operas, including *Die Leiden des jungen Werthers* (after Goethe; Schwetzingen, 1986), *63: Dream Palace* (Munich, 1990), and *Schlachthof V* (after Kurt Vonnegut's *Slaughterhouse-Five*; Munich, 1996). He has also written ballets, orchestral music, three string quartets and other chamber music, and a cycle of *Sappho-Gesänge* for mezzo-soprano and ensemble (1983). ABur

Bösendorfer. Austrian firm of piano makers founded in Vienna in 1828 by Ignaz Bösendorfer (1796–1859). Liszt's endorsement brought the company international renown and royal patronage, its 33 models winning many prizes and being among the best pianos ever built. A Bösendorfersaal opened in Vienna in 1872. AL

Bossi, (Marco) Enrico (*b* Salò, Lake Garda, 25 April 1861; *d* at sea, Atlantic Ocean, 20 Feb. 1925). Italian organist and composer. He studied with Amilcare Ponchielli at the Milan Conservatory (1873–81) and then embarked on a career as a teacher in musical academies, becoming director of the Accademia di S.

Cecilia in Rome in 1916. He also enjoyed success as a recital organist, and died while returning from appearances in the USA. Unlike most Italian composers of his generation, he paid little attention to opera, instead cultivating a severe contrapuntal style in his many organ works, orchestral pieces, and oratorios. PG

Boston Handel and Haydn Society. The oldest oratorio society in the USA, founded in 1815 for the purpose of 'cultivating and improving a correct taste in the performance of sacred music'; it gave first American performances of many major European works and now presents about six concerts a year. JBo

Bottesini, Giovanni (*b* Crema, nr Milan, 22 Dec. 1821; *d* Parma, 7 July 1889). Italian double-bass player, conductor, and composer. He was given a scholarship to the Milan Conservatory at a very early age on condition that he take up the double bass, this offering the only vacant place. He became a leading virtuoso on the instrument and travelled the world, being for a time principal double bass at the Teatro Tacón, Havana, where his first opera, *Cristoforo Colombo* (1848), was given. He visited England frequently, writing an oratorio—*The Garden of Olivet*—for the 1887 Norwich Festival; he was also a prolific composer of virtuoso double-bass pieces and a distinguished conductor, giving the first performance of Verdi's *Aida* in Cairo (1871). He died shortly after being appointed director of the Parma Conservatory. DA/RP

bottleneck. A device used by blues guitarists to achieve a smooth *portamento* effect. The open strings of the guitar are tuned to a chord (typically E or G), and the neck of a bottle is used to stop the strings. In this way players can produce the primary chords of a particular key without the need for fingering patterns. A metal slide is sometimes used in place of glass, although the original bottleneck is still often encountered. SM

bouche fermée (Fr.). '[With the] mouth closed', i.e. humming. See also BOCCA CHIUSA.

bouchés, sons. See SONS BOUCHÉS.

Boucourechliev, André (*b* Sofia, 28 July 1925; *d* Boulogne-Billancourt, 13 Nov. 1997). Bulgarian-born French composer and writer. In 1946 he entered the Sofia Conservatory to study the piano and after three years went to the École Normale de Musique, Paris. After obtaining his 'licence de concert' in 1951 he remained at the École Normale for another eight years, teaching the piano. Meanwhile he began to compose, attending the summer course in Darmstadt in 1954. An early work, *Texte 1*, uses tape to explore indeterminacy in pitch, dynamic, and rhythm. A series of nine pieces called *Archipels* took this principle further: each is written on a single, vast sheet over which the performer(s) have to navigate, taking their cue (in the larger pieces) from the other musicians. Among other works that attracted attention were *Grodek* (1963, rev. 1969), a dramatic setting of Georg Trakl for soprano, flute, and percussion, *Faces* (1971–2) for chamber orchestra, and *Amers* (1972–3) for large orchestra. Boucourechliev's books include a study of Schumann (1956), a pictorial biography of Chopin (1962), and volumes on Beethoven (1963) and Stravinsky (1982).

MA

Bouffons, Les (Fr.) [matassins, mattachino]. A sword dance for four described in some detail by Arbeau in his dance manual *Orchésographie* (1588). See also MORESCA.

Bouffons, Querelle [Guerre] des (Fr.). A dispute, between the supporters of serious French opera and Italian comic opera, that raged in Paris between 1752 and 1754. It was provoked by a performance on 1 August 1752 of Pergolesi's *La serva padrona* by Eustachio Bambini's visiting troupe (the 'Bouffons'), but its roots lay in the discontent that was widely felt by intellectuals, especially Rousseau and the Encyclopedists, with the state of French opera, and more generally with the degree of control exercised by the king, both over the Opéra and in constitutional matters. Supporters of French opera came to be identified as the 'coin du roi' and of Italian as the 'coin de la reine'. Religious issues (Jesuits v. Jansenists) were also involved. The musical dispute, though vigorously argued by Grimm, Rousseau (notably in his *Lettre sur la musique française*, 1753), Diderot, and others, who saw Italian comic opera, with its greater simplicity and more natural expression, as a breath of fresh air, was in a sense unreal, since comparison between the exalted *tragédie lyrique* and the Italians' skittish *opere buffe* and intermezzos was essentially meaningless; but it served to symbolize a wider dispute that affected many aspects of French political and intellectual life at the time.   SS

Boughton, Rutland (*b* Aylesbury, 23 Jan. 1878; *d* London, 25 Jan. 1960). English composer. He studied for a short period at the RCM with Stanford and Walford Davies (1900–1) and, rescued from poverty by Granville Bantock, taught at the Midland Institute School of Music in Birmingham (1904–11). His attraction to Morrisonian socialism and Wagner's music dramas led to the creation of an English Bayreuth at Glastonbury (though plans for a theatre were unfulfilled) with a strong English choral dimension. He produced a cycle of Arthurian operas (written between 1908 and 1945), but his most famous work for the stage was his Celtic romance *The Immortal Hour* (1914), which received hundreds of performances in Bir-

mingham and London between 1921 and 1926. Boughton's style ranges from the genuinely symphonic (as in the Third Symphony of 1937) to the naively simple (e.g. his choral drama *Bethlehem* of 1915), underpinned by a conservative harmonic vocabulary symptomatic of his socialist realism. He remained politically active for much of his life as a member of the Communist Party, published books, and wrote articles for *The Sackbut*. He was granted a civil list pension in 1937.   PG/JD1

📖 M. HURD, *Immortal Hour: The Life and Period of Rutland Boughton* (London, 1962, enlarged 2/1993 as *Rutland Boughton and the Glastonbury Festivals*)

Boulanger, Lili (*b* Paris, 21 Aug. 1893; *d* Mézy, 15 March 1918). French composer. Influenced in her childhood by Fauré and by her elder sister Nadia, she went on to study at the Paris Conservatoire. She was the first woman to win the Prix de Rome, in 1913. She composed prolifically, in spite of the ill health that led to her early death. Her works include a few orchestral and instrumental pieces; much choral music, including the powerful setting of Psalm 130, *Du fond de l'abîme* (completed 1917); and the song cycle *Clairières dans le ciel* (completed 1914).   ABur

Boulanger, Nadia (Juliette) (*b* Paris, 16 Sept. 1887; *d* Paris, 22 Oct. 1979). French conductor, pianist, organist, and teacher. She studied at the Paris Conservatoire with Fauré and others. Her career included notable successes as a conductor: she was the first woman to conduct an entire concert of the Royal Philharmonic Society (1937); she was active in reviving Monteverdi between the wars; she was a celebrated interpreter of the Fauré Requiem, making a pioneering recording (1948); and she was a loyal advocate of the music of her friend Stravinsky and her sister Lili.

Her outstanding contribution, however, was in teaching, at the Paris Conservatoire and, from 1921, at her own American Conservatory in Fontainebleau, as well as in the USA between 1940 and 1946. 'Mademoiselle', as she was known, imparted the qualities of discipline, clarity, and coherence to many distinguished composers in several generations: among Americans, Aaron Copland, Roy Harris, and Elliott Carter all studied with her; so did Europeans including Igor Markevitch and Jean Françaix, and British composers from Lennox Berkeley to James Wood.   PG/ABur

📖 L. ROSENSTIEL, *Nadia Boulanger: A Life in Music* (New York, 1982)

Boulevard Solitude. Opera in seven scenes by Henze to a libretto by Grete Weil after Walter Jockisch's *Boulevard Solitude*, itself based on Antoine-François

Prévost's novel *L'Histoire du chevalier des Grieux et de Manon Lescaut* (1731) (Hanover, 1952).

Boulez, Pierre (*b* Montbrison, 26 March 1925). French composer and conductor. He studied at the Paris Conservatoire with Messiaen (1942–5) and privately with Andrée Vaurabourg for counterpoint and René Leibowitz for serial technique. In 1946 he was appointed musical director of the Renaud–Barrault company, with which he toured internationally during the early 1950s. At the same time he was rapidly developing his musical style on the basis of Schoenberg's *serialism, the rhythmic methods of Stravinsky and Messiaen, and Webern's tightly integrated approach to composition. His first works, which include two piano sonatas (1946 and 1948) and the cantata *Le Soleil des eaux* (1948), show an awesome intellectual command allied with an expressive force capable of both lyrical ecstasy and intransigent violence.

With the first book of *Structures* for two pianos (1951–2) Boulez achieved a definitive conjunction of the methods of his predecessors, creating and transcending a 'total serial' style in which every musical aspect—pitch, duration, loudness, and attack—is organized according to serial rules. Having thus laid the foundations for a new musical language, he went on to show the power and suppleness of that language in *Le Marteau sans maître* for contralto and six instrumentalists (1953–5), where three short poems by René Char form the basis for an elaborate, densely polyphonic, and fugitively coloured cycle of movements.

Boulez's next departure was to introduce chance into his music, following the work of Cage but with strict limitations. In the Third Piano Sonata (1955–7) he allows abundant choices to the performer, concerning tempos and dynamics, and also the order of the material. The second book of *Structures* (1956–61) takes advantage of extra possibilities available with a duo: the score provides musical cues and allows a loosening of ensemble at some points. Both of these works indicate the importance to Boulez of Stéphane Mallarmé's aesthetics, and in *Pli selon pli* for soprano and orchestra (1957–62) he created a 'portrait' of the poet, again permitting various kinds of aleatory mobility. Equally striking here is the finesse of Boulez's orchestration, and in particular his poetic use of the glittering sonorities of tuned percussion, which is also a feature of his *Éclat/multiples* for orchestra (1965–).

Éclat/multiples, like many of Boulez's later compositions, remains 'work in progress'; indeed, of his works since 1962 only the orchestral *Rituel* (1974–5) has been published in a complete form. To some extent this diminished rate of output may be attributed to Boulez's increased activity as a conductor. In 1954 he founded the Domaine Musical concerts in Paris, their programmes including new scores and music from the Renaissance and Baroque, and from 1957 to 1967 he conducted many of them himself. He also became increasingly in demand as a guest conductor throughout Europe and the USA, and was eventually appointed chief conductor of both the BBC Symphony Orchestra (1969–74) and the New York Philharmonic (1969–77).

Since then he has curtailed his conducting commitments in order to concentrate again on composition. He was the founder-director of the *Institut de Recherche et de Coordination Acoustique/Musique (IRCAM) in Paris, where work on digital sound transformation enabled him to embark upon several long-developing projects, among them '... *explosante-fixe* ...' for electronic flute and chamber orchestra (1971–93), *Répons* for six tuned percussion soloists, similarly wired and accompanied by a similar ensemble (1981–), and *Dialogue de l'ombre double* for clarinet and electronics (1982–5). Other works of this period include *Notations* for orchestra (1977–).

Boulez's abilities, his energy, and his multiple activities—as composer, theorist, conductor, and advocate—have resulted in his having great influence on fellow composers and on musical life generally.

PG

📖 P. BOULEZ, *Boulez on Music Today* (Eng. trans., London, 1971) · *Pierre Boulez: Conversations with Célestin Deliège* (Eng. trans., London, 1976) · P. GRIFFITHS, *Boulez* (London, 1978) · P. BOULEZ, *Orientations* (Eng. trans., London, 1986) · L. KOBLYAKOV, *Pierre Boulez: A World of Harmony* (Chur, 1990) · P. BOULEZ, *Stocktakings from an Apprenticeship* (Eng. trans., Oxford, 1991) · D. JAMEUX, *Pierre Boulez* (Eng. trans., London, 1991) · J.-J. NATTIEZ (ed.), *The Boulez–Cage Correspondence* (Eng. trans., Cambridge, 1993) · G. BORN, *Rationalizing Culture: IRCAM, Boulez, and the Institutionalization of the Avant-Garde* (Berkeley, CA, 1995) · J. VERMEIL, *Conversations with Boulez: Thoughts on Conducting* (Eng. trans., Portland, OR, 1996)

Boult, Sir **Adrian** (Cedric) (*b* Chester, 8 April 1889; *d* Farnham, 24 March 1983). English conductor. After studying with Hugh Allen at Oxford he spent a year at the Leipzig Conservatory (1912–13), where he was deeply influenced by Nikisch's flexible style. He was a répétiteur with the Covent Garden Opera in 1914, and in 1918 gained recognition when he gave the premiere of Holst's *The Planets*. In 1924 he became music director of the City of Birmingham Symphony Orchestra, and in 1930 was appointed the first music director of the BBC Symphony Orchestra. For 18 years he was internationally revered in this post, performing an enormous repertory, including many premieres, and nurturing a finely balanced and stylistically aware ensemble, one of the best in the world. A keen advocate of British music, especially that of Elgar, Vaughan Williams, Holst, and Bliss (whose music he introduced to foreign audiences), he was also acclaimed in Schubert, Brahms, Tchaikovsky, and Ravel. He gave the first British performances of Berg's *Wozzeck* (1934) and wrote an autobiography (*My Own Trumpet*, 1973). He was knighted in 1937. JT

📖 M. KENNEDY, *Adrian Boult* (London, 1987)

bourdon (Fr.). 'Drone', 'drone pipe', or 'drone string'. The term also sometimes denotes the lowest pipe, string, voice, or register whether used for a drone or for a low, often repetitive accompaniment. Depending on the nature of the instrument or music, bourdons can be incessant or intermittent and may, for example when humming while blowing a flute, change from one pitch to another. The word is also used for the lowest bell in a ring without implying a drone. JMo

Bourgeois gentilhomme, Le ('The Would-be Gentleman'). *Comédie-ballet* in five acts by Molière, for which Lully wrote the music for the first performance (Chambord, 1670). Richard Strauss wrote incidental music for Hugo von Hofmannsthal's adaptation of Molière's play (Berlin, 1918), later arranging it as a suite (1920).

bourrée (Fr.; It.: *borea*) [borre, borree]. A dance that probably originated in the Auvergne, where it was accompanied by such folk instruments as the musette or the hurdy-gurdy. It was adapted into fashionable French social life during the 17th and 18th centuries as a couple dance in quick duple metre with a characteristic single upbeat. Michael Praetorius mentions the dance in his *Syntagma musicum* (1615) and included an example in his *Terpsichore* (1612), but it does not seem to have been used as an instrumental form until the second half of the 17th century. The bourrée occurs frequently in operas and ballets by French court composers including Lully, Charpentier, Campra, and Rameau. Like the gavotte, it later found its way into the *suite as an optional movement, where it often followed the sarabande. Handel included two bourrées in his *Water Music*, and pairs of bourrées occur in Bach's French Suites and orchestral suites. —/JBE

boutade (Fr.). An improvised composition, usually a dance. Rousseau's *Dictionnaire de musique* (1768) defines it both as an extemporized ballet and as an instrumental caprice or fantasia.

Boutique fantasque, La ('The Fantastic Toyshop'). Ballet in one act arranged by Respighi from Rossini's *Soirées musicales* and other pieces to a scenario by André Derain; it was choreographed by Leonid Massine for Diaghilev's Ballets Russes (London, 1919).

bouts. The curved sections of the *ribs of a stringed instrument such as a violin or a viol. The concave sections that form the waist are the middle bouts, and the convex sections either side are the upper and lower bouts.

bouzouki. A Greek long-necked lute with a bowl resonator and wire strings plucked with a plectrum, deriving from the Turkish *saz but now resembling a long-necked mandolin, with fixed metal frets instead of movable gut, and machine tuning-heads instead of pegs. Older instruments have three double courses, but present-day ones usually have four courses, tuned *d/d′– g–b–e′* or *c/c′–f–a–d′*. A very similar smaller instrument is the *baglamas*. In the late 20th century the bouzouki was adopted by players of Irish traditional music, and a version was developed with a pear-shaped, flat-backed body (similar in shape to the flat-backed mandolin), played in a variety of tunings. JMo

bow (Fr.: *archet*; Ger.: *Bogen*; It.: *arco*). A rod, normally of wood, with horsehair stretched between each end, used to apply friction to fiddle strings, causing them to vibrate. The hair must be tensioned and be rubbed with *rosin or a similar compound to grip the string. The development of the bow began in Central Asia about AD 800, first as a friction-stick or roughened grass-stem. Simple bows are tensioned by the natural spring of the stick, bent like an archer's bow, which can be enhanced by the fingers of the bowing hand acting on the stick and the hair. In some areas of Asia and Europe early bows consisted of a straight stick with the hair loosely attached; the player would tighten the hair with the fingers of the bowing hand while playing.

In Renaissance Europe the stick became straighter, and a wooden *frog was wedged between stick and hair to hold them apart at the *heel. The early 'clip-in' frog rested in a slot in the stick, but tensioning by drawing the frog back with a screw was introduced during the 18th century. A typical Baroque violin or viol bow had a finely tapered snakewood stick, almost straight or slightly curved outwards.

In the latter part of the 18th century, makers including François Tourte in Paris and John Dodd in London developed the modern violin bow, now known by Tourte's name, with a stronger head that holds the hair further from the wood, and an inward curve giving greater strength. Modern bows are made of pernambuco, but as this becomes increasingly expensive and difficult to obtain some makers are experimenting with carbon fibre and other synthetics. For cheap bows, fibreglass sticks and nylon hair are popular, but nothing as yet compares with pernambuco and horsehair.

When the bow is held with an overhand grip, as it always is when the instrument is held horizontally (e.g. the violin), the down-bow (when the bow is pulled across the strings) is the stronger stroke, but the up-bow (or push-bow) is stronger when the bow is held with an underhand grip, as with many types of fiddle that are held vertically, including viols (but with the notable exceptions of the cello and, sometimes, the double bass).   AB/JMo

bow, musical. The simplest, and earliest, stringed instrument (whether the archer's bow or the musical bow came first is debated). Found throughout the world, it consists solely of a flexible stick with a string (or strings) stretched between its ends. Selective overtones of the string can be made to resonate if the bow is held against the mouth; or a gourd resonator can be more or less widely opened against the player's chest, allowing different harmonics to resonate. A second fundamental can be obtained if the string is stopped with the thumb or a stick. Different types may be sounded by the player plucking, tapping, or rubbing the string, or scraping across serrations cut along one side of the stick.   JMo

Bowen, (Edwin) York (*b* London, 22 Feb. 1884; *d* London, 23 Nov. 1961). English composer and pianist. He studied at the RAM (1898–1905) with Frederick Corder and Tobias Matthay, and, like his contemporaries Bax and Holbrooke, fell under the spell of the German progressives, Wagner, Liszt, and Richard Strauss. He produced three piano concertos between 1904 and 1908 (in two of which he appeared as soloist under Hans Richter at the Queen's Hall) and a fourth in 1929. There are also two symphonies and solo concertos for violin and viola. The most substantial part of his output is taken up with solo piano music, much of which he, as a virtuoso, played himself. He also wrote six sonatas (three are unpublished), suites, *ballades*, *romances*, 24 preludes in all major and minor keys, and numerous other miniatures. Bowen published two books on piano technique (1936, 1961).   JD1

   M. WATSON, *York Bowen: A Centenary Tribute* (London, 1984)

Bowles, Paul (Frederic) (*b* Jamaica, NY, 30 Dec. 1910; *d* Tangiers, 18 Nov. 1999). American composer and writer. He went to Paris in 1929, returned to New York in 1930–1 to study with Copland, and then went back to Paris. There he moved in expatriate artistic circles, from which he escaped for periods of travel, until making a more or less permanent home in north Africa in 1947. He wrote two operas based on plays by Lorca (*The*

Wind Remains, New York, 1943; *Yerma*, Denver, 1958), ballets (*Yankee Clipper*, 1936), chamber pieces, and songs, but virtually abandoned composition after *Yerma* to concentrate on writing. His distinction as a novelist overshadowed his musical achievements until there was a revival of interest in the latter in the 1990s.   PG

   C. SWAN (ed.), *Paul Bowles: Music* (New York, 1995)

Boyce, William (*b* London, *bapt.* 11 Sept. 1711; *d* Kensington, 7 Feb. 1779). English composer, organist, and scholar. He was a chorister at St Paul's Cathedral and then became an organ pupil of Maurice Greene. In 1734 he gained the post of organist to the chapel of the Earl of Oxford, and two years later was made composer to the Chapel Royal, succeeding John Weldon. He was also a conductor at the Three Choirs Festival. Among his major early works are the small-scale oratorio *David's Lamentation over Saul and Jonathan* (1736), the masque *Peleus and Thetis* (before 1740), the serenata *Solomon* (1742), and *The Secular Masque* (*c.*1746). The first volume of his collection of songs, *Lyra britannica*, and 12 trio sonatas were published in 1747, and in 1749 his ode *Here all thy active fires defuse* was written for the installation of the Duke of Newcastle as chancellor of Cambridge University. At this time too Boyce received his Cambridge doctorate, and several of his compositions were performed there in what was effectively a one-man festival.

For the next few years Boyce worked for Garrick at Drury Lane, composing everything from short operas to songs and instrumental music. After Maurice Greene's death he was made Master of the King's Music, in which post he produced two odes each year— one for the new year and one for the king's birthday. The overtures to these, some quite extensive, formed the basis of his *Twelve Overtures* (1770), and two others were included in the *Eight Symphonys* (1760).

Increasing deafness caused Boyce to withdraw from his duties as organist at various churches, although he became an organist at the Chapel Royal in 1758 and spent the latter part of his life compiling three volumes of *Cathedral Music* (1760, 1768, 1773), a collection covering 200 years that subsequently provided much of the repertory of English cathedral and church choirs. He was buried in St Paul's Cathedral. *Cathedral Music* kept his name alive during the 19th century, but many of Boyce's own compositions have been successfully revived and published in more recent years.

DA/PL

   H. D. JOHNSTONE and R. FISKE (eds.), *The Eighteenth Century*, The Blackwell History of Music in Britain, iv (Oxford, 1990)

Boyd, Anne (Elizabeth) (*b* Sydney, 10 April 1946). Australian composer. She studied with Peter

Sculthorpe at Sydney University and with Wilfrid Mellers and Bernard Rands at York University (1969–72), after which she stayed in England as a lecturer at the University of Sussex (1972–7). During these years in England she wrote her first important works, including *Angklung* for piano. She then returned to Australia before becoming head of music at the University of Hong Kong (1981–90), and returned again to take a similar position at Sydney University. Much of her music has to do with Australian and Asian subjects and musical traditions.　　　　　　　　　　　PG

Bozay, Attila (*b* Balatonfűzfő, 11 Aug. 1939; *d* Budapest, 14 Sept. 1999). Hungarian composer. He studied at the Budapest Academy of Music with Ferenc Farkas, and from 1963 to 1966 worked for Hungarian Radio. His music combines modernist and folk influences, and shows a particular sensitivity to timbre; he wrote several times for the zither, an instrument he himself played.　　　　　　　　　　　　　　　　　　ABur

Br. (Ger.). Abbreviation for *Bratschen*, 'violas'.

Brabançonne, La ('Après des siècles d'esclavage'). Belgian national anthem. It was written in 1830 during the struggle with Holland for independence. The music is by François van Campenhout (1779–1848) and the original text was by Hippolyte Louis Alexandre Dechet (1801–30); the present words, by Charles Rogier, were substituted in 1860. The Flemish population had their own anthem until 1951, when they adopted *La Brabançonne*.　　　　　　　　　　　　　　　AL

brace (Fr.: *accolade*). The perpendicular line and bracket connecting two or more staves in piano or orchestral scores; also a name for the staves thus connected.

Brade, William [Wilhelm] (*b* 1560; *d* Hamburg, 26 Feb. 1630). Violinist and composer. He was probably born and trained in England, but was later based in Germany and Denmark. Nothing certain is known about his early career. By 1594 he had left England, and over the course of the next 30 years he held various court and civic appointments in Copenhagen, Berlin, Hamburg, and Halle, and in the service of the Brandenburg and Brunswick courts, among others. At the outbreak of the Thirty Years War he settled in Hamburg, where he died. Brade's compositions, written for instrumental consort, reflect the international tastes of the courtly circles in which he worked. Dances predominate, in a variety of styles, English, French, German, and Italian.　　　　　　　　　　　　　　　　　　　JM

Braga Santos, (José Manuel) **Joly** (*b* Lisbon, 14 May 1924; *d* Lisbon, 18 July 1988). Portuguese composer. His output covered a wide range of forms including stage

and film work, with six powerfully argued symphonies at the core. The first four, written between 1946 and 1951, are couched in a conservative, polyphonic-modal idiom reminiscent of Sibelius or Vaughan Williams. A sabbatical break devoted to travel and conducting (1955–61) nurtured a much tougher, atonal style which was fully developed in his massive Symphony no. 5 (1965–6), with its percussive Mozambique rhythms, and the aphoristic no. 6 (1972), in one movement with a choral finale.　　　　　　　　　　　　　　　　　　CW

Brahms, Johannes (*see page 160*)

Braille notation. A system of musical notation for the blind devised by Louis Braille (1809–52). Successive six-dot clusters have different members raised so as to indicate (by the top four dots) pitch, and (by various other combinations) duration, rests, and the correct octave. Several variants of the system are in use, and there are now computerized methods for producing Braille notation from conventional scores. Some recent avant-garde works are resistant to translation into the Braille system.　　　　　　　　　　　　　AP

Brain, Dennis (*b* London, 17 May 1921; *d* Hatfield, Herts., 1 Sept. 1957). English horn player. A son of the great horn player Aubrey Brain (1893–1955), he made his debut with the Busch Chamber Players in 1938; he became principal of the original Royal Philharmonic Orchestra and the Philharmonia as well as establishing a celebrated solo career, which did much to popularize the instrument. Britten, Hindemith, Malcolm Arnold, Lutyens, and Gordon Jacob wrote works for him. He had a phenomenal technique, a rounded tone, eloquent phrasing, and felicitous tonguing in a concerto repertory ranging from Mozart to Richard Strauss.　　CF

📖 S. Pettitt, *Dennis Brain: A Biography* (London, 1976, 2/1989)

Brand, Max (*b* Lemberg [now L'viv, Ukraine], 26 April 1896; *d* Langenzersdorf, nr Vienna, 5 April 1980). Austrian-born American composer. He studied in Vienna with Franz Schreker and Alois Hába, and worked there in ballet and film. In 1938 he moved via Brazil to the USA; he returned to Austria in 1975. His 'machine age' opera *Maschinist Hopkins* was first performed in Duisburg in 1929; it was produced in 37 European theatres but was banned by the Nazi regime. Brand also wrote other operas, ballets, the scenic cantata *The Gate* (1944), some orchestral music, and *The Astronauts: An Epic in Electronics* (1962).　　ABur

Brand, Michael. See Mosonyi, Mihály.

Brandenburg Concertos. Six concerti grossi by Bach, BWV1046–51 (1711–20), dedicated to Christian Ludwig, (*cont. on p. 164*)

Johannes Brahms (1833–97)

The German composer Johannes Brahms was born in Hamburg on 7 May 1833 and died in Vienna on 3 April 1897.

Brahms was one of the greatest composers of the 19th century. His music unites lyrical Romanticism with the rigours of Baroque and Classical forms. His many masterpieces are part of the standard repertory for symphony orchestras, pianists, singers, choral societies, vocal ensembles, chamber ensembles, and the solo instruments he favoured: piano, violin, cello, and clarinet.

The early years

Brahms was born to a respectable family of limited means. His father, Johann Jakob, earned a living as a freelance musician playing the flute, violin, cello, horn, and double bass, as needed. Arriving as a young man in Hamburg from Schleswig-Holstein, Johann Jakob saved enough money within a few years to apply for Hamburg citizenship and soon afterwards moved to a better part of the town. There he married his landlady, Christiana Nissen, a seamstress 17 years his elder, intelligent and steady. Within five years there were three children, the second of whom was Johannes, born in Hamburg's old district of narrow streets, the Gängeviertel. The family remained there for only six more months, moving away before it gained its later unsavoury reputation, but the address of Brahms's birth has led to a long-standing misconception that his early life was lived in poverty.

In fact, Brahms spent his formative years away from the Gängeviertel and far from the infamous docks of the Elbe, in a small house on the Dammtorwall, the northern perimeter of Hamburg near the Inner Alster. The house overlooked a tree-lined street and the fields beyond the city walls. With his brother, he was educated at his parents' expense at a middle school for 'boys of the general middle class', conducted according to the most up-to-date educational theories. One of his teachers, to whom Brahms gave piano lessons while he was still a student there, described him as conscientious and hard-working, if not brilliant. Brahms graduated at 14 with some knowledge of Latin, French, English, natural sciences, history, mathematics, and gymnastics. This last remained a hobby until he was about 30. A powerful interest in history, the visual arts, and literature remained with him for life.

Brahms's precocious display of musical talent was nurtured by his father. By seven he was receiving the piano lessons he so wanted, and later had lessons on the horn and cello (cello lessons stopped when his teacher absconded with the instrument). His piano teachers laid the foundation for a first-rate technique: Otto Cossel (1813–65) taught him until he was ten, then sent him to his own teacher, the highly regarded Eduard Marxsen (1806–87), who taught both Johannes and his brother Fritz without charge. Marxsen also gave Brahms his only formal lessons in theory and composition.

He gave his first performance at ten. He appeared in public from his 13th year and made an auspicious debut as a virtuoso pianist just before his 16th birthday (April 1849), with a programme that included one of his own compositions. Nothing came of the splendid reviews. Nor was his passion to compose welcomed by his parents. Lacking concert engagements, he contributed to the family finances by playing in taverns, in dance halls, for the Hamburg City Theatre, and at the occasional musical evening at a fine house, where he earned good money. He arranged operatic potpourris for a local publisher, and earned additional money by giving piano lessons. Many biographies of Brahms mention poverty and the consequent necessity for him to earn money playing in brothels and unsavoury 'Lokals'. Although money was always an issue for the Brahms family, there is no good evidence for these stories, and much to challenge them. Recent searches of historical records disclose the picture of a family at the lower end of the middle class, labouring—succeeding—to make ends meet. The shortage of money in the Brahms household came not from insufficient income, but from Johann Jakob Brahms's propensity for unwise spending.

The making of a composer

At 19, in an attempt to satisfy his parents and build a concert career, Brahms embarked on a short tour to a few small towns in northern Germany, accompanying the brilliant Hungarian violinist Eduard Reményi. Rather than launching him as a pianist, however, the tour marked the start of his life as a composer. Reményi took him to Hanover to meet his compatriot Joseph Joachim, one of the greatest violinists of the 19th century and even at 22 the friend of many renowned artists. The two immediately struck up a friendship, which lasted, with one painful break, for the rest of their lives. Through Joachim, Brahms met Liszt and Berlioz, and most important, Robert and Clara Schumann, who instantly recognized his talent ('Visit from Brahms, a genius', reads Schumann's diary entry for 1 October 1853, as Brahms appeared at their door in Düsseldorf). When Brahms returned to Hamburg in December 1853 he was the most feted young composer in Germany, with seven works about to be issued by leading publishers.

This meteoric rise was the result of his meeting with the Schumanns, the single most momentous occurrence of his life, personally and musically. Schumann promoted his interests with extreme vigour; his panegyric 'Neue Bahnen', published in the *Neue Zeitschrift für Musik*, called Brahms the long-awaited saviour of music and propelled the 20-year-old into the limelight. More beneficially, both Schumanns broadened Brahms's musical and literary horizons and introduced him to friends and acquaintances who would figure in his life for the next four decades. The Schumanns' Düsseldorf home introduced Brahms to a world in which a love of books and culture and a passionate devotion to music were the norm and where his creative gifts were esteemed and encouraged.

The compositions Brahms took when he left home included a range of works for solo piano and a sample of the kind of music that gained him later fame: chamber music, a violin sonata, and lieder. Much that has survived from the period is stormy, passionate, even unruly, the piano works of enormous difficulty (Piano Sonatas opp. 1, 2, and 5, Scherzo op. 4). Cossel and Marxsen had raised him on Bach, Clementi, some Mozart, Beethoven, Mendelssohn, and a wide assortment of virtuoso salon composers of the day, but he must have known music by Schumann, Chopin, and Liszt. His interest in folksongs and early music was already evident, and he was buying books which would eventually form part of a considerable library. The Romantic novels of Jean Paul and stories of E. T. A. Hoffmann were among his favourites.

Brahms's involvement with the Schumann family quickly led to years of personal turmoil, as Schumann, unbeknown to all, was suffering from the late stages of neurosyphilis. His suicide attempt in February 1854 and subsequent admission to hospital signalled the end of Brahms's first period of productivity. In coming to Clara's aid Brahms fell in love with her, while maintaining a reverential love and active concern for her husband, now in an asylum. The story, which has the makings of a soap opera, has been treated with varying degrees of luridness by novelists and screenwriters but perhaps never with more feeling than in some of Brahms's own music of the time: the First Piano Concerto op. 15, and two movements of the Piano Quartet in C minor op. 60. The possibility of a real romance between Clara and Brahms is remote, given their characters and circumstances. The friendship, however, which went through many phases and endured many tensions, was lifelong, and was for each the most important one of their lives.

With Schumann's death (1856), Brahms returned to Hamburg. Although he never ceased composing, his published works trickled to a stop. Not until 1860 did he publish again. In the intervening years, he engaged in counterpoint studies with his friend Joachim, studied old masters assiduously, edited the first of his many publications of the works of earlier composers (in this case C. P. E. and W. F. Bach, 1859, published 1864), and wrote music along archaic or classic lines (e.g. *Begräbnisgesang* op. 13, First Serenade op. 11, First String Sextet op. 18, Handel Variations op. 24). For three seasons (September–December 1857–9) he was choral conductor of the private chorus of Count Leopold III zur Lippe in Detmold and piano teacher to the Royal Princess and some of her friends and family. During the rest of the year he worked to establish a professional career in Hamburg, founding a women's chorus (1859), teaching, conducting, and even attempting, with Clara's help, to revive his virtuoso piano career. An exploratory trip to Vienna in 1862 coincided with his rejection for the post of conductor of the Hamburg Philharmonic and Choral Society, a blow he never forgot and one that closed the doors to Hamburg for ever.

Unsettled years

In Vienna came quick success. Two concerts led to Brahms's selection as conductor of the Vienna Singverein (1863). Although he resigned after only a year to devote himself to composing, performing, and getting his music published, his career never faltered again. He had no fixed domicile and little money, but he was composing one great work after another. The next summers were spent mostly in Baden-Baden, where Clara and her children had their only real home. Works from this time include some of his best chamber music: the Piano Quintet op. 34, the First Cello Sonata op. 38, the Second String Sextet op. 36, the Horn Trio op. 40, the Waltzes for piano four hands op. 39. Some of his most beloved songs (*Von ewiger Liebe, Heimweh*

II: 'O wüsst ich doch den Weg zurück', *Mondnacht*) date from this time. But the crowning work of the period is *A German Requiem* op. 45, begun about 1865 and performed in Bremen in 1868. It was soon given in many cities, establishing broad acceptance for his music at last, and the large fee paid by his publisher marked the end of Brahms's financial problems. Published at virtually the same time are his two most popular works, the Lullaby and the Hungarian Dances.

Vienna

With an offer to conduct the orchestra and chorus of the Gesellschaft der Musikfreunde, Brahms settled in Vienna in 1871. His Viennese audience had to get used to more serious fare, as Brahms indulged his antiquarian tastes and gave Vienna its first hearing of Bach's cantata *Christ lag in Todesbanden* (bwv4), along with other rarely heard Baroque works. He was sought out as editor for some of the many authoritative editions then being published, preparing the *Pièces de concert* for the complete edition of Couperin's music and contributions to the complete editions of Chopin, Mozart (his portion was the Requiem k626), Schubert, and Schumann. In 1875 he resigned his orchestral post and established the pattern of living he maintained for the rest of his life: touring as performer and conductor of his own works during autumn and winter, travelling in the spring, and composing during the summer, usually in the mountains.

Brahms was frequently attacked in the press for his 'conservatism' by Wagner and his followers. In contrast, while Wagner's personal style was inimical to Brahms, he appreciated Wagner's music, invariably defending it and even calling himself 'the best Wagnerite of all'. Brahms's own fame continued to grow. Among his many medals and honours are the Maximilian Order (Bavaria, 1873), Pour le Mérite (Prussia, 1887), Commander of the Order of Leopold (Austria, 1889), and Austrian Order for Art and Science (1895). In 1879 the University of Breslau awarded him an honorary doctorate, after he declined to travel to England to accept one from Cambridge University.

For the last 20 years of his life, Brahms was the dominant musical figure in Vienna. When he died of cancer just before his 64th birthday, the city declared a day of mourning and buried him in an honorary grave between Beethoven and Schubert.

Brahms's music

Brahms's association with the Schumanns had a profound effect on his music. If for a brief time he had identified himself with the 'Musicians of the Future', a reference to Liszt and his circle who were looking for new forms and who favoured literary connections to their music, Brahms's reverence for the old masters grew so that by 1860 he was 'itching' to declare his opposition to the futurists in a public declaration. Although the quarrel may now seem puzzling, Brahms and his friends felt deeply that the circle round Liszt was undermining the future of music by claiming that it could attain its greatest potential only if allied with a literary or programmatic idea: in their view, the symphony and chamber music of Mozart and Beethoven's day were finished. To Brahms, the independence of the art of music was at stake. Although he rounded up 20 composers to sign it, the declaration was published prematurely with only his name and three others and was an embarrassment. Brahms never publicly expressed his views on music again. They are, however, easy enough to discern from his work: an enormous reverence for the great composers from the late Renaissance onwards; instead of discarding their techniques for something new, he made them his own and infused them with his personal brand of lyric Romanticism.

The characteristic qualities that identify Brahms's music are present from the first to the last of his works, giving his output unusual unity. His skill at harnessing rhythmic and harmonic motion imparts what Joachim likened to a 'force of nature'. His practice of making every note count, of developing material so that it is varied and reused throughout a piece, makes his work compact and durable. This manner of using musical material richly and economically is also what aroused the admiration of Schoenberg, who surprised the musical world with his essay 'Brahms the Progressive' (1933). In spite of those unifying characteristics, Brahms's work falls into identifiable periods, the earliest comprising compositions with a sometimes unruly exuberance of musical ideas (e.g. the piano sonatas opp. 1, 2, and 5, the Piano Trio op. 8 in its original version, the great Piano Concerto op. 15, and the Piano Quartet op. 26). By the time of the Piano Quintet op. 34, he had developed a masterful ability to fit musical idea to appropriate form.

A long series of large works followed over the next 20-odd years. Among the best-known compositions for chorus and orchestra are *A German Requiem* (1865–8), the *Alto Rhapsody* (1869)—an unusual work for orchestra, contralto, and men's chorus—and the *Schicksalslied* (1871). The first mature large work for orchestra (1873) was the *Variations on a Theme by Haydn* op. 56a, still one of his most popular. The symphonies appeared between 1876 and 1885, the Violin Concerto in 1878, the *Tragic* and *Academic Festival* Overtures in 1880, the Second Piano Concerto in 1881, the Double Concerto in 1887. Although there has been much speculation that Brahms hesitated to publish his first symphony for fear of failing to live up to Beethoven's examples, a more likely explanation is that Brahms postponed publishing for orchestra until he had had the experience of working with one. Throughout his life he wrote and published music for instrumental and vocal combinations with which he was familiar: his first published works are for piano, the first choral works are for women's voices, and his first duo sonata is for cello and piano.

Full-scale chamber works are equally evident in this middle period of maturity: the three string quartets, the Second String Sextet, two piano trios, the two string quintets. The two Rhapsodies for piano also appeared at this time. So did much of his vocal chamber music—best known is the first set of *Liebesliederwalzer* op. 52, but there are many others, rich additions to an otherwise small repertory. And during these years, as in all others, Brahms composed songs, of which there are over 200. He is one of the four great 19th-century German lied composers, and the only one to have lived a relatively long life. His songs express a wide range of colour and character, though he is possibly best known for his settings of melancholy, of unrequited love, and for transcendent settings of nature poetry. Among his most delightful are artful settings of folk melodies, reflecting his intense interest in what he saw as the essence of German music and his belief that untrained people should enjoy them.

One senses Brahms's desire from about 1880 to condense his thought and shed all superfluity. Some of his starkest choral music dates from this time, as do the compact late piano pieces opp. 116–19. By 1890 Brahms was ready to retire from composing. After so informing his friend and publisher, Fritz Simrock, and sending him his will for safekeeping, he was suddenly moved to write for Richard Mühlfeld, the solo clarinettist of the court orchestra at Meiningen. This surge of creative energy resulted in a unique contribution to the clarinet literature, enriching the repertory as never before or since: two Sonatas for clarinet op. 120 nos. 1 and 2, the Clarinet Trio op. 114 and the Clarinet Quintet op. 115, for many people the final great chamber work of the 19th century. The last piece he published, *Vier ernste Gesänge* for solo voice and piano op. 121 (1896), is the profoundest music expressed with the sparsest sound.

In spite of stringent personal artistic standards and unyielding refusal to publish any but the music that met his approval, Brahms amassed a considerable fortune from the fees his publishers paid him (he never earned royalties but was paid a flat fee for each of his works). By the middle of his life his music had come to appeal to a musically educated audience in England, the USA, and the German-speaking countries, who not only attended concerts of his works but bought the printed music for home use, either in four-hand editions of the orchestral and choral music, or in the original versions of the smaller combinations.

Personal life

Brahms never married, although he had several serious attachments to women (besides Clara Schumann) and numerous flirtations. He often referred to himself as 'The Outsider' and sometimes complained of loneliness, but in fact had a need for solitude. At the same time, he was a sociable person. His considerable circle of friends, attested to by his thousands of letters, included leading scientists, musicologists, poets, writers, journalists, artists, conductors, performers, and music lovers, women as well as men, and he spent almost 20 summers in the fashionable spas of Baden-Baden and Ischl. He was instrumental in founding the Vienna Composers' Society (the Tonkünstlerverein), of which he was Honorary President. Some of his most important friendships suffered celebrated rifts (notably with the conductor Hermann Levi, Joachim, and the surgeon Theodor Billroth); much less well known are the lifelong, faithful friendships. In the same way, there are endless stories of Brahms's well-known prickliness, sarcasm, irony, and tactlessness. Less well known, but just as well documented, are accounts of his great generosity, kindness, loyalty, and good humour. Brahms was godfather to at least 15 children, a responsibility not normally offered to an ogre. Perhaps it is that very complexity of character that gives his music such range.

One story indicates both the quality of his music and his character. Brahms once criticized a composition because the individual parts were unpleasant to play. 'You give people individual notes like the little pins in a musical box', he chided the composer. 'But a musician is not a musical box, he is a human being; he must always have something to say. If you give him the dissonance, you must also give him the resolution.'   SA

📖 K. Geiringer, *Brahms: His Life and Work* (Eng. trans., London, 2/1948) · H. Gál, *Johannes Brahms* (Frankfurt, 1961; Eng. trans. 1963) · K. Stephenson, *Johannes Brahms in seiner Familie* [family correspondence] (Hamburg, 1973) · M. Musgrave, *The Music of Brahms* (London, 1985, 2/1994) · K. Hofmann, *Brahms und Hamburg* (Reinbek, 1986) · M. MacDonald, *Brahms* (London and New York, 1990, 2/2001) · W. Frisch, *Brahms: The Four Symphonies* (New York, 1996) · S. Avins, *Johannes Brahms: Life and Letters* (Oxford, 1997) · L. Botstein (ed.), *The Compleat Brahms: A Guide to the Musical Works* (New York, 1999) · M. Musgrave, *The Cambridge Companion to Brahms* (Cambridge, 1999); *A Brahms Reader* (London and New Haven, CT, 2000)

Margrave of Brandenburg; Bach described them as 'Concerts avec plusieurs instruments'. They are significant for their unusual combinations of instruments and textures and for the way in which Bach moved away from conventional concerto grosso form; for example, no. 3 is for three groups of strings (a violin, viola, and cello in each), and no. 4 is for a violin and two recorders in the concertino and strings and continuo in the ripieno.

branle (Fr., also *bransle*; It.: *brando*) [brawl, brangill]. Originally a sideways step in the *basse danse, it became established as a popular circle dance by the 16th century. Its only Renaissance source is Arbeau's *Orchésographie* (1588) which describes over 20 dances in four main forms: the *branle simple* and *double* in duple time; the *branle gai* in triple time; and the *branle de Bourgogne* in a mixture of metres. There are many regional versions, such as the *branle d'Écosse* (Scottish branle) and the *branle de Malte* (Maltese branle) which, like the Italian *brando*, required the performer to make mimed gestures and facial expressions. It was absorbed into the repertory of court dances and was taken up with enthusiasm in England; Shakespeare mentions it in *Love's Labour's Lost*. —/JH

Brant, Henry (Dreyfuss) (*b* Montreal, 15 Sept. 1913). Canadian-born American composer. He studied at the McGill Conservatorium before settling in 1929 in New York, where he continued formal studies while taking private lessons with Wallingford Riegger and George Antheil. Earning his living as an arranger, and later also as a college teacher, he began writing works for unconventional forces, such as *Angels and Devils* for solo flute and ten other flutes (1931) and *Music for a Five and Dime Store* for violin, piano, and kitchen hardware (1932). From *Antiphony I* (1953) he was principally concerned with ensembles separated in space and in style, though also still with unusual combinations, as in *Orbits* for 80 trombones and organ (1979). PG

Brassart, Johannes (*b* c.1405; *d* after 1445). Flemish cleric and composer. His career was largely spent in and around Liège, but he also served at the papal chapel in Rome, where he was a colleague of Dufay. Some 30 works by him have survived, including individual mass movements and several large-scale ceremonial motets. JM

brass band. An ensemble of brass instruments and percussion. Brass bands began as military bands in the 19th century, initially with keyed bugles, serpents, bass horns, and other keyed brass instruments, changing to valved brass once these became available. Civilian bands, especially those connected with factories and mines, quickly followed their example. The Salvation Army established its first band in 1878 and remains an important influence on the movement, commissioning its own music and maintaining instrument manufactures. Today the number and type of instruments vary from country to country.

In Britain the instrumentation became codified in about 1850 with the establishment of national contests. The full brass band consists of 25 or 26 players: one E♭ soprano cornet, three or four B♭ solo cornets, one repiano cornet in B♭, two each of 2nd and 3rd B♭ cornets, one B♭ flugel horn, three E♭ tenor horns (solo, first, and second), two B♭ baritones (first and second), one euphonium (which often has an important solo part), two tenor trombones and one bass trombone, two E♭ basses (tuba or bombardon), and two BB♭ basses, as well as one or two percussionists. All the parts except the bass trombone are written in treble clef and transposed to make it easy for players to change from one instrument to another. The standard of technique is often fully comparable to that of the best orchestral players. Brass band contests (see COMPETITIONS IN MUSIC) always include an obligatory test piece, often specially written by a major composer. Holst, Elgar, Bliss, Arnold, and Birtwistle have all composed important brass band works. JMo

📖 M. H. and R. M. HAZEN, *The Music Men: An Illustrated History of Brass Bands in America, 1800–1921* (Washington, DC, 1987) · T. HERBERT (ed.), *The British Brass Band: A Musical and Social History* (Oxford, 2000)

brass instruments. A term applied to those instruments of the Western orchestra or band made of brass or other metal (excluding the flute), and extended in common usage to apply to all instruments, of whatever material, sounded by the lips buzzing into a hole at the end or side. Serpents and cornetts are made of wood (or plastic), horns of ivory, animal horn, wood, gourd, or metal, and conches of shell, but all are called brass instruments; an alternative term is 'lip-reeds'. Brass instruments are classified in *organology as *aerophones (see INSTRUMENTS, CLASSIFICATION OF). The brass section of an orchestra typically consists of trumpets, horns, trombones, and tubas.

A 'natural' brass instrument—one without valves, slides, or fingerholes—can sound only the notes of the *harmonic series, and the number available depends on the instrument's length. A tube 4′ 6″ (137 cm) long, the length of a B♭ trumpet or bugle, can sound the first six easily, the eighth with some skill (the seventh does not fit into the Western musical scale), and the higher ones only with difficulty. A 12′ (366 cm) tube, the length of an F horn or a Swiss alphorn, can sound up to the 16th harmonic or beyond.

The gaps between these notes can be filled only by opening holes in the side of the tube (*cornett, *serpent), by lengthening the tube with a slide (*trombone), by adding short lengths of extra tubing with valves (many modern instruments), or by partly closing the bell with the hand (the Classical French horn).

The facility with which high or low notes can be played is greatly affected by bore profile and mouthpiece shape. A wide conical bore with a deep mouthpiece, such as on the tuba, helps low notes. A narrow, mainly cylindrical bore with a sharp cup mouthpiece, such as on the Baroque natural trumpet, helps high notes. A long, mainly conical bore with a deep funnel-shaped mouthpiece, such as on the Classical horn, helps the full range. In all cases, the shape of the bell is critical in projecting the sound, giving it much of its characteristic tone-colour and stabilizing its pitch.

JMo

Bratsche (Ger.). 'Viola'.

Braunfels, Walter (*b* Frankfurt, 19 Dec. 1882; *d* Cologne, 19 March 1954). German composer and pianist. His musical talent was fostered by his mother, a friend of both Liszt and Clara Schumann. From 1902 he studied the piano in Vienna, subsequently taking composition lessons with Ludwig Thuille. His first major work, the opera *Prinzessin Bambilla* (1909), was strongly post-Wagnerian, though he was a passionate admirer of Berlioz's music, paying homage to his hero in *Fantastic Apparitions of a Theme by Hector Berlioz* for orchestra (1917). His greatest successes coincided with the early years of the Weimar Republic. His opera *Die Vögel* ('The Birds', after Aristophanes) was fiercely championed by Bruno Walter after its 1920 premiere. Its sequel *Don Gil von den grünen Hosen* ('Don Gil of the Green Trousers', 1924) drew comparable enthusiasm, and by 1925, when he was invited to become co-director with the conductor Hermann Abendroth of the new Hochschule in Cologne, Braunfels was established as one of Germany's most popular operatic composers.

Yet about this time a note of austerity began to creep into his music, notably in the Great Mass of 1926. Part-Jewish by birth (though a Christian by creed), Braunfels, a fierce opponent of the Nazis, was dismissed from his post in Cologne when the party came to power in 1933. His works were proscribed during the Third Reich, and he withdrew from public life to an isolated house on Lake Constance, where he continued to compose. His opera *Verkündigung* ('Tidings'), an imposing setting of Paul Claudel's play *L'Annonce faite à Marie*, was completed in 1935 but remained unperformed until 1948. In the immediate postwar years, Braunfels turned primarily to the composition of chamber music. In 1945 he was asked to resume work at the Cologne Hochschule, becoming professor emeritus in 1950. Though little of his work is now performed, *Die Vögel* has re-entered the repertory as a result of recent interest in *Entartete Musik*.

TA

Brautlied (Ger.). 'Bridal song'.

bravura (It., 'skill'; Fr.: *bravoure*). A term used to describe showmanship in performance; *aria di bravura*, a brilliant virtuoso aria making great demands on a singer's vocal technique.

Brazil. See LATIN AMERICA, 4.

break. 1. In jazz, a brief, fast, extemporized solo, often for clarinet, saxophone, or trumpet, played while the rest of the band is temporarily silent; it serves as an introduction to an extended solo or between passages for the whole band.

PGa

2. The point of change between vocal and instrumental registers, especially important on clarinets.

3. A momentary silence after a musical phrase, normally indicated by a comma above the staff. No loss of time must occur, the break being made by slightly shortening the last note of the phrase.

breathing. See VOICE, 2.

breathing, circular. See CIRCULAR BREATHING.

breit (Ger.). 'Broad', i.e. *largo*. In string playing, *breit gestrichen* means 'broadly bowed'.

Breitkopf & Härtel. German firm of music printers and publishers. Founded in Leipzig in 1719 by the printer Bernhard Christoph Breitkopf, it achieved special eminence after 1745 under his son Johann Gottlieb Immanuel Breitkopf (1719–94), an exceptional innovator who developed a new music type of great clarity. He published music by nearly all the leading composers of the second half of the 18th century, including Haydn, Leopold Mozart, and C. P. E. Bach. Gottfried Christoph Härtel (1763–1827) succeeded as director in 1796, introducing Senefelder's lithographic printing method and publishing collected editions of the works of Mozart, Haydn, Clementi, Dussek, and Cramer, as well as 25 first editions of Beethoven's works. He founded the *Allgemeine musikalische Zeitung* (1798–1848), a major critical journal. Later generations of the Härtel family consolidated the company's position as a leading European publishing house with instrumental works by Mendelssohn, Schumann, Brahms, Berlioz, Liszt, Wagner, and Chopin, and operas by Meyerbeer, Cherubini, Donizetti, and Bellini. Landmark publications included the first complete editions of Bach (1851–99) and of Beethoven (1862–5). The firm issued many important music books, acquired such composers as Busoni and Sibelius, and continued to expand up to 1914, opening branches in Brussels, London, and New York.

After the publishing house was destroyed in World War II, and following the division of Germany, the Leipzig side became state-owned and a West German branch was established in Wiesbaden. Contemporary German composers (Lachenmann, Huber, Höller) were acquired in Wiesbaden through the catalogue of Edition Gerig, Cologne, to which were added works by Hans Zender and others. A Paris branch opened in 1984, and in 1991 the Leipzig firm was reincorporated into the business following the reunification of Germany. The acquisition of Deutscher Verlag für Musik (founded in Leipzig in 1954) brought works by Gesualdo, Mendelssohn, Eisler, Matthus, and Udo Zimmermann into the catalogue. Complete editions of Mendelssohn and Sibelius appeared in 1997 and 1998 respectively. In 2000 Breitkopf took over the French publishing house Musica Rara.   HA

Bretón (y Hernández), **Tomás** (*b* Salamanca, 29 Dec. 1850; *d* Madrid, 2 Dec. 1923). Spanish conductor and composer. His works include two symphonies, tone-poems, a Violin Concerto dedicated to Sarasate, and the delicate orchestral serenade *En la Alhambra* (1888), as well as some finely crafted chamber music. His operas *Los amantes de Teruel* (1889) and *La Dolores* (1895) are still occasionally heard in Spain and abroad, but the most successful of his many stage works is the classic one-act zarzuela *La verbena de la paloma* ('The Festival of the Dove', 1894), composed in 19 days and hugely popular throughout the Spanish-speaking world.   WT/CW

breve (from Lat. *brevis*, 'short'; ▭ or ◫). Formerly, as its name suggests, the shortest time-value in musical notation, but now (the longer note-values having gradually fallen into disuse) the longest—twice the length of the semibreve. The breve is now rarely encountered, except in church music.

breve, alla. See ALLA BREVE.

breviary (Lat.: *breviarum*). A book containing the chants, prayers, and lessons for the Office; see PLAINCHANT, 4.

Brewer, Sir (Alfred) **Herbert** (*b* Gloucester, 21 June 1865; *d* Gloucester, 1 March 1928). English organist and composer. A chorister at Gloucester Cathedral, he returned there as organist in 1896. An able performer, church musician, and composer of oratorios (including *Emmaus*, orchestrated by Elgar), songs, and church music, he is best remembered for his work as conductor of the Gloucester Three Choirs Festivals (1898–1925)

and for their innovatory programmes. He was knighted in 1926.   JDı

Brian, **Havergal** (*b* Dresden, Staffs., 29 Jan. 1876; *d* Shoreham, 28 Nov. 1972). English composer. He first made a reputation as a composer of festival choral pieces with *By the Waters of Babylon* (Hanley, 1907) and *The Vision of Cleopatra* (Southport, 1909), and Henry Wood conducted his *English Suite* no. 1 (completed in 1904) at the Queen's Hall. After World War I interest in his music declined but he went on composing, undaunted by public neglect. In all he produced 32 symphonies including the 'Gothic' (1919–27, for large orchestra, quadruple chorus, children's chorus, and four brass bands), symphonic poems, orchestral suites, five large-scale operas, and the lyric drama *Prometheus Unbound* (1937–44). A revival of interest in his music began in the 1950s and a number of his symphonies were broadcast by the BBC, but his work is still generally neglected.   JDı

📖 R. MATTHEW-WALKER, *Havergal Brian: Reminiscences and Observations* (St Austell, 1995) · J. SCHAARWAECHTER (ed.), *HB: Aspects of Havergal Brian* (Aldershot, 1997)

bridge. 1 (Fr.: *chevalet*; Ger.: *Steg*; It.: *ponticello*). On stringed instruments, the piece of carved wood which supports the strings and transmits their vibrations to the belly. The sounding length of a string runs from the front edge of the bridge to the nut (for an open string) or to the finger or tangent (if the string is stopped).

JMo

2. A 'bridge passage' serves as a link between two other passages of greater prominence in the piece as a whole. Thus in *sonata form a transition may be described as a bridge passage, as its function is to link the first group to the second, often modulating from the first tonal centre to the next.

Bridge, **Frank** (*b* Brighton, 26 Feb. 1879; *d* Eastbourne, 10 Jan. 1941). English composer. He studied the violin and composition at the RCM (1899–1903). The main emphasis of his studies was composition, under Stanford, though his violin playing enabled him to make a living after he left the RCM. He switched to the viola and did a great deal of quartet playing in London; he deputized for Emanuel Wirth of the Joachim Quartet in 1906 and was a member of the English String Quartet until 1915. He was also an active orchestral and opera conductor, making five concert tours to the USA to conduct his works and to hear performances of his new commissions financed by the wealthy American patron Elizabeth Sprague Coolidge. She became a close friend and established a Trust Fund to support Bridge in the 1920s; he reciprocated by dedicating several works to her. After spending his professional life in London, he moved to the South Downs during the mid-1920s and died in relative obscurity.

Bridge's early chamber works—the single-movement 'phantasies' written for the Cobbett Chamber Music Medal (awarded by the *Worshipful Company of Musicians)—have a Brahmsian fluency and a fresh, distinctive lyric impulse that he learnt from Stanford. This is apparent in the Quartet no. 1 (1906) and the *Phantasy Piano Quartet* (1910), and more so in the Suite for strings (1908), *The Sea* (1910–11), and the *Dance Poem* (1913), a symphonic waltz. During World War I, which profoundly affected him, Bridge's style began to assimilate a new chromatic intensity (embracing to some extent those post-Romantic languages of Debussy, Delius, Ireland, and Bax), which is first heard in the symphonic poem *Summer* (1914) and evolved steadily through the poignant *Lament* for strings (1915), the *Two Poems of Richard Jefferies* (1915), the Quartet no. 2 (1915), and the brooding Cello Sonata (1913–17).

After the war, and several years of near-silence, the modernity in the Piano Sonata (1921–4) signalled a further stylistic departure. This work, which exhibited new harmonic processes involving bitonality in particular, initiated a new momentum in his instrumental essays. The chamber compositions, notably the Third and Fourth Quartets (1926 and 1937), the Piano Trio no. 2 (1929), and the Violin Sonata (1932), have a Bergian concentration, while the orchestral music—*Enter Spring* (1927), the threnody *There is a Willow Grows Aslant a Brook* (1928), the *Rebus Overture* (1940), and the two concertante works, *Oration* (1930) for cello and *Phantasm* (1931) for piano—retains the rich sonorities of his earlier works but exhibits a more focused intellectualism. None of these works appealed to English audiences of the time, and Bridge's importance came to be recognized only a generation after his death, thanks in part to the efforts of his pupil Benjamin Britten.

PG/JD1

📖 A. Payne, *Frank Bridge, Radical and Conservative* (London, 1984) · K. R. Little, *Frank Bridge: A Bio-Bibliography* (Westport, CT, 1991)

bridge harp. A group of West African instruments of which the best known is the Mandinka *kora. These instruments were classified as *harp-lutes by Hornbostel and Sachs (see INSTRUMENTS, CLASSIFICATION OF), but as the neck performs no other function than that of string-holder, and they conform in other respects to the definition of harp (they are closely related, structurally and historically, to other African harps), the name 'bridge harp' was proposed for them by scholars in the 1970s.

Brigg Fair. Orchestral work (1907) by Delius; subtitled 'An English Rhapsody', it is a set of variations on an English folksong, to which Delius's attention had been drawn by Grainger.

brillante (Fr.). 'Brilliant', 'sparkling'. Many 19th-century concert pieces have 'brillante' or 'brillant' in their titles.

Brindisi (It., 'toast'). A term, perhaps connected with the Italian town of that name, applied to a drinking-song. Such pieces are often found in 19th-century opera, e.g. 'Libiamo' ('Let's drink') in Verdi's *La traviata* and Iago's drinking-song in *Otello*.

brio (It.). 'Vivacity', 'liveliness'; *con brio*, *brioso*, 'with fire', 'with spirit'.

brisé (Fr.). 'Broken'; it is used of a chord played in *arpeggio fashion or of string music played with short, detached bowstrokes; see also STYLE BRISÉ.

British Federation of Festivals for Music, Dance and Speech. An organization of amateur competitive music festivals in Britain and the Commonwealth, founded in 1921 as the British Federation of Music Festivals. See COMPETITIONS IN MUSIC.

British Grenadiers. The regimental march of the Grenadier Guards. The origin of the tune is unknown but it may date from the second half of the 16th century. The original words are from the end of the 17th century (hand grenades, to which the words refer, were in use from *c*.1678). A later version, alluding to the Battle of Waterloo, is sometimes substituted.

British Society for Music Therapy (BSMT). Founded in 1958 as the Society for Music Therapy and Remedial Music, it promotes the use and development of music therapy; its sister organization, the Association of Professional Music Therapists, was formed in 1976 to assist in the creation of new posts and foster the exchange of professional information both in Britain and abroad.

JBo

Britten, (Edward) Benjamin [Lord Britten of Aldeburgh] (*b* Lowestoft, 22 Nov. 1913; *d* Aldeburgh, 4 Dec. 1976). English composer, pianist, and conductor. He was the outstanding British musician of his generation both as creator and as executant, for his brilliance as a pianist (especially as accompanist) and as an interpreter of his own and other composers' music would have ensured him a major career even if he had not been so great a composer.

1. The early years; 2. After *Peter Grimes*

1. The early years

Britten was the youngest of four children of a dentist and his musical wife. He was taught the piano from the age of five and began to compose (prolifically) at the same age. At ten he began viola lessons. A major childhood event was a visit to the 1924 Norwich Festival when he was 'knocked sideways' by hearing Frank Bridge conduct his suite *The Sea*. At the same festival three years later Bridge's *Enter Spring* made a similar impression on the boy, who then became his pupil, learning from him the elements of composition and also the principles of pacifism which remained his creed to the end of his life. After his public school—Gresham's, Holt, Norfolk—Britten entered the RCM in 1930 where he found the teaching and general conservative atmosphere uncongenial. Several of his early compositions were played in London while he was at the RCM but only one of them, the Sinfonietta, at the college itself. In 1934 his *Phantasy Quartet* was selected for performance at the ISCM Festival in Florence and his choral variations, *A Boy was Born*, were broadcast by the BBC. The following year he began to write music for a small documentary film company and collaborated with the poet W. H. Auden, who became an influential friend. He became associated with various left-wing theatre companies and in 1936 went to Barcelona, where his Suite for violin and piano was played at the ISCM Festival.

Britten's first large-scale work was the symphonic cycle for voice and orchestra, *Our Hunting Fathers*, to a text compiled by Auden. At its first performance, at the 1936 Norwich Festival, the audience was scandalized both by the audacity of the harmonies and vocal writing and by the verbal satire, which savagely indicted the hunting and shooting of animals. Warmer acclaim greeted the *Variations on a Theme of Frank Bridge* (composed for the 1937 Salzburg Festival) in which Britten combined his talent for parody with a deeper vein owing something to Mahler's influence. His extraordinary sensitivity to instrumental timbres was also apparent in his Piano Concerto (1938).

In 1937 he met the tenor Peter Pears, who became his lifelong artistic and domestic partner, the inspirer of much of his vocal music. They sailed to North America in spring 1939 intending to forsake Britain altogether as Auden, Christopher Isherwood, and others had done, but in 1942 homesickness and the war persuaded them to return and to go before a conscientious objectors' tribunal. While in America Britten completed the song cycle *Seven Sonnets of Michelangelo* (1940), the Violin Concerto (1939), and the *Sinfonia da requiem* (1940).

With Auden as librettist, he composed an operetta *Paul Bunyan* (1941) which he put aside after its first performances until he revised it in 1974–5. On returning to England, Britten wrote two fine works—*Hymn to St Cecilia* (1942) and *Serenade for Tenor, Horn, and Strings* (1943)—but most of his energy was concentrated on the opera *Peter Grimes*, based on George Crabbe's poem about the fisherfolk of Aldeburgh. This was produced in London in June 1945 and was immediately hailed as the first indisputably great English opera since Purcell's *Dido and Aeneas*. From then on, in Britain and often elsewhere, every new work by Britten, especially if it was an opera, was regarded as a major musical event.

2. After *Peter Grimes*

Although Britten wrote a second string quartet in 1945, opera increasingly occupied his attention. *The Rape of Lucretia* (1946) and *Albert Herring* (1947) were produced at Glyndebourne and led to the formation of the English Opera Group. Having settled at Aldeburgh in 1947, Britten and Pears, with others, founded a festival there in 1948. Many of Britten's subsequent works (such as the delightful *Let's Make an Opera*) were written for Aldeburgh festivals and he persuaded outstanding musicians to appear there, so that it soon became one of the notable events in the calendar, combining the highest artistic merit and professionalism with a charming homeliness and improvisation. Between 1950 and 1960 Britten wrote four major operas—*Billy Budd* (1951), *Gloriana*, for Elizabeth II's coronation (1953), *The Turn of the Screw* (1954), and *A Midsummer Night's Dream* (1960)—as well as his Thomas Hardy settings, *Winter Words* (1953), two canticles (1952 and 1954), the full-length ballet *The Prince of the Pagodas* (1957), and *Noye's Fludde*, based on a Chester miracle play (1958), in addition to many shorter works.

Britten reached his widest audience when his *War Requiem* was performed during celebrations to mark the dedication of the new Coventry Cathedral in 1962. In this large-scale choral work, combining the Latin Mass with war poems by Wilfred Owen, Britten's pacifism found its most public and eloquent outlet. It was an immense popular success, to such an extent that he retreated afterwards, as if alarmed, into a barer, more private style. Friendship with the Russian cellist Mstislav Rostropovich led to a Cello Sonata (1961), the Cello Symphony (1963), and three unaccompanied suites for cello (1964, 1967, and 1971). Another feature of the 1960s was the trilogy of church parables, *Curlew River* (1964), *The Burning Fiery Furnace* (1966), and *The Prodigal Son* (1968). These were a variety of chamber opera, performed in a highly stylized manner, the music reflecting the influence of the gamelan, which Britten had heard on a visit to East Asia. His next large-scale opera, also on an anti-war theme, was *Owen Wingrave*, like *The Turn of the Screw* an adaptation of Henry James. This was first produced on television in 1971, the year in which Britten began to compose his last opera, *Death in Venice* (1973), based on Thomas Mann's story. In 1973 he underwent an operation, not wholly successful, to replace a heart valve. For the last three years of his life Britten was an invalid, able to work for only short periods of each day and no longer able to play the piano. Yet he revised some earlier compositions and composed several vocal works, the orchestral *Suite on English Folk Tunes* (1974), and the Third String Quartet (1975). In 1976, six months before his death, he was created a life peer. In 1953 he had been made Companion of Honour and in 1965 a member of the Order of Merit.

Although in earlier works such as the Sinfonietta Britten showed an interest in Schoenbergian methods and wanted at one time to study with Berg, and although he sometimes wrote themes using 12 notes of the scale, he never embraced serialism. To the avantgarde he was always a 'conservative' composer in harmonic terms, but the freshness of his approach to everything he undertook (particularly where children were involved), his ability to find new but not freakish ways to write for instruments and voices, and his obvious delight in being able to provide music for friends or for particular occasions ensured a ready and immediate response from a public generally inclined to be wary of 'modern music'. His choice of operatic subjects reflected his preoccupation with innocence betrayed and with cruelty and his sympathy with the 'outsider' in society, something of which he had personal experience as conscientious objector and homosexual. Probably as a result of his formative years with the documentary film team, he enjoyed working as one of an artistic group and was fortunate in gathering round himself an array of gifted and like-minded collaborators as singers, instrumentalists, librettists, directors, and designers. If there are some works in which the desire to serve these talents led to a perhaps superficial application of his undoubted genius, there are many more where his vision, compassion, and astounding technical competence produced enduring masterpieces of a rare kind.

MK

📖 D. MITCHELL and H. KELLER (eds.), *Benjamin Britten: A Commentary on his Works from a Group of Specialists* (London, 1952) · I. HOLST, *Britten* (London, 1966, rev. edn 1980) · E. W. WHITE, *Benjamin Britten: His Life and Operas* (London, 1970) · D. MITCHELL and J. EVANS, *Benjamin Britten: Pictures from a Life 1913–76* (London, 1978) · P. EVANS, *The Music of Benjamin Britten* (London, 1979) · D. HERBERT (ed.), *The Operas of Benjamin Britten* (London, 1979) · C. HEADINGTON, *Britten* (London, 1981) · A. BLYTH (ed.), *Remembering Britten* (London, 1981) · M. KENNEDY, *Britten* (London, 1981, 2/2000) · D. MITCHELL, *Britten and Auden in the Thirties* (London, 1981) · R. DUNCAN, *Working with Britten* (London, 1982) · A. WHITTALL, *The Music of Britten and Tippett* (Cambridge, 1982, 2/1990) · D. MITCHELL and P. REED (eds.), *Letters from a Life: Selected Letters and Diaries of Benjamin Britten* (London, 1991) · H. CARPENTER, *Benjamin Britten: A Biography* (London, 1992)

Britton, Thomas (*b* Rushden, Northants., 14 Jan. 1644; *d* London, 27 Sept. 1714). English patron of music and amateur musician. Though employed as a coal dealer, Britton held weekly music meetings in a narrow room over his shop in Clerkenwell, and also amassed a fine library embracing divinity, chemistry, astrology, and music. His performers included the best professionals of his day, such as John Banister (ii) and Handel, together with accomplished amateurs. He counted book-loving noblemen among his friends, and his concerts were well patronized by the aristocracy. Some music manuscripts from his collection are extant.

AA

Brixi, František [Franz Xaver] (*b* Prague, *bapt.* 2 Jan. 1732; *d* Prague, 14 Oct. 1771). Czech composer and organist. His family, related to the Bendas, included several composers and organists of whom he was the most prominent. After musical training at the Piarist Gymnasium, Kosmonosy (1744–9), and a series of church organist posts in Prague, in 1751 he was appointed Kapellmeister of St Vitus Cathedral. Enormously prolific, he wrote some 500 religious works including masses and oratorios. His music, like that of many of his Czech contemporaries, embraced the Viennese characteristics of Fux and the Neapolitan style of Alessandro Scarlatti; his lively rhythmic writing and melodic inventiveness continued to exert an influence on Czech music into the 19th century.

JSM

broadcasting. Radio emerged as a serious means of dissemination, of both speech and music, immediately after World War I. This period was the heyday of radio hobbyists: former soldiers' interest in wireless had been aroused in the forces, and ample supplies of ex-government equipment and amateur crystal receivers were cheaply available. By early 1920 the main radio manufacturers were putting out daily programmes, though programming was haphazard. Possibly the most notable was on 15 June 1920, when Nellie Melba broadcast on the Marconi transmitter at Writtle, near Chelmsford. What were seen as excesses in the USA, resulting from fierce competition, persuaded the General Post Office in Britain to set up the British Broadcasting Company in 1922—the first national broadcasting organization in Europe. Thus a controlled monopoly embracing all the previous station operators began transmitting programmes in its own right from Marconi's London station 2LO from November 1922, and public service broadcasting was born. This soon developed into an active regional network with a national focus. Receiving licences were introduced, and grew rapidly in numbers from half a million at the end of 1922 to two million by 1926 and four and a half million by 1931.

1. The BBC: early history; 2. New music; 3. Concert-promoting and -recording; 4. World War II; 5. Postwar developments; 6. Festivals; 7. Television; 8. Conclusion

1. The BBC: early history

In 1927 the British Broadcasting Company became the British Broadcasting Corporation (BBC), a non-commercial organization 'acting as a trustee for the national interest', intentionally independent of both government and commerce. Its money came from licence fees from the outset. John Reith, who had been General Manager of the old Company since 1922, became the Corporation's Director General from its inception until 1938, and was central to its elevated policies, strong religious ethic, and high moral tone.

A wide range of music figured large in BBC schedules from the first, and as the technology of broadcasting developed it was recognized as a major opportunity for the development of the audience for classical music. Serious men (and at that stage they were all men) sought what they considered the best music for listeners. The BBC also became the showcase for new music at a time when the repertory showed significant development by both British and foreign composers, and when a wide range of composers were producing what are now regarded as the classics of the 20th century. However, there was hostility from many listeners both to the new music and to the more esoteric branches of the repertory, particularly chamber music, which became the regular butt of variety show comedians.

In the late 1920s the BBC recognized the potential of broadcasting as a tool for educating its musical public. Articles (notably by Percy *Scholes) in the *Radio Times* were soon supplemented by regular radio talks, notably Walford Davies's long-running series *Music and the Ordinary Listener* at which he spoke informally at the piano. This established a format emulated and developed by many distinguished speakers including Herbert Howells and George Dyson, and later given a new personal voice by Antony Hopkins in *Talking about Music*.

The first BBC Director of Music was Percy Pitt, previously at Covent Garden and a minor composer. Setting up almost from scratch, he moulded a BBC music policy that set high standards and soon expanded to provide an astonishing quantity of music-making. The inception of broadcasting made possible the dissemination on a national scale of an art which had previously appealed to a comparatively restricted audience. Opera was broadcast from an early date, with a quickly developed in-house capability (Armstrong Gibbs's comic opera *The Blue Peter* appearing as early as 1924), and the BBC published printed librettos for many of the works relayed. In 1929 it was d'Erlanger's opera *Tess*. Even music on the most massive scale was heard in the early years, probably crowned by the broadcast from Queen's Hall of Schoenberg's *Gurrelieder* conducted by the composer in 1928.

Adrian Boult, who succeeded Pitt as Director of Music in 1930, set about consolidating BBC music. From the first he faced problems of standards, particularly of soloists and orchestral performance, and met continuing hostility from some of the profession—principally Beecham, who regarded the BBC as a threat rather than an opportunity. It was the performing standards issue, and the concomitant employment of distinguished continental artists, on which Boult crossed swords with the profession almost more than on the vexed question of new music. Boult was intimately associated with the formation of the BBC Symphony Orchestra, becoming its conductor from its foundation in 1930. He thus doubled the two most important full-time jobs. During his tenure the BBC Music Department developed out of all recognition.

2. New music

The BBC (as did radio stations worldwide) quickly became the focus for many composers' aspirations, and a rapidly growing number of new scores were submitted. In 1926 it ran a composition competition but did not award a prize, considering none of the 240 entries good enough. The first BBC commission to be broadcast was Holst's *The Morning of the Year* in 1927. In taking over the Henry Wood Promenade Concerts in 1927 the BBC also adopted Wood's practice of inviting composers to submit new works for each season, a practice that developed into formal commissions. A procedure evolved whereby unsolicited music submissions were considered anonymously by an independent panel, but the assessment criteria were never stated and the reasons for rejection never given. However, the amount of new music performed was impressive, and growing (most recently documented by Mitchell and Poulton).

Later broadcasting organizations worldwide commissioned new works, one of the earliest being the radio cantata *Der Lindberghflug* (1929) by Weill and Hindemith for Baden-Baden, broadcast subsequently by the BBC in 1930. The newly founded Australian Broadcasting Commission ran an Australian Composers competition in 1932. In Canada, Healey Willan with his librettist John Coulter was commissioned to write the first Canadian radio operas: the one-act *Transit through Fire* (1942), set in the Depression, and *Deirdre* (1946), telling the Irish legend of Deirdre of the Sorrows. By appointing key music staff, particularly Edward Clark (a Schoenberg disciple) and Adrian Boult, the BBC championed new music on a scale that was not (one suspects) envisaged by the Director General and the Board.

3. Concert-promoting and -recording

Having established the BBC Symphony Orchestra the BBC systematically presented and broadcast high-profile public concerts, often of repertory that other organizations would not risk, a pattern followed by many broadcasting orchestras across the world. Notable series in London included a festival of new British music in 1934, and concert performances of British premieres of major new operas from Europe, requiring expenditure on a scale not possible from private promoters. This started with Berg's *Wozzeck* in 1934, and later included Shostakovich's *The Lady Macbeth of the Mtsensk District*, Hindemith's *Cardillac*, Milhaud's *Christophe Colomb*, Busoni's *Doktor Faust*, and Hindemith's *Mathis der Maler* in 1939.

In the mid-1930s radio stations, particularly in the USA, began using acetate direct-cut disc recordings to time-shift music broadcasts; large numbers of these have survived, providing an invaluable archive which is gradually reaching a wider public on compact disc as the originals go out of copyright. The BBC's Watts disc-cutting equipment was operational from 1934; among recordings that have survived are the second act of the first broadcast of *Wozzeck* and many first performances from the 1930s. Possibly the most prized is Toscanini's celebrated Queen's Hall performance of Beethoven's *Missa solemnis* with BBC forces in 1939, which reappeared on CD from BBC Legends in 1999.

4. World War II

During the war music became a significant tool of cultural diplomacy, an activity which in most countries was carried on with a less than sympathetic attitude to the avant-garde that was later reinforced from eastern Europe in an age of *socialist realism. The war initially interrupted BBC musical activities, but these were soon resumed. There was a great expansion of the Overseas Music Department, in which the composer Arthur Bliss was a leading light until he became Director of Music in 1942. In both capacities his belief in promoting the living composer was paramount; he included the music of those leading European composers living in the USA, arranging an early BBC performance of Stravinsky's Symphony in C, for example, and ensuring that Shostakovich's two wartime symphonies (the 'Leningrad' and no. 8) were performed as soon as materials could be obtained.

Radio stations at this time, notably the BBC, were also responsible for creating an entirely new genre, albeit a short-lived one: the radio drama with an extensive specially commissioned score. Notable among BBC commissions were several from Britten, whose music for Edward Sackville-West's *The Rescue*, first broadcast in 1943, was styled 'a melodrama' by its author.

5. Postwar developments

After the war the BBC Music Department sought to reflect what had been going on in Europe during the interim and also to represent the new British music (notably Britten and Tippett) to a European audience. The launch of the Third Programme in 1946 created a forum for the airing of the latest discoveries—not only new music but also (largely through the influence of Denis Stevens as programme planner) early music, in which there was a rapidly developing interest focused particularly on the activities of the group round Tippett at Morley College. This led to revivals of both Monteverdi and Purcell featuring the voice of the countertenor Alfred Deller. The music of Mahler, too, seldom played before the war, began to be heard.

The 1950s saw an increasing tendency in Europe, particularly Germany, but also France and Italy, for radio stations and their orchestras to promote the most advanced music, often late at night—an activity which, though carrying prestige, appealed to a tiny clique, then portrayed as mainstream. With the appointment in 1959 of William Glock (1908–2000) as Director of Music at the BBC there was an expansion of repertory exemplified by the Thursday Invitation Concerts, which set classical works beside the Second Viennese School and the postwar European avant-garde. This characterized his approach of 'creative unbalance'. Invigorating at the time, it eventually generated a public reaction against much new music.

The wider acceptance of broadcast music was driven by technical developments, the first being the implementation of FM (or VHF) broadcasting, which gave much greater fidelity, wider frequency range, and a cleaner signal (from the mid-1950s); this led to the introduction of stereophonic broadcasting (from the mid-1960s), which increased the realism of outside broadcasts especially. At the beginning of the 21st century the arrival of digital broadcasting heralded a further gain in fidelity and immediacy without interference.

After the war BBC broadcasting was streamed into 'Light' (later Radio 2), 'Home' (later Radio 4), and Third (later Radio 3); Radio 1 was later added for pop music. The BBC had spread its music programming across its various wavelengths, but the late 1960s and the 1970s saw a movement for stations to be subject-specific. In the UK this meant most serious music was on Radio 3, reflecting similar patterns elsewhere in the world.

While the BBC was a monopoly it more or less dictated popular music policy, but the popular English-language commercial stations founded in Europe, notably Radio Luxembourg, and the pirate radio stations broadcasting illegally from ships offshore attracted an enormous following and set the agenda for future BBC pop music provision. In 1992 Classic FM, the first classical commercial station in Britain, began broadcasting; it was perceived to be taking a significant proportion of Radio 3's audience, stimulating the BBC to respond with a more populist stance.

6. Festivals

The jewel in the BBC Music Department's crown has long been the Henry Wood *Promenade Concerts held every summer in the Royal Albert Hall and broadcast live to a wide audience. From Glock's time as Director of Music this has been consciously built into a major summer festival attracting leading soloists and orchestras and underlining the BBC's continuing pre-eminent position in the provision of music in the UK.

BBC Radio 3 designated 1995 as a festival of British music under the title 'Fairest Isle' and used a wide range of BBC resources to explore the more obscure corners of the repertory in a revelatory way. This prizewinning activity was on a scale that would have been impossible for any other organization to accomplish. Piquantly, it was followed by a noticeable contraction of the repertory offered and the cessation of in-house opera productions as it attempted to compete with Classic FM. This resulted in a widely reported uproar from regular listeners.

7. Television

Though trailing behind sound radio as a practical medium for communication and entertainment, television can trace its theoretical ancestry well back into the 19th century. In 1929 the Baird Television Company and the BBC began daily half-hour transmissions from London. The first television receiver to go on sale to the public, in 1930, was the Baird Televisor costing 25 guineas (£26.25). The BBC took over responsibility for the transmissions in 1932, though only about 500 sets could have been in use. Even then there was a great deal of backroom activity, notably by the Marconi-EMI team led by Isaac Shoenberg, so that when the government approved the inauguration of the world's first regular public television service, on 2 November 1936, the companies were authorized to share the transmissions on an alternate-week basis. However, the Crystal Palace fire destroyed all the Baird Company equipment and soon afterwards it was decided to settle on a single standard: that of Marconi-EMI. A boom period followed the successful televising of the coronation of George VI and his queen consort on 12 May 1937. When war broke out in 1939, the television service was closed down promptly as transmissions on the VHF band would have provided too accurate a navigational aid for German aircraft.

Televised music usually consisted of a studio concert or a relay of a prestigious public concert. For many years broadcasts were circumscribed by the limitations of television sound. The need to create meaningful television images meant that the orchestra would be represented by a variety of held or panning shots including close-ups of individual instruments and the conductor. Non-musical images were also included, particularly shots of the countryside and archive footage of the composer or contemporary events. Until the 1990s televised music was a regular weekly feature on BBC2. From the outset the BBC had designated opera producers and a television orchestra. During the early period operas were televised at the rate of one a month, in specially excerpted versions lasting about half an hour. The first was Albert Coates's *Pickwick* in 1936 at the time of its Covent Garden production.

After the war it was another coronation, in 1953, which again stimulated demand for television sets, and at that time the only service was the BBC. With the subsequent introduction of new channels (initially ITV, then BBC2 and later, in 1982, Channel 4) opportunities for televising music increased, and until the late 1980s music was an important item on the agendas of television managements; but after that there was a change as more populist policies began to predominate and audience rating became the paramount consideration. In 2000 Jeremy Isaacs, the first director of Channel 4 and a champion of arts broadcasting, established Artsworld, a satellite channel devoted to arts programmes including much music.

The first opera commissioned for television was Menotti's *Amahl and the Night Visitors* for the American NBC in 1951. The first in the UK was Arthur Benjamin's one-act *Mañana* broadcast in 1956 and soon followed by Malcolm Arnold's *The Open Window* and Joan Trimble's *Blind Raftery*. Few operas presented on television have made the transition to the stage, apart from *Amahl and the Night Visitors*, reputedly long the most performed opera in the USA. Britten's *Owen Wingrave* has been widely staged but was arguably surpassed on television by John Culshaw's haunting production of *Peter Grimes*, since widely disseminated on video. Others who wrote television operas included Stravinsky (*The Flood*; CBS, 1962) and Bliss (*Tobias and the Angel*; BBC, 1960).

It is reported that during the 1980s no operas were commissioned for television. At Christmas 1992, seeking a wider non-specialist audience, BBC2 presented Marschner's *Der Vampyr* recast as a thriller, set in modern dress with new words and shown in short instalments. In 1994 Channel 4 revived the concept of television opera, televising five specially written short operas from young composers. In 1999 the BBC reaffirmed its ability to make television music programmes of the highest quality with a series of six programmes each concerned with a performance of an important British 20th-century work filmed in a prime location, such as Vaughan Williams's Tallis Fantasia memorably shot in Gloucester Cathedral.

8. Conclusion

The accountancy-driven revolution of the 1990s coincided with a crisis in the arts generally, resulting from changes and reductions in funding worldwide and a sudden shift in long-held certainties. Many radio orchestras disbanded or amalgamated and there was much talk of 'dumbing down'. In spite of a brief period in the mid- and late 1990s when BBC radio music programmes replaced many long-established presenters, adopted a more populist style, and lost some of their breadth of repertory, the BBC orchestras remained active, enjoying an enhanced profile with their public on CD as a result of new arrangements for 'shared sessions' with record companies. Thus, for the first time, outside entrepreneurs were dictating a certain proportion of the more pioneering BBC broadcast repertory. JBo/LF

W. GLOCK, *The BBC's Music Policy* (London, 1963) · J. BORNOFF, *Music and Twentieth Century Media* (Florence, 1972) · N. KENYON, *The BBC Symphony Orchestra: The First Fifty Years, 1930–1980* (London, 1981) · W. GLOCK, *Notes in Advance* (Oxford, 1991) · H. CARPENTER, *The Envy of the World: Fifty Years of the BBC Third Programme and Radio 3* (London, 1996) · J. DOCTOR, *The BBC and Ultra-Modern Music, 1922–1936: Shaping a Nation's Tastes* (Cambridge, 1999) · J. DRUMMOND, *Tainted by Experience: A Life in the Arts* (London, 2000) · A. MITCHELL and A. POULTON, *A Chronicle of First Broadcast Performances of Musical Works in the United Kingdom, 1923–1996* (Aldershot, 2001)

Broadwood. English firm of piano makers founded in London in 1728 by Burkat *Shudi, whose daughter married John Broadwood (1732–1812) who continued the business after Shudi's death in 1773. The company's earliest instruments were improved versions of *Zumpe's square pianos but by the 1790s Broadwood's grand pianos, triple-strung and with increased dynamic flexibility, were the favourites of many leading composers including Haydn, Clementi, and Beethoven (to whom the firm gave a piano). AL

D. WAINWRIGHT, *Broadwood by Appointment: A History* (London, 1982)

Brod, Max (*b* Prague, 27 May 1884; *d* Tel Aviv, 20 Dec. 1968). Czech-born German-Israeli writer, composer, and librettist. He studied law and worked for a time as a state employee in Prague. A writer of poetry, novels, and opera librettos, he was also a renowned music and theatre critic. His friends among the German-Jewish writers' community in Prague included Franz Kafka, whose biography he later wrote. Best known for his translations into German of Janáček's operas, he also wrote the first substantial biography of the composer. In 1939 Brod left Czechoslovakia for Palestine. His book *Die Musik Israels* (1951) covers the early development of Israeli music and discusses Jewish elements in the works of Mendelssohn and Mahler. LC

Brodsky, Adolph (*b* Taganrog, 21 March/2 April 1851; *d* Manchester, 22 Jan. 1929). Russian violinist. He studied in Vienna and rose to fame by giving the premiere of Tchaikovsky's concerto in Vienna under Hans Richter in 1881, then led the New York Symphony Orchestra for Damrosch before being called by Hallé in 1895 to Manchester. He succeeded Hallé as principal of the new Royal Manchester College of Music (appointing Wilhelm Backhaus, Egon Petri, and Carl Fuchs as teachers) and founded the Brodsky Quartet. CF

broken cadence. See CADENCE.

broken chord. The playing of a chord as individual notes rather than simultaneously—usually as an accompanying figure, as in the *Alberti bass.

broken consort. See CONSORT.

broken octave. 1. A variant of *short octave.

2. The playing of octaves as single notes, sounded separately rather than simultaneously (see Ex. 1).

broken octave, Ex. 1

rather than

Brossard, Sébastien de (*b* Dompierre, Orne, *bapt.* 12 Sept. 1655; *d* Meaux, 10 Aug. 1730). French lexicographer, theorist, and composer. Educated as a priest, he held various ecclesiastical and musical posts in Paris, Strasbourg (1687–98), and Meaux (1698–1730) and composed a considerable amount of church music. His main importance is as the writer of one of the earliest music dictionaries, first published in 1701. A second edition, entitled *Dictionaire de musique, contenant une explication des termes grecs, latins, italiens et françois* (Paris, 1703/*R*1964), includes a catalogue of more than 900 writers and remains a valuable source for understanding 17th-century music. His library, which he left to Louis XIV in exchange for an annuity in 1724, is still in the Bibliothèque Nationale.   DA/LC

Brouček, The Excursions of Mr. See EXCURSIONS OF MR BROUČEK, THE.

Brouwer, (Juan) Leo(vigildo) (*b* Havana, 1 March 1939). Cuban composer and guitarist. As a pupil of Emilio Pujol he inherited the Cuban guitar tradition; he then studied in the USA at the Juilliard School and Hartt College. Back in Cuba, he soon had a place at the forefront of the avant-garde, though his sympathies are broad and his copious output testifies to his facility and freedom. His guitar works, which include five concertos, numerous solo pieces, and arrangements, are part of the international repertory. Among his other works are orchestral compositions and film scores.
                                                        PG

Brown, Earle (*b* Lunenburg, MA, 26 Dec. 1926; *d* Rye, NY, 2 July 2002). American composer. He studied mathematics and engineering at Northeastern University, Boston, and composition with Joseph Schillinger (1946–50) and Roslyn Brogue Henning. After two years as a teacher of Schillinger methods in Denver he settled in New York, where he associated with John Cage and with such artists as Jackson Pollock and Alexander Calder. Influenced as much by them as by Cage, he produced one of the first graphic scores (see GRAPHIC NOTATION), *December 1952* (1952), a design of thin black rectangles on a white ground. Then, in *25 Pages* (1953), he provided material that can be used in any manner by from one to 25 pianists. While working as a producer for Time Records (1955–60) Brown came into contact with members of the European avant-garde, and he returned to conventional notation, though often in mobile forms. *Available Forms II* (1961–2), for instance, has a variety of musical events to be set in order by two conductors, each working independently of the other with a group of 49 players.   PG

📖 M. NYMAN, *Experimental Music: Cage and Beyond* (London, 1974, 2/1999)

Browne, John (*fl* late 15th century). English composer. Although he was perhaps the greatest English composer between Dunstaple and John Taverner, nothing is known for certain about his life, and only 13 works by him survive, most of them in the *Eton Choirbook. These include a group of celebrated antiphons on texts concerned with the Passion, of which the powerful *Stabat mater* is regarded as his masterpiece. Browne's output also includes *Magnificat* settings, most of which are now lost, as well as some of the finest carols of the period; two of these, *Woefully arrayed* and *Jesu, mercy, how may this be*, are remarkable for their use of expressive musical effects and even occasional word-painting.   JM

Browning. The name given to a number of English 16th- and 17th-century instrumental compositions based on a tune associated with such texts as 'The leaves be greene, the nuts be browne', mostly elaborate sets of variations (e.g. those in five parts by Byrd).

Bruch, Max (Christian Friedrich) (*b* Cologne, 6 Jan. 1838; *d* Berlin, 2 Oct. 1920). German composer. At 14 he won the coveted Frankfurt Mozart Foundation Prize and studied with Ferdinand Hiller and Carl Reinecke. His long career included appointments as a conductor at the German courts of Coblenz and Sondershausen and in such cities as Liverpool and Breslau; work as a freelance composer; and latterly, 1890–1911, the post of professor of composition at the Berlin Academy. Much influenced by Schumann and Mendelssohn's music, Bruch achieved early fame in 1868 with his First Violin Concerto op. 26, which largely overshadows his 100 published works. His predilection for violin music grew out of his friendships with Ferdinand David, Joachim, Sarasate, and Willy Hess. His further output includes three symphonies, three operas, chamber music, many songs, eight more concerted works for violin, four for cello (among them *Kol Nidrei*), and several choral works including large-scale oratorios on the subject of Greek myths.

Bruch's music is notable for its melodic strength, its harmonic weakness being due to a lack of inventiveness and a resistance to the progressive ideas of Wagner and Liszt. Bruch loved folksong as a melodic source, and many of his works were derived from such countries as Scotland (*Scottish Fantasy* op. 46), Sweden, and Russia.

His precocious gifts remained largely unfulfilled because he lived in the shadow of his greater contemporary Brahms and because he resisted current changes in musical development, but his name will endure thanks to one superb violin concerto.   CF

C. Fifield, *Max Bruch: His Life and Works* (London, 1988)

Bruckner, (Josef) Anton (*b* Ansfelden, 4 Sept. 1824; *d* Vienna, 11 Oct. 1896). Austrian composer and organist. He initially intended to become a village schoolmaster, and might have remained in that occupation for the rest of his life had not circumstances and his own inner determination led him to embark on an exclusively musical career. While retaining strong connections with his roots, he progressed inexorably from unexceptional beginnings to a position of some eminence in Vienna. As a church composer, he brought the Viennese Classical mass of Haydn, Mozart, Beethoven, and Schubert to its final stage of development; as a symphonist, he was conscious of following in the footsteps of Beethoven (as was his great contemporary, Johannes Brahms), but he enlarged the structure of the genre to match the harmonic and melodic eloquence of its enriched content.

1. The early years; 2. Linz; 3. Vienna; 4. Bruckner as symphonist

1. The early years

From a rural, working-class background, Bruckner received his first music lessons from his father and his talented cousin, Johann Baptist Weiss, and in the mid- to late 1830s began to show a modest but unmistakable aptitude for organ-playing, sufficient to allow him occasionally to deputize for his father. When his father died in 1837 the family moved to Ebelsberg, a small village near St Florian. One of the fortunate consequences was that the young Bruckner was accepted as a choirboy in this great Augustinian monastery, where he received a thorough musical and general education; it was to become his spiritual home for the rest of his life.

After training as a teacher in Linz (about 13 km from St Florian), by far the largest town in Upper Austria, Bruckner took a post as a schoolteacher, thus intending to follow his father and grandfather. This first appointment in the remote village of Windhaag (1841–3) was not a happy experience, but his next two posts—in Kronstorf (1843–5) and St Florian (1845–55)—were much more rewarding. Bruckner attempted to improve his standing as a teacher by taking more examinations, but the call of music was irresistible. During his ten years at St Florian he took the opportunity of playing the splendid Chrismann organ in the abbey and of

studying the numerous manuscripts and printed volumes in the large library. He became a fine organist, able to hold his own with the recognized organ virtuosos of the day.

Bruckner's development as a composer, slow at first during the Windhaag and Kronstorf years and resulting almost entirely in short sacred pieces including two mass settings, began to take wing at St Florian; and his earliest large-scale works—the Requiem in D minor (1849) and the *Missa solemnis* in B♭ minor (1854)—belong to these 'apprentice years'. They are clearly derivative, but the fingerprints of the mature Bruckner are already much in evidence. At the end of 1855 the post of cathedral organist in Linz fell vacant; Bruckner was the unanimous choice. This was the first watershed: schoolteaching was left behind and he could now devote himself to music.

2. Linz

Although fully involved in the musical life of Linz, as a church musician and occasional conductor of the Frohsinn choral society, Bruckner made significant progress as a composer. Initially, during a remarkable six-year course of harmony and counterpoint studies with the great Viennese theoretician Simon Sechter—a mixture of 'distance learning' and extended visits to Vienna—he wrote little, so great was his desire to acquire a firm grounding and to improve his technical facility. But in Vienna in 1861, at an examination, he so impressed his examiners with his skills as an improviser that he gained a qualification as a recognized harmony and counterpoint teacher. He continued his long and rigorous self-imposed musical education, taking lessons in form and orchestration from Otto Kitzler (1834–1915) and studying scores of modern works (Berlioz, Schumann, Wagner) with Ignaz Dorn in Linz.

The *Kitzler Studienbuch* is essentially a diary of progress, containing many examples of Bruckner's attempts to master different forms and culminating in the String Quartet in C minor (1862), the Three Orchestral Pieces (1862), the Overture in G minor (1862), the Symphony in F minor (*Studiensymphonie*, 1863), and a setting for choir and orchestra of Psalm 112 (1863). It was as if the shackles of academic constraint were now cast off. In his last four or five years in Linz there was an outpouring of music, including three fine mass settings, in D minor (1864), E minor (1866), and F minor (1868)—the splendid culmination of the Viennese Classical mass and a testament to Bruckner's great faith—and the Symphony no. 1 in C minor (1865–6), as well as a number of sacred and secular choral works and some modest instrumental and chamber music pieces. The symphony was inspired by his hearing *Tristan und*

Isolde at its premiere (Munich, 1865), to which Wagner had invited him.

With this increase in compositional output came a restlessness with his situation in Linz, where Bruckner felt ever more restricted by lack of opportunity. Recovery from a catastrophic nervous breakdown in 1867 no doubt helped him concentrate seriously on his future: Vienna was clearly the place to be if he was to develop as a composer and gain any kind of national, let alone international, recognition. After making a few unsuccessful attempts to establish a foothold in the Austrian capital, he was encouraged by Johann Herbeck, one of his examiners in 1861 and now court music director, to apply for the post of harmony and counterpoint teacher at the conservatory, in succession to Sechter. He was successful, and Herbeck demonstrated commendable tact and patience in dealing with Bruckner's vacillating response, reassuring him of the advantages of the move and, not least, securing him an unpaid but prestigious position as supernumerary organist at the Hofkapelle. In summer 1868 Bruckner moved to Vienna.

3. Vienna

Following this second watershed, Bruckner now embarked on the final stage of his career. His activities were threefold. As an organist he played at services in the Hofkapelle and was eventually 'promoted' to a paid position, though he never secured the more senior posts of assistant or chief music director. He also had the opportunity to direct performances of his own church music and, for a time, was responsible for coaching the choirboys. He briefly considered a career as a concert organist, particularly after his successes in representing Austria as an international soloist in concerts in Nancy and Paris in 1869 and in London in 1871 at the Albert Hall and Crystal Palace, after which his fame spread.

As a teacher, not only did Bruckner continue in his post at the conservatory until 1891 but he taught privately and, from 1875 to 1894, was lecturer in harmony and counterpoint at the University of Vienna; his methods were orthodox but the way he presented them was often extremely unorthodox, though effective. He nevertheless established a rapport with his students and young supporters, many of whom devoted much energy to playing his orchestral works in solo piano and piano-duet arrangements at a time when they were otherwise rarely performed. Gustav Mahler may have gone on to become the most prominent of these young 'disciples' as a conductor and composer in his own right, but the Schalk brothers (Joseph and Franz) and Löwe were the most active. Bruckner's pupils were to include several people who later became leading conductors.

It was essentially to hone his skills as a symphonist and develop his career as a composer that Bruckner had moved to Vienna, one of the musical capitals of the world. While he clearly enjoyed most aspects of teaching, he often complained that it left him little time and energy for composition. Most of his summer vacations, spent in St Florian and, latterly, in Steyr, were devoted to intensive work on his symphonies, beginning with the Janus-faced Symphony no. 'o' in 1869 and continuing with Symphonies nos. 2–5 in the 1870s, nos. 6–8 in the 1880s, and culminating in the unfinished no. 9.

Recognition did not come quickly. Both the String Quintet (1879) and the *Te Deum* (1884) were accepted as outstanding works almost immediately, but the infrequent performances of his symphonies led the extremely self-critical Bruckner, often aided and abetted by his interfering, albeit well-meaning, friends, to revise them persistently. In 1876 and 1877, for instance, several of his works underwent close rhythmical scrutiny. Two events that particularly shook Bruckner's confidence were the disastrous first performance of the second version of his Third Symphony in December 1877 and the cool reception given to the first version of his Eighth by his friend Hermann Levi (1839–1900) ten years later.

Levi, a great Wagner conductor and champion of Bruckner's music, and Nikisch, a pupil of Bruckner's, had already helped to secure him some measure of international recognition by conducting performances of his Seventh Symphony in Munich and Leipzig in 1884 and 1885 before the work was finally performed by Hans Richter and the Vienna Philharmonic in Vienna in 1886. (In 1882 Bruckner had been to Bayreuth to hear *Parsifal* and, much moved by Wagner's death, composed the last pages as a tribute.) But Bruckner, after some profound inner struggles, responded positively to Levi's criticism and revised his remarkable Eighth Symphony, which was given its belated first performance to great acclaim in Vienna in December 1892.

The huge amount of revision undertaken by Bruckner in the late 1880s and early 90s, some in collaboration with Josef Schalk, resulted in alterations to the Mass in F minor and new versions of the First, Third, and Fourth Symphonies. The now ailing composer exhibited marked symptoms of depression and anxiety, this revision process leaving him little time and energy to devote to new compositions. In 1892 and 1893, however, he wrote three large-scale choral pieces, a majestic setting of Psalm 150, *Das deutsche Lied* for male chorus and brass, and *Helgoland* for male chorus and orchestra.

For the last ten years of his life, his insecurities unalleviated and his religious convictions intensified,

Bruckner withdrew from teaching and organ-playing and was occupied to a greater or lesser degree with the Ninth Symphony, of which he completed the first three movements. Granted the use of a small house on Emperor Franz Josef I's Belvedere estate in 1895, Bruckner was working on the finale right up to his death. The appreciable number of surviving sketches are a poignant testimony to a mind that remained remarkably active and inventive to the last. Bruckner was much honoured in his lifetime and was buried at St Florian.

4. Bruckner as symphonist

The creative energy of Bruckner's Symphony no. 1 in C minor (1865–6) is well summed up in his own nickname for the work—the 'saucy little besom'. While lacking the breadth of the later symphonies, it more than makes up for that in its rugged grandeur. The 'sauciness' perhaps lies particularly in Bruckner's handling of symphonic form and development of thematic material: there is a confidence he did not possess in the somewhat tentative, albeit promising, F minor Symphony (1863). With this C minor symphony Bruckner signalled to the musical world that he was a force to be reckoned with.

Symphony no. '0' in D minor was written in 1869 (i.e. after no. 1) during Bruckner's first year in Vienna. He showed it to the court music director, Otto Dessoff, in the early 1870s and Dessoff's astonished reaction, 'Where is the main theme, then?', was perhaps one of the reasons why Bruckner set the work aside and 'nullified' it when he organized his manuscripts in 1895. While the symphony undeniably draws on ideas from works of the 1860–8 period, particularly the E minor and F minor Masses to which there are thematic references in the first and second movements, its opening and the bustling quaver activity in the Scherzo clearly point to later works, Symphony no. 3 in particular.

Symphony no. 2 in C minor (1871–2) marks a significant advance in Bruckner's symphonic thinking. There is a much closer thematic–motivic relationship within and between the movements. The short time between the work's gestation and the first performance of the F minor Mass in Vienna in June 1872 is underlined by quotations from the latter in the symphony's slow movement and finale. Between its first performance in October 1873 and publication in 1892, Bruckner made several cuts and alterations in scoring, though these were not as extensive as those he made to some of the later symphonies.

Bruckner dedicated his Symphony no. 3 in D minor (1873) to Wagner, to whom he showed it when he visited Bayreuth. It underwent a number of revisions both before and after the Vienna performance of its second version in December 1877 (incorporated in the first edition of 1879) and the Vienna performance of its third version in December 1890 (incorporated in the second edition of the same year). When he revised it in 1876–7, for instance, he retained most of the self-quotations but eventually eliminated all but one of the Wagner quotations in the original version. Nevertheless there is still a wealth of thematic material in the first movement which is matched by the Schubertian prodigality of invention in the slow movement. One of Bruckner's happiest inspirations occurs in the second subject group of the finale: the combination of a polka-like theme in the strings and a chorale in the brass.

Symphony no. 4 in E♭ (1874), like its predecessor, was substantially altered in subsequent years, the most significant changes being a new Scherzo added in December 1878, a second finale entitled 'Volksfest' which was written in the late summer of 1878, and a third finale composed in 1879–80; further changes, essentially involving structural tautening and textural thinning, were made before the printing of the first edition in September 1889. The first movement already has the famous atmospheric opening with a horn call over *tremolando* strings in the original version.

Bruckner's great contrapuntal skills are in evidence throughout Symphony no. 5 in B♭ (1875–8), a work of epic proportions. In the finale he intertwines elements of sonata form and fugue. Not content to use his two main fugal themes in double counterpoint, he eventually reintroduces the main theme from the first movement and brings the work to a magnificent conclusion by combining all three themes in triple counterpoint. In contrast, Symphony no. 6 in A (1879–81) is much more compact structurally, but there is no corresponding decrease in the wealth of thematic invention. Of the (by now standard) three subject groups in the first movement, the first is particularly rich motivically. The Adagio second movement is a jewel among Bruckner's slow movements.

From the expansive theme for cellos and violas at the very outset, the Symphony no. 7 in E (1881–3) introduces us to a new, even richer sound world. The four Wagner tubas add a distinctive colour and lend nobility to the closing Adagio, which is essentially one long elegy for Wagner. The tonal plan of this movement is also one of Bruckner's finest. The Symphony no. 8 in C minor (1884–7, rev. 1889–90) represents the essential Bruckner: great climactic surges, grand melodic sweep, particularly in the slow movement whose poignant, bitter-sweet harmonies both hark back to Schubert and foreshadow Mahler, and assured contrapuntal mastery, notably in the coda of the finale in which themes from different parts of the work are magnificently combined.

Bruckner's Symphony no. 9 in D minor, begun in August 1887 and left incomplete on his death in October 1896, is a remarkably forward-looking work, presaging the 20th century in its obsessive, driving rhythms in the second movement and wrenching dissonances in the third movement and the finale sketches. The elegiac coda of the third movement is an eloquent summing-up of Bruckner's achievements as a composer for the church and the concert hall in that it not only recalls material from earlier in the symphony but quotes themes from other works, including the D minor Mass which, more than 30 years earlier, had signalled his emergence from relative obscurity to national and, eventually, international recognition.   CH

📖 R. SIMPSON, *The Essence of Bruckner* (London 1967, 2/ 1992) · D. WATSON, *Bruckner* (London, 1975, 2/1996) · P. HAWKSHAW, *The Manuscript Sources for Anton Bruckner's Linz Works: A Study of his Working Methods from 1856 to 1868* (Ann Arbor, MI, 1984) · T. JACKSON and P. HAWKSHAW (eds.), *Bruckner Studies* (Cambridge, 1997) · S. JOHNSON, *Bruckner Remembered* (London, 1998) · C. HOWIE, T. JACKSON, and P. HAWKSHAW (eds.), *Perspectives on Anton Bruckner* (Aldershot, 2001) · C. HOWIE, *Anton Bruckner: A Documentary Biography* (Lampeter, 2001)

Bruhns, Nicolaus (*b* Schwabstedt, nr Husum, 1665; *d* Husum, 29 March 1697). German organist and composer. He came from a family of professional musicians: after learning the organ with his father he went to Lübeck in 1681 to study the violin and viol with his uncle. He also had organ and composition lessons from Buxtehude, soon becoming so skilled that he was able, according to Mattheson, to provide a pedal obbligato to his own violin playing. Buxtehude persuaded him to undertake further studies in Copenhagen. He later returned to Schleswig-Holstein as organist of the parish church in Husum, where he settled and married, only to die at the age of 32.

Bruhns was one of the greatest organists of his time, second only to his teacher Buxtehude in northern Germany. Of his compositions only five organ pieces and 12 sacred vocal works survive.   WT

bruitism (from Fr. *bruit*, 'noise'). The use in music of sounds taken from an extra-musical source or context. The term is used most often of percussion or of electronic music that suggests the sounds of machinery. See also FUTURISM.

Brumel, Antoine (*b* c.1460; *d* ?1512). French church musician and composer. Nothing certain is known about him until 1483, when he is listed as a singer at Chartres Cathedral. Between 1486 and 1498 he held posts at the cathedrals of Geneva and Laon, and visited the court of Savoy. From 1498 until 1500 he was given charge of the choristers at the Cathedral of Notre Dame, Paris; he then returned to the Savoy court as a singer. He spent his final years in Italy, first as choirmaster at the ducal court at Ferrara (1506–10), later in the vicinity of Mantua. Brumel is important for his church music, especially his masses; the 12-voice *Missa 'Et ecce terrae motus'* in particular is celebrated for its spectacular sonorities and rhythmic energy. His *Magnificat* settings are also especially lively. Comparatively few secular works by him survive.   JM

Bruneau, (Louis Charles Bonaventure) Alfred (*b* Paris, 3 March 1857; *d* Paris, 15 June 1934). French composer. He began his career as a cellist and subsequently became a composition pupil of Massenet, who was highly influential on his style. In 1881 his cantata *Geneviève* gained second prize in the Prix de Rome and in 1887 the success of his first opera *Kérim* was enough to persuade him to devote himself to opera; as he was to do in several later operas, he incorporated folksong. His middle years were dominated by his collaborations with Émile Zola, the central figure of French naturalism. Politically important was his unfailing support of Zola in the infamous Dreyfus affair.

These factors led Bruneau to write about a dozen operas with lifelike plots, politically sensitive themes, and characters in contemporary dress. *Le Rêve* (1891) was the first opera based on Zola, its libretto adapted by the writer and librettist Louis Gallet. *L'Attaque au moulin* (1893) is also to a Gallet adaptation of Zola. Thereafter the collaborations became more direct, with Zola himself fashioning the librettos. The first of these, *Messidor* (1901), was perhaps the most important and has been the most performed. *L'Ouragan* ('The Hurricane') and *L'Enfant roi* (1902) followed. After Zola's death Bruneau himself wrote the librettos for operas based on Zola. From 1913 he turned to different subjects, *Virginie* (1928) being the most successful. Of his other works, his songs deserve more attention; his Requiem is sometimes performed, and his copious writings give a perspective on the period not found elsewhere.   RLS

📖 S. HUEBNER, *French Opera at the Fin de Siècle: Wagnerism, Nationalism, and Style* (Oxford, 1999)

brunette (Fr.). A French popular song on an idyllic, pastoral, or amorous text. The genre flourished in the 17th and 18th centuries, and some of the tunes were later used in harpsichord suites and comic operas. The songs frequently featured a 'jolie brunette', hence the title.

Brunetti, Gaetano (*b* ?Fano, 1744; *d* Colmenar de Orejo, nr Madrid, 16 Dec. 1798). Italian composer. From about 1762 he was in Spain, in the service of Charles III and later of Charles IV, for whom he built up an extensive music library. His output of over 400 works includes 28 symphonies, six overtures, several marches, minuets, galops, church music, and a great deal of chamber music (sextets, quintets, quartets, trios, and violin sonatas). One of Brunetti's most interesting works is a 'programme symphony' ('Il maniatico', 1780) in which a cello is used to portray the hero's madness, rather in the manner of Richard Strauss's *Don Quixote*.   WT

brush. A device made from thin strands of wire, used to play drums. Brushes have been used since the 1920s, especially by kit-drummers in jazz and dance bands, to produce a softer sound than ordinary side-drum sticks.

brusque (Fr.). A 17th-century dance form used by Chambonnières.

Bruststimme (Ger.). *'Chest voice'. See also VOICE, 4.

Brustwerk (Ger.). That department of a German Baroque organ immediately in front of the player, below the *Hauptwerk* or Great organ. It was approximately equivalent to a small *chamber organ, usually had its own manual, and was often used to accompany singers.   JMo

Bryars, (Richard) Gavin (*b* Goole, 16 Jan. 1943). English composer. He read philosophy at Sheffield University, then studied composition privately and at the Northern School of Music. His early compositional activities were in popular and experimental music. While a lecturer at the Portsmouth College of Art in 1970 he co-founded the Portsmouth Sinfonia, specifically for untrained performers, and he was an important figure among those British musicians who rejected the complexity and seriousness of the continental avant-garde, and whose heroes were Satie and Cage. With *The Sinking of the Titanic* (1969–75) and *Jesus' Blood Never Failed Me Yet* (1971) Bryars demonstrated an ability to rethink the elements of music drama that bore fruit in his later operatic ventures, including *Medea* (Lyons, 1984) and *Doctor Ox's Experiment* (ENO, 1998). He has also composed much instrumental and vocal music which connects the repeated rhythmic and harmonic patterns of the minimalist style with broader and more lyrical melodic writing.   AW

buccin (Fr.). A trombone with dragon-head bell, made for 19th-century military bands.

Buch der hängenden Gärten, Das ('The Book of the Hanging Gardens'). Songs for voice and piano, op. 15 (1908–9), by Schoenberg, settings of 15 poems by Stefan George.

bucina (Lat.). A Roman cavalry trumpet of oxhorn, decorated with silver.

buffo, buffa (It., 'comic'). See OPERA BUFFA.

Buffoon, The Tale of the. See CHOUT.

bugaku. The traditional court music of Japan, performed with dance. There are two genres, characterized by the musical repertory and the colour of the costumes. 'Dances of the Left' (with mainly red costumes) are performed to music of the *tōgaku* repertory, and 'Dances of the Right', in blue and green, primarily to that of the *komagaku* repertory.   KC

bugle. 1 (Fr.: *clairon*; Ger.: *Signalhorn*; It.: *cornetto da segnale, tromba*). A simple brass instrument used for signalling and military calls. British military bugles are in B♭ with conical bore, whereas the American are more often bored cylindrically (like trumpets) and have, like the Italian type, a single valve to lower the pitch a 4th. The first 18th-century bugles were semicircular. By the end of the century they were built in a single loop, the modern twice-coiled pattern appearing in about 1860, though the single loop is still common elsewhere in Europe. In 1810 Joseph Haliday of Dublin devised a keyed bugle with five keys, to which a sixth was added later. This became the leading melody instrument of military bands and was enormously popular, especially in America, where many more keys were used.

2 (Fr.). 'Flugel horn'.   JMo

Bühnenmusik (Ger., 'stage music'). *Incidental music for a play; also any music played on stage as part of the drama or opera.

Bühnenweihfestspiel (Ger., 'stage-dedication festival play'). A term coined by Wagner to describe *Parsifal*, in which he hoped to restore the idea of the sacred to drama. See also FESTSPIEL.

buildings and music. The shape, dimensions, and furnishings of large auditoria and small rooms have a significant effect on the characteristics of both live and reproduced music. See ACOUSTICS; ARCHITECTURAL ACOUSTICS.   JBo

buisine (Fr.). See BUYSINE.

Bull, John (*b* Old Radnor, Radnorshire, *c*.1562; *d* Antwerp, 12 or 13 March 1628). English keyboard player, church musician, and composer. He was a chorister at Hereford Cathedral in 1573, and a year later became one of the Children of the Chapel Royal, where he studied with the organist William Blitheman. His connection with Hereford Cathedral resumed in 1582, when he was appointed organist and, a year later, Master of the Choristers; but these positions lapsed as he spent increasing periods of time in London, and in 1586 he was made a Gentleman of the Chapel Royal. In the same year he was awarded the degree of B.Mus. at Oxford, and would have taken the D.Mus. if Oxford had not had 'Clownes & rigid Puritans that could not endure Church music' (in Anthony Wood's colourful phrase). Bull eventually achieved the Oxford doctorate by taking the degree at Cambridge by 1589 and then 'incorporating' in 1592. In 1597 he was elected Public Reader in music at Gresham College, London, a well-salaried position that did much to relieve his acknowledged poverty; he was obliged to resign in 1607 after fathering a daughter out of wedlock, and subsequently married the child's mother, Elizabeth Walter.

Bull was probably the greatest English keyboard virtuoso of his age. Though never officially employed as a private musician to Queen Elizabeth, he played for her on occasions of state and before important foreign visitors. He was valued, too, by James I, and held a position in the short-lived court of Henry, Prince of Wales. In 1612 he was appointed music master to Princess Elizabeth; the famous collection *Parthenia, or The Maydenhead of the First Musicke that Ever Was Printed for the Virginalls*, which includes several pieces by Bull, was dedicated to her and the Elector Palatine, Prince Friedrich, at about the time of their marriage in 1613. In addition to performing, Bull built keyboard instruments, and served as an adviser on the building of organs.

In 1613 he was charged with adultery—having become, in the words of George Abbott, Archbishop of Canterbury, 'as famous for marring of virginity as he is for fingering of organs and virginals'—and fled to Brussels. There he entered the service of Archduke Albert, and worked alongside other leading organists of the day, including Peter Philips and Peeter Cornet. His sudden departure from the Chapel Royal was resented by James I, who caused him to be dismissed from the archduke's chapel. His last years were spent in Antwerp, as organist of the cathedral and an adviser on organ construction.

There can be no doubting Bull's prowess as a keyboard player; his variations on the *Walsingham* tune test finger dexterity to the full. His skill as a composer of keyboard music, however, is equally great. His interest in counterpoint is shown in a set of 120 canons, most of them on the 'Miserere' plainsong, which use such techniques as augmentation, diminution, and retrograde motion. This skill informs many of his compositions, especially the great A minor *In nomine*, with its complex rhythmic proportions. His linked pavans and galliards are treated less as music for dancing than as miniature variation sets, each phrase decorated on its repeat so as to heighten the emotion; similarly his

arrangements of John Dowland's *Piper's Galliard* glow with a dark passion. Among his fantasias are several derived from continental models, but he also wrote typically English short genre pieces with such titles as *My Self*, *My Jewel*, and *My Grief*.

The grave-faced portrait in the Faculty of Music at Oxford has round its edge the rhyme:

> The Bull by force
> In field doth Raigne
> But Bull by Skill
> Good will doth Gayne.

DA/JM

📖 P. CHAPPELL, *A Portrait of John Bull* (Hereford, 1970) · W. CUNNINGHAM, *The Keyboard Music of John Bull* (Ann Arbor, MI, 1984)

Bull, Ole (Bornemann) (*b* Bergen, 5 Feb. 1810; *d* Lysøen, nr Bergen, 17 Aug. 1880). Norwegian violinist and composer. A seminal figure in 19th-century Norwegian musical life, he also experimented with modifications to the shape of the bow and to the height of the bridge while developing a new manner of holding both. His performing career took him throughout Europe (he played with Liszt and Mendelssohn) and to the USA. In his homeland he established the Norwegian Theatre, appointing the young Henrik Ibsen as resident dramatist, and later encouraged Grieg to study in Leipzig. His playing skills were comparable to Paganini's, and Schumann was struck by his beautiful tone. His compositions, which include the song *Saeterjentens Søndag*, are rich in melody and harmony.   CF

📖 E. HAUGEN and C. CAI, *Ole Bull* (Oslo, 1992; Eng. trans. 1993)

Buller, John (*b* London, 7 Feb. 1927). English composer. He studied with Anthony Milner, and worked professionally as an architectural surveyor until the mid-1970s. His principal compositions since that date include *Proença* for soprano, electric guitar, and orchestra (Proms, 1977) and an opera *The Bacchae* (ENO, 1992), which impress through their textural subtlety and vivid sense of drama. James Joyce was an important influence during the 1970s: *The Mime of Mick, Nick, and the Maggies* (1978) remains one of the most convincing compositions to owe its derivation to the enigmatic *Finnegans Wake*.   AW

bullroarer [thunderstick, whizzer] (Fr.: *rhombe, planchette ronflante*; Ger.: *Schwirrholz*). A wooden blade with a hole through which a cord is tied, swung round the player's head so that the blade spins with a sound like that of a roaring bull or thunder. Used worldwide from earliest times as a ritual instrument, often representing an ancestral or spirit voice, it has been adopted latterly in many areas as a noise-maker to protect crops and has now become a child's plaything, so embodying the classic cycle of ritual, tool, and toy.

JMo

Bülow, Hans (Guido) **von** (*b* Dresden, 8 Jan. 1830; *d* Cairo, 12 Feb. 1894). German pianist and conductor. Hearing Wagner conduct in 1849, then attending the premiere of *Lohengrin* under Liszt in 1850, led him to abandon a career in law: he went to Zürich to become a disciple of Wagner, and gained some conducting experience there before studying with Liszt (whom he greatly impressed) in order to become a concert pianist. In 1854 he married Liszt's daughter Cosima. He spent 1855–6 as a teacher at the Stern Conservatory in Berlin.

In 1864, when Ludwig II called Wagner into his service in Munich, Bülow was engaged as a conductor. He put into practice his detailed methods of preparing an opera for performance, giving the premieres of *Tristan und Isolde* (1865) and *Die Meistersinger von Nürnberg* (1868). He stayed in Munich until 1869, in spite of Wagner's seduction of his wife, which finally led to divorce. Anguished by this relationship, Bülow nevertheless behaved with dignity and remained a firm supporter of Wagner's music. Having left Munich, he spent some time in Florence, also undertaking extremely demanding concert tours that included giving (in Boston in 1875) the first performance of Tchaikovsky's First Piano Concerto, which was dedicated to him. He was in Hanover from 1878 to 1880 as conductor, then from 1880 to 1885 in Meiningen, where he raised the orchestra to one of world class. Quarrelsome by nature, with an acerbic tongue, he was none the less a fine conductor as well as a pianist who, especially through his lucid, intellectual performances, did much to establish and extend the standard repertory. His own piano compositions reflect the bravura of Liszt.

DA/JW

📖 R. DU MOULIN ECKART, *Hans von Bülow* (Munich and Berlin, 1921)

bumbass [bladder and string]. A home-made bass instrument consisting of a long pole, often with cymbals or other jingles on the top, with a single string attached at each end and stretched over a resonator made of a pig's bladder, tin can, small drum, or wooden box. It is usually played as a rattling drone, bowed with a saw-toothed wooden stick, and is sometimes called 'devil's fiddle'.

JMo

Bund (Ger.). 'Fret'.

Buonamente, Giovanni Battista (*b* Mantua, late 16th century; *d* Assisi, 29 Aug. 1642). Italian composer, violinist, and singer. He was a member of the Fran-

ciscan order and worked at the imperial court in Vienna in the 1620s. He stayed for a short time at S. Maria Maggiore, Bergamo, and was a violinist in Parma before becoming *maestro di cappella* at S. Francesco, Assisi, in 1633. A follower of Monteverdi and Salamone Rossi, he wrote some fine trio sonatas, and is noted for the development of idiomatic violin music, using such techniques as tremolando and cross-string writing.   DA

burden [burthen]. 1. A term for a refrain repeated after the verses (or at other points) of a song, carol, etc. Shakespeare used the term in Act II scene 7 of *As You Like It*: 'I would sing my song without a burden'.

2. A drone; see BOURDON.

3. The lowest of three voices singing together; see FABURDEN.

Burgmüller, (Johann) **Friedrich** [Frédéric] (*b* Regensburg, 4 Dec. 1806; *d* Beaulieu, 13 Feb. 1874). German composer and pianist. He settled in Paris after 1832, making a living as a teacher and composer. As well as the numerous piano studies and other pedagogical pieces for children for which he is well known he composed songs and a ballet, *La Péri* (1843). His brother **Norbert** (*b* Düsseldorf, 8 Feb. 1810; *d* Aachen, 7 May 1836), a child prodigy, studied the piano with Spohr in Kassel and composed two symphonies, a piano concerto, and other orchestral pieces, as well as piano sonatas and many keyboard miniatures—all typical of the early 19th-century German Romantic style. He was much admired by his close circle of acquaintances including Schumann, who thought highly of his melodic gifts and compared him to Schubert. Mendelssohn composed a march (op. 103) for Burgmüller's funeral.

—/SH

Burgon, Geoffrey (*b* Hambledon, 15 July 1941). English composer. He studied composition at the Guildhall School in London with Peter Wishart and privately with Lennox Berkeley. After working as a freelance trumpeter until 1971 he made his reputation as a concert composer with a series of vocal and choral works including a Requiem (1976), then enjoyed great success with many film and television scores including *Tinker, Tailor, Soldier, Spy* (1979) and *Brideshead Revisited* (1981).

ABur

Burgundian school. A term occasionally used, somewhat misleadingly, to refer to the great succession of 15th- and 16th-century composers who were born and trained in the Low Countries (present-day Holland, Belgium, and northern France) but were often resident elsewhere in Europe during their adult careers. The succession certainly existed, probably as a result of the rigorous training that boy choristers received in the churches and cathedrals of the Low Countries. However, the area involved extends beyond the regions governed by the dukes of Burgundy (which included, at various times, Flanders, Artois, Brabant, Hainaut, Holland, Limbourg, and Luxembourg), and it is clear that the Burgundian court itself was only partly responsible for fostering this rich musical tradition. More inclusive terms, although again not wholly accurate, are 'Franco-Flemish' and 'Franco-Netherlandish'. JM

Burkhard, Willy (*b* Leubringen bei Biel, 17 April 1900; *d* Zürich, 18 June 1955). Swiss composer and teacher. After attending the Berne Conservatory he studied with Karg-Elert and Teichmüller in Leipzig (1921), Walter Courvoisier in Munich (1922–4), and Max d'Ollone in Paris (1924). Returning to Switzerland, from 1926 he was active as a choirmaster. He taught composition and theory at the Zürich Conservatory from 1942 until his death.

Burkhard composed prolifically in spite of spells of illness. His style, superficially similar to Hindemith's, is vigorously contrapuntal, with a strong sense of impetus. The idiom is essentially tonal though dissonance, bitonality, and, occasionally, polytonality are liberally used. He wrote an opera, *Die schwarze Spinne* ('The Black Spider', 1947–8), two symphonies (1926–8, 1944), many concertante works, chamber and instrumental pieces, and much liturgical and secular choral music. MA

burla (It.). 'Jest'; *burlando*, 'jestingly'.

burlesque (Fr.; It.: *burlesca*; Ger.: *Burleske*). An entertainment with music that had a brief vogue before *operetta and *musical comedy were developed to suit popular tastes in the mid-19th century. It was generally a parody or skit on more serious opera, a forerunner of the satirical *revue. Burlesque flourished in England; one of its most important creators was J. R. Planché (1796–1880), whose first burlesque, *Olympic Revels*, was given at Drury Lane in 1831. A leading producer was John Hollingshead (1827–1904), manager of the old Gaiety Theatre, where some of the last true burlesques, including *Little Jack Sheppard* (1885) and *Carmen-up-to-Data* (1890), made popular stars of J. L. Toole (1830–1906), Nellie Farren (1845–1904), and others.

Originally the music was an arrangement of the work being 'burlesqued', but soon such composers as Meyer Lutz (1822–1903), musical director at the Gaiety, were writing original scores like *Ruy Blas and the Blasé Roué* (1889); these were close in spirit to the musical comedies of the 1890s, which would succeed and extinguish the burlesque tradition in England. In America, burlesque (or 'burlycue') had a similar vogue in the same period and with much the same repertory; but through such shows as *The Black Crook* (1866) it developed into a kind

of spectacular revue or variety show and lingered there for much longer. PGA

burletta (It.). A name used in England from the late 18th century for Italian comic operas, then for English imitations of them (by such composers as Samuel Arnold and Charles Dibdin).

Burney, Charles (*b* Shrewsbury, 7 April 1726; *d* Chelsea, 12 April 1814). English music historian. His father was a dancer, violinist, and portrait-painter. Charles Burney, one of 20 children, was educated at Shrewsbury School, then at what is now the King's School, Chester, where he began to play the organ. At Chester he met Arne, who was returning from Dublin, and was taken on by him as an apprentice, living in his house in London and sometimes playing in Handel's orchestra. Thereafter (apart from some years in King's Lynn) he spent most of his life as a teacher, composer, and organist in London, until in the early 1770s he travelled extensively in Europe, collecting information for his four-volume *General History of Music* (London, 1776–89). Almost every member of his family achieved some distinction, and his second daughter was the novelist Fanny Burney (Madame d'Arblay).

Burney was one of the first and finest of English musical historians. As well as his history and his travel diaries, from 1801 onwards he wrote the musical articles for the 45-volume *Rees's Cyclopaedia* (1819–20). He became friendly with Haydn on the latter's London visits, and was much involved with the Handel Commemoration of 1784. He had become a D.Mus. of Oxford University in 1769 and was made a Fellow of the Royal Society in 1773. In 1810 he was elected a Correspondant of the Institut de France (Classe des Beaux-Arts). PS/DA/LC

📖 P. A. SCHOLES, *The Great Dr Burney* (London, 1948/R) · P. A. SCHOLES (ed.), *Dr. Burney's Musical Tours in Europe* (London, 1959) · R. LONSDALE, *Dr Charles Burney: A Literary Biography* (Oxford, 1965) · H. E. POOLE (ed.), *Music, Men and Manners in France and Italy* (London, 1969) · K. S. GRANT, *Dr. Burney as Critic and Historian of Music* (Ann Arbor, MI, 1983)

Burning Fiery Furnace, The. Church parable, op. 77, by Britten to a text by William Plomer based on the book of Daniel (Aldeburgh, 1966).

burrasca (It., 'storm'). Music that illustrates a storm, such as the opening of Verdi's *Otello*.

Burrell, Diana (*b* Norwich, 25 Oct. 1948). English composer. While working as a teacher and viola player she gave increasing attention to composition, developing a style that offers immediately appealing, striking musical images by means of textures in which the distinction between the fundamental and the decorative is always crystal clear. The success of the 50-minute *Missa Sancte Endeliente* (1980) has been followed by a sequence of noteworthy orchestral compositions, including *Landscape* (1988), *Symphonies of Flocks, Herds and Shoals* (1995–6), and concertos for viola (1994), clarinet (1996), and flute (1997). Burrell is particularly adept at involving youthful and amateur performers in music whose freshness and vitality are genuinely contemporary in style.   AW

burthen. See BURDEN.

Busch, Fritz (*b* Siegen, Westphalia, 13 March 1890; *d* London, 24 Sept. 1951). German conductor. He studied at the Cologne Conservatory, becoming conductor in 1918 of the Stuttgart Opera and in 1922 of the Dresden State Opera, where he gave the world premieres of Strauss's *Intermezzo* (1924) and *Die ägyptische Helena* (1928), Busoni's *Doktor Faust* (1925), and Hindemith's *Cardillac* (1926). A fierce critic of the Nazis, he was subjected to harassment when the party came to power in 1933, and renounced his German citizenship in protest. He was appointed music director at Glyndebourne when the theatre opened in 1934, retaining the post until his death: his Mozart interpretations, many of which were recorded, became the stuff of legend. After World War II he lived in Copenhagen, where he was conductor of the Danish State Radio Orchestra.
                                                                                              TA

   📖 B. DOPHEIDE, *Fritz Busch* (Tutzing, 1970)

Bush, Alan (Dudley) (*b* London, 22 Dec. 1900; *d* Watford, 31 Oct. 1995). English composer. He studied composition with Frederick Corder at the RAM (1918–22) and privately with John Ireland (1922–7). In 1925 he was appointed to teach harmony and composition at the RAM. He spent the years 1929–31 studying musicology with Johannes Wolf and Friedrich Blume in Berlin, where he came into contact with Hanns Eisler. This last association encouraged his determination to assist the socialist movement, with which he had already allied himself in England. Early experimentation, as in the strenuous *Dialectic* for string quartet (1929), gave place to a strong diatonic style and to an emphasis on choral music and operas. Of the latter, *Wat Tyler* (1953) and its three full-scale successors were all introduced in East Germany. Bush wrote two volumes of autobiography, *In my Seventh Decade* (London, 1971) and *In my Eighth Decade and Other Essays* (London, 1980).   PG/AW

   📖 R. M. SCHAFER, *British Composers in Interview* (London, 1963)

Bush, Geoffrey (*b* London, 23 March 1920; *d* London, 24 Feb. 1998). English composer. He was a chorister at Salisbury Cathedral and studied at Oxford University, where in 1947 he was appointed lecturer in music within the extra-mural department. After holding other university posts he became visiting professor of music at King's College, London, in 1969. His compositions include three operas, two symphonies, choral pieces, and chamber music, couched in a straightforward, conservative style and occasionally drawing on English predecessors. His writings included *Left, Right and Centre: Reflections on Composers and Composing* (1983) and *An Unsentimental Education* (1990).   PG/AW

Busnois [Busnoys], **Antoine** [Antonius] (*b* c.1430; *d* early Nov. 1492). French composer. Nothing certain is known about his origins or early training. By 1461 he was resident in Tours as a chaplain at the cathedral. In 1465 he was in charge of the choristers first at the collegiate church of St Martin in Tours (where his senior colleagues included Johannes Ockeghem), then at St Hilaire-le-Grand in Poitiers. By 1467 he had moved into the service of the Burgundian court, and he became an official member of the chapel staff in 1470. This position involved extensive travel in northern France and the Low Countries, both in peacetime and during military campaigns. The last payments to him occur in 1483, after which his biography is again obscure.

Busnois is famous above all for his many polyphonic chansons, sophisticated works that reflect not only the Burgundian milieu but also the French royal court circle in which he moved during his years at Tours. Some of their poetic texts are almost certainly his own work. Fewer sacred works by him survive, but they are of high quality and often ingenious construction. One motet, *Anthoni usque limina*, is composed round a tenor line that invokes the tolling of a bell; another, the nonreligious *In hydraulis* (*c*.1467), pays tribute to Ockeghem in both words and music. Busnois was among the first in a long line of composers to write a mass based on *L'*Homme armé*, a melody thought to have had symbolic meaning to the Burgundian dukes.

                                                                                              JM

   📖 P. HIGGINS (ed.), *Antoine Busnoys: Method, Meaning, and Context in Late Medieval Music* (Oxford, 1999)

Busoni, Ferruccio (Dante Michelangiolo Benvenuto) (*b* Empoli, 1 April 1866; *d* Berlin, 27 July 1924). Italian composer, pianist, and teacher. As his parents were both musicians, he grew up with music all around him and soon manifested prodigious abilities: he gave a recital in Vienna at the age of ten, and by 13 had 143 compositions to his credit, among them a *Stabat mater* which he conducted in Graz (whither his family had moved in 1877) when he was 12. When he was 15 he became a member of the Accademia Filarmonica in

Bologna, the youngest since Mozart, and in 1883 conducted his oratorio *Il sabbato del villaggio* there.

From 1886 Busoni spent three years in Leipzig, where he deepened his knowledge of Bach—an enthusiasm his father had inculcated in him—after which he went to Helsinki to teach the piano at the conservatory. There he became friends with Sibelius (his pupil, though he was a few months older than Busoni) and married Gerda Sjöstrand, the daughter of a sculptor; she was to outlive him by three decades. When, in 1890, Busoni won the Rubinstein Competition in St Petersburg (with his *Konzertstück* for piano and orchestra), he was offered a post as professor of piano at the Moscow Conservatory (1890–1), which was succeeded by an appointment at the New England Conservatory in Boston; he combined the position with a number of lucrative American tours, reinforcing the internal conflict between performing and composing. He had maintained his base in Berlin but, as a pacifist, refused to live or perform in any of the belligerent countries and, after another American tour, settled in Zürich for the duration of World War I; he returned to Berlin only in 1920 and died there, of nephritis, in 1924.

Although for much of his life, and for some decades thereafter, Busoni's name was current more for his editions of Bach for the piano, his own powerful music began to win acclaim in the last decades of the 20th century, and his visionary ideas were acknowledged: his writings foresaw, for example, the arrival of electronic music and adumbrated other later developments. He composed five operas including *Die Brautwahl* (1912), *Arlecchino* (1917), *Turandot* (1917), and *Doktor Faust* (1925); the last was completed after his death by his pupil Philipp Jarnach, and with it, Dallapiccola later commented, '*Doubt* has entered the opera house'. His orchestral music ranges from the brilliant *Comedy Overture* (composed overnight in July 1897), via the luminously sepulchral *Berceuse élégiaque* (1909), to the epic, five-movement Piano Concerto (1901–4), which requires a male-voice chorus in the finale.

Busoni's hitherto unparalleled magnificence as a pianist was naturally reflected in a substantial amount of music for piano. His early, childhood works reflect the influence of Brahms; later, Bach became a stronger model, reinforcing Busoni's own tendency towards contrapuntal thought. It reached its culmination in the commanding, architecturally conceived *Fantasia contrappuntistica* (three versions for solo piano, 1910–12, one for two pianos, 1921), which began life as an attempt to complete the unfinished *Contrapunctus XIV* in Bach's *Art of Fugue*. Another of Busoni's many major piano works is the *Fantasia after J. S. Bach* (1909), inspired by the death of his father.

Busoni was an important piano teacher: his pupils in Berlin included Egon Petri, Rudolf Ganz, and Grainger. His composition students numbered Weill and Vogel among them, and Varèse was much marked by his contact with Busoni. Busoni's two principal concerns met in a series of compositions intended to transmit the art of playing the piano, not least *An die Jugend* (1909), *Klavierübung* (1897–1923), and *5 kurze Stücke zur Pflege des polyphonischen Spiels* (1923).

As Busoni's huge output is gradually becoming better known, his status in the history of Western music is slowly being acknowledged, though his ability to synthesize its major developments—from medieval music, via the Baroque and Classical periods, and stretching into the imagined trends of the future—in his own works has yet to be fully appreciated.   MA

📖 E. J. DENT, *Ferruccio Busoni* (London, 1933) · A. BEAUMONT, *Busoni the Composer* (London and Boston, 1985)

Busser [Büsser], **Henri** (*b* Toulouse, 16 Jan. 1872; *d* Paris, 30 Dec. 1973). French conductor, teacher, and composer. He attended the École Niedermeyer (1885–9) and the Paris Conservatoire (1889–93), where he studied the organ with Franck and Widor. He won the Prix de Rome in 1893. On his return to Paris he conducted at the Opéra and the Opéra-Comique, taking over from Messager after the first four performances of *Pelléas et Mélisande* in 1902. For many years he taught composition at the Conservatoire, where his pupils included Dutilleux, Gaston Litaize, and Marcel Landowski. He wrote organ and piano pieces and five operas. His memoirs, *De 'Pelléas' aux 'Indes galantes'* (Paris, 1955), are readable but not wholly reliable.   RN

Bussotti, Sylvano (*b* Florence, 1 Oct. 1931). Italian composer. He entered the Florence Conservatory in 1940 and studied the piano there with Dallapiccola but left before graduating. After several years of self-tuition, in 1957–8 he had lessons from Max Deutsch in Paris. He first attracted attention with his *Five Piano Pieces for David Tudor* (1959), a graphic score, and for a while his works remained remarkable for notational idiosyncrasy. Equally characteristic is the high eroticism of his imagery, graphic, musical, and theatrical, as in the 'staged concert' *La Passion selon Sade* (1965–6). There is also a vein of flamboyant egotism in his creative nature: his opera *Lorenzaccio* (1972) was conceived for himself as composer, designer, producer, and star. Later compositions include further operas, ballets, and concert pieces of all kinds.   PG

Butler, Martin (*b* Romsey, 1 March 1960). English composer. He studied at Manchester and Princeton universities. The character of his musical style is suggested by such titles as *Bluegrass Variations* and *Jazz*

Machines. The orchestral work *O Rio* (1991) builds on an interest in Latin American dance music, the rhythms and textures of which provide the basis for subtle yet colourful processes of transformation and elaboration. Butler's operas *Craig's Progress* (1994) and *A Better Place* (2001) were both staged in London.

AW

Butt, Dame Clara (Ellen) (*b* Southwick, Sussex, 1 Feb. 1872; *d* North Stoke, Oxon, 23 Jan. 1936). English contralto. She won a scholarship to the RCM, where she took lessons from John Blower, and in 1892 made her debut at the Royal Albert Hall singing Ursula in Sullivan's *The Golden Legend*. A few days later she drew praise for her singing of Gluck's Orpheus at the Lyceum. She quickly rose to fame as a concert singer, specializing in English ballads and oratorios. Elgar particularly admired her unusually powerful voice and meticulous enunciation, and composed his *Sea Pictures* (1899) for her. In 1902 she gave the first performance of his *Land of Hope and Glory*. She made many recordings and was created DBE in 1920.   JT

Butterley, Nigel (*b* Sydney, 13 May 1945). Australian composer, pianist, and teacher. He studied at the New South Wales Conservatorium, and later with Priaulx Rainier in London. He worked for the Australian Broadcasting Commission, and has taught in Sydney and Newcastle (NSW) as well as organizing and performing in many contemporary concerts. Butterley's music—including an opera, ballets, orchestral and choral works, and piano pieces—reflects the influence of several 20th-century traditions, and also of medieval and Renaissance music, allied to a strong Christian faith.   ABur

Butterworth, George (Sainton Kaye) (*b* London, 12 July 1885; *d* Pozières, 5 Aug. 1916). English composer. He was educated at Eton, where he had lessons from Thomas Dunhill, and at Trinity College, Oxford (1904–8). After a brief period as a music critic on *The Times*, and teaching at Radley College, he went to the RCM (1910–11), where he studied composition with Charles Wood and the organ with Walter Parratt but did not complete the course. A keen folksong collector, he assisted Cecil Sharp with dance demonstrations and summer schools. He formed a friendship with Vaughan Williams and helped him with the reconstruction of *A London Symphony*. Soon after war was declared in 1914 he joined the army and was killed in the Battle of the Somme in 1916. A slender output reveals a refined sensibility inspired by the folksong movement. His orchestral works include *Two English Idylls* (1911), the rhapsody *A Shropshire Lad* (1912), and *The Banks of Green Willow* (1913). He produced three song cycles,

two from Housman's *Shropshire Lad* collection (1911–12) and one with string quartet, *Love Blows as the Wind Blows* (c.1914).   PG/JDi

📖 I. Copley, *George Butterworth and his Muse: A Centennial Tribute* (London, 1985) · M. Barlow, *Whom the Gods Love: The Life and Music of George Butterworth* (London, 1997)

Buus, Jacques (*b* ?Ghent, c.1500; *d* Vienna, Aug. 1565). Flemish organist and composer. From 1541 to 1550 he served as organist at St Mark's, Venice, as a colleague of Adrian Willaert, and from 1550 to his death he was employed at the imperial court at Vienna. Although his output includes motets and secular music, he is remembered today largely for his long polyphonic organ ricercars.   JM

Buxheimer Orgelbuch (Buxheim Organ-Book) (Munich, Bayerische Staatsbibliothek, Cim. 352*b*). An important manuscript source of early German organ music, written down c.1470. It contains more than 250 works, notated in German organ tablature, including intabulations of French and German songs, liturgical compositions, preludes, and dances, as well as Conrad Paumann's *Fundamentum organisandi* and four or five collections of teaching pieces similar to it. A modern edition was published in 1958–9.

Buxtehude, Dietrich [Diderik] (*b* Oldesloe [now Bad Oldesloe], Holstein, c.1637; *d* Lübeck, 9 May 1707). Danish composer. In 1660 he was appointed organist at the German church in Helsingør (Elsinore), and eight years later succeeded Franz Tunder as organist of the Marienkirche, Lübeck, a post he was to retain for the rest of his life. Among his chief concerns at Lübeck were the *Abendmusiken* concerts, held annually on five Sundays between Martinmas and Christmas, which Tunder had initiated in 1646. Under Buxtehude's direction the concerts, raised in contemporary estimation to 'stärke Musiken' (powerful music), featured sacred vocal works (mainly dramatic or vividly allegorical dialogues), organ recitals, and chamber concerts.

Typical of Buxtehude's most spacious 'cantatas' are their sectional structures, in which arioso settings are linked with ritornello and choral passages, often with variation or ostinato systems to impart unity. These procedures, together with his use of chorale melodies to interrelate significantly with his free poetic texts, made a potent impression on succeeding generations of German 'cantata' composers, including Krieger, Schelle, Kuhnau, and J. S. Bach. Hardly less influential was his expertise in the grand polychoral style, shown by his motet *Benedicam Dominum* (for two vocal and four instrumental choirs), a work designed probably for some major festival. His instrumental compositions include chamber music for strings and continuo and numerous organ works—fantasias, fugues, chorale settings, and variations—many of them virtuoso compositions from which a clear line of descent can be traced to the great organ works of Bach. Such was his fame as an organist that Bach, in 1705, walked some 400 km from Arnstadt to Lübeck to study his technique, and overstayed his leave by three months.

Many of Buxtehude's works were left unpublished in his lifetime. Of those that survive, most owe their preservation to a collection (now housed in Uppsala University library) made by Gustaf Düben (1624–90), Kapellmeister to the Swedish court. In a dedication to Düben of his 'rhythmica oratio' *Membra Jesu nostri* Buxtehude calls him his 'amico plurimum honorando', a phrase that seems to indicate a close relationship between the two men.   WT/BS

📖 K. J. SNYDER, *Dietrich Buxtehude, Organist in Lübeck* (New York, 1987) · C. WOLFF, 'Buxtehude, Bach, and seventeenth-century music in retrospect', *Bach: Essays on his Life and Music* (Cambridge, MA, 1991), 41–55

buysine [buisine] (Fr.). A name for the medieval straight trumpet (see TRUMPET, 2). It derived from the Latin *bucina*, as did the German *Bosaun*, the word for 'trumpet' in German translations of the Bible.

BVM. Abbreviation for Blessed Virgin Mary; see ANTIPHONS OF THE BLESSED VIRGIN MARY.

BWV. Abbreviation for Bach-Werke-Verzeichnis, an informal title given to the *thematic catalogue of J. S. Bach's works drawn up by the German music librarian Wolfgang Schmieder (1901–90) and published in Leipzig in 1950. Bach's works are usually referred to by BWV number, though 'Schmieder' (sometimes abbreviated to s) is still occasionally used.

Byrd, William (*b* London, *c*.1540; *d* Stondon Massey, Essex, 4 July 1623). English composer. He was the foremost English composer during the reigns of Elizabeth I and James I. His large output, which includes masses, motets, polyphonic songs, and works for keyboard and instrumental consort, ranks among the most individual and inspired of the late Renaissance, on a level with that of Palestrina, Lassus, or Victoria.

It is thought likely that Byrd was a pupil of Tallis in the Chapel Royal, becoming Tallis's assistant after his voice broke; he would thus have been well placed to secure the position of organist and choirmaster of Lincoln Cathedral, which he occupied from 1563 to 1570. Much of his English-texted church music was written in Lincoln; even after he moved back to London, the cathedral authorities continued to pay a

quarter of his former salary on condition that he provide them with 'church songs and services' on regular occasions.

Early in 1572 Byrd was sworn in as a Gentleman of the Chapel Royal in succession to Robert Parsons, also becoming joint organist with Tallis. Five years later, Elizabeth granted the two composers exclusive rights to print music in England and import foreign publications; the monopoly made little profit but resulted in the publication that year of a book of *Cantiones sacrae* to which both composers contributed 17 works, one each for every year of the queen's reign.

During his career in London, Byrd devoted a great deal of time to the composition of motets, Latin having been officially sanctioned by Elizabeth for the services of the Chapel Royal. It seems likely, however, that Byrd's increasing interest in motet production reflects his personal religious beliefs, which conflicted with the prevailing Anglicanism of the court. He was almost certainly a practising Catholic throughout his life, evading threats of persecution purely on account of his acknowledged excellence as a composer. His commitment is confirmed not only on grounds of biographical evidence—in particular, his close association with the powerful Catholic nobility of the day, to whom most of his subsequent publications were dedicated—but also by the nature of the religious texts which he chose to set to music.

In 1589 and 1591 Byrd issued two further collections of *Cantiones sacrae*, many of which stand as moving testaments of his personal convictions. Their texts, most of them biblical, dwell largely on themes of lamentation, oppression, and entreaty, set to richly polyphonic music which combines a wholly modern approach to the clear and expressive enunciation of the words with a deep respect for the contrapuntal and textural idioms of the past. If Byrd's sacred music sometimes appears conservative, it is because he found deeper inspiration in his heritage than in the newer Italianate fashions which so captivated younger English contemporaries such as Weelkes and Morley.

Byrd's secular vocal music also has its roots firmly in the past. He wrote few madrigals, preferring the medium of the consort song—settings of serious verse for solo voice with instrumental accompaniment, most commonly a consort of viols. He published three collections of English songs to a variety of secular and devotional texts (1588, 1589, 1611); many of the songs were printed with words underlaid to the instrumental parts in order to make them entirely suitable for vocal performance. Madrigalian touches are uncommon in Byrd's songs; he shunned extensive word-painting in favour of a counterpoint which is often learned and purely musical in its inspiration, mirroring the overall sentiment of the text rather than details of individual words or phrases.

Byrd was a prolific composer of keyboard music. Although indebted to the idioms of the past, much of his output was radically new in both spirit and technique, and had a profound influence on younger contemporaries writing for the virginals. He produced many fine sets of variations on popular melodies and ground basses as well as stylized dance music (especially pavans and galliards) and such abstract pieces as fantasias and preludes. A smaller quantity of consort music has survived, mostly fantasias and works constructed round a plainchant cantus firmus, in particular settings of the *In nomine*. Little of his instrumental music was published during his lifetime; it survives instead in manuscripts compiled for patrons or by admirers, such as the exquisite *My Ladye Nevells Booke* and the vast Fitzwilliam Virginal Book.

Although Byrd composed instrumental and secular vocal music in later life, he became increasingly preoccupied with Latin church music for the Roman rite. By 1591 he had effectively abandoned court life, turning instead to the patronage and protection of the Catholic nobility. Taking up residence in Stondon Massey, a village in Essex close to Ingatestone Hall, seat of the Petres, Byrd set to work on his largest project: a cycle of music for the Roman Catholic Mass, intended for use in the private chapels of English recusants. Three settings of the Ordinary were completed and published in the early 1590s, one each for three, four, and five voices, while music for the Proper was composed over a period of some 20 years, published cumulatively in two books of *Gradualia* (1605, 1607). Compared with the earlier, highly emotional *Cantiones sacrae*, Byrd's later Catholic church music is more often joyful, meditative, and serene in spirit, reflecting the security and stability offered him by his patrons. He appears to have written little music after 1611, the year in which his final collection, the *Psalmes, Songs, and Sonnets*, was published.

Byrd's impact on his contemporaries was profound; his pupils included Morley and Tomkins, and there can have been few English composers of the period who failed to learn by his example. With the exception of the madrigal and ayre, he contributed significantly to all the major genres of his day, establishing in each new standards of excellence. His output was widely admired, and served as a secure foundation for the work of a whole generation of younger composers.   JM

📖 O. Neighbour, *The Consort and Keyboard Music of William Byrd* (London, 1978) · J. Kerman, *The Masses and Motets of William Byrd* (Berkeley, CA, and London, 1981) · A. M. Brown and R. Turbet (eds.), *Byrd Studies* (Cambridge, 1992) · J. Harley, *William Byrd, Gentleman of the Chapel Royal* (Aldershot, 1997)

Byttering (*fl c.*1420). English composer. Five works by him are included in the Old Hall Manuscript (1415–early 1420s); one of them is a wedding motet for Henry V and Catherine Valois, who married in June 1420. He has not been positively identified, but he may be the Thomas Byteryng who was a canon at Hastings Castle in 1405–8 and a rector in London in 1414.   —/JM

Byzantine chant. The plainchant of the Byzantine rite. Originating in late antique Constantinople and Palestine, it has continued to develop until the present day. Medieval Byzantine chant underlies Russian and Serbian chant, while the received tradition of Byzantine chanting is today used by the Eastern Orthodox churches of Alexandria, Antioch, Bulgaria, Constantinople, Greece, Jerusalem, and Romania.

The Byzantine rite's three eucharistic liturgies come from Justinian's Great Church of Hagia Sophia. Possessing relatively modest cycles of proper psalmody—the prokeimenon, alleluiarion, and koinonikon, corresponding respectively to the Roman gradual, alleluia, and communion—these services are dominated by such hymns as the *Trisagion and the *Cherubic Hymn. Before the Latin conquest of 1204, Constantinople Cathedral also possessed an elaborate stational liturgy and a Liturgy of the Hours known as the 'Sung Office' (Asmatike Akolouthia), both of which were characterized by their archaic antiphonal psalmody and sparing use of non-scriptural hymnography. The strophic form of Constantinopolitan hymnody known as the *kontakion was originally paraliturgical.

Other elements of Byzantine chant, including its system of eight modes (*oktoechos*), are of Palestinian origin. During the 7th and 8th centuries a school of prolific composers led by St Sophronios of Jerusalem, St Andrew of Crete, and St John of Damascus wrote kanons and other proper hymns to farse the psalms and canticles of the Palestinian Book of the Hours (Horologion). The adoption of the Palestinian Divine Office by the Constantinopolitan monastery of Studios in 799 was followed over the next four centuries by the completion of its hymnodic cycles, thereby creating the 15 volumes of proper hymns currently in use.

Early Byzantine musical notations appearing in the 9th and 10th centuries were dependent on oral tradition and give no precise indications of pitch. By the later 12th century the so-called 'Coislin' family of neumes had developed into a fully diastematic system—known today as 'Middle Byzantine' or 'Round' notation—of quantitative signs ('bodies') indicating the succession of intervals and qualitative signs ('spirits') supplying ornaments and other nuances, the realization of which continued to be transmitted orally.

The period following the recapture of Constantinople in 1261 was marked by liturgical consolidation and musical creativity, processes in which monasticism played a leading role. St John Koukouzeles (*c.*1280–*c.*1360), a cantor, theorist, and monk, not only re-edited the central chant repertory, but was also one of many Late Byzantine composers to contribute elaborate new settings in a virtuoso 'kalophonic' style to the recently codified *All-Night Vigil.

Musical activity after 1453 in areas not under Ottoman control gave rise to the Westernized chant dialects surviving today in southern Italy, Corsica, and the Ionian Islands. The revival and gradual reshaping of the central Constantinopolitan tradition by patriarchal cantors of the 17th and 18th centuries culminated in 1814 with the notational reform of the 'Three Teachers' Chrysanthos, Gregorios, and Chourmouzios. Their 'New Method', which remains in use with minor modifications, drastically reduced the number of quantitative neumes and introduced a Westernized solmization system, exact tunings for the scales of each mode, and characters precisely regulating rhythmic subdivision and chromaticism.   ALi

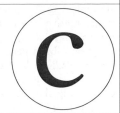

C. The first degree (tonic) of the scale of C major (see SCALE, 3).

c.a. Abbreviation for *coll'arco*.

cabaça. See CABAZA.

cabaletta (It.). The term has several meanings. It is usually applied to a short aria of simple reiterated rhythm, with repeats. Rossini, whose operas have many, told Clara Novello that the first statement should be sung as written; thereafter the singer could embellish as he or she pleased. In the 18th century the term grew to mean the final section only of an aria in several parts, usually quick and brilliant but now actually written down. It has also been used to describe the first section of an aria; this would, on its reappearance, be varied and often with triplets in the accompaniment (suggesting a possible derivation from *cavallo*, 'horse', from the galloping movement). One of the earliest examples of the cabaletta is the aria 'Le belle imagini' in Gluck's *Paride ed Elena*. Famous cabalettas include 'Ah! non giunge' in Bellini's *La sonnambula*, 'Sempre libera' in Verdi's *La traviata*, and 'Di quella pira' in *Il trovatore*.
JW

Caballero, Manuel Fernández (*b* Murcia, 14 March 1835; *d* Madrid, 26 Feb. 1906). Spanish composer. His early failure in Madrid led him to emigrate to Cuba. His success after his return in 1871 was partly attributable to his introduction of Caribbean dance rhythms, notably the habanera, into Spanish music. His zarzuelas—including *Los sobrinos del capitán Grant* ('Captain Grant's Nephews', 1877), *La viejecita* ('The Little Old Woman', 1897), and above all *Gigantes y cabezudos* ('Carnival Giants and Dwarves', 1898)—are central to the Spanish repertory, their popularity assured by Caballero's unfailing theatricality, distinguished melodic invention, and orchestral vigour.
CW

Cabanilles, Juan Bautista José (*b* Algemesí, nr Valencia, 4 Sept. 1644; *d* Valencia, 29 April 1712). Spanish organist and composer. At the age of 21 he succeeded his teacher as organist of Valencia Cathedral, where he stayed until his death. He was ordained priest in 1668.

Cabanilles was the most famous and important Spanish organist and organ composer of the second half of the 17th century, and one of the greatest European organists before Bach. His surviving works, which include about 200 tientos, six toccatas, keyboard dances, and sets of variations, are simple in style, being written for the rather primitive Spanish organ without pedal keyboard, yet highly expressive. Most of his vocal music is lost.
WT

cabaret (Fr., 'little bar'). A word loosely applied either to a place of informal musical entertainment (e.g. a bar, café, or nightclub), or to a specific mode of performance consisting of a sequence of short, simply structured, self-contained numbers in which textual projection is paramount. The term was first used in 18th-century France to denote a café or tavern regularly frequented by writers, where music was provided by ballad singers or street musicians. The first modern cabaret, the Chat Noir, was founded in Paris by the painter Rodolphe Salis on 18 November 1881; it served as an informal venue for the artistic avant-garde, at which poetry readings and performances of short musical works took place. The stance of the Chat Noir was inherently anti-bourgeois, and a number of features gradually emerged which defined the cabaret style up to the years before World War II.

The quintessential cabaret song is a strophic ballad in which the text—usually satirical, erotic, or sentimental—is as important as its musical content, and is frequently delivered in a style poised between speech and song. In Germany, where the first cabaret, the *Überbrettl, was founded in Berlin in 1901, a strong political element was added, with the result that cabaret became a major attraction for the political left as well as the avant-garde. Numerous composers were drawn to cabaret. Satie played the piano at the Chat Noir. Schoenberg conducted the small orchestra at the Überbrettl and composed cabaret songs of his own, while his use of *Sprechstimme* in, most notably, *Pierrot lunaire* was strongly influenced by the cabaret style. The music of the young Kurt Weill is frequently considered to embody German cabaret at its best—though it should be remembered that his work constitutes an attempt to fuse cabaret with operatic structure. More representative German cabaret composers include Friedrich Hollaender and Mischa Spoliansky. Among the great cabaret performers may be mentioned Yvette Guilbert, Claire Waldoff, Trude Hesterberg, Marlene Dietrich, and Kurt Gerron. Cabaret was banned in Germany by the Nazis in 1935, and after World War II it lost much of its political force. Towards the end of the 20th century, the word 'cabaret' became synonymous with 'theatrical revue'. TA

📖 L. APPIGNANESI, *The Cabaret* (London, 1975, 2/1984) · P. JELAVICH, *Berlin Cabaret* (Cambridge, MA, 1993)

cabaza [cabaça]. A gourd rattle with an external network of beads, used in Latin American music.

Cabezón, Antonio de (*b* Castrillo de Matajudíos, nr Burgos, 1510; *d* Madrid, 6 Feb. or 26 March 1566). Spanish keyboard player and composer. Blind from childhood, he was apparently in Palencia before he joined the chapel of the Empress Isabella, wife of Charles V, in 1526. He served Isabella as organist and in 1538 is also listed among Charles's musicians. After Isabella's death in 1539 Cabezón worked for Prince Philip and his sisters, and from 1543 was in the service of Philip alone. He accompanied the prince on his journeys to Italy, Germany, and the Netherlands, and to England in 1554.

About 40 keyboard pieces attributed to 'Antonio'—generally accepted as referring to Cabezón—were published in Venegas de Henestrosa's *Libro de cifra nueva* (1557), but the majority of Cabezón's works were issued by his son, Hernando, in 1578. His output includes many liturgical items such as hymns, Kyries, and versets for psalms and canticles. In addition, there are tientos, glosas on sacred and secular Franco-Netherlandish pieces, and several sets of variations. OR

caccia (It., 'chase', 'hunt'). 1. A 14th- and 15th-century Italian vocal genre. The text describes the hunt in vivid, programmatic terms, including the cries of the huntsmen, the barking of the dogs, etc. The music sets the text as a two-part canon, to which is added a third part—with longer note-values, apparently intended for an instrument—in the tenor (which, in most vocal music of the time, was the first part to be composed). The master of the genre was Jacopo da Bologna, in the mid-14th century.

2. The *horn came into the orchestra from the hunting field as a simple coiled instrument played with the bell pointing upwards and called the corno da caccia or *cor de chasse*. Bach's tenor *oboe, curved and with a flared bell of brass or wood, was called oboe da caccia. JMo

Caccini, Francesca (*b* Florence, 18 Sept. 1587; *d* Florence, after 1637). Italian singer and composer, the elder daughter of Giulio Caccini. Like the rest of her family, she was instructed in singing by her father, and became a notable performer with the nickname 'La Cecchina' (a diminutive of Francesca). She married twice, the first time to Giovanni Battista Signorini, an instrumentalist and minor composer in Florence. Her own compositional abilities were far superior. Her songbook, *Il primo libro delle musiche* (Florence, 1618), contains powerfully expressive pieces; she also wrote a number of dramatic works, most notably the short opera *La liberazione di Ruggiero dall'isola d'Alcina* (Florence, 1625). DA/TC

Caccini, Giulio (*b* Rome, 8 Oct 1551; *d* Florence, Dec. 1618). Italian composer and singer. He studied with Giovanni Animuccia in Rome before being recruited to sing in a set of wedding festivities in Florence in late 1565, after which he stayed in Florence for most of his life. He was famous as a singer (tenor), taking part in the celebrated performances of *intermedi* for the wedding festivities of Francesco de' Medici and Bianca Cappello in 1579 and of Ferdinando de' Medici and Christine of Lorraine in 1589. During the 1570s and 80s he was much involved with the *camerata sponsored by Giovanni de' Bardi and its discussions concerning the nature of Greek music. As a result he evolved a new style of singing which approached the naturalness of speech—hence a kind of recitative.

Caccini was temporarily exiled from Florence in the 1590s but returned to play a leading role in the festivities for the wedding of Maria de' Medici and Henri IV of France in October 1600. Thus he became involved in the rise of opera in Florence: he forced his own singers to sing his rather than Jacopo Peri's music in *Euridice* (Florence, 1600; libretto by Ottavio Rinuccini), and he beat Peri to the press (although Caccini's *Euridice* was not performed complete until December 1602). However, his talents are best revealed in his two collections of solo songs: *Le nuove musiche* (Florence, 1602) and *Nuove musiche e nuova maniera di scriverle* (Florence, 1614). They contain madrigals and strophic arias, with lyrical melodies and discreet ornamentation. *Le nuove musiche* is also important for its preface on vocal technique and for its development of the figured bass. One of the songs in it, *Amarilli mia bella*, was immensely popular: a six-voice version had been published in 1601 (it was arranged for keyboard by Peter Philips in the *Fitzwilliam Virginal Book*), and the piece was well known throughout Europe, whether in its original form (a version was included in Robert Dowland's *A Musicall Banquet* of 1610) or in spiritual *contrafacta*.

Caccini was a first-rate singing teacher, his pupils including his two wives, his two daughters, Francesca (see above) and Settimia, and his son, and also Francesco Rasi—one of the most celebrated singers of the early 17th century. Caccini and his family were invited to spend the winter of 1604–5 at the French court, and in his later years he received other invitations to work outside Florence. He nevertheless continued in the service of the Medici, and was buried with all honour in the church of Ss. Annunziata.   DA/TC

cadence [close] (Fr.: *cadence*; Ger.: *Kadenz, Schluss*; It.: *cadenza*). A melodic or harmonic motion conventionally associated with the ending of a phrase, section, movement, or composition. The implied connection between 'cadence' and falling is most explicitly realized in music where a melodic line descends conclusively to the modal final or tonal tonic. But cadential closure in modal and tonal music has more to do with a sense of emphasized arrival on the interval or chord most fundamental to the work in question than with literal and uniform descent. In post-tonal music, the sense of cadence can be achieved by forms of emphasis and resolution which have varying degrees of explicitness or ambiguity, but it is not possible to classify post-tonal cadences in the way that types of modal and tonal cadence are defined below. Often, of course, post-tonal composers demonstrate their independence of traditions by avoiding cadential effects and ending with what can sound like arbitrary abruptness.

1. The early cadence; 2. Standard types of cadence

1. The early cadence

In plainchant melodies the commonest cadential close is a descending step to the final from the note above (see Ex. 1*a*); other formulas, such as a descending 3rd (Ex. 1*b*) or an ascending 2nd (Ex. 1*c*), are also found. In early polyphony, for example in 11th- and 12th-century or-ganum, cadences consist of the resolution either of a perfect interval between the voices (4th or 5th) into another perfect one (unison or octave; see Ex. 2*a*), or of an imperfect interval (3rd or 6th) into a perfect one (unison or octave; see Ex. 2*b*). The latter formulation also became common practice in the 13th century.

In 14th- and early 15th-century polyphony cadences were still almost invariably of this linear type, usually based on the descending step of a 2nd in the tenor—the main structural voice. Some common cadences in music of this period are shown in Ex. 3. Of these, two have gained identifying names: Ex. 3*d* became known as the Phrygian cadence, from its implications (the minor 2nd F–E in the tenor, the major 2nd D–E in the upper part) of the Phrygian mode (corresponding to the scale on the white notes of the piano beginning on E), and has persisted into later music (see below); and Ex. 3*c*, characterized by the insertion in the top voice of the sixth degree of the scale between the leading note and the tonic, is traditionally known as the Landini cadence (after Francesco Landini, although the device is equally common in the music of Machaut, Dufay, Binchois, and other Burgundians).

In the later 15th century, with an increased freedom in polyphonic part-writing, a growing emphasis on vertical thinking instead of horizontal melodic progression, and the addition of a more freely moving voice part—the tenor—below the tenor, the bass line became an important factor in shaping cadences, and new formulas developed in association with a new, disjunct bass line (see Ex. 4). As 3rds and 6ths became more common between voice parts, the final chord, formerly consisting of 'bare' 5ths or octaves, came increasingly to include the third degree of the scale; in the 16th century this was frequently sharpened in minor modes (Ex. 5) and became known as the *tierce de Picardie* ('Picardy 3rd').

The 16th and 17th centuries extended the harmonic approach of the late 15th and saw the introduction of such elaborations as suspensions in cadences (Ex. 6) and the device of anticipation (Ex. 7*a*). The latter

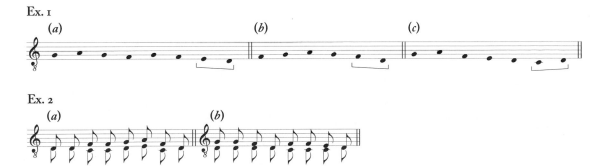

Ex. 1
  (*a*)   (*b*)   (*c*)

Ex. 2
  (*a*)   (*b*)

Ex. 3

often involved striking dissonances which gave rise to such names as the Corelli cadence, or 'Corelli clash', from its special association with the violin repertory of the Corelli school (Ex. 7b), and the English cadence, from its persistent appearance in English 17th-century music by Purcell and his contemporaries (Ex. 7c).

As the Baroque era advanced and modality was all but ousted by tonality, the distinctive characteristics of cadences were principally harmonic, and they also began to carry important structural implications. The cadences commonly found in music of the Classical period largely conform to the standard types discussed below. In various extended and decorated guises these went on to form the basis of all cadences in tonal music until the early 20th century, when post-tonal developments transformed harmonic practices and overthrew the traditions of tonal thinking.

2. Standard types of cadence

Cadences commonly in use in the 18th and 19th centuries are defined and described in terms of their degree of finality. Variations in terminology, however, have sometimes led to confusion; the discussion below attempts to clarify the terms most frequently encountered for the four most basic and important types of cadence.

A cadence is normally called 'perfect' if it consists of a tonic chord preceded by a dominant chord (Ex. 8a). This may also be known as a final, full, or complete cadence, or a full close, and it is considered to have the greatest degree of finality of all the cadences. Some theorists claim that for the cadence to be perfect the final chord must have the tonic in the top part and that both chords must be in root position (Ex. 8b).

An 'imperfect' cadence normally consists of the dominant chord preceded by any other chord (most commonly I or IV; Ex. 9). This lacks the finality of the perfect and plagal cadences and is therefore often used

Ex. 4

Ex. 5

Ex. 6

Ex. 8

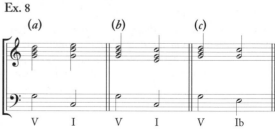

Ex. 7

in the course of a composition, at the end of a phrase, and more particularly half-way through a section or period, whence it has acquired conventional musical settings of the word 'Amen'. Some American theorists view this cadence only as a variation of the perfect cadence, distinguishing the dominant–tonic cadence described above by the term 'authentic'; by extension, they term the closing harmonic progression IV–V–I or IV–Ib–V–I, with its mixture of subdominant and dominant elements, a mixed cadence (Ex. 10).

A cadence is normally called 'plagal' if it consists of a tonic chord preceded by a subdominant chord (Ex. 11). This is traditionally known as an 'Amen' (less commonly 'church' or 'Greek') cadence, from its association with the additional names 'half', 'semi-', or 'demi-cadence', or 'half close'. Again, American usage differs, reserving the name 'imperfect' for any cadence in which the final chord either does not have the root in the top part (also called semi-perfect; Ex. 8a) or is not in root position (also called inverted; see Ex. 8c), and describing a cadence ending with a dominant chord as a half-cadence or semi-cadence.

A cadence is called 'interrupted', 'deceptive', or 'false' where the penultimate, dominant chord is followed not by the expected tonic but by another chord, often the submediant (Ex. 12). Other, less common names for this cadence are 'abrupt', 'avoided', 'broken', 'evaded', irregular', or 'surprise'.

The Phrygian cadence, common in modal polyphony (see above), has survived in later music in various forms (Ex. 13). In a tonal context, however, its Phrygian-mode connotations are less obvious, and in a major key it is often regarded as a variety of imperfect cadence resolving on the dominant of the relative minor.

Any of the four main types of cadence—perfect, plagal, imperfect, and interrupted—can be decorated or extended in a variety of ways, for example by adding a 7th (or other interval) to the dominant (Ex. 14), or by inverting either chord, which has the effect of reducing the cadence's finality (Ex. 15). In that connection, other terms sometimes used to qualify a cadence in terms of its chord positions include 'radical' (both chords in root position), 'medial' (the penultimate chord inverted), and 'inverted' (the final chord or both chords inverted). A 'suspended' cadence is one involving a delay (often on the second inversion of the tonic chord) before the two main cadential chords, such as may occur immediately before a soloist's cadenza or other elaborative passage (Ex. 16, overleaf).   JN/AW

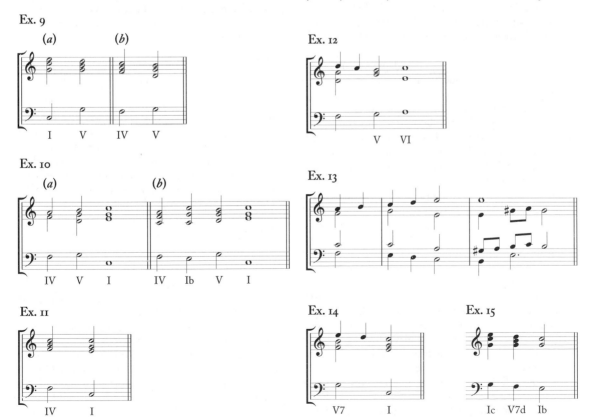

Ex. 9

(a)   (b)

I   V   IV   V

Ex. 10

(a)   (b)

IV   V   I   IV   Ib   V   I

Ex. 11

IV   I

Ex. 12

V   VI

Ex. 13

Ex. 14

V7   I

Ex. 15

Ic   V7d   Ib

cadence, Ex. 16

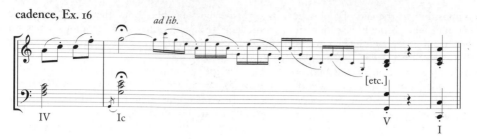

cadenza. A cadenza is best defined as a decorated cadence, though the most extensive examples obscure this
fact. During the Baroque era a singer would embellish a cadence near the end of an aria. Such 'cadences'
were improvised (though it is likely some had been
prepared in advance), and although we have no information on most of them they were probably quite short.
By the 18th century, however, they became much
extended. This custom continued in Italian opera until
at least the time of Rossini. In the early 18th century it
was transferred to the concerto, Vivaldi occasionally
writing out an extensive brilliant passage for violin over
a held dominant pedal (a fine example is the C major
Concerto 'fatto per la solennità della S. Lingua di S.
Antonio in Padova 1712'). Other composers provided
opportunities for improvisation, no doubt sometimes
with disastrous results; but when the composer was
playing his own work, presumably they were effective
and in scale.

   In the concerto of the Classical period, there was
usually a place for a cadenza at the end of the recapitulation and before the concluding tutti of the first
movement. It is clear from examples written out by
Mozart for his pupils that these were sometimes quite
long and consisted not only of brilliant passage-work
but also of a 'working out' of the themes of the
movement. With the composer at the keyboard this
process was appropriate, but when other performers
came to improvise—or more often to write out—a
cadenza for another composer's concerto, problems
arose, because the musical styles did not always match.
Clara Schumann's cadenzas to Mozart's D minor Piano
Concerto K466, for example, though delightful, are too
near her husband's manner not to seem out of place. In
the 20th century some players inserted wildly inappropriate cadenzas in Classical concertos, either
displaying flashy technique or modulating to keys so
remote as to wreck the tonal balance of the movement.

   Cadenzas were sometimes played in movements
other than the first, notably in rondo finales where the
restatement of the main theme is intended to be preceded by a flourish, although this is more properly
called a 'reprise' or 'fermata'. Here substantial development is inappropriate, as is great length (even

Beethoven's own cadenza in the finale of his Third
Piano Concerto, before the final change of metre, can
seem tedious in the hands of an inferior player).
Clementi's *Musical Characteristics* (1787) is a set of
preludes and cadenzas in the styles of six contemporary
composers. Cadenzas at this date were used even in
pieces for piano solo. The 'concerted cadenza' was also
found, where several instruments took part; this obviously could not be improvised. There is an excellent
example in Mozart's Quintet for Piano and Winds
K452.

   The improvised cadenza largely disappeared in the
19th century, when composers tended to write out what
they wanted to hear. Beethoven instructs the soloist of
the 'Emperor' Concerto not to improvise but to play the
provided cadenza. One of the last concertos to leave a
pause for an improvised cadenza was Brahms's Violin
Concerto (1876).   DA/NT

cadenzato (It.). 'Rhythmical'.

Caecilienverein. See Cecilian Movement.

caesura. A term sometimes used interchangeably with
'pause' to indicate a note that is held for longer than its
written value. More specifically it was used in the
Viennese Classical tradition in its German form, *Cäsur*
or *Zäsur*, to indicate where a singer or wind player
should take a breath (shown by a comma or a 'v' above
the staff); it is also used to denote the holding up of the
metre, often heard in the Viennese waltz.

   The term may also signify a pause in poetic metre,
frequently near the middle of a line; such pauses are
often reflected in musical settings.   ABul

Cage, John (Milton) (*b* Los Angeles, 15 Sept. 1912; *d*
New York, 12 Aug. 1992). American composer. He
studied with Henry Cowell in New York (1933–4) and
Schoenberg in Los Angeles (1934) and began to write
chromatic pieces based on long repeating strings of
notes (Sonata for solo clarinet, 1934). In 1937 he moved
to Seattle, where he organized a percussion orchestra,
as he did again in San Francisco (1939–41), Chicago
(1941–2), and New York (his home from 1942). The
medium enabled him to concentrate on rhythm, and
to develop new methods of construction based on

temporal proportions. The *First Construction (in Metal)* for six players (1939), for instance, has a rhythmic structure operating on two levels: there are 4+3+2+3+4 units, each of 16 bars, and these 16-bar units are similarly proportioned. Pulsation, heterophony, percussive scoring, and repetition all make for a suggestion of Balinese gamelan music.

At the same time, these percussion pieces show a willingness to accept the unorthodox: home-made instruments (tin cans) and sometimes electrical devices (frequency recordings on variable-speed turntables in *Imaginary Landscape no.1*, 1939). Another innovation was the prepared piano: a piano with objects (bolts, pieces of felt, etc.) inserted between its strings, converting its sounds into clunks and rattles, and so making available a one-person percussion orchestra. In the 1940s this was his chief resource, used in dance scores (he worked closely with choreographers, and not only with Merce Cunningham, his life's partner) and in the major concert works that culminated in the hourlong *Sonatas and Interludes* (1946–8). The prepared piano's confinement to a relatively small repertory of sounds also had its effect on the austere, mesmeric String Quartet (1949–50). More far-reaching was the idea—made inevitable by the prepared piano, on which sounds would be grossly changed in timbre and pitch—that musical notation was an invitation to action and not necessarily an image of sounds.

During the late 1940s Cage's growing interest in Asian philosophies led him to a study of Zen, and thus to an art of non-intention, an ideal he realized by tossing coins to make choices about pitches, durations, and attacks (*Music of Changes* for piano, 1951, which initiated a long-standing relationship with the pianist David Tudor), by writing for the unpredictable sounds of radio receivers (*Imaginary Landscape no.4*, 1951), and by providing just silence (*4'33"*, 1952, a score asking the performer or performers to make no sound). Soon after he began introducing new kinds of notation that could be read in many different ways or that indicated actions without prescribing the resultant sounds. Many of these he compiled in a masterpiece of indeterminacy, the *Concert for Piano and Orchestra* (1957–8), in which he also found numerous means by which sounds could be made on the piano other than by striking the keys (though that too).

In the 1960s Cage's focus moved to live electronic music (*Cartridge Music* for amplified small sounds, 1960) and later to mixed-media pieces embracing as much as possible (*HPSCHD* for amplified harpsichords, tapes, and other means ad lib, 1967–9)—pieces that celebrated not only his growing reputation but the libertarian mood of the time. In *Cheap Imitation* (1969) he made a surprising return to conventional notation,

and though this was at first for practical reasons—copyright problems had left Cunningham's company with the need for a 'cheap imitation' of Satie's *Socrate*—he went on to find new uses for notation, sometimes in music of extreme virtuosity (*Freeman Etudes* for violin, 1977–90), and finally, in the 'number' series of his last years (e.g. *Four* for string quartet, 1989), in music where notes hang free in unmeasured time.

Cage's influence, especially in the 1950s and 60s, was potent and widespread, mediated not only through his music but through his writings, especially those contained in the anthologies *Silence* (Middletown, CT, 1961) and *A Year from Monday* (Middletown, 1967).

PG

📖 R. Kostelanetz (ed.), *John Cage* (New York, 1970) · D. Revill, *The Roaring Silence: John Cage: A Life* (London, 1992) · J. Pritchett, *The Music of John Cage* (London, 1993)

Cajun music. The traditional music of French-speaking settlers in Louisiana; the term is a corruption of 'Acadian', from the original name for Nova Scotia, where the Cajuns' ancestors first settled.

cakewalk. A 19th-century African-American dance. It originated among plantation slaves (*c*.1850), reputedly to parody the promenades that opened the plantation owners' formal balls. In the 1890s it became commercial entertainment, and it was used for social dancing at the turn of the 20th century. The music is a syncopated march and is a forerunner of ragtime and jazz. It was first brought to prominence in Europe by Sousa during his band's 1899 tour. Debussy's *Golliwogg's Cake-Walk* (1907) reflects its wide appeal in the early 20th century.

PGa

calando (It.). 'Lowering', 'dropping', i.e. gradually dying away in volume and sometimes also tempo.

calata (It.). A 16th-century Italian dance, resembling the *basse danse, known from 13 examples in Petrucci's *Intavolatura de lauto* (1508).

calathumpian concert. See CHARIVARI.

Caldara, Antonio (*b* Venice, *c*.1670; *d* Vienna, 28 Dec. 1736). Italian composer. A choirboy at St Mark's, Venice, and probably a pupil there of Legrenzi, in 1699 he became *maestro di cappella* to the dissolute and extravagant Duke of Mantua. In 1708, the duke's financial problems having obliged Caldara to leave Mantua, he settled in Rome, where he probably met Handel and the Scarlattis, and served various patrons, including Cardinal Ottoboni, Prince Ruspoli, and Charles III of Spain (brother of the Habsburg Emperor Joseph). An opera by Caldara for Charles's marriage celebrations was probably the first Italian opera performed in Spain. Charles succeeded as emperor in 1711, and in 1715 Caldara was appointed court vice-Kapellmeister; by 1729 he was receiving a higher salary than the Kapellmeister, J. J. Fux.

Caldara was one of the most prolific and influential composers of his time, and one of the few lesser-known figures whose music is not largely forgotten today. Most of his output consists of vocal music, including nearly 100 operas and more than 40 oratorios written over a period of some 40 years, cantatas, and a large quantity of church music, most of which dates from his time in Vienna. His earlier oratorios especially show an unusual ability to write dramatic and strongly characterized music as well as attractive melodies, though his later operas and oratorios tend to be more facile, perhaps because of the speed with which he had to work. His orchestrally accompanied church music, including festive masses and a fine *Stabat mater* for the 1726 canonization of St John Nepomuk, is among the best and most forward-looking of its period; he was also an extremely skilful practitioner of the polyphonic *a cappella* style of church music, and a 16-part *Crucifixus* is still occasionally performed.   DA/ER

     📖 B. W. PRITCHARD (ed.), *Antonio Caldara: Essays on his Life and Times* (Aldershot, 1987)

calenda [calinda] (Sp.). A dance form from the Guinea coast of Africa that spread through South America. Drums and other percussion instruments are much used in the accompaniment. In the 16th century it was performed in religious processions and inside churches on Christmas Eve. Delius used a piece based on the calenda in his opera *Koanga*.

Calife de Bagdad, Le ('The Caliph of Bagdad'). Opera in one act by Boieldieu to a libretto by Claude de Saint-Just [Godart d'Aucourt] (Paris, 1800).

Calisto, La. Opera in a prologue and three acts by Cavalli to a libretto by Giovanni Faustini after Ovid, first performed in Venice in 1651. It was probably not heard again until 1970, when it was given in Raymond Leppard's realization at Glyndebourne.

Callas [Kalogeropoulou], (Cecilia Sophia Anna) **Maria** (*b* New York, 2 Dec. 1923; *d* Paris, 16 Sept. 1977). Greek soprano. When she was barely 16 she sang Santuzza in the Athens Conservatory's performance of *Cavalleria rusticana*. She then studied with the coloratura expert Elvira de Hidalgo and in 1941 made her professional debut singing Beatrice in Suppé's *Boccaccio* in Athens, where she went on to sing a number of dramatic roles. Her international debut was in Verona in 1947, when she took the title role in *La Gioconda*, then in 1949 she appeared at La Fenice, Venice, singing Elvira in *I Puritani*. This prompted a sensational response of a kind that was to accompany most of her appearances. At this time, remarkably, she sang Wagnerian roles as well as the bel canto repertory. With Serafin, she revived neglected operas including Spontini's *La Vestale* and Bellini's *Il pirata*.

Following her debut at La Scala, Milan (1950), Callas was for a decade the most acclaimed soprano, making her Covent Garden debut in 1952 and her American debut two years later. She became famous for such *spinto* roles as Norma, Tosca, Lucia, and Violetta, in which she commanded an exceptional range of colours and dynamics. Her vocal timbre had an individual edge which was not to everyone's taste, but even her critics conceded her outstanding coloratura technique, her remarkable breath control, and exceptional acting ability. From the early 1960s she began to experience difficulties, and in 1965 she retired from the stage (as Tosca at Covent Garden). After a turbulent life she became reclusive and died alone.   JT

     📖 M. SCOTT, *Maria Meneghini Callas* (Boston and London, 1991) · D. BRETT, *Maria Callas: The Tigress and the Lamb* (London, 1998)

calmando, calmato (It.). 'Becoming calm'.

calore, con (It.). 'With warmth', 'with passion'; *caloroso*, 'passionately'.

Calvé [Calvet de Roquer], (Rosa-Noémie) **Emma** (*b* Decazeville, 15 Aug. 1858; *d* Millau, 6 Jan. 1942). French soprano. She studied in Paris with Jules Puget, Mathilde Marchesi, and Rosina Laborde and made her debut in Brussels in 1881 as Marguerite in Gounod's *Faust*. Three years later her dramatic singing and colourful acting began to make a strong impression in Paris when she appeared at the Opéra-Comique. A watershed was her performance of Ophélie in Thomas's *Hamlet* at La Scala, Milan, in 1890. Subsequently she was successful at Covent Garden and at the Metropolitan Opera, New York, where she was acclaimed as Santuzza in *Cavalleria rusticana* and was considered the finest interpreter of the title role of Bizet's *Carmen*, which she performed 1000 times until 1904. She continued to give concerts until 1927.   JT

calypso. Originally a West Indian folk dance, the sung calypso was developed mainly in Trinidad, where its relaxed, syncopated duple-time rhythm provides a medium for comment in racy language on current events, scandal, sport, or politics. Texts use a mixture of English and patois and are freely set to a body of traditional melodies. Calypso became popular in Europe shortly after World War II. It continues to have an important social function on Trinidad, in the carnival period from the end of Christmas to Ash

Wednesday, and a calypso king is chosen on the last Sunday in Lent. KC

cambiare (It.). 'To change'; an instruction in an instrumental part for a woodwind player to change to another instrument, a brass player to change crook, or a timpanist to alter the tuning.

cambiata. 1. See ÉCHAPPÉE.

2. See NOTA CAMBIATA.

Cambini, Giuseppe Maria (Gioacchino) (*b* Livorno, ? 13 Feb. 1746; *d* ?Paris, ?1825). Italian violinist and composer. He studied the violin and music theory in Naples, *c*.1763–6. The story that on his return journey he and his fiancée were captured by Barbary pirates, sold as slaves, and bought and released by a Venetian merchant is unlikely to be true. In the early 1770s Cambini made his way to Paris, where he was befriended by Gossec and had several works performed at the Concert Spirituel. Over the next 20 years he wrote a great deal of music, including about 60 symphonies, 30 *symphonies concertantes*, 144 string quartets and about 400 other pieces of chamber music, two oratorios, and over 20 operas and ballets. He was conductor at several minor theatres in Paris. Towards the end of his life he became poverty-stricken and resorted to arranging popular *airs*. Fétis wrote that Cambini spent his last ten years in the Bicêtre almshouses in Paris, but more recent research indicates that he may have gone to the Netherlands.
WT/RP

camera (It., 'chamber'; Fr.: *chambre*; Ger.: *Kammer*). In the early Baroque era, a designation often attached to music to be performed in a setting other than a church (*chiesa*) or theatre, usually a domestic room. A musical distinction was drawn between pieces, for instance sonatas or concertos, considered appropriate for performance in a sacred place and those intended for a secular context. A *sonata da camera*, for example, usually consisted of a slow prelude and a sequence of dance movements (as in the later *suite), whereas a *sonata da chiesa* alternated slow and fast movements with no connection to dancing and generally used the organ as continuo. Corelli's works provide good examples of the distinction.

See also CHAMBER MUSIC. JBe

camerata (It., 'club', 'society'). A term used in 16th-century Italy for a small, informal *academy or group of intellectuals who met to discuss particular aspects of a subject. In music the term refers in particular to the Florentine Camerata, a group made up chiefly of literary figures who met in the 1570s and 80s to discuss the music of the Ancient Greeks. The leader and host of the Camerata was Count Giovanni de' Bardi, and among its members were the musicians Vincenzo Galilei, Piero Strozzi (*c*.1550–1609), and Giulio Caccini; the poet and librettist Ottavio Rinuccini was associated with the Camerata, though he may not have been a member. In 1592 Bardi went to Rome and Jacopo Corsi became the leader of the group. Two years later, Corsi and Jacopo Peri set to music Rinuccini's *Dafne* (performed 1598); this was effectively the first opera, though only fragments of the music survive. The Camerata was important mainly for the development of *monody and of the *stile rappresentativo*; Galilei, in his *Dialogo della musica antica et della moderna* (1581), advocated these techniques as having been those of the Greeks and being more effective at moving the passions of the hearers, and Caccini was a pioneer in the composition (and performance) of monodic songs. —/JJD

Camidge. English family of organists. **John Camidge** (i) (*b* York, *bapt.* 8 Dec. 1734; *d* York, 25 April 1803) was a chorister at York Minster before going to London to study with Greene and Handel. In 1756 he succeeded James Nares as organist of York Minster, holding the post until 1799. He was active throughout his life in York musical circles. His son **Matthew Camidge** (*b* York, *bapt.* 25 May 1764; *d* York, 23 Oct. 1844) was educated in the Chapel Royal before succeeding to the position of organist at York Minster. He published sonatas and other keyboard pieces, concertos for piano or organ, and church music. Matthew's son **John Camidge** (ii) (*b* York, 1790; *d* York, 21 Sept. 1859) graduated Mus.D. at Cambridge and in turn succeeded his father at York Minster in 1842. He became paralysed in 1848, and his son **Thomas Simpson Camidge** (1828–1912) took over as deputy organist for ten years until his father's official resignation. WT

Cammerton (Ger., 'chamber pitch'). The concert pitch standard prevailing in Germany from about 1740 to 1820; see PITCH, 3.

camminando (It.). 'Walking', i.e. moving on.

campana (It.). 'Bell'.

Campanella, La. Transcription for piano by Liszt of the 'Rondo alla campanella' ('Ronde à la clochette'; 'Bell' Rondo) from Paganini's Violin Concerto in B minor (1826). Liszt first used the theme in the *Grande fantaisie de bravoure sur La clochette* (*La campanella*) (1833). The most popular version is 'La Campanella' from the *Études d'exécution transcendante d'après Paganini* (1851), itself a revision of a version dating from 1838–9.

campanelli (It., 'bells'). See GLOCKENSPIEL; TUBULAR BELLS.

Campiello, Il ('The Small Venetian Square'). Opera in three acts by Wolf-Ferrari to a libretto by Mario Ghisalberti after Carlo Goldoni's play *Il campiello* (1756) (Milan, 1936).

Campion [Campian], Thomas (*b* London, *bapt.* 12 Feb. 1567; *d* London, 1 March 1620). English composer and poet. Although he did not earn his living solely by writing poetry and music, it is clear that both played a prominent role at every stage of his life, including his days at Peterhouse, Cambridge (1581–4); at Gray's Inn, where he studied for the legal profession; and during his practice as a London physician—he received his MD in France, at the University of Caen in 1605.

Campion regarded his English ayres as less serious than his Latin poems—'superfluous blossoms of his deeper Studies'—yet he is primarily remembered as a fine English poet, whose literary output is inseparable from the other art in which he excelled, music. His treatise on metre, *Observations in the Art of English Poesie* (London, 1602), for instance, is subtly influenced by his musical mind, and the result is more than simply an exposition on 'quantity' and an attack on rhyming metres. His purely musical treatise, *A New Way of Making Fowre Parts in Counter-Point* (London, ?1614), was one of his best-known works in the 17th century; in it he recognized, much ahead of his time, the harmonic function of the bass part. He also outlined a scale system closer to the modern major–minor form than the old *hexachord, and an embryonic pattern for related keys which became standard in the Baroque era.

His music, all for voices, is immediately attractive. It is especially tuneful, restrained though rarely melancholic, and marked by sectional repetition and the occasional sequence. His masques are distinguished by their musical and poetic content, especially the first, the *Lord Hayes* (1607), where music and poetry not only adorn the masque but also direct the whole movement of the work. Herein lie the seeds of opera, which unfortunately Campion did not nurture. In his later masques, *Lords* (1613) and *Somerset* (1614), music and poetry are incorporated in a more formal manner into the now conventional Jonsonian design, and Campion seems to have lost interest. In his ayres the vocal line is all-important, the lute acting very much as an accompaniment—in contrast to, say, some of Dowland's or Daniel's songs. In his five books of ayres, and other single examples, can be found a perfect union of music and poetry.   CRW

📖 C. WILSON, *Words and Notes Coupled Lovingly Together: Thomas Campion: A Critical Study* (New York, 1989)

Campra, André (*b* Aix-en-Provence, *bapt.* 4 Dec. 1660; *d* Versailles, 29 June 1744). French composer. He was the son of an Italian professional violinist. In 1674 he was a choirboy at St Sauveur in his native town under a distinguished teacher, Guillaume Poitevin. In 1681 he was made *maître de musique* at Ste Trophime, Arles, moving in 1683 to a similar position at Toulouse. It was here that he began to make his name as a composer, of both sacred and secular music, but by 1694 he had moved again to Paris as director of the song school at Notre Dame. In 1697 he wrote his first substantial works for the theatre, using his brother's name because he feared the disapproval of the church authorities. These works—especially *L'Europe galante*, an *opéra-ballet* staged in 1697—were so well received that by the turn of the century Campra felt confident enough to use his own name. He was granted a pension of 500 livres by Louis XV in 1718 and in 1723 was appointed one of three *sous-maîtres* at the royal chapel.

Campra was one of the major composers for the French theatre, writing greatly successful divertissements, *tragédies lyriques*, ballets, and *opéras-ballets*. He can be credited with the invention of the French *opéra-ballet*; the introduction by him and his contemporaries of elaborate *airs* of the *da capo* type is the direct result of Italian influence, while the use of dance, which assumed a greater importance than hitherto, was a purely French innovation (a similar mix of French popular music and Italian aria characterizes his sacred motets). He went beyond Lully in his dramatic use of the orchestra and sometimes anticipated ideas later used by Rameau (the use of an offstage chorus, for instance). He also introduced elements of operatic style into his secular cantatas, and into several *grands motets* written for the royal chapel towards the end of his life.

DA/PW

Camptown Races ('Gwine to run all night'). Song (1850) by Stephen Foster.

Canada. Canada is culturally distinct from the USA in that original traditions—British, French, and Amerindian—have developed more independently. There are records of music in Canada going back to Jacques Cartier's landing in 1535. In the next century French missionaries translated hymns into Amerindian languages, and some music was composed for church and theatre. Even after the British conquest, the French province remained musically ahead: two Mozart string quintets were performed at a subscription concert in Quebec in 1793, five years after the appearance of Joseph Quesnel's comic opera *Colas et Colinette*. Only in the 1850s did Toronto become a musical centre of comparable importance, visited by Jenny Lind, Ole Bull, Henri Vieuxtemps, and Adelina Patti.

A little later, professional composers began to appear in Canada, especially in Quebec, one of the first being

Calixa Lavallée (1842–91), followed by his pupil Alexis Contant (1858–1918) and the Paris-educated Guillaume Couture (1851–1915). Given the importance of choirs in the country, it was natural that big choral works were the major endeavours of both Contant and Couture. But the foundation of university music departments and conservatories during their lifetimes, notably in Montreal and Toronto, prepared for a more various and vigorous musical life, signalled by the establishment of symphony orchestras in Toronto (1922), Vancouver (1933), and Montreal (1934). Meanwhile, Healey Willan arrived in Toronto in 1913, already fully trained and prepared to take a leading role in music education and church music, alongside Ernest MacMillan (1893–1973), the country's first outstanding conductor. Their Quebecois contemporary Claude Champagne was also an important teacher.

Leading composers of the next generation included Violet Archer, Jean Papineau-Couture, Barbara Pentland, and John Weinzweig. Open to advanced European influences—Archer studied with Bartók, and Papineau-Couture with Boulanger—they brought Canadian music into the modern mainstream while also striving, often through the absorption of folk music, to make it distinctively Canadian. That aim was realized in Willan's opera *Deirdre* (1945), Champagne's *Symphonie gaspésienne* (1945), and Weinzweig's ballet *Red Ear of Corn* (1949).

The collecting of Amerindian and French Canadian folk music had begun in earnest in 1910 at the National Museum of Canada in Ottawa (now the National Museum of Man), led by Edward Sapir and C. Marius Barbeau, who was active at the museum between 1911 and 1948. During the same period other collectors, working in Nova Scotia and Newfoundland, gathered folk music of English, Scottish, and Irish origin.

Musical life, in terms of performance and composition, moved forward strongly after World War II. In 1950 regular opera performances began in Toronto, leading to the creation of the Canadian Opera Association in 1960, and in 1951 the Canadian League of Composers was formed, with Weinzweig as founder president. Teaching at the University of Toronto from 1939 to 1978, Weinzweig also influenced many leading composers, among them John Beckwith, Norma Beecroft (*b* 1934), Harry Freedman, Bruce Mather (*b* 1939), Murray Schafer, and Harry Somers. In Montreal his role was paralleled in the work of Champagne and Papineau-Couture, whose pupils included François Morel (*b* 1926), Serge Garant, Jacques Hétu (*b* 1938), André Prévost (1934–2001), and Gilles Tremblay.

Canadian composers, unlike their American counterparts, tended to seek further training in Europe, often in Paris—those from Toronto as much as those from Montreal, though the French influence was strongest on the latter group: Garant gained from Boulez and Tremblay from Messiaen. Also, as in European countries, music enjoyed state support, notably through the Canadian Broadcasting Corporation (CBC), founded in 1936, and the Canada Council, established in 1957. In 1963 and 1964 Stravinsky visited Toronto to make recordings with the CBC Symphony Orchestra. Jazz in Canada, too, was encouraged by the CBC, with whom Oscar Peterson (*b* 1925) began his career. And the Montreal International Jazz Festival has helped maintain a vibrant jazz culture.

The gifted generation of musicians born in the 1920s and 30s—including Glenn Gould, the most celebrated musician the country has produced—provided for a rich musical life in the 1960s. Schafer, in addition to his compositions, produced handbooks on music education, noise, and sound design that had a wide influence. Gould and Peterson, in their different ways, made piano recordings that reached wide audiences. Beckwith, like Weinzweig, had a long tenure at the University of Toronto (1952–90), while students in Montreal were exposed to the teaching of Garant, Tremblay, and Hétu, and thereby to the tradition of Messiaen and Boulez. Garant was also active in conducting and presenting new music, and in 1966 founded the first Canadian institution for concerts of new works, the Société de la Musique Contemporaine Québécoise. The next year, that of Canada's centenary as a dominion, was marked by the first performance of Somers's opera *Louis Riel*.

Among younger composers who emerged from the thriving new-music culture in Montreal in the 1960s and 1970s were Denys Bouliane (*b* 1955), Serge Provost (*b* 1952), and Claude Vivier. Vivier's singular music has received more widespread attention than that of any other Canadian composer.   GP/PG

📖 H. KALLMANN, *A History of Music in Canada, 1534–1914* (Toronto, 1960) · H. KALLMANN, G. POTVIN, and K. WINTERS (eds.), *Encyclopedia of Music in Canada* (Toronto, 1981, 2/1992) · T. J. McGEE, *The Music of Canada* (New York, 1985) · M. MELHUISH, *Oh What a Feeling: A Vital History of Canadian Music* (Kingston, ON, 1996)

canarie (Fr.). A 17th-century French dance derived from rituals indigenous to the Canary Islands. It is danced in a fast, often dotted, triple metre. The earliest example is to be found in Arbeau's **Orchésographie* (1588); later ones occur in the harpsichord suites of Chambonnières and Louis Couperin, and in such operas as Lully's *Armide et Rénaud* (1686) and Purcell's *Dioclesian* (1690). It is mentioned in Shakespeare's *All's Well that Ends Well*.   —/JH

can-can. A lively dance, developed from the quadrille, usually performed by a troupe of women in flouncy dresses, its acrobatic steps, high kicks, and splits, revealing the upper thigh. It became very popular in the music halls of mid-19th-century Paris, and was given a degree of respectability by the French operetta composers, notably Offenbach, who used it most effectively in his *Orphée aux enfers* (1858). The word 'can-can' originally meant tittle-tattle of a scandalous nature.

PGa

canción (Sp.). 'Song'. The term refers particularly to a 15th-century type of serious song, in contrast to the popular *villancico*; *canción danza*, 'dance-song'.

cancionero (Sp.). A 'songbook' or, in modern usage, a collection of poetry. The word is used for the monophonic songbooks of the Iberian Middle Ages (mostly with texts in Portuguese-Galician), for poetry collections, whether printed or manuscript, for the Spanish polyphonic songbooks of the years after about 1490—most notably the enormous *Cancionero de palacio* of soon after 1500—and, particularly from the 19th century, for collections of Spanish folksongs.   DF

cancrizans (Lat., 'crab-like'). See RETROGRADE.

Candide. Operetta in two acts by Bernstein to a libretto by Lillian Hellman after Voltaire, with lyrics by Richard Wilbur, John Latouche, Dorothy Parker, Hellman, and Bernstein, orchestrated by Bernstein and Hershy Kay (Boston, 1956); it was revised into one act to a libretto by Hugh Callingham Wheeler, with lyrics by Wilbur, Latouche, Bernstein, and Stephen Sondheim, orchestrated by Kay (New York, 1973).

Cannabich, (Johann) Christian (Innocenz Bonaventura) (*b* Mannheim, *bapt.* 12 Dec. 1731; *d* Frankfurt, 20 Jan. 1798). German composer, violinist, and conductor. The son of a flautist in the Mannheim orchestra, he joined the ensemble when he was 12. He studied composition with Johann Stamitz and, from 1752 to 1754, with Jommelli. Following Stamitz's death in 1757 Cannabich became joint Konzertmeister at Mannheim, writing large numbers of symphonies and ballets for the court and directing the orchestra with a brilliance that drew the highest praise from his contemporaries. During the 1760s he gained an international reputation as a composer with the publication of symphonies and chamber works in Paris, London, and Amsterdam. When the Palatine and Bavarian courts merged in 1778 he moved to Munich as director of the combined orchestras, a post he held for the rest of his life. Many of his symphonies show strong Italian influences, though the exposure he gave to the wind instruments and his imaginative use of dynamic contrasts no doubt reflect the strengths of his orchestra. His last symphony (1794) is in the mature Classical style of works by his friend Mozart.   DA/TRJ

canon. A device in *counterpoint whereby a melody in one voice (or part) is imitated throughout, note for note, by one or more other voices, which normally begin after the first voice and overlap it. The word 'canon' (from the Greek *kanōn*) means 'rule' or 'precept' and was first used in the 15th century as an inscription or 'rule' of instruction in connection with any piece of music which was intentionally written out in an obscure or enigmatic way and required resolution before it could be performed. At that time a piece that was strictly canonic in the present-day sense was more commonly called a *rota*, chace, *fuga* (whence the term *fugue, which now has a distinct meaning), *rondellus*, or *caccia (whence the more familiar English *catch, or *round, e.g. *Three Blind Mice*). Contrapuntal writing that is not strictly canonic is usually termed imitation; the composition of a true canon, however, has traditionally been regarded as among the most highly skilled compositional techniques.

A wealth of terminology surrounds the study of canons. The first voice to enter with the melody is called the *dux* ('leader') or antecedent, and any imitating voice is called the *comes* ('companion') or consequent. Canons may be described in terms of the distance (in bars or fractions of bars) between the imitating parts; for example, 'canon of two bars' means that the second voice enters with the melody two bars after the first, the third voice two bars after the second, and so on. They may also be described in terms of the interval between the voices: the commonest is the canon in unison or at the octave, but canons at the 4th and 5th are also common, and theoretically any interval is possible. Rounds and catches are in effect canons in unison, and they also exemplify the principle of perpetual or infinite canon: when each voice reaches the end it immediately begins again, so that the piece is self-perpetuating and can be repeated as many times as desired. A canon with a separately composed ending may be termed a finite canon.

A canon for two voices using one line of melody is called a canon two in one, three voices with one melody a canon three in one, and so on. Sometimes two canons are carried on simultaneously (e.g. first and third voice in canon with one melody, second and fourth in canon with another): such group canons are defined as canon four in two, as appropriate to the number of voices and melodies involved.

A canon in which the imitating voice or voices gives out the melody in notes of longer rhythmic value than the original is called a canon by augmentation; one in which it imitates in shorter note-values is a canon by diminution. A canon in which the imitating voice gives out the melody backwards (both voices usually starting together) is called variously a retrograde canon, *canon recte et retro*, *canon rectus et invertus*, or *canon cancrizans* ('crab canon'). A canon by inversion is one in which any ascending interval in the first voice becomes a descending one in the second. These last two devices may be combined to form a mirror canon or canon in retrograde inversion, where the second voice has the melody backwards and with the intervals inverted.

A canon described as *per arsin et thesin* ('raising and lowering') may be a canon by inversion or, more usually, one in which notes on naturally accented (strong) downbeats in the first voice are displaced to unaccented (weak) upbeats in the second voice. A canon that includes 'free' parts (e.g. a four-voice piece that combines a canon two in one with two freely moving voices) is called a mixed or accompanied canon.

Canons are described as strict or free according to whether or not each pitch interval is imitated exactly. All canons at the unison and octave are necessarily strict, but at any other interval the relative position of tones and semitones in the scale used by the imitating voice is different from that in the original. In order to reproduce strictly the intervals of the melody, some notes in the imitating voice must be adjusted by accidentals; in tonal canons these will imply modulations that the continuing first voice cannot fulfil without itself modulating, which may lead to still further difficulties. Hence free canon, which allows the imitating voice to alter some intervals so as to avoid unwanted modulation, is commoner than strict (Ex. 1).

Ex. 1

Opening of Fugue VIII from Bach, '48', book 1.

The earliest known wholly canonic piece is the 13th-century *rota Sumer is icumen in*. Several 14th-century composers, notably Machaut, used extended canonic passages in their motets, masses, and chansons, but it

was the Flemish composers active in the late 15th century (Ockeghem, Josquin) who brought canonic composition to a peak. The 16th century saw a growing aversion among writers on music to an abstract composition technique which they claimed obscured both text and any real musical invention. Canonic writing nevertheless persisted as an intellectual pursuit: a composer would set down a melodic line and call it 'canon', giving no indication (except perhaps in the form of an abstruse riddle) as to how many voices should take part, where each should enter, or what sort of imitation (strict, inverted, retrograde, etc.) was required to 'solve' it. Byrd is reputed to have written 40 such canons on the *Miserere* plainchant, in friendly competition with Alfonso Ferrabosco (i).

Progressive Baroque composers of the 17th century regarded canon as a somewhat outdated and irrelevant device, although it was still advocated for didactic purposes by theorists. In England at that time, however, the catch was experiencing a considerable revival in the wake of the madrigal's decline. By the mid-18th century canonic composition had reached another peak in the music of Bach (notably in the 'Goldberg' Variations, *Musical Offering*, and *The Art of Fugue*), after which it again came to be viewed more as an academic exercise than as a viable composition procedure.

Composers of the Classical period made some use of canon, although in string quartet and symphony movements by Haydn and Mozart it appears a somewhat self-conscious device. Among the greatest 19th-century composers only Schumann and Brahms showed any concern with what had by then become largely an academic exercise. In the 20th century, however, there was a renewed interest in canon as a means of establishing kinship with tradition, and from Schoenberg and Webern to Maxwell Davies and beyond the principle has offered valuable form-building properties, on both small and large scales. The idea of the post-tonal canon, in which melodic lines imitate one another in the traditional fashion while observing none of the traditional rules of voice-leading (as in Webern's op. 16), is often deemed of dubious value in that no rules of contrapuntal procedure apply beyond the composer's instinct for balance and interaction. That may be one reason why later post-tonal composers (Maxwell Davies, for example) prefer to write rhythmic canons in which the pitch materials are not constrained by the need for melodic correspondence.   PS/JN/AW

canon cancrizans. See CANON.

canonical Hours. Alternative name for *Office Hours.

canso. Troubadour name for a strophic song taking courtly love as its theme.

cantabile (It.). 'Singable', 'in a singing style'. Beethoven often used the term to qualify a slow or moderate tempo indication, such as *adagio* or *andante*.

cantando (It.). 'Singing', *cantabile.

cantata (It.; Fr.: *cantate*; Ger.: *Kantate*). Literally a piece to be sung, as opposed to a 'sonata', an instrumental work to be played. The term applies to a variety of genres, but most usually to ones featuring a solo voice, with instrumental accompaniment and quite often of a quasi-dramatic character.

> 1. The secular cantata of the Baroque era; 2. The origins of the sacred cantata; 3. The Protestant tradition; 4. After 1750; 5. The 20th century

1. The secular cantata of the Baroque era

The form first appeared in the 1620s in song collections, entitled *Cantade et arie*, by various Venetian composers, most notably Alessandro Grandi and Giovanni Berti. The earliest examples involved the use of strophic variation; but a division soon began to appear (as also in operas of the period) between sections in which the text was set syllabically without much repetition (anticipating recitative) and ones where repeated and balanced phrases provided a more tuneful, aria-like character. A second generation, largely of Roman composers such as Rossi and Carissimi, produced longer and more sectionalized settings with frequent alternation between the incipient recitative and aria of the period, and using an intermediate stage similar to arioso. Many of these works involved verse of a trivial, pastoral-amorous character, but some, for example Carissimi's *Il lamento di Maria di Scozia*, provided dramatic treatment of historical themes, with vivid word-painting and unusual turns of melody and harmony. Towards the end of the century the cantata gained greater substance, mainly through the works of Alessandro Stradella, who increased the instrumental involvement with ritornellos and provided the arias with clearer formal patterns.

By 1700, in works by Alessandro Scarlatti and others, the cantata comprised—like the operas of the time—a clear-cut alternation between rapidly declaimed recitatives and *da capo* arias, often with three pairings of each. Designed to appeal to connoisseurs, Scarlatti's cantatas generally showed more complexity of melody and harmony, and richness of orchestration, than his operas, and provided a model for many early 18th-century composers, including Vivaldi and Handel. It was during his time in Rome (1707–9) that Handel wrote his many distinguished cantatas—some lyrical, some dramatic, some for voice and continuo, and others with rich orchestral support. At this time he also produced several extended serenatas, notably *Apollo e Dafne* and *Aci, Galatea e Polifemo*, which resemble short operatic scenes, with finely drawn musical character-sketches.

Because of the popularity abroad, from about 1660, of Italian opera and visiting opera singers, the cantatas of such composers as Giovanni Bononcini, Antonio Caldara, and Attilio Ariosti became well known in Germany and England, and thus a separate development, in those countries, of secular cantatas in the vernacular was limited. English composers preferred on the whole to cultivate their own song traditions, though Purcell's chamber cantatas—such as his setting of Abraham Cowley's *How pleasant is this flow'ry plain* (*c*.1683), for soprano and tenor with two flutes and continuo—provide fine examples of the genre. In France, from about 1710, for some 20 years, important, and truly French, contributions to the cantata genre were made by such composers of stature as André Campra, M. P. de Montéclair, and L.-N. Clérambault. Dramatic scenes were favoured, sometimes with mood-painting sinfonias, and much use made of obbligato instruments. Bible stories also proved popular, in settings akin to miniature oratorios.

2. The origins of the sacred cantata

In parallel with the development of the secular cantata there gradually arose that of the solo motet to a sacred text. Works of this type were of particular value to churches and confraternities with modest performing resources, and were much favoured by students at the Italian conservatories. A set of 21, similar in form to the Roman cantatas of the time, was published in 1655 by Natale Monferrato, music director at the Mendicanti in Venice; and large numbers were composed over the following two decades in the Bologna–Modena area, most notably by G. B. Bassani.

In the early 18th century it was not unusual for Italian church composers to be opera composers too, and consequently their solo motets often differed little from operatic scenes. In the opera-style motets of Vivaldi a preference is evident for a tripartite structure (aria–recitative–aria, often with a brilliant final 'Alleluja' setting), the arias of which are in *da capo* form and much given to vocal display. Although the texts adopted were usually in dog Latin, some liturgical passages, such as the *Salve regina* and the *Stabat mater*, were also set in cantata style, the former notably by Vivaldi and Galuppi and the latter, most splendidly, by Domenico Scarlatti.

3. The Protestant tradition

Most influential on the Protestant cantata was the concertato chorale, a form derived from the early

17th-century practice of setting hymns with a different combination of voices, solo and choral, for each verse. J. S. Bach's *Christ lag in Todes Banden* (BWV4), in which the chorale melody is infused, whole or in small segments, into the vocal and instrumental lines, is a setting of this type. It was on this basis, and that of the secular cantata with recitatives and arias, that the church cantata of the first 30 years of the 18th century developed, eventually attaining its climax with the large-scale works of Bach. The union of its elements resulted largely from the work of Erdmann Neumeister, a Hamburg poet and pastor who, from 1700, published cycles of freely poetic sacred texts, clearly modelled on those of Italian cantata and opera, and providing scope for alternating recitative and aria treament. These were set by a number of composers, including J. P. Krieger, F. W. Zachow, and Christoph Graupner, in their later cantatas, and J. S. Bach in his earliest ones.

With an expansion of Neumeister's basic scheme to include biblical passages and chorales, the ground was laid for the grand church cantata, which typically involved an orchestral prelude, a chorus (on a chorale or biblical text), two pairs of recitatives and arias, separated by a further chorus (often using the same chorale), and a final chordal setting, again of the basic chorale, for congregational use. Some of Bach's cantatas are quite short and require only modest resources; one example is *Liebster Jesu, mein Verlangen* (BWV32), a dialogue for soprano and bass soloists which has the ground plan aria–recitative–aria–recitative–duet–chorale, with oboe, solo violin, strings, and continuo in accompaniment. Others are longer and need altogether larger forces. A notable example is *Herz und Mund und Tat und Leben* (BWV147), which is scored for SATB soloists and chorus, with accompaniment for trumpet, two oboes, oboe d'amore, two oboes da caccia, bassoon, solo violin, strings, and organ continuo, and is divided into two substantial parts (each ending with the famous chorale setting 'Jesu, Joy of Man's Desiring'), intended for performance before and after an hour-long sermon.

Bach is known to have composed over 300 church cantatas, many of which have been lost, together with a number of secular works including the well-known 'Peasant' and 'Coffee' cantatas. His total may seem modest when compared to those of Telemann and Graupner, each of whom wrote well over a thousand cantatas. But, to be valid, any comparison must take into account the altogether grander scale and richness of technique apparent in the great majority of Bach's settings. C. P. E. Bach also wrote some cantatas, and the genre continued among composers in smaller towns; but by 1750 it was definitely in decline.

4. After 1750

The decline of the cantata had several causes: a decrease in the number and quality of school and civic choirs; changes in musical taste; and a break with the high Baroque style in works that rejected the complex polyphony of traditional writing, or replaced it with stiffly academic counterpoint, and allowed the brilliantly ornate or emotional arias of the past to be supplanted by simple 'moral' songs. In the secular sphere some excellent works were written, such as Haydn's *Arianna a Naxos* (*c*.1790), for voice and piano; but it was chiefly within church composition that the cantata concept survived.

The growth of antiquarianism and the rediscovery of Bach's music during the 19th century brought a new awareness of the church cantata. As a result the middle-class choral societies in Germany, and their subsequent followers in England, encouraged the production of new choral works which, cast mainly in the style of the Handelian oratorio, used soloists, chorus, and orchestra, but placed particular emphasis on the chorus. Cantatas thus became miniature versions of the oratorio. Some, for example Dvořák's *Stabat mater* (1877), were based on religious texts, and others, such as Mendelssohn's settings of Goethe, *Die erste Walpurgisnacht* (1832), and Brahms's *Rinaldo* (1863), on secular ones. Various occasional pieces for grand ceremonies were also produced, a noteworthy example being Wagner's *Weihegruss* (1843), written for the unveiling of a memorial to Friedrich August I of Saxony.

5. The 20th century

During the 20th century, 'cantata' became an umbrella term under which there sheltered many choral and orchestral works. Notable examples, of greatly varied character, include Rakhmaninov's *Spring* (*Vesna*) op. 2 (1902), Bartók's *Cantata profana* (*The Nine Enchanted Stags*, 1930), Prokofiev's Cantata for the 20th Anniversary of the October Revolution op. 74 (1936–7), Webern's two cantatas (1939, 1943), Tippett's *Boyhood's End* (1943) for tenor and piano, Petrassi's *Noche oscura* (1950–1), Stravinsky's *Cantata* (1952), and Britten's *Cantata academica* op. 63 (1959) and *Cantata misericordium* (1963).

In the course of the century, the 'choral society' cantata became less popular, largely because most recent music of high quality is written in an idiom unsuitable for amateur choirs. However the concept of a choral or solo vocal piece in several movements, linked by a continuous verbal text, is too useful to disappear completely, and the cantata, by whatever name it is known, seems likely to continue for some time yet.

DA/BS

M. F. BUKOFZER, *Music in the Baroque Era* (New York, 1947) · W. G. WHITTAKER, *The Cantatas of J. S. Bach, Sacred and Secular* (London, 1959) · G. ROSE, 'The Italian cantata of the Baroque period', *Gattungen der Musik in Einzeldarstellungen: Gedenkschrift Leo Schrade*, ed. W. Arlt and others (Berne and Munich, 1973), 655–77 · D. TUNLEY, *The Eighteenth-Century French Cantata* (London 1974, 2/ 1997) · G. WEBBER, *North German Church Music in the Age of Buxtehude* (Oxford, 1996)

cantatorium (Lat.) [cantatory]. A kind of chant book; see PLAINCHANT, 4.

cante flamenco. See FLAMENCO, CANTE FLAMENCO.

cante hondo [cante jondo] (Sp., 'deep song'). A popular Spanish singing style; the term is used to identify a strain of *flamenco song.

Cantelli, Guido (*b* Novara, 27 April 1920; *d* Paris, 24 Nov. 1956). Italian conductor. He studied at the Milan Conservatory and made his debut in opera in Novara in 1943, becoming internationally celebrated after his American debut with the NBC Symphony Orchestra in 1949. He conducted at the Salzburg Festival from 1953. A fanatical perfectionist, he achieved his demands with fierce concentration and a vivid baton technique. His wide repertory included contemporary and American music. He died in an air crash a few days after he was appointed music director of La Scala, Milan.   JT

L. LEWIS, *Guido Cantelli: Portrait of a Maestro* (San Diego and London, 1981)

Canteloube (de Malaret), (Marie) **Joseph** (*b* Annonay, 21 Oct. 1879; *d* Paris, 4 Nov. 1957). French composer and collector of folksongs. A native of the Auvergne, he became a leading figure in the regionalist movement in France. In 1902 he met d'Indy, who became his teacher and shared his deep respect for folk music. To the end of his life Canteloube believed that contemporary music had lost its way because it had turned its back on folksong. As well as his celebrated *Chants d'Auvergne*, which appeared in five books between 1923 and 1954, he published many collections of songs from various regions of France. Although the *Chants d'Auvergne* have subtly orchestrated and harmonized accompaniments, many of Canteloube's arrangements are for amateurs and simply accompanied, or for voice alone. He defended his more sophisticated treatments, and his 'folklore imaginaire', by claiming that their accompaniments captured the atmosphere surrounding those who originally sang them. Among his original works are two operas, Verlaine settings, and two orchestral song cycles dedicated to Maggie Teyte.   RLS

canti carnascialeschi (It., pl. of *canto carnascialesco*). *Carnival songs'.

canticle (from Lat. *canticulum*, dim. of *canticum*, 'song'). 1. A song or prayer (other than a psalm) derived from the Bible and used in the liturgical worship of Eastern and Western Christian Churches. Early Greek manuscripts of the Bible present a series of 14 canticles or 'odes' including the *Gloria in excelsis* and the apocryphal Prayer of Manasseh. The modern Eastern Orthodox office of Orthros features a Palestinian series of nine biblical odes (eight Old Testament canticles and a composite New Testament ode consisting of the *Magnificat* and the Benedictus), to which are affixed the troparia of kanons. Outside monasteries, only the *Magnificat* is regularly sung in full.

The three canticles drawn from the New Testament used daily in the medieval and modern offices of the Roman rite are the Benedictus (see BENEDICTUS, 2), the *Magnificat*, and the *Nunc dimittis*. Medieval Lauds featured a weekly cycle of seven canticles (taking the fourth place in the sequence of psalms) beginning on Sunday with the *Benedicite*. The Breviary of Pius X (1911) supplemented the original series with seven others for use in Lent. Variable New and Old Testament canticles are appointed for use at morning and evening prayer, respectively, in the Liturgy of the Hours promulgated after the Second Vatican Council.

In the Anglican *Book of Common Prayer* the term applies strictly only to the *Benedicite*, but common usage applies it also to the Benedictus, the *Magnificat*, and the *Nunc dimittis*, as well as to the psalms *Venite*, *Jubilate*, *Cantate Domino*, and *Deus misereatur* and the hymn *Te Deum* (all known by their Latin names, though they are given in English).

2. The Book of Canticles is another name for the Song of Solomon.   —/ALi

Canticum sacrum (ad honorem Sancti Marci nominis) ('Sacred Song to the Honour of the Name of St Mark'). Choral work (1955) by Stravinsky, a setting of a biblical text for tenor and baritone soloists, chorus, and orchestra.

Canti di prigionia ('Songs of Imprisonment'). Work (1938–41) by Dallapiccola for chorus, two pianos, two harps, and percussion, to texts by Queen Mary Stuart, Boethius, and Savonarola; it was composed as a protest against Mussolini's adoption of Hitler's racial policies, which threatened Dallapiccola's Jewish wife.

cantiga (Sp., Port.). 'Song'. A term usually taken to refer to the 13th-century Spanish monophonic song in honour of the Virgin Mary. The most famous of these are the *Cantigas de Santa Maria*.

Cantigas de Santa Maria (Sp., 'Canticles of the Virgin Mary'). A collection of 420 songs about the Virgin

Mary made between about 1270 and 1290 under the direction of King Alfonso X. Most of the *cantigas* recount miracles accomplished through the intervention of the Virgin, and some are hymns in her praise. The locale of the miracles extends from Syria to Scotland, and one, set in England, reappears as Chaucer's *Prioress's Tale*. The Portuguese-Galician text of the *cantigas*, much influenced by the art of the troubadours, is set in metrically irregular stanzas of from four to ten lines. The chief musical form is that of the **virelai*. The manuscripts are famous for their pictorial representations of medieval instruments and performers.   AL

cantilena (It.; Fr.: *cantilène*). 1. A lyrical vocal melody or instrumental passage performed in a smooth style, particularly in the 18th century.

2. A short song or, in medieval times, any secular piece, such as a *ballade*, *virelai*, or *rondeau*.

3. In choral music, the part that carries the main tune.

4. A type of *solfeggio, or vocal exercise, using the whole scale.

cantillation. The chanting of a text in a plainchant style. The term is used primarily in connection with the performance of Jewish liturgical music.   —/ALI

cantional (From Lat. *cantio*, 'song'; Ger.: *Kantional*). A hymnbook or collection of sacred songs. In Germany the word meant a collection of hymns or chorales usually printed in a large-format choirbook for use by the whole choir, as in Schein's *Cantional, oder Gesangbuch* (Leipzig, 1627).

Cantiones sacrae ('Sacred songs'). A term used by many composers, including Byrd for two books of motets: the first (1589) contains 29 for five voices, the second (1591) 20 for five voices and 12 for six voices. Byrd and Tallis jointly published a volume of *Cantiones sacrae* (1575) for five to eight voices.

cantique (Fr.). 'Canticle', 'hymn'.

canto (It., Sp.). 'Song', 'melody'; *col canto*, 'with the melody', i.e. the accompanist should follow closely any fluctuations in tempo etc. made by the performer of the melodic line.

canto carnascialesco (It.). *'Carnival song'.

canto de órgano (Sp.). Spanish term for polyphony in the Renaissance and Baroque periods (as opposed to *canto llano*, 'plainchant').

cantor. 1. In modern Anglican and Roman Catholic usage, the singer who is charged with the duty of intoning the first words of psalms, antiphons, and hymns. Cantors, especially on feast days, often work in pairs at the desk in the middle of the choir. See also KANTOR.

2. The leading singer in a synagogue.

Cantorei. See KANTOREI.

cantoris (Lat., 'of the singer'). The side of the choir on which the *precentor sits, now normally the north side. Choral music sometimes has passages marked *cantoris*, indicating that the singers on that side should take the passage. See also DECANI.

cantus (Lat.). 'Song', 'melody'. The term has been used more specifically to denote the highest voice-part in a polyphonic work; see PART, 1.

cantus firmus (Lat., 'fixed melody' or 'firm melody', pl. cantus firmi; It.: *canto fermo*). The term is most commonly used for the melodies in even semibreves that formed the basis of the contrapuntal training in J. J. Fux's *Gradus ad Parnassum* (1725) but drew on a theoretical tradition reaching back to Zarlino (1558) and Banchieri (1610). More loosely, however, it denotes a pre-existing melody taken as the basis of a new polyphonic composition. Such melodies can be of three basic types: plainchant, secular, and invented themes. The cantus firmus was usually 'held' in long notes in the lower voice, and the Latin verb *tenere*, 'to hold', led to this part being called the tenor.

Plainchant melodies, or sections of them, were taken as cantus firmi in the earliest forms of polyphony (e.g. *organum, *clausula) and in the 13th- and 14th-century *motet and some early mass movements. Secular melodies were used very occasionally in the 13th- and 14th-century motet, and frequently in the mass from at least the mid-15th century. Invented themes are those originally derived from the hexachord or from the vowels of a group of words (usually a name) by applying *solmization syllables; the latter is sometimes described as a *soggetto cavato* (It., 'extracted subject')—a term derived from Zarlino, who used it specifically to describe the tenor of Josquin's *Missa 'Hercules dux Ferrarie'* (rendering the vowels as *re–ut–re–ut–re–fa–mi–re*), his only mass with an even-note cantus firmus (see MASS, Ex. 1).

In some early settings the notes of the cantus firmus have no fixed rhythm, their individual lengths being determined by the extent to which the composer chose to elaborate polyphony over them. This could lead to a single note of the cantus firmus being held in the tenor for well over a minute in performance. This way of setting cantus firmi, with long notes, usually applied to sections of plainchant that were syllabic. However, sometimes the chosen plainchant was melismatic, with perhaps as many as 30 notes to a melisma; to keep the performance time within reasonable bounds the tenor part would move at more or less the same pace as the upper parts, and like them would be written in one of the rhythmic modes (see NOTATION, 2). In the 13th century there was an increasing use within the melody of repeated patterns. These were either derived from a straightforward repetition of the melody, or they were the result of large-scale recurrent rhythmic patterns derived from repetitions of the rhythmic mode. From these repetition patterns grew the practice of *isorhythm, which dominated the treatment of cantus firmi from the time of Philippe de Vitry to that of Josquin.

Although the cantus firmus usually appeared in the tenor part (on the Continent this was the lowest, but in England it was frequently the middle of three parts), there were alternatives. Around 1400 the English developed a custom of moving the cantus firmus melody between the parts; this is often described as a 'migrant' cantus firmus and the Old Hall Manuscript contains many examples. Another possibility was to place the cantus firmus in the highest voice and elaborate (or 'paraphrase') the original melody. Usually a well-known plainchant was chosen for this treatment and the text kept, so that such elaborations are easily identified.

By the mid-15th century two important developments in the use of cantus firmi had begun. The earliest cyclic masses using the same tenor for each movement appeared in about 1430, and soon after that composers began to turn to secular melodies in their mass compositions. This contributed to a new kind of treatment of the cantus firmus, whereby its structure was governed by the phrasing of its secular model, rather than by an abstract technique such as isorhythm, determined by number and proportion. From about 1480 there was a gradual decline in the use of a cantus firmus as an important structural component, and allusions to a cantus firmus melody occurred in a way that was virtually incidental in works whose organization was basically much freer. By the 16th century strict cantus firmus masses and motets were seen as old-fashioned, and were composed only rarely—for example for special occasions, or in honour of an individual.

In spite of this decline the cantus firmus principle underpins much of late Renaissance and early Baroque instrumental and keyboard music. The best-known examples are the settings of the sacred cantus firmi *Felix namque* and *In nomine*, but secular tunes (e.g. Dowland's *Lachrimae*) were also used as a subject in this way. A late flowering of the cantus firmus manner of composition was in the use of chorale melodies as the basis of such forms as the *chorale cantata and the *chorale prelude.   —/DF

📖 E. H. SPARKS, *Cantus Firmus in Mass and Motet* (Berkeley, CA, 1963)

cantus fractus (Lat., 'broken song'). A rhythmicized form of plainchant used in the 15th century, particularly for new melodies for the Credo and certain antiphon, sequence, and hymn texts.   IR

cantus planus (Lat.). 'Plainchant'.

Canyons aux étoiles, Des. See DES CANYONS AUX ÉTOILES.

canzona (It., 'song') [canzona francese, canzona da sonar]. The most important instrumental form of the late 16th and early 17th centuries. The earliest canzonas, generally for lute or keyboard instruments, were arrangements of such vocal works as French chansons from the first half of the 16th century. These chansons, with their lively rhythms and melodies, often imitative openings (typically beginning with a minim and two crotchets or similar motif), and their simple, distinctive structure (with repeated sections at the beginning or end to give an AABC, ABCC, or even ABCA pattern), translated well from a vocal to an instrumental idiom. Important examples from the early 16th century are the keyboard canzonas of M. A. and Girolamo Cavazzoni.

At first the arrangers did little more than add a few trills at cadences, but later they embellished their models quite elaborately, thus completely transforming their nature. This led to the composition of pieces that, though maintaining the general manner of the chanson, were conceived wholly in instrumental terms. From the 1570s several north Italian composers wrote such pieces, which could be played either by an ensemble (perhaps a viol consort or a group of cornetts and sackbuts) or on a keyboard instrument. They still used contrapuntal writing, but they were able to include intervals that would have been awkward to sing, and high registers uncomfortable for the voice. By the end of the century such works had become extremely popular, especially among composers in Venice, including Claudio Merulo (for keyboard) and Giovanni Gabrieli. Gabrieli's canzonas, for example those published in his *Sacrae symphoniae* (1597), were written for the large instrumental ensemble at St Mark's, adapting the idiom of *cori spezzati* to bring a grand scale into instrumental music. Some of these works are extremely complicated in form, using rondo and even simple concerto patterns, with virtuoso parts for such instruments as cornetts and violins.

Among the most important collections of canzonas from early 17th-century Italy are those by Frescobaldi, and Alessandro Raverii's anthology *Canzoni per sonare* (1608), which includes pieces by composers working mainly in Venice and Brescia. Thereafter this type of canzona declined, though it survived longer in Germany than in Italy. The use of a continuo part transformed the texture of music for smaller ensembles, the older canzona for four melody instruments giving way to works usually for one or two upper instruments with continuo, the bass line frequently being played by a bass viol or a cello. Keyboard canzonas continued to be popular for as long as contrapuntal writing was maintained—again the Italians gave up earlier than the Germans, such composers as Froberger, Muffat, and Buxtehude continuing to write keyboard canzonas until the later 17th century.

The sectional nature of the canzona proved useful in conveying the contrasts of emotions that were so much to the taste of Baroque composers. Different sections came to be contrasted so that they either brought new counterpoints or harmonies to a single unifying theme—in effect, sets of free variations—or were essentially diverse in texture and musical material. This second manner, aptly called by Hugo Riemann a *Flickkanzone* ('patch canzona' or, as Manfred Bukofzer described it, **quilt canzona'), soon led to individual sections becoming almost independent units or movements, a trend intensified when Frescobaldi began marking them 'Adagio' and 'Allegro' in a number of pieces published about 1630. By that time any resemblance to the older vocal form had totally disappeared; and, since the term 'sonata' was by then in common use and had similar connotations to 'canzona', by about 1650 most such pieces were called, more logically, 'sonata'. Thus the canzona had become the solo or trio sonata. However, fugal movements in sonatas were sometimes entitled 'canzona' (for example in Purcell's Trio Sonata in G minor), and many movements both in sonatas and in later concertos—for instance the first movement of Bach's Third Brandenburg Concerto—betray their origins in the canzona by their use of themes with some variation of the motto rhythm described above.   DA/EW

canzone (It.). 'Song'. 1. The canzoni of Dante and Petrarch were lyric poems written in such a way as to be apt for musical setting. Petrarch's *Vergine bella* (canzone 49), for example, was set by Dufay (stanza 1 only) in the 15th century, and by Rore, Merulo (both stanza 1 only), and Palestrina (eight stanzas, each as a separate piece) in the 16th.

2. In the 16th century, 'canzone' was frequently used as a title, or as part of a title (see, for ex-

ample, VILLANELLA), for a popular or folk-like secular song.

canzonetta (It., dim. of **canzone'). 'Canzonet'. From the late 16th century to the 18th, the term was applied to short vocal pieces in a light, often dance-like, style, for example by Marenzio, Vecchi, Banchieri, or Felice Anerio. The term found its way to England mainly through the collections of Italian canzonettas made by Thomas Morley (the first appeared in 1597), whose own canzonets tended to match the seriousness and the form (single-stanza, through-composed) of the madrigal. Germans, for example Hassler, also used the term.

In the 18th century, 'canzonetta' came to be used as a title for a light, lyrical kind of solo song, as in Haydn's *Six Original Canzonettas* (London, 1796). The word has also occasionally been borrowed for instrumental pieces, for example by Tchaikovsky in the slow movement of his Violin Concerto.

caoine (Irish, 'weeping') [keen]. An ancient Irish funeral lament, usually performed by women. See also CORRANACH.

capella. Common misspelling of **cappella*.

Caplet, André (*b* Le Havre, 23 Nov. 1878; *d* Neuilly-sur-Seine, 22 April 1925). French composer and conductor. He studied at the Paris Conservatoire and won the Prix de Rome in 1901, but soon established himself as a conductor, both in France and for the Boston Opera (1910–14). A friend of Debussy, he orchestrated part of *Le Martyre de Saint Sébastien*, of which he conducted the premiere in 1911, and most of *La Boîte à joujoux* (1919). Having been gassed in World War I, he gave up conducting to concentrate on composition. He wrote some highly original chamber works, songs, and deeply felt sacred music.   PS/ABur

capo (It.). See DA CAPO.

capo tasto (It., 'top of the fingerboard'). A bar covered with felt, leather, cork, or rubber which can be clamped over the neck of a plucked string instrument (e.g. lute or guitar) just behind a fret to convert that fret temporarily into the **nut. The player can thus transpose a piece of music into a higher key without altering the fingering. Various spellings of the word are encountered.   JMo

cappella (It.). 'Chapel' (for the origin of the word, see CHAPEL); *a cappella*, *alla cappella*, 'in the church style', meaning that a piece of choral music is to be sung unaccompanied (or, if accompanied, the instrument—probably an organ—should simply double the voice parts). A rare application of the term makes it a synonym for **alla breve*.

Capriccio. Opera in one act by Richard Strauss to a libretto by the composer and Clemens Krauss (Munich, 1942).

capriccio (It., 'whim', 'fancy'; Fr.: *caprice*). 1. A term applied to a piece of music, vocal or instrumental, of a fantastical or capricious nature. Rousseau defined it in his dictionary (1768) as 'A kind of free music, in which the composer, without subjecting himself to any theme, gives loose rein to his genius, and submits himself to the fire of composition'.

In the 16th century the name was sometimes given to madrigals, but in the early 17th it was used more for keyboard pieces employing fugal imitation, though not necessarily following the rules of strict counterpoint. Frescobaldi's capriccios (1624) vary widely in character: they have several contrasting sections, with sudden fluctuations of tempo, and some are based on unusual melodic ideas, for example the call of the cuckoo, or the *hexachord. In the works of some Baroque composers the capriccio closely resembles the keyboard *canzona, *toccata, or *ricercar, while other examples are related to dance forms (e.g. the final movement of Bach's keyboard Partita no. 2). Programmatic elements are also common in many capriccios, with pieces imitating such sounds as birdsong or horn calls.

Other keyboard capriccios were often in the style of free fantasias (e.g. J. S. Bach's *Capriccio sopra la lontananza del suo fratello dilettissimo*). Later, the term was used by composers including Brahms and Mendelssohn to describe short, humorous pieces, while Rimsky-Korsakov (*Spanish Capriccio*), Tchaikovsky (*Italian Caprice*), and Walton (*Capriccio burlesca*) are among those who applied the title to orchestral works.

2. In the 18th century the direction 'a capriccio' was sometimes used to indicate a *cadenza. Often written out in full, such passages were occasionally published as separate pieces in their own right, usually as virtuoso technical studies. Locatelli's 24 Capriccios for violin (1733), one in each key, were originally concerto cadenzas, and his set provided a model for other composers, notably Veracini (op. 2, 1744), Rodolphe Kreutzer (1796), and Paganini (op. 1, c.1805).

WT/JBE

Capriccio italien. See ITALIAN CAPRICE.

capriccioso (It.), **capricieux** (Fr.). 'Capricious'; *capricciosamente*, in a lively, informal style.

Caprioli, Carlo (*fl* Rome, 1643–91). Italian composer, violinist, and organist. His first known post was as second organist at the Collegio Germanico in Rome (1643–5). He had become attached to the papal Pamphili family by 1653. Already an established composer, through the agency of Antonio Barberini he was invited by Cardinal Mazarin to produce an opera at the French court in 1654. As a violinist he took part in the festivities at S. Luigi dei Francesi from 1649 to 1670, and periodically for the Lenten devotions at S. Marcello—highlights of the Roman musical year. He achieved the distinction of *guardiano* of the instrumentalists' section of the musicians' guild of S. Cecilia in 1664. The bulk of his surviving works are secular cantatas, but much confusion has been caused by the fact that both he and his close associate Carlo Mannelli bore the sobriquet 'Carlo del violino'.

PA

Capriol Suite. Suite for string orchestra (or piano duet) by Warlock, composed in 1926 and arranged for full orchestra in 1928; its six movements are based on old French dances from Thoinot Arbeau's *Orchésographie* (1588), a manual on dancing in which 'Capriol' is a character.

Capuleti e i Montecchi, I ('The Capulets and the Montagues'). Opera in two acts by Bellini to a libretto by Felice Romani based on Italian Renaissance sources (Venice, 1830).

Capuzzi, Giuseppe Antonio (*b* Brescia, 1 Aug. 1755; *d* Bergamo, 28 March 1818). Italian violinist and composer. He was active in Venice, where he was leader of the orchestra at the Teatro S. Samuele, 1780–6, and later director at the S. Benedetto. In 1796 he travelled to London, where his ballet *La Villageoise enlevée* was well received. From 1805 he was in Bergamo, teaching the violin and directing the orchestra of S. Maria Maggiore. In addition to his stage works, he wrote chamber music and a *sinfonia concertante*. His double bass (violone) concerto is now a standard practice work.

WT/RP

Cara, Marchetto [Marco] (*b* Verona, *c.*1465; *d* Mantua, 1525). Italian singer, lutenist, and composer. Trained as a cleric, he changed his profession to music in 1497, shortly after entering the service of the Gonzaga court in Mantua. He remained with the Gonzaga for the rest of his life, serving initially as a performer and composer, from 1511 additionally as *maestro di cappella* to the court. Like his colleague Bartolomeo Tromboncino, Cara is remembered today as a prolific composer of frottolas, tuneful Italian-texted secular songs with chordal support that can be sung either to the lute or accompanied by a consort of instruments or voices. The majority of these were published in Venice by Ottaviano Petrucci and circulated far beyond Mantua. During his early years in Verona, Cara also composed religious *laude*.

JM

Caractacus. Dramatic cantata (1898) by Elgar, for soprano, tenor, baritone, and bass soloists, chorus, and orchestra, to a text by H. A. Acworth. Several composers have written works based on the story of the British king who, during the reign of Claudius, put up almost the last resistance to the Romans, and was eventually captured and taken to Rome in AD 51, but whose nobility of spirit so impressed the emperor that he was set free.

Cardew, Cornelius (*b* Winchcombe, Glos., 7 May 1936; *d* London, 12 Dec. 1981). English composer. He was a chorister at Canterbury Cathedral and studied at the RAM (1953–7). From 1958 to 1960 he served as assistant to Stockhausen, particularly on the score of *Carré*, for four orchestral groups. His earliest works were influenced by Stockhausen, but from 1960 he moved more towards Cage, this period culminating in the beautifully drawn *Treatise* for unspecified forces (1963–7). In 1969 he founded the Scratch Orchestra, a group of amateurs who gave rough and ready performances of music new and old. Out of this came a militant Maoist group, and from the early 1970s Cardew directed his efforts to arrangements of numbers from Peking operas, revolutionary songs, and other such music. He wrote a *Treatise Handbook* (Buffalo, NY, 1970) and *Stockhausen Serves Imperialism* (London, 1974), and also edited *Nature Study Notes* (London, 1971) and *Scratch Music* (London, 1972).   PG

Cardillac. Opera in three acts by Hindemith to a libretto by Ferdinand Lion after E. T. A. Hoffmann's *Das Fräulein von Scuderi* (1818) (Dresden, 1926); Hindemith revised it in four acts, to his own libretto (Zürich, 1952).

Cardine, Dom Eugène (*b* Courseulles, Calvados, 11 April 1905; *d* Solesmes, 24 Jan. 1988). French scholar. He built on the foundations laid by André Mocquereau through study of the notational signs of the earliest manuscripts of plainchant, with the aim of rediscovering aspects of its performance, particularly its rhythm, melody, and vocal nuances. Cardine became a monk of *Solesmes in 1928 and was appointed professor at the Pontificio Istituto di Musica Sacra at Rome in 1952.   PW

Cardoso, Manuel (*b* Fronteira, nr Portalegre, *bapt.* 11 Dec. 1566; *d* Lisbon, 24 Nov. 1650). Portuguese composer. From 1574 or 1575 he attended the choir school of Évora Cathedral, and in 1588 entered the Carmelite Convent in Lisbon, where he became *mestre da capela* and sub-prior. He was held in high regard by both John IV of Portugal and Philip IV of Spain. His printed works include masses, *Magnificat* settings, and motets.

Within richly contrapuntal textures, displaying traditional skills of the kind valued by John IV, Cardoso exploited chromatic inflections to create highly charged music.   WT/OR

Cardus, Sir Neville [John Frederick] (*b* Rusholme, Manchester, 2 or 3 April 1888; *d* London, 28 Feb. 1975). English critic and writer. Largely self-educated, he wrote music criticism from 1913, and from 1920 wrote about both music and cricket for the *Manchester Guardian*. His writing avoided technicalities and is noted for its supreme ability to capture the essence of music in words. Mahler, Strauss, Delius, and Elgar were among his specialities. He was knighted in 1967.   ALa

carezzando, carezzevole (It.). 'Caressingly', 'soothingly'.

carillon. A chime of bells, normally in a tower, played either from a keyboard or mechanically by a barrel (like that of a *barrel organ, but larger) or similar device. The bells are not swung as in change-ringing but are struck by pulling their clappers or moving external hammers, with a simple mechanical action using trackers and wires, from the keyboard or barrel; this makes it possible to play tunes. Traditionally the keyboard, of well-spaced wooden batons laid out in the standard pattern, is struck with the fists to impart enough energy to the trackers to move the clappers, but modern instruments have been made using a smaller, finger-played keyboard powered with servo-motors.

The carillon developed from 16th- and 17th-century clock chimes. The technique of grinding the bells to bring overtones into tuneful and harmonic relationships was developed in the Low Countries in the mid-17th century by Jacob van Eyck, the Hemony brothers, and their colleagues. Belgium and the Netherlands retain the largest number of carillons, though many have been built in the USA, and some in Britain and elsewhere.

The largest carillons today have 70 or more bells, and a skilled carillonneur, using a manual and a pedalboard, can play transcriptions of keyboard sonatas and fugues, and the growing repertory of music specially composed in a style idiomatic to the carillon.   JMo

📖 A. LEHR, W. TRUYBEN, and G. HUYBENS, *The Art of the Carillon in the Low Countries* (Tielt, 1991) · K. and L. KELDERMANS, *Carillon: The Evolution of a Concert Instrument in North America* (Springfield, IL, 1996)

Carissimi, Giacomo (*b* Marini, nr Rome, *bapt.* 18 April 1605; *d* Rome, 12 Jan. 1674). Italian composer. He was one of the finest of the 17th century and of great importance in the history of the oratorio (see ORATORIO, 2). The youngest child of a cooper, he became a singer at Tivoli Cathedral in his late teens and was appointed organist there before 1627. In about 1628 he was *maestro di cappella* at Assisi Cathedral, but he left soon after to assume the same position at the Collegio Germanico in Rome. There he remained until his death, despite tempting offers from the imperial court at Vienna and St Mark's, Venice (as Monteverdi's successor). The Collegio Germanico was one of the main schools for training Jesuit priests to be sent to northern Europe, and Carissimi was thus in a position of considerable influence.

His reputation rests on his religious dialogues and oratorios, in which he adopted the operatic idiom of Monteverdi to the purpose of sacred drama. For the most part he set Latin texts, taking Old Testament stories and bringing the characters alive with remarkable vividness. The seascape in *Jonas* and the elegiac beauty of the sacrifice in *Jephte* are fine examples of his dramatic power, in which he uses not only the expressive aria and arioso developed by Monteverdi in his later operas, but also the sonorous madrigalian choruses favoured in Rome. He also composed masses and motets, some quite old-fashioned (as in his *Missa 'L'*Homme armé'*—probably the last work to be based on this 15th-century tune) and some in the more modern concertato style. The cantata was another favourite genre of Carissimi's: he wrote over 100, many of them for Queen Christina of Sweden, a convert to Roman Catholicism who set up a brilliant court in Rome and in 1656 made Carissimi her 'maestro di cappella del concerto di camera'.

Under his direction the music at the Collegio Germanico became sumptuous. For a time Carissimi's own music was banned from publication—apparently because it encouraged elaboration in liturgical music. Nevertheless, pupils flocked to him, the most distinguished being Charpentier, who introduced the religious dialogue and oratorio into France. Carissimi died of a stroke, his will indicating that he was a rich man.

DA/TC

📖 A. V. JONES, *The Motets of Carissimi* (Ann Arbor, MI, 1982) · G. DIXON, *Carissimi* (New York, 1986)

Carlton, Richard (*b* c.1558; *d* ?1638). English cleric and composer. A graduate of Cambridge University, he was vicar of St Stephen's church, Norwich, and a minor canon at Norwich Cathedral, where he took responsibility for the upkeep of the choristers. In 1601 he published a set of English madrigals and contributed one piece to Morley's anthology *The Triumphes of Oriana*.   JM

carmagnole. An 18th-century popular dance. A 'carmagnole' was originally a short coat worn by workers in Carmagnola in northern Italy, introduced into France in the 18th century. The name was subsequently given to a round dance which became identified with French Revolutionary festivities in the 1780s (including executions); these are described by Thomas Carlyle in *The French Revolution* (1837) and Charles Dickens in *A Tale of Two Cities* (1859). Honegger included the *carmagnole* in his *Danse des morts* (1938).   —/JH

Carmelites. See DIALOGUES DES CARMÉLITES.

Carmen. Opera in four acts by Bizet to a libretto by Henri Meilhac and Ludovic Halévy after Prosper Mérimée's novel (1845) (Paris, 1875).

carmen (Lat.). 'Song', 'poem'. The word was used during the Middle Ages and the Renaissance to refer to various kinds of vocal music; it has also been used in connection with instrumental music derived from vocal chansons. See also CARMINA BURANA.

Carmina burana (Lat., 'Songs of Beuron'). 1. The title given by J. A. Scheller to his edition (1847) of a 13th-century German manuscript containing over 200 Latin secular poems, found at the monastery of Benediktbeuren (where, however, it probably did not originate); it is now in the Bavarian State Library, Munich. Most are love poems (some obscene), some in French and German, and several are provided with music in neumatic notation.

2. Scenic cantata by Orff, for soprano, tenor, and baritone soloists, boys' choir, chorus, and organ, a setting of 24 Latin poems from the *Carmina burana* with optional mimed action (Frankfurt, 1937); it is the first part of his trilogy **Trionfi*.   AL

Carnaval ('Carnival'). Schumann's op. 9 (1833–5), for piano; it is subtitled 'Scènes mignonnes sur quatre notes' ('dainty scenes on four notes'), the notes being A–S–C–H (A–E♭–C–B). Asch was the home town of Ernestine von Fricken, with whom Schumann was in love, and its four letters were the only 'musical' letters of his own name. Each of the work's 21 pieces has a descriptive name (e.g. 'Papillons'—'Butterflies'). An orchestral version of *Carnaval* by Glazunov and others was used for a ballet by Mikhail Fokine performed in St Petersburg in 1910.

Carnaval des animaux, Le ('The Carnival of the Animals'). 'Grand zoological fantasy' by Saint-Saëns (1886), originally for two pianos, string quintet, flute, clarinet, glockenspiel, and xylophone, but also for two pianos and orchestra; it is in 14 movements, each representing a different animal, no. 13 being the famous *Le Cygne* ('The Swan'). Performance was forbidden in the composer's lifetime.

Carnaval romain, Le ('The Roman Carnival'). Overture, op. 9 (1844), by Berlioz; it uses material from his opera *Benvenuto Cellini*.

Carnival of the Animals, The. See CARNAVAL DES ANIMAUX, LE.

Carnival song (It.: *canto carnascialesco*, pl. *canti carnascialeschi*). A secular song performed in late 15th- and early 16th-century Florence as part of the festivals of Carnival (before Lent) and Calendimaggio (from 1 May). One of the most common types of Carnival song was the *mascherata: often setting comic or suggestive texts and satirizing notable local characters, mascheratas were performed by masked singers as they processed through the city's streets. More serious texts were set as *carri* and *trionfi*, performed by costumed singers on decorated carts.

Music survives in various Florentine manuscripts for about 70 Carnival songs. Their texts are mainly strophic with a refrain, and the musical settings are for three or four voices, generally chordal in style and setting each line of text to a distinct musical phrase. Instruments may have been added to swell the sound for outdoor performance. Whereas Lorenzo de' Medici (ruled 1469–92) supported the performance of Carnival songs and was the author of several texts, Savonarola banned the songs in favour of the sacred *lauda; after he was burnt at the stake in 1498 and the Medici returned to power, however, the secular songs flourished again.

—/EW

carol. A term generally associated with Christmas song but which has been used to denote various different genres.

In the Middle Ages the term 'carol' referred to a song in a particular musical form peculiar to England, though in the late Middle Ages carols were classified according to their various uses. Carol form begins with a refrain known as a 'burden', and is followed by verses (stanzas) of uniform structure; the burden is repeated after each verse. It seems likely that the alternation between burden and verse originally implied a responsorial performance, with chorus and soloist(s) in alternation. However, in later carols the method of performance is more difficult to interpret, for example in carols of the Fayrfax manuscript (late 15th–early 16th centuries) which sometimes had two burdens. The text could be in English, Latin, or a macaronic mixture of several languages. Not all songs in carol form had Christmas words (the *Agincourt Song celebrates the English victory over the French in 1415, for instance), but many had Mariological texts which would tend to associate them with Advent and Christmas, and others made more direct reference to

the Christmas season, so that eventually the term came to be applied to any Christmas song, whether or not in carol form.

It is most probable that the carol began as a monophonic dance-song (Fr.: *carole*), in both courtly and popular forms; few written monophonic examples have survived, though there is much indirect evidence for their existence. However, the medieval carol as recorded in surviving manuscripts is neither monophonic, nor popular in origin, though destined for popular consumption. It was not composed for the liturgy, but would appear sometimes to have been used liturgically, especially as a processional song. Although a few carol texts survive from 14th-century sources, the earliest extant musical settings date from the 15th century. From this time carols became polyphonic and gradually discarded any characteristics of dance. By the late 15th century the musical form was increasingly elaborate; not only could there be more than one burden, but successive verses might have different music.

After the Reformation, elaborate compositions retaining some of the formal characteristics of the pre-Reformation carol were still used in courtly and aristocratic circles (e.g. those by Byrd and Weelkes). The Puritans vigorously suppressed Christmas customs in the 17th century, and the 'high-status' carol was not revived at court after the Restoration.

However, the term 'carol' was also applied to Christmas 'folk' songs and occasionally to those of certain other festivals, for example May Day. Of these we know nothing until surviving written records first appear. Educated circles took no interest in the subject until the 19th century. Popular Christmas songs were published immediately after the Restoration, many of them in broadsheets, especially in the 18th and early 19th centuries. These so-called carols were not in medieval carol form, but were either folk *ballads or strophic hymns with Christmas words, though some had a refrain. The hymns tended stylistically to resemble the prevailing parish church music of any given time. Thus, in the 18th and early 19th centuries, the carols sung by the village quire at Christmas were often indistinguishable in style from the metrical psalms, *fuging tunes, and evangelical hymns they sang during the rest of the year; these are the carols of Thomas Hardy's Mellstock Quire.

In spite of the later suppression of this repertory, it has sporadically and independently survived to the present day, outside a church context, in some rural areas, especially Yorkshire and Cornwall. In the later 19th century, the *embourgeoisement* of the church led to the replacement of the old village quires with new church choirs, and to the development of the modern hymnbook, from which the carols of the later 19th century took their musical style; a few of these are still popular and remain in currently used hymnbooks. Christmas, having declined as a communal celebration, was 'reinvented' as a private, family celebration, which led to the publication of carol collections that could serve both for church choirs and for the domestic market of the new middle classes, for example Bramley and Stainer's *Christmas Carols, New & Old* (1871).

The carol collections of the 20th century were informed by the agenda of the composer-collectors of the 'folk music' movement, whose legacy is still influential at the beginning of the 21st. A landmark publication of this movement was *The Oxford Book of Carols* (1928, 25/1964), responsible for the popularization of many now well-known examples. It included medieval carols, folksongs, and new 'art' compositions (these last are particularly associated with the modern 'carol service', developed in cathedral and collegiate choirs and still a growth industry), as well as many Christmas songs from other countries, so that the term 'carol' became applied in an informal way also to the French **noël* and the German *Weihnachtslied*.

The repertories of both the Victorians and the 18th- and 19th-century village quires were rejected; admitted, however, were choral arrangements of ancient house-visiting **wassail* or *quête* songs (the *God rest you merry* tune-type, versions of which are found all over Europe), which might have been sung by the poor, and similar arrangements of originally monophonic folk ballads with Christmas words. The texts of the latter sometimes betray a Catholic theology suggestive, perhaps, of an origin among migrant labourers and beggars of Irish descent rather than of the survival of medieval English piety. The Christmas music of the 18th- and 19th-century village quire, and its surviving American descendants, were finally admitted to a mainstream publication with *The New Oxford Book of Carols* (1992), which also added some well-known Victorian carols that the 1928 edition had banished to hymnbooks.

PW

📖 J. STEVENS, 'Carols and court songs of the early Tudor period', *Proceedings of the Royal Musical Association*, 77 (1950–1), 51–62 · E. ROUTLEY, *The English Carol* (London, 1958) · D. BRICE, *The Folk Carol of England* (London, 1967) · C. IDLE, *Christmas Carols and their Stories* (Oxford, 1989)

carole (Fr.). A medieval French name for a round dance (see ROUND, 2).

Carpenter, John Alden (*b* Park Ridge, IL, 28 Feb. 1876; *d* Chicago, 26 April 1951). American composer. After studying with John Knowles Paine at Harvard he joined the family firm. His works include a charming Ravelian

orchestral suite, *Adventures in a Perambulator* (1914), two ballets coloured by jazz (*Krazy Kat*, 1921, and *Skyscrapers*, 1922–3), two symphonies, and the tone-poem *Sea Drift* (1933).   PG

Carreño, (Maria) Teresa (*b* Caracas, 22 Dec. 1853; *d* New York, 12 June 1917). Venezuelan pianist and composer. Her father, a leading politician and musician, arranged for his daughter to study with Louis Moreau Gottschalk in New York and Anton Rubinstein in Paris, where she spent much of her working life. The third of her four husbands was Eugen D'Albert. She wrote a string quartet, and quantities of piano music in a brilliant, virtuoso style.   CW

Carter, Elliott (Cook) (*b* New York, 11 Dec. 1908). American composer. While still at school he received encouragement from Charles Ives, and at Harvard, where his principal studies were literary, he had tuition from Walter Piston. All along he enjoyed frequent trips to Europe with his parents, who were lace importers, and he maintained close contacts with European musicians, especially in France, Italy, and Britain. He studied in Paris with Nadia Boulanger (1932–5) and returned to America a fluent neo-classicist. His early works, which include the ballet *Pocahontas* (1936–9) and the *Holiday Overture* (1944), show a post-Stravinsky style characteristic of American Boulanger pupils, but with a rhythmic life that is Carter's own. With the Piano Sonata (1945–6) there began a process of growth which continued in the Cello Sonata (1948) and reached fruition in the First String Quartet (1951).

In these works Carter progressively extended his harmonic range, introduced a new rhythmic fluidity by means of **metric modulation*, and began to create forms which are conversations of musical characters, these being defined by their harmonic nature. 'Movement' is redefined as a kind of musical motion unfolding throughout a work, rather than of tempo within a fixed span of time: a work might have two or more 'movements' in this sense proceeding simultaneously, or might, like the First Quartet, have pauses within rather than between movements. Movement—nearly always fast, energetic—and character became the hallmarks of his style.

During the next two decades and more Carter worked slowly, producing a major work every few years and confining himself to instrumental genres: the string quartet (no. 2, 1959; no. 3, 1971) and the orchestra (Variations, 1955; Double Concerto for piano, harpsichord, and two chamber orchestras, 1961; Piano Concerto, 1965; Concerto for Orchestra, 1969). In these works the neo-classical inheritance has been left far behind; the language is tough but elegant, complex but inviting because the musical ideas are so pregnant. The

Double Concerto was hailed by Stravinsky as an American masterpiece, and performances of this and other works began to be regular on both sides of the Atlantic.

Carter next made a surprising return to vocal music, in three works for soloists and chamber orchestra: *A Mirror on Which to Dwell* (1975), *Syringa* (1978), and *In Sleep, in Thunder* (1981), setting contemporary American poetry (by Elizabeth Bishop, John Ashbery, and Robert Lowell). At the same time he began to compose more abundantly. Big instrumental compositions continued to appear—including *A Symphony of Three Orchestras* (1976), *Night Fantasies* for piano (1980), Triple Duo for six players (1983), two more string quartets (1986 and 1994), concertos for oboe (1987), violin (1990), and clarinet (1996), and the *Symphonia* for orchestra (1994–7)—but so did smaller pieces for solo instrument or ensemble, many of them tributes or memorials, but done with a characteristic lightness and exhilaration: the middle section of the *Symphonia*, Adagio tenebroso, is one of the composer's rare slow movements. During this late period Carter's music became looser, its expressive balance shifted from energy towards humour, and as he approached 90 he wrote his first opera, the one-act comedy *What Next?* (Berlin, 1999).   PG

 📖 D. SCHIFF, *The Music of Elliott Carter* (London, 1983, 2/1998) · C. ROSEN, *The Musical Languages of Elliott Carter* (Washington, DC, 1984) · J. W. BERNARD (ed.), *Elliott Carter: Collected Essays and Lectures, 1937–1995* (Rochester, NY, 1997) · J. F. LINK, *Elliott Carter: A Guide to Research* (New York, 2000)

Caruso, Enrico (*b* Naples, 25 Feb. 1873; *d* Naples, 2 Aug. 1921). Italian tenor. He was one of the most celebrated dramatic singers in history. He sang in local churches, and his exceptional vocal potential was noticed by Guglielmo Vergine, who took him on as a pupil. In 1894 he made his debut in Naples in Morelli's *L'amico Francesco*, after which he appeared in small theatres, though with varying success. In 1897 he made his debut at Palermo in Ponchielli's *La Gioconda*. The following year he was acclaimed for his performance as Loris in the premiere of Giordano's *Fedora* in Milan.

This marked the start of Caruso's international career, which took him to Buenos Aires, Rome, Monte Carlo, London, and New York. He achieved his greatest fame at the Metropolitan Opera, New York, where he appeared every season from 1902 to 1920. In 1902 he made his historic set of ten aria recordings for the Gramophone Company in Milan (see RECORDING AND REPRODUCTION, 1); they were an unprecedented commercial success and the first to create an international demand for recording. It was the combination of extremely forceful projection and gentle lyricism that made him famous, as did his mastery of bel canto style and the imaginative detail he brought to nuances of music and word.   JT

 📖 M. SCOTT, *The Great Caruso* (New York, 1988) · E. CARUSO JR and A. FARKAS, *Enrico Caruso: My Father and my Family* (Portland, OR, 1991)

Carver, Robert (*b* c.1490; *d* after 1546). Scottish composer. He may have been a canon of Scone Abbey, near Perth. His music, which survives in a large choirbook now at the National Library of Scotland, includes the *Missa 'Dum sacrum mysterium'* for ten-part choir, which may have been written for the coronation of James V in 1513, and a huge 19-part motet, *O bone Jesu*. They reveal an ingenious if somewhat unsophisticated imagination.   JM

Casadesus, Robert (Marcel) (*b* Paris, 7 April 1899; *d* Paris, 19 Sept. 1972). French pianist and composer. His pianism was renowned for its clarity of touch and for his affinity with the works of Ravel. He was also a distinguished teacher at the American Conservatory at Fontainebleau. His solo career took him throughout the world, and he played in partnership with the violinist Zino Francescatti and in a piano duo with his wife Gaby (née Gabrielle L'Hôte; 1901–99). Much of his music remains unpublished; his piano and chamber works are often complex and dissonant, yet musically thoughtful. Several members of the Casadesus family were musicians, notably his uncles Francis (1870–1954), Henri (1879–1947), and Marius (1892–1981).   CF

 📖 S. STOOKES, *The Art of Robert Casadesus* (London, 1960) · C. TIMBRELL, *French Pianism: A Historical Perspective* (White Plains, NY, and London, 1992, enlarged 2/1999)

Casals, Pablo [Pau] (*b* Vendrell, 29 Dec. 1876; *d* Puerto Rico, 22 Oct. 1973). Catalan cellist, conductor, pianist, and composer. He studied in Barcelona and made his international debut in 1899. The greatest cellist of his generation, he focused in his programmes on Beethoven, Brahms, and the unaccompanied works of Bach, while also reviving the concertos of Haydn, Dvořák, and Lalo. He refined the use of portamento, shaped his phrasing with warmth and his tone with a singing style, and freed the arm in its control of the bow. Like his pianist friend Cortot, with whom he joined in 1905 to form a trio with the violinist Jacques Thibaud, Casals was also an able conductor, of orchestras in Barcelona and those at his own Prades and Puerto Rico Festivals.   CF

 📖 P. CASALS and A. E. KAHN, *Joys and Sorrows* (London, 1970) · R. BALDOCK, *Pablo Casals* (London, 1992) · H. GARZA, *Pablo Casals* (New York, 1993)

Casella, Alfredo (*b* Turin, 25 July 1883; *d* Rome, 5 March 1947). Italian composer. He was born into a musical home in which the playing of chamber music was commonplace. At the age of 12 he was sent to study at the Paris Conservatoire, where he was a pupil of Fauré. In 1902 he began his career as a pianist and conductor, living in Paris from 1912 to 1915. His works from this period show the expected influences of Debussy, Ravel, and early Stravinsky but also, more unusually, those of Mahler and Strauss; the sensuous *Notte di maggio* ('May Night') for voice and orchestra (1913) is a typical work of the time.

After World War I Casella was quick to take up Stravinsky's neo-classical approach. He composed divertimentos based on earlier music, *Scarlattiana* (1926) and *Paganiniana* (1942), and also a host of original works using older forms and manners, beginning with such works as the Concerto for string quartet (1923–4) and the Partita for piano and orchestra (1924–5). On occasions he used unusual combinations, as in the Symphony for piano, cello, clarinet, and trumpet (1932), but his intention was not so much to shock as to provide opportunities for his cool-headed craftsmanship. An objective tone prevails even in his stage works, of which the most ambitious is the fairy opera *La donna serpente* ('The Snake-Woman'; Rome, 1932).

While composing his large output Casella was also active as a teacher, concert organizer, and promoter of new music. He gave piano master classes at the Accademia di S. Cecilia in Rome (1932–47), and his work with the Corporazione delle Nuove Musiche, founded in 1924, had a lasting effect in acquainting Italian audiences with radical developments. His autobiography (1941) has been translated into English as *Music in my Time* (Norman, OK, 1955).   PG

Cashian, Philip (John) (*b* Manchester, 17 Jan. 1963). English composer. His studies with Oliver Knussen and Simon Bainbridge encouraged an approach to composition in which poetic images are projected through materials of strong character and forms of impressively sustained coherence. Although the images are often sombre (*Nightmaze* for orchestra, 1991, *Dark Inventions* for ensemble, 1992), Cashian can also compose ebullient and entertaining music, as in the Chamber Concerto for large ensemble (1995).   AW

Casken, John (Arthur) (*b* Barnsley, 15 July 1949). English composer. He studied at Birmingham University, and in Poland with Andrzej Dobrowolski and Lutosławski. Early works of the 1970s (*Music for the Crabbing Sun*, *Tableaux des trois âges*) revealed a refined and personal way with the favoured modernist techniques of the time, and two vocal works, *Ia orana, Gauguin* (1978) and *Firewhirl* (1980), displayed a special sensitivity to the colouristic and dramatic potential of texts; this was developed further in the opera *Golem* (Almeida, 1989), which won the first Britten Award. Casken's close association with the Northern Sinfonia while teaching at Durham University produced several works, including a passionately reflective Cello Concerto (1991). His second opera, *God's Liar*, had its premiere in London in 2001. In 1992 he was appointed professor of music at Manchester University.   AW

cassation (Ger.: *Kassation*; It.: *cassazione*). An 18th-century instrumental form, especially popular in Vienna and elsewhere in Austria. It is related to the *divertimento and *serenade, and consists of a variable series of movements for strings and wind in sonata or dance form, each shorter but more numerous than the corresponding movements of a symphony. Cassations were intended purely for entertainment and thus were light in character; unlike the serenade, their performances were not restricted to the evenings, though they were usually performed in the open air. There are examples by Dittersdorf, Haydn, and Mozart (K63, K99/63*a*).

cassette. A recording tape completely enclosed in a shell. Although in the late 1950s various manufacturers marketed recording systems that used such tapes, the Philips Compact Cassette system, introduced in 1963, became the *de facto* world standard, using narrow (3.8 mm) tape running at the low speed of 4.75 cm/second, anchored at each end to a pair of tiny spools. Mechanical improvements to cassette players and the use of Dolby B encoding meant that it became an acceptable medium for recording music, and a substantial catalogue of pre-recorded cassettes soon appeared. Blank cassettes customarily come in 30 ('C60'), 45 ('C90'), and 60 ('C120') minutes per side, and are widely used for personal recording. The development by Sony of the 'Walkman' resulted in a substantial range of portable machines normally used with headphones.

See also RECORDING AND REPRODUCTION.   LF

castanets. Small *clappers consisting of pairs of shallow cup-shaped pieces of wood, each with a hollow carved in the struck faces as resonance chambers. They are normally played as a pair in each hand, each pair being strung together with a cord looped over the thumb or middle finger; the shells are struck together by the fingers. Usually the pairs differ slightly in pitch, the 'female' sounding higher than the 'male'. Orchestral and children's castanets are tied on a handle, with a wooden plate between the two shells. Castanets are associated most strongly with Spain but are also used in southern Italy and were known in ancient Egypt.

                    JMo

Castelnuovo-Tedesco, Mario (*b* Florence, 3 April 1895; *d* Los Angeles, 17 March 1968). Italian composer. He studied composition with Pizzetti at the Cherubini Institute in Florence (1913–18) and quickly showed his talent for sensitive word-setting in, for example, the song cycle *Coplas* (1915). This was followed by settings of all of Shakespeare's songs in the original English (1921–5). The melodic breadth that Castelnuovo-Tedesco developed in his songs is also a feature of his orchestral works, which include a popular Guitar Concerto (1939), while his feeling for his native city is evident in the opera *La mandragola* ('The Mandrake Root', 1920–3; Venice, 1926), after Machiavelli's comedy. In 1939 Castelnuovo-Tedesco emigrated to the USA, where he taught at the Los Angeles Conservatory and composed much film music. The voluminous output of his American years includes two Shakespeare operas and several large-scale choral works, such as the Sacred Service (1943) and the oratorio *Saul* (1960), based on Jewish chant. PG

Castiglioni, Niccolò (*b* Milan, 17 July 1932; *d* Milan, 7 Sept. 1997). Italian composer. He studied composition with Giorgio Ghedini at the Milan Conservatory, with Boris Blacher at the Salzburg Mozarteum, and from 1958 at the Darmstadt summer courses. An early and unfashionable interest in late Romanticism (*Aprèslude* for orchestra, 1959) led, through a strong identification with Boulez (*Aleph* for oboe, 1964), to a music of very precise artifices, typically of elaborate structures working themselves out in the high treble and of wilfully heterogeneous doublings. PG

Castor et Pollux. Opera in a prologue and five acts by Rameau to a libretto by Pierre-Joseph Bernard (Paris, 1737); Rameau revised it, without the prologue and with a new first act (Paris, 1754).

castrato (It.). A male singer who kept the soprano or alto range of his voice into adulthood as a result of having been castrated before puberty, usually between the ages of six and eight. The practice of preserving boys' voices by this means originated in Italy and Spain in the 16th century. Castratos were present in the Sistine Chapel choir by 1565, and continued to sing in the choir, in the face of growing moral opposition, until the late 19th century. The last surviving castrato from the Sistine choir was Alessandro Moreschi (1858–1922). Castratos reached the summit of their popularity in 18th-century *opera seria*, when such singers as Senesino (for whom Handel wrote many leading roles), Nicolini, and Farinelli were feted like present-day pop stars. The operatic castrato survived into the age of Rossini, whose *Il crociato in Egitto* (1824) was the last major opera to contain a castrato role. Castratos were famed for their brilliant, penetrating timbre and their extraordinary breath control, facilitated by the combination of the small larynx and the larger than normal chest.

See also SINGING. RW

Catalani, Alfredo (*b* Lucca, 19 June 1854; *d* Milan, 7 Aug. 1893). Italian composer. After early studies in Lucca he completed his education at the Paris and Milan conservatories, graduating from the latter with a one-act opera, *La falce* (1875), to a libretto by Arrigo Boito. He composed various operas and orchestral works during the 1880s, notably *Dejanice* (1883), as well as being closely involved in the latter stages of Italy's bohemian movement, known as the *scapigliatura*. Dogged by ill health, he was nevertheless appointed composition professor at the Milan Conservatory in 1888. His most famous opera, *La Wally*, was successfully performed at La Scala, Milan, in 1892 and retains a tenuous hold on the repertory even today, its anticipations of verismo and prominent harmonic influence of Wagner proving that Catalani was an important representative of the Italian *fin de siècle*. RP

catalogue, thematic. See THEMATIC CATALOGUE.

Catalogue Aria. Nickname for Leporello's aria in Act I scene 2 of Mozart's *Don Giovanni* in which he recounts to Donna Elvira a list of Don Giovanni's amorous conquests in various countries, ending each instalment with the words 'but in Spain, a thousand and three' (*mille e tre*); it was probably modelled on a similar aria in Gazzaniga's *Don Giovanni*, the rapid singing of a list of items being a popular feature of 18th-century comic opera. AL

Catalogue d'oiseaux ('Catalogue of Birds'). Piano work (1956–8) by Messiaen; each of the 13 pieces includes the notated song of a different bird.

catch. A variety of English *round, with the additional feature that the words are so treated as to introduce some point of humour (often a pun). The origin of the term is unknown; it was first applied to music in a manuscript collection of rounds of 1580. A typical example is *Ah, how, Sophia, can you leave your lover?* by J. W. Callcott (1766–1821), which in singing suggests 'Our house afire'; later in the song 'Go fetch the Indian's borrowed plume, yet richer far than that you bloom' suggests 'Go fetch the engines . . .'. Another well-known catch by the same composer exploits the appearance in the same year (1776) of both Hawkins's and Burney's histories of music, the words 'Have you Sir John Hawkins' History? Some folks think it's quite a mystery' being followed by 'Burney's history I like best', with the effect that as the voices are singing together one comes in with 'Sir John Hawkins' and another with 'burn 'is history'.

Catches were popular between the late 16th century and the 19th and were usually performed by three or more men. Many written in the Restoration period set indecent, not to say obscene, texts. Several by Purcell, in particular, are especially bawdy. In the 18th century societies were founded for the singing of catches, the best known being the Noblemen's and Gentlemen's Catch Club in London (established 1761).

See also GLEE.   PS/AL

catechumens, Mass of the. See MASS, 1.

Cathédrale engloutie, La ('The Submerged Cathedral'). Piano piece (1910) by Debussy, no. 10 of his *Préludes*, book 1; it is based on the legend of the Cathedral of Ys with its tolling bells and chanting under the sea. Debussy quoted from it in his Cello Sonata (1915).

cathedral music. The musical repertory and traditions associated with English choirs of men and boys. Of the many choral foundations established to perform sacred polyphony before the English Reformation, approximately 40 survived in Anglican cathedrals (some of which had previously been monastic churches), colleges, and chapels. Their maintenance of daily services over the centuries resulted in the composition of a rich repertory of music for choir and organ, especially canticles, responses, and anthems for Matins and Evensong. Spread to parish churches by the Oxford Movement during the 19th century, cathedral music underwent a major revival throughout the 20th century.   ALi

Cato, Diomedes (*b* Venice, before 1560–5; *d* after 1607 or 1618). Italian lutenist and composer. He composed a great deal of music, mainly for his instrument. He is always referred to as a Venetian but spent most of his life in Poland. One of his fantasias was published as far abroad as London in Robert Dowland's *Varietie of Lute-Lessons* (1610).   DA

Catoire [Katuar], Georgy Lvovich (*b* Moscow, 27 April 1861; *d* Moscow, 21 May 1926). Russian composer and theorist of French descent. While studying mathematics at the universities of Moscow and Berlin, he also took private piano lessons from Karl Klindworth (1830–1916), from whom he inherited his Wagnerian sympathies. He later studied with Lyadov and Rimsky-Korsakov in St Petersburg. His first compositions won the approval of Tchaikovsky in 1886; together with Wagner, Tchaikovsky became a major influence on his music, though Catoire was most accomplished in the field of chamber music. He is best remembered as a

professor at the Moscow Conservatory (from 1917) who contributed significantly to the development of Russian music theory through his books on harmony and musical form.   MF-W

Cat's Fugue. Nickname of the keyboard sonata in G minor K30 by Domenico Scarlatti, so called because the fugue subject consists of wide, irregular leaps, as though created by a cat padding over the keyboard.

Catulli carmina ('Songs of Catullus'). Scenic cantata by Orff for soloists, chorus, four pianos, four timpani, and up to 12 percussionists, a setting of 12 Latin poems by Catullus, with opening and closing Latin choruses by Orff (Leipzig, 1943); it is the second part of his trilogy *Trionfi*.

Cavaillé-Coll, Aristide (*b* Montpellier, 4 Feb. 1811; *d* Paris, 13 Oct. 1899). French organ builder. From a family of organ builders, he studied in Paris and was joined there by his father and brother. They built over 500 organs, including those at Notre Dame, Ste Clotilde, and the Madeleine. By making technical improvements to the controls and introducing many new stops, they created the quintessential French Romantic organ, capable of subtle expressiveness and great volume, which profoundly influenced the school of French organ composers from Franck to Messiaen.   AL

 F. DOUGLASS, *Cavaillé-Coll and the Musicians: A Documented Account of his First Thirty Years in Organ Building* (Raleigh, NC, 1980) · C. NOISETTE DE CRAUZAT, *Cavaillé-Coll* (Paris, 1984)

Cavalieri, Emilio de' (*b* Rome, *c*.1550; *d* Rome, 11 March 1602). Italian composer. Of noble birth, he was involved with the Roman Oratorio del Crocifisso in his early years. He met Cardinal Ferdinando de' Medici when the latter was resident in Rome, and, after the cardinal became Grand Duke of Tuscany in 1587, Cavalieri moved to Florence the next year as superintendent of the court artists and musicians. There he organized, and wrote some of the music for, a series of spectacular entertainments, including the grand *intermedi* for the marriage of Ferdinando to Christine of Lorraine in 1589; the final 'Ballo del Granduca' became famous both as a new kind of sung and danced entertainment and as a popular tune. In the 1590s, he provided the music for a number of pastoral entertainments in Florence (now lost), and later he claimed precedence for the invention of the recitative style.

Of his surviving works, the best-known is the *Rappresentatione di Anima, et di Corpo*, given at the Oratory in Rome in April 1600. It is often described as the first *oratorio*, but was performed in the manner of an opera, albeit with a spiritual theme and an allegorical plot. Much of its music is in the 'speech-song' of the *stile rappresentativo* (as the title has it, 'per recitar cantando'), but there are also madrigalian, strophic, and dance-like songs and simple, effective choruses. Another remarkable work is a setting of the Lamentations for Holy Week (*c.*1599) for one to five voices and continuo.   DA/TC

Cavalleria rusticana ('Rustic Chivalry'). Opera in one act by Mascagni to a libretto by Giovanni Targioni-Tozzetti and Guido Menasci after Giovanni Verga's play (1884), based on his story (1880) (Rome, 1890).

Cavalli [Caletti], (Pietro) **Francesco** (*b* Crema, 14 Feb. 1602; *d* Venice, 14 Jan. 1676). Italian composer. He was the son of Giovanni Battista Caletti, *maestro di cappella* at Crema Cathedral, and his early musical promise earned him the patronage of Federico Cavalli, the governor of Crema, whose name Francesco adopted in the 1630s as a mark of respect and gratitude. He entered the choir of St Mark's, Venice, as a soprano in 1616 and soon became well known as a singer; in 1620 he also became organist at SS Giovanni e Paolo, remaining in the post until 1630 when he married a wealthy widow, Maria Sozomeno. His first published work, the solo motet *Cantate Domino*, appeared in 1625; it seems reasonable to assume that many of the compositions printed in a grand retrospective volume of his church music in 1656 date from these early years. They show the influence of Monteverdi, but are melodious and pleasant rather than powerfully emotional, and contain little to suggest Cavalli's future fame.

This came suddenly after the opening of the first Venetian opera houses in 1637. Cavalli's *Le nozze di Teti e di Peleo* ('The Marriage of Thetis and Peleus', performed at the Teatro S. Cassiano in January 1639) was the first of many operas produced over the next 20 years. Most were given first in Venice, where at one time he had a contract with the Teatro S. Apollinare for 400 ducats an opera (the annual salary of the *maestro di cappella* at St Mark's). Several works went on to be staged abroad, notably *Egisto* (1643), which was given in Paris and perhaps also in Vienna. Cavalli's popularity must be attributed to his combination of a good dramatic sense (again showing the influence of Monteverdi) with the gift of writing memorable arias. These are usually short, often working out a motif or rhythmic figure, and he was a master of the lament over an ostinato bass (there is a particularly fine example with a chromatic bass in *Egisto*); at the same time his recitatives are rarely perfunctory, and they express the emotions of the individual phrase or word.

At the height of his fame, in 1660, Cavalli was invited to compose an opera for the wedding of Louis XIV and Maria Theresa of Spain. However, the theatre was nowhere near ready on his arrival in Paris and the production suffered innumerable delays and political intrigues. When *Ercole amante* ('Hercules in Love') was finally given in 1662 it was not a great success, Lully's ballets winning most acclaim. Cavalli returned to Venice later that year; although he had vowed never to produce another dramatic work, he composed several operas on quasi-historical themes which look forward to the late Baroque style.

Cavalli had been appointed second organist at St Mark's in 1639 and became first organist in 1665; three years later he was *maestro di cappella*. Although his fame was won in the theatre, he composed a great deal of music for St Mark's. His motets for a small number of voices with organ accompaniment are notable for their delicate word-painting, while the *Messa concertata* (in *Musiche sacre*, Venice, 1656) mixes the double-choir style traditional in Venice with melodious duets and trios. He published another volume of church music in 1675, and then a Requiem which he intended to be sung twice yearly after his death. He died the following year, leaving a large part of his substantial estate to the church of S. Lorenzo, where he was buried.

DA/TC

📖 J. GLOVER, *Cavalli* (London, 1978) · E. ROSAND, *Opera in Seventeenth-Century Venice: The Creation of a Genre* (Berkeley and Los Angeles, 1991)

cavaquinho. A small Portuguese four-string *guitar, also called *machête*, carried worldwide by early explorers and traders. It is ancestral to the South American *charango* and to the *ukulele.   JMo

cavata (It., 'epigram'). In musical usage, a short *arioso at the end of a passage of recitative. There are several examples in Bach's cantatas.

cavatina (It., dim. of *cavata*). In 18th- and 19th-century opera, a short solo song, simple in style and lacking the *da capo*, often consisting of a short instrumental introduction to a single sentence or statement set to music. Examples are the Countess's 'Porgi amor' and, in more elaborately developed form, Figaro's 'Se vuol ballare', both from Mozart's *Le nozze di Figaro*. Later examples include Agathe's 'Und ob die Wolke' (*Der Freischütz*), Norma's 'Casta diva', and Faust's 'Salut! demeure'. Verdi wrote many such numbers up to Leonora's 'Tacea la notte' (*Il trovatore*), after which he abandoned the description; in 19th-century Italian opera the music often demanded quite elaborate virtuosity on the part of the singer. The term is sometimes applied to a songlike air included as part of a long scena or accompanied recitative, or to a songlike piece of music, e.g. the fifth movement of Beethoven's op. 130 String Quartet and Raff's *Cavatina*.   JW

Cavazzoni, Marco Antonio [da Bologna] (*b* Bologna, *c*.1490; *d* Venice, *c*.1560). Italian organist and composer. His career was spent in Urbino, Rome, Padua, and Venice. A volume of his music published in 1523 contains the earliest known keyboard ricercars; unlike later works of this kind, they contain a mixture of chordal, imitative, and improvisatory elements.

His son, **Girolamo Cavazzoni** [da Bologna] (*b c*.1525; *d* Venice, after 1577), had two volumes of music published in Venice in the 1540s. They include some ricercars in a fully imitative style which was to lead to the monothematic ricercar, and ultimately to the fugue.

JM

Cave, The. Work by Reich for two solo sopranos, solo tenor, percussion, keyboards, string quartet, woodwind, and videotape; a 'documentary drama' lasting a whole evening in performance, it mixes fragments of interviews with Israelis, Palestinians, and Americans with purely musical material (Vienna, 1993).

Cavendish, Michael (*b c*.1565; *d* London, ?5 July 1628). English gentleman-composer, related to the Cavendishes of Chatsworth and Hardwick, and later a courtier to Prince Charles, son of James I. His secular works, a mixture of madrigals and lute-accompanied ayres, were published in 1598 in a volume dedicated to his second cousin, Lady Arabella Stuart. One of the madrigals, *Come, gentle swains*, was subsequently rewritten for inclusion in Morley's tribute to Elizabeth I, *The Triumphes of Oriana* (1601).

JM

Cavos, Catterino Al'bertovich (*b* Venice, 19/30 Oct. 1775; *d* St Petersburg, 28 April/10 May 1840). Italian-born Russian composer and conductor. He studied with Francesco Bianchi and made his debut in 1797 when his Patriotic Hymn was performed at La Fenice, Venice. In 1799 he moved to St Petersburg to take up an administrative post for the Imperial Theatres; he became director of the Russian Opera in 1806 and from 1832 was also director of music at the imperial court (see RUSSIA, 3). He wrote over 50 stage works including operas, vaudevilles, and ballets. His most celebrated piece was the patriotic opera *Ivan Susanin* (1815; staged 1822), which held its place in the repertory even after the appearance of Glinka's opera on the same plot, *A Life for the Tsar*, conducted by Cavos at its premiere in 1836.

JWAL

Cazzati, Maurizio (*b* Lucera, nr. Guastalla, *c*.1620; *d* Mantua, 1677). Italian composer. After being ordained priest, he was in charge of the music for various organizations, including the Accademia della Morte at Ferrara, S. Maria Maggiore in Bergamo, and S. Petronio, the largest church in Bologna. There he was largely responsible for increasing the scale of music for festivals, using huge choirs and orchestras. His large output includes much attractive instrumental music, consisting mainly of dances and sonatas: it was Cazzati who initiated the S. Petronio repertory of sonatas with a trumpet part, of which there are three in his op. 35 (Bologna, 1665). He was also the first Bolognese composer to publish solo violin sonatas (op. 55, Bologna, 1670). His church music is solemn rather than deeply felt, but none the less worthy of revival. After a professional argument over 'errors' in his counterpoint he left S. Petronio and spent his last years as *maestro di cappella* to the Duchess of Mantua.

DA

cb. (It.). Abbreviation for *contrabasso* ('double bass') or *col basso* ('with the bass').

C clef. See CLEF.

CD. See COMPACT DISC.

c.d. (It.). Abbreviation for **colla destra*.

CD-ROM. A type of *compact disc (developed from the technology of the CD) that may be installed on a computer in order to interact, as a primary resource, with multimedia information; the initials ROM stand for 'read-only memory'. In an educational context the CD-ROM medium allows musical extracts to be easily linked together as either a score or a performance (or both), accompanied by an explanatory narrative as printed text or speech.

PM

cebell [cibell]. A type of gavotte, found mainly in late 17th-century English harpsichord music. The name comes from an *air* in gavotte style from Lully's opera *Atys* (1676) that accompanies the descent to earth of one of the main characters, the goddess Cybele. This *air* became very popular and subsequently found its way into printed collections, appearing in England under the title 'Cebell' or 'Cibell' in keyboard pieces by such composers as Purcell and Jeremiah Clarke. The first English example of the cebell, however, is a lute piece, *My Mistress*, which was published in Mace's *Musick's Monument* in the same year as Lully's opera.

Cecilia. Saint of the early Christian Church, venerated as a martyr from the 5th century and honoured as patron saint of music from the 15th. A long poem published at Florence in her honour in 1594 does not mention her musicianship, though by this time she sometimes appeared in Italian paintings with harp, organ, and other musical instruments: it was probably the painters who were responsible for dissemination of the belief that St Cecilia was a musician. She even came to be spoken of as the inventor of the organ. Her reputation as patron of music grew in the 16th century and she was portrayed by leading artists (including Raphael, Rubens, and Poussin) and celebrated by poets.

The first known music festival in honour of St Cecilia was at Évreux, in Normandy, in 1570. It was a 'puy de musique', and part of the celebration took the form of a competition in composition; among those who won prizes in 1575 was Lassus, with the motet *Cantantibus organis*.

The date when British celebrations of St Cecilia's Day (22 November) began is not known. The first of which record exists was in London in 1683, but they had already been held annually for some time. From that year the programme comprised a church service followed by an entertainment, an important part of which was an ode, written and composed for the occasion. Purcell composed two such odes (1683, 1692), and his *Te Deum and Jubilate* in D were written for the celebration of 1694. Dryden was the poet in 1687 and 1697. Odes were subsequently written by Thomas Shadwell, William Congreve, D'Urfey, Alexander Pope, and others, and composers included John Eccles, Jeremiah Clarke, Handel, Boyce, Samuel Wesley, and Hubert Parry.

These London celebrations became merely occasional until 1905, when a revival took place under the auspices of the ancient Musicians' Company. The Musicians' Benevolent Fund now organizes a concert each St Cecilia's Day.

In the late 17th century and the 18th, the musicians of several English cities (Wells, Oxford, Salisbury, Winchester, Devizes) held celebrations of St Cecilia's Day. From 1726 Dublin did so too, as had Edinburgh since 1695, when what appears to be the first public concert in that city was given. The St Cecilia Hall in Edinburgh was built in 1762. Musical celebrations have also taken place annually in many European cities, notably Paris, where from the mid-19th century a new mass was composed for the occasions.

Many musical societies, from the early 16th century onwards, have adopted the name of St Cecilia. Palestrina founded one in Rome: in 1847 Pius IX turned it into an academy for the furtherance of church music and it still exists. In 1867 a 'Cecilia Society for German-speaking Countries' was founded; three years later it received papal patronage (see CECILIAN MOVEMENT).

PS/AL

Cecilian Movement. A 19th-century movement for the reform of Roman Catholic church music; its roots lay in the late 18th century. It sought the integration of music and liturgy, and to this end promoted the *a cappella* polyphony and Gregorian chant of the age of Palestrina, together with new polyphonic compositions in-

spired by this model, and opposed music for solo voice accompanied by orchestra, which had become commonplace following an edict in 1749 of Pope Benedict XIV. The movement was successful in developing church choirs and congregational singing, and was also influential on the church music of other denominations.

There were many influences towards the development of Cecilian philosophy from the early 18th century onwards: the 'Caecilien-Bündnisse' in Vienna and Passau, which kept *a cappella* singing alive, contemporary theological and theoretical writings, editions of Renaissance polyphony, the incorporation of Gregorian chant into compositions; discussions of Gregorian chant paved the way for the abandonment of modernized 'Baroque' chant, culminating in the 'Mechlin' edition and, later, the Regensburg Edition, both based on the *Editio medicaea* of the chant (1614), prepared by Palestrina and his pupils. This preference of the Cecilians was eventually overridden, however, since under Pope Pius X the Solesmes monks' 'medieval' *Editio vaticana* replaced all previous arrangements of the Gregorian melodies; at the same time, their espousal of *a cappella* polyphony as the ideal liturgical music was for a time vindicated.

The beliefs of the Cecilians had little effect in practice until the second half of the 19th century. Results came first through the efforts of Guéranger in France, and Geissel, Diepenbrock, and Sailer in Germany, and gained ground after F. X. Witt (1834–88) founded the Allgemeiner Deutscher Cäcilien-Verein in 1869, given official approval by the Holy See in 1870; thereafter, similar organizations sprang up in other European countries and in the USA. In spite of changes of emphasis after the Second Vatican Council (1962–5), the intellectual principles of the movement have held firm.   PW

cédez (Fr.). 'Yield', i.e. slow down; *cédant*, 'slowing down'.

celere (It.). 'Quickly', 'swiftly'; *celeramente*, 'with speed'.

celesta (Fr.: *céleste*). A keyboard instrument resembling a small upright piano. Its steel bars, each resting on felt supports over an individual wooden resonator box, are struck with small piano hammers, thus making a much gentler sound than that of the *glockenspiel. Unlike that instrument it has a damper pedal. The celesta was invented in Paris in the 1880s by Victor Mustel. After hearing it there Tchaikovsky wrote its best-known orchestral part, in the 'Dance of the Sugar Plum Fairy' in the ballet *Nutcracker*. Many other composers have scored it since, including Bartók in his *Music for Strings,*

Percussion, and Celesta. The range is five octaves from *c*, and parts are written an octave lower than sounding pitch. A predecessor, patented by Mustel in 1865, was the *typophone*, with tuning-forks instead of steel bars. A later instrument of this type was Thomas Machell of Edinburgh's 'dulcitone' of 1880.   JMo

céleste (Fr.). A soft pedal on some pianos, similar to the moderator or practice pedal, that slips a cloth between the hammers and the strings.

Cellier, Alfred (*b* London, 1 Dec. 1844; *d* London, 28 Dec. 1891). English organist, conductor, and composer. After an early career in church music, and a brief period as director of the Belfast Philharmonic Society, he turned his attention to the theatre as both composer and conductor. Appointments in Manchester (Prince's Theatre, 1871–5) and London (the Opera Comique, Criterion, and St James's) culminated in a long association with the Savoy Theatre and Richard D'Oyly Carte, not least as his representative in the USA and Australia. Cellier was closely linked with Sullivan: he conducted many of the Savoy operas, including *HMS Pinafore* and *Iolanthe* (in the USA), composed the overture for *The Sorcerer*, and helped the composer with the score of *The Pirates of Penzance*, as well as presiding over the first performance of *Ivanhoe* (1891).

Cellier wrote numerous comic operas, vaudevilles, one grand opera, *The Masque of Pandora* (Boston, 1881), and a few instrumental works. His comic opera *Dorothy* (1886) was a huge triumph, outstripping all the Savoy operas with 931 performances. *Doris* (1889) was less successful, and Cellier did not live to see the result of his collaboration with W. S. Gilbert, *The Mountebanks* (1892).   PGA/JDI

cello. See VIOLONCELLO.

Celtic Requiem. Work (1969) by Tavener for soprano, children's chorus, chorus, and orchestra, to a text compiled from the Requiem Mass, poems by Henry Vaughan, Cardinal Newman, and Blathmac, and children's singing-games.

cembalo (It.). 'Harpsichord'.

Cendrillon ('Cinderella'). Opera in four acts by Massenet to a libretto by Henri Cain after Charles Perrault's fairy tale (Paris, 1899). Isouard (1810) and Rossini (*La Cenerentola*, 1817) wrote operas on the same subject.

Cenerentola, La (*La Cenerentola, ossia La bontà in trionfo*; 'Cinderella, or Goodness Triumphant'). Opera in two acts by Rossini to a libretto by Jacopo Ferretti after Charles Perrault's *Cendrillon* and librettos by Charles-Guillaume Étienne for Isouard's *Cendrillon*

(1810) and Francesco Fiorini's for Stefano Pavesi's *Agatina, o La virtù premiata* (1814) (Rome, 1817).

cent. A unit of scientific method for measuring musical intervals. It was introduced by A. J. Ellis (1804–90) and adopted in acoustics and ethnomusicology. One cent is equal to 0.01 of a semitone.

centonization. Composing by patchwork (Lat.: *cento*), using pre-existent material. The term *cento* has been used in literature since classical times to describe a poem built of received matter, particularly from Homer and Virgil. It was imported to the study of music by Paolo Ferretti (1934) to explain the recurrence of certain melodic shapes in different Gregorian chants. While his views are no longer favoured, the term proves useful for studies of Byzantine and other Eastern chant traditions.   DF

Central Park in the Dark (in the Good Old Summertime) (A Contemplation of Nothing Serious). Work (*c*.1909) for chamber orchestra by Ives; it is the second of *Two Contemplations*, the other being *The Unanswered Question*.

Ce qu'on entend sur la montagne ('What one Hears on the Mountain'; *Bergsymphonie*, 'Mountain Symphony'). Symphonic poem by Liszt after Victor Hugo's *Feuilles d'automne*, orchestrated by Raff in 1848–9 and revised in 1850, later revised again by Liszt in 1854.

cercar la nota (It., 'look for the note'). In vocal technique, a slight anticipation of the following note.

Ceremony of Carols, A. Settings of carols, op. 28 (1942), by Britten, for treble voices and harp, in 11 movements; Julius Harrison arranged it for mixed chorus and harp or piano.

Cererols, Joan (*b* Martorell, nr Barcelona, 9 Sept. 1618; *d* Montserrat, 28 Aug. 1676). Spanish singer, instrumentalist, and composer. He was educated in the school at Montserrat, and became a monk there after 1636. For 30 years he was a celebrated teacher at the monastery, as well as being a fine violinist and organist. He composed much sacred music including a 'battle' mass and some interesting villancicos.   WT

Cerha, Friedrich (*b* Vienna, 17 Feb. 1926). Austrian composer. He studied at the Vienna Academy of Music with Joseph Polnauer, a pupil of Schoenberg, while simultaneously taking a degree in philosophy and German literature at Vienna University. He became a lecturer at the Vienna Academy in 1959 and professor ten years later. In 1958, with the composer Kurt Schwertsik, he founded the chamber ensemble Die Reihe, largely to promote the music of the Second Viennese School. His early instrumental music focuses on the experimental expansion of sonority, though from the early 1960s he embarked on a series of abstract musico-dramatic works, such as *Spiegel* (Graz, 1972) and *Netzwerk* (Vienna, 1981), cyclic collections of pieces for instrumentalists, singers, and actors.

A turning-point in Cerha's career came in 1962, when he was asked by Universal Edition to prepare a performing edition of the incomplete final act of Berg's *Lulu* (the 1949 Vienna premiere of the two-act version had been one of his formative experiences). The completion of *Lulu*, first performed in Paris in 1979, was undertaken without the knowledge of Helene Berg, the composer's widow, and was subsequently opposed by the Berg Foundation, though it is now widely accepted as the definitive performing version. Berg's influence on Cerha's own music is apparent in his first opera, *Baal* (Salzburg, 1981), based on the play by Bertolt Brecht. His second opera *Der Rattenfänger* ('The Rat-Catcher') was first performed in Graz in 1987.   TA

   📖 H. LANDESMANN (ed.), *Projekt Friedrich Cerha* (Salzburg, 1996)

Černohorský [Czernohorsky], **Bohuslav Matěj** (*b* Nymburk, ? 16 Feb. 1684; *d* Graz, Feb. 1742). Bohemian composer and organist. He became a Franciscan in 1704, then studied in Italy, also serving as cathedral organist in Assisi (1710–15) and Padua (1715–20). In 1720 he returned to Prague, later working in Horažd'ovice (1727–30) and, again, Assisi (1732–41). Much of his music was destroyed in a fire at St Jakub's church in Prague in 1754, but his surviving choral works (the ten published organ works are of doubtful attribution) show a distinctive mastery of counterpoint and a synthesis of Italian and German elements.   JSM

Certon, Pierre (*d* Paris, 23 Feb. 1572). French composer. He was a clerk at Notre Dame, Paris, in 1529, and from 1532 he belonged to the Sainte Chapelle, where in 1536 he became Master of the Choristers. He was a celebrated chanson composer, his 285 pieces having great influence on the development of the genre. One of the earliest Catholic composers to write psalm tunes, which were arranged for solo voice and lute, he also wrote masses and motets.   DA

Ces (Ger.). The note C♭; *Ceses*, the note C♭♭.

Cesti, Antonio [Pietro] (*b* Arezzo, *bapt.* 5 Aug. 1623; *d* Florence, 14 Oct. 1669). Italian composer. He was a choirboy at Arezzo and in 1637 became a member of the Franciscan order at Volterra, where after a period of study in Florence he was appointed first organist, then *maestro di cappella* at the cathedral. He was ordained as a priest, but this does not seem to have prevented him from travelling round Italy as an opera singer during the next few years. He entered the service of the Archduke Ferdinand Karl in Innsbruck in 1652 and remained technically a member of that court for many years, even though for about three years from 1659 he was a singer in the papal chapel, apparently drawing two stipends. His early operas such as *Alessandro vincitor di se stesso* (1651), *L'Argia* (1655), and *Orontea* (probably 1656) established his reputation as one of the best-known composers for the theatre. He spent his last years at the imperial court in Vienna, where his *Il pomo d'oro* ('The Golden Apple') was given a sumptuous production (requiring 24 stage sets) in 1668. Later that year he moved to Florence as *maestro di cappella* at the court, where he died ('poisoned by his rivals' according to one report).

Cesti's success as an opera composer was due partly to his ability to write attractive arias, which made it possible to produce his operas in countries where Italian was not the native tongue, and partly to his mastery of comic elements, which previously had made only a small contribution. His melodic gift was also used to good effect in his 61 cantatas.   DA

Chabrier, (Alexis-)**Emmanuel** (*b* Ambert, Puy-de-Dôme, 18 Jan. 1841; *d* Paris, 13 Sept. 1894). French composer. The son of a barrister, he studied the piano with two Spanish musicians who had settled in his native town. In 1856 his parents moved to Paris, and he became a civil servant there, with no thought of becoming a professional musician. His circle of friends included many of the Impressionist painters, of whose works he built up a fine collection, as well as such literary figures as Villiers de l'Isle Adam, Catulle Mendès, and Verlaine, with whom he collaborated on two operettas in 1864. Among his musical acquaintances was Duparc, who persuaded him to go to Munich to hear *Tristan* in 1879. The experience affected Chabrier so much that he resigned his post in the civil service (not too great a hardship, since he had a private income) in order to compose. Although he had been writing songs and piano music since his teens, he first made his mark in 1881 with the ten *Pièces pittoresques*, which Franck felt to signal a return to the spirit of Couperin and Rameau. Wider success came with the orchestral rhapsody *España*, composed after a visit to Spain in 1882, which remains his best-known work.

In 1886 his opera *Gwendoline* received its premiere in Brussels, followed by performances throughout Germany. Although Chabrier admitted in his letters that he was finding it hard to keep clear of Wagner's influence, *Gwendoline* is a good deal less Wagnerian than has often been supposed; certainly the modal, asymmetrical, loosely articulated theme of the overture is individual to a degree. Some of his best music went into the comic opera *Le Roi malgré lui* (Opéra-Comique, 1887), but unfortunately the work is saddled with one of the most complex and incomprehensible librettos of all time. His final opera, *Briséis*, another serious work, was left unfinished at his death, though the complete first act is available on CD. His last years were clouded by syphilis, which eventually paralysed him. But he lived to attend the triumphant premiere of *Gwendoline* at the Opéra in 1893.

Although he was one of the 'modern' French Wagnerians, Chabrier's gifts lay not in profound, philosophic music but in the genial, dynamic pieces which echoed his own sympathetic character. Having avoided the conventional musical education of the conservatoire, he was able to bypass the normal paths of French music of the 1860s, and to explore a new harmonic idiom and especially a novel way of writing for the piano. A delightful description by Alfred Bremner of 'Chabrier, in a drawing-room full of elegant women, advancing towards the fragile instrument and then playing his *España* in a blaze of broken strings, hammers reduced to pulp and splintered keys' gives some idea of his opposition to French salon politeness, and helps to explain why he was admired by d'Indy, Debussy, Ravel, Satie, Stravinsky, and Poulenc, who wrote a short biography of him (1961).   DA/RN

📖 R. MYERS, *Emmanuel Chabrier and his Circle* (London, 1969) · F. ROBERT, *Emmanuel Chabrier: L'Homme et son oeuvre* (Paris, 1970) · D. PISTONE, 'Emmanuel Chabrier, opera composer', *Opera Quarterly*, 12/3 (1996), 17–25

chace (Fr.). A type of French 14th-century canon, usually for two or three voices; see CACCIA.

chaconne (Fr.; It.: *ciaccona*; Sp.: *chacona*) [chacony]. A form of continuous variation, similar to the *passacaglia, which became popular during the Baroque era; in the 20th century the term was sometimes used to denote an instrumental piece of a particularly austere character using ground-bass variations.

The chaconne originated in Latin America in the late 16th century as a lively dance in triple metre which had both instrumental and vocal accompaniment. The name derives from the appearance of the word *chacona* (of uncertain meaning) in the refrain. Although no music for the Latin American type survives, it is most likely that the refrain was constructed on one of a series of typical harmonic patterns. During the early 17th century the chaconne appeared in Spain and Italy, where it became popular as both a dance and an instrumental form.

The first notated examples were Italian guitar tablatures that present only a series of harmonic schemes (e.g. I–V–VI–V; I–VI–IV–V; I–V–V–V) over which variations were composed. These works were soon followed by fully notated pieces, almost always in triple metre and displaying a dance-like character, for violin, voice, chitarrone, or keyboard. Some Italian composers used the same melody throughout the piece, repeating it continually in the manner of a *ground bass; others repeated the same melody but moved it into other parts as well as the bass; still others used a series of different melodies. Italian composers who wrote vocal or instrumental *ciaccone* include Monteverdi (*Zefiro torna* from *Scherzi musicali*, 1632), Corelli (Sonata op. 2 no. 12, 1685), and Frescobaldi, who was among the first to associate the *ciaccona* closely with the passacaglia (e.g. in *Cento partite sopra passacaglia*, 1637).

The chaconne also became popular in France and, towards the middle of the 17th century, in Germany and England. In France, the dance became slower and more stately, as did the *sarabande on its removal to France from Spain. There are many chaconnes for harpsichord by Chambonnières, the Couperins, and others, and orchestral chaconnes occur frequently in the stage works of Lully, Rameau, and Campra. The French chaconne was often in rondeau form with the repeated chaconne melodies being restricted to the refrain sections (this was true also of the passacaglia).

In Germany the chaconne flourished particularly in the later 17th century and in the first half of the 18th. Several chaconnes were written for solo organ (e.g. by Buxtehude and Pachelbel): these were often highly contrapuntal and used newly composed bass patterns. Bach wrote a Chaconne in D to close his second Partita for solo violin. The form was less popular in England, though there are some fine examples of 'chacony': Purcell wrote one in G minor for string consort and another for two violins, bass viol, and continuo (no. 6 in the posthumous *Ten Sonata's in Four Parts*), and chaconnes also appear in his semi-operas *Dioclesian* (1690) and *King Arthur* (1691).

The chaconne fell from favour in the Classical period but appeared occasionally in the late 19th century and during the 20th. Brahms's finale to his Fourth Symphony was composed in deliberate imitation of the Baroque chaconne, but has some features more typical of the passacaglia. 20th-century examples include the last movement of Britten's Second String Quartet ('Chacony') and Busoni's *Toccata: Preludio, Fantasia, Ciacona*.   —/JBE

📖 R. HUDSON, *Passacaglio and Ciaccona: From Guitar Music to Italian Keyboard Variations in the 17th Century* (Ann Arbor, MI, 1981); *The Folia, the Saraband, the Passacaglia, and the Chaconne*, Musicological Studies and Documents, 35 (Rome, 1982) · A. SILBIGER, 'Passacaglia and ciaccona: Genre pairing and ambiguity from Frescobaldi to Couperin', *Journal of Seventeenth-Century Music*, 2/1 (1996)

chacony. Old English term for *chaconne.

Chadwick, George (Whitefield) (*b* Lowell, MA, 13 Nov. 1854; *d* Boston, 4 April 1931). American composer and teacher. After starting a career in business he went, at the age of 23, to Germany to study music. He returned to Boston in 1880, joined the faculty of the New England Conservatory two years later, and stayed there as director from 1897 until his death. His works, in the highly traditional, German-influenced New England style, include three symphonies, five quartets, and choral pieces.   PG

Chailley, Jacques (*b* Paris, 10 March 1910; *d* Montpellier, 21 Jan. 1999). French musicologist and composer. He took lessons from Nadia Boulanger (1925–7) and studied composition at the Paris Conservatoire with Busser (1933–5) and, privately, with Delvincourt; his conducting teachers were Mengelberg and Walter in Amsterdam (1935–6) and Monteux (1936–7). He also studied musicology (1930–6). He taught at the Sorbonne from 1952, and later at the Conservatoire and the university. In 1969 he became the founder and first director of the department of music and musicology at the Sorbonne (now Paris IV), retiring in 1979 to begin composing again.

Chailley wrote not only technical, analytical papers but also books and articles for the general musical public, on a wide range of composers. His *Traité historique d'analyse musicale* (1951) contains many novel theoretical insights. Chailley's own music is in a style that owes something to Duruflé, Ravel, and Honegger, with a flavouring of Fauré and Françaix. His earliest works are informed with elements of Gregorian chant and French folk music; modality, a fairly constant feature, brings a timeless quality to many of his scores, which include two symphonies (1942–47, 1980), two operas, *Pan et la Syrinx* (1946) and *Thyl de Flandre* (1949–54), a ballet, *La Dame à la licorne* ('The Lady with the Unicorn', 1953), and smaller-scale instrumental works. His religious conviction was given voice in many choral works, some on a large scale, such as the *Missa solemnis* (1947), the *Messe française* (1976), and the oratorio *Casa Dei* (1991).   MA

chains. Heavy iron chains shaken or dropped into a bucket or on to a metal plate on the floor. Schoenberg used them in *Gurrelieder* at the climax of the 'Wild Hunt', and Litolff for the fall of the guillotine in his overture *Maximilian Robespierre*. Varèse, Havergal Brian, and other composers have also scored them.   JMo

chair organ (Ger.: *Rückpositiv*). An organ chest secondary to the *Great organ, with its own separate case and keyboard. It is placed behind the organist's chair, and is often referred to by its German name (meaning

'back positive'). This form was common in the 15th and 16th centuries; later both chests were more often placed within a single case, the secondary department becoming known in England as the choir organ and in Germany as the *Brustwerk*.   JMo

chaleur (Fr.). 'Warmth', 'passion'; *chaleureux*, *chaleureusement*, 'with warmth'.

Chaliapin [Shalyapin], **Fyodor** (Ivanovich) (*b* nr Kazan, 1/13 Feb. 1873; *d* Paris, 12 April 1938). Russian bass. He was born into poverty and initially taught himself how to sing; he began his career in 1891 in a small provincial opera company in Ufa. His first formal training was in 1892, when he took lessons for a year in Tbilisi with Dmitry Usatov, who had sung at the Bol'shoy Opera. In Tbilisi he became a member of the opera company, and this led to an appointment with the Imperial Opera in St Petersburg (1894–6). It was during his time in Savva Mamontov's private company in Moscow (1896–9) that he consolidated his innovatory style and became famous for his dramatic intensity, imagination, and subtlety as a singer-actor unprecedented on the opera stage. He became internationally in demand, especially in Italy, London, New York, and Paris. He sang in four of Diaghilev's Ballets Russes seasons in Paris (1908–13), gave frequent recitals, and appeared in two films. Of his wide repertory he was inextricably associated with the roles of Boris Godunov in Musorgsky's opera, Philip II in *Don Carlos*, and Méphistophélès in Gounod's *Faust*. His vocal and theatrical style exerted a lasting influence on generations of basses.   JT

📖 V. BOROVSKY, *Chaliapin: A Critical Biography* (New York, 1988)

chalumeau (Fr., from Latin *calamus*, 'reed'). 1. A single-reed wind instrument with a tied-on reed (rather larger than that of the clarinet), seven fingerholes and a thumbhole, and two keys. Also known as the mock trumpet, it seems to have been invented in about 1700 by J. C. Denner of Nuremberg, who later also developed the clarinet, with which the chalumeau coexisted for some time.

2. The chanter of a *bagpipe.

chamber music (*see page 224*)

chamber opera. An opera written for small forces, especially instrumental ones. Economical to stage, it also has the advantage of being suited to small theatres. Strauss's *Ariadne auf Naxos*, in its original version of 1912, is one of the first examples of the genre, which subsequently proved particularly appealing to 20th-century composers. It encapsulates a number of key features of the nascent form, not least its reduced forces—a band of 36 players, in contrast to the massive

(*cont. on p. 230*)

chamber music

Chamber music is music written for a small ensemble, either for private (domestic) performance or, if in the presence of an audience, for a relatively small hall. This definition excludes solo music, for an essential ingredient of chamber music is the pleasure of playing together. It also excludes music for virtuoso display in the large concert hall, even though only a few instruments may be involved. The term is sometimes defined as music in which there is only one player to each part, thus in contrast to orchestral music, but this is not entirely adequate, since such a piece as Richard Strauss's *Metamorphosen* for 23 solo strings is certainly not chamber music in the conventional sense. The usual combinations are those for from two to ten instruments, which may include the piano, all stringed instruments, woodwind, and, occasionally, brass instruments. Much of the repertory was written to give pleasure to amateurs, and still does so, but some works are more intimate expressions of emotion which the composer could not put into orchestral terms. There is also a considerable repertory of music for voices which fulfils these basic criteria, but since vocal genres developed in different ways because of their dependence on words, the reader is referred to the article on song.

Early forms

It was in fact with vocal music that chamber music in one sense began, in the days of the later Renaissance when, to quote from Baldassare Castiglione's *Il libro del cortegiano* ('The Book of the Courtier', 1528), a gentleman was expected to have 'understanding and cunning upon the book, have skill in like manner on sundry instruments' (i.e. to be able to sight-read and to play several instruments). No doubt not every gentleman could, but there is a great deal of evidence to show that music was considered an important social accomplishment, and that many men learnt music seriously and enjoyed playing or singing in ensembles. Women, too, participated in music-making in private

chambers. Outside the courts, domestic music began to flourish in the homes of the wealthy classes, aided in particular by the wider dissemination of music that followed the advent of music printing.

The first music to cater for the growing numbers of amateur musicians was the polyphonic *chanson, written in a style that did not make great demands on musical experience (difficult rhythms and phrases needing large breath capacity were avoided). These were often performed by a mixture of voices and instruments (so that those unable to sing but wishing to take part could do so) or by instruments alone (a practice that led to the rise of the *canzona, one of the most popular forms of instrumental music until well into the 17th century). A similar function was fulfilled by the Italian *madrigal (though not all madrigals were chamber music), known throughout Europe, but the greater emphasis placed on madrigal texts meant that purely instrumental performance of madrigals was probably much rarer. In fact the most sophisticated instrumental music came to be written in the country where the madrigal arrived late: England.

In England, consorts of viols were in existence early in the 16th century and were provided with a fine repertory, made up partly of dance music and partly of *fantasias and *In nomine settings. Most English composers contributed, especially Byrd and Gibbons, both masters of the fantasia. This tradition survived longer in England than anywhere else, viol playing remaining popular throughout the Commonwealth until the 1680s, and Purcell, Jenkins, and William Lawes wrote some superb fantasias in a style entirely different from that of the Continent.

The Baroque era

In the early 17th century the genres and styles of chamber music began to change radically. The pragmatic mixing of instruments and voices in the madrigal fell away, to be replaced by specifically vocal and instrumental genres, of which the *cantata and duet (for voices), and the solo *sonata and *trio sonata (for instruments), are the best known. At the courts, this repertory was often performed by specially employed chamber musicians—a necessity in the case of some of the new music, which presented considerable technical challenges. The violin, lacking frets and demanding a larger tone than the viol, was not easily mastered by amateurs, and such virtuoso violinists as Marini, Buonamente, and Farina (the last, significantly, called 'suonatore di violino da camera') were in demand by European princes. In wealthy middle-class circles, private music-making continued to expand as a socially desirable leisure pursuit, with some publishers and composers often showing themselves sharply aware of the domestic market. At the same time, gender distinctions crystallized: the violin family was typically the province of men, whereas plucked strings and keyboards were dominated by women, who also sang.

Sonatas at this time were usually written for one or two violins, these combinations (and their vocal equivalents) being possible only because the harmonies could be provided by the continuo part, normally played in these works by a cello or bass viol with harpsichord, organ, or lute. Thus a solo sonata could be performed by three players (melody instrumentalist with two continuo players), and a duet sonata by four (though this latter type is mainly called a 'trio sonata', with two violins and continuo). The trio sonata was one of the most favoured genres of the period until about 1750, with all the major continental composers contributing appealing works. They include Purcell, Legrenzi, Vitali, and especially Corelli, whose op. 1 trio sonatas (1681) set the fashion and were widely emulated, particularly in England. Corelli and others labelled their sonatas according to function, some *da chiesa*, for use in church as voluntaries or interludes, and others (usually including dance movements) *da camera*, literally 'for the chamber'; however, in practice such distinctions were often meaningless.

In Italy the most popular instruments were strings. By contrast, the Germans, notably Telemann, liked using wind instruments as well as strings, so that a trio sonata might well be for flute or oboe, violin, and continuo, or for two flutes and continuo; or it might even allow players to make their own choice about which instruments to use, thus limiting the style of figuration to what was possible on virtually any melody instrument. Even in France, where there was considerable opposition to Italian music, the trio sonata eventually came into fashion. Couperin's *Le Parnasse, ou L'Apothéose de Corelli* (1724) attempted a union of the national styles, and his *Concerts royaux* (1722), like Rameau's *Pieces de clavecin en concerts* (1741), exploited the expert playing of the bass viol still available in France, through the unusual combination of harpsichord, violin, and obbligato bass viol.

But in general, French composers (e.g. Hotteterre and Leclair) and many of the Germans who imitated them tended towards the *galant* style, in which florid melody forced the harmonic instruments into a very subsidiary role—the cello parts especially being rather dull, however attractive the result may be for the listener. Easy elegance is the hallmark of much of the period *c.*1725–60, though in Berlin the ultimate conservative Frederick the Great still enjoyed Bach's music (as well as the extensive output of the *galant* Quantz), and thus experienced the equality of part-writing that is the stuff of genuine chamber music. Bach's trio sonata and the old-fashioned but magnificent ricercars included in the *Musical Offering*, as well as his solo sonatas for flute and for violin, are notable examples of such repertory.

The Classical period

In the later 18th century the market for domestic music-making continued to expand, though chamber music, with the attendant costs of instruments and lessons, was considered a luxury, beyond many people's purses. A body of such works as instrumental duets and arrangements of theatrical tunes for small ensembles was tailored to amateur musicians of limited abilities. Alongside this developed what is now considered the mainstream Classical chamber repertory of quartets, quintets, and trios; much of it was produced in or near Vienna (though London and Paris were also important centres, certainly for publication), and it was directed at connoisseur players and listeners.

Two related phenomena, the disappearance of the basso continuo and the rise of the piano, shaped the nature of chamber music of the later 18th century. Although both the trio sonata and the harpsichord lingered for some time (Haydn, Gluck, and Mozart all wrote in the old manner, and harpsichords continued to be played), the increasing popularity of the piano meant that the nature of keyboard accompaniment had to change, since the crisp chordal patterns for the harpsichord did not come off well on the newer instrument, and it was clearly a waste not to exploit the expressive and brilliant character for which the piano had been developed. As early as the 1760s a new type of chamber music came into being. This was, in effect, a keyboard piece to which were added one or more subsidiary parts for strings. This arrangement was reflected in such titles as Schobert's *Sonates pour le clavecin avec accompagnement d'un violon et basse.*

The relationship between the bass instrument and the left hand of the keyboard part in such pieces was often not very different from that in the old basso continuo era; and frequently the violin part was not completely independent of the right hand (though a skilful composer would produce a certain amount of interesting counterpoint to relieve typical accompanying figurations). This is not only the nature of early piano trios by Haydn, Mozart, and (to a lesser extent) Beethoven; most of Mozart's violin sonatas are also conceived in this way. It was not until later, for instance in Mozart's sonata K454 for the famous violinist Regina Strinasacchi (1784), and in Haydn's piano trios of the 1790s, presumably for performers in Vienna and London, that the independence of the stringed instruments was asserted; and even in Beethoven's sonatas for violin and, especially, those for cello, where the piano occasionally has a cadenza while the cello is subordinated, the relics of the old 'accompaniment' sonata still appear. Finally, by the time of Beethoven's middle-period works (*c.*1802–1814), there is absolute equality of the instruments: such pieces as the 'Kreutzer' Sonata were written for professionals to play at concerts rather than as works to be published in sets for the dilettante.

Music without keyboard raised other problems. Lacking the in-filling keyboard of the continuo ensemble, the old trio-sonata texture of two equal melody instruments and bass was difficult to make convincing, though there were a few attempts. The seemingly natural substitute of violin, viola, and cello (known today as a 'string trio') proved almost as unsatisfactory, and—in spite of Mozart's celebrated Divertimento in E♭ K563, a number of works by Boccherini, and an interesting set of three by Beethoven (op. 9)—was little cultivated.

The string quartet had the advantage of retaining the two violins and cello of the trio sonata while adding the viola. The earliest works to use this combination were really divertimentos (and some symphonies), but composers soon realized the potential of working with four instruments of similar tone-colour and great expressiveness, and the repertory burgeoned. Some composers, for instance Boccherini and the young Haydn, made the individual parts suitable for amateurs of limited abilities, but by about 1770 Haydn was composing more intricate works that needed at least a leader with advanced technical skills. What is more, when four competent players were envisaged, composers could exploit such contrapuntal textures as fugue (as found in works by F. X. Richter, Mozart, and Haydn himself in his op. 20). Thereafter the quartet became for Haydn a genre in which to express his most intimate thoughts, confident that his Viennese audiences would be able to follow him. From his op. 33 quartets (1781) all the instrumentalists are treated as equally competent (unless he was writing for a particularly brilliant player such as Johann Tost, the dedicatee of opp. 54 and 55).

Mozart is known to have played the viola in quartets with Haydn (alongside Vanhal and Dittersdorf), and he admired the older man's work so much that he wrote a set of six quartets between 1782 and 1785 and dedicated them to him. They use most of the devices of Haydn's mature style (the G major K387, for example, has a fugal finale), but add a touch of drama—as in the famous 'Dissonance' Quartet K465, with its passionate and strange slow introduction. These quartets, with Haydn's later works written after Mozart's death, are in a style in which thematic development achieves the height of subtlety, and are widely considered some of the glories of chamber music.

It was probably the sophistication of the medium that attracted Beethoven to the quartet. His first quartets, op. 18, published as a set of six according to 18th-century practice, do little technically that Haydn did not, but expand both the scale and the emotional potential. For example, where Haydn had speeded up the minuet to what he called a scherzo, Beethoven seized on the possibility for aggressive, un-dancelike accentuation; and the quartet is persuaded to give a more ample sound by means of strong unison passages and an increased use of extreme registers. After about 1800, when he was occupied with orchestral and solo music, Beethoven returned to chamber music only intermittently; but on each occasion he increased its scope. The three 'Razumovsky' Quartets op. 59 (dedicated to the Russian ambassador to Vienna) are on a grand scale, employing quasi-orchestral sonorities and rhetorical gestures that address the concert hall rather than the drawing-room, and demand expert playing.

Beethoven's last quartets used to be described as attempting to take the medium beyond its real capacity. Technically, they make extreme demands on all four performers. As compositions they are complex, pushing previous concepts to their ultimate (the 'Grosse Fuge' op. 133 is the *ne plus ultra* of the tradition of fugal finales begun in the 1760s). Emotionally, they express the most intimate feelings, as in the 'Hymn of Thanksgiving to the Divinity, from a Convalescent, in the Lydian mode' ('Heiliger Dankgesang', the third movement of op. 132). This was the 'music of the future'—incomprehensible to many contemporary players and audiences—and it is significant that Beethoven chose chamber music to express his innermost thoughts.

No other combination was as popular as the quartet. The quintet of strings, with either a second cello as favoured by Boccherini or a second viola as preferred by Mozart, was much less common. The advantage of Boccherini's combination is the release of one cello to play melodies independent of the bass, which the composer exploited for charming *galant* touches. Mozart's preference gives a chiaroscuro effect that is heard at its best in his passionate and tragic G minor Quintet (K516). Larger combinations were occasionally met with, and works including wind instruments were common. Those for wind sextet or octet are really for outdoor performance (see CASSATION; DIVERTIMENTO; SERENADE), but there are a number of captivating pieces that mix wind and strings or piano. Mozart's oboe quartet, quintets with horn, and clarinet quintet, each written for a particular soloist, tend to stress the concertante element in the relationship, whereas the two fine quintets for piano and wind by Mozart and Beethoven put the emphasis on the piano part, in the tradition described above.

The Romantic period

The work of the great Viennese Classical composers has been described in some detail because it has long been considered the highpoint of the repertory. In the Romantic period, which followed, forms dependent on the union of words and music came into view and, in a sense, song now became the real chamber music, for the German lied composers evolved a true and intimate partnership between singer and pianist. A large part of the instrumental repertory (much of it the 19th-century quartets, piano trios, etc., known today) was written with professional players and the newly emerging concert setting in mind, and incorporated extrovert idioms and thick textures that emphasized the repertory's arrival in the public arena.

Concerts given over to chamber music became ever more part of the musical calendar in many European cities (though there were as yet no permanent professional ensembles to speak of). With their audiences usually characterized as comprising devotees, the events themselves quickly took on associations of high seriousness. Meanwhile, music for the home centred on the piano, which was now the quintessential domestic instrument, badge of female gentility and social respectability. Piano solos, duets, and accompanied songs were the mainstays, joined by novelties for concertinas and harmoniums, and, later on, the pianola.

As the century progressed, the repertory in the concert hall became increasingly fixed on the Viennese Classics and on the later music that emulated them, with modern works added only gradually. New pieces were certainly being written, but many composers faced challenges in merging the chamber music ideal with the musical language of Romanticism. From the 1820s, chamber music was largely the intermittent preoccupation of the more conservative German composers and their foreign disciples.

Schubert's three mature quartets (in A minor, D minor, and G major) are clearly indebted to Beethoven. The first movements are on a symphonic scale, using a greater range of keys than was usual in Classical quartets, and sometimes achieving sonorities that are orchestral rather than intimate. His interest in lyrical melody and beauty of sound are most clearly displayed in the String Quintet in C, where the addition of a second cello to play the bass line frees the first cello to play long-breathed melodies, while the whole ensemble creates a peculiarly rich sound.

Brahms found difficulty in composing in the quartet idiom, destroying a number of works before eventually publishing his op. 51. His earliest extant chamber music for strings comprises the two sextets: in these the additional instruments give a full sound, which he achieved eventually in the quartets composed in middle life. His two late quintets, one with an additional viola, the other with clarinet used in the concertante manner of Mozart's Clarinet Quintet, though exploiting the instrument's mellow qualities rather than brilliant sounds, are often considered his finest chamber works. Among other staples of the German repertory are

Mendelssohn's op. 44 and op. 80, which display a mastery of counterpoint and delicate textures, and Wolf's witty *Italienische Serenade*, one of the few 'characteristic pieces' for quartet.

Works using unusual combinations, such as Beethoven's Septet (for violin, viola, clarinet, bassoon, horn, cello, and double bass); Schubert's Octet (for string quartet, double bass, clarinet, horn, and bassoon); Hummel's Septet (for piano, flute, oboe, horn, violin, cello, and double bass); Spohr's Nonet (for violin, viola, cello, double bass, flute, oboe, clarinet, horn, and bassoon) and 'double quartets' (two string quartets playing antiphonally); and Mendelssohn's Octet (for strings) gained popularity in some concert programmes. These colourful ensembles allowed pleasantly lyrical themes to be displayed with different sonorities, sometimes poured into the mould of sonata form, but often lacking truly rigorous development.

In spite of the textural freedom in Beethoven's mature chamber music with keyboard, the pianist continued to dominate in the works of Mendelssohn, whose well-known Trio in D minor gives the string players material essentially designed for the piano; while in Schumann's Piano Quintet the strings could almost be omitted without loss of musical content. Only later did a non-virtuoso pianist, Dvořák, exploit the distinctive colour of the piano's upper octaves, supporting it by the strings rather than by its own lower register, and lending a novel sound to his Piano Quartet and Quintet.

A more congenial use of piano and strings for the Romantics was possible in the violin sonata, where the singing quality of the violin could be matched by the newly developed sustaining potential of the piano. Schumann wrote two sonatas using some excellent effects, while Brahms's three sonatas combine lyrical melody with the sonata principle in masterly fashion. The nationalists, with folksongs as part of their idiom, also found the genre to their liking, Grieg and Dvořák (an exquisite Sonatina) contributing to the repertory.

Although there was a movement in Italy in the 1860s and 70s to form 'quartet societies' to play the Classical repertory, chamber music was overshadowed there by operatic traditions and considered a foreign form of art, especially by Verdi who, in spite of some acid but Germanic inhibitions, composed a single quartet of great charm. In 19th-century Hungary, Bohemia, Poland, and Russia, chamber-music composition was limited. Dvořák's contributions to the quartet

and quintet repertory—very much in the German tradition—have already been mentioned, though Smetana achieved more personal expression in his First String Quartet, 'From My Life', in which the high E at the end of the final movement is an agonizing representation of the onset of his deafness.

In Russia there was no creative tradition of chamber music for much of the century. As late as 1880 the critic César Cui remarked that 'Russian composers began to cultivate chamber music only recently; Glinka, Dargomïzhsky, and Serov have written nothing in this genre, save a few youthful attempts, very imperfect and by no means worthy of attention'. Dargomïzhsky had been concerned primarily with vocal writing, Serov with opera, and even Glinka's *Gran sestetto originale* and *Trio pathétique* pale in comparison with his orchestral music and stage works. Nor had the 18th century produced much of more than academic interest, the ensemble music of Bortnyansky, for instance, being notable more for its rarity than for any artistic merit or originality in the instrumental writing. Tchaikovsky's and Borodin's quartets, composed in the 1870s and 80s, were the first Russian quartets to secure a place in the repertory; in the 1890s Taneyev began to exploit his contrapuntal skills in his own group of quartets.

Music for ensembles other than the quartet seemed to fare even less well in Russia. Rimsky-Korsakov acknowledged that his Quintet for piano and wind, attractive as it is, did not represent him at his most characteristic, though the piano did feature more prominently (and with more idiomatic writing than Rimsky could muster) in a number of important Russian works, notably in Nikolay Rubinstein's Piano Trio, Tchaikovsky's Piano Trio (written in memory of Rubinstein), and Rakhmaninov's second *Trio élégiaque* (written in memory of Tchaikovsky). Aleksandr Gol'denveyzer extended the chain by writing a trio in memory of Rakhmaninov, and the genre was later chosen as a vehicle for mourning by Shostakovich, whose Piano Trio op. 67 was dedicated to the memory of his friend Ivan Sollertinsky.

In France a substantial flowering of chamber music came after the Franco-Prussian War of 1870. The Société Nationale de Musique was founded in 1871 to encourage works from young French composers. The results included Saint-Saëns's Septet for trumpet, strings, and piano, and works by Fauré, whose chamber output embraces two violin sonatas and two piano quartets, distinctly lyrical in melody with elegant piano writing. Franck was more influenced by the Lisztian methods of thematic transformation, as he shows in his Piano Quintet, while his Violin Sonata (also arranged for cello and for flute) is one of the most interesting and satisfying for both players. A group of composers sprang up, all writing good chamber music: Chausson, Lekeu, Florent Schmitt, and Debussy, whose early String Quartet (1893) was strongly influenced by Franck.   DA/CBA

The 20th century

The growth in size and importance of the orchestra during the late Romantic period left little room for chamber music, and it is noteworthy that Mahler and Richard Strauss, for example, contributed almost nothing of importance to the genre. Yet at the same time the turn of the century saw the beginnings of a revival, for several reasons. In the first place, chamber music had come to seem the apt repository for a composer's deepest musical thoughts: this was a view implicit in the late works of Beethoven and Brahms, endorsed by Reger, and vigorously propounded by Schoenberg in his creative work and his teaching. Secondly, composers came to chamber music as a disciplined, economical medium when, after World War I, there was a reaction against late Romantic self-indulgence. And thirdly, the rise of permanent professional quartets—many of which gained international reputations—stimulated new contributions to their medium, though at the expense of the amateur musician: Hindemith and some others wrote works expressly for home use, but in general 20th-century chamber music was a field for the virtuoso ensemble. For instance, the Kolisch Quartet in the 1920s and 30s were able to give the first performances of works by Schoenberg (Third and Fourth Quartets), Bartók (Fifth and Sixth Quartets), Berg (*Lyric Suite*), and Webern (String Quartet op. 28)—all pieces that very few amateurs could contemplate performing.

At about the same time, the innovations of sound recording and broadcasting took chamber music back into the domestic environment, to a potentially wider audience than ever before, and many enthusiasts got to know a broad chamber repertory, through listening, in the home. Chamber music continued to be played in private throughout the century for social and intellectual pleasure by a small section of society, but only the most highly skilled (e.g. conservatory-trained players) could attempt most 20th-century works.

Part of the reason for the difficulty of this repertory lay in the new resources it demanded—*sul ponticello*, harmonics, various kinds of pizzicato—all of which were freely used by Schoenberg and his pupils in their quartets of about 1910 (see especially Webern's tiny Bagatelles, 1913) and developed by Bartók. But there were also other features introduced by these composers that removed their quartets from the sphere of amateur competence: the stamina and concentration required of all four players in the immense single movement that is Schoenberg's First Quartet (1901); the problems of intonation in atonal works for strings; the dense, strenuous writing of Berg's String Quartet op. 3 (1910); the exposed lines of Webern's quartets; the use of a soprano soloist for the last two movements of Schoenberg's Second Quartet (1907–8); or the difficulties of ensemble in the irregular rhythms of Bartók's quartets. The string quartets of these four composers, and particularly those of Bartók, have thus become cornerstones of the professional repertory, while remaining beyond most amateurs.

Although Bartók's six are the outstanding quartet cycle of the 20th century, Shostakovich's 15 also command attention for their variety of design and their expressive power. Among other composers who contributed notably to the genre are Britten with three quartets, Carter also with three, Babbitt with four, Tippett with five, Ives, Janáček, and Szymanowski with two, and Sibelius, Ravel, Fauré, Elgar, and Boulez each with one. Important works in other standard chamber forms include two piano quintets by Fauré, one each by Elgar and Shostakovich, single piano trios by Ives and Ravel, and string trios by Schoenberg and Webern.

In contrast, especially since the coming of neo-classicism in the 1920s, there was a great deal of interest on the one hand in the duo sonata and on the other in chamber ensembles of heterogeneous constitution. Debussy, following a common pattern in concentrating on chamber music late in his career, heralded both trends, for his set of sonatas (1915–17) was created in conscious imitation of the Baroque while also including a work for the unusual trio of flute, viola, and harp. Few later composers touched by neo-classicism failed to produce a fair quantity of duo sonatas, though few equalled the record of Hindemith, whose large output of chamber music includes sonatas for most of the orchestral instruments with piano, not omitting the cor anglais or the double bass. Other composers whose works entered the repertory include Poulenc (sonatas for flute, oboe, and clarinet), Prokofiev (two violin sonatas, of which the second is also available for flute), Ravel (sonatas for violin with cello and with piano), Ives (four violin sonatas), and Kodály (cello sonata).

Perhaps the first notable work for a mixed ensemble was Schoenberg's *Pierrot lunaire* for reciter with flute (doubling piccolo), clarinet (doubling bass clarinet), violin (doubling viola), cello, and piano (1912). It was a precedent Schoenberg himself followed in such later works as his Serenade (1920–3) and his Suite for septet (1924–6), and one which opened the way, more or less directly, to Prokofiev's Quintet for oboe, clarinet, violin, viola, and double bass (1924), Stravinsky's Septet (1952–3), Messiaen's *Quatuor pour la fin du temps* (1941), and Maxwell Davies's *Ave maris stella* for sextet (1975). Indeed, from the early 1950s mixed ensembles became so much the norm that this list of examples could be extended indefinitely. But what distinguishes the Davies and Messiaen works is that they are true chamber music, designed to be performed without a conductor, for while Schoenberg's *Pierrot lunaire* enlarged the boundaries of chamber music it also changed the nature of the genre, which is that of a discourse between musicians as equals. When a conductor is involved, as in Schoenberg's First Chamber Symphony (1906) or *Pierrot lunaire*, there can be no question of chamber music proper, and, though the First Chamber Symphony was successfully rescued for chamber music by Webern in his arrangement of the work for quintet, Schoenberg's innovation has done more for conducted ensembles than chamber groups.

In the second half of the 20th century other new directions for chamber music opened up. Such works as Roger Reynolds's *The Emperor of Ice Cream* (1965), which requires the players to change their positions on stage during performance, emphasized a theatricality at odds with the essential spirit of chamber music, and some composers went further still by asking the players deliberately to avoid coordination (e.g. Lutosławski's String Quartet, 1964). On the other hand, works that combined acoustic instruments with live electronic manipulation (e.g. Stockhausen's *Solo* for instrument and tape feedback, 1966) retained something of chamber music's conversational essence. The string quartet repertory continued to be extended and developed by such composers as Henze (five works), Ligeti (two), Stockhausen (*Helikopter*, in which each of the players is placed in a helicopter, connected by television and audio relay), Ferneyhough (four), and the American minimalists Reich (*Different Trains* and *Triple Quartet*, both with tape) and Glass (five). Some ensembles, such as the Arditti and Kronos Quartets, devoted themselves to the performance and recording of new music, the Kronos imaginatively bridging gaps between popular, classical, and non-Western musics by issuing a series of thematic 'crossover' CD albums.

PG/CBa

W. W. Cobbett (ed.), *Cobbett's Cyclopedic Survey of Chamber Music* (London, 1929–30; new edn, rev. C. Mason, London, 1963) · A. Robertson (ed.), *Chamber Music* (Harmondsworth, 1957) · K. Geiringer, 'The rise of chamber music', *The Age of Enlightenment, 1745–1790*, The New Oxford History of Music, vii (Oxford, 1973), 515–73 · M. Berger, *Guide to Chamber Music* (London, 1985) · J. McCalla, *Twentieth-Century Chamber Music* (New York, 1996) · J. H. Baron, *Intimate Music: A History of the Idea of Chamber Music* (Stuyvesant, NY, 1998)

orchestra of Strauss and Hofmannsthal's previous collaboration, *Der Rosenkavalier*. The many layers of *Ariadne* (the 18th century, classical mythology, and *commedia dell'arte*) were a feature of chamber opera as it developed over its first half-century: Busoni's *Arlecchino* (1917) continued the exploration of *commedia dell'arte*, and the neo-classical spirit set the tone for later works from Hindemith (*Cardillac*, 1926) to Stravinsky (*The Rake's Progress*, 1951). By analogy, 18th-century operas for small forces, such as Pergolesi's *La serva padrona*, which is strictly speaking an intermezzo, have retrospectively attracted the description 'chamber opera'.

The emergence of chamber opera in the years leading up to World War I was an expression of the general reaction against late Romantic luxuriance (though Strauss himself returned to full-scale forces in *Die Frau ohne Schatten*, 1919), contemporary with the aesthetic shift represented by Stravinsky's work after *The Rite of Spring*. A similar shift, but born of practical considerations, is found in the work of Britten, who, immediately after the success of *Peter Grimes* in 1945, also turned to chamber scoring in *The Rape of Lucretia* (1946), which has a band of 12 instrumentalists and piano. This marked the beginning of a series of chamber operas by Britten which includes *Albert Herring* (1947) and *The Turn of the Screw* (1954). The personal choice of instrumentation that chamber opera offered merged with more radical musical and dramatic ideas to produce *music theatre in the 1960s and 70s.

Chamber opera, however, has survived as a showcase for an emerging composer (e.g. Adès's *Powder her Face*, 1995).   KC

chamber orchestra. A small orchestra, usually with the forces that predominated in the second half of the 18th century: pairs of oboes, bassoons, and horns with a small body of strings (six to eight first and second violins, four violas, four cellos, and one or two basses). Flutes, clarinets, trumpets, and timpani are added as required. Such orchestras play music of the Baroque and Classical eras on modern instruments (as distinct from 'early music orchestras' or 'period instrument ensembles') and also have a considerable modern repertory. A great deal of music was written in the 20th century for string orchestras of this size.   JMo

chamber organ [cabinet organ]. A small *organ housed in a compact cabinet, intended for use in domestic settings or in small churches or chapels. Such instruments were popular in the 18th and early 19th centuries.   JMo

Chamber Symphony (*Kammersymphonie*). Title of two works by Schoenberg for small orchestra: no. 1 (op. 9) was composed in 1906 and arranged for full orchestra in 1922 and again in 1935; no. 2 (op. 38) was begun in 1906 and completed in 1939. Webern made a simplified arrangement of the first. Other composers have used this title, including Schreker; but many have preferred the term 'Chamber Concerto'.

Chambonnières, Jacques Champion, Sieur de (*d* Paris, 1672). French composer. His family name was Champion, and he came from a long line of musicians—his grandfather was a keyboard player of some distinction and his father a member of the royal household as 'joueur d'espinette'. Chambonnières was himself a famous harpsichordist, and took over his father's appointment about 1643. For many years he was highly favoured, but intrigues caused him to retire from the court of Louis XIV in 1662.

His surviving works show him to be a founder of the French school of harpsichord composers. In 1670 two books of his *Pièces de clavessin* were published. They consist mainly of dances in the *style brisé* arranged, perhaps for publication, in suites. Some have titles, but there is no suggestion of programme music. Their delicate and elegant style reveals much of the man whose 'beauty of rhythm, fine touch, lightness and rapidity of hand' (according to Marin Mersenne) were admired throughout Europe.   DA

Chaminade, Cécile (Louise Stéphanie) (*b* Paris, 8 Aug. 1857; *d* Monte Carlo, 18 April 1944). French pianist and composer. She had considerable success in the early 20th century and even had a perfume named after her, sold with her portrait. She studied privately with various composers at the Paris Conservatoire. Often dismissed as a salon composer, she in fact left several substantial pieces including an early Piano Trio, a Piano Sonata, and a Concertino for flute and orchestra. Her many piano pieces were technically within reach of the aspiring amateur; their covers were particularly elaborately designed, either giving the impression of a nostalgic reverie or bearing a portrait of Chaminade herself composing at the piano—a role-model for her enthusiasts. Her piano piece *Automne* at one time sold more than 6000 copies a year. Her recitals of her own music were particularly well received in the USA, where her rarity as a female composer was a distinct advantage, and where clubs were set up for the promotion of her music.   RLS

Champagne, Claude (Adonai) (*b* Montreal, 27 May 1891; *d* Montreal, 21 Dec. 1965). Canadian composer and educationist. He received a diploma from the Dominion College of Music in 1906 and graduated from the Montreal Conservatory in 1909, then studied in Paris (1921–8) where he was influenced by Fauré and Debussy. He taught at the Collège de Varennes, the École de Musique d'Outrement, and McGill Conservatorium. He was also assistant director of the Quebec Provincial Conservatory of Music and Dramatic Arts. Champagne taught an entire generation of Canadian composers including Serge Garant, Violet Archer, and Gilles Tremblay. His interest in folk music is evident in the *Symphonie gaspésienne* (1945), a symphonic poem, but his last major work, *Altitude* (1959), moves towards a new acoustic world. He was not a prolific composer but his works have found a secure place in the Canadian symphonic repertory.   HRe

📖 M. NEVINS (ed.), *Claude Champagne 1891–1965: Composer, Teacher, Musician* (Ottawa, 1990)

champêtre (Fr., 'rural', 'rustic'). A *danse champêtre* is a peasant dance performed in the open air. The celebrated 'Fête champêtre' in Act IV of Lully's opera *Roland* depicts a rustic wedding.

chance operations. A term introduced by John Cage for techniques that open the compositional process to chance, for example the tossing of a coin to determine pitches. See also INDETERMINATE MUSIC.

Chandos Anthems. 12 anthems by Handel for soloists, chorus, and orchestra, on religious texts, composed in 1717–18 for James Brydges, Earl of Carnarvon, later the Duke of Chandos, at Cannons (his palace near Edgware, Middlesex).

change-ringing. A style of ringing church bells or handbells, organized into a musical structure, which originated in the Church of England in the 17th century.

The tolling of bells has always been linked to Christian worship; bells of various kinds have often been sounded in combination with liturgical actions. But change-ringing, though associated with church bells, originally had no connection with Christian worship. After the Reformation the use of bells in the context of the liturgy was considered 'Popish', and change-ringing thus originated as a secular pastime; it became associated with calling people to worship only as a result of church reform in the 19th century, but this practice was not initiated by the ringers themselves.

The number of bells in a peal varies from three to 12, usually tuned to a diatonic major scale, or part of one. In the simplest form of change-ringing, called a 'plain hunt', each bell follows a path among others. In the following schematic representation of a plain hunt involving three bells the top bell of the peal (the 'treble') is represented by the number 1, and the bottom bell (the 'tenor') by the number 3:

```
1 2 3 (rounds)
2 1 3
2 3 1
3 2 1
3 1 2
1 3 2
1 2 3 (rounds)
```

Here the start and finish, in which the bells are rung in descending order from the highest to the lowest pitch, is known as 'rounds'. A line can be drawn charting the course of bell 1 from its first position among the others through the sequence and back again. The same procedure can be followed using a greater number of bells. It produces twice as many changes as there are bells.

However, when four or more bells are used the plain hunt cannot produce all possible combinations, so more complex methods of changing are required. There are two main ways of doing this, one for an even number of bells (Table 1), the other for odd numbers (Table 2).

TABLE 1

Even-bell

name	number of bells
minimus	4
minor	6
major	8
royal	10
maximus	12

The simplest variation of a plain hunt which extends its possibilities is 'Plain Bob', in which some bells 'bob' (meaning dodge, or change places) to avoid repetition. Thus a Plain Bob performed on four bells is 'Plain Bob Minimus', performed on six bells it is 'Plain Bob Minor', and so on. The effect of hearing the tenor bell at the end of each row is pleasing to the ear. In order to produce this effect with an even number of bells, it is necessary that only the remaining bells change; hence the schemes for ringing an odd number of bells shown in Table 2.

TABLE 2

Odd-bell

name	number of bells
doubles	5
triples	7
caters (from Fr. *quatre*)	9
royal	11

In the 'Grandsire' (odd-bell) system bells follow courses among other bells as in Plain Bob, but this time in pairs: two pairs in 'Grandsire Doubles', three in triples, and so forth. There are other, more complex odd-bell systems, for example 'Stedman', in which one group of bells follows a plain hunt while others dodge among themselves and, during the course of ringing, those in the first group change places with those in the second.

The principles of ringing were first described in *Tintinnalogia* (1668/*R*1970, 2/1671) by Richard Duckworth, an Oxford clergyman; this was followed by *Campanologia* (1677/*R*) by C. R. Fabian Stedman, a Cambridge printer who had joined the Ancient Society of College Youths (founded in London in 1637 and still active). Ringing societies still flourish and the Central Council of Bellringers publishes a weekly newspaper, *The Ringing World* (founded in 1911). Dorothy L. Sayers's detective novel *The Nine Tailors* (1934) contains much technical detail concerned with change-ringing. Maxwell Davies's *Stedman Caters* for chamber ensemble and *Stedman Doubles* for clarinet and percussion (both 1968) are based on bell peals.   PW

📖 J. SANDERSON, *Change Ringing: The History of an English Art*, 3 vols. (Guildford, 1987–94) · S. COLEMAN, *The Bellringer's Bedside Companion* (Gloucester, 1994)

changing note. See NOTA CAMBIATA.

chanson (Fr., from Lat. *cantio* via Provençal *canso* and It. *canzon*, 'song'). A song setting French words. The term is used chiefly of French polyphonic songs of the

Middle Ages and Renaissance, and the following discussion will be largely confined to that application (though 'chanson' has also been in continuous use since the Middle Ages to denote art song or folksong with French words, including *trouvère monophony, through to accompanied song from the 17th century to the 20th).

From the 12th century survive such narrative genres as the *chanson de geste* (epic song)—with many lines (*laisses* or *tirades*) sung monophonically to repeated melodic formulas—and such shorter lyrical forms as the *chanson de toile* (spinning song), divided into strophes sometimes including a refrain. Between the 13th and 15th centuries most of the shorter lyric forms, derived from the round-dance (*carole*), were designated by their fixed rhyme form—*rondet, rondel, *rondeau (ABaAabAB), *ballade (ababbcCC), or *virelai/ bergerette (ABccabAB)—and were set to music for two, three, or four voices. Although the troubadours and trouvères occasionally invented new melodies, their verse was often sung to tunes derived from plainchant or popular song, played on the fiddle (*vielle*) or other instruments by the minstrels (*jongleurs*). Few chanson melodies survive from the Middle Ages, when oral transmission ruled art song as well as folksong, but many have been reconstructed from later indirect polyphonic sources including 13th-century Latin or polytextual motets and instrumental music.

Direct polyphonic setting burgeons in the work of such 14th-century poet-musicians as Adam de la Halle, Jehan de L'Escurel, and particularly Guillaume de Machaut. Whereas the earliest examples generally have a relatively unadorned melody in the upper voice, with lower voices moving in parallel harmony, during the 14th century there is increasing melismatic elaboration, rhythmic complexity, and independence of part-writing. In the 15th century a reaction to the mannered complexity of such Ars Nova or *ars subtilior* composers as Jaquemin de Senleches and Baude Cordier is found in the chansons of Dunstaple and other English composers who showed the way to musicians associated with the court of Burgundy—for example, Dufay, Binchois, and Busnois—who wrote mostly fixed-form poems for three parts. Although the lower parts were frequently conceived for and played on instruments, these chansons achieve greater clarity of melody and counterpoint—based generally on *fauxbourdon (6-3) rather than root-position (5-3) harmony.

The highpoint of the polyphonic chanson as an international form was reached in the 16th century, when an enormous repertory of three-, four-, and five-part pieces appeared from the new printing presses of Venice (Petrucci and Gardano), Rome (Antico), Paris (Attaingnant, Du Chemin, and Le Roy), Lyons (Moderne), Antwerp (Susato), and Louvain (Phalèse). Josquin, Compère, and Févin abandoned the fixed repetitive forms of their predecessors and concentrated on setting single strophes in a way that more clearly reflects the verse's natural prosody and syntax. This is even more marked in the work of their successors Sermisy, Janequin, Jacotin, Certon, Sandrin, and others who refine the art of balancing homophony with light motivic counterpoint. Josquin's northern disciples— Gombert, Clemens non Papa, Crecquillon, and others—generally pursue a denser contrapuntal approach, passing short motifs between the voices while setting the same kind of (mostly amorous courtly) epigrams and strophic pieces by such poets as Clément Marot and Mellin de Saint-Gelais.

Whereas constant or unrequited love had long remained the favourite subject of courtly chanson, more anacreontic, carnal, humorous, or satirical themes are exploited in the narrative anecdotes of Marot and his less well-known contemporaries, admirably set in syllabic counterpoint by Janequin, Jacotin, Passereau, Certon, and others. Janequin used the same deft counterpoint, alternating with varied homophony, and light, frequently syncopated rhythms in his onomatopoeic sound-pictures of birds and battles. Simple strophic pieces of popular language were adapted for courtly use in the 'chansons' of Marot and in the 'voix de ville' of Saint-Gelais and others, set for four voices by such composers as Certon, Antoine Mornable, and Arcadelt; these were often arranged and sung for solo voice and lute or guitar, with the instrument generally condensing the lower voices.

During the second half of the 16th century more sophisticated verse, based on classical or Petrarchan models, came to the fore with the odes and sonnets of Pierre de Ronsard and the poets of the Pléiade, set mostly for four or five voices with increasingly colourful word-painting by Arcadelt, Clereau, Goudimel, Costeley, Lassus, Monte, Jean de Castro, Bertrand, Guillaume Boni, Le Jeune, and many others. Lassus's chansons in particular are notable for their complexity, encompassing a broad range of moods and displaying great subtlety and depth (see Ex. 1). Meanwhile a preference for monodic performance of the simpler strophic verse led to the designation 'chanson en façon d'air' (Costeley, 1570) or simply 'air' (Adrian Le Roy, 1571) replacing that of 'voix de ville', though such pieces continued to be published as homophonic partsongs rather than lute-songs. The latter do not begin to predominate until the 17th century, when the Ballard press mastered the technique of printing French lute tablature.

With French thus supplanting Latin as the leading European language of the late Middle Ages, the

Ex. 1

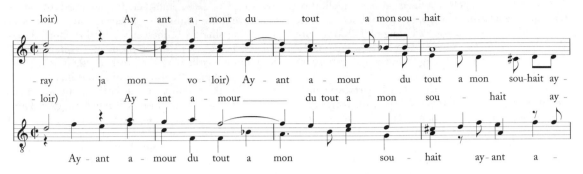

Lassus, *Helas quel jour*, bars 6–16.

chanson became the main type of secular music sung or played by amateur or professional musicians in the homes, palaces, theatres, schools, and streets of Renaissance Europe. Not only were chansons widely sung, they were also frequently arranged for instrumental solo or ensemble, inspiring such new forms as the canzona, fantasia, and variations. They also provided the melodic and even harmonic substance for much new sacred music—notably 'imitation' or 'parody' masses and *Magnificat* settings, as well as vernacular psalms, chorales, and other spiritual contrafacta.

During the 16th century the French chanson paralleled its Italian counterpart, the *madrigal, becoming more responsive to the expression of the text as well as to its form and metre, which had hitherto been its primary concern. This new attention to *word-painting, heightened by the greater contrast in rhythm and texture, as well as by chromatic melody and harmony, is demonstrated particularly in the mannerist settings of Ronsard and Joachim Du Bellay. A more independent French innovation is seen in the *musique mesurée* of Lassus, F. M. Caietain, Le Jeune, Mauduit, and Du

Caurroy, which sets the verse that Jean-Antoine de Baïf and his colleagues of the Académie de Musique et Poésie (1570–) modelled on classical metres (*vers mesurés*).

See also AIR, 2; AIR À BOIRE; AIR DE COUR; CHANSON SPIRITUELLE; LIED; MÉLODIE; MONODY, 2; ROMANCE; SONG.
FD

📖 H. M. BROWN, 'The genesis of a style: The Parisian chanson, 1500–1530', *Chanson and Madrigal, 1480–1530*, ed. J. Haar (Cambridge, MA, 1964) · J.-M. VACCARO (ed.), *La Chanson à la Renaissance* (Tours, 1981) · J.-P. OUVRARD, *La Chanson polyphonique française du XVIe siècle: Guide pratique* (Paris, 1982) · G. DOTTIN, *La Chanson française de la Renaissance* (Paris, 1984) · F. DOBBINS (ed.), *The Oxford Book of French Chansons* (Oxford, 1987) · D. FALLOWS, *Songs and Musicians in the Fifteenth Century* (Aldershot, 1996)

chanson de croisade (Fr., 'crusade song'). A type of song written by medieval singer-performers in the expectation of, or in reaction to, going on crusade. Most frequently associated with troubadours (as in the works of Peirol), such songs are also found among the works of Minnesinger, in which case they are known as *Kreuzlieder*.
ABul

chanson de geste. A French medieval epic poem, often of considerable length and divided into sections. The poem was sung to short musical phrases, probably involving a certain amount of repetition, of a simple nature so as not to distract the listener from the narrative. One of the most celebrated *chansons de geste* is the *Chanson de Roland*, but no complete examples survive with music.

chansonnier. A book (either manuscript or printed) whose principal content is chansons (French lyric poetry), either in their text form or set to music. In these terms the earliest chansonniers are the manuscripts transmitting the works of the troubadours and trouvères, but the word is more normally used with reference to polyphonic song manuscripts of the 15th and 16th centuries. The great flowering of the Franco-Flemish chanson during this period led to the production of numerous chansonniers, many of them quite small and some beautifully decorated. Several of these manuscripts contain works in other languages, and a surprising number were produced outside France, in places where French culture was still predominant. Collections containing popular monophonic songs were also produced in the Renaissance; later printed chansonniers contained songs for popular entertainment, in contrast to the more private function of earlier manuscript collections.
ABul

chanson sans paroles (Fr.). 'Song without words'; see CHARACTER PIECE.

Chansons de Bilitis. Three songs (1897–8) by Debussy for voice and piano to prose poems by Pierre Louÿs. Maurice Delage made an orchestral version of them in 1926. In 1900–1 Debussy arranged the music for two flutes, two harps, and celesta to accompany readings of the poems; the celesta part was lost but was reconstructed by Boulez (1954) and Arthur Hoérée (1971). Debussy recomposed the music as part of *Six épigraphes antiques* (1914) for piano duet.

chanson spirituelle (Fr., 'spiritual song'). A type of French secular *chanson of the second half of the 16th century, the texts of which are spiritual or moralistic in tone. Most examples were written by Protestants, though similar chansons by Catholics also exist. In many cases existing chansons were simply given new words, as happened with a large number of Lassus's polyphonic songs. One of the most influential collections was *Chansons spirituelles* (1548) with texts by Guillaume Guéroult and music by Didier Lupi Second; it contains the well-known *Suzanne ung jour*, which was reworked many times by later composers. Other notable contributors to the genre include Hubert Waelrant, Jean Pasquier, Simon Goulart, and Claude Le Jeune, who composed many three- and four-part settings of texts by Calvinist authors including Antoine Chandieu.
JBe

chant. See ANGLICAN CHANT; PLAINCHANT.

chantant, chanté (Fr.). 'Singing', 'in a singing style'.

chanter. The melody pipe of a *bagpipe.

chanterelle (Fr.). The highest or melody string of any stringed instrument.

Chants d'Auvergne ('Songs of the Auvergne'). Traditional dialect songs of the Auvergne region of France which have become well known through four collections (1923–30) of arrangements by Canteloube from which a suite of nine songs for solo voice and orchestra (or piano) is frequently performed.

chanty. See SHANTY.

chapel (Fr.: *chapelle*; Ger.: *Capelle, Kapelle*; It.: *cappella*). St Martin's famous cloak (Lat.: *cappa*), which he divided with the beggar, was preserved by the Carolingian kings in a reliquary, whose custodians were called *cappellani* and thence gave the name of *cappella* (or *capella*) to the church where it was housed. Thus any smallish place of worship, whether a free-standing structure or within a larger edifice such as that of a cathedral or palace, came to take the name. The whole staff of priests, musicians, and other functionaries attached to such places then came to be called 'the king's chapel', 'the pope's chapel', and so on.

Chapels grew in importance as institutions for the cultivation of music during the late 14th and the 15th centuries, when demand by patrons eager to enhance their reputations created an international market for singers and composers of polyphony. The papal chapel and the royal chapels of English, French, Spanish, and Habsburg monarchs were also important as models for emulation both at home by lesser nobles and abroad. In Italy, ducal chapels organized in imitation of northern courts began to appear after the mid-15th century in such cities as Milan and Ferrara, with that of Venice achieving prominence in the 16th century. One result of these developments was that, in common usage, the term was restricted to the musicians, so that the German 'Kapellmeister', the French *maitre de chapelle*, the Italian *maestro di cappella*, and so on came to be applied to the musical director.

In Germany the term 'Kapelle' eventually was applied to any organized musical group, of voices or of instruments, in the church, the concert hall, or the opera house, and the term 'Kapellmeister' to the musical director of any such group. Up to the 19th century, the position generally involved composition, and many famous composers were Kapellmeister. Thereafter, however, composition was thought to be better left to independent visionaries, and the duties of Kapellmeister were largely restricted to the organization of the music. Thus *Kapellmeistermusik* became a derogatory term denoting technical proficiency without inspiration. The equivalent French, Italian, and English terms continued to be used to describe only sacred musical establishments.   —/ALı

Chapel Royal. The English Chapel Royal is strictly a body of persons rather than any particular building; the term denotes the personnel maintained by the successive sovereigns of England as members of the royal household, to order and perform divine service for the good estate of the royal family at all times, and in the royal presence when required. Until the later 16th century, the Chapel was a largely peripatetic body, travelling with the royal household. Under the Stuart dynasty, however, it was rarely required to follow the king away from London or Windsor, and since 1702 it has been established permanently in Kensington Palace, London; nevertheless, a remnant of its former nature survives in its practice of attending the sovereign at the annual distribution of the Royal Maundy, wherever that ceremony may be held.

The fluctuating fortunes of the Chapel Royal over its long history reflect fairly faithfully the degree of authority in national life exercised by the monarchy and the national church of the day, and, more recently, the amount of interest taken by successive sovereigns in liturgical worship and the music associated with it. The Chapel first took shape during the reigns of Edward I and Edward II (1272–1307, 1307–27). The performance of the services of the Latin liturgy required groups of priests, clerks in non-priestly orders, and boys, for which purpose Edward II's Chapel by 1318 consisted of a chief chaplain (later called Dean), five other priest-chaplains, six clerks, and three or four choristers. This staff was classified on standard medieval lines, and to this day the terms Gentlemen and Children remain in use to designate the singing-men (i.e. lay clerks) and choristers. Furthermore, they continue to wear the resplendent uniforms appropriate to their status in the royal household, rather than the more usual ecclesiastical garb.

From these modest beginnings, successive sovereigns expanded the Chapel until, from the 15th to the 17th centuries, it stood as one of the foremost secular liturgical choirs in Europe, presenting to the world at large an ostentatious and overtly propagandist image of the piety and wealth of the English monarch, and of the pool of musical talent, both creative and executive, available to him in the ordering of his religious devotions. Henry IV (1399–1413) maintained a Chapel of 16 Gentlemen and four Children, and himself composed church music, presumably for his Chapel to perform. Some idea of the breadth of its repertory at this influential period may be derived from study of the Old Hall Manuscript. Under Henry V and Henry VI (1413–22, 1422–61), the Chapel grew to as many as 32 Gentlemen and 16 Children, and accompanied the monarchs to the conquered regions of northern France.

Between the majority of Henry VI (1436) and the outbreak of the Civil War (1642) the staff of the Chapel Royal rarely fell below 32 men and from ten to 12 boys, dimensions which permitted its composers to write music conceived on the grandest scale, since its personnel were not only numerous, but also of the highest calibre. After 1558 the patronage offered by Elizabeth I maintained the Chapel's pre-eminence, even while elsewhere in England the practice of church music was contracting almost into insignificance, and her interest was maintained by the first two Stuart kings. Composers who wrote the great bulk of their church music for the Chapel Royal at this time included Robert Fayrfax, Thomas Tallis, John Sheppard, William Byrd, John Bull, Orlando Gibbons, and Thomas Tomkins.

The final adoption in 1559 of vernacular services from the *Book of Common Prayer* in place of the Latin rite appears to have had no adverse effects on musical standards. Nevertheless, the change reduced the number of services from up to ten to only three a day, leaving the members of the Chapel with much free time; for a short period the Children came to be employed as actors in dramatic presentations at court and at the Blackfriars Theatre, while the Gentlemen commonly obtained additional posts at provincial cathedrals or Westminster Abbey. Nevertheless, members of the Chapel took the lead in devising novel musical forms to meet the demands made by the new vernacular liturgy, largely inventing the Short and Great Services, and also the verse anthem and service.

After the restoration of Charles II in 1660, the Chapel was reconstituted and enjoyed some 40 more years of pre-eminence, drawing on the talents of Pelham Humfrey, John Blow, and Henry Purcell. However, with the accession of the largely unmusical Hanoverian dynasty in 1714, and in tune with the general 18th-century attenuation of religious concern and fervour, the Chapel Royal entered a rapid and comprehensive decline, and sadly it has been given little opportunity to make much positive mark on the musical scene during the last 200 years. Its choir school was closed in 1923, and its ten choristers are now drawn from the City of London Boys' School; there are six Gentlemen and an organist.   RB

Chapí (y Lorente), Ruperto (*b* Villena, nr Alicante, 27 March 1851; *d* Madrid, 25 March 1909). Spanish composer. The son of a village barber, he studied at the Madrid and Paris conservatories and in Rome. Several of his many zarzuelas, including *La bruja* ('The Witch', 1887) and *La revoltosa* ('The Troublemaker', 1897) are staples of the Spanish repertory. He also wrote operas, chamber music, and orchestral works, including a Berlioz-influenced *Fantasia morisca* (1876) and a tripartite tone-poem *Los gnomos de la Alhambra* (1899), both of which are effective examples of *alhambrismo*, the picturesque imitation of Moorish music that attracted many of his Spanish contemporaries. He also founded the Sociedad de Autores (1899) to safeguard copyright for all Spanish artists.   WT/CW

Chappell. English firm of music publishers, concert agents, and piano manufacturers. Founded in 1810 by J. B. Cramer, F. T. Latour, and Samuel Chappell, it has always taken a pioneering role in popularizing music and it played a large part in the formation of the Philharmonic Society in 1813. In the 1840s the firm began making pianos and publishing dance music and light opera, beginning in 1843 with Balfe's *The Bohemian Girl*. From 1870 it issued the operas of Gilbert and Sullivan, and financed the Comedy Company which performed them until D'Oyly Carte took over in 1877. Between 1858 and the end of the century Chappell promoted a huge number of popular concerts—the forerunners of the Queen's Hall Promenade Concerts—which the firm ran from 1915 until the BBC assumed control in 1927. Chappell also led the campaign against musical piracy which prefaced the introduction of the Copyright Act of 1911.

The firm's activities in light music continued in the 20th century with the publication of musical comedies by British and American composers (Coward, Novello, the Gershwins, Berlin, Kern, Porter, Rodgers and Hammerstein). Alongside its vast catalogue of educational and band music, it ran a hire library of background music for films and television and these activities led to its merger with the American Warner Bros. Music in 1988. The new company, Warner/Chappell Music, continues the tradition of promoting popular music and is active in television, film, and commercial music. It retains an extensive music hire library and owns rights in many stage musicals.

HA

character dance. A folk dance adapted to balletic style. The term is also used for dances evoking stereotypical characters (e.g. beggar, soldier). In the classical repertory, character dances are generally intended to give a sense of national character and colour, an example being the mazurka in Delibes's *Coppélia* (1870).   JH

character piece (Ger.: *Characterstück*). A piece designed to convey a specific allusion, atmosphere, mood, or scene, such as pastoral serenity, agitation, or rustic ceremony, without the benefit of text, programme, or stage action. Strictly speaking, character pieces—unlike funeral marches, military marches, or dances—are not functional but are intended only to arouse, through the performer, a passive listener's feelings and associations. Such goals have been present in Western music from the earliest times, as for example in the medieval *caccia* ('hunt'), or in pieces by the Elizabethan virginalists or François Couperin. But they held a uniquely important place in the piano music of the 19th century, a time when purely abstract forms lost much of their appeal, *Romanticism encouraged literary influences on music, and *nationalism led composers to evoke the folk music of nations or ethnic groups.

Older genres such as the capriccio (Fr.: *caprice*), fantasia (Fr.: *fantaisie*), prelude, and toccata took on new characteristics in the hands of the Romantic composers. In addition to the ballroom dances of the age, such as the *écossaise*, galop, mazurka, polka, polonaise (It.: *polacca*), quadrille, *redowa*, *Schottische*, and waltz (Fr.: *valse*), many of which could also serve as character pieces, other dance types were cultivated purely to evoke the antique (gavotte, *contredanse*, pavane), the exotic (bolero, cakewalk, *krakowiak* or *cracovienne*, tarantella), or the rustic (jig, ländler, tyrolienne), or to express nationalism.

Of the newly invented genres, one group could suggest a literary connection without specifying any actual story or subject matter (*ballade*, eclogue, *élégie*, novelette, *romance*); another established the idea of song (chanson, *Lied ohne Worte*, *mélodie*, *Volkslied*). Visual images could be called forth by a title (arabesque, aubade, nocturne, *scène*, *sérénade*, *tableau*). Others suggested action (*bacchanale*, barcarolle or *Gondellied*, berceuse, *chasse*, *fête*, *Wanderlied*) or merely state of mind (*consolation*, humoresque, *méditation*, *réminiscence*, *rêverie* or *Träumerei*, *rapsodie*). Finally, some generic titles seem designed to define the composer's or performer's attitude to the music, generally a casual one (album-leaf, bagatelle, divertissement, *étude*, impromptu, intermezzo, lyric piece, *moment musical*, *morceau*, *perpetuum mobile* or *moto perpetuo*, scherzo).

Even with the rise of nationalism, the French language continued to predominate in the names of keyboard pieces, much as the Italian did for operatic and vocal genres. This was doubtless because of its social cachet, which led publishers to hope it would attract the all-important market of young ladies. There was a tradition of using French generic titles for keyboard music going back at least to the time of Bach.

Few of the titles (other than those of dances) call for any specific musical structure, though character pieces are typically in a single movement, and involve in some way the return of the opening theme after a digression. The promise of the title is fulfilled by means of rhythmic gestures (especially, of course, in dances or action pieces), non-standard scales for exotic cultures, and textures consistently maintained for moods and visual images. Here the rapid development of the piano was important, with its expanding range of pitch and dynamics and the effects made possible by pedalling. Imitation of actual sounds such as bells, birdsong, water in various forms, hunting-horns, galloping horses, or machinery sometimes played a part. But the character piece is best distinguished from the descriptive piece with a specific programme (see PROGRAMME MUSIC), for example Liszt's *Années de pèlerinage* or Musorgsky's *Pictures at an Exhibition*, and from pieces based on pre-existing musical themes.

Character pieces of a single genre were frequently published in sets, those of mixed genres as suites or under a collective title. Some of the main types are now strongly associated with particular composers: the bagatelle with Beethoven, the impromptu with Schubert and Chopin, the nocturne with Field, Chopin, and Fauré, the *Lied ohne Worte* (Ger., 'song without words') with Mendelssohn, the *ballade* with Chopin and Brahms, the prelude with Chopin, Debussy, Skryabin, and Rakhmaninov, the novelette with Schumann, the rhapsody with Liszt and Brahms, the capriccio and intermezzo with Brahms, the 'lyric piece' with Grieg. Some composers invented whimsical or satirical generic titles, like the 'Pause' and triple-time 'march' that conclude Schumann's *Carnaval*, or the 'gnossiennes' and 'gymnopédies' of Satie: the latter suggest that the character piece was beginning to lose ground as serious music. But examples continued to appear through much of the 20th century. Character pieces are also found for other instruments, alone or in combination, and for orchestra.   NT

charango. A small fretted lute of the Andes. Its shallow resonator may have a flat back of wood or a round back made of armadillo shell or carved wood. Most commonly it has five double (sometimes single or triple) courses of metal strings (sometimes nylon or gut), which give a dense, high-pitched sound.

charivari (Fr.). A noisy and violent ceremony involving improvised music performed with household utensils capable of making the maximum amount of noise. It was originally given as a public expression of disapproval. Thomas Hardy described an incident along similar lines in *The Mayor of Casterbridge*; when the 'skimmington ride' takes place, it is accompanied by 'the din of cleavers, tongs, tambourines, kits, crouds, humstrums, serpents, ramshorns, and other historical kinds of music'. Later, however, the charivari took the form of a mock serenade performed beneath the windows of newly married couples. It is an ancient custom that was evidently practised in many countries, for most languages include a term for it: in Germany it is known as *Katzenmusik* ('cats' music'), in England 'rough music', in Italy *chiasso* ('hubbub'), and in the USA as a shivaree or a calathumpian concert.

Charleston. A dance, probably of African origin, that started its vogue in American dance halls from about 1905; it became a craze once it had been introduced into various musical shows in the 1920s. A catchy tune written by the jazz pianist James P. Johnson (1894–1955) gave it its musical character and it was seen and prospered in such shows as *Runnin' Wild* (1923) and *Ziegfeld Follies of 1923*. Joan Crawford spread its delights in the film *Our Dancing Daughters* (1925) and many popular songs of the times were designed to fit it. It was slightly too athletic for most amateur dancers, with its side-kicks and syncopated steps, and it soon gave way to the more manageable *quickstep. It remains a popular symbol of the frivolous but turbulent 1920s.
                                    PGA

Charpentier, Gustave (*b* Dieuze, Moselle, 25 June 1860; *d* Paris, 18 Feb. 1956). French composer. Although he entered the Paris Conservatoire in 1879 and soon developed a love of Montmartre and bohemian life, his career did not really blossom until in 1884 he joined the composition class of the sympathetic Massenet, who taught him 'the love of loving and the love of being loved'. Charpentier's other main influences were Wagner, from whom he adopted the use of the leitmotif, and Berlioz, who awakened him 'to the sense of the picturesque and the unexpected'. He was awarded the coveted Prix de Rome for his cantata *Didon* in 1887.

During the next three unusually prolific years at the Villa Medici in Rome, Charpentier composed the nucleus of his life's work: the orchestral suite *Impressions d'Italie* (1889–90), the symphonic drama *La Vie du poète* (1888–9, rev. 1890–2, a latterday equivalent of Berlioz's *Lélio*), and the overall plan and first act of his opera *Louise*. The last was inspired by one of perhaps many romantic liaisons, with a young Montmartre seamstress in about 1885, and thus predates the successful verismo operas of Mascagni, Leoncavallo, and Puccini, even though it was not completed until 1896 (with clandestine assistance on the libretto from the Symbolist poet Saint-Pol-Roux, who infused Charpentier's often crude realism with the lyricism that has helped ensure *Louise*'s survival). In January 1898 Albert Carré decided to inaugurate his directorship of the Opéra-Comique with a production of *Louise*, and Charpentier's growing reputation during the 1890s with such open-air extravaganzas as the *Sérénade à Watteau* (1896) and *Le Couronnement de la muse* (1897), coupled with the promiscuous theme of *Louise* and the excitement of the Paris Exhibition, ensured a box-office triumph in February 1900.

Perhaps out of gratitude, in 1902 Charpentier founded the Conservatoire Populaire Mimi Pinson, which successfully gave free musical tuition to poor working girls until World War II, supported by the income from Charpentier's popular festivals of his own compositions. Communication rather than composition dominated the rest of his long life, and after the short-lived success of his last opera, *Julien* (1913), none of his many projects seems to have reached fruition. He became increasingly interested in the development of the gramophone, radio, and film as means of bringing music to a wider audience, and in 1938 he supervised the recording of a film version of *Louise*, directed by Abel Gance. Perhaps the phenomenal triumph of *Louise*, whose real heroine is Paris herself, overwhelmed Charpentier's creative talents. Certainly he became increasingly self-critical and given to self-borrowing, and it was on *Louise* that the reputation of this social idealist (and ideal socialist) was to rest.

RO

📖 M. DELMAS, *Gustave Charpentier et le lyrisme français* (Paris, 1931) · F. ANDRIEUX (ed.), *Gustave Charpentier: Lettres inédites à ses parents* (Paris, 1984) · J. FULCHER, 'Charpentier's operatic "roman musical" as read in the wake of the Dreyfus affair', *19th-Century Music*, 16 (1992), 161–80 · S. HUEBNER, *French Opera at the Fin de Siècle* (Oxford, 1999)

Charpentier, Marc-Antoine (*b* Paris, 1643; *d* Paris, 24 Feb. 1704). French composer. Following a Jesuit education in Paris, he ventured to Rome at some time in 1666 to study with Carissimi at the Collegio Germanico, mastering counterpoint as well as the polychoral techniques practised at that time by Francesco Beretta. Returning to Paris in 1670, he entered the service (as composer and *haute-contre*) of Mademoiselle de Guise, the cousin of Louis XIV and an ardent admirer of Italian sacred music. He remained in her service—throughout the years of Lully's monopolistic reign at the Académie Royale de Musique, which saw both his own collaboration with Molière's troupe on revivals of earlier plays (as well as on *Le Malade imaginaire* in 1673) and the expansion of the *musiques de cour*—until shortly before her death in 1688. During his prolific tenure at the Hôtel de Guise in Paris, he composed often experimental musical entertainments (such as his cantata *Orphée* and the sonata for eight instruments) for the friends of Mlle de Guise as well as sacred music for the religious occasions she celebrated and the organizations she supported.

Simultaneously, Charpentier also held appointments at several Jesuit institutions: the Collège d'Harcourt, the Collège de Clermont (Collège Louis-le-Grand), for which he composed *David et Jonathas* (1688) to complement a sacred drama, and St Louis (St Paul–St Louis). In the course of his career he took pupils and left in manuscript rules for composition and accompanying. Charpentier provided music for the dauphin (1679–83) before entering the competition for four quarterly appointments as *sous-maîtres* of the royal chapel, but had to drop out when he became ill; in 1692–3 he taught the Duke of Chartres (later Duke of Orléans and regent) composition, and his motets were known to the king.

Charpentier's *Médée* (a *tragédie lyrique* on a libretto by Thomas Corneille) was staged by the Académie Royale de Musique in 1693, with sets by Jean Berain and with Marthe Le Rochois in the title role. But, in common with other new operas of the post-Lully era, it was not well received by Parisian audiences owing to the 'cabals of the envious and ignorant' (according to Brossard, 1724). In 1698, with the intercession of the powerful Duke of Orléans, Charpentier was made *maître de musique* of the Sainte Chapelle on the Île de la Cité, where he remained until his death.

Charpentier was Lully's most important contemporary in France, and in many ways his music is better crafted, wider-ranging, and decidedly more interesting. With the exception of the score of *Médée* and a handful of *airs*, none of Charpentier's music was published during his lifetime and was really revived only in the late 20th century, contributing to a belated assessment of his place in French history and appreciation of his music.   DA/JAS

    📖 H. W. HITCHCOCK, *Marc-Antoine Charpentier* (Oxford, 1990) · J. R. ANTHONY, *French Baroque Music from Beaujoyeulx to Rameau* (Portland, OR, enlarged 3/1997)

Chasse, La ('The Hunt'). Haydn's Symphony no. 73 in D major (probably 1781), so called because of the style of its last movement.

Chasseur maudit, Le ('The Accursed Huntsman'). Symphonic poem, op. 44 (1882), by Franck, based on Gottfried Bürger's ballad *Der wilde Jäger*.

Chausson, (Amédée-)**Ernest** (*b* Paris, 20 Jan. 1855; *d* Limay, nr Mantes, Yvelines, 10 June 1899). French composer. His private education and upbringing among cultured people older than himself turned him into a serious-minded, introspective, often melancholy adult, who set himself the highest artistic standards and was plagued by self-doubt. In deference to family pressure he first studied law and qualified as a barrister in 1877, though in this same year he finally decided on a musical career and composed his first song, *Les Lilas*. He studied composition at the Paris Conservatoire with Massenet (1879–81), though he benefited more by sitting in on Franck's classes. His other main formative influence was Wagner, and he made pilgrimages to Munich (from 1879) and even spent his honeymoon with Jeanne Escudier in 1883 at Bayreuth in order to hear *Parsifal*.

Chausson's composing career divides into three periods. The first (1877–86) shows his musical style evolving as he moved away from the elegant charm of Massenet (1879–80) towards the bolder harmonic language and sonorities of Wagner (as in his symphonic poem *Viviane* of 1882), and towards the chromaticism of Franck, which lent greater emotional depth to such works as the choral *Hymne védique* (1886). The second period (1886–94) began when Chausson became secretary of the Société Nationale and entered more fully into Parisian intellectual circles. He now struggled to dispel the image of the wealthy 'amateur' composer by turning to more substantial dramatic works like the intense and metrically fluid *Poème d'amour et de la mer* (1882–93), the incidental music for Bouchor's *La Légende de Sainte Cécile* (1891), and his heroic opera *Le Roi Arthus* (1886–95) with its Wagnerian leitmotifs and orchestration; his Franckian side is best seen in the cyclical form and modulations of the Symphony in B♭ (1889–90).

In his third period (1894–9) Chausson, encouraged by Debussy, sought to purge his music of external influences, though his output remained serious (even pessimistic). He lacked Chabrier's gift for mischievous humour, even if he shared his perfect prosody, orchestral virtuosity and 'French' harmonic subtlety and refinement. Chausson's sensitivity to Symbolist poetry is evident in his masterful Maeterlinck cycle *Serres chaudes* (1893–6), and his discovery of the Russian novelists resulted in his well-known *Poème* (1896) for violin and orchestra based on a story by Turgenev. In 1897 Chausson returned to chamber music and adopted an increasingly pure classical approach, achieving greater clarity and concision in his Piano Quartet, and in his String Quartet, the Scherzo of which he was working on at the time of his premature death in a cycling accident. If Chausson's career in many ways parallels (and was overshadowed by) that of Debussy, his varied and imaginative music has in recent times happily received more of the recognition it deserves.   RO

    📖 G. SAMAZEUILH and others, 'Ernest Chausson', *Revue musicale*, 6/Dec. (1925) [special issue] · J.-P. BARRICELLI and L. WEINSTEIN, *Ernest Chausson: The Composer's Life and Works* (Norman, OK, 1955/R1973) · R. S. GROVER, *Ernest Chausson: The Man and his Music* (London, 1980) · J. GALLOIS, *Ernest Chausson* (Paris, 1994)

Chávez (y Ramírez), **Carlos** (Antonio de Padua) (*b* Mexico City, 13 June 1899; *d* Mexico City, 2 Aug. 1978). Mexican composer. He studied the piano and harmony as a child but was essentially self-taught as a composer, though he gained much from contact with Varèse and others in New York during the 1920s. As conductor of the Mexico Symphony Orchestra (1928–48) and director of the Mexican National Conservatory (1928–35) he did much to invigorate musical life in his home country, while his international tours took his own and other Mexican music to the world. He incorporated native instruments into the ballet *Toxcatl* (1952), and many of his works, including the second of his six symphonies, the *Sinfonía india* (1935–6), evoke the ritual splendour of pre-Columbian America, with vigorous rhythms, intricate percussion scoring, and atmospheric woodwind solos.   PG/CW

Chaykovsky, Pyotr Il'yich. See TCHAIKOVSKY, PYOTR IL'YICH.

Checkmate. Ballet in one act by Bliss to his own scenario; it was choreographed by Ninette de Valois and first performed by the Sadler's Wells company (Paris, 1937). Bliss arranged a suite from the score (1939).

chef d'attaque (Fr.). 'Leader'.

chekker (Fr.: *eschaquier, eschiquier*). Some kind of stringed keyboard instrument, first mentioned in 1360 as a novelty from England. Whether it was a clavichord, a key-hammered dulcimer, or an upright harpsichord is disputed.   JMo

chelys (Gk., 'tortoise'). The small Greek *lyre with a soundbox made from a tortoise shell, used for domestic and informal music-making. The term came to be used in medieval and Renaissance Latin for the lute, and by the viol player Christopher Simpson for the viol (1665).

Chemins ('Paths'). A series of orchestral and ensemble works by Berio, many based on his *Sequenze* (see SEQUENZA); *Chemins I* dates from 1964, *Chemins V* from 1992.

cheng. See ZHENG.

Cherepnin. See TCHEREPNIN.

Cherevichki ('The Slippers'). Opera in four acts by Tchaikovsky to a libretto by Yakov Polonsky, amplified by Nikolay Chayev and the composer, after Nikolay Gogol's story *Noch' pered rozhdestvom* ('Christmas Eve') (Moscow, 1887); it is a revision of *Vakula the Smith*.

Cherry Ripe. Song by Charles Edward Horn, a setting of a poem by Robert Herrick (published in *Hesperides*, 1648), apparently first performed in 1826.

Cherubic Hymn. Offertory chant of the Byzantine Divine Liturgy accompanying the transfer of the eucharistic gifts of bread and wine to the altar (the 'Great Entrance').   ALI

Chérubin. Opera in three acts by Massenet to a libretto by Henri Cain and Francis de Croisset after the latter's play (Monte Carlo, 1905).

Cherubini, (Maria) Luigi (Carlo Zanobi Salvadore) (*b* Florence, 8 or 14 Sept. 1760; *d* Paris, 15 March 1842). Italian composer active mainly in France. He received his earliest musical education in Florence, and by the age of 16 he had composed an oratorio, several masses, and other choral works. He studied for a time with Sarti in Bologna and Milan, and received his first commission for a full-length opera, *Il Quinto Fabio*, in 1779. Following the success of several other *opere serie*, in 1784 he went to London, where he composed an *opera buffa* and an *opera seria*—*La finta principessa* and *Il Giulio Sabino*—for the King's Theatre. Neither was particularly successful so, encouraged by Viotti, in 1786

he settled in Paris, where he was to spend much of the rest of his life.

In 1789 Cherubini became music director of the newly opened Italian Opera at the Théâtre de Monsieur (later the Théâtre Feydeau). The post, which involved conducting a range of works by his compatriots and writing separate pieces for insertion in operas, allowed him the time to familiarize himself with the French language and with the taste of the Parisian public. His first French opera, *Démophon*, was coolly received at the Opéra in 1788, though in many ways it foreshadowed his mature style with its rich orchestration and dramatic conclusion. In 1792 he signed a new contract with the Théâtre Feydeau, which had now dropped Italian opera in favour of French works. This provided him with financial security and the opportunity to experiment, and his reputation as a composer rests essentially on the *opéras comiques* he wrote at the theatre during the next ten years. His serious treatment of topical subjects, as well as his dramatic writing, rich orchestral textures, and skilful ensembles, helped to transform the genre and belied his (largely unsuccessful) ambitions in serious opera.

It was *Lodoïska* (1791), a rescue opera set in Poland, that established his name when it was given at the Théâtre Feydeau. It responded to the public's new taste for subjects involving highly charged action and catastrophic finales: Cherubini's symphonic style (notably his use of motivic development) and imaginative use of orchestral colour were particularly suited to such themes. *Lodoïska* effectively set new standards for French opera in terms of size and complexity, and it was a model for Beethoven's *Fidelio*. *Éliza, ou Le Voyage aux glaciers du Mont St Bernard* (1794) also gained immediate success, and with its transposition of the rescue theme to an alpine setting it can be regarded as the first Romantic opera to depict the tension between the outward calm and the underlying menace of nature.

After the Revolution, in spite of undertaking engagements for the provisional government, including choruses for the commemorative spectacle *Mirabeau à son lit de mort* (1791), Cherubini found himself out of favour with the authorities. However, he joined the staff of the recently established Institut National de Musique in 1794, and the following year (when the Institut was renamed the Conservatoire) he was appointed an inspector of instruction. There, as well as teaching, he selected and composed ceremonial republican hymns (such as the *Hymne à la victoire*, 1796), and benefited from some financial security. He continued to find success—particularly in Europe—with his new operas. *Médée* (1797) is considered his masterpiece for its dramatic and musical range and intensity; in many ways, not least through its psychological force and emotional tension, it anticipates 19th-century tragic opera. In contrast, *Les Deux Journées, ou Le Porteur d'eau* (1800) was in a simpler, brighter style, at a time when themes of peace were beginning to replace those of violence in works for the theatre. In 1805 Cherubini visited Vienna, where several of his operas were staged, including the specially commissioned rescue opera *Faniska* (1806). He met Beethoven—who acclaimed him as the foremost dramatic composer in Europe— and was greeted enthusiastically by Haydn. But when Napoleon invaded Austria he ordered Cherubini to organize his concerts at Schönbrunn and then to return to Paris.

Cherubini arrived back in France penniless and suffering from severe depression, and temporarily abandoned music, turning instead to painting and botany. Most of his important compositions after this time were sacred, with the exception of a set of six string quartets (1814–37), a symphony (1815, commissioned by the Philharmonic Society in London), and two *tragédies lyriques*. *Les Abencérages* (1813), based on a medieval Spanish theme, was poorly received, in spite of its colourful score, and *Ali-Baba* (1833), a reworking of earlier material, was a failure. His sacred works, however, were much admired; the critic Fétis noted how he could 'blend the austere beauties of counterpoint and fugue with dramatic expressiveness, enhanced by rich instrumentation'. Though inspired by Haydn and Mozart in his mass settings, he showed a more meticulous concern for tailoring the music to the meaning of the text. The C minor Requiem (1816) achieved particular success and was praised by Beethoven, Schumann, and Brahms.

With the fall of Napoleon, Cherubini's professional fortunes had begun to improve: in 1814 he was made a member of the Institut and a Chevalier of the Légion d'Honneur, and two years later he was appointed, with Le Sueur, superintendent of Louis XVIII's chapel. In 1822 he was made director of the Conservatoire, where he remained for a further 20 years and published a counterpoint and fugue method (with Halévy, 1835) and a composition treatise (1837). After 1837 he abandoned composition altogether to devote himself to teaching; his pupils included Auber, Halévy, and Boieldieu.

WT/SH

📖 B. Deane, *Cherubini* (London, 1965) · M. Boyd (ed.), *Music and the French Revolution* (Cambridge, 1992)

Chester Music. English firm of music publishers. It was founded in 1860 by John and William Chester of Brighton. In 1915 it was bought by Otto Kling, the former London director of Breitkopf & Härtel, and moved to London where it quickly established its reputation for publishing a distinctive list of composers, including Bax, Ireland, Falla, Poulenc, and Stravinsky. In the late 1950s, Chester merged with the Danish house of Wilhelm Hansen, the largest music publisher in Scandinavia. Chester/Wilhelm Hansen joined the worldwide Music Sales Group of companies in 1988 and Chester Music continues to promote such leading contemporary composers as Weir, Tavener, Nyman, Saariaho, and Maxwell Davies. Its catalogue includes educational tutors and music for film and television. Music Sales's hire library, an offshoot of the well-known Chester Music Lending Library, is one of the largest in Britain.

HA

chest of viols. A term used in 16th- and 17th-century England for a matched set of *viols, typically comprising two trebles, two or three tenors, and one or two basses, so called because they were kept in a specially built chest or press.

chest voice. A term used to denote the lower part of the male and female voice, in contradistinction to the head voice. Female singers tend to make use of the chest voice below d' or e'. From the mid-19th century onwards tenors began to use the full chest voice, rather than the head voice, to produce powerful, ringing high notes.

RW

chevalet (Fr.). 'Bridge'.

chevrotement (Fr.). 'Goat's trill'.

chiamata (It., 'call', 'summons'; Fr.: *chamade*). In early Venetian opera, a fanfare-like piece written in imitation of hunting horns.

chiaro, chiaramente (It.). 'Clear', 'clearly'.

chiasso (It.). See CHARIVARI.

chiave (It.). 'Clef'.

Chichester Psalms. Work (1965) by Bernstein for countertenor, chorus, and orchestra (originally organ, harp, and percussion), a setting of a Hebrew text; Bernstein composed it for Chichester Cathedral, where it was first performed.

chiesa (It., 'church'). For *concerto da chiesa* see CONCERTO, 2; for *sonata da chiesa* see SONATA, 3.

Chihara, Paul (Seiko) (*b* Seattle, 9 July 1938). American composer of Japanese extraction. He studied with Robert Palmer at Cornell (1960–5), with Gunther Schuller at Tanglewood, with Nadia Boulanger in Paris (1962–3), and with Ernst Pepping in Berlin (1965–6). He then taught at the University of California at Los

Angeles (1966–75) and, from 1976, the California Institute of the Arts. Much of his music shows an oriental quality of refined immediacy and closeness to nature, the latter reflected in some of his titles: *Logs* for double bass (1966), *Branches* for two bassoons and percussion (1966), *Grass* for double bass and orchestra (1971), *Sequoia* for string quartet and tape (1984). He has also written ballets, including *The Tempest* (1980).   PG

Chilcot, Thomas (*b* Bath, *c*.1707; *d* Bath, 24 Nov. 1766). English organist and composer. From 1728 he was organist of Bath Abbey, and he was an important figure in the secular life of the city. The elder Thomas Linley was one of his pupils. His surviving works are a set of 12 songs, six keyboard suites, and two sets of six keyboard concertos that show the influence of Domenico Scarlatti's harpsichord style.   WT/PL

Child, William (*b* Bristol, 1606 or 1607; *d* Windsor, 23 March 1697). English organist and composer. He was trained in Bristol, and in 1631 took the degree of B.Mus. at Oxford University. His adult career was spent at St George's Chapel, Windsor, where he was organist from about 1630 until his death, a span of more than 60 years that was interrupted only by the suspension of choral services during the Civil War. Following the Restoration, he additionally held appointments as one of the organists of the Chapel Royal, and private organist to Lord Sandwich (through whom he became a friend of Samuel Pepys). He was awarded the degree of D.Mus. by Oxford University in 1663. Child is remembered principally for his church anthems and service music, written in a conservative polyphonic style. He also composed more Italianate psalm settings for use at 'private meetings' during the interregnum. Very little instrumental music by him survives.   JM

Childhood of Christ, The. See ENFANCE DU CHRIST, L'.

Child of our Time, A. Oratorio (1939–41) by Tippett for soprano, alto, tenor, and bass soloists, chorus, and orchestra, a setting of his own text prompted by the persecution of Jews that followed the assassination in 1938 of a Nazi diplomat by Herschel Grynsban, a 17-year-old Jewish boy; in it Tippett uses spirituals in the same way that Bach used chorales in his Passions.

children and music. Children sometimes show aptitude for music at a remarkably early age. A few can sing in tune before the age of two, while some studies suggest that children may able to respond to music even before they are born. Certainly by the age of three or four most children are able to take part in elementary music-making, and in some cultures they do so alongside adults as soon as they are capable, though they may not be given any special or distinctive role to play.

In the European art-music tradition of recent centuries children's contributions have been more restricted, and have largely been confined to certain specific contexts. The earliest use of children for a distinct purpose in written-down music came with the rise of religious part-music covering a wide pitch range between the highest and the lowest voices; boy choristers were required to sing the highest part, since women (and girls) were not normally permitted to sing in church. This type of music made its appearance, along with trained boy choristers, during the 15th century, and since then boys have been used—at least in some churches and denominations—for this purpose.

As instrumental music gained importance during the 17th and 18th centuries, increasing numbers of children learnt to play. Eventually music was written specifically for children, and designed to suit their world. The earliest notable examples are perhaps Schumann's *Kinderszenen* (1838) and *Album für die Jugend* ('Album for the Young', 1848). These were followed by such works as Debussy's *Children's Corner* (1906–8) and vast amounts of children's music, often with an educational purpose, during the rest of the 20th century.

Children have also figured prominently in many operas. In some cases children's roles have been played by women, as in Humperdinck's *Hänsel und Gretel* (1893); in others real children are used, as in Puccini's *Tosca* (1900); while some children's roles are mute, for example Butterfly's son in Puccini's *Madama Butterfly* (1904). On the other hand, children have sometimes played adult roles. Purcell's *Dido and Aeneas*, for example, was performed in 1689 at a girls' school, for which it may have been composed. Several operas with mainly adult characters have also been written in recent years for school performance.

Since the mid-18th century, children with exceptional ability have sometimes been recognized as outstanding performers on their instrument from an early age. Mozart was the first to achieve noteworthy success as a child 'prodigy', and by the age of nine he had been widely admired as a performer in several countries, including England, France, Germany, and the Netherlands. He was soon followed by others, for example William Crotch, who was already attracting attention at the age of two, and began his first concert tour at the age of three. In more recent years there have been many notable child performers, among them Paganini, Andrés Segovia, Yehudi Menuhin, and Yo-Yo Ma. Most of the outstanding ones have continued as adults, though they are often emulated in later life by others who had earlier shown far less precocity.

Some children have begun composing at a remarkably early age. The youngest to have written a properly constructed piece of music appears to be Frederick Ouseley (1825–89), whose first known composition was created at the piano when he was 39 months old, and was written down by an older sister. Mozart began at the age of five; he composed several substantial works while still a child, including the full-length operas *La finta semplice* (1769) and *Mitridate, re di Ponto* (1770). Other noteworthy child composers include Samuel Wesley, Mendelssohn, Saint-Saëns, Richard Strauss, and Korngold. As in the case of child performers, most notable child composers develop into successful, though not necessarily outstanding, adult composers.

Music written by children of the past is often either dismissed without proper examination or ignored altogether. Yet this music is not necessarily of inferior quality, and the level of originality, imagination, and compositional technique in the best of these works is remarkably high. Many of them also display features that became characteristic of the composer's adult works. For example, Beethoven's first known composition, a set of variations written when he was 11, moves from C minor to C major towards the end, like his Fifth Symphony and several other works. And Strauss's first orchestral work, a *Festmarsch* (1876) written at a similar age, displays a lush orchestration that is strongly prophetic of his later works. Further study of such works is clearly needed.   BC

📖 C. KENNESON, *Musical Prodigies* (Portland, OR, 1999)

Children's Corner. Suite of piano pieces (1906–8) by Debussy; dedicated to his daughter, and with English titles, they are *Doctor Gradus ad Parnassum* (see GRADUS AD PARNASSUM), *Jimbo's Lullaby* ('Jimbo' is the composer's mistake for 'Jumbo'), *Serenade for the Doll*, *The Snow is Dancing*, *The Little Shepherd*, and *Golliwogg's Cake-Walk*.

Childs, Barney (Sanford) (*b* Spokane, WA, 13 Feb. 1926; *d* Redlands, CA, 11 Jan. 2000). American composer. He studied at Oxford, the University of Nevada, and Stanford, and had lessons with Carlos Chávez, Copland, and Carter. He then taught at the University of Arizona (1959–65), Deep Springs College, California (1965–9), and Redlands University (1973–94). His works include two symphonies and eight quartets, though he also composed in less traditional formats.   PG

Chile. See LATIN AMERICA, 3.

chime. 1. A generic term for a set of tuned instruments, normally *idiophones, for example stationary bells

struck by hammers or by pulling the clapper, or similar-sounding instruments such as the *tubular bells (also known as 'orchestral chimes'). Wind chimes are sets of tubes or rods of any material (usually metal, bamboo, or wood, but sometimes of glass, stone, or shell), hung to clatter in the wind.

2. Any instrument that emits a bell-like sound may be called a chime, including the 'chime bar', consisting of a single tuned metal plate fixed above a tubular resonator, used by children.

3. Clock chimes are a sequence of notes sounded on a ring of bells automatically at fixed intervals, a famous example being the 'Westminster Quarters' or 'Cambridge Chime' of the clock tower of the Houses of Parliament in London.   JMo

Chin, Unsuk (*b* Seoul, 14 July 1961). Korean composer. She studied composition at the National University in Seoul with Sukhi Kang, and from 1985 to 1988 with Ligeti in Hamburg. In 1988 she settled in Berlin. She has worked with tape and live electronics, and has a special interest in microtonal tuning. Her works include *Akrostichon-Wortspiel* for soprano and ensemble (1991, revised 1993), *Xi* for ensemble and electronics (1999), *Miroirs des temps* for vocal ensemble and orchestra (1999), which incorporates reworkings of medieval songs, and a continuing series of *Études* for piano.   ABur

Chinese block. See WOODBLOCK.

chin rest. Originally a curved piece of wood (now usually made of plastic) clamped to the lower part of violins and violas to help players grip the instrument with the chin, so freeing the left hand from supporting it. It was introduced by Spohr in about 1820.   JMo

chironomy (from Gk. *kheir*, 'hand', *nomos*, 'law'). The practice of indicating the changing pitches of a melody by regulated movements of the hand, or (less commonly) by pointing to various positions on the hand (for the latter, see GUIDO OF AREZZO). The earliest, albeit comic, account of the former is in Herodotus' *Histories* (iv.129) dating from the 5th century BC, and the practice seems to have been known throughout the ancient and medieval worlds. Since the hand signals gave only a general idea of the shape of the melody rather than exact pitches, they were probably used as a memory aid. Chironomy is still used in teaching (see TONIC SOL-FA) and in conducting Gregorian chant.
                                                         AP

Chisholm, Erik (*b* Cathcart, Glasgow, 4 Jan. 1904; *d* Rondebosch, South Africa, 7 June 1965). Scottish composer and educationist. While studying in Glasgow, London, and Edinburgh he revolutionized concert life in Glasgow, founding the Active Society for the Propagation of Contemporary Music in 1929 and inviting many of the leading figures of the day—Bartók, Schmitt, Szymanowski, and Casella among them—to give or hear concerts of their music. He was also active as a conductor and critic. He was appointed director of the South African College of Music, Cape Town University. A book on the operas of Janáček was published posthumously in 1971. Chisholm wrote over 100 works, including nine operas, seven ballets, and 35 works for orchestra (two symphonies and a Concerto for Orchestra). Evidence of his precocity is given by the Chaconne, Triple Fugue and Epilogue he wrote as a 16-year-old, each fugue subject representing a different girlfriend.   MA

chitarrone (It.). A name used from about 1580 to about 1650 for the *theorbo, derived from the Greek *kithara* (the concert *lyre).

chiuso (It., 'closed'). 1. In horn playing, the same as *stopped.

2. See OUVERT AND CLOS.

Chlubna, Osvald (*b* Brno, 22 July 1893; *d* Brno, 30 Oct. 1971). Czech composer. A pupil of Janáček, he is remembered chiefly for his arrangements of his teacher's music, including the last act of *Šárka*, the unfinished symphony *The Danube*, and *From the House of the Dead*, to which he added a cheerful ending at variance with Janáček's original intentions. Chlubna's own music, heard at its best in the orchestral work *To je má zem* ('This is My Country'), is warmly Romantic.   JSM

choeur (Fr.). 'Chorus' or 'choir'. In addition, the term *grand choeur* is used to denote a group of stops added to the *fonds d'orgue* on French post-classical organs.

choir, chorus (Fr.: *choeur*; Ger.: *Chor*; It.: *coro*). Both terms denote a body of singers performing as a group, normally, though not necessarily, in parts. The English language appears to be alone in perpetuating a useful distinction between 'choir' and 'chorus'. The latter is commonly used to denote larger groups of singers—especially amateur enthusiasts, but also professionals in the theatre and opera house. 'Choir' is applied mostly to smaller bodies of singers—to ecclesiastical groups, and to small, expert groups such as are often composed of professionals and called 'chamber choirs'. In addition, the term 'consort of voices' began to be used in the mid-20th century to denote a specialized choir formed to sing, for instance, the repertory of Renaissance madrigals, with only one or two voices to each part.

1. The early church choir; 2. The choir in opera and oratorio; 3. Recent developments

1. The early church choir

Classical and biblical sources abound in references to choral singing. In the modern Western art-music tradition, its practice has always been especially fostered by the Christian Church—indeed, knowledge of the extent of choral singing before about the 16th century is limited by the fact that only its ecclesiastical use was systematically documented. The standard vehicle for the Christian liturgy was monophonic plainchant, though in general this was cultivated in only the corporate ecclesiastical institutions—the monastic, cathedral, and collegiate churches, and the private household chapels of royalty and aristocracy—which could deploy large numbers of voices. Following the cessation of child oblation in the 12th century, monastic choirs consisted only of adult men, in many instances numbering over 50. Cathedral and collegiate churches and household chapels were staffed both by men (canons and their substitutes under many different names, numbering up to 50) and by boy choristers (up to 16); nunneries deployed women's voices alone. These rendered plainchant in unison (the boys, where available, singing an octave above the men), either as a body or antiphonally across the choir. No matter how great, these corporate churches and chapels were essentially the private chapels of their immediate members; the lay public was not normally admitted to their services.

From an early date responsorial performance of the chant was introduced to inject variety into its execution, the choral chant alternating with passages sung by either one soloist or a unison group of up to four. The contrast was heightened when, from about the 11th century onwards, such soloist passages began to be enhanced, on feast days, by the addition of newly composed polyphonic counterpoints. The medieval church knew no choral polyphony, only the ensemble of three or four soloists, drawn from alto, tenor, and baritone voices. However, around the turn of the 15th century, the practice began of having a small chorus sing polyphonically. The steady increase through the century in the proportion of the singers expected to be capable of joining the polyphonic chorus can be traced in the corresponding increase in size of the choirbooks from which they sang. In England, boys' and bass voices were added to the ensemble from *c*.1450, and the principle of the SATB chorus of up to 25 voices had become established well before the end of the century. In many European countries, however, the use of adult male sopranos or (later) castratos instead of boys, and the recruitment of small specialized groups, in preference to using the larger foundation choir, produced for a time a distinctive and—in the case of the Sistine Chapel choir—long-enduring vocal sound.

The early Renaissance choir performed unaccompanied, but accompanying instruments began to be used between about 1510 and 1520, and by the end of the 16th century the practice was widespread, though far from universal. In 16th-century Germany, and subsequently also elsewhere, the application of Reformation principles encouraged unison congregational participation in the singing of hymns and metrical psalms during services. Nevertheless, the performance of choral polyphony during the Baroque period remained the preserve of the professional church choir. Indeed, in Lutheran churches the employment of a trained choir was long perpetuated, now under the auspices of either clerical or municipal authorities. In Leipzig, Bach could call on the services of up to 36 musicians.

2. The choir in opera and oratorio

In numerous Italian (and some south German) cathedrals and court chapels, the multiplicity of singers and instrumentalists enabled composers to experiment with the sonority created by *cori spezzati*—two or more choirs of equal or contrasting composition, placed in different parts of the building. It was in Italy also that a yet more dramatic use for the vocal chorus was pioneered. Monteverdi and the earliest Mantuan and Roman opera composers had employed a chorus, but their Italian successors did not persevere with this departure (unlike Lully and Rameau in France); instead it was taken up by oratorio composers, who for the first time took the chorus outside the simple context of the liturgical service to give it the role of narrator and commentator in large-scale dramatic works.

For Italian oratorio (like the German cantata) the chorus was supplied by established professional church choirs, and this remained the case in England when Handel first transplanted the genre there. After his death, however, an unprecedented interest in choral singing emerged among amateur enthusiasts, leading to the creation of gentlemen's madrigal societies and catch clubs, and of parish church 'west gallery' bands devoted to singing Handel choruses, and also to the accumulation of enormous choirs to sing oratorio—especially Handel's—in public. Subsequently, in both Britain and Germany, such ad hoc choruses began, around the turn of the 19th century, to achieve greater continuity of organization through being brought under the auspices of permanent mixed-voice choral societies. In Britain many were based on parish churches or, especially, Nonconformist chapels; the celebrated Huddersfield Choral Society was founded in 1836. Large-scale choral festivals further nourished the amateur choral movement, reaching their apogee in the gigantic Handel Festivals held triennially at the Crystal Palace (1859–1926).

3. Recent developments

The rise of the mixed amateur chorus largely reduced church choirs to singing the liturgy; in the late 18th century some German court chapels could do justice to the masses of Haydn, Mozart, and Beethoven, but elsewhere revolutionary fervour extinguished much liturgical observance. Even in England performance standards declined, until the mid-19th-century ritualistic Oxford Movement stimulated a revived interest in the surpliced chancel choir. Many provincial cathedrals and Oxford and Cambridge college chapels now maintain choirs of high standard; and sporadic examples elsewhere, such as Regensburg Cathedral in Germany and Montserrat Abbey in Spain, show that the tradition is not limited to England.

At most periods in the history of opera, composers have valued and exploited the scope of the chorus for complementing and heightening the functions of principals and orchestra. Since the early 19th century the chorus has been a standard character in the operatic conception, and every major opera house maintains its resident professional chorus.

Perhaps the most intriguing departure in recent years has been the rise of the chamber choir specializing in Renaissance, Baroque, or contemporary music. Many leading composers, including Birtwistle, Boulez, Bryars, Ferneyhough, Pärt, and Xenakis, have deployed the expertise of these bodies in novel approaches to the setting and projection of words, and in exploring an almost orchestral range of vocal sound, sonority, and timbre. Indeed, in its many guises—as large amateur chorus, church choir, opera chorus, vocal consort, children's choir, or chamber choir—the chorus of human voices continues to offer composers a varied and challenging medium of performance.   RB/RW

choirbook. A term generally used to denote a book from the 14th–17th centuries in which all the voices of a polyphonic composition are written separately. The upper voice is always on the top of the left-hand page, the lowest is usually at the bottom of the right-hand page, and so on. Since choirbooks are often a mere 30 cm high they are useful only for relatively small 'choirs', perhaps with just one singer to a voice, though occasional examples can be up to 80 cm high. From about 1500, as choirs grew larger, individual partbooks gradually took over, but many of the masses of Lassus and Palestrina, for example, were originally published in choirbook format.   DF

choir organ (Ger.: *Chororgel*). See CHAIR ORGAN. The name is also given to a small organ in the chancel of a church, used to accompany the choir.

Chopin, Fryderyk (*see page 248*)

Chor (Ger.). 'Chorus' or 'choir'.

Choralbearbeitung (Ger., 'chorale reworking'). Specifically, a work—vocal or instrumental—based on a Protestant chorale melody (e.g. *chorale cantata, *chorale prelude). However, the term has also been applied more widely to pieces based on any kind of pre-existing sacred melody, particularly plainchant, and therefore embraces Notre Dame *organum as well as many late medieval and Renaissance motets.

chorale (from Ger. *Choral*). The strophic congregational hymn of the Protestant Church in Germany. The German term originally signified a plainchant melody sung chorally, but from the late 16th century its meaning was widened to include vernacular hymns. However, the term most commonly used for such hymns in early Reformation times was *geistliche* (or *christliche*) *Lieder* ('spiritual songs'). Strictly speaking, the word 'chorale' means both the text and the melody of a hymn, considered as a unit, but not infrequently the term is used to describe the music alone—either a single-line melody or a fully harmonized version as in the four-part settings of Bach.

From the outset of the *Reformation the chorale proved to be one of the most powerful means of disseminating the ideals of the new Confession, crystallizing its message in simple language and providing an opportunity for congregations to take a central role in liturgical worship. Martin Luther was much involved in the creation of the new hymns, writing some 36 himself and encouraging others (notably Justus Jonas, Lazarus Spengler, and Paul Speratus) to follow his example. The texts and melodies of most of the earliest chorales, however, were adaptations of various older sources, particularly Gregorian hymns, antiphons, and sequences, and medieval German religious songs—the latter frequently requiring radical 'purification' from a doctrinal point of view. In addition to translating and adapting Latin hymns Luther produced some magnificent psalm paraphrases, such as 'Aus tiefer Not' (Psalm 130), and a number of hymns based on the medieval *Leise* (e.g. 'Nun bitten wir den heiligen Geist'). In addition, he wrote several liturgical hymns designed as substitutes for parts of the Latin Ordinary of the Mass, such as 'Wir glauben all' an einen Gott' to replace (or, at times in the liturgy, to supplement) the Credo.

No doubt the musically gifted Luther was responsible for the tunes to many of his own chorales, though few of them can be regarded as wholly original. Even the most famous of the melodies attributed to him, that set to *'Ein' feste Burg', appears to be modelled on the tune called *Silberweise* ('Silver Tone') written in 1513 by the renowned Meistersinger Hans Sachs (which in turn shows signs of having been based on an earlier model). One characteristic feature of many of the melodies, which stems from Meistersinger practice, is the use of *Bar* form.

Two main types of chorale book were published during the 16th century, one containing polyphonic settings for use by trained choirs, with the melody normally placed in the tenor voice (as was customary in the standard cantus firmus practice of the time), and the other with single-line melodies only, for the use of congregations. The earliest example of the first type was Johann Walter's *Geystliches gesangk Buchleyn* (Wittenberg, 1524), while the most renowned of the early congregational books were those of Joseph Klug (Wittenberg, 1529) and Valentin Babst (Leipzig, 1545). A step of major significance was taken in 1586 when Lukas Osiander published a book of fully harmonized chorales with the melody in the treble line. This method of harmonization, created partially in imitation of Calvinist singing and known as 'Cantionalsatz', was designed to facilitate congregational participation.

The Thirty Years War severely disrupted German liturgical life and fostered the composition of comparatively subjective chorales which could also be used for personal devotions. Particularly influential in this regard were the meditations on sin, death and suffering by Paul Gerhardt (1608–76), author of *'O Haupt voll Blut und Wunden'. Johannes Crüger, Gerhardt's colleague at the Nikolaikirche in Berlin and composer of the melodies to 'Nun danket alle Gott' and 'Jesu meine Freude', also made important contributions to the re-shaping of the received tradition through his work as an editor of hymnbooks. Crüger published harmonizations consisting of a melodic line with figured-bass accompaniment, a format which became standard during the 18th century. He also incorporated the new devotional hymns alongside the older Reformation chorales, updating the latter with accidentals reflecting the influence of contemporary Italian tonal and harmonic procedures. Further emphasis on the individual's emotional experience in German hymnody was subsequently heightened by the emergence of Pietism as a theological movement.

J. S. Bach, perhaps the last great exponent of the chorale before it entered into decline during the Enlightenment, produced a monumental collection of

(*cont. on p. 249*)

Fryderyk Chopin
(1810–49)

The Polish composer and pianist Fryderyk (Frédéric) Franciszek Chopin was born in Żelazowa Wola, near Warsaw, probably on 1 March 1810, and died in Paris on 17 October 1849.

Chopin spent his early life in Warsaw, where he studied privately with Adalbert Żywny (1756–1842) and at the High School of Music with Józef Elsner (1769–1854). From an early age his talents were much in demand in the leading aristocratic households in Warsaw, and he continued to move freely in such circles when he moved to Paris in 1831. Although he clearly drew much of his inspiration from a private, idealized image of Poland, Chopin found his way of life in Paris congenial and soon put to the back of his mind any thoughts of returning to his homeland. He made a comfortable living from teaching and from sales of his published music, and he enjoyed the friendship of some of Europe's most eminent artists and composers.

After the failure in 1837 of his plans to marry Maria Wodzińska, a Polish girl of good family, Chopin found himself increasingly involved with the novelist George Sand; the next ten years of his life were dominated by that relationship, though it seems that they were lovers in the accepted sense for only a short time. These were productive years for Chopin, and when the relationship ended in 1847 (partly as a result of family intrigues involving George Sand's children from her marriage to Casimir Dudevant) he composed little more.

Chopin's legendary reputation as a performer, and above all improviser, was based almost exclusively on his frequent appearances in fashionable society drawing-rooms, for, unlike most composer-pianists of the day, he disliked the public concert. Contemporary accounts of his playing stress its lyrical, flowing quality, the remarkable delicacy of his touch, and the subtlety of his dynamic shading and pedalling. His compositions rarely ventured beyond the world of the piano, for he drew much of his inspiration directly from the exploration of its sonorities, translating into its idiomatic language gestures culled from symphonic and operatic literature as well as from popular and folkloristic materials. The extra-musical, and specifically literary, sources of inspiration that were so fashionable in the early 19th century held little attraction for him, and if his music reflects, in its sheer intensity of feeling, the restless, yearning spirit of the age, it does so without resort to cheap emotional effects or extravagant rhetoric and certainly without the aid of a programme.

The works composed in Warsaw (polonaises, rondos, variations) reflect above all the influence of such composer-virtuosos as Hummel, Weber, and Kalkbrenner. The three early compositions for piano and orchestra are typical of this *stile brillante*, both in their forms—rondo, variations, and fantasia—and in their links with opera (op. 2), and with 'national' airs (op. 13) and dances (op. 14). Even the two piano concertos (1829–30), in which the composer's personal voice is a great deal stronger, belong to this world in their overall style and conception. The concertos marked the end of Chopin's apprenticeship. With the *Études* op. 10, completed in 1832, he achieved the fully integrated style of his maturity, a style characterized by a marked refinement of detail within prevailing melody and accompaniment textures, often involving a subtle mixture or 'counterpoint' of fragmentary motifs—melodic, rhythmic, and textural.

As the conventional rhetoric of *stile brillante* faded from Chopin's musical language, other, more lasting, influences gained ground. His affinity with Bach, especially clear in the preludes and studies, is revealed in figurative patterns which imply a strong harmonic foundation while at the same time permitting linear-melodic elements to emerge through the pattern. Bach is recalled also in the increasingly close-knit, intricate textures of Chopin's later music and in his preference for unitary formal schemes—often a single impulse of departure and return.

Early 19th-century Italian opera too played a part in shaping Chopin's musical language, both directly and mediated through the cantilenas of Hummel and Field. The nocturnes in particular respond to Italian bel canto, in their widely spanning melodic arcs, their *fioriture*, and their stylization of such vocal embellishments as portamento and parlando repetitions of a single note. Even more characteristically, the modal and rhythmic structures, melodic intonations, and harmonic asperities of Mazovian folk music permeate the mazurkas which preoccupied Chopin throughout his life and which embody some of his most private thoughts.

Chopin has frequently been criticized for a weak, even primitive, sense of form. Yet the relatively static ternary design favoured in many of his shorter pieces creates a necessary foil or counterpoint to dynamic and carefully graded tension–release patterns, achieved principally through harmony. This counterpoint of external pattern and intensity curve is anything but primitive, and it is seen again in single-movement extended works such as the four ballades, the *Fantasy* op. 49, and the *Polonaise-fantaisie* op. 61. Even more than the sonatas, these works are triumphs of architecture, blending and adapting elements of Classical formal archetypes—sonata, rondo, and variations—to give structural strength to the composer's 'narrative' manner.

Chopin's influence was immense, and it acted on several different levels. The external characteristics of his style were appropriated by many composers of light 'salon' pieces, designed primarily for the Victorian musical soirée. More crucially, his innovatory harmonic language foreshadowed Brahms, Wagner, and other late Romantics, while his approach to thematic working informed several composers working outside the Austro-German mainstream, notably in Russia. Most influential of all was his development of a new soundscape of highly idiomatic piano textures, essentially distinct from the pianism of Beethoven, Schumann, Mendelssohn, and Brahms.

The differentiation within these textures, and the detail and subtlety of their composition, were unprecedented in keyboard music. In general, the style is characterized by a transparency and lightness of sound, by a thinning-out of density across the whole range of the keyboard, and by a sensitivity to nuances of dynamics and articulation. Its legatees were above all Russian and French composers and its influence was still clearly discernible in the early years of the 20th century, in the piano music of Rakhmaninov, Lyadov, and Skryabin, for example, and of Fauré and Debussy. The link with Debussy extends beyond such textural parallels, moreover. In Chopin texture and configuration gain a new structural status, at times even superseding harmony as the formal determinant of a work. His music takes a decisive step towards the eventual liberation of texture and colour as structural agents more than half a century later. JS

F. NIECKS, *Frederick Chopin as a Man and Musician*, 2 vols. (London, 1888, 3/1902/R1973) · G. ABRAHAM, *Chopin's Musical Style* (London, 1939, 4/1960) · A. HEDLEY, *Chopin* (London, 1947) · A. HEDLEY (ed.), *Selected Correspondence of Fryderyk Chopin* (London, 1962) · J. SAMSON, *The Music of Chopin* (London, 1985, 2/1994) · J.-J. EIGELDINGER, *Chopin: Pianist and Teacher*, trans. N. Shohet with K. Osostowicz and R. Howat, ed. R. Howat (Cambridge, 1986) · J. SAMSON (ed.), *The Cambridge Companion to Chopin* (Cambridge, 1992) · J. SAMSON, *Chopin* (Oxford and New York, 1996) · J. KALLBERG, *Chopin at the Boundaries: Sex, History and Musical Genre* (Cambridge, MA, and London, 1996) · J. RINK, *Chopin: The Piano Concertos* (Cambridge, 1997)

choral and instrumental settings, including a valuable body of four-part harmonizations. Bach's example was of fundamental importance to the musicologists and liturgiologists who carried out the restoration of the tradition during the 19th and 20th centuries.

BS/ALi

K. AMELN, *The Roots of German Hymnody of the Reformation Era* (St Louis, MO, 1964) · J. RIEDEL, *The Lutheran Chorale: Its Basic Traditions* (Minneapolis, 1967) · R. L. MARSHALL, *Luther, Bach, and the Early Reformation Chorale* (Atlanta, GA, 1995)

chorale cantata (Ger.: *Choralkantate*). A cantata with two or more movements based on chorale texts (and usually also melodies). There are three main types: those in which one chorale is used for all the movements; those in which some movements use texts from other sources; and those in which some chorale verses are paraphrased as free poetry, in the form of recitatives and arias. The last type was of Bach's own devising and occurs in his cantatas of the 1720s, for example in *Ach Gott von Himmel* (BWV2).

chorale fantasia. An organ work in the free style of a fantasia based on a chorale melody (see ORGAN CHORALE). Chorale fantasias, often large-scale works, were composed by north German 17th- and 18th-century composers, notably Buxtehude and Bach, and the genre was revived in the late 19th century by such composers as Reger.

chorale fugue (Ger.: *Choralfuge*). An organ fugue taking as its subject the first line (or two lines) of a chorale melody (see ORGAN CHORALE). Chorale fugues were composed in Germany from the late 17th century by such composers as Pachelbel.

chorale mass. A mass based on the German chorales appropriate to the items of the Lutheran liturgy.

chorale motet (Ger.: *Choralmotette*). A polyphonic composition based on a chorale melody. At first the melody was treated as a *cantus firmus, but from the end of the 16th century it became more usual to use each line as a subject for fugal imitation. Sometimes the organ may replace one or more of the voice parts. Two fine examples of chorale motets are Scheidt's *Fantasia super 'Ich ruf zu dir'* and Bach's *Nun komm der Heiden Heiland*.

chorale partita. See CHORALE VARIATIONS.

chorale prelude (Ger.: *Choralvorspiel*). A setting of a chorale melody, usually for organ, and originally having the function in the Lutheran service of introducing congregational singing of that same melody. It could, however, particularly by the 18th century, take on an independent role, allowing for domestic study and enjoyment for professionals and amateurs alike.

See also ORGAN CHORALE. DY

chorale trio. A type of *organ chorale devised by J. S. Bach.

chorale variations. A set of variations, usually for keyboard, on a chorale melody (see ORGAN CHORALE). The genre developed during the 17th century, modelled on the secular variation sets of Sweelinck, Froberger, and Scheidt, among others. Pachelbel wrote seven sets of chorale variations, while Bach wrote three sets called *Partite* (BWV766–8) and the Canonic Variations on *Vom Himmel hoch*. Buxtehude's variations on *Auf meinen lieben Gott* incorporate secular dance forms borrowed from the *suite, a procedure followed in the 20th century by Ernst Krenek.

Choral Fantasia. 1. Beethoven's op. 80 (1808), for piano, chorus, and orchestra, a setting of a poem by Christoph Kuffner; it consists of variations on Beethoven's song *Gegenliebe* (1794–5), a melody that resembles that of the principal theme of the finale of his Ninth Symphony, for which this fantasia seems to have been a preliminary study.

2. Holst's op. 51 (1930), for soprano, chorus, organ, strings, brass, and percussion, a setting of words by Robert Bridges.

Choralfuge (Ger.). 'Chorale fugue'.

Choralmotette (Ger.). 'Chorale motet'.

'Choral' Symphony. Popular name for Beethoven's Symphony no. 9 in D minor (1823–4), which includes a setting for chorus and soloists of Schiller's *An die Freude* ('Ode to Joy') in the last movement. Other symphonies

using choral forces include Berlioz's *Roméo et Juliette*; Liszt's *Dante Symphony* (1856) and *Faust Symphony* (1854); Holst's First Choral Symphony (1923–4), a four-movement setting for soprano, chorus, and orchestra of four poems by John Keats; Mahler's Second ('Resurrection'), Third, Fourth (a solo soprano appears in the final movement), and Eighth symphonies; Vaughan Williams's *A Sea Symphony*; Britten's *Spring Symphony*; and Shostakovich's Second, Third, 13th, and 14th symphonies.

Choralvorspiel (Ger.). 'Chorale prelude'.

chord (Fr.: *accord*; Ger.: *Akkord, Klang*; It.: *accordo*). Two or more notes sounded together. The different types are named according to the *intervals they span: the *triad, for example—the fundamental chord in Western harmony—is built from a 'root' note with two superposed 3rds; the *dominant 7th consists of a triad on the dominant of the diatonic major scale with the addition of the note a 7th above the dominant.

See also INVERSION, 1; ROOT, ROOT POSITION.

PFa

chordophone. A term used in *organology for all instruments sounded by the vibration of strings, whether they are plucked (e.g. *guitar, *lute), bowed (e.g. *violin), blown (e.g. *aeolian harp), struck (e.g. *dulcimer, *piano), or electronically amplified (e.g. *electric guitar). See INSTRUMENTS, CLASSIFICATION OF. JMo

choreographic poem. A piece of music originally designed as a ballet, but which can also stand as an orchestral work in its own right. Famous examples include Debussy's *Prélude à 'L'Après-midi d'un faune'*, and Ravel's *Boléro* and *La Valse* (subtitled 'poème chorégraphique'). The designation was used more loosely by Maxwell Davies for *The Beltane Fire* (1995). JBe

choreography (from Gk. *khoreia*, 'choral dancing to music', and *graphē*, 'writing'). The art of composing dance or ballet. The term was first used in a French treatise on dance by Raoul-Auger Feuillet and Pierre Beauchamp (1700) to denote graphic symbols representing the movement of the feet. Its better-known, current meaning is thought to have originated in 1777 with J. C. Feldstein's *Die Kunst nach Choregraphie zu Tanzen und Tänze zu schrieben* ('The art of dancing from choreography and writing dances'). The notation of dances is known as *choreology.

Choreography usually falls into one of three categories: narrative, mood, or abstract. Narrative choreography has recognizable, named characters and a conventionally linear plot, as in *Swan Lake*; it borrows from drama and pantomime the gestures and mime needed to convey feelings and responses. Mood choreography is highly expressive and although it has no plot it evokes a sense of situation or atmosphere: for example, Christopher Bruce's *Ghost Dances* (1981). Abstract choreography is entirely non-representational, exploring dance as an art in itself, as in George Balanchine's choreography of Stravinsky's *Agon* (1957) or Paul Taylor's *Aureole* (1968).

The term 'choreographer' denotes an artist who creates dances, whether in ballet, modern, or popular form. In the 16th and 17th centuries, such an artist would have been designated a dancing master, later replaced with the title 'ballet master', and in the 20th century with that of choreographer. In modern usage, a ballet master or ballet mistress is the person in day-to-day charge of the company, who gives daily classes, assigns roles, and takes rehearsals of established works.

Before the 20th century, the overwhelming majority of choreographers were male. This may, at least in the 19th century, owe something to the lack of challenge for male dancers in the repertory, where the focus was firmly on the star ballerinas. However, in the 20th century there were as many significant female choreographers as male. Male choreographers have, to some extent, continued to dominate ballet (for example, Mikhail Fokine (1880–1942), Vaslav Nijinsky, Leonid Massine (1895–1979), George Balanchine (1904–83), David Tudor, Serge Lifar, Frederick Ashton (1904–88), and Kenneth MacMillan, with Bronislava Nijinska, Marie Rambert (1888–1982), and Ninette de Valois (1898–2001) standing out as female pioneers in ballet choreography); in modern dance, however, most choreographers until the middle of the century were women, most notably Isadora Duncan (1878–1927), Ruth St Denis (1877–1969), Mary Wigman (1886–1973), Martha Graham (1894–1991), and Doris Humphrey.

Most social dances, both historically and currently, need no choreographer as they are based on a limited number of steps and conventions. Choreography is brought into play only when dance's primary function becomes spectacle rather than participatory activity. Choreography, therefore, is the art of combining and extending the basic vocabulary of steps and gestures within a dance genre to create an original work which, at its best, communicates thought and feeling through the structuring of movement in time and space.

The main genres of choreographed dance are ballet, modern dance, and jazz dance. Jazz dance is an umbrella term for genres largely derived from 20th-century American social dances, including tap, swing dance, and the style of dancing popularized in musical theatre. Florenz Ziegfeld's *Follies* were one of the earliest examples of this on Broadway, further popularized in film by Fred Astaire, Ginger Rogers, and Gene Kelly.

George Balanchine choreographed the musical *On your Toes* (1936) and influenced the development of theatrical jazz dance by introducing ballet steps without ballet's conventionally turned-out positioning of the legs. Some of the most influential choreographers in this genre have come from ballet and modern dance backgrounds. Jerome Robbins (1918–98), the choreographer of *West Side Story* (1957), was a classical dancer who choreographed works for American Ballet Theatre and New York City Ballet; Agnes de Mille (1905–93), trained with Marie Rambert, choreographed Copland's *Rodeo* in 1943 and, later, *Oklahoma!*, with its famous dream-sequence ballet.

Dance in all genres is usually accompanied by music, but modern choreographers are more willing to replace music with other sounds, such as those generated by the dancers themselves as they move. This is notable in the work of Pina Bausch (*b* 1940) who regularly incorporates alternative sonic accompaniments into her work, such as the sound of chairs being knocked over in *Café Müller* (1978), or of alsatians barking on stage in *Nelken* (1982). The use of speech in dance works is also more common as in the British company Second Stride's *Escape at Sea* (1993), breaking the long-held ballet convention that dancers should be seen but not heard.

The changing nature of the performing space has also had an impact on choreography. In the 16th century social dances were often performed as entertainments, with the audience viewing from all sides and often from above; this led to choreography concentrating on creating geometric floor-patterns. This continued in such genres as **ballet de cour*. Performances increasingly moved to theatres with proscenium arches, so the audience now viewed the dancers from the front, though no two spectators would have an identical view. The new dimension of stage depth and the resulting sight-lines, therefore, needed to be accounted for in choreography, along with the move away from abstract social dances to more narrative forms. More recently, theatres have experimented with a number of different configurations such as thrust stages and theatre in the round, as well as site-specific works in such venues as galleries and warehouses, where the space itself becomes a feature of the choreography. Dance works have also been created for or adapted to television and video, such as Lloyd Newson's film version of *Strange Fish* with DV8 (1992), the new media freeing choreography from the restriction of a single enclosed stage.

See also BALLET AND THEATRICAL DANCE.

NG/JH

📖 P. Van Praagh and P. Brinson, *The Choreographic Art: An Outline of Its Principles and Craft* (New York, 1963) · E. Sawyer, *Dance with the Music: The World of the Ballet Musician* (Cambridge, 1985) · S. L. Foster, *Choreography*

& *Narrative: Ballet's Staging of Story and Desire* (Bloomington, IN, 1996) · J. ANDERSON, *Art without Boundaries* (London, 1997) · M. BREMSER, *Fifty Contemporary Choreographers* (London and New York, 1999)

choreology. A system of dance notation. The recording on paper of movement patterns has taken many forms over several centuries. Choreology was developed by Rudolph and Joan Benesh and first made public in 1955, when it was adopted by the Royal Ballet. The Benesh Institute (formerly the Institute of Choreology) was founded in 1962 and merged with the Royal Academy of Dance in 1997. Choreology is the more widely used of two principal dance notation systems, the other being Labanotation. It aims to provide a visual representation of the dancer's position, as viewed from behind, using a five-line staff to notate the positions of the head, shoulders, waist, knees, and feet. Additional symbols indicate the position of limbs, direction and dynamics of movement, and group formations. The first score fully notated in this way was Serge Grigoriev's re-creation of Fokine's original choreography for Stravinsky's *Petrushka*, staged by the Royal Ballet in 1957 and notated by Joan Benesh.

JH

chorister. A boy or, more rarely, a girl singer in an English cathedral choir or university choir school.

Chororgel (Ger.). 'Choir organ'. See also CHAIR ORGAN.

Chorton (Ger., 'choir pitch'). The term used by 18th-century German theorists to denote a pitch standard higher than normal in Italy and in organs; see PITCH, 3.

Chout (*Skazka pro shuta*; 'The Tale of the Buffoon'). Ballet in six scenes by Prokofiev to his own scenario after Nikolay Afanas'yev; it was composed in 1915 and revised in 1920 and was first performed by Diaghilev's Ballets Russes (Paris, 1921). Prokofiev arranged an orchestral suite from the score (1920).

Chou Wen-chung (*b* Chefoo [now Yantai], 29 June 1923). Chinese-born American composer. He emigrated in 1946 and studied at the New England Conservatory, at Columbia University, and privately with Varèse (1949–54). As the latter's musical executor, he completed *Nocturnal* and edited other scores. His own works show the influence of Varèse, but more deeply that of Chinese music. In 1972 he was appointed professor at Columbia.

PG

Chowning, John (*b* Salem, NJ, 22 Aug. 1934). American composer. He studied at Stanford University and in Paris with Nadia Boulanger (1959–62). In 1975 he became director of the Center for Computer Research in Music and Acoustics at Stanford, and he advised Boulez on the setting up of a similar institution in Paris—IRCAM. His few works are among the most beautiful and sophisticated achievements in computer music, and include *Stria* (1977) and *Phoné* (1981).

PG

'Christmas' Concerto. Popular name for Corelli's Concerto Grosso in G minor op. 6 no. 8, for strings and continuo, published in Amsterdam in 1714; it was intended as a *concerto da chiesa* (for church use) and was inscribed 'fatto per la notte di Natale' ('made for Christmas night').

Christmas Eve (*Noch' pered rozhdestvom*). Opera in four acts by Rimsky-Korsakov to his own libretto after the story in Nikolay Gogol's *Evenings on a Farm near Dikanka* (ii, 1832) (St Petersburg, 1895).

Christmas Oratorio (*Weinachts-Oratorium*). Oratorio by J. S. Bach to texts, possibly by Picander, relating the biblical story of the Nativity with a commentary; it comprises six cantatas designed for performance in Leipzig on the six feast-days between Christmas Day and Epiphany (1734–5) and includes music adapted from his secular cantatas. Schütz also wrote a *Christmas Oratorio* (1664).

Christoff, Boris (Kirilov) (*b* Plovdiv, 18 May 1914; *d* Rome, 28 June 1993). Bulgarian bass. After studying law in Sofia, he impressed the King of Bulgaria when he sang solos in the Gusla Choir, and in 1941 the king awarded him a scholarship to study with the baritone Riccardo Stracciari in Rome. He continued his studies in Salzburg but was interned in a wartime labour camp. In 1946 he made his debut in Rome, first as a concert singer, then as Colline in *La bohème* at Reggio Calabria. In 1949 he was engaged to sing his first Boris Godunov for his Covent Garden debut, creating a sensation that made him world-famous overnight. He was compared to Chaliapin and was soon engaged by international opera houses to sing the roles that had made Chaliapin famous, notably Philip II in *Don Carlos* and Méphistophélès in *Faust*. He also sang Wagner. His voice was not large but it projected powerfully and conjured up a range of colours and nuances. He was an intensely charismatic actor and conveyed the meanings of words as dramatically and sensitively as the music.

JT

📖 A. BOZHKOV, *Boris Christoff* (Sofia, 1985; Eng. trans. 1991)

Christophe Colomb ('Christopher Columbus'). Opera in two acts by Milhaud to a libretto by Paul Claudel (Berlin, 1930; revised Graz, 1968); on an enormous scale, it is in 27 scenes and incorporates film. Pietro Ottoboni (1690), Morlacchi (1828), Franchetti (1892), and Egk (1933) also wrote operas on the subject.

Christou, Jani (*b* Heliopolis, Egypt, 8 Jan. 1926; *d* Athens, 8 Jan. 1970). Greek composer. He studied philosophy at Cambridge (1938–44) and remained in England to take composition lessons with Hans Redlich (1945–8). Influenced by his elder brother Evanghelos, a psychoanalyst, he studied with Carl Jung (1948) before completing his musical education in Italy (1949–50). During the 1950s, in such works as the First Symphony (1949–50), he worked with the advanced serialism of the period, but with the orchestral *Patterns and Permutations* (1960) that style began to give way to one fiercely driven by mystical ideas; the Pentecost oratorio *Tongues of Fire* (1964) shows this style at its height. In 1965–6 Christou sketched a large number of psychological 're-enactments' for stage performance. The magnum opus of his last years, an operatic setting of the *Oresteia*, was left unfinished when he died in a car crash. PG

Christus. 1. Oratorio (1862–7) by Liszt for soprano, alto, tenor, baritone, and bass soloists, chorus, organ, and orchestra, a setting of a biblical and liturgical text.

2. Oratorio, op. 97, by Mendelssohn to a text by Chevalier Bunsen; it was begun in 1844 but left unfinished at Mendelssohn's death.

Christus am Ölberge ('Christ on the Mount of Olives'). Oratorio, op. 85 (1803; revised 1804), by Beethoven for soprano, tenor, bass, chorus, and orchestra, a setting of a text by Franz Xaver Huber; the English version, called *Engedi*, changes the subject to the story of David.

Chromatic Fantasia and Fugue. Keyboard work by J. S. Bach, BWV903 (*c.*1720); the fantasia makes remarkable chromatic modulations and the fugue subject is highly chromatic.

chromaticism (from Gk. *khroma*, 'colour'). In the modern sense, the use of a scale that divides the octave into 12 equal intervals of a semitone (see SCALE, 4). Chromaticism has been a feature of music since its origins in ancient Greece, however, in the sense of the 'colouring' of intervals by non-diatonic subdivision. Greek theory recognized a partly chromatic *tetrachord involving two adjacent semitones. There was discussion in the 14th century about the value of incorporating all possible *musica ficta* notes into the diatonic series to make a complete chromatic scale, already a feature in keyboard instruments of the time. In the later 16th century chromatic inflection was exploited by Italian

madrigalists, notably Marenzio and Gesualdo (see MADRIGAL, 3). In the Baroque period, chromaticism was an important source of *Affekt* (see AFFECTIONS, DOCTRINE OF), not only as an expressive device in vocal music but also in such instrumental works as fugues and other contrapuntal forms on chromatic subjects.

Against the background of a universal tonal language, chromaticism in the Classical and Romantic periods is usually interpreted as a steady historical progress towards the dissolution of tonality. Whereas the extremes of tonal chromaticism in Classical music—for example in the Introduction of Mozart's 'Dissonance' Quartet K465—elaborated a decisive tonal centre, so that the fundamentally diatonic harmonic structure of a piece was never in question, the richer tonal palette of such early 19th-century composers as Chopin brought chromatic ambiguity into the basic material of composition. Wagner's chromatic harmony (though itself owing much to Liszt) was the principal influence over this process. His increasing emphasis on non-diatonic chords (especially in *Tristan und Isolde* and *Parsifal*) and his use of complex chromatic alterations obscuring the immediate sense of diatonic reference, with the 'classical' distinction between closely and distantly related keys becoming less salient, all prepared for the appearance of 'total chromaticism'.

By 1909 Schoenberg and his pupils were writing music whose characteristics were post-tonal—relatively free of the constraints of major–minor tonality, functional harmony, and the concepts of dissonance and consonance as separate, complementary harmonic phenomena (see, for example, Schoenberg's *Erwartung* and Webern's Six Pieces for Orchestra op. 6). A more ordered kind of chromaticism appeared in the 1920s in the form of *twelve-note music, in which the repeated permutations of the chromatic scale are one organizing element of the pitch structure. Although the extreme heterogeneity of later 20th-century music embodied resistance to such total chromaticism as much as perpetuation of it, the most vital tonal music being written at the turn of the millennium was undoubtedly more chromatic than diatonic. JD/AW

chromatic scale. See SCALE, 4.

Chronochromie ('Time Colouration'). Orchestral work (1960) by Messiaen; it is permeated by birdsong, and the sixth of its seven movements ('Épode') is for 18 solo strings, each playing a different birdsong.

Chrysander, (Karl Franz) **Friedrich** (*b* Lübtheen, Mecklenburg, 8 July 1826; *d* Bergedorf, nr Hamburg, 3 Sept. 1901). German music scholar. A pioneer musicologist, he is known for his editions of Handel, Corelli, and other Baroque composers. In 1855 he embarked on a vast biography of Handel, intended as his life's work. The first volume was published in 1858, the second in 1860, and the third in 1867, but the study was abandoned in favour of his monumental collected edition of Handel's works. This was issued through the Händel-Gesellschaft, which Chrysander and the literary historian Gottfried Gervinus founded in 1856, and funded by a grant from the Hanoverian crown. When the money ran out, Chrysander took sole responsibility for the edition and set up a printing press in his garden. In 1875 he was forced to sell part of his personal library to the Hamburg state. Although his Handel edition, which was left incomplete at his death, has since been superseded, it remains a remarkable memorial to his ingenuity, dedication, and perseverance.   JMT/LC

Chueca, Federico (*b* Madrid, 5 May 1846; *d* Madrid, 20 June 1908). Spanish composer. The foremost zarzuela composer of his day, he was discovered by Barbieri while imprisoned after an uprising in 1865. His strong melodic talent but initially modest grasp of compositional technique led him to work closely with the more polished Joaquín Valverde between 1875 and about 1890. The partnership produced the cult one-act zarzuela *La canción de la Lola* (1880) as well as the revue *La Gran Vía* (1886), which remains one of the few native stage works to have achieved fame outside Spain. His later, unaided works include *El bateo* ('The Baptism', 1901) and the brilliant *Agua, azucarillos y aguardiente* ('Water, Sweets, and Spirits', 1897), a vivid celebration of Madrid life. Always immensely popular, Chueca is now acquiring academic respectability for the subtle musical organization of his one-act zarzuelas into effective dance suites.   CW

Church, John (*b* ?Windsor, 1675; *d* London, 6 Jan. 1741). English composer. By 1695 he was singing in London theatres. He became a Gentleman of the Chapel Royal and lay vicar at Westminster Abbey in 1697, and Master of the Choristers at the abbey from 1704. He wrote anthems and services.   WT/AA

church drama. The earliest deliberate representation of divine persons within Latin worship appears to have been performed in the 9th century, when it became customary to recreate the visit of the Marys to the tomb of Christ on Easter Eve. At its simplest this ceremony, usually known as the *Visitatio sepulchri* ('Visit to the Sepulchre'), consisted of a brief dialogue initiated by the Angels ('Whom seek ye in the sepulchre, followers of Christ?'). Versions also survive of the same dialogue adapted for the Christmas season (*Midwives*: 'Whom seek ye in the manger, shepherds?', etc.).

The 11th and 12th centuries witnessed the composition of new liturgical dramas, including plays about Herod and the Wise Men, and the *Sponsus* drama about the Wise and Foolish Virgins. The limit of what could be accommodated within the framework of medieval church services is reached with such long verse dramas of the 13th century as the Passion Play in the *Carmina burana* manuscript (from Austria) and the *Play of Daniel* (from Beauvais).

The music of the earliest dramas was written in traditional plainchant style, often drafting in chants from the regular liturgy. But from the *Sponsus* play onwards the text was frequently versified, and the music was in a distinctly new idiom. The *Play of Daniel* is particularly remarkable for its vigorous, strongly rhythmic conductus (Ex. 1).

Ex. 1

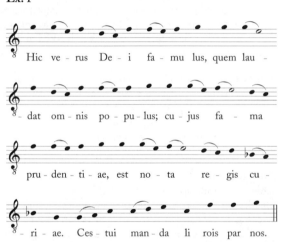

Hic ve-rus De-i fa-mu lus, quem lau-dat om-nis po-pu-lus; cu-jus fa-ma pru-den-ti-ae, est no-ta re-gis cu-ri-ae. Ces-tui man-da li rois par nos.

Since the chief function of liturgical drama was didactic, it is not surprising that many of the later dramas strike a popular note. Daniel is sometimes addressed in medieval French (see the last line of Ex. 1); and many German *Visitatio* ceremonies from the 12th century onwards conclude with the singing of *Christ ist erstanden* ('Christ is risen'). Most were copied without indications of 'staging', but there is occasional evidence of the wearing of costumes and the erection of some basic scenery.   DH/ALı

church modes. See MODE, 2.

church music 1. Introduction; 2. Christian chant; 3. Polyphony

1. Introduction

Music gained ready acceptance from the earliest Christians as an essential component of worship. References to its use can be found in the New Testament, as well as in such early sources as the letter from Pliny the Younger to the Emperor Trajan, which contains an allusion to the Christian practice of singing 'hymns to Christ, addressing him as God'. And from the 4th century onwards references to singing, particularly the singing of the psalms, are found with increasing frequency in patristic writings. However, not all music dating from the first Christian era was soberly religious in character: some forms, particularly those involving instruments, were associated with paganism and magic, or with other activities capable of arousing the baser passions; these were attacked with vehemence by Church Fathers. Consequently there arose, even from the earliest times, discussions regarding the place of music in Christian worship and life.

Saints Athanasius, Augustine, and Jerome were among those who tended to regard liturgical music in a somewhat equivocal light, on the one hand as an indispensable handmaid to worship, and on the other as a potentially dangerous distraction to the worshipper, to be countenanced only under conditions of careful control. At various times these conditions have involved the exclusion of instruments, the limitation of Christian song to biblical psalmody, the formation of canonical repertories of texts and melodies, and the delegation of musical leadership to particular individuals within the assembly, or conversely the abolition of such liturgical ministries in favour of exclusively congregational singing.

The forms of church music and their application have been similarly diverse: pastorally minded bishops of late antiquity and Protestant reformers introduced music to encourage congregational participation; civil and ecclesiastical authorities have supported the performance of elaborate music within the context of impressive ceremonial to project images of power and piety; and monks have sung the psalter in course as a contemplative exercise. Liturgical music also has an important theological component. The psalmodic propers of certain plainchant repertories, for example, enumerate the biblical typology associated with particular feasts, while hymnodic repertories often fulfil not only devotional but also homiletic or hermeneutic roles, offering theological explanations of the above-mentioned typologies.

2. Christian chant

The history of church music during the first millennium of Christianity's existence is essentially coterminous with that of plainchant, in which words and music enjoy a particularly intimate relationship. Even after the rise of cultivated forms of polyphony, chant long continued to be the primary medium for the celebration of common worship, and has remained so until the present day in many of the Eastern Christian churches. Christian plainchant offers melodic settings of varying complexity for the Ordinary and Proper texts of their parent rites, which may consist of psalmody and other scriptural texts or freely composed hymnody. Intended for performance by soloists, choirs, or congregations, the melodies of individual chants may be classed stylistically as syllabic, neumatic or melismatic.

The major traditions of Christian chant may be grouped according to language and liturgical rite in the following manner:

(*a*) *Armenian chant: the plainchant of the non-Chalcedonian Armenian Apostolic Church.

(*b*) Coptic chant: the orally transmitted plainchant of the non-Chalcedonian Coptic Church of Egypt, sung in a mix of Coptic (demotic Egyptian), Greek and, increasingly, Arabic.

(*c*) Ethiopian chant: the orally transmitted plainchant of the non-Chalcedonian Churches of Ethiopia and Eritrea, sung in Ge'ez.

(*d*) Syriac chant: this term today embraces three musico-liturgical traditions spanning multiple ecclesiastical jurisdictions: the East Syrian (including the ['Nestorian'] Church of the East, as well as the Chaldean and Malabar churches in union with Rome); the West Syrian (embracing the non-Chalcedonian Syrian Orthodox Church, Mar Thomas Protestants, and Syro-Antiochene and Malankar uniates); and the Maronite.

(*e*) Latin chant: the *Beneventan, Gallican, and *Old Roman chants are the most important Latin repertories to have been permanently suppressed as a result of the imposition of Roman chant in its Frankish recension (i.e. Gregorian chant). *Mozarabic chant initially suffered the same fate, but was partly restored in 15th-century Toledo, while Ambrosian chant has survived in the Archdiocese of Milan until the present day. Notwithstanding occasional attempts at standardization, considerable variety persisted in Latin plainchant until the beginning of the 20th century, when the monks of *Solesmes published uniform editions based on medieval manuscripts. See also PLAINCHANT.

(*f*) *Byzantine chant: the plainchant of the Byzantine rite, used in its received form to varying extents by the modern Orthodox churches of Albania, Alexandria, Antioch, Cyprus, Bulgaria, Constantinople, Greece, Jerusalem, and Romania, as well as by Melkite uniates. Western dialects of Byzantine chant are found in the Ionian Islands, southern Italy, and Corsica.

(*g*) Slavonic chant: most Slavonic plainchant belongs liturgically to the rite of Byzantium, where the earliest strata of its melodies and musical notation also originated: the lost tradition of Kondakarion singing is related to the choral traditions of the cathedral rite of the Great Church Hagia Sophia, and early *znamennïy* chant (chanting 'by signs') was recorded in palaeo-Byzantine 'Coislin' neumes. Long after the Byzantines developed notation precisely indicating a melody's succession of intervals, *znamennïy* chant continued to be recorded in archaic non-diastematic neumes, thus allowing the meaning of its signs and the melodies they conveyed to diverge significantly from their Greek prototypes. Supplemented by the virtuoso *demestvennïy* chant (probably from the Russian term for 'precentor') in the 16th century, the *znamennïy* repertory was stabilized during the early 17th century through the addition of signs permitting the exact notation of pitch. The new 'Kievan', 'Greek', and 'Bulgarian' repertories of Russian chant created during the 17th century were recorded directly in Western staff notation. This period also witnessed the emergence of variant traditions in Ukraine, Carpatho-Rus, and Galicia known collectively as 'Carpatho-Rusyn' chant. Modern Serbian plainchant is a more recent hybrid tradition in which Byzantine chant has been transformed by a variety of influences. Exceptionally, the oral tradition of Glagolitic chant of Croatia and Slovenia consists of music for the Roman rite in Church Slavonic translation.

3. Polyphony

The rise in medieval Europe of cultivated forms of sacred polyphony occurred against a background of unnotated polyphonic and heterophonic practices associated with the performance of plainchant, remnants of which still survive in Corsica and other communities on the periphery of Western art music. Some of these orally transmitted practices, especially the use of drones and singing in parallel perfect consonances, were logical extensions of modal systems organized by tetrachords in which the concept of octave equivalency was also extended to the 4th or 5th. Known collectively as organum, they were described by early theorists of Western plainchant, including the anonymous authors of the *Enchiriadis* treatises (9th century) and the *Summa musice* (13th century).

Notated polyphony for liturgical use featuring extended passages of contrary motion appears in the early 11th-century Winchester Troper, assuming a more developed form with melismatic passages in Aquitanian sources dating from the late 11th to the 13th centuries. The most influential early collection of artistic polyphony was the Parisian *Magnus liber organi* (later 12th–early 13th century), which contains liturgical cycles of florid organa and clausulae based on solo plainchants of the Mass and Office, as well as paraliturgical con-

ductus and motets. Its compilation was attributed to *Léonin by Anonymous IV, who also ascribed its augmentation with pieces for three and four voices to a certain *Pérotin.

The appearance in early 14th-century France of the rhythmic and metric innovations which historians identify by the term **'Ars Nova' provoked Pope John XXII to issue his edict *Docta sanctorum* of 1324–5, denouncing the modern school for 'preferring their new inventions to the ancient chants of the Church' and for producing 'a multitude of notes so confusing that the seemly rise and decorous fall of the plainchant melody . . . is entirely obscured'. In actuality, however, continental composers of artistic polyphony generally ignored liturgical texts until later in the century, concentrating instead on motets and secular songs. Even then—by which time Machaut had produced his landmark Notre Dame Mass and other composers were writing settings of single or paired items from the Mass Ordinary—the most solemn occasions at the papal chapel in late 14th-century Avignon continued to be celebrated with monophony.

The inundation of Latin worship with artistic polyphony waited until the 15th and 16th centuries, when such composers as Josquin and Palestrina wrote numerous cyclical mass Ordinaries, as well as many settings of other service texts, the dissemination of which was facilitated by the invention of music-printing. During the same period the liturgical use of the organ and other instruments also became firmly established. Nevertheless, chant and improvised polyphony of various kinds remained in widespread use, particularly outside the chapels maintained by the social elite. Popular piety was also expressed through repertories of paraliturgical devotional songs in Latin or the vernacular.

The fate of established musical traditions in the new churches of the *Reformation depended to a large extent on their respective founders' views regarding the utility of music in Christian worship. Luther retained the received musical tradition almost intact, supplementing it with vernacular settings and congregational hymnody. On the other hand, John Calvin restricted song to congregational renditions of metrical psalms. The Church of England swung back and forth between these two extremes until Anglicanism came to accommodate both models simultaneously: elaborate music was preserved in some colleges and cathedrals, while Anglican parish music was generally reduced to metrical psalmody. Yet the Counter-Reformation did comparatively little in response to change the course of Catholic church music. New service books suppressing certain additions to the Roman rite (including nearly the entire repertory of sequences) were issued following the

Council of Trent, which had also made some general recommendations advocating purity and intelligibility in sacred music.

In churches which continued to promote art music, the 17th and 18th centuries were marked by the canonization of 16th-century forms of imitative polyphony (the *stile antico*) alongside, and sometimes in combination with, newer styles of concerted vocal music. Lutheran music flourished as its composers made ever more sophisticated use of chorales in cantatas, passions, and works for organ. Also at this time, Western music infiltrated Russia through Poland and Ukraine, inspiring such Ukrainian and Russian musicians as Nikolay Diletsky (*d* after 1680) and Vasily Titov (*c*.1650–*c*.1715) to apply Western techniques to the composition of Orthodox liturgical music. Thus was initiated a process of musical Westernization that ultimately marginalized Russian plainchant and the native styles of polyphony based on it.

During the half-century after J. S. Bach's death in 1750, musical standards in Lutheranism declined rapidly in the face of triumphant Enlightenment rationalism and pietism. Meanwhile, concerted forms of Catholic church music drew ever closer to contemporary operatic and instrumental music. Perhaps this was not altogether inappropriate, for popular piety had come to place greater emphasis on the adoration of the Host in such paraliturgical rites as Benediction of the Blessed Sacrament than on its personal reception, thereby relegating the celebration of High Mass to the realm of religious spectacle.

The general reconsideration of the immediate past that followed the collapse of the Enlightenment in the conflagrations of the French Revolution and Napoleonic Wars was marked in several denominations by efforts to re-evaluate the musical and liturgical present in the light of the more distant past. Mendelssohn's 1829 revival of Bach's *St Matthew Passion* presaged later scholarly and practical work by Protestants to recover earlier layers of their tradition. The *Cecilian Movement promoted the renewal of Catholic church music through the replacement of 'theatrical' settings with imitative polyphony in the style of Palestrina, while the Benedictine monks of Solesmes presided over the restoration of the medieval versions of Gregorian melodies. Both movements were given official sanction by Pius X in his **motu proprio* of 1903. In England, the Oxford Movement and its musical offshoots fostered the recovery of Anglicanism's Catholic heritage and the dissemination of cathedral styles of worship to parishes (see ANGLICAN PARISH CHURCH MUSIC; HYMN, 4). In the later 19th century the 'New Russian' choral school rejected the Italianate and Germanic idioms of Bortnyansky and L'vov. Redis-

covered by scholars and composers, Russian plainchant served as the basis for *All-Night Vigils by Tchaikovsky and Rakhmaninov.

Those seeking the renewal of Christian worship through the study and recovery of early documents, a group that came to include some Calvinists, eventually joined forces across ecclesiastical boundaries to form an ecumenically inclusive Liturgical Movement. Conflicts with traditionalists, however, arose during the latter half of the 20th century when some musicians and liturgists began to advocate the replacement of art music in worship with radically acculturated forms of 'pastoral' music. Examples of the latter include 'ethnic', 'folk', and commercial (e.g. 'praise music') styles of sacred song.   BS/ALi

📖 R. A. LEAVER and J. A. ZIMMERMAN (eds.), *Liturgy and Music: Lifetime Learning* (Collegeville, MN, 1998)

ciaccona (It.). See CHACONNE.

Ciampi, Vincenzo (Legrenzio) (*b* Piacenza, ?1719; *d* Venice, 30 March 1762). Italian composer. A representative of the Neapolitan school, he was a pupil of Leo and Durante and had six operas performed in Naples before moving to Venice, where he was appointed *maestro di coro* at the Ospedale degli Incurabili in 1747. However in 1748 he was in London with the company responsible for the first season of Italian comic opera there. He remained in England until about 1756, when he returned to Venice, resuming his post at the Incurabili in 1760. His operas were widely successful, especially in Paris, but the aria for which he is best known, 'Tre giorni son che Nina', was probably added to his opera *Gli tre cicisbei ridicoli* by another hand. He also published sonatas and concertos.

DA/ER

cibell. See CEBELL.

Ciconia, Johannes (*b* Liège, *c*.1370; *d* Padua, June or July 1412). Liégeois composer and theorist, active largely in Italy. For many years the date of his birth was placed some 35 years earlier, at about 1334; but it is now widely believed that this conflates his biography with that of his father (also named Johannes Ciconia). A later birthdate would explain why so few works by him can be dated before 1390. Very little is known about his origins and early career. It is likely that he was the illegitimate son of a priest, and himself took holy orders. By the 1390s he was in Italy, certainly in Rome, and possibly also linked in some way to the Visconti court. His connections with Padua Cathedral began in 1401; he held a benefice there, and occupied various official positions, as both a cleric and a musician, until his death.

Ciconia's is the largest surviving output of any composer between Machaut and Dufay, and stylistically is very varied. It includes mass movements (all Glorias or Credos), motets, and a variety of secular songs in French and Italian. Some of the motets can be dated by their references to important personages and occasions; *O felix templum jubila*, for instance, was probably written when Stefano Carrara became Bishop of Padua in 1402. The songs are more difficult to place; although one French piece, *Sus une fontayne*, brings to mind the complexity of the late 14th-century *ars subtilior*, it does so through the quotation of works by an earlier composer, Philippus de Caserta. Elsewhere a more modern style is evident in the use of imitation and sequential melodic writing.

It is not easy to assess Ciconia's importance. Clearly he was one of the first northern composers to settle in Italy and, in a sense, to 'marry' the French and Italian traditions. On the other hand, his music mostly survives in manuscripts emanating from only a relatively small area around Padua and Venice. Whatever the case, his open melodic style, clarity of texture, and 'modern' sense of harmonic direction make him an attractive and accessible composer.　　　　AP/JM

Cid, Le. Opera in four acts by Massenet to a libretto by Adolphe d'Ennery, Édouard Blau, and Louis Gallet after the play by Pierre Corneille (1637) (Paris, 1885). Gasparini (1717), Piccinni (1766), Paisiello (1775), Aiblinger (1821), and Cornelius (1865) are among those who also wrote operas on the subject.

Cifra, Antonio (*b* Terracina, 1584; *d* Loreto, 2 Oct. 1629). Italian composer. He was a choirboy at S. Luigi dei Francesi in Rome, and subsequently directed the music at the Collegio Germanico (1608–9), St John Lateran (1622–6), and the Santa Casa, Loreto (from 1609 until his death, with a break of four years when he returned to Rome). He was a prolific composer and one of the earliest to write motets for a solo voice; in his songs he developed the use of the *ground bass, particularly over the *romanesca. His music was well known in England, and Henry Lawes set the song titles and one or two performing directions from his *Scherzi et arie* (Venice, 1614) with the intention of mocking his fellow countrymen's adulation of Italian music.　　DA

Cikker, Ján (*b* Banská Bystrica, 29 July 1911; *d* Bratislava, 21 Dec. 1989). Slovak composer and teacher. A talented pianist, he studied at the Prague Conservatory, working eventually in composition with Novák. As a teacher at the College of Performing Arts of Bratislava (1949–77) he influenced several generations of Slovak composers and was one of the founding fathers of modern Slovak music. His highly individual style was built variously from the late Romanticism of Novák, folk-influenced rhythm and modality, and even aspects of serialism. His nine completed operas show a sophisticated approach to music drama; several, notably *Vzkriesenie* ('Resurrection', 1962), *Hrá o láske a smrti* ('The Play of Love and Death', 1968), and *Coriolanus* (1974), met with considerable success.

　　　　JSM

Cilea, Francesco (*b* Palmi, Reggio Calabria, 23 July 1866; *d* Varazze, Savona, 20 Nov. 1950). Italian composer. An early meeting with the Neapolitan librarian Francesco Florimo, a friend of Bellini, led to his enrolment in the Naples Conservatory in 1879. He wrote both piano and orchestral music, and a student opera, *Gina* (1889), attracted the attention of the publisher Sonzogno, who commissioned a series of dramatic works over the next two decades. *L'arlesiana* (Milan, 1897, rev. 1898) was well received (and in 'È la solita storia' has one of the best-known tenor arias of the current recital repertory). Cilea's most successful opera was *Adriana Lecouvreur* (1902), which assured his position as a leading figure of the so-called Giovane Scuola ('young school') of Italian composers. Subsequent operas did not equal this success. Cilea was also a distinguished teacher, ending his career as director of the Naples Conservatory.　　　　RP

Cima, Giovanni Paolo (*fl* 1610–22). Italian composer. He was the most notable of a family of organists and composers active in Milan and Rome in the 17th century. In 1610 he was organist and director of music at S. Celso, Milan. Most of his music is for the organ or for instrumental ensemble; his *Concerti ecclesiastici* (Milan, 1610) includes a very early example of a trio sonata. He also left some interesting instructions on tuning keyboard instruments at the end of his *Partito di ricercari, canzoni alla francese* (Milan, 1606). He is last documented as contributing to a counterpoint treatise published in 1622.　　　　DA

Cimarosa, Domenico (*b* Avera, nr Naples, 17 Dec. 1749; *d* Venice, 11 Jan. 1801). Italian composer. The son of a working couple, he studied music and singing at the Conservatorio di S. Maria di Loreto, Naples, from 1761 to 1771. In 1772 his first opera was produced in Naples, and he was soon famous in the city and elsewhere in southern Italy, especially for his comic works. He was *maestro* at the Ospedaletto, a Venetian conservatory for girls, from about 1782, and five years later his fast-growing European reputation led to an invitation from Catherine II to work as *maestro di cappella* in St Petersburg. He left Russia in 1791, travelling to Vienna, where he was Kapellmeister for two years. It was there, in 1792, that his most famous opera *Il matrimonio segreto* was first performed at the Burgtheater. Returning to Naples later that year, he became *maestro* of the royal chapel. In 1796 his *Gli Orazi ed i Curiazi*, written for La Fenice in Venice, showed republican sympathies, and when the French army took Naples in 1799 he composed a patriotic hymn. After the departure of the French he was imprisoned for a time and narrowly escaped execution. On his release he left to return to St Petersburg but got only as far as Venice, where he died preparing an opera for the Carnival season.

Cimarosa was one of the most successful composers of *opera buffa* of his time, completing about 60 stage works, many of which were performed frequently in the principal centres of Europe. Admired by Goethe and Stendhal, he excelled in the emerging sentimental style, and like Mozart helped develop a form of opera in which ensembles were as important as solo arias, and in which the multi-section finale was an important focus of dramatic attention. Though by no means as musically complex as Mozart's mature operas, particularly in harmonic terms, Cimarosa's best work was enormously popular both during his lifetime and into the early 19th century, a vogue that went into decline only with the rise of Rossini after 1815. Cimarosa also wrote a good deal of sacred vocal music, secular cantatas, and instrumental and keyboard music.

DA/RP

cimbalom. Hungarian *dulcimer. The big concert cimbalom, developed about 1870 by Jozsef V. Schunda, has a compass of *D–e‴*. It appears in orchestral works by Kodály, Stravinsky, and other composers. Smaller, closely related, traditional forms are used all over southeastern and eastern Europe. JMo

cimbasso. A name used for a number of brass bass instruments in Italian opera scores. From about 1827 it was an upright *serpent, later it was an *ophicleide or early *tuba, and eventually it denoted a bass valved *trombone, subsequently made with two valves and a bass slide.

Cinderella. 1. See CENERENTOLA, LA; CENDRILLON.
2. (*Zolushka*). Ballet in three acts by Prokofiev to a scenario by Nikolay Volkov; it was choreographed by Rostislav Zakharov (Moscow, 1945).

cinema organ [theatre organ]. An organ with high wind pressure and many stops imitating other instruments, including percussion and other special effects. Designed originally to accompany silent films, and so saving the cost of an orchestra, it became popular for solos between the films, played from an ornate console which rose into view on a hydraulic lift with the organist already playing. JMo

Cinesi, Le ('The Chinese Ladies'). Opera in one act by Gluck to a libretto by Pietro Metastasio (Vienna, 1754).

Cinq rechants. Five works (1949) by Messiaen for three sopranos, three altos, three tenors, and three basses, settings of his own texts; like *Harawi* and *Turangalîla-symphonie*, they were inspired by the legend of Tristan and Isolda.

circle of fifths. A graphic representation, in the shape of a circle, of key notes with their signatures (Fig. 1). C is placed at the top of the circle, from where the notes progress clockwise in ascending 5ths (C–G–D, etc.). At the bottom of the circle, the note F♯ is called also by its *enharmonic name, G♭, and the same happens with the next note, C♯/D♭; the notes on the return to C are then called by their flat names (A♭, E♭, etc.). The return to C can be made only in *equal temperament; if Pythagorean 5ths were used, the series would be infinite. The key signatures are placed against their respective key notes, the major keys being shown in the outer circle, the minor ones (in lower-case letters) in the inner one.

The circle of 5ths shows the relative 'closeness' and 'distance' of one key from another: for example, C major and F♯ major, at opposite ends of the circle, have not one triad in common (see MODULATION, Ex. 1*d*). It also provides the basis for the compositional idea of the 'cycle' of 5ths, when music moves consistently through a smaller or larger segment of the tonal structural resource which the circle abstractly represents. AW

Fig. 1.

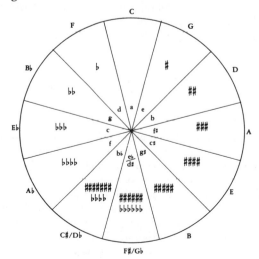

Circles. Work (1960) by Berio for female voice, harp, and two percussionists, a setting of texts by e. e. cummings from his *Poems 1923–54*.

circular breathing. A technique by which a continuous tone is sustained on a wind instrument. While it is physiologically impossible to breathe in and out simultaneously, a player may, by filling the cheeks and squeezing the air from them, maintain air pressure, and therefore tone, while taking a breath through the nose. This technique is crucial in playing the *didjeridu and can be used with other instruments, for example the clarinet and oboe. BW

Circus Polka (for a young elephant). Piece by Stravinsky composed for the Barnum and Bailey Circus; it was first performed, danced by a troupe of young elephants, in New York in 1942, scored for wind band by David Raksin. Stravinsky made a version for symphony orchestra and a piano reduction.

Cis (Ger.). The note C♯; *Cisis*, the note C𝄪.

cithara (Lat., from Gk. *kithara*, 'lyre'). In the earlier Middle Ages *cithara anglica* was a harp and *cithara teutonica* a lyre. In early medieval biblical illustrations King David is always shown playing a lyre, but after about 1100 the harp became more common. David's own instrument, the *kinnor*, was certainly a lyre. JMo

citole. A medieval plucked string instrument. The flat-backed citole had various body shapes. A common type resembled a holly-leaf from in front, with little trefoil wings, a remnant of which survived at the base of the neck of the later *cittern. On some types the pegbox curved backwards from the neck and was reinforced by a bracket or arm connecting it to the body, or the neck was a solid mass with a hole carved out for the player's thumb. The identity of the citole has often been confused with that of the *gittern. JMo

 📖 L. WRIGHT, 'The medieval gittern and citole: A case of mistaken identity', *Galpin Society Journal*, 30 (1977), 8–42

cittern (Fr.: *cistre*; Ger.: *Cister, Sister*; It.: *cetra, cetera*). A wire-strung plucked instrument of the Renaissance. The body is pear-shaped, flat-backed, and with sides narrowing from the neck block to the bottom. The neck is half cut away under the bass side of the fingerboard, leaving a channel along which the player's left thumb can run. Citterns were typically given *re-entrant tunings: Italian citterns had six double courses tuned *a*–*c′*–*b*–*g*–*d′*–*e′*, but English and French types had four, tuned *b*–*g*–*d′*–*e′* and *a*–*g*–*d′*–*e′* respectively. Some of the

courses were tuned in octaves. The cittern was popular for both informal and formal music-making. JMo

City Glee Club. A London club for music-making founded in the 1670s as the Civil Club; it adopted its new name in 1853. Its membership was fixed at 200, and most of the singers who performed at meetings were from the choirs of St Paul's Cathedral, the Chapel Royal, and Westminster Abbey.

cl. Abbreviation for 'clarinet'.

Clair de lune ('Moonlight'). 1. Third movement of Debussy's *Suite bergamasque* (1890) for piano; it was orchestrated by André Caplet and exists in several other arrangements, none by Debussy.

 2. Song (1891) by Debussy to a poem by Paul Verlaine, the third of his *Fêtes galantes*.

 3. Song, op. 46 no. 2 (1887), by Fauré to the same poem by Verlaine.

cláirseach (Irish Gaelic). The small, diatonic Irish harp of medieval origin (see HARP, 2a), the ancestor of the modern 'Celtic' harp.

clappers. Instruments of concussion: any two similar objects, of any material, that are struck together. The commonest are sticks (e.g. *claves) or plaques (e.g. *bones). Vessel clappers have a hollow in the surface, and include *cymbals and *castanets. Clappers may be hinged at one end. Some used in ancient Egypt were carved in the shape of human forearms and hands, often of ivory or bone. Clappers in the form of sticks or stones may be the oldest of all the world's instruments, and are still in use. JMo

claque (from Fr. *claquer*, 'to clap'). A group of people paid to *applaud at concerts.

Clari, Giovanni Carlo Maria (*b* Pisa, 27 Sept. 1677; *d* Pisa, 16 May 1754). Italian composer. He studied with G. P. Colonna in Bologna and was elected to the Accademia Filarmonica in 1697. In 1703 he was appointed *maestro di cappella* at Pistoia Cathedral, for which he wrote much liturgical music, and in 1724 he became *maestro* at Pisa Cathedral. He enjoyed the favour of the Medici family, for whom he wrote a number of oratorios, but was chiefly celebrated for his chamber cantatas, which circulated widely and were especially popular in England; Handel used material from five of them in his oratorio *Theodora*. ER

clarinet. A woodwind instrument played with a single reed. It was developed from the chalumeau (see CHALUMEAU, 1) by J. C. Denner in Nuremberg in about 1700. Because it has a cylindrical bore it *overblows to the 12th, the third harmonic, and other odd-numbered harmonics (rather than to the octave and all harmonics, which are produced by such conical-bore reed instruments as the oboe, bassoon, and saxophone). As a result, the fingering differs in each octave and the clarinet is less happy in keys with many sharps or flats than are the other woodwinds. For that reason clarinets have been built since their early days in different keys.

The standard treble is available in B♭, sounding a tone below written pitch and best for flat keys, or in A, sounding a minor 3rd lower and better for sharp keys. The C clarinet, sounding as written, is less often seen today, though its characteristic tone-colour, brighter than that of the B♭, differs enough from that of the others to be a loss from the orchestral palette. In contrast the A clarinet sounds smoother and rounder, which is why Mozart among others chose it for solo works. In earlier times the D soprano was the favourite soloist, sounding not unlike the clarino range of the trumpet (hence the instrument's name). This size is seldom seen today, though its E♭ brother is common in military bands and the larger orchestral works.

The clarinet has long been the mainstay of the *military band, where it is used in several sizes, from the small A♭ sopranino, through the E♭ and B♭, to the E♭ alto and the B♭ bass, which also appears in the orchestra. Less often encountered are the E♭ contralto and the B♭ contrabass, though these giant sizes play as freely as any other size of clarinet. A size specially favoured by Mozart and his contemporaries was the *basset horn, pitched in F alto with an extended range at the bottom to written c (sounding F). All other clarinets have e as their lowest written note, with the exception of B♭ models made with an extension to written e♭ to obviate the necessity of buying an A, and the occasional bass clarinets made to cope with the demands of composers who thought there was a bass in A. Mozart's Clarinet Concerto and other solo works were written for clarinets with a similar extension to low C.

The earliest clarinets had two or three keys, but those from the second half of the 18th century were built with five or six. It was probably this extra keywork—needed to fill the interval of a 12th with only ten fingers available, compared with the one-key flute and the two-key oboe—combined with the different fingering in each octave (and perhaps the extra expense of needing three instruments, in B♭, A, and C), that delayed the clarinet's general adoption as an orchestral instrument, for until Beethoven's time it is much less common in scores than the oboe and flute. Once fully adopted, it rapidly acquired extra keywork for greater facility. The 13-key, 'simple system' clarinet was established before 1830, initially devised by the German clarinettist Iwan Müller and later improved by Charles-Joseph Sax.

Further improvements in about 1860 by Eugène Albert in Brussels created what has often been called the 'Albert system', which retains a few devotees. Later, more complex clarinets based on the simple system and devised by Oscar Oehler, Schmidt-Kolbe, and others remain the most popular in Germany and eastern Europe.

Another complex system, taking advantage of the keywork Boehm had devised for the 1832-system *flute (though not adopting his acoustical theories for fingerhole diameter and placement), was patented by the player H. E. Klosé working with the maker L.-A. Buffet in Paris in 1844. The Boehm-system clarinet is used by most players in western Europe and North America.

Because the bore is cylindrical, clarinets are much cheaper to make than oboes. The traditional material for modern clarinets is African blackwood, though moulded plastic is a less expensive alternative. Clarinet reeds, being a single slip of cane backed by the strong support of a wooden or plastic mouthpiece, to which they are secured by a metal 'ligature' with two screws, are much less delicate than those of the oboe, and may more easily be bought ready-made.   JMo

📖 A. R. RICE, *The Baroque Clarinet* (Oxford, 1992) · C. LAWSON (ed.), *The Cambridge Companion to the Clarinet* (Cambridge, 1995)

clarion. A medieval term for a trumpet. How it differed from any other form of trumpet is unknown, though it may have been higher in pitch.

Clarke, Jeremiah (*b* c.1674; *d* London, 1 Dec. 1707). English composer. He began his career as a Child of the Chapel Royal under Blow, singing at the coronation of James II in 1685. From 1692 to 1695 he was organist at Winchester College, and in 1699 he was made a vicar choral and organist of St Paul's Cathedral. He became Master of the Choristers there in 1704, later that year becoming joint organist, with Croft, at the Chapel Royal. According to Hawkins, Clarke shot himself when in a state of acute mental depression after an unhappy love affair. He was buried in St Gregory's vault in the crypt of St Paul's.

Clarke seems to have shared in composing music for court or state, such as the anthems *Praise the Lord, my Soul* for the coronation of Queen Anne and *I will love thee* after the English victory at Elixem in 1705. However, Clarke was also associated with the theatre and collaborated with many of the leading playwrights and theatre composers of the day, notably Daniel Purcell. Among his other works are instrumental music (including *The Prince of Denmark's March*, better known as the 'Trumpet Voluntary' and formerly attributed to Purcell), songs, odes, and other choral music. His first ode was *Come, come along*, on the death of Henry Purcell, and he later composed a curious ode for the 'Gentlemen of Barbados', probably another Cecilian ode but also commemorating a hurricane in the West Indies in 1705.   WT/AA

Clarke, Rebecca (*b* Harrow, 27 Aug. 1886; *d* New York, 13 Oct. 1979). English viola player and composer. After withdrawing from the RAM in 1905, she studied at the RCM (1907–10) with Stanford, who persuaded her to take up the viola. She played in the Queen's Hall Orchestra from 1912 and was in many chamber groups, some exclusively of women. A recital career took her in 1916 to the USA, where she stayed until after World War I. She revisited America in 1939, this time remaining there and marrying a fellow RCM student and composer, James Friskin (1886–1967), in 1944. Among her output is a series of lullabies (including the exquisite *Morpheus*) for viola, written between 1909 and 1918, the highly acclaimed Viola Sonata (1918–19), submitted under the pseudonym 'Anthony Trent' for the Coolidge Competition, in which it won second prize, a piano trio (1921), a rhapsody for cello and piano (1923), and many songs. Her output declined markedly in later life.   JDı

📖 D. KOHNEN, *Rebecca Clarke, Komponistin und Bratschistin* (Egelsbach, 1999)

clàrsach (Scots Gaelic). The small, diatonic Scottish harp of medieval origin (see HARP, 2a). The modern *clàrsach* stands about 1 metre tall and has blades to alter the pitch of each string.   JMo

class. A theoretical term, most common in writings about post-tonal music. The pitch class C is used to refer to Cs in general, with no particular C implied. 'Interval class' refers to the number of semitones between the constituent pitches, with the first pitch as 0: interval class 2 is C–D, or the equivalent; interval class 6 is C–F♯, C♯–G, and so on. The intention is to provide an alternative to terms from tonal theory, for example major 2nd, which have functional implications.   AW

Classical era, the (*see opposite page*)

Classical Symphony. Prokofiev's Symphony no. 1 in D major op. 25 (1916–17), written in the style of Haydn.

classification of instruments. See INSTRUMENTS, CLASSIFICATION OF.

clausula (Lat.). 1. A term usually related to medieval music, particularly that of the Notre Dame period, denoting either the concluding of a passage or the passage itself so concluded. It is often thought to mean 'cadence', but differs from the modern definition of that term in that it refers to the melodic formulas of the individual voices, with no implication of typical harmonic progressions. In the 18th century this distinction was lost, and 'clausula' became synonymous with 'cadence'; the *clausula vera* came to be seen as the equivalent of the perfect cadence, *clausula falsa* the interrupted cadence, *clausula plagalis* the plagal cadence, and so on.

2. A polyphonic composition based not on an entire chant, as was the case with organum, but on a short portion of one. Clausulae may originally have been composed as passages for substitution in organum compositions, but if so they soon acquired their own position as self-sufficient pieces to be sung at appropriate points in the liturgy. The clausula used melismatic fragments of chant, and at first would be vocalized to the syllable or syllables concerned (e.g. 'Virgo'); on being given words of its own, the clausula developed into the 13th-century *motet.

clavecin (Fr.). 'Harpsichord'.

claves. A pair of short hardwood sticks, the principal time-keepers in much Latin American dance music. Other percussion instruments (e.g. the *maracas and the *güiro) may vary their rhythms, but the claves maintain a steady ostinato. One stick rests on the fingertips, with the cupped palm acting as a resonance chamber, and is struck by the other.   JMo

clavicembalo (It.). 'Harpsichord'.

clavichord (Fr.: *clavicorde, manicorde*; Ger.: *Klavier, Clavichord, Klavichord*; It.: *clavicordo, manicordo*). The simplest, one of the first, and the most expressive of all stringed keyboard instruments. A brass blade or 'tangent' standing on the inner end of each key rises, when the key is depressed by the finger, to touch a pair of strings (from the earliest times the strings were in pairs) with enough force to make them vibrate. As long as the tangent remains in contact with the strings it defines one end of the vibrating length (and thus its pitch), the bridge defining the other, and the strings continue to vibrate. When the key is released, the tangent falls away from the strings, and the cloth 'listing', wound over the left-hand end of the strings, dampens their vibration.

The strings are tuned in a sequence of 3rds (on the earliest clavichords they were tuned in unison), and there are never more than two naturals on one string, so that the notes of every white-note common chord, and of many which include a black note, can be sounded together. *Monochord interval measurements were used to determine the position of each tangent along the strings. The clavichord was, in effect, a series of

(*cont. on p. 266*)

The Classical era

The Classical era (or Classic era, a usage generally preferred in the USA) is usually understood to mean the period in which the central 'classics' of the standard repertory—essentially, the works of Haydn, Mozart, and Beethoven—were composed: that is, from about 1750 or soon after to some time between 1800 and 1830. Whether this is truly a 'style period', in the sense that the style of the three 'classical composers' was a universally used one, or simply a period in which those three great composers worked, has been a matter of some contention among students of the period and of musical history.

The word 'Classical', which is derived from the Latin *classicus* (meaning 'of the first class'), is defined in the *Oxford English Dictionary* as 'Of the first rank or authority; constituting a standard or model . . .'; further definitions refer to kinship with Greek and Latin antiquity (including 'conforming in style or composition to the rules of or models of Greek or Latin antiquity'). The relevant definition of 'Classic' is 'Of the first class, of the highest rank or importance; approved as a model; standard, leading'. In common parlance, the word is used primarily to distinguish cultivated music that is not popular or traditional, and probably has its historical roots in ecclesiastical or courtly traditions; it is thus used in a sense that implies acknowledgment of some kind of authority, seriousness of purpose, and perhaps superiority, and certainly of the idea that it has stood the test of time. In this sense it is applied to the music of composers of any era, from the Middle Ages to the present day, and might even be understood to include 'serious' music of the avant-garde. The term is also often applied, in the discussion of non-Western music, to courtly music traditions of such cultures as those of East and South-East Asia and the Middle East. In France, the phrase 'French Classical Tradition' does not normally indicate music of the late 18th century but of the age of Louis XIV, an era regarded as a 'classical' one.

Drawing on the association of merit with the ancient civilizations, the term was initially used in musical discourse in the sense of 'classics of their kind', or works widely recognized as models of excellence within their own genre. Forkel, writing in 1802, referred to Bach's keyboard works as classics; Palestrina's masses and Corelli's concertos have been similarly described, as representing an outstanding group of examples of a particular genre. Mozart's first biographer, F. X. Niemetschek, wrote of the 'classical value' of his music, and indeed hinted at the idea of Mozart's belonging to a 'classical era' when he wrote that 'The masterpieces of the Romans and Greeks please more and more through repeated reading, and . . . the same applies for both connoisseur and amateur with regard to the hearing of Mozart's music'.

The earliest manifestations of the attitude that made this usage possible were the 'classicizing' of certain repertories: the music of Handel (and to a lesser extent Corelli) in England from the mid-18th century onwards, and Lully's operas at the Paris Opéra (and to some extent Lalande's motets at the Concert Spirituel). These were among select audiences; it was only towards the end of the 18th century and especially in the early 19th, with the rise of canonical repertories and the concomitant development of concert life and large-scale music publishing, that this usage could become widespread. The idea of a specific 'Classical school', referring to Haydn, Mozart, and Beethoven, took firm root in German writings about music during the 1830s, as a German or Viennese phenomenon, parallel to the Weimar Classics of Goethe and Schiller; only later did it come to be called the 'Viennese Classical School' (and later 'First Viennese School', to distinguish it from the Second Viennese School of Schoenberg, Berg, and Webern).

It was in the early 19th century that a need was felt for a terminology that would differentiate the new Romantic movement from what had gone before. The word 'Romantic', as a term to describe a musical style or an approach to music, seems to have entered the musical vocabulary earlier than the word 'Classical', which was now invoked as an antithesis to describe the music of the preceding era. It was appropriate for a number of reasons, three in particular, of which the first is that the music of Haydn and Mozart (and in effect no other composer) had remained in the repertory and had come to achieve a canonical or classical status.

Secondly, it is apt because of the curiosity and the kinship felt by artists of the second half of the 18th century, and its final quarter especially, for the ancient classical civilizations and their art. This was an age during which Greek and Roman literature, art, and architecture were re-examined, more scientifically than before. Archaeologists had excavated Pompeii beginning in 1748; the visible remains were drawn, engraved for wider circulation, and their design analysed. The austere temple at Paestum, already known, was sketched and engraved, and imitated for operatic stage sets. Writers, of whom the most influential was J. J. Winckelmann in the 1750s, discovered a 'noble simplicity' in classical architecture. G. B. Piranesi's collections of engravings of Rome had a wide circulation and influence, and Joshua Reynolds stressed that the highest achievement in painting depended on the use of Greek or Roman subjects and their representation of heroic or suffering humanity. Jacques-Louis David, inspired by Pompeii and Rome, provided eloquent paintings of Socrates and Brutus in the 1780s and, following classical principles, went on to become the official artist of the French Revolution. The sculptor Antonio Canova used classical statues as the basis for his figures of modern men and women. At the end of his career, the poet and librettist Pietro Metastasio wrote a survey of Greek drama and Aristotelian theory of tragedy, and made a translation of Horace's *Ars poetica*, as models for operatic practice. (The turn of the century is sometimes described as a 'neo-classical' era, but that term is more appropriate to the visual arts than to music, where it is more aptly and usefully saved for the stylistic events of just over a century later.)

What grounds, one may ask, might composers of this era have had for regarding themselves as heirs to, or revivers of, some kind of classical tradition? There were no musical models for them to imitate, as there were in the literary and the visual arts. Any answer to this question (which of course is an unreal one, since the composers were dubbed 'classical' only retrospectively)—and this is the third reason referred to above—must be concerned with the formal and structural features of the music of the era and its relation to expression: the traditional Classic–Romantic antithesis,

which, to present it in grossly oversimplified form, defines the precedence given by the Classical composer to formal matters and by the Romantic composer to expressive ones.

There are in fact a number of important stylistic features common to a high proportion of the music composed, in all genres, during the period in question. The so-called pre-classical period, in which features of the Baroque are softened and heavily decorated (the *rococo style) and features of the Classical era are adumbrated, had begun by 1730; some writers see it as continuing until the 'high' Classical period of the 1770s or 80s and including all the work of such composers as Pergolesi, C. P. E. Bach, J. C. Bach, and Hasse, as well as the early and even the middle works of Haydn. By 1750 many composers were using patterns of symmetrical phrase structure, coupled to cadential harmony, with increasingly static bass lines, of the kind that would underlie much Classical composition, and soon after that date the basic Classical formal pattern—known as sonata form—evolved from its binary-form precursors.

Sonata form, involving the presentation of two contrasting groups of material in complementary keys, and their later recapitulation in the same key, is fundamental and permeates virtually all the music of the Classical period (excepting only pieces in variation form, the occasional fugue, and certain types of dance and vocal composition, although the underlying presence of its procedures is rarely absent), and it continued in use—of a more self-conscious kind—long thereafter. In this intermediate pre-classical period various other stylistic characteristics, or mannerisms, are found: those of the primarily north German *empfindsamer Stil*, with its intensely expressive 'sighing' clichés, those of the *Sturm und Drang* period, marked by their stormy outbursts and passionate tone, and the light *galant* manner, with its aura of gracious, courtly charm, and its standardized cadence patterns. All these had to be synthesized for the universal style of the high Classical era to be achieved.

It was Haydn and Mozart who achieved that synthesis in its fullest form: and therein lie the arguments, forcefully propounded by Charles Rosen (1971) in particular, that the Viennese Classical style is the style of Haydn, Mozart, and, in a later extension, Beethoven, and accordingly that it is not appropriate to talk of a 'Classical period'. It has been argued by Friedrich Blume (1970) that 'there is no "Classic" style period in the history of music, only a "Classic-Romantic" one'—although he continues to refer to it. Nevertheless, many writers have felt that it is realistic, not to say convenient, to accept that the period of the Classical composers, however few they are in number, can fairly be reckoned a 'Classical period'. In any case, most of the composers active in this period wrote in styles that are in a general sense indistinguishable from those of the great men. It is however incontestable that their own personal languages lack the breadth and the richness of those of Haydn, Mozart, and Beethoven, or their universality: for between them these three reached heights far beyond any others of their time (and arguably of any time) in all the central genres of music—the symphony, the concerto, the string quartet (and quintet), the piano sonata, opera (both comic and serious), and sacred music.

Another composer with a claim to be regarded as Viennese Classical, although far more limited than these three, was Gluck. His central contribution was the creation (in which he was not alone but was the most prominent) of a new operatic style, which renounced the extravagances, vocal and decorative, of serious Italian opera in favour of a Winckelmann-like 'noble simplicity'. In *Orfeo ed Euridice* (1762) he concentrated on a single subject and the emotions of just two characters, and devised a language, less convention-ridden than the prevailing one, to heighten its expression; his later operas, especially *Iphigénie en Tauride* (1779), develop his principles while maintaining a powerful focus on the emotions of the central characters. Few other composers (among them was Salieri) were strongly or directly influenced by Gluck, at least for a generation; Mozart showed a way in his last classical opera, *La clemenza di Tito* (1791), of achieving a classical synthesis by means of a less radical simplification of the Metastasian operatic tradition, and his type of 'reform' was closely in line with Italian operatic developments in the 1790s.

The placing of Beethoven within the Viennese Classical school raises difficult issues. To those who first described the school, immediately after his lifetime, his gigantic status demanded his inclusion as an instant classic. Yet he is clearly at least on the verges of Romanticism, with his wildness and extravagance, his refusal to observe the proprieties, his concern for extra-musical meanings to his music, his intentness on originality (forswearing the traditionally classical ease of communication), his heroic attitude to his art, and his personal suffering. It is the fact of his clear departure point in Haydn and Mozart, and the sense of Classical form that he always retained (possibly his deafness to innovations played a role in this), that justifies his inclusion. There are arguments too for including Schubert in this select group (as does Rushton, 1986), since he maintains Classical proportions in his mature compositions in a sense that later Romantics do not; yet it is clear especially from his handling of form and incident that his priorities are not the same as those of Haydn, Mozart, or Beethoven and that his musical thought, once past the early works, is that of the new era. Among other composers of the time, a strong case can be made out for regarding Rossini as Classical rather than Romantic in his compositional thinking.

The great social developments concurrent with the Classical era had a profound influence on musical life and musical composition. First, the lot of the composer underwent considerable charge. In 1750, most composers were employed by private patrons or by the church; by 1800, private patronage was greatly diminished and increasing numbers of composers now had to make their living on a freelance basis, composing and performing for a wider public. This, generally speaking, was made easier by the growth of concert life, which had developed substantially since the 1760s; by the growing market for teachers, with the large increase in numbers of middle-class daughters and the greater availability of instruments; and by the changes in methods of music-printing and -publishing, with cheaper editions poured out in quantity by numerous firms in the leading centres (London, Paris, Vienna, Leipzig, Amsterdam). By the end of the Classical period, instrumental music enjoyed a new primacy, as a direct consequence of the changes in patronage, and sacred music was never again to enjoy the centrality that had been taken for granted up to the end of the Baroque era.

SS

F. Blume, *Classic and Romantic Music: A Comprehensive Survey* (New York, 1970) · C. Rosen, *The Classical Style: Haydn, Mozart, Beethoven* (New York and London, 1971, enlarged 3/1997) · R. G. Pauly, *Music in the Classic Period* (Englewood Cliffs, NJ, 1965, 3/1988) · J. Rushton, *Classical Music: A Concise History from Gluck to Beethoven* (London, 1986) · D. Heartz, *Haydn, Mozart, and the Viennese School* (New York, 1995) monochords placed in a single box, and it was called *monochordia* (*manicorde*, etc.) by many 15th- and 16th-century writers.

Early (15th-century) clavichords were 'fretted' (Ger.: *gebunden*), being so constructed that each pair of strings was shared by the tangents of three or four adjacent keys, each touching at the appropriate point along its length. Each key-bar had to be bent to reach the right point, and only one note at a time could be sounded from a single pair of strings. In the 16th century triple fretting was still sometimes used, but by the end of the 17th, clavichords were usually arranged so that no more than two adjacent notes shared a string; seldom did one need to play a chord with notes a semitone apart. Some instruments, and most by the mid-18th century, were completely 'unfretted', every tangent having its own string. Advantages of fretting are in economies of cost, for fewer strings are needed; space, because the instruments are compact; time, because there are fewer strings to tune; and downward tension, allowing the soundboard to vibrate more freely. The disadvantages are the impossibility of playing some chords and the need to be neat-fingered when playing trills on two notes which share a string.

An important part of 18th-century clavichord technique was the *Bebung, a vertical vibrato on the key while the tangent remains in contact with the string, by means of which the sound is kept alive and the impression of a slight crescendo given. During the vibration the point of contact with the string becomes a node (point of least amplitude)—hence the soft, intimate tone of the clavichord; even the larger instruments are not designed to be played to large audiences. In compensation for this lack of volume the player can exert sensitivity of control through touch and, within small limits, can command a dynamic range from *piano* to *forte* unequalled on any other keyboard instrument before the invention of the piano. This is why the clavichord remained a favourite practice instrument well into the 19th century. It is said that both Mozart and Chopin carried small clavichords for practising on long coach journeys.

Bach's *The Well-Tempered Clavier* (the '48') was probably written for the clavichord. *Clavier* or *Klavier* normally meant the clavichord, whereas the harpsichord was usually called *Instrument* or *Cembalo*. Certainly it was the clavichord which was intended by C. P. E. Bach in his famous treatise on keyboard-playing (*Versuch über die wahre Art das Clavier zu spielen*, Berlin, 1753, 1762).

Clavichords were particularly popular with organists because they could practise on them at home instead of in a cold church, and without the need to pay someone to pump the organ bellows. One clavichord could rest on top of another to simulate two different manuals, and some makers provided a pedal clavichord with long bass strings. Although the instrument was common throughout Europe in the 16th century, it was used after that time mainly in Germany, Spain, Portugal, and Scandinavia; clavichords were still being made by some makers in the 1820s, long after the invention of the *square piano. It was however in England that the clavichord was revived, by Arnold Dolmetsch in the 1890s. Today many makers are producing them and the clavichord has to some extent recovered its rightful place as an ideal domestic instrument and, in a hall with sympathetic acoustics, one suitable for public recitals.

JMo

📖 B. BRAUCHLI, *The Clavichord* (Cambridge, 1998)

clavier (Fr., 'keyboard'; Ger.: *Klavier*). A term used to denote both manual and pedalboard, as well as keyboard instruments in general, including in France the modern piano. In 18th-century Germany it was used specifically for 'clavichord', as distinct from *Instrument* or *Cembalo*, both of which meant 'harpsichord'.

The term is also sometimes used for practice instruments such as the dumb clavier, or *silent keyboard, and at least one electronic keyboard instrument has been marketed under the name of Clavier.   JMo

Clavier-Büchlein (*Clavierbüchlein*; 'Little Keyboard Book'). Title given by J. S. Bach to three of his collections of keyboard music: the first (1720), for his son Wilhelm Friedemann, contains early versions of the inventions and sinfonias and some preludes from book 1 of the '48', as well as pieces that may be by Wilhelm Friedemann; the second (1722) and third (1725), for his second wife Anna Magdalena (the 'Anna Magdalena Books'), include the first five French Suites, and the third and sixth partitas, as well as other pieces by J. S. Bach, C. P. E. Bach, and other composers.

Clavier-Übung ('Keyboard Practice'). Title given by J. S. Bach to four volumes of keyboard music: the first (1731) contains six partitas, BWV825–30, for harpsichord; the second (1735), also for harpsichord, consists of the Italian Concerto BWV971 and the Ouverture in the French Style BWV831; the third (1739) is mainly of liturgical organ music, BWV552, 669–89, and 802–5 (a prelude and fugue, 21 chorale preludes, and four duets); and the fourth (1741) the 'Goldberg' Variations for harpsichord. Kuhnau, Bach's predecessor at Leipzig, had used the title for two volumes of keyboard music (1689, 1692).

clef (Fr., 'key'; Ger.: *Schlüssel*; It.: *chiave*). A sign written at the beginning of the staff to indicate the pitch of the notes. There are three signs in present-day usage (Fig. 1). The G (or treble) clef marks the second line up on the staff, and indicates that the pitch of that note is *g'*; the F (or bass) clef marks the fourth line up on the staff, and indicates that the pitch of that note is *f*. The C clef is movable, and may be found marking either the middle line of the staff (alto or viola clef), or the fourth line up (tenor clef); in each case it indicates that that particular note is *c'*.

Fig. 1.

The G clef is used for the upper staff of keyboard music, the soprano voice, and the high instruments (e.g. violin or flute). When the G clef appears with a figure '8' attached to its tail the pitch of the note is *g* (an octave below that of the ordinary G clef); this is the tenor G clef, and it is often used in vocal music. The F clef is used for the lower staff of keyboard music and for all bass voices or instruments. The alto clef is used for the viola and similar instruments, and the tenor for the high notes of the cello, bassoon, tenor trombone, etc.

The clef signs evolved from the letters for which they stand. It was Guido of Arezzo (*c.*991–after 1033) who, in his *Aliae regulae* (*c.*1030), recommended that a staff should be used with spaces as well as lines indicating pitches, and that at least one of the lines should be identified by a pitch letter (i.e. clef). In practice he used a red line to indicate F and a yellow one for C, and before long a four-line staff was established for the writing down of plainchant. Standard clef combinations began to appear in 15th- and 16th-century vocal music which probably indicated the usual voice ranges. In early printed sources, for example, soprano, alto, tenor, and bass were often signalled by three C clefs (on the lowest, third, and fourth lines up) and an F clef (on the fourth line up). Sometimes the standard combinations would appear transposed up or down a 3rd (as in Palestrina's *Missa Papae Marcelli*) with the F clef on line 3, for example. This system is known as *chiavette* ('key code') and may have been used to signal transposition down a 4th or 5th.

The modern treble (or G) clef became fairly well established after about 1580; it is made up of two elements: 𝄞 for *signum* ('sign') and the letter 𝄞 underneath: 𝄞→𝄞. In music before 1750 clefs occurred in various different positions; for example, in the music of 17th-century French composers (e.g. Lully) the G clef invariably marked the bottom line of the staff, whereas in Italian music it marked the second line, as at present. The C clef could mark any line. The reason for the frequent changes of clef encountered in early music seems to have been a desire to avoid using ledger lines. It is only in recent years that composers have shown an overwhelming preference for G and F clefs. C clefs are found in much music by Wagner, Brahms, and Schoenberg, in all kinds of Italian vocal music, and for certain instruments (e.g. violas, bassoons) or parts of their ranges.

See also NOTATION, 1.   AP

Clemens (non Papa), Jacobus [Clement, Jacob] (*b c.*1510–15; *d c.*1555–6). Franco-Flemish composer. He was succentor at St Donaas, Bruges, in 1544, but otherwise little is known of his life. He was a popular and prolific composer, writing chansons both to bawdy and to more elegant texts, and church music, including some fine motets in the imitative contrapuntal manner. He was the first to set Dutch translations of the psalms ('souterliedekens') polyphonically, using popular melodies taken from love songs and drinking songs, ballads, and sacred tunes. His works were known throughout Europe. There seems to be no very serious reason for the words 'non Papa' ('not the Pope') appearing on the title pages of his publications.

DA/TC

Clementi, Muzio (*b* Rome, 23 Jan. 1752; *d* Evesham, 10 March 1832). Italian-born British composer, pianist, teacher, and piano manufacturer. At 13 he was organist at at a minor church in Rome but was soon 'discovered' by a travelling English gentleman, Peter Beckford, who persuaded Clementi's father (with difficulty) to allow his son to go to England. Clementi lived for seven years at Beckford's estate near Blandford Forum, Dorset, where he studied in isolation. About 1774 Clementi left for London, where, though he initially attracted little attention, his work as conductor at the King's Theatre and his technically brilliant sonatas op. 2 (published 1779) began to establish his reputation. In 1780 he toured Europe, playing before Marie Antoinette in Paris and taking part in the famous contest with Mozart in Vienna. Mozart, however, thought that in spite of his technical gifts he was 'a mere mechanicus' and 'a charlatan like all Italians'. By contrast Clementi was complimentary of his younger 'competitor'.

In 1783 he returned to London, where he accepted the young J. B. Cramer as a pupil, but by the end of the year he was back in France, having eloped to Lyons with the 18-year-old Victoire Imbert-Colomés, a former pupil. However, her father, a wealthy Swiss merchant, intervened and prevented the marriage. After some time in Berne, in 1785 he returned to London and enjoyed great success as a player and teacher. In the period 1779–90 he published about 60 sonatas, many of which were admired—and to some extent imitated—by

Beethoven. He was a soloist at the Hanover Square Grand Professional Concerts and the rival La Mara–Salomon series (1786–90) and conducted his symphonies (from the keyboard) until 1796, though the visits of Haydn to London (1791–2 and 1794–6) overshadowed his music and playing. As part compensation, Clementi still commanded high fees as a teacher and invested the money he earned in piano manufacturing and publishing.

In 1802 he embarked again for Europe to promote his firm abroad, to sell pianos, and to acquire the publishing rights to new music; among those he negotiated were the British rights to some of Beethoven's principal works. Between 1802 and 1810 he visited Russia and Italy twice and Vienna four times, though his plans were hampered by the Napoleonic wars. Three years after he returned to London, he was named as one of the six directors of the newly founded Philharmonic Society (1813). This association marked a new period of productivity as an orchestral composer and conductor (he was one of the last to direct from the keyboard) which, with four further visits to the Continent to conduct his works, continued until 1824. In 1830 he retired with his second wife and family to the country, where he died. He was buried in the cloisters of Westminster Abbey with great ceremony and adulation.

Clementi's famous *Gradus ad Parnassum* op. 44 (Leipzig and Paris, 1817, 1819, 1826), a comprehensive set of 100 keyboard studies, is best known for its five-finger exercises, but the more advanced pieces in the collection belong to the musical tradition that was to lead to Chopin's piano music. Although there is a certain amount of commercial music in his output, there is also much that is rewarding, notably the sonatas opp. 13, 25, 33, 40, and 50, which a show a fertile and original imagination.   DA/JDi

📖 L. PLANTINGA, *Muzio Clementi: His Life and Music* (London, 1977).

Clemenza di Tito, La ('The Clemency of Titus'). Opera in two acts by Mozart to a libretto by Pietro Metastasio adapted by Caterino Mazzolà (Prague, 1791). Metastasio's libretto was set by some 20 other composers, including Gluck (1752).

Clérambault, Louis-Nicolas (*b* Paris, 19 Dec. 1676; *d* Paris, 26 Oct. 1749). French organist and composer. The son of Dominique Clérambault (*c*.1644–1704), one of the Vingt-Quatre Violons du Roi, and a pupil of Raison, he began composing at an early age, writing a motet for large choir when only 13. From 1707 he was organist of the Grands-Augustins in Paris, later undertaking the organization of Madame de Maintenon's chamber music concerts at Versailles during the last years of Louis XIV's reign. In 1714 Clérambault took over Nivers's posts as organist at St Sulpice and as organist and teacher at Mme de Maintenon's school for the daughters of military officers at St Cyr, and in 1719 he succeeded Raison at St Jacques in Paris. He in turn was succeeded by two of his own sons.

While maintaining a busy career as a performer, Clérambault also composed. During the 1690s he experimented with the sonata (a single manuscript of solo and trio sonatas survives) and published *airs* in the Ballard series. In 1704 he published a collection of *pièces de clavecin* and about 1710 a *Livre d'orgue*. In tune with the prevailing fashion he published five collections of French cantatas, several of which—*Orphée* and *Médée*, for example—are considered the finest of their genre between 1710 and 1726. Clérambault also composed divertissements as well as numerous motets and a *Te Deum*.   DA/JAS

clerk, lay. See VICAR CHORAL.

cloche (Fr., 'bell'). See BELL, 1; TUBULAR BELLS.

clock chimes. See CHIME, 3.

'Clock' Symphony. Nickname of Haydn's Symphony no. 101 in D major (1794), so called because of the 'tick-tock' accompaniment to the first subject of the second movement.

clos (Fr.). See OUVERT AND CLOS.

close. See CADENCE.

close harmony. A passage of music is said to be in 'close' harmony when the notes of the chords are all fairly closely spaced, not extending beyond the interval of about a 12th. Various vocal groups have made singing in close harmony a feature of their style, for example the King's Singers, and the technique appears also in *barber-shop ballads. When the notes are fairly widely spaced, a passage is said to be in 'open' harmony. See also POSITION, 2.

clubs for music-making. Musical clubs have long played a considerable part in the cultural and social development of music among European communities. The earliest of which we have much knowledge were the German guilds of *Meistersinger, apparently first organized in 14th-century Mainz though best known from 16th-century Nuremberg. Protestant Germany also gave rise in the 16th and 17th centuries to a variety of non- or semi-professional musical societies such as the Kantorei (for recreational singing of sacred music) and the less specialized *collegium musicum. In early modern Italy and France a similar kind of music-making was the province of *academies (which were more literary in scope) and salons (which were more informal in organization). The English model (see below) was influential in Germany from the late 18th century and in France and Italy after the Napoleonic era; North America has built on both the English and the earlier German patterns.

In England many musical clubs originated in the 17th and 18th centuries as gatherings of amateur singers and instrumentalists that met regularly for the purpose of performing madrigals, glees, catches, and chamber music. Among the earliest such clubs was one mentioned in the dedication of the first book of madrigals ever published in England: *Musica transalpina*, issued in London in 1588 by Nicholas Yonge; he stated that a body of merchants and gentlemen was accustomed to gather at his house in the parish of St Michael, Cornhill, 'for the exercise of musicke daily'. In the 17th century some clubs met weekly, such as those in Oxford described by the chronicler Anthony Wood as 'Musick Meetings', and the meetings held in London by the composer Edmund Chilmead. 'Musique Meetings' in London were described in some detail by both Samuel Pepys and the music publisher Henry Playford.

Professional musicians were increasingly admitted to the ranks of club members, and they soon began to organize music-making along more sophisticated and more ambitious lines, encouraging clubs to give public concerts. Several of those clubs that survived into the late 18th and the 19th centuries developed into fully fledged concert organizations, which supported orchestras and choirs and ran entire seasons of professional concerts and recitals. There has always been a place for the amateur music-making club, however, and many survive to this day in the form of orchestral and choral societies and sponsoring organizations.

See also CATCH; CONCERT; GLEE; MADRIGAL; SOCIETIES; and see names of individual clubs and societies.   —/JJD

cluster. A group of adjacent notes, usually on the piano, where clusters may be performed with the fist, palm, or forearm. Piano clusters were introduced by Henry Cowell in *The Tides of Manaunaun* (1912).

coach-horn. See POSTHORN.

Coates, Albert (*b* St Petersburg, 23 April 1882; *d* Cape Town, 11 Dec. 1953). English conductor. He studied at the Leipzig Conservatory, where he was influenced by Nikisch. From 1906 he held posts in German opera houses and at the Mariinsky Theatre in St Petersburg (1911–18), where he became a friend of Skryabin, whose music he advocated. After 1918 he became revered in Britain, Europe, and the USA for his orchestral and opera conducting, especially of Wagner and Musorgsky,

and he gave several premieres. He settled in South Africa in 1946. He composed a number of works including the first opera shown on television.   JT

Coates, Eric (*b* Hucknall, Notts., 27 Aug. 1886; *d* Chichester, 23 Dec. 1957). English composer. He studied the violin and composition in Nottingham, then switched to the viola, studying with Lionel Tertis and becoming principal viola in Henry Wood's Queen's Hall Orchestra in 1912. By then he had begun to compose regularly, and after 1919 he became a freelance composer of light music, achieving fame largely through the new medium of radio. Although he had great success in his lifetime as a songwriter, he is best remembered for his tuneful, picturesque, and beautifully orchestrated suites, including *London* and *The Three Elizabeths*.   PGa/ABur

cobla. 1. The Catalan dance band, consisting of shawms, flugel horns, pipe and tabor, string double bass, and other wind instruments, which plays, usually outdoors, for the traditional *sardana* dance.

2. A Provençal term, meaning 'stanza', frequently found in medieval treatises on the composition of verse.

Coccia, Carlo (*b* Naples, 14 April 1782; *d* Novara, 13 April 1873). Italian composer. He studied at the Naples Conservatory and wrote his first opera in 1807. His early efforts were in the vein of Paisiello, in particular in a fondness for *opera semiseria* subjects; but in the next decade—like all Italian opera composers—he came under the influence of Rossini. In the 1820s he took positions in Lisbon and then London, returning to Italy in 1828. During the 1830s he showed that he could adapt to a post-Rossinian operatic style, writing some highly praised works for La Scala, Milan, notably *Caterina di Guisa* (1833) and *La solitaria delle Asturie* (1838). His last opera was written in 1841, and he spent his remaining years as *maestro di cappella* in Novara.   RP

Cockaigne (In London Town). Concert overture, op. 40 (1901), by Elgar; it is dedicated to his 'friends the members of British orchestras'. The title refers to the imaginary land of idleness and luxury from which the word 'cockney' is said to be derived.

coda (It., from Lat. *cauda*, 'tail'). An addition to a standard form or design, occurring after the main structure of a piece or melody has been completed with a cadence in the home key. In *strophic form, for instance, the coda would occur after the last verse, in *variation form after the last variation, in *binary form after the second section has ended (generally with a repeat mark), and in *sonata form after all the material of the exposition has been recapitulated. Beethoven greatly expanded the coda in some of his sonatas and quartets, and Schumann often allotted the piano an important coda in his songs and song cycles.

—/NT

codetta (It., dim. of 'coda'). 1. A brief *coda or conclusion.

2. In *fugue the term is used to describe any passage in the exposition that links two entries of the theme, provided that the theme ends with a definite cadence, giving the impression that what follows is in the nature of a link.

3. A short cadential passage at the end of a *sonata-form exposition.

Coelho, Manuel Rodrigues (*b* Elvas, *c*.1555; *d* ?Lisbon, *c*.1635). Portuguese organist and composer. He began as an organist in his native town, moving to Lisbon in 1602 and working there until 1633 as chaplain and organist in the royal chapel. His influential collection of 24 tentos and variations for keyboard, entitled *Flores de musica pera o instrumento de tecla e harpa* (Lisbon, 1620), was the first instrumental music to be printed in Portugal.

WT

Coffee Cantata (*Kaffeekantate*). Nickname of J. S. Bach's cantata no. 211, *Schweigt stille, plaudert nicht* ('Be silent, don't chatter'), to a text by Picander; it was probably composed in 1734 and refers to the growing passion for coffee in Leipzig at the time.

cog rattle. See RATCHET.

col, coll', colla, coi, colle (It.). 'With', 'with the'.

colascione (Fr.: *colachon*; Ger.: *Gallichona*, *Galizona*, etc.). An Italian long-necked lute, with two or three courses of gut strings played with a plectrum. It was introduced through Naples in the late 15th century, deriving from the Turkish *saz, whose early forms it resembles. Popular in the Renaissance and Baroque, it survived as a folk instrument in southern Italy and Sicily.

The German and French forms of the name were also applied to a large 18th-century German bass lute, used for playing thoroughbass and also known as the *mandora.

JMo

Colasse, Pascal. See COLLASSE, PASCAL.

Colbran, Isabella (Angela) (*b* Madrid, 2 Feb. 1785; *d* Castenaso, Bologna, 7 Oct. 1845). Spanish soprano. She studied with Gaetano Marinelli and Girolamo Crescentini. Her concert debut was in Paris in 1801 and five years later she performed on stage for the first time in Spain. After appearances in Bologna and at La Scala,

Milan, her debut in Naples in 1811 marked the start of her fame as a dramatic singer with a powerful stage presence; she was especially acclaimed in tragic roles. Her singing exerted a strong influence on Rossini, who wrote coloratura roles for her in *Otello*, *Armida*, *Mosè in Egitto*, *La donna del lago*, and *Zelmira*. For her he also composed *Semiramide*, one of the most demanding of all coloratura parts. It was completed in 1823, one year after she and Rossini were married (they separated in 1837). She composed four volumes of songs.

JT

Coleman, Cy [Kaufman, Seymour] (*b* Bronx, New York, 14 June 1929). American composer. A musical child prodigy, he turned in his teens to jazz and began writing songs. He achieved his first major success with *Sweet Charity* (1966; filmed 1969), from which come the songs 'If my Friends Could See me Now', 'Rhythm of Life', and 'Big Spender'. Later successes include *On the Twentieth Century* (1978) and the circus-based *Barnum* (1980). His score to *City of Angels* (1989) exemplifies his jazz-inflected, harmonically advanced, and rhythmically supple style.

JSN

colenda. See KOLĘDA.

Coleridge-Taylor, Samuel (*b* London, 15 Aug. 1875; *d* Croydon, 1 Sept. 1912). English composer. He was the son of a doctor who was a native of Sierra Leone, and an Englishwoman. He entered the RCM in 1890 as a violin student and became a composition pupil of Stanford two years later. Several of his works were performed while he was at the college, notably a clarinet quintet, clarinet sonata, and piano quintet. In 1898, a year after he had left the RCM, his *Ballade* in A minor for orchestra was commissioned by the Gloucester Festival at the instigation of Elgar, whose attention had been drawn to Coleridge-Taylor's music by A. J. Jaeger of Novello. But a greater success came two months later when Stanford conducted the first performance of the cantata *Hiawatha's Wedding Feast* at the RCM. Both in Britain and in the USA this Longfellow setting became a favourite; it was followed in 1899 with *The Death of Minnehaha* and in 1900 with *Hiawatha's Departure*. He composed incidental music for plays by Shakespeare, Stephen Phillips, and Alfred Noyes at Herbert Beerbohm Tree's His Majesty's Theatre, but nothing approached the popularity of *Hiawatha*, though his *Petite Suite de concert* (1910) and his Violin Concerto (1912) are more representative of his charming if limited talent.

Coleridge-Taylor was a fine conductor, being known by New York orchestral players as 'the black Mahler'. He made three visits to the USA, where he helped to demonstrate that a black man could be the equal of the whites. Although he encountered colour prejudice in

Britain, he endured it with patience and dignity. He was professor of composition at Trinity College of Music, London, in 1903, and at the Guildhall School of Music in 1910. MK

📖 G. SELF, *The Hiawatha Man: The Life and Work of Samuel Coleridge-Taylor* (Aldershot, 1995)

Colista, Lelio (*b* Rome, 13 Jan. 1629; *d* Rome 13 Oct. 1680). Italian lutenist and composer. He enjoyed the patronage of Pope Alexander VII from 1656 and became one of the most renowned musicians of his day, amassing a considerable fortune, helped by a lucrative sinecure as *custode delle pittore* at the Sistine Chapel. He worked periodically at the chief Roman churches, notably S. Luigi dei Francesi and S. Marcello, and accounts survive of his performance at 'academies'. Like some other Roman contemporaries he felt no need to publish his works, which circulated across Europe in manuscript, and this no doubt contributed to his oblivion soon after his death. He was well received at the French court in 1664, and his sonatas were acclaimed by Purcell. PA

colla destra, colla sinistra (It.). 'With the right (hand)', 'with the left (hand)'.

colla parte, colla voce (It.). 'With the part', 'with the voice'. An indication to play another, written-out part, or to an accompanist to look to the main part for guidance on tempo, etc.

colla punta dell'arco (It.). In string playing, an instruction to play 'at the point of the bow'.

coll'arco (It., 'with the bow'; sometimes abbreviated to *c.a.*). A direction to string players to resume playing with the bow after a pizzicato passage.

colla sinistra. See COLLA DESTRA, COLLA SINISTRA.

Collasse [Colasse], **Pascal** (*b* Reims, *bapt.* 22 Jan. 1649; *d* Versailles, 17 July 1709). French composer. By 1651 he had moved to Paris, and in 1677 became Lully's secretary. At the same time he was conductor at the Opéra, and six years later obtained the post of *sous-maître* in the royal chapel. He was appointed *compositeur de la musique de la chambre* in 1685 and *maître de la musique* and *maître des pages* there in 1696. After Lully's death in 1687 Collasse began composing operas on his own account, but with relatively little success. For a short time he managed an opera house in Lille, but it burnt down in 1700. His most successful work was *Thétis et Pélée* (1689), a *tragédie lyrique* notable for its vivid depiction of a storm in Act II. He was much in demand for occasional music but died in poverty, ruined by his attempts to find the philosopher's stone. DA

colla voce. See COLLA PARTE, COLLA VOCE.

collect. 1. Short prayers sung or said before the scripture readings of the Roman *Mass (now usually referred to as 'opening prayer') or Anglican Holy Communion.

2. In the Anglican liturgy the collect is sung at the conclusion of the offices of Morning and Evening Prayer. In the Roman Office this is referred to as 'oratio' (in English, 'concluding prayer').

collected editions. See EDITIONS, HISTORICAL AND CRITICAL.

collection. A term used in the discussion of atonal music to denote a group of different notes without making any implication about that group. Thus a *set is a collection, but a collection is not necessarily a set.

collegium musicum. An organization of professional musicians and capable amateurs who met regularly to sing and play music privately, either for their own enjoyment in such informal settings as coffee-houses or public gardens, or in the homes of noble patrons. The *collegium musicum* originated in 16th-century Germany and spread to other German-speaking Protestant regions and to the Netherlands. Leipzig became a thriving centre of student *collegia musica*, celebrated examples being those established by Telemann in 1702 and Fasch in 1708.

During the 18th century the *collegium musicum* evolved into a body that performed in public before a paying audience, many of the players being drawn from the town musicians. From there it was a short step to concerts becoming fully professional affairs, and the *collegium musicum* retreated once more into its academic surroundings, all but dying out as its name came to denote a university music lecture. During the 20th century it underwent a revival, not only in Germany but, through the influence of German scholars and musicians who emigrated in the years before World War II, also in the USA. It was this regeneration that gave much of the initial impetus to the organ movement and the early music revival. PFA

col legno (It., 'with the wood'). A direction to string players to strike the strings with the stick of the bow, rather than with the hair. It was used to imaginative effect by Saint-Saëns in his *Danse macabre*, to suggest the rattling of skeletons.

Colonna, Giovanni Battista (*b* Bologna, 16 June 1637; *d* Bologna, 29 Nov. 1695). Italian composer and organist. He studied with Abbatini, Benevoli, and Carissimi in Rome while serving as organist at S. Apollinare. On returning to his native Bologna in 1659 he took posts as organist at various churches, finally becoming *maestro di cappella* at S. Petronio from 1674 until his death. He committed the blunder of publicly criticizing some obvious (but deliberate) consecutive 5ths in a work of Corelli, whereon he incurred the wrath of the entire Roman School. No doubt to regain some of his lost prestige he dedicated his op. 11 Psalms to Pope Innocent XII, who in 1694 offered him the post of *maestro di cappella* at the Vatican, which he declined. In fact, Colonna's works in the polychoral style favoured in both Rome and Bologna are outstandingly impressive, and earned the recognition of Emperor Leopold I. Of particular interest is the orchestration specifying 'concertino' and 'concerto grande', perhaps employing trumpets, well before the rise of the instrumental concerto grosso.   PA

Colonne, Édouard [Judas] (*b* Bordeaux, 23 July 1838; *d* Paris, 28 March 1910). French conductor and violinist. He studied at the Paris Conservatoire and became leader of the Paris Opéra orchestra. In 1873, with the Hartmann publishing company, he founded a series of concerts in Paris, which he conducted to promote new French music and the works of Berlioz; they became known as the Concerts Colonne. He toured as a conductor in England, Russia, and the USA, and exerted an important influence on performing standards and musical taste in France.   JT

colophony. See ROSIN.

coloration. A device used in early music notation to reduce the normal value of a note by a third. Before about 1450 'colored' (*sic*) notes were usually red. Later, the note-heads of colored notes were normally filled in black. Coloration produced two slightly different rhythmic effects: in music in duple time (modern 2/4, 4/4) it was used to write down triplets; but, for music with triple-time elements (3/4, 6/8), colored notes produced a *hemiola effect of three against two, equivalent either to three straight crotchets in a modern 6/8 bar, or to three undotted minims across two bars of 3/4.   AP

coloratura (It., 'colouring'). A term applied to elaborate decoration, either extemporized or notated, of a vocal melody (by figuration, ornamentation, etc.). A coloratura soprano is one with a high, light, agile voice capable of singing such virtuoso arias as the two written by Mozart for the Queen of Night in *Die Zauberflöte*. See VOICE, 7.

colour and music. The connection between colour and music takes several forms: the whimsical, the aesthetic, the symbolic, and the synaesthetic. Of these the syn-aesthetic is probably most notorious. The brain's ability, in certain circumstances, to connect the perception of different senses (to experience, for example, taste as shape, colour as sound, or sound as colour) was observed in ancient times and has recently been much studied. The 12th-century abbess Hildegard of Bingen apparently associated her prophetic visions, which included hearing music, with shapes and sometimes blinding colours. Occasional references to similar transferred or linked perceptions are found in later theoretical writings, especially on occasions when such links appear to support a Pythagorean explanation of the laws of creation. Isaac Newton, for example, actively sought reflections of celestial mechanics in supposed correspondences between colour and sound, and his ideas in turn were pursued by Louis-Bertrand Castel (1688–1757), who built an 'ocular harpsichord' to demonstrate such notions. Castel's writings were then translated into German by Telemann himself and may even have had some influence among German theorists. But it does not seem to have been until the later 19th century, perhaps with the relative popularization of such scientific knowledge of synaesthesia as there was at the time, that composers began to make definite claims to hear music as specific colours.

Suddenly the idea became quite widespread, most notably in Russia with Rimsky-Korsakov and Skryabin both describing the experience and even using it as a part of the composing process. Skryabin in particular attempted to write the element of colour into the very musical fabric of his orchestral work *Prometheus, the Poem of Fire* (1909–10). In this score, the required changing colours, to be played by a musician on a 'colour organ' or 'tastiera per luce', are actually notated in musical terms. However, although Skryabin attempted to build his own instrument to play this element of his orchestration, complete with painted light bulbs mounted on a wooden stand, serious realization of his vision had to wait until the late 20th century and advanced laser technology.

Reports of synaesthesia show little consistency in sound–colour associations. Different composers describe perceiving different colours with different keys, instrumental timbres, or harmonic structures. And even at the time of the special Russian vogue for such things before World War I, there were those who doubted whether some were really as synaesthetic as they claimed. Rakhmaninov recalled a hilarious discussion in a café in Paris in 1906 between Rimsky-Korsakov, Skryabin, and himself. Skryabin and Rimsky-Korsakov had been attempting to dissuade him from his sceptical attitude towards their ideas about colour and music: 'The fact that Rimsky-Korsakov and Skryabin differed over the points of contact between the sound- and colour-scale seemed to prove that I was right. Thus, for instance, Rimsky-Korsakov saw F♭ major as blue, while to Skryabin it was red-purple. In other keys, it is true, they agreed.' But in spite of his careful arguments, Rakhmaninov tells us, 'I could not prevent my two colleagues from leaving the café with the air of conquerors who were convinced that they had thoroughly refuted my opinion'.

Nonetheless, in the later 20th century, several more composers claimed they were synaesthetic. Most notably, Messiaen linked sequences of well-defined colours with particular modes. For him the octatonic scale 'turns through certain violets, certain blues, and violet-purple', while the scale tone–semitone–semitone, tone–semitone–semitone 'corresponds to an orange with tints of red and black, touches of gold and milky white with iridescent reflections, like opals'. The very titles of such pieces as *Couleurs de la cité céleste* ('Colours of the Celestial City', 1963) and *Chronochromie* ('Time Colouration', 1960) give a vivid flavour of the nature of his commitment to this idea.

In more recent years the American composer Michael Torke has made his synaesthetic instincts the very subject of his art in a series of mostly orchestral works with titles like *Ecstatic Orange* (1984), *Bright Blue Music* (1985) and, simply, *Green* (1987). He has commented, with a certain charm and no apparent irony:

> It's been an involuntary reaction, ever since I can remember. I read somewhere that it's a primitive part of your brain which mixes the senses synaesthetically without meaning to. *Bright Blue Music* begins and stays in D major. 'Why didn't you modulate?' people ask … well, I see blue when I listen to D major.

At the time of the early 20th-century vogue for such ideas, there were also many composers who made looser but enthusiastic colour–music associations of this kind, usually without quite seeming to claim specific synaesthetic experiences. Bartók, for example, specified the changes in lighting for *Bluebeard's Castle* (1918) as the door to each chamber is opened; and Schoenberg in the text and score of his opera *Die glückliche Hand* (1924) makes detailed descriptions of the different and changing colours he requires on the stage: 'a dark-violet velvet curtain … from which green-lit faces peer … The light very weak … The rest is swathed in soft red veiling, and this too reflects the greenish light'.

Such combinations of colours seem to have been imagined by Schoenberg as precisely correlated to similarly vivid and sumptuously orchestrated musical textures, and it would seem from the music itself that in his imagination the composer associated the colours he asks for less with keys (which are merely transitory and fleeting presences in this music) than with chord-structures, timbres, densities, and textures, as well as with the symbolic content of the psychological drama depicted on the stage.

At about the same time the abstract painter Wassily Kandinsky (later a friend of Schoenberg's) revealed similar preoccupations in his dramatic text in the form of a would-be opera libretto *Der gelbe Klang* ('The Yellow Sound', 1909) and even more so in the manifesto-introduction to that work. There he makes explicit his desire to take further Wagner's idea of the 'total work of art' and also notes that in *Der gelbe Klang* 'music' is 'the principal element', but at the same time 'colour-tones take on an independent significance and are treated as a means of equal importance'.

Dukas attempted something similar in his Maeterlinck-inspired opera *Ariane et Barbe-bleue* (1906), specifically in the scene where the heroine unlocks a series of six doors, to reveal behind each one a glittering treasure of precious stones (behind the seventh door are Bluebeard's previous wives). Dukas's most famous pupil, Messiaen, adored this music and pointed out that as each successive door is opened, each new colour of jewel is marked by its own distinctive orchestration, its own key, and sometimes its own rhythmic character (B major and brass fanfares for amethyst; A♭ major with woodwind and pizzicato strings for sapphire; C major and solo flute and string harmonics for pearl; D major and triplet rhythms for emerald; B♭ major, trombones, and touches of the whole-tone scale for ruby; and F♯ major and orchestration of what Messiaen calls 'incredible brilliance' for diamond).

In Stravinsky's ballet *The Firebird* (1910) we also find timbre (string and harp harmonics and even harmonic glissandos and touches of celesta) associated with the bright colours of the firebird's feathers and the gleaming gold of the magic apples in the garden of Kashchey the Immortal. And similar effects can be found in the dramatic and programmatic scores of many other composers of this period.

In the late 20th century the Russian composer Gubaidulina became interested in a rather different connection between colour and music. After reading an essay about how different colours are created when white light hits a particular surface and loses proportionally different amounts of itself, she attempted to reinvent those same proportional differences between the colours in the structural and rhythmic aspects of her choral and orchestral work *Alleluia* (1990). In effect she came up with a proportional 'scale' (white = 0:8, yellow = 1:7, orange = 2:6, light blue = 3:5, green-purple = 4:4 etc., ending with black = 8:0). Her musical exploitation of this proportional scale concentrates on the drama of the way white 'sacrifices' ever greater portions of itself until it becomes black. Her connection between music and colour is therefore essentially symbolic and religious.

Gubaidulina intended that *Alleluia* should be performed, as Skryabin's *Poem of Ecstasy* has been several times in recent years, with elaborate changing colours and laser effects suffusing the auditorium as a counterpoint to the experience of the music's sound. She took this idea further in her String Quartet no. 4 (1987), written for the Kronos Quartet who had already worked extensively with their own lighting effects. Unfortunately it has proved so far technically impossible to realize the composer's complete intentions in either work: such a marriage of colour and sound would seem to be harder in the fulfilment than in the intention.

The 20th century also gave us what, in the English language, is probably the most celebrated of all associations of colour and music: the idea of the blues and the *blue note'. While this world-famous resonance would appear to originate from the centuries-old slang equating of 'blue' with melancholy, its embodiment in a certain kind of jazz harmony (with roots in both black music and klezmer), not to mention its frequent essentialization in the shape of a single chord (usually, depending on context, of a flattened 7th or other flattened or added note), has by now come to carry enormously rich associations for almost anyone who listens to music. Indeed these musical associations are so familiar that they can be triggered almost in the absence of the music itself, just by a trick of words or a characteristic look.

There remains to mention the looser and more general use of the word 'colour' to mean timbre. Those who talk about music, especially orchestral or electronic music (where timbre is a particularly complex matter), frequently speak of the music's 'colour', and of that 'colour' being bright or dark, heavy or light. While such talk is usually assumed by commentators to be simply metaphorical, the general habit of talking in this way, of using the idea of colour as a metaphor for sound, is a persistent one and may well reflect habitual and ancient anxieties about the limits of our control and understanding of the difference between what we see and what we hear, and also our fascination with the idea of possible connections between all the different ways in which we sense the world around us.   GMcB

📖 D. S. Schier, *Louis Bertrand Castel, Anti-Newtonian Scientist* (Cedar Rapids, IA, 1941) · K. Peacock, 'Synaesthetic perception: Alexander Scriabin's colour hearing', *Music Perception*, 2/2 (1984–5), 483–506 · J. W. Bernard, 'Messiaen's synaesthesia: The correspondence between the color and sound structure in his music', *Music Perception*, 4/1 (1986–7), 41–68 · R. Cytowic, *Synaesthesia* (New York, 1989) · M. Franssen, 'The ocular harpsichord of Louis-Bertrand Castel', *Tractrix*, 3 (1991), 15–77 · S. Baron-Cohen and J. E. Harrison (eds.), *Synaesthesia: Classic and Contemporary Readings* (Cambridge, 1997)

colpo d'arco (It.). 'Bowstroke'.

Combattimento di Tancredi, e Clorinda ('The Combat of Tancred and Clorinda'). Dramatic cantata by Monteverdi to a text from Torquato Tasso's *Gerusalemme liberata;* partly acted and partly narrated, it was first performed in Venice in 1624 and was published in *Madrigali guerrieri e amorosi* (1638).

combination tone. See ACOUSTICS, 8.

combinatoriality. In *twelve-note music, that property of a set which makes one part of it complementary to another under the serial procedures of transposition, inversion, or retrograding (see SERIALISM). The term, a mathematical one, was first used in a musical context by Milton Babbitt in the 1950s, although earlier 12-note compositions, including many by Schoenberg, use the principle in a straightforward way. In the most common case, each hexachord of a 12-note set is combinatorial with the same hexachords of a transposed inversion: that is, each pair of hexachords combines to give all 12 notes. In Schoenberg's Variations for Orchestra op. 31 (1926–8), the hexachords of the prime or principal set form, starting from B♭, are identical in total content (not literal order) with those of the inverted form beginning on G (Ex. 1). In works by Babbitt, combinatorial relations between three- and four-note segments of the set are exploited.   AW

Ex. 1

prime

inversion

combo. An abbreviation for 'combination', generally applied to a small jazz group.

come (It.). 'As', 'like'; *come prima*, 'as at first', i.e. to be performed as it was the first time; *come stà*, 'as it stands'; *come sopra*, 'as above'.

comédie-ballet (Fr.). A genre of music theatre cultivated at the French court during the late 17th century. Devised by Molière and Lully, it attempted to link the content of the ballet and song presented in the *intermèdes* to the plot of the principal (spoken) drama.

comes. See CANON.

Come ye sons of art. Ode (1694) by Purcell for soprano, two altos, and bass soloists, chorus, and orchestra, composed for the birthday of Queen Mary, wife of William III; it contains the song 'Sound the trumpet'.

comic opera. See OPERA, 6; OPERA BUFFA.

comma. A minute interval (generally taken to be a ninth of a whole tone) which results when a succession of untempered 5ths and a similar succession of octaves arrive at what is ostensibly the same note, but is not really quite such. See TEMPERAMENT.

commedia dell'arte. A form of semi-improvised Italian comic theatre popular in the 16th and 17th centuries. It made use of stock scenes (*lazzi*), characters, and masks. The plots usually concerned customs surrounding marriage and procreation, while mocking the earthier aspects of love and sex, and punning on gender reversals. Much of the humour was physical, ranging through gesture, dance, and acrobatics. Modern companies like the Cirque du Soleil still model their practices on the *commedia dell'arte*, but perhaps the best-known form in which it survives is the Punch and Judy show.

The entertainment often had a musical performance as its climax, and dances and songs were usually performed both within the plays (often villanellas and scherzos) and between acts (madrigals). The itinerant players were frequently virtuoso singers, such as Virginia Andreini, who created the leading role in Monteverdi's opera *Arianna* at short notice; others (e.g. Giovanni Gabrielli and his son Francesco) carried large numbers of musical instruments with them. Music from the *commedia dell'arte* survives in print, notably in early 17th-century song anthologies.

The episodic form of the genre influenced 17th-century Venetian opera and the madrigal comedy, and its conventions and characters—Arlecchino, Scaramuccia, Pantalone—informed a range of comic operas including Pergolesi's *La serva padrona*, Mozart's *Le nozze di Figaro*, and Strauss's *Ariadne auf Naxos*, as well as Stravinsky's *Pulcinella* and Schoenberg's *Pierrot lunaire*.   SH

📖 E. ROSAND, *Opera in Seventeenth-Century Venice: The Creation of a Genre* (Berkeley, CA, 1991)

commedia per musica (It., 'comedy through music'). A term used in the 18th century, particularly in Naples, to refer to **opera buffa*.

commemoration. In the Roman rite, either an observance of low rank or the **memorial appended to an office in honour of such an observance.

commodo. See COMODO, COMODAMENTE.

common chord. A triad in which the 5th is perfect, i.e. the major or minor triad. In American usage, only the major triad is so described.

Common Prayer, Book of. The traditional service book of the Anglican Church, containing everything permanently authorized for use in its worship except the variable items: lessons (which are regulated by the Lectionary), anthems, and hymns. In this it fulfils the same purposes as the Missal, Breviary, Pontifical, and Ritual of the Roman Catholic Church. Most editions have also included a Psalter—either Coverdale's prose translation from the Great Bible of 1535 or the metrical version of Sternhold and Hopkins—as an integral part of the volume. The 39 Articles representing the doctrinal positions taken by the Church of England at the Convocation of 1563 and finalized in 1571 are customarily included as an appendix.

Thomas Cranmer, Archbishop of Canterbury 1533–53, was the primary architect of the Church of England's reformed vernacular liturgy. The first Prayer Book prepared under his direction and promulgated by Edward VI in 1549 presents in English translation an abridgment, made according to a combination of pastoral and theological criteria, of the Sarum 'Use' of the Roman rite. Drawing on the breviary of Quiñones, Cranmer created a streamlined Divine Office of two similarly structured services of Matins and Evensong in which the number of Propers was drastically reduced, the cycle for the recitation of the psalter was stretched to one month, and the proclamation of scripture was emphasized by the inclusion of two lessons at each Office. Uniquely Protestant concerns are more evident in the revisions to the Mass, which followed Luther in preserving its sung portions with few alterations while censoring its theology of sacrifice. Merbecke's *The Booke of Common Praier Noted* (1550) was one of several attempts to provide plainchant settings for the new Anglican liturgy.

Criticism by Martin Bucer (1491–1551) and other reformers led to the preparation of a more explicitly Protestant Service of Holy Communion, in which most of the propers and anything reminiscent of transubstantiation were removed, for a revised Prayer Book issued in 1552. Although suspended during the Catholic restoration and the Commonwealth, this second Prayer Book was enshrined with minor amendments in the 1559 and 1662 Acts of Uniformity. It was also the basis for the prayer books of the non-English churches of the Anglican Communion.

Efforts to recover elements of medieval worship provided the initial impetus for increasingly thorough revisions of Anglican service books during the 20th century. These eventually embraced texts in modern

English, the incorporation of material from ancient Christian liturgies, and the flexible use of multiple orders of service. The Church of England formally placed traditional and contemporary forms of worship on a roughly equal footing with the publication of *Common Worship* (2001), which unites revised services with those of the *Book of Common Prayer* in a single volume.   ABo/ALı

common time. Another name for 4/4 time. It is sometimes denoted by the letter **C**, which does not stand for 'common' but dates back to the period of mensural notation when triple (or perfect) time was indicated by a full circle, and duple or quadruple (imperfect) time by a semicircle (C).

communion. 1. Chant sung during the Communion in the Roman *Mass.

2. For the Anglican Holy Communion service, see COMMON PRAYER, BOOK OF.

comodo, comodamente (It.). 'Comfortable', 'convenient'; *tempo comodo*, 'at a comfortable, moderate speed'.

compact disc [CD]. A 12-cm plastic disc on which digitally encoded signals are recorded in the form of a spiral pitted track running from the centre outwards. Compact discs, coated in a reflecting metal (usually aluminium) and sealed by a protective layer to prevent oxidization, are read by a precisely focused laser. Corrosion of the reflective surface caused by faults in the protective layer is known as 'bronzing'. Discs are manufactured by stamping and pressing into a plastic sheet. The capacity of commercially manufactured discs allows up to 79 minutes per disc. Compact discs were developed jointly by Philips and Sony and introduced in 1983. They quickly became the *de facto* world standard recorded-music carrier, and long-playing records and pre-recorded cassettes were discontinued in all but specialized markets within seven years.

See also RECORDING AND REPRODUCTION.   LF

compass (Fr.: *étendue*; Ger.: *Umfang*). The range of pitches obtainable from an instrument or voice.

Compère, Loyset (*b* Hainaut, *c*.1445; *d* Saint Quentin, 16 Aug. 1518). French church musician and composer. His earliest known position, in the mid-1470s, was in the *cappella* of Galeazzo Maria Sforza in Milan. Following the duke's murder in 1476 he established links with the French court, and later held posts in Cambrai and Douai. His last years were spent at the collegiate church in Saint Quentin, where he is buried. Compère

has long been overshadowed by his younger contemporary, Josquin des Prez. His works bridge the stylistic gap between the late medieval sound world of Busnois and Ockeghem and, at the other extreme, the declamatory imitative texture typical of 16th-century polyphony. His surviving output consists principally of motets and chansons. During his Milanese years he also wrote motet cycles ('motetti missales') to be sung, according to local custom, in place of the words of the Mass.   JM

competitions in music. The human instinct for competition has not been applied solely to physical or sporting activities. Musical contests of different sorts date back to ancient times, from the Pythian Games held in Delphi in the 6th century BC, through the meetings of Welsh bards known as *eisteddfodau (said to date from the 7th century AD), to the medieval *puys and other competitions made famous by Wagner in *Tannhäuser* and *Die Meistersinger von Nürnberg*. However, in the 19th and 20th centuries competitions for performers and composers became part of musical life.

History reports many well-known contests between individual musicians aiming to win appointments or patronage. In 1557 Claudio Merulo won a competition for the post of organist of St Mark's, Venice, in which Andrea Gabrieli was an unsuccessful candidate. Handel and Domenico Scarlatti competed as organists in Rome in 1708. In the 1790s, competition with Joseph Wölfl and J. B. Cramer, the leading piano virtuosos in Vienna, led Beethoven to strive harder for pre-eminence as a performer.

1. Amateur competitions in Britain; 2. Amateur competitions outside Britain; 3. Band contests; 4. Competitions for performers; 5. Competitions for composers; 6. Recording industry prizes

1. Amateur competitions in Britain

By the end of the 18th century, rural publicans organized singing contests as attractions. At the beginning of the 19th century, vocal competitions were being held in towns and villages, perhaps under the influence of the modern *eisteddfodau*, established in 1817. By the middle of the century similar contests between bands, and singing competitions in cities, began to attract more attention—not only for their competitive interest, but also as opportunities for audiences to hear good performances. In Manchester a 'Prize Glee-Singing' contest was held in the Belle Vue Gardens in 1855, and competitions in madrigal and choral sight-singing at the Royal Pomona Palace in 1874. Choral competitions were organized in Liverpool, Bradford, Sheffield, and in London at the Crystal Palace.

The Curwen family were influential in what was to become a competition movement. John Curwen, the renowned music educationist and proponent of Tonic Sol-fa, organized competitions for choirs in London during the 1860s. His son, Spencer Curwen, inaugurated the Stratford Festival in east London in 1882; this event, which included classes for solo instrumental, ensemble, solo vocal, and choral performance, became the model for all subsequent local competitive festivals.

In the early years of the 20th century an Association of Competitive Festivals was formed; it was succeeded in 1921 by the British Federation of Music Festivals, now the British Federation of Festivals for Music, Dance and Speech, which organizes over 300 local amateur competitive festivals in Britain and the Commonwealth as well as running summer schools of music. The federation publishes a handbook, organizes an annual conference, and maintains the standards of festivals affiliated to it. Most British towns hold annual competitive festivals in which thousands of schoolchildren have been presented as candidates, as soloists and ensembles in various classes. Some musicians object to the spirit of rivalry engendered by such events, but the movement as a whole helped to raise of standards in amateur performance. By the 1920s, for example, British composers were taking advantage of the fact that amateur choirs could perform far more difficult music than they could at the end of the 19th century.

2. Amateur competitions outside Britain

During the 19th century, singing and band competitions grew in popularity on the Continent. Leading composers, among them Schumann, were often required to adjudicate. In Ireland the Feis Ceoil, the Irish national music competition, was first held in Dublin in 1897. The British competition movement extended to Commonwealth countries, where local festivals are organized on British lines, often with British adjudicators; many such festivals are affiliated to the British Federation of Festivals.

In the USA the earliest recorded musical contests were those between rival church choirs held in the 1790s. During the 19th century competitions between school bands and choirs became the most common. The competition movement expanded greatly in the 20th century: in 1924 school band contests were held in only five states, but by 1931 all but five states organized them, with 1100 bands and 770 orchestras taking part. National contests were established for bands (1926) and orchestras (1929). Inter-collegiate singing contests (between 'glee clubs') are also widespread in the USA.

3. Band contests

Since the early 19th century, *brass bands have flourished in the northern industrial towns of Britain. Closely associated with what became a brass band movement has been the cultivation of band contests, which had become widespread by the 1840s. The British Open Brass Band Championship, now one of the most celebrated, was first held at Belle Vue, Manchester, in 1853. In 1898 some of the prizewinning bands from Belle Vue gave a concert in London, at the Royal Albert Hall; Arthur Sullivan, who conducted them, suggested establishing a similar contest in London. The National Brass Band Championships were first held at the Crystal Palace, where they were an annual event until 1936. By the mid-1930s nearly 200 bands took part each year, in ten classes.

Since the 1940s, with the enormous increase in participating bands, the preliminary rounds of the National Championship have been held locally and the final is at the Royal Albert Hall. By the 1970s about 500 bands took part each year. Bands also compete internationally, and the European championship is held annually in London. The national contests have a tradition of commissioning specially composed set pieces, which now provide a valuable repertory of band music. Elgar's *Severn Suite* was composed in 1930 for the Crystal Palace competition.

4. Competitions for performers

During the 20th century a great number of international competitions for aspiring virtuosos were established. Most are devoted to a single instrument or discipline (e.g. conducting) and are held annually or biennially. There is normally an age limit for entrants, who perform pieces from a given list to a jury of professional musicians. After the preliminary rounds, the finalists are usually expected to give a public recital and a concerto performance. Winners are assured not only of a cash prize but also of a considerable boost to their careers: increasing commercial involvement guarantees concert tours and recording contracts. The foundation of a major music prize or scholarship has become a common way for a commercial organization to sponsor the arts.

Among the internationally known competitions held in Britain are the City of London Carl Flesch International Violin Competition (biennial), the Leeds International Piano Competition (triennial), and the St Albans International Organ Festival Competition (annual). The donors of some scholarships and awards arrange their final stages as public events similar to competitions, for example the Kathleen Ferrier and Maggie Teyte/Miriam Lycette awards for singers.

Some national organizations in Britain and several regional arts associations organize 'musicians' platforms' or name 'musicians of the year' after preliminary contests, the winners usually being given financial assistance with a debut recital or with further study. Among such schemes are two major competitions sponsored by the BBC: BBC Young Musicians (established 1978) and Cardiff Singer of the World (a biennial competition established in 1983, coinciding with the opening of the new St David's Hall).

Many competitions open to international entry are affiliated to the Fédération des Concours Internationaux de Musique, an organization based in Geneva which issues an annual booklet giving details of venues, entry requirements, prizes, closing dates, addresses, etc. Some competitions for performers are not devoted to any one instrument and vary their classes from year to year, for example the International Tchaikovsky Competition (Moscow), the Geneva International Competition, the Gaudeamus Competition for the Interpretation of Contemporary Music (Rotterdam), and the Queen Elisabeth International Competition (Brussels). Other contests include classes for ensembles.

Like the Carl Flesch competition, many international competitions have been founded to commemorate a renowned musician. Among them are those in honour of Chopin (Warsaw), Paganini (Genoa), Mitropoulos (New York), and Callas (Athens).

5. Competitions for composers

Many prizes for composers are awarded by conservatories or are for graduates of musical institutions. The *Prix de Rome was instituted in 1803 and until 1968 was awarded annually by the French Académie des Beaux-Arts to the composition student at the Paris Conservatoire judged to have written the best cantata to a commissioned text; the first prize allowed the winner to live at the Villa Medici, Rome, and to study in the city for two years (followed by a further two years either in Rome or in another cultural centre). Berlioz (1830), Bizet (1857), and Debussy (1884) were among the winners. There is a Belgian Prix de Rome and an American one (established in 1905).

Composition contests arouse less public interest, but the guarantee of a professional performance of a new work is an attraction for aspiring composers. Such competitions are often organized in association with a festival (e.g. the Huddersfield Contemporary Music Festival) or with a performers' contest for which there is a separate competition for the composition of a test piece (e.g. the Carl Flesch competition). Many competitions for composers held in Britain are open only to British composers or those who have studied in the UK,

for example the Royal Philharmonic Society Composition Prize. The best-known international contests are the Queen Elisabeth International Competition (Brussels), the Prince Pierre of Monaco Prize (Monaco), and the Geneva International Competition for the Composition of Opera and Ballet; several are affiliated to the Fédération des Concours Internationaux de Musique. Some are organized on similar lines to literary awards, for example the Britten Award (UK, established 1990) and the American Grawemeyer Award. Some organizations for promoting new music (e.g. the ISCM) arrange events that are not competitions in the accepted sense but at which scores selected from many submitted are included in a festival-like programme.

Following the success and public interest in its performing competitions, the BBC has jointly sponsored two composing competitions: since 1998, in partnership with EMI, the LSO, and *BBC Music Magazine*, it has sponsored 'Masterprize', giving the winning works maximum public exposure through concerts, broadcasts, and the production of a compact disc. In conjunction with the *Guardian* newspaper the BBC has organized a Young Composer Competition, with the winning pieces being played at the Proms; the competition embraces classical, jazz, rock, and pop styles. This development may reflect the increased importance attached in education to composing, which has been a compulsory component in the British National Curriculum since 1991.

6. Recording industry prizes

The recording industry has started sponsoring competitions. The annual Technics Mercury Music Prize (organized in conjunction with the British Phonographic Industry and the British Association of Record Dealers) is awarded to a recorded album (a CD) from a shortlist of 12, rather than a performance; aiming 'to celebrate the best in British music', it is open to all types of music. It remains to be seen whether, even in a 'postmodern' era, a competition can apply an agreed set of criteria to make musically valid judgments about entries in radically differing styles.

British competitions are listed in *The British and International Music Yearbook*, and details of individual international ones can be found on the Internet.

AL/PSp

complete cadence. See CADENCE.

Compline (from Lat. *completorium*, 'completion'). Originally the last of eight hours of the Divine *Office in the medieval Roman rite, sung before retiring to bed. 'Night prayer' is an alternative name in both the Anglican and Roman rites.

Composers' Guild of Great Britain. Society founded in 1944 to protect composers' interests; Vaughan Williams was its first president.

composition 1. Introduction; 2. History; 3. Form, genre, style; 4. Study and method; 5. Expression and evaluation

1. Introduction

Composition is both the activity of composing and the result of that activity. It is not an exclusively musical term—applications to prose, poetry, painting, architecture, and a variety of other media are common—and in all cases it describes a process of construction, a creative putting together, a working out and carrying through of an initial conception or inspiration. This conception or inspiration may itself take a variety of forms, from a complete structural outline to the briefest thematic, harmonic, or rhythmic idea whose structural implications and potential remain to be worked out, and whose generic context may be at first unclear. The initial conception may be purely musical, or it may derive from a literary, dramatic, or scenic stimulus. But such initial conceptions will always need to be consciously worked on, even if their first appearance is spontaneous, unbidden, and not the result of conscious thought.

A composition may come into being because it is commissioned for a specific function, and for particular performers, or because the composer determines to create it even with no hope of immediate, adequate performance. It may be simple or complex in form, with a duration of seconds or hours, accessible to the most inexperienced amateur or taxing for the most expert professional. It may be abstract or programmatic, vocal or instrumental, laid out for any grouping or combination of voices or instruments, live or electronic. A composition may allude directly or tangentially to a familiar genre (dance, song), and composers may work with particular precedents or models in mind, or aim as far as possible to avoid such connections. They may call upon some kind of system in their work, to provide certain established procedures and materials—modes of pitch or rhythm, the conventions of tonal harmony, the 12-note method. Composers may regard the expression of feeling as a primary aim, or give greater emphasis to the intellectual creation of satisfying, coherent forms—always assuming that they accept the validity of attempts to verbalize about their creative instincts and processes.

Because of the closeness of the words 'composition' and 'composure', it might seem that the intellectual aspect of the activity is what matters most, and that even the initial conception or inspiration is in some respects intellectually determined. But most composers would disagree. Schoenberg made a celebrated distinction between pupil and master, student and composer, in his *Harmonielehre*, where he asserted that 'the pupil should think, but the artist, the master, composes by feeling. He no longer needs to think, for he has reached a higher kind of response to his need for self-expression.' In any case, it is scarcely possible to quantify the relation between instinct and intellect, conscious and unconscious, in the composition process. It is possible to subject the results of that process—the completed work—to close examination or *analysis, but it is a great deal more difficult to reproduce the stages of the process with any certainty of accuracy; it is also difficult to recapture the immediate effects of listening to a composition on any individual member of an audience.

2. History

The further back in time one goes, the more likely it is that a composition had a definite social or religious function, rather than existing primarily as the self-expression of a composer—but 'self-expression' intended to be communicated to others by interpreters. The term 'composition' has been traced back as far as an 11th-century Latin treatise, the *Micrologus* (*c*.1030) by Guido of Arezzo, which contains a chapter called 'De commoda vel componenda modulatione' ('On grateful melodic lines, and composing them'). The term may first have been applied to polyphonic music by Johannes de Grocheo, in whose *Ars musice* (*c*.1290) the author of a piece for two or three voices ('Musica composita') is called 'compositor'. And towards the end of the 15th century Tinctoris used the verb 'componere' and the noun 'compositor' to reinforce the distinction between music which was written down and music which was improvised. It became increasingly possible to think of composers as individuals who wrote down music for others to perform, rather than as performers improvising their own compositions. Tinctoris also indicated that a composer was likely to be concerned with novelty, originality: writing down music was a way of giving permanent form to a personal statement.

Of course, a written-down composition may itself provide the basis for improvisation or ornamentation, most familiarly in the *da capo* forms of the Baroque era. But a composer normally writes down music in order to provide materials to be realized as accurately as possible in performance, while accepting that the interpretation of a sensitive performer is likely to involve rather more than a mechanical reproduction of what is notated on the printed page. A composition in this sense cannot exist without notation, and musical notation has indeed evolved as a means of enabling composers to present their ideas in visible, readable form, and to allow performers to interpret the intentions of composers as precisely or as freely as composers desire. However, certain conventions of style—*rubato in Chopin, for example—will be implicit in the character of the music rather than explicit in the notation, and to this extent 'realizing the intentions of composers' on the basis of what is actually written down will always be a delicate and controversial task (see NOTATION, 5).

The writing down of music in score, with all parts aligned, can be traced back at least as far as the late 14th century, in manuscripts of instrumental compositions set out on two staves with regular bar-lines. The use of score notation became general only in the mid-16th century (see NOTATION, 3), and it was during the same century that scores began to be used for study. The writing down of music in score naturally affected the development of the art of composition in crucial and far-reaching ways, effecting a shift from the successive addition of complete parts to a complete single line, to working on all parts or voices simultaneously. The motivic processes of Beethoven or Wagner represent very different kinds of basic compositional techniques from the use of a tenor as *cantus firmus by Machaut or Dufay—even though all four composers were doubtless concerned in their different ways with the fundamental task of balancing unity and diversity, and achieving a necessary coherence.

The varied and complex changes through which the art of composition developed after the 16th century—in particular, the emergence of instrumental styles and genres in which a polarity between the outer parts, melody and bass, came to dominate—clearly cannot be ascribed solely to the fact that composers had begun to work in score. Changes in the nature of musical materials and techniques, and especially in the progress towards a fully developed sense of tonality and harmonic rhythm which stressed equality and regularity, were even more important. But the characteristic post-Renaissance concept of the composer as an individual who sought a perceptible degree of originality through works given permanent form in score stems essentially from such new possibilities of publication and transmission. Only rarely is a composition a composite—the work of several hands. Collective improvisation survives, both in art music and in jazz, but in the broadest sense a 'composite composition' is a contradiction in terms; the most highly regarded compositions are those in which a single individual has achieved the most memorable fusion of construction and expression, individuality and communication.

It has been argued that a composition is normally capable of being written down in such a way that different performances of it will resemble each other closely. But many 20th-century composers grew impatient of the fact that their attempts at precise notation of rhythmic subtleties or pitch inflections proved too complex for performers to realize accurately. Such composers as Lutosławski, Ligeti, and Stockhausen, aware of the subtle inflections present in traditional and non-Western music, therefore developed notations which were *indeterminate in various ways, with respect both to the duration of individual pitches and to the order in which the various events of the composition actually occurred (see NOTATION, 5). Moreover, with experimental composers like *Cage, the unforeseen and unforeseeable became part of the creative act and its subsequent realizations in performance. Even with pieces that offer only the slightest of verbal instructions in place of conventional musical notation, it is still possible to detect the presence of a composer. That composer may be more of an initiator than a completer, but the initial, generative idea is the composer's alone. In his 'silent' piano piece, *4′33″* (1952), Cage decided that the piano should not be played for the period indicated in the title, and his score is notated accordingly. But without Cage's compositional concept the piece would not exist and could not knowingly be performed. Even when there are no intentional sounds, therefore, a composer's decisions will still determine the character and, to a degree, the content of a work.

3. Form, genre, style

Compositions are often named according to the generic family to which they belong: and even a work that appears to reject generic attribution—beyond the apparently neutral title 'piece'—may well have explicit generic associations: for example, the sixth of Schoenberg's Six Little Piano Pieces op. 19 can be linked with the lament, and also the chorale. Such generic connections are vital aspects of music's ability to communicate in a social context. Yet the materials a composer assembles and exploits to make a composition, even when the work's source, or its central element, is primarily a text or libretto, are commonly described in terms of particular formal features: motif, theme, subject, or *melody (something stated, and likely to be elaborated or varied); *harmony (the vertical relations, both small- and large-scale); *rhythm; *tone-colour; and *texture (polyphonic or homophonic, predominantly close-position, or widely dispersed). The identification and description of these formal features is complicated by the obvious fact that they are interdependent rather than distinct. In discussing such features and attempting to define how they function—to create continuity and contrast, unity and diversity—we are defining *form; while in describing the expressive or emotional character of musical ideas and processes we are dealing more directly with genre and style.

In his *Fundamentals of Musical Composition*, Schoenberg declared that 'the chief requirements for the creation of a comprehensible form are logic and coherence'. This had been a common perception ever since Aristotle built classical aesthetics round his dislike of the episodic, and the formal ideal of Western art, at least until the 19th century, remained one in which diversity was subordinated to unity, discontinuity to continuity. Yet the emphasis on unity in this sense has always been more appropriate for some musical forms and genres than others—for a fugue more than a large-scale symphony, an aria or a song than a full-length opera; and the conclusion that an emphasis on diversity or contrast can lead to incoherence in a composition has been challenged during the modernist era, variously defined as beginning with the radically innovatory compositions of late Beethoven, or with the collapse of tonal structuring after Wagner. As noted earlier, many 20th-century composers adopted a more flexible, even indeterminate approach to musical form than their Classical and Romantic predecessors, but this did not mean that Boulez or Lutosławski were no longer concerned with the balance and coherence of the work as a whole: they simply believed that such qualities could be achieved in a more flexible way than formerly.

Form can also be defined in terms of various form-building procedures—for example, statement, development, variation, contrast—which establish either the goal-directed logic most evident in tonal music, or the more multivalent qualities of much earlier and more recent music, in which the composition may seem to float in space rather than advance determinedly in time. But whereas these strategies represent compositional technique, the personality of a work's creator will be more immediately detectable in the style which informs materials and compositional structuring alike.

Even so, a style that is aurally detectable may be hard to define in words. The term 'style' is therefore often used as a synonym for 'technique', yet if style is personality, character, manner, then it comprises not only the presence of particular techniques but also the expressive essence, purpose, or consequence of those techniques. The interpretation of style thus requires a combination of the interpreter's aesthetic and analytic responses. For example, to state that Palestrina's style does not include the frequent use of the tritone as a melodic interval is another way of saying that he found this interval technically and aesthetically undesirable—whereas Webern, three and a half centuries later, gave the tritone the greatest prominence and significance.

The technical result in each case is clear-cut and easy to demonstrate. The aesthetic result is aurally explicit to the extent that we are unlikely ever to confuse one composer with the other. But putting the difference into words is worthwhile only as part of a much broader account of the stylistic and generic imperatives governing the compositional activity of two such different masters.

Style may well be sensed initially through distinctions between historical periods in which certain qualities come to be seen as representative. The differences between Byrd and Bach, or Beethoven and Boulez, are likely to be evident to the least experienced listener, even if that listener finds it difficult—and unnecessary—to describe the differences in words. General definitions of period styles—medieval, Renaissance, Baroque, Classical, Romantic, modernist, and their various tributaries—are not particularly difficult to devise. But nowhere is the inadequacy of words as a medium for explaining and justifying musical perceptions more clear than in any attempt to provide detailed accounts of the difference in style between masters of the same period—Bach and Handel, Schoenberg and Stravinsky. It can be even harder to convey differences in style (if any) between two minor composers of the same period—Vanhal and Dittersdorf, for example—or to judge, on grounds of style, whether a composition is by, say, a late 19th-century radical or a mid-20th-century conservative.

Style is something to be sensed through informed instinct, a matter of mood as much as of texture or technique. And it is so closely related to surface features, particularly those of rhythmic character, that it is as hard to evaluate as it is to analyse. Comparisons can be especially misleading: for example, to argue on stylistic grounds that Telemann is a more coherent composer than Cage—or, more broadly, that because it sets less store by surface continuities 20th-century music is in general less logical than 18th-century music, risks taking oversimplification to excess. Without a positive sense of style a composition would be of little value, the work of an individual which succeeds only in sounding anonymous. But detailed examination of a composition's materials and procedures, as distinct from its character and effect, tends to focus on matters of structure. Such structural matters may ultimately be interpreted stylistically, and may be linked to broader topics in generic and cultural history, but they can usefully be considered without close reference to such wider issues.

4. Study and method

In section 2 the origin and early history of the term 'composition' were outlined. Like many other disciplines, composition eventually became something which was not simply 'done' but which was studied and taught. Treatises were needed as teaching material, and many hundreds have been compiled over the centuries, some concentrating on exercises of the author's own devising, others using examples from 'real' music. Textbooks do not invariably shun the term 'composition' in their titles, but only rarely do they claim to be directly concerned with the practice of a 'free' or original style. Their concern is with technique rather than style, with the beginner rather than the expert, and although in one case, at least—*Simple Composition* (1979) by Charles Wuorinen—the author claims that his text 'can also be employed in composing "real music"', this is because he is concerned with a particular 20th-century technique, the 12-note system.

Opinions vary about the extent to which talented fledgling composers benefit from working at other academic musical subjects—the techniques of strict counterpoint, imitative studies of Palestrina, Bach, etc., as well as history, analysis, or orchestration. It is nevertheless generally accepted that an original gift can be nurtured, encouraged, and to some extent shaped by a good teacher (not necessarily a composer). Originality is more likely to be stifled by lack of direct stimulus, of both criticism and encouragement, than by any particular teaching 'philosophy'; and if the most highly regarded teachers of composition are often composers of some stature themselves (Messiaen, Petrassi, and Babbitt are three examples from the post-1950 period), it is probably as much because of the personality that informs their creative work as through any specific insights they could offer student composers about their own efforts.

Nadia Boulanger (1887–1979) is perhaps the most celebrated example of a 20th-century composition teacher who was not herself a major composer. It may be difficult to prove conclusively that the development and achievement of the likes of Aaron Copland and Elliott Carter would have been radically different had they not studied with her, but the impressions such students have conveyed of her teaching give some indication of what they found most valuable. All stress the combination of strictness and tolerance, her instant understanding of a composer's intentions and motivations. As Copland commented,

> it begins, perhaps, with the conviction that one is in the presence of an exceptional musical mentality. By a process of osmosis one scales up attitudes, principles, reflections, knowledge. The last is a key word; it is literally exhilarating to be with a teacher for whom the art one loves has no secrets.

Not all pupils will respond positively to such apparent omniscience, of course, and on occasion the personality which makes the teacher so powerful an example can come dangerously close to stifling the most talented pupils: such was the case of Schoenberg and his relationship with both Berg and Webern. But although the argument that great composers have been decisively influenced by anything other than their own inner resources is never easy to prove, it is certain that a multitude of lesser talents, and many musicians who have not attempted to become serious composers at all, have benefited greatly from the study of composition, and also from study with composers.

Another issue of absorbing interest, and still greater complexity, is that of how a composition comes into being, from conception to completion. As composers became independent of church and court, and more reliant on the support of public and patrons—whether individuals, publishers, broadcasting organizations, or arts councils—so their work became less obviously 'functional' and more the expression of an individual sensibility, even if it also demonstrated awareness of the need to conform to the expectations aroused by acknowledgment of a parent genre of some kind. Documentary evidence about the workings of the compositional process is always tantalizing: it may offer a graphic picture of slow, gradual evolution of large structures from small ideas, as with Beethoven's sketches—in which case commentators can speculate over the reasons for each and every change, cancellation, and variant reading. More often, however, surviving drafts and manuscripts give very little indication of the mental effort, and the probably extensive mental preliminaries, which preceded the putting of pen to paper—in which case commentators feel even more justified in speculating about the 'why' of the music, as if there must ultimately be a rational explanation for every flicker of the creative consciousness.

Composers' own reminiscences tend naturally to be more concerned with the most general, fundamental matters of inspiration and effort, and to avoid blow-by-blow accounts of techniques being tried and applied. Brahms stressed the contrast between the initial, unbidden inspiration, quoting the first vocal phrase of his song *Die Mainacht*, and the hard work of actual composition, which might not begin for a long time after the initial inspiration had occurred, in order to give it time to mature and germinate. For Schoenberg, however, there was no real separation of idea from working out: 'The composer ... conceives an entire composition as a spontaneous vision' and 'proceeds like Michelangelo, who chiselled his Moses out of the marble directly, without sketches, complete in every detail, directly forming his material'. Hindemith made a similar point:

If we cannot, in the flash of a single moment, see a composition in its absolute entirety, with every pertinent detail in its proper place, we are not genuine creators . . . In working out his material [the composer] will always have before his mental eye the entire picture. In writing melodies or harmonic progressions he does not have to select them arbitrarily, he merely has to fulfil what the conceived totality demands.

Most composers are understandably irritated by what they see as an impertinent and counter-productive obsession with 'how it is done'; and they tend to compose their statements and reminiscences accordingly. Occasionally a Maxwell Davies or a Ferneyhough proves willing to provide at least some salient technical details in programme notes or lectures. But Stravinsky is probably more representative. In discussing the genesis of *The Rite of Spring*, he stressed the difficulty and novelty of the enterprise: 'I had only my ear to help me. I heard and I wrote what I heard. I am the vessel through which [*The Rite*] passed.' It has been left to later scholars to discover the extent of Stravinsky's use of published Russian folk material in the work and to argue that such information is of legitimate interest to the listener. Such information is, after all, more likely to strengthen admiration for the quality of Stravinsky's inspiration, and for his technical skill, than to undermine it. The discovery of sources may render a composition less purely original than the composer wishes it to be known. Yet skill in the treatment of existing material can count for as much as, if not more than, the quality of utterly unprecedented musical thinking.

5. Expression and evaluation

There is often considerable agreement, bolstered of course by 'historical' knowledge, as to the stylistic, technical, formal, and generic aspects of a composition: for example, few would care to dispute that Haydn's 'London' Symphony is a Classical composition using the tonal system and the formal conventions associated with sonata-type structures, to produce a concert work appropriate for late 18th-century London. But it is much more difficult to pin down a single interpretation of musical meaning as emotional expression, especially when the composition has no text or illustrative programme—hence the difficulties, outlined above, with respect to 'style analysis'. And while the presence of such performing instructions as 'con fuoco' or 'tranquillo' may encourage the assumption that the composition to which these are applied possesses such qualities in ways that all attentive listeners will inevitably experience in performance, it would be difficult to argue that all other examples of similar thematic, harmonic, and rhythmic events necessarily possess the

same attributes. A composition is less a series of linguistic statements than a succession of expressive gestures. Music communicates less like prose, or even poetry, and more like choreography, with its 'vocabulary' of facial and bodily expressions.

Compositions are experienced as expression in sound, and in performance even the most thoroughly trained and committed analyst is likely to respond emotionally rather than intellectually to the music. Compositions are nevertheless evaluated both analytically and aesthetically: in respect of the techniques and forms involved, and as 'good' or 'bad'. But the two approaches are not mutually exclusive, since the critic's aesthetic criteria are bound to include analytical elements—matters of proportion, balance, diversity, unity, coherence. And it has already been argued that, save for the more experimental modern composers, the processes associated with these elements—repetition, variation, decoration, contrast, evolution, contradiction—have consistently concerned composers of all periods and in all forms. The listener's response to and awareness of such fundamentals will vary enormously. There is no single formula guaranteed to produce a great composer, or a good composition, and there is no single way in which music must be heard in order that its capacity to communicate may function. The listener's experience is a putting together of all the diverse responses which occur as the composer's own putting together unfolds in time. In this sense, at least, the listener is a composer too.   AW

compound interval. An *interval larger than an octave.

compound time [compound metre]. A time signature having a triple pulse within each beat, such as 6/8, 6/4 (respectively, two beats of three quavers each, and two beats of three crotchets each; both called compound duple time), 9/8 (three beats of three quavers each; compound triple time), or 12/8 (four beats of three quavers each; compound quadruple time).

comprimario (It.). In opera, a role of secondary importance, or a singer taking such a part.

computers and music. Computers first appeared on the commercial market in 1951, designed to serve the needs of business and commerce and to further scientific research and development. The legacy of this digital revolution influences the daily lives of almost everyone, from the multimedia environment of the personal computer to the world of digital radio, television, and the mobile phone. There are few areas of the art and practice of music that have not been affected by this technology either directly or indirectly. Some of the more significant applications are summarized below.

In the case of music-printing, computer typesetting has now replaced traditional engraving in the production of new scores. The evolution of software for music notation has proved especially challenging, since there is no obvious correlation between the graphic symbols of a music score and the alphanumeric code traditionally used by computers to represent information internally. The difficulties encountered here extend not only to music-printing but also to other applications that require the digital manipulation of music data. Early attempts to produce a comprehensive representational language for music met with varying degrees of success. In many instances the results fell short of a precise representation of every nuance encountered in the visual mapping of a conventional music score and involved complicated and error-prone manual coding procedures. The subsequent development of graphics-driven notation programs for personal computers was altogether more successful, and this has put increasing pressure on the industry to develop a universal standard for representing common music notation as digital data. One such format, known as NIFF (Notational Interchange File Format), was proposed in 1995 but has yet to achieve universal acceptance.

Music research is another sphere that has derived considerable benefit from the computer, both as a means of cataloguing reference material and as an aid to music analysis. Computers are well suited to tasks of a repetitive nature and are thus ideal tools for studying features such as the frequency and distribution of musical elements within one or a number of scores. Statistical investigations have been carried out on a wide variety of musical materials from many periods of history, generating data to support hypotheses concerning the nature of the compositional process. Such techniques have proved especially successful with medieval and Renaissance music, identifying the underlying characteristics of variation and invention, and also with more modern music based on compositional procedures that have a mathematical basis, for example the serial works of Schoenberg or Webern.

Much progress has been made in recent years in the development of software to assist the processes of teaching and learning in music, ranging from inter-active aural training programs to *CD-ROMs which provide complete tutorials on individual works. The use of this multimedia environment to interleave elements of speech, text, music score, and acoustic performance in a highly structured manner illustrates the versatility of the modern computer as a study aid.

Extensive use has been made of the computer as a tool for generating new music, in terms of both electronic synthesis and the underlying processes of composition itself. In the latter context mathematical models are sometimes used to calculate the detailed results to a series of musical propositions, for example the frequency and distribution of events according to a set of probabilities. In the former context the computer becomes directly involved in the processes of sound-generation, generating acoustic wave functions either from first principles or by extracting features from naturally produced sounds, captured by a microphone and input to the computer in a digital format.

Early computers lacked both the processing power and the supplementary technology necessary for generating and converting digital functions into acoustic sound waves, and the pioneers of computer music faced considerable difficulties in overcoming these short-comings. Such problems are rarely encountered with a modern computer, which has the capacity to compute and process music information at speeds representing many orders of magnitude when compared to a typical mainframe computer of the 1960s. In addition, high-quality interfaces for the input and output of audio information are now standard features. Such developments, however, are a relatively recent phenomenon, and it is important to recognize the significance of the *synthesizer as an alternative means of generating and processing sound material. All-digital synthesizers were strongly in evidence by the mid-1980s, using hardware specially designed to compute music audio functions. It took a further decade for the personal computer to achieve an equivalent functionality, but this tool now represents a serious alternative to the synthesizer for composers and performers alike.   PM

📖 *Computer Music Journal* (1977–) · *Computers in Music Research* (1989–) · A. MARSDEN and A. POPLE (eds.), *Computer Representations and Models in Music* (London, 1992) · P. MANNING, *Electronic and Computer Music* (Oxford, 1993) · D. COPE, *Experiments in Musical Intelligence* (Madison, WI, 1996) · E. SELFRIDGE-FIELD (ed.), *Beyond MIDI: The Handbook of Musical Codes* (Cambridge, MA, 1997) · R. L. WICK, *Electronic and Computer Music: An Annotated Bibliography* (Westport, CT, 1997)

Comte Ory, Le ('Count Ory'). Comic opera in two acts by Rossini to a libretto by Eugène Scribe and Charles-Gaspard Delestre-Poirson after their own play (Paris, 1828). It uses much music from Rossini's *Il *viaggio a Reims*.

Comus. Masque in three acts by John Milton performed at Ludlow Castle in 1634 with music by Henry Lawes. Arne composed new music for John Dalton's adaptation of Milton's verse, a version first performed in London in 1738. In 1942 Lambert arranged music by Purcell for a ballet in which some of Milton's verse was spoken. Another ballet was produced in 1946 with music by Handel and Lawes, arranged by E. Irving.

concentus. See ACCENTUS.

concert. A musical performance given for an audience, generally by relatively large numbers of players or singers; for performances by small groups or soloists, the term *'recital' is preferred. In the classical tradition, concerts are normally as untheatrical as possible, given without action, in 'concert dress' (white tie and tails for men, long gowns for women: the evening attire of the upper classes in the late 19th century) and with merely functional lighting and stage set-up. The audience is invited to respond to an experience that is principally auditory, and to do so in a rather formal manner. Concerts generally take place in purpose-built halls. They also have their rituals: applause for the arrival of the principal musicians, who may come on in succession (orchestra leader then conductor, for instance); silence during the performance; applause afterwards (but only after whole works). And these rituals are generally maintained even for performances of music far outside the orchestral tradition that gave birth to them: Renaissance church music, for example.

1. Renaissance and Baroque beginnings; 2. 1750–1850; 3. Since 1850

1. Renaissance and Baroque beginnings

The idea of musical performance as an art in itself, and not as an element of liturgy or drama, a support for words, or an accompaniment to dancing, is one that has probably come and gone in different cultures at different times. In western Europe it was revived as a product of Renaissance humanism, within the 'academies' named after the garden where Plato taught (see ACADEMY). The earliest of these, the Accademia Platonica, appeared in Florence in 1470 and was devoted to speculative pursuits of all kinds: literary, dramatic, scientific, philosophical, musical. Similar institutions—clubs for artists, scholars, and connoisseurs—were founded in other Italian cities, and by the mid-16th century they had begun to sponsor musical performances. What they gave rise to, however, was not the concert but opera. In Paris the Académie de Poésie et de Musique was formed in 1570, though again its interests were more in music theory and music theatre than in concert-giving. At about the same time many of the princely courts of Germany and Austria gained musical establishments, but generally for service at table and in the chapel rather than to perform concerts.

The concert, implying an audience able to pay for admission, naturally arose first in England, where a middle class appeared earlier than in other European countries—especially in London, much the largest European city in the 16th, 17th, and 18th centuries. Music was sometimes a prefatory entertainment in the theatres of Shakespeare's times, and there were more or less regular performances by viol consorts in colleges and taverns in Oxford, Cambridge, and London during the first half of the 17th century. However, the first record of clearly recognizable concerts, open to whoever could afford the shilling ticket price, is that of those given by the violinist John Banister (i) in London between 1673 and 1678, and advertised in the *London Gazette* of 26–30 December 1672:

> These are to give notice that at Mr John Banister's House (now called the Music School) over against the George Tavern in Whyte Fryers, this present Monday, will be musick performed by excellent Masters, beginning at four o'clock in the afternoon and every afternoon for the future precisely at the same hour.

Banister had several immediate successors. Thomas Britton presented weekly concerts in a room above his small-coal shop for 36 years, from 1678 until his death in 1714. And, about the time of Britton's first concerts, the earliest concert hall in Europe was opened, at York Buildings in Villiers Street, seating 200. By 1700 there were at least three series of public subscription concerts being held in concert halls, tavern rooms, theatres, and guild halls. Concerts were also given at the pleasure gardens, of which Marylebone and Vauxhall opened about 1660. Whether in rooms or garden pavilions, concerts would offer assortments of orchestral pieces, solo instrumental items, and songs, as remained the norm until the mid-19th century. This thriving musical life attracted many musicians to London—notably Handel, who played at Britton's concerts and presented his own, to perform his oratorios and concertos.

Elsewhere in Europe concerts remained semi-private, arranged in the palaces of noblemen and high church officials, though the advent of orchestral music—Corelli's concertos, for example—indicates they were becoming bigger.

The English social fabric, with its relatively large leisured class, was replicated in the 18th century in Italy, France, and Germany. Public concert life followed. Music was normally part of the curriculum at the 'orphanages' in Venice that housed illegitimate children: Vivaldi was musical director at one, for girls, and his pupils would give public performances. Generally in Catholic countries concerts particularly flourished in Lent, when theatrical performances were forbidden:

that was the origin of the Concert Spirituel, founded in Paris by Anne Danican Philidor in 1725 and continuing until 1791. In Germany the leading orchestras remained court institutions, those of Berlin and Mannheim becoming pre-eminent in the first half of the 18th century, but public concert series were founded in cities without a court: Frankfurt (1712), Hamburg (1721), and Leipzig (1743).

2. 1750–1850

In the second half of the 18th century concerts became larger and more regular occurrences across Europe. Indeed, the development of the Classical style, with its non-verbal language of form and rhetoric, took place largely in concert music, for example in Haydn's quartets, many of which were written for public performance, and in Mozart's piano concertos. Large concert halls were built during this period, including the *Hanover Square Rooms in London (1775) and the *Gewandhaus in Leipzig (1781). Concert series were arranged by local musicians in such large cities and might well involve gentlemen amateurs as well as professionals—Mozart took part in several concert ventures of this kind in Vienna—but touring performers would also contribute, as Mozart did on his visits to Paris and Prague, for example. Haydn, his reputation established by the increasingly important medium of music publishing, was invited to London to take part in J. P. Salomon's concerts in 1790–1 and 1794–5. He also wrote for the prominent Paris concert series, the Concert de la Loge Olympique. Still at this time most music in performance was new, though in London in 1776 the Earl of Sandwich and other noblemen founded the Concert of Ancient Music to keep alive the works of Handel and others.

In general, concerts remained under the protection of aristocratic support well into the 19th century, and composers wishing to put on concerts—as Mozart and Beethoven did in Vienna—had to find patronage before they could reach an audience. Gradually, however, the responsibility shifted. The London pattern of the impresario presenting concerts for profit—a pattern going right back to Banister's initiative—became more widespread. Concert series were also established by bourgeois societies, such as the Philharmonic (later Royal Philharmonic) Society of London (which commissioned Beethoven's Ninth Symphony) and the Gesellschaft der Musikfreunde of Vienna, both founded in 1813, or the Société des Concerts du Conservatoire in Paris (1828). In the 1820s, when Liszt and Paganini began their international careers, the phenomenon of the touring virtuoso added a new flavour to concert life. Orchestras began to be organized as permanent institutions a little later, the Vienna

Philharmonic and the New York Philharmonic both dating from 1842.

3. Since 1850

With the arrival of the symphony orchestra, concert life settled into the shape it has retained. Programmes ceased to be potpourris: the orchestral concert, with two halves each about an hour long, became the norm everywhere during the third quarter of the 19th century. Beethoven's symphonies were the central repertory of the professional orchestra from the first, and round them was gradually established a core of classics. Generally each concert would feature a soloist—perhaps a singer, more likely a pianist or violinist in a concerto. Thanks to improvements in transport (railways, transatlantic steamships), soloists were able to pursue enormously successful and wide-ranging careers, and so contribute to the increasing professionalization of musical life, if also to its increasing homogenization. Some local particularities, however, remained. In England, especially, large choral works were an essential element.

As the orchestra became the centre of concert life, and grew, and as its audience also grew, so larger concert halls were built. In London, Louis Jullien's promenade concerts (1841–59) were followed by August Manns's concerts in the Crystal Palace (from 1855), by daily concerts organized by the music-publishing firm of Novello in the Royal Albert Hall (from 1874), and by Henry Wood's Promenade Concerts in the Queen's Hall (from 1895—a series still continuing in the summer Proms given at the Albert Hall). There were similar developments in New York (opening of Carnegie Hall, 1891), Paris (Pasdeloup's concerts of 1861–84, Lamoureux's begun in 1881), and Vienna.

One major change since the 19th century has been in the economics of concert-giving. While Jenny Lind's American tour at the behest of P. T. Barnum (1850–2) had a close parallel a century and half later in the Three Tenors concerts given by José Carreras, Plácido Domingo, and Luciano Pavarotti, concert promotion gradually, towards the mid-20th century, moved from being a profitable enterprise to one requiring—as often it had in earlier times—patronage. In the USA, orchestras came to depend increasingly on private donors; elsewhere support has generally come from the state, either directly or through state-funded broadcasting authorities (such as the BBC, which assumed responsibility for the Proms in 1927).

Perhaps partly for economic reasons, but also because of changes in taste, smaller concert venues reasserted themselves at about the beginning of the 20th century. Carnegie Hall was built to embrace a recital room as well as its 3000-seat auditorium, and in London the

500-seat Wigmore Hall opened (as the Bechstein Hall) in 1901. These were places for chamber music, for song recitals, and for unusual repertory. As the common orchestral repertory became increasingly fixed, admitting very few works written after 1914, the chamber-scale hall became the main forum for new music, and was there also for the revival of pre-Classical music. In London, for example, the opening of the Queen Elizabeth Hall (1967) helped foster the growth of new-music groups and early-music ensembles that were conspicuous in the city's concert life during the next decades.

But concerts need not take place in concert halls. Concerts in churches and theatres, or out of doors, have a continuous history, and may reach audiences daunted by the formality and the middle-class propriety of traditional concert halls. It was in order to find a new, working-class audience that Luigi Nono began giving concerts in Italian factories in the 1960s. Also, the growing importance since 1945 of festivals as against regular concert series—of music as special, away from home—has opened the possibilities of the concert, which may be encountered in a disused warehouse or on a beach.

Even when taking place in a purpose-designed auditorium, the concert may be recovering its 18th-century miscellaneous character, though in new ways. Boulez's Domaine Musical concerts in Paris (1954–67) began by putting together old music (Machaut, Bach), modern classics (Schoenberg, Varèse), and new works. Other examples include the series given by Maurizio Pollini in Salzburg and New York in the late 1990s and early 2000s, when an evening might include choral music from Schubert to Ferneyhough along with piano solos, or chamber music from Mozart to Sciarrino.

See also PROMENADE CONCERT. MH/PG

📖 W. WEBER, *Music and the Middle Class: The Social Structure of Music in London, Paris and Vienna, 1830–48* (London, 1975) · D. COX, *The Henry Wood Proms* (London, 1980) · H. HASKELL, *The Early Music Revival* (London, 1988) · M. S. MORROW, *Concert Life in Haydn's Vienna* (Stuyvesant, NY, 1989) · J. HOROWITZ, *Understanding Toscanini: A Social History of American Concert Life* (New York, 1993) · S. MCVEIGH, *London Concert Life from Mozart to Haydn* (London, 1993)

concertante (It., from *concertare*, 'to agree', 'to act together'). A term used to describe music that has a solo element or is in some other way concerto-like. In common with *concertato, it was used in the Baroque period to describe a group of soloists, instrumental or vocal, in works such as the concerto grosso or in a motet where one (usually smaller) body of performers is contrasted with another. In the 18th century, 'concertante' was linked with the symphony in such titles as *symphonie concertante* (indicating a symphonic work with a number of parts for soloists), and with the string quartet to form the 'concertante quartet' (more usually found in the French form *quatuor concertant*), denoting that all four parts should be regarded as equal in status (not, as in the 19th-century use of the same title, indicating special brilliance in the first violin). In the context of accompanied keyboard sonatas, the label 'concertante' distinguishes an obbligato violin accompaniment from an optional one. In 20th-century instrumental works the term implies a soloistic element that falls short of what would be expected in a full concerto.

concertato (It., from *concertare*, 'to agree', 'to act together'). A term, related to 'concerto', used in the 17th century to describe music that involves some element of contrast in its performance. In instrumental music, a number of concertato soloists might be required to play in contrast to, as well as in combination with, a larger body of *ripieno players. In vocal works, a small *coro concertato* might be set against the full complement of singers (called ripieno or *cappella*).

concert band. An offshoot of the *military band, developed for concert tours by such bandmasters as Sousa.

Concert de la Loge Olympique. Concert series established in Paris in 1769 as the Concert des Amateurs, renamed in 1780. See CONCERT, 2.

Concert des Amateurs. Concert series established in Paris in 1769, later renamed Concert de la Loge Olympique. See CONCERT, 2.

concert grand. The largest size of piano, some 3 metres long. See PIANOFORTE.

concert halls. In the early days of concert-giving, performances took place in any available suitably large room or hall. Where there was royal or wealthy patronage the choice could range from a grand audience chamber to an intimate drawing-room. Less favoured audiences might meet in a 'Musick House' attached to an alehouse.

The earliest room in London designed as a public concert hall was in York Buildings, off the Strand. Built in 1678, it could accommodate an audience of 200. Later, John Hickford's dancing school, where the young Mozarts appeared in 1765, offered a much larger room. The *Hanover Square Rooms, where Salomon presented his 12 Haydn concerts in 1791, housed 900. A similar pattern of development took place on the Continent, with autonomous principalities providing the salons of great palaces. Typical was the Grosser Redoutensaal in the Hofburg, Vienna, where much of the music of Haydn, Mozart, and Beethoven was first performed.

As orchestras grew in size and public concerts became more popular, more concert halls were designed and built. The Royal Albert Hall in London (1871) is a famous example, though its large dimensions and oval plan produced uneven acoustic results. The best halls were rectangular, with a platform at one end and the audience seated in rows facing it. A few halls, including the old Gewandhaus in Leipzig, retained the older seating plan with the rows facing inwards towards a central aisle. The decorative style was generally ornate, with pillars, statues, and scrollwork helping to produce a pleasing diffusion of sound.

More informal designs were adopted in the 20th century. In the new Philharmonie in Berlin (1957) the orchestra is almost surrounded by the audience for greater intimacy. In the USA, the Hollywood Bowl (1922) is nearly open-air, with the orchestra in an acoustic shell and the audience in a vast amphitheatre.

Since music from all periods now commands a ready audience, modern concert halls have to provide different acoustic specifications. Architects often incorporate movable screens or acoustic panels to vary the reverberation time, or resort to such electronic aids as 'assisted resonance' (as, for example, in the Royal Festival Hall in London) or sound reinforcement.

See also ARCHITECTURAL ACOUSTICS.   MH/JBo

concertina. A small free-reed organ of the *accordion type, held in the hands. The two hexagonal or square wooden endpieces, which carry the reeds and the buttons that control them, are linked by folded cardboard bellows. The 'Chemnitz' or German concertina, developed by C. F. Uhlig in 1834, had rectangular ends with a diatonic action, each button giving two notes, differing with push from pull. A slightly altered version of this form is found widely in the USA as the lead instrument in polka bands. The bandoneon, especially popular in the tango orchestras of Latin America, was derived from the Chemnitz concertina in the 1840s by Heinrich Band of Krefeld, who modified the button layout. Chromatic versions of both the Chemnitz concertina and the bandoneon have been made. Concertina bands were particularly popular in 19th-century Germany.

The hexagonal English concertina introduced by Charles Wheatstone in 1844 produces the same note from each button on both push and pull and has a chromatic range, the notes of the scale being placed alternately on either side. On the 'Duet' concertina, patented in 1884 by J. H. MacCann of Plymouth, the left side produces bass notes and the right treble. A modified version of the duet concertina was adopted by the Salvation Army. Another system popular in England, and also hexagonal in shape, is the diatonic Anglo-German (or 'Anglo') concertina, much loved by English folk musicians for its rhythmic capabilities.

JMo

📖 S. EYDMANN, 'The concertina as an emblem of the folk music revival in the British Isles', *British Journal of Ethnomusicology*, 4 (1995), 41–50 · A. W. ATLAS, *The Wheatstone English Concertina in Victorian England* (Oxford, 1996)

concertino. 1. The group of soloists in a *concerto grosso.

2. In the first half of the 18th century, a term denoting an orchestral work in the form of a small-scale symphony, having several movements but no soloists (see SYMPHONIE CONCERTANTE). Since the 19th century the word 'concertino' (Ger.: *Konzertstück*) has often been applied to orchestral compositions in the style of a small concerto. Such works are usually in only one movement but may contain sections of contrasting speed and character; they are sometimes for chamber ensemble rather than orchestra. Weber composed several concertinos: for horn (1806), clarinet (1811), and piano (*Konzertstück*, 1821). Other notable examples include Schumann's *Conzertstück* for four horns (op. 86, 1849), Bruch's *Konzertstück* for violin (1911), Milhaud's *Concertino de printemps* for violin (1936), and Stravinsky's Concertino for string quartet (1920).   —/JBE

concert master. See LEADER.

concerto. A concerto is generally held to be a piece for one or more soloists and orchestra. However, the term has been applied to a wide variety of music, some of it not fulfilling this basic criterion. 'Concerto' is probably derived from the Latin *concertare*, which can mean 'to dispute' or 'to work together'; in Italian the same word means 'to agree' or 'to get together'. These dual concepts of competition and collaboration have underpinned the genre from its earliest history, though at different periods the emphasis has changed from one to the other.

1. Origins and early history; 2. The concerto grosso; 3. The 'ritornello' concerto; 4. The Classical concerto; 5. The 19th century; 6. The 20th century

1. Origins and early history

At the end of the 16th century the term 'concerto' was most often used in the sense of collaboration, denoting music for vocal ensembles or for mixed vocal and instrumental forces. The earliest publication with the title is *Concerti di Andrea, et di Gio. Gabrieli, organisti* (Venice, 1587), a collection of church music and madrigals for large forces. Viadana's *Cento concerti ecclesiastici* (Venice, 1602) applied the same principle to smaller ensembles, and throughout the 17th century the term was used in this sense not only in Italy but also in Germany, where the *geistliches Konzert* became an important genre in Protestant church music. The purely instrumental concerto has its origins in the last two decades of the 17th century, when composers in various Italian cities began to exploit technical and textural contrasts between solo and tutti in sonatas performed by string orchestras. Particularly influential were the orchestral trumpet sonatas by such Bolognese composers as Cazzati and Torelli, pieces in which abrupt textural contrasts, brilliant passage-work, and thematic dialogue replaced the contrapuntal idiom of the solo sonata. The clear and vigorous melodic style that characterized idiomatic trumpet writing was quickly transferred to solo violin writing in concertos for strings alone, as in Torelli's op. 6 (Augsburg, 1698), and became a hallmark of the later Baroque concerto.

2. The concerto grosso

Two distinct types of instrumental concerto soon evolved in Italy. In the north the basic four-part string orchestra was complemented by a soloist drawn from its ranks (usually the principal violin); but in Rome the core of the orchestra was a concertino ensemble of two violins, cello, and continuo which could be strengthened, as occasion demanded, by a larger group of strings (the ripieno). From this Roman practice the concerto grosso emerged. Corelli was writing concertos as early as the 1680s, and 12 of these were published in a revised form as his op. 6 in 1714. In spite of textural contrasts between concertino and ripieno there is little difference in the style or substance of solo and tutti writing, and these works have, with some justification, been described as 'amplified' trio sonatas. As in his sonatas, Corelli maintained a distinction between 'chamber' concertos and 'church' concertos (with and without dance movements respectively). But in neither type is there a fixed number and order of movements.

Even before they were published, Corelli's concertos established a vogue that spread rapidly throughout northern Europe. As early as 1682 Georg Muffat's *Armonico tributo* (published in Salzburg) introduced the Roman-style concerto to Germany. In England Corelli became a cult figure and was followed by Geminiani and Handel, whose own *Twelve Grand Concertos* op. 6 (1739) constitute a brilliant and original conspectus of Baroque concerto styles with a Corellian core.

3. The 'ritornello' concerto

A more far-reaching development of the concerto was achieved by a group of Venetian composers at the start of the 18th century. In 1700 Albinoni issued a collection of solo violin concertos (part of his op. 2) that reflected the mannerisms of the contemporary operatic sinfonia and are mostly cast in three movements (fast–slow–fast). His example was followed by Vivaldi, whose 600 concertos exploit a vivid orchestral language of simple effects and memorable ideas, coupled with new standards of virtuosity in his solo parts. Vivaldi's revolutionary set of 12 string concertos *L'estro armonico* (op. 3, 1711) was the first to make regular and sophisticated use of the ritornello principle. The ritornello—a refrain of one or more ideas played by the orchestra—is stated in full at the start of the movement and returns at various times, in whole or in part, to punctuate the solo sections and underline the various tonal centres through which the music passes.

The attraction of this principle lay in its power to dramatize the 'competition' between solo and tutti in connection with a movement's tonal plan, and in its flexibility as a means of organizing musical ideas. The pattern could be used for any combination of instruments (and, for that matter, voices): while the violin was the solo instrument in most concertos at the start of the century, repertories quickly developed for almost all other orchestral instruments. Conversely, the principle could be applied to pieces that lacked an obvious soloist, such as Bach's Brandenburg Concerto no. 3, and those that lacked a tutti, as in the same composer's Italian Concerto for harpsichord.

Vivaldi's concertos were admired throughout Europe, especially in Germany, where they were widely imitated. Bach's development of Vivaldian principles was not in itself unusual, but the complexity and subtlety of his concertos are unique, marking the highpoint of the Baroque ritornello concerto. He was one of the earliest composers to write concertos for one or more harpsichords, thus laying the foundation for the primacy of the keyboard concerto during the second half of the 18th century.

4. The Classical concerto

Although the symphony replaced the concerto during the Classical period as the pre-eminent orchestral genre, the concerto continued to flourish in different guises. The elegance and melodic fluency of the *galant* style did not lend themselves to overt displays of virtuosity, and many composers wrote concertos for domestic consumption, making modest demands on amateur techniques. The best examples of this type, such as the keyboard concertos of Wagenseil and J. C. Bach, were widely admired in England and Germany. In contrast, concertos written for professional virtuosos made greater technical demands and were often musically more ambitious. Concertos by Mannheim composers showed off to best advantage the talents of members of the famous orchestra; at Eszterháza Haydn wrote his fine cello concertos for his colleague Anton Kraft; and leading players inspired Mozart's concertos for horn (Ignaz Leutgeb) and clarinet (Anton Stadler).

Many critics made stinging diatribes against 'empty' virtuosity in the concerto, but others were careful to distinguish between the best and worst examples. H. C. Koch, having C. P. E. Bach's striking keyboard concertos in mind, asked his readers to imagine a well worked-out concerto in which 'there is a passionate dialogue between the concerto player and the accompanying orchestra'. He emphasized the dignity of which the genre was capable by comparing it to 'the tragedy of the ancients, where the actor expressed his feelings not towards the pit, but to the chorus'.

The concept of a dialogue was enhanced in the Classical period by a growing distinction in 'public' concertos between the grand symphonic manner of orchestral tuttis and the more intimate sonata style of solo passages. The mixture of symphony and sonata was most perfectly realized in Mozart's concertos. In childhood he arranged sonata movements by the Bachs and others as concertos, and his violin concertos (all from the 1770s) show the influence of a wide range of south German and Italian models. But it was in his piano concertos, culminating in a great series of works from his Viennese heyday (1782–6), that he made his most important contribution to the genre.

Mozart was himself the original soloist in most of these pieces, and the piano writing has an unprecedented spontaneity and brilliance. In his autograph scores the solo part is often only sketched in or partly notated, and it is clear that he improvised throughout a performance, not just in his cadenzas. He made his orchestra sound symphonic in complex tuttis, but treated accompaniments with a chamber-like finesse: the complex interplay between solo and orchestra stemmed from his unprecedentedly rich writing for the wind section, begun in K450 and K451 (both 1784) and reaching its apogee in K482 (1785) and K491 (1786). Above all, Mozart invested the concerto with a renewed sense of theatricality, invoking the human comedy and pathos of his great operas.

The finest composer to continue Mozart's line of thinking was Beethoven. His admiration for his predecessor is clearly evident in his first three piano concertos (no. 1, 1795, rev. 1800; no. 2, before 1793, rev. 1794–5; no. 3, 1800–3). The Fourth and Fifth Piano Concertos (1806 and 1809), together with the Violin Concerto (1806), owe much to his experience as a composer of symphonies and extend the scope of Classical concerto form: both piano concertos start with solo statements (undemonstrative in the Fourth,

commanding in the Fifth), and in all three works the slow movement runs into the finale. The Fifth Concerto is one of the most powerful statements in Beethoven's 'heroic' style: the wit of Mozart's solo writing is replaced by the galvanizing, energetic elaboration of a few pregnant motifs.

5. The 19th century

In the decades after Beethoven's death the concerto was increasingly affected by the pre-eminence in concert life of the virtuoso composer-performer and the symphony. A constant factor in the 19th-century concerto was the drive to redefine the boundaries of virtuosity. In violin music the key figure was Paganini, whose three violin concertos (no. 1, c.1815; no. 2, 1826; no. 3, 1826) stand at the peak of the 'display' repertory. To an even greater degree than Chopin's two piano concertos (no. 1, 1830; no. 2, 1829–30), the orchestra is pushed into the background so that the solo instrument may be given the audience's undivided attention. Paganini cast aside any sense of musical 'competition' in favour of the thrills of solo wizardry, though Chopin's solo lines exhibit a far more refined grace and sensibility. Liszt's revolutionary piano technique is compelling in his two piano concertos (no. 1, 1849; no. 2, 1839; both revised later), the *Totentanz* (1849, later revised), and the Hungarian Fantasy (?1853); it was widely admired, and echoes through many piano concertos from the second half of the century.

The symphony's dominance of concert programmes inevitably meant that the concerto played a smaller part in the expressive armoury of most composers. It became a genre that composers might now take up only a few times during their creative lifetime, and many works originated as gifts for favoured performers. Several such relationships were particularly fruitful: Schumann wrote his Piano Concerto for his wife Clara; Mendelssohn and Brahms wrote their violin concertos for Ferdinand David and Joseph Joachim respectively. The symphony also had a more tangible effect on the style and form of the concerto. Its characteristic ideal of a sustained elevated discourse can be heard in many concertos from this period. Brahms constructed massive symphonic structures in his two piano concertos (no. 1, 1854–8; no. 2, 1878–81)—indeed, the first movement of the First Concerto had previously been considered as material for a symphony, and the Second Concerto is in four movements, including the most Beethoven-like scherzo in all his orchestral music.

Brahms's Violin Concerto (1878) begins with a long ritornello, but for most 19th-century composers sonata form and the fantasia were more important than the ritornello principle. Thus many concertos that are otherwise utterly different begin with the sustained participation of the soloist (for example, Mendelssohn's E minor Violin Concerto and Tchaikovsky's Piano Concerto no. 1). The symphony had a profound effect on orchestral writing in the 19th-century concerto. With technical changes making solo instruments more powerful, composers increasingly exploited symphonic orchestral textures. This especially suited the competition with more sonorous pianos, but it is equally evident in the violin concertos of Mendelssohn (1844), Bruch (no. 1, 1868), Brahms, Tchaikovsky (1878), and Dvořák (1879–80), as well as in Dvořák's Cello Concerto (1894–5).

6. The 20th century

Having been eclipsed by the symphony in 19th-century concert life, the concerto underwent a remarkable renaissance. The perennial attraction of virtuosity was as strong as ever, and the commercial draw of star performers became increasingly significant in the commissioning of new works. In an age of extreme and rapid social change composers became fascinated by the relationship between the individual and the group; and the flexibility of the concerto's fundamental principles became more attractive at a time when there was an increasing fragmentation of musical style and form.

The diversity of musical responses to these issues is, perhaps, the defining feature of the 20th-century concerto. The repertory expanded to include concertos for instruments that had previously been neglected, many clustering round such leading performers as the trombonist Christian Lindberg and the saxophonist John Harle. And composers widened textural possibilities, from novel orchestral colours and extended playing techniques through to the abandoning of solo–tutti contrasts altogether. However, four broad generic trends can be identified: the appropriation of elements from the 19th-century concerto; reactions against that tradition; a renewed interest in the ensemble concerto; and the development of the concerto for orchestra.

No doubt the longevity of the solo concerto can be attributed to its ability to transcend changes in taste and style. Several early 20th-century works drew on Romantic models, notably the violin concertos of Sibelius (1903, rev. 1905) and Elgar (1909–10), and Rakhmaninov's four piano concertos (no. 1, 1890–1, rev. 1917; no. 2, 1900–1; no. 3, 1909; no. 4, 1926, rev. 1941). But the tradition also proved adaptable to modernism and coexisted with more radical musical styles and forms in the concertos of Schoenberg, Berg, Bartók, Prokofiev, Ravel, and Shostakovich. Others reacted against this tradition and sought alternative sources for inspiration. For example, Stravinsky turned to Bach for his Violin Concerto (1931) and to jazz for his *Ebony Concerto* for clarinet and jazz orchestra (1945).

In an age of increasing democratization, many composers looked for alternatives to the solo concerto. The conversational and antagonistic possibilities of the concerto for two solo instruments were widely pursued, notably in Carter's for piano and harpsichord (1961) and Ligeti's for flute and oboe (1972). Ensemble concertos explored the principles of competition and collaboration in many new ways, from the neo-classicism of Hindemith's *Kammermusik* no. 1 (1922) and Stravinsky's 'Dumbarton Oaks' Concerto (1937–8), through the austere serialism of Webern's Concerto op. 24 (1931–4) and subtle textural experiments of Ligeti's Chamber Concerto (1969–70), to the balanced *cori spezzati* of Tippett's Concerto for Double String Orchestra (1938–9). Reflecting the rise of virtuoso ensembles, the concerto for orchestra is the most democratic development of the genre. The repertory is dominated by Bartók's work of 1944, though there are important examples by Lutosławski (1954), Tippett (1962–3), and Carter (1969).   DA/TRJ

📖 D. F. Tovey, *Essays in Musical Analysis*, iii (London, 1936/*R*1972) · R. Layton (ed.), *A Guide to the Concerto* (Oxford, 1988, 2/1996) · M. T. Roeder, *A History of the Concerto* (Portland, OR, 1994)

Concert of Ancient Music. A society established in London in 1776 to perform music of the recent past. See CONCERT, 2.

concerto form. At each stage of its development the *concerto has adopted the forms characteristic of the epoch. Nevertheless all works possessing the character of a concerto have to use their form to exploit the generic principles of competition and collaboration. It is the late 18th-century solution to these issues, most commonly found in the opening movements of concertos, that has generally become known as concerto form.

During the last three decades of the 20th century there was considerable controversy over the nature and origins of Classical concerto form. Earlier editions of this *Companion* described it as a modified sonata form with a double exposition. The first exposition is played by the orchestra in the tonic key; the second is led by the soloist and modulates to the dominant or (in a minor key) the relative major, culminating in another orchestral passage before the development section begins. The development is dominated by the soloist, and only in the recapitulation is there a true sense of collaboration between the two. There is some historical evidence to support this theory, since during the Classical period sonatas were often arranged as concertos by adding an orchestral introduction to the sonata exposition.

However, this view has come under increasing attack as an anachronistic distortion of 18th-century ideas. Musicians writing in the late 18th century described concerto form as a ritornello form with alternating orchestral and solo sections. After texture, theorists were most interested in the form's tonal plan; they rarely commented on the number of themes in each section. Nevertheless, many writers made careful stylistic distinctions between the symphony-like ritornellos (R) and the sonata-like solo sections (S). A typical first movement might have the sections shown in Table 1.

TABLE 1

R^1	S^1	R^2	S^2	R^3	S^3	cadenza	R^4
I	I–V	V	V–vi	vi–V–	I		I

Classical concerto form shared the clear tonal plan of symphony and sonata movements. It may be seen from the model illustrated that the first, second, and fourth ritornellos emphasize the main tonal centres of the tonic and dominant, while the first and second solo sections modulate between these key areas. Some composers omitted the modulating R^3 and linked the second and third solos with a brief confirmatory tutti in the tonic. This was Mozart's usual procedure, though he retained a modulating ritornello in the first movement of his Clarinet Concerto K622. Taking 18th-century writings into account, some scholars have therefore viewed concerto form as a reinterpretation of the Baroque ritornello principle within a Classical stylistic framework.

Yet not all musicologists have been convinced that the origins of concerto form lie in the Baroque concerto. In the 1990s attention usually focused on the relationship between concerto form and the form of certain mid-18th-century *opera seria* arias, and many similarities of style and structure have been noted: the clear tonal structure, the proportion of orchestral to solo material, and the move from 'thematic' ideas to bravura passage-work in solo sections. But obvious differences, such as the texted nature of the aria, suggest that it would be most incautious to regard Classical concerto form as an expanded aria form.

In summary, it is problematic to view concerto form as an adaptation of other forms. Rather, it was a unique, if contingent, solution to the generic issues of concerto writing during the Classical period.   TRJ

concerto for orchestra. In the 20th century, a name given to large-scale works in which the orchestra itself and various instruments or sections within it are given a prominent virtuoso role. A well-known example is Bartók's Concerto for Orchestra (1943).

concerto grosso (It., 'large concerto'). In Baroque music, a concerto (see CONCERTO, 2) in which a small ensemble of soloists (concertino) is contrasted with a larger group (ripieno).

concert overture. See OVERTURE, 2.

concert pitch. The internationally accepted pitch standard, according to which $d' = 440$ vibrations per second. See PITCH, 2.

Concerts Lamoureux. A concert series established in Paris by Charles Lamoureux in 1897 through the amalgamation of his Société des Nouveaux Concerts (founded 1881) with the Concerts de l'Opéra. See CONCERT, 3.

Concert Spirituel. A society formed in Paris in 1725 to provide concerts during Lent. See CONCERT, 1.

Concerts Populaires de Musique Classique. A concert series established in Paris by Jules Pasdeloup in 1861 and continuing until 1884. See CONCERT, 3.

Concertstück (Ger.). 'Concert piece'. See CONCERTINO, 2.

conch. A seashell with a hole pierced in the side or the tip so that it may be blown as a trumpet, either for signalling, both at sea and on land, or for rituals. Many species of gastropod are used from Europe to Oceania (where side-blowing is common; elsewhere they are end-blown). Most conches produce only one note, but in Fiji a fingerhole is bored in the parietal wall, and in several areas hand-stopping is used to alter the pitch.
JMo

Concierto de Aranjuez ('Aranjuez Concerto'). Concerto (1939) for guitar and orchestra by Rodrigo; he also arranged it for harp and orchestra.

concitato (It.). See STILE CONCITATO.

concord. A consonant chord or interval; see CONSONANCE AND DISSONANCE.

Concord Sonata. Piano work (*c.*1916–19) by Ives (its full title being Second Piano Sonata 'Concord, Mass., 1840–60'); it was written in honour of the Concord group of writers, whom Ives admired, and its movements are entitled 'Emerson', 'Hawthorne', 'The Alcotts', and 'Thoreau' (with optional flute).

concrete music. See MUSIQUE CONCRÈTE.

condensed score. See SHORT SCORE.

conducting. The art of directing an ensemble of instrumentalists or singers, or both, in such a way as to produce a unified, balanced performance of a given piece of music. Today the conductor is considered one of the most important figures in musical performance. On the covers of modern recordings the conductor's name is often printed as large as, or larger than, the composer's, and it is the conductor who typically receives the highest payment for concerts and recordings. He or she is the centre of attention in most orchestral and choral concerts, yet until less than 200 years ago music was directed only lightly—if at all—and usually by its composer: a conductor's interpretative role was less developed than it is today, as a brief survey of the history of this art will show.

1. Early history; 2. 19th-century developments; 3. The 20th century; 4. Technique

1. Early history

Although it is almost impossible to trace the first instances of the practice of beating time for an ensemble, it is known that early plainchant (composed before precise musical notation had been developed) was directed by an individual who used his hands to indicate the general contours of the melody, a kind of melodic mnemonic by which the rhythm would also be suggested. By the 15th century it had become common practice to direct polyphony by indicating accented beats with a downward gesture and unaccented beats with an upward one (the precursor of the modern conductor's 'down' and 'up' beats). Iconographical evidence suggests that these gestures were given in a number of ways: with the hands alone, with the staff held by the cantor to indicate his seniority, or with a roll of paper.

By the beginning of the 17th century the increase in the size of ensembles, particularly choirs, led to a need for firmer direction. Praetorius, for example, suggested that, when *cori spezzati* were indicated by a composer, a *maestro* should lead the first choir and sub-directors should conduct one or more of the other choirs. Conductors would commonly direct from a basso continuo part, with indications of important vocal entries. Subsequently, it was the continuo player himself (*maestro al cembalo*) who became the director, notably in the opera house, and hints on beating time are given in some of the later continuo-playing instruction manuals. The conductor's role as interpreter probably began in this period, since it was often a condition of an opera composer's contract that he be available to teach the singers their parts and to direct the first three performances.

In about 1700 the establishment of string-dominated orchestras, in contrast to the somewhat ad hoc ensembles of earlier times, led to a new type of directing.

Although the rather disagreeable French custom of banging the floor with a large staff (the manner in which Lully directed the famous *Vingt-Quatre Violons du Roi) continued into the 19th century, in other countries—Italy in particular—the first violinist became increasingly responsible for maintaining a satisfactory ensemble. This responsibility explains the title given to this player in the modern orchestra: 'leader' or 'concert master' (Ger.: *Konzertmeister*). The violinist would typically direct the ensemble with the bow, though some contemporary accounts describe how he kept time by waving his instrument on the first beat of the bar. The keyboard player still had an important role, however: Haydn directed even his late symphonies from the keyboard, and Clementi conducted from the keyboard in London in 1828.

2. 19th-century developments

The 19th century saw the rise of the specialist conductor, particularly of orchestral music and opera. Music was becoming too complex, and orchestras too large, to rely on an often indistinct beat from a violinist or keyboard player.

The earliest of these specialist conductors included such important composers as Spohr, Weber, and Mendelssohn; they were followed by Berlioz and Wagner, who in turn had their own disciples. Neither Berlioz nor Wagner was an instrumental virtuoso, and both therefore paid greater attention to the problems of the relatively new art of orchestral conducting. These problems were a direct result of the new freedoms inherent in their own music, above all the constant fluctuation of the tempo and the complexity of the orchestration. Wagner addressed both issues in his book *Über das Dirigieren* ('On Conducting', 1869), stating that the conductor must 'find the tempo' and 'find the melody' (i.e. the correct balance).

Even more important, conductors were clearly taking on a more interpretative role than in previous generations, and certain figures became renowned for their individual renditions of great works. Powerful interpretations demanded greater control and the ability to communicate subtle nuances by gesture alone; technique therefore improved immensely. Increased rehearsal time was also necessary, and orchestras generally engaged a permanent conductor whose stylistic fingerprint often became unmistakable; thus one could speak of the Furtwängler Berlin Philharmonic sound, the Richter Hallé sound, and so on.

3. The 20th century

During the 20th century a number of important changes to musical performance greatly affected the art of conducting. Rehearsal time with orchestras and choirs became expensive owing to the unionization of music, and a conductor was therefore compelled to impose his style on an orchestra very rapidly. 'Stick technique' became a matter of obsession to many, so that every fine detail of the music could be communicated with little or no verbal instruction to highly trained musicians. Numerous conductors therefore became even more entrenched in individual styles, since there was often insufficient time to explore new interpretations. The development of high-quality sound recording contributed to this trend, and audiences came to expect perfect or near-perfect renditions of complex works, even in live performances.

The increased costs in the 20th century also saw the return of conductorless ensembles (an early example was Persimfans in Soviet Russia in the 1920s), especially in early music, where 'historically informed' performances became popular. Moreover, much contemporary music contains improvisatory elements, allowing the individual performer greater interpretative freedom in place of a director's imposed reading; in this respect, history has come full circle with regard to conducting.

4. Technique

It may be said that really great conductors are born and not made, but it is also the case that many of today's greatest conductors have received some level of training, whether formal or informal. Most competent musicians, with a little guidance and a great deal of practice, can attain a level of conducting technique adequate for the majority of amateur purposes. It is therefore worth considering certain elements of technique to assist readers who may be called on to conduct ensembles.

Probably the most essential requirement is clarity, whether of beat or of spoken instruction. Conductors should learn and practise the basic beat patterns from a book or a colleague until they become second nature, so that they may concentrate on monitoring and improving the sound produced by the ensemble. The left hand (for right-handed conductors) should be used sparingly for expressive purposes, and should never simply mirror the baton hand. Certain general principles can be applied to beating time: large, fast gestures will lead to loud playing, and slower, smaller gestures will produce quieter results. Particular attention should be paid to the upbeat, since it is this preparatory gesture that will give the music its initial character. The importance of breathing with the ensemble on the upbeat cannot be overestimated, and an accurate opening attack can often be attained through this means alone, even if the ensemble consists only of string players and no winds. Above all, through his or her gestures the conductor must give performers the confidence to play to the best of their ability, whatever that level may be.

Technique, of course, counts for nothing if the conductor has little to say in rehearsal. It is essential that the conductor never stops an ensemble unless he or she needs to give verbal instruction; embarrassing silences will soon lead to a loss of respect on the part of the ensemble. The conductor should express instructions and opinions in as constructive a tone as possible, and never as personal criticism. As Pierre Monteux, conductor of the premiere of *The Rite of Spring*, suggested, 'don't be disrespectful to your players (no swearing); don't forget individuals' rights as persons; don't undervalue members of the orchestra simply because they are "cogs" in the "wheels"'. This is particularly important for conductors of amateur groups, whose members may be paying for the pleasure of making music.

The greatest disservice that a conductor can do to an ensemble is to show a lack of knowledge of the score. Preparation is therefore of the utmost importance, and the old adage that 'the good conductor should have the score in his head and not his head in the score' is a pertinent one. A conductor's eyes are among his most powerful assets. Leopold Stokowski once said that 'conducting is only to a small extent the beating of time; it is done more through the eyes', and establishing eye contact with players (something that naturally requires a thorough knowledge of the score) is an excellent way of ensuring that they are following the conductor. A certain facility at the keyboard will assist in the learning of the music, and the score may be marked up with symbols to assist the conductor in rehearsal. As well as knowing the notes, rhythms, texts, and orchestration of the score, the conductor must decide in advance on such interpretative matters as tempo, articulation, ornamentation, bowing, and dynamics in order not to waste precious rehearsal time. The conductor in an amateur setting must also often act as impresario, arranging rehearsals as efficiently as possible, booking venues, hiring music, engaging soloists, and soothing wounded egos, even before the music has begun. Tact and persistence are therefore invaluable assets.

Berlioz believed that the conductor should 'possess almost indefinable gifts, without which an invisible link cannot establish itself between him and those he directs'. But conducting does not have to be the impenetrable mystery it is sometimes thought to be. There will always be great maestros, but there will also always be a need for hard-working, competent, and, above all, enthusiastic amateurs who possess the ability to communicate their love for music to others.

DA/SM

📖 E. GALKIN, *A History of Orchestral Conducting in Theory and Practice* (New York, 1988) · K. PHILLIPS, *Basic Techniques of Conducting* (Oxford, 1997)

conductor. The director of an ensemble, responsible for all aspects of performance. See CONDUCTING.

conductus (Lat., pl. conductus). Latin medieval song. The literary and musical types to which the term was applied in the Middle Ages are several and varied; pieces called 'conductus' in one manuscript are found in another with different appellations. The term seems to have been favoured chiefly in northern France in the 12th and 13th centuries.

The earliest pieces labelled 'conductus' are Latin songs on sacred topics (principally Christmas), with several stanzas (quite often with a refrain) in regular, strongly accented, rhyming poetry. The melodies are simple and direct. They are found in a mid-12th-century manuscript from Norman Sicily (probably indicating now lost sources from Normandy), and in a manuscript containing music for St James's Day, compiled probably at Vézelay *c.*1160–70 and known as the Codex Calixtinus. The songs appear to have been used for processional and recessional purposes. This function is maintained not only in early 13th-century festival services of the Christmas season that have survived from Beauvais, Sens, and Laon, but also, interestingly, in the famous *Play of Daniel* from Beauvais of the same period (e.g. 'conductus of the Queen as she comes to the King', 'conductus of Daniel as he comes to the King'; see CHURCH DRAMA, Ex. 1).

Some of the same pieces, and others in exactly the same style, survive in an early 12th-century Aquitanian manuscript, where they are called 'versus'. But the latter term may have covered a wider variety of songs; one is an exhortation to a crusade, another a Provençal song to the Virgin Mary. Many have elaborate melodies.

Another class of sacred song in exactly the same style as the Sicilian conductus has a text wherein were introduced the closing words of Matins, Lauds, and Vespers: 'Benedicamus Domino', 'Deo gratias'. This may indicate that the songs functioned as a sort of closing anthem.

Some of the Aquitanian and Calixtine conductus are set for two voices, and this development was followed up with great energy and brilliance by the late 12th- and early 13th-century Parisian composers of the so-called Notre Dame School. Their compositions are for from one to four voices, and great variety of textual genre and musical style is displayed. Besides sacred conductus (including 'Benedicamus' songs) there are polemical, political, and other topical pieces, and laments (*planctus*) on the deaths of notable figures. Some conductus are written with only one note (or chord) to each syllable of text; others are much more ornate, containing long melismas to certain syllables (particularly opening and penultimate or final syllables of lines). An anonymous theorist of the 1270s attributes several of these conductus to Pérotin.

In Paris, conductus seem to have dropped out of fashion by the mid-13th century, probably because of the popularity of the motet, but a few (not, however, called conductus) were still copied outside France as late as the 15th century.   DH

Conforto [Conforti], Nicola (*b* Naples, 25 Sept. 1718; *d* Madrid, 16 March 1793). Italian composer. He studied at the Conservatorio di S. Maria di Loreto in Naples, where his first opera, *La finta vedova*, was staged at the Teatro dei Fiorentini in 1746. He then worked in various Italian theatres including S. Carlo, where his *Antigono*, to a libretto by Pietro Metastasio, was given in 1750. Between 1752 and 1754 he wrote two operas and two serenatas, at Farinelli's instigation, for the Spanish court; these were so successful that he moved in 1755 to Madrid as court composer. From the operas he wrote there may be singled out *Nitteti* (1756) and *Adriano in Siria* (1757). After the death of Fernando VI in 1759 Conforto's activity as a composer diminished (he wrote only two serenatas and a set of Lamentations) and he devoted himself to teaching. His music displays a happy melodic vein and expressive use of harmony, with the frequent minor inflections typical of the Neapolitan school.   GGS

congas [conga drum]. Afro-Cuban drums with a tall, narrow, barrel-shaped body, used either singly or in pairs and played with the fingers. They are highly tensioned and can produce wide varieties of sounds and pitches, using hand pressure and different types and placements of strokes. Pairs of congas are usually tuned a 5th apart.   JMo

conjunct motion. See MOTION.

Conon [Quennon] de Béthune (*b* ?Béthune, nr Lille, *c.*1160; *d* 17 Dec. 1219 or 1220). Trouvère poet and composer. He was of noble birth, and from the age of 20 was associated with the French court. In later life he became active as a soldier and politician. Like many contemporary trouvères he took part in the crusades, and he was present at the siege of Constantinople in 1204; several of his poems are *chansons de croisade*, describing or commenting on current events. Some ten songs have been attributed to him, all of them composed in a modest style with much repetition.   JM

Consecration of the House, The. See WEIHE DES HAUSES, DIE.

consecutive interval. An interval which occurs between the same two parts in two consecutive chords, for example A and C between tenor and soprano in one chord followed by B and D in the same parts in the next chord, this being an instance of consecutive minor 3rds. In traditional harmonic teaching there are two 'forbidden' consecutive intervals: the 5th and the octave. In practice, the term 'consecutives' is used pejoratively, implying consecutive 5ths or octaves. American usage prefers 'parallel' to 'consecutive'.

consequent. See ANTECEDENT AND CONSEQUENT.

conservatories. The earliest formal schools of music were those organized by the medieval church in connection with training singers in the performance of plainchant (see SCHOLA CANTORUM). Specialist schools, where students could receive a thorough professional training in several branches of music, originated in the orphanages and other institutions of medieval foundation which cared for needy children ('conservatorio'). In the late 16th century and the early 17th, those in Naples and Venice began to concentrate on teaching music, partly as a means of raising money through having their pupils sing at weddings and in public performances. Institutions for boys in Naples (e.g. the Conservatorio di S. Onofrio, Conservatorio dei Poveri de Gesù Cristo) and those for girls in Venice (e.g. Ospedale della Pietà, Ospedale degli Incurabili) gained wide recognition and an enviable reputation for their music teaching; they soon began to admit fee-paying pupils as well as children in need. Each institution had a *maestro* in charge of specific parts of the music curriculum, and there were specialist teachers for singing and instrumental tuition. The conservatories aimed to include on their staff a number of notable composers (for example Vivaldi, at the Pietà in Venice).

In the later 18th century the idea of music conservatories began to spread. After visiting Italy, Burney in 1774 produced a plan for a music school, but neither this nor an earlier plan devised by John Potter in 1762 bore fruit in England. In Leipzig a private singing school was founded in 1771 and other similarly limited schools sprang up. A larger-scale project was the first French conservatory, founded in 1783 as the École Royale de Chant (and closely associated with the Opéra), which taught singing, theoretical subjects, and performance. In 1795, however, it was superseded by the Conservatoire National de Musique et de Déclamation, which expanded rapidly and, in spite of its reputation for a certain conservatism, was distinguished throughout the 19th century; its teaching staff included Gossec, Méhul, and Cherubini.

After the decline of the charitable institutions in Italy in the late 18th century and the upheavals of the Napoleonic wars, Italy was slow to develop new schools of music. The surviving Naples conservatories eventually merged in the early 19th century to form the Real Collegio di Musica; a part-time college of music was established in Bologna in 1806 and one in Milan in 1807; but it was only in 1824 that Milan had its first large-scale school of music, the Regio Conservatorio di Musica, and other Italian cities eventually followed suit (Genoa, 1829; Florence, 1861; Turin, 1867; and Rome, 1877).

Central and northern European countries have many notable conservatories, the oldest of which are Prague (1811) and Vienna (1817). The Leipzig conservatory, founded by Mendelssohn in 1843, also included among its teachers Schumann, Moscheles, and Joachim; with its broadly based curriculum in all theoretical and practical areas of music, it attracted young students from throughout Europe and the USA. The Munich conservatory was established along similar lines in 1846 and was closely followed by Berlin (1850), Dresden (1856), Frankfurt (1861), Moscow (1862), St Petersburg (1866), Weimar (1872), Budapest (1875), and many others. Brussels has had a conservatory since 1813 (reconstituted in 1832 as the Conservatoire Royal and led for many years by Fétis), and Geneva since 1835.

In Britain it was almost 50 years after Burney's plan before the first academy of music was founded (1822) and opened (1823) in London. It was soon granted a royal charter, and in 1830 it became the Royal Academy of Music. Pupils were admitted at an early age and many boarded on the premises until 1853, after which a series of government grants enabled the Academy to survive and flourish up to the present day in a much enlarged and diversified form.

Other London schools of music included the Church Choral Society and College of Church Music, which specialized in sacred music; it was founded in 1872 and was renamed Trinity College of Music in 1875. The National Training School of Music was established in 1876 to train performers for the profession; in 1883 it became the Royal College of Music, with George Grove as its first director. The Guildhall School of Music was established by the City of London in 1880 as a municipal institution for training musicians.

Among important British schools of music outside London are the Birmingham School of Music (founded 1859), the Royal Scottish Academy of Music and Drama in Glasgow (founded in 1890 as the Athenaeum School of Music), the Welsh College of Music and Drama in Cardiff (founded 1949), the Leeds College of Music (founded 1968) and the Royal Northern College of Music in Manchester, which was formed in 1972 from an amalgamation of the Royal Manchester College of

Music (founded in 1893 by Charles Hallé) with the Northern School of Music (founded in 1942). As the *Associated Board of the Royal Schools of Music, those institutions with royal charter (as well as Trinity College) have long exerted influence throughout Britain and in English-speaking countries abroad by administering series of local graded examinations in instrumental playing, singing, and the theory of music. Other British conservatories, notably the Guildhall and Trinity College, also administer local examinations.

Specialist schools of music in Britain include the Royal Military School of Music, Kneller Hall, Twickenham (founded in 1857 as the Military School of Music), the Royal College of Organists in London (founded in 1864 as the College of Organists), and the Royal School of Church Music at Addington Palace, Croydon (founded in 1927 as the School of English Church Music).

The USA has an immense number of conservatories, some independent and others attached to universities and colleges. They first appeared in the 1860s (Oberlin, Ohio, 1865; Peabody Conservatory, Baltimore, 1866; New England Conservatory, Boston, 1867), but the early 20th century saw the establishment of the greatest numbers (Juilliard School of Music, New York, 1905; Eastman School of Music, Rochester, 1921; Curtis Institute of Music, Philadelphia, 1924). The close association between American conservatories and university departments allows generous provision for talented young musicians, who can often combine training in musicology with developing practical skills in solo and ensemble playing (as is also possible at several British conservatories).

While schools of music in the USA were much influenced by those in Europe, particularly Germany, conservatories in other English-speaking countries naturally tended to follow the lead of the London institutions. The first Australian conservatories independent of university music departments were established in Melbourne (1895) and Adelaide (1898), and Sydney followed in 1916 with the New South Wales State Conservatorium. In New Zealand, however, professional training in music has traditionally remained the responsibility of the university music departments. In Canada, as in the USA, schools of music more often take the form of university music departments than of independent conservatories, but some of the older schools (Royal Conservatory of Toronto, 1886; McGill School of Music [now McGill Conservatorium], Montreal, 1904) continue to play an important role in teaching and examining students preparing for performing careers.

During the second half of the 20th century, conservatories worldwide developed and modified their traditional range of activities. The curricula have broadened to embrace studies in jazz, musical theatre, composing for films and other broadcast media, music therapy, and arts administration. The divide between universities and conservatories has become less marked. Conservatories now place greater emphasis on a broader range of studies for all students, embracing the academic as well as the practical, while nearly all British universities support some training in performance. Although their initial purpose was to promote performing within the Western tradition, many conservatories now include some elements of non-Western music in their curricula. The techniques of professional presentation and communication have been given greater attention in recent years.

Until the last quarter of the 20th century, the difference between universities and conservatories was most keenly reflected in the kinds of qualification they awarded: universities offered academic degrees and conservatories practical diplomas with less demanding academic content. This divide has been bridged and conservatories now offer degrees as the main qualifications for undergraduate and postgraduate students. There has also been an increasing promotion of research in conservatories, both by staff and postgraduate students, and the establishment of welcome links between conservatories and universities, formally and informally.

See also EDUCATION.   PS/JN/PSp

Consolations. Six pieces for solo piano (1844–8) by Liszt; the best known is no. 3, for which Liszt later recommended the use of the (then newly invented) sostenuto pedal.

console. That part of the *organ, sometimes well separated from the instrument, which includes the manual and pedal keyboards, stops, tabs, and other controls.

consonance and dissonance. Consonance (or concord) is the quality inherent in an interval or chord which, in a traditional tonal or modal context, seems satisfactorily complete and stable in itself. In traditional contrapuntal and harmonic theory, consonant intervals comprise all perfect intervals (including the octave) and all major and minor 3rds and 6ths, but what constitutes a consonant sonority is not strictly laid down and has varied over time. Since the early 20th century many composers have accepted the Schoenbergian concept of the 'emancipated' dissonance, in which traditionally dissonant intervals and chords could be treated as relatively stable harmonic entities, functioning in effect as 'higher' or more remote consonances.

The opposite of consonance is dissonance (or discord): the quality of tension inherent in an interval or chord which, in a traditional tonal or modal context, involves a clash between adjacent notes of the scale and creates the expectation of resolution on to consonance by conjunct motion, as when the 7th in a *dominant 7th chord (in C major, the F, which is dissonant with the G) moves to a note within the consonant tonic major triad (E, in the case of C major). The term is ambiguous to the extent that one chord held to demand resolution on to consonance, the diminished 7th (e.g. D, F, A♭, B), is not strictly dissonant, since it contains no pitches a major or minor 2nd apart. See also INTERVAL.   AW

con sordino (It.). 'With the *mute'.

consort. A group of players or singers, their music, or their performance. The word was in common use from the late 16th century to the early 18th in English musical life. One of the commonest consorts in the Elizabethan period was the combination of treble viol or violin, flute or recorder, bass viol, lute, cittern, and bandora, for which Morley wrote his *Consort Lessons* in 1599. A tendency has arisen to refer to this as a 'broken consort', in contrast to the 'whole consort' of like instruments—a consort of viols or a violin band, for instance—but it is now thought more likely that 'broken consort' referred to music that was broken into divisions or variations. This is the more likely because consort was also used in much the same sense as the Italian term 'concerto': a piece of music for a group of players.   JMo

consort song. A song for solo voice and a *consort of some kind, usually of viols, that flourished in England from the mid-16th century to shortly before the mid-17th. The texture is polyphonic, usually in five parts (including the voice), so that the consort cannot be described as an 'accompanying' body; indeed, the instrumental parts were sometimes underlaid with words, so that entirely vocal performance was a possibility. The master of the genre was William Byrd, whose consort songs are mostly strophic and syllabic, often use imitative textures, and are relatively restrained in style compared to some of his church music. The consort song survived the huge popularity of the madrigal and the lute-song in England and outlived those genres by some years, sometimes incorporating from them such elements as *word-painting.   —/EW

Constant, Marius (*b* Bucharest, 7 Feb. 1925). French composer and conductor. He had contacts with George Enescu during World War II but received his higher musical education in Paris at the Conservatoire and the École Normale de Musique (1946–9), his teachers including Messiaen, Nadia Boulanger, and Honegger for composition and Jean Fournet for conducting. He was

musical director both for Roland Petit's Ballets de Paris (1956–66), composing several scores for the company, and of the Ars Nova new music ensemble (1963–71). In addition to his own works, he has made reduced versions of Bizet's *Carmen* and Debussy's *Pelléas et Mélisande* for Peter Brook productions, as *La Tragédie de Carmen* (1981) and *Impressions de Pelléas* (1992).
                                                                    PG/ABur

Construction (in Metal). Three works for percussion by Cage; the *First Construction* is for six players and was composed in 1939 and the other two are for four players and date from 1940 and 1941 respectively.

Consul, The. Opera in three acts by Menotti to his own libretto (Philadelphia, 1950).

conte (Fr., 'tale'). A title sometimes given to an instrumental piece. See MÄRCHEN.

Contes d'Hoffmann, Les ('The Tales of Hoffmann'). Opera in a prologue, three acts, and an epilogue by Offenbach to a libretto by Jules Barbier and Michel Carré after E. T. A. Hoffmann's stories *Der Sandmann*, *Die Abenteuer der Sylvester-Nacht*, *Rat Crespel*, and others (Paris, 1881); Offenbach died during rehearsals and it was completed by Ernest Guiraud.

Conti, Francesco Bartolomeo (*b* Florence, 20 Jan. 1682; *d* Vienna, 20 July 1732). Italian composer and theorbo player. A theorbist at the Habsburg court in Vienna from 1701, he achieved international celebrity; Quantz in his autobiography (1754) called him the 'best theorbo player of all time'. Ill health forced him to abandon his virtuoso career in 1726, but by then he had secured lifetime employment as court composer in Vienna (succeeding J. J. Fux), having achieved prominence with his opera *Clotilde* and the oratorio *Il Gioseffo* (both 1706). His earnings made him one of the wealthiest musicians of his day, a situation enhanced by his three marriages to rich widows.

Conti was pre-eminent as a court composer of dramatic music for almost two decades, composing most of the Carnival operas from 1714 until his death and setting texts by such famed librettists as Silvio Stampiglia, Apostolo Zeno, Pietro Metastasio, and Pietro Pariati. *Don Chisciotte in Sierra Morena* (1719), to a text by Pariati, allowed his talent for comic writing free rein and brought him international renown, as did numerous intermezzos (also with Pariati), which significantly influenced such composers as Telemann and Keiser.

Conti's sacred music often borders on the operatic in the expressiveness of its solo arias, and a concern for orchestral sonority and texture is evident in his operas and oratorios. Bach edited and performed the offertory *Languet anima mia* during his residency in Cöthen, and the *Missa Sancti Pauli* was repeated regularly for well over 150 years at the Schottenkirche in Vienna.

MHE

📖 H. WILLIAMS, *Francesco Bartolomeo Conti* (Aldershot, 1999)

continuo (It., abbreviation of *basso continuo*, 'continuous bass'; Ger.: *Generalbass*) [thoroughbass]. A term meaning either the group of instruments (or single instrument) used to provide the bass line in a musical work or the notated bass line from which those instruments play, in which case it is more accurately called the basso continuo.

1. Introduction; 2. History; 3. Instrumentation; 4. Realizing a figured bass

1. Introduction

Though still used in subsequent periods for special purposes (e.g. recitative in opera), continuo belongs above all to the Baroque era as one of its most important defining characteristics. The bass line, properly speaking when it is 'figured' (i.e. with sets of numerals appended), was also known as thoroughbass or *bassus generalis*, indicating both its 'continuity' and pervading presence. This bass, when 'realized', completes the harmonic part of the polyphonic whole by supplying chords and contrapuntal extras notated only in shorthand in the score.

The realization of the continuo by various, originally mainly unspecified, instruments is a serious performance issue which affects not only the sound but the entire interpretation of a musical work. Instruments capable of playing polyphonically, namely harpsichord, organ, and plucked strings (lute, guitar, lyra viol, etc.),

would realize the figures (the harmony), while others (e.g. cello, bassoon, violone) would reinforce the bass line. Although we know in general what constituted a continuo group, in no case do we know what specific combination of instruments was used for a particular piece or how it was used. Iconographic evidence, contemporary records, and individual composers, however, do give some clues to what is required in certain works. But there is by no means any uniformity. Almost without exception, written continuo parts, whether figured or not, do not distinguish between the keyboard player and the single-line bass players. In essence, the characteristic of the continuo is entirely dependent on its realization. Little indication is provided about its instrumentation.

2. History

The prerequisite for the evolution of the continuo was the increasing tendency in the early 17th century towards bass-upwards harmony, and the contrapuntal orientation of treble melody and bass. During the late 16th century, instruments came increasingly to be used to accompany polyphonic choral works, mainly doubling the voice parts. Organs were nearly always present in church music, as manuscript sources indicate. In the first decade of the 17th century, bass (organ) parts began to be printed separately from the voices, as in Viadana's *Cento concerti ecclesiastici ... con il basso continuo* (1602)—the first publication to use the term 'basso continuo'. Although the organ part incorporates much of the vocal line it accompanies, it also acts as a continuous instrumental 'voice', not dependent on the solo vocal part (Ex. 1). In Monteverdi's fifth book of madrigals (1605) the publisher has wrung a continuo bass out of him, in response to current fashion starting

Ex. 1

Basso per sonar nell'organo

Viadana, *Exaudi me Domine* (*Cento concerti ecclesiastici*).

with Luzzaschi's *Madrigali per cantare et sonare* (1601), but it mostly doubles the vocal part (*basso seguente*) and is therefore not a proper continuo bass.

The practice of printing a separate bass part was to have far-reaching consequences, including the eventual disintegration of the polyphonic Renaissance madrigal and the emergence of the new concertato madrigal, notably in Monteverdi's sixth book (1614). Meanwhile continuo-accompanied *monody (influenced by the Florentine *Camerata), in which the solo voice with its word-expressive capability was harmonically supported by the continuo, was developed by Caccini (*c*.1550–1618) and d'India (1580–1629) (see Ex. 2). These monodies,

when transferred to opera, gave rise to the declamatory aria for solo voice and continuo alone. This texture was also crucial to what became known as *recitativo secco* (see RECITATIVE), in which the unmetred vocal line accompanied only by the basso continuo advanced the dramatic content (see Ex. 3).

Another important province of the continuo was the sonata notated for one, two, or sometimes three solo voices or melody instruments (e.g. violins, recorders), or both, with bass, for example *Nigra sum*, *Pulchra es*, and *Duo seraphim* in Monteverdi's Vespers (1610). This evolved into the solo *sonata and *trio sonata of the later Baroque, the latter being emblematic of the period. In

Ex. 2

Caccini, opening of *Sfogava con le stelle*.

Ex. 3

Monteverdi, recitative from *L'incoronazione di Poppea*.

Corelli's concerti grossi the trio-sonata instrumentation of two violins and continuo was used for the concertino sections, contrasting with the full string ensemble. The continuo became an important feature of both the concerto grosso and the solo concerto. By the 1650s it was integral to virtually all Baroque ensemble music, whether sacred or secular. Only in archaic pieces (e.g. Purcell's viol fantasias of the 1680s) and in such exceptional works as Bach's motets is the continuo absent. Elsewhere it is all-pervading until the 1750s.

The decline in importance of the basso continuo is evident in the increasing number of pieces with notated four-part texture or with non-harmonic accompanying bass from the earlier part of the 18th century. This can be seen especially in orchestral music (early Haydn) and in solo sonatas (e.g. Bach, sonata for violin and harpsichord BWV1016). The string quartet began to displace the trio sonata, and the continuo texture was superseded by the *galant*-style melody with bass accompaniment. It is noticeable that in the improvisatory years of the Baroque period a significant part of the art of continuo playing was sensitivity to how solo instruments or voices, or both, ornamented their parts. Consequently, the demise of the continuo and the end of extempore ornamentation were more or less contemporaneous.

In the Classical period the continuo lost favour except in opera and oratorios, where it was still used in recitatives. Mozart's masses contain continuo parts. The direction 'senza cembalo' at certain points in Haydn's *The Creation* implies that a keyboard instrument is used elsewhere and is essential in the recitatives. Evidence from the Salomon concerts in London in the 1790s suggests that Haydn directed his symphonies from the fortepiano. Several of Mozart's piano concertos include figured continuo basses. And when Spohr went to London to conduct the Philharmonic Society concerts in the 1820s he was placed, at least initially, 'at the fortepiano'. The first print of Beethoven's Piano Concerto no. 1 has continuo figurings under the bass part, implying, as in the case of the Mozart concertos, that the soloist might function as a continuo player during the orchestral passages. Continuo did not die out completely in the 19th century: it is found, for example, in Italian opera recitative or such church music as Bruckner's *Requiem* (1849), in which the organ part is figured. Neo-classical uses of the continuo for recitative in the 20th century include Britten's *Cantata academica* (1960, piano) and Stravinsky's *The Rake's Progress* (1951, piano).

3. Instrumentation

For the most part continuo instruments are not specified. Exceptionally, Monteverdi indicates harpsi-

chords, chitarroni, harp, regals, and two *organi di legno* in his opera *Orfeo* (1607) following the practice of late 16th-century music for weddings and other festivities. Agostino Agazzari notes in his *Del sonare sopra il basso* (1607) that there were two kinds of continuo instrument: the 'Instruments of Foundation', or harmony instruments (e.g. organ, cembalo, lute, theorbo); and 'elaborating instruments' (cittern, chitarrone, harp, mandore, lirone, etc.). Later commentators observe that the bass viol, cello, bassoon, dulcian, trombone, or violone may reinforce the continuo bass. Throughout the Baroque era a harmony instrument on its own or in combination with an elaborating instrument or two would realize the continuo. Small groups, according to contemporaneous commentary, were more common.

The culmination of the basso continuo tradition is arguably seen in the works of J. S. Bach, who also represents the end of the Baroque compositional style based on the thoroughbass. Questions of correct practice in Bach continuo performance are frequently revisited. Which keyboard instrument is to be used, organ or harpsichord? The received wisdom—organ for church and harpsichord for chamber—is now seriously challenged and clear delineations redefined. When should we use cello, bassoon, or violone? Did such instruments as the lute, viol, or violoncello piccolo play a role as continuo instruments? There are no definitive answers, but evidence from documents, parts, and scores gives some indicators. The organ is predominant in church works, but that does not rule out the harpsichord. All the doubling bass instruments occur, but there is no standardized procedure. Certain instruments, for example the lute and viol, are used for special, often symbolic, purposes whereas others, notably the cello, become the conventional doubling bass instrument, particularly during the last period of Bach's life at Leipzig.

4. Realizing a figured bass

This can be a dry, mathematical exercise, as generations of music students have found while wrestling with artificial figured-bass keyboard tests. In performance, however, true art and invention can be shown as the player becomes musically involved in the contrapuntal and harmonic intricacies of the ensemble. Continuo playing requires spontaneity, discretion, and imagination. The style and manner of playing should be in keeping with function, location, date of the music, and the composer's individual traits.

The general principle of the figured bass is for the numerals to indicate the essential intervals above the bass, giving a clue as to the chord required. In early 17th-century basses, intervals are sometimes specified literally, e.g. as '11' (as in Peri's *Euridice*, 1600), which

Ex. 4

Handel, 'Amen', *Messiah*.

later became '4' when compounds were not indicated and numbers above 9 not used. In general the 5th and 3rd were to be assumed when not indicated. No numbers meant a chord in root position. An accidental by itself referred to the (major or minor) 3rd of the chord. When linked with other figures it indicated the inflection of that interval. An occasional horizontal line under a series of notes directed the player not to change the harmony. 'Tasto solo' is an instruction to play only the bass line without realizing the harmony (Ex. 4).

Various 18th-century treatises and manuals attempt to describe the art of continuo playing. Perhaps the most famous is in part 2 of C. P. E. Bach's *Versuch über die wahre Art das Clavier zu spielen* (1762). Earlier German treatises, in which guidance on how to embellish the realized harmonies of the continuo was provided, were largely influenced by Heinichen's *Neu erfundene und gründliche Anweisung* (Hamburg, 1711) and *Der Generalbass in der Composition* (Dresden, 1728). For the Italian Baroque, the most useful is Francesco Gasparini's *L'armonico pratico al cimbalo* (1708). Among the numerous French treatises and manuals, Denis Delair's *Traité d'accompagnement pour le théorbe, et le clavessin* (1690) and D'Anglebert's 'Principes de l'accompagnement' in his *Pièces de clavecin* (1689) are the most lucid and valuable contributions to the art of idiomatic keyboard continuo playing. Nicolo Pasquali's *Thorough-Bass Made Easy* (1763) for the most part justifies its title with its basic exercises and simple realizations of song and *secco* recitative (Ex. 5).

Modern tutors include, from the 20th century, F. T. Arnold's extensive *The Art of Accompaniment from a Thorough-Bass* (1931/R1965 in 2 vols.), Hermann Keller's systematic *Schule des Generalbass-spiels* (1931; Eng. trans. 1966 as *Thoroughbass Method*), Peter Williams's *Figured Bass Accompaniment* (1970), and David Ledbetter's *Continuo Playing According to Handel* (1990), a clearly presented modern edition of the eminently practical and musical figured-bass exercises that Handel devised between 1724 and 1735 when he was harpsichord tutor to the royal children. All tutors, old and modern, describe the chords and basic progressions on a figured bass, but few lead the student on to the more elaborate and stylistically sophisticated manner of realization which we know to have been the practice in true continuo playing. Once the rudiments have been acquired, much is left to the skill and imagination of the individual player. There is no one correct way to perform a thoroughbass according to rules or a set formula.

CRW

📖 T. BORGIS, *The Performance of the Basso Continuo in Italian Baroque Music* (Ann Arbor, MI, 1987) · L. DREYFUS, *Bach's Continuo Group* (Cambridge, MA, 1987) · N. NORTH, *Continuo Playing on the Lute, Archlute and Theorbo* (London, 1987) · P. J. ROGERS, *Continuo Realization in Handel's Vocal Music* (Ann Arbor, MI, 1989) · M. CYR, *Performing Baroque Music* (Aldershot, 1992)

continuo lied (Ger.: *Generalbasslied*). A type of strophic song with continuo accompaniment that became popular in Germany during the Baroque period, especially in the mid-17th century. Aimed primarily at amateur performers, continuo lieder were usually simple in style with a limited vocal range, regular phrase lengths, and general attitude of subservience to the text; many examples are based on dance tunes. They were customarily for solo voice with continuo, but pieces for up to five voices were also composed and obbligato parts sometimes included. The first collection of such lieder was Johann Nauwach's *Erster Theil teutscher Villanellen* (1627), and other composers of the genre include Heinrich Albert, Andreas Hammerschmidt, Johann Rist, and Adam Krieger. In the later 17th and early 18th centuries the continuo lied became more elaborate as it was increasingly influenced by Italian operatic styles and forms. Such developments, however, led to a decline in its popularity. —/JBE

contrabass (It.: *contrabasso*). See DOUBLE BASS.

contrabassoon [double bassoon] (Fr.: *contrebasson*; Ger.: *Kontrafagott*). A large bassoon, usually sounding an octave lower than the normal instrument and an octave lower than written. Richard Strauss required *A''*, for which a special extended bell is needed. Many 18th- and 19th-century instruments were smaller and went

continuo, Ex. 5

Nicolo Pasquali, *Thorough-Bass Made Easy.*

only to *F′*, *C′*, or *D′* below the bassoon's lowest note of *B♭*. The modern contrabassoon is closely folded with several U-bends to make it more manageable than some 18th-century examples built simply like a double-size bassoon. Seldom playing solos, it has a valuable function enriching the bass line: Beethoven, for example, used it more to double the string double basses than the bassoons.   JMo

contrafactum (from medieval Lat. *contrafacere*, 'to counterfeit'). A vocal piece in which the original text is replaced by a new one. In Latin plainchant, texts for new feasts were frequently adapted to the melodies of existing chants. Contrafacta make up a significant portion of the surviving repertories of 12th- and 13th-century Western monophonic secular song (i.e. of the troubadours, trouvères, and Minnesinger), enabling a limited group of melodies to be applied to a much larger body of texts with the same rhyme scheme. The motet and other genres of medieval polyphony also include many adaptations of sacred compositions to secular texts and vice versa. After the mid-15th century, however, contrafacta tended to replace a secular text with a sacred one. At the end of the 15th century, for example, the fierce attacks of the monk Savonarola on the often licentious *Carnival songs led to their having penitential religious texts fitted to their tunes. In the Reformation the texts of many Lutheran chorales and Calvinist metrical psalms were fitted to existing melodies.

Hymnody in the Christian East has historically depended heavily on the setting of texts to certain model melodies. Used by 4th-century Syrian hymnographers, contrafacta were are also written by the later authors of the Byzantine *kontakion. The prolific Palestinian and Constantinopolitan hymnographers of the 7th–11th centuries developed elaborate schemes of original melodies ('automela' or, in kanons, 'heirmoi') and contrafacta ('prosomoia' and 'troparia' respectively). Most of the texts in the 15 volumes of proper hymns appointed for use in modern Eastern Orthodox services are contrafacta.   —/ALi

contralto (from It. *contra alto*, 'against the alto', i.e. contrasting with the high voice; Ger.: *Alt*). The lowest female voice, with a range of roughly *g* to *g″*. It is characterized by a dark, rich tone-quality. In the 19th and early 20th centuries most female singers were described as either soprano or contralto, but from the mid-20th century *mezzo-soprano' was increasingly used for lower female voices as the true, deep contralto became ever rarer.   —/RW

contrapunctus (Lat.). 'Counterpoint'. The term was used in the Baroque period either in this general sense or more specifically to denote a fugal movement.

contrapuntal. Adjective formed from *counterpoint'.

contrary motion. See MOTION.

Contrasts. Work (1938) by Bartók for violin, clarinet, and piano, composed for the jazz clarinettist Benny Goodman; the violinist uses two instruments, the second in *scordatura tuning.

contratenor (Lat., 'against the tenor'). In early vocal music, the name for a voice part with roughly the same range as the tenor, but composed after, or 'against', that part (see TENOR, 2). When four-part writing became common around the mid-15th century, the contratenor was divided into the *contratenor altus* ('high [part] against the tenor') and *contratenor bassus* ('low [part] against the tenor'), which in turn eventually became the alto and bass parts in the standard four-part (SATB) choir.   —/RW

contredanse (Fr.), **contradanza** (It.). See COUNTRY DANCE.

Converse, Frederick Shepherd (*b* Newton, MA, 5 Jan. 1871; *d* Westwood, MA, 8 June 1940). American composer. He studied with John Knowles Paine at Harvard and Josef Rheinberger in Munich, then worked as a teacher (at the New England Conservatory, 1920–38) and opera administrator (with the Boston Opera, 1908–14). His *The Pipe of Desire* was the first American opera staged at the Metropolitan (1910); other works include five symphonies and tone-poems (*The Mystic Trumpeter*, 1904).   PG

Conyngham, Barry (*b* Sydney, 27 Aug. 1944). Australian composer. After playing jazz piano at school and as a law student, he studied composition with Raymond Hanson and Peter Sculthorpe. A visit to Japan for Expo 70 led to fruitful encounters with Takemitsu and Stockhausen; study in the USA from 1972 to 1974 prompted an interest in electronic music. He has taught at the universities in Melbourne and Wollongong (NSW), and in 1993 was appointed vice-chancellor of the new Southern Cross University at Lismore (NSW). His works include an opera, the full-length ballet *Vast* (1988), orchestral and chamber music, and tape compositions.   ABur

Conzertstück (Ger., 'concert piece'). See CONCERTINO, 2.

cool jazz. The most intellectual styles of jazz, originally applied to a variant of *bebop at the end of the 1940s that played down the 'hot' aspects of that style and earlier jazz. The term is sometimes associated with the West Coast musicians of the 1950s and 60s but is more meaningfully applied to the styles of such jazz musicians as Miles Davis.   PGa

Cooper, John. See COPRARIO, JOHN.

coperto (It.). 'Covered'; e.g. drums muffled by being covered with a cloth, in funeral music.

copla (Sp.). A type of popular Spanish sung poem, generally improvised; the term is also applied to a couplet or stanza in Spanish and Latin American forms such as the *villancico. KC

Copland, Aaron (*b* Brooklyn, New York, 14 Nov. 1900; *d* Westchester, NY, 2 Dec. 1990). American composer. The son of immigrant Jewish parents from Lithuania, he learnt the piano from the age of 13 and had theory lessons from Rubin Goldmark. He then studied with Nadia Boulanger in Paris (1921–4) and, as one of her first American pupils, gained a facility for neo-classicism which he skilfully and brashly combined with jazz in his Piano Concerto (1926). This and other early works, including the *Dance Symphony* (1925) and Piano Variations (1930), quickly gained him a reputation in America as a daring modernist. He taught at the New School for Social Research in New York (1927–37) and did much to promote contemporary music in the city: to the end of his professional life he was exceptionally generous to other composers.

Visits to Mexico gave rise to the picturesque *El salón México* for orchestra (1936), which was followed by a series of ballets in which Copland used American material (New England hymns, folksongs, jazz): *Billy the Kid* (1938), *Rodeo* (1942), and *Appalachian Spring* (1944). In doing so he was motivated partly by a patriotic wish to create a distinctively American music (reflected also in his concern for jazz) and partly by a democratic determination to communicate with a large audience. *Appalachian Spring*, originally a chamber score for Martha Graham, gained enormous popularity in its orchestral version and proved that Copland had indeed found an American style, spare in harmony and sensitively coloured.

Meanwhile, the entry of the USA into World War II had sharpened his sense of national duty, expressed in *Lincoln Portrait* for speaker and orchestra (1942) and *Fanfare for the Common Man*, from the same year. His Third Symphony (1944–6) was an attempt to use a similar style—public, American—on the most ambitious plane. He also wrote an opera, *The Tender Land* (New York, 1954), though his more successful works of the decade or so after the war are on a smaller scale: the 12 Emily Dickinson songs (1949–50), Piano Quartet (1950), and Piano Fantasy (1952–7). From this point his output declined as he struggled to come to terms with postwar developments—in which he took a keen interest—until he arrived at a personal use of Stravinsky-like *serialism in his orchestral works *Connotations* (1961–2) and *Inscape* (1967).

While pursuing his career as a versatile composer Copland taught composition at Tanglewood (1940–65) and appeared internationally as a conductor of his own

music and that of younger Americans from 1956 until the early 1970s, the period of his last compositions: *Night Thoughts* for piano (1972) and *Two Threnodies* for flute and string trio (1971–3). His later years were clouded by mental decline. PG

📖 A. COPLAND, *Our New Music* (New York, 1941), rev. as *The New Music* (New York, 1968); *Music and Imagination* (Cambridge, MA, 1952) · H. POLLACK, *Aaron Copland: The Life and Work of an Uncommon Man* (New York, 1999)

Coppélia, ou La Fille aux yeux d'émail ('Coppélia, or The Girl with Enamel Eyes'). Ballet in two acts by Delibes to a scenario by Charles Nuitter and Arthur Saint-Léon after E. T. A. Hoffmann's story *Der Sandmann*; it was choreographed by Saint Léon (Paris, 1870). Delibes arranged a suite from the ballet, of which there are now many different choreographic versions.

Coprario [Cooper], John [Giovanni] (*b* c.1570–80; *d* ?June 1626). English viol player and composer. He adopted the Italian form of his name as a mark of respect for Italian fashions. Coprario moved in the circles of the English aristocracy and nobility; his patrons included Sir Robert Cecil, Earl of Salisbury, and Edward Seymour, Earl of Hertford. From 1618 he was salaried as a composer by Charles, Prince of Wales (later Charles I). Coprario's early works include Italian-texted villanellas and madrigal-like instrumental fantasias. He also composed for the lyra viol, and was a pioneer in the development of the fantasia-suite. Two sets of his elegies appeared in print, *Funeral Teares* (1606) and *Songs of Mourning* (1613). His unpublished treatise *Rules how to Compose*, written before 1617, may have been intended to instruct his pupil William Lawes. JM

copyright. In its earliest manifestation dating back to the 16th century, copyright literally meant the right to copy, a right reserved at that time to publishers in respect of their books. Modern copyright law is commonly described as a bundle of rights, having evolved to embrace virtually every form of reproducing and using creative works in both the physical and the online worlds, ranging from photocopying sheet music to downloading music from the Internet and from performing a musical work to webcasting a performance. This is by necessity a very brief overview only of the law of copyright and related rights and should not be relied upon other than for general information. Consultation with a specialist lawyer is vital for anyone requiring advice on the full implications of the law of copyright in relation to any particular circumstances.

1. Basic principles of copyright

Rights of copyright are exclusive to the owner of copyright. This exclusivity means that anyone wanting to use a copyright work in one or more defined ways (known as restricted acts) must first secure the permission of the copyright owner. Failure to do so will result in such use being an infringement of copyright. Copyright therefore provides a mechanism by which the copyright owner can control the use of a copyright work through licensing. The terms of the licence will govern, for example, the period for which the work may be used and the territory of use. The copyright owner can also require payment in return for a licence, whether in the form of a one-off fee or of a royalty being a share of a revenue stream derived, for example, from sales or advertising.

Copyright attaches only to a work which is in a material form—that is, the form in which an idea is expressed rather than the idea itself. A composer who composes a musical work in his or her head cannot therefore rely on copyright protection for that composition until it is expressed in some tangible way, for example on paper or as a recording.

A further fundamental principle is that copyright protection is available only for a creative work which is 'original' to its creator in the sense that it has not been copied, whether directly or indirectly or consciously or subconsciously, from any other work and providing the creator has invested sufficient skill and labour in its creation. Issues of novelty, quality, or merit therefore have no place in copyright law.

In developing the copyright framework, legislators have always sought to strike a balance between protecting the interests of the copyright owner and the right of others to have access to creative works for particular purposes such as private study. This has resulted in the development of a number of exceptions to copyright and defences to infringement of it.

2. Chronology of UK copyright law

Copyright legislation in the UK dates back to the Statute of Anne of 1709. This provided protection against making print copies of works for a maximum of 28 years. Common law copyright developed alongside this and sometimes in conflict with the Statute of Anne and other statutes passed in the 19th century.

The 20th century saw the passing of three major copyright statutes, the pace of legislative change being forced by the continual development of new means of exploiting creative works. The 1911 Copyright Act served to consolidate existing common law and legislation and brought within the copyright fold the right to perform a creative work. It also introduced new rights that took into account the development of sound recordings and film. Interestingly, the 1911 Act enshrined the statutory duty for publishers of books and music to deposit a copy of every publication with the British Library and other libraries, an obligation now enshrined in other legislation. The 1956 Copyright Act took account of broadcasting and was later amended to provide protection for cable programming.

The current law is to be found in the Copyright, Designs and Patents Act 1988 ('the 1988 Act') as varied by Statutory Instruments (often implementing EU Directives) and Orders in Council (extending the 1988 Act to works created overseas). Although the 1988 Act repeals the earlier legislation, some parts of the former statutes still govern the copyright protection afforded to works created during the life of those statutes. The interpretation of the prevailing statutes is embodied in case law developed over time and this applies equally to the 1988 Act where appropriate.

3. International perspective

Copyright laws vary from one country to another. An international copyright framework developed through conventions ensures certain minimum standards of copyright protection in all participating countries. The Berne Convention, originally ratified in 1886, established a minimum term of protection of life of the author plus 50 years, while the Universal Copyright Convention of 1952 sets a minimum term of life of the author plus 25 years. Both Conventions have been periodically revised. Most countries that have a significant production of copyright works have now adhered to them.

To qualify for copyright protection under the Berne Convention there must be no requirement to register or deposit copies of a work. It is noteworthy that the USA did not ratify the Berne Convention until 1989 following relaxation of their registration rules. In contrast, the Universal Copyright Convention does allow the imposition of registration formalities as a prerequisite for copyright protection within contracting states but, most important, only works that bear the copyright symbol © followed by the name of the copyright owner and the year of first publication are eligible for protection. It is common practice today to use this form of copyright notice as a warning to others, particularly those who may be considering using the work in some way, that the work is thought to be protected by copyright even though the notice itself does not confer or guarantee protection under UK law.

A fundamental principle of both Conventions is 'national treatment' whereby each contracting state agrees to accord the same copyright protection to works by authors of other contracting states as it would to works by its own nationals. Works created by authors not resident in a Berne Convention country can be brought within the scope of the convention if they are first or 'simultaneously' (i.e. within 30 days) published in a Berne Convention country.

The 1961 Rome Convention and the 1971 Geneva Convention govern international protection of performers, phonogram producers, and broadcasters. Recordings are protected when they bear the symbol Ⓟ followed by the year of first publication, the name of the owner of the phonogram producer rights, and the names of the performers.

An integral part of the World Trade Organization Agreement signed in 1994 was the agreement on Trade-Related Aspects of Intellectual Property Rights (TRIPS) which had as its purpose the reduction of distortions and impediments to international trade. It aims to balance the need for effective and adequate protection of intellectual property rights against the needs of legitimate trade.

In 1996 the above Conventions were revised in two WIPO treaties. They include provisions to bring the Conventions into line with TRIPS and also heralded in legislative terms the dawn of the digital era. The treaties have still to be fully ratified (by 30 countries) to be effective. Those countries which have so far ratified include the USA with the passing of the Digital Millennium Copyright Act 1998 and the 15 member states of the European Union (EU) through the Copyright Directive. The Copyright Directive is to be implemented in each member state by late 2002.

4. Essentials of UK copyright law

(a) Which creative works qualify for copyright protection? Copyright protection is afforded to musical works, dramatic works, literary works (which include computer programs and certain databases), artistic works (which include photographs, drawings, and many other graphic and three-dimensional works), sound recordings, films, broadcasts, cable programmes, and typographical arrangements of published editions. These are protected to the extent that they are in a material form and original (see above, 1). For example, a CD recording of a song could contain several different copyright works, including a musical work, a literary one (the words of the song), the sound recording, a further literary work in respect of the words of any notes on the cover and, finally, an artistic work in respect of any photograph or drawing on the cover. For any of the above to qualify for protection under UK law,

either the author must be a British citizen or domiciled or resident in the UK at the time of making the work, or the work must be first published in the UK. If none of these criteria are met the work may nevertheless qualify under the international Conventions (see above). Copyright protection is not dependent on publication, registration, or deposit of a work.

(b) Who is the copyright owner? The first owner of copyright is the author unless he or she was employed at the time of creating the work, in which case the employer becomes the first owner in the absence of any agreement to the contrary. The producer is regarded for these purposes as the author of a sound recording or film and the publisher as the author of a typographical arrangement. Copyright in a work may be wholly or partly assigned with the result that the assignee becomes the owner of the rights assigned. An assignment must be in a written document signed by the person assigning the work. Copyright ownership may also be passed by will.

(c) How long does copyright last? In the case of most types of work copyright endures for 70 years from the end of the year of death of the author. In the case of a work created by more than one author, the period is calculated by reference to the last to die.

The term of protection was increased in 1996 from the life of the author plus 50 years in accordance with the Term Directive which harmonized the term of protection throughout the EU. One of the effects of this was that works which had fallen into the public domain after the life plus 50-year period, but which were still within the life plus 70-year period, were effectively brought back into copyright ('revived copyright'). This applies to the works of any author who died between 1925 and 1945.

The copyright in sound recordings, broadcasts, and cable programmes remains unchanged at 50 years from the end of the year of being made (or, in the case of sound recordings which are released, from the end of the year of release) and the copyright in the typographical arrangement of a published edition remains limited to 25 years.

(d) The restricted acts: Permission is required from the copyright owner to do any of the following 'primary' restricted acts in relation to the whole or a substantial part (measured by reference to quality rather than quantity) of a copyright work: to copy it (i.e. to reproduce it in a material form which includes storing the work electronically); to issue copies to the public; to rent or lend copies to the public; to perform, show, or play the work in public; to broadcast it or include it in a cable programme service; to make an adaptation of the

work or to do any of the above acts in relation to an adaptation of it.

Anyone who does or authorizes the doing of any of the above without permission will incur civil liability for infringement of copyright, regardless of whether they intended to or knew that they were infringing copyright. The copyright owner would be entitled to apply to the courts for an injunction to stop the infringer from continuing to do such acts, for an order that the infringer pays damages, for delivery up of the infringing copies, and for an account of any profits made.

Liability for 'secondary' restricted acts arises when someone who knows or has reason to believe that they are dealing with infringing copies of a work does any of the following: imports an infringing copy into the UK for non-private use (a copy imported from another part of the EU when it has been lawfully circulated in the EU is not infringing for these purposes)*; possesses or deals with an infringing copy of a work in the course of business*; distributes an infringing copy otherwise than in the course of business to the prejudice of the copyright owner*; provides the means for making infringing copies*; allows premises to be used for an unlicensed performance; provides the means for an unauthorized performance of a sound recording or film or for the electronic reception of sound or visual images. Such a person will be considered to have the necessary knowledge once put on notice by the copyright owner of the fact that they are dealing in infringing copies.

In addition to civil liability all the acts marked above with an asterisk are criminal offences for which the offender may be fined or imprisoned, or both.

(e) *Exceptions and defences*: In certain prescribed circumstances a copyright work can be used without needing the prior permission of the copyright owner. The fair dealing exceptions, for example, allow works to be used for private research and study and, subject to acknowledging the copyright owner, for criticism, review, and the reporting of current events. There are also certain exceptional activities permitted under the 1988 Act for educational purposes and by libraries.

All exceptions are subject to an overarching 'three-step test' set out in the Berne Convention even though it is not currently expressly provided for in the 1988 Act. Its effect is to confine any exceptions to certain special cases provided such excepted use does not conflict with a normal exploitation of the work and does not unreasonably prejudice the legitimate interests of the author.

The Copyright Directive provides for a much broader range of exceptions than currently exist under the 1988 Act and it remains to be seen to what extent these will be incorporated into UK law.

5. Moral rights

The 1988 Act introduced moral rights into UK copyright law. They are personal to the author and cannot be assigned, although they can be waived. They have no economic basis, in contrast to copyright.

The moral rights recognized under UK law are the paternity right (the right to be identified as the author of the work), the integrity right (the right to object to derogatory treatment of the work), false attribution (the right not to have a work falsely attributed to one), and the right of privacy in photographs or films commissioned for private purposes. With the exception of the false attribution right, which expires 20 years after death, moral rights endure for the full period of copyright. They do not apply to works whose authors died before the 1988 Act came into force.

6. Rights in performances

The 1988 Act confers rights on performers analogous to rights of copyright. These include the right to prevent the recording or transmission of their performances or the use of or dealing in recordings of their performances without their consent. Performers also enjoy a right to a share of the income when a recording of one of their performances is played in public or broadcast.

The owners (in most cases, the record company) of the right to make recordings of a performance by virtue of an exclusive recording contract with a performing artist also have the right to prevent others from recording the performer's performance and making use of such recording without their permission.

These so-called neighbouring rights last for 50 years from the end of the year in which the performance takes place or, if a recording of it is released, from the end of the year of release. They can be assigned or bequeathed in the same way as can copyright.

7. Collective administration of rights

The business of licensing copyrights throughout the world, monitoring usage, and collecting in royalties is increasingly complex and, in many cases, impractical for individual copyright owners. A system of collective administration of rights has therefore developed over the last 150 years with the establishment of collecting societies in each country. Rights owners register their works with their local collecting societies who take on the responsibility for licensing the works and collecting in the royalties. The collecting societies have reciprocal agreements with societies in other countries.

Collecting societies play a particularly prominent role in the music business. They include the Mechanical Copyright Protection Society (MCPS) which licenses the recording of musical works; the Performing Right Society (PRS) which licenses the public performance and broadcast of musical works; Phonographic Performance Limited (PPL) which licenses the broadcast and public performance of sound recordings; Association of United Recording Artists (AURA) and Performing Artists Media Rights Association (PAMRA) which administer the equitable remuneration due to performers in respect of the use of recordings of their performances; Video Performance Limited (VPL) which licenses the broadcast and performance of videos; and Christian Copyright Licensing Inc. (CCLI) which licenses limited photocopying associated with religious services.

Copyright owners maintain control over certain rights which they generally license directly, including photocopying, some synchronization licensing (the application of music or sound recordings to moving picture, whether in film or commercials), and certain performances of dramatico-musical works (such as operas and ballets).

The Copyright Tribunal exists to oversee licensing schemes operated by the collecting societies. Users of copyright can refer a licensing scheme to the Tribunal if they consider any of the terms to be unreasonable.

SFa

Coq d'or, Le. See GOLDEN COCKEREL, THE.

cor (Fr., 'horn'). A horn of any sort. The term embraces *bugles* ('oxhorns'), oliphants of ivory, the *cor anglais, and the orchestral French *horn. *Cor de chasse, cor d'harmonie* (Fr.), 'natural horn'; *cor à pistons* (Fr.), 'valved horn'.

cor anglais (Fr., 'English horn'; Ger.: *englisches Horn*; It.: *corno inglese*). Neither English nor a horn but a tenor *oboe in F with a bulbous bell, which gives a somewhat hollow sound. The second half of the name may be a corruption of *anglé* ('bent'), for early examples were curved or angled. It is a transposing instrument, sounding a 5th lower than written. As a solo orchestral voice it has been widely popular with composers from the early 19th century onwards, especially in pastoral or romantic roles. It derived from the 18th-century tenor oboe and first appeared later in that century in works by Haydn and his contemporaries.   JMo

coranto (It.). See COURANTE.

corda (It., 'string'; Fr.: *corde*). In piano music *una corda* denotes the 'soft' pedal, which shifts the action on grand pianos so that the hammer strikes only one of the three strings. Similarly, *due corde* indicated two strings on early pianos. Each is cancelled by the instruction *tre corde* or *tutte le corde* (It., 'three strings' or 'all the strings'). See PIANOFORTE, 7.   JMo

corde, à la (Fr., 'on the string'). In string playing, a direction to keep the bow on the string, to produce a legato effect.

Corder, Frederick (*b* London, 26 Jan. 1852; *d* London, 21 Aug. 1932). English conductor and composer. He studied at the RAM (1873–5) and in Cologne (1875–8) and Milan (1878–9), returning to England to become conductor at the Brighton Aquarium (1880–2). His opera *Nordisa* (1886), commissioned by Carl Rosa, met with some success, but Rosa's untimely death caused him to abandon all aspiration to a career as an opera composer. A champion of Wagner, he translated *Parsifal* (1879) and the *Ring* (1882) into English, his versions being widely used for many years. He also wrote composition primers, books on Beethoven, Liszt, and Wagner, and a useful if outdated monograph on the RAM. In 1888 he was appointed to teach composition at the RAM, where he passed on his affinity for German progressivism to pupils who included Bantock and Bax.   JDi

Cordier, Baude (*fl c.*1400). Composer. All that is known of his life is that he was born in Reims and was a university graduate. He may be the same person as Baude Fresnel, who served as harpist and organist to the court of Philip the Bold, Duke of Burgundy. Most of Cordier's dozen surviving works are secular songs. Several are notable for their rhythmic complexity and notational ingenuity; one of them is written in the form of a circle, another in the shape of a heart.   JM

Corelli, Arcangelo (*b* Fusignano, nr Faenza, 17 Feb. 1653; *d* Rome, 8 Jan. 1713). Italian violinist and composer. His life has been subjected to considerable misrepresentation, not least, initially, by the English historians Burney and Hawkins in the late 18th century. Marc Pincherle did much to rectify this, but a great deal of misinformation remains: Corelli's upbringing was humble, not noble; he arrived in Bologna not in 1666 but about 1670; it seems that his teachers there were the violinists Benvenuti and Brugnoli—he is not known to have studied composition; he never acknowledged membership of the Bolognese Accademia Filarmonica; he associated himself entirely with the Roman School, having received a rigorous training in counterpoint under Matteo Simonelli; in Rome he composed in a wide variety of media possibly including vocal works; he was particularly renowned for his use of wind and brass instruments; and his abilities on the violin were incomparable.

Corelli was in Rome by 1675, working periodically at S. Luigi dei Francesi and for the Lenten devotions at S. Marcello. At this time he confined himself to the composition of virtuoso solo sonatas, which he would not have contemplated publishing since elaborate violin idioms were beyond the capability of the primitive printing technology still prevailing in Italy into the 18th century. About 1679 he became *musico da camera* to ex-Queen Christina of Sweden, a connoisseur of young talent. However, by 1684 he had entered the service of Cardinal Benedetto Pamphili, with whom he remained until the latter's appointment as papal legate to Bologna in 1690. He was soon adopted by Cardinal Pietro Ottoboni, in whose household he spent the rest of his life, together with his close friend and colleague Matteo Fornari. He certainly performed outside Rome, but the account of a debacle in Naples over his inability to play a work of Alessandro Scarlatti's (an associate in Rome) is as unlikely as a similar confrontation with Handel at the Ruspoli palace in 1707, given that Corelli was universally regarded as the finest violinist of his age. Until late in his life he led an immensely active career: as a performer and impresario presiding at the lavish festivities that formed so prominent a feature of Roman life, involving him in public opera, massive oratorios, and secular cantatas; at such societies as the Academia del Disegno; and finally as one of a few select musicians to be admitted to the illustrious Arcadian Society.

During his lifetime he published five sets of sonatas, although this must represent but a small part of his output, as suggested by the mountain of apocryphal works. The first four sets are sonatas *a* 3, op. 2 alone being styled 'da camera'—Corelli never used the term 'sonata da chiesa', this being added in the 19th century. The free sonatas were intended originally as concert music (op. 1 was composed specifically for the academies of its dedicatee, Queen Christina), although this would not exclude their use in church. Contrary to popular belief his op. 5 sonatas are not solo works but duos for violin and violone, which, like the opp. 2 and 4 dance suites, require no keyboard accompaniment. They achieved immense status as didactic works, aided by Estienne Roger's edition embellishing the slow movements as he claimed with 'Corelli's graces'. His op. 6 concerti grossi were published in 1714 shortly after his death and enjoyed huge popularity in northern Europe for almost 100 years, becoming the standard fare of concert societies then flourishing particularly in Britain. Today the title evokes comparison with the concerto genre, but they should rather be regarded as a colouristic orchestral medium, of which solo–tutti contrast is a possible but not essential element. Nor should they be thought of as enlarged trio sonatas, since many of the most substantial movements have no parallels in any of Corelli's sonatas and, furthermore, his concertino grouping varies from true solo (no. 12) or duo (no. 2) to trio as well as quartet. By far the most famous of the set was the so-called Christmas Concerto (no. 8, 'fatto per la notte di Natale'), most probably performed, as was customary, in the Ottoboni palace on Christmas Eve rather than at midnight Mass. It actually contains a prelude and three dances a well as the pastorale movement—a popular idiom of the period.

Extravagant claims have been made for Corelli's music, especially in regard to his treatment of harmony and tonality, but there is no doubt of his immense influence, as attested by the acknowledgments of such composers as Tartini, Couperin, and Telemann. PA

📖 M. PINCHERLE, *Corelli et son temps* (Paris, 1954; Eng. trans. 1956) · P. ALLSOP, *Arcangelo Corelli: 'New Orpheus of Our Times'* (Oxford, 1999)

Corelli clash. See CADENCE.

Corigliano, John (Paul) (*b* New York, 16 Feb. 1938). American composer. The son of a professional violinist, he studied with Otto Luening at Columbia University and Vittorio Giannini at the Manhattan School, graduating in 1959. He then worked in radio, television, and the theatre in New York, before taking teaching posts at the Manhattan School (1971) and at Lehman College (1973). In 1991 he began teaching also at the Juilliard School. He made his reputation as a composer with his Clarinet Concerto (1977), a fiercely dramatic piece in which avant-garde techniques are at the service of a broadly traditional kind of expression. His Symphony no. 1 (1988–9), written as a memorial to AIDS victims during the period he was composer-in-residence with the Chicago Symphony (1987–90), continued in that style and brought him an international audience. Other works include the 'grand opera buffa' *The Ghosts of Versailles* (Metropolitan, 1991), a part-pastiche fantasy in which characters from Mozart mingle with the French court, the choral symphony *A Dylan Thomas Trilogy* (1960–76), the Beethoven-inspired *Fantasia on an Ostinato* for piano (1985) or orchestra (1986), chamber and piano pieces, choral settings and songs, and film scores (*Altered States*, *The Red Violin*). PG

Coriolan ('Coriolanus'). Overture, op. 62, by Beethoven, composed in 1807 for a revival in Vienna of Heinrich Joseph von Collin's play *Coriolan* (on the same subject as Shakespeare's).

cori spezzati (It., 'broken choirs'). A term used to describe the division of musical forces into musically, and sometimes also spatially, distinct groups. Such antiphonal use of two groups of singers is traceable to Jewish and early Christian liturgical music, but the deliberate, artistic development of the practice dates from the later years of the 15th century. It is associated particularly with psalm settings by composers in and around Venice in the mid-16th century, notably

Willaert, whose *Salmi spezzati* (1550) ushered in a period of great popularity for polychoral music. These works, characterized by simple, diatonic harmonies and clear text-setting, do little to exploit contrast or 'dialogue' effects. Lassus's *cori spezzati* music, sacred and secular, features both contrapuntal textures and contrast between the complete forces and the separate choirs, to more striking effect.

Andrea and Giovanni Gabrieli continued the *cori spezzati* tradition at St Mark's, Venice, in their ceremonial motets, introducing bold harmonic gestures and using instruments to exploit contrasts of register between vocal and instrumental groups and between full choir and a solo voice (or group of soloists) with continuo. The contrasting groups engage in a musical dialogue, in phrases of varying lengths and degrees of overlap. Echo effects such as those found in Monteverdi's *Vespers* (1610) became common and led to contrasting dynamics being considered a useful device even when there was no spatial separation. Here again the harmonic flow provided by a continuo was important.

The *cori spezzati* technique spread from northern Italy to Rome, where it is found in works by Palestrina and his pupils and by Victoria, through whom it reached Spain. It also caught on in Germany, through the influence of Lassus and the Gabrielis, among composers including Hassler and Schütz. Praetorius in *Syntagma musicum* (1619) advocated the singing of individual chorale verses by different forces placed around the church. A well-known but comparatively rare example in English music is Tallis's *Spem in alium*, for 40 voices in eight five-part choirs. On an even bigger scale is the grand ceremonial *Missa salisburgensis*, written (probably by Biber) for performance in Salzburg Cathedral. In 53 parts distributed among eight choirs, it is necessarily in a simple harmonic style, its interest lying in spatial and textural effects.

Cori spezzati continued to be used in Italy into the 18th century, in concertos, cantatas, and motets, where the contrast between choruses and solo voices or duets became increasingly sectionalized. Bach explored polychoral effects in some of his motets and the *St Matthew Passion*. Developments in electronic and computer music increased the possibilities of spatial effects still further in the 20th century.   DA/EW

Cornago, Johannes (*b* *c*.1400; *d* after 1474). Spanish church musician and composer. He graduated in theology from the University of Paris in 1449. Soon afterwards he entered the service of King Alfonso I of Naples, and within a few years commanded a large salary that implies high status. Later in life he sang with the court chapel of King Ferdinand II of Spain.

Cornago is the first in the long and distinguished line of Spanish Renaissance composers. His few surviving works include a handful of polyphonic songs in Spanish, and one of the earliest known cyclic masses based on a secular cantus firmus.   JM

cornamuse. An early Baroque *wind-cap instrument described by Michael Praetorius (*Syntagma musicum*, 2/1619) as resembling a straight *crumhorn, cylindrical in bore, but with a closed distal end except for two small vents in the sides, and therefore a quieter sound. No such instrument is known to have survived, though modern reconstructions have been made. Italian concert accounts mention it, sometimes with the *dolzaina* (*douçaine*), but whether a crumhorn or Praetorius's instrument was meant is unknown.   JMo

Cornelius, (Carl August) Peter (*b* Mainz, 24 Dec. 1824; *d* Mainz, 26 Oct. 1874). German composer. Like Wagner and Lortzing, he came of an acting family, also possessing literary gifts whose admirers included Berlioz. He had little formal musical training in his youth, studying with Siegfried Dehn in Berlin only in 1844. Moving to Weimar in 1852, he became part of Liszt's circle, writing much in support of their ideas while retaining his independence. He also came to know Berlioz, for whom he translated *Benvenuto Cellini* and who thereby influenced his charming and witty comedy *Der Barbier von Bagdad* (1858). Through no fault of Cornelius, the premiere precipitated Liszt's departure from Weimar, and to escape Liszt's influence Cornelius moved to Vienna. There he came under the still more powerful influence of Wagner. Although *Der Cid* (1865) has elements in common with *Lohengrin*, it can stand independently as one of the most remarkable German grand operas of the day. Following Wagner to Munich in 1868 with some reluctance, Cornelius taught composition at the conservatory. He remained a strong supporter of Wagner and the Bayreuth enterprise, also always appreciating the best in Wagner's character. His ability to detach himself, for fear of being stifled, without damaging their friendship was a reflection of his unusually amiable nature and to the credit of them both. Cornelius also wrote many excellent songs, some of which reflect his strong Christian faith (for instance, his *Vater unser* cycle, which makes creative use of plainchant). A third opera, *Gunlöd*, was left unfinished.   DA/JW

cornemuse (Fr.; It., Sp.: *cornamusa*). Generic term for bagpipes.

cornet [cornopean] (Fr.: *cornet à pistons*, *cornet*; Ger.: *Cornett*, *Kornett*; It.: *cornetta*). A high-pitched, three-valve brass instrument in B♭, the same pitch as the modern trumpet. Invented in Paris by Halary in the

1820s as a valved version of the coiled *posthorn, it was originally supplied with a set of shanks and crooks from Bb down to F. It became immediately popular, replacing the keyed *bugle as a melodic instrument for bands and winning a place in the French orchestra, where it contrasted with the more majestic *trumpet. Because of its greater facility, players began to use it for trumpet parts; in rivalry, the trumpet was modified into an instrument resembling it to the extent that today there is little difference between the two in either construction or sound.

The cornet became the leading instrument of British and American brass bands. It was the principal instrument in early jazz bands (though the trumpet became more popular from the 1920s) and has now once again found its main home in the brass band.   JMo

Cornet, Peeter [Pierre, Pietro] (*b* ?Brussels, 1570–80; *d* Brussels, 27 March 1633). Flemish organist and composer. All that is known of his early career is that he came from a family of professional musicians. In about 1606 he was appointed one of the organists to the royal chapel of Archduke Albert and Archduchess Isabella at Brussels, where he worked alongside the English émigré musicians John Bull and Peter Philips. His surviving works, all for keyboard, are few in number but impressive in scope.   JM

cornett (Fr.: *cornet à bouquin*; Ger.: *Zink*, *Cornett*; It.: *cornetto*). A Renaissance wind instrument. It is spelt 'cornett' to distinguish it from the brass-band cornet. The standard cornett is made from a curved piece of wood split longitudinally, hollowed out, glued back together, and covered with a sleeve of leather to seal it against air leakage. Like a woodwind instrument it has six fingerholes and a thumbhole; like a brass instrument it has a cupped mouthpiece, often shaped like the cup of an acorn, and its performance combines the best features of both woodwind and brass. It was the principal virtuoso instrument of the Renaissance. Immensely flexible, when played from towers with sackbuts it could be heard above the clamour of a marketplace; in the choir it could support the treble voices; and played in chamber or church it was capable of the most subtle and florid playing.

Descant (*cornettino*) and tenor (S-shaped, and called lysarden in English) cornetts also existed, as well as a (very rare) bass, from which the later *serpent derived. The most important variant was the mute cornet (Ger.: *stiller Zink*), a straight, lathe-turned instrument with an integral, horn-type mouthpiece carved into the top of the bore, and with a much gentler sound. The cornett has been successfully revived for modern performance of Renaissance music.   JMo

Cornish, William. See CORNYSH, WILLIAM.

cornopean. A mid-19th-century English name for the valved *cornet, now normally reserved for those with Stölzel *valves.

cornu (Lat., 'horn'). A Roman bronze horn, curved over most of a circle, the supporting crossbar held so that the bell came over the player's head. It was used by both cavalry and infantry.

Cornysh [Cornish], **William.** There were two English musicians of this name, possibly father and son. William Cornysh (i) (*d* c.1502) was Master of the Choristers at Westminster Abbey from 1479 to 1491; William Cornysh (ii) (*d* 1523) was a Gentleman of the Chapel Royal, and Master of the Children there from 1509 until his death. Of the two, only Cornysh (ii) is known to have been a composer. He was also a poet, dramatist, actor, and producer of theatrical entertainments, many of which involved the choirboys for whom he bore responsibility; none of his plays survive. His most securely attributed compositions are his songs, which shed vivid light on the court cultures of Henry VII and especially Henry VIII. Some of them, including *Ah, Robin, Blow thy horn, hunter*, and *Woefully arrayed*, are still popular today. Less securely his is the church music attributed to 'William Cornysh', some of which survives in the Eton Choirbook of c.1500–5. This ranks among the most spectacular music of its age, with its thrilling textures and virtuoso vocal lines. Neither man is to be confused with the composer John Cornysh (*fl* 1500), who has not been positively identified but may have had connections with Winchester College, and later New College, Oxford.   JM

corona. A symbol found above some long notes in early sources that resembles the modern 'pause' sign. Its meaning is not clearly explained by theorists, though sometimes it seems plausible that the performer should have decorated the note with an improvised ornament (perhaps in a style known as 'cantus coronatus'). Alternatively it may simply indicate a pause (or 'fermata').   AP

coronach. See CORRANACH.

'Coronation' Concerto. Nickname of Mozart's Piano Concerto no. 26 in D, K537 (1788), so called because it was performed at the coronation of Leopold II (1790) but it had in fact been performed by Mozart in 1789.

'Coronation' Mass. Nickname of Mozart's Mass in C, K317 (1779), so called because it is believed to have been composed for, or associated with, the annual crowning of a statue of the Virgin in a church near Salzburg.

Haydn's *Nelsonmesse* is sometimes referred to as the Coronation Mass.

Coronation Ode. Choral work, op. 44, by Elgar, for four soloists, chorus, and orchestra, a setting of words by A. C. Benson. It was commissioned for the Covent Garden gala performance to celebrate Edward VII's coronation in June 1902; the gala was cancelled because of the king's illness and the work was given its premiere at the Sheffield Festival in October that year. The finale, 'Land of Hope and Glory', is to a melody adapted from the trio section of Elgar's first *Pomp and Circumstance* march.

Coronation of Poppaea, The. See Incoronazione di Poppea, L'.

Corps glorieux, Les ('The Glorious Hosts'). Organ work (1939) by Messiaen, in seven movements.

Corradini [Coradigni, Coradini], **Francesco** [Francisco] (*b* Venice, *c*.1690; *d* Madrid, 14 Oct. 1769). Italian composer. His early works—an oratorio and operas—were written for Naples, but he spent most of his career in Spain (initially as a *maestro de capilla* in Valencia), dominating the country's musical scene for about 15 years. In 1734 he moved to Madrid, where he composed a run of popular operas and other stage pieces in the modern style that united Spanish librettos with Italian music. His surviving works (much of his output is lost) are characterized by tunefulness and harmonic simplicity, though with an over-reliance on predictable if pleasing phrase structures. The comedy *Don Juan de Espina en Madrid* (1740) is typical. In 1747 Corradini was appointed one of the orchestral directors in the royal theatre at the palace of Buen Retiro, and contributed the second act for a Spanish version of Pietro Metastasio's *La clemenza di Tito*. In his later years he retired from opera composition and devoted himself to his duties as *maestro de música* to the Queen Dowager Isabella Farnese.   MHE

corranach (Gaelic) [coronach]. A Scottish funeral dirge, originally chanted by a bard to the accompaniment of a harp but later performed by women. Tobias Smollett, in *Humphrey Clinker* (1771), describes one such ceremony: 'the coronach, composed of a multitude of old hags, who tore their hair, beat their breasts and howled most hideously ... At the ... panegyric of the defunct, every period [was] confirmed by a yell of the coronach'. The *caoine* is the Irish equivalent.

Correa (de Araujo [de Acevedo]), **Francisco** (*b* Seville, *bapt*. 17 Sept. 1584; *d* Segovia, 6 Oct. – 18 Nov. 1654). Spanish organist, composer, and theorist. He became organist of the collegiate church of S. Salvador in Seville on 1 September 1599. In 1536 he moved to Jaén

Cathedral as organist, and from 1540 was organist at Segovia Cathedral. His *Libro de tientos y discursos ... intitulado Facultad orgánica* (Alcalá, 1626), incorporating information on music theory and performance, presents organ pieces graded by technical difficulty. Most of these works exploit the division of organ stops into separate registers, allowing solos for the right or the left hand. Correa made liberal use of false relations and augmented intervals, and his extravagantly varied passage-work includes irregular groupings of short notes.   OR

Corregidor, Der ('The Magistrate'). Opera in four acts by Wolf to a libretto by Rosa Mayreder after Pedro Antonio de Alarcón's novel *El sombrero de tres picos* ('The Three-Cornered Hat', 1874) (Mannheim, 1896). Falla's ballet *El sombrero de tres picos* is based on the same story.

corrente (It.). See courante.

Corrette, Michel (*b* Rouen, 10 April 1707; *d* Paris, 21 Jan. 1795). French organist and composer. Little is known of his life before 1732 when he became music director of both the Foire St Germain and the Foire St Laurent, producing vaudevilles and divertissements. He held organ posts at Ste Marie (1737–90) and the Jesuit college (*c*.1738–62) and enjoyed the patronage of the Prince of Conti and the Duke of Angoulême. A prolific composer, he was one of the first in France to write concertos in the Italian manner, among them 25 'concertos comiques', some of which are descriptive; many are based on popular tunes of the day. Corrette also composed sacred music: masses, motets, *leçons de ténèbres* and a *Te Deum*. A dedicated teacher, he published an astonishing number of 'methods' which provide interesting information about 18th-century French performance practice; the best known is the violin method, *L'École d'Orphée* (1738), with its illustrated discussion of French and Italian styles.   DA/JAS

Corsaire, Le ('The Corsair'). Overture, op. 21, by Berlioz, based on Byron's poem; it was composed in 1844 and revised some time before 1852. It was first performed with the title *La Tour de Nice*, then as *Le Corsaire rouge* (the French title for Fenimore Cooper's *The Red Rover*).

Corsaro, Il. Opera in three acts by Verdi to a libretto by Francesco Maria Piave after Byron's poem *The Corsair* (1814) (Trieste, 1848).

Corselli, Francesco. See Courcelle, Francesco.

Corsi, Jacopo (*b* Florence, 17 July 1561; *d* Florence, 29 Dec. 1602). Italian patron and prominent supporter of Florentine poets and musicians in the 1590s. He was closely involved in the first operas, composing some of the music for Peri's *Dafne* (1598) and playing the harpsichord in *Euridice* (1600).   TC

Corteccia, (Pier) Francesco (*b* Florence, 27 July 1502; *d* Florence, 7 June 1571). Italian organist and composer. He was a choirboy at S. Giovanni Battista, Florence, and held various posts there until his death. In 1531 he became organist and *maestro di cappella* at S. Lorenzo, the Medici chapel, and in 1540 at the court. In 1539 he composed madrigals and *intermedi* for the wedding celebrations of Cosimo I, Duke of Florence, and Eleonora di Toledo. His liturgical music includes some of the earliest extant Italian Passion settings.   DA

cortège (Fr., 'procession'). A title given to a piece of music suitable for accompanying, or illustrative of, a procession.

Cortot, Alfred (Denis) (*b* Nyon, 26 Sept. 1877; *d* Lausanne, 15 June 1962). French pianist, teacher, and conductor. He studied at the Paris Conservatoire with Chopin's disciple Émile Descombes and with Louis Diémer, winning a first prize in 1896. He worked as a répétiteur at Bayreuth and in 1902 conducted the first Paris performance of *Götterdämmerung*. In 1905 he formed a famous piano trio with Jacques Thibaud and Casals and in 1907 was given a senior class at the Conservatoire which he held until 1923. He was cofounder in 1918 of the École Normale de Musique, where he was insistent on student pianists being well grounded in history and aesthetics. His pupils there and at the Conservatoire numbered many names to become celebrated subsequently, including Vlado Perlemuter, Magda Tagliaferro, Marcelle Meyer, Dinu Lipatti, Samson François, Eric Heidsieck, and Yvonne Lefébure.

Cortot's own repertory was centred on Chopin, Schumann, and Debussy. Later in his career he tended to make errors, but in his prime his technique was stupendous: no one has ever matched the wild fury of his Chopin B♭ minor Prelude. Nor, at the other end of the scale, has anyone approached his imagination and control of touch in 'Der Dichter spricht' from Schumann's *Kinderszenen*. His tone was sonorous and produced without apparent effort—he had no time for players who banged. All in all, he was one of the greatest pianists of his age.   RN

📖 C. TIMBRELL, *French Pianism: A Historical Perspective* (White Plains, NY, and London, 1992, enlarged 2/ 1999) · T. MANSHARDT, *Aspects of Cortot* (Hexham, 1994)

Cosens, Benjamin. See COSYN, BENJAMIN.

Così fan tutte (*Così fan tutte, ossia La scuola degli amanti*; 'All Women Do the Same, or The School for Lovers'). Opera in two acts by Mozart to a libretto by Lorenzo Da Ponte (Vienna, 1790).

Costa, Sir Michael (Andrew Agnus) [Michele Andrea Agniello] (*b* Naples, 4 Feb. 1808; *d* Hove, 29 April 1884). Italian-born British conductor and composer. After studying composition and singing in Italy, in 1829 he went to England, where he made his permanent home. A forceful, even despotic personality, he quickly abolished the common orchestral practice of divided leadership (between presiding pianist and leading violinist) at the King's Theatre (later Her Majesty's), becoming its conductor and director of Italian Opera in 1833. The discipline he instilled by using a baton was widely praised and emulated. He resigned from Her Majesty's in 1846 and went on to found the Royal Italian Opera at Covent Garden (1847–68). He was also conductor of the Philharmonic Society (1846–54), the Sacred Harmonic Society (1848–82), and the grand Triennial Handel Festivals at the Crystal Palace (1847–80), again at Her Majesty's Theatre (1871–81), and of the Birmingham Festival (1849–80), for which he wrote two oratorios, *Eli* (1855) and *Naaman* (1864); like his earlier operas, they were of limited appeal, as Rossini's comment suggests: 'Good old Costa has sent me an oratorio score [*Eli*] and a Stilton cheese; the cheese was very fine.' He was knighted in 1869.   JD1

Costeley, Guillaume (*b* Fontanges, Auvergne, *c*.1530; *d* Évreux, 28 Jan. 1606). French composer. He moved to Paris about 1554, and in 1560 became organist and composer at the French court. He was a member of Baïf's *académie* and played a part in the development of *musique mesurée. His chansons include settings of verse by Ronsard and are composed in a style that allows the words to be clearly heard. He was also one of the first to write *airs de cour* (called 'chansons en façon d'airs'). In 1570 Le Roy & Ballard published nearly all his vocal works in a volume entitled *Musique de Guillaume Costeley*. Costeley was the first president of a society sponsoring masses in honour of St Cecilia at Évreux.

Cosyn [Cosens], **Benjamin** (*b c*.1570; *d* ?London, 1652 or later). English composer. He served as organist at Dulwich College in London from 1622 and at Charterhouse from 1626. His famous manuscript collection of keyboard music (London, British Library, R.M.23.L.4) contains works by Gibbons and Bull as well as by himself.   JM

cotillon [cotillion]. A ballroom dance that originated in France at the beginning of the 18th century and reached Germany a little later; a German publication of 1769 refers to it as a type of country dance. In the 19th century it became more elaborate, often ending an evening's entertainment. Any number of couples followed the movements of the leading couple. The cotillon was not associated with a particular musical style but could be danced to waltzes, mazurkas, polkas, etc.

Cotter, Hans. See KOTTER, HANS.

Coucou, Le. Harpsichord piece (1735) by Daquin.

coulé (Fr.). 1. 'Flowing', i.e. slurred, *legato.
   2. See SLIDE, 2.
   3. An 18th-century term for the *appoggiatura.

Coulthard, Jean (*b* Moncton, NB, 10 Feb. 1908; *d* Vancouver, 9 March 2000). Canadian composer. In 1928 she won a scholarship to study in London: the piano with Kathleen Long, composition with Vaughan Williams, and theory with R. O. Morris. She further studied with Arthur Benjamin in London (1939), with Bernard Wagenaar in New York (1945, 1949), and with Gordon Jacob in London as late as 1965–6. She also submitted her compositions for criticism during lessons with Milhaud (1942), Bartók (1944), and Boulanger (1955). In 1947 she was appointed to the University of British Columbia, Vancouver, where she taught composition and analysis until 1973.

Coulthard was a prolific composer, the final tally of her works reaching 350, in virtually every genre. For the stage there are two ballets (*Excursion*, 1940; *The Devil's Fanfare*, 1958) and a large-scale opera after Hardy, *Return of the Native* (1956–79). Her orchestral output includes three symphonies (1950–1, 1967, 1975) and concertante works for various instruments. There are many piano pieces, choral works, songs, and chamber music. Her idiom was conservative but in her later works she experimented with aleatory passages, clusters, microtones, etc. in textures that are contrapuntal in manner and lyrical in tone.   MA

Council of Trent. A council of the Roman Catholic Church convened by Pope Paul III in 1545 in Trent (then in the South Tyrol, now in northern Italy); it concluded the last of its 25 sessions in 1563. It was an important embodiment of the ideals of the Counter-Reformation, held with the intention of clarifying doctrine and legislating disciplinary reforms within the church. The council's pronouncements on music included rather general condemnations of unintelligible and 'impure' settings. The implementation of its liturgical directives was left to the papacy, which issued uniform editions of the Breviary (1568) and the Missal (1570). Celebration from these volumes, which eliminated most of the tropes and sequences in liturgical use, was compulsory for those not possessing a rite more than 200 years old or otherwise granted a special dispensation. Despite several attempts, a comparable standardization of Roman chant was never achieved. A project undertaken by Palestrina and Annibale Zoilo for Pope Gregory XIII was left incomplete, while the humanistically inspired *Editio medicaea* of Felice Anerio and Francesco Soriano (printed 1614–15) was never imposed throughout the church. (The story that Palestrina 'saved' church music by composing the *Missa Papae Marcelli*, which overwhelmed the cardinals with its beauty, is untrue.)   —/AL1

countermelody. A melodic line, more extended or expansive than a fugal countersubject, which is subordinate to, and combines contrapuntally with, a principal line.

counterpoint 1. Introduction; 2. Early history; 3. Theory; 4. Later history; 5. Post-tonal counterpoint

1. Introduction

Counterpoint is the coherent combination of distinct melodic lines in music, and the quality that best fulfils the aesthetic principle of unity in diversity. Before the 20th century, coherence and unity were achieved in contrapuntal music by adherence to rules of voice-leading predicated on the distinction between *consonance and dissonance, and the need for the latter to resolve on to the former. In post-tonal music, contrapuntal lines may follow principles of symmetry (often mirror symmetry) and complementation, the pitches of one voice not duplicating those of other voices, within the span of a phrase or other structural unit. But for music to be truly contrapuntal there must always be a balance between independence and interdependence, and this is as true of a canon by Webern as of a fugue by Bach.

2. Early history

Counterpoint arises when the natural procedure of two or more voices singing exactly the same melody an octave or some other interval apart is modified, so that the voices are no longer heard in rhythmic unison. For counterpoint to be aesthetically and technically acceptable, however, the differences between the contrapuntal voices must not undermine the perceived coherence of the musical result.

Counterpoint is likely to be most immediately perceptible when the distinct voices use the same material in close proximity. This is the case when a texture is *heterophonic, or when the form is that of *round, *canon, *fugue, or some other genre in which the imitation of a leading voice by others is fundamental. But there is another kind of counterpoint, in which unity in diversity is achieved differently. Here there might be a single, slow-moving line, a *tenor or *cantus firmus, round which other more florid lines are arranged in ways that make it clear to the ear that these lines are decorating or embellishing the framework provided by the principal line (Ex. 1, from the Credo of Dufay's *Missa 'L'Homme armé'*). The chaconnes and passacaglias of the tonal era also acknowledge this principle of decorative counterpoints moving against a recurrent pattern. In such counterpoint, it is all the more important that some governing principle, ensuring that the independent lines still combine to make musical sense, should be apparent to the ear; and for most of the history of music that principle has been subsumed under basic rules of voice-leading which embody perceptions about the distinctions between *intervals that are stable (consonant, or perfect) and those that are unstable (dissonant, imperfect).

3. Theory

Counterpoint came to prominence in music as a means whereby composers could exploit the ability of singers to demonstrate their skills at carrying independent lines in combination. The sacred vocal polyphony of medieval and Renaissance times, culminating in the masses and motets of Palestrina, was a powerful embodiment of the ability of music to reflect the sublimity and intensity of religious belief, and also of the increasing perception that such a sense of ritual depended on a no less intense need for order and control. (Ex. 2, from the Credo of Palestrina's *Missa 'Quando lieta sperai'*, illustrates the balance of independence and interdependence typical of Renaissance counterpoint.) It was therefore natural and right that, as society came to recognize the role of composers as individuals dedicated to the provision of music which served its

purposes in the most efficient and effective manner, the need arose for manuals that identified the ways in which such provision could be guaranteed and offered methods of procedure to aspiring composers, derived where possible from study of the works of well-established masters. Such treatises would usually seek to establish the legitimacy of their subject matter by recounting the history, as it was then known, of the ways in which musical intervals and modes, or scales, had evolved from the time of the Ancient Greeks and early fathers of the church, in order to ground prescriptions for contemporary practice in the most convincing way.

The culmination of this process during the 16th-century High Renaissance was Gioseffo Zarlino's *Le istitutioni harmoniche* (1558), the title of which in English translation, *The Art of Counterpoint* (not 'harmony'), offers a neat confirmation of the ambiguity of basic musical terminology. At the heart of Zarlino's treatise is the attempt to define how 'an artful union of diverse sounds reduced to concordance' could be achieved, and Zarlino's four basic principles not only codified existing practice but set the standards which have remained valid for any composer wishing to remain within the framework of the traditional modal or tonal language.

In brief, these principles require: the subordination of dissonance to consonance, within clearly defined rhythmic and metrical contexts; the creation of an equable balance between difference and similarity of direction and melodic shape in all the independent voices; the use of specific modes to govern the harmonic, vertical relations between voices, and within which the main cadences of a work are placed; and

Ex. 1

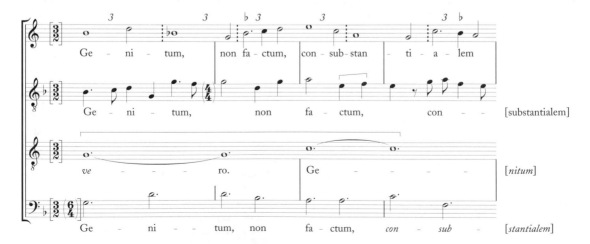

Ex. 2

Ex. 3

control over rhythmic diversity by means of regular successions of strong and weak beats. As is usual with pedagogical prescription encoding existing practice, such strategies were likely to be resisted and rejected by the radicals of the time, and as new vocal genres (opera, cantata) came into being around 1600, and instruments gained new prominence in music of all kinds, laws relevant to purely vocal polyphony might be deemed archaic and irrelevantly restrictive. In fact, Zarlino's

laws were no less adaptable than the modal system itself, and as modality transmuted into tonality, so the laws of vocal counterpoint became relevant to the bass-orientated, chordally conceived harmonic-contrapuntal complexes of the Baroque era, which reached their technical and stylistic fulfilment in the passacaglias and fugues of J. S. Bach. (See Ex. 3, from Bach's great G minor Fugue for organ BWV542.)

It was part and parcel of the intellectual ferment of the 18th century that an element of principled antiquarianism should become increasingly influential over ideas about education and creativity. Johann Joseph Fux's *Gradus ad Parnassum* (1725) is notable for stepping back from any primary concern with contemporary compositional practice, and even though the *a cappella* style of unaccompanied vocal polyphony was still in use in the early 18th century, Fux included no analyses of Handel or Bach in his text. Instead he sought to create an ideal world of basic contrapuntal practice in terms of elementary yet fundamental principles involving mode, cantus firmus, and contrapuntal voices, governed, in the simplest rhythmic and formal contexts, by the laws of voice-leading. Fux's treatise was not a composition manual to the extent that those later theory texts which referred in considerable detail to actual works by composers of the time aspired to be. But the clarity and conviction with which *Gradus ad Parnassum* defined and demonstrated basic contrapuntal practices ensured its long life and immense influence, culminating in Schenker's incorporation of Fuxian principles in his theoretical exposition of 'free composition'.

4. Later history

The forms and procedures of contrapuntal composition survived the development of more chromatic harmonic perspectives and the new generic and textural initiatives of the 19th century. A fugue, or some other multi-voice design, like the extended vocal and orchestral ensemble which ends Act II of Wagner's *Die Meistersinger von Nürnberg*, was still an appropriate way of achieving the composer's aesthetic goals: and the basic musical laws governing tonality—whether conceived primarily as chordal and harmonic, or as contrapuntal—remained in force. Moreover, the 19th century's strong feeling of respect for tradition meant that some of its most powerful products—Beethoven's *Grosse Fuge*, *Bruckner's symphonic developments, *Brahms's many elaborate polyphonic structures—served to reinscribe the virtues of a contrapuntal practice which took legitimacy from the way it built new and even radical structures on recognizably ancient foundations.

5. Post-tonal counterpoint

With the Schoenbergian 'emancipation of the dissonance'—something evident in Debussy, Ives, Skryabin, and other early 20th-century composers as much as in Schoenberg himself—the old Fuxian rules were swept away, and it has often been argued that there has been no more obvious and inept demonstration of the horrors of 'wrong-note composition' than in thoroughgoing post-tonal polyphony, like Webern's Movement for String Trio of 1925 (Ex. 4), or in imitative textures where obvious similarity of melodic shape is cut adrift from the laws of good combination which governed them in tonal times. Such criticism denies to post-tonal music the capacity for suggesting the ebb and flow of tension and release: but the counter-argument is that these qualities can still be achieved, even in the absence of the consonance–dissonance relation and the rhythmic conventions of tonal counterpoint.

In any case, many 20th-century composers of post-tonal music alluded to the contrapuntal strategies of earlier times, from cantus-firmus-based polyphony to canon and fugue, in ways which make determined efforts to free such procedures from the constraints of traditional tonal voice-leading, while not suggesting that the resulting polyphony is merely arbitrary, governed by no elements of aural discrimination. In this respect, 20th-century counterpoint, like that of Peter Maxwell *Davies, has more in common with the pioneering, visionary polyphony of a *Machaut or *Dufay (see Ex. 1) than with the more explicitly integrated procedures which replaced them. The crucial point is that coherence can be achieved even when the constraints in operation are not those of traditional modal or tonal practice.

It nevertheless remains true that we cannot abstract general principles of contrapuntal procedure from Webern or Maxwell Davies which are comparable to

Ex. 4

those deducible from Palestrina or Bach. At the same time, post-tonal composers recognize the value of the kind of rhythmic controls that balance the voices against each other, and they also seek to ensure that the succession of intervals, from both linear and vertical viewpoints, balances similarity and difference while creating a musical atmosphere appropriate to the chosen text. Coherence in Webern is as much to do with equilibrium as it is in Bach, and even though Webern's counterpoint crosses the great divide from something recalling the 'natural' polyphonic practice of singers who start from the absolute authority of perfect intervals (particularly the octave), it can often be perceived in terms of a stable axis of symmetry, which functions as a centre and point of focus for the polyphonic lines that move above and below that centre.

With more experimental kinds of 20th-century composition, like that of Cage, the mutually supportive yet independent lines of traditional counterpoint transmute into the elements of collage or montage in which conjunction is accidental and even arbitrary. To the extent that the listener can still find these unexpected combinations stimulating and attractive, the contrapuntal principle remains positively at work, and only when clashes arise through simultaneities that appear pointless and unpleasant might counterpoint be felt to have been definitively abandoned.   AW

countersubject. See FUGUE.

countertenor. The adult male voice with a range corresponding roughly to that of the female *mezzo-soprano or *contralto. It is usually produced by developing the *falsetto register, though occasionally it is a naturally very high, light tenor. Sometimes the term 'male alto' is used for the latter (see ALTO VOICE), but the terms are usually interchangeable. See also CONTRATENOR.

Count of Luxembourg, The. See GRAF VON LUXEMBURG, DER.

country and western. See COUNTRY MUSIC.

country dance (Fr.: *contredanse*; Ger.: *Kontretanz*; It.: *contradanza*). A dance that originated in English folk tradition but that found its way into more refined circles by the 16th and 17th centuries. John Playford's *The English Dancing Master* (1651) was the first published collection of such dances, using folk and popular tunes and a variety of steps. The music was in binary form, with repeats, and generally in 2/4 or 6/8 time; a set figure was danced to it nine times. In France, where it was very popular, the *contredanse* became increasingly formalized during the 18th century, giving rise to *contredanse* suites by several composers including Mozart, Haydn, and Beethoven. The dance survived into the 19th century, when it gave way to the waltz, polka, and quadrille, though the Sir Roger de Coverley remained popular in England as the traditional way to finish an evening. Other country dances survived only in folk tradition but were revived in the 20th century through the efforts of such bodies as the English Folk Dance and Song Society.   —/JH

Country Gardens. English country-dance tune. It first appeared in print in *The Quaker's Opera* (1728) and became well known through the orchestral piece *Country Gardens* by Grainger, who also arranged it for piano solo, piano duet, and two pianos (four hands or eight hands).

country music [country and western]. An American style of popular music, the origins of which lay in the folksong brought by early settlers from the British Isles. Derived from the folk music of the isolated Appalachian regions, it has been transformed into a multimillion dollar industry by radio broadcasting. The most important early radio show was the *Grand Ole Opry*, based in Nashville, Tennessee, from 1926, which produced arguably the first ever pop star, Jimmie Rodgers (1897–1933). For a time the folk idiom was lost in a welter of commercial imitations but gradually the 'hillbilly' craze was eased aside by a more folk-based country and western idiom that combined authenticity and popularity. This included the music from the Blue Mountains of Virginia, given the label 'bluegrass' when popularized by Bill Monroe (1911–96).

The style is still centred on Nashville and has continued to produce performers who achieve cult status, including the Carter Family, Roy Acuff (1908–92), Hank Williams (1923–53), Patsy Cline (1932–63), Johnny Cash (*b* 1932), Tammy Wynette (1942–98), and Dolly Parton (*b* 1946).   PGa

   📖 B. McCLOUD and others, *Definitive Country: The Ultimate Encyclopedia of Country Music and its Performers* (New York, 1995)

coup d'archet (Fr.). 'Bowstroke', 'bowing'. The orchestra of the Parisian Concert Spirituel was famous for its strong, unanimous attack at the beginning of a piece, known as the *premier coup d'archet*; however, Mozart saw nothing very new about it, remarking in a letter to his father, 'These oxen here make such a to-do about it! What the devil! I can see no difference—they merely begin together—much as they do elsewhere.'

coup de glotte (Fr.). See VOICE, 3.

coupé (Fr., 'cut'). See PAS, 2.

Couperin. French family of musicians. It included two first-rate composers and several excellent performers. The family can be traced back to the 16th century, but of particular interest were three brothers born at Chaumes-en-Brie to the organist Charles Couperin (i) (*c*.1595–1654).

The eldest, **Louis Couperin** (*b c*.1626; *d* Paris, 29 Aug. 1661), was a composer, viol player, and among the most skilled keyboard players of his day. According to Titon du Tillet (1732), in about 1650 Louis and his brothers serenaded Chambonnières, who invited them to travel to Paris where they might seek their fortunes. With introductions from Chambonnières, Louis became organist of St Gervais (a post the Couperins held for the next 175 years) and a treble viol player at the court in 1653. None of his works were published; the surviving music is restricted to three manuscripts containing music of astonishing quality and breadth: *pièces de clavecin* (including a dozen unmeasured preludes and even more chaconnes and *passacailles*), organ music (including 33 fugues), and fantasies for two viols, for shawm band, and for five-part strings. His keyboard music shows the influence of Chambonnières, but he also knew Froberger, who was in Paris in 1651–2 and by whom he may well have been introduced to Italian music.

The second brother, **François Couperin** (i) (*b c*.1631; *d* Paris, 1708–12), achieved much less after his arrival in Paris. His daughter **Marguerite-Louise** (*b* 1675–6 or 1678–9; *d* 30 May 1728) was an excellent singer and harpsichordist, according to Titon du Tillet. She became an *ordinaire de la musique de la chambre* in 1702, performing at Versailles with her cousin François Couperin (ii). The youngest brother, **Charles Couperin** [*le jeune*] (*b* 9 April 1638; *d* Paris, 1679), became organist of St Gervais on Louis's death. By 1679 he had also become an *officier* in the service of the Duchess of Orléans. No music by him survives. His main claim to fame is that he was the father of the most illustrious member of the family.

Musically precocious, **François Couperin** (ii) [*le grand*] (*b* Paris, 10 Nov. 1668; *d* Paris, 11 Sept. 1733) was at the age of ten promised the post of organist at St Gervais on his father's death (Lalande assumed the day-to-day duties until the young Couperin came of age). He obtained permission to publish two organ masses in 1690 (though he had insufficient money to complete the project) and in 1693 he was appointed an *organiste du roi*. At much the same time, he experimented clandestinely with composing trio sonatas (seen as an Italian genre), a number of which he published only in the 1720s. Meanwhile—long before any of his music appeared in print—he was ennobled (1696) and, in 1702, made Chevalier de l'Ordre de Latran.

Over the next years Couperin published small-scale church music originally composed for the private worship of the king: three collections each, all for solo voices, of *versets* (1703–5) and of *Leçons de ténèbres* (1713–17). The mixture of Italian and French styles results in a delicate sensuousness quite unlike anything else in the history of church music. Couperin also composed chamber music for the Sunday concerts at which Madame de Maintenon was host, including *Concerts royaux* and two masterly suites for bass viol.

In 1713 Couperin began publishing his secular music with a view to capitalizing on his legacy. First came the first of four books of *pieces* [*pièces*] *de clavecin*, grouped in *ordres*, or suites (none of the books uses the modern orthography *pièces*). Most of their movements are in dance rhythms, a fact disguised by their highly ornamented melodies and equally complex accompaniments, many of which adapt the 'broken' figuration of lute playing to the keyboard (a technique that came to be known as *style brisé*). The movements are given titles: some have a programmatic purpose while others are musical portraits, their subjects now long forgotten. Well mannered, rarely passionate, yet keenly felt, Couperin's keyboard music truly merits the description **'rococo'*, and comparisons with Watteau's paintings are apt.

Alongside the second book in 1716 came his keyboard treatise, *L'Art de toucher le clavecin*, reflecting his experience as a performer and teacher; of particular significance is his discussion of ornamentation. With the third book in 1722 he published the *Concerts royaux* (for instruments and/or harpsichord), inaugurating an important series of chamber music publications charting Couperin's assimilation of Italian elements into a new, more cosmopolitan French style: *Les Goûts-réunis, ou Nouveaux concerts* (1724), *Le Parnasse, ou L'Apothéose de Corelli* (1724), *Concert instrumental sous le titre d'Apothéose composé à la mémoire immortelle de l'incomparable Monsieur de Lully* (1725), and *Les Nations* (1726). The fourth book of harpsichord *ordres* appeared in 1730, as did the two suites of *pieces* [*sic*] *de violes*.

In later years Couperin suffered ill health. His second daughter, **Marguerite-Antoinette** (*b* Paris, 19 Sept. 1705; *d c*.1778), succeeded him at court, becoming the first woman *ordinaire de la chambre pour le clavecin*. The organ post at St Gervais was taken over by his cousin **Nicolas** (*b* Paris, 20 Dec. 1680; *d* Paris, 25 July 1748), to whom was entrusted the publication of the remaining manuscript works by Couperin *le grand*—a task in which he failed. Nicolas's son **Armand-Louis** (*b* Paris, 25 Feb. 1727; *d* Paris, 2 Feb. 1789) succeeded to the post at St Gervais in 1748. The composer of harpsichord pieces, *cantatilles*, and motets, he died after being knocked down by a horse, leaving two sons: **Pierre-Louis** (*b* 14 March 1755; *d* Paris, 10 Oct. 1789) and **Gervais-François** (*b* Paris, 22 May 1759; *d* 10 Oct. 1826), the last Couperin to be organist at St Gervais. DA/JAS

📖 D. TUNLEY, *Couperin* (London, 1982) · W. MELLERS, *François Couperin and the French Classical Tradition* (London, 2/1987) · J. CLARK, *François Couperin: Pièces de clavecin: The Background* (Oxford, 1992)

coupler. On an organ or harpsichord, a mechanism which connects one department or manual to another, allowing notes to sound simultaneously on more than one pipe or string when keys are depressed. A greater range of tone-quality and volume is thus made possible; couplers are therefore an important element in *registration.

couplet. 1 (Fr.). A term used to describe the stanza of a poem (not necessarily two rhyming lines). In 17th-century *rondeaux, the term was used for the various sections which are connected by a repeated refrain. It is often found in the keyboard pieces of François Couperin.

2 (Fr.). In 18th- and 19th-century light opera, a *couplet* is a strophic song of a humorous character. There are many examples in Offenbach's operettas.

3. A term for *duplet.

4. The 'two-note slur', i.e. two notes of equal value slurred together. The second note is often slightly shortened to accentuate the phrasing.

courante (Fr., 'running'; It.: *corrente, coranto*) [corant]. A dance type that first appeared in 16th-century French sources. Its popularity lasted until the mid-18th century, and as an instrumental form it was one of the standard movements of the Baroque *suite. According to Arbeau (*Orchésographie*, 1588), it involved jumping movements and largely improvised figuration, but Thomas Morley (*A Plaine and Easie Introduction*, 1597) said it was a 'running' dance.

In the 17th century the dance took two distinct national forms: the Italian *corrente*, and the French courante. The Italian version was a fast, lively dance in triple metre (3/4 or 3/8), in binary form, basically homophonic in style, and moving continuously in short note-values, especially in the upper part. It was a courtship dance, involving a combination of hops and steps. Several pieces called 'coranto' appear in the Fitzwilliam Virginal Book, mostly anonymously, and in 3/4 or 6/8 time. There are also *correnti* in such German and Italian sources as Praetorius's *Terpsichore* (1612), Schein's *Banchetto musicale* (1617), Scheidt's *Tabulatura nova* (1624), and Frescobaldi's *Il secondo libro di toccate*

. . . correnti, et altre partite (1627). Later examples are found in Italian violin music, for instance the sonatas of Corelli and Vivaldi.

The French courante was more elegant and stately than its Italian counterpart. It also consisted of two repeated halves in triple time (usually 3/2), but the pace was much slower (it was described as the slowest of all the court dances) and there was greater rhythmic variety than in the evenly flowing *corrente*. Typical features of the courante were the use of hemiola, especially at cadence points, and a contrapuntal and imitative texture. Courantes first appeared in the works of early 17th-century French lutenists, and were often found in *ballets de cour*. Lully, surprisingly, made little use of the dance—only five examples occur in his works—but during the reign of Louis XIV it was the most important courtly dance, with the king himself often performing the opening courante at balls.

The courante (in one form or the other) became a standard component of the *suite, generally placed between the allemande (to which it was often thematically related) and the sarabande. Handel's courantes, though they bear the French title, are more like *correnti*: they are usually found after the opening allemande. Bach used both types: in the original edition of the keyboard partitas, he clearly differentiated between the two, but later editors tended to call them all 'courantes'. WT/JBE

📖 W. HILTON, 'A dance for kings: The 17th-century French *courante*', *Early Music*, 5 (1977), 160–72

Courcelle [Corselli, Corcelli], **Francesco** [Francisco] (*b* Piacenza, 19 April 1705; *d* Madrid, 3 April 1778). Italian composer and conductor, of French extraction. His first significant appointment was as *maestro di cappella* to the Duke of Parma (later Charles III of Spain), 1727–33. He spent the rest of his career in Spain, initially as music master to the royal children in Madrid (from 1734), then for 40 years from 1737 as *maestro de capilla* of the royal chapel and rector of the choir school. He soon established a formidable reputation as a composer of opera and sacred music. Unlike his Italian contemporaries in Spain, he produced almost exclusively Italian *drammi per musica* (mostly on librettos by Metastasio), thus paving the way for the flourishing of Italian opera during the reign of Ferdinand VI.

Although many of Courcelle's operas are now lost, the most popular, *Farnace* (1739), is extant and displays a lively dramatic sense, a fondness for chromaticism, and wide-ranging vocal writing. Courcelle's dramatic proclivities are also evident in his more than 400 sacred works. Although fugal textures predominate in many movements of his almost 30 masses (written for adult male voices), elsewhere in his later church music he displays the rhythmic vitality, periodic melodic writing, and attention to orchestral colour characteristic of the developing Classical style. MHe

course. A rank of strings on a plucked instrument. A 12-string guitar, which has six paired ranks of strings, would be described as having six double courses. A four-course mandolin sometimes has triple courses, and a 13-course archlute might have six stopped double courses and eight long, unstopped single diapasons. Modern pianos are strung with single courses in the bass range, double courses in the tenor, and triple courses in the treble.

Courtois, Jean (*fl* 1516–40; *d* before 1568). ?Franco-Flemish composer. He is known for his masses, motets, and witty chansons. He was *petit vicaire* at Cambrai in 1516–17 and 1534–5, and his four-part motet *Venite populi terrae* was performed at Cambrai Cathedral in 1540, during his tenure as director of music, to welcome Charles V on a visit to Cambrai. DA

Covent Garden. London *opera house, opened in 1732.

cover version. A recording of a popular song by a performer or performers other than those responsible for the original version; it can be a re-creation of the original or a radical reworking. Cover versions can direct a song towards a new audience: for example, in the 1960s Eric Clapton presented as rock music blues songs which had originally been recorded by black rural blues singers in the 1920s. KG

Coward, Sir Noël (Peirce) (*b* Teddington, 16 Dec. 1899; *d* Port Maria, Jamaica, 26 March 1973). English songwriter. Although he came from a naturally musical family he had little formal musical training, but he pursued a dazzling career as an actor, playwright, and composer. His songs include *I'll see you again*, *Some day I'll find you*, and *Mad Dogs and Englishmen*. He reached his peak in the shows *Bitter-Sweet* (1929), *Words and Music* (1932), and *Conversation Piece* (1934). He was knighted in 1970. PGa/ALa

cowbells. Bells hung from the necks of domestic animals of all kinds worldwide, both to aid location and for magical protection against evil. They are commonly forged from folded sheet iron, though in Africa they are often carved from wood, in South-East Asia they may be of bamboo or wood, in Switzerland cast bronze, and in other areas cast brass. Composers including Mahler and Webern have scored cowbells, but their commonest musical use is as part of the *drum kit. See also BELL, 1. JMo

Cowell, Henry (Dixon) (*b* Menlo Park, CA, 11 March 1897; *d* Shady, NY, 10 Dec. 1965). American composer. He spent his boyhood near San Francisco and in the Midwest, being exposed to traditional music, American and Asian, which permanently influenced him. On the day after his 15th birthday he gave his first performance as a composer-pianist, in San Francisco, his programme including *The Tides of Manaunaun* (1912), in which he introduced 'clusters' of notes to be played with the fist, palm, or forearm. Later he used the inside of the piano in such pieces as *The Banshee* (1925), which is played throughout on the strings. These and other works formed the repertory for his concert tours of Europe and America during the 1920s and 30s.

After the publication of his influential book *New Musical Resources* (1930; reprinted with commentary by David Nicholls, Cambridge, 1996) Cowell did not stop experimenting. He introduced 'elastic' forms in works like the String Quartet no. 3, 'Mosaic' (1935), requiring the performers to assemble given fragments in any order. He devised a machine, the rhythmicon, for realizing the complex rhythms he was demanding in his music. And his prodigious output of orchestral music, including 20 symphonies, shows his wide interests in musical cultures: there are, for example, works with solo parts for Persian, Indian, and Japanese instruments, as well as a set of 18 *Hymns and Fuguing Tunes* relating to American traditions. Cowell also had a significant effect on American musical life as propagandist and teacher. His New Music Edition published works by Ives, Schoenberg, and others, while his composition pupils included musicians as diverse as Gershwin and Cage. PG

📖 W. LICHTENWANGER, *The Music of Henry Cowell: A Descriptive Catalog* (New York, 1986)

Cowen, Sir Frederic (Hymen) (*b* Kingston, Jamaica, 29 Jan. 1852; *d* London, 6 Oct. 1935). English composer, conductor, and pianist. A child prodigy pianist and composer, he had a piano trio performed professionally in 1865. After studying in Germany he launched himself in England in 1869 with a symphony and a piano concerto. His extensive compositional output includes an opera *Signa* (1894), six symphonies (of which no. 3, the 'Scandinavian', was most successful), incidental, choral, and chamber music, and some 300 songs. His conductorships included those of the Philharmonic Society and the Hallé, Liverpool Philharmonic, and Scottish orchestras. He was knighted in 1911. ALa

cowhorn. A bovine horn with the tip removed for blowing. Brass imitations have been made for Wagner, and for Britten's *Spring Symphony*.

Cozzolani, Chiara Margarita (*b* Milan, 27 Nov. 1602; *d* Milan, 1676 or 1678). Italian composer and singer. A Benedictine nun from 1619, she helped make S. Radegonda, Milan, one of the principal musical attractions of the city, which later gave cause for ecclesiastical complaint. She was also an accomplished composer, and, unusually, she published four volumes of sacred and spiritual pieces (1640–50) dedicated to prominent patrons. Her works are remarkable not just for their expressive power but also for her seemingly wide knowledge of the contemporary musical scene.

TC

crab canon. See CANON.

cracovienne (Fr.). See KRAKOWIAK.

cradle-song. See BERCEUSE.

Cramer (i). German family of musicians of Silesian descent who settled in England. **Wilhelm Cramer** (*b* Mannheim, *bapt.* 2 June 1746; *d* London, 5 Oct. 1799) was a violinist in the Mannheim orchestra. After working in Stuttgart (for the Duke of Württemberg) and Paris, in 1772 he went to London, where, encouraged by J. C. Bach, he settled. He was chamber musician to the king and leader of several important orchestras, including those of the Ancient Concerts and Professional Concerts.

His eldest son, **Johann Baptist Cramer** (*b* Mannheim, 24 Feb. 1771; *d* London, 16 April 1858), was a composer, pianist, and publisher. He was a piano pupil first of J. D. Benser and later of J. S. Schroeter, before completing his studies with Clementi (1783–4); from 1785 he also learnt theory from C. F. Abel. He made his formal debut on 5 April 1781, having attracted attention as a child virtuoso. In 1788 he embarked on the first of several continental tours (others followed in 1799 and 1816), performing in France, Germany, Austria, and the Netherlands, and meeting such composers as Hummel, Weber, Cherubini, and Beethoven, who greatly admired him. In later years he came to know Moscheles, Mendelssohn, Liszt, and Berlioz. In London he was a celebrated pianist—known to his admirers as 'Glorious John'—and championed the work of Bach, Mozart, and Beethoven. He was a founder member of the Philharmonic Society in 1813 and was appointed to the board of the newly created Royal Academy of Music in 1822. He retired officially in 1835, after which he continued to travel abroad, spending some time in Paris. He returned to England in 1845.

Cramer was a hugely prolific composer. He produced no fewer than 124 piano sonatas, nine piano concertos (which compare interestingly with those of Clementi, Griffin, Dussek, and Field, his London contemporar-

ies), and a celebrated set of 84 studies, *Studio per il pianoforte*, in two books (1804, 1810), used by Beethoven and Schumann. Cramer was also involved in various publishing activities, founding the firm J. B. Cramer & Co. (which also manufactured pianos) in 1824; see CRAMER (ii). His brother, **Franz Cramer** (*b* Schwetzingen, nr Mannheim, 1772; *d* London, 1 Aug. 1848), was Master of the King's Music from 1837 until his death.

DA/JD1

Cramer (ii). English firm of music publishers and piano manufacturers. Founded in 1824 by the pianist and composer J. B. Cramer (see CRAMER (i)), Robert Addison, and Thomas Beale, the firm (known as Cramer, Addison & Beale) first concentrated on publishing piano music. The acquisition of many of the plates of the Royal Harmonic Institution—works by Beethoven, Haydn, Dussek, Clementi, and others—strengthened its catalogue. After various reorganizations and changes of name, it turned to making pianos while continuing its publishing activities by issuing Italian songs and duets and English operas. Like Chappell and Boosey, the firm published and promoted ballads through concerts. In 1964 it sold the piano business and concentrated on the publication of choral, piano, organ, and educational music. In 1992 the firm became an independent company again, trading as Cramer Music Limited and broadening its activities.

HA

Crawford Seeger, Ruth (Porter) (*b* East Liverpool, OH, 3 July 1901; *d* Chevy Chase, MD, 18 Nov. 1953). American composer. She studied in Jacksonville, in Chicago, and in New York with Charles Seeger, whom she married in 1931, after a year in Berlin and Paris. Her few works, of which the most important date from the period 1930–2, show a delight in adventure and abstract pattern-making: her String Quartet of 1931 has numerical and serial systems applied to duration as well as pitch. In later years she and her husband, as socialists, devoted themselves to collecting, arranging, and publishing American folk music.

PG

📖 J. N. STRAUS, *The Music of Ruth Crawford Seeger* (Cambridge, MA, 1995)

Creation, The (*Die Schöpfung*). Oratorio (1796–8) by Haydn, for soprano, tenor, and bass soloists, chorus, and orchestra, to a text by Gottfried van Swieten after a poem by an unknown English author ('Mr Lidley', possibly Thomas Linley) based on John Milton's *Paradise Lost*.

Création du monde, La ('The Creation of the World'). Ballet in one act by Milhaud to a scenario by Blaise Cendrars; it was choreographed by Jean Börlin (Paris, 1923).

'Creation' Mass (*Schöpfungsmesse*). Haydn's Mass no. 13 in B♭ major (1801), so called because there is a quotation from his oratorio *The Creation* in the 'Qui tollis'.

Creatures of Prometheus, The. See GESCHÖPFE DES PROMETHEUS, DIE.

Crecquillon, Thomas (*b* c.1480–c.1500; *d* ?1557). Franco-Flemish composer. He was in the service of Emperor Charles V in the 1540s and early 1550s, and from 1555 held a canonicate at Béthune. Although an excellent and prolific composer of church music, especially of highly expressive motets, he is now best known for his witty and elegant chansons. His works were known (and frequently arranged) throughout Europe for many years after his death.   DA

Credo (Lat., 'I believe'). Part of the Ordinary of the Roman *Mass, sung between the gospel and the offertory. The Nicene version is the one usually said at this service; the shorter 'Apostles' Creed' is sometimes recited at the *Divine Office (see CREED).

creed (from Lat. *credo*, 'I believe'). A confession of the Christian faith. Originating as declarations of belief recited by candidates for baptism, creeds were later issued as conciliar statements. The most important example is the Nicene–Constantinopolitan Creed (381), which was adopted for recitation during the Eucharist at Antioch (473) and Constantinople (6th century). Its decisive introduction as an ordinary chant of the Western Mass occurred in 798, when Carolingian reformers mandated its performance with a still controversial addition (the 'filioque') affirming the double procession of the Holy Spirit. Two other ancient confessions used by Western Christians, the so-called Apostles' and Athanasian Creeds, are of little musical significance.   —/ALɪ

Creole music. See ZYDECO.

crescendo (It.). 'Growing', 'increasing', i.e. gradually getting louder. The term is often represented by the 'hairpin' sign (see DYNAMIC MARKS, Table 1) or by the abbreviation *cresc.* The opposite is *decrescendo*.

Cresswell, Lyell (*b* Wellington, 13 Oct. 1944). New Zealand composer. The vividness and passion of his music may reflect his Salvation Army upbringing, though Xenakis provides another point of comparison. After studies in Wellington, Toronto, Aberdeen, and Utrecht, he taught at Glasgow and Edinburgh universities, settling in 1980 in Edinburgh. He has concentrated mostly on electronic, instrumental, and orchestral music, his works in the last category including *O!* (1982) for the Salvation Army centenary and concertos for cello (1984) and accordion (*Dragspil*,

1994–5); he has also written large-scale vocal works, among them *A Modern Ecstasy* for mezzo-soprano, baritone, and orchestra (1986).   PG

cries. See STREET MUSIC.

Cristo, Pedro de (*b* Coimbra, c.1550; *d* Coimbra, 16 Dec. 1618). Portuguese composer. In 1571 he took his vows at the monastery of Santa Cruz in Coimbra, where he later became *mestre de capela*. At times he held the equivalent post at the monastery of S. Vicente de Fora in Lisbon. He played the harp, flute, and dulcian, as well as keyboard instruments. His numerous works—many preserved in autograph copies—are mainly for four or five voices in a concise style, with frequent use of sequence, and some rhythmically animated declamation of text.   OR

Cristofori, Bartolomeo (*b* Padua, 4 May 1655; *d* Florence, 27 Jan. 1732). Italian keyboard instrument maker. He served at the Medici court in Florence from 1690. He experimented with harpsichord construction and in 1700 created an instrument in which the strings were hit with hammers rather than plucked—a forerunner of the piano (see PIANOFORTE). He refined this method and produced several pianos of which three dating from the 1720s survive.   AL

📖 H. HENKEL, 'Bartolomeo Cristofori as harpsichord maker', *The Historical Harpsichord*, 3, ed. H. Schott (Stuyvesant, NY, 1992), 1–58

critical editions. See EDITIONS, HISTORICAL AND CRITICAL; see also EDITING.

criticism of music. Broadly speaking, criticism of music is the intellectual activity of formulating judgments on the value and degree of excellence of individual works of music, or whole groups or genres. Because music exists not only in performance but also in written (or printed) form, music criticism covers several related fields of activity: evaluation of the achievement of individual composers, critical commentary and analysis of works in scores, appraisal of newly created works, accounts of public performances and of recordings in electronic form. Although the existence of several or all of these fields may be tacitly accepted by many, it has become a popular convention to understand 'music criticism' to mean only one of the above activities—'reviews of concerts published in the daily press'—and a 'music critic' is often understood to be a kind of journalist.

    The reasons for thus unjustly narrowing the field are to be found in the nature of music. Since it is a non-conceptual art in which the organization of the material (i.e. the sound) follows an intricate internal logic, the description of this logic is hard to achieve in terms of conceptual language. An adequate process of 'translation' has never been satisfactorily formulated; whenever it is attempted it tends to contain a great deal of technical discussion which makes it accessible only to a relatively narrow reading public. An easy solution has often been sought in the description of the most obvious elements of the composition or in the description of its impact on the emotions and the imagination of the listener.

Criticism is often mentioned in the same breath as *aesthetics, and indeed in the early stages of Western thought in ancient Greece it is difficult to distinguish between one and the other. However, a useful practical distinction is that aesthetic theory is concerned with general speculation on the nature of art or an art form, whereas criticism applies some of the ideas established in aesthetics to individual works. Another important distinction is that the concept of value does not necessarily figure prominently in aesthetic investigation, whereas it occupies an important position in critical judgment.

1. The early history of music criticism; 2. The 19th century; 3. The 20th century: divisions and schools; 4. The role of critics and criticism

1. The early history of music criticism

The earliest instances of music criticism are no more than isolated passages from longer works, often voicing censure or disapproving comments. Thus Plato, in the *Laws*, condemned the naturalistic imitations produced by the players of the aulos, while the early 14th-century theorist Johannes de Muris objected to the new style of motet composition. In the 15th century Johannes Tinctoris praised, among others, Dufay, Dunstaple, Binchois, and Ockeghem, and in the following century Heinrich Glarean (*Dodecachordon*, 1547) paid attention to many individual works of the past, not only discussing their technical features, but often praising in non-technical language those of which he approved.

At the turn of the 17th century stylistic innovations provoked intense controversy and caused many composers to defend their style by the written word (e.g. prefaces to Caccini's *Le nuove musiche*, 1602; Monteverdi's fifth book of madrigals, 1605, and *Madrigali guerrieri et amorosi*, 1638). This pattern, of composers accepting the dual role of creator and polemicist, has persisted to our own day.

In the 18th century music came to be seen as an art form with social implications and not just a technical skill for the initiated. As the opera in Paris was the centre of musical life in France, most of the polemical activity—particularly by the Encyclopedists—

developed round it (see BOUFFONS, QUERELLE DES; FRANCE, 4; OPERA, 6). Various opinions on the merits of Italian and French styles (the so-called Querelle des *Bouffons) came from the pens of the men of letters of the time, some of whom possessed little musical knowledge and regarded opera as a social rather than an artistic phenomenon. In Germany a new genre of dedicated music periodicals emerged as the preferred medium for critical opinion. England had neither the periodicals of Germany nor the powerful focus of musical life of France, and critical writings were either the work of dedicated practitioners, such as Charles Avison's *Essay on Musical Expression* (1752), or of polymaths like Burney and Hawkins who set themselves the task of writing comprehensive histories of music.

2. The 19th century

Germany's tradition of music periodicals continued; soon after its foundation in 1834, Schumann's *Neue Zeitschrift für Musik* established itself as one of the most influential vehicles for musical opinion. The *Revue musicale*, founded in 1827, was in 1834 combined with the *Gazette musicale de Paris* to form the *Revue et gazette musicale de Paris*. The English periodicals that survived more than a few issues included *The Quarterly Musical Magazine* (1818–28), *The Harmonicon* (1823–33), and *The Musical World* (1836–91). They were followed in 1844 by a periodical which, after several changes of name, is still flourishing as *The Musical Times*.

The magazines published essays which remain an important part of the cultural history of the 19th century, while many daily papers offered regular columns to contributors whose task it was to describe the concerts as social events and to evaluate the performance of music. One distinguished representative of newspaper criticism, Eduard Hanslick, battled throughout the second half of the 19th century in the Viennese press against the Romantic notion of music as a vehicle for the transmission of hidden poetic or extra-musical content. His criticism, although at times over-harsh, nevertheless shows a profound musical intelligence and a sharp wit. The latter quality, as well as often strong, even abusive, language characterizes the music criticism of Bernard Shaw, who wrote regular reviews during the period 1888–94.

Throughout the century an especially important contribution to criticism was made by composers, Schumann, Liszt, Berlioz, and Wagner particularly distinguishing themselves in these dual roles. In Bohemia, Russia, and Hungary several composers were active as critics and propagandists for a national style in music (Smetana in Prague, Cui and Serov in St Petersburg, Tchaikovsky in Moscow, and Mihály Mosonyi in Budapest).

The discipline of *musicology, which came into existence at about this time, was not simply a history of music under a different name, but an intellectual activity concerned with a complex set of subjects ranging from acoustics to aesthetics. Musicological criticism was distinct from the activity of instructing the layman in the art of enjoying music and gained it a depth of learning which newspaper criticism by its very nature could not have. Carl von Winterfeld's study of Giovanni Gabrieli (1834) opened a new vista to the public whose knowledge of music did not stretch back beyond some works of Bach and Handel. Important studies were written on Mozart by Otto Jahn (1856), on Beethoven by Wilhelm von Lenz (1855–60) and A. W. Thayer (1866–79), and on Bach by Philipp Spitta (1873–80). Friedrich Chrysander and especially Spitta were pioneers in the tiresome but valuable process of establishing a correct musical text in which the conventions of the past were to be explained to the modern performer. A. B. Marx (?1795–1866) and Hugo Riemann (1849–1919) achieved an encyclopedic breadth combining historical and theoretical studies with criticism.

3. The 20th century: divisions and schools

Innovations in the musical language of the 20th century caused a profound division in the ranks of the critics. In the 1920s and 30s some established and respected critics found themselves unable to accept the increasing demand on listening capacity and concentration required by the music of Stravinsky, Schoenberg, Hindemith, and Bartók, and the papers for which they wrote became vehicles for decidedly conservative criticism, claiming to be the expression of true public opinion. The more enlightened among them often had to retreat into the territory of magazines specially created to advance the cause of new music (such as *Musikblätter des Anbruch*, published in Vienna, 1919–37).

A number of critics have made significant contributions both as newspaper reviewers and as authors of lasting critical studies. Notable examples have been Ernest Newman, Alfred Einstein, Roman Vlad, Massimo Mila, and Adolfo Salazar. For some of them criticism was a practical application of philosophical and aesthetic theory. Thus Henri Bergson's speculations on the nature of time and consciousness produced an echo in the work of several French critics, Benedetto Croce's ideas about intuition and expression influenced the writing of Massimo Mila, whereas the ideas of Theodor W. Adorno were shaped on the rich foundations of German philosophy including the thought of Hegel, Marx, and Nietzsche. Initially, critics in the English-speaking world showed little or no interest in the link between aesthetic theory and criticism, preferring a more pragmatic approach. The situation

changed in the second half of the 20th century with the activity of, among others, Deryck Cooke in England and Joseph Kerman and Charles Rosen in the USA.

4. The role of critics and criticism

The increasing complexity of new music, with rapid changes in stylistic orientation, have made the critics' tasks more difficult, and the nature of criticism and reviewing more complex, but essentially not different from that of their predecessors, some of whom also witnessed profound stylistic changes in their time. There has been an increased tendency for the critics to specialize in their coverage of separate fields such as early music, opera, or avant-garde music. However, the essence of their task remained unchanged. Critics, whether writing reviews for newspapers, essays, or extended critical works, have to be aware of their complex role as mediators between the composer or performer and the public. Reviewing, if it is only a description of obvious outward features of a composition or mere reporting of 'what it was like to be there', will remain shallow unless the critic's arguments are based on a consistently upheld set of musical criteria and an understanding of music as a social force rather than a pleasant social custom or pastime. Absence of such understanding led in the past to the intensely emotionalist approach which set the vague notion of 'feeling' as an arbiter. This does not mean that a critic must be detached and cool. His or her objectivity is limited, which is in itself no failing, but the critic's understanding of implications must be thorough.

After all this a sceptic may conclude that music criticism is not possible. It is truer to say that, although there is no scientific objectivity in music criticism, the act of translating from a musical to a verbal mode of thinking ought to be, for both the critic and his reader, an experience almost as profound and vital as the experience of the music itself, and the best music criticism reveals this clearly. In other words, the critic should be an artist in his or her own right.   BB

Croatia. A republic in the western part of the Balkan Peninsula, a successor state to Yugoslavia. In the past, Hungary, Austria, Venice, and Turkey all sought to establish their supremacy in this part of the world and the area lacked stable sources of patronage. Periods of lively musical activity were interspersed with periods of stagnation. In the Middle Ages monasteries and churches along the Adriatic coast were the main musical centres. The medieval tradition of plainchant sung in the vernacular church Slavonic, known as the Glagolitic chant, survives in certain coastal locations. The ideas of Italian humanism were evident in 16th-century Dalmatia, resulting in a rich flowering of architecture, painting, and Croat literature. In the late 16th century Dubrovnik attracted Lambert Courtois (*fl* 1542–83) and other members of his family. Giulio Schiavetto, composer of some fine five- and six-part motets, was active in the service of the Bishop of Šibenik. In the late 16th and the early 17th centuries the cathedral churches of Split and Hvar fostered an active local school of composers (Ivan Lukačić, ?1587–1648; Tomaso Cecchino, c.1582–1644; Marcantonio Romano, c.1552–1636), whose music reflected the characteristics of early monody and the Venetian style of the time. Paskoj Primović's 1617 translation of Rinuccini's *Euridice* is probably the earliest translation into any language of an Italian opera libretto. Luka Sorkočević (1734–89) wrote symphonies in an Italianate manner.

In the 19th century most of the musical activity was centred on Zagreb. The first Croatian national opera, Vatroslav Lisinski's *Ljubav i zloba* ('Love and Malice'), was produced in 1846, though operatic life was dominated by visiting Italian companies until 1870, when the opera of the Croatian National Theatre was formed. Under the directorship of Ivan Zajc (1832–1914), himself a prolific opera composer, its repertory included nearly all the major works soon after their premieres in the big European opera houses. The singing class at the Music School of the Croatian Musical Institute (still extant, originally founded as the Musikverein in 1827, later acting as the founder of the Academy of Music) and the Opera produced a number of excellent singers, among whom Milka Ternina, Zinka Milanov, and Sena Jurinac achieved world fame.

The advent of modernism was somewhat delayed but Josip Stolzer-Slavenski (1896–1955) came closest to the style and outlook of Bartók, combining a feeling for the Balkan folk tradition with an awareness of the avant-garde spirit of the time. In the second half of the century Ivo Malec (*b* 1925) and Milko Kelemen (*b* 1924) established an international reputation. The Zagreb Biennale of Contemporary Music, founded by Kelemen in 1961, is an important focus for younger composers. At the start of the 21st century, Croatian music reflects all the major stylistic tendencies of European music.   BB

Croce, Giovanni (*b* Chioggia, nr Venice, c.1557; *d* Venice, 15 May 1609). Italian composer. He was a pupil of Zarlino and a member of the choir of St Mark's, Venice, eventually becoming director of music there. His church music includes both small-scale motets and splendid works in the grand manner, using *cori spezzati; but he was best known for his extremely singable madrigals and canzonettas, which were closely imitated by Thomas Morley in England. His contri-

bution to *Il trionfo di Dori* (1592) was the inspiration for *The Triumphes of Oriana*.   DA/TC

croche (Fr., 'hook'). Quaver. (The French for 'crotchet' is *noire*.)

Crociato in Egitto, Il ('The Crusader in Egypt'). Opera in two acts by Meyerbeer to a libretto by Gaetano Rossi (Venice, 1824).

Croft, William (*b* Nether Ettington, Warwicks., *bapt.* 30 Dec. 1678; *d* Bath, 14 Aug. 1727). English composer. A chorister in the Chapel Royal and pupil of Blow, he became in 1700 a Gentleman-Extraordinary of the chapel, with Jeremiah Clarke. Four years later Croft and Clarke were appointed joint organists there, and after Clarke's death in 1707 Croft became sole organist. The following year he succeeded Blow as composer and Master of the Children at the Chapel Royal and as organist of Westminster Abbey. He graduated D.Mus. from Oxford in 1713 and was among the first members of the Academy of Vocal Music.

Croft is the most significant composer of English church music between Purcell and Greene. His principal importance lies in his anthems (he wrote more than 80, mostly verse anthems), which integrate both Purcellian and more modern Italianate characteristics. His sectional verse anthems incorporate solos, duets, trios, and passages for organ alone. He also wrote services, including a fine Burial Service, some theatre music, instrumental pieces, songs, and odes, including one for Queen Anne's birthday and two celebrating the Treaty of Utrecht. In 1724 he published a selection of his church music in score in two books, entitled *Musica sacra*.   WT/PL

croiser (Fr.). 'To cross'; *croiser les mains*, in keyboard playing, a direction to cross the hands.

cromatico, cromatica (It.). 'Chromatic'.

Cronaca del luogo ('Chronicle of the Place'). Opera in a prologue and five scenes by Berio to a libretto by Talia Pecker Berio (Salzburg, 1999).

crook. On reed instruments, a curved metal tube (Amer.: bocal) between the reed and the instrument. On brass instruments, coils of tubing (called a 'shank' when straight) to alter the tube length and thus the pitch. Natural and early valved horns, trumpets, and cornets had full sets of crooks, one for each key.   JMo

crooning. A style of soft, deep-throated, sentimental singing, introduced in the USA in the 1920s by male radio entertainers, notably Rudy Vallee; its best-known exponent was Bing Crosby (1904–77).   PGA

cross-accent. A way of varying the expected accentuation of notes by placing stresses on the 'weak' beats of the bar, and detracting from the 'strong' beats by substituting rests for them or by holding over a note from the previous beat. See also SYNCOPATION.

Crosse, Gordon (*b* Bury, 1 Dec. 1937). English composer. He studied with Edmund Rubbra and Egon Wellesz in Oxford and with Goffredo Petrassi in Rome. His early works show a mixture of medieval and serial thought suggesting comparison with Maxwell Davies, though the harmony is more straightforward and the feeling correspondingly more relaxed. In later works he developed a rich, eclectic style anchored more firmly in tonality. His output includes several operas, among which his setting of Yeats's one-act *Purgatory* (Cheltenham, 1966) is outstanding, as well as two symphonies, two violin concertos, other orchestral and chamber works, and music for children. Crosse ceased composing during the 1990s, though without excluding the possibility of returning to composition in the future. AW

cross-fingering. A technique that enables keyless woodwind instruments to play certain chromatic notes, since a note may be flattened by covering the soundhole two below the one sounding. From about 1760, keys were added to improve the quality of chromatic semitones. Cross-fingerings are now used to correct naturally occurring tuning problems in upper registers. SM

crossover. A term used to describe either work by a performer or composer in a musical genre different from that with which he or she is usually associated, or the merging or hybridization of different musical genres. KG

cross-relation. See FALSE RELATION.

cross-rhythm. The regular use of conflicting rhythmic groupings, for example of three notes against four. The Minuet of Bach's fifth keyboard Partita has a conflict of two-against-three almost throughout.

crotal [pellet bell]. A small closed bell (e.g. a *sleigh bell) containing one or more loose pellets, clusters of which are used as *jingles. See BELL, 1.

crotala (Lat.). Ancient Roman and Greek *clappers consisting of two pairs of slivers of wood or bone, held one in each hand.

crotales. See ANTIQUE CYMBALS.

Crotch, William (*b* Norwich, 5 July 1775; *d* Taunton, 29 Dec. 1847). English composer, organist, teacher, and theorist. He was a remarkable child prodigy, giving his first concert some months before his third birthday; he played before the king and queen when he was three (his name was brought before the Royal Society by Charles Burney shortly afterwards), then toured Britain with his mother. At the age of 11 he went to Cambridge, playing for services at Trinity and King's colleges and Great St Mary's Church and assisting the professor of music, John Randall.

Moving to Oxford in 1788, Crotch began his education in earnest. From 1790 he was organist at Christ Church, and in 1794 he graduated B.Mus. He composed the 'Westminster Chimes' for a clock installed in 1793 at Great St Mary's, Cambridge (they were put on the clock of St Stephen's Tower in the Houses of Parliament in 1860). In 1797 he succeeded Philip Hayes as professor of music at Oxford, a position he held until his death. He took the D.Mus. in 1799. Between 1800 and 1804 he delivered a series of lectures at the university (a noted innovation); he also lectured at the Royal Institution.

Crotch left Oxford about 1807 for London, where he composed his popular oratorio *Palestine* (1805–11) and wrote *Elements of Composition* (1812); some of his Oxford lectures were published in 1831 as *The Substance of Several Courses of Lectures*. His *Specimens of Various Styles of Music* (1808–15) were also regarded as an important pedagogical aid. He was an active member of the Philharmonic Society, for which he conducted concerts. His Symphony in F was performed by the society in 1814. He was appointed principal of the RAM on its foundation in 1822, resigning ten years later. His last public appearance was as organist at the Handel Festival in Westminster Abbey in 1834. His works, which show an awareness of both modern and ancient styles, include glees, organ works, choral odes, three oratorios, and anthems. WT/JDI

crotchet (♩). The note having a quarter of the value of the semibreve, or whole note; hence the American usage 'quarter-note'.

crowd. 1. See CRWTH.
　2. See TURBA.

Crown Imperial. March by Walton, composed for the coronation of George VI in 1937; the score is headed by a line from the poem *In Honour of the City* by William Dunbar (1465–1520): 'In beautie beryng the crone imperiall'. It has been arranged for military band, for piano, and for organ.

Crown of India, The. Imperial masque, op. 66, by Elgar to words by Henry Hamilton; it was written to celebrate the Delhi Durbar in 1912. Elgar made an orchestral suite from it the same year.

Cruce, Petrus de. See PETRUS DE CRUCE.

Crucifixion, The. Oratorio (1887) by Stainer to a text by J. Sparrow-Simpson with extracts from the Bible; it is for tenor and bass soloists, chorus, organ, and orchestra, and the congregation may join in five hymns (omitted in some performances).

Crucifixus. The article of the Nicene–Constantino-politan *Creed beginning with the phrase 'Crucifixus etiam pro nobis' ('He was crucified also for us'). The tendency of Baroque composers to treat the Credo as a string of self-contained movements led to the composition of both free-standing and integral settings of the Crucifixus.   ALI

Crüger, Johannes (*b* Gross-Breesen, nr Frankfurt an der Oder, 9 April 1598; *d* Berlin, 23 Feb. 1662). German composer and theorist. After studying theology at Wittenberg, he was elected Kantor in 1622 at St Nicolai, Berlin, a post he held until his death. He is remembered as the composer of such well-known chorale melodies as 'Nun danket alle Gott', 'Jesu meine Freude', and 'Schmücke dich, O liebe Seele', published in his renowned collection *Praxis pietatis melica* (1644, with numerous further editions). Several of his later hymns (from 1649) are set in four-part harmony, with added lines for two violins or trumpets.
                                                 DA/BS

Crumb, George (Henry) (*b* Charleston, WV, 24 Oct. 1929). American composer and teacher. He studied with Ross Lee Finney at the University of Michigan and taught at Boulder, Colorado, before joining the University of Pennsylvania in 1965. During the next few years he was, with Penderecki, one of the pioneers in using avant-garde gestures for their immediate expressive effects, weird or touching, with an effectiveness guaranteed by his precise judgment of sonority. Notable works include *Echoes of Time and the River* for orchestra (1967), *Ancient Voices of Children* for soprano, treble, and ensemble (1970, a nocturnal and at times fiercely dramatic setting of poems by Lorca), *Black Angels* for amplified string quartet (also 1970), and *Vox balaenae* for three masked players (1971). After this period of productivity and success, he became less prolific.   PG

📖 D. GILLESPIE (ed.), *George Crumb: Profile of a Composer* (New York, 1985)

crumhorn (from Ger. *Krummhorn*, 'crooked horn'). A double-reed *wind-cap instrument with a narrow, cylindrical bore. It produces a buzzing sound. The distal end is bent like the crook of a walking-stick, hence its name. It was used from about 1480 to 1660, mainly in Germany, Italy, and the Low Countries, but has been revived for much early music. Like a recorder it has a thumbhole and seven fingerholes; on larger instruments the lowest hole is controlled by a key. The range is limited to a 9th, though some instruments have additional keys that extend the range downwards. As with most Renaissance instruments, crumhorns were made in different sizes, from soprano to great bass.
                                                 JMo

Crusell, Bernhard (Henrik) (*b* Nystad, 15 Oct. 1775; *d* Stockholm, 28 July 1838). Finnish composer, clarinet-tist, and conductor. He moved to Stockholm when he was 15 and made a career as a virtuoso there and, later, on the Continent. His three clarinet concertos, all composed as a vehicle for his own prowess, were the first Nordic concertos to enter the international repertory. Urbane and mellifluous, fertile of invention, and fluent, they are close in idiom to the music of Spohr and Weber. On settling back in Sweden, in addition to composing and teaching, Crusell translated the librettos of Mozart and Rossini operas into Swedish for the Royal Opera in Stockholm.   WT/RLa

crwth [crowd]. The traditional Welsh bowed *lyre, with a neck and fingerboard similar to those of the Baroque *violin (though deriving from a medieval form) running between the resonator and the crossbar of the yoke. Two *bourdon strings running beside the neck were bowed, or plucked with the thumb, as drones. Use of the *crwth* died out in the 19th century, though attempts to revive it persist.   JMo

Cry. Work (1976–9) for 28 amplified voices by Giles Swayne.

cryptography. The encoding of words and symbols in music goes back to the Renaissance: the use of triple time, three-part forms, and three-voice textures would commonly symbolize perfection or, in particular, the Trinity, and the works of Obrecht go much further in representing sacred numbers. Similar procedures have been uncovered in the music of J. S. Bach, who also signed some pieces with the motif *B–A–C–H, a musical idea taken up by later composers in homage to him, including Liszt, Schoenberg, and Webern. Schumann used the same principle in writing into his music the names of Meta Abegg (A–B♭–E–G–G) or Clara (C–A–A) Wieck. Berg used both note-name and numerical cryptograms in nearly all his music: for example, his *Lyric Suite* interlaces his initials (A–B♭) with those of his lover Hanna Fuchs-Robettin (B–F) and uses numbers he associated with the two of them, 23 and 10, in its formal divisions. Shostakovich used his own musical monogram (in German transliteration), D–Sch (D–E♭–C–B).

German note names allow the encrypting of nine letters, as shown in the above examples. To these may be added French note names for L (*la*: A), M (*mi*: E), and R (*ré*: D), as in Boulez's encoding of the name of Paul Sacher (E♭–A–C–B–E–D). Alternatively, the traditional equivalences of notes and letters can be recycled through the alphabet, so that H = A, I = B, J = C, etc. (English–American system), or I = A, J = B, K = C, etc. (German system). These codes were used by several French composers in homages to Haydn, Fauré, and Roussel.

Honegger's Roussel tribute, however, is based on an alphabet of 26 defined pitches, and Messiaen used a rather similar technique—though with durations fixed as well—to inscribe lines from Thomas Aquinas across his *Méditations sur le mystère de la Sainte Trinité* and other works. Messiaen's music is also full of formal, rhythmic, and textural ideas based on the holy numbers three, seven, nine, and 12. PG

csárdás (Hung., from *csárda*, 'tavern'). A 19th-century Hungarian ballroom dance, supposedly derived from a country dance performed in taverns; it was especially fashionable from the 1850s to the 1880s. Musically, the csárdás is very similar to the fast (*friss*) section of the **verbunkos* and is characteristically in duple time with many syncopations. A slow (*lassú*) version appeared during the second half of the 19th century. Liszt included a csárdás in several of his works, notably the 19 Hungarian Rhapsodies (1846–85) and *Csárdás macabre* (1881–2), all for piano. —/JBe

Cuba. See LATIN AMERICA, 5.

Cuckoo, The. See COUCOU, LE.

cue. 1. In an orchestral or vocal part, an extract from another, prominent part (usually printed in small notes), to warn a performer of an approaching entry, usually after a long rest.

2. A gesture from a conductor to signal the entrance of a player or a section.

Cui, César [Kyui, Tsezar'] **Antonovich** (*b* Vilnius, 6/18 Jan. 1835; *d* Petrograd, 26 March 1918). Russian composer and critic, of French descent. His father, an officer in Napoleon's army, remained in Russia after the French retreat in 1812. Cui had his early education in Vilnius, where he was also given a few lessons by Moniuszko. In St Petersburg in the 1850s he met Balakirev, who introduced him to the circle of nationalist composers, The Five. Cui was himself subsequently accepted as one of the group. Like his colleagues, he combined musical activities with a career in another sphere: he was an expert on military fortifications, and from 1857 taught at the St Petersburg Academy of Military Engineering (he was professor from 1878).

Within The Five, Cui was initially acknowledged as the authority on opera, and on vocal writing in general. His opera *William Ratcliff* (1869, after Heinrich Heine) was praised by Vladimir Stasov as 'one of the most important compositions of our time'; its extensive declamatory scenes and bold harmonic progressions had a significant impact on the development of The Five's operatic ideals. In 1872 Cui composed Act I of the collective opera *Mlada*, in collaboration with Rimsky-Korsakov, Borodin, Musorgsky, and Minkus (only Cui and Minkus ever completed their allotted portions); here he demonstrated his command of The Five's 'Russian' manner, giving the lie to the lingering allegations of 'Frenchness' levelled by friends and critics alike.

Cui's next opera, *Angelo* (1876, after Victor Hugo), was widely discussed by The Five, but they showed little interest in his later works, which they considered insufficiently nationalist and progressive. Cui did, however, make substantial contributions to the nationalist cause when he completed Dargomïzhsky's *The Stone Guest* and Musorgsky's *Sorochintsy Fair*, which had both been left unfinished on the death of their composers. Nevertheless, his influence was felt primarily through his critical writings rather than his work as a composer. From 1864 he joined Stasov in advertising The Five's achievements and promoting their views at every opportunity. The negative side of this activity was his coverage of those whom he saw as rivals to the nationalist school proper: his criticisms of Tchaikovsky, Anton Rubinstein, and even Rakhmaninov were often caustic. His book *La Musique en Russie* (Paris, 1880, repr. 1974) enjoyed a wide readership in the West and played a significant role in conditioning Western opinion to the views of the Russian nationalist school, greatly facilitating Diaghilev's task when he began promoting Russian music in Western concert halls and opera houses.

After 1880 Cui's relations with the other members of The Five became more distant. Outliving them all, he composed prolifically up to his last days. He wrote 13 operas, most of which received performances but met with only limited success; among them were four expressly for children, a popular genre at the beginning of the 20th century. He also composed numerous piano pieces and about 300 songs, often marked by Schumann's influence. None of his operas and few of his smaller works remain in the repertory, but Cui's name is saved from oblivion through his association with the other, more distinguished members of The Five.

MF-W

📖 M. O. Zeitlin, *The Five* (New York, 1959) · R. Taruskin, ' "Kuchkism" in practice: Two operas by César Cui', *Opera and Drama in Russia as Preached and Practiced in the 1860s* (Ann Arbor, MI, 1981), 341–426 · S. Campbell (trans. and ed.), *Russians on Russian Music, 1830–1880: An Anthology* (Cambridge, 1994)

cuivre (Fr.). 'Copper', 'brass'. *Les cuivres*, the brass instruments; *cuivré*, 'brassy', playing with a forced, strident tone, especially on the horn, often combined with hand-muting.

Cunning Little Vixen, The (*Příhody Lišky Bystroušky*; 'The Adventures of the Vixen Bystrouška'). Opera in three acts by Janáček to his own libretto after Rudolf Těsnohlídek's novel *Liška Bystrouška* (originally texts to go with drawings by Stanislav Lolek, published in the Brno newspaper *Lidové noviny* in 1920) (Brno, 1924).

Cupid and Death. Masque by James Shirley, performed in 1653 with music probably by Christopher Gibbons; it was revived in 1659 with music by Christopher Gibbons and Matthew Locke.

cupo (It.). 'Dark', 'sombre'. The term was much used by Verdi.

Curlew, The. Song cycle (1920–2) by Warlock for tenor, flute, cor anglais, and string quartet, a setting of four poems by W. B. Yeats.

Curlew River. Church parable, op. 71, by Britten to a text by William Plomer after the Japanese *nō* play *Sumidagawa* by Jūrō Motomasa (1395–1431) (Aldeburgh, 1964).

curtal. Alternative name for the *dulcian, the ancestor of the bassoon.

Curwen. English family of music educationists and publishers. It was founded by John Curwen (1816–80), a Congregational Church minister, who adopted and modified the *Tonic Sol-fa system devised by Sarah Glover as a means of teaching the rudiments of music. J. Curwen & Sons became a vital force in educational music with succeeding generations of the family developing the catalogue to include piano tutors, choral music, music for amateurs, and a diverse range of orchestral music ranging from Holst to Varèse. The catalogue was divided between Faber Music and Roberton Publications in 1971 and since 1986 has been part of the Music Sales Group.   HA

Curzon, Sir Clifford (Michael) (*b* London, 18 May 1907; *d* London, 1 Sept. 1982). English pianist. His career was launched by Henry Wood in 1923, but he then studied further with Schnabel, Landowska, and Boulanger. Initially a virtuoso concerto soloist, he undertook extensive tours of Europe and America but from 1945 turned to solo recitals and played chamber music interrupted by prolonged periods of study. His sensitively direct yet beautiful playing style made him a particularly renowned Mozartian. He was knighted in 1977.   CF

cushion dance (Ger.: *Kissentanz*). A dance, popular in England and Scotland in the 17th century, in which the participants selected a partner by dropping a cushion before him or her.

custos. See DIRECT.

Cutting, Francis (*bur.* London, 7 Jan. 1596). English lutenist and composer. He may have been employed by the Howards of Arundel House in London. About 50 of his compositions for lute survive. Some of them were published in the year of his death, alongside works by his younger contemporary John Dowland.

Cuzzoni, Francesca (*b* Parma, 2 April 1696; *d* Bologna, 19 June 1778). Italian soprano. After studying with Francesco Lanzi, she sang in Parma in 1716 and the same year in Bologna. In 1718 she made an auspicious debut in Venice as Dalinda in Pollarolo's *Ariodante*; the role of Ginevra was taken by the mezzo-soprano Faustina Bordoni, with whom she was to enter into bitter rivalry, leading to a fight on the stage of the King's Theatre, London. She made her London debut in 1723 in Handel's *Ottone*, for which she received high praise from both the audience and the press. She became the star of all the operas performed there, acclaimed in works by Handel, Ariosti, and Bononcini and earning unprecedented fees. In Bath, Paris, and Vienna she was equally sought after for concerts, oratorios, and recitals, but because the Vienna Court Opera would not meet her exorbitant fees she never sang there. During the 1730s her success spread to Naples, Florence, and Genoa but by the 1740s her voice began to decline as she sought an ever more extravagant way of life. She began to incur huge debts, and was arrested in London in 1750. She spent her last 20 years in prison, then in obscurity and poverty.

                JT

cyclic form. In a general sense the word 'cyclic' applies to any work in several movements, for example a suite, symphony, sonata, or string quartet. More particularly, however, the term is used to describe any such work in which the movements are connected by some musical theme or themes common to all. Berlioz's *Symphonie* *fantastique*, where the *idée fixe* appears in each of the five movements, is in this sense in cyclic form, though the theme itself is in some movements not an essential part of the structure but rather an inserted musical quotation. Numerous examples of cyclic form are found in the music of other 19th- and 20th-century composers, for instance Liszt (B minor Piano Sonata), Franck (D minor Symphony), and Rakhmaninov (First Symphony). In some cases (there are examples among the symphonies of Brahms, Bruckner, and Elgar), the sense of cyclicity is emphasized by closing the finale with a theme from the start of the work.

A related use of the term is found in sacred music (see CYCLIC MASS).   GMT/RP

cyclic mass. A setting of the Mass Ordinary that links its movements through the use of common musical material, for instance a *motto or a cantus firmus. The earliest known complete example is the *Missa 'Caput'*, an anonymous 15th-century English setting for four voices using the same plainchant cantus firmus for the tenor of each movement. Such tenor masses eventually gave way to *parody masses, in which movements were linked by their derivation from a common polyphonic model. Although existing material was often chosen for its symbolic value, modern scholars (particularly those seeking the origins of autonomous musical art) have tended to value cyclic masses for their unity of form.

—/ALı

cylinder. A recording device patented by Thomas Alva Edison in 1877. It consisted of a cylinder covered with aluminium foil, the recording being indented on its surface. The sound thus preserved was very crude and wax was soon adopted as the recording medium. At first cylinders had to be recorded individually, mass production becoming possible only with the introduction of a moulding process in 1904. Cylinders continued in parallel with disc recordings during the acoustic period, finally disappearing about 1924. The Edison Cylinder *Phonograph was used particularly for folk and ethnomusicological recordings, most notably by Bartók in central Europe and Grainger in England and Denmark.

See also RECORDING AND REPRODUCTION.   LF

cymbals (Fr.: *cymbales*; Ger.: *Becken*; It.: *piatti, cinelli*). Bowls or concave plates of bronze (*c*.80% copper and 20% tin). Individual cymbals may be suspended on a stand or a cord and struck with a stick or other implement; pairs may be clashed together. Evidence of cymbals goes back to the 2nd millennium BC in Anatolia and the Middle East. These were often quite small (5–15 cm in diameter); the smaller instruments were

sometimes fixed to the ends of wooden or metal tongs, as are the modern Turkish *zilli massa*.

Cymbals were used throughout Europe in the Middle Ages and experienced a renaissance in Western art music in the mid-18th century after the wars with the Turks, when they were adopted by European military bands (and later orchestras) among the 'alla turca' percussion instruments (see JANISSARY MUSIC). The Turkish-style cymbal (Fig. 1a) is still the main one used in the West, a major manufacturer being the family firm of Zildjian (the name means 'cymbal-maker'), established in 1623 in Constantinople and now also based in Norwell, Massachusetts. Less common is the Chinese type of cymbal (Fig. 1c), which has a more brittle sound and is used in the Western orchestra only for special effects. Cymbals are widely used elsewhere in Asia, especially in India (*tal*) and Tibet (Fig. 1d). 'Antique cymbals'—small, thick tuned cymbals, sometimes fixed on stands and struck with beaters, and sometimes played in pairs—go back to Berlioz's reproductions of Roman cymbals from Pompeii. Egyptian dancers use small 'finger cymbals', *c*.5 cm across, attached with gut loops; similar instruments are found in India (Fig. 1b).

A variety of suspended cymbals is made for the drum kit. The 'ride cymbal' is designed so that repeated strokes do not build up into an overpowering roar, as can happen when the suspended cymbal is played with hard felt beaters. The light 'snap cymbal' makes a quick splash of sound, rather like the 'Chinese crash' used in the older jazz band and in pairs for processional music in China. The 'sizzle cymbal' has a series of holes drilled in it, each loosely holding a rivet; a sizzling sound is produced when the cymbal is struck, an effect that can be simulated by resting a chain on a crash cymbal.   JMo

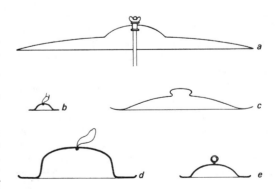

Fig. 1. (a) 50-cm suspended cymbal; (b) Egyptian dancer's cymbal; (c) 30-cm Chinese cymbals; (d) Tibetan 'bowler hat' cymbal; (e) bronze cymbal, Roman period.

Czech Republic. The present Czech Republic was founded in 1992 after the breakup of the two states constituting Czechoslovakia, which was made up of two ethnic subgroups, Czechs and Slovaks. Czechoslovakia was established in 1918 and comprised the former Habsburg territories of Bohemia, Silesia (Czech), Moravia, and Slovakia, during whose long history boundaries had been drawn and redrawn with bewildering frequency. The early 10th century saw the growing dominance of the western area, Bohemia, over Greater Moravia. Slovakia came under Hungarian rule in 1906 and in spite of strong linguistic and cultural links remained politically separate until the 20th century. In 1948 Czechoslovakia became a socialist republic, and from 1968 it was a federation of two states. After the fall of the Communist government in 1989, the two states formally separated into the Czech and Slovak republics. The cultural history of all three regions has been varied and interesting with art music fertilized at many stages by a rich indigenous folk tradition. At various periods Czech music and musicians touched on the European mainstream, particularly in the 18th century when Bohemian and Moravian composers and performers populated the musical establishments of many capitals; in the 19th century Bohemia was a major centre of musical nationalism.

1. Bohemia and Moravia: the Middle Ages and Renaissance; 2. Bohemia and Moravia: the Baroque and Classical eras; 3. Bohemia and Moravia: Romanticism and nationalism; 4. Slovakia to 1918; 5. Czechoslovakia from 1918; 6. The Czech Republic from 1992

1. Bohemia and Moravia: the Middle Ages and Renaissance

Apart from sources of the Gregorian chant repertory, the earliest original Czech music appears in late 14th- and 15th-century manuscripts, though both the setting of 'Hospodine, pomiluj ny' ('Lord, have mercy') and the St Wenceslas Hymn probably date from much earlier. The cathedral in Prague was the major centre of ecclesiastical music-making, and with the elevation of Prague to an archbishopric in 1346 there was greater liturgical variety, including the reappearance of the Slavonic rite which had earlier been superseded by the Gregorian.

First references to secular music indicate little more than clerical disapproval, but the Přemyslid court of the 11th to early 14th centuries encouraged the performances of the *jongleurs* and later Minnesinger. The university in Prague, founded by Charles IV in 1348, took that of Paris as its model; surviving documents show that scholars were aware of Johannes des Muris' treatise *Musica speculativa* (1323).

The 15th-century sacred song repertory shows distinct folk traits and reflects the teachings (aimed largely against the laxity and corruption of the church) of the religious reformer Jan Hus. The music inspired by his reforms was monodic, polyphony and instrumental participation being discouraged. The melodies show the influence of secular and Gregorian models, but like the Lutheran chorale they possess great individuality and strength, the most famous—*Ktož jsú Boží bojovníci* ('You who are warriors of God')—coming to be a symbol of national identity and defiance in the 19th and 20th centuries. These songs accorded well with liturgical practice, which in many areas remained Protestant in character until the 17th century. Partly as a result of this, an interest in newer styles of polyphony was slow to develop, but it increased towards the end of the 16th century, stimulated by the arrival of distinguished foreign composers at the court of the Habsburg monarchs. That of the splendidly eccentric Rudolf II (1576–1612) was especially lavish, attracting musicians of the quality of Kerle, Regnart, Philippe de Monte, and Luython. Domestic polyphony at the beginning of the 17th century was not without distinction and may be seen at its best in the surviving work of the nobleman Kryštof Harant (1564–1621).

Although Moravia had lost its primacy to Bohemia in the 10th century, becoming a margravate in 1029, it maintained separate musical interests. At an early stage the Moravians favoured Byzantine chant, but in the 11th century they were subject to the same constraints as the church in Bohemia. In Brno, the capital, the first musical references are to the church of St James and the Cathedral of St Peter, and records of payment to town musicians in the 15th century suggest secular music on similar lines, if on a smaller scale, to that of Prague. Musical establishments in the provinces developed rather later than Brno, the most spectacular belonging to the Prince-Bishop of Olomouc at Kroměříž.

2. Bohemia and Moravia: the Baroque and Classical eras

The Battle of the White Mountain in 1620 was as much a watershed for Czech culture as it was for the nation's political fortunes. With the move of the imperial capital to Vienna, the variety and wealth of musical life in Prague declined. Elsewhere in Bohemia and Moravia the imposition of Roman Catholicism signalled a change in the nature of music-making and musical education. The opening of numerous Jesuit schools and seminaries was responsible for much of the increase in quality of musical training. But the beautiful palaces and churches built by the new Habsburg nobility were the only permanent evidence of their presence, since, like the court, they were usually away in Vienna. Poor employment prospects and high taxation meant that soon after 1620 there was a steady trickle of performers and composers to the courts and capitals of Europe. By the 18th century the exodus was in full spate, giving rise to Burney's comment that Bohemia was the 'Conservatoire of Europe'.

The *Missa concertata* of Jakub Rybnický (*c.*1600–39) is indicative of a growing appreciation of the concertato style, as are the more developed church works of the Jesuit-trained Adam Michna (*c.*1600–76), though of greater interest are his idiosyncratic settings of hymns and psalm paraphrases, *Loutna česká* (1653), for soloists, strings, and organ. In Moravia, the last four decades of the 17th century witnessed a remarkable flowering of talent. The musical establishment kept by the Prince-Bishop Karl Lichtenstein-Kastelcorn at Kroměříž surpassed earlier and contemporary chapels in Bohemia and Moravia, with composers of the quality of Schmelzer, Poglietti, and Bertali composing for his large body of musicians. The first Kapellmeister was Biber, succeeded by the Moravian Pavel Vejvanovský, whose compositions for strings and trumpets show an individual use of instruments and a characteristic use of folk elements.

The 18th century saw an increase in opera performances, though works on Czech subjects—Bartolomeo Bernardi's *La Libussa* (Prague, 1703) was one of the first—were exceptions. Productions in Prague for the visiting imperial court were geared to their Italian tastes: the operatic fare comprised works by Fux, Bioni, Pollarolo, Porta, Albinoni, Vivaldi, and Gluck. Count Sporck's (1662–1738) Italian opera was the first permanent company in Prague, and in 1783 Count Nostitz (1725–94) opened the first genuine opera house with a resident company. Pasquale Bondini (?1737–89), the director of the company, and the Bohemian Estates which later took over the theatre commissioned respectively Mozart's *Don Giovanni* (1787) and *La clemenza di Tito* (1791).

Although traditions of excellent tuition continued in the 18th century—Gluck, Johann Stamitz, and Zelenka among others studied at the Clementinum in Prague—few musicians who learnt their craft in Bohemia remained to work. Among those who did the church musicians Bohuslav Matěj Černohorský and František Brixi were the most successful, the latter bringing a distinctive accent to the Viennese musical vernacular. Later in the century F. X. Dušek (noted for the originality of his piano sonatas as much as for offering Mozart hospitality) and Tomášek were important in providing a focus for musical life. Instrumental concerts in the early and mid-18th century had tended to be as seasonal as the visits of the nobility, but by the end

travelling virtuosos—among them Mozart, Stadler, and Beethoven—were finding ready and discriminating audiences.

The courts of Europe were the main beneficiaries of the Bohemian and Moravian educational system, and by the end of the 18th century there was hardly an orchestra without one or more Czech musicians. Among the first to leave was Jan Dismas Zelenka, who worked principally at the court of Dresden, though his festive *Melodrama de Sancto Wenceslao* (1723) was one of the few native operatic presentations given in Prague in the period. However, Josef Mysliveček, the major operatic talent, had most of his successes in Italy and Austria. Johann Stamitz in Mannheim, Franz and Georg Benda at the courts of Potsdam and Gotha, and later Antoine Reicha in Paris all produced work of importance and originality, but by far the chief centre of attraction was Vienna. František Tůma and Josef Antonín Štěpán worked for the royal family, and Adalbert Gyrowetz became conductor of the court theatre in 1804. Leopold Kozeluch and Franz Krommer held successively the posts of *Kammer Kapellmeister* and *Hofmusik Kompositor* to the emperor, and J. B. Vanhal and Paul Wranitzky pursued independent careers as teachers and performers; the last named also organized much of the concert life in Vienna.

3. Bohemia and Moravia: Romanticism and nationalism

The major feature of artistic life among the Czech-speaking community in the 19th century was the growth of a national identity. Fostered by the liberalizing influence of the Enlightenment, an interest arose in Czech culture. After nearly two centuries of political domination by Austria a process of recovery was initiated. The work of M. A. Voight (1733–87) did much to encourage an enthusiasm for older Czech church music and in 1815 Bohumir Dlabač (G. J. Dlabačz, 1758–1820) published his *Allgemeines historisches Künstler-Lexikon*, the first systematic consideration of Czech cultural history. 1784 had seen the founding of the Royal Bohemian Academy of Sciences, followed in 1791 by a chair in Czech language and literature at the Charles University. The work of Dobrovský and Jungmann in linguistics and grammar was vital in encouraging an interest in a language which had long suffered from scholarly neglect. In 1830 Josef Wenzig (1807–76) published a German translation of Czech folksongs as a counterpart to *Des Knaben Wunderhorn* (1806–8); it was followed in 1835 by František Sušil's Moravian folksongs in the vernacular and a formative collection by Karel Erben in 1842. Extended settings of Czech had been known in the 18th century, but the participation of composers was by no means general. The *pastorellas were a rich source of Czech settings and made use of folksong; these were interpolations into the Christmas liturgy (sometimes entirely replacing the Latin) in a pastoral vein.

Opera translations were used towards the end of the 18th century, but a collection of standard works did not appear until the first decades of the 19th. *Dráteník* ('The Tinker', 1826), a *Singspiel* by František Škroup, had local success and may fairly claim to be the first Czech opera of any substance. The greatest single impetus to the creation of a national opera came with the opening of the Provisional Theatre in 1862 for the production of plays and opera exclusively in Czech. Austrian power had been fundamentally weakened in the late 1850s, and with the prospect of a genuine national revival the response of the Czech-speaking population of Prague was favourable to requests for subscriptions. However, apart from Škroup's work there were no indigenous operas ready at the theatre's opening, and its repertory comprised mainly translations of French, Italian, German Romantic, and Mozart operas.

Matters improved with offerings from František Skuherský (1830–92), Vilém Blodek, Karel Šebor, Karel Bendl, and Josef Richard Rozkošný (1833–1913), but the eight operas of Smetana provided the real backbone of the repertory. During the 1870s–90s operas by Dvořák, Fibich, and Karel Kovařovic among the younger generation further expanded the showing of Czech works in performance at the Provisional Theatre, which was converted into the larger National Theatre in 1881 (rebuilt 1883). The operas favoured folk-inspired or patriotic-historical themes. This tendency continued until the 20th century, but the works of Rozkošný and the younger composers J. B. Foerster and Celanský (1870–1931) indicate verismo tendencies carried into the 20th century most memorably by Janáček. Opera remained central to the national movement and was cultivated assiduously by a wide variety of composers; but another theatrical genre which also received the attention of musicians was melodrama, of which Fibich's cycle *Hippodamie* (1888–91) was the most remarkable example.

19th-century Czech piano music shows a fondness for shorter forms, as initiated by Tomášek and Voríšek in their eclogues and impromptus. Smetana, Dvořák, and Fibich in his unique *Piano Diary* cultivated the miniature, expanding its terms of reference by composing pieces based on national dance forms. The instrumental sonata was largely neglected by major composers. The symphony fared better with distinctive contributions from Voríšek, Kittl, Smetana, Fibich, and Foerster, though Dvořák's later efforts in the form were the most consistent and had the greatest international impact. With *Má vlast* (1874–9) Smetana produced arguably the most national of 19th-century symphonic poems, and Czech interest in the form continued in the 20th century with works by Novák and Suk. Chamber music took an idiosyncratic turn in the G minor Trio and two string quartets of Smetana, though these were balanced by the more classically oriented works of Dvořák, who provided the most substantial Czech contributions to the medium. As in opera, the introduction of folk elements into instrumental works became a regular if not ubiquitous feature at this time.

In common with other European capitals, the 19th century saw the rise of musical institutions. The Prague Conservatory was founded in 1811, the Prague Organ School in 1830. They were amalgamated in 1890, and Dvořák was appointed to teach composition. The university offered music courses in Czech by the influential critic and aesthetician Otakar Hostinský (1847–1910) and in German by A. W. Ambros. In the provinces choral societies reflected more organized musical interests, and towards the end of the century Bohuslav Jeremiáš (1859–1918) founded the South Bohemian Conservatory. In Prague a Czech Artistic Society (Umělecká Beseda) was founded in 1863 followed by a publishing house (Hudební Matice) in 1871. The pages of the principal musical journal *Dalibor* give ample evidence of the vitality of musical life in Bohemia and Moravia during the period of national revival.

The rivalry between the Czech and German communities did much to uphold standards of performance, not least in the two theatres, though under Kovařovic the National Theatre achieved pre-eminence in the early years of the 20th century. The German Chamber Music Society (1876) and its Czech counterpart (1894) ensured the quality of chamber performances, and the foundation of the Czech Quartet in 1891 initiated a line of similarly distinguished groups which are still a major ornament of Czech musical life. The 1890s also saw the formation of the Czech Philharmonic, soon followed by the start of its career as an independent orchestra in the early 1900s.

New musical styles apparent after the turn of the century are typified in the work of two of Dvořák's pupils, Josef Suk and Vitězslav Novák. They show a perceptible lessening of German influences matched by a growing interest in Impressionism and a softening of the folk element (though in Novák's case there was a conscious reorientation towards Slovak folk models). If composition lacked the enormous energy of the early days of nationalism it offered compensations in sophistication and originality.

In opera, Moravia lagged somewhat behind Bohemia with no regular company until 1882 and no national theatre until the opening of the Provisional Theatre in

Brno in 1884. But in other respects Moravian musical life was in advance of the western Czechs. A major figure was the teacher and composer Pavel Křížkovský, whose choruses, many of which were based on Moravian folksong, attracted the favourable attention of Smetana and served as a model for similar works by Bendl, Foerster, Dvořák, and Janáček. More modest in scope than the early operas, these works were nevertheless fundamental to the national musical revival.

As in Prague, the music-making of the Czech and German-speaking communities remained separate. Křížkovský started a music society (Beseda Brněnská) and encouraged choral singing among the Czech community. Janáček built on Křížkovský's achievement, founding an Organ School (1882; in 1919 it became the State Conservatory) and in 1884 the musical journal *Hudební listy*. But Janáček's most lasting contribution to the national heritage was his work as a composer: a late developer, he forged a style in part based on a systematic study of Moravian folksong which, coupled with an acute dramatic instinct, produced some of the most remarkable operatic and instrumental music of the 20th century.

The folk music of Bohemia and Moravia began to be collected systematically in the 19th century. Bohemian and western Moravian folksong tended towards a regularity of metre and a simplicity of melodic outline based on the triad. In contrast, the folksong of the eastern parts of Moravia, remote from German and Austrian influence, is often more rhapsodic, the melody characterized by resonant open intervals, sharpened 4ths, and flattened 7ths with irregular metres and snapped rhythms common to Slovakian and Hungarian folk music. Violins and clarinets were used in instrumental combinations in all areas, with the bagpipe (ubiquitous since the Middle Ages) prevalent in Bohemia, and the double bass and dulcimer in Moravia. Of the rich repertory of folk dances the *furiant*, with its characteristic hemiola rhythm, appears most frequently in art music though the *sousedská* (a ländler type) was also common. Though not of folk origin the polka became a favourite duple-time dance in both popular and sophisticated society and best typifies the mobility of the folk element in music-making.

4. Slovakia to 1918

Early musical survivals from Slovakia in the 11th century show that the region shared the Byzantine interests of Moravia. Later liturgical sources from the capital Bratislava and Košice in the east of the country from the mid-14th to late 15th centuries suggest a local tradition of troping. From 1302 much of the responsibility for music in Bratislava was in the hands of the parish minister, and the cathedral of St Martin con-

tinued as the major centre of liturgical music-making until the 17th century. Indigenous polyphonic music reveals a rather old-fashioned approach in both Bratislava and provincial towns up to the end of the 15th century. The 16th century witnessed a broadening of attitudes, and a list of the cathedral repertory from 1616 shows a wide range of polyphony including works by Lassus, Marenzio, and Hassler. Secular music-making in Slovakia went largely unrecorded, though as a city of strategic importance Bratislava doubtless had itinerant musicians, and with the formation of guilds in 1376 presumably enjoyed the craft of the Meistersinger. The contribution of town musicians to church services was recorded from 1448 and appears to have continued substantially.

In spite of the continuity afforded by a line of distinguished organists at the cathedral, the major musical developments of the 17th century in Bratislava seem based on the Protestant Church, which flourished briefly between 1635 and 1673, culminating in the work of Samuel Friedrich Capricornus (1628–65) and his successor Johann Kusser (*fl* 1659–74). In addition to producing their own works in concertato style, the Lutheran community possessed a large number of accompanying instruments and performed compositions ranging from Praetorius and Schütz to Viadana and Carissimi. Similarly Lutheran-oriented was the principal exponent of provincial church composition, Ján Šimbracký (*fl* 1635–48), the organist of Ľubica and Spišské Podhradie. Indigenous sacred music in the 18th century varied from the pastorella (which reflected the simplicity of its Bohemian counterpart) to the more sophisticated Italianate work of J. P. Roškovský (1734–89) and F. X. Budinský. Congregational hymns also played an important part in the preservation of the vernacular in music. The native element is present in some of the keyboard collections of the 17th and 18th centuries in simple arrangements and harmonizations, though foreign dance suites predominate.

Although there were few outstanding local figures, Bratislava boasted a musical culture of some sophistication and seems to have been on the itinerary of travelling concert artists including Mozart and Beethoven, and later Liszt and Brahms. The Austrian Anton Zimmermann (*c*.1741–81) did much to improve standards of performance in the orchestra of Archbishop Josef Batthyany, and the composer Franz Rigler (1747 or 1748–96) was important in stimulating the musical life of the city both as a teacher and theorist. Like Tomášek in Prague, Henrik Kelin (1756–1832) offered a focus for musicians in Bratislava in the early 19th century.

Unlike that of Bohemia in the 19th century, opera in Slovakia did not become identified with the rise of a national movement. Opera in the 17th century had been confined to performances for the visiting imperial court by its own company and in the 18th and 19th centuries consisted of Italian and (later) German and Hungarian offerings. Performances of operas in Slovak became a regular occurrence only after the founding of the Slovak National Opera society in Bratislava in 1919. In general, musical nationalism in Slovakia remained less well developed than in Bohemia and Moravia in the 19th century: as musical activity was less centralized, with strong Hungarian leanings, a clearly defined Slovakian voice did not emerge until quite late, and notwithstanding the earlier work of men like Viliam Figuš (1875–1937), Mikuláš Schneider-Trnavský (1881–1958), and Ján Bella (1843–1936) in folksong-collecting and song-setting, a true flowering of Slovak nationalism occurred only after the founding of Czechoslovakia in 1918.

5. Czechoslovakia from 1918

The traditions of 19th-century nationalism effectively ended with the death of Dvořák's pupil Novák in 1949 and of his friend Foerster in 1951, though throughout the 1920s and 30s such composers as Jeremiáš, Otakar Zich (1879–1934), Ladislav Vycpálek (1882–1969), and later Boleslav Vomáčka (1887–1965) continued to compose in what had come to be regarded as the classical, folk-influenced manner. The younger generation of composers in Prague favoured experiment ranging from the microtone compositions of Alois Hába to the Parisian neo-classicism of Iša Krejčí (1904–68) and Martinů. There was also an interest in *socialist realism apparent before the war, manifested most memorably in the work of the pianist and composer Erwin Schulhoff (1894–1942). In Moravia, Janáček remained the dominant figure but had few successors, owing to his highly personal style. Pavel Haas amalgamated a variety of influences, including that of Janáček, in an effective musical language, as did Milan Harašta (1919–46).

After 1918 Slovak musical life began a steady development spurred on by the opening of a Slovak School of Music in 1919 and a National Opera (1920), and after World War II the founding of the High School of Musical Arts (1949) and the Slovak Philharmonic (1949). The major Slovak composers since World War I—Ján Cikker, Alexander Moyzes, and Eugen Suchoň—all studied in Prague, but each showed an individual handling of Impressionist and atonal techniques in combination with national elements. Among the younger composers there has been a willingness to experiment, though many maintain the national orientation of their elders.

While there was a tendency for the Czech musical elite to divide into factions over the relative standing of Smetana and Dvořák, the 1930s were marked by co-operation between Czech and German composers in Prague, which did much to encourage the performance of new works. The German Theatre under George Szell and the National Theatre under Václav Talich kept a varied repertory of new Czech and foreign works. Prague Radio also showed imagination in experimenting with broadcast opera, and commissioning radio operas from Martinů among others. Provincial radio stations were important in broadening the platforms of several performing groups, and the Moravian Municipal Theatre in Brno was hardly less ambitious in performing new works than the main theatres of Prague.

After the end of World War II and the setting up of a socialist state (1948) the musical life of the republic was marked by greater centralization and the nationalization of institutions and performing bodies. State support for the arts increased considerably, though church music and choral societies suffered temporarily. New symphony orchestras were set up in the provinces, and comprehensive concert series (with the aid of state subsidies) brought good performances of a wide range of music before a large audience. Practical music was taught in a number of academies; the universities of Prague, Brno, Bratislava, and several regional cities offered courses in musicology, while the Institute for the Theory and History of Art fostered a growing scholarly interest in Czech music.

Although composition in the 1950s was dominated to a large extent by the exigencies of socialist realism, the latter part of the 20th century witnessed greater interest in experiment. While the majority of composers avoided serial techniques there was a move towards the avant-garde. State concert-promotion helped new composers find a platform (through the Union of Czech Composers), not least in the annual Week of New Compositions held in Prague. But in spite of the variety of talent, no major figures of comparable stature to Novák, Suk, Janáček, or Martinů emerged after the war. Instead, the principal representatives of Czechoslovak musical culture were performers: the Czech and Slovak Philharmonic orchestras, numerous remarkable chamber groups ranging from the Czech Nonet and string quartets to the Suk Trio, and instrumental and vocal soloists.

6. The Czech Republic from 1992

Since the founding of the Czech Republic in 1992 the musical institutions of the country have seen rapid change. Free-market economics have forced many organizations to look for sponsorship and performers have increasingly looked abroad for employment opportunities. Interest in early music, present from the

1960s, has greatly intensified. The Prague National Theatre and the Czech Philharmonic Orchestra remain at the heart of Czech music-making, but the former now has competition from the Prague State Opera, based in the former Smetana Theatre.   JSm

📖 R. NEWMARCH, *The Music of Czechoslovakia* (London, 1942/*R*) · V. ŠTĚPÁNEK and B. KARÁSEK, *An Outline of Czech and Slovak Music* (Prague, 1960–4) · J. TYRRELL, *Czech Opera* (Cambridge, 1988) · C. HOGWOOD and J. SMACZNY, 'The Bohemian lands', *The Classical Era*, ed. N. Zaslaw, Man and Music/Music and Society (London, 1989), 188–212 · J. SMACZNY, 'The Czech symphony', *A Guide to the Symphony*, ed. R. Layton (London, 1993, 2/1995), 221–61

Czernohorsky, Bohuslav Matěj. See ČERNOHORSKÝ, BOHUSLAV MATĚJ.

Czerny, Carl (*b* Vienna, 21 Feb. 1791; *d*. Vienna, 15 July 1857). Austrian piano teacher, composer, and performer. He was Beethoven's most celebrated pupil. As a theorist he was influential in the codification of sonata form and other musical structures. His musical talents were discovered early, and by the age of ten, when he became a pupil of Beethoven, he could perform the Pathétique Sonata. Later, he was famously capable of playing all the master's solo piano music from memory, and gave the first performance of the 'Emperor' Concerto in 1812.

Beethoven's piano teaching emphasized legato playing but otherwise followed the precepts of C. P. E. Bach's *Versuch*. In his own teaching, Czerny adopted a policy of rigorous codification of technical difficulty, the fruits of which are seen in the massive *Pianoforte-Schule* op. 500 and in the numerous books of studies such as *School of Velocity* op. 299. He was one of the most important 19th-century teachers, his famous charges including Heller, Theodor Döhler, Theodor Kullak, Leschetizky, and Liszt. Although Czerny's studies are still sometimes used in teaching, their musical value is too slight for them to be viable concert works; ironically, their didactic purpose is often compromised by the composer's attempt to make each a rounded piece of music, even if of staggering banality, for the tonal scheme rarely allows the figuration to adopt every useful permutation.

Czerny was a prolific composer, writing over 1000 works in most genres apart from opera, and transcribed for the piano many pieces by Handel, Haydn, Mozart, and Beethoven as well as now more obscure composers such as Halévy, Hérold, and Mercadante. His more ambitious compositions show fluent craftsmanship but suffer fatally from what Schumann described as 'imaginative bankruptcy'. In spite of recent attempts to rehabilitate Czerny as a serious composer, Schumann's verdict has been shared by posterity. The works at their best—such as the Piano Sonata in A♭ op. 7—are competently written and pleasant, but offer little to incite a second hearing. Czerny's career as a virtuoso failed to progress beyond Vienna, owing to a lack of extrovert brilliance in both his playing and his character, yet the example of his dedication and sincerity proved crucial in channelling the talents of many more successful pianists—among them the young Liszt, whose playing gained immeasurably from an infusion of his teacher's more sober qualities.   KH

D. 1. The second degree (supertonic) of the scale of C major (see SCALE, 3).

2. Abbreviation for *Deutsch, used as a prefix to the numbers of Schubert's works as given in the standard *thematic catalogue of O. E. Deutsch.

da capo (It., 'from the head'). An instruction to go back to the beginning of a piece, sometimes abbreviated to *d.c.* The indication of where to stop is usually provided by the word *fine*, or a pause mark (⌒). Sometimes the expression used is *da capo al segno*, 'from the beginning to the sign' (𝄋), or *da capo al fine*, 'from the beginning to the end'. Sometimes, also, to one of these expressions is added *poi segue la coda*, 'then follows the coda'—meaning that, the point indicated having been reached, a jump is made to the final section of the piece, usually marked 'coda'.

The term was commonly used in Baroque instrumental music, such as concertos, and regularly in minuet-and-trio structures, to indicate the repeat of the minuet. A '*da capo* aria' is an *aria that has two sections, followed by a repetition of the first, thus making a tripartite structure ABA.

dactyl. A rhythmic pattern, or foot in prosody, consisting of three values, the first stressed (strong), the others unstressed (weak).

dada-mama. A rudimentary side-drum technique in which the hands produce a bouncing stroke in alternation (LLRR or RRLL).

Dafne ('Daphne'). Opera in a prologue and six scenes by Peri to a libretto by Ottavio Rinuccini (Florence, 1597). *Dafne* is generally supposed to be the earliest opera, but most of the music is now lost. It was first performed in Jacopo Corsi's house, and from one of the surviving manuscripts of fragments of the music it appears that Corsi collaborated with Peri.

Dahl, Ingolf (*b* Hamburg, 9 June 1912; *d* Frutigen, 6 Aug. 1970). German-born American composer. He studied in Cologne with Philipp Jarnach (1930–2), in Zürich (1932–6), and in California, where he settled in 1938, becoming an American citizen in 1943. From 1945 until his death he taught at the University of Southern California. He was close to Stravinsky, musically as well as personally, and in his Piano Quartet (1957) followed Stravinsky from neo-classicism into serialism. Most of his small output consists of instrumental music.

PG

Dalayrac [d'Alayrac], Nicolas-Marie (*b* Muret, Haute-Garonne, 8 June 1753; *d* Paris, 26 Nov. 1809). French composer. He was trained as a lawyer before turning to music as a career, and was fortunate in attracting the patronage of Marie Antoinette before the Revolution and that of Napoleon later. He composed nearly 60 *opéras comiques*, which were hugely successful in the 1790s. An inheritor of the tradition of Grétry, he similarly set a range of dramatic subjects—from historical romance to Gothic fantasy to lighthearted comic intrigue—and cultivated an increasingly lyrical, Italianate melodic style. His operas reveal careful dramatic planning, and his use of recurring themes and motifs frequently creates conceptual and musical unity within a work. In *Deux mots, ou Une nuit dans la forêt* (1806), for example, the fragment of a *romance* returns in different guises and comes to represent the voice of the mute heroine, functioning as a warning signal to the hero in its final appearance. Dalayrac was also a resourceful orchestrator. Among his most popular operas were *Nina, ou La Folle par amour* (1786), *Raoul sire de Créqui* (1789), *Camille, ou Le Souterrain* (1791), and *Maison à vendre* (1800). His other works include violin duos, string quartets, trios, instrumental overtures, and songs.

WT/SH

D'Albert, Eugen. See ALBERT, EUGEN D'.

Dalcroze method. A teaching method developed by the Swiss educationist and composer Émile Jaques-Dalcroze (1865–1950). He worked at the Geneva Conservatory, where he found the teaching failed to give students a living experience of music. Inspired by the rhythms of oriental music and the metres of classical poetry, Dalcroze developed a system of coordinating music with bodily movements. This method, which may be used with adults and children, aims to promote alertness, expressiveness, and a sense of phrasing and musical structure.

Dalcroze's ideas spread quickly and gained both official and international recognition during the early years of the 20th century. He visited England in 1912 and soon afterwards the London School of Dalcroze Eurhythmics was established. Similar schools were started in centres across Europe and the USA and training in his method is now worldwide. Dalcroze was one of the 20th century's major contributors to the development of musical education. PSP

Dalibor. Opera in three acts by Smetana to a libretto by Josef Wenzig translated from German into Czech by Ervín Špindler (Prague, 1868).

Dall'Abaco, Evaristo Felice (*b* Verona, 12 July 1675; *d* Munich, 12 July 1742). Italian composer and violinist. He worked at the Este court at Modena from 1696 until at least 1701, and is next heard of in 1704 at the Bavarian court of Elector Maximilian II. After the Battle of Blenheim (1704) Maximilian spent several years in exile, and Dall'Abaco went with him to Brussels, Paris, and various other French cities. He wrote attractive sonatas and concertos, and the rhythmic quality of his themes is sometimes reminiscent of Vivaldi. Signs of his sojourn in France can be seen in his liking for dance rhythms (sarabande, gavotte, passepied, etc.), especially in the chaconnes, which he often wrote as slow movements. DA

Dallapiccola, Luigi (*b* Pisino, Istria, 3 Feb. 1904; *d* Florence, 19 Feb. 1975). Italian composer. In 1922 he settled in Florence, where he studied composition with Vito Frazzi at the Cherubini Conservatory. During this period he was powerfully impressed by Debussy's *Pelléas et Mélisande* and Schoenberg's *Pierrot lunaire*, but he later disowned all his youthful works. He received his diploma in 1931 and immediately joined the staff as a teacher of piano as a second subject—a modest position in which he remained throughout his career. His first acknowledged works, which include the *Sei cori di Michelangelo* (1933–6), show a fluent, neo-classically tinged style influenced by Malipiero, Casella, and Ravel. Gradually—through such works as his first opera, the one-act *Volo di notte* (Florence, 1940)— the harmonic and expressive tensions of his music began to increase, a process culminating in the *Canti di prigionia* for chorus and instruments (1938–41), which make an impassioned plea for liberation from suffering.

The next step was a full adoption of 12-note serialism, which came in 1942 and was assisted by his contacts with Webern. This new technique sharpened Dallapiccola's technique without fundamentally altering his harmonic style, and made possible a still more moving treatment of the prisoner's predicament in the

opera *Il prigioniero*, again in one act (Florence, 1950). The harmonic turbulence of this work suggests Schoenberg, but the piece is thoroughly Italian in its emphasis on the voice, and thoroughly typical of the composer in its effective orchestration.

Refinement of his serial manner during the next years brought Dallapiccola closer to Webern, particularly in such works as the *Cinque canti* for baritone and eight instruments (1956), one of many contributions to vocal chamber music. Others include his *Liriche greche*, a triptych setting texts by Sappho, Alcaeus, and Anacreon (1942–5), *Goethe Lieder* for mezzo-soprano and three clarinets (1953), and *Parole di San Paolo* (1964). Among his rather few purely instrumental scores are the *Due studi* for violin and piano (1946–7), *Tartiniana* and *Tartiniana seconda* for violin and orchestra (1951, 1955–6), *Quaderno musicale di Annalibera* for piano (1952), *Piccola musica notturna* for orchestra (1954), and *Three Questions with Two Answers* for orchestra (1962). Dallapiccola's distinctive synthesis of Webern, Debussy, and bel canto, and also the depth of his philosophical thought, contributed to the success of his opera *Ulisse* (1960–8; Berlin, 1968), where the wanderings of Odysseus become a metaphor for man's spiritual search. PG

📖 R. SHACKELFORD (ed.), *Dallapiccola on Opera: Selected Writings*, i (London, 1987)

dal segno (It.). 'From the sign'; an indication that a passage is to be repeated not from the beginning but from the place marked by the sign 𝄋 , then continued to the end, to the word *fine*, or to a double bar with a pause sign over it; it is often abbreviated 'D.S.'

Dame blanche, La ('The White Lady'). Opera in three acts by Boieldieu to a libretto by Eugène Scribe after Walter Scott's novels *Guy Mannering* (1815), *The Monastery* (1820), and *The Abbot* (1820) (Paris, 1825).

Damnation de Faust, La ('The Damnation of Faust'). Cantata ('dramatic legend'), op. 24 (1845–6), by Berlioz, for mezzo-soprano, tenor, baritone, and bass soloists, chorus, and orchestra, to a libretto by the composer and Almire Gandonnière after Gérard de Nerval's French translation of Johann Wolfgang von Goethe's *Faust*; it incorporates the earlier *Huit scènes de Faust* (1828–9). It was adapted as a fully staged opera (Monte Carlo, 1893) and is often given as an opera. See also RÁKÓCZI MARCH.

damper. The device which stops ('damps') the vibration of strings on keyboard instruments or of the membrane of a drum. On *harpsichords it is a cloth flag in the top of the jack, on pianos it was originally cloth but is now a pedal-controlled felt pad (see PIANOFORTE), and on *clavichords it was the listing woven round the strings. On a drum it denotes a pad pressing on one or both heads.   JMo

Dämpfer (Ger.). *'Mute'; *mit Dämpfern*, 'with mutes'; *Dämpfung*, 'muting' or (on the piano) 'soft-pedalling'.

Damrosch, Walter (Johannes) (*b* Breslau, 30 Jan. 1862; *d* New York, 22 Dec. 1950). German-born American conductor. He was the son of the conductor Leopold Damrosch (1832–85), with whom he went to New York in 1871. He studied conducting with his father and in 1884 began assisting him in his German opera seasons at the Metropolitan Opera, New York. He succeeded him in 1885 as the conductor of the New York Symphony Society and conducted at the Metropolitan Opera and with the Philharmonic and Symphony Orchestras before they merged in 1928. He formed and conducted the Damrosch Opera Company (1894–9). When the National Broadcasting Company (NBC) was formed he was appointed director of classical music and began a long-running weekly music appreciation hour for children. He introduced many works to the USA, including Mahler's Fourth Symphony, and composed operas and choral works. His autobiography, *My Musical Life*, was published in 1923.   JT

dance. See BALLET AND THEATRICAL DANCE.

Dance before the Golden Calf (*Der Tanz um das goldene Kalb*). The central part of Act II of Schoenberg's opera *Moses und Aron*.

dance notation. See CHOREOLOGY.

Dance of Death (Fr.: *danse macabre*; Ger.: *Totentanz*). The idea of Death as a dancer or as a skeletal fiddler of dance tunes was particularly important during the Middle Ages, especially following the Black Death in the 14th century. In the 19th and 20th centuries it was an influential concept in art and literature and also inspired several composers. Liszt's *Totentanz* for piano and orchestra (1849) drew on a poem by Goethe, and Saint-Saëns's symphonic poem *Danse macabre* (op. 40, 1874) was based on poetry by Henri Cazalis; both these works use the *Dies irae*, the traditional plainchant of the Requiem Mass. The *Danse des morts* for solo voices, chorus, and orchestra (1938) by Honegger was inspired by Hans Holbein's famous series of woodcuts *Imagines mortis* (Lyon, 1538).

Dance of the Blessed Spirits. Slow dance episode in Act II of Gluck's *Orfeo ed Euridice* (1762) characterized

by a lyrical flute solo; it is often performed as a concert item.

Dance of the Hours. A ballet in Act III of Ponchielli's *La *Gioconda*, often played as a separate orchestral piece; an entertainment staged by one of the characters for his guests, it symbolizes the conflict between darkness and light.

Dance of the Seven Veils. Popular name for Salome's dance before Herod in Richard Strauss's opera *Salome* (1905); for orchestra alone, it is often performed as a concert item.

Dance of the Sylphs. Orchestral episode in the second part of Berlioz's *La Damnation de Faust*; it is often played separately.

Dances of Galánta (*Galántai táncok*). Orchestral suite (1933) by Kodály; based on Gypsy tunes collected in the market town of Galánta, it was composed for the 80th anniversary of the Budapest Philharmonic Society.

Dance Suite (*Táncszvit*). Orchestral work (1923) by Bartók, composed to celebrate the 50th anniversary of the merging of Buda and Pest; Bartók also arranged it for piano (1925).

Dandrieu [d'Andrieu], **Jean-François** (*b* c.1682; *d* Paris, 17 Jan. 1738). French composer. He was an infant prodigy, playing in public before the age of five, and later became the most celebrated harpsichordist after Couperin and Rameau. He was appointed organist at St Merry in 1705 and one of the organists of the royal chapel in December 1721. He composed exclusively for the organ and harpsichord, and according to Rameau was best remembered for his 'ingenious' *noëls*. Dandrieu explicitly intended his pieces to be descriptive and gave them appropriate titles: *Les Caractères de la guerre*, written as an orchestral piece to be danced in an unidentified opera, and later transcribed for harpsichord, imitates the sounds of cannon fire in what was probably the first use ever of a note *cluster. It seems likely that Dandrieu often reworked pieces by his uncle, Pierre Dandrieu (1664–1733); the authorship of the *airs* and *noëls* especially is uncertain.   PW

D'Anglebert, Jean-Henry (*b* Bar-le-Duc, *bapt.* 1 April 1629; *d* Paris, 23 April 1691). French organist and harpsichordist. He may have been a pupil of Chambonnières before becoming organist to the Jacobins in the rue St Honoré in the 1650s. In 1660 he was appointed harpsichordist to the Duke of Orléans (the brother of Louis XIV) and two years later took over Chambonnières's duties as court harpsichordist.

D'Anglebert's *Pieces de clavecin* (Paris, 1689), which includes brilliant arrangements of Lully overtures and ballet music as well as an important table of ornaments, inspired the next generation of keyboard players, including François Couperin, Rameau, and J. S. Bach.

D'Anglebert's son, **Jean-Baptiste Henry** (*bapt.* 26 March 1662; *d* 1735), succeeded him at court in 1674 and was in turn succeeded in 1736 by Couperin's daughter, Marguerite-Antoinette.   DA/JAS

> 📖 B. SCHEIBERT, *Jean-Henry D'Anglebert* (Bloomington, IN, 1986)

Danican. See PHILIDOR.

Daniel [Danyel], John (*b* Wellow, nr Bath, *bapt.* 6 Nov. 1564; *d c.*1626). English lutenist and composer. He took the degree of B.Mus. at Oxford University in 1603, and thereafter held various appointments as a teacher of the lute. From 1617 he was a court musician; he was also involved in the production of choirboy plays in Bristol. His works include a set of lute-accompanied songs, published in 1606, and music for solo lute.   JM

Daniel-Lesur, Jean Yves (*b* Paris, 19 Nov. 1908). French composer and administrator. He studied at the Paris Conservatoire, taking private composition lessons with Charles Tournemire, to whom the rhapsody *La Vie intérieure* for organ (1932) is dedicated. In 1936 he joined Messiaen, André Jolivet, and Yves Baudrier to form the *Jeune France group. Among his most attractive works is the set of Variations for piano and strings (1943), which fully reflects the cherished French tradition of clarity and elegance. Above all Daniel-Lesur excelled in writing for the human voice, notably in *Quatre lieder* (1934–9) to poems by Cécile Sauvage and Heinrich Heine, *Le Cantique des cantiques* for 12-part mixed choir (1953), and the opera *Andrea del Sarto* (Marseilles, 1969).   AT

Dannreuther, Edward (George) (*b* Strasbourg, 4 Nov. 1844; *d* London, 12 Feb. 1905). British pianist, writer, and teacher of German origin. His family emigrated to the USA in 1846 and he grew up in Cincinnati. After studying the piano with Moscheles in Leipzig (1860–3) he moved to London, eventually settling there after his marriage in 1871. A virtuoso pianist, he introduced English audiences to concertos by Grieg, Liszt (no. 2), Tchaikovsky (no. 1), Scharwenka (no. 1), and Parry, his most prominent pupil. His home in Bayswater was the setting for a series of semi-public chamber concerts promoting contemporary music (1876–93), and it was where Wagner stayed during the London Wagner Festival (1877). Wagner's theories of opera and drama were the subject of several important writings by Dannreuther, including *Wagner and the Reform of Opera*

(1873) and a lengthy article for the first edition of Grove's *Dictionary of Music and Musicians*. In later life he taught at the RCM (from 1895), edited Liszt's piano works, and wrote two important reference books: *Music Ornamentation* and volume 6 (*The Romantic Period*) of The Oxford History of Music.   JD1

Danse macabre ('Dance of Death'). Symphonic poem, op. 40 (1874), by Saint-Saëns, based on a poem by Henri Cazalis in which Death the Fiddler summons skeletons from their graves at midnight to dance; it includes the *Dies irae* (Saint-Saëns had already set the poem as a song). Liszt made a piano transcription of it. See also DANCE OF DEATH; TOTENTANZ, 2.

Dante Sonata. Piano work by Liszt, the first version (in two movements) dating from 1839; it was revised twice and became, in one movement, the final piece in book 2 of the *Années de pèlerinage*, the full title of this version being *Après une lecture du Dante, fantasia quasi sonata*.

Dante Symphony. Orchestral work (1855–6) by Liszt, based on Johann Wolfgang von Goethe's play, its full title being *Eine Symphonie zu Dantes Divina commedia* ('A Symphony to Dante's Divine Comedy'); it is in two movements, 'Inferno' and 'Purgatorio', the latter concluding with a choral *Magnificat*. Tchaikovsky's *Francesca da Rimini* was heavily influenced by its first movement.

Dantons Tod ('Danton's Death'). Opera in two parts (six scenes) by Einem to a libretto by Boris Blacher and the composer after Georg Büchner's play (1835) (Salzburg, 1947).

Danyel, John. See DANIEL, JOHN.

danza tedesca (It., 'German dance'). The Austrian *ländler, or an early type of waltz.

Danzi, Franz (*b* Schwetzingen, 15 June 1763; *d* Karlsruhe, 13 April 1826). German composer and conductor. He studied with his father Innozenz and with the Abbé Vogler, then joined the Mannheim orchestra as first cellist in 1783. There he was encouraged to compose operas. He had already written a successful melodrama in the Benda vein, *Cleopatra* (1780), and went on to achieve his greatest operatic success with *Die Mitternachtsstunde* ('The Midnight Hour', 1789), an entertaining, artificial light comedy that includes some original harmonic touches. In 1790 he married the soprano Margarethe Marchand, with whom he toured. Her death in 1800 threw him into a deep depression, and he did not resume operatic duties until 1807, when he became Kapellmeister at Stuttgart. There he wrote a German grand opera, *Iphigenia in*

Aulis (1807), which was favourably reviewed but is unfortunately now lost. He also befriended the young Carl Maria von Weber, encouraging performances of his work. His own *Rübezahl* (1813), on a subject abandoned by Weber, includes some anticipations of the Wolf's Glen scene in *Der Freischütz*. Danzi is less well known today for his operas than for his attractive chamber music for wind instruments and for his concertos.   DA/JW

Daphne. Opera in one act by Richard Strauss to a libretto by Joseph Gregor (Dresden, 1938).

Daphnis et Chloé. Ballet ('choreographic symphony') in three movements by Ravel to a scenario by Mikhail Fokine, who choreographed it for Diaghilev's Ballets Russes (Paris, 1912); the score includes a part for wordless chorus. Ravel made two orchestral suites from it (1911, 1913).

Daquin [D'Aquin], Louis-Claude (*b* Paris, 4 July 1694; *d* Paris, 15 June 1772). French organist and composer, of part-Jewish ancestry. His great-uncle was physician to Louis XIV, and at the age of six Daquin was taken to play before the king. His godmother was the harpsichordist Élisabeth Jacquet de la Guerre. A renowned improviser and virtuoso performer, Daquin competed successfully against Rameau for the post of organist at St Paul in 1727, succeeding Marchand at the Cordeliers in 1732 and Dandrieu at the royal chapel in 1739; in 1755 he took on one quarter-share of the prestigious organ post at Notre Dame. His works include suites of descriptive harpsichord pieces (Paris, 1735), of which the best known is *Le Coucou*, and a book of *noëls* (Paris, 1757).   DA/JAS

Dardanus. Opera in a prologue and five acts by Rameau to a libretto by Charles-Antoine Le Clerc de La Bruère (Paris, 1739). Sacchini wrote an opera on the same subject (Versailles, 1784).

Dargomïzhsky, Aleksandr Sergeyevich (*b* Troitskoye, Tula district, 2/14 Feb. 1813; *d* St Petersburg, 5/17 Jan. 1869). Russian composer. He was born into a cultured household but, like many of his Russian contemporaries, he had little formal training in music; however, he studied the piano and was much in demand as a singing teacher, and acquired a knowledge of the classics through his friendship with Glinka. But music was little more than a sideline, and he earned his living in government service. Dargomïzhsky had already composed two conventional operas, *Ésmeralda* (1847) and *Rusalka* (1856), before taking a radically new direction in *Kamenniy gost'* ('The Stone Guest'), a word-for-word setting of Pushkin's poem on the Don Juan legend; like some of his songs, *The Stone Guest* reflects

Dargomïzhsky's quest for 'truth in art', which led him to mould the musical lines closely to the inflections of the Russian text instead of fitting the Russian into melodic patterns more appropriate to Italian speech rhythms. The opera was left incomplete at Dargomïzhsky's death but was soon completed by Cui and Rimsky-Korsakov and was performed in 1872. Although by general consent the result of Dargomïzhsky's experiment is rather dry, the opera became highly influential among the advocates of musical realism in 19th-century Russia.

GN/MF-W

Darke, Harold (Edwin) (*b* London, 29 Oct. 1888; *d* Cambridge, 28 Nov. 1976). English organist and composer. He studied at the RCM with Walter Parratt (organ) and Stanford (composition). As organist of St Michael's Cornhill in London from 1916 to 1966, he gained a reputation for his playing of Bach (in the style of Albert Schweitzer) and his regular Monday recitals; he also founded the St Michael's Singers (1919–66), whose festivals featured works by Parry, Vaughan Williams, and Howells. During World War II he was acting organist of King's College, Cambridge, while Boris Ord was on war service. His large output of church music includes three settings of the Anglican Communion service, anthems, and motets, but he is perhaps best known for his popular setting of the carol *In the bleak mid-winter*. He also composed chamber music and an unpublished symphony.   PG/JDi

Dart, (Robert) Thurston (*b* Kingston upon Thames, 3 Sept. 1921; *d* London, 6 March 1971). English musicologist, harpsichordist, and teacher. From about 1947 he was the leading light in the revival of early music, and his book *The Interpretation of Music* (London, 1954, 4/1967) inspired much investigation into performance practice. He wrote numerous articles, edited a great deal of 17th-century music, and made many recordings. He taught at Cambridge and at King's College, London; his pupils included many of the best English musicologists of the next generation.   DA/LC

Daser, Ludwig (*b* Munich, *c*.1525; *d* Stuttgart, 27 March 1589). German composer. Trained at the Munich court chapel, he was Kapellmeister there from 1552 until supplanted by Lassus in 1563. In 1572 he transferred to the Lutheran court at Stuttgart. His compositions include 22 masses, numerous motets, and an impressive through-composed *St John Passion* (1578).   DA/BS

dauernd (Ger.). 'Enduring', i.e. continuing, lasting.

Daughter of the Regiment, The. See FILLE DU RÉGIMENT, LA.

Dauprat, Louis-François (*b* Paris, 24 May 1781; *d* Paris, 17 July 1868). French horn player, teacher, and composer. He spent much of his career as principal horn at the Paris Opéra, and though a successful soloist preferred orchestral work, teaching, and composing for the horn. His *Méthode pour cor alto et cor basse* remains an important teaching manual, and he published much music for the instrument.   CF

David, Félicien(-César) (*b* Cadenet, 13 April 1810; *d* St Germain-en-Laye, 29 Aug. 1876). French composer. He studied at the Paris Conservatoire, then joined the *Saint-Simonians, becoming the most prominent musician in the order. Following the dissolution of the community by the government in 1832, he travelled in the Middle East, finding in it a fascinating source of musical inspiration. Back in France, he achieved great success with his 'ode-symphonie' *Le Désert* (1844), which includes a prayer to Allah and a muezzin's call. He then wrote a series of pieces evoking Eastern subjects that were to influence later composers, including Delibes and Saint-Saëns. Other concert works and songs were successful, but the *opéra comique Lalla-Roukh* (1862), which held the stage for 20 years, is recognized as his masterpiece. Although David may be regarded in some respects as a successor to Berlioz, his evocative, strongly coloured music does not explore the rich harmonies favoured by other mid-19th-century French composers.   SH

   📖 D. V. HAGAN, *Félicien David, 1810–1876: A Composer and a Cause* (Syracuse, NY, 1985)

Davidde penitente ('David the Penitent'). Oratorio by Mozart, K469 (1785), to a text probably by Lorenzo Da Ponte; it is for two sopranos and a tenor soloist, chorus, and orchestra and incorporates material from an unfinished Mass in C minor, K427/417a (1782–3).

Davidovsky, Mario (*b* Medanos, Buenos Aires, 4 March 1934). Argentine-born American composer. He studied in Buenos Aires before settling in New York (1960), where he studied with Milton Babbitt, taught at City College (1968–80), and worked at the Columbia–Princeton Electronic Music Center. His best-known works are the fluent and characterful *Synchronisms* that create blendings and dialogues for live performers (instrumental soloists, chamber groups, chorus, or orchestra) and tape, but his non-electronic pieces—chamber works and rare orchestral pieces—show the same pregnancy of idea, vigour of growth, and joyful musicality.   PG

Davidsbündlertänze. Schumann's op. 6 (1837), a set of 18 character pieces for piano.

Davies, Sir **Peter Maxwell** (*b* Manchester, 8 Sept. 1934). English composer. He studied at Manchester University and with Richard Hall at the RMCM, as well as with Goffredo Petrassi in Rome and Roger Sessions at Princeton. Together with his fellow Manchester students Harrison Birtwistle and Alexander Goehr he developed an interest in connections between intricate serial techniques and medieval contrapuntal and rhythmic practices, evident in such early works as *Alma Redemptoris mater* for wind sextet (1957) and *Prolation* for orchestra (1959).

Davies first came to prominence during his years as music director at Cirencester Grammar School (1959–62), where he pioneered many imaginative musical activities. He has remained strongly committed to education through creativity ever since, and this has in no way compromised the often complex techniques and elaborate textures of his own compositions. His fascination with the life and music of John Taverner gave rise to two orchestral fantasias (1962, 1964) and the opera *Taverner* (Covent Garden, 1972); many other works besides these have used segments of plainchant as the source of their serial materials. Such methods, similar to those used in 15th- and 16th-century parody masses, led him to parody in the modern sense: for example, *St Thomas Wake* (1969) is a 'foxtrot for orchestra' in which a pavan by John Bull is heard in its original form alongside violent distortions in 1920s foxtrot style.

In 1968 Davies co-founded the Pierrot Players (renamed the Fires of London in 1970). His extensive output for this group includes many of his most uncompromisingly dramatic works, for example *Eight Songs for a Mad King* and *Vesalii icones* (both 1969). With his move to the Orkney island of Hoy in 1971, and the later disbanding of the Fires, Davies's music became less overtly parodistic, while retaining the intense emotional charge special to his particular brand of expressionism, as well as its technical basis in chant-derived serial matrices structured according to the arithmetical principle of the magic square (for illustration see SERIALISM, Ex. 2).

Since the mid-1970s Davies's energies have focused primarily on a series of large-scale symphonies and concertos, including the ten *Strathclyde Concertos* written for the Scottish Chamber Orchestra between 1987 and 1996 and the *Symphonia antarctica* (2001). In these and other later compositions, like the ballet score *The Beltane Fire* (1995), the presence of Scottish material, often folk-like in character, reinforces the more broadly lyrical manner of the music written since 1970. These works are also notable for the consistent presence of his personal concept of tonality, which provides a strong harmonic framework for the music's elaborately wrought melodic and contrapuntal processes. Davies's tonality differs from traditional diatonicism in giving primary importance to symmetrical divisions of the octave, and associating tonal centres a minor 3rd or tritone apart; the clearly perceptible prominence given to D, F, G♯, and B in the Symphony no. 3 (1984) at important points in the structure is a good example. Davies was knighted in 1987. **PG/AW**

   📖 P. GRIFFITHS, *Peter Maxwell Davies* (London, 1982) · M. SEABROOK, *Max: The Life and Music of Peter Maxwell Davies* (London, 1994) · R. McGREGOR (ed.), *Perspectives on Peter Maxwell Davies* (Aldershot, 2001)

Davies, Sir (Henry) Walford (*b* Oswestry, 6 Sept. 1869; *d* Wrington, Som., 11 March 1941). English composer, organist, and broadcaster. He was a choirboy and pupil assistant at St George's Chapel, Windsor (1882–90). He studied at the RCM with Parry, Stanford, and W. S. Rockstro (1890–4) and taught counterpoint there (1895–1903). As organist of the Temple Church (1898–1923) he rapidly developed a career as choral conductor and composer. He was professor of music at the University of Wales (1919–26) and organist at St George's, Windsor (1927–32), before retiring, though he accepted the position of Master of the King's Music (1934–41). His large-scale choral works, notably *Everyman* (1904), *Lift up your hearts* (1906), and *Noble Numbers* (1909), reveal his admiration for the ethical preoccupations of Parry, whom he much respected. He is best known today for *Solemn Melody* (1908) for organ and strings, an attractive setting of *O Little Town of Bethlehem*, the introit *God be in my head* (1908), and the *RAF March Past* (1921). He also played an important part in popular musical education through his many broadcast talks for the BBC. **PG/JDi**

   📖 H. C. COLLES, *Walford Davies: A Biography* (London, 1942)

Davis, Carl (*b* New York, 28 Oct. 1936). American composer. He studied with Paul Nordoff, Hugo Kauder, and, in Copenhagen, with Per Nørgård. In 1961 he went to the Edinburgh Festival as co-author of a revue, and from that time made his career in Britain, especially as a composer for films both old (Abel Gance's *Napoléon*, 1980) and new, television, the theatre, and ballet, and as an arranger (Paul McCartney's *Liverpool Oratorio*). **PG**

Davy, Richard (*b* c.1465; *d* ?Exeter, c.1507). English composer. He worked as choirmaster and organist at Magdalen College, Oxford, from 1490 to 1492, and at Exeter Cathedral from 1497 to 1506. His works include a four-part setting of the Passion according to St Matthew, masses, and votive antiphons (many of which are now lost), as well as some songs and carols. **JM**

d.c. Abbreviation for *da capo*.

Dean, Brett (*b* Brisbane, 23 Oct. 1961). Australian composer and viola player. He studied at the Queensland Conservatorium in Brisbane, and in Berlin. He was a permanent member of the Berlin Philharmonic Orchestra from 1985 to 2000, when he left to return to Australia and concentrate on composition. Many of his works have been written for himself or for performing colleagues. Larger-scale works include *Ariel's Music* for clarinet and orchestra (1995), *Carlo* for strings, sampler, and tape (1997), *Beggars and Angels* for orchestra (1999), inspired by paintings by his wife Heather Betts, and *Pastoral Symphony* for ensemble and tape (2001). **ABur**

Death and the Maiden. See TOD UND DAS MÄDCHEN, DER.

Death and Transfiguration. See TOD UND VERKLÄRUNG.

Death in Venice. Opera in two acts (17 scenes) by Britten to a libretto by Myfanwy Piper after Thomas Mann's novella *Der Tod in Venedig* (1911) (Snape, 1973).

Death of Klinghoffer, The. Opera in two acts by Adams to a libretto by Alice Goodman (Brussels, 1991).

De Béthune, Conon. See CONON DE BÉTHUNE.

De Boësset, Antoine. See BOËSSET, ANTOINE DE.

Deborah. Oratorio (1733) by Handel to a biblical text compiled by Samuel Humphreys.

De Brossard, Sébastien. See BROSSARD, SÉBASTIEN DE.

Debussy, Claude (*see page 346*)

debut (from Fr. *début*). 'Beginning', or 'opening', i.e. the first public appearance of an artist.

decani (Lat., 'of the dean'). The side of the choir on which the dean sits, now normally the south side. Choral music sometimes has passages marked *decani*, indicating that the singers on that side should take the passage. See also CANTORIS.

decay. The more or less gradual fall in intensity of a musical note, or of any sound in a hall or room, after the source has stopped vibrating (see ARCHITECTURAL ACOUSTICS, 3 and 4). **JBo**

deceptive cadence. See CADENCE.

decibel. A unit of transmission (abbreviated to dB) giving the ratio of two powers or sound intensities. There are 10 decibels in a Bel, the basic logarithmic unit

(*cont. on p. 348*)

Claude Debussy
(1862–1918)

The French composer Achille-Claude Debussy was born at St Germain-en-Laye on 22 August 1862 and died in Paris on 25 March 1918.

The early years

Debussy's early life was unsettled because of his father's numerous occupations and his imprisonment after the Commune of 1871, and he received no formal education until he entered the Paris Conservatoire the following year. Piano lessons with Mme Mauté, who claimed to be Chopin's pupil, led to early hopes of a virtuoso career, but Debussy decided in favour of composition with Ernest Guiraud in 1880 and won the Prix de Rome in 1884 with his cantata *L'Enfant prodigue*. He regarded the Villa Medici in Rome as a prison, and his 'envois' (*Zuleima*, 1885–6, now lost; *Printemps*, 1887, reorchestrated by Busser, 1912; *La Damoiselle élue*, 1887–8) received little approval from the Académie des Beaux-Arts. The most promising work to emerge was a setting of part of Act II of Banville's *Diane au bois* (1883–6), which anticipated the forest dream world and seductive flute writing of the *Prélude à 'L'Après-midi d'un faune'* (1894), his first great success. Earlier, Debussy had attempted conventional opera with *Rodrigue et Chimène* (libretto by Catulle Mendès, after Guillén de Castro and Pierre Corneille, 1890–2), which he found grandiose and uncongenial. But both that and the *Cinq poèmes de Baudelaire* (1887–9) were the vehicles whereby he was able to compose the superficial aspects of Wagnerism out of his system, though a deeper-seated influence and a love–hate relationship with both Wagner and the theatre persisted through to his ballet *Jeux* (1913).

The year 1893 proved a turning-point for Debussy: *La Damoiselle élue* at the Société Nationale on 8 April brought his music to public attention, and on 17 May he saw the premiere of Maurice Maeterlinck's Symbolist play *Pelléas et Mélisande* (1892) at the Théâtre des Bouffes-Parisiens. In the shadowy, suggestive, and apparently simple world of *Pelléas*, Debussy realized he had found his ideal opera libretto, and he set the play directly, in prose (with only four scenes cut), between August 1893 and 17 August 1895. After Albert Carré finally agreed to produce *Pelléas* at the Opéra-Comique in May 1901, Debussy completed its orchestration, adding extra (Wagnerian) interludes at the last moment to facilitate the complex scene changes. Difficulties with Maeterlinck came to a head at the stormy dress rehearsal on 28 April 1902, chiefly because he had tried to insist that his mistress Georgette Leblanc play Mélisande, instead of Mary Garden who was Debussy's choice. Badly copied parts, injunctions, the sale of defamatory librettos, Garden's Scottish accent, and the completely new operatic conception of *Pelléas* did little to ease its birth, but in spite of being thought formless, monotonous, decadent, and technically incomprehensible by many of its audience, the younger enthusiastic element prevailed and the opera entered the repertory. Like Wagner, Debussy gave the orchestra a substantial commentatorial role and used recurring themes. But the latter were subtly adapted to the characters' changing states of mind and feelings rather than being mere 'visiting-cards' announcing their entry. The main influence was more Musorgsky in the precise prosody and naturalness of the recitative-like vocal lines.

Otherwise, Debussy's theatrical career was one of 'compulsive inachievement' (Holloway). He never again found his ideal poem or poet, and his one-act Edgar Allen Poe operas *Le Diable dans le beffroi* (1902–?12) and *La Chute de la maison Usher* (1908–17) remain unfinished, as does his music for *Le Roi Lear* (1904) and *No-ja-li* (1913–14). Other dramatic projects were, like his uncongenial foreign conducting tours, accepted for financial reasons and often required outside assistance to complete their orchestration. *Le Martyre de Saint Sébastien* (a five-act mystery by Gabriele D'Annunzio mixing Christianity with paganism) was completed in 1911 with André Caplet's help; *Khamma* (a 'ballet pantomime' commissioned by the exotic dancer Maud Allan) was finished by Charles Koechlin in 1912–13; and *La Boîte à joujoux* (1913, a children's ballet by André Hellé) was completed by Caplet in 1919.

After 'Pelléas'

In almost every respect the performance of *Pelléas et Mélisande* forms a watershed in Debussy's career. While his songs are evenly spread before and after in terms of quality (compare the two sets of Paul Verlaine's *Fêtes galantes* of 1891 and 1904), his best piano music dates from after he left his first wife Rosalie (Lilly) Texier for Emma Bardac in June 1904. Their daughter Claude-Emma (Chouchou) was born on 30 October 1905 and her parents married on 20 January 1908. The piano pieces inspired by their 'honeymoon' in Jersey and Dieppe in the summer of 1904 included *Masques* and the unusually extrovert *L'Isle joyeuse*, and these, like Debussy's two series of *Images* (1905, 1907), were first performed by Ricardo Viñes. Chouchou's infant world inspired the *Children's Corner* suite (1906–8) with its celebrated *Tristan* parody in *Golliwogg's Cake-Walk*, but Debussy is best known for his two books of *Préludes* (1909–10, 1911–13), which evoke a series of widely varied natural subjects from the antics of Christy 'minstrels' at Eastbourne in 1905 and the American acrobat 'Général Lavine' to dead leaves and the sounds and scents of the evening air. They are wrongly termed impressionistic, for Debussy's inspiration owed far more to the painter J. M. W. Turner and to the literary *Symbolist movement. But in his orchestral *Images* (*Gigues*, 1909–12; *Ibéria*, 1905–8; and *Rondes de printemps*, 1905–9), Debussy told his publisher Jacques Durand that he was 'attempting something different—in a sense, *realities*', and he delightedly described to Caplet in 1910 how natural the join between the last two parts of *Ibéria* sounded, almost as if it were improvised. He claimed he could actually hear 'the watermelon merchant and the whistling urchins' at the start of 'Le Matin d'un jour de fête', though such moments of complete artistic optimism were sadly rare.

Debussy's style

'Music is made up of colours and barred rhythms', Debussy told Durand in 1907, and in his experiments with timbre and his efforts to free music from formal convention he tried many different solutions—from proportional structures based on the Golden Section (*La Mer*, *L'Isle joyeuse*) to the cinematographic form of *Jeux*, with its constant motivic renewal in which undulating fragments gradually evolve into a scalar theme which is itself broken off at its violent climax. As elsewhere in Debussy's works, this climax is approached by a series of lesser ones and is placed as near to the end as he dared. Debussy's earlier orchestral music includes the *Nocturnes* (1897–9), with their exceptionally varied textures ranging from the Musorgskian start of *Nuages*, through the approaching brass band procession in *Fêtes*, to the wordless female chorus in *Sirènes*, whose study of 'sea-textures' is a kind of preparation for *La Mer* (1903–5). Here the ever-changing moods of the sea are fully explored and the three 'symphonic sketches' together make up a giant sonata-form movement with its own Franckian cyclic theme. The evocative central 'Jeux de vagues' is a sort of development section leading into the final 'Dialogue du vent et de la mer', a powerful essay in orchestral colour and sonority.

After *La Mer*, the woodwind increasingly carried the main thematic burden, and the percussion gradually gained in importance via *Ibéria* to the subtleties of *Jeux*. Here, Debussy attempted to find an orchestra 'without feet . . . lit from behind' as in Wagner's *Parsifal*. In spite of its radical nature, *Jeux* was overshadowed in Diaghilev's Ballets Russes season (15 May 1913) by the *succès de scandale* of Stravinsky's *The Rite of Spring* a fortnight later. The cordial relations between the two composers deteriorated after this, though Stravinsky's rising genius had earlier influenced Debussy: *Khamma* (1911–12), for instance, shows how well Debussy had learnt the lesson of *Petrushka*. Whereas Debussy's early songs, inspired by his affair with a Madame Vasnier, included much showy vocalise, his settings were more mature and restrained from the *Ariettes oubliées* (1885–7) onwards. He wrote his own poems for the *Proses lyriques* (1892–3) and for the recently rediscovered *Nuits blanches* (1898–1902) but, as in *La Chute de la maison Usher*, his literary talents were not on a par with his musical imagination. His career as a songwriter culminated in the sensitive and witty *Trois ballades de François Villon* (1910) and in the *Trois poèmes de Stéphane Mallarmé* (1913). Two of the latter (*Soupir* and *Placet futile*) were also set by Ravel in the same year (to Debussy's annoyance), both composers finding inspiration in the atmospheric qualities and formal subtlety of Mallarmé's poetry.

Debussy's career in chamber music had had an auspicious beginning with his cyclic String Quartet (1893), the influential scherzo of which, with its cross-rhythms and flying pizzicatos, recalled the gamelan sonorities he had heard at the Paris Exhibition of 1889. But apart from the *Première rapsodie* for clarinet and piano (1909–10), written for the Paris Conservatoire, it was not until his final years that Debussy reverted to the medium. Ever concerned with the necessity for French music to be true to itself, he planned a series of six chamber sonatas in a nationalistic spirit looking back to Rameau. Before finally succumbing to rectal cancer, he completed three of them: the Cello Sonata (1915, contemporary with *En blanc et noir* for two pianos and the 12 *Études* in memory of Chopin), the Sonata for flute, viola, and harp (1915), and the Violin Sonata (1916–17). The finale of the last sonata caused the ailing Debussy enormous difficulty, though there is virtually no evidence of declining powers in any of his wartime music. All three sonatas anticipated neo-classicism in their simplicity, clarity, and stylistic restraint.   RO

📖 E. Lockspeiser, *Debussy: His Life and Mind*, 2 vols. (London, 1962, 1965/R1979) · R. Langham Smith, *Debussy on Music* (London, 1977) · R. Holloway, *Debussy and Wagner* (London, 1979) · R. Orledge, *Debussy and the Theatre* (Cambridge, 1982) · R. Howat, *Debussy in Proportion* (Cambridge, 1983) · F. Lesure and R. Nichols (eds.), *Debussy Letters* (London, 1987) · R. Nichols, *Debussy Remembered* (London, 1992, 2/1998) · F. Lesure (ed.), *Claude Debussy: Correspondance 1884–1918* (Paris, 1993) · F. Lesure, *Claude Debussy: Biographie critique* (Paris, 1994) · M. Cobb, *The Poetic Debussy* (Rochester, 2/1994) · R. Langham Smith, *Debussy Studies* (Cambridge, 1997) · R. Nichols, *A Life of Debussy* (Cambridge, 1998)

named after the inventor Alexander Graham Bell. See ACOUSTICS, II.   JBo

décidé (Fr.), **deciso, decisamente** (It.). 'Decided', i.e. resolutely.

declamation. Emphatic or heightened speech; declamation might therefore be thought of as a transitional mode of expression between speech and music. In this sense a musical text setting is likely to be regarded as declamatory if it seeks to preserve something of purely verbal accentuation in the musical setting, as in *recitative or *arioso, but in a context where the mood is forceful or even aggressive rather than reticent or understated.   AW

decoration. See ORNAMENTS AND ORNAMENTATION.

Decoration Day. Orchestral work by Ives (*c*.1915–20); it became the second movement of *Holidays*.

decrescendo (It.). 'Decreasing', i.e. gradually getting quieter. The term is often represented by the 'hairpin' sign (see DYNAMIC MARKS, Table 1) or by the abbreviations *decr.* or *decresc.* The opposite is *crescendo*.

Deering, Richard. See DERING, RICHARD.

De Fesch, Willem (*b* Alkmaar, *bapt.* 26 Aug. 1687; *d* London, 3 Jan. 1761). Dutch composer and violinist. He may have been a choirboy in Liège during the 1690s. By about 1710 he had moved to Amsterdam, where he married Anna Maria Rosier, daughter of the composer Carl Rosier, and gave several concert performances on the violin. He spent six years as *kapelmeester* at Antwerp Cathedral but resigned in 1731 after several quarrels with the church authorities (apparently due to his poor conduct). He then moved to London, where he appeared as a concert violinist, led and directed various orchestras, and wrote the oratorio *Judith* (performed 1733), which had some success. His works include concertos showing Vivaldi's influence, violin and trio sonatas, and Italian and English songs.   LC

degree. In general parlance, a term for indicating which note of the musical scale one is referring to (first degree, second degree, etc). In music analysis there are special terms for these degrees of the scale which convey their harmonic functions when they are used as the bottom notes of chords: tonic (first degree); supertonic (second); mediant (third); subdominant (fourth); dominant (fifth); submediant (sixth), and leading note (seventh).   AP

degrees and diplomas. Strictly speaking, a degree is a qualification and a diploma is a document certifying that a person is entitled to a qualification. However, in the UK, both words are generally taken to refer to qualifications, with degrees seen as more substantial in both breadth and depth of study. It is only recently that the British Quality Assurance Agency (QAA) for Higher Education has published criteria that help to define and clarify this distinction. According to the QAA, five levels of certification apply in higher education:

(a) Certificate level. The holder of a Certificate of Higher Education will have a sound grasp of basic skills and concepts.

(b) Intermediate level. The intermediate level includes non-honours degrees, Diplomas of Higher Education (Dip.H.E.), and other higher diplomas. Nearly all diplomas in music awarded by conservatories or such consortia as the Associated Board of the Royal Schools of Music or the Royal College of Organists fall into this category (see Table 1). Examples include: (i) Licentiate diplomas of the Royal Academy of Music (LRAM) and Trinity College of Music (LTCL); (ii) Associate diplomas of the Royal College of Music (ARCM) and the Guildhall School of Music and Drama (AGSM) (these have largely been superseded by, or absorbed into, degree programmes); (iii) Certificate in Teaching of the Associated Board of the Royal Schools of Music (CTABRSM), aimed at the continuing professional development of experienced instrumental teachers; (iv) Associateship and Fellowship diplomas of the Royal College of Organists (ARCO and FRCO).

(c) Honours level. Honours courses normally require three or four years of full-time study and lead to a Bachelor's degree with Honours. In music this can be a Bachelor of Music (B.Mus. or Mus.B.) or a Bachelor of Arts (BA), where students can pursue music either as a

TABLE 1

Bodies granting diplomas in music (conservatories, etc.)

BSM	Birmingham School of Music [Conservatoire]
CLCM	City of Leeds College of Music
GSM	Guildhall School of Music and Drama
LCM	London College of Music
NSM	(former) Northern School of Music
RAM	Royal Academy of Music
RCM	Royal College of Music
RCO	Royal College of Organists
RMCM	(former) Royal Manchester College of Music
RNCM	Royal Northern College of Music
RSM	Royal Schools of Music
RSAM	Royal Scottish Academy of Music and Drama
TCL	Trinity College of Music, London
WCMD	Welsh College of Music and Drama

L = Licentiate, A = Associate, G = Graduate, F = Fellow
(e.g. ABSM = Associate of the Birmingham School of Music)

single subject or in combination with other disciplines. British universities have been awarding degrees in music for over 500 years. However, until the last decade of the 20th century, conservatories mostly awarded 'Graduate Diplomas': qualifications, reflecting a practical rather than academic bias, which were given 'pass degree' rather than 'Honours' status. Following the lead of the Royal Academy of Music in 1991, all conservatories have now replaced graduate diplomas with honours degrees. Reciprocally, nearly all British university courses in music now include practical performance in their degree programmes.

(d) Master's level. Master's degrees are awarded after completion of taught courses, programmes of research, or a mixture of both. Longer, research-based programmes often lead to the degree of MA, M.Mus., or M.Phil. They require at least one year of full-time study by Honours graduates (or people with equivalent achievement). Also at this level are advanced short courses leading to Postgraduate Diplomas (PG.Dip.) and such qualifications as the certificate offered by the Royal Military School of Music for Honours graduate bandmasters wishing to be considered for promotion to the rank of captain and the post of director of music.

(e) Doctoral level. Doctorates in music (Ph.D., D.Phil., or D.Mus.) are awarded for substantial work in original research or composition. A doctorate normally requires the equivalent of three years' full-time study, and the writing of an extended dissertation.

In addition to the above, universities award honorary doctorates to distinguished composers, performers, and scholars, and conservatories grant honorary diplomas, usually called 'fellowships', to eminent former students and members of their teaching staff.

As a result of a custom dating from the 13th century, the Archbishop of Canterbury (through his former office of Legate of the Pope) can grant degrees; these doctorates are known as 'Canterbury Degrees' or 'Lambeth Degrees'.

See also CONSERVATORIES.   PSp

dehors, en (Fr.). 'Outside', i.e. emphasized or prominent.

Deidamia. Opera in three acts by Handel to a libretto by Paolo Antonio Rolli (London, 1741).

De la Halle, Adam. See ADAM DE LA HALLE.

Delalande, Michel-Richard. See LALANDE, MICHEL-RICHARD DE.

Delibes, (Clément Philibert) **Léo** (*b* Saint Germain du Val, Sarthe, 21 Feb. 1836; *d* Paris, 16 Jan. 1891). French composer. He had his first musical training from his mother and uncle. After his father's death in 1847 the family moved to Paris and he entered the Conservatoire, studying the organ with François Benoist and composition with Adam. A chorister at the Madeleine church, he sang in the premiere of Meyerbeer's *Le Prophète* at the Opéra in 1849 and, from the age of 17, was organist at various churches. His early compositions included one-act operettas for Offenbach's Bouffes-Parisiens, of which *Deux vieilles gardes* (1856) enjoyed particular success. He wrote music criticism under the anagrammatic name Éloi Delbès, and became chorus master at the Théâtre Lyrique (where he worked on Gounod's *Faust*) and later at the Opéra.

In 1866 Delibes first gained wide attention for the ballet *La Source*, written jointly with Léon Minkus. He also composed a 'Pas des fleurs' for Adam's ballet score *Le Corsaire* in 1867, and this was later combined with Delibes's half of *La Source* to form the ballet *Naila*. In 1869 he composed his final operetta, *La Cour du roi Pétaud*, after which the Opéra staged his most celebrated creation, the classic ballet *Coppélia* (1870). Its success enabled him from 1871 to concentrate fully on composition, including the further full-scale ballet success *Sylvia* (1876). This led directly to his decoration as a Chevalier of the Légion d'Honneur in 1876. His operas *Le Roi l'a dit* (1873), *Jean de Nivelle* (1880), and *Lakmé* (1883), the last named an essay in the then popular 'French oriental' style, ensured even greater honours.

Delibes also composed a set of period dances for Victor Hugo's *Le Roi s'amuse* (1882), various choruses, and songs including the brilliant soprano bolero *Les*

Filles de Cadiz (1874). His last opera, *Kassya* (1893), based on a story by Sacher Masoch and orchestrated after his death by Massenet, was an attempt at something more weighty; but it is his lightness of touch, melodic facility, deftness of theme, and orchestration that ensure his music's survival.

DA/ALa

📖 W. E. STUDWELL, *Adolphe Adam and Léo Delibes: A Guide to Research* (New York, 1987)

delicato (It.). 'Delicate'. The opening movement of Beethoven's 'Moonlight' Sonata is marked 'Si deve suonare questo pezzo delicatissimamente' ('this piece must be played most delicately').

délié (Fr.). 'Untied', i.e. detached, or *staccato*; it also implies 'free'. Czerny used it in his *L'Art de délier les doigts* ('The Art of Freeing the Fingers').

Delius, Frederick (Theodore Albert) (*b* Bradford, Yorks., 29 Jan. 1862; *d* Grez-sur-Loing, 10 June 1934). English composer. He had one of the most individual and easily recognizable harmonic and melodic styles, artistically successful within a strictly defined and narrow emotional and expressive range. He was the son of a German wool merchant who had settled in Yorkshire and played a part in the city's musical life but who did not regard music as a suitable profession. Delius entered the family business but was a failure; in 1884 he went to Florida to grow oranges, managing (or neglecting to manage) a plantation at Solano Grove, near Jacksonville. He studied music with Thomas Ward and in 1886 entered the Leipzig Conservatory, where he was befriended by Grieg. On leaving, he settled in Paris, where he joined the circle of Paul Gauguin, August Strindberg, and Edvard Munch.

Delius's earliest compositions were songs, chamber works, and orchestral pieces such as the *Florida* suite (1887, rev. 1889), but after 1890 he concentrated on operas, completing *Irmelin* in 1890–2, *The Magic Fountain* (1893–5), *Koanga* (1895–7), and *A Village Romeo and Juliet* (1900–1). Only the two last of these were produced in his lifetime, *Koanga* at Elberfeld (1904) and *A Village Romeo and Juliet* in Berlin (1907). In 1897 Delius settled at Grez-sur-Loing with an artist, Jelka Rosen, whom he married in 1903. Apart from a London concert in 1899, his music was almost unknown in Britain until 1907 when his Piano Concerto (1897, rev. 1906) and the set of variations for chorus and orchestra, *Appalachia* (1896–1903), were performed. The latter was heard by Thomas Beecham, who thereafter became Delius's most ardent champion, poetic interpreter, and loyal friend.

Delius's largest work outside the opera house was his Nietzsche setting *A Mass of Life* (1904–5), for soloists, choir, and orchestra. But his best-known works are his exquisite, sensuous orchestral idylls: the 'English Rhapsody' *Brigg Fair* (1907), *In a Summer Garden* (1908), *North Country Sketches* (1913–14), the magnificent *Song of the High Hills* (1911) for wordless chorus and orchestra, and the two short tone-poems, *On Hearing the First Cuckoo in Spring* (1912) and *Summer Night on the River* (1911). In all these, Delius's use of a late Romantic style—dominant discords, secondary 7ths, chromatic harmonies—is at its most supple. He also wrote a Requiem (1914–16), a Violin Concerto (1916), Cello Concerto (1921), Violin and Cello Concerto (1915–16), and the opera *Fennimore and Gerda* (1909–10, performed Frankfurt, 1919).

Always susceptible to women, Delius contracted syphilis probably in Florida. The physical effects began to tell in about 1920, and the fine incidental music for Flecker's *Hassan* (1920–3) was the last music he wrote in his own hand. In 1928 Eric Fenby became his amanuensis and enabled him to complete *A Song of Summer* (1929–30) for orchestra, the Third Violin Sonata (1930), and the *Songs of Farewell* (Whitman) for chorus and orchestra (1930). Delius, blind and paralysed, last visited England in 1929 for Beecham's festival of his music. He was made Companion of Honour that year. He died in France but was buried at Limpsfield, Surrey. His music is principally concerned with nostalgia for lost love, and perhaps the finest example of it is his Whitman setting for baritone, chorus, and orchestra, *Sea Drift* (1903–4).

MK

📖 P. HESELTINE, *Frederick Delius* (London, 1923, 2/1952/R1974) · E. FENBY, *Delius as I Knew him* (London, 1936, 3/1966/R1981) · T. BEECHAM, *Frederick Delius* (London, 1959, 2/1975) · C. REDWOOD (ed.), *A Delius Companion* (London, 1976, 2/1980) · C. PALMER, *Delius: Portrait of a Cosmopolitan* (London, 1976) · L. CARLEY, *Delius: A Life in Letters, i: 1862–1908* (London, 1983); *ii: 1909–1934* (London, 1988) · J. B. SMITH, *Frederick Delius and Edvard Munch* (London, 1983) · L. CARLEY (ed.), *Frederick Delius: Music, Art and Literature* (Aldershot, 1998)

Deller, Alfred (George) (*b* Margate, 31 May 1912; *d* Bologna, 16 July 1979). English countertenor. He was one of the most celebrated countertenors of recent times, exerting a strong influence on the latter-day revival of interest in the art of the castrato. After singing in the choir of Canterbury Cathedral, he formed the Deller Consort principally for the performance of 16th- and 17th-century music. Its success was an important catalyst in the early music movement and its appeal was strengthened by Deller's dramatic and colourful performances, which aroused the enthusiasm of many who had hitherto considered early music a mainly academic art form. His influence extended to contemporary composers; Britten wrote the part of Oberon in *A Midsummer Night's Dream* for him. He sang with florid virtuosity, which some found mannered, but also lyrically with a gently supple delivery.   JT

Del Tredici, David (Walter) (*b* Cloverdale, CA, 16 March 1937). American composer. He studied at Berkeley and with Roger Sessions at Princeton, and has taught at Harvard (1966–72), Boston University (1973–84), and City College, New York (from 1984). In 1968, after some vivid James Joyce settings, he began a long series of works based on Lewis Carroll's *Alice* books, often using large-scale and diverse resources to the ends of surrealist whimsy. These works include *The Lobster Quadrille* for folk group and orchestra (1969), the misleadingly titled *Final Alice* for amplified soprano, folk group, and orchestra (1976), *Child Alice* for orchestra (1977–81), and *Haddock's Eyes* for soprano and chamber orchestra (1985–6).   PG

Delvincourt, Claude (*b* Paris, 12 Jan. 1888; *d* Orbetello, 5 or 15 April 1954). French music administrator and composer. He studied composition at the Paris Conservatoire with Henri Busser and in 1913 shared the Prix de Rome with Lili Boulanger. He was seriously wounded during the war and took some years to recover, but in 1931 was appointed director of the Versailles Conservatoire. In 1941 he succeeded Henri Rabaud at the Paris Conservatoire and proved to be an inspiring and innovatory director. In 1943 he formed the orchestra Les Cadets du Conservatoire to prevent the institution's best players being deported to Germany and commissioned up-and-coming composers, including Messiaen, Jolivet, and Dutilleux, to write test pieces for a number of the final *concours*. His own music, lacking any marked individuality, has not stood the test of time. But after his death in a car crash, his administrative gifts at the Conservatoire were greatly missed.   RN

démancher (Fr.). In string playing, a direction to the player to move along the neck (Fr.: *manche*) of the instrument into a higher position. Its use is documented by Rabelais in the 16th century.   DMi

Demantius, Johannes Christoph (*b* Reichenberg [now Liberec], Bohemia, 15 Dec. 1567; *d* Freiberg, Saxony, 20 April 1643). German composer and writer on music. He studied at the University of Wittenberg, moved to Leipzig, then became Kantor at Zittau (1597) and Freiberg (1604), where he remained until his death. His personal life was blighted: he was married four times and most of his children died during his lifetime.

Demantius was one of the most versatile composers of his day. His sacred music, which includes important Lutheran motets, is often strongly descriptive and emotional, showing especially anguished word-painting in the works for Passiontide. His secular music is influenced by Italian models and he was one of the first to introduce elements of Polish dance. He was the author of the first German music dictionary, published as a supplement to his *Isagoge artis musicae* (Freiberg, 1632).   DA/AL

📖 B. SMALLMAN, *The Background of Passion Music* (London, 1957, enlarged 2/1970)

demi-pause (Fr.). 'Half-rest', i.e. the minim or half-note rest.

demisemiquaver (𝅘𝅥𝅯). The note having ¹⁄₃₂ of the value of the semibreve, or whole note; hence the American usage '32nd-note'.

demi-ton (Fr.). 'Semitone'.

demi-voix (Fr., 'half-voice'). In vocal music, a direction to sing at half the vocal power; see also MEZZO, MEZZA.

Dench, Chris (*b* London, 10 June 1953). English composer, resident in Australia. He was self-taught as a composer, and his work derives principally from that of the postwar European avant-garde. While unambiguously complex in its refracted, highly unstable instrumental lines, and often darkly expressionistic in tone, his music explores a wide range of expression and evokes many powerful images. '*atsiluth* for flute with bass clarinet and piano (1991) is characteristic in the way it deals with elaborate, densely compacted musical ideas suggesting the archetypal forces of cosmic creation.   AW

Denisov, Edison Vasil'yevich (*b* Tomsk, 6 April 1929; *d* Paris, 23 Nov. 1996). Russian composer. He graduated in mathematics from Tomsk University in 1951; after corresponding with Shostakovich he received Shostakovich's encouragement to go to Moscow, where he studied composition at the conservatory with Shebalin and privately with Filip Gershkovich, a pupil of Webern. His early major work, the cantata *Sun of the Incas* (1964), was one of the first 12-note works written in the USSR, and through the advocacy of Maderna and Boulez it earned him international recognition. Denisov's commitment to modernist techniques soon soured his relations with the Composers' Union, so his most important works were subsequently first performed in the West: the *Requiem* (1980) in Hamburg, the opera *L'Écume de jours* (1986) and the Symphony (1987) in Paris. In 1990 Boulez invited him to Paris to work at IRCAM; the most important electronic composition from this period is *Sur la nappe d'un étang glacé* (1991). For many years Denisov taught instrumentation at the Moscow Conservatory (he was not allowed to teach composition until his last years), but this class nevertheless attracted most adventurous young musicians (including Firsova, Smirnov, and Tarnopol'sky), who can be said to constitute a Denisov school.　　　　　　　　　　　　　　　　　JWAL

📖 S. BRADSHAW, 'The music of Edison Denisov', *Tempo*, 3 (1984), 2–9

Denmark. Music flourished in Rome and Vienna long before it did in Copenhagen and Stockholm. With the possible exception of the Swedish Baroque master Johan Helmich Roman, the wider musical public is scarcely conscious of any Scandinavian composer before the mid-19th century, when an upsurge of national feeling created the climate in which Grieg emerged. Yet considering the extent of Scandinavia's power in the 10th century, it would be surprising if its musical procedures had not had some influence, however modest, on those parts of northern Europe with which it had contact. They certainly played some part at least in the development of polyphony. The practice of *gymel (two-part singing based partly on parallel 3rds) may well be Scandinavian in origin. Traces of skaldic chant can be discerned in the two-part hymn *Nobilis, humilis*, and Giraldus Cambrensis ascribed the part-singing practised in northern Britain to the influence of the invading Vikings.

1. The Danish court in the late Renaissance; 2. Song and theatre; 3. Denmark after Nielsen; 4. Bentzon, Holmboe, and their successors

1. The Danish court in the late Renaissance

As a vital force, the Scandinavian countries were comparatively dormant in the Renaissance, and although many of the famous Flemish and Italian masters were heard in the northern courts, no great indigenous composer appeared. The Danish court maintained a large musical establishment, reaching the height of its importance at the time of King Christian IV (1588–1648). He was an accomplished amateur musician, attracting such figures as Dowland and Schütz and extending his patronage to many others, including Michael Praetorius and Orazio Vecchi. He also sent a few of his most promising young musicians to study in Italy, among them Melchior Borchgrevinck (*c.*1570–1632), Mogens Pedersøn (*c.*1583–1623), and Hans Nielsen (*c.*1580–1626 or later). All three composers wrote madrigals in the Italian style and to Italian texts, Nielsen even going so far as to publish them under an Italian name, Giovanni Fonteijo. Pedersøn also pub-

lished madrigals in Venice showing a good command of the techniques perfected by Marenzio. His most important work was the *Pratum spirituale* (1620), which includes a Latin mass as well as motets and psalm settings in Danish. Yet no distinctive Danish voice can be discerned in Pedersøn's finely crafted music. The lavish musical resources of the court were dispersed after King Christian's death.

2. Song and theatre

There were few indigenous masters in 18th-century Denmark, and the country tended to import its opera. *Syngespil* and operas on national historic themes were performed, including *Holger Danske* by Friedrich Ludwig Aemilius Kunzen (1761–1817). However, it was Kuhlau's operas *Lulu* (1824) and *Elverhøj* ('The Elf Hill', 1828) that opened the door to Romantic opera and paved the way for such works as *Liden Kirsten* ('Little Christine', 1846) by J. P. E. Hartmann, later Niels Gade's father-in-law. The turn of the century had also seen an upsurge of interest in song, which flourished in both Denmark and Sweden. Perhaps the greatest figure was Christoph Ernst Friedrich Weyse (1774–1842), who settled in Copenhagen in 1789. His works, and those of his successor Peter Heise (1830–79), show spontaneity and inventiveness. Heise's opera *Drot og marsk* ('King and Marshal') is his masterpiece and the only Danish opera of real stature before Nielsen. Copenhagen became a thriving musical centre in the latter half of the 19th century and produced a number of composers besides Gade. Both C. F. E. Horneman (1840–1906) and Peter Lange-Müller (1850–1926) possessed a fresh melodic charm and great facility. Although Horneman had some influence on Nielsen, neither his symphonies nor those of Hartmann have a more than peripheral hold on the repertory, and neither is likely to experience a revival such as that enjoyed by the Gade symphonies.

3. Denmark after Nielsen

Like Sibelius in Finland, Nielsen loomed so large on the horizon that younger Danish composers could hardly escape his magnetism. This is certainly the case with Jeppesen and Høffding. Others such as Riisager and Jørgen Jersild (*b* 1913) turned to French models. Denmark also produced its 'outsider' in Rued Langgaard, who composed no fewer than 450 works and has been compared to Ives and Havergal Brian, though his achievement is more questionable. However, few of Nielsen's contemporaries have made much of an impression outside Denmark. The six symphonies of Louis Glass (1864–1936), a composer of distinct quality, remain on the fringes of the repertory while the three of Peder Gram (1881–1956) are totally neglected. A more peripheral but gifted figure whose musical outlook was formed by the diatonicism of Nielsen is Leif Keyser (*b* 1919), whose remarkable First Symphony was first performed in Göteborg when he was only 20 and whose Second, composed a year later, is hardly less impressive in its sense of pace and feeling for organic growth. However, the enormous promise of these early works did not develop into a comparable fulfilment, and Keyser's creative work was interrupted by his call to the priesthood.

4. Bentzon, Holmboe, and their successors

It is in the music of Herman D. Koppel (1908–98), Vagn Holmboe, and Niels Viggo Bentzon that Nielsen's influence is assimilated alongside that of such neoclassical figures as Hindemith and Stravinsky. Holmboe proved the most consistent stylistically. His world of feeling is as disciplined as the expressive means he chooses. There is an inexorable sense of forward movement in the symphonies and an organic coherence that place him in the tradition of Sibelius, though there is no trace of Sibelius's influence in his sound world. Neither Koppel's nor Bentzon's symphonies have quite the same concentration. Although Bentzon, who was descended from J. P. E. Hartmann, may not have shown comparable stylistic consistency, his Third, Fourth, and Seventh Symphonies are remarkably imaginative and possess real vision. Both Holmboe and Bentzon were fascinated in the postwar years by thematic metamorphosis and both show remarkable resource. Holmboe also enriched the repertory of choral music, as has his younger contemporary Bernhard Lewkovitch (*b* 1927). Bentzon, a fine pianist in his youth, composed over 20 piano sonatas, the first seven of which exhibit a masterly control of keyboard writing and much originality of mind. Of the next generation to come to the fore, two of Holmboe's pupils stand out: Per Nørgård (*b* 1932) and Ib Nørholm (*b* 1931). Nørgård's early music was greatly influenced by Holmboe's teaching, but by the late 1960s he had broken loose from this tradition. His extra-musical inspiration and often pleasing sound world has served to overshadow Nørholm's symphonies. The most acclaimed of the younger generation, Poul Ruders (*b* 1949), has drawn widely on different stylistic impulses and has been compared to Xenakis, Tippett, and Dutilleux. RLA

📖 K. KETTING (ed.), *Music in Denmark* (Copenhagen, 1987) · A. ØRBAK and O. KONGSTED (eds.), *Heinrich Schütz und die Musik in Dänemark zur Zeit Christians IV* (Copenhagen, 1989) · K. A. RASMUSSEN, *Noteworthy Danes: Portraits of Eleven Danish Composers* (Copenhagen, 1991) · L. D. McLOSKEY, *Twentieth Century Danish Music: An Annotated Bibliography and Research Directory* (London, 1998)

density. An informal measure of polyphonic complexity, chord content, or general sound, chiefly used of 20th-century music where a more precise vocabulary does not exist. One may thus speak of 'dense textures', 'dense harmonies', etc. PG

Dent, Edward J(oseph) (*b* Ribston, Yorks., 16 July 1876; *d* London, 22 Aug. 1957). English musicologist. He spent most of his academic life at Cambridge, where he became professor in 1926. He was mainly interested in opera, especially the works of Alessandro Scarlatti and Mozart, and he translated about 25 librettos for Sadler's Wells Opera. He enjoyed being mischievous and at times outré—footnotes in his book *Mozart's Operas* (1913) are occasionally delightfully outrageous—but his work was essentially serious and deservedly admired. DA/LC

Denza, Luigi (*b* Castellamare di Stabia, 24 Feb. 1846; *d* London, 26 Jan. 1922). Italian composer. He studied at the Naples Conservatory with Mercadante and Paolo Serrao. In 1879 he settled in London, where he was a director of the London Academy of Music and professor of singing at the RAM. He wrote more than 500 songs, of which *Funiculì, funiculà* (1880) is by far the best known. PG

déploration (Fr.). A mourning poem. In music, the term generally refers to a song composed on the death of a celebrated musician by one of his pupils or fellow composers. Two well-known examples are *Mort, tu as navré*, written by Ockeghem on the death of Binchois, and *Nymphes des bois*, written by Josquin on the death of Ockeghem.

De profundis (Lat., 'Out of the depths'). One of the seven Penitential Psalms (no. 130 in the English numbering, 129 in the Vulgate). It has a place in the Office of the Dead of the Roman Catholic Church and has been set polyphonically many times, notably by Lassus.

De Reszke, Jean [Mieczisław, Jan] (*b* Warsaw, 14 Jan. 1850; *d* Nice, 3 April 1925). Polish tenor. He was the most celebrated in a family of singers that included the bass Édouard de Reszke (1853–1917). He studied with the baritone Antonio Cotogni and in 1874 made his debut as a baritone singing Alfonso in *La favorita* at La Fenice, Venice. That year he sang Valentino in *Faust* and the title role of *Don Giovanni* in London. In 1876 he began studying as a tenor and three years later made his stage debut as a tenor in the title role of *Robert le diable*, without success. In 1884 he created a remarkable impression in Paris when he sang John the Baptist in Massenet's *Hérodiade*. Thereafter he was internationally one of the most sought-after tenors of his time, excelling in both Italian and French dramatic roles and, later, in heavy Wagnerian parts. Among his successes were his creation of Roméo in Gounod's *Roméo et Juliette* in Paris in 1888, his performances of Don José and Otello at Covent Garden in 1890 and 1891, and his Tristan and Siegfried at the Metropolitan Opera, New York, in 1895 and 1896. He had an impressive stage presence.   JT

Dering [Deering, Diringo], **Richard** (*b* c.1580; *d* London, March 1630). English organist and composer. He supplicated for the degree of B.Mus. from Oxford University in 1610, claiming to have studied music for a decade. In 1612 he was in Rome, where he converted to Roman Catholicism, and in 1620 he was organist at a convent of English nuns in Brussels. Five years later he returned to England, serving as a musician to Charles I and organist of Queen Henrietta Maria's chapel. Dering was a versatile composer. The motets he composed while living abroad (published in 1617 and 1618) bring to mind the manner of Sweelinck, but he also wrote anthems, consort songs, and instrumental fantasias that are idiomatically English. Other works by him include Italian-texted canzonets, and the declamatory *Cantica sacra*, published posthumously in 1662.   JM

D'Erlanger, Frédéric. See ERLANGER, FRÉDÉRIC D'.

De Rore, Cipriano. See RORE, CIPRIANO DE.

Des (Ger.). The note D♭; *Deses*, the note D♭♭.

descant. See DISCANT.

Des canyons aux étoiles ('From the Canyons to the Stars'). Work (1970–4) by Messiaen for piano, horn, and orchestra; it was inspired by the American landscape.

descort. The Provençal word for **lai*. It was also used for French works and (as *discordio*) for some Italian pieces. Whether there is any difference between the *lai* and the *descort* is a matter for debate. Some scholars have argued that the term *descort* implies a 'discord' of some kind in the textual content of a work, while a few have contended that it has some bearing on musical content; yet others maintain that there is no difference and that the terms were fully interchangeable.   ABUL

Desert Music, The. Work (1982–4) by Reich for small, amplified chorus and large orchestra, a setting of poems by William Carlos Williams.

desiderio (It.). 'Desire'; *con desiderio*, 'longingly'.

Des Knaben Wunderhorn ('The Boy's Magic Horn'). A collection of the texts of over 700 German folksongs, assembled between 1804 and 1807 by the poets Achim von Arnim (1781–1831) and Clemens Brentano (1778–1842) and published, with a dedication to Goethe, in three volumes between 1805 and 1808. Both writers made substantial adjustments to the original material, and their editorial work is now regarded as suspect and unscholarly. The collection, however, had a powerful impact on composers and writers and is widely regarded as one of the most important documents in the history of both German Romanticism and German nationalism. Schumann, Mendelssohn, Brahms, and Richard Strauss all set individual texts as lieder, though the composer most closely associated with the work is Mahler, who set nine poems for voice and piano, and 13 for voice and orchestra. His Second (*'Resurrection'), Third, and Fourth Symphonies rework thematic material from his *Wunderhorn* songs and draw on further texts for their vocal and choral sections.   TA

Desmarets, Henri (*b* Paris, Feb. 1661; *d* Lunéville, Lorraine, 7 Sept. 1741). French composer. A court page and a pupil of Lully, he became an *ordinaire* in 1680. In 1683 he competed for one of the posts of *sous-maître* to the royal chapel without success (he was considered too young), but he occupied himself composing motets for one of the winners, Goupillet—an arrangement not made public until a decade later. He turned his hand to opera, but was only moderately successful, being overshadowed by Collasse and Campra. In 1699 he eloped and was forced into exile in Brussels, but in 1701 he was offered the post of *maître de musique* to Philip V at the Spanish court. Meanwhile, his friends promoted his music in Paris by publishing and producing it (Ballard issued his *airs* and Philidor a *grand motet*; Campra completed and staged his opera *Iphigénie en Tauride* in 1704). Hoping to gain a royal pardon from the French regent, Desmarets took up a post at the court of Lorraine, where he revived his own *Vénus et Adonis* (1697) and several of Lully's operas; the pardon finally came in 1720.   DA/JAS

Desprez, Josquin. See JOSQUIN DES PREZ.

Dessau, Paul (*b* Hamburg, 19 Dec. 1894; *d* Berlin, 28 June 1979). German composer. He was trained as a conductor, beginning to compose seriously only when he was about 30. An exile from the Nazis, he went to the USA, where the most decisive event in his career was his meeting with Brecht in 1942. He attached himself to the Brechtian style of Eisler and began to produce a great range of vocal, choral, and dramatic works to texts by Eisler, including most importantly the oratorio-like *Deutsches Miserere* (1944–7) and the incidental music for *Mother Courage* (1946). In 1948 he returned with Brecht to Germany, settling in East Berlin. In his opera *Das Verhör des Lukullus* ('The

Interrogation of Lukullus', to a libretto by Brecht, 1955) he blended Eislerian technique with elements of serialism, which initially led to charges of *formalism. After Eisler's death in 1962 he became the leading figure in East German musical life. His Marxist humanism, much admired by Henze, finds its most powerful expression in his opera *Einstein* (1976), a probing parable about the nature of scientific responsibility.   PG/TA

dessous (Fr.). 'Below', 'under'. A term used in 17th- and 18th-century French instrumental music for the lower part (the equivalent of a modern viola part).

dessus (Fr., 'above', 'over'). Treble, i.e. the highest part in an ensemble. In 17th- and 18th-century French instrumental music it meant the violin; a *dessus de viole* is a treble viol.

Destinn, Emmy [Kittlová, Ema; Destinnová, Ema] (*b* Prague, 26 Feb. 1878; *d* České Budějovice, 28 Jan. 1930). Czech soprano. She studied with Marie Loewe-Destinn, the latter part of whose name she adopted. In 1898 she made her debut in Berlin as Santuzza in *Cavalleria rusticana* and created such a powerful impression that she was immediately engaged by the company, performing a large number of parts in the next ten years. She was highly acclaimed at Bayreuth in 1901 when she sang Senta in *Der fliegende Holländer*, going on to elicit a similar reaction at Covent Garden in *Aida* and *Madama Butterfly* and at the Metropolitan Opera, New York, as Aida and Minnie. She created the latter role in *La fanciulla del West* in 1910. Her deeply musical and expressive singing can be heard in over 200 recordings.   JT

Destouches, André Cardinal (*b* Paris, *bapt.* 6 April 1672; *d* Paris, 7 Feb. 1749). French composer. He was educated by the Jesuits and visited Siam when he was 15. He joined the army, but left in 1694 to take up music; he studied with Campra and had a *pastorale–héroïque*, *Issé*, performed to Louis XIV's delight at Fontainebleau in 1697. He held several court positions: *inspecteur général* of the Académie Royale de Musique in 1713, *surintendant de la musique de la chambre* in 1718, and in 1727 *maître de musique de la chambre*; from 1728 until his resignation in 1730 he was director of the Opéra. Although some of his contemporaries considered him (no doubt because of his aristocratic birth and connections) an amateur, his operas, which include *tragédies* and ballets of various types, are noted for their keen theatrical sense, their flexible declamation and their attractive and colourful dances; three *airs* in Campra's *L'Europe galant* are Destouches's work. He also composed *grands motets* but all are now lost.

WT/SS

destro, destra (It.). 'Right'; *mano destra*, 'right hand'.

détaché (Fr.). 'Detached'; in string playing it is almost the equivalent of **staccato*.

Dettingen Te Deum and Anthem. Choral works by Handel composed to celebrate the British victory over the French at Dettingen, near Frankfurt, in 1743; the anthem is to the text 'The king shall rejoice'.

deuterus. See MODE, 2a.

deutlich (Ger.). 'Distinct'.

Deutsch. Abbreviation for the standard *thematic catalogue of the works of Franz Schubert drawn up by the Austrian biographer and bibliographer Otto Erich Deutsch (1883–1967) and published in London in 1951 (enlarged Ger. edn, 1978). Schubert's works, especially those without distinguishing title or opus number, are often referred to by Deutsch number (usually further abbreviated to 'D').

Deutsches Requiem, Ein. See GERMAN REQUIEM, A.

Deutschland über alles. See EINIGKEIT UND RECHT UND FREIHEIT.

deux (Fr.). 'Two'; *à deux*, either an abbreviation for *à deux temps* (see DEUX TEMPS, 2) or 'for two (voices or instruments)'. See also À DEUX, A DUE, A 2.

Deux Journées, Les (*Les Deux Journées, ou Le Porteur d'eau*; 'The Two Days, or The Water Carrier'). Opera in three acts by Cherubini to a libretto by Jean-Nicolas Bouilly (Paris, 1800); in England it is generally known as *The Water Carrier* and in Germany as *Der Wasserträger*.

deux temps (Fr., 'two time'). 1. In 2/2 time.

2. A *valse à deux temps* is either a quick waltz in which there are only two steps, falling on the first and last of the three beats of each bar; or, as the word *temps* can also mean 'beat', a waltz in two simultaneous time-values (there is an example in Gounod's *Faust* where the melody is in 3/2 time and the accompaniment in 3/4 time).

development. A process by which musical materials, generally melodic themes, are changed and extended; or a section of a piece in which this process takes place. The purpose of development is to lead the listener through an intellectual and emotional experience that could be described metaphorically as exploration, adventure, or transformation. From the starting-point of a readily grasped theme, which may have been heard more than once, the listener is drawn into less predictable situations where the theme, or part of it, is still recognizable but has taken on new characteristics and is perhaps combined with other materials or with other versions of itself. Development, then, has to be audible: it is not merely a method of construction, like the 12-note *series.

Among the many ways of developing a theme are (1) sequence (see SEQUENCE, 1), either diatonically within a key or through a succession of keys; (2) rhythmic displacement, so that the metrical stress occurs at a different point in the otherwise unchanged theme; (3) alteration of pitch *intervals while retaining the original rhythm (a special case of this is inversion); (4) alteration of rhythm while retaining the original pitches (this is often called transformation of themes). (5) Treating a theme in contrapuntal *imitation can also be a feature of development. Perhaps the most powerful and varied technique, however, is (6) the division of a theme into parts, each of which can be developed in any of the above ways or recombined in a new way. Similarly, (7) two or more themes can be developed in combination; in some cases, themes are composed with this possibility in mind.

Composers specially noted for their powers of development are Bach, Haydn, Beethoven, Wagner, and Brahms. It is no accident that all five are of Germanic background. Building large and imposing structures by means of development in tonal music was a technique in which German composers excelled, and it played an important part in their hegemony during the Classical and Romantic periods.

A 'development section' follows the close of the exposition in a piece in *sonata form, and typically develops one or more themes from the exposition through neighbouring or remote keys before returning to the home key for the recapitulation. The same term can be used appropriately for sections of sonata rondos or concerto movements. But in some cases, for instance in many Classical concertos and in some of Mozart's sonatas, the 'development section' contains little actual development, consisting instead of new melodies or virtuoso passage-work (or both) passing through various keys. NT

Devienne, François (*b* Joinville, Haute-Marne, 31 Jan. 1759; *d* Paris, 5 Sept. 1803). French composer. He joined the Paris Opéra orchestra in 1779 before entering the service of Cardinal de Rohan. In the 1780s his works began to be performed in various concert series, including the Concert Spirituel, but he became famous as a composer only after the Revolution. He wrote his first *opéra comique* in 1790; two years later came the popular *Les Visitandines*, which enjoyed performances throughout the 19th century. Devienne had joined the National Guard military band in 1790, and when it became the Institut National de Musique (1793) and

then the Paris Conservatoire (1795) he stayed on, at first as a sergeant in charge of administration, and finally as professor of flute; his flute method remained in use until recent times. His many compositions include chamber music and concertos for wind instruments. DA/RP

Devil and Kate, The (*Čert a Káča*). Opera in three acts by Dvořák to a libretto by Adolf Wenig after a Czech folk tale (Prague, 1899).

'Devil's Trill' Sonata. Nickname of a violin sonata in G minor (*c.*1714) by Tartini, first published in J. B. Cartier's *L'Art du violon* (Paris, 1798), so called because of the long trill in the last of its four movements. Legend has it that Tartini dreamt he had made a deal with the Devil, to whom he gave his violin; the Devil played such a beautiful solo that when Tartini woke, he tried to play it himself. He failed, but composed the 'Devil's trill'. This legend is the subject of Cesare Pugni's ballet *Le Violon du diable* (1849).

Devin du village, Le ('The Village Soothsayer'). Opera in one act by Rousseau to his own libretto (Fontainebleau, 1752). The libretto of Mozart's *Bastien und Bastienne* is based on a parody.

devotion. A term used to describe a number of private or paraliturgical meditations and rituals arising from the subjective piety of late medieval Western Christianity. The Stations of the Cross, the Rosary, Benediction of the Blessed Sacrament, and other devotions became occasions for the performance of Latin and vernacular hymns. ALi

devoto (It.). 'Devoutly'.

Dia, Comtessa [?Beatrix] de (*fl* late 12th–early 13th centuries). *Trobairitz* (woman troubadour). Nothing certain is known about her life; she may have been the daughter of Count Isoard II of Dia. Only one song by her survives with music (*A chanter m'er de so qu'en no volria*). It is the sole extant song by a *trobairitz*; all others are known only from their poetry. JM

Diabelli, Anton (*b* Mattsee, nr Salzburg, 5 Sept. 1781; *d* Vienna, 7 April 1858). Austrian music publisher and composer. In 1803 he set himself up as a teacher of the piano and guitar and as a proofreader in Vienna. In 1818 he joined the music publishing firm of Cappi, which later (1824) became Anton Diabelli & Cie. The firm existed under the Diabelli name until 1852 and numbered many of Schubert's works among its publications. Apart from publishing, Diabelli is chiefly remembered for having prompted composition of Beethoven's *33 Variations on a Waltz by Diabelli*. WT/JWA

Diabelli Variations. Beethoven's *Variations on a Waltz by Diabelli* op. 120 (1819–23), for piano. The publisher Diabelli commissioned 51 composers to write a variation on his waltz tune, as a means of creating an anthology of contemporary Austrian music. The collection, entitled *Vaterländischer Künstlerverein* ('Society of Artists of the Fatherland'), was published in two volumes, the first containing Beethoven's variations—he provided 33, the second those of the other 50 composers, including Schubert, Moscheles, Kalkbrenner, Czerny, and the 11-year-old Liszt.

diabolus in musica (Lat., 'the devil in music'). A late medieval nickname for the disruptive interval of the *tritone, or diminished 5th.

dialogue. 1. Spoken dialogue is used in place of recitative in certain types of opera, for example the French *opéra comique, the German *Singspiel*, the Spanish *zarzuela, and the English *ballad opera. In some cases recitative written by another composer is substituted for the original dialogue (e.g. Ernest Guiraud's recitatives for Bizet's *Carmen*).

2. A vocal work that contrasts or alternates two sung parts in a way that resembles spoken dialogue. Examples range from the dialogues for different singers found in medieval *church dramas (e.g. the *Visitatio sepulchri*) to such folksongs as *Soldier, soldier won't you marry me?*, in which a single voice takes both parts.

Dialogues des Carmélites ('Dialogues of the Carmelites'). Opera in three acts by Poulenc to his own libretto after Georges Bernanos's play (Milan, 1957).

Diamond, David (Leo) (*b* Rochester, NY, 9 July 1915). American composer. He studied at the Eastman School, with Roger Sessions in New York (1935), and with Nadia Boulanger in Paris (1936–7). Influenced by the composers he met in Paris—Ravel, Stravinsky, Roussel—he established a lucid neo-classical style, marked by lithe counterpoint, and devoted himself especially to symphonies (11 of them), concertos, quartets, ballet scores, and songs. After a period in Italy (1951–65) he returned to New York, where he was head of the composition department at the Manhattan School, 1965–7.   PG

diapason (from Gk., 'through all'). 1. The whole octave.

2. The entire compass of an instrument.

3. The foundation or unison stops of the organ at 8′ pitch (i.e. the open and stopped Diapasons), so called because they extended over its whole compass whereas other stops did not.

4. The diatonically tuned bass strings of a lute, theorbo, or archlute, etc.

5. (Fr.). 'Pitch': the concert *pitch (*diapason normal*) of the note *a*′ was fixed at 435 Hz by the Académie Française in 1858; *diapason à bouche*, 'pitchpipe'; *diapason à branches* or simply *diapason*, 'tuning-fork'.

diapente (Gk.). Ancient Greek and medieval name for the interval of the 5th.

diaphonia, diaphony. 1. In Greek theory, 'dissonance', as opposed to *symphonia*, 'consonance'.

2. From the 9th century to the 12th the word was commonly used by such theorists as Guido of Arezzo to mean two-part polyphony.

Diary of One who Disappeared (*Zápisník zmizelého*). Song cycle (1917–20) by Janáček for tenor, contralto (or mezzo-soprano), three women's voices, and piano, settings of 21 poems by O. Kalda.

diastematic neumes (from Gk. *dia-*, 'through', 'across', *stema*, an 'interval', 'gap'). A type of early plainchant notation used before the invention of the staff. The dots and squiggles ('neumes'; see NOTATION, 1) were arranged carefully in relation to each other so as to show their relative pitch. Occasionally the pitches were further clarified by the addition of a faintly scratched line representing the final note of the modal scale in which the chant was written. Neumes written without any attempt to show relative pitch are known as 'adiastematic'.   AP

diatonic (from Gk. *dia tonikos*, 'at intervals of a tone'). In the major–minor tonal system, a diatonic feature—which may be a single note, an interval, a chord, or an extended passage of music—is one that uses exclusively notes belonging to one key. In practice, it can be said to use a particular scale, but only with the proviso that the alternative submediants and leading notes of harmonic and melodic minor allow up to nine diatonic notes, compared with the seven available in a major scale. Few pieces of tonal music are without tonal elaboration, the suggestion of different keys in the course of the music: thus a piece in C major that appears to modulate to its dominant, G major, and return to the tonic may be called diatonic if it uses only the eight notes—C, D, E, F, F♯, G, A, and B—belonging to the two keys.

The earliest concept of diatonicism is found in Greek music theory of about the 5th century BC, which recognized scales built from *tetrachords of three classes, of which the diatonic class had the descending interval pattern tone–tone–semitone. Medieval diatonicism, which did not include the principle of octave equivalence, was codified by Guido of Arezzo in the early 11th century: it acknowledged notes from *G* to *e*″, arranged in seven overlapping hexachords (see SOLMIZATION).

The spread of *equal temperament in the 17th and 18th centuries confirmed the modern transpositional diatonic system.

There have been many attempts to argue that modern diatonicism is based on acoustic fact, an attractive proposal in the sense that the major scale and major triad are sounded by the 11 lowest overtones (see HARMONIC SERIES), though there is no such convenient explanation of the components of the minor scale. The strength of this affinity between art and nature is undeniable, however. It is represented in the acoustics of instruments, where open strings and natural notes on wind and brass articulate diatonic reference points. The theorist Josef Hauer (1883–1959) went so far as to maintain that orchestral instruments are fundamentally diatonic, as opposed to the genuinely chromatic keyboard: 'every note of an orchestral instrument has a quality and quantity either closer to or further from that of the "freely" resonating string or column of air, and the player is quite unable to even this out' (*Vom Wesen des Musikalischen*, 1920).

See also PANDIATONICISM. JD

diatonic scale. See SCALE, 3.

Dibdin, Charles (*b* Southampton, *bapt.* 15 March 1745; *d* London, 25 July 1814). English composer and dramatist. As a composer he was largely self-taught, and he doubtless learnt much from his early experiences in the chorus at Covent Garden. He took a few solo operatic roles, but most of his life was devoted to composing and supervising music for various London theatres (including Covent Garden and Drury Lane). During an enterprising and colourful career he fell out with almost every impresario, actor-manager, singer, librettist, and composer in town; yet he was enormously prolific, composing some 60 stage works (including operas, pantomimes, and dialogues, many to his own librettos) as well as writing several music textbooks, novels, and other prose works. Dibdin's songs were immensely popular, and he frequently sang them himself; some are characterful and imaginative, but they are uneven in quality. Two of his illegitimate sons, Charles Isaac Mungo (1768–1833) and Thomas John (1771–1841), also had careers in the theatre. JN/PL

Dichterliebe ('Poet's Love'). Song cycle, op. 48 (1840), by Schumann for voice and piano, settings of 16 poems by Heinrich Heine.

Dichtung (Ger., 'poem'). A term found in such compounds as *symphonische Dichtung*, *'symphonic poem'*, or *Tondichtung*, 'tone-poem'.

dictionaries of music. The purpose of dictionaries and encyclopedias of music, like those of other disciplines, is to collect, organize, and explain existing knowledge concerning their subject. They may be aimed at the specialist or the amateur: and the study of them as a genre can reveal much about changes in taste, thought, and musical competence among their readers, and in the development of the discipline of music itself.

Music is well known for its multilingual terminology, and for its use of a large number of specialized technical terms: the need for explanation of this terminology meant that the first music dictionaries, including the first printed example, Johannes Tinctoris's *Terminorum musicae diffinitorium* of 1495, were devoted to this area of the subject. In the early 18th century a demand arose for information about those who created music, resulting in the first biographical dictionaries of musicians. All these early biographical publications, including J. G. Walther's *Musicalisches Lexicon* (1732), Johann Mattheson's *Grundlage einer Ehrenpforte* (1740), and E. L. Gerber's *Historisch-biographisches Lexicon der Tonkünstler* (1790–2), were German in origin. However, both Charles Burney and John Hawkins included much biographical information, in English, in their histories of music from the mid-1770s onwards, and biographical writing began to flourish in all parts of Europe. The 18th century also saw publication of many instrumental 'tutor' books, in which students would be introduced to the principles of playing their instrument and presented with some simple tunes on which to practise, and then, frequently, with an appendix setting out, in alphabetical order and with explanations, terms concerning performance that they might encounter in their musical studies. Such publications were the precursors of the rather more sophisticated musical primers aimed at the amateur market that appeared from the 19th century onwards, especially from such companies as Novello, whose musical publications relied in large part on such a market.

The 19th century witnessed a rapid increase in the publication of music dictionaries of all types—general, biographical, terminological, national—the most important of which are F.-J. Fétis's monumental *Biographie universelle des musiciens* (1835–44), John Moore's *Musician's Lexicon* (1845; the first American music encyclopedia), and the first edition of George Grove's *Dictionary of Music and Musicians* (1879–90); of Hugo Riemann's *Musik-Lexikon* (1882), and of Theodore Baker's *Biographical Dictionary of Musicians* and Robert Eitner's *Biographisch-bibliographisches Quellen-Lexikon* (both 1900). While Grove in his original dictionary still aimed to maintain contact with the musical amateur, Eitner's work in particular reflected the rise of the new discipline of musicology (*Musikwissenschaft*, literally 'musical science'), whose leaders were more likely to present musical knowledge in such a way as to make comprehension by the lay person a difficult undertaking. *The New Grove Dictionary of Music and Musicians* of 1980, edited by Stanley Sadie, also reflected this move away from the musical amateur to some extent.

Such dictionaries were counterpoised by approachable volumes, among them those by Percy Scholes, whose *Oxford Companion to Music*, first published in 1938, was only one of a number of highly successful music-appreciation books he wrote. Scholes was one of the last to produce a large music dictionary on his own: from the time of the massive German-language *Die Musik in Geschichte und Gegenwart* (1949–68, edited by Friedrich Blume; 2/1994–, edited by Ludwig Finscher) there has been a trend away from the single editor towards a committee of several editors and the commissioning of articles from many different authorities. Individuals have, none the less, continued to produce music dictionaries on a small scale, notable examples being Eric Blom's *Everyman's Dictionary of Music* (1947, 6/1988), and Arthur Jacobs's *Penguin Dictionary of Music* (1958, 6/1996).

As musical knowledge has broadened and deepened, dictionaries have been devoted to specialized areas. Macmillan, publishers of Grove's dictionary since its first edition, were pioneers in this field, producing dictionaries of musical instruments (1984), American music (1986), jazz (1988, 2nd edn in progress), opera (1992), and women composers (1994), as well as dictionary-based handbooks on performance practice, ethnomusicology, and music printing and publishing.

Individual countries have issued compilations of biographical information on composers of their own territories, a process helped in many cases by the rise of music information centres, which are often state-sponsored. Richard Dobson's *A Dictionary of Electronic and Computer Music Technology* (Oxford, 1992) answered a need raised by the spread of technology in musical endeavour, while Graham Strahle's *An Early Music Dictionary* (Cambridge, 1994) and Nicholas Temperley's *The Hymn Tune Index* reflect the development of other special areas. The launch of the second edition of *The New Grove Dictionary* in both print and online versions in 2001 suggests the way ahead for future dictionary and encyclopedia publishing that has also been used for the *Performance Practice Encyclopedia*, edited by Roland Jackson (1997–), which is available only through the Internet.

The list below is classified by category. It is intended to include all pioneer works in each category and thereafter the most important historically and those of the most practical use to the musician (though some works may be defective in certain areas). The list

excludes manuscript works, as well as general dictionaries and encyclopedias that embrace extensive information on music but are not primarily concerned with it.

1. Comprehensive dictionaries; 2. Non-biographical dictionaries; 3. Biographical dictionaries; 4. Terminological dictionaries; 5. National dictionaries; 6. Dictionaries of instruments, performers, and makers; 7. Dictionaries of opera; 8. Dictionaries of church music and hymnology; 9. Dictionaries of chamber music; 10. Dictionaries of early music; 11. Dictionaries of contemporary music; 12. Dictionaries of dance; 13. Dictionaries of jazz, popular music, and musical theatre; 14. Dictionaries of music publishers; 15. Thematic dictionaries; 16. Miscellaneous dictionaries

1. Comprehensive dictionaries

(all fields, including biography)

WALTHER, J. G., *Musicalisches Lexicon* (Leipzig, 1732); 666 pages; 86 pages of suppl. on busts and statues of musicians, lists of organists, instruments, inventors; letter 'A' previously published 1728; facs. repr. 1953

FRAMERY, N. E., and GINGUENÉ, P. L., *Dictionnaire de musique* (Paris, 1791); part of the general *Encyclopédie méthodique* (1782–1832); 2nd vol. published in Paris in 1818, ed. J. J. de Momigny; facs. repr. 1971

SCHILLING, G., *Encyclopädie der gesammten musikalischen Wissenschaften, oder Universal-Lexikon der Tonkunst* (Stuttgart, 1835–8, suppl. 1841–2); facs. repr. 1973

ESCUDIER, L. and M., *Dictionnaire de musique d'après les théoriciens, historiens et critiques les plus célèbres* (Paris, 1844, 5/1872); facs. repr. 1974

GASSNER, F. S., *Universal-Lexikon der Tonkunst* (Stuttgart, 1849); résumé of Schilling

MOORE, J. W., *Complete Encyclopaedia of Music* (Boston, 1854, suppl. 1875, 2/1880); facs. repr. 1973

MENDEL, H., and REISSMANN, A., *Musikalisches Conversations-Lexikon* (Berlin, 1870–9, 2/1880–3 with suppl., 3/1890–1); facs. repr. 1969

GROVE, G., *A Dictionary of Music and Musicians* (London, 1879–90, with appendix by J. A. Fuller Maitland, 2/1904–10 ed. Fuller Maitland, 3/1927–8 ed. H. C. Colles, 4/1940 ed. Colles, 5/1954 ed. E. Blom with suppl. 1961, rev. and enlarged 6/1980 by S. Sadie as *The New Grove Dictionary of Music and Musicians*, 2/2001; Amer. suppl. 1920 by W. S. Pratt, 2/1928)

MATHEWS, W. S. B., *Dictionary of Music and Musicians* (New York, 1880)

RIEMANN, H., *Musik-Lexikon* (Berlin, 1882, 9–11/1910–29 ed. A. Einstein, 12/1959–67 ed. W. Gurlitt, suppls. 1972– by C. Dahlhaus); also trans. into

Eng. (1893–7), Fr. (1895–1902), Nor. (1888–92), Russ. (1901–4)

LAVIGNAC, A., and DE LA LAURENCIE, L., *Encyclopédie de la musique et dictionnaire du Conservatoire* (Paris, 1920–31)

DELLA CORTE, A., and GATTI, G. M., *Dizionario di musica* (Turin, 1926, 6/1959); Sp. trans. (1949)

SCHOLES, P. A., *The Oxford Companion to Music* (London, 1938, 10/1970 ed. J. O. Ward); Sp. trans. (1983)

THOMPSON, O., *The International Cyclopedia of Music and Musicians* (New York, 1939, further edns by N. Slonimsky and R. Sabin, 10/1974 ed. B. Bohle)

BLOM, E., *Everyman's Dictionary of Music* (London, 1947, enlarged 5/1971 by J. A. Westrup, 6/1988 ed. D. Cummings)

MORIN, G., NORRBY, J., and TÖRNBLOM, F. H., *Sohlmans musiklexikon* (Stockholm, 1948–52, enlarged 2/1975–9 by H. Åstrand)

BLUME, F., *Die Musik in Geschichte und Gegenwart* (Kassel, 1949–68, suppls. 1973–86; 2/1994– ed. L. Finscher)

DUFOURCQ, N., *Larousse de la musique* (Paris, 1957–8)

JACOBS, A., *A New Dictionary of Music* (Harmondsworth, 1958, 6/1996 as *The Penguin Dictionary of Music*)

SARTORI, C., *Enciclopedia della musica* (Milan, 1963–4, 2/1972–4)

GATTI, G. M., and BASSO, A., *La musica: enciclopedia storica* (Turin, 1966)

——, *La musica: dizionario* (Turin, 1968–71)

HONEGGER, M., *Dictionnaire de la musique* (Paris, 1970–6; new edn 1993)

RANDEL, D. M., *Harvard Concise Dictionary of Music* (Cambridge, MA, 1978)

ARNOLD, D., *The New Oxford Companion to Music* (Oxford, 1983)

KENNEDY, M., *The Oxford Dictionary of Music* (Oxford, 1985, 2/1994)

MOREHEAD, P. D., and MacNEIL, A., *The Bloomsbury Dictionary of Music* (London, 1992)

2. Non-biographical dictionaries

(all fields, excluding biography)

JANOVKA, T. B., *Clavis ad thesaurum magnae artis musicae* (Prague, 1701, 2/1715 as *Clavis ad musicam*); facs. repr. 1974

BROSSARD, S. DE, *Dictionaire de musique* (Paris, 1703, 2/1705, 3/c.1715); facs. repr. 1965

Kurzgefasstes musikalisches Lexikon (Chemnitz, 1737, 2/1749); attributed to 'Barnickel'; facs. repr. 1975

GRASSINEAU, J., *A Musical Dictionary of Terms* (London, 1740, enlarged 2/1769, 3/1784); partly based on Brossard, not solely terminological

TANS'UR, W., *A New Musical Grammar* (London, 1746, 5/1772 with preface dated 1766 as *The Elements of Musick Display'd*, 7/1829 as *A Musical Grammar*)

ROUSSEAU, J.-J., *Dictionnaire de musique* (Paris, 1768, many further edns; Eng. trans. 1771, 2/1779); facs. repr. 1975

HOYLE, J., *Dictionarium musica* [sic] (London, 1770, 2/1790, 3/1791); facs. repr. 1976

BUSBY, T., *An Universal Dictionary of Music* (London, 1786; complete edn 1801 as *A Complete Dictionary of Music ... with the Assistance of Samuel Arnold*, 6/1827); facs. repr. 1973

KOCH, H. C., *Musikalisches Lexikon* (Frankfurt, 1802, 3/1865 ed. A. VON DOMMER; abridged 1807 as *Kurzgefasstes Handwörterbuch der Musik*); facs. repr. 1964

CASTIL-BLAZE, *Dictionnaire de musique moderne* (Paris, 1821, 2/1825, 3/1828 ed. J.-H. Mees)

LICHTENTHAL, P., *Dizionario e bibliografia della musica* (Milan, 1826); facs. repr. 1970

STAINER, J., and BARRETT, W. A., *A Dictionary of Musical Terms* (London, 1876, 4/1889, rev. 1898); facs. repr. 1971, 1974

APEL, W., *Harvard Dictionary of Music* (Cambridge, MA, 1944, 2/1969; relaunched 1986 as *The New Harvard Dictionary of Music*, ed. D. M. Randel)

3. Biographical dictionaries

MATTHESON, J., *Grundlage einer Ehren-Pforte* (Hamburg, 1740); ed. M. Schneider, (1910); facs. repr. 1969

GERBER, E. L., *Historisch-biographisches Lexicon der Tonkünstler* (Leipzig, 1790–2, enlarged 2/1812–14 as *Neues historisch-biographisches Lexikon der Tonkünstler*)

CHORON, A.-E., and FAYOLLE, F. J. M., *Dictionnaire historique des musiciens* (Paris, 1810–11, 2/1817; Eng. trans. 1824); facs. repr. 1971

BINGLEY, W., *Musical Biography* (London, 1814, 2/1834); facs. repr. 1971

SAINSBURY, J. H., *A Dictionary of Musicians* (London, 1824, repr. 1825, 2/1827); facs. repr. 1966

FÉTIS, F.-J., *Biographie universelle des musiciens* (Brussels, 1835–44, enlarged 2/1860–5, suppls. 1878–80 by A. Pougin); facs. repr. 1972

EITNER, R., *Biographisch-bibliographisches Quellen-Lexikon* (Leipzig, 1900–4, suppl. 1912–16 as *Miscellanea musicae bio-bibliographica*, both enlarged 2/1959–60); facs. repr. 1947

BAKER, T., *Baker's Biographical Dictionary of Musicians* (New York, 1900, enlarged 3/1919 by A. Remy, enlarged 4/1940 by C. Engel, 8/1991 ed. N. Slonimsky)

SAERCHINGER, C., *International Who's Who in Music and Musical Gazetteer* (New York, 1918)

Who's Who in Music and Musicians' International Directory (New York, 1935)

COHEN, A. I., *International Encyclopedia of Women Composers* (New York, 1984, 2/1987)

CUMMINGS, D., *International Who's Who in Music and Musicians' Directory (in the Classical and Light Classical Fields)* (Cambridge, 1990; since 1996 includes a 2nd vol. covering popular music, ed. Tyler)

RANDEL, D. M., *The Harvard Biographical Dictionary of Music* (Cambridge, MA, and London, 1996)

4. Terminological dictionaries

(see also sections 1 and 2 above)

TINCTORIS, J., *Terminorum musicae diffinitorium* (Treviso, 1495); ed. A. Seay (1975); Eng. trans. (1964)

A Short Explication of Such Foreign Words, as are made Use of in Music Books (London, 1724); facs. repr.

CALLCOTT, J. W., *An Explanation of the Notes, Marks, Words, &c. used in Music* (London, 1793, 2/c.1800)

KOCH, H. C., *Kurzgefasstes Handwörterbuch der Musik* (Leipzig, 1807)

JOUSSE, J., *A Compendious Dictionary of Italian and other Terms used in Music* (London, 1829, rev. 1907; published Boston, 1866, as *A Catechism of Music*, rev. 1874)

BAKER, T., *A Dictionary of Musical Terms* (New York, 1895; many later edns)

WOTTON, T. S., *A Dictionary of Foreign Musical Terms* (Leipzig, 1907); facs. repr. 1972

MOSER, H. J., *Musikalisches Wörterbuch* (Leipzig and Berlin, 1923)

GAMMOND, P., *Terms Used in Music* (New York, 1959, 2/1971)

EGGEBRECHT, H. H., *Handwörterbuch der musikalischen Terminologie* (Wiesbaden, 1972–)

LEUCHTMANN, H., *Terminorum musicae index septem linguis redactus* (Kassel, 1978); polyglot dictionary

5. National dictionaries

(excluding regional dictionaries)

Australia

GLENNON, J., *Australian Music and Musicians* (Adelaide, 1968)

McCREDIE, A. D., *Catalogue of 46 Australian Composers* (Canberra, 1969)

MURDOCH, J., *Australia's Contemporary Composers* (Melbourne, 1972)

SAINTILAN, N., SCHULTZ, A., and STANHOPE, P., *Biographical Dictionary of Australian Composers* (Rocks, NSW, 1996)

Belgium

GREGOIR, E., *Les artiste-musiciens belges* (Brussels, 1885–90, suppl. 1887)

VANNES, R., and SOURIS, A., *Dictionnaire des musiciens (compositeurs)* (Brussels, 1947)

CeBeDeM, *Music in Belgium: Contemporary Belgian Composers* (Brussels, 1964)

Britain

ABC Dario Musico (Bath, 1780)

BAPTIE, D., *Musical Scotland Past and Present* (Paisley, 1894); facs. repr. 1972

CROWEST, F., *Dictionary of British Musicians* (London, 1895)

BROWN, J. D., and STRATTON, S. S., *British Musical Biography* (Birmingham, 1897); facs. repr. 1971

PULVER, J., *A Biographical Dictionary of Old English Music* (London, 1927); facs. repr. 1969

Canada

KALLMANN, H., *Catalogue of Canadian Composers* (Ottawa, 1952; rev. edn 1972)

KALLMANN, H., POTVIN, G., and WINTERS, K., *Encyclopedia of Music in Canada* (Toronto, 1981, 2/1992)

Czech Republic and Slovakia

DLABACŽ, G. J., *Allgemeines historisches Künstler-Lexikon für Böhmen ... Mähren und Schlesien* (Prague, 1815); facs. repr. 1973

GARDAVSKY, C., *Contemporary Czechoslovak Composers* (Prague, 1965)

Finland

HILLILA, R.-E., *Historical Dictionary of the Music and Musicians of Finland* (Westport, CT, 1997)

France

Tablettes de renommées des musiciens (Paris, 1785); facs. repr. 1961

Dictionnaire des musiciens français (Paris, 1961)

Germany

LIPOWSKY, F. J., *Baierisches Musik-Lexikon* (Munich, 1811); facs. repr. 1971

MÜLLER VON ASOW, E. H., *Deutsches Musiker-Lexicon* (Dresden, 1929, 2/1954 as *Kürschners deutscher Musiker-Kalendar 1954*)

Komponisten und Musikwissenschaftlicher der Deutschen Demokratischen Republik (Berlin, 1959, enlarged 2/1967)

Iceland

PODHAJSKI, M., *Dictionary of Icelandic Composers* (Warsaw, 1997)

Italy

GERVASONI, C., 'Descrizione generale dei virtuosi filarmonici italiani', *Nuova teoria di musica* (Parma, 1812)

DE ANGELIS, A., *L'Italia musicale d'oggi* (Rome, 1918, 3/1928)

Latin America

MAYER-SERRA, O., *Música y músicos de Latinoamérica* (Mexico City, 1947)

Compositores de América, Pan-American Union (Washington, DC, 1955–72)

Netherlands

GREGOIR, E., *Biographie des artistes-musiciens néerlandais des XVIIIe et XIXe siècles* (Brussels, 1864)

LETZER, J. H., *Muzikaal Nederland* (Utrecht, 1911, 2/1913)

DE SCHRIJVER, K., *Levende componisten* (Louvain, 1954–5)

Poland

SOWIŃSKI, W., *Les musiciens polonais et slaves* (Paris, 1857); facs. repr. 1971

CHOMIŃSKI, J. M., *Słownik muzyków polskich* (Kraków, 1964–7)

Portugal

MAZZA, J., *Diccionário biográfico de músicos portugueses*, compiled *c*.1790; ed. J. A. Alegría (Lisbon, 1944–5)

VIEIRA, J., *Diccionário biográfico de músicos portuguezes* (Lisbon, 1900–4)

Spain

VILLAR, R., *Músicos españoles* (Madrid, 1918–27)

Diccionario de la música Labor (Barcelona, 1954)

68 compositores Catalans, Associació Catalana de Compositors (Barcelona, 1989)

CASARES RODICIO, E., *Diccionario de la música española e hispanoamericana* (Madrid, 1999–)

Switzerland

REFARDT, E., *Historisch-biographisches Musikerlexikon der Schweiz* (Zürich, 1928)

SCHUH, W., and REFARDT, E., *Schweizer Musikbuch* (Zürich, 1939, enlarged 1964 as *Schweizer Musik-Lexikon/Dictionnaire des musiciens suisses*)

Forty Contemporary Swiss Composers, Swiss Composers' League (Amriswil, 1956)

USA

JONES, F. O., *A Handbook of American Music and Musicians* (Canaseraga, NY, 1886); facs. repr. 1971

HUBBARD, W. L., *The American History and Encyclopedia of Music* (New York, 1908–10)

PRATT, W. S., *American Supplement to Grove's Dictionary of Music and Musicians* (New York, 1920, 2/1928)

REIS, C., *American Composers of Today* (New York, 1930, 2/1932 as *American Composers*, 3/1938 as *Composers in America*, enlarged 4/1947)

HANDY, W. C., *Negro Authors and Composers of the United States* (New York, 1935); facs. repr. 1976

ELLINWOOD, L., and PORTER, K., *Bio-Bibliographical Index of Musicians in the United States of America since Colonial Times* (Washington, DC, 1941, 2/1956); facs. repr. 1971

The ASCAP Biographical Dictionary (New York, 1948, 4/1980)

CLAGHORN, C. E., *Biographical Dictionary of American Music* (Nyack, NY, 1973)

HITCHCOCK, H. W., and SADIE, S., *The New Grove Dictionary of American Music* (London, 1986)

DUPREE, M., *Musical Americans: A Biographical Dictionary, 1918–1926* (Berkeley, CA, 1997)

USSR and Russia

VODARSKY-SHIRAEFF, A., *Russian Composers and Musicians* (New York, 1940, repr. 1969)

BELZA, I. F., *Handbook of Soviet Musicians* (London, 1943, 3/1945)

BERNANDT, G. B., and DOLZHANSKY, A. N., *Sovetskïye kompozitory* (Moscow, 1957)

HO, A., and FEOFANOV, D., *Biographical Dictionary of Russian/Soviet Composers* (New York, 1989)

6. Dictionaries of instruments, performers, and makers

General

JACQUOT, A., *Dictionnaire pratique et raisonné des instruments de musique anciens et modernes* (Paris, 1886)

SACHS, C., *Real-Lexikon der Musikinstrumente* (Berlin, 1913, enlarged 1964); facs. repr. 1962

WRIGHT, R., *Dictionnaire des instruments de musique* (London, 1941)

MARCUSE, S., *Musical Instruments: A Comprehensive Dictionary* (Garden City, NY, 1964); facs. repr. 1975

SADIE, S., *The New Grove Dictionary of Musical Instruments* (London, 1984)

BAINES, A., *The Oxford Companion to Musical Instruments* (Oxford, 1992)

Keyboard instruments

PAUER, E., *Dictionary of Pianists and Composers for the Pianoforte* (London, 1896)

BOALCH, D. H., *Makers of the Harpsichord and Clavichord, 1440 to 1840* (London, 1956, 3/1995 ed. C. Mould)

CLINKSCALE, M. N., *Makers of the Piano* (Oxford, 1993–)

Organ

WEST, J. E., *Cathedral Organists Past and Present* (London, 1899, 2/1921)

THORNSBY, F. W., *Dictionary of Organs and Organists* (Bournemouth, 1912, 2/1921)

AUDSLEY, G. A., *Organ Stops and their Artistic Registration* (New York, 1921)

IRWIN, S., *Dictionary of Pipe Organ Stops* (New York, 1962, 2/1965)

——, *Dictionary of Electronic Organ Stops* (New York, 1968)

Stringed instruments

PEARCE, J., *Violins and Violin Makers: A Biographical Dictionary* (London, 1866)

VIDAL, A., *Les Instruments à archet* (Paris, 1876–8); facs. repr. 1961

CLARKE, A. M., *A Biographical Dictionary of Fiddlers* (London, 1895); facs. repr. 1972

STAINER, C., *A Dictionary of Violin Makers* (London, 1896, rev. edn 1956); facs. repr. 1977

LÜTGENDORFF, W. L. VON, *Die Geigen- und Lautenmacher vom Mittelalter bis zur Gegenwart* (Frankfurt, 1904, 6/1922); facs. repr. 1968

EMERY, F. B., *Violinist's Dictionary* (London, 1912, 3/1928 as *The Violinist's Encyclopedic Dictionary*)

BACHMANN, A., *An Encyclopedia of the Violin* (New York, 1925); facs. repr. 1975

HENLEY, W., *Universal Dictionary of Violin and Bow Makers* (Brighton, 1959–65, appendix 1969; 2/1973)

Wind instruments

GORGERAT, G., *Encyclopédie de la musique pour instruments à vent* (Lausanne, 1955)

LANGWILL, L. G., *An Index of Musical Wind-Instrument Makers* (Edinburgh, 1960, 6/1980; relaunched 1993 as *The New Langwill Index*, ed. W. Waterhouse)

SUPPAN, W., *Lexicon des Blasmusikwesens* (Freiburg, 1971, 2/1976)

7. Dictionaries of opera

ALLACCI, L., *Drammaturgia* (Rome, 1666, 2/1755); facs. repr. 1966

DUREY DE NOINVILLE, J.-B., *Histoire du Théâtre de l'Opéra en France* (Paris, 1753, 2/1757); facs. repr. 1958, 1972

CLÉMENT, F., and LAROUSSE, P., *Dictionnaire lyrique, ou Histoire des opéras* (Paris, 1867–9, suppls. to 1881; 2/1897 ed. A. Pougin, suppl. 1904; 3/1905); facs. repr. 1969

RIEMANN, H., *Opern-Handbuch* (Leipzig, 1887–93); facs. repr.

TOWERS, J., *Dictionary-Catalogue of Operas and Operettas* (Morgantown, WV, 1910); facs. repr. 1967

LOEWENBERG, A., *Annals of Opera, 1597–1940* (Cambridge, 1943, enlarged 3/1978); facs. repr. 1971

ROSENTHAL, H., and WARRACK, J., *Concise Oxford Dictionary of Opera* (London, 1964, 2/1979, 3/1996 with E. West); Fr. trans. (1974)

ORREY, L., and CHASE, G., *The Encyclopedia of Opera* (New York, 1976)

Who's Who in Opera: An International Biographical Dictionary (New York, 1976)

DAHLHAUS, C., and DÖHRING, S., *Pipers Enzyklopädie des Musiktheaters* (Munich, 1986–97)

PARSONS, C. H., *The Mellen Opera Reference Index* (Lewiston, NY, 1986–97)

SADIE, S., *The New Grove Dictionary of Opera* (London, 1992)

8. Dictionaries of church music and hymnology

ORTIGUE, J. D', *Dictionnaire liturgique* (Paris, 1854, 2/1860); facs. repr. 1971

KÜMMERLE, S., *Encyklopädie der evangelischen Kirchenmusik* (Gütersloh, 1888–95); facs. repr. 1974

JULIAN, J., *A Dictionary of Hymnology* (London, 1892, 2/1907); facs. repr. 1957

HUGHES, A., *Liturgical Terms for Music Students* (Boston, 1940; London, 1941); facs. repr. 1971

STUBBINGS, G. W., *A Dictionary of Church Music* (London, 1949)

THOMSON, R. W., *Who's Who of Hymn Writers* (London, 1967)

PORTE, J., *Encyclopédie des musiques sacrées* (Paris, 1968–70)

DAVIDSON, J. R., *A Dictionary of Protestant Church Music* (Metuchen, NJ, 1975)

TEMPERLEY, N., *The Hymn Tune Index* (Oxford, 1997)

9. Dictionaries of chamber music

ALTMANN, W., *Kammermusik-Literatur* (Leipzig, 1910, 6/1945; Eng. trans. 1923)

COBBETT, W. W., *Cobbett's Cyclopedic Survey of Chamber Music* (London, 1929–30, enlarged 2/1963 ed. C. Mason)

10. Dictionaries of early music

PADELFORD, F. M., *Old English Musical Terms* (Bonn, 1899); facs. repr. 1976

PULVER, J., *A Dictionary of Old English Music and Musical Instruments* (London and New York, 1923); facs. repr. 1969

CARTER, H. H., *A Dictionary of Middle English Musical Terms* (Bloomington, IN, 1961)

ROCHE, J. and E., *A Dictionary of Early Music* (London, 1981)

STRAHLE, G., *An Early Music Dictionary: Musical Terms from British Sources, 1500–1740* (Cambridge, 1994)

11. Dictionaries of contemporary music

SLONIMSKY, N., *Music Since 1900* (New York, 1937, 5/1994)

THOMPSON, K., *A Dictionary of Twentieth-Century Composers, 1911–1971* (London, 1973)

VINTON, J., *Dictionary of Contemporary Music* (New York, 1974)

GOUBAULT, C., *Vocabulaire de la musique à l'aube du XXe siècle* (Paris, 2000)

12. Dictionaries of dance

COMPAN, C., *Dictionnaire de danse* (Paris, 1787); facs. repr. 1974

BEAUMONT, C. W., *A French–English Dictionary of Technical Terms used in Classical Ballet* (London, 1931, enlarged 2/1939); facs. repr. 1951

CHUJOY, A., *The Dance Encyclopedia* (New York, 1949, enlarged 2/1967)

WILSON, G. B. L., *A Dictionary of Ballet* (London, 1957, 3/1974)

CLARKE, M., and VAUGHAN, D., *The Encyclopedia of Dance and Ballet* (London and New York, 1977)

KOEGLER, H., *The Concise Oxford Dictionary of Ballet* (London, 1977, enlarged 2/1982, rev. 1987)

BREMSER, M., and NICHOLAS, L., *International Dictionary of Ballet* (Detroit and London, 1993)

COHEN, S. J., *International Encyclopedia of Dance* (New York and Oxford, 1998)

CRAINE, D., and MACKRELL, J., *The Oxford Dictionary of Dance* (Oxford, 2000)

13. Dictionaries of jazz, popular music, and musical theatre

KERNFELD, B., and SADIE, S., *The New Grove Dictionary of Jazz* (London, 1988; 2nd edn forthcoming)

CLARKE, D., *The Penguin Encyclopedia of Popular Music* (Harmondsworth, 1989)

GAMMOND, P., *The Oxford Companion to Popular Music* (Oxford and New York, 1991)

LARKIN, C., *The Guinness Encyclopedia of Popular Music* (London, 1992, 2/1995)

GÄNZL, K., *The Encyclopedia of the Musical Theatre* (Oxford and New York, 1994)

14. Dictionaries of music publishers

KIDSON, F., *British Music Publishers, Printers and Engravers* (London, 1900); facs. repr. 1967

HOPKINSON, C., *A Dictionary of Parisian Music Publishers, 1700–1950* (London, 1954)

HUMPHRIES, C., and SMITH, W. C., *Music Publishing in the British Isles* (London, 1954, 2/1970)

SARTORI, C., *Dizionario degli editori musicali italiani* (Florence, 1958)

LESURE, F., and DEVRIÈS, A., *Dictionnaire des éditeurs de musique français* (Geneva, 1979–88)

KRUMMEL, D. W., and SADIE, S., *Music Printing and Publishing* (London, 1990)

ANTOLINI, B. M., *Dizionario degli editori musicali italiani, 1750–1930* (Pisa, 2000)

15. Thematic dictionaries

BURROWS, R., and REDMOND, B. C., *Symphony Themes* (New York, 1942)

BARLOW, H., and MORGENSTERN, S., *A Dictionary of Musical Themes* (New York, 1948; It. trans. 1955); facs. repr. 1975

——, *A Dictionary of Vocal Themes* (New York, 1950, repr. 1976 as *A Dictionary of Opera and Song Themes*)

BURROWS, R., and REDMOND, B. C., *Concerto Themes* (New York, 1951)

LARUE, J., *A Catalogue of 18th-Century Symphonies*, i: *Thematic Identifier* (Bloomington, IN, 1988)

16. Miscellaneous dictionaries

NULMAN, M., *Concise Encyclopedia of Jewish Music* (New York, 1975)

SPIEGL, F., *Music Through the Looking-Glass: A Very Personal Kind of Dictionary of Musicians' Jargon, Shop-Talk and Nicknames* (London, 1984)

DOBSON, R., *A Dictionary of Electronic and Computer Music Technology* (Oxford, 1992)   PS/JWa

diddley bow. A home-made plucked *monochord of the southern USA, consisting of a length of wire attached to a wall of a frame house, the house itself acting as a resonator. An object such as a cotton-reel might be used as a bridge. The string is stopped using a slide made from a bottleneck or nail. Many blues guitarists, including Muddy Waters, learnt to play the diddley bow first.

diddling. A Lowland Scottish practice similar to the Highland practice of *puirt-a-beul, in which dance tunes are sung to meaningless vocables.   KC

didjeridu. The only melodic instrument of the Australian Aborigines. It consists of a long wooden tube, usually of eucalyptus, blown as a trumpet and simultaneously sung into, using *circular breathing; it is often accompanied by clapping-sticks. The mixture of blown fundamentals and overtones with sung and spoken rhythms produces resultant tones in a rich harmony unrivalled by any other instrument.   JMo

Dido and Aeneas. Opera in three acts by Purcell to a libretto by Nahum Tate after his play *Brutus of Alba, or The Enchanted Lovers* (1678) and book 4 of Virgil's *Aeneid* (London, 1689).

Dido's Lament. The lament 'When I am laid in earth', in Act III of Purcell's *Dido and Aeneas*, which Dido sings before she dies.

Dienstag aus Licht ('Tuesday from Light'). Opera in a greeting and two acts by Stockhausen to his own libretto (Leipzig, 1993), the 'fourth day' of *Licht.

Dieren, Bernard (Hélène Joseph) **van** (*b* Rotterdam, 27 Dec. 1887; *d* London, 24 April 1936). Dutch composer and writer, active in England. With little means he settled in London in 1909 and wrote criticism for continental newspapers and periodicals. He spent 1912 in Berlin, where he attended Busoni's orchestral concerts of contemporary music; indeed, the Italian's preoccupation with counterpoint may well have influenced van Dieren's own fascination with contrapuntal intricacy, clearly evident in the six string quartets he wrote between 1912 and 1928. His highly chromatic harmonic palette and metrical freedom profoundly affected the young Philip Heseltine (Peter Warlock), and he was admired by Lambert, Moeran, and Walton for his broad knowledge and critical independence. His *Chinese Symphony* (1914), Overture for 16 instruments (1916), and Serenade (*c*.1923) are worth reviving, though the intensity of his contrapuntal idiom and the unremitting chromatic language are exceptionally demanding. He published a study of the sculptor Jacob Epstein (1920) and the volume of essays *Down Among the Dead Men* (1935).   JDi

 📖 A. CHISHOLM, *Bernard van Dieren: An Introduction* (London, 1983)

dièse (Fr.). 1. The sharp sign (see SHARP, 1).
2. In 17th-century, usage, 'major', e.g. *mi dièse*, E major.

Dies irae (Lat., 'Day of wrath'). The sequence of the pre-Vatican II *Requiem Mass, attributed to Thomas of Celano (*d* c.1250). Occasional efforts to set the text polyphonically by composers of the 15th–17th centuries were succeeded by often highly dramatic settings with instrumental accompaniment, including those by Mozart, Verdi, and Ligeti. The plainchant melody has been used in instrumental music for its inherent symbolism, for example by Berlioz in the *Symphonie fantastique* and Saint-Saëns in the *Danse macabre* (see DANCE OF DEATH).   —/ALi

diesis (It.). The sharp sign (see SHARP, 1).

Dies natalis ('Birthday'). Cantata, op. 8 (1926–39), by Finzi for soprano or tenor and strings; it is in five movements, the first instrumental, the second a setting of a prose passage from *Centuries of Meditation* by Thomas Traherne (1638–74), and the last three being settings of Traherne poems.

Dieupart, Charles (*d* London, *c*.1740). French composer, violinist, and keyboard player. He settled in England about 1700. He wrote and arranged music for various plays and entertainments, and, together with other musicians, gave series of concerts. His *Six suittes de clavecin* (Amsterdam, 1701) may have been the models for Bach's English Suites.   DA

diferencia (Sp.). 1. A term used for a kind of ornamentation in which a melody is broken up by fast figuration.
2. 16th-century name given to variations. Some of the earliest known *diferencias* are in Luis de Narváez's *Los seys libros del Delphín* (Valladolid, 1538) for vihuela; other famous examples are those by Antonio de Cabezón for keyboard. *Diferencias* are generally longer and more elaborate than *glosas.

difference tone. See ACOUSTICS, 8.

Different Trains. Work (1988) by Reich for string quartet and tape; the taped material consists of fragments of interviews linking the composer's memories of rail journeys made in his childhood to the trains that transported Holocaust victims to their death in concentration camps.

Dillon, James (*b* Glasgow, 29 Oct. 1950). Scottish composer. His early involvement in music came about through playing in Scottish pipe bands and rock groups, and though he later studied music in London he received no formal training in composition. From the beginning his sympathies were with the postwar European avant-garde and with such British composers as Michael Finnissy and Brian Ferneyhough who were building radical and challenging musical edifices on avant-garde foundations. Relatively early pieces like *Ti-re-Ti-ke-Dha* for solo drummer (1979) and *Spleen* for solo piano (1980) display a rugged vitality stemming from Varèse and Xenakis, while *Überschreiten* for 16 players (1986) and *helle Nacht* for orchestra (1986–7) extend Dillon's characteristically elaborate and taxing textural tapestries on to a larger scale. He can nevertheless complement an aggressive percussiveness with more sustained linear writing and more mellow sonorities, as in *La Femme invisible* for 12 players (from the *Nine Rivers* cycle, 1989) and *Vernal Showers* for solo violin and ensemble (1992). And although he can use traditional instruments and voices in startlingly novel ways (with or without electroacoustic manipulation) he does not reject all contact with the kind of generic heritage, up to and including Bartók, that can be heard in his String Quartet no. 3 (1998).   AW

diluendo (It.). 'Dissolving', i.e. dying away.

diminished interval. A major or perfect *interval decreased by a semitone.

diminished seventh chord. The chord of the diminished 7th usually appears on the seventh degree of the scale. It spans the interval of a diminished 7th and is made up of a succession of minor 3rds (thus in C major the chord is B–D–F–A♭). The diminished 7th usually resolves on to the tonic chord (Ex. 1a), but because the intervals of the chord are all the same, any one of its notes may be treated as the root, and modulation to other keys is easily effected (Ex. 1b; the modulation can be to either major or minor). The chord of the diminished 7th is often thought of as a dominant 9th chord with its root missing (see DOMINANT SEVENTH CHORD).

diminished triad. See TRIAD.

diminuendo (It.). 'Diminishing', i.e. gradually getting quieter. The term is often represented by the 'hairpin' sign (see DYNAMIC MARKS, Table 1) or by the abbreviations *dim.* or *dimin.* It is the equivalent of *decrescendo* but seems to have been in use earlier than the corresponding *crescendo*.

diminution. A melodic device, often found in fugal compositions, in which the time-values of the melody notes are proportionally shortened. For example, a melody moving in minims, crotchets, and quavers could undergo diminution to move in crotchets, quavers, and semiquavers (each value diminishing by half).

diminutions. See ORNAMENTS AND ORNAMENTATION.

Dimitrij. Opera in four acts by Dvořák to a libretto by Marie Červinková-Riegrová (Prague, 1882; revised Prague, 1894).

di molto (It.). 'Very'; *allegro di molto*, 'very fast'.

D'India, Sigismondo. See INDIA, SIGISMONDO D'.

D'Indy, Vincent. See INDY, VINCENT D'.

Dioclesian (*The Prophetess, or The History of Dioclesian*). Semi-opera in five acts by Purcell to a libretto by Thomas Betterton after the play by John Fletcher and Philip Massinger (London, 1690).

direct (Fr.: *guidon*; Ger.: *Wachte*; It.: *guida*; Lat.: *custos*). The sign (∿) occasionally used at the end of a page or line of music to give an indication of the pitch of the next note. It is most often found in early music.

direct psalmody. The singing of a psalm without any textual additions or other alterations, as opposed to antiphonal and responsorial psalmody (see ANTIPHON; RESPONSORY), for example the psalmody sung at Compline by Benedictine monks.

dirge (Lat.: *naenia*; It.: *nenia*). A vocal or instrumental composition performed at a funeral or memorial service. Britten set one of the best-known English dirges, the 15th-century *Lyke-Wake-Dirge*, as the fourth song of his *Serenade for Tenor, Horn, and Strings* (1943); the *Lyke-Wake-Dirge* was also used by Stravinsky, as a framework for his Cantata (1952).

Dirigent, dirigieren (Ger.). 'Conductor', 'to conduct'.

Dis (Ger.). The note D♯; *Disis*, the note D𝄪. In earlier music *Dis* sometimes meant the enharmonic equivalent E♭, and as late as 1805 Beethoven's 'Eroica' Symphony (in E♭) was described as being 'in Dis'.

discant [descant] (from medieval Lat. *discantus*, 'sounding apart'). A medieval technique of composition in which one voice is added to a plainchant part, usually note against note and usually in contrary motion. The term 'discantus' was first used by 12th-century theorists, and there survive musical examples from the beginning of that century onwards. The large 12th-century repertory of settings of Latin sacred songs from France (usually called *conductus or versus), though not settings of plainchant, may also be regarded as examples of discant, at least in harmonic style.

In the remarkable corpus of polyphony of the so-called Notre Dame School, composed in 12th- and 13th-century Paris, discant technique was employed in two parts of the repertory: in conductus (an anonymous theorist of the 1270s attributed some of these to Pérotin), and for setting phrases of plainchant (more specifically, those phrases of the original plainchant which were a melisma on one syllable, rather than syllabic sections). Parisian chant settings of this time actually alternate passages of discant (such passages are also known as *clausulae) with passages where the original chant is heard in long held notes, beneath an onward-moving upper part or parts (see ORGANUM, 4). The above-mentioned theorist calls Pérotin 'optimus discantor' ('the best singer [composer] of discant'),

diminished seventh chord, Ex. 1

(a)   (b)

E♭ major   F♯ major   A major

implying that he was responsible for those parts of plainchant settings that are in discant style.

By the second half of the 13th century, discant was the chief style of polyphony in existence, and therefore also the most common term for polyphony itself; the long-held-note style was more or less obsolete. Techniques of part-writing became more complex, however, and mere two-part writing less predominant. In the 14th century, therefore, 'discantus' was often used simply as a label for an extra accompanying part added above the main (cantus and tenor) voices (as in chansons by Machaut, for instance).

At its simplest, discant was no more than a set of rules-of-thumb for the improvisation of two-part polyphony. Interesting and relatively late sets of rules of this type are found in treatises written in England in the 14th and 15th centuries, by Leonel Power among others. The dependence of discant on contrary motion differentiates it decisively from parallel-motion techniques such as *faburden.   DH

disc jockey. See DJ.

disco. A form of dance music with roots in *soul and *funk which predominated in the late 1970s, having emerged from the black, Latino, and gay clubs of New York earlier in the decade. A repetitive bass drum pattern on each beat was perhaps its most characteristic sound. Earlier disco retained some of the rhythmic and harmonic complexities of jazz funk; later, however, the leaner rhythmic and harmonic structures of 'Eurodisco' became dominant. Disco entered the mainstream in 1977 following the success of the film *Saturday Night Fever*. Although it was comparatively short-lived, aspects of its style, particularly bass and drum patterns, passed into subsequent dance styles, especially *house music and its subgenres.   PW

discography. A purposeful, critical list or catalogue of sound recordings. A discography may include recordings in any medium, not merely those on some form of disc. The crucial distinction between a discography and a library or manufacturer's catalogue is the critical selection and organization of its information for a distinct purpose.

The earliest discographies in the 1930s were devoted to particular performers (W. H. Seltsam, 'A [Geraldine] Farrar Discography', *Phonograph Monthly Review*, Jan. 1931) or to the deeply confusing typology of jazz recordings (Charles Delaunay, *Hot Discography*, Paris, 1936). These established a method for the arrangement of discographies of vernacular musics, in which the chief performer or performing group was the primary basis of organization, the chronological sequence of his or her recordings being next in importance. Chron-

ology is the principal factor in discographies of record labels. Discographies of classical music, on the other hand, are typically organized first by composer and second by some conventional arrangement of his or her works, with performers and date of recording being lower in the hierarchy, though there are many discographies devoted to particular performers of classical music, arranged like the first class.

The crucial constituent of well-made discographies is the standardization of information. In classical music, composers' names (especially in transliteration, or before 1600) are subject to great variation on record labels and liners; incompatible numbering systems are in place for many composers' works (e.g. the symphonies of Haydn or Dvořák); many recordings embody distinct versions of a work (Bruckner's symphonies) or make varying selections from multiple versions (Handel's *Messiah*, many operas); the same work may be attributed to different composers; and so on. Many early jazz recordings were anonymous; some were reissued with different performers credited or with new titles, and popular music of all kinds has frequently been repackaged. A good discography must bring order into all these areas. Details of recording sessions and matrix and take numbers are invaluable pieces of documentation in this endeavour, and such collateral information as biographical facts and correspondence is often included.   JJD

📖 J. A. BOWEN (ed.), *Guide to Discography* (Berkeley, CA, forthcoming)

discord. A dissonant chord or interval; see CONSONANCE AND DISSONANCE.

disinvolto (It.). 'Free', 'jaunty'.

disjunct motion. See MOTION.

dismissal. A formula, generally including a response, sung or spoken to dismiss the congregation at the end of a service (e.g. *Ite missa est, Deo gratias*).

dissonance. See CONSONANCE AND DISSONANCE.

'Dissonance' Quartet (*Les Dissonances*; *Dissonanzen-Quartett*). Nickname of Mozart's String Quartet in C major, K465 (1785); one of the 'Haydn' Quartets, it is so called because the introduction contains a remarkable use of dissonance.

Distler, Hugo (*b* Nuremberg, 24 June 1908; *d* Berlin, 1 Nov. 1942). German composer, choral conductor, organist, and teacher. He was organist at St Jakobi in Lübeck (1931); from 1937 he was lecturer and choir conductor at the Württemberg Hochschule für Musik, Stuttgart, before going on to the Hochschule für Musik in Berlin. His sympathy for early German masters such as Schütz and Lechner allowed him to coexist uneasily with the Nazis, who found his music bordering on the unacceptably modern; and though he shared their enthusiasm for choral singing, his Lutheran faith invited official suspicion. Well-placed friends initially enabled him to avoid call-up; when in 1942 he received the order to join a panzer division, he committed suicide. His music is liberally dissonant within a strongly tonal framework, the asperity resulting from the play of contrapuntal lines rather than from wilful experiment. His output includes two harpsichord concertos (the second only recently rediscovered) and a number of organ works; the bulk of it is for chorus, setting both religious and secular texts.   MA

Distratto, Il ('The Distraught Man'). Haydn's Symphony no. 60 in C major (1774), so called because it includes the incidental music Haydn wrote for the comedy *Der Zerstreute* (after J. F. Regnard's *Le Distrait*) (Eszterháza, 1774).

dithyramb (from Gk. *dithyrambos*; Fr.: *dithyrambe*; It.: *ditirambo*). An ancient Greek song in honour of Dionysus, the god of wine and good living. Originally a choral strophic song, it gradually became more elaborate, combining instrumental accompaniment, soloists, and groups of dancers. By the end of the 4th century BC it had become virtually a theatrical performance.

The name is sometimes given to modern compositions of a free and passionate character.

ditonus (Lat.). Medieval name given to the major 3rd (i.e. equal to two whole tones).

Dittersdorf, Carl Ditters von [Ditters, Carl] (*b* Vienna, 2 Nov. 1739; *d* Neuhof, Pilgram, Bohemia, 24 Oct. 1799). Austrian composer. Born plain Carl Ditters, he studied in Vienna and played the violin in a local church orchestra. From 1751 to 1761 he was a member of the orchestra of the Prince of Sachsen-Hildburghausen, studying music with Giuseppe Bonno. After the prince left Vienna, Dittersdorf was successful as a solo and orchestral violinist; he went with Gluck to Italy in 1763. He next worked as Kapellmeister to the Bishop of Grosswardein (now Oradea) from 1765 to 1769, succeeding Michael Haydn, then entered the service of the Prince-Bishop of Breslau at Johannisberg (now Jánský Vrch).

Dittersdorf ran an efficient and lively musical establishment there; he composed several works to Italian texts for the theatre, but a larger number of German stage works, most for Vienna, his *Singspiel Der Apotheker und der Doktor* (later known as *Doktor und Apotheker*) being especially popular. In 1770 he was made a Knight of the Golden Spur, and in 1773 he was

ennobled by Empress Maria Theresa, gaining the additional surname 'von Dittersdorf'. After the prince-bishop's death in 1795 Dittersdorf received only a small pension. He wrote some *Singspiele* for a new court theatre at Oels (now Oleśnica) in Silesia, but in 1797 retired to the estate of Baron Ignaz von Stillfried in Bohemia. His autobiography was published two years after his death.

Dittersdorf composed in all the main musical genres of his day. His *Singspiele* are written, like Mozart's, in a variety of idioms borrowed from Italian opera, but they have a more pronounced folk element; they can still provide an excellent evening's entertainment. He was also an important and prolific composer of symphonies, sometimes using programmatic titles (for example in the 12 based on the *Metamorphoses* of Ovid), and at his most attractive when adopting a Haydnesque vigour and sense of humour. Many of his concertos are for violin, and these too resemble Haydn's, while his chamber music, especially the string quartets, is equally worthy of revival.   DA/FL

📖 C. DITTERS VON DITTERSDORF, *The Autobiography of Karl von Dittersdorf*, trans. A. D. Coleridge (London, 1896/ R1970)

div. Abbreviation for **divisi*.

diva (It., 'goddess'). See PRIMA DONNA.

divertimento (It.). 'Diversion', 'recreation'. The 18th-century divertimento, which was usually scored for a combination of solo instruments, was related to such genres as the **cassation*, **Nachtmusik*, **notturno*, and **serenade*, in that all were light in approach and intended to serve as entertainment pieces. Vienna was the divertimento capital, but the term was also widely used in southern Germany, Bohemia, and Italy.

The keyboard divertimento resembled the sonata, and was composed mainly by Austrians such as Wagenseil and Haydn. Haydn's divertimentos have three movements: quick–slow–quick. Some keyboard divertimentos have accompaniments for other instruments, as do many contemporary keyboard sonatas. There were also divertimentos for wind ensemble (often pairs of oboes, horns, and bassoons), or for strings (trio, quartet, quintet), sometimes with added wind instruments. Mozart and Haydn each wrote several for wind alone, while the wind and string repertory includes pieces by all the major Viennese composers of the mid- to late 18th century, including the Haydn brothers and Leopold and Wolfgang Mozart, as well as Jommelli, Boccherini, and some of the Mannheim composers.

The 18th-century divertimento could have up to nine movements, but more commonly only five or so were used (opening and closing Allegro movements in sonata form, two minuets, and a central slow movement). Haydn used the five-movement scheme for his string and wind pieces, as did Mozart for his string divertimentos; his wind divertimentos are in four movements only. This arrangement of movements played an important role in the development of the four-movement Classical string quartet, achieved by the omission of one minuet (Mozart's *Eine kleine Nachtmusik* originally had a second minuet).

The genre proper died out at the beginning of the 19th century (an exception is Weber's Divertimento for guitar and piano, 1816), but the term was occasionally used in the 20th for works of a light, brilliant character, such as Bartók's Divertimento for strings, Rawsthorne's for orchestra, Berkeley's for chamber orchestra, and Tippett's *Divertimento on Sellinger's Round*.

WT/NT

divertissement (Fr., 'diversion', 'entertainment'). 1. In opera, a portion of a *tragédie lyrique* or *opéra-ballet* composed mainly of songs and dances and accompanied by spectacular stage effects, often having little connection with the main plot. Rousseau, in his dictionary of music (1768), scathingly defined the divertissement as 'Certain collections of dances and songs which it is the rule in Paris to insert in each act of an opera, ballet, or tragedy to break the action at some interesting moment'. In some of Lully's *tragédies lyriques* the divertissement is purely decorative, but in others it forms an integral part of the action (e.g. during the village wedding scene in Act IV of *Roland*, when the shepherds' celebrations reveal to the hero his betrayal by his loved one). Lully's divertissements often occur at the end of the opera, as a grand closing gesture, but in his masterpiece *Armide* the final divertissement occurs halfway through the last act, leaving the end free for the tragic denouement.

In French *opéra-ballet* of the early 18th century, in which dance and spectacle played a greater part than in the *tragédie*, each act (or *entrée*) had its own divertissement of dances. The spectacular element in French opera became increasingly important in the early 18th century, often at the expense of the drama, and still flourished in the works of Rameau and Gluck. The divertissement persisted far into the 19th century; Rossini, Verdi, and Wagner all had to add one when their operas were performed in France. It was also a feature of Russian ballet; a good example is in the last act of Tchaikovsky's *Nutcracker*. What all these meanings have in common is the idea of a break or diversion from the main plot.

2. An all-purpose entertainment lasting an entire evening or even for several days or weeks. At the height of the *grand siècle* spectacular divertissements were arranged at court to celebrate royal births, marriages, and victories (the one given at Versailles in 1674 by Louis XIV after his successful Franche-Comté campaign lasted nearly a month, and included two Lully operas and two *comédies-ballets* by Molière and Lully). The Duchess of Maine held a famous series known as the Grandes Nuits de Sceaux at her chateau in 1714 and 1715, but by this time such entertainments were rare.

3. In the early 19th century, a light *character piece, generally in several sections (the term was more or less interchangeable with 'divertimento', used in this sense by J. B. Cramer). An unusually serious example is Schubert's extraordinary *Divertissement à la Hongroise*, a set of linked dances in 'Gypsy' style for piano duet. The term was occasionally revived in the 20th century, for example by Ibert, for a medley based on his music for *The Italian Straw Hat*.

WT/NT

Divine Office. See OFFICE.

Divine Poem, The (*Bozhestvennaya poema*; *Le Divin Poème*). Skryabin's Symphony no. 3 in C minor op. 43 (1902–4); it illustrates the composer's theosophical ideas, the three movements being called 'Struggles', 'Delights', and 'Divine Play'.

divisi (It.). 'Divided'. An indication in ensemble and orchestral scores that players who normally have the same part should divide into groups to play that part, often notated on the same staff; for string players, this is a practical alternative to using double or triple stopping, the number of 'divisions' required indicated by 'div. a 2', 'div. a 3' etc. See À DEUX, A DUE.

divisions. 1. A term used in the 17th and 18th centuries for a kind of ornamentation in which a melody is broken up by fast figuration. *Coloratura vocal runs by Handel and others may be regarded as written-out divisions.

2. More specifically, the performance of 'divisions upon a ground' was a characteristic English practice in the 17th century. Over a recurrent *ground bass, provided by a harpsichord or another instrument, a viol player would improvise variations or 'divisions'— splitting up the notes of the ground into shorter notes or providing a counter-melody to it 'as his skill and present invention do then suggest unto him' (Christopher Simpson, *The Division-Violist*, London, 1659).

SMcV

division viol. See VIOL.

dixieland. The early style of New Orleans jazz as played by white musicians, originally distinguished from black jazz by less use of rhythmic *swing and *blue notes and by a somewhat different melodic and harmonic idiom. The name was at first applied to black marching jazz around 1900, but was popularized by the white Original Dixieland Jazz Band, which toured and recorded widely from 1917 (the term 'Dixie' for the Old South of the USA comes from Dan Emmett's 1859 minstrel song of the same name). Dixieland was revived along with black New Orleans jazz in the 1950s and remains a popular style. PGA/JJD

DJ. Abbreviation for 'disc jockey', a term coined in the 1950s to describe presenters who provided the link between records on pop music broadcasts. It came to apply to anyone who fulfilled such a linking function, especially in clubs. The role of the DJ increasingly involved an element of performance, influencing Caribbean 'toasting' (speaking in rhythm over recordings) and American hip-hop, in which combining records using such techniques as scratching and fading created new effects from existing music. A club DJ is responsible for building and maintaining an increasing level of excitement throughout an evening, and is now sometimes better known than the performers on the records being played. JSn

Dobro. Resonator guitar; see GUITAR, 4.

Dobrowolski, Andrzej (*b* Lwów [now L'viv, Ukraine], 9 Sept. 1921; *d* Graz, 8 Aug. 1990). Polish composer and teacher. After establishing his name in neo-classical pieces, in the late 1950s he adopted serial procedures as well as exploring sonoristic textures. He was a pioneer of works involving live performance and electronics (*Music for Tape and Oboe*, 1965). Most of his music is orchestral (*Music for Orchestra* nos. 1–7, 1968–87), in which contrasted sound-blocks dominate his structural thinking. ATH

doctrine of affections. See AFFECTIONS, DOCTRINE OF.

doctrine of figures. See FIGURES, DOCTRINE OF.

Dodecachordon. Treatise on modal theory by Heinrich *Glarean, published in Basle in 1547. Its significance lies in Glarean's introduction and application of a new theory of 12 modes, with the addition of four modes—an Ionian and Hypoionian with finals on C, and an Aeolian and Hypoaeolian with finals on A—to the existing system of eight (see MODE, 2*b*). The work had a profound influence on Renaissance theory and composition, and is also important as an anthology, containing over 120 compositions by Josquin des Prez, Ockeghem, Isaac, and others.

dodecaphonic (from Gk., literally 'twelve-sound'). A term used to describe *twelve-note music. For the dodecaphonic scale, see SCALE, 4.

dodecuple [duodecuple]. Alternative word for *dodecaphonic.

Dodge, Charles (Malcolm) (*b* Ames, IA, 5 June 1942). American composer. He studied with Otto Luening at Columbia University (1964–70) and with Godfrey Winham at Princeton (1966–7), and has taught at Columbia University (1967–77) and Brooklyn College (from 1977). With *Changes* (1967–70) and *Earth's Magnetic Field* (1970) he was one of the pioneers of computer-synthesized music, which he has continued to produce, sometimes also using instrumental soloists. An entertaining example is *Any Resemblance is Purely Coincidental* for piano and computer-made Caruso voice (1980). PG

Dodgson, Stephen (Cuthbert Vivian) (*b* London, 17 March 1924). English composer. He studied at the RCM, where he was later appointed to the staff. A prolific composer, he has proved adept at producing likable, well-crafted music to order, often for unusual chamber ensembles (he has some claim, for instance, to being the first composer since the 18th century to write for baryton trio). PG

doh [do]. The first degree of the scale in the *Tonic Sol-fa system. Two methods of applying these *solmization syllables are in use: the *fixed-*doh* principle, in which they are applied to fixed notes of the C major scale—thus *doh* is always the note C; and the movable-*doh* principle, in which *doh* may be the tonic of any major scale.

Dohnányi, Ernő [Ernst von] (*b* Poszony [now Bratislava], 27 July 1877; *d* New York, 9 Feb. 1960). Hungarian composer. In 1893 he entered the Budapest Academy to study with István Thomán (piano) and Hans Koessler (composition); in not seeking his education outside Hungary he set a precedent that was followed by his younger friend Bartók. He made his debut as a pianist in Berlin in 1897 and then enjoyed a career as a virtuoso; he also served as director of the Budapest Conservatory from 1919. In 1948 he left Hungary for political reasons and settled in the USA. Unlike Bartók, he showed little interest in folksong and none in the advanced musical trends of the time, preferring a Romantic style rooted in the music of Brahms and Liszt. His compositions include two piano concertos and the popular *Variations on a Nursery Song* for piano and orchestra (1913), three symphonies, three operas, and chamber music. PG

Doktor Faust. Opera in eight scenes by Busoni to his own libretto after the 16th-century puppet plays; the final scene was completed by Jarnach (Dresden, 1925).

dolce (It.). 'Sweet', sometimes 'soft'; *dolcemente*, 'sweetly', *dolcissimo*, 'very sweet'.

dolente (It.). 'Doleful', 'sad'; *dolentamente*, 'dolefully'.

Dolly. Suite for piano duet, op. 56 (1894–7), by Fauré.

Dolmetsch, (Eugène) Arnold (*b* Le Mans, 24 Feb. 1858; *d* Haslemere, 28 Feb. 1940). Swiss musician and maker of early instruments. He studied the violin with Vieuxtemps in Brussels and, from 1883, at the RCM in London. In 1889 he began investigating English viol music and renovating early instruments, making a lute (1893), clavichord (1894), and harpsichord (1896). He worked in Boston and Paris, returning to England in 1914. The following year he published the pioneering *The Interpretation of the Music of the XVII and XVIII Centuries*. He settled in Haslemere, where he founded (1925) a festival, established a workshop for making and repairing early instruments (notably recorders), and collected and edited manuscripts. Several members of the family were well-known players and his son Carl (1911–97), a virtuoso recorder player, carried on his father's work.   DA/AL

📖 M. CAMPBELL, *Dolmetsch: The Man and his Work* (London, 1975)

doloroso (It.). 'Sorrowful', 'painful'.

dolzaina [dulzaina, dulzan, etc.] (It., Sp.). A reed instrument of the 14th–17th centuries. It may have been the same as the **douçaine*, or possibly a crumhorn or another unknown reed instrument. See also DULZAINA.

dolzana. See DOUÇAINE; DOLZAINA.

dominant. The fifth degree of the major or minor scale.

dominant seventh chord. The dominant chord with the note a 7th from its root added (thus in C major the chord is G–B–D–F). The dominant 7th normally resolves on to the tonic chord, or the submediant chord, the added 7th note falling a semitone (Ex. 1*a*); it can be used in root position or in any one of its three inversions (Ex. 1*b*). Further additions can be made to the chord to produce the dominant 9th, 11th, and even 13th.

Ex. 1

dompe. See DUMP.

Donato [Donati], Baldassare (*b* c.1530; *d* Venice, 1603). Italian singer and composer. He was active in Venice from about 1550 until his death. As a singer at St Mark's he was several times in trouble with the authorities for being disorderly and rebellious, but he succeeded Zarlino in the post of *maestro* there in 1590, and seems to have done good work in reorganizing the *cappella*. He was a well-known madrigalist, two of his works being included in the English **Musica transalpina*, but his real gift was as a composer of popular villanellas in a witty, sometimes licentious, style. His surviving works also include motets and psalms, and in 1599 his church music was collected together in a retrospective volume.   DA

Donatoni, Franco (*b* Verona, 9 June 1927; *d* Milan, 17 Aug. 2000). Italian composer. He studied at the conservatories of Milan (1946–8) and Bologna (1948–51), and at the Accademia di S. Cecilia, Rome, with Pizzetti (1952–4). An influential teacher himself, in Italy (particularly at the Accademia Chigiana in Siena) and abroad, he went through successive stages of nihilistic modernism in his music to arrive in the mid-1970s at a playful style most often and variously expressed in small instrumental pieces. In later years he began to write for the voice, producing *Arie* for soprano and orchestra (1978) and reworking earlier pieces as an opera, *Atem* (La Scala, Milan, 1985).   PG

Don Carlos. Opera in five acts by Verdi to a libretto (in French) by Joseph Méry and Camille Du Locle after Friedrich von Schiller's dramatic poem (1787) (Paris, 1867); Verdi revised it into four acts (dropping Act I of the French version), with a revised libretto by Du Locle translated into Italian (as *Don Carlo*) by Achille de Lauzières and Angelo Zanardini (Milan, 1884).

Don Giovanni (*Il dissoluto punito, ossia Il Don Giovanni*; 'The Libertine Punished, or Don Giovanni'). Opera in two acts by Mozart to a libretto by Lorenzo Da Ponte after Giovanni Bertati's libretto for Gazzaniga (1787) (Prague, 1787).

Donizetti, (Domenico) Gaetano (Maria) (*b* Bergamo, 29 Nov. 1797; *d* Bergamo, 8 April 1848). Italian composer. With Bellini, he was the leading Italian opera composer in the generation between Rossini and Verdi.

1. Life; 2. Naples; 3. Paris; 4. Style and reputation

1. Life

Donizetti was born in extremely modest circumstances, his early encounters with music made possible by his first composition teacher and lifelong mentor, Simon Mayr, a native of Bavaria who was *maestro di cappella* at the cathedral in Bergamo. At the age of nine

Donizetti was admitted to the Lezioni Caritatevoli, a school founded by Mayr, taking classes in singing, keyboard, and later composition with Mayr himself. In 1815 Mayr arranged (and provided financial support) for him to continue his studies at the Liceo Filarmonico Comunale in Bologna under Padre Mattei, Rossini's teacher. From this period comes the one-act dramatic scene *Il Pigmalione* (1816), which exhibits a strong influence of Mayr but as yet little trace of Rossini.

When Donizetti concluded his studies in Bologna in 1817, Mayr helped him obtain a commission that resulted in *Enrico di Borgogna*, given its premiere in Venice in November 1818. More commissions followed, though during this period he also composed a large proportion of his sacred works and several string quartets. In 1821 he wrote *Zoraida di Granata* for the Teatro Argentina, Rome: it was Donizetti's most successful yet, winning him an invitation to write for Naples from the leading impresario of the time, Domenico Barbaia. While in Rome for rehearsals of *Zoraida*, Donizetti met the Vasselli family, whose daughter Virginia would become his wife in 1828.

Donizetti settled in Naples in February 1822 and was based there for the next 16 years, writing many operas for the city but also receiving performances and commissions across a wide area. In 1825–6 he experienced a disastrous year at the Teatro Carolino, Palermo, a position that paid him only 45 ducats a month. On returning to Naples in 1827 he signed a new contract with Barbaia, for four new operas a year over three years. Even while fulfilling the Naples contract he accepted commissions from other Italian cities as his reputation grew. Among the most important was an invitation in 1828 to participate in the opening season of the new Teatro Carlo Felice in Genoa, for which he supplied *Alina, regina di Golconda*.

After more than a decade in the theatre, Donizetti's reputation was established, nationally and internationally, by his 31st opera, *Anna Bolena* (Milan, 1830). From then until his departure for Paris in 1838 he produced 25 operas, among which are many of his most famous: he composed with equal facility overtly 'Romantic' works, those on historical or classical subjects, and comic pieces. A major preoccupation was obtaining a commission for Paris. The long-awaited opportunity finally arrived in 1835 when Rossini commissioned new works for the Théâtre Italien from both Donizetti and Bellini. Donizetti's effort, adapted from Byron's play, was *Marin Faliero*. A series of personal blows struck in the late 1830s. In 1835–6 his parents died within a few weeks of each other, and in July 1837, at the age of only 29, Virginia died after giving birth to a stillborn child. Discouraged by a sequence of professional disappointments and personal tragedy, Donizetti left

Naples in October 1838 and settled permanently in Paris.

The rate of his production hardly slowed in this new atmosphere. He wrote several grand works for the Paris Opéra, *La Fille du régiment* appeared at the Opéra-Comique, and the Théâtre de la Renaissance presented the French premiere of *Lucie de Lammermoor*. In 1842 he accepted the far more prestigious position of Hofkapellmeister to the Habsburg court in Vienna and court composer to the Austrian emperor, an appointment that was assured by the success of *Linda di Chamounix* (1842), his first opera written expressly for Vienna. Further Viennese operas appeared, the ultra-melodramatic *Maria di Rohan* and the classically comic *Don Pasquale*, and Donizetti completed a last grand opera, *Dom Sébastien*, late in 1843. His health had been declining for some years, and by 1844 the syphilis that was eventually to kill him had become serious enough to slow his furious productivity to a crawl. Early in 1846 he was confined in an asylum in Paris. In the autumn of 1847 he was moved back to Bergamo, where he died on 8 April 1848.

2. Naples

Donizetti's long sojourn in Naples in the 1820s certainly affected the style of his first operas, in particular his early taste for *opere buffe* and *semiserie*, which were becoming less popular elsewhere. But wherever he had been in Italy, the musical possibilities available to him were constrained above all by the wild popularity of Rossini. Rossinian influence can be heard most immediately in a wealth of vocal display, at first indulged equally in all voice types and in all sections of an aria, and gradually (by about 1827) restricted to higher voices and confined to cadential passages. However, even purely comic works demonstrate that Donizetti's early style was less slavishly Rossinian than is often asserted. His approach to the duet, for example, shifts from the Rossinian model—in which both characters sing together throughout the usually very brief movement—to a more extended slow movement that begins with parallel solo statements and reserves the impact of the two voices blended in harmony for a few concluding phrases.

Although *Anna Bolena* (1830) is usually marked as a watershed in Donizetti's progress, a cluster of operas written in about 1828 attest to a comparable change of style. Such works as *Alina, regina di Golconda*, *Il paria*, and especially *L'esule di Roma* ('The Exile from Rome') all show a reduction of vocal ornament, especially for the male voices, and an exploration of new plot types and new approaches to musical structure. However, *Anna Bolena* is remarkable for the increased pace of its recitatives and orchestral introductions, and its elimination of repetition and predictable turns of phrase from cabalettas. At least some of *Anna Bolena*'s remarkable innovation is due to the presence of a much-anticipated Bellini premiere at the same theatre in the same season. Bellinian inspiration can be heard in the blurring of boundary between aria and recitative and in the obscuring or modifying of the opera's division into discrete 'numbers'.

Not all the works that followed *Anna Bolena* were as adventurous. Similar innovations can be heard in *Lucrezia Borgia* (1833), *Maria Stuarda* (1835), and *Maria de Rudenz* (1838), but these alternated with such works as *Parisina* (1833) and *Pia de' Tolomei* (1837), which enjoyed equal success while repeating the 'portrait gallery' structure and highlighting florid solo singing over ensembles and extended scenic units. Traditional approaches are particularly tenacious in the *opere buffe* and *semiserie*: works like *Torquato Tasso* and *Il furioso all'isola di San Domingo* tend to combine the old free-form comic patter numbers with elaborate double arias for the *seria* characters. Donizetti's best-known opera of this period, *Lucia di Lammermoor*, represents more of a conservative extreme than a measure of his standard practice. Its famous mad scene apart, *Lucia* is surprisingly Classical, based on a succession of conventional (if beautifully conceived) double arias and bipartite duets. Even the psychological and musical disruptions of the mad scene are confined to the extended recitative that begins the scene, never seriously derailing the logic of the double aria.

Partly in response to French models, aria forms in the 1830s move in two divergent directions, either towards greater discursive freedom or towards the increased patterning of strophic forms. Another novelty involves harmony and tonal motion, with a growing tendency to modulate to distant keys within movements and, in rare instances, to attach dramatic meaning to specific keys or pitches.

3. Paris

The operas of Donizetti's final period do not exhibit a 'late style' as traditionally understood. New stylistic directions were prompted above all by the international milieu in which he now worked. The play with Parisian models took on greater importance, not only because Donizetti was now resident in Paris, but because he began to write for the (French-language) Opéra, which imposed a specific set of stylistic requirements: all three works for the Opéra—*Les Martyrs* and *La Favorite* (both 1840), and *Dom Sébastien* (1843)—feature ballets and elaborate choral tableaux. While many traces of the French encounter also inform operas for other cities, the predominant impression of the works written for Vienna and Italy is of reserve, even conservatism: more

modest orchestral and choral forces, and a novel but less ostentatious approach to staging. In contrast to some of the rebellious pronouncements made at the beginning of his career, Donizetti now sometimes returned to such conventions as the *rondò* finale for the prima donna, even complaining that the original endings of both *Adelia* (1840) and *Maria Padilla* (1841) dispatched the heroines too quickly for a final cabaletta.

Donizetti's first opera for Vienna, *Linda di Chamounix* (1842), represents a return to the rather old-fashioned genre of *opera semiseria* but within this framework invents a radical new sense of atmosphere and of stage space. His other opera for Vienna, *Maria di Rohan* (1843), demonstrates his continuing willingness to adhere to the traditional outlines of 'number opera', especially in presenting the principal characters. However, the conventionality sounds more self-consciously classicizing than regressive, as if Donizetti had set himself the challenge of writing an aria for each character in turn without sacrificing forward motion.

4. Style and reputation

Some of Donizetti's greatest successes were comic operas and he continued to compose in the comic vein throughout his career, even when the genre began to lose prestige. In addition to such full-length works as *L'elisir d'amore* (1832), *La Fille du régiment* (1840), and *Don Pasquale* (1843), all of which enjoyed immediate and lasting success, he produced a steady stream of comedies in one act. Although they proceed from the plot types and musical conventions traditional to *opera buffa*—*Don Pasquale* is based on a libretto first set to music in 1810—he injects a new strain of sentiment into the old forms. Both operas set up more natural—but ultimately no less 'Romantic'—alternatives to artifice, as if to revise but not wholly reject the earlier tradition. Indeed, his playful stance towards conventions of tragedy and romance suggests that Donizetti's periodic turns to comedy fulfilled a rejuvenating function, providing a distanced perspective from which to comment on the established idioms of serious opera.

By the time of Donizetti's death, more than a score of his 65 completed operas were enjoying strong careers across Europe, a situation that would endure until the last quarter of the 19th century. While most fell out of the repertory by the turn of the century, a handful—*L'elisir d'amore*, *Lucrezia Borgia*, *Lucia di Lammermoor*, *La Fille du régiment*, *La Favorite*, and *Don Pasquale*—enjoyed uninterrupted popularity. He was undoubtedly a major influence on Verdi, and in France his operas quickly came to represent the Italian vocalism that both attracted and alarmed critics and composers. The early 20th century was a lowpoint, but beginning with a centenary season in Bergamo in 1948, the so-called

Donizetti renaissance brought many forgotten works back to the stage, often as vehicles for such sopranos as Maria Callas, Joan Sutherland, and Montserrat Caballé. The revival continues: today there are more Donizetti operas in the repertory than at any time since the 1840s.   MAS

📖 H. WEINSTOCK, *Donizetti and the World of Opera in Italy, Paris and Vienna in the First Half of the Nineteenth Century* (New York, 1963) · W. ASHBROOK, *Donizetti and his Operas* (Cambridge, 1982) · A. BINI and J. COMMONS (eds.), *Le prime rappresentazioni delle opere donizettiani nella stampa coeva* (Rome, 1997)

Don Juan. 1. Tone-poem, op. 20 (1887 or 1888–9), by Richard Strauss, based on a poem by Nikolaus Lenau.

2. The legend of the libertine Don Juan has been the basis of many plays since that of Tirso di Molina, *El burlador di Sevilla y confidado di piedra* (1630), and of many operas, the best known being Mozart's *Don Giovanni*. Other composers who have treated the subject include Alessandro Melani (1669), Gazzaniga (1787), Vincenzo Fabrizi (1787), Pacini (1832), Dargomïzhsky (*The Stone Guest*, 1872), Alfano (1914, revised 1941), and Goossens (1937).

3. *Don Juan, ou Le Festin de Pierre.* Ballet-pantomime in one act and three scenes by Gluck to a scenario by Gasparo Angiolini, who also choreographed it (Vienna, 1761).

Donna del lago, La ('The Lady of the Lake'). Opera in two acts by Rossini to a libretto by Andrea Leone Tottola after Walter Scott's poem *The Lady of the Lake* (Naples, 1819).

Donnerstag aus Licht ('Thursday from Light'). Opera in a greeting, three acts, and a farewell, by Stockhausen to his own libretto (Milan, 1981), the 'first day' of *Licht*.

Don Pasquale. Opera in three acts by Donizetti to a libretto by Giovanni Ruffini and the composer after Angelo Anelli's libretto for Stefano Pavesi's *Ser Marcantonio* (1810) (Paris, 1843).

Don Quichotte. Opera in five acts by Massenet to a libretto by Henri Cain after Jacques Le Lorrain's play *Le Chevalier de la longue figure* (1904), itself based on Miguel de Cervantes's novel *Don Quixote* (Monte Carlo, 1910).

Don Quichotte à Dulcinée. Three songs by Ravel (1932–3) for voice and orchestra, settings of poems by Paul Morand; Ravel arranged them for voice and piano (1932–3). They were written for a film based on Miguel de Cervantes, starring Chaliapin, and were Ravel's last works.

Don Quixote. 1. Tone-poem, op. 35 (1896–7), by Richard Strauss, subtitled 'Fantastische Variationen

über ein Thema ritterlichen Charakters' ('Fantastic Variations on a Theme of Knightly Character'); it has an introduction, theme and ten variations, and finale, with solo parts for cello and viola.

2. Miguel de Cervantes's novel, published in two parts (1605, 1615), has inspired many works for the stage. Operas on the subject have been composed by, among many others, J. P. Förtsch, F. B. Conti, Boismortier, Paisiello, Piccinni, Salieri, García, Mendelssohn, Mercadante, Donizetti, Macfarren, and Falla. Purcell wrote incidental music to a play by D'Urfey. Ballets include Petipa's (1869), with music by Minkus, and those with music by Petrassi, Ibert, and Gerhard.

doo-wop. A style of singing in harmony by groups of four or five singers, current in the rock and roll era, derived from 19th-century barber-shop singing and such black vocal groups as the Ink Spots in the 1930s and the Orioles in the 1940s. These had many white imitators, particularly among Italian Americans. The style is still heard in rock and roll revivals.   PW

dopo (It.). 'After'.

Doppel (Ger.). 'Double'; *doppeln*, 'to double'.

Doppelfagott (Ger.). 'Contrabassoon'.

Doppelflöte (Ger., 'double flute'). An organ pipe with two mouths, front and back, producing a loud, pure flute tone.

Doppelfuge (Ger.). 'Double fugue'.

Doppelhorn (Ger.). 'Double horn' (see HORN, 2).

Doppelschlag (Ger., 'double stroke'). *Turn.

doppelt so schnell (Ger.). 'Twice as fast', i.e. at double speed.

Doppelzunge (Ger., 'double tongue'). Double *tonguing.

doppio (It.). 'Double'; *doppio movimento*, 'double the speed'.

Dorian mode. The mode represented by the white notes of the piano beginning on D. See MODE, 2.

'Dorian' Toccata and Fugue. Nickname of Bach's Toccata and Fugue in D minor for organ, BWV538 (1708–17), so called because the original copy omitted a B♭ from the key signature, thus suggesting the Dorian mode.

dot (Fr.: *point*; Ger.: *Punkt*; It.: *punto*). 1. A dot placed above or below a note normally indicates that the note is to be played *staccato or (in string music, when slurs are also present) *portato; in some early keyboard music, however, it may instead signify chromatic alteration.

2. In early mensural notation, a dot (Lat.: *punctum*) placed between notes may be used to mark off groups of notes into rhythmic divisions. In such cases it acts rather like the modern bar-line.

3. A dot placed immediately after a note normally makes the note half as long again (Ex. 1*a*); a second dot added after the first ('double-dotting') effectively adds half the value of the first dot (Ex. 1*b*). In modern notation dotted notes are used only when their value is contained within one bar, otherwise a *tie is used.

In musical notation during the Baroque period, the rhythmic value of dotted notes was more approximate than it is today and might vary in accordance with a number of performing conventions or expressive considerations. A dot after a note ordinarily meant that it was half as long again as its normal value, but otherwise the dot simply signified that the notes on either side were irregular in some way. A dotted note might be used to assimilate duple to triple rhythms (see Ex. 2*a*). The use of the dot was necessary here because the notational conventions of ♩♪ and ♩♩ did not exist until the 19th century. The only alternative was to use such devices as introducing passages of 9/8 into music

Ex. 1

Ex. 2

(*a*) *Assimilation of duplet to triplet rhythm*

played

(from C. P. E. Bach, *Versuch über die wahre Art das Clavier zu spielen* (1753), pt 1, ch. 3, 27)

(*b*) *Dot used as a tie of irregular length*

(from C. P. E. Bach, *Versuch*, pt 1, ch. 3, 23)

(NB. Dot increases quaver length by a quarter, not a half)

meaning

(from F. Couperin, *Nouveaux concerts* (1724), no. 14, Prelude, bar 1)

(NB. Dot increases length of crotchet by nine-sixteenths)

(*c*) *Dot used as a tie across the bar-line*

... an-xious care   and   strife ...   etc.

(from Purcell, *The Fairy Queen* (1692), 'Thrice Happy Lovers'; London, Royal Academy of Music, MS 1)

(*d*) *Double dot*

(from Chambonnières, *Pieces de clavecin*, bk 1 (1670), Courante, p. 51)

Irregular and novel uses of the dot in the 17th and 18th centuries.

written in 3/4. It is by no means certain that the as-similation of dotted duplets in one part to triplets in another was always intended; Quantz (*Versuch einer Anweisung die Flöte traversiere zu spielen*, chapter 5, part 22) argues against it and, at a later date, Czerny in his account of Beethoven's playing of the 'Moonlight' Sonata felt it necessary to point out that the dotted and triplet rhythms were not synchronized. A dot might also be used to increase the length of a note by more or less than the usual half (see Ex. 2*b*), or be used to show that a note is tied across a bar-line (Ex. 2*c*).

The possible application by the performer of dotted or unequal rhythms to undotted notes (*notes inégales) creates problems best approached through the history of *performance practice, since it is precisely the lack of notational guidance that leads to difficulties in resurrecting this practice. For the question of over-dotting in the so-called French-overture style the notational evidence is a little more suggestive. It was Ebenezer Prout who, in his late 19th-century Handel editions, first established the idea that rhythms written as ♩. ♪ and ♫ in French overture movements should be played as ♩.. ♪ and ♫. However, Handel's copyist, John Smith the younger, when transcribing the overture to *Amadigi*, for example, made a careful distinction between the two rhythms ♩. ♪♪ and ♩. ♪ in both notation and spacing. The over-dotting of single dotted notes is clearly mentioned by such writers as Quantz (*Versuch*, chapter 5, part 21), but there is no reference to the French style, and Quantz is writing of soloistic rather than orchestral or ensemble music.   AP

double. 1. When applied to instruments, the English word 'double' indicates either low pitch (the double bass is the lowest member of the violin family, the double bassoon of the bassoons, etc.) or a combination of two instruments in one, such as the double horn, or the duplication of elements such as keyboards (e.g. double-manual *harpsichord) or ranks of strings (double *harp). In the first case, the prefix 'contra' is sometimes used (e.g. contrabassoon, contrabass clarinet).   JMo

2. To take more than one singing role or to play more than one instrument in the same work. Opera singers have 'doubles', or understudies, who are able to take over a role in case of the principal's absence.

3 (Fr.). In 17th- and 18th-century French music, a simple variation, usually consisting simply of an elaborated version of the melody, while the original harmony and rhythm are retained. A *double* often appears in keyboard suites as an ornamented reprise of the preceding dance (e.g. Bach's English Suite no. 1 BWV806).

doublé (Fr., 'doubled'). See TURN.

double action. See HARP, 2*d*.

double appoggiatura. See APPOGGIATURA.

double bar. The double perpendicular line placed at the end of a complete work, or of a movement or section of one. Unless it coincides with a single bar-line, the double bar has no rhythmic value. When the double bar is preceded by two dots, placed one above the other, a repeat is indicated. If the repeat bar is marked 'prima volta' or simply '1' and is followed by a bar marked 'seconda volta' or '2', the repeat should be made, and at the end of it the player should take the second bar, which will lead into the next section of music. The two bars are sometimes called the first-time and the second-time bar.

double bass [contrabass, string bass, bass] (Fr.: *contrebasse*; Ger.: *Kontrabass*; It.: *contrabasso*). The largest and lowest-pitched member of the violin family. The modern double bass has four strings tuned in 4ths (*E'–A'–D–G*), and music for the instrument is notated an octave higher than actual pitch. Since the early 20th century some basses have been made with either a fifth string at *C'* or an extension to lower the E string to *C'*; Mahler is among those who have written works demanding this compass.

The bass usually (though not always) has sloping shoulders, making it easier for the player to reach the upper ranges of the fingerboard, and a flat back, which economizes on wood and saves the labour required in carving out a 'swell back' from expensive maple (the other members of the violin family have rounded shoulders and curved back). These characteristics are shared with the *viol family, though this is purely through the coincidence of desirable factors. Tuning the double bass in 4ths (unlike the rest of the violin family) is also a matter of convenience, as the wide finger-stretches involved make tuning in 5ths impractical. Basses may also be made from plywood that is steam-pressed to shape, thus making a cheaper though durable construction, adequate for many circumstances.

The number of strings on earlier basses varied from four to six. Basses have ranged greatly in size and shape, especially in the 16th and 17th centuries when some five- or six-string 'violoni' were constructed as double bass viols (see VIOLONE), having frets and viol tunings (a combination of 4ths and 3rds). During the 18th century most players settled on three strings, tuned *A'–D–G* or *G'–D–G*. It was said in late 18th-century Germany that the tone of the three-string bass was richer than that of older types with five, presumably because of the lesser strain on the body. The body size of the modern standard three-quarter-size double bass, used in orchestras, jazz, and popular music, is about 115 cm, the instrument standing 180 cm tall (excluding the endpin). Smaller chamber basses are common, with body lengths of about 90 cm. Even smaller processional basses, supported by a strap so that the player can walk while playing, have been widely used in central European folk bands. Larger basses have been made: in 1848 the Parisian maker Vuillaume produced a monstrous three-string 'octobass' about 4 metres tall (it is now in the Musée de la Musique, Paris).

Two styles of bow are in use. The French or 'Bottesini' bow, named after the great 19th-century virtuoso Giovanni Bottesini, resembles a cello bow but is shorter and heavier; the German 'Simandl' or 'Butler' bow owes something to another virtuoso, Domenico Dragonetti (1763–1846), and has a wider frog so that it can be grasped from the side, rather like a saw. For jazz and many forms of popular music, the double bass is mostly played pizzicato.

The invention of the double bass cannot have been much later than that of the rest of the violin family, for examples survive by some of the earlier makers including Gasparo da Salò (1540–1609) and Maggini (c.1581–c.1632). The main function of the double bass in the early orchestra was to double the cello line at the octave. Until the 19th century most scores simply said 'bassi' on the bottom line, to cover both cellos and basses—and often bassoons too. When the music descended below the range of the double bass (the bottom note for the cello is C), the bass player would simply transpose up an octave. Beethoven was one of the first to provide a separate double-bass line in his scores but, except for a few obbligato passages, it was many years before composers normally wrote a fully independent part for the bass. Solo concertos were written in the late 18th century by Haydn and Dittersdorf among others, and many solo works have been written by soloists themselves. The versatile double bass has been used wherever a deep bass instrument has been needed, vying since the late 19th century with the bass tuba and since the 1950s with the electric bass guitar.   JMo

📖 T. COOLMAN, *The Bass Tradition: Past, Present, Future* (New Albany, IN, 1985) · P. BRUN, *A New History of the Double Bass* (Villeneuve d'Ascq, 2000)

double bassoon. See CONTRABASSOON.

double choir, double chorus. A choir arranged in two equal and complete bodies, usually with the aim of providing a spatial effect.

double concerto. A concerto for two solo instruments and orchestra or other instrumental ensemble, for example Bach's Concerto in D minor, for two solo violins with strings, or Brahms's Concerto in A minor, for violin and cello with orchestra.

double counterpoint. Alternative name for *invertible counterpoint.

doubled leading-note cadence. A three-voice progression in 14th-century vocal polyphony in which the outer voices move by step from leading notes (upper or lower) on to the octave (or 5th).   AW

double flat. The sign (♭♭) that, when placed before a note, lowers it by one tone. See also ACCIDENTAL.

double fugue. A *fugue in which two subjects are presented and developed simultaneously from the start.

double mordent. A *mordent with two repercussions.

double pedal. See PEDAL POINT.

double reed. The *reed used on the aulos, most bagpipe chanters, bassoon, contrabassoon, cor anglais, crumhorn, curtal, *cornemuse*, *douçaine*, heckelphone, *Kortholt*, musette, oboe, sarrusophone, racket, *Rauschpfeife*, and shawms.

double sharp. The sign (𝄪) that, when placed before a note, raises it by one tone. See also ACCIDENTAL.

double stopping. In string playing, bowing two strings simultaneously to produce intervals or chords. In spite of the use of the word *'stopping', one or both of the strings may be open.

double tonguing. See TONGUING.

double trill. A trill performed simultaneously on two separate notes, usually a 3rd apart.

double whole-note (Amer.). Breve.

douçaine (Fr., 'gentle shawm'). A medieval cylindrical-bore *shawm with a more limited range and softer sound than normal shawms. Tinctoris's description (c.1480) was tantalizingly vague until the unique surviving example was found in Henry VIII's ship *Mary Rose*. See also DOLZAINA; DULZAINA.   JMo

douloureux (Fr.). 'Sorrowful', 'painful'.

doux, douce (Fr.). 'Sweet'; *doucement*, 'sweetly'.

Dove, Jonathan (*b* London, 18 July 1959). English composer. He studied with Robin Holloway at Cambridge. He is notable for his concern with accessibility and his involvement with community projects. His work for the City of Birmingham Touring Opera includes reduced versions of Wagner's *Ring* and Janáček's *The Cunning Little Vixen*. He has written film and theatre music, especially for the Almeida Theatre, London, and also opera (*Flight*, Glyndebourne, 1998; *Tobias and the Angel*, Almeida, 1999). He provided a fanfare and a new arrangement of the national anthem for the opening ceremony of the Millennium Dome.   AW

Dowland, John (*b* ? London, 1563; *bur.* London, 20 Feb. 1626). English composer and lutenist. At the age of 17 he went to Paris for a year as 'servaunt' to Sir Harry Cobham, and in 1588 he was admitted to Christ Church, Oxford. In 1592 he played before Queen Elizabeth at Sudeley Castle. One major frustration seems to overshadow Dowland's professional life: his inability to secure a position in the Queen's Music in 1594. Soon after this disappointment he set out on his European travels, visiting Germany and Italy, and eventually, in 1598, securing an appointment as court lutenist to King Christian IV of Denmark. Although this position paid far more than any of Elizabeth's musicians received, Dowland still bitterly regretted his earlier failure, for his heart was set on a position at the English court. This he finally achieved in October 1612. Once appointed, he remained settled in London, but became increasingly introspective, and possibly also intensely religious, as the ayre *If that a sinners sighes* (from *A Pilgrimes Solace*, London, 1612), with its unsettling discords, would suggest.

Dowland's religion has been put forward as one reason for his failure in 1594. On his visit to Paris in 1580 he had become a Catholic. However, in view of Elizabeth's flexible approach to religion—witness her tolerance of Byrd—Dowland's sympathies cannot have interfered with his career to any great extent. Clearly religion played a major part in his life, however; he contributed to Thomas East's *The Whole Booke of Psalmes* (1592) and wrote some spiritual songs which were printed in Leighton's *The Teares or Lamentacions of a Sorrowfull Soule* (1614), of which *An heart that's broken and contrite* is particularly moving.

One of the most famous composers and lutenists of his day, Dowland also represented the Elizabethan artistic temperament. He was especially sensitive to criticism, and given to melancholy, but at the same time he was ambitious, self-centred, and often naive. He was notably conservative: he preferred, for example, the old-fashioned style of Giovanni Croce to that of Giovanni Gabrieli when he visited Venice, and his choice of the German textbook by Andreas Ornithoparcus, *Musice active Micrologus* (1517), to translate and publish in 1609 is similarly unadventurous.

Some of Dowland's finest songs have a quality of sadness—for example, *In darknesse let me dwell* (from Robert Dowland's *A Musicall Banquet*, London, 1610) and *Sorrow, sorrow stay* (from his own *Second Booke of Airs*, London, 1600). Neither is melancholy ever far away in his music for solo lute and string consort, and it

is particularly evident in his *Lachrimae, or Seaven Teares* (London, 1604), a collection of pavans, galliards (his favourite form), and almands for five-part string consort.

If in his day England did not afford Dowland the position and respect his talent merited, and his life was fraught with disappointment, introspection, and petty rivalries, time has generously corrected any such injustice, and today Dowland is ranked among England's finest composers.   CRW

 📖 D. Poulton, *John Dowland* (London, 1972, 2/1982) · I. Spink, *English Song: Dowland to Purcell* (London, 1974, repr. 1986 with corrections) · J. M. Ward, 'A Dowland miscellany', *Journal of the Lute Society of America*, 10 (1977), 5–152 · P. Holman, *Dowland: Lachrimae (1604)* (Cambridge, 1999)

downbeat (Fr.: *temps fort*; Ger.: *Niederschlag*). The first, 'strong', beat of the bar; see BEAT, 1.

Down by the Greenwood Side. Dramatic pastoral in one act by Birtwistle to a libretto by Michael Nyman after an English Mummers' Play and 'The Ballad of the Cruel Mother'; it is for soprano, mime, and speech, and chamber ensemble (Brighton, 1969).

doxology (from Gk. *doxa*, 'glory', and *logos*, 'word'). A liturgical formula of praise. Jewish precedents were imitated by the authors of the New Testament and other early Christian texts, who regularly used them as concluding formulas punctuated by an 'Amen'. In reaction to the Arian controversies of the 4th century, the Trinitarian *Gloria Patri* ('Glory be to the Father', etc., called the Lesser Doxology in Western usage) achieved ubiquity in Christian worship with slight regional variations in the text of its second phrase. The *Gloria in excelsis Deo* ('Glory to God in the highest') is described by the Eastern and Western churches as the 'Great(er) Doxology'.

In the non-liturgical Protestant churches 'The Doxology' usually means a metrical form of the Lesser Doxology, generally that sung to the tune *Old Hundredth*—'Praise God from whom all blessings flow', etc., from Bishop Ken's (1637–1711) Morning and Evening Hymns 'Awake, my soul' and 'Glory to thee'. In the 1640s there was great strife in certain parts of Scotland over the abandoning of the 1595 psalter's use of a doxology of this kind after the metrical psalms.   PS/ALi

drag. One of the ornamental rudiments of side-drum playing, notated as illustrated. Tight execution of the grace notes (by either hand) is required to introduce militaristic connotations.   SM

L L R
R R L

Draghi, Antonio (*b* Rimini, 1634 or 1635; *d* Vienna, 16 Jan. 1700). Italian composer and librettist. He spent most of his life in Vienna. He was a singer at the Teatro S. Apollinare in Venice in 1657, but the following year was in Vienna in the service of the dowager Empress Eleanor, widow of Ferdinand III. Draghi was one of the most prolific composers of his day: there are, for instance, 59 three-act operas. Of his sacred music, besides oratorios he particularly cultivated the *sepolcro*—a dramatic presentation of the Passion or Crucifixion, peculiar to the imperial court.   DA/PA

Dragonetti, Domenico (Carlo Maria) (*b* Venice, 7 April 1763; *d* London, 16 April 1846). Italian double-bass player and composer. In 1787 he began to play in the orchestra of St Mark's. His fame as a performer soon spread beyond Italy, and in 1794 he was invited to London, where he was engaged at the King's Theatre. For the next 52 years he played regularly in London orchestras. He was a good friend of Haydn's, and Beethoven learnt much about double-bass technique from him. He was active as a player into his 80s, when Berlioz reported hearing him. Dragonetti was an incomparable virtuoso on his instrument, which was usually a three-string bass (tuned *A'–D–G*). His many compositions for it include concertos, chamber music, and numerous occasional works.   WT/RP

Dramaturg (Ger.). A term denoting a person, often of scholarly background, employed by an opera house to suggest repertory, to advise on the suitability of competing editions of operas, and sometimes to edit or write material for programme books, etc. Although a position of some influence in 20th-century German theatres, the post has been slower to establish itself elsewhere.   RP

drame lyrique (Fr., 'lyric drama'; It.: *dramma lirico*). A modern name for a serious opera, generally implying a more intimate mode of expression than that of *grand opera or Wagnerian music drama. Debussy called his *Pelléas et Mélisande* a 'drame lyrique'.

dramma giocoso (It., 'jocular drama'). In the 18th century, a name often given to Italian comic operas. It is particularly associated with the works of Carlo Goldoni, where it commonly occurs in librettos in which standard character types from *opera seria* appear together with those from *opera buffa*. Lorenzo Da Ponte labelled his libretto for Mozart's *Don Giovanni* a *dramma giocoso*. See also OPERA, 6.   JBE

dramma per musica (It., 'drama for music', 'drama in music'). See OPERA, 2.

drängend (Ger.). 'Pressing on', 'hurrying'.

drawing-room ballad. A type of song designed primarily for domestic performance by amateurs. The genre has little connection with the traditional *ballad, except that some examples tell a story in their verses. Drawing-room ballads are mainly strophic and generally of a romantic, sentimental nature. Their origins lie in the kind of songs sung at the music evenings in the London *pleasure gardens, but they began to flourish with the advent of cheaper music-printing in the early 19th century and continued to be performed well into the 20th. Such publishing houses as Chappell encouraged their popularity by organizing series of concerts featuring them. A particularly famous example is *Home, Sweet Home* by Henry Bishop, which, like many drawing-room ballads, was originally composed as part of an opera.   —/JBE

draw stops. Knobs on each side of organ manuals, drawn out by organists to allow air to reach each rank of pipes.

Dream of Gerontius, The. Choral work, op. 38 (1900), by Elgar, for mezzo-soprano, tenor, bass, chorus, semi-chorus, and orchestra, a setting of Cardinal Newman's poem (1866). Although it is frequently described as an oratorio, the term does not appear on the score and Elgar did not approve of it being referred to as such.

Dreigroschenoper, Die ('The Threepenny Opera'). Play with music in a prologue and three acts by Weill to a libretto by Bertolt Brecht, translated by Elisabeth Hauptmann, after John Gay's *The Beggar's Opera*, with additional poems by François Villon and Rudyard Kipling (Berlin, 1928).

Drei Pintos, Die ('The Three Pintos'). Comic opera in three acts by Weber to a libretto by Theodor Hell [Carl Gottfried Theodor Winkler] after Carl Seidel's story *Der Brautkampf*. Weber worked on it in 1820–1 but left it unfinished; his grandson Carl showed the sketches to Mahler, who completed the score (Leipzig, 1888).

Dresden Amen. A threefold setting made by J. G. Naumann (1741–1801) for the royal chapel in Dresden which achieved celebrity after being quoted by Mendelssohn in his 'Reformation' Symphony (1832) and later by Wagner in *Parsifal* (1882). In both cases it symbolizes the solemnity of religious faith.   AW

Drigo, Riccardo (*b* Padua, 30 June 1846; *d* Padua, 1 Oct. 1930). Italian conductor and composer. He was in St Petersburg from 1878 to 1920, first as conductor of the Italian Opera, then from 1886 as conductor and composer to the Imperial Ballet, for which he conducted premieres of ballets by Tchaikovsky and Glazunov. As a composer of operas and ballets he is best known for the

Serenade from his ballet *Arlekinada* (*Les Millions d'Harlequin*, 1900).   ABur

drone (Fr.: *bourdon*). A steady or constantly reiterated note, usually on the keynote. It is the simplest of all accompaniments. Drones can be sounded through additional pipes (e.g. on *bagpipes) or by bowing or plucking strings (e.g. on a *hurdy-gurdy, *crwth, or *sitar), or by humming while playing. Tuning can be more precise when playing or singing against a drone and musical tension is enhanced by contrasting with the drone, as in Indian music.   JMo

Druckman, Jacob (*b* Philadelphia, 25 June 1928; *d* New Haven, CT, 24 May 1996). American composer. He studied at the Juilliard School with Vincent Persichetti, Peter Mennin, and Johan Wagenaar, and in Paris (1954), and taught at Juilliard (1956–72), Brooklyn College, and Yale (1976–96). In 1965 he started work at the Columbia–Princeton Electronic Music Center in New York, where he composed a series of dramatic encounters for live musicians and tape (*Animus I–III*, 1966–9). Later works are no less strongly figured but often on a larger scale; they include the orchestral pieces *Windows* (1972), *Lamia* (1974, with soprano), *Prism* (1980, based on the Medea operas of Cavalli, Charpentier, and Cherubini), *Brangle* (1988–9), and *Counterpoise* (1994, again with soprano). In the mid-1980s Druckman was artistic director of the New York Philharmonic's 'Horizons' festivals of new music.
                                                                PG

drum (Fr.: *tambour, caisse*; Ger.: *Trommel*; It.: *tamburo*). Although the word 'drum' can be used for almost any object that is struck to produce sound (e.g. *slit drum, *steel drum: both *idiophones), most drums are *membranophones: instruments with membranes (the 'head') of skin, parchment, or plastic tensioned over a resonating cavity, usually sounded by striking or, more rarely, by rubbing (*friction drums). The principal categories are: *kettledrums, where the body is a bowl, vessel, or 'shell' (e.g. *timpani, *tablā); *frame drums, where the membrane is stretched over a shallow frame (*tambourine, *rototoms, bodhrán); and tubular drums, either with a skin or 'head' stretched over one end of the shell and the other end open (*congas, *bongos) or with a head at either end (*side drum, *bass drum). Tubular drums are the commonest type worldwide, and are found with bodies of various shapes: cylindrical (bass drum), barrel-shaped (congas), hourglass-shaped (Korean *changgo*, *hutumba* of Sierra Leone), conical (found in India), and goblet-shaped (the Middle Eastern and North African *darabukka*).

The traditional material for drum-heads is animal skin, but plastic has become common, partly because it is unaffected by changes of temperature and humidity (natural skin slackens disastrously in damp conditions and may split if it becomes too dry), and partly because the preparation of parchment or vellum is a highly skilled and time-consuming operation, making these materials expensive. Many timpanists have nevertheless returned to calfskin because it produces noticeably better tone-quality than does plastic. The tension of the head can be controlled by metal screws, as on most modern orchestral or band drums, or by ropes, as on older military drums and many African and Indian drums. Other drums have fixed heads: this is done by a variety of methods, including stretching the wet skin tight and nailing it to the shell (as with the tambourine and most Chinese drums) or gluing it to the shell (as with many Middle Eastern drums). Hourglass drums have tension cords which pass from head to head and can be pressed into the waist by the player's arm or hand, so raising the pitch by increasing the tension of the heads. They can be made to imitate the pitch and rhythmic pattern of words in a tonal language, as in parts of Africa (though all kinds of drum can be, and are, used as 'talking drums').

Pitch is controlled by the diameter and tension of the drum-head. Volume and resonance depend on the amount of air inside the shell: if it is coupled to the head by the shape of the body (as with the bowl of a kettledrum, or with goblet and hourglass drums, which have necks that are narrow in proportion to the body-length) the resonance will be strong enough for the pitch to be more easily perceived than, for example, with a side drum. Most drums can be tuned to some degree by adjustment of the head's tension. On timpani this is so precise that specific notes may be written for them to play. Side and bass drums, however, are intended to sound independently of the harmony of the rest of the music, so identifiable pitch is rigorously avoided; 'pitchlessness' is here helped by a second head off-tuned to the first, and further, on the side drum, by the vibrating snare.

The sound produced by drums is short; thus, any continuous sound can be produced only by rapid repetition. On the timpani and bass drum this is done with alternate strokes from each hand, fast enough to give the illusion of continuity but not so fast that each stroke kills the vibration of the preceding one. The side drum's sound is so short that hand-to-hand reiteration cannot be fast enough; the so-called *dada-mama bouncing stroke (LLRR or RRLL, repeated as often as necessary) is therefore used (see also DRAG; FLAM; PARADIDDLE; RUFF). Great relaxation of the wrists and hands are needed to produce a smooth roll in this way. Much greater tonal variety is possible when a drum is played with the fingers (the Indian *tablā*; Middle

Eastern goblet drums, e.g. the *darabukka*; Latin American drums, e.g. the congas; many frame drums) rather than with sticks.

Although it is possible to 'drum' on any object, anthropological evidence suggests that membrane drums of hollowed wood or pottery with heads stretched across them were first made in the neolithic period. Drums in a variety of shapes and sizes appear in the art of ancient Mesopotamia, India, Persia, China, Africa, Egypt, Israel, Greece, and Rome. In Europe, evidence for the use of drums is hazy before the 13th century, when small kettledrums (*nakers) and tabors of Arab or Saracen origin were brought back from the Crusades. No information has survived from before the 16th century about the kinds of rhythm played.

The side drum was introduced by Swiss and German mercenaries shortly before 1500 as a military instrument for keeping time on the march. Few earlier armies tried to march in step; drums had been used in battle both for signalling and to produce an encouraging uproar, but there seems to have been no conception of the military march. By the late 1500s, however, it was assumed that drummers would mark the time for every step of the march, and precise details of what they played were written down, at least in France.

The *pipe and tabor, and probably the tambourine, were essential accompaniments to the dance, and trumpets and timpani were from the early 16th century emblematic of royalty, ceremonial, and pageantry. But drums played little part in concerted music until the introduction of timpani into the orchestra in the second half of the 17th century. Other drums appeared occasionally from the late 18th century, normally to imitate the military band or for operatic effects. The bass drum became a regular member of the opera orchestra (not, however, without objections from critics) from about 1800, but it was not until the late 19th century, in works by such composers as Rimsky-Korsakov, that the side drum, bass drum, and tambourine became regular members of the concert orchestra.

In the 20th century the use of drums on the Western concert stage increased to such an extent that other musicians sometimes found themselves outnumbered. Now that music from so many cultures and traditions has become more widely known and available, there is no limit to the types of drum that composers can specify, and percussionists are expected both to own and to be able to play a vast range of instruments.   JMo

📖 J. BLADES and J. MONTAGU, *Early Percussion Instruments* (London, 1976) · J. HOWARD, *Drums: From the Tropics to the Arctic Circle* (Los Angeles, 1982) · A. J. BERNET KEMPERS, *The Kettledrums of South-East Asia* (Rotterdam, VT, 1988) · E. A. DAGAN (ed.), *Drums: The Heartbeat of Africa* (Montreal, 1993)

drum kit [drum set, trap set]. A set of drums, suspended cymbals, and other percussion instruments forming the basic equipment of the jazz, rock, and dance-band drummer. The basic elements are the bass drum, cymbal, and side (snare) drum, all of which, in the late 19th and early 20th centuries, were placed so that they could be struck with side-drum sticks, skilled players being able to sustain a side-drum roll while marking the rhythm with flicked strokes to bass drum and cymbal. Such 'double drumming' was rendered unnecessary with the invention of the bass-drum pedal in the mid-1920s.

Several types of suspended *cymbals ('snap', 'ride', 'crash', and 'sizzle') were added for different sounds. The hi-hat, consisting of a pair of cymbals mounted on a stand and operated by a pedal, but at a height where it could also be played with drumsticks, was introduced in 1927. One or two tom-toms were added, and sets of woodblocks, cowbells, and other idiophones, all mounted along the rim of the bass drum. One or more floor tom-toms followed and by 1940 the drum kit had reached its present form, though any number of peripheral instruments may be added by the player. A wide variety of drumsticks, including hard sticks, soft mallets, and brushes, is used.   JMo

'Drum' Mass. See PAUKENMESSE.

Drumming. Work (1971) by Reich for two solo women's voice (wordless), piccolo, four pairs of tuned bongos, three marimbas, and three glockenspiels; a 90-minute work written in response to Reich's visit to Ghana, it was highly influential in the last quarter of the 20th century.

'Drumroll' Symphony (*Paukenwirbel-Symphonie*). Nickname of Haydn's Symphony no. 103 in E♭ major (1795), so called because it opens with a roll on the kettledrums.

drumstick. See BEATER.

D.S. Abbreviation for *dal segno*.

D–S–C–H. Shostakovich's musical monogram, derived from the German transliteration of his name, Dmitry SCHostakowitsch, which in German pitch nomenclature reads D–E♭–C–B. He used it in many of his works, notably the String Quartet no. 8 (1960), the so-called 'Autobiographical Quartet', and the Symphony no. 10 (1953), where it permeates the whole work and is powerfully driven home at the climax of the finale.

Dubois, Théodore (*b* Rosnay, 24 Aug. 1837; *d* Paris, 11 June 1924). French composer and organist. Of humble origins, he rose through the meritocratic system of the Paris Conservatoire, winning the Prix de Rome in 1861.

He became organist of the Madeleine in Paris and a highly respected professor of harmony, counterpoint, and fugue at the Conservatoire, producing standard textbooks on these subjects. Of his compositions, little besides an organ Toccata is known today. In 1896 he was appointed director of the Conservatoire, but his reputation never recovered from Ravel's notorious 1905 failure in the Prix de Rome. AT

duct flute. A general term for a flute with air blown through a narrow duct to impinge at the correct angle on a lip or edge at the base of a mouth. The duct can be formed in many ways: the 'beak' of the mouthpiece may be moulded from plastic (modern *penny whistles) or clay (some types of *ocarina), carved from bone or wood, or created by the insertion in the mouthpiece of a block (the *recorder), a metal plate (the languid of an *organ flue pipe), or even the player's tongue. Because it is easy to sound, the duct flute is the most common form of flute found throughout the world. JMo

ductia. A medieval vocal (*cantilena ductia*) or instrumental dance form, related to the *estampie.

due (It.). 'Two'; *a due*, see À DEUX, A DUE, A 2.

Due Foscari, I. Opera in three acts by Verdi to a libretto by Francesco Maria Piave after Byron's play *The Two Foscari* (1821) (Rome, 1844).

Duenna, The. 1. Opera (*The Duenna, or The Double Elopement*) in three acts by Thomas Linley (i) and Thomas Linley (ii) to a libretto by Richard Brinsley Sheridan (London, 1775).

2. Opera in three acts by Gerhard to his own libretto after Sheridan (broadcast 1949; first staged Madrid, 1992).

3. Opera by Prokofiev; see BETROTHAL IN A MONASTERY.

duet (Fr.: *duo*; Ger.: *Duett*; It.: *duo*, *duetto*). Any combination of two performers (with or without accompaniment), or a piece or passage written for such a combination. The most important forms are the vocal duet (discussed below) and the instrumental *duo; see also PIANO DUET.

The earliest unaccompanied duets are found in the more elaborate 13th-century *conductus. In 1545 the first printed collections of *bicinia, also unaccompanied, with French, German, or Latin texts, were published by Georg Rhau; many were used in German-speaking areas for teaching and moralistic purposes. Passages for two voices with accompaniment occur both in opera (e.g. the final moments of Monteverdi's *L'incoronazione di Poppea*, the end of Act I of Verdi's *Otello*, much of Act II of Wagner's *Tristan und Isolde*) and in non-operatic contexts, for example in cantatas and other choral works by Bach, Berlioz, or Fauré, or in songs by Schubert, Schumann, or Brahms. The chamber duet (a chamber cantata for two singers and accompaniment) was a favourite 17th-century form cultivated by, among others, Monteverdi, Frescobaldi, and Steffani. WT

Dufay, Guillaume (*b c*.1400; *d* Cambrai, 27 Nov. 1474). French composer. He is the most acclaimed musician of the 15th century. Almost 200 of his works survive, including 84 songs, eight complete masses, 13 isorhythmic motets, and numerous hymn settings, single mass movements, and works in honour of the Virgin Mary and various saints and liturgical feasts. He is often described as a Burgundian composer, but in spite of well-attested contacts with Burgundian composers (e.g. Binchois) and the fact that his home town of Cambrai was under Burgundian control, he was never a resident member of that court.

1. Life; 2. The music

1. Life

Dufay is first heard of as a choirboy at Cambrai Cathedral in 1409, and there he was perhaps instructed by the composers Grenon, Lebertoul, and Loqueville. In his early 20s he apparently moved to Italy, since two motets (*Vasilissa ergo* and *Apostolo glorioso*), a chanson (*Resvelliés vous*), and possibly his *Missa sine nomine* commemorate events connected with the Pesaro branch of the Malatesta family. He then seems to have returned to France for a time, as in 1426 he was writing the song *Adieu ces bons vins*, which bids farewell to the people and wines of the north. He is next found in Bologna in 1427.

The ten years between 1428 and 1438 must have been unsettled times for Dufay. Bologna was under the control of the Pope, held for him by the Malatesta, but in 1428 it revolted and Dufay, together with his patron Cardinal Aleman, had to flee to Rome. The *Missa Sancti Jacobi* may have been written during his time in Bologna. Dufay stayed in Rome until 1433, and sang in the papal chapel. In 1431 Pope Martin V died and was succeeded by Eugenius IV. Several of Dufay's works commemorate this Pope and his deeds, including the motets *Balsamus et munda cera*, *Supremum est mortalibus bonum*, and the famous *Nuper rosarum flores*, written for the dedication of Florence Cathedral by Eugenius in 1436.

Throughout the 1430s Dufay seems to have been torn between two patrons, Eugenius IV (whom he served 1431–3 and 1436–7) and Duke Amadeus VIII of Savoy (where he worked 1433–5 and 1438–9). It was at the wedding of Amadeus's son Louis in 1434 that

Dufay's first recorded meeting with the Burgundian court and Binchois, described by the Savoy poet Martin le Franc in *Le Champion des dames* (*c.*1440), seems to have taken place. In 1438 a church council deposed Eugenius and elected Felix V—alias Duke Amadeus of Savoy—in his place. The election was strongly opposed by Philip the Good of Burgundy, and had Dufay remained in Savoy he would have been barred from visiting Cambrai and from collecting his benefices in Burgundian territory. Thus in 1439 Dufay returned to the north.

His temporary separation from the Savoy court and his final departure from Italy seem gradually to have turned his attention away from secular song and the ceremonial motet. Instead, he expanded his technique to include the more Gothic northern form of the cyclic mass based on a tenor cantus firmus. The masses on *Se la face ay pale*, *L'Homme armé*, *Ecce ancilla Domini*, and *Ave regina coelorum* are of this type; the *Missa 'Caput'* sometimes attributed to Dufay is now thought instead to be by an English composer.

For the next 11 years Dufay was back in Cambrai. It seems that one of the buildings belonging to the cathedral was called the Maison L'Homme Armé. The coincidence of this name with the title of a famous melody is intriguing, as the *L'Homme armé* tune formed the basis of masses by many composers with Cambrai connections, including Dufay, Busnois, Ockeghem, Tinctoris, and Regis. Dufay visited the Burgundian court a couple of times during these years, but his connection with the famous Burgundian Feast of the Pheasant, held in 1454 as part of a rescue campaign for Constantinople, now seems doubtful. His Lamentation on the Fall of Constantinople was written too late for the feast, and the song *Je ne vis oncques* sung there is probably by Binchois rather than Dufay.

The last major upheaval for Dufay came in 1450, when Felix V stepped down and Philip of Burgundy reopened contacts with the Savoy court. Immediately Dufay is found in Savoy territory, and in 1452–8 he went for a long stay at the court itself.

2. The music

Dufay was one of the last continental composers in the medieval churchly tradition. In spite of this, some of his works (particularly the chansons and mass movements from his middle years) display the warm harmonies, symmetrical phrasing, and directly expressive melodies characteristic of the early Renaissance. Moreover, Dufay provides us with the earliest example of close harmonies derived from *fauxbourdon technique (in the *Missa Sancti Jacobi*), some of the earliest completely integrated four-voice textures (in the *Missa 'Ave regina coelorum'*), and a movement towards richer sonorities

based on the intervals of the 3rd, 6th, and 10th. His preferred forms were conservative in outline rather than in detail; for example, his masses were perhaps the first to employ secular tunes as cantus firmi. Some of his stylistic features, such as his melodic clarity, can be linked with his experience of Italian music, while his harmonic sonority may have been derived from developments in English music.

In spite of his secular output, Dufay was a cosmopolitan rather than a worldly composer. In the course of a long illness he requested that his motet *Ave regina coelorum*, with its mention of his name in a personal supplication, should be sung at his deathbed. This was not possible, but the motet and his Requiem Mass (the earliest of its kind, unfortunately now lost) were sung at his funeral.   AP/DF

📖 D. Fallows, *Guillaume Dufay* (London, 1982, 2/1987)

Dugazon. A term used in French opera to denote the types of role sung by the famous soprano Louise-Rosalie Dugazon (1755–1821). The light, romantic roles she sang early in her career were dubbed 'jeune Dugazon', while the matrons she impersonated from about 1790 were known as 'mère Dugazon'.   RW

Dukas, Paul (Abraham) (*b* Paris, 1 Oct. 1865; *d* Paris, 17 May 1935). French composer, critic, and teacher. He entered the Paris Conservatoire at the age of 16 and came second in the Prix de Rome competition of 1888, but did not compete in subsequent years. After a period of military service, he began to obtain performances of his music, starting with the overture *Polyeucte* (1892), a work with a strong flavour of Franck and Wagner. A Symphony in C (1897) also uses Franckian themes, but his popular *L'Apprenti sorcier* (1897), a 'symphonic scherzo after a ballad of Goethe', has a vivid realistic quality and a mastery of the orchestra.

Rather than adopting a fashionable 'Impressionist' idiom Dukas was more interested in Classical forms, in which he was virtuoso, as is testified by his *Variations on a Theme of Rameau* and the monumental Sonata, both for piano. His opera *Ariane et Barbe-bleue* (finished in 1906 and produced at the Opéra-Comique the following year) follows Debussy's *Pelléas et Mélisande* (which it quotes) as a musical setting of Maeterlinck; its harmony and brilliant orchestration were widely admired and influenced such composers as Schoenberg and Berg. Dukas's last major work was the 'poème dansé' *La Péri* (1912), a short ballet in which the orchestra and the harmonic usage are reminiscent of Ravel, but with a rhythmic drive and oriental atmosphere that bring to mind Strauss's then fashionable *Salome*.

Curiously, Dukas thereafter published virtually nothing. He wrote a number of pieces, including a Violin Concerto, and worked for several years on a symphony inspired by Shakespeare's *The Tempest*; but he destroyed them all shortly before his death. During these later years he taught at the Conservatoire and the École Normale de Musique, wrote a great deal of sapient criticism in various Paris journals (revealing a broad cultural outlook), and edited music by Beethoven, Rameau, Couperin, and Scarlatti. He was much honoured and was a member of the Académie Française. Musically conservative and a fine craftsman, Dukas upheld a structural, classical strand of French music which he passed on to his many pupils, who included Messiaen.   DA/RLS

Duke, Vernon [Dukelsky, Vladimir Aleksandrovich] (*b* Parfianovka, nr Pskov, 10/23 Oct. 1903; *d* Santa Monica, CA, 16 Jan. 1969). Russian-born American composer. He studied at the Kiev Conservatory (1916–19) with Glière and Marian Dombrovsky. After the Revolution he left Russia, eventually settling in New York, where he studied orchestration with Joseph Schillinger (1934–5). In 1936 he became an American citizen, adopting the name 'Vernon Duke' at Gershwin's suggestion. Among his works are the ballet *Zéphyr et Flore* (produced by Diaghilev, 1925), a musical *Cabin in the Sky* (performed on Broadway, 1940, with choreography by Balanchine and an all-black cast), film scores including *April in Paris* (1952), operettas and further musicals, songs, and orchestral works.   JK

Duke Bluebeard's Castle. See BLUEBEARD'S CASTLE.

dulcian. 1. An ancestor of the bassoon, developed in the mid-16th century. Two parallel bores are drilled in a piece of wood and connected at the bottom, creating a single, conical tube. Like the bassoon and the larger shawms, the reed was placed on a crook inserted in the top of the instrument. The dulcian was widely used in a family of sizes, though most commonly the bass, up to about 1700; it survived much longer in Spain. It was also known in England as the curtal.

2. A narrow-scaled, gentle-sounding, flue organ stop.
JMo

dulcimer (Fr.: *timpanon*; Ger.: *Hackbrett*; It.: *salterio*; Hung.: *cimbalom*). A *zither whose strings, normally in multiple courses of two to four to each note, are struck by light beaters (or 'hammers'). It is sometimes called 'hammer dulcimer' to distinguish it from the plucked *Appalachian dulcimer. The soundbox is usually trapeziform, the long or bass side positioned towards the player. There are commonly two long bridges on the soundboard, or two rows of individual bridges like chess pawns, in addition to the nut at each side. The right-hand bridges usually carry the bass strings, which run across the soundboard to the nut on the opposite edge. The left-hand bridge divides each alto and treble string in two, with two thirds of its length, running to the right-hand nut, usually an octave above the neighbouring bass string, and one third, on the left, a 5th higher.

The dulcimer appeared in Europe in the mid-1500s; whether it derived from or was the model for such instruments as the Persian *santūr* is debated. It became a popular folk instrument throughout Europe, including parts of Britain, its most elaborate form being the Hungarian concert *cimbalom, the only one with pedal-operated dampers. From Persia it also spread eastwards to Central Asia, India, Korea, and China (where the *yangqin* holds an important position in ensemble music).   JMo

dulzaina (Sp.). A *shawm of Spain and of the Basque region. See also DOLZAINA.

'Dumbarton Oaks' Concerto. Popular name for Stravinsky's Concerto in E♭ for chamber orchestra; 'in the style of the Brandenburg Concertos', it was commissioned by Mr and Mrs R. W. Bliss and first performed in 1938 at Dumbarton Oaks, their house in Washington, DC.

dumb keyboard. See SILENT KEYBOARD.

dumka (from Cz. *dumat*, Pol. *dumać*, 'to ponder'; pl. *dumky*). A Slavonic folk ballad from Ukraine, with a lamenting quality. In the 19th century the name was also given to a type of instrumental music, most notably by Dvořák, whose sympathies were more pan-Slavonic than narrowly Bohemian. He interpolated faster, cheerful passages, breaking up the prevailing melancholy mood, and his 'Dumky' Piano Trio op. 90 consists of a string of six movements of this nature.   KC

dummy keyboard. See SILENT KEYBOARD.

Du Mont [de Thier], **Henry** (*b* Looz [now Borgloon], nr Hasselt, *c*.1610; *d* Paris, 8 May 1684). French composer, organist, and harpsichordist. He and his brother Lambert entered the choir school at Maastricht, where in 1629 Henry became organist, then studied at the Jesuit College. From 1643 until his death he was organist of St Paul, Paris, and he was granted French nationality in 1647. In 1652 he was named harpsichordist to the Duke of Anjou, in 1660 organist to the queen, and in 1663 one of the four *maîtres* of the royal chapel. He became *compositeur de la musique de la chapelle royale*, and, in 1673, *maître de la musique de la reine*. Additional ecclesiastical responsibilities enhanced his distinguished career. Du Mont composed chansons, *airs*, and keyboard music, but is best known for his prolific output of sacred music, notably his *petits motets* and *grands motets*. The latter, highly influential in the development of the genre, were for a *petit choeur* of up to seven voices, a five-part *grand choeur*, and an orchestra of varying sizes; choruses, solo *récits*, vocal ensembles, and instrumental ritornellos alternate within these large-scale works, many of which were composed for the royal chapel.   AL

    📖 J. R. ANTHONY, *French Baroque Music from Beaujoyeulx to Rameau* (London, 1973, 3/1997)

dump [dompe, dumpe]. A 16th- and 17th-century English dance form that survives in about 20 examples, all instrumental (for keyboard, lute, or viol), the earliest being *My Lady Carey's Dompe* (*c*.1540). Most of the pieces share a variation structure, over a tonic–dominant harmonic scheme, and are slow and sad in character; they may have been composed as mourning pieces. Their character is recalled in the expression 'down in the dumps', describing an unhappy state of mind.

Dunhill, Thomas (Frederick) (*b* London, 1 Feb. 1877; *d* Scunthorpe, 13 March 1946). English composer, writer, and teacher. He studied at the RCM (1893–1901) with Stanford (composition) and Franklin Taylor (piano). He taught at Eton College (1899–1908 and 1939–45) and at the RCM (1905–22), was an examiner for competitive festivals and the Associated Board, and wrote much pedagogical music for student instrumentalists. He also published books on chamber music (1912), Sullivan's comic operas (1928), and Elgar (1938). Early in his career Dunhill produced a sizable corpus of chamber works, of which the Violin Sonata no. 2 (1916) is arguably the finest; in 1924 he was the first winner of the Cobbett Chamber Music Medal. He enjoyed some success with songs, light opera, notably *The Enchanted Garden* (1924) and *Tantivy Towers* (1931, with words by A. P. Herbert), and the ballet *Gallimaufry* (Hamburg, 1937).   JDi

    📖 D. DUNHILL, *Thomas Dunhill, Maker of Music* (London, 1997)

Duni, Egidio Romoaldo (*b* Matera, *bapt.* 11 Feb. 1708; *d* Paris, 11 June 1775). Italian composer. His career began in Rome with *Nerone* (1735), and he had operas performed in Milan, Florence, London, and other centres. He was appointed *maestro di cappella* in Parma towards the end of the 1740s and collaborated with Goldoni on *La buona figliuola* (1756). In 1757 he moved to Paris to produce *Le Peintre amoureux de son modèle*, and in 1761 he became music director of the Comédie-Italienne. He was the first major composer of *opéra comique*, his Italianate music delighting the public; his collaborations with Louis Anseaume, C.-S. Favart, and M.-J. Sedaine became staple repertory for over 30 years in spite of the rival talents of Philidor, Monsigny, and Grétry.   JR

Dunstaple [Dunstable], **John** (*b c*.1390; *d* 24 Dec. 1453). English composer. His biography is obscure. According to his epitaph (which firmly establishes the date of his death), he was respected in his lifetime as an astronomer and mathematician as well as a 'prince of music'; he seems also to have practised astrology. His earliest known music dates from about 1420, suggesting a birthdate in the late 14th century. Documentary sources link his name with some of the leading political figures of the day, including John, Duke of Bedford (*d* 1435), the dowager Queen Joan (*d* 1437), and Humfrey, Duke of Gloucester, but it is unclear in what capacity. Some of his musical works also imply a connection with England's royal and noble households; for example, the motet *Preco preheminencie* may have been written for the marriage of Henry V and Catherine Valois in 1420. Although many of his works are found in manuscripts copied in Italy and Germany, this is not to be taken as evidence that Dunstaple travelled extensively abroad. Instead, their transmission is proof principally of England's political, diplomatic, intellectual, and cultural exchanges with the Continent during the era of the Hundred Years War. Dunstaple appears not to have been in clerical orders, and may have been married. He was buried in the parish of St Stephen Walbrook in the City of London, and probably had a residence there, though he seems also to have owned property in Cambridgeshire and elsewhere.

Dunstaple was the most eminent English composer in the first half of the 15th century. His surviving works consist chiefly of polyphonic masses, single mass movements, mass pairs (Gloria–Credo), and motets, mostly for three or four voices; there are also a few secular songs. Many are anonymous in one source but have been attributed to him on the strength of an ascription against the same piece in another; and some pieces with conflicting attributions are allocated to Dunstaple on grounds of style, though these ascriptions can rarely if ever be certain, since so many stylistic features of Dunstaple's music are in fact typically English traits found also in the works of others, for example his contemporary, Leonel Power. Particularly attractive to continental composers was the characteristically English sonority of texture caused by frequent juxtapositions of 3rds and 6ths between voices, instead of the barer, and more common, 'open' intervals of 5ths and octaves. In the works of Dunstaple and his English contemporaries there is also a feeling for chords and chordal progression—a concern for vertical (harmonic) as well as horizontal (melodic) logic—together with a greater than usual equality among the voices.

From the present-day listener's point of view, one of the most striking features of the best of Dunstaple's music is its lyrical freshness, airiness, and sheer 'singability'. Many of the treble-dominated pieces have smooth, stepwise-moving melodies with few leaps (such as the motet *Salve regina mater mire*). Some use repetition in short, easily identifiable melodic figures, or in imitative interplay (as in the motet *Sancta Maria, non est tibi similis*). The text-setting is often clearly syllabic or even declamatory, as in the motet *Quam pulchra es*, a largely chordal setting in which musical and textual accents are carefully aligned. Several of the more complex motets have lengthy sections for two voices, where parallel motion in 3rds or 6ths has a particularly sonorous effect. Dunstaple was singled out for praise by a number of 15th-century writers, including the poet Martin le Franc and the music theorist Johannes Tinctoris, both of whom imply that his works were influential even on composers as eminent as Dufay, Binchois, Ockeghem, and Busnois. Although his music ceased to be performed regularly after 1500, it continued occasionally to be cited with respect by music theorists in the 16th century. Today, Dunstaple is often mentioned alongside Byrd and Purcell as one of the great names in the early history of English music.

JN/JM

📖 M. BENT, *Dunstaple* (London, 1981)

duo. A piece of music for two performers. Although it is sometimes applied to early vocal duets, including the Renaissance *bicinium, and itself is French for 'duet', the word is now normally used exclusively for instrumental music. The numerous 18th- and 19th-century works for violin and keyboard can correctly be described as duos, but the term 'sonata' is generally preferred where appropriate. 'Duo' is more often used for music written for two equal or two melody instruments, such as two violins, two flutes, or violin and cello.

A substantial number of such duos were composed in the 18th century, chiefly for amateur performance, by English composers, among them Charles Burney and William Shield; in France, Leclair wrote two sets; and in Italy, Boccherini wrote one. Mozart wrote two duos for violin and viola (K423 and 424) and a duo for bassoon and cello is attributed to him (K292/196c). Three duos for clarinet and bassoon have been improbably ascribed to Beethoven. Weber wrote a *Grand duo concertant* for clarinet and piano, and Stravinsky a *Duo concertante* for violin and piano. The outstanding 20th-century duos are the 44 by Bartók for two violins. Duos are extensively used for didactic purposes and many have been written by composer-teachers.

The term is occasionally applied to performers who play such works: *piano duets ('duo' is rarely used for a work for two pianos or piano duet) might be played by a 'piano duo', and a pair of performers who regularly play music for two instruments might be described as a 'violin and piano duo'.

SS

duodrama. A *melodrama for two speakers.

Duparc, (Marie Eugène) **Henri** (Fouques) (*b* Paris, 21 Jan. 1848; *d* Mont-de-Marsan, 12 Feb. 1933). French composer. He was educated at the Jesuit College at Vaugirard, where he showed little inclination for music; but César Franck was a visiting piano teacher at the college, and it was with him that Duparc studied composition. Duparc tried, with varying success, to destroy many of his earliest efforts and this spirit of fierce self-criticism remained with him. The 16 solo songs and one duet on which his reputation rests were written between 1868 and 1884.

In 1871 Duparc joined Saint-Saëns and Romain Bussine in founding the Société Nationale, with the aim of promoting contemporary French music. At the same time he was a keen Wagnerian (though by no means as idolatrous as some of his contemporaries) and Wagner's chromatic harmonies contribute much to the passion and sweep of his finest songs, such as *L'Invitation au voyage* (1870), *Extase* (1872) (written apparently in deliberately Tristanian vein as a hit against anti-Wagnerian critics), *Phidylé* (1882), and *La Vie antérieure* (1884). Yet in spite of Wagner's influence his songs never seem to attempt to go beyond the limits possible on the smaller scale, since even the most widely exploratory harmony is based on a clear key structure underlined by pedal notes. The result is an art that has made *fin de siècle* ennui palatable to the 20th century and beyond, whether in rescuing poems by minor artists or in matching the qualities of Gautier, Leconte de Lisle, and Baudelaire.

Duparc also wrote a few short orchestral works, of which the symphonic poem *Lénore* (1875) is the most often heard. But in 1885 a deterioration in his nervous system put an end to composing, and the last half-century of his life was spent in retirement in the country, where for a time he was mayor of Marnes-les-Coquette. He brought out a definitive edition of his songs in 1911 but, after working on an opera *Roussalka* (based on Pushkin) from 1885 to 1895, he finally burnt the score. The best of his songs, though, rival any in either the French or German repertory, so that he must be regarded as a major composer of his time.

DA/RN

📖 S. MORTHCOTE, *The Songs of Henri Duparc* (London, 1949) · B. MEISTER, *Nineteenth-Century French Song: Fauré, Chausson, Duparc, and Debussy* (Bloomington, IN, 1980) · R. STRICKER, *Les Mélodies de Duparc* (Arles, 1996)

Duphly, Jacques (*b* Rouen, 12 Jan. 1715; *d* Paris, 15 July 1789). French harpsichordist and composer. He was organist of Évreux Cathedral *c.*1732, then of the two principal churches in Rouen. In 1742 he settled in Paris, where he published four books of harpsichord pieces (1744–68); each piece is named after a pupil or a friend. His works represent a fusion of French and Italian styles—the *goûts *réunis* attempted by many mid-18th-century composers. They consist of a mixture of dances and musical portraits or *character pieces.   WT

duplet. A term for two notes that are to be performed in the time of three; they are indicated by the figure '2' placed above or below the two notes (see Ex. 1).

Ex. 1

duple time. See TIME SIGNATURE.

duplex long. A note-value (▬) found in medieval music.

duplum (Lat.). 1. In two parts; used in medieval polyphony to describe a composition for two voices, e.g. *organum duplum*.

2. In the 13th and 14th centuries, the 'second' voice-part in a polyphonic work—that is, the voice immediately above the tenor. In a motet this part was also called 'motetus'. See also PART, 1.

Du Pré, Jacqueline (*b* Oxford, 26 Jan. 1945; *d* London, 19 Oct. 1987). English cellist. From 1955 she studied with William Pleeth, later with Tortelier, Casals, and Rostropovich, and began her short but hugely successful career with a recital in 1961 at the Wigmore Hall, London. Married to the pianist and conductor Daniel Barenboim (*b* 1942), she played in concerts throughout the world. Her distinctively physical playing style was eloquently suited to the Schumann and Elgar concertos. In 1973 multiple sclerosis forced her to retire from the concert hall, but her beauty of tone and dazzlingly natural technique is preserved on many recordings.   CF

📖 E. WILSON, *Jacqueline du Pré* (London, 1998)

Dupré, Marcel (*b* Rouen, 3 May 1886; *d* Meudon, nr Paris, 30 May 1971). French composer and organist. The precocious son of Albert Dupré, organist of St Ouen, Rouen, he studied the organ with Alexandre Guilmant and composition with Charles-Marie Widor at the Paris Conservatoire. In 1906 he became Widor's assistant organist at St Sulpice, succeeding him in 1934.

As organ professor at the Conservatoire (1925–54) he formed a most distinguished line of students, among them Messiaen, Jean Langlais, Jehan Alain, and Pierre Cochereau; in later years he was briefly director there (1954–6). His teaching methods were strict and dogmatic, and he wrote several treatises on organ playing; he also made editions of Bach and Franck.

Dupré was world-famous as a recitalist, his supreme technical brilliance characterizing many of his organ compositions, notably the well-known Three Preludes and Fugues (1912), *Variations sur un vieux noël* (1922), and *Deux esquisses* (1945). By contrast, deeper, more spiritual qualities are evident in such works as *Cortège et litanie* (1921), *Évocation* (1941), *Le Tombeau de Titelouze* (1943), and above all the magnificent *Symphonie-Passion* (1924), whose dissonant harmonic idiom and intensive ostinato patterns profoundly influenced Messiaen. Notable, too, are the superb *Quatre motets* (1916) for mixed voices and organ.   PG/AT

📖 M. MURRAY, *Marcel Dupré: The Work of a Master Organist* (Boston, 1985)

dur (Ger.). 'Major', in the sense of key (e.g. *A-dur*, 'A major', *dur Tonart*, 'major key'); however, 'major triad' is *harter* (not *dur*) *Dreiklang*. The French word *dur* means 'hard', *majeur* being used for 'major'. See also DURUM AND MOLLIS.

Durand. French firm of music publishers. It was founded by the organist, critic, and composer Auguste Durand (1830–1909) in Paris in 1869 as Durand-Schoenewerk. After Schoenewerk withdrew in 1891, Durand took his son Jacques (1865–1928) into the firm, renaming it A. Durand & Fils, and after Auguste's death it became Durand & Cie. Auguste Durand owned the extensive catalogue of the publisher Gustave-Alexandre Flaxland. He also acquired many piano works, songs, and chamber music by Schumann and Chopin, as well as the early works of Saint-Saëns and Duparc; he later obtained the French and Belgian rights to several Wagner operas.

In 1894 the company initiated a complete edition of Rameau, with Saint-Saëns as general editor. In 1914 there began the collection Édition Classique Durand & Fils, which included editions of Chopin by Debussy, of Mendelssohn by Ravel, and of Schumann by Fauré. Auguste and Jacques Durand strongly supported French music and were the original publishers of most of the music of Saint-Saëns, Debussy, and Ravel. From 1910 to 1913 they promoted concerts of new music, in 1927 they established a composition prize, and they have continued to publish music by Milhaud, Poulenc, d'Indy, Messiaen, Auric, Ibert, Jolivet, and others. In 2000 the firm was acquired by BMG.   JMT/JWA

Durante, Francesco (*b* Frattamaggiore, nr Naples, 31 March 1684; *d* Naples, 30 Sept. 1755). Italian composer and teacher. He studied at the Conservatorio di S. Onofrio in Naples, where his uncle was director, and taught there briefly in 1710–11. After that nothing is heard of him until 1728, when he became *primo maestro* at the Conservatorio dei Poveri di Gesù Cristo, though he may have studied in Rome at some point. In 1742 he moved to the equivalent post at the Conservatorio di S. Maria di Loreto, to which he later added that at S. Onofrio.

As a composer he was known mainly for his contrapuntal church music, based on the style of Palestrina though using a more up-to-date harmonic language, but he also wrote keyboard music of considerable virtuosity which may have influenced Domenico Scarlatti. His chief fame, however, was as an exceptional teacher; his pupils included such important figures as Pergolesi, Jommelli, and Paisiello. DA/ER

durch (Ger.). 'Through'; *durchaus*, 'throughout'.

durchdringend (Ger.). 'Piercing', 'shrill'.

Durchführung (Ger., 'through-leading'). The development in a sonata-form movement or the exposition of a fugue; *Durchimitation*, 'through-imitation', i.e. imitation systematically applied to all parts of a polyphonic piece, a technique developed at the end of the 15th century and a particular feature of the 'Palestrina style'.

durchkomponiert (Ger.). *'Through-composed'.

duret [duretto]. A dance named in English masques and in Michael Praetorius's *Terpsichore* (1612), where it is described as a *courante.

Durey, Louis (Edmond) (*b* Paris, 27 May 1888; *d* Saint Tropez, 3 July 1979). French composer. He came late to music, studying at the Schola Cantorum from 1910 to 1914. He was a member of Les *Six, but he was the first to secede from the group in 1921, going to live in seclusion in the south of France. In any case, he had little in common with Poulenc or Milhaud. He was influenced more by the determined simplicity of Satie than by his insouciance, and he produced his best music in serious chamber works, including three string quartets (1917, 1922, 1928). In later years he aligned himself with socialism and devoted much of his attention to folksong arrangements and works of propaganda, such as the cantata *La Longue Marche* to words by Mao (1949). PG/ABur

durezza (It.). 'Harshness'; *con durezza* is an indication to play in a severe and determined manner. In the 17th century *durezza* meant dissonance and hence a style of keyboard writing which featured chromaticisms and dissonance.

Durkó, Zsolt (*b* Szeged, 10 April 1934; *d* Budapest, 2 April 1997). Hungarian composer. He studied with Ferenc Farkas in Budapest and Petrassi in Rome; later he taught at the Budapest Academy of Music and worked for Hungarian Radio. His music is essentially modernist, though written with an awareness of Hungarian tradition, and is notable for its imaginative textures. It includes an opera, *Mózes* (Budapest, 1977), *Halotti beszéd* ('Burial Prayer', 1975) and other choral works, orchestral pieces, and much chamber music. ABur

Durón, Sebastián (*b* Brihuega, *bapt.* Guadalajara, 19 April 1660; *d* Cambó, 3 Aug. 1716). Spanish composer. He held organist's posts at the cathedrals of Zaragoza (1679), Seville (1680), Burgo de Osma (1684), and Palencia (1686), and at the royal chapel in Madrid (1691). A favourite at the Madrid court, in 1701 he was named *maestro de capilla* and rector of the royal choir school; he also became the 'official' composer of zarzuelas and court comedies. However, in 1706 he was banished by Philip V for supporting the Habsburgs in the War of the Spanish Succession; from then until his death he was chaplain to Mariana of Neuburg, the widowed queen of Carlos II, in southern France.

Durón's many sacred works include villancicos and lamentations in which he displayed his particular synthesis of the Spanish traditional style and recent Italian developments. His distinguished theatre music is well represented by *Salir el amor al mundo* (1696) and *La guerra de los gigantes* (composed 1700–7). In spite of being exiled in France he wrote the music for several comedies given in public theatres in Madrid in 1710–11. P-LR

📖 L. K. STEIN, *Songs of Mortals, Dialogues of the Gods: Music and Theatre in Seventeenth-Century Spain* (Oxford, 1993)

Duruflé, Maurice (*b* Louviers, 11 Jan. 1902; *d* Paris, 16 June 1986). French composer and organist. He studied the organ with Charles Tournemire and Louis Vierne, who influenced him profoundly. On entering the Paris Conservatoire, he joined Eugène Gigout's organ class. After deputizing at Ste Clotilde and Notre Dame, he was appointed organist of St Étienne-du-Mont in 1930. A notable recital career followed, during which he gave the premieres of Vierne's Symphony no. 6 and Poulenc's Organ Concerto.

Duruflé's output as a composer, though highly regarded, is remarkably small, and exemplifies the extreme self-criticism and superb craftsmanship of his composition professor Paul Dukas. His principal organ works are the *Scherzo* (1924), *Prélude, adagio et choral varié sur le 'Veni Creator'* (1930), *Suite* (1933)—ending with a scintillating Toccata which he subsequently rejected—and *Prélude et fugue sur le nom d'Alain* (1942). Duruflé's comparable ability in writing for the orchestra is revealed in the sensuous *Trois danses* (1932). The large-scale Requiem for soloists, chorus, orchestra, and organ (1947), which achieved considerable popularity, treats the traditional Gregorian themes with considerable harmonic and contrapuntal elaboration. His valuable transcriptions of Tournemire's *Cinq improvisations* from gramophone records were published in 1958.

In 1953 Duruflé married the distinguished organist Marie-Madeleine Duruflé-Chevalier; his own performing career was effectively terminated in 1975 by a serious car accident.　　　　　　　　　　　　　AT

durum and mollis. In the letter notation used in medieval times, 'b' was written in one of two ways. The square, 'hard' (Lat.: *durum*) form (♮) stood for B♮, and this letter type became the basis of the modern 'natural' and 'sharp' signs in music. The rounded, 'soft' (Lat.: *mollis*) form (♭) stood for B♭, and the modern flat sign is a version of this letter. Since music in minor keys was originally written using flat key signatures, while major keys tended to have sharp signatures, the Germans use *dur* to indicate a major key (*C-dur*, etc.) and *moll* to indicate the minor (*A-moll*, etc.).　　　　　　AP

Dušek [Dussek], **František Xaver** (*b* Chotěborky, Bohemia, *bapt.* 8 Dec. 1731; *d* Prague, 2 Feb. 1799). Czech pianist and composer. After studying with Wagenseil in Vienna, he settled in Prague. He was a good friend of Mozart, who completed *Don Giovanni* in Dušek's suburban Prague villa, Bertramka. Mozart also wrote the concert aria *Bella mia fiamma* (K528) for Dušek's wife, the soprano Josefa Dušek (née Hambacher; 1754–1824). Dušek's own compositions, including some 40 symphonies, keyboard concertos, and much chamber music, show a command of the Classical vernacular sometimes coloured by Baroque features.　　　　JSM

Dussek [Dusík], **Jan Ladislav** [Johann Ludwig] (*b* Čáslav, 12 Feb. 1760; *d* St Germain-en-Laye or Paris, 20 March 1812). Bohemian pianist and composer. The son of a well-known musician, Jan Dussek (1738–1818), he studied in Prague (1776–8) and in Hamburg (1782), possibly with C. P. E. Bach. He visited Germany, Russia, Lithuania, Italy, and France before settling in London in 1789. There he set up a music-publishing business with his father-in-law, Domenico Corri, and gave many concerts. By 1799 the publishing business was bankrupt, and Dussek took refuge from his creditors in Hamburg; from 1804 he was Kapellmeister

to Prince Louis Ferdinand of Prussia. After his patron's death in 1806, he turned to concert promotion and teaching. He worked for a number of other wealthy and influential patrons including Talleyrand, in whose service he spent his last years.

Haydn played with Dussek in London, describing him as 'one of the most upright, moral, and, in music, most eminent of men'. With the exception of a mass and some music for the stage, Dussek's output comprises mainly keyboard and chamber music. He wrote many keyboard sonatas including the famous 'Elegiac' Sonata on the death of Louis Ferdinand, 17 concertos (some now lost), and numerous smaller pieces. His works, while firmly rooted in the Classical style, foreshadow the Romantic period in their use of expressive chromatic harmonies. His important treatise on piano playing, *Instructions on the Art of Playing the Piano Forte or Harpsichord* (London, 1796), was translated into French and German.　　　WT/JSM

dutār (Persian, 'two strings'). A long-necked lute similar to the Turkish **saz*, with two or three single or double courses. It and similar instruments are used throughout Central Asia.　　　　　　　　JMo

Dutilleux, Henri (*b* Angers, 22 Jan. 1916). French composer. He studied with Henri Busser and Maurice Emmanuel at the Paris Conservatoire (1932–8) and in 1938 won the Prix de Rome. His stay in Rome was cut short by the war and he returned to Paris, taking up various posts including that of chorus master at the Opéra. In 1943 he joined French Radio as a music producer, remaining there until 1963 when he became a full-time composer.

His early works show the predominant influence of Ravel, but also of Stravinsky and Poulenc, and he later disowned many of them as being uncharacteristic. His first major success came with the Piano Sonata, written for his wife Geneviève Joy, who gave its first performance in 1948. Here Dutilleux turned his back decisively on the world of *petits maîtres*, as he did again with his First Symphony (1950–1), in which he also showed his independent streak by making the first movement a passacaglia.

He then set about a thorough and painstaking exploration of what an orchestral work of the late 20th century might be. From his earliest orchestral pieces the listener is seduced through the sounds conjured up by Dutilleux's fastidious and imaginative ear; at the same time he was always equally concerned over the structure of his music and over the relevance and consistency of its procedures and developed a technique he called 'croissance progressive', in which proliferation and memory combine in what he acknowledged to be a Proustian manner.

In the Second Symphony (1957–9) the argument is shared between a chamber orchestra and a larger body, while in *Métaboles* (1961–4) Dutilleux explored contrasts between orchestral families. Other sources of inspiration have included the visual world (van Gogh's painting *Nuit étoilée à Saint Rémy* for *Timbres, espace, mouvement* (1976–8), where the gap between the village and the stars is mirrored by the absence of violins and violas) and literature, his Cello Concerto, *Tout un monde lointain* (1967–70), being the offshoot of an abandoned ballet to mark the centenary of the death of Baudelaire. In this work, dedicated to Rostropovich, and in his Violin Concerto, *L'Arbre des songes* (1979–85), dedicated to Isaac Stern, Dutilleux wrote music of considerable technical difficulty (for both soloists and orchestra), but without ever losing sight of his poetic premises: in the Cello Concerto, a celebration of the cello as an essentially feminine instrument (Rostropovich's wonderfully characteristic tone high on the A string was one source of inspiration) and, in the Violin Concerto, the image of the tree as a strong, coherent structure, with a capacity for almost infinite proliferation.

In *Mystère de l'instant* (1986–9), one of Paul Sacher's last commissions, Dutilleux temporarily abandoned 'croissance progressive' in favour of a series of 'snapshots'. But the technique reappeared in *The Shadows of Time* (1995–7), where Proustian ideas of memory are engaged in a deeply moving tribute to Anne Frank and other victims of the Holocaust. In 2000 Dutilleux was working on settings of letters to musicians for soprano and orchestra. The letters themselves were to be linked by more amorphous, atmospheric sections. This technique of separating 'active' sections from 'reflective' or 'prospective' ones is to be found in many of his works, notably the string quartet *Ainsi la nuit*, a classic of 20th-century quartet literature.

Although Dutilleux occasionally used 12-note techniques, he kept aloof from what he called the 'serial terror' of the 1950s and 60s. His music makes much use of pivot-notes and -chords, and embodies his belief that a hierarchy of pitches is essential. He is not afraid of repetition or, at times, of extreme simplicity (he has a penchant for sudden, menacing octaves that transform the texture). But overall his music is subtle, brilliantly coloured, technically demanding, and above all deeply human. If it is less well known than it deserves, the composer's own gentle, undemonstrative nature is no doubt partly responsible. The integrity and imaginative power of his oeuvre dictate that this state of affairs will surely change. RN

📖 C. POTTER, *Henri Dutilleux: His Life and Works* (Aldershot, 1997)

dux. See CANON.

Dvořák, Antonín (*see opposite page*)

Dwarf, The. See ZWERG, DER.

dyad. A pair of notes. The term is sometimes found in writings on serial music.

Dykes, John Bacchus (*b* Hull, 10 March 1832; *d* Ticehurst, Sussex, 22 Jan. 1876). English composer. After classical studies at Cambridge, where he was also a pupil of T. A. Walmisley, he became precentor and a minor canon of Durham Cathedral (1849) and later vicar of St Oswald's Church, Durham (1862). Of the 60 hymns he contributed to the first edition of *Hymns, Ancient & Modern* (1861)—many of which are now much admired for their distinctive, chromatic harmony and fertile melodies—such tunes as *Strength and Stay*, *St Cross* ('O come and mourn'), *Nicaea* ('Holy, holy, holy'), *Gerontius* ('Praise to the holiest'), *Melita* ('Eternal Father, strong to save'), and *St Cuthbert* ('Our blest Redeemer') are still frequently sung. Dykes was awarded the honorary D.Mus. at Durham in 1861. JD1

dynamic accent. An *accent produced by an increase in volume.

dynamic marks. The terms, abbreviations, and signs used in musical notation to indicate relative intensity (loudness) and degree of accentuation. The most common are listed in Table 1. Composers have occasionally expanded these, using *fff*, *ffff*, *ppp*, *pppp*; Tchaikovsky went so far as to mark the end of his Sixth Symphony *pppppp*.

See also PERFORMANCE PRACTICE.

TABLE 1

Dynamic marks

pp	*pianissimo*	very soft
p	*piano*	soft
mp	*mezzopiano*	moderately soft
mf	*mezzoforte*	moderately loud
f	*forte*	loud
ff	*fortissimo*	very loud
fp	*fortepiano*	loud, then immediately soft
fz	*forzato* ⎱	forced
sf ⎱	*sforzato* ⎰	
sfz ⎰		
<	*crescendo*	getting louder
>	*decrescendo, diminuendo*	getting softer
◆		attack
		agogic accent

(*cont. on p. 392*)

Antonín Dvořák
(1841–1904)

The Czech composer Antonín Leopold Dvořák was born in Nelahozeves, near Prague, on 8 September 1841 and died in Prague on 1 May 1904.

Early years and first successes

Dvořák was the eldest son of an innkeeper in Nelahozeves, a village some 15 km north of Prague. He began his musical education in the village school in 1847 and made good progress on the violin. Contrary to accounts in many standard biographies, his parents did not intend him to be a butcher but did what they could, with severely limited means, to encourage his musical talents. He studied the organ in both Zlonice (1853–6), where he also had lessons in music theory and figured bass, and Česká Kamenice (1856–7). In the autumn of 1857 he enrolled at the Organ School in Prague, graduating second in his class in 1859. Having performed as an orchestral viola player in Prague from 1857, he joined Karel Komzák's dance orchestra in 1859 and continued to work with this group when it came to provide the basis of the new Prague Provisional Theatre orchestra on its opening in November 1862. Dvořák stayed with the theatre orchestra until the summer of 1871, acquiring a solid knowledge of French grand opera, operetta, Verdi, and Mozart.

Dvořák's first serious compositions, including chamber music, a song cycle (*Cypresses*), a cello concerto, and the first two symphonies, date from the early to mid-1860s. With his first-hand experience of the growing Czech operatic repertory it is unsurprising that he also turned to opera, composing *Alfred* to a German text (1870) and the comedy *Král a uhlíř* ('The King and the Charcoal-Burner', 1871). The latter was rejected as too difficult for the company during rehearsals at the Provisional Theatre in 1873; a much simpler, note-for-note recomposition of the score was given there with moderate success in 1874. On leaving the theatre Dvořák supported himself by teaching. During the next two years he became known in the Czech musical salons of Prague as a composer of chamber music and songs, but he attracted far more public attention with the success of his patriotic cantata *Dědicové bílé hory* ('The Heirs of the White Mountain') in 1873. In the same year he married his piano pupil Anna Čermáková.

1874 saw rather more financial independence with Dvořák's appointment as organist of St Vojtěch (1874–7). In 1875 he was awarded an Austrian state stipendium of 400 gulden, on the basis of 15 compositions including the Third and Fourth Symphonies, which he received for a further three years. This greater pecuniary security unleashed a wealth of creativity: in 1875 alone he wrote the G major ('Double Bass') String Quintet, the B♭ Piano Trio, the D major Piano Quartet, four Moravian Duets, the E major string Serenade, the Fifth Symphony, and the five-act grand opera *Vanda*.

International fame: the American years

On the recommendation of Brahms, who sat on the state stipendium committee from 1875, the Berlin publisher Simrock published a set of Moravian Duets in 1879 and prompted Dvořák to compose the first set of Slavonic Dances. These were published in 1878 and marked a spectacular increase in Dvořák's fortunes, resulting in commissions and numerous performances abroad. At home, his tragic grand opera *Dimitrij* was a success in 1882. In 1883 he was invited by the Philharmonic Society of London to conduct performances of his works in England the following year. English enthusiasm for his music, fired by performances of the *Stabat mater* and the Sixth Symphony, resulted in commissions for a choral work for the Birmingham Festival (*Svatební košile*, 'The Spectre's Bride') and a symphony (no. 7 in D minor) for the Philharmonic Society in 1885. Further works for England followed, including the oratorio *St Ludmila* (Leeds, 1886) and the Requiem Mass (Birmingham, 1891). In 1887 Dvořák returned to opera with *Jakobín* ('The Jacobin'), though he also continued to compose instrumental and orchestral works, notably the A major Piano Quintet (1887) and the Eighth Symphony (1889).

At the height of his international popularity in 1892, Dvořák took up an invitation to become director of the National Conservatory of Music in America (New York) and professor of composition with an annual salary of $15,000. There, in spite of teaching and administrative duties, he composed his Ninth Symphony ('From the New World', 1893) and, while on holiday in the Czech-speaking community of Spillville, Iowa, the F major String Quartet ('American', op. 96) and the E♭ major String Quintet op. 97. During a return visit to New York in 1894–5 Dvořák composed the *Biblical Songs* (op. 99), the Violin Sonatina in G major (op. 100), and the B minor Cello Concerto. On returning to Prague, and after completing two string quartets (opp. 105 and 106), he immersed himself in Bohemian folklore, composing four symphonic poems based on folk tales from Karel Erben's *Kytice* which use lines of poetry as the rhythmic basis for melody. His last years were devoted to opera: he revised *The Jacobin* (1897) and composed two works based on Czech legend, *Čert a Káča* ('The Devil and Kate', 1899) and his operatic masterpiece *Rusalka* (1900). Both were highly successful with Prague audiences, and though his last opera, *Armida*, a four-act grand opera to an archaic text, was far less popular, Dvořák was still considering more texts at the time of his death in 1904 from a stroke.

Musical style

Dvořák was one of the most versatile composers of the 19th century, writing successfully in a wide range of genres. After the influence of Mozart, Beethoven, Mendelssohn, and Schumann in his earliest work, he embarked between 1869 and 1874 on a highly experimental phase of composition, coloured by Wagner and Liszt but showing a remarkable and challenging individuality, notably in such pieces as the E minor String Quartet and the first version of *The King and the Charcoal-Burner*. From the time of the Fifth Symphony (1875) this experimentalism gave way to a greater attention to Classical form, more symmetrical melody, and less exploratory harmony. Also apparent is the influence of his musical education: in essence this was little different from that given to Dvořák's 18th-century predecessors, and manifests itself in an interest in firm, continuo-like bass lines and in Baroque *Figuren*, found notably in his setting of the *Stabat mater* (1877). While the Sixth and Seventh Symphonies and the F minor Piano Trio (op. 65), all from the early to mid-1880s, exhibit Brahmsian features, Dvořák preserved a strongly individual style of melody and development. Ultimately the compositional manners of Beethoven, Smetana, and Wagner proved most enduring as a resource. His response to American popular styles during his stay in New York led to an intensification of certain characteristics, notably pentatonicism and ostinatos. Wagner returned as a stimulus in the late operas, though his influence hardly impairs Dvořák's lyrical genius, at its height in these works.

The perceived native element in his music results from a manner Dvořák inherited largely from Smetana. He almost never quoted folksong, though he frequently alluded to popular styles. His methods of composition, often belied by the apparent spontaneity of his inspiration, could be painstaking, and many of his works were subject to revision and sometimes extensive recomposition. Although he is best known today for orchestral and chamber music, he enriched many genres and towards the end of his life considered opera to be his major area of endeavour. Dvořák cultivated the popular image of himself as a simple Czech 'musikant', but this masked aspects of a complex personality often prey to neurosis. A devout Roman Catholic, he was loyal to church—though not to its trappings—and country, and he resisted more than one attempt to persuade him to settle in Vienna. Though remarkably consistent, Dvořák's output addressed a wide variety of audiences, a characteristic that has assured the lasting success of many of his works.   JSм

📖 J. Clapham, *Antonín Dvořák, Musician and Craftsman* (London, 1966); *Dvořák* (London, 1979) · J. Tyrrell, *Czech Opera* (Cambridge, 1988) · M. Beckerman (ed.), *Dvořák and his World* (Princeton, NJ, 1993) · B. Beveridge (ed.), *Rethinking Dvořák: Views from Five Countries* (Oxford, 1996)

dynamics. The aspect of musical expression concerned with the variation in the volume of sound. See PERFORMANCE PRACTICE, 9.

Dyson, Sir George (*b* Halifax, 28 May 1883; *d* Winchester, 28 Sept. 1964). English composer and teacher. He studied composition with Stanford at the RCM (1900–4), after which he travelled as a Mendelssohn Scholar to Italy and Germany. He returned in 1907 to embark on a career as a public-school music master, teaching at Osborne (1908), Marlborough (1911), and Rugby (1914). In 1914 he joined the infantry and wrote a 'Manual of Grenade Fighting'. Shell-shocked in 1916, he transferred to the Air Ministry. After the war he taught at Wellington College and at the RCM, where he returned as director (1938–52) after a period as head of music at Winchester College (1924–37). He was knighted in 1942.

In the tradition of Parry, Elgar, and Vaughan Williams, Dyson produced large-scale choral works for provincial festivals, the best known of which was *The Canterbury Pilgrims* (1931). A master of colourful instrumentation (after Richard Strauss, whom he greatly admired), he composed a symphony (1937), works for string orchestra, and a fine Violin Concerto (1942) given its premiere by Albert Sammons. He was also the author of two influential books, *The New Music* (1924) and *The Progress of Music* (1932), a study of music in social history. JD1

📖 C. PALMER (ed.), *Dyson's Delight: An Anthology of Sir George Dyson's Writings and Talks on Music* (London, 1989); *George Dyson: Man and Music* (London, 1996)

Dzerzhinsky, Ivan Ivanovich (*b* Tambov, 27 March/9 April 1909; *d* Leningrad, 18 Jan. 1978). Russian composer. He studied music in Moscow and Leningrad, latterly with the composers Pyotr Ryazanov (1899–1942) and Boris Asaf'yev (1884–1949). His output (which includes operas, concertos, symphonic poems, and piano music) is relatively small, but in 1936 he was raised from potential obscurity by his opera *Tikhiy Don* ('The Quiet Don'), based on episodes from the then incomplete novel by Mikhail Sholokhov known in English as *Quiet Flows the Don*. Dzerzhinsky had submitted the score to a Bol'shoy Theatre competition in 1932, when the jury, while acknowledging his 'undoubted talent', commented that 'the composer's craftsmanship is on a very low level'. But, largely through the intervention of Shostakovich, the opera was staged at the Malïy Theatre, Leningrad, in 1935. Stalin saw it in 1936, identifying in it the traits of *socialist realism which he was encouraging in the arts: a simple, direct musical language and an upliftingly patriotic plot. In the furore surrounding the condemnation of Shostakovich's *The Lady Macbeth of the Mtsensk District*, *The Quiet Don* emerged as a model of Soviet opera, achieving 200 performances by mid-1938. From 1936 Dzerzhinsky held important administrative posts, his subsequent works failing to make much impression. GN

📖 G. ABRAHAM, *Eight Soviet Composers* (London, 1943)

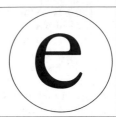

E. The third degree (mediant) of the scale of C major (see SCALE, 3).

ear and hearing. Scientific studies of the human ear and the ways in which the brain interprets sounds have increased in recent years. The subject is complex and the following article summarizes present knowledge of only those aspects that bear on musical performance and reproduction.

1. Physical description; 2. The perception of pitch; 3. Absolute pitch; 4. Interaction of notes; 5. The perception of loudness; 6. Directional hearing; 7. Hearing defects and deafness.

1. Physical description

The train of varying pressures in the air that constitute sound waves (see ACOUSTICS) enter through an opening in the outer ear or pinna. The ear canal or meatus is about 2.5 cm long and behaves like an organ pipe, resonating to produce an increase in hearing acuity in the range 2000–5500 Hz. The ear canal is closed at its inner end by a thin diaphragm of stretched skin known as the eardrum or tympanic membrane, which vibrates as the air pressure changes.

The inner face of the eardrum acts on the air in a cavity known as the middle ear, which communicates with the atmosphere through the eustachian tube, thus equalizing the average pressures on the two sides of the eardrum. Suspended in the middle ear is a system of levers comprising three tiny bones or ossicles. These act as a protection device and help to transmit vibrations more efficiently. They are given the descriptive names hammer, anvil, and stirrup, the last being attached to a further membrane, the oval window, which leads to a complex labyrinth, the cochlea. This structure, shaped like a snail shell, is a coiled tube filled with fluid and divided into two galleries connected by a small opening at the narrow end.

Vibrations of the oval window set the fluid in motion, and a third membrane, the round window in the lower gallery, allows the incompressible fluid to move. The partition between the two galleries contains some 2400 fibres, scaled in length and connected to nerve endings and to the auditory nerve, which is linked to the brain. It is movement of these fibres that produces the sensation we call hearing.

2. The perception of pitch

The German scientist Hermann von Helmholtz (1821–94) first suggested that these fibres were tuned to different frequencies and responded selectively to provide the sense of pitch. A more probable explanation is given in the travelling-wave theory of the Hungarian acoustician Georg von Békésy (1899–1972), which associates pitch with amplitude peaks at different lengths along the cochlear canal. The range of frequencies audible to young ears covers a ratio of about 1000:1, i.e. 20–20,000 Hz.

The human nervous system acts like a telecommunications network of great sophistication, enabling us to recognize not only different notes on the musical scale but different instruments and performers, while decoding millions of other impulses from all five senses. The basic interval of a semitone is a feature of Western music and corresponds to a frequency change of about 25 per cent (see ACOUSTICS). Human hearing extends over about ten octaves and, since there are 12 semitones to the octave, only 120 different musical notes need to be distinguished by the listener. However, some 1400 smaller intervals can be detected by keen ears.

3. Absolute pitch

Some people—not all of them musicians—can identify any note heard, or sing any note on demand, without the need for a pitch reference. This facility is called absolute (or perfect) pitch and was possessed, for instance, by Mozart, who correctly identified pitch errors at the age of seven. It seems that this gift is hereditary and cannot be acquired in later life.

4. Interaction of notes

Sounds consisting of a single frequency are the exception rather than the rule (see ACOUSTICS, 5 and 6) and so the ear's response to more than one note sounding simultaneously is of special interest. Musicians can develop astonishing powers of selection in identifying the separate component notes and instruments in a complex sound mixture. When two notes are separated by only a few Hertz, the effect is of a single note at an intermediate frequency fluctuating in loudness ('beats'). When those notes are separated by more than about 20 Hz, the sensation of beats disappears but, when loud, the actual difference frequency may become audible as a third note and play a part in tuning. Another aspect of the interaction of notes is the 'masking' of one note by another, more usually with a lower note masking a higher one. Exposure to very loud sounds introduces a 'masking' shift like a temporary hearing loss or listening fatigue.

5. The perception of loudness

A scale of loudness was first suggested by G. T. Flechner based on a unit step of 'just noticeable differences'. A given step in perceived loudness comes from multiplying the existing intensity by some factor—that is, the relationship is logarithmic rather than linear. For example, increasing the sound intensity by a factor of 10 produces about twice the loudness. To double the loudness again would require a further tenfold increase in intensity. This is the basis for the decibel scale (see ACOUSTICS, 11). It should be noted that the electrical signals from the inner ear to the brain do not themselves vary greatly in amplitude. Nor do they form an imitation (analogue) of the original waveform. It is a coded stream of impulses which carries the information as to the frequencies and intensities present, for interpretation by the brain.

6. Directional hearing

The spread of stereophonic recording and broadcasting has made it common knowledge that we are able to locate or sense the direction of a sound source by comparing the sounds reaching our two ears ('binaural hearing'). If someone directly in front of me claps his hands, the sound reaches both my ears at the same instant and the same intensity. My brain would easily deduce that the source was straight ahead. If the source now moves to the left of centre, the sound will reach my left ear earlier than the right, giving a clue to its direction. The sound will also be slightly louder, not so much because of the shorter distance travelled but because my head casts an acoustic 'shadow' in the region of my right ear. Both the time difference and the intensity difference contribute to directional hearing ability. Time difference is more important at frequencies below about 1000 Hz, and intensity difference is a stronger clue from 4000 Hz upwards. Small head movements assist the brain in locating source direction more accurately.

7. Hearing defects and deafness

In the world of music, the devastating effect of deafness on such key figures as Beethoven and Smetana comes to mind first, but some degree of hearing impairment affects a great many people of all ages. The sudden onset of deafness is comparatively rare, a gradual loss being more usual. Two broad types can occur: conduction-hearing loss in the mechanisms of the outer and middle ear, and sensory-neural loss in the inner ear and auditory nerve. The former affects all frequencies, the commonest cause being wax accumulation, with infections in the inner ear being more serious. Sensory-neural loss may affect all sounds or only those in a narrow band. It is a hazard of old age, particularly at high frequencies, but may also be caused by exposure to loud explosions or long periods in a noisy environment. Excessive noise can be dangerous as well as irritating, and regulations exist in many countries aimed at reducing both 'community noise', in cities and aircraft flight paths, and industrial noise that puts workers' hearing at risk.

See also PSYCHOLOGY OF MUSIC, 1.   JBo

📖 C. E. SEASHORE, *Psychology of Music* (New York, 1938/R1967) · M. CAMPBELL and C. GREATED, *The Musician's Guide to Acoustics* (London, 1987)

Earth Dances. Orchestral work (1985–6) by Birtwistle.

ear-training. In its simplest sense, ear-training, or 'aural perception', aims to improve communication between the ear and the brain, thus improving the listener's conscious and intellectual grasp of what the ear hears.

The broader implications of ear-training and aural perception go to the very roots of the different stages in the phenomenon of music. Within the Western classical tradition, these could be said to begin with the process of gestation on the part of the composer; the conversion of the music into symbols on paper (we are disregarding here music which misses out this stage, namely improvisation); the transference of these written symbols into actual sound via performance; and finally the reception of the sounds by the listener's ear.

No performer, teacher, or leader of an ensemble could function properly without a high degree of aural perception. Indeed, teachers and leaders would be of little help to their pupils and ensembles if their aural perception were inadequate to allow them to spot and correct wrong pitches and rhythms. Similarly, string, wind, and brass players must, like singers, create their own pitches. It requires a well-developed ear to guarantee that the pitches they create are in tune— not only relative to each other, but also to whatever other instruments or voices are sounding at the same time.

For music students, a traditional way of doing this has been through 'ear-training classes'. These have long been part of the curricula of conservatories and university music departments, both in Britain and abroad. In such classes students are systematically trained to identify pitches and rhythms and, by practice and guidance, to learn to write them in musical notation. (This, incidentally, is the converse of *sight-singing.) Students must learn to listen 'horizontally' in order to follow melody or rhythm, and 'vertically' so as to separate mentally the various sounds that combine to form a chord or note cluster. They must also understand the grammar of written music in order to express these sounds as symbols on paper.

However, research has resulted in criticism of established methods of ear-training as being inadequate and inappropriate in meeting students' professional needs. Ear-training exercises in the past have confined themselves only to features that can be rendered in notation and, consequently, readily assessed. Other characteristics, such as timbre, density of texture, spatial location of sounds, dynamics, articulation, and phrasing, tend to be overlooked. Also, traditional ear-training does not promote the perception of those fine shadings of pitch and rhythm that notation is inadequate to convey. The note G♯ in the key of A should, for example, sound at a slightly different pitch from an A♭ in the key of E♭; an educated ear can guide the player's fingers or lips towards making these subtle intonations. (Only keyboard instruments lack the facility to distinguish between pitches in this way.)

Where rhythm is concerned, aural acuity and observation are strongly bound up with matters of performing style. What appears on paper as a sequence of notes of equal duration may be interpreted with minute adjustments to length depending on whether the performer is playing a Baroque concerto, a piece of Romantic music demanding a flexible rubato, or a jazz 'standard' that needs to swing. Such minute adjustments to pitch and rhythm may seem intuitive, but authentic ways of creating them can be learnt only through observation and practice. Recent research into ear-training, such as the 'Research into Applied Musical Perception' project led by George Pratt at Huddersfield University, has aimed to broaden its scope and make it more useful to students in its application to their day-to-day work as musicians.

There seems to be a wide range of natural ability and disability in the field of aural perception. On the one hand are those who maintain that they are 'tone deaf' (a difficult phenomenon to define, suggesting as it does that, to the sufferer, all sounds are meaningless or chaotic); on the other, the world of music has from time to time been amazed by the seemingly uncanny ability of a musician such as the great Italian conductor Arturo Toscanini to hear a single wrong note played by some hapless musician within the welter of sound of an orchestral tutti. However, whether applied to the making of music or the listening to it, a properly trained ear is not only an essential part of every musician's technical armoury, but is also a considerable advantage to even the most casual listener.

CFr/PSp

   📖 G. PRATT, with M. HENSON and S. CARGILL, *Aural Awareness: Principles and Practice* (Milton Keynes and Philadelphia, 1990)

East, Michael (*b* c.1580; *d* Lichfield, 1648). English church musician and composer. He contributed a madrigal to Morley's anthology *The Triumphes of Oriana* in 1601, five years before taking the degree of B.Mus. at Cambridge University. After working in London and as a lay clerk at Ely Cathedral, he settled in Lichfield, where he was Master of the cathedral choristers. He was a prolific but conservative composer of madrigals, songs, and instrumental music. The printer Thomas *East may have been his uncle.   JM

East, Thomas (*b* ?Swavesey, Cambs., c.1540; *d* London, 1608). English music printer and publisher. He was a member of the Company of Stationers from 1565 and the most important printer in England from 1588 until his death. He published the works of all the principal composers of madrigals and ayres, including the madrigal collection *The Triumphes of Oriana* (1601). He also collected (and perhaps commissioned) settings for his *Whole Booke of Psalmes* (London, 1592), which went to six further editions and was corrected and enlarged by Thomas Ravenscroft in 1621, being known thereafter as 'Ravenscroft's Psalter'.   DA/JWa

Eben, Petr (*b* Zamberk, 22 Jan. 1929). Czech composer and pianist. He studied composition with Bořkovec and the piano with František Rauch at the Prague Academy of Musical Arts. A sensitive accompanist, he had considerable success in chamber music. The large body of works to religious texts is testament to Eben's profound beliefs. Influences range widely, from early musics to Messiaen and Britten. Nevertheless his pungent and individual style, heard at its finest in such pieces as the orchestral *Noční hodiny* ('Night Hours', 1975) and the cycle for trumpet and organ *Okná* ('Windows', 1976), have ensured lasting success and international recognition.   JSm

Eberl, Anton (*b* Vienna, 13 June 1765; *d* Vienna, 1807). Austrian composer and pianist. He showed conspicuous musical ability as a child. Mozart may have taught him in the 1780s, and some of Eberl's early compositions were published under Mozart's name. Eberl's first opera, *Die Marchande des Modes* (1787, lost), was praised by Gluck. Apart from two stays in St Petersburg (1796–1800, 1801–2) and concert tours in Germany, he worked in Vienna, where he was seen as a serious rival to Beethoven, as both pianist and composer. His surviving opera *Die Königin der schwarzen Inseln* (1801), his chamber works, piano works, and two mature symphonies contain music of striking quality and individuality, belied by his current neglect.   CB

Eberlin, Johann Ernst (*b* Jettingen, Bavaria, *bapt.* 27 March 1702; *d* Salzburg, 19 June 1762). German composer and organist. In 1726 he entered service in Salzburg as fourth organist at the cathedral, and 23 years later eventually attained the rank of court and cathedral Kapellmeister. His vocal works include operas, intermezzos, and oratorios, in a mainly Italianate manner, together with numerous church compositions (including some 70 masses), several of which were admired and imitated by Leopold Mozart. In addition to keyboard toccatas and fugues, he composed music for the mechanical organ at Hellbrunn Castle, the summer palace of the archbishop.   DA/BS

Ebony Concerto. Concerto by Stravinsky for clarinet (an 'ebony stick' in jazz slang) and orchestra, composed for the jazz musician Woody Herman, who gave its first performance with his band (New York, 1946).

Eccard, Johannes (*b* Mühlhausen, Thuringia, 1553; *d* Berlin, 1611). German composer. He was a choirboy in the Weimar court chapel before becoming a singer at the Munich court under Lassus. From 1579 he was in the service of Margrave Georg Friedrich of Prussia, becoming his Kapellmeister in 1604. He wrote some agreeable lieder but is most famous for his hymn tunes, setting chorale melodies so that the accompanying parts expressed the meaning of the text and thus prefiguring Bach's technique.   DA

Eccles. English family of musicians. **Solomon Eccles (i)** (*b c.*1617; *d* London, 2 Jan. 1682) was its most eccentric member. About 1660 he became a Quaker and abandoned his profession as a music teacher, publicly burning his music books and instruments on Tower Hill in London. His 1667 tract, *A Musick-Lector*, is a theoretical argument concerning the function of music in religion that describes some of his travels abroad as a proselytizing Quaker.

Solomon Eccles (ii) (*bapt.* ?1649; *d* Guildford, 1710) may have been his nephew. A court musician, he also wrote incidental music for two plays staged in London in 1682, Aphra Behn's *The City Heiress* and Thomas Otway's *Venice Preserv'd*. **Henry Eccles (i)** (*b* ?1640–50;

d London, 1711), possibly his brother, was also a court musician, from 1689, and in 1691 he accompanied William III to Holland.

John Eccles (*b c.*1668; *d* Hampton Wick, 12 Jan. 1735), a theatre composer, was in 1700 appointed Master of the King's Music, in which capacity he composed many occasional odes. In 1701 he won second prize in a competition for his setting of Congreve's *The Judgement of Paris*. Eccles wrote the music for some 12 masques and other dramatic pieces, including the English opera *Semele* (1707), which was not produced, and incidental music for more than 50 plays.

Another member of the family, **Henry Eccles (ii)** (*b* ?1675–85; *d* after 1735), was a violinist and composer who by 1720 was living in Paris, where he published 12 violin sonatas.   WT/PL

ecclesiastical modes. Alternative name for church modes; see MODE, 2.

échappée (Fr.). 'Escaped (note)'. A melodic progression in which an unaccented passing note (i.e. a note that intervenes between two chords but does not form part of the harmony of either of them) appears outside the interval formed by the notes on either side of it, approached in the opposite direction to the resolution (Ex. 1*a*). When such a passing note is made in the same direction as the resolution, it is called a 'changing' note (It.: *cambiata*, not to be confused with *nota cambiata) (Ex. 1*b*).

Ex. 1

échelle (Fr.). 'Scale' (but the more usual word for the musical scale is *gamme*).

echo. 1. See ACOUSTICS, 10.

2. The imitation in music of a natural echo effect, often used in vocal music during the late 16th and 17th centuries. It was especially associated with the madrigal; Lassus wrote one called *O la, o che bon echo*. Subsequently the effect was assimilated into theatre music; examples occur in early Italian oratorios and in French operas by Lully, Rameau, and Gluck. Lully went so far as to set up two distinct groups within his orchestra, a concertante group (*petit choeur*) and the main ensemble (*grand choeur*); in addition to accompanying recitatives and *airs* the *petit choeur* was used to echo the *grand choeur*. In England, Purcell used echo techniques in his stage works to heighten the sense of drama. There is an 'echo dance and chorus' in *Dido and Aeneas* ('In our deep vaulted cell', and 'Echo dance of Furies'), in which the end of each phrase is repeated softly. A similar piece is 'May the god of wit inspire' in *The Fairy Queen*.

The echo effect also permeated instrumental music; it is found in some English consort dances, and in Venice, where the Gabrielis exploited the special acoustic qualities of St Mark's in their antiphonal instrumental and choral music (see CORI SPEZZATI). It was also used in keyboard music designed for two-manual harpsichords, and in organ music, where it was achieved by the use of contrasting stops. In French Baroque harpsichord music the 'petite reprise' was an echo device whereby a short phrase at the end of a binary form movement was repeated. The soft repetition of phrases ultimately became a common feature of Baroque instrumental music, not just confined to 'echo' movements.   —/LC

Eckhardt-Gramatté, Sophie-Carmen [Fridman-Kochevskoy, Sonia de] (*b* Moscow, 25 Dec. 1898/6 Jan. 1899; *d* Stuttgart, 2 Dec. 1974). Russian-born Canadian composer, pianist, and violinist. A childhood prodigy rumoured to be the daughter of Tolstoy (her mother was governess to the Tolstoy children), she studied, *inter alia*, chamber music with d'Indy at the Paris Conservatoire (1909–13). In 1914 she and her mother moved to Berlin, living in some poverty until Joachim's daughter-in-law heard her and enabled her to study with Huberman. She married the painter Walter Gramatté in 1920 (he died in 1929) and Ferdinand Eckhardt, an art critic, in 1934. They moved to Vienna in 1939 and to Winnipeg in 1953; she became a Canadian citizen in 1958. Her death was the result of a road accident. Her music is highly contrapuntal and charged with rhythmic energy. She wrote orchestral music including two symphonies (1939, 1969–70) and chamber and instrumental works.   MA

éclatant (Fr.). 'Brilliant', 'dazzling'.

Éclat/multiples ('Fragment/Multiples'). Orchestral work by Boulez, expanded from his *Éclat* (1965) for 15 instruments; he made this second version in 1971 and it remained a 'work in progress'.

eclogue [eglogue]. A short pastoral poem involving shepherds' dialogue, after the model of Theocritus' *Idylls* and Virgil's *Eclogues*. From the late 15th century to the 17th, notably in Spain, poems of this type were written in the form of plays and performed with incidental music on the stage: such productions were among the forerunners of opera. The most significant composer of these *eglogas* was Juan del Encina, whose works were performed from 1492 onwards. Later composers, for example Liszt and Dvořák, gave the title 'Eclogue' or 'Eglogue' to works of an idyllic, pastoral nature.

écossaise (Fr., 'Scottish'). A quick dance in 2/4 time, popular in France and England in the early 19th century. Despite its name it seems to have no connection with Scotland. Beethoven, Schubert, and Chopin all wrote collections of *écossaises*.

See also SCHOTTISCHE.

Ecuatorial. Work (1932–4) by Varèse for bass (solo or unison chorus), four trumpets, four trombones, two ondes martenot, and percussion (six players), a setting of a prayer from the *Popol Vuh* of the Maya Quiché, translated by Jimines.

Edgar. Opera in three (originally four) acts by Puccini to a libretto by Ferdinando Fontana after Alfred de Musset's dramatic poem *La Coupe et les lèvres* (1832) (Milan, 1889; four-act version, Buenos Aires, 1905).

editing. The editing of music is its preparation for publication, performance, and study, usually by someone other than the composer. Editions satisfy two needs: students, scholars, and music-lovers require authoritative scores for consultation; and performers need reliable performing materials. These two aims are not incompatible, and a number of fine editions, particularly those issued since World War II, succeed in fulfilling both. Moreover, the growing enthusiasm for cultivating early music, the original notation of which is no longer familiar to many practising musicians, has stimulated the need for clear, usable, and modernized editions.

An editor has several specific tasks. He or she must collect the sources of the work in question, evaluate them, and collate them to create a version that most closely reflects the composer's intentions. The variant readings should be described and listed. The collated version is then transcribed into modern notation, indicating any editorial changes or additions to the original material. The editor may also include suggestions for ornamentation, realization of a basso continuo, and accentuation marks; add bar-lines in music before 1600; and transfer music from obsolete clefs to modern ones. He or she must also underlay the text and may make transpositions (if the pitch in use in early times is known to be different from today's).

Musicology can claim an illustrious history of editorial practice. Since the formation in 1850 of the Bach-Gesellschaft, for the production of a complete edition of the music of J. S. Bach, musicologists have produced a vast array of distinguished editions (see EDITIONS, HISTORICAL AND CRITICAL). Much of this enterprise was driven by the sheer necessity of making the music accessible. But an equally strong motive was the creation of a canon, a central core of repertory, containing texts that carried the same philological weight as their rivals in literature and political history. These editions constitute a statement, by the purveyors of the young academic discipline of music, of musicology's place in the academy. Even their presentation, in imposing folio volumes, reflects the gravity of their intent.

The accomplishments of these initial efforts led to three subsequent developments in the scholarly editing of music. The first was the production of editions labelled 'Urtext' to distinguish them from 'performing' or interpretative editions. Scholars complained that the numerous performance instructions added in the latter (usually prepared by famous performers) obscured the original notation, and that, because little effort was expended in differentiating editorial marks from those in the source, the users of such editions had no means of distinguishing between them. Although the term 'performing edition' is now largely discredited by scholars, the original conception was honourable: to provide texts that allowed the composer's notation to speak for itself. Even the most devout exponents of the concept, however, acknowledge that editorial intervention is unavoidable.

As research, largely made possible by the first wave of scholarly editions, contributed to a deeper knowledge of repertories and their sources, and critical appraisals of that knowledge continued, new editions were needed to reflect the latest developments. These later editions present substantial refinements in virtually every respect: editors were urged to jettison some of the philological purity of their texts (old clefs, for example) to make editions more accessible to performers.

Far from being simply the mechanical reconstruction of compositional intentions, final or otherwise, editing requires the critical engagement of the editor. It is interpretative, and therefore cannot claim to be a precise science or to produce definitive documents. No two editors will edit the same piece in precisely the same way. Moreover, every piece of music is created in a unique combination of cultural, social, historical, and economic circumstances. An acknowledgment of those circumstances, and thus of the uniqueness of each creative product, affects the conception of all editorial projects: each piece, source, and edition is thus a special case. The corollary of this is that different repertories require different editorial methods—even that each edition calls for a unique approach. Every project generates the editorial procedure that best represents the editor's critical engagement with the subject of the edition and its sources.

One principle of editing arises from the rich tradition of textual criticism in philology. Every editorial decision is taken in the context of the editor's understanding of the work as a whole; and that understanding can be achieved only through critical evaluation. The meaning of the work and the reading of the text are complementary and interdependent. Each work and each source originated in a particular historical situation that directly impinges on the editor's understanding and interpretation. The editor assesses the value of source evidence against the background of the larger historical context in which the piece was created.

The meaning of each reading depends on the semiotic nature of musical notation. Notation addresses not the listener but the performer, who stands as the essential intermediary between composer and audience. The written text thus functions as a set of instructions for the performer. These are encoded in notational symbols that carry no intrinsic meaning but depend entirely on their context. For example, the addition of a stem carries no essential meaning that requires a minim to last half as long as a semibreve, but convention dictates it. These conventions operate within a historical framework, so the evaluation of each reading in each source is combined with an understanding of historical context.

Editing depends on the evaluation of readings as good, bad, and indifferent. Some are rejected, others retained. The final arbiter is the editor's taste and his or her sensitivity to musical style, which also exists within historical determinants. What is acceptable for the music of one period does not automatically translate into another. An editor might unhesitatingly supply a missing leading note in a piece by Mozart, for example, but question its necessity in one by Josquin.

From this conceptual framework, a generalized theory for editing can be proposed, within which each editor can develop a particular methodology. While each repertory—indeed, each piece—presents special challenges, there is a common group of problems that underlies the process of editing, irrespective of repertory: the nature and historical situation of the sources; how they relate to one another; the nature and historical situation of the work; how the sources shape editorial decisions; the most effective way of presenting the edited text.

No edition is definitive. New investigations of well-known sources continue to yield insight into the works they transmit in direct proportion to the imagination and erudition of the investigators. Moreover, though few startling discoveries remain to be made, many known sources suffer from unjust neglect or under-appreciation. All sources have a dual existence: as historical documents and as the repositories of readings. Each, as a physical artefact, originated in a particular historical context which affects its value and significance. The authenticity of individual readings, however, still needs verification, regardless of the authenticity of the source: not every reading in a given source carries equal merit.

The principal task when primary sources are used in editing is transcription. No transcription is objective. Scholars form and impose their interpretations as they transcribe, applying sense, reason, and logic to the notational symbols. That imposition, however, has the potential to distort the source's evidence and so make it that much more difficult to assess its importance. A diplomatic transcription (one that records the information given in the source exactly as it appears with as many details as possible) is one solution.

Tracing the relationships between sources and the historical assessment of readings can be facilitated by stemmatic filiation. This often controversial process, while providing a powerful tool for the classification of readings and sources, by no means constitutes a mechanical method for reconstructing lost sources. In its simplest form, textual errors that are shared by two or more sources allow the editor to deduce the existence of a single ancestor common to those sources that share the error and unknown to those that do not. The identification of error depends on the editor's sensitivity to style, so this process too is interpretative.

The editor has a mass of material from which the text is now extracted. The evidence collected is not simply a set of neutral facts but has been shaped by the critical processes involved in its collection, from the selection of sources to the methods of transcription and the classification of the sources.

Because the relationship between the act of composition and the transmission of the resulting piece is infinitely variable, the procedure followed in treating the sources and their readings will vary according to the editor's perception of that relationship. Accordingly no attempt is made to acknowledge every possibility. Moreover, no single editorial theory can satisfactorily accommodate the multiplicity of situations that arise in editing, even though each of the proposed theories of textual criticism has some value in particular contexts. Compositional autographs contain errors; scribes, typographers, and engravers introduce corruptions; and the performing tradition can substantively alter the written record. The attempt, therefore, to reproduce an 'original' or 'definitive' text is often made in vain. Editors are continually asked to reconcile the circumstances of transmission with their historical conception of the piece. The edition, then, marries the most complete knowledge of the text, its composer, and their histories, with the creative and imaginative faculties of the humanistic scholar. Editors should be scientific in their methodology and humanistic in its application.

Critical and historical engagement persists into the phase of shaping the presentation of the text. The first priority is clarity. The editor communicates many different types of information, including pitch, rhythm, metre, instrumentation, tempo, dynamics, articulation, and even greater particulars like bowing, pedalling, registration, breathing, or, in vocal music, literary text. It is the responsibility of the editor to present these disparate elements in such a way that the user can immediately comprehend and coordinate them. A musical score or part is an extremely complex piece of visual communication; the editor should not reduce that complexity but should enable the user to grasp it efficiently.

Critical editions should generate critical users. A critical edition offers guidance from a scholar who has devoted time, energy, and imagination to a piece and whose opinion is therefore worth considering. That is not to say that users must agree with the editor in every particular. But a critical attitude should stimulate a critical response, of which one possible manifestation is a competing edition. And that is the goal of editing: it is the critical investigation of a text and its readings in order to establish the likelihood of their truth within a piece's historical context.

See also AUTOGRAPH; PALAEOGRAPHY; RASTROLOGY; SOURCES.   JG

📖 P. BRETT, 'Text, context, and the early music editor', *Authenticity and Early Music*, ed. N. Kenyon (Oxford, 1988), 83–114 · J. CALDWELL, *Editing Early Music*, Early Music Series, 5 (Oxford, 2/1995) · J. GRIER, *The Critical Editing of Music: History, Method, and Practice* (Cambridge, 1996)

Editio medicaea. The Tridentine gradual. See COUNCIL OF TRENT; PLAINCHANT, 3.

editions, historical and critical. A historical edition may be generally defined as one devoted to a body of work of the past; a critical edition is one based on scholarly evaluation and collation of sources, taking into account variant readings and innumerable aspects of contemporary performance practice (see EDITING). Throughout their existence, historical and critical editions have balanced the dual functions of practical performance and academic study. Different editions strike different balances, and one function usually predominates, but the other is never lost sight of. The model for historical and critical editions of music has always been the critical editing of the literary classics, and it is no accident that they first came into existence only after a widespread sense of a 'classical' tradition of music had been evolved, in mid-18th-century England.

The first example of a critical, historical edition of music was William Boyce's collection *Cathedral Music* (London, 1760–73), which assembled a repertory of anthems and services representing the classical canon of English church music from Tallis, Tye, and Byrd to the recent works of Croft and Weldon. Boyce specifically stated his purpose of publishing this music 'in its original purity', critically edited in score so as to supplant the corrupt versions then current in manuscript parts. Boyce's *Cathedral Music* inaugurated a tradition of historical collections for practical use devoted to particular genres that remains vigorous to the present day. Distinguished collections of continental sacred music from the 16th and 17th centuries were edited by Franz Commer (*Musica sacra*, 1839–42; *Collectio operum musicorum Batavorum saeculi XVI*, 1844–58; *Cantiones XVI, XVII saeculorum*, 1860–87) and Carl Proske (*Musica divina*, 1853–61; continued by J. Schrems and F. X. Haberl, 1865–77). Jean-Baptiste Cartier's *L'Art du violon* (Paris, 1798) includes a wide range of 17th- and 18th-century violin music from Italy, France, and Germany, much of it derived from manuscript sources. *Le Trésor des pianistes*, edited by Aristide and Louise Farrenc (Paris, 1861–74), contains harpsichord and piano music spanning 300 years and had an enormous influence on the reception of early music in the later 19th century.

Another type of historical and critical edition is the didactic anthology. An early example, G. B. Martini's *Essemplare, o sia Saggio fondamentale pratico di contrappunto* (Bologna, 1774–6), is a collection of excerpts from historical works exemplifying advanced contrapuntal techniques. 'Histories of music in examples' form a larger genre. At the beginning of the 19th century the Viennese music-lover Joseph Sonnleithner projected a *Geschichte der Musik in Denkmäler*, which was to be edited by J. N. Forkel; unfortunately the project was abandoned when the plates of the first volume were destroyed in the Napoleonic occupation of Vienna in 1805 (though Forkel's proof copy survived). Other early examples that came to fruition are William Crotch, *Specimens of Various Styles of Music* (London, c.1808–15), and John Stafford Smith, *Musica antiqua: A Selection of Music … from the Commencement of the 12th to the Beginning of the 18th Century* (London, 1812), the latter especially careful and imaginative in its critical methods. Influential later anthologies include Riemann's *Musikgeschichte in Beispielen* (Leipzig, 1912), Arnold Schering's *Geschichte der Musik in Beispielen* (Leipzig, 1931), and Willi Apel's *Historical Anthology of Music* (Cambridge, MA, 1946–50).

A few early composers had issued carefully prepared and controlled editions of their own collected works,

notably Machaut in the mid-14th century and Carpentras in the mid-16th—and arguably Corelli in the early 18th century. The first attempt at an independent edition of the complete works of a major composer was Samuel Arnold's edition of Handel (London, 1787–97), which included most of the oratorios as well as the instrumental and orchestral music before it was suspended for lack of subscribers. Other early efforts towards collected editions of recent composers were also left incomplete, including a somewhat more critical edition of Handel's works based on his autographs (English Handel Society, London, 1843–58).

A new direction and new momentum were given by the project of the Bach-Gesellschaft, which began in 1851 to issue a meticulously prepared edition of the complete works of J. S. Bach. The publishers of this edition, Breitkopf & Härtel in Leipzig, also began truly complete editions (Ger.: *Gesamtausgaben*) of numerous other composers from Palestrina, Lassus, and Victoria to Berlioz, Chopin, and Schumann before the end of the 19th century. Two 20th-century composer editions before World War II that were important forerunners of postwar work were Albert Smijers's edition of Josquin des Prez (Amsterdam, 1921–69) and Friedrich Ludwig's of Machaut (Leipzig, 1926–34), which extended the field of composer editions much earlier than had hitherto been the case.

The last major category of historical and critical editions comprises the national collections of 'monuments' or *Denkmäler*. These open-ended series tend to comprise editions organized according to several different principles, including for example the complete works of national composers (e.g. Cristóbal de Morales within the *Monumentos de la música española*) as well as editions of complete anthological sources (e.g. the *Cancionero musical de palacio* in the same series). An early instance is the publications of the Musical Antiquarian Society (London, 1841–8), which published English secular vocal and instrumental music from the Elizabethan period to Purcell. Most of the monumental series belong to the 20th century, however: the *Denkmäler der Tonkunst in Österreich* and *Les Maitres musiciens de la Renaissance française* began to publish in 1894, *Denkmäler deutscher Tonkunst* in 1901, *I classici della musica italiana* in 1918.

The period after World War II was one of enormous expansion on nearly all fronts. More and more national series were begun, including *Musica britannica* (1951) and *Music of the United States of America* (1977). Series of practical editions of early music, including the pre-war series *Das Chorwerk* (1929) and *Hortus musicus* (1936), continued strongly and were added to by new series such as the *Recent Researches in Music* group (1964) and *Le Pupitre* (1967). Perhaps most important has been the rise of comprehensive international series. A leader in this movement was Les Éditions de l'Oiseau-Lyre, founded in Paris in 1932 by the Australian Louise B. M. Dyer to promote neglected early music from all over Europe; it was followed in 1946 by the American Institute of Musicology, founded by Armen Carapetyan and based in Rome. Both institutions have outlived their founders and continue strongly to the present day, having published an enormous quantity of music from before 1600 in editions of the highest quality. The AIM's most important series, *Corpus mensurabilis musicae*, comprises complete editions of composers' works; it also publishes the *Corpus of Early Keyboard Music*, *Corpus scriptorum de musica* (critical editions of music theory), the monograph series *Musicological Studies and Documents*, and the annual *Musica disciplina*.

Two types of historical and critical edition that have become widespread only during the last half-century or so are editions based on integral sources, which have been particularly encouraged by the series *Monuments of Renaissance Music* (Chicago, 1964–) but are also included in many national monumental collections, and facsimiles of original sources, now published in too many series to name, often with valuable commentaries and indexes.   JJD

📖 J. COOVER, *Gesamtausgaben: A Checklist* (Buffalo, NY, 1970) · S. R. CHARLES, *A Handbook of Music and Music Literature in Sets and Series* (New York, 1972) · A. H. HEYER, *Historical Sets, Collected Editions, and Monuments of Music: A Guide to their Contents* (Chicago, 3/1980) · G. R. HILL and N. L. STEPHENS, *Collected Editions, Historical Series, & Sets & Monuments of Music: A Bibliography* (Berkeley, CA, 1997)

education. 1. Historical background; 2. Philosophies of music education; 3. Principles of music education

1. Historical background

Education and music are closely related. Instances of music-making or writing and talking about music where there is no intended educational outcome are as rare as educational institutions and general curriculum programmes where music has no part.

Many musicians, in any case, are declared teachers, deriving their income partly from initiating others into music; but even those who would deny that they ever 'teach' are not exempt from serving educational purposes. The pianist who adjudicates at a music festival influences the attitudes, skills, and musical understanding of those taking part, whether entrants or audience. An orchestral player may make no direct attempt to educate his or her immediate partner, but may still be a very influential model of tone-quality, phrasing, precision in ensemble, and even of attitude towards the particular pieces in the repertory. The recording-studio engineer who helps a band secure clarity of ensemble, the writer of programme notes, the opera translator, the critic and reviewer, the composer trying to say something new in a work—all these are instances of musicians influencing, or attempting to influence, other people. To attempt to change people by leading them towards some knowledge or skill, or by extending their understanding, is what we mean by education. Viewed in this broad way, education thus inevitably includes a great deal that musicians say and do.

It is equally true that liberal or general educational provision makes room for music. In ancient Greece, its status was possibly higher than at any subsequent period of Western civilization. While today the word 'arts' covers music, dance, the visual arts, and drama, for the Greeks 'music' was the generic term embracing these pursuits. For Plato, physical exercise and music were crucial for the development of young people. The person educated in music would be able to discriminate between the ugly and the beautiful in art and in nature, and rhythm and harmony are thought to enter the soul, 'bearing grace with them'. There are also social and political implications, a belief that any alteration in the modes of music is inevitably followed by radical changes in the laws of the state. We do not know what less exalted Greeks thought about this, but it seems certain that music was widespread and highly regarded, and was taught in more or less systematic ways.

This is not the place for a comprehensive history of music education. It will suffice to note, along with Scholes in earlier editions of this *Companion*, that courtiers in feudal times were instructed in music as one of the arts of chivalry, and that the monasteries and choir schools exerted an educational influence from the 4th to the 16th centuries. In medieval universities, music ranked with arithmetic, geometry, and astronomy in the higher division of the 'seven liberal arts', in marked contrast to its lowly status in present-day curricula. However, in both the Christian and the Islamic worlds, it was the theory, not the practice of music that held sway as an intellectual pursuit. On music in British education during the 16th and 17th centuries, Scholes writes:

> *Mulcaster*, headmaster of Merchant Taylors' School (1561–86) and of St. Paul's School (1596–1608), says of music: 'For my own part I cannot forbear to place it among the most valuable means in the upbringing of the young', and then enlarges on this, discussing the musical curriculum—prick-song (i.e. sight-singing), harmony and composition, virginals and lute, etc. ...
> *Locke* (1693) thinks less of Music: 'A good hand upon some instruments is by many people mightily valued:

but it wastes so much of a young man's time, to gain but a moderate skill in it, and engages often in such odd company ...' and so on! The Golden Age of British music was just ending and the dull 18th century beginning, a century during which music largely dropped out of the British educational curriculum, except as an 'accomplishment' for the young ladies of gentility, or those who wished to be considered such.

These are indeed two contradictory positions with regard to the value of music. Some consider music (among the other arts) essential to a person's education; others believe it to be a pastime, 'innocent luxury'. For the first view it can be argued that music helps to develop general intellectual and social accomplishments and that to study music improves attention and concentration, advancing reading and writing, and even numerical ability. There is some slight evidence that this may be so, but probably 'transfer' effects of this kind result less from the intrinsic nature of music than from any well-structured programme of work, especially with committed and experienced teachers. Besides, such effects should not be used as justification for including a subject in the curriculum. Music is a worthwhile pursuit in its own right, not a 'service activity' helping to secure basic literacy and numeracy.

2. Philosophies of music education

Questions as to the nature and value of music may not always seem of great importance for professional musicians, but teachers are required to negotiate with other colleagues for time, money, and resources: there is a real need to be articulate as to the need for music education and the necessary conditions for bringing it about. On a superficial level it is fairly easy to promote the idea that music has intrinsic value by observing that musical activities, sometimes linked with ceremony, ritual, dance, storytelling, and even magic, can be found in practically all cohesive communities—in other words, in all cultures. If schools and colleges are to base their curricula on the important activities in a culture, then music is an obvious candidate. The real difficulty occurs when we ask the reason why music is so valued. If we are to believe, with Plato, that music's importance lies in its moral effect and that the influence of music on the moral character of people can be ascertained, even down to the level of which particular scale structure underlies particular melodies, then we might decide that some modes are 'slack', while others are acceptable. Immediately a great deal of music becomes unworthy—including all that is written within the framework of what we call the major scale. Although this case is extreme, the past 100 years have witnessed similar forms of musical censorship, including restrictions imposed in Stalinist Russia (see FORMALISM; SOCIALIST

REALISM), approved styles in Communist China, and the widespread disapproval among 'classical' musicians of jazz and the popular musical styles that it influenced.

Where music in schools and colleges is concerned, three less extreme attitudes can be detected, sometimes in public statements and writings but at other times buried in practice and a multitude of curriculum decisions, undeclared, perhaps even unrecognized, as value-systems by those directly involved. The most familiar of the three positions might be called 'subject-centred' or 'traditional'. Pupils are regarded primarily as inheritors of a culture that has grown through the years and been distilled by time. Schools and colleges are seen as important agents in this process of transmission, and teachers are crucial agents in the selection of activities and materials. The teacher decides what is worthwhile, taking into account the wishes of parents, the nature of the institution in which he or she works, and the constraints of other bodies, such as examination boards. Several British educational philosophers have supported this view, which identifies certain forms of knowledge involving characteristic processes and criteria. For example, scientific, mathematical, and philosophical forms of knowledge involve different procedures and tests for truth. Music belongs in the domain of aesthetic or artistic knowledge, and musical education must initiate pupils into recognized musical traditions.

An important feature of this view of the curriculum is that there is no controversy about what is to be learnt. There is a clear commitment to the value of such established skills as playing instruments and gaining musical literacy and familiarity with the masterworks of Western high culture—opera, the symphony, church music, etc. A good example is to be found in the work of *Kodály and the extensive materials which form his choral method. This highly structured, sequential approach aims primarily to develop musicianship through singing, especially sight-singing, but it also involves initiating pupils into folk music (the Hungarian tradition) and the elements of Western instrumental and choral music. In the less rigorous atmosphere of many British classrooms, teachers feel that children should at least come into contact with some 'good' music, should have some idea of how notation functions, should learn to discriminate between the standard instruments, and should know something about important composers and their work. Whenever possible, children are encouraged to take up an instrument, and this is thought to give direct access to the accepted musical tradition.

Another characteristic of this view of music education is an emphasis on testing and examining. Of all the arts, music is the most often and most rigorously examined. Not only does the system of school-leaving examinations embrace music, but there are also vast and independent examination structures for instrumental and vocal performance across the English-speaking world and other parts of the globe, from Britain to Australia. In this examination system the traditional virtues are clearly enshrined. A repertory, which until quite recently was largely rooted in Western art music, is performed on traditionally important instruments, and knowledge of conventional notation is tested under the heading of 'theory'.

A further concern of those committed to the 'subject-centred' or 'traditional' view is the identification of musical potential in the young, in order to foster and develop it through the provision of specialized musical activities, often in specialist schools. This is clearly important, not only for the children concerned but also for the musical life of a country and its standards of excellence.

A number of influential figures have contributed to music education and in particular have reinforced and developed 'traditional' philosophy and practice. Kodály has already been mentioned in connection with singing and sight-singing, but he was influenced by John Curwen's development of *Tonic Sol-fa as a device to develop the ability to read music, particularly by his emphasis on starting with sound, rather than sign, and building up musical imagery, the 'inner ear'. Curwen is often thought to have tried to develop an alternative notation to the staff. This is not so. He emphasized that the object of his method was 'to enable the pupil, more speedily than is usual, to sing at sight from that notation'.

Concern with notation and what has come to be called musical literacy did, however, lead J.-J. Rousseau to devise an alternative system, where pitch relationships were signified by numbers, and durations by lines and dots. Staff notation, he thought, could then be dispensed with, and the processes of printing and reading music made easier. The direct educational implications of this idea for sight-singing were taken up in the 19th century by Pierre Galin, Aimé Paris, and Émile Chevé in France (see GALIN-PARIS-CHEVÉ SYSTEM). In their teaching method there is again a stress on imagery: even the elementary pupils of Chevé were required to 'think' notes, as well as to sing them. Since that time there have been several attempts to develop systematic courses of music training, usually linked to notation and related to the mainstream of Western music. The American music educationist Justine Ward (1879–1975) produced a vocally based method, which has been influential in several countries, especially among teachers of younger children.

Perhaps the largest single influences on music education were the development of the radio and gramophone during the first half of the 20th century and of computer technology during the second. For many teachers, the advent of radio and gramophone indicated a change in the balance of classroom activities, though at that time no revision of the traditional aims of music teaching was suggested. In particular, the work of Stewart Macpherson (1865–1941) and Scholes himself directed attention to the possibilities of developing informed and discriminating listening. Scholes believed that the dissemination of music through the new media opened up tremendous possibilities for mass education, not only in schools and colleges but also more generally through the radio. (*The Oxford Companion to Music* itself was intended to be read with profit by both the expert and the amateur; one of its functions was to illuminate and inform those who were becoming aware of a world of music hitherto unavailable.) The 'listener' came into being along with what has been called the *'appreciation' movement.

This electronic revolution also nurtured seeds that were eventually to grow into challenging alternatives to the traditional view of music education. Music itself began to change rapidly once electronic transmission, recording, and sound generation became possible. On another level, Carl Seashore (1866–1949) systematically devised *tests of what he called musical 'talent', including measures of pitch, timbre, and loudness discriminations, all made possible by electronics and the availability of calibrated sound sources. Music educationists began to consider more precise assessments of pupil potential and the diagnosis of problems using quasi-scientific methodologies. At this time, then, we perceive an opening up of infinite and often controversial possibilities as composers begin to 'experiment' with sound, and simultaneously a tendency to identify ability on what is usually regarded as a sub-musical level. Both developments seem more concerned with isolated notes than musically coherent tunes.

At first, electronic hardware and its necessary and related skills had little effect on music education. However, the 1960s saw the emergence of a new generation of musical educationists keen to embrace the new opportunities for electronic composing which challenged teachers to extend their repertory and even to redefine the musical tradition. The advent of cheap and easily available synthesizers, computers, and digital technology rapidly accelerated this development and created opportunities for making music more widespread than ever before. There is a bigger sound palette now accessible on a typical home computer than was ever available to the pioneering composers working in German electronic studios in the 1950s. In the 1980s, British schools and colleges embraced the musical possibilities afforded by the new technology, supported by grants for computer equipment and software that vastly exceeded anything that had been given for the more traditional 'acoustic' musical activities.

The 20th century saw major advances in technology, which assisted in the 'democratization' of musical learning. Equally important, however, was the influence of thinkers who reflected on the way in which we can all learn to enhance our musicality. The Swiss educationist Émile Jaques-Dalcroze (1865–1950) is best known for his development of *'eurhythmics', which many people take to be an educational method linking physical movement and music. This is partly true, but his thinking was more complex. He found music students lacking in fluency and expressiveness. Certain techniques might have been mastered, but where was the feeling of musical involvement and sensitivity? Dalcroze observed that musical performance fundamentally depended on movement and that when students moved with music they performed in a more vital way. He wanted his pupils to 'feel' music through movement.

Over 100 years previously, Rousseau, in a broader educational context, sowed the seeds of what is sometimes called the 'child-centred' view of education. It is easy to oversimplify here, but basically the emphasis is away from the tradition, or the subject, and towards the natural development of children, towards those same things that Dalcroze valued: expression, feeling, involvement. With the younger child in mind, and with no particular focus on music, Johann Heinrich Pestalozzi (1746–1827) and Friedrich August Wilhelm Froebel (1782–1852) took up these ideals. In the 20th century, teachers of art and drama have developed similar ideas and, eventually, music found its first 'progressive' educationist, Carl *Orff (1895–1982).

Orff was born in Germany and first became known as a composer. Between 1948 and 1954 his reputation as an educationist began to spread internationally. His ideas were coloured by those of Dalcroze and involve a synthesis of performance through instruments and voice, aural training, movement, and improvisation. His approach is based on direct and immediate involvement with music from the first encounter, and it is music for everyone, in classes, with contributions at whatever level an individual can offer. The prime aim is to develop improvisation through the gradual extension of performing skills and the development of musical imagination.

The materials developed by Orff in the late 1940s derived from folksong traditions of both East and West, especially the use of the pentatonic scale. 20 years later, and in other hands, this emphasis had changed, though the improvisatory or 'creative' principles were carried forward. It began to be argued that music education had lagged behind the other arts and was living in the past. Children should not only be creative but should also use the techniques and sound resources of contemporary composers. In Britain the most influential advocate was John Paynter, a composer who worked at York University and directed the Schools Council Project, Music in the Secondary School Curriculum, from 1973 to 1982. Like Orff, Paynter was committed to the ideal of music education for everyone, not just the gifted or socially advantaged. In Canada, Murray Schafer took up the same cause, adding to it a particular emphasis on respect for an acoustic environment that was becoming increasingly polluted by noise. In the USA, Ronald Thomas articulated in detail the implications for the school music curriculum in the *Manhattanville Music Curriculum Program* (1970).

One consequence of these developments is a change in the teacher's role. The traditional view that teachers knew what pupils had to learn, and would direct and organize the activities through which learning was to take place, has given way to the view that pupils should take the initiative, making decisions about what is required in their composition, rehearsing it, and often performing to other groups who will have been working at the same time. The teacher's role is to stimulate—to question and advise, rather than to show and tell. These group compositions may or may not be notated; if they are, a variety of notations may be used, from the staff to grids or graphic analogies to the sounds. Such scores sometimes may resemble those of the so-called European and American avant-garde composers of the 1950s and 60s.

So far we have considered aspects of the 'traditional' view of music education and the 'child-centred' view. There remains a third and more recent concept of music education. With the progressive raising of the school-leaving age, with the growth and decay of inner-city areas, and with the increased migration of people into Europe, Australia, and the USA, it is often impossible to specify the common cultural tradition of a school community. The divergent musical interests of older students, especially those from differing ethnic and social backgrounds, have presented teachers with problems. If there is a common culture, it is transmitted through the media of radio, television, and the compact disc. What is the music teacher to do when students come to school and college steeped in current popular musical styles? The traditional answer is to ignore it, hoping that it will go away. Another solution has been to sidestep the issue, by assuming that such music is a 'social' rather than an artistic phenomenon, and to concentrate instead on beginning again with the exploration of 'sound' rather than specific, recognizable idioms. Yet since the 1960s, when the Beatles demonstrated beyond contention that commercial styles and artistic quality were compatible, there has been a growing acceptance of the richness to be found in students' diverse backgrounds. The mass media go some way towards making a general, communal, shared experience—an amplified folk culture, orally transmitted and aurally received, woven into the fabric of people's daily lives. A teacher would surely be wrong to ignore this widely shared tradition. In any event, it is salutary to observe how much children learn through the mass media without anyone to teach them.

3. Principles of music education

In the UK, during the closing years of the 20th century, there was an increasing pressure on educational institutions to be publicly accountable. Far-reaching reforms in school assessment and examining procedures, and the establishment in 1991 of a National Curriculum, gave music educationists an opportunity to establish principles that would form a basis for musical education. The 'attainment targets' set out in the National Curriculum—performing, composing, listening, and appraising—gave a clear planning structure that focused on gaining musical experience rather than transmitting second-hand information. The National Curriculum draws on best practice in schools, carefully combining elements of a range of educational philosophies. Underpinning its thinking, as with all schemes to promote useful learning, are some fundamental principles to guide teachers, whether working with the well motivated, the reluctant, or the talented, with the individual pupil, classes in school, or in further education.

Everyone needs to experience achievement, and people taking part in music lessons are no exception. This does not necessarily mean achievement in terms of tests or examinations, but in day-to-day encounters with music. If motivation is to be sustained there has to be an increasing sense of mastery and understanding. All normal human beings need and want to learn, unless repeated failure distorts this drive. Schools have sometimes been places where pupils learn to fail—indeed where teachers also fail—because of the great difficulties involved in organizing learning for large groups of people whose attendance may be reluctant but compulsory.

The effective teacher recognizes what the psychologist Jerome Bruner has called 'the natural energies that sustain spontaneous learning'—curiosity, a desire to be competent, a strong tendency to emulate others, and a need for social interaction. Curiosity is not aroused by dictating notes on the history of music, or by telling pupils what to listen for, or by treating a performing group as a kind of mechanical organ; it can be aroused by asking questions, by discussion, by listening to music before talking about it, by involving people in making decisions about the music they perform, and through composing or improvising. The National Curriculum has assisted teachers by creating a framework of clear and manageable objectives. Above all, learning about music involves having good models: does a pupil hear others perform or listen to their compositions? Is the teacher a model of sensitive musical behaviour? Would recognition of the need for social interaction cause us to organize more ensembles or to teach instruments in groups?

That music-teaching must involve direct musical experience may seem obvious, but research has indicated that teachers often avoid music itself, emphasizing instead such features as historical periods, analysis of form, instruments of the orchestra, acoustics, the lives of famous musicians, the theory of notation. Music thus becomes something to be talked about rather than experienced as composer, performer, and listener. Even when music teachers have striven to engage students in creating and handling sounds in the classroom, often using a wide range of acoustic and electronic resources, the results have often been less than musical. But when such activities have been undertaken in a structured way, as part of a broad programme, and when the teacher has expected progression and development, children have gained a great deal.

In a similar way, the teaching of instruments has often concentrated on the acquisition of notational, aural, and technical skills—an overemphasis noted by Scholes. Skills are important, but more so are musical understanding, sensitivity, and enjoyment. If a pupil can only just manage the technique required for a difficult work it is unlikely that there will be a capacity for making musical decisions. There may be only one speed at which the playing is secure, the rhythms may be so tenuously grasped that any suggestion of rubato would be fatal; there will hardly be time to listen. Yet a number of smaller works, below a student's technical ceiling, would give endless scope for musical development and help technical security. What would happen if we played a work quicker or slower, louder or softer, more or less legato? Could we make up a short piece using some of the techniques and ideas found in a particular composition? Can we write down one of the themes from memory? Can we transpose it? What kind of chords are used? Is one piece like or unlike another? In this way we are looking for a broad musical education, developing a range of skills, understanding, and attitudes.

Not only should direct experience of music be a prime concern, but this experience should be over the widest possible range. We are bombarded with music from over the centuries and across a vast social and cultural spectrum. Our environment is now more polluted with noise than at any previous time. Do we listen, or merely overhear? It is all too easy to muster music under this or that stylistic flag without giving any attention to the qualities of a particular work, the integrity of this fugue or that slow passage. Listening critically is an act of the imagination, and education must have a crucial role in informing and promoting this skill.

If we reflect on the work of the best teachers, the most influential music educationists, we find that the principle of achievement and the principle of direct musical experience are fundamental to their success. Some system (any method will do provided it is systematic) gives shape and purpose to the teaching and learning and makes achievement possible, and recognizable. The effective teacher is also realistic in assessing what pupils can do and is ambitious for their development. But running in counterpoint with any system or way of working will be the question: is it musical? Is there a sense of structure and a feeling for expressive character in what is done or said? To watch an effective music educationist at work (rather than a mere trainer) is to observe a strong sense of musical intention linked with educational purpose: skills are used for musical ends, factual knowledge informs musical understanding.

The ultimate aim is the development of a rich and wide appreciation, whether the student becomes a professional musician, a gifted amateur, or a responsive listener. Such appreciation offers not only instantaneous delight, but also gives insights into the realm of human feeling. Among the other arts, music can truly claim to be a way of knowing. However, such knowing is not purely instinctive or inherited. The ability to appreciate music is largely learnt, beyond certain fairly basic responses. Music educationists have the task of bringing about such learning: in doing so they inevitably and incidentally bring about initiation into traditions, the development of imaginative and creative potential, and insights into and empathy with a range of other cultures.   KS/PSp

📖 B. RAINBOW, *Music in Educational Thought and Practice* (Aberystwyth, 1989) · K. SWANWICK, *Musical Knowledge: Intuition, Analysis and Music Education* (London, 1994)

Edwards [Edwardes], Richard (*b* Somerset, March 1525; *d* London, 31 Oct. 1566). English writer and musician. From Oxford, where he was educated, he moved to London, becoming a member of the Chapel Royal by 1558, and Master of the Choristers in 1561. Edwards is best known today as a poet, and in his lifetime was also

prominent as a dramatist, writing and producing plays and other entertainments for his choirboys to perform. A few songs by him survive, and there is a Latin-texted motet that may be his work.   JM

effects. A term used for the many noise-makers in the percussionist's kit. In jazz bands it includes *cowbells, *woodblocks, *temple blocks, *washboards, and so on. In the nightclubs of the 1930s, and still in pit orchestras, the term embraces hooters, whistles, squeakers, *whips, *rattles, and other sound effects to enliven the musical scene, as well as special instruments for solo 'spots', such as the musical *saw.   JMo

Egdon Heath. Orchestral work, op. 47 (1927), by Holst; subtitled 'Homage to Hardy', it was inspired by a passage in Thomas Hardy's *The Return of the Native* (1878) describing the Dorset landscape.

Egk [Mayer], Werner (*b* Auchsesheim, Bavaria, 17 May 1901; *d* Inning, nr Munich, 10 July 1983). German composer. Though briefly a pupil of Orff, he was largely self-taught. He worked for Bavarian radio (1923–33) and came to prominence with his radio opera *Columbus* (1932, revised for the stage in 1942). His opera *Die Zaubergeige* ('The Magic Violin', 1935) made him successful in the Third Reich, though some have seen elements of subversion in his work from the period. Adverse critical reaction to his opera *Peer Gynt* (1938, after Ibsen) was quashed when the Nazi authorities championed the piece. Egk was appointed Kapellmeister at the Berlin Staatsoper, 1936–40, then in 1941 head of the composers' section of Goebbels's Reichsmusikkammer. From 1950 to 1953 he was director of the Berlin Hochschule für Musik. He was primarily a dramatic composer drawing on mainstream European literature, his style, influenced by Stravinsky, being essentially polytonal and often marked by caustic wit. His later operas include *Irische Legende* (1955, after Yeats), *Der Revisor* ('The Government Inspector', 1957, after Gogol), and *Die Verlobung in San Domingo* ('The Betrothal in Santo Domingo', 1963, after Kleist).
                                                                   PG/TA

églogue (Fr.). 'Eclogue'.

Egmont. Overture and incidental music, op. 84 (1809–10), by Beethoven, composed for Johann Wolfgang von Goethe's play; the overture is often performed separately.

eguale (It., 'equal'). See EQUALE.

Egyptian music. See ANCIENT MESOPOTAMIAN AND EGYPTIAN MUSIC.

E.H. Abbreviation for *englisches Horn* or English horn, i.e. cor anglais.

Eichner, Ernst (Dietrich Adolph) (*b* Arolsen, *bapt*. 15 Feb. 1740; *d* Potsdam, early 1777). German bassoonist and composer. He was a member of the orchestra at Zweibrücken in 1762, becoming its Konzertmeister in 1769. In 1770 he travelled to Paris with Duke Christian IV of Zweibrücken, but two years he later left the duke's service and made an extended tour to London, where he played the bassoon in J. C. Bach's subscription concerts. In 1773 he joined the musical establishment of Prince Friedrich Wilhelm (later King of Prussia). According to Burney, Eichner was an excellent bassoonist; he was also a composer of merit, writing several symphonies (which show a highly developed conception of sonata form) and concertos.   DA

1812. Concert overture, op. 49 (1880), by Tchaikovsky; written for the Moscow Exhibition, it commemorates Napoleon's retreat from Moscow in 1812 and incorporates *La Marseillaise* and the Tsarist national anthem. The original idea was for it to be performed in a Moscow square with large orchestra, military band, cathedral bells, and cannon fire. It is sometimes still performed with a cannon (especially at the popular Tchaikovsky evenings in the Royal Albert Hall, London, and at summer concerts outdoors).

eighth-note (Amer.). Quaver.

Eight Songs for a Mad King. Music-theatre piece by Maxwell Davies to a libretto by Randolph Stow and King George III; in eight movements, it is for a male actor-singer and ensemble (including railway whistle, didjeridu, and chains) (London, 1969).

Eile, mit (Ger.). 'With haste'; *eilend*, 'hurrying'; *eilig*, 'quick'.

Eimert, Herbert (*b* Bad Kreuznach, 8 April 1897; *d* Cologne, 15 Dec. 1972). German composer. He studied in Cologne at the Musikhochschule and the university (1919–30). In 1924 he published a treatise on atonality, and he used serial techniques in his First String Quartet (1925). Later writings included two books on 12-note procedures and many influential articles on electronic music. His output remained small until, in 1951, he helped found a studio for electronic music at the Cologne radio station, where he was soon joined by Stockhausen; together they edited the important journal *Die Reihe*, and their joint efforts placed Cologne in a central position for avant-garde developments. There Eimert produced some of the first works in which sound is synthesized purely by electronic means (*Glockenspiel*, 1953; *Etüde über Tongemische*, 1953–4) and made effective use of the speaking voice as a sound source in *Epitaph für Aikichi Kuboyama* (1958–

62). He later taught at the Cologne Conservatory and ran the electronic music studio there (1965–71).   PG

Einem, Gottfried von (*b* Berne, 24 Jan. 1918; *d* Oberdürnbach, nr Maissau, 12 July 1996). Austrian composer. He studied with Boris Blacher (1941–3) and worked as a lecturer for the Vienna Konzerthaus Gesellschaft (1946–66), an administrator of the Salzburg Festival (1946–66), and a teacher of composition at the Vienna Music Academy (1963–72). He gained early success with his ballet *Prinzessin Turandot* (Dresden, 1944) and opera *Dantons Tod* (Salzburg, 1947) and repeated those successes with later works for the theatre, especially the operas *Der Prozess* (after Franz Kafka; Salzburg, 1953), *Der Zerrissene* (Hamburg, 1964), and *Der Besuch der alten Dame* (Vienna, 1971). His music is sharply dramatic, with an extended tonality that stems from Stravinsky, modified by his involvement at Salzburg with Mozart's operas.   PG

📖 D. HARTMANN, *Gottfried von Einem* (Vienna, 1968)

einfach (Ger.). 'Simple'.

Ein' feste Burg (ist unser Gott) ('A safe stronghold (is our God)'). Lutheran Reformation hymn, a setting of Psalm 46 to a tune adapted from a plainchant melody. Bach used it in his Cantata no. 80 and it has been quoted in several other works including Meyerbeer's *Les Huguenots*, Mendelssohn's 'Reformation' Symphony, and Wagner's *Kaisermarsch*.

Einigkeit und Recht und Freiheit ('Unity, justice, and freedom'). German national anthem. The words, from a poem of aspiration for the unity of the German peoples, written before the revolutions of 1848, are by August Heinrich Hoffmann von Fallersleben (1798–1874) from a poem by Walther von der Vogelweide. It is sung to the tune Haydn wrote for the Austrian national anthem (see EMPEROR'S HYMN). In 1922 it was adopted by Germany, Hoffmann von Fallersleben's poem beginning with the words 'Deutschland über alles', and from 1933 it was sung in conjunction with the Nazi party Horst Wessel Song. In 1950 the Federal Republic replaced the first verse with the third; the German Democratic Republic the previous year adopted its own anthem, *Auferstanden aus Ruinen*. *Einigkeit und Recht und Freiheit* is the anthem of the reunited Germany.   AL

Einklang (Ger.). 'Unison'.

Einleitung (Ger.). 'Introduction'.

Einsatz (Ger.). 'Attack', 'entrance' (of an orchestral part).

Einstein on the Beach. Opera in four acts and five 'knee plays' (intermezzos) by Glass and Robert Wilson to a libretto by Christopher Knowles, Lucinda Childs, and Samuel M. Johnson (Avignon, 1976).

einstimmig (Ger.). 'One-voiced', i.e. *monophonic.

Eintritt (Ger.). 'Entrance', of a fugue subject or a soloist in a concerto.

Eis (Ger.). The note E♯; *Eisis*, the note E✗.

Eisler, Hanns (*b* Leipzig, 6 July 1898; *d* Berlin, 6 Sept. 1962). German composer. He was brought up in Vienna and initially studied there at the conservatory. From 1919 to 1923 he was a pupil of Schoenberg, whose influence is strong in his early works, such as *Palmström* ('Palm Stream', 1924) for reciter and instrumentalists. A committed socialist, he believed that music should be accessible to the proletariat; this led him away from the Second Viennese School, and in 1929 he began to work with Brecht, turning to the composition of political choruses, protest songs, theatre music, and film scores in a pungent, combative style.

With the Nazi acquisition of power in 1933 Eisler was obliged to leave Germany, and after various travels arrived in New York in 1938. While in the USA he taught and continued to compose in his political style. Moving to Los Angeles in 1942, he also experimented with new techniques of film composition, though the masterpiece of his American period is *The Hollywood Songbook* (1942–3), a powerful musical diary of his experience of exile. He was called to account by Senator McCarthy in 1947 and forced to leave the USA the following year, returning first to Vienna, then, in 1950, to East Berlin, where he renewed his collaboration with Brecht and created music in a popular style for immediate use. His late output included the national anthem for the German Democratic Republic and over 600 songs of various types. Charges of *formalism forced him to abandon his opera *Johannes Faustus* in 1953, though the Communist authorities continued to treat him as a national figure. He died disillusioned after the revelation of Stalinist atrocities.　　PG/TA

eisteddfod (Welsh, 'session', from *eistedd*, 'to sit'). A competitive festival devoted to music, dance, and poetry, held generally throughout Wales and among Welsh communities. Its origins lie in the irregular gatherings of medieval bards, and attempts to revive that tradition in the late 18th and early 19th centuries, allied to an evocation of bardic ritual, led to the establishment of the annual National Eisteddfod in 1880. See WALES, 3.　　KC

élargissant (Fr.). 'Broadening', i.e. *allargando.

electric bass guitar [bass guitar]. A solid-bodied *electric guitar with four strings, tuned like the *double bass (*E′–A′–D–G*). The first bass guitar, the Fender Precision Bass designed by Leo Fender, was introduced in 1951, with a string length of 34″ (865 mm, rather shorter than that of the double bass). It was designed to match the volume and complement the powerful tone of the electric guitar. It has been widely adopted in most forms of popular music. Fretless electric basses were introduced in 1966 by Ampeg, and 'headless' models, with the headstock removed and tuners set in the body, were introduced in 1979 by Ned Steinberger. Acoustic bass guitars, which combine the stringing of the bass guitar with the resonator of the acoustic guitar, began to appear in the 1970s.　　RPA

electric guitar. An electronically amplified guitar. The vibrations of the strings are converted into electrical impulses by transducers consisting of built-in electromagnetic pickups; the impulses are passed via a cable to an external amplifier, and thence to a loudspeaker. The pickups usually consist of six magnetic polepieces surrounded by a coil of wire, one under each string. Special effects (reverb, overdrive, wah-wah, and fuzz, for example) may be added by pedals plugged between the instrument and the amplifier, or in some cases they may be incorporated into the amplifier.

Experiments with crude pickups and air microphones on guitars go back to the early 1920s, and the first commercially manufactured electric guitars, the Rickenbacker A22 and A23, were introduced in 1931 by the Electro String Instrument Company. These were hollow-bodied 'lap steel' or Hawaiian guitars, played with the instrument resting on the player's lap and the strings stopped with a steel bar held in the left hand. The Gibson company introduced an electric Spanish guitar in 1935 or 1936. Hollow-bodied (or 'semi-acoustic') electric guitars, such as those made by Gretsch, have continued to be used, particularly in jazz and country music, though fashion soon turned towards solid-bodied electric guitars. Acoustic guitars may be amplified by placing a contact microphone inside the body. In 1969 Ovation introduced their electric–acoustic hybrid with a shallow, plastic-backed resonator and a built-in pickup.

Solid-bodied electric guitars, where the body contributes little resonance of itself but simply anchors the strings under tension and carries the bridge and the electronic parts, were first marketed in 1948 by Fender (the Fender Broadcaster, renamed the Telecaster in 1950). This was followed by the Gibson Les Paul guitar (1952), designed by Gibson for the American jazz guitarist and inventor Paul, and the Fender Stratocaster (1954). The latter had three pickups and a 'tremolo arm' for pitch-bending effects. These three models are still made, almost unchanged except for a few refinements. Their designs have been copied continually, with or without variation, by countless makers. Perhaps the most important subsequent development is the 'humbucking' pickup, invented in 1955 by Seth Lover and introduced on most Gibson electric guitars; it uses two coils instead of one to eliminate interference and hum, and changes the sound by reducing the response to high frequencies. The electric guitar has become a ubiquitous presence in virtually all forms of popular music. RPA

electric piano. An electronically amplified keyboard instrument which produces piano-like sounds. The Neo-Bechstein piano of the 1930s, developed under the direction of Walther Nernst in Berlin, had strings but no soundboard; electromagnets picked up the vibration of each string, as on an electric guitar. Oska Vierling's Elektrochord of 1936 was similar. A later development, the most widely used of which was the Rhodes (or Fender-Rhodes) electric piano introduced in 1965, had tuned steel bars or reeds instead of strings; when struck by a felt-covered hammer, these vibrated in a polarized electrical field.

Electric pianos have been almost entirely superseded by fully electronic pianos, introduced in the 1980s; in these the sound is generated by electronic oscillators, originally by digital synthesis but now using sampled sounds, which can accurately reproduce the tone of both acoustic and electric pianos. 'Classic' electric pianos such as the Fender-Rhodes, with their characteristic sounds, have become collectors' items and are occasionally used by musicians wishing to replicate the sounds of the 1960s and 70s. JMo, RPA

Electrification of the Soviet Union, The. Opera in two acts by Osborne to a libretto by Craig Raine after Boris Pasternak's novel *The Last Summer* and his poem *Spectorsky* (Glyndebourne, 1987).

electroacoustic music. Music that puts electro-acoustics, defined in *Chambers Dictionary* as 'the technology of converting acoustic energy into electrical energy and vice versa', to creative, artistic use. It is now the preferred term for music which involves the combination of instrumental or vocal sounds with the electronic (often computer-assisted) manipulation of those sounds, or with sounds pre-recorded on tape. 'Electroacoustic' may, strictly speaking, be a tautology, since all sound, electronic or otherwise, has an acoustic element; but dictionaries increasingly include 'of mu-

sical instruments, not electric' (e.g. an acoustic guitar or piano) in their definitions of 'acoustic', to underline the sense of opposition as much as connection between the two components of the term in a post-1950 context. Other aspects of the varied terminologies applied to this repertory will be noted below.

The experience of listening to music changed radically during the 20th century as the result of developments in sound reproduction and transmission that had, by the end of the century, reached the relative sophistication of digital recording and compact- or mini-disc reproduction. These developments would have been impossible without electricity as prime power source, and with hindsight it seems inevitable that composers would follow performers and recording engineers into the increasingly complex and ever-changing world of electronic reproduction and information technology. Changes in ways of reproducing and transmitting musical sounds generated interest in new ways of creating sounds themselves and of organizing them into musical compositions. As early as 1907, reports about the American inventor Thaddeus Cahill's 200-ton dynamophone, or telharmonium, excited the interest of Busoni, as he sought, in his *Sketch for a New Aesthetic of Music*, to envisage how the art might progress in a genuinely modern manner.

From the time, during the first half of the 20th century, when instruments powered by electricity—not just the organ, but the ondes martenot and vibraphone, among others—were used alongside traditional instruments and voices (in Messiaen's *Turangalîla-symphonie*, 1946–8, for example), there was a tendency to regard instruments dependent on electric power as more artificial, more mechanical, less responsive to human touch, than the traditional, purely acoustic kind. The eagerness with which the possibilities of brashly amplified sound were taken up by pop and rock musicians—even the relatively gentle vibraphone was first used in jazz—was one reason for regarding their potential in more 'serious' contexts with deep suspicion. By contrast, composers sympathetic to electronic or electrically powered instruments—Stockhausen, above all—tended to regard them as extending and transforming traditional sounds in well-nigh visionary ways. It was this view of electroacoustic techniques which, in the later decades of the century, superseded the more radical attitudes of the 1950s, when it had been possible to believe that electronic sound might need to replace traditional sound altogether if music were to move forward in an appropriately progressive manner.

The early experiments of the postwar decades in Europe (Paris, Cologne) and the USA (Princeton) had their origins in the exploration of *musique concrète*, the making of compositions from the juxtaposition and manipulation of what were often 'everyday' sounds, recorded 'in the field' and taken into the studio for reassembly on to tape or disc, or both. Even at this stage, however, the initiatives of Pierre *Schaeffer and his colleagues at the Club d'Essai in Paris from 1948, beginning with various 'concrete' tape pieces, such as *Étude violette* and *Étude aux tourniquets*, were soon complemented by initiatives in the combination or juxtaposition of taped and live sounds; Maderna's *Musica su due dimensioni* for flute and tape (1952) and Varèse's *Déserts* (1949–54) for orchestra and organized sound on tape are the earliest significant instances.

Such pioneering works can appear primitive by the technological standards of later decades. Yet one can still marvel at the aesthetic impact of what could be achieved with relatively limited resources—for example, by Varèse in his tape piece *Poème électronique* (1957–8), or by Stockhausen in *Gesang der Jünglinge* (1955–6), conceived and executed within four short years of the composer's first encounter with the medium. Fundamental to the success of this work is Stockhausen's technical mastery of the means of 'modulating' between electronically generated sounds (sine tones and other materials) and the recorded voice of the boy soprano, and the building up of a multi-layered form to be projected over five (originally six) channels in the auditorium.

Significantly, however, Stockhausen himself soon moved away from the idea of keeping electronic and 'live' music separate. *Kontakte* (1959–60) was first conceived as a self-contained work on four-channel tape, but Stockhausen also devised a version in which piano and percussion play along with the tape. Such a hybrid concept has its limitations, not least because the pre-recorded tape could obviously not adapt itself in performance to any momentary inflections from the live players—a factor which irritated Boulez in particular. From the mid-1960s, therefore, Stockhausen's energies were devoted to the possibilities of what is often termed—with due acknowledgment of the ambiguity—live electronic music. The first example, *Mikrophonie I* (1964), involves the real-time transformation and manipulation of the sound produced by (and from) a large tam-tam. *Mikrophonie I* set the standard for a type of performance in which one individual, often the composer, controls the sound-diffusion from a mixing desk at the centre of the auditorium; despite the enormous changes in technology since the 1960s, this has remained the most common mode of electroacoustic musical performance, giving audiences a vivid visual sense of the interaction, and symbiosis, between technology and human performers.

Later composers have occasionally sought to make aesthetic capital from the relative purity of a conception committed to tape which is then transmitted in concert with no 'performer' involved other than the sound engineer; Jonathan Harvey's *Mortuos plango, vivos voco* (1980) is a notably successful example. Nevertheless, the subtitle of that work—'for computer-manipulated concrete sounds on pre-recorded quadraphonic tape'—points to the fundamental technological changes that had been taking place since the 1950s. In 1964 the first commercial, mass-produced, transistorized synthesizer became available, and in 1976 Boulez founded the Institut de Recherche et de Coordination Acoustique/Musique (IRCAM) in Paris, specifically to explore the possibilities of then-new computer technology to advance beyond what from Boulez's point of view had, until that point, been an impossibly primitive phase in the development of essentially new ways of creating sounds and composing with those sounds. IRCAM has offered many composers, from Berio to George Benjamin, Harvey to York Höller, unrivalled opportunities to experiment and to complete important projects. Though subject to the political pressures and ideological tensions of any large-scale institution at the heart of contemporary culture, it has done much to ensure that electroacoustic music has not only survived but prospered, artistically as well as technologically.

With various major, ongoing works—'. . . *explosante-fixe* . . .', *Répons*—Boulez himself has shown how he sees the possibilities for cooperation and interaction between live sounds and 'real-time' computer manipulation of those sounds. The effect in *Répons* (begun in 1981), for example, is of 'normal' instrumental sonorities enhanced and extended, and of compositional processes which are in no way cancelled out or contradicted by technological priorities. Such works offer enthralling aural experiences to a 'live' audience, and, to the extent that they depend on live performance and diffusion, they also reinforce the validity of traditional concert contexts and venues. For other composers, too, the experience of working at IRCAM (or at other well-endowed institutes like that at Stanford University, California) has encouraged explorations of the acoustic formation of sound itself—its reverberations or spectra. The more recent compositions of Harvey, Tristan Murail, and Kaija Saariaho share this fascination with the complex inner structures of particular sonorities, and the ways in which those structures can be exploited in compositions involving the manipulation and transformation of instrumental and vocal sounds. The fact that such technical work on sound spectra has influenced the sonorities and structures of purely acoustic music is testimony to the healthy state of stylistic pluralism at the beginning of the new millennium, and the stimulus provided to all kinds of music by electroacoustic technology is a vital contributor to this plurality.   AW

📖 P. MANNING, *Electronic and Computer Music* (Oxford, 1993)

electronic music. See ELECTROACOUSTIC MUSIC.

electronic musical instruments. A large group of instruments comprising those in which sound is generated by conventional means but then amplified, moderated, and otherwise manipulated electronically ('electroacoustic' instruments), and those in which sound is generated purely by electronic means. In a middle ground are those instruments in which sound, though produced purely electronically, was initially provided by recording (*'sampling') some other instrument. Some electronic organs, for example, contain the complete repertory of sounds recorded from a normal pipe organ, and regurgitate these on demand. Many samplers depend on sounds recorded or installed from other instruments.

The best-known electronically amplified instrument is the *electric guitar, but most instruments have been so amplified in one way or another. The electric violin (more rarely viola and cello) can, in skilled hands, produce a range of sounds undreamt of by Stradivari. Flutes can be fitted with a microphone in place of the cork in the head joint, and many instruments can have a microphone attached, though it often takes considerable trial and error to determine the best type of microphone and its most effective position. Once this is done, the initial sound is fed through amplifiers, fuzz boxes, reverberation and delay circuits, and all the other tools of the sound engineer to produce a wide variety of effects. With digital computerization most instruments can now be incorporated into *MIDI systems so that what starts as a single sound can be transmuted into that of a full orchestra or almost anything the player or controller can imagine.

The first electronic instrument was Thaddeus Cahill's dynamophone or telharmonium, made in three versions between 1895 and 1911, which produced musical sounds by rotating toothed wheels near electromagnets, the resulting pure sounds being combined in appropriate combinations to resemble those of ordinary instruments. Weighing over 200 tonnes, the machine was not really practicable as a musical instrument. Its principal function, the imitation of other instruments, has bedevilled the world of musical electronics to the present day: to most musicians there seems very little point in going to such trouble to do what can be better done on the normal instrument. Hence it was chiefly in

the imitation of organs with machines that cost a tenth or hundredth of the price of a pipe organ that electronic instruments had their widest successes, until instruments were devised that could create truly new and exciting sounds.

The earliest such instruments were the *theremin, Sphärophon, and *ondes martenot of the 1920s. They were based on heterodyning, one electric current interfering with another (familiar from placing a microphone too close to a speaker). In spite of producing new sounds, these instruments have been of limited use, partly because of their inherent glissandos and partly because they are monophonic, little or no tonal variety is possible, and they have seldom been widely available.

One of the early electronic keyboards which had a limited success was the neo-Bechstein *electric piano of the 1920s. Like the electric guitar, this used electromagnets (instead of a soundboard) to pick up the vibrations of the strings. Far more popular, as it still is, was the *Hammond organ introduced in the mid-1930s, which worked on a principle not unlike that of the original telharmonium, but with all the advantages of the thermionic valve and more recently the transistor, neither of which had been available to Cahill. A series of tone wheels rotates close to magnets, each wheel producing a specific pitch. These pitches are combined to create musical sounds by controls operated by the player. The keyboard specifies the fundamental pitch in the normal way and the spectrum of harmonic overtones formed from the other pitches available is controlled by draw-bars. The resulting sound is not unlike that of an organ, and different settings imitate different registrations while a reverberation unit can simulate different acoustic conditions.

Other electronic organs work by using electronic oscillators, rather than revolving wheels, to produce the basic pitches and frequency dividers to derive further pitches from them, resulting in instruments sufficiently complex to justify consoles as full as those of the largest pipe organs, with three or four manuals, pedalboard, and rows of stops, levers, and pistons. Their makers claim that anything a pipe organ can do an electronic organ can do at a fraction of the cost. Organists are sharply divided over the truth of such claims, particularly regarding the quality, but the cost-saving is undeniable and has led to their installation in many churches and concert halls.

There is no doubting their utility at the more modest end of the market. The pipe organ today cannot compete with the electronic instrument for domestic and studio use. Instruments costing very little have a range of a couple of octaves, a choice of half a dozen instrumental sounds, and a built-in drum machine to provide a rhythm accompaniment in a wide range of metres and dance rhythms. More elaborate, and more expensive, instruments have a full-size keyboard and sometimes a second manual, with either full or half range, and even an octave of pedals. Almost all have an earphone socket so that the player can revel in sound sufficient to fill a cathedral without disturbing the peace of family and neighbours.

Instruments of this sort have been built to imitate pianos and harpsichords, though with rather less success; the ictus of a quill plucking a string, or a hammer striking one, is much more difficult to reproduce than the sound of an organ (though there too it is the commencement of the sound that is most likely to reveal that one is hearing an electronic simulation). Again, economy is the outstanding advantage, for the initial cost is substantially less than that of the real instrument and there is no need for regular tuning or other maintenance.   JMo

📖 R. H. Dorf, *Electronic Musical Instruments* (Mineola, NY, 1954, 2/1958) · N. H. Crowhurst, *Electronic Musical Instruments* (Blue Ridge Summit, PA, 1971, 2/1975) · T. Darter and G. Armbruster (eds.), *The Art of Electronic Music* (New York, 1984) · J. Appleton, *Twenty-First Century Musical Instruments: Hardware and Software* (Brooklyn, NY, 1989) · H. A. Deutsch, *Electroacoustic Music: The First Century* (Miami, 1993) · P. Manning, *Electronic and Computer Music* (Oxford, 1993) · M. Vail, *Vintage Synthesizers: Groundbreaking Instruments and Pioneering Designers* (San Francisco, 1993) · J. Chadabe, *Electric Sound: The Past and Promise of Electronic Music* (Upper Saddle River, NJ, 1997)

electrophone. See ELECTRONIC MUSICAL INSTRUMENTS.

elegy (Fr.: *élégie*; It.: *elegia*). A song of lament, or an instrumental composition of mournful character. In the Renaissance, composers often wrote an elegy or *déploration* on the death of a colleague or teacher. Dowland's *Lachrimae, or Seaven Teares* has the character of an elegy. Fauré wrote an *Élégie* for cello and piano (1880).

Elegy for Young Lovers. Opera in three acts by Henze to a libretto by W. H. Auden and Chester Kallman (Schwetzingen, 1961).

Elektra. Opera in one act by Richard Strauss to a libretto by von Hugo von Hofmannsthal after his play (1903), itself based on Sophocles' tragedy *Electra* (*c*.410 BC) (Dresden, 1909).

elevation (Lat.: *elevatio*). The music played during the Elevation of the Host (the lifting up of the consecrated bread and wine) in the Roman Mass, which before the reforms of the Second Vatican Council was said silently. Such music consists usually of a motet or an organ piece or improvisation. In Masses where a polyphonic setting of the Ordinary (as opposed to the plainchant) was sung, an extended setting of the *Benedictus performed this function, separated from the Sanctus. Frescobaldi's *Fiori musicali* (1635) contains some organ pieces for this purpose.

Elfenreigen (Ger.). 'Elfin dance'. See REIGEN.

Elgar, Sir **Edward** (William) (*b* Broadheath, Worcs., 2 June 1857; *d* Worcester, 23 Feb. 1934). English composer. He rose from obscure beginnings and a long apprenticeship to become the pre-eminent figure in British music for the first three decades of the 20th century.

1. The early years; 2. The years of maturity

1. The early years

Elgar was the fourth child and second son of a Worcester piano tuner and music-shopkeeper and his Roman Catholic wife. Although he showed musical promise at an early age and learnt the piano, violin, and organ, he first worked briefly as a solicitor's clerk. But at 16 he became a freelance musician, playing in many local orchestras for which he arranged and composed. Apart from violin lessons he had no formal musical education. His instruction in counterpoint and orchestration came from reading books and from his own practical experiments. From 1878 he was a violinist in the orchestra for the Three Choirs Festival when it was held triennially in Worcester. At about this time, too, he established himself as a violin teacher. In 1884 his *Sevillana* was conducted by August Manns at the Crystal Palace, Elgar's first London performance. But the next five years, taking Elgar beyond his 30th birthday, saw little significant advance in his fortunes. In 1889, however, he married Alice Roberts, daughter of an Indian Army general. She was nine years older than Elgar and met him when she took lessons in piano accompaniment. She believed implicitly in his ability to become a great composer and they settled first in London, hoping to interest publishers and conductors in his work. They had little success, and ironically it was the Worcester Festival, in 1890, which commissioned from Elgar an orchestral work, the overture *Froissart*.

Elgar settled in Malvern in 1891, resuming his teaching. *Froissart* was published by Novello, chief suppliers to the market for cantatas. Elgar therefore set to work on a Longfellow setting, *The Black Knight* (1893). This was followed by an oratorio *The Light of Life* (1896) and by another Longfellow cantata, *King*

Olaf (1896). The latter gave Elgar his biggest success to date and was again taken up by Manns. But Elgar's name was still not widely known outside the Midlands. For this to change it needed Queen Victoria's Diamond Jubilee in 1897 and the success of his *Imperial March*, which led to a commission from the 1898 Leeds Festival for the cantata *Caractacus*. However, it was with a wholly orchestral work, the *Variations on an Original Theme* ('Enigma'), that Elgar in 1899 achieved a significant breakthrough, for the first performance was conducted in London by Hans Richter, whose championship of Elgar was emulated by several of his fellow conductors in Europe. From 1900 to 1914 Elgar's fame on the Continent and in Russia was as widespread as any English composer has achieved, not excluding Britten.

2. The years of maturity

The years 1899–1919 were the zenith of Elgar's creativity and success. In these two decades he composed three large-scale religious choral works—*The Dream of Gerontius* (1899–1900), a setting of Newman's poem, which many regard as Elgar's masterpiece, and two biblical oratorios *The Apostles* and *The Kingdom* (1902–3, 1901–6)—two symphonies (1907–8, 1909–11), the *Introduction and Allegro* for strings (1904–5), the concert overtures *Cockaigne* (1900–01) and *In the South* (1903–4), the first four *Pomp and Circumstance* marches (nos. 1 and 2, 1901; no. 3, 1904; no. 4, 1907), the *Coronation Ode* (1901–2), the *Wand of Youth* Suites nos. 1 and 2 (1907, 1908), based on music he had written when a child, the Violin Concerto (1909–10), the ode *The Music Makers* (1912), the wartime cantata *The Spirit of England* (1915–17), the Violin Sonata and String Quartet (1918), Piano Quintet (1918–19), and the Cello Concerto (1919). In addition there were many songs, partsongs, occasional pieces, and incidental music. With the song *Land of Hope and Glory*, adapted from the trio of the *Pomp and Circumstance* march no. 1 in D in 1902, Elgar became unofficial national musical laureate, although he did not succeed to the post of Master of the King's Music until 1924.

The death of his wife in 1920 provided Elgar with an excuse to retreat from the musical world except as a conductor of his own works at concerts and in the recording studio. He was out of key with the postwar world and felt 'unwanted'; in addition he had long been disillusioned by the financial returns on his work. In the last 14 years of his life he completed no major works, and the two with which he came nearest to doing so, the *Severn Suite* (1930) and the *Nursery Suite* (1931), were largely constructed from material in old sketchbooks. But in 1932 and 1933 he worked on an opera, *The Spanish Lady*, with a libretto adapted from Ben Jonson by Barry Jackson, and a third symphony which was commissioned by the BBC. He left copious sketches of both works. A performing version of the opera was concocted by Percy Young and of the symphony by Anthony Payne. The latter, first performed in 1997, was an immediate success and, although misgivings had been expressed, was judged to be a remarkable achievement. Elgar received many honours, including a knighthood in 1904, the Order of Merit in 1911, and a baronetcy ('of Broadheath') in 1931.

His personality was complex: his appearance, that of a country squire with dogs at heel, was a consciously adopted pose which complemented his frequent defence-mechanism assertions that he had no interest in music. His early struggles and the prejudices against his religion left wounds that success and honours never healed. His music combines instant popular appeal with the loftiest, most visionary *raptus*. There are lofty, visionary moments in such slight pieces as *Chanson de nuit*; the fresh insouciant charm of the slighter pieces invades the symphonies and concertos. His gift for melody is at the root of all his work; his harmony is sometimes richly chromatic, at others simply and touchingly diatonic; his use of tonality is often unstable and elusive, lending an airy, fantastic tone to the music; his scoring is brilliant and colourful, with particularly impressive use of string textures; his compositional style is based on a fondness for sequences, for rising 3rds, falling 7ths, and parallel triads. His style is a highly individual compound of influences as various as Schumann, Wagner, Gounod, Saint-Saëns, Franck, Liszt, and Brahms. With such a pedigree, the specific 'Englishness' ascribed to him is hard to define and it is therefore not surprising that the extremely powerful and affecting impression made by his music on those responsive to it requires the adjective 'Elgarian'.

MK

📖 W. H. Reed, *Elgar as I Knew him* (London, 1936, 2/1973) · D. McVeagh, *Edward Elgar: His Life and Music* (London, 1955) · P. Young, *Elgar O.M.: A Study of a Musician* (London, 1955) · P. Young (ed.), *Letters of Edward Elgar and Other Writings* (London, 1956) · M. Kennedy, *Portrait of Elgar* (London, 1968, 3/1987) · J. Northrop Moore, *Edward Elgar: A Creative Life* (Oxford, 1984) · J. Northrop Moore (ed.), *Elgar and his Publishers: Letters of a Creative Life*, 2 vols. (Oxford, 1987); *The Windflower Letters: Correspondence with Alice Stuart Wortley and her Family* (Oxford, 1989); *Edward Elgar: Letters of a Lifetime* (London, 1990) · R. Monk (ed.), *Elgar Studies* (Aldershot, 1990) · R. Anderson, *Elgar in Manuscript* (London, 1990) · J. Rushton (ed.), *Elgar: Enigma Variations* (Cambridge, 1999)

Elias, Brian (David) (*b* Bombay, 30 Aug. 1948). British composer. He studied with Elisabeth Lutyens and at the Juilliard School, New York. His early works tended to be intensely economical in the materials and forces required, but he gradually developed a more expansive and lyrical voice, impressively apparent in *Somnia*, settings of Petronius for tenor and orchestra (1983), and the *Five Songs to Poems by Irina Ratushinskaya* (1989).

AW

Elijah (*Elias*). Oratorio, op. 70 (1846), by Mendelssohn for soprano, contralto, tenor, bass, and treble soloists, boys' chorus, chorus, and orchestra, a setting of a text by Julius Schubring after 1 Kings 17–19.

Elisabetta, regina d'Inghilterra ('Elizabeth, Queen of England'). Opera in two acts by Rossini to a libretto by Giovanni Schmidt after Carlo Federici's play based on Sophia Lee's novel *The Recess* (Naples, 1815).

Elisir d'amore, L' ('The Love Potion'). Opera in two acts by Donizetti to a libretto by Felice Romani after Eugène Scribe's libretto for Auber's *Le Philtre* (1831) (Milan, 1832).

Ella, John (*b* Leicester, 19 Dec. 1802; *d* London, 2 Oct. 1888). English violinist, conductor, and critic. He studied at the RAM and with Fétis in Paris before earning his living as an orchestral player at the King's Theatre, the Philharmonic Society, and the Ancient Concerts. He retired from orchestral playing in 1848. With the support of wealthy patrons he attempted to generate enthusiasm for chamber music through concerts at the home of Lord Saltoun (1826–46), the Musical Union subscription concerts (1845–80), and his Musical Winter Evenings (1852–9), providing his own 'analytical programmes'. The concerts attracted prominent performers, notably Hallé, Alfredo Piatti, and Prosper Sainton, and Ella counted Meyerbeer, Thalberg, and Wagner among his acquaintances. He wrote criticism for *The Athenaeum*, *The Morning Post*, and *The Musical World* and was appointed lecturer at the London Institution in 1855. He was known for his outspoken views on standards of performance and interpretation, considering those on the Continent to be higher than in Britain; he lent his impassioned support to a state-sponsored National Academy of Music.

JDI

Eller, Heino (*b* Tartu, 7 March 1887; *d* Tallinn, 16 June 1970). Estonian composer and teacher. In St Petersburg he studied the violin (1907–8), then composition, at the conservatory (with Vasili Kalafati, 1913–15, and Maximilian Steinberg, 1919–20), and law at the university. He taught at the Tartu Higher School of Music (1920–40) before moving to Tallinn as professor of composition at the State Conservatory. Eller was a vital element

in the establishment of the Estonian national school: his outlook as a teacher was more open and internationally inclined than the 'rival' school of the more conservative Artur Kapp, and the three generations of his pupils include Tubin, Pärt, and Lepo Sumera.

Eller's own music emerges from late Romanticism, but without a trace of sentimentality. His tone-poem *Koit* ('Dawn', 1918) shows an exquisite sense of orchestral colour that allies him to Rakhmaninov; his early piano music, by contrast, reveals an affinity with Skryabin, while the *Elegy* for harp and strings (1931) has an Elgarian nobility. He composed over 30 orchestral works, including three symphonies ('In modo mixolydio', 1936; 1947; 1961), seven concertante pieces, and eight symphonic poems, most of which lie unpublished in pencil manuscripts in a museum in Tallinn. His chamber and instrumental music includes five string quartets, four piano sonatas, and two sonatas for violin and piano.

MA

Ellis, Vivian (John Herman) (*b* London, 29 Oct. 1903; *d* London, 19 June 1996). English composer and lyricist. He studied the piano with Myra Hess but was attracted by the theatre and went on to compose *Mr Cinders* (1929), *Jill Darling* (1933), *Streamline* (1934), and *Bless the Bride* (1947). His orchestral works include *Coronation Scot* (1948).

PGA/ALA

Éloy, Jean-Claude (*b* Mont-Saint-Aignan, nr Rouen, 15 June 1938). French composer. He studied composition at the Paris Conservatoire with Milhaud, at the Darmstadt summer courses with Hermann Scherchen and Henri Pousseur, and in Basle with Boulez, who conducted and recorded his *Équivalences* (1963). He was invited by Stockhausen to work at the Cologne electronic music studio, producing *Shanti* for voices, instruments, and electronics (1974). Éloy's music has been strongly influenced by Eastern (especially Hindu) music and aesthetics.

ABUR

embellishments. See ORNAMENTS AND ORNAMENTATION.

embolada (Port.). A Brazilian folksong in which each syllable of the text is set to one note in a semiquaver pattern and sung rapidly. Villa-Lobos also used the term for some of his instrumental pieces.

embouchure (Fr.). 1. The manner in which a player's mouth and lips are placed when playing flutes, reeds, or brass instruments; the word has been used in English in this sense since the 18th century.

2. The mouth-hole of a flute.

3. In France also the mouthpiece of a brass instrument (whence *instruments à embouchure*, 'brass instruments').

AB

Emerald Isle, The. Opera in two acts by Sullivan to a libretto by Basil Hood; it was unfinished when Sullivan died and was completed by Edward German (London, 1901).

'Emperor' Concerto. Nickname of Beethoven's Piano Concerto no. 5 in E♭ major op. 73 (1809); the title may have been added by the pianist and publisher J. B. Cramer.

'Emperor' Quartet (*Kaiserquartett*). Nickname of Haydn's String Quartet in C major op. 76 no. 3 (1797), so called because the slow movement is a set of variations on the *'Emperor's Hymn'.

Emperor's Hymn. Austrian national anthem from the time of its composition (1797) by Haydn to 1918, when the Austro-Hungarian Empire was replaced by the new Austrian Republic. A new anthem was chosen, *Deutsch-Österreich, du herrliches Land*, but it was never popular and Haydn's melody was reinstated with new words. As Germany had also selected Haydn's tune, which it still uses (see EINIGKEIT UND RECHT UND FREIHEIT), in 1947 Austria chose another anthem, *Land der Berge*.

Haydn was originally commissioned to write the tune to words by Lorenz Leopold Haschka (1749–1827), 'Gott erhalte Franz den Kaiser', for the emperor's birthday; he subsequently used it as the basis of a set of variations in his String Quartet op. 76 no. 3 (1797), thereafter called the 'Emperor' Quartet or *Kaiserquartett*.

AL

Empfindsamkeit (Ger., 'sentiment', 'sensitivity'). A term applied to an aesthetic movement that flourished in Europe and especially north Germany in the mid-18th century. Its origins lay partly in the English cult of 'sensibility', as seen in Samuel Richardson's *Pamela* (1741), one of several works which stressed the importance of a personal, emotional response. In music its most important exponent was C. P. E. Bach, who emphasized in his *Versuch über die wahre Art das Clavier zu spielen* (1753) that the highest aim of music was to touch the heart and move the affections. His favourite instrument was the soft-toned, expressive clavichord, and it is his clavichord pieces that best exemplify the *empfindsamer Stil*, for example his six 'Prussian' Sonatas (1740–2), and the F♯ minor Fantasia (1787).

The *empfindsamer Stil* which Bach cultivated in music was favoured by other north German composers, among them C. H. Graun, whose *Der Tod Jesu* (1755), to a libretto by K. W. Ramler in imitation of Friedrich Klopstock (the leading German poet in the style), was admired above all works for its ability to move the passions with its intensely expressive text-setting, replete with musical 'sighs', chromatic harmonies, and other clichés.

—/SS

Empfindung (Ger.). 'Expression', 'feeling'; *empfindungsvoll*, 'with feeling'. See EMPFINDSAMKEIT.

empressé (Fr.). 'Eager', 'hurrying'.

enchaînez (Fr.). 'Chain up', 'join together', i.e. the next movement should start immediately without a break (the same as *attacca*).

Enchiriadis. See MUSICA ENCHIRIADIS.

Encina, Juan del [Fermoselle, Juan de] (*b* Salamanca, 12 July 1468; *d* León, 1529 or 1530). Spanish poet, dramatist, and composer. The son of an artisan called Fermoselle, he was a choirboy at Salamanca Cathedral and studied at the university there. On graduating he may have been a magistrate in northern Spain. By 1495 he was in the service of the Duke of Alba, and became famous as a writer of plays, on both secular and sacred themes. By 1500 Encina was in Rome; he was favoured by Pope Julius II, who granted him the archdiaconate of Málaga Cathedral. He was ordained in 1519, and celebrated his first Mass in Jerusalem that year. His remains are now buried in Salamanca Cathedral. More than 60 villancicos by Encina survive, and he is considered the finest master of the genre.

DA/JM

encore (Fr., 'again'). A word adopted into English and called out by audiences to demand that a performer or performers should return to the stage to give an additional performance—sometimes of the same piece, but more usually of another. Such an additional piece is itself referred to as an 'encore'. The use of the term dates back to the 18th century, when it was common in concerts and operas for performances to be interrupted for the repetition of movements and arias. The French themselves, and the Italians, use the word *bis* (Lat., 'twice'), whereas the Americans prefer 'bravo'.

—/LC

encyclopedias. See DICTIONARIES OF MUSIC.

end-blown flute. Any flute blown from the end, including *duct flutes, but specifically one blown across the open end. The end is usually chamfered externally to form a sharp edge, either all round the circumference ('rim-blown flutes', e.g. the Arab *nāy* or the *kaval* of south-eastern Europe and Turkey) or at the base of a notch ('notched flutes', e.g. the *shakuhachi* or the Peruvian *kena*). *Panpipes consist of several rim-blown flutes tied together in the form of a raft.

JMo

en dehors. See DEHORS, EN.

Endless Parade. Work (1986–7) by Birtwistle for trumpet, vibraphone, and strings.

Enescu, George [Enesco, Georges] (*b* Leveni-Vîrnav [now George Enescu], nr Dorohoi, 19 Aug. 1881; *d* Paris, 4 May 1955). Romanian composer. He made his debut as a violinist at the age of seven and began studies at the Vienna Conservatory in 1890. In 1895 he went to the Paris Conservatoire to continue his violin studies, but concentrated instead on composition under Massenet and Fauré. He quickly achieved success in Paris with such works as the first two violin sonatas (1897 and 1899) and the two *Romanian Rhapsodies* for orchestra (1901 and 1902), all of which he performed himself as violinist, pianist, or conductor. As a violinist he made many international tours, winning renown for his playing of Bach and of contemporary works. He was also active as a teacher in Paris and Bucharest, his pupils including Yehudi Menuhin and Arthur Grumiaux.

Enescu's early works, which have remained the most frequently played, make use of Romanian folk themes in an opulent late Romantic manner. Later he approached Bartók's more incisive treatment, notably in the Third Violin Sonata (1926); he also looked back to Bach in such grandly conceived works as the Second Suite for orchestra (1915). His small output (33 opus numbers) also includes a four-act opera, *Oedipe* (1921–31; Paris Opéra, 1936).   PG

 📖 N. MALCOLM, *George Enescu: His Life and Music* (London, 1990)

Enfance du Christ, L' ('The Childhood of Christ'). Oratorio, op. 25 (1850–4), by Berlioz for seven soloists, chorus, and orchestra, to his own text.

Enfant et les sortilèges, L' ('The Child and the Spells'). Opera ('lyric fantasy') in one act by Ravel to a libretto by Colette (Monte Carlo, 1925).

Enfant prodigue, L' ('The Prodigal Son'). **1**. Cantata by Debussy for soprano, tenor, and baritone soloists, chorus, and orchestra, to a text by Ernest Guiraud. With it Debussy won the *Prix de Rome in 1884; it was first performed in Paris that year with a two-piano accompaniment and was revised in 1906–8.

2. Opera in five acts by Auber to a libretto by Eugène Scribe (Paris, 1850).

3. Ballet by Prokofiev; see PRODIGAL SON, THE.

Engeführung (Ger.). The equivalent of *stretto in fugal writing.

England. 1. Introduction; 2. From the beginnings to the Reformation; 3. From the Reformation to the Restoration; 4. From 1660 to the accession of Queen Victoria; 5. Victorian and Edwardian England; 6. The 20th century; 7. Conclusions

1. Introduction

England's long and distinctive musical history has been coloured throughout by three factors: its complex relations with states bound to it by historical ties; the changing pattern of its relationships with its immediate neighbours in the islands of Britain and Ireland; and a strong tradition of centralization that has often made England seem synonymous with London. After the invasions that began the process of turning Britannia into England, the territory was invaded first by Scandinavians and later by the Normans, to be ruled by a French-speaking monarchy and nobility until the 15th century. The unity of Catholic Europe facilitated the exchange of music and musicians, with England being a net exporter, as it were, during the 15th century; after the Reformation, when alliances shifted, its music became influential in the Netherlands and Germany, while drawing heavily on Italian music for inspiration.

From the 17th to the 19th centuries London was a Mecca for European musicians, many of whom stayed on for the rest of their lives. The British Empire proved not to be a source of cultural unity, however, and the once-dependent nations have since proclaimed their cultural independence. On the other hand, the greatly improved communications of the 20th century called into question the legitimacy of a purely national framework for musical history, a factor that might be countered by an appeal to the specifically local inspiration of so many English composers. Wales, Scotland, and Ireland have their own distinctive traditions that have resisted integration with those of England, notwithstanding a tendency since World War II to advance the cause of 'British' music.

As for the centrality of London, a closer investigation reveals that until the Reformation highly professional standards were maintained in numerous other centres; after the Reformation, when the profession came to be centred on an increasingly static court and the capital's principal churches, theatres, and (eventually) concert halls, a certain marginalization can be observed. In the 20th century good communications and advances in broadcasting once again brought the whole country into a beneficial symbiosis.

2. From the beginnings to the Reformation

Christianity was re-established in Britain by St Augustine, who arrived in 597. Bede records the frequent efforts made to ensure that liturgical chant accorded with Roman practice, and in due course *'Gregorian' chant in its standard form, together with a partly indigenous repertory of *tropes and *sequences, became the norm, as a number of pre-Conquest manuscripts make clear. During the 10th century several cathedrals received a monastic constitution, among them Canterbury, Winchester, and Worcester, a principle extended after the Conquest to others such as Durham. The rest were secular cathedrals, governed by a chapter consisting of a dean and canons whose duty to maintain the Divine *Office in choir was carried out by deputies or vicars, normally in priests', deacons', or subdeacons' orders. Somewhat later their own musical duties came to be performed by clerks in lower orders, together with the boy choristers provided for in the founding statutes.

Many other collegiate churches were founded on this model, or on a similar one that provided for a number of chaplains to fulfil the duty of celebrating Masses for the departed. Many such churches provided an education that by the 15th century had led to a high standard of musicianship among boy choristers throughout the country; this in turn led to a wider cultivation of *polyphony in the liturgy and an increasingly sophisticated style of polyphonic composition. The larger monasteries maintained their own polyphonic choirs, and by the Reformation many parish churches also provided for polyphonic music either regularly or intermittently. Religious guilds and hospitals often made similar provision, together with the educational colleges of Oxford, Cambridge, Eton, and Winchester, and the chapels of royalty and the nobility. The *Chapel Royal itself was refounded as a permanent institution by Edward IV.

Medieval manuscripts of *plainchant and polyphony are in fairly short supply, mainly it would seem owing to the wave of destruction that followed on the Reformation, though other factors such as obsolescence and normal physical degradation should be borne in mind. However, enough remains for the chant traditions of medieval England to be reconstructed almost completely, the principal Uses being those of Salisbury (used in most parts of southern England), Hereford, and York, together with that of the Benedictine monasteries and cathedrals. Only in the case of York is there a substantial lacuna.

Polyphony was cultivated at Winchester before the Conquest (see MIDDLE AGES, THE) and in several other monastic churches. The St Andrews manuscript (13th century) contains a version of the polyphonic repertory of Notre Dame in Paris, together with an appendix of locally composed music. While this manuscript undoubtedly belonged to the monastery of St Andrews in the 14th century it is not certain that the music unique to it originated there. The largest source of fragments from the 13th and 14th centuries is Worcester, the manuscripts having been dismembered in the Middle Ages in order to strengthen the bindings of books then belonging to the cathedral library. The music itself, however, seems to have been collected together from a wide area. The style of this and of music from similar sources is noteworthy for its exploitation of full triads, the 3rd being then considered by theorists to be a dissonance. The musical forms are those of the Ordinary and Proper of the Mass, the *conductus, and the *motet, the last being almost always a sacred form in England.

During the 14th century there is evidence of a simpler, strictly functional style of composition alongside an increasingly sophisticated type of motet-writing. The latter owed much to French influence, partly it seems through the capture of the French king John II and the establishment of his court in London (1357–60). These tendencies are evident in the oldest more or less complete manuscript to have survived since that of Winchester. This is the *Old Hall Manuscript, now in the British Library, dating from the early 15th century and thought to have belonged originally to Lionel, Duke of Clarence, the brother of Henry V. The composers include Leonel Power and, as a later addition, John Dunstaple, the two most famous of a large galaxy. The music is for the Ordinary of the Mass (though without any settings of the Kyrie), together with a small number of antiphons and motets.

Dunstaple's music enjoyed a considerable reputation on the Continent; he was singled out by the Burgundian court poet Martin le Franc (c. 1440) as exhibiting the contenance angloise ('English aspect', identifiable perhaps with euphony), and later by *Tinctoris as the leading light of an older generation. Much of his music, like that of some of his contemporaries, survives only in Italian manuscripts. A slightly later group including Walter Frye is represented by manuscripts now in Brussels and Lucca, both of Burgundian origin.

While a certain amount of music from the middle and later years of the 15th century has survived, it has a somewhat parochial flavour. Among the genres cultivated was that of the polyphonic *carol, a formal derivative of the French carole, a popular dance-song with refrain. The English polyphonic type, however, was used mainly for serious purposes, having English or Latin texts or a combination of the two, and was no longer intended for dancing. Its style, nevertheless, is melodious and accessible, at least to begin with; later examples are more contrapuntal, while those of the 16th century are often deeply felt. Their function has been much debated; there may have been an informal place for some of them in the liturgy, but they may equally have served for the domestic entertainment of religious and clerical communities. The 'Deo gratias' refrain of the *Agincourt Song ('Owre kinge went forth to Normandy') has suggested to some the expansion of a liturgical response, but a text of this kind, while not exactly secular, has very little religious feeling in it. A certain amount of wholly secular polyphonic song has come down to us, some in the style of the contemporary French chanson.

Some of the finest English music of the late 15th and early 16th centuries was little known if at all outside England, and not much influenced by Continental composers either. A highly florid style developed in the hands of such composers as William Cornysh (almost certainly the younger of the two composers of that name) and Robert Fayrfax, both members of the Chapel Royal. They, and many of their contemporaries, are represented in the Eton Choirbook (MS 178 of the college library), one of the few medieval manuscripts to remain in the possession of the institution for which it was compiled, shortly before and after 1500. This volume is devoted almost exclusively to *Magnificat* settings (for Vespers) and antiphons (or motets), the latter being sung at the conclusion of the daily Office before the statue or in the chapel of the saint being addressed (usually Our Lady). The statutes of many institutions, Eton among them, specified the singing of an antiphon at the close of the liturgical day, though not necessarily in polyphony.

The other principal musical form was the large-scale mass. The finest composer of the epoch was undoubtedly John Taverner, Master of the Choristers at Cardinal College (later Christ Church), Oxford, from 1526 to 1530. For that institution he composed the three magnificent six-part masses that are among the glories of the period; among his other compositions is his Mass on *Western Wynde*, a secular song later used for the same purpose by John Sheppard and Christopher Tye. A great deal of music was also written for other liturgical forms such as the responsory and the Office hymn.

The most elaborate polyphonic music seems to have been written not for the cathedrals but for more recent foundations, such as the Chapel Royal, collegiate churches, the colleges, and in some cases the secular choirs of the greater monasteries. Their singers could also be borrowed for special occasions by lesser institutions, or by organizations like the Guild of the Holy Name, which met in the crypt of St Paul's Cathedral and made use of the singers of the Chapel Royal as well as its own choirboys. Standards of musicianship must have been impressive, the music being read from individual parts written in a complex notational system. Never before or since has a rigorous musical education been so pervasive in society; and to such performers and composers must be added the secular musicians ('minstrels') of the court and of the major towns, educated by a system of apprenticeship and organized in companies or guilds with their own privileges and responsibilities. It was these musicians, sometimes assisted by the boys and singing-men of the local church, who provided the musical element in the performances of popular plays, chief among these being the outdoor religious cycles given at or around the feast of Corpus Christi in such cities as York, Coventry, and Chester. A cooperation between the chapel and non-chapel musicians of a secular establishment, including those of the monarch's own household, was often effected to provide the live entertainment that was so important a constituent of medieval life.

3. From the Reformation to the Restoration

The English *Reformation was a protracted affair. Initially political, being driven by Henry VIII's wish for a divorce from (in modern terms, the annulment of his marriage to) Catherine of Aragon, it led to the disavowal of the Papacy and its replacement by the Royal Supremacy; this in turn paved the way for religious reform, resisted at first but allowed full sway during the short reign of Edward VI, 1547–53. When Mary came to the throne, steps were taken to restore the Latin rite and papal authority; but on her death late in 1558 Elizabeth, daughter of Ann Boleyn, succeeded her and brought about the final establishment of Anglicanism. Elizabeth's skill in striking a balance between Catholic and Protestant sentiment cannot be denied, but her settlement proved unacceptable to Catholics and initiated a religious divide that has existed ever since.

Henry VIII saw an opportunity to replenish his coffers and reward his servants through the dissolution of the monasteries, beginning with the smaller ones in 1536 and concluding with the larger ones in 1538–40. The later round of suppressions was particularly damaging to music, since it was the greater monasteries that were foremost in providing for musical education and performance, not to mention composition. But the dissolution of the chantries (by Acts of 1545 and 1547), which included almost all non-educational collegiate churches, was even more destructive in this respect. A few such foundations, converted or restricted to parochial use, survived the onslaught and continued their educational role; its musical content, however, was severely diminished when it did not disappear entirely.

In the later 1540s various experiments were carried out in the use of English in the liturgy; on the death of Henry these gained momentum and went hand in hand with a simplification that led in 1549 to the first *Book of *Common Prayer. Not only were many elements of the Latin rite expunged, but the music deemed suitable for worship was much simplified. Even plainchant was reduced, in John Merbecke's *The Booke of Common Praier Noted* (1550), to a small number of chants (some newly composed) and an entirely syllabic setting of the texts. Polyphonic music was mostly homophonic, often with a chant in the tenor part. Merbecke's publication, and much of the earliest polyphony, had a rather short life, since the 1549 book was replaced by another, still further removed from the letter and spirit of the Latin rite, in 1552.

The revival of Catholic worship by Mary Tudor led to the renewed composition of complex polyphony. It is difficult always to be certain about the dating of such music, but much of the Latin work of Tallis, Sheppard, Tye, William Mundy, and Robert White will have belonged to her reign. The same is true of some of the extant liturgical organ music, in which the organ acted as a substitute for singing, often in alternation with a vocal group. On the other hand the composing careers of Tallis, Sheppard, and Tye started well before 1549, and there were various possible reasons for composing non-liturgical Latin polyphony during the reigns of Edward VI and Elizabeth (and indeed liturgical polyphony too, for unofficial and secret celebrations of the Latin rite). Psalm-motets in particular were neutral in status and were probably composed for both Catholic and Anglican dispensations. Even such a composition as Tallis's outstanding set of Lamentations may well have been composed in Elizabethan times.

Elizabeth introduced a slightly revised version of the second Prayer Book in 1559, and again the problem of dating occurs, since it is often hard to tell whether a particular piece was composed in Edwardian or early Elizabethan days. While a small number of Edwardian manuscripts do survive, there is very little, apart from one printed collection (the publisher John Day's *Certaine Notes*, 1560, reissued as *Mornyng and Evenyng Prayer and Communion* in 1565) from the earlier part of Elizabeth's reign. Indeed, much of Tallis's music, for example, survives only in 17th-century sources. However, it is possible to chart a course whereby in the Chapel Royal and the major London establishments a more elaborate style of writing came to be accepted, one that exploited the seating of the Anglican choir on two sides of the chancel, known respectively as *decani* and *cantoris*. This arrangement encouraged antiphonal writing and a varied approach to vocal scoring. The use of the organ for accompanimental purposes (notwithstanding Puritan objections to the instrument) allowed the development of the 'verse anthem', in which accompanied solos alternated with choral sections. In the provinces, however, such ideals were not always attainable, and Puritan sentiment encouraged the use of metrical psalms, sung in unison, in public worship.

The middle years of the 16th century saw an increase in the production of written music for domestic purposes. The great houses, for many of which a musical chapel establishment had become otiose, continued to support professional musicians for entertainment and for the teaching of their children and servants. Musical forms such as the *partsong and *consort song (in which solo voices were supported by a consort of instruments) flourished. Towards the end of the century, lute-accompanied song enjoyed a spectacular upsurge, and the partsong was often transformed into the madrigal, a vernacular imitation of the Italian model. However, we should not assume that the more difficult pieces were intended to be sight-read by all and sundry after meals, as the introductory dialogue in Thomas Morley's *A Plaine and Easie Introduction to Practicall Musicke* (1597) might seem to imply. It is quite likely that harmonized metrical psalms, and the simpler kinds of consort song and partsong, were pressed into service on such occasions in civilized households, and no doubt purely instrumental music, whether for whole or mixed consort, was often played, either for dancing or for attentive listening; and keyboard music was certainly much cultivated by both lady amateurs and professional gentlemen.

Catholic society, under severe legal disadvantages as it was, brought into being an impressive repertory of sacred music to Latin texts, above all by the long-lived William Byrd (*c*.1540–1623). Tallis and Byrd, who had been granted a monopoly of music-printing, issued a joint set of *Cantiones sacrae* in 1575, and Byrd went on to produce two more sets of his own. In many of these, as well as in works surviving only in manuscript, an element of lamentation over the situation of the Catholics can be detected, though only occasionally were the texts such as to raise Protestant eyebrows. However, Byrd also issued three printed masses, the surviving copies of which are bound up with his two books of *Gradualia* (1605, 1607). The *Gradualia* consist mostly of settings of the Proper of the Mass, and were doubtless intended for liturgical use in Catholic households, though the complexity of some of those in the second book makes one wonder if they could ever have been put fully into use.

The first part of the 17th century saw a movement towards greater ritual elaboration in the Anglican Church, and the final flowering of the Elizabethan tradition in the composition of service music and anthems. In secular music, too, the reign of James I was as much of a Golden Age as the later Elizabethan. Under the musically adventurous Charles I, who had enjoyed his own private music on becoming Prince of Wales, the supremely imaginative William Lawes benefited from royal patronage. The masque flourished in both reigns, but it is the chamber music of Lawes and John Jenkins that gives the period its distinctive stamp. Solo song also entered into new territory with the affective declamatory idiom of Nicholas Lanier (the first Master of the King's Music) and Henry Lawes, William's older brother.

Both sacred and secular music suffered with the Civil War and the subsequent interregnum. The distinctive character of the Church of England was destroyed, while the withdrawal of royal patronage severely limited the opportunities for composers of secular music in all its forms. Much now depended on private patronage, while private music meetings (for example at Oxford) came to play a part and led in due course to more formal and public concert-giving. Even opera of a kind (William Davenant's *The Siege of Rhodes*, set to music by several composers) was experimented with in private houses.

4. From 1660 to the accession of Queen Victoria

The restoration of the monarchy brought about the resumption of Anglican worship and its musical traditions. Charles II set up a large Chapel Royal complete with a band of 'violins' (i.e. strings) in emulation of the orchestra of Louis XIV's chapel. Cathedral music was re-established at Westminster Abbey and at St Paul's Cathedral, and court music was revived. Henry Cooke became Master of the Choristers at the Chapel Royal and trained a new generation of choirboys that included John Blow and Henry Purcell. Foreign musicians, including Louis Grabu and Giovanni Battista Draghi, settled in England for a time; foreign music was imported and sometimes published in England, while young musicians like Pelham Humfrey were sent abroad to study. For the Chapel Royal, anthems with orchestral accompaniment were composed by Cooke himself, Matthew Locke, Humfrey, Blow, Purcell, and many of their contemporaries. However, they also wrote more reflective, sometimes rather archaic, church music, and after the reign of James II, under the puritanical and parsimonious William III, the chapel ceased to be a focus for elaborate settings, although it continued to employ the finest English composers. From then on, spectacular church music was reserved for special occasions.

The emancipation of the theatres might have seen the establishment of opera in London, but while operas by Grabu and Cambert were given in 1674, the English did not really take to 'true' opera. The earliest artistically worthwhile English examples, Blow's *Venus and Adonis* and Purcell's *Dido and Aeneas*, were written for private occasions in the 1680s. The public preferred to watch spoken plays, usually with a substantial amount of music, and sometimes supported by elaborate 'masques' to create a genre known as 'dramatic opera' or 'semi-opera'. The masque at this period could indeed be a dramatic action told in music—a miniature opera, in fact—and such pieces were often inserted within plays or were added to the end of an evening's entertainment. *Dido* itself was revived in 1700 as a series of masques to be performed between the acts of Shakespeare's *Measure for Measure*.

Public concerts began, modestly enough, and while some families continued to support professional musicians the emphasis shifted towards an entrepreneurial society, creating a divide between the public professional and the private amateur, the latter relying more and more on published music by famous names. Foreign musicians, such as the Italian violinist Nicola Matteis, were much admired, while Corelli's concertos, once they had arrived in England, became immensely popular. The French style favoured by Charles II had long given way to the Italian by 1700, and formed the foundation for musical development in the 18th century.

Though he was by no means the first foreigner to settle in England, the arrival of Handel in the early 18th century decisively altered the balance of power between native and European composers. His effortless technical superiority took the city by storm in his opera *Rinaldo* (produced in the 1710–11 season, though based largely on his earlier music); he quickly found favour with Queen Anne, and was able to make peace with her successor George I, the Elector of Hanover from whose employ Handel had outstayed his leave. While English composers such as Maurice Greene retained the formally prestigious posts, Handel was given the commissions that brought his name into the public eye. His further operatic ventures, however, were only intermittently successful, and he turned almost accidentally to oratorio through unstaged performances of his masque *Acis and Galatea* and of *Esther*. The latter, being on a biblical subject, was the ancestor of all his oratorios properly so called, although he wrote further dramatic works on secular subjects and a number of pieces that altogether lack the dramatic structure of the original model. *Messiah*, the most famous of all these, was first performed in a Dublin theatre but later became associated above all with church and chapel performances. It became enormously influential and could be said to be the prototype for the large majority of later English oratorios.

Theatrical and concert life flourished throughout the 18th century, particularly but not exclusively in London. English composers were rarely successful in serious opera, but they fully exploited the vogue for comic opera with spoken dialogue following the phenomenal success of *The Beggar's Opera* by John Gay, with music arranged by J. C. Pepusch (1728). At first these were merely pasticcios, based on ballads or borrowed music (or both), but Thomas Arne started writing comic operas with wholly original music and achieved a noteworthy success with his serious opera *Artaxerxes* (1762); his oratorio *Judith* (1761), moreover, was one of the few really worthy successors to those of Handel. The national song 'Rule, Britannia!', from his masque *Alfred* (1740), has been sung ever since, usually in a corrupt form.

Concerts were often miscellaneous affairs, but orchestral music came to predominate in the later 18th century. The then current fashion for 'ancient' music prefigures the later English tendency to prefer the tried and tested to the novel; most audiences, however, still preferred the offerings of the new virtuosos and their own music. In the provinces, concerts were often managed by local amateurs, and the performances 'stiffened' by professionals. Madrigal societies and glee clubs were popular. Domestic music came to be served more and more by printed music aimed at the amateur market; by 1800 enormous numbers of songs and instrumental works of all kinds had been published.

The established Church, in a period of relative stagnation, managed to maintain a decent level in much of its music; the needs of country parishes, however, led to the publication of a repertory of music by local composers, some of it technically unconventional but often persuasive in its ad hoc solution to compositional problems. Among a great quantity of worthwhile writing on music the *Histories* of John Hawkins (1776) and Charles Burney (1776–89) stand out for their painstaking and wide-ranging scholarship.

The early 19th century at first saw the continuation of the previous century's traditions; the quantity of published music continued to increase, and a tendency to triviality was maintained in, for example, a large amount of theatre music, published song, and popular piano music. At the same time, however, a new seriousness was beginning to emerge. The foundation of the Philharmonic Society in 1813 helped to enhance the prestige of orchestral music, while Londoners were able to enjoy a wider range of foreign opera than hitherto. Thomas Attwood enlarged the expressive range of church music and song, while William Crotch, a true polymath, wrote compelling orchestral and choral music as well as contributing splendidly to musical scholarship in his lectures and the accompanying published *Specimens of Various Styles of Music* (1808).

5. Victorian and Edwardian England

One of the impediments to the international recognition of English music in this period was the long-standing lack of a truly competitive system of musical education. Outside the church, apprenticeship was still the norm, and the Royal Academy of Music (founded in 1822) catered originally only for junior pupils. The English musical public came more and more to appreciate European composers and performers to the detriment of those born and trained in England; such earlier figures as the pianist-composers Clementi and Cramer were followed in public esteem by Thalberg and Moscheles, and later on Clara Schumann, with Joachim the most popular violinist and Michael Costa, followed by August Manns and Hans Richter, favourite conductors. Mendelssohn became not only a highly popular composer in England but one of the most influential musicians in the 19th century. English performers lacked the virtuoso skills to maintain their appeal, while composers, unless like Sterndale Bennett they studied abroad, tended to be limited in their vision. Even Bennett became absorbed in administrative routine as principal of the RAM, and his later music suffered as a result.

Opera, too, was dominated by continental composers, and the most successful 'English' composers were of either German or Irish origin. Opera in English was revived in 1834 at the Lyceum Theatre and flourished intermittently thereafter, almost always in a form with spoken dialogue. There is nothing intrinsically inferior about this, but the subject matter and the stilted diction of the librettos make revival of even the best of them (such as Balfe's *The Bohemian Girl* or Julius Benedict's *The Lily of Killarney*) a dubious proposition nowadays. Otherwise opera was mainly given in Italian, even in works of German or French origin, at first at Covent Garden and from 1847 at Her Majesty's in the Haymarket. Later in the century, the operettas of Gilbert and Sullivan brought into being a new genre of gentle musical and verbal satire, especially popular with the middle classes and the ancestor of early 20th-century musical comedy. More traditional comic operas fared less well, and serious English opera even worse, notwithstanding two lengthy seasons devoted to Sullivan's *Ivanhoe*.

Towards the end of the century new ideals, spearheading what has usually been called 'the English Renaissance', came to the fore. The RAM had been transformed into a conservatory of international standing under George Macfarren and the Scotsman Alexander Mackenzie, while Hubert Parry and Charles Stanford, as director and professor of composition respectively, made the Royal College of Music (founded in 1883) an effective nursery for budding composers. Parry and Stanford themselves were closer in spirit to Brahms (and to a lesser extent Wagner) than to Mendelssohn, with Stanford's Irish background providing a further distinctive element. Edward Elgar achieved recognition only after years of struggle; but when he did at last become a widely known figure with his 'Enigma' Variations (1899), it was as a composer of international distinction.

6. The 20th century

There is no doubt that the 20th century, building on the achievement of Elgar in the years up to World War I, was the most innovatory since the 17th. While English composers were not normally at the forefront of technical developments, they explored the potential of such developments, often after some lapse of time, in highly individual ways—for example in the use of serialism during and after World War II by Elisabeth Lutyens, Humphrey Searle, and Benjamin Frankel. Earlier still, the highly eclectic Frank Bridge had experimented with 12-note themes.

More characteristic of the English genius, many would judge, was the folk-imbued idiom of Ralph Vaughan Williams and Gustav Holst, an idiom that sometimes masks their profound originality. Both covered an enormous range, from music for amateurs and children to works of great symphonic scope, though it was Vaughan Williams in particular who achieved a substantial canon of large-scale masterpieces. Only in opera did success elude both composers and indeed most of their contemporaries with the exception of Frederick Delius, whose operas and other major works had been performed in Germany before World War I. Between the wars, the influence of French-style neo-classicism and of jazz permeated the youthful work of Constant Lambert, Arthur Bliss, and William Walton.

Operatic maturity came to England with Benjamin Britten's *Peter Grimes*, produced in London in 1945 shortly after the end of the war. It was the beginning of a second wave of regeneration in English music, which drew much of its inspiration but little of its technical apparatus from the European pre- and postwar avant-garde. Apart from serialism in its various forms, the influences of such composers as Stravinsky and Hindemith can be seen, above all in the textural clarity and classicism of much of Britten, who became a major player on the operatic scene, eclipsing all his contemporaries in the number of his productions and the majority of them in terms of convincing musical dramaturgy. Only Michael Tippett approached him in the latter respect, above all in his first two operas, *The Midsummer Marriage* and *King Priam*.

These relatively conventional works were succeeded by a period of experiment in musical theatre, to which such works as Britten's church parables are a noteworthy contribution. But the concept of music theatre owes more to the innovations of a trio of close contemporaries, Alexander Goehr, Peter Maxwell Davies, and Harrison Birtwistle. Not only did they create a

genre characterized by a free approach to dramatic and narrative form, the two principles often being inextricably merged, but their methods also came to be widely adopted in more consistently operatic music. Their innovations from the 1960s onwards have parallels in such European composers as Berio but seem to have been developed independently; indeed these three composers are among the first since the 16th century to have made a significant impact on the development of music outside England. They and many of their younger colleagues have experimented in turn with, for example, total *serialism, *aleatory music, *minimalism, and the postmodern tendency towards cross-culturalism and polystylism.

To emphasize the innovatory aspects of English music in the later 20th century is not to ignore the equally powerful forces of conservatism. Until fairly recently, advanced study in performance, and the culture of festivals and prizes, was directed largely towards a conventional interpretation of the established classics. Before the 1970s, little was done to prepare most pupils for the demands either of new music or for a style-conscious approach to pre-Classical music; concert programmes and opera-house seasons remained largely predictable. This conservatism was challenged, though never fully overcome, by a number of pioneering spirits of whom William Glock (1908–2000), appointed Head of Music at the BBC in 1959, should be especially mentioned (see BROADCASTING). His appointment of Pierre Boulez as conductor of the BBC Symphony Orchestra in the 1970s did much to improve standards in the performance of contemporary music, while a growing interest in the early music movement sustained the increasing demand for historically informed performance. The traditional choral repertory of the Anglican cathedrals and similar foundations surprisingly secured a new lease of life after the war; a reduction in the number of services permitted a gradual improvement in the quality of performance and a wider choice of music, extending both to the Tudor period and to new work, some of it specially commissioned.

Apart from the disruptions caused by military conflicts involving whole populations, the 20th century saw an ever-increasing institutionalization and commercialization of music. Technological advances, above all in recording and broadcasting, stimulated the demand for music and went a long way towards satisfying it, to the partial detriment, it may be, of 'live' music and theatre. This applied even more to popular music, often driven by American fashions in jazz, rock, and the musical, so that 'music' is now as likely to refer to a multi-million-pound industry as to a demanding and uniquely satisfying art form.

Music has also been affected by the growing role of the nation-state in providing for the needs of its citizens. In the latter half of the 20th century the place of music in state-funded education was significantly enhanced, spurred on perhaps by the early high profile of the enormously successful National Youth Orchestra of Great Britain, founded in 1947 by Ruth Railton. Similarly the study of music in universities benefited from the massive expansion of higher education in the 1960s. But the serious performing arts have required increasingly large amounts of national subsidy to keep them alive, especially after World War II. Changes in society have reduced the element of private patronage, this being directed most often in any case towards conventional activities. The predominantly social-democratic politics of postwar England (still more those of the Thatcher years, 1979–90) have led to a much lower level of public support of the arts than in western Europe, and the state subsidy of high-profile endeavours seen as elitist (opera in particular) has been the subject of sustained attack in the populist press. Governments try to square the circle by insisting on greater access to the arts, but in the last resort there is an inevitable conflict between the support of major institutions in the capital and the spending priorities demanded by the majority of voters.

7. Conclusions

The end of a millennium is a time to take stock. For well over 1000 years England has not merely enjoyed a strong musical culture but has contributed distinctively and permanently to the established repertory. While England has not usually been perceived as part of the 'central' tradition represented by Italy, France, and Germany, it should be remembered that until the Reformation it was an integral part of Catholic Europe and a more central player than a fragmented Germany. Austro-German musical leadership was a comparatively recent and relatively short-lived phenomenon, but it has led to a sustained mythology about the status of music in other countries, not least England. Now that that is at an end, and with the exponential increase in the status and influence of America on European music, both serious and popular, a wholesale reordering of the global culture-chart seems inevitable. Modern England is both multicultural and socially mobile, and it is inevitable that its music in the future will increasingly reflect this. There is every reason for that music to be as diverse as society requires, but there is no need for it to remain the class-ridden battleground that it has been all too apt to become. The hope for the future lies in the hands of the educationists and in the imaginations of the composers, performers, and commentators that they produce.   JCa

F. Ll. Harrison, *Music in Medieval Britain* (London, 1958, 4/1980) · J. Stevens, *Music and Poetry in the Early Tudor Court* (London, 1961, repr. with corrections, 1979) · P. le Huray, *Music and the Reformation in England, 1549–1660* (London, 1967, 2/1978) · B. Rainbow, *The Land without Music: Musical Education in England, 1800–1860, and its Continental Antecedents* (London, 1967) · R. Fiske, *English Theatre Music in the 18th Century* (London, 1973, 2/1986) · C. Ehrlich, *The Music Profession in Britain since the Eighteenth Century: A Social History* (Oxford, 1985) · J. Caldwell, *The Oxford History of English Music*, 2 vols. (Oxford, 1991–9) · P. Holman, *Four and Twenty Fiddlers: The Violin at the English Court, 1540–1690* (Oxford, 1993) · S. McVeigh, *Concert Life in London from Mozart to Haydn* (Cambridge, 1993)

English cadence. See CADENCE.

English Folk Dance and Song Society. A society formed in 1932 when the Folk Song Society (founded 1898) and the English Folk Dance Society (1911) combined; it has a library and archives in London (at Cecil Sharp House).

English guitar [guittar]. See GUITAR, 4.

English horn. See COR ANGLAIS.

English Hymnal. A collection of English hymns and tunes published in 1906 (revised in 1933), edited by Percy Dearmer with Vaughan Williams as music editor. It includes several hymn tunes by Vaughan Williams, and others by his English contemporaries, some of which are adaptations of folksongs.

English Suites. Six keyboard suites by J. S. Bach, BWV806–11 (*c*.1715); the source of the title is unknown but it may refer to an English dedicatee.

Englund, (Sven) Einar (*b* Ljugarn, Gotland, 17 June 1916; *d* Ljugarn, 27 June 1999). Finnish composer, pianist, teacher, and critic. Childhood ability as a pianist led him to enrol at the Sibelius Academy in Helsinki, where besides the piano he studied composition (with Bengt Carlson and Palmgren) and orchestration (with Leo Funtek). Immediately after graduating in 1941 Englund joined the Finnish army and fought in the 'Winter War' against the invading Soviet army. When his troop, guarding a lighthouse, was caught in an ambush, Englund had to leap from the top to avoid being shot, damaging the little finger of his left hand; regret at the loss of a virtuoso career was put aside when he discovered a bullet-hole through his beret.

His wartime experiences were reflected in his first two symphonies (1946, 1947), which are permeated with march rhythms; their assertiveness and robust anti-sentimentality made a considerable impact in postwar Finland. Englund composed vigorously throughout the 1950s but at the end of the decade, disconcerted by the increasing dominance of serialism, he stopped, turning instead to music criticism (for the Swedish-language Helsinki daily *Hufvudstadsbladet*, 1956–76) and teaching (lecturing in composition and theory at the Sibelius Academy, 1957–81). His compositional silence ended with the Third Symphony (1969–71); four more were to follow, as well as concertos for cello (1954), violin (1981), flute (1985), and clarinet (1990–1); there is also a Concerto for 12 Cellos (1980–1). Englund's neo-classical style bears the imprint of Shostakovich and Prokofiev, but his music is more rigorously contrapuntal, and his elusive harmonic idiom is entirely his own.   MA

engraving. The process of cutting music notation into copper plates, from which the music is printed. See PRINTING AND PUBLISHING OF MUSIC, 2c.

enharmonic (from Gk. *en*, 'in', and *harmoniā*, 'harmony'). 1. In the music theory of the Ancient Greeks, a scale containing intervals smaller than a semitone.

2. In modern harmonic music theory, taking account of *equal temperament, notes that differ from each other in name but not in pitch (e.g. C♯/D♭); on a keyboard instrument these notes are genuinely identical in all but name, but on any other instrument an inflection can slightly sharpen or flatten the note so that there is a difference in pitch. Keys, intervals, and chords can also be described as enharmonic.

enigmatic scale (It.: *scala enigmatica*). A *scale consisting of the notes C–D♭–E–F♯–G♯–A♯–B–C, used as a cantus firmus by Verdi in his 'Ave Maria' (one of the *Quattro pezzi sacri*, 1898).

'Enigma' Variations. Popular name for Elgar's orchestral work, op. 36 (1899), the *Variations on an Original Theme* ('Enigma'). Dedicated 'to my friends pictured within', the work consists of 14 musical portraits, each headed with initials or a pseudonym from which the subjects' identities have been deduced; the last is a portrait of the composer himself. Elgar revised the finale for the third performance. Frederick Ashton choreographed a one-act ballet, *Enigma Variations* (1968), using the original finale.

En saga ('A Saga'). Symphonic poem, op. 9 (1892, revised 1902), by Sibelius.

ensalada (Sp., 'salad'). A type of 16th-century *quodlibet. The best-known *ensaladas* are those in Mateo Flecha's collection of 1581. Such pieces were often humorous or programmatic (e.g. *La guerra*, 'The Battle', and *El fuego*, 'The Fire'), but some were longer, with religious subject matter.

ensemble (Fr., 'together'). 1. A group of instrumentalists or singers, of any size from two players to an entire orchestra, though the term is most often applied to a chamber-music group or a small chamber orchestra.

2. By extension, the degree of unanimity of timing, balance, and style between the members of such a group: the subordination of the preference of the individual to that of the group.

3. In opera, an ensemble is an item for two or more soloists.   JMo

Entartete Musik. Originally, the name given to a propagandistic, racist exhibition, which opened in Düsseldorf on 24 May 1938, featuring the works of composers and musicologists proscribed and banned by the Nazi party on the grounds that they were 'entartet'. The word is frequently translated as 'decadent' or 'degenerate', though it derives from the science of genetics, where it means 'mutant', and hence was appropriated by the Nazis to signify either 'racially inferior' or 'mentally deficient'. The aim of the exhibition was the defamation of modernism, and the exhibits, many of which were daubed with obscene graffiti, consisted of scores, books, and recordings, the last of which could be switched on by the public at random. The featured writers and composers were all deemed to have affected German culture detrimentally during the years of the Weimar Republic (1918–33) by introducing 'non-Aryan' or 'anti-nationalistic' elements into music. Jewish writers and composers, those specifically open to jazz or American influences, communists or socialists, composers of Slavonic origin, and those who adopted atonality and serial techniques (the last considered by the Nazis to be the musical embodiment of 'Jewish Bolshevism') were the primary targets. The composers featured included Berg, Bloch, Eisler, Hindemith, Korngold, Krenek, Schoenberg, Schreker, Stravinsky, Toch, and Weill; the musicologists and critics included Adorno, Paul Bekker, and Alfred Einstein.

The designation *entartet* was, however, taken up by some modernists as an expression of anti-Fascist resistance, accompanied by demands for freedom of individual expression. Bartók famously wrote to Goebbels complaining that his music had not been included in the original exhibition. Henze and Kagel subsequently adopted the term as a protest against the normative cultural values of the German Federal Republic. In the last two decades of the 20th century *Entartete Musik* gained the symbolic resonance of a demand for musical pluralism as the result of an important and painstaking reappraisal of the works of those composers who suffered most deeply under Fascism, or who were profoundly affected by it. A reconstruction of the exhibition, together with considerable documentary evidence concerning its background, was undertaken in

Düsseldorf in 1988 by the musicologists Albrecht Dummling and Peter Girth. It was subsequently shown in Los Angeles in 1991 and London in 1995. Its appearance coincided with that of Decca's pioneering series of recordings issued on its own Entartete Musik label. The series commemorates both the murdered victims of Nazism and those whose careers and potential international reputations were curtailed or destroyed by it. The recordings have resulted in a major re-evaluation both of composers whose works were featured in the original exhibition (Eisler, Korngold, and Krenek) and of those whose works did not, including Goldschmidt, Wilhelm Grosz, Schulhoff, Ullmann, Wolpe, and Zemlinsky.   TA

📖 E. LEVI, *Music in the Third Reich* (London, 1994)

entfernt (Ger.). 'Distant'.

Entführung aus dem Serail, Die ('The Abduction from the Seraglio'). Opera in three acts by Mozart to a libretto by Christoph Friedrich Bretzner (*Belmont und Constanze, oder Die Entführung aus dem Serail*), adapted and enlarged by Gottlieb Stephanie the younger (Vienna, 1782).

entr'acte (Fr.). A piece of music, usually instrumental, played 'between the acts' of a play or opera (e.g. the music Schubert wrote to be played between the acts of *Rosamunde*, D797, 1823). The orchestral version of the famous Barcarolle from Offenbach's *Les Contes d'Hoffmann* (1881) serves as an entr'acte between Acts II and III, and Puccini's opera *Manon Lescaut* includes an entr'acte between Acts II and III to prepare the audience for Manon's transformation from successful courtesan to condemned criminal. The four Sea Interludes in Britten's *Peter Grimes* are another well-known example. Purcell's entr'actes were known as 'act tunes'.

See also INTERLUDE; ACT TUNE.

entrada. See INTRADA.

entrata (It., 'entrance', 'beginning'). An introduction or prelude.

entrée (Fr.; Sp.: *entrada*). A 17th- and 18th-century term, defined by Rousseau in his *Dictionnaire de musique* (1768) as: (1) an instrumental piece before a ballet (in which capacity it often occurs in the operas of Lully), or a march-like piece played to introduce an important character or group of dancers; (2) an act in an *opéra-ballet*, in which each act is self-contained and devoted to its own subject (as in Rameau's *Les Indes galantes*); (3) the moment of commencement of any part of a work.

The term *entrée* has also been applied to instrumental pieces such as Bach's Suite in A minor for violin and keyboard, probably because its march-like character suggests the operatic type of *entrée* described in (1) above.

In 17th- and 18th-century ballet, an *entrée* may also be a subdivision of an act, corresponding to a 'scene' in opera.

entremés (Sp.). Originally a comic musical interlude performed between the acts of a play (see INTERMEZZO, 2); the term came to be applied to a brief and independent musical entertainment of a humorous nature.

entschieden, entschlossen (Ger.). 'Decided', 'resolute', 'determined'.

envelope. The naturally occurring variation in amplitude of a sound wave; see ACOUSTICS, 4.

envoi [envoy]. 1. A short stanza added to the end of a strophic trouvère song.

2. A name for the works that the winners of the French *Prix de Rome for composition were required to submit to the Paris Conservatoire, as proof of progress during their three-year stay in Rome. One of the most celebrated was Debussy's *Printemps*.

Eötvös, Péter (*b* Székelyudvarhely, Transylvania, 2 Jan. 1944). Hungarian composer and conductor. He studied at the Budapest Academy of Music and in Cologne, where in 1968 he joined Stockhausen's performing group. There he also worked in the electronic music studio and began a career as a conductor that led to his appointment as music director of the Ensemble InterContemporain in Paris from 1980 to 1991. Eötvös began composing music for theatre, films, and television in his teens, and many of his concert works have an element of theatre. His opera *Drei Schwestern*, after Chekhov, was produced in Lyons in 1998.   ABur

epicedium (Lat., from Gk. *epikēdeion*). 'Funeral ode'. On the death of Queen Mary II (1694) George Herbert's *The Queen's Epicedium* was set by both Blow and Purcell.

epidiapente (Gk.). 'A fifth above', a direction to give a part or parts of a *canon a 5th above.

epilogue. Alternative name for *coda.

episode. 1. A section of a *fugue between subject entries.

2. The thematically and tonally contrasting sections in *rondo form.

epithalamium (Lat., from Gk. *epithalamion*). 'Wedding song'. The name is sometimes used for a piece of organ music to be performed at a wedding. A well-known example of a wedding song is 'Thrice happy lovers', from Act V of Purcell's *The Fairy Queen*.

equale [aequale] (Lat., 'equal'; It.: *eguale*). A work in which instruments or voices of the same type play each part (see EQUAL VOICES). In Austria during the 18th century and the early 19th the term denoted a type of short piece played, usually by four trombones, at a funeral service. Beethoven composed three *Equali* for use in Linz Cathedral on All Souls' Day 1812; two of these, with added vocal parts, were performed at his own funeral in 1827. In their instrumental form they were also played at William Gladstone's funeral in Westminster Abbey (1898). Bruckner's *Aequali* in C minor (1847) are scored for three trombones, and an echo of the tradition may be seen in Stravinsky's *In memoriam Dylan Thomas* (1954) for tenor, string quartet, and four trombones.   —/JBE

equal temperament. A system of tuning the scale whereby the octave is divided into 12 equal semitones. It is based on a cycle of 12 identical 5ths, each slightly smaller than 'pure', the reason being that a chain of 12 pure 5ths exceeds the equivalent of seven octaves by an interval known as the 'Pythagorean comma'. To compensate for this, and in order for the circle of 5ths to arrive at a perfect unison, in equal temperament each 5th is smaller than pure by ¹⁄₁₂ of a Pythagorean comma. Another important aspect of equal temperament is the adjustment of the 3rds, so that three major 3rds, or four minor 3rds, are equal to an octave. To achieve this, major 3rds must be tuned slightly larger than pure, minor 3rds smaller.

Equal temperament appears to have been used by makers and players of fretted instruments at least as early as the 16th century, and some 16th-century composers evidently favoured the enharmonic advantages of the system. It was slower to gain acceptance among keyboard musicians, though Frescobaldi gave it his approval in the 1630s and it was taken up by his pupil Froberger in his later keyboard works. Most Baroque keyboard musicians preferred such alternatives as *mean-tone temperament or other slightly irregular tunings. One argument against equal temperament was that the major 3rds sounded too high, and the minor 3rds too low, though it was conceded that using the system in ensemble music would result in a more satisfactory blending of different instruments. Bach's famous 48 preludes and fugues, the first book of which was published under the title *Das wohltemperirte Clavier*, were not necessarily conceived with equal temperament in mind, for though Bach evidently intended the term *wohltemperirte* to signify a tuning system suitable for all 24 keys, equal temperament was not the only such system in use at that time.

In the late 18th century, the German theorist F. W. Marpurg put forward a strong case in favour of equal temperament, and as a result of his influence the system eventually became the standard tuning for keyboard instruments. It was adopted by the Broadwood firm of piano makers in the 1840s, and used by the organ builder Cavaillé-Coll in his later instruments. Contemporary German organ builders followed Cavaillé-Coll's lead, but in England it was largely resisted until after the Great Exhibition of 1851. Equal temperament is now widely regarded as the standard tuning of the Western 12-note chromatic scale.

See also TEMPERAMENT.   LC

equal voices (It.: *voci eguali*; Lat.: *voces aequales*; Ger.: *gleiche Stimmen*). A choral composition for voices of the same kind, such as two or three sopranos. The parts are normally arranged so that the top line is divided among the participating voices. Occasionally the term is used less correctly in contradistinction to 'mixed voices', meaning for children's voices alone, women's voices alone, or men's voices alone, rather than a combination of men's and women's voices.

Érard. French firm of piano and harp makers founded in Paris in *c*.1780 by Sébastien Érard (1752–1831). His invention of the *clavecin mécanique* (1779) and royal patronage led him, with his brother Jean-Baptiste (1745–1826), to manufacture pianos. They moved to London (1886–96), where they opened a shop. Their improvements to pianos (double escapement and key repetition) and harps (single- and double-action) made them one of the most successful firms of their day.

AL

ergriffen (Ger.). 'Deeply moved', 'stirred'.

Erkel, Ferenc (*b* Gyula, county of Békés, 7 Nov. 1810; *d* Budapest, 15 June 1893). Hungarian composer, pianist, conductor, and teacher. His first studies were in Poszony (now Bratislava), where his family had long-standing roots. In 1827 he took up a position in an aristocratic household in Koloszvár (now Cluj-Napoca, Romania), where he established a reputation as a pianist and gained experience as a conductor of the local opera company with which, in 1835, he moved to Buda. There and in Pest he remained until his retirement in 1874.

Erkel was fundamental in the awakening of Hungarian musical life: he was music director at the National Theatre from its foundation until he retired; he founded (1853) and conducted the Philharmonic concerts until 1871; he was the first professor of piano and instrumentation at newly established Academy of Music and then its director (1875–88); and he composed the Hungarian national anthem and the first national opera, *Hunyadi László* (both 1844). He played a Mozart concerto at his own 80th birthday concert and made his final appearance as a conductor in 1892. Many of his nine operas, several of which were written in collaboration with his sons, take up national themes; the most successful of them was *Bánk bán* (1861).   MA

Erlanger, Baron Frédéric d' (*b* Paris, 29 May 1868; *d* London, 23 April 1943). British composer, of German-American parentage. Born into a well-known family of bankers, he studied in Paris with Anselm Ehmant, then moved to London, taking British nationality. Notable among his four operas is *Tess* (Naples, 1906), with a libretto by Luigi Illica based on Thomas Hardy's *Tess of the d'Urbervilles*. His essentially conservative output also includes a ballet, orchestral and chamber music, and a Requiem for soloists, chorus, and orchestra (1931).   ABur

Erlebach, Philipp Heinrich (*b* Esens, Friesland, *bapt.* 25 July 1657; *d* Rudolstadt, 17 April 1714). German composer. He was Kapellmeister for 33 years at the ducal court in Rudolstadt. His surviving works include *Six ouvertures* (Nuremberg, 1693), six sonatas for violin, bass viol, and continuo (Nuremberg, 1694), two volumes of songs with instrumental ritornellos entitled *Harmonische Freude* (Nuremberg, 1697, 1710), cantatas, motets, and sacred songs.   WT

Erleichterung (Ger.). 'An easing', i.e. a simplified version.

Erlkönig ('The Erl-King'). Song (1814) by Schubert to a poem from Johann Wolfgang von Goethe's ballad opera *Die Fischerin* (1782). Several composers set the poem, including Reichardt, Zelter, and Loewe, and Beethoven left sketches of a setting.

erlöschend (Ger.). 'Dying out'.

ermattend (Ger.). 'Tiring', 'weakening'.

Ermione ('Hermione'). Opera in two acts by Rossini to a libretto by Andrea Leone Tottola after Jean Racine's *Andromaque* (1667) (Naples, 1819).

Ernani. Opera in four parts by Verdi to a libretto by Francesco Maria Piave after Hugo's play *Hernani* (1830) (Venice, 1844).

erniedrigen (Ger.). 'To lower', i.e. flatten in pitch.

Ernste Gesänge, Vier. See Vier ernste Gesänge.

'Eroica' Symphony. Beethoven's Symphony no. 3 (1803–4); he composed it in honour of Napoleon and planned to call it *Bonaparte*, but when he heard that Napoleon had declared himself emperor, in 1804, he changed the title to *Sinfonia eroica, composta per festiggiare il sovvenire di un grand uomo* ('Heroic Symphony, composed to celebrate the Memory of a Great Man') and dedicated it to Prince Franz Joseph von Lobkowitz. The finale is a set of variations on a theme Beethoven had used in earlier works, notably *Die *Geschöpfe des Prometheus* (1801) and the **'Eroica' Variations*.

'Eroica' Variations. Beethoven's Piano Variations in E♭ major op. 35 (1802), so called because he used the theme in the finale of the **'Eroica' Symphony*. Beethoven had used the theme in the seventh of his *Contredanses* for orchestra (1802) and in *Die *Geschöpfe des Prometheus* (1800–1); the work is therefore also known as the *Prometheus Variations*.

eroticism in music. The inherent irrationalism of music, its dependence on effective patterns of tension and release, pulse and rhythm, and its emphasis on emotion and feeling have always allowed it to give voice to the ebb and flow of human sexuality and its yearning for consummation in physical reality. The oldest extant erotic music is found in the works of the trouvères and the Minnesinger (the word itself literally means 'singers of sexual love') as well as in the earthiness of such manuscripts as *Carmina burana*, in which sexuality is extolled as a valid alternative to spiritual austerity.

Eroticism was a central subject for the 16th-century Italian and English madrigalists, who exploited the sexual conceits of contemporary poetry, with its metaphoric equation of 'sighing' and 'dying' with ecstasy and orgasm (see SYMBOLISM). It is with the emergence of opera, however, in which music is linked to individual psychology, that sexual expression begins to gain its greatest force. The final duet of Monteverdi's *L'incoronazione di Poppea* (1642), itself a study of the sexuality of power in which love is rendered redundant, forms an effective prototype for much erotic music in its reliance on closely entwined vocal lines and harmonies that arouse desire by repeatedly delaying melodic and harmonic resolution. The psychological bifurcation between desire and love, already present in *Poppea*, is integral to opera's exploration of the splits in the human psyche between subconscious thought and conscious action. Mozart's operas to librettos by Da Ponte examine attempts to constrain the irrationality of desire within the artificial boundaries of class and society. Monteverdi's methodology, meanwhile, is not in fact far removed from that of Wagner in *Tristan und Isolde* (1865), considered by many to be the most erotic work in musical history, in which tonality itself seems suspended in chromatic irresolution as the lovers strive for a level of erotic fulfilment that is impossible in life.

Conflicting sexual attitudes have frequently led to inherent musical or dramatic tensions. The 19th century, though it shirked pleasure, was obsessed by desire. Wagner, avoiding all depiction of physical sex, relentlessly balances eroticism with prudishness, most notably in *Tannhäuser* (1845, rev. 1861), which also polarizes women as saints or demonic whores. Elsewhere in Wagner's output the expression of desire is equated with emotional or physical catastrophe. Many 19th-century works that dared to suggest or imply pleasurable sexual activity (Verdi's *Rigoletto* and *La traviata*, Bizet's *Carmen*, for instance) met with a considerable outcry, and it is not until Strauss's tone-poem *Don Juan* (1889) that an element of genuine hedonism, absent since Mozart, re-enters music. Strauss is the first composer to portray not only desire but also the sexual act itself, beginning with his opera *Feuersnot* (1901) and continuing with the *Symphonia domestica* (1902–3), *Der Rosenkavalier* (1911), and *Arabella* (1933).

Strauss's work also coincided with the Freudian revolution that constrained sexuality within the parameters of psychoanalytic pathology. The erotic and harmonic extremism of *Salome* (1905) and *Elektra* (1909) have been seen as a parallel development along similar lines, as have the operas of Franz Schreker and, most notably, the profound sexual expressionism of Berg's *Lulu* (1937), written after the Schoenbergian redefinition of tonality and depicting an incarnate sex goddess whose principal theme is the note row from which the musical structure of the entire work is derived. In France the heady sensuousness of Debussy, Ravel, and early Roussel retains the emphasis on sexual pleasure and hedonism. The radical re-evaluation of sexual attitudes in the second half of the 20th century brought with it a new sexual frankness, found in such works as Stockhausen's *Stimmung* (1968), Zimmermann's *Die Soldaten* (1965), and Ginastera's *Bomarzo* (1967), and witnessed the emergence of powerful trends in both feminist and gay musicology.   TA

📖 L. MACY, 'Speaking of sex: Metaphor and performance in the Italian madrigal', *Journal of Musicology*, 14 (1996), 1–34

erotikon (Gk.). A love song, or its instrumental equivalent.

Ersatz (Ger.). 'Substitute'.

Erste Walpurgisnacht, Die ('The First Walpurgis Night'). Cantata, op. 60 (1832, revised 1843), by Mendelssohn, a setting for chorus and orchestra of Johann Wolfgang von Goethe's ballad. Walpurgis Night is the spring festival when witches ride to the Brocken in the Harz Mountains.

ersterbend (Ger.). 'Dying away'.

Erwartung ('Expectation'). Monodrama (composed in 1909) in one act by Schoenberg for soprano and orchestra, to a libretto by Marie Pappenheim (Prague, 1924). See also EXPRESSIONISM.

erweitert (Ger.). 'Expanded', i.e. broadened (at a steadier pace).

Es (Ger.). The note E♭; *Eses*, the note E♭♭.

escapement. A mechanism on the piano that prevents the hammer from rebounding on to the string after it falls away. See PIANOFORTE.

Esclarmonde. Opera in four acts by Massenet to a libretto by Alfred Blau and Louis de Gramont after *Parthenopoeus de Blois*, a medieval *chanson de geste* (Paris, 1889).

Escobar, Pedro de [Pedro del Puerto] (*b* Oporto, *c*.1465; *d* after 1535). Portuguese church musician and composer. He worked in Spain for much of his adult career, first in the chapel choir of Queen Isabella (1489–99), then as Master of the Choristers at Seville Cathedral (1507–14). Most of Escobar's surviving works are liturgical, but he also wrote Spanish-texted villancicos.   JM

Escurel, Jehannot d'. See L'ESCUREL, JEHAN DE.

esercizio (It.). *Exercise'.

España ('Spain'). Rhapsody (1883) by Chabrier for orchestra.

Espansiva, Sinfonia. See SINFONIA ESPANSIVA.

Esplá (y Triay), Oscar (*b* Alicante, 5 Aug. 1886; *d* Madrid, 6 Jan. 1976). Spanish composer. He studied philosophy and engineering at Barcelona University, 1903–11, but at the age of 20 he won first prize in an international composition contest, subsequently studying with Reger and, later, Saint-Saëns. On the outbreak of the Civil War he left Spain for Brussels, eventually returning to Spain in the 1950s. He made use of Mediterranean folk culture, inventing a 'Levantine' scale (C–D♭–E♭–E–F–G♭–A♭–B♭) which pervades much of his music. His works include symphonic poems and suites, the *Sonata del sur* (1943) for piano and orchestra, a choral symphony, chamber music, operas and ballets, and a harmonically refined Requiem (1949).

WT/CW

espressivo (It.). 'Expressive', 'with expression'; it is abbreviated *espr*.

esquisse (Fr.). 'Sketch'. Debussy described the three movements of his *La Mer* (1903–5) as 'trois esquisses symphoniques'.

Esquivel (Barahona), **Juan** (*b* Ciudad Rodrigo, *c.*1560; *d* after 1615). Spanish composer. He was *maestro de capilla* successively at the cathedrals of Oviedo (from 1581), Calahorra, and (possibly from 1591) Ciudad Rodrigo. Three collections of his music were published in Salamanca: masses (1608), motets (also 1608), and an enormous collection of psalms, hymns, canticles, Marian antiphons, and masses (1613). Chromaticism features prominently in some of his works.

OR

essential note. A note belonging to the chord in question, as opposed to a passing note, a suspension, an appoggiatura, etc., which are all 'unessential notes'.

essercizio. An old spelling of *esercizio* (*'exercise').

Estampes ('Engravings'). Three piano pieces by Debussy (1903): *Pagodes* ('Pagodas'), *La Soirée dans Grenade* ('Evenings in Granada'), and *Jardins sous la pluie* ('Gardens in the Rain'); the first was orchestrated by Caplet, and the second by Busser.

estampie (Fr.; It.: *istampita, stampita*; Provençal: *estampida*). A type of textless melody popular during the 13th and 14th centuries; the name was also applied to poetry. In melodies designated as *estampies* the absence of words suggests that the performance was purely instrumental and as such the genre may be the earliest known instrumental music in the West. Some scholars believe it was intended for dancing. The form, which is similar to that of the *lai, consists of a series of phrases (*puncta*), each of which is repeated immediately using a first- (*ouvert) and a second-time (*clos*) ending. The two endings are usually the same throughout the piece (i.e. AxAy, BxBy, CxCy, etc.). The best-known example is the song *Kalenda maya*, said to have been written by the troubadour Raimbaut de Vaqueiras (*c.*1150–1207) to an instrumental *estampie* he had heard performed. The earliest extant melodies are in French early 14th-century manuscripts. —JBE

Esterházy. Hungarian noble family, patrons of the arts. **Pál** [Paul] **Esterházy** (*b* 7 Sept. 1635; *d* 26 March 1713), who succeeded to the principate in 1687, consolidated the family's wealth and power. A general, poet, artist, and composer, he published a collection of 55 sacred cantatas, *Harmonia caelestis*, in 1711. His grandson, **Paul Anton** [Pál Antal] (*b* 22 April 1711; *d* 18 March 1762), assumed the title in 1734. Adept in German and French and married to an Italian, he oversaw the Europeanization of the court at Eisenstadt. He renovated the palace garden, built an extensive library, initiated theatrical presentations, assembled an orchestra, and engaged Joseph Haydn as vice-Kapellmeister in 1761.

In 1762 Paul Anton was succeeded by his younger brother, **Nicolaus Joseph** [Miklós] 'the Magnificent' (*b* 18 Dec. 1714; *d* 28 Sept. 1790), who oversaw the renovation of an old hunting-lodge in Süttör, western Hungary, into a miniature Versailles called Eszterháza. He maintained a large musical establishment, including an orchestra, an opera house, and a marionette theatre. For his music-loving prince, Haydn wrote numerous symphonies, operas, and chamber pieces, including over 160 works for the baryton.

Nicolaus was succeeded by his son, (Paul) **Anton** (*b* 11 April 1738; *d* 22 Jan. 1794), who disbanded the orchestra and opera troupe in the year of his accession but retained Haydn as Kapellmeister. His son and heir, **Nicolaus Esterházy** (*b* 12 Dec. 1765; *d* 25 Nov. 1833), reconstituted the orchestra, replacing Haydn as head of the Kapelle in 1802. Haydn wrote six masses for him, and Beethoven the Mass in C op. 86 (1807). Other members of the Esterházy family include Count Franz [Ferenc] Esterházy (1715–85), at whose memorial service Mozart's *Masonic Funeral Music* was performed; Count Johann [János] Esterházy (1754–1840), for whom Mozart played in 1784 and gave his arrangement of Handel's *Messiah* in 1789; Count Johann (Karl) Esterházy (1755–1834), who employed Schubert as music teacher to his daughters; and Count Michael Esterházy (1783–1874), for whom Liszt played as a boy.

WT/CC

Esther. Oratorio (1732) by Handel to a text after Jean Racine; in its first version it was a masque (?Cannons, ?1718); Handel revised and expanded it into an oratorio, with additions to the text by Samuel Humphreys.

estinguendo (It.). 'Extinguishing', i.e. dying away.

estinto (It.). 'Extinguished', i.e. barely audible.

estompé (Fr.). 'Toned down'.

estribillo (Sp.). A 17th-century term for a refrain in a song (for example in the *villancico).

Estro armonico, L' ('The Harmonious Inspiration'). Vivaldi's op. 3 (Amsterdam, 1711 and 1712), 12 concertos for different solo combinations of violin, two violins, four violins, and cello, with orchestra and continuo. Six of them were transcribed by J. S. Bach.

Eszterháza. Country palace of the *Esterházy family.

éteint (Fr.). 'Extinguished', i.e. barely audible.

Et exspecto resurrectionem mortuorum ('And I look forward to the resurrection of the dead'). Work (1964) by Messiaen for 18 woodwind, 16 brass, and three percussionists (scoring which makes it suitable for vast spaces); each of its five movements is headed with a biblical quotation.

ethnomusicology. A term first used by the Dutch scholar Jaap Kunst in the subtitle of his book *Musicologica: A Study of the Nature of Ethno-musicology, its Problems, Methods, and Representative Personalities* (1950). The discipline's objects of study, methodologies, lineages, and histories have varied according to the perspectives of ethnographically and historically situated scholars and schools. Initially a discipline within universities in the USA, Canada, and Europe, ethnomusicology had as its objects of study the traditional art and folk musics of the exotically removed 'other', whether the 'other' was in relation to geography (e.g. non-Western music), ethnicity (e.g. music of 'oriental' peoples and 'primitive' tribes), or class (e.g. 'folk' music). Kunst, for instance, delineated the field as 'the music and the musical instruments of all non-European peoples, including both the so-called primitive peoples and the civilized Eastern nations', and Nettl (1964) as 'the music of non-literate cultures, the music of advanced oriental societies, and the folk music of Western and oriental civilizations'.

During the second half of the 20th century, scholars began to suggest that a discipline of ethnomusicology should be distinguished by its methodology rather than its object of study. Alan P. Merriam (1923–88) in the USA and John Blacking (1928–90) in Britain pioneered 'fieldwork' and 'ethnography' as essential methodological tools. Merriam attempted to redress the theoretical balance within ethnomusicology, which appeared at that time to be weighted in favour of musicological perspectives, by advocating an anthropological approach. Ethnomusicologists gradually distanced themselves from the German school of 'comparative musicology' (*vergleichende Musikwissenschaft*), with its emphasis on the music itself, its evolutionary, diffusionist theories, and comparative methods, and aligned themselves more with the methods of British 'social' anthropology and American 'cultural' anthropology. Merriam's dynamic four-part model for ethnomusicological research (conceptualization of music, human behaviour, sound, and aesthetics), as outlined in *The Anthropology of Music* (1964), became seminal to the discipline's development on both sides of the Atlantic. Intellectual perspectives mirrored those used in anthropology, and the process of integrating the two disciplines began: American ethnomusicologists studied music 'in culture' then 'as culture' (Merriam), reintroduced the comparative study of musical cultures (Nettl, 1975), and, through Mantle

Hood's notion of 'bi-musicality', reasserted the importance of the musical object; British ethnomusicologists stressed that music was 'humanly organized sound' based both in experience of society and in the body and, as ethnomusicology gradually found its place in university music departments, began to reintroduce the musical note as an object of study. Anthropological models continued to be used. The Swiss scholar Hugo Zemp, trained by Claude Lévi-Strauss in Paris, and the Canadian Jean-Jacques Nattiez introduced French structural theories to the discipline.

Notation and transcription became an issue as scholars realized the inherent subjectivity of these processes and the shortcomings of a standard system such as that devised in 1909 by Hornbostel and Abraham. The distinction made in 1908 by B. I. Gilman between observational theories and facts as transcription was formulated as 'prescriptive' and 'descriptive' music writing by Seeger (1958). Various solutions to the problem of transcribing the sounds of other cultures have been sought: adapting their own traditional notations (Hood), using sol-fa notation (Kara), producing multi-dimensional (Wade) or conceptual (Ellingson) transcriptions, and involving musicians in the transcription process (Widdess).

Two early publications were significant in recognizing the 'cultural' rather than 'natural' production and evaluation of musical sounds: Jean-Jacques Rousseau's *Dictionnaire de musique* (1768), which included the musics of Swiss, Iranian, Chinese, and Canadian first-nation peoples, suggested that different peoples react differently to 'diverse musical accents'; and the British philologist and phonetician A. J. Ellis (1814–90), in his work on the scales of various nations (1885), suggested that 'acoustical phenomena' should be studied by scientists rather than musicians, since the latter tended to consider 'familiar' sounds as 'natural'. Moreover, Ellis's system of pitch measurement, which divided the Western tempered semitone into 100 cents, made possible a less ethnocentric analysis of scales and modes.

In the post-World War II modernist era, the establishment of ethnomusicology as an independent discipline led to the creation of a lineal history in which the discipline grew from two 'schools': the German school of comparative musicology and the American school of musicological and anthropological methods. Theodore Baker's doctoral dissertation *Über die Musik der nordamerikanischen Wilden* (Leipzig, 1882; Eng. trans. 1982) has been cited as the first contribution to the German school, though 'vergleichende Musikwissenschaft' is first found in Adler's famous discussion of the term three years later. Scholars of the German school, who included E. M. von Hornbostel

(1877–1935), Carl Stumpf (1848–1936), Otto Abraham (1872–1926), Robert Lachmann (1892–1939), Curt Sachs (1881–1959), and George Herzog (1901–84), focused on the structural aspects of non-Western musics—the study of musical systems, styles, and tunings—by transcribing recordings made in the German colonies and from visitors to Europe. Scholars included in the early lineage of the American school are the anthropologist Franz Boas (1858–1942), George Herzog, Alice Cunningham Fletcher (1838–1923), Frances Densemore (1867–1957), and Charles Seeger (1886–1979).

Towards the end of the 20th century ethnomusicology developed into a worldwide network of disciplines, with different nations and regions asserting their own histories, fields, methods, and terminologies in response to their own needs. With the post-cold war realignment of political relations, scholars in former Soviet-bloc countries, with their methods of musical folklore and evolutionary history, began to participate more actively in international ethnomusicological discourse. British ethnomusicologists began to look back for their discipline's beginnings not only to Ellis's theories but also to the French sociologist Émile Durkheim's concepts of 'emotional effervescence' and 'social solidarity' generated during ritual (1915) and to the early work of British anthropologists—for example the filmed dance sequences of the Malu-Bornai ceremonies during A. C. Haddon's 'Cambridge Anthropological Expedition to the Torres Strait' in 1898, and A. R. Radcliffe-Brown's interpretation (1922) of the music and dance of the Andaman Islanders as a moral force acting on the individual—as well as to the folk music collections of Cecil Sharp and Percy Grainger.

Each nation has its specialists whose perspectives not only form part of that nation's own lineage but who often influence the lineages of others. The organologist André Schaeffner (1895–1980), for example, who worked with the Dogon of Mali (formerly French Sudan), is an important figure in French ethnomusicology but also taught and influenced John Blacking; the Romanian Constantin Brăiloiu, who argued that music is indissolubly attached to social phenomena, is an essential influence in French and Swiss as well as Romanian ethnomusicologies. Differing perspectives are expressed in national terminologies. Bulgarian and Ukrainian scholars, for instance, equate ethnomusicology with *muzikal'naya etnografiya* (musical ethnography), and *muzikal'naya fol'kloristika* (musical folklore) respectively.

Ethnomusicology's perceptions of its field as the music of 'others' was linked to the colonial historical period, and the discipline's origins were back-projected on to writings about music in colonial holdings. (Often cited, for instance, are the Swiss theologian Jean de Léry's writings about Brazil (1578); the French missionary Joseph Amiot's work on Chinese music (1779); Sir William Jones's writings about Hindu music in India (1792); the Dutch philologist J. A. Wilkens's description of the gamelan orchestra (1850); and the work of E. Coart and A. de Haulleville (1902) on the music of the Belgian Congo.) In the post-colonial era, the establishment of many new national and regional schools and institutions in ethnomusicology has highlighted different voices. Some, such as those in Japanese ethnomusicology (*minzoku ongakugaku*), embrace Western theoretical models; others, such as ethnomusicologists in Africa (e.g. Agawu and Masolo), Latin America (Béhague), and China (Witzleben), contest the hegemony of Western ethnomusicological theories, practices, and terminologies.

European and American ethnomusicologies incorporated into their histories collections of national folk musics made by scholars and classical musicians—for instance those of the British-American ballad collector F. J. Child (1883–98), the English folksong collector Cecil Sharp (1907), and the Hungarians Béla Bartók (1924) and Zoltan Kodály (1937)—even though their activities pre-date the establishment of ethnomusicology, and the individuals involved would have viewed themselves and their activities differently. This harmonized with the rise of the nation-state as a site for musical research from the 1950s and acquired renewed importance during the rise of national schools of ethnomusicology during the 1990s.

Before World War II, musical scholars were influenced by theories from a range of disciplines, for instance acoustics, anthropology, ethnology, folklore, linguistics, musicology, psychology, physics, and sociology. Ethnomusicology has continued to cross-fertilize in intra- and interdisciplinary ways. As the 20th century progressed, close links were established between British and American ethnomusicologies and their national anthropologies that eventually reached a mutual accommodation: North Americans incorporated British social perspectives under the overarching concept of 'musical culture' as part of a 'study of music in the context of human life' (Todd Titon), and British ethnomusicologists took into consideration cultural as well as social aspects of music and dance. New interdisciplinary relationships have been established—for example with popular music studies, performance studies, performing arts, archaeo-musicology, and cultural studies—in addition to the continuing traditional ones.

For contemporary British and American ethnomusicologists, the ethnomusicological field now embraces 'human musical life in its full richness and diversity' (British Forum for Ethnomusicology, 2001)—

that is, the study of the local and global musics of individuals, communities, and societies throughout the world (including traditional art and folk musics, rural and urban musics, pop and world musics, micromusics, and Western art music). Theoretical perspectives have expanded from static functional or structural models in which music was perceived as a reflection of other aspects of homogeneous society and culture, to embrace emotion, experience, practice, and the power of music and performance to create society and culture. Social, cultural, biological, and musical aspects of music and dance are investigated, and a range of issues including ethnicity, nationalism, colonialism, diaspora, globalization, race, sexuality, gender, and the new historicism are addressed. Such concepts as 'culture', 'society', and 'fieldwork' have themselves become areas of contention; and the subjectivity of scholarly evaluations, radical changes in the discipline, and the need to reassess its histories and methods have been acknowledged. A fierce debate concerning the value and use of the term 'ethnomusicology' has provoked renewed discussion about the central object of ethnomusicological study and the nature of the discipline—or disciplines.

Ethnomusicological methods have been consistently influenced by technology. The invention by Thomas Edison of the phonograph in 1877 was soon put to use in the field (e.g. J. W. Fewkes's recordings in Maine in 1890, Béla Vikár's in Hungary in 1896, and Evgeniya Linoyova's in Russia in 1897), as were photographic equipment, cine-cameras, and magic lantern projectors (e.g. the Torres Strait Expedition). As new technologies such as cassette machines, CD, DVD and video recorders, and the World Wide Web have been assimilated, and as increasing globalization has facilitated access to the world's musics, debate continues about the politics and ethics of representation, the appropriation of other peoples' musics, the preservation of the world's musics, and the aims and methods of ethnomusicology.

International societies include the Society for Ethnomusicology (SEM; formed in Philadelphia in 1955), which publishes the journal *Ethnomusicology*, and the International Council for Traditional Music (ICTM), which was founded as the International Folk Music Council in 1947 with 'folk music' as the prime object of study but which changed its title in 1982. The ICTM maintains national committees throughout the world and publishes a *Yearbook for Traditional Music*. The UK and Ireland affiliated committee of ICTM, the British Forum for Ethnomusicology, remains linked but independent, publishing its own journal, *The British Journal of Ethnomusicology*. The European Seminar in Ethnomusicology (ESEM) was founded in Belfast in 1981 with the aim of counteracting the American domination of the SEM and

produces *Information Bulletins*. Online journals include *Ethnomusicology Online* and *Music and Anthropology*.

CP

📖 G. ADLER, 'Umfang, Methode und Ziel der Musikwissenschaft', *Vierteljahrsschrift für Musikwissenschaft*, 1 (1885), 5–20 · A. J. ELLIS, 'On the musical scales of various nations', *Journal of the Society of Arts*, 33 (1885), 485–527 · J. W. FEWKES, 'A contribution to Passamaquoddy folklore', *Journal of American Folklore*, 3 (1890), 257–80 · E. M. VON HORNBOSTEL and O. ABRAHAM, 'Vorschläge für die Transkription exotischer Melodien', *Sammelbände der International Musikgesellschaft*, 2 (1909), 1 · É. DURKHEIM, *The Elementary Forms of Religious Life* (London, 1915) · A. R. RADCLIFFE-BROWN, *The Andaman Islanders* (Cambridge, 1922) · R. LACHMANN, 'Musiksysteme und Musikauffassung', *Zeitschrift für vergleichende Musikwissenschaft*, 3 (1935), 1–23 C. SEEGER, 'Prescriptive and descriptive music writing', *Musical Quarterly*, 44 (1958), 184–95 · B. NETTL, *Reference Materials in Ethnomusicology* (Detroit, 1961, 2/1967); 'Symposium on Transcription and Analysis', *Ethnomusicology*, 8/3 (1964), 223–77 · A. P. MERRIAM, *The Anthropology of Music* (Evanston, IL, 1964) · B. NETTL, *Theory and Method in Ethnomusicology* (New York, 1964) · G. KARA, *Chants d'un barde mongol* (Budapest, 1970) · M. HOOD, *The Ethnomusicologist* (New York, 1971) · H. ZEMP, *Musique Dan: La Musique dans la pensée et la vie sociale d'une société africaine* (Paris, 1971) · J. BLACKING, *How Musical is Man?* (Seattle, 1973) · J.-J. NATTIEZ, *Fondements d'une sémiologie de la musique* (Paris, 1975) · B. NETTL, 'The state of research in ethnomusicology, and recent developments', *Current Musicology*, 20 (1975), 67–81 A. P. MERRIAM, 'Definitions of "comparative musicology" and "ethnomusicology": An historical-theoretical perspective', *Ethnomusicology*, 21/2 (1977), 189–204 · S. FELD, *Sound and Sentiment: Birds, Weeping, Poetics, and Song in Kaluli Expression* (Philadelphia, 1982, 2/1990) · B. C. WADE, *Khyāl: Creativity within North India's Classical Music Tradition* (Cambridge, 1984) · A. SEEGER, *Why Suyá Sing: A Musical Anthropology of an Amazonian People* (Cambridge, 1987) · P. V. BOHLMAN, *The Study of Folk Music in the Modern World* (Bloomington, IN, 1988) · R. H. FINNEGAN, *The Hidden Musicians: Music-Making in an English Town* (Cambridge, 1989) G. BÉHAGUE, 'Reflections on the ideological history of Latin American ethnomusicology', *Comparative Musicology and Anthropology of Music*, ed. B. Nettl and P. V. Bohlman (Chicago, 1991) · V. K. AGAWU, 'Representing African music', *Critical Inquiry*, 18/2 (1992), 245–66 · T. ELLINGSON, *Transcription*, The New Grove Handbooks in Music (London, 1992) · H. MYERS (ed.), *Ethnomusicology: An Introduction* (London, 1992) · M. SLOBIN, *Subcultural Sounds: Micromusics of the West* (Hanover, 1993) · T. RICE, *May it Fill your Soul: Experiencing Bulgarian Music* (Chicago, 1994) · R. WIDDESS, 'Involving the performers in transcription and analysis: A collaborative approach to *dhrupad*', *Ethnomusicology*, 38/1 (1994), 59–80 · J. BLACKING, *Music, Culture, and Experience* (Chicago, 1995) J. TODD TITON (ed.), *Worlds of Music: An Introduction to the Music of the World's Peoples* (New York, 1996) · G. F. BARZ and T. J. Cooley (eds.), *Shadows in the Field: New Perspectives for Fieldwork in Ethnomusicology* (New York, 1997) · J. L. Witzleben, 'Whose ethnomusicology? Western ethnomusicology and the study of Asian music', *Ethnomusicology*, 41 (1997), 220–42 · D. A. Masolo, 'Presencing the past and remembering the present: Social features of popular music in Kenya', *Music and the Racial Imagination*, ed. R. M. Radano and P. V. Bohlman (Chicago, 2000) · C. Pegg, *Mongolian Music, Dance and Oral Narrative: Performing Diverse Identities* (Seattle, 2001)

ethos. In the theory of ancient Greek music, 'ethos' refers to the character conveyed by an entire piece of music or by one of its component parts. Thus, an individual *tonos*, a rhythmic pattern, a particular instrumental timbre, and the text itself convey varying ethoses, and their mixture in a musical composition conveys an overall ethos. Theoretical descriptions of the working of musical ethos begin to appear in the 5th century BC and are developed throughout the Hellenistic period.   TM

Étoile, L' ('The Star'). Opera in three acts by Chabrier to a libretto by Eugène Leterrier and Albert Vanloo (Paris, 1877).

Étoile du nord, L' ('The North Star'). Opera in three acts by Meyerbeer to a libretto by Eugène Scribe (Paris, 1854).

Eton Choirbook (Windsor, Eton College Library, 178). The most important surviving source of early Tudor church music, written down *c*.1500–5 for use at Eton College; the manuscript is large enough for about 20 choirboys to sing from. It contains about 50 complete works (a further 40 or so are fragmentary or have been lost altogether), most of them elaborate antiphons and settings of the *Magnificat* for four, five, six, or more voices. The composers represented include John Browne, William Cornysh, Richard Davy, Robert Fayrfax, and Walter Lambe. A modern edition by Frank Ll. Harrison has been published in the *Musica britannica* series (1956–61, rev. 1969–73).

étouffer (Fr., 'to damp', 'to stifle'). Direction to mute a violin, to damp a kettledrum, or to apply the soft pedal on a piano; *étouffoir*, a piano damper.

étude (Fr.). 'Study'. The essence of the genre is revealed in the title of one of J. B. Cramer's sets, 'Dulce et utile' ('sweet and useful'), as distinct from an 'exercise' which is merely useful. The study was above all designed to encourage amateurs by wrapping up the necessary technical practice in a piece that was interesting to play and tolerable to listen to, whereas a would-be professional might prefer to work on purely mechanical exercises such as those of Czerny, Dohnányi, or C.-L. Hanon. The first set using the term

(actually named *Studio per il pianoforte*) was published by Cramer in London in 1804. Each piece generally concentrates on a particular aspect of instrumental or compositional technique, often by the repetition of the same figure or feature at various pitches. Earlier examples had used other terms, such as 'esercizio' (It.), 'exercice' (Fr.), 'lesson' (Eng.), or 'Übung' (Ger.).

Piano studies were published in the early 19th century by Clementi (*Gradus ad Parnassum*), Hummel, and Henselt, among others. As the century progressed, they began to be written for professional concert use as well as for private practice, resulting in works of such virtuosity as Liszt's two *Études de concert* and his *Études en forme de 12 exercices* (revised first as *Grandes études*, and then as *Études d'exécution transcendante*), dedicated to Czerny; Chopin's 12 *Grandes études* op. 10, dedicated to Liszt, and his *12 études* op. 25; and Schumann's *Études symphoniques* op. 13, dedicated to Sterndale Bennett. Liszt also transcribed some of Paganini's virtuoso violin music for piano as the *Études d'exécution transcendante d'après Paganini*. Later composers who have written notable sets of piano *études* include Alkan, Saint-Saëns, and Debussy. Studies for solo violin include Paganini's brilliant *24 caprices*, which provided a fertile source of inspiration for other composers.

In the 20th century, studies continued to be written both for professional concert use and for private amateur practice; of course, they can be for any instrument, or even for the voice or orchestra. The piano study has been especially cultivated by eastern European composers, notably Skryabin, Rakhmaninov, Prokofiev, Bartók, and Ligeti. Stravinsky wrote one for pianola, which he later orchestrated; other orchestral examples have been contributed by Henze, Rawsthorne, and Milhaud.   WT/NT

Études d'exécution transcendante d'après Paganini ('Transcendental Studies after Paganini'). Work for solo piano by Liszt, transcriptions of six of Paganini's violin caprices, including *La campanella*; they were composed in 1838–9 and revised in 1851 as *Grandes études de Paganini*. Liszt also composed a set of 12 *Études d'exécution transcendante* ('Transcendental Studies') in 1851.

Études symphoniques (*Symphonische Etüden*; 'Symphonic Studies'). Schumann's op. 13 (1834–7), for solo piano; it was originally called *Etüden im Orchestercharakter für Pianoforte von Florestan und Eusebius* and was revised in 1852 as *Études en formes de variations* as a theme, 12 variations, and a finale. Five variations that were originally suppressed were published posthumously in 1873.

etwas (Ger.). 'Somewhat'.

Eugene Onegin (*Yevgeny Onegin*). Opera in three acts by Tchaikovsky to a libretto by the composer and Konstantin Stepanovich Shilovsky after Pushkin's novel in verse (1833) (Moscow, 1879 (privately); Moscow, 1881).

Eulenburg. Anglo-German firm of music publishers. It was founded by Ernst Eulenburg (1847–1926) in Leipzig in 1874. In 1891 he acquired the *miniature score series (comprising over 200 chamber works) published as Payne's Pocket Scores in Leipzig, and in 1894 he took over the series of orchestral scores (about 100 titles) published by Donajowski in London, combining the two series under the Eulenburg imprint. It soon became the world's leading publisher of *miniature scores. Over 1200 works have appeared in the familiar yellow covers of the Eulenburg Miniature Scores series, an unrivalled study resource of authoritative editions, sold at reasonable prices. Kurt Eulenburg (1879–1982), son of the founder, became a partner in 1911 and in 1926 sole proprietor. Under his influence the catalogue expanded to include Wagner operas and hitherto unpublished contemporary music. He moved the firm to London in 1939 in response to the political conditions in mainland Europe. After World War II the original Leipzig firm ceased to exist. Branches were formed in Zürich (1947) and Stuttgart (1950). The London firm was taken over by *Schott in 1957 (and remains a wholly owned subsidiary) with Kurt Eulenburg in charge of production until his retirement in 1968; he greatly extended the scope of the catalogue, particularly in the area of preclassical music, with the help of musicologists. From 1968 to 1975, under the general editorship of Roger Fiske, the series was substantially revised and many new works were added.   HA

Eulenspiegels lustige Streiche, Till. See TILL EULENSPIEGELS LUSTIGE STREICHE.

euphonium (Amer.: baritone; Fr.: *basse en si bémol*; Ger.: *Baryton*; It.: *bombardino*). A tenor *tuba invented in about 1843 by F. Sommer of Weimar. The euphonium differs from the B♭ baritone *saxhorn at the same pitch in being considerably wider in bore. In many countries the two instruments have merged into one, but in Britain, where each has its own place in the *brass band, they remain quite distinct. The euphonium is appropriately named (from Gk. *euphonos*, 'well-' or 'pleasant-sounding') and has one of the most flexible voices in the band. It is an important soloist in both brass and *military bands, often taking the melodic lead in the trio or second section of a march, or the solo part in a band transcription of a vocal work.

The euphonium is often used in the orchestra when the score calls for a tenor tuba, for example in Holst's *The Planets*; where a *Wagner tuba is clearly intended, as in some works by Richard Strauss, it should be substituted only if no Wagner tuba is available.

JMo

eurhythmics (Fr.: *eurythmie*). A method invented by Émile Jaques-Dalcroze for expressing the rhythmic aspects of music by physical movements (see DALCROZE METHOD). The German philosopher Rudolf Steiner (1861–1925) applied the term to movements striving to express the content not only of music but also of poetry.

Euridice. 1. Opera in a prologue and six scenes by Peri, with some arias and choruses by Caccini, to a libretto by Ottavio Rinuccini (Florence, 1600). It is the first opera of which the music is extant.

2. Opera in a prologue and six scenes by Caccini, to a libretto by Rinuccini (Florence, 1602).

Euryanthe. Opera in three acts by Weber to a libretto by Helmina von Chézy after the early French romance *L'Histoire du très-noble et chevalereux prince Gérard, comte de Nevers, et de la très-virtueuse et très chaste princesse Euriant de Savoye, sa mye* (Vienna, 1823).

Evangelist. The *narrator in a *Passion, who recounts the Gospel story either in plainchant or, as in most Passion settings from the mid-17th century onwards, in continuo-accompanied recitative. In 17th- and 18th-century German Passions, most famously those of J. S. Bach, the part of the Evangelist was traditionally taken by a tenor.   RW

Evensong. A synonym for Vespers, the service of the Christian Office hours celebrated daily near sunset. After the English Reformation, the name was applied in the *Book of Common Prayer* (1549) to the Anglican service of Evening Prayer, the basis of which are the ancient Sarum offices of Vespers and Compline.

—/ALi

evirato (It., 'unmanned'). A synonym for *castrato.

Evovae, Euouae. An artificial 'word' comprising the vowels of '*seculorum Amen*', the last words of the Latin Lesser *Doxology (*Gloria Patri*), used as an abbreviation in medieval sources when giving the psalm tone with its appropriate cadence (*differentia*) at the end of an *antiphon. Some 19th-century scholars, misunderstanding the 'word', falsely supposed that *Evovae* derived from the Greek *evoe*, a bacchanalian exclamation of joy.

See also AEVIA.   —/ALi

Excursions of Mr Brouček, The (*Výlety páně Broučkovy*). Opera in two parts by Janáček to his own libretto, with contributions from František Gellner, Viktor Dyk, and F. S. Procházka after Svatopluk Čech's *Brouček* novels (1888, 1889) (Prague, 1920).

exequiae (Lat.). Music for funeral rites (exequies).

exercise. 1. A passage specifically designed for the practice of vocal or instrumental technique and with no aesthetic intent, as for example in C.-L. Hanon's *Le Piano virtuose* (1873).

2. A piece of a technical character, often intended to improve the performer's ability, but which is also a fully worked-out composition. Examples include Domenico Scarlatti's keyboard sonatas, a selection of which was published as *Essercizi* (1738), and the works in Bach's *Clavier-Übung*. Such pieces are usually given a title other than 'exercise' (e.g. toccata or *étude*).

3. A piece of work, usually a composition, submitted by a candidate for a university degree in music.   JBE

exit aria (It.: *aria di sortita*). In Italian 18th-century *opera seria*, the first aria sung by each leading character. It invariably occurred at the end of a scene, after which the singer left the stage.   JBE

Exody (23.59.59). Orchestral work (1996–7) by Birtwistle.

exoticism. The 'exotic' sound of other musical traditions has been one of the resources of Western music since about 1500. Perhaps the earliest example is Heinrich Isaac's *La la hö hö*, based on a Dervish song. Isolated instances occur in the 16th and 17th centuries, but the increasing knowledge of Chinese and other cultures that influenced literature and the visual arts in the late 17th and the 18th centuries had an impact on music too. Rameau, for instance, attempted to suggest the alien music of his oriental and American settings in *Les Indes galantes*. The late 18th-century vogue for 'Turkish' music (see JANISSARY MUSIC) is especially notable, as is the way Gluck used that style in *Iphigénie en Tauride* to characterize the ancient Scythians.

The growing sophistication of European knowledge of other cultures in the 19th century made many more exotic options available. Composers made free use of Middle Eastern idioms (*Aida*, *Samson et Dalila*) or Japanese tunes (*The Mikado*, *Madama Butterfly*) to give 'authenticity' (or *couleur locale*) to operas set in distant places. The European past ('another country') could also be a source of 'exotic' historical tunes (*Les Huguenots*, *Die Meistersinger von Nürnberg*). While musical *nationalism in the 19th century is the opposite of exoticism, many composers adopted alien European national traditions as exotic; Spanish dance tunes were especially popular, from *Carmen* to the orchestral Spanish rhapsodies by Russian composers from Glinka

to Stravinsky. Among the most fruitful sources of exotic sounds in late 19th- and 20th-century music were the gamelan and jazz.

The view of exoticism expressed here emphasizes the 'otherness' of the musical effects produced. It seems important to distinguish composers' purpose in this practice from the complementary one of drawing on outside musical traditions in order to enrich one's own music. Debussy's style, for instance, was founded in part on the integration of resources learnt from Asian musics, without the intention of evoking the cultures in which they originated. Since his time composers in the Western tradition have made use of materials (sounds, techniques, instruments, etc.) from all the other musical traditions of the world.

The same distinction holds in popular music. It has been a matter of convention in the musical theatre and in film music to signal exotic locations with appropriate music. Besides the long tradition of exotic novelty songs, popular musicians have often drawn on exotic resources, such as the Beatles' use of the Indian sitar or Paul Simon's collaboration with musicians from southern Africa. At the same time an analogous enriching of the materials of Western popular music by drawing on outside traditions has taken place. For instance, Louis Armstrong and Charlie Parker introduced 'exotic' quotations from Chopin and Stravinsky into their solos; later jazz musicians have integrated avant-garde techniques from the Western art-music tradition into their own. And while on the whole the more sophisticated musical traditions outside the West have resisted incorporating Western elements, non-Western cultures have found Western pop music a useful foundation on which to build their own pop traditions.   JJD

📖 J. BELLMAN (ed.), *The Exotic in Western Music* (Boston, 1998) · P. HAYWARD (ed.), *Widening the Horizon: Exoticism in Post-War Popular Music* (Sydney, 1999)

experimental. With regard to music, making some radical departure in technique. During the 1960s the word came to have a more specific meaning, being used to distinguish anti-traditional composers, such as Cage, from the established *avant-garde of Boulez and Stockhausen.

'… explosante-fixe …'. Work by Boulez for electronic flute and chamber orchestra, composed between 1971 and 1993.

exposition. The opening portion of a fugue or sonata movement, in which the principal thematic material is introduced. 1. In a *fugue, each voice enters in turn with a statement of the subject or answer, then continues with the countersubject or other contrapuntal material until the last voice has completed its statement. There the exposition ends.

2. In a movement in *sonata form, the first subject (or theme group) is stated in the main key; then there is a modulation to the complementary key, usually the dominant or relative major, in which key the second subject (or theme group) follows. There may be a series of cadences in the new key, the last of which marks the end of the exposition. This is often followed by a double bar and repeat mark, sometimes with a first ending providing a link back to the opening.   NT

expression. A term that may denote either the expressive qualities of a performance or those inherent in a piece of music. In performance, expression is created through a complex interaction of a variety of discrete technical devices and practices used by the performer, such as dynamic variation, choice of tempo, rubato, phrasing, articulation, variations in the use of vibrato, changes of instrumental or vocal timbre, body movement, or any number of similar devices. By these means a performance may be invested with emotion, and hence 'playing expressively' may be synonymous with 'playing with emotion'.

Over time, composers have become increasingly concerned with suggesting or even prescribing expressive aspects of performance. Baroque composers tended to provide few, if any, indications concerning dynamics or tempo in their manuscripts and publications, but in the Classical era these and articulation markings became common. 19th-century composers sometimes gave extremely detailed instructions for tempo and dynamic changes (Tchaikovsky, for instance, towards the end of his Sixth Symphony, indicates a decrescendo from *p* to *pppppp* over the course of five bars), and in the 20th century some felt the need to preface their works with precise instructions to the performer about the way in which expression marks (sometimes newly created) should be realized.

Expression may also be inherent in a musical work. A melody, a harmonic progression, a dissonance, or another device or combination of devices may be said to give a work expression.   BW

Expressionism. An artistic movement concerned with the ruthless expression of disturbing or distasteful emotions, often with a stylistic violence that may involve pushing ideas to their extremes or treating the subject matter with incisive parody. The term is especially associated with the 'Blaue Reiter' group of painters, including Wassily Kandinsky and Franz Marc, who worked in Munich in the years before World War I, but it has been extended to cover also, for example, the poetry of Georg Trakl and some of the music of Schoenberg and his pupils, particularly the atonal, non-serial works they composed from 1908 to *c.*1920.

This is a not inappropriate extension of meaning, for Schoenberg took a close interest in the work of the 'Blaue Reiter' group. He was influenced by Kandinsky's thinking; he took up painting in an Expressionist manner, producing numerous vivid if amateurish self-portraits; and he published an article in the yearbook *Der blaue Reiter* (1912), which also included songs by him and his pupils *Berg and *Webern. Moreover, a work such as Schoenberg's Five Orchestral Pieces (1909) bears comparison with Expressionist painting in its lack of conventional logic, its emotional turbulence, and its bewildering variety of colours and shapes. Schoenberg here allies himself with Kandinsky in a mistrust of rules, a belief that the artist must begin afresh with each work, allowing it to take a form concordant with his inner vision, unrestricted by anything external.

Kandinsky's influence on Schoenberg's work is evident in practical terms in the case of *Die glückliche Hand* (1910–13; staged 1924), which follows the painter's requirements for 'stage composition' in music, words, and light. Following the Expressionist belief that the artist must be true to his vision in its wholeness, Schoenberg not only composed the text and music of *Die glückliche Hand* but also designed the costumes, the setting, and an elaborate lighting scheme.

The portrayal of characters in extreme or psychotic states, a feature of Expressionist drama, is to be found not only in *Die glückliche Hand* but also in Schoenberg's *Erwartung* (1909; staged 1924), a musical 'monodrama' for a woman seeking her lover in a forest at night. The crazed figures and menacing situations of Berg's *Wozzeck* (1917–22; staged 1925) are also typically Expressionist, as is the opera's reliance on such ominous symbols as the blood-red moon. Schoenberg's *Pierrot lunaire* (1912), though often satirical and ironic in tone, is no less characteristic of Expressionist art in the violence of its gestures and in its deep psychological penetration, exposing feelings of longing, abandonment, and murderousness that border on insanity.

Since Expressionism demanded such intense self-examination, it is not surprising that, in the raw state, it was a short-lived movement. Schoenberg, again like Kandinsky, began to codify his language in the early 1920s, developing serialism just as Kandinsky was moving into geometric purity. However, some later composers, for example Peter Maxwell Davies, have sometimes been seen as perpetuating the Expressionism of Schoenberg, Berg, and Webern.

See also OPERA, 15.   PG

📖 K. LANGHEIT (ed.), *The Blaue Reiter Almanac* (London, 1947)

Exsultate, jubilate ('Rejoice, be Glad'). Motet by Mozart, K165/158a (1773), for soprano, organ, and orchestra; the second part is the famous setting of the 'Alleluia'. It was written for the castrato Venanzio Rauzzini.

extravaganza. A term often applied to musical works written in a spirit of caricature or parody. Gilbert and Sullivan described their *Trial by Jury* as an 'extravaganza'.

Eybler, Joseph Leopold (*b* Schwechat, nr Vienna, 8 Feb. 1765; *d* Vienna, 24 July 1846). Austrian composer. He studied with Albrechtsberger and Haydn. Befriended by Mozart, he was at first entrusted with the task of completing the Requiem, but yielded this to Süssmayr. In 1792 he became choirmaster of the Carmelite Church in Vienna, and from 1794 that of the Schotten monastery, where he remained for 30 years. He was court music master and, from 1804, first deputy Hofkapellmeister under Salieri, whom he succeeded in 1824. He was a proficient instrumentalist and singer whose compositions, including masses, oratorios, symphonies, chamber and piano music, and operas, were praised by both Haydn and Mozart.   WT/JW

eye music (Ger.: *Augenmusik*). A term used to describe musical notation that portrays an idea visually but has no aural effect. It was much used in 15th- and 16th-century madrigals and sacred music, such words as 'black', 'darkness', or 'night' being set to black notes, and 'day', 'light', 'white', etc. to white ones. Songs of mourning were often written in black notation.

Although eye music flourished particularly in late medieval and Renaissance music, there are occasional examples of its later use; in the 20th century Dallapiccola coined the term 'idiogram' to describe pieces such as his 'Christmas' Concerto, *fatto per la notte di Natale 1956*, in which the staves are shaped like the branches of a Christmas tree, and the third of his *Cinque canti*, in which the staves take the form of a cross.

F. 1. The fourth degree (subdominant) of the scale of C major (see SCALE, 3).

2. Abbreviation for *forte*.

fa. The fourth degree of the scale in the *solmization system. In French and Italian usage it has become attached, on the fixed-*doh* principle, to the note F, in whichever scale it occurs. See TONIC SOL-FA.

Faber Music. English firm of music publishers. It is the sister company of the book publisher Faber & Faber and was established in 1965 primarily to issue the new and previously unpublished works of Benjamin Britten. Its catalogue now includes a notable group of British composers, among them Vaughan Williams, Holst, Bridge, Britten, Arnold, and such leading contemporary figures as Harvey, Knussen, Benjamin, and Adès. Faber Music also publishes a number of music-theatre works, notably Lloyd Webber's *Cats*, and has a small but active film music division. Its wide range of printed music includes an extensive educational catalogue, a strong and varied choral list, and scholarly performing editions (e.g. Dowland's collected lute music and Mahler's Tenth Symphony). In 1971 it acquired part of the *Curwen catalogue. Its publications, like Faber's books, enjoy a reputation for good design.

HA

faburden. A type of improvised polyphony, chiefly in parallel motion, in 6-3 chords with 8-5 chords at the beginnings and ends of phrases, popular in England from the 15th century to the Reformation. The origins and significance of the term have been much disputed. It has in the past been mistakenly equated with English *discant, and it has also been seen as an offshoot of *fauxbourdon, again almost certainly incorrectly.

The term 'faburden' first appears in two references dating from about 1430: a statement of the skills required of a prospective vicar at the Yorkshire collegiate church of Hemingborough, and a list of the teaching duties of the choirmaster of Durham Cathedral. At some time between 1430 and 1450 John Wylde, precentor of the Augustinian Abbey of Holy Cross, Waltham, copied several anonymous treatises on im-

provised polyphony; the last of these, *The Sight of Faburden*, is the first known full description of the technique.

The purpose of faburden is to add two voices to a plainchant. The 'faburden' part begins a 5th lower than the chant, moves up to a 3rd below it, and remains at that interval for succeeding notes until the final note of a phrase, where the interval of the 5th is regained. A top part, called a 'treble', sings in parallel 4ths above the chant throughout. The 'faburdener' is recommended to avoid 5ths below E and B, but these are necessary at the end of E-mode pieces. Ex. 1 shows the start of a well-known chant harmonized according to these rules.

The sonorities of faburden were not unknown to earlier English musicians: many 14th-century English compositions make abundant use of parallel 6-3 chords, although they are hardly more common than parallel 5-3 and 10-5 chords. However, most of the 14th-century pieces using these harmonies are not based on chant but are completely original compositions, mostly Latin songs of one type or another. Perhaps, then, at the beginning of the 14th century it was realized that to the current techniques of improvised choral polyphony (parallel 5ths, octaves, and so on) could be added the more pungent sonority of the 6-3 chord, which was obviously already popular with composers of 'art music'; the practice of faburden may have been the result.

It is understandable that an improvisation technique practised by lesser singers should have made little impression on the high art music of the time. As the 15th century wore on, however, more and more faburden-influenced pieces are to be found. Ex. 2 gives a simple example of polyphony from the Cambridge manuscript Pepys 1236 that is nothing more than written-out, lightly ornamented faburden. Even more unexpected than this is the fact that there survive numerous examples of faburden parts notated alone (usually lightly ornamented, and given measured rhythm), and also complete polyphonic compositions based not on a plainchant but on a faburden part, the real chant being quite absent.

Faburden was most popular for processional music: litanies, antiphons, psalms, and hymns. It was used for alternate verses of hymns and canticles, as a contrast to

Ex. 1

Treble (improvised)

(words as below)

Meane (chant, given)

Sal — ve fes — ta di — es to — to ve — ne — ra — bi — lis e — vo

Faburden (improvised)

(words as above)

Ex. 2

Treble

Tenor (plainchant) faburden   etc.

Tri — ni — tas san — cta u — ni — tas fir — ma

plainchant verses. The majority of the fine polyphonic *Magnificat* settings which are among the highlights of early 16th-century English music are based on faburden parts, not on plainchant.   DH

Façade. 'Entertainment' (1921–2) by Walton for reciter and ensemble (flute doubling piccolo, clarinet doubling bass clarinet, saxophone, trumpet, percussion, and cello); the speaker, or speakers, declaim in notated rhythm poems by Edith Sitwell. It has undergone several revisions, the last in 1942; the final published version (*Façade I*) comprises 21 items. Eight unpublished numbers were performed in 1977 under the title *Façade Revived*, three of them having been rejected before publication and three others (nos. 4, 6, and 7) having been substituted by the composer; this version was revised, and performed in 1979 as *Façade II*. Walton arranged the work without the poems as two orchestral suites (1926 and 1938). The score has been used by several choreographers (including Frederick Ashton)

and many numbers from it have been arranged by different composers for a variety of instruments.

facile (Fr., It.). 'Easy'; *facilement* (Fr.), *facilmente* (It.), 'easily', i.e. fluently and effortlessly.

Fackeltanz (Ger., 'torch dance'). A torchlight procession with music and dancing, part of the celebrations at German royal weddings. Spontini and Meyerbeer each wrote four for Prussian royal weddings. The music is scored for military band.

fado (Port.). A popular type of Portuguese strophic solo song, usually urban, which originated in Lisbon in the 19th century. A guitar provides harmonic support, and the lute-like *guitarra portuguesa* plays a counterpoint to the voice.   KC

fa fictum. See MUSICA FICTA.

Fagott (Ger.). 'Bassoon'. The term was used originally for the *dulcian, perhaps because of its resemblance to a bundle of sticks (It.: *fagotti*).   JMo

Faidit, Gaucelm (*b* Uzerche, nr Limoges, mid-12th century; *d* ?*c*.1220). Troubadour poet and composer. According to his *vida*, which is not necessarily factually dependable, he began his career in poverty, and for 20 years roamed without receiving recognition. Later Boniface, Marquis of Montferrat, became his patron. 68 poems are attributed to him, of which 14 have music. One of them, *Fortz causa*, laments the death of Richard the Lionheart in 1199.   DA/JM

Fairfax, Robert. See FAYRFAX, ROBERT.

fairground organ. See MECHANICAL MUSICAL INSTRUMENTS.

Fair Maid of Perth, The. See JOLIE FILLE DE PERTH, LA.

Fairy Queen, The. Semi-opera in five acts by Purcell to a libretto anonymously adapted from Shakespeare's *A Midsummer Night's Dream* (London, 1692). The score was lost by 1700 but was found in the library of the Royal Academy of Music in 1901.

Fairy's Kiss, The. See BAISER DE LA FÉE, LE.

Fall, Leo(pold) (*b* Olomouc, 2 Feb. 1873; *d* Vienna, 16 Sept. 1925). Austrian composer. The son of a military bandmaster, he became a cabaret composer and conductor. His operettas, in the style of Lehár and Oscar Straus, include *Der fidele Bauer* ('The Merry Peasant', 1907), *Die Dollarprinzessin* (1908), *Die Rose von Stambul* (1916), and *Madame Pompadour* (1922). ALa

Falla (y Matheu), **Manuel de** (*b* Cádiz, 23 Nov. 1876; *d* Alta Gracia, Argentina, 14 Nov. 1946). Spanish composer. After studying the piano at the Madrid Conservatory in the mid-1890s he tried to establish himself as a composer of zarzuelas. Of the five he wrote the only one to reach the stage was *Los amores de la Inés* (1902), which was not a success. Of much greater importance to his development was the friendship of Felipe Pedrell, from whom he took composition lessons, 1901–4. Pedrell, who was working his way towards a specifically Spanish style based on folk music, also introduced Falla to the polyphonic music of Spain's golden age. His influence was decisive, and Falla was able to overtake his teacher in the short opera *La vida breve* ('The Short Life', 1904–5), to a libretto by Carlos Fernández Shaw, which also owes something in theme, content, and musical ambience to Gerónimo Gímenez's one-act zarzuela *La tempranica* ('The Headstrong Girl', 1900). In spite of its uneven musical quality *La vida breve*, in two short acts, is the first of Falla's works to reveal his personality, in its imaginative, atmospheric scoring as much as its driving Spanish rhythms and brooding melody.

La vida breve was not produced until 1913, when it was warmly received in France, and especially in Madrid. Falla, however, had already left Spain, moving to Paris in 1907, where he lived in straitened circumstances until the financial success of the opera. There he was befriended by Debussy, Ravel, and Dukas, and the four *Pièces espagnoles* for piano solo (1909) reflect their influence. The famous piano concerto *Noches en los jardines de España* ('Nights in the Gardens of Spain', 1911–15) marries French Impressionism to Spanish

alhambrismo, the exotic imitation of Moorish music popular with Albéniz and other composers of the previous generation, though harmonic spice and sensuous orchestral exuberance are firmly reined in by taut construction. The resulting, paradoxically calm, meditation on beauty was probably inspired by Falla's reading of poems by the Nicaraguan writer Rubén Darío, a series of melancholy 'Night Thoughts' that lament the passing of youth and yearn for what might have been.

At the outbreak of World War I Falla returned to Spain, where he wrote two ballet scores, *El amor brujo* ('Love, the Magician', 1915, rev. 1916) and *El sombrero de tres picos* ('The Three-Cornered Hat', 1917–19), the latter given its premiere in London by Diaghilev's company. Both works contain vocal numbers, derived from Andalusian *cante jondo* (as opposed to the better-known flamenco style). Suites of dances from the revised scores soon became staple orchestral showpieces; but the *Danza ritual del fuego* ('Ritual Fire Dance') from *El amor brujo*, in particular, gains from being heard in the context of the complete work. Pungent orchestration and pulsing rhythms combine with terse, economical writing in this powerful nocturnal incantation, to which the sunny, more relaxed *El sombrero* makes a genial foil.

Instead of building on these colourful successes, Falla began to condense and purify his style, influenced by Stravinsky but taking Domenico Scarlatti as his model. The percussive *Fantasía baetica* (1919) for piano solo, a bravura piece of almost aggressively Bartókian austerity, is still comparatively neglected. In 1920 he returned to Spain, living in Granada. The major works of his 'Spanish neo-classical' period are the one-act chamber opera *El retablo de Maese Pedro* ('Master Peter's Puppet Show', 1919–22, performed 1923) and the Concerto for Harpsichord and five instruments (1923–6). The opera, based on an episode from Cervantes's *Don Quixote*, surprised Falla's admirers with its spare textures and delicate use of courtly Spanish Baroque figuration. The concerto, written for the pioneering harpsichordist Wanda Landowska, continues the refining process in a work notable for elliptic wit and rigorous thematic compression.

Most of the remaining 20 years of Falla's life were devoted to work on the 'cantata scenica' *Atlántida*, a setting of the Catalan poet Jacint Verdaguer's epic retelling of the destruction of Atlantis and foundation of Spain, which remained unfinished at his death. (A concert version made by his pupil Ernesto Halffter was presented in 1962, rev. 1976–7.) Strong religious faith played a part in his increasingly self-critical asceticism, and the only other published works of the period are the exquisite miniatures *Psyche* (1924), for voice and chamber ensemble, and *Soneto a Córdoba* (1927), for voice and harp. Ill, and unhappy with the political state of Spain under Franco, Falla emigrated in 1939 to Argentina, where he published his last orchestral score *Homenajes* (1920–38), a collection of pieces written over the years to commemorate E. F. Arbós, Debussy, Dukas, and Pedrell, and orchestrated for publication in 1939. The fact that Falla's reputation continues to grow, in spite of the limited size of his published output, testifies to the quality and diversity of his creative work.

PG/CW

📖 J. B. Trend, *Manuel de Falla and Spanish Music* (New York, 1929, 2/1935) · J. Pahissa, *Manuel de Falla* (London, 1954) · S. Demarquez, *Manuel de Falla* (Paris, 1963; Eng. trans. 1968) · R. Crichton, *Manuel de Falla: Descriptive Catalogue of his Works* (London, 1976) · R. Crichton, *Falla* (London, 1982)

Fall and Resurrection. Work (1999) by Tavener, to biblical texts, for chorus and orchestra.

falsa (Sp., Port.). 'Dissonance'. In 17th-century organ music, an *obra de falsas* was a composition which deliberately exploited dissonance; many such pieces were composed by Sebastián Aguilera de Heredia, J. B. J. Cabanilles, Francisco Correa, and others.

false close. Alternative name for an interrupted *cadence.

false relation. The simultaneous or adjacent appearance in different voices of two modally conflicting notes with the same letter name, often the major and minor 3rds of the same triad. This effect was much exploited by the madrigal composers of the late 16th century and the 17th, and became prominent again in the 20th century, especially in the neo-classical works of Stravinsky. By then, however, the more pervasive use of dissonance made any frisson of 'falseness' less powerful than in earlier times.

AW

falsetto. The vocal register used by adult male singers to sing in the alto and treble ranges. The highest register of the female voice is often also called falsetto. A falsetto is produced when the vocal folds vibrate only at their edges (see VOICE, 3 and 4). Tenors who cannot, or choose not to, produce a full-blooded top note slip into falsetto. In opera falsetto is sometimes used for comic effects, as in Verdi's *Falstaff*.

RW

falsobordone (It., from Fr. *fauxbourdon*, 'false bass'). A technique of singing psalms in harmony, following simple chord progressions. The earliest *falsobordoni* were harmonizations of Gregorian plainchant psalm tones and appeared in Italy and Spain in the 1480s; they were for four voices and used what are now called root-position chords. The name was probably derived from

**fauxbourdon': both fauxbourdon and *falsobordone* involved a type of choral, chordal declamation, though achieved by quite different means.

The Gregorian melodies were gradually abandoned after the 1560s. Figured-bass parts were provided from about 1600, and at the beginning of the 17th century there was a vogue for dramatic and colourful new *falsobordoni*. Keyboard embellishments of *falsobordoni* were composed by Antonio de Cabezón and others. The use of *falsobordone* gradually declined during the 17th century (though it was maintained, among other places, at the Sistine Chapel), but its English form, *Anglican chant, has survived to the present day. The most celebrated example of *falsobordone* is Gregorio Allegri's *Miserere*, in which choral *falsobordone* alternates with solo sections.

DH

Falstaff. Opera in three acts by Verdi to a libretto by Arrigo Boito after Shakespeare's *The Merry Wives of Windsor* (1600–1) and *Henry IV*, parts 1 and 2 (1597–8) (Milan, 1893).

Fanciulla del West, La ('The Girl of the Golden West'). Opera in three acts by Puccini to a libretto by Guelfo Civinini and Carlo Zangarini after David Belasco's play *The Girl of the Golden West* (1905) (New York, 1910).

fancy. See FANTASIA.

fandango (Sp.). An energetic Spanish dance for a single couple, accompanied by guitars and castanets alternating with sung couplets (cf. **seguidilla*). It originated in the early 18th century and is in quick triple time; its performance is characterized by a steady acceleration and by abrupt pauses in the music, with the dancers freezing in position until it starts again. Gluck's ballet *Don Juan* (1761) contains a fandango based on an authentic Spanish melody and subsequently borrowed by Mozart for the Act III finale of *Le nozze di Figaro*. The third movement of Granados's *Goyescas* (1912) is in the style of a fandango, and Rimsky-Korsakov introduced one into his *Spanish Capriccio*.

—/JH

fanfare. A flourish of brass instruments, usually trumpets, sometimes also with percussion. Originally improvised (as distinct from military signals), fanfares are used for ceremonial purposes, for example to announce the entrance of a dignitary, and are characterized by reliance on the harmonic series. Fanfares are now often fully composed, not only for state (natural) trumpets, but also for various brass instruments in six or more parts. 'Fanfare trumpets' and trombones are valved instruments built in a long, straight 'herald's *trumpet' format. In the 20th century fanfares were composed by Copland (*Fanfare for the Common Man*, 1942) and Stravinsky (*Fanfare for a New Theatre*, 1964). In France the word 'fanfare' denotes a call executed by either the large circular *hunting horn or, more usually, a *brass band.   AB/JBe

Fanfare for the Common Man. Work (1942) by Copland for brass and percussion, one of a series of wartime fanfares commissioned by Eugene Goossens.

fantasia (It.; Fr.: *fantaisie*; Ger.: *Fantasie*, *Phantasie*) [fantasy, fancy]. A title often given to pieces of no fixed form, implying that a composer wishes to follow the dictates of his or her freely ranging imagination. By its very nature the term is difficult to define, but it is possible to distinguish various types of fantasia through the ages, and some of the music written in this 'anti-form' is extremely fine.

The word begins to appear fairly frequently in the early 16th century, when lutenists used it in their tablature books as a title for pieces that were not simply transcriptions of vocal music but were conceived originally for the instrument. Such pieces vary from short studies of an improvisatory nature (not dissimilar to the *ricercar of the time) to extended works in which contrapuntal and chordal passages alternate, and sections of brilliant passage-work demonstrate the skill of the player. In this latter sense the word was also used by keyboard composers, whose works in this vein are the precursors of the *toccata.

About the middle of the 16th century, fantasias for instrumental ensemble were written. Again like the ricercar at this period, they borrow vocal idioms currently in use in the motet, though because instruments can play angular melodic lines and need no rests for breath, composers were freer to develop a distinctive style. Unlike the ricercar the fantasia had no didactic purpose, so there was no attempt to display contrapuntal skill, the ability to work out a theme, or proficiency of any other kind. Willaert was one of the first composers to write such pieces, and a number of Italians (e.g. Bassano, Vecchi, and Andrea Gabrieli) followed in his path, sometimes also adapting the manner for keyboard instruments.

It was at this stage that the fantasia became known in England. There are many fine examples for keyboard by such composers as Byrd, Gibbons, and Tomkins, while John Dowland wrote some masterly pieces for the lute. However, it was in the realm of viol consort music that the most significant developments took place. Thomas Morley defined the genre admirably in *A Plaine and Easie Introduction to Practicall Musicke* (1597): 'a musician taketh a point at his pleasure and wresteth and turneth it as he list ... and what you list'. In practice this meant that the English adapted to instrumental music the various traits of the *madrigal, which they had recently adopted, adding these to their experience of viol consort music in stricter genres like the *In nomine*. Fantasias (often known as 'fancies') of admirable emotional range were written by Byrd, Gibbons, and Ward, the last two particularly exploiting the capabilities of string instruments to advantage; Morley himself published some two-part pieces that are especially attractive offshoots of his canzonet style. A number of Byrd's fantasias show a tendency towards a sectional construction, as well as the introduction of dance rhythms and even popular tunes. Such works led to the popular fantasia-suite, in which a large-scale polyphonic movement in the quasi-madrigalian manner was followed by dances.

The instrumentation of fantasias and fantasia-suites varied. Any combination of viols could be used, from a full six-part consort comprising two trebles, two tenors (or alto and tenor), and two basses, down to two bass viols (e.g. by Coprario and Jenkins). As the 17th century progressed, violins may have been used instead of treble viols, particularly in three-part works scored for two trebles and bass, by such composers as Lupo, Tomkins, Jenkins, and Hingston. The last is unusual in that his output includes a few examples of fantasia-suites scored for cornetts and sackbuts; Hingston was employed as Cromwell's chief musician, so these pieces may have been composed for some specific function. William Lawes was a master of the fantasia-suite, writing not only for viol consorts but also for unusual combinations of violins, viols, and harmony instruments such as the harpsichord, organ, and harp. Thomas Mace (*Musick's Monument*, 1676) recorded the practice of accompanying a viol consort with the chamber organ; in some cases the organ did more than merely double the string parts, being given an independent role integral to the composition as a whole.

The taste for fancies persisted throughout the Civil War (when chamber music was so much more attractive because of the danger of being 'knock'd on the head' when venturing out, according to the devotee Roger North) and into the Commonwealth. On the Restoration the taste for modern French music made them seem old-fashioned, and few were written; these, however, include some fine examples by Locke and a set of masterpieces by Purcell, which exploit the by now archaic idiom with unique power. The genre died regretted by lovers of chamber music. As Christopher Simpson put it in 1667, 'this kind of music is now much neglected, by reason of scarcity of auditors that understand it; their ears being better acquainted with light and airy music'.

On the Continent the fashion for violin music and the use of continuo parts led to the demise of the polyphonic fantasia early in the 17th century. Works for keyboard with this title were, however, still to be found. Sweelinck wrote fantasias in a strict contrapuntal manner that differ from the canzona and ricercar mainly in their exploitation of various effects such as 'echoes' made possible on double-manual organs. Froberger and other Germans also wrote polyphonic fantasias, but J. S. Bach used the title for vast improvisatory preludes set before fugues, the best known being the *Chromatic Fantasia*, which precedes a lengthy D minor fugue. It is this sense of the word that C. P. E. Bach favoured, defining it as an expression 'not of memorized or plagiarized passages, but rather of true musical creativeness [in] which the keyboardist more than any other executant can practise the declamatory style, and move audaciously from one emotion to another'. Thus, anything is allowed: rhythmically free arpeggiando sections, recitative-like passages, and brilliant displays of finger dexterity, as well as more organic, thematic sections. Mozart's improvisatory techniques are demonstrated in two keyboard fantasias (K396/385*f*, K397/385*g*) built up in a number of contrasting sections, and Beethoven used a similarly extended improvisation in his *Choral Fantasia* (op. 80) to precede, not a fugue, but a massive hymn setting in the manner of the finale of the Ninth Symphony.

Mozart wrote one of his free fantasias as an introduction to his C minor Piano Sonata K457, and Beethoven developed the concept in his two sonatas op. 27, each of which is called 'Sonata quasi una fantasia' (the second is commonly known as the 'Moonlight' Sonata). These sonatas, with their improvisatory first movements, led to still freer works in which formal pattern and improvisation combine. The most influential was Schubert's 'Wanderer' Fantasia, an extended working out of ideas from his song *Der Wanderer*, and the tradition culminated at about the middle of the century with such pieces as Liszt's Piano Sonata in B minor, using *cyclic form, and Schumann's fine Fantasia in C.

In general, however, the fantasia became a potpourri of themes from operas compiled by virtuoso pianists as display pieces. Henry Wood's *Fantasia on British Sea Songs* (1905) for orchestra was conceived in a similar vein. In the 20th century, concepts of formal pattern became so fluid that the idea of an 'anti-form' was largely unnecessary. Vaughan Williams's *Fantasia on a Theme of Thomas Tallis* proved that the improvisatory tradition could result in serious, rhapsodic music.

DA/LC

📖 I. Spink (ed.), *The Seventeenth Century*, The Blackwell History of Music in Britain, iii (Oxford, 1992) · A. Ashbee and P. Holman (eds.), *John Jenkins and his Time: Studies in English Consort Music* (Oxford, 1996)

Fantasia Concertante on a Theme of Corelli. Work (1953) by Tippett for strings; the theme is from Corelli's Concerto Grosso op. 6 no. 2 and the work quotes Bach's Fugue on themes of Corelli; it was composed in the tercentenary year of Corelli's birth.

Fantasia contrappuntistica. Work (1910) by Busoni for solo piano; a second version was composed also in 1910, a third in 1912, and a fourth (for two pianos) in 1922. It is subtitled 'Preludio al corale "Gloria al Signori nei Cieli" e fuga a quattro soggetti obbligati sopra un fragmento di Bach'. Busoni based it on the Contrapunctus XVIII from *The Art of Fugue* in a desire to complete Bach's unfinished fugue; he created a fourth subject (Bach composed only three) and added a fifth. Wilhelm Middelschulte, the work's dedicatee, adapted it for organ.

Fantasia on a Theme by Thomas Tallis. Work by Vaughan Williams for double string orchestra and string quartet; it was composed in 1910 and later revised, the last revision being in 1919. The theme is the third (*Why fumeth in fight*) of nine psalm tunes Tallis composed in 1567 for Archbishop Parker's psalter. See also Tallis's Canon.

Fantasia on British Sea Songs. Henry Wood's orchestral arrangement of traditional and other songs, made in 1905 to celebrate the centenary of Nelson's victory at Trafalgar. Malcolm Sargent added a solo contralto to the last of the nine songs, 'Rule, Britannia!', when they were first performed at the Promenade Concerts in London, and they became the traditional finale to the last night of the Proms.

Fantasia on 'Greensleeves'. Ralph Greaves's arrangement (1934) for one or two flutes, harp, and strings of an interlude from Vaughan Williams's opera *Sir John in Love*, the middle section being based on the folksong *Lovely Joan*. There are several other arrangements, none by Vaughan Williams.

fantasia-suite. A suite of dances preceded by a large-scale polyphonic *fantasia.

Fantasiestücke. See Phantasiestücke.

fantasy-suite. A suite of dances preceded by a large-scale polyphonic *fantasia.

farandole (Fr.). A traditional dance that originated in regions of southern France (especially Provence) and northern Spain. In 6/8 time, it is danced through the streets by chains of people to the accompaniment of the *galoubet* and *tambourin* (pipe and tabor), and is thought to have its origins in ancient times. Bizet composed a farandole in his incidental music to *L'Arlésienne* (1872), as did Gounod in his opera *Mireille* (1864). —/JH

Farbe (Ger., 'colour'). In musical terminology, tone-colour. See KLANGFARBENMELODIE.

farce (It.: *farsa*). An 18th-century term denoting a short comic play with music, generally in two (sometimes three) acts, and often consisting of spoken dialogue interspersed with arias. Such pieces were performed as intermezzos between the acts, or at the end, of a larger opera or play. In the late 18th and early 19th centuries the term embraced a lighter kind of *opera buffa*. Today it means a light comedy, often with slightly risqué subject matter, with no specific musical associations.

'Farewell' Symphony (*Abschiedsymphonie*). Nickname of Haydn's Symphony no. 45 in F♯ minor (1772); in the extra (Adagio) finale, the orchestra is gradually reduced until only two violins are left. Haydn composed it to persuade Prince Nicolaus, his employer, not to prolong the court musicians' stay at the prince's summer residence at Eszterháza but to allow them to return to their families at Eisenstadt. At the symphony's first performance the players left as their music finished, leaving only Haydn and the violinist Luigi Tomasini.

Farina, Carlo (*b* Mantua, *c*.1600; *d c*.1640). Italian composer and violinist. He worked for most of his life in Dresden (where he was a colleague of Schütz), and wrote a great deal of violin music, some of it using the then novel effects of double stopping, glissando, tremolo, *col legno*, and *sul ponticello*. As well as dance movements and canzonas, Farina wrote ten sonatas for one or two violins and continuo, and he was influential in the spread of the genre in Germany and Austria.

DA

Farinelli [Farinello; Broschi, Carlo] (*b* Andria, Apulia, 24 Jan. 1705; *d* Bologna, 15 July 1782). Italian soprano castrato. He took lessons from Porpora, in whose *Angelica e Medoro* he made his public debut in Naples in 1720, with such success that Porpora created for him the demanding title role of *Adelaide* (Rome, 1723). The following year Farinelli began his international travels, which for 13 years brought him the highest acclaim, especially when he appeared in London at the Opera of the Nobility. Although he had been criticized for poor acting, his singing created a sensation, its ornate style probably the most important influence on the development of the new florid writing in Italian *opera seria* after 1730.

In 1737 Farinelli left the public stage and entered the private service of the Spanish court in Madrid, where he was the prized employee of Philip V and then Ferdinand VI. There he was also in charge of a variety

of administrative matters, including the redirection of the river Tagus, the importation of Hungarian horses, the redesigning of the opera house, and the production of many Italian operas. In 1759 he settled in Bologna, where he collected pictures and played the harpsichord and viola d'amore. From his own day to the present, Farinelli's life has been the subject of numerous fictional accounts including a film (1994). JT

Farkas, Ferenc (*b* Nagykanisza, 15 Dec. 1905; *d* Budapest, 10 Oct. 2000). Hungarian composer and teacher. He studied at the Budapest Academy of Music, and in Rome with Respighi. He worked as a film composer in Vienna and Copenhagen before returning to Hungary in 1935 and beginning a teaching career. From 1949 to 1975 he was professor of composition at the Budapest Academy, teaching most of the leading Hungarian composers of two generations. Farkas's prolific output, of eclectic inspiration, includes operas, ballets, orchestral works, chamber and instrumental music, songs, and many choruses. His set of *Antiche danze ungheresi* for wind quintet (1953) is widely performed. ABur

Farmer, John (*fl* 1591–1601). English church musician and composer. In 1595 he was appointed organist and choirmaster at Christ Church Cathedral, Dublin; four years later he moved to London. His earliest published work (1591) is a set of canons, composed 'in youth' and dedicated to Edward de Vere, Earl of Oxford. The same dedication heads his 1599 set of madrigals, some of which remain popular today—notably *Fair Phyllis I saw sitting all alone*. He also wrote metrical psalms, and contributed a piece to Morley's *The Triumphes of Oriana* (1601). JM

Farnaby, Giles (*b c*.1563; *d* London, Nov. 1640). English composer. A joiner by trade, in 1592 he took the degree of B.Mus. at Oxford University, and by 1602 was resident in Lincolnshire, where he was music tutor to the children of Sir Nicholas Saunderson of Fillingham. His unconventional background may explain the peculiar charm of his works, which include keyboard pieces, canzonets, madrigals—including the chromatic *Construe my meaning*, published in 1598—and psalm settings. His son **Richard** (*b* London, *c*.1594) also wrote keyboard music, in a style reminiscent of his father's.

JM

Farrant. There were at least four Tudor musician-composers of this name. Their separate biographies can be distinguished, but it is not always clear which compositions should be assigned to each man. The most senior of them, **Richard Farrant** (*b c*.1525–30; *d* 30 Nov. 1580), was a Gentleman of the Chapel Royal from 1552, then Master of the Choristers successively at St

George's Chapel, Windsor (1564–9), and at the Chapel Royal. He wrote and produced choirboy plays, but none has survived. He is remembered chiefly for his anthems, including the popular *Hide not thou thy face*. Conceivably descended from Richard are the two church musicians called **John Farrant**, possibly father and son, who were associated with Salisbury Cathedral in the late 16th and early 17th centuries. They are contenders for some of the church music attributed in the sources only to 'Farrant'. **Daniel Farrant** (*b c.*1575; *d* July 1651), possibly Richard's son, was a string player at the court of James I as well as an instrument maker and the composer of a few works for instrumental consort.

JM

Farrar, Geraldine (*b* Melrose, MA, 28 Feb. 1882; *d* Ridgefield, CT, 11 March 1967). American soprano. She studied in Boston and Berlin, where she made her debut as Marguerite in Gounod's *Faust* in 1901. She then took lessons with Lilli Lehmann, while continuing to perform in Berlin. In 1906 she was engaged as a member of the Metropolitan Opera, New York, making her successful debut as Juliette in Gounod's *Roméo et Juliette*. Subsequently she was acclaimed in a variety of roles, particularly in Mozart, Gounod, Bizet, and Puccini. She was considered an outstanding interpreter of Madama Butterfly and Carmen. Her artistic imagination and supple voice can be heard on her many recordings. She also appeared in films.   JT

📖 E. NASH, *Always First Class: The Career of Geraldine Farrar* (Washington, DC, 1982)

farruca (Sp.). An Andalusian dance of Gypsy origin. Falla included a farruca in his ballet *El sombrero de tres picos* (1919).

farse (from Lat. *farcire*, 'to stuff'). Words (in Latin or the vernacular) introduced into set texts, usually liturgical. The term is virtually synonymous with *trope' but is mostly used only for simpler chants such as lessons.

Fasch, Carl Friedrich Christian (*b* Zerbst, 18 Nov. 1736; *d* Berlin, 3 Aug. 1800). German composer, harpsichordist, and conductor, son of Johann Friedrich Fasch. He became second harpsichordist to Frederick the Great (C. P. E. Bach was first harpsichordist), but his main claim to fame was his part in reviving the tradition of choral singing in Germany through the foundation of the Berlin Singakademie in the 1790s. The Singakademie's performances of works by J. S. Bach contributed greatly to the *Bach Revival. Much of Fasch's own music is lost, for he destroyed any work that failed to come up to his high standards.

DA/LC

Fasch, Johann Friedrich (*b* Buttelstedt, nr Weimar, 15 April 1688; *d* Zerbst, 5 Dec. 1758). German composer. He was educated at the Thomasschule and the university in Leipzig, and in 1708 he instituted a *collegium musicum* there in modest rivalry with the one formed six years earlier by Telemann and later directed by Bach. In 1722 he was appointed court Kapellmeister at Zerbst, where he wrote much sacred music, including 12 cantata cycles and a *Passio Jesu Christi* (1723), as well as symphonies, concertos (in the Vivaldi manner), and chamber works, many of which provide notable links between the Baroque and early Classical styles.

DA/BS

Faschingsschwank aus Wien ('Viennese Carnival Pranks'). Schumann's op. 26 (1939–40), for solo piano; subtitled 'Fantasiebilder', it is in five movements.

fasola. See SHAPE NOTE.

fastoso (It.). 'Pompous'; *fastosamente*, 'pompously'.

Fate. See OSUD.

Faugues, Guillaume (*fl c.*1460). French or Flemish composer. He was roughly contemporary with Ockeghem and Busnois. Of his works only four masses have survived: *Missa 'Le Serviteur'*, *Missa 'Je suis en la mer'*, *Missa 'L'Homme armé'*, and *Missa 'La Basse danse'*. They were discussed by the theorist Johannes Tinctoris.

JM

Fauré, Gabriel (Urbain) (*b* Pamiers, Ariège, 12 May 1845; *d* Paris, 4 Nov. 1924). French composer. He trained as a church musician at the École Niedermeyer in Paris (1854–65), and his study of plainchant and modal harmony considerably influenced his later compositions. He was introduced to contemporary music through the piano classes of Saint-Saëns (from 1861) who also helped launch his composing career in the 1870s in Parisian salons such as that of Pauline Viardot. Fauré 'graduated' with a first prize in composition for his *Cantique de Jean Racine* (1865), and though he produced much religious music— notably the Requiem, which was mostly written in January 1888 after his mother's death—his heart was not in this, or in organ-playing, choir-training, or private teaching, all of which he abandoned after he was appointed director of the Paris Conservatoire in 1905. He held this post until deafness forced his retirement in 1920.

On 9 March 1903 in *Gil Blas*, Debussy branded Fauré 'the Master of Charms', an epithet which stuck, to the detriment of powerful later works such as the *Fantaisie* for piano and orchestra (1918), the Second Piano

Quintet (1919–21), and the Piano Trio (1922–3). It arose from the popularity of early songs such as *Lydia* (*c*.1870) and *Clair de lune* (1887, which marked Fauré's discovery of Verlaine and the beginning of his mature, second period), and instrumental gems such as the *Pavane* (1887) and the *Sicilienne* (1893) for cello and piano. With his song cycle *La Bonne Chanson* (1892–4) and *Prométhée* (1900, an impressive lyric tragedy with spoken interludes), Fauré began to leave fashionable taste (and Saint-Saëns) behind. The gap widened with the cycle *La Chanson d'Ève* (Van Lerberghe, 1906–10), in which he reduced the number of recurring themes from six to two. In the last song cycles, *Le Jardin clos* (1914), *Mirages* (1919), and *L'Horizon chimérique* (1921), the move towards simplicity was carried still further, and the unity derives rather from the subject and the restrained style. In his piano music written between 1905 and 1909 Fauré experimented with the whole-tone scale (Impromptu no. 5, 1909) and with basing entire compositions on a short, single idea developed sequentially (Nocturnes 9–10). But the crowning achievement of his later years was his opera *Pénélope* to a libretto by René Fauchois, which occupied him during the summers of 1907–12. It was performed in Monte Carlo and Paris in 1913, but the war, and the opera's status as pure music which disdains theatrical effect, prevented its entering the repertory.

As Nectoux wrote, 'Fauré's work is a work of transition; he is a musician of the 19th century, but also a classic of the 20th'. For Fauré, art and music existed 'to elevate mankind as far as possible above everyday existence', but in his oeuvre the Hellenic aspect of calm, philosophical serenity has been overstressed. This should be regarded as secondary to the joyous strength, sustained intensity, and supreme manifestations of diversity within unity that are his lasting contributions to the 20th century. Only piano works such as the early Nocturnes show any sign of influence (in this case Chopin, Saint-Saëns, and Liszt), and Fauré was almost alone among his generation in not coming under Wagner's spell. His lack of interest in orchestration and deliberate virtuosity have not assisted his popularity, though his *Shylock* suite (1889) and Nocturne no. 13 (1921) show his skill with both. His genius was one of synthesis: he reconciled such opposing elements as modality and tonality, anguish and serenity, seduction and force within a single non-eclectic style, as in the *Pelléas et Mélisande* suite (1898), his symphonic masterpiece. The quality of constant renewal within an apparently limited range (chiefly two hands at a piano) is a remarkable facet of his genius, and the spare, elliptical style of his single String Quartet (1923–4) suggests that his intensely self-disciplined style was still developing at the time of his death.   RO

📖 R. ORLEDGE, *Gabriel Fauré* (London, 2/1983) · J.-M. NECTOUX (ed.), *Gabriel Fauré: His Life through his Letters* (London and New York, 1984) · J.-M. NECTOUX, *Gabriel Fauré: A Musical Life*, trans. R. Nichols (Cambridge, 1991) · T. GORDON (ed. and trans.), *Regarding Fauré* (Amsterdam, 1999)

fausset (Fr.). 'Falsetto'.

Faust. Opera in five acts by Gounod to a libretto by Charles-François Barbier and Michel Carré after Carré's *Faust et Marguerite* and Johann Wolfgang von Goethe's *Faust* part 1 (in the French translation by Gérard de Nerval) (Paris, 1859).

'Faust', Scenes from Goethe's. Overture and six movements (1844–53) by Schumann, for soloists, chorus, and orchestra, settings of texts by Johann Wolfgang von Goethe.

Faust Symphony, A (*Eine Faust-Symphonie*). Symphony (1854–7) by Liszt, based on Johann Wolfgang von Goethe's play. It is subtitled 'in drei Charakterbildern' ('in three character studies'), the movements being 'Faust', 'Gretchen', and 'Mephistopheles'; the last has alternative endings, one purely orchestral, the other a setting for tenor, men's chorus, and orchestra of the final words of Goethe's play.

Fauvel, Roman de. A long poem by Gervais du Bus, completed in 1316. It is an allegorical satire on the Roman Church, the character of Fauvel being a horse. One of the 12 manuscripts in which it survives contains numerous textual and 167 musical interpolations. This 13th- and 14th-century monophonic and polyphonic music—motets, *lais*, *ballades*, *rondeaux*, sequences, conductus, refrains, and chants—includes pieces by Philippe de Vitry and from the Notre Dame repertory and is of great historical significance.

fauxbourdon. A technique of singing improvised polyphony, associated particularly with 15th-century Franco-Burgundian sacred music. It has many similarities to English *faburden, but the derivation of either from the other has not been established, and there are significant differences between them.

The origins of the term are obscure. Whereas *faux* ('false') is clear enough, the word *bourdon* cannot be traced in 15th-century France; it may be related to *bourde*, meaning 'lie' or 'error'. (In 14th- and 15th-century English, 'burden' meant a low voice in part-music.) The word 'fauxbourdon' (in the form *faulx bourdon*) is first encountered as an instruction in Dufay's *Missa Sancti Jacobi* and in another piece in the same manuscript, both compositions probably dating from the 1420s or 30s. Evidence from choir archives of the practice of fauxbourdon, of the sort common for faburden, has so far not been discovered. Theoretical descriptions are rather late, beginning with Guillelmus Monachus, an Italian writer of the 1480s; they continue throughout the 16th century, although the practice of fauxbourdon in its original form probably died with the 15th century.

The compositions of Dufay and his contemporaries show that fauxbourdon meant improvising a supplementary voice in parallel 4ths below a given voice (often a decorated plainchant). A third, composed, part would complete the texture. Ex. 1 gives the opening of verse 2 of Dufay's setting of the hymn *Conditor alme siderum*. In the manuscript only the top and bottom parts are copied out; the simple instruction 'faulx bourdon' next to the top part indicates that the middle voice is to be supplied in performance.

Like faburden, the technique of fauxbourdon was used as the starting-point for more sophisticated compositions. Some fauxbourdon pieces survive side by side with alternative versions, where fully composed parts are provided in place of the improvised line. Other compositions are written-out decorations of fauxbourdon. Some of these practices are described by Guillelmus Monachus in *De preceptis artis musicae*. Guillelmus' descriptions have given rise to much discussion, because they do not wholly agree with what appears in musical sources. He gives two ways of creating fauxbourdon by improvisation: (*a*) by adding two voices above a cantus firmus, in 8-5 chords at the beginnings and ends of phrases and in 6-3 chords elsewhere; and (*b*) by adding two voices below. It is possible that we have here evidence of choirmen's rules of thumb for improvising polyphony, which may have existed before, and therefore have given rise to, the specially composed pieces of Dufay and his contemporaries.   DH

Favola d'Orfeo, La. See ORFEO, L'.

Favorite, La (*La favorita*; 'The Favoured One'). Opera in four acts by Donizetti to a libretto by Alphonse Royer and Gustave Vaëz with additions by Eugène Scribe, partly after *L'Ange de Nisada* (derived from Baculard d'Arnaud's *Le Comte de Comminges*) on which the story of Eleonora di Guzman is grafted (Paris, 1840).

Fayrfax [Fairfax], Robert (*b* Deeping Gate, Lincs., 23 April 1464; *d* ? St Albans, 1521). English composer. He was a leading figure at the courts of Henry VII and Henry VIII. From the late 1490s until his death he served as a Gentleman of the Chapel Royal, not only as a composer but also as a singer and music scribe. He was also associated, perhaps in an honorary capacity, with St Albans Abbey. As well as holding two Cambridge degrees—the Mus.B. (1501) and Mus.D. (1504, for which he submitted the *Missa 'O quam glorifica'*)—Fayrfax was awarded the first D.Mus. to be conferred by the University of Oxford. His output of church music, which includes six masses, two *Magnificat* settings, and ten antiphons, is characterized by its restraint and economy of style, lacking the florid display of many of his contemporaries. Two of his masses are unusual in design: the *Missa Albanus* uses a nine-note motto which is treated as a cantus firmus, sometimes presented in inversion or retrograde motion; while the *Missa 'O bone Jesu'* is composed without a cantus firmus, instead sharing material with two other works by the composer, a *Magnificat* and the motet *O bone Jesu*. Fayrfax also wrote partsongs, mostly in a simple syllabic idiom, whose texts reflect the culture of the early Tudor court.   JM

F clef. See CLEF.

Fedeltà premiata, La ('Fidelity Rewarded'). Opera in three acts by Haydn to a libretto by Giambattista Lorenzi (Eszterháza, 1781).

Ex. 1

Cantus (*=original chant notes): Qui con do lens in te ri tu Mor tis pe ri re se cu lum

Improvised reading: (words as above)

Tenor: Qui condolens

Fedora. Opera in three acts by Giordano to a libretto by Arturo Colautti after Victorien Sardou's play (1882) (Milan, 1898).

Feen, Die ('The Fairies'). Opera in three acts by Wagner (his first) to his own libretto after Carlo Gozzi's *La donna serpente* (1762) (Munich, 1888).

feierlich (Ger.). 'Solemn', 'festive'; a term associated with public celebrations, either 'solemn' religious festivals and holy days or 'festive' secular celebrations and holidays.

Felciano, Richard (James) (*b* Santa Rosa, CA, 7 Dec. 1930). American composer. He studied with Milhaud at Mills College and in Paris, and with Dallapiccola in Florence (1958–9). During his student years he sang plainchant in a Catholic church choir, and the experience had a lasting effect on his music, as well as on his view of music as having religious or social functions. Back in California he taught at Lone Mountain College (1959–67) and Berkeley (from 1967), while pursuing creative projects with institutions of diverse kinds. His works make use of avant-garde techniques and sometimes include electronic or other non-traditional means.   PG

Feldman, Morton (*b* New York, 12 Jan. 1926; *d* Buffalo, NY, 3 Sept. 1987). American composer. He studied with Wallingford Riegger and Stefan Wolpe but was influenced more by his association with John Cage in the early 1950s. His earliest published scores, the *Projections* series (1950–1), introduced notation on squared paper, each square representing a time unit and specifying the sound only in general terms (for example, asking for a pizzicato note in the low register of the cello). Soon he began to notate his music more conventionally, but the absence of dynamism remained the same. The music is usually very quiet and transparently scored, and one event follows another with no sense of purpose. In some cases, instrumental parts are not synchronized, and the effect is of delicate lines moving in unpredictable combinations towards silence. Often the titles are abstract, indicating just the instrumentation (*Four Instruments*, 1965), but they may also be poetic evocations of the music's nature (*Between Categories* for eight players, 1969) or puzzling allusions (*The King of Denmark*, 1964, surely the gentlest percussion solo ever written).

In the 1970s and 80s Feldman received numerous orchestral commissions, and at the same time he became fascinated by possibilities of irregular repetition ('crippled symmetry', to quote another title), influenced by the irregular weave of Islamic carpets, which he collected. Works of luminous drift thus gave way to pieces featuring ostinatos that are slow, not quite matched, and harmonically non-progressive (*Triadic Memories* for piano, 1981; *Coptic Light* for orchestra, 1986), but again there was no essential change in the goal-less effect. In his hugely productive last decade or so he also wrote a monodrama to a text by Samuel Beckett (*Neither*, 1976–7) and some works of enormous length, outstandingly String Quartet II (1983), which plays for five hours without interruption.   PG

Feldmusik (Ger., 'field music'). The general name given to 17th- and 18th-century music for brass instruments (*Feldpartiten*, *Feldstücke*, etc.) designed for outdoor performance. The earliest types were simply fanfares in four parts, played by military trumpeters (*Feldtrompeter*); later compositions included the more sophisticated *partita or *divertimento. Haydn wrote several *Feldpartiten*.

Felix namque (Lat., 'For thou art happy'). The title of a large number of 15th- and 16th-century English keyboard pieces (by Redford, Tallis, Blitheman, and Tomkins among others) that set the plainchant *Felix namque es*, an offertory for certain Marian Masses. These vary from the densely polyphonic to those using brilliant (if sometimes mechanical) figuration; there is even an early 16th-century setting in quintuple time.
—/ALı

feminist musicology. Scholarship dedicated to the role of women in music. It focuses on women composers, traditionally excluded from the Western canon, and examines their music within its social context, both at the time of its composition and through its subsequent interpretation. Such study followed feminist research in the other humanities and the social sciences. The first attempts to investigate the history of women in music began in the 1970s. Previously, women's roles within Western music had been considered almost exclusively with reference to the men with whom they were associated, as in the case of Clara Schumann, wife of Robert. Extensive research into previously undiscovered works by women composers—Lili Boulanger, Amy Beach, Ruth Crawford Seeger, Cécile Chaminade—led musicologists including Marcia Citron and Karin Pendle to call into question the linear formulation of the Western canon and its authority on aesthetic value and talent.

*Postmodernism brought about a number of changes in *musicology generally: it became more pluralistic, and perspectives altered on the approach to *ethnomusicology and theory: music was no longer studied in isolation but set in a broader context. For feminist musicology this involved changing the way women composers and their works were studied: the women's lives and careers became part of the investigation and it thus became possible to create a clearer picture of how present-day music practice evolved. By examining patterns of female experience and bringing them to the fore, feminist musicology questions the previous acceptance of male experience as universal.

There are many approaches that feminist musicologists can take, as well as debate over which should be given precedence: recovering the work of women composers or establishing a feminist critique of the canon. Some hold the view that a separate canon should be pieced together, taking into account a new aesthetic based on historical differences in conditions for women composers and including other women whose roles were instrumental in the progress of Western music.

Feminist criticism can take many forms. It may simply be the study of gender and sexuality within dramatic music (especially opera), in the roles the female characters play. Or it may be the study of the melodic lines they are given: the musical association between chromatic, meandering melodic lines and the 'otherness' (from the male perspective) of the female character. It has successfully examined how music scholarship and music itself can be recognized not only as a mere reflection of sociological values but as a confirmation and imperative of social behaviour. Feminism uncovers the loaded gender implications within traditional analysis of autonomous musical form. If the 'feminine' subject is so called because it is romantic, chromatic, and meandering, and the 'masculine' subject labelled such for being strident and centred on the tonic, the language of so-called objective analysis uses, and hence condones, sexual stereotyping to make its case.

Feminist musicology extends to analysis of the texts or lyrics of classical and popular songs, examining musical performance as the codifying of gender relationships within popular music culture, for example in gangsta rap, pop, blues, rhythm and blues, and swing. Similarly, the role of women within the music industry is of prime interest to feminists, who are concerned to understand how music continues to be presented as a male-oriented and male-dominated art.

See also WOMEN IN MUSIC.   LD

📖 S. McCLARY, *Feminine Endings: Music, Gender, and Sexuality* (Minneapolis, 1991); 'Reshaping a discipline: Musicology and feminism in the 1990s', *Feminist Studies*, 19 (1993), 399–423 · S. G. CUSICK, 'Gender, musicology, and feminism', *Rethinking Music*, ed. N. Cook and M. Everist (Oxford, 1999)

Fenby, Eric (William) (*b* Scarborough, 22 April 1906; *d* Scarborough, 18 Feb. 1997). English composer and writer on music. Largely self-taught in music, he served

as Delius's assistant from 1928 until his death in 1934 and was responsible for taking down the blind composer's late works. He also published arrangements of works by Delius and two books: *Delius as I Knew him* (London, 1936, 2/1966) and *Delius* (London, 1971). His own compositions include the overture *Rossini on Ilkla Moor*. He taught composition at the RAM.

PG/AW

Fennimore and Gerda. Opera in 11 pictures (scenes) by Delius to his own libretto after Jens Peter Jacobsen's novel *Niels Lyhne* (1880) (Frankfurt, 1919). The intermezzo performed as a concert item is based on material in the last scene.

Ferguson, Howard (*b* Belfast, 21 Oct. 1908; *d* Cambridge, 2 Nov. 1999). English composer and musicologist. He studied at the RCM and began a career as a composer and pianist. He produced a number of craftsmanlike scores, including an Octet (1933), Piano Sonata (1938–40), and *Amore langueo* for tenor, chorus, and chamber orchestra (1956), before abandoning composition to concentrate on editing keyboard music.

AW

ferial (from Lat. *feria*, 'festival'). A term originally applied by the Romans to a holy day, but which from the 3rd century was used by Latin Christians to mean exactly the opposite—a weekday when no feast falls. Today the term is applied by some (incorrectly) also to Sundays, provided they are not special feast days.

—/ALi

fermata (It.). The *pause sign (𝄐).

Ferne (Ger.). 'Distance'; *wie aus der Ferne*, 'as if from a distance'.

Ferne Klang, Der ('The Distant Sound'). Opera in three acts by Schreker to his own libretto (Frankfurt, 1912).

Ferneyhough, Brian (*b* Coventry, 16 Jan. 1943). English composer. He studied with Lennox Berkeley at the RAM, then with Ton de Leeuw in Amsterdam and Klaus Huber in Basle. He taught at the Musikhochschule in Freiburg, at The Hague, and in the USA at San Diego and Stanford universities. He has also taught regularly at the Darmstadt summer courses.

As early as the *Sonatas* for string quartet (1967) and the *Missa brevis* for 12 voices (1969) Ferneyhough showed a determination to extend the expressionistic aspects of the postwar avant-garde style in the direction of still greater technical and notational complexity, in order to do justice to the poetic, philosophical topics that concerned him. Most of his works require relatively small forces: individual virtuosity and commitment to meeting the considerable technical challenges can yield the most positive results. Between 1981 and 1986 he composed the seven separate works of the *Carceri d'invenzione* cycle for large chamber orchestra and various soloists, including flute, violin, and soprano. The nature of Ferneyhough's continuing creative concerns can be gauged from such later titles as *On Stellar Magnitudes* (1994) and *Indissolubility* (1999). In spite of the demands these compositions make on performers and listeners alike, they carry great conviction as appropriately intense statements, often inspired by the profound and mysterious forces at work in the cosmos.

AW

📖 J. Boros and R. Toop (eds.), *Brian Ferneyhough: Collected Writings* (Amsterdam, 1995)

Ferrabosco. Italian family of musicians.

Domenico Maria Ferrabosco (*b* Bologna, 14 Feb. 1513; *d* Bologna, Feb. 1574) was a town musician in Bologna; he was also a singer at, and later *maestro di cappella* of, S. Petronio. He spent short periods in Rome, and in the 1550s was a colleague of Palestrina's in the papal chapel. He was well known as a composer of madrigals, and Palestrina based two masses on his *Io mi son giovinetta*.

His eldest son, **Alfonso Ferrabosco** (i) (*b* Bologna, *bapt.* 18 Jan. 1543; *d* Bologna, 12 Aug. 1588), travelled with his father to Rome, and in the late 1550s was in the service of Charles of Guise, Cardinal of Lorraine. In 1562 he was in England, where Elizabeth I granted him an annuity, and where he made his home until 1578, spending substantial periods in Italy and France (he may have been a spy in the English service, but this is not certain). In 1577 he was accused of robbing and murdering a young foreigner in the service of Sir Philip Sidney, after which he left England (protesting his innocence) to become, by 1582, a musician in the service of the Duke of Savoy at Turin. Queen Elizabeth's attempts to gain his return were unsuccessful. He was a highly competent composer, both of Latin church music and of Italian madrigals. His sacred music reveals a sound knowledge of counterpoint and an appreciation of chromaticism. His madrigals, composed before it became fashionable to express, or 'paint', each detail of the verse, were influential in the development of the English school, and were probably the first to be known to English composers before the importation of madrigals from Italy was customary.

Alfonso Ferrabosco (ii) (*b* ?Greenwich, before 1578; *d* Greenwich, March 1628) was the (probably natural) son of Alfonso (i). He was brought up by a musician at the English court after his father had departed for Italy. He remained in the service of the court all his life, receiving various annuities and pensions for teaching the young princes, Henry and Charles (the future Charles I). With Ben Jonson and Inigo Jones he was responsible for the production of court masques; he succeeded Coprario as Composer in Ordinary and Composer to the King in 1626.

Like his father, Alfonso the younger was well known as a composer of church music, writing English anthems for the Anglican Church as well as motets to Latin words. His secular songs are mainly either *madrigalette* (short, light partsongs), which were copied by Tregian into his manuscript anthology (London, British Library, Egerton 3665), or solo songs with lute accompaniment that show the influence of the declamatory style then becoming fashionable in England. The best of his music, however, is for viols, especially the imaginative fantasias and *In nomine* settings in which each performer was expected to show his skill in fast-moving scale passages, broken chords, and the like. His court appointments passed to his sons **Alfonso** (iii) (*c*.1610–60) and **Henry** (*c*.1615–1658), while his youngest son, **John** (1628–82), was organist of Ely Cathedral from 1662 and composed some Anglican church music.

DA/TC

📖 I. Spink (ed.), *The Seventeenth Century*, The Blackwell History of Music in Britain, iii (Oxford, 1992)

Ferrari, Benedetto (*b* Reggio nell'Emilia, ? 1603 or 1604; *d* Modena, 22 Oct. 1681). Italian composer, librettist, singer, and theorbo player. He wrote the libretto for *L'Andromeda*, the opera that opened the Teatro S. Cassiano in Venice to the paying public in 1637 (the music was by Francesco Manelli). He also wrote librettos for other composers, and several operas, but most of his own music is now lost save for three attractive books of chamber songs.

DA

Ferrari, Luc (*b* Paris, 5 Feb. 1929). French composer. He studied at the Versailles Conservatoire (1946–8), with Honegger and Alfred Cortot at the École Normale de Musique, Paris (1948–50), with Messiaen (1953), and with Varèse in New York (1954). In 1958, with Pierre Schaeffer, he set up the Groupe de Recherches Musicales, which he briefly directed. His output is divided evenly between works for electronic resources and those for more conventional forces. *Presque rien no. 1* (1970) is a compilation of everyday sounds recorded in a Yugoslav village, and in other works too he has used the tape recorder to explore the place of music and sound generally in life. Works for live performance include the orchestral *Histoire du plaisir et de la désolation* (1979–81) and two music-theatre pieces: *Journal intime* (Paris, 1982) and *Cahier du soir* (Strasbourg, 1994).

PG

Ferretti, Giovanni (*b* *c*.1540; *d* after 1609). Italian composer. In 1575 he was *maestro di cappella* at Ancona Cathedral and then moved to other positions in northern Italy, ending up at the Santa Casa in Loreto (1596–1603). He may also have had connections with Rome. His five volumes of *canzoni alla napolitana* for five voices (1567–85), and two for six (1573, 1575), were widely reprinted across Europe and influenced the English madrigalists, not least Morley.   TC

Ferrier, Kathleen (Mary) (*b* Higher Walton, 22 April 1912; *d* London, 8 Oct. 1953). English contralto. She began to study singing relatively late, at the age of 25, having been a telephone switchboard operator. On the advice of Malcolm Sargent she moved to London and took lessons with John Hutchinson and Roy Henderson. During World War II she began to attract considerable attention while singing for the armed forces and for workers in factories, and when the war ended she quickly rose to world fame for the strength and beauty of her singing. Bruno Walter engaged her to sing in performances and recordings of Mahler's songs. Her operatic appearances were few but acclaimed, beginning with the premiere of Britten's *The Rape of Lucretia* (Glyndebourne, 1946) and ending with her only other operatic role, Gluck's Orpheus (Covent Garden, 1953). She was a leading concert and oratorio singer, notably in *The Dream of Gerontius*, and an admired recitalist. The beauty of her voice and warm personality endeared her to audiences.   JT

📖 N. Cardus (ed.), *Kathleen Ferrier: A Memoir* (London, 1954, 2/1969)

Fes (Ger.). The note F♭; *Feses*, the note F♭♭.

Fesch, Willem de. See De Fesch, Willem.

Festa, Costanzo (*b* *c*.1490; *d* Rome, 10 April 1545). Italian composer. He was a member of the Sistine Chapel in Rome from 1517 until his death. His attractive madrigals are important early examples of the genre and are in widely diverse manners, sometimes simple and homophonic, sometimes elaborately contrapuntal, with lively rhythms and effective climaxes. He also wrote many sacred works. His music was singled out for praise by several contemporaries.   DA

festal. A term used to distinguish ecclesiastical feast days from ordinary, or *ferial, days.

festa teatrale (It., 'theatrical celebration'). A genre of 18th-century music theatre especially popular at Viennese courts. It was usually performed in celebration of an important occasion (e.g. a birthday or wedding) and generally treated a mythological or allegorical subject. It shared some of the characteristics of contemporary Italian opera and the *serenata. The court poet Pietro Metastasio wrote nine such works, most of them for Vienna (e.g. *Egiria*, 1764).   JBE

Feste romane ('Roman Festivals'). Symphonic poem (1928) by Respighi.

Festgesang ('Festive Hymn'). Work (1840) by Mendelssohn for male voices to words by A. E. Prölss; it was composed for the festival in Leipzig to celebrate the 400th anniversary of the invention of the Gutenberg printing press (*Lobgesang* was composed for the same occasion). The second number of *Festgesang* was adapted by W. H. Cummings to the words of the hymn *Hark, the herald angels sing*.

Festing, Michael Christian (*b* London, 29 Nov. 1705; *d* London, 24 July 1752). English composer and violinist. He studied the violin with Geminiani and first played in public in 1724. In 1735 he was appointed Master of the King's Music, and during the 1730s and 40s he played an important part in London concert life: he was leader of the Philharmonic Society, director of the Hickford's Room subscription concerts, and from 1742 director also of the newly opened Ranelagh Gardens, for which he composed instrumental and vocal music. His violin music demonstrates his comprehensive knowledge of string technique.   WT/PL

festivals (from Lat. *festivitas*, 'merriment') have a long history as gatherings where the arts, including music, are presented during a relatively short 'season'. The early ritual associations have broadened to include links to specific composers, musical genres, artists' workshops, and *competitions, and festivals now inevitably reflect a desire to market packages promoting the arts and tourism in equal degree.

1. Early history; 2. Choral festivals; 3. North America; 4. Europe

1. Early history

The Olympic Games, beginning in Greece in 776 BC and held every four years until the end of the 4th century AD, combined music and dancing, athletics, and religious celebrations. The Romans and some Middle Eastern cultures held regular festivities, and the tradition continued throughout early Christian Europe, for example with the Welsh *eisteddfodau (first documented in 1176), the Irish festivals for St Patrick's Day (17 March), and the *puys of northern France (*c*.1570).

In the Middle Ages, festivals were mainly associated with courtly pageantry. The Renaissance saw a rise of composers cultivating a 'festal' style for royal and other noble occasions but, beginning in Italy, there followed a move towards processions and events for the common people. In England, St *Cecilia's Day (22 November) was marked by sacred and secular musical festivities arranged in the late 17th century by the Musical Society (and revived in 1905 by the Musicians' Company).

During the 19th century, festivals commemorating composers in their native cities began to be held; many of these continue today (see below, 4).

2. Choral festivals

The Three Choirs festival was established in about 1715 when the choirs of Gloucester, Worcester, and Hereford Cathedrals began meeting for two days each year to perform together to raise money for the widows and orphans of clergy. Secular as well as sacred music was performed by the mid-18th century, and Handel's oratorios became regular features (as are the works of Elgar and other English composers to this day).

The popularity of Handel's oratorios heralded a growth of choral festivals throughout England, and the Handel commemorations in London in 1784, using enormous forces, inspired the formation of numerous choral societies and set a fashion for large-scale performances. However, by the mid-19th century the need to attract paying audiences as well as scores of singers was recognized, and a gradual change to smaller choirs or even ensembles with only a few singers to each part took place during the 20th century. In Germany and Austria too, the choral music of Handel, Haydn, and others grew in popularity and led to the formation of festival-organizing choirs. The first true German festival at Frankenhausen in 1810 included a performance of Haydn's *The Creation* directed by Spohr. The Lower Rhine Festival, established in 1817, resembled the Three Choirs festival in Britain with the combined choirs of Düsseldorf, Aachen (Aix-la-Chapelle), and Cologne performing in each city in turn; Mendelssohn directed this festival from 1833 to 1847.

3. North America

German immigrant communities in the USA in the 19th century fostered the performance of choral works. The Handel and Haydn Society of Boston led the way in 1858 with festivities in Boston and Worcester (Massachusetts), and since 1873 there has been an annual festival in Cincinnati, which now includes opera and concerts. In Canada, British communities have influenced music festivals, beginning in Montreal in 1860, while the French connection was first demonstrated in Quebec with the launch of the Fête Nationale des Canadiens-Français (1880).

The expansion of festivals in the USA was slow, but there are now many important examples, notably the annual Tanglewood Festival (Lenox, MA), established in 1937 by Serge Koussevitzky after the Boston Symphony Orchestra made its permanent home there.

Mention should also be made of the festivals at Ravinia Park, near Chicago (1915), Aspen, Colorado (1949), and Marlboro, Vermont (1950), the Coolidge Summer Music Festival in Washington (1950), the New York Jazz Festival (formerly the Newport, Rhode Island, Festival, 1954), and the opera festivals at Santa Fe, New Mexico (1957), Wolf Trap Farm Park (Vienna, VA, 1971), and Glimmerglass (Cooperstown, NY, 1975). In San Juan, Puerto Rico, a festival of concerts and opera was established in 1957 under the direction of Casals.

4. Europe

During the 20th century the term 'festival' applied to many kinds of events: venues ranged from cities and spas to picturesque rural retreats. The special interests or 'themes' were expanded to include every musical genre from opera through chamber, contemporary, and early music to jazz; musical events are often supported by theatre, film, art exhibitions, master classes, and lectures or discussions. The tourism industry has woken up to the attractions of 'festivals', whether they are genuine gatherings of top musicians bringing high standards of interpretation for aficionados or merely groupings of routine concerts in attractive locations.

A useful guide to the more serious events presented by its many festival-organizing members is published annually by the Association Européenne des Festivals de Musique (122 rue de Lausanne, CH-1200 Geneva). The major international festivals are generally held during the summer months. Among those that present a range of events, including opera, are the Maggio Musicale Fiorentino (founded in 1933), the Edinburgh Festival (1947), the Holland Festival (1947, held in Amsterdam, The Hague, and Rotterdam), and the festivals at Dresden (1934), Dartington (1948), Brighton (1967), Buxton (1978), and Canterbury (1984).

Festivals devoted almost exclusively to opera include the Bayreuth Festival (1876), where several of Wagner's operas are staged annually in July and August in the Festspielhaus specially designed for his music dramas. The Glyndebourne Festival (1934, new opera house opened 1994) presents operas from May to August in a small opera house in the grounds of an Elizabethan manor near Lewes, Sussex. Other notable opera festivals are those at Munich (1875), Zürich (1909), the open-air Roman arena in Verona (1913), Salzburg (1920), Bregenz (1946, staged beside Lake Constance), Wexford, Eire (1951), Drottningholm (1766, relaunched 1953), Santa Fe (1957, outdoor theatre built 1968), Savonlinna, Finland (1912, relaunched 1967), Garsington, Oxford (1989), and Aix-en-Provence (1948, relaunched 1998).

Festivals featuring contemporary music and regularly commissioning new works have included those in

Venice (1930–73), Cheltenham (1945), and Donaueschingen (1950), the Warsaw Autumn (1956), the Festival of Two Worlds (1958, held in Spoleto and Charleston, SC), the English Bach Festival (1963, London and Oxford), the Journées de Musique Contemporaine, Paris (1968), the Styrian Autumn Festival (1968, Graz), the Rencontres Internationales d'Art Contemporain, La Rochelle (1973–7, successor to the Royan Festival, 1964), and the Huddersfield Contemporary Music Festival (1978). The ISCM has organized a festival (including a competitive element), held in a different country each year, since 1923. The Almeida Festival in London, with links to Aldeburgh, has featured new operas since 1992.

Some festivals were inaugurated to celebrate a particular composer associated with the location, such as those held in Bonn (1845, Beethoven), Zwickau (1847, Schumann), Halle (1858, Handel), Salzburg (1870, Mozart), Torre del Lago (1930, Puccini), Aldeburgh (1948, Britten), Rio de Janeiro (1966, Villa-Lobos), Linz (1974, Bruckner), Pesaro (1980, Rossini), Eisenstadt (1987, Haydn), and Catania (1989, Bellini).

Other themed festivals may specialize in early music (Haslemere, founded by Arnold Dolmetsch in 1925; Innsbruck, 1977; York, 1977) or Baroque music (Beaune, Brescia); or they may be used as an expression of nationalism, for example at Llangollen (1947), Dublin (biennial since 1969), or Madrid; in the Nordic Music Days held throughout Scandinavia, Finland, and Iceland (c.1950); and at the east European festivals in Bratislava, Prague, Sofia, Szeged, and Wrocław.

In short, music festivals can now be enjoyed in almost any town in Europe and in many locations throughout the world. Musical directories, including those on the Internet, and most tourist offices provide easy guidance. AL/JBo

📖 D. G. STOLL, *Music Festivals of the World* (Oxford, 1963) · S. HUGHES, *Glyndebourne: A History of the Festival Opera* (London, 1965, 2/1981) · R. T. WATANABE, *American Composers' Concerts, and Festivals of American Music, 1925–1971* (Rochester, NY, 1972) · R. ADAMS, *A Book of British Music Festivals* (London, 1986) · A. BODEN, *Three Choirs: A History of the Festival* (Stroud, 1992) · B. A. HANAWALT and K. L. REYERSON (eds.), *City and Spectacle in Medieval Europe* (Minneapolis, 1994) · F. SPOTTS, *Bayreuth: A History of the Wagner Festival* (New Haven, CT, 1994)

festivo, festoso (It.). 'Festive'; *festivamente*, 'in a festive manner'.

Festschrift (Ger.). A collections of essays published in honour of a particular individual or institution, usually in celebration of a significant anniversary. The majority of musical *Festschriften* (the *Festschrift* is not, of course, exclusively a musical phenomenon) contain essays written for an influential individual—often a scholar, composer, or performer—by friends and pupils. The most common anniversaries seem to occur at five-year intervals between the ages of 60 and 80. Increasing specialization among musicologists is perhaps the main reason for a development whereby certain *Festschriften* are dedicated to a central theme such as opera, an individual composer, or the music of a particular country, though modern publishers' dislike of the miscellany may also be a factor. Institutions and organizations, including music publishers themselves, have also inspired *Festschriften*, though the distinction between a volume produced by admirers, and a self-congratulatory set of essays published by a firm to celebrate its own longevity, can become somewhat blurred. In any case, both probably fit the spirit, if not the letter, of the definition. Essays published to celebrate anniversaries of the death of particular figures should strictly be known as *Gedenkschriften* (memorial writings), though they too are often designated *Festschrift*. JWA

Festspiel (Ger., 'festival play'). A term sometimes applied to musical stage works or to plays with incidental music. August von Kotzebue's play *Die Ruinen von Athen*, to which Beethoven wrote incidental music, is called a 'Festspiel'. Wagner, recalling that all ancient Greek stage performances were called 'festival performances', attached the title to his *Ring* tetralogy, which he called a 'Bühnenfestspiel' (stage festival play), while *Parsifal* bears the grand title of 'Bühnenweihfestspiel' (stage-dedication festival play). Wagner's theatre at Bayreuth is thus called a 'Festspielhaus' (festival playhouse).

Fêtes galantes. Two sets of three songs (1891, 1904) by Debussy to poems by Paul Verlaine; the second of the second set was orchestrated by Roland-Manuel (1923) and the third by Louis Beydts (1929).

Fétis, François-Joseph (*b* Mons, Hainaut, 25 March 1784; *d* Brussels, 26 March 1871). Belgian scholar, critic, teacher, and composer. He came from a musical family and in 1800 entered the Paris Conservatoire, where he developed a special interest in 16th-century contrapuntal music, especially that of Palestrina. After a spell of teaching elsewhere (1811–18) he returned to Paris and from 1821 taught counterpoint at the Conservatoire. In 1833 he became the first director of the Brussels Conservatory.

Though a prolific composer who made his living mainly by teaching, Fétis is chiefly important for his critical writing and theoretical treatises. His eight-volume *Biographie universelle des musiciens* (Brussels, 1835–44) was the most comprehensive biographical dictionary of musicians of its time and is still a standard source of information, particularly on French musicians of his own day. Fétis built up an extensive library and a fine collection of instruments. He founded (1827) and for six years edited the famous journal *Revue musicale*, through which he encouraged interest in music of the past while showing a somewhat conservative attitude to contemporary music.   JN

Feuer (Ger.). 'Fire'; *mit Feuer, feuerig*, 'with fire', 'passionate'.

Feuersnot ('Fire Famine'). Opera in one act by Richard Strauss to a libretto by Ernst von Wolzogen after a Dutch legend (Dresden, 1901).

feuille d'album (Fr.). 'Album-leaf'.

Feux d'artifice ('Fireworks'). Piano piece by Debussy, no. 12 of his *Préludes* book 2.

Févin, Antoine de (*b* ?Arras, *c*.1470; *d* Blois, 1511 or 1512). French church musician and composer. He is mentioned in connection with the French royal court in a letter from Louis XII in 1507. On his death he was commemorated in song by another court composer, Jean Mouton. Févin was one of the earliest composers of parody masses, and wrote polyphonic arrangements of popular songs. His most celebrated work, however, is the crisply declamatory motet *Sancta Trinitas*. **Robert de Févin** (*fl* 1500–15), probably his brother, was also a singer and composer.   JM

ff, fff. Abbreviations for **fortissimo*.

Fg. (Ger.). Abbreviation for *Fagott*, 'bassoon'.

f-hole. See SOUNDHOLE.

fiati (It., 'breaths'). Wind instruments.

Fibich, Zdeněk [Zdenko] (*b* Všebořice, Bohemia, 21 Dec. 1850; *d* Prague, 15 Oct. 1900). Czech composer. After Smetana and Dvořák he is the principal representative of Czech Romantic music. Encouraged to compose from childhood, he had written a great deal by the end of his schooling in Prague in 1865. Between 1865 and 1867 he studied in Leipzig with E. F. Richter and Moscheles. After stays in Paris and Mannheim he settled in Prague in 1871. Although he conducted in the Provisional Theatre (1875–81) and the Russian Orthodox Church (1878–81), from 1881 Fibich sustained himself by composition and teaching. After the death of his first wife, Růžena Hanušová, he married, at her request, her sister Betty (1846–1901), an admired operatic contralto. An affair with the writer Anežka Schulzová (1868–1905) provided inspiration for the music of his final decade. After increasing ill health, he died of pneumonia.

Fibich's music is the least consciously national of major Czech composers. His German training prompted an inclination towards Schumann in instrumental music and Wagner in dramatic works. In spite of a fine melodic instinct, his music lacks the character of Smetana's and the appeal of Dvořák's. However, Fibich was always prepared to experiment. His three completed symphonies contain much fine music, while his symphonic poems (especially the influential *Záboj, Slavoj a Luděk*, 1873, and *Toman a lesní panna*, 'Toman and the Wood Nymph', 1875) are genuinely innovatory, and he made the first use of the polka in an instrumental work (String Quartet in A major, 1874).

The almost 400 miniatures making up Fibich's vast *Piano Diary* (most were published as *Moods, Impressions and Reminiscences*, 1892–9) have attracted considerable notoriety since they chart his relationship with Schulzová and are used extensively in his later music. His eight operas show a preoccupation with tragedy; the third, *Nevěsta messinská* ('The Bride of Messina', 1883), was an attempt to provide the Czechs with music drama in the Wagnerian manner. His literary bent led him to several fine texts including *Bouře* ('The Tempest', 1893) and three by Schulzová, the second of which, *Šárka* (1897), remains his most popular. Fibich's cultivation of melodrama led to a resurgence of interest in the form and culminated in the epic trilogy of stage melodramas, *Hippodamie* (1888–91).   JSM

📖 J. TYRRELL, *Czech Opera* (Cambridge, 1988)

fiddle (Fr.: *vielle, vièle*; Ger.: *Fiedel*; It.: *viola*; Lat.: *viella*). A generic term for any bowed instrument, including the violin. It is used especially for the medieval European bowed instruments with oval or waisted bodies. These were mostly flat-backed, the neck, back, and sides being carved from a single piece of wood, and commonly (though with frequent exceptions) had five strings, one of them often a bowed or plucked drone. The fiddle was distinct from the pear-shaped **rebec*, which usually had three strings. Some fiddles were held against the chest, others downwards.

A wide variety of fiddles is used around the world, with bodies of bamboo, gourd, or wood, bellies of skin or wood, and one or more strings.   JMo

'Fiddle' Fugue. Nickname of J. S. Bach's Fugue in D minor for organ, BWV539:2 (1720), so called because it is an arrangement of the second movement of the Sonata in G minor for solo violin (1720).

Fidelio (*Leonore, oder Der Triumph der ehelichen Liebe*; 'Leonore, or The Triumph of Married Love'). Opera in two (originally three) acts by Beethoven to a libretto by Joseph von Sonnleithner (1805), with revisions by

Stephan von Breuning (1806) and Georg Friedrich Treitschke (1814), after Jean-Nicolas Bouilly's French libretto *Léonore, ou L'Amour conjugal*; the first version was given its premiere in Vienna in 1805, the second version in 1806, and the final version in 1814. Beethoven wrote four overtures for the opera: the first three are known as the **Leonore* overtures; the fourth, the *Fidelio* overture (the one now usually played), was composed for the final version.

Field, John (*b* Dublin, 26 July 1782; *d* Moscow, 23 Jan. 1837). Irish composer and pianist. He was a pioneer in the development of a Romantic style of piano music that reached its zenith in the works of Chopin, and he is best remembered today for his nocturnes, written between 1812 and 1836. A prodigy by the age of ten, he made his debut at the Rotunda Assembly Rooms in Dublin in March 1792. The following year he was taken to London by his father, a professional violinist; by the end of 1793 he had become a pupil of Clementi and was said by Haydn to play the piano 'extremely well'. For seven years he studied with Clementi and enjoyed a close friendship with Dussek, whose ground-breaking exploration of idiomatic piano textures was to be of considerable importance to Field's later development. In 1799 his First Piano Concerto was performed at the King's Theatre, marking an important stage in his career. A year later, having concluded his apprenticeship with Clementi (to whom he dedicated the three piano sonatas, his official op. 1), he was in great demand in London as a concert pianist.

In 1802 Field accompanied Clementi on a continental business tour, to Paris, Vienna (where he turned down counterpoint lessons with Albrechtsberger, Beethoven's teacher), and finally St Petersburg. There he became the darling of Russian aristocratic society and earned a comfortable living as a pianist and teacher of wealthy pupils. After visiting Riga and Mitau (now Jelgava) in 1805 he arrived in Moscow, where he made his first public appearance in March 1806. Moscow and St Petersburg alternately were his home for the next 29 years. In 1831 he returned to London seeking medical attention for cancer and was operated on with partial success. He then undertook concerts in London and Manchester, as well as playing his Seventh Piano Concerto (his last substantial work, though he wrote some further nocturnes) in Paris in December 1832. After concerts in France, Belgium, Switzerland, and Italy he became increasingly ill but gave three concerts in Vienna (as Czerny's guest) before arriving back in Moscow in September 1835. He died there 16 months later.

Field regarded himself as a pianist who composed rather than a composer first and foremost: his virtuoso career left him little scope for sustained creative effort.

By about 1810 the familiar style, featuring a widely spread left-hand accompaniment and singing melody heavily ornamented by chromatically inflected figuration, had begun to crystallize in his Divertissement no. 2 for piano and string quartet. Having explored various titles for his piano pieces, he settled on 'Nocturne' with the publication in 1812 of his first three nocturnes (the last were published in 1836). His seven piano concertos are of mixed quality but contain several charming movements, notably the variations on James Hook's *Within a mile of Edinboro' town* (no. 1), an exquisite Siciliano (no. 4), and the virtuoso first movement of the Fifth Concerto, called 'L'Incendie par l'orage'. Perhaps most impressive is the first movement of the Second Concerto, which most successfully combines the roles of piano and orchestra. Field also wrote fantasies and rondos (using popular melodies), *études*, waltzes, and works for piano duet.   RL/JD1

📖 P. PIGGOTT, *The Life and Music of John Field* (London, 1973)

field trumpet. See BUGLE.

Fierrabras (*Fierabras*). Opera in three acts by Schubert to a libretto by Josef Kupelwieser after J. G. G. Büsching and F. H. von der Hagen's story in *Buch der Liebe* (1809) and Friedrich de la Motte Fouqué's *Eginhard und Emma* (1811); commissioned in 1823, it was not performed until after Schubert's death, in a revised form (Karlsruhe, 1897).

Fiery Angel, The (*Ognennïy angel*; 'The Flaming Angel'). Opera in five acts by Prokofiev to his own libretto after the novel by Valery Bryusov (1907); it was composed between 1919 and 1923 and revised in 1926–7 (Paris, 1955). Prokofiev used material from the opera in his Symphony no. 3 in C minor (1928).

fife. A small transverse **flute with a shrill sound, associated particularly with military music. In modern British fife and drum bands it has six keys and a conical bore, and is pitched in B♭. Fife and drum corps are common in the USA.

'Fifths' Quartet. Nickname of Haydn's String Quartet in D minor op. 76 no. 2 (1797), so called because the opening theme begins with melodic leaps of a 5th.

figura (Lat.). In medieval musical theory, the generic term for notational symbols.

figural (Lat.: *figuratus*; Fr.: *figuré*; Ger.: *figuriert*). Literally, florid or elaborately conceived. In their most general sense the adjectives 'figural', 'figurate', and 'figured' have been used somewhat indiscriminately to draw a distinction between polyphony (*musica figurata*) and plainchant (*musica plana*) and hence to distinguish any florid style of writing from a simpler one or a single florid polyphonic voice from a less elaborate one. The term *musica figurata* was also used in a more specialist sense in the 15th and 16th centuries to denote the florid complex polyphony of some early Flemish composers (e.g. Ockeghem or Obrecht) as distinct from the generally more sober *musica reservata* of Josquin and later composers. In the 17th and 18th centuries the terms 'figural' and 'figured' were applied to music containing *figuration. (See also FIGURE, 1.)

figuration. A term used loosely to describe passage-work or accompaniment with a distinctive shape (e.g. scales, arpeggio patterns) often derived from the repetition of an easily identifiable figure or motif. It is particularly common in working out variations and in the elaboration of a chorale or hymn tune (sometimes called a 'figured chorale').

See also FIGURE, 1.

figure. 1. A brief, easily distinguishable melodic or rhythmic motif, which may be as long as a few bars or as short as two notes. On its own or along with more substantial ideas it may form the basis for the construction of a piece or movement; the first prelude of Bach's *The Well-Tempered Clavier* is built entirely on one such musical figure. Used repetitively, often at varying pitches, a figure may play an important part in sections of thematic development. A persistent use of figures in keyboard accompaniment for songs (e.g. the leaping triplet figure in the piano part of Schubert's *Die Forelle*) is particularly common. Such repetition of figures in accompanying parts or in passage work is sometimes termed *figuration.   —/JBe

2. An arabic number placed beneath a line of music to indicate (in terms of intervals from the bass) all or part of the implied accompanying harmonies. See CONTINUO.

figured bass [thoroughbass, general bass] (Fr.: *basse chiffrée, basse continue*; Ger.: *Generalbass, bezifferter Bass*; It.: *basso continuo*). A bass line with figures indicating the required harmonies. The figured bass was a feature of the Baroque period. Usually a bass instrument, for example the bass viol or cello, would play the single bass line while a keyboard or plucked instrument filled in the harmonies. For the history and an example of the figured bass, see CONTINUO.

figures, doctrine of (Ger.: *Figurenlehre*). A term formulated in the early 20th century by German musicologists, notably Arnold Schering, to describe a theory of composition of the late Baroque period in Germany which relates *rhetorical figures of speech to musical figures. Just as Ancient Greek and Roman orators might decorate their speeches with rhetorical language, so it

had become common for composers to use musical imagery and specific devices, or figures, to illustrate textual ideas. Although this practice had its precursors in the *word-painting of Renaissance music, it was the German theorist-musicians of the 17th and 18th centuries who first formulated a system of musical figures and attempted to rationalize their use. Such writers as Joachim Burmeister and Johannes Nucius in the early 17th century began to list and describe musical-rhetorical figures, and the terminology that they and their successors devised persisted in use until the mid-18th century (Mattheson).

By analogy with the theory's classical origins, Latin and Greek names were used to codify musical figures, though several names might serve for the same figure and there was little uniformity of terminology among composers, who might invent new figures as required and name them at will. The sorts of device covered by the terminology of the doctrine of figures range from broad compositional styles such as types of fugal imitation (*apocope, hypallage*), chordal writing (*noema*), and word-painting in general (*hypotyposis*) to more specific details such as a substantial melodic leap (*exclamatio*), an unexpected pause (*abruptio*), and the repetition of the same melodic formula to begin successive phrases (*anaphora*). The doctrine of figures, like the closely related doctrine of *affections, was very much a product of the age of rationalism that nurtured it. It enjoyed something of a revival in those 20th-century theoretical and analytical studies (by Leonard Ratner, for example: see, in particular, *Classic Music: Expression, Form and Style*, 1980) which aimed to apply historically appropriate criteria and terminology to particular compositions.   JN/AW

filar il suono [la voce] (It.), **filer le son** [la voix] (Fr.). 'To spin the sound (of the voice)': in singing, an instruction to sustain a note without taking a breath; it can be a similar instruction to wind players and to string players not to use a change of bow. In modern times the term has been taken to imply a constant level of sound but it has also implied a gradual *crescendo* and *diminuendo*. The same effect is known as *messa di voce*.

Fille aux cheveux de lin, La ('The Girl with the Flaxen Hair'). Piano piece (1910) by Debussy, no. 8 of his *Préludes* book 1; it was suggested by a poem by Leconte de Lisle.

Fille du régiment, La ('The Daughter of the Regiment'). Opera in two acts by Donizetti to a libretto by Jules-Henri Vernoy de Saint-Georges and Jean-François-Alfred Bayard (Paris, 1840). It was later revised to an Italian translation by Calisto Bassi (Milan, 1840).

Fille mal gardée, La ('The Unchaperoned Girl'). Ballet in two acts to a scenario and with choreography by Jean Bercher Dauberval, originally to a potpourri of French songs and *airs* (Bordeaux, 1789). Hérold created a new score, using some of the earlier music, extracts from Donizetti and Rossini, and his own contributions (Paris, 1828). Peter Ludwig Hertel provided music for a new version (Berlin, 1864). The ballet was recreated with a new score by John Lanchbery, based on Hérold but with Hertel's 'Clog Dance', choreographed by Frederick Ashton (London, 1960).

film music. Music that accompanies films, whether specifically composed or assembled from existing sources. In the days of the silent film, background music was simply a practical necessity: it not only obscured the distracting sound of the early projectors, but also helped to underline and illuminate the significance of the images being projected. Equally, the conventional use of incidental music in the theatre was a precedent for its transferral into the cinema. At first the music was improvised by a pianist or organist, and pieces from the piano repertory were called into use for this purpose. Subsequently, genre pieces with titles indicating their mood and broad dramatic application were provided by specialist composers, in books of selections for piano and organ. When orchestras were introduced in the larger cinemas, complete scores were distributed with a given film. D. W. Griffiths selected the music that accompanied his epic *The Birth of a Nation* (1915) in association with Joseph Breil. The following year *The Fall of a Nation* opened in New York with music by the popular operetta composer Victor Herbert which may be the first complete orchestral film score.

The advent of sound in film in the late 1920s saw a continuation of the practice of using classical music, now contained on the soundtrack. A brief period of experiment with different levels of musical intervention gave way to the successful and effective integration of music into film, in Germany in the work of Wolfgang Zeller and Herbert Windt, in France where, from the outset, prestigious figures were involved, and in Hollywood, where the arrival of composers trained in the Austro-German tradition such as the Austrians Erich Korngold and Max Steiner established an idiom strongly conditioned by their cultural inheritance.

The output of such Hollywood composers was considerable: in 1933 Steiner wrote scores for some 37 films, including *King Kong* and George Cukor's adaptation of *Little Women*. Korngold's contribution, though much smaller, was no less influential, and includes the scores for many of Errol Flynn's films, for example *Captain Blood* (1935) and *The Adventures of Robin Hood* (1938). The highly detailed textures and

tireless descriptive commentary of these scores exemplifies the Hollywood style of the period. Other leading figures included Franz Waxman, who had begun his career in the German film industry (arrangement credit for *Der blaue Engel*) and left Germany in 1934, arriving the following year in Hollywood, where he scored many of Hitchcock's first American films (*Rebecca*, 1940) and wrote the lurid, Oscar-winning score for Billy Wilder's *Sunset Boulevard* (1950); the versatile Hungarian composer Miklós Rózsa; and the Russian-born Dimitri Tiomkin.

American composers were also active, such as the prolific Alfred Newman, who had studied with Schoenberg and whose career spanned almost 40 years, from *The Devil to Pay* in 1931 to *Airport* in 1970. The scores of Bernard Herrmann, born in New York and one of the composers associated with Copland in the 1930s, represent a later stage in the development of Hollywood film scores, from *Citizen Kane* in 1941 to his work with Hitchcock in the 1950s and 60s; these provide a crucial commentary on the visual imagery, most notably in the use of a string orchestra and a stylized musical violence in *Psycho* (1960), and in Herrmann's swansong, the obsessive and dreamlike score for Martin Scorsese's *Taxi Driver* (1976).

In France, Georges Auric, one of Les Six, provided scores for Jean Cocteau and René Clair among other directors, while the Hungarian émigré Joseph Kosma worked with Jean Renoir and, under a pseudonym, collaborated on the music for Marcel Carné's *Les Enfants du paradis* (1945). In Britain, well-known composers were tempted into trying their hand at film music, a notable early example being the score that Bliss supplied for the 1936 film *Things to Come*, based on H. G. Wells's book. The music director on this film, Muir Mathieson, had a significant influence on the direction taken by British film music and subsequently commissioned scores from many leading figures, including Bax for David Lean's *Oliver Twist* (1948). Walton was the most successful and prolific of British composers to write for film, most notably with scores for Laurence Olivier's three Shakespeare adaptations, *Henry V* (1944), *Hamlet* (1944), and *Richard III* (1955).

In the USSR, Eisenstein's silent films, such as *Battleship Potemkin*, for which Edmund Meisel provided scores, were followed by classic collaborations with Prokofiev in the dangerous, politicized circumstances of the later 1930s (*Alexander Nevsky*, 1938). In postwar Italy, the neo-realism initiated by Roberto Rossellini's *Roma, città aperta* (1945) saw the emergence of a number of composers who went on to play a significant role in Italian cinema (Rota, Alessandro Cicognini). Many composers for whom cinema music was an adjunct to their work for the concert hall were tempted to reuse their scores: Prokofiev's cantata *Alexander Nevsky* (1939), Bliss's suite *Things to Come*, and Vaughan Williams's *Sinfonia antartica*, derived from his music for *Scott of the Antarctic* (1948).

A break with the late Romantic idiom in Hollywood movies was announced in the postwar era by the score supplied by Alex North for *A Streetcar Named Desire* (1951), where sparer textures and jazz instruments and motifs replaced orchestral richness. While the epic film-making of the period called up epic scoring from North and Rózsa, a more contemporary idiom, with or without jazz elements, was soon established (Henry Mancini's score for Orson Welles's *Touch of Evil*, 1958). Elmer Bernstein, one of the most gifted and prolific Hollywood composers, first rose to prominence in the 1960s for his 'action' scores for *The Magnificent Seven* (1960) and *The Great Escape* (1963).

In France, the regenerative impulse of the 'New Wave' of film makers brought new composers to prominence, among them Georges Delerue (a pupil of Milhaud), who provided the music for Alain Resnais's *Hiroshima mon amour* (1959) and was subsequently François Truffaut's long-term collaborator. As the 1960s progressed, such innovation as the chilly, disengaged organ soundtrack for Resnais's *L'Année dernière à Marienbad* (1961) gave way to a trend for epic, romantic scores, such as those of Maurice Jarre for Lean's *Lawrence of Arabia* (1962) and *Doctor Zhivago* (1965), which, through the use of a memorable theme, stamped their personality on the identity of the film as a whole. The trend continued in the work of the prolific John Williams, in his romantic scores for the adventure films *Star Wars* (1977), *Superman* (1978), and *Raiders of the Lost Ark* (1981), among others. Peter Greenaway's films too have been lent a strong musical identity through the director's collaboration with Michael Nyman (beginning with *The Draughtsman's Contract*, 1982), whose scores for other directors include most notably that for Jane Campion's *The Piano* (1992).

The wholesale use of existing pieces from the concert repertory did not end with the advent of the specialist film composer. Rakhmaninov's Second Piano Concerto, for instance, served as a backdrop for the unfulfilled love story of the British classic *Brief Encounter* in 1945. The uses to which classical works were put became increasingly sophisticated in postwar cinema: a piece of sacred music, such as Mozart's C minor Mass, can provide a complex counterpoint to Robert Bresson's austerely told prison drama *Un condamné à mort s'est échappé* (1956) or form a shocking part of a film-maker's personal vision (the ironic use of the 'Hallelujah' chorus in Luis Buñuel's *Viridiana*, 1961). More recently, operatic arias have been used for their textual significance—'Questa o quella' (*Rigoletto*) in

Wall Street (1988) and 'La mamma morta' (*Andrea Chénier*) in *Philadelphia* (1993), for example. The use of Handel's music in *The Madness of King George* (1994) illustrates the effectiveness of contemporaneous music in evoking the period in which a historical film is set.

Stanley Kubrick rejected a score by Alex North in favour of a compilation of famous works for *2001: A Space Odyssey* (1968), most strikingly the opening of Strauss's *Also sprach Zarathustra*. Later examples of Kubrick's use of existing music include that of Bartók and Ligeti in *The Shining* (1980). The Adagietto of Mahler's Fifth Symphony encapsulates the mood of Luchino Visconti's *Death in Venice* (1971), and Mozart's Piano Concerto no. 21 is insistently used throughout Bo Widerberg's tragic romance *Elvira Madigan* (1967). The music of J. S. Bach has been treated in various ways to telling effect in a number of films including Steven Spielberg's *Schindler's List* (1993) and Anthony Minghella's *The English Patient* (1996).

Film biographies of composers and musicians, once a regular feature of Hollywood output, have returned in Miloš Forman's adaptation of Peter Shaffer's play *Amadeus* (1984), in Alain Corneau's *Tous les matins du monde* (1991), on the 17th-century French composer and viol player Marin Marais, and in the 1994 Beethoven film *Immortal Beloved*, helping to popularize the music involved—significantly so in the case of Mozart.

Particularly in the 1950s, it was not uncommon for classical masterpieces to be evoked in pastiche. In early postwar Japanese cinema, Fumio Hayasaka's score for Akira Kurosawa's *Rashomon* (1950) can be cited; Kurosawa later worked regularly with Tōru Takemitsu, who introduced a contemporary sound world and also used traditional Japanese instruments in Kurosawa's *Ran* (1985). The habitual approach of Federico Fellini was to use a 'temp track'—playing his own selection of music while the camera was running—and to commission the composer (usually Nino Rota) to emulate this in the score he subsequently composed. After independence in 1947, India saw the emergence of a realist school of film directors influenced by contemporary Italian cinema. Prominent among these was Satyajit Ray, who used music by Ravi Shankar for his *Apu* trilogy of 1956–60; thereafter Ray himself composed the music for his films. Indian commercial cinema has since given rise to a flourishing song culture.

In recent years Hollywood has relied increasingly on classics of popular music in assembling a soundtrack and in establishing a musical character for a given film. Uninterrupted pop songs make up an at times barely audible soundtrack in George Lucas's nostalgic *American Graffiti* (1972), while an interlude in the narrative scripted round a pop song can be found in such later films as *Witness* (1985). Latterly, the exploitation of a familiar song has become an important part of the commercial possibilities offered by the cinema. In counterpoint to this, expansive orchestral scores are being written by a new generation of film composers, including James Horner (*Titanic*) and Michael Kamen. Among such scores by composers not exclusively associated with films may be mentioned those of Philip Glass (*The Secret Agent*, 1996; *Kundun*, 1997) and Tan Dun (*Crouching Tiger, Hidden Dragon*, 2000).

PGa/KC

📖 H. EISLER and T. ADORNO, *Composing for the Films* (London, 1947/R1971) · M. CHION, *Le Son au cinéma* (Paris, 1985; Eng. trans. 1990) · C. McCARTY (ed.), *Film Music 1* (New York and London, 1989) · M. CHION, *L'Audio-vision* (Paris, 1990; Eng. trans. 1994) · W. JEFFERSON and J. DU BOIS, *American Film Music* (Jefferson, NC, and London, 1990) · C. PALMER, *The Composer in Hollywood* (London and New York, 1990) · W. KALINAK, *Settling the Score: Music and the Classical Hollywood Film* (Madison, WI, 1992) · G. BRUT, *The Art of Film Music* (Boston, 1994) · D. KERSHAW, 'Film and television music', *The Twentieth Century*, ed. S. Banfield, The Blackwell History of Music in Britain, vi (Oxford, 1995), 125–44

Fils, (Jan) Antonín [Filtz, (Johann) Anton] (*b* Eichstätt, Bavaria, *bapt.* 22 Sept. 1733; *bur.* Mannheim, 14 March 1760). Bohemian composer and cellist. A pupil of Johann Stamitz, he played in the famous Mannheim orchestra from 1754 until his death, and as a composer was one of the first members of the so-called Mannheim school. He wrote over 60 symphonies, a large quantity of chamber music, and a few concertos for flute, for harpsichord, and for cello. His works were noted for their humorous use of Bohemian melodies and rhythms in conjunction with more traditional writing.   DA

Filtz, Anton. See FILS, ANTONÍN.

fin (Fr.). 'End'.

final (Lat.: *finalis*). The concluding pitch of a modal melody, and effectively equivalent to the tonic of a tonal scale, even though the differences between modal and tonal composition are probably more important than their similarities. The concept of the final as possessing a decisive role in determining the nature of the mode in use, by fulfilling the need for clear cadencing, appeared gradually as modal composition became more polyphonic and more systematic in its contrapuntal and harmonic procedures.   AW

final cadence. See CADENCE.

finale. The last movement of a multi-movement instrumental work (e.g. a symphony, concerto, or sonata), or the closing section of an act of an opera or other stage work. As used by 18th-century composers, notably Haydn (in both his orchestral and his chamber music) and Mozart (chiefly in his symphonies), the term 'finale' was usually associated with a lightweight, tuneful movement, often in rondo or sonata form and typically in a fast, energetic 6/8 tempo. Later in the century the finale increased in scale and musical weight, and gained a new seriousness which both counterbalanced the first movement and afforded the opportunity for the sort of triumphant, consummating conclusion that characterizes many of Beethoven's symphonies.

In the 19th century, with Schumann, Brahms, Bruckner, and Tchaikovsky, the finale continued to expand in breadth and musical significance: symphonic finales tended to embrace a wider variety of types and structures (e.g. theme and variations), admit of slower, more grandiose tempos, and allow a review or even development of the thematic material of earlier movements (e.g. Brahms's Third, Dvořák's Ninth). In chamber music, the term 'finale' is less common and tends to be reserved for serious, large-scale works (e.g. Brahms's Piano Quintet, Franck's Violin Sonata). In later music, 'finale' has been applied generally to any concluding movement or section: the last section of a suite (or other loosely linked series of movements) or of a set of variations (e.g. Elgar's 'Enigma' Variations) might be termed 'finale'.

Developed in the 18th century by Italian composers such as Alessandro Scarlatti and Galuppi, and perfected by Mozart, the operatic finale was an important precursor of the more continuous style of writing that was to characterize 19th-century opera as a whole. The 18th-century finale is usually on a larger scale than the opera's other numbers: it may include extensive ensemble passages and is often divided into contrasting sections (e.g. the finale of Act II of Mozart's *Le nozze di Figaro*) that parallel the dramatic elements as the plot unfolds or resolves.   JN

Finalmusik (Ger., 'end music'). A type of piece related to the *divertimento, *serenade, or *cassation, played as the last item in an outdoor concert such as the end-of-term ceremonies at Salzburg University in the 18th century. Examples by Mozart include K100/62a, K185/167a, and K251.

fin'al segno (It.). 'As far as the sign', i.e. repeat a piece up to the sign 𝄋 .

Finck, Heinrich (*b* ?Bamberg, 1444 or 1445; *d* Vienna, 9 June 1527). German composer. He was a student in Leipzig in 1482, but otherwise spent much of his life in Poland. Later he served the emperors Maximilian I and, for the last five months of his life, Ferdinand I. Finck was one of the earliest major composers. Although his composing career was a long one, relatively few works by him survive; those that do demonstrate his adaptability to changing stylistic trends. In addition to writing masses and motets, he was an important composer of hymns and polyphonic lieder.

His great-nephew, **Hermann Finck** (*b* Pirna, 21 March 1527; *d* Wittenberg, 29 Dec. 1558), was also a composer but is better known as the author of an informative theoretical work, *Practica musica* (Wittenberg, 1556), which mentions many contemporary musicians.   DA/JM

Finck, Herman (*b* London, 4 Nov. 1872; *d* London, 21 April 1939). British composer and conductor. The son of a German-born theatre conductor, he played in London theatre orchestras from the age of 14 and became musical director of the Palace Theatre in 1900. He did much to raise the standard of theatre and music-hall conducting, composed many attractive orchestral pieces—for example, *In the Shadows* (1910), a lasting best-seller—and contributed to and composed many theatre scores.   PGa/ABur

fine (It.). 'End'; *al fine*, an indication to repeat a passage, but only to the place marked *fine*.

Fine, Irving (Gifford) (*b* Boston, 3 Dec. 1914; *d* Boston, 23 Aug. 1962). American composer. He studied at Harvard University (1933–9) and then in Paris with Nadia Boulanger before returning to Harvard as director of the glee club (1939–46) and assistant professor of music (1946–50). In 1950 he moved to Brandeis University as chairman of the School of Creative Arts. Although, like other Boulanger pupils, he was influenced by Stravinsky's neo-classicism, he used that influence to create carefully worked compositions in which serial methods also had a part. His small output includes a string quartet, a symphony, and various vocal works.   PG

Fine, Vivian (*b* Chicago, 28 Sept. 1913; *d* Bennington, VT, 20 March 2000). American composer. She studied with Ruth Crawford Seeger at the American Conservatory in Chicago (1925–31) and with Roger Sessions in New York (1934–42), then worked as a teacher, notably at Bennington College (1964–87). Her earliest works, such as the Four Songs for voice and strings (1933), were strenuously dissonant and contrapuntal, but in New York she fell more under Copland's influence. Later works include a ballet for Martha Graham (*Alcestis*, 1960) and an opera (*The Women in the Garden*, San Francisco, 1978).   PG

Fingal's Cave. See HEBRIDES, THE.

Finger, Gottfried [Godfrey] (*b* ?Olmütz [now Olomouc], *c*.1660; *d* Mannheim, Aug. 1730). Moravian composer. He went to England about 1687, serving as a musician in the Catholic chapel of James II. After James's reign he worked in London as performer and composer, but left England in a huff in 1701 after being awarded only fourth prize for a competition setting of Congreve's masque *The Judgement of Paris* (the first, second, and third prizes went to John Weldon, John Eccles, and Daniel Purcell). He spent his later life first in north Germany, and then as musician to the Innsbruck court, which moved to Heidelberg and Mannheim. As well as dramatic music, he wrote some pleasant sonatas in the Italian style.   DA/AA

fingerboard (Fr.: *touche*; Ger.: *Griffbrett*; It.: *tastiera, tasto*). A strip of hardwood, for example ebony, glued to the neck of a stringed instrument to provide a surface against which to stop the string with the fingers. Most plucked instruments, and some bowed, have *frets tied over or set into the fingerboard; some have inset dots to mark frequently used positions. A *capo tasto* may be fixed over the fingerboard to provide an alternative *nut in a higher position, thus acting as a transposing device.   JMo

finger cymbals. Small *cymbals used by Egyptian dancers; see also ANTIQUE CYMBALS.

fingering. Numerical notation recommending which fingers should be used in performance. It is found chiefly in music for keyboard and stringed instruments, whose technique allows some choice—usually determined by artistic licence and compositional context—in such matters; for many other instruments, fingering is related to the means of producing the note required and therefore rarely notated. See also KEYBOARD FINGERING.   DMi

finite canon. See CANON.

Finland 1. From the Renaissance to the 19th century; 2. The influence of Sibelius; 3. The 1960s and 70s; 4. Recent developments

1. From the Renaissance to the 19th century

For many centuries Finland was a Swedish province, with no independent musical life. The main cultural centre and capital during the late Renaissance was Åbo (now Turku), where Didrik Peter of Nyland compiled the celebrated *Piae cantiones* (1582). But apart from Åbo in the southwest, Uleåborg (Oulu) in the north and Viipuri (Vyborg) in the south-east, there was relatively little musical activity outside the church. In Åbo a musical society was founded in 1790 but the two best-known composers of this period—Crusell, renowned for his clarinet concertos, and Erik Tulindberg (1761–1814), who composed a number of string quartets—were essentially Swedish in culture.

When, in 1809, Finland became a grand duchy of the tsarist empire, the first seeds of national self-consciousness were sown. They first bore fruit in literature with Elias Lönnrot's publication of folk poetry, *Kantele* (1831), and the *Kalevala* (1835). The so-called 'Father of Finnish music', however, was Fredrik Pacius (1809–91), German-born and a pupil of Spohr, who spent some years with the Stockholm court orchestra before settling in 1835 in Helsinki, which had by then become the capital. Pacius and Sibelius's teacher Wegelius galvanized musical life in the city. However, it was not until 1882 that Robert Kajanus (1856–1933) established the Helsinki Orchestra on a permanent footing, and a further 30 years elapsed before the Finnish national opera was founded by the soprano Aïno Ackté. The extent of Sibelius's achievement can be measured against this provincial background and the relatively pale, wholly conventional work of such predecessors as Filip von Schantz (1835–65), Axel Gabriel Ingelius (1822–68), and Pacius himself.

2. The influence of Sibelius

Such was the genius of Sibelius and the power of his musical personality that only the hardiest plant could flourish in his shadow. Many of the composers writing in his immediate wake reflect some measure of intoxication with his idiom: Leevi Madetoja (1887–1947) and Erkki Melartin (1875–1937) did not escape his magnetic pull, though Madetoja's feeling for French culture surfaces in his Third Symphony. Sibelius's influence extended far beyond Finland's borders, to Sweden (Wirén, Larsson), England (Walton, Moeran), and even the USA (Barber, Roy Harris). Only one of Sibelius's younger contemporaries, Yrjö Kilpinen, carved himself a special place in Finnish music by avoiding the symphonic challenge—indeed, the orchestral canvas altogether—and concentrating on songs, of which he wrote more than 600.

Few have matched Kilpinen's skill in distilling a powerful atmosphere with such economy of means. But the Expressionist Aarre Merikanto is increasingly perceived as the most interesting and independent figure to appear in Sibelius's wake. His opera *Juha*, to a libretto that Sibelius also considered, reveals a striking and vivid personality that offers some curious parallels with Janáček, while one of his violin concertos almost suggests Szymanowski. *Juha* serves as a reminder that although Sibelius chose not to pursue an operatic path after *The Maiden in the Tower* there were the beginnings of a lively native tradition: Madetoja's *Pohjalaisia* ('The Ostrobothnians', 1924) was a vigorous, pioneering work and laid the foundations for the resurgence of interest in opera in the 1970s.

3. The 1960s and 70s

Among the middle and younger generation of composers there is as broad a spectrum of sympathies and as wide a variety of styles as may be found in any Western country. The works of Joonas Kokkonen are among the most highly regarded. His alert and intelligent scores with their refined craftsmanship and well-calculated textures combine cosmopolitan neo-classicism with an inward-looking Nordic intensity. But the very existence of such diverse musical personalities as Erik Bergman, more receptive to radical musical thinking, Bengt Johansson (1914–89), Einar Englund, and Einojuhani Rautavaara points to an exceptional musical vitality. Opera has flourished in a way which has few parallels in other countries of a similar size; its renaissance owes much to the success of Aulis Sallinen, who has produced an impressive series of dramatically effective and musically accessible scores. Mention should also be made of Paavo Heininen, the composer of the opera *The Damask Drum* (1983).

4. Recent developments

Of the composers to emerge in the 1970s and 80s, the most important are Kalevi Aho (*b* 1949) and Magnus Lindberg (*b* 1958). Inventive and prolific, Aho shows in his early works a debt to Shostakovich, as does Englund, but he quickly found his own voice. Lindberg is innovatory and powerful, and arguably the strongest talent among his generation. The growth of the Helsinki Philharmonic and the Finnish Radio Orchestra into first-class orchestras has coincided with the coming to international prominence of a large number of gifted Finnish conductors including Paavo Berglund, Esa-Pekka Salonen, Leif Segerstam, Petri Sakari, and Sakari Oramo.   RLa

📖 A. Hodgson, *Scandinavian Music: Finland and Sweden* (Rutherford, NJ, 1984) · L. de Gorog, *From Sibelius to Sallinen: Finnish Nationalism and the Music of Finland* (New York, 1989) · K. Aho and others, *Finnish Music* (Helsinki, 1996)

Finlandia. Orchestral work, op. 26 (1899, revised 1900), by Sibelius; it was written as the final tableau of a nationalist pageant to raise money for a press pension fund in Helsinki. Its patriotic fervour (though no folksong material was used) has led to its adoption as a symbol of Finnish nationalist aspirations.

Finney, Ross Lee (*b* Wells, MN, 23 Dec. 1906; *d* Carmel, CA, 4 Feb. 1997). American composer. He studied with Nadia Boulanger in Paris (1927–8), Roger Sessions at Harvard (1928–9), and Berg in Vienna (1931–2), and taught at the University of Michigan (1949–74). His music exhibits strong rhythmic propulsion and a passion for dialectic, together, from the 1950s, with serial techniques. A large output includes four symphonies, concertos, large-scale choral works, eight quartets, and much other chamber music.   PG

Finnissy, Michael (*b* London, 17 March 1946). English composer. He studied with Bernard Stevens and Humphrey Searle at the RCM, and with Roman Vlad in Italy. He has taught in schools, colleges, and universities in England and Australia, and has been active as performer and composer with several dance companies and ensembles. His earliest extant compositions, from the mid-1970s, exploited avant-garde style in ways that linked him with the 'new complexity', and many of his works present formidable technical challenges to performers. These compositions, like the *Verdi Transcriptions* for piano (1986), are often based on earlier, very different music and transform rather than simply transcribe their sources. Finnissy's openness to the entire span of musical history and to the wealth of different musics to be found throughout the world has also led him to work on a smaller, simpler, often explicitly folk-like scale, and he is as capable of approachable sacred pieces (the choral sections of *Anima Christi*, 1991) as he is of challenging modernist scores like the short opera *Shameful Vice* (1994), which deals with the last days of Tchaikovsky's life.   AW

   📖 H. BROUGHAM, C. FOX, and I. PACE (eds.), *Uncommon Ground: The Music of Michael Finnissy* (Aldershot, 1997)

Finta giardiniera, La ('The Feigned Gardener's Girl'). Opera in three acts by Mozart to a libretto of unknown authorship which had been set by Anfossi (1774) (Munich, 1775).

Finta semplice, La ('The Feigned Simpleton'). Opera in three acts by Mozart to a libretto by Carlo Goldoni with alterations by Marco Coltellini (Salzburg, 1769).

Finzi, Gerald (Raphael) (*b* London, 14 July 1901; *d* Oxford, 27 Sept. 1956). English composer of Italian-Jewish extraction. He studied privately with Ernest Farrar (1914–16) and, after Farrar joined the army, with Edward Bairstow (1917–22). He also studied counterpoint with R. O. Morris (1925). The death of his three elder brothers and Farrar in World War I inclined him to introspection. For much of his life he lived in the country—in Gloucestershire (1922–5) and, after a period in London (1925–35), in Wiltshire and Hampshire—pursuing his interests in the cultivation of apples and book-collecting and conducting the Newbury String Players, the amateur orchestra he founded in 1940. Between 1930 and 1933 he taught composition at the RAM, and during World War II he worked for the Ministry of Transport (1941–5).

Though thoroughly aware of the contemporary music around him, Finzi preferred to fashion his style in the tradition of Parry, Elgar, and Vaughan Williams, to whom he owed much in terms of melodic phraseology, harmony, and artistic ethics. His larger choral works, notably *Intimations of Immortality* (written between 1936 and 1950) and the deeply affecting *In terra pax* (1954), reveal his indebtedness to the grandeur of Parry's broad architectural writing. His two more ambitious instrumental works, the Clarinet Concerto (1948–9) and the Cello Concerto (1951–5), exhibit respectively a natural affinity for lyricism and a passion expressed by a more dissonant language. But Finzi's most personal utterances may be found in his miniatures—the *New Year Music* op. 7, the *Eclogue* for piano and strings op. 10, and the *Romance* op. 11—and even more intensely in his songs, notably his settings of Thomas Hardy (for whom he admitted a special empathy), among which *A Young Man's Exhortation* op. 14, *Earth, Air and Rain* op. 15, and *Before and After Summer* op. 16 are especially fine, though even these are outshone by his masterpiece, the cycle of Thomas Traherne poems *Dies natalis* op. 8.

JD1

   📖 S. BANFIELD, *Gerald Finzi: An English Composer* (London, 1997) · J. C. DRESSLER, *Gerald Finzi: A Bio-Bibliography* (Westport, CT, 1997)

Fioravanti, Vincenzo (*b* Rome, 5 April 1799; *d* Naples, 28 March 1877). Italian composer. His father was also a composer and, after some resistance, became his teacher. Fioravanti's first opera was written in 1819 and for the next 35 years he produced a steady stream of *opere buffe*, almost all for the Neapolitan market. Though rarely staged in the most prestigious theatres, his operas were remarkably popular, perhaps especially in the 1840s, when his *Il ritorno di Pulcinella dagli studi di Padova* (1837) rivalled even early Verdi in the extent of its dissemination in the Italian peninsula. He served for some years as *maestro di cappella* of the cathedral in Lanciano, and wrote sacred as well as secular music.

RP

fioritura (It., 'flourish', 'flowering'). A general term denoting embellishment of a melodic line (or a part of one), either notated by the composer or added at the discretion of the performer. It is commonly used to describe extended or complex embellishments rather than standard localized ornaments such as trills, mordents, or appoggiaturas. *Fioritura* consists of passage-work of varying degrees of intricacy which enhances colour and gives variety to simple melodic figurations. Its use is documented as early as the 13th century, and it featured prolifically in the composition and playing of many 19th-century virtuosos, particularly (though not exclusively) Chopin and Liszt. NPDC

fipple flute. An older term for *'duct flute'.

Firebird, The (*Zhar'-ptitsa*). Ballet in two scenes by Stravinsky to a scenario by Mikhail Fokine, who also choreographed it for Diaghilev's Ballets Russes (Paris, 1910). The original score was in 19 sections but Stravinsky wrote a five-movement suite from the ballet in 1911 and revised it in 1919; he composed a ten-movement version in 1945.

Fireworks Music (*Music for the Royal Fireworks*). Instrumental suite (1749) by Handel written for and played at the fireworks display at Green Park, London, to mark the Peace of Aix-la-Chapelle; Handel composed it for wind band but later added string parts. It has become well known in modern orchestrations by Hamilton Harty and Charles Mackerras.

Firsova, Elena (Olegovna) (*b* Leningrad [St Petersburg], 21 March 1950). Russian composer. She studied composition with Aleksandr Pirumov at the Moscow Conservatory and (informally) with Denisov, who became a great influence. Her style is marked by novel timbral contrasts, usually for combinations of instruments within chamber ensembles or small orchestral forces (the string quartet and concerto are her favoured genres); elements of serialism and irregular rhythms are usually organized within tightly constructed forms. In 1991 she emigrated to England with her husband, the composer Dmitry Smirnov. Her chamber opera *The Nightingale and the Rose* (after Oscar Wilde) was given its premiere in London in 1994. JWAL

first inversion [6-3 chord]. A term describing the vertical presentation of a chord when the 3rd rather than the root is the lowest note, the other notes being a 3rd and a 6th above it (hence 6-3). See also INVERSION, I.

first-movement form. See SONATA FORM.

First Post. See TATTOO.

first subject. The first or principal theme of the first group of a *sonata-form movement.

first-time bar. See DOUBLE BAR.

Fis (Ger.). The note F♯; *Fisis*, the note F♯♯.

Fischer, Carl. American firm of music publishers. Carl Fischer (1849–1923), a trained musician, emigrated from Germany to the USA in 1872 and began business as a music retailer and arranger in New York. He catered for the contemporary popular taste in band music and eventually became chief publisher of John Philip Sousa and other important figures in the band world. In 1885 he started a journal for bandleaders, *The Metronome*. His son Walter S. Fischer, who took over in 1923, published excellent educational music and many successful arrangements. Frank H. Connor, who succeeded him in 1946, was particularly interested in young composers, and the firm's catalogue now includes works by Dello Joio, Foss, Randall Thompson, and Virgil Thomson. The firm remains a family concern— Charles Abry, great-grandson of its founder, took over in 1996—and it is still pre-eminent as a publisher of band music. JMT/JWa

Fischer, Johann Caspar Ferdinand (*b* c.1670; *d* Rastatt, nr Karlsruhe, 27 March 1746). German composer. From 1695, as Kapellmeister to the Baden court, he composed much instrumental and theatre music. Most noteworthy are his Lullian orchestral suites (in *Le Journal de printemps*, 1695) and his organ preludes and fugues in 19 different keys (*Ariadne musica*, 1702), in which the plan, and in two cases actual themes, of *The *Well-Tempered Clavier*, book 1 (1722), are foreshadowed. DA/BS

Fitkin, Graham (*b* Crows-an-Wra, Cornwall, 19 April 1963). English composer. He studied at Nottingham University, and in the Netherlands with Louis Andriessen, whose forceful, expansive minimalism provides the basis for Fitkin's own compositions. In a series of works written for ensembles including Icebreaker and Ensemble Bash, the emphasis on electronic instruments and percussion creates links with rock music. In such works as *Cud* (1988), *Hook* (1991), and *Stub* (1992), Fitkin has combined galvanic rhythmic energy with harmony that, while repetitive, is sonorous and richly coloured. Works for more traditional orchestral forces include a number of pieces written in the mid-1990s during his residency with the Royal Liverpool Philharmonc Orchestra, and a Clarinet Concerto (1998). AW

Fitzwilliam Virginal Book (Cambridge, Fitzwilliam Museum, 32.g29, Mus. MS 168). A manuscript volume left to Cambridge University in 1816 by Viscount Fitzwilliam as part of a valuable collection of books, music, and paintings. It was once called 'Queen Elizabeth's Virginal Book', but it is now known not to have belonged to her. The manuscript constitutes the largest single collection of Jacobean keyboard music (not only for the virginals), containing nearly 300 pieces. It was once thought to have been compiled by Francis *Tregian, a Catholic recusant, between 1609 and 1619, but the nature of its connection with his family is now unclear. Although most of the major keyboard composers of the time are represented (e.g. Byrd, Bull, and Farnaby), there are some surprising omissions, for example Orlando Gibbons. A modern edition was published in 1894–9 (rev. 1979–80).

Five, The. A group of 19th-century Russian composers who shared the common ideal of creating a distinctively Russian school of composition. They were Balakirev (the group's often despotic musical mentor), Borodin, Cui, Musorgsky, and Rimsky-Korsakov. 'The Five' is used interchangeably with 'the Mighty Handful' or 'the Kuchka' as a rendering of the Russian name, Moguchaya Kuchka ('mighty little heap'), which was humorously and affectionately coined in 1867 by the critic Vladimir Stasov, the group's main ideologist. The Five combined musical nationalism, founded on models provided by Glinka and Dargomïzhsky, with a doctrine of musical progress inspired by the examples of Berlioz, Schumann, and Liszt.   GN/MF-W

Five Orchestral Pieces. Orchestral work, op. 16 (1909), by Schoenberg; he arranged it for a much smaller orchestra in 1949 and it was arranged for chamber orchestra by Felix Greissle and for two pianos by Webern.

five-three chord. A chord in *root position, so called because the largest interval is a 5th and the middle one a 3rd (in close position). See INVERSION, 1.

fixed doh. A term applied to the system of sight-singing in which C is called *doh* in whichever key it appears (and D is called *re*, etc.). The opposite system is the movable *doh* system, in which *doh* is the name applied to the keynote of every major scale, *re* to the second note, and so on. See TONIC SOL-FA.

fl. Abbreviation for 'flute'.

flagellant songs (Ger.: *Geisslerlieder*). Vernacular songs sung by flagellants of the 13th and 14th centuries during their acts of pilgrimage and penance. In 13th-century Italy, where the flagellant movement arose, the songs were associated with the *lauda, but only one flagellant melody has survived from this period. In the 14th century, particularly following the Black Death of 1349, the movement spread to other areas as numerous penitential processions, often led by singers, were formed for the confession of sins and acts of flagellation. In Germany some of the processional songs were notated (in neumes) by Hugo Spechtshart of Reutlingen in 1349. These *Geisslerlieder* were religious folksongs following an essentially strophic framework.
                                                         —/JBE

flageolet. A *duct flute. Simple versions, often known today as tin whistles or *penny whistles, have been used worldwide since the Stone Ages. The term was used particularly for two varieties, French and English, differing mainly in the layout of the fingerholes. French

flageolets originated in about 1600 with two thumbholes and four fingerholes; in the 19th century they were made with as many as six keys for chromatics. The 'beak' was replaced in about 1750 by a slender mouthpiece, often of ivory, that covered the windway. The 19th-century English flageolet, as made by William Bainbridge, had six fingerholes and a thumbhole, and additional keys. Double and triple flageolets were also made, with the mouthpipe attached to a stock into which two or three pipes were inserted. Flageolets were often elegantly made and were popular among amateurs. A similar instrument was the Hungarian *czakan*.   JMo

flageolet notes [flageolet tones]. *Harmonics produced on stringed instruments.

Flagstad, Kirsten (Malfrid) (*b* Hamar, 12 July 1895; *d* Oslo, 7 Dec. 1962). Norwegian soprano. She made her debut in Oslo in 1913 and sang regularly in Scandinavia until 1930, when her first appearance at Bayreuth established her as one of the most remarkable Wagner interpreters of the 20th century. She first sang at the Metropolitan Opera, New York, in 1935 and appeared regularly at Covent Garden in 1936–7 and between 1948 and 1951. In 1950 she gave the world premiere of Strauss's *Vier letze Lieder* in London. She possessed a voice of immaculate beauty and evenness of tone and was famous for the aristocratic dignity of her singing. In addition to Wagnerian roles, she was outstanding as Beethoven's Leonore (in *Fidelio*), Purcell's Dido, and Gluck's Alceste, as well as being a noted exponent of Brahms's lieder.   TA

📖 H. VOGT, *Flagstad: Singer of the Century* (London, 1987)

flam. A rudimentary side-drum technique, notated as illustrated. The two notes should strike almost simultaneously, either hand leading.

L R
R L
♪♩

flamenco, cante flamenco (Sp.). In its purest sense *cante flamenco* is the name for the songs and dances of Andalusia, but is now more widely used to cover the genre that is simply thought of as the folk music of Spain. To the original Andalusian strains were added Gypsy elements derived from invading musicians of either Flemish or Moorish origin, or possibly both; and there is much discussion as to whether the name 'flamenco' derives from one or the other of these sources. Varied styles and different songs and dances developed in different regions. Basically, however, there are two broad divisions: *cante hondo, jondo,* or *grande,* implying a deeper strain of music dealing with the themes of love, sorrow, and death and covering such forms as the *martinetes, serrana, siguiriya,* and *soleraes*; and *cante chico* or *pequeño,* which covers the lighter entertainment side of the music and such forms as the *alegria, buleria,* fandango, habanera, and tango.

Flamenco was exploited by professional entertainers who performed in an increasingly stylized way in the cafés and night haunts of Spanish cities. It then became a theatrical entertainment with troupes of performers including musicians, singers, dancers, and the percussion chorus which introduced the characteristic heel-tapping, hand-clapping, and castanet-clacking that is now familiar throughout the world.

Flamenco-style guitar playing became highly developed through such pioneering virtuosos as Ramón Montoya and Andrés Segovia, as well as non-Spanish musicians. In whatever form flamenco appears, it is an art based on established rules which are the platform for variation and improvisation (*falseta*) in the spirit of each regional style.   PGA

flat (Fr.: *bémol*; Ger.: *Be*; It.: *bemolle*). **1.** The sign (♭) that, when placed before a note, lowers it in pitch by a semitone. In English terminology the verb is 'to flatten' and the adjective 'flattened'; in American usage the corresponding terms are 'to flat' and 'flatted'. See ACCIDENTAL; for the origins of the flat sign and its early use, see DURUM AND MOLLIS; NOTATION, 1.

2. An adjective applied to vocal or instrumental performance, denoting inexact intonation on the low side.

flatté (Fr.). The telescopic slide of a trombone or slide trumpet.

Flatterzunge (Ger.). 'Flutter-tongue'. See TONGUING.

flat trumpet. The English slide trumpet (see TRUMPET, 2) of Purcell's time, with a backward-moving slide.

flautando, flautato (It.). 'Flute-like': an instruction to a violinist to produce flute-like tones by bowing very lightly over the end of the fingerboard or using harmonics.

flauto (It.). 'Flute'. Until the mid-18th century the unqualified term meant 'recorder'; the flute was specified as *flauto traverso* or 'German flute'.

Flavio (*Flavio, re di Longobardi*; 'Flavio, King of the Lombards'). Opera in three acts by Handel to a libretto by Nicola Francesco Haym adapted from Matteo Noris's *Il Flavio Cuniberto* (1682, rev. 1696) (London, 1723).

flebile (It.). 'Mournful', 'plaintive'; *flebilmente,* 'mournfully', 'plaintively'.

Fledermaus, Die ('The Bat'). Operetta in three acts by Johann Strauss to a libretto by Carl Haffner and Richard Genée after Henri Meilhac and Ludovic Halévy's vaudeville *Le Réveillon* (1872) (Vienna, 1874).

flexatone. A flexible metal blade fixed in a frame, shaken so that balls on wire springs strike it on each side, producing an eerie tremolo, while the thumb controls the flexure, and thus the pitch.   JMo

flicorno (It.). 'Flugel horn'. The word is also used for a full range of instruments similar to *saxhorns, from high treble to contrabass, devised by Giuseppe Pelitti in Milan.

Fliegende Holländer, Der ('The Flying Dutchman'). Opera in one act, later three acts, by Wagner to his own libretto after Heinrich Heine's *Aus den Memoiren des Herren von Schnabelewopski* (1831) (Dresden, 1843).

fliessend (Ger.). 'Flowing'; *fliessender,* 'more flowing'.

Flight of the Bumble Bee, The. Orchestral interlude in Rimsky-Korsakov's opera *The Tale of Tsar Saltan* (1899–1900) in which a prince becomes a bee and stings his villainous relatives. Many (often spurious) arrangements have been made for a variety of solo instruments.

fling. A vigorous and energetic *reel danced in the Scottish Highlands.

Flood, The. Musical play by Stravinsky to a libretto arranged by Robert Craft from the book of Genesis and the York and Chester mystery plays; for three speakers, tenor and two basses, chorus, orchestra, and actors, it was performed on television in 1962 and staged in Hamburg in 1963.

floral dance [flora]. See FURRY DANCE.

Florentinische Tragödie, Eine ('A Florentine Tragedy'). Opera in one act by Zemlinsky to his own libretto after Oscar Wilde's play fragment *A Florentine Tragedy* (1908) (Stuttgart, 1917).

florid. A term applied to highly embellished music. It is particularly used of 18th-century vocal music, with its passage-work ('divisions') and ornamentation, but is also applied to the elaborate polyphony of such composers as Ockeghem and Obrecht.

Flos campi ('Flower of the Field'). Suite (1925) by Vaughan Williams for solo viola, (wordless) chorus, and small orchestra; each of the six movements is prefaced by a Latin quotation from the Song of Solomon.

Flöte (Ger.). 'Flute'.

Flotow, Friedrich von (*b* Toitendorf, 27 April 1812; *d* Darmstadt, 24 Jan. 1883). German composer. He studied with Reicha and Pixis in Paris, where his first ten operas, mostly *opéras comiques*, were produced. A number of them were later rewritten, enlarged, or given different plots, especially when he began writing German opera. His first major German Romantic opera was *Alessandro Stradella* (1844), based on an episode in that composer's adventurous life. Though French-influenced, notably in extended choral and ballet scenes in the manner of *grand opéra*, the work shows its German heritage in the rich orchestration and in the skilful motivic preparation for the hymn that Stradella sings at the climax of the opera.

Flotow's greatest success was *Martha* (1847), in which *opéra comique* provides the main influence, though some of the vocal writing is strongly Italianate. He again holds the work together motivically, here by the repeated appearance of the folksong 'The Last Rose of Summer' but more subtly, by integrating its melodic ingredients into the fabric of the score. The 1848 Revolution led him to return to Germany. *Sophia Catharina* (1850) is in some ways a return to the manner of *Alessandro Stradella*, without that work's charm, though neither here nor in *Rübezahl* (1852) does his ear for the orchestra fail him. He moved to Vienna in 1852, then became director of the grand-ducal court opera in Mecklenburg, 1855–62. He settled on the family estate at Toitendorf in 1873. None of his later works, whether French or German, achieved anything like the success of *Stradella* or *Martha*.   JW

flott (Ger.). 'Brisk', 'lively'.

flottant (Fr.). 'Floating': an instruction to a violinist to use a smooth, flowing bow movement.

flourish. A trumpet call of the *fanfare type. In Restoration England the term also denoted a brief improvisatory passage that preceded the work proper and consisted largely of scales and arpeggios. In a more general sense, the word has come to mean any florid instrumental passage.   —JBE

Flowers o' the Forest. Scottish lament of which the original words are lost; the forest is a district of Selkirk and Peebles and the flowers are young men killed in battle. The tune is played by pipers at the Remembrance Day ceremony.

Floyd, Carlisle (Sessions) (*b* Latta, SC, 11 June 1926). American composer. He studied with Ernst Bacon at Syracuse University (1945–9) and has taught at Florida State University (1947–76) and the University of Houston (from 1976). His opera *Susannah* (Tallahassee, FL, 1955), telling the biblical story in a 19th-century Tennessee context with a smooth folksong lyricism, became a staple of the American repertory and was staged by the Metropolitan in 1999. Later operas include *Wuthering Heights* (Santa Fe, 1958), *The Passion of Jonathan Wade* (New York, 1962), *Of Mice and Men* (Seattle, 1970), *Bilby's Doll* (Houston, 1976), and *Willie Stark* (Houston, 1981).   PG

flugel horn (Fr.: *bugle*; Ger.: *Flügelhorn*; It.: *flicorno*). A valved bugle in B♭. It is at the same pitch as the *cornet but has a wider conical bore, which gives it a fuller tone. In the British *brass band it plays a subsidiary role in unison with one of the cornets, but in central and southern Europe it is a leading brass instrument.   JMo

flüssig (Ger.). 'Flowing'.

flute (Fr.: *flûte*; Ger.: *Flöte*; It.: *flauto*). Any instrument sounded by a stream of air crossing a hole in either a tube or a vessel (e.g. the *ocarina). The hole may be at the end (*end-blown flute) or in the side, or the air may be led through a duct (*duct flute) as on a *recorder or *flageolet.

Since the end of the 18th century the standard European flute has been the side-blown instrument. Before that time, the word 'flute' meant the recorder, and the side-blown flute was called either transverse flute or German flute, the latter alluding to its use as a military instrument by German mercenaries. The name *traverso*, from the Italian *flauto traverso*, has become accepted as meaning the one-key Baroque-style instrument in early-music performances.

The Renaissance flute was a one-piece cylindrical tube with six fingerholes and a somewhat limited range. In the second half of the 17th century the Baroque *traverso* was devised, by makers at the French court, in three pieces or joints: a cylindrical head; a conical body, with the six fingerholes, narrowing from the head towards the foot; and a foot joint, which carried a single key. The lowest note was d', and the key was opened to obtain $e♭'$; all other chromatic notes were obtained by cross-fingering (i.e. closing holes below the lowest open hole to flatten the pitch).

After about 1720 the body was divided into two halves, each with three fingerholes; the advantages this brought were that the bore could be reamed more accurately, with shorter tools, and that a series of interchangeable upper-body joints (*corps de rechange*), each differing slightly in length, could allow the production of different pitches. Extra keys for F, G♯, and B♭ were added by the 1780s and the range was extended by adding keys for c' and $c♯'$; these were followed by a key for c'', creating the eight-key flute, which remained available into the 20th century. A tuning-barrel between the head and the upper body with a brass tuning-slide saved the cost of the extra upper-body joints.

In the 1830s there was demand for flutes with a louder and more equal sound, for notes produced by cross-fingering or from the rather small key-covered holes were quieter than those from the six fingerholes. Theobald Boehm (1794–1881), a Munich craftsman-inventor and flautist, devised a system in which all the holes were nearer to their ideal size and position. Because this put many beyond reach of the fingers, he also had to invent a mechanism to control the keys and rings that covered the holes. Ring-keys allow fingers to cover holes and at the same time, by means of rod-mechanisms, to close or open other holes further away. The mechanism of the conical-Boehm flute, or 1832 system, has been adapted to control the keywork of all other woodwind instruments.

In 1847 Boehm produced an entirely new model, with a head joint which narrowed parabolically towards its top, a one-piece cylindrical body, and a cylindrical foot. All the holes were covered by open-standing keys, all were roughly equal in size, and each as nearly as possible in its correct acoustical position. The flute was preferably made of metal—silver or gold for professionals, cheaper metals for students and amateurs—and was, with slight subsequent improvements, in all essentials the modern concert flute.

Flutes are made in a variety of sizes. The concert flute, which is the same size as the old Renaissance tenor, is in C. The piccolo (It., 'small') is an octave higher, but it rarely has the C foot of the concert flute and so its lowest note is *d''*. The alto flute in G was sometimes confusingly called a bass flute, but the French name, *flûte en sol*, avoids any ambiguity. Less common, and used mainly in recording studios, is the true bass flute, an octave below the concert flute. This often has its head curved back over the body, but it remains awkward to hold and heavier to support than is comfortable. It also suffers from having too narrow a bore for the best sound.

Different sizes were made for military bands. The standard fife, the old Renaissance treble, is pitched in B♭ and has six fingerholes; later models with added keys are called B♭ flutes in Britain and A♭ flutes in the USA even though they very seldom have the C foot needed to take them down to *d♭'*. This flute has its own piccolo, usually in E♭, an alto (the F flute; called E♭ in the USA), and a tenor in B♭, a tone below the concert flute. 19th-century tenors are often confused with the classical flûte d'amour, which was about the same size. Basses and even occasionally contrabasses are also made for flute bands.

The flute's repertory is vast, for as well as being a professional's instrument it was very popular with amateurs including royalty and aristocrats—so much so that flutes built into walking-sticks were a common novelty. Frederick the Great of Prussia played and composed music for the flute, and many composers wrote solos for him, including J. S. Bach and Frederick's resident teacher and house composer, J. J. Quantz, who also wrote one of the most famous treatises on the instrument (*Versuch einer Anweisung die Flöte traversiere zu spielen*, 1752).

Globally, transverse flutes are less common than end-blown or duct flutes. Instruments up to 3 metres long are used in New Guinea, and quite short ones, much the size of a fife, in Japan. In China flutes have extra holes: one between the blowing hole and the first fingerhole is covered by a thin membrane to add a kazoo-like buzz, and two or more at the foot are tuning-vents to which a decorative tassel may be attached, for hanging up the instrument when not in use. The flute was known in Mesopotamia and Egypt in the 3rd millennium BC and is depicted in Etruscan and Roman artefacts, though it fell out of use in Europe after the fall of Rome. In India the flute has long been associated with Krishna and also widely used in classical music, and it was from there that it reached Byzantium in the 10th and 11th centuries, thence making its way again into Europe.　　　　JMo

📖 N. TOFF, *The Development of the Modern Flute* (New York, 1979, 2/1986) · A. COOPER, *The Flute* (London, 1980, enlarged 2/1984) · J. SOLUM, *The Early Flute* (Oxford, 1992) · J. M. THOMSON (ed.), *The Cambridge Companion to the Flute* (Cambridge, forthcoming)

flutter-tonguing. A variety of *tonguing introduced by Richard Strauss.

Flying Dutchman, The. See FLIEGENDE HOLLÄNDER, DER.

focoso (It.). 'Fiery'; *focosamente*, 'in a fiery manner'.

Foerster, Josef Bohuslav (*b* Prague, 30 Dec. 1859; *d* Vestec, nr Stará Boleslav, Bohemia, 29 May 1951). Czech composer, teacher, and writer. He received his earliest training from his father Josef (1833–1907), himself a composer and one of Prague's most respected choirmasters and organists. Later he studied at the Prague Organ School and in 1893 moved to Hamburg where his wife, the soprano Berta Lautererová (1869–1936), had been engaged at the Stadttheater. In 1903 the couple moved to Vienna where Foerster continued working as a critic and teaching composition. Throughout this time he maintained links with his native land, providing critiques and articles for Czech newspapers, many of which were aimed at raising the standard of repertory in the National Theatre; several of his works were given their premieres in Prague, including his best-known opera *Eva* (1899).

In 1918 Foerster returned to Prague, teaching composition at the Prague Conservatory and later in the master school and the university where he influenced many of the succeeding generation of Czech composers. His large output has a firm bias towards vocal and choral music, much of which shows a clear affinity with Czech national styles. His strongly lyrical idiom betrays the influence of his countrymen Fibich and Smetana, and in his orchestral music that of his friend Mahler. The finest of his six operas, *Eva* and *Jessika*, not only display a melodic gift but also show genuine dramatic abilities.   JSM

📖 J. TYRRELL, *Czech Opera* (Cambridge, 1988)

folia [follia, folies d'Espagne]. A dance, probably Portuguese in origin, the characteristic harmonic framework of which was adopted by several 17th- and 18th-century composers as the basis of sets of variations. The name 'folia' is first mentioned in late 15th-century Spanish and Portuguese documents in connection with both singing and dancing, the latter reputed to be wild, frenzied, and 'folly-like'. During the early 17th century the *folia* became popular as a sung dance with guitar accompaniment in Spain, from where it spread to Italy, France, England, and elsewhere, and was scored for various instrumental combinations.

The bass line of the *folia*, which established the characteristic harmonic pattern, eventually became standardized as a sort of *ground bass, and, as with other Renaissance ground-bass dances such as the *romanesca*, a particular melodic outline was commonly attached to it; this outline (or a rhythmic or melodic variant of it) eventually earned equal status with the bass line and the chordal structure as an identifying feature of the *folia* (Ex. 1).

Ex. 1

Composers who wrote variations on the *folia* tune include Frescobaldi (keyboard, 1630), Corelli (violin, 1700), Marais (viol, 1701), Vivaldi (chamber ensemble, 1737), J. S. Bach ('Peasant' Cantata, 1742), C. P. E. Bach (keyboard, 1778), and Liszt (*Rapsodie espagnole*, *c*.1863). The enormous popularity of Corelli's set in the 19th century led to the mistaken belief that the tune itself was originally his, hence the title of Rakhmaninov's *Variations on a Theme by Corelli* (1932).   JN

folies d'Espagne. See FOLIA.

folk dance. A participatory dance originating within an ethnic culture. Most folk dances are rural, with their origin in pre-industrial cultures. The 20th century saw the establishment of many folk-dance societies, one of the earliest being the English Folk Dance Society, founded by Cecil Sharp in 1911.

folk music 1. History of the 'folk' concept; 2. Music associated with the 'folk' concept

1. History of the 'folk' concept

The use of the idea of 'the folk' to describe the 'essence' of a nation originated in European Romanticism. Early in the 19th century, however, 'popular song' had been synonymous with 'peasant', 'national', and 'traditional' song; towards the end of the century the term 'folk' took on these connotations, and 'popular' came to be reserved for more recent urban popular music, from the music-hall repertory onwards. The song-collecting pioneer of the 'first folk revival', Cecil Sharp, restricted the meaning of the term 'folk', so that it no longer conveyed the vague notion of a 'national essence' but was concerned solely with the disappearing rural labouring classes, who were seen as illiterate, and uncontaminated either by commercial ('popular') music or by 'art'.

However, the drawing of boundaries between 'folk' and 'popular' musics has never been satisfactorily resolved, and the difficulty of doing so has only increased since the advent of broadcasting, which has led to all kinds of music being heard by everyone. This problem led to a change of emphasis, towards identifying 'folk music' in the cultural processes claimed by Sharp to distinguish it from art or popular music; hence the classic definition of folk music by the International Folk Music Council (set out in its *Journal*, 7 (1955), 23):

> Folk music is the product of a musical tradition that has been evolved through the process of oral transmission. The factors that shape the tradition are: (i) continuity which links the present with the past; (ii) variation which springs from the creative impulse of the individual or the group; and (iii) selection by the community which determines the form or forms in which the music survives.

However, there are many who believe that this definition raises more problems than it resolves. A. L. Lloyd recognized that those who performed 'folk' music, far from being illiterate, were often readers of music notation, and therefore did not rely exclusively on oral transmission. Harker asks, 'Why do not continuity, variation and selection represent the conditioning factor for *all* musical production, amateur or professional?', since such processes might apply equally to the whole (popular and classical) musical field. For Harker, the musical practices of working people have been so 'mediated' by 'bourgeois' collectors and publishers that 'folksong' can be no more than an ideological construction of their making, and can therefore be used only in a figurative sense.

Moreover, the term did not stay within the bounds set for it by the song collectors of the first revival. Lloyd expanded the conception of 'the folk' to include industrial workers, though Harker maintains that the preferred music of the working class was more typically derived from the music hall, and questions whether the 'folk' repertory identified by Lloyd was really representative of working-class taste. In the USA the use of the term has been more fluid; in a relatively new country, several 'folk' traditions of European origin were implanted, together with African music, all of which have been interacting and producing new hybrids. The development of ethnomusicology in the 1950s brought about a willingness to extend the 'folk' concept into the hybrid forms, and a recognition of the many urban musical subcultures among various immigrant groups. Since the 'second' folk revival of the 1950s, the tendency of folksingers to sing their own songs as well as traditional ones has blurred the distinction in America between folk and pop styles.

In this situation, many of those concerned with 'traditional' music felt that current usage of the term 'folk' was too vague to specify their area of interest without ambiguity. So, for example, the International Folk Music Council, which had produced the definition of 'folk music' cited above, changed its name in 1981 to the International Council for Traditional Music; more recently, the British world-music periodical *Folk Roots*, intending by the term 'roots' to make clear its concern with music 'rooted' in a tradition, felt it necessary to remove its title's reference to 'folk' by calling itself *fRoots*. Thus the meaning of the term 'folk' has been considerably broadened during the history of its usage, and as a result other terms are competing with it for its conventionally accepted domain.

2. Music associated with the 'folk' concept

Some of the oldest musical types which have been called 'folksong' reach back into musical prehistory, though of course they were not so named until much later. This includes survivals of early song forms in eastern Europe (though not in western Europe), collected and studied particularly by Hungarian musicians and composers in the 20th century. Their melodic character is of an oft-repeated, but varied, single melodic phrase ('variative' song). They are not yet organized into a regular metrical structure, nor are they 'strophic' (i.e. the text is not arranged into regular strophes, or verses, which coincide with a complete statement of the melody, as occurs in the later ballad). However, what appear to be later versions also survive; although the melodic material is recognizably similar, in these the structure of the song has become strophic and is arranged in verses of regular length, the melody more or less exactly repeated for each verse.

From such evidence the Hungarian musicologist János Maróthy developed a theory of the relationship between musical form and social structure, according to which the earlier 'variative' tunes were used in tribal society for the recitation of long epic tales (the surviving epics of the Balkan countries have been compared in form to those of Homer); and the later strophic ballads, sung by a solo singer, were associated with the development of feudal society, their texts self-contained stories extracted from the earlier epics; thus the epic is said to have developed into the *ballad. This eastern European evidence can be taken to suggest the prehistory of the ballad in western Europe, where the earlier layer of tune types does not survive. Study of early European melodic types remains a continuing interest among eastern European scholars. Their research also shows how a linear, vocal ballad melody can be taken up by instrumental players and turned into a more angular dance tune, a phenomenon also observable in tunes of Anglo-Celtic origin.

Interest in the ballad was awakened two centuries earlier, and pre-dates the advent of the 'folk' concept. Harker views the term 'ballad' as he does 'folksong', an ideological construction; yet, while 'folk music' is a rather loose category comprising many different musical genres, it can be countered that, unlike 'folk', the term 'ballad' corresponds fairly straightforwardly to an identifiable song form. 18th-century antiquarian interest produced such publication titles as D'Urfey's *Collection of Old Ballads* (1723–5) and Percy's *Reliques of Ancient English Poetry* (1765), 'consisting of Old Heroic Ballads'. Interest in Scottish and Welsh traditional song in the drawing-rooms of London led to the publication of arrangements by Haydn. The Romantic composers were influenced by the ballad; some German composers set translations of traditional English ballads to music, a model that influenced Schubert.

Although the concept of 'the folk' is associated with the Romantic movement, ballads were not yet 'folksong'; this would wait until the end of the 19th century. The association of 'folk' music with 'national essence' is demonstrated by the conscious use of the music of 'the folk' for such a purpose in the Romantic era (by such composers as Weber, Schubert, Liszt, Chopin, Glinka, and Smetana). However, the involvement of classical composers of the 'first folk revival' at the beginning of the 20th century (e.g. Vaughan Williams and Bartók) cannot be simply reduced to the musical expression of political nationalism. As Vaughan Williams (*National Music*, 1935, p. 85f.) was later to write:

> If we look at a collection of German *Volkslieder* we are apt to be disappointed because the tunes look exactly like the simpler Mozart, Beethoven and Schubert tunes. The truth is of course the other way out. The tunes of Mozart, Beethoven and Schubert are so very much like *Volkslieder* . . . What we call the classical idiom . . . is as narrowly national as that of Grieg or Mussorgsky.

Here the classical tradition is revealed as having been already a national tradition (based on German 'folk') before the advent of other national styles, rather than a universal musical language. Its capacity for further development was uncertain, so that composers sought in modality a direction alternative to the endless extrapolation of tonality; the use of other 'folk' styles thus broadened the classical idiom. Moreover, Vaughan Williams's view of the relationship between composer and audience came from his socialism, and this was both the well-spring of his accessible compositional style, and the primary reason, rather than nationalism, for arranging folksongs for popular consumption. For composers of this period, the discovery of new sonorities was at least as important as nationalism: such composers include Sibelius, Prokofiev, Khachaturian, Janáček, Bartók, Debussy, Ravel, Falla, Villa-Lobos, Copland, and Ives.

If the first folk revival was led by classical musicians, producing classical arrangements of folk music for the concert hall and for music education in schools, the second, whose heyday was the 1950s, had a different emphasis, attempting to return to a performance style resembling that of the 'folk' from whom the material had been collected, and was typically performed in 'folk clubs'. Leading performers of this revival were (in the USA) Woody Guthrie, Pete and Peggy Seeger, Joan Baez, and Judy Collins, and (in Britain) Ewan MacColl, Alex Campbell, Peter Bellamy, the Copper family, Martin Carthy, and the Watersons.

In Britain in the 1960s, some performers began to fear for the survival of the traditional song repertory, largely confined to folk clubs, while Western youth turned to commercial pop music. This led to the production of various hybrid forms; for example, the group Steeleye Span used the electric instruments of a rock band for arrangements of traditional ballads; some American 'folk blues', first recorded in the 1920s, had always remained in the popular repertory and now turned up in rock versions, by Eric Clapton, for instance. Since that time, the styles of pop music have changed, and the focus of youth music has shifted from song to dance. There are some examples of the hybridization of youth dance culture with traditional British music, for example the Scottish band Shooglenifty.

Traditional music is a minority interest in England, though very much a living tradition in Scotland and Ireland. There has been a liberal suspicion of anything that might be perceived as 'nationalist' in England; however, the Scottish experience might suggest that a positive role for national identity marginalizes the negative aspects of nationalism. If the traditional music of Britain is less strong in pop music than it was, the influence of non-European traditional music is felt in the 'world music' phenomenon, for example through the WOMAD festivals.

In many European countries, particularly those of the former Eastern bloc, folk music has been 'professionalized', so that trained dancers tour the world, acting as cultural ambassadors for their countries by performing often highly choreographed 'traditional' dances in stylized 'traditional' costumes. Many such dances have their origin in social dance. Folk dance in Britain is exclusively amateur, and, while the ritual Morris dance is deemed worthy of public performance, social dance is rarely performed for spectators.

Although the categorization of music as 'folk' is of European origin, there are other places in the world where a similar distinction is made between art and folk music, India being one of them. Sometimes, however, the West has inappropriately applied the 'folk' category to non-Western musics that are regarded as art music in their native country (for example those of India, Indonesia, China, Japan, or Korea), and to the music of countries where there is no conceptual distinction between 'folk' and 'art' music (e.g. African countries). The advent of ethnomusicology, however, brought an awareness that the relationship between music and social organization is different from one culture to another, and that the 'folk' concept cannot be universally applied.

It is now recognized that folksongs, like art songs, have an author, even though anonymous, and are not 'communally' created, though the community has a role in adopting or rejecting songs. It is also recognized that not all songs are ancient, and that folk repertories are constantly changing. Change may be spontaneous (innovation) or stimulated by contact with another group of people (acculturation); new songs are composed, and old ones discarded or put to new uses; modes, scales, and rhythms may be changed. There is still interest in tracing back melodies to an archaic layer, particularly in eastern Europe, but field-workers today have come to focus on the self-identification of the folksinger and the singer's perhaps changing repertory, rather than, as in the early 20th century, on material useful only for some ulterior purpose of the collector.

HM/PW

📖 C. J. Sharp, *English Folk Songs: Some Conclusions* (London, 1907, rev. 4/1965 by M. Karpeles) · A. L. Lloyd, *Folk Song in England* (London, 1967) · D. Harker, *Fakesong: The Manufacture of British 'Folksong', 1700 to the Present Day* (Milton Keynes, 1985) · P. V. Bohlman, *The Study of Folk Music in the Modern World* (Bloomington, IN, 1988) · N. MacKinnon, *The British Folk Scene: Musical Performance and Social Identity* (Buckingham, 1993) · R. Cantwell, *When We Were Good: The Folk Revival* (Cambridge, MA, 1996)

folk rock. A term used not only for rock arrangements of traditional song and dance, but also more broadly for a range of interpretations of traditional music, or of contemporary songs in a 'folk' idiom, using amplified instruments and modern technology, some of which might more appropriately be termed 'electric folk'. It was first applied to the music of the Byrds in the USA in 1965. Other American exponents include Bob Dylan and Simon and Garfunkel. British pioneers were Fairport Convention and Steeleye Span. There are also mainland European and Latin American examples, and recent fusions of 1950s folk with black American *rap.

KG

Folquet de Marseille [Fulco Anfos] (*b* ?Marseilles, *c.*1150–60; *d* Toulouse, 25 Dec. 1231). Troubadour, later a cleric and bishop. He may have been born in Genoa, the son of a merchant. As a troubadour his career spanned only the period *c.*1180–95; 29 songs by him survive, half of them with their music intact. In later life he entered the church, rising to become Bishop of Toulouse. He established the university in that city, and was one of the founders of the Dominican order.

JM

Fomin, Yevstigney Ipat'yevich (*b* St Petersburg, 5/16 Aug. 1761; *d* St Petersburg, 16/28 April 1800). Russian composer. He received a thorough education in music, first at the Academy of Fine Arts in St Petersburg, then in Italy, where he was elected a member of the Accademia Filarmonica of Bologna in 1785. He returned to Russia the following year, and at first

probably earned his living in government administration, later coaching singers for the court theatre. As a composer he is known chiefly for his operas which, though generally lightweight, were later seen as important forerunners of 19th-century Russian opera because of their attempts to create Russian national colouring: the opening chorus from *Yamshchiki na podstave* ('Coachmen at the Inn', 1787), for example, is often cited as an early and artistically successful (albeit inaccurate) representation of Russian choral folksong. Perhaps his most powerful work is the melodrama *Orpheus and Euridice* (1792), which is marked by a sure feel for dramatic situation and tragic expression. Many of Fomin's scores were lost during a long period of oblivion; his work was rediscovered only in the 1950s.

GN/MF-W

Fontana, Giovanni Battista (*b* Brescia; *d* Padua, *c.*1630). Italian composer and violinist. He is known only by a posthumous collection (1641) of six sonatas for solo violin (or cornett) and continuo and 12 for two, some with an additional part for bassoon or cello. Its preface says that he was from Brescia and worked in Rome, Venice, and Padua. They are fine virtuoso works that mark an important contribution to a developing genre.

TC

Fontane di Roma ('Fountains of Rome'). Symphonic poem (1914–16) by Respighi; its four sections depict the sensations of the composer when he was contemplating four of the city's most famous fountains—Valle Giulia at dawn, Tritone in mid-morning, Trevi at noon, and Villa Medici at sunset.

foot. 1. The unit or group in the rhythmic make-up of a poem. See metre.

2. Applied to instruments, 8′ denotes the written pitch, 4′ an octave higher, 16′ an octave lower, etc. The usage derives from the nominal lengths of organ pipes sounding *c*′.

3. The lowest joint (that furthest from the player's mouth) on flutes and recorders.

Forbes, Sebastian (*b* Amersham, 22 May 1941). Scottish composer. He studied at the RAM and Cambridge University. He then worked as a BBC producer before becoming a university teacher at Bangor and Surrey (Guildford), where he was professor of music. His many works in 'mainstream' instrumental, orchestral, and vocal genres include three symphonies and three string quartets.

PG/AW

Force of Destiny, The. See Forza del destino, La.

Ford, Thomas (*d* London, ?12 Nov. 1648). English lutenist and composer. He was in the service of Henry, Prince of Wales, in 1610, and later in that of Charles I. His songs, published in 1607, are his best work. They vary between those, like *Since first I saw your face*, that have simple but memorable tunes, and others, such as *Go, Passion*, in the more emotional manner of John Dowland. He also wrote anthems, and music for viols. He was buried in St Margaret's, Westminster.

DA/JM

forefall. A 17th-century English term for an ascending *appoggiatura, notated and performed as in Ex. 1.

Ex. 1

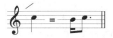

Forelle, Die ('The Trout'). Song (1817) for voice and piano by Schubert to words by Schubart; it exists in five versions that differ only slightly, the last version (1821) having a five-bar piano prelude. Schubert used the theme for variations in his Piano Quintet in A major D667, known as the *'Trout' Quintet.

Forgotten Rite, The. Orchestral work ('prelude') by Ireland (1913); the unspecified rite is associated with the Channel Islands.

Forkel, Johann Nicolaus (*b* Meeder, nr Coburg, 22 Feb. 1749; *d* Göttingen, 20 March 1818). German theorist and music historian. The son of a shoemaker, box maker, and tax collector, he was enabled to study law by a noble patron but turned to music, becoming university organist and director of music at Göttingen. He was one of the earliest to lecture on music history and theory at a university; his *Allgemeine Geschichte der Musik* (Leipzig, 1788–1801) was the first German comprehensive history of music. He was also active as a music critic, and his biography of J. S. Bach (Leipzig, 1802) won much acclaim.

DA/LC

forlana [furlano] (It.; Fr.: *forlane*). An Italian dance dating from the 16th century. During the Baroque period it became a lively dance similar to the *gigue, in triple or compound-duple time, with dotted rhythms and repeated motifs. It was particularly popular in Venice and in 18th-century *opéras-ballets* such as Campra's *Les Fêtes vénitiennes* (1710). Bach's Orchestral Suite no. 1 in C (BWV1066) and Ravel's *Le Tombeau de Couperin* both include a forlana.

form. The shape or structure of a musical work.

1. Introduction; 2. Strophic forms; 3. Variation forms; 4. Continuation or contrasting forms; 5. Binary form and allied concepts; 6. Sonata form; 7. Ritornello and concerto forms; 8. Contrapuntal forms; 9. Forms with extra-musical elements; 10. The 20th century

1. Introduction

Form can be said to be the way in which the various elements in a piece of music—its pitches, rhythms, dynamics, timbres—are organized in order to make it coherent to a listener. The definition of the word 'form' has been the subject of aesthetic debate for centuries, and in a musical context 'form' cannot be separated from content. In his *Fundamentals of Musical Composition* (written between 1937 and 1948), Schoenberg stated that 'form means that a piece is organized: i.e. that it consists of elements functioning like those of a living organism … The chief requirements for the creation of a comprehensible form are *logic* and *coherence*. The presentation, development, and interconnection of ideas must be based on relationship'. Percy Scholes, writing in the first edition of this *Companion* (1938) about (chiefly) the music of the 18th to the early 20th centuries, found that there was a limited number of moulds into which composers poured their music. Since that first edition, however, interest in earlier music and the explosion of new attitudes to formal patterns by 20th-century composers have widened our approach to form. The present article will discuss some general principles by which music is given clarity and unity. Individual forms referred to in the text are described in more detail in separate entries, in conjunction with which this article should be read; the most important are also listed at the end.

Since music is essentially a temporal art, in live performance there is no chance for the listener to rehear a detail or part of a work. This is not the case with painting or literature, for example, where the eye can continue to study a whole work or a detail of it for any length of time. In music a substitute for that property is some kind of repetition. It may be a short sequence of sounds that is repeated, or a long and complex section which most people would find impossible to remember exactly. Nevertheless, the effect of such repetition will be registered, at least by the experienced listener, and will give him or her a sense of order. However, repetition alone would be monotonous. Musical form also consists of the relationship between different patterns of sound.

Works may be classified as single or compound forms. Single forms are formally complete and tonally self-contained and are not divisible into smaller units. Compound forms include two or more single forms;

they are usually multi-movement works (*sonata, *symphony, string quartet, *suite).

2. Strophic forms

The simplest structural procedure in music is the exact repetition of an idea. The rhythm of a drummer keeping men marching in step is often no more than a basic idea reiterated as long as necessary. Similarly the melody of a hymn, for congregational singing, may be repeated for several verses. Folksongs embody repetition. Strophic art songs, after the manner of folksongs, commonly repeat the same music to different words. For example, in Schubert's *Heidenröslein* three verses, or strophes, are set to the same melody, with no alterations to the voice part or the piano accompaniment. In the art song the limit of this technique is reached in, for example, 'Das Wandern', the first song of Schubert's cycle *Die schöne Müllerin*, which consists of five verses without change. Strophic forms can be made more elaborate by repetitions of phrases or sections within each verse. Many medieval and Renaissance songs have more or less complicated structures of this kind (see BALLADE; RONDEAU; VIRELAI). The strict strophic pattern may also be abandoned for a single verse, which nevertheless maintains roughly the same dimensions as the other verses (see BAR FORM).

3. Variation forms

Methods of varying material can be subtle and almost endless and several may be present at any one time. Rough divisions may be made between those that alter melody, harmony, rhythm, and texture or quality of sound. Changing melody is the most elementary way of creating musical variation. A folksinger will rarely sing exactly the same notes for each verse of a song but will add new embellishments; hence there is rarely a 'true' version of a folk tune but several equally valid variants. Frequently these variants will be sung by a number of performers simultaneously, the result being *hetero-phony. In art music, this simple concept of decoration results in *divisions: the tune is taken as a basic outline and quicker notes are added or gaps between leaps are filled, to give a sense of continuous flow.

Variation and decoration, however, are not synonymous. A melody may be kept plain but changed in a more basic way, for example by switching its mode from major to minor (or vice versa). This may alter its emotional significance completely and is often used by composers to provide vivid contrast. The idea of a change of mode in a melody implies some harmonic considerations: an unaccompanied melody rarely uses this device, whereas an accompanied one frequently does. The most elementary kind of 'harmonic variation' is made by adding fresh harmonies to the same tune,

much practised by organists (with mixed success) in trying to alleviate the tedium of repeating a hymn tune for many verses. (Bach, however, an organist of genius, exploited harmonic variation to marvellous effect in the *St Matthew Passion*.)

More sophisticated use of harmonic variants goes back to the 16th century—or even earlier. It is to be found in the *basso ostinato*, a repeated bass line over which a keyboard player or lutenist improvises chords and a singer or player evolves a melody. Even if the basic chords are unchanged, the melody almost inevitably adds passing notes which effectively alter the chords. The possibilities of this kind of variation for emotional expression are the more attractive since the juxtaposition of consonance and dissonance gives immediate and strong contrasts.

Variations in which rhythm is the changing element are rarer. Rhythm as the stable element is fundamental to dance music (Ravel's *La Valse*, with its frequently vague melody, would seem formless without it). In *isorhythm it is a rhythmic pattern which is repeated while the melody changes. Nevertheless, a basic melody can be changed by altering rhythm or metre, a device explored by composers of variation suites and linked pavans and galliards in the 16th and 17th centuries; Dowland, for example, used this technique in his *Lachrimae*. Such variations can be produced in a freer way (as in the seventh variation of Brahms's 'St Anthony' Variations), provided the phrase and harmonic structures of the original melody remain recognizable.

Variety can also be obtained without affecting the musical substance simply by repeating a melody with different dynamics or instruments (see KLANG-FARBENMELODIE). The *ne plus ultra* of this technique is Ravel's *Boléro*, in which the same tune is repeated many times, each with a different combination of instruments and gradually getting louder (this piece also perhaps shows the limitations of the device). More subtle variation can be achieved by changes in figuration. Thus a tune may be harmonized in block chords on the piano and then given an *Alberti bass-type accompaniment; counterpoints may be written against it; certain notes of the melody may be transferred to a different octave (a common device for piano composers): the possibilities are practically endless.

All the above techniques are in constant use in all kinds of music. Their distillation is the form known as 'Air (or Theme) and Variations', which has been used by many great composers, notably Bull, Byrd, Bach, Handel, Beethoven, Schubert, and Brahms. This form has the advantage of immediate recognition on the part of all listeners, since the pattern of phrase lengths remains reasonably constant, even in otherwise complex works (such as Elgar's 'Enigma' Variations).

4. Continuation or contrasting forms

It takes a great composer to create a fine set of variations, because this does not demand pure invention so much as the ability to see the underlying possibilities of a single idea. Lesser composers can construct their music by the use of more material, which provides the opportunity for contrast. Nevertheless, a continuous succession of new ideas will not prove satisfying, so repetition of some sort is necessary.

The most common way of achieving this is to repeat the opening material at the end of a piece, a structure that can be represented by the letter scheme ABA. *Ternary form, as this is known, has been in use since the 17th century, when the *da capo* aria became prevalent. Here there is an extended opening section, a middle section which may or not be in the same mood but provides new material, then an exact return of the opening section. The contrasts of the middle section may be any of those used in variations (changes of mode, time, texture). During the 18th century, when minuets were arranged in pairs—Minuet 1–Minuet 2–Minuet 1—the second minuet was occasionally written in just three instrumental parts (as opposed to the full band) and was called a *trio; it was sometimes appropriate for the first minuet to be in the minor key and the second in the major, thus providing contrasts of sonority, texture, and mode (an example is the third movement of Mozart's Symphony no. 40 in G minor). The basic pattern is not obscured by some variations in the repeat of the first section (it was customary, for example, for singers to embellish their reprise in the *da capo* aria) provided that it does not change radically in tonality or scale.

An extension of this form is the *rondo, where there are two sections using new material, in the pattern ABACA. These sections involve the same principles as the middle sections of ternary form, the desire for variety encouraging composers to change mode, tonality, texture, and so on for at least one episode. However, the principle of the main theme recurring in the same key is usually adhered to. Rondo form was popular for keyboard music in the 17th century, especially in France (*rondeau*). Composers also found it conveniently light, but not too lightweight, for the final movements of symphonies and sometimes created from it quite complicated patterns (see also below, 6).

5. Binary form and allied concepts

Although the principles so far described apply both to extended pieces and to small sections of music, they have mainly been explained in terms of what might be called macroforms, or overall patterns, simply because they are more easily perceived when the scale is not too restricted. Others, however, are more obvious on a small scale, or microform.

In ternary form, the concept of tonality assumes importance (see above): its function is at the heart of other forms. Tonality, by its nature, provides a place of rest, places of less rest, and places of discomfort. In any tune the place of rest is the tonic; places of a little less rest are the other notes of the tonic chords (III and V); places of still less rest are notes IV and VI (and perhaps II); and discomfort surrounds the leading note, which, as its name implies, needs to go somewhere (to the tonic). If a piece ends in the tonic key, all is resolved; but if it ends in any other, discomfort results—the degree of discomfort depending largely on which key it is.

At the end of the 17th century, composers (notably Corelli) discovered that this could be exploited, and they began writing pieces in two sections. The first ended in a foreign key (often the dominant or relative minor); the second progressed from this new key back to the tonic. This was known as *binary form. Such pieces may be short (Baroque dances) or extremely long (the larger movements in J. S. Bach's partitas). Long movements are often hard to follow, simply because they rely not on pure melody but on a combination of melody and harmony that it is impossible to sing. Nevertheless, the attentive listener will recognize the feeling of satisfaction when the final tonic is reached. Also, for reasons of historical evolution, the two parts are both repeated. This further helps to orient the listener.

The thinking behind binary form is the basis of so much music of the 18th and 19th centuries that many of the details of other forms have to be explained from it. The most important of these is **development' or 'working out', which occurs most often at the beginning of the second section. Development draws together the twin processes of variation and contrast. A theme (often with a strong, memorable rhythm) will be repeated, either exactly or in varied form, perhaps transferred to another key. It can be shortened, by being interrupted by new contrasting material, or achieve extension with similar but new material. In the process of shortening or extension, new harmonies, especially those modulating to a new key, will often be used. Akin to development is the 'bridge passage', which does not introduce memorable new ideas but forms a link between two themes in different keys; a bridge passage may embody development techniques and it can be vital in large-scale forms.

Another formal element is that of the 'coda' or tailpiece. At the end of a rondo, the last repetition of the theme may not give a suitable sense of finality, so the composer may add a few bars to confirm the tonic key. Something of this sort is even more essential in long movements in binary form, where the simple return to the home key is not enough to bring a work to a satisfactory conclusion. However, Beethoven and others used the coda as an additional opportunity for development in a large-scale movement in the most complex form built from these ingredients: *sonata form.

6. Sonata form

*Sonata form is sometimes known as 'first-movement form' since it is used in the opening movements of sonatas and symphonies (though it is also sometimes found in other movements). It is a mixture of binary and ternary principles, for, although its essence is to move out of the tonic and return to it, it sounds to the listener as an ABA structure: the recapitulation repeats the opening material, albeit with changes. Because of its origins in binary form, the exposition will usually be marked with repeats in a Classical work; the development-cum-recapitulation sometimes also has them.

Any description of sonata form is necessarily an outline, since the musical material in a sonata-form movement can vary enormously. The 'subjects' are often not tunes or lengthy themes but short, memorable ideas; because there is often more than one, subjects are sometimes called 'groups'. The first subject will usually blend into the bridge passage almost unnoticed. The second subject may be of contrasting material; Haydn, however, often uses first-subject material in the second subject. The essential feature is that it should be in a different key from the first subject in the exposition but be in the tonic in the recapitulation (following the principle of binary form).

In the development, there may be a new theme. Mozart sometimes opens with one (as in the Piano Sonata in F major K332/300k) and Beethoven and Brahms occasionally use one in the later part of the development section (as in their violin concertos). But on the whole the material will be derived from the exposition and may include parts of the bridge passage. The development explores different keys, usually avoiding the tonic so that its return at the opening of the recapitulation provides a satisfying sense of homecoming. One of the main features of the recapitulation is the alteration of the bridge passage which necessarily occurs because the key of the second subject is changed to the tonic. The composer here has the opportunity to provide new interest, since the attentive listener will be subconsciously comparing what is being heard with what was heard in the exposition, as in variations. Similarly, although the coda in a short movement will usually merely reiterate cadential for-

mulas in the tonic, in an extended one it may begin in much the same way as the development, providing a dramatic element by arousing expectations of something very long, which is then curtailed.

Sonata form is the most complex and most adaptable of forms, capable of sustaining music for up to half an hour, as in the first movement of Beethoven's Ninth Symphony and in some symphonies by Mahler and Bruckner. It makes demands on the listener's attention simply because it uses the variation/development principle so constantly. A form that keeps many of its virtues but relieves them with the greater straightforwardness of the rondo is the *sonata rondo, often used for the finales of sonatas and symphonies.

7. Ritornello and concerto form

Sonata and sonata rondo form are used in concertos for one or more soloists and orchestra, but the special circumstances caused by contrasting two distinctive bodies of sound make their own demands. The *concerto exploits the contrasts between a single instrument (or a small group) and a larger group, and calls on the skill of a soloist in elaborate and technically more demanding music. However, if there is no thematic rapport between soloist and orchestra the work becomes dull (as in the case of many 19th-century virtuoso violin concertos). The best concertos, therefore, have a form in which the qualities of both bodies are developed but both have enough music in common to create a sense of unity.

In the Baroque era, the first movements of solo concertos were written in *ritornello form, in which a refrain recurs several times, as in rondo form (see also CONCERTO, 3). The ritornello differs from the rondo in several ways: it is usually made up of several ideas which can be detached from each other; it appears complete only at the beginning and end—both times in the tonic; the 'episodes' for soloists often make use of the ritornello material, after the manner of a development section, these episodes being designed to demonstrate the soloists' virtuosity. This is the plan adopted by Vivaldi in his best concertos, such as those of *L'estro armonico*, and by Bach.

When sonata form became standard for symphonic movements, the ritornello scheme was modified in various ways, and the pattern of the first movement of the Mozart/Beethoven concerto often shows a mixture of ritornello and sonata procedures (see CONCERTO FORM); some commentators prefer to discuss it more in terms of the former than the latter. Nevertheless, many of Mozart's concertos sound as if they are in sonata form, and there is evidence that by 1800 many other composers were conceiving their concerto movements as sonata-form structures.

8. Contrapuntal forms

So far we have discussed structures which will work for music with an unaccompanied melody (strophic, variation, ternary, and rondo) or based on harmonic concepts (binary and sonata form). In the context of variations (above, 3) we mentioned heterophony, which arises when a melody and its variations are sung simultaneously. From this concept come a number of forms the pattern of which is constructed by the simultaneous performance of several melodic strands. The earliest historically, and the easiest to understand, is the use of the *cantus firmus, often a piece of plainchant sung in long notes, round which other voices weave faster-moving parts. This differs from heterophony in that the surrounding parts are not necessarily derived from the cantus firmus: they obey laws of harmony and are not haphazard. In extended pieces, the cantus firmus could be repeated, in which case it was sometimes treated in *isorhythm.

A later development was the use of what one scholar has called 'syntactic imitation'. Each line of verse in a madrigal or each separate phrase in a Latin motet is set to a musical figure. This is announced by one voice and then imitated by the others. There is thus a succession of musical phrases used 'in imitation'; but since in a vocal ensemble of four voices each has a different range, these themes have to be altered in pitch, the alto usually being a 4th below the soprano, the tenor an octave below, and the bass a 4th below the tenor. The use of fresh points of imitation for each line fulfils the same function as does the end of a line in verse, or the punctuation—syntax—of prose. This idiom was transferred to instrumental music, as in the *canzona francese* and *ricercar. Since these lack words, the principle was modified to make more obvious shapes for the listener, the canzona often using a kind of ternary form, the ricercar tending to use a single theme for all the 'lines' or sections, providing variety with new melodic accompaniments and new sonorities.

It was from this that the *fugue was developed. This is not strictly a form so much as a 'concept' or 'texture'. Fugues as complete and independent entities are comparatively rare, though Bach's '48' are obvious examples. More often they are part of a larger work. In mass settings, the section 'Cum Sancto Spiritu' in the Credo is often a fugue. Sometimes a fugue has to be integrated into a larger pattern. In the last movement of Mozart's G major String Quartet (K387) a fugue is subsumed into sonata form, with a non-fugal second subject.

9. Forms with extra-musical elements

The forms so far described are what some commentators might categorize as those of 'absolute' music.

However, non-musical factors influence the form of some works: the structure of vocal music is often dependent on the text being set, and visual or literary elements can determine the shape of programme music.

The simplest of such forms is the *'through-composed' song (a term derived from the German *durchkomponiert*)—a work without an obvious strophic construction. Schubert's *Erlkönig* is a good example, the melody being set to bring out the dialogue between the different characters—the child, the father, and the menacing spectre of the Erlking—all unified by the piano accompaniment's continuous suggestion of galloping horses. Even so, it is only the outline of the song which is 'through-composed'; in detail there are many repetitions using subtle changes of tonality and of theme. Similarly Schubert's *Gretchen am Spinnrade*, though not falling into the usual strophic or ternary forms, repeats its initial phrase at the end, using the lack of its extension into the second phrase to evoke the unease suggested by the poem.

On a larger scale, the linking of movements of symphonies or sonatas by giving them themes in common is known as *cyclic form. Among the best-known examples is Berlioz's *Symphonie fantastique*, where a single theme, the 'idée fixe', represents the composer's beloved, imagined in various circumstances (in the country, at a ball, at the witches' sabbath, etc.). While certain movements of the symphony are in 'pure' forms, the work does not make sense as a whole without a knowledge of the programme. Most works that use such links have a literary foundation (see SYMPHONIC POEM). Similarly in oratorio, though each individual movement may be studied from an abstract point of view, the macroform depends on the narrative.   DA/AL

10. The 20th century

The explosion of compositional novelty that historians both then and now have diagnosed in the music of the last century led to the need for an exceptionally clear sense of the balance of old and new. Thus for example in Schoenberg's early 12-note works, offering pioneering melodic and harmonic universes the likes of which had never been heard before, the composer tended to compensate by using such traditional forms as sonata, variation, and even the neo-Baroque forms implied by movements called 'Sarabande' or 'Gigue'. The same balancing impulse can be discerned even in *'moment' form, one of the avant-garde forms that became recognized from the 1960s, first exposed conspicuously in the works of Stockhausen and still a principle in some sense in Boulez's long-term, monumental work-in-progress *Répons*. Moment form is an ideal, in which the composer aims—and the open-minded listener is supposed to aim—at an intense concentration on the present rather than on formal connections between antecedents and consequents. *'Mobile' form, also conceived of as a novelty in the 20th century, offered performers a free or a guided choice of paths through different composed musical elements, most famously perhaps in some of Cage's works. While introducing a refreshing improvisatory impulse into post-tonal music, mobile form nevertheless rekindled the spirit of 18th-century improvisation, a spirit also to be found in jazz, especially the 'aleatory' and 'free' jazz fashions of the post-World War II period.   JD

See also BAR FORM; BINARY FORM; CANON; CANTUS FIRMUS; CONCERTO FORM; CYCLIC FORM; DA CAPO; FUGUE; GROUND, GROUND BASS; HETEROPHONY; ISORHYTHM; MOBILE FORM; MOMENT FORM; RITORNELLO; RONDO FORM; SONATA FORM; SONATA RONDO FORM; STROPHIC; STROPHIC VARIATIONS; TERNARY FORM; THROUGH-COMPOSED; TRIO, 2; VARIATION FORM.

formalism. Although the original Formalists were a group of Russian literary theorists active in the early Soviet period, the term was soon used by Soviet critics to condemn composers (or other artists) whose work did not conform ideologically to the materialist tenets of Marxist–Leninist aesthetics. Formalist composers were therefore accused of working within the bourgeois category of the autonomous art work, according to which art had no necessary causal relationship with the economic and social context in which it was produced.

During the period of Stalin's rule (1927–53), the term became a mere buzzword, albeit very dangerous to those on the receiving end, and served as the opposite pole to *socialist realism, the official aesthetic doctrine. Formalist music, in these years, could be written in an idiom that Stalin disliked, a work which a critic thought it prudent to condemn (for fear of being wrong-footed), or by a composer the Party wished to discipline. It would therefore be misleading to define formalism solely in terms of any particular stylistic features, though dense textures, the avoidance of melody, elusive rhythms, and the absence of a firm tonal framework would often (but not always) invite condemnation.

After a period of relative artistic freedom during and after the war years, in 1948 Andrey Zhdanov, in charge of cultural affairs, oversaw a carefully orchestrated backlash which led to the condemnation of, among others, Shostakovich, Prokofiev, Khachaturian, and Myaskovsky as formalists whose music was often 'radically wrong[—]it is anti-People and prefers to cater for the individualistic experience of a clique of aesthetes'. After the Khrushchev thaw (in the late 1950s), the Stalinist usage of 'formalism' was itself condemned, and from the 1960s onwards many features of 'formalist' Western modernism were tolerated, if not always encouraged, in Soviet music.   JWAL

formant. See ACOUSTICS, 7.

formes fixes (Fr., 'fixed forms'). The three chief forms of the late medieval chanson: the *ballade, *virelai, and *rondeau.

Forqueray. French family of virtuoso viol players and composers.

Antoine Forqueray [*le père*] (*b* Paris, 1672; *d* Mantes, 28 June 1745) played the *basse de violon* to Louis XIV as a child and was taken into the court as a page and taught to play the bass viol; in 1689 he was appointed an *ordinaire de la chambre du roi*. In Paris he and his wife, the harpsichordist Henriette-Angélique Houssu, lived and performed at the *hôtel* of the Prince of Carignan; their son, Jean-Baptiste-Antoine, was born there. However, Forqueray neglected his family and in 1710 he and his wife separated. He had his teenage son imprisoned (*c*.1715) and later banished from France (1725). When he also lost 100,000 livres by speculating in the Mississippi Company, the regent underwrote his debt.

Forqueray was admired for his performances of Italian violin sonatas on the bass viol and his ability to improvise. His playing was often compared with that of his elder colleague Marin Marais—they were likened to a devil and an angel by Hubert Le Blanc (1740). Forqueray had many aristocratic pupils, among them the Dukes of Orléans, Bavaria, and Burgundy. He never published and only a few manuscript pieces survive; he left it to his son to publish an edition of their *pièces de viole* in 1747.

Jean-Baptiste(-Antoine) **Forqueray** [*le fils*] (*b* Paris, 3 April 1699; *d* Paris, 19 July 1782) was the son of Antoine. He too was a virtuoso viol player, who as a child played for Louis XIV. By 1726 he was playing in the *petit chœur* of the Académie Royale as well as in the salons of wealthy Parisians; after his marriage in 1732 he lived with his wife at the *hôtel* of the Chevalier Étienne Boucon, where he played with Jean-Pierre Guignon and Rameau. When Telemann visited Paris in 1737 Forqueray took part in the performances of his 'Paris' Quartets. After the death of his wife in 1740 he married the harpsichordist Marie-Rose Dubois. During the 1740s they were much in demand as a duo and it would seem probable that she had a hand in the harpsichord transcription of the Forquerays' *pièces de viole*, which was published simultaneously. Forqueray *le fils* dedicated the 1747 edition to his pupil Princess Henriette-Anne, the daughter of Louis XV.   WT/JAS

fort (Ger.). 'Onward', 'away': an instruction in organ music to silence a stop.

forte (It.). 'Strong', i.e. loud; it is abbreviated *f*.

fortepiano. A term sometimes used to distinguish the 18th- and early 19th-century piano from the modern instrument.

fortissimo (It.). Very loud; it is abbreviated *ff*.

Fortner, Wolfgang (*b* Leipzig, 12 Oct. 1907; *d* Heidelberg, 5 Sept. 1987). German composer. He studied composition with Hermann Grabner at the Leipzig Conservatory and taught at the Heidelberg Church Music Institute (1931–54), the North-West German Music Academy in Detmold (1954–7), and the Freiburg Musikhochschule (from 1957). In 1946 he helped to establish the Darmstadt summer courses. As one of the pre-eminent composition teachers of his time he was hugely influential on large numbers of young composers, his pupils including Henze and Rudolf Kelterborn.

Among Fortner's earlier works are many church compositions and instrumental pieces (two string quartets, various concertos) influenced by the neo-classicism of Hindemith and Stravinsky. Immediately after World War II he began to incorporate a modified form of *serialism into his music, and his works from that time on—the Symphony (1947), several sacred cantatas, and the opera *Bluthochzeit* (after Lorca; Cologne, 1957)—tend to be made up of tight, symmetrical structures. In his later dramatic works he began to use electronic resources, both pre-recorded (*Elisabeth Tudor*, Berlin, 1972) and live (*That Time*, Baden-Baden, 1977).   PG

Fortspinnung (Ger.). The development, or 'spinning out', of a short melodic motif to form a complete phrase, often using sequences.

'Forty-Eight, The'. Popular title of Bach's collection of 48 preludes and fugues *The *Well-Tempered Clavier*.

Forty-part motet. See SPEM IN ALIUM NUNQUAM HABUI.

forza (It.). 'Force', 'strength'; *forzando, forzato*, 'forcing', 'forced', i.e. strongly accented.

Forza del destino, La ('The Force of Destiny'). Opera in four acts by Verdi to a libretto by Francesco Maria Piave after Angel de Saavedra, Duke of Rivas's play *Don Alvaro, o La fuerza del sino* (1835), with a scene from Friedrich von Schiller's play *Wallensteins Lager* (1799), translated by Andrea Maffei (St Petersburg, 1862); Verdi revised it, with additional text by Antonio Ghislanzoni (Milan, 1869).

Foss [Fuchs], Lukas (*b* Berlin, 15 Aug. 1922). German-born American composer. He studied in Berlin and Paris before moving in 1937 with his family to the USA, where he was a pupil of Thompson at the Curtis Institute and Hindemith at Yale (1939–40). He started composing as a neo-classicist, inclining towards Copland's popular manner in such works as his cantata *Prairie* (1944), to words by Carl Sandburg; during this period he was also a pianist with the Boston SO (1944–50). A post as professor of composition at the University of California in Los Angeles (1951–62) took him to a different climate, and in 1956 he began improvising with his students and writing aleatory scores, including *Time Cycle* for soprano and orchestra (1960) and *Echoi* for four instruments (1961–3). He was then appointed conductor of the Buffalo Philharmonic (1962–70), and during this period produced an early example of postmodernism in his *Baroque Variations* for orchestra (1967), in which music by Handel, Scarlatti, and Bach is subject to distortion, multiple imaging and 'composition by deletion' (i.e. composing holes into the originals). Latterly he has worked as a teacher and conductor in Cincinnati and New York, and continued his quirky compositional life.   PG

 📖 K. J. PERONE, *Lukas Foss: A Bio-Bibliography* (Westport, CT, 1991)

Foster, Stephen (Collins) (*b* Lawrenceville, PA, 4 July 1826; *d* New York, 13 Jan. 1864). American composer. While working in his brother's business in Cincinnati he wrote many songs for amateurs and managed to sell some to publishers. These were soon being sung in popular minstrel shows all over America, but Foster gained little reward, preferring to try to make his name with more serious and sentimental ballads. For many of his now world-famous songs he received only a few dollars in outright payment, but eventually he was well enough known to be able to bargain for royalties and, by now living in Pittsburgh, composed prolifically for several years. An incorrigible spendthrift, he became incapable of supporting his family and went to New York, where he began to drink heavily and to turn out mediocre songs. He died in hospital after collapsing in his hotel room and wounding his head. Owing to the folksong-like qualities of such lasting favourites as *Oh! Susanna* (1848), *Camptown Races* (1850), *Old Folks at Home* (*Swanee River*) (1851), *My Old Kentucky Home* (1853), and *Jeanie with the Light Brown Hair* (1854), he still receives small credit as their composer.

                  PGA/PFA

Foulds, John (Herbert) (*b* Manchester, 2 Nov. 1880; *d* Calcutta, 24 April 1939). English composer and conductor. A cellist in the Hallé Orchestra (1900–6), he left to concentrate on composition. He was a composer of light music for the theatre, a silent-film pianist in France, and Director of European Music for All-India Radio in Delhi until his death from cholera. He enjoyed success with his theatre scores and his gargantuan *A World Requiem* (1919–21). Influenced by theosophy, he went to India where he collected folksongs and attempted to syncretize Indian and Western musical practices. The results are evident in *Three Mantras* for orchestra with female voices ad lib and the *Symphony of East and West*, and his penchant for experimental techniques can be observed in the *Essays in the Modes* for piano (1920–7). He wrote *Music To-day* (1934).   JDi

📖 M. MacDonald, *John Foulds: His Life in Music* (Rickmansworth, 1975, enlarged 2/1989 as *John Foulds and his Music*)

Fountains of Rome. See Fontane di Roma.

Four Last Songs. 1. See Vier letzte Lieder.
2. Songs (1954–8) for voice and piano by Vaughan Williams to words by Ursula Vaughan Williams.

4′ 33″. Piece (1952) by Cage consisting of four minutes and 33 seconds of silence for any instrument or instruments.

Fournier, Pierre (Léon Marie) (*b* Paris, 24 June 1906; *d* Geneva, 8 Jan. 1986). French cellist. His career was based largely in France between 1925 and 1939 but internationally thereafter, particularly with Schnabel, Szigeti, and Primrose at the Edinburgh Festivals in chamber music by Schubert and Brahms. Known as the aristocrat of cellists, he had a broad repertory and his playing was notable for its beauty and the graceful poise of its phrasing. He gave the premieres of concertos by Roussel, Martin, and Martinů.   CF

Four Sacred Pieces. See Quattro pezzi sacri.

Four Saints in Three Acts. Opera in a prologue and four acts by Virgil Thomson to a libretto by Gertrude Stein with a scenario by Maurice Grosser (Hartford, CT, 1934).

Four Sea Interludes. Orchestral work, op. 33*a* (1945), by Britten, consisting of the descriptive orchestral interludes from his opera *Peter Grimes* ('Dawn', 'Sunday Morning', 'Moonlight', and 'Storm'); the Passacaglia (op. 33*b*) from the opera is often performed with the interludes.

Four Seasons, The (*Le quattro stagioni*). Four violin concertos by Vivaldi, the first four of his *Il cimento dell'armonia e dell'inventione* op. 8, a set of 12 violin concertos published in two volumes (Amsterdam, 1725); they are 'Spring' in E major, 'Summer' in G minor, 'Autumn' in F major, and 'Winter' in F minor.

Four Serious Songs. See Vier ernste Gesänge.

Four Temperaments, The. 1. Subtitle (*De fire Temperamenter*) of Nielsen's Symphony no. 2, op. 16 (1901–2); it was inspired by a painting of that name, each movement being descriptive of one of the medieval 'temperaments' of human character: choleric, phlegmatic, melancholic, and sanguine.
2. Subtitle of Hindemith's Theme and Variations for piano and strings (1940), the four variations denoting the melancholic, sanguine, phlegmatic, and choleric.

Fox, Christopher (*b* York, 10 March 1955). English composer. He studied with Hugh Wood, Jonathan Harvey, and Richard Orton and has taught at Huddersfield University as well as at the Darmstadt summer courses. While avoiding the extremes of fragmented complexity on the one hand, and hyper-repetitive minimalism on the other, Fox builds extended forms out of simple yet strongly characterized material and its progressive evolution. The piano piece *More Light* (1987–8) is a good example of his distinctive and absorbing style.   AW

foxtrot. A ballroom dance that developed from the one-step, becoming known as the foxtrot about 1914. By 1924 the original smooth, gliding dance was labelled the slow foxtrot to distinguish it from the simplified and faster foxtrot, which became known as the *quickstep. It is danced to music in common time at about 30 to 32 bars a minute. The foxtrot became popular in England when it featured in *Tonight's the Night* at the Gaiety Theatre (1915) and in various spectacular revues of the time.   PGa

Fra Diavolo (*Fra Diavolo, ou L'Hôtellerie de Terracine*; 'Brother Devil, or The Inn of Terracina'). Opera in three acts by Auber to a libretto by Eugène Scribe (Paris, 1830).

frame drum (Ger.: *Rahmentrommel*). Any drum with a body-depth measuring less than the radius of the head. Frame drums may be single- or double-headed; the latter often have a jingle (e.g. a pellet bell) rolling freely inside the drum. Some (e.g. the *tambourine) have jingles set in the rim, and others have a snare of some sort. Some are fitted on a handle. Larger frame drums (e.g. the bodhrán) are often played with a stick, but smaller ones are usually beaten by hand. Frame drums are used throughout the world, including the Arctic Circle; they are found among Native Americans, where they are played especially by shamans, and all round the Mediterranean, where since ancient Egyptian times they have been played particularly by women.   JMo

française (Fr.). A round dance in triple or compound-duple time, popular in the 1830s. It is a later development of the *contredanse* (see COUNTRY DANCE).

Françaix, Jean (René Désiré) (*b* Le Mans, 23 May 1912; *d* Paris, 25 Sept. 1997). French composer and pianist. His parents were musical and gave him an early training before he moved to Paris to study with Nadia Boulanger. His Piano Concertino (1932) won acclaim at a contemporary music festival in Baden-Baden, even though the other entries were atonal and 12-note pieces, and effectively launched his career. He remained largely within the neo-classical tradition, writing for various chamber combinations and producing many concertos. His music is vivacious, witty, and elegant, but his slow movements may display haunting harmonies. Though criticized by some for his conservatism and lightness, he is one of the most frequently performed French composers of the 20th century, particularly outside France. Film scores, ballets, and a handful of operas may be counted among his successes, which also include a more serious and substantial religious work *L'Apocalypse de St Jean* (1939). He performed widely as a pianist, and recorded his double piano concerto with his daughter Claude.   RLS

France. Throughout the ages France has had music which seems to reflect a national character. This comes in part from its early foundation as a political entity and its comparatively early centralization on a single city, Paris. There has been also a persistent delight in orderliness, which has given French music and architecture a classical balance at times when wild abandon has been rampant throughout the rest of Europe. The French have never been good internationalists, and when they have taken in foreign composers, whether Lully, Gluck, Meyerbeer, or Stravinsky, those composers have largely adopted French attitudes and complied with French institutional traditions. France's musical history is therefore interesting for its continuity rather than for its diversity, at least in mood, while in style, French conservatism has sometimes led to revolution, in art as in politics.

1. The Middle Ages; 2. Ars Nova and Renaissance; 3. 1600–1715; 4. From Louis XV to the Revolution; 5. The First Republic; 6. The Restoration and the Second Empire; 7. 1870–1914; 8. From World War I to 1945; 9. Since 1945; 10. Conclusion.

1. The Middle Ages
Clovis, King of the Franks 481–511, laid the foundations of the French state; he also embraced Christianity in about 496. Charlemagne (*d* 814) extended the Frankish kingdom over much of Western Europe, and was crowned Emperor of the West in 800. After his death, the Treaty of Verdun (843) divided the Carolingian Empire into three parts, the western area, approximating to medieval France, being ruled over by Charles the Bald.

As in most of Europe, medieval France's contribution to art music was made through monasteries. Choir schools (*maîtrises*) were attached to cathedrals, mainly in the north of France. In addition, a handful of Saintes Chapelles operated under the control of the royalty or princes of high standing. The liturgy observed was that of the Gallican rite until Pepin and Charlemagne imposed the Roman rite (see PLAINCHANT, 2). Several of the great monasteries, especially that of St Martial in Limoges, were noted during the 9th and 10th centuries for their development of the *sequence and the *trope. France was also important in another means of elaborating plainchant—that of adding a musical part to the chant melody to produce polyphony (see ORGANUM).

During the 12th century, Paris became an important centre for art and culture, especially after the building of Notre Dame was completed in the 1180s. A new school of composers grew up there, including Léonin, whose *Magnus liber organi* provided a magnificent and distinctive repertory, and his successor Pérotin. The heyday of Paris persisted until about 1250, the Notre Dame composers playing a substantial part in the development of the *motet.

Meanwhile, secular music was flourishing in the south of France, especially in Provence, where the 'langue d'oc' (or Provençal) was spoken, the language of the courtly poetry of the *troubadours. Their art is typically French in being highly organized, the rhyme schemes of the verses acting as a basis for sectional musical repetitions. A similar body of poet-musicians, the *trouvères (whose 'langue d'oil' was to develop into modern French), came into being in the north and north-east, to make France the most flourishing of all musical centres at this time.

2. Ars Nova and Renaissance
The early 14th-century *Ars Nova period takes its name from the title of Philippe de Vitry's treatise on innovations to previous notational practice (the Ars Antiqua). During this time Vitry rationalized rhythmic notational potential and introduced the intellectual device now known as *isorhythm. The melodic style of both motets and secular songs became rhythmically complex, especially with the use of such techniques as *hocket and *canon. Secular genres, such as the chace (similar to the Italian *caccia), the *lai, and the *formes fixes* of *ballade, *rondeau, and *virelai, became highly sophisticated in musical structure. That liturgical music also responded to these innovatory times can be seen in

Machaut's Notre Dame Mass, which unifies the sections of the Ordinary of the Mass and uses both isorhythm and hocket.

The second half of the 14th century saw this artistic excitement deflected into other areas. The Hundred Years War with England (1337–1453) resulted in the temporary capture of Paris, and the Black Death and civil war accelerated the decline of the French court. The Burgundian dukes rose to power, taking over large areas of north-eastern France and the Low Countries, becoming allies of the English, and also becoming involved in taking Joan of Arc prisoner. Choir schools flourished in Cambrai, Dijon, and Lille, with Dufay and Binchois becoming renowned throughout Europe for the brilliance and sophistication of their *chansons.

The death of Charles the Bold in 1477 ended this brilliance, but it was not immediately transferred to Paris, for the return of the papal court from Avignon to Rome had taken many French musicians to Italy, where humanist ideals gave a new impetus to music. By the early 16th century France was known less for church music than for domestic music. While Louis XII's reign ended with an impoverished *chambre*, subsequent monarchs rekindled both sacred and secular music. François I introduced French violinists, Italian trumpeters, and oboists into the *écurie*, and Henri II employed Arcadelt and Janequin, celebrated for the chanson.

Paris became an important centre for the chanson, which was widely disseminated after the granting of royal warrants to printers (see PRINTING AND PUBLISHING OF MUSIC, 4), notably to Attaingnant and the house of Le Roy & Ballard. Numerous chanson collections were printed from the 1520s to the 1550s, by such composers as Sermisy, Certon, and Janequin. Chansons lent themselves to arrangement for lute and keyboard, and dances based on them provided much of the European instrumental repertory throughout the 16th century (see CANZONA); instrument-making, especially of lutes, flourished in Paris and Lyons.

In the second half of the century, humanistic thinking led to the founding (by Courville and Baïf) of the Académie de Poésie et de Musique, devoted to recreating the Roman and ancient Greek styles of setting words to music, on the premise that music should follow the metrical patterns of classical verse (see MUSIQUE MESURÉE). As far as grander spectacle was concerned, elaborate court ballets (such as the *Balet comique de la Royne* of 1581) resulted in entertainments not dissimilar to the Italian *intermedio* (see BALLET AND THEATRICAL DANCE, 1). This love of ballet led to a demand for French dancing masters in courts throughout Europe, as well as to the writing of treatises on the subject, such as Arbeau's famous *Orchésographie* (1588).

3. 1600–1715

From c.1580 to c.1640 the charmingly tuneful and rhythmically ordered *air de cour* was fashionable, and treatises on singing (e.g. Bénigne de Bacilly's *L'Art de bien chanter*, 1668) began to appear. Lute music, represented by such composers as Denis Gaultier and Charles Mouton, influenced several generations of keyboard composers. Ballet continued to be the main dramatic entertainment.

French travellers in Italy, such as André Maugars, were impressed by the rapid developments there. During the reign of Louis XIV (1643–1715) the powerful Cardinal Mazarin tried to introduce Italian opera but, though the elaborate machines pleased, the music did not, and ballet continued to dominate. A young Florentine, Jean-Baptiste Lully, was one of the principal dancers and composers, collaborating with Molière in the 1660s to produce highly successful *comédies-ballets* (plays with elaborate interludes of dancing and music).

Lully, who was appointed director of the state music in 1661, established the Petite Bande, an elite string group that supplemented the *Vingt-Quatre Violons du Roi. Additionally there was the Musique de la Grande Écurie, a wind group used for outdoor occasions, and the royal chapel had a choir at one time of more than 60 and its own orchestra, intended for the *grands motets* which Louis delighted to hear in the chapel of Versailles. To these establishments was added France's first opera company, the Académie Royale de Musique (the Paris Opéra), founded in 1669 by Pierre Perrin and Robert Cambert and taken over in 1672 by Lully, whose *tragédies lyriques* to librettos by Philippe Quinault were a foundation stone of French opera. A related genre, the *opéra-ballet* (more ballet than opera), enjoyed some success in the hands of Campra. Lully's influence on church and instrumental music was also considerable. The solemn, splendid style of his motets for the royal chapel, using soloists, chorus, and orchestra, was expanded by Lalande and Charpentier, resulting in some of the most impressive church music of the period. Other sacred music, such as Charpentier's for the Jesuit church of St Louis or Couperin's for the nuns of Longchamp Abbey, is more intimate, and was often written for virtuoso forces.

French instrumental music was represented by the Lullian overture, the sharp, dotted rhythms of its slow introduction succeeded by a mock-fugal quicker section, followed if desired by dances. Chamber music offered more variety. Lute music flourished, and was imitated by a host of excellent keyboard players—

Chambonnières, the Couperins, D'Anglebert, and Lebègue—whose highly ornamental melodies and subtle textures provide the first distinctive keyboard music since the English virginalists. Most notable in both the lute and keyboard repertories are the *préludes non mesurés*, written in free notation without bar-lines. Virtuoso players of the viol (Marais) and flute (the Hotteterre family) encouraged the cultivation of a similarly arcane chamber music, at its height in François Couperin's *Concerts*. His *Parnasse* was a fusion of the French style with the Italian trio sonata, exemplified in his two *Apothéoses*, one for Lully and one for Corelli. Fine organ music was heard in many Paris churches, with such composers as Lebègue, Couperin, and Raison playing large instruments noted for their nasal reed, trumpet, and cromorne stops (typically French is the standardization of specification), and outside Paris with Titelouze at Rouen and Grigny at Reims. Louis XIV's reign was indeed a *grand siècle*.

4. From Louis XV to the Revolution

As Louis XIV became more withdrawn in his last years and less willing to attend public functions, opera declined and chamber music became increasingly popular. The lack of artistic vitality in court circles persisted under Louis XV. Conservatism at the Opéra continued until the 1730s, when the 50-year-old Rameau composed *Hippolyte et Aricie* (1733), his first *tragédie lyrique*, essentially bringing up to date Lully's conception, but musically much more alive. Rameau was highly criticized both for being too modern and, by a faction favouring Italian music that grew up in the 1740s and 50s, for being old-fashioned. The pro-Italians were encouraged by the success of Pergolesi's *La serva padrona* in 1752, and this led to a fierce polemic (the Querelle des *Bouffons) concerning the respective merits of French and Italian music, resulting in a new genre that was to prove extremely fecund: *opéra comique*. One of the most successful examples was Rousseau's *Le Devin du village* (1752). Among those in favour of the new genre were Denis Diderot and Jean Le Rond d'Alembert, the editors of the huge and influential *Encyclopédie, ou Dictionnaire raisonné des sciences, arts, et metiers*, with musical entries by Rousseau. The latter produced his own *Dictionnaire de musique* (Paris, 1768), which had a considerable influence on French, and European, musical thought in the later 18th century.

More constant and flourishing than opera was concert life. The famous Concert Spirituel was founded by Anne Danican Philidor in 1725 and lasted until 1790. The repertory initially consisted largely of *grands motets* by Lully and Lalande (and, later, Rameau), but there were some orchestral pieces, and great violinists in-

cluding Leclair both led and composed concertos for the concerts. The orchestra was much admired for its disciplined style, and the wind players especially attracted a concerto repertory.

A new wave of internationalism came in the 1770s, when Louis XVI, with his Viennese wife Marie Antoinette, succeeded his father. One visitor to France was Gluck, who in Vienna had grafted an Italian style on to what were essentially French *tragédies lyriques* in *Orfeo* and *Alceste*. He developed the form further in his Iphigénie operas, in general pleasing the old-fashioned rather than the modern critics. The *opéra comique* flourished, Grétry's *Richard Coeur-de-lion* (1784) showing that the genre could serve political ends. Most of all, the concert series were enterprising; Mozart's 'Paris' Symphony (K297/300a) was given by the Concert Spirituel in 1778, and Haydn's symphonies were given by the Concert de la Loge Olympique. Even a new school for opera singers, the École Royale de Chant, was opened in 1784.

5. The First Republic

The grand *fêtes* of the Revolution inspired a new style of civic, outdoor music of which the most celebrated example is Rouget de Lisle's *Marseillaise*. Gossec's hymns and choruses were also highly important in this repertory, which not only inspired Berlioz's *Grande symphonie funèbre et triomphale* but also found an echo in the funeral march of Beethoven's 'Eroica' Symphony. At first, the Revolution affected musical institutions surprisingly little. The opera houses continued, and the royal family attended them until 1791. The preferred repertory was French, even in the Théâtre Italien (most Italians had left the country), and works extolling patriotism or liberty (e.g. Kreutzer's *Jeanne d'Arc* and Grétry's *Guillaume Tell*) came to the fore. The power of the Roman Catholic Church rapidly diminished, and church music was replaced by hymns to 'the Supreme Being', or 'Reason', or 'Liberty'. During the years of the Terror (1792–3), operatic activity diminished, but military campaigns diverted political activity abroad, and by 1797 the new shape of musical institutions was being established.

The Opéra-Comique was the liveliest of the theatres. The flourishing concert series of the 1780s disappeared almost completely, but the École Royale de Chant was replaced in 1795 by the Conservatoire de Musique, which recruited its students on a regional basis throughout France by competitive examinations, and eventually issued textbooks to unify tuition. Thus state control of all the major musical institutions was assured. Napoleon's rule both stabilized and broadened activity. Italian by birth, he enjoyed the music of Paisiello, whereas the Empress Josephine favoured that of Spontini. Thus, though the Opéra-Comique continued to flourish with a French-language repertory, the massive *tragédie lyrique* returned to the Opéra, while the Théâtre Italien, directed from 1810 to 1812 by Spontini, kept alive the *opera buffa* tradition. The competitive spirit of the Conservatoire was crowned by the tradition of the *Prix de Rome in 1803, a scholarship much coveted throughout the 19th century.

6. The Restoration and the Second Empire

On Napoleon's abdication, activity ceased for about a year until the Restoration of the Bourbon monarchy was complete. The Paris Opéra became the most heavily subsidized opera house in Europe, and mounted immense spectacles after the French taste. Rossini's *Moïse et Pharaon* proved a great success and, together with *Guillaume Tell*, offered a compromise between the conservative tradition and the 'novel' Italian style. After the 1830 Revolution the operas of Meyerbeer and Halévy enjoyed much success. The Opéra-Comique continued in its liveliness, while the Théâtre Italien produced the latest Italian operas, including works by Verdi. Thus Paris became the centre of the operatic world.

Orchestral concert life was less rich. Its mainstay was the orchestra of the Conservatoire. Presided over by Cherubini (1822–42), and then by Auber (1842–70), the Conservatoire's composition professors were mainly conservative, and extremely influential. The Société des Concerts du Conservatoire, founded by Habeneck in 1828, performed works by Haydn, Mozart, and Beethoven, but little really modern music. The institutionalization of music caused difficulties for those outside the charmed circle, notably Berlioz, who was disliked by Cherubini and forbidden access to the Opéra after the disastrous premiere of his *Benvenuto Cellini* in 1838. His earlier music was better known in Germany, where it suited the Romantic taste, than at home. The real moderns were heard more often in the private concert rooms of such piano manufacturers as Pleyel and Érard and in the salons of rich bankers (e.g. the Rothschilds) or the nobility. Here Chopin and Liszt were heard, and even the late quartets of Beethoven were played.

The 1848 Revolution, the Second Republic, and the subsequent Second Empire of Louis Napoleon made surprisingly little difference to the musical institutions. The Opéra, having found no replacement for Meyerbeer, imported Verdi and Wagner, while the Opéra-Comique introduced Ambroise Thomas. The new Théâtre Lyrique, founded in 1851, had an interesting foreign repertory including several Mozart operas, and enterprisingly tried new French composers including the Prix de Rome winners Gounod and Bizet. In 1863 it

attempted Berlioz's *Les Troyens*, which in spite of cuts and inadequate production achieved some success. But such modernity was rare, even at the concerts of the Société des Jeunes Artistes du Conservatoire, founded by Pasdeloup in 1852, and classics remained the staple fare. The Second Empire also opened yet another opera house, the Théâtre des Bouffes-Parisiens, where the delicious musical soufflés of Offenbach needed no subsidies.

7. 1870–1914

The defeat of France by the Prussians in 1870 resulted in a new national awareness and determination, which encouraged the formation of the Société Nationale de Musique (1871) and the Concerts de l'Association Artistique (founded by Édouard Colonne in 1874). This led to a resurgence of instrumental music by, among others, Saint-Saëns, Franck, d'Indy, and Chausson.

Something of this resurgence was felt at the Opéra-Comique, which, in spite of the initial lack of success of Bizet's *Carmen* in 1875, provided a new repertory of Massenet, Delibes, and more progressive composers such as Chabrier. By contrast, the Opéra was less adventurous in its choice of repertory; however, it staged the premieres of 17 new operas in the 16 years until 1892. Of these, the most enduring success was Massenet's *Le Cid* in 1885. The Opéra took up Wagner in the 1890s but mounted the entire *Ring* cycle only in 1911, even though an enormous vogue for Wagner had sprung up in both intellectual and musical circles in Paris during the 1880s. France was affected as much by Wagner's ideas of the fusion of the arts as by his musical techniques, though his leitmotif technique was adopted by many subsequent composers antipathetic to other aspects of his music.

One result of the Wagner cult was the further alienation of artists from the Establishment. The Conservatoire did its best to improve the teaching but it now had rivals: the École Niedermeyer, founded in the 1850s for the study of 'old' church music and directed for a time by Saint-Saëns; and the *Schola Cantorum, which offered compositional training based on a wide spectrum of the history of music. Neither trained virtuoso singers and players, but they had enormous influence on composers, directing their attention to the old modal system as a way of avoiding the lush, chromatic music of Wagner's *Tristan*. This typically French liking for classical restraint is shown at its best in the work of Fauré and Duparc, who transformed the salon *mélodie into an art song worthy of the great German lieder composers, and helped create a new style of piano music. The teaching of post-Wagnerian techniques was largely in the hands of Franck, whose Symphony in D minor shows his interest in both chromatic harmony and thematic transformation. From him, d'Indy, Duparc, Vierne, and others learnt a broader outlook.

The catalyst for a really new French style came with the Paris Exposition Universelle in 1889, which featured a Javanese gamelan orchestra. On hearing this, Debussy realized that there were sonorities and attitudes other than Wagner's. Debussy's love–hate relationship with Wagner's music resulted in an opera—*Pelléas et Mélisande* (1902)—which became one of the most frequently performed of the 20th century. It is Wagnerian in its use of symbolic leitmotifs but quite the reverse in its delicate orchestration and speech-like declamation.

Debussy's importance lay also in his works for piano and for orchestra, in a style commonly known today as *Impressionism, using parallel chords, unresolved discords, and non-tonal modes such as the *octatonic, pentatonic, and whole-tone scales (see SCALE, 5 and 6). This, not Wagner's, turned out to be the 'music of the future', and made French values once more the centre of intellectual interest. Debussy's younger contemporary, Ravel, used many similar techniques but was more classical in attitude and technique, deliberately working in such old forms as the pavane, minuet, and sonatina. Thus, when Diaghilev launched his revolutionary Ballets Russes in Paris in 1909, he was able to find suitably modern composers to provide the music, which included Ravel's *Daphnis et Chloé* (1912), Debussy's *Jeux* (1913), and Satie's *Parade* (1917). Diaghilev also brought the music of Stravinsky and Prokofiev to Paris.

8. From World War I to 1945

War broke out when the arts were thriving, and though this time France was on the winning side, the country nevertheless suffered three million casualties and a ruined economy from which it did not really recover during the 21 years of peace. The establishment was now nearly irrelevant to Paris's musical life, though the Conservatoire had some more up-to-date composition professors (including Dukas and Roger-Ducasse) and its librarians included some distinguished musicologists.

The influence of Wagner and Germanic music in general disappeared with the war. In 1917, at the end of his life, Debussy completed a set of sonatas that deliberately look back to 18th-century French music—not in idiom, but in the ideals of clarity, charm, and classical restraint. In the 1920s, Stravinsky's *neo-classicism was taken up by a group of composers called Les *Six. There was a certain desire to shock in French music and literature at this time, spurred on by Satie, Jean Cocteau, and Guillaume Apollinaire. Satie was adopted as their father figure; his ballet *Parade*, with cubist cos-

tumes by Picasso, was seen as the embodiment of the 'new spirit'. Piano pieces and songs by Poulenc and the jazz-influenced ballet music of Milhaud reflect the sophistication of Parisian society at this time. Foreign composers including Bliss and Prokofiev found it their spiritual home, while others, especially such Americans as Copland, came to study with a remarkable teacher, Nadia Boulanger, who insisted on clarity of orchestration, good construction, and mastery of technique.

The lack of a serious philosophy of music in the 1930s led to another manifestation, this time from a new group called La *Jeune France, whose members—Jolivet, Baudrier, Daniel-Lesur, and Messiaen—were all about 30 years old. Intense and interested in religion, they had no time to develop their attitudes before the outbreak of World War II, which led to a national humiliation worse than that of 1870. Paris was taken, the radio and Opéra were controlled by the Germans, Messiaen was a prisoner of war, and other young composers joined the Resistance. Nevertheless, in certain ways music flourished under the control of the Vichy government.

9. Since 1945

In 1945 Paris regained its reputation as an avant-garde centre, with Messiaen especially admired by the younger generation, of whom Boulez, Stockhausen, and Nono were only three of many to attend his courses at Paris or Darmstadt. But it was through the efforts of René Leibowitz that *serial music was brought to the attention of the French, and it had an effect, notably on Boulez, which has changed the attitudes of the new avant-garde. Today Paris, with its state support for an institute for research into the potentialities of musical sound, the *Institut de Recherche et de Coordination Acoustique/Musique (IRCAM), is an international centre. IRCAM is inextricably linked with Boulez, who directed the institute from 1977 to 1992. Electroacoustic music emanating from the institute has led the field internationally and has resulted in part in a post-Boulez school of spectral music, pioneered by such figures as Murail and Grisey, in which the harmonic make-up of particular sounds has been a force in compositional technique. After 1945, Boulez's uncompromising attitude towards non-serial music caused some composers to feel overshadowed by his modernist developments. More traditional voices emerging from France in the postwar years included Jolas, Dutilleux, and Ohana.

In opera, the construction of a new opera house in Lyons, opened in 1993, has been a significant step in the cause of decentralization. Festivals have particularly flourished, several of them with 'niche' specialities, for example Avignon (music theatre), Versailles and

Saintes (early music), and Aix-en-Provence (opera premieres).

10. Conclusion

Its very continuity has ensured that French music has been one of Europe's most distinctive cultural activities, and while it has taken many shapes there is no doubt that its nationality is often instantly recognizable. The French genius seems to like order—from the isorhythmic motet of the Ars Nova period to Messiaen's 1949 piano piece *Mode de valeurs et d'intensités*. It is rationalist rather than religious; its greatest church music, by Lalande and Berlioz, has been ceremonial rather than mystical; it likes clarity—in rhythm (as in *musique mesurée* and the dance music to which it has been addicted for several centuries) and in colour (as in the orchestration of Rameau, Debussy, and Messiaen).

Above all, French music is strongly linked to its literature. Few traditions of song have had such distinguished verse as that used from the troubadours to Debussy. Few opera librettos have such well-wrought verse as Quinault's, and few have been so little ravaged by the composers. Instrumental music is rarely abstract, be it the titled keyboard pieces of Couperin or the *Miroirs* of Ravel. And as a concomitant, few countries have so strong a tradition of polemic concerning music, from the squabbles of the Querelle des Bouffons to those of the 20th-century avant-garde. Significantly, France has resisted foreign intrusions, be they Italian or German—and when they have been too strong to discount entirely, they have been influenced considerably by French taste. In a world of rapid communications and international commitments, it remains to be seen whether this can continue.   DA/RLS

📖 N. WILKINS, *The Lyric Art of Medieval France* (Cambridge, 1978, 2/1989) · E. BRODY, *Paris: The Musical Kaleidoscope, 1870–1925* (New York, 1987) · J. F. FULCHER, *The Nation's Image: French Grand Opera as Politics and Politicized Art* (Cambridge, 1987) · C. PAGE, *The Owl and the Nightingale: Musical Life and Ideas in France, 1100–1300* (London, 1989) · *150 ans de musique française, 1789–1939* (Lyons, 1991) · M. BENOIT (ed.), *Dictionnaire de la musique en France aux XVIIe et XVIIIe siècles* (Paris, 1992) · M. BENOIT, 'Paris, 1661–87: The age of Lully', *The Early Baroque Era*, ed. C. Price, Man and Music/Music and Society (London, 1993) · M. DEVOTO, 'Paris, 1918–45', *Modern Times: From World War I to the Present*, ed. R. P. Morgan, Man and Music/Music and Society (London, 1993) · *Early Music History*, 13 (1994) [French music in the late 16th century, ed. I. Fenlon]

Francesca da Rimini. The story of the adulterous lovers Paolo and Francesca in canto V of Dante Alighieri's *Inferno* (*c.*1307–21) has been the basis of several compositions, the best known being the following.

1. Symphonic fantasia by Tchaikovsky, op. 32 (1876), based on a picture by Gustave Doré.

2. Opera in a prologue, two scenes, and an epilogue by Rakhmaninov to a libretto by Modest Tchaikovsky (Moscow, 1906).

3. Opera in four acts by Zandonai to a libretto by Tito Ricordi (ii) from the play by Gabriele D'Annunzio (Turin, 1914).

Francesco (Canova) **da Milano.** See MILANO, FRANCESCO DA.

Francés de Iribarren, Juan (*b* Sangüesa, nr Pamplona, *bapt.* 24 March 1699; *d* Málaga, 2 Sept. 1767). Spanish composer and organist. Trained as a choirboy at the Colegio de Cantorcicos in Madrid, he became organist at Salamanca Cathedral (1717–33) and *maestro de capilla* at Málaga Cathedral (1733–66). His style is characterized by occasional use of polychoral writing, figured continuo parts (uncommon in Spanish music of the time), and idiomatic writing for the violin and oboe, then rarely heard in churches. His output exceeds 800 works including more than 500 villancicos—the largest corpus in 18th-century Spain, providing a conspectus of the evolution of the genre. Francés de Iribarren's music survives mainly at Málaga Cathedral, with some works in other Iberian and Latin American archives.

MAM

Franchetti, Alberto (*b* Turin, 18 Sept. 1860; *d* Viareggio, 4 Aug. 1942). Italian composer. After studies in Turin and Venice he completed his education in Dresden and Munich, the resulting influence of German musical manners being an important aspect of his operatic style. His operas, composed between 1888 and 1922, are frequently grandiose in their scenic effects, with prominent use of symphonic interludes and extensive use of musical local colour. His most acclaimed works, *Cristoforo Colombo* (Genoa, 1892) and *Germania* (La Scala, Milan, 1902), were written to texts by Puccini's librettist Luigi Illica.   RP

Franchomme, Auguste (Joseph) (*b* Lille, 10 April 1808; *d* Paris, 21 Jan. 1884). French cellist and composer. After occupying orchestral posts in Paris he turned to solo work and chamber music (the Alard Quartet) as well as becoming a significant teacher (developing the light, so-called 'French' bow technique). A friend of Mendelssohn and intimate of Chopin (who dedicated his cello sonata to him), Franchomme also composed several works for the cello.   CF

Franck, César(-Auguste-Jean-Guillaume-Hubert) (*b* Liège, 10 Dec. 1822; *d* Paris, 8 Nov. 1890). Belgian-born French composer. The sons of a banker, he and his younger brother Joseph were both driven towards a musical career by their father, who arranged a concert tour for César when he was only 11. The family moved to Paris in 1836 with a view to César's entering the Conservatoire, which he did the following year. He studied both composition and the piano and achieved distinction as a writer of fugues. He was preparing for the Prix de Rome competition when, in 1842, his father removed him from the Conservatoire, intending him for a career as a piano virtuoso, in obvious imitation of Liszt. It was at this time that he composed his First Piano Trio, much admired by various critics and later by d'Indy, who thought it important in having established the *cyclic form for which Franck became celebrated. Two further trios followed, taking their place in the French chamber repertory in spite of being such youthful works. Franck, however, met with little success and for some years had a difficult time, earning his living by teaching and giving recitals; he married in 1848 during the Revolution.

That year he was appointed organist at Notre Dame de Lorette, where he remained until 1853 when a better post at St Jean-François-du-Marais became vacant; he finally moved to the larger Ste Clotilde in 1858. Eventually this church would be furnished with an organ by the celebrated French builder Aristide Cavaillé-Coll, but its construction fell behind schedule and Franck had to make do with a harmonium until December 1859. The dazzling Louis Lefébure-Wély, famous for his opera transcriptions and light music, was engaged to inaugurate the instrument alongside Franck, who played Bach. Franck later participated in the inauguration of other Cavaillé-Colls, including the celebrated instrument at St Sulpice. He was, however, more a Bach player and an improviser than a virtuoso, though compositions for the organ began to appear at this time. Franck's Mass for three voices and *Six pièces pour grand orgue* achieved success, the latter making a profound impression on Liszt, who visited Ste Clotilde in 1866.

Growing fame led to Franck's appointment in 1872 as professor of organ at the Conservatoire. Subsequently he produced a steady stream of compositions until the end of his life. His appointment (obtained by Théodore Dubois who recommended him to the principal, Ambroise Thomas) led to his works being more widely performed; his cantata *Ruth*, which had failed at its first airing (1846), received a warmer reception in 1872, but circumstances conspired against a successful premiere of his major oratorio *Rédemption* and it was soon overshadowed by Gounod's piece of the same name. Franck's training in fugue and his natural predilection (as an organist) for Bach left their mark on most of his compositions; but the fact that he worked in genres

that had achieved their latest development in Germany ensured that his idiom was in many ways up to date.

This tendency was reinforced by a lively group of pupils and his association with various musicians who were interested in Wagner's latest works (the music dramas were beginning to be known through performances in Munich in about 1870). Franck was more influenced by Liszt, however, than directly by Wagner. His symphonic poems *Les Éolides* (1876), *Le Chasseur maudit* (1882), and *Les Djinns* (1884) are among the earliest French attempts at the form, the last named being a work for piano and orchestra after the manner of Liszt's *Malédiction*. Franck did make a few attempts to reach the operatic stage—*de rigueur* for any French composer seeking real success. Fragments from the opera *Hulda*, on a subject from Nordic mythology, were given in his lifetime, but it was staged complete only posthumously.

Apart from the best of his organ works—the *Prélude, fugue et variation*, the *Prière* (both 1860–2), and the *Trois pièces* (1878)—Franck's real genius is to be found in a handful of compositions in purely musical genres: a String Quartet (1889), Piano Quintet (1879), Violin Sonata (1886), and Symphony (1886–8). These all use the Lisztian concept of thematic transformation and are cyclic in structure. Franck often starts with a germinal motif from which the rest of the material develops. His themes frequently centre on a single note, with the intervals between statements growing longer, giving the effect of yearning and incompleteness. His idiom is extremely chromatic, with extraordinarily frequent and free modulations and a tendency to veer between major and minor which he perhaps took from Schubert. His best music is probably that in which the form dictates a controlled harmonic scheme, as in the canonic final movement of the Violin Sonata and in the *Variations symphoniques* (1885) for piano and orchestra. His orchestration owes something to the organ loft, his piano writing to the enormous hands which allowed him to create large organistic sonorities: both are extremely effective. The *Prélude, choral et fugue* (1884) and the *Prélude, aria et finale* (1886–7) have secured a place in the piano repertory, the former in particular commanding some legendary performances such as those of Blanche Selva and Alfred Cortot.

Known as Père Franck because of the simplicity of his nature (made explicit in his music), he was much loved by his pupils and colleagues; many of the former officially studied the organ with him but, through his insistence on fluent improvisation, were in fact composition students. His formal pupils included d'Indy, Vierne, and Lekeu, and both Bizet and Debussy attended his classes for a short time. Franck died as a result of a road accident, having been struck by a horse-bus.   DA/RLS

   📖 L. VALLAS, *César Franck*, trans. H. Foss (London, 1951) · L. DAVIES, *César Franck and his Circle* (London, 1970); *Franck* (London, 1973) · J.-M. FAUQUET, *César Franck* (Paris, 1999)

Franck, Johann Wolfgang (*b* Unterschwaningen, *bapt.* 17 June 1644; *d c.*1710). German composer. From 1666 he served the royal court at Ansbach. Accused of murdering a fellow musician in 1679, he fled to Hamburg, where he was accorded asylum. In Hamburg he composed, for the Theater am Gänsemarkt, some 17 German operas, of which only one has survived in score, *Die drey Töchter des Cecrops* ('The Three Daughters of Cecrops', 1680; rev. ?1686). His last years were spent in London, where he published numerous songs and gave concerts in association with Robert King.   BS

Franck, Melchior (*b* Zittau, *c.*1580; *d* Coburg, 1 June 1639). German composer. He was the son of a painter, and was taught possibly by J. C. Demantius, and certainly by Hans Leo Hassler, before he entered the service of the Prince of Coburg in 1603. A prolific composer, he wrote church music for both large and small forces, but is best remembered for his lively dance music and his mastery of the *quodlibet.   DA

Francoeur. French family of musicians active in Paris throughout the 18th century.

   Joseph Francoeur (*b c.*1662; *d* Paris, 1741) played the bass violin in the Vingt-Quatre Violons du Roi from 1706 and in the Opéra orchestra from 1713. His son, **Louis Francoeur** [*le fils aîné*] (*b* Paris, 1692; *d* Paris, before 18 Sept. 1745), was a violinist and composer who joined the Opéra orchestra in 1704. Six years later he joined the Vingt-Quatre Violons, eventually becoming its leader. He published two books of technically demanding violin sonatas in Italianate style (1715, 1726).

   His brother, **François Francoeur** [*le cadet*] (*b* Paris, 21 Sept. 1698; *d* Paris, 5 Aug. 1787), entered the Opéra orchestra as a first violin at the age of 12 and then joined the royal chamber music. In 1726 he began a lifelong musical partnership with François Rebel, whom he had met in 1723. In 1727 Francoeur was appointed *compositeur de la chambre du roi* and in 1730 he became a member of the Vingt-Quatre Violons, along with his father and brother. He was promoted to *maître de musique* at the Opéra in 1739 and (jointly with Rebel) *inspecteur général* in 1743; in 1744 he became *surintendant de la musique de la chambre du roi*. 13 years later he and Rebel together undertook the direction of the Opéra, a move which both had reason to regret.

   The venture was doomed from the start: the Opéra burnt down in 1763 and in 1767 they were forced to resign. However, Francoeur retained his royal appointment until his retirement in 1776. Most of his music was written in collaboration with Rebel; over half a century, composing in the post-Lully tradition of French opera, they jointly produced *tragédies*, ballets, and divertissements for the Opéra (including *Pirame et Thisbé*, 1726; *Scanderberg*, 1735; *Les Génies tutélaires*, 1751), as well as ballets and other works for performance at the various royal residences, particularly Versailles and Fontainebleau. Francoeur's main contribution, it was said, was the more expressive music.

   Louis's son **Louis-Joseph Francoeur** (*b* Paris, 1738; *d* Paris, 10 March 1804) was only seven when a royal decree awarded him the right to take his late father's place in the Vingt-Quatre Violons. He joined the Opéra orchestra in 1752 and took a court post in 1754. He was appointed assistant *maître de musique* at the Opéra in 1764, rising to *maître* three years later and director of the orchestra in 1779. He then became an administrator; his career was hindered by the political events of the time (he spent several months in prison), but after resuming it he stayed until 1799. He composed a handful of stage works, other vocal pieces, and some theoretical works.   WT/SS

Franconian notation. A type of notation codified in about 1260 by Franco of Cologne. It was the true precursor of modern notation in that the rhythm of a note could now be read solely from its shape, rather than construed from the pattern of the other notes in the vicinity.   AP

Francs-juges, Les ('The Judges of the Secret Court'). Overture, op. 3 (1826), by Berlioz, composed for an opera he later abandoned.

Frankel, Benjamin (*b* London, 31 Jan. 1906; *d* London, 12 Feb. 1973). English composer. Largely self-taught in music, he earned his living first as a jazz violinist and teacher, then as an orchestrator and conductor in the West End theatre of Noël Coward and C. B. Cochran, and from 1934 by writing film scores. Meanwhile he struggled for acceptance as a composer of serious music, producing a variety of chamber works and a Violin Concerto (1951) that fuse influences from Bartók, Berg, and Walton. In 1958 he adopted 12-note serialism without abandoning tonality; his chief works from this period were eight symphonies and the unfinished opera *Marching Song*.   PG

Frankfurt Group. A term used collectively of four English composers (Norman O'Neill, Roger Quilter, Cyril Scott, and H. Balfour Gardiner) and one Australian (Percy Grainger) who studied at the Hoch

Conservatory, Frankfurt, in the late 1890s with Iwan Knorr, though at no time were they all there together.

JD1

Franz [Knauth], Robert (*b* Halle, 28 June 1815; *d* Halle, 24 Oct. 1892). German composer. Overcoming paternal opposition, he studied with Friedrich Schneider in Dessau, then returned to Halle, eventually obtaining a post as organist in 1841 and as conductor of the Singakademie the following year. Having sent some songs to Schumann, he was surprised to find them immediately published. He suffered from deafness and nervous disorders, and in 1868 had to give up all paid employment and to rely on support from colleagues including Liszt, who gave concerts in his aid and who published a book on him in 1872. He composed many songs, admired more in Germany than elsewhere, simply because his flair was less to create strong music than to find a setting that reflected both the mood and the accentuation of German lyrics.

DA/JW

Fratres. Work (1977) by Pärt for chamber ensemble, later arranged for several smaller-scale instrumental combinations.

Frauenliebe und -leben ('Woman's Love and Life'). Song cycle, op. 42 (1840), by Schumann for female voice and piano, settings of eight poems by Adalbert von Chamisso.

Frauenlob [Heinrich von Meissen] (*d* Mainz, 29 Nov. 1318). German Minnesinger. He was probably born in Meissen in the mid-13th century, and at some stage had connections with the Přemyslid court at Prague. Peter van Aspelt, Bishop of Mainz from 1306, is thought to have been his patron. His name may reflect his many songs in praise of women in general, and the Virgin Mary in particular. Frauenlob is known to have been profoundly influential on the later *Meistersinger tradition. His musical achievements are not easy to assess, partly because some of the songs attributed to him are of doubtful authenticity, partly because many survive as texts only, lacking the melodies to which they were originally sung.

JM

Frau ohne Schatten, Die ('The Woman without a Shadow'). Opera in three acts by Richard Strauss to a libretto by Hugo von Hofmannsthal after his own story (1919) (Vienna, 1919).

Frederick II, King of Prussia [Frederick the Great; Friedrich der Grosse] (*b* Berlin, 24 Jan. 1712; *d* Sanssouci, nr Potsdam, 17 Aug. 1786). German emperor (from 1740) and an important patron of the music of his time. His earliest musical grounding (in thorough bass) came from the Berlin cathedral organist, Gottlieb Heyne,

after which, from 1728, he received instruction in flute playing and composition from J. J. Quantz. As crown prince he assembled, at Ruppin and Rheinsberg, several leading musicians, including Franz and Joseph Benda, Carl and Johann Graun, and C. P. E. Bach; on his accession, freed at last from his father's rigidly militaristic regime, he made these associates the basis of his Kapelle at Sanssouci, the royal palace near Potsdam where the intelligentsia of the day often met. C. H. Graun was appointed as his Kapellmeister, C. P. E. Bach as his accompanist, and, from 1741, Quantz as his chamber composer and director of the musical soirées.

Frederick's own compositions include flute sonatas and concertos (modelled on those of Quantz), arias for some of Graun's operas, and military marches extolling his triumphs in the War of the Austrian Succession (1740–8) and the Seven Years War (1756–63). He made his principal mark in musical history on 7 May 1747 when he welcomed J. S. Bach on a visit to Potsdam and offered him a 'royal theme' on which to improvise a fugue on the 'forte e piano'. On this theme Bach subsequently based the canons, ricercars, and trio sonata of his *Musical Offering*, which he dedicated to the king in July 1747.

WT/BS

fredonner (Fr.). 'To hum'.

Freedman, Harry (*b* Łódź, 5 April 1922). Canadian composer, cor anglais player, and educationist. His family moved to Canada when he was three. He was trained as a painter in Winnipeg and played in jazz bands there. After serving in the Royal Canadian Air Force during World War II, he studied composition with Weinzweig at the Royal Conservatory of Music in Toronto (1945–51) and took summer classes in composition with Copland, Messiaen, and Krenek in Tanglewood and Toronto. In 1951 he was a co-founder of the Canadian League of Composers. He played the cor anglais with the Toronto Symphony Orchestra (1946–71) and wrote *Graphic I* for the orchestra's 50th anniversary (1971). Many of his compositions are influenced by the visual arts and Canadian landscapes: *Tableau* (1952), *Images* (1958), and *Klee Wyck* (1970, rev. 1986). *The Tokaido* (1964) resulted from his study of Japanese sumi painting. From the 1960s Freedman also wrote music for ballet (*Oiseaux exotiques*, 1984), film, television, and the theatre.

HRE

📖 G. Dixon, 'Harry Freedman: A survey', *Studies in Music from the University of Western Ontario*, 5 (1980), 122–44

free jazz. The avant-garde jazz style of the 1960s associated with Ornette Coleman, John Coltrane, and others, where the performers were given a free reign with regard to tonality and chord sequences. The freedom it accorded resulted in jazz that was extreme even by most modern jazz standards.   PGa

freemasonry and music. Music has long held a place in masonic activities. The secrecy that surrounds masonry precludes the possibility of analysing the place of music in the craft with any exactitude. The repertory intended for use in masonic lodges cannot therefore be fully described; it would however seem, from the publications that survive, that the chief kinds of music used at lodge meetings were first hymns and secondly songs appropriate for unison singing. Substantial repertories with such titles as *La Lire maçonne* (1766) or *Freimaurerlieder im Musik* (1785) indicate that adaptations, especially of opera airs, were commonly sung.

Several well-known composers have been freemasons. Freemasonry played a considerable part in Mozart's life and drew several important works from him. Attracted by the ideals and the comradeship of freemasonry, he joined a Viennese lodge in 1784 and remained a member for the rest of his life. He had earlier composed music with masonic significance, and during his period as a freemason wrote several further works, including the cantatas *Dir, Seele des Weltalls* K429/468a and *Die Maurerfreude* K471 and the song *Gesellenreise* K468, all for use in masonic contexts; two later cantatas, *Die ihr des unermesslichen Weltalls* K619 and *Laut verkunde unsre Freude* K623, were intended for use within masonic ritual. The so-called *Masonic Funeral Music* K477/479a, supposedly written in memory of two brother masons but dated several weeks before their deaths in Mozart's own catalogue, is now thought to have been designed for other purposes.

The libretto of *Die Zauberflöte* was written by a sometime mason, Emanuel Schikaneder; the work embodies masonic symbolism in the temples and the 'enlightened' brotherhood led by Sarastro, as well as the ordeal scenes, while the music, in its use of keys (much of Mozart's masonic music is in E♭ major) and its threefold repetitions, reflects various aspects of masonic thought. His masonic music has a distinctive tone, solemn yet exalted and often joyous. Mozart quoted from masonic teachings in the moving letter he wrote to his dying father, and he called on a brother mason, Michael Puchberg, for financial help when he found himself in difficulties. It has been suggested that he is depicted in a painting, now in the Historisches Museum der Stadt Wien, of a meeting of the lodge Zur gekrönten Hoffnung in 1790.

It is known that Haydn was a member of a Viennese lodge, at least briefly, and so possibly was Beethoven. In France, Clérambault and Rameau are among those who at least had connections with freemasonry. 19th-century composers believed to have been freemasons include Spohr, Ole Bull, and Puccini; Liszt also had an interest in the craft. The main composers of music for actual use in masonic gatherings have however been minor figures.   SS

free reed. The type of *reed used in the accordion, American organ, bandoneon, concertina, harmonica, harmonium, and melodica, and in such East Asian mouth organs as the *shō* and the *sheng*.

frei (Ger.). 'Free'.

Freischütz, Der ('The Freeshooter'). Opera in three acts by Weber to a libretto by Johann Friedrich Kind after Johann August Apel and Friedrich Laun's *Gespensterbuch* (1811) (Berlin, 1821).

Freitag aus Licht ('Friday from Light'). Opera in a greeting, two acts, and a farewell by Stockhausen to his own libretto (Leipzig, 1996), the 'first day' of *Licht.

Fremstad, Olive [Rundquist, Olivia] (*b* Stockholm, 14 March 1871; *d* Irvington, NY, 21 April 1951). Swedish-born American soprano, originally mezzo-soprano. Brought up by adoptive parents in Minnesota, she was trained as a pianist before taking up singing in 1890. In 1893 she studied in Berlin with Lilli Lehmann. She made her debut as Azucena in *Il trovatore* in Cologne in 1895, later gravitating towards the dramatic soprano repertory. She was a member of the ensemble at the Metropolitan Opera, New York (1903–14), where she became an outstanding Wagner performer. Her Isolde, a role she sang regularly with Mahler, was considered definitive by many. Her career inspired Willa Cather's novel *The Song of the Lark* (1915), widely regarded as one of the finest of all literary portrayals of the artistic temperament.   TA

📖 M. W. Cushing, *The Rainbow Bridge* (New York, 1954, repr. 1977)

French horn. See HORN, 2.

French overture. See OVERTURE, 1.

French pitch. An 18th-century pitch standard about a tone below modern pitch; see PITCH, 3.

French sixth chord. An *augmented 6th chord.

French Suites. Six keyboard suites, BWV812–17 (1722–5), by J. S. Bach; first drafts for several of them are in the first *Clavierbüchlein* (1722) for Anna Magdalena Bach. The title does not appear in any source traceable to Bach and the suites are not in the style of Bach's French contemporaries.

French time names. See GALIN–PARIS–CHEVÉ SYSTEM.

frequency. The rate of repetition of the cycles in any periodic quantity such as sound, radio, or light waves. The unit is the Hertz (Hz).   JBo

fresco (It.). 'Fresh'; *frescamente*, 'freshly'.

Frescobaldi, Girolamo (*b* Ferrara, Sept. 1583; *d* Rome, 1 March 1643). Italian organist and keyboard composer. His father was a well-established musician in Ferrara, where he studied with the famous organist Luzzaschi. By 1604 he was in Rome as a member of the Accademia di S. Cecilia, and three years later he became organist of S. Maria in Trastevere. He was taken up by the wealthy and influential Cardinal Guido Bentivoglio and went with him to Brussels, returning to Rome as organist of St Peter's in 1608. In the same year he published his first volume of keyboard music, containing fantasias which show a remarkable grasp of counterpoint, and a book of madrigals of no great quality. In 1612 he married the mother of his two illegitimate children. A volume of toccatas and partitas published in 1615 shows his gifts as an improviser, using unusual harmonies and turns of phrase. The preface tells us that he avoided the use of *tempo rubato*, *notes inégales* in scale passages, and ritardandos at cadence points.

Between 1615 and 1624 there was a pause in publications of his music. The capriccios of 1624, and especially the magnificent toccatas of 1627, show a considerable stylistic advance. Among the toccatas are some composed for performance during Mass, at the Elevation of the Host; their rich harmonies convey a mystical attitude to religious ceremonial. In 1628 Frescobaldi left Rome to become organist at the Florentine court of Grand Duke Ferdinando II de' Medici, where he stayed until 1634. During his time in Florence he composed two books of *Arie musicali* (Florence, 1630). His final years were spent in Rome, again as organist at St Peter's, where he was greatly admired and honoured.

In 1635 he published his most famous volume, the *Fiori musicali*, a collection of music for use in the Mass. Here he displays the same delight in contrapuntal skill that Bach showed at the end of his life. 60 years after Frescobaldi's death the young Bach copied and studied the pieces, an acknowledgment of the earlier composer's status as the finest Italian keyboard composer of his time. His many pupils included Michelangelo Rossi and Froberger, and there is no doubt of his influence on such other organ composers as Buxtehude.   DA/TC

   📖 F. HAMMOND, *Girolamo Frescobaldi* (Cambridge, MA, 1983) · A. SILBIGER (ed.), *Frescobaldi Studies* (Durham, NC, 1987)

Fresnel, Baude. See CORDIER, BAUDE.

fret (Fr.: *touche*; Ger.: *Bund*; It.: *tasto*). A strip of gut, bone, ivory, wood, or metal placed across the fingerboard of certain stringed instruments. Like the *nut, a fret provides a sharper cut-off point to define one end of the vibrating string than would the finger against a bare fingerboard. Thus on the *viol (unlike the violin) all notes have something of the quality of an open string.

Frets may be movable, with pieces of gut or wire tied round the neck so that tuning may be adjusted, or they may be set into the fingerboard, as on the modern guitar. On some instruments, such as the *sitar, the frets are raised high off the fingerboard so that notes may be 'bent' by pulling the string along them.   JMo

frettevole, frettoso, frettoloso (It.). 'Hurried'.

fricassée (Fr., 'jumble', 'medley'). A 16th-century name for a humorous *quodlibet, in which melodies from various sources, including chansons, folk tunes, urban popular songs, and street cries, are assembled for comic effect. Henri Fresneau composed one that drew on more than 100 different melodies; other examples include pieces by Clément Janequin and Jean Servin.

—/JBE

Fricker, Peter Racine (*b* London, 5 Sept. 1920; *d* Santa Barbara, CA, 1 Feb. 1990). English composer. His studies at the RCM were cut short by war service, after which he took composition lessons from Mátyás Seiber. He was music director at Morley College (1953–64), then moved to the University of California, Santa Barbara. His early works, including the Wind Quintet (1947) and Symphony no. 1 (1948–9), are in an intense polyphonic style recalling Bartók and Hindemith. His subsequent music used serial methods in a free manner, often combined with a degree of tonal harmonic movement. He concentrated on instrumental genres, his works including five symphonies and a wide variety of chamber pieces.   PG/AW

   📖 R. M. SCHAFER, *British Composers in Interview* (London, 1963)

friction drum. A drum sounded by rubbing on the skin, or more frequently on a stick or a string standing on or passing through the skin, making a growling noise. It is found in most parts of the world, including Europe (e.g. the Flemish *rommelpot*), and in Latin American dance orchestras (the Brazilian *cuíca*). See also STRING DRUM.   JMo

Friedenstag ('Day of Peace'). Opera in one act by Richard Strauss to a libretto by Joseph Gregor (Munich, 1938).

Friml, (Charles) Rudolf (*b* Prague, 7 Dec. 1879; *d* Los Angeles, 12 Nov. 1972). Czech-born American composer. He studied at the Prague Conservatory, then became accompanist to the violinist Jan Kubelík; in 1904 they visited the USA, where Friml settled. He appeared as soloist in his own Piano Concerto with the New York Philharmonic, but gravitated to the musical theatre with *The Firefly* (1912), *Rose Marie* (1924), *The Vagabond King* (1925), and *The Three Musketeers* (1928).

PGA/ALA

Froberger, Johann Jacob (*b* Stuttgart, May 1616; *d* Héricourt, nr Belfort, 6 or 7 May 1667). German composer. In 1637 he settled in Vienna as court organist, and from there (*c*.1641) was given leave of absence to study with Frescobaldi in Rome. Later, after conversion to Catholicism, he went to Brussels, Paris, and London where, having been robbed by pirates during his Channel crossing, he composed his *Plainte faite à Londres, pour passer le mélancholie*. The insight he gained into different keyboard styles during his travels had a profound influence on his own work. In 1658 he retired from his Habsburg post and moved to Héricourt, to the estate of his friend and pupil Princess Sibylla of Württemberg-Montbéliard.

Froberger was the leading German keyboard composer of his time. His works in the Italian style comprise expansive toccatas—full of imaginative chromatic harmony and eloquent passage-work—together with canzonas and ricercars built effectively on the style of Frescobaldi, and with elegantly chiselled thematic ideas which point forward to those of Bach. His French-style contributions, comprising suites and character-pieces for harpsichord, show the influence of Chambonnières and, in their use of **style brisé*, Denis Gaultier. Of particular note are his 'laments', such as the *Lamentation faite sur la mort très douloureuse de Sa Majesté Imperiale* (Ferdinand III, who died in 1657) with its exquisitely beautiful representation of the soul rising to heaven.

DA/BS

frog [heel, nut]. On a bow used for stringed instruments, the block that secures the hair and holds it away from the stick at the handle end. Early frogs were clipped into a notch on the side of the bow. On modern bows the hair tension may be increased by a screw mechanism set in the frog, regulated by a screw button in the end of the stick.

'Frog' Quartet (*Froschquartett*). Nickname of Haydn's String Quartet in D major op. 50 no. 6 (1787), which has a 'croaking' theme in the finale.

fröhlich (Ger.). 'Joyful'.

Froissart. Concert overture, op. 19 (1890), by Elgar; the title refers to a passage in Walter Scott's *Old Mortality* in which Claverhouse speaks of his enthusiasm for the historical romances and *Chronicles* of the French writer Jean Froissart (1337–1410) and the score is headed by a quotation from John Keats: 'When chivalry lifted up her lance on high'.

From Bohemia's Woods and Fields (*Z Českých luhů a hájů*). Symphonic poem (1875) by Smetana, the fourth of his cycle **Má vlast* and often played separately.

From My Life (*Z mého života*). Smetana's String Quartet no. 1 in E minor (1876); although he gave the same title to his other string quartet, no. 2 in D minor (1882–3), which is similarly autobiographical, it is now used only for the first, which culminates in a sustained high E in the finale, representing the whistling in the Smetana's ear which heralded his deafness.

From the House of the Dead (*Z mrtvého domu*). Opera in three acts by Janáček to his own libretto after Fyodor Dostoyevsky's *Zapiski iz myortvogo doma* ('Memoirs from the House of the Dead', 1862) (Brno, 1930).

From the New World. See NEW WORLD, FROM THE.

Froschquartett. See 'FROG' QUARTET.

frottola (It.). A form of secular song popular in Italy in the late 15th and early 16th centuries, the most important forerunner of the madrigal. The frottola developed from the widespread practice of reciting poetry to an improvised musical accompaniment. Frottolas set verse, often lighthearted love poetry, in many different forms and rhyme schemes, some lighter, bawdy or sentimental, such as the frottola or barzelletta, *oda*, and *capitolo*, and some more serious, such as the sonnet, **strambotto*, and canzone. Frottolas are generally strophic, repeating the same music for successive stanzas, and may include repeated lines of verse and their accompanying music within each strophe, often in the form of a refrain.

Because the same music was used for every stanza, the possibilities for detailed **word-painting* were limited: this is the key difference between the frottola and the through-composed madrigal. Frottolas generally follow the structure of their texts closely, however. Settings are for three or four voices, mainly syllabic and homophonic, with the melody in the top voice. Often the text is written out only in the top voice, which suggests that as well as being performed by a group of singers frottolas could be performed by one singer with the three lower parts taken by viols or by a single instrument such as a lute or keyboard.

Two of the foremost frottola composers, Bartolomeo Trombomcino and Marchetto Cara, worked at the Mantuan court, which was one of the leading centres for the form in the decades around 1500. Many other frottola composers remain unknown. Collections of frottolas were among the earliest printed music books: the Venetian printer Ottaviano Petrucci published 11 books of frottolas between 1504 and 1514.   DA/EW

📖 J. HAAR (ed.), *Chanson and Madrigal, 1480–1530* (Cambridge, MA, 1964) · W. F. PRIZER, *Courtly Pastimes: The Frottole of Marchetto Cara* (Ann Arbor, MI, 1981) · F. LUISI, *Frottole di B. Trombomcino e M. Cara 'per cantar et sonar col lauto'* (Rome, 1987) [incl. facsimiles and transcriptions]

Frühlingslied (Ger.). 'Spring song'.

Frühlingssonate. See 'SPRING' SONATA.

Frye, Walter (*d* before June 1475). English church musician and composer. He may have worked at Ely Cathedral and in London before moving into the service of Anne of Exeter, elder sister of Edward IV. Through this latter connection he visited the Burgundian court, where his works were known and copied in manuscript. Several of his motets were unusually widely circulated in his lifetime; one of them, *Ave regina celorum*, even features in paintings of angel musicians, where the piece is notated on a scroll. Frye also composed some impressive cyclic masses, and rare early examples of English-texted polyphonic songs.   JM

Fuenllana, Miguel de (*b* Navalcarnero, nr Madrid, early 16th century; *d* ?1578–91). Spanish vihuelist and composer. Blind from infancy, he worked for the Marchioness of Tarifa and then for Philip II, to whom he dedicated his *Orphenica lyra* (Seville, 1554). This includes both vihuela fantasias and transcriptions of vocal music in which—in addition to the vihuela part—one or two parts are intended to be sung. From 1562 to 1568 he was chamber musician to Philip's third wife, Élisabeth de Valois, and a 'Folhana', who may well have been Fuenllana, served King Sebastian of Portugal in 1574.   WT/OR

fuga (Lat., It.). 'Fugue'.

fugato (It.). A passage in fugal style introduced into a non-fugal composition. For example, the *allegro* section of Mozart's overture to *Die Zauberflöte* begins fugally but soon turns into a sonata-form movement rather than working itself out entirely as a fugue.

fughetta (It.). A short *fugue.

fuging tune [fuguing tune]. A style of singing metrical psalms and hymns used in English parish churches in the 18th and early 19th centuries and still found in parts of the USA. A typical fuging tune is constructed of alternating homophonic and contrapuntal musical phrases; in the latter, voices enter in imitation of each other in the manner of a fugue.   PW

fugue (Lat., It.: *fuga*; Fr.: *fugue*; Ger.: *Fuge*). Literally, 'flight' or 'escape'. In music the word denotes a composition in which three or more voices (very rarely two) enter imitatively one after the other, each 'giving chase' to the preceding voice. Fugue is a style of composition rather than a fixed structure, but all fugues have features in common, and there is an accepted terminology to describe the roles of individual voices, the component parts of the fugue, and certain technical devices.

The first voice to enter carries the principal theme, known as the 'subject'. After this theme has been presented the second voice enters, transposing the subject to the dominant; the dominant entry is called the 'answer'. The third voice enters with the original subject (in a different octave), and so on. This opening section is called the 'exposition'; it concludes when each voice has presented the subject or answer. It is usual to allocate the same version of the theme to alternate voices (in a typical four-voice fugue soprano and tenor have the subject, and alto and bass the answer, or vice versa), and to introduce the voices in an alternating sequence of subject and answer. Occasionally an exposition ends with an extra statement of the theme known as a 'redundant entry'.

As the second voice enters (with the answer) the first voice provides a counterpoint against it; similarly the second voice provides a counterpoint to the third voice (subject), and so on. When this counterpoint is identical at each appearance in the exposition it is called a regular 'countersubject'; when either the subject (or answer) or the countersubject can serve as the bass line without grammatical error the counterpoint is said to be invertible. Additional counterpoint is called 'free', but such material may be restated in an identical form, as if it were a second countersubject. The exposition of a typical three-voice fugue could be represented as in Table 1. Sometimes a link is inserted between successive entries, most commonly the second (answer) and third (subject).

The answer may be 'real' or 'tonal'. A real answer is one that exactly transposes the subject to the dominant; a tonal answer modifies it in some way. The latter is most commonly used when a dominant note appears

TABLE 1

1st voice	subject	countersubject	free counterpoint
2nd voice		answer	countersubject
3rd voice			subject

prominently at or near the beginning of the subject: this note is answered not with the home key's supertonic (an exact transposition) but with its tonic. In a C major fugue an initial G would become a C at the beginning of the answer, not a D. Similarly a leap from tonic to dominant (C–G) would be answered with a leap from dominant to tonic (G–C, not G–D). There are examples of tonal answers in the D♯ minor, F minor, and F♯ major fugues in book 1 of J. S. Bach's '48'. A tonal answer is also needed if the subject ends in the key of the dominant. A real answer would modulate to the supertonic key, far from the tonic in which the subject is about to return; an adjustment is made so that the answer ends in the tonic key. The E♭ major and G♯ minor fugues in book 1 of the '48' have modulating subjects.

After the exposition most fugues continue with an alternating sequence of episodes and middle entries—the latter in related keys—and conclude with a final entry in the tonic. (The first fugue of the '48' is exceptional in containing no episodes.) Episodes are generally based on the thematic material of the subject or countersubject (or both), developing it in various ways and effecting a modulation for the next entry of the subject. Middle entries may incorporate counterpoints from the exposition or introduce new ones.

Sometimes after the exposition the composer creates excitement by bringing the entries of the subject nearer to each other so that they overlap. This device is called 'stretto' (It., 'close' or 'compressed'); it is used with unusual frequency in the C major fugue of book 1 of the '48'. Other technical devices are *inversion, *diminution, *augmentation, and more rarely *retrograde.

Occasionally one or more countersubjects appear simultaneously with the subject at the beginning of the fugue. Such a fugue is often called a double (or triple, etc.) fugue; but this term is more properly applied to a fugue in which a second (third, etc.) independent subject appears in the course of the fugue and may subsequently be combined with the first subject.

Bach's C minor Fugue from book 1 of the '48' illustrates some of the characteristic features of a fugue (Ex. 1; see previous pages). The eight-bar exposition opens with the subject in the middle voice. The soprano enters in bar 3 with a tonal answer (the fourth note is *c″*, not *d″*), while the middle voice continues with the countersubject. A two-bar link (derived from subject and countersubject) intervenes before the entry of the subject in the bass in bar 7, where the soprano continues with the regular countersubject. The three contrapuntal strands heard in bars 7¹–9¹ (countersubject, free voice, and subject) reappear in invertible counterpoint at every middle entry, though with small modifications; all but one of the six possible permutations are used. A two-bar episode leads to the soprano middle entry in the

relative major. In the second episode the soprano inverts the bass line from the first episode. The alto middle entry in bar 15 presents the theme in the dominant minor in its 'answer' form, and the third episode develops the counterpoint of the link (bars 5–6). A tonic middle entry at bar 20 is followed by the fourth episode, which develops and extends material from the first episode. Both the bass entry in bar 26 and the soprano entry in bar 29 have the effect of final entries. The dramatic break in bar 28 and the concluding tonic pedal signal the end of the fugue. GMT/AVJ

fuguing tune. See FUGING TUNE.

full anthem. An anthem written for full choir; see ANTHEM, 1.

full close. See CADENCE.

full organ. In Britain, usually all the stops of the *Great organ.

full score. A *score in which each instrumental or vocal part is separately displayed.

Füllstimme (Ger.). 1. A 'filling' part, without independent or functional significance, for example an extra orchestral part.

2. The mixture stop of an organ.

functional harmony. A theory of tonal harmony established by Hugo Riemann (1849–1919), who devised the term. The theory is that each chordal identity within a tonality can be reduced to one of three harmonic functions—those of tonic, dominant, and subdominant. Thus, for example, a supertonic chord has the function of a subdominant. AW

fundamental bass (Fr.: *basse fondamentale*). An imaginary bass line, consisting not of the actual lowest notes of a series of chords but of the roots of those chords. In Ex. 1, the fundamental bass notes are shown in black beneath the actual lowest note; where no black note appears, the root itself is the lowest note. The fundamental bass was a demonstration of one of Rameau's most important theories: that, even when inverted, a chord retains its harmonic nature and function.

Ex. 1

funèbre (Fr.), **funebre** (It.). 'Funereal', 'gloomy'.

Funiculì, funiculà. Song (1880) by Denza composed in honour of the opening of the Naples funicular railway. It was quoted in *Aus Italien* (1886) by Richard Strauss, who apparently thought it was a genuine folksong.

funk. A musical style derived from *rhythm and blues and *soul, characterized by repeated rhythmic figures and a strong bass line. The term was first used in the 1950s, and in the 1960s became associated with the Black Power movement through James Brown's *Say it Loud, I'm Black and I'm Proud*. It became an identifiable genre only in the 1970s, when it was made popular by such performers as Kool and the Gang, Earth Wind and Fire, Stevie Wonder, Miles Davis, Herbie Hancock, and Weather Report.   KG

fuoco, con (It.). 'With fire', i.e. wild and fast.

Für Elise ('For Elise'). Beethoven's Bagatelle in A minor for piano (1808–10), of which the autograph score is inscribed 'Für Elise am 27. April zur Erinnerung von L. v. Bthvn'.

furiant (Cz.). A quick, exhilarating Bohemian folk dance characterized by the alternation of 3/4 and 2/4 time. It was frequently used by Dvořák (*Two Furianty* op. 42; *Furiant and Dumka* for piano op. 12; and in place of the scherzo in his Piano Quintet op. 81, String Quartet op. 105, and Symphony in D op. 60) and also by Smetana (*The Bartered Bride*), both composers writing in 3/4 metre but with a strong hemiola pattern to emphasize the shifting beats.   —/JBE

furioso (It.), **furieux** (Fr.). 'Furious'; *furiosamente* (It.), *furieusement* (Fr.), 'furiously'.

furlano (It.). See FORLANA.

furry dance. An ancient processional dance to celebrate the coming of spring, still practised annually at Helston in Cornwall. It is sometimes called the 'floral dance' or 'flora', and is danced through the streets to instrumental accompaniment.

Furtwängler, (Gustav Heinrich Ernst Martin) **Wilhelm** (*b* Berlin, 25 Jan. 1886; *d* Baden-Baden, 30 Nov. 1954). German conductor. He studied in Munich with Rheinberger and Schillings and obtained the first of several posts as a répétiteur in 1905. He became conductor of the Lübeck Orchestra (1911–15), Mannheim Opera (1915–20), and the Tonkünstler Orchestra, Vienna (1919–24). In 1922 he succeeded Nikisch at both the Leipzig Gewandhaus Orchestra (until 1928) and the Berlin Philharmonic Orchestra, where he conducted for most of his life. He toured widely and conducted at Salzburg and Bayreuth, becoming one of the great Wagner conductors of his day. He was among the most influential conductors of the century, though his interpretations were often idiosyncratic. He gave numerous premieres, including Bartók's First Piano Concerto, Hindemith's symphony *Mathis der Maler*, and Strauss's *Vier letzte Lieder*. Controversy over his position under the Nazi regime led him to resign his posts; he fled to Switzerland in 1944. He was tried as a Nazi collaborator in 1946 but was acquitted and allowed to resume his career. He composed three symphonies, a piano concerto, and chamber music.   TA

   📖 H.-H. SCHÖNZELER, *Furtwängler* (London, 1990) · S. SHIRAKAWA, *The Devil's Music Master: The Controversial Life and Career of Wilhelm Furtwängler* (New York, 1992) · J. ARDOIN, *The Furtwängler Record* (Portland, OR, 1994)

fusa (Lat.). An early note-value, from which the modern *quaver derives; see NOTATION, Fig. 6.

fusion. An abbreviated variant of *jazz-rock fusion.

Futurism (It.: *Futurismo*; Russ.: *Futurizm*). An artistic movement that saw the 20th century as a new age, a future it vigorously embraced. It was specially prominent in Italy and Russia, and was at its height in the second and third decades of the century. In Italy, Futurist artists were stimulated by the speed and energy of mechanized technology and of 20th-century city life. Their principal spokesman was the writer Filippo Tommaso Marinetti (1876–1944), who delivered the classic statement of Futurist aesthetics: 'A roaring motor car . . . is more beautiful than the *Victory of Samothrace*' (1909). Debussy, no Futurist in practice, wrote that 'the century of the aeroplane will require its own music', indicating that Futurist ideals were widely shared.

In Russia, during the same period, Futurists were concerned more with spiritual regeneration: Skryabin's example was crucial for such Futurist composers as Arthur Lourié and Nikolay Roslavets. The Revolution then prompted a Futurist movement more akin to the Italian one, joined by composers who identified themselves with the country's technological and social change: Aleksandr *Mosolov's orchestral piece *The Iron Foundry* (1926–8) is a classic example of Soviet Futurism. Shostakovich, too, was involved in the movement, before it was officially suppressed at the beginning of the 1930s.

The principal musicians of the Italian movement were Francesco Balilla *Pratella, whose *Musica futurista* for orchestra (1912) was one of the few Futurist scores to be published, and Luigi *Russolo, who designed mechanical percussion instruments which he called *intonarumori* ('noise makers'). Concerts he gave in

London (1914) and Paris (1921) excited the interest of Stravinsky, Varèse, Antheil, and others, and thereby contributed to the development of the percussion ensemble as a musical force. The original Futurist group was in decline by the time of the Paris concert, but their musical means and ideals, transmitted through the scores of Stravinsky and Prokofiev, had a strong influence on the Russian futurists of the 1920s. The term also entered popular journalism of the 1920s and 30s, used of composers as unalike as Varèse and Bartók, generally with opprobrious intent. Since then it has normally been reserved for the original Italian and Russian movements.

See also TWENTIETH CENTURY, THE.   PG

📖 L. RUSSOLO, *L'Art des bruits* (Paris, 1954) · V. MARKOV, *Russian Futurism: A History* (Berkeley, CA, 1968) · M. KIRBY, *Futurist Performance* (New York, 1971) · G. WATKINS, 'The music of Futurism', *Soundings: Music in the Twentieth Century* (New York and London, 1988)

Fux, Johann Joseph (*b* Hirtenfeld, nr Graz, 1660; *d* Vienna, 13 Feb. 1741). Austrian composer and theorist. In the 1690s he settled in Vienna, first as organist at the Schottenkirche and, with increasing renown, as composer (from 1698), vice-Kapellmeister (from 1713), and principal Kapellmeister (from 1715) to the Habsburg court. From 1705 to 1715 he was also engaged as assistant, and eventually principal, director of music at St Stephen's Cathedral. His astonishingly large output comprises over 400 church compositions, including some 80 masses—a few in a mock-Palestrina style, but the majority with supporting instruments in the late Baroque *stylus mixtus*—together with operas and oratorios of majestic character, and a wide variety of chamber works. The most celebrated of his masses, the *Missa canonica*, provides a searching study in canonic techniques and is often regarded as a 'spiritual precursor' of J. S. Bach's *Art of Fugue*. Fux's festive operas include *Julio Ascanio, re d'Alba*, written for the emperor's name-day in March 1708, and *Costanza e Fortezza* ('Constancy and Fortitude'), a work of exceptional splendour for the coronation festivities of Charles VI at Prague in August 1723. Noted as much for his cultivation of the mature Austro-Italian Baroque manner as for his absorption of the techniques of Palestrina into his unaccompanied polyphony, he provided a crucial link between the two stylistic eras.

In 1725 Fux published his renowned treatise, *Gradus ad Parnassum* (in Latin, but subsequently translated into German by Lorenz Mizler), which, for his pupils and for numerous later composers, provided an exposition of traditional contrapuntal theory of unusual clarity. A copy of the treatise (in its original Latin) formerly in the possession of J. S. Bach has survived, and it has been surmised that it was his admiration for this work, and for Fux's achievements as a composer in general, which prompted Bach to work so inventively with the *stile antico in his later works.   BS

📖 E. WELLESZ, *Fux* (London, 1965)

fz. Abbreviation for *forzando* or *sforzando.

g

G. The fifth degree (dominant) of the scale of C major (see SCALE, 3).

Gabrieli, Andrea (*b* Venice, *c*.1533; *d* Venice, 30 Aug. 1585). Italian composer. He was organist at S. Geremia (now S. Lucia) in Cannareggio, northern Venice, in 1557, when he took part unsuccessfully in the competition for the post of organist at St Mark's. Five years later he went to Munich to work in the Bavarian court chapel under Lassus, and the two composers became friends. Gabrieli returned to Venice in 1566 and this time was successful when he applied for a position as one of the organists at St Mark's. He remained there until his death.

Gabrieli became very popular with the Venetian publishing houses, contributing to many anthologies of madrigals as well as producing his own books of motets, madrigals, and lighter forms. He was both prolific and versatile, and a master of the caricatures embodied in villanellas, mascheratas, and giustinianas. He also wrote some fine church music, notably two books of motets (1565, 1576), in which the long, flowing lines of traditional polyphony in the style of Palestrina are replaced by shorter motifs. He composed pieces for instrumental ensemble and some attractive organ music, notably the canzonas, some of which are arrangements or imitations of French chansons.

Gabrieli's most famous work, however, is his grand music for the splendid festivals of St Mark's, using the *cori spezzati* arrangement which he had learnt from the former Venetian *maestro*, Willaert, and from Lassus. By adding an instrumental ensemble to the choir, contrasting solo voices with the chorus and highvoices with low ones, and simplifying the harmony to avoid problems occasioned by performing with forces separated by quite large distances, he wrote music that was perfectly suited to state occasions—neither too difficult for the relatively unmusical listener, nor lacking in splendour to impress visiting statesmen. This music was published in a posthumous collection called *Concerti* (1587), assembled by his nephew Giovanni, and was widely imitated throughout Europe.

DA/TC

Gabrieli, Giovanni (*b* Venice, *c*.1555; *d* Venice, Aug. 1612). Italian composer, nephew of Andrea Gabrieli. He was almost certainly a pupil of his uncle and followed him by going to Munich about 1575; he remained there as organist in the court chapel under Lassus. By 1584 he was back in Venice at St Mark's, and was made permanent organist the following year: uncle and nephew were now colleagues. He continued to work at St Mark's until his death. Also in 1585 he was appointed organist to the religious confraternity of the Scuola Grande di S. Rocco, for which he regularly arranged the sumptuous music given on the day of its patron saint.

Even before his return to Venice Gabrieli had acquired a reputation as a madrigal composer, but his interest in secular music declined. Much of what survives from these earlier years seems to be occasional music, such as the grand choruses for plays given in the courtyard of the doge's palace. In church music he took over his uncle's role as provider of large-scale stately works, many of them for *cori spezzati*. He developed the idiomatic use of instruments, made the contrasts of sound and texture more acute, increased the use of dissonance, and wrote in a less simple, more devotional style than had Andrea. His first book of *Sacrae symphoniae* (1597) includes a mass and motets; there are some especially fine works for Christmas in this volume, such as *Hodie Christus natus est* and *O Jesu mi dulcissime*. He also wrote music for instrumental ensemble, again using *cori spezzati*.

An impressive stream of pupils (including Schütz) came from all over Europe to study with Gabrieli. He directed their attention to the modern madrigalian techniques developed by Monteverdi, and his own later church music—published posthumously in a second volume of *Sacrae symphoniae* (1615)—mirrors this interest, several motets using discords and jagged melody for the expression of the anguish of sin (his setting of *Timor et tremor* shows this at its most extreme). He moved away from *cori spezzati* in favour of contrasts between solo voice, chorus, and instruments, deploying them in separate sections unified by refrains. This technique can be seen at its best in the famous motets *In ecclesiis* and *Quem vidistis pastores*. His later instrumental music explores new formal patterns as well as exploiting the virtuosity of cornettists and violinists. Most of his later music was not published until after his death, and he had little influence on the younger Italians. In Germany, however, he was revered for many years through the enthusiasm of Schütz, and it was a German scholar, Carl von Winterfeld (1784–1852), who was responsible for the revival of interest in him in the 19th century.   DA/TC

📖 D. ARNOLD, *Giovanni Gabrieli and the Music of the Venetian High Renaissance* (London, 1979)

Gabrielli, Domenico (*b* Bologna, 15 April 1651; *d* Bologna, 10 July 1690). Italian composer and cellist. He studied composition with Legrenzi in Venice and the cello with the eminent player Petronio Franceschini in Bologna. He was in the orchestra of S. Petronio from 1680 until his death, except for a few months in 1687 when he was temporarily dismissed for not attending to his duties—not surprisingly, for by that time he had become a sought-after opera composer who was frequently in Venice, Modena, or Turin to supervise productions of his works. He was also a member of the Bologna Accademia Filarmonica and in 1683 became its president. Today some historical importance attaches to his *Ricercari* of 1689 which, together with the two sonatas for cello and continuo, are among the earliest contributions to the cello repertory. This adds weight to the theory that developments in the art of string making which made possible the construction of the small bass violin or violoncello occurred primarily in Bologna. Gabrielli also added to the important repertory of Bolognese trumpet pieces.   DA/PA

Gace Brulé (*b* c.1160; *d* after 1213). Trouvère. Born probably in Champagne, he moved in the circles of the nobility and other early trouvères, and may have participated in the Third or Fourth Crusade. His many songs, which are clearly indebted to the troubadour tradition, were widely disseminated during the 13th century, and are sometimes cited in the contemporary romance literature.   JM

Gade, Niels (Wilhelm) (*b* Copenhagen, 22 Feb. 1817; *d* Copenhagen, 21 Dec. 1890). Danish composer. The son of an instrument maker, he studied with Andreas Peter Berggreen (1801–80) and first attracted attention with his music to Adam Oehlenschläger's play *Aladdin* (1839) and the overture *Efterklange af Ossian* ('Echoes of Ossian', 1840). Mendelssohn was so much taken with his First Symphony ('Pa Sjölands fagre sletter'—'From the beautiful plains of Sjøland') that he conducted its first performance, and Gade also had the support of Schumann, writing in the *Neue Zeitschrift für Musik*, which served to put him on the musical map. He briefly

succeeded Mendelssohn as conductor of the Gewandhaus Orchestra, but in 1848 the outbreak of war between Prussia and Denmark forced him to resign his Leipzig post and return home.

In 1851, by the time he was 34, Gade held several key positions in Copenhagen musical life; he also founded its orchestra. In 1866 he became head of the newly established Royal Danish Music Conservatory. His eight symphonies span three decades (1841–70) and offer few formal surprises, though they are full of fresh, attractive ideas and are beautifully proportioned and crafted: new ideas enter at what seem precisely the right points (as in the finely paced Third Symphony, in A minor) and rarely outstay their welcome. The captivating Fifth Symphony, for piano and orchestra, written as a wedding present for Gade's wife, has an evident sense of mastery and command of pace. He wrote a number of choral works, the best known of which is *Elverskud* ('The Elf-King's Daughter', 1853), and a considerable quantity of chamber and instrumental music. His work inhabits a polite and well-regulated world, and any Nordic accents are muted. For all his charm and skill, his music rarely makes any significant escape from the orbit of Mendelssohn.   RLa

Gafori, Franchino (*b* Lodi, 14 Jan. 1451; *d* Milan, 25 June 1522). Italian theorist and composer. The son of a soldier and a noblewoman, he soon entered the church. After service at Lodi, Verona, Genoa, Naples, and Bergamo, he was appointed *maestro di cappella* at Milan Cathedral in 1484 and remained in that position for the rest of his life. In 1492 he was also appointed to lecture at the gymnasium in Milan.

His main theoretical publications are *Theorica musice* (Milan, 1492), *Practica musice* (Milan, 1496), and *De harmonia musicorum instrumentorum* (Milan, 1518). Smaller publications and manuscript treatises are in general either invective or preparatory work for the larger treatises, though he was also the main contributor to an intriguing series of letters that survive, discussing many astonishing details of music theory in the early 16th century. Much of his theory draws on earlier writers, most particularly Tinctoris. But in an age of burgeoning music theory and harsh disagreements, the clarity and solidity of Gafori's main writings are like a breath of fresh air: more than any other writer of the time, he seems to react to actual compositions with an immediacy and a musical instinct that make his writings particularly valuable.

Gafori's many surviving compositions, which include at least 15 mass cycles, show far less individuality. But when he became choirmaster at Milan Cathedral he began to assemble a series of choirbooks, apparently for cathedral use. Three of these survive complete; one more was severely burnt in the fire of 1906, though enough of it survives to give a reasonably clear idea of its contents. Much of this material was copied by Gafori himself, who was an inveterate scribe, though many others also contributed. Between them, these four choirbooks contain well over 300 works and give our best view of Italian cathedral polyphony in the years round 1500, perhaps reaching back to the 1470s. Much work is still to be done in evaluating these choirbooks and understanding the repertory they present.   DF

gagaku (Jap., 'elegant music'). An umbrella term covering the various repertories of Japanese traditional court music. These include music originally imported from China (*tōgaku*) and Korea (*komagaku*), which flourished during the Heian period (794–1185). Preserved during the following centuries at court in Kyoto, and at Nara and Osaka, the repertory was standardized after the Meiji restoration of 1868, but contemporary composers continue to compose new pieces for the traditional *gagaku* orchestra.   KC

Gagliano, Marco da (*b* Florence, 1 May 1582; *d* Florence, 25 Feb. 1642). Italian composer. A pupil of Luca Bati, the *maestro di cappella* of Florence Cathedral and S. Lorenzo, he succeeded his master in 1608, and spent his life in church service. His real achievements, however, lay in his secular music. He was a fine composer of madrigals in a modern style and of songs in the new monodic manner (see MONODY, 2); six volumes of madrigals for five or more voices (Venice, 1602–17) and one including also monodies, duets, and trios (Venice, 1615) were published in his lifetime. One of the first Italian opera composers, he is remembered today mainly for his opera *La Dafne*, which was a great success at its first performance in Mantua in 1608. He also wrote other music for court entertainments. In 1607 Gagliano founded the Accademia degli Elevati, which included many of the best-known musicians and musically inclined literary figures of Florence, and for the rest of his life he was considered one of the city's most distinguished musicians.

His brother **Giovanni Battista Gagliano** (*b* Florence, 20 Dec. 1594; *d* Florence, 8 Jan. 1651) was also a composer active in Florence, publishing both songs and church music.   DA/TC

gagliarda (It.). See GALLIARD.

gaillard (Fr.). See GALLIARD.

Gál, Hans (*b* Brünn [now Brno], 5 Aug. 1890; *d* Edinburgh, 3 Oct. 1987). Austrian composer. He studied with Eusebius Mandyczewski in Vienna, where he was lecturer in music theory at the university from 1919 to

1929. He directed the Mainz Musikhochschule until 1933, then worked as a conductor in Vienna until the *Anschluss*, when he moved to Edinburgh as a university lecturer. There he remained, a well-loved teacher and presence in the city's musical life, also producing a large amount of choral, orchestral, and chamber music in a well-wrought conservative style. His books included several perceptive studies of composers, including *Johannes Brahms* (London, 1964), *Franz Schubert* (London, 1974), and *Richard Wagner* (London, 1976).   PG/JW

Galán, Cristóbal (*b* ?Valencia, *c*.1615; *d* Madrid, 24 Sept. 1684). Spanish composer. He may have been trained in Valencia under Juan Bautista Comes. Until 1640 he was *maestro de capilla* at the College of Morella (Castelló), then held similar positions at Teruel Cathedral (1646) and at the civic chapel in Cagliari, Sardinia (1653); he was in the choirs of the Buen Retiro in Madrid (1657) and the cathedrals of Sigüenza (1663) and Segovia (1664). The queen appointed him *maestro de capilla* at the convent of the Descalzas Reales, Madrid (1667), and of the royal chapel (1680). His many sacred works include villancicos for several voices and *tonos* with violins. He also wrote incidental music for Calderón's *autos sacramentales* and for secular court plays.
                                          P-LR

📖 R. STEVENSON, *Renaissance and Baroque Musical Sources in the Americas* (Washington, DC, 1970) · L. K. STEIN, *Songs of Mortals, Dialogues of the Gods: Music and Theatre in Seventeenth-Century Spain* (Oxford, 1993)

galant (Fr.). A term used to describe the elegant style popular in the 18th century, not only in music but also in literature and the visual arts (as in Watteau's *Fêtes galantes*, for example). The *style galant* (Ger.: *galanter Stil*) was typical of Rococo rather than Baroque attitudes, and it served the Enlightenment ideals of clarity and naturalness. In music it resulted in an emphasis on melody with light accompaniment rather than on equal-voiced part-writing and fugal texture. Many composers, Italian and German as well as French, aimed at the light, deliberately pleasing effects of the *style galant*, ranging from François Couperin, Pergolesi, Telemann, and Muffat to J. C. and W. F. Bach, Galuppi, and Sammartini. In the 1770s the simple and attractive, but by then rather superficial, *galant* style was given a new lease of life in Germany in the sensitive, emotional *empfindsamer Stil* (see EMPFINDSAMKEIT), particularly by C. P. E. Bach.
                                          —/PL

Galanterien (Ger.; Fr.: *galanteries*). In the early 18th-century *suite, the *Galanterien* are extra movements not essential to the usual scheme of allemande, courante, sarabande, and gigue. They are generally taken from such dance forms as the minuet, gavotte, bourrée, or passepied and are mostly in a lighter vein than the larger-scale suite movements.

galanter Stil (Ger.). See GALANT.

Galilei, Vincenzo (*b* S. Maria a Monte, nr Florence, ? late 1520s; *d* Florence, 1591). Italian theorist, composer, lutenist, singer, and teacher. He was a member of the Florentine *Camerata and became interested in its discussions on the nature of ancient Greek music, travelling widely to study it and publishing his views in a book, the *Dialogo della musica antica et della moderna* (Florence, 1581). He was critical of the contrapuntal style, advocating *monody in its place. His own compositions in the new style have not survived, but his views were eventually embodied in the Florentine operas. He wrote some pleasant lute music (mainly arrangements of madrigals), improvisatory fantasies, and dances with fanciful titles. In his later years he wrote a number of shorter essays on acoustics. The eldest of his six or seven children was the astronomer and philosopher Galileo Galilei (1564–1642).

DA/LC

Galin–Paris–Chevé system. A method of teaching sight-singing devised by Pierre Galin (1786–1821), Aimé Paris (1798–1866), and Émile Chevé (1804–64). They used a figure notation, originally proposed by J.-J. Rousseau in 1742, in which 1 represented the tonic, 5 the dominant, and so on, but in practice sang the sol-fa syllables (*do, re, mi, fah, sol, la, si*). Their most important contribution was a series of note names for durations, pronounced rhythmically so as to represent the sound of the notes themselves. Commonly known as 'French time names' (Fr.: *langue des durées*), these were adopted by John Curwen in his sight-singing method (see TONIC SOL-FA).

PSp

gallarda (Sp.). A Spanish 16th- and 17th-century dance, often used as the basis for a set of variations.

galliard (Fr.: *gaillarde*; It.: *gagliarda*; Sp.: *gallarda*). A lively dance of Italian origin popular during the 16th and 17th centuries. It is a sectional dance very similar to the *saltarello and *tordion, with a five-step pattern, and is usually in moderate triple or compound duple time; bars in hemiola rhythm frequently occur, especially near cadence points. The galliard was normally paired with the *pavan (with the galliard placed second as the afterdance), and the two sometimes used the same melodic material. It was also popular in theatrical presentations: examples occur in French ballets, English masques, and Italian *intermedi* (including some by Monteverdi).

Galliards first appeared in print in the *Dix-huit basses dances* for lute and *Six gaillards et pavanes* for keyboard issued by Attaingnant (both 1530), with the earliest Italian examples dating from the mid-16th century. In England galliards flourished during the period 1590–1625, both for keyboard and for instrumental consort. Many appear in such keyboard sources as the Fitzwilliam Virginal Book and *Parthenia* as independent pieces (i.e. not coupled with pavans), while there are two galliards attached to the well-known *Earl of Salisbury's Pavan* by Byrd. The galliard survived, like the pavan, in Italy, France, Germany, and England up to the second half of the 17th century, when Thomas Mace described it as 'perform'd in a slow, and large triple-time, and (commonly) Grave and Sober' (*Musick's Monument*, 1676).

WT/JBe

Gallus Carniolus, Jacobus. See HANDL, JACOB.

galop (Fr.). A fast and lively ballroom dance in 2/4 time which became popular in Paris and Vienna in the 1820s. It derived from an earlier German dance, the hopser, and was popular in England in the mid-Victorian era, either as an individual dance or as a *quadrille movement.

PGa

Galpin Society. A society formed in 1946 to continue the work of Francis William Galpin (1858–1945), an authority on ancient musical instruments. It publishes the annual *Galpin Society Journal*.

Galuppi, Baldassare (*b* Burano, nr Venice, 18 Oct. 1706; *d* Venice, 3 Jan. 1785). Italian composer. He is often known as 'Il Buranello' after his birthplace. The son of a violin-playing barber who gave him his earliest music lessons, he composed his first opera at the age of 16; it was a failure, and on Benedetto Marcello's advice he became a pupil of Antonio Lotti for several years. After a brief spell as a harpsichordist in Florence he returned to Venice and successfully relaunched his operatic career. In 1740 he became *maestro di musica* at the Ospedale dei Mendicanti, where he did much to raise the musical standards, but in 1741 he went to London to compose *opera seria* for the King's Theatre; he remained one of England's favourite Italian composers long after his return to Italy in 1743. Here he gradually adopted the new Neapolitan style of *opera buffa*, with which he became even more successful than with *opera seria*, setting many librettos by Carlo Goldoni. In 1748 he became *vicemaestro* at St Mark's, Venice, and in 1762 succeeded to the post of *maestro*, from which in 1765 he obtained three years' leave to go to Moscow as *maestro di cappella* to Catherine the Great. On his return to Venice he added to his work at St Mark's the post of *maestro di coro* at the Ospedale degli Incurabili, and for the rest of his life composed church and keyboard music rather than opera.

Galuppi was the most important Venetian musician of his time. He was widely admired and respected by his peers, not only as a composer but also as a keyboard player—his virtuosity was greatly acclaimed in Russia—and as a conductor whose firm discipline made the orchestra at St Mark's one of the best in Europe. His most important single contribution was to the development of *opera buffa*—*Il filosofo di campagna* (1754) was the first such work to be a resounding international success—in which he matched witty texts (often commenting on Venetian social mores) with attractive music that included not only tuneful arias, to suit both comic and semi-serious characters, but also ensemble finales of the kind later used by Mozart. His considerable output of *opere serie*, oratorios, and church music is largely forgotten, but some of his keyboard music, which combines the language and structural principles of *opera buffa* with idiomatic keyboard writing, is still played today. It is not known which of these works inspired Robert Browning's poem *A Toccata of Galuppi's*. DA/ER

📖 M. T. MURARO and F. ROSSI (eds.), *Galuppiana: studi e ricerche* (Florence, 1986)

gamba (It., 'leg'). Contraction of *'viola da gamba'. See VIOL.

gambang kayu. The wooden or bamboo xylophone of the Javanese *gamelan. One of the elaborating instruments, with the *suling* (flute) and *rebab* (fiddle), it weaves a decorative pattern round the nuclear melody played on bronze *sarons*. JMo

Gambler, The (*Igrok*). Opera in four acts by Prokofiev to his own libretto after Fyodor Dostoyevsky's short story (1866) (Brussels, 1929). Prokofiev arranged *Four Portraits* for orchestra from the score (1931).

gamelan. A general term for instrumental ensembles throughout Indonesia and Malaysia. The two best-known forms of gamelan are the Balinese and the Central Javanese. Both consist mainly of percussion instruments.

In the Central Javanese gamelan, *metallophones with a series of bronze bars (*sarons* and *slentem*) play the nuclear melody (*balungan*) while horizontal gong chimes (*bonangs*), other types of metallophone (*gender*), xylophones (*gambang*), flutes (*suling*), and a fiddle (*rebab*) decorate it, and other horizontal gongs (*kenong*, *ketuk*, and *kempyang*) and hanging gongs (*kempul*, *gong ageng*, and *gong suwukan*) provide rhythmic punctuation. Singers, both solo and in chorus, are frequently an important part of the gamelan and the ensemble is

controlled by the *kendang* (drum) player, who signals changes of speed, mood, and music. The gamelan frequently plays by itself and with dancers, but is also used to accompany the *wayang*: dramatic performances, most commonly given in Java today with shadow puppets, all controlled by a single puppeteer (the *dalang*) who also takes all the vocal roles and directs the musicians by signals with a metal beater held between his toes and struck against the wooden box in which the puppets are stored. With his other foot he strikes two metal plates together to add dramatic impulse to the story.

There are two tuning systems: *slendro* with five almost equal steps to the octave, and *pelog* with five steps chosen from seven unequal steps. Because only one pitch is common to both systems, all instruments save the drums, fiddle, and the two great gongs are duplicated in each gamelan. They are normally set out at right angles to each other so that players face forward for *slendro* and turn to face right or left for *pelog*. The Balinese instruments and scales are similar in principle but differ in pattern and detail. Musical styles show a sharper difference, and Balinese gamelans are often louder and play faster than the Javanese. Dance dramas are more common than the shadow plays.

Other ensembles proliferate in the islands with local instruments and styles, but the Javanese hegemony is such that its style is supplanting the regional forms. It is this form that is the most popular abroad, with gamelans in active use in universities, museums, and other musical centres throughout Europe and the Americas. JMo

📖 N. SORRELL, *A Guide to the Gamelan* (London, 1990, 2/2000) · M. TENZER, *Balinese Music* (Berkeley, CA, 1991) · SUMARSAM, *Gamelan: Cultural Interaction and Musical Development in Central Java* (Chicago, 1995)

Game of Cards. See JEU DE CARTES.

gamme (Fr.; It.: *gamma*). 'Scale'; see GAMUT, 3.

gamut. 1. The note G, at the pitch indicated by the bottom line of the bass staff. The word is a contraction of *gamma ut*, which might literally be translated as 'G-doh', the *solmization name for the lowest note recognized in the medieval *hexachord.

2. By extension, the whole hexachordal system. The term was used in this sense (in the form 'gamme') at the end of the 14th century by John Gower, and there are several such uses in 15th-century writings. It also occurs in Shakespeare (discussed in some detail in *The Taming of the Shrew*, Act III scene 1) and as late as Pepys. Although the hexachordal system was no longer in use at the end of the 17th century, hexachordal names for notes were common and the term 'gamut' (which seems

to be peculiar to English) was still used to refer collectively to them.

3. By further extension, range, compass (as in the modern French *gamme* and the Italian *gamma*). From an early association with the range of the Guidonian hand (see GUIDO OF AREZZO), the term came to be used figuratively to refer to any extended range of musical sounds reckoned from the lowest to the highest.

See also SOLMIZATION.   —/AL

Ganassi dal Fontego, Sylvestro (di) (*b* Fontego, nr Venice, 1492; *d* mid-16th century). Italian musician. He was employed as an instrumentalist at St Mark's, Venice. His two treatises—one on playing the recorder (Venice, 1535), the other on viol technique (Venice, 1542–3)—are valuable sources of information about embellishment, tuning, fingering, and so on.   DA

ganz (Ger.). 'Whole'; e.g. *ganzer Bogen*, 'whole bow', *gänzlich*, 'completely'; *ganze Note*, 'whole note', i.e. semibreve; *ganze Pause*, 'whole-note rest'.

gapped scale. A pentatonic scale; see SCALE, 6.

garage. A term originally applied to certain 1960s American bands seen as outside the mainstream of pop music, and therefore as precursors of *indie music. Its current usage is derived from the Paradise Garage Club in New York, and refers to a style prevalent in dance-club culture.   KG

Garant, Serge (Albert Antonio) (*b* Quebec City, 22 Sept. 1929; *d* Sherbrooke, PQ, 1 Nov. 1986). Canadian composer. He studied composition with Claude Champagne in Montreal (1946–50) and attended courses with Messiaen in Paris (1951–2). On his return to Montreal in 1954, he organized concerts of new music and performed Schoenberg's piano music. Acknowledging early influences including Messiaen and Webern, he developed a musical language and style similar to that of Boulez, using serialism. Garant was the first Canadian composer to combine magnetic tape and instruments (*Nucléogame*, 1955) and was noted for his experimental music; his aleatory pieces include *Pièces pour quatuor à cordes*. He spent scholarship years in Basle (studying conducting with Boulez), Bali, and Rome. In 1966 he founded the Société de Musique Contemporaine du Québec (SMCQ), directing it from its inception until his death. He was appointed professor at the University of Montreal in 1967. Among his most important works are *Phrases II* (1968), *Offrande II* (1970), *Cage d'oiseau* (1962), and *Chant d'amours* (1975). He was also active as a conductor.   HRe

   📖 M.-T. LEFEBVRE, *Serge Garant et la révolution musicale au Québec* (Montreal, 1986)

garbo, con, garbato (It.). 'Graceful', 'elegant'.

García, Manuel (del Pópulo Vicente Rodríguez) (*b* Seville, 21 Jan. 1775; *d* Paris, 10 June 1832). Spanish tenor, composer, and director. He was in the choir of Seville Cathedral when he was six and made his solo debut in Cádiz when he was about 17, by which time he was known in Spain as a composer. He left Spain in 1807 and settled in Paris, where he made his debut and spread his popularity and influence, as he had done in Madrid. In 1811 he took lessons from Giovanni Ansani in Naples. His outstanding agility and even greater flexibility brought him the creation of the baritone role of Almaviva in the premiere of *Il barbiere di Siviglia* in Rome in 1816. For the next nine years he enjoyed the highest acclaim in Paris and London, especially in Rossini roles.

In 1825 García moved to New York to establish a company to perform opera in Italian. While touring to Mexico in 1827–8 he was robbed of all his earnings. In 1829 he returned to Paris, where he continued to perform, compose, and teach. His many operas and operettas were highly popular, but many remain unpublished. He was a highly influential teacher, his pupils including his daughters, Maria Malibran and Pauline Viardot, and his son, Manuel (Patricio Rodríguez) García (1805–1906), whose *Mémoire sur la voix humaine* and *Traité complet de l'art du chant* (1840) were for many years the most influential publications on vocal technique.   JT

   📖 J. RADOMSKI, *Manuel García (1775–1832): Chronicle of the Life of a 'bel canto' Tenor at the Dawn of Romanticism* (Oxford, 2000)

Gardano. Italian family of music printers. Their printing operation was established in 1538 in Venice by Antonio Gardano (1509–69), who printed nearly 450 music books, mostly of secular music, by such composers as Arcadelt, Lassus, Rore, and Willaert. He was succeeded by his sons Alessandro (*b* before 1540; *d* ?1591 or 1603) and Angelo (*c*.1540–1611). The success of the Gardano business was due to cheap mass production of music printed by single impression, and to the family's connections with the leading composers of their day, who provided them with salable material for publication.   JWA

Garden, Mary (*b* Aberdeen, 20 Feb. 1874; *d* Inverurie, 3 Jan. 1967). Scottish-born American soprano. She had singing lessons in Chicago, then moved to Paris, where she studied with Lucien Fugère. She made her debut at the Opéra-Comique in 1900 in the title role of Charpentier's *Louise*, a role she took over halfway through a performance when Marthe Rioton collapsed. She was acclaimed for her flexible and agile singing and her subtly evocative acting and within two years had become world-famous for her creation of Mélisande in Debussy's opera; she later recorded a fragment from her historic performance with the composer at the piano. Her success as Manon led Massenet to write *Chérubin* for her. In 1907 she was received with similar acclaim at her American debut as Thaïs at the Manhattan Opera. From 1910 she was the Chicago Grand Opera's leading soprano, and for a year was also the director of the company. She returned to Scotland in 1939.   JT

📖 M. T. R. B. TURNBULL, *Mary Garden* (Aldershot, 1997)

Garden of Fand, The. Symphonic poem (1913) by Bax; Fand is a heroine of Irish legend whose garden was the sea.

Gardiner, H(enry) Balfour (*b* London, 7 Nov. 1877; *d* Salisbury, 28 June 1950). English composer. He studied in Frankfurt with Iwan Knorr. In the earlier part of his career he achieved success with works including the *Overture to a Comedy* (1906), *Evening Hymn* (1908), *Shepherd Fennel's Dance* (1911), and *News from Whydah* (1912), together with songs and piano pieces. Becoming dissatisfied with his music, he withdrew from composition but used his private means to support his English contemporaries, with a series of concerts in London in 1912–13 and with a private performance of Holst's *The Planets* in 1918. A kindly and well-loved figure, he then spent much time busying himself with forestry in Dorset.   PG/JW

Gardner, John (Linton) (*b* Manchester, 2 March 1917). English composer. He studied at Oxford and, after war service in the RAF, joined the staff at Covent Garden; later he taught at the RAM and elsewhere. He first attracted attention with his Symphony (1946–7), written in a graceful neo-classical style; his opera *The Moon and Sixpence* was produced at Sadler's Wells in 1957. Later works include another opera, *The Visitors* (Aldeburgh, 1972), and some church music.   PG

Gaspard de la nuit. Three piano pieces (1908) by Ravel: *Ondine*, *Le Gibet*, and *Scarbo*; the title of the set is from Aloysius Bertrand's *Histoires vermoulous et poudreuses du Moyen Âge.*

Gasparini, Francesco (*b* Camaiore, nr Lucca, 5 March 1668; *d* Rome, 22 March 1727). Italian composer. After studying with Legrenzi in Venice he went to Rome, where he knew and may have studied with Corelli and Pasquini, and where he wrote his first operas. In 1701 he returned to Venice as *maestro di coro* at the Ospedale della Pietà (he was responsible for Vivaldi's appointment as violin teacher there). He returned to Rome in 1713, becoming *maestro di cappella* at S. Lorenzo in Lucina in 1717; though appointed to St John Lateran in 1725 he was prevented by poor health from taking up the post. He was extremely active as an opera composer in both Venice and Rome, and made important contributions to the cantata repertory. Domenico Scarlatti, Benedetto Marcello, and J. J. Quantz were among his pupils. His textbook on playing from figured bass, *L'armonico pratico al cimbalo* (Venice, 1708), continued in use for more than a century and is still a valuable source of information on contemporary continuo-playing practice.   DA/ER

Gaspar van Weerbeke. See WEERBEKE, GASPAR VAN.

Gassenhauer (Ger.). In 16th-century publications, a popular song. The term now means a vulgar street song.

Gassmann, Florian Leopold (*b* Brüx [now Most], Bohemia, 3 May 1729; *d* Vienna, 20 Jan. 1774). Bohemian composer. The little that is recorded of his early life is in itself uncertain: he may have been educated at the Jesuit Gymnasium in Komotau (now Chomutov), just as Gluck may have been, and when he went to Italy in about 1732 he may have studied with Padre Martini. He spent some time in Venice, in the service of Count Leonardo Veneri, and his success as an opera composer led to his appointment in Vienna in 1763 as a ballet composer in succession to Gluck. In 1772 he became the imperial Hofkapellmeister, but he died only two years later after a fall from a carriage.

Gassmann wrote some *opere serie*, but his later comic operas for Vienna were more modern with a clear focus on ensemble finales; they may have had some influence on Mozart's early operas and are among his best works, especially *L'amore artigiano* (1767) and *La contessina* (1770). With *Ezio* (Rome, 1770) he returned to *opera seria*, and the piece shows that he must have known of and appreciated Gluck's 'reforms' in opera.

DA/JSM

Gastoldi, Giovanni Giacomo (*b* Caravaggio, Lombardy, 1554; *d* Mantua, 4 Jan. 1609). Italian composer. He was first a singer and later *maestro di cappella* in the Gonzaga chapel of S. Barbara, Mantua. He was famous for his ballettos, which were published in a multitude of editions in the Netherlands, Paris, and Scotland, as well as in Italy. They were also widely imitated, notably by Thomas Morley, who borrowed (and even pirated) the words and sometimes the music for his own volume of balletts.   DA

gathering note. In hymn-singing, a note played by the organist before the first (or each) verse of a hymn to alert the congregation and establish the pitch. In the late 16th century and the 17th a gathering note often prefaced each line of the tune.

Gaucelm Faidit. See FAIDIT, GAUCELM.

Gaultier, Denis (*b* ?Marseilles, 1597 or 1603; *d* Paris, 1672). French composer. The finest lutenist of his time, he played mainly in the Paris salons and held no place at court. His compositions show a superb grasp of the potential sonorities of his instrument, and in his use of the *style brisé and the construction of his suites he had a considerable influence on such keyboard composers as Couperin and Froberger.   DA

Gaveaux [Gavaux, Gaveau], Pierre (*b* Béziers, 9 Oct. 1760; *d* Charenton, nr Paris, 5 Feb. 1825). French singer and composer. He sang in Béziers, then Bordeaux, where he was appointed as conductor and tenor at the Grand Théâtre. In 1789 he went to Paris to sing major roles at the Théâtre de Monsieur. When the company moved to the Théâtre Feydeau he began composing *opéras comiques* and during the Revolution he wrote a number of patriotic songs, many of which he published himself. One of his most successful works, to a libretto by Jean-Nicolas Bouilly, was *Léonore* (1798), which later provided Beethoven with the subject of *Fidelio*.
                                                                SH

gavotte (Fr.; It.: *gavotta*). A French folk dance of Breton origin, absorbed into the repertory of court dances in the 16th century; in the Baroque era it also developed into an instrumental form. Baroque gavottes were in moderate duple metre and generally followed a simple binary structure with two repeated halves (some, however, are in *rondeau* form). They usually begin with an upbeat of two crotchets and the melodies move in stepwise quavers. Just as a minuet was generally followed by another minuet in contrasting style (see TRIO, 2), so the gavotte acquired a second gavotte, often in the style of a *musette.

Before the mid-17th century a gavotte usually followed a series of *branles, a dance to which it was closely related, and was performed in a line or circle. During the latter half of the century, however, a different type emerged at the French court: a social couple dance, it seems to have been unrelated to the branle. It was also adapted for inclusion in many dramatic works and ballets by such composers as Lully, Campra, and especially Rameau, and was often associated with pastoral scenes. In England, Purcell included a gavotte in *Dido and Aeneas*, and Handel placed one at the end of some of his opera and oratorio overtures.

As an instrumental form, especially for keyboard, the gavotte appears as an optional movement in the 18th-century *suite, where it usually follows the sarabande, and as an independent piece. It was also used as a movement in many 18th-century solo and trio sonatas. Composers who wrote instrumental gavottes include François Couperin, Rameau, Purcell, Pachelbel, and J. C. F. Fischer. J. S. Bach included one in each of the first two English Suites.

In the 19th century, many lightweight drawing-room pieces were written in gavotte style, and the form was revived in the 20th century, for example by Prokofiev (*Classical Symphony*) and Schoenberg (Suite for Piano op. 25).   WT/JBe

Gawain. Opera in two acts by Birtwistle to a libretto by David Harsent after the anonymous Middle English poem *Sir Gawain and the Green Knight* (London, 1991).

Gay, John (*b* Barnstaple, *bapt.* 16 Sept. 1685; *d* London, 4 Dec. 1732). English playwright and poet. His musical importance lies in his libretto for *The Beggar's Opera*, which was first performed on 29 January 1728 and sparked a decade of public enthusiasm for ballad opera. *The Beggar's Opera* was immensely popular, owing to its colourful portrayal of the low life of contemporary London, a subject that provided Gay with ample opportunity for political satire. The public found the mixture of dialogue in English and music based on simple, well-known tunes (including some by such composers as Purcell and Handel) a refreshing change from the fashionable but often incomprehensible Italian *opera seria*, and its success is said to have made 'Gay rich, and Rich [the impresario] gay'. A sequel, *Polly*, was banned by the Lord Chamberlain and not performed until 1779.   WT/PL

Gayané (*Gayaneh*). Ballet in four acts by Khachaturian to a scenario by Konstantin Derzhavin, choreographed by Nina Anisimova (Molotov-Perm, 1942); it was revised in 1945 (Leningrad). In 1943 Khachaturian made three suites from the score, which includes the famous Sabre Dance.

Gazza ladra, La ('The Thieving Magpie'). Opera in two acts by Rossini to a libretto by Giovanni Gherardini after the comedy *La Pie voleuse* (1815) by J. M. T. Badouin d'Aubigny and Louis-Charles Caigniez (Milan, 1817). Although the opera was not revived until the mid-20th century, the overture, in Rossini's most brilliant style, always remained very popular.

Gazzaniga, Giuseppe (*b* Verona, 5 Oct. 1743; *d* Crema, 1 Feb. 1818). Italian composer. He studied with Porpora and Piccinni but remained a minor member of that brilliant generation which included Paisiello and Cimarosa. After beginning his career in Naples in 1768 he went on to present comic and serious operas at various Italian theatres. He is most associated with Venice where his best-known work, *Don Giovanni*, was performed as part of a 'dramatic caprice' in 1787. Giovanni Bertati's libretto was useful to Da Ponte, but neither text nor music can survive comparison with

Mozart's opera. Gazzaniga became *maestro di cappella* in Crema in 1791 and composed several liturgical works, his theatrical activity ceasing in 1801.   JR

G clef. See CLEF.

Gebrauchsmusik (Ger., 'music for use'). Music designed for children or amateurs and thus, by implication, simpler than that which the composer would write for concert performance (*Hausmusik*). The term arose in Germany during the 1920s, when *Hausmusik* gained political and social importance. Hindemith wrote many such pieces.

gebunden (Ger.). 'Bound', 'tied', i.e. *legato*.

gedämpft (Ger.). 'Muted': an indication that an instrument should be muffled, damped, or deadened, by the appropriate means, i.e. muted (string and brass instruments), muffled (drums), or damped (keyboard instruments).

gedehnt (Ger.). 'Prolonged', 'sustained', i.e. slow.

gefällig (Ger.). 'Agreeable', 'pleasant'.

gefühlvoll (Ger.). 'With feeling'.

gehalten (Ger.). 'Sustained'.

gehend (Ger.). 'Going', i.e. at a moderate pace, **andante*.

Geisslerlieder (Ger.). 'Flagellant songs'.

Geistertrio. See 'GHOST' TRIO.

geistlich (Ger.). 'Spiritual', 'sacred'; e.g. *geistliches Lied*, 'spiritual song'. Schütz's *Geistliche Konzerte* are vocal and instrumental pieces for sacred use.

gekoppelt (Ger.). 'Coupled', as applied to organ stops.

gelassen (Ger.). 'Calm', 'quiet'.

Geläufigkeit (Ger.). 'Fluency', i.e. technical ability.

Gelinek [Jelínek], Josef (*b* Sedlec, nr Sedlčany, 3 Dec. 1758; *d* Vienna, 13 April 1825). Czech composer, teacher, and pianist. After a time at the Jesuit college at Svatá Hora near Príbram, and tuition in composition in Prague, he entered the general seminary, taking holy orders in 1786. As a musician he was noted at an early age for his abilities as a keyboard player and his skill at improvisation. He impressed Mozart sufficiently for the latter to recommend him to Count Philipp Kinsky, in whose service in Vienna Gelinek fulfilled the dual role of chaplain and family music master. In about 1805 he entered the service of Prince Nicolaus Esterházy, again as chaplain-cum-pianist, though by this time he was in great demand in Vienna as a teacher, composer, and arranger.

Gelinek was acquainted with most of his major musical contemporaries, and many of his extant compositions are fluent and technically demanding piano variations on melodies from both stage and instrumental works. His transcriptions of music by Haydn, Mozart, and Beethoven among others were of a high standard, and his own compositions show skill and taste. The surviving piano trios bear witness to a pleasing melodic gift, readily displayed though rarely enhanced by effective development. Gelinek's popularity ensured the publication of most of his music during his lifetime, and his contemporary reputation encouraged the misattribution of a multitude of keyboard works.   JSM

gemächlich (Ger.). 'Comfortable', i.e. unhurried; *gemächlicher*, 'at a more leisurely pace'.

gemässigt (Ger.). 'Moderate', i.e. at a moderate speed.

gemendo (It.). 'Moaning', i.e. lamenting.

gemessen (Ger.). 'Measured', 'restrained', i.e. precise (in time values), at a moderate speed, or in a restrained style.

Geminiani, Francesco (Xaverio) (*b* Lucca, *bapt.* 5 Dec. 1687; *d* Dublin, 17 Sept. 1762). Italian violinist, composer, and theorist. After studying in Rome with Corelli (violin) and Alessandro Scarlatti (composition) he played in the Lucca theatre orchestra from 1707 to 1710. In 1711 he became leader of the opera orchestra in Naples where, it is said, the other players found his *tempo rubato* difficult to follow. In 1714 he went to London, where with the aid of considerable aristocratic patronage he established himself as a popular and highly successful player, composer, and teacher; his pupils included Charles Avison, Michael Festing, and Matthew Dubourg. He also dabbled, less successfully, in picture-dealing. As well as travelling to France and the Netherlands he paid two long visits to Ireland in the 1730s, settling there (though prevented by his Catholicism from obtaining the post of Master of the State Music in Ireland) in 1759.

Geminiani was acknowledged as one of the greatest virtuoso violinists of his time, and though his sonatas and concertos follow the Corellian four-movement pattern the violin writing is far more technically advanced, using much higher positions, multiple stops, and difficult figurations such that some of his solo sonatas were beyond the abilities of all but a few of his contemporaries. He enlarged the normal solo group of two violins and cello in concerti grossi by the addition of a viola, and his works are notable for their fluent command of counterpoint and bold use of chromatic harmony. The most important and influential of his theoretical works is *The Art of Playing on the Violin*, published in 1751 and the first such work to be aimed at advanced professional players rather than amateurs; many of its suggestions regarding such matters as chromatic fingering and vibrato are standard ingredients in modern violin technique. DA/ER

gemshorn. An *ocarina made from an animal horn, blown through a duct cut in the block that plugs the wider end, known from depictions of the 14th–16th centuries; also a similar-sounding organ stop. JMo

genau (Ger.). 'Exact'.

Generalbass (Ger.). See CONTINUO.

Generalbasslied (Ger.). 'Continuo lied'.

Generali, Pietro (*b* Masserano, nr Vercelli, 23 Oct. 1773; *d* Novara, 3 Nov. 1832). Italian composer. He studied in Rome and Naples, and his first compositions were mostly sacred. After 1800 he mainly wrote operas, producing more than 50 by the end of his long career. His early works were predominantly *opere buffe* and *farse*, most notably *Pamela nubile* (Venice, 1804), written after Goldoni. His later production included *opere serie*, but after about 1815 he inevitably suffered from comparisons with the all-conquering Rossini. He spent his last years as *maestro di cappella* at the cathedral in Novara. RP

Generalpause (Ger.) An indication in orchestral scores, often abbreviated to G.P., that all the players are silent at that point. It commonly occurs after a climactic passage, and was one of the notable innovations of the 18th-century *Mannheim school of orchestral playing.

General William Booth Enters into Heaven. Song (1914) by Ives for voice and piano, a setting of lines from a poem by Vachel Lindsay; it also exists in a version for bass soloist, chorus, and chamber orchestra.

Genoveva. Opera in four acts by Schumann to his own libretto after Ludwig Tieck's *Leben und Tod der heiligen Genoveva* and Friedrich Hebbel's *Genoveva* (Leipzig, 1850).

Genzmer, Harald (*b* Blumenthal, nr Bremen, 9 Feb. 1909). German composer and teacher. He studied in Berlin with Hindemith and worked as a chorus répétiteur and teacher. He also took part in research into electronic instruments, which led him to compose two concertos for trautonium (1940, 1952). After the war he taught composition at the Musikhochschulen in Freiburg and Munich. His craftsmanlike output consists of ballets, orchestral works, a Mass in E (1953) and other choral music, pieces for piano and organ, and chamber music for many different instrumental combinations, including several works featuring the saxophone. ABur

Gerhard, Roberto (*b* Valls, Catalonia, 25 Sept. 1896; *d* Cambridge, 5 Jan. 1970). Spanish-born British composer. He studied with Granados and Pedrell in Barcelona and with Schoenberg in Vienna and Berlin (1924–8). His Wind Quintet (1928) tests the possibilities of a synthesis of Schoenbergian and Spanish elements, but it remained without notable successors until the 1940s, by which time Gerhard had settled in Cambridge. Then in three stage works, the ballets *Don Quixote* (1940–1) and *Pandora* (1944–5) and the opera *The Duenna* (composed 1945–7; Madrid, 1992), he used Spanish idioms together with a variety of harmonic styles.

From that time on, Gerhard gradually pulled away from Iberian influences to forge a highly individual musical argument based not on development of themes but on contrasts of characteristic detail. Landmarks on the way to the late style include three symphonies (1952–3, 1957–9, 1960), of which the Third sets the orchestra against electronic sounds on tape. There followed a sequence of bold and colourful works, sometimes suggesting Varèse in their jagged edges but distinctly original in their warmth and vigour; notable among them are the Concerto for Orchestra (1965), the Fourth Symphony (1967), and a zodiac cycle of chamber pieces, of which only three—*Gemini*, *Libra*, and *Leo*—were completed. PG

📖 M. BOWEN, *Gerhard on Music: Selected Writings* (Aldershot, 2000)

German, Sir Edward [Jones, German Edward] (*b* Whitchurch, Shropshire, 17 Feb. 1862; *d* London, 11 Nov. 1936). English composer. He studied the organ, violin, and piano at the RAM (1880–7), then supported himself by playing in theatre orchestras and conducting. He first attracted attention with incidental music for *Henry VIII* (1892) and *English Nell* ('Nell Gwyn', 1900), together with the orchestral *Gipsy Suite* (1892) and *Symphonic Suite* (1894). In 1901 he completed Sullivan's last comic opera, *The Emerald Isle* (left unfinished at the composer's death), and he confirmed his position as Sullivan's heir with his comic opera *Merrie England* (1902), an Elizabethan extravaganza set to tuneful and effective music. Of his later works in this manner only *Tom Jones* (1907) enjoyed much success. He also wrote two symphonies and other serious orchestral works as well as such songs as *Glorious Devon* (1905). PG/ALa

German Requiem, A (*Ein deutsches Requiem*). Choral work, op. 45 (1865–8), by Brahms for soprano and baritone soloists, chorus, and orchestra; it is so called because the text is not that of the Roman Catholic liturgy but passages selected by Brahms from Luther's translation of the Bible.

German sixth chord. An *augmented 6th chord.

Germany. Although the German-speaking lands have been considered 'the musical countries *par excellence*', this was true only for the 250 years from *c*.1650. Whereas English commentators of the 19th and early 20th centuries regarded Germany (and Austria) as Mecca for music, a broader view shows that both France and Italy have perhaps made more substantial contributions over a longer period of time, while the Low Countries, England, and Russia, if possessing less sustained traditions, have, in their own ways, made incursions into the course of Western music. The interest of Germany's musical history lies in its diversity and capacity to assimilate, rather than in its nationalism. Such a view would have been anathema to Wagner and his followers, as well as to the 1933–45 regime, but is more in line with today's perception of internationalism as a virtue.

1. The Middle Ages to 1520; 2. 1520 to the Thirty Years War; 3. The German Baroque; 4. 1750–1815; 5. 1815–70; 6. United Germany; 7. Since 1914

1. The Middle Ages to 1520

Much of present-day Germany and Austria came under the jurisdiction of Charlemagne, the first Holy Roman Emperor (crowned 800). After the Treaty of Verdun in 843 the Carolingian Empire was divided, the eastern part including Saxony and Bavaria. There were many huge monasteries in the area, producing some notable music theorists, from Hucbald to Wilhelm of Hirsau (*d* 1091). Some monasteries had song schools, but these propagated plainchant and overlooked the developments in polyphony taking place in France and Flanders.

At first, secular music was of little significance. The spread of the chivalric ideal from France in the 12th century inspired the courtly songs of love sung by such wandering musicians as Walther von der Vogelweide; the Hohenstaufen ducal courts in Franconia and Swabia were centres for this music. In addition to courtly love, the poetic material of the German *Minnesinger dealt sometimes with rural and religious matters. The tradition of *Frauenlob*, worship of the noble lady, lasted until the 14th century. German society was distinguished not so much by the aristocratic court as by the free town, of which there were many. Unions of tradesmen formed conservative guilds of *Meistersinger (realistically depicted in Wagner's opera *Die Meistersinger von Nürnberg*), their rules largely perpetuating the old Minnesinger ideals, especially with regard to their adherence to monophony.

Polyphony was slow to take over and is first found in organ music. Organs were being built in Germany at Aachen, Strasbourg, and Freising in the 9th century, and Cologne in the 10th. The blind organist Conrad Paumann, employed at Munich, travelled widely in the 15th century, gaining a knowledge of Italian and Burgundian music. His influence encouraged the pre-eminence of organ music in Germany that was to continue well into the 18th century. The Buxheimer Orgelbuch gives a good idea of the style and forms of the music composed by the 15th-century school of German organists. Polyphonic techniques are found in vocal music of this period where the German equivalent of the chanson is commonly called the *Tenorlied because the principal melody is 'held' in one of the voices. Such songs, together with French and Burgundian chansons, are found in several important songbooks compiled in the second half of the 15th century, bringing German music abreast of the international scene. Nevertheless, the influence of Renaissance ideas had made little headway in Germany, and it is symptomatic that German writers today describe their country's music at this time as 'late Gothic' rather than 'Renaissance'.

2. 1520 to the Thirty Years War

The German Renaissance was hindered by religious trouble. In 1517 Martin Luther posted his famous 95 theses on the door of the Schlosskirche at Wittenberg, and the *Reformation soon split Germany into many factions. Some of the northern principalities and most of the independent cities became Protestant, while the majority of southern states remained Catholic. Although various Protestant sects did not approve of elaborate church music, Luther did, and retained much of the Roman Catholic Mass, using German translations. His principle of congregational participation resulted in the *chorale, in which new words were frequently set to older secular tunes. The importance of music in the vernacular stimulated the new generation of German composers, as did the growing number of German printing houses (see PRINTING AND PUBLISHING OF MUSIC, 4). Of the new generation, Stoltzer and Senfl composed for the Reformed Church but did not openly embrace the new faith; however they did provide polyphonic settings of the Kyrie, Gloria, and *Magnificat*, as well as motets, mostly in the vernacular but occasionally in Latin. Another important figure was Johann Walter, Luther's musical adviser and the first of the great Protestant Kantors. Music for the Lutheran service tended to be conservative, in contrast to that of composers writing for the Roman Catholic churches who still maintained contact with Italy and France.

The free cities had maintained groups of civic musicians known as *Stadtpfeifer* (town pipers) since the 14th century. Such groups (*Stadtpfeifereien*) comprised mainly wind players and inspired a great deal of instrumental music, as well as encouraging the industry of instrument making. Nuremberg became famous for its trumpets and trombones, as well as lutes and viols, while Paumann's tradition flourished in the organ music of Arnolt Schlick and Paul Hofhaimer.

The years between the Treaty of Augsburg in 1555 and the beginning of the Thirty Years War in 1618 were among the most peaceful in German history, and established the basic pattern of music-making for the next two centuries. In the south, the predominantly Catholic courts imitated the Italian princedoms by having many Kapellen and employing as Kapellmeister composers who had been trained in or visited Rome. In Munich, Lassus was in charge from 1563 to his death in 1594, employing a number of young Italians; some of his music has been discussed in connection with the concept of *musica reservata*. At Dresden, the court music was directed by the Italian Antonio Scandello from 1568 until his death in 1580, and Philippe de Monte, who had spent many years in Italy, was Kapellmeister to the imperial court of the Habsburgs in Vienna and Prague.

Protestant princes much admired the splendid church music of the Catholic courts and sent their young men to study in Italy. The most famous of these was Heinrich Schütz, a pupil of Giovanni Gabrieli from 1609 to 1612 whose mastery of the grand Venetian manner is typical of a whole generation of German musicians in the early 17th century. This knowledge of modern Italian music combined with the older traditions of chorale and polyphony gave German Protestant music a richness of style that such theorists as Michael Praetorius attempted to categorize in the first half of the 17th century. The second volume of his *Syntagma musicum* contains an invaluable pictorial record of virtually every instrument known at the time. There was also some polemic about the emotional effects of music arising from the discussions concerning *musica reservata*, which eventually led to the so-called doctrine of *affections.

3. The German Baroque

The Thirty Years War ruined the German economy, and artistic life was seriously compromised almost everywhere. The dividing lines between Protestant and Catholic, with centres in Berlin and Vienna respectively, were finally settled. There remained 350 smaller courts that provided employment for many musicians.

There was a general shift of population towards the free cities, and large Protestant churches, which had song schools attached and which effectively organized the music of the whole community, became increasingly influential. One of the most sought-after posts was that of Kantor, implying not just a choirmaster or organist, but also the director of music in a school, even with the right to run other organizations in the town. The cities also maintained 'town musicians'. Their virtuosity as trumpeters was especially valuable, but their general quality as wind players helps to account for the popularity in Germany of such minor members of the double-reed family as the oboe d'amore and oboe da caccia. Finally, it was in the cities that the universities were situated, often with flourishing music clubs.

The prestige of the large courts, the proliferation of the small ones, and the power of the free cities brought forth the great period of German music, though Italian influence continued to be strong in the southern courts. The Thirty Years War delayed the arrival of opera: Schütz's lost setting of *Dafne* (1627) seems to have been an isolated example. When peace was declared, companies established in Venice and northern Italy soon ventured to Innsbruck and Vienna. Cesti's *Il pomo d'oro* (1668) marked the beginning of a strong operatic tradition in Vienna, where the court employed Draghi as well as Caldara and Fux. Their operas were in Italian, and court poets such as Apostolo Zeno and Pietro Metastasio were specially commissioned to write librettos. Salzburg, Dresden, Munich, and Hanover followed suit, to the extent that church music was also Italian in style, and remained more opulent. Large forces were involved in masses in the Venetian polychoral manner: one, written for a grand occasion in Salzburg, required no fewer than 53 voices and instruments, disposed in eight groups.

The first German public opera house opened in Hamburg in 1678 with a performance of Theile's *Adam und Eva*, and a lively, independent German tradition was established in spite of the use of Italian for the arias in some works. Composers included Keiser, Telemann, and Handel. Leipzig established its own opera house in May 1693 with Nicolaus Strungk's *Alceste*. Over 100 operas were produced there between 1693 and 1720, but opera was not a commercial proposition and survived only in the Italianate houses of the larger courts. The lesser courts were notable for their orchestras. In the early 18th century the repertory was probably Italian and the works of Corelli and Vivaldi were especially popular. This vogue was stimulated by the visits of the violinists Veracini, Locatelli, and Vivaldi himself. But native Germans were often in charge; among others, J. S. Bach shows the emergence of a new school of German composers.

From the 1670s and 80s onwards the courts imitated French as well as Italian models. Germany's unique contribution, at this time, lay in the music for the great Protestant churches of northern Germany. The organ continued to play an important part, and the splendid music for it included virtuoso toccatas, learned fugues, and arrangements of chorale tunes. A long line of organists, from Buxtehude in Lübeck, Pachelbel in Nuremberg and Vienna, and Georg Böhm in Lüneburg, to J. S. Bach at Weimar, provided what has become the basic repertory of the organist. There is also a rich German repertory of music for harpsichord, sometimes mirroring French tastes (as in the works of Froberger and some suites of J. S. Bach) but at other times showing off the executant's skills, as exemplified in Bach's *The Well-Tempered Clavier*. These composers also wrote extremely elaborate church music, which owed little to Catholic models, although Bach's great Mass in B minor admittedly follows the outline of the fashionable Neapolitan style mass (see MASS, 3). Buxtehude's famous *Abendmusiken* set a vogue for what might almost be called religious concerts, including lengthy cantatas. This fashion was eventually incorporated into liturgical use, and can be seen at its height in the cantatas of J. S. Bach for his Leipzig churches (see CANTATA, 3). The vernacular liturgy and its concentration on the Bible also encouraged church music, rather than oratorios, in a dramatic style. *Passion music, essentially the setting to music of one of the biblical descriptions of the events leading to the Crucifixion, brought together a range of musical styles in a way impossible anywhere except in Protestant Germany.

4. 1750–1815

The richness of this native tradition, with its ability to assimilate Italian and French elements, continued over the next 65 years, though with changes of emphasis and place. Various wars established still further the strengths of the Prussian kings in Berlin and the Habsburg emperors in Vienna, but another group of states began to emerge as a third force: Saxony, Württemberg, Bavaria, and various duchies in Thuringia. Some of their rulers became great patrons of music. At Mannheim, a fine orchestra was established under Johann Stamitz, with which several important composers were associated (see MANNHEIM SCHOOL; SYMPHONY, THE), but this ensemble decreased in importance when the court moved to Munich in 1778. Italian poets and composers acquired permanent positions. This was especially the case in Vienna, where Lorenzo Da Ponte and Giovanni Casti succeeded Metastasio as librettists, while Piccinni, Paisiello, Sarti, and Salieri were among the more popular composers in

spite of Mozart's immense superiority over them, which was not appreciated at the time.

By the end of the Seven Years War in 1763, more attention had to be paid to a wider audience, and the popularity of Italian *opera buffa* was soon transferred to Germany and Austria. There had been a hiatus during the war, but the *Singspiel* was revived in the 1760s, and such works as Goethe's *Erwin und Elmire* and *Claudine von Villa Bella* (set to music by Reichardt) proved popular. In the years immediately preceding the French Revolution, German composers progressively superseded foreigners in most of the major cities. In Berlin, the conservatism of Frederick the Great (reigned 1740–86) is reflected in his choice of composers: Hasse, the Graun brothers, and W. F. and C. P. E. Bach. The stability achieved by the Empress Maria Theresa and her son Joseph II in Vienna resulted in a prosperity that allowed many noblemen to maintain private orchestras and regular concerts, while both Italian and German opera flourished. At the lesser German courts the symphony was taken up with tremendous enthusiasm, and thousands were composed by the Stamitz brothers and their contemporaries. With the development of the piano the solo concerto became popular, especially at public concerts for which such virtuosos as Mozart hired halls and orchestras in the hope of attracting large audiences and so that their new works could be heard.

It was probably these opportunities for employment at court, as much as the philosophy of the Enlightenment, that caused the decline of the Protestant Kantor, and the glories of church music at Lübeck and Hamburg disappeared. The best examples were written for the Roman Catholic Church, mainly in southern Germany and Austria, in spite of a period of austerity in ceremonial during the 1780s. The Haydn brothers and Mozart composed brilliant masses, using orchestra, soloists, and choir (see MASS, 4).

The French Revolution and subsequent Napoleonic Wars completed the movement away from foreign domination. The income of the nobility fell, causing them to reduce their musical establishments of which Haydn's retirement from Eszterháza is a sad example. In place of orchestras there were subsidized string quartets, no longer requiring salaried Kapellmeister. Instead, the nobility commissioned music from individual composers. The Napoleonic campaigns that raged across Germany increased anti-French feeling, disrupted relationships with Italian states, and so encouraged the native German musician.

If it was the French who conceived the main elements of Romantic thought—the glorification of nature, of the simple man, of the people as opposed to the nobility, of the hero—the Germans developed them most vigorously (see ROMANTICISM). There was a new flowering of lyric verse, particularly in the work of Goethe. This awakened interest inspired such composers as Beethoven and Schubert to write a new type of song, breaking away from the traditions of the Italian cantata, in a simple melodic style, with much of the musical interest given to the piano accompaniment (see LIED). *Singspiel* was by this time considered as respectable as Italian opera. The first performance of Mozart's *Die Zauberflöte* at Emanuel Schikaneder's Theater auf der Wieden in 1791, rather than at one of the court opera houses, brought *Singspiel* to a new level of seriousness, which Beethoven maintained in *Fidelio*.

5. 1815–70

After the Treaty of Vienna in 1815 much of northern Italy came under Austrian rule, but instead of the former 300 German states there were now only about 30, with Prussia in the ascendancy. Many of the nobles were subjects of others and a new middle class came into being, reinforced by wealthy industrialists and merchants. The tastes of this middle-class society are sometimes called Biedermeier, denoting a worthy, even cosy art rather than the revolutionary extravagances of the Romantics. The comfortably-off bourgeoisie bought pianos for their drawing-rooms and required music which lay within their technical means, such as the short genre pieces called *Moments musicaux*, bagatelles, or *Albumblätter*, examples of which can be found among the late music of Beethoven and, especially, of Schubert. The song with piano accompaniment was equally popular, the verse often reflecting middle-class life, as in Schumann's *Frauenliebe und -Leben* and *Dichterliebe* cycles. The concept of the Schubertiad, an informal meeting of friends to sing, play, and listen, is the essence of this bourgeois art.

The middle classes preferred the German light or comic operas of Nicolai and Lortzing to the French or Italian heroic works. These survived only at the large, state-supported opera houses in Berlin, Dresden, and Vienna while elsewhere the municipally supported theatres alternated spoken drama and opera. Standards were often not very high and it is noticeable that many ambitious German composers, such as Meyerbeer and the young Wagner, looked abroad for success. Nevertheless, the opportunities for opera composition were numerous, and there were also many orchestras, though less wealthy towns had to be content with a mixture of professional and amateur players. At Leipzig, the Gewandhaus orchestra had consistently good players led by famous violinists, and by 1840 they were being conducted by Mendelssohn. Small orchestras occa-sionally joined forces to give a festival. The Lower Rhine Festival took place in turn at Düsseldorf, Aachen, and Cologne with the standard repertory including concertos for virtuoso performers so as to attract audiences. Symphonic music tended to be retrospective, with Mozart, Haydn, and Beethoven forming the staple fare and accounting for the conservative forms of Schumann's and Mendelssohn's orchestral compositions.

The German interest in the past now flourished and gave rise to such early monuments of musicology as Carl von Winterfeld's books on Palestrina and Giovanni Gabrieli and the complete editions of Handel, Bach, and earlier composers. The middle-class amateur choral society, of which over 150 existed in Germany before 1933, was exemplified by the Berlin Singakademie, and all found this music to their taste. Mendelssohn's revival of Bach's *St Matthew Passion* in 1829 was a manifestation of generally deepening knowledge and understanding. For Catholics, the *Cecilian Movement kept alive interest in old polyphony and plainchant.

The establishing of German teaching institutions—of which that founded by Mendelssohn at Leipzig in 1843 was the most famous—and a strong national consciousness meant that students were no longer sent to the Italian conservatories. Music schools were founded between 1845 and 1869 in Cologne, Munich, Dresden, Stuttgart, and Berlin, and foreigners flocked there, confident that Germany was the centre of musical life, a view that every German shared. The first great so-called scientific musicologists were at work on the historical aspect from the 1860s, and many musical journals were launched in the 1830s and 40s to deal with the critical viewpoint. The most important was Schumann's *Neue Zeitschrift für Musik*, first published in Leipzig in 1834.

Just as the 1848 revolutions challenged the comfort of bourgeois life, so there were rumblings of musical discontent around the 1850s. Weimar became the centre for a New German school of composers, influenced by the anti-Classical ideas of Liszt, which included Bülow and Cornelius. Liszt conducted performances of operas by Verdi, Donizetti, Berlioz, and Wagner, including the first performance of *Lohengrin*. In 1861, Liszt helped to establish the Allgemeiner Deutscher Musikverein, a society devoted to furthering modern German music and looking after musicians and their families. In the previous year, the young disciples of Schumann, among them Brahms and Joachim, had issued a manifesto against these moderns, but it only encouraged the New Germans.

Wagner was the foremost exception to the generally conservative Germanic music culture, being the most consciously German composer of the 19th century. His opera *Der fliegende Holländer* takes its subject matter from northern legend and personal experience of a raging storm in the North Sea, while *Tannhäuser* and *Lohengrin* look back to the German Middle Ages in a highly romanticized form. He became the greatest polemicist of German music; his theories of the theatre and the music drama, determinedly based on German literature and traditions, were influenced by the philosophers Hegel and Schopenhauer and worked out from the musical standpoint of Beethoven. Wagner was, however, unacceptable to the established institutions; his attempts at reorganizing German musical education failed, and he had comparatively little success in raising standards at opera houses. It was not until the first festival of his operas at Bayreuth had amazed the musical world in 1876 that Wagner acquired enormous influence by creating new standards of performance and conditions of working, as well as demanding a new seriousness from the audience. The essentially religious German approach to the theatre and music now reached its apotheosis.

6. United Germany

The Austro-Prussian War of 1866 effectively put Prussia at the head of a united Germany, a position confirmed by the Franco-Prussian War of 1870–1 and the end of the French Second Empire when the German Empire came into being with the Hohenzollern dynasty as its monarchy.

The impact of Wagnerism was by no means confined to Germany and received various degrees of acceptance throughout the Western world and Russia. Within Germany the new seriousness of Wagnerian opera was impossible to reconcile with the *Singspiel*. As a direct result, the Volksoper repertory turned to *operetta, inspiring some charming works in Vienna from Johann Strauss the younger, Lehár, Oscar Straus, and others. Those influenced by Wagner included Weingartner, Siegfried Wagner, and Humperdinck; however, the only composer to put Wagner's methods to original use was Richard Strauss, whose *Salome* and *Elektra* combine the methods of the music drama with an interest in perverse characterization. After reaching the utmost threshold of tonality with *Elektra*, Strauss turned back to create the imperishable *Der Rosenkavalier*, and never returned to atonality.

All Strauss's songs are influenced by the poets' ethos or by the singers for whom they were intended and only occasionally did he nod deferentially towards Wagner. Wolf, the composer of more than 600 skilfully fashioned lieder, was devoted to Wagner, but imbued many of his songs with an ironic quality that reflects the growing distance between the sensitive artist and the interests of Prussian-led Germany. The symphonies and song cycles of Mahler, director of the Vienna State Opera between 1897 and 1907, similarly show the increasing alienation of the despised minorities (he was Jewish-born) from the 'master race'. They also show a constant awareness of the imperfection and the fleeting nature of existence, derived from Schopenhauer's philosophy as revealed in *Tristan*.

Only the Austrian Bruckner managed to preserve some of the confidence of the Wagnerian manner in his symphonies and church music, the latter retrospective in outlook and using a contrapuntal style influenced by the now very active Cecilian Movement. By the first decade of the 20th century the real progressives, Debussy and Skryabin, were working outside Germany, whose position as a musical haven was dependent on the widespread concert life, the opera houses, and the educational institutions. The nationalism of the later 19th century is reflected in the printed editions of past German composers such as Bach, Handel, Schütz, and many others in the series *Denkmäler deutscher Tonkunst* and *Denkmäler der Tonkunst in Österreich*. The publications of Ambros and Riemann were more internationally minded and still provide the framework of music history as we know it today.

7. Since 1914

Germany's position as the centre of musical activity in Europe was seriously affected by World War I. The main musical institutions suffered little physical hardship, but the ignominy of defeat and the end of Prussian control, as well as damage to the old style of concert life in central and southern Germany, was hard to bear. Austria was reduced to a small strip of mainly mountainous country with only Vienna capable of sustaining large-scale artistic institutions.

There were different reactions in different places. Austria's traditional conservatism was reflected in the Salzburg Festival, founded in 1920 (with the first concert series given in 1921) by Max Reinhardt, Richard Strauss, and Strauss's librettist Hugo von Hofmannsthal. The departure of the Hohenzollerns from Berlin, on the other hand, gave the Kaiser's old city a new liveliness. Berlin's three serious opera companies were the Staatsoper, directed by Max von Schillings; its subsidiary the Kroll Oper under Klemperer; and the Städtische Oper with its music director Bruno Walter. The adventurous Kroll included much contemporary music, with works by Weill and Hindemith, but it was too advanced for general comfort and became part of the Staatsoper company. Social commitment was to be found in a group of composers working in Vienna, led by Schoenberg with his pupils Berg and Webern. Schoenberg and Berg extended late Romanticism into

*Expressionism. Berg's two operas, *Wozzeck* and *Lulu*, were in the tradition of early Strauss, but with a distinctive social awareness.

In 1930, Hitlerite students demonstrated against Weill's opera *Aufstieg und Fall der Stadt Mahagonny* at Leipzig because of the composer's Jewish 'impurity'. With the onset of Nazi rule in 1933, such incidents became more frequent; Jewish artists were dismissed from official positions and Nazi anti-intellectualism resulted in the banning of all music by Jewish composers. By 1935 many Jewish instrumentalists, now not allowed even to play in orchestras, had fled abroad. By 1938, with the *Anschluss* (takeover) of Austria, it was almost too late to obtain an exit visa. Among distinguished composers, only Strauss and Orff stayed put; Furtwängler and Knappertsbusch were among the older generation of conductors who remained. In a few years, Germany's vigorous musical life had been destroyed, leaving only the nationalist haven of Bayreuth and the major opera companies intact, but with increasing Gestapo surveillance everywhere. World War II completed this process, even though those opera houses which still stood continued to function until 1944, when all artistic enterprises were banned in the atmosphere of all-out war. The historic and lovely houses at Munich, Vienna, and Dresden were among those destroyed, the Berlin Staatsoper was twice bombed and once rebuilt, while most of the famous old music-publishing and printing works had been obliterated.

Rapid revival after the war owes as much to musical tradition as to the regionalism of German life, divided between West and East, with the capitals of both Austria and Germany occupied by American, British, and French allies on one side and Communists on the other. Theatres and orchestras were soon re-established in most West German cities. Even in its postwar poverty Austria signalled its commitment to music, one of its first public acts being to lay plans for rebuilding the Vienna State Opera. Bayreuth escaped almost unscathed but was used by American troops and abused by refugees. Wagner's two grandsons controlled the first postwar festival in 1951 at which Furtwängler conducted the opening concert and Knappertsbusch and Karajan directed the opera performances.

The Salzburg Festivals, by contrast, had never stopped and were given every encouragement to resume, under American patronage, only three months after the Nazi surrender in August 1945. Salzburg has been followed by more specialized festivals, such as the Ansbach Bach Week and the contemporary music festival at Donaueschingen. Early music has flourished, encouraged by the growth of musicology and by the interest of recording and television companies. Today in comparatively small cities (e.g. Kassel), where the old

tradition of patronage was well established, opera houses are large, well equipped, and intent on producing the most complex works. In the larger cities of Hamburg, Munich, Stuttgart, and Vienna some of the most lavish opera productions still take place. The Berlin Philharmonic is still considered by many to be the world's finest orchestra.

The effect of the exodus of artists during the 1930s has been more difficult to reverse. Few intellectuals returned from England and the USA where they taught the next generation of composers and scholars. These countries have exported some of their own singers and instrumentalists to German opera houses and orchestras. Stockhausen was the first major composer of the postwar period. Although he sought his point of departure in electronic music in France, his musical aims and attitudes are nevertheless very 'German'. Other German composers whose music has been performed internationally include Henze, Zimmermann, and Rihm.

Any summary of German musical achievement must first stress its essentially religious approach. Denied the Renaissance, Germany made the Enlightenment a continuation of Protestant aims and beliefs, and in the Romantic era made art itself a religion. Stockhausen has turned to Eastern philosophy, but maintains the serious approach. Secondly, German music at its height has generally tended to the abstract and the logical: fugue, symphonic form, and the doctrine of affections are notably German, as is the number-symbolism of the late Baroque. In opera, it has been the philosophic rather than the personal that has inspired composers, notably Beethoven, Wagner, and even Richard Strauss, although he was more concerned with the individual than were the others. South German and Austrian composers, particularly Mozart and Schubert, have generally been more personal and capable of a lighter touch, possibly through the influence of Italian artists.   DA/AJ

📖 B. Hosler, *Changing Aesthetic Views of Instrumental Music in 18th-Century Germany* (Ann Arbor, MI, 1981) · T. Baumann, *North German Opera in the Age of Goethe* (Cambridge, 1985) · D. Parr and P. Walker, *German Sacred Polyphonic Vocal Music between Schütz and Bach* (Warren, MI, 1992) · J. Daverio, *Nineteenth-Century Music and the German Romantic Ideology* (New York, 1993) · G. Webber, *North German Church Music in the Age of Buxtehude* (Oxford, 1996) · D. Wyn Jones (ed.), *Music in Eighteenth-Century Austria* (Cambridge, 1996) · M. H. Kater, *The Twisted Muse: Musicians and their Music in the Third Reich* (New York, 1997); *Composers of the Nazi Era* (New York, 2000)

Gershwin, George [Gershvin, Jacob] (*b* Brooklyn, New York, 26 Sept. 1898; *d* Hollywood, CA, 11 July 1937).

American composer. He studied the piano from 1912 with Charles Hambitzer and had lessons in theory and composition from Henry Cowell and Joseph Schillinger, among others. These lessons, however, came only after he had begun to make a reputation as a composer of popular music. In 1916 he started work as a song plugger (house pianist) for Jerome Remick's publishing company and had a song of his own published, *When you Want 'em you Can't Get 'em*. Swanee, sung by Al Jolson in a Broadway musical, was his first hit, and in 1919 he wrote a score for an entire show of his own, *La, La, Lucille*. Another show, *Blue Monday*, gained him a commission from Paul Whiteman's band, resulting in the one-movement piano concerto *Rhapsody in Blue* (1924). That year he began working with his brother Ira as his lyricist: their first show, *Lady Be Good*, included 'Fascinatin' Rhythm' as well as the title song and was followed by a series of Broadway successes, among them *Tip-Toes*, *Oh Kay!*, *Strike Up the Band*, *Funny Face*, *Girl Crazy*, and *Of Thee I Sing*.

Following common Broadway practice, these shows were orchestrated by others, as was *Rhapsody in Blue* in its versions for band and symphony orchestra. But Gershwin was eager to master classical techniques and establish himself as a composer of concert music, a dual process he began in the Piano Concerto in F (1925) and the tone-poem *An American in Paris* (1928), the latter written after a visit during which he had sought, but not received, tuition from Ravel. In 1930 he and Ira moved to Hollywood, where they worked on the film of *Girl Crazy* and also on *Shall We Dance?*, with Fred Astaire and Ginger Rogers. Continuing his quest to create an American contribution to the classical tradition, he also produced the opera *Porgy and Bess* (New York, 1935), which was his biggest achievement and among his last. This, like the concert pieces, depends largely on the genius for melody that sparked his songs and was, indeed, unrivalled, even in that golden age of songwriting. In the many numbers the Gershwin brothers wrote together (e.g. *Someone to Watch Over Me*, *Let's Call the Whole Thing Off*, *Our Love is Here to Stay*, *I Got Rhythm*), Ira's verbal sophistication is matched by George's musical ingenuity and the distinctive subtlety he brought to the jazz style of the interwar American musical theatre.   PG

📖 I. GERSHWIN, *Lyrics on Several Occasions* (New York, 1959) · R. GREENBERG, *George Gershwin* (London, 1998)

Gervaise, Claude (*fl* Paris, 1540–60). French composer and arranger. He made popular arrangements of dance tunes for Pierre Attaingnant, and composed one book of these *Danceries* himself (Poulenc made use of them in his *Suite française*, 1935).   DA

Ges (Ger.). The note G♭; *Geses*, the note G♭♭.

Gesamtausgabe (Ger.). A 'collected edition' of the complete works of a single composer. See EDITIONS, HISTORICAL AND CRITICAL.

Gesamtkunstwerk (Ger., 'total work of art'). Although the ideal of an art form unifying music, poetry, and painting is as old as opera, and particularly absorbed German composers and writers from the mid-17th century, the term is associated with Wagner. It was formulated in his essay *Das Kunstwerk der Zukunft* ('The Art-Work of the Future', 1849), where, in the course of his argument about the ideal unification of the arts in the theatre, he makes his sole use of the term 'Gesamtkunstwerk der Zukunft', also referring to the projected drama as 'das künstlerische Gesamtwerk'. The essence of his idea was that the 'three purely human arts' (music, poetry, and dance) should be united with 'the ancillary aids of drama' (architecture, sculpture, and painting), not merely in association but in a single expressive aim.   JW

Gesang (Ger., 'song'). See LIED.

Gesang der Jünglinge ('Song of the Young Boys'). Electronic work (1955–6) by Stockhausen in which a boy's voice, speaking and singing the *Benedicite*, is transformed, multiplied, and combined with electronic sounds; it is played by five spatially separated loudspeaker groups.

gesangvoll (Ger.). 'Songlike'.

Geschöpfe des Prometheus, Die ('The Creatures of Prometheus'). Ballet in an overture, introduction, and 16 numbers by Beethoven, choreographed by Salvatore Viganò (Vienna, 1801). Beethoven used two themes from the finale in other works: one in G major is no. 11 of his *12 contredanses* for orchestra (1802); another in E♭ is used in no. 7 of the *Contredanses*, as the theme of the 'Eroica' Variations, and in the finale of the 'Eroica' Symphony. The overture is often performed as a concert item.

geschwind (Ger.). 'Quick', 'agile'.

Gesellschaft der Musikfreunde. A concert society formed in Vienna in 1812. See CONCERT, 2.

Gesellschaftslied (Ger., 'society song'). A song originating among the middle classes of Renaissance society, as opposed to *Hoflied* (a court or aristocratic song) or *Volkslied* (a folksong). It applies especially to the German polyphonic songs of such composers as Senfl and Hofhaimer.

gesteigert (Ger.). 'Increased', i.e. *crescendo*.

gestopft (Ger.). 'Stopped': in horn-playing, notes produced when the bell of the instrument is more or less completely closed by the player's fist; the term is sometimes used interchangeably with *gedämpft*.

Gesualdo, Carlo, Prince of Venosa (*b* ?Naples, *c*.1561; *d* Gesualdo, Avellino, 8 Sept. 1613). Italian madrigal composer. He was of noble birth and inherited the principality of Venosa on his father's death in 1586. In the same year he married his cousin, Maria d'Avalos, but four years later had her and her lover assassinated. He then retired to his estate at Gesualdo. In 1593 he began negotiations to marry the niece of Alfonso d'Este, Duke of Ferrara and a notable patron of music. He travelled to Ferrara to wed Lucrezia d'Este the following year, but the marriage was not a success, and in his last years he suffered from a pathological masochistic melancholia.

Gesualdo's links with Ferrara brought him into association with Luzzasco Luzzaschi, Alfonso Fontanelli, and other composers who were experimenting with chromaticism. In his own six books of five-voice madrigals he took chromatic harmony to extremes, often creating striking dissonances. More startling, his manic-depressive nature is expressed by sudden changes of tempo, juxtaposing passages in semiquavers with slow-moving minims and semibreves. His texts are frequently erotic, and the emotional meaning of each phrase is conveyed with maximum intensity. These works achieved some fame, and after his death they were published together in 1613 as one of the earliest printed full scores (and one of the earliest collected editions). Gesualdo also wrote church music, in a style only marginally more restrained than that of his madrigals. His eventful life has attracted much attention: Stravinsky, for example, was fascinated by his music, and orchestrated and completed some of his works. DA/TC

    📖 G. E. WATKINS, *Gesualdo: The Man and his Music* (London, 1973) · D. ARNOLD, *Gesualdo* (London, 1984)

geteilt (Ger.). 'Divided': the same as *divisi*; it is sometimes abbreviated to *get*.

getragen (Ger.). 'Solemn', 'slow'.

Gewandhaus. Concert hall in Leipzig. Formerly a drapers' hall, from which it took its name, in 1781 it became the venue for annual concerts which had been held in a private house since 1743, during the time when Bach was Kantor of the Thomasschule. A new building with excellent acoustics was opened in 1884. JBo

gewöhnlich (Ger.). 'Usual', 'normal': it is used to countermand a previous instruction that an instrument should be played in an unusual way, e.g. bowing on the fingerboard of a stringed instrument.

Ghedini, Giorgio Federico (*b* Cuneo, 11 July 1892; *d* Nervi, nr Genoa, 25 March 1965). Italian composer and teacher. He studied at the Turin Conservatory (piano, organ, cello, composition), then at the Liceo Musicale in Bologna (composition, with Bossi, graduating in 1911), but learnt as much as an autodidact, from examining scores by earlier Italian composers including Frescobaldi, Monteverdi, and Vivaldi. His teaching—at his alma mater in Turin (1918–37) and at the conservatories in Parma (1938–41) and Milan (from 1941), where he became director (1951–62)—sought to infuse the best of the past into current practice; his own musical language, not surprisingly, was essentially neoclassical, in the Busonian sense of 'new classicality', though he later began to embrace more modern techniques.

Ghedini was a productive composer, writing seven operas (one of them after Herman Melville's *Billy Budd*), and a generous quantity of orchestral, chamber, and choral music. Many of his orchestral pieces are concertante (16 out of 25 scores), a series that begins with his Concerto Grosso for wind quintet and strings (1927) and *Pezzo concertante* for two violins, viola, and orchestra (1931) and ends with *Contrappunti* for violin, viola, cello, and strings and *Musica concertante* for cello and strings (both 1962); among his purely orchestral works, there is a single symphony (1938). His breakthrough came only after 1941, with the success of his *Architetture* for orchestra (1940). When 20th-century Italian orchestral music after Respighi attracts the attention it deserves, Ghedini will be seen to be one of its most important figures. MA

Gherardello da Firenze [Niccolò de Francesco] (*b c*.1320–5; *d* Florence, 1362 or 1363). Florentine composer. He was an ordained priest, and served at several churches in Florence. During his lifetime he was best known for his liturgical works, but of these only two mass movements have survived. He also wrote madrigals, *ballate*, and a *caccia*. DA/JM

ghichak. A three-string spike fiddle of Central Asia, with a bowl resonator and a skin belly.

Ghiselin [Verbonnet], **Johannes** (*fl* early 16th century). Flemish composer. He is first recorded in 1491 at the court of Ercole I d'Este, Duke of Ferrara, and he served at the French court some ten years later, coming into contact with Josquin. His works include a set of masses published by Petrucci (Venice, 1503), as well as many motets and chansons. JM

Ghizeghem, Hayne van. See HAYNE VAN GHIZEGHEM.

Ghosts of Versailles, The. Opera in two acts by Corigliano to a libretto by William M. Hoffman after Beaumarchais's play *La Mère coupable* (1792) (New York, 1991).

'Ghost' Trio (*Geistertrio*). Nickname of Beethoven's Piano Trio in D major op. 70 no. 1 (1808), so called because of the atmosphere of the slow movement which includes 'mysterious' chromatic chords and tremolos.

Giacetto de Berchem. See BERCHEM, JACQUET DE.

Gianni Schicchi. Opera in one act by Puccini to a libretto by Giovacchino Forzano after a passage from Dante Alighieri's narrative poem *Commedia* part 1: 'Inferno' (*c*.1307–21), the third part of Puccini's *Il trittico* (New York, 1918).

'Giant' Fugue. Nickname of J. S. Bach's organ chorale *Wir gläuben all an einen Gott* BWV680, from part 3 of the *Clavier-Übung*, so called because of the giant strides of the bass figure played on the pedals.

Giardini, Felice (de) (*b* Turin, 12 April 1716; *d* Moscow, 8 June 1796). Italian violinist and composer. A choirboy at Milan Cathedral, he studied the violin with G. B. Somis in Turin and by the age of 12 was playing in an opera orchestra in Rome. Later in Naples he became a leader of the Teatro S. Carlo orchestra, gaining a reputation for embellishments and cadenzas. In 1748 he began an extended concert tour which took him in 1750 to England. He was involved in many London concert series, directed the Italian Opera at the King's Theatre, contributed to various English stage works, and led the orchestra for the Three Choirs Festival, 1770–6. He returned to Naples in 1784 but went back to London in 1790 to direct the opera at the Little Theatre in the Haymarket. Having little success he set out on his travels again, dying in poverty shortly after leaving St Petersburg. He wrote three operas, the oratorio *Ruth* (with Avison), and much chamber music.

DA

Gibbons, Christopher (*b* Westminster, *bapt.* 22 Aug. 1615; *d* Westminster, 20 Oct. 1676). English organist and composer, son of Orlando Gibbons. He was probably a chorister at the Chapel Royal, and briefly served as organist of Winchester Cathedral. During the Civil War he made a living as a player and teacher of the organ; following the Restoration he held positions at Westminster Abbey and the Chapel Royal. Although principally a performer, he also composed anthems and music for instrumental consort.

JM

Gibbons, Orlando (*b* Oxford, *bapt.* 25 Dec. 1583; *d* Canterbury, 5 June 1625). English keyboard player and composer. He was the youngest child of William Gibbons, a musician who had been a member of the Cambridge waits. In 1596 he became a chorister at King's College, Cambridge, and he took the Cambridge degree of Mus.B. in 1606. From 1603 he was a member of the Chapel Royal, and served as organist there (jointly with Thomas Tomkins) possibly from 1605, certainly from 1615 until the end of his life. In 1606 he married Elizabeth Patten; they lived in Westminster. He was well connected in court circles and in 1619 was appointed 'one of his Majesty's musicians for the virginelles to attend in his Highness' privy chamber'. In 1623 he became joint organist and Master of the Choristers (with Thomas Day) at Westminster Abbey; he took part in James I's funeral in March 1625. He died of a brain haemorrhage during preparations for the reception into England of Charles I's royal bride, Henrietta Maria.

Gibbons was one of the most versatile composers of his generation. He was a serious madrigalist, shunning the frivolous pastoral style of the Italian-influenced Morley and Weelkes in favour of a moralizing, strictly contrapuntal manner in the tradition of Byrd and the consort song; his setting of *The Silver Swan*, for instance, is a lament for modern life in which 'More geese than swans now live, more fools than wise'. His sacred music was written either for the Anglican Church or for occasions of state; his best work is found in such large-scale pieces as the anthems *Hosanna to the son of David* and *O clap your hands together*, yet even his most modest works are perfectly shaped and finely expressive. His contrapuntal skills are particularly evident in his pieces for viol consort. Above all, however, Gibbons was celebrated during his lifetime as an organist and virginalist. His keyboard works use virtuosity for expressive ends, not for its own sake, and they often have considerable emotional power. The best known of them is *The Lord of Salisbury, his Pavan and Galliard*, first published in *Parthenia* (London, 1613).

DA/JM

  📖 J. HARLEY, *Orlando Gibbons and the Gibbons Family of Musicians* (Aldershot, 1995)

Gibbs, Cecil Armstrong (*b* Great Baddow, 10 Aug. 1889; *d* Chelmsford, 12 May 1960). English composer. Enjoying a private income from the family toothpaste business, he studied music at Cambridge with Dent and Charles Wood. After a period as a schoolteacher (1915–19) he worked with Vaughan Williams at the RCM, where he later taught (1921–39). Among his large-scale works are three orchestral symphonies, a choral symphony *Odysseus*, six string quartets, many works for chorus and orchestra, incidental music for plays, comic operas, and much *Gebrauchsmusik*. His reputation, however, has rested essentially on his songs, notably his many settings of Walter de la Mare (such as the exquisite *Silver* and the songs from his music to de la Mare's children's play *Crossings* of 1919).   JDı

Gigli, Beniamino (*b* Recanati, 20 March 1890; *d* Rome, 30 Nov. 1957). Italian tenor. He took lessons in Rome with Agnese Bonucci and won a scholarship to the Liceo Musicale, where he studied with Antonio Cotogni and Enrico Rosati. After winning an international competition in Parma in 1914, he made his debut in Ponchielli's *La Gioconda* at Rovigo and the following year won acclaim for the ardour and beauty of his Faust in Boito's *Mefistofele* in Bologna. Repeating the part at La Scala, Milan, in 1918 and at the Metropolitan Opera, New York, for his debut there in 1920, brought him international fame.

For over 30 years Gigli enjoyed celebrity status in predominantly lyrical parts, such as the principal tenor roles in *La bohème*, *La Gioconda*, *Rigoletto*, *L'Africaine*, *Andrea Chénier*, and *Tosca*. He was especially lauded at Covent Garden in the 1930s. In spite of an association with Mussolini, he made a triumphant return to Rome as Cavaradossi in 1945 and to London as Rodolfo in 1946. The strength and beauty of his mellifluous voice and his perfect intonation made him one of the most popular of all 20th-century artists, and a successor to Caruso.   JT

Gigout, Eugène (*b* Nancy, 23 March 1844; *d* Paris, 9 Dec. 1925). French composer and organist. He studied at the École Niedermeyer in Paris with Saint-Saëns and Clément Loret, and was subsequently appointed professor of organ and composition there; his pupils included Fauré, André Messager, and Léon Boëllmann. From 1863 until his death he was organist at St Augustin. A distinguished teacher, he succeeded Alexandre Guilmant in 1911 as organ professor at the Paris Conservatoire. He wrote a great deal of organ music, including *Poèmes mystiques* (1893), *Album grégorien* (1895), and *Cent pièces nouvelles* (1922). But little of this is played today, apart from the Toccata, composed in the conventional French style.   WT/AT

gigue (Fr., 'jig'; It.: *giga*). A dance of British origin (see JIG), imported into France in the mid-17th century; as an instrumental form the French gigue was one of the four standard movements of the Baroque *suite.

Two distinct styles of the dance emerged during the 17th century: the French gigue and the Italian *giga*. The former was typically in triple or compound duple metre, moderate to quick time, and with predominantly dotted rhythms—rather more elegant than its British forebear. The dance was popular with lutenists: later in the century it appeared in the harpsichord suites of such composers as Lebègue and D'Anglebert, and it is also found in the stage works of Lully and his contem-

poraries. Some 18th-century French composers (e.g. D'Anglebert, François Couperin, and Rameau) used only this French version, but others (e.g. Leclair and Mondonville) adopted the Italian *giga* too.

The Italian *giga* was nearly always in 12/8 time, much quicker and less contrapuntal than its French cousin. There are examples in the solo and trio sonatas of G. B. Vitali, Corelli, Geminiani, and Tartini among others. In Germany, the French version was the first to appear and from the late 1660s onwards was commonly used as the last movement of keyboard suites. Bach and Handel used both the French and the Italian forms.

The dance fell out of use in the Classical period, but instances of its influence can be seen in the late 18th and early 19th centuries, for example in the finale of Haydn's 'Military' Symphony, no. 100. The title appeared occasionally in the 20th century, for example in the first of Debussy's three orchestral *Images*.   —/JBE

Gilbert, Anthony (*b* London, 26 July 1934). He studied in London with Mátyás Seiber, Anthony Milner, and Alexander Goehr, and taught in London, Lancaster, and Australia before moving to the RNCM, where he became head of composition. His early works, such as *Nine or Ten Osannas* for five instruments (1967), have a bold, even brash quality typical of British composers of the generation of Maxwell Davies and Birtwistle. During and after the 1970s Gilbert's music became less abrasive, reflecting an interest in Indian rhythmic structures (*Towards Asavari*, 1978) and finding room for a more lyrical tone.   PG/AW

Gilbert, Henry F(ranklin Belknap) (*b* Somerville, MA, 26 Sept. 1868; *d* Cambridge, MA, 19 May 1928). American composer. He studied at the New England Conservatory (1886–7) and with Edward MacDowell (1889–92), but did not devote himself to composition until after seeing Charpentier's *Louise* in 1901. He then departed from the German-impressionist mainstream of New England music to use spirituals, ragtime, and Amerindian music in his compositions, which include orchestral works (*Comedy Overture on Negro Themes*, c.1906; *The Dance in Place Congo*, c.1908), piano pieces, and songs.   PG

Gilbert, Sir W(illiam) **S**(chwenck) (*b* London, 18 Nov. 1836; *d* Harrow Weald, London, 29 May 1911). English dramatist and librettist. After unsuccessful careers as a government clerk and barrister he turned to writing in the early 1860s as a contributor to the comic journal *Fun* and soon afterwards as a playwright. By 1871 he had become extremely productive (with the premieres of no fewer than seven plays) and worked with Sullivan for the first time on *Thespis*. Two further collaborations, *Trial by Jury* (1875) and *The Sorcerer* (1877), were modest successes, but it was the commercial windfalls brought by *HMS Pinafore* (1878) and *The Pirates of Penzance* (1879) that induced Gilbert to abandon serious drama in favour of satirical comedy. Of his 11 premieres in the 1880s, seven had music by Sullivan. After *The Gondoliers* (1889) the partnership dissolved amid animosity, bitterness, and the law courts; though the two worked together again on *Utopia Limited* (1893) and *The Grand Duke* (1896), the old creative fire had been extinguished. Gilbert went on to collaborate with Alfred Cellier and Edward German among others, and continued to write plays until the year of his death, notably *The Hooligan*, in which his deeply entrenched iconoclasm was rekindled. He was knighted in 1907.   JD1

Gilels, Emil (Grigor'yevich) (*b* Odessa, 19 Oct. 1916; *d* Moscow, 14 Oct. 1985). Russian pianist. A prizewinner in competitions in the USSR and Europe during the 1930s, he did not appear professionally outside Russia until 1947 (1955 in the USA). Gifted with a flawless technique and considerable power, he could also produce the most delicate of touches in his thoughtful and considered interpretations of the widest repertory from Bach to Bartók and the music of his Russian contemporaries.   CF

Giles, Nathaniel (*b* in or nr Worcester, *c*.1558; *d* Windsor, 24 Jan. 1634). English composer, organist, and choirmaster. His career, after early years at Worcester Cathedral, was spent at St George's Chapel, Windsor. He was also a Gentleman of the Chapel Royal, and played an active part in organizing choirboy plays at the Blackfriars Theatre, London. He received the B.Mus. from Oxford in 1585 and was awarded a doctorate in 1622. His works include many verse anthems, as well as services and a few Latin motets.   JM

gimel. See GYMEL.

Ginastera, Alberto (Evaristo) (*b* Buenos Aires, 11 April 1916; *d* Geneva, 25 June 1983). Argentine composer. He studied at the National Conservatory in Buenos Aires (1936–8), where apart from a period of exile in New York (1945–7) he lived as an influential composer and teacher. His earlier works, including the seminal ballet *Estancia* (1941) and the Piano Sonata (1952), use elements of folk music. Later these were fused into a vigorous and colourful style, drawing on Schoenbergian serialism, Bartók, and other modern masters. The main works of the second period are the *Cantata para América mágica* for voice and percussion orchestra (1960), the First Piano Concerto (1961), and the Violin Concerto (1963). Ginastera's three operas, *Don Rodrigo* (Buenos Aires, 1964), *Bomarzo* (Washington, 1967), and *Beatrix Cenci* (Washington, 1971), exploit perverse and violent emotions. *Bomarzo* was described by the *Neue*

Zeitschrift für Musik as 'Porno in Belcanto', which neatly summarizes its lyrical power as well as its sensationalism.   PG/CW

📖 P. SUÁREZ URTUBEY, *Alberto Ginastera* (Buenos Aires, 1967)

Gioconda, La ('The Joyful Girl'). Opera in four acts by Ponchielli to a libretto by 'Tobia Gorrio' (Arrigo Boito) after Victor Hugo's play *Angélo, tyran de Padoue* (1835) (Milan, 1876); the third act includes the Dance of the Hours.

giocoso (It.). 'Playful', 'humorous'.

Gioielli della Madonna, I (*Der Schmuck der Madonna*; 'The Jewels of the Madonna'). Opera in three acts by Wolf-Ferrari to a libretto by Carlo Zangarini and Enrico Golisciani (Berlin, 1911); the text was revised in 1933.

gioioso (It.). 'Joyfully'.

Giordani, Tommaso (*b* Naples, *c*.1730–3; *d* Dublin, Feb. 1806). Italian composer. He toured with his father's opera company and presented six operas in Dublin. In 1768 he moved to London where he remained for 15 years, composing, adapting, and conducting operas at the King's Theatre and writing other vocal and instrumental works in the *galant* style. He returned to Dublin, continued to compose, and opened the shortlived English Opera House before becoming musical director of the Theatre Royal, Crow Street (1788).   SH

Giordano, Umberto (Menotti Maria) (*b* Foggia, 28 Aug. 1867; *d* Milan, 12 Nov. 1948). Italian composer. He studied at the Naples Conservatory, and in 1899, while still a student, won sixth prize in a one-act opera competition sponsored by the publisher Sonzogno (the winner was Mascagni's *Cavalleria rusticana*). This led to further commissions, among which the most successful was *Andrea Chénier* (1896), one of the few verismo operas to remain in the repertory (chiefly as a vehicle for star tenors). Several further operas now find occasional revival, including *Fedora* (Milan, 1898, on a play by Victorien Sardou) and *Siberia* (La Scala, Milan, 1903). *Andrea Chénier* and *Siberia* had librettos by Luigi Illica, the co-librettist of Puccini's greatest successes of about the same period. Giordano's later operas were less well received, though *La cena delle beffe* (La Scala, 1924) is still sometimes seen.   RP

Giorno di regno, Un ('King for a Day'). Opera in two acts by Verdi to a libretto by Felice Romani (probably revised by Temistocle Solera) from his libretto for Gyrowetz's *Il finto Stanislao* (1818) after Alexandre

Vincent Pineu-Duval's play *Le Faux Stanislas* (1808) (Milan, 1840).

Giovanna d'Arco ('Joan of Arc'). Opera in a prologue and three acts by Verdi to a libretto by Temistocle Solera partly after Friedrich von Schiller's play *Die Jungfrau von Orleans* (1801) (Milan, 1845).

Giovannelli [Giovanelli], **Ruggiero** (*b* Velletri, nr Rome, *c*.1560; *d* Rome, 7 Jan. 1625). Italian composer. He became *maestro di cappella* at the Cappella Giulia on the death of Palestrina, and then moved to the Cappella Sistina; he was also much in demand from other Roman institutions and patrons. He wrote church music, some in the style of Palestrina and some more modern in approach, as well as several volumes of attractive madrigals.   DA

Giovanni da Cascia [Giovanni da Firenze] (*fl* northern Italy, 1340–50). Italian composer. He was organist of Santa Trinità, Florence, and was also associated with the courts of Milan and Verona. He was one of the earliest known Italian composers. Some 20 works by him have survived; they are cast in the typical forms of the day, the two-voice madrigal and the *caccia*.   JM

Giovanni da Firenze. See GIOVANNI DA CASCIA.

Gipsy Baron, The. See ZIGEUNERBARON, DER.

Girl of the Golden West, The. See FANCIULLA DEL WEST, LA.

Giroust, François (*b* Paris, 10 April 1737; *d* Versailles, 28 April 1799). French composer. He was appointed *maître de musique* of Orléans Cathedral in 1756 and of the Saints Innocents in Paris 13 years later. In 1775 he entered the royal chapel at Versailles, writing a *Missa brevis* for Louis XVI's coronation. He was *surintendant* of the king's music, 1785–92, but during the Revolution he suppressed his royalist loyalties and wrote revolutionary songs and choruses. His sacred works include over 70 motets, six masses, a Requiem, and four oratorios.   WT

Gis (Ger.). The note G♯; *Gisis*, the note G𝄪.

Giselle, ou Les Wilis ('Giselle, or The Wilis'). Ballet in two acts by Adam to a scenario by Jules-Henri Vernoy de Saint-Georges and Théophile Gautier after a story by Heinrich Heine; it was choreographed by Jean Coralli and Jules Perrot (Paris, 1841); modern productions are based on Petipa's last St Petersburg production of 1884. The Wilis are the ghosts of girls who die before their intended marriages.

gitano, gitana (It., Sp.). 'Gypsy'; *alla gitana*, 'in Gypsy style'.

gittern. A medieval plucked string instrument. Seen from the front it resembled a small lute but with no clear division between the body and neck, both being carved (like the *rebec) from a single piece of wood; some examples may have had a rounded back (side views are seldom seen). An ancestral link with the later *mandolin is possible. The identity of the gittern has often been confused with that of the *citole.

The early four-course *guitar was also known as 'gittern' (*guiterne, gyttron,* etc.) in France and in Elizabethan and Stuart England.   JMo

📖 L. WRIGHT, 'The medieval gittern and citole: A case of mistaken identity', *Galpin Society Journal*, 30 (1977), 8–42

giù (It.). 'Down'; e.g. *arcata in giù*, 'down-bow'.

Giuliani, Mauro (Giuseppe Sergio Pantaleo) (*b* Bisceglie, nr Bari, 27 July 1781; *d* Naples, 8 May 1829). Italian singer, guitarist, and composer. From 1806 to 1819 he taught and played the guitar in Vienna, later making concert tours abroad. The greatest guitarist of his day, he also wrote a great deal of guitar music.   WT

Giulio Cesare (*Giulio Cesare in Egitto*; 'Julius Caesar in Egypt'). Opera in three acts by Handel to a libretto by Nicola Francesco Haym adapted from Giacomo Francesco Bussani's *Giulio Cesare in Egitto* (1677) and a later version of the same libretto (1685) (London, 1724).

giustiniana (It.). A term derived from the name of the poet Leonardo Giustiniani. In the 15th century it was applied to songs setting texts by or ascribed to him, some of the earliest polyphonic examples being by Ciconia. Other settings (labelled 'justiniane') are found in Ottaviano Petrucci's sixth book of *Frottole* (Venice, 1506). In the 16th century the term was applied to a popular, comic type of villanella or *canzone napolitana*; Andrea Gabrieli's *Greghesche et iustiniane* for three voices (1571) are typical. See also VILLANELLA.   EW

Giustiniani [Giustinian], **Leonardo** (*b* Venice, *c*.1383; *d* Venice, 10 Nov. 1446). Italian statesman and poet. A number of poems by or attributed to him survive with music; they include devotional *laude* and lyric verses. His more extended poems may also have been performed by solo voice with lute accompaniment, but in an unwritten tradition that has left no trace in music notation.   JM

Giustino ('Justin'). Opera in three acts by Handel to a libretto adapted anonymously from Pietro Pariati's *Giustino* (1711) as revised for Vivaldi (1724), after Nicolò Beregan's *Il Giustino* (1683) (London, 1737).

giusto (It.). 'Just', 'exact'; *tempo giusto*, either the usual tempo for the type of music in question, or the return to a regular tempo after a passage of flexible tempo.

Glagolitic Mass (*Glagolská mše*; *Mša glagolskaja*). Cantata (1926) by Janáček for soprano, alto, tenor, and bass soloists, chorus, orchestra, and organ, a setting of an old Slavonic church text adapted by Miloš Weingart.

glam rock [glitter rock]. A theatrical and gender-bending style of rock and pop presentation (of a certain 'glamour') rather than a musical style; it is sometimes seen as an expression of dissatisfaction with the macho image of heavy rock (though not necessarily less 'heavy' in musical content), and also as prefiguring the presentational style of *punk. Associated with glam are the New York Dolls, T. Rex, Slade, Sweet, Gary Glitter, Roxy Music, and David Bowie. Bowie consciously used image subversively as part of his work and experimented with make-up and cross-dressing.   PW

Glanert, Detlev (*b* Hamburg, 6 Sept. 1960). German composer. He studied composition from the age of 12; his principal teacher was Henze. In 1987 he settled in Berlin. Many of his works are commentaries on the music of the past: he has said that 'a symphony of today can only be a discussion of the symphonies of yesterday'. A strong dramatic sense animates his orchestral and chamber music, as well as his operas *Leyla und Medjnun* (Munich, 1988), a 'musical fairy tale' with a Turkish setting, *Der Spiegel des grossen Kaisers* ('Mirror of the Great Emperor'; Mannheim, 1995), *Joseph Süss* (Bremen, 1999), and *Scherz, Satire, Ironie und tiefere Bedeutung* ('Jest, Satire, Irony, and Deeper Meaning'; Halle, 2001).   ABur

Glanville-Hicks, Peggy (*b* Melbourne, 29 Dec. 1912; *d* Sydney, 25 June 1990). Australian composer. She studied with Fritz Hart at the Melbourne Conservatorium and later at the RCM (1931–5) with Vaughan Williams (composition), Arthur Benjamin (piano), Lambert, and Sargent (conducting). She also worked with Wellesz in Vienna and Boulanger in Paris. She began to develop her reputation as a composer with the *Three Gymnopedie* (1934) and the *Choral Suite* (1938); the latter was given at the London ISCM Festival under Adrian Boult. Between 1948 and 1959 she lived in the USA where in addition to composing she was an influential journalist. *Letters from Morocco* (1952), the *Sinfonia da Pacifica* (1953), and her first opera *The Transposed Heads* (1953) show a penchant for orientalism, a preoccupation that persisted after she settled in Athens in 1953. Her interest in Aegean demotic music and the folklore of East Asia is evident in her operas *Nausicaa* (1961) and *Sappho* (1965). She also produced orchestral works and ballet scores.   JDi

📖 D. Hayes, *Peggy Glanville-Hicks: A Bio-Bibliography* (Westport, CT, 1990) · W. Beckett, *Peggy Glanville-Hicks* (Sydney, 1992)

glänzend (Ger.). 'Brilliant'.

Glarean, Heinrich [Glareanus, Henricus; Loriti] (*b* Molles, canton of Glarus, June 1488; *d* Freiburg, 28 March 1563). Swiss music theorist, educationist, poet, and humanist. The son of a prosperous landowner, he studied philosophy, theology, mathematics, and music at the University of Cologne. He first went to Basle in 1514; his subsequent travels round Europe introduced him to many humanists. He taught at the universities of Basle and Freiburg and throughout his life was involved with numerous educational projects, including plans to establish a Swiss Catholic Hochschule. He produced an edition of Boethius' *De musica*, from which he developed his own system of 12 modes. His theories formed the basis of a vast treatise, *Dodecachordon* (Basle, 1547), which had a considerable impact on Renaissance musical thought.   LC

Glass, Philip (*b* Baltimore, 31 Jan. 1937). American composer. He played the violin and flute as a boy, and studied at the University of Chicago (1952–6) and the Juilliard School (1958–62), and with Nadia Boulanger in Paris (1964–6). While in Paris he was engaged by a film-maker to transcribe some of Ravi Shankar's music into Western notation, whereupon he made a new beginning as a composer. He travelled in north Africa and India, then returned to New York, where he introduced his distinctive style of repeated arpeggio figures building long tracts of essentially unchanging sound. At first he wrote only for himself, for performers he knew, or for his own ensemble of amplified keyboard and wind instruments, which he founded in 1968 and with which he toured internationally, presenting such works as *Music in Twelve Parts* (1971–4).

Einstein on the Beach (Avignon, 1976), a four-hour theatre piece created in collaboration with the director Robert Wilson, demonstrated the power of such music to sustain a kind of decelerated, near-static drama, and led to several works closer to conventional opera, including *Satyagraha* (Rotterdam, 1980, on the subject of Gandhi), *Akhnaten* (Stuttgart, 1984), *The Making of the Representative for Planet 8* (1988, based on a science-fiction novel by Doris Lessing), and *The Voyage* (1992, staged by the Metropolitan to mark the 500th anniversary of Columbus's arrival in the western hemisphere). At the same time, the success of *Einstein* brought him numerous commissions both from the established musical world and from figures in rock music, theatre, and film, and he has been prolifically active in all these areas. His works include string quartets, symphonies (*The Low Symphony*, 1992, based on a David Bowie album), a Violin Concerto (1987), scores for films both new (*Koyaanisqatsi*, 1982) and old (*La Belle et la bête*, 1996; *Dracula*, 1999), *Itaipuu* for chorus and orchestra (1988), and further collaborations with Wilson (*The Civil Wars*, 1982–4; the video opera *Monsters of Grace*, 1998).   PG

□ P. GLASS, *Music by Philip Glass*, ed. R. T. Jones (New York, 1987), repr. as *Opera on the Beach* · R. KOSTELANETZ (ed.), *Writings on Glass* (New York, 1997) · K. POTTER, *Four Musical Minimalists: La Monte Young, Terry Riley, Steve Reich, Philip Glass* (Cambridge, 2000)

glasses, musical. Sets of wine glasses, often arranged to stand in a box in scalar order, which are rubbed by moistened fingers or tapped by light beaters. The glasses are tuned approximately by size and then with precision, being filled with as much water as necessary; on better instruments, the tuning is done by grinding the bowls. Because players can strike or rub only two glasses at a time, the instrument's scope is limited, unlike that of the *glass harmonica.   JMo

glass harmonica [armonica]. A series of glass bowls in graduated sizes mounted concentrically on a horizontal spindle. The spindle is turned by a treadle and the player's fingers are kept moist by water in a trough below the bowls. The glass harmonica was invented by Benjamin Franklin in 1761. Because the bowls fit closely together, keyboard-like parts can be played. Mozart composed an Adagio and Rondo (K617) for armonica, flute, oboe, viola, and cello. The instrument was revived in the USA in the late 20th century.

JMo

Glazunov, Aleksandr Konstantinovich (*b* St Petersburg, 29 July/10 Aug. 1865; *d* Paris, 21 March 1936). Russian composer. He had lessons in theory and composition from Rimsky-Korsakov, who reports that he progressed 'not by the day but by the hour', and at the age of 16 he scored a success with his First Symphony (1881–2, rev. 1885 and 1929), which reveals skilful orchestration and a pleasing melodic strain owing much to the music of The Five. This work attracted the attention of the wealthy industrialist Mitrofan Belyayev, who became a tireless promoter of Glazunov's music. Belyayev arranged for the symphony's publication in 1884, and that year took the composer to Europe, where he arranged a meeting with Liszt and had the symphony performed in Weimar. The First Symphony also inspired Belyayev to institute the Russian Symphony Concerts series and gave Glazunov his debut as a conductor in 1888; from 1896 he became a regu-

lar conductor for the concert series. His First String Quartet (1882) followed swiftly after the Symphony.

Glazunov's early style betrays the young composer's enthusiasm for Borodin's music, and he later had a chance to repay the debt when he orchestrated Borodin's Third Symphony, which was incomplete at the time of the older composer's death in 1887; later still, he collaborated with Rimsky-Korsakov in producing a completed version of Borodin's opera *Prince Igor*. Tchaikovsky was to be the next major influence. Glazunov's Third Symphony (1890) unfolds at Tchaikovsky's more leisurely pace and displays that composer's warm lyricism. In the following years Glazunov suffered a creative crisis, but he emerged with renewed vigour and soon produced a further three symphonies, which number among his finest works: they are endowed with broad melodies, masterful orchestration, balanced forms, and an abundance of elaborate thematic development.

Glazunov also became acquainted with Wagner (he was to be found poring over the scores during rehearsals of the *Ring*), and his new symphonies bear eloquent witness to this new influence in much of their harmonic and melodic writing, as well as in their orchestration (as in the slow movements of the Fourth and Fifth Symphonies, for example). Between 1898 and 1900 St Petersburg saw the premieres of Glazunov's three ballets, *Raymonda*, *Les Ruses d'amour*, and *Vremena goda* ('The Seasons'), which earned their composer lasting success both on stage and on the concert platform; *The Seasons* was especially popular, thanks to such memorable items as the Waltz of the Cornflowers and Poppies and the invigorating Bacchanale.

By the end of the 1890s Glazunov was established in Russian musical life as a composer and conductor, but in 1899 he added a third strand to his career by accepting a professorship at the St Petersburg Conservatory. During the Revolutionary upheavals of 1905 he resigned in protest at Rimsky-Korsakov's politically motivated dismissal, but in the ensuing peace he was able to return as the conservatory's new director, a position he retained well into the Soviet era. Glazunov continued to produce some of his most significant works during this period: the Seventh and Eighth Symphonies (1902 and 1906) combine monumentality (e.g. the towering finale of the Eighth) with dramatic pathos (e.g. the slow movement of the Seventh). The Violin Concerto (1904) found a firm place in the repertory thanks in equal measure to its inspired writing and its stringent demands on the soloist's virtuosity; the cadenza even includes an unaccompanied fugue, which pushes the instrument to its limits.

During the following decade, however, Glazunov's productivity was more sporadic, since he was now burdened by his duties as director of the conservatory and distracted by World War I and the Revolution. In the 1920s he still enjoyed a public profile, and his directorship of the conservatory was not under threat. Nevertheless, the comforts of his private life had deteriorated severely: for example, he had to accept several families of strangers to live with him in his apartment. By 1928 he was using any excuse to travel outside the USSR, and he embarked on a conducting tour that took him across Europe and the USA.

Glazunov eventually settled in Paris, but continued to justify his absence from the USSR on grounds of ill health. Although he spent some eight years outside the country before his death, his increasingly transparent excuse preserved his reputation from the stigma of émigré status; his music therefore retained its respected place in the Soviet repertory, in contrast to that of official émigrés like Stravinsky and Rakhmaninov. Among the works of his last years only the Saxophone Concerto (1934) became well known; its jazz-type syncopations show that Glazunov was not oblivious to the culture of his new Western environment. Nevertheless, the musical revolutions of the previous decades had passed him by, and he never ventured far from the polished manner he had perfected at the turn of the century.   GN/MF-W

📖 G. Abraham, *On Russian Music* (London, 1939/R) · B. Schwarz, *Music and Musical Life in Soviet Russia, 1917–1970* (London, 1972)

Glebov, Igor'. See Asaf'yev, Boris Vladimirovich.

glee. A type of unaccompanied English *partsong composed in the 17th, 18th, and 19th centuries. The word derives from Old English *gliv* or *glēo*, meaning 'music'. Numerous glee clubs formed for the performance of such partsongs still survive in Britain and the USA, often attached to universities.

The most characteristic and productive period of the English glee was 1760–1830. An estimated 10,000 glees were composed during this 70-year period. Among these a sizable corpus of masterpieces is revealed. The finest composers of glees worked in London. Many had connections with Westminster Abbey, St Paul's Cathedral, and the Chapel Royal, as either choirboys, lay clerks or organists. Notable glee composers include Thomas Arne, the Earl of Mornington, Jonathan Battishill, Samuel Webbe (i), John Stafford Smith, Richard Stevens, Thomas Attwood, John Wall Callcott, and Samuel Webbe (ii). Glees were written also outside London, in provincial areas of England, Lowland Scotland, and Dublin, but these are usually of poorer quality.

In the early 18th century the predominant English partsong form was the male-voice *catch—a kind of short humorous round, generally with words celebrating the joys of drink, male conviviality, hunting, or lechery. Glees were also at first a male-voice genre, usually for TTB, ATB, or ATTB (the alto parts being sung by countertenors). Later, boys were paid to sing treble parts at meetings of glee clubs, and glees for SATB became more common. From about 1740, English madrigals began to be rediscovered and reprinted; this inspired composers to create new partsongs which would be longer than catches, more expressive and elegant, wider ranging in subject matter, and suitable for women to hear and take part in. Some were even called madrigals.

Not surprisingly, glees are in certain respects similar to the earlier English madrigals. They were mainly written for from three to five voices, exceptionally for from six to eight; the lyrics were set not strophically, but one phrase at a time, with special attention to word-painting; and they contained a mixture of homophonic and contrapuntal writing. Some glees from this period are almost madrigal pastiches. Others, however, have up-to-date 18th-century features, often falling into several contrasted sections, like compressed Baroque sonatas or miniature cantatas, and including modern *sf* and *fp* dynamic markings and Handelian fugues.

Between 1800 and 1820 composers experimented with 'virtuoso' glees specifically designed for professional singers, and with glees accompanied by piano and harp; but these experiments were not sustained. After 1830 the balance between old and new musical elements in the glee shifted. A few composers (notably Robert Lucas Pearsall, 1795–1856) continued to compose in a madrigalian manner, but in general English partsongs became shorter and less contrapuntal, and were influenced by the dramatic modulations and chromatic harmonies of Weber and Mendelssohn. Other descendants of the glee are the close-harmony folksong arrangement and the American *barber-shop quartet.

From the later 18th century, it was common for one glee to be included in an English opera; Bishop was a skilled composer of such pieces, and they are still to be found in most of Sullivan's operas, sometimes under the name of madrigal (e.g. 'Strange Adventure' in *The Yeomen of the Guard*).   DJ/NT

📖 W. A. Barrett, *English Glees and Part-Songs* (London, 1886) · D. Baptie, *Sketches of the English Glee Composers* (London, 1896) · D. Johnson, 'The 18th-century glee', *Musical Times*, 120 (1979), 200–2 · M. Hurd, 'Glees, madrigals and partsongs', *Music in Britain: The Romantic Age*, ed. N. Temperley (London, 1981), 242–65

Glière, Reinhold [Glier, Reyngol'd] **Moritsevich** (*b* Kiev, 30 Dec. 1874/11 Jan. 1875; *d* Moscow, 23 June 1956).

Russian composer. He studied at the Moscow Conservatory and later taught composition there (1920–41). His international reputation has long rested on the epic Third Symphony, 'Il'ya Muromets' (1909–11), though its predecessors have recently enjoyed some success. For many years the ballets *Krasnïy mak* ('The Red Poppy', 1927; rev. as *Krasnïy tsvetok*, 'The Red Flower', 1949) and *Mednïy vsadnik* ('The Bronze Horseman', 1949) held the stage in the USSR for their lyrical warmth, dramatic effectiveness, and rich orchestration, and his late concertos maintained their popularity; however, his pre-Revolutionary works, more immediate offshoots of late Romanticism, are now eclipsing them in interest.

GN/DN

📖 S. D. KREBS, *Soviet Composers and the Development of Soviet Music* (London and New York, 1970)

Glinka, Mikhail Ivanovich (*b* Novospasskoye [now Glinka], nr Smolensk, 20 May/1 June 1804; *d* Berlin, 15 Feb 1857). Russian composer. He was born into a noble family, the income from his estate obviating the need for employment. Like many Russian gentlemen of his generation he began to compose romances (settings of lyric poetry for voice and piano) as a dignified pastime, but he soon came to see composition as his vocation. He spent his youth in St Petersburg, where his romances won some attention in salon society. His musical education was erratic: after a few piano lessons with John Field he travelled to Italy in 1830 to study vocal composition; for a more rigorous grounding in theory he later turned to Siegfried Dehn in Berlin. During his Italian sojourn, though he had written a number of Italian arias and had been received warmly by Bellini and Donizetti, he decided that he did not want a career as an Italian opera composer, however promising his prospects. As he recounts in his memoirs, the imperatives of national character drove him to plan the composition of a Russian opera, whereupon he returned to St Petersburg.

Two years later, in 1836, *A Life for the Tsar* (also known as *Ivan Susanin* in its Soviet adaptation) was given a lavish premiere, the inaugural performance marking the opening of a new opera house in the presence of Tsar Nicholas I. For various reasons this event is taken as marking the beginning of Russian national music: *A Life for the Tsar* was the first all-sung opera by a Russian composer; its patriotic and nationalist plot (about the invasion of Russia by the Poles and the installation of the Romanov dynasty in the 17th century) resonated well with the current moods of the court and the intellectual elite; most important, it skilfully combined the Italian operatic style with the idioms of the drawing-room romance and Russian popular song, creating an impression of native art. Its

success won Glinka the directorship of the Court Cappella Choir, a post he relinquished after three years.

His second opera followed in 1842: *Ruslan and Lyudmila*, based on Pushkin's narrative poem, was less explicitly Russian in its musical detail; its more complex idiom, slow pace, and great length pleased neither the court nor the public. This indifference to the work he considered his true masterpiece—far superior to *A Life for the Tsar*—caused Glinka to fall silent. Embittered, he left Russia and spent most of his remaining years abroad, first in Paris, where he enjoyed the company of Berlioz, and then in Spain. His travels inspired him to write two Spanish overtures, *Capriccio brillante* (1845) and *Recuerdos de Castilla* (1848; final version, *Souvenir d'une nuit d'été à Madrid*, 1851). In 1848 he returned to Russian material in *Kamarinskaya*, a brilliant orchestral fantasy which later influenced The Five. Only in the last year of his life did he resume his ambition of forging a Russian national music: taking Palestrina as his model, he set out to remould Russian church music into a contrapuntal art, hoping that Russian music history could follow the course the West had taken earlier. He therefore returned to Berlin to resume his studies with Dehn, but died there shortly afterwards.

The next two generations of Russian nationalist composers revered Glinka as the 'father of Russian music' and mined his works endlessly for ideas. *Ruslan and Lyudmila* was taken as a model for Russian epic and fairy-tale operas, and its musical representations of the oriental and the supernatural were developed by The Five. *Kamarinskaya* inspired them to base pieces on folk melody and to adopt Glinka's characteristic 'changing-background' variation technique, which left the melody intact but reclothed it in an array of colourful new harmonizations and textures. Glinka's scant knowledge of Russian folksong was presented retrospectively as a lifelong intimacy, and various novel features of his compositions were interpreted, posthumously, as the natural product of this supposed intimacy, or simply of his Russian blood. But the importance of his contribution to Russian music lay not only in his exploration of nationalism but in the artistic precedent he set: after Glinka, there could be no return to the bland competence of the gentleman amateur. His works are invariably graceful, with tasteful and transparent orchestration (he was the author of the first Russian orchestration manual); he sought out fresh harmonies and enriched his textures with contrapuntal interest, and his more daring novelties—the whole-tone scale and 5/4 metre—contributed to the 'progressive' character of later Russian nationalist music.   MF-W

📖 D. BROWN, *Mikhail Glinka: A Biographical and Critical Study* (London, 1974) · M. FROLOVA-WALKER, 'On *Ruslan* and Russianness', *Cambridge Opera Journal*, 9 (1997),

21–45 · R. Taruskin, 'M. I. Glinka and the state', *Defining Russia Musically* (Princeton, 1997), 25–47

glissade. See SLIDE, I.

glissando (It.). A sliding movement from one note to another. The term is not an authentic Italian word but an Italianization of the French verb *glisser*, 'to slide'. On the piano the effect is achieved by drawing the thumb or the side of the index finger quickly up or down a series of adjacent notes (double glissandos, usually in octaves, and, very occasionally, triple ones also exist). Ravel and Debussy used glissandos in their piano music. The technique is also much used in harp music, for example in Ravel's *Introduction and Allegro*). With bowed instruments and voices, an infinite number of microtones are passed through in a glissando. The technique is also effective on the trombone (for example in Stravinsky's *Pulcinella*) and on the pedal timpani (as in Bartók's *Music for Strings, Percussion, and Celesta*).

A glissando may be notated either by means of a written-out ascending or descending chromatic scale in the smallest note-values (in which case the composer generally intends each note to be heard), or by a diagonal straight or wavy line connecting the highest and lowest notes (in which case a *portamento is intended).
AL

glissé (Fr.). 'Slid': in harp playing, a *glissando.

Globokar, Vinko (*b* Anderny, Meurthe-et-Moselle, 7 July 1934). Slovenian composer and trombonist. He studied at the conservatories of Ljubljana and Paris and later with Berio, who, in *Sequenza V*, became one of many composers to exploit his extraordinary virtuosity and new playing techniques on the trombone. Between 1973 and 1979 he was head of vocal and instrumental research at IRCAM in Paris. His own creative activity has been bound up with his life as a performer, whether as trombone soloist or as a member of New Phonic Art, an improvisation quartet founded in 1972. His works, many incorporating elements of theatre and humour, include *Fluide* for brass and percussion ensemble (1967), *res/as/ex/ins-pirer* for brass soloist (1973), and a series of nine works for different instrumental combinations called *Discours*.
PG/ABur

glockenspiel (Ger., 'play of bells'; Fr.: *jeu de clochettes*, *jeu de timbres*; It.: *campanelli*) [orchestral bells]. A *metallophone consisting of a graduated series of steel bars, usually arranged like the piano keyboard, struck with hard beaters of brass, plastic, or wood. The instrument's range is usually two or two and a half octaves, and its music is written two octaves lower than it sounds. Marching bands use the *bell lyra.

Some such instruments, played from a keyboard, were used by Handel (*Saul*) and Mozart (*Die Zauberflöte*). In the 20th century composers including Dukas (*L'Apprenti sorcier*) wrote for small keyboard glockenspiels, though most such works are now played on the normal instrument. (A more sophisticated keyboard metallophone is the *celesta.) In the 19th century glockenspiels were often made of glass under the name 'harmonica' or 'armonica', as used by Saint-Saëns in *Le Carnaval des animaux* for 'Oiseaux'.
JMo

Gloria in excelsis Deo (Lat., 'Glory to God in the Highest'). The Great(er) *Doxology, an ancient hymn of Christian praise beginning with the words of the angelic host to the shepherds (Luke 2: 14). The *Apostolic Constitutions* (*c*.380) appoints a version of the text for morning prayer, a usage also observed in 6th-century Gaul. A long redaction appearing in the Codex Alexandrinus (5th century) is still sung at the climax of Byzantine Orthros on Sundays and feasts. Since the 8th century it has been a part of the Ordinary of the Roman *Mass, sung between the Kyrie and the collect except in Advent and Lent, when it is omitted. After the Reformation, vernacular versions were retained at the Eucharists of the Anglican and Lutheran Churches.
—/AL1

Gloriana. Opera in three acts by Britten to a libretto by William Plomer after Lytton Strachey's *Elizabeth and Essex*; it was commissioned by Covent Garden for the coronation of Queen Elizabeth II, who attended its first performance on 8 June 1953.

Gloria Patri (Lat., 'Glory to the Father'). The *Lesser Doxology, added as a final verse to all psalms.

'Gloria tibi Trinitas', Missa. Mass for six voices by Taverner that uses the antiphon *Gloria tibi Trinitas* as a cantus firmus.

glosa (Sp., 'gloss'). 1. A term used from the 16th century to the 18th for a kind of ornamentation in which a melody is broken up by fast figuration.

2. A 16th-century term for the technique of writing variations, usually on a religious theme; in Cabezón's *Obras de música* (Madrid, 1578) it is used to describe simple figurative variations of harmonized psalm tones. Such variations are generally simpler and less extensive than *diferencias*.

Gluck, Christoph Willibald Ritter von (*b* Erasbach, Upper Palatinate, 2 July 1714; *d* Vienna, 15 Nov. 1787). Austrian composer. His father worked for the Bohemian nobility, and the precocious son took advantage of noble contacts to develop his career by studying music and law in Prague, probably sponsored by Prince

Lobkowitz. Gluck learnt to play the violin and keyboard instruments, but his later appearances as a virtuoso were on the glass harmonica. He may have studied singing as well; Burney records that in 1772 he sang 'with as little voice as possible', but with such expression that 'it was a defect which was soon entirely forgotten'. In his early 20s he went by way of Vienna to Milan, where he was probably a pupil of Sammartini. His first eight operas, of which the music is mostly lost, appeared rapidly, during 1743 and 1744, in Milan and Venice. Six are based on librettos by Pietro Metastasio and all are *opere serie*; Gluck wrote no *opera buffa*. In 1746 he presented two operas in London, with scant success; but he improved his musical understanding, as he later told Burney, by contact with Handel and English taste. Handel's disparaging remark to the effect that Gluck knew no more counterpoint than his cook may be apocryphal. Gluck's music first appeared in print from the London publisher Walsh; this included 'favourite airs' from *La caduta de' giganti*, an opera whose subject relates to the recent Jacobite rising, and a set of trio sonatas which are his only independent instrumental work.

From his earliest operas Gluck engaged in the habit of recycling his best ideas. Less fluent than his Italian contemporaries, and more dependent on striking originality, he was certainly justified in seeking better dramatic contexts for his most challenging pieces, such as Sesto's aria 'Se mai senti spirarti' from *La clemenza di Tito*, which as 'O malheureuse Iphigénie' became the highpoint of his final masterpiece, *Iphigénie en Tauride*. Since most Italian opera productions lasted no more than one season, and scores were seldom printed, few in the audiences will have been aware of this compositional economy. In later years, however, it was brought into the open when he revised operas for Paris, where controversies about plagiarism from and by Gluck made excellent journalistic copy.

Returning to Germany, Gluck worked with Pietro Mingotti's travelling company in Dresden, Vienna, Denmark, and Prague. He produced a courtly opera (*Le nozze d'Ercole e d'Ebe*) in Dresden in 1747, and further Metastasio librettos were set for Vienna (1748, *La Semiramide riconosciuta*) and Prague (1750, *Ezio*). In 1750 he married and settled in Vienna, where in spite of scepticism from the Empress Maria Theresa and hostility from the court poet Metastasio, who found his music bizarre, he established himself at the centre of theatrical life. Some important works were commissioned elsewhere; in 1752, *La clemenza di Tito* caused controversy in Naples because of daring harmony in 'Se mai senti spirarti'. *Antigono* (1756) was composed for Rome. Several works were written for the imperial family, who frequently participated; these include the

satirical Metastasio libretto *Le cinesi* (1754). Already, however, in *L'innocenza giustificata* (1755) Gluck was party to the devices of the theatre Intendant Count Durazzo in undermining Metastasio's supremacy by adapting his aria texts to a new plot, and in the final crucial aria Gluck demonstrated his ability to achieve dramatic potency by the simplest of music.

Before the celebrated 'reform' of Italian opera, Durazzo's principal enterprise was the production of ballets and French *opéra comique*, for which Gluck arranged and, increasingly, composed the music (some ballets to which he contributed have only recently been identified). The dramatic ballet, including mime, came to a head in Gluck's collaboration with Gasparo Angiolini in *Don Juan* (1761), followed in 1764–5 by *Alessandro*, *Sémiramis*, and *Iphigénie*. Music from these ballets has been identified in later operas, but *Don Juan* remains one of Gluck's most impressive scores, concluding with a ghostly statue scene and an extended dance (chaconne) for the furies, in D minor; plagiarized in a symphony by Boccherini and recycled for Paris in *Orphée*, this surely influenced Mozart's treatment of the same subject in *Don Giovanni*.

Opéra comique trained Gluck in setting the French language. At first he included traditional melodies, but increasingly he took a musical role, and the fine storm overture in *L'Île de Merlin* (1758) was later adapted for *Iphigénie en Tauride*. *L'Ivrogne corrigé* ('The Drunkard Reformed', 1760) contains a mock hell scene in which the musical style, though satirically applied, anticipates *Don Juan*, *Orfeo ed Euridice*, and *Alceste*. The last of Gluck's comedies, *La Rencontre imprévue* ('The Unexpected Encounter, or The Pilgrims to Mecca', 1764), is a masterpiece of the genre. The plot is a paradigm of the oriental type, involving a rescue from a harem; translated into German for Joseph II's National Singspiel, it became a direct model for Mozart's *Die Entführung aus dem Serail*.

Gluck did not emulate Traetta by setting Italian translations of French *tragédie lyrique*, but the influence of the serious French genre clearly inspired Durazzo and a new arrival from Paris, the Italian poet Ranieri Calzabigi, who had had a hand in the scenario of *Don Juan*. *Orfeo ed Euridice* (1762) is the earliest opera never entirely to have left the repertory. What appears in retrospect as a decisive reform of Italian opera, however, had at the time a mainly local impact. In its dramatic integrity (except perhaps the arbitrary happy ending) *Orfeo* transcends genre, but if anything it is not an *opera seria* but an *azione teatrale*, a court genre which already included dance and chorus. The most novel element, the simplified vocal style, owes much to *opéra comique*, and the recitative is entirely accompanied by orchestra. The first Orfeo, the castrato Gaetano

Guadagni, had worked with Handel and learnt acting with David Garrick. The blend of chorus and dance (Angiolini was the choreographer) reflects *tragédie lyrique*, with a possible musical influence from Rameau. Calzabigi's claim to have dictated to Gluck how to set his verses may be discounted: he could have achieved nothing without Gluck's musical inspiration. Exceptionally, the score was published (in 1763); Gluck included a reduced version as an act of *Le feste d'Apollo* (Parma, 1769), and an expanded version for Paris (*Orphée*, 1774).

After *Orfeo* Gluck composed no more *opera seria*, though subsequent court commissions appear conventional in comparison. *Telemaco* (Vienna, 1765, to a libretto by another reformer, Marco Coltellini) restores simple recitative and some coloratura singing but retains choral and dance scenes, forming a hybrid between reform and convention within the context of court opera. With *Alceste* (1767) Gluck and Calzabigi made a more decisive break with the past, despite restoring simple recitative. The monumentality and unrelenting seriousness of this opera led to a mixed reception, but in publishing the score in 1769 Calzabigi wrote, and Gluck signed, the dedication to the Grand Duke of Tuscany (later Leopold II) which is the manifesto of reform: denouncing the abuses of composers and singers, the authors 'have striven to restrict music to its true office of serving poetry' by means of expression and by following the situations of the story, without interrupting the action or stifling it with useless superfluity of ornaments'. Gluck made the overture integral to the opera, through its sombre character and by linking it to the first scene. At its first production *Alceste* dispensed with the castrato (it was performed by a troupe more practised in *opera buffa*, but the castrato Giuseppe Millico replaced the tenor in a revival). In 1770 *Paride ed Elena* restored the castrato lover and included lighter elements in its intrigue. Another preface complained that *Alceste* had found no imitators, but *Paride*, one of his most attractive works, was undervalued by Gluck who did not adapt it for France, instead borrowing several numbers.

Diplomatic connections played a major role in the last, French, stage of Gluck's campaign of reform, and the dauphine, later Queen Marie Antoinette, had once been his pupil. Gluck was committed to produce six serious operas for Paris because the management rightly predicted that works of such novelty and energy would kill the old repertory. By 1772 he had already set an adaptation of Racine's *Iphigénie* by F. L. G. Leblanc Du Roullet, attaché at the French embassy in Vienna. *Iphigénie en Aulide* was performed in Paris to a mixed reception in 1774, but overcame opposition following the triumph of *Orphée* in the same year. The castrato

title role was adapted for high tenor, and the new dances included the famous Dance of the Blessed Spirits and the Furies' Dance from *Don Juan*; a virtuoso aria added to the first act was—wrongly—claimed by the composer Bertoni.

Gluck next adapted and enlarged two of his *opéras comiques* and revised *Alceste* (1776), making it less monumental but more theatrical. *Armide* (1777) uses an almost unaltered libretto by Philippe Quinault, set by Lully nearly a century before. The magical scenes rival those of *Orfeo* and, with *Iphigénie en Aulide*, this is Gluck's main appropriation of French tradition, successfully adapted to his own Italian-based (but highly personal) style. In 1778 Piccinni produced *Roland*, in which Quinault's libretto is partly modernized; the clear success of Piccinni may have led Gluck to incorporate more Italian elements into *Iphigénie en Tauride* (1779), by recycling several longer arias as well as incorporating much of the ballet *Sémiramis*. A German version, *Iphigenia auf Tauris*, was presented in Vienna in 1781.

From one angle *Iphigénie en Tauride* is an inspired pastiche; but its dramatic force and intelligence make it a crowning masterpiece, which overshadowed the delicate, and more French, pastoral of the same year, *Écho et Narcisse*. Poor health (he suffered his first stroke at this time) and the failure of *Écho* drove Gluck back to Vienna, before the successful confrontation between his penultimate opera and Piccinni's *Iphigénie en Tauride*. Gluck added some songs to poetry of F. G. Klopstock and a *De profundis* to his slight output of smaller vocal works but retired from opera, though he allowed his name to be used to promote the Paris operas of Salieri and J. C. Vogel.

Gluck's greatness depends on his restoration of the balance between music and poetry, with due attention to visual elements (the Paris Opéra personnel complained of his interventionist stage direction). In striving for 'beautiful simplicity' in melody, by working closely with his collaborators, and by moulding his music to enhance the drama without regard to convention, he nevertheless established the composer as the dominant dramatic force in the creation of opera, a position endorsed from their diverse points of view by Mozart, Verdi, and Wagner, as well as his disciples Spontini and Berlioz.   JR

📖 P. Howard, *Gluck and the Birth of Modern Opera* (London, 1963) · P. Howard (ed.), *C. W. von Gluck: Orfeo* (Cambridge, 1981) · B. A. Brown, *Gluck and the French Theatre in Vienna* (Oxford, 1991) · P. Howard, *Gluck: An Eighteenth-Century Portrait in Letters and Documents* (Oxford, 1995) · D. Heartz, *Haydn, Mozart and the Viennese School, 1740–1780* (New York, 1995) · J. A. Rice, *Antonio Salieri and Viennese Opera* (Chicago, 1998)

Glückliche Hand, Die ('The Fortunate Hand'; 'The Knack'). Drama with music in one act by Schoenberg to his own libretto (Vienna, 1924); it contains mimed parts for a man and a woman, and the use of coloured lights is of fundamental importance (see also COLOUR AND MUSIC; EXPRESSIONISM).

Glyndebourne Festival Opera. English festival established in 1934. See FESTIVALS, 4.

Gnossiennes. Three piano pieces (1890) by Satie; their 'oriental' flavour was influenced by a visit to the Paris Exposition in 1889.

G.O. (Fr.). Abbreviation for *Grand orgue*, 'Great organ'.

goat's trill (Fr.: *chevrotement*; Ger.: *Bockstriller*, *Geisstriller*). A badly performed vocal trill, reminiscent of the bleating of a goat.

Gobbi, Tito (*b* Bassano del Grappa, 24 Oct. 1913; *d* Rome, 5 March 1984). Italian baritone. He studied with Giulio Crimi in Rome and in 1935 made his debut there as Rodolfo in *La sonnambula*. From 1938 he sang regularly at the Rome Opera, where his highly dramatic but strikingly natural presence in many roles attracted international attention. In 1942 he sang the title part in the first Italian performance of *Wozzeck*. He also excelled in such comic roles as Belcore in *L'elisir d'amore*, with which he made his La Scala debut in 1942.

From the early 1950s Gobbi became one of the most sought-after artists with an extremely wide repertory of nearly 100 roles. He was particularly celebrated for his Scarpia, Gianni Schicchi, Iago, Rigoletto, Falstaff, Posa, and Don Giovanni. Some of his outstanding successes were at Covent Garden, where a new generation of directors such as Luchino Visconti and Franco Zeffirelli made strong use of his charismatic and intelligent acting. He was a frequent television broadcaster, director of a number of operas, and a star of 26 films. JT

Godard, Benjamin (Louis Paul) (*b* Paris, 18 Aug. 1849; *d* Cannes, 10 Jan. 1895). French composer and viola player. He studied composition at the Paris Conservatoire and played the viola in various instrumental groups. His first great success came in 1878 with a prizewinning 'dramatic symphony' *Le Tasse*, on the life of the poet Torquato Tasso. He went on to write operas of limited distinction, for which he is remembered largely by the berceuse from *Jocelyn* (1888) and an aria from *La Vivandière* (1895). He also wrote much instrumental music and songs, and his Suite for flute and orchestra (1890) is still played. DA/ALA

Godefroid, Jules(-Joseph) (*b* Namur, 23 Feb. 1811; *d* Paris, 27 Feb. 1840). French harpist and composer. He was taught music by his father before entering the Paris Conservatoire in 1826 to study the harp with Nadermann and composition with Le Sueur. In the 1830s two of his operas (*La Diadesté* and *La Chasse royale*) were staged in Paris, but without success. His brother **Félix** (Dieudonné Joseph Guillaume) Godefroid (*b* Namur, 24 July 1818; *d* Villers-sur-Mer, 12 July 1897) was also a harpist and composer. He too was trained by his father, and entered the Paris Conservatoire in 1832 as a pupil of Nadermann. Three years later he left to study the double-action harp with Théodore Labarre. He became a virtuoso performer, touring in Europe and the Middle East, and composed much music for the harp. His opera *La Harpe d'or* (1858) was given with some success at the Théâtre Lyrique in Paris. WT/SH

God Save the King [Queen]. British national anthem. Its origins are obscure but the tune seems first to have appeared in print in 1744 and is the first national anthem. The earliest recorded performances of it were in an arrangement by Thomas Arne in 1745 at the Theatre Royal, Drury Lane, London, following Sir John Cope's defeat at Prestonpans. In the 19th century the tune was used as the national anthem of many other countries, including Denmark, Sweden, Switzerland, Russia, and the USA, with many different texts. It has been incorporated into works by several composers including Beethoven, Weber, Paganini, Marschner, Brahms, and Debussy; Ives used it as the theme for his *Variations on 'America'* for organ (1891–2). Several composers have made choral arrangements of it, notably Elgar (1902) and Britten (1961). AL

📖 P. SCHOLES, *God Save the Queen! The History and Romance of the World's First National Anthem* (London, 1954)

Goebbels, Heiner (*b* Neustadt Weinstrasse, 17 Aug. 1952). German composer. He studied sociology as well as music, and has worked with rock and progressive groups. Early in his career he wrote music for the theatre, film, and ballet; since the 1980s, though he has composed several works for chamber ensembles, he has concentrated on music theatre, including collaborations with Heiner Müller (on radiophonic works) and Michael Simon. Among his stage works are *Ou bien le débarquement désastreux* (1993), *La Reprise* (1995), *Schwarz und Weiss* (1996), and *Max Black* (1998), and the music-theatre piece *Hashirigaki* (2001). His orchestral works include *Surrogate Cities* (1993–4). ABur

Goehr, (Peter) Alexander (*b* Berlin, 10 Aug. 1932). German-born British composer. The son of the conductor Walter Goehr, who took the family to England in 1933, he studied with Richard Hall at the RMCM and with Messiaen at the Paris Conservatoire. He worked as a BBC producer and taught in the USA before becoming professor of music at Leeds University in 1970. He was professor of music at Cambridge from 1976 to 1999.

Goehr's early music was closer to the 12-note traditions of Schoenberg than was that of his Manchester colleagues Maxwell Davies and Birtwistle, and his respect for established musical genres (Violin Concerto, 1961–2, *Little Symphony*, 1963) enabled him to exploit a strong vein of lyricism alongside more concentrated dramatic ideas. These qualities are particularly apparent in his music-theatre pieces and operas, which include *Arden Must Die* (Hamburg, 1967), *Arianna* (1994–5), described as 'lost opera by Monteverdi composed again by Alexander Goehr', and *Kantan and Damask Drum* (2001).

A strong sense of tradition, as embodied in contrapuntal, canonic technique and modally based harmony, permeates Goehr's mature work and underpins the many distinctive features of such substantial vocal compositions as *Babylon the Great is Fallen* (1979), *Sing, Ariel* (1989–90) and *The Death of Moses* (1991–2). His later instrumental works include *Symphony—with Chaconne* (1985–6), String Quartet no. 4 (1990), and *Schlussgesang* for viola and orchestra (1996).   PG/AW

   📖 B. Northcott (ed.), *The Music of Alexander Goehr* (London, 1980) · D. Puffett (ed.), *Finding the Key: Selected Writings of Alexander Goehr* (London, 1998)

Goetz, Hermann (Gustav) (*b* Königsberg [now Kaliningrad], 7 Dec. 1840; *d* Hottingen, nr Zürich, 3 Dec. 1876). German composer. He studied in Berlin, winning good opinions for his first works from his teacher Bülow. Developing tuberculosis, he took up a post as organist in the favourable climate of Winterthur, where he managed to pursue a career as conductor, composer, critic, and teacher. He was highly successful with his comic opera *Der Widerspenstigen Zähmung* ('The Taming of the Shrew'), a lively work resisting Wagner's influence, which was produced in 1874 and soon given throughout Europe. He also wrote an attractive symphony, as well as chamber music and concertos for piano and violin, on which the principal influence is that of Mendelssohn. A second opera, *Francesca da Rimini*, was completed after his death by Ernst Frank.   DA/JW

Goeyvaerts, Karel (*b* Antwerp, 8 June 1923; *d* Antwerp, 3 Feb. 1993). Belgian composer. He studied at the Paris Conservatoire with Messiaen and Milhaud. In 1951 he composed a Sonata for two pianos, a pioneering exercise in total serialism; at the Darmstadt summer courses it made a significant impact on Stockhausen. Goeyvaerts later experimented with tape composition, the combination of instruments with electronics, and

the psychology of performance and perception. From 1970 he worked at IPEM in Ghent, and from 1974 to 1987 he was a producer for Belgian Flemish Radio. His opera *Aquarius* was performed in Rotterdam in 1990.   ABur

'Goldberg' Variations. Work for harpsichord by J. S. Bach, BWV988, 30 variations on an original theme, published in part 4 of the *Clavier-Übung* (1741–2); Bach gave a copy of them to Johann Gottlieb Goldberg (1727–56), harpsichordist to Count Keyserlingk, but it is unlikely that they were commissioned by him.

Golden Cockerel, The (*Zolotoy petushok*). Opera in a prologue, three acts, and an epilogue by Rimsky-Korsakov to a libretto by Vladimir Bel'sky after Pushkin's poem (1834), itself based on 'The House of the Weathercock' and 'Legend of the Arabian Astrologer' from Washington Irving's *The Alhambra* (Moscow, 1909); it was completed in 1907 but its performance was banned during the composer's lifetime because of its satire on autocracy. The habit of referring to it as *Le Coq d'or* arose from Diaghilev's production, choreographed by Mikhail Fokine, in which the roles were enacted by dancers while singers sat at the side of the stage (Paris and London, 1914).

'Golden' Sonata. Nickname of Purcell's Trio Sonata in F for two violins and continuo, the ninth of *Ten Sonata's in Four Parts* published posthumously in 1697.

Goldmark, Karl [Károly] (*b* Keszthely, 18 May 1830; *d* Vienna, 2 Jan. 1915). Hungarian composer. The son of a poor Jewish cantor, he was sent at the age of 14 to study in Vienna, which with few interruptions remained his home. He worked as a theatre violinist, and began to teach (his pupils briefly included Sibelius), compose, and work as a music critic. His support for Wagner brought him into conflict with Hanslick, among others. An early success with a String Quartet (1860) won him a following, and later his *Sakuntala* overture (1865) helped to gain him a government grant in support of his first opera, *Die Königin von Saba* ('The Queen of Sheba', 1875), the most popular of his six. He also wrote a number of concert works, including the popular *Ländliche Hochzeit* ('Country Wedding', 1877).

His nephew **Rubin Goldmark** (*b* New York, 15 Aug. 1872; *d* New York, 6 March 1936) studied in Vienna and New York, where his teachers included Dvořák. He taught at the College Conservatory in Colorado and later at the Juilliard School in New York. His pupils included Gershwin and Copland.   DA/JW

Goldschmidt, Berthold (*b* Hamburg, 18 Jan. 1903; *d* London, 17 Oct. 1996). German-born British composer and conductor. He took private lessons in counterpoint and harmony with Werner Wolff, who conducted at the Hamburg Opera. It was through Wolff that Goldschmidt met Busoni. He then studied composition (with Schreker) and conducting at the Berlin Hochschule für Musik (1922–4). He also played the keyboard in the Berlin Philharmonic and was répétiteur and celesta player in the premiere of Berg's *Wozzeck* under Kleiber in 1925. In 1927 Carl Ebert engaged him as assistant conductor at the Darmstadt Opera, where he stayed for two years, and in 1931, the year he made a guest appearance in Leningrad (where he met Shostakovich), he joined the Städtische Oper in Berlin. As a Jew, he was dismissed by the Nazis and eked out a living before fleeing to Britain in 1935.

Goldschmidt survived largely from private teaching until, in 1944, he was put in charge of the music broadcasts of the BBC European Service to Germany. In 1947 his conducting career resumed: he conducted Verdi's *Macbeth* at the Edinburgh Festival, and in 1960 the first performance of Deryck Cooke's completion of Mahler's Tenth Symphony. By that point he had already observed five years' silence as a composer, a response to critical indifference to his three concertos (1953–5, for violin, cello, and clarinet). He composed almost nothing until the Clarinet Quartet of 1984, when he was 81. Now began an Indian summer of extraordinary vigour, as the rediscovery of his music was matched by a renewed flow, chiefly of chamber works, that continued until his death: as part of that late harvest he added a Third and Fourth String Quartet (1988–9, 1992) to his first two (1926, 1936).

The 'middle period' concertos apart, most of Goldschmidt's orchestral music dates from the beginning of his career, as does his first opera, *Der gewaltige Hahnrei* (based on Fernand Crommelynck, 1929–30); his second opera, *Beatrice Cenci* (Shelley), was composed in 1951 though not performed until 1988. His music is characterized by a steely, contrapuntal strength, its tendency towards darkness offset by a ready sense of irony; its grim humour and utter lack of sentimentality reflect the outlook of its creator.   MA

> S. Hilger and W. Jacobs (eds.), *Berthold Goldschmidt* (Bonn, 1993, 2/1996)

Golem. Opera in two parts by Casken to a libretto by the composer with Pierre Audi (London, 1989). Several composers have written operas on the subject, notably Sitsky (1993).

goliard songs. Latin poems on secular and sacred themes written by the 'goliards', wandering scholars and clerics of the late 10th to mid-13th centuries who played an important part in the dissemination of culture in the Middle Ages. The most famous collection of goliard songs (also containing other types of vocal music) is the late 13th-century anthology *Carmina burana*.

Golliwogg's Cake-Walk. The sixth piece of Debussy's piano suite *Children's Corner*.

Gombert, Nicolas (*b* c.1495; *d* after 1556). Flemish composer. Possibly a pupil of Josquin (on whose death he wrote a *déploration*), he was a member of the royal chapel of Emperor Charles V and travelled widely with the court, spending much time in Spain. He seems to have retired to his native Flanders, where he had been awarded several benefices by his master, and probably died at Tournai. Although he was an excellent writer of polyphonic chansons, his finest music lies in his motets and *Magnificat* settings, composed not only with a mastery of counterpoint comparable to that of Palestrina but also with a rich expressiveness. Despite their dense textures, these works are highly singable. Gombert was a major figure of the early 16th century: his works continued to be published, parodied, and arranged long after his death, and as late at 1610 Monteverdi chose one of his motets as the basis for his *Missa 'In illo tempore'*.   DA/TC

Gomes, (Antônio) Carlos (*b* Campinas, 11 July 1836; *d* Belém, 16 Sept. 1896). Brazilian composer, of Portuguese parentage. He studied with his father, a bandmaster, and began composing at the age of 15. He then entered the conservatory at Rio de Janeiro, where in 1861 he wrote his first opera. Two years later he went to Italy on an imperial scholarship to study at the Milan Conservatory. There he embarked on a highly successful career as a composer of operas in robust, lyrical Italian style. His best-known work, *Il Guarany*, was produced at La Scala in 1870. About 1890 Gomes returned to Brazil, but his monarchist leanings made him unpopular with the new republic, and no significant appointment came his way until a few months before his death, when he was appointed director of the Belém Conservatory (1895).   WT/CW

gondola song (Ger.: *Gondellied*). See BARCAROLLE.

Gondoliers, The (*The Gondoliers, or The King of Barataria*). Operetta in two acts by Sullivan to a libretto by W. S. Gilbert (London, 1889).

gong, tam-tam. In general terms, a gong is any percussion *idiophone in the form of a circular metal disc, which may be of definite or indefinite pitch. Its surface may be flat or curved, or may have a pronounced central boss; its edges may be flat or flanged. It is hung vertically and struck with a beater. Gongs differ from bells in that the vibrations are greater at the centre than at the edges. Western orchestral usage differentiates between gongs, having a deep turned-down rim and often a protruding central boss, and tuned to definite pitch, and tam-tams (the more common type in the West) which have a flat surface and only a shallow lip and are of indefinite pitch. A tam-tam may be struck anywhere on its surface, but a gong must be struck in the centre. Both are widely used in modern scores. Their first orchestral appearance seems to have been in Gossec's *Marche lugubre* (1790).

Bossed gongs entered Europe from Indonesia and South-East Asia (gongs are important members of the *gamelan) whereas tam-tams came from China, though there is evidence for their use in ancient Greece, India, and elsewhere, and their name is of Malay origin.

JMo

Goodall, Sir Reginald (*b* Lincoln, 13 July 1901; *d* Bridge, nr Canterbury, 5 May 1990). English conductor. After studying in Munich and Vienna, he began his career with the London Theatre Mozart Concerts and the British National Opera Company in the 1920s. He joined Sadler's Wells Opera in 1944 and the following year conducted its historic premiere of Britten's *Peter Grimes*. In 1946 he joined the Covent Garden Opera, but went abroad to assist Furtwängler, Clemens Krauss, and Knappertsbusch; he was greatly in demand by singers as a coach. Late recognition came in 1968, when he conducted Wagner with the Sadler's Wells company. He was knighted in 1985.

JT

📖 J. LUCAS, *Reggie: The Life of Reginald Goodall* (London, 1993)

Good Friday Music (*Karfreitagzauber*). The music in Act III of Wagner's *Parsifal* heard as Parsifal is anointed in preparation for his entry into the castle of the Grail; it is sometimes performed as a separate concert piece.

Good-Humoured Ladies, The (*Le donne di buon umore*). Choreographic comedy in one act by Tommasini based on harpsichord sonatas by Domenico Scarlatti to a scenario after Goldoni; it was choreographed by Leonid Massine (Rome, 1917). Tommasini arranged a suite for orchestra from the score.

Goossens, Sir (Aynsley) Eugene (*b* London, 26 May 1893; *d* Hillingdon, 13 June 1962). English conductor and composer. The son and grandson of conductors, he studied composition at the RCM with Stanford and Charles Wood (1907–10) and the violin with Achille Rivarde. He played the violin in the Queen's Hall Orchestra (1911–15), with which he later worked as assistant conductor. His early career as a conductor included the first English performance of *The Rite of Spring* in 1921. His career blossomed through appointments with the Rochester Philharmonic Or-

chestra (1923–31) and the Cincinnati Symphony (1931–46). In 1947 he moved to Australia where he was director of the New South Wales Conservatorium and resident conductor of the Sydney Symphony Orchestra (1947–56).

Between the wars Goossens was highly regarded as a composer, and such works as the Sinfonietta (1922), the *Phantasy Sextet* (1922–3), written for the wealthy musical patron Elizabeth Sprague Coolidge, and the Concertino for string octet (1928) are highly attractive in their eclectic mixture of post-Romanticism and wiry neo-classicism. He also produced two operas, *Judith* (1929) and *Don Juan de Maañara* (1937), and the oratorio *The Apocalypse* (1953), though these technically demanding works have fallen into neglect. His brother was the oboist Leon Goossens (1897–1988) and his sister the harpist Sidonie (1899–).

PG/JDı

📖 E. GOOSSENS, *Overture and Beginners* (London, 1951) · C. ROSEN, *The Goossens: A Musical Century* (London, 1993)

gopak. See HOPAK.

Gordon, Michael (*b* Miami, 20 July 1956). American composer. He grew up in Nicaragua and studied with Martin Bresnick at Yale. He then settled in New York, where in 1983 he formed his own performing group. In 1987 he was a co-founder, with David Lang and Julia Wolfe, of Bang on a Can, a performance organization that presented everything from near-rock to Milton Babbitt. He has written operas (*Chaos*, 1994) and orchestral pieces (*Sunshine of your Love*, 1999), but most of his works are for non-standard groups, and include *Trance* for an ensemble based on winds, keyboards, and electric guitars (1995).

PG

Górecki, Henryk (Mikołaj) (*b* Czernica, nr Rybnik, 6 Dec. 1933). Polish composer. While he was still a student in the late 1950s his music came to the forefront of the Polish avant-garde, culminating in the orchestral *Scontri* (1960). After a period of intense reflection (*Elementi*, 1962), he emerged with clear-headed and expressively direct music (*Refrain*, 1965). In the late 1960s he developed a language based on modal idioms, references to Polish sacred and folk music, and iconographic quotations of such composers as Beethoven and Chopin. The music was customarily slow-moving, repetitive, and strongly contrasted in its blocked dynamics (Symphony no. 2, 'Copernican', 1973).

The Third Symphony, 'Symphony of Sorrowful Songs' (1976), is the epitome of this period, with its three slow laments for solo soprano and orchestra. It hovered on the edge of the contemporary orchestral repertory until 1993, when the fourth recording—by

Dawn Upshaw and the London Sinfonietta, conducted by David Zinman—burst into the classical and popular charts in many countries. Its belated success (this recording sold over a million copies worldwide) was unprecedented for a contemporary work, and not without controversy among critics and musicians. It marked a pivotal moment when new music reached out beyond its often narrow confines to the wider public.

Górecki's music in the 1980s concentrated on choral and chamber genres, culminating in two string quartets (1988, 1991) in which he pursued a more classical, developmental approach to material and structure. From the Harpsichord Concerto (1980), he also demonstrated a keen sense of wit and pace, which resulted in 1993 in *Little Requiem for a Certain Polka*, with its idiosyncratic combination of reflection and exuberance.　　ATH

 📖 B. JACOBSON, *A Polish Renaissance* (London, 1996) · A. THOMAS, *Górecki* (Oxford, 1997)

gorgheggio (It., from *gorgheggiare*, 'to trill'). A modern term applied to a long, rapid vocal passage in which one vowel takes many notes.

gorgia (It.). A term given to the art of improvised vocal ornamentation practised around 1600 in the performance of madrigals, motets, and other pieces. Caccini, in his preface to *Le nuove musiche* (1602), gives a detailed explanation of the various types of ornament required.

Goss, Sir John (*b* Fareham, Hants., 27 Dec. 1800; *d* London, 10 May 1880). English organist and composer. A Child of the Chapel Royal under John Stafford Smith and a pupil of Attwood, he was an operatic tenor before devoting himself to church music. He was appointed organist at St Paul's (1838) and composer to the Chapel Royal (1856). His output consisted mainly of sacred music, *If we believe* (for the funeral of the Duke of Wellington in 1852) and *O Saviour of the world* (1869) being among several fine examples. Goss also edited three collections of hymns, and published *An Introduction to Harmony and Thorough-Bass* (1833) and *The Organist's Companion* (1864).　　WT/JD1

Gossec, François-Joseph (*b* Vergnies, Hainaut, 17 Jan. 1734; *d* Passy, 16 Feb. 1829). French composer of Walloon origin. A chorister at Antwerp Cathedral from 1742, he went to Paris in 1751 and through Rameau's influence joined the orchestra of the tax-gatherer La Pouplinière, which Johann Stamitz directed in 1754–5. Gossec was soon publishing chamber music and beginning his prolific career as a symphonist. He showed a predilection for unusual orchestration, using clarinets in a symphony in 1761; his *Messe des morts* (1760) exploits spatial disposition of orchestral and choral forces. His long association with the stage began with arias for Sophie Arnould and an *opéra comique* for a private theatre (1761). After La Pouplinière's death (1762) he found other patrons, and composed several successful works for the Comédie-Italienne. He continued to write instrumental music and in 1769 founded the Concert des Amateurs, performing his own and Haydn's symphonies. His symphonies, in four movements, are the most important French works of his generation.

In 1773 Gossec became a director of the Concert Spirituel. He was also employed by the Opéra, in 1779 supplying a ballet for Gluck's *Iphigénie en Tauride*. The rising stars of Grétry in *opéra comique* and Gluck at the Opéra stood in the way of his own success, in spite of the pioneering instrumentation (with trombones) of his nationalistic *Sabinus* (for the dauphin's marriage, 1773). His *Thésée* (1782) set a version of a text used by Lully, but both serious operas, and the fashionably sentimental *Rosine* (1786), failed and, unusually, were not published. Although he received royal patronage he favoured the Revolution, and with Bernard Sarrette directed performances of the National Guard for revolutionary ceremonies, composing fine wind music such as *Marche lugubre* and several revolutionary hymns. He was among the founding directors of the Paris Conservatoire and devoted most of his energy after 1795 to teaching.　　WT/JR

 📖 J. MONGRÉDIEN, *La Musique en France, des Lumières au Romantisme: De 1789 à 1830* (Paris, 1986; Eng. trans. 1996)

Gothic Symphony. Havergal Brian's first symphony (1919–27); the last of its four movements is a setting of the 'Te Deum' for soprano, alto, tenor, and bass soloists, quadruple chorus, children's chorus, four brass bands, and large orchestra.

Götterdämmerung ('The Twilight of the Gods'). Opera in three acts by Wagner to his own libretto, the 'third day' of *Der *Ring des Nibelungen*.

Gottschalk, Louis Moreau (*b* New Orleans, 8 May 1829; *d* Tijuca, Brazil, 18 Dec. 1869). American pianist and composer. His life reads like a romantic novel, and much of his music bears the same colourful and fantastic traits. Born of English-Jewish and French Creole parents, Gottschalk left New Orleans at the age of 13 to study the piano and composition in Paris. He soon drew acclaim for both his playing and his Creole-inspired compositions (*Bamboula*, *La Savane*, *Le Bananier*). After several years spent giving concerts in Europe, he returned to America in 1853 an international celebrity, touring extensively and impressing audiences with his good looks, charm, and wide-ranging repertory. The last 13 years of his life were characterized by intensive periods of work and travel punctuated by interludes of languorous dissipation in the Caribbean region. He organized 'monster concerts' in Cuba and South America, and died during a strenuous concert tour.

Although he spoke English with an accent and never settled anywhere in the USA, Gottschalk was hailed as the first virtuoso performer-composer of international repute that America had produced. Apart from two symphonies and a one-act 'opera' *Escenas campestres* (1860), he mainly wrote shorter piano compositions. His output ranges from uninspired salon trifles to miniature masterpieces whose effect is fresh and immediate (*Souvenir de Porto Rico*, *Berceuse*, *The Banjo*), but in spite of that unevenness and the variety of stylistic influences, Gottschalk's music is unified by its ability to evoke the vitality, grace, and élan of 19th-century America, and animated by the spirit of its composer.   MT

Goudimel, Claude (*b* Besançon, *c*.1514; *d* Lyons, 28–31 Aug. 1572). French composer. His early works include masses and motets for the Catholic rite, as well as many chansons. Following his conversion to the Protestant faith in *c*.1560 he turned his attention to setting the words and tunes of the Genevan Psalter in a variety of styles, the simplest of which remained in congregational use in France until the 19th century. One of the foremost French composers of his time, he died in the St Bartholomew's Day massacre of the Huguenots.

                                                                 JM

Gould, Glenn (Herbert) (*b* Toronto, 25 Sept. 1932; *d* Toronto, 4 Oct. 1982). Canadian pianist, writer, composer, and broadcaster. A teenage prodigy in Canada, he made his American debut in 1955 and first appeared in New York playing Bach's 'Goldberg' Variations, a risky choice but one that brought him immediate acclaim and a recording contract. He then toured Europe and the USSR, but in 1964 forsook the concert platform for the recording and radio studios. His performing mannerisms, eccentric behaviour, and unorthodox repertory did not obscure the clarity of his pianism, and his written and broadcast legacy is both profound and provocative.   CF

📖 T. PAGE (ed.), *The Glenn Gould Reader* (New York, 1984) · K. BAZZANA, *Glenn Gould: The Performer in the Work* (Oxford, 1997)

Gould, Morton (*b* Richmond Hill, NY, 10 Dec. 1913; *d* Orlando, FL, 21 Feb. 1996). American composer. He studied at the Institute of Musical Art in New York and with Vincent Jones for composition and Abby Whiteside for the piano. During the Depression he found work in vaudeville theatres and cinemas, and in the 1940s his radio programmes, mixing classical and popular music, had enormous audiences. Thereafter, as composer and conductor, he recognized no boundaries. He made ground-breaking recordings of Ives's music, wrote shows and film scores, and produced a large output of orchestral concert pieces, usually drawing on American sources (jazz, folk music, hymns, parlour songs).   PG

Gounod, Charles (François) (*b* Paris, 17 June 1818; *d* Saint Cloud, 18 Oct. 1893). French composer. After entering the Paris Conservatoire in 1836, to study with Halévy (counterpoint) and Le Sueur (composition), he won the Prix de Rome in 1839. In Rome his musical scope was broadened by his discovery of Palestrina and 16th-century polyphony, together with Bach, Beethoven, and Mendelssohn (to whose music he was introduced by Fanny Hensel, Mendelssohn's sister). On his return to France he stood somewhat apart from his operatically oriented contemporaries: visits to Vienna (1842) and Leipzig (1843) had given him a wider understanding of European music past and present; and his life (like Liszt's) was a curious mixture of the sacred and profane, for he began training for the priesthood (1846–8) and remained an insatiable womanizer.

In 1849 he met Pauline Viardot, who assisted his entry into the Parisian operatic world by promising to sing the title role in his first opera, *Sapho* (1851). Like his next Meyerbeerian *grand opéra*, *La Nonne sanglante* (1854), *Sapho* was a failure, and it was not until he moved from the Opéra to Carvalho's more forward-looking Théâtre Lyrique that he produced the five more successful operas (four with librettos by Barbier and Carré) on which his reputation now rests: *Le Médecin malgré lui* (1858); *Faust* (1859); *Philémon et Baucis* (1860); *Mireille* (1864, libretto by Carré alone); and *Roméo et Juliette* (1867). In these operas Gounod moved away from the predominant spectacular tradition of Meyerbeer towards a mixture of tender, lyrical charm, consummate craftsmanship, and genuine musical characterization. *Faust* remains one of the landmarks of French 19th-century opera, full of variety and with an underlying sensuality that saved it from the sentimentality and banality to which Gounod's later works (especially his oratorios) often descended in his quest for inspired simplicity. Gounod always needed words to create his best music, and again his early masses are his best, though he moved away from Palestrinian austerity towards a more fluid, operatic style in his *Messe solennelle de Sainte Cécile* (1855); in general his music of the 1860s became more Italianate, while retaining its French attributes of precision, taste, and elegance.

The turning-point in Gounod's life and music came with the war of 1870–1, which forced him to seek refuge in England and resulted in his disastrous liaison with the possessive and trouble-prone singer Georgina Weldon. After this his music became increasingly repetitive and platitudinous, even if his numerous songs and oratorios (e.g. *La Rédemption*, 1881, and *Mors et vita*, 1885) were immensely popular. Gounod's influence on Bizet and Massenet, on Fauré's early songs, and on English choral music was considerable. *Faust* brought him international fame, but even at the height of his powers (1855–65) Gounod seldom rose far above the rank of *petit maître*.   RO

📖 C. Gounod, *Mémoires d'un artiste* (Paris, 1896) · M. Cooper, *French Music from the Death of Berlioz to the Death of Fauré* (London, 1951/R1961) · F. Noske, *French Song from Berlioz to Duparc*, trans. R. Benton (London and New York, 1970) · J. Harding, *Gounod* (London, 1973) · S. Huebner, *The Operas of Charles Gounod* (Oxford, 1990)

goûts réunis, les (Fr., 'reunion of tastes'). See réunis, 3.

Goyescas (*Los majos enamorados*; 'Pieces in the Style of Goya'; 'Youth in Love'). 1. Suite for piano (1911) by Granados, six pieces in two sets, inspired by the paintings of Francisco Goya; it is usually performed with the addition of 'El pelele' ('The Worthless Man').

2. Opera in one act (three scenes) by Granados to a libretto by Fernando Periquet (New York, 1916); it was expanded and scored from the above piano pieces.

G.P. 1. Abbreviation for *Generalpause*.

2. In French organ music, an abbreviation for *Grand-positif*, the 'Great' and 'choir' organs coupled together.

Grabovsky, Leonid [Hrabovs'ky, Leonid (Oleksandrovych)] (*b* Kiev, 28 Jan. 1935). Ukrainian composer. He studied economics at Kiev University, then composition with Levko Revuts'ky and Lyatoshyns'ky at the Kiev Conservatory, where he subsequently took up a teaching post. He was briefly resident in Moscow before emigrating to the USA in 1990; he now lives in New York. His style developed under the influence of such European postwar modernists as Lutosławski and Penderecki, and he characteristically explores unusual timbral combinations. He has also taken an innovatory approach to Ukrainian folk music in various works.
                                                        JWal

Grabu, Louis [Luis] (*fl* 1665–94). Catalan composer. Appointed as composer to Charles II in 1665, he soon became Master of the King's Music and later displaced John Banister (i) as director of the select violin band at court. Grabu, with other Roman Catholics, was dismissed from his place at court in 1673. Thereafter he wrote much music in the French style for London theatres until, in 1694, he left England permanently for the Low Countries.   AA

grace notes. A term used generally for ornamental notes printed in small type and not included in the sum of notes in the bar. The simplest example is the *appoggiatura, especially in its short form (often called *acciaccatura). Some composers, for instance Chopin, wrote long chains of grace notes, to be performed lightly and freely while maintaining a steady tempo overall.

gradatamente (It.). 'Gradually'.

gradevole (It.). 'Pleasing', 'agreeable'.

gradito (It.). 'Pleasant'.

gradual (from medieval Lat. *graduale*, a chant sung 'on the steps' (*gradus*) of the altar). 1. The liturgical book containing the chants of the Mass. It is used by the choir, whereas the words spoken by the priest during Mass are found in the Missal (now called the Sacramentary). The modern gradual is divided into two sections: one contains a series of Ordinary chants common to almost all Masses (Kyrie, Gloria, Credo, Sanctus, Agnus Dei, *Ite missa est*) and is called the Kyriale; the other has groups of chants for the changing, or Proper, part of the Mass (introits, graduals (see below, 2), alleluias, tracts, offertories, and communions) arranged for services throughout the church year. It also includes special Masses, such as the Requiem Mass. The earliest surviving graduals (8th century) contained only the Proper chants, but from the 10th century they are together with the Kyriale chants. Many of the earliest sources of polyphonic music (the 11th-century Chartres Manuscript, the Winchester Troper, the Codex Calixtinus, and the earliest Notre Dame source) are centrally concerned with setting items from the Gradual and Kyriale—particularly alleluias, graduals, and troped settings of the Ordinary of the Mass.

The first modern printed Gradual, the *Liber gradualis*, was produced in 1883 by the monks of Solesmes. Their work was approved by Pope Pius X in 1904, and in 1908 the first official Vatican Gradual was produced (revised 1948). Following the Second Vatican Council (1962–5) changes were made in the content and importance of certain Masses; a new Missal appeared in 1970 and a new Gradual in 1974.

See also Liber usualis.   —/ALi

2. A responsorial chant, part of the Proper of the Mass, one of the chants between the readings; since the Second Vatican Council it is usually replaced by a longer text (a 'responsorial psalm'). It is sometimes also known as *responsorium graduale*, or simply *graduale*,

perhaps because it was performed on the steps (Lat.: *gradus*) leading to the altar. Graduals are among the most elaborate of all chants and are performed by soloists and choir in alternation.

Gradualia. Latin motets by Byrd: the first book (1605) contains 32 for five voices, 20 for four voices, and 11 for three voices; the second (1607) contains nine for six voices, 17 for five voices, and 19 for four voices.

Gradus ad Parnassum ('Steps to Parnassus'). A title, referring to the mountain sacred to Apollo and the Muses, given from the early 18th century onwards to dictionaries of Latin prosody. It was also given to two musical publications, each designed to lead to a form of musical perfection: *Fux's treatise on counterpoint (Vienna, 1725, rev. 1842) and Clementi's three-volume collection of piano studies op. 44 (Leipzig and Paris, 1817, 1819, 1826). The first piece in Debussy's *Children's Corner* (1906–8) for piano is called *Doctor Gradus ad Parnassum* and is a parody of a child's attempt to play a Clementi study.

Graf, Conrad (*b* Riedlingen, 17 Nov. 1782; *d* Vienna, 18 March 1851). Austrian piano maker. In Vienna from 1804 he made fine, almost entirely wooden pianos which were admired by Beethoven, Chopin, the Schumanns, and Liszt.   AL

Graf von Luxemburg, Der ('The Count of Luxembourg'). Operetta in three acts by Lehár to a libretto by A. M. Willner and Robert Bodanzky (Vienna, 1909).

grall. 1. English name for a gradual (see GRADUAL, 1).
2. The Holy Grail was the vessel said to have been used by Christ at the Last Supper and then by Joseph of Arimathea to receive Christ's blood at the Crucifixion; it features in Wagner's opera *Parsifal*.

Grainger, (George) Percy (Aldridge) (*b* Brighton, Melbourne, 8 July 1882; *d* White Plains, NY, 20 Feb. 1961). Australian-born American composer, pianist, writer, and ethnomusicologist. Best known for much of his life as a pianist, he was long celebrated as a composer for what he called his 'fripperies'—such short orchestral works as *Handel in the Strand* (1911–30), *Molly on the Shore* (1907–14), *Country Gardens* (1908–18), and *Mock Morris* (1910–12)—which in their day enjoyed popularity as piano solos and in instrumental arrangements. It was only when Britten featured Grainger at the 1966 Aldeburgh Festival that the variety of the latter's folksong settings, from the sombre and impressive power of *Shallow Brown* (1910, rev. 1923–5) to the fine wind-band arrangement *Lincolnshire Posy* (1937–8, 1940), was revealed; and since the appearance in 1976 of Bird's pioneering biography, Grainger's

reputation as one of the most significant early Australian composers has been consolidated.

With his mother, Grainger emigrated to Europe in 1895; until 1899 he studied composition with Knorr at the Hoch Conservatory, Frankfurt, where he became associated with the *Frankfurt Group. In 1901 he moved to London. After taking piano lessons with Busoni in Berlin in 1903 he immediately established a reputation as a concert pianist, but also found time to collect 500 English folksongs, particularly in Lincolnshire, and pioneered the use of the wax-cylinder phonograph for field recording. It was on one of those tunes—*Brigg Fair*—that Delius's orchestral rhapsody was based.

In 1914 Grainger went to New York, primarily as a virtuoso pianist. He served as a bandsman in the US Army, 1917–19, and took American citizenship in 1918. After his mother's suicide in 1922 he became restless and travelled widely in Scandinavia, collecting folksongs in Jutland and meeting Grieg; the two men became close friends, and Grainger championed Grieg's Piano Concerto. On one of his return journeys to the USA he met the Swedish painter and poet Ella Ström, whom he married in 1928 before an audience of thousands in the Hollywood Bowl. He taught at the Chicago Musical College, 1919–28, and in 1932–3 was chairman of New York University music department; in 1934–5 he returned to Melbourne, where in 1938 he inaugurated an ethnomusicological research centre at the university and built the Grainger Museum, to which he was to leave his skeleton.

Grainger's music is notable for his use of unusual instruments (e.g. harmonium, saxophones); he also wrote and arranged extensively for wind band. His largest-scale symphonic work *The Warriors*, subtitled 'Music for an Imaginary Ballet' (1913–16), is dedicated to Delius; for a large orchestra, it is music of typical athleticism, contrasting the pungent rhythms of the outer sections with a slow, anguished string melody.

As a pioneer ethnomusicologist, Grainger had a natural interest in Pacific cultures, but he also experimented in what later became *musique concrète* and electronic music, striving to fulfil his lifelong conception of 'free music' with a succession of home-made machines. The sonorities of unusual instruments were a constant preoccupation, demonstrated in his orchestrating for flexible ensembles often dominated by tuned percussion.   MK/LF

📖 J. BIRD, *Percy Grainger: The Man and the Music* (London, 1976, 2/1999) · L. FOREMAN (ed.), *The Percy Grainger Companion* (London, 1981) · K. DREYFUS, *The Farthest North of Humanness: The Letters of Percy Grainger, 1901–1914* (Melbourne, 1985) · T. BALOUGH (ed.), *A Musical Genius from Australia: Selected Writings About and By Percy*

Grainger (Perth, W. Australia, 1986) · M. GILLIES and B. C. Ross (eds.), *Grainger on Music* (Oxford, 1999)

gramophone. A recording device patented by Emile Berliner in 1888. It used as its medium a shellac disc (rather than the *cylinder favoured by Thomas Alva Edison) which could be mass produced by stamping from a metal master. Because Edison owned exclusive rights in 'phonograph' Berliner coined the term 'gramophone', which became the accepted colloquial usage in the UK for all disc recordings. It was later adopted (1923–) as the name of the principal British journal for reviewing recordings.

See also RECORDING AND REPRODUCTION.   LF

Granados (y Campina), Enrique (*b* Lérida, 27 July 1867; *d* at sea, English Channel, 24 March 1916). Spanish composer and pianist. He studied composition in Barcelona with Felipe Pedrell and the piano in Paris with Charles de Bériot from 1887. On returning to Barcelona in 1889 he gave some recitals, performing a number of his works with success. In spite of the popular fame of his zarzuela *Maria del Carmen* in Madrid (1898) most of his time was devoted to teaching, and it was not until the success of his piano suite *Goyescas* (1911, inspired by the paintings of Goya) that he gained much recognition as a serious composer. After performing *Goyescas* in Paris in 1914, he was invited to compose an opera based on it for the Paris Opéra, but the war intervened, and it was eventually given by the New York Metropolitan Opera in 1916, in the composer's presence. He lost his life on his return to Europe, when his ship, the *Sussex*, was torpedoed in the English Channel.

Much of Granados's music is for his own instrument, the piano. Though inevitably influenced by that of his compatriot Albéniz, it is generally less flamboyant, less overtly nationalist, relying more for its inspiration on early Romantic, even non-Hispanic models. The best pieces, for example *Goyescas* and the exquisite *Danzas españolas* (1892–1900), much admired by his contemporaries, show a characteristic simplicity and a sensitive, restrained approach to the highly decorative figuration usually associated with Spanish nationalist music. Of his other works, his delicate songs are mainstays of the Spanish repertory, and the opera version of *Goyescas*, though not conventionally theatrical, is sensuously evocative of 18th-century Madrid. Granados's early Piano Quintet (1898), neat and aphoristic, is among the most memorable of Spanish chamber works.   JN/CW

📖 C. A. HESS, *Enrique Granados: A Bio-Bibliography* (New York, 1991)

grand choeur (Fr.). 'Full choir', 'full organ', sometimes used as the title of a loud organ piece; it may be abbreviated *gd choeur* or *gd ch*.

Grand Duo. Subtitle given by the publisher (in 1838) to Schubert's Sonata in C major for piano duet, D812 (1824); it was once thought to be a piano version of a 'lost' symphony but that theory has been discredited. There are orchestral versions of the work by Joachim and Anthony Collins.

Grande Bande. See VINGT-QUATRE VIOLONS DU ROI.

Grande-Duchesse de Gérolstein, La ('The Grand-Duchess of Gerolstein'). Opera in three acts by Offenbach to a libretto by Henri Meilhac and Ludovic Halévy (Paris, 1867).

Grande Messe des morts ('High Mass for the Dead'). French title of Berlioz's Requiem op. 5 (1837), for tenor solo, boys' chorus, chorus, and orchestra; it was revised in 1852 and 1867.

grandezza, con (It.). 'With grandeur'.

Grandi, Alessandro (*b* ?1575–80; *d* Bergamo, 1630). Italian composer. From about 1597 to 1617 he held various posts at churches in Ferrara. He was then appointed a singer at St Mark's, Venice, subsequently becoming Monteverdi's assistant. In 1627 he became *maestro di cappella* at S. Maria Maggiore, Bergamo, where he died, with his family, of the plague. He was probably the first composer to use the designation 'cantata', but his finest work lies in his superb motets for one, two, and three voices. His music was widely disseminated across Europe; clearly he was one of the most popular composers of the day.   DA/TC

grandioso (It.). 'Grandiose'.

Grand Macabre, Le ('The Grand Macabre'). Opera in two acts by Ligeti to a libretto by the composer and Michael Meschke after Michel de Ghelderode's play *La balade du Grand Macabre* (Stockholm, 1978).

grand opera. In common English usage, serious opera without spoken dialogue. In French, more precisely, *grand opéra* (as opposed to *opéra comique*) means a serious, epic work on a historical, mythic, or legendary subject, usually (though not exclusively) in five acts, which uses the chorus actively and includes a ballet, and frequently dramatizes the conflict between private emotion and public, religious, or political responsibility. It was the characteristic form of the Paris Opéra until the late 19th century, originating during the first Napoleonic Empire and coinciding with the emergence of a wealthy *grande bourgeoisie* devoted to spectacle. Great importance was therefore attached to magnificence of effect, both on stage with the reforms of the stage designer Pierre-Luc-Charles Cicéri (1782–1868), and among singers with the disappearances of the castrato and the emergence of a new type of heroic dramatic singer.

The composer who first answered these demands and set new standards was Spontini, with *La Vestale* (1807), *Fernand Cortez* (1809), and *Olimpie* (1819). Among the most important grand operas in the years that followed at the Opéra were Auber's *La Muette de Portici* (1828) and Rossini's *Guillaume Tell* (1829). The archetypal five-act form of *grand opéra* became fixed in the works of Meyerbeer (*Robert le diable*, 1831, *Les Huguenots*, 1836, and *Le Prophète*, 1849) and Halévy (*La Juive*, 1835). The form and style of French *grand opéra*, often rigidly imposed by the Paris house, has come to be regarded as normative, formulaic, and constricting, though its influence was enormous and many 19th-century composers produced works that may be seen as either adhering to, or adapting, its demands. The style left its mark on Wagner's early operas, especially *Rienzi* (1842). His second version of *Tannhäuser*, prepared for the Paris Opéra in 1861, is widely regarded as a radical attempt to break down the constraints of the genre. In spite of Wagner's frequent attacks on the Opéra, his later demands for scenic spectacle, notably in *Der Ring des Nibelungen* (1850–76), may be seen as derived from French theatricality.

The two greatest works in the traditional form of *grand opéra*, both unsuccessful in their day, are now considered to be the original French version of Verdi's *Don Carlos* (1867) and Berlioz's *Les Troyens* (1856–8). Many Italian composers produced works that are effectively variants on the French structure—frequently in four acts, though making powerful use of spectacle, ballet, and the dramatization of the conflict between private and public interests—many of which are regarded as 'grand opera' in the English sense of the term. Verdi's *Aida* (1871) is the most popular example, though the description also pertains to Ponchielli's *La Gioconda* (1876), and Boito's *Mefistofele* (1868) and *Nerone* (1918).   JW/TA

📖 J. F. FULCHER, *The Nation's Image: French Grand Opera as Politics and Politicized Art* (Cambridge, 1987)

grand piano. A piano in a horizontal, wing-shaped case. See PIANOFORTE.

Grange, Philip (Roy) (*b* London, 17 Nov. 1956). English composer. He studied composition with David Blake at the University of York and with Maxwell Davies at the Dartington Summer School. In 2001 he took up a teaching post at Manchester University. While profoundly influenced by the expressionistic aspect of Maxwell Davies's style, he has sought to preserve a more direct, even simpler lyricism, notably in his settings of Edward Thomas (*On this Bleak Hut*, 1981, *As it Was*, 1985) and Robert Louis Stevenson (*A Puzzle of Shadows*, 1997). Grange's vivid response to specific texts is no less apparent in his instrumental compositions, which, while often dark in tone, are volatile and intricate in texture (*Cimmerian Nocturne*, 1979, *The Dark Labyrinth*, 1987, *In Spectre Search*, 1994).   AW

graphic notation. A system developed in the 1950s by which visual shapes or patterns are used instead of, or together with, conventional musical notation. Graphic scores tend to fall into one of two categories. First there are those which attempt to communicate particular compositional intentions. Examples include Feldman's pioneering *Projection* (1950–1) and Stockhausen's *Prozession* (1967). Second there are those in which visual, often aesthetically pleasing, symbols are presented so as to inspire the free play of the performer's imagination in unstipulated ways. Earle Brown's *December 1952* is an early example, and Cardew's *Treatise* (1967) has the status of a classic in this idiom.   AP

Graun, Carl Heinrich (*b* Wahrenbrück, nr Dresden, 1703 or 1704; *d* Berlin, 8 Aug. 1759). German composer. He came from a family of musicians; both he and his brother Johann Heinrich served with distinction at the court of Frederick the Great. After service as a tenor in the opera chorus at Dresden, he transferred in 1725 to Brunswick, where he wrote six operas for the court, notably *Pharao Tubaetes*, in which Italian arias are linked with German recitatives. In 1733 he composed the opera *Lo specchio della fedeltà* ('The Mirror of Fidelity') for the marriage of Frederick, Crown Prince of Prussia, to Princess Elisabeth Christine of Brunswick, and on Frederick's accession in 1740 he became Kapellmeister to the Prussian court. During the next 15 years Graun dominated opera in Berlin (though not without some interference in artistic decisions by his royal patron), writing 15 new works, including *Cesare e Cleopatra* (1742) for the opening of the Royal Opera House (the renowned Lindenoper), and *Montezuma* (1755), to a libretto by Frederick; the latter was unusual for its time in being based on a non-classical theme. In 1756, however, Graun's activities were halted by the outbreak of the Seven Years War, and thereafter he wrote no further operas. Among his other works the most enduring are his Passion oratorio *Der Tod Jesu* (1755) and his *Te Deum* in celebration of Frederick's victory at Prague in 1756.   DA/BS

Graun, Johann Gottlieb (*b* Wahrenbrück, nr Dresden, 1702 or 1703; *d* Berlin, 27 Oct. 1771). German violinist and composer, brother of Carl Heinrich Graun. He was appointed (*c.*1726) Konzertmeister at Merseburg, where he met J. S. Bach and for a short period taught Wilhelm Friedemann Bach. In 1732 he joined the musical coterie of the Prussian Crown Prince Frederick at Ruppin and, on the latter's accession in 1740, became leader of the new Berlin Opera orchestra. His numerous instrumental works—symphonies, concertos, and trio sonatas—display striking individuality.   DA/BS

Graupner, (Johann) Christoph (*b* Kirchberg, 13 Jan. 1683; *d* Darmstadt, 10 May 1760). German composer. As a pupil at the Thomasschule in Leipzig from about 1697, he studied for nine years under the Kantors, Schelle and Kuhnau. In 1706 he moved to Hamburg, where he was befriended by Telemann and, from 1707, acted as harpsichordist for the Theater am Gänsemarkt. Among the operas he wrote for Hamburg *Bellerophon* (1708) enjoyed particular success. In 1709 he was appointed vice-Kapellmeister (under Wolfgang Briegel) to the Darmstadt court of the Landgrave Ernst Ludwig, becoming Kapellmeister in 1712. In 1722 he applied for the vacant post of Kantor at the Thomasschule but withdrew at the request of his employer, thus making way for Bach's appointment. His impressive output included some 1400 church cantatas, close in style to those of Bach, together with 113 symphonies, 40 concertos, and numerous chamber and solo keyboard works.   DA/BS

grave (Fr.). 1. 'Serious', 'solemn': a tempo indication which in the 17th century meant very slow but which by the 18th came to mean the same as *andante*.

2. When applied to pitch, 'low'.

grazioso (It.). 'Graceful'; *graziosamente*, 'gracefully'.

Great organ. The main section of an organ, controlled by the lower manual and equivalent to the German *Hauptwerk* and *Oberwerk*. It includes diapasons and reeds, and is distinct from the *chair, *swell, and pedal departments (see also ORGAN, 5 and 8).

great service. See SERVICE.

Grechaninov, Alexander (Tikhonovich) (*b* Moscow, 25 Oct. 1864; *d* New York, 4 Jan. 1956). Russian composer. He studied at the Moscow Conservatory, but, finding his composition teacher Anton Arensky unsympathetic to his music, he moved to St Petersburg, where his studies with Rimsky-Korsakov were to have a lasting impact. After the Revolution he settled for a while in Paris (from 1925) and in 1939 moved to the USA. He is known specially for his liturgical music, his piano works for children, and his many songs, but he also wrote much music for the theatre (including the opera *Dobrïnya Nikitich*, Moscow, 1903), some chamber music, and a number of orchestral works, among them

four symphonies of which even the last (composed in 1924) reveals Grechaninov's essential conservatism of language, albeit marked by deeply felt lyricism (particularly in the slow third movement) and invigorated by a lively rhythmic sense and a flair for apt, assertive orchestration.   GN

Greece. 1. See ANCIENT GREEK MUSIC.

2. The music of present-day Greece—remarkable for both its abundance and its diversity—has developed over many centuries and has been subject to a variety of historical and geographical influences. The different regions of Greece have absorbed elements of the music of their Turkish, Balkan, and Italian neighbours, so that it is impossible to speak of a single tradition. Until the mid-20th century the survival of a rich musical culture was assured by the continuation of age-old pastoral, agricultural, and maritime patterns of existence. Equally, the individuality of music in different regions has been protected by the country's mountainous terrain, its poor communications, and the isolation of communities from one another.

Since the end of World War II Greece has undergone enormous social and economic changes, the single most significant factor being the mass migration from the countryside to the towns. Music, dance, and song continue to play a central role in both urban and rural life, and musical traditions are being maintained to a striking degree. Chief among these is the *rebetiko* song repertory, originally associated with hashish-smoking urban communities in low-life areas; the songs are accompanied by groups of plucked string instruments, principally the *bouzouki.

Western art music did not gain a foothold in Greece until after the foundation of the independent Greek kingdom (1832). Efforts to promote interest in it were almost entirely privately inspired and the growth of an audience was slow. Touring European musicians—most of them Italian opera and operetta companies—visited Greece from the late 1830s onwards. Such 19th-century composers of the 'Ionian school' as Nikolaos Mantzaros (1795–1872; composer of the national anthem), Spyridon Xyndas (?1812–1896), and Pavlos Carrer (1829–196) were unable to rise above overwhelming Italian influences and failed to establish independent styles of their own. Although the Athens Conservatory was established in 1871, promising musicians were still obliged to look outside Greece for musical education and experience.

It was not until after World War I that such composers as Manolis Kalomiris (1883–1962) and Petro Petridis (1892–1977) demonstrated Greece's ability to make a valuable and original contribution to Western music. Skalkottas, who studied with Schoenberg, is undoubtedly the foremost avant-garde Greek composer of the period, though the extent of his output in atonal music did not become apparent until after his death in 1949.

After World War II, Xenakis (resident outside Greece from his mid-20s) achieved international renown, producing a large body of orchestral, choral, and chamber music as well as a number of works for tape. Prominent among his contemporaries were Jani Christou and Yannis Andreou Papaioannou (1910–89), both of whom adopted serial procedures. Arghyris Kounadis (*b* 1924) has written extensively for the stage, but his operas have found more success in Germany than in Greece. He and other composers of his generation found inspiration in *rebetiko* melodies, rhythms, and instrumentation: Manos Hadjidakis (1925–94) and Mikis Theodorakis combined urban and rural traditional styles extensively in their music, the best-known examples being the film scores for *Never on Sunday* (Hadjidakis) and *Zorba the Greek* (Theodorakis).

The oustanding figures of the next generation, including Logothetis and Aperghis, became known largely through the activities of the Studio für Neue Musik (founded 1962) and the Hellenic Association for Contemporary Music; the latter, with the Greek section of the ISCM, organized five Hellenic Weeks of Contemporary Music between 1966 and 1976.

Most concerts given by the Athens State Orchestra are held in the Megaro Moussikis Athinon (Athens Concert Hall), opened in 1991. Opera productions at the Megaro have included many specially commissioned works as well as the Greek premieres of *Die ägyptische Helena*, *Wozzeck*, and *Pelléas et Mélisande*. The Institute of Research in Music and Acoustics, founded in 1989, is devoted to contemporary music, fostering technological experiment and serving as an information centre.   RCM/PFA

Greek. Opera in two acts by Turnage to a libretto by the composer and Jonathan Moore after Steven Berkoff's play *Greek* (Munich, 1988).

Greek Passion, The (*Řecké pašije*). Opera in four acts by Martinů to his own libretto with Nikos Kazantzakis after Jonathan Griffin's translation (1954) of Kazantzakis's novel *Christ Recrucified* (1948) (Zürich, 1961).

Greene, Maurice (*b* London, 12 Aug. 1696; *d* London, 1 Dec. 1755). English organist and composer. The son of a clergyman, he was a chorister at St Paul's Cathedral and was subsequently articled to the organist there. He worked as an organist at St Dunstan-in-the-West, Fleet Street, and at St Andrew's, Holborn, before becoming organist at St Paul's in 1718. In the 1720s he

cultivated the friendship of Handel and of Handel's great rival, Bononcini. When Bononcini was expelled from the Academy of Ancient Music for musical fraud Greene also withdrew his membership, establishing a rival concert society, the Apollo Academy, at the Devil Tavern, near Temple Bar. Handel, who by this time had cooled considerably towards Greene, is said to have remarked that Greene had 'gone to the devil'. On the death of Croft in 1727, Greene was appointed organist and composer to the Chapel Royal. He became professor of music at Cambridge University in 1730, and in 1735 succeeded John Eccles as Master of the King's Music.

Greene's reputation as a composer rests chiefly on his *Forty Select Anthems* (1743). He devoted his last years to compiling a collection of English church music, which was taken over and completed after his death by his friend William *Boyce and published as the monumental *Cathedral Music*. Greene's other compositions include odes for royal occasions, church music, three oratorios, keyboard works, and much secular vocal music, notably the dramatic pastorals *Florimel, or Love's Revenge* (1734) and *Phoebe* (1747).   WT/PL

Greensleeves. Old English tune. It was twice mentioned by Shakespeare in *The Merry Wives of Windsor* and by other writers of this and later periods. The first known reference to it occurs in 1580 in the Registers of the Stationers' Company, where it is called 'a new Northern Dittye'. There are ballads to the tune, which was also adopted for sacred use (e.g. 'Green Sleeves moralised to the Scriptures', 1580). During the 17th-century Civil War it was adopted by the Cavaliers, who set many political ballads to it. From this period the tune was sometimes known as *The Blacksmith*; Pepys alluded to it under that name in his diary (23 April 1660). In the 20th century it was used by Vaughan Williams in his opera *Sir John in Love*, by Holst in his *St Paul's Suite* and Suite no. 2 for military band, and by Busoni in *Turandot*.   AL

greghesca (It.). A light song of the mid-16th century, so called because the texts, by Antonio Molino (under the pseudonym Manoli Blessi), are in a 'language' derived from the dialect of the Veneto region and Greek. In 1564 Molino published a collection of *greghesche* with contributions from such composers as Willaert, Andrea Gabrieli, and Rore.

Gregorian chant. See PLAINCHANT.

Gretchen am Spinnrade ('Gretchen at the Spinning-Wheel'). Song (1814) for voice and piano by Schubert (D118) to words from Johann Wolfgang von Goethe's *Faust*,

Grétry, André-Ernest-Modeste (*b* Liège, 8 Feb. 1741; *d* Montmorency, Paris, 24 Sept. 1813). Flemish-born French composer. His father was a violinist at a Liège church, and Grétry became a choirboy there. He composed a set of six symphonies and a Mass, which earned him a scholarship to study at the Collège Darchis in Rome. A first operatic intermezzo, *La vendemmiatrice*, was performed in Rome in 1765; but the next year he moved to Geneva, where he met Voltaire and had his first exposure to *opéra comique*. He moved to Paris in 1767, and after a couple of years had become so popular that he received regular commissions to write two or three operas a year for various theatres. Early on he established a fruitful relationship with Jean François Marmontel, who had been Rameau's librettist some years previously. By the 1770s and 80s he was internationally famous, as well as having been appointed to several important official posts.

Of Grétry's comic operas, the relatively short and light *Zémire et Azore* (1771, libretto by Marmontel) and *Richard Coeur-de-lion* (1784, libretto by M.-J. Sedaine, another prominent librettist of the period) were among the most famous. He was also successful with serious opera, in particular *La Caravane du Caire* (1783). However, after the mid-1780s his operas became somewhat outmoded, at least until he revamped his style with more ambitious *opéras comiques*, and with *Guillaume Tell* (1791), a *drame mis en musique*. Many of his later works had subject matter obviously designed for the audiences of Revolutionary France, perhaps most blatantly *Joseph Barra* (1794)—an openly propagandistic *fait historique*. He was admired by Robespierre, appointed one of the inspectors of the Institut de France in 1795, and granted a pension by Napoleon. His *Mémoires* (Paris, 1789) are full of interesting details of late 18th-century life and music, as well as theories on how drama should be realized in music.

One of Grétry's most important contributions was, in common with many of his contemporaries, to open up French opera to the influence of Italian operatic style, thus attempting to compete with the latter in popularity. This can be seen in his fondness for multi-section arias and, most notably, extended ensemble numbers. However, he was also adept at supplying his best work with a distinctive (and distinctively French) sense of *couleur locale* and, perhaps most famously in *Richard Coeur-de-lion*, with recurring musical material to articulate the drama. In both these developments he was an important precursor of so-called 'Romantic' opera. Several of Grétry's works continued to be performed regularly up to the French Revolution, and some were even revived in the early 19th century.

DA/RP

 D. CHARLTON, *Grétry and the Growth of Opéra-Comique* (Cambridge, 1986)

Gr. Fl. (Ger.). Abbreviation for *grosse Flöte* ('large flute'), the standard concert flute, as distinct from the piccolo (*kleine Flöte*, Kl. Fl.).

Grieg, Edvard (Hagerup) (*b* Bergen, 15 June 1843; *d* Bergen, 4 Sept. 1907). Norwegian composer. He was not only the foremost composer Norway has produced but the first Scandinavian composer to win universal acceptance abroad—indeed, he is one of the handful of popular composers through whom many find their way to music. The family originally came from Scotland, his great-grandfather changing the spelling of his name from Greig to Grieg on assuming Norwegian nationality in 1779. Hagerup was his mother's maiden name and also that of his cousin Nina. He showed early talent as a pianist, and when in 1858 the violinist-composer Ole Bull, a distant relative of his mother, heard him play he persuaded Grieg's parents to send the 15-year-old to Leipzig. There he studied with E. F. Wenzel, a keen advocate of Schumann, Moscheles, and Reinecke, and heard Clara Schumann playing her husband's Piano Concerto in A minor, on which his own was later to be modelled. But he was not happy there and in 1860 was afflicted by an attack of pleurisy which resulted in a collapsed lung. For the rest of his days he was plagued with respiratory problems and struggled through life on one lung.

Grieg's early training and his immersion in the Leipzig tradition of Mendelssohn and Schumann formed the basis for his musical grammar, but Norwegian folksong—whose treasures he discovered some years later in Lindeman's *Norske Fjeldmelodier* ('Norwegian Mountain Melodies') and through his friendship with Rikard Nordraak (1842–66)—was the foundation on which his distinctive musical language developed. After Leipzig he went to Copenhagen and took lessons from Gade who, on being shown some of Grieg's smaller pieces, told him to write a symphony; this he finished in 1864. He often complained in later life that his early studies at the Leipzig Conservatory left him with little understanding of the orchestra, and after hearing Svendsen's D major Symphony in 1867 he withdrew his own and forbade its performance. (However, a photocopy of the autograph was surreptitiously spirited away to the USSR and played on Moscow Radio, so the case for upholding Grieg's ban went by default. The work was performed at the 1981 Bergen Festival and subsequently recorded, and is included in the complete edition currently in progress.) The concert overture *I Høst* ('In Autumn'), which followed two years later, was not much more successful. Grieg was in his early 20s at the time and finished it in

March 1866 while staying in Rome. Later in life he related that he showed the piece to Gade, who dismissed it as 'a load of rubbish' and urged him to go home and think of something better. Before presenting it at the Birmingham Festival in 1888 he completely rescored it.

His reputation at the time was primarily as a miniaturist, resting on the piano music and songs, though this should not be allowed to obscure the fact that in the G major Violin Sonata op. 13 or the A minor Piano Concerto op. 16 he was able to handle longer-breathed musical ideas and think in terms of paragraphs rather than sentences, to commanding effect. But the concerto was the last work of any scale that Grieg attempted, and only three others were to follow: the C minor Violin Sonata op. 45, the Cello Sonata, and the fine G minor String Quartet, which served as a model for Debussy's quartet in the same key. The Piano Concerto, composed in 1868, survives unceasing exposure only to emerge perennially and indestructibly fresh. Yet it is in the ideas themselves rather than the ingenuity of their development that its strength lies.

In 1867 Grieg married his cousin, the singer Nina Hagerup, for whom he composed many of his songs and who was their most persuasive advocate. He set many of the great Norwegian poets of the day including Bjørnstjerne Bjørnson and, of course, Ibsen. In 1872 he composed music for a production of Bjørnson's play *Sigurd Jorsalfar* in Christiania (as Oslo was then known). Although Grieg had met Ibsen in Rome in 1866 they had not become close. But it was obvious to Ibsen from the comments Grieg had made about his early play *Brand* that he had a real understanding of and feeling for his work. Ibsen had never intended *Peer Gynt* to be staged, but in 1874 when his 'dramatic poem' was going into its third printing he decided to adapt it as a play, and it was to Grieg that his thoughts turned when the idea of incidental music first surfaced in his mind. The great success of their enterprise in 1876 took both author and composer by surprise, and neither expected the play to make any headway outside Norway. Grieg's score is more extensive than is popularly believed, and runs in its entirety to no fewer than 32 numbers, amounting to almost 90 minutes of music. Later productions in Copenhagen (1886) and Oslo (1892) entailed revision of the score and in some places extra musical numbers.

In the 1880s Grieg briefly directed the Bergen Harmonien (now known as the Bergen Philharmonic), but in the latter part of that decade and throughout the next he vigorously pursued the life of the travelling concert virtuoso, playing and conducting his own music. He visited England in 1888, and it was there that he gave his last concert in 1906. More than any other

artist before him (with the exception of Musorgsky) he evokes the character of a nation's music. Yet in his songs he hardly ever quotes folk music directly, though his music breathes its spirit. Only 'Solveig's Song' uses a borrowed tune. Throughout his life, both in the songs and in the piano music there is a growing response to the musical language of Norway, and his awareness of its harmonic originality deepened continually. The harmonic astringency of the *Slåtter* ('Norwegian Dances' op. 72, 1902) even suggests Bartók at times. Here and in the ten books of *Lyric Pieces* there is an undying freshness and directness of utterance.

RLa

📖 J. HORTON, *Grieg* (London, 1974) · F. BENESTAD and D. SCHJELDERUP-EBBE, *Grieg: Man and Artist* (London, 1988) · R. LAYTON, *Grieg* (London, 1998)

Griffbrett (Ger.). 'Fingerboard'.

Griffes, Charles T(omlinson) (*b* Elmira, NY, 17 Sept. 1884; *d* New York, 8 April 1920). American composer. He studied with Humperdinck in Berlin (1903–7) and taught from 1908 at a private boys' school in Tarrytown, New York. There he moved on from the solidly Germanic style of his first works to produce a small number of works influenced—as Szymanowski was at the same time—by Debussy, Skryabin, and Asian music, among them *Four Roman Sketches* for piano (1916–18), a Piano Sonata (1918–19), Three Preludes for piano (1919), and the symphonic poem *The Pleasure-Dome of Kubla Khan* (1919). PG

📖 E. M. MAISEL, *Charles Tomlinson Griffes* (New York, 1943)

Griffin, George (Eugene) (*b* London, 8 Jan. 1781; *d* London, 28 May 1863). English pianist and composer. In 1813 he was one of the 30 founder members of the Philharmonic (later Royal Philharmonic) Society. He appeared in some of the society's concerts, performing his own Piano Quartet in 1817, and was invited to write a new piece in 1832 (though he does not appear to have fulfilled the commission). His compositions, in a conservative style, include two piano concertos, four piano sonatas, and a number of shorter piano pieces, arrangements, and songs. Abandoning composition, in the early 1830s he turned instead to teaching. SH

Grigny, Nicolas de (*b* Reims, *bapt.* 8 Sept. 1672; *d* Reims, 30 Nov. 1703). French composer. Like his grandfather and father, he became an organist, and from 1693 to 1695 served in that capacity at the abbey of St Denis, Paris. By 1696 he was at Reims Cathedral, where he remained until his death. He was one of the finest composers of organ music of his time: his work shows a mastery of counterpoint and a grasp of audacious, expressive harmony. Bach made a copy of his *Premier livre d'orgue* (Paris, 1699) in *c*.1703. DA

Grisélidis. Opera in a prologue and three acts by Massenet to a libretto by Armand Sylvestre and Eugène Morand after their dramatization (1891) of the medieval French story (Paris, 1901).

Grisey, Gérard (*b* Belfort, 17 June 1946; *d* Paris, 11 Nov. 1998). French composer. He studied with Messiaen at the Paris Conservatoire (1965–7, 1968–72), with Dutilleux at the École Normale (1968), and with Xenakis and Ligeti at the Darmstadt summer courses. He won the Prix de Rome, and while at the Villa Medici (1972–4) became friendly with Murail; with Murail and Michaël Lévinas in 1973 he founded the ensemble L'Itinéraire. He taught at Darmstadt (1976–82), the University of California, Berkeley (1982–6), and the Paris Conservatoire (1987–98), becoming an admired teacher whose pupils included Eric Tanguy and Lindberg. Grisey's early works, notably *Dérives* (1973–4) for orchestra, explore the acoustic properties of sound and the nature of musical perception (so-called 'spectral music'); he took this idea further in the huge cycle *Les Espaces acoustiques* (1974–85), which ranges from pieces for solo viola to large orchestra. The psychological properties of tempo, sound, and pulse was another preoccupation, explored musically in *Tempus ex machina* (1979) for six percussion and theoretically in an essay of the same title (1988). From the mid-1980s Grisey's musical style changed (*Vortex temporum* (1994–6), for example, is harmonically simpler) and he began to include vocal writing; *L'Icone paradoxale* (1992–4) sets texts on perspective by Piero della Francesca. Grisey was one of the most original composers in the generation after Boulez and won international acclaim; his influential career was cut short by his early death. AL

   📖 R. ROSE, 'Introduction to pitch organization in French spectral music', *Perspectives of New Music*, 34/2 (1996), 6–39

Grisi, Giulia (*b* Milan, 22 May 1811; *d* Berlin, 29 Nov. 1869). Italian soprano, younger sister of the mezzo-soprano Giuditta Grisi (1805–40). She made her debut in Bologna as Emma in Rossini's *Zelmira* in the 1828–9 season and made a strong impression there as Rosina in *Il barbiere di Siviglia*. Two years later she made her debut at La Scala, Milan, where she went on to create the role of Adalgisa in *Norma*. She was the first Giulietta, opposite her sister, in *I Capuleti e i Montecchi*. She left Italy and her career then flourished in Paris (1832–49) and London (1834–61). She was one of the finest singers of her day and often appeared with Giovanni Mario, her lifelong companion. JT

   📖 E. FORBES, *Mario and Grisi* (London, 1985)

groppo (It.). A cadential *trill.

gros, grosse (Fr.). 'Great', 'large'; when used of an organ stop it means 'of low pitch'; *grosse caisse*, *gros tambour*, 'bass drum'.

gross, grosse (Ger.). 'Great', 'large'; e.g. *grosse Flöte*, 'flute'; *grosses Orchester*, 'full orchestra'; *grosse Trommel*, 'bass drum'. When applied to intervals, it signifies 'major', or 'perfect' in the case of 4ths and 5ths.

Grosse Fuge ('Great Fugue'). Beethoven's fugue for string quartet, op. 133 (1825–6), composed as the last movement of his String Quartet op. 130; Beethoven wrote another finale for op. 130 in 1826 and published the *Grosse Fuge* separately in 1827.

Grosse Orgelmesse ('Great Organ Mass'). Haydn's Mass no. 4 in E♭ major (1768 or 1769), so called because of its prominent organ part; its full title is *Missa in honorem Beata Virgine Mariae* or *Missa Sancti Josephi*. See also KLEINE ORGELMESSE.

ground, ground bass. A short melody, usually in the bass, repeated continually with changing upper parts. The term 'ground' first appeared in England in the late 16th century and referred variously to the melody itself, the harmonic framework constructed round it, or the entire composition. One of the best-known examples of the ground bass is Dido's Lament 'When I am laid in earth' from Purcell's opera *Dido and Aeneas*; the bass (Ex. 1) is heard once alone and is then repeated six times with varied harmonies over it. Above these there is a vocal line so free and continuous that the strictures imposed by the repetition of the bass are scarcely felt. It was this contrast between a fixed bass and freely moving upper parts that so attracted 16th- and 17th-century composers to the ground, particularly in England, where elaborate extemporization in an upper part or parts above a ground bass earned the name 'divisions' and became a highly valued performing technique among viol players (see DIVISIONS, 1). Christopher Simpson's, *The Division-Violist* (1659), for example, contains instructions for playing diminutions and other embellishments over the ground melody.

Ex. 1

A ground bass may vary in length from a few notes (as in some of Byrd's keyboard pieces) to a full-length, extended melody (Dido's Lament and countless other vocal works by Purcell). In practice its repetitions need not be rigidly fixed: modifications are possible to allow, for example, for changes of key; the entire ground may shift to a different pitch for a section of the composition; it may be fragmented, with its phrases broken up by rests; or it may fail to coincide with an exact number of bars, so that its notes appear in different positions in the bar (and are thus differently accented) at each repetition.

In Renaissance and Baroque dance music a ground bass was sometimes allied to a particular melody (e.g. in the *romanesca and *folia), and these paired tunes, often together with their implied harmonic scheme, formed the basis of a number of theme and variation sets which were occasionally described as grounds (e.g. 'Farinelli's Ground', actually the *folia).

The ground is in effect an element of *variation form. It can be regarded as an extension of *ostinato, and the *passacaglia and *chaconne can both be considered types of ground, even though their repeated motifs may be in parts other than the bass. It was indeed as a variation technique that the ground persisted beyond the Baroque period, though often under the more specific title of chaconne or passacaglia (e.g. the finale of Brahms's Fourth Symphony or Britten's Passacaglia from the *Four Sea Interludes* from *Peter Grimes*). The ground, together with related ostinato and passacaglia techniques, held some fascination for 20th-century composers, particularly those interested in neo-classicism, notably Bartók (Concerto for Orchestra and many of the piano pieces in *Mikrokosmos*), Stravinsky (*Symphony of Psalms*, Cantata), Hindemith (piano and organ music), and Britten.   PS/JN

Groupe de Recherches Musicales. Electronic music studio in Paris (the first), established in 1951 by Pierre Schaeffer; many leading composers (e.g. Messiaen, Boulez, Berio, Stockhausen, Xenakis) have worked there.

Grove, Sir George (*b* Clapham, 13 Aug. 1820; *d* Sydenham, 28 May 1900). English writer on music. A civil engineer by profession, he built lighthouses in the West Indies and became secretary successively to the Society of Arts (1850) and the Crystal Palace (1852); in the latter position he valuably added to the influence of the conductor August Manns by writing programme notes. He helped to edit Smith's *Dictionary of the Bible* and to found the Palestine Exploration Fund, and wrote articles and books on a variety of subjects, including a geography primer. For 15 years he was editor of *Macmillan's Magazine*, until, in 1883, he became the first

director of the Royal College of Music; he was knighted that year.

Grove's *Dictionary of Music and Musicians* appeared in four volumes, 1879–89, and since his death has appeared in further and enlarged editions: in 1904–10 (ed. J. A. Fuller Maitland), 1927–8, 1940 (both ed. H. C. Colles), and 1954 (ed. Eric Blom; supplement 1961). In 1980 the dictionary, newly conceived and rewritten, was published in 20 volumes as *The New Grove Dictionary of Music and Musicians* (ed. Stanley Sadie). A revised and enlarged edition appeared in both print (29 volumes) and online versions in 2001 under the editorship of Stanley Sadie and John Tyrrell.   PS/LC

📖 P. M. YOUNG, *George Grove* (London, 1980)

Gr. Tr. Abbreviation for *grosse Trommel* (Ger., 'large drum', i.e. *bass drum).

Grua [Pietragrua]. Family of Italian and German musicians. **Carlo Luigi Pietragrua** (*b* Florence, *c*.1665; *d* Venice, 27 March 1726) was vice-Kapellmeister at several German courts. He wrote five Italian operas, sacred music, and chamber duets. Later he returned to Italy. His son, **Carlo Grua** (*b* ?Milan, *c*.1700; *d* Mannheim, 11 April 1773), was Kapellmeister at the Mannheim court *c*.1734. He composed oratorios, church music, and two operas, *Meride* (1742) and *La clemenza di Tito* (1748). His son, **Franz Paul** [Francesco da Paula] **Grua** (*b* Mannheim, 2 Feb. 1753; *d* Munich, 5 July 1833), studied with Holzbauer in Mannheim, and in Italy. Returning to Mannheim, he entered the court chapel as a violinist; he moved to Munich with the court in 1778, becoming Kapellmeister in 1784. He composed orchestral and much sacred music, and an opera, *Telemaco* (Munich, 1780).   WT/RP

Gruber, H(einz) K(arl) (*b* Vienna, 3 Jan. 1943). Austrian composer. He was a member of the Vienna Boys' Choir and later studied composition at the Hochschule für Musik there under Hanns Jelinek and Gottfried von Einem. His first works, dating from the early 1960s, were serial, but then he changed tack and developed an individual style of surreal tonality, the harmonic linkages strained and tantalizing. Among his works are the grotesque *Frankenstein!!* for baritone reciter and orchestra (1976–7) and several music-theatre pieces, and concertos for violin (1977–8 and 1988), cello (1989), and trumpet (1999).   PG

Gruenberg, Louis (*b* nr Brest-Litovsk, 3 Aug. 1884; *d* Los Angeles, 9 June 1964). American composer. His family emigrated to the USA when he was two. At the age of 19 he went to Berlin to study with Busoni, and he stayed in Europe working as a pianist and teacher. His compositions of this period include the unperformed opera *The Bride of the Gods* (1913), to a libretto by Busoni. In 1919 he returned to New York, where he was a founder of the League of Composers and a leader of jazz-based modernism, of which *The Daniel Jazz* for tenor and sextet (1924) was a notable example. Jazz and spirituals also influenced his opera *The Emperor Jones* (Metropolitan, 1931), successful in its time, and his Violin Concerto (1944). In later years he moved to California and wrote film music.   PG

grunge. A style of 1990s pop music involving heavy, distorted guitar sound and an image and attitude reflecting *punk. It originated in Seattle and is typified by the band Nirvana, especially their *Smells like Teen Spirit* (1991).   KG

Gruppen ('Groups'). Work (1955–7) by Stockhausen for three orchestras; they are placed in different parts of the hall and each plays different music.

gruppetto (It.). 'Small group'; in the 16th century, a *trill, but thereafter a *turn.

gruppo (It.). A cadential *trill.

guajira (Sp.). A type of Cuban rural narrative song. Its characteristic features are texts improvised on traditional Spanish melodies, alternating use of 3/4 and 6/8 metre, and tonic and dominant melodies. The generally high-lying vocal line is accompanied by guitars, lute, and clappers.   KC

Guami, Gioseffo (*b* Lucca, *c.*1540; *d* Lucca, 1611). Italian organist and composer. One of a much travelled family of musicians, he was organist at the Bavarian court in Munich from at least 1568, then at St Mark's, Venice (1588–91), and at Lucca Cathedral. He was a brilliant player. He wrote many madrigals and some canzonas for instrumental ensemble, some of which have written-out embellishments.   DA

Guarany, Il (*O Guarani*; 'The Guaraní').Opera in four acts by Carlos Gomes to a libretto by Antonio Scalvini and Carlo D'Ormeville after José de Alencar's novel (1857) (Milan, 1870).

Guarneri. Italian family of violin makers. Andrea (*c.*1626–98) learnt his craft with Nicola *Amati and opened a workshop in Cremona in 1654. His son Pietro Giovanni (1655–1720), known as 'di Mantova', had moved by 1683 to Mantua, where he worked as a court musician and violin maker. Pietro's brother Giuseppe Giovanni Battista (1666–1739 or 1740) inherited the firm and developed an admired and individual style. His elder son Pietro (1695–1762), 'di Venezia', established a workshop in Venice in about 1718. It was Pietro's brother Bartolomeo Giuseppe (1698–1744) who was the most celebrated member of the dynasty; he

used the letters I.H.S. on his labels and therefore became known as 'del Gesù'. He was one of the greatest makers ever: his violins, renowned for their rich, powerful tone, have been favoured by virtuosos from Paganini to Pinchas Zukerman.   AL

📖 C. Chiesa and others, *Giuseppe Guarneri del Gesù* (London, 1998)

Gubaidulina, Sofia (Asgatovna) (*b* Chistopol', Tatarstan, 24 Oct. 1931). Russian composer. Born to a Russian-Tatar family, she studied the piano at the Kazan' Conservatory, then composition at the Moscow Conservatory with Nikolay Peyko and Shebalin. In the early 1960s she enthusiastically absorbed the music of the European avant-garde, and at the end of the decade she worked in the Moscow experimental electronic music studio with Schnittke and Denisov.

Most of her compositions attempt to convey a religious or moral message, and her texts are drawn from many different cultures: *Noch' v Memfise* ('Night in Memphis', 1968) is based on ancient Egyptian poetry, *Rubayyat* (1969) on texts by Khakani, Hāfiz, and Omar Khayyám; *Chas dushi* ('Hour of the Soul', 1974) sets the poetry of Marina Tsvetayeva, and there is a *Posvyashcheniye T. S. Eliotu* ('Homage to T. S. Eliot', 1987). In her untexted works, a message is conveyed no less expressively through musical symbolism or elements of instrumental theatre (where individual instruments behave like different characters in a drama), as in *In croce* for cello and organ (1979) or *Sem' slov na kreste* ('Seven Last Words on the Cross') for bayan, cello, and string orchestra (1982). She often uses numerical symmetries as the basis of her musical structures: *Quasi hoketus* for viola, bassoon, and piano (1984) and the symphony *Slïshu ... umolklu ...* ('I hear ... silence ...', 1986), for example, are based on the Fibonacci series. Although Gubaidulina was a member of the Composers' Union, her works were often treated with suspicion or even suppressed. She sprang to international fame in the late 1980s, and in 1991 emigrated to Germany.   JWAL

Guerre des Bouffons. See Bouffons, Querelle des.

Guerrero, Francisco (*b* Seville, 1527 or 1528; *d* Seville, 8 Nov. 1599). Spanish composer. He was taught music by his brother (also a composer) and Morales, a number of whose works he directly emulated in his own. He learnt to play several instruments, including the vihuela, cornett, and harp, and in 1542 was employed as a singer by Seville Cathedral. In 1546 he was appointed *maestro de capilla* of Jaén Cathedral, but he returned to Seville Cathedral in 1549 and—having been sought after by Málaga Cathedral for the post of *maestro* there—was put in charge of the choirboys at Seville in 1551.

Although he was officially no more than assistant to the aged *maestro de capilla* until 1574, it is clear that Guerrero acted as *maestro* long before that, and he remained in the service of the cathedral for the rest of his life.

Guerrero began publishing his music in the 1550s, and his masses and motets rapidly brought him a considerable reputation. He was allowed extended leave to visit Italy in 1581–2 and 1588–9 in order to publish his works; on the second occasion the time required by the Venetian printer afforded him the opportunity for a trip to the Holy Land, his published account of which achieved widespread fame. He was a prolific composer, producing settings of both Latin and Spanish texts, whose aim in sacred works was 'not to caress the ears of pious persons with song, but to excite their . . . souls to worthy contemplation of the sacred mysteries' (*Liber vesperarum*, Rome, 1584). His music frequently combines technical sophistication (for example, canonic writing) and intense expressiveness.   DA/OR

Guglielmi, Pietro Alessandro (*b* Massa, 9 Dec. 1728; *d* Rome, 19 Nov. 1804). Italian composer. He presented his first operas in Naples and Rome (1757–63), then spent four years in northern Italy, mainly in Venice. In 1767 he went to London as joint composer and music director of the King's Theatre; his *I viaggiatori ridicoli tornati in Italia* (1768) achieved great success. In 1772 he returned to Italy and in 1776 to Naples, where he challenged the popularity of Cimarosa and Paisiello. Of his 50 comic operas, over a dozen were international successes; his oratorio *Debora e Sisara* (1789) was also universally admired.   SH

guida (It.). 1. A fugue subject.

2. A *direct.

Guido of Arezzo (*b* c.991; *d* after 1033). Italian theorist and music teacher. A Benedictine monk, he invented the musical staff from which the modern form is descended, using a four-line staff with *f* and *c'* marked by clefs or by the colouring of the line in question, or both. He notated a complete antiphoner in this way and was invited to Rome to show it to Pope John XIX. Guido also taught the aural analysis of melodies in terms of the *hexachord. Used in conjunction, the staff and the hexachord facilitated both the singing of melodies from notation, and the notation of melodies from hearing them; hence they were of incalculable benefit for the teaching and learning of Gregorian chant. Guido's treatise *Micrologus* also explains how to sing a second voice accompanying a plainchant melody, creating two-part *organum. The teaching aid known as the Guidonian hand (see Fig. 1 overleaf), showing the notes of the scale and their *solmization syllables at specific points on the human hand, dates from after Guido's time.   DH

📖 D. Hiley, *Western Plainchant: A Handbook* (Oxford, 1993)

Guildhall School of Music and Drama. British conservatory founded in London in 1880. See DEGREES AND DIPLOMAS.

Guillaume Tell (*Guglielmo Tell*; 'William Tell'). Opera in four acts by Rossini to a libretto by Étienne de Jouy and Hippolyte-Louis-Florent Bis, assisted by Armand Marrast and Adolphe Crémieux, after Friedrich von Schiller's play *Wilhelm Tell* (1804) (Paris, 1829); the opera's four-movement overture is a popular concert item. Grétry (1791) wrote an opera on the same subject.

Guilmant, (Félix) Alexandre (*b* Boulogne-sur-Mer, 12 March 1837; *d* Meudon, 29 March 1911). French organist, composer, and editor. He came from a family of organists and organ builders and had his first lessons with his father; in 1860 he went to Brussels to study with J. N. Lemmens. In the 1860s he inaugurated several organs, including the Cavaillé-Coll instruments in Paris at St Sulpice (1862) and Notre Dame (1868), and in 1871 became organist at La Trinité. He also pursued an international career as a concert recitalist with an extraordinarily wide repertory, which he did much to popularize through his colourful performances and numerous editions. He succeeded Widor as organ professor at the Paris Conservatoire (1896–1911) and was a founder of the Schola Cantorum (1894). His compositions include eight organ sonatas.   AL

📖 L. Archbold and W. J. Peterson (eds.), *French Organ Music: From the Revolution to Franck and Widor* (Rochester, NY, 1995)

guimbarde (Fr.). 'Jew's harp'.

güiro [reco-reco]. A South American gourd with a series of grooves cut in one side which are scraped in both directions with a wooden or wire rod. Bamboo or wooden tubes are sometimes used in dance bands, as was a washboard in skiffle groups. Stravinsky scored for it (as *rape*) in *The Rite of Spring*.   JMo

guitar (Fr.: *guitare*; Ger.: *Gitarre*; It.: *chitarra*; Port.: *viola*, *violão*; Sp.: *guitarra*). A fretted plucked string instrument, related to the lute, but with a waisted body and often a flat or gently curved back. Instruments with some of these characteristics, usually with a small body and a long pole-neck, are of great antiquity, appearing in ancient Central Asian, Mesopotamian, and Egyptian carvings and wall-paintings. Such instruments are still found in many parts of the world. Variants with an oval or waisted body were depicted in early medieval iconography, but it was not until the end of the 15th

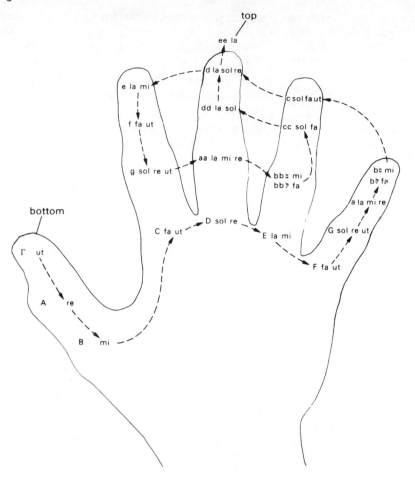

top

ee la

d la sol re

e la mi

c sol fa ut

f fa ut

dd la sol

cc sol fa

g sol re ut

aa la mi re

bb♮ mi
bb♭ fa

b♮ mi
bb♭ fa

a la mi re

bottom

C fa ut

D sol re

E la mi

G sol re ut

Γ ut

F fa ut

A re

B mi

Guido of Arezzo, Fig. 1. The Guidonian hand (the dotted line shows the order in which the notes are to be read).

century that an instrument recognizable as an early version of the modern guitar first appeared.

1. Four- and five-course guitars; 2. The six-string classical or Spanish guitar; 3. Metal-strung plectrum guitars, variants, and hybrids

1. Four- and five-course guitars

The early guitar was smaller in all dimensions than both the modern instrument and the contemporary Spanish *vihuela, but was otherwise similar to them. The upper and lower bouts ('shoulders' and 'hips') were about equal in width, the body was shallow, and it had four double courses of gut strings, tuned to intervals of a 4th, a 3rd, and a 4th, from a flat pegboard with pegs inserted from the back. Like the lute it had movable gut frets tied round its neck, a bridge and string-holder glued to the belly, and a single round soundhole filled with a decorative *rose, though guitar roses were often

of elaborate tracery, cut and glued from several layers of parchment, rather than carved from the wood of the soundboard as on the lute. The four-string guitar was usually called *guiterne* in France and *gittern in England, though it had no direct connection to the medieval instrument of that name. Similar instruments (though with fixed metal frets and an open soundhole), some smaller still, survive quite widely with various names including *cavaquinho, *charango, cuatro, machête, tiple, and *ukulele.

The five-course guitar seen in paintings by Vermeer and others and in numerous surviving examples (often known as the Baroque guitar even though such instruments were in use by the end of the 15th century) was considerably larger than the four-course instrument and deeper in the body, often with a slightly arched back built up from staves rather than the normal flat back (a typical body outline is shown in Fig. 1a for comparison with later outlines). A fifth course was

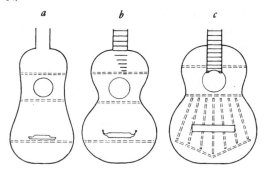

Fig. 1.

added in the bass. The instrument was superseded by the six-course guitar.

2. The six-string classical or Spanish guitar

The sixth course was added to the guitar in the late 18th century, and by the early 19th most makers had abandoned the old double or triple courses and adopted the modern pattern of six single strings. At the same time the movable gut frets were replaced by ivory, ebony, or brass wire set into the neck, and additional wooden frets were glued to the soundboard, extending the range of the instrument upwards. During much the same period the lower bout was widened and, presumably to counteract the resulting lowering of the air-resonance pitch of the body, the decorative rose was abandoned and the soundhole became an open hole as it is today. The outline of a typical early to mid-19th-century guitar is shown in Fig. 1b.

In Spain at the turn of the 19th century José Pagés replaced the old horizontal bars under the belly with fan-barring, making the instrument far more responsive. This improvement was carried further in about 1870 by Antonio de Torres Jurado, who at the same time greatly increased the size of the body, especially that of the lower bout, and effectively created the modern form of the Spanish or 'classical' guitar (see Fig. 1c). This is the instrument for which the modern solo concert repertory was written. The flamenco guitar of southern Spain is similar, though of lighter construction, with a lower action (the strings lying nearer the frets), and it often retains the older wooden tuning-pegs instead of geared 'machines'.

3. Metal-strung plectrum guitars, variants, and hybrids

The *chitarra battente* or plectrum ('beaten') guitar of the 17th and 18th centuries shares many characteristics with the slightly later Neapolitan *mandolin. Like the mandolin it had wire strings that ran down to the end of the body (sometimes in triple courses), a movable bridge, fixed metal frets, and a deep, vaulted body,

sometimes with the belly bent downwards from the bridge to the end. Various instruments of this type are still used in southern Italy and Portugal.

In the late 18th and early 19th centuries a wide variety of guitar hybrids appeared. Some were purely cosmetic variations: a lyre-shaped body with a guitar neck running up between the arms, for example (see LYRE GUITAR); but others, for example the harp-lute (see HARP-LUTE, 2), which had extra bass strings, were more radical.

There was also a group of instruments now regarded as possible late descendants of the *cittern, with its characteristic pear-shaped body, but with full depth of body from top to bottom like the guitar. One such instrument, the English guitar or guittar, was widely popular and made its way to Portugal (as the *guitarra*), perhaps through the Napoleonic Wars or the port trade; it is still associated with such Portuguese music as *fado*. English guittars originally had normal tuning-pegs, but later ones had machine tuning with worm screws turned by a watch-key. The Portuguese *guitarra* has the same worm-screw mechanism but turned with knurled knobs fanning out from the tuning-head. Instruments of similar shape but with more conventional tuning-pegs or machines were used also in France (*cistre*), Germany, and Sweden.

In the early 20th century many changes were made, mainly in the USA, to the design of the classical guitar, usually in order to produce the greater volume and penetration required by guitarists playing such popular forms as jazz, blues, folk, dance music, and rock and roll. The 'Jumbo' and 'Dreadnought' models (introduced by Martin of Nazareth, Pennsylvania, in the 1930s, though based on instruments being made since 1916) are flat-top, six-string 'folk' guitars, with a larger body than the classical guitar, broader in the waist, and with a larger expanse of belly behind the bridge. Other important modifications include: playing with a plectrum; using higher-tension steel strings that stand up to the wear of a plectrum and produce a brighter sound; structural alterations to withstand the higher tension of the strings, including reinforcing the neck with a steel truss-rod inside and more complex internal bracing; a narrower fingerboard and neck, making chords easier to finger; the junction of the neck and the body being moved from the 12th (octave) fret, as in the classical guitar, to the 14th, making the neck longer and bringing the bridge closer to the soundhole.

The basic tuning is the same as that of the Spanish guitar (*E–A–d–g–b–e'*), though many alternatives have been developed. 12-string versions of the flat-top 'folk' guitar have adopted the old idea of double courses, the upper three pairs of strings tuned in unison and the lower three usually tuned in octaves. Another design of six-string acoustic guitar was developed by the Gibson company in the 1920s. Like their new designs of mandolin, it had an arched top, and *f*-shaped sound-holes. The steel strings pass over a relatively high bridge to a steel tailpiece, and again the 14th fret is at the edge of the body. The arched-top ('cello-style') guitar came to the fore as the regular plectrum guitar for jazz, giving chords of a penetrating, rather metallic quality. As acoustic instruments they were largely superseded when electrical pickups were added to them and they became 'hollow-bodied' *electric guitars.

Another solution to the search for greater volume was provided by the 'resonator guitar', commonly known by one of its trade names, 'Dobro'. This had one or more steel resonator discs built in the belly to support the bridge (in some models the entire body is of metal). As with the *Hawaiian guitar, it is often played across the lap and with a slide, using an 'open tuning' (all the strings tuned to a major chord). Electrical pickups were added early (about 1935) to both of these guitars.   JMo

  D. Brosnac, *The Steel String Guitar: Its Construction, Origin, and Design* (San Francisco, 1973, 2/1975) · H. Turnbull, *The Guitar from the Renaissance to the Present Day* (London and New York, 1974) · T. and M. A. Evans, *Guitars: Music, History, Construction and Players from the Renaissance to Rock* (New York, 1977) · J. Tyler, *The Early Guitar: A History and Handbook* (London, 1980) · R. Denyer, *The Guitar Handbook* (London, 1982) · J. Schneider, *The Contemporary Guitar* (Berkeley, CA, 1985) · J. Huber, *The Development of the Modern Guitar* (Westport, CT, 1991) · J. Morrish (ed.), *The Classical Guitar: A Complete History* (London, 1997)

Gungl, Joseph (*b* Zsámbék, Hungary, 1 Dec. 1809; *d* Weimar, 1 Feb. 1889). Hungarian bandmaster and composer. He completed his musical education in Buda, and in 1834 began a career as military musician and bandmaster. He formed his own dance orchestra, and in 1843 established himself in Berlin as a counterpart to the Strauss family in Vienna. He made extensive tours, including to the USA in 1849 and England in 1873. Though lacking the Strausses' invention, his waltzes long enjoyed wide popularity, among them *Träume auf dem Ozean* (1849), *Immortellen* (1849), *Die Hydropathen* (1858), and *Amorettentänze* (1860).
                ALa

Guntram. Opera in three acts by Richard Strauss to his own libretto (Weimar, 1894).

Guo Wenjing (*b* Chongquing, Sichuan, 1 Feb. 1956). Chinese composer. He studied composition at the Central Conservatory in Beijing, where from 1990 he taught. With his chamber opera *Wolf Cub Village* (1994) he became recognized as an innovator and established

an international reputation. His music reflects his upbringing in rural south China, with its absorption of the supernatural elements of Chinese folklore; but it also admits Western influences, notably in *Suspended Ancient Coffins on the Cliffs in Sichuan* (1983). His second opera, *Ye Yan*, had its premiere in London in 1998.
                AL

Guridi (Bidaola), Jesús (*b* Vitoria, 25 Sept. 1886; *d* Madrid, 7 April 1961). Basque composer. He was a pupil of Vincent d'Indy. Although his chamber and keyboard (especially organ) music is esteemed, Guridi's reputation is founded on his sensitively nationalistic orchestral and operatic scores, especially *Euzko irudiak* ('Basque Scenes', for choir and orchestra, 1922) and the zarzuela *El caserío* ('The Homestead', 1926). These sound closer to Slav than Spanish models, while the marvellously orchestrated *Diez melodias vascas* ('Ten Basque Songs', 1941) and *Homenaje*, a homage to Walt Disney for piano and orchestra (1955), add astringent harmonic touches to Guridi's customarily lyrical canvas.
                CW

Gurney, Ivor (Bertie) (*b* Gloucester, 28 Aug. 1880; *d* Dartford, 26 Dec. 1937). English composer. He was an articled pupil of Herbert Brewer at Gloucester Cathedral (1906–11) before gaining an open scholarship in composition to study with Stanford at the RCM in 1911. In World War I he served in France until he was wounded, gassed, and shell-shocked in 1917. After discharge from the army he returned to the RCM to study with Vaughan Williams. He left in 1921 but was unable to find employment. Serious deterioration in his mental condition led to his admission to mental hospital, where he died of tuberculosis. A songwriter of rare distinction (and a poet of considerable ability), who looked more to the German lied tradition than to the folksong manner then becoming popular, he showed early promise in his thoroughly 'English' *Five Elizabethan Songs* (1912); the songs written in the trenches— for example *In Flanders* and *By a Bierside*—possess an extraordinary haunting power. But perhaps his finest works date from the period 1919–22, notably the two Housman cycles for voice and piano quintet, *Ludlow and Teme* and *The Western Playland* (both 1919).
                JD1

  M. Hurd, *The Ordeal of Ivor Gurney* (Oxford, 1978) · R. K. R. Thornton (ed.), *Ivor Gurney: Collected Letters* (London, 1991)

Gurrelieder ('Songs of Gurra'). Work (1900–11) by Schoenberg for solo voices, choruses, and orchestra to a text translated into German by R. F. Arnold from Jens Peter Jacobsen's poems; it is scored for a huge orchestra (including ten horns, four Wagner tubas, six timpani, and iron chains). Gurra is the castle where the 14th-century heroine Tove lived. Schoenberg arranged the *Lied der Waldtaube* ('Song of the Wood Dove') for voice and chamber orchestra in 1922.

gusle. One- or two-string fiddle of the Balkan countries, used to accompany epic songs.

gusli. Central Russian plucked zither of bicorn shape (a trapezium with a rounded treble end and extended flanks at the bass end). It is made in various sizes according to the number of strings (11 to 36). In Baltic Russian, *gusli* is the name for the **kantele*. JMo

gusto (It.). 'Taste', i.e. with appropriate speed, phrasing, etc.; *gustoso*, 'tastefully'; *con gusto*, 'with style', 'with zest'.

Guy, Barry (John) (*b* London, 22 April 1947). English composer. He worked as a double bass player while studying composition with, among others, Buxton Orr and Patric Standford, and his involvement with jazz and improvisation had a strong effect on his own compositions. He came to prominence with *D* for amplified solo strings (1972), and his later works, including *After the Rain* for strings, *Bird Gong Game* for improvising soloist and ensemble (both 1992), and *Remembering Earth* for tenor, bass, lute, bass viol or guitar, and synthesizer (1992), continue to explore the possibilities for interaction between strongly contrasted source elements, including early-music instruments and electronics. AW

Gwendoline. Opera in three acts by Chabrier to a libretto by Catulle Mendès (Brussels, 1886).

gymel [gimel] (from Lat. *gemellus*, 'twin'). A term used to describe a technique of late medieval and Renaissance polyphonic composition where one contrapuntal voice-part temporarily divides to form two of equal range. The word first appeared in mid-15th-century continental manuscripts of English music, but there is an important English source for gymels in the (slightly later) Eton Choirbook: here there are a number of examples of a melodic line, evidently designed for two unison singers, splitting into two separate contrapuntal lines each labelled 'gymel' (rather like the modern 'divisi').

It was long thought that 15th-century theorists had used 'gymel' to describe a type of 13th- and 14th-century English polyphony characterized by consecutive 3rds between the upper parts (possibly improvised, as in **faburden); but after further study of the appropriate music manuscripts scholars now believe that this interpretation is no longer tenable. The word 'semel', formerly thought to indicate a return to unison singing after a passage of gymel, is simply an alternative to that term.

Gymnopédies. Three piano pieces by Satie (1888); the first and third were orchestrated by Debussy in 1896, and the second by Roland-Manuel and Herbert Murrill. The title is said to refer to the ancient Greek annual festival in Sparta in honour of Apollo.

Gypsy Baron, The. See Zigeunerbaron, Der.

Gyrowetz, Adalbert [Jírovec, Vojtěch Matyáš] (*b* Česke Budějovice, 20 Feb. 1763; *d* Vienna, 19 March 1850). Czech composer and conductor. He was one of the most widely travelled Bohemian musicians of his day, and one of the few who spoke his native language and showed an interest in his country's music. Having displayed a remarkable talent at an early age, he studied with his father and in Prague. His linguistic gifts encouraged him to seek his fortune abroad, and he travelled first to Vienna, then to Italy, Paris, and England, where he met his musical idol, Haydn. He successfully established himself in London in 1789 and, with his knowledge of the city's concert life and his fluency in English, was of considerable help to Haydn on his first London visit.

After three years he returned to Bohemia, then settled in 1803 in Vienna, where he became composer and conductor at the Court Theatre in 1804. Modelling his style on Haydn and even on earlier 18th-century music, Gyrowetz had already cultivated a pleasing and undemanding idiom which guaranteed the popularity of his op. 1 String Quartets (1788) and numerous symphonies. With little modification, this refined Classicism continued to serve him well, even in the face of 19th-century musical advances which he found unsympathetic. At the Court Theatre, he first made a name with *Agnes Sorel* (1806), an attempt at German grand opera. Out of his depth here, he capitalized on the success of Weigl's sentimental comedies with one of his own, *Der Augenarzt* ('The Oculist', 1811). This mild, tuneful work, with melodious arias and some tempo-linked ensembles, achieved wide popularity but drew down on itself a withering review from E. T. A. Hoffmann. While he admired Beethoven and generously encouraged younger composers, Gyrowetz's heart and to a large extent his style remained rooted in the late 18th century. JSm/JW

H (Ger.). The note B (*H-dur*, 'B major'; *H-moll*, 'B minor'); B♭ is called B in German.

Haas, Pavel (*b* Brno, 21 June 1899; *d* Auschwitz [Oświęcim], ? 18 Oct. 1944). Czech composer. He studied with Janáček (1920–2) and taught music in Brno from 1935. Janáček's influence on his music, heard perhaps at its clearest in parts of the Second String Quartet, including ad lib jazz band (op. 7, 1925), and the opera *Šarlatán* ('The Charlatan') was strong, but Moravian folksong and Gregorian and Jewish chant made significant contributions to his style. Along with other Jewish artists he was incarcerated in *Terezín (1941–4), where he composed, among other works, the increasingly well-known Study for Strings (1943). In 1944 he was transported to Auschwitz and killed.

JSM

Hába, Alois (*b* Vizovice, Moravia, 21 June 1893; *d* Prague, 26 Nov. 1973). Czech composer. He studied with Vitězslav Novák at the Prague Conservatory (1914–15) and with Franz Schreker in Vienna and Berlin (1918–22). In his Second String Quartet (1920) he began to use quarter-tones, and though he was not the first composer to do so, the innovation has become associated with his name. He founded and directed a department of microtonal music at the Prague Conservatory (1923–51), and in some later works he used sixth-tones and fifth-tones. He also designed versions of the piano, clarinet, and other instruments to play these small intervals. In style his music relates to the Czech folk-music traditions of Novák and Janáček, with occasional influences from the atonal and serial styles of Schoenberg. Apart from the quarter-tone opera *Matka* 'The Mother'; Munich, 1931) his most important works were for chamber forces.

PG

habanera (Sp.; Fr.: *havanaise*). A Cuban dance, possibly of African origin, that became popular in Spain. In slow 2/4 time, with the first quaver of the bar dotted, it was further developed in South American music as the quicker but similar *tango. One of the earliest published examples was *El arreglito* composed by Iradier in 1840; this was the source of inspiration for the popular habanera song 'L'Amour est un oiseau rebel' in

Bizet's *Carmen*. The habanera was also used by Debussy, Ravel, and Chabrier at a time when French music was regularly absorbing Spanish musical idioms.

PGA

Habeneck, François-Antoine (*b* Mézières, 22 Jan. 1781; *d* Paris, 8 Dec. 1849). French conductor, composer, and violinist. He studied at the Paris Conservatoire and joined the Paris Opéra orchestra, becoming director (1821–4), then conductor (1824–47). He gave premieres of operas by Rossini, Meyerbeer, and Halévy, and Berlioz's *Benvenuto Cellini*. He founded the Société des Concerts du Conservatoire in 1828, introducing Beethoven's symphonies to France. The leading French conductor of his day, he achieved new standards of orchestral execution, though Berlioz considered him somewhat pedantic.

JT

Hadley, Patrick (Arthur Sheldon) (*b* Cambridge, 5 March 1899; *d* Heacham, 17 Dec. 1973). English composer. After war service in France during which he lost a leg, he went to Cambridge (1919–22), then to the RCM (1922–5), where he studied composition with Vaughan Williams and conducting with Boult. From 1925 to 1938 he taught at the RCM before returning to Cambridge, first as lecturer and later (1946–62) as professor. His most effective works, assimilating folksong and the music of Delius, are the symphonic ballad *The Trees So High* (1931) based on a Somerset folk tune, an exquisite setting of the carol *I sing of a maiden* (1936), the anthem *My beloved spake* (1938), and the deeply personal cantata *The Hills* (1944).

PG/JDi

📖 W. TODDS, *Patrick Hadley: A Memoir* (London, 1974) · E. WETHERELL, *'Paddy': The Life and Music of Patrick Hadley* (London, 1997)

'Haffner' Serenade. Nickname of Mozart's Serenade in D major K250/248b (1776), so called because it was composed for a marriage in the Haffner family of Salzburg.

'Haffner' Symphony. Nickname of Mozart's Symphony no. 35 in D major K385 (1782); it was originally intended as a serenade (but not the 'Haffner' Serenade, K250/248b) and was written for the Haffner family.

Hahn, Reynaldo (*b* Caracas, 9 Aug. 1874; *d* Paris, 28 Jan. 1947). Venezuelan-born French composer, singer, and critic. His family moved to Paris in 1878 and Hahn entered the Paris Conservatoire in 1885, studying with Dubois and Massenet among others. His early reputation as a composer was assured by the song *Si mes vers avaient des ailes*, written before he was 15; but he plumbed far greater depths with later settings of Verlaine, Banville, and Leconte de Lisle. He was much in demand as a salon singer and as a singing teacher. Happily, a good number of his recordings are available on CD. He took a particular interest in Mozart, conducting *Don Giovanni* at Salzburg in 1906 and in 1925 writing an operetta *Mozart*, following the success of *Ciboulette* (Paris, 1923). Perhaps the best of his more serious works are the powerful Piano Quintet (1922) and the opera *Le Marchand de Venise* (Paris, 1935). In 1945 he was made a member of the Institut and appointed director of the Paris Opéra.   RN

Haieff, Alexei (Vasilievich) (*b* Blagoveshchensk, Siberia, 25 Aug. 1914; *d* Rome, 1 March 1984). Russian-born American composer. He emigrated to the USA in 1932 and studied with Frederick Jacobi and Rubin Goldmark at the Juilliard School (1934–8), going on to study further with Nadia Boulanger in Paris (1938–9). His music owes much to Stravinsky's neo-classicism, and includes ballets, three symphonies, piano and violin concertos, chamber music, and songs.   PG

halrpIns. A colloquial term for *crescendo and *decrescendo signs; see DYNAMIC MARKS.

halb, Halbe (Ger.). 'Half'; e.g. *Halbe-Note*, 'half-note', i.e. minim; *Halbe Pause*, 'half-note rest'.

Halévy, Jacques (François) **Fromental** (Élie) [Levy, Elias] (*b* Paris, 27 May 1799; *d* Nice, 17 March 1862). French composer. Born into a Jewish family, he entered the Paris Conservatoire at the age of ten; his teachers included Berton for harmony and Cherubini for counterpoint. He won the Prix de Rome in 1819, having previously twice been placed second. On his return from Italy he determined to concentrate on music for the stage, and in 1827 his opera *L'Artisan* was first performed at the Théâtre Feydeau. Two years later *Clari* was accepted for performance at the Théâtre Italien.

During the next 30 years Halévy composed over 35 operas, of which the most successful was undoubtedly *La Juive*, first performed at the Paris Opéra in 1835; it ranks among the most important examples of French grand opera and remains the work on which his fame rests. Unlike the operas of Meyerbeer, *La Juive*, a brooding study of anti-Semitism in medieval Europe,

continued to be a critical as well as a public success for nearly a century, numbering both Wagner and Mahler among its admirers. The role of Éléazar, a persecuted Jewish goldsmith and the heroine's father, was long regarded as among the finest and most demanding in the tenor repertory. Ten months later *L'Éclair*, for four performers and no chorus, was given its premiere at the Opéra-Comique, the first of the series of comic operas that formed the bulk of Halévy's output. The success of both works gained him entrance to the French Institute, and in 1854 he was elected to the influential post of its secretary. In 1840 he became professor of composition at the Conservatoire, where he had taught counterpoint since 1816—a position he probably owed to Cherubini, to whom *La Juive* is dedicated. Halévy's pupils included Gounod, Bizet, and Saint-Saëns.

His most successful works at the Opéra after *La Juive* included *Guido et Ginevra* (1838), *La Reine de Chypre* (1841), and *Charles VI* (1843). *La tempesta*, based on Shakespeare, was written for London in 1850. Many of his best works were to librettos by Eugène Scribe, but after the success of Meyerbeer's *Les Huguenots* in 1836 (to a libretto by Scribe) he became less concerned with the quality of his chosen texts, and the plots of some of his later works are cluttered and over-complicated.

Towards the end of his life Halévy wrote two volumes of memoirs and musical criticism under the titles *Souvenirs et portraits* and *Derniers souvenirs* (1863), which possess great charm and erudition and which were critically admired at the time. He died of tuberculosis. Little of his music is now performed, though *La Juive* remained in the repertory until the 1930s and is still occasionally revived as a vehicle for a great tenor. His nephew, Ludovic Halévy (1834–1908), was a novelist and dramatist who collaborated with Henri Meilhac on the texts of operettas by Lecocq and Offenbach, including *La Vie parisienne* and *La Belle Hélène*, as well as writing the libretto for Bizet's *Carmen*.   WT/TA

📖 J. F. FULCHER, *The Nation's Image: French Grand Opera as Politics and Politicized Art* (Cambridge, 1987)

half-close. See CADENCE.

half-coloration. A term applied to a two-note *ligature in which only one of the notes is in *coloration. The 'uncolored' note has its normal length, the 'colored' note loses a third of its value.   AP

half-diminished seventh chord. The diminished 7th is a full diminished chord, comprising three minor 3rds which together span a diminished 7th interval (e.g. D–F–A♭–C♭). A half-diminished chord spans a minor 7th, and is built from two minor 3rds and a major 3rd, as in D–F–A♭–C. The *'Tristan' chord is half-diminished, and may also be termed a 'secondary 7th': that is, a 7th chord on a degree of the scale other than the dominant.   AW

Halffter, Cristóbal (*b* Madrid, 24 March 1930). Spanish composer, nephew of Ernesto Halffter. He studied with Conrad del Campo at the Madrid Conservatory (1947–51), an institution he later directed (1964–6). His early works, for example the Piano Concerto (1953), are in the neo-classical manner of his uncle and late Falla, but from the mid-1960s Halffter wholeheartedly embraced the European avant-garde. *Lineas y puntos* ('Lines and Points', 1967) for 20 instruments and tape was one of the first works to demonstrate his often delicate, painterly abstraction, but later works, such as the Second Cello Concerto (1985), are epic in scale and dramatic in content.   CW

Halffter, Ernesto (*b* Madrid, 16 Jan. 1905; *d* Lisbon, 5 July 1989). Spanish composer. In 1923 he met Falla, who became his teacher and his most influential champion. Halffter's music, notably the popular Sinfonietta (1923–7), shares the neo-classical clarity of his master's later work, and Halffter repaid the debt by spending many years completing Falla's sketches for *Atlántida* (1956–76). His own work developed an increasingly detached mysticism, as in the *Canticum para el Papa Juan XXIII* (1964), but towards the end of his life his individuality re-emerged in sunnier works, notably the Guitar Concerto (1969) and *Nocturno y Serenata* (1981).   CW

half-note (Amer.). Minim.

half-trill. See TRILL.

Halle, Adam de la. See ADAM DE LA HALLE.

Hallelujah. See ALLELUIA.

Hallelujah Chorus. Popular name for the chorus that closes part 2 of Handel's *Messiah* in which the word 'Hallelujah' is repeated many times.

halling. A lively Norwegian folk dance in duple or quadruple time, normally a solo dance for men. Grieg wrote several, including his op. 47 no. 4 and op. 71 no. 5.

Halstan. English firm of typesetters. See PRINTING AND PUBLISHING OF MUSIC, 2*d*.

Hamerik [Hammerich], **Asger** (*b* Copenhagen, 8 April 1843; *d* Frederiksborg, 13 July 1923). Danish composer, conductor, and educationist. In spite of parental opposition to his musical career (his father was a theologian), he studied with Gade and J. P. E. Hartmann in Copenhagen, with Bülow in Berlin, and finally (1864–9) with Berlioz in Paris—he seems to have been Berlioz's only pupil. His *Hymne à la paix*, written for the

World Exposition in Paris in 1867 (and now lost), showed his teacher's influence: it was scored for wind band, chorus, two organs, and 12 harps. After Berlioz's death, Hamerik visited Italy and Austria, where the American consul in Vienna proposed that he take up the directorship of the Peabody Institute in Baltimore. Hamerik moved to Baltimore in 1871, returning to Copenhagen only in 1898.

Although Hamerik was the most prominent Danish symphonist between Gade and Nielsen, the early focus of his career was on opera (he wrote four). With the move to the USA, where he had an orchestra at his disposal, he began to concentrate on orchestral music, and many of his works—seven symphonies (excluding a youthful, unnumbered effort from 1860) and five *Nordic Suites*—were written for himself to conduct; he wrote little after his return to Europe. His music, which emerges from that of Gade and Hartmann, and has a hint of Schumann, often uses the Berliozian *idée fixe*; his Requiem (1886–7) echoes Berlioz's in its sense of scale and space.   MA

Hamilton, Iain (Ellis) (*b* Glasgow, 6 June 1922; *d* London, 21 July 2000). Scottish composer. After early training in engineering he studied composition with William Alwyn at the RAM (1947–51), then worked in London as a composer, teacher, pianist, and music administrator. In 1962 he moved to the USA, where he served as professor of music at Duke University (Durham, North Carolina) and the City University of New York; he returned to England in 1981. His early works, which include two symphonies (1949, 1951), are in vigorous, often harsh style influenced by Bartók, Hindemith, and Stravinsky. During the 1950s Hamilton came gradually to a full adoption of serial methods, though the pull of tonality continued to be felt, particularly in the works of the 1970s. His large output embraces a variety of chamber and orchestral pieces as well as several operas, including *The Royal Hunt of the Sun* (composed 1967–9; ENO, 1977), *The Catiline Conspiracy* (Stirling, 1974), and *Anna Karenina* (ENO, 1981).   PG

   📖 R. M. SCHAFER, *British Composers in Interview* (London, 1963)

Hamlet. Opera in five acts by Thomas to a libretto by Michel Carré and Jules Barbier after Shakespeare's play *Hamlet, Prince of Denmark* (*c.*1602) (Paris, 1868).

Hammerich, Asger. See HAMERIK, ASGER.

'Hammerklavier' Sonata. Beethoven's Piano Sonata no. 29 in B♭ major op. 106 (1817–18). Beethoven used the word 'Hammerklavier' (Ger., 'pianoforte') in the subtitle of other piano sonatas, but this is the only one commonly referred to by this appropriate title.

Hammerschmidt, Andreas (*b* Brüx, 1611 or 1612; *d* Zittau, 29 Oct. 1675). Bohemian-born organist and composer. As Protestants, he and his family were forced by the Thirty Years War to migrate from Brüx to Freiberg in Saxony. His most important organist post was at the Johanniskirche in Zittau, which he held from 1639 until his death. A prolific church composer, he is renowned for his four sets of *Musikalische Andachten* ('Musical Devotions') of 1639–46, comprising over 150 works, many of them close in style to Schütz, and for his *Dialogi, oder Gespräche zwischen Gott und einer gläubigen Seel* ('Conversations between God and a Believing Soul'), set in the form of dramatic dialogues on biblical themes with two or more voices representing the interlocutors.   DA/BS

Hammond organ. An electronic organ, invented by Laurens Hammond in 1933–4 for church and domestic use, and much used in jazz and popular music. The sound is created by toothed steel tone-wheels rotating in front of magnets. A series of draw-bars, moved in and out, controls the intensity of the harmonic content of the sound and thus the tone-quality.   JMo

handbell. A small bell with a handle. In Britain and the USA sets of tuned handbells of up to five chromatic octaves (occasionally more) are played by handbell 'choirs', each ringer playing one or two bells, held by the handle, or lifting appropriate ones from a table as specific notes are required by the music. Melodic handbell music consists of original compositions and arrangements, and *change-ringing is also practised on handbells. The soft felt clappers are fixed to swing in only one direction and have a spring mechanism, allowing greater control of striking.   JMo

Handel, George Frideric (*see page 554*)

hand horn. The valveless natural horn (see HORN, 2). Partly closing the bell with the hand allowed players from about 1750 onwards to play a fully chromatic range from the third harmonic upwards.

Handl, Jacob [Gallus Carniolus, Jacobus] (*b* ? Ribnica, 15 April – 31 July 1550; *d* Prague, 18 July 1591). Slovene composer. Because the two forms of his name mean 'rooster' ('Handl' being the German diminutive), it is conjectured that his original name may have been Petelin. He spent much of his life travelling in Austria, Moravia, Bohemia, and Silesia, staying in various monasteries. In 1579 or 1580 he was appointed choirmaster to the Bishop of Olomouc, and in about 1586 Kantor at the Prague church of St Jan na Brzehu, where he supervised the publication of *Opus musicum* (four

volumes, 1586–91) containing 445 motets, psalms for All Saints, three Passions, and settings of the Lamentations. He also composed 20 masses; most of his secular music sets the Latin poets of classical antiquity. Handl's compositional style was a mixture of the new and the old, encompassing both polyphonic music in the Netherlands style, perhaps influenced by Lassus, and polychoral works after the Venetian manner.

DA/PW

Handy, W(illiam) C(hristopher) (*b* Florence, AL, 16 Nov. 1873; *d* New York, 28 March 1958). American composer. The son of freed slaves, he left home at the age of 18 for a vagrant career as a trumpeter, and eventually had his own orchestra, with which he toured the South between 1903 and 1921, as well as a share in a Memphis publishing firm. His *Memphis Blues* (1912) and *St Louis Blues* (1914) were among the earliest examples of the blues to appear in print.   PG

Hanover Square Rooms. A suite of rooms in the West End of London, at the north-west corner of Hanover Square. It included a lofty room, about 27 by 9 metres, with high windows and an arched ceiling, and seating up to 900, which became the premier concert room in London. It had excellent acoustics but was sometimes criticized for its poor amenities.

Originally owned by Giovanni Gallini, initially in partnership with J. C. Bach and C. F. Abel, the Hanover Square Rooms opened in 1775 and housed the Bach–Abel concerts until Bach's death in 1782. The Professional Concerts were given there, 1783–93, and from 1786 the Salomon series at which Haydn appeared in the early 1790s. Other notable series include the Concert of Ancient Music, 1804–48, and the Philharmonic Society concerts, 1833–69. Among the artists to appear at the Hanover Square Rooms were Mendelssohn, Paganini, Liszt, Clara Schumann, Jenny Lind, Anton Rubinstein, and Joachim. The last concert there was given in 1874 by the Royal Academy of Music, which had used the rooms since 1823. The premises were sold the following year and converted into a club.   SS

Hänsel und Gretel. Opera in three acts by Humperdinck to a libretto by Adelheid Wette after a fairy tale by the Brothers Grimm (1812–14), Jacob Ludwig, and Wilhelm Carl (Weimar, 1893).

Hans Heiling. Opera in a prelude and three acts by Marschner to a libretto by Eduard Devrient (Berlin, 1833).

Hanslick, Eduard (*b* Prague, 11 Sept. 1825; *d* Baden, nr Vienna, 6 Aug. 1904). Austrian music critic, aesthetician, and historian. He received his early musical

(*cont. on p. 557*)

George Frideric Handel
(1685–1759)

George Frideric Handel (born Georg Friederich Händel), an English composer of German birth, was born in Halle on 23 February 1685 and died in London on 14 April 1759.

Halle, Hamburg, and Italy

The son of a 63-year-old barber-surgeon and his much younger wife (the daughter of a pastor), Handel was found to have musical talent at an early age. He studied with a local organist, F. W. Zachow, who taught him keyboard and composition. Visiting Berlin, where he met his future colleagues Attilio Ariosti and Giovanni Bononcini, he made such an impression that the elector offered to send him to study in Italy, an offer not taken up by his family. It was intended that Handel would enter the legal profession. He studied at the grammar school and university in Halle, but was appointed organist at the cathedral in 1702; the following year he decided to seek his fortune in Hamburg.

Hamburg's main attraction was the opera, directed by Reinhard Keiser. Handel played second violin in the orchestra before becoming *maestro al cembalo*. He became friendly with the singer, composer, and (later) critic Johann Mattheson, with whom he fought a duel in 1704 as the result of a quarrel over the continuo part in one of Mattheson's operas. He also had the opportunity to write his first operas, of which *Almira*, though a strange mixture of German and Italian, was evidently successful at its performance in 1705. *Nero*, performed soon after, was a failure, however, and by the time the huge score (now mostly lost) of Handel's third opera was ready he had decided to learn his craft in Italy.

Although the details of Handel's stay in Italy are unclear, it is likely that he first visited Florence. He was however in Rome by January 1707, when he played the organ at St John Lateran. There he enjoyed the patronage of several distinguished and art-loving cardinals and became acquainted with Corelli, Alessandro and Domenico Scarlatti, and probably Pasquini too. He composed many secular cantatas and some fine church music: the psalm setting *Dixit Dominus* (1707), displaying a formidable array of choral textures and an impressive handling of the concerted style, suggests the high standards of the singers at his disposal. He also wrote his first oratorio, *Il trionfo del Tempo e del Disinganno* (1707). Notable among his compositions

from the next couple of years are two splendid quasi-dramatic cantatas, *Aci, Galatea e Polifemo* (1708) and *Apollo e Dafne* (1709–10). He visited Florence again, as well as Naples and Venice, where he met Cardinal Grimani (who provided the libretto for the opera *Agrippina*) and the composers Vivaldi and Albinoni. The production of *Agrippina* in Venice in the winter of 1709–10 was a great success, and the work itself contains many of the components of Handel's mature operatic style. In Venice Handel also met Prince Ernst August of Hanover, whose brother the elector was looking for a new Kapellmeister. Handel travelled to Hanover and accepted the post on condition that he be allowed first to visit England.

Hanover and early London years

Handel arrived in London in autumn 1710 and discovered a city ripe for Italian opera, in spite of the objections of London's literati to such entertainments. He was employed at the Queen's Theatre in the Haymarket and wrote *Rinaldo*, which was produced in February 1711. Though some of the music had originated in earlier compositions—it was Handel's common practice throughout his career to recycle music, and not just his own—its fine arias and especially its elaborate staging (involving a flock of sparrows, waterfalls, thunder effects, and fireworks) caused a sensation, and the publisher John Walsh senior printed the popular arias. Handel duly returned to Hanover in summer 1711 and there spent a year or so writing chamber and orchestral music, but he was in London again by mid-October 1712.

For three years Handel lived in Piccadilly at the home of Lord Burlington. For the 1712–13 season he wrote *Il pastor fido*, which was a failure; but *Teseo*, based on the plot of Lully's *Thésée*, was more successful. At the same time Handel cultivated connections outside the opera house: his grand *Te Deum and Jubilate*, composed to celebrate the Treaty of Utrecht in 1713, as well as his *Ode for Queen Anne's Birthday*, helped to establish a favourable relationship with the English court and with the queen, who awarded him a pension of £200.

When Queen Anne died in 1714 Handel's employer, George of Hanover, succeeded as king. There seems to be no truth in the legend that Handel, having exceeded his leave from Hanover, provided the *Water Music* to make his peace with him (it was performed during a royal serenade on the Thames in July 1717). In fact George doubled his pension, and a further amount was added later when Handel became music master to the royal children. In the 1714–15 season *Rinaldo* was revived and *Amadigi* composed. Handel may have visited Germany briefly in 1716, but at any rate was presumably back in London in January 1717 for revivals of *Rinaldo* and *Amadigi*. That he prospered in his first years in London is suggested by the fact that he was able to invest £500 in the South Sea Company.

There followed a gap in Handel's operatic career. He composed nothing fresh in the genre until 1720, and during this time stayed at Cannons, near Edgware, as resident composer to the Earl of Carnarvon (from 1719 Duke of Chandos). There Handel composed the Chandos anthems, revealing a flair for creating splendid sonorities with small resources, and two English masques, *Acis and Galatea* (1718) and the first version of *Esther* (?1718).

Opera

In 1718–19, in an effort to create a more secure footing for Italian opera in London, members of the nobility, with the backing of the king, formed an opera syndicate on strictly commercial lines, known as the Royal Academy of Music. Handel was appointed musical director, and he immediately went to Düsseldorf and Dresden to recruit singers. The academy opened on 2 April 1720 and ran for nine seasons, mixing new works with revivals. There was some rivalry between the resident composers—who included Bononcini and Ariosti—and Bononcini was particularly successful between 1720 and 1722, but the Academy was to stimulate Handel to a series of masterpieces. His first work there, *Radamisto* (1720), though not his finest, had the ticket touts charging astronomical prices, and later works such as *Giulio Cesare*, *Tamerlano* (both 1724), and *Rodelinda* (1725) were written for a stunning cast—including the celebrated castrato Senesino, Giuseppe Boschi, and Francesca Cuzzoni.

Modern research has established Handel as a master of dramatic technique within the constraints of stylized Italian *opera seria*. Although his operas are conventionally based on a series of recitatives and arias, with few ensembles or orchestral movements, his subtle manipulation of musical form underpins dramatic progress, and the breadth of his characterization, aided by an intensity of emotional expression, tonal control, and variety of scoring, transcends the limitations of the genre. The range of music, from simple songs on dance rhythms to brilliant concerto-like movements, is astonishing.

Paradoxically, the presence of star singers, one of the trump cards of the Royal Academy, became one of the reasons for its decline and subsequent collapse, as their inflated fees contributed to financial difficulties, and internal squabbling undermined the whole enterprise. Hardly any more helpful was the success of Gay's *The *Beggar's Opera* (1728). In the 1727–8 season Handel presented a patriotic opera that happily coincided with the accession of the new king, *Riccardo primo* (1727), and two other new works, but at the end of that season the doors were closed and the company disbanded. Handel himself was not financially embarrassed, nor did his reputation suffer. He was still favoured at court and had in 1723 become a composer to the Chapel Royal: his four anthems for the coronation of George II are among his best-known contributions to English ceremonial. In 1727 he became a naturalized English citizen.

Handel set up a new company at the King's Theatre in 1729 with Johann Heidegger, the erstwhile manager of the Royal Academy, and both travelled abroad to recruit singers. Handel's first operas for the new venture, *Lotario* and *Partenope*, were not successful. Revivals of such old favourites as *Giulio Cesare* and *Scipione* were interspersed with new operas, including *Poro* (1731), *Ezio*, and *Sosarme* (both 1732), which had mixed receptions, and *Orlando* (1733), which was a triumph. But at the end of the 1732–3 season the Opera of the Nobility was set up, a rival company supported by the Prince of Wales. This company poached some of Handel's best singers and engaged the famous composer Nicola Porpora. In spite of their rivalry, by the end of the next season both companies were playing to empty houses, and the existence of other companies, including one giving opera in English, contributed to their difficulties. In July 1734 Heidegger dissolved the partnership and handed over the lease of the King's Theatre to the Opera of the Nobility.

Undeterred, Handel moved to the theatre at Covent Garden and produced several operas, including two masterpieces, *Ariodante* and *Alcina* (both 1735). But the strain of giving operas was beginning to tell, and, in spite of a hit with *Atalanta* (1736), declining fortunes led to both theatres closing—the Opera of the Nobility for good. In April 1737 Handel suffered a stroke, and he retired to take the waters at Aix-la-Chapelle in September. After his return to London in October or November, apparently recovered, he was employed by Heidegger, at the King's Theatre, and produced the operas *Faramondo*, *Alessandro Severo* (a pasticcio), and *Serse*.

Oratorio

Although Handel doggedly persisted with opera, the public reception of which was unpredictable at best, his dramatic interests found further outlet in oratorio, a genre new to England that was created almost by accident. Handel's masque *Esther* had been given private performances by Bernard Gates in London in 1732. Such was its success that it was presented in public at the King's Theatre in May that year, though, on the orders of the Bishop of London, who objected to the staging of a sacred drama in a secular space, it was given without staged action. Thus performed it was the first oratorio to be heard in London, and it inevitably encouraged the production of others, among the first of which were *Deborah* (1733) and *Athalia*. *Athalia* was first performed in Oxford, at the Sheldonian Theatre, during summer 1733, when Handel visited the city and, according to reports, turned down an honorary doctorate.

Unbound by operatic convention and the egotistical whims of top Italian singers, Handel was able to develop in his oratorios a potent and flexible dramatic style that was adequate compensation for the lack of visual drama. Although he drew substantially on techniques honed in opera, his formal freedom was much greater and his characterization benefited considerably from extensive use of the chorus. An incidental attraction at oratorios was the interval entertainment, for which Handel played his organ concertos; Walsh junior published six of them as op. 4 in 1738 (a further set of six followed in 1761). Also used were the 12 concerti grossi op. 6, an outstanding collection of works which ranks as one of the highpoints of the genre in the late Baroque period.

In 1738 Handel wrote *Saul*, a remarkably dramatic piece with a massive orchestra (including huge kettledrums borrowed from the Tower of London). This was followed by *Israel in Egypt*, which did not find initial popularity: it is an untypical oratorio dominated by choruses and with a text derived directly from the Bible. In the winter of 1739–40 Handel presented a complete series of oratorio concerts at the theatre in Lincoln's Inn Fields; it included *L'Allegro, il Penseroso, ed il Moderato* and revivals of *Esther*, *Saul*, and *Israel*. But in spite of the attractions of oratorio, the public reaction to Handel's works still varied, and Handel himself was not yet ready to abandon opera. He returned to it for the last time in 1740 with *Imeneo* and *Deidamia*, but they were both met with indifference.

By summer 1741 there were rumours that Handel intended to return to Germany, but an invitation from the lord-lieutenant of Ireland to give a series of concerts in Dublin seems to have fired his enthusiasm. He composed *Messiah* before leaving London in November, and in Dublin he gave a successful series of concerts, including the premiere of *Messiah*, which made large sums of money for local charities. *Messiah* is uncharacteristic of Handel's oratorios in part because of its largely undramatic, more contemplative, nature and its text, which is compiled from passages in the Bible. In London it flopped; it was not appreciated there until the Foundling Hospital performances in the 1750s, since when it has remained by far his best-known, if unrepresentative, oratorio.

Handel returned to London with his confidence restored, and finished a new oratorio, *Samson*, which takes its text from Milton rather than from the Old Testament. Although it was popular with the public, Handel was still not out of the woods. In the 1743–4 and 1744–5 seasons he presented a mixed bag: the secular oratorio *Semele*, the uneven *Joseph and his Brethren*, and two splendid dramatic works, *Hercules* and *Belshazzar*, the latter one of his finest oratorios. By summer 1745 he was again ill. However, the events of the Jacobite rising inspired a series of militaristic oratorios, beginning in 1746 with the patriotic *Occasional Oratorio*, hastily compiled from existing works, followed by *Judas Maccabaeus* (1747), and continuing in 1748 with a sequel to *Judas*, *Alexander Balus*, and *Joshua*.

In 1749 Handel composed the *Music for the Royal Fireworks* for the celebrations of the Peace Treaty of Aix-la-Chapelle. He also gave two new oratorios, *Susanna* and *Solomon*, and composed another, *Theodora*. In 1751 he embarked on *Jephtha*, his final masterpiece with superb dramatic arias and recitatives. But in the middle of its composition he began to suffer from eye trouble and, although he evidently still managed to play his organ concertos—they had in any case always relied heavily on extemporization—he was totally blind by January 1753. *Jephtha* effectively marks the end of his creative career.

Handel's reputation

Handel died a national figure and was buried at Westminster Abbey in the presence of about 3000 people. Though his operas were soon all but forgotten, he was remembered in the years after his death through some of his instrumental music, such as the concertos, and some of the ceremonial church music, but particularly as an oratorio composer. His oratorio seasons were maintained from 1760 by J. C. Smith and John Stanley. Handel's music, always the dominant model for his English contemporaries, remained a strong influence not only on English musicians (both in London and in the provinces) but also on such composers as

Mozart and Haydn. In England a collected edition of his works was proposed in 1786 but not completed. However, 18th-century reverence for him is seen most clearly in the massive Handel Commemoration events mounted in 1784 at Westminster Abbey, which in turn helped to establish a fashion for the large-scale performance of just a handful of choral works—notably *Messiah*—that persisted, and shaped Handel's reputation, until the mid-20th century.   PL

📖 W. DEAN, *Handel's Dramatic Oratorios and Masques* (Oxford, 1959/R1990) · D. BURROWS, *Handel* (Oxford, 1994) · W. DEAN and J. M. KNAPP, *Handel's Operas, 1704–1726* (Oxford, 2/1995) · D. BURROWS (ed.), *The Cambridge Companion to Handel* (Cambridge, 1997)

training from Tomášek before becoming a law student in Vienna. There he spent much of his spare time studying music and writing criticism, and from the mid-1840s contributed to several journals including the *Wiener Allgemeine Musik-Zeitung*, which published his highly favourable review of Wagner's *Tannhäuser*. In 1854 his treatise on *aesthetics in music, *Vom Musikalisch-Schönen*, appeared, to great acclaim. From 1856 he held a series of posts at the University of Vienna, becoming professor of music history and aesthetics in 1870. A strong supporter of Brahms, he is perhaps best known (his early enthusiasm having cooled) as the leading critical opponent of Wagner of his time.   LC

Hanson, Howard (Harold) (*b* Wahoo, NE, 28 Oct. 1896; *d* Rochester, NY, 26 Feb. 1981). American composer of Swedish descent. He studied with Percy Goetschius at the Institute of Musical Art in New York and with Arne Oldberg at Northwestern University. During his long career as director of the Eastman School of Music in Rochester, New York (1924–64), he had a notable influence on many younger American composers. His works include seven symphonies, in a style close to that of Sibelius. He also wrote a treatise, *The Harmonic Materials of Modern Music* (New York, 1960).   PG

Hanuš, Jan (*b* Prague, 2 May 1915). Czech composer. He studied composition privately with Jeremiáš in 1934 and trained as a conductor at the Prague Conservatory, then worked as a music editor for some years. He was in charge of the complete editions of the music of Dvořák and Fibich and was involved in the critical edition of Janáček's works. He was also prominent in the Union of Czechoslovak Composers and a number of other Czech musical institutions, but on the fall of the Communist regime returned all his state distinctions. His own music, though distantly rooted in the tradition of Smetana and Dvořák, emerges from that of the subsequent generation, such as his teacher, Jeremiáš, and Ostrčil. It is loosely tonal, allowing itself a considerable degree of liberty to accommodate Hanuš's sense of the dramatic, with his natural lyricism often punctuated by pungent dissonance. His output includes seven symphonies (written between 1942 and 1990) and a good number of other orchestral works, often with a concertante element, four operas—*Plameny* ('Flames', 1942–4; staged 1956), *Sluha dvou pánů* ('Servant of Two Masters', 1959), *Pochodeň Prométheova* ('The Torch of Prometheus', 1965), and *Pohádka jedné noci* ('The Story of One Night', 1961–8)—seven masses and other vocal pieces, much chamber music, and works for piano and organ.   MA

Happy End. Comedy with music in three acts by Weill to a book by Elisabeth Hauptmann (as Dorothy Lane) and with lyrics by Bertolt Brecht (Berlin, 1929).

Harawi, chant d'amour et de mort ('Harawi, Song of Love and Death'). Song cycle (1945) by Messiaen for soprano and piano, settings of 12 of his own texts; like *Cinq rechants* and the *Turangalîla-symphonie*, they were inspired by the legend of Tristan and Isolda, as well as by Peruvian mythology.

Harbison, John (Harris) (*b* Orange, NJ, 20 Dec. 1938). American composer. He studied at Harvard (1956–60), in Berlin (1960–1) and at Princeton with Earl Kim and Roger Sessions (1961–3). In 1969 he began teaching at the Massachusetts Institute of Technology. His music skilfully blends aspects of modernism into a broadly traditional, lyrical discourse, and his large output covers all the usual genres, from piano and chamber music through three symphonies and a spectrum of concertos (for violin, viola, cello, piano, flute, and oboe) to opera (*Winter's Tale*, San Francisco, 1974; *Full Moon in March*, Boston, 1977; *The Great Gatsby*, Metropolitan, 1999).   PG

Hardanger fiddle. Norwegian traditional violin, with four wire *sympathetic strings below the fingerboard in addition to the four bowed strings above. Elements of early Baroque violins are preserved in its design, with its short, straight neck, wedge fingerboard, and high-arched belly and back. The body is often elaborately inlaid with bone and the scroll carved with an open-jawed dragon head.   JMo

hard bop. The kind of hard-driven modern jazz of the 1950s and 60s as played by Art Blakey and Cannonball Adderley, which brought more blues inflections (see BLUE NOTE) into the music than usually found in the cooler manifestations.   PGA

hard hexachord. See HEXACHORD; SOLMIZATION.

hard rock. See HEAVY METAL.

Hark, the herald angels sing. Hymn originally written by Charles Wesley in 1743; it appeared in various hymn publications between 1760 and 1782. W. H. Cummings, organist of Waltham Abbey, set the words to the melody of the second number of Mendelssohn's *Festgesang* and published it in 1856; it soon became very popular.

harmonica [mouth organ]. A mouth-blown instrument sounded with *free reeds (one for each note). The simplest instruments are diatonic, with a single row of ten channels cut into a block of cedar or now often of plastic. Two metal plates, one mounted above the block and the other below, carry a reed for each note (making 20 reeds in all), the upper plate with the reeds set to sound on blow, the lower plate to sound on draw. A metal covering plate on each side protects the reeds and provides a 'tone-chamber'. The reeds that sound on the blow give the notes of the common chord of the keynote of the instrument (thus a C major harmonica sounds C, E, and G), whereas sucking produces the dominant 7th (D, F, A, and B). Chromatic harmonicas have a double row of 12 holes and a spring-controlled slider to open one row or the other. If one row had reeds for C as above, the other would be a semitone sharper, from C♯.

Vibrato and other variations of tone can also be produced by cupping and moving the hand round the instrument and by the use of such breath techniques as *overblowing (which can also be used to 'bend' a note off pitch by as much as a tone). Numerous varieties of harmonica are available. Some have two reeds to each note, one set tuned fractionally sharper than the other to produce a tremolo. Harmonicas can be obtained in almost any key. Tenor and bass instruments, and instruments designed for giving simple chords, are made for harmonica bands. The *melodica, a variant of the harmonica, has been made by Hohner since about 1959.

Mouth organs originated in East Asia some thousands of years ago. The introduction into Europe of the Chinese *sheng in the late 18th century led to various experiments in the use of free reeds. The history of the harmonica itself began in about 1821, with the 'Aura' of C. F. L. Buschmann of Berlin, designed mainly as a tuning instrument. Christian Messner developed this idea further in Trossingen, the German town that was to become the centre of harmonica production. There in 1857 Matthias Hohner founded the firm that eventually acquired a virtual monopoly in harmonica manufacture, having absorbed many of the smaller firms.   JMo

📖 A. BAINES (ed.), *Musical Instruments through the Ages* (Harmondsworth, 1961, 2/1966) · K. FIELD, *Harmonicas, Harps and Heavy Breathers: The Evolution of the People's Instrument* (New York, 1993) · M. HÄFFNER and C. WAGNER, *Made in Germany, Played in the USA: The History of the Mouth Organ in the USA* (Trossingen, 1993)

harmonic minor scale. See SCALE, 3.

harmonic rhythm. The rhythm articulated by changes of harmony within a given phrase or structure. As such, harmonic rhythm offers important indications about the relative weight and stability of harmonic events in a composition, and whereas rhythmic motifs may move across the surface of the music, with repetitions of the same chord a prominent feature (see, for example, the opening of Beethoven's 'Waldstein' Sonata), harmonic rhythm has a sub-surface function in distinguishing between chord repetitions which prolong the function of a single harmony and genuine changes of chord which create changes of function.   AW

harmonics. See ACOUSTICS, 5; HARMONIC SERIES.

harmonic series. A series of frequencies that underlies music in many ways (see ACOUSTICS, 5; EAR AND HEARING, 4) and features in the playing technique of stringed and wind instruments.

The series 1, ½, ⅓, ¼, etc. is musically represented in the divisions of the length of a string or, in wind instruments, of an air column. The corresponding frequency-values (and therefore the musical pitch) follow a reciprocal series 1, 2, 3, 4, etc., since twice the

Ex. 1

♭ = quarter-flat   ♯ = quarter-sharp

TABLE I

Comparison of intervals in the equal-tempered scale and the harmonic series (cent values shown in parentheses)

equal temperament	harmonics				
C (0)	1	2	4	8	16
C♯ (100)					17 (105)
D (200)				9 (204)	18
E♭ (300)					19 (298)
E (400)			5 (386)	10	20
F (500)					21 (471)
				11 (551)	22
F♯ (600)					23 (628)
G (700)		3 (702)	6	12	24
G♯ (800)					
				13 (840)	
A (900)					
B♭ (1000)			7 (969)	14	
B (1100)				15 (1088)	
c (1200)					

wavelength corresponds to half the frequency, and so on. To demonstrate the series musically, the note C (C below the bass staff) is conventionally taken as the root or fundamental. Ex. 1 illustrates the series up to the 24th harmonic, since this is found in some 18th-century music for brass instruments.

Except for certain stringed instruments, on which natural harmonics are produced by touching the string at particular points along its length, the standard scheme numbers the octave harmonic '2' (as in Ex. 1); this has the great advantage of bringing the numbers in line with the interval ratios. For example, the Cs 1, 2, 4, 8, etc. are each an octave apart, i.e. in a ratio of 1:2. Every interval in the series is expressible as the ratio of the two notes involved: for example, the interval G–E (3:5) is the natural or 'just' major 6th, as is D–B (9:15 = 3:5).

The higher one goes through the series, the smaller the successive intervals become; thus, in Ex. 1, the intervals between harmonics decrease progressively from an octave (1:2) to about three-quarters of a semitone (23:24). This means that the series does not line up with a musical scale, in which the intervals are repeated in each octave. In practical music-making the differences are evened out by either *mean-tone or *equal-temperament tuning (see TEMPERAMENT).

The differences between intervals in the harmonic series and in the equal-temperament scale can be shown in terms of cents, a cent being ¹⁄₁₀₀ of an equal-

temperament semitone. This is illustrated in Table 1, again based on C below the bass staff, and beginning each octave from zero cents. These are calculated values and may differ in practice. For example, harmonics (partials) of a stretched string may become increasingly sharp at higher frequencies because of string stiffness.

AB/JBo

Harmonie (Fr., Ger.), **Harmoniemusik** (Ger.). A term used in France and Germany for a wind band, wood-wind or mixed (as opposed to the French *fanfare*, a brass band). The wind section of an orchestra is sometimes referred to as the 'harmonie'. In France, *pièces d'harmonie* were generally collections of opera *airs* arranged for wind. The main tradition is however German and central European. In the late 18th century 'Harmonie' or 'Harmoniemusik' denoted a group of wind players—from the 1780s, ideally two oboes or clarinets (or both), two bassoons, and two horns, following the make-up of Emperor Joseph II's Harmonie from the early 1780s (the tradition centred on Vienna)—or the music they played. Such bands were maintained by wealthy courts for performing serenades during dinner and on festive occasions, as a background to social activity; they were imitated by street bands, such as the one that famously serenaded Mozart with his own music on his nameday in 1781.

The repertory of serenades for *sextet or *octet by Mozart, Haydn, Beethoven, Krommer, Schubert, and many minor composers belongs to this category of *Harmoniemusik*, which also includes transcriptions of operas. Mozart considered making such an arrangement of *Die Entführung aus dem Serail* but was probably anticipated by one of the professional Viennese arrangers of the time, prominent among whom were the imperial Harmonie oboists Johann Wendt and Joseph Triebensee, who also transcribed several of his later operas. *Fidelio* was similarly treated, by Wenzel Sedlak, with Beethoven's approval. Mozart himself noted the tradition in his use, during the supper scene of *Don Giovanni*, of a stage wind band to play excerpts from his own opera *Le nozze di Figaro* and from operas by Sarti and Martín y Soler.

Some of the later music for Harmonie, including selections from operas by Spontini and others, is for larger combinations, adding flute, basset horns, trumpets, and so on in step with the growth of the *military band itself. Haydn's *Harmoniemesse* is so called because of the prominence of wind instruments in the score; Mendelssohn wrote *Harmoniemusik* in 1824 for 23 wind instruments and percussion. The tradition died out soon after that date, to be replaced by that of the full military band.

AB/SS

Harmonie der Welt, Die ('The Harmony of the World'). Opera in five acts by Hindemith to his own libretto based on the life of the 17th-century astronomer Johannes Kepler, author of *De harmonia mundi* (Munich, 1957). Hindemith had previously written a three-movement symphony with the same title (1951).

Harmonielehre. Orchestral piece (1984–5) by Adams.

Harmoniemesse ('Wind-Band Mass'). Haydn's Mass no. 14 in B♭ major (1802), so called because it makes fuller (though not exclusive) use of wind instruments than do Haydn's other masses.

Harmonious Blacksmith, The. Nickname for the air and variations in Handel's Harpsichord Suite no. 5 in E from the first set of eight suites (1720); the title was first used after Handel's death and has no connection with the circumstances of the work's composition.

harmonium, American organ [reed organ]. An organ with a *free reed for each note, activated by air pumped usually by pedal-operated bellows. Inspired by the Chinese *sheng*, many 18th-century makers experimented with the possibilities of free reeds. A prototype reed organ was invented in the 1780s by C. G. Kratzenstein in St Petersburg, and in the first decade of the 19th century several makers invented true reed organs more or less simultaneously, including Bernhard Eschenbach and J. C. Schlimbach in Germany, Ebenezer Goodrich in the USA, and G.-J. Grenié in Paris. Many makers followed their example but it was A. F. Debain who first used the term 'harmonium', in about 1840. This name was patented for a delicate instrument using only one set of reeds, but by 1842 Debain was making larger models using different registers or stops to produce different tone-colours. His main competitors in Paris were Jacob Alexandre and Victor Mustel. In Germany Schiedmayer of Stuttgart was the largest producer.

The harmonium became widely popular both as a domestic instrument and as a substitute for pipe organs in smaller churches and chapels (and was strongly recommended by Berlioz for use in opera houses), because in it the range of a true organ could be covered by an instrument smaller than an upright piano—and costing rather less, for reeds were cheaper than strings.

Alexandre invented the expression stop, which allowed the player to control the air pressure directly and thus play more loudly or softly at will. He also adopted the percussion stop, with which a tiny hammer strikes the reed to give it an initial ictus and so avoid the characteristic rather mushy beginning of the sound.

Other standard stops are similar to those of the *organ, including 16' and 4' ranks which add lower and higher octaves. The 'Voix Céleste' is a slightly off-tuned rank which combines with the 'Clarinette' to give a constant vibrato from the beats between the two ranks, whereas the 'Tremolo' produces pulsating wind.

In the harmonium the action of the bellows blows air past the reeds. American makers generally preferred the contrasting action of suction bellows, which suck it past the reeds. 'American organs' (which are also made in Europe) have greater stability of tone and pitch, thicker reeds, and sound rather more like a pipe organ, but they are less capable of expression than the harmonium.

Rather simpler reed organs with electric blowers were produced in the mid-20th century, often with chord buttons like a piano accordion, but they were rapidly replaced by the various types of electronic organ. In India small harmoniums are widely used both as drone instruments, replacing the *tambūra*, and to accompany singers and instrumentalists.

Many composers wrote specifically for the harmonium, including Rossini, Franck, and Saint-Saëns; Dvořák composed a set of *Bagatelles* for two violins, cello, and harmonium.   JMo

📖 A. W. J. G. Ord-Hume, *Harmonium: The History of the Reed Organ and its Makers* (London, 1986) · R. F. Gellerman, *The American Reed Organ and the Harmonium: A Treatise on its History, Restoration and Tuning* (Vestal, NY, 1996)

harmony 1. Introduction; 2. History and theory to 1900; 3. History and theory since 1900; 4. Practice and principle; 5. Harmony since 1900

1. Introduction

The range of dictionary definitions of this most familiar of musical terms points to its essential, abiding ambiguity. Such definitions tend to proceed from textural to aesthetic interpretation: 'combination of simultaneously sounded musical notes to produce chords and chord progressions': 'pleasing effect of apt arrangement of parts; agreement; concord' (*Pocket Oxford Dictionary*). The ambiguity is partly aesthetic, in the implication that only pleasing concords can be properly harmonious, and partly textural, in that it seems possible to distinguish (in real music, not just technical exercises) between the *harmonic* ways in which simultaneous sounds relate and the *contrapuntal* ways in which successive sounds relate. While the entire history of music theory appears to depend on just such a distinction between harmony and *counterpoint, it is no less evident that developments in the nature of musical composition down the centuries have presumed the interdependence—at times amounting to integration, at other times a source of sustained tension— between the vertical and horizontal dimensions of musical space.

It seems natural and right that music which is not merely harmonic, but harmonious, should be highly regarded in civilized societies. Even though pure, unaccompanied vocal melody may historically have preceded it, and such music was the repository of particularly strong spiritual and lyrical qualities (plainchant, folksong), there is a clear correspondence between the concept of society as a mutually supportive commonwealth, and those manifestations of concert and theatre music which attract the collective approbation 'civilized'. Collective performance, as in singing the same text to different but interdependent vocal lines, can be regarded as the musical correlate of civilized democracy. A hymn, or a national anthem, embodies the harmoniousness of shared rituals and beliefs, and certain instruments—organ, piano, guitar—are often known as 'harmony instruments', providing that chordal support without which the top-line melody on its own would seem incomplete. 20th-century developments in popular music helped to reinforce the role of basic, chordal harmonic support as an inseparable part of the musical statement, and of musical communication. Here, as in churches, the 'harmony instruments' may well be electronic.

2. History and theory to 1900

Since the time of the Ancient Greeks, writers on music have dealt with the acoustical nature of harmony alongside its physical and emotional effects. Discussions of how musical intervals occur, and of how particular scales or modes can be constructed, have a much longer history than studies of more than two notes in vertical combination: and it was more than a hundred years after those early 17th-century developments that brought the chordally accompanied music of recitative into the forefront of cultural practice before a major text with 'harmony' in its title was written. Nevertheless, the theoretical exploration of harmony began well before that text by Rameau (*Traité de l'harmonie*, 1722), just as it has continued after what many feel to be the last significant example of a comparable initiative— Schoenberg's *Harmonielehre* of 1911.

Such texts tend to share ideas and values which were closely bound up with the evolution of tonality and tonal composition between 1700 and 1900, from Monteverdi to Richard Strauss. The governing principle is that harmony embraces harmoniousness—that is, creates a pleasing effect—by observing certain compositionally established conventions. Those conventions derive from the perception that not all chords are the same and that combining different selections of notes of the scale creates different degrees of stability and instability, consonance and dissonance. The feeling that music communicates both its processes and effects through the distinction between consonance and dissonance, and through generally accepted ways of moving between these two types of harmony, had become well established before 1700, at a time when compositions were primarily contrapuntal.

But the shaping of musical forms and phrases in relation to the means of achieving convincing closure, or cadence, was a fruitful source of development in promoting harmonic theory, and the interaction between the two principles reached the height of technical sophistication and expressive power in the music of Handel and Bach. Study of the consistent procedures followed by these masters enabled Rameau, and later theorists, to codify harmonic practice, and the increasing 18th-century tendency to think of music as founded on a *fundamental bass of chordal roots, moving harmonic analysis away from the *figured bass, also contributed to the idea that rules of harmonic practice were not merely acceptable but desirable. Talented students were encouraged to proceed from simple technical exercises in the resolving of dissonances and the construction of coherent progressions to real, free composition in which those rules were still honoured, even when occasionally breached. Foremost among those rules was the celebrated prohibition of parallel movement in 5ths and octaves, aimed at promoting that degree of independence in part-writing which reinforces the interdependence of harmony and counterpoint.

3. History and theory since 1900

The potential for a realistic exploration of the nature of harmonic structures and functions in tonal composition was fully realized only in the 20th century when Heinrich Schenker gave priority to basic, background contrapuntal processes in determining those structures (see ANALYSIS, 3). The notion that the chordal progressions and relations on the musical surface, with all their particular doublings, spacings, and instrumental colourings, were less significant, less essential, than elemental two-voice fundamental structures was one of the most radical formulations of 20th-century music theory, and its presentation by Schenker was the more telling for his determination to restrict his focus to 'masterworks' of the Baroque, Classical, and Romantic canon. The no less radical alternative offered by *Schoenberg, that the surface was of the essence, and that—in contradiction of Schenker's elaborately wrought concepts of prolongation, of the contrapuntal elaboration of background harmony—there was no such thing as a 'non-harmonic' note, raised the prospect of categorizing every conceivable chordal simultaneity from three notes to 12 in terms of the disposition of intervals above the bass. But to function as the basis of effective pedagogical routine, harmonic theory always depended more on principles of progression than on strategies for chord classification.

4. Practice and principle

In many ways the most important prescription for tonal harmonic practice has to do with horizontal progression, not vertical disposition. Good harmony, the textbooks teach—and Bach's chorale harmonizations are held to demonstrate this to perfection—moves in such a way that the constituent voices of each individual chord balance independence against interaction (Ex. 1). To a remarkable extent, Baroque, Classical, and Romantic harmonic practice kept to essentially vocal ideas about acceptable principles of motion, even in a bass line that was understood to need to move more by leap than by step. And such dominant harmoniousness was reinforced by principles of rhythmic structuring and formal organization that emphasized regularity of

phrase structuring as the norm and made clearly hierarchical distinctions between stronger, accented events within the prevailing metre and those weaker events which were inevitably perceived as moving between and therefore linking the strong ones in ways with which the hierarchies of tonal harmonic relationships could engage.

The devising of rule-based exercises in harmonic practice helped to reinforce the evident fact that the acceptance of harmonic laws imposed no particular stylistic constraints on the composer. Nor was it the case that composers moving from small-scale to large-scale works needed to move from harmonic conformity to harmonic freedom, or from one set of rules to another. A 20-minute symphonic movement by Mahler will range far more widely across the tonal spectrum than a ten-minute movement by Haydn, and will use a more elaborate, more chromatic harmonic palette with a higher proportion of dissonance to consonance; as the felt need to resolve the one on to the other relatively explicitly becomes increasingly eroded, the basic harmonic grammars of Haydn and Mahler are

Ex. 1

Bach, harmonization of chorale *Nun ruhen alle Wälder.*

comparable—as, in the operatic sphere, are those of Handel and Verdi, Mozart and Richard Strauss. The idea that 19th-century composers were engaged in a systematic undermining of traditional harmonic principles, in order to ease Schoenberg's ultimate path to their destruction, is simplistic, since the total effect—in Wagner, above all, and also, more often than not, in Liszt, despite his late experiments—is to enhance the ultimate, delayed (but never to be doubted) arrival at consonant closure. The chromatic chords and dissonant strategies of the Romantic composers served in this way to enrich tonality, and such enrichments continued to be explored and used during the 20th century alongside more radical initiatives.

5. Harmony since 1900

Those radical initiatives are generally associated with moves from tonal to post-tonal harmony, and evolutionary models of music history explain this development in terms of the inevitability of change and the decline in concepts that had become over-familiar and—in some sense—worn out. As soon as it was possible for Mahler to end a work—*Das Lied von der Erde* (1908–9)—on a chord other than a pure, root-position triad (Ex. 2), or for Debussy in a piano piece from much the same time—*Mouvement*—to compose out a change from diatonic major tonality to whole-tone modality, then, logically, the evolutionary process could continue until tonality, and harmony, were replaced by their opposites. This model appeared to be supported by Schoenberg's 'emancipation of the dissonance'. Nevertheless, in attempting to argue that absolute distinctions between consonance and dissonance were no longer meaningful, Schoenberg never sought to jettison the much more basic musical opposition, and alternative, between stability and instability. In 'freeing' the dissonance, he aimed to develop new ways of establishing coherence and stability by harmonic means: or, if it was felt that coherence could be achieved without harmonic stability, then stability, or consistency—the means whereby the music could have the potential for pleasing its listeners—must be introduced in other ways.

The simplest indication of such developments is found in a work like the third of Schoenberg's Five

Orchestral Pieces op. 16 (1909), in which a single chord, dissonant by traditional standards, provides a contextually established standard of stability against which other events can be perceived as decorative, unstable (Ex. 3). Stylistically, such music is evidently not so far removed from the highly expressive continuities of late Romantic and Impressionist works which still use tonal harmony; and music since 1909 has varied greatly in the way it approaches the creation or rejection of stability and coherence in harmonic terms. Whereas many individual if not radical composers from Stravinsky to Schnittke use chords which are close enough to traditional types to set up associations with those types and their distinct functions as consonances or dissonances (even if divorced from the 'functional', scale-degree differentiation of truly tonal chords), others have succeeded in escaping from the need for coherence through harmony, understood as some kind of consistent chordal vocabulary. Such music (see for example Stockhausen's *Klavierstück III*, quoted in RHYTHM, Ex. 2) uses shapes, gestures, even contrapuntal relationships in ways that set up textural strategies independent of harmonic thinking. The sense of such music as extreme nevertheless offers the prospect of the judgment that an element of harmonic stability in the creation of compositional coherence could always remain a necessity for music if it is to please, and not just stimulate through provocation, more than a very small number of listeners: and this will be so even if the time-honoured harmonic distinction between consonance and dissonance is definitively set aside.   AW

Ex. 3

harmony of the spheres. See SPHERES, MUSIC OF THE.

Harold en Italie ('Harold in Italy'). Symphony, op. 16 (1834), by Berlioz for viola and orchestra, inspired by Byron's *Childe Harold*; it was composed at Paganini's request for a work in which he could display his newly acquired Stradivari viola, but Paganini rejected it because the viola part gave him little opportunity for displays of virtuosity. See also PROGRAMME MUSIC.

harp (Fr.: *harpe*; Ger.: *Harfe*; It.: *arpa*). An instrument with its strings standing free, to be plucked with the hands from both sides; they are attached at one end to a 'string bar' which runs along a sloping soundboard from

Ex. 2

end to end. From this they rise in a perpendicular plane to a neck, where they are tuned with a key or by other means. European harps are generally 'frame harps', having the structural support of a forepillar between the distal ends of the neck and resonator that helps to bear the tension of the strings. Most harps in Asia and Africa, including those of antiquity, are 'open harps', lacking the forepillar. Open harps may be 'arched' or 'angular'.

1. Open harps; 2. European frame harps: (a) Medieval diatonic harps (b) Two- and three-rank chromatic harps (c) Hook harps (d) Pedal harps

1. Open harps

Arched, or 'bow', harps may be seen as elaborations of the musical bow (see BOW, MUSICAL), with the bass of the curved neck inserted in one end of a resonator of gourd or carved wood, and a string-holder stick lodged near the base of the neck and running under the sound-skin under tension. Such instruments were used in the Middle East and Egypt in the 3rd millennium BC and are still widely played in East and Central Africa. Arched harps also appeared in ancient India and were carried with Buddhism to Myanmar (Burma), Indo-China, and Indonesia. The *saùng-gauk* arched harp is still played in Myanmar.

Angled harps have the neck set into the top of the resonator at a sharp angle; such instruments appeared in Mesopotamia in about 1900 BC; they were used throughout the Hellenistic period, and later spread along the Islamic and Buddhist trade routes to East and South Asia. They ceased to be used in China by the 12th century and in South and South-East Asia, Persia, and Turkey in the 17th century, but they remain widely used in Central Africa and survive in isolated cases in Georgia and Western Siberia. Tuning is effected, on both arched and angled harps, either by rotating collars ('tuning-nooses') encircling the neck or by tuning-pegs of some kind.

2. European frame harps

(a) Medieval diatonic harps: A disadvantage on all such harps is a certain amount of flexibility in the joint between neck and resonator, so that tightening one string brings the neck fractionally forward, slackening the others enough to throw them out of tune. The solution is to insert a forepillar between the distal ends of the resonator and neck. With the exception of stone carvings of harps with forepillars dating from about 2500 BC in the Greek Cycladic Islands, this device first appears in Europe on Picto-Scottish stone carvings from the late 8th century AD, and also, rather less clearly, in the Utrecht Psalter (816–35). The main source

of information on the harp is Christian iconography, usually illustrations of the Psalms and depictions of King David. Open harps continue to be shown until the 12th century; thereafter only frame harps are shown.

On frame harps the strings rise vertically from the centre of the soundboard, passing to the wrest pins in the neck. The graceful dip, or 'harmonic curve', in the neck is the natural result of the strings rising from the sloping soundboard, following the principle that their length should double for each octave difference (Fig. 1). In practice the strings also increase in thickness, and somewhat in tension too, allowing the curve to flatten out towards the bass end—markedly so in such smaller instruments as some medieval harps (dotted lines in Fig. 1).

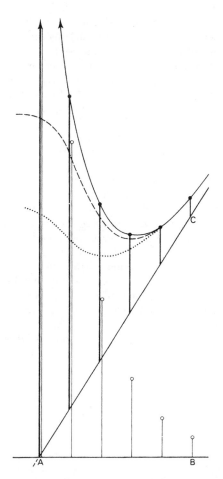

Fig. 1. Diagram of strings an octave apart, doubling in length for each octave. Shown in fine line: perpendicular to horizontal base AB; in heavy line: the same lengths rising from slope AC (representing the soundboard), producing a curve with a dip. The modified curves (broken and dotted lines) are also based on AC.

Medieval European iconography shows three distinct types of harp: that which became known as the Irish harp (modern 'Celtic' harps are also based on this type), though the first extant evidence for it is in Lincoln *c.*1270, and it was also known elsewhere in Europe; the Gothic harp, widespread in Europe, with a gracefully curved forepillar and a pointed crest to the neck near its joint with the soundbox; and a lighter medieval harp, also widely used, with a shorter forepillar, merging in a smooth curve into the end of the neck with a lower head. All three were normally diatonic only, though players could raise the pitch by a semitone by stopping a string near the neck.

The surviving Irish and Scottish harps in Dublin and Edinburgh, from the 14th and 15th centuries, are the oldest extant harps in Europe. They are small enough to be played on the knee or on a low table. The belly and sides of the resonator are carved from a solid block of wood, traditionally willow or hornbeam, with a separate back. The resonator is wide in the bass, with a substantial, strongly curved pillar and neck. Irish harps had strings of brass or silver, whereas in Wales, where the belly was of skin instead of wood, strings were of braided horsehair. The original tradition of playing these harps (often known by the Gaelic name *clàrsach* or *clàirseach*) persisted in Wales, Ireland, and Scotland, dying out by the end of the 18th century, though revivals began in the 19th century.

The Gothic and light medieval harps had resonators probably of box construction, built up from staves, with (like all modern harps) a softwood belly. The necks and forepillars were also lighter. An extra effect on the diatonic harp was the use of brays: angled wooden belly pins which, when turned to touch the string, gave a strong buzzing sound, replete with overtones.

(b) Two- and three-rank chromatic harps: As polyphonic music began to demand a greater range of chromatic notes, and keyboard instruments became fully chromatic in the 14th century, greater chromaticism was also required of the harp. The *arpa doppia* ('double harp'), with two or three ranks of strings, one of which was tuned to the chromatic notes, was introduced in Spain or Italy. On two-rank harps the chromatic and diatonic ranks were either parallel to each other, crossing over at about *c'* so that the fingers of both hands had to reach through the diatonic rank to play the chromatic strings, or, as in Spain, crossed in an X shape. On the triple harp the diatonic scale was duplicated in the two outer ranks, and the chromatic notes were in the middle rank. It was particularly popular in southern Italy in the 17th century, and it remained the standard concert harp into the 18th century (e.g. in Handel's Harp Concerto). The 'arpa doppia' used in Monteverdi's *Orfeo* (1607) was probably the triple harp, which survived into the 20th century in Wales and has been revived there. Single- and double-rank harps are also used in Central and South America, derived from the Spanish instruments of the Renaissance and Baroque periods.

(c) Hook harps: Two- and three-rank harps were expensive to maintain, for harp strings have never been cheap, and the German hook harp, with a single rank of strings and a series of hooks set into the neck below some of the wrest pins, was a strong competitor from the late 17th century. Each hook could be turned to press against its string at the correct point to shorten it by a semitone. It needed a hand free for long enough to turn the necessary hooks in each octave, but it was a great deal lighter and cheaper than the triple harp. A similar system, with blades or levers instead of hooks, is used today on the popular 'Celtic' harp introduced in the 1960s (the first being the 'Troubadour' model by Lyon & Healy of Chicago).

(d) Pedal harps: Early in the 18th century several Bavarian and French makers thought of using pedals, with trackers inside the forepillar, to move the hooks. This had the dual advantage of allowing both hands to remain on the strings, and of the F pedal (for example) being used to raise all the F strings to F♯, instead of each hook having to be moved individually. F.-J. Naderman's system in France worked by a *crochet* pulling the string in towards the neck so that it rested against a fixed metal nut as a cut-off bar. Georges and J.-G. Cousineau's system, for the type of harp for which Mozart wrote, had pairs of *béquilles* that turned in opposite directions to grip the string between them. At the end of the century Sébastien Érard produced his *fourchettes* ('forks'): two pins, fixed to a disc, that gripped the string as the disc revolved. In the mid-19th century John Egan of Dublin invented the first modern 'Irish' harp, copied from Érard's harp but with ditals in the forepillar instead of pedals.

Meanwhile, Érard had moved to London and in 1810 invented the double-action harp, which is still the standard concert instrument. The strings are tuned to the diatonic scale of C♭, and each string is provided with two *fourchettes* (Fig. 2). Each pedal can be depressed twice: moving it into the first notch turns the upper *fourchette* (Fig. 2*b*), sharpening the string by a semitone; in the second notch the lower *fourchette* also turns and the pitch is raised by a further semitone (Fig. 2*c*). There are seven pedals—one for each note of the scale—so each note can be played flat, natural, or sharp. The modern concert harp has 46 or 47 strings and a compass of six and a half octaves.

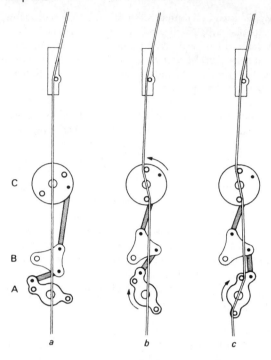

Fig. 2. Pedal-harp mechanism as visible on the neck. The bridge pin at the top is shown (a) with pedal up; (b) in first notch; (c) in second notch.

The pedal harp was not without rivals. Gustave Lyon commissioned Debussy to write the *Danse sacrée et danse profane* for his double harp, made by Pleyel with 76 strings crossing in an X, a reinvention of the old Spanish double harp. Érard retaliated by commissioning Ravel's *Introduction and Allegro* for his pedal harp.

A new generation of pedal harps was introduced in 1996 by the French firm Camac, which reduced the weight and strengthened and stabilized the pedal, tracker, and forked-disc mechanism by using light modern materials and modifying the design. The strings fan out, especially in the higher octaves, rather than being parallel to each other, and the neck and resonator joint is lower down, making the higher reaches of the instrument more comfortable to play.

On the modern harp, players pluck the strings near the middle with the pads of their fingers. The traditional technique on the Welsh harp, and presumably on the classical triple and double harps too, was to pluck, or 'strike the strings' as the last traditional player said, close to the soundboard. Irish harpers used their fingernails on the wire strings of their harps, again probably near the soundboard.   JMo

📖 J. Rimmer, 'Harps in the Baroque era', *Proceedings of the Royal Musical Association*, 90 (1963–4), 59–75 · R. Rensch, *The Harp: Its History, Technique and Repertoire* (London and New York, 1969) · J. Rimmer, *The Irish Harp* (Cork, 1969, 3/1984) · O. Ellis, *The Story of the Harp in Wales* (Cardiff, 1980, 2/1991) · B. Lawergren, 'Acoustics and evolution of arched harps', *Galpin Society Journal*, 34 (1981), 110–29 · C. Bordas Ibañez, 'The double harp in Spain from the 16th to the 18th centuries', *Early Music*, 15 (1987), 148–63 · M. van Schaik, *The Harp in the Middle Ages: The Symbolism of a Musical Instrument* (Amsterdam, 1992) · R. Jackson, 'Performance practice and the harp: Twelfth to nineteenth centuries', *Historical Harp Society Bulletin*, 6/3 (1996), 2–13 · P. Bruguière and J.-L. Grootaers (eds.), *Song of the River: Harps of Central Africa* (Paris, 1999)

harp-lute. 1. Generic term formerly used for a group of West African instruments of which the best known is the Mandinka *kora*. They have now been reclassified as *bridge harps.   RPA

2. Generic term for a group of hybrid guitars in vogue during the early 19th century, especially among lady amateurs in France and England. They were slightly shorter than conventional guitars, and had stave-built, vaulted soundboxes, usually in the shape of a trapezium with a rounded bottom. The earliest, Edward Light's harp-guitar invented in 1798, had eight gut strings tuned to a C major chord. Later models, for instance Light's harp-lute of 1811 and his dital harp of 1819, had extra bass strings to the side of the fingerboard (like a *theorbo); these were attached to a harp-style 'neck' rising from the top of the fingerboard to a 'forepillar' that came out of the bass side of the body. There was also a mechanism to raise the strings by a semitone. The most complex of these instruments, which were decorative rather than practical and were used to accompany songs, was Angelo Benedetto Ventura's Harp Ventura of 1828. Another contemporary hybrid with a similar function was the *lyre guitar.

                    JMo

'Harp' Quartet. Nickname for Beethoven's String Quartet in E♭ major op. 74 (1809), so called because of the harp-like pizzicato arpeggios in the first movement.

harpsichord, virginals, spinet. A class of keyboard string instruments, on all of which sound is produced by the plucking of the strings with a plectrum of quill, leather, or today often plastic.

1. General description; 2. Harpsichords; 3. Virginals and spinet

1. General description

The plectrum is mounted in the tongue of a jack, a rectangular slip of wood (Fig. 1) standing on the end of a key. The tongue (A) must be free to pivot against a

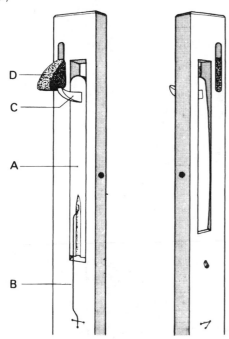

Fig. 1.

spring (B), usually of hog bristle, so that the plectrum (C) can slide back past the string on the return journey without plucking it. A damper of cloth in a slot at the top of the jack (D) touches the string to stop it vibrating when the key is released. A padded wooden bar, the jack-rail, runs across the instrument from side to side above the jacks to prevent them jumping out, for they are not attached to the keys but stand in individual slots in a strip of wood (the jack-slide) which runs under the strings to stop the jacks falling sideways and to guide their vertical motion.

2. Harpsichords

Although some harpsichords have only a single set of strings and jacks, most have at least two sets of each, the jacks resting on the keys one behind the other, facing in opposite directions. A set of jacks may be engaged or disengaged by moving the jack-slide laterally, so bringing the plectra in and out of reach of the strings. As each plectrum always produces the same sound on a string, regardless of the force with which the key is struck, this mechanism is incapable of producing any degree of dynamic or tonal variation from a single set of strings. Volume can be increased only by engaging more sets of strings and jacks. Single-manual harpsichords usually have two unison (8′) registers and often a third an octave higher (4′), which players can select or combine at will by shifting the jack-slide, either directly

(where the end of the slide protrudes through a slot in the side wall) or with a lever controlled by a stop-knob on the front of the instrument. The two 8′ registers contrast in tone because the plectra of two jacks standing even as little as 2.5 cm apart on the key will produce two different tone-qualities by plucking at different points along the string.

On single-manual instruments, one hand must be free to make the change of register. On a two-manual harpsichord these different sonorities are available simply by moving one or both hands from one manual to the other. Typical French two-manual harpsichords of the 17th and 18th centuries have one 8′ register played from the upper manual and the other from the lower, with the 4′ also on the lower, its jacks standing between the two 8′ jacks so that they are further apart. A coupler allows the lower manual to pluck all three registers. English 18th-century harpsichords often have a 'lute stop', an extra set of jacks played from the upper manual and plucking the same 8′ strings as the ordinary set on that manual. The extra set is placed close to the nut to produce a penetrating, nasal sound (hence the French and German terms *nasale* and *Nazard*). Another stop, common in all periods, was the buff stop (also known as harp stop and, confusingly, in French as *registre de luth* and in German as *Lautenzug*), consisting of a sliding batten fitted with a row of soft-leather pads that could be pressed against the strings to mute them slightly.

Thus there were considerable differences in national styles, each having its own characteristic sound as well as its own characteristic construction and appearance. Italian harpsichords were usually single-manual, light and very responsive, sometimes with only one 8′ register. From the end of the 16th century to the end of the 17th, harpsichord-building in northern Europe was dominated by Flemish builders, particularly the Ruckers dynasty of Antwerp. Early 17th-century Flemish two-manual instruments used the second manual to transpose, so that, for example, the C keys of the upper manual plucked the same strings as the F keys of the lower. The reason for this arrangement is still disputed. The great French two-manual harpsichords of the 18th century are those most often copied today. The early German harpsichords seem to have been based on the light Italian models. Later instruments, in Bach's time, were bigger and heavier than the French, sometimes with a low 16′ register or even a high 2′ register. Later English instruments, built in the days when harpsichords were competing with pianos, had such devices as a swell to allow crescendo and diminuendo and a pedal-operated machine stop, functioning like an organ pre-set, allowing instantaneous changes from one registration to another. The range of tonal contrasts between one set of strings and another is one of the harpsichord's great advantages over the piano and the reason why harpsichord music can sound dull when played on the piano.

The earliest harpsichord of which we have any detailed knowledge is the *clavisimbalum* described by Henri Arnaut de Zwolle in his treatise of *c.*1440. It was quite small with a three-octave compass and four types of jack, one of which had a hammer action foreshadowing that of the piano. This and contemporary iconography suggests that the harpsichord was first devised around 1400. The only surviving 15th-century instrument is a *clavicytherium* or upright harpsichord in the Royal College of Music in London, dating from about 1480. It has a slightly larger compass of 40 notes, F–g'' without $F\sharp$ (omitting the lowest sharp remained a common practice). When the missing chromatics in the bass were needed, some makers provided a 'broken octave' by splitting keys, the front half giving the short-octave note and the back half the nominal note. The compass was increased in the 16th century by using the C/E *short octave. It was then further increased, becoming G/B–c''' in the 17th century and F'–f'' in the 18th.

The modern revival of the harpsichord began with the growing interest in Baroque music in the mid-19th century, when A. J. Hipkins and others began to play on original instruments. Pleyel in Paris built a harpsichord in 1882, and Arnold Dolmetsch made his first in 1898. Many of these incorporated 'improvements' drawn from piano-building, such as metal frames and thick strings at high tension, and elaborate pedal mechanisms for changing registration. Under the influence initially of Hugh Gough, Frank Hubbard, and William Dowd in the 1950s, almost all makers are now copying original technology as closely as possible, and it is extremely rare to see instruments of the type made in the late 19th and early 20th centuries, though there is an important corpus of music written specifically for them which cannot be played on old harpsichords because the pedals are essential for it.

3. Virginals and spinet

The harpsichord, wing-shaped like the later grand piano, was always a large and expensive piece of furniture. Smaller domestic instruments were also made. The terms 'harpsichord', 'virginals', and 'spinet' have been interchangeable almost throughout their history, or have varied in meaning in different countries and at different periods. In modern times the following distinctions are made (illustrated in Fig. 2). The harpsichord has strings running from front to back. The virginals (normally pluralized in English, though nobody knows why) has a polygonal or rectangular case

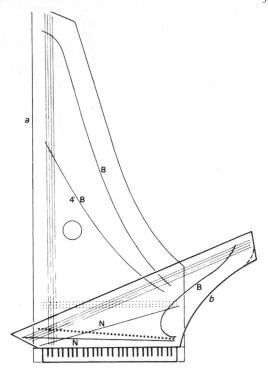

Fig. 2. Schematic views from above showing bridge (B), nut (N), and rows of jacks (indicated by dotted lines) on (a) harpsichord, including 4' bridge; (b) spinet; (c) virginals, rectangular and polygonal forms.

with strings running across the instrument at right angles to the keys, the jacks in a line diagonally from back to front so that bass keys are longer than the trebles. In the spinet, the strings run obliquely away from the player, producing a wing-shaped ('bentside' or 'leg of mutton') case, or a trapezoid case in smaller instruments. As on the harpsichord, the line of jacks lies parallel to the keyboard and all the keys are the same length. The spinet was therefore a small harpsichord in style and sound, with a single manual. Smaller instruments that fit this description date from early 17th-century Italy. The invention of the 'bentside' spinet, which became the standard domestic instrument in 18th-century England, has been attributed to the Italian maker Girolamo Zenti, whose earliest surviving spinet is dated 1637.

The virginals (Fr.: *épinette*; It.: *spinetto*) was a subtly different instrument with its own distinctive tone-quality, though seldom equipped (unlike the harpsichord) with the means to change timbre. Having originated in the mid-15th century, virginals are depicted more frequently in 16th- and 17th-century paintings, etc., than are harpsichords, indicating their importance as domestic instruments. Flemish virginals, mostly rectangular in shape, were made either with the keyboard placed in the centre (or left of centre) in one of the long sides of the case ('spinetten') so that the jacks plucked the strings close to the end and gave a bright and clear sound, or with the keyboard located towards the right-hand end of the case ('muselars') so that the strings were plucked in the middle, giving a full, dark, and hollow sound. Some Flemish 'mother and child' virginals were made effectively double-manual by having a small 4′ virginals tucked away in a drawer beside the keyboard. If this was taken out and placed over the jacks of the main instrument, after removing the jack-rail both could be played together, the jacks of the 'mother' pushing up the jacks of the 'child'. The 'child' could also be played on its own.

JMo

📖 R. Russell, *The Harpsichord and Clavichord* (London, 1959, rev. 2/1973 by H. Schott) · F. Hubbard, *Three Centuries of Harpsichord Making* (Cambridge, MA, 1965, 2/1967) · E. M. Ripin (ed.), *Keyboard Instruments* (Edinburgh, 1971, 2/1977) · L. Palmer, *Harpsichord in America: A Twentieth-Century Revival* (Bloomington, IN, 1989) · P. Dirksen (ed.), *The Harpsichord and its Repertoire* (Utrecht, 1992)

Harris, Renatus [René] (*b* ?Quimper, *c*.1652; *d* Bristol or London, 1724). English organ builder. His father, Thomas (*d c*.1684), built the organs in Gloucester, Salisbury, and Chichester cathedrals. Renatus was a colourful figure and rival of 'Father' *Smith; he built 39 organs, among them those in Bristol Cathedral (1685) and St Bride, Fleet Street (1694).   AL

Harris, Roy (Ellsworth) (*b* Lincoln County, OK, 12 Feb. 1898; *d* Santa Monica, CA, 1 Oct. 1979). American composer. He had lessons in Los Angeles from Arthur Farwell, Modest Altschuler, and Arthur Bliss, and studied in Paris with Nadia Boulanger (1926–9). His First Symphony (1933) established his reputation and also proposed a model of specifically American symphony writing to which other composers have aspired; his Third Symphony (1937) is the classic work of this type, and one of the most frequently played American compositions. Harris's style is strong and assertive, imbued with an American melos of hymn tunes and folksongs, and using the orchestra to create powerful effects of block antiphony. Besides the 15 symphonies

his output includes many other orchestral works, numerous choral pieces, songs, and chamber compositions. He taught at several colleges and universities in the USA.   PG

Harris, Sir William (Henry) (*b* London, 28 March 1883; *d* Petersfield, 6 Sept. 1973). English organist and composer. He entered the RCM in 1899, studying the organ with Walter Parratt and composition with Charles Wood and Walford Davies. He held organist appointments at Lichfield (1911–19), New College, Oxford (1919–29), Christ Church, Oxford (1929–32), and finally St George's Chapel, Windsor (1933–61). He was a professor at the RCM (1923–53) and conductor of the Bach Choir (1926–33). His best-known works are the double-choir motets *Faire is the Heaven* (1925) and *Bring us, O Lord* (1959), in the mould of Parry's *Songs of Farewell*. He also wrote music for the cornonations of 1937 and 1953 and for the Three Choirs Festival.

PG/JD1

Harrison, Lou (Silver) (*b* Portland, OR, 14 May 1917). American composer. He studied in San Francisco with Cowell (1934–5) and worked there with Cage writing and performing percussion music (1939–41), then had lessons with Schoenberg (1941) before moving to New York in 1943. There he worked as a critic and edited and performed some of Ives's scores. After returning to the west coast he taught at San José State University (1967–82) and Mills College (1980–5). His large and happy output includes works of many different kinds, often drawing a tuneful, modal line from American folk music to Baroque, medieval, or Asian traditions, scored for media including symphony orchestra, gamelan, and specially built percussion instruments, some made by his life partner William Colvig. Long a fringe composer, he began to be more widely performed and recorded in the 1980s.   PG

Härtel, Gottfried Christoph. See Breitkopf & Härtel.

Hartke, Stephen (Paul) (*b* Orange, NJ, 6 July 1952). American composer. He sang in choirs as a boy treble and later studied with James M. Drew at Yale, George Rochberg at the University of Pennsylvania, and Ed Applebaum at the University of California at Santa Barbara, where he taught from 1981 to 1987, moving then to the University of Southern California. His music continues the freshness of imagination, the rhythmic élan, and the quizzical historicizing of such Stravinsky pieces as *Agon*, and includes two symphonies, a Violin Concerto (1992), other orchestral pieces, chamber music, and instrumental solos.   PG

Hartmann, Johann Peter Emilius (*b* Copenhagen, 14 May 1805; *d* Copenhagen, 10 March 1900). Danish composer and teacher. He was a scion of the most important family in Danish musical history: his grandfather, his father, his son, his son-in-law (Niels W. Gade), and his great-grandson (Niels Viggo Bentzon) were all composers. After taking a degree in law, he became a prosperous civil servant, retiring in 1870; but he was also a leader of Danish musical life. Appointed organist of Garnisons Kirke when he was 19, in succession to his father, he resigned the post in 1843 on becoming organist at Copenhagen Cathedral; he held the two appointments for a total of 76 years. From 1827 he taught at the Copenhagen Conservatory. He helped found the Musikforening (Music Society) in 1836 and the Studentersangforening (Students' Choral Society) in 1839.

Hartmann was a prolific composer, writing several hundred works in all genres, including three operas, several ballets, two symphonies, chamber and instrumental music (including a good deal for piano), and songs. Although his music shows an affinity with the idiom of Schumann, he was one of the first to introduce a genuinely Nordic tone into music, in his early melodrama *Guldhornene* ('The Golden Horns', 1832).

MA

Hartmann, Karl Amadeus (*b* Munich, 2 Aug. 1905; *d* Munich, 5 Dec. 1963). German composer. He studied with Joseph Haas at the Munich Music Academy (1923–7) and with Scherchen, who did much to promote his music at the outset of his career. During the Nazi years he withdrew from public musical life, studying with Webern in 1941–2. He also continued to compose, recording his opposition to the regime privately, as when he incorporated a Hussite chorale, 'Ye who are warriors of God', into his *Concerto funebre* for violin and strings (1939) to protest against Hitler's annexation of Czechoslovakia. In 1945 he took up his public activities in Munich, becoming Dramaturg at the Bavarian State Opera and founding the Musica Viva concert series (which he supervised for the rest of his life) to introduce the music of Schoenberg, Stravinsky, Bartók, and others.

Hartmann's essentially contrapuntal approach to the generation of symphonic momentum places him in the line that passes through Beethoven and Brahms; his avoidance of sentimental gesture suggests Hindemith's influence; and his orchestration reveals a fondness for the music of Stravinsky. His eight symphonies compensate for an overtly intellectual impulse with a sense of seething energy that gives them direct impact. For the stage he wrote the five short operas of his *Wachsfigurenkabinett* (1929–30) and *Simplicius*

Simplicissimus (1934–5, rev. 1956–7); his concertos include the Chamber Concerto for clarinet, string quartet, and strings (1930–5) and works for trumpet (1933) and viola (1954–6); and among his chamber music are two string quartets (1933, 1945–6). He was a productive composer, but he was also self-critical, and many works failed to see the light of day or were recycled into other compositions.

PG/MA

📖 A. McCredie, *Karl Amadeus Hartmann* (Wilhelmshaven, 1980) · G. Rickards, *Hindemith, Hartmann and Henze* (London, 1995) · M. Kater, *Composers of the Nazi Era: Eight Portraits* (New York, 2000)

Harty, Sir (Herbert) Hamilton (*b* Hillsborough, Co. Down, 4 Dec. 1879; *d* Hove, 19 Feb. 1941). Irish composer and conductor. He studied and worked as an organist in Ireland before moving to London in 1900. There he gradually established a reputation as a conductor which led to his appointment to the Hallé Orchestra (1920–33). He produced a number of original compositions, including an Irish Symphony and many songs, but achieved most success with his arrangements for the modern orchestra of Handel's *Music for the Royal Fireworks* and *Water Music*.

PG

Harvey, Jonathan (Dean) (*b* Sutton Coldfield, 3 May 1939). English composer. His main composition studies were with Erwin Stein, Hans Keller, and Milton Babbitt, and he has taught at Southampton, Sussex, and Stanford universities. His earlier works reflect the impact of composers as diverse as Britten, Messiaen, and Stockhausen (on whom he published a study in 1974), but it was the last named who was decisive in turning Harvey in the direction of electronic techniques, often in the context of subject matter with a strong spiritual dimension.

These concerns are evident as early as *Cantata IV: Ludus amoris* (1969), but they deepen in the large-scale *Inner Light* trilogy (1973–7) and many subsequent works, several of which originated in time spent at IRCAM (e.g. *Mortuos plango, vivos voco*, 1980, and *Advaya*, 1994). Harvey has also produced a series of impressive symphonic compositions, including *Madonna of Winter and Spring* (1986) and concertos for cello (1990) and percussion (1997), as well as the full-length opera *Inquest of Love* (ENO, 1993).

PG/AW

📖 A. Whittall, *Jonathan Harvey* (London, 1999)

Harwood, Basil (*b* Woodhouse, Olveston, Glos., 11 April 1859; *d* London, 3 April 1949). English organist and composer. He studied at Oxford (1878–81) and briefly in Leipzig with Salomon Jadassohn and Robert Papperitz (1882–3). He was organist at Ely Cathedral (1887–92), but most of his professional career was spent in Oxford, where he was organist of Christ Church (1892–1909) and university choragus. His compositions include an organ concerto (written for the Gloucester Festival in 1910), cantatas, church music, and a corpus of technically demanding organ music, notably the Organ Sonata no. 1 in C♯ minor op. 5 (1886), the *Dithyramb* op. 7 (1892), *Paean* op. 15 no. 3 (1902), and the Toccata op. 49 (1929). In 1909 he retired from the music profession in order to manage his inherited Gloucestershire estate. PG/JDı

📖 V. RUDDLE, *The Life and Hymn Tunes of Basil Harwood* (Sutton Coldfield, 1996)

Háry János (*Háry János kalandozásai Nagyabonytul a Burgváráig*; 'János Háry: His Adventures from Nagyabony to the Vienna Burg'). Opera in a prologue, four adventures (five at the first three performances), and an epilogue by Kodály to a libretto by Béla Paulini and Zsolt Harsányi after János Garay's comic epic *Az obsitos* ('The Veteran') (Budapest, 1926). Kodály arranged a suite (1927) from the opera's orchestral music.

Hasse, Johann Adolf (*b* Bergedorf, nr Hamburg, *bapt.* 25 March 1699; *d* Venice, 16 Dec. 1783). German composer. From the 1730s he was the leading German exponent of Italian opera, with some 62 *opere serie* and numerous shorter dramatic works to his credit. After service as a tenor at the Hamburg opera (1718) he transferred to Brunswick (1721), where he sang the title role in his first opera, *Antioco*. Subsequently he moved to Naples (1722), where he converted to Roman Catholicism, studied with Porpora and Alessandro Scarlatti, and in 1725 mounted his serenata *Antonio e Cleopatra* (1725), with Carlo Broschi (Farinelli) and Vittoria Tesi in the title roles. In Naples during the next four years he composed his first seven *opere serie*, including *L'Astarto* (1726) and *Tigrane* (1729); and at Venice in 1730 he produced *Artaserse*, his first setting of a Metastasio libretto. Also in Venice he met, and soon after married, the mezzo-soprano Faustina Bordoni, one of the finest singers of her time. In 1731 the couple travelled to Dresden, where Hasse was installed as Kapellmeister to the royal court, an occasion enhanced by a performance of his opera *Cleofide* (1731) at which J. S. Bach and his son Wilhelm Friedemann were reportedly present. From the 1730s Hasse and Metastasio, with increasing admiration of each other's skills, became ever more closely associated, the composer eventually setting all the poet's texts except *Temistocle*.

From their Dresden base Hasse and Bordoni visited several other European cities—Turin, Rome, Milan, and, particularly, Venice and Vienna—where they presented new operas, often in response to royal commissions. In 1745, on the occasion of a state visit by Frederick the Great to Dresden, Hasse provided a festal *Te Deum* and the heroic opera *Arminio*; in later years the composer and his wife were frequently invited to perform for the king at Potsdam. However, this harmonious relationship was strained in 1760 when, on returning to Dresden from Vienna, the couple found the opera house, the court library, and their home destroyed by Frederick's artillery. With musical activities at court severely curtailed, Hasse and his wife were dismissed without pensions and moved to Vienna. In 1773, in serious financial straits, and already largely forgotten, they retired to Venice, where Bordoni died in November 1781, and Hasse just over two years later.

The Neapolitan type of opera that Hasse cultivated, with its ordered recitative–aria patterns, provided him with an ideal vehicle for the promotion of *bel canto aria. His simplicity of harmony, delicacy of orchestration, and suppleness of melodic line all serve to highlight the role of the solo singer, while at the same time giving subtle emphasis to changes in dramatic expression suggested by the text. Furthermore, in his treatment of recitative sections he provides precisely for the pitch inflections and natural rhythms of speech, while skilfully marshalling his keys and cadences so as to underpin variations of mood and character.

JN/BS

📖 F. L. MILNER, *The Operas of Johann Adolf Hasse* (Ann Arbor, MI, 1979)

Hassler, Hans [Johann] **Leo** (*b* Nuremberg, *bapt.* 17 Aug. 1562; *d* Frankfurt, 8 June 1612). German composer. He was the second of three sons (all of whom became organists) of a Nuremberg organist. In 1584 he went to Venice to study with Andrea Gabrieli. He returned to Germany two years later to become organist to the banker Octavian II Fugger; this was his most productive composing period. After Octavian's death in 1600 he left Augsburg, returning for four years to Nuremberg, after which he moved to Ulm (where he married at the age of 46) before ending his life as organist to the Elector of Saxony at Dresden.

Hassler was a leading composer of his day. His Latin polyphonic and polychoral works were influenced by Lassus and his circle and by the Venetian school. His secular compositions include Italian madrigals and rhythmic *Tanzlieder* ('dance-songs'). A Protestant, he published some significant hymn and psalm settings for the Lutheran liturgy. The well-known 'Passion Chorale' *O Haupt voll Blut und Wunden* was adapted from one of his German love songs; his *All Lust und Freud* was used by Schütz for a psalm setting still sung by Protestant congregations today. PW

hastig (Ger.). 'Hurried', 'impetuous'.

Haubenstock-Ramati, Roman (*b* Kraków, 27 Feb. 1919; *d* Vienna, 3 March 1993). Polish-born Austrian composer. He studied in Kraków and Lwów, and from 1947 to 1950 was head of the music department of Polish Radio, while also writing music criticism. From 1950 to 1957 he was in Tel Aviv, where he was director of the music library and also worked as a teacher. In 1957 he returned to Europe, working in Vienna for the publisher Universal Edition, and also lecturing widely. Haubenstock-Ramati's music reflects many late 20th-century trends, including serialism, mobile forms, and graphic scores. It includes an opera, *Amerika* (after Franz Kafka; Berlin, 1966), as well as orchestral, vocal, and ensemble works. ABur

Haunted Manor, The (*Straszny dwór*). Opera in four acts by Moniuszko to a libretto by Jan Chęciński after a story from Kazimierz Wójcicki's *Stary gawędy i obrazy* ('Legends and Pictures') (Warsaw, 1865).

Haupt (Ger.). 'Head', 'principal'; e.g. *Hauptthema*, the 'principal theme' of a composition.

Hauptstimme (Ger.). 'Principal voice': the leading part, often the soprano. Schoenberg used the term to denote the principal part in a complex polyphonic texture, often marked in the score by a bracket symbol formed from the letter H (see MELODY).

Hauptwerk (Ger.). The principal division of a German organ, the Great organ.

Hausmusik (Ger.). See GEBRAUCHSMUSIK.

Haussmann, Valentin (*b* Gerbstedt, 1565–70; *d* c.1614). German composer. He became independent of aristocratic patronage unusually early, and this is reflected in his choice of compositional genres, the large number of bourgeois dedicatees of his compositions, and his varied, peripatetic employments. He published 148 Polish dances collected on his travels. Other publications included Italian, English, and Polish vocal music to which he supplied his own poetry. He was an accomplished exponent of the Italian musico-poetic style then current in Germany. His varied output reflects the shift from religious to secular music in his time: as well as sacred pieces he composed songs, *Tanzlieder*, dances in both German and Polish styles, fugues, and fantasias. PW

haut, bas (Fr.). Terms used to describe early instruments and ensembles by their loudness, not their pitch. *Haut* ('loud') instruments such as shawms and slide trumpets played outdoor, festive music; *bas* ('soft') instruments—recorders, fiddles, lutes, and harps—

played more intimately. A few instruments, for example cornetts, sackbuts, and percussion, could play in both styles. JMo

hautbois (Fr.). 'Oboe' or, before the mid-17th century, 'shawm'. The term was formerly used in English in the same two senses, frequently written 'hautboy' or 'hoboy'. JMo

haute-contre (Fr.). A high tenor voice (or instrument of similar range), neither castrato nor falsetto, with a range of roughly *d–b′*. It was the leading male solo voice in French opera from Lully to Rameau; by about 1820 it had been superseded by the normal tenor voice.

haute danse (Fr., 'elevated dance'). The opposite of *basse danse, i.e. a dance in which the feet were lifted off the ground as opposed to being kept close to it.

havanaise (Fr.). The *habanera.

Hawaiian guitar [lap steel guitar]. A guitar held flat, across the knees or resting on a table or stand; the player stops the strings by sliding a bar along the neck with the left hand. The playing style originated when Hawaiians took up the guitar in the 19th century, but it became popular in the USA early in the 20th century, and American manufacturers began making Hawaiian guitars. The rectangular, solid-bodied, electric Hawaiian guitar was introduced in the 1930s. A common variant is the 'pedal steel guitar' (or simply 'steel guitar'), a Hawaiian guitar with knee-levers and pedals that alter the tuning. JMo

Hawes, William (*b* London, 21 June 1785; *d* London, 18 Feb. 1846). English musician. A chorister of the Chapel Royal (1795–1801), he became a professional violinist and played in the orchestra at Covent Garden. He sang in the choirs of Westminster Abbey and St Paul's, the latter appointing him almoner and Master of the Choristers in 1812; at the Chapel Royal he was also lutenist and Master of the Children (1817). He was active in other areas of musical life: as a publisher in London; as an associate of the Philharmonic Society; as conductor of the Madrigal Society; as organist of the Lutheran Church in the Savoy; and as director of the English Opera House at the Lyceum Theatre (1824–36), where many of his adaptations (including Weber's *Der Freischütz* and Mozart's *Così fan tutte*) were staged. In addition to several operettas, Hawes published editions of madrigals (including *The Triumphes of Oriana*) and composed two collections of glees, the best known of which is *The bee, the golden daughter of the spring* (1836). He was the father of the contralto Maria Hawes (1816–86). JDi

Hawkins, Sir John (*b* London, 29 March 1719; *d* London, 21 May 1789). English music historian. He was the son of a Freeman of the Haberdashers' Company and became an attorney, spending some of his spare time on music—Handel was among his friends. In 1753 he married the daughter of an attorney; she came into money, allowing Hawkins to give up his legal practice, but he continued as a magistrate (becoming chairman of the Middlesex Quarter Sessions) and achieved eminence through his public services, for which he was knighted in 1772.

From at least as early as 1761 Hawkins had carried out research on music history. This resulted in the five-volume *A General History of the Science and Practice of Music* (London, 1776), which appeared just after Charles Burney's *History*. Burney's work was undoubtedly better organized and had benefited both from his greater musical knowledge and from his research abroad. Hawkins was criticized during his day for concentrating more on 16th- and 17th-century music than on modern musical styles; he apparently found trends in 18th-century opera 'most unnatural and absurd'. Nevertheless, his work is full of useful information, especially about musical society in early 18th-century London. He died of a stroke and was buried in the cloisters of Westminster Abbey.   DA/LC

hay [haye, hey]. A late 16th-century dance, mentioned by Arbeau in his *Orchésographie (1588), in which a chain of dancers follow each other through various figurations and conclude by forming a circle. The origin of the name is unknown. Samuel Johnson suggested in his dictionary (1755) that the name came from the practice of 'dancing round a haycock', while others have suggested that it derived from the French *haie* ('hedge'), because the dancers were aligned in hedge-like rows.

Haydn, Joseph (*see page 574*)

Haydn, (Johann) Michael (*b* Rohrau, Lower Austria, *bapt.* 14 Sept. 1737; *d* Salzburg, 10 Aug. 1806). Austrian composer, younger brother of Joseph Haydn. Like his brother, he became a choirboy in about 1745 at St Stephen's Cathedral, Vienna, where he studied singing and composition, including the music and counterpoint treatise of Fux. After his beautiful soprano voice changed, he worked as a freelance musician in the capital until in 1757 he became Kapellmeister to the Bishop of Grosswardein in the Romanian–Hungarian border town of Oradea (Nagyvárad). There he wrote several masses and began to compose symphonies.

In 1763 Haydn became Konzertmeister to the Archbishop of Salzburg. He remained in Salzburg for the rest of his life, serving two archbishops during a 37-year career at court. In 1777 he assumed the post of organist at the Dreifaltigkeitskirche and in 1781 succeeded Mozart as organist at Salzburg Cathedral, where he was also responsible for training the choristers. He married the soprano Maria Magdalena Lipp, daughter of the court organist, in 1768; they had one daughter, who died in infancy.

During his lifetime, Michael Haydn was considered a better composer of church music than his famous brother. A master of the *stile antico, he wrote some 400 sacred works. The best known of his masses (over three dozen of them) is the Requiem in C minor composed for the death of Archbishop Sigismund in 1771 and performed at the funeral of Joseph Haydn. Mozart's own Requiem written two decades later bears many similarities to this work. Both Mozart and his father copied out several sacred works by Michael Haydn, whose pupils included Weber and Diabelli. Among Haydn's impressive ceremonial masses with orchestra and soloists is the 'Spanish' Mass commissioned by the Spanish court in 1786, perhaps on the recommendation of his brother.

Haydn composed many symphonies, divertimentos, and chamber pieces for secular entertainments; several of the late symphonies from the 1780s are in three movements without minuet and some contain fugal finales. Among his dramatic works are Italian cantatas, German oratorios, and *Singspiele*; he also wrote incidental music, including instrumental interludes for Voltaire's drama *Zaïre* (1777) featuring Turkish effects. In 1804 he was made a member of the Royal Swedish Academy of Music. He died following a year of illness and hardship and was buried in St Peter's cemetery in Salzburg.   DA/CC

'Haydn' Quartets. Name given to six string quartets by Mozart: no. 14 in G major K387 (1782); no. 15 in D minor K421/417*b* (1783); no. 16 in E♭ major K428/421*b* (1783); no. 17 in B♭ major K458, the 'Hunt' Quartet (1784); no. 18 in A major K464 (1785); and no. 19 in C major K465, the 'Dissonance' Quartet (1785). They are so called because he dedicated them to Haydn, who played the first violin in performances in Mozart's house (Mozart played the viola).

Haym, Nicola Francesco (*b* Rome, 6 July 1678; *d* London, 11 Aug. 1729). Italian cellist, composer, and librettist. Between 1694 and 1700 he played the 'violone' (probably the cello) in Cardinal Ottoboni's orchestra in Rome under Corelli, who is named as his teacher in one document. The future Duke of Bedford, in Rome on his grand tour, then persuaded him to enter his service in England (1701–11). From 1718 he was in the employ of Handel's patron, the Duke of Chandos, and became one of the chief providers of librettos for Italian operas (including Handel's), then in vogue in London. Thus

(*cont. on p. 577*)

Joseph Haydn
(1732–1809)

The Austrian composer Franz Joseph Haydn was born in Rohrau, Lower Austria, on 31 March or 1 April 1732 and died in Vienna on 31 May 1809.

The early years

Haydn's ancestry was once a subject of considerable controversy. A mixture of Middle European settlers inhabited the region of Lower Austria where he was born, suggesting that the child Haydn, whatever his exact heritage, was exposed to a variety of folk musics and cultural traditions. Born into a humble family of modest means, Haydn was the second child of Mathias Haydn, a master wheelwright by trade and village magistrate, and Anna Maria Koller, a former cook at the nearby castle of Count Harrach, a local landowner. His first musical instruction was at home where, according to his earliest biographers, G. A. Griesinger and A. C. Dies, his father often played the harp and accompanied himself while singing, a pastime shared with all the children. At about the age of six Haydn went to live with a distant relative, Joseph Mathias Franck, a schoolmaster in the nearby town of Hainburg. At the church school the young Haydn, who may have been in training for the clergy, received further musical instruction. Although he would later complain of getting 'more thrashings than food' in the Franck household, his music education progressed rapidly during the Hainburg years; as well as learning several musical instruments he developed a sonorous soprano voice. Recognizing his 'pleasant voice' and 'studious diligence', Georg Reutter, Kapellmeister at St Stephen's Cathedral in Vienna, accepted the young Haydn into his choir school in 1740.

In Vienna, capital city of the Habsburg empire, Haydn's musical world expanded immensely. Lessons in singing, the violin, and the harpsichord augmented those in languages and other traditional subjects. At St Stephen's, where he was required to perform services twice daily, he sang masses and sacred compositions by Caldara, Fux, and other lesser contemporaries of the late Baroque era. Celebrations of the many feast days and events of the Catholic liturgical year were offset by occasional concerts at court and other private entertainments. Although Haydn claimed to have learnt more from singing and hearing the music he was making than from formal lessons, he did receive limited instruction in theory and composition from Reutter. A prankster by nature, he was frequently out of favour with his teacher, who abruptly dismissed him from the choir school when he lost his soprano voice at about the age of 16.

In the late 1740s Haydn suddenly found himself without food, lodging, or a source of income. Biographical details are slim and often contradictory for this next decade, but Haydn continued to nurture his talent through diligence and perseverance. At first he eked out a meagre existence in his adopted city by giving keyboard lessons, performing in ad hoc orchestras, and playing the violin and organ in churches and private chapels. He furthered his education through self-study, acquiring a copy of Mattheson's *Der vollkommene Capellmeister* and Fux's *Gradus ad Parnassum* and studying the works and theoretical writings of C. P. E. Bach. Many compositions from this period are now lost, including *Der krumme Teufel*, a *Singspiel* to a libretto by Kurz-Bernardon, first performed at the Kärntnertortheater in the early 1750s. During this period he made the acquaintance of the imperial court poet and librettist Pietro Metastasio and other inhabitants of the Michaelerhaus where he was living, including the dowager Princess Maria Octavia Esterházy (mother of Paul Anton and Nicolaus), the talented young pianist Marianne von Martinez to whom he gave lessons, and Nicola Porpora, the Neapolitan opera composer and singing instructor. As Porpora's accompanist and apprentice, Haydn gained invaluable insight into vocal composition and the Italian language.

The year 1759 marked a turning-point for the young composer. On the recommendation of Count von Fürnberg, for whom he wrote some of his earliest string quartets (subsequently published as opp. 1 and 2), Haydn was appointed Kapellmeister to Count Carl Joseph Franz Morzin. The count, who maintained residences in Vienna and Lukavec, Bohemia, retained a small string orchestra and a wind band for which Haydn composed serenades and divertimentos, including the symphony Hob. I: 1 in D major (see HOBOKEN), which features an opening rocket theme. With free board and lodging, and a yearly salary of 200 gulden, Haydn was now an established musician.

Having secured full-time employment, Haydn married Maria Anna Keller in St Stephen's Cathedral in 1760. The elder sister of his former pupil and first love, Therese Keller, who entered a convent, Maria Anna turned out to be a poor match for the aspiring composer. Although they maintained a joint household until her death in 1800, both sought relationships outside marriage (she most notably with the painter Ludwig Guttenbrunn, and he, after 1779, with Luigia Polzelli, a young, married opera singer at the Esterházy court). The circumstances surrounding Haydn's termination of employment with Count Morzin are unclear, but he was certainly in Esterházy service by 1 May 1761, the date of his contract with Prince Paul Anton.

Eszterháza, 1761–90

During the almost 30 years he worked at the court of Hungary's wealthiest family, Haydn developed and consolidated many of the genres and stylistic features identified with Classical composition. Though engaged primarily as an instrumental composer by Prince Paul Anton, for whom he wrote the innovatory concertante Symphonies nos. 6–8, 'Le Matin', 'Le Midi', and 'Le Soir', Haydn in effect assumed responsibility for all musical activities at court. In addition to composing 'such music as His Serene Highness may command' and directing performances from the violin or keyboard, Haydn was in charge of overseeing the large collection of musical manuscripts and instruments, and of managing the resident musicians, with whom he was to 'abstain from undue familiarity'. He was to report twice daily in livery to the prince and, as a senior officer of the house, was to set an example for other court employees. Although these conditions seem strict by today's standards, they were typical of the time and earned the composer some 600 gulden a year with other benefits.

After Paul Anton's death in 1762, control of the large family estate passed to his younger, music-loving brother Prince Nicolaus, in whose service Haydn remained until 1790. As vice-Kapellmeister, Haydn had devoted himself to instrumental composition in deference to the ageing court Kapellmeister, G. J. Werner, who specialized in church music. At the request of his gifted patron, Haydn composed numerous baryton solos, duets, and trios, but with his promotion to full Kapellmeister after Werner's death in 1766 he also took up sacred composition, producing the *Missa cellensis* (1766), *Stabat mater* (1767), and *Applausus* cantata (1768). New too is the heightened drama associated with several symphonies in the minor mode composed between about 1768 and 1772, including no. 49, 'La Passione' in F minor, no. 52 in C minor, and the 'Farewell', written in the highly unusual key of F# minor. 18 string quartets also date from this fertile period, of which the six 'Sun' Quartets op. 20 best demonstrate the composer's increasing prowess. Their rapid scherzos, fugal finales, and dependence on four equally engaging string players attest as much to the virtuosity of the instrumentalists employed at court as to Haydn's accomplishment. The leading violinist Luigi Tomasini and the cellist Joseph Weigl, both first-class musicians, probably helped Haydn in his experiments to 'observe what created an impression, and what weakened it, thus improving, adding to, cutting away and running risks'. As Haydn later reported to Griesinger, 'I was set apart from the world, there was nobody in my vicinity to confuse and annoy me in my course, and so I had to be original'.

By the late 1760s Prince Nicolaus was spending less time at the Esterházy residences in Vienna and Eisenstadt, some 50 km south-east of the capital, and instead was devoting considerable time and expense to the renovation of a rural hunting-lodge, called Eszterháza, in nearby Süttör. Associated with this palace, a symbol of the wealth and power of Prince Nicolaus 'the Magnificent', are Haydn's many works for the theatre. *Lo speziale*, an *opera buffa*, opened the 400-seat opera house in 1768; *Philemon und Baucis*, a *Singspiel*, launched the grotto-like marionette theatre in 1773; and *La fedeltà premiata* (1781) inaugurated the new opera house built to replace the one destroyed by fire in 1779. Instrumental pieces written to accompany productions of German plays put on by travelling theatre troupes were reworked into symphonies, of which no. 60, subtitled 'Der Zerstreute' or 'Il distratto', is an example.

Although the demands of theatrical composition, revision, rehearsing, and conducting left Haydn little time for instrumental composition following the introduction in 1776 of a regular operatic season at the court, his reputation continued to grow through wide circulation of his works. In 1780 the Viennese firm Artaria published six keyboard sonatas (XVI: 35–9 and 20) and in 1782 it issued six new string quartets 'written in a new and special way', the op. 33 'Russian' Quartets that were the stimulus for Mozart's six string quartets dedicated to Haydn in 1785. (At a quartet party held during Leopold Mozart's visit to Vienna in February 1785, Haydn met the young composer's father and heard the last three quartets, of which he would later be the dedicatee.) Several prestigious foreign commissions also ensued after 1785. The Concert de la Loge Olympique in Paris commissioned six symphonies (nos. 82–7), which admirably combine popular and learned styles in their slow introductions, colourful orchestration, and grand scale. From Cádiz Cathedral came the request for seven orchestral Adagios, a 'passione istrumentale' to accompany meditations on the Seven Last Words of Our Saviour on the Cross, which Haydn later arranged for string quartet and for chorus. For King Ferdinand of Naples, Haydn wrote several works for the esoteric *lira organizzata*, similar to a hurdy-gurdy. On the death of Prince Nicolaus Esterházy in September 1790, the heir to the title, Paul Anton II, disbanded the orchestra and opera troupe, leaving Haydn free to return to Vienna. Although he remained in Esterházy service, he was able to accept the invitation of the violinist and impresario J. P. Salomon to visit London.

The London visits, 1791–5

When Haydn arrived in London in January 1791, he was already a celebrity. After his years of isolation, the social whirlwind and appreciative audiences awaiting him rejuvenated his spirit and stimulated his creativity, and his letters and personal notebooks dating from this period detail many new friendships and activities. His lucrative contract with Salomon called for a new opera, six 'grand' symphonies, and other smaller compositions and concert engagements, but only the opera *L'anima del filosofo*, a *seria*-style work based on the Orpheus theme, failed to reach the stage because of intrigues against John Gallini and the Pantheon opera house. Salomon's public concerts, held in the Hanover Square Rooms with Haydn directing from the fortepiano, were a resounding success, quelling the opposition mounted by the rival Professional Concerts. The Symphony no. 92 in G major, warmly received at the first concert in March 1791, was repeated that July when Haydn received an honorary doctorate in music from the University of Oxford. The 1792 concert season saw the performance of the cheery Concertante in B♭ for violin, cello, oboe, bassoon, and orchestra, symphonies nos. 93, 97, 98, and Haydn's best-known composition, the 'Surprise' Symphony (no. 94), whose nickname derives from the sudden *fortissimo* sounded by the full orchestra following a *pianissimo* statement of the main theme of the Andante.

After a successful 18-month stay in England, Haydn returned to Vienna, where he instructed Beethoven in composition and introduced the rising young star to several aristocratic patrons. With his wife he bought a small house in the Viennese suburb of Gumpendorf, but Vienna held little allure now that his musical

colleague Mozart was dead. Following the death of his close friend and confidante, the pianist Marianne von Genzinger, Haydn negotiated a second contract with Salomon and returned to London in February 1794 accompanied by his long-time copyist and assistant, Johann Elssler.

With England at war with France, audiences enthusiastically greeted his 'Military' Symphony (no. 100), a Turkish-style work depicting a mock battle. On the cessation of Salomon's concert series in January 1795, Haydn joined ranks with the large orchestra of the Opera Concerts led by the violinist Viotti, who gave the premieres of his last three symphonies. Nos. 102–4 complete the set of 12 'London' Symphonies designed to please and edify connoisseurs and amateurs alike, and mark the end of Haydn's long and remarkable career as a symphonist. Other works written in conjunction with the composer's second London visit are the 'Apponyi' Quartets (op. 71 and op. 74), the piano trios (XV: 24–6) dedicated to his pupil and admirer Rebecca Schroeter—including the spritely 'Rondo all'ongarese'—and the last three piano sonatas (XVI: 50–2), written for the resonant English instruments. Long after leaving London, Haydn continued to make arrangements of British folksongs to meet the demands of an insatiable middle-class audience and publishing industry.

The late years

Haydn returned to Vienna in 1795 a wealthy man with an unrivalled international reputation. Dividing his time between Vienna and Eisenstadt at the request of his new patron, Prince Nicolaus II, he wrote a series of six masses for the nameday celebrations of the prince's wife between 1796 and 1802. Although they were originally deemed insufficiently ecclesiastical, their symphonic style and varied choral writing parallel those of *The Creation* (1798) and *The Seasons* (1801). The arias and ensembles of these two great oratorios, composed to texts fashioned by the Viennese court official Baron Gottfried van Swieten, are indebted to Haydn's London experience of Handelian oratorio; unprecedented is *The Creation*'s evocative 'Representation of Chaos'. The patriotic Emperor's Hymn, inspired by the English national anthem, was first performed at the Burgtheater in honour of the emperor's birthday in February 1797 and became the basis for the slow variation movement of the String Quartet op. 76 no. 3 which, together with the two op. 77 quartets, crown Haydn's achievements in this genre.

Forced by deteriorating health to give up conducting and composition late in 1803 (leaving unfinished the String Quartet op. 103), Haydn settled into retirement. Assisted by Elssler, he began drawing up a catalogue of the works 'he could approximately recall having composed', while awards and accolades poured in from across Europe. To mark Haydn's 76th birthday in March 1808, Antonio Salieri conducted a performance of *The Creation* in the great marble hall of the old university before an exclusive audience of admirers that included Princess Esterházy and Beethoven. In May the following year, as Napoleonic troops bombarded Vienna, Haydn died at his small home and was buried in Gumpendorf cemetery. At the behest of Prince Nicolaus his remains were moved to the Bergkirche in Eisenstadt.

Haydn's reputation

Since Haydn and his music were antithetical to the ideals of Romanticism, his reputation waned in the 19th century. Caricatured as a man of innocence and simplicity because of his humble origin, years of servitude, endearing musical wit, and use of folk music idioms, Haydn assumed the sobriquet 'Papa'—a label his long

life, late fame, and fecundity could do little to counter. Mythologizing of this kind dissipated as 20th-century scholarship concentrated on unearthing archival documents and determining the authenticity and chronology of the composer's canon. The complete edition of his works (*Joseph Haydn Werke*, 1958–) and the historical performance movement are fostering many new interpretative, analytic, and contextual studies of Haydn and his oeuvre.   CC

M. HORÁNYI, *The Magnificence of Eszterháza* (London, 1962) · H. C. R. LANDON, *Haydn: Chronicle and Works*, 5 vols. (Bloomington, IN, and London, 1976–80) · K. GEIRINGER, *Haydn: A Creative Life in Music* (London, 3/1982) · J. P. LARSEN, with G. FEDER, *The New Grove Haydn* (London, 1982) · H. C. R. LANDON and D. WYN JONES, *Haydn: His Life and Music* (Bloomington, 1988) · J. WEBSTER, *Haydn's 'Farewell' Symphony and the Idea of Classical Style* (Cambridge, 1991) · C. ROSEN, *The Classical Style* (New York, 3/1997) · E. SISMAN (ed.), *Haydn and his World* (Princeton, NJ, 1997) · W. D. SUTCLIFFE (ed.), *Haydn Studies* (Cambridge, 1998) · D. WYN JONES (ed.), *J. Haydn* (Oxford, 2002)

he was among the first wave of Italian immigrants who disseminated the Corellian style in England, producing two sets of trio sonatas modelled on those of his master. He was a member of the Academy of Ancient Music, 1726–7.   PA

Hayne van Ghizeghem (*b* c.1445; *d* before 1497). Franco-Burgundian composer. A contemporary of Ockeghem, he spent at least 15 years in the service of Charles the Bold, Duke of Burgundy. His *rondeaux* were exceptionally popular during the late 15th and early 16th centuries and served as models for many of his successors.   JM

Hb. (Ger.). Abbreviation for *Hoboe*, 'oboe'.

Head, Michael (Dewar) (*b* Eastbourne, 28 Jan. 1900; *d* Cape Town, 24 Aug. 1976). English composer. He studied composition with Frederick Corder at the RAM (1919–25), returning to teach the piano there in 1927. He also served widely as an examiner and adjudicator. His reputation as a composer rests on a body of almost 100 songs, fastidiously written in a manner suggesting Gerald Finzi and often designed for himself to perform to his own accompaniment.   PG

head-motif. See MOTTO THEME.

hearing. See EAR AND HEARING.

Hear my Prayer. Hymn (1844) by Mendelssohn for soprano solo, choir, and organ, composed for Bartholomew's concerts in Crosby Hall, London, where it was first performed in 1845.

heavy metal. A term with a meaning not clearly distinguishable from 'hard rock'. The two styles exist on a continuum but are none the less distinct from styles outside that continuum. Characteristic of both is the surprising rarity of blues chords and the 12-bar structure, and the alternation of plucked bass and power chord. Heavy metal, which originated in the 1970s, is represented by Iron Maiden, Black Sabbath, Motörhead, Metallica, and Alice Cooper; exponents of hard rock, which developed in the late 1960s, are Deep Purple, Led Zeppelin, Meatloaf, and Bon Jovi.

Heavy metal overwhelmingly concentrates on frenetic pace; it generally confines itself to a trio of guitar, bass, and drums; guitar solos focus on distortion. Its lyrics are often about violence, Satanism, and the occult. Hard rock bands, on the other hand, often perform in something more akin to ballad style; they add Hammond organ and synthesizer to the instrumental mix, sometimes to provide 'atmospheric' interludes; frequent use is made of high male vocalizing with vibrato on long notes; in guitar solos, virtuosity is more important than distortion. Misogyny and macho sexuality dominate the lyrics. PW

📖 M. HALE, *Headbangers* (Ann Arbor, MI, 1993)

Hebrides, The (*Die Hebriden*; *Fingals Höhle*; 'Fingal's Cave'). Overture, op. 26 (1830), by Mendelssohn; it was based on an earlier version (1829) called *Die einsame Insel* ('The Lonely Island'), and was revised in 1832. It is said that Mendelssohn conceived the principal theme while on a visit to the Hebrides and the Isle of Staffa in 1829, but he had in fact jotted it down before that visit.

heckelphone. A wide-bore bass oboe with a spherical bell, devised by the bassoon makers Heckel in 1904 and sounding an octave below the standard oboe (extended to *A*). Played with a reed similar to that of a bassoon, it has a considerably louder and fuller sound than that of the French bass oboe developed by Guillaume Triébert. The two instruments are therefore not properly interchangeable, but because of their rarity this often happens, upsetting the orchestral balance. JMo

heel. See FROG.

heftig (Ger.). 'Violent', 'impetuous'.

Heidenröslein ('Little Rose on the Heath'). Song (1815) for voice and piano by Schubert (D257) to words by Johann Wolfgang von Goethe.

Heifetz, Jascha (*b* Vilnius, 2 Feb. 1901; *d* Los Angeles, 10 Dec. 1987). Russian-born American violinist. He joined Auer's class in St Petersburg at the age of ten, played under Nikisch in 1912, and emigrated to the USA in 1917, making his New York debut that year. His flawless technique made him ideal for recording all the great concertos. His stance was immobile, the instrument held high, the face directed towards his fingers. He commissioned concertos from Walton and Korngold and was a renowned player of chamber music with Piatigorsky and Rubinstein. Withdrawing from the concert platform in the 1960s, he then taught at the University of Southern California. He published numerous transcriptions. CF

📖 A. WESCHLER-VERED, *Jascha Heifetz* (New York and London, 1986)

heighted neumes. Neumes placed in such a way as to give an idea of their relative pitch. See NOTATION, 1.

Heiligmesse ('Holy Mass'). Nickname of Haydn's Mass no. 10 in B♭ major (1796), so called because of the special treatment of the words 'Holy, Holy' in the Sanctus; its full title is *Missa Sancti Bernardi von Offida*.

Heiller, Anton (*b* Vienna, 15 Sept. 1923; *d* Vienna, 25 March 1979). Austrian composer and organist. He studied with Friedrich Reidinger (theory) and Bruno Seidlhofer (organ) at the Vienna Music Academy (1941–2), where in 1945 he was appointed professor of organ. He was an admired exponent of Bach, and was influenced by that composer and by Hindemith in his music, which includes sacred choral pieces, organ works, and the secular oratorio *François Villon* (1956). PG

Heinichen, Johann David (*b* Krössuln, nr Weissenfels, 17 April 1683; *d* Dresden, 16 July 1729). German composer and theorist. After practising law at Weissenfels he embarked on a career in music, primarily as an opera composer. In 1710 he settled in Venice where, during the Carnival season of 1713, he achieved his greatest operatic successes, with *Mario* and *Le passioni per troppo amore*. He spent his final years at Dresden, as Kapellmeister to the Elector of Saxony, and there in 1728 he produced his treatise *Der Generalbass in der Composition*, a valuable study of continuo realization, particularly as practised in Italian opera houses of the time. DA/BS

Heininen, Paavo (Johannes) (*b* Helsinki, 13 Jan. 1938). Finnish composer and teacher. He studied with Aarre Merikanto at the Sibelius Academy in Helsinki, and also with Rautavaara, Englund, and Kokkonen. After graduating he studied with Zimmermann in Cologne (1960–1), with Persichetti and Edward Steuermann in New York (1961–2), and with Lutosławski in Poland. After a year on the staff of the Sibelius Academy (1962–3) he taught at Turku (1963–6), then returned to the Sibelius Academy, where he has remained. His teaching career has been vastly influential in the history of modernism in Finland: many of the most prominent composers of the younger generation studied under him. His own compositions are mostly serialist in style, and are characterized by a sense of line, colour, and luminosity. They include the opera *Silkkirumpu* ('The Damask Drum', 1984), four symphonies (1958–73), and a number of other orchestral works; he has also composed much chamber, keyboard, and vocal music. MA

Heinrich von Meissen. See FRAUENLOB.

heiter (Ger.). 'Cheerful', 'serene'.

Heldenleben, Ein ('A Hero's Life'). Tone-poem, op. 40 (1897–8), by Richard Strauss; the 'hero' is Strauss himself, and one of the work's six sections contains several self-quotations.

Heldentenor (Ger., 'hero tenor'). A big-voiced tenor suitable for such heavy operatic roles as Siegfried in Wagner's *Ring* cycle.

Hellendaal, Pieter (*b* Rotterdam, *bapt.* 1 April 1721; *d* Cambridge, 19 April 1799). Dutch violinist, organist, and composer. He studied in Italy with Tartini but by 1744 was again living in the Netherlands, in Amsterdam. In 1751 he left for London, where he gave several concerts. He settled in England, becoming organist of Pembroke College, Cambridge, in 1762. He was well known as a teacher and took an active part in musical life in Cambridge, Oxford, and Norwich. His published works include two books of violin sonatas (Amsterdam, *c*.1745, *c*.1750), *Six Grand Concertos* and *Six Solos* for violin (London, 1758, 1761), and *Eight Solos for the Violoncello with a Thorough Bass* (Cambridge, *c*.1780). The written-out cadenzas to his autograph violin sonatas, now in the Fitzwilliam Museum, Cambridge, provide valuable insights into late 18th-century performance practice.   WT/LC

Heller, Stephen [István] (*b* Pest, 15 May 1813; *d* Paris, 14 Jan. 1888). Hungarian-born French pianist and composer. At the age of 14 he began a two-year concert tour of central Europe, the strain of which resulted in his collapse from nervous exhaustion. In 1830 he obtained a post as piano teacher to a wealthy family in Augsburg, where he remained for eight years, studying composition and writing numerous lieder. Schumann admired his works and invited him to be the Augsburg correspondent of the *Neue Zeitschrift für Musik*. In 1838 Heller moved to Paris, where he made a living as a critic and a composer of salon music and enjoyed the friendship of Berlioz. Though remembered today for his studies, he was an important transitional figure between German Romanticism and French Impressionism, as is demonstrated in his character pieces of the 1850s (e.g. *Im Walde* opp. 86, 128, and 136) and by his later, more exploratory works including the Barcarolles op. 141 and the Sonata in B♭ minor op. 143.   DA/SH

Hely-Hutchinson, (Christian) **Victor** (Noel Hope) (*b* Cape Town, 26 Dec. 1901; *d* London, 11 March 1947). English composer, pianist, and administrator. Son of the last governor of Cape Colony, he was educated at Eton and Oxford. He was a lecturer at the South African College of Music (1922–6) before joining the staff of the BBC, first in London and later in Birmingham. He succeeded Bantock as professor of music in Birmingham University (1934–44) before becoming Director of Music at the BBC. He produced several chamber works, a piano sonata, a set of Variations for Orchestra (1927), film music, and some entertaining settings of Edward Lear and Lewis Carroll. His most enduring composition, however, is the *Carol Symphony* (1927), a masterpiece of the light music genre.   PG/JD1

hemidemisemiquaver (𝅘𝅥𝅲). The note having ¹⁄₆₄ of the value of the semibreve, or whole note; hence the American usage '64th-note'.

hemiola [hemiolia] (from Gk. *hemiolios*, 'the whole and a half'). A term denoting the ratio 3:2. In modern notation, a hemiola occurs when two bars in triple metre (e.g. 3/2) are performed as if they were notated as three bars in duple metre (6/4), or vice versa (Ex. 1). This rhythmic device is common in music of the Baroque period, especially in the *courante. It was later used by Schumann and particularly by Brahms.

In early mensural music, the equivalent situation prevails when three imperfect notes are substituted for two perfect ones (see NOTATION, 3). In the early theory of musical pitch, 'hemiola' meant an interval of a 5th: the two lengths of vibrating string that produce this interval are in the ratio 3:2.

Ex. 1
(*a*)

Bach, French Suite no. 3, Courante.

(*b*)

Sibelius, Violin Concerto, last movement.

Hen, The. See POULE, LA.

Henle. German firm of music publishers. Founded in Munich in 1948 by the industrialist and amateur musician Günter Henle (1899–1979), it has a reputation based on its reliable, beautifully produced *Urtext editions of the standard piano and chamber music repertory of the 18th, 19th, and early 20th centuries. It publishes scholarly new complete editions of Haydn, Beethoven, and Brahms and associated material as well as a series of historical anthologies and other academic music publications.   HA

Henry VIII (*b* Greenwich, 28 June 1491; *d* Windsor, 28 Jan. 1547). King of England from 1509 to 1547. Like many Renaissance monarchs and magnates, Henry nurtured music as part of the courtly culture that surrounded him. He significantly increased the number of professional instrumentalists and singers who served or performed before him, and also built up a large collection of musical instruments. He was a singer, a proficient lutenist, and a keyboard player. Unusually, he also composed; more than 20 songs and consort pieces by him survive, and he is reported to have written church music. Henry's children were in turn instructed in music, ensuring succession in the patronage of music by the Tudors up to the death of Elizabeth I.   JM

Hensel, Fanny. See MENDELSSOHN, FANNY.

Henselt, (Georg Martin) **Adolf** (von) (*b* Schwabach, Bavaria, 9 May 1814; *d* Bad Warmbrunn, Silesia, 10 Oct. 1889). German pianist and composer. He was a pupil of Abbé Vogler, and later of Hummel and Sechter. He was widely regarded as one of the leading piano virtuosos of his era, notable for his silken tone and his ability to negotiate wide stretches. Another famous feature of his performances—chronic stage fright—was perhaps a less useful model for his numerous students. From 1838 his career was centred on St Petersburg, where he developed an outstanding reputation as a performer and teacher. His compositional output is chiefly devoted to piano music. The attractive, if slight, concert study *Si oiseau j'étais* remained in the repertory for years after his death; but his most ambitious piece is the massive, and structurally novel, Piano Concerto in F minor op. 16, which strikingly displays his propensity for extended figuration.   KH

Henze, Hans Werner (*b* Gütersloh, 1 July 1926). German composer. He studied at the Brunswick Staatsmusikschule (1942–4) before he was called up for military service; after the war he attended the Heidelberg Church Music Institute (1946–8) and received instruction from Wolfgang Fortner and René Leibowitz. He held theatre appointments in Konstanz (1948–50) and Wiesbaden (1950–3) before the success of his first two operas, *Das Wundertheater* (Heidelberg, 1949) and *Boulevard Solitude* (Hanover, 1952), allowed him to leave Germany and settle in Italy.

There he rejected the doctrinaire *serialism to which he had been drawn in such works as his Third Symphony (1949–50) and began instead to draw into his music an Italianate melodic grace together with a harmonic lushness redolent of the Mediterranean. Among the first works to show the change of style were the Fourth Symphony (1955), the opera *König Hirsch* (Berlin, 1956; rev. 1962 as *Il re cervo*), and the *Fünf*

neapolitanische Lieder for voice and chamber orchestra (1956). The ease and confidence of the new manner were then celebrated in three further operas—*Der Prinz von Homburg* (Hamburg, 1960), *Elegy for Young Lovers* (Schwetzingen, 1961), and *Der junge Lord* (Berlin, 1965)—and several vocal works of exalted lyricism. This style came to a climax in *The Bassarids* (Salzburg, 1966), a reworking of Euripides' *Bacchae* to a libretto by W. H. Auden and Chester Kallman, who had provided the text for *Elegy*.

Up to that point Henze's multi-faceted professional life, as teacher and conductor as well as composer, all necessitating much travelling, had been led at a frenetic pace. He found himself at a crisis, both personally and in his compositional activity, and sought a change of direction. During the next few years he became politically aware: he visited Cuba, and expressed a commitment to revolutionary socialism in most of his works, essays, and interviews. His excursions into concerto form—*Musen Siziliens* (1966), in which two pianos and instrumental group are pitted against chorus and orchestra, and the concertos for double bass (1966), oboe and harp (1966), and piano (1967)—arose from his consciousness of the conflict between individuals and society. This period culminated in his opera *We Come to the River* (1976), after which political issues retreated behind the sensuous allure and psychological sophistication he has retained and developed from his earlier music. Works of this later period include *The English Cat* (Stuttgart, 1983), *Das verratene Meer* (Berlin, 1990), and *Venus and Adonis* (Munich, 1997), as well as his Seventh, Eighth, and Ninth symphonies.   PG

📖 H. W. HENZE, *Music and Politics* (London, 1982) · G. RICKARDS, *Hindemith, Hartmann and Henze* (London, 1995) · H. W. HENZE, *Bohemian Fifths* (London, 1998)

Herabstrich (Ger.). In string playing, 'down-bow'.

Heraufstrich (Ger.). In string playing, 'up-bow'.

Herbert, Victor (August) (*b* Dublin, 1 Feb. 1859; *d* New York, 26 May 1924). Irish-born American composer. Sent to study in Europe, he became a cellist in Stuttgart and married a singer, with whom he went to the USA. He was conductor of the Pittsburgh Symphony Orchestra (1898–1904) and a prolific composer, his works including two cello concertos and the shows *Babes in Toyland* (1903), *Mlle Modiste* (1905), *The Red Mill* (1906), and *Naughty Marietta* (1910).   PGA/ALA

Herbstlied (Ger.). 'Autumn song'.

Herman, Jerry [Gerald] (*b* New York, 10 July 1933). American composer and lyricist. His first successful Broadway musical was *Milk and Honey* (1961), but it was with *Hello, Dolly!* (1964; filmed 1969) that he established his accessible and optimistic style, characterized by the title number. *Mame* (1966; filmed 1974) continued Herman's distinctive combination of a rousing title song, emotional ballads ('If he Walked into my Life'), and revue-style numbers ('Bosom Buddies'). *La Cage aux folles* (1983), which included the anthemic 'I Am what I Am' and evocative 'Song on the Sand', affirmed Herman's popular appeal.   JSN

hermeneutics. An approach to the analytical interpretation of music that emphasizes meaning and context rather than structure or technique. The term derives from the Greek word for interpretation and was revived during the 17th and 18th centuries for studies in classical literature, the Bible, and the law. Its application to music dates from the 19th and early 20th centuries: for example, in Wilhelm Dilthey's essay 'Das musikalische Verstehen' ('On musical understanding'; *c.*1910) and the writings of Hermann Kretzschmar (1848–1924). The concept was revived by musicologists in the later 20th century as part of a renewed emphasis on the importance of acknowledging the relevance of matters of meaning and context to musical analysis.   AW

Hérodiade ('Herodias'). Opera in four acts by Massenet to a libretto by Paul Milliet and Henri Grémont (Georges Hartmann) after the story by Gustave Flaubert (1877) (Brussels, 1881; revised Paris, 1884).

Hérold, (Louis Joseph) Ferdinand (*b* Paris, 28 Jan. 1791; *d* Paris, 19 Jan. 1833). French composer. One of a long line of musicians, he was first taught music by his father, François-Joseph (1755–1802), who had been a pupil of C. P. E. Bach. At the Paris Conservatoire he studied the violin with Kreutzer and composition with Méhul. In 1812 he won the Prix de Rome, which took him to Rome for a year. He stayed for a time in Naples, and on his way back to Paris visited Vienna, where he met Hummel and Salieri and heard operas by Mozart.

Hérold began his career as an opera composer in 1815, when Boieldieu asked him to write part of a privately commissioned opera, *Charles de France* (1816). This led to a long series of pieces for the Opéra-Comique, which he wrote while he was working as accompanist at the Théâtre Italien; *Marie* (1826), one of his most popular works, was praised for its elegance and skilful orchestration. In 1826 he was appointed singing master at the Opéra. The larger theatre gave him the opportunity to compose a number of ballets, including *La Somnambule* ('The Sleepwalker', 1827), which inspired imitations in the secondary theatres and was recognized as the first Romantic ballet. (It was also the source of the libretto for Bellini's *La sonnambula*, 1831.) As a ballet

composer Hérold was influential in breaking away from the tradition of quoting known opera airs (to aid audiences' comprehension of mime scenes) and making more subtle use of original material. *La Fille mal gardée* (1828) and *La Belle au bois dormant* ('Sleeping Beauty', 1829) were also popular. His two major operatic successes, *Zampa* (1831), a version of the Don Juan legend, and *Le Pré aux Clercs* (1832), a more intimate treatment of the events later to be portrayed in Meyerbeer's *Les Huguenots* (1836), came too late for him to enjoy their fruits. But the power of *Le Pré aux Clercs* in particular suggests that he might have fulfilled his ambition to compose a *grand opéra* had he lived. He died of tuberculosis shortly before his 42nd birthday.   SH

📖 I. GUEST, *The Romantic Ballet in Paris* (London, 1966)

Herrmann, Bernard (*b* New York, 29 June 1911; *d* Hollywood, CA, 25 Dec. 1975). American composer and conductor. He studied with Bernard Wagenaar at the Juilliard School, then embarked on a dual career as a radio conductor for CBS and as a film composer. In the latter capacity he worked with many leading directors, including Orson Welles (*Citizen Kane* and *The Magnificent Ambersons*) and Alfred Hitchcock (*Vertigo* and *Psycho*), frequently producing scores of a postmodern nature in which subject is pinned to style through a complex web of allusions. He also composed a symphony, various instrumental works, and an opera based on *Wuthering Heights* (1948–50, though not staged until 1982). During his last years he worked as a conductor, principally in England, returning to film music, shortly before he died, with the score for Martin Scorsese's *Taxi Driver*.   TA

Herstrich (Ger.). In cello and double-bass playing, 'down-bow'.

Hertel, Johann Christian (*b* Oettingen, 1699; *d* Strelitz, Mecklenburg, Oct. 1754). German viol player, violinist, and composer. After studying theology at Halle University with a view to taking holy orders, he turned to music and took lessons in viol playing from Ernst Christian Hesse at Darmstadt. In 1733 he was appointed Konzertmeister and director of music at Eisenach and from 1742 held similar posts at Strelitz. He composed numerous instrumental works, only one of which, a set of six violin sonatas, was published (Amsterdam, 1727).   WT/BS

Hertel, Johann Wilhelm (*b* Eisenach, 9 Oct. 1727; *d* Schwerin, 14 June 1789). German violinist, keyboard player, and composer. He studied originally with his father, the distinguished string player Johann Christian Hertel, whom he accompanied as harpsichordist on concert tours. From 1744 he held appointments at

Strelitz, and from 1754 was court composer at Schwerin, a post he left in 1770 (apparently because of weakening eyesight) to become private secretary to Princess Ulrike of Mecklenburg. He was a prolific and, in his lifetime, highly esteemed composer. His output includes masses, Passions, cantatas, and other church music for the court, as well as numerous keyboard concertos, symphonies, chamber works and two sets of *Oden und Lieder*. His writings embrace a treatise on thorough bass and two autobiographies.   WT/BS

Hertz. A unit of frequency (abbreviated to Hz), equal to one cycle per second, named after the German physicist Heinrich R. Hertz (1857–94).   JBo

Hervé [Ronger, Florimond] (*b* Houdain, 30 June 1825; *d* Paris, 3 Nov. 1892). French composer, conductor, organist, and singer. He studied briefly at the Paris Conservatoire and was organist at St Eustache. He then wrote and appeared in small-scale theatrical entertainments that pre-dated, but were soon eclipsed by, those of Offenbach. Less ambitious musically than Offenbach's, his works nevertheless proved enormously popular. Above all *L'Oeil crevé* (1867), *Chilpéric* (1868), *Le Petit Faust* (1869), and *Mam'zelle Nitouche* (1883) are still seen in France today. Hervé also conducted his own ballets at the Folies-Bergère in Paris and the Empire Theatre, London.   ALa

hervorgehoben (Ger.). 'Prominent', 'emphasized'.

hervortretend (Ger.). 'Brought out', 'prominent'.

Herz, Henri [Heinrich] (*b* Vienna, 6 Jan. 1803; *d* Paris, 5 Jan. 1888). Austrian pianist, composer, teacher, and piano manufacturer. A child prodigy, he showed musical gifts from the age of eight. In 1816 he entered the Paris Conservatoire to study the piano and composition; he later spent over 30 years as a piano teacher there. In 1851 he founded his own piano factory, producing instruments highly regarded by his contemporaries. As a performer he toured widely in Europe and the Americas, but as a composer his output—chiefly for piano—was intimately linked to the needs of his virtuoso career. For Schumann, writing in the *Neue Zeitschrift für Musik*, Herz's music was merely vapid, meretricious display, without originality or enduring qualities. Time has proved him correct on the last feature, though we can see in Herz's variation sets and piano concertos a fertile keyboard imagination, if never allied to a comparable musical inventiveness.   KH

herzlich (Ger.). 'Heartfelt', 'affectionate'.

Hes (Ger.). The note B♭. It is, however, more usually called B in German (see also H).

Heseltine, Philip. See WARLOCK, PETER.

Hess, Dame Myra (*b* London, 25 Feb. 1890; *d* London, 25 Nov. 1965). English pianist. A pupil of Tobias Matthay, she first appeared in 1907 but it took years for her career to develop (her American debut was in 1922). She played much chamber music, culminating in the lunchtime concerts at the National Gallery in London during World War II. She was much admired in Bach, Scarlatti, Mozart, and Beethoven, but music from Schumann and Brahms to Debussy also featured in her programmes. Her playing was notable for its warmth, charm, and inner poetry, while her transcriptions (particularly Bach's *Jesu, Joy of Man's Desiring*) became extremely popular. She was created DBE in 1941.

CF

📖 D. LASSIMONNE and H. FERGUSON (eds.), *Myra Hess by her Friends* (London, 1966) · M. C. MCKENNA, *Myra Hess* (London, 1976)

heterophony. A term first used by Plato when differentiating between voice and lyre parts in the accompanied vocal music of ancient Greece. It is now used to describe the simultaneous sounding of a melody with an elaborated variant of it, and also the quasi-canonic presentation of the same or similar melodies in two or more vocal or instrumental lines. Such heterophony is a particular feature of 20th-century music influenced by Indonesian or other East Asian ensemble music—Britten's church parables, for example—in which such textures are a common occurrence.   AW

Heugel. French firm of music publishers. In 1839 Jacques-Léopold Heugel (1815–83) became a partner of Jean-Antoine Meissonnier (1783–1857), a publisher of light music, and on Meissonnier's retirement in 1842 became sole owner. In 1840 the firm had acquired the popular weekly journal *Le Ménéstrel* (which it continued to issue for the next hundred years). Heugel published instrumental, sacred, and pedagogical works, but it was for theatre music that his firm became one of the most important in Paris, issuing the works of David, Offenbach, Thomas, Delibes, and others. It was carried on by his son and later by his descendants. Among the 20th-century composers in the catalogue are Auric, Fauré, Hahn, Ibert, d'Indy, Milhaud, Poulenc, and Widor, and, later, Amy, Boulez, Dutilleux, and Jolas. The firm also developed a catalogue of scholarly editions of early music, including the series *Le Pupitre* (1967–), and issued publications for the Société Française de Musicologie. Leduc acquired Heugel in 1980.   AL

Heure espagnole, L' ('The Spanish Hour'). Opera in one act by Ravel after the play by Franc-Nohain (Paris, 1911).

hexachord (from Gk. *hex*, 'six', *chordē*, 'string'). A scale segment consisting of six adjacent notes. Although the term could denote such a series from any scale (just as 'tetrachord' means four adjacent notes from any scale), since the Middle Ages it has been used almost invariably to refer to six notes with the interval pattern tone–tone–semitone–tone–tone: the 'natural' hexachord (*hexachordum naturale*) C–D–E–F–G–A, the 'soft' hexachord (*hexachordum molle*) F–G–A–B♭–C–D, and the 'hard' hexachord (*hexachordum durum*) G–A–B–C–D–E. The notes of the hexachord were labelled *ut–re–mi–fa–sol–la*, a practice known as *solmization.

DH

Hexaméron. Six variations for piano on a march from Bellini's *I Puritani*; they are by Liszt, Thalberg, Pixis, Herz, Czerny, and Chopin, Liszt also contributing an introduction and a finale. They were composed for a Paris charity concert in 1837 but not finished in time.

hey. See HAY.

Hiawatha. Cantata in three parts by Coleridge-Taylor to a text from H. W. Longfellow's poem of the same title; the three parts are *Hiawatha's Wedding Feast* (1898), *The Death of Minnehaha* (1899), and *Hiawatha's Departure* (1900).

hichiriki. Japanese cylindrical oboe with seven fingerholes and two thumbholes, played with a large double reed in *gagaku* court music.

Hidalgo, Juan (*b* Madrid, 1614; *d* Madrid, 30 March 1685). Spanish composer. A harpist in the royal chapel by 1631, he dominated the provision of stage music at the Spanish court, and was the leading Spanish composer for the theatre of his time. The principal librettist with whom he worked was Calderón de la Barca. Hidalgo wrote two all-sung operas, but provided music mainly for partly sung works: semi-operas, *zarzuelas, comedias, and *autos sacramentales*. There survive many other songs (*tonos humanos*) besides those known to be associated with plays, and *villancicos. His music for semi-operas includes recitative (reserved for divine characters), declamatory airs, more lyrical songs and dance-songs (often of a popular cast), and choruses. The songs are typically strophic, with refrains.   OR

hi-fi. See HIGH FIDELITY.

Higglety Pigglety Pop! Opera in one act by Knussen to a libretto by Maurice Sendak after his book (incomplete version, Glyndebourne, 1984; preliminary version, Glyndebourne, 1985; definitive version, Los Angeles, 1990); it was conceived as a companion-piece to *Where the Wild Things Are*.

high fidelity [hi-fi]. A term used to refer to a standard of excellence in sound reproduction on records, tape, and film; it has come to be applied to the reproduction

equipment itself. See also RECORDING AND REPRODUCTION.

Highland bagpipe. The *piob mhór*, with a chanter, two tenor drones, and one bass drone, whose use has been spread worldwide by Scottish regiments of the British army. See BAGPIPE.   JMo

highlife. An African style of popular music developed in Ghana and Nigeria, which took its name by association with 'high society' (i.e. party-going). Its origins lay in the importation of European military band instruments to the coastal forts of Ghana during the 19th century. It was a blend of African, black American, and European idioms. Its popularity eventually declined in the 1960s in favour of string bands.   PW

hi-hat. A pair of cymbals mounted on a post, with a pedal by which the upper one may be made to clash against the lower. See DRUM KIT.

Hildegard of Bingen (*b* Bermesheim, nr Alzey, 1098; *d* Rupertsberg, nr Bingen, 31 Oct. 1179). Benedictine abbess, writer, and composer. Of noble birth, she entered religious life at the age of 14 and rose to become prioress of her convent at Disibodenberg. In 1150 she moved to the newly established convent at Rupertsberg, near Bingen. She experienced visions (induced possibly by migraine), and recorded these with the aid of her amanuensis, Volmar. She wrote works on medical, scientific, and hagiographical subjects, and entered into correspondence with political and spiritual leaders of the day, including emperors and popes. Her prophecies led to her being described posthumously as the 'Sybil of the Rhine'. She has never been formally canonized by the Roman Catholic Church.

Hildegard's religious poetry has long been recognized for its vivid imagery, visionary qualities, and deep spirituality. Intended for liturgical use, her verses fall into the familiar categories of antiphon, respond, sequence, and hymn, and cover the cycle of the church year. She also wrote a morality play, *Ordo virtutum*. The music to which many of these words are set is also highly original and is widely believed to be by Hildegard herself, even though there is no proof that she had a developed understanding of music and its notation.

JM

📖 S. FLANAGAN, *Hildegard of Bingen, 1098–1179: A Visionary Life* (London, 1989, 2/1998) · F. MADDOCKS, *Hildegard of Bingen* (London, 2001)

Hill. English family of organ builders. The firm was founded in 1825 and in 1832 managed by William Hill (1789–1870), who built the organs in York Minster (1829–33) and Birmingham Town Hall (1832–4); he then made great design changes, incorporating elements of

German instruments and adding new registers, an example being in Worcester Cathedral (1842). His son Thomas (1822 or 1823–93) carried on the business, which passed to his son Arthur George (1857–1923); it amalgamated in 1916 with Norman & Beard and continues to restore and build, notably at Norwich Cathedral.

AL

Hill, Alfred (Francis) (*b* Melbourne, 16 Nov. 1870; *d* Sydney, 30 Oct. 1960). Australian and New Zealand composer, conductor, and teacher. He studied at the Leipzig Conservatory and played the violin in the Leipzig Gewandhaus Orchestra. He spent the rest of his life conducting in New Zealand and Australia. He was the first composer to use Maori material, in his cantata *Hinemoa* (1896). His vast output, over 500 works, includes 13 symphonies and nine operas.

📖 J. M. THOMSON, *A Distant Music: The Life and Times of Alfred Hill, 1870–1960* (Auckland, 1981)

hillbilly. A term used to describe the songs of the farming communities of the south-eastern USA. Originating in the 1920s and supplanted after World War II by the description 'country music', it now generally designates the songs of that period before the commercialization of country music.   KC

Hiller, Ferdinand (von) (*b* Frankfurt, 24 Oct. 1811; *d* Cologne, 11 May 1885). German pianist, conductor, and composer. He studied with Alois Schmitt in Frankfurt and Hummel in Weimar. He then made occasional concert tours and in the late 1820s and early 30s lived in Paris, where he gave recitals, composed, and became one of the circle round Berlioz, Liszt, and Chopin. His replacing of another friend and supporter, Mendelssohn, as conductor of the Leipzig Gewandhaus orchestra led to a split between them. He also conducted in Dresden (where he was befriended by the Schumanns), Düsseldorf, and Cologne. During 30 years in the Rhineland he organized and conducted at many festivals and competitions, and was an influential teacher. His numerous compositions include chiefly songs and piano pieces, but he also wrote choral and orchestral music; among his operas is *Die Katakomben* (1867), an overambitious attempt at German grand opera. Hiller's critical writings, though conservative in spirit, show his appreciation of Liszt and Wagner; they also shed light on the German musical circles in which he moved.   JN/JW

Hiller, Johann Adam (*b* Wendisch-Ossig, nr Görlitz [now Gorlice, Poland], 25 Dec. 1728; *d* Leipzig, 16 June 1804). German composer and writer on music. He studied in Dresden and Leipzig, and played an important part in Leipzig's musical life, organizing subscription concerts, founding a singing school, and

directing the music at several city churches. In 1781 he became director of the Gewandhaus concerts, and in 1789 Kantor of St Thomas's. His popularity rested chiefly on the lively, touching *Singspiele* he wrote for the comedies of C. F. Weisse. Their appeal lay in their combination of plain situations—often rustic young lovers triumphing over resistance from their elders—with fully developed melody that well characterized both simple folk close to nature and more sophisticated urban or aristocratic figures. In this, Hiller added a French melodic elegance to the manner of German folksong. Many of his pieces, of which the most successful was *Die Jagd* (1770), entered a wide repertory. He wrote much other music, and his important writings include articles on music and aesthetics in the journal he founded, *Wochentliche Nachrichten*.   JN/JW

Hiller, Lejaren (Arthur) (*b* New York, 23 Feb. 1924; *d* Buffalo, NY, 26 Jan. 1994). American composer. He studied chemistry at Princeton, though he also had composition lessons with Milton Babbitt and Roger Sessions, and joined the chemistry department at the University of Illinois in 1952. There, with Leonard Isaacson, he created the first digitally programmed composition, the *Illiac Suite* for string quartet (1957), named after its computer. He moved to the university's music department (1958–68), then to Buffalo, continuing to work on composition with computers. He assisted Cage in the programming of *HPSCHD* for harpsichords and tapes (1967–9), and wrote, with Isaacson, *Experimental Music: Composition with an Electronic Computer* (New York, 1959).   PG

Hilton, John (i) (*d* Cambridge, 1609). English church musician and composer. He was a chorister and lay clerk at Lincoln Cathedral before taking up the post of organist at Trinity College, Cambridge, in 1594. Three years later he supplicated for the Cambridge degree of Mus.B. His best-known work is the anthem *Call to remembrance*; he also contributed a madrigal to Morley's anthology *The Triumphes of Oriana* (1601). Some of the church music attributed ambiguously to 'Hilton' is probably by his son, John Hilton (ii).

Hilton, John (ii) (*b* ? Cambridge, 1599; *d* 1657). English church musician and composer, son of John Hilton (i). He took the Cambridge degree of Mus.B. in 1616, and from 1628 was organist of St Margaret's Church, Westminster. Many more works can be attributed to him than to his father; in addition to the disputed anthems and canticles, he wrote canons, partsongs, and consort music. There are also solo songs and dialogues by him, cast in a more modern idiom.   JM

Himmel, Friedrich Heinrich (*b* Treuenbrietzen, 20 Nov. 1765; *d* Berlin, 8 June 1814). German composer. He was taken up at an early age by Friedrich Wilhelm II, who sent him to study in Italy. He then succeeded Reichardt as Kapellmeister in Berlin, where his plans for opera led to debts which he had to pay off by means of a tour to Russia and Scandinavia in 1797–9. Back in Berlin, his rivalry with Reichardt divided the city. His operas include the light, elegant *Fanchon* (1804), in *Liederspiel* vein, and a striking Romantic opera, *Die Sylphen* (1806), mingling comic and dark elements and influenced by *Die Zauberflöte*. Himmel retained royal support throughout his career, in spite of testing loyalties by his drunkenness, even at his own rehearsals.

DA/JW

Hindemith, Paul (*b* Hanau, 16 Nov. 1895; *d* Frankfurt, 28 Dec. 1963). German composer. A gifted child, he played the violin in the Frankfurt Children's Trio, founded by his impoverished, exploitative father, before entering the Hoch Conservatory in Frankfurt as a scholarship pupil at the age of 12; there he was taught composition by Arnold Mendelssohn and Bernhard Sekles. A period of employment in the orchestra at the Frankfurt Opera (1915–23) was interrupted by his conscription into the German army, in which he served as a regimental bandsman (1917–18). He also played second violin in the quartet of his violin teacher Anton Rebner; his first published works include a quartet (no. 1, 1918) and a set of four sonatas, one for each instrument in a quartet (1918). These, and other early works such as the op. 9 *Orchestral Songs* (1917), are richly chromatic, influenced by Reger and, above all, by Strauss.

A new phase opened between 1919 and 1921 with the composition of a trilogy of violent, expressionistic one-act operas—*Mörder, Hoffnung der Frauen* ('Murderer, Hope of Women'), *Das Nusch-Nuschi* ('Nuts'—slang for 'testicles'), and *Sancta Susanna*—which earned him notoriety in the early years of the Weimar Republic and which are now widely regarded as being among the most important of his early works. In 1922 Hindemith became second violinist in the Amar Quartet (he later switched to the viola), with which he played a considerable amount of contemporary music. In the same year he wrote the piano suite *1922*, fashionably including 'shimmy' and 'ragtime' movements, and *Kammermusik* no. 1 for small orchestra, which marked a turning towards neo-classicism.

During the next few years, Hindemith produced a large number of similar suite-like works, often loosely based on Bach but expressing a modernist urgency in their motor rhythms and their chords rich in 4ths. He later used the same style, determinedly anti-Romantic, in his opera *Cardillac* (1926), though a more reflective element had entered his music with the song cycle *Das Marienleben* ('The Life of Mary', 1923), to a text by

Rainer Maria Rilke, which also marks the beginning of Hindemith's attraction to visionary, almost mystical subject matter. Many of his works from the 1920s aim to assault bourgeois values; he worked with Bertolt Brecht on the 'scenic cantata' *Lehrstück* ('Lesson', 1929) and with Brecht and Weill on the cantata *Das Lindberghflug* ('The Lindbergh Flight', 1929), later collaborating with the right-wing avant-gardist Gottfried Benn on the oratorio *Das Unaufhörliche* ('The Perpetual', 1931), when his relationship with Brecht turned sour.

Prolific and versatile, Hindemith was concerned that his music should serve a functional purpose: his *Kammermusik* series, for instance, includes chamber concertos for piano, cello, violin, viola, viola d'amore, and organ. The word *Gebrauchsmusik* ('functional music' or 'utility music'), a term Hindemith detested, is commonly applied to the educational works he wrote for children and amateurs, including choral songs, cantatas, orchestral pieces, and chamber music, much of this large output dating from the years 1927–38.

After 1933 Hindemith's music increasingly became the subject of Nazi opprobrium, in spite of the fact that he initially showed no resistance to the regime, possibly out of the belief that its term of office would be short. His satirical one-act opera *Neues vom Tage* ('News of the Day', 1929), which featured nudity on stage, had caused particular offence to Hitler at the time of its premiere and was one of the first works to be proscribed after the Nazi seizure of power. His greatest opera, *Mathis der Maler* ('Mathis the Painter'), which yielded material for a symphony, was composed to his own libretto in 1934–5; it asserts the ethical primacy of the artist's spiritual duty to bear witness to human suffering, and makes a powerful demand for the right to individual conscience at a time of political brutality. In spite of the championship of Wilhelm Furtwängler, the opera remained unperformed in Germany until after World War II, though fierce controversy in the press over a projected radio broadcast of the symphony in 1934 forced Hindemith to take a six-month leave of absence from the Staatliche Musikhochschule in Berlin, where he had taught composition since 1927.

Between 1935 and 1937 he spent considerable time abroad: first in Ankara, to which he was invited by the Turkish government to assist in the foundation of a new musical academy; then in Italy, where he worked with the choreographer Leonid Massine on the ballet *Nobilissima visione*, inspired by the life of St Francis of Assisi. By 1937 the threat to both his personal life (his wife was Jewish) and his music could no longer be ignored and he finally resigned his teaching post in Berlin, leaving Germany for Switzerland the following year. In 1940 he settled in the USA as professor of theory at Yale, taking American citizenship six years later.

Hindemith's major theoretical work was *Unterweisung im Tonsatz* (1937–8, translated as *The Craft of Musical Composition*), which draws heavily on planetary and cosmological imagery, posits the idea of the chromatic scale as a reflection of divine harmony, and advocates a revised tonality—blurring the distinction between major and minor keys—as the basis of composition; the book, reflecting qualities already apparent in both the libretto and the score of *Mathis*, effectively served as a preface to the more lyrical, less strident style of his later music. The works he composed in the USA included *The Four Temperaments* for piano and strings (1940), *Ludus tonalis*, an ambitious cycle of 'studies in counterpoint, tonal organization, and piano technique' (1942), the ebullient *Symphonic Metamorphosis on Themes of Carl Maria von Weber* (1943), the ballet *Hérodiade* (1944, commissioned by Martha Graham), and the symphony *Die Harmonie der Welt* ('The World's Harmony', 1951). This last work was extended after Hindemith returned to Europe in 1953, to form an opera of the same title on the life of the astronomer Johannes Kepler. He also revised some of his earlier works, notably *Das Marienleben* and *Cardillac*, in the light of his harmonic theories. Hindemith spent his last years teaching at Zürich University, no longer composing so speedily; his last work was an unaccompanied Mass (1963).   PG/TA

  📖 P. Hindemith, *The Craft of Musical Composition* (Eng. trans., London, 1941–2); *A Composer's World* (Cambridge, MA, 1952) · I. Kemp, *Paul Hindemith* (London, 1952) · G. Skelton, *Paul Hindemith: The Man Behind the Music* (London, 1975) · D. Neumeyer, *The Music of Paul Hindemith* (New Haven, CT, 1986) · G. Rickards, *Hindemith, Hartmann and Henze* (London, 1995)

Hingston, John (*b* ?York, early 17th century; *d* London, *bur.* 17 Dec. 1683). English organist, viol player, and composer. A pupil of Orlando Gibbons, he was in the service of the Clifford family until 1645, and later (*c.*1654–7) in that of Oliver Cromwell. After the Restoration, Hingston became tuner of the organs and a viol player to Charles II. He presented six volumes of his compositions, which include some fine fantasias for viols, to the Music School at Oxford.   WT/AA

Hinrichsen. See Peters.

hinsterbend (Ger.). 'Dying away'.

Hinstrich (Ger.). In cello and double-bass playing, 'up-bow'.

Hin und zurück ('There and Back'). Opera in one act by Hindemith to a libretto by Marcellus Schiffer (Baden-Baden, 1927); the plot and, in part, the music go into reverse at the halfway point.

hip-hop. A term embracing various aspects of black American cultural life, including *rap, music created by DJs, graffiti art, and acrobatic break-dancing ('breaking'). Since 1979 the term has tended to be most commonly associated with *rap.   KG

  📖 S. H. Fernando, *The New Beats: Exploring the Music Culture and Attitudes of HipHop* (New York, 1994)

Hippolyte et Aricie ('Hippolytus and Aricia'). Opera in a prologue and five acts by Rameau to a libretto by Simon-Joseph Pellegrin after Jean Racine's *Phèdre* (1677), Euripides' *Hippolytos* (428 BC), and Seneca's *Phaedra* (Paris, 1733).

Hirt auf dem Felsen, Der ('The Shepherd on the Rock'). Song (1828) by Schubert for soprano and piano, with clarinet obbligato, to words by Wilhelm Müller and possibly Helmina von Chézy.

His (Ger.). The note B♯; *Hisis*, the note B𝄪.

Histoire du soldat ('The Soldier's Tale'). Work in two parts by Stravinsky, 'to be read, played and danced', to a French text by Charles-Ferdinand Ramuz based on a Russian tale; it is for three actors, female dancer, clarinet, bassoon, cornet, trombone, percussion, violin, and double bass (Lausanne, 1918). Stravinsky arranged a five-movement suite from it for violin, clarinet, and piano (1919) and an eight-movement one for the original instrumental ensemble (1920).

Histoires naturelles ('Natural Histories'). Song cycle by Ravel (1906), settings for voice and piano of five poems by Jules Renard. Manuel Rosenthal made a version for voice and orchestra.

historical editions. See EDITIONS, HISTORICAL AND CRITICAL; see also EDITING.

historic instruments. A term used for instruments current in earlier periods which survive to the present day in collections or in use. 'Historical instruments', on the other hand, are those made in recent times as copies or reconstructions of these, whether for display, research, or performance.   JMo

Hlzbl. (Ger.). Abbreviation for *Holzbläser* ('wood blowers', i.e. the woodwind section).

HMS Pinafore (*HMS Pinafore, or The Lass that Loved a Sailor*). Operetta in two acts by Sullivan to a libretto by W. S. Gilbert (London, 1878).

Hoboken. Abbreviation for the standard *thematic catalogue of the works of Joseph Haydn drawn up by the Dutch collector and bibliographer Anthony van

Hoboken (1887–1983) and published in Mainz, 1957–78. Haydn's works, especially those without distinguishing title or opus number, are often referred to by Hoboken number, as in the form 'Hob. XVII: 6' (the so-called Variations in F minor for piano).

höchst (Ger.). 'Highest', 'in the highest degree'.

Hochzeitsmarsch (Ger.). 'Wedding march'. Celebrated examples were composed by Mendelssohn (in his incidental music to *A Midsummer Night's Dream*) and Wagner (in *Lohengrin*); *Hochzeitszug*, a wedding procession.

hocket [hoquet]. A device of medieval polyphony whereby a melody is divided between two (or occasionally three) contrapuntal voice parts. One part rests while the other sounds, giving a fast alternation of single notes (or small groups of notes) and rests in each part and producing the effect of a vocal line 'jumping' from one voice to another (Ex. 1).

Many motets by Machaut and other 13th- and 14th-century composers include passages in hocket between the upper parts, but after about 1400 it was superseded by other contrapuntal developments and tended to be reserved for special effects. It reappeared in works by a number of 20th-century composers (Webern, Maxwell Davies) and is also a feature of some African and Indonesian antiphonal performance practices.

Ex. 1

Hoddinott, Alun (*b* Bargoed, 11 Aug. 1929). Welsh composer. He studied at University College, Cardiff, and with Arthur Benjamin in London. He taught at Cardiff (Welsh) College of Music and Drama from 1951 and at Cardiff University, as professor of music, from 1959 until his retirement. His early success, with works suggesting the influence of Bartók and Hindemith (e.g. the Clarinet Concerto, 1950), led to a prolific output of orchestral and vocal compositions including, besides many concertos and symphonies, the operas *The Beach of Falesá* (Cardiff, 1974), *The Trumpet Major* (Manchester, 1981), and *Tower* (Swansea, 1999). While certain works effectively incorporate Welsh folk music and idioms, Hoddinott's style is notable for its synthesis of progressive post-tonal techniques with traditional formal frameworks.   PG/AW

📖 B. DEANE, *Alun Hoddinott* (Cardiff, 1977)

Høffding, Finn (*b* Copenhagen, 29 March 1899; *d* Frederiksberg, 29 March 1997). Danish composer and teacher. After learning the violin, he studied composition and harmony with Knud Jeppesen (1918–21) and took courses in organ and music history; in 1921–2 he studied with Joseph Marx in Vienna. His long career as a teacher at the Royal Danish Conservatory of Music (1931–69; director from 1954) made him one of the most influential figures in 20th-century Danish music. His own music has made less of an impact, though it has considerable power and a ready humour, expressed with consummate craftsmanship. His output includes four symphonies (1923, 1924, 1928, 1934) and four Symphonic Fantasies, of which the second, *Det er ganske vist* ('It is Perfectly True', 1940), is his best-known work. There is also much chamber and choral music, and music for use in schools.   MA

Hoffmann, E(rnst) **T**(heodor) **A**(madeus) [originally Wilhelm; Amadeus adopted in homage to Mozart] (*b* Königsberg [now Kaliningrad], 24 Jan. 1776; *d* Berlin, 25 June 1822). Though chiefly remembered as a writer of fantastic tales, Hoffmann was also a composer, conductor, and a highly influential writer on music. After working as a government official in Poland and Prussia, he became director of the Bamberg theatre, where he conducted a wide repertory that included his own operas. He later lived in Berlin. His works include a lively comedy, *Die lustigen Musikanten* ('The Merry Musicians', 1805), an impressive German grand opera, *Aurora* (composed 1811–12), much influenced by Gluck, and a key work of Romantic opera, *Undine* (1816), in which the exemplar is Mozart. He also composed a symphony, piano sonatas, songs, and chamber music.

Hoffmann's own influence as a writer was profound. In two important tales, *Ritter Gluck* (1809) and *Don Juan* (1813), he uses fiction to make points about music as a mediation between human experience and the mysterious or infinite, and sets out a claim for Mozart and Gluck as exemplars for German opera composers. In *Der Dichter und der Komponist* (1813) he uses a fictional dialogue to discuss thoughts about the interaction of words and music in opera. He also argued for opera as a unified work of art. His critical articles on Beethoven and Gluck were highly significant. Many of his tales, typically fantastic in their mingling of normality and reality, sometimes in weird forms, provided subjects for many later works, among them Offenbach's opera *Les Contes d'Hoffmann* and Tchaikovsky's ballet *Nutcracker*.   WT/JW

Hoffmeister, Franz Anton (*b* Rothenburg am Neckar, 12 May 1754; *d* Vienna, 9 Feb. 1812). Austrian music publisher and composer. After studying law in Vienna he turned to music, becoming well known as a composer of *Singspiele* and instrumental music. His publishing firm, founded in 1784, included some of Mozart's music in its catalogue: Mozart's String Quartet in D K499 is often known as the 'Hoffmeister' Quartet. At about the turn of the 18th century he founded a 'bureau de musique' with Ambrosius Kühnel in Leipzig: this eventually became the publishing house C. F. *Peters Verlag.   —/JWA

Hoffnung, Gerard (*b* Berlin, 22 March 1925; *d* London, 28 Sept. 1959). German-born British humorist. He made his name first as a musical cartoonist and then, from 1956, as the organizer of 'Hoffnung Music Festivals', concerts of spoofs, pastiches, and musical jokes.   PG

Hoffstetter, Roman (*b* Laudenbach, Württemberg, 4 April 1742; *d* Miltenberg, 21 June 1815). German composer. He entered the Benedictine monastery at Amorbach in 1763 and remained there until its dissolution in 1803, when he moved to Miltenberg. His compositions include six String Quartets op. 3 (formerly ascribed to Haydn), three viola concertos, and some sacred works, including ten masses.   DA/SH

Hoflied (Ger.). A Renaissance song emanating from courtly or aristocratic circles, as opposed to *Gesellschaftslied*, a middle-class song, or *Volkslied*, a folksong.

ho-hoane. A corruption of the Gaelic *ochóin* ('oh, alas'), i.e. a lament (see LAMENT, 2).

Holberg Suite (*Fra Holbergs tid*; *Aus Holbergs Zeit*; 'From Holberg's Time'). Piano suite, op. 40 (1884), by Grieg, orchestrated for strings the same year and for full orchestra in 1885; in five movements, it was written to celebrate the bicentenary of the birth of the Norwegian dramatist Ludvig Holberg (1684–1754).

Holborne, Anthony (*d c.*1 Dec. 1602). English courtier and musician. His biography is obscure, but he may have been the Anthony Holborne who was educated at Cambridge and admitted to the Inner Temple in 1565; in 1584 he married in Westminster. He is known to have acted on behalf of Sir Robert Cecil in 1599, and in his publications styles himself 'gentleman and servant' to Queen Elizabeth. His compositions, all of which are instrumental, include pieces for the cittern, lute, and bandora, and a collection of dance music 'both grave and light' for five-part consort, published in 1599. Three small pieces also survive by his brother, William Holborne, about whom nothing is known.   JM

Holbrooke, Joseph (Charles) (*b* Croydon, 5 July 1878; *d* London, 5 Aug. 1958). English composer. He studied

with Frederick Corder at the RAM and was heavily influenced by Wagner and Richard Strauss. His large output is dominated by music for the stage, the orchestra, and for chamber ensembles. Obsessed with the work of Edgar Allan Poe, he had his first success with the symphonic poem *The Raven* (1900). His works were performed at Leeds (*Queen Mab*, 1904) and Birmingham (*The Bells*, 1906), and he produced four symphonies (several others are in manuscript), concertos for piano, violin, and cello, and many symphonic poems, all written for huge orchestra. His largest project was a commission from Lord Howard de Walden to set his epic poem, *The Cauldron of Annwn*, which resulted in a trilogy of operas, *The Children of Don* (1912), *Dylan* (1914), and *Bronwen* (1929).   JDi

hold. Another term for a fermata or *pause, mainly an American usage.

Holidays (*New England Holidays*). Orchestral work by Ives assembled *c.*1917–19 from four pieces previously published separately; they are *Washington's Birthday* (*c.*1915–17), *Decoration Day* (*c.*1915–20), *The Fourth of July* (*c.*1914–18), and *Thanksgiving and Forefathers' Day* (*c.*1911–16).

Holland. See LOW COUNTRIES.

Höller, York (*b* Leverkusen, 11 Jan. 1944). German composer. He studied in Cologne with Bernd Alois Zimmermann and Herbert Eimert. He first worked at the Cologne electronic music studio in 1971, with Stockhausen; he became its director in 1990. He has also had a close association with Boulez, and has created several works at IRCAM. Höller has developed a technique in which a basic cell provides the inspiration for the free development of all aspects of a work. Many of his compositions combine instruments with tape or live electronics. His opera *Der Meister und Margarita*, after Mikhail Bulgakov, was performed in Paris in 1989; his orchestral works include concertos for piano (1970), MIDI-piano (*Pensées*, 1991), and two pianos (*Widerspiel*, 2000).   ABur

Holliger, Heinz (*b* Langenthal, 21 May 1939). Swiss oboist and composer. He studied at the conservatories of Berne, Basle, and Paris, his teachers including Émile Cassagnaud and Pierre Pierlot for the oboe, and Sándor Veress and Pierre Boulez for composition. One of the leading wind virtuosos of his time, he has had works written for him by Berio, Henze, Penderecki, and many others. His own compositions show a fascination with extreme situations, both psychological and musical, and include several works for his own instrument, operas (*Schneewittchen*, Zürich, 1998, and smaller-scale settings of Samuel Beckett plays), and *Scardanelli-Zyklus*

(1975–91), a concert of choral and instrumental pieces based on the poetry of Friedrich Hölderlin.   PG

Holloway, Robin (Greville) (*b* Leamington Spa, 10 Oct. 1943). English composer. His principal studies were at Cambridge, where he became a lecturer after completing a doctoral dissertation, *Debussy and Wagner*. His early compositions reflect the concentrated serial thinking of his main teacher, Alexander Goehr, and the later Stravinsky. But Holloway soon developed a more lyrical, romantic, and allusive idiom (*Scenes from Schumann*, 1970; *Evening with Angels*, 1972), which has evolved over the years to embrace a whole range of sources from Wagner and Brahms to Britten and Gershwin. Among his most important works are the opera *Clarissa* (composed 1968–76; ENO, 1990), the Violin Concerto (1990), and the Concerto for Orchestra no. 3 (completed 1994).   AW

Holmboe, Vagn (*b* Horsens, Jutland, 20 Dec. 1909; *d* Ramløse, 1 Sept. 1996). Danish composer and teacher. He studied music theory with Knud Jeppesen and composition with Høffding at the Royal Conservatory in Copenhagen (1926–30) and with Toch at the Berlin Hochschule für Musik (1930). In 1933–4 he travelled in Romania, studying folk music—an important influence on his own compositions, as was Bartók. After returning to Denmark he taught and published articles, many on ethnomusicological subjects. He taught in Copenhagen at the Institute for the Blind (1940–9) and the Royal Conservatory (1950–65) and was a music critic for the newspaper *Politiken* (1947–55). His 'retirement' in 1965 allowed him to devote himself to composition.

Holmboe's musical style turned its back on both national Romanticism and the symphonic tradition of Nielsen: he retained the energy of Nielsen's symphonism, stripping down the orchestration to produce textures of exemplary clarity; he was also a supremely skilled contrapuntist. He developed a technique he called 'metamorphosis', in which larger structures evolve out of small groups of notes. His output was prodigious: 13 symphonies and many other orchestral pieces, two operas and a ballet, concertante works including one of the earliest concertos for orchestra (1929), 20 string quartets (and ten incomplete ones), choral music, including the large-scale *Requiem for Nietzsche* (1963–4) and 12 cantatas, solo songs, and much piano music, including the 'symphonic suite' *Suono da bardo* (1949–50). Holmboe was the most important 20th-century Danish composer after Nielsen's death and an influential teacher, whose pupils include Nørgård.   PG/MA

📖 P. Rapoport, *Vagn Holmboe* (London, 1974; Copenhagen, 3/1996, as *The Compositions of Vagn Holmboe*) · V. Holmboe, *Experiencing Music: A Composer's Notes*, trans. P. Rapoport (London, 1991)

Holmès [Holmes], Augusta (Mary Anne) (*b* Paris, 16 Dec. 1847; *d* Paris, 28 Jan. 1903). French composer, of Irish descent. Rumour had it that her true father was her godfather, the poet Alfred de Vigny. A childhood prodigy on the piano, she was giving concerts at an early age and was soon composing songs, using the pseudonym Hermann Zenta. After she had become a pupil of Franck, her composing grew more ambitious and she wrote four operas, several symphonic poems, the dramatic symphony *Les Argonautes*, and a number of cantatas. Her music is conventional but has a rough vigour which saves it from banality. A society beauty, she was the mistress of Catulle Mendès and at one point had to fend off an offer of marriage from Saint-Saëns.   MA

holograph. A manuscript wholly in the hand of its composer. See also AUTOGRAPH.

Holst, Gustav (Theodore) (*b* Cheltenham, 21 Sept. 1874; *d* London, 25 May 1934). English composer. The son of a piano teacher, he conducted village choirs when he was 17 and won a scholarship to the RCM at the second attempt in 1895, becoming a pupil of Stanford. He played the trombone in seaside bands before joining the orchestra of Carl Rosa Opera. In 1903 he began teaching and two years later became director of music at St Paul's Girls' School, Hammersmith, a post he held all his life. In 1907 he also became music director at Morley College. A love of folksong, stemming from his friendship with Vaughan Williams, resulted in the *Somerset Rhapsody* (1906–7). In order to set some Hindu poetry to music, he had lessons in Sanskrit, making his own translations for his *Choral Hymns from the Rig Veda* (four groups, 1908–12). Another product of this enthusiasm was the chamber opera *Sāvitri* (1908, first staged in 1916). He did not enjoy a major success with the public until 1919, when his large-scale orchestral suite *The Planets* (1914–16) was performed. This was followed in 1920 by his choral masterpiece *The Hymn of Jesus* (1917).

Holst suffered from poor eyesight and neuritis in his arm, and his health was further affected by a fall in 1923. The effect on his music was that it was pared to the bone: the effort of writing it down compelled an artistic economy which some felt was carried too far. His Keatsian *Choral Symphony* (Leeds, 1925) took many years to become established, and the austere bitonality of the Fugal Concerto (1923) and the Double Concerto for two violins (1929) puzzled even his admirers. A richer, more lyrical vein began to return with the orchestral landscape *Egdon Heath* (1927), the *Moorside Suite* for brass band (1928), and the *Lyric Movement* for viola and chamber orchestra (1933).

Besides *Sāvitri*, Holst wrote three operas, *The Perfect Fool* (Covent Garden, 1923), *At the Boar's Head*, a Falstaff episode (Manchester, 1925), and *The Wandering Scholar* (1929–30; Liverpool, 1934). Some of his most characteristic and powerful music is in the choral works, such as the *Choral Fantasia* (1930) for soprano, chorus, organ, and orchestra, and the *Ode to Death* (1919), while the beauty of his solo songs, particularly the 12 Humbert Wolfe settings of 1929, and the 12 Welsh folksong settings for unaccompanied chorus (1930–1), shows that allegations of a lack of warmth in his music originate in superficial assessment.

Even towards the end of his life Holst's works were rejected by publishers, but after his untimely death following an operation his work gradually intensified its grip on a new generation of listeners, who recognized in Holst the fount of much that they admired in the music of Britten and Tippett. It would be difficult, too, to exaggerate his influence as a teacher with a genius for encouraging amateurs and beginners to strive after the highest and most uncompromising standards. This integrity is reflected in some of the choral works he wrote for his pupils to sing, often demanding a subtlety and discipline which would tax professionals. But in such a partsong as *This Have I Done for my True Love* (1916), the practical musician and the visionary idealist meet on equal terms.   MK

    📖 I. HOLST, *Gustav Holst: A Biography* (London, 1938); *The Music of Gustav Holst* (London, 1951, 2/1975, 3/1986 with *Holst's Music Reconsidered*) · M. SHORT (ed.), *Gustav Holst (1874–1934): A Centenary Documentation* (London, 1974); *Gustav Holst: Letters to W. G. Whittaker* (Glasgow, 1974) · M. SHORT, *Gustav Holst: The Man and his Music* (Oxford, 1990) · A. E. F. DICKINSON, *Holst's Music: A Guide*, ed. A. Gibbs (London, 1995)

Holt, Simon (*b* Bolton, 21 Feb. 1958). English composer. He studied art, then composition in Manchester with Anthony Gilbert. Of all the English composers of the generations following those of Maxwell Davies (1934–) and Brian Ferneyhough (1943–), Holt has been one of the most resourceful in developing an essentially expressionistic tradition in ways that combine allusiveness and intensity, avoiding extreme fragmentation while preserving taut structures and often febrile textures. Notable works are the chamber compositions *Shadow Realm* (1983) and *Sparrow Night* (1990), while the Viola Concerto (1990–1) and the opera *The Nightingale's to Blame* (Opera North, 1998), after Lorca, demonstrate Holt's ability to work on a relatively large scale.

AW

Holy Week. The week preceding Easter, traditionally marked in Christian liturgy by services recalling the events surrounding the Passion and Resurrection of Jesus Christ. Holy Week begins with Palm Sunday and concludes with the ancient *Triduum* ('three days') of Maundy Thursday (the institution of the Eucharist), Good Friday (the Crucifixion), and Holy Saturday.

ALI

Holz (Ger., 'wood'). *Holzbläser*, 'woodwind players'; *Holzblasinstrumente*, 'woodwind instruments'; *Holzflöte*, 'wooden flute', an organ stop; *Holzharmonika*, 'xylophone'; *Holzschlägel*, 'wooden drumsticks'.

Holzbauer, Ignaz (Jakob) (*b* Vienna, 17 Sept. 1711; *d* Mannheim, 7 April 1783). Austrian composer and conductor. Largely self-taught, he developed his composing skills by directing the music at the Burgtheater in Vienna. After three years in Italy with his wife, the singer Rosalie Andriedes, he moved to Stuttgart and then Mannheim (1753–78). Here he wrote his most important opera, *Günther von Schwarzburg* (1777), a pioneering German grand opera both in its choice of a German historical theme and in the fluency of much of its handling and its expressive orchestration. It was admired by Mozart, and influenced him in a number of specific ways (including in *Idomeneo* and *Die Zauberflöte*). Holzbauer also composed much interesting church and chamber music.

JW

Home, Sweet Home. Melody (1821) by Bishop composed for an album of national airs described as 'Sicilian'; with words by J. H. Payne (1791–1852) it was incorporated in 1823 into Bishop's opera *Clari*. The tune occurs in an altered version in Donizetti's *Anna Bolena*.

Homme armé, L' (Fr., 'The Armed Man'). A 15th-century melody which was used extensively as the tenor *cantus firmus of polyphonic masses between about 1450 and 1600 by such composers as Dufay, Busnois, Ockeghem, Obrecht, Tinctoris, Josquin, La Rue, Senfl, Morales, and Palestrina. Carissimi composed an example in the 17th century. There are also several polyphonic chanson settings, by Morton and Josquin among others. The origin of the melody is uncertain; it has been suggested that it first appeared in a French chanson composed by Robert Morton, an English member of the Burgundian chapel, 1457–75, but it has also been attributed to Busnois; research has revealed that it may have been named after a popular tavern (see DUFAY, GUILLAUME, 1). Maxwell Davies used the tune as the basis of a dramatic chamber piece (1968), later revised (1971) for speaker and ensemble.   AL

homophony. A term used to describe music in which one voice or part is clearly melodic, the others accompanimental and chiefly chordal. The converse is *polyphony, where the parts tend towards independence and equality. The term 'homophony' has also been used to describe part-writing where all the parts move in the same rhythm; a more precise term for this is *homorhythm.

See also MONOPHONY.

homorhythm. A term used to describe music in which all the voices or parts move in the same rhythm (e.g. hymns, chorales, early organum).

Honegger, Arthur (*b* Le Havre, 10 March 1892; *d* Paris, 27 Nov. 1955). Swiss composer. Of Swiss Protestant parentage, he studied at the conservatories in Zürich (1909–11) and then Paris, where his teachers included Widor for composition and d'Indy for orchestration. While at the Paris Conservatoire he came into contact with a group of young composers, including Poulenc and Milhaud—the group which in 1920 was christened Les *Six. Honegger, however, never joined in the other members' regard for Satie nor, by and large, did he subscribe to the heart-on-the-sleeve aesthetics propounded by the group's self-appointed spokesman Jean Cocteau, though lightheartedness breaks through occasionally, as in the Clarinet Sonatina (1922) and the Piano Concertino (1924).

His first great success came with the 'dramatic psalm' *Le Roi David* (1921), even if some of his fellow composers, including Milhaud and Poulenc, thought it over-conventional. *Pacific 231* (1923), an orchestral picture of a steam locomotive, *Rugby* (1928), and *Mouvement symphonique* no. 3 (1933) form a triptych showing Honegger's relish of powerful, almost physical gestures given weight by his chromatic harmony. And a similar strength of design, idea, and feeling makes his cycle of five symphonies one of the most important of the century. The Third, *Symphonie liturgique* (1945–6), evokes recent history in its development from forceful striving to peace, and contrasts with the lightness of the Fourth, *Deliciae basilienses* (1946); the Fifth, *Di tre re* (1950), takes its name from the fact that each movement is based on the note D.

Honegger's other works include several ballets and operas, as well as the 'dramatic oratorio' *Jeanne d'Arc au bûcher* (1935), a massive fresco for speaking and singing voices, chorus, and orchestra. He pioneered a style of French text-setting in which the accentuation of weak syllables made for unusual forcefulness and clarity. He also wrote numerous scores, especially in the 1930s, for plays and films. He was a dedicated crafts-man and an extremely hard worker; his studio door in Montmartre bore the injunction 'Do not disturb' in more than 50 languages. His book *I Am a Composer* (Eng. trans., London, 1966), written in 1951 when he was already a sick man, takes a gloomy view of the prospects for serious composers, belying the widespread early fame accorded to Honegger himself.

PG/RN

📖 G. K. SPRATT, *The Music of Arthur Honegger* (Cork, 1987) · H. HALBREICH, *Arthur Honegger* (Paris, 1992)

Hook, James (*b* Norwich, ? 3 June 1746; *d* Boulogne, 1827). English organist and composer. He appeared as a soloist in concertos at the age of six and composed a ballad opera at eight. In London he worked at Marylebone Gardens and then for almost 50 years at Vauxhall Gardens, where he composed numerous organ concertos and more than 2000 songs. He also wrote dramatic works, such as the successful comic opera *The Double Disguise* (1784), a huge quantity of instrumental music, and a celebrated instruction book, *Guida di musica* (issued in two parts, *c*.1785, *c*.1794). He was a notable exponent of the *galant* style.

WT/PL

Hooper, Edmund (*b* North Halberton, Devon, *c*.1553; *d* London, 14 July 1621). English church musician and composer. He may have been a choirboy at Exeter Cathedral. By 1582 he was a singer in the choir of Westminster Abbey; six years later he was appointed Master of the Choristers there. In 1604 he became a Gentleman of the Chapel Royal, and in 1615 was promoted to the position of joint organist, working alongside Orlando Gibbons. In addition to anthems and canticles, he wrote sacred songs for domestic use and some keyboard dance movements.

JM

hopak [gopak]. A Ukrainian folk dance, apparently deriving its name from the exclamation 'hop' uttered during performance. It is usually in a major key and fast duple metre. Originally for men, it is now danced by mixed couples and male soloists; the solo dancing is improvised and acrobatic. There are examples in Musorgsky's unfinished opera *Sorochintsy Fair* (1874), Tchaikovsky's *Mazeppa* (1881–3) and Rimsky-Korsakov's *May Night* (1878). It is in the repertory of numerous folk-dance companies and traditionally ends a performance.

GN/JH

Hopkins, Bill [George William] (*b* Prestbury, 5 June 1943; *d* Newcastle upon Tyne, 10 March 1981). English composer. He studied with Egon Wellesz and Edmund Rubbra at Oxford, then took lessons from Messiaen and Jean Barraqué in Paris; his compositions derived from the avant-garde world of both Barraqué and

Boulez while achieving a distinctive tone of voice of well-nigh ecstatic intensity. Among the most memorable are *Sensation* (1965) for soprano and four instruments and *En attendant* (1976–7) for instrumental quartet.   AW

hopser. See GALOP.

horn (Fr.: *cor, cor d'harmonie*; Ger.: *Horn, Waldhorn*; It.: *corno*). 1. A general term for an animal horn adapted for blowing through buzzing lips by cutting off the tip or piercing a hole in the side, or for similar instruments of other materials (e.g. wood, ivory, ceramic, metal, or shell). Horns are favourite signalling instruments because the sound carries over long distances. More than one note can be produced by altering the lip tension, by partly covering the distal end, or by opening a fingerhole.

2. [French horn]. A coiled brass instrument with a wide bell, originally developed for the hunting field in 17th-century France, but then refined into the orchestral instrument in Germany. The horn was probably the first brass instrument to acquire *valves (1814). Unlike other valved brass instruments, these are played by the left hand.

The Baroque natural (valveless) horn, made in the shape of a broad circle or hoop, appeared in France in the second half of the 17th century and was probably used by Lully in a *comédie-ballet* at Versailles in 1664. It was a true hunting horn (Fr.: *cor de chasse, trompe de chasse*; It.: *corno da caccia*) with the mouthpiece soldered to the body, made with one, two, or three coils; as with the natural *trumpet, the notes it could play were restricted to the *harmonic series of a single key, giving only consecutive pitches from the 8th harmonic upwards. Such instruments were held in one hand and with the bell turned upwards.

Early in the 18th century, horns began to be made on which separate coils of tubing of different lengths, called crooks, could be inserted at the mouthpipe to give the horn a different key. The system was first to supply two conical 'master crooks' into which the mouthpiece fitted and to add separate cylindrical 'couplers' for the lower keys. This was superseded later in the century, on the Continent at least, by a set of nine or more separate crooks for each of the main keys from 'C alto' down to B♭ *basso*. As these developments were taking place, players were cultivating the lower and middle registers of the horn. The instrument was now being held with the bell downwards as it is today, partly so that the left hand could secure the crooks and mouthpiece; gaps in the harmonic series were filled by the partial occlusion of the bell with the right hand. The use of the hand allowed composers including Mozart to write melodically in the middle register of

the 3rd to 12th harmonics; the change in tone between the natural 'open' notes and the hand-stopped notes was thought to add to rather than detract from the beauty of a performance. Orchestral players, who worked in pairs, specialized either in high-register *cor alto* or in low-register *cor basso* with its hand-horn technique. Even today the right hand is used in the bell to control the tone-quality and tuning and, when required, as a mute (see STOPPED NOTES, 2; the technique is known in French as *sons bouchés*, in German as *gestopft*, and in Italian as *chiuso*).

Later in the 18th century the *Inventionshorn* was devised by the Dresden horn player A. J. Hampel, with a series of tuning-slides inserted into the body of the instrument. This was improved by the Parisian Joseph Raoux, whose *cor solo* was provided with only five crooks; these were in the most important keys for the concert soloist—G, F, E, E♭, and D—and were made more rigid by being crossed over themselves.

With valves the horn became a fully chromatic instrument, and composers speedily took advantage of its ability to play freely over the full compass, though it is clear that many players regarded valves initially as instantaneous crook changes, still relying on their hands for any non-harmonic notes. In France and Britain the horn remained narrow in bore and retained both valves and crooks, and the hand horn was taught in French conservatories into the 20th century. Many instruments were made with a pair of slides—one plain, the other with valves—giving players the choice of which to use and the option of changing crook to avoid transposing. In Germany, on the other hand, where the horn was wider in bore, the mouthpipe was fixed and the key of the instrument established as F, sounding a 5th lower than written. Music written for horns in other keys had to be transposed accordingly by the use of valves. The French instruments used piston valves, initially the narrow pistons of H. D. Stölzel and later the wider ones of François Périnet. In Germany rotary valves were more popular and have now become almost ubiquitous there and in Austria, except in Vienna where the double piston is still used.

In 1897 the horn maker Fritz Kruspe of Erfurt introduced the double horn in F/B♭. An extra valve for the thumb cuts out a third of the tubing, raising the basic pitch from F to B♭ *alto* and thus making high-lying parts more secure. It requires more complex valve systems, however, because the length of the extra tubing opened by operating a valve must be proportionate to the length of the main tubing. On the earlier compensating double horn, therefore, one set of valve loops was made long enough for the B♭ side, while the other added sufficient length to be in tune for the F horn. The slightly later full double, the instrument most often used today, has two independent sets of valve loops for each key. In each case, the valve rotors were deep enough to carry two sets of ports and auxiliary tubing.

In the second half of the 20th century various other combinations were designed, including double horns in Bb/F *alto* and triple horns in F/Bb/F *alto* or F/Bb/Bb soprano.

3. In jazz and traditional music 'horn' is often used as a general name for any lip-vibrated ('brass') instrument. JMo

📖 R. MORLEY-PEGGE, *The French Horn* (London, 1960, 2/ 1973) · H. FITZPATRICK, *The Horn and Horn-Playing and the Austro-Bohemian Tradition* (London, 1970) · A. C. BAINES, *Brass Instruments: Their History and Development* (London, 1976) · T. HERBERT and J. WALLACE (eds.), *The Cambridge Companion to Brass Instruments* (Cambridge, 1997) · E. H. TARR, *East Meets West* (Stuyvesant, NY, forthcoming)

Horn, Charles Edward (*b* London, 21 June 1786; *d* Boston, 21 Oct. 1849). British composer and singer, of German parentage. Taught by his father, Charles Frederick Horn (1762–1830), and Venanzio Rauzzini, he became a professional cello and double-bass player in London theatres as well as a singer, making his debut in June 1809. In 1827 he visited New York where he sang and directed operas including his own *The Devil's Bridge*; he visited Boston and Philadelphia the following year. After a three-year interlude in London, during which he was musical director of the Olympic Theatre (1831–2), he returned to the USA to become director of the Park Theatre, New York. There he was a successful music publisher, conductor, and participant in the foundation of the New York Philharmonic Society (1842). His oratorio *The Remission of Sin* (1835), the first written in the USA, brought his name before the American public. He was in England again in 1843, but after four years travelled back to the USA, settling in Boston as conductor of the Handel and Haydn Society. Horn's technique was inadequate in large-scale forms, as his second oratorio, *Daniel's Prediction* (1847) shows, but he had a gift for charming melody (as demonstrated by *Cherry Ripe* and *On the Banks of Allen Water*), folksong imitation, and attractive orchestration, couched in an essentially 18th-century harmonic style strongly influenced by Mozart. JDi

Horne, David (*b* Tillicoultry, 12 Dec. 1970). Scottish composer and pianist. He won the 1988 BBC Young Musician of the Year Award in the keyboard section and played at the Proms in 1990. He studied composition with Rorem at the Curtis Institute (1989–93), then at Harvard (1993–9). Much of his music is in abstract, instrumental forms, and, outside the mod-

ernist mainstream, is often very lyrical. He has also written two chamber operas and a music-theatre piece, as well as a full-scale opera, *Friend of the People* (Glasgow, 1999), on the subject of the 18th-century parliamentary reformer Thomas Muir. AL

hornpipe. 1. A single-reed pipe, made of wood or cane with up to six fingerholes. The name comes from the use of a horn bell to project the sound and often a horn reed cap as well. Examples are the Welsh pibcorn (or pibgorn) and, with geminate pipes, the Basque *alboka* and the Tunisian *zukra* (with bag like a *bagpipe). JMo

2. A British dance similar to the jig, but usually in 3/2, 2/4, or 4/4 time, especially popular between the 16th and 19th centuries. It was usually performed by one person (though versions for several people are found) and was generally accompanied by bagpipes and fiddles. From the 16th century onwards, hornpipes appeared in dance suites and incidental music for the stage by such composers as Anthony Holborne, Byrd, Purcell, Arne, and Handel (*Water Music*, nos. 9 and 12). By the end of the 17th century the 2/4 or 4/4 variety was the norm.

The traditional association of the hornpipe with British seamen seems to have begun in the late 18th century. By far the best-known example is the so-called College Hornpipe, also known as 'The Sailor's Hornpipe' and traditionally played on the Last Night of the Proms. It is not, however, typical. WT/JBe

Horn Signal. Nickname of Haydn's Symphony no. 31 in D major (1765), so called because the slow movement includes calls for four horns.

Hornwerk. A small barrel organ set in a tower to announce the hours and important church services in Germany and Austria in the 16th and 17th centuries. A surviving example is the *Stierorgel* (Ger. *Stier*, 'bull') in Salzburg, dating from 1502, so called because all the pipes sounded together at the end of each piece.

Horowitz, Vladimir (Samoylovich) (*b* ?Kiev, 18 Sept./1 Oct. 1903; *d* New York, 5 Nov. 1989). Ukrainian-born American pianist. His international career began in the 1920s but from 1936 he began a series of retirements from the concert platform. His appearances were always sensational events for, in personifying the eccentric virtuoso, he captivated audiences with his steely control, powerful climaxes, and dazzling technique. Though less comfortable in Beethoven and notoriously unauthentic in Scarlatti he excelled in the great Romantics, particularly Liszt, Tchaikovsky, Rakhmaninov, Prokofiev, and Skryabin, all composers whose music accorded perfectly with his temperament. CF

📖 G. PLASKIN, *Horowitz: A Biography* (New York and London, 1983) · H. C. SCHONBERG, *Horowitz: His Life and Music* (New York and London, 1992)

Hosanna. Hebrew exclamation of praise to God, adopted also in the Greek and Latin languages. It was the cry of the multitudes on Christ's entry into Jerusalem (Matthew 21: 9) and has been taken into many liturgies. In the Roman *Mass it concludes the Sanctus and the Benedictus.

Hosokawa, Toshio (*b* Hiroshima, 23 Oct. 1955). Japanese composer. He studied the piano and composition in Tokyo, then continued his composition studies in Germany with Isang Yun, Klaus Huber, and Brian Ferneyhough. In 1989 he was appointed artistic director of the Akiyoshidai International Contemporary Music Seminar and Festival. His works include series of pieces called *Fragmente*, *Vertical Time Study*, and *Landscape*; *Landscape V* (1993) combines string quartet with the Japanese *shō*.   ABur

Hotteterre, Jacques(-Martin) ['Le Romain'] (*b* Paris, 29 Sept. 1674; *d* Paris, 16 July 1763). French wind player, instrument maker, and composer. By 1708 he was a bassoonist and flautist at the French court and he also played the musette. Much sought after as a teacher, he wrote the first treatise on flute-playing, *Principes de la flûte traversière* (1707; Eng. trans. 1968), a treatise on flute improvisation (1719), and a musette method (1737). His compositions include suites for flute and bass (1708, 1715), the first French pieces for unaccompanied flute, and trio sonatas. He was one of a large family of woodwind players and makers who are best known for the improvements they made to the *hautbois* which led to the development of the modern oboe.   AL

Hours, Liturgy of the. See OFFICE.

Housatonic at Stockbridge, The. Third movement of Ives's First Orchestral Set *Three Places in New England*; it was composed *c*.1912–17 and is sometimes performed separately.

house. A style of late 20th-century club dance music, which took its name from the Warehouse club in Chicago. It grew out of *disco, but whereas disco was typically song-based, and was played on a variety of instruments, early house records usually consisted only of a drum machine playing a common-time rhythm, with synthesized bass line. Most subsequent dance styles have developed from it.   PW

Hovhaness [Chakmakjian], **Alan** (Vaness Scott) (*b* Somerville, MA, 8 March 1911; *d* Seattle, 21 June 2000). American composer, of Armenian-Scottish parentage. He studied with Frederick Converse at the New England Conservatory and Martinů at Tanglewood (1942). His enormous output—over 400 opus numbers, covering nearly all genres—includes more than 60 symphonies (well over half of them composed after his 60th birthday), many to programmes of an exotic, religious, or philosophical character; he also wrote 12 operas, mostly to his own librettos, six ballets, and chamber works for a large variety of instrumental combinations. Richly imbued with Armenian modality, his music tends to be colourful and massive.   PG

Howells, Herbert (Norman) (*b* Lydney, Glos., 17 Oct. 1892; *d* London, 23 Feb. 1983). English composer. An articled student of Herbert Brewer at Gloucester Cathedral (1909–12), he studied with Stanford and Charles Wood at the RCM (1912–17); he joined the teaching staff in 1920, remaining there until 1979. Succeeding Holst, he was director of music at St Paul's Girls' School, Hammersmith (1936–62), and during Robin Orr's absence on active service during World War II, he acted as organist at St John's College, Cambridge, which made him a Fellow in 1962.

Much of Howells's finest music was composed between 1915 and 1930. The chamber music, notably the Piano Quartet (1916), the *Rhapsodic Quintet* (1917), the *Fantasy String Quartet* (1918), the three violin sonatas (1918–23), and the string quartet *In Gloucestershire* (1923), show a remarkable facility and inventiveness, while the orchestral works—the Three Dances for violin and orchestra (1915), the suite *The B's* (1916), *Merry Eye* (1920), the *Pastoral Rhapsody* (1923), and the Piano Concerto no. 2 (1924)—evince an individual flair for instrumentation and form. An intuitive spiritual connection with his Tudor forebears is evident in many of his vocal and organ works, as is his regard for Parry's spacious architecture in such works as *Hymnus paradisi* (1938), the *Missa sabrinensis* (1954), and the *Stabat mater* (1963). His smaller works have a polish and finesse. Among his songs *King David* (1921), *Come Sing and Dance*, and the cycle *In Green Ways* (both 1928) are the finest of their period, as are his exquisite *Three Carol-Anthems* (1918–20) including 'A Spotless Rose'. After the success of his canticles for King's College (the *Collegium regale*, 1944), he wrote many services for cathedral and college choirs which continue the legacy of Stanford's symphonic settings.   JDi

📖 C. PALMER, *Herbert Howells: A Centenary Celebration* (London, 1992) · P. SPICER, *Herbert Howells* (Bridgend, 1998)

Hoyland, Vic (*b* Wombwell, 11 Dec. 1945). English composer. His studies included composition with Bernard Rands at York. Rands's contacts with Italian composers influenced many of his pupils, and Hoyland first became known as the composer of subtly textured chamber scores (*Jeux-thème*, 1973; *Andacht zum Kleinen*, 1980). He also produced strongly wrought, dramatic vocal pieces, in particular *Michelagniolo* (1984), in which the example of Berio and Franco Donatoni, though detectable, is transmuted and developed. Hoyland also composed the orchestral works *In Transit* (Proms, 1987) and *Vixen* (Cheltenham, 1997).   AW

Hr. (Ger.). Abbreviation for 'horns'.

Hrabovs'ky, Leonid. See GRABOVSKY, LEONID.

Hrf. (Ger.). Abbreviation for *Harfe*, 'harp'.

Hubay [Huber], Jenő [Eugen] (*b* Budapest, 15 Sept. 1858; *d* Budapest, 12 March 1937). Hungarian violinist and composer. He was a pupil of Joseph Joachim from 1870 at the Berlin Hochschule für Musik. He returned to Budapest and in 1878 visited Paris, where he worked with Henri Vieuxtemps. In 1882 he became first violin professor at the Brussels Conservatory (a post earlier held by Henryk Wieniawski), but in 1886 he returned to Budapest and eventually directed the Academy of Music there (1919–31). He played a fine Amati violin; his pupils include Jenő Vécsey, Josef Szigeti, and Jelly d'Aranyi. He composed operas, symphonies, four violin concertos, songs, and much chamber music.

Huber, Klaus (*b* Berne, 30 Nov. 1924). Swiss composer. He studied at the Zürich Conservatory with Willy Burkhard for theory and Stefi Geyer for violin (1947–9), and had private composition lessons from Burkhard and, in 1955–6, Boris Blacher. His works are structurally elaborate and often have some connection with the involutions of 16th-century theological and metaphysical thought: the oratorio *Soliloquia* (1959–64), based on texts of St Augustine, is typical. As a teacher, notably at the Basle Conservatory from 1961, he had a notable influence on younger Swiss and foreign composers.   PG

Hucbald of Saint-Amand (*b* northern France, *c*.840; *d* Saint-Amand, 20 June 930). Monk, composer, and music theorist. He composed several liturgical chants, including a sequence, a set of Gloria tropes, a versified Office for St Peter, and two hymns. He is primarily known as the author of the treatise *Musica* (called *De harmonica institutione* in the edition by Martin Gerbert, *Scriptores ecclesiastici*, i, 1784); it discusses the practical aspects of teaching psalmody, including the notation of chant, and its importance lies in the establishment of a system for defining the pitches used in the plainchant repertory. Several other early medieval treatises that have sometimes been attributed to Hucbald, including *Musica enchiriadis*, *Commemoratio brevis*, and *Alia musica*, are now no longer thought to be by him.

JBE

Hugh the Drover (*Hugh the Drover, or Love in the Stocks*). Ballad opera in two acts by Vaughan Williams to a libretto by Harold Child (London, 1924).

Huguenots, Les ('The Huguenots'). Opera in five acts by Meyerbeer to a libretto by Eugène Scribe and Émile Deschamps (Paris, 1836).

Hullah, John (Pyke) (*b* Worcester, 27 June 1812; *d* London, 21 Feb. 1884). English educationist. He was an exponent of the continental ('fixed-*doh*') method of teaching sight-singing, which is attractively easy for the beginner and reveals its difficulties only later. His system was superseded by John Curwen's *Tonic Sol-fa. Hullah held several eminent teaching positions in London and became government inspector of music in 1872. He also wrote books on music history, edited collections of early vocal music, and composed some songs, of which *O that we two were a-Maying* and *The Three Fishers*, to poems by his friend Charles Kingsley, were especially popular.   —/LC

humanism. A movement, grounded in scholarly studies of ancient literary texts, that informed the ideals and aims of the *Renaissance.

Humble, (Leslie) Keith (*b* Geelong, Victoria, 6 Sept. 1927; *d* Geelong, 23 May 1995). Australian composer, pianist, and conductor. He studied in Melbourne, in London with Howard Ferguson, and in Paris with René Leibowitz. He taught in Europe, Australia, notably at La Trobe University, and the USA; he was also active in the performance and promotion of new music. Humble's more experimental works involve mixed media, tape collages, electronics, and chance techniques; he also composed a series of piano sonatas.

ABUR

Hume, Tobias (*b* ?*c*.1579; *d* London, 16 April 1645). English soldier, musician, and composer. He served as an officer in the Swedish and Russian armies, and considered music 'the onely effeminate part of me'. He published two collections of music, *The First Part of Ayres* (London, 1605), a large and often witty set of pieces for lyra viol, and *Captaine Humes Poeticall Musicke* (London, 1607), 'so contrived, that it may be plaied 8 severall waies upon sundry Instruments'. The collections are interesting both for their idiosyncrasy and for the variety of their invention.   DA/JM

Humfrey [Humphrey], Pelham (*b* 1647; *d* Windsor, 14 July 1674). English composer. He was one of the first set of choirboys recruited for the Chapel Royal on the Restoration of Charles II. A precocious composer (his earliest anthems date from *c*.1663), he was sent to

France and Italy about 1664 to study the latest fashions in music. He returned to England in 1667, according to Pepys 'an absolute monsieur as full of form and confidence and vanity, and disparages everything and everybody's skill but his own'. During his absence he was appointed a singer-lutenist in place of Nicholas Lanier and a Gentleman of the Chapel Royal, taking up the posts on his return. When Henry Cooke died in 1672, Humfrey was granted four more places which Cooke had held, including Master of the Children of the Chapel Royal; that year he also married Cooke's daughter Katherine. Furthermore from 1672 he shared two posts of 'Composer for the Violins' with Thomas Purcell. He died aged 27 and is buried in Westminster Abbey.

Humfrey's greatest achievement lies in his church music, showing a mastery of both French and Italian styles. He had a particular gift for word-setting, in which he shows a perceptive knowledge of the recitative manner of Italy and of the more melodious idiom of his English forebears. This is well displayed in a miniature masterpiece, his setting of John Donne's *Hymne to God the Father*. His music for *The Tempest*, written in the last year of his life, displays a considerable flair for dramatic atmosphere, and it may be that his premature death deprived England of a talented opera composer. He was highly influential, and led the way to Purcell's assimilation of continental styles into the English tradition.   DA/AA

  📖 P. DENNISON, *Pelham Humfrey* (Oxford, 1986)

Hummel, Johann Nepomuk (*b* Pressburg [now Bratislava], 14 Nov. 1778; *d* Weimar, 17 Oct. 1837). Austrian composer and pianist. In 1785 his family moved to Vienna, where he gained useful experience through his father's post as director of the Theater auf der Wieden. An infant prodigy, he impressed Mozart, who gave him lessons. A four-year concert tour with his father took him through Bohemia, Germany, Denmark, and Britain. He was in London from 1790 to 1792 but returned in 1793 to Vienna, where he studied with Albrechtsberger, Salieri, and Haydn, and began his close and sometimes stormy relationship with Beethoven; they were to be both friends and rivals until Beethoven's death. In 1804 Haydn recommended Hummel as Konzertmeister to Prince Nicolaus Esterházy at Eisenstadt; he was eventually dismissed in 1811 when he returned to Vienna. In 1813 he married the singer Elisabeth Röckel, whose encouragement led to his triumphant return to the concert platform in 1814 in time for the Congress of Vienna. After an unsatisfactory sojourn as Kapellmeister in Stuttgart, he moved to Weimar in 1818. He remained there until his death, though he continued to tour widely. He was finally

reconciled to Beethoven, at whose wish he improvised at the funeral concert, and his friendship with Schubert won him the original dedication of the last three piano sonatas.

Growing up in the world of Haydn and Mozart, living in the Vienna of Beethoven, and eventually settling in a Weimar that saw the burgeoning of Romanticism, Hummel not only ranged across many European countries as a virtuoso but bestrode several musical ages. His early music grew out of Classicism, to whose principles he remained attached, while he was able to accommodate various Romantic gestures, especially harmonic, without seriously disturbing Classical equilibrium. Yet his music has an instinctive warmth, and sometimes a striking originality, which enabled him to move with ease in Romantic territory. It is naturally in his piano music, but no less in his chamber music, that his quality is best discerned. Always excellently written, it is almost invariably attractive without achieving a profundity that greater mastery of form might have allowed.   WT/JW

  📖 J. SACHS, *Kapellmeister Hummel in England and France* (Detroit, 1977)

humoresque (Fr.; Ger.: *Humoreske*). A name used as a title in the 19th century for a lively instrumental composition, often 'good-humoured' rather than 'humorous'. Schumann, Dvořák, and Grieg, among others, used the French or the German title. Humoresques are generally short and in one movement, but Schumann's op. 20 is one of his largest piano works and is more like a suite.

Humperdinck, Engelbert (*b* Siegburg, nr Bonn, 1 Sept. 1854; *d* Neustrelitz, 27 Sept. 1921). German composer. The son of a grammar-school master, he was a choirboy at the local cathedral, then won various prizes which allowed him to study in Cologne and Munich. Here he met Wagner, who invited him to Bayreuth to help with the preparations for *Parsifal*. He spent some time in Spain, and showed an interest in Moorish music before returning to Germany. He conducted, wrote criticism, and taught until his greatest success, the opera *Hänsel und Gretel*, was produced in Weimar in 1893, conducted by Richard Strauss. A fairy-tale opera for children, it has also found a steady adult following, in part for its skilful use of folk or folk-like songs in a simple motivic technique derived from Wagner. His only other significant success came with *Königskinder* (1897, rev. 1910).   DA/JW

hundred-and-twenty-eighth-note (♬). American term for the note having ¹⁄₁₆ of the value of a quaver (i.e.

¹⁄₁₂₈ of that of a semibreve, or whole note). There is no established English term for this note.   AP

Hungarian Dances (*Ungarische Tänze*). Piano duets by Brahms, published in four volumes between 1852 and 1869; he orchestrated three of the 21 (nos. 1, 3, and 10; 1873) and arranged some for piano solo.

Hungarian Rhapsodies. A group of works for solo piano by Liszt, nos. 1–15 composed between 1846 and 1853, nos. 16–19 composed about 30 years later; they are based on an earlier set (1839–47) of 21 pieces (some also called Hungarian Rhapsodies, others *Magyar dallok*) that draw on Hungarian Gypsy music. Several were orchestrated by Franz Döppler with advice from Liszt. The Hungarian Fantasy (1853) for piano and orchestra is based on no. 14.

Hungary 1. Introduction; 2. From the Middle Ages to 1848; 3. 1848–1945; 4. Since 1945

1. Introduction

Hungary was settled by the Magyar people in the 9th century. Christianity was established in the 11th century by István (Stephen), who was crowned king using a crown sent by Pope Sylvester II. During the Middle Ages the country was settled by foreigners from neighbouring territories, and by the 13th century the Finno-Ugric Hungarian tongue was only one of several languages spoken within its borders. After the defeat of the Hungarian forces by the Turks at Mohács in 1526 and the fall of Buda in 1541 the country was divided between the Ottoman Empire and the Habsburgs, with an independent Hungarian principality in Transylvania.

Eventual liberation from Turkish rule at the end of the 17th century brought colonization by the Habsburgs, and profound and lasting German influence. The Reform period of the second quarter of the 19th century and the revival of the Hungarian language reached a climax in the revolution of 1848, suppressed by Austria, but succeeded by an accommodation with the Habsburgs (the Compromise of 1867) which established the dual monarchy. After the union of Buda and Pest into a single capital of Budapest (1873) there was a period of urbanization and industrialization.

Defeat in World War I and the collapse of the Austro-Hungarian Empire was followed by two short-lived republics, then the authoritarian regency of Horthy de Nagybánya, which allied the country to Germany. A republic was again instituted after defeat in 1945, and the Communist People's Republic was established in 1949. The 1956 uprising, crushed by Russian troops, was followed by economic reform in 1968, accelerated after 1985, and led to the opening of the frontier with the West in 1989.

2. From the Middle Ages to 1848

In the Middle Ages Hungary was a country of peasants, governed by the king and a number of noble families. The presence of foreign musicians from the 12th century onwards is a sign that the music of the *troubadours and the German *Minnesinger was cultivated by the court. King Matthias Corvinus (1458–90), a great supporter of the arts, had at his court Italian, Burgundian, Flemish, and German musicians. Many native musicians chose to work abroad during the Turkish occupation of the 16th and 17th centuries; no sources of courtly secular music survive from that period. Collections printed in Transylvania, where Protestantism, particularly Calvinism, took root during the Turkish period, have, however, survived, and include the earliest printed Hungarian music.

During the 18th century many German musicians were active in major centres from Pozsony (Bratislava), the notional seat of government, to Nagyvárad (Oradea). Music was cultivated in great houses, most notably the opulent palace of Eszterháza, east of Sopron, built by Prince Nicolaus Esterházy and the home of Haydn for three decades (1761–90). The characteristic Hungarian dance style, later known as *verbunkos*, emerged in the 18th century; its adoption by Gypsy bands and exploitation by such composers as Liszt and Brahms in the following century gave the country a folkloric musical identity.

The main events and institutions of the Reform period were strongly associated with Pest, where concerts were regularly given from the 1830s, and the Nemzeti Szinház (National Theatre) opened in 1837; its conductor from 1838 was Ferenc Erkel (1810–93), composer of the national anthem, and creator of a Hungarian musical idiom that fused *verbunkos* and the newer csárdás dance-style with Italian and Viennese elements. For his visit in 1846 Berlioz made the arrangement of the Rákóczi March later used in *La Damnation de Faust*.

3. 1848–1945

The importance of Pest in musical life continued to increase after the 1848 revolution was crushed by Austria, and though Philharmonic Concerts began in 1853, under Erkel, Austrian oppression outlawed a Philharmonic Society until 1867. Similarly, Erkel could only make his operatic setting of the nationalist play *Bánk bán* (1861) after restrictions were eased. Many foreign musicians visited the country, including Wagner, and Mahler, who was for a time music director of the imposing Royal Hungarian Opera House (opened 1884). Liszt was born in Hungary but lived abroad for most of his career and was not a Hungarian speaker; nevertheless, he had a great impact on the development of Hungarian music. After 1869 he was more regularly resident in Budapest, and in 1875 he became the first president of the newly formed Academy of Music, which was subsequently renamed after him. Among those who trained and taught there, Bartók and Kodály occupy a special place in the history of 20th-century Hungarian music: together they undertook research into the folk music traditions within Hungary's pre-1918 borders (covering areas now in Slovakia and Romania), publishing the fruits of their work (Kodály, *A magyar népzene*, 1937) and absorbing folk styles into their personal contemporary musical idiom. The roll-call of musicians trained at the Liszt Academy of Music includes some of the greatest names in 20th-century music: the violinist Joseph Szigeti, pianist Annie Fischer, and conductors Eugene Ormandy, Fritz Reiner, Antal Dorati, and Georg Solti.

4. Since 1945

Bartók left Hungary for the USA in 1940, but Kodály remained at home, and his song-based educational ideas were highly influential in the postwar period. In common with the other countries of the Warsaw Pact, much foreign recent contemporary music, including a number of Bartók's scores, were unheard in the 1950s, and like many Hungarians the composer György Ligeti left the country in 1956 to pursue a career abroad. The situation relaxed with subsequent political changes; Bartók's more demanding music was rehabilitated and avant-garde styles found acceptance. In recent years the music of Ligeti's contemporary György Kurtág (born in Romania, in 1926, but resident in Hungary) has found a wide international audience. An outstanding figure of the middle generation is Peter Eötvös (*b* 1944), as well known for his conducting of contemporary music as his own compositions, and there is an active younger generation of composers born in the 1950s and 60s.

PS/KC

📖 *Studia musicologica Academiae scientiarum hungaricae* (Budapest, 1961–) [quarterly journal with articles in Eng., Fr., Ger., and It.] · L. Dobszay, *Magyar zenetörténet* [A History of Hungarian Music] (Budapest, 1984; Eng. trans. 1993) · R. Gates-Coon, *The Landed Estates of the Esterházy Princes: Hungary during the Reforms of Maria Theresia and Joseph II* (Baltimore, 1994)

Hunnenschlacht ('Battle of the Huns'). Symphonic poem (1856–7) by Liszt; it was inspired by Wilhelm von Kaulbach's painting depicting the combat in the air between the ghosts of the slain Huns and the Christian armies of Emperor Theodoric after the battle of the Catalanian Fields in AD 451.

hunting horn (Fr.: *cor de chasse, trompe de chasse*; Ger.: *Jagdhorn, Waldhorn*; It.: *corno da caccia*). A signalling

instrument. Originally a cow- or oxhorn (Fr.: *bugle*), it was later made of metal in a half-moon shape. By the 17th century in France, from where it spread throughout Europe, it was a large circular instrument, precursor of the orchestral *horn. In Britain the hunting horn is more often short and straight, but in Germany it is coiled like a *posthorn.   JMo

'Hunt' Quartet. Nickname of Mozart's Quartet no. 17 in B♭ major K458 (1784); one of the 'Haydn' Quartets, it is so called because of the hunting motifs which introduce the first movement.

hüpfend (Ger., 'hopping'). In string playing, with a springing bow (i.e. *spiccato).

hurdy-gurdy (Fr.: *vielle à roue*; Ger.: *Leier, Radleier*; It.: *ghironda*). An instrument with strings sounded by a rosined wheel instead of a bow. One or two *chanterelles* or melody strings are encased in a box that houses a set of tangents fixed on sliding bars terminating in touch-pieces or keys; when a key is depressed, the tangent stops the string. Up to four drone strings run outside the box; they can usually be silenced by being moved away from the wheel. One drone, the *trompette*, has a trembling bridge like that of the *trumpet marine: one leg rattles against the belly causing a buzzing sound. The wheel is turned by a crank in the right hand; the player may articulate notes by rhythmically interrupting the wheel's rotation. The body of the French hurdy-gurdy is often in the shape of a deep guitar or lute (see Fig. 1).

A large medieval form, the 12th-century *organistrum*, needed two players: one to turn the wheel and the other to work the keyboard. The 13th- and 14th-century 'symphony' (Fr.: *chifonie*; Lat.: *symphonia*) was box-shaped and small enough for a single player. The

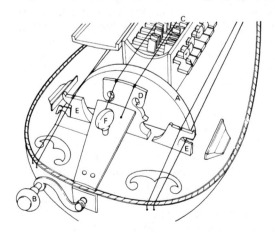

Fig. 1. French hurdy-gurdy: general view of the right-hand half of the instrument.

hurdy-gurdy's popularity has fluctuated. The instrument was normally associated with itinerant musicians, peasants, and blind beggars, but was briefly adopted by the French aristocracy during the 18th century when the pastoral ideal was in vogue; much music was published for it at that time, and increasingly elaborate instruments were made in France. Hurdy-gurdies continued to be played in rural France and eastern Europe throughout the 19th century. A more general revival began in the 20th century, especially in playing instruments of the French model.

See also LIRA ORGANIZZATA.   JMo

hurtig (Ger.). 'Quick', 'agile'.

Husa, Karel (*b* Prague, 7 Aug. 1921). Czech-born American composer. He studied at the Prague Conservatory (1941–5) and with Nadia Boulanger and Honegger in Paris (1946–51), where he remained before embarking on his long career at Cornell University (1954–92). His music is in a rhythmically dynamic neoclassical style, with roots in Honegger and Bartók, and later in Viennese serialism. Nearly all his works are instrumental; they include two symphonies, several concertos, pieces for concert band, four string quartets, and other chamber compositions.   PG

Hüttenbrenner, Anselm (*b* Graz, 13 Oct. 1794; *d* Oberandritz, 5 June 1868). Austrian composer. He studied in Vienna with Salieri and made a modest reputation as a composer. He was also friendly with Beethoven and Schubert. Probably in 1823, Schubert gave Hüttenbrenner's brother Felix the score of the 'Unfinished' Symphony, whence it eventually passed to Anselm, who made a piano duet arrangement. In 1865 Johann Herbeck retrieved the score from him and conducted the belated premiere in Vienna.   JW

Huygens, Constantijn (*b* The Hague, 4 Sept. 1596; *d* The Hague, 29 March 1687). Dutch diplomat, poet, and composer. As part of his broad education he was taught to play the lute, viol, organ, and harpsichord. He claimed to have written almost 1000 works, but very few of them survive; his *Pathodia sacra et profana* includes settings of his own poetry. He is remembered today mainly for his correspondence with, among others, Chambonnières, Froberger, and Gaultier, which gives interesting information about musical life in the various cities he visited.   DA/JM

hydraulis. The earliest form of organ, its invention attributed to Ctesibius in Alexandria about 300 BC. It had up to four ranks, each with four to 18 pipes, averaging about eight. How these were tuned is unknown. A pump on each side provided the air, the pressure being stabilized by a tank of water, hence the name (Gk. *hydor*, 'water', *aulos*, 'pipe'). The keys were spring-controlled. Mosaics show the hydraulis in the Roman Circus, often with trumpets, but detailed information on how it was used has not survived.

See also ORGAN, 1, and Fig. 1.   JMo

hymn (from Gk. *humnos*; Lat.: *hymnus*). A term deriving from ancient Greek pagan religious song, later applied to (especially strophic and metrical) genres of Latin Christian song, and thence vernacular Christian song.

1. Antiquity and the Latin hymn; 2. The Reformation; 3. The psalms and psalm tunes of England and Scotland; 4. The English hymn; 5. Recent developments

1. Antiquity and the Latin hymn

The term 'hymn' is now usually applied to Christian songs for worship, written in metrical verse in lines of regular length, whereas 'psalm' refers to the 'Psalms of David' in the Old Testament, whose poetry is neither metrical nor regular. In earliest Christian usage, however (from the epistles of the New Testament to the 4th-century period of the Church Fathers, including such writers as St John Chrysostom, Eusebius of Caesarea, John Cassian, and St Ambrose of Milan), the terms 'psalm' and 'hymn' were often interchangeable. One of the earliest liturgical songs dating from the end of this period is the non-metrical *Te Deum*, which is still referred to in liturgical books even after the Second Vatican Council as 'Hymnus'. Also from this early period come the first surviving metrical hymns of the Western church, some of which are attributed to St Ambrose; they are constructed of iambic strophes of four octosyllabic lines each (no melody survives from this time):

> Splendor paterne gloriae,
> de luce lucem proferens,
> lux lucis et fons luminis,
> diem dies illuminans.

Latin hymns are sung at the Divine Office, and are assigned to different liturgical occasions, according to time of day, season of the year, or Holy Day. The first known such assignment is found in the 6th-century Rules of Caesarius of Arles and Aurelian of Arles. The repertory of late antiquity, consisting of only 16 hymns, was designated the 'Old Hymnal' by Gneuss (*Hymnar und Hymnen im englischen Mittelalter*, 1968). To this was added the 'Frankish Hymnal' in the 8th century (contemporaneous with the establishment of 'Gregorian' chant), and the 'New Hymnal' in the 9th. By the 11th century, there were between 200 and 300 hymns in use. These remain in current liturgical books. From the 15th century, the melodies of

Gregorian hymns often appeared in polyphonic arrangements.

2. The Reformation

The earliest Protestant hymns often made use of Gregorian melodies. In Bohemia, the followers of the religious leader Jan Hus (1369–1415), known as the Bohemian Brethren, published in 1501 what is thought to be the first Protestant collection of hymns and psalms in the vernacular. Hussite songs were like the Lutheran chorales and hymns in that only a few were given original tunes, most of them being taken from Gregorian chant and secular song.

Luther made great use of hymns: he was a musician himself and was greatly helped by his musical colleague Johann Walter. The first Lutheran hymnbook appeared in Wittenberg in 1524; other books quickly followed (see CHORALE). The poetry and tunes of the German hymns have been a great source of inspiration to German composers. Bach, two centuries after Luther, followed the custom of his period by introducing chorales into his church cantatas and his settings of the Passion. He also harmonized many of them for four-part singing. It would be difficult to overestimate the importance of the place the chorale has occupied in German life (chiefly, of course, in the Protestant north, but also in certain Catholic parts of the country where it has been adopted). See also REFORMATION.

3. The psalms and psalm tunes of England and Scotland

Many English and Scottish divines fled to Geneva, the headquarters of Calvinism, to escape the persecutions of the times. They took some of the English psalm paraphrases and their tunes and brought back other tunes; from Geneva thus came a number of the metrical psalm tunes now most dear to English and Scottish congregations. Examples include the *Old Hundredth* (which appears to derive from a Dutch traditional tune in the *Souterliedekens*, 'Little Psalm-Songs', of 1540), the *Old 113th*, the *Old 124th*, and others frequently found in the hymnbooks of today; their titles refer to those psalms to the metrical versions of which they were originally attached. Calvinistic practice, unlike Lutheran, restricted congregational singing to metrical versions of the psalms; this restriction operated in England and for a much longer period in Scotland.

The metrical psalter of Thomas Sternhold and John Hopkins was completed and published by John Day in London in 1562. Day published it with melodies taken from French and German sources, and the following year brought out a harmonized edition of the tunes. Other tune books that followed as companions for Sternhold and Hopkins's version were East's (1592),

Ravenscroft's (1621), and Playford's (1677). Playford's was the first popular book to put the melody in the treble.

Sternhold and Hopkins was the chief book authorized in the Church of England for well over a century—up to 1696, when Nahum Tate and Nicholas Brady's version appeared and was used by a number of churches in preference; many however continued to use Sternhold and Hopkins for over a century longer, its phraseology having acquired almost the authority of holy writ, so that it passed through 600 editions. After 1696 Sternhold and Hopkins was spoken of as the 'Old Version' and Tate and Brady as the 'New Version', and this 'New Version' (or, rather, the two versions together) held the field right up to the introduction of the modern hymnbook.

In ordinary parish churches the psalms for the day were read in prose, and in cathedrals they were sung to the Anglican chants; a metrical psalm would be sung in a service as a kind of religious relaxation. Psalm books made a great contribution to popular musical education and included instructions on the reading of vocal music by the use of a kind of sol-fa. During the 18th century, itinerant psalmody teachers were extremely common and were often engaged by village communities to give a course of class lessons in singing.

The early psalm tunes of the Genevan type were congregational, and generally in a simple syllabic style. At the beginning of the 18th century there was a new development: parish 'quires' were formed and initiated a new and elaborate style of singing, which was none the less distinct from 'art' music, typified by the *fuging tune. Such parish quires also contained players of stringed and woodwind instruments. Stylistically, although the fuging tune did not obey all the rules of conventional harmony, it was usually in the diatonic major–minor idiom of its age. When taken to America, however, the form was enhanced by an injection of the modalism of folksong. There was also an American evangelical tradition equivalent to that of Wesley in Britain. The development of 'shape-note' notation in about 1800 allowed the publication in accessible format of psalms, hymns, fuging tunes, and anthems. Among the most important were William Walker's *Southern Harmony* (1835) and E. J. King's *The Sacred Harp* (1844). From the 'Camp Meetings' came the tradition of *spirituals; alongside these developed the urban hymnody of 'gospel music', which, in its black American form, eventually developed into a type of popular music (see SOUL).

4. The English hymn

John and Charles Wesley represent a new movement, away from the Calvinist metrical psalm towards a means of expressing the personal emotion of an evangelical congregation. Wesley sought something other than the formal old-style psalm tunes or the florid fuging tunes. Early Methodist tunes use the fashionable *galant* style of the time, and some of Wesley's texts are intended to borrow contemporary secular tunes; for example, the well-known 'Love Divine, all loves excelling' is a textual parody of Dryden's 'Fairest Isle, all isles excelling', itself associated with a tune by Purcell.

In the established church, such experiments could not be made, because only metrical psalms were authorized for use; some churches still used Sternhold and Hopkins's 'Old Version' because the Brady and Tate 'New Version' was still frowned on as being too 'free'. A court case in 1819 had the unexpected result that an incumbent could introduce any hymns or psalms at his discretion. From this moment on, the established church took the lead. Bishop Heber wrote a book of hymns in 1827 assigning a different hymn to each day of the church calendar. This liturgical principle was carried further by the High Church Oxford Movement; in 1851 Thomas Helmore and J. M. Neale published English versions of the pre-Reformation Latin Office Hymns with their plainchant melodies. Evangelical publications include those by the two Bickersteths (1833 and 1838), and the middle ground was occupied by the Society for the Promotion of Christian Knowledge and others. The Lutheran chorale and the early English psalm tune were rediscovered.

All this activity culminated in *Hymns, Ancient & Modern* (1861), a publication that saw off every one of its rivals. It was an Anglo-Catholic initiative, but it was decided that its contents should be comprehensive, with the result that the ideas of the Oxford Movement became part of the general tradition of the Church of England. The book popularized a new kind of Victorian hymn tune, typified by those of J. B. Dykes. During this period, in Britain and America, different denominations developed their own hymnbooks in similar formats.

The English Hymnal (1906) was the first publication to introduce a 'folk' element into Anglican worship; edited by Vaughan Williams, it also had the highest musical ambitions. It might well have replaced *Hymns, Ancient & Modern* altogether had its stance not been too uncompromisingly High Church for some.

5. Recent developments
Since the 1960s there has been an upheaval: first, the Roman Catholic Church allowed congregational hymn-singing, which has led to the development of a popular style of Catholic hymn; the charismatic movement has led to the development of the 'worship song', which in some quarters has replaced hymn-singing altogether. 'Worship songs' are in various popular styles, including *rock; the organ is replaced by a small band, including guitars, and the congregation are encouraged to move and clap their hands.

The hymn has fought back in a movement to renew the traditional form; new hymns have appeared first as supplements to the established hymnbooks, and then incorporated into new editions. Writers associated with this are Fred Pratt Green, Brian Wren, and Timothy Dudley-Smith.   PW

R. Stevenson, *Protestant Church Music in America* (New York, 1966) · N. Temperley, *The Music of the English Parish Church* (Cambridge, 1979) · E. J. Lorenz, *Glory Hallelujah! The Story of the Campmeeting Spiritual* (Nashville, TN, 1980) · E. Routley, *The Music of Christian Hymns* (Chicago, 1981) · M. L. West, *Ancient Greek Music* (Oxford, 1992), 288–308, 317–18 · I. Bradley, *Abide With Me: The World of Victorian Hymns* (London, 1997) · J. R. Watson, *The English Hymn: A Critical and Historical Study* (Oxford, 1997) · N. Temperley, *The Hymn Tune Index: A Census of English-Language Hymn Tunes in Printed Sources from 1535 to 1820* (Oxford, 1998)

Hymnen ('Anthems'). Work (1966–7) by Stockhausen for four-track tape, composed using national anthems. Stockhausen also made a version with solo instruments (1966–7) and a shortened version with orchestra (1969).

Hymn of Jesus, The. Choral work, op. 37 (1917), by Holst to a text he translated from the apocryphal Acts of St John, for two choruses, female semi-chorus, and orchestra.

Hymns, Ancient & Modern. English hymnbook first issued in 1861. It was intended to help minimize the differences that existed between the various church denominations of the time and therefore included hymns and hymn tunes from a variety of sources. Its enormous popularity meant that by the early 20th century most parish churches were using it.   JBe

Hymns from the Rig Veda. Settings (1907–12) by Holst of his translations of words from the Sanskrit; there are 23, in five sets, for different combinations of voices and instruments.

Hymn to St Cecilia. Choral work, op. 27 (1942), by Britten, a setting of a text by W. H. Auden.

Hymnus paradisi ('Hymn of Paradise'). Requiem (1938) by Howells to texts from the Latin Mass for the Dead, Psalm 23, Psalm 121, the Burial Service, and the Salisbury Diurnal (translated by G. H. Palmer); composed in memory of Howells's son, it was not released for performance until 1950.

Hz. Abbreviation for Hertz.

iambus. A poetic foot of two syllables, weak–strong. The adjective is 'iambic'. For its equivalent in the rhythmic modes, see NOTATION, 2.

Iberia. Suite of 12 piano pieces by Albéniz, published in four sets of three (1906–8), with titles evoking Spanish scenes or places; Albéniz orchestrated two of them but the five orchestrated by his friend Enrique Arbós are better known.

Ibéria. Orchestral work by Debussy, the second of his *Images*.

Ibert, Jacques (François Antoine Marie) (*b* Paris, 15 Aug. 1890; *d* Paris, 5 Feb 1962). French composer. He studied at the Paris Conservatoire (1909–13) with Paul Vidal, Émile Pessard, and André Gedalge. His early orchestral works, notably the suite *Escales* (1922), are in a lush Impressionist style, but he was mainly known for pieces that display a witty frivolity, for example the Divertissement for small orchestra (1930) and the Flute Concerto. He also wrote a short operatic farce, *Angélique* (1927), and collaborated with Honegger on the opera *L'Aiglon* (1937). Less well known are such pieces as the String Quartet, which shows a mastery and individuality of harmony and a more serious side to his musical personality. Ibert's professional career included periods as director of the French Academy in Rome (1937–60) and of the Paris Opéra (1955–6).

PG/RLS

Ice Break, The. Opera in three acts by Tippett to his own libretto (London, 1977).

iconography. Music iconography is concerned with the visual representation of musical topics. The primary materials studied include portraits of performers and composers, illustrations of instruments and occasions of music-making, and the use of musical imagery for purposes of metaphorical or allegorical allusion. Iconography is thus an important resource for the study of music and the visual arts, including questions of patronage, reception history, social and intellectual history, philosophy, and aesthetics, as well as more strictly technical matters such as organology, music theory, performance practice and contexts, and the study of artistic styles and symbolic meanings. Depictions of musical scenes may also include representations of such associated performance arts as dance and drama, as well as of the kinds of space in which such activities took or take place. Bringing musicological knowledge to bear on the analysis of images can contribute valuable insights both to art history and to drama and theatre studies.

Music as visual icon may be studied in three contexts: (1) organology: the history and technology of musical instruments; (2) performance practice and socio-cultural aspects; (3) symbolic uses of musical imagery. Both organological and performance-practice questions may be greatly assisted by iconographic study, but they depend also on other types of documented information. This is most critical in the case of organology, for example in identifying the number of strings on a harp, the position of a bow on a fiddle or viol, the number of players in an ensemble, or, indeed, the precise groupings of instrumental ensembles. Visual accounts alone may often be determined by restrictions of space, the limitations of the medium, or the fact that the artist's purpose in using such imagery was an extra-musical one—for instance as a motif in abstract design, as in the case of choirs of angels in some medieval and Renaissance sources; or for symmetry, as in Greek Geometric pottery. Imagery is also used to underline the importance of number symbolism: the 24 Elders of the Apocalypse (over the front portal at Santiago de Compostela); the mystical number 9: nine choirs of angels, the nine Muses, a nine-string *lira da braccio*; or the Ten Commandments symbolized by a ten-string psaltery or harp.

Irrespective of whether instruments and scenes of performance are represented in accurate technical detail, the primary purpose of visual representation of music (unless the sources have a theoretical or pedagogical function) is to convey extra-musical messages—for example, in the depiction of dancers performing round- and chain-dances, to symbolize civic harmony; or, in still-life images, to embody a certain atmosphere or illustrate a metaphor. Hence musical instruments may be introduced to express some aspect of cultural symbolism *per se*, their precise technical details being of secondary interest. Examples include the erotic associations of wind instruments (the oboe in ancient Egypt, the flute in classical Greece) or the association of particular instruments with social status (bagpipes for shepherds, hurdy-gurdies to denote beggars). Music iconography, like all the visual arts, is thus primarily a medium used to convey particular socio-cultural messages, including information on contexts and cultural ideas about music; as a source of precise information on the technical aspects of music, it necessarily depends on, and may complement, other types of data.   ABu

📖 H. M. BROWN and J. LASCELLE, *Musical Iconography: A Manual for Cataloguing Musical Subjects in Western Art before 1800* (Cambridge, MA, 1972) · E. WINTERNITZ, *Musical Instruments and their Symbolism in Western Art: Studies in Musical Iconology* (New Haven, CT, and London, 1979) · A. BUCKLEY, 'Music iconography and the semiotics of visual representation', *Music in Art: International Journal for Music Iconography*, i/1–2 (1998), 7–12

idée fixe (Fr., 'fixed idea', 'obsession'). The name given by Berlioz to the theme in his *Symphonie fantastique* (1830) that represents 'the beloved'. It recurs in all the movements, undergoing various transformations. The use of this device is related to *cyclic form, and is a forerunner of Wagner's technique of *leitmotif.

idiophone. A term used in *organology for all instruments made of materials sufficiently rigid to sound of themselves without skins or strings; they are mostly percussion instruments. See INSTRUMENTS, CLASSIFICATION OF.   JMo

Idomeneo, re di Creta ('Idomeneus, King of Crete'). Opera in three acts by Mozart to a libretto by Giovanni Battista Varesco after Antoine Danchet's *Idoménée* (1712) (Munich, 1781).

idyll. A literary description (in prose or verse) of happy rural life, applied by extension to a musical composition of a peaceful, pastoral character, for example Wagner's *Siegfried Idyll* or Janáček's *Idyll* for string orchestra.

Illuminations, Les ('The Illuminations'). Song cycle, op. 18 (1940), by Britten for soprano or tenor solo and orchestra, settings of nine prose poems (1872–3) by Arthur Rimbaud.

Images ('Pictures'). 1. Orchestral work by Debussy consisting of *Gigues* (1909–12), *Ibéria* (1905–8), and *Rondes de printemps* (1905–9).
2. Six piano pieces by Debussy in two sets of three: the first (1905)—*Reflets dans l'eau* ('Reflections in the Water'), *Hommage à Rameau*, and *Mouvement*; the second (1907)—*Cloches à travers les feuilles* ('Bells through the Leaves'), *Et la lune descend sur le temple qui fut* ('And the moon descends on the temple that used to be'), and *Poissons d'or* ('Goldfish').

Imaginary Landscape. The title of five pieces by Cage (1939, 1942, 1942, 1951, 1952) for different forces, including turntables and other electrical equipment; the fourth is for 12 radios with two players at each, one operating the volume and the other the wavelength, and the fifth is for tape.

Imbrie, Andrew (Welsh) (*b* New York, 6 April 1921). American composer. He studied with Roger Sessions at Princeton and Berkeley, where he joined the faculty in 1948. His music follows that of Sessions in its lucid, purposeful 12-note harmony and its large, strongly shaped forms, though the sensibility is gentler. He has worked in every standard genre, producing operas, choral music (Requiem for soprano, chorus, and orchestra, 1984), three symphonies, three piano concertos, and five string quartets.   PG

Imeneo ('Hymen'). Opera in three acts by Handel to a libretto adapted anonymously from Silvio Stampiglia's *Imeneo* (1723) (London, 1740).

imitation. 1. The representation in music of extra-musical sounds. There are obvious analogies between musical sounds and phrases and sounds in nature and the external world, from birdsong and flowing water to rumbling traffic and the inflections of human discourse. Among the most tantalizing aspects of music are the degree to which its gestures and structures are widely held to imitate, or at least reflect, identifiable emotions and states of mind, and the extent to which musical works are expected to create appropriate emotional states in the listener. At the very least, it must be acknowledged that imitation in this sense is highly subjective, and for many music lovers the beauty of music involves its resistance to such direct translation into the specifics of feeling, given the extreme improbability that everyone would always respond to the same music in precisely the same way.
2. The repetition—a process more technical than aesthetic—of a motif or idea in other voices: in fugal expositions, for example, the initial subject statement is answered and repeated as a way of reinforcing its importance to the contrapuntal structure. Controversy may arise in this context when the relationship between statements and their imitative variants is less precise. Nevertheless, the question of when something ceases to be a variant and becomes a new idea is unlikely to arise in contexts where imitation is a fundamental feature of the musical argument.   AW

immer (Ger.). 'Always', 'ever', 'still', e.g. *immer belebter*, 'ever more lively'; *immer schnell*, 'always quick'.

Immortal Hour, The. Music drama in two acts by Boughton to his own libretto after plays and poems by 'Fiona Macleod' (the pseudonym of William Sharp) (Glastonbury, 1914).

imperfect cadence. See CADENCE.

imperfect interval. An *interval of a 2nd, 3rd, 6th, or 7th.

Imperial, The (*L'Impériale*). Nickname of Haydn's Symphony no. 53 in D major (1778 or 1779); the name was first used, for an unknown reason, in a 19th-century Paris catalogue of Haydn's symphonies.

Imperial Mass. See NELSONMESSE.

Impresario, The. See SCHAUSPIELDIREKTOR, DER.

Impressionism. A term used for a style of late 19th-century French painting and extended to apply to music of a generation later. Monet's *Impression: Lever du soleil* ('Impression: Sunrise'), exhibited in 1874, was a key work and led to the coinage of the term by the critic Louis Leroy. It was first used pejoratively for a school of painting concerned with urban (often Parisian) and landscape subjects treated in a particular way: suffused and reflected light (the impression), sometimes hazy or smoky, is more important than outline or detail. Its principal exponents include Camille Pissarro, Auguste Renoir, Alfred Sisley, and Edgar Degas. The movement was imitated outside France, particularly in England and the USA.

The term was applied to early 20th-century French music that was similarly concerned with the representation of landscape or natural phenomena, particularly the water and light imagery dear to Impressionists, through subtle textures suffused with instrumental colour. Debussy has traditionally been described as an 'Impressionist' (he himself disapproved of the term); he wrote many piano pieces with titles evocative of nature, for example *Reflets dans l'eau* ('Reflections in the Water', 1905), *Les Sons et les parfums tournent dans l'air du soir* ('Sounds and Perfumes Swirl in the Evening Air', 1910), and *Brouillards* ('Mists', 1913). The Impressionists' use of brush-strokes or dots ('pointillism') is also reflected in the music of Debussy and Ravel, for example in Ravel's ballet *Daphnis et Chloé* (1912), in which static sections are built up from slow-moving harmonies arpeggiated with fast-moving 'dots' of sound, akin to the broad washes of colour in the paintings. 'Impressionist' has been applied loosely to several later composers, notably Bartók, Delius, and Szymanowski.

RLS

📖 C. PALMER, *Impressionism in Music* (London, 1973) · R. BYRNSIDE, 'Musical Impressionism: The early history of the term', *Musical Quarterly*, 66 (1980), 522–37

impromptu. An instrumental composition, not necessarily (despite its name) of an improvisatory character. 'Impromptu' was used as a title for short piano pieces in the 19th century, the earliest known examples being by the Czech composer Voříšek (1822). The most famous are those of Schubert (he adopted the name only after his publisher, Haslinger, had called the first four of his 1827 set 'impromptus') and Chopin (opp. 29, 36, 51, and 56—the last better known as the 'Fantaisie Impromptu', 'Fantaisie' having been added to the title by Chopin's editor).

Improperia (Lat., 'reproaches'). A series of chants sung in the Roman rite during the Veneration of the Cross on Good Friday. In modern books there are three greater Reproaches based on passages from the Prophets, which are preceded by the verse 'Popule meus, quid feci tibi?' ('O My people, what have I done to you?') and responded to by the *Trisagion in Greek and Latin, and nine lesser Reproaches which usually have the 'Popule meus' verse as a refrain.   —/ALı

improvisation. Dictionary definitions of this term invariably stress the idea of composing or performing 'extempore', without preparation. The implication is that improvisation is the freest kind of creative activity, in which spontaneity and lack of forethought displace the long and often tortuous processes which compositional acts are traditionally assumed to involve, as well as displacing the painstaking learning and processing of a printed text which performance normally presumes.

As is often the case with categorizations in music, however, absolute distinctions between improvisation and non-improvisatory activities cannot be sustained. Where performance is concerned, it is obvious that printed compositional texts leave many interpretative aspects undefined. Hence the fact that valid performances of the same text can differ markedly without one being deemed irrefutably more accurate or authentic than another. Indeed, an 'improvisatory' quality—a feeling that the player is in some sense inventing the music there and then—is often regarded as a positive interpretative factor.

Nevertheless, just as a written composition is regarded as providing performers with something fundamental to work with, so that every other interpretation of the same text, however variable in its details of expression, will count as the same piece, so performances called 'improvisations' can scarcely avoid relying on formal models or generative materials which, to significant degrees, constrain the musical result. This is particularly the case with jazz performance, which commonly involves a balance between fixed materials or frameworks and the specific lines and patterns floated against and around the framework by the players.

Composers occasionally indulge in the paradox of giving the title of 'Improvisation' to something fully notated (even if aspects of coordination and the order of events may be varied from performance to performance)—as in Boulez's *Improvisations sur Mallarmé* (1958–9). Here the implication is not simply that the character of the music has something of the unconstrained quality of 'real' improvising, but that the composer's thoughts themselves have an improvisatory character, seeking to replace the logical and rational with something more spontaneous and freely associative.

The ability to improvise has long been regarded as one indication of good musicianship, but the skill it represents has as much to do with memory as with genuine creativity. Most improvisations, especially by organists needing to fill in time during services and ceremonies, are likely to be, if only vaguely, 'in the style of' Bach, Elgar, or whomever; but only rarely would such improvisations count as examples of that style superior to, or even equal to, that shown in written compositions. Similarly, it is notable that the encouragement of spontaneous improvisation within certain contexts of 20th-century experimental music—that of *Cage and *Stockhausen, for example—has remained subordinate to activities which preserve the distinction between the roles of composer and interpreter.

AW

IMS. See INTERNATIONAL MUSICOLOGICAL SOCIETY.

in alt, in altissimo. See ALT, 1.

In C. Work (1963) by Riley for an unspecified number of instruments; it consists of 53 simple melodic phrases each repeated as many times as desired, at a mutually agreed pace. It was the work that defined *minimalism and brought it to a wide audience.

incalzando (It.) 'Pressing on', 'chasing', i.e. increasing the tempo.

incantation. In opera or oratorio, a scene in which spirits are conjured, for example the Witch of Endor scene in Handel's *Saul* (1738). Other notable examples occur in Cavalli's *Il Giasone* (1649), Massenet's *Le Roi de Lahore* (1877), and the Wolf's Glen scene in Weber's *Der Freischütz* (1821). Sullivan's early operetta *The Sorcerer* (1877) includes a parody of an operatic incantation scene.

incidental music (Fr.: *musique de scène*; Ger.: *Bühnenmusik*; It.: *musica di scena*). Music played during a performance of a spoken drama. Incidental music is of secondary importance to the speech (though this does

not necessarily mean it has no dramatic significance) and thus the term is not used with reference to such forms as the operetta, musical, *Singspiel*, or masque. It embraces both the music 'outside' the drama, including the overture before the play and the *entr'actes, *interludes, or *act tunes between the acts, as well as the music performed as part of the action (fanfares, songs, dances, marches, and supernatural and mood music) whether on or off the stage. Such music was first used to accompany plays in ancient Greece.

Incidental music has often taken the form of arrangements of popular tunes. Many composers and theatre directors, however, have been concerned that all the music contributes directly to the drama, for example by reflecting the mood of the action in interludes or illustrating an event occurring between acts (e.g. the storm scene in *The Tempest*, music for which was composed by Matthew Locke in 1674). Composers who wrote incidental music include Henry Purcell (13 plays and semi-operas), Mozart (*Thamos, König in Ägypten*), Beethoven (*Egmont*), Schubert (*Rosamunde*), Schumann (*Manfred*), Mendelssohn (*A Midsummer Night's Dream*), Grieg (*Peer Gynt*), Debussy (*Le Martyre de Saint Sébastien*), Elgar (*The Starlight Express*), and Sibelius (*Stormen*, for *The Tempest*). Many of these works, particularly those on a large scale, have a life independent of the play for which they were originally composed and are now more often heard in the concert hall than in the theatre. Film scores are a type of incidental music.

JBE

incipit (Lat., 'begins'). 1. The opening words or music of a work as presented in a catalogue or index.

2. Occasionally, a synonym for intonation (see INTONATION, 1).

3. The preliminary staff in modern editions of early music, giving the original clefs and time and key signatures, the opening note or notes in their original notation, and occasionally the range of the part.

Incontro improvviso, L' ('The Unexpected Meeting'). Opera in three acts by Haydn to a libretto by Carl Friberth after L. H. Dancourt's *opéra comique La Rencontre imprévue* (Eszterháza, 1775).

Incoronazione di Poppea, L' ('The Coronation of Poppaea'). Opera in a prologue and three acts by Monteverdi to a libretto by Giovanni Francesco Busenello after Tacitus; it was first produced in Venice in 1642.

Incorporated Society of Musicians (ISM). British association founded in 1882 to represent the interests of professional musicians and to uphold the standards of music education. It adopted its present title in 1892.

Indes galantes, Les ('The Amorous Indies'). *Opéra-ballet* in a prologue and four *entrées* by Rameau to a libretto by Louis Fuzelier (Paris, 1735); it was first performed with three *entrées*, the fourth being added in 1736.

indeterminate music. Music over which the composer has to some degree relinquished control, perhaps by leaving some aspects to chance or to the performer's decision. All music falls within this definition, since musical notation, however detailed, can never prescribe a performance with complete precision; but the term is normally reserved for cases of a conscious abstention from creative choice.

A composer may, for example, involve chance in the process of composition. Techniques of this kind have been much used by John *Cage, whose piano work *Music of Changes* (1951) was largely determined by the results of tossing coins. Other pieces by Cage were composed by placing notes on physical imperfections in the manuscript paper, by tracing musical patterns from star maps, and so on.

Alternatively, composers may present their work in such a way that the result is bound to be unpredictable. They may, for example, substitute graphic designs for conventional notation, allowing performers to decide how to interpret the score; again, Cage's output offers many instances. A second possibility is the use of texts to prompt a collective musical response, as in Stockhausen's *Aus den sieben Tagen* (1968).

There are also numerous examples of more closely defined indeterminate music. The works of Lutosławski and Henze, for example, contain passages which leave some decisions to performers. They may have to repeat a fragment an indefinite number of times or choose a rhythm for a given set of pitches, and by loosening control in this manner the composer can create a texture which is fixed in broad terms but variable in detail.

The opposite approach, providing fixed material which may be played in alternative sequences, is particularly associated with *Boulez. For instance, the completed segments of his Third Piano Sonata (1955–7) allow the player to decide the order of movements, and of fragments within them, to omit certain passages, to choose between alternative tempos and dynamics, and so on. PG/AW

India, Sigismondo d' (*b* Palermo, *c.*1582; *d* ?Modena, before 19 April 1629). Italian nobleman and composer. The origin of his unusual name is unknown; it has been suggested that India may have been the name of a village near Palermo, but there is no sign of such a place on any map. In 1606 he was in Mantua, where he may have met Monteverdi, and between 1608 and 1611 he visited Florence, Rome, Naples, Parma, and Piacenza. He became director of the chamber music at the court of Carlo Emanuele I, Duke of Savoy, at Turin in 1611, moving to the Este court at Modena in 1623 after malicious gossip had forced his departure. In 1624 he went to Rome, where his sacred opera *Sant'Eustachio* was performed in the palace of Cardinal Maurizio of Savoy, but he returned to Modena, and probably died there, although he may have taken up an appointment offered him at the Bavarian court of Maximilian I.

D'India was an important composer of monodic songs and madrigals; they are remarkable for their powerful use of dissonance and angular melody, and have been compared with the madrigals of Gesualdo. His secular vocal music, monodic and polyphonic, is mainly contained in five volumes of *Musiche* (Milan, Venice, 1609–23), and ten volumes of madrigals and villanellas (Milan, Naples, Venice, Rome, 1606–24).
—/TC

Indian Queen, The. Semi-opera in a prologue and five acts by Purcell adapted from the play by John Dryden and Robert Howard, with a final masque by Daniel Purcell (London, 1695).

indie. A term that refers to record labels rather than a musical style. Until the mid-1970s, six large record labels monopolized the dissemination of rock and pop music. 'Indie' refers to the 'independent' labels which, in the wake of punk, broke this monopoly, especially Stiff Records, Rough Trade, Creation, 4AD, and Kitchenware. In the late 1980s the term was particularly associated with a new wave of Manchester bands: Inspiral Carpets, Happy Mondays, New Order, and Stone Roses. Indie bands were mainstays of the 1990s rock festivals—Glastonbury and Reading in the UK, and Lollapalooza in the USA. KG

📖 C. LARKIN, *The Virgin Encyclopedia of Indie & New Wave* (London, 1998)

In dulci jubilo ('In Sweet Joy'). German 14th-century macaronic carol; the English version dates from *c.*1540.

Indy, (Paul Marie Théodore) Vincent d' (*b* Paris, 27 March 1851; *d* Paris, 2 Dec. 1931). French composer. Born into a military aristocratic family, he entered the Paris Conservatoire, where Franck's unique organ and composition class made a lifelong impression on him. Eager to widen his experience, he visited Liszt at Weimar and heard Wagner's *Ring* and *Parsifal* at Bayreuth. He was highly critical of the Conservatoire's limited methods and general outlook, so he joined Charles Bordes and Alexandre Guilmant in 1894 in founding the rival Schola Cantorum. His own composition classes were solidly based on a historical foundation of Gregorian chant, Palestrinian and Bachian polyphony, Beethoven's symphonic language, and Franck's technique of cyclic themes. This culminated in the widely influential treatise *Cours de composition musicale* (1903–51).

Professing Roman Catholic beliefs and right-wing political views, d'Indy was involved in numerous controversies, and his name has unjustly become synonymous with reaction and dogma. In reality, however, much of his work was admirably open and progressive. An interesting variety of pupils included Roussel, Albéniz, Turina, Satie, and Varèse, and as secretary of the Société Nationale he generously encouraged other young composers of advanced tendencies, notably Debussy and Dukas. He was also active in reviving the operas of Monteverdi and Rameau, making new editions and directing performances.

D'Indy's early compositions are largely derivative, but the breakthrough came with *Symphonie sur un chant montagnard français* for piano and orchestra (1886), inspired by his native Cevennes. Indeed, he particularly excelled in the evocation of nature and in his imaginative command of the orchestra. These aspects are also found in *Jour d'été à la montagne* (1905), and the late works *Poème des rivages* (1921) and *Diptyque méditerranéen* (1926). Bold formal experiment characterizes the Orient-inspired *Istar* (1896), a set of symphonic variations in reverse order, ending with the theme itself. The cyclic Symphony in B♭ (1903), on the other hand, exemplifies the more conservative aspects of his teaching. Other compositions include three operas and a quantity of chamber music. AT

📖 A. THOMSON, *Vincent d'Indy and his World* (Oxford, 1997)

inégales. See NOTES INÉGALES.

inequality. The convention, established during the Baroque period in France, whereby a sequence of notes written as equal in durational value was performed as alternately long and short. See NOTES INÉGALES.

AW

Inés de Castro. Opera in two acts by MacMillan to a libretto after J. Clifford (Edinburgh, 1996).

Inextinguishable, The (*Det Uudslukkelige*). Nielsen's Symphony no. 4 op. 29 (1914–16).

Infedeltà delusa, L' ('Deceit Outwitted'). Opera in two acts by Haydn to a libretto by Marco Coltellini, possibly revised by Carl Friberth (Eszterháza, 1773).

inflection [inflexion]. A term referring to those parts of the melody that move away from the reciting tone in the simpler forms of plainchant, recitation, or cantillation; see PLAINCHANT, 5.

Ingegneri, Marc'Antonio (*b* Verona, after 1547; *d* Cremona, 1 July 1592). Italian composer and organist. He worked for most of his life in Cremona, where he became *maestro di cappella* about 1579. Most of his surviving madrigals are contained in seven volumes published in Venice between 1572 and 1587 (one volume is known to be lost), and one published posthumously in 1606. They are rather old-fashioned, although chromaticism is used occasionally, but were popular during Ingegneri's lifetime and after his death, and influenced his most important pupil, Monteverdi, with their clear, well-worked-out structures. His church music is similarly constrained, although this probably has more to do with the reforms suggested by the *Council of Trent than with an innate conservatism. His 27 responsories for Holy Week were for some time attributed to Palestrina. —/TC

innig (Ger.). 'Heartfelt', 'sincere'.

In nomine (Lat.). A peculiarly English form of instrumental *cantus-firmus composition that flourished during the 16th and 17th centuries. The cantus firmus is the Sarum antiphon *Gloria tibi Trinitas* (Ex. 1). The title 'In nomine' is explained by the fact that the genre derives from John Taverner's cantus-firmus mass (written probably before 1528) based on that antiphon: in the latter section of the Benedictus the words 'In nomine Domini' are set for four voices, with the cantus firmus in breves, and this passage gained separate currency in various arrangements, both vocal (with new texts) and instrumental (for keyboard and for lute). Over 150 *In nomine* settings survive, up to the genre's late flowering with Purcell.

There are two main *In nomine* traditions: the first for consort (these seem sometimes to have been sung) and the second (composed rather than arranged) for keyboard. (The latter is really a descendant of the earlier liturgical keyboard settings of plainchant, and indeed many of these pieces are called *Gloria tibi Trinitas*.) The *In nomine* tradition from Taverner seems to have been established by 1560: there are settings by Thomas Preston and Robert Golder (both died in the mid-1560s), and the Mulliner Book (*c*.1560) is the earliest surviving source for *In nomine* settings (it includes Taverner's 'original' *In nomine* in keyboard transcription, though there is no reason to associate the arrangement with the composer). After an early preference for four parts, five became the norm for the consort *In nomine*. There are various connections between the settings of different composers. Many, including Byrd, made reference to Taverner's own

Ex. 1

accompanying material, and in his fifth five-part *In nomine* Byrd was also indebted (like others) to Robert Parsons's settings. The largest contribution to the repertory was made by Christopher Tye, of whose settings over 20 are extant. Composers of the *In nomine* were developing a more instrumental style than is naturally found in their model, and there are already extreme instances of this in Tye's angular lines and extravagant leaps. Some of his settings are strikingly original; many bear idiosyncratic titles, for example *Beleve me* and *Howld fast*. Composers including Tallis, Strogers, and Alfonso Ferrabosco (i) continued to develop the style, using instrumental melodic devices to structural ends. The 16th-century consort *In nomine* culminated in Byrd's seven settings, unrivalled in invention and expressive control.

Remarkably, the consort tradition persisted through the 17th century. With the diminution of note-values and the elaboration of rhythms, such composers as Alfonso Ferrabosco (ii), Gibbons, and Tomkins restored the genre to a new mastery, while innovations by others included having the cantus firmus migrate and putting it into the major mode. As if echoing Byrd, Purcell rounded off the *In nomine* in about 1680 with two settings, in six and seven parts, of an extraordinary and fitting archaic intensity.

In the keyboard tradition, among the earliest examples are six settings by Blitheman. The keyboard *In nomine* frequently aspired to virtuosity (and the cantus firmus was generally based on the semibreve rather than the breve). Bull's 12 settings include one effectively in 11/4. The last extant examples are by Tomkins and date from the mid-17th century.

Among present-day composers, Peter Maxwell Davies has shown a special fascination with the *In nomine*: the plainchant and various settings of it inform much of his output, in particular the two Taverner fantasias, *Seven In Nomine*, and the opera *Taverner*.

In seculum (Lat.). A popular *cantus firmus in the 12th and 13th centuries, consisting of the melisma to the words 'in seculum' from the Easter gradual *Haec dies*.

insieme (It.). 'Together'.

Institut de Recherche et de Coordination Acoustique/Musique (IRCAM). Organization initiated in 1976 in Paris, at music studios in the Centre Pompidou (with Boulez as director), to experiment with and develop techniques of electronic composition; the organization, best known by its acronym, was profoundly influential on music in the last quarter of the 20th century. See also ELECTROACOUSTIC MUSIC.   AL

📖 G. BORN, *Rationalizing Culture: IRCAM, Boulez, and the Institutionalization of the Musical Avant-Garde* (Berkeley, CA, 1995)

instrumentation. See ORCHESTRATION.

instruments, classification of. There are innumerable ways of classifying instruments, for example by sound, colour, material, size, or use. Many of these are, or have been, used in common speech, such as *haut and bas, brass or woodwind, jazz or orchestral. Other systems have been invented throughout the world according to the needs of particular cultures.

The only system to have stood the test of time—one that can cover all instruments worldwide—is one that categorizes instruments solely according to what it is that vibrates to create the sound. This was first developed in India many centuries ago, refined by the 19th-century organologist Victor-Charles Mahillon, and put on a culture-free basis by Erich von Hornbostel and Curt Sachs in 1914 (translated into English by Anthony Baines and Klaus Wachsmann in 1961) through the adoption of the Dewey decimal system. Because they used numbers, the definition in German could be converted into any language. For example, the description *Rahmentrommel (ohne Stiel), einfellige* ('single-skin frame drum (without handle)') and its number, 211.311, may be applied to any such instrument throughout the world, including the English tambourine, the Arabic *duff*, and the Irish bodhrán. No people is forced to use any language but its own, provided that it also uses the Hornbostel–Sachs number.

There are five main classes of instrument (initially four, with the fifth added by F. W. Galpin in 1937): 1, idiophones, where 'the substance of the instrument itself yields the sound'; 2, membranophones, whose 'sound is excited by a stretched membrane'; 3, chordophones, with a 'string stretched between fixed points'; 4, aerophones, where 'the air itself forms the vibrator'; 5, electrophones, or better electronophones, to distinguish between ordinary instruments amplified and those whose sound is generated electronically. This section has as yet no agreed structure.

Within the first two classes, the second and third levels are categorized by how the instrument is made to sound. Idiophones may be struck (11), plucked (12), made to sound by friction (13; e.g. musical *glasses, *nail violin), or, rarely, blown (14). Struck idiophones may be struck directly by the performer (111) or indirectly (112). Clappers or concussion idiophones (111.1) are directly struck idiophones consisting of two or more complementary objects being struck together (e.g. *castanets or *cymbals); percussion idiophones (111.2) are struck with or against a non-sonorous object such as a beater (e.g. *xylophones and *bells). Indirectly struck idiophones may be shaken (112.1; e.g. *maracas), scraped (112.2; e.g. *güiro), or sprung together (112.3). Membranophones may also be struck (21) or plucked (22), though those instruments originally classed as plucked drums have more recently been recognized as chordophones. Membranophones may also be made to sound by friction (23) and by singing (24; kazoos). A membrane may be made of paper, plastic, or onion skin, or even be a diaphragm of thin metal, as well as animal skin.

The third class, the chordophones or stringed instruments, is divided first by type of construction rather than playing method, as many may be played in several ways (a violin string can be bowed, plucked, or tapped with the bow). Simple chordophones or zithers (31) consist solely of a string-bearer, or of a string-bearer with a resonator that can be detached without destroying the sound-producing apparatus. One could remove the sides and bottom (which form the resonator box) from an Alpine zither without dismantling the board, which carries the strings. Composite chordophones (32), however, have a resonator that is integral to the structure: detaching the resonator from a lute or a harp would destroy the instrument.

Zithers are subdivided according to the type of string-bearer and, further, according to whether they have a resonator. Bar zithers (311) include musical *bows (311.1: where the string-bearer is flexible) and stick zithers (311.2: where the string-bearer is rigid); tube zithers (312) have a vaulted surface which may be a complete tube (312.1; e.g. the Malagasy valiha) or half or less of the tube (312.2; e.g. *koto, *kayagŭm), with the strings on the outer, convex side. Most European zithers, including the dulcimer and the piano, are box zithers (314.122), having a resonator box made from

slats; they are a subclass of board zithers (314), where the string-bearer is a flat board.

Composite chordophones (32) comprise lutes (321), where the plane of the strings runs parallel with the sound-table, and harps (322), where the plane of the strings runs perpendicular to the sound-table. According to this system, the *lyre is a subdivision of lute (a 'yoke lute'; 321.2) because the strings run perpendicular to the sound-table, though they are attached to a yoke (consisting of two arms and a crossbar) rather than to a pegbox at the end of a neck. The Western lute, guitar, *bouzouki, violin, *rebec, and viol, which have necks, are all types of 'handle lute' (321.3). Suffixes to the class number indicate how the strings of a chordophone are made to sound: with the fingers like a *theorbo (321.322–5), with a plectrum like a *mandolin (321.322–6), or rubbed with a bow like a rebec (321.322–71) or with a wheel like a hurdy-gurdy (321.322–72). The West African *kora was originally classed as a harp-lute (323), but has been reclassed as a *bridge harp, a new subcategory of harp.

Aerophones or wind instruments are divided into free aerophones (41) and wind instruments proper (42). In free aerophones the air is not confined by the instrument; they include instruments with *free reeds (e.g. mouth organs, harmoniums), except for those South-East Asian instruments (e.g. the *sheng) where a free reed is coupled to an air column exactly as double or single *reeds are. Rotating and whirling aerophones (e.g. sirens and bullroarers), and even plosive aerophones (e.g. pop-guns), are also in this category.

In wind instruments proper, the vibrating air is confined within the instrument itself. Edge instruments or flutes (421) are those in which an airstream is directed against an edge. They are subdivided into flutes without ducts (421.1) and *duct flutes (421.2). Flutes without ducts may be end-blown (e.g. empty bottles, *panpipes) or side-blown (e.g. the Western transverse flute). Duct flutes include the recorder, penny whistle, flageolet, and also 'vessel flutes' or *ocarinas. Reedpipes (422) are divided into oboes (422.1) or double-reed aerophones (thus also including the bassoon and the crumhorn), clarinets (422.2) or single-reed aerophones, and free-reed pipes with a coupled air column (e.g. sheng). 423 comprises trumpets and horns, where the airstream passes through the player's vibrating lips (hence the term 'lip-reed').

The Hornbostel–Sachs system avoids such imprecise terms as 'woodwind' and concentrates first on the way sound is produced rather than on materials or manner of playing. All flutes, for example, whether they are made of glass, ivory, ebonite, or metal, or whether they have a duct, are classified as 421. Piano strings are struck with hammers (-4) and harpsichord strings are plucked with a plectrum (-6), but both are classified as box zithers (314). Composite instruments may be classified simply by combining several class numbers separated by a slash (/), and new numbers may be added as instruments are discovered or invented. JMo

intabulation (Ger.: *Intabulierung*; It.: *intavolatura*). An arrangement, usually for keyboard or plucked string instruments (e.g. lute), of an existing polyphonic vocal piece. Normally, all the voices of the original model were retained, though small omissions might occur, and the parts might be differently distributed for the convenience of a single player. In short, intabulations were the medieval and Renaissance equivalents of modern piano arrangements of orchestral scores, except that, in the earlier examples, the highest part was frequently embellished. The earliest surviving keyboard source, the Robertsbridge Codex (*c*.1320), contains intabulations of two motets from the *Roman de Fauvel* which clearly demonstrate the practices that were to become general.

The term 'intabulation' was also commonly applied to any piece written in a particular type of instrumental notation known as *tablature (which used letters or figures). The intabulated arrangements of early music provide valuable evidence for the addition of ornamentation in performance, and also (since the tablature notation tells the string player exactly where on the fret to put the fingers) for the use of accidentals in earlier times (see MUSICA FICTA). AP

intavolatura (It.). **1.** 'Intabulation'. When used to describe late 16th- and 17th-century Italian keyboard pieces, 'intavolatura' implies that the music was printed in 'keyboard score' format, that is, with all parts compressed on to just two staves (*d'intavolatura*), rather than with each part allocated to a separate staff (*partitura*, 'score'). The term also generally indicates that such publications contain compositions originally written for voices but now arranged for instrumental performance.

2. Any collection of solo instrumental music printed in *tablature. AP

Intégrales. Work (1924–5) by Varèse for 11 wind instruments and percussion.

Intendant (Ger.). A term denoting a person who has administrative and often also artistic control over an opera house. Of late, responsibility for artistic matters has come to be shared usually with the theatre's chief conductor. The equivalent term in English is usually General Manager. RP

interference pattern. More or less complex acoustic disturbance caused when more than one sound wave passes through a given space. In the special case of waves at the same frequency, the pattern may be stationary; it is then called a *standing wave. JBo

interlude. Music, usually instrumental, played between the sections of a work. In church music, interludes are often short improvisatory passages played on the organ between the verses of a hymn or psalm. In stage works, particularly operas, interludes are performed between scenes or acts and often serve to further the progress of the drama, as in the four Sea Interludes in Britten's *Peter Grimes* (see also ENTR'ACTE and ACT TUNE). The term is also used as a title of a musical work without the above connotations.

intermède. In the French theatre of the 16th and 17th centuries, music and dance performed between the acts of a play or opera—the French equivalent of the Italian *intermedio. Intermèdes* were spectacular presentations, often on mythological themes, in which, from the early 17th century, ballet was an important element. Although many *intermèdes* were unconnected to the plays and operas to which they were attached, several by Lully are closely related to the main work; his *intermède* for Molière's *La Princesse d'Élide* (1664), for example, concerns the actions of minor characters in the play.

In the 18th century the term was also used to refer to a short one- or two-act comic opera in French. JBe

intermedio (It.). A type of entertainment popular in the 16th and 17th centuries, particularly in Italy; it could involve music, drama, and dance and was performed between the acts of a play. The first known *intermedio* performances took place at the Ferrarese court in the late 15th century. They functioned as a means of distinguishing one act from the next, perhaps setting the scene or indicating the passage of time, and could consist simply of instrumental music performed by players who were not in view of the audience; *intermedi* were later added before and after the play as well. The more popular type of *intermedio*, however, involved singing, acting, and dancing and was usually based on a pastoral or mythological theme. *Intermedi* were not necessarily linked to the play they accompanied, or even to each other, though during the 16th century they tended to display greater unity or closer connection with the play.

Descriptions survive of many of the elaborate and spectacular *intermedi* performed in Florence in the 16th century, but a complete record of the music survives for just two. In 1539, as part of the celebrations for the marriage of Cosimo I de' Medici and Eleonora of Toledo, a five-act comedy, *Il commodo*, was staged with six *intermedi* written by G. B. Strozzi and set to music by Francesco Corteccia. The opening and closing *intermedi*, representing Dawn and Night respectively, were for a solo singer whereas the central ones were for groups of singers and instrumentalists and generally on pastoral themes. In 1589 the wedding of Ferdinando de' Medici and Christine of Lorraine was celebrated with the most lavish and expensive *intermedi* yet, the scale of which completely overshadowed the play, Girolamo Bargagli's *La pellegrina*. The *intermedi* texts, by Giovanni de' Bardi, Ottavio Rinuccini, and Laura Guidiccioni, were set to music by Marenzio and Malvezzi, with contributions also from Peri, Caccini, Cavalieri, Bardi, and others. As well as the texts and music (published in 1591), the designs for the costumes and sets for these spectacular *intermedi* survive. They are linked by a strong thematic unity, and their music embraces a wide variety of styles, from virtuoso solo songs to large-scale polychoral madrigals, each *intermedio* beginning with an instrumental sinfonia.

Intermedi such as these exerted considerable influence on the first operas, which themselves were developed in Florence and involved many of the same musicians and librettists. This is seen particularly in Monteverdi's *Orfeo* (1607), which (unlike the pared-down early Florentine music dramas of Caccini and Peri) includes such elements from the *intermedio* tradition as pastoral, allegorical, and infernal scenes, spectacular stage effects, a rich orchestral accompaniment, and musical forms ranging from solo songs to large-scale choruses that use dance rhythms. *Intermedi* continued to be performed even after opera was no longer a new genre: in the 1670s Stradella wrote some for the performances in Rome of operas by Cavalli, Cesti, and others. The tradition was taken up in 17th-century France by such composers as Charpentier. The French *intermède* tended to include more ballet than the Italian *intermedio*.

See also OPERA.   EW

📖 D. P. WALKER, *Musique des intermèdes de 'La Pellegrina'*, Les Fêtes du mariage de Ferdinand de Médicis et de Christine de Lorraine, Florence, 1589, i (Paris, 1963) · H. M. BROWN, *Sixteenth-Century Instrumentation: The Music for the Florentine Intermedi* (Rome, 1973) · A. M. CUMMINGS, *The Politicized Muse: Music for Medici Festivals, 1512–1537* (Princeton, NJ, 1992)

Intermezzo. Opera in two acts by Richard Strauss to his own libretto (Dresden, 1924).

intermezzo (It., 'in the middle'). 1. The 18th-century term for an *intermedio*.

2. In the first half of the 18th century, a type of entr'acte performed between the acts of a spoken play or *opera seria*. The intermezzo was a development of the Italian 16th- and 17th-century *intermedio* but differed from its predecessor in having a single comic plot, usually presented in two parts, and the same cast of two or three characters. Although the first examples came from Venice (the earliest is thought to be *Frappolone e Florinetta*, 1607, for which the music is lost), the genre was especially popular in Naples, where, in the 1720s, it acquired independence from the *opere serie* and spoken dramas to which it had formerly been attached. Pergolesi's *La serva padrona* of 1733 is a well-known example of the independent, Neapolitan *intermezzo*. After about 1750 the intermezzo evolved further into *opera buffa*. See also OPERA, 6.

3. In the 19th century, a term occasionally used as the title of a movement, usually of a light character, contained within a larger work. Examples can be found in Brahms's Piano Quartet op. 25 and Schumann's *Kreisleriana*. Brahms and Schumann also wrote short, independent piano pieces called Intermezzo.

4. The term acquired a meaning similar to that of *interlude, and sometimes denoted a short orchestral piece inserted into an opera to indicate a lapse of time, as in Mascagni's *Cavalleria rusticana*, or to summarize events, as in the 'Walk to the Paradise Garden' in Delius's *A Village Romeo and Juliet*.   —/JBE

International Inventory of Musical Sources. See RISM.

International Musicological Society (IMS). An organization formed in 1927, as the International Society for Musical Research, to carry on the work of the defunct International Musical Society (a German scholarly organization that flourished from 1899 to 1914). Its most notable publication is the biannual bulletin *Acta musicologica*. The headquarters are in Basle.   JBo

International Society for Contemporary Music (ISCM). An organization that sponsors an annual 'World Music Days' Festival, in one of its national sections, to bring composers together and present performances of recently composed works (up to six can be submitted by each country). It was founded in Salzburg in 1922 by a group that included Bartók, Kodály, Hindemith, Milhaud, and Webern, and its festivals have seen the premieres of many important works. Its member countries (*c*.50) have autonomous chapters that organize concerts, lectures, symposia, and other activities.   JBo

Internet, music on the. See MUSIC ON THE INTERNET.

interpretation. The process by which a performer translates a work from notation into artistically valid sound. Because of the ambiguity inherent in musical notation, a performer must make important decisions about the meaning and realization of aspects of a work which the composer cannot clearly prescribe. These may include discrete choices about dynamics, tempo, phrasing, and the like, or large-scale judgments concerning the articulation of formal divisions, pacing of musical climaxes, and so on. These determinations reflect the performer's understanding of the work, as conditioned by musical knowledge and personality, and result in an interpretation. Whereas every performance of a work is a unique event, since the exact reproduction of all elements of a performance is impossible except through a recording, an interpretation can be repeated. Furthermore, musical works generally allow a variety of interpretations, including some that differ radically, which may nonetheless be equally valid.

The interpretation of a musical work is in many ways analogous to the stage representation of a play. Two actors may declaim a soliloquy from *Hamlet* at different speeds, and with different tones and inflections, yet the text they reproduce is the same. Similarly, musicians may decide on divergent presentations of a work which reflect the meaning each discerns within it, though they use the same set of instructions contained in the score. Interpretation is susceptible to fashion; the degree of licence that may be taken in performing a work in one era may be found unacceptable in another.   BW

   📖 M. KRAUSZ (ed.), *The Interpretation of Music: Philosophical Essays* (Oxford, 1993) · P. KIVY, *Authenticities: Philosophical Reflections on Musical Performance* (Ithaca, NY, and London, 1995)

interrupted cadence. See CADENCE.

interval. The distance in pitch between two notes. Precise measurement of intervals is expressible acoustically in terms of frequency ratios (see ACOUSTICS, 4), but for ordinary purposes the diatonic scale is taken as a convenient yardstick. Table 1 shows examples of the most common intervals.

Each interval is named according to the number of notes of the scale it spans. Thus C–D (above) or C–B (below) is a 2nd (two notes), C–E (above) or C–A (below) is a 3rd (three notes), and so on. Intervals larger than an octave are 'compound' intervals: thus C–D (in the next octave above) or C–B (in the next octave below) may be referred to either as a compound 2nd or, more usually, as a 9th, and so with compound 3rds (10ths), compound 4ths (11ths), and so on.

The intervals of a 4th, 5th, or octave are called 'perfect'; they have a purity of tone and a bareness that makes them quite different from the others. The 'imperfect' intervals—the 2nd, 3rd, 6th, and 7th—may be of two types, according to the number of semitones they span. Thus C–E and C–A, which both occur in the major scale on C, are a major 3rd (four semitones) and a major 6th (nine semitones) respectively, whereas C–E♭ and C–A♭, which both occur in the minor scale on

C, are a minor 3rd (three semitones) and a minor 6th (eight semitones) respectively. By extension, any major interval reduced chromatically by a semitone at either end becomes minor: thus C–D is a major 2nd, and C–D♭ and C♯–D are minor 2nds.

All intervals, perfect or imperfect, major or minor, may also be 'augmented' or 'diminished'. A major or perfect interval increased chromatically by a semitone at either end becomes augmented: thus C–G, a perfect 5th, becomes an augmented 5th in either of the forms C–G♯ or C♭–G, and C–A, a major 6th, becomes an augmented 6th in either of the forms C–A♯ or C♭–A. Similarly, any minor or perfect interval reduced chromatically by a semitone at either end becomes diminished: thus C–G, a perfect 5th, becomes a diminished 5th in either of the forms C–G♭ or C♯–G, and C–A♭, a minor 6th, becomes a diminished 6th in either of the forms C–A♭♭ or C♯–A♭. Very occasionally augmented or diminished intervals are increased or reduced by a further semitone, to become 'double augmented' or 'double diminished'.

It should be noted that, while C–A♭ and C–G♯ are identical intervals on modern keyboard instruments, they none the less have different names: C–A♭ is a minor 6th (six note-names embraced) and C–G♯ an augmented 5th (five note-names). Although on the keyboard G♯ and A♭ are the same note, they are acoustically distinct; such intervals as that between G♯ and A♭ are called *enharmonic.

Intervals may be 'inverted' by reversing the positions of the two notes relative to one another (i.e. if the upper note remains in position and the lower one steps over it to the pitch an octave above its previous position, or if the lower note remains in position and the upper one steps over it to the pitch an octave below its previous position). It will be seen that inverted intervals, except for the unison and octave, change their quality and size on inversion: inverted major intervals become minor, minor become major, augmented become diminished, and diminished become augmented; and the size of an interval plus the size of its inversion always total nine, an inverted 4th becoming a 5th, a 6th becoming a 3rd, and so on.

In the context of modal or tonal composition, some intervals (3rds, 6ths, and all perfect intervals) are consonant, and others (2nds, 7ths, and all augmented or diminished intervals) are dissonant (see CONSONANCE AND DISSONANCE). Although these distinctions have an acoustical basis, they have been called into question by many composers since 1900, for whom Schoenberg's 'emancipation of the dissonance' has been of central importance. In post-tonal music, degrees of harmonic stability and instability do not normally depend on regarding single intervals as either consonant or

TABLE 1

Intervals from middle C

	DIMINISHED	MINOR	MAJOR	PERFECT	AUGMENTED
UNISON					
2nd					
3rd					
4th					
5th					
6th					
7th					
OCTAVE					

dissonant. In addition, much 20th-century music, electroacoustic as well as for conventional voices or instruments, has made use of non-standard intervals—three-quarter-tones, quarter-tones, and even smaller intervallic distances, thus enriching the range of materials available to the composer.   PS/JN/AW

In the Steppes of Central Asia (*V sredney Azii*; 'In Central Asia'). 'Orchestral picture' by Borodin, composed in 1880 to accompany a *tableau vivant* at an exhibition marking Alexander II's silver jubilee; it represents the approach and passing of a caravan.

Intimate Letters (*Listy důvěrné*). Subtitle of Janáček's String Quartet no. 2, composed in 28 days in 1928; it is autobiographical, the letters concerned being those he wrote to Kamila Stösslová between 1917 and 1928.

Intolleranza 1960 ('Intolerance 1960'). Opera in two parts by Nono, after an idea by Angelo Maria Ripellino,

to texts by Ripellino, Henri Alleg, Bertolt Brecht, Aimé Césaire, Paul Éluard, Vladimir Mayakovsky, Julius Fucik, and Jean-Paul Sartre, assembled by the composer (Venice, 1961); because of its use of contemporary references, Nono revised it for a performance in 1974, changing its name to *Intolleranza 1970*.

intonation. 1. The opening phrase of a plainchant melody, perhaps so called because it was sung by the priest or cantor alone, giving the pitch and, in the psalms, the 'tone' (see TONUS, 3) of what was to follow.

2. The term used for identifying the state of a performer's tuning. It is thus possible to distinguish between 'good' and 'poor' intonation.

intonazione [intonatione] (It., 'intonation'). In the works of Andrea and Giovanni Gabrieli, the name given to a type of short organ piece used as an introduction to a vocal item in the church service. It was designed to establish the pitch and mode of the following work; the left hand usually played chords and the right-hand scalar passages.   —/JBE

intoning [monotoning]. Singing on one note, as practised by the clergy in parts of the Roman, Anglican, and other liturgies. See also INTONATION, 1.

Intrada (Ger., from Sp. *entrada*, 'entrance', 'beginning'). An instrumental piece played as a prelude to an occasion, the entrance of a character on stage, or to introduce choral items in the church service. In Spain the term was associated with the 'entries' of different polyphonic voices. In 17th-century Germany an *Intrada* was often included in the orchestral suite.   —/JBE

introduction (Ger.: *Einleitung, Eingang*; It.: *introduzione*). Any musical material that precedes the main structural substance of a composition. Introductions are usually slow and range from a single chord to a lengthy passage that develops its own theme. In sonata-form movements of the late 18th and early 19th centuries, introductions often precede the exposition, as for example in Mozart's symphonies nos. 38 and 39 and Beethoven's Seventh Symphony. Composers have sometimes used the designation 'introduction' for a slow section of a work—Beethoven, for instance, labelled the slow movement of his 'Waldstein' Sonata 'Introduzione'.   JBE

Introduction and Allegro. Elgar's op. 47 (1905) for string quartet and string orchestra.

introit. 1. A chant accompanying the entrance of the clergy in Christian worship. The term most frequently refers to the initial chant of the Roman *Mass, normally consisting of an antiphon with one verse (usually of a psalm) and the *Gloria Patri* (see DOXOLOGY) in the order: antiphon–verse–antiphon–*Gloria Patri*–antiphon. The introit is a part of the Proper of the Mass, and several Sundays are named after the first word of their introit. The introit (*eisodikon*) is no longer functional at Divine Liturgies of the Byzantine rite celebrated only by a priest, who leaves and re-enters the sanctuary in a symbolic 'Little Entrance'.   —/ALı

2. An organ piece replacing all or part of the sung introit of the Mass.

invariance. The property of remaining the same after some operation has been completed; the term is normally used in connection with atonal music. For instance, the set C–E–A♭ may be said to be invariant in content under transposition by a major 3rd, since such transposition results in the set E–G♯(A♭)–C.   PG

invention (It.: *inventione, invenzione*). A name sometimes given to a short, instrumental piece with no specified musical characteristics but which displays some kind of novelty; in the 20th century the term was occasionally applied to works of a contrapuntal nature (e.g. by Martinů and Blacher). The word appears in the title of Janequin's first madrigal book (1555) and also occurs in many Italian works from the 17th and 18th centuries.

J. S. Bach used the term for a set of 15 short, two-part keyboard pieces in his *Clavier-Büchlein* for his son Wilhelm Friedemann (1720). The 15 three-part pieces in the same book are now known as 'three-part inventions', though Bach himself called them either 'sinfonias' or 'fantasias'. In a preface added later (1723) Bach states that the inventions provide instruction in 'learning to play distinctly in two parts ... and in addition, not only of arriving at good original ideas [*inventiones*], but also of developing them satisfactorily; and most of all of acquiring a cantabile style of playing and at the same time of receiving a strong foretaste of composition'. Each invention is highly contrapuntal and most are imitative in texture, developing a short melodic motif.   —/JBE

inversion. 1. Chords. According to theories of harmony that became prominent during the 18th and 19th centuries, chord construction was not simply a matter of particular intervals arranged in ascending order, but of particular intervals placed above a governing or *fundamental bass. This theory, associated principally with Rameau (*Traité de l'harmonie*, 1722), contended that the fundamental bass note, or *root, does not simply change when, for example, a *triad changes in vertical presentation from C–E–G to E–G–C. Rather, the functions of the notes in the chord that obtain when its fundamental bass note is the actual bass—the so-called *root-position chord (root, 3rd, 5th)—are retained even though the notes change position in the chord when read upwards. So, with E–G–C the bass (lowest) note remains the 3rd of the chord, and the position of the root is changed. Strictly speaking, this procedure is one of permutation in musical space, but in a simple sense, best experienced at the keyboard, shifting the root from bottom to top inverts the chord, turning it upside down. This, a first inversion (E–G–C), can in turn be inverted to give a second inversion (G–C–E). For chords with four different notes (e.g. secondary or dominant 7ths) a *third inversion is possible. Chordal inversion has primary relevance to the harmonic constructions of tonal music, with its individually differentiated scale degrees and hierarchical distinctions between consonance and dissonance.   AW

2. Intervals. Inversion can be applied to intervals by reversing the positions of the two notes: the upper note remains and the lower note moves to the pitch an

octave above its original position, or the lower note remains and the upper one moves to the pitch an octave below its original position. This is not literal inversion (see 4 below) but a complementation within the octave, and is the basis of *invertible counterpoint. See also INTERVAL.

3. Melodies. An inverted melody follows the shape of the original in mirror image; where the original melody rises, the inversion descends, and vice versa. In tonal music the intervals between the successive pitches are not literally replicated (see 4 below) but become the equivalents within the diatonic scale. For example, the melody F–G–E–F would become F–E–G–F. Melodic inversion is a common feature of imitative forms, particularly fugue. There are numerous examples in J. S. Bach's '48' and The Art of Fugue.

4. 12-note rows. Inversion of a row or series of notes is fundamental to *twelve-note, or serial, music (see SERIALISM). Such inversions are literal: an ascending major 3rd becomes a descending major 3rd, a descending minor 2nd becomes an ascending minor 2nd, and so on. For example the inversion of F–G–E–F is F–E♭–G♭–F. In serial music any note in the series may occur at any octave register, so the inversion of a row may not necessarily be an inversion of its melodic contour.   AL

inverted cadence. See CADENCE.

inverted interval. See INTERVAL.

inverted mordent. A *mordent that includes the upper rather than the lower auxiliary note.

invertible counterpoint. A technique of contrapuntal writing that allows the voices to change places (the higher becoming the lower, and vice versa) and still make musical sense.

Invisible City of Kitezh and the Maiden Fevroniya, The Legend of the. See LEGEND OF THE INVISIBLE CITY OF KITEZH AND THE MAIDEN FEVRONIYA.

Invitation to the Dance. See AUFFORDERUNG ZUM TANZ.

invitatory (Lat.: *invitatorium*). In the Divine Office of the Roman and monastic rites, the opening chant of Matins, consisting of the psalm *Venite* (Psalm 95 in the English numbering and Hebrew Old Testament, 94 in the Vulgate and Greek Old Testament) and its corresponding antiphon. Since the Second Vatican Council, Matins in the Roman rite has become the Office of Readings, and the invitatory can now open either this or Lauds (Morning Prayer), and one of four psalms may be used. In the Anglican liturgy and the Lutheran and Methodist Churches the *Venite* has traditionally occupied an equivalent position.

Iolanta ('Iolanthe'). Opera in one act by Tchaikovsky after Henrik Hertz's play *Kong Renés Datter* ('King René's Daughter'), translated from the Danish by Fyodor Miller, adapted for Moscow by Vladimir Rafailovich Zotov (St Petersburg, 1892).

Iolanthe (*Iolanthe, or The Peer and the Peri*). Operetta in two acts by Sullivan to a libretto by W. S. Gilbert (London, 1882).

Ionian mode. The name given by Heinrich Glarean (in his treatise *Dodecachordon*) to the authentic mode on C; it has the same distribution of tones and semitones as the major scale. See MODE, 2.

Ionisation ('Ionization'). Work (1929–31) by Varèse for 13 percussion instruments.

Iphigénie en Aulide ('Iphigenia in Aulis'). Opera in three acts by Gluck to a libretto by Marie François Louis Gand Leblanc Roullet after Jean Racine's *Iphigénie en Aulide*, itself based on Euripides (Paris, 1774).

Iphigénie en Tauride ('Iphigenia in Tauris'). Opera in four acts by Gluck to a libretto by Nicolas-François Guillard after Guymond de la Touche's *Iphigénie en Tauride*, itself based on Euripides (Paris, 1779). Piccinni wrote an opera on the same subject (Paris, 1781).

Ippolitov-Ivanov, Mikhail Mikhaylovich (*b* Gatchina, 7/19 Nov. 1859; *d* Moscow, 28 Jan. 1935). Russian composer and conductor. He was a pupil of Rimsky-Korsakov at the St Petersburg Conservatory, graduating in 1882. From 1882 to 1893 he lived in Tbilisi, directing the local division of the Russian Music Society and teaching (among his students were Zakharia Paliashvili and Dimitri Arakishvili). From 1893 he taught at the Moscow Conservatory, of which he was director from 1905 to 1922, and he simultaneously worked as an opera conductor (from 1899 to 1906 with the Mamontov and Zimin private opera companies, and from 1925 to his death at the Bol'shoy). His music is heavily influenced by The Five, especially by the orientalist aspect of their style, and also, to a lesser extent, by Tchaikovsky. He composed several operas, including the three missing acts for Musorgsky's *Marriage* (1931), chamber ensembles, a symphony, and many programmatic orchestral works on oriental themes—the *Kavkazskiye eskizï* ('Caucasian Sketches', 1894) remain in the repertory. His interest in Georgian music is reflected in his book *Gruzinskaya narodnaya* *pesnya i eyo sovremennoye sostoyaniye* ('Georgian Folksong and its Present State', Moscow, 1895).

PS/MF-W

Iradier [Yradier], **Sebastián** (*b* Sauciego, Álava, 20 Jan. 1809; *d* Vitoria, 6 Dec. 1865). Spanish composer. After working in Madrid, Paris (as singing teacher to the Empress Eugénie), and Cuba, he ended his career as professor of singing at the Madrid Conservatory. His chief claim to fame was as the composer of the song *El arreglito*, which Bizet adapted as the Habanera in Act I of *Carmen*, thinking it was a genuine folksong.

WT/CW

IRCAM. See Institut de Recherche et de Coordination Acoustique/Musique.

Ireland. The history of music in Ireland has been profoundly affected by invasion and colonization, and a long-standing oral tradition has led to a lack of documentary evidence. After the adoption of Christianity in the 5th century a strong monastic culture developed, but few written records of the music of the Celtic Church survive. Equally, there is no trace of the music sung at court to harp accompaniment. The 12th-century Anglo-Norman invasion brought English culture and liturgy to Ireland, and Gaelic traditions faded from the cities that had developed after the earlier Viking invasions.

Much of the country was now under control of the English crown. In Dublin a choir school was founded at St Patrick's Cathedral in 1423, and there is record of an organist appointed there in 1509; the Sarum rite was in use, and English church music performed. The Reformation was imposed on, rather than accepted by, Ireland. As in England and Scotland the monasteries were suppressed, and the churches and cathedrals were deserted by all but a fraction of the population. The resources for fine musical performance were left in the hands of the politically dominant culture, and English musicians and music were imported for the cathedrals. With the defeat of the last area of Irish resistance, in Ulster in 1603, Gaelic patronage of secular music disappeared.

Much of the culture of Irish traditional music has its origins in this period. It was only in Irish-speaking areas, in the west of the country, that Gaelic songs survived; these are generally lyrical, and few examples of work song are found. Importation of songs in English pre-dates the 17th century, but many English and Scottish songs circulated from this point on, while elements of Gaelic poetry and song survived in new Irish songs to English words. Isolated Irish folk tunes were first published in 17th-century English collections, and the earliest purely Irish collection dates from 1726;

during the 18th century the tunes became increasingly current, and in the early part of the 19th century were popularized through the work of the poet Thomas Moore, who wrote new words to many melodies collected by Edward Bunting (1773–1843). Subsequent collections appeared by George Petrie (*The Ancient Music of Ireland*, 1853–5) and Patrick Joyce (1873).

The country's national emblem, the harp, saw a decline after the disappearance of Gaelic patronage: the Belfast Harp Festival of 1792, which provided Bunting with much of his material, was a conscious effort to revive the instrument. The other instruments of traditional music are the bellows-blown *uilleann* pipes (a bagpipe), the bodhrán (a frame drum), and the fiddle, supplemented by accordion, melodeon, flutes, and whistles; the postwar upsurge in folk music has seen the adoption of many other instruments.

In the stable political circumstances of the 18th century, Dublin, as the capital city and seat of government, was a considerable centre of musical culture generally. Such societies as the Academy of Music (1757) were established, and composers and performers from England paid lengthy visits; Handel was there from November 1741 to August 1742, and *Messiah* had its first performance during his visit. Foreign composers including Geminiani settled in the city, and Dublin appears to have been one of the musical centres of Europe. This period came to an end with the Union of 1801 and the consequent disappearance of the city's residential importance as the seat of parliament.

In the 19th century, the chief composers of Irish and Anglo-Irish origin mainly lived and worked abroad, Field, Balfe, and Wallace being the most prominent; Stanford studied at the Royal Irish Academy of Music (founded 1848) before leaving for England. Dublin was a favoured destination for touring Italian opera companies in the mid-century, and a cult of Italian opera flourished for several decades. Two festivals established in 1897, Feis Ceoil and Oireachtas, are still in existence.

The National University of Ireland was established in 1908, with provision for music at degree level; its constituent colleges in Cork and Dublin, together with the older Trinity College, Dublin, produced many of the first generation of Irish composers of the Free State, including Ó Riada. An active younger generation of composers born in the 1950s includes such figures as Gerald Barry and Raymond Deane, and a further generation is represented by Deirdre Gribbin (*b* 1967).

The national broadcasting company, RTE (Radio Telefís Éireann), supports two orchestras and a chamber choir and is increasingly active in commissioning new work. The Wexford Festival, established in 1951, is a major event in the international opera calendar. Dublin is home to two opera companies, Opera

Ireland and the touring Opera Theatre Company, and to the Contemporary Music Centre founded in 1986 by the Arts Council.

The first professional orchestra in Northern Ireland, the BBC Northern Ireland Orchestra (founded 1924), was amalgamated in 1981 with the chamber-sized Ulster Orchestra (founded in 1966 to replace the City of Belfast Orchestra) to form a full symphony orchestra, which retains the name Ulster Orchestra. With the building of the Waterfront Hall in 1997 it acquired a concert hall seating 2500. Both the University of Ulster and Queen's University, Belfast, have attracted students wishing to specialize in composition with degree courses focusing on analysis and electronic music. Queen's University organizes an annual three-week festival (established 1964) embracing all genres, as well as smaller festivals devoted to early and to contemporary music. PS/KC

📖 C. ACTON, *Irish Music and Musicians* (Dublin, 1978) · B. BOYDELL (ed.), *Four Centuries of Music in Ireland* (London, 1979) · G. GILLAN and H. WHITE (eds.), *Music and Irish Cultural History* (Blackrock, 1995) · H. WHITE, *The Keeper's Recital: Music and Cultural History in Ireland, 1770–1970* (Cork, 1998)

Ireland, John (Nicholson) (*b* Bowdon, Cheshire, 13 Aug. 1879; *d* Rock Mill, Washington, Sussex, 12 June 1962). English composer. At the RCM (1893–1901) he studied composition with Stanford and the piano with Frederick Cliffe. He was organist of St Luke's, Chelsea (1904–26), and taught at the RCM, numbering among his pupils Moeran, Alan Bush, Searle, and Britten. His most important early compositions were chamber works: the *Phantasie Trio* (1906) and the prizewinning Violin Sonata no. 1 (1908–9), though it was with the striking Violin Sonata no. 2 (1917), championed by its first executant, Albert Sammons, that Ireland's name rose to fame. Other chamber works—the Cello Sonata (1923) and *Fantasy-Sonata* for clarinet and piano (1943)—are of similar stature.

Ireland's orchestral output is slender but no less distinguished. The prelude *The Forgotten Rite* (1913) shows an awareness of European Expressionism in its angular thematic material and advanced harmonic language. Its preoccupation with myth and pagan mysticism (inspired by the literary works of Arthur Machen) also found voice in the symphonic rhapsody *Mai-Dun* (1920–1) and the *Legend* for piano and orchestra (1933). Ireland showed a flair for orchestral colour in *A London Overture* (1936), the overture *Satyricon* (1946), and the music for the film *The Overlanders* (1946–7), but his most successful and frequently played large-scale work is the Piano Concerto (1930), which fuses most convincingly the Brahmsian rigour of his youth (filtered through Stanford) with the iridescent, bitter-sweet palette of his later development.

His most intimate music is to be found in his songs and solo piano works which, at their best, are some of the finest utterances by any English composer of the period. Among his best piano pieces are the Debussy-inspired *Decorations* (1912), the two miniatures *For Remembrance* and *Amberley Wild Brooks* (1921), the Sonatina (1926–7), and *Sarnia* (1940–1), while some of his finest songs can be found in the Housman cycle *The Land of Lost Content* (1920–1), the *Five Poems by Thomas Hardy* (1926), and *Songs Sacred and Profane* (1929–31). Ireland's retirement to Guernsey was truncated by World War II and the Nazi invasion of the Channel Islands in June 1940. After the war he returned to his home in Chelsea but spent his time increasingly in Sussex, where he eventually settled in 1953. JDᴵ

📖 M. V. SEARLE, *John Ireland: The Man and his Music* (Tunbridge Wells, 1979) · F. RICHARDS, *The Music of John Ireland* (London, 2000)

Iribarren, Juan Francés de. See FRANCÉS DE IRIBARREN, JUAN.

Iris. Opera in three acts by Mascagni to a libretto by Luigi Illica (Rome, 1898).

Irish Symphony. Sullivan's Symphony in E major (1864). It is also the subtitle of Stanford's Symphony no. 3 in F minor (1887) and the title of a symphony by Harty (1904).

Isaac, Heinrich [Henricus] (*b* Flanders, *c.*1450; *d* Florence, 26 March 1517). Flemish composer. Beyond the fact that he was writing music in the mid-1470s, almost nothing is known about him until July 1485, when he became one of the singers at the baptistry of S. Giovanni in Florence. The position brought him into the orbit of the Medici, whose patronage he enjoyed for the next eight years. By November 1496 he had moved into the service of Emperor Maximilian I, as court composer and a member of the chapel choir. In 1502 he was considered for a post at the Este court of Ferrara, but the position was given instead to Josquin des Prez. Between 1505 and 1508 Isaac was resident in Konstanz, where the cathedral chapter commissioned him to write a cycle of liturgical works. He returned to Florence for his last years, possibly acting as a diplomat to Maximilian.

Isaac was one of the most prolific and influential composers of his time, and is unusual for having been employed principally for his compositional skills rather than as a performer. 36 masses by him survive, based variously on secular material—songs, dances, and mottoes—or on plainchant; in many of the latter settings, Isaac set only portions of the liturgical texts to music, these to be sung in alternation with either chant or organ music. His massive cycle of mass Propers, built round plainchant melodies, was composed partly in response to the Konstanz commission, partly for use by the imperial chapel choir. His large output of motets and secular works is extremely varied, and reflects his international career and outlook. Isaac's best-known work is also one of his shortest and simplest, the lied *Innsbruck, ich muss dich lassen.*   JM

   📖 W. SALMEN and R. GSTREIN (eds.), *Heinrich Isaac and Paul Hofhaimer im Umfeld von Kaiser Maximilian I.* (Innsbruck, 1997)

ISCM. See INTERNATIONAL SOCIETY FOR CONTEMPORARY MUSIC.

Islamey. 'Oriental fantasy' for piano by Balakirev, composed in 1870 and revised in 1902. Lyapunov made an orchestral version of it.

Isle of the Dead, The (*Ostrov myortvïkh*). Symphonic poem, op. 29 (1909), by Rakhmaninov, inspired by Arnold Böcklin's painting *Insel der Toten.*

ISM. See INCORPORATED SOCIETY OF MUSICIANS.

Isola disabitata, L' ('The Deserted Island'). Opera in two acts by Haydn to a libretto by Pietro Metastasio (Eszterháza, 1779).

isomelic (from Gk. *isos*, 'equal', *melōidiā*, 'melody'). A term referring to repeated uses of the same pitch contour, though with variations in rhythm. The technique was much used by English and continental composers (e.g. Walter Frye, Johannes Ciconia, Dufay) in the 15th century.

isometric (from Gk. *isos*, 'equal', *metron*, 'measure'). A term used to describe either works that have one rhythm simultaneously in all voices (i.e. homorhythm) or works that have the same time signature throughout.

isorhythm (from Gk. *isos*, 'equal', *rhythmos*, 'rhythm'). A modern term for the technique of using a repeated rhythmic and melodic pattern as a main structural component. In the 13th century the tenor part of a motet would frequently be organized according to a short repeated rhythmic pattern, derived from the *ordines* of the rhythmic modes (see NOTATION, 2). These patterns increased in length as the century progressed. The melody in the tenor part was also often repeated, but not always to synchronize with the rhythmic repeat. The term *color* was often used for the melodic pattern and *talea* for the rhythmic pattern. The two patterns were not necessarily the same length, however, so successive statements of the *talea* may occur with different pitches.

Two of the most important composers of isorhythmic motets in the 14th century were Philippe de Vitry and Machaut. Their compositions display to good effect some of the variations and extensions possible with isorhythm. One of the most common was the repetition of the rhythm pattern not in the same note-values but in proportional diminution: for example, the original values could be halved or reduced by a third. Moreover, the technique was not restricted to the tenor part: in some motets it was extended to upper voices, particularly for passages in *hocket.

Towards the end of the 14th century the use of isorhythm in all voices ('panisorhythm') was developed, especially by English composers; it was also used by Machaut in some of his motets, and by Ciconia, Dunstaple, and Dufay. Isorhythmic structuring is not commonly found in music of the tonal era (*c*.1700–1900). It has however been revived, as a means of generating substantial musical paragraphs, by several important post-tonal composers including Messiaen and Maxwell Davies.

   📖 U. GÜNTHER, 'The 14th-century motet and its development', *Musica disciplina*, 12 (1958), 27–58 · D. LEECH-WILKINSON, *Compositional Procedure in the Four-Part Isorhythmic Works of Philippe de Vitry and his Contemporaries* (New York, 1989)

Isouard, Nicolas [Nicolò de Malte] (*b* Valletta, 18 May 1773; *d* Paris, 23 March 1818). French composer. He studied in Paris, Malta, Palermo, and Naples; his first opera, *L'avviso ai maritati* ('Warning to Married Couples'), was written for Florence in 1794. He was then appointed organist to the Order of St John of Malta, composing serious and comic Italian operas until the French invasion in 1798. In 1799 Isouard arrived in Paris, where he collaborated on two *opéras comiques* and reworked two of his earlier operas before achieving success with *Michel-Ange* (1802). Thereafter his popularity continued with a stream of works for the Opéra-Comique, including the fairy-tale opera *Cendrillon* ('Cinderella', 1810) and *Joconde* (1814), which confirmed his international reputation. He also composed masses, motets, cantatas, duets, and songs, but his reputation is founded on his contribution to the genre of *opéra comique* and the Italian influence he brought to French music.   SH

Israel in Egypt. Oratorio (1739) by Handel to a text probably compiled by the composer.

istesso (It.). 'Same'; *l'istesso tempo*, 'the same tempo' as before. See also STESSO, STESSA.

Italiana in Algeri, L' ('The Italian Girl in Algiers'). Opera in two acts by Rossini to a libretto substantially derived from Angelo Anelli's libretto for Luigi Mosca's *L'italiana in Algeri* (1808) (Venice, 1813).

Italian Caprice. Orchestral work, op. 45 (1880), by Tchaikovsky, often known as the *Capriccio italien*.

Italian Concerto. Work for harpsichord, BWV971, by J. S. Bach, published with the Ouverture in the French Style BWV831 to form the second part of the *Clavier-Übung* (1735). Bach intended to highlight the contrast between the two national styles: the concerto is in three movements like the Italian concerto grosso and imitates tutti–solo contrasts and colourful orchestral effects.

Italian Girl in Algiers, The. See ITALIANA IN ALGERI, L'.

Italian overture. See OVERTURE, 1.

Italian sixth chord. An *augmented 6th chord.

Italian Symphony. Mendelssohn's Symphony no. 4 in A major, which he began during a trip to Italy in 1830–1 and completed in 1833, subsequently revising it several times; it contains allusions to Italian folk music, notably in the finale, a 'Saltarello'.

Italienische Serenade ('Italian Serenade'). Work for string quartet (1887) by Wolf; it was arranged for orchestra in 1892 and by Reger for piano duet.

Italienisches Liederbuch ('Italian Songbook'). Collection of 46 songs for voice and piano by Wolf, settings of German translations by Paul Heyse of anonymous Italian poems; they were published in two volumes (1892, 1896). Some were later orchestrated by Wolf, others by Reger.

Italy 1. Introduction; 2. To *c.*1500; 3. 1500–1640; 4. From 1640 to the Napoleonic invasion; 5. The Napoleonic invasion to World War I; 6. Since 1914

1. Introduction

Like Germany, Italy as a nation was born in the 19th century from a number of more or less small states, but, unlike Germany, Italy has always been a geographical unit. Surrounded by the Mediterranean on three sides and the Alps on the fourth, it seems a natural division of Europe; it was first united by Rome in the 3rd century BC. However, Italy's very length and diversity, the waves of invasion, and different political and cultural experiences of the various regions after the fall of the Roman Empire have resulted in a strong sense of regionalism, with an attendant risk of parochialism (*campanilismo*). Differences in prosperity, culture, and politics, most notably between the south and north, continue to dog the republic. A tradition of family enterprise and individualism has, however, benefited

music in producing players, singers, composers, and instrument makers of the highest rank, and the country has one of the richest of musical traditions.

2. To *c.*1500

We know little about the earliest music of the Christian Church, but by the second half of the 4th century the importance of Rome as a liturgical centre meant that there was a song school—the original Schola Cantorum—near St John Lateran (the seat of the Bishop of Rome, i.e. the Pope). The aural tradition of Christian chant is, according to convention, said to have been put in order during the reign of Pope Gregory (590–604), but the unifying trend this represents is now thought to have been instituted under the Carolingian kings in the 8th and 9th centuries.

Separate traditions existed and survived in other parts of Italy, most enduringly in and around Milan, where St Ambrose, Bishop of Milan (374–97), is said to have encouraged the antiphonal singing of hymns and psalms to fortify the morale of Christians under siege from the forces of the Empress Justina in the 4th century. Also in northern Italy, an independent rite was practised at Aquileia, seat of the most important patriarchate outside Rome, from the 7th century until its abolition in 1751. In the south, the Beneventan rite (so named after the location of its most important manuscripts, Benevento, in the present-day province of Campania) flourished at the Benedictine monastery of Monte Cassino. The different traditions also varied in the notation used, until the adoption of that of Guido of Arezzo (see NOTATION, 1); there are hints that some form of polyphony was in use from the 11th century.

Information about secular music is sketchy. Some *jongleur* songs survive from the 12th century, and troubadour music was well known during the 13th. Monophonic dance-songs known as *ballate were also popular at this time, as was their religious counterpart, the responsorial *laude sung by the lay brothers of the Franciscan communities and the flagellant confraternities in the religious fervour of the later 13th century. Manuscripts have survived of 14th-century secular polyphonic music, practised at the northern courts of the Scaligeri in Verona, and the Visconti in Milan, and elsewhere; these contain lively pieces called 'madrigals', typically Italian in their demand for virtuosity (see MADRIGAL, 2) by such composers as Gherardello da Firenze, Giovanni da Cascia, and Jacopo da Bologna, the outstanding figure of the day, to whom the treatise *L'arte del biscanto* is attributed. Other forms are the *caccia, originally a madrigal using canon whose texts describe lively, outdoor scenes, particularly hunting, and the polyphonic *ballata* which, towards the end of the century, began to replace the madrigal in popularity.

The style of the French *Ars Nova composers began to affect Italy only in the mid-14th century. The great Italian master of the second half of the century, Francesco Landini, used French notation and even very occasionally *isorhythm, but he never adopted the complexities of the French, and Italian Ars Nova remained independent of contemporary French styles, though *subtilitas* was used latterly (see ARS SUBTILIOR), and French models were followed in the period of the Great Schism (1378–1417).

After this period, whose richness of activity is perhaps erroneously suggested by the survival of manuscripts, there is a significant lack of source material which makes 15th-century Italy seem empty of native genius. Certainly there was an oral tradition of singing various kinds of song to the lute or viol, and Leonardo Giustiniani, a Venetian nobleman, had a genre of such songs, typical of the newly prevalent humanistic outlook, named after him. There were also players of lutes and keyboard who were favourites at the various courts. Even so, music came to be increasingly directed by foreigners. The return of the popes to Rome after their exile in Avignon in the second decade of the century probably encouraged a new internationalism, as Dufay's career in Rome and his relations with Florence, Ferrara, and Rimini show.

The *cappella* set up in Naples by Alfonso I of Aragon was imitated by other noble houses, notably the Sforza in Milan and the Este in Ferrara; the Medici encouraged music in Florentine churches, but for them to have established a *cappella* would have offended the sensibilities of republican Florence. Alfonso's employment of a northerner, Johannes Tinctoris, in his chapel was similarly imitated by these families, and Dufay and Josquin were active in Milan and Isaac in Florence, thus encouraging the spread of the kind of polyphony developed in the Low Countries. If these composers had little influence on the native art of song, they certainly had a great effect on other areas of Italian musical life.

3. 1500–1640

By 1500 a new pattern of musical institution was established in Italy. Although in Rome and the Papal States a number of churches had excellent choirs directed by a (frequently foreign) *maestro di cappella*, a transfer of patronage had already taken place. Princes and their families of the wealthy northern courts had been affected by the new humanistic education (see RENAISSANCE, THE), and they vied with each other to find composers, players, and singers of quality not so much to direct the music of their chapels as to be part of

their retinue. The musical establishment of the Este family was lively throughout the century until the lack of a male heir caused Ferrara to be absorbed into the Papal States in 1597. The marriage of Isabella d'Este to Francesco II Gonzaga in 1490 stimulated a similar enthusiasm at Mantua, though here it was more intermittent. It was the Mantuan musicians Cara and Tromboncino who brought new sophistication to native song, in the form of the *frottola. In addition to this and the similarly light form of the *strambotto*, more literary texts, such as those by Petrarch, were set for voice and lute.

Venice followed the prevailing trend for employing northern European musicians when Willaert was appointed *maestro di cappella* at St Mark's in 1527. The city's importance for music had begun earlier, when the first music-printing house of any size was set up there in 1498 by *Petrucci, who for the next 20 years printed mainly secular music in some quantity. In addition to many French chansons, his collections included a considerable number of frottolas (their printing can be said to reveal the repertory of native Italian song of the late 15th century). By the mid-century Venice's printing trade was the most important in Italy.

Patronage and printing between them turned the country into the centre of European music for the rest of the 16th century. The nobility followed the model of the perfect courtier expressed in Baldassare Castiglione's *Il libro del cortegiano* (1528), and learnt to play instruments and sing their part in the madrigals that flourished from the 1530s. Moreover, since the humanistic nobles began to meet in academies to discuss the philosophical ideas of the Ancient Greeks, musicians were led to examine whether Greek music (or a modern equivalent) could be recreated. Thus the madrigal acquired more complex and subtle idioms, and this in turn encouraged virtuoso singing, resulting in the setting up of professional ensembles; the most famous of these was the *concerto delle dame* at Ferrara from the 1580s, a group of women who sang elaborately ornamented music at regular court concerts. In addition, new, lighter genres together with narrative madrigal comedies arose. While in Venice the trend in sacred music was towards sumptuous sound and polychoral writing (*cori spezzati), in Rome, anticipating the thrust of the deliberations of the *Council of Trent (concluded 1563), and its demands that the words of the Mass should be heard clearly, a style of polyphony freed from complexity was perfected by Palestrina and Victoria.

Instrument-making also flourished. Italian harpsichords by such makers as Giovanni Baffo in Venice were light in weight and bright in tone. Lutes were made at Bologna, Venice, Padua, and Rome, and the

Amati family was making string instruments at Cremona at least from the 1560s; and in 1568 Gasparo da Salò described himself as 'maestro di violini'.

A confluence of concern with word-setting in the vernacular, the discussions held between approximately 1573 and 1587 in the Florentine *camerata of Count Bardi on the role of music in ancient Greek tragedy, and the fashion for brilliant courtly entertainments in the closing decades of the 16th century (*intermedi* in which songs, madrigals, and instrumental music were performed by large forces) led to the creation of the *stile rappresentativo*, or recitative, of Peri's pastorals *Dafne* and *Euridice* (1600), the first opera. The vocal style was essentially the same as set out by Caccini in his own *Euridice* and *Le nuove musiche* of 1602, whereby words were naturally declaimed with light accompaniments notated chord by chord in the system known today as 'figured bass' (see CONTINUO). Opera was taken up by Monteverdi in Mantua (*Orfeo*, 1607) and in Rome, under the auspices of the Barberini family; that working practices were soon established is clear from the directions in the anonymous manual of opera production *Il corago*, written some time before 1637, the year the first public opera house opened in Venice, a city which became the leading operatic centre of the next half-century.

4. From 1640 to the Napoleonic invasion

The popularity of opera was so great that its composition and performance became the most financially rewarding activity for musicians. Such composers as Cavalli and Legrenzi used their church appointments virtually as sinecures from which to launch their theatrical ventures. Other dramatic, but generally unstaged genres were the *cantata and serenata, and the sacred equivalent of opera, oratorio, given in Lent when theatres were closed. The *stile concertato* traceable back to Giovanni Gabrieli and Monteverdi (*Vespro della Beata Vergine*, 1610), with its vivid differentiation between the constituent elements of a piece, lines, instruments, or sonic space, dominated both vocal and instrumental music. In the latter, the concertato style and the move towards the warmer and more resonant sound of the violin resulted in the works of Arcangelo Corelli, and the Venetian school of concerto writing, led by Vivaldi.

The training of musicians was undertaken within professional musical families, in the conservatories in Naples and Palermo, or at the chapels of the leading cathedrals. The Venetian Ospedali, orphanages for girls where music was taught to the young charges, did not produce professional musicians. Many composers, such as Scarlatti and Tartini, taught privately. Lombardy had a high reputation for instrumental teaching, Bologna

for singing. Because of this training, Italian composers and performers virtually dominated Europe, from Dublin to St Petersburg. Few Italian musicians of real quality did not travel abroad. The result was that Italy was considered the musical centre *par excellence*, as the diaries of those who undertook the Grand Tour show, and this remained the case into the early 19th century.

In the public sphere, opera experienced a continuous development, from the time of the reforms introduced by Apostolo Zeno (significantly, a librettist and not a composer) and perfected by Pietro Metastasio, to the end of the 18th century. There were two basic genres: *opera seria*, from which all the comic characters of Venetian opera had been expunged, and *opera buffa*, derived from comedies in Neapolitan, translated into Italian and exported throughout the peninsula and beyond. The interaction of characters from different social levels was already reintroduced in Pergolesi's *Lo frate 'nnamorato* (1732). This, together with the greater use of ensembles in *opera buffa*, the reforms of Ranieri Calzabigi and Gluck to the established format of recitative and *da capo* aria, and the fashion for pathetic subjects introduced by Piccinni's *La buona figliuola* (1760, based on Samuel Richardson's *Pamela*) all affected the path taken by the serious genre. Opera also exerted a profound influence on church music, and composers and singers operated in both spheres. Instrumental music was generally played in the context of private academies, and thus the province of a select audience.

In mid-century Milan, under Austrian rule from 1706, such composers as Sammartini began to write sinfonias for strings, which marked a departure from Baroque instrumental forms and served as models for J. C. Bach and others. However, the exodus of instrumentalist-composers, most notably the cellist Boccherini and pianist Clementi, demonstrates that little priority was given to instrumental music in a culture dominated by opera.

5. The Napoleonic invasion to World War I

Opera continued to hold sway over Italian musical life after the Napoleonic invasion, which completed the decay of the old court structure. The number of opera houses increased steadily, and the advent of Rossinian comic opera encouraged a renewal of the genre. While Napoleon was emperor, such Italian composers as Paisiello, Paër, and Spontini were in favour in Paris, and Italian singers were constantly heard there. The emergence of the patriotic movements of the 1820s and 30s, after the Treaty of Vienna had placed most of northern Italy under the repressive Austrian regime, saw this trend increased: Rossini moved to Paris, and his successors Bellini and Donizetti were also drawn to the French capital, which, with its skilled orchestras and sophisticated audiences, became a mecca for Italian composers.

By the mid-1830s, the movement towards Italian independence known as the Risorgimento was well under way, and its major composer was already at work. The accident whereby Verdi's name formed an acronym used in a revolutionary slogan—'Vittorio Emanuele Re D'Italia'—made his reputation as a political figure, a role that he more or less consciously fulfilled, at least in retrospect. However, his true genius lay not in the support of political movements, but in the portrayal of character. More than any other composer, he brought Italian music into the Romantic movement, exploiting the traditional musical forms for his own purposes, and transforming them to create a real music drama in Italian (not Wagnerian) terms. He also did much to improve the performance of operas, insisting on good productions and orchestral playing. His development as a composer, however, took place outside the general trend of Italian music during the years immediately before and after unification (1861); shunning La Scala for a quarter of a century, his operas of the period were increasingly written for theatres abroad, principally Paris.

Interest in French music before unification had its counterpart in an openness to European cultural trends afterwards. The Milanese Società del Quartetto (founded 1864) promoted composition competitions and orchestral concerts; in 1870 Hans von Bülow conducted the La Scala orchestra in all-Beethoven concerts. *Tannhäuser* and *Lohengrin* received their Italian premieres (in Florence and Bologna respectively), orchestral concerts began in Turin and Rome, and the single post of conductor was established at La Scala, in place of the old division of roles between conductor and coach, laying the foundations for the power that the holder of the post would wield in the person of Toscanini at the end of the century.

In place of the 'travelling composer' system under which Rossini and Donizetti had operated, the major publishing houses—especially Ricordi, Lucca, and Sonzogno in Milan—promoted their own composers, taking advantage of the newly established copyright convention and the abolition of government subsidy to opera houses. An intellectual reaction against opera in the 1880s saw Milan again a centre for instrumental music (the most prominent figures being Sgambati and Martucci) and the beginnings of Italian musicology. In opera a flirtation with German Romanticism was submerged by the so-called Giovane Scuola of Mascagni, Leoncavallo, Puccini, and Giordano, who all came to prominence in the 1890s, writing in a vein influenced by Bizet and Massenet. The school, known by the shorthand term of verismo, was short-lived, and by World War I was already excoriated by the younger generation of Italian musicologists who were laying the foundations for research into Italy's forgotten past.

6. Since 1914

World War I punctured the self-confidence of what became known as 'Italietta'—the apparently prosperous Italy of the first decade of the century. A certain dissatisfaction with Italian society and its institutions found expression in a variety of musical manifestations, from Futurist experiments to the establishment of Alfredo Casella's Società Italiana di Musica Moderna. Many members had been born in the 1880s and the group of composers covering Respighi, Pizzetti, Malipiero, and Casella himself was later defined as the 'generazione dell'ottanta'. The search for an Italian musical identity was a new goal for the country's composers, but there was little of a shared aesthetic, aside from finding inspiration in Italy's past. Before World War I the rediscovery of earlier Italian music, especially that of the 16th and 18th centuries, had already resulted in the first attempt to catalogue Domenico Scarlatti's keyboard music; subsequently such series as the *Istituzioni e monumenti dell'arte musicale Italiana* and Malipiero's collected edition of Monteverdi's music appeared.

The death of verismo, which had staggered on into the 1920s and the new Fascist regime in the works of minor composers, signalled the death of opera as a culturally unifying phenomenon, and the move towards modernism was condemned in a manifesto printed in the leading newspapers in 1932 and signed by Respighi and Pizzetti among others. The Fascist state's involvement in music is not comparable to that of Nazi Germany, and much contemporary music continued to be played; the performers and composers of postwar Italy were all trained in institutions operating under the prevailing ideology, and anti-Fascist composers like Dallapiccola and Petrassi, with a European outlook, emerged in the 1930s.

However, it was not until after the devastation of World War II that 12-note techniques were widely adopted. The war impoverished Italy but generated great self-respect, the defeat of the nation being considered as really the defeat of Fascism and to have been redeemed by the bravery of the partisans. The compromised royal family was exiled, and a republic instituted in 1946. Postwar Italy saw the expansion of the orchestras set up by the national broadcasting organization (RAI) to Turin, Milan, Rome, and Naples, the establishment of an electronic music studio at the Milan branch of the RAI, and a mushrooming of summer festivals, such as that at Spoleto, directed by Menotti.

Bruno Maderna played a key role in the development of postwar Italian composition and was closely involved with the Darmstadt summer courses, attended by most of the new generation, including Berio, Nono, Donatoni, and Bussotti. Nono's 'engaged' work exemplifies a politicized music, while Bussotti has explored music theatre in a highly personal manner. Berio is the composer who has most acquired a following outside Italy, from the experimental days of the 1950s to the pluralistic 1990s, and he has latterly approached opera from a 'critical' perspective. Composers including such leading figures as Azio Corghi and Giorgio Battistelli continue to produce operas, but the genre does not dominate and stagings of contemporary operas in the leading theatres are relatively rare.

A Vivaldi revival, begun before the war, took off in the 1950s, and has been followed by increasingly thorough exploration of Italy's patrimony of Renaissance and Baroque music. Such enterprises as the Rossini Opera Festival in Pesaro (established 1980) have provided a showcase for musicological research and historically informed singing, but Italian performers have been slower to follow the lead of northern European ensembles in embracing original instruments. DA/KC

📖 A. Casella, *I segreti della giara* (Florence, 1941; Eng. trans. as *Music in my Time*, London, 1955) · N. Fortune, 'Italian secular monody from 1600 to 1635: An introductory survey', *Musical Quarterly*, 39 (1953), 171–95 · N. Pirrotta and E. Povoledo, *Li due Orfei: Da Poliziano a Monteverdi* (Turin, 1969, enlarged 2/1975; Eng. trans. as *Music and Theatre from Poliziano to Monteverdi*, Cambridge, 1982) · E. Selfridge-Field, *Venetian Instrumental Music from Gabrieli to Vivaldi* (Oxford, 1975, 3/1994) · D. Arnold, *Giovanni Gabrieli and the Music of the Venetian High Renaissance* (London, 1980) · I. Fenlon, *Music and Patronage in Sixteenth-Century Mantua* (Cambridge, 1980–2) · J. Rosselli, *The Opera Industry in Italy from Cimarosa to Verdi* (Cambridge, 1984) · H. Sachs, *Music in Fascist Italy* (London, 1987) · D. Kimbell, *Italian Opera* (Cambridge, 1991) · J. Rosselli, *Music and Musicians in Nineteenth-Century Italy* (London, 1991)

Ite missa est (Lat., 'Go, you are dismissed'). The final chant of the *Mass. Although strictly part of the Ordinary, with an unchanging text, it is rarely set to music.

Ivanhoe. Opera in three acts by Sullivan to a libretto by Julian Sturgis after Walter Scott's novel (1819) (London, 1891): Sullivan's only 'serious' opera.

Ivan IV. Opera in five acts by Bizet to a libretto by François-Hippolyte Leroy and Henri Trianon (Württemberg, 1946).

Ivan Susanin. See Life for the Tsar, A.

Ives, Charles (Edward) (*b* Danbury, CT, 20 Oct. 1874; *d* West Redding, CT, 19 May 1954). American composer. His music, almost all of it written before he suffered a heart attack in 1918, abounds in unconventional ideas and audacious experiments: atonality, quotation, simultaneous clashing metres, quarter-tones, the use of spatially separated groups of instruments—all of these he pioneered with extraordinary imagination, working in isolation and obscurity, ignorant of what was being achieved by his contemporaries in Europe. His daring was not, however, that of a naive amateur. He did not pursue a musical career, preferring to earn his living by setting up a successful insurance business, but he had studied with Horatio Parker at Yale (1894–8).

Ives's taste for musical experiment was stimulated in his boyhood by his father, George Ives, who taught him the rudiments of music but also encouraged him to be open-minded and independent. This seems to have started when he was still in his teens. His father gave him the means to hold down jobs as a church organist, and also a querulous, inventive spirit that made him look for his own ways of doing things. At Yale that spirit was somewhat curbed. Parker, like Dvořák, advocated Classical Germanic principles admixed with local material: the melody of American folksongs and hymns. Ives, during and after his Yale years, composed readily along those lines in such works as his First Quartet (*c*.1897–*c*.1900, *c*.1909), First Symphony (*c*.1898–*c*.1901, *c*.1907–8), and church cantata *The Celestial Country* (1898–1902, *c*.1912–13). But at the same time he was continuing his explorations: his unaccompanied setting of Psalm 67 (*c*.1898–9) is in two simultaneous keys throughout, and he tried different unconventional ideas in other psalms of around this period.

By not seeking a musical appointment he gave himself the liberty to compose as he wanted: he set up his own office in 1906, and composed during evenings and weekends. But his work in insurance also had its own justification. Through insurance, he felt, free individuals could protect themselves against the vagaries of fate, which alone, in his optimistic vision, could put the members of a democratic society at risk. His music was also an expression of his democratic ideals. It was rooted in the parlour musicales, the outdoor sing-songs, the marching bands, the hymns stoutly sung in church, and other impressions of his boyhood; its poetry is that of a pastoral New England before the motor car. But at the same time it passionately speaks out for the individual's right to a point of view, however eccentric.

Many of Ives's subsequent innovations were carried out in his songs, which are of an astonishing variety.

They range from imitations of German lieder (*Feldeinsamkeit*) to powerful declamations that are virtually atonal (*Paracelsus*), from serene hymn-tune pieces (*At the River*) to boyishly humorous ones (*The Circus Band*), from strident epigrams (*Duty*) to homely numbers (*Songs my Mother Taught me*). Often these songs were derived from chamber or orchestral pieces, or else they were later arranged for different forces. Ives's music, so diverse in style, was also mutable in detail.

This has caused some difficulty in the publication of his works, for his scores tend to be crowded with revisions, alternatives, and deliberate impossibilities: what mattered was, in his terms, the 'substance' of the music, not its realization. His approach to the art was influenced by New England transcendentalism, the thought of the 19th-century writer-philosophers who lived around the town of Concord in Massachusetts, and it was on their work that he based his Second Piano Sonata (*c.*1916–19), subtitled 'Concord'. Other compositions, notably the orchestral *Three Places in New England* (*c.*1912–17), evoke the landscape and history of Ives's native region. The symphony *Holidays* (1909–13), which includes the uproarious 'Fourth of July', is particularly rich in quotations of this kind, developing to collages of impenetrable density.

However, other orchestral works, for example the overture *Browning* (*c.*1912–14), achieve their effects by entirely original means, including a vigorous use of dissonant harmony. Ives also investigated new, atonal ways of organizing music in his pieces for small instrumental ensemble, which include *The Unanswered Question* for trumpet, four flutes, and strings (1908) and *Tone Roads no. 1* for flute, clarinet, bassoon, and strings (*c.*1913–14). The latter piece contains some anticipation of serialism; the former has the trumpet pose the question, unanswered by vain scurryings in the flutes while the strings, representing the silence of metaphysical wisdom, play discreetly off stage. Ives's Fourth Symphony (*c.*1912–18) is similar in its philosophical ambitions but much grander in conception. A short prelude is followed by an enormously complex second movement (developed from the corresponding movement in the 'Concord' Sonata), a fugue (also used in the Second Quartet of *c.*1913–15), and a finale which is an apotheosis on a serenely spiritual plane. In its diversity and its vision this work could well stand as Ives's most complete achievement.

Having virtually given up composing—perhaps on account of discouragement as much as poor health—Ives had his 'Concord' Sonata, its accompanying *Essays Before a Sonata*, and a volume of 114 songs privately printed in 1920–2. (He also provided funds to support the publication, performance, and recording of works by other American composers.) In about 1930 the sonata was taken up by John Kirkpatrick and *Three Places* by Nicolas Slonimsky, but most of Ives's scores remained unheard until after World War II.   PG

📖 H. and S. Cowell, *Charles Ives and his Music* (New York, 1955, 2/1969) · C. Ives, *Essays Before a Sonata and Other Writings*, ed. H. Boatwright (New York, 1962, 2/1970 as *Essays Before a Sonata, The Majority and Other Writings*); *Memos*, ed. J. Kirkpatrick (New York, 1971) · H. W. Hitchcock, *Ives* (London, 1977) · J. P. Burkholder (ed.), *Charles Ives and his World* (Princeton, NJ, 1996) · J. Swafford, *Charles Ives: A Life with Music* (New York, 1996)

I was glad. Anthem (1902) by Parry, with processional music, composed for the coronation of Edward VII.

I Was Looking at the Ceiling and then I Saw the Sky. 'Songplay' in two parts by Adams to texts by June Jordan (Berkeley, CA, 1995).

jácara [xácara] (Sp., Port.). An old Spanish ballad or dance tune. In the 17th century the *jácara* was often used in the theatre, and it eventually developed into the **tonadilla*.

Jacchini, Giuseppe Maria (*b* Bologna, *c.*1663; *d* Bologna, 2 May 1727). Italian cellist and composer. A pupil of Domenico Gabrielli, he was a member of the *cappella* at S. Petronio and, from 1688, of the Accademia Filarmonica. His sonatas, concertos, and sinfonias for trumpet and strings were well known in his lifetime, and many include obbligato parts for his instrument; his op. 4 (1701) contains some of the earliest concertos with obbligato solos for cello, albeit of a fairly rudimentary nature. DA/PA

Jachet Berchem. See BERCHEM, JACQUET DE.

Jachet [Jacquet] **of Mantua** [Colebault, Jacques] (*b* Vitré, Brittany, *c.*1483; *d* Mantua, 2 Oct. 1559). French composer. He worked at the Cathedral of SS Peter and Paul, Mantua, from *c.*1526 until his death, first as a singer and then as *maestro di cappella*. He was one of the most important composers of church music of the generation before Lassus and Palestrina; his works include cycles of hymns, vesper psalms for the entire church year (some written in collaboration with Willaert and others), motets, and masses (including 16 parody masses based on his own works and on secular and sacred works by other composers). In the 16th century he was frequently confused with his contemporary, Jacquet de Berchem. JM

Jacob, Gordon (Percival Septimus) (*b* London, 5 July 1895; *d* Saffron Walden, 8 June 1984). English composer. He studied with C. V. Stanford and Charles Wood at the RCM, where he was an influential teacher of composition from 1924 to 1969. His large output includes various concertos and other orchestral works, choral music, and chamber pieces, usually in a straightforward, even ebullient style; his is music for performers to enjoy. He is also the author of *Orchestral Technique* (London, 1931, 2/1982), *How to Read a Score* (London, 1944), and *The Composer and his Art* (London, 1954). PG

Jacobin, The (*Jakobín*). Opera in three acts by Dvořák to a libretto by Marie Červinková-Riegrová (Prague, 1889; revised Prague, 1898).

Jacopo da Bologna [de Bononia] (*fl* mid-14th century). Italian composer and music theorist. Little is known about his life beyond what can be gleaned from the texts he set to music; these point to a link with the Visconti court at Milan in the 1340s and 50s. He appears to have known the poet Petrarch, and to have written the words of some of his own madrigals. More than 30 compositions by him survive, the majority of them secular; they stand out from other Italian works of the period for their skill and invention. His theoretical writings show an understanding of the notational principles of the French Ars Nova. JM

Jacquet de Berchem. See BERCHEM, JACQUET DE.

Jacquet de La Guerre, Élisabeth (*b* Paris, *bapt.* 17 March 1665; *d* Paris, 27 June 1729). French harpsichordist and composer. The younger daughter of the Parisian organist Claude Jacquet (*d* Paris, 6 Nov. 1702), she came to the attention of Louis XIV and Madame de Montespan when she played the harpsichord and sang at court at the age of five. She later spent three years as the ward of Mme de Montespan before marrying another Parisian organist, Marin de La Guerre, in 1684. They had one son, who died at the age of ten.

As well as performing, Jacquet de La Guerre taught and also composed: in 1687 she published her first collection of *pièces de clavecin*, which includes unmeasured preludes. During the 1690s she composed a ballet, *Les Jeux à l'honneur de la victoire* (*c.*1691; lost), and a *tragédie lyrique*, *Céphale et Procris*, which was performed at the Opéra in 1694. Alongside Couperin, Rebel, and Clérambault, she also experimented with Italian genres, principally the sonata and the cantata. However, it was only in 1707 that her six violin sonatas appeared in print, together with her second book of *pièces de clavecin*; the first of her two collections of biblical cantatas followed in 1708. A third collection—of secular cantatas and a 'raccommodement comique' composed for the Foire St Germain—appeared in 1715.

Her *Te Deum* of 1721 is lost. She died a widow, in wealthy circumstances.   JAS

> 📖 C. CESSAC, *Élisabeth Jacquet de La Guerre: Une femme compositeur sous le règne de Louis XIV* (Arles, 1995)

Jacquet of Mantua. See JACHET OF MANTUA.

Jakob Lenz. Opera in one act by Rihm to a libretto by M. Fröhling after Georg Büchner's play *Lenz* (Hamburg, 1979).

Jakobsleiter, Die ('Jacob's Ladder'). Unfinished oratorio by Schoenberg, a setting of his own text for solo voices, chorus, and orchestra; he worked on it between 1917 and 1922 and the scoring was completed posthumously by Winifred Zillig. The first part was first performed in Hamburg in 1958 and the work was given complete in Vienna in 1961.

Jamaican Rumba. Piece for two pianos (1938) by Benjamin; it has been arranged for many other combinations, particularly small orchestra.

jam session. A jazz get-together, where the players improvise in an informal and unstructured way. The word 'jam' had at times been used as a synonym for 'jazz', but in the 1930s it became specifically attached to these improvisatory sessions where musicians, often working within the constraints of the *big-band world, could enjoy more creative freedom.   PGA

Janáček, Leoš [Leo Eugen] (*b* Hukvaldy, Czechoslovakia, 3 July 1854; *d* Ostrava, 12 Aug. 1928). Czech composer. The son of a Moravian schoolmaster and organist, he studied at the Augustinian 'Queen's' Monastery and the German Realschule in Brno and in 1869 prepared himself to follow his father's career, attending the Brno Teacher Training College (1869–74) and the Prague Organ School (1874–5). In 1875 he joined the staff at the former institution. He was now beginning to make his mark locally as a composer, particularly with choral pieces influenced by the director of the abbey school, Pavel Křížkovsky. He went for brief periods to study at the conservatories of Leipzig (1879–80) and Vienna (1880) but gained little from the experience. In 1881 he became founder and first director of the Brno Organ School.

For the next 30 or so years Janáček lived in Brno in relative obscurity: his first mature works, such as the *Lachian Dances* for orchestra (1889–90), suggested only that he would develop as a gifted follower of Dvořák. Gradually, however, his music began to be infused with Moravian folksong, which he had started to collect in 1885. He was also noting down the pitch inflections and rhythms of speech in his native region,

preparing to emulate Musorgsky in finding a vocal style to suit the particular qualities of his language. All these studies bore fruit in his opera *Jenůfa* (1904), a passionate tale of love and jealousy set in a Moravian village.

The Prague premiere of this opera in a revised version, given in 1916, belatedly established Janáček's reputation, both nationally and soon internationally. In a sense this marked the beginning of his career, for almost all his important works were written in the next dozen years. A major influence on the music of this time was Janáček's passionate friendship with Kamila Stösslová, 35 years his junior. In many ways she became his muse, and his love for her is commemorated in several of his later works. From this period came his orchestral rhapsody *Taras Bulba* (1915–18) and his boldly scored Sinfonietta (1926), his two String Quartets (1923 and 1928), and a variety of other chamber pieces. All of this music is highly individual, sometimes even quirky, based as it is on short, irregular phrases of modal character and strong personality.

Janáček's greatest achievements, however, came in a rapid succession of operas: *Výlety páně Broučkovy* ('The Excursions of Mr Brouček', 1920), *Káťa Kabanová* (1921), *Příhody Lišky Bystroušky* ('The Cunning Little Vixen', 1924), *Věc Makropulos* ('The Makropulos Affair', 1926), and *Z mrtvého domu* ('From the House of the Dead', unfinished, posthumously produced in 1930). Widely varied in dramatic tone and setting, these show his unerring ability to depict characters by means of swift, imaginative strokes, to follow the words (usually his own) naturally yet with high intensity, and to achieve potent dramatic effects through his very personal use of the orchestra, involving stark sonorities and rapid developments of pungent motifs.

These later operas also display Janáček's relish of the bizarre and unusual. *Mr Brouček* is a comic fantasy which finds an ordinary man transported first to the moon and then to the 15th century, while *The Cunning Little Vixen* is a quite unpatronizing tale of animals; *The Makropulos Affair* reveals the empty fate of a woman who has magically prolonged her existence for 300 years, and *From the House of the Dead* is an austere setting of incidents from Dostoyevsky's prison-camp novel. Yet, as *Káťa Kabanová* eloquently proves, Janáček was stimulated above all by the inner lives of real human beings, and by the tragedy of their destinies.   PG/JSM

> 📖 J. VOGEL, *Leoš Janáček* (Eng. trans., London, 1962, 3/1997) · J. TYRRELL (trans. and ed.), *Intimate Letters: Leoš Janáček to Kamila Stösslová* (London, 1994); *My Life with Janáček: The Memoirs of Zdenka Janáčková* (London, 1998) · P. WINGFIELD (ed.), *Janáček Studies* (Cambridge, 1999)

Janequin [Jannequin], Clément (*b* Châtellerault, nr Poitiers, *c*.1485; *d* Paris, 1558). French composer. He spent his early years in the region of Bordeaux, at the same time studying for the priesthood. In the 1530s he moved to Angers, serving as *maître de chapelle* at the cathedral from 1537. During those years he built up a considerable reputation as a chanson composer, and had some works published by Pierre Attaingnant (including *Chantons, sonnons, trompettes*, written for a visit to Bordeaux by François I); at least four volumes of his works were published. In 1549 he settled in Paris, becoming *chantre ordinaire du roi* and then *compositeur du roi*; he also registered as a student at the university. In spite of the fact that in 1555 he was a singer in the royal chapel, he died a poor man.

Janequin's over 250 chansons form easily the greater part of his output (although he also wrote many psalm settings and *chansons spirituelles*), and even his two masses are of the parody kind, based closely on two of his chansons (*Missa super 'L'Aveuglé dieu'* and *Missa super 'La Bataille'*). Many of them set the verse in a programmatic way, imitating birdsong, the chattering of women, and so on. His well-known *La Bataille de Marignan* (probably written soon after the Battle of Marignano, 1515), using warriors' cries, the clashing of swords and other battle sounds, was a favourite throughout Europe, and provoked many imitations.

DA/TC

janissary music [Turkish music] (Fr.: *bande turque*; Ger.: *Janitscharenmusik*; It.: *banda turca*). Literally, a Turkish wind and percussion band of the Ottoman Empire. The term has however come to be used to describe supposedly Turkish elements in music of the Classical period. The original janissary band (the word is of Turkish derivation) dates back to 1329, when it was founded, although the tradition of military percussion and wind groups (the Turkish term is *mehter*) is much older. Such bands, sometimes including more than 30 musicians, were popular in the 16th and 17th centuries. They became known in Europe during the 17th century and in particular in Austria after the wars which culminated in the Turkish defeat following the siege of Vienna in 1683. Janissary instruments came to be added to some Western military bands during the 17th century and especially the 18th, in particular the bass drum, and towards the end of the century the triangle and cymbals.

These instruments, and musical styles associated with them, came into occasional use in music of the Classical period, for example in Mozart's *Die Entführung aus dem Serail* (1782, set in Turkey), Haydn's Symphony no. 100 ('Military', 1794), and Beethoven's Ninth Symphony (1825: the *alla marcia* section of the finale) as well as works by Michael Haydn and Gluck, who called on them for the Scythian music in *Iphigénie en Tauride* (1779). Composers used them to evoke a Turkish or a more generally *exotic setting, or simply for military imagery. The instruments soon gained a regular place in the orchestra as well as the military band. Supposedly Turkish effects were also used by Classical composers without the use of janissary instruments: famous examples are Mozart's Violin Concerto in A K219 (the finale) and the Rondo alla turca of his Piano Sonata in A K331/300*i*, in which flourishes in the left hand imitate the roll of the drum and the clash of the cymbals.

The original janissaries were disbanded in 1826. Recreations of janissary bands show *bass drums played with stick and cane, pairs of small *kettledrums held on the left arm (see also TIMPANI), cymbals, and *zūrnā* (see SHAWM) for the melodies, doubled by Western valved trumpets (since no record survives as to what the original trumpets did). In front are singers, each with a 'Turkish crescent', a staff surmounted by a brass crescent and hung with horsetails (and sometimes small bells, hence the nickname 'jingling johnny': it was used by Berlioz in his *Grande symphonie funèbre et triomphale*, 1840); this could be raised and thumped down in time with the music. A later addition was the tambourine.

AB/SS

M. PIRKER, 'Pictorial documents of the music bands of the janissaries (mehter) and the Austrian military music', *RIdIM Newsletter*, 15/2 (1990), 2–12

Jannequin, Clément. See JANEQUIN, CLÉMENT.

Jarnach, Philipp (*b* Noisy-le-Sec, nr Paris, 26 July 1892; *d* Börnsen, nr Bergedorf, 17 Dec. 1982). German composer. Of Spanish–German parentage, he studied at the Paris Conservatoire with Édouard Risler (piano) and Albert Lavignac (theory). In 1914 he moved to Zürich, where he became an associate of Busoni's; on that composer's death in 1924 he completed his opera *Doktor Faust*. He then worked as a music critic in Berlin (1927–45), as professor of composition at the Cologne Musikhochschule (1949–59), and as director of the Hamburg Musikhochschule (1959–70). His compositions include orchestral and chamber works in a neoclassical style influenced by Busoni.

PG

Jaufre Rudel. See RUDEL, JAUFRE.

jazz. A popular music of black American origin, distinguished by its characteristic rhythms and harmonies and typically involving improvisation. The word originally signified liveliness, and may have had particular reference to sexual excitement. Although many elements went into the making of jazz—*ragtime, field hollers, work songs, *spirituals, *vaudeville songs, street marches, the *blues, and so on—it developed its own distinctive character by about 1900. Despite the claims of certain individuals (among them Jelly Roll Morton and Nick La Rocca) to have 'invented' it, jazz began as a social music, the natural response of the black population, especially in the southern American states, to their situation, their sorrows and oppressions, their hopes and aspirations. Song and dance were natural means of expression, and jazz emerged as both an expressive and a functional music: the vocalized melodies of work songs formed the basis of its instrumental style, and a combination of the dance and the march its rhythms.

It is usually said that jazz originated in New Orleans, but in fact it was springing up all over the USA in the second decade of the 20th century; it was simply that in New Orleans it first found its natural habitats—in brothels, clubs, dance halls, *barrelhouses, and other haunts of low life, as well as on the colourful riverboats that carried the music up the river to places like Memphis, St Louis, and Chicago. New Orleans has always been a polyglot city, the meeting-place of many different races, and many cultures were involved in the development of jazz—French, Spanish, Creole, and Latin American, as well as black American—so that, although it was and remains essentially a black music, its popular appeal was such that it was taken up by white musicians, even if often (though not always) in a debased and devitalized form. And being a popular music, jazz has been closely involved with commercial entertainment, with the inevitable result of frequent dilution. But the hard core of the music remains and is not corrupted.

1. Early days; 2. The Depression and after; 3. Bop; 4. From the 1950s

1. Early days

The history of jazz is short but by no means uneventful. In less than half a century it evolved from a simple folk music into an art form of considerable sophistication, drawing on sources unknown to and unsuspected by many of its early practitioners. While black songs, and another of their offspring, the blues, formed a basis for many of the instrumental techniques, others derived from brass- and wind-playing in the aftermath of the Civil War, when the military bands broke up and left many of their instruments lying around, battered and discarded, to be picked up by poor folk and used in street parades, funeral processions, and the like.

When jazz went indoors it sometimes met the gentle but spirited bands of strings, piano, and drums with banjo or guitar playing the dance music of the day. It was in this environment that one of the great original

talents of jazz, Jelly Roll Morton, began to shape and define the jazz idiom proper. In many ways Morton was a maverick: he hated jazz that was merely loud and brash, as much of it was in the early days, and insisted on the importance of melody. As a pianist he played in a style that drew on both ragtime and authentic jazz, thus forming one of the principal links between the two genres.

The 'classic' jazz style, born of and in New Orleans, is essentially a linear, melodic music, played on trumpet, trombone, and clarinet with piano, drums, banjo or guitar, and bass (brass at first, string later). There were additions and substitutions, but the true New Orleans style adheres to this basic instrumentation, just as it adheres to the principle of collective improvisation. New Orleans jazz reached its peak with King Oliver's Creole Jazz Band during the early 1920s. It was in the Oliver band that the young Louis Armstrong learnt many of his early lessons, as second cornet to Oliver himself, and it was on this instrument that he was soon to base one of the two most original and influential virtuoso solo styles in jazz history. The best Oliver recordings of this period have a coherence and co-ordination, a feeling of genuine partnership, that typifies the New Orleans style at its best.

But jazz did not stay long in New Orleans. In the 1920s many of its leading figures began a northward migration to Chicago and New York, where the seeds of jazz were already flowering, the money was good, and the pre-Depression high life offered ample rewards. The era of Prohibition and bootlegging had a marked effect on the dissemination of jazz in the USA, and also on its character. As life became harder and tougher, so did the music. Nor did jazz confine itself, either stylistically or geographically, to one or two centres only: distinctive styles emerged not only in New Orleans, Chicago, and New York but also in Kansas City, St Louis, and Memphis.

Oliver and Armstrong, with their colleagues from New Orleans, won new fame and reputation in Chicago. In New York Duke Ellington, perhaps the one indisputable genius of the jazz tradition, came to international recognition and worldwide fame at the Cotton Club in Harlem (which admitted only a white clientele) in the years after 1927. Fletcher Henderson led a band that was also to be a major influence. At the same time, a school of white jazz grew up in New York, led by Red Nichols, the Dorsey brothers Tommy and Jimmy, and others. A distorting element came in with the 'symphonic jazz' of Paul Whiteman, who at various times employed a number of the leading white jazzmen, including two of the greatest: the trumpet player Bix Beiderbecke, whose early death (largely caused by drink) turned him into a legend, and the trombonist

Jack Teagarden. Most of Whiteman's music was commercial dance music and entertainment material, though some was jazz-inflected; he won himself the accolade 'King of Jazz' (the title of a celebrated film of the period), even though it was Duke Ellington who was creating the original and authentic jazz at the Cotton Club. The conditions of the time gave white musicians infinitely more publicity and nationwide exposure.

About the same time, a white style of a different kind was evolving in Chicago in the hands of such players as Bud Freeman, Max Kaminsky, Frank Teschemacher, Eddie Condon, and Teagarden (who played both styles, old and new). Chicago jazz was harder, more brittle, and generally more frenetic than the New York variety, yet both remained important and influential.

2. The Depression and after

Jazz rode high in the 1920s, spreading everywhere. The social cleavages and distinctions did not hinder its dissemination. Then, in 1929, came the Wall Street crash and the beginnings of the Depression. This was a major setback, less for jazz itself than for its practitioners, many of whom went out of the business, some never to return. Those who combined toughness and shrewdness with genuine talent managed to survive, but plenty went under. And black musicians were always vulnerable, barred by their colour from the most lucrative jobs in hotels and on radio. As long as the good times had lasted this did not matter too much; there was work and money enough to go round. But when both were tight the black people suffered first.

Fortunately the worst effects of the Depression did not last indefinitely. In 1934 came a change. Jazz, which had been for the most part a minority taste among whites, made a sudden leap forward in general appeal. It began when Benny Goodman, who had long been prominent in 'name' bands and in making records with small groups under his own leadership, formed a new big band, engaged Fletcher Henderson to do the arrangements, and suddenly discovered a new generation of young Americans who wanted to dance to his music and were prepared to pay for it. The 'swing' era was born, and Goodman was proclaimed its king. Goodman achieved a hitherto unimagined popularity, and other bands quickly followed his lead: Tommy and Jimmy Dorsey were now leading their separate bands, as were Artie Shaw, Glenn Miller, and many others.

Small-group jazz continued to flourish alongside the big bands. A new development was what later came to be called 'mainstream' jazz, which brought the swing idiom into the smaller ensemble. Older styles were perpetuated and extended by musicians like the New Orleans clarinettist Sidney Bechet, the *stride pianist Fats Waller, or the white cornettist Muggsy Spanier. Spontaneous, unrecorded *jam sessions encouraged the development of considerable technical virtuosity, which would bear fruit somewhat later in bebop (see below, 3).

Swing was not in itself new; nor, indeed, was the word: it had always been one of the basic ingredients of jazz (hence Duke Ellington's *It Don't Mean a Thing (if it Ain't got that Swing)*, 1932), and Henderson had been playing much the same music with his band for some years without marked success. But Goodman, more by accident than design, gave it a new twist and caught the mood and enthusiasms of the young. Although the great black bands continued to reap their share of the rewards, swing was essentially a white music appealing to a white audience, not only in the USA but very soon all over the world. Thus jazz, or a form of it, became in the fullest sense the international popular music of the era.

In the unfolding of jazz history, the swing period can now be seen as a kind of consolidation and expansion, a summing up of the formal and technical developments up to that time. Because it was based primarily on technique, it could be played—and well played—by many musicians, both inside and outside the USA, who were not by nature or inheritance outstanding jazz musicians. Goodman was a perfectionist who demanded the best from every member of his bands; he thus set new standards of polish and sophistication, based on his own clarinet technique, which he had deliberately refined and extended (including the classical repertory). Because of Benny Goodman, jazz found a new and vastly increased audience.

Goodman and swing achieved another important breakthrough. Until the mid-1930s black and white musicians were not allowed to appear together in public, although they frequently played together privately. Now Goodman (prompted by the impresario John Hammond) employed first Teddy Wilson and then Lionel Hampton in the small groups that had featured from the beginning alongside the big band. Not much later black musicians including the ex-Ellington trumpet star Cootie Williams and guitarist Charlie Christian sat in the band itself as permanent members. From then on it was customary for black and white musicians to appear together on stage.

By the end of the 1930s swing had become a mass-produced music for a mass-produced audience. In the hands of its leading lights, the big white bands, it had become stereotyped, a matter mostly of mechanical exercises. Something new was needed to rejuvenate jazz from within itself. Duke Ellington somewhat acidly summed it up: 'Jazz is music, swing is business'. Swing had become altogether too much business. All the same, it had had a profound influence on *popular music. Frank Sinatra, after Bing Crosby the most widely influential of popular singers, worked in his early days with the Tommy Dorsey orchestra and learnt his perfection of timing and phrasing from listening to Dorsey's immaculate trombone playing. All popular singing in fact tended to benefit from its contact with jazz via swing.

3. Bop

A fresh direction was not only needed but inevitable. It came in the early 1940s, led by another of jazz's seminal figures and influential soloists: the alto saxophonist Charlie Parker. Parker and his colleagues, notably the trumpeter Dizzy Gillespie, the pianists Bud Powell and Thelonious Monk, and the drummers Max Roach and Kenny Clarke, gathered at Minton's Playhouse in New York and virtually inaugurated a new jazz era. The style they introduced, which was avidly taken up by young musicians everywhere (and by some of the older ones too), was known as 'bebop', or simply 'bop', largely (it is said) after Gillespie's *scat-singing syllables. Essential to bop were chromatic harmony and a new, more complex system of rhythms. Hitherto jazz had been primarily a diatonic music with a straight 4/4 beat: if there was chromatic harmony, it was incidental; if there was rhythmic complexity, it was a deviation from the norm. Now, in Charlie Parker's hands, jazz became predominantly chromatic with frequent cross-rhythms, interchange of metre, division of beat between bass and drums, and so on. Just as in classical European music, when chromaticism began to break down tonal thinking, traditional forms continued alongside the new, so in jazz the older forms held their place, though because of the compressed history of jazz and its strong social involvement the rift seemed at the time deeper and more permanent than it really was.

Indeed, during the same period, and in one sense as a kind of counter-revolution, there arose a 'revivalist' movement in which some of the old jazzmen were brought out of retirement (notably Bunk Johnson, who had been playing before World War I) to 'recreate' their music, and new groups, almost entirely white, played 'traditional' jazz and made it an article of faith as vigorously proclaimed as bop was on the other side. The 'revivalist' or 'trad' movement contributed nothing to jazz history, and little of musical value, though it did spark off a 'trad' boom in popular music.

Bop, on the other hand, was crucial to the development of jazz, and produced some of its greatest music. Parker himself died young, the victim of drugs and drink, but while he lived he not only altered the entire conception of jazz playing but also laid his influence on virtually everything and everyone except the dedicated 'traditionalists'. Parker's work transformed the playing of all kinds of instrumentalists. Trumpet players tended to follow Gillespie's flashing technique, brilliant articulation, and exceptional quickness of mind. The problem for those who came up at the same time or just after was how to get out from under the Parker–Gillespie umbrella. Among those who did was Miles Davis, who played the trumpet in some of Parker's groups, in a sensitive if rather hesitant and unformed style; but he went on to become one of the outstanding modern jazz figures with a series of records that continually broke new ground.

Part of this modernist revolution, as it was called—though not the Parker side—was the emergence of the so-called 'cool' school. This replaced the open emotional force and physical excitement of 'hot' jazz with deliberate understatement and restraint. In 1949–50 Davis led a group, which included French horn and tuba (then quite outside the jazz line-up), with arrangements by Davis himself, Gerry Mulligan, John Lewis, and Gil Evans, in a series of recordings collectively known as 'The Birth of the Cool'. This was of great and decisive importance directing the development of jazz along a path quite different from that of Parker. While 'The Birth of the Cool' was taken from band sessions (a nine-piece unit, in fact, but used like a big band), the modern tendency was, with one or two exceptions like the big bands Dizzy Gillespie led whenever he had the chance, to use a small group of players. Now these groups were becoming more diverse in their choice of instruments. One of the most important was the Modern Jazz Quartet, which lasted for 22 years, led by the pianist John Lewis with Milt Jackson on vibraharp, as well as bass and drums. The Modern Jazz Quartet specialized in quiet, unforced jazz, making frequent use of classical forms (fugue, canon, etc.) and even drawing on the works of such composers as Bach. Sometimes their music tended towards the pretty and merely decorative, but beneath the outward restraint and sometimes assumed solemnity was an essentially jazz-inspired, deep, earthy swing.

4. From the 1950s

After the Parker revolution, which was the centre of the modernist movement, jazz continued with considerable vitality through the 1950s, sometimes relying on or extending the Parker style, sometimes looking back to its past, sometimes searching for new ground, whether 'cool' or 'hot' or 'pseudo-hot'. And all the time the old masters continued to work. Ellington was still producing new music that proved him time and again the most original, genuinely progressive, and creative of all jazz musicians; Louis Armstrong, long established as a popular as well as a connoisseur's favourite, went back to small groups (mostly) on the New Orleans pattern but modified by his own exceptional virtuosity and following the path he had laid down with pianist Earl Hines in 1928 (Hines played again with Armstrong for a while in the 1950s). Some of the more adventurous of the older men adapted themselves to the new ways, like Coleman Hawkins, who had formed virtually single-handed the role of the tenor saxophone in jazz with Fletcher Henderson in the 1920s. The powerful Count Basie band had to break up briefly when the big band slump arrived, but was reformed and has gone on ever since, even after Basie's death.

In spite of all this activity the years were beginning to tell and the obituary columns were filling. New names appeared, one or two of them genuine pathfinders, like John Coltrane, a saxophonist of brilliance and originality whose early death in 1967 was a sad blow, and Ornette Coleman, who began experimenting with 'free jazz' as did Joe Harriot in England. But as the 1960s progressed tastes changed, and preference was given to pop. Jazz for the first time found itself in a backwater, partly because of changing taste and fashion, partly because in its own evolution it began to lose touch with its younger audience. And as pop and rock took more and more of the limelight—partly because, as with the swing bands of the 1930s, they were successfully promoted and given commercial exposure—jazz appeared to decline into a minority cult of the middle-aged. There was always that audience, but the nature of jazz itself in its latest manifestations has placed it at a disadvantage in popular terms. Much avant-garde jazz (to use an unsatisfactory term) is as 'difficult' for the traditional lover of jazz as much contemporary art music is to the lover of Mozart; it is all too likely to appear an incomprehensible succession of unconnected squeaks, squawks, grunts, silences, and minor explosions. In one sense the adoption by jazz of these modern means of expression is a token of its inner vitality, its ability to grow, borrow, absorb, and develop. But from another point of view it is ominous: jazz is essentially a popular music, and when it loses touch with its natural audience—the people—it is in danger of extinction.

Even the revival of jazz in recent years at the hands of Wynton Marsalis and others marks the transferral from its role as entertainment music to a more esoteric position, close to the revered heights of 'serious', classical music. One of the leading modern practitioners, Roland Kirk, once defined jazz as 'black classical music'. It is a good definition, but it does indicate a shift in emphasis from the time when it was the popular music of an age. BJ/JJD

📖 N. SHAPIRO and N. HENTOFF, *Hear me Talkin' to ya: The Story of Jazz as Told by the Men who Made it* (New York, 1955) · M. STEARNS, *The Story of Jazz* (New York, 1956, 3/1970) · W. MELLERS, *Music in a New Found Land* (London, 1964) · E. SOUTHERN, *The Music of Black Americans: A History* (New York, 1971, 3/1997) · B. KERNFELD and S. SADIE (eds.), *The New Grove Dictionary of Jazz* (London, 1988) · B. KERNFELD, *What to Listen for in Jazz* (New Haven, CT, 1995) · T. GIOIA, *The History of Jazz* (New York, 1997) · G. GIDDINS, *Visions of Jazz: The First Century* (New York, 1998)

jazz-rock fusion. A style from the late 1960s and early 70s that combined modern jazz techniques with the then current style of soul and rock; it thus brought jazz for a time nearer to the commercial tastes of the day, including the use of electronic instruments.

Jeanne d'Arc au bûcher ('Joan of Arc at the Stake').
1. Dramatic oratorio (1934–5) by Honegger, for four speakers, three sopranos, contralto, tenor, bass, ondes martenot, chorus, and orchestra, a setting of a text by Paul Claudel.
2. Scena (1845) by Liszt for mezzo-soprano and piano, a setting of a text by Alexandre Dumas; Liszt later arranged it for voice and orchestra.

Jeep, Johannes [Johann] (*b* Dransfeld, 1581 or 1582; *d* Hanau, 19 Nov. 1644). German composer and organist. He wrote some spirited student songs before marrying (successively) two widows, and became a respected composer and organist to the Count of Hohenlohe in 1613. He is mentioned by James Joyce in *Ulysses*. DA

Jeffreys, George (*b* c.1610; *d* Weldon, Northants., 4 or 5 July 1685). English composer and organist. From about 1631 until his death he served as a musician and administrator to the Hatton family, both in Northamptonshire and, during the Civil War, in Oxford, where he assisted as organist in chapel services for King Charles I. Jeffreys is one of the first English composers to have paid close attention to Italian declamatory song with continuo accompaniment, and his own vocal music often fuses that style with more characteristically English polyphony. His works include English-texted anthems, Latin-texted motets, and settings of English and Italian verse. JM

Jehan de L'Escurel. See L'ESCUREL, JEHAN DE.

Jehan des Murs. See JOHANNES DE MURIS.

Jelínek, Josef. See GELINEK, JOSEF.

'Jena' Symphony. Name given to a symphony by Friedrich Witt (1770–1836) found in 1909 in Jena, Germany, and long attributed to Beethoven.

Jenkins, John (*b* Maidstone, 1592; *d* Kimberley, Norfolk, 27 Oct. 1678). English composer. He was chiefly employed by noble families in East Anglia as their resident musician. A fine viol player, he took part in the masque *The Triumph of Peace* in London in 1634. In 1660 he was appointed as theorbo player in Charles II's 'Private Musick', but spent more time at Kirtling, Cambridgeshire, with the family of Roger North, who wrote warmly about him. Jenkins composed over 800 instrumental pieces, including superb fantasias for three, four, five, and six viols. Around 70 fine 'fantasia-suites' are more modern in style and, like his pieces for bass viol(s), often feature florid divisions (see DIVISIONS, 3). The best of his music is distinguished by its lyrical invention, emotional intensity, and adventurous tonal schemes, and his first-hand knowledge of the viol allowed him to exploit its expressive and technical capabilities to the full. He also wrote a few sacred and secular vocal pieces.   JN/AA

Jensen, Adolf (*b* Königsberg [now Kaliningrad], 12 Jan. 1837; *d* Baden-Baden, 23 Jan. 1879). German composer. He worked as a piano teacher until ill health compelled him to retire to various south German and Austrian resorts. His early music—mainly songs and piano music—recalls Schumann, but he was later influenced by Liszt and Wagner. Some of his songs show his intention 'to translate Wagner's ideas of beauty and truth into music in the smaller forms', and reflect or even anticipate Tristanesque harmony. His brother **Gustav Jensen** (*b* Königsberg, 25 Dec. 1843; *d* Cologne, 26 Nov. 1895) was a violinist and composer who also made editions of old violin music.   DA/JW

Jenůfa (*Její pastorkyňa*; 'Her Stepdaughter', 'Her Foster Daughter'). Opera in three acts by Janáček to his own libretto after Gabriela Preissová's play (1890) (Brno, 1904).

Jephtha. Oratorio (1752) by Handel to a biblical text by Thomas Morell.

Jeremiah, Lamentations of. See LAMENTATIONS.

Jeremiáš, Otakar (*b* Písek, 17 Oct. 1892; *d* Prague, 5 March 1962). Czech composer and conductor. He came from a musical family; his father, who gave Otakar his earliest tuition, founded the South Bohemian Conservatory at České Budějovice. The son studied in Prague with Novák (composition) and Jan Burian (cello). He accompanied his pianist-composer brother on foreign tours, returning in 1918 to succeed his father as director of the conservatory. In 1929 he was appointed conductor of the newly formed radio symphony orchestra in Prague, and in 1945 became opera director of the National Theatre. As a composer he was strongly aware of his nationalist heritage. An unqualified admiration for Smetana's music helped mould his style, and an interest in Wagner marks his larger choral and theatrical works. By the 1920s he had developed a musical language of some individuality, heard at its best in his opera *Bratři Karamazovi* (1928) and his unaccompanied choral works.   JSm

Jeritza, Maria [Mizzi] [Jedlitzká, Marie] (*b* Brno, 6 Oct. 1887; *d* Orange, NJ, 10 July 1982). Czech soprano. She studied in Brno, then sang in the chorus of the Brno Opera before making her solo debut in Olmütz (Olomouc) in 1910. From 1913 to 1938 she was a member of the Vienna State Opera ensemble; she appeared regularly at the Metropolitan Opera, New York, between 1921 and 1932, returning sporadically as a guest until 1951. A great beauty, she was a compelling, if idiosyncratic, singing actress, much admired by Puccini and Strauss. She created the title role in Strauss's *Ariadne auf Naxos* (1912) and the Empress in *Die Frau ohne Schatten* (1919). Both Puccini's *Turandot* (1924) and Strauss's *Die ägyptische Helena* (1928) were written for her, but she sang neither title role at the respective premieres. Her commercial recordings generally failed to do her justice, though pirated tapes of her performances in Vienna and New York testify to the overwhelming excitement she could generate in the theatre. The manuscript of Strauss's last completed song, *Malven* ('Mallows', 1948), dedicated 'to beloved Maria', was found among her possessions after her death. She published her autobiography, *Sunlight and Song: A Singer's Life* (New York, 1924/R).   TA

📖 R. WERBA, *Maria Jeritza, Primadonna des Verismo* (Vienna, 1981)

Jerusalem. Choral song for unison voices (1916) by Parry to William Blake's short poem beginning 'And did those feet . . .' (not his long poem *Jerusalem*); Elgar orchestrated it for the 1922 Leeds Festival.

Jérusalem. Opera in four acts by Verdi to a libretto by Alphonse Royer and Gustave Vaëz from Temistocle Solera's libretto for Verdi's I *Lombardi alla prima crociata* (1843) (Paris, 1847).

Jessonda. Opera in three acts by Spohr to a libretto by Eduard Gehe after Antoine-Marin Lemièrre's play *La Veuve de Malabar* (Kassel, 1823).

Jesu, Joy of Man's Desiring. The title of a piano transcription by Myra Hess of J. S. Bach's chorale 'Wohl mir, dass ich Jesum habe' which ends each part of his cantata no. 147, *Herz und Mund und Tat und Leben*; the hymn text, from which the English title derives, is Martin Jahn's *Jesu, meine Seelen Wonne*. Hess's transcription was published in 1926 and for piano duet in

1934; it has since been arranged in various ways. In spite of its bright original scoring—for trumpet, oboes, strings, and continuo—arrangements are often played slowly and solemnly.

jeté (Fr., 'thrown'). In string playing, a bowstroke (also known as *ricochet) in which the bow is dropped on to the string so as to bounce several times.   DMi

Jeu de cartes ('Game of Cards'). Ballet 'in three deals' by Stravinsky to a scenario by the composer and M. Melaïeff; it was choreographed by George Balanchine (New York, 1937).

jeu de clochettes (Fr.). 'Glockenspiel'.

Jeu de Robin et de Marion, Le ('The Play of Robin and Marion'). Pastoral play with music, written by Adam de la Halle during the period 1283–5, while he was in the service of the French court at Naples. Its blend of rustic spoken comedy and simple songs has been seen as one of the elements from which grew the concept of opera, particularly *opéra comique*. But in fact the birth of opera was a peculiarly Renaissance phenomenon, and Adam's *Robin et Marion* had no immediate successors. See OPERA, I.

jeu de timbres (Fr.). 'Glockenspiel'.

Jeune France, La (Fr., 'Young France'). A group of composers formed in 1936 and including Yves Baudrier, Jean Yves Daniel-Lesur, André Jolivet, and Olivier Messiaen. They were opposed to the neo-classicism current in Paris at the time, and the aesthetic of Les *Six, determining that their music should serve higher goals; otherwise the grouping has little significance.

Jeunesses Musicales (Fédération Internationale des Jeunesses Musicales; FIJM). An international organization whose stated purpose is 'to enable young people to develop through music across all boundaries' both as audiences and as performers. It boasts nearly half a million members in over 40 countries. Founded during World War II by the Belgian musician Marcel Cuvelier, it inspired Robert Mayer to found the British organization Youth and Music, with which it has links. Jeunesses Musicales spread rapidly after the war, organizing such events as international summer camps, festivals, and competitions for young musicians. It promotes an international youth orchestra and choir, both of which meet annually under the direction of world-renowned conductors. Its Imagine Festivals promote workshops, concerts, and competitions in a wide range of styles, including classical, jazz, folk, and rock. The organization's 'Crossroads' work embraces the rich musical heritage of African countries.   PSp

jeu-parti [partimen]. A type of troubadour or trouvère poetry cast in the form of a dialogue; as in the *tenso*, its most common topic is love. However, it is unlike the *tenso* in that the first speaker allows his opponent the choice of which of two positions he wishes to defend, then takes the opposite side.   AL

Jeux ('Games'). Ballet ('danced poem') by Debussy to a scenario by Vaslav Nijinsky; it was choreographed by Nijinsky, with designs by Léon Bakst, and performed by Diaghilev's company (Paris, 1913).

Jeux d'eau ('Fountains'). Piano piece (1901) by Ravel.

Jeux vénitiens. See VENETIAN GAMES.

Jewels of the Madonna, The. See GIOIELLI DELLA MADONNA, I.

Jewish music 1. Ancient Hebrew music; 2. The rise of synagogue song. 3. The 19th and 20th centuries

1. Ancient Hebrew music

A vivid picture of a musical culture in the making is given in the Old Testament. During the 2nd millennium BC the tribes of Israel—first as nomadic shepherds and later as farmers of the Judaean heights—passed on their traditions in song or recitation. Maidens went out to the fields to sing mythical songs and *maḥol* (rounds). Victories were celebrated with women's choirs and the beating of tambourines. The combined sound of harp, drum, flute, and lyre enraptured the bands of early prophets and turned young Saul 'into another man'. By contrast, the music of the lyre soothed the melancholy of the old King Saul. 200 years later, the prophet Elisha called for a lyre player to evoke the ecstatic spirit of prophecy.

The first instruments of religious worship were the *shofar* (horn of the ram or ibex) and a silver trumpet. Their sound may once have been connected with magic but it soon became associated with calling on the help of God. Both were also used for signalling, in peace and war, and for paying homage to the kings; the *shofar* continues to be used in worship to this day. The Bible mentions several stringed instruments, for example the *kinnor* or lyre, played with a plectrum. The *nevel* was another type of lyre, plucked with the fingers. *Ḥalil* was a generic name for pipes (probably reed instruments). It was a popular instrument with phallic associations, symbolizing fertility, life, and resurrection: thus it was played at weddings as well as funerals (Matthew 9: 23), and accompanied prayers for rain. Of the idiophones, only the *zalzal* and the *m'ziltayim* (cymbals) were sounded in the temple to separate the sections of psalm singing. The *tof* (frame drum) was the standard instrument of women in joy and mourning. *Azey broshim* (clappers) and *m'nànaìm* (rattles) were also played. Many instruments accompanied the solemn escort of the Holy Ark to Jerusalem (2 Samuel 6: 5).

Canaanite urban civilization imprinted its mark on Judaean musical life, as did Hellenism later. But genuine Hebrew music came into its own and achieved legendary fame as it was performed in the Temple of Jerusalem. It was established there, and given a royal charter by King David between 1002 and 970 BC. The Levite clan was entrusted with the vocal and instrumental performance for generations. We will never know how the much-praised psalm choirs and interludes sounded, but we can imagine the nature of their sonority as calm and restrained: a small male choir (occasionally heightened by boys' descants), accompanied simply by the plucked strings of lyres and harps. Cymbals, trumpets, and horns sounded only between the musical sections marked in the Psalm text with the word *sela*. This reserved character of Hebrew Temple music contrasted sharply with the drumming, rattling, and ecstatic clamour heard in most of the heathen cult rituals.

2. The rise of synagogue song

The music of the Temple was abolished, and its instruments banned until the coming of the Messiah, after the destruction of the Judaean state and its sanctuary by the Romans in AD 70. These events made synagogue song, together with poetry, the most characteristic expression of Jewish art. The sacrifices and other ceremonies were replaced by individual and congregational prayer associated with the study and exegesis of the Bible. Thus the singing had to make transparent the Word and its spiritual message and express religious feeling, while remaining within reach of lay musical comprehension and ability.

Three particular synagogue styles can safely be ascribed to the first centuries AD. These forms are a common heritage of synagogues all over the world, but their modern realization in melody differs widely according to local taste.

First, *psalmody, the sung recitation of psalms, generally on a single pitch, with melodic figures (cadences) attached to the middle and the end of the verse. Verses usually begin with an intonation (Ex. 1). This modest configuration is repeated throughout the entire psalm. Psalmody is frequently responsorial or antiphonal. The simple melodic pattern of psalmody is often embellished, varied, or extended to generate more elaborate forms.

The second vocal form of the early synagogue is Bible reading. The liturgical recitation of the Bible and other texts such as prayers were originally performed in a style similar to psalmody. The logical division of every sentence was clarified by musical cadences which interrupted the flow of words. These cadences were indicated by conventional gestures of the hand and fingers. This old instructional method, called *chironomy, is still practised in some Jewish communities. After about AD 500, teachers assigned written accent-signs to the points where the cadence motifs occurred. An intricate and still widespread system of scriptural accents, *Te'amim*, was drawn up by the Tiberias school of grammarians and concluded *c*.900. Particular combinations of accents divide the verse into word-groups: thus the tune of the reading is formed from a series of motifs repeated in various sequences (Ex. 2). Prayer modes are the third vocal form of the synagogue. Modes are based on a specific scale in conjunction with characteristic motifs, elaborated and varied by the singer.

During the second half of the 1st millennium AD, synagogue singers composed a rich repertory of hymns to accompany the prayers. These hymns perpetuated the free rhythm of biblical poetry and old Hebrew music. The role of ḥazan (precentor), which persists to the present day, grew from the increased demand for the professional composition and performance of hymns.

Attracted by the smooth flow and formal consistency of Arabic metrical verse, Hebrew poets adopted its rhythmical patterns, and some tunes also acquired measured rhythms. The metrically patterned tune was a new element in Jewish music. An unceasing search for an equilibrium between the old Hebrew rhythmic freedom and the metrical tunes of the host cultures is a recurring theme of Jewish musical history.

Ex. 1

L'Da - vid. A - do-shem ó - ri w'yish-ì, mi-mi __ í - rá,

A - do-shem ma-òz ha - yay, mi - mi éf - had.

Ex. 2

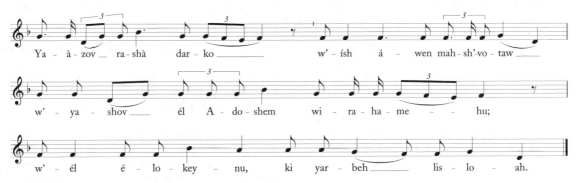

Ya - à - zov ra-shà dar - ko_____ w' - ísh á - wen mah - sh'vo - taw_____ w' - ya - shov_____ él A - do-shem wi - ra - ha - me - - hu; w' - él é - lo - key - nu, ki yar - beh_____ lis - lo - ah.

During the Middle Ages, a threefold pattern of musical life emerged in the dispersed Jewish communities. First was the established repertory of sacred song. Second was the profane art of itinerant minstrels, jugglers, and folk musicians. Third was contemporary art music. Jewish musical history demonstrates a continuing interplay of these three types, leading, for instance, to the adoption of secular art music in the synagogue, or the acceptance of folk-tunes for hymns.

Jewish integration at different levels of secular music is best illustrated during the late Italian Renaissance. An elite of Jewish minstrels rose to the rank of court musician (as had occurred formerly in Spain and other countries). Others practised as singers, dancers, and dancing-masters. Musical theory was advocated as a part of Jewish studies by the Mantuan rabbi Juda Moscato (d 1590). At least four Jewish composers had their madrigals published between 1575 and 1628. Salamone Rossi's choral compositions for the synagogue (Venice, 1622) were a genuine innovation.

During the Middle Ages, sacred song was influenced by the steady growth of mystical movements. Jewish mystics used song to prepare themselves for visionary states. With the spread of mysticism, precentors extend the vocalises in their melodies to suggest nuances hidden in the prayer text; by the use of leading motifs they hinted at secret meanings ascribed to certain words.

According to mystical tenets, prayer had to be offered in a joyful mood. The ordinary man was advised to overcome distress and gloom by singing his prayer to melodies close to his heart. The mystics of Safed in Galilee during the 16th and 17th centuries, who originated mainly from the Jews exiled from Spain, adopted for the synagogue song features of their vast repertory of Mediterranean folksong. Poets like Israel Najara (d 1628) composed a wealth of Hebrew hymns, some of which fit the tunes of well-known *romances*, villancicos, or oriental songs (Ex. 3, from a 1587 print giving the Spanish tune *Linda era y fermosa*).

Ex. 3

Refrain
Ku - mi yo - nah ye - ku' - shah / ú - ri é - ven ha - ró - shah!

Stanza
1. Yo - nah ze - í mi - ke - vel /
wa - he - gi shir aley ne - vel /
Ki á - shiv le - vat ba - vel / hish à - ma - lah be - ró - shah.

The latest ramification of Jewish mysticism is the Ḥasidic movement of eastern Europe (mid-18th century onwards), which emphasizes music as a direct mode of communication between the soul and the divine. Ḥasidic melodies (niggunim) are usually sung without words, cheerfully, and in an enthusiastic mood. They may use dance rhythms and typical modes (Ex. 4, ascribed to Rabbi Michal of Złoczew, d 1781).

The Ḥasidic style of singing influenced synagogue song in eastern Europe, and helped consolidate the very special style of its precentors (Ex. 5). This profession had always attracted and absorbed the musical talents of the isolated Jewish communities. Precentors often developed a virtuoso vocal style of great public appeal; their performance was accompanied by the improvisations of a descant and a bass singer. The more ambitious precentors strove to absorb the art music of the host cultures. In the East, for example, they adopted the maqām system during the 16th century. In Western countries, the late Baroque devices of ornamental diminution and variation techniques attracted some alert singers.

3. The 19th and 20th centuries

Early in the 19th century, the Jewish striving for social and political emancipation led to the assimilation of Western conventions. In the liturgy the process started with extreme reforms. Fervent disputes were aroused by prayer in the vernacular, chorales after Protestant models, mixed choirs, and organ-playing. Although most synagogues retained the traditional liturgy, they decided to change the performance practice of music, chiefly through the introduction of part-singing and permanent choirs (Paris, 1822; Vienna, 1826; Munich, 1832). The most influential innovator of synagogue music was Solomon Sulzer (1804–90), chief cantor of the Viennese Jewish community. He was a singer and arranger who laboured hard to reach his goal of 'satisfying musical demands while remaining Jewish'. In this respect, Louis Lewandowski of Berlin (1821–94) found musically more convincing solutions.

Many 20th-century composers, of varying standards and artistic convictions, contributed to synagogue music. They either explored the eastern European tradition using a quasi-improvisatory style for male choir, or expressed traditional moods in a contemporary

Ex. 4

Ex. 5

Ya - dà - ti, A - do-shem, ki⸺ ze - deq mish-pa - -tey - kha, w'ém-u - nah⸺ ini - ta - ni.

musical language. The sacred works of Bloch, Schoenberg, and Milhaud, however, are intended for the concert hall rather than the synagogue. The rich and diversified legacy of precentors' interpretations and compositions continues to grow.   HAv/JJD

jew's harp [jaw's harp, jew's trump] (Fr.: *guimbarde*; Ger.: *Maultrommel, Mundgeige*). A small metal hoop with two parallel arms between which a spring-steel reed with an up-bent end is closely set (Fig. 1). The arms are held between the player's lips. As the free end of the reed is twanged, the player may cause overtones to resonate selectively by changing his or her mouth-shape as though forming different vowels; a harmonic series is produced and tunes played. In Asia and Oceania, 'idioglot' jew's harps are made by slitting a reed in a piece of bamboo, palm-rib, or bone.   JMo

Fig. 1. The jew's harp.

jig. 1. A traditional dance of the British Isles, probably dating back to the 15th century. The word may be derived from the Old French verb *gigner* ('to leap', 'to gambol'). It is characterized by lively jumping steps, the only common feature of its many varieties. The best-known jig is the Irish, danced solo or by a couple to the accompaniment of the pipe and fiddle and usually in compound duple or triple time. The jig appears in the Fitzwilliam Virginal Book and other contemporary keyboard collections, with examples by Byrd, Bull, and Farnaby. Shakespeare mentioned the 'Scotch jig' in *Much Ado about Nothing*. See also GIGUE.

2. From the 16th century to the 18th, the jig (or jigg) was also an often bawdy farce in rhyme, sung and danced to popular tunes, performed both in England and on the Continent.   —/JH

jingle. A short and easily identifiable melody used to characterize a product or a broadcast programme. Jingles are used by radio and television stations to provide instant recognition of the station or an individual programme. In advertising, the jingle adds an aural trigger to a visual one.   JSɴ

jingles. A cluster of objects, for example small *crotal bells (*sleigh bells), miniature cymbals, bottle-tops, or

shells, that jangle against each other. They can be used as separate rattles or can be attached to other instruments (e.g. the *tambourine). See SISTRUM.   JMo

jingling johnny. See TURKISH CRESCENT.

Joachim, Joseph (*b* Kitsee, nr Pressburg [now Bratislava, Slovakia], 28 June 1831; *d* Berlin, 15 Aug. 1907). Austro-Hungarian violinist. A child prodigy, he studied the violin in Pest and Vienna. In 1843 he went to Leipzig, where he became a protégé of Mendelssohn, who arranged for him to study theory and composition with Moritz Hauptmann at the recently founded Leipzig Conservatory, accompanied him in most of his public appearances, and negotiated his first visit to England in 1844. Joachim was appointed by Liszt as leader of his orchestra in Weimar (1850–3), then became leader and Kapellmeister of the court orchestra in Hanover. In keeping with his affinity for the music of Beethoven, Mendelssohn, Schumann, and Brahms, Joachim broke with Liszt in 1857 and was one of four signatories to Brahms's declaration against the 'Musicians of the Future' (1860), directed at Liszt and his followers.

From 1866 Joachim's annual visits to England exerted enormous influence on English concert life. His concert career also included engagements as a conductor, particularly of Brahms's symphonic music. It was Joachim who first provided the encouragement for Brahms to start his career as a composer, and for years he was Brahms's confidant. Their friendship survived a rupture when Brahms sided with Joachim's wife in the violinist's unsuccessful suit for divorce in 1881; Joachim suffered from extreme jealousy, a trait that clouded his life more than once, and not until Brahms's Double Concerto op. 102 was being rehearsed (1887) did the two men meet again.

Involved with the foundation in 1868 of the Royal Conservatory in Berlin, Joachim was its only director from 1869 until his death, building an institution of the first rank. Among his most famous students were Leopold Auer, Bronislav Hubermann, and one of the first women violin virtuosos, Marie Soldat. In 1869 he founded the Joachim Quartet, whose celebrated performances were a dominant feature of musical life in much of Europe for over 30 years.

Joachim was a skilful composer (his *Hungarian Concerto* op. 11 for violin and the *Hebrew Melodies* op. 9 for viola and piano are returning to the repertory), and the standard cadenzas to the Brahms and Beethoven concertos are by him. He also acted as adviser to other composers—Bruch, Dvořák, and Brahms dedicated their concertos to him—and was the inspiration for Schumann's late violin works. Joachim was famous for his tone and the purity of his intonation, and he placed faithful interpretation above virtuosity for its own sake. His playing is well described by contemporary critics, notably his fine interpretation of Beethoven's Violin Concerto.   SA

📖 A. MOSER, *Joseph Joachim: Ein Lebensbild* (Berlin, 1898, 5/1910; Eng. trans. 1900) · J. A. FULLER MAITLAND, *Joseph Joachim* (London and New York, 1905) · JOHANNES JOACHIM and A. MOSER (eds.), *Briefe von und an Joseph Joachim* (Berlin, 1911–13; abridged Eng. trans. 1913/R1972) · B. SCHWARZ, 'Joseph Joachim and the genesis of Brahms's Violin Concerto', *Musical Quarterly*, 69/3 (1983), 503–26

Job. 1. 'Masque for dancing' in nine scenes and an epilogue by Vaughan Williams to a scenario by Geoffrey Keynes and Gwen Raverat after Blake's *Illustrations of the Book of Job*; it was performed first as an orchestral work (Norwich, 1930) and staged the following year in London.

2. Oratorio by Parry (Gloucester, 1892).

3. Opera (*sacra rappresentazione*) by Dallapiccola to his own libretto after the book of Job (Rome, 1950).

Jodel (Ger.). See YODEL.

Johannes de Lymburgia [Johannes Vinandi] (*fl* 1420–35). Composer and church musician. He was probably of French origin but was active in Padua and Vicenza. More than 40 compositions by him survive. They include pieces written in honour of the city of Padua, as well as liturgical hymns, *Magnificat* settings, and mass movements.   JM

Johannes de Muris (*b* nr Lisieux, *c*.1300; *d c*.1350). French theorist. A student in Paris from 1318, he spent periods also at Évreux, Fontevrault, and Mézières-en-Brenne and wrote at least three highly influential treatises on music in the early 1320s: *Ars nove musice* (*c*.1321), on definitions and acoustics; *Musica pratica* (*c*.1322), on notation; and *Musica speculativa* (1323), a distillation of Boethian theories of consonance. He also wrote works on mathematics and astronomy.
                                                        IR

John Brown's Body. American popular song; the tune is that of a well-known 19th-century camp-meeting and revival hymn written by a Philadelphia musician and still sung to the words 'Mine eyes have seen the glory of the coming of the Lord', a poem (1862) by Julia Ward Howe (the 'Battle Hymn of the Republic').

John Chrysostom (*b* Antioch, *c*.345; *d* Komana, 407). Saint ('golden-mouthed' homilist) and Archbishop of Constantinople (398–404). He studied rhetoric with Libanius in Antioch, where, after a period as a monk, he was ordained deacon and priest. He attacked contemporary pagan music and, in Constantinople, promoted stational processions with psalmody. The main

Eucharist ('Divine Liturgy') of the modern Orthodox Church is attributed to him.   ALi

John [João] **IV, King of Portugal** (*b* Vila Viçosa, 19 March 1604; *d* Lisbon, 6 Nov. 1656). Collector of music and composer. He studied music at an early age, and on becoming Duke of Bragança (1630) began to build up a substantial collection of music. This avid collecting activity—resulting in probably the largest music library of the time—continued after John became king in 1640. His collection was destroyed in the Lisbon earthquake of 1755, but a partial catalogue (Lisbon, 1649) reveals its enormous scope, with masses, motets, villancicos, madrigals, chansons, and instrumental works, by composers from many parts of Europe. Numerous pieces by Spanish and Portuguese composers do not survive. Only two motets preserved in a fragmentary state may be attributed to John with confidence (although other works are ascribed to him or to 'the king'). He was an important patron of Portuguese and Spanish composers, and published two musical treatises.
                                                     WT/OR

Johnson, Robert (*b* ?London, *c*.1583; *d* London, *c*.26 Nov. 1633). English composer and lutenist, the son of the lutenist John Johnson. He was in the service of Sir George Carey from 1596 until 1603. In 1604 he was appointed lutenist to James I, and was responsible for the upkeep of the king's lutes. He is best known for the songs he wrote for plays performed at the Globe and Blackfriars theatres; they include the popular 'Where the bee sucks' and 'Full fathom five' for Shakespeare's *The Tempest* (1611), as well as songs for *Cymbeline* (*c*.1609) and *A Winter's Tale* (*c*.1611), for Webster's *The Duchess of Malfi* (*c*.1613), and for several plays by Beaumont and Fletcher. He also wrote dance music for court masques, and dance-inspired pieces for solo lute.   DA/JM

'Joke' Quartet. Nickname of Haydn's String Quartet in E♭ major op. 33 no. 2 (1781), so called because at the end of the finale Haydn teases the listener's expectations with rests and repeated phrases.

Jolas, Betsy [Illouz, Elizabeth] (*b* Paris, 5 Aug. 1926). French-American composer. She studied in the USA (1940–6) and with Messiaen and Milhaud at the Paris Conservatoire (1948–55), then worked for French radio (1955–70) and as Messiaen's deputy at the Conservatoire. Boulez was a strong influence, though her music tends to be softer and smoother than his. Her works include operas (*Schliemann*, Paris, Bastille, 1990), symphonic pieces, others for smaller ensemble (*Points d'aube* for viola and 13 winds, 1968; *États* for violin and six percussionists, 1969), and chamber music (five quartets, of which the second, 1966, has a soprano replacing one of the violins).   PG

Jolie Fille de Perth, La ('The Fair Maid of Perth'). Opera in four acts by Bizet to a libretto by Jules-Henri Vernoy de Saint-Georges and Jules Adenis after Walter Scott's novel *The Fair Maid of Perth* (1823) (Paris, 1867).

Jolivet, André (*b* Paris, 8 Aug. 1905; *d* Paris, 20 Dec. 1974). French composer. He studied literature at the Sorbonne, also taking composition lessons with Paul Le Flem (1927–32) and Varèse (1928–30). His early works, including *Mana* for piano (1935) and the *Cinq incantations* for flute (1936), show a fascination with exotic religious beliefs and with irregular, flowing rhythms. In 1936, together with Messiaen and others, he formed the *Jeune France group in opposition to the flip aesthetic of Les *Six. He was conductor and later music director of the Comédie Française (1943–59), adviser to the French Ministry of Cultural Affairs (1959–62), and professor of composition at the Paris Conservatoire (1965–70). His large output includes many concertos and other orchestral works, often showing his facility for writing long, modal lines.
                                                                                      PG

Jommelli [Jomelli], Nicolò (*b* Aversa, 10 Sept. 1714; *d* Naples, 25 Aug. 1774). Italian composer. From 1725 he studied in Naples, where he was influenced by Hasse and Leo; in 1741 he went to Bologna, where he became a pupil and friend of Padre Martini and was admitted to the Accademia Filarmonica. He was *maestro di cappella* at the Ospedale degli Incurabili in Venice from 1741 to 1743, when he moved to Rome, in 1749 becoming *maestro coadiutore* to the papal chapel. In 1753 he was appointed *Ober-Kapellmeister* to the Duke of Württemberg at Stuttgart, where the court theatre was particularly lavishly equipped. In 1768 problems with the duke caused him to secure a non-resident appointment to provide operas for the royal court at Lisbon that enabled him to return to Naples.

Jommelli wrote operas for many Italian cities, and also for Vienna, where Metastasio, then court poet, greatly admired his tuneful and expressive melodies. His great achievement was to loosen the straitjacket of *opera seria* convention by increasing the dramatic importance of the orchestra, especially in accompanied recitative—the Stuttgart orchestra was among the finest in Europe—and by making more use of ensembles and also of ballet; in so doing he created operas that are integrated artistic works rather than vehicles for individual star singers and which have something in common with those of Gluck. He also wrote a substantial quantity of orchestrally accompanied church music in which solo, ensemble, and choral textures are effectively mixed in a way that to some extent foreshadows Haydn.   DA/ER

Jones, Daniel (Jenkyn) (*b* Pembroke, 7 Dec. 1912; *d* Swansea, 23 April 1993). Welsh composer. He studied at University College, Swansea, the RAM, and in Vienna. In Swansea he was an associate of Dylan Thomas, whose verse he set, and whose complete poems he edited in 1971. His compositions included nine symphonies and eight string quartets, as well as operas, choral pieces, and chamber music.   PG/AW

Jones, Robert (i) (*fl c.*1520–35). English church musician and composer. He was a Gentleman of the Chapel Royal during the reign of Henry VIII. Three works by him survive: a Mass, a votive antiphon, and a fragmentary song.   JM

Jones, Robert (ii) (*fl* 1597–1615). English composer. He took the B.Mus. at Oxford in 1597. In 1610 he was granted a patent, together with Philip Rosseter and two others, to train the 'Children of the Revells of the Queene'. He composed madrigals, but is principally known for his five books of ayres (London, 1600–10), which are retrospective in style.   DA/JM

jongleur (Fr.). A medieval entertainer or minstrel. The word derives from the Latin *jocus* ('jest') and has many variants within the Romance languages, not all of which imply musicianship.   JM

Jongleur de Notre-Dame, Le ('The Juggler of Notre Dame'). 1. Opera in three acts by Massenet to a libretto by Maurice Léna after the medieval legend recounted by Anatole France in his *L'Étui de nacre* (1892) (Monte Carlo, 1902).

2. Masque in one act by Maxwell Davies to his own libretto (Kirkwall, 1978).

Jonny spielt auf ('Jonny Strikes Up'). Opera in two parts (11 scenes) by Krenek to his own libretto (Leipzig, 1927).

Joplin, Scott (*b* north-east Texas, July 1867 – mid-Jan. 1868; *d* New York, 1 April 1917). American composer and pianist. He came from a musical family, and during the 1880s worked as a travelling musician. In the mid-1890s he settled in Sedalia, Missouri, and wrote songs and *ragtime pieces for piano. The second of these to be published, *Maple Leaf Rag*, eventually became so successful that it provided him with a steady though modest income. Out of a desire to see ragtime accepted as an art form and not simply popular entertainment, Joplin embarked on the composition of a ragtime opera (a ballet and an earlier opera had been staged in 1899 and 1903 respectively), but the result, *Treemonisha*, completed in 1910, failed to reach the stage in his lifetime; it was eventually given in 1972 (when his piano rags were attracting renewed and widespread attention) and won a posthumous Pulitzer Prize in 1976.　　PFA

　　📖 E. A. BERLIN, *King of Ragtime: Scott Joplin and his Era* (New York, 1994)

Joseph. 1. (*Joseph and his Brethren*). Oratorio (1744) by Handel to a biblical text by J. Miller.

2. Opera in three acts by Méhul to a libretto by Alexandre Duval after Genesis 37–46 (Paris, 1807).

Josephs, Wilfred (*b* Newcastle upon Tyne, 24 July 1927; *d* London, 17 Nov. 1997). English composer. He studied at Durham University and in Paris. The powerful Romantic style of his Requiem (1963) won him an international award, and he wrote many scores for films and television programmes as well as making substantial contributions to traditional instrumental and vocal genres. His works include ten symphonies and several operas, notably *Rebecca* (Opera North, 1983).

PG/AW

Josephslegende ('The Legend of Joseph'). Ballet in one act by Richard Strauss to a scenario by Harry Graf Kessler and Hugo von Hofmannsthal; it was choreographed by Mikhail Fokine for Diaghilev's Ballets Russes (Paris, 1914).

Joshua. Oratorio (1748) by Handel to a text probably by Thomas Morell.

Josquin des Prez [Jossequin Lebloitte] (*b* c.1450; *d* Condé-sur-Escaut, 27 Aug. 1521). Franco-Flemish composer. The towering composer of the Renaissance, he was profoundly influential on 16th-century music. His biography, which has never been easy to pin down, was substantially revised during the 1990s through the discovery that it conflated the lives of two different musicians; the other Josquin, variously called 'Judocus de Francia', 'Joschino di Picardia', etc., can now be isolated with certainty, and he appears not to have been a significant composer. As a result of this disentanglement, it is now clear that Josquin des Prez was born at a later date, and resident in Italy for far fewer years, than had previously been thought.

Josquin probably came from the region of Saint Quentin, and at an early age had connections with Condé-sur-Escaut (near Valenciennes), the town where he lived in his later years. Nothing is known about his early training or career. In 1477 he is recorded as a singer in the choir of René of Anjou; he may also have spent some time in Budapest. By 1484 he was in the service of Cardinal Ascanio Sforza, and from 1489 until about 1495 was a member of the papal choir in Rome. His exact whereabouts are unknown for the next seven years. Between June 1503 and April 1504 he was a member of the chapel choir of Ercole d'Este, Duke of Ferrara, an important position to which he was recruited in preference to Heinrich Isaac. From Ferrara he moved to the collegiate church of Notre Dame in Condé-sur-Escaut, where in May 1504 he was installed as canon and provost, posts he held until his death.

The collected edition of Josquin's music gives the impression of a prolific composer. Opinions vary, however, about the authenticity of many of the works attributed to him in 16th-century sources; doubts have even been cast over pieces that were once thought to be firmly his, such as the motet *Absalon fili mi*, which has now been tentatively reassigned to Pierre de la Rue. The problem arises from the fact that Josquin's music won international recognition during his lifetime, and was widely imitated. This was true especially in Germany, where the demand for 'new' works by Josquin continued long after his death; many of the disputed pieces are found only in posthumous German sources. Compounding the problem of attribution is the fact that Josquin's compositions are often individually idiosyncratic, making it hard not only to be sure what he might or might not have written, but also to place his works in chronological order. Josquin scholarship therefore has to consider four interrelated issues: biography, problems of attribution, the question of chronology, and Josquin's reputation and reception.

A few of his works can be linked with specific patrons, employers, or colleagues, and they provide some pillars of certainty. For example, the solemn five-voice motet *Miserere mei, Deus* belongs to the year Josquin spent at Ferrara (1503–4), and was written expressly for Ercole d'Este. *Virgo salutiferi*, a vigorous five-voice motet quite different in style from *Miserere*, probably dates from the same year. Josquin also paid homage to Duke Ercole in one of his Mass settings; it is built round an eight-note melody derived from the syllables 'Her-cu-les Dux Fer-ra-ri-e' ('Ercole, Duke of Ferrara'), which are translated by assonance of vowels into the solmization syllables *re–ut–re–ut–re–la–mi–re* (see MASS, Ex. 1). The resulting melody, which is used throughout as a cantus firmus, thus becomes an emblem of Ercole himself. What is not clear, however, is whether this work too dates from Josquin's year in Ferrara. Most authorities place it earlier on stylistic grounds, and this raises the possibility that Josquin's links with Ercole d'Este began some years before his actual residence in Ferrara.

The *Missa 'La sol fa re mi'*, too, is built round a motto derived from words; according to Glarean they echo the phrase 'Laise faire moy' ('Leave it to me'). For many years both this saying and Josquin's Mass were associated with Cardinal Ascanio Sforza. However, one manuscript copy of the work shows a turbaned figure bearing the words 'Lesse faire a mi', and this has led to the suggestion that both saying and Mass refer in some way to Prince Djem (half-brother of Sultan Bayezit II), who was courted by the popes during Josquin's years in Rome. Other works linked to specific persons include *Nymphes des bois*, the *déploration* which commemorates Johannes Ockeghem (*d* 1497)—though it is not known how soon after Ockeghem's death Josquin wrote the piece—and the late five-voice *De profundis*, which is clearly a memorial work for an unidentified French magnate. Examples such as these show how pieces of apparently firm attribution may nevertheless resist precise dating. Even the paired settings of 'Pater noster'/'Ave Maria', which Josquin intended to be sung after his death in front of his house on days in the church calendar when processions passed by, could have been written many years before 1521. What these and other works of secure authorship do make possible, however, is the task of sketching a profile of Josquin's musical personality. They provide benchmarks against which to judge pieces that are less certainly by him.

Josquin was a singer by profession, and virtually all his music is vocal in conception. His interest lay principally in three genres: the mass, the motet, and the French-texted chanson. He was an important contributor to all three; the masses in particular are striking, and were widely circulated at the time, but if impact on later generations is to be taken as a guide to significance, then Josquin's motets must be reckoned the works on which his reputation is most firmly anchored. This is partly because of their sheer number, partly because of their varied range of style and structure (compared, for instance, with the more homogeneous motet outputs of contemporaries such as Isaac and Pierre de la Rue), and partly on grounds of their intrinsic interest and quality. Even in early motets such as the popular *Ave Maria . . . virgo serena* Josquin shows true independence of mind, strongly innovatory tendencies, and a concern for the clear, rhetorical declamation of the words. Viewing his motets as a whole, it is remarkable how Josquin seems constantly to have reinterpreted and reinvented the genre, in ways that clearly stimulated his successors. In particular his interest in expressive text-setting was singled out for comment and praise by 16th-century writers; the great *Miserere mei, Deus* provides a magnificent example.

The masses are very varied indeed. They include works based on plainchant (the *Missa 'Pange lingua'*), monophonic songs (the two *L'Homme armé* masses), or voice parts extracted from polyphonic chansons (*Missa 'Faisant regretz'*). One, the *Missa ad fugam*, is an exercise in continuous canon. The chansons, too, cover a wide range, from lively little arrangements of popular songs to sombre, densely scored settings of languorous

love poetry, and the *déploration* in memory of Ockeghem, mentioned above. A few wordless pieces, such as *La Bernardina* and *Ile fantazies de Joskin*, were probably meant for instrumental consort. The garrulous *El grillo* is one of three Italian-texted songs attributed to him. Placed side by side, these works cover such a wide range of style and substance that they are barely credible as the work of one composer; in time, some may even be removed from him. Nevertheless it is clear that Josquin's genius extends beyond wit, inventiveness, and technical skill to include a striking characteristic: an extreme reluctance to repeat himself. 16th-century reports speak of him as a composer who wrote when he chose, not when asked, and who released new pieces only when fully satisfied with them. Apocryphal or not, these anecdotes chime in well with the evidence of the music itself.   JM

📖 R. SHERR (ed.), *The Josquin Companion* (Oxford, 2000)

Joubert, John (Pierre Herman) (*b* Cape Town, 20 March 1927). British composer. He studied at the South African College of Music and, after moving to England, at the RAM. He taught first at the University of Hull and from 1962 until his retirement at Birmingham University. His compositions include operas and large-scale symphonic works, and he has been particularly successful with sacred choral music, written in an uncomplicated yet vigorously contemporary style.   PG/AW

jouer (Fr.). 'To play'.

Jubilate (Lat., 'O be joyful'). The 100th Psalm (in the Hebrew and English numbering; 99 in the Greek Old Testament and the Vulgate). In the *Book of Common Prayer* it is provided as an alternative to the *Benedictus* (see BENEDICTUS, 2) at Morning Prayer; in the Roman Office since the Second Vatican Council and in the Anglican *Common Worship* it is an *invitatory alternative to the Venite.

jubilus. The name given in Latin antiquity to a joyful work song without text. First applied to melismatic Christian chant by Amalarius of Metz (9th century), it has customarily been defined narrowly by modern scholars as the long melisma on the final syllable of the refrain 'alleluia' in the alleluia chant. These melismas are often much freer in melody than the rest of the chant and have their own internal forms based on various patterns of repetition.   —/ALı

Judas Maccabaeus. Oratorio (1747) by Handel to a text by Thomas Morell based on biblical incidents; composed to celebrate the English victory at Culloden and the return to London of the victorious general, the

Duke of Cumberland, it contains the chorus 'See, the conquering hero comes'.

Judenkünig, Hans (*b* Schwäbisch Gmünd, mid-15th century; *d* Vienna, March 1526). German lutenist and composer. He was based in Vienna for at least the last eight years of his life. His two instruction manuals for amateur lutenists (*c.*1515–19, 1523) are among the first of their kind. They include, in addition to dances, arrangements of vocal settings of the odes of Horace.

JM

Judith. 1. Oratorio (1888) by Parry to a biblical text.

2. Biblical opera in three acts by Honegger to a libretto by René Morax (Monte Carlo, 1926).

3. Oratorio (1761) by Arne to a text by Isaac Bickerstaff.

Juditha triumphans. Oratorio (1716) by Vivaldi to a text by Giacomo Cassetti.

Juive, La ('The Jewish Woman'). Opera in five acts by Halévy to a libretto by Eugène Scribe (Paris, 1835).

jukebox. An automatic gramophone or record player, usually coin-operated, often placed in bars or cafés. A number of discs or tapes are racked and can be selected individually by customers. It has now been succeeded by devices that store the music digitally to be selected via microchips.

JMo

Julietta (*Snář*; 'The Dream-Book'). Opera in three acts by Martinů to his own libretto after Georges Neveux's play *Juliette, ou La Clé des songes* (Prague, 1938).

Julius Caesar. See GIULIO CESARE.

Jullien, Louis (George Maurice Adolphe Roch Albert Abel Antonio Alexandre Noé Jean Lucien Daniel Eugène Joseph-le-brun Joseph-Barême Thomas Thomas Thomas-Thomas Pierre Arbon Pierre-Maurel Barthélemi Artus Alphonse Bertrand Dieudonné Emanuel Josué Vincent Luc Michel Jules-de-la-plane Jules-Bazin Julio César) (*b* Sisteron, 23 April 1812; *d* Paris, 14 March 1860). French conductor and composer. After serving in the army he studied at the Paris Conservatoire, then conducted dance-music entertainments in Paris and London, thus establishing the early promenade concert. He also toured the USA (1853–4) and the Netherlands (1857). His programmes consisted largely of such popular numbers as quadrilles, galops, waltzes, and overtures, but he also performed more substantial works, including symphonies by Beethoven and Mendelssohn. A great showman with a talent for publicity, he attracted the best players into his orchestras.

SH

Junge Lord, Der ('The Young Lord'). Opera in two acts by Henze to a libretto by Ingeborg Bachmann after Wilhelm Hauff's story 'Der Affe als Mensch' from *Der Scheik von Alexandria und seine Sklaven* (1826) (Berlin, 1965).

'Jupiter' Symphony. Nickname of Mozart's Symphony no. 41 in C major K551 (1788). It is not known why or when the name originated but it was possibly first used in a programme for a Philharmonic Society of London concert, conducted by Bishop, on 26 March 1821; according to Mozart's son F. X. Mozart, the nickname was coined by Salomon.

just intonation. A system of tuning the scale to perfection, based on the ratios of the natural harmonics. Because there are two sizes of whole tone, the major tone 9:8 and the minor tone 10:9, keyboard instruments cannot change key and therefore require a tempered scale (see TEMPERAMENT). Other instruments and singers use just intonation whenever possible.

JMo

K. Abbreviation for *Köchel and *Kirkpatrick, used as a prefix to the numbers of Mozart's works and Domenico Scarlatti's keyboard sonatas respectively, as given in the standard *thematic catalogues of Ludwig Köchel and Ralph Kirkpatrick.

Kabalevsky, Dmitry Borisovich (*b* St Petersburg, 17/30 Dec. 1904; *d* Moscow, 14 Feb. 1987). Russian composer. He was destined for a career in mathematics and economics, but a flair for the arts encouraged him to devote himself to learning the piano. He also studied composition with Catoire and Myaskovsky at the Moscow Conservatory (1925–9), and from about that time began to produce his earliest important works, including the First Piano Concerto (1928), First String Quartet (1928), *Three Blok Poems* (1927), and First Piano Sonatina (1930); this last heralded an important facet of Kabalevsky's later writing, his music for young people, which included much piano music and a series of concertos for violin (1948), cello (1948–9), and piano (his Third Piano Concerto, 1952). He also became active as a writer on music from 1927 (a collection of his articles was published in Moscow in 1963), and was a key figure in the Union of Soviet Composers, established in 1932.

During the 1930s Kabalevsky wrote his Second Piano Concerto (1936)—perhaps the most striking and invigorating of the three—and launched into writing for the theatre, both incidental music and opera. His first opera was the three-act *Colas Breugnon* (Leningrad, 1938), in which his gifts for lyrical melody, transparent orchestration, and vivid choral writing combined to make an effective stage piece, though it attracted criticism (primarily for certain aspects of the libretto) and Kabalevsky revised the score for its revival in 1971. A poor libretto dogged his next opera, *V ogne* ('Into the Fire'; Moscow, 1943), and Kabalevsky eventually withdrew it, incorporating some of the music into *Sem'ya Tarasa* ('The Family of Taras'; Leningrad, 1947, rev. 1950 and 1967). He composed one other opera, *Nikita Vershinin* (Moscow, 1955), and two lightweight operettas, *Vesna poyot* ('Spring Sings'; Moscow, 1957) and *Syostri* ('Sisters'; Perm', 1967). In his later years Kabalevsky devoted much attention to choral works and solo songs, though he continued to contribute to the instrumental repertory such works as the deeply felt, but tough and cogent Cello Sonata (1962).   GN

📖 G. ABRAHAM, *Eight Soviet Composers* (London, 1943) · S. D. KREBS, *Soviet Composers and the Development of Soviet Music* (London and New York, 1970)

kabuki. A form of Japanese theatre that originated in the Edo period (1603–1868). It is traditionally performed by males. Music is played both off stage and on: off stage, the *geza* ensemble of percussion, flutes, *shamisen*, and singer sets the mood and location, provides interludes, and performs songs which may accompany mime. A similar onstage ensemble (*debayashi*), without a singer, provides a commentary on the narrative, and accompanies dance.   KC

Kaddish. A Jewish doxology in Aramaic and Hebrew sanctifying the name of God, used liturgically in the synagogue to punctate sections of services. Other versions of the Kaddish, including one traditionally recited at a funeral by the sons of the deceased, are associated in Jewish practice with prayer for the dead.   ALi

Kadenz (Ger.). 1. 'Cadence'.
2. 'Cadenza'.

Kadosa, Pál (*b* Léva [now Levice, Slovakia], 6 Sept. 1903; *d* Budapest, 30 March 1983). Hungarian composer, pianist, and teacher. A piano pupil of Arnolf Székely and Kodály at the Academy of Music in Budapest (1921–7), he embarked on a short career as a pianist before concentrating on teaching, in Budapest, at the Fodor Music School (1927–43), the Goldmark Music School (1943–4), and the Academy of Music (from 1945); many of the leading Hungarian pianists of the present day studied with him. He was a productive composer, his music influenced by Bartók, though his output has yet to be fully investigated. It includes eight symphonies and other orchestral pieces, four piano concertos, two for violin and a concertino for viola, three string quartets and other chamber works, and much music for piano, not least four sonatas.   MA

Kagel, Mauricio (Raúl) (*b* Buenos Aires, 24 Dec. 1931). Argentine composer. He studied literature and philosophy at the University of Buenos Aires (1950–5) and took private music lessons. In 1955 he began organizing concerts at the university while working as a choral coach and conducting at the Teatro Colón. His early works show an awareness of advanced European serial techniques (String Sextet, 1953, rev. 1957) and a willingness to experiment with electronics (*Música para la torre*, 1952). He was therefore equipped to join the international avant-garde when he moved to Cologne in 1957. However, he quickly showed a taste for the bizarre or absurd which distanced him from such colleagues as Stockhausen.

Although he explored new sounds and new formal procedures in, for example, *Transición II* for pianist, percussionist, and tapes (1958–9) and *Sur scène* for speaker, mime, singer, and three instrumentalists (1958–60), Kagel was also attracted by the theatrical potential of unusual performance situations. This he has exploited in many subsequent works for the concert hall, opera house, cinema, and radio. Often the intention is to question common musical conventions: *Staatstheater* (1967–70), for instance, requires the performing personnel of an opera house—soloists, chorus, ballet, orchestra—to engage in activities right outside their norms, while the *Sankt-Bach Passion* (1981–5) is an oratorio on the life and music of J. S. Bach. In some later works, though, the irony is at a lower level, almost covered by a rich inventiveness of sound and gesture: examples include several orchestral scores of the 1990s.

Kagel has appeared widely as a performer (with his own Cologne New Music Ensemble since 1961), lecturer, and teacher; in 1974 he was appointed professor of music theatre at the Cologne Conservatory.

PG

📖 D. SCHNEBEL, *Mauricio Kagel: Musik, Theater, Film* (Cologne, 1970) · M. KAGEL, *Kagel ... /1991* (Cologne, 1991); *Worte über Musik: Gespräche, Aufsätze, Reden, Hörspiele* (Cologne, 1991)

Kaisermarsch ('Emperor March'). Work (1871) by Wagner for unison male voices and orchestra, composed to celebrate the German victory in the Franco-Prussian War (1870) and the election of Wilhelm I as emperor.

Kaiserquartett. See 'EMPEROR' QUARTET.

Kaiser von Atlantis, Der (*Der Kaiser von Atlantis, oder Der Tod dankt ab*; 'The Emperor of Atlantis, or Death Abdicates'). Opera ('legend') in four scenes by Ullmann to a libretto by Petr Kien, composed in 1943 at *Terezín (Amsterdam, 1975).

Kaiser-Walzer ('Emperor Waltz'). Waltz, op. 437 (1888), by Johann Strauss (ii), composed in honour of Emperor Franz Joseph. Schoenberg arranged it for chamber ensemble (1925).

Kakadu Variations. Beethoven's variations for piano trio, op. 121*a* (1803), on Wenzel Müller's song 'Ich bin der Schneider Kakadu' ('I am the tailor Kakadu') from the musical play *Die Schwestern von Prag* ('The Sisters from Prague', 1794).

Kalabis, Victor (*b* Červený Kostelec, 27 Feb. 1923). Czech composer. He studied at the Prague Conservatory (1945–8) and at the Academy of Musical Arts (1952), concurrently studying philosophy and musicology at the university. From 1953 he worked for Czech radio, leaving in 1972 to devote himself to composition. He is one of the most prominent Czech composers of his generation, and among the few to have achieved international renown. His music shows influences of Bartók and Honegger, as well as of Czech and Moravian folklore. An admirer of Brahms, he initially wrote in a late Romantic idiom, but developed an individual style characterized by avoidance of expressive excess and attention to concision and proportion. Many of Kalabis's works have been the result of important commissions (the Violin Concerto no. 2 from Josef Suk, Symphony no. 4 for the Dresden Staatskapelle). He won recognition with his monothematic String Quartet no. 2 (1962); his best-known pieces also include the Symphony no. 2 (*Sinfonia pacis*, 1961) and the Harpsichord Concerto (1975)—the latter, like the Piano Concerto no. 1 (1954), written for his wife Zuzana Růžičková.

MHE

Kalevala. Finnish epic songs from the Kalevala region, transmitted orally for several centuries. In 1835 Elias Lönnrot published an edition of 12,000 verses, and in 1949 a second edition of 23,000, in trochaic verse, unrhymed, divided into 50 cantos or runes; it has been translated into Swedish, German, English, and French. Several Finnish composers have based works on parts of this epic, notably Sibelius, in his *Kullervo*, *Pohjola's Daughter*, *Tapiola*, and the *Lemminkäinen Suite*.

kalimba. See MBIRA, KALIMBA, LIKEMBE.

Kalinnikov, Vasily Sergeyevich (*b* Voiny, Oryol district, 1/13 Jan. 1866; *d* Yalta, 29 Dec. 1900/11 Jan. 1901). Russian composer. He grew up in impoverished circumstances, and it was probably during his youth that he contracted consumption, the cause of his early death. He studied music in Moscow, and in 1893 was appointed conductor of the Italian Opera. However, he had to resign through ill health, and he spent the rest of

his life in the warmer climate of the Crimea. There he devoted himself to composition, making his name especially with his accomplished First Symphony (1894–5), which displayed the influence of Tchaikovsky and The Five. He also composed a Second Symphony (1895–7), some stage music, chamber works, piano pieces, and songs. In his final years he was sustained by the generosity of friends, especially the critic Semyon Kruglikov (1851–1910); he also received the attention of Rakhmaninov, who in 1900 persuaded Pyotr Jürgenson to publish his First Symphony and some other works.
PS/GN/MF-W

Kalkbrenner, Frédéric [Friedrich Wilhelm Michael] (*b* between Kassel and Berlin, Nov. 1785; *d* Enghien-les-Bains, 10 June 1849). French pianist, composer, and teacher, of German extraction. He was one of the earliest outstanding students of the Paris Conservatoire, where he studied the piano and composition. It was during his decade in England, where he moved in 1814, that he established an international reputation. In 1824 he returned to Paris, now recognized as a leading virtuoso, and also attracting attention as a composer. Chopin's two piano concertos show the influence of Kalkbrenner's concertos, and his Preludes also had an antecedent in Kalkbrenner's *24 préludes dans tous les tons* op. 88. Few of Kalkbrenner's own works transcend the clichés of the brilliant early Romantic style that he helped to popularize.

Kalkbrenner was a part-owner of the Pleyel firm of piano makers. In 1831 he published a *Méthode pour apprendre le pianoforte à l'aide du guide-mains*, a piano tutor to accompany his invention of a set of parallel metal rails attached to the keyboard in an attempt to force the hapless piano student to use only finger action while practising. Leaving aside the many cases of paralysis no doubt caused by the *guide-mains*, the tutor offers a useful insight into early Romantic concepts of playing and teaching.
KH

Kalliwoda, Johann Wenzel [Kalivoda, Jan Křtitel Václav] (*b* Prague, 21 Feb. 1801; *d* Karlsruhe, 3 Dec. 1866). Bohemian composer and violinist. He studied at the Prague Conservatory, then joined the orchestra of the Estates Theatre, where Weber was still conductor. In 1821 he toured Germany, Switzerland, and Holland, and the next year became conductor to the Prince of Fürstenberg at Donaueschingen, remaining there for the rest of his life. Kalliwoda was a prolific composer: he wrote over 300 works, including seven symphonies, concertos for various instruments including the violin, oboe, and bassoon, and an opera *Blanda, oder Die silberne Birke*. His son Wilhelm (1827–93) was a pianist, conductor, and composer.
WT

Kálmán, Emmerich [Imre] (*b* Siófok, 24 Oct. 1882; *d* Paris, 30 Oct. 1953). Hungarian composer. After studying at the Budapest Academy of Music, his interests centred increasingly on the theatre. He had his first real success with *Tatárjárás* ('The Gay Hussars', 1908) and became one of the leading figures of Viennese operetta, retaining a strongly Hungarian flavour in his works, which included *Der Zigeunerprimas* ('The Gypsy Chief', 1912), *Die Csárdásfürstin* ('The Csárdás Princess', 1915), *Gräfin Mariza* ('Countess Mariza', 1924), and *Die Zirkusprinzessin* ('The Circus Princess', 1926).
PGa/ALa

Kalmus, Alfred. See Universal Edition.

Kamarinskaya. Orchestral piece (1848) by Glinka, arranged for piano duet in 1856.

Kaminski, Heinrich (*b* Tiengen, Baden, 4 July 1886; *d* Ried, Bavaria, 21 June 1946). German composer and teacher. He studied at the Stern Conservatorium in Berlin and in 1930 succeeded Pfitzner as professor at the Prussian Academy of Fine Arts in Berlin, leaving in 1933 with the Nazis' accession to power and returning to Ried to compose. His music is powerfully polyphonic, with a sense of architecture inherited from Bruckner and of purposeful counterpoint acquired from Bach. His output is small but of high quality; there are two operas (*Jürg Jenatsch*, 1929; *Das Spiel vom König Aphelius*, 1950) and a *Passionspiel* (1920), a setting of Psalm 69 and a *Magnificat*, and organ music.
MA

Kammer (Ger.). 'Chamber', e.g. *Kammermusik*, 'chamber music'; *Kammersymphonie*, 'chamber symphony'; *Kammerton*, 'chamber pitch' (see Cammerton; pitch, 3).

Kammermusik ('Chamber Music'). Title given by Hindemith to seven instrumental works (1922–7): no. 1 (1922) is for small orchestra; no. 2 (1924) is a piano concerto; no. 3 (1925) is a cello concerto; no. 4 (1925) is a violin concerto; no. 5 (1927) is a viola concerto; no. 6 (1927) is a viola d'amore concerto; and no. 7 (1927) is an organ concerto.

Kancheli, Giya (*b* Tbilisi, 10 Aug. 1935). Georgian composer. He studied under Iona Tuskiya at the Tbilisi Conservatory, where he taught composition from 1970. In 1971 he became musical director of the Rustaveli Theatre in Tbilisi, for which he wrote a number of musicals. At the centre of his more serious output are the seven symphonies, which characteristically proceed at slow tempos with striking textural and dynamic contrasts and many interspersed silences. Elements of Schnittke-like polystylism, allusions to the sounds of Georgian folk music, and influences of film music also feature in much of his output. In 1992 he settled in Berlin.

JWAL

Kander, John (*b* Kansas City, MO, 18 March 1927). American composer. He studied music at Oberlin College and Columbia University, and worked as a vocal accompanist. In 1962 he began collaborating with the lyricist Fred Ebb. After the pop successes *My Colouring Book* and *I Don't Care Much* they began to work on musicals, and with *Flora the Red Menace* (1965) began a long relationship with the singer Liza Minnelli. Their most successful shows include *Cabaret* (1966; filmed 1972) and *Chicago* (1975), both exploiting an astringent style that often refers to period popular music. Their songs for film include the title song of *New York, New York* (1977).

JSN

kanon. A Byzantine poetic form consisting of nine odes, or biblical canticles. Each ode begins with a model stanza (heirmos), followed by three or four further stanzas (troparia), the last (theotokion) in praise of the Virgin. The kanon is sung at the morning Office of the Greek Orthodox Church in three stages of three odes. Each ode is provided with a different melody to which the heirmos is sung, the remaining stanzas being recited.

PFA

kantele. A wing-shaped *psaltery of Finland, with five wire strings (up to 13 on modern instruments) plucked by the fingers. It is analogous to the *kokle* (Latvia), *kannel* (Estonia), *kanklės* (Lithuania), and *gusli* (Baltic Russia).

Kantional. See CANTIONAL.

Kantor [Cantor] (Ger.). The director of music at a German Protestant church and usually also of any choir school or similar institution attached to such a church. Bach, for example, was Kantor of the church and school of St Thomas, Leipzig.

Kantorei [Cantorei] (Ger.). In the 15th and 16th centuries, a group of professional singers employed by a church or at a court.

Kapelle (Ger.). *'Chapel'; *Hofkapelle*, 'court chapel'.

Kapellmeister (Ger., 'chapel master'). See CHAPEL.

Kapralová, Vítězslava (*b* Brno, 24 Jan. 1915; *d* Montpellier, 16 June 1940). Czech composer. Her father, the composer Václav Kaprál (1889–1947), prompted her to compose from an early age. She studied composition and conducting in Brno (1930–5) and continued in Prague with Novák and Talich respectively. This was followed by further study in Paris with Martinů, with whom she developed a close personal and professional relationship, and Charles Münch. In 1940 she

married the writer Jiří Mucha, dying shortly afterwards from tuberculosis. Her best-known work is the *Vojenská symfonietta* ('Military Sinfonietta'), but a number of compositions, some touched by the influence of her teachers Novák and Martinů, indicate a fine potential talent sadly cut short.

JSM

Karajan, Herbert von (*b* Salzburg, 5 April 1908; *d* Anif, 16 July 1989). Austrian conductor. He studied at the Salzburg Mozarteum and made his debut in Salzburg in 1927 with *Fidelio*. He soon made a strong impression in Germany as a brilliant and original conductor, who achieved great polish and refinement in his performances. After early appointments at Ulm (1929) and Aachen (1934), he came to high prominence as music director of the Berlin State Opera from 1939 to 1945. He formed an important association with the Philharmonia Orchestra (1948–60) and was a powerful music director of the Vienna State Opera (1956–64), but it was as music director of the Berlin Philharmonic (1955–89) that he achieved his greatest prowess. With it he developed his unmistakably individual style, noted for its opulent sonorities and dynamic extremes that blended together seamlessly. He was influential in opera, being artistic director of the Salzburg Festival (1956–60, 1964–88) and founding the Salzburg Easter Festival, where he staged his own productions. He also made many films of operas. His international career was halted until 1947 because of his Nazi affiliations. A charismatic individual, he was one of the outstanding conductors of the second half of the 20th century.

JT

📖 K. LANG, *The Karajan Dossier* (London, 1992) · R. OSBORNE, *Karajan: A Life in Music* (London, 1998)

karaoke (from Jap. *karappo*, 'empty', and *okesutura*, 'orchestra'). Invented in Japan in about 1980, karaoke was formed of a hybridization of traditional 'folk' culture with modern technology. It began its life in places of evening entertainment: a tape would be played containing only the accompaniment of a popular song, giving customers a chance to sing into a microphone. More specifically designed equipment has since allowed 'home karaoke'. Because the Japanese often live in densely populated accommodation, the public roadside 'karaoke box' and soundproofed 'karaoke rooms' have also been developed.

PW

Karel, Rudolf (*b* Plzeň, 9 Nov. 1880; *d* Terezín, 6 March 1945). Czech composer. He studied law at the Prague Conservatory (1901–4), where in his final year he was taught by Dvořák, whose last pupil he thus became. He threw himself into composition, writing a number of chamber works and orchestral scores, of which the symphonic poem *Ideály* (1906–9) was particularly well received. He had also written an opera, *Ilseino srdce* ('Ilsea's Heart', 1906–9; staged 1924), before going to Russia for the summer in 1914, only to find that the outbreak of war prevented him from returning home. Arrested as a suspected Austrian spy and sent to Irkutsk, he escaped and joined the Czech Legion, for which he organized and conducted a symphony orchestra. He continued to compose but had to abandon all but a single work, the orchestral *Démon* (1918–20).

After his return to Prague in 1920 Karel taught at the conservatory (1923–43), also writing a second opera, *Smrt kmotřička* ('Godmother Death'; Brno, 1933) and a second symphony, 'Spring' (1935–8), a third string quartet (1935–6), and much else, not least a number of choral pieces and songs. With the Nazi invasion, the socialist Karel gave vent to his feelings both in music, with the *Revolutionary Overture* (1938–41), and by joining the resistance and acting as a go-between for undercover groups. In March 1943 he was arrested by the Gestapo, imprisoned, and tortured. His spirit undimmed, he began in his prison cell to compose a third opera, *Tři zlaté vlasy děda vševěda* ('Three Golden Hairs of the Wise Old Man', 1944–5), committing the music to memory and writing the short score on hundreds of scraps of paper. In these conditions he managed also to compose a nonet for wind quintet and string quartet before being transferred in February 1945 to *Terezín, where he died a month later of dysentery.   MA

📖 J. KARAS, *Music in Terezín, 1941–1945* (New York, 1985)

Karelia. Overture and suite for orchestra, opp. 10 and 11 (1893), by Sibelius. Karelia is a province in southern Finland.

Karetnikov, Nikolay Nikolayevich (*b* Moscow, 28 June 1930; *d* Moscow, 10 Oct. 1994). Russian composer. He studied at the Moscow Conservatory under Shebalin. During the 1960s he joined many of his fellow Soviet composers in adopting serialism; he was exceptional, however, in continuing to use this technique for the rest of his career. His output displays an uncompromising seriousness, and chamber genres predominate. Only the ballet *Vanina Vanini* (1962), performed at the Bol'shoy Theatre, won him substantial success; his works generally met with indifference from the public, and some were banned by the authorities. His first opera, *Til' Ulenshpigel'*, was completed in 1985 but staged in Germany only in 1993; the opera-oratorio *Misteriya apostola Pavla* was written between 1972 and 1987.   JWAL

Karg-Elert, Sigfrid (*b* Oberndorf am Neckar, 21 Nov. 1877; *d* Leipzig, 9 April 1933). German composer and organist. He studied at the Leipzig Conservatory with Carl Reinecke and Salomon Jadassohn, and taught there from 1919. His creative output was enormous, but he is remembered chiefly for his organ works, which themselves constitute a considerable body, and secondarily for his pieces for harmonium. Unusually among German composers of his time he was influenced by Debussian harmony, and his organ pieces range from chorale improvisations (66 dating from 1908–10, 20 chorale preludes and postludes from 1912) to Romantic impressions.   PG

Karłowicz, Mieczysław (*b* Warsaw, 11 Dec. 1876; *d* Tatra mountains, 8 Feb. 1909). Polish composer. The son of a leading figure in Warsaw musical life, he studied in Berlin and Leipzig, and was an inspiration to the 'Young Poland' group of composers who came to prominence in the early years of the century, including Szymanowski. Karłowicz's early songs and orchestral works suggest influences from Brahms and Tchaikovsky, but in a later series of tone-poems, including *Powracające fale* ('Returning Waves'), *Odwieczne pieśni* ('Eternal Songs'), *Stanisław i Anna Oświecimowie*, and *Epizod na maskaradzie*, his allegiance to 'New German' music is clear. In spite of their overt dependence on Straussian orchestral polyphony, these works are increasingly recognized as masterly, and it is regrettable that Karłowicz's promise was cut short by his early death in an avalanche.   JS

📖 A. WIGHTMAN, *Karłowicz, Young Poland and the Musical Fin-de-Siècle* (Aldershot, 1996)

Kassation (Ger.). See CASSATION.

Kát'a Kabanová. Opera in three acts by Janáček to his own libretto after Alexander Ostrovsky's play *Groza* ('The Storm', 1859) (Brno, 1921).

Kate and the Devil. See DEVIL AND KATE, THE.

Katerina Izmaylova. A revision of Shostakovich's *The *Lady Macbeth of the Mtsensk District*.

Kats-Chernin, Elena (*b* Tashkent, 4 Nov. 1957). Uzbek-born Australian composer. She studied in Tashkent and Moscow, and, after her family had emigrated to Australia, at the Sydney Conservatorium with Richard Toop. After further study from 1981 with Helmut Lachenmann in Hanover she remained in Germany, working with theatre and dance companies. In 1994 she returned to Australia, where her works have included two chamber operas, *Iphis* (1997) and *Matricide* (1998). She has also written orchestral and chamber music, and many piano pieces. Her music is quirky and often humorous, reflecting diverse influences including those of Stravinsky, Weill, tango, klezmer, and ragtime.

ABur

Katuar, Georgy Lvovich. See CATOIRE, GEORGY LVOVICH.

Katzenmusik (Ger.). See CHARIVARI.

Kay, Ulysses (Simpson) (*b* Tucson, AZ, 7 Jan. 1917; *d* Englewood, NJ, 20 May 1995). American composer. A nephew of the jazz musician King Oliver, he studied at the Eastman School (1938–40), with Hindemith, and with Otto Luening at Columbia University (1946–9). The American Prix de Rome took him to Italy (1949–52), after which he worked in New York for Broadcast Music Inc. (1953–68) and at Lehman College (1968–88). His works include operas, much choral music, orchestral pieces, and chamber music. PG

kayagŭm. Long zither of Korean classical music, similar to the Japanese *koto*, with 12 strings, each standing on its own bridge.

kazoo. An instrument that imparts a rasping, buzzing quality to the human voice. It now consists of a cigar-shaped tube of metal or plastic (sometimes amplified by a trumpet-like bell). A disc-shaped membrane fixed over a large hole in the top of the tube vibrates as the performer sings or hums into the mouth-hole at the other end. The term is sometimes used generically of all *'mirlitons' or 'singing membranes' (see INSTRUMENTS, CLASSIFICATION OF). JMo

Kb. (Ger.). Abbreviation for *Kontrabass*, 'double bass'.

Keel Row. English north-country song. Its origin is unknown but it first appeared in print in *A Collection of Favourite Scots Tunes* (Edinburgh, 1770); it is, however, principally associated with the Tyneside district (where 'keel' means boat in the local dialect). Debussy quoted it in *Gigues*, the first of his **Images* for orchestra.

keen. See CAOINE.

Keiser, Reinhard (*b* Teuchern, nr Weissenfels, *bapt.* 12 Jan. 1674; *d* Hamburg, 12 Sept. 1739). German composer. After service (from about 1692) as court composer at Brunswick, where he wrote the first of his 60 operas, he transferred in 1696 to Hamburg. There, as director of the Theater am Gänsemarkt, he mounted many of his finest works, including *Masagniello furioso* (1706) and *Croesus* (1711). Following visits to Stuttgart and Copenhagen from 1718, he returned to Hamburg in 1723 to further his operatic career. In addition to his operas and other stage works, he composed much church music, including Passions, oratorios, and cantatas. BS

Kelly, Michael (*b* Dublin, 25 Dec. 1762; *d* Margate, 9 Oct. 1826). Irish tenor, actor, and composer. He studied singing with various Italians living in Dublin, notably Giuseppe Passerini and Venanzio Rauzzini. After making his debut in the city, in 1779 he left for Naples, where he studied with Fedele Fenaroli and Giuseppe Aprile. Recruited by the Austrian Emperor Joseph I for his Italian opera company at court—the Austrian ambassador had heard Kelly sing in Venice—he moved to Vienna, where he remained for four years (1783–7). There he became friendly with Mozart and appeared in *Le nozze di Figaro* as Don Curzio and Don Basilio. On returning to London in 1787 (with Attwood and the Storaces) he became principal tenor at Drury Lane, staying until his retirement in 1811. He was stage manager of the King's Theatre (1793–1824), and from 1801 until he went bankrupt ten years later he ran a music shop in Pall Mall and was involved in the wine trade. His volume of *Reminiscences*, published in 1826, is both entertaining and fascinating for its detail, recollection, and cultural insight. Kelly wrote music for 61 dramatic pieces including *Blue Beard* (1798), *Cinderella* (1804), *The Forty Thieves* (1806), and *The Lady and the Devil* (1820), though his gifts as a composer were limited to the creation of popular melody rather than anything more searching or technically demanding. Sheridan, suspecting that some of Kelly's compositions borrowed material from foreign sources, suggested that his music shop should carry the inscription: 'Michael Kelly, Composer of Wines and Importer of Music'.

WT/JDi

Kelterborn, Rudolf (*b* Basle, 3 Sept. 1931). Swiss composer, conductor, and teacher. He studied in Basle, and later with Willy Burkhard, Boris Blacher, Wolfgang Fortner, and Günter Bialas. He taught from 1960 in Detmold, Germany, and from 1968 at the Zürich Musikhochschule; in 1983 he became director of the Basle Academy of Music. Kelterborn's early neo-Baroque style was affected by his absorption of serial techniques, though he has remained independent of the avant-garde. His works include five operas, many cantatas, four symphonies and other orchestral music, five string quartets, and many pieces for various chamber ensembles. ABur

kemençe. Short-necked bowed fiddle of Turkey, with a narrow trough-shaped carved resonator and three strings, played held downwards with the body resting on the knee.

Kempe, Rudolf (*b* Niederpoyritz, Saxony, 14 June 1910; *d* Zürich, 11 May 1976). German conductor. He studied with Busch and began his career as an oboist, in 1929 joining the Leipzig Gewandhaus Orchestra. He became a répétiteur at the Leipzig Opera and in 1935 conducted his first performance there at short notice. He soon acquired a reputation as a disciplined but sensitive conductor and took several important posts, notably at the Dresden State Opera (1950–3), and the

Munich Opera (1952–4). At Covent Garden he made a deep impression in the 1950s and 60s with his refined, lyrical performances of Wagner and Strauss. He succeeded Beecham as principal conductor of the Royal Philharmonic Orchestra, with which he had a long association.   JT

Kempff, Wilhelm (Walter Friedrich) (*b* Jüterbog, 25 Nov. 1895; *d* Positano, 23 May 1991). German pianist and composer. His career began in Berlin in 1917; thereafter he toured Europe, South America, and Japan, but made his debuts in London only in 1951 and New York in 1964. His fame rests on his interpretation of the Classical and Romantic repertory, primarily on his unflamboyant playing of Beethoven and his natural affinity for Schumann's music; he recorded the complete sonatas of Beethoven and Schubert. He was an acclaimed pedagogue and chamber music player (with Casals, Fournier, and Menuhin). He composed many large-scale works, including four operas.   CF

📖 J. Hunt, *Giants of the Keyboard* (London, 1994)

Kempis, Nicolaes a. See A Kempis, Nicolaes.

Kerle, Jacobus de (*b* Ieper, 1531 or 1532; *d* Prague, 7 Jan. 1591). South Netherlands composer. He was one of the leading composers of the Counter-Reformation. During his career he worked at Orvieto, Rome, Dillingen, Augsburg, and, from 1583 until his death, at the imperial court at Prague. His output, which includes masses, motets, and a cycle of hymns for the church's year, conforms to the requirements of the *Council of Trent in its economy, restraint, and emphasis on the correct declamation of the text.   JM

Kerll, Johann Kaspar (*b* Adorf, Saxony, 9 April 1627; *d* Munich, 13 Feb. 1693). German organist and composer. His first employer, Archduke Leopold William at Vienna, sent him to Rome to study with Carissimi. In 1656 he was appointed Kapellmeister at the Bavarian court in Munich, and there he wrote a number of operas (including *L'Oronte* for the opening of the opera house) and ballets, apparently with some success. In 1673 he gave up his job, probably because of the current vogue for Italian musicians, and moved to Vienna, becoming court organist at St Stephen's Cathedral in 1674 and at the imperial court in 1677. His works include masses (including the splendid Mass for three four-part choirs) and keyboard pieces, but his dramatic works are now lost. Handel appears to have thought enough of Kerll's music to 'borrow' from it: the choruses 'Egypt was glad' from *Israel in Egypt* and 'Let all the angels' from *Messiah*, for example, both had their origins in keyboard canzonas by Kerll.   DA

Kern, Jerome (David) (*b* New York, 27 Jan. 1885; *d* New York, 11 Nov. 1945). American composer. He was at the forefront of the American dominance in musical theatre, his first big success being *Sally* (1920), which was followed by the classic *Show Boat* (1927). His 1930s shows produced such songs as 'Smoke Gets in your Eyes', and he wrote others for the Hollywood films *Swing Time* (1936), *You Were Never Lovelier* (1942), and *Cover Girl* (1944).   PGa/ALa

Kernis, Aaron Jay (*b* Philadelphia, 15 Jan. 1960). American composer. He studied at the San Francisco Conservatory, the Manhattan School, and Yale, his teachers including John Adams, Charles Wuorinen, and Jacob Druckman. After completing his studies he settled in New York. His music is always vivid and often passionately expressive, drawing on a variety of American influences, but it can also be humorous and, in the detail, intriguing. Most of his works are instrumental, presenting a strong sense of harmonic progression. They include three symphonies, *Colored Field* for cor anglais and orchestra (1994), two string quartets, *Still Movement with Hymn* for piano quartet, and songs both comic and touching.   PG

Ketèlbey, Albert W(illiam) (*b* Birmingham, 9 Aug. 1875; *d* Cowes, 26 Nov. 1959). English composer. He studied composition at Trinity College of Music, London, and his proficiency on the piano, cello, clarinet, oboe, and horn contributed to the development of his career as a composer and conductor. His tuneful, sentimental compositions *In a Monastery Garden* (1915), *In a Persian Market* (1920), and *Sanctuary of the Heart* (1924) became immensely successful. Some of Ketèlbey's piano works were published under the pseudonym Anton Vodorinski.   PGa/ALa

kettledrum. A *drum with a single skin membrane ('head') stretched over a hemispherical or egg-shaped resonator; a note of definite pitch is produced. The membrane may be tensioned by various means. Kettledrums are known from antiquity onwards. Often used for martial music, they have also been played on horse- or camelback. Small kettledrums were introduced from the Middle East (*naqqāra*) to Europe during the 13th-century Crusades; in England they came to be known as *nakers. Large European cavalry kettledrums, which were later put to orchestral use (see TIMPANI), were also inspired by Middle Eastern or Ottoman models. The larger of the two Indian *tablā* is a kettledrum. Kettledrums with shells made from hollowed tree trunks are found in Africa.   JMo

Keuris, Tristan (*b* Amersfoort, 3 Oct. 1946; *d* Amsterdam, 15 Dec. 1996). Dutch composer and teacher. He studied in Utrecht with Ton de Leeuw, and taught composition in the conservatories in Amsterdam, Hilversum, and Utrecht, also frequently lecturing abroad. Keuris's Sinfonia (1975) established him internationally as a composer with a distinctive neoromantic voice and a highly individual orchestral sound—a reputation enhanced by later works including concertos for piano (1980), violin (1984 and 1997), saxophone quartet (1987), alto saxophone (*Three Sonnets*, 1989), two cellos (1992), and organ (1993), a choral symphony, *Laudi* (1993), and a classically oriented Symphony in D (1995).   ABur

key. 1. As a compositional principle, the adherence in any passage to the elements of one of the major or minor *scales, or *tonalities. Compositions using the tonal system (and the separate movements of compositions) will normally have a principal key, understood as the one in which a movement begins and ends, and even those large areas of the music which deviate from the diatonic elements of the principal key may be regarded as ultimately dependent on it.   AW

2. A lever on an instrument which is depressed by finger or foot to produce a note, for example on a piano by finger, on an organ by foot, on woodwind by finger (the levers covering the airholes).

keyboard (Fr.: *clavier*; Ger.: *Klaviatur*; It.: *tastiera*; Sp.: *teclado*). The manual or pedalboard allowing players to control an instrument's action and select the required notes. The earliest surviving keyboard, from 3rd-century Aquincum, Hungary, was diatonic. In the Middle Ages B♭ was added, allowing both hard and soft tetrachords. By the mid-15th century, keyboards were fully chromatic, laid out as they are today.

Attempts have been made to realize purer intonation by splitting the chromatic keys so that, for example, the front part controls G♯ and the back A♭. Nicola Vicentino's arcicembalo of 1555 had 35 keys to the octave, giving quarter-tones. Other makers have sought to systematize fingering or to reduce the orientation of the keyboard to C major by making 'sequential keyboards' with several rows of keys. The best known of these is the Janko keyboard of 1887–8; such instruments have had their devotees, but generally their success has been limited.   JMo

keyboard fingering. In the modern system of keyboard fingerings an octave is divided into one group of three notes and another of four, representing two distinct hand positions. The aim is to connect these as imperceptibly as possible by passing the thumb under the long fingers, or the fingers over the thumb. Although many different methods have been used to indicate keyboard fingerings the system known as 'continental fingering', which numbers the thumb as 1

and the fingers 2 to 5, is now used exclusively by composers, teachers, and publishers.

1. Early methods; 2. The evolution of modern scale fingerings; 3. Fingering and articulation

1. Early methods

In scales with sharps or flats, the change of hand position is made most comfortably where long and short keys occur contiguously (Ex. 1). The little finger is generally reserved for the highest note in the right hand or the lowest in the left. This method has come to seem most natural and it is therefore difficult to imagine any other viable system. However, for over two centuries after the appearance of the earliest extant teaching manual, Buchner's *Fundamentbuch* (c.1520), fingerings radically different from today's were used.

Ex. 1

16th- and 17th-century sources consistently recommend that extended scale passages should use pairs of fingers, for example by passing the third finger over the fourth when ascending with the right hand, or the third over the second when ascending with the left. The shallower touch and longer chromatic keys of early keyboards compared with modern counterparts probably facilitated this method. The choice of paired fingerings was not arbitrary, being closely governed by accentuation. Many pedagogues advised that 'good' or strong fingers should coincide with accented beats. Two schools emerged: in the Italian tradition, represented by Girolamo Diruta, the second and fourth fingers were considered strong (Ex. 2a), whereas the English virginalists' tradition treated the third finger as strongest (Ex. 2b).

The latter mode of fingering reappears in many later sources including Purcell's *A Choice Collection of Lessons* (1696) and J. S. Bach's 'Applicatio' from the *Clavier-Büchlein vor Wilhelm Friedemann Bach* (1720). Even in the second half of the 18th century, C. P. E. Bach provides alternative fingerings in which the paired method appears most practical. Evidently such fingerings caused little difficulty at the time: D. G. Türk (*Clavierschule*, 1789) recalled W. F. Bach's ability to play the most complicated figurations smoothly and

Ex. 2

(a)

[Good Bad G B G B G B G]

(b)

[G B G B G B G B G]

(a) From Diruta, *Il transilvano*.
(b) From Bull, Prelude.

with astounding speed merely by using the three middle fingers.

2. The evolution of modern scale fingerings

The thumb was not entirely neglected by earlier musicians. Santa Maria (*L'arte de tañer fantasia*, 1565) recommended thumbs for fast scale passages (Ex. 3*a*) and many English virginalists notated for all five fingers (Ex. 3*b*). As the use of remote tonalities increased, fingering patterns were reconceived. C. P. E. Bach declared that his father had been the first to devise an approach exploiting the potential of the thumbs. François Couperin provided a system which, however, did not secure a smooth connection of the two hand positions. C. P. E. Bach's influence in developing a

Ex. 3

(a)

(b)

(a) Santa Maria
(b) Bull

Ex. 4

Couperin 1 2 3 4 2 3 4 5 (R.H.)

C. P. E. Bach 2 1 3 2 1 4 3 2 } (L.H.)
5 4 3 2 1 3 2 1

more sophisticated system was considerable, though some variants came to be regarded as unnatural and were dismissed by the 1790s. Evidently Beethoven adhered closely to Bach's method, and the second suggestions shown in Ex. 4 have become widely adopted.

3. Fingering and articulation

Since the mid-19th century pianists have been more flexible, often even placing the thumb on the raised chromatic keys. In 1839 Henri Herz observed that it was no longer necessary to 'avoid placing the thumb or little finger on black notes', and pianists were subsequently encouraged to practise all scales with the conventional C major fingering.

The principle that fingering can enhance articulation appears to have been observed in earlier keyboard performance, though the extent of its application is disputed. Many believe, for example, that paired fingerings imply a detached style or even a degree of rhythmic inequality. While this may be the result of such fingerings (Ex. 5), C. P. E. Bach's dictum that paired fingerings were often 'better suited for the attainment of unbroken continuity' is significant. Other early fingerings, however, give clearer indication of the required articulation and provide valuable insights into past performance ideals (Ex. 6). During the early 19th

Ex. 5

Ex. 6

(a)

(b)

(c)

(a) From Bull, Fantasia.
(b) From Couperin, *L'Art de toucher le clavecin*.
(c) From Milchmeyer, *Die wahre Art das Pianoforte zu spielen* (1797).

century the growing preference for *legato* style placed greater emphasis on simplicity of fingering. Unnecessary changes of hand position were avoided, and wherever possible the fingers were applied in their natural order. WGJ/NPDC

📖 H. FERGUSON, *Keyboard Interpretation from the 14th to the 19th Century* (London, 1975) · M. LINDLEY and M. BOXALL (eds.), *Early Keyboard Fingerings* (London, 1992)

key signature. A group of sharp or flat signs placed at the beginning of a composition (after the clef) or during a composition (normally after a double bar) to indicate the *key of the music that follows. By their positions on the staff the signs show which notes are to be consistently sharpened or flattened throughout, in all octaves, thus establishing the prevailing tonality of the music. Ex. 1 shows the 14 common key signatures, relating to all the diatonic major and minor keys. Each signature indicates one of two keys: the white note represents the major key, the black the minor key with the same signature (the 'relative' minor, its key note a minor 3rd below the major).

Key notes for the 'sharp' signatures rise a perfect 5th as each sharp is added, and the major key note is always a semitone above the last sharp; key notes for the 'flat' signatures fall a perfect 5th as each flat is added, and the major key note is always a perfect 4th below the last flat (i.e. the same pitch as the penultimate flat). The order of sharps in the signature is also by rising 5ths, the order of flats by falling 5ths and equivalent to the order of sharps reversed.

Keys with six sharps (F♯ major and D♯ minor) are the *enharmonic equivalents of keys with six flats (G♭ major and E♭ minor); keys with seven sharps (C♯ major and A♯ minor) are the enharmonic equivalents of keys with five flats (D♭ major and B♭ minor). Composers use either signature according to convenience and familiarity, but 'key colour' may also play a part in their choice: for example, sharp keys are thought to suggest bright colours, flat keys sober ones (see COLOUR AND MUSIC).

Although the use of one flat as a key signature is found in the earliest staff notation (11th–12th centuries),

the association of a prefatory signature with a particular tonality came only in the 18th century. The modal principles of medieval music often resulted in 'partial' signatures where different voice parts had different signatures, the lower ones often with one more flat than the upper ones. Sharps in signatures did not become common until the 17th century. Throughout the Renaissance and Baroque periods a wider range of keys was used than signatures suggest: pieces in minor keys were often written with one less flat and in major keys with one less sharp in the signature than is normal today, the 'missing' accidentals appearing regularly in the course of a piece where modern notation would include them in the key signature.

In the late 19th century and the 20th, chromaticism and atonality contributed to the demise of the key signature's usefulness. At the same time, some composers experimented with 'hybrid' signatures, including both sharps and flats, to draw attention to special features of tonality in their music.

See also ACCIDENTAL; CIRCLE OF FIFTHS; MUSICA FICTA; TONALITY. PS/JN

Khachaturian, Aram (*b* Tbilisi, 6 June 1903; *d* Moscow, 1 May 1978). Armenian composer. He studied in Moscow, at the Gnesin Institute of Music and then at the conservatory with Myaskovsky. His international reputation rests largely on the Piano Concerto (1936, introduced to England by Moura Lympany in 1940) and on the ballets *Gayane* (1942, from which comes the famous Sabre Dance) and *Spartak* ('Spartacus', 1954, rev. 1968). But within Russia he is more widely regarded as one of the chief exponents of 20th-century Armenian 'nationalist' music. He wrote about 25 film scores, including *Vladimir Ilyich Lenin* (1948) and *Stalingradskaya bitva* ('The Battle of Stalingrad', 1949). These intensely patriotic films were made in the wake of the 1948 Zhdanov purges, when Khachaturian attracted criticism for some of his recent work, notably the Third Symphony (1947), written for the 30th anniversary of the October Revolution—a work marked not so much by musical substance as by spectacular celebratory effects (the symphony calls for a large

Ex. 1

orchestra, including organ, and 15 extra trumpets). Later, however, he achieved considerable success with a series of concert rhapsodies—for violin (1961–2), cello (1963), and piano (1965)—characterized by vitality of rhythm, rich orchestration, and intoxicating, highly spiced, and distinctive melody owing much to the inflections of Armenian folk music. GN

📖 G. SHNEYERSON, *Aram Khachaturyan* (Moscow, 1958; Eng. trans. 1959) · V. YUZEFOVICH, *Aram Khachaturian* (New York, 1985)

Khovanshchina ('The Khovansky Affair'). Opera in six scenes, usually given in five acts, by Musorgsky to his own libretto compiled with Vladimir Stasov from historical sources. It was left unfinished at the composer's death and was completed and orchestrated by Rimsky-Korsakov (St Petersburg, 1886); there is a version by Ravel and Stravinsky (Paris, 1913) and one by Shostakovich (Leningrad, 1960).

Khrennikov, Tikhon Nikolayevich (*b* Elets, 28 May/10 June 1913). Russian composer. He studied the piano and composition in Moscow, graduating from Shebalin's composition class at the conservatory in 1936. He made his mark as a composer with his spirited First Piano Concerto (1932–3), which owes much to Prokofiev in its energy, rhythmic drive, and broad, lyrical sweep; his Second Piano Concerto (1971) and succinct First Cello Concerto (1964) are written in much the same vein, though the music is tougher, more rhetorical in its gestures, and shows a liking for muscular melody and vivid orchestral colours. His orchestral works also include three symphonies and two violin concertos, but most of his creative work has been done in the theatre. Of his several operas, *V buryu* ('Into the Storm', 1939, rev. 1952) and *Mat'* ('Mother', 1957) were held up as examples of 'song' operas in the tradition of *socialist realism; the former is particularly notable in being the first Russian opera to feature Lenin as a character, in a brief speaking role.

Khrennikov also wrote incidental music and some film scores, but his name is known especially in connection with his administrative work at the Union of Soviet Composers. In the shake-up of personnel during the 1948 Zhdanov purges Khrennikov became secretary of the union, a position he retained until its dissolution following the collapse of the USSR in 1991. Younger composers accused Khrennikov of obstructing performances of their works and preventing them from touring abroad; his memoirs *Tak èto bïlo* were written in response to a wave of post-Soviet hostility. GN

📖 V. RUBTSOVA (ed.), *Tak èto bïlo: Tikhon Khrennikov o vremeni i o sebe* [How it Really Was: Tikhon Khrennikov on Himself and his Times] (Moscow, 1994)

Kilar, Wojciech (*b* Lwów [now L'viv, Ukraine], 17 July 1932). Polish composer. Though best known for his substantial contribution since 1958 to both the Polish film industry and Hollywood, he has a distinct place in the history of Polish contemporary music. After an initial exploration of avant-garde idioms, he came into his own with the orchestral *Krzesany* ('Sparking Dance', 1974), the first of several pieces based on Polish mountain culture. His music is expressively direct and is based on rhythmic repetition and diatonic harmony; some works draw on Polish religious traditions or imagery. His music treads a fine line between kitsch and naivety. ATh

Kilpinen, Yrjö (Henrik) (*b* Helsinki, 4 Feb. 1892; *d* Helsinki, 2 May 1959). Finnish composer. He was largely self-taught and his output is predominantly for the voice. He wrote more than 600 songs to Finnish, Swedish, and German poetry. His best-known German settings are of Christian Morgenstern (*Lieder um den Tod* op. 67) and possess remarkable concentration and atmosphere. His settings of both Swedish and Finnish poems are highly economical and strongly characterized. He is undoubtedly the greatest song composer that Scandinavia has produced since Grieg, and his style reflects something of his admiration for Hugo Wolf and even Musorgsky. His output also includes six piano sonatas, a cello sonata, and some choruses, but no orchestral music. RLa

Kindermann, Johann Erasmus (*b* Nuremberg, 29 March 1616; *d* Nuremberg, 14 April 1655). German organist and composer. In *c*.1635 he was sent by the Nuremberg city council to study in Italy. He returned in 1636 and spent most of his remaining years there, from 1640 as organist at the Egidienkirche. His works include motets, cantatas, and dialogues (some of them showing Italian influence in the use of a continuo part and concertato writing), some beautiful chorale settings, and the *Harmonia organica* (1645), a collection of organ music including improvisatory preludes and fugal fantasias on chorale melodies. DA

Kinderstück (Ger.). 'Piece for children'.

Kinderszenen ('Scenes from Childhood'). Schumann's op. 15 (1838), for piano, a set of 13 pieces (for adults); the seventh piece is *Träumerei.

Kindertotenlieder ('Songs on the Death of Children'). Song cycle (1901–4) by Mahler for baritone or contralto and orchestra, settings of five poems by Friedrich Rückert.

King, William (*b* Winchester, 1624; *d* Oxford, 17 Nov. 1680). English composer. He was the son of George

King, the organist at Winchester Cathedral, and was admitted to Magdalen College, Oxford, in October 1648. He graduated less than a year later, and spent the rest of his life at Oxford, from 1664 as organist of New College. He composed services, anthems, and a volume of *Poems of Mr. Cowley and Others, Composed into Songs and Ayres* (Oxford, 1668) for solo voice and continuo.   WT

King Arthur (*King Arthur, or The British Worthy*). Semi-opera in five acts by Purcell and John Dryden (London, 1691).

Kingdom, The. Oratorio, op. 51 (1906), by Elgar, for four soloists, chorus, and orchestra, to a biblical text compiled by the composer; Elgar composed it as a sequel to *The *Apostles*.

King Goes Forth to France, The (*Kuningas lähtee Ranskaan*). Opera in three acts by Sallinen to a libretto by Paavo Haavikko (Savonlinna, 1984).

'King of Prussia' Quartets. See 'Prussian' Quartets.

King Priam. Opera in three acts by Tippett to his own libretto after Homer's *Iliad* (Coventry, 1962).

King Roger (*Król Roger*; *Pasterz*; 'The Shepherd'). Opera in three acts by Szymanowski to a libretto by Jarosław Iwaszkiewicz and the composer, loosely based on Euripides' *Bacchae* (Warsaw, 1926).

King Stag. See König Hirsch.

Kirbye, George (*d* Bury St Edmunds, Oct. 1634). English composer. He spent much of his life in the household of Sir Robert Jermyn of Rushbrooke in Suffolk. His collection of madrigals (London, 1597) is written largely in a serious vein that owes much to Marenzio. He also contributed a madrigal to Morley's collection *The Triumphes of Oriana* (1601), and psalm settings to Thomas East's metrical psalter of 1592.
                                                          DA/JM

Kirchencantate (Ger.). 'Church cantata'; see Cantata, 2 and 3.

Kirchner, Leon (*b* Brooklyn, NY, 24 Jan. 1919). American composer. The child of Russian Jewish immigrants, he studied with Bloch and Schoenberg in Los Angeles, and with Roger Sessions in New York. After a decade teaching at Mills College (1952–61) he was appointed to Harvard, where he remained until he retired in 1989. His music is large in gesture, of strong melodic movement and in a harmonic realm close to Schoenberg and Berg, with echoes also of Stravinsky and Skryabin. Among his works are two piano concertos (1953, 1963), other orchestral works, three string quartets (1949, 1958, 1966, the third with tape), and pieces written towards the opera *Lily* (New York, 1977), based on Saul Bellow's *Henderson, the Rain King*.
                                                          PG

Kirkpatrick. Abbreviation for the standard *thematic catalogue of the keyboard sonatas of Domenico Scarlatti drawn up by the American keyboard player and scholar Ralph Kirkpatrick (1911–84) and published in his study of the composer (Princeton, NJ, 1953, 3/1968). There have been other attempts to catalogue Scarlatti's many sonatas, by Alessandro Longo (Naples, 1906–8) and by Giorgio Pestelli (Turin, 1967), but Kirkpatrick's is the one in common use. The sonatas are often referred to by Kirkpatrick number, usually further abbreviated to 'κ' or 'Kk'.

Kirnberger [Kernberg], **Johann Philipp** (*b* Saalfeld, *bapt.* nr Weimar, 24 April 1721; *d* Berlin, 26 or 27 July 1783). German theorist and composer. According to Marpurg, he became a pupil of J. S. Bach in 1739. He joined the orchestra of Frederick the Great as a violinist in 1751 and later became music director to Princess Anna Amalia of Prussia, in whose service he remained until his death. One of several important theorists associated with the Berlin court, he advised J. G. Sulzer on the music articles for his encyclopedia, the *Allgemeine Theorie der schönen Künste* (1771–4), and wrote treatises on composition and pedagogy, of which the most significant is the counterpoint method *Die Kunst des reinen Satzes* ('The Art of Strict Musical Composition', 1771–9).   DA/TRJ

Kiss, The (*Hubička*). Opera in two acts by Smetana to a libretto by Eliška Krásnohorská after the story by Karolina Světlá (Prague, 1876).

kit (Fr.: *pochette*). Small dancing-master's fiddle, made in a variety of shapes from the 16th century to the 19th. Most have either boat-shaped bodies like a small *rebec or body shapes derived from the violin or viol families. Kits were small enough to be kept in the tail-pockets (Fr.: *poche*). They had three or four strings tuned in 4ths or 5ths, sometimes at the same pitch as the violin, sometimes an octave higher, adequate for playing dance music while demonstrating and teaching steps.
                                                          JMo

kithara. The ancient Greek concert *lyre.

Kittl, Jan Bedřich [Johann Friedrich] (*b* Orlík nad Vltavou, 8 May 1806; *d* Lissa, Prussia [now Leszno, Poland], 20 July 1868). Czech composer. A pupil of Tomášek, he was one of the earliest Czech nationalist composers to achieve a measure of international success. It was his second symphony (*Jagdsymphonie*) that established him, performances being given by Spohr in Kassel (1839) and Mendelssohn in Leipzig (1840), the latter no doubt recognizing certain similarities to his own music. As director of the Prague Conservatory (1843–65), Kittl had an enormous influence on the development of music in the city, showing interest in the works of Liszt and Berlioz, and supporting the Prague premieres of Wagner's *Tannhäuser* and *Lohengrin*. Wagner himself wrote the libretto for Kittl's opera *Bianca und Giuseppe* (1848), one of the most successful operas composed in Bohemia before Smetana. In spite of his Germanophile orientation, Kittl also contributed to the Czech national renaissance. He was forced by ill health and financial difficulties to retire in 1865 and spent his final years in exile, teaching the piano privately.   MHe

Kl. (Ger.). Abbreviation for *Klarinette*, 'clarinet'.

klagend, kläglich (Ger.). 'Lamenting', 'plaintive'.

Klagende Lied, Das ('The Song of Sorrow'). Cantata (1880) by Mahler, a setting of his own text for soprano, alto and tenor soloists, chorus and orchestra; he composed it in three parts—*Waldmärchen* ('Forest Legend'), *Der Spielmann* ('The Minstrel'), and *Hochzeitsstück* ('Wedding Piece')—but revised it in 1892–3 and 1898–9 omitting *Waldmärchen*.

Klang (Ger.). 1. 'Sound', 'sonority'.
2. 'Chord'.

Klangfarbenmelodie (Ger., 'sound-colour melody'). A term introduced by Schoenberg in 1911 for a 'melody' of timbre, in which the instrumentation of a piece is as important as the pitch and rhythm and has its own structural function. Schoenberg himself attempted this in the central movement of his Five Orchestral Pieces (1909), and the idea was taken up by Webern and by many composers after 1950.

klar (Ger.). 'Clear', 'distinct'.

Klavierbüchlein. See CLAVIER-BÜCHLEIN.

Klavierstücke I–XI ('Piano Pieces I–XI'). 11 piano pieces by Stockhausen, composed between 1952 and 1956 (*IX* and *X* were revised in 1961); *XI* is *aleatory, allowing the pianist to choose the order of its component sections and the tempos.

Klavierübung. See CLAVIER-ÜBUNG.

Klebe, Giselher (*b* Mannheim, 28 June 1925). German composer. After studying at the Berlin Conservatory with Kurt von Wohlfurt, Josef Rufer, and Boris Blacher, he worked from 1946 to 1949 for Berlin Radio. The 12-note serial techniques that he studied with Rufer were demonstrated in such early orchestral pieces as *Das Zwitzermaschine* (1950). But later, as he became one of the most prolific of postwar German opera composers, he developed a more flexible language. As well as ten operas, Klebe has composed ballets, orchestral music, chamber music, and music for piano solo, duet, and duo.   ABur

Kleiber, Erich (*b* Vienna, 5 Aug. 1890; *d* Zürich, 27 Jan. 1956). Austrian conductor. After studying in Prague, he was appointed to the Darmstadt Opera in 1912. Through a succession of appointments at German opera houses he rose to fame as a meticulous ensemble builder and a conductor of great brilliance and high discipline. From 1923 to 1934 he was music director of the Berlin State Opera, where he gave premieres of many works, including Berg's *Wozzeck*. Opposing the Nazi regime, he lived in exile, exerting great influence at the Teatro Colón in Buenos Aires (1936–49) and, after the war, as a guest at Covent Garden. His son Carlos is also a conductor.   JT

  📖 J. RUSSELL, *Erich Kleiber: A Memoir* (London, 1957)

klein (Ger.). 'Small'; when applied to intervals, 'minor'.

Klein, Gideon (*b* Přerov, Moravia, 6 Dec. 1919; *d* ?Fürstengrube, nr Katowice, Poland, end of Jan. 1945). Czech composer and pianist. He studied the piano with Vilém Kurz in Prague. The Nazi occupation prevented his taking up a scholarship to the RAM in London; in 1941 he was deported to *Terezín and finally to Fürstengrube where, almost certainly, he met his end early in 1945. In Terezín his presence proved an inspiration and encouragement to other composers and he himself continued to compose. Some of his finest music was written at the camp, among it the Piano Sonata (1943) and a String Trio (1944) including superbly expressive variations on a Moravian folksong. In general his music is modernist with some affinity with serial methods.   JSm

Kleine Nachtmusik, Eine ('A Little Night Music'). Mozart's title for his Nocturne in G major K525 (1787); it is scored for string quartet and double bass and was originally in five movements but the second, a minuet, is lost. It is now often performed with orchestra.

Kleine Orgelmesse ('Little Organ Mass'). Haydn's Mass no. 7 in B♭ major (*c*.1775); its full title is *Missa brevis Sancti Joannis de Deo*. See also GROSSE ORGELMESSE.

Klemperer, Otto (*b* Breslau, 14 May 1885; *d* Zürich, 6 July 1973). German conductor and composer. He studied in Frankfurt with James Kwast and in Berlin with Pfitzner, making his debut in Berlin in 1906 with

Offenbach's *Orphée aux enfers*. At Mahler's recommendation, appointments in Prague (1907–10) and Hamburg (1910–12) followed, though he was forced to resign from the latter owing to public scandal concerning his liaison with the soprano Elisabeth Schumann. After working as Pfitzner's assistant in Strasbourg, he was appointed director of the Cologne Opera (1917–27), then of the Kroll Opera in Berlin (1927–31). In both posts he became known as a fierce champion of contemporary music and avant-garde theatrical production.

Klemperer transferred to the Berlin State Opera in 1931 but left Germany after the Nazi acquisition of power in 1933 and emigrated to the USA, where he conducted the Philadelphia and Los Angeles Orchestras. After the war he worked briefly in Budapest (1947–50), but much of his later life was spent in London, where he first conducted the Philharmonia in 1951. He was appointed conductor for life in 1964 at a time when the orchestra was threatened with disbandment, and continued to appear with the Philharmonia even when his health had been impaired by a series of strokes. Famous for his slow tempos and his cultivation of a titanic, monumental style, he was a superlative interpreter of Mozart, Beethoven, Brahms, and Mahler. He began composing late in life, completing six symphonies and nine string quartets.

TA

📖 P. HEYWORTH, *Conversations with Klemperer* (London, 1973, 2/1985); *Otto Klemperer: His Life and Times*, 2 vols. (Cambridge, 1983–96)

klezmer. Originally a Yiddish term meaning 'musician' (pl. *klezmorim*), 'klezmer' now denotes a musical tradition cultivated by Ashkenazi Jews in the east European diaspora, where it absorbed many local influences. Performed by Polish, Romanian, Russian, and Ukrainian immigrants it made its way to the USA, where it enjoyed a huge revival in the late 20th century. Klezmer bands, characteristically consisting of a combination of instruments drawn from clarinets, trumpets, violins, and plucked string instruments (including double bass), and often with a singer, perform music that embraces a wide range of moods from the soulful to the energetic. They are popular entertainers at weddings and other family celebrations particularly, though by no means exclusively, in Jewish communities.

PFA

Kl. Fl. (Ger.). Abbreviation for *kleine Flöte*, 'piccolo'.

klingen (Ger.). 'To sound'; e.g. *klingen lassen*, 'allow to sound'; *klingend*, 'resonant'.

Knaben Wunderhorn, Des. See DES KNABEN WUNDERHORN.

Knappertsbusch, Hans (*b* Eberfeld, 12 March 1888; *d* Munich, 25 Oct. 1965). German conductor. He studied in Bonn and Cologne, made his debut at Mülheim in 1910, and held several posts before becoming music director of the Munich Opera in 1922. He stayed there for 14 years, then conducted at the Vienna State Opera, returning to Munich in 1945. From 1951 until his death he conducted at Bayreuth, where he became famed for his expansive performances. He was also an esteemed interpreter of Richard Strauss.

JT

Knayfel′, Aleksandr Aronovich (*b* Tashkent, 28 Nov. 1943). Russian composer. He studied the cello with Rostropovich in Moscow, then composition with Boris Arapov at the Leningrad Conservatory. His early works were heavily influenced by Shostakovich, the best-known being his comic opera *Kentervil'skoye privideniye* ('The Canterville Ghost', after Oscar Wilde), written during his student years and performed in Leningrad in 1974. Later he explored a wide range of new techniques, seeking out unusual timbres, using numerical sequences to organize different musical parameters, and introducing theatrical elements into performance. Prominent among his later works is a series of lengthy, static, single-movement pieces including *Nika* (1984; duration 140′) and the *Agnus Dei* (1985; 120′).

JWAL

Knorr, Iwan (Otto Armand) (*b* Mewe, W. Prussia, 3 Jan. 1853; *d* Frankfurt, 22 Jan. 1916). German composer and teacher. After holding teaching appointments in Kharkiv, in 1883 he was recommended by Brahms for a post at the Hoch Conservatory in Frankfurt. He was a distinguished teacher noted for fostering individual talent, his pupils including Hans Pfitzner, Ernst Toch, and the so-called Frankfurt Group, consisting of the English composers Cyril Scott, Norman O'Neill, Roger Quilter, and H. Balfour Gardiner, together with the Australian Percy Grainger.

JW

Knot Garden, The. Opera in three acts by Tippett to his own libretto (London, 1970).

Knussen, (Stuart) Oliver (*b* Glasgow, 12 June 1952). English composer and conductor. He studied in London with John Lambert and at Tanglewood with Gunther Schuller. He conducted the LSO in the premiere of his First Symphony at the age of 16 and since then has worked slowly as a composer owing to the demands of his conducting career, in which he has achieved worldwide renown as a specialist in contemporary music. His compositions include two further symphonies (completed in 1971 and 1979 respectively) and two operas: *Where the Wild Things Are* (London, 1984) and *Higglety Pigglety Pop!* (Los Angeles, 1990). Among smaller-scale instrumental and vocal works

Four Late Poems and an Epigram of Rainer Maria Rilke (1988) and *Songs without Voices* (1992) stand out for their technical refinement and expressive power.

PG/AW

Koanga. Opera in a prologue, three acts, and an epilogue by Delius to a libretto by the composer and Charles F. Keary after George W. Cable's novel *The Grandissimes* (Elberfeld, 1904).

Köchel. Abbreviation for the standard *thematic catalogue of the works of Mozart drawn up by the Austrian music historian Ludwig Köchel (1800–77) and published in Leipzig in 1862. The catalogue has been revised several times, notably by Alfred Einstein for the third edition (1937, often referred to as 'K-E') and by Franz Giegling, Alexander Weinmann, and Gerd Sievers for the sixth (1964, often referred to as 'K6'). A further revision, *Der neue Köchel* ('NK'), was begun in the closing years of the 20th century under the editorship of Neal Zaslaw. Mozart's works, especially those without distinguishing title, are nearly always referred to by Köchel number, usually further abbreviated to 'K'.

Koczwara, František [Franz; Kotzwara, Francis] (*b* ?Prague, *c*.1750; *d* London, 2 Sept. 1791). Czech composer and instrumentalist. Of uncertain origins, he was one of the community of émigré musicians who made an itinerant orchestral career in Britain, playing a variety of wind and string instruments, the fortepiano, and the cittern. At the time of his death he was a double bass player at the King's Theatre. His compositions comprise mainly chamber music, including string quartets and accompanied keyboard sonatas. His contemporary reputation, however, was secured by his spectacularly successful programme sonata *The Battle of Prague* (*c*.1788) for piano, cello, and violin with drum ad lib (later arranged for solo keyboard). This work, replete with a bevy of appropriately militaristic effects, was sufficiently popular to run to some 40 editions and to sire an army of comparably noisy offspring. Koczwara's notoriety was further advanced by the bizarre circumstances of his death, the unsuccessful conclusion of an erotic experiment.   JSM

Kodály, Zoltán (*b* Kecskemét, Hungary, 16 Dec. 1882; *d* Budapest, 6 March 1967). Hungarian composer. The son of a railway official and enthusiastic amateur musician, Kodály began to compose in his boyhood. In 1900 he went to Budapest to study modern languages at the university and composition, with Hans Koessler, at the Academy of Music. He took the D.Phil. in 1906 with a dissertation on Hungarian folk music, and from that time he began to collaborate with his friend Bartók, both in collecting folksong and in pressing for a new vitality in Hungarian musical life. Like Bartók he

was appointed to a professorship at the Budapest Academy in 1907, and he remained in the city for the rest of his life.

Kodály's early works, for example the sonatas for cello and piano (1909–10) and for unaccompanied cello (1915), can be compared to Bartók's of the same period in their successful attempt to create a style on the basis of Hungarian folk music. However, Kodály was the more conservative musician; he did not share Bartók's rigorousness, and he was content to develop at a slower pace. His style changed little after he had established himself in Hungary and abroad with the *Psalmus hungaricus* for tenor, chorus, and orchestra (1923)—a powerful work composed, like Bartók's *Dance Suite*, for the 50th anniversary of Budapest as a unified city—and the witty, brilliant score for his opera *Háry János* (1926), from which he extracted a popular orchestral suite.

The experience of preparing the *Psalmus hungaricus*, which includes a boys' choir, led Kodály to concern himself with musical education. He was instrumental in developing a school music curriculum which ensured that every child learnt to sing at sight, and he wrote an enormous quantity of choral music and exercises for children and amateurs. In other fields he became much less prolific. All of his important chamber works, including two quartets (1908–9, 1916–18), were composed before 1920, and he wrote only a few orchestral pieces after *Háry János*. Of these few, the colourful and dynamic works founded in folk music—*Dances of Marosszék* (1930, after the piano version of 1927), *Dances of Galánta* (1933), and 'Peacock' Variations (1938–9)—have proved more lasting than the more ambitious but long-winded Concerto for Orchestra (1939) and Symphony (1961).   PG

📖 L. Eősze, *Zoltán Kodály* (London, 1962) · P. M. Young, *Zoltán Kodály* (London, 1964) · L. Eősze, *Kodály's Life in Pictures and Documents* (Eng. trans. 1971, enlarged 2/1982)

Koechlin, Charles (Louis Eugène) (*b* Paris, 27 Nov. 1867; *d* Le Canadel, Var, 31 Dec. 1950). French composer. A pupil of Massenet, Fauré, and André Gedalge at the Paris Conservatoire, he was a late developer whose career began with song-writing, progressed through chamber music after 1911, and reached its full maturity in symphonic works like *La Course de printemps* (completed in 1927) in the 1920s. In the 1930s he became fascinated with the early sound film and especially the now-forgotten Lilian Harvey, who appears in his *Seven Stars' Symphony* (1933). The 1940s saw a bifurcation into powerful symphonic poems, for example *Le Buisson ardent* (1938–45), and monodies including the 96 *Chants de Nectaire* for flute (1944).

Like Milhaud, Koechlin was extremely prolific (he reached op. 226) and seldom self-critical. Paradoxically, he was a disciplined libertarian, an eclectic original, and a subjective composer who proved the most objective of critics (like Berlioz). In spite of his Romantic attitudes to inspiration and composition, he was a pioneer of polytonality in the early 1900s and remained dedicated to its exploration throughout his *Jungle Book* cycle (1899–1940). This culminated in his scherzo *Les Bandar-log* (1939–40), an orchestral *tour de force* in which Kipling's chattering monkeys parody all that Koechlin despised in modern music (e.g. academic serialism), while the all-knowing jungle restores order in music of diaphanous, almost cosmic luminosity that shows him at his best. His reputation as a visionary independent has been much enhanced by the CD, for during his lifetime the difficulty and expense of performing his larger works caused him to become better known as a pedagogue and enlightened teacher (of Poulenc, Tailleferre, and Cole Porter).   RO

   📖 M. Li-Koechlin (ed.), *Catalogue de l'oeuvre de Charles Koechlin* (Paris, 1975); *Charles Koechlin (1867–1950), La Revue musicale*, 340–1 (1981) [autobiography and articles] and 348–50 (1982) [letters] · R. Orledge, *Charles Koechlin (1867–1950): His Life and Works* (Luxembourg, 1989, 2/1995)

Koenig, Gottfried Michael (*b* Magdeburg, 5 Oct. 1926). German composer. He studied at the Brunswick Staatsmusikschule (1946–7), the North-West German Music Academy in Detmold (1947–50, composition with Günter Bialas), and the Cologne Musikhochschule (1953–4). He first encountered electronic music at the 1951 Darmstadt summer courses, and was close to Stockhausen in the development of serialism, and in instrumental and electronic compositions; as a leading member of the electronic music studio of Cologne Radio (1954–64) he assisted Stockhausen and others. Thereafter he was artistic director of the studio at Utrecht University, where he worked on computer music and was an influential teacher.   PG

Kokkonen, Joonas (*b* Iisalmi, 13 Nov. 1921; *d* Järvenpää, 2 Oct. 1996). Finnish composer. He studied the piano at the Sibelius Academy, Helsinki, and musicology with Ilmari Krohn at Helsinki University, returning to the Sibelius Academy as lecturer (1950–9), then as professor of composition (1959–63). As a composer he was largely self-taught. Sibelius and Bartók are the most obvious influences on Kokkonen's music, and in his early works he also experimented with serialism. He wrote four symphonies and three string quartets, but his most successful and influential work has been the opera *Viimeiset kiusaukset* ('The Last Temptations', 1975), inspired by the life of the 19th-century Finnish revivalist preacher Paavo Ruotsalainen.   SJ

Kolb, Barbara (*b* Hartford, CT, 10 Feb. 1939). American composer. She studied at Hartford University (1957–64), in Vienna, and with Lukas Foss and Gunther Schuller at Tanglewood. Besides composition, her musical activities have included playing the clarinet and teaching. A residency at IRCAM led to the composition of *Millefoglie* for computer tape and ensemble (1984–5). Other works include orchestral pieces, chamber music, and piano pieces.   PG

kolęda (Pol.; Rom.: *kolenda*). A Christmas song, the Polish counterpart of the carol. The *kolęda* was particularly popular in Poland during the 17th and 18th centuries, from which period many collections (including the music) are extant. Similar songs are found in many other east European countries.   —/JBe

Kol Nidrei (*Kol Nidre*; 'All Vows'). 1. Bruch's op. 47 (1881) for cello and orchestra, an Adagio on Hebrew melodies which was also arranged for cello and piano.
   2. Schoenberg's op. 39 (1938) for speaker, chorus, and orchestra, a setting of the *Kol Nidre*, the opening prayer of the Jewish service on the evening of the Day of Atonement (Yom Kippur), which has tragic associations with the Spanish persecution of Jews in the 17th century.

König Hirsch ('King Stag'). Opera in three acts by Henze to a libretto by Heinz von Cramer after the fable by Carlo Gozzi (cut version, Berlin, 1956); Henze revised it as *Il re cervo, oder Die Irrfahrten der Wahrheit* ('King Stag, or The Meanderings of Truth') (Kassel, 1963) (complete score, Stuttgart, 1985).

kontakion. A Byzantine form of stanzaic hymnody for urban vigils perfected by St Romanos the Melodist (6th century). Most kontakia were later abbreviated to their prologue (koukoulion) and first stanza (oikos).

Kontakte ('Contacts'). Work (1959–60) by Stockhausen for four-track tape alone and, in another version, with piano and percussion; the tape was used in the music-theatre piece *Originale* (1961).

Kontrabass (Ger.). 'Double bass', 'contrabass'.

Kontra-Punkte ('Counterpoints'). Work (1952, revised 1953) by Stockhausen for ten instruments; it is a revision of the orchestral work *Punkte* (1952), itself revised in 1962, 1964, and 1966.

Kontretanz (Ger.). See COUNTRY DANCE.

Konzert (Ger.). 1. 'Concert'.
   2. 'Concerto'.

Konzertmeister (Ger., 'concert master'). See LEADER.

Konzertstück (Ger.). See CONCERTINO, 2.

kora. *Bridge harp of the West African Manding. The neck is a long pole that passes diametrically through a skin-covered gourd. Over 20 strings are attached to the neck at the base and, via tuning-collars, at the upper end. They are arranged in two parallel ranks at right angles to the soundboard, and held in notches cut in each side of a tall bridge. Two poles, stuck in the sound-skin at either side of the neck, serve as handles, and the strings are plucked with the thumbs and index fingers. The *kora* is played by professional musicians to accompany songs and narrations, and in virtuoso solo performances.   RPA

Korndorf, Nikolay (Sergeyevich) (*b* Moscow, 23 Jan. 1947; *d* Vancouver, 30 May 2001). Russian composer. He studied composition with Sergey Balasanyan and conducting with Lev Ginzburg at the Moscow Conservatory, graduating in 1972 and gaining a postgraduate diploma in 1979. He was appointed lecturer in instrumentation at the conservatory in 1975. In 1991 he emigrated to Canada. He was awarded the Duisburg City Prize (1990) and the Hindemith Prize (1991). His works include an opera *Pir vo vremya chumï* ('Feast in the Time of Plague', 1973), *Yarilo* for prepared piano and tape (1981), four symphonies, many chamber and solo instrumental works, and music-theatre pieces.
                                                          JK

Korngold, Erich Wolfgang (*b* Brno, 29 May 1897; *d* Hollywood, CA, 29 Nov. 1957). Austrian-born American composer. The son of the music critic Julius Korngold (1860–1945), he was a remarkable child prodigy. When he was ten his cantata for voices and piano, *Gold*, brought him to the attention of Mahler, who recommended him to Zemlinsky as a pupil. At 11 he completed the ballet *Der Schneemann* ('The Snowman'), which caused a sensation at its premiere at the Vienna Court Opera in 1910; his Second Piano Sonata, composed the same year, was enthusiastically championed by Schnabel. A pair of one-act operas, *Der Ring des Polykrates* and *Violanta*, had their premieres in 1916. Characterized by a sensuous, post-Romantic chromaticism, they reveal an astonishing emotional maturity in one so young, though their obvious debts to Strauss and Puccini (both of whom admired Korngold intensely) cannot be overlooked. *Die tote Stadt* ('The Dead City'), a Symbolist study of morbid sexual obsession, widely regarded as the finest of Korngold's operas, received a dual premiere in Hamburg and Cologne in 1920. *Die Wunder der Heliane* ('The Miracle of Heliane') was no less successful at its first per-

formance in 1927. In 1928, a poll taken from among the readers of the *Wiener Tageblatt* revealed that Korngold was considered one of the two greatest contemporary Austrian composers, Schoenberg being the other. In 1927 he was appointed professor at the Vienna State Academy.

In 1934 Korngold was invited to the USA by Max Reinhardt to adapt Mendelssohn's incidental music for *A Midsummer Night's Dream* as a film score. In 1935 he elected to remain in Hollywood, a decision partly provoked by the worsening political situation in Europe. Korngold was Jewish, and his works were therefore deemed *Entartete Musik* by the Nazis and were subsequently suppressed in the German-speaking world. His last opera *Die Katrin*, written for the Vienna State Opera, was withdrawn after the Anschluss in 1938 and received its premiere in Stockholm the following year. During World War II Korngold concentrated on film music, producing some 19 scores, though he returned to absolute music in later life with his Violin Concerto (1946) and the Symphony in F♯ (1951–2). His reputation suffered in the years after his death largely because of his association with the American film industry. A revival of *Die tote Stadt* in New York in 1975, followed by growing interest in the exploration of *Entartete Musik*, led to a major reappraisal of his work. He is now regarded by many as one of the finest post-Romantic composers.   TA

  📖 B. G. CARROLL, *The Last Prodigy* (Portland, OR, 1997)

Kortholt. Generic term for several double-reed instruments with a cylindrical bore drilled in a single piece of wood: the early bassoon (the English term 'curtal' derives from *Kortholt*), racket, *sordun*, and the *sordun* with a *wind cap, described by Michael Praetorius.

koto. Japanese zither with 13 silk strings plucked with ivory plectra on the thumb and the index and middle fingers of the right hand. Each string has its own movable bridge, standing on the curved paulownia wood soundboard. The *koto* derived from the Chinese *zheng*; 8th-century examples are preserved in the Shōsōin Repository at Nara, Japan. The *kayagŭm* is the Korean equivalent.   JMo

Kotoński, Włodzimierz (*b* Warsaw, 23 Aug. 1925). Polish composer, writer, and teacher. He was one of the first Polish composers to explore pointillistic serialism and music for tape (*Study on One Cymbal Stroke*, 1959). In the 1960s he made use of extended instrumental techniques, with an emphasis on chamber ensembles, especially percussion. Later pieces adopt more traditional formats and language, some with electroacoustic input. He is particularly noted as the teacher of many younger Polish composers, including Kulenty and Szymański.   ATH

Kotter [Cotter], Hans [Johannes] (*b* Strasbourg, *c*.1485; *d* Berne, 1541). German organist and composer. He was a pupil of Paul Hofhaimer. In 1514 he was organist of St Nikolaus in Fribourg; there he turned Protestant and was expelled from the town. He spent his later years in Berne. His works, which survive only in manuscript, include preludes, dances, and arrangements of vocal pieces by Hofhaimer and Isaac.   DA/JM

Koussevitzky, Serge [Kusevitsky, Sergey Aleksandrovich] (*b* Vyshny-Volochok, 14/26 July 1874; *d* Boston, MA, 4 June 1951). Russian-born American conductor, composer, and double-bass player. He studied the double bass at the Moscow Philharmonic School, played widely in Russia, and made international debuts in Berlin (1903) and London (1907). The following year he made his conducting debut with the Berlin Philharmonic Orchestra. In 1909 he set up a publishing business (Éditions Russes de Musique) to help publicize new Russian music, and in 1914 bought up the firm of Gutheil for 300,000 rubles; Rakhmaninov was already on Gutheil's books, and Koussevitzky added such composers as Prokofiev, Stravinsky, and Skryabin, for whose music he had particular enthusiasm. He left Russia after the 1917 Revolution and attained yet higher fame as a conductor on being appointed to the Boston Symphony Orchestra (1924–49). In 1942 he created the Koussevitzky Music Foundation, which (among other activities) commissions works by composers on both sides of the Atlantic.   PS/PG

Kovařovic, Karel (*b* Prague, 9 Dec. 1862; *d* Prague, 6 Dec. 1920). Czech composer, conductor, and accompanist. He studied the piano, harp, and clarinet at the Prague Conservatory, and composition with Fibich. In the 1880s, while he was harpist of the National Theatre orchestra, he regularly accompanied the violinist František Ondříček and made a guest appearance in 1885 with Sarasate. Kovařovic worked as a répétiteur in Prague, and as an opera conductor at the Czech Theatre in Brno (1885–6). He composed stage works including the operas *Psohlavci* ('The Dog Heads', 1897) and *Na starém bělidle* ('At the Old Bleaching House', 1901) and the ballet *Hašiš* (1884), each exploiting a rich, occasionally French-influenced, lyrical vein. After being appointed chief conductor of the Czech National Theatre in 1900 he devoted himself to improving standards in the theatre. He gave premieres of operas by Dvořák, Foerster, Novák, and Ostrčil, and the first performance in Prague of Janáček's *Jenůfa* (1916). He also revived interest in the 19th-century Czech classics.

His performances remained a model for Czech operatic conductors for many years.   JSM

Kozeluch [Kotzeluch, Koželuh], Leopold (*b* Velvary, 26 June 1747; *d* Vienna, 7 May 1818). Czech composer, pianist, teacher, and publisher. Baptized Jan Antonín, he later took the name Leopold to avoid confusion with his cousin, the composer and teacher Jan Antonín Kozeluch (1738–1814). His earliest musical training in Velvary was followed by tuition from his cousin in Prague and lessons with F. X. Dušek. After considerable success with theatre music in Prague, Kozeluch left in 1778 for Vienna, where he forged a career as pianist, teacher, and composer; in 1785 he founded his own publishing house. His contacts with British publishers were especially good, and many of his works were issued simultaneously in England and Vienna. Later, in common with Haydn and Beethoven, he made folksong settings for the Scottish publisher George Thomson.

In 1792 Kozeluch succeeded Mozart as *Kammer Kapellmeister* and *Hofmusik Compositor*, posts which occupied his time and energy until his death. He was influential in diverting attention from the harpsichord to the fortepiano: his 49 sonatas and numerous solos were important in cultivating a style of writing suited to the latter. The best of his early work reflected current rococo and Classical trends, and later (Three Caprices for fortepiano, *c*.1797) an anticipation of pre-Romantic styles is perceptible. Kozeluch was prolific in other genres producing symphonies, concertos, cantatas, songs, and a large number of accompanied keyboard sonatas (trios), but it was for his distinguished fortepiano music that he was widely popular.   JSM

kräftig (Ger.). 'Strong', 'vigorous'.

krakowiak [krakoviak] (Fr.: *cracovienne*). A lively Polish dance, named after the Kraków region. It is in quick duple time with syncopated rhythms and has been described as a simple type of *polonaise. It is danced by several couples who strike their heels together, shout, and sing. The *krakowiak* became popular in the early 19th century, when the dancer Fanny Elssler introduced it to western Europe. Chopin's op. 14, the Grand Concert Rondo for piano and orchestra, is a *krakowiak*.

Krása, Hans [Johann; Jan] (*b* Prague, 30 Nov. 1899; *d* Auschwitz [Oświęcim], 18 Oct. 1944). Czech composer. From a wealthy Jewish family, he studied composition with Zemlinsky and worked briefly as a répétiteur at the German Theatre in Prague. His Symphony for Small Orchestra (1926) and his first opera, *Verlobung im Traum* ('The Betrothal in a Dream', 1933), were notable successes. In 1941 he was sent to *Terezín, where he continued to compose, among other works a fine *Dance for string trio*. His early works show the influence of both Schoenberg and Stravinsky, but his later music has a clear personal accent, notably the remarkable children's opera *Brundibár* ('Bumble-Bee', 1938), which also makes use of popular idioms. In 1944 he was transported to Auschwitz and killed. JSM

Kraus, Joseph Martin (*b* Miltenberg am Main, nr Darmstadt, 10 June 1756; *d* Stockholm, 15 Dec. 1792). German composer. He was educated in Mannheim. In 1778 he went to Sweden and, as the most gifted composer working there, he eventually became musical director of the Stockholm theatre and Kapellmeister to Gustav III. His C minor symphony was admired by Haydn and attributed to Mozart; his operas include the fine *Aeneas i Carthago*. When the king was assassinated, Kraus composed a magnificent funeral cantata; he himself died soon afterwards. —/JR

Krauze, Zygmunt (*b* Warsaw, 19 Sept. 1938). Polish composer and pianist. His early music stands out from that of his compatriots for its deliberate avoidance of contrast, drawing inspiration from the 'unistic' paintings by Władysław Strzemiński (1893–1952). He often uses sequences of quiet, static tableaux (*Piece for Orchestra no. 1*, 1969). In the 1970s he incorporated not only folk themes (*Aus aller Welt stammende* for string chamber ensemble, 1973) but also folk and mechanical instruments (*Idyll* and *Automatophone*, 1974). He is interested in theatre music and spatial 'happenings' (*La Rivière souterraine* for seven tapes and optional instruments, 1987). Krauze is an advocate of contemporary music, and many of his works anticipate postmodernist and post-Romantic trends in Polish music. ATH

Krebs, Johann Ludwig (*b* Buttelstedt, nr Weimar, *bapt.* 12 Oct. 1713; *d* Altenburg, 1 Jan. 1780). German organist and composer. He was the most prominent member of a family of musicians: his father, **Johann Tobias Krebs** (*b* Heidelheim, Weimar, 7 July 1690; *d* Buttstädt, 11 Feb. 1762), was an organist and composer who (at Weimar, 1710–17) learnt the harpsichord with J. G. Walther and studied composition with J. S. Bach; a few organ pieces by him have survived. Johann Ludwig attended the Thomasschule in Leipzig from 1726 and became an admired pupil of Bach, who allegedly referred to him as 'the only crayfish [Krebs] in my brook [Bach]'. In 1737 he was appointed organist at the Marienkirche, Zwickau, and later held court posts at Zeitz and Altenburg. On Bach's death in 1650 he applied unsuccessfully for the vacant post at Leipzig. His surviving output consists solely of instrumental music, including organ preludes and fugues, concertos for two harpsichords, and trio sonatas, much of it strongly influenced by Bach.

Krebs's eldest son, **Johann Gottfried Krebs** (*b* Zwickau, *bapt.* 29 May 1741; *d* Altenburg, 5 Jan. 1814), spent his working life in Altenburg as an organist and city Kantor; his surviving works include over 70 church cantatas and other sacred music. WT/BS

Krebsgang (Ger., 'crab motion'). See RETROGRADE.

Krein. Russian family of composers. **Grigory Abramovich Krein** (*b* Nizhniy Novgorod, 6/18 March 1879; *d* Komarovo, nr Leningrad, 6 Jan. 1955) studied with Glière at the Moscow Conservatory (1900–5) and with Reger in Leipzig (1907–8). He lived in Vienna and Paris between 1926 and 1934 before returning to Russia, where he held various administrative posts. Unlike his brother, he was not concerned with exploring the musical heritage of his Jewish roots; the dense, chromatic harmonic textures in his music testify primarily to Skryabin's influence. His compositions include three symphonic poems (1922, 1923, 1934), two violin sonatas (1913, 1923), three piano sonatas (1906, 1924), and incidental music.

Aleksandr Abramovich Krein (*b* Nizhniy Novgorod, 8/20 Oct. 1883; *d* Staraya Ruza, Moscow district, 21 April 1951), younger brother of Grigory Krein, entered the Moscow Conservatory at the age of 14, studying with Taneyev and Boleslav Yavorsky and later teaching there (1912–17). He was a member of the Society for Jewish Folk Music and secretary of Muzo-Narkompros, and his music is strongly coloured by Jewish modes and rhythms, often combined with the chromatic complexity of late Skryabin. His works include two symphonies (1923–5, 1944–6), two sets of *Yevreyskiye éskizi* ('Jewish Sketches', 1910) for clarinet and string quartet, a string quartet, song cycles, ballets, an opera, and incidental music.

Yulian Grigor'yevich Krein (*b* Moscow, 20 Feb./5 March 1913; *d* 28 May 1996), a composer, pianist, and musicologist, was the son of Grigory Krein. He studied at the École Normale in Paris with Dukas, graduating in 1932 and returning to Moscow in 1934. Influences of French and Russian idioms are combined in his music. His works include concertos for cello (1926), piano (1929, 1942, 1943), and violin (1959), four string quartets (1925, 1927, 1936, 1943), a vocal-symphonic poem *Rembrandt* (1962–9) and three symphonic poems (1943, 1953, 1954), and two piano sonatas (1924, 1955). He has published books on Debussy, Falla, and Ravel and on orchestration. PF

📖 L. SABANEYEV, *Modern Russian Composers* (New York, 1927) · I. BÈLZA, *Handbook of Soviet Musicians*

(London, 1943) · L. Sitsky, *Music of the Repressed Russian Avant-Garde, 1900–1929* (Westport, CT, 1994)

Kreis (Ger.). 'Circle', 'cycle'; *Liederkreis*, **song cycle*.

Kreisler, Fritz (*b* Vienna, 2 Feb. 1875; *d* New York, 29 Jan. 1962). Austrian-born American violinist and composer. The son of a distinguished doctor, he was an infant prodigy as a violinist, entering the Vienna Conservatory at the age of seven and winning the *premier prix* of the Paris Conservatoire at 12. He toured the USA in 1889, then returned to Vienna, where for a time he studied medicine and did his military service before resuming his career as a concert violinist. He followed that career for the rest of his life except for a short period in the Austrian army in 1914, being wounded soon after his entry. Between the two world wars he lived first in Berlin, then in Paris. In 1939 he went to the USA, taking up American citizenship in the following year.

Kreisler was a renowned interpreter of the standard classics, and also performed some new works, notably the Concerto by Elgar (1910). His sweetness of tone, using continuous vibrato, was unmatched; his technical polish was legendary. As one of the first great instrumentalists in the age of recording he had an enormous influence on later generations. He was also a composer: as well as an operetta, *Apple Blossoms* (with Victor Jacobi, 1919), he wrote a String Quartet (1919) and many charming salon pieces. Some of these he passed off as transcriptions of various 'old masters'; by his own account, he did this out of modesty rather than with any deliberate intention to deceive.

DA/ABur

📖 L. P. Lochner, *Fritz Kreisler* (New York, 1950, 2/1951) · A. C. Bell, *Fritz Kreisler Remembered* (Braunton, Devon, 1992)

Kreisleriana. Schumann's op. 16 (1838, revised 1850), for piano, consisting of eight fantasies; it is dedicated to Chopin. The title refers to Kreisler, a character in E. T. A. Hoffmann's stories.

Krenek, Ernst (*b* Vienna, 23 Aug. 1900; *d* Palm Springs, CA, 23 Dec. 1991). Austrian-born American composer. A prolific composer, he was a restless, eclectic experimenter throughout his life. He studied with Franz Schreker in Vienna and Berlin (1916–23). His early works, which include two symphonies and his first string quartet, show the influence of his teacher along with that of Bartók and Mahler. Encounters with Busoni and Hermann Scherchen, together with a number of extended trips to Paris between 1923 and 1925, led to the evolution of a harmonically astringent neo-classicism, typified by the Concerto Grosso no. 2

(1924) and the Concerto for flute, violin, harpsichord, and strings (1924).

Elements of jazz entered Krenek's work as early as 1924 with the opera *Der Sprung über den Schatten* ('Jumping over the Shadow'), though the work that made him famous was *Jonny spielt auf* ('Jonny Strikes Up'), which caused a sensation at its Leipzig premiere in 1927 and remains one of the key works of the Weimar Republic. Combining jazz with Puccinian lyricism, it marks a drastic simplification of Krenek's harmonic idiom. The opera's vision of a jaded European culture revivified by American music—the hero is a black jazz bandsman on tour in Europe—made it anathema to the emerging Nazi party, which later deemed it to be the embodiment of **Entartete Musik*. The opera made Krenek financially secure and he settled in Vienna.

A trilogy of one-act operas followed, of which the finest, *Der Diktator* (1928), reveals a strong anti-Fascist streak (the central character is based on Mussolini), while the song cycle *Reisebuch aus den österreichischen Alpen* ('A Travel Diary from the Austrian Alps', 1929), partly modelled on Schubert's *Winterreise*, expresses Krenek's fears for European culture. A second song cycle *Gesänge des späten Jahres* ('Songs as the Year Draws to a Close', 1931) explicitly warns of the dangers of Nazism.

In the early 1930s Krenek encountered the works of Berg and Webern and was strongly drawn to serial techniques, which form the foundation for his opera *Karl V*. Commissioned by the Vienna State Opera, it was written between 1930 and 1934 but withdrawn on political grounds during its initial rehearsal period, the premiere taking place in Prague in 1938. During its composition Krenek had reaffirmed his lapsed faith in Roman Catholicism, and the opera posits the idea of the Universal Church as a political alternative to contemporary dictatorships. Its theatricality, using split stages and simultaneous action, was ahead of its time, anticipating Zimmermann's *Die Soldaten* by over 30 years.

Krenek first visited the USA in 1937, and after the Anschluss he made his home there, taking American citizenship in 1945 and settling in California in 1966 after an itinerant period that included teaching posts at Vassar College and at Hamline University, St Paul, Minnesota. His searing choral masterpiece *Lamentatio Jeremiae Prophetae* (1942) both reflected his anguished experience of exile and affirmed his commitment to advanced serial techniques. He did not resume contact with Europe until 1950. His opera *Pallas Athene weint* ('Pallas Athena Weeps'), a scathing satire on the collapse of democracy, was first performed in Hamburg in 1955. Though he was awarded the Gold Medal of

Vienna in 1960, he never returned to live in Europe. In his later works he experimented with electronic music, while aleatory techniques form the basis of two major orchestral scores from 1967, *Horizons Circled* and *Perspectives*. Krenek was a prolific author as well as a composer, his books including *Music Here and Now* (1939) and *Studies in Counterpoint, Based on Twelve-Tone Technique* (1940).   TA

   📖 G. H. BOWLES, *Ernst Krenek: A Bio-Bibliography* (New York and London, 1989) · J. L. STEWART, *Ernst Krenek: The Man and his Music* (Berkeley, CA, 1991)

Kreutzer, Conradin (*b* Messkirch, Baden, 22 Nov. 1780; *d* Riga, 14 Dec. 1849). German composer and conductor. He produced several successful operas in Vienna before embarking on a career as musical director to several of the smaller German courts. From 1822 he worked again in Vienna, where *Libussa* (1822), an uneven but not uninteresting work on the founding of the Bohemian state, gained him the directorship of the Kärntnertortheater. He also held appointments at the Theater in der Josefstadt. His greatest success was *Das Nachtlager in Granada* ('A Night's Shelter in Granada', 1834), which includes some striking Romantic elements among more conventional *Singspiel* gestures, as does *Der Verschwender* ('The Spendthrift', 1834).

DA/JW

Kreutzer, Rodolphe (*b* Versailles, 16 Nov. 1766; *d* Geneva, 6 Jan. 1831). French violinist and composer. He worked mainly in Paris, before the Revolution in the chapel of Louis XVI, afterwards in that of Louis XVIII. During the Republic he worked for Napoleon and as professor of violin at the Institut National de Musique, remaining there when it became the Conservatoire in 1795. He met Beethoven in Vienna while on a concert tour in 1798, but Beethoven's 'Kreutzer' Sonata op. 47 was composed and dedicated to him after his return to Paris, and he is thought never to have played it in public. Kreutzer composed several concertos, *études*, and chamber music, and wrote a violin method (Paris, 1803); he also composed *opéras comiques* and other dramatic works for theatres in Paris.   DA/RP

'Kreutzer' Sonata. 1. Popular name for Beethoven's Violin Sonata in A major op. 47 (1802–3), dedicated to the violinist Rodolphe Kreutzer, who is believed never to have played it.

   2. Subtitle of Janáček's String Quartet no. 1 (1923); it incorporates part of a scrapped piano trio of 1908–9 and on the score the composer wrote 'Inspired by L. N. Tolstoy's *Kreutzer-sonata*', a novel published in 1890.

Kreuz (Ger., 'cross'). The sharp sign (see SHARP, 1).

Krieger, Adam (*b* Driesen, nr Frankfurt an der Oder, 7 Jan. 1634; *d* Dresden, 30 June 1666). German composer. He was one of the greatest songwriters of his time. While studying at Leipzig he founded the university musical society, and in 1655 he became organist at the Nikolaikirche. After failing to gain the post of Thomaskantor in 1657 he moved to Dresden, where he served as organist to the electoral chapel until his death. With his *Arien* (1657–67) he provided a vast treasury of songs for solo voice, or small ensemble, and continuo.

DA/BS

Krieger, Johann Philipp (*b* Nuremberg, Feb. 1649; *d* Weissenfels, 6 Feb. 1725). German composer and organist. After early studies at Copenhagen he entered service at the court of Bayreuth. In 1677 he became organist at Halle, and in 1680 moved to Weissenfels as Kapellmeister. His output (most of which is now lost) included 2000 cantatas, 18 operas, and much chamber music. His surviving sacred works show his mastery of the mixed-text (Bible and free poetic) setting, typical of the pre-Bach 'cyclic' cantata. His brother, **Johann Krieger** (*b* Nuremberg, *bapt.* Jan. 1652; *d* Zittau, 18 July 1735), followed Johann Philipp to Bayreuth in 1672, where he deputized for him as organist during his absences. He is noted for his keyboard suites, and for the preludes, fugues, and ricercars published in his *Anmuthige Clavier-Übung* ('Agreeable Keyboard Exercises') of 1698.

DA/BS

Křižkovský, (Karel) Pavel (*b* Holasovice, Silesia, 9 Jan. 1820; *d* Brno, 8 May 1885). Czech choirmaster and composer. He received basic training in Neplachovice and later as a chorister in Opava. He studied philosophy in Olomouc and finally Brno where he settled in 1843, founding a student choir and studying composition. In 1848 he took holy orders in the Augustinian monastery where he also became choirmaster, influencing a generation of Moravian composers including Janáček and Vojáček. Křižkovský greatly expanded Brno musical life, promoting the Viennese Classics and Czech composers, but above all cultivating an interest in Moravian folksong. As choirmaster of the Brno Beseda musical society he gave concerts in Moravia and Bohemia, and his performances and settings of folksong and poetry attracted the attention of Smetana. Křižkovský's exclusively vocal output embodied the contours and harmonic characteristics of Moravian folk music, and his secular choruses were a stimulus and model for Smetana, Dvořák, Janáček, and many others. He thus helped mould a style of choral writing which formed an important part of his nation's musical revival.

JSM

Krommer, Franz [Kramář, Krommer-Kramář, František Vincenc] (*b* Kamenice u Trebíce, 27 Nov. 1759; *d* Vienna, 8 Jan. 1831). Czech composer and Kapellmeister. Although he studied the organ and the violin with his uncle, Krommer was largely self-taught as a composer. He was an organist in Turan for a few years before following the well-worn path to Vienna in 1785. After pursuing a career as Kapellmeister to various of the Hungarian nobility and Duke Ignaz Fuchs in Vienna, he succeeded his compatriot Kozeluch as the emperor's *Kammer Kapellmeister* and *Hofmusik Compositor* in 1818. Krommer's music, in particular his many quartets and quintets, were admired in Vienna and disseminated widely throughout Europe. He was held in high regard in England, France, and Italy. His musical style faithfully reflected the changing tastes of his day, from rococo to early Romantic, and though his contemporary reputation was founded mainly on his chamber music, interest today focuses on his solo wind concertos and occasional wind ensemble pieces. JSM

Krumpholtz, Jean-Baptiste [Johann Baptist, Jan Křtitel] (*b* Prague, 5 Aug. 1747; *d* Paris, 19 Feb. 1790). Bohemian harpist, composer, and instrument designer. He entered the chapel of Prince Nicolaus Esterházy in 1773 as a harpist and a composition pupil of Haydn. In 1777 he went to Paris, making his debut at the Concert Spirituel with one of his own harp concertos. His was one of the first harpists to use harmonics and devise designs to increase the range and facility of the instrument. His works include sonatas, variations, and concertos (mainly for the harp), and two 'symphonies' for harp and orchestra.

His brother, **Wenzel Krumpholtz** (*b* ?Budenice, *c.*1750; *d* Vienna, 2 May 1817), was a violinist in the Esterházy chapel and, from 1796, in the court opera in Vienna. He was also a minor composer. WT/JSM

Kubelík, (Jeronym) Rafael (*b* Bychory, 29 Jan. 1914; *d* Lucerne, 8 Nov. 1996). Czech conductor. The son of the violinist Jan Kubelík (1880–1940), he studied conducting at the Prague Conservatory. Prodigiously talented, he began regularly conducting the Czech Philharmonic Orchestra at the age of 21 and was its music director from 1941 to 1948, attracting international attention for his colourful, volatile, and vivacious performances. From 1955 to 1958 he was music director at Covent Garden (where he gave the first virtually complete performance of Berlioz's *Les Troyens*), and, from 1961 to 1985, of the Bavarian Radio Orchestra. A romantic and poetic interpreter, he inspired orchestras to play with a rare combination of warmth and discipline. His wide repertory included contemporary music, and he gave premieres of works by Schoenberg, Martinů, Martin, K. A. Hartmann, and himself. JT

Kuchka. See FIVE, THE.

Kuhlau, (Daniel) Friedrich (Rudolph) (*b* Uelzen, nr Hanover, 11 Sept. 1786; *d* Copenhagen, 12 March 1832). German-born Danish composer. The son of a military bandsman, in 1810 he avoided conscription in Napoleon's army by fleeing to Copenhagen, where he made a career as a pianist and teacher and found success with his Piano Concerto no. 7 and *Røverborgen* ('The Robbers' Castle', 1814), a *Singspiel*. Kuhlau toured as a pianist in Scandinavia and visited Austria, meeting Beethoven in Vienna in 1825. His compositions include many works for the flute and for the piano; he also wrote operas for the Royal Theatre in Copenhagen as well as the hugely successful incidental music *Elverhøj* ('The Elf Hill', 1828), which contains the melody used for the Danish national anthem. DA/SH

Kuhnau, Johann (*b* Geising, Harz Mountains, 6 April 1660; *d* Leipzig, 5 June 1722). German composer. In 1684, while pursuing legal studies at Leipzig, he was appointed organist, and seven years later Kantor, at St Thomas's—two posts in which he was Bach's immediate predecessor. His compositions include Latin and German motets, a fine *St Mark Passion* (1721), and innovatory keyboard works. Among the latter are two sets of suites (in his *Neue Clavier-Übung*, 1689, 1692) and his six Biblical Sonatas (1700), in which such Old Testament accounts as 'David and Goliath' and 'The Mortal Illness and Recovery of Hezekiah' are illustrated by simple but effective musical detail. A noted polymath, he gained renown not only as a musician but also as a lawyer, a translator from Hebrew, Greek, and other languages, a poet, and as author of the satirical novel *Der musikalische Quacksalber* ('The Musical Quack'). WT/BS

Kuhreigen [Kuhreihen] (Ger.). See RANZ DES VACHES.

Kulenty, Hanna (*b* Białystok, 18 March 1961). Polish composer. She established a distinctive voice early in her career, influenced in part by her studies with Louis Andriessen in Holland. Her music is characterized by strong rhythmic, gestural, and propulsive forces, habitually structured in what she calls the 'polyphony of arcs' (*Trigon* for chamber orchestra, 1989); elsewhere she explores spectral harmony, glissandos, and microtones (Violin Concerto no. 1, 1992). More recent pieces, such as *Sinequan forte* (1994), use electronic delay and more popular idioms. ATH

Kullervo. 1. Symphonic poem, op. 7 (1892), by Sibelius for soprano, baritone, male chorus, and orchestra, based on the *Kalevala*; it was withdrawn after its first performance and not played again until 1958.

2. Opera in two acts by Sallinen to his own libretto after a play by Aleksis Kivi (Los Angeles, 1992).

Kunst der Fuge, Die. See ART OF FUGUE, THE.

Kurtág, György (*b* Lugoj, Transylvania, 19 Feb. 1926). Hungarian composer. He studied with Sándor Veress and Ferenc Farkas at the Budapest Academy of Music (1946–55), and spent a year in Paris (1957–8), where he attended Messiaen's and Milhaud's classes at the Conservatoire, copied out Webern's output in its entirety, and was treated by the psychiatrist Marianne Stein, to whom he dedicated his op. 1, a string quartet written back in Hungary in 1959. Webern's influence, with Bartók's, was crucial to this piece and to those that followed, but what Kurtág appreciated in Webern, unusually for the time, was not so much the structure as the intensity and compression of feeling. He required his own music to be similarly compact and vivid, and little of it met his standards. By 1963 he had published only four more small-scale instrumental pieces; the next five years he devoted to *The Sayings of Péter Bornemisza*, a highly charged setting for soprano and piano of fragments from a Reformation preacher. All the time he stayed in Budapest, in spite of difficulties.

In the mid-1970s Kurtág began to compose more abundantly, thanks partly to the creative release he discovered in writing children's piano pieces exploring a wide range of compositional techniques, historical models, and sonic possibilities (*Játékok*, 'Games'; several volumes, 1973–), and partly to international interest. Pierre Boulez commissioned *Messages of the Late Miss R. V. Trusova* for soprano and small orchestra (1976–80), Kurtág's first work for larger forces and one of several written for Adrienne Csengery. All this time he was teaching chamber ensembles at the academy where he had studied, and in the performance of his own music he has preferred long, intensive periods of preparation. Orchestral works from him have remained rare, and in several of them the 'orchestra' is splintered into an ensemble of ensembles placed round the auditorium (*. . . quasi una fantasia . . .* for piano and instrumental groups, 1987–8). More typical are collections of small, often tiny, movements, for small instrumental formations (*Officium breve* for string quartet, 1988–9), with solo voice (*Kafka-Fragmente* for soprano and violin, 1986–7), or for chorus (*Songs of Despair and Sorrow*, 1980–94). From 1990 Kurtág lived largely abroad, moving from one great west European city to another.   PG

kurz (Ger.). 'Short'.

Kusevitsky, Sergey Aleksandrovich. See KOUSSEVITZKY, SERGE.

KV. Abbreviation for *Köchel-Verzeichnis, sometimes used as a prefix to the numbers of Mozart's works as given in the standard *thematic catalogue of Ludwig Köchel.

Kvapil, Jaroslav (*b* Fryšták, Moravia, 21 April 1892; *d* Brno, 18 Feb. 1958). Czech composer, conductor, pianist, organist, and pedagogue. A pupil of Janáček at the Brno School of Organists, he went on to study with Reger at the Leipzig Conservatory (1911–13) before returning to Moravia. From 1920 he taught at the Brno School of Organists and the conservatory, and in 1947 he was appointed professor of composition at the Brno Academy. His music is chiefly in a late Romantic style with occasional references to folk idioms, and displays a fluent contrapuntal facility, particularly in more ambitious pieces such as the oratorio *Lví srdce* ('The Lionheart', 1931). As a conductor, Kvapil gave the Czech premieres of several notable contemporary works, including Honegger's *Judith* (1933) and Szymanowski's *Stabat mater* (1937), but perhaps most remarkably was responsible for the first Czech performance—as late as 1923—of Bach's *St Matthew Passion*.   MHE

Kyrie eleison (Gk., 'Lord, have mercy'). An ancient acclamation adopted for use in Christian worship. In the Eastern Churches it is primarily used as a response in diaconal litanies. Imitation of this practice led to its adoption as part of the Ordinary of the Roman *Mass between the introit and the Gloria, where it was supplied with Latin verses (abolished after the Council of Trent) and sung in alternation with 'Christe eleison'. By the 10th century a ninefold pattern of performance ('Kyrie eleison' three times, 'Christe eleison' three times, 'Kyrie eleison' three times) had become customary for the Roman Kyrie. Various forms of the Kyrie were retained in the Eucharists of the Anglican and Lutheran Churches.   —/ALI

Kyui, Tsezar' Antonovich. See CUI, CÉSAR ANTONOVICH.

la [lah]. The sixth degree of the scale in the *solmization system. In French and Italian usage it has become attached, on the fixed-*doh* principle, to the note A, in whichever scale it occurs. See TONIC SOL-FA.

Lablache, Luigi (*b* Naples, 6 Dec. 1794; *d* Naples, 23 Jan. 1858). Italian bass, of French and Irish parentage. He studied at the Naples Conservatory and made his debut in Fioravanti's *La molinara* in 1812. He continued his studies and was engaged in Palermo. Word spread of his extraordinary singing and acting, and in 1817 he was acclaimed in his debut at La Scala, Milan, as Dandini in *La Cenerentola*. At the S. Carlo, Naples, he created many new roles, both comic and dramatic, in operas by Bellini and Donizetti. In 1827 he sang in Mozart's Requiem at Beethoven's funeral. From 1830 to 1856 he enjoyed outstanding success almost every year in London and Paris, where he created many more important new roles, such as Giorgio in *I Puritani* and the title role in *Don Pasquale*, one of his greatest successes. He was a fine actor by the standards of his time and had a powerful voice of exceptional range. Among his many singing pupils was Queen Victoria. JT

Lachenmann, Helmut (Friedrich) (*b* Stuttgart, 27 Nov. 1935). German composer and teacher. He studied at the Stuttgart Academy of Music, at the Darmstadt summer courses, and with Nono in Italy. He taught in several German cities before returning to the Stuttgart Academy as professor of composition in 1981. Lachenmann's works are concerned with what he describes as 'music as existential experience', focusing attention on the materials of music and the processes of sound production; they have been characterized as 'meta-music'. They include orchestral, choral, and ensemble pieces, and an opera, *Das Mädchen mit den Schwefel-hölzern* (Hamburg, 1997), after Hans Christian Andersen's *The Little Match Girl*. ABur

Lachner, Franz (Paul) (*b* Rain am Lech, Upper Bavaria, 2 April 1803; *d* Munich, 20 Jan. 1890). German composer and conductor, brother of Ignaz Lachner. His brother Vincenz (1811–93) and step-brother Theodor (1788–1877) were also composers. His first studies were with his father, Anton Lachner, the town organist of Rain am Lech, after whose death in 1822 he moved first to Munich, then (in 1823) to Vienna, on his appointment as organist of the Lutheran Church there. He became a friend of Schubert and a pupil of Sechter. In 1827 he was appointed Kapellmeister at the Kärntnertortheater and in 1834 at the opera house in Mannheim; from 1836 he was court conductor in Munich and from 1852 *Generalmusikdirektor* until, in 1865, he was forced from office (but not from public esteem) by Wagner. He published his memoirs of Schubert in 1881. His music—which injects the influence of his friend, Schubert, into a Mendelssohnian classicism—includes four operas, eight symphonies (1828–51), seven orchestral suites, two concertos for harp and one for flute, eight masses and other choral works, a considerable quantity of chamber music, and piano pieces. MA

Lachner, Ignaz (*b* Rain am Lech, Upper Bavaria, 11 Sept. 1807; *d* Hanover, 24 Feb. 1895). German composer, conductor, and organist, brother of Franz Lachner. Like his brothers, he had his first training from his father, who wanted him to become a teacher. Only after his father's death in 1822 was he able to begin a career as a musician, working as a violinist in Munich until 1826, when his brother Franz brought him to Vienna. He followed Franz through a number of positions, succeeding him as organist of the Lutheran Church, then becoming assistant conductor at the Kärntnertortheater (1825–8) and thereafter at the Court Opera. From there he became court conductor in Stuttgart (1831–6), Munich (1836–53), and Stockholm (1858–61), after a spell (1853–8) as conductor of the Hamburg Opera. His final appointment was as principal conductor at Frankfurt.

Lachner's output has been even less thoroughly investigated than that of his brother Franz, but what little has come to light in modern times has revealed a thorough and inventive craftsman, of a Classical bent but open to the innovations of the early Romantics. There are three operas as well as a number of *Singspiele* and other dramatic works, ballets, symphonies, choral and chamber music, and piano pieces. MA

Lachrimae, or Seaven Teares. A collection (1604) of 21 pieces for five viols and lute by Dowland; the 'teares' are seven 'passionate' pavans, each a set of variations on Dowland's song *Flow my Teares*, and the other 14 pieces are dances. They were transcribed for keyboard by several composers, notably Byrd.

lacrimoso, lagrimoso (It.). 'Lachrymose', 'tearful'.

Lady Macbeth of the Mtsensk District, The (*Ledï Makbet Mtsenskogo uyezda*). Opera in four acts by Shostakovich to a libretto by the composer and Aleksandr Preys after the short story by Nikolay Leskov (1865) (Leningrad, 1934). Shostakovich revised it as *Katerina Izmaylova* (Moscow, 1963) but for reasons of political compromise; the original version is regarded as definitive.

Lady Mass. A votive Mass with propers in honour of the Blessed Virgin Mary. It is often celebrated daily in the 'lady chapels' of medieval cathedrals of the Western church.

Lady Nevell's Book. See MY LADY NEVELLS BOOKE.

Lage (Ger.). 'Position'. In string playing, the position: *erste Lage*, 'first position', *zweite Lage*, 'second position' etc. Of a chord, the spacing: *enge Lage*, 'close position', *weite Lage*, 'wide (open) position'. In reference to an instrument or voice, the register: *hohe Lage*, 'high', *tiefe Lage*, 'low'.

lah. See LA.

lai [lay] (Fr.; Ger.: *Leich*). A term used in a variety of ways in the Middle Ages. It usually denotes an extended song form featuring several stanzas ('strophes'), each using a different metrical form, rhyme scheme, and melody (the 'lyric *lai*'). However, *lai* might also be used merely as a synonym for 'song'; moreover, songs in similar form appear under different names, especially *descort*. In spite of the formal variety embodied in a *lai*, however, formal symmetries are often provided by the subdivision of strophes into versicles which may be repeated a number of times (a device known as 'lesser responsion'), and sometimes by the use of the same musical and metrical scheme for two strophes, especially for the first and last strophes (known as 'greater responsion').

As well as the lyric *lai*, there existed also the 'narrative *lai*', a different poetic and musical form. The earliest known to have been recorded in writing (though no written music survives), by Marie de France, date from after 1160. References to Tristan and Arthur in some narrative *lai* texts and the use of the term *lai* in Celtic sources, together with the attribution of Marie de France herself, have suggested to some a Celtic origin for the *lai*; however, this would not apply to the lyric *lai*. Some narrative *lais* have survived in Scottish oral tradition.

The troubadour and trouvère 'lyric *lai*' repertory of the 12th and 13th centuries comprises over 30 pieces, which exhibit considerable variety in number and length of stanzas. The four *lais* in the early 14th-century *Roman de *Fauvel* are more standardized in these respects; their rhythm is unambiguous and the scheme of repetitions is more regular. They form the immediate background to the *lais* of Guillaume de Machaut. Machaut's *lais* exhibit the formal developments present in the *lais* of the *Roman de Fauvel* but also explore new directions resulting from the development of the mensural system, which made possible the use of a greater variety of tempos. The *lai* was essentially a monophonic form; however, Machaut departed from tradition by composing four polyphonic *lais* of different kinds: in *Le Lay de confort* each stanza is written as a three-part canon, while monophonic and canonic stanzas alternate in *Le Lay de la fonteinne*. In *Le Lay de consolation* both halves of each stanza have different music, these together forming a two-part texture, and the three-part writing of *En demantant* is a result of the combination of each group of three stanzas.

After Machaut, there survive a few formulaic compositions in *lai* form; it is not entirely clear whether these are isolated survivors of a lost tradition, or whether, by the 15th century, composers abandoned the *lai*, perhaps because an essentially monophonic form was outmoded in the age of polyphony.

PD/PW

📖 G. REANEY, 'Concerning the origins of the medieval lai', *Music and Letters*, 29 (1958), 343–6 · S. N. ROSENBERG and H. TISCHLER, *The Monophonic Songs in the Roman de Fauvel* (Lincoln, NE, 1991) · A. BUCKLEY (ed.), *Lyric Lais* (Newton Abbot, 1992–4)

laisser (Fr.). 'To allow', 'to leave'; *laisser vibrer*, 'allow to sound, do not damp'.

Lakmé. Opera in three acts by Delibes to a libretto by Edmond Gondinet and Philippe Gille after Pierre Loti's novel *Rarahu* (Paris, 1883).

Lalande, Michel-Richard de [Delalande, Michel-Richard] (*b* Paris, 15 Dec. 1657; *d* Versailles, 18 June 1726). French composer. The son of a Parisian tailor, he was a choirboy at St Germain-l'Auxerrois, 1667–72; he evidently had a fine voice and was also a violinist, but he 'renounced the violin for ever' when refused a place in the opera orchestra under Lully. He was however an accomplished organist and harpsichordist: he taught the royal princesses the harpsichord, and Louis XIV was impressed by his organ playing when he heard him in 1678 but thought him too young for a royal appointment. He held posts at four Paris churches and in 1683 took up his first royal position, as one of the four *sous-maîtres* (each serving for one quarter) at the royal chapel.

Lalande gradually acquired more court posts: in 1685 he became *compositeur de la musique de la chambre* (for a quarter of the year, by 1700 three quarters, by 1709 all four) and in 1689 *surintendant de la musique de la chambre* (half the position, in 1695 the whole) and by 1714 he had collected all four quarters as *sous-maître*. He was much favoured by the king, who directed that all his *grand motets* should be copied by the court copyists. After Louis's death, in 1715, Lalande gradually relinquished his posts, handing some of them on to his best pupils and his brother-in-law, Jean-Féry Rebel. His wife, Anne-Renée Rebel, died in 1722; their two daughters, both gifted singers, died young, in a smallpox epidemic in 1711. Lalande remarried in 1723.

His central achievement lies in the *grands motets* he composed for the royal chapel. He wrote 77 in all; many exist in multiple versions as he often revised them. These are extended works, settings of Latin psalms (mostly in several movements) for five-part choir and orchestra with solo voices. They are noted for the richness of their harmony and their textures and for the intensely expressive quality of their solo numbers; the sombre *De profundis* is particularly admired. For their variety, their emotional force, and their technical skill they crown the French Baroque motet tradition. Unlike almost all other music of the period, they were kept alive after Lalande's death, partly through the appearance of a lavish new edition in 1729—exceptional at the time and especially for a composer no longer living—and they were much performed at the Paris Concert Spirituel for many years after his death.

Lalande also wrote a considerable quantity of theatre music, including several operas and ballets (the few that survive show a competent composer with an attractive vein of melody and feeling for orchestral colour), and also instrumental works, among them *Symphonies pour les soupers du roi* (mainly dances from his theatre music), a *Concert de trompettes*, some *Caprices*, and the *Symphonies des noëls*, versions of Christmas carols.   SS

Lalo, Édouard (Victoire Antoine) (*b* Lille, 27 Jan. 1823; *d* Paris, 22 April 1892). French composer. He studied in Lille, then moved to Paris at the age of 16. There he lived as a violinist and teacher, playing in some of Berlioz's concerts and composing two symphonies which he destroyed. His chamber music of the 1850s received some attention. Following his marriage to a singer in 1865 he wrote a grand opera, *Fiesque*, but he

was deeply dispirited when it failed to win a competition and when lukewarm interest from the Paris and Brussels opera houses came to nothing.

The founding of the Société Nationale de Musique, dedicated to the performance of French music, was partly responsible for the series of concertos Lalo produced during the 1870s, given their premieres by such celebrated violinists as Armand Marsick and Sarasate (for whom he wrote the celebrated *Symphonie espagnole*) and by the cellist Adolphe Fischer, who not only gave the first performance of the Cello Concerto in 1877 but also of a *Fantaisie norvégienne* which followed it. Lalo then turned to the ballet *Namouna* (1881), greatly admired by Debussy, and the opera *Le Roi d'Ys* (1888), which firmly established his reputation. Based on the Breton myth of the legendary submerged city of Ys, the opera blends Breton folk music with his habitual style: a love of compound-time signatures, surprise chords, and an idiosyncratic dark and turbulent harmonic language. It is one of the strongest regionalist French operas of the period.   RLS

📖 S. HUEBNER, *French Opera at the Fin de Siècle: Wagnerism, Nationalism, and Style* (Oxford, 1999)

Lambe, Walter (*b* ?Salisbury, 1450 or 1451; *d* after 1499). English composer. He may have been a scholar at Eton College in 1467. His career was largely spent at St George's Chapel, Windsor, first as a singer and later as Master of the Choristers. Little of his music survives, but he was an important contributor to the *Eton Choirbook, and some of his votive antiphons are of extraordinary length and complexity.   JM

Lambert, (Leonard) **Constant** (*b* London, 27 Aug. 1905; *d* London, 21 Aug. 1951). English composer. He studied with R. O. Morris and Vaughan Williams at the RCM, showing great promise as a student with his ballet scores *Prize Fight* (1924–5) influenced by Satie, *Romeo and Juliet* (1924–5) commissioned by Diaghilev, and *Pomona* (1926), modelled to a large extent on Stravinsky's *Pulcinella*. The late 1920s and early 30s proved to be Lambert's most fertile period. His *Elegiac Blues* (1927) and ever-popular *The Rio Grande* (1927) show a fascination with jazz and black music, as does the Piano Concerto (1931); but the concerto also exhibits a darker, more acerbic, astringent, and often disturbingly melancholy dimension to the composer's personality which is also evident in the *Music for Orchestra* (1927) and the Piano Sonata (1928–9).

Appointed conductor of the Carmargo Society in 1930 and musical director of the Vic-Wells (later Sadler's Wells, still later Royal) Ballet in 1931, Lambert gave much time to the conducting of ballet and the arrangement of ballet scores which inevitably precluded time for composition. He wrote two further large-scale ballets for Frederick Ashton—*Horoscope* (1937) and *Tiresias* (1951)—the cantata *Summer's Last Will and Testament* (1932–5), an urban pastoral with words from Thomas Nashe's *Pleasant Comedy* of 1593, and a hauntingly beautiful orchestral miniature, *Aubade héroïque* (1942). Satirical, witty, and hugely knowledgeable of the other arts, he held unconventional and independent views, evident from his criticism, his writing for magazines and national newspapers, and his one book, *Music Ho! A Study of Music in Decline* (1934, 3/1966). JDt

📖 R. SHEAD, *Constant Lambert* (London, 1973)

lamellophone. A term used in *organology for all instruments sounded by the plucking—or, more rarely, striking—of thin lamellae or tongues of metal, wood, reed, plastic, or other suitable material; examples include the *mbira, *jew's harp, and musical box (see MECHANICAL MUSICAL INSTRUMENTS). Such instruments are classified in *organology as plucked *idiophones (see INSTRUMENTS, CLASSIFICATION OF), though it is arguable that blown *free-reed instruments (which are *aerophones), for example mouth organs or harmoniums, should also come under this head. JMo

lament. 1. Specifically, music for bagpipes at Scottish clan funerals.

2. Any piece of music expressing grief, usually at the loss of a friend or a famous person. A well-known example in opera is Dido's lament 'When I am laid in earth' from Purcell's *Dido and Aeneas*. Laments associated with leave-taking rituals—for example before weddings, or on the departure of young men for war service—are found in the traditional music of many countries. See also APOTHÉOSE; DÉPLORATION; DIRGE; DUMP; ELEGY; EPICEDIUM; LAMENTO; PLAINTE; THRENODY; TOMBEAU.

Lamentations. The Lamentations of the prophet Jeremiah. Before the Second Vatican Council, readings from Jeremiah were sung at *Matins during the week before Easter (known as 'Tenebrae'); they had their own proper plainchant melodies and were often set polyphonically for choir (for example the great settings by Tallis). The Greek word *Threni* is sometimes used.

'Lamentation' Symphony. Nickname of Haydn's Symphony no. 26 in D minor (late 1760s), so called because some of its themes resemble the plainchant melodies sung in Roman Catholic churches in the week before Easter. It is also sometimes referred to as *Weihnachtssymphonie* ('Christmas Symphony'), but that title has no apparent relevance.

lamento (It.). A song of mourning. The *lamento* was often an important item in 17th-century Italian opera, usually placed before the emotional climax of the plot. Such tragic arias were vehicles for the composer's skills of expression and word-setting. A famous example is Monteverdi's *Lamento d'Arianna* (1708), which was the model for many later *lamenti*. —/JBE

Lamento d'Arianna. The only surviving music from Monteverdi's opera *L'Arianna* (1608); Monteverdi arranged it as a five-part madrigal, *Lasciatemi morire* ('Leave me to die'), published in 1623.

Lamoureux, Charles (*b* Bordeaux, 28 Sept. 1834; *d* Paris, 21 Dec. 1899). French conductor and violinist. He studied the violin at the Paris Conservatoire and played in the Paris Opéra orchestra. In 1872 he was appointed assistant conductor of the Société des Concerts du Conservatoire but soon began to organize his own concerts of large-scale choral works. After short seasons conducting at the Opéra-Comique and the Opéra, in 1881 he began giving weekly symphony concerts, later known as the Concerts Lamoureux. He was a passionate advocate of Wagner, including single acts of his operas in concert performances; in the theatre he conducted the first Paris performances of *Lohengrin* and *Tristan und Isolde*. He also conducted works by such young French composers as Lalo, Dukas, and Chabrier. The Lamoureux Orchestra remained a leading European ensemble. JT

Lampugnani, Giovanni Battista (*b* Milan, 1706; *d* ?Milan, after autumn 1780). Italian composer. Nothing is known of his life before 1732, when he began a successful career as an opera composer in Milan and other north Italian cities. In 1743 he went to London as composer to the King's Theatre, returning to Italy in 1746. He continued to write operas until 1769, including another for London and one for Barcelona, but whether he travelled to those cities is not known. About 1758 he settled permanently in Milan, where he taught singing and became a harpsichordist at La Scala. He also published instrumental music. DA/ER

lancers. A simplified version of the *quadrille.

lancio, con (It.). 'With vigour'.

Land der Berge. Austrian national anthem. See EMPEROR'S HYMN.

Land des Lächelns, Das ('The Land of Smiles'). Operetta in three acts by Lehár to a libretto by Ludwig Herzer and Fritz Löhner (Berlin, 1929).

Landi, Stefano (*b* Rome, 1586 or 1587; *d* Rome, 28 Oct. 1639). Italian composer and teacher. He was a boy soprano at the Collegio Germanico in Rome, and then became organist at S. Maria in Trastevere and, in 1611, a singer at the Oratory of Ss. Crocifisso. He left Rome to become *maestro di cappella* to the Bishop of Padua, but soon returned to become one of the favourite musicians of the Barberini family. Landi was one of the most notable of the early school of Roman opera composers. His *La morte d'Orfeo* ('The Death of Orpheus', 1619) is unusual for having comic characters, while *Il Sant'Alessio* (1632, perhaps preceded by a performance the previous year) is a grand spectacular opera, using big choruses and elaborate machines and scenery.

DA/TC

Landini, Francesco (*b* Fiesole or Florence, *c*.1325; *d* Florence, 2 Sept. 1397). Italian composer and organist. An attack of smallpox left him blind from childhood. He became a skilled performer on the *organetto* or portative organ, and designed and built musical instruments. He also sang, composed poetry, and possessed a keen mind with a deep knowledge of philosophy and politics. Little is known of his early career, but to judge from the texts of his motets he probably spent some time in Venice and elsewhere in northern Italy. In 1361 he was appointed organist at the monastery of Santa Trinità in Florence. He is buried in the church of S. Lorenzo, where a monument depicts him playing a portative organ.

Landini was the leading composer of the Italian Ars Nova; more works by him survive than by any of his Italian contemporaries. They include 140 *ballate* for two or three voices, 12 madrigals, and four motets, three of which are fragmentary. These works draw on a wide range of styles, and no certain chronology can be made of his artistic development, though the works for two voices are probably mostly earlier than those for three. Landini's music is noted for its fluid melodiousness and rhythmic grace, in contrast to the more angular manner of his French contemporary, Guillaume de Machaut. At least some of the texts he set to music are likely to be his own work, since they include autobiographical references.

JM

Landini cadence. See CADENCE.

ländler (Ger.). A rustic German and Austrian dance in slow *waltz tempo. It originated in the Landel district of Austria (now Upper Austria) and was popular in the early 19th century: Mozart, Beethoven, and Schubert all wrote collections of ländler. In its early form it was a hearty country dance, with stamping and clapping; the dancers sometimes sang or yodelled, while the typical instrumental accompaniment consisted of violin and double bass. A more refined version became popular in Vienna, and the dance soon began to resemble the waltz, which eventually superseded it. The symphonies of Mahler and Bruckner use the characteristic rhythms and spirit of the dance, and Berg quoted a ländler tune in his Violin Concerto and in his opera *Wozzeck* (Act II scene 4).

Land of Hope and Glory. The title of the finale of Elgar's **Coronation Ode*, for alto, chorus, and orchestra, a setting of words by A. C. Benson to a melody adapted from the trio section of Elgar's first **Pomp and Circumstance* march. It was also published as a separate song, for alto and orchestra, with words different from those in the *Coronation Ode*; this is the version sung generally and communally.

Land of my Fathers (*Hen wlad fy nhadau*). Welsh national anthem. The music is by James James (1832–1902) and the words are by Evan James (1809–93) and it was composed in 1856; it first appeared in print in John Owain's *Gems of Welsh Melody* (1860).

AL

Land of Smiles, The. See LAND DES LÄCHELNS, DAS.

Land of the Mountain and the Flood, The. Overture (1887) by MacCunn.

Landowska, Wanda (*b* Warsaw, 5 July 1879; *d* Lakeville, CT, 16 Aug. 1959). Polish keyboard player. A pioneer of harpsichord-playing, she first played the instrument in public in 1903, having developed an enthusiasm for Bach and undertaken extensive research into 17th- and 18th-century music. She commissioned a two-manual harpsichord from Pleyel, established a course in Berlin, played the harpsichord continuo in Bach's Passions, took the instrument to the USA, made early gramophone recordings, and founded a music school in France. She later moved to the USA and in 1949 recorded Bach's '48'. Poulenc and Falla wrote concertos for her.

CF

📖 D. RESTOUT (ed.), *Landowska on Music* (New York and London, 1965)

Lang, David (*b* Los Angeles, 8 Jan. 1957). American composer. He graduated from Stanford (1978), the University of Iowa (1980), and Yale (1989), as a doctoral pupil of Martin Bresnick, then settled in New York, where in 1987 he founded, with Michael Gordon and Julia Wolfe, the unbounded performance organization Bang on a Can. His works include the opera *Modern Painters* (Santa Fe, 1994) and orchestral pieces, but most of his music is for soloists (*The Anvil Chorus* for percussionist, 1990) or small ensembles, combining elements from minimalism and the more hard-edged avant-garde with a streetwise sense of musical drama.

PG

Lang, Josephine (Caroline) (*b* Munich, 14 March 1815; *d* Tübingen, 2 Dec. 1880). German composer. She made her debut at the age of 11, playing a set of piano variations by Herz, and four years later met Mendelssohn, who gave her lessons in theory. During the 1830s she taught singing and the piano, sang in the royal Vokalkapelle, and composed. She wrote some 150 songs, most of which deal with themes of love or nature; they contain daring melodies with independent accompaniments. SH

Lange, (Maria) **Aloysia** (Louise Antonia) [née Weber] (*b* Zell or Mannheim, *c.*1761; *d* Salzburg, 8 June 1839). German soprano. She studied with Georg Vogler in Mannheim and took lessons from Mozart, who in 1777–8 wrote concert arias for her. Mozart, who was in love with her, later married her sister Constanze. In 1779 she made her debut in Munich, as Parthenia in Schweitzer's *Alceste*, and in Vienna, and the following year she married the painter and actor Joseph Lange. It was at the Kärntnertortheater that she achieved her greatest fame, notably creating the role of Konstanze in *Die Entführung aus dem Serail*; she also sang Donna Anna in the Viennese premiere of *Don Giovanni* in 1788. Her voice was light but expressive. JT

Langgaard, Rued (Immanuel) (*b* Copenhagen, 28 July 1893; *d* Ribe, 10 July 1952). Danish composer and organist. Grounded in music by his parents, he made his debut as a virtuoso organist at the age of 11, and his precocious First Symphony (1908–11) was performed by the Berlin Philharmonic Orchestra. But Langgaard's romantic mysticism and aggressively eccentric behaviour condemned him to life as an outsider in Denmark. His output is bizarrely inconsistent in style and quality, but at his best—as in the Fourth (1916) and Sixth (1919) Symphonies, the Third Quartet (1924), and above all the visionary *Sfaerenes musik* ('Music of the Spheres', 1918)—he could be strikingly original. SJ

Langlais, Jean (François) (*b* La Fontenelle, 15 Feb. 1907; *d* Paris, 8 May 1991). French organist and composer. Blind from childhood, he studied at the Institut National des Jeunes Aveugles (1917–30) and the Paris Conservatoire (1927–34), where his teachers included Marcel Dupré and Charles Tournemire for the organ and Paul Dukas for composition. In 1945 he was appointed organist of Ste Clotilde, and he also taught at the Institut (from 1931) and the Schola Cantorum (from 1961). Influenced chiefly by Tournemire and Messiaen, he produced a large output of organ music, including three concertos with orchestra, as well as several liturgical choral works. PG/ABur

langsam (Ger.). 'Slow'; *langsamer*, 'slower'; *sehr langsam*, 'very slow'.

Lanier, Nicholas (*b* London, *bapt.* 10 Sept. 1588; *d* Greenwich, Feb. 1666). English singer, lutenist, and composer. He was of French descent, his family having settled in London in the second half of the 16th century. In his early years he served the Cecils, through whom he forged connections with the court, and in 1616 he was appointed lutenist to the King's Music. In that role he collaborated with Ben Jonson, writing music (now lost, but reportedly in the Italian recitative style) for the masque *Lovers Made Men* (1617). On Charles I's accession he was made Master of the King's Music. He was knowledgeable about painting, and travelled to Italy to purchase pictures on the king's behalf; Hampton Court contains some of the fruits of his labours. He was later appointed Master of the King's Miniatures, and during the Civil War made a living trading in pictures and musical instruments. Little of Lanier's music survives. He wrote some of the earliest English examples of declamatory song, and his recitative *Hero and Leander* shows a close knowledge of the Italian lament. He was evidently a talented artist, and left a delightful self-portrait; Van Dyck also painted him. DA/JM

Laporte, André (*b* Oplinter, Limburg, 12 July 1931). Belgian composer. He studied in Mechelen with Flor Peeters and Marinus de Jong, and at the summer courses in Darmstadt and Cologne. He has worked as a producer for Belgian Radio, and taught at the Brussels Conservatory. His works include the large-scale cantata *La vita non è sogno* (1972), and the opera *Das Schloss* (after Kafka; Brussels, 1986). ABur

lap steel guitar. See Hawaiian guitar.

largamente (It.), **largement** (Fr.). 'Broadly', i.e. slow and dignified. See also largo.

largando. See allargando.

larghetto (It.). 'Slow', but less so than **largo*.

largo (It.). 'Broad'. A tempo indication which, when it first appeared in the early 17th century, was considered the slowest. Rousseau listed it as such in his dictionary (1768), but Purcell and his contemporaries considered it to be between *adagio* and *andante*. The term 'largo' is often also used as the title of a slow movement or piece. The work known as Handel's 'Largo' is the aria 'Ombra mai è fù' from his opera *Xerxes*, played in various instrumental arrangements; the original aria, however, is marked *larghetto*.

Lark Ascending, The. Romance (1914) by Vaughan Williams for violin and orchestra, inspired by the poem of that name by George Meredith; it was revised in 1920.

'Lark' Quartet (*Lerchenquartett*). Nickname of Haydn's String Quartet in D major op. 64 no. 5 (1790), so called because of the soaring violin theme of its opening; the rhythm of the last movement has given rise to another, less frequently used nickname, the 'Hornpipe' Quartet.

Larsen, Libby [Elizabeth Brown] (*b* Wilmington, DE, 24 Dec. 1950). American composer. She studied with Dominick Argento, Paul Fetler, and Eric Stokes at the University of Minnesota (1968–78). Her music is generally bold, clear, and colourful, and includes three symphonies, operas (*Mrs Dalloway*, Cleveland, 1993), chamber music (*Schoenberg, Schenker, Schillinger* for string quartet, 1991, in three movements following those respective masters), and vocal compositions.

PG

Larsson, Lars-Erik (Vilner) (*b* Åkarp, nr Lund, 15 May 1908; *d* Hälsingborg, 27 Dec. 1986). Swedish composer, teacher, and conductor. After success in examination as an organist, he enrolled at the Stockholm Conservatory, studying composition with Ernst Ellberg and conducting with Olalla Morales (1924–9) before further instruction in Vienna with Berg (1929–30) and in Leipzig with Reuter (1930–1). Back in Stockholm he worked for Swedish Radio (1937–53). In the mean time he had become professor of composition at the Musikhögskola in Stockholm, and was later appointed director of music at the University of Uppsala.

Larsson was a Romantic composer: although his idiom was neo-classical (with some investigation of dodecaphonic technique later in his work), his was a lyrical instinct and his music is tuneful and direct. His breakthrough as a composer came in 1938 with his *Pastoral Suite* and was consolidated in 1940 with the 'lyric suite' *Förklädd Gud* ('God in Disguise') for narrator, soprano, baritone, and orchestra. He also composed three symphonies (1927–8, 1936–7, 1945) as well as a number of other orchestral works, and his concertante music includes 12 concertinos op. 45, for various solo instruments, all with string accompaniment (1954–7); there are three string quartets (1944, 1955, 1975) in his chamber output.

MA

La Rue, Pierre de [Pierchon] (*b* ?Tournai, *c*.1452; *d* Kortrijk, 20 Nov. 1518). Franco-Flemish church musician and composer. His career, which was spent almost entirely in the Low Countries, began with appointments as a singer in Brussels, Ghent, Nieuwpoort, Cologne, and 's-Hertogenbosch. In 1492 he became a member of the Habsburg–Burgundian chapel, and travelled twice to Spain on diplomatic missions. Many of his works were copied into exquisite manuscripts produced by the court scriptorium, some of which were destined to become gifts to political leaders across Europe. He retired from his position in 1516.

Like his immediate contemporary Jacob Obrecht, la Rue is a composer of major stature who remains overshadowed by the towering figure of the age, Josquin des Prez. His surviving output also resembles Obrecht's in being dominated by masses; more than 30 settings survive, the majority based on plainchant melodies. There are fewer motets, but in that area his achievement has been boosted by the discovery that the powerfully expressive *Absalon fili mi*, long thought to be a work of Josquin's, may in fact be by la Rue. A very different motet, the ingenious six-voice triple canon *Ave sanctissima Maria*, served as the starting-point for one of his own *parody masses. Considerable problems of attribution surround the chansons, and it is likely that many of the anonymous pieces in the beautiful chansonniers made for Marguerite of Austria, including settings of texts by Marguerite herself, are his work.

JM

📖 H. MECONI, *Pierre de la Rue* (Oxford, forthcoming)

'La sol fa re mi', Missa. Mass for four voices by Josquin des Prez based entirely on a five-note solmization.

Lasso, Orlando di. See LASSUS, ORLANDE DE.

Lass of Richmond Hill, The. Song by James Hook to words by L. McNally; it is a reference to Richmond, Yorkshire, not Surrey.

lassú (Hung.). 'Slow'; see CSÁRDÁS; VERBUNKOS.

Lassus, Orlande [Roland] **de** [Orlando di Lasso] (*b* Mons, *c*.1532; *d* Munich, 14 June 1594). Franco-Flemish composer. He was a choirboy at St Nicolas, Mons, and tradition has it that he was kidnapped three times for the beauty of his voice. At the age of 12 he was allowed by his parents to enter the service of Ferrante Gonzaga, with whom Lassus went to Paris, Mantua, Palermo, and Milan. When his voice broke he went to Naples in the service of a minor nobleman, and there he became a member of the Accademia de' Sereni, a literary and artistic circle. He then visited Rome as a guest of the influential Archbishop of Florence and obtained the important post of *maestro di cappella* at St John Lateran when he was only 21. In Rome he was again involved with a group of intellectuals, who were interested in modern ideas including the use of chromaticism in music. He stayed in this post only briefly before being called home to visit his parents who were ill; they had both died by the time he arrived in Mons. In 1555 he was in Antwerp, and it was at that time that he began to publish his works, showing an extraordinary versatility in putting together a book of elegant madrigals for Antonio Gardano in Venice and a mixed set of madrigals, bawdy villanellas to Neapolitan dialect texts, French chansons, and Latin motets for Tylman Susato in Antwerp.

Lassus's reputation was well established by the publications of the 1550s, and in 1556 he was invited to become a singer at the Bavarian court of Duke Albrecht V in Munich. Within a few years he was head of the musical establishment, in the place of the then unfashionably Protestant Ludwig Daser; he held the position until his death. In 1558 he married Regina Wäckinger, the daughter of a court official, and resumed publishing his works on a massive scale, books of sacred and secular music appearing in Antwerp, Venice, Paris, Munich, and Frankfurt. In the early Munich years he proved himself a master of both the witty chanson and the more serious madrigal, giving in the madrigal a musical expression of the texts which few could equal, and not indulging in the less subtle word-painting which was soon to become fashionable. He took an active part in the celebrations for the royal wedding of Wilhelm V and Renée of Lorraine in 1568 as an actor in a traditional *commedia dell'arte* performance. He also travelled widely in search of singers and instrumentalists for the rapidly expanding musical establishment, to Flanders, Frankfurt, and especially northern Italy. He built up his *cappella* such that Munich became the most famous musical centre in Europe, inspiring a host of young composers (including the Gabrielis) to study with him there.

Some of Lassus's church music from this period reflects the good fortune he was enjoying. The parody masses are based so closely on their models that the secular words must often have sprung to mind. However, it was also about this time that the gloominess and intensity of Counter-Reformation ideas began to affect his music, most especially in his settings of the seven Penitential Psalms.

In 1579 economic circumstances and the accession of the new duke, Wilhelm V, dictated a reduction in the *cappella*. Shortly after this Lassus was offered the post of *maestro* at the Saxon court at Dresden, but he refused it, partly because Albrecht had granted him an ample pension for life, but mainly because he was settled in Munich, with two town houses and one in the country. The effect of the new atmosphere is none the less noticeable in his music. The publications of the 1580s are largely concerned with church music, including settings from the book of Job, the Penitential Psalms, and the Lamentations of the prophet Jeremiah. His

fifth book of madrigals (Nuremberg, 1585) sets verses by Petrarch on the passing of youth and religious sonnets by Gabriele Fiamma. In 1585 he made a further visit to Italy, significantly making a pilgrimage to Loreto (the Lourdes of its time); a couple of years later he dedicated a madrigal volume to the Munich court physician, who was growing concerned for Lassus's mental state. By 1590 Lassus was suffering from melancholia, sometimes scarcely recognizing his wife, and was beset by thoughts of death. In 1594 he published a volume of six-part motets which the preface refers to as his swansong. Nevertheless, he accompanied his master to Regensburg in the same year, and was preparing for publication his cycle of religious madrigals, the *Lagrime di S. Pietro*, when he died. Of his four sons, two— **Ferdinand** (*b* Munich, *c*.1560; *d* Munich, 27 Aug. 1609) and **Rudolph** (*b* Munich, *c*.1563; *d* Munich, 1625)— became musicians and were in the service of the Bavarian court.

Lassus was acknowledged in his lifetime as one of the great masters of music. In 1604 a collected edition of his motets was published by his sons, and his church music, known from England to Poland, continued to be performed, especially in France, where his connection with the publishing house of Le Roy & Ballard had been very strong. Several more posthumous editions were published before 1650, an unusual tribute to a composer's popularity at this period. Nevertheless, his music has not latterly received the attention it deserves, perhaps because of his eclecticism but also, it seems, because of the 'canonization' of Palestrina to the exclusion of other, arguably more gifted, contemporaries. Even so, Lassus's excellence in virtually all genres deserves recognition. He is especially fine in the subtle expression of moods, in both church and secular music, and his chansons and villanellas can be seen as the equivalent of a great master's drawings or etchings, capturing the character of the grotesque or unusual in his fellow men.   DA/TC

📖 J. ROCHE, *Lassus* (New York, 1982) · P. BERGQUIST (ed.), *Orlando di Lasso Studies* (Cambridge, 1999)

Last Post. British army bugle call. The First Post at 9.30 p.m. calls all men back to their barracks; the Last Post ends the day. By a natural and poetical association, it has become the custom to sound the Last Post at military funerals. See also TATTOO.

Last Rose of Summer, The. Irish air, originally *Castle Hyde*, which became R. A. Millikin's *The Groves of Blarney* (*c*.1790). Thomas Moore included it, with his own, new words, in his *Irish Melodies* (1813). Beethoven set it, Mendelssohn wrote a piano fantasia on it, and it is used extensively by Flotow in his opera *Martha* (1847).

Last Supper, The. Opera (dramatic tableaux) by Birtwistle to a libretto by Robin Blaser (Berlin, 2000).

Latin America 1. Diversity of traditions; 2. Mexico and Central America; 3. Spanish-speaking South America; 4. Brazil; 5. The Caribbean area

1. Diversity of traditions

Latin America, with a population of over 340 million, stretches from Mexico and Cuba south to Cape Horn. In general, Latin American music can be said to blend native Indian, transported African, and imported European elements. What gives each regional music its distinctive flavour is the relative strength of these three traditions in the mixture. The rural musics in highland areas of nations that still boast a large Indian population (e.g. Mexico, Guatemala, Peru, Bolivia, Ecuador) integrate various aboriginal traits. These include 'tight', 'out of tune' melodies, and ritualistic festive performances. Prominent 20th-century Mexican (Carlos Chávez, Candelario Huízar, Daniel Ayala), Guatemalan (Jesús and Ricardo Castillo), and Peruvian (Daniel Alomía Robles, Teodoro Valcárcel, Andrés Sas) composers have effectively incorporated Indian and pseudo-Indian tunes in their works.

On the other hand, African influences now dominate both folk and art music in Caribbean island nations where before 1550 sub-Saharan Africans began replacing Indians in the labour force. Among Spanish-speaking nations, African influences have affected the folk music of coastal Mexico, Guatemala, Honduras, Panama, Venezuela, Colombia, Ecuador, and Peru. The marimbas of southern Mexico and Guatemala and the leg drums played by blacks in coastal Colombia and Ecuador are generally conceded to be African-derived. Portuguese-speaking Brazil (which constitutes half of South America in population and territory) testifies even more strongly to African intermixture. The works of the Brazilian mulattos José Joaquim Emerico Lóbo de Mesquita (*c.*1745–1805) and Nunes Garcia (see below, 4) may not sound in any way idiomatically African, but Brazilian *samba de roda* song repertories and Brazilian *maracatu* dance processions exemplify undeniable African traits persisting to the present day.

As well as the (relatively weak) Indian element in Latin American music as a whole, and the African component in Caribbean and Brazilian areas, Latin American music everywhere betrays thoroughgoing indebtedness to European models. The many varieties of guitar that abound in the regional folk musics of Latin America are all adaptations of European models.

Even the *charango*, a small fretted lute backed with an armadillo shell, popular in the Andes, had as predecessor a double-string, five-course, discontinuously tuned guitar described by Mersenne. The violins and trumpets that give Mexican *mariachi* music its characteristic flavour are entirely European instruments— even though not played in a European manner. Latin rhythms and especially harmonies also rely heavily on European models. The fast hemiola rhythms (6/8 alternating with 3/4) which lend vivacity to the *son jarocho* performed in the region of Veracruz, Mexico, accompanied by harps and guitars, are Spanish-derived, as are the hemiolas in the Peruvian *marinera* and Argentine *vidalita*. Latin harmony is similarly conventional in chordal structure.

2. Mexico and Central America

Long before Spaniards arrived, Mexican territory was the home of successive high civilizations. When organum was just coming to birth in Europe the Totonacs in the Veracruz region were already favouring quadruple and triple clay tube flutes that sounded four- and three-note chords. A protuberance at the necks of some archaic clay flutes excavated in Tabasco deflected the air through an 'oscillating air chamber', giving them a reedy timbre. The Mayas with their delicate six-fingerhole flutes found in excavations of Jaina island were the Greeks of ancient Mexico; the Aztecs with their four-fingerhole flutes were the Romans. Between Mayas and Aztecs came the Toltecs, who incised five holes on their human-bone flutes.

Aztec sages taught that duality, maleness and femaleness, engendered the universe. In accordance with that principle, the greatest importance among Aztec instruments attached to the wooden *teponaztli*, struck with two rubber-tipped mallets, and the upright cylindrical *huehuetl*, tipped with jaguar skin, played with two bare hands. These two percussion instruments, each sounding two pitches, were customarily joined for ceremonial use. Aztec musicians enjoyed high social prestige and exemption from tribute payments.

The Aztecs immediately took to European music in all its aspects. By 1561 Indian instrumentalists were so rife that Philip II issued a decree against 'the present excessive number of musicians who consume their time playing trumpets, clarions, shawms, sackbuts, flutes, cornetts, dulzainas, fifes, viols, rebecs, and other kinds of instrument, in inordinate variety'. In 1865 Mexican ecclesiastical authorities petitioned the crown for 'a further abatement in the excessive number of Indian singers'.

Because the Indians learnt almost at once to make clever imitations of European instruments while continuing to produce their own, they were able as early as the mid-16th century to develop instrumental accompanying ensembles with hitherto unknown tone-colour possibilities. They also began to write down their music. According to Juan de Torquemada (1565–1624), 'their villancicos, their polyphonic music in four parts, certain masses and other liturgical works, all composed with adroitness, have been adjudged superior works of art when shown to Spanish masters of composition'. Among Indian composers whose works have been published, Tomás Pascual (*fl* Guatemala, 1595–1635) and Juan Mathías (*fl* Mexico, mid-17th century) prove Indian mastery in smaller forms. The greatest colonial composer identifiable as an Indian, however, was Don Juan de Lienas (active at Mexico City 1630–50), who wrote sublime *Salve* settings, masses, and Lamentations; a five-voice mass and four-voice *Salve* have been published and recorded. Much of his music discovered in the 1970s is for double choir.

The leading Spanish-born or Spanish-descended composers in Mexico City before 1800, all of whom left sizable repertories, were Hernando Franco (*maestro de capilla* of the cathedral 1575–85), Antonio Rodríguez de Mata (1625–43), Luis Coronado (1643–8), Francisco López Capillas (1654–74), Antonio de Salazar (1688–1715), and Manuel de Zumaya (1715–39). Both López Capillas and Zumaya were born in the city. Zumaya, who ranks as one of the paramount composers in New World annals, composed the first Mexican opera, *Il Partenope* (1711), to the libretto by Silvio Stampiglia later used by Handel. Ignacio Jerusalem (1749–69), a master of charming melody born in Lecce, was the first Italian to direct Mexico City cathedral and theatre music simultaneously.

At Puebla, Mexico, the leading composers included the Portuguese-born Gaspar Fernandes (organist and *maestro de capilla* 1606–29) and his successor Juan Gutiérrez de Padilla (1629–64), born in Málaga. Fernandes left in autograph over 250 festal *chanzonetas* and villancicos, many highly spiced with Negro-dialect text and Negro-influenced rhythms. Padilla presided over Puebla music during its heyday, bequeathing a large body of sumptuous double-choir music (including four masses for eight voices). An excellent teacher, he counted among many illustrious pupils his successor, Juan García Zéspedes (1619–78).

After independence, social and political unrest played havoc with music educational opportunities in Mexico as elsewhere in Spanish America. The roll of renowned 19th-century Mexican composers, all of whom made their reputations in opera—in their century the one sure passport to fame—ranges from Cenobio Paniagua (1812–82), Aniceto Ortego (1825–75), and Ricardo Castro (1864–1907) to Gustavo Emilio Campa (1863–1934). The waltz *Sobre las olas* ('Over the Waves'), by the Otomí Indian Juventino Rosas (1868–94), remains one of the most famous Latin American pieces worldwide. Next to the Mexican national anthem, composed in 1854 by Jaime Nunó (1824–1908), the best-known song written in 19th-century Mexico is Narciso Serradell's *La golondrina* ('The Swallow', 1862), encapsulating the sorrow felt at the departure of a beloved friend.

The most widely known Mexican concert song of the 20th century is Ponce's *Estrellita* ('Little Star'); his larger works include the *Concierto del sur* (1941), written for Segovia. The chief exponent of Indian themes and subjects in 20th-century Mexico was Carlos Chávez. His contemporaries and pupils include Revueltas, whose symphonic poem *Sensemayá* (1938) crowned his output; José Pablo Moncayo (1912–58), whose coruscating *Huapango* (1941) catches all the colour of folk-loric dancing; and Blas Galindo Dimas (1910–93), a Huichol Indian. Rodolfo Halffter (1900–87) emigrated from Spain in 1940 to become the teacher and prophet of a new generation not wedded to Mexican folklore or Aztec evocations. The younger composers Manuel Enríquez (1926–94), Héctor Quintanar (*b* 1936), Mario Lavista (*b* 1943), and Juan Trigos (*b* 1965) eschew anything locally Mexican, and instead flow with prevalent international currents.

3. Spanish-speaking South America

The favourite instruments of the Andean indigenes were *antaras* (panpipes) and *quena-quenas* (vertical flutes). Although panpipes excavated along the Peruvian coast testify to a Nazca musical system that allowed for microtones in upper registers, the Incas favoured pentatonic melodies. The colour and number of drums counted as heavily in ritual performances at their capital, Cuzco, as the timbre of the *qquepas* (trumpets) and *pincollos* (flutes) heard during ceremonies honouring their sun deity or their deceased rulers. By 1560 European music of the highest quality was being brought to Cuzco. Morales's printed masses (1544) were imported to the Inca capital only a decade after publication. The most distinguished composer in 16th-century South America was Gutierre Fernández Hidalgo (*c*.1547–1623), whose extant liturgical works, of surpassing beauty and intensity, include *Salve* and *Magnificat* settings and psalms. The first polyphonic composition published in the New World, a delightful marching song for mixed choir with a text in Quecha, the language of the Incas, appeared at Lima in 1631.

The Spanish-descended composers at Lima, capital of the viceroyalty of Peru (the richest dominion in the Spanish empire), included the erstwhile organist of the Portuguese royal chapel, Estacio de la Serna (active at Lima 1612–14), and Tomás de Torrejón y Velasco (1676–

1728). Using a libretto written in 1660 by Pedro Calderón de la Barca, Torrejón y Velasco composed the earliest extant New World opera-zarzuela, *La púrpura de la rosa*, mounted at the viceroyal palace in Lima in 1701. Like other New World centres racked by revolutions and wars, Peru lost its musical pre-eminence after 1821. José Bernardo Aizedo (1788–1878), who composed the Peruvian national anthem that year, emigrated to Chile where he conducted the cathedral music at Santiago de Chile. 20th-century Peruvian music benefited from the leadership of such European immigrants as the Belgian Andrés Sas (1900–67) and the German Rodolfo Holzmann (1910–92).

In 1717 Argentina welcomed the Italian Domenico Zipoli (1688–1726). Through his published keyboard works Zipoli was the most renowned of the numerous Jesuit musical missionaries sent to Argentina and Paraguay before 1767. Buenos Aires, capital of a viceroyalty established in 1776, came into its own during the 19th century as the centre of music publishing, opera, and concert life in Spanish South America. The present Teatro Colón (seating 3950), opened in 1908, was preceded by the old Teatro Colón (1857–88), Teatro de la Ópera (1872), Teatro Nacional (1882), and other theatres showing Italian, French, and to a limited extent Argentine operas. The most acclaimed South American composer of his generation, Alberto Ginastera, made his international reputation in opera; and other prominent Argentinians who gained fame with operas include Arturo Berutti (1862–1938), Constantino Gaito (1878–1945), and Juan José Castro (1895–1968). Even the tango composer Piazzolla eventually turned to opera in his most ambitious work, *María de Buenos Aires* (1967).

Such Chilean 20th-century composers as Enrique Soro (1884–1954), Alfonso Leng (1894–1974), Domingo Santa Cruz (1899–1987), Alfonso Letelier Llona (1912–84), and Juan A. Orrego-Salas (*b* 1919), however, eschewed all stage music. Santiago de Chile is the brightest centre for musicological research in South America. The *Revista musical chilena*, founded in 1945, remains the most significant and respected musicological periodical published in Latin America.

4. Brazil

The earliest extant dated piece of Brazilian music is a recitative and aria composed in 1759 by Caetano de Mello Jesus, *maestro de capilla* at Bahia Cathedral. In 1763 the capital moved to Rio de Janeiro, where the mulatto priest José Maurício Nunes Garcia (1767–1830) became *maestro de capilla* of the cathedral in 1798. Garcia's rich surviving repertory of liturgical music in all genres recalls Haydn and Mozart, whom he idolized, but he had none the less his own rich vein

of melody. His pupil, Francisco Manuel da Silva (1795–1865), composed the Brazilian national anthem in 1831.

During the Brazilian empire (1822–89, ending with the abdication of Pedro II), Rio de Janeiro boasted the best library in South America, the most flourishing music publication industry in Latin America, concert seasons that attracted such virtuosos as Thalberg and Gottschalk, and above all a flourishing operatic life. Carlos Gomes, a protégé of Pedro II, composed two operas for Rio before transferring to Milan, where eight of his operas were produced between 1867 and 1891.

Villa-Lobos, who overshadowed all other South Americans of his generation, was alone among Brazilians in making a strong impact in Europe. Aware of what was needed to impress European critics, he invented new musical forms in his *Chôros* and *Bachianas brasileiras*, spiced his works liberally with tunes imitating popular Brazilian music, and posed as a descendant of an Indian tribe. Other 20th-century Brazilians who necessarily suffer in comparison but who individually merit acclaim include Oscar Lorenzo Fernândez (1897–1948), Camargo Guarnieri (1907–93), Cláudio Santoro (1919–89) Édino Krieger (*b* 1928), and Marlos Nobre (*b* 1939).

5. The Caribbean area

The immense wealth of its mainland colonies caused Spain to neglect its Caribbean outposts. Before Esteban Salas y Castro (1725–1803) Cuba lacked a first-rate composer. During the 19th century no Cuban dramatic composer impressed Europe until Caspar Villate (1851–91) had three operas mounted, at Paris, The Hague, and Madrid. Eduardo Sánchez de Fuentes (1874–1944), Alejandro Garcia Caturla (1906–40), and Amadeo Roldán (1900–39) typified right, centre, and left in Cuban music of their generation. Of these, Roldán, who wrote *Danza negra* (1928) and *Poema negro* (1930), took Cuba's black heritage the most seriously, and therefore enjoys greatest prestige in Havana today. The expatriate Ernesto Lecuona published zarzuelas, fine piano music, and songs which continue to rank among the best-known Latin American compositions.

Haiti (Saint-Domingue) during the second half of the 18th century witnessed a constant round of operas and other stage works by Gluck, Piccinni, Monsigny, Duni, Blaise, Rousseau, and their like. After Toussaint l'Ouverture and Henri Christophe, all such French stage traditions fled the island, to be replaced by a vigorous African-oriented musical culture emphasizing drums.

At the head of Venezuelan musicians during that nation's period of colonial musical glory stood the mulatto Juan Manuel Olivares (1760–97). His pupils included Juan José Landaeta (1780–1814), to whom is attributed the music of the Venezuelan national anthem, *Gloria al bravo pueblo*, and Lino Gallardo (1773–1837). The renowned Venezuelan composer and cathedral-music director Cayetano Carreño (1774–1836) was the grandfather of the celebrated pianist Teresa Carreño. José Ángel Lamas (1775–1814), generally considered the most gifted composer in Venezuelan music, gave his name to the national conservatory at Caracas. The foremost 19th-century Venezuelan composer, José Angel Montero (1832–81), wrote the first opera by a native Venezuelan mounted in Caracas, *Virginia* (1873, revived there 1969).   RSt/CW

📖 R. Stevenson, *Music in Mexico: A Historical Survey* (New York, 1952); *The Music of Peru* (Washington, DC, 1960) · G. Chase, *A Guide to the Music of Latin America* (Washington, DC, 1962) · R. Stevenson, *Music in Aztec and Inca Territory* (Berkeley, CA, 1968); *Foundation of New World Opera* (Lima, 1973) · D. Malmström, *Introduction to Twentieth Century Mexican Music* (Uppsala, 1974) · R. Stevenson, *A Guide to Caribbean Music History* (Lima, 1975); *Latin American Colonial Music* (Washington, DC, 1975) · G. Béhague, *Music in Latin America: An Introduction* (Englewood Cliffs, NJ, 1979) · C. E. Robertson (ed.), *Musical Repercussions of 1492: Encounters in Text and Performance* (Washington, DC, 1992)

Lauda Sion (Lat., 'Praise, O Sion'). One of the four *sequences allowed to remain in the liturgy of the Roman Catholic Church after the *Council of Trent (1542–63). The words are traditionally held to have been written by Thomas Aquinas (*c*.1264) at the request of Pope Urban IV for the feast of Corpus Christi (on which they are still sung). It has its own traditional plainchant (a pre-existing melody, originally used for several Victorine sequences), but has also been set to music by composers, for example Palestrina, Mendelssohn (who used a contemporary form of the plainchant), and Rubbra.   —/ALi

lauda spirituale (It., 'spiritual praise', pl. *laude spirituali*; the form *laude*, pl. *laudi*, is also found). A type of sacred song, usually with Italian words though sometimes partly or wholly in Latin, cultivated in Italy from the 13th century to the 16th. Like the Spanish *cantiga and the English *carol, *laude* belong to the category of popular religious music sung by the laity, and never formed part of the formal worship of the church. Their performance was fostered by guild-like fraternities of singers (called *laudesi*), which existed throughout Italy; *laude* were also popular within monastic communities, and were sometimes included in religious plays.

The earliest *laude* were penitential in tone; they were sung at times of warfare, plague, or other affliction, and were usually addressed to the Virgin or one of the saints, especially St Francis of Assisi. Later, verses of a more generally devotional or seasonal nature (concerning the Christmas story, the Passion, etc.) were also set. The poetry is homely and stereotyped in nature, and is rarely of any great literary distinction.

For its musical substance, the early *lauda* drew on a wide variety of sources, its basic idiom owing much to folk and popular elements, but with the influence of plainchant and the songs of the troubadours also apparent. These *laude* were monophonic at first, with syllabic melodies moving largely by step, unsophisticated rhythms, and often also short refrains. During the 15th century, accompanying lines came to be improvised or composed around the original melody, most often in a note-against-note fashion, giving rise by the early 16th century to simple chordal works for four voices with an emphasis on the melody and bass, in a style not unlike that of the contemporary *frottola. The market for *laude* was apparently large at this time, for the Venetian printer Petrucci published two collections. Although the *lauda* itself declined in importance later in the 16th century, some of its characteristic features were taken over in the music of the *rappresentazione sacra* and the early oratorio (see ORATORIO, 1).   JM

laudesi (It.). See LAUDA SPIRITUALE.

Laudon Symphony (Loudon Symphony). Haydn's Symphony no. 69 in C major (mid-1770s), so called because it is dedicated to the Austrian field marshal Ernst Gideon Freiherr von Loudon (1716–90).

Lauds. The second of eight hours of the Divine *Office in the medieval Roman rite, celebrated at daybreak, and so called because it featured the ancient morning 'Praises' (Lat.: *laudes*; Gk.: *ainoi*), Psalms 148–50. It is known in the Anglican Church as Morning Prayer.

laut (Ger.). 'Loud'.

Laute (Ger.). 'Lute'.

lavolta. See VOLTA, 1.

Lawes, Henry (*b* Dinton, Wilts., *bapt.* 5 Jan. 1596; *d* London, 21 Oct. 1662). English singer and composer, the elder brother of William Lawes. He was brought up in Salisbury, and may have been a chorister in the cathedral there. In 1626 he was made a Gentleman of Charles I's Chapel Royal, and five years later was appointed one of the king's musicians 'for the lutes and voices'. He wrote the music for John Milton's masque of *Comus*, produced at Ludlow Castle on Michaelmas Night 1634, of which only five songs survive. During the Commonwealth he became a fashionable teacher;

his pupils included the daughters of the Earl of Bridgewater, dedicatees of his first book of *Ayres and Dialogues* of 1653. He contributed to Davenant's lost opera *The Siege of Rhodes*, first performed at Rutland House in 1656. At the Restoration he was reinstated to his court positions, and wrote a setting of *Zadok the Priest* for the coronation of Charles II. He was buried in Westminster Abbey.

Lawes was one of the most important songwriters of the 17th century. More than 400 songs by him survive, to verses by contemporary poets including Thomas Carew, John Suckling, and Richard Lovelace. John Milton's sonnet 'To Mr. H. Lawes on his Aires' commends his word-setting:

> Harry, whose tuneful and well-measured song
> First taught our English music how to span
> Words with just note and accent.

He also wrote anthems and psalm settings. Despite his interest in the declamatory style, Lawes remains a thoroughly English composer in outlook, and in the preface to his 1653 *Ayres* openly deplores the current taste for Italian music at the expense of that of English composers.   WT/JM

Lawes, William (*b* Salisbury, *bapt.* 1 May 1602; *d* Chester, 24 Sept. 1645). English court musician and composer, the younger brother of Henry Lawes. He was a pupil of Coprario, and in 1635 joined his brother as a 'musician in ordinary for the lute and voices' at Charles I's court. A royalist, he enlisted as a soldier during the Civil War; he was shot at the Battle of Chester, 'betrayed thereunto by his own adventuresness' (Fuller).

Unlike his brother, Lawes published nothing during his lifetime. His most important achievements lie in instrumental rather than vocal music. His works for viol consort include sets of fantasias and stylized dances that show the influence of Italian madrigalists such as Monteverdi, with their expressive dissonances and melodic leaps. The violin works, conversely, come closer to the worlds of the solo and trio sonata after the more modern Italian style. The pieces grouped together under the title 'The Royall Consort', composed in the mid-1630s but subsequently reworked, won particular acclaim. Lawes also wrote songs and incidental music for plays, masques, and other entertainments by Ben Jonson, William Davenant, Francis Beaumont, John Fletcher, and other leading authors of the day. His position at court did not require Lawes to compose for the church, and his only surviving sacred music is a set of psalm settings, using the metrical translations of George Sandys.   DA/JM

📖 A. Ashbee (ed.), *William Lawes (1602–1645): Essays on his Life, Times and Work* (Aldershot, 1998)

lay clerk, lay vicar. Alternative titles for a *vicar choral, a layman serving in the Anglican Church.

Layolle, Francesco de (*b* Florence, 4 March 1492; *d* Lyons, *c*.1540). Italian composer and organist. He was a pupil of Bartolomeo degli Organi in Florence, and himself taught Benvenuto Cellini. He left Florence in 1518, and in 1521 moved to Lyons, where he was an associate of the publisher Jacques Moderne, editing and composing for him volumes of sacred music in the 1530s. He wrote masses and motets, but most of his surviving music is secular, comprising chansons, canzonas, and madrigals. Andrea del Sarto depicted him in a fresco for the Florentine church of Ss. Annunziata, and Jacopo da Pontormo painted his portrait, which now hangs in the Uffizi.   DA

leader [concert master] (Fr.: *chef d'attaque*; Ger.: *Konzertmeister*). The principal first violinist in an orchestra, who plays the violin solos in orchestral works and is often a considerable virtuoso. He or she represents the orchestra in any discussion or dispute with conductors and is responsible for phrasings and bowings in the string parts.   JMo

leading motif. See LEITMOTIF.

leading note. The seventh degree of the scale, a semitone below the tonic. It is so called because of its tendency to rise, or 'lead', to the tonic. In a minor key it is sometimes flattened in the descent, and is then called a 'flattened leading note'.

Lear. Opera in two parts by Reimann to a libretto by Claus H. Henneberg after Shakespeare's *King Lear* (Munich, 1978).

Lebègue, Nicolas (*b* Laon, *c*.1631; *d* Paris, 6 July 1702). French composer. The son of a miller-baker, he left Laon for Paris when he was in his 20s; he may have studied there with Chambonnières. In 1664 he was appointed organist of St Merri, and in 1678 he joined Nivers, J.-D. Thomelin, and J.-B. Buterne as one of four organists to the royal chapel. Much sought after as an adviser on organ-building, he also had many pupils including Grigny. In his later years he was swindled of his life savings, and at the age of 69 underwent successful surgery for a kidney stone. His published volumes of harpsichord pieces (Paris, 1677, ?1687) helped to standardize the number and order of dances in the suite, and his collections of organ works (Paris, 1676, ?1678, ?1685) contain a wide range of pieces, from virtuoso keyboard trios to simple Mass versets and arrangements of popular *noëls*.   DA/JAS

lebendig (Ger.). 'Lively'.

Lebewohl, Das ('The Farewell'). Beethoven's title for his Piano Sonata no. 26 in E♭ major op. 81*a*, usually known as *Les *Adieux*.

lebhaft (Ger.). 'Lively', *vivace*.

Lechner, Leonhard (*b* South Tyrol, *c*.1553; *d* Stuttgart, 9 Sept. 1606). German composer. He served under Lassus at the Bavarian court chapel. After converting to Protestantism (*c*.1568) he became a schoolmaster in Nuremberg and, in 1583, joined the Catholic court at Hechingen. However, religious problems led him to make further moves—to Tübingen, and finally to Stuttgart, where he became Hofkapellmeister in 1594. His works embrace masses, *Magnificat* settings, and motets, including *Quid chaos*, a polychoral setting in the Venetian manner. Particularly noteworthy are his *St John* motet *Passion (1594) and a choral cycle, *Sprüche von Leben und Tod* ('Sayings of Life and Death'), completed shortly before his death.   DA/BS

Leclair, Jean-Marie [*l'aîné*] (*b* Lyons, 10 May 1697; *d* Paris, 22 Oct. 1764). French composer and violinist. The son of Antoine Leclair, a Lyons lace-maker and amateur cellist, he was one of eight children, six of whom became violinists. He intended to follow his father's profession, but in 1722 he was engaged as a dancer and ballet-master at Turin, where he seems to have studied the violin with G. B. Somis. In 1723 he went to Paris, securing a patron in Joseph Bonnier and publishing his first book of violin sonatas. From 1726 to 1728 he was again in Turin, studying with Somis while continuing to earn his living as a dancer and composer of ballet music for the Teatro Regio.

On his return to Paris, Leclair published a second book of violin sonatas and made his debut at the Concert Spirituel, performing his own sonatas and concertos. Between 1733 and 1737 he held a post at the court of Louis XV, but from 1738 he spent three months a year at the court of Orange, and from 1740 the remaining nine months in the service of François Du Liz at The Hague. In 1743 he settled in Paris, where in 1746 his *Scylla et Glaucus*, an *opéra tragédie*, was performed by the Académie Royale de Musique. Shortly before his death he separated from his second wife and went to live in an insalubrious suburb of Paris. On the morning of 23 October 1764 he was found murdered on his own doorstep, almost certainly by his own nephew, though the culprit was never brought to justice.

In addition to violin sonatas (1723–67) Leclair's published music includes several collections of violin duets (1730), trio sonatas (*c*.1731–66), and concertos (1737, 1745); of his theatre music only *Scylla et Glaucus*

survives. As a violinist Leclair was renowned for his musicianship and his technical brilliance; he was also regarded as a difficult colleague. His chamber and orchestral works represent a synthesis of the best elements from the French and Italian styles, while his opera compares favourably with similar works by Rameau.   WT/JAS

📖 A. BOROWITZ, 'Finale marked "Presto": The killing of Leclair', *Musical Quarterly*, 72 (1986), 228–38 · N. ZASLAW, '*Scylla et Glaucus*: A case study', *Cambridge Opera Journal*, 4 (1992), 199–228

Lecocq, (Alexandre) Charles (*b* Paris, 3 June 1832; *d* Paris, 24 Jan. 1918). French composer. He studied the organ and composition at the Paris Conservatoire with François Benoist and Halévy but, physically handicapped from birth and dependent on crutches, he found organ playing increasingly arduous. After leaving the Conservatoire he helped support his parents by teaching the piano and accompanying dances and dancing classes. In 1856 he and Bizet shared first prize in a competition sponsored by Offenbach for an operetta entitled *Le Docteur Miracle*, but his first major success came with the fashionably oriental *Fleur-de-thé* (Paris, 1868). This was followed by *Les Cent Vierges* and the classic *La Fille de Madame Angot* (both staged in Brussels in 1872). Later successes included *Giroflé-Girofla* (1874), *La Petite Mariée* (1875), *Le Petit Duc* (1878), and *Le Jour et la nuit* (1881). Lecocq's music is characterized by a gift for melody and an inventive use of rhythm to great dramatic effect. He was made a Chevalier of the Légion d'Honneur in 1900 and an Officier in 1910.   ALa

Lecuona, Ernesto (*b* Guanabacoa, 6 Aug. 1895; *d* Tenerife, 29 Nov. 1963). Cuban composer. A prolific composer of songs and film music, he also produced the *Rapsodia negra* for piano and orchestra (1943), such colourful zarzuelas as *Maria la O* (1930), and many piano pieces, notably the suite *Andalucia* (1929) incorporating the vivid *Malagueña* (1919).   CW

Ledenyov, Roman Semyonovich (*b* Moscow, 4 Dec. 1930). Russian composer. He studied with Anatoly Aleksandrov at the Moscow Conservatory, where he later became a professor of composition. In the 1960s, like many other Soviet composers, he experimented with serialism, and was influenced especially by Webern; he later returned to tonality and melodic writing, occasionally producing polystylistic and even minimalist works. His output consists predominantly of chamber music and is characterized by a graceful lyricism and formal elegance.   JWal

ledger lines [leger lines]. Short extra lines added below or above the staff to accommodate notes that are too low or too high to be placed on the staff itself.

Leeuw, Reinbert de (*b* Amsterdam, 8 Sept. 1938). Dutch conductor, pianist, writer, and composer. He studied the piano and theory in Amsterdam, and composition with Kees van Baaren in The Hague. In 1974 he became director of the Schoenberg Ensemble, and he has conducted many orchestras and ensembles in the Netherlands and abroad. As a pianist he has specialized in the music of Satie. He is noted for his innovatory programme-planning, and was a guest artistic director of the 1992 Aldeburgh Festival. His compositions include works for orchestra and chamber ensemble, and a share in two collective operas, *Reconstructie* (1969) and *Axel* (1977), both staged in Amsterdam.   ABur

Leeuw, Ton de (*b* Rotterdam, 16 Nov. 1926; *d* Paris, 31 May 1996). Dutch composer and teacher. He studied composition with Henk Badings, and with Messiaen and Thomas de Hartmann in Paris; he also made a study of ethnomusicology, supplemented by a journey to India in 1961. He taught in Utrecht, and was director of the Amsterdam Conservatory from 1971 to 1973; he spent the last ten years of his life in Paris. De Leeuw's work was influenced by Eastern thought, alongside serialism and more avant-garde procedures; he frequently used electronics, and composed many pieces involving antiphonal layouts and movement, including a series called *Spatial Music*. He wrote an oratorio, *Job* (1956), a television opera, *Alceste* (1963), and the opera *De droom* (Amsterdam, 1963).   ABur

LeFanu, Nicola (Frances) (*b* Wickham Bishops, Essex, 28 April 1947). English composer. The daughter of the composer Elizabeth Maconchy, she studied at Oxford, in Italy with Goffredo Petrassi, and in the USA. She has taught in schools and universities, and in 1994 was appointed professor of music at the University of York. Her earliest works, for example *Soliloquy* (1966) for oboe and *But Stars Remaining* (1970) for solo soprano, reveal a gift for sinuous, strikingly dramatic melody, and she has given much emphasis to vocal music, including the operas *Dawnpath* (London, 1977), *The Green Children* (King's Lynn, 1990), and *Blood Wedding* (London, 1992). There is also a radiophonic opera for solo soprano and 16 voices, *The Ballad of Mary O'Neill* (1986).   PG/AW

legato (It.). 'Bound', i.e. played smoothly with no noticeable breaks between the notes. This may be indicated either by the use of a phrase mark over the passage in question or by placing the word *legato* at the

beginning of it. The term does not imply an absence of articulation. The term *legatissimo*, 'extremely smoothly', is sometimes used. The opposite of *legato* is **staccato*.

legatura (It.). 'Ligature'.

legend (Fr.: *légende*; Ger.: *Legende*). A name given to a short composition of lyrical or epic character. Well-known examples are Dvořák's *Legends* op. 59 and Sibelius's four *Legends* for orchestra op. 22, which include *The Swan of Tuonela*.

Legend of the Invisible City of Kitezh and the Maiden Fevroniya, The (*Skazaniye o nevidimom grade Kitezhe i deve Fevronii*). Opera in four acts by Rimsky-Korsakov to a libretto by Vladimir Bel'sky drawn from E. S. Meledin's 'Kitezh Chronicle', Pavel Mel'nikov's novel *V lesakh* ('In the Woods'), and songs, epics, and traditional tales (St Petersburg, 1907).

léger, légèrement (Fr.). 'Light', 'lightly'.

leger lines. See LEDGER LINES.

leggero, leggeramente (It.). 'Light', 'lightly', a direction that also implies a detached style of playing in quick passages.

leggiadro, leggiadretto (It.). 'Graceful'; *leggiadramente*, 'gracefully'.

leggio (It., from *leggere*, 'to read'). 'Music desk'.

legno (It.). 'Wood'; *col legno*, 'with the wood', a direction to string players to tap the strings with the wood of the bow instead of playing with the hair; *strumenti* [*stromenti*] *di legno*, 'woodwind instruments'.

Legrant, Guillaume (*fl* 1418–56). French composer. He worked at the chapel of Pope Martin V from 1418 until at least 1421, and later at Rouen. His surviving works include chansons and mass movements.   JM

Legrenzi, Giovanni (*b* Clusone, nr Bergamo, Aug. 1626; *d* Venice, 27 May 1690). Italian composer. The son of a violinist, in 1654 he became organist at the civic church of S. Maria Maggiore in Bergamo, where in all likelihood he had received his early education. He remained until 1656, when he was appointed director of music at the Accademia dello Spirito Santo in Ferrara. There he began to compose opera. He stayed for about 11 years, but a period of some 12 years follows when his whereabouts are not known for certain. In the early 1670s he moved to Venice, where he was in charge of music at the Conservatory of the Mendicanti and, from 1685, *maestro di cappella* at St Mark's. His last years were clouded by illness.

Legrenzi wrote church music throughout his career; his motets for solo voice or small ensemble are particularly attractive. His sonatas favour the trio ensemble of two violins and string bass with continuo at a time when the duo medium without melodic bass was more popular, thus displaying an inclination towards contrapuntal textures. Unlike the works of his older contemporary in Bergamo, Tarquinio Merula (in other respects a cogent influence), his sonatas show considerable fluidity of structure, especially in the multi-sectional middle sections. But his most distinguished work lies in opera. The individuality of his melody with its fluid continuity, his harmonic idiom, richer in dissonance and chromaticism than was normal in mid-century Italy, and an instrumental style benefiting from his expertise as a sonata composer account for his enormous success both in Italy and beyond.

DA/PA

Lehár, Franz [Ferenc] (*b* Komárom, 30 April 1870; *d* Bad Ischl, 24 Oct. 1948). Austro-Hungarian composer and conductor. He studied at the Prague Conservatory with Antonín Bennewitz (violin) and J. B. Foerster (theory) and began a career as a theatre violinist and military bandmaster (1890–1902). Alongside dances and marches he made unsuccessful early attempts at serious works, including songs and an opera *Kukuschka* (1896). In 1902 his waltz *Gold und Silber* was well received in Vienna and he embarked on a career in operetta there with *Wiener Frauen*. Of its successors, *Die lustige Witwe* (1905) proved an international sensation and gave Viennese operetta a new lease of life. Further successes included *Der Graf von Luxemburg* (1909), *Zigeunerliebe* (1910), and *Eva* (1911).

The outbreak of World War I restricted the international currency of his works, but another phase of success arrived in the 1920s after the tenor Richard Tauber sang in *Zigeunerliebe* and *Frasquita* (1922). Lehár thereafter wrote more serious operettas with key roles and powerful arias for Tauber, notably *Paganini* (1925), *Der Zarewitsch* (1927), *Friederike* (1928), *Das Land des Lächelns* (1929), and finally *Giuditta* (1934), which was composed for the Vienna State Opera. Lehár then retired to concentrate on leaving definitive versions of his works for posterity. He was a superb melodist and a brilliant orchestrator, with fine feeling for the human voice, and his works rise consistently above the operetta norm.

ALa

📖 B. GRUN, *Gold and Silver: The Life and Times of Franz Lehár* (London, 1970)

Lehmann, Lilli (*b* Würzburg, 24 Nov. 1848; *d* Berlin, 17 May 1929). German soprano. She studied in Prague with her mother, Marie Loewe, and made her debut there in 1865 as the First Boy in *Die Zauberflöte*. Her debut at the Berlin Hofoper as Marguerite de Valois in *Les Huguenots* established her as an outstandingly musical coloratura soprano with technical brilliance and flexibility, and she was engaged as a permanent member of the company (1869–85). Her fame spread: at the first Bayreuth Festival she sang two of the Rhinemaidens and the Woodbird in the first complete performance of Wagner's *Ring*, and, in marked contrast, she made her successful London debut in the role of Violetta in *La traviata*. She moved to New York in 1885 and after her debut as Carmen gained fame in a variety of roles, notably as Brünnhilde and Isolde. She was a fine Mozart singer and sang at the Salzburg Festival, of which she became artistic director. A remarkable actress, she had a huge repertory: 170 roles in 119 operas. She was an admired teacher and translator; among her own books is an autobiography *My Path through Life* (Eng. trans. 1914).

JT

Lehmann, Liza [Elizabeth] (Nina Mary Frederica) (*b* London, 11 July 1862; *d* Pinner, 19 Sept. 1918). English soprano and composer. The daughter of a painter and a musician, she grew up in artistic surroundings. She studied singing with Alberto Randegger and Jenny Lind in London, and composition in Rome, Wiesbaden, and (with Hamish MacCunn) in London. After making her singing debut in London in 1885 she forged a career in oratorio and recitals, in which she was a notable exponent of Schumann's lieder. In 1894 she retired from singing, later becoming known for her setting of *In a Persian Garden* (1896) for four solo singers with piano. She composed a number of song cycles including *The Daisy Chain* (1893) and *In memoriam* (1899), over 150 individual songs, a light opera *The Vicar of Wakefield* (1906), and the one-act opera *Everyman* (1915). Lehmann briefly resumed her singing career in 1910, accompanying herself on two successful tours of the USA. In 1911–12 she was the first president of the Society of Women Composers. Her autobiography was published in 1919.

JD1

Lehmann, Lotte (*b* Perleberg, 27 Feb. 1888; *d* Santa Barbara, CA, 26 Aug. 1976). German-born American soprano. She studied in Berlin and in 1914 joined the Vienna State Opera, where she was discovered by Richard Strauss, who insisted she replace the soprano initially scheduled to create the role of the Composer in the revised version of *Ariadne auf Naxos* (1916). Strauss regarded her as 'the ideal interpreter of [his] operas', and she subsequently created the Dyer's Wife in *Die Frau ohne Schatten* (1919) and Christine in *Intermezzo* (1924), in addition to becoming the definitive Marschallin in *Der Rosenkavalier*. She was also an outstanding Wagner singer, remaining unsurpassed as Sieglinde (in *Die Walküre*) and Elsa (in *Lohengrin*).

Lehmann refused to perform in Germany after the Nazis came to power in 1933, though she remained in Vienna until the *Anschluss*, after which she left Europe for the USA, settling in California in 1939 and not retiring until 1951. She was one of the greatest artists of the 20th century, equally at ease in lieder and on the operatic stage. The psychological perception evinced by her singing matched the extraordinary warmth of her voice. She also wrote an affectionate memoir of her work with Strauss.   TA

📖 B. GLASS, *Lotte Lehmann: A Life in Opera and Song* (Santa Barbara, CA, 1988) · A. JEFFERSON, *Lotte Lehmann, 1888–1976* (London, 1988)

Lehrstück (Ger., 'teaching-piece'). A 20th-century musical work of a didactic, and often political, nature. The term first gained currency in the theatre, through the work of Bertolt Brecht, and acquired a musical dimension in his collaborations with Hindemith, Weill, and Eisler.

Leibowitz, René (*b* Warsaw, 17 Feb. 1913; *d* Paris, 29 Aug. 1972). Polish-born French composer, conductor, writer on music, and teacher. He studied composition with Webern (1930–1) and Schoenberg (1932), orchestration with Ravel (1933), and conducting with Pierre Monteux (1934–6). After settling in France in 1945, he worked as a conductor, performing many works of the Second Viennese School for the first time in France and, as a teacher, introducing Boulez and others to serial methods of pitch organization. He wrote several influential books, including *Schoenberg et son école* (1946; Eng. trans. 1948), *Introduction à la musique de douze sons* (1949), and, with Jan Maguire, *Thinking for Orchestra* (1961). His compositional output includes several operas, various concertos and other orchestral pieces, and chamber and piano works, all written in the 12-note technique of which he was such a fervent advocate.
                                              PG/ABur

leicht (Ger.). 'Light', i.e. popular; 'easy'; *Leichtigkeit*, 'lightness', 'easiness'.

leidenschaftlich (Ger.). 'Passionately'.

Leigh, Walter (*b* Wimbledon, 22 June 1905; *d* nr Tobruk, Libya, 12 June 1942). English composer. An organ scholar at Christ's College, Cambridge (1923–6), he later studied in Berlin with Hindemith (1927–9), who decisively influenced his style. Having a flair for light music, he composed several theatre scores including *Jolly Roger* (Savoy Theatre, London, 1933), which ran for six months, and *The Frogs* (Cambridge, 1936), music for films and radio, *Music for String Orchestra* (1931), an overture *Agincourt* (1935), and a concertino for harpsichord and strings (1936). His few

chamber works include a fine trio for flute, oboe, and piano (1936) and a sonatina for treble recorder (1939). He was killed in action.   PG/JD1

Leighton, Kenneth (*b* Wakefield, 2 Oct. 1929; *d* Edinburgh, 24 Aug. 1988). English composer. He studied classics at Oxford University (1947–51) and composition in Rome with Petrassi (1951). From 1953 to 1956 he held a composing fellowship at Leeds University; thereafter he taught at Edinburgh University, apart from a period back at Oxford (1968–70). His large output includes two symphonies, several concertos, and much church music, the style owing something to Bartók and Hindemith in its bold use of expanded diatonic and polytonal harmonies.   PG

Leighton, Sir William (*b* ?Plash, Shropshire, *c*.1565; *d* London, July 1622). English editor and composer. finding himself in ill repute and debt, he attempted to show 'the least part of my unfained and true repentance' by publishing a collection of penitential songs entitled *The Teares or Lamentacions of a Sorrowfull Soule* (London, 1614), with works by himself, Bull, Byrd, John Milton, Martin Peerson, and others.   JM

Leise (Ger.). A medieval German devotional song, perhaps owing its name to the frequent use made of the refrain 'Kyrie eleison', abbreviated to 'kirleis' or 'leis'. The oldest known *Leise* dates from the 9th century.

leise (Ger.). 'Soft', 'gentle'; *leiser*, 'more softly'.

leitmotif (from Ger. *Leitmotiv*, 'leading motif'). A term coined in the mid-1860s by the music historian A. W. Ambros to describe a musical motto or theme which recurs in a piece of music (usually an opera) to represent a character, object, emotion, or idea. It is particularly associated with the later operas of Wagner, though he did not use the term himself, preferring to call the themes *Hauptmotiv* ('principal motif'), *thematisches Motiv* ('thematic motif'), *Grundthema* ('basic theme'), and so on. The term should be distinguished from 'reminiscence motifs', which had been used in opera at least as far back as the 18th century. While reminiscence motifs are also associated with characters, objects, and so on, they typically stand out from their musical context, and are used sparingly to point up a particular dramatic situation. Leitmotifs, on the other hand, tend to be used much more frequently, to the extent of becoming part of the basic thematic material of the work in question.

Wagner's early operas, up to *Lohengrin* (1848), make increasingly liberal use of reminiscence motifs, but the turning-point into leitmotif technique is generally agreed to be *Das Rheingold*, the first opera of the *Ring* cycle. From here onwards, all of Wagner's operas have a dense web of leitmotifs, usually borne by the orchestra rather than the voices. The precise association that such musical ideas carry has always been a matter of debate. In certain operas, notably the *Ring*, many of the motifs are straightforwardly associated with a particular object, character, or place, famous examples being the 'ring' motif itself, or the 'Valhalla' motif. Even here, however, some stretches of the music are without leitmotifs, and some recurring ideas are difficult to attach to anything specific. In *Tristan und Isolde* labelling becomes an even greater problem: the famous opening bars undoubtedly present the central motif of the entire opera, but precisely what it represents remains unclear.

Almost all opera composers after Wagner, sometimes influenced as much by the critical literature as by the operas themselves, made some use of leitmotif, perhaps the most successful being Richard Strauss in his early operas *Salome* and *Elektra*. Debussy in *Pelléas et Mélisande* was much more sparing. Puccini and other Italians experimented briefly, but largely returned to 'reminiscence motif' techniques. RP

📖 C. ABBATE, *Unsung Voices: Opera and Musical Narrative in the 19th Century* (Princeton, NJ, 1991) · H. M. BROWN, *Leitmotiv and Drama: Wagner, Brecht, and the Limits of 'Epic' Theatre* (Oxford, 1991)

Le Jeune, Claude (*b* Valenciennes, *c.*1530; *d* Paris, Sept. 1600). French priest and composer. About 1580 he was master of the children at the court of the Duke of Anjou. Because of his Protestant sympathies he had to flee Paris in 1589, taking refuge in La Rochelle for a time, but later he was in the service of Henri IV. He was notable for his experiments in recreating the music of the Greeks, using chromaticism and the principles of *musique mesurée*; he was a member of Baïf's *académie*. He also composed chansons, madrigals, and some church music; his metrical settings of the Psalms were used extensively by Protestant churches during the 17th and 18th centuries. DA/TC

Lekeu, Guillaume (*b* nr Verviers, 20 Jan. 1870; *d* Angers, 21 Jan. 1894). Belgian composer. He moved to Paris in 1888, and studied composition privately with Franck, and after Franck's death with d'Indy, who encouraged him to enter for the Belgian Prix de Rome in 1891, in which he received second prize. Ysaÿe heard the cantata he submitted and commissioned the Violin Sonata (1892), his best-known work. He produced several chamber pieces, including a piano sonata in the fugal style and a piano trio, and a violin sonata. His music, characterized by feverish intensity, was admired by most of his French contemporaries. He died of typhoid fever. DA/AL

📖 P. VENDRIX (ed.), *Guillaume Lekeu et son temps* (Liège, 1995)

Lélio, ou Le Retour à la vie ('Lélio, or The Return to Life'). Monodrama, op. 14*bis* (1830–2), by Berlioz to his own text but with one number by Albert DuBoys after Johann Wolfgang von Goethe; for soloists, chorus, and orchestra, it was composed as a sequel to the *Symphonie fantastique*.

Lemminkäinen Suite (*Lemminkäis-sarja*). Four symphonic poems, op. 22, by Sibelius on legends in the *Kalevala* of the warrior Lemminkäinen; they are *Lemminkäinen and the Maidens of the Island* (1895; revised 1897, 1939), *Lemminkäinen in Tuonela* (1895; revised 1897, 1939), *The Swan of Tuonela* (1893; revised 1897, 1900), and *Lemminkäinen's Return* (1895; revised 1897, 1900).

Leningrad Symphony. The subtitle of Shostakovich's Symphony no. 7 in C major op. 61 (1941), composed during the German siege of Leningrad and dedicated to the city.

lent, lentement (Fr.). 'Slow', 'slowly'; *lenteur*, 'slowness'.

lento, lentamente (It.). 'Slow', 'slowly'; *lentando*, *lentato*, 'slowing', 'slowed' (the same as *rallentando*); *lentezza*, 'slowness'. *Lento* is one of the earliest tempo marks, appearing from the early 17th century.

Lenya [Lenia, Lenja], **Lotte** [Blamauer, Karoline Wilhelmine] (*b* Vienna, 18 Oct. 1898; *d* New York, 27 Nov. 1981). Austrian-born American singer and actress. Trained as a dancer in Zürich, she moved in 1920 to Berlin, where she worked as an actress. She married Kurt Weill in 1926 and became one of the most important interpreters of his work. She created Jenny in *Die Dreigroschenoper* (1928), repeated the role in Georg Pabst's 1931 film, and combined it with the role of Polly in the work's first recording. She subsequently sang in the first performances of Weill's *Die sieben Todsünden* (1933), *The Eternal Road* (1937), and *The Firebrand of Florence* (1945).

When the Nazis came to power Lenya emigrated to the USA, and after Weill's death in 1950 she assiduously promoted many of his works, placing a strong emphasis on music from his German period which has been deemed controversial by some. Her early recordings reveal a soprano of shimmering sexuality, though later in life she adopted a low, husky, gravelly tone and the sharp textual delivery of a *diseuse*, which for many remains the quintessence of the German cabaret style. She was an outstanding actress, and her late films include *The Roman Spring of Mrs Stone* (1961) and *From Russia with Love* (1963). TA

📖 D. Spoto, *Lenya: A Life* (New York, 1989) · L. Symonette and K. Kowalke (eds.), *Speak Low (when you Speak Love): The Letters of Kurt Weill and Lotte Lenya* (Berkeley, CA, 1996)

Leo, Leonardo (Ortensio Salvatore de) (*b* San Vito degli Schiavi [now San Vito dei Normanni], nr Brindisi, 5 Aug. 1694; *d* Naples, 31 Oct. 1744). Italian composer and teacher. He studied at the Conservatorio S. Maria della Pietà dei Turchini in Naples, where he had a sacred opera performed in 1712, and in 1714 became an organist in the royal chapel. In 1725 he succeeded Alessandro Scarlatti as first organist; he was appointed *pro-vicemaestro* in 1730 and *vicemaestro* in 1737, and finally became *maestro* in 1744, shortly before his death. He was active as a teacher from 1737, becoming *primo maestro* at the Conservatorio S. Onofrio in 1739 and at the Turchini in 1741.

Leo was one of the leading Neapolitan composers of his time and was especially active in opera, writing both comic operas in the manner of Pergolesi to suit Neapolitan taste and serious ones for such cities as Venice and Rome; he left a total of over 70. His other works include oratorios and much church music, some of it in the polyphonic *a cappella* style, and some with orchestral accompaniment. As a theorist and teacher he had considerable influence, his pupils including Jommelli and Piccinni.   DA/ER

Leoncavallo, Ruggero (*b* Naples, 23 April 1857; *d* Montecatini, 9 Aug. 1919). Italian composer and librettist. The son of a police official, he studied at the Naples Conservatory, graduating in 1876. He went on to study literature at Bologna University, attending lectures by the poet Giosuè Carducci and becoming acquainted with Wagner's music. He started work on the libretto of an operatic trilogy on the Italian Renaissance, and composed an opera, *Chatterton*, to prepare himself, but failed to get this performed.

He then fell on bad times, working in Paris, London, and Egypt as a café pianist. He composed light songs for the Eldorado in Paris; there he met the famous baritone Victor Maurel, who introduced him to Ricordi, the leading publisher in Milan. Ricordi disapproved of *I Medici* (the first opera of the 'Renaissance' trilogy), which was grandly Wagnerian in conception. Leoncavallo then turned to the *verismo vein of *Pagliacci*, the story based on one of his father's criminal cases. This was published by Sonzogno (Ricordi's rival), performed in Milan under Toscanini in 1892, and was immediately successful. Designed originally in a single act, it suited Leoncavallo's talents by allowing his short-breathed melodic ideas to express the violent emotions of theatrical characters who need not be seen in the round.

In 1893 it was announced that operas on Henry Murger's *Scènes de la vie de bohème* were being composed by both Puccini (for Ricordi) and Leoncavallo (for Sonzogno). Leoncavallo's *La bohème* was performed in Venice in 1897, some months after Puccini's. At first both were successful, but Puccini's finally drove his rival's off the stage; although Leoncavallo's is an effective piece, it tends to melodrama rather than evoking the delicate, even humorous atmosphere of Puccini's. Leoncavallo's next venture was a comedy, *Zazà*, an immediate success showing some signs of Massenet's influence. Though often successful in Germany, his later operas were not popular in Italy, and in later life he turned principally to operetta.

DA/RP

Leoni, Franco (*b* Milan, 24 Oct. 1864; *d* London, 8 Feb. 1949). Italian composer, resident in England for some years. A pupil of Cesare Dominiceti and Amilcare Ponchielli at the Milan Conservatory, he had his first opera, *Raggio di luna*, produced in Milan in 1890. From 1892 to 1917 he was in London, where he composed operas and oratorios and conducted the Queen's Hall Choral Society. After 1917 he divided his time between Italy, France, and England, continuing to write operas, though increasingly out of fashion. Leoni's most celebrated opera was the one-act *L'oracolo*, which was produced in London in 1905 with the baritone Antonio Scotti as the opium dealer Cim-Fen, revived as a vehicle for Scotti at the Metropolitan Opera in New York, and recorded with Tito Gobbi in the role in 1975.

ABur

Leoni, Leone (*b* Verona, *c*.1560; *d* Vicenza, 24 June 1627). Italian composer. He was associated with the prominent patron Count Mario Bevilacqua in Verona, and from 1588 until his death was *maestro di cappella* at Vicenza Cathedral. He published a fair amount of sacred music, some of which embraces the newer styles, and five volumes of five-voice madrigals. His popularity in anthologies, and the fact that his printed music was often copied into north European manuscripts, suggest that he was very highly regarded.

TC

Léonin [Leoninus] (*b c*.1135; *d* 1201 or shortly after). Canon, poet, and composer. Evidence of his activities as canon of St Benoît and later of Notre Dame, Paris, priest, and poet are found in numerous archival documents. His chief poetic work is *Hystorie sacre gestas ab origine mundi* ('Acts of Sacred History from the Origin of the World'), in over 14,000 hexameters. (His name was given to a common type of hexameter with internal rhyme, though not before the 17th century.) Léonin's compositional activity is mentioned by the

English theorist known as Anonymous IV (*fl c.*1270), who states that he was 'optimus organista' ('the best composer [or singer] of *organum'), and that he made a 'big book' (*magnus liber*) of settings of Mass and Office chants used at Notre Dame.

The only surviving copies of music which might be by Léonin date from the mid-13th century; they give no composers' names, and they contain music that is much later stylistically than anything Léonin is likely to have written. He probably contributed some of the earliest music in the manuscripts, 60 years or so before the surviving copies were made. Anonymous IV also implies that one of Léonin's successors, *Pérotin, revised some of the earlier music, and the surviving copies do indeed bear evidence of a process of revision. It is therefore impossible to be certain of exactly what Léonin composed.

His *magnus liber* contained polyphonic settings of those portions of plainchant that were reserved for solo singers. The chants set were Vespers responsories, Mass graduals, and alleluias, and perhaps some processional antiphons. Only chants for the major festivals of the church year were set—between 40 and 50 compositions in all. Léonin probably took as a starting-point music like that in the Codex Calixtinus (*c.*1160; see ORGANUM, Ex. 2), where the chant is placed beneath a more florid upper voice, with its notes consequently often lengthened and sustained. Such a chant setting for two voices is known as *organum duplum*. Léonin's settings appear to have been on a more extended scale than earlier ones, with an increased proportion of notes in the upper voice to those in the lower.

It is not clear whether Léonin's chant settings contained any sections in *discant style, or whether these sections, numerous in the surviving copies, are the work of later composers. In them the chant is disposed in regular rhythm, moving in step with the upper voice. This occurs usually when there is a melismatic flourish in the original chant, as in Ex. 1. If such music really is by Léonin, then he probably played a part in the evolution of modal rhythm (see NOTATION, 2).

Léonin is also likely to have composed in such other popular forms of the time as the *conductus, but no examples attributed to him are known.   DH

📖 C. WRIGHT, *Music and Ceremony at Notre Dame of Paris, 500–1500* (Cambridge, 1989)

Leonore. The original title of Beethoven's opera *Fidelio. Beethoven wrote three overtures with this title: no. 2 for the first production (1805), no. 3 (a revision of no. 2) for the 1806 revival, and no. 1 (1806–7) for a proposed production in Prague that never took place. He composed the *Fidelio* overture for the final version (1814).

Leopold I (*b* Vienna, 9 June 1640; *d* Vienna, 5 May 1705). Holy Roman Emperor and composer. He was crowned in 1658. In spite of a turbulent reign, during which Vienna was besieged by the Turks in 1683, he continued the Habsburg tradition of music patronage, expanding the Hofkapelle until it employed over 100 musicians, including performers and composers from Italy, and especially encouraging Italian opera; Cesti's *Il pomo d'oro* was commissioned for the celebrations surrounding his marriage to Margherita of Spain in 1666 (but probably not performed until 1668). He was himself a more than competent composer, and many of his works were performed at court. They include ballet music, oratorios, and other sacred music, most notably an impressive *Miserere* in G minor.   DA

Lerchenquartett. See 'LARK' QUARTET.

Le Roy & Ballard. French firm of music printers founded in Paris in 1551 by the lutenist-composer Adrian Le Roy (*c.*1520–1598) and his cousin Robert Ballard (*b* ?1525–30; *d* 1588). They were the most important music printers of their day and held a monopoly over music-printing in France for more than 200 years. They received an exclusive privilege from Henri II and in 1553 succeeded Pierre Attaingnant as music printers to the king, a monopoly the Ballard family zealously guarded until the 18th century. The partnership successfully combined Le Roy's artistic sense with Ballard's business acumen, and the firm produced elegant editions of a remarkably high quality: their title pages and fine initial letters provide a conspectus of accomplished Renaissance design.

Their repertory ranged widely: between 1551 and 1598 they issued some 3000 works in 350 editions, including

Ex. 1

From *Alleluia Ascendens Christus.*

nearly 2000 chansons, over 600 motets, nearly 500 psalms and *chansons spirituelles*, over 200 Italian and Spanish pieces, masses, music for plucked string instruments (including instruction books), and theoretical treatises. They published many works by Lassus, a friend of Le Roy, as well as music by Arcadelt, Goudimel, Janequin, Le Jeune, and Sermisy.

After Le Roy's death the business was continued by Robert Ballard's descendants, but from the 1670s it met opposition to its monopoly and criticism of its unwillingness to adapt to new techniques and styles. Its privilege was abolished in 1790.

See also PRINTING AND PUBLISHING OF MUSIC, 4.

JMT/JWA

📖 F. LESURE and G. THIBAULT, *Bibliographie des éditions d'Adrian Le Roy et Robert Ballard (1551–1598)* (Paris, 1955; suppl. in *Revue de musicologie*, 40, 1957, pp. 166–72) · D. HEARTZ, 'Parisian music publishing under Henry II', *Musical Quarterly*, 46 (1960), 448–67

Les Adieux. See ADIEUX, LES.

Leschetizky, Theodor (*b* Lancut, Galicia, 22 June 1830; *d* Dresden, 14 Nov. 1915). Polish teacher, pianist, and composer. He was a child prodigy, making his public debut at the age of nine and soon afterwards becoming a pupil of Czerny in Vienna. Czerny's precepts stayed with him for the rest of his life, but an equally powerful impact was made by the playing of Chopin's pupil Julius Schulhoff, whom he heard in the 1840s. Schulhoff's emphasis on beauty of tone and prominent delineation of the principal melody were to become central to Leschetizky's pedagogy. After a career as a touring virtuoso, Leschetizky moved to Russia, where, at the invitation of Anton Rubinstein, he became head of the piano department of the St Petersburg Conservatory at its founding in 1862. His comic opera *Die erste Falte* (1867) was produced in Prague, but as a composer he merely displayed a modest imagination harnessed to a deft technical confidence.

On his return to Vienna 16 years later Leschetizky set up as a private teacher and soon began to attract a legion of talented students: he was one of the most celebrated, successful, and influential piano teachers of the late Romantic period, with an astonishingly long list of famous pupils, including Paderewski, Ignacy Friedman, Schnabel, Mark Hambourg, Benno Moiseiwitsch, Alexander Brailowsky, Ossip Gabrilovich, and Vasily Safonov. The colossal international success of Paderewski, who began to study with him in 1885, set the seal on his worldwide reputation, and it is fitting that Paderewski's performance style was perhaps the closest to Leschetizky's own (from the evidence of Leschetizky's piano rolls and Paderewski's recordings) in its focus on melodic projection and copious use of arpeggiation and rubato. In spite of books dubiously claiming to expound 'The Leschetizky Method' of piano teaching, he stated that such a template never existed; rather, his approach varied pragmatically according to the needs of each pupil.

KH

L'Escurel, Jehan de (*d* Paris, 13 May 1304). French poet and composer. He appears to have been a cleric at Notre Dame Cathedral, Paris, and to have been hanged for debauchery. A small number of his monophonic chansons in the courtly tradition of the trouvères has survived; they show him to be, with Adam de la Halle, one of the most important precursors of Machaut.

JM

lesto (It.). 'Agile', 'quick'; *lestamente*, 'agilely', 'quickly'.

Le Sueur, Jean-François (*b* Drucat-Plessiel, nr Abbeville, 15 Feb. 1760; *d* Paris, 6 Oct. 1837). French composer. After attending choir school he obtained the post of choirmaster of Notre Dame de Paris in 1786, but lasted only a year; he was dismissed because he attempted to modernize church music by engaging large orchestras and opera singers, turning the Mass into a 'theatrical representation'. Under the Revolution he had some successes in the theatre, including *La Caverne* (1793), a powerful and sometimes harsh work, produced—as were *Paul et Virginie* (1794) and *Télémaque* (1796)—at the Théâtre Feydeau. He met the demand for revolutionary 'hymns' and was among the first directors and teachers at the Paris Conservatoire, contributing to pedagogical publications. Another quarrel with management interrupted his teaching career, but with Napoleon's support he produced his greatest success, *Ossian*, at the Paris Opéra (1804, though composed earlier), capitalizing on popular enthusiasm for the mythical Gaelic bard. The work he considered would be his masterpiece, *La Mort d'Adam* (libretto by Guillard, Paris Opéra, 1809), was too theologically ambitious to succeed.

Le Sueur returned to sacred music, acting as director of music at the Tuileries for Napoleon and, alongside Cherubini, for the restored Bourbons; he recycled music composed for Napoleon's coronation for that of Charles X in 1825. His large output of sacred music, which he prepared for publication in his last years, includes masses, oratorios, canticles, and motets in which he treats the Latin texts with considerable freedom. He also wrote somewhat eccentric works of theory and history and, having once again joined the musical establishment, became a well-known teacher with many pupils who succeeded in winning the Prix de Rome; the most celebrated are Berlioz and Gounod, Berlioz being the pupil who came closest to realizing his teacher's lofty ideals.

JR

W. DEAN, 'Opera under the French Revolution', *Proceedings of the Royal Musical Association*, 94 (1967–8), 77–96 · D. CHARLTON, *French Opera, 1730–1830: Meaning and Media* (Aldershot, 2000)

Let's Make an Opera. 'An entertainment for young people' by Britten to a libretto by Eric Crozier (Aldeburgh, 1949); it incorporates as its third act the opera The *Little Sweep*. Britten composed it to involve local young people and adult amateurs, who, in the first two acts, plan the opera of the third act and rehearse four songs with the audience.

letzt (Ger.). 'Last'.

levalto. See VOLTA, 1.

levare (It.). 'To lift', 'to take off'; e.g. *si levano i sordini*, 'the mutes are taken off'; *levate*, 'take off'.

levet (? from It. *levata*, 'rising', 'getting up'). A trumpet call or musical strain to raise soldiers and others in the morning. On New Year's Day 1696, Judge Sewall of Boston, New England, recorded in his diary: 'One with a Trumpet sounds a Levet at our window just about break of day, bids me good morrow, and wishes health and happiness to attend me.'

Levinson, Gerald (*b* New Hyde Park, NY, 22 June 1951). American composer. He studied with George Crumb, George Rochberg, and Richard Wernick at the University of Pennsylvania, Ralph Shapey at the University of Chicago, and Messiaen at the Paris Conservatoire. In 1977 he started teaching at Swarthmore College, from which he took leave for two visits to Bali (1979–80, 1982–3). Balinese music has influenced him, along with Messiaen's clarity of timbre and the long, expressive line of Mahler. His works include two symphonies (1984–6, 1992–4) and other orchestral pieces, several compositions for mixed ensemble, and chamber music (*Dreamlight* for cello, piano, and percussion, 1990).   PG

L.H. Abbreviation for left hand, *linke Hand* (Ger.).

L'Homme armé. See HOMME ARMÉ, L'.

liberamente (It.). 'Freely', i.e. in a free rhythm or tempo.

Liber usualis (Lat., 'Book of Common Practice'). A compendium of prayers, lessons, and especially chants for the most important services of the Roman Catholic liturgy, issued by the monks of *Solesmes from 1896 up to the time of the Second Vatican Council (1962–5). It was published in editions with rubrics in French or English as well as Latin, and because of this and its comprehensive (though far from exhaustive) contents it became widely used as a convenient standard collection

of *plainchant. Its historical value, however, is negligible.   JJD

libitum, ad (Lat., 'at pleasure'). An indication that a performer is at liberty, according to the context, to vary the tempo, or to improvise, embellish, or devise a cadenza; it was often used in the late 18th century to indicate that a part so marked could be omitted (the opposite of *obbligato).

libraries. There are many types of music library; each has a different purpose and contains different kinds of material.

    1. History; 2. Types of library; 3. Bibliographies and online resources

1. History

The earliest collections of music were compiled for the singing schools (*scholae cantorum*) of the great cathedrals and abbey churches, in the form of manuscript plainchant antiphoners and, later, polyphonic choirbooks. Because the music was for current use, its survival once it became obsolete was a matter of chance, often helped by the conservative nature of the church and the facilities for storing unused material in an odd corner of a large building. Needless to say, more has been lost than has survived. That performance material is ephemeral is even more evident from the survival of secular music. Only after 1500 does the printing of instrumental and secular vocal music result in the existence of a significantly increased amount, and even then not because it was specifically collected for preservation.

In England one of the earliest collections of secular music to have survived intact is that of the Music School of Oxford University, begun by the presentation in 1627 of several sets of madrigal and motet partbooks by the first professor of music, William Heather. That the Music School was actively concerned with the performance of both instrumental and vocal music throughout the 17th century gives its collection, now in the Bodleian Library, particular importance.

The 17th and 18th centuries saw the development of court orchestras and public opera houses. The archives of both types of institution have not been well documented, but some survive, notably that of the Opéra in Paris, now part of the Bibliothèque Nationale de France. All too often these archives have been lost in the fires that destroyed theatres, or have simply been thrown away when a new management has taken over.

Libraries for performance are often 'private', tend to specialize in one form of music, and have little care for what is not in the current repertory. Even today there are many collections belonging to string quartets, professional and amateur choirs and orchestras, chamber ensembles, and early music groups that will disappear when the group disbands. Some may be given to a similar group, others will be broken up and sold; some will be put in the rubbish bin and some consigned to the attic or cellar.

The collection of music for the study of its history began in the late 17th century.

2. Types of library

Public libraries, by their nature, supply current needs and discard the obsolete. The largest collections easily available are to be found in the great metropolitan centres. Most contain music in some form or other, and printed music and performing sets of orchestral and choral music are made widely available through interlibrary loan, for which there are regional and national networks. Many public libraries also have local history sections containing archives relating to local musical activities and famous musicians.

Music colleges have extensive collections of music in all genres, often receiving valuable bequests from former pupils, and many house valuable antiquarian collections. Universities provide material for study of the history of music, for analysis of composition, and increasingly for study of both popular and non-European musics. Their libraries concentrate on scores (rather than parts), literature, and sound recordings.

Since the 18th century national libraries have received music through legal deposit arising out of various licensing and *copyright laws. Until the 1840s the deposit of music was haphazard, but since then the continued receipt of British publications and the purchase and gift of foreign and antiquarian material has made the magnificent collections now in the British Library. Libraries naturally have a particular duty towards housing the music of their own countries, and today every state has a library or group of libraries for that purpose. Paris, Vienna, and Madrid have national libraries, Berlin the Deutsches Musikarchiv as well as the Staatsbibliothek, Copenhagen, Brussels, and Stockholm their Royal Libraries, and the USA has the Library of Congress.

The collection of sound recordings, both commercially published and privately made, is widespread. Public libraries are now more likely to have currently available sound recordings than printed scores. Other institutional libraries house older recordings, though the technical problems of playing and preserving wax cylinders, 78, 45, and 33 rpm black discs, reel-to-reel tapes, and cassettes are considerable. Nevertheless the growing interest in the sound recordings of the past will no doubt increase demand on the few archives of sound recordings, of which the British Institute of Recorded

Sound and the BBC Sound Archives are the most important. There are also sound archives within the major national libraries.

A new form of library is the Music Information Centre, for the promotion of new music by local or national composers. Each has a library of scores and sound recordings of published and unpublished music supplied by the composers for other musicians' use. The MICs in some countries take an active role in music publishing.

3. Bibliographies and online resources

Locating copies of music, books, or recordings is not always easy. For music there is the International Inventory of Musical Sources (better known by its French acronym *RISM). Series A/I is a vast union catalogue of all printed music to 1800, while Series A/II covers musical manuscripts from 1600 to 1800 and is available both on CD-ROM and online, though it is in progress and by no means complete. Series B covers a range of specialized areas, including early polyphony to 1600, medieval theory, Arabic writings, etc. There are no specialized resources for locating 19th-century music or books.

For locating music literature to 1800 there is RISM Series B/VI, but nothing specific for later periods. Imogen Fellinger's *Verzeichnis der Musikzeitschriften des 19. Jahrhunderts* locates all 19th-century periodicals. The *Music Index* has listed the contents of many periodicals since it started in 1949, and *RILM Abstracts of Music Literature* provides abstracts of both monographs and periodical articles since 1967. *RIPM (Répertoire International de la Presse Musicale) offers lists of the contents, with quoted abstracts and contextual indexes, of the most important musical periodicals of the 19th century.

The Internet offers access to both catalogues and indexes for finding music scores, books on music, periodical articles, and sound recordings. Music and music literature are included in the online union catalogues of British universities (COPAC, the Consortium of University Research Libraries) and in the consortium of British music colleges (MLO, Music On Line). American multi-campus state universities also usually have union catalogues (e.g. MELVYL for the University of California). These are currently free, as are the online catalogues of most national, state university, and individual university libraries. However, the most important American-based international union catalogues (OCLC, RLIN), and specialist indexes of periodicals (*RILM, RIPM) and dissertations (e.g. Dissertation Abstracts), are often available only by subscription, though often accessible at the larger libraries.

These are only the more important bibliographies available in the larger music libraries. For more detailed lists of libraries see the article on Libraries in *The New Grove Dictionary of Music and Musicians* (London, 2/2001), and for a guide to the many bibliographies see Vincent Duckles, *Music Reference and Research Material* (New York, 5/1997, ed. M. Keller and L. S. Blotner).

RA

libre, librement (Fr.). 'Free', 'freely'.

libretto (It., 'little book', dim. of *libro*, 'book'; Fr.: *livret*; Ger.: *Textbuch*). The name generally given to the book of the words of an opera, or other vocal dramatic work, and consequently to the text itself. The earliest were over 20 cm in height, and the Italian diminutive refers to the reduced measurement of 14 cm, introduced when the first public opera houses opened in Venice. The term has been current in English since about the mid-18th century.

The first libretto ever written was Rinuccini's text for *Dafne*, set by Peri; the earliest verifiable performance took place in Florence in 1598. Early librettos usually began with a title page followed by a preface in which the writer made obsequious dedication to his patron, then by a few words addressed to the reader. The *argomento* (literally 'argument'), which also preceded the actual text in early librettos, was a summary of the events leading up to the action of the opera: these tended to increase in complexity, and even to take their place in the opera itself as a prologue (e.g. Verdi's *Il trovatore*). After the list of the characters in the opera came a catalogue of the scene changes, dances, and perhaps also the scenic effects: this trait survives on to playbills of the English music theatre of the 19th century. Until about the end of the 18th century there would also be a *protesta*, in which the author affirmed his good Roman Catholic faith in spite of the opera's pagan references to *numi* ('gods'), *fati* ('fates'), and so on: this arose from the necessity of having the libretto approved in cities under papal domination.

Essentially, a good libretto has always been a story, whether dramatic in origin or not, moulded to the needs of music drama. The sources of successful librettos have ranged from great dramatic masterpieces (*Othello* for Verdi) and great novels (*War and Peace* for Prokofiev) to *romans-à-clef* (*Scènes de la vie de bohème* for Puccini) and narrative poems (*Eugene Onegin* for Tchaikovsky), from heroic legend (most of Metastasio's librettos) to real-life incident (perhaps *Pagliacci*, Janáček's *Osud*), from metaphysics and questions of belief (*Parsifal*) to farce (most of Offenbach), from artistic enterprises (Hindemith's *Mathis der Maler*, Pfitzner's *Palestrina*) to comic strip (Janáček's *The Cunning Little Vixen*), from history or biography (*Rienzi*, and much French grand opera) to fairy tale (Russian opera in both categories). There are no rules of origin but a number of successful methods of their application, of which most composers have singled out conciseness and a capacity to depict human emotions in a dramatic context as prime but not exclusive virtues.

As operatic structures became standardized in the 18th century, the pattern of recitative, aria, and chorus made special demands on the librettist and determined the course of the action. The argument about the supremacy of music or words has been raging ever since, and found operatic expression (if not resolution) in Strauss's *Capriccio*. Though conventions have naturally changed—with the virtues of formality and the contrasting virtues of freedom exchanging precedence—the vital element has remained dramatic potency as it charges a composer's imagination. The status of the libretto in 18th-century opera is indicated by the fact that it was the text, rather than the score, that was printed, and with only the author's name appearing. Collaboration has thus not proved indispensable: Metastasio is the great example of a librettist, 27 of whose works did duty for 1000 settings by 50 composers at least. At the other extreme, fruitful results have come from the careful mutual planning of Quinault and Lully, Boito and Verdi, Gilbert and Sullivan, and Hofmannsthal and Strauss. Berlioz, Wagner, Berg, and Menotti are among the most successful of those composers who have preferred to shape, and indeed write, their own librettos, which further suggests that any rules must follow rather than precede example.

The popularity of printed librettos is undiminished, and many opera lovers, if in lesser numbers outside Italy, still provide themselves with copies both to study at home and to take to the performance. Candlegrease spots on early specimens are evidence of the audience's habit of consulting the libretto during a production, with the aid of *cerini* (tapers) on sale at the door. Librettos were also, however, published as part of a poet's collected works, in well-printed and handsomely bound editions. Again, Metastasio's works were particularly well served in this way, and their wide dissemination contributed to the nascent unitary Italian language. The translation of librettos became widespread during the 19th century, and it is now customary for commercial recordings of complete operas to be accompanied by a full libretto (with parallel translations), as well as synopses and notes.

JW/KC

📖 P. J. Smith, *The Tenth Muse: A Historical Study of the Opera Libretto* (New York, 1970) · C. H. Parsons (ed.), *Opera Librettists and their Works* (New York, 1987)

Libuše. Opera in three acts by Smetana to a libretto by Josef Wenzig (Prague, 1881).

licenza (It.). 1. 'Licence', 'freedom'; *con alcuna licenza*, 'with some licence', i.e. freedom with regard to tempo and rhythm. The term was used in the 17th and 18th centuries for a passage or cadenza improvised by the performer.

2. An epilogue added to a stage work in honour of a patron's birthday or wedding or for some other festive occasion.

Licht: Die sieben Tage der Woche ('Light: The Seven Days of the Week'). A cycle of seven operas by Stockhausen to his own librettos, begun in 1977 and scheduled for completion in 2002; their order of performance is *Donnerstag aus Licht, *Samstag aus Licht, *Montag aus Licht, *Dienstag aus Licht, *Freitag aus Licht, *Mittwoch aus Licht, *Sonntag aus Licht.

Lidholm, Ingvar (Natanael) (*b* Jönköping, 24 Feb. 1921). Swedish composer. He studied at the Royal Swedish Academy in Stockholm (1940–6) and privately with Rosenberg and Seiber (1954). He held posts as conductor of the Örebro Orchestra (1947–56), as teacher of composition at the Royal Swedish Academy (1965–75), and in radio. His early works show the influence of Nielsen, Hindemith, and Stravinsky, but he then entered the avant-garde mainstream; such works as *Ritornell* for orchestra (1955) and *Nausikaa ensam* for soprano, chorus, and orchestra (1963), display a typically Scandinavian feeling for musical poetry. *Kontakion* (1979) shows his brilliant orchestration. His first opera *Ett drömspel* had its premiere in Stockholm in 1990.

PG/MA

📖 B. E. Brolsma, *The Music of Ingvar Lidholm: A Survey and Analysis* (Ann Arbor, MI, 1981)

lié (Fr., 'bound'). Slurred or tied, i.e. *legato*.

Liebe der Danae, Die ('The Love of Danae'). Opera in three acts by Richard Strauss to a libretto by Joseph Gregor (Salzburg, 1952); there was a public dress rehearsal in Salzburg in 1944 but the opening performance was cancelled.

Liebermann, Lowell (*b* New York, 22 Feb. 1961). American composer. He wrote a piano sonata when he was 15 and played it the next year at his debut recital in New York, but continued formal studies at the Juilliard School until 1987. His music is fluent and tonal, and continues a tradition of latterday Romanticism inherited from Barber and Prokofiev. Among his works are two symphonies, two piano concertos, concertos also for flute, for flute and harp, for piccolo, and for

trumpet, and the opera *Dorian Gray* (Monte Carlo, 1996). PG

Lieberson, Peter (*b* New York, 25 Oct. 1946). American composer. The son of Goddard Lieberson, president of Columbia Records, and Vera Zorina, a dancer, he studied composition with Milton Babbitt and with Charles Wuorinen at Columbia University (1972–4), then went to Boulder, Colorado, to study with Chogyam Trungpa, a Tibetan Buddhist master. He resumed composition studies at Brandeis, with Donald Martino and Martin Boykan, after which he directed Shambhala Training, a meditation and cultural programme, in Boston in the 1980s and Halifax, Nova Scotia, in the 1990s; he also taught at Harvard (1984–8). His music often has to do with Buddhist myths and concepts, though the means will generally be Western, and highly sophisticated. Major works include the Piano Concerto (1980–3), his breakthrough piece, other concertos for viola (1992–4) and horn (1999), *Drala* (1986) and *World's Turning* (1991) for orchestra, the opera *Ashoka's Dream* (Santa Fe, 1997), chamber music, and solo piano pieces. PG

Liebesliederwalzer ('Love-Song Waltzes'). 18 waltzes, op. 52 (1868–9), by Brahms, for two pianos, with soprano, alto, tenor, and bass soloists, settings of texts from Georg Friedrich Daumer's *Polydora*; a version was published (op. 52a) without the vocal parts. In 1874 Brahms composed 15 more, *Neue Liebesliederwalzer* (op. 65), for the same forces (op. 65a without voices).

Liebesmahl der Apostel, Das ('The Love Feast of the Apostles'). 'Biblical scene' (1843) for male chorus and orchestra by Wagner to his own text.

Liebestod ('Love-Death'). Isolde's final aria at the end of Act III of Wagner's *Tristan und Isolde* (or the orchestral arrangement of it, often played as a concert item with the Prelude to Act I); Wagner applied the term to the love duet in Act II.

Liebesträume ('Dreams of Love'). Three nocturnes for solo piano by Liszt, composed *c*.1850; they are transcriptions of his songs *Hohe Liebe*, *Gestorben war ich*, and *O Lieb, so lang du lieben kannst*, the third (in A♭) being one of the best-known Romantic melodies.

Liebesverbot, Das (*Das Liebesverbot, oder Die Novize von Palermo*; 'The Ban on Love, or The Novice of Palermo'). Opera in two acts by Wagner to his own libretto after Shakespeare's *Measure for Measure* (Magdeburg, 1836).

lied (Ger.). The German word for 'song' that came into general acceptance in the 15th century. *Gesang*, also meaning 'song' (as in *Meistergesang*, the art of the

Meistersinger), became used less frequently. The greatest age of the lied was the 19th century, with Schubert, Schumann, Brahms, and Wolf being the supreme masters.

1. Before the 19th century; 2. The 19th and 20th centuries

1. Before the 19th century

The early 15th-century Tyrolean poet and composer Oswald von Wolkenstein has been claimed as the creator of the lied for his pioneering marriage of text and music. Important song collections from later in the century are the Lochamer Liederbuch (*c*.1452–60), with 44 mostly monophonic lieder; the Schedelsches Liederbuch (1460s) with 128 pieces, 68 of which are polyphonic; and the Glogauer Liederbuch (*c*.1480), including 70 polyphonic lieder but many more pieces with French or Italian texts. The influence of composers from the Low Countries, France, and Italy on the late flowerings of vocal polyphony is strong, but the Lochamer Liederbuch contains an early example—the anonymous three-part *Der wallt hat sich entlawbet*—of an indigenous genre, the **Tenorlied*.

The composers of these 15th-century songs, where they are named at all, are usually obscure figures, and it is only in the 16th century that more important names begin to be regularly associated with German song: notably Paul Hofhaimer, Heinrich Finck, and Isaac (whose *Innsbruck, ich muss dich lassen* is probably the best-known lied from this period). The relative popularity of the lied in the 16th century owed much to the advances made at the beginning of the century in the printing industry, particularly in Augsburg, Cologne, and Mainz. In the second half of the century, Lassus, H. L. Hassler, and Leonhard Lechner can be seen as the last great masters of the tradition.

The solo lied with continuo accompaniment, known as the **continuo lied* or *Generalbass* lied, began to supersede polyphonic song in Germany in the 1620s. On the whole, the music of the 17th- and 18th-century lied was subservient to its text. Berlin was an important centre of lied composition in the second half of the 18th century, with Frederick the Great's patronage encouraging what was later known as the First Berlin School, formed by C. G. Krause on precepts that the lied should be folk-like and easily singable, express the text, and have a simple accompaniment. Composers associated with him included J. F. Agricola, Franz Benda, C. H. Graun, and C. P. E. Bach. A move away from the limitations of these strophic songs was initiated chiefly by C. G. Neefe, whose songs are generally in modified strophic form so as to match the progress of the text.

About 1770 there arose the Second Berlin School, whose composers included J. A. P. Schulz, and especially J. F. Reichardt and C. F. Zelter. They turned increasingly to better poems, the latter two setting many by Goethe, who believed that his lyric verse should be completed in music but who did not care for music to take a dominant role. The best lieder by Reichardt and Zelter provide an accompaniment that enriches the poetry but is musically distinguished in its own right. A Swabian School included C. F. Schubart and J. R. Zumsteeg, the latter interested especially in ballads set in quasi-cantata form with varied and linked movements. His influence on the early songs of Schubert, who greatly admired him, is very marked. The lieder of Haydn and Mozart, for all their beauties, are mostly simple and strophic.

2. The 19th and 20th centuries

Beethoven's contribution to the lied was weightier. At first influenced by his teacher Neefe, his songs grew in range with his growing care for tonal structure and for more extended forms that included scena (*Adelaide*, 1794–5) and the pioneering **song cycle An die ferne Geliebte* (1816). Important contributions to the Romantic lied were also made by Weber and Spohr.

Schubert wrote more than 600 songs, varying in size from a few bars to 20 or more pages. The vocal line can range from very simple in the vein of 18th-century domestic song (*Heidenröslein*, 1815) to the virtuosity of *Der Hirt auf dem Felsen* (1828), and can encompass the dramatic urgency of the ballad *Erlkönig* (1815), with a lyrical grace that is entirely his own. His greatest contribution to the lied was to give the piano part a new significance, characteristically by setting the scene of a poem with expressive figuration suggesting water or rustling leaves, the chirrup of a cricket, a galloping horse, or a leaping trout and developing this with harmonic and motivic subtlety in support of the vocal melody. These gifts are most amply displayed his two great song cycles on the loss of love, touching in *Die schöne Müllerin* (1823) and tragic in *Winterreise* (1828). His poets range from Goethe to dozens of minor artists whose imagery caught his imagination. With Schubert, the lied becomes a major art form.

About half Schumann's 300 songs were written in 1840. To this year, that of his long-frustrated marriage to Clara Wieck, belong the Eichendorff and Heine *Liederkreise, Dichterliebe* (also Heine), and the song cycle *Frauenliebe und -leben*. Less pictorially inclined than Schubert, Schumann can, with his acute literary sense, respond to a poem's essence, whether with the irony that he found in Heine, sometimes the pain of seeing the beloved happy in another's arms, or the subtleties of Eichendorff, with Romantic evocations of a bygone age or of the darker aspects of the natural world. The piano again plays a crucial role, sometimes continuing the song after the voice has ceased.

Brahms's output included over 200 songs. The few sketches he left show how carefully he planned tonal and metrical strategies to give the poem its greatest musical potential. He responded to the stimulus of unusual or uneven metres, and tended to draw on minor poets or folksong texts that he felt had expressive possibilities which the music could realize. He published his songs in groups, sometimes with a connecting emotional link such as the passionately romantic set of op. 43 (which includes 'Von ewiger Liebe', 1864) or the more inward and death-haunted *Vier ernste Gesänge* (op. 121, 1896) to biblical texts.

Hugo Wolf's reputation rests almost entirely on his songs, in a short creative career lasting from about 1888 to his death in 1903. Possessing great poetic sensibilities, he sometimes chose a single poet (Eichendorff, Goethe, Mörike) for volumes entitled *Gedichte von ...* ('Poems by ...') or a specifically national collection (Spanish and Italian songbooks). He further extended keyboard virtuosity as an aspect of song and, with Wagnerian tendencies that set him in opposition to Brahms, made use of motif and advanced chromatic harmony to compress a drama into the framework of song. He rarely set poems which he felt had been successfully treated by his predecessors, and then only when he believed he had more to say, as he does with one of his greatest songs, Mignon's 'Kennst du das Land?' from Goethe's *Wilhelm Meister*.

Other significant lieder composers of the century include Mendelssohn, with numerous gracefully turned songs that he published in groups, and especially Carl Loewe. Though particularly associated with the ballad, which he brought to new artistic maturity (his setting of *Erlkönig* is of similar date to Schubert's, and can well stand beside it), he also wrote numerous fine songs that respond sensitively to poems by, especially, Goethe, Heine, and Byron. Among minor masters may be mentioned Peter Cornelius, with some excellent religious songs, Robert Franz, a gentle and sensitive talent, and Adolf Jensen, another composer who responded intelligently to the harmonic explorations of Wagner and Liszt. Wagner himself wrote a number of songs, of which the five setting poems by Mathilde Wesendonck in an orchestral cycle are the most important; Liszt's songs range far wider (encompassing settings of several languages besides German) and though sometimes prolix reveal a true lyric gift, associated with the keyboard virtuosity he himself commanded.

Mahler is especially significant for his settings of poems from *Des Knaben Wunderhorn* and his absorption of the lied into orchestral cycles, notably the *Lieder eines fahrenden Gesellen* (1883–5) and *Kindertotenlieder*

(1901–4), and into symphony. Most of Richard Strauss's songs were written early in his career, and were often either conceived for orchestra or later orchestrated by himself or others. They can reflect his love of the human voice, especially the soprano, which is so manifest in his operas. His *Vier letzte Lieder* (1946–8) are in some ways a farewell not only to his own creative life but to the long tradition of lied that he inherited.

LO/JW

📖 R. H. THOMAS, *Poetry and Song in the German Baroque: A Study of the Continuo Lied* (Oxford, 1963) · K. WHITTON, *Lieder: An Introduction to German Song* (London, 1984) · R. HALLMARK (ed.), *German Lieder in the Nineteenth Century* (New York, 1996) · E. F. KRAVITT, *The Lied: Mirror of Late Romanticism* (New Haven, CT, 1996)

Liederbuch (Ger., 'songbook'). A word used for the songbooks of the German Middle Ages (most of which survive without music), for later poetry collections, whether printed or manuscript, for the German polyphonic songbooks of the 15th and 16th centuries, and for many later collections of songs with German text. This last obviously includes songs for voice and piano, most notably Hugo Wolf's *Spanisches Liederbuch* and *Italienisches Liederbuch*, setting German translations of Spanish and Italian poems. The 'Glogauer Liederbuch' (*c*.1480) is a special case, being a set of three partbooks containing mostly non-German repertory.

DF

Lieder eines fahrenden Gesellen ('Songs of a Wayfarer'). Cycle of four songs (1883–5) by Mahler for baritone or mezzo-soprano and orchestra (or piano), settings of his own poems based on, or imitative of, **Des Knaben Wunderhorn*; he revised them 1891–6, and orchestrated them 1891–3. The second and fourth songs are linked thematically with the first and slow movements of his First Symphony.

Liederkreis. The German term for ***song cycle', first used by Beethoven to describe his *An die ferne Geliebte*. Schumann used it for two song cycles for voice and piano: op. 24, settings of nine poems by Heinrich Heine, and op. 39, settings of 12 poems by Joseph von Eichendorff, both composed in 1840.

Lieder ohne Worte ('Songs without Words'; *Romances sans paroles*). 48 piano pieces by Mendelssohn, in which a songlike melody progresses against an accompaniment, published in eight books of six each: 1, op. 19 (1830); 2, op. 30 (1835); 3, op. 38 (1837); 4, op. 53 (1841); 5, op. 62 (1844); 6, op. 67 (1845); 7, op. 85 (1850); 8, op. 102 (*c*.1845). Most of the individual titles were not Mendelssohn's, the exceptions being the three *Auf einer Gondel* (nos. 6, 12, and 29), the *Duetto* (no. 18), and

Volkslied (no. 23). He also wrote a *Lied ohne Worte*, op. 109 (*c*.1845), for cello and piano.

Liedertafel (Ger., 'song table'). A name given to many German male-voice singing societies that flourished in the nationalistic climate of the early 19th century. They were originally conceived as informal, convivial occasions at which members sat round a table with refreshments, but with the establishing of the more serious-minded *Männergesangvereine* ('male song societies') the aims became more artistic: about the middle of the century huge annual competitive festivals were held, notably the Lower Rhine Festivals (from 1817). The French equivalent of the *Liedertafel* is the **orphéon*.

Liederzyklus (Ger.). 'Song cycle'.

Lied von der Erde, Das ('The Song of the Earth'). Cycle of six songs (1908–9) by Mahler for tenor and alto or baritone soloists and orchestra, settings of poems from Hans Bethge's *Die chinesische Flöte*, German translations of 8th- and 9th-century Chinese poems; Mahler called it a 'symphony'.

lieto, lietamente (It.). 'Joyful'; *lietissimo*, 'most joyful'; *lieto fine*, 'happy ending' as of an opera.

Lieutenant Kijé (*Poruchik Kizhe*). Orchestral suite, op. 60 (1934), by Prokofiev; it is derived from the music he wrote for the film of the same name and has an optional baritone part.

lieve, lievemente (It.). 'Light', 'lightly'; 'easy', 'easily'.

Life for the Tsar, A (*Zhizn' za tsarya*; *Ivan Susanin*). Opera in five acts (or four acts and an epilogue) by Glinka to a libretto by Baron Yegor Fyodorovich Rozen, Vladimir Sollogub, Nestor Vasil'yevich Kukol'nik, and Vasily Andreyevich Zhukovsky (who suggested the subject) (St Petersburg, 1836). In the Soviet era Sergey Gorodetsky rewrote the libretto, refocusing interest on the leaders of the uprising against the Poles rather than the Romanov dynasty, and it was given as *Ivan Susanin* (Moscow, 1939). Cavos wrote an opera on the same plot (1815).

Life with an Idiot (*Zhizn's idiotom*). Opera in three acts by Schnittke to a libretto by Viktor Yerofeyev (Amsterdam, 1991).

ligature (from Lat. *ligare*, 'to bind'). A note form representing two or more notes. The use of ligatures was common in the medieval period, but the advent of music printing and other factors led to their demise in about 1600. Ligatures originated in neumatic plainchant notation (see NOTATION, 1), where a single ligature contained a group of notes sung to just one syllable of text. At about the beginning of the 13th century, set ways of combining ligatures were established so as to indicate clearly the rhythmic patterns of the music. These set patterns were called 'rhythmic modes'; in the basic system, there were six of them (see NOTATION, 2). Later, from the 14th century to the 16th, the rhythmic meaning of individual ligatures became fixed irrespective of their combination with other ligatures. A summary explanation of these 'fixed rhythm' ligatures is given in Fig. 1 (overleaf). In the 16th century it became common for several notes setting a single syllable to be written not as a ligature but as individual notes under a slur sign, just as is done today. The ligature equivalent to two semibreves persisted for some time and is still found in the early 18th century in the works of J. J. Fux. Modern editors of early music indicate groups of notes originally written as a single ligature by enclosing them under a square bracket.

AP

Ligeti, György (Sándor) (*b* Dicsőszentmárton, Transylvania [Diciosânmartin, now Tîrnăveni, Romania], 28 May 1923). Hungarian composer. His early conservatory studies were disrupted by the war; he then studied with Ferenc Farkas, Sándor Veress, and Pál Járdányi at the Budapest Academy of Music (1945–9), to which he returned in 1950 to teach counterpoint. While still a student he had begun writing adventurous pieces, but these could not be published or performed under the Stalinist despotism of 1949–53. Privately he went on with his explorations (*Musica ricercata* for piano, 1951–3), but he also produced choral songs more suited to the political climate. In 1956, following the collapse of the liberal revolution, he left for the West; he went first to Cologne, to make contact with Stockhausen.

For a year Ligeti did little but listen and study. He was fascinated by Webern, in whom he found a model of manifest construction allied with extreme expressive effect, and he familiarized himself with the thinking of his Western contemporaries. He then worked on three electronic pieces and on realizing his dream of unmeasured rhythm, fantastical complexity, and sonic drama in *Apparitions* for orchestra (1958–9), in which he introduced orchestral clusters. In 1959 he settled in Vienna, his base until 1973 when he began teaching at the Hamburg Musikhochschule, but from this time on he travelled often to teach and to attend performances.

Apparitions led to a more homogeneous and static handling of orchestral clusters in *Atmosphères* (1961), which is almost a single cloud, drifting through different regions of colour, harmony, and texture, whether in the form of sustained notes or of what

ligature, Fig. 1

(a) Two-note ligatures, basic forms

⬚ long, long ⬚ breve, breve ⬚ or ⬚ long, breve

⬚ ⬚ ⬚ ⬚ are all equivalent to two semibreves (note the up-stem to the left).

(b) The addition of down-stems to the breve and long

down-stem to the right lengthens a note: ⬚ breve, long ⬚ long, breve

⬚ long, long

down-stem to the left reduces a note: ⬚ breve, long ⬚ breve, breve

⬚ breve, breve ⬚ long, breve

(c) Ligatures of more than two notes

(i) Treat the first two and the last two notes as if they are two-note ligatures; this gives the value of the first and last note.

Example:

breve long

(ii) All middle notes are breves *unless* they have a down-stem to the right, *or* they are semibreves, *or* they are maximas (i.e. the note form twice as long as the long: ⬚).

Examples:

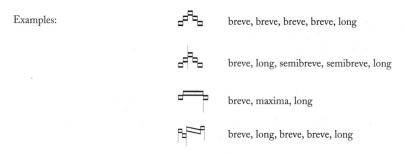

breve, breve, breve, breve, long

breve, long, semibreve, semibreve, long

breve, maxima, long

breve, long, breve, breve, long

Ligatures in the 14th, 15th, and 16th centuries.

Ligeti called 'micropolyphony', consisting of dense weaves of canons at the unison, in which the lines move at different speeds and are not separately identifiable. But he was also master of a quite different style, of abrupt gestures, intensely expressive and comic at the same time, as shown in *Aventures* and *Nouvelles Aventures* (1962–5), quasi-operatic situations for three singers and seven instrumentalists. His Requiem (1963–5) embraces both styles and also points towards the recuperation of elementary harmonies in *Lux aeterna* for unaccompanied voices (1966) and *Lontano* for orchestra (1967). This was not a return to conventional tonality—he preferred chords with no clear diatonic sense (e.g. a major 2nd superimposed on a minor 3rd)—but, together with the principle of canon, it allowed him access to the continuity of conventional tonal music. In the orchestral *Melodien* (1971) well-defined melodies emerge from and fold back into more characteristic textures of held chords and fast arpeggios. Ligeti then put everything he had discovered into his opera *Le Grand Macabre* (1974–7; staged Stockholm, 1978), in which a mysterious stranger arrives in 'Breughelland' to announce the end of the world: the piece is at once extravagantly comic and monitory, and it marked a real ending, for after it the composer found himself at an impasse.

This he resolved in his Horn Trio (1982) and the first six in a continuing series of virtuoso *Études* for piano (1985), unfolding a new complexity of polymetre, ambiguous modality (assisted in the non-piano works by disintonations both deliberate and accidental), and rich form, without losing his brilliance and clarity of sound. His music began to echo with resonances—from Debussy, Chopin, and Nancarrow, as well as from folk music from around the world, but especially from central Europe, Indonesia, and the Caribbean—while being unlike anything else in its precision and imaginative fantasy. Other works in the new style include concertos for piano (1985–8) and violin (1989–93), choral pieces, and a Sonata for solo viola (1991–4).

PG

📖 *György Ligeti in Conversation* (London, 1983) · P. GRIFFITHS, *György Ligeti* (London, 1983, 2/1996)

light. An adjective applied loosely (often pejoratively) to music deemed of no great intellectual or emotional depth, intended for light entertainment, and usually for orchestra. There is a large repertory of British light music, much of it witty, imaginative, and skilfully orchestrated, by such composers as Ketèlbey, Coates, Ronald Binge, Robert Farnon, and Gilbert Vinter. Elgar and Britten composed in the genre, which flourished from the 1950s with the expansion of radio broadcasting. Such music is often played by 'light orchestras'. See also POPULAR MUSIC; OPERETTA.

AL

📖 G. SELF, *Light Music in Britain Since 1870: A Survey* (Aldershot, 2001)

Light Cavalry (*Leichte Cavallerie*). Operetta in two acts by Suppé to a libretto by C. Costa (Vienna, 1866); its overture is popular as a concert item.

Lighthouse, The. Chamber opera in a prologue and one act by Maxwell Davies to his own libretto (Edinburgh, 1980).

Lighthouses of England and Wales. Orchestral work (1988) by Benedict Mason.

likembe. See MBIRA, KALIMBA, LIKEMBE.

Lilburn, Douglas (*b* Wanganui, 2 Nov. 1915; *d* Wellington, 6 June 2001). New Zealand composer. He studied in Canterbury and with Vaughan Williams and R. O. Morris at the RCM in London. He returned to New Zealand in 1940, becoming an influential figure in the country's musical life. He has composed many orchestral and chamber works, and since 1965 mostly electronic pieces. His music reflects many 20th-century influences, and the landscape and culture of New Zealand and the Pacific environment.

ABUR

Lilliburlero. Tune of unknown origin which first appeared in print in 1686 in a book of 'lessons' for the recorder or flute, where it is styled 'Quickstep'. The following year it achieved popularity when sung to satirical verses, with the mock Irish word 'Lilliburlero' as a refrain. It has remained a song of the Orange party, set to different words as 'Protestant Boys'. In Purcell's *Musick's Hand-Maid* (1687) it appears under the title 'A New Irish Tune' for harpsichord; Purcell also used it as a ground bass in his incidental music for the play *The Gordian Knot Unty'd* (1691).

Lily of Killarney, The. Opera in three acts by Benedict to a libretto by John Oxenford and Dion Boucicault after Boucicault's play *The Colleen Bawn, or The Brides of Garryowen* (London, 1862).

Lincoln Portrait, A. Work (1942) for speaker and orchestra by Copland, with words taken from Abraham Lincoln's speeches and letters; it was proposed for performance at Dwight Eisenhower's inauguration as president (1953) but was rejected because of Copland's alleged Communist sympathies. In performance it has attracted a wide range of speakers including Copland himself, Adlai Stevenson, Eleanor Roosevelt, Henry Fonda, John Gielgud, Katharine Hepburn, Margaret Thatcher, and Norman Schwarzkopf.

Lind [Lind-Goldschmidt], **Jenny** [Johanna Maria] (*b* Stockholm, 6 Oct. 1820; *d* Wynds Point, Herefordshire, 2 Nov. 1887). Swedish soprano. She was celebrated for her virtuoso technical agility and the purity of her singing, which gained her the nickname 'The Swedish Nightingale'. When she was ten, she enrolled at the Royal Opera School in Stockholm. In 1838 she made her debut in Stockholm as Agathe in *Der Freischütz*. To remedy weaknesses in her middle register she went to Paris to take lessons from the younger Manuel García. In 1842 she sang the title role in *Norma*, and in spite of reports of her excessive ornamentation she became greatly in demand for her coloratura brilliance. For the next five years she sang in Stockholm, Berlin, Hamburg, Vienna, and London, her most acclaimed roles being Amina in *La sonnambula* and Marie in *La Fille du régiment*. She created a sensation everywhere. In London she also sang Alice in *Robert le diable* and created the role of Amalia in *I masnadieri*. Her acting abilities were limited and her finest achievements were in her recitals and oratorio performances, to which the purity and steadiness of her voice were ideally suited.

JT

📖 G. DENNY, *Jenny Lind, the Swedish Nightingale* (New York, 1962)

Linda di Chamounix ('Linda of Chamonix'). Opera in three acts by Donizetti to a libretto by Gaetano Rossi after Adolphe-Philippe d'Ennery and Gustave Lemoine's play *La Grâce de Dieu* (1841) (Vienna, 1842).

Lindberg, Magnus (*b* Helsinki, 27 June 1958). Finnish composer. He studied at the Sibelius Academy, Helsinki, and at the EMS studio in Stockholm. He was influenced early on by central European modernism, but he quickly rejected the constraints of serialism. His award-winning *Kraft* (1985) is a riotous cornucopia of modernist sounds and devices, but in more recent orchestral works (e.g. *Arena*, 1995; *Feria*, 1997) he has moved closer to the Sibelian tradition of organic development, based on memorable short motifs. SJ

Lindpaintner, Peter Joseph von (*b* Coblenz, 9 Dec. 1791; *d* Nonnenhorn, 21 Aug. 1856). German composer and conductor. He studied with Peter Winter. Kapellmeister in Stuttgart from 1819 to his death, he was widely admired as a conductor ('the best in Germany', wrote Mendelssohn). After some early success with operas in various genres, he turned to horror opera in the manner popular in the 1820s. *Der Bergkönig* ('The Mountain King', 1825) includes some powerful music influenced by Weber's *Euryanthe*, as well as attractive rustic scenes. *Der Vampyr* (1828) suffered by comparison with Marschner's opera, but makes powerful use of Spohr-influenced chromatic harmony set against diatonic innocence and develops scene complexes well. Lindpaintner's considerable talent was really better suited to the charming little oriental comedy *Die Macht des Liedes* ('The Power of Song', 1836) than to his essays in German grand opera, such as *Die sizilianische Vesper* (1843), which find him overstretching his resources. JW

lining out. A method of performing metrical *psalmody.

Linley. English family of musicians. **Thomas Linley** (i) (*b* Badminton, Glos., 17 Jan. 1733; *d* London, 19 Nov. 1795) taught singing and directed concerts in Bath before becoming a musical director at Drury Lane Theatre in London. In 1775 he and his son Thomas composed and compiled music for a performance of *The Duenna* by his son-in-law, the playwright Richard Brinsley Sheridan. Linley provided music for over 20 more dramatic works.

Thomas Linley (ii) (*b* Bath, 5 May 1756; *d* Grimsthorpe, Lincs., 5 Aug. 1778) was a talented violinist and composer. He studied with Boyce and later with Nardini in Florence, where he met Mozart. Burney reported that Linley and Mozart were 'talked of all over Italy as the most promising geniuses of their age'. Linley's surviving music includes the *Ode on the Spirits of Shakespeare* (1776), an orchestral anthem *Let God arise* (1773), an oratorio *The Song of Moses* (1777), and the comic opera *The Cady of Bagdad* (1778). His career was tragically cut short when he drowned while on holiday.

The elder Linley's daughters **Elizabeth Ann** (1754–92), **Mary** (1758–87), and **Maria** (1763–84) were all singers, and of his other sons **Ozias Thurston** (1765–1831) was an organist and **William** (1771–1835) a writer and composer. WT/PL

'Linz' Symphony. Nickname of Mozart's Symphony no. 36 in C major K425 (1783), so called because it was composed and first performed in Linz.

Lipatti, Dinu [Constantin] (*b* Bucharest, 19 March 1917; *d* Geneva, 2 Dec. 1950). Romanian pianist and composer. In Paris he studied the piano with Cortot, conducting with Münch, and composition with Dukas and Boulanger. His career developed after World War II, but with the onset of a rare cancer it was immediately limited to European appearances and the recording studio (to which, as a perfectionist, he was eminently suited). His playing was notable for its great clarity of detail, delicate sensitivity, and virtuoso brilliance, and his recording legacy includes major works of Bach, Mozart, Chopin, and Schumann. CF

liquescent neume. A form of neume associated with plainchant to indicate certain consonants and diphthongs. The singer produces a semi-vocalized sound when moving from one note to the next. See NOTATION, 1, and Fig. 1.

lira [lyra]. A short-necked, three-string bowed fiddle of Greece, played held downwards with the body resting on the knee. Like those of the *rebec and the North African *rebab* (see RABĀB), its pear-shaped body and neck are carved from a single piece of wood. Similar instruments are played throughout the Balkans and eastern Europe.

lira da braccio. A Renaissance bowed string instrument. Played on the shoulder, it had five stopped strings tuned in 5ths and a pair of *bourdon (drone) strings lying off the fingerboard. It was used in the 15th and 16th centuries for the chordal accompaniment of songs and recitations, and had a flattish bridge so that the bow could play on several strings at once. The drone strings could be plucked or stopped by the left thumb. The *lira da braccio*, regarded as the equivalent of the lyre of Apollo and Orpheus, was the most respectable bowed instrument of its day. See also LIRONE. JMo

lira da gamba. See LIRONE.

lira organizzata. A *hurdy-gurdy with built-in organ pipes sounding at the same time as the strings. Both the rosined wheel that bowed the strings, and the bellows for the organ pipes, were operated by the hand-crank. The instrument was in use during the latter half of the 18th century; Haydn composed five concertos for the *lira organizzata* for Ferdinand IV, King of Naples.

JMo

lirone [lira da gamba]. A bowed string instrument, the bass counterpart to the *lira da braccio*. It was held between the knees like a *viol, and had nine to 14 strings tuned to facilitate the playing of chords. The bridge was only gently curved, so that the bow could play on several strings at once. The lirone was in use from the mid-16th century to the end of the 17th, mainly in Italy, especially to accompany singing and as part of the continuo group for sacred operas and oratorios.

RPa

liscio, liscia (It.). 'Smooth', 'even'.

Liszt, Franz (*see page 698*)

litany (Lat.: *litania*, *letania*, from Gk. *litaneia*, 'prayer'). A form of prayer consisting of a series of petitions to God, the Virgin Mary, or the saints, or the procession during which such supplications are made. The earliest Christian litanies are sets of diaconal petitions with a congregational response such as 'Kyrie eleison' or 'Grant this, O Lord'. Litanies of this type are frequently encountered in the services of the Orthodox Church and in the non-Roman rites of the Latin West. In Roman usage, these were overshadowed by litanies of the saints, whose intercession the congregation invoked with the phrase 'ora pro nobis' ('pray for us'). One of the most popular of these litanies was the *Litaniae lauretanae* ('Litany of Loreto') in honour of the Virgin Mary. It has attracted numerous polyphonic settings, by such composers as Victoria, Palestrina, and Mozart.

A theologically revised German litany was issued by Luther in 1529, while in 1544 Thomas Cranmer wrote an English litany for use in processions ordered by Henry VIII. The latter was subsequently published in the *Book of Common Prayer* without its original references to the saints. Western service books of the 20th century include many new litanies, some borrowed from Eastern liturgies and others recently composed.

—/ALi

literature and music. See NOVEL, MUSIC IN THE.

Literes (y Carrión), Antonio (de) (*b* Artá, Mallorca, 18 June 1673; *d* Madrid, 18 Jan. 1747). Spanish composer. In 1686 he won a place as a choirboy at the Colegio de Cantorcicos in Madrid, a college linked to the royal chapel, before being appointed a violinist at the chapel itself in 1693. He remained in that post until his death, combining his performing duties with the composition of sacred music and stage works. During his long tenure in Madrid he established influential contacts with eminent musicians including Sebastián Durón and José de Torres. His skill in absorbing Italian stylistic elements contributed to his reputation as a composer of standing.

MAM

lithography (from Gk. *lithos*, 'stone', and *graphein*, 'to write'). The principal technology for printing music and other writings. At the turn of the 18th century the Bavarian actor and playwright Alois Senefelder wished to find a means of printing his plays that was less expensive than the traditional technologies of metal type and engraving. After briefly experimenting with other methods, he discovered that it was possible to use the extremely fine-grained Solnhofen limestone in a chemical rather than physical process to define where ink should go on the printed paper. The fundamentals of lithography were arrived at by 1798, and Senefelder rapidly acquired patents throughout Europe. The new printing technology was adopted for all manner of purposes, eventually encompassing virtually all printing (except for high-volume colour printing, e.g. of catalogues), but from the outset one of its most important uses was for music.

The essence of Senefelder's discovery was that if the stone is written on with a grease-based ink and then wetted, the ink will repel the water, which in turn repels the printing ink from all but the marks first made. The resulting two-dimensional printing surface is more durable than the three-dimensional surface of engraved plates or type. Three fundamental improvements have been made to the original technique: the stone has been replaced by cheaper treated-metal or resin plates; instead of being written directly on the surface, the image is transferred (chiefly photographically) from a more easily managed medium (increasingly at the beginning of the 21st century printers are fabricating plates directly from computer files); the ink is 'offset' from the printing plate on to a rubber blanket and thence to the paper, making the surface last even longer.

See also PRINTING AND PUBLISHING OF MUSIC, 2*d*.

JJD

lithophone (from Gk. *lithos*, 'stone'). Any instrument made of resonant stone plaques.

Litolff, Henry (Charles) (*b* London, 7 Aug. 1818; *d* Bois-Colombes, 5 Aug. 1891). French pianist, music publisher, and composer. After studying the piano in London with Moscheles he went to Paris (1835) and, with Fétis's encouragement, to Brussels (1839–41) to

(*cont. on p. 702*)

Franz Liszt
(1811–86)

The Hungarian composer Franz (Ferenc) Liszt was born in Raiding on 22 October 1811 and died in Bayreuth on 31 July 1886.

Introduction

Liszt was regarded by many as the supreme piano virtuoso of the 19th century, but he was also active as a conductor, teacher, and author. In his music and his life, he typifies the image of the Romantic artist: his career as a performer met with unparalleled success and adulation, his personal life seemed torn between the worldly passions and religious mysticism so vividly expressed in his music. His creative imagination, despising routine, gave birth to some of the most daring and progressive compositions of the era. An active proselytizer for new music, he was an ardent supporter of the works of Wagner and Berlioz, among others. With his fervent advocacy of programme music, he attempted to revitalize symphonic composition, drawing inspiration from art and literature. Combining his dramatic instincts with a sincere religious faith, he endeavoured to revolutionize church music and oratorio. His striking sensitivity to keyboard tone-colour and sonority ensured that his piano music exploited the resources of the instrument to an unprecedented degree. Even Brahms, who scarcely admired Liszt's musical style, declared that if Mozart represented musical classicism, Liszt represented 'the classicism of piano technique'. In later years his master classes bestowed his insights as an interpreter to a new generation of pianists, many to become celebrated in their own right.

Liszt's vast output of music traverses virtually every genre, though opera is represented only by the juvenile and insignificant *Don Sanche* (a mature opera on Byron's *Sardanapalus* was begun but never completed), and chamber music plays a minimal role. His works abound with formal and harmonic innovations—many of them anticipating 20th-century developments—but ironically the oft-repeated statement that he 'invented' the symphonic poem does not survive scrutiny (he initially attached the title to pieces that he himself had previously called concert overtures), nor does the idea that 'thematic metamorphosis', a prominent feature of so much of his output, represents anything more novel than the principle of thematic variation found in music from time immemorial. Liszt's repeated assertions as to the originality of his programme music ('new bottles for new wine'—'forms, not formulas') should also not blind us to the importance of sonata form to the structure of many of the larger works, or to the influence of such composers as Beethoven, Berlioz, Chopin, and Weber.

Youth

Liszt's father, a failed trainee for the Catholic priesthood and an amateur musician, was a clerk on the Esterházy estates near Raiding (a German-speaking part of Hungary), his mother a chambermaid from lower Austria. Though proud of his Hungarian origins, their only child never learnt the Hungarian language: Liszt initially spoke German but became fluent in French as a teenager (at one point even drawing a rebuke from an Italian newspaper that he was 'a Hungarian masquerading as a Frenchman'). His musical talents were soon discovered to be prodigious, and he made his debut as a pianist in Ödenburg (now Sopron) at the age of nine playing a concerto by Ries. A subsequent concert in Pressburg (now Bratislava) attracted the attention of several Hungarian noblemen, who agreed to finance his musical studies in Vienna, where he became a pupil of Czerny (piano) and Salieri (composition). One of Liszt's proudest memories was of his meeting with Beethoven during this period (the exact venue is disputed), and his first published composition was a modest variation on the same waltz by Diabelli that Beethoven made the basis of one of his most ambitious works. Astonishingly, Czerny was Liszt's only notable piano teacher, though his studies with him lasted scarcely more than a year. Throughout his life Liszt remained grateful for Czerny's rigorous training, later dedicating the 12 *Grandes études* to him as the fruits of his teaching.

In 1823, seeking a larger orbit for their son's talents, the family moved to Paris, where an attempt to enrol him as a student at the Conservatoire was refused by the director, Cherubini (Liszt, as a foreigner, was ineligible). Instead, his father engaged Paër as a composition teacher and Reicha to give a grounding in theory. Liszt also began a mutually beneficial association with the firm of Érard, whose pianos were to become his preferred instrument. With ever-increasing concert appearances, the child prodigy began to establish a notable reputation as a pianist, and he made three successful visits to England between 1824 and 1827. His reputation as a composer, too, was burgeoning, and was given greater impetus by the Parisian production of his opera *Don Sanche* in October 1825. This was added to an ever-increasing portfolio of compositions that included sonatas, piano concertos, and (in 1826) the 'Étude en douze exercices' that was later to be the basis of the 12 *Grandes études* and their revision as the *Études d'exécution transcendante*. Those juvenile pieces of Liszt that survive (including the opera and several piano works) display a precocious fluency, but nothing on the level of the adolescent Mozart or Mendelssohn. Even a decade later, Schumann claimed that Liszt's pianistic flair would always overshadow his compositional achievements.

The heady progress of Liszt's career was brought to an abrupt halt by the unexpected death of his father in 1827. This event, coupled with a thwarted liaison with one of his pupils, Caroline de Saint-Cricq (whom Liszt always regarded as his first love), led him into a spiral of depression and illness. In 1828 the journal *Le Corsaire* even published his obituary. Although rumours of his death had indeed been greatly exaggerated, Liszt retreated ever more from the public eye and into religious contemplation. He was finally wakened from this condition by the July Revolution of 1830—'The cannons cured him!' his mother later said, with obvious relief—which elicited an almost chaotic sketch of a 'Revolutionary' symphony, and spurred an interest in the reformation of society through art (ideals shared by such contemporary writers as Félicité de Lamennais, Alphonse de Lamartine, Victor Hugo, and George Sand).

Liszt, painfully aware of his lack of formal schooling, now began an intensive course of self-education and became involved with the Saint-Simonian movement, whose precepts were based on a near-socialist interpretation of the gospel of Christ. At this period too he became associated with fellow composers including Chopin, Berlioz, and Alkan, and with such painters as Eugène Delacroix and Ary Scheffer: all contributed to create in Liszt an artist of wide humanitarian interests and cosmopolitan idealism. Musically, his encounter in 1832 with the quasi-demonic virtuosity of Paganini galvanized him to reconsider his approach to performance, and he became fired with the desire to achieve for piano technique what Paganini had for the violin. The fantasy on *La Clochette*, written the following year, was the first of his creative tributes to Paganini to display this new pianistic ambition; it was later followed by reworkings of some of the violin caprices as *Études d'exécution transcendante d'après Paganini*.

1832 saw another encounter, as significant for Liszt's personal life as Paganini was for his artistic: his meeting with Marie, the wife of Count Charles d'Agoult. A turbulent relationship developed, and the adulterous lovers eloped to Geneva in 1835, scandalizing sections of the Parisian society they had left behind and making Liszt's love-life the source of gossip for the first, but not the last, time. They had three children together—including Cosima, who was to become the wife of Richard Wagner. Travels in Switzerland and Italy with Marie d'Agoult inspired the piano pieces of the *Album d'un voyageur* (eventually revised as the first volume, 'Switzerland', of *Années de pèlerinage*), and work on the Italian volume was also begun at this time, but Liszt's compositional activity was soon to be diverted by the resumption of his concert career and the start of his 'Glanzperiode' ('glory days') as a travelling virtuoso.

From 1839 to 1847 he toured most of Europe (including Russia and Turkey) as the most celebrated pianist the musical world had seen—feted and idolized by audiences, admired with less than decorous, but welcome, passion by many women. A new term, 'Lisztomania', was aptly coined. Of his contemporaries, only Sigismond Thalberg (with whom he had a famous piano 'duel' in 1837) came close to rivalling his success. Liszt established the solo 'recital' (hitherto most concerts had been variety acts), and composed a plethora of dextrous transcriptions and fantasies for his own performance. Many of these pieces (such as the fantasy on *Don Juan*) display an imagination and creativity that raises them to the level of original works of art, but by 1847 Liszt felt that his incessant touring was a hindrance to sustained compositional work (it had already contributed to the breakdown of his relationship with Marie d'Agoult). In 1842 he had accepted a position of 'Kapellmeister in ausserordentlichem Dienst' in Weimar without placing much significance on it, but in 1848 he settled permanently in the town, soon to be joined by Princess Carolyne zu Sayn-Wittgenstein, his new lover and a fervent worshipper at the shrine of his compositional genius. In Weimar he aimed to usher in a new era of artistic achievement.

Creative maturity

Liszt's period as Kapellmeister in Weimar was the most musically productive of his life, and finally established his reputation as a significant composer. He effectively made the small town a centre for avant-garde music (giving, for example, the first performance of Wagner's *Lohengrin* in 1850 and organizing two Berlioz festivals), developed his conducting technique, and composed a vast body of harmonically radical music, including 12 symphonic poems (*Les Préludes, Orpheus, Tasso, Mazeppa, Prometheus, Festklänge, Hungaria, Heroïde funèbre, Ce qu'on entend sur la montagne, Die Ideale, Hunnenschlacht,* and *Hamlet*), *A Faust Symphony* (1854–7), a symphony on Dante's *Divine Comedy* (1855–6), *Two Episodes from Lenau's 'Faust',* two piano concertos, *Totentanz* for piano and orchestra, the Piano Sonata in B minor, and a host of other important piano works, such as the final versions of the *Transcendental Studies,* Paganini Studies, and the first two volumes of *Années de pèlerinage.* The oratorio *St Elizabeth* was begun in 1857 while Liszt still held his post in Weimar but was not finished until 1862, by which time he had resigned as Kapellmeister, feeling stifled in his musical aims by what he regarded as irremediable provincialism.

Liszt moved to Rome in 1861, initially prompted by his intention to marry Princess Carolyne there on his 50th birthday, but the ceremony was abandoned after machinations within the Vatican by Monsignor Gustav Hohenlohe, whose youngest brother had married Princess Carolyne's daughter and whose inheritance might have been imperilled by her mother's remarriage. His original purpose unachieved, Liszt however remained in Rome, motivated by an ambition to reform church music. This was not realized, in spite of his personal friendship with Pope Pius IX (who referred to him as 'my dear Palestrina'). To the astonishment of some of his contemporaries, Liszt began to contemplate a religious vocation, took minor orders in 1865, and completed his largest work, the oratorio *Christus,* in 1867.

From 1869 onwards Liszt visited Hungary every year (establishing a music academy in Budapest), spent most summers in Weimar and winters in Rome. This 'vie trifurquée' became the general pattern of his life until his death. Meanwhile, his compositional style was undergoing a profound change, prompted partly by his love of experimentation, but largely by an increasing bitterness and frustration at the course of his life. The dreams of a new golden artistic age in Weimar had not been fulfilled, the vision for the revivification of church music had come to nothing. His most ambitious music was abominated by conservative critics and also baffled concert audiences. His son Daniel had died prematurely in 1859, his daughter Blandine in 1862. His only surviving child, Cosima, had been involved in an adulterous affair with Wagner. This, and Cosima's eventual conversion to Protestantism in order to remarry, pained Liszt deeply, in spite of the parallels with his own situation with her mother. Liszt and Wagner

were eventually reconciled in 1870, but relations between father and daughter remained uneasy, especially after Wagner's death in 1883. In his very last years Liszt began to recover some optimism: his music gradually seemed to be making headway with the public ('I can wait', he told his pupils), and the admiration of a younger generation of pianists (including Ignacy Friedman, Emil Sauer, and Frederic Lamond) was close to idolatry. During a visit to Britain in 1886 he was lionized with genuine enthusiasm and affection. He died in Bayreuth later that year.

The musical legacy

Liszt's music is valuable both for what it is, and for what it prompted others to become. Wagner freely admitted (but only in private) that the development of his style was heavily indebted to Liszt's works of the 1850s. Subsequent composers including Debussy, Bartók, Busoni, and Schoenberg found inspiration in his harmonic daring and structural experimentation. The final decades in particular 'threw their lance far into the future' (Princess Carolyne's phrase) with use of whole-tone harmonies (*Der traurige Mönch, Nuages gris*), acerbic dissonant clashes and tritones (*Unstern*), chords built on 4ths (third *Mephisto* Waltz), and avoidance of tonal stability (*Bagatelle sans tonalité*). The questing, fragmentary nature of much of Liszt's later music has sometimes seemed a bizarre departure after the grandiose canvases of his Weimar years, or the bravura swagger of the music of his Glanzperiode, but we can perhaps better see it as a return to aspects of his style in the early 1830s. Pieces like the three *Apparitions,* or the first version of *Harmonies poétiques et religieuses,* are admittedly couched in a different harmonic language from the late music, but they share the same Romantic intimacy and almost wilful evanescence of mood.

The music of the 1850s—extrovert, confident, and written on a heroic scale—seems like that of another composer. It is here that the influence of Beethoven is most keenly felt, not only at individual points (compare the opening of Liszt's *Missa solemnis* in D minor, or of *Ce qu'on entend sur la montagne,* with the opening of Beethoven's Ninth Symphony) but also in structural terms (the sonata form of *Les Préludes* is obviously modelled on the first movement of Beethoven's 'Waldstein' Sonata). Indeed, sonata form is much more important for Liszt's music than is often acknowledged. The first version of *Vallée d'Obermann* is a sonata form based on the first movement of Weber's E minor Piano Sonata, while several of the symphonic poems (*Les Préludes, Orpheus, Festklänge, Tasso*) and the first movement of the *Faust* Symphony are also sonata designs. The structure of the Piano Sonata in B minor (which contains elements of a slow movement and scherzo within a single-movement plan) is more innovatory, as is the first movement of the 'Dante' Symphony, where the normal contrast of key in the sonata archetype is replaced by a contrast of mode (first group a highly chromatic D minor, second group D major), and the development section is replaced by an independent, programmatic episode (illustrating the love of Francesca da Rimini and Paolo). In general, the later group of symphonic poems are more distant from the sonata archetype, although *Ce qu'on entend* does sport a massive three-key exposition that recalls the tonal procedures of both Beethoven and Schubert.

Liszt achieved a mastery of orchestration relatively late in life—the orchestral scores and sketches of the 1820s to 40s are competent, but nothing more. After settling in Weimar he initially used the minor composers August Conradi (1821–73) and Raff as amanuenses and orchestration assistants, though later he acquired enough experience to dispense with any help. The final versions of all the orchestral music were scored by Liszt alone, and the style of orchestration he eventually developed is clear and practical, even if it does not have the opulence of Wagner or the novelty of Berlioz. At its best, Liszt's orchestration displays a fine colouristic imagination (the 'March of the Three Kings' from *Christus* is an impressive example), but sometimes (as in the frequent use of basses in striding octaves) the hint of the virtuoso pianist is difficult to ignore.

In the piano music itself, a complete understanding of the resources of the instrument and an acute ear for contrast allowed Liszt to produce a quasi-orchestral palette of tone-colours, lending a coruscating brilliance and variety to both his original music and his transcriptions. As the foremost keyboard technician of his day (Thalberg himself admitted Liszt's superior dexterity), he devised effects hitherto considered impossible—such as the climax of the *Fantasy on 'La Sonnambula'*, where, in addition to a thematic combination in the centre of the texture, the hands simultaneously play bass harmonies and a trill high in the treble. Liszt's command of the keyboard contributes significantly to the appeal of his illustrative music, with pieces such as *Les Jeux d'eau à la villa d'Este* or *Orage* ('storms', Liszt told Amy Fay, 'are my speciality') gaining much of their impact from the manipulation of piano sonority.

Liszt's harmonic style oscillates between diatonic verities (the Prelude to *Christus*) and intense chromaticism (the Agony in the Garden scene from the same work). His melodic style too is distinctive by its very eclecticism: Italian cantilena mingles with ecclesiastical plainchant, tunes reminiscent of French grand opera are treated to the motivic development of German symphonic music. Liszt had a fertile lyric gift (witness the all-too-famous third *Liebestraum*), and although his metamorphosis-of-themes technique was hardly original in itself (compare Schubert's 'Wanderer' Fantasia), the scale on which he attempted the procedure was unusual (the third movement of the *Faust* Symphony is a completely transformed recomposition of the first). Liszt's use of this device generally had a dramatic or programmatic purpose (Mephistopheles, as the 'spirit of negation', contorts and distorts Faust's themes), and in many ways it is the dramatic immediacy of Liszt's music that is its most striking feature, and the force that welds all its disparate elements into an unmistakeable individuality.

Few composers encompass such a stylistic range as Liszt's music traverses—in some ways it is difficult to believe that the *Grand galop chromatique* and *Via crucis* were written by the same composer, but no more difficult than accepting the carnal and the mystic together as equally important aspects of the man himself. Musical analysis by character traits is as deeply unfashionable in certain quarters now as it was commonplace in Liszt's day, but in his case, as with Berlioz and Schumann, the life and music are inextricably linked. It is the personality of the man that seems to explain, and give unity to, the work. In this respect, Liszt is a true Romantic icon. KH

📖 P. RAABE, *Franz Liszt: Leben und Schaffen* (Stuttgart, 1931, 2/1968) · D. WATSON, *Liszt* (London, 1983, 2/1990) · A. WALKER, *Franz Liszt*, 3 vols. (London, 1988–97) · A. WILLIAMS, *Portrait of Liszt* (Oxford, 1990) · M. SAFFLE, *Franz Liszt: A Guide to Research* (New York, 1991) · K. HAMILTON, *Liszt: Sonata in B minor* (Cambridge, 1996)

compose and to pursue a solo career. In the 1840s and 50s he gave concerts in Germany and the Netherlands. In 1849 he settled in Brunswick, acquiring through his marriage the publishing firm of Gottfried Meyer; he renamed it Henry Litolff's Verlag and soon became an important figure in local musical life. His connections with Moscheles, Fétis, Berlioz, Liszt, and others contributed to the firm's success, but it was chiefly later under Theodor Litolff (1839–1912), Meyer's son whom Litolff adopted, that the firm gained a flourishing reputation as a publisher of piano music and teaching material, including notable collections of the classics.

Litolff returned to Paris in 1858 and took up conducting and teaching, organizing the official musical celebrations during the siege of Paris in 1871. Meanwhile his compositions were fast accumulating: he wrote operas, choral and orchestral works, songs, and chamber music, but today is remembered chiefly for his brilliant piano music, especially the *Concertos symphoniques* for piano and orchestra (no. 4 includes the famous Scherzo). His solo piano music, written mainly for the salon, combines simple lyricism with brilliant bravura passages. A colourful figure who was married four times, Litolff was much admired by his contemporaries, especially Liszt.   JN/SH

'Little Russian' Symphony. Nickname of Tchaikovsky's Symphony no. 2 in C major op. 17 (1872), so called because it uses folksongs from Ukraine ('Little Russia').

Little Sweep, The. 'An entertainment for young people' by Britten to a libretto by Eric Crozier, the third act of *Let's Make an Opera* (Aldeburgh, 1949).

liturgy (Gk., 'public service'). 1. In its broadest sense, the forms and patterns of worship employed by any faith community. The term is more commonly used in a narrower sense with reference to the established forms of public worship historically used by Jews and Christians. Many of the more precise definitions offered by Christian theologians and liturgiologists tend to speak of liturgy's ecclesiological and theological significance: e.g. as an eschatological 'convocation' (Gk.: *ekklesia*) of the members of Christ's mystical body (i.e. the Church), as the instrument for imparting grace through the Word or sacraments, or as a symbolic epiphany of the heavenly hierarchies. Other definitions relate to the special status assigned by individual religious communities to particular forms of corporate worship, whether formally by means of legislation or decrees issued by church or civil authorities, or informally through repeated use. Services or devotions falling outside such juridical definitions of liturgy have consequently often been labelled 'paraliturgical'.

Before the destruction of Jerusalem by the Romans in AD 70, Judaism possessed an elaborate Temple liturgy that is described extensively in the Old Testament. Its cycle of daily morning and evening sacrifices was maintained by hereditary priests and musicians. During the centuries that followed the cessation of sacrificial worship, new forms of Jewish liturgy consisting of psalmody, readings, and prayers arose within the context of the synagogue.

Jewish patterns of informal daily prayer and temple worship furnished Christianity with precedents for the establishment of its own liturgical life during the first centuries of its existence. Although it is clear that Early Christian worship centred on the weekly celebration of the Eucharist on the day of Christ's resurrection (i.e. Sunday), relatively little detailed information about Christian liturgy survives from before the legalization of Christianity by the Roman Emperor Constantine in 313. From then on, however, a host of regional urban and monastic liturgical usages or 'rites' using the local vernacular (Greek, Latin, Syriac, Armenian, etc.) are documented. These encompassed forms of daily common prayer (i.e. a 'Liturgy of the Hours' or 'Divine Office'), the Eucharist, rites of initiation (Baptism and Chrismation) and other services. The subsequent multiplication of holy days celebrating events in the life of Christ and the saints resulted in the formation of annual fixed and movable cycles of worship based respectively on the solar calendar and the changeable date of Easter. The superimposition of these feasts on the existing daily and weekly cycles was complemented by the creation of variable ('Proper') texts for insertion among the invariable ('Ordinary') liturgical texts of particular services.

Among the rites of late antiquity, those of the imperial capitals of Rome and Byzantium subsequently underwent particularly complex processes of development, emerging from the Middle Ages as the dominant liturgies of Eastern and Western Christianity. The *Reformation brought forth numerous forms of Protestant worship that to a greater or lesser degree rejected the theology, ritual, and music of Roman Catholic liturgy (see also LUTHERAN CHURCH MUSIC). Although the number variants has increased commensurately with the proliferation of denominations, centrifugal tendencies have recently been balanced by consensuses forged through ecumenical scholarship.

AP/ALi

📖 J. HARPER, *The Forms and Orders of Western Liturgy from the Tenth to the Eighteenth Century* (Oxford, 1991)

2. In the Eastern Christian Church, a synonym for the Eucharist (e.g. the Divine Liturgy of St John Chrystostom).

Liturgy of the Hours. See OFFICE.

lituus (Lat.). An Etruscan and Roman bronze ritual trumpet. It has a hooked bell and resembles the letter J in shape. From Roman imperial times onwards the name referred instead to the cavalry trumpet of oxhorn, the *bucina, and it was used for brass instruments of uncertain type by Bach and his contemporaries.

JMo

livret (Fr., 'little book'). *Libretto.

Lloyd, George (Walter Selwyn) (*b* St Ives, Cornwall, 28 June 1913; *d* London, 3 July 1998). English composer. At the RAM he studied the violin with Albert Sammons, counterpoint with C. H. Kitson, and composition with Harry Farjeon. He enjoyed some success with his first opera *Iernin* (1934) which led to two further operatic ventures, *The Serf* (1938), given at Covent Garden under Albert Coates, and *John Socman* (1951) for the Festival of Britain. Composition was interrupted by World War II, during which Lloyd served in the Royal Marines. Severely shell-shocked, he was invalided out in 1942. Between 1945 and 1948 he lived with his wife in Switzerland and resumed composition. The backbone of his output, in a more conventional tonal idiom, consisted of 12 symphonies, four piano concertos, and two violin concertos, though he also wrote choral works (including a symphonic mass) and chamber and piano music.

JDɪ

Lloyd, Jonathan (*b* London, 30 Sept. 1948). English composer. He studied at the RCM with John Lambert and Edwin Roxburgh, and later in Paris and at Tanglewood. He writes music of deceptive simplicity, often including elements of popular music. His compositions include five symphonies, *Tolerance* (1994) and other orchestral works, a Violin Concerto (1995), choral and ensemble music, a community opera, *The Adjudicator* (1986), and music for theatre, films, and radio.

ABUR

Lloyd Webber, Andrew [Lord Lloyd-Webber of Sydmonton] (*b* London, 22 March 1948). English composer. He studied at the RCM and wrote the musicals *Joseph and the Amazing Technicolor Dreamcoat* (1968), *Jesus Christ Superstar* (1971), and *Evita* (1978) with the lyricist Tim Rice. Exploiting commercial opportunities, these works were hugely successful, as, later, were *Cats* (1981), *Starlight Express* (1984), *The Phantom of the Opera* (1986), *Aspects of Love* (1989), *Sunset Boulevard* (1993), and *Whistle Down the Wind* (1998). Lloyd Webber has also written film scores, a Requiem, and Variations for cello and rock band. The recipient of many awards, he was knighted in 1992 and was created a life peer in 1997.

ALᴀ

Lobgesang ('Hymn of Praise'). Symphony-cantata by Mendelssohn, his Symphony no. 2 (1840), with solo voices, chorus, and organ in the last movement. It was composed for the same occasion as *Festgesang*.

Lobo, Alonso (*b* Osuna, *bapt.* 25 Feb. 1555; *d* Seville, 5 April 1617). Spanish composer. Having been a canon of the collegiate church at Osuna, in 1591 he became master of the choirboys and assistant to Francisco Guerrero at Seville Cathedral. He was elected *maestro de capilla* at Toledo Cathedral in 1593, and in 1604 returned as *maestro* to Seville, where his music (notably the *Credo romano*) continued to be sung long after his death. He is best known for the motet *Versa est in luctum*, written on the death of Philip II, and published—with six other motets and six masses—in his only printed collection, the *Liber primus missarum* (Madrid, 1602).

OR

Lobo, Duarte (*b* c.1565; *d* Lisbon, 24 Sept. 1646). Portuguese composer. In his youth he attended the choir school of Évora Cathedral, and was taught by Manuel Mendes. He subsequently became *mestre de capela* at Évora and later in Lisbon, at the Hospital Real and at the cathedral. Lobo was celebrated both as a teacher and as a composer of sacred music. His works—published by the Plantin firm in Antwerp, and including two books of masses and one of *Magnificat* settings—display a wide range of styles, from traditional counterpoint to rhythmically animated homophony in some polychoral works. For his parody masses he favoured the works of Guerrero and Palestrina as models.

OR

Locatelli, Pietro Antonio (*b* Bergamo, 3 Sept. 1695; *d* Amsterdam, 30 March 1764). Italian composer and violinist. In 1711 he went to Rome, where he studied the violin (probably with Giuseppe Valentini rather than Corelli) and seems to have enjoyed the patronage of Cardinal Ottoboni between 1717 and 1723. In about 1725 he embarked on a career as a travelling virtuoso violinist, visiting Venice, Munich, and Berlin, and in 1729 he settled permanently in Amsterdam. There he gave concerts, taught, entered the publishing business, and from 1741 ran a thriving business importing violin strings from Italy.

Locatelli was one of the finest violinists of his time and has been called 'the 18th-century Paganini'. His playing was notable for its combination of sweetness and brilliant virtuosity, the latter quality being reflected in the technical demands of his own violin writing, which goes up to the 16th position and contains extremely difficult figurations and multiple stops. His concertos and sonatas show both Roman and Venetian influences; a set of concertos published in 1733 contains written-out cadenzas.   DA/ER

Locke, Matthew (*b* ?Devon, 1621 or 1622; *d* London, Aug. 1677). English composer. He was trained as a choirboy at Exeter Cathedral, where his name is carved in the stone of the organ screen. He may have been taught by Orlando Gibbons's brother Edward and by John Lugge, and it is likely that in 1644 he met his future employer, the young Prince Charles (later Charles II), who stayed at Exeter for a time. Locke probably followed Charles into exile in the Low Countries and perhaps accompanied the Duke of Newcastle to Antwerp in 1649; he seems to have converted to Catholicism there. By 1651 he was again in England, perhaps at Exeter, since his *Little Consort* was 'made att the request of Mr Wake [possibly William of Exeter] for his Schollars 1651'. Duos for bass viols followed in 1652. He may have been in Herefordshire about 1654–6: *The Flat Consort for my Cousin Kemble* probably belongs to this time.

By 1656 Locke was in London, singing in and composing part of Davenant's opera *The Siege of Rhodes*; he contributed to other Davenant productions in the following years. His music for James Shirley's masque *Cupid and Death* was probably written for a 1659 performance. At the Restoration he was appointed as composer to the 'Private Musick' of Charles II and also as composer for the court violin band. Music by him was played in the streets of London during Charles II's progress the day before his coronation. He was appointed organist in the new Chapel of Catherine of Braganza in 1662, but Roger North wrote that 'the Italian masters, that served there, did not approve of his manner of play', and he was confined to playing a small chamber organ. He was among a small group of musicians who journeyed with the royal family to escape the plague in 1665–6 and wrote some compositions at Oxford when they stayed there. Although the Gentlemen of the Chapel Royal objected to singing his varied Kyrie settings on 1 April 1666 and sabotaged the performance, Pepys noted 'a special good Anthemne' performed by them on 14 August following—Locke's *Be thou exalted*, a thanksgiving for victory over the Dutch.

Locke seems to have been somewhat prickly by nature, publishing a pamphlet attacking the Chapel Royal debacle noted above and others concerning Thomas Salmon's *An Essay to the Advancement of Music*. His *Melothesia*, published in 1673, contains preludes and dances for harpsichord by himself and other court composers, with seven organ voluntaries as well as the earliest known printed rules for realizing a figured bass. Locke continued to compose for the stage, too, and in 1674 was one of five composers invited to write music for Thomas Shadwell's adaptation of *The Tempest*. His *Psyche* of 1675 is an important forerunner of the *semi-operas later taken up by Purcell and others. The young Purcell, who succeeded Locke as composer for the violin band, wrote an ode on his death, *What hope for us remains now he is gone?*

Many of Locke's compositions survive in autograph copies. In addition to his dramatic music, he was a notable composer of chamber music for strings. His extensive output includes several collections of dances, grouped in suites, and scored for various combinations of treble and bass viols (or violins). He seems to have supervised *Tripla concordia*, a collection of airs for two trebles and bass by himself and others published in 1676. His surviving sacred music consists of about 60 works, including over 30 anthems and various pieces to Latin texts. Many of these conform to the prevailing taste at court for incorporating substantial instrumental parts.   WT/AA

loco (It.). 'Place': an instruction to return to the normal register after a passage marked to be played in a different one, for example an octave higher or lower; it is also given in the form *al loco*, 'at the place'.

Lodoïska. Opera in three acts by Cherubini to a libretto by Claude-François Fillette-Loraux after an episode from Jean-Baptiste Louvet de Couvrai's novel *Les Amours du chevalier de Faublas* (Paris, 1791). Kreutzer (1791), Storace (1794), and Mayr (1796) wrote operas on the same subject.

Loeffler, Charles Martin (Tornow) (*b* Mulhouse, 30 Jan. 1861; *d* Medfield, MA, 19 May 1935). French-born American composer. He studied the violin and composition in Berlin and Paris, and in 1881 settled in the USA, where he was assistant leader of the Boston Symphony Orchestra (1882–1903), then lived as a composer and teacher. He was influenced by contemporary French music and classical subject matter (*A Pagan Poem* for orchestra with obbligato piano, cor anglais, and trumpets), though in later years he became an admirer of Gershwin.   PG

Loeillet. Flemish family of musicians. **Jean Baptiste Loeillet** (i) (*b* Ghent, *bapt.* 18 Nov. 1680; *d* London, 19 July 1730) was the son of a barber-surgeon who died in 1685. He may have been brought up by his uncle, **Pieter Loeillet** (*b* Ghent, *bapt.* 21 May 1651; *d* Ghent, 2 Nov. 1735), a violinist and concert master. In about 1705 he settled in London, where he changed his Christian name to John. From about 1707 to 1710 he made frequent appearances as an oboist and flautist in the London opera orchestras, and from 1710 ran a series of highly profitable weekly concerts at his house in Hart

Street, Covent Garden. It was at one of these concerts that Corelli's concerti grossi op. 6 were first performed in England, probably in December 1714. Loeillet is credited with popularizing the side-blown flute in England. He was a renowned harpsichord teacher, and his works include nine suites of lessons for harpsichord or spinet, as well as trio and solo sonatas for recorder, flute, oboe, and violin.

His half-brother **Pierre** (*b* Ghent, *bapt.* 20 April 1674; *d* Ghent, 24 Nov. 1743) was a violinist, while his younger brother, **Jacques Loeillet** (*b* Ghent, *bapt.* 7 July 1685; *d* Ghent, 28 Nov. 1748), was an oboist to the Elector of Bavaria in the Netherlands and at Munich; later he was a musician at the French court. His works include concertos for oboe and for flute, and sonatas for flute or violin with continuo and for two solo flutes or violins.

Jean Baptiste Loeillet (i) is sometimes confused with his uncle Pieter's son, **Jean Baptiste Loeillet** (ii) (*b* Ghent, *bapt.* 6 July 1688; *d* Lyons, *c.*1720). The latter entered the service of the Archbishop of Lyons, where he remained until his early death. He composed some 48 sonatas for recorder and continuo (Amsterdam, 1710–17) in the style of Corelli; they were reprinted in London by Walsh & Hare. In his works he styled himself 'Loeillet de Gant'. His half-brother **Étienne Joseph Loeillet** (*b* Mâcon, *bapt.* 18 Sept. 1715; *d* Brussels, 10 Dec. 1797) served as a violinist and organist at the collegiate church of St Michel and Ste Gudule in Brussels for about 40 years.   WT/LC

Loesser, Frank (Henry) (*b* New York, 29 June 1910; *d* New York, 28 July 1969). American songwriter. He made his initial steps in popular music as a lyricist before composing his first Broadway musical, *Where's Charley?* (1948). His greatest success, *Guys and Dolls* (1950), was followed by songs for the film *Hans Christian Andersen* (1952) and the shows *The Most Happy Fella* (1956), *Greenwillow* (1960), and *How to Succeed in Business Without Really Trying* (1962).   PGA/ALA

Loewe, Carl (*b* Loebjuen, nr Halle, 30 Nov. 1796; *d* Kiel, 20 April 1869). German composer. He studied with his father, then at Halle University, showing an early talent for singing and composition. In 1820 he became professor and Kantor at the Stettin Gymnasium, where he remained, apart from successful tours as a singer and composer, until a stroke in 1865 forced him to resign. His reputation rests on his many ballads, narrative songs in which his melodic gift, grasp of dramatic effect, and skilful use of motif can sustain interest across lengthy structures. Among the best of these is *Erlkönig*, a setting that can stand beside Schubert's, as can some of his finest songs. He had less

success with his oratorios, or with his operas, in which his mastery of dramatic narrative does not translate into dramatic action.   WT/JW

Loewe, Frederick (*b* Berlin, 10 June 1904; *d* Palm Springs, FL, 14 Feb. 1988). German-born American composer. The son of an operetta singer, he moved with his father to the USA and worked as a pianist and composer—with little success until he began to work with the lyricist Alan Jay Lerner. Their collaboration produced the hugely popular shows *Brigadoon* (1947), *Paint your Wagon* (1951), *My Fair Lady* (1956), and *Camelot* (1960), and the film *Gigi* (1958).   ALA

log drum. A large form of *slit drum made from a hollowed-out log up to 9 metres long, found in Asia, the Americas, and the South Seas.

Logothetis, Anestis (*b* Pyrgos, 27 Oct. 1921; *d* Vienna, 6 Jan. 1994). Greek-born Austrian composer. He moved to Vienna in 1942, studying mechanical engineering before turning to composition at the Music Academy and, later, on courses in Rome and Darmstadt. His early works used serial techniques, and he also created tape compositions. Most of his works after 1959, however, were in graphic notation, allowing freedom of interpretation to performers, and in many cases also some freedom in the choice of instruments. He composed ballets and other stage works, and some of his concert works specify orchestral forces.

                    ABUR

Lohengrin. Opera in three acts by Wagner to his own libretto after the anonymous German epic (Weimar, 1850).

loin, lointain (Fr.). 'Distant'.

Lombardi alla prima crociata, I ('The Lombards at the First Crusade'). Opera in four acts by Verdi to a libretto by Temistocle Solera after Tommaso Grossi's poem (1826) (Milan, 1843); Verdi revised it as *Jérusalem* (1847).

Lombardy style. See SCOTCH SNAP.

London College of Music. British conservatory founded in 1887. See DEGREES AND DIPLOMAS.

Londonderry Air. Irish folk tune first published in the Petrie collection (1855). Several sets of words have been fitted to it: 'Would I were Erin's apple blossom' and 'Emer's Farewell', both by Alfred Perceval Graves, and 'Danny Boy' by F. E. Weatherly. Stanford used it in his *Irish Rhapsody* no. 1 and Grainger made several arrangements of it (as *Irish Tune from County Derry*).

London Overture, A. Orchestral work (1936) by Ireland; it was originally written for brass band (1934) under the title *Comedy Overture*, and one of its principal themes is said to have been inspired by a bus conductor's call of 'Piccadilly'.

'London' Symphonies ('Salomon' Symphonies). Haydn's last 12 symphonies, nos. 93–104 (1791–5), composed for the impresario Salomon and first performed during Haydn's visits in 1791–2 and 1794–5. The last, no. 104 in D major (1795), is known as the 'London' Symphony, or the 'Salomon' Symphony.

London Symphony, A. Vaughan Williams's second symphony; it was composed in 1912–13, revised substantially in 1920, and finally in 1933. It is not a programmatic work but it includes evocations of London life, such as Westminster chimes, a lavender-seller's cry, the jingle of hansom cabs, and the sounds of street musicians.

long. A note-value (¶) used in medieval and Renaissance music. See NOTATION, 2.

Long, Marguerite [Marie-Charlotte] (*b* Nîmes, 13 Nov. 1874; *d* Paris, 13 Feb. 1966). French pianist. She won a first prize at the Paris Conservatoire in 1891, then studied with Antonin Marmontel. She taught at the Conservatoire, 1906–40, and in 1920, after a long campaign, took over a senior class on the death of Louis Diémer. Among her pupils there, and at her own school which she opened in 1941, were Jean Doyen, Jacques Février, Gaby Casadesus, and Gabriel Tacchino. Her playing, coming mostly from the finger, knuckle, and wrist, was light and sparkling rather than powerful, and she gave first performances of Ravel's *Le Tombeau de Couperin* and G major Concerto. As a person, she roused strong emotions, for and against.   RN

   📖 C. TIMBRELL, *French Pianism: A Historical Perspective* (White Plains, NY, and London, 1992, enlarged 2/1999) · C. DUNOYER, *Marguerite Long: A Life in French Music* (Bloomington, IN, 1993)

long-playing record. See LP.

Lontano. Orchestral work (1967) by Ligeti.

lontano (It.). 'Distant'.

Loqueville, Richard (*d* Cambrai, 1418). French harpist, composer, and music tutor. In the early years of the 15th century he taught the choristers at Cambrai Cathedral, where his pupils included the young Guillaume Dufay. A few polyphonic songs, motets, and mass movements by him survive.   JM

Lord's Prayer. See PATER NOSTER.

Lorelei. The legendary figure who sings on a mountain by the Rhine, luring sailors to their death on the rocks below, has been the subject of several operas, including

an unfinished one by Mendelssohn to a libretto by Emanuel Geibel, dating from 1847 (the 'Ave Maria' is sometimes given in the concert hall); among others are those by Wallace (1860), Bruch (1863), and Catalani (1890).

Lortzing, (Gustav) Albert (*b* Berlin, 23 Oct. 1801; *d* Berlin, 21 Jan. 1851). German composer. He spent much of his early life touring with his family in a travelling opera company, where he found time to have occasional lessons and to begin composing for the stage as well as acting and singing. His first opera, *Ali Pascha von Janina* (1824)—written to his own text and reflecting the language of Mozart, to which he remained loyal—set the pattern of spoken dialogue opera. With *Die beiden Schützen* ('The Two Riflemen') and *Zar und Zimmermann* (both 1837) he made his reputation with works in his characteristic vein of light tunefulness (based on German popular song), expert stage sense, a touch of sentimentality in the drawing of character, and inventive handling of stage convention. His greatest success in this vein came with *Der Wildschütz* ('The Poacher', 1842), which adds a salting of satire to a rustic tale with echoes of Weber. In 1844 Lortzing became Kapellmeister in Leipzig, but he was forced to leave and encountered much difficulty in fending for his large family.

His next work, *Undine* (1845), was a magic opera that accommodates some Romantic gestures, including use of motif, to his by now tried operatic methods. In 1846 he moved to Vienna, where he strengthened his popularity with *Der Waffenschmied* ('The Armourer', 1846). When he attempted to capitalize on the revolutionary events of 1848 with *Regina*, however, he found the idea too subversive in uneasy times. He lost his post, but was called to Leipzig to supervise *Rolands Knappen* (1849), an impressive work which includes some original use of chromatic harmony. However, these and other novelties are usually incidental or decorative rather than representing a serious advance in his language. Similarly, his characterization did not greatly develop during his career but rested on the singer types of German musical theatre, handled with such skill and charm as to make a wide appeal in his day and since. His last work, *Die Opernprobe* (1851), satirizes some of the stage and operatic conventions he knew so well, especially the Italian recitative he disliked.

An appointment in Leipzig fell through, and in 1850 Lortzing moved to Berlin as conductor of a small theatre. There he and his family lived in poverty in spite of the frequent performance of his works, and he died, unable to afford a doctor, when about to be dismissed from even this modest post.   JW

Lost Chord, The. Song (1877) by Sullivan, a setting of a poem by Adelaide Anne Procter; composed in sorrow at his brother's death, it is regarded as the archetypal Victorian drawing-room ballad.

Lotti, Antonio (*b* Venice or Hanover, *c.*1667; *d* Venice, 5 Jan. 1740). Italian composer. He may have been born in Hanover, where his father was Kapellmeister, but by 1683 he was in Venice studying with Legrenzi. In 1689 he joined the choir of St Mark's, holding various organist's posts there from 1690 and becoming *maestro di cappella* in 1736. He wrote many operas for the Venetian stage and also for Dresden. He was one of the few composers of his time to be equally successful with opera and with contrapuntal sacred music in the neo-Palestrina style, some of which has remained in use. Lotti was an influential teacher whose pupils included Galuppi.   DA/ER

Loudon Symphony. See LAUDON SYMPHONY.

Louise. Opera in four acts by Charpentier to a libretto by the composer with assistance from Saint-Pol-Roux (Paris, 1900).

Louis Ferdinand, Prince of Prussia (*b* Friedrichsfelde, nr Berlin, 18 Nov. 1772; *d* Saalfeld, 13 Oct. 1806). German composer and pianist. The nephew of Frederick the Great, he showed early musical promise and, having proved himself on the battlefield by the age of 20, settled down to musical studies. He was taught by Dussek (who entered his service in 1804) and quickly acquired a considerable reputation as a pianist. Among his admirers was Beethoven, who dedicated the Fourth Piano Concerto to him. Louis Ferdinand's music, almost entirely for the piano, reflects his Romantic interests, and had an influence on Weber, who built the third book of his *Leyer und Schwert* songs round quotations of the prince's music. He was killed in a skirmish at Saalfeld before the battle of Jena.
                                          WT/JW

lourd, lourde (Fr.). 'Heavy'; *lourdement*, 'heavily'.

loure (Fr.). 1. A bagpipe used in 16th- and 17th-century Normandy.

2. A dance popular in the late 17th and early 18th centuries. It resembles the *gigue, but the speed is slower. It is characteristic in moderate triple time, with dotted and syncopated rhythms. There is a loure in the prologue to Lully's opera *Alceste*, but the best-known example is by Bach, in his fifth French Suite.

louré (Fr.). 1. (It.: *portato*). In string playing, a type of bowing where several notes are taken in the same direction, but slightly detached from one another.

2. See NOTES INÉGALES.

Lourié, Arthur (Vincent) (*b* St Petersburg, 2/14 May 1892; *d* Princeton, NJ, 12 Oct. 1966). Russian-born American composer. He studied at the St Petersburg Conservatory but disliked the formal teaching and turned to his own methods of composing; a prominent member of the *Futurist movement in Russia, he produced a number of experimental atonal vocal and piano pieces. In 1918 he was appointed commissar for music, but in 1922 he left for Berlin, where he was befriended by Busoni, and in 1924 arrived in Paris, where he first met Stravinsky, an acquaintance he was later to renew. He emigrated to the USA in 1941, taking American citizenship in 1947. Lourié was prolific, producing two operas, two symphonies, chamber music, piano pieces, songs, and a large number of sacred choral works which show some influence of Orthodox Russian liturgical music. In his later works he abandoned the atonality of his early years, preferring a modal style of writing, as typified in the *Sonata liturgica* (1928) for alto voices and chamber orchestra, and the *Concerto spirituale* (1929) for voices, solo piano, brass, double basses, and percussion.   JN

Love for Three Oranges, The (*Lyubov' k tryom apel'sinam*). Opera in a prologue and four acts by Prokofiev to his own libretto after Carlo Gozzi's play *L'amore delle tre melarance* (1761) adapted by Vsevolod Meyerhold, Vladimir Solov'yov, and Konstantin Vogak (Chicago, 1921, as *L'Amour des trois oranges*). Prokofiev arranged an orchestral suite from the score (1919, revised 1924).

Love in a Village. Comic opera in three acts by Arne to a libretto by Isaac Bickerstaff after Charles Johnson's *The Village Opera* (1729); it is a pasticcio of 42 items, of which Arne composed five, borrowed 13 from his earlier works and arranged the rest from several composers including C. F. Abel, Geminiani, and Galuppi (London, 1762).

Love Potion, The. See ELISIR D'AMORE, L'.

Love-Song Waltzes. See LIEBESLIEDERWALZER.

Low Countries. For all its inexactitude as a geographical and political designation, the term 'Low Countries' is particularly useful in music history, suggesting as it does a region with a relatively unified cultural identity while avoiding the matter of its complex history of changing national boundaries. Only in the 19th century were the territories of Belgium, Luxembourg, and the Netherlands finally established in their present form, and it would be misleading to apply these names anachronistically to the Low Countries as they existed, for example, during the 15th and 16th centuries when much of the area, including the northernmost part of France, was governed first by the Dukes of Burgundy and later absorbed into the Holy Roman Empire. Because of this political instability through the centuries, no term exists which adequately describes the regional identity of composers and musicians emanating from the Low Countries from the Middle Ages to the present day; such words as 'Burgundian', 'Franco-Flemish', 'Netherlandish', 'Dutch', and 'Walloon' are loaded with specific geographic and temporal implications and need to be used with caution if their precise meanings are to be respected.

1. To 1500; 2. The 16th century; 3. Religious diversity; 4. The 17th and 18th centuries; 5. The 19th and 20th centuries

1. To 1500

Little as we know about the development of music-making in the Low Countries before the 14th century, it does seem likely that foreign influences played an important part in shaping its initial course. Books of plainchant from the region contain the more or less international repertory of Gregorian chant, though as in most other parts of Europe this gradually acquired a distinctive 'dialect' as local variants emerged and new chants were added, in particular hymns, *sequences, and liturgical drama. Courtly song in the vernacular was also in widespread use by the 14th century, its development almost certainly stimulated by the *trouvère tradition of northern France, and a small number of monophonic Netherlandish songs have come down to us with their music intact.

There is little evidence of early polyphony in the Low Countries, the few motets which survive today again attesting to the influence of French models. If sources of actual music are scarce, however, documentary evidence suggests that music—and the arts in general—gradually won an important place in the civic life of the region as the textile trade brought increasing prosperity during the later Middle Ages; by the end of the 14th century, sophisticated music was being cultivated not only in churches and monastic communities but also by the nobility and wealthy educated class of the great weaving towns.

Although music has continued to occupy an important position in the cultural life of the Low Countries to the present day, there can be no doubt that the 14th and 15th centuries stand out as a true 'golden age'. During a period of almost 200 years the region nurtured an extraordinary dynasty of talented composers and musicians, the majority of them born and trained in the southern counties of Hainaut, Artois, Flanders, and Brabant—for which reason they are commonly described as being of 'Franco-Flemish' origin. While no simple reason can be offered for the initial rise of this movement, it is clear that choir schools, with their emphasis on theory and rigorous instruction, played an important part in maintaining a strong musical tradition. Equally significant was the acquisition of much of the Low Countries during the late 14th and 15th centuries by the dukes of Burgundy. With their sumptuously elaborate style of courtly life and sophisticated tastes, the dukes were liberal patrons of the arts and eagerly exploited the stock of native talent in their northern territories. Composers associated specifically with the Burgundian court during the 15th century include Tapissier, Binchois, Busnois, and Hayne van Ghizeghem.

As the reputation of Franco-Flemish composers strengthened, so the demand for composers trained in the region spread, and increasingly large numbers were attracted abroad. This tendency to migrate can be discerned as early as 1350, when the Liégeois composer Johannes Chiwagne—better known today as Ciconia—entered the circle of Pope Clement VI in Avignon, the first stage in a career which took him to most of the principal cities in northern Italy. Many others followed him: Dufay, for example, spent virtually all of his early career in Italy or at the court of Savoy; Ockeghem worked almost exclusively for the French royal chapel; Josquin enjoyed the patronage of the Italian nobility for almost 40 years.

Highly influential as these composers were abroad, however, experience of foreign styles played an equally important part in shaping their musical language, and ultimately that of Franco-Flemish music in general. By the end of his career, Ciconia had absorbed many Italianate features into his essentially French style, while in the early years of the 15th century Dufay encountered—and thoroughly digested—the richly triadic, consonant music of such Englishmen as Power and Dunstaple, imported to the Continent by the household chapels of the English nobility during their campaigns in France and northern Italy. Through this process of cultural cross-fertilization the music of Franco-Flemish composers gradually acquired a broadly cosmopolitan flavour which, together with its high level of craftsmanship, certainly helped to widen its international appeal.

Throughout the 15th and early 16th centuries, composers from the Low Countries, whatever their place of employment, were particularly recognized for their ability to write skilful, elegant counterpoint. At first the emphasis was on fluidity and expansiveness, heard to its best advantage in the works of Dufay, Binchois, and Ockeghem; but as the 15th century progressed, Franco-Flemish composers gradually established a new musical idiom in which audible unity rather than variety was the goal, achieved through the use of imitation and canon. In many cases compositions were also carefully planned to reflect geometric or arithmetic proportions or significant numbers from Christian theology in their design, adding a mystical or symbolic dimension: music to stimulate not only the ear but also the intellect.

As well as contributing significantly to the development of musical style throughout Europe, Franco-Flemish composers played a major part in the evolution of the three principal forms of the early Renaissance: *mass, *motet, and *chanson. Through their efforts isorhythm was gradually abandoned in favour of less rigid methods of incorporating plainchant into polyphony—free cantus firmus, for example, or paraphrase. They were the first to compose masses based on secular models, whether single lines extracted from polyphonic chansons or the tunes of popular songs, and the first to write *parody masses. The chanson, though changing less rapidly, had by the end of the 15th century shed its medieval exterior as the *formes fixes* were replaced by looser, less artificial verse, allowing scope for greater variety of musical setting.

But above all it was the motet which attracted a spirit of exploration, particularly evident in the works of such men as Josquin and Isaac whose careers brought them into contact with Italian humanism. By rejecting the traditional backbone of a plainchant cantus firmus and concentrating entirely on the syntactical structure and word-rhythms of the text, their motets acquired a new declamatory, rhetorical manner—one of heightened naturalism—which has been valued in Western music ever since.

2. The 16th century

By 1500 the works of composers from the Low Countries virtually dominated music-making throughout Europe. Although the ensuing century saw the emergence (or, in the cases of France and Italy, resurgence) of more obviously national schools of composition, all were heavily indebted to the Franco-Flemish idiom, accepting to a large extent the structural norm of a contrapuntal texture unified by imitation and sometimes canon. Even with this rise of native talent, however, the demand for musicians trained in the north was slow to wane, and many of the leading 16th-century composers were émigrés of the Low Countries: Willaert in Venice; Cipriano de Rore in Parma and Venice; Vaet at the Habsburg court; Philippe de Monte variously in Naples, London, Vienna, and Prague; and,

above all others, Lassus who, in spite of a career spent largely at Munich, was universally admired and widely influential.

None the less, the 16th century was essentially a period of decline in the Low Countries after its ascendancy in the early Renaissance. A number of political and religious factors contributed to this downward course: the merging of the Duchy of Burgundy with the Kingdom of Spain and the Holy Roman Empire to form a single political unit under Charles V; a drop in economic prosperity throughout the region, resulting in a decline in the quality of education; above all, the divisive effect of religious dissension between Protestant sympathizers in the north and Catholics in the south. Although former standards were for a while upheld—by Clemens non Papa and the two principal imperial composers, Gombert and Crecquillon, for example—musical life in the Low Countries lost much of its former splendour and by the end of the 16th century appears peripheral beside the lively culture of Italy.

The rise of vernacular song in the Low Countries during the 16th century can be seen as evidence of a new spirit of regional identity, in contrast to the international outlook of the French-speaking Burgundian court. This trend can already be perceived in the output of Jacob Obrecht, one of the few late 15th-century composers associated with the area north of the Burgundian ambit and the first to write a substantial corpus of Dutch songs. In 1540 Symon Cock of Antwerp printed a collection of *souterliedekens* (translations of the psalms into Dutch verse, set to popular or folk melodies); 11 years later the Antwerp publisher Tylman Susato issued the first of his *Musyck boexken* ('music booklets'), a series devoted to Flemish songs and dances and polyphonic arrangements of the *souterliedekens* by Clemens non Papa and Gherardus Mes. Perhaps most patriotic of all in tone, however, was the *Neder-landtsche gedenck-clanck* of Adriaen Valerius, published posthumously in 1626: a historical account of the dispute between the Netherlands and Spain during the mid-16th century, illustrated by Dutch popular songs with lute and cittern accompaniment and including the present Dutch national anthem.

3. Religious diversity

Following decades of conflict, the northern counties of the Low Countries, with their Protestant outlook, finally won a degree of political autonomy from the Catholic south through the establishment of the 'Republic of the Seven United Provinces' in 1588, a claim for independence fully realized only in 1648 with the signing of the Treaty of Westphalia at the end of the

Thirty Years War. The new religion of the north followed Calvinist principles, Dutch translations of the Genevan Psalter having been adopted by the church in 1568, though the original French texts of Clément Marot and Théodore de Bèze were used locally, and were set to polyphony by Sweelinck in a vast cycle published between 1604 and 1621.

The use of the organ to accompany the singing of psalms was banned by the Dutch Reformed Church in 1572, a prohibition which remained in force until 1680 in spite of the eloquent arguments put forward by Constantijn Huygens, one of the leading musicians and intellectuals of the early 17th century. Instead, the organ was used as a solo instrument, playing before and after church services, at festivals, and in weekday recitals. Sweelinck's important output of keyboard works, written for the Oude Kerk in Amsterdam and one of the chief peaks in the tradition, was in fact composed to satisfy the requirements of the civic authorities rather than the Church. Later developments in organ music and the manufacture of organs can similarly be attributed to municipal pride and a state of rivalry between town councils.

In the southern Low Countries the sense of tradition was at first stronger. Under the rule of the Spanish Habsburgs Roman Catholicism remained the official religion, flirtation with Calvinism being discouraged by the threat of the Inquisition; only during 1566 was this state of repression temporarily relaxed, but quickly reinstated when the true extent of popular support for the Protestant faith became fully apparent. Soon after, the singing of metrical psalms again became an act of heresy and punishable by death. During this time the royal chapel at Brussels emerged as an important centre for Latin church music, especially in the early 17th century under the leadership of Gery de Ghersem (c.1573–1630), whose colleagues included two Catholic refugees from England, Peter Philips and John Bull, as well as the organist Peeter Cornet. As in the United Provinces, keyboard music flourished and the region became an important centre for the development of virginals and harpsichord manufacture, especially in the hands of the Ruckers family of Antwerp, whose activities can be traced back to 1579.

4. The 17th and 18th centuries

The 17th and 18th centuries witnessed a further decline in the musical traditions of the Low Countries as foreign music—especially French and Italian—gradually saturated the market. Courtly patronage during these centuries was on the whole insubstantial, the impetus for musical activity lying with the church and above all the bourgeoisie. Particularly important was the rise of *collegia musica* (amateur music societies devoted to the performance of vocal and instrumental works, often aided by professional civic musicians), which sprang up throughout the Low Countries during the early 17th century. Organ recitals remained common, while the popularity of another civic instrument, the carillon, also grew rapidly at this time.

Local composers such as Jacob van Eyck of Utrecht—who is also remembered today for his works for solo recorder based on tunes popular in the Netherlands at this time—soon provided the basis of a repertory for the carillon which reached its peak in the virtuoso contrapuntal showpieces of the Louvain composer Matthias van den Gheyn. But if the carillon repertory of the Low Countries evinces a strong regional identity, the general trend was towards a more cosmopolitan style, discernible in the works of Constantijn Huygens, whose contact with Monteverdi in Venice assisted the introduction of the monodic style to the Netherlands.

The presence of the Fiocco family (Pietro Antonio, c.1650–1714; Jean-Joseph, 1686–1746; and Joseph-Hector, 1703–41) at the royal court and chapel in Brussels from the 1680s to 1744 is symptomatic of the growing taste for Italian music, while the Amsterdam-based publishing firm of Estienne Roger and Le Cène, with its pioneering use of the engraving process, thrived on editions of works by Corelli, Vivaldi, Albinoni, and Locatelli (the last-named was a resident of Amsterdam from 1729 until his death 35 years later). Ironically, two of the most talented composers born in the Low Countries during this period, Henry Du Mont and Jean Baptiste Loeillet, worked exclusively abroad, in Paris and London respectively.

Opera was late to arrive in the Low Countries, though once established it quickly gained widespread popularity. Brussels and Amsterdam were the principal early centres, with productions dating from the early 1680s, but from the start their repertories were almost exclusively imported, primarily from France and Italy, and translations into Dutch or Flemish were rare. Few local composers turned their hands to opera, the one major exception, Grétry, writing largely for Parisian audiences, who regarded him as a leader of French comic opera. The early 18th century also saw the rise of public concerts, especially in Amsterdam and The Hague; here as in the theatre foreign music predominated, and the one major local composer of the period, Gossec, again left the region to work almost exclusively in Paris, where he became one of the most popular composers during the Revolution.

5. The 19th and 20th centuries

In 1815, following the Napoleonic wars, north and south were brought together to form the 'United Kingdom of the Netherlands'; however, the union was dissolved in 1830, creating the kingdoms of Belgium and the Netherlands as they exist today. Foreign music continued to exert a strong influence throughout the Low Countries during the 19th century, though a certain degree of nationalist fervour can be detected in the works of Peter Benoit, who was instrumental in raising the standards of Flemish music to a more international level. At the Brussels Conservatory, founded in 1832, François-Joseph Fétis provided another form of leadership through his influential work as a teacher, critic, theorist, and musicologist.

Important Belgian composers of the period were César Franck, Guillaume Lekeu, and the violinist-composers Henri Vieuxtemps and Eugène Ysaÿe. In the Netherlands the impact of German music was especially profound, evident in the works of Johannes Verhulst (1816–91), the leading Dutch composer of the mid-19th century, though several of his younger contemporaries aimed at a more self-consciously Dutch idiom, especially through the use of folk material. Musical life in Amsterdam acquired a new sense of focus with the inauguration of the Concertgebouw—one of the finest concert halls in northern Europe—in 1888, and the establishment of a permanent orchestra there in the same year.

During the 20th century the Low Countries once again became an important centre of European music. Among the most celebrated 20th-century Belgian composers were Paul Gilson (1865–1942), Jean Absil, Marcel Poot (1901–88), Flor Peeters, Karel Goeyvaerts, Henri Pousseur, and Lucien Goethals (b 1931), while in the Netherlands Willem Pijper, Henk Badings, Ton de Leeuw, Louis Andriessen, and Tristan Keuris won widespread acclaim. The region was also the site of notable developments in electroacoustic music. In 1958 Pousseur established the first Belgian electronic music studio, APELAC, which became part of the Centre de Recherches Musicales de Wallonie founded in Liège in 1970, also under Pousseur's direction. Its counterpart in the Flemish area, the Institut voor Psychoacoustica en Electronische Muziek (IPEM) in Ghent, was set up in 1962 by Louis de Meester (1904–87).

There was a revival of interest in both the organ and the carillon; in addition, the region became a centre for music education, and was especially active in the rediscovery of early music. In the Netherlands, ethnomusicology attracted much scholarly attention, while the creation of the Donemus Foundation in 1947 greatly assisted the promotion of Dutch music. The Holland Festival (centred on Amsterdam) and, in Belgium, the Flanders Festival, are two of the outstanding events of the European cultural year, standing as eloquent testimony to the healthy state of music in the Low Countries at the beginning of the 21st century.   JM

📖 L. SAMAMA, F. ABRAHAMS, and M. DE REUTER, *Music in the Netherlands* (The Hague, 1985) · F. NOSKE, *Music Bridging Divided Religions: The Motet in the Seventeenth-Century Dutch Republic* (Wilhelmshaven, 1989) · R. A. RASCH, 'The Dutch Republic', *The Late Baroque Era*, ed. G. J. Buelow, Man and Music/Music and Society (London, 1993), 393–410

Lowe & Brydone. English firm of typesetters. See PRINTING AND PUBLISHING OF MUSIC, 6.

lower mordent. See MORDENT.

Lower Rhine Festival. German choral festival established in 1817. See FESTIVALS, 2.

Lowland pipe [Border pipes]. Bellows-blown *bagpipe of Scotland, sounding similar to, but rather quieter than, the Highland pipe.

LP [long-playing record]. A type of long-playing microgroove record pressed in vinyl. It was introduced by Columbia in the USA in 1948, after an unsuccessful attempt in 1931. Decca produced the first British LPs in 1950. More prone to wear than the shellac records they replaced, they required the use of new reproducing equipment with a lightweight pickup arm. At first they were issued in 10- and 12-inch formats (25 and 30 cm), used respectively for shorter and longer repertory, but 10-inch LPs quickly died out.

See also RECORDING AND REPRODUCTION.   LF

Lualdi, Adriano (b Larino, Campobasso, 22 March 1885; d Milan, 8 Jan. 1971). Italian composer. He studied in Rome and Venice, and in his early career divided his time between composition, conducting, and writing music criticism. His operas, representative of one strand of Italian modernism, were much feted in the 1930s, during which time he served as a member of the Fascist parliament; they have since fallen into neglect. He also served in several important administrative posts, both before and after the Fascist period.   RP

Lübeck, Vincent (b Paddingbüttel, nr Bremen, 1654; d Hamburg, 9 Feb. 1740). German composer, organist, and teacher. His first appointment, at the age of 20, was at Stade, where he remained for nearly 30 years. In 1702 he became organist at St Nicolai, Hamburg, where he spent the rest of his working life. His few known compositions include three cantatas, one of which, *Willkommen süsser Bräutigam* ('Welcome, Sweet Bridegroom'), for Christmas, remains popular in Germany, and nine large works for organ—preludes, fugues, toccatas, and chorale settings—of a quality to rival those of Buxtehude.   DA/BS

Lucia di Lammermoor ('Lucy of Lammermoor'). Opera in three acts by Donizetti to a libretto by Salvadore Cammarano after Walter Scott's novel *The Bride of Lammermoor* (1819) (Naples, 1835).

Lucier, Alvin (Augustus) (*b* Nashua, NH, 14 May 1931). American composer. He studied at Yale (1950–6), Brandeis (1958–60), and Darmstadt (1961), and has taught at Brandeis (1962–70) and Wesleyan University (from 1970). He was a member, with Robert Ashley and others, of the Sonic Arts Union (1966–73), performing live electronic pieces that included his own *Vespers* (1968) for people in the dark using echo-location devices to explore the acoustic environment. Later works have also used electronics in live performance, often involving interaction between slow electronic glissandos and instrumental sounds.   PG

Lucio Silla ('Lucius Sulla'). Opera in three acts by Mozart to a libretto by Giovanni De Gamerra (Milan, 1772). Anfossi (1774) and J. C. Bach (1775) also wrote operas on the subject.

Lucrezia Borgia. Opera in a prologue and two acts by Donizetti to a libretto by Felice Romani after Victor Hugo's play *Lucrèce Borgia* (1833) (Milan, 1833).

Ludford, Nicholas (*b c*.1485; *d* ?London, *c*.1557). English composer. He was a singer at the collegiate chapel of St Stephen, Westminster, until its dissolution by Henry VIII in 1547. His output included at least 17 masses—more than by any other English composer—of which three are now lost and three survive incomplete. Seven of them form a unique cycle of *Lady masses for three voices, written in a manuscript that once belonged to Henry VIII and Catherine of Aragon. Like his more famous contemporary, John Taverner, Ludford wrote mostly in an idiom that emphasized abstract grandeur and exuberance of florid detail, rather than humanistic expressiveness or concision.   JM

Ludus tonalis ('The Play of Notes'). Piano studies (1942) by Hindemith; consisting of a prelude, 12 fugues with 11 interludes, and a postlude (an inverted version of the prelude), they are studies in counterpoint, tonal organization, and piano technique.

Luening, Otto (Clarence) (*b* Milwaukee, WI, 15 June 1900; *d* New York, 2 Sept. 1996). American composer and teacher. He studied in Munich (1915–17) and in Zürich (1919–20), where he had private lessons with Philipp Jarnach and Busoni. In 1920 he moved to Chicago and embarked on a career as a teacher, notably at Columbia University (1944–68), where in 1952 he and Vladimir Ussachevsky set up the studio that became the Columbia–Princeton Electronic Music Center. During the 1950s and 60s he wrote electronic pieces, sometimes in collaboration with Ussachevsky, but his output was large and diverse, and included the opera *Evangeline*, orchestral works, string quartets, and other chamber pieces.   PG

Luftpause (Ger., 'air break'). A pause for breath in wind playing or singing, often indicated by a V-shaped mark above the staff. See also ATEMPAUSE.

Luisa Miller. Opera in three acts by Verdi to a libretto by Salvadore Cammarano after Friedrich von Schiller's play *Kabale und Liebe* (1784) (Naples, 1849).

lullaby. See BERCEUSE.

Lully, Jean-Baptiste [Lulli, Giovanni Battista] (*b* Florence, 29 Nov. 1632; *d* Paris, 22 March 1687). French composer of Italian origin. The son of a miller, he had only simple instruction in music during childhood, from a monk who taught him the guitar and the violin. He was taken to France in 1646 as *garçon de chambre* and Italian teacher to Louis XIV's cousin, Anne-Marie-Louise d'Orléans. At her court in the Tuileries his musical talents soon attracted attention and he became famous for his skill as a violinist; he probably also studied with the organists Nicolas Métru, Nicolas Gigault, and François Roberday.

By the time, in 1652, that Mademoiselle d'Orléans was exiled from Paris because of her sympathy with the Fronde uprising Lully had made an impression at court for his dancing, and the next year he was taken into court employment as *compositeur de la musique instrumentale* to Louis XIV, a position that involved writing music for the court ballets and dancing in them, bringing him into close contact with Louis XIV. He was admitted to the Vingt-Quatre Violons du Roi but found the band lacking in discipline and obtained permission to set up his own Petits Violons of 16 players. From 1656 to 1664 he trained this band, which became widely famous for its precision.

Meanwhile Lully was becoming known as a composer, especially of ballet. In 1660 his ballet *entrées* for Cavalli's *Xerse* and *Ercole amante* attracted more attention than the operas themselves, and the following year Louis made him *surintendant de la musique de la chambre du roi*. He became a naturalized French citizen, and a further mark of the royal favour, his appointment as *maître de musique* to the royal family, enabled him to marry the daughter of the composer Michel Lambert. They had three sons, all of whom became musicians, and three daughters. Lully continued to compose ballets and in 1664 he wrote *entrées* for a revival of Pierre Corneille's *Oedipe* and his first *comédie-ballet* in partnership with Molière (in some of which he sang), a collaboration which was to culminate in 1670 with *Le*

Bourgeois gentilhomme, a minor masterpiece of witty words with music to match.

By the end of the 1660s the idea of opera was growing increasingly popular in Paris. A privilege to establish opera academies in France was granted in 1679 to Pierre Perrin; in spite of Lully's initial scorn at the idea of large-scale dramatic works sung in French he was quick to take advantage of Perrin's fall from favour at court and bought his privilege in 1672. Soon after, and following some vicious intriguing, he was granted the right to compose and produce opera at the Académie Royale de Musique, a monopoly he held for the rest of his life. He went into partnership with the designer Carlo Vigarani, obtained premises in a tennis court, and staged the first *tragédie en musique*: *Cadmus et Hermione*, produced in 1673. The libretto was provided by Philippe Quinault, who also wrote texts for ten further *tragédies* for Lully in spite of the composer's constant criticisms and cuts. Louis then provided him with a theatre, at the Palais Royal. Lully stifled any potential rivals by imposing arbitrary and often crippling limits, as his privilege entitled him to do, on any other theatrical productions: for example, no one was permitted to use dancers, more than two voices, or more than six violins.

Lully was unscrupulous in his greed and ambition and capable of ruthless plotting against his rivals. He made numerous enemies. Royal favour saved him from prosecution for homosexual practices, though even Louis reprimanded him on this account in 1685. In the 1680s the court became more sober and restrained in its entertainments, and Lully turned his attention to church music. It was during a performance of his monumental *Te Deum* before the king in 1687 that Lully struck his foot with his conducting cane (it was normal practice to keep time by striking it upon the floor), and later that year he died after the foot had turned gangrenous. He left a considerable fortune, including five houses in Paris and the monopoly of the performing rights to his music. His greater legacy was a series of traditions that died hard and transformed the face of French music.

Lully's central achievement was the creation of French opera, and with it he established a style tradition that continued to dominate French musical theatre for more than a century—indeed his operas were unique at this time in retaining a place in the performing repertory for several decades after his death. They inspired several controversies among Paris intellectuals (French v. Italian; Lully v. Rameau; French *tragédie* v. Italian comedy; even Gluck v. Piccinni was affected by his shade).

Lully brought to the composition of lyric drama in French an acute understanding of French declamatory traditions and the non-metric structure of the language, devising a new musical style to accommodate them, one in which a uniquely flexible form of recitative (much slower-moving than its Italian counterpart, and unfettered by rhythmic constraints) could give full value to the words and their sense. He devised too a simple form of *air*, often using a dance rhythm, that could capture faithfully the nature of the sentiment expressed. He also created, using chorus and dancers, spectacular and effective divertissements, often with picturesque effects (tempests, sleep scenes, the underworld, for example). His dances, which abound in the operas, are often highly attractive melodically, with unusual rhythmic structures; and his five-part orchestration (even if he may have engaged assistants to fill in the *parties de remplissage*, the inner voices) is rich and resourceful.

Lully's musical gifts as such have sometimes been questioned, but recent revivals of his operas (among them *Atys*, *Alceste*, and *Armide*) have shown them to be more appealing in the theatre than the printed page seems to promise. Lully's works for the church consist mainly of *grands motets* (among which the *Miserere* of 1663 and the 1677 *Te Deum* are the most famous and admired), which have a grandeur and formal solemnity appropriate to the context for which they were composed.   DA/SS

📖 R. M. Isherwood, *Music in the Service of the King: France in the Seventeenth Century* (Ithaca, NY, 1973) · J. H. Heyer and others (eds.), *Jean-Baptiste Lully and the Music of the French Baroque: Essays in Honor of James R. Anthony* (Cambridge, 1989) · J. R. Anthony, *French Baroque Music from Beaujoyeulx to Rameau* (Portland, OR, enlarged 3/1997)

Lulu. Opera in a prologue and three acts by Berg to his own libretto after Frank Wedekind's plays *Erdgeist* and *Die Büchse der Pandora* (Acts I and II, Zürich, 1937); Berg died before the final act was finished and it was completed by Friedrich Cerha (Paris, 1979).

Lumsdaine, David (*b* Sydney, 31 Oct. 1931). British composer. He studied at the New South Wales Conservatorium and at Sydney University, and then in London with Lennox Berkeley at the RAM and with Mátyás Seiber privately. He was appointed lecturer in music at Durham University in 1970 and senior lecturer at King's College, London, in 1981, retiring in 1993. Two impressive early works—*Annotations of Auschwitz* (1964) and *Easter Fresco* (1966)—introduced a style of strong gestures and firmly directed argument. Later compositions include meditations on Bach and on the natural world.   PG

lungo, lunga (It.). 'Long'; *lunga pausa*, 'long rest'.

Luonnotar. Tone-poem, op. 70 (1913), by Sibelius for soprano and orchestra; it is a setting of words from the *Kalevala* telling of the creation of the world.

Lupi, Johannes (*b* ?Cambrai, *c.*1506; *d* Cambrai, 20 Dec. 1539). Franco-Flemish composer. His career was spent mainly at Cambrai Cathedral, where he served as choirboy, singer, and, from 1527, choirmaster—a post from which he was almost dismissed on several occasions because of his lack of control over the choirboys. His surviving works include two masses, motets, and chansons; they are notable for their high quality.

JM

Lupo. Jewish family of string players active in England in the 16th and 17th centuries. Three musicians of this name became instrumentalists at Henry VIII's court in about 1540; they were recruited in Venice, and are described as being 'de Milano'. The most important member of the family, **Thomas Lupo** (*bapt.* 7 Aug. 1571; *d* ?Dec. 1627), like his father Joseph Lupo (*d* 1616) and grandfather Ambrose Lupo (*d* 1591), was a member of the court string consort. In 1619 he received a royal warrant as 'composer for our violins'; his music for violin consort, much of which would have been created for dancing and masques, must either survive anonymously or be lost. He was also an important composer of music for viol consort in the tradition of Gibbons and Coprario, and wrote some motets and secular songs.

JM

lur (Swed.). 1. A Scandinavian wooden *alphorn covered with a spiral of bark and used by herdsmen.

2. A long bronze horn of the 10th–6th centuries BC. Large numbers of *lurs* have been discovered in Danish peat bogs since 1797. Most of them had been deposited in pairs in what were lakes at the time, presumably in the course of some ritual. Each *lur* of a pair produces much the same pitch, and each is coiled in a double curve in the opposite direction to its fellow so that the resemblance is to a pair of great oxhorns. Later examples have a trombone-like mouthpiece, and some Danish composers have written for them.

JMo

lusingando (It.). 'Flattering', 'coaxing'. Debussy misspelt it 'lusigando'.

lustig (Ger.). 'Merry', 'cheerful'; *Lustspiel*, 'comedy'.

Lustigen Weiber von Windsor, Die ('The Merry Wives of Windsor'). Opera in three acts by Nicolai to a libretto by Salomon Hermann Mosenthal after Shakespeare's play (?*c.*1597) (Berlin, 1849).

Lustige Witwe, Die ('The Merry Widow'). Operetta in three acts by Lehár to a libretto by Victor Léon and Leo Stein after Henri Meilhac's *L'Attaché d'ambassade* (Vienna, 1905).

lute (Fr.: *luth*; Ger.: *Laute*; It.: *liuto*; Sp.: *laùd*). A plucked string instrument with a large half-pear body, frets, and a pegbox turned back at a right angle from the neck. In instrument classification any stringed instrument with a resonator and a neck, whether plucked or bowed, is categorized as a lute (see INSTRUMENTS, CLASSIFICATION OF).

The medieval lute came from the Arabic-speaking world in the 13th century, deriving both its form and its name from the Arabic *al *'ūd*, which was introduced to Europe during the Moorish conquest and occupation of Spain (711–1492). The vaulted back was built up from thin staves of wood, and a tracery-filled soundhole was usually carved integrally with the belly. Gut frets were tied round the neck so that all the notes would have the ring of an open string rather than being partly muted by the flesh of the finger on the fingerboard. The early lute was played with a plectrum and had four double courses of strings; during the 15th century a fifth course was added.

By 1500 the lute had acquired a more elaborate musical role and was plucked with the fingers so that it could play polyphonically and with more complex chords, though the plectrum also continued to be used for some time. A sixth course was added, the top course or *chanterelle* often single, the others in pairs, with the three lowest courses tuned in octaves. This was necessary because thick plain gut strings are somewhat dull in tone, and the octave pair gave a brighter ring. Covered strings, with an overlay of thin wire, did not become available until the mid-1600s.

Music for the lute was written in *tablature, indicating which strings were to be stopped on which frets, with the rhythm noted above. Besides being much easier to learn to read than staff notation, tablature has the extra advantage that, provided the intervals between the strings remain constant, the music will come out the same no matter what size of lute is being used (though transposed to suit different vocal or instrumental ranges). It also allows the easy use of different tunings. Folk and jazz guitarists use similar tablature.

The golden age of the lute, when it was regarded as the 'queen of instruments all', was the 16th and early 17th centuries. The *lute-song was then one of the leading musical genres, and vast numbers of lute solos were written. Many lute tutors were also compiled. Larger forms of lute were developed for continuo playing and accompaniment from about 1600, usually with some extra courses. The *archlute and the *chitarrone or *theorbo had, in addition to the strings on the fingerboard, open bass strings on an extended neck with a second pegbox. By the 18th century composers in Germany and Bohemia were writing music for 13-course lutes. Treble lutes also existed but seem to have been little used save for the smallest, which merged with the *mandolino* (see MANDORE; MANDOLIN).

The basic tuning for the six-course lute has the following intervals, from the bottom up: 4th–4th–3rd–4th–4th. The most common tunings were either in A (*A–d–g–b–e'–a'*) or in G (*G–c–f–a–d'–g'*); this basic tuning became known as *vieil ton*. Many variant tunings were used, especially ones where the lowest one, two, or three courses were lowered to give drone-like 5ths and 4ths. A seven-course lute in the late 15th century lowered the compass of the bass by another 4th, but on later lutes with more than six courses the open bass courses were usually tuned diatonically downwards.

The European lute ceased to be used at the end of the 18th century, until Arnold Dolmetsch led its revival in the 1890s. The *'ūd* still survives over all the Arab world, where it is used as a solo instrument and for accompanying song, though it no longer has frets. It has its own variants, all still plectrum-played, in the areas of Europe once dominated by the Ottoman Empire. The *cobza* is an important member of Romanian traditional ensembles, as is the *laouto* in Greece and Crete, though the latter has been supplanted in urban music by the bouzouki.   RPA

📖 I. HARWOOD and M. PRYNNE, *A Brief History of the Lute* (Richmond, 1975) · D. POULTON, 'The lute in Christian Spain', *Lute Society Journal*, 19 (1977), 34–49 · L. P. GRIJP and W. MOOK (eds.), *Proceedings of the International Lute Symposium* (Utrecht, 1988) · B. BADLEY, 'The *oud*', *Songlines*, 5 (1999), 42–8 · D. A. SMITH, *History of the Lute from Antiquity to the Renaissance* (forthcoming)

lute-song. The accompanied song or ayre of the late 16th and early 17th centuries is peculiar to England. Although it is similar to the French *air de cour*, its inception (unlike that of its counterpart, the English madrigal) was not dependent on continental influences—indeed, manuscript sources show the independent and continued existence of the form from the 1560s. The genre is related to the native mid-16th-century partsong and near contemporary consort song. The partsong is the forerunner of the simple or 'light' ayre with its hymn-like melody and homorhythmic texture, whereas the consort song prefigures the more elaborate and contrapuntal ayres of John Dowland, John Daniel, and Philip Rosseter. In the lute-song the vocal line—mostly solo but sometimes duet—is dominant, unlike in the partsong and consort song.

The genre flourished most in the period 1597–1622, when the printed books of ayres appeared. These were all similar in size and format, following the model of Dowland's *The First Booke of Songes or Ayres of Fowre Parts with Tableture for the Lute* (1597), its published format confirming as it were a homogeneous movement. During this period over 600 songs were published, of which a third were provided with partsong arrangements so that 'all the parts together, or either of them severally may be sung to the Lute, Orpherian or Viol de gambo' (Dowland, 1597).

In contrast to the madrigal, the lute-song is generally strophic and musically concise. The musical structure is often directly related to the poetic form without reproducing inner details. Moreover, the vocal line usually attempts to embody the mood and content of the poem it sets. In most songs continuity is largely dependent on sectional repetition, the commonest form being ABB. Campion, exceptionally, likes to repeat the first strain, thus AABB. The musical styles of Dowland, Morley, Daniel, and Francis Pilkington are clearly more elaborate than those of Campion, Thomas Ford, and Robert Jones (ii). But all lute-song composers, including such theatre composers as Alfonso Ferrabosco (ii), John Coprario, and Philip Rosseter, mix elaborate 'serious' styles with simple melodic and chordal types.

Lute-song composers appear more discerning than madrigal composers in their treatment of texts, for the most part (though by no means always) eschewing mannerism and affectation. Moralizing and serious subjects contrast with amorous and light 'conceits'. Most of the poetry set, like madrigal verse, is anonymous. Campion is exceptional in setting only his own poetry, which was also used by his contemporaries. Among the better-known poets chosen by lute-song composers were Nicholas Breton, Fulke Greville, Ben Jonson, John Donne, Samuel Daniel, and Philip Sidney.

The lute-song lost its identity when the lute was replaced by the lyra viol, and as the declamatory continuo song of the Baroque era displaced the simple English Renaissance ayre. Though a miniature genre and comparatively short-lived in its original form, the lute-song has achieved a prominent place in England's musical heritage.   CRW

Lutheran church music. Lutheranism possesses a rich musical tradition, the breadth of which may traced to its founder's own love of music and his deeply pastoral approach to the question of its role in a reformed liturgy. Martin Luther (*b* Eisleben, 10 Nov. 1483; *d* Eisleben, 18 Feb. 1546) was an admirer of Josquin's polyphony and believed that services should continue to be celebrated in Latin where the language was understood. At the same time he advocated the use of the vernacular as a means of imparting the Word of

God, notably through the medium of congregational hymnody. These ideals are embodied in his two formularies for the Eucharist: the Latin *Formula missae* (1523), which removed the theology of sacrifice from the pre-Tridentine Roman Mass but retained most of its sung portions supplemented by German hymnody; and the *Deutsche Messe* (1526), a much simpler order replacing much of the ordinary with German hymns, some of which were chorales paraphrasing their Latin counterparts. Never imposed uniformly in Germany and the Nordic countries, these formularies were applied flexibly to the point of total conflation, resulting by the end of the 16th century in the emergence of bilingual celebrations of the Sunday Eucharist (*Hauptgottesdienst*), a process mirrored in the parallel transformation of Roman Vespers into Lutheran *Vespergottesdienst*.

The types of music employed in early Lutheran worship were similarly diverse and continuous with the Roman Catholic past. The music used in a single service could range from Latin and vernacular plainchant or imitative polyphony to chorales and instrumental music. Such Lutheran composers as Schütz and Michael Praetorius fully kept pace with the technical innovations of their Catholic colleagues in Italy, composing works in the Venetian polychoral idiom and adopting continuo-based monody, while also creating distinctly Lutheran repertories. Out of the Renaissance tradition of polyphonic gospels, for example, emerged the repertory of Lutheran Passions and *historiae* to which Schütz and J. S. Bach made important contributions. Chorales provided composers with particularly rich material for further elaboration, beginning with the polyphonic settings of Johann Walter's *Geystliches gesangk Buchleyn* (1524) and continuing in such concerted and instrumental forms as the *cantata and the *chorale prelude.

The flexibility allowed in practice by Orthodox Lutheranism's consignment of liturgy and its music to the category of 'adiaphora' (i.e. matters not explicitly defined as essential for salvation in such repositories of doctrine as the *Book of Concord*, 1580) ultimately left the tradition vulnerable to those indifferent or actively hostile to its more elaborate elements. Plainchant and other relics of Roman Catholic worship gradually disappeared during the 17th and 18th centuries as Calvinism subtly influenced the form and content of Lutheran church music. The subjective spirituality of Pietism transformed the chorale and promoted disregard for ritualized worship, a tendency that only increased during the Enlightenment. Renewed interest in earlier layers of the tradition during the 19th century was marked by the study, imitation, and revival in performance of works by J. S. Bach and others. The

restoration of Lutheran worship and music continued well into the 20th century, during which Lutheranism fully engaged with such ecumenical phenomena as the liturgical and pastoral music movements.   ALi

R. A. LEAVER, 'The Lutheran Reformation', *The Renaissance: From the 1470s to the End of the 16th Century*, ed. I. Fenlon, Man and Music/Music and Society (London, 1989), 263–85 · G. WEBBER, *North German Church Music in the Age of Buxtehude* (Oxford, 1996)

luthier (Fr., from *luth*, 'lute'; Ger.: *Lautenmacher*). Originally a maker of stringed instruments (lutes, harps, viols, etc.) but later particularly of instruments of the violin family.

Lutosławski, Witold (*b* Warsaw, 25 Jan. 1913; *d* Warsaw, 7 Feb. 1994). Polish composer and conductor. He studied composition and the piano but was prevented by World War II from studying in Paris. During the war he eked out a living as a café pianist (*Variations on a Theme by Paganini* for two pianos, 1941) with his fellow-composer Panufnik. After the war he completed his first major orchestral work, the First Symphony (1941–7), whose concept and language owed much to Bartók, Roussel, and Prokofiev. When it was inexplicably banned by the Stalinist authorities in 1949, Lutosławski tried to keep a low profile, complying like many others with mass songs and small-scale occasional pieces. Nevertheless his folk-based works of the early 1950s, such as his music for children, the *Tryptyk śląski* ('Silesian Triptych', 1951), and, most notably, the Baroque-influenced Concerto for Orchestra (1954), are acknowledged highlights of the period of *socialist realism in Poland.

With the cultural thaw initiated by the Warsaw Autumn festival in 1956, Lutosławski felt able to bring to fruition ideas on which he had been quietly working in preceding years. Initially these revolved round new ways of formatting the 12 pitches of the chromatic scale, both vertically (Five Songs, 1957) and horizontally (*Muzyka żałobna*, 'Funeral Music', 1954–8). In response to internal and external stimuli he introduced elements of controlled chance—what he termed 'aleatory counterpoint'—in his most experimental piece, *Gry weneckie* ('Venetian Games') for chamber orchestra (1960–1). As a result he was able to manipulate his multi-hued harmonic designs with extraordinary flexibility, performability, and dramatic effect and began to realize his ambition for sustained symphonic thought. He explored these new techniques on the small scale (String Quartet, 1964) and the large (Symphony no. 2, 1965–7). His orchestral palette and structural invention in *Livre pour orchestre* (1968) are particularly alluring. As in many of his works of the 1960s and 70s, his favourite formal procedure was to create a number of inconclusive preliminary sections or movements. These would lead to the main body of the work, where the music was propelled towards a cataclysmic climax and a balancing quiet coda.

By this stage in his career Lutosławski had achieved international recognition, with commissions and performances from the world's leading artists. He worked slowly, composing on average one major work every two years in the 1970s. The Cello Concerto (1970), written for Rostropovich, is a major rethinking of the dramatic potential inherent in the concerto genre. In Preludes and Fugue for 13 solo strings (1970–2) he carried out a controlled experiment in *mobile form, while *Les Espaces du sommeil*—one of several subtle works in which he set French texts—brings together in seamless fashion the horizontal and vertical aspects of the pitch organization he had initiated in the 1950s. But he felt that his music was still lacking in inner momentum and melodic appeal. In the opening of *Mi-parti* (1976) he attempted to create melodies out of an evolving sequence of 12-note chords. The breakthrough came in the tiny *Epitaph* for oboe and piano (1979), whose chamber proportions compelled him to dispense with dense chording. The ensuing Third Symphony (1981–3), written for the Chicago Symphony Orchestra and Georg Solti, synthesizes his harmonic and melodic impulses in a highly colourful texture where newly romantic melodic ideas jostle with more familiar aleatory passages.

In his final decade Lutosławski relaxed his expressive guard and created a series of works in which he sometimes approached the sound world of Ravel (the song cycle *Chantefleurs et chantefables*, 1990) and Rakhmaninov (Piano Concerto, 1988). The underlying impulse, however, became increasingly 18th century, reverting in distinct ways to the 18th-century procedures which underpinned some of his concert music before 1956, notably the Concerto for Orchestra. This is epitomized by the Partita for violin and piano (1984). Lutosławski's last orchestral work, the Fourth Symphony (1988–92), set the seal on his reputation as one of Europe's leading 20th-century composers, whose distinctive techniques were always at the service of expressivity. He was, in many ways, the embodiment of the classical modernist.   ATн

📖 B. A. VARGA, *Lutosławski Profile* (London, 1976) · S. STUCKY, *Lutosławski and his Music* (Cambridge, 1981) · C. B. RAE, *The Music of Lutosławski* (London, 1994, enlarged 3/1999) · B. JACOBSON, *A Polish Renaissance* (London, 1996) · Z. SKOWRON (ed.), *Lutosławski Studies* (Oxford, 2001)

Lutyens, (Agnes) Elisabeth (*b* London, 6 July 1906; *d* London, 14 April 1983). English composer. The daughter of the architect Edwin Lutyens, she studied composition with Harold Darke at the RCM (1926–30). In 1931 she helped found the Macnaghten–Lemare Concerts, which offered a platform to young composers. Her first acknowledged works, for example the Chamber Concerto no. 1 (1939), were among the earliest serial pieces composed in England, and she kept abreast of younger contemporaries in most of her subsequent large output.

Most of Lutyens's music, whether vocal or instrumental, was sparked off by literature, and she set an extraordinary range of texts, from Chaucer to Stevie Smith, from African poems to letters of Gustave Flaubert, and from Japanese haiku to Ludwig Wittgenstein, usually preferring a chorus or small ensemble of voices and instruments. Her many theatre works, however, usually employ her own words, whether the subject is ritual drama (*Isis and Osiris*, 1969–70; London, 1976) or an intimate play of contemporary mores (*Infidelio*, 1954; Sadler's Wells, 1973).   PG

📖 M. and S. HARRIES, *A Pilgrim Soul: The Life and Work of Elisabeth Lutyens* (London, 1989)

Luzzaschi, Luzzasco (*d* Ferrara, 10 Sept. 1607). Italian composer. A distinguished organist, he worked at the Este court at Ferrara from the early 1560s until the secession of the city to the papacy in 1597, probably staying there until his death. He was also organist at Ferrara Cathedral and in charge of the music at the religious confraternity of the Accademia della Morte. He wrote seven books of madrigals for five voices, and although his style is in the main unremarkable he was capable of startling chromatic harmonies (he was one of the few players of the famous *arcicembalo); he also proclaimed an adherence to the text in ways that became associated with Monteverdi's *seconda pratica* (see PRIMA PRATICA, SECONDA PRATICA). His most striking surviving music is the set of highly ornamented *Madrigali … a uno, e doi, e tre soprani* (Rome, 1601), comprising works written several years earlier for the ensemble of women's voices for which Ferrara was famous. Most of his instrumental music has disappeared. Frescobaldi was one of his pupils.   DA/TC

L'vov, Aleksey Fyodorovich (*b* Reval [now Tallinn, Estonia], 25 May/5 June 1798; *d* nr Kovno [now Kaunas, Lithuania], 16/28 Dec. 1870). Russian composer and violinist. His father, Fyodor Petrovich L'vov (1766–1836), was director of the court chapel choir in St Petersburg, a post in which Aleksey succeeded him in 1837. He had pursued a military career from 1818, and in 1834 was appointed adjutant to the tsar, who in 1833 invited L'vov to write the Russian national anthem, *Bozhe, tsarya khrani* ('God Save the Tsar'). Though known today chiefly for that one work, he also composed some delightful violin music (including 24 solo caprices, and a concerto, 1840), three operas, and a number of sacred choral works. He was also well known as a violin virtuoso, winning praise from Schumann and playing Mendelssohn's Violin Concerto at the Leipzig Gewandhaus in 1840, with Mendelssohn himself conducting. GN

Lyadov, Anatoly Konstantinovich (*b* St Petersburg, 29 April/11 May 1855; *d* Polïnovka, Novgorod district, 15/28 Aug. 1914). Russian composer. It is perhaps significant that he is known chiefly for failing to produce a score for Diaghilev's *The Firebird*, thus giving Stravinsky his first important opening in the theatre. Lyadov was somewhat disorganized in his approach to composition: as a student he was expelled from Rimsky-Korsakov's composition class at the St Petersburg Conservatory because of absenteeism, and even as a mature composer he produced a relatively small number of works (though this was also due in part to his self-critical attitude). In his day Lyadov was valued both as a teacher—Prokofiev and Myaskovsky were among his pupils—and as an establishment figure. He was one of the composers who gathered round the wealthy publisher Mitrofan Belyayev, and he acted as an adviser for Belyayev's publishing activities and for the Glinka Awards. Of his few orchestral works, *Baba-Yaga* (1904), the *Eight Russian Folksongs* (1905), *Kikimora* (1909), and *Volshebnoye ozero* ('The Enchanted Lake', 1909) have retained a precarious hold on the repertory, revealing a certain tasteful lyricism and an ability for clear orchestration in the Rimsky-Korsakov vein. GN

Lyapunov, Sergey Mikhaylovich (*b* Yaroslavl, 18/30 Nov. 1859; *d* Paris, 8 Nov. 1924). Russian composer and pianist. He studied at the Moscow Conservatory (composition with Taneyev, the piano with Karl Klindworth and Pavel Pabst). Later he moved to St Petersburg, where he came under the influence of Balakirev, hence his many virtuoso piano pieces in the Lisztian tradition (such as the *12 études d'exécution transcendante* op. 11) and his symphonies set firmly in the mould established by The Five (no. 1, 1887; no. 2, 1917). He succeeded Balakirev at the Free Music School, completing some of his mentor's unfinished works after his death and producing a popular orchestration of Balakirev's most celebrated piano work, the 'oriental fantasy' *Islamey*. Lyapunov taught the piano and composition at the St Petersburg Conservatory until 1923, when he left Russia on the pretext of a European concert tour. He died from a heart attack just before one of his concerts and was buried in Paris. MF-W

Lyatoshyns'ky, Borys (*b* Zhytomyr, 22 Dec./3 Jan. 1895; *d* Kiev, 15 April 1968). Ukrainian composer. In 1913 he began studying with Glière, at first privately, then at the Kiev Conservatory, where he taught from 1919 to 1968, becoming professor in 1935. He also taught orchestration at the Moscow Conservatory (1935–7, 1943–4). He was director of the Ukrainian Association of Contemporary Music (1922–5) and president of the Ukrainian Composers' Union (1939–41).

Lyatoshyns'ky's work falls into three periods; most of his chamber music dates from the first, post-Skryabin romantic period of the 1920s and 30s, of which the outstanding masterpiece was his Second Symphony (1935–6). The second period, of the 1940s and 50s, saw a handful of less successful works as he struggled with the constraints of *socialist realism, its heroic, pseudofolkloric style being in direct opposition to his subtle blend of late Romantic chromaticism and Ukrainian folk idioms. In the 1960s, supported by some of his pupils (including Valentyn Sil'vestrov), Lyatoshyns'ky returned to his earlier style, most notably in his Fourth Symphony (1963) and *Polish Suite* (1961).

His works include five symphonies (1918–19; 1935–6, rev. 1940; 1951, rev. 1954; 1963; 1965–6), a four-act music drama *Zolotoy obruch* ('The Golden Ring', 1930, rev. 1970), two piano trios (1922, 1942), and four string quartets (1915, 1922, 1928, 1943). PF

📖 V. SAMOKHVALOV, *B. Lyatoshyns'ky* (Kiev, 1970, 2/1974)

Lydian mode. The mode represented by the white notes of the piano beginning on F. See MODE, 2.

Lydian tetrachord. A *tetrachord spanning an augmented 4th, as in the first four notes of the Lydian mode (see MODE, 2). Fauré's song *Lydia* makes poignant use of the Lydian tetrachord.

lyra. See LIRA.

lyra viol. A small bass *viol, and a style of playing it using a range of *scordatura tunings, popular in England (and having considerable influence on violplaying in continental Europe) during the 17th century. The extent to which the lyra viol differed from the normal bass viol is debated: it is perfectly possible to perform the repertory on a bass viol played 'lyra-way' (i.e. with the appropriate tuning and in the lyra style). A sizable repertory exists, both in printed publications and in manuscript, of music for solo lyra viol, for lyra viol in combination with other instruments, and to accompany song; some 70 different tunings have been uncovered. Lyra viol music is an attempt to mimic polyphonic textures on a bowed instrument; like lute music, it contains a mixture of chords and melodic lines. RPA

lyre. 1. A *chordophone on which the strings run across a skin-covered resonator to a yoke consisting of a crossbar held by two arms coming out of the resonator. The earliest evidence for the lyre comes from the 3rd millennium BC, in Mesopotamia. From there it spread throughout the Middle East, Anatolia, and North Africa, and it was the most important stringed instrument in ancient Greece and Rome. It also spread throughout medieval Europe, particularly among Germanic peoples, who also developed bowed variants (see CRWTH; ROTTE). Apart from a few survivals, particularly in Scandinavia, it has now all but died out. However, an unbroken tradition of lyre playing, as a solo instrument or to accompany song, persists to the present day in East Africa.

The lighter Greek lyres, the *phorminx, barbiton*, and *chelys*, had bodies made from a tortoise shell. The big concert *kithara* used by professional bards was a heavier instrument with a wooden body and an elaborate form. Through its association with the Apollo and Orpheus myths and with the Homeric epics the lyre was accorded high status in Greek and Roman society. The Hebrew and Egyptian *kinnor* associated particularly with King David was also a lyre, probably with a wooden body. Because of its classical and biblical associations the lyre has been a potent musical symbol in Western culture since the Renaissance.

See also ANCIENT GREEK MUSIC, 2; ANCIENT MESOPOTAMIAN AND EGYPTIAN MUSIC. JMo

2. See BELL LYRA.

lyre guitar. A guitar with lyre-shaped 'wings' projecting from the soundbox, made from about 1780 to about 1820, mainly in France and England. Decorative rather than practical, it was played in much the same way and with the same tuning as an ordinary guitar, mainly by lady amateurs to accompany songs. See also HARP-LUTE, 2.

lyric. 1. Strictly speaking, vocal performance accompanied by the lyre, but in fact broadened in meaning to denote any kind of accompanied vocal music, e.g. *drame lyrique* (Fr., 'lyric drama', i.e. opera).

2. A short poem, i.e. not epic or narrative. Composers including Grieg adapted this meaning to music, e.g. *Lyric Piece* (Ger.: *Lyrisches Stück*).

3. A description of a voice-type, e.g. lyric tenor or lyric soprano, meaning somewhere between light and heavy in style.

4. The words of a song, especially used of popular 20th-century song and musical comedy.

Lyric Suite. 1. Orchestral work (1904) by Grieg, arranged from four of his six *Lyric Pieces* (book 5) op. 54.

2. Work (1925–6) for string quartet by *Berg.

lyrisches Stück. See LYRIC, 2.

Lyrische Symphonie. Zemlinsky's op. 18 (1922–3), seven songs for soprano, baritone, and orchestra, settings of the composer's German translations of poems by Rabindranath Tagore. It is dedicated to Berg, who quoted from it in his *Lyric Suite*.

lysarden. See CORNETT.

Macbeth. 1. Opera in four acts by Verdi to a libretto by Francesco Maria Piave (with additional material by Andrea Maffei) after Shakespeare's play (1605–6) (Florence, 1847); Verdi revised and expanded it, using Piave's libretto translated into French by Charles-Louis-Étienne Nuitter and Alexandre Beaumont (Paris, 1865).

2. Tone-poem, op. 23 (1886–8), by Richard Strauss, revised in 1889–90.

McCabe, John (*b* Huyton, Lancs., 21 April 1939). English composer. He studied at the RMCM and in Germany. Besides composing he has been active as a pianist and writer and was director of the London College of Music from 1983 to 1990. His compositions reveal a concern to fuse and develop from the achievements of such mid-century figures as Bartók, Hindemith, and Karl Amadeus Hartmann; energetic symphonic working can be offset by warmer lyrical melody, as in *Notturni ed alba* for soprano and orchestra (1970). His instrumental works include *The Chagall Windows* for orchestra (1974) and *Red Leaves* for chamber ensemble (1990). PG/AW

MacCunn, Hamish (*b* Greenock, 22 March 1868; *d* London, 2 Aug 1916). Scottish composer, conductor, and teacher. In 1883, at only 15, he won an open scholarship to the newly founded Royal College of Music, where he studied composition with Parry and Stanford. He taught harmony at the RAM (1888–94) and composition at the Guildhall School of Music (1912–16). He was an active, efficient conductor, working for the Carl Rosa Company (from 1898), the Moody–Manners Company, the Savoy Theatre, and for Beecham's operatic productions. He died prematurely from cancer.

MacCunn's early and skilfully executed overture *The Land of the Mountain and the Flood* (1887), with its pleasing amalgam of Brahmsian qualities and Scottish folk tunes, has proved to be his most enduring legacy; some of his most imaginative invention, however, is found in the orchestral ballad *The Ship o' the Fiend* (1888) and the opera *Jeanie Deans* (Edinburgh, 1894), arguably his finest work, created from a much broader palette influenced by Liszt and Wagner. JD1

MacDowell, Edward (Alexander) (*b* New York, 18 Dec. 1860; *d* New York, 23 Jan. 1908). American composer, pianist, and teacher. He received musical training as a boy, then moved with his mother to Europe in 1876, returning to the USA 12 years later. A successful performance of his First Piano Concerto at Weimar in 1882 encouraged the young pianist to think of himself primarily as a composer. For the rest of his life he struggled to find time and energy to compose while making a living as a teacher and performer.

Settling in Boston in 1888, MacDowell taught privately and composed his two orchestral suites (no. 1, 1888–91, 1893; no. 2, 1891–5) as well as many piano works. Public appearances as a pianist heightened his impact on American musical life. By 1896, when Columbia University named MacDowell its first professor of music, the trustees' claim that he was 'the greatest musical genius America has produced' did not seem an exaggeration. His years at Columbia, however, proved frustrating. Throwing himself into his new job, he found that it consumed almost all his time and that only in the summers could he compose seriously. A conflict with university authorities brought about his resignation in 1904. Soon afterwards he showed signs of mental collapse, and he spent the last years of his life in a state of childlike insanity.

To the public of his day, expectantly awaiting the appearance of a 'great' American composer, MacDowell's music seemed more strikingly original than it does now. Nevertheless, works like *Woodland Sketches* for piano (1896, which include the well-known *To a Wild Rose*) blend diatonic melody with chromatically tinged harmony, communicating a quality of restrained lushness and revealing MacDowell's distinctive, secure voice—a perfect exemplar of turn-of-the-century American Romanticism. RC

Mace, Thomas (*b* 1612 or 1613; *d* ?Cambridge, ?1706). English writer on music and composer. He seems to have spent much of his life in Cambridge. His *Musick's Monument* (London, 1676) is a verbose but important book: part 1 deals with psalmody, part 2 is a major study of the lute and how to play it, while part 3 explores 'The Generous Viol, in its Rightest Use' and includes performance suggestions for consort music. Some pieces in the book, used as music examples, were composed by Mace.   WT/AA

McEwen, Sir John Blackwood (*b* Hawick, 13 April 1868; *d* London, 14 June 1948). Scottish composer and teacher. He studied at the RAM with Frederick Corder (1893–5), returning as professor of harmony and composition in 1898 and succeeding Alexander Mackenzie as principal in 1924. His large-scale works include a Viola Concerto (1901), three *Border Ballads* (1906–8), the 'Solway' Symphony (1911), and the choral-orchestral *Hymn on the Morning of Christ's Nativity* (1901–5), but his output is dominated by the 17 string quartets written between 1893 and 1947. He was knighted in 1931.

JD1

Macfarren, Sir George (Alexander) (*b* London, 2 March 1813; *d* London, 31 Oct. 1887). English composer. He studied with Cipriani Potter at the RAM (1829–36), returning as a professor in 1837 and remaining there for the rest of his life, apart from an absence from 1847 to 1851. He founded the Society of British Musicians (1834) and the Handel Society (1844), and was a conductor at Covent Garden from 1845. In 1875 he suceeded Sterndale Bennett as professor of music at Cambridge and principal of the RAM. He was knighted in 1883.

In spite of his poor eyesight—he became blind in 1860—Macfarren was immensely prolific in all areas of composition. His nine symphonies (1828–74), strongly Classical in orientation, failed to attract public attention, and he abandoned opera, his first love, when opportunities dwindled. In later years he turned to choral music, where his natural sense of drama found voice in cantata and oratorio, notably *St John the Baptist* (1873). One of his best-known works was the overture *Chevy Chase*, much admired by Wagner (who conducted it) for its 'wild, passionate character'.   JD1

Machaut [Machault], **Guillaume de** (*b* ?Reims, *c.*1300; *d* ?Reims, 13 April 1377). French composer and poet. He now appears as the most important French composer of the 14th century. Certainly he was influential in establishing polyphonic song in France, and his is the earliest known complete setting of the Mass by a single composer. He took great care to preserve his complete works and they have survived more or less intact in six copies; this has undoubtedly favoured his reputation as compared with that of his near contemporary Philippe de Vitry. Altogether 141 of Machaut's works remain: they include 23 motets, 19 *lais*, 33 *virelais*, 21 *rondeaux*, 42 *ballades*, a Mass, and an instrumental hocket.

Machaut seems to have been brought up in Reims. His earliest datable composition, the motet *Bone pastor Guillerme/Bone pastor qui pastores*, was probably written for the election of Guillaume de Trie as Archbishop of Reims in 1324. In the same year Machaut received his first recorded appointment when he became secretary to King John of Bohemia. He followed the king on military expeditions to Silesia, Poland, Prussia, and Lithuania. John of Bohemia was killed by the English at the Battle of Crécy in 1346. After John's death Machaut was employed by his daughter, Bonne, but he retained his connections with Reims and was apparently based there for the rest of his life.

His later patrons included King Charles of Navarre (for whom he wrote the poem *Le Confort d'ami*), the Dauphin of France (who became King Charles V in 1364), Pierre I of Cyprus (Machaut tells of his exploits in *La Prise d'Alexandrie*), and Jean Duc de Berry (for whom he wrote the poem *La Fonteinne amoureuse* and from whose library a complete copy of Machaut's work survives). In later life Machaut acquired various ecclesiastical positions: he was canon both of Saint Quentin, whose patron saint is celebrated in the motet *Martyrum gemma latria/Diligenter inquiramus/A Christo honoratus*, and of Reims, where he lived his last days writing and supervising the copying of his works.

Machaut, though a cleric, wrote relatively little for the church. Only three of his 141 surviving works (the Notre Dame Mass and two of his Latin motets) have a specific place in the church service. The Mass is the earliest setting for four voices. It has six movements (Kyrie, Gloria, Credo, Sanctus, Agnus, and Ite missa est); all except the Gloria and Credo are based on plainchant and some of the movements share common melodic material. Machaut's motets make full use of the new rhythms and more flexible notation developed in the 14th century; they are true examples of the *Ars Nova style, with many syncopations, small note-values (the minim appears for the first time), and complex repetitions of the tenor part in diminished note-values. A typical example is the motet *De bon espoir/Puisque la douce rousee/Speravi*, which is divided into two sections. The tenor tune is stated twice in each section but the two statements in the final section are twice the speed (half the note-values) of those in the first. Another characteristic is the use of two French texts against the Latin tenor. This feature, and Machaut's preference for relatively few subdivisions within the main section, stands in contrast to earlier motets by Vitry and others.

Machaut's most acclaimed achievement is in the realm of secular song. Almost all of his *virelais* and *lais* are monophonic, and his interest in these outmoded genres was somewhat unusual. However, his treatment of the polyphonic *ballades* and *rondeaux* was clearly innovatory: he greatly expanded the length of songs compared with earlier examples by Adam de la Halle and L'Escurel and introduced much more complex textures. Perhaps the most famous of his songs is *Ma fin est mon commencement*, a *rondeau* in which the second voice sings the music of the first voice backwards.

A more typical example, among the *ballades*, is *Nes que on porroit*, of which the opening of the top voice and tenor are shown in Ex. 1 (the contratenor is omitted). This shows a new, melismatic approach to polyphonic vocal writing, the fluid top part contrasting with the syncopated tenor. The example contains several of Machaut's melodic fingerprints: the fragment marked 'x' is found in almost a dozen other works and is transposed in several more, and the motif 'y' is one of Machaut's most characteristic melodic shapes. Incidentally, we are told in Machaut's autobiographical poem *Le Voir dit* (*c.*1365) that he wrote this song for his lover Peronne, that it should be performed without ornamentation, and that it can be played on the organ or bagpipes.

Ex. 1

Soon after Machaut's death the poet Eustache Deschamps wrote a moving lament, *Armes, amours/O flour des flours*, praising him as the 'master of all melody'. The lament was set to music by Franciscus Andrieu; he borrowed chords from the Gloria and Credo of Machaut's Mass to set the poignant words 'la mort Machaut'. Machaut was the last major figure to imitate the aristocratic poet-musicians of the 12th and 13th centuries by writing both monophonic songs and poems, and yet he also excelled in the new rhythmically varied style of polyphonic music which had been developed in Paris while he was still a young man.

AP

📖 G. REANEY, *Machaut* (London, 1971) · D. LEECH-WILKINSON, *Machaut's Mass: An Introduction* (Oxford, 1990) · L. EARP, *Guillaume de Machaut: A Guide to Research* (New York, 1995)

machicotage (Fr.). Extempore embellishment of sections of plainchant by a soloist, usually through the addition of passing notes. The practice was common in France and Italy in the Middle Ages, and continued until the adoption of the Solesmes versions of plainchant early in the 20th century.

Machover, Tod (*b* New York, 24 Nov. 1953). American composer. He studied at Columbia University (1973–5) and with Carter and Roger Sessions at the Juilliard School, then worked on computer composition at Stanford. After a time on the staff at IRCAM (1976–85) he joined the Massachusetts Institute of Technology. Most of his works have used sophisticated computer applications, as in the science-fiction opera *Valis* (Paris, 1987), but he espoused a much more traditional style in a second opera, *Resurrection* (Houston, 1999).

PG

Mackenzie, Sir Alexander (Campbell) (*b* Edinburgh, 22 Aug. 1847; *d* London, 28 April 1935). Scottish composer and conductor. From a family of musicians, he studied music in Schwarzburg-Sondershausen in Germany before gaining the King's Scholarship to the RAM (1862–5). After 14 years in Edinburgh (1865–79) he moved to Florence. In Italy he was highly productive, with choral works including *The Bride* (1881), *Jason* (1882), and (arguably his masterpiece) *The Rose of Sharon* (1884), such orchestral works as *La Belle Dame sans merci* (1883) and the Violin Concerto (1884, written for Sarasate), and the opera *Colomba* (Drury Lane, 1883), which brought his name before the public.

On being elected principal of the RAM Mackenzie returned permanently to London. He was conductor of the Philharmonic Society (1893–9) and general president of the International Musical Society (1908–12), and played an important role in the foundation of the Associated Board of the Royal Schools of Music in 1889. He retired from the RAM in 1924. He was knighted in 1895 and created KCVO in 1922, the year of the RAM's centenary.

Mackenzie is remembered mainly for his Scottish works—the three rhapsodies and the *Scottish Concerto* for piano—but his range was much wider and shows influences of Liszt and Wagner, his gifts being essentially dramatic rather than symphonic. He was however a fine orchestrator, as is demonstrated in his patriotic overture *Britannia* (1895) and the incidental music to *Coriolanus* (1901). JDi

Mackey, Steve(n) (*b* Frankfurt, 14 Feb. 1956). American composer. He studied at the University of California and at Brandeis, and began teaching at Princeton in 1985. His music is rich in allusions, to popular culture as much as to Western classical music, and often quirky.

Many of his pieces he wrote for himself to play on the electric guitar, whether as soloist, with the Kronos Quartet (*Physical Property*, 1993), or with orchestra (*Deal*, 1995). Other works include *Eating Greens* for orchestra (1993) and a music-theatre piece, *Ravenshead* (1998).   PG

MacMillan, James (Loy) (*b* Kilwinning, Ayrshire, 16 July 1959). Scottish composer. He studied at Edinburgh and Durham universities, and was active as a teacher and performer while laying the foundations for a successful career as a composer. In 2000 he took up visiting appointments in Manchester with the BBC Philharmonic and at the RNCM. Since setting William Soutar's *The Tryst* in Scottish ballad style (1984) he has developed an idiom that blends allusion to his ethnic roots with more mainstream modernist qualities deriving from (among others) Penderecki and Lutosławski. Roman Catholicism is another important part of his creative make-up and does much to determine the atmosphere of such large-scale works as *Triduum* (1995–7), comprising *The World's Ransoming* for orchestra with obbligato cor anglais, the Cello Concerto, and the *Symphony: Vigil*. With such works as his 1990 Proms success *The Confession of Isobel Gowdie*, the percussion concerto *Veni, veni, Emmanuel* (1993), and the opera *Inés de Castro* (Scottish Opera, 1996) MacMillan has reinforced his prominent if at times controversial position on the British compositional scene.   AW

Maconchy, Elizabeth (*b* Broxbourne, Herts., 19 March 1907; *d* Norwich, 11 Nov. 1994). English composer. She studied at the RCM with Vaughan Williams and later in Prague. Her music always tended to focus on European toughness rather than English lyricism, and at its most original owed more to Bartók and Hindemith than to Vaughan Williams or Britten. Her series of 13 string quartets (1932–84) is an outstanding 20th-century contribution to the genre, worthy to stand alongside the cycles of Shostakovich and Robert Simpson.   PG/AW

McPhee, Colin (Carhart) (*b* Montreal, 15 March 1900; *d* Los Angeles, 7 Jan. 1964). Canadian-born American composer and ethnomusicologist. He studied at the Peabody Conservatory, in Toronto, and with Paul Le Flem and Isidore Philipp in Paris (1924–6), then moved to New York, where he had lessons with Varèse. From 1934 to 1936 he lived on Bali, whose music was the source for his *Tabuh-Tabuhan* for two pianos and orchestra (1936) and *Balinese Ceremonial Music* for two pianos (1940). After World War II he lived in Los Angeles and worked on his study *Music in Bali* (New Haven, CT, 1966).   PG

Macque, Giovanni de (*b* Valenciennes, *c*.1550; *d* Naples, Sept. 1614). Flemish composer and organist. After serving as a choirboy in the imperial chapel at Vienna he studied with Philippe de Monte. He then moved to Rome where, with Nanino and Marenzio among others, he was a member of the Compagnia dei Musici. He went to Naples about 1585 and remained there for the rest of his life. His activities included taking part in the music-making of the academy of Don Fabrizio Gesualdo, father of Carlo Gesualdo, and serving as organist at Ss. Annunziata and the chapel of the Spanish viceroy. He was also an important teacher; his pupils included Luigi Rossi.

Macque's style of composition changed noticeably after he arrived in Naples. From having been relatively conservative, he began to write madrigals, motets, *laudi*, and canzonettas in an advanced idiom, and his organ works from these years are full of chromatic harmonies and dissonances, probably reflecting the influence of Gesualdo.   DA/TC

Madama Butterfly ('Madam Butterfly'). Opera in two acts by Puccini to a libretto by Giuseppe Giacosa and Luigi Illica after David Belasco's play *Madame Butterfly* (1900), itself based on John Luther Long's short story, which in turn was based partly on Pierre Loti's story *Madame Chrysanthème* (Milan, 1904; revised Brescia, 1904).

Maddalena. Opera in one act by Prokofiev to his own libretto (concert performance, Manchester, 1978; staged Graz, 1981).

Maderna, Bruno (*b* Venice, 21 April 1920; *d* Darmstadt, 13 Nov. 1973). Italian composer and conductor. He studied composition and conducting at conservatories in Milan, Siena, and Rome, but the more significant influence on him was that of his private conducting teacher Hermann Scherchen. Still more important were his contacts with Stockhausen and Boulez, made in the early 1950s. He soon settled in Darmstadt, the Mecca of the international avant-garde, and there worked as composer, conductor, and teacher. In 1955 he assisted Luciano Berio in founding the electronic music studio in Milan. His works have a bigness characteristic of the man; they include various concertos, among them three for oboe, as well as *Hyperion* (1963–5), an aleatory theatre piece after Friedrich Hölderlin. Among smaller compositions, his *Musica su due dimensioni* for flute, percussion, and tape (1952) was the first to combine live and electronic resources.   PG

📖 R. FEARN, *Bruno Maderna* (London, 1990)

madrigal 1. Introduction; 2. The 14th-century Italian madrigal; 3. The Italian madrigal in the 16th and early 17th centuries; 4. The madrigal beyond Italy

1. Introduction

The term 'madrigal' has two distinct applications. One is to a poetic form and its musical setting as a secular song cultivated in Italy in the 14th century; the other is to a type of secular song that flourished in Italy in the 16th and early 17th centuries, also spreading to most other European countries, one of the most important genres of the late Renaissance. These two types are not related in anything other than name.

The origin of the word is a matter for dispute. Various derivations have been suggested—including *mandra* (Italian, 'flock'), which would imply a pastoral song—but the most likely is *matricale* (Italian, 'of the womb'), referring to the fact that madrigal texts are in the mother tongue, rather than in Latin; another possible derivation is from 'materialis', suggesting a poem that is in a free form.

2. The 14th-century Italian madrigal

This earlier kind of madrigal did not adopt a more or less fixed form until the 1340s, some 20 years after its first appearance. From having a musical form that basically followed that of the verse, it settled into a standard length of two or three stanzas, each of three lines and each being set to the same music, the final stanza closing with a 'ritornello' of one or two lines, usually in a contrasting metre. The music is commonly in two, sometimes three, parts and is highly melismatic, particularly in the upper voice. The rhythms are often lively, and though imitative textures are rare, some madrigals use canonic techniques.

The most famous composers of the early madrigal were north Italians, for example Giovanni da Cascia, Gherardello da Firenze, and Jacopo da Bologna, but there are also some fine examples by Landini and Ciconia. Towards the end of the 14th century the madrigal yielded in popularity to the **ballata*—only 12 madrigals by Landini, for example, survive, compared to roughly 140 *ballate*. The early madrigal is characteristically bright and attractive, apt for virtuoso singing and playing (the lower part, or parts, may have been performed by instruments). The 14th-century madrigal died out after about 1415.

3. The Italian madrigal in the 16th and early 17th centuries

In contrast to the earlier madrigal, which followed the structure of a specific poetic form, the 16th-century madrigal set a variety of verse types, usually a single verse without a refrain. These included the serious and lighter types, such as sonnets, canzoni, and a poetic form known in the 16th century as 'madrigale', which consisted of one stanza of an unspecified number of lines of seven and 11 syllables in a free rhyme scheme. The first publication of pieces called 'madrigals' is *Madrigali de diversi musici: libro primo de la Serena* (Rome, 1530); it includes songs by Verdelot and others.

In the early years the madrigal was essentially a serious form, setting verse of a high quality, much of it the courtly love poetry of Petrarch, which was enjoying a new wave of popularity. Madrigals were composed by Italians, particularly those based in Rome and Florence, such as Costanzo and Sebastiano Festa, and by northern musicians employed at Italian courts and churches including Verdelot, Arcadelt, and Willaert (see ITALY, 3). The style is formed from a mixture of elements: the contrapuntal writing and smoothly flowing melodic lines of the motet; the more lively and rhythmic melodies and tendency towards harmonic thinking derived from the frottola; and from the chanson short, memorable themes and chordal textures that made the music easy for amateur musicians to perform, combined with such programmatic writing as the imitation in music of sounds of nature. The result is a work that is typically for between three and six voices, uses both polyphonic, often imitative textures and chordal writing, and places strong emphasis on tunefulness and on reflecting the mood and meaning of the text in its music. The passage from Arcadelt's popular *Il bianco e dolce cigno* shown in Ex. 1 is a fine example, the sudden E♭ chord used to highlight the key word *piangendo* ('weeping').

The work of these early madrigalists gained increasing popularity during the 1530s and 40s until, by the mid-century, madrigals dominated secular music in Italy. There was evidently a great demand for this music, and many volumes of madrigals, both anthologies and the works of single composers, were published during these decades, with the Venetian printing firms of Gardano and Scotto leading the way.

Several important developments in the madrigal occurred at about this time. The range of note-values available increased with a new style of notation that involved the used of *note nere* ('black notes', i.e. crotchets and quavers) in addition to the existing 'white notes' (minims, semibreves, breves). This allowed composers greater flexibility in text-setting, making rapid declamatory patterns and quick imitative entries possible, and also increased the possibilities for contrast against slower, sustained notes. Madrigals that used these free declamatory rhythms in a chordal texture were known as *madrigali ariosi*; several anthologies of such madrigals were issued in Rome in the 1550s. As a result of the experiments of Nicola Vicentino, a pupil of

Ex. 1

Willaert's who worked at the Ferrarese court, the madrigal's melodic and harmonic resources expanded to include chromaticism, a new expressive tool which composers exploited to the full over the years.

The master of these new resources, and the most renowned composer of the mid-century style, was Cipriano de Rore, and it is no coincidence that he worked at Ferrara at just this time of experimentation and revolution. He chose poetry a little away from the elegant tradition of Petrarch, often with many more emotional words, and this allowed him to develop a more concentrated and intense musical style. Almost every significant word seems to suggest a corresponding image in sound. Minor intervals express sadder emotions, major ones joy; ascending notes symbolize such words as 'heaven', low registers 'earth'. Rore uses dissonance and wide, jagged leaps to express pain or struggle, and places melismas on words, which, though not suggesting programmatic expression, require emphasis. Lines of verse could be run together or cut short. The second section of his madrigal *Mia benigna Fortuna* became a classic and much-imitated example of

such music: it opens with a 'forbidden' ascending major 6th, its relentless dissonant suspensions expressing the 'cruel, bitter, inexorable death' of the text (Ex. 2).

Other important composers active after the mid-16th century include Lassus, who wrote both serious madrigals that show the influence of Rore's style and lighter, often humorous Neapolitan *villanescas, and Monte, whose output was prolific. Both composers worked in Italy as young men before returning to northern Europe, where they continued to publish Italian madrigals. In Rome, Palestrina wrote both secular and spiritual madrigals, published in his own collections and in anthologies.

By the time of Rore's death in 1565, the range of expression possible in the madrigal was widening rapidly, and the genre developed in several different directions. One involved a rapprochement between the serious madrigal and such lighter forms as the *canzonetta and *villanella. Giovanni Ferretti and Andrea Gabrieli were key contributors to this development. Gabrieli's madrigals often set lighthearted, pastoral, and amorous texts full of words and images suitable for

Ex. 2

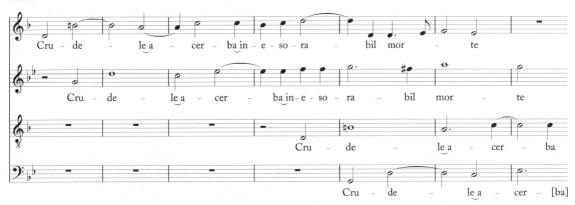

*word-painting; musically they are an attractive combination of imitative passages and chordal declamatory phrases, lively rhythms, and clear textures. Gabrieli and other Venetian composers also wrote larger-scale ceremonial madrigals and small-scale, satirical *giustiniane* and similar pieces for three voices. Gabrieli's 'hybrid' madrigal style was taken up in the 1580s by northern Italian composers including Orazio Vecchi, who played an important role in the evolution of the lighthearted madrigal comedy. At the same time a similarly light madrigal style was also popular among composers working in Rome, for example G. M. Nanino, Felice Anerio, and Marenzio. This lighter madrigal style remained very popular for several decades both in Italy and in northern European countries.

The madrigal also developed in a more serious direction. In the 1580s two of the most important centres for madrigal composition and performance were the courts at Mantua and Ferrara. Stimulated by the presence there of groups of virtuoso singers (e.g. the Ferrarese *concerto delle dame*, whose female singers were renowned as much for their grace and beauty as for their singing), such composers as Luzzasco Luzzaschi at Ferrara and Giaches de Wert at Mantua cultivated rich, ornamented, and highly expressive styles also seen in the later madrigals of Marenzio. Wert's madrigals (from the 1560s onwards) are particularly intense and dramatic, using chromaticism, dissonance, and sudden and extreme contrasts of range, rhythm, and harmony to portray every nuance of the text; he also used a pared-down, chordal declamatory style. His *Giunto alla tomba* is a fine example.

The 1590s saw the further exploitation of this range of expressive devices at the hands of Marenzio, Luzzaschi, Gesualdo, and Monteverdi, among others. Some of the best madrigals from this time set texts that were not merely 'poesia per musica' but poems of the highest quality by such contemporary poets as Torquato Tasso and G. B. Guarini. Monteverdi coined the term *seconda pratica* to describe the new expressive style of composition, which originated with the madrigals of Rore, in which, as Monteverdi put it, 'the words are mistress of the harmony'. The aim was for music to express as richly as possible the words being sung, and composers achieved this by developing an expanded and more complex musical language that more conservative critics (notably G. M. Artusi) considered a violation of the rules of harmony and counterpoint. Whereas the madrigal of earlier decades had been a popular form of entertainment among amateur musicians as well as courtly and professional musicians (indeed, the lighter 'hybrid' style continued to be popular), these madrigals were more likely to be performed by professional singers.

Gesualdo's madrigals are well known today for their extreme style: his chromatic melodies create dissonant and disjointed harmonic progressions that explore the most melancholy aspects of the dark texts he set. Monteverdi's madrigals, while equally expressive, use a greater variety of technical and emotional resources. Chromaticism, dissonance, wide melodic leaps, and bold harmonies all have their place in Monteverdi's musical language, but are combined with a strong dramatic sense, the use of declamatory rhythms and recitative-like passages, and a focus on large-scale structures as well as on small-scale attention to individual words. The result, notably in his fourth and fifth books (1603 and 1605), is a constantly evolving style that, unlike Gesualdo's, was full of potential for future musical developments.

While polyphonic madrigals continued to be written into the 17th century, the rise of the basso *continuo (or more accurately the *basso seguente*) and of *monody had important implications for the madrigal's development as a piece for one or two voices (sometimes more) with continuo. In fact, it is likely that ensemble madrigals had been performed throughout the 16th century not just by groups of unaccompanied singers but also in arrangements for different forces, with such instruments as viols or lute or chitarrone doubling or replacing some vocal parts—even replacing all but the top line and acting as an accompaniment to a solo voice. Monteverdi's fifth and sixth books of madrigals contain a mixture of ensemble madrigals, in which an added *basso seguente* part is optional, and new 'concerted' madrigals, which include sections for vocal solo or duet with continuo accompaniment. The presence of the continuo part (sometimes using strophic basses) and the reduced textures left the solo voice(s) free to explore much more virtuoso embellishment or dramatic representations of speech than was possible in the ensemble madrigal, as such works as Monteverdi's *Zefiro torna* and his *Lamento d'Arianna* demonstrate.

By the mid-17th century the possibilities of madrigal writing had more or less been exhausted; composers of secular vocal music extended the techniques of ensemble writing in the dialogue and the cantata, and those of the solo madrigal in the solo cantata and the aria.

4. The madrigal beyond Italy

(a) England: The lighter madrigal style that flourished in Italy in the 1580s enjoyed great popularity in England in the 1580s and 90s, though in terms of numbers of publications the madrigal was a very much smaller phenomenon in England than in Italy. Italian madrigals had been available in England in manuscript copies in earlier decades, but it was in the 1580s that the genre

began to flourish in print. One of the most important publications was Nicholas Yonge's anthology *Musica transalpina* (1588), which contains madrigals by such composers as Marenzio, Palestrina, and Ferrabosco (as well as two by Byrd) with their texts translated into English. According to Yonge the collection reflected the tastes of the group of amateur musicians, 'Gentlemen and Merchants of good accompte', who met regularly at his house. It was followed two years later by a similar collection of *Italian Madrigalls Englished*, issued by Thomas Watson; this is made up mainly of madrigals by Marenzio, but again includes two pieces by Byrd.

The popularity of these Italian madrigals in translation, combined with developments in English poetry seen, for example, in the sonnets of Edmund Spenser and Philip Sidney, encouraged English composers to write madrigals setting English verse. Such songs are typically lighthearted in tone, setting pastoral and amorous texts full of Petrarchan imagery suitable for depicting in music, and use a mixture of light imitative and chordal writing. Byrd wrote no pieces labelled 'madrigal', but the genre's stylistic influence can be found in his consort songs. Thomas Morley, however, was the master of the English madrigal style. Morley's books of *Canzonets*, *Madrigalls*, and *Balletts* published in the 1590s contain a mixture of his own works and transcriptions of pieces by Italians including Felice Anerio and Gastoldi. Morley's own light, lively style was taken up by other English composers, and in 1601 Morley published *The Triumphes of Oriana*, an anthology of madrigals by English composers in honour of Elizabeth I.

The more serious Italian madrigal of the later 16th century had no great influence in England, though some composers, notably Weelkes, Wilbye, and Ward, did develop this style, setting darker texts and using chromaticism and dissonance. Walter Porter's collection of 1632 shows the influence of Monteverdi's concerted madrigal style, particularly in the use of more virtuoso solo and duet passages with continuo. By this time, however, the madrigal in England was being superseded by the native *lute-song and ayre.

(b) Northern Europe: The influence of the Italian madrigal spread to northern Europe in two main ways: by the travels of musicians between the various courts and cathedrals of Europe, and by dissemination via the main centres of printing and publishing. Such Franco-Flemish composers as Lassus and Monte worked in Rome in the mid-16th century before returning to the north, to Munich and Vienna respectively, where they continued to publish Italian madrigals. In the later 16th and early 17th centuries, such German composers as H. L. Hassler, Grabbe, and Schütz travelled to Venice

and studied with Andrea and Giovanni Gabrieli, and Christian IV of Denmark sent young composers such as Mogens Pedersøn and Hans Nielsen to study with Giovanni Gabrieli. The influence of contemporary Italian styles is very clear in the works of all these composers, those of Pedersøn and Schütz in particular bearing comparison with Monteverdi's in their expressive musical language. Nuremberg and Munich were the main centres of publishing in Germany, and printers based there issued not just books of madrigals by German composers, setting German and Italian texts, but reprints of collections by Italian composers too.

The Netherlands played a particularly important role in disseminating the Italian madrigal style, particularly through the work of printers and publishers based in Antwerp. Anthologies of Italian madrigals, often also including some pieces by such local composers as Waelrant and Verdonck, were published there from the mid-16th century and into the 17th. Poland and Spain also enjoyed strong commercial and cultural links with Italy in the 16th century, and the influence of the Italian madrigal, though not as widespread as in other European countries, is still evident.   DA/EW

📖 A. EINSTEIN, *The Italian Madrigal* (Princeton, NJ, 1949/R1971) · J. KERMAN, *The Elizabethan Madrigal* (New York, 1962) · J. ROCHE, *The Madrigal* (London, 1972, 2/1990) · A. NEWCOMB, *The Madrigal at Ferrara, 1579–1597* (Princeton, NJ, 1980) · K.-S. TEO, *Chromaticism in the English Madrigal* (New York, 1989)

madrigal comedy. A musical entertainment made up of a series of madrigals or lighter vocal forms that illustrate a story or a group of characters. The first work to use the title 'commedia musicale', and certainly the best known, was Orazio Vecchi's *L'Amfiparnaso* (1597). Madrigal comedies are generally, though not necessarily, comic in tone. Vecchi intended his to portray what he called 'the great theatre of the world', and both *L'Amfiparnaso* and his *Le veglie di Siena* (1604) contrast *piacevole* (light) with *grave* (serious) moods. Other madrigal comedies, such as those by Adriano Banchieri and Alessandro Striggio (i), are more lighthearted, and may make use of the stock characters associated with *commedia dell'arte*.   —/EW

Madrigali guerrieri ed amorosi ('Madrigals of Love and War'). Monteverdi's eighth book of madrigals (1638).

Maelzel, Johann Nepomuk (*b* Regensburg, 15 Aug. 1772; *d* at sea off Charleston, SC, 21 July 1838). German inventor. In 1792 he settled in Vienna, where in 1804 he exhibited his *panharmonicon, a mechanical 'orchestra' for which his friend Beethoven later wrote his *Battle Symphony* (1813). In 1808 he was appointed court mechanician. Beethoven owned one of Maelzel's ear trumpets and was interested in his musical chronometer. Maelzel went on to develop the metronome, which he began manufacturing in Paris in 1816. He travelled widely demonstrating his curiosities and was found dead on board ship. AL

maestoso (It.). 'Majestic'; *maestevolmente, maestosamente,* 'majestically'.

maestro (It., 'master', 'teacher'). The *maestro di cappella* (Ger.: *Kapellmeister*) was the director of music at courts and churches. Today 'maestro' is customarily used as a mark of respect or courtesy when addressing or referring to a conductor or soloist of high professional standard of any nationality. JMo

Magalhães, Filipe de (*b* Vila Nova de Azeitão, nr Lisbon, *c*.1563; *d* Lisbon, 17 Dec. 1652). Portuguese composer. Apparently the favourite pupil of Manuel Mendes at the choir school of Évora Cathedral, he succeeded Mendes as *mestre da claustra* there. Moving to Lisbon, he directed the choir of the Capela da Misericórdia and served in the royal chapel, from 1623 to 1641 as its *mestre de capela*. A collection containing eight masses, dedicated to Philip IV of Spain, was issued in 1636, and Magalhães also published a book of *Magnificat* settings dedicated to John, Duke of Braganza. OR

maggiore (It.). 'Major'.

maggot. In Old English, a fanciful idea. In the 16th and 17th centuries it was used as a title for a pleasant piece of music, such as a dance, with the name of a person attached, e.g. 'My Lady Winwood's Maggot', and, on a less exalted level, 'Dick's Maggot'. In the 20th century, Peter Maxwell Davies revived the word in his theatre piece *Miss Donnithorne's Maggot*.

Magic Flute, The. See ZAUBERFLÖTE, DIE.

Magnard, (Lucien Denis Gabriel) **Albéric** (*b* Paris, 9 June 1865; *d* Baron, 3 Sept. 1914). French composer. His father was the director of *Le Figaro*, but Magnard directed much of his energies in his early years towards making his own way and refusing anything that might be construed as a favour. He studied at the Paris Conservatoire with Dubois and Massenet, winning a *premier prix* in harmony. But he gained more from later private studies with d'Indy (1888–92), whose intransigent outlook on life and veneration for Beethoven he shared. In 1892 his articles in *Le Figaro* on the Chanteurs de Saint-Gervais did much to popularize those early proponents of 19th-century choral music, whose performances were admired by Debussy.

Magnard himself was a natural contrapuntist, often seeming wilfully to shun the blandishments of orchestral colour. At other times, as in the scherzo of the Fourth Symphony (1911–13), he turns his back on civilized Paris and allows his music to galumph: Milhaud was one of the earliest supporters of his four symphonies, saying they 'smelt of the French countryside'. For all that, Magnard had a considerable lyrical gift, even if he seems to have exercised it somewhat reluctantly.

In *Bérénice*, a *tragédie en musique* after Racine (Paris, 1911), the presence of a canon in the love music and the casting of the hero's meditation as a fugue indicate that perhaps the opera house was not his natural home. But his opera *Guercoeur* (Paris, 1931), reconstituted after his death, is both passionate and powerful, with passages of radiant beauty in the final act.

If Magnard is never an 'easy' composer, with rather too much Franckian seriousness for some modern tastes, the Fourth Symphony is a deeply impressive work, suggesting that by his mid-40s he was coming to terms with his own psychological problems and that his death, met while defending his property against German soldiers, was a great loss to French music. RN

Magnificat. The *canticle of the Virgin Mary (Lat.: 'Magnificat anima mea', 'My soul magnifies the Lord'), Luke 1: 46–55. Delivered in response to the greeting of Elizabeth, this song of thanksgiving echoes the Old Testament prayer of Hannah (1 Samuel 2: 1–10). The *Magnificat* became a fixed element of Vespers in the medieval Roman rite, where its verses were sung to special psalm tones, the choice of which was determined by an accompanying proper antiphon. Following the Protestant Reformation, the canticle passed into the evening offices of the Anglican and Lutheran Churches. Since late antiquity in the Byzantine, Armenian, and Syrian Orthodox rites, however, the *Magnificat* has been an element of the morning Office. At Byzantine monastic Orthros, it is sung on ordinary days with the Marian refrain 'Greater in honour than the cherubim' as the last in the series of nine biblical canticles ('odes'), to which are also attached the poetic stanzas of the kanon.

Between the 15th and 17th centuries, Western composers including Dunstaple, Dufay, Binchois, Lassus, Palestrina, Monteverdi, and Schütz set the *Magnificat* to polyphony more frequently than any other liturgical text outside the Mass Ordinary. These works range from *alternatim* settings of the psalm tone in fauxbourdon or imitative style to continuous compositions with instrumental ritornellos. Anglican composers often set the *Magnificat* and *Nunc dimittis* together, either on their own or as part of a full service. During the Baroque era, continental composers began to set the verses of the *Magnificat* as a series of discrete choruses and arias, a sectional approach followed for instance by Bach. The Classical period saw the emergence of unified 'symphonic' settings such as that of Mozart's *Vesperae solennes de confessore* (K339). Modern settings diverge greatly in scale and complexity, with those by Pärt and Penderecki representing opposite ends of the spectrum.   —/ALı

Magnus liber organi ('Great Book of Organum'). A collection of two-voice plainchant settings for liturgical use, dating from the early Notre Dame period (*c.*1170). It has been attributed to *Léonin and said to have been revised by *Pérotin. The most important surviving work of the period, it is arranged for the church year in cycles of polyphonic settings of the Office and the Mass. Its title is taken from the description by the 13th-century theorist Anonymous IV: 'Magnus liber organi de graduali et antifonario'.

Mahagonny. 'Songspiel' in three parts by Weill after poems from Bertolt Brecht's *Hauspostille* (Baden-Baden, 1927); the title is also sometimes used to refer to *Aufstieg und Fall der Stadt Mahagonny*.

Mahler, Gustav (*see page 730*)

Mahler-Werfel, Alma (Maria) (*b* Vienna, 31 Aug. 1879; *d* New York, 11 Dec. 1964). Austrian writer and composer. The daughter of the painter Emil Schindler, she had a private education, supervised by her mother after Schindler's death in 1892. She studied with Joseph Labar, then with Zemlinsky, who was the first in a sequence of important artistic figures to fall in love with her. In 1900–1 she wrote a number of songs, the bulk of which are now believed lost, the manuscripts having been destroyed in the bombing of Vienna during World War II. Those that survive reveal an intense chromatic sensuality and a vocal style poised between declamation and lyricism.

Alma Schindler met Gustav Mahler in 1901 and married him a year later, abandoning composition at his request. Like many of her relationships, the marriage was stormy. During the couple's marital crisis in 1910 Mahler rescinded his edict against her composing and selected five of her songs for publication. Four more of her early songs appeared in 1915. After Mahler's death in 1911 she returned sporadically to composition, publishing a further set of songs in 1924. The same year she edited Mahler's letters and the manuscript of his incomplete Tenth Symphony for publication. After an intense, troubled relationship with the painter Oskar Kokoschka, she married and subsequently divorced the Bauhaus architect Walter Gropius.

Her third husband, whom she married in 1929, was the novelist Franz Werfel, one of whose poems she had set in 1915. In 1938 the couple left Nazi-occupied Austria, eventually arriving in the USA in 1940 and settling in California, where Alma was hostess to many members of the émigré artistic community. After Werfel's death in 1945 she moved to New York. Her reputation as artistic muse and *femme fatale* rests partly on Mahler's music and partly on her two volumes of autobiography: *Gustav Mahler: Erinnerungen und Briefe* (1940) and *Mein Leben* (1960), an abridgment of which had been published in English as *And the Bridge is Love* in 1958. Though they make colourful reading, their veracity has often been called into question. Berg's Violin Concerto (1935) was inspired by the death from polio of Manon, her daughter by Walter Gropius.

TA

📖 S. Filler, *Gustav and Alma Mahler: A Guide to Research* (New York and London, 1989) · S. Keegan, *The Bride of the Wind: The Life and Times of Alma Mahler-Werfel* (London, 1991)

Maid of Orléans, The (*Orleanskaya deva*). Opera in four acts by Tchaikovsky to his own libretto after Friedrich von Schiller's tragedy translated by Vasily Andreyevich Zhukovsky, Jules Barbier's *Jeanne d'Arc*, and Auguste Mermet's libretto for his own opera, after Barbier (1876), with details from Henri Wallon's biography of Joan of Arc (St Petersburg, 1881).

Maid of Pskov, The (*Pskovityanka*). Opera in three acts by Rimsky-Korsakov to his own libretto after Lev Mey's play (1860), with additions by Vsevolod Krestovsky and Musorgsky (St Petersburg, 1873); it was revised (St Petersburg, 1895) and a prologue was added (Moscow, 1901).

Maid of the Mill, The. See Schöne Müllerin, Die.

main (Fr.). 'Hand'; *main droite*, 'right hand'; *main gauche*, 'left hand'; *à deux mains*, 'both hands'; *à quatre mains*, 'four hands', i.e. piano duet.

mainstream jazz. A term for present-day jazz improvised on chord progressions in a chiefly solo style. It is no longer confined to jazz in the swing idiom (the sense for which it was coined in the 1950s), and is sometimes extended to fusion styles, but it excludes both free and avant-garde jazz as well as dixieland and other traditional styles.   JJD

maîtrise (Fr.). 'Choir school', usually attached to a cathedral. The word can also apply, by extension, to the body of choristers in a church choir or to their choirmaster.

majeur (Fr.). 'Major'.

major interval. See Interval.

major scale. See Scale, 3.

(*cont. on p. 732*)

Gustav Mahler
(1860–1911)

The Austrian composer and conductor Gustav Mahler was born in Kaliste, Bohemia, on 7 July 1860 and died in Vienna on 18 May 1911.

Mahler's ten symphonies are among the finest monuments to the declining years of the Austro-German domination of European music and adumbrate developments that were to revolutionize the Viennese tradition in the works of Berg, Schoenberg, and Webern. In four of the symphonies he used the human voice and achieved a synthesis of song and symphonic form which, though not unique, has remained inimitable. He was a great conductor, especially of opera, his decade as director of the Vienna Court Opera being regarded as the zenith of that house's achievement.

The early years
Mahler was the second of 14 children born to a Jewish distillery owner, Bernhard Mahler, and his wife Marie. His parents were ill-matched in spite of their fertility, and he was an introspective child. Shortly after his birth the family moved to Iglau (Jihlava). The bugles at the local barracks and the folksongs sung to him by maidservants made an indelible impression. His father encouraged his obvious musical talent and in 1870 Mahler gave a piano recital in Iglau. The following year he was sent to school in Prague, where he was ill-treated; he was fetched home in 1872.

In 1875, on the advice of a farm manager who had heard him play, Mahler was taken to Vienna to play to Julius Epstein, piano professor at the conservatory. He was accepted as a student, but though successful in piano competitions at the conservatory, he abandoned playing in favour of composing. While in Vienna he attended lectures on philosophy at Vienna University and some of Bruckner's lectures. In the course of the next two years he worked as a piano teacher and wrote the libretto and music of his first major work, the dramatic cantata *Das klagende Lied*, which contains many of the individual features of his later style.

Mahler's career as a conductor began in operetta in 1880 at a small summer theatre at Bad Hall, Upper Austria. In 1883 he was appointed to a post at Olmütz (Olomouc). Already his exacting approach to his work

was earning him notoriety among those singers who objected to the standards he imposed. His next appointment was at Kassel (1883–5). There he had a love affair with a singer, the unhappy end of which was sublimated in his song cycle *Lieder eines fahrenden Gesellen* (1883–5, voice and piano, orchestrated 1891–3), for which he again wrote the texts. Themes from this work were also used in his First Symphony.

Dissatisfied with Kassel, he moved to Prague for the 1885–6 season. There for the first time he conducted the Mozart and Wagner operas in which he was to excel. Prague was merely a marking-time operation before he took up the post of second conductor to Arthur Nikisch at Leipzig in 1886. There he conducted several Weber operas and was invited by the composer's grandson to 'complete' Weber's comic opera *Die drei Pintos* from the surviving sketches. This had a successful premiere in January 1888 and made Mahler famous.

Mahler's next two operatic posts were of more significance. From 1888 to 1891 he reinvigorated the Royal Opera at Budapest. While there he conducted the first performance of his First Symphony (under the title Symphonic Poem) but it was not liked. At Hamburg in 1891 he encountered international singers for the first time and conducted up to 19 operas a month, including Wagner's *Tristan und Isolde*. In summer 1892 he made his only visit to London, where he conducted at Drury Lane and Covent Garden.

The years of maturity
From 1893 Mahler spent his summers at a retreat in the Salzkammergut (and later in Carinthia) where he devoted his time to composition. The Second and Third Symphonies were completed in the years 1893–6. The Second Symphony was performed complete in Berlin in 1895, Mahler's first real success as a composer. Among champions of his work at this time was Richard Strauss. In 1897, when the possibility of his appointment to the Vienna Court Opera arose, he fulfilled a necessary condition by being baptized as a Catholic. He was appointed director of the Opera that autumn and

in 1898 conductor of the Vienna Philharmonic (an appointment which ended in 1901 after friction).

Mahler's achievement in Vienna was his sensational raising of standards in all aspects of opera production—not only singing, but acting, lighting, and stage design. In 1902 he married Alma Schindler, herself a composer and the daughter of an artist. Through her he became associated with the Sezession movement and, through the encouragement he gave them, he became the focal point of the younger generation of composers such as Schoenberg, Berg, Webern, and Zemlinsky.

Between 1899 and 1907 Mahler composed his Symphonies nos. 4–8 and two big song cycles. In 1907 the anti-Semitic faction opposed to him secured his departure from the Opera. During this year his elder daughter, aged four, died from scarlet fever, and he was told that he had a malfunction of a heart valve. He left Europe for New York, where he conducted at the Metropolitan Opera from 1908 to 1910, leaving when Toscanini arrived. From 1909 he was conductor of the New York Philharmonic Orchestra, where neither his strict standards of discipline, his concentration on unfamiliar works, nor his retouching of the orchestration of Beethoven's symphonies met with general approval.

Each summer he returned to Europe, composing *Das Lied von der Erde* and the Ninth Symphony (1908–9), conducting his own works in major cities, and in 1910 supervising and conducting the first two performances at Munich of his enormous choral work, the Eighth Symphony. This was the crowning public triumph of his career. Back in New York for the 1910–11 season, he became seriously ill in February. He expressed a wish to return to Vienna where his 50 years of life, lived at an incredible pitch of intense activity, ended in a clinic.

Mahler's style

The importance of the influence of the folk-tale anthology *Des Knaben Wunderhorn* on Mahler's musical style cannot be exaggerated. The elements of satire, parody, and grotesquerie which are such a prominent feature derive from these tales and poems. Early audiences were repelled by Mahler's highly organized settings: the brilliance and clarity of the orchestration seemed to those accustomed to more conventional means to be at variance with the true nature of the material. Not only are the settings remarkable in themselves, but they spilt over into Mahler's symphonic works. Thus, in the First Symphony, the funeral march is based on a parody of the children's round *Bruder Martin*; in the scherzo of the Second the song about St Anthony preaching to the fishes is quoted instrumentally, and the contralto sings the poem *Urlicht* as a prelude to the 'Resurrection' finale; in the Third, the children's vision of heaven *Es sungen drei Engel* is a principal motif, as is the song *Das himmlische Leben* which provides the last movement of the Fourth. Both the Second and the Third Symphonies are on an enormous scale structurally, and their musical content is an extraordinary and convincing juxtaposition of military marches, fanfares, ländler, and popular songs.

The Fifth, Sixth, and Seventh Symphonies are purely instrumental but are also linked with song settings, in their cases the *Kindertotenlieder* (1901–4), the *Five Rückert Lieder* (1901–2), and the last two *Wunderhorn* settings, *Revelge* (1899) and *Der Tamboursg'sell* (1901). The Fifth may be defined as Mahler's 'Eroica', but the Sixth is his most tragic and classically formal symphony. It is also unusual in being concerned with one tonality, A minor, whereas in the other works a system of 'progressive tonality' is used. The Seventh is a reversion to the earlier manner, but presented in a more sophisticated way. In these three central symphonies, a large orchestra is used economically, with passages of delicacy and refinement akin to chamber music.

With the Eighth Symphony, Mahler again called upon the human voice. This work, nicknamed the 'Symphony of a Thousand' because of the number of performers engaged at the Munich premiere, is in two parts, the first a gigantic Bach-inspired polyphonic setting of the hymn *Veni Creator Spiritus*. The second half is a setting of the final scene of Goethe's *Faust*, a long movement in which elements of cantata, symphony, song cycle, and even oratorio are merged. The result is undeniably impressive, but the song-symphony *Das Lied von der Erde*, its six movements based on the German translation of Chinese texts, is artistically more successful as an amalgam of the most potent aspects of Mahler's art.

For his last two symphonies, the Ninth and Tenth, Mahler returned to wholly instrumental forces. Like *Das Lied von der Erde*, the Ninth is emotionally concerned with farewell, a reaction to the knowledge of his heart condition, but this aspect of the music can be over-stressed and sentimentalized. As a symphonic construction it shows Mahler looking ahead both harmonically and formally, for the opening slow movement is a novel structure in which a recurring crescendo governs the development—more properly fragmentation—of the material. The Tenth Symphony (1910–11), made available in a reconstruction by Deryck Cooke (1964, published 1976) of the short score, proves that Mahler had conquered the spiritual desolation implicit in the Ninth. His creative powers were undiminished: the first movement of the Tenth goes further along the path pioneered in the Ninth, and in the huge concluding movement he redevelops earlier themes in a way that transfigures them far beyond the normal recapitulatory process.   MK

📖 N. Bauer-Lechner, *Recollections of Gustav Mahler* (Vienna, 1923; Eng. trans., ed. P. Franklin, London, 1980) · A. Mahler (ed.), *Selected Letters of Gustav Mahler* (Berlin, 1924; Eng. trans., enlarged, ed. K. Martner, London, 1979) · B. Walter, *Gustav Mahler* (Vienna, 1936; Eng. trans. 1937, 2/1941/R1970) · A. Mahler, *Gustav Mahler: Memories and Letters* (Amsterdam, 1940; Eng. trans. 1964, rev. and enlarged, ed. D. Mitchell and K. Martner, London, 1975) · D. Mitchell, *Gustav Mahler: The Early Years* (London, 1958, 2/1980) · D. Cooke, *Gustav Mahler, 1860–1911* (London, 1960, enlarged 2/1980) · H.-L. de La Grange, *Mahler* (New York, 1973; London, 1974) · D. Mitchell, *Gustav Mahler: The Wunderhorn Years* (London, 1975); *Gustav Mahler: Songs and Symphonies of Life and Death* (London, 1985) · H.-L. de La Grange, *Gustav Mahler: Vienna: The Years of Challenge, 1897–1904* (Oxford, 1995) · J. Carr, *The Real Mahler* (London, 1997) · P. Franklin, *The Life of Mahler* (Cambridge, 1997) · D. Mitchell and A. Nicholson (eds.), *The Mahler Companion* (Oxford, 1999) · H.-L. de La Grange, *Gustav Mahler: Vienna: Triumph and Delusion, 1904–1907* (Oxford, 1999)

Makropulos Affair, The (*The Makropulos Case*; *Věc Makropulos*). Opera in three acts by Janáček to his own libretto after Karel Čapek's comedy *Věc Makropulos* (1922) (Brno, 1926).

Mal (Ger.). 'Time'; *das erste Mal*, 'the first time'; *einmal*, 'once'; *zweimal*, 'twice', etc.

malagueña. An improvised Spanish song in free style and rhythm but based on a repetitive chordal accompaniment.

Maldere, Pierre van (*b* Brussels, 16 Oct. 1729; *d* Brussels, 1 Nov. 1768). Flemish composer. In 1746 he was a violinist in the royal chapel at Brussels; he seems to have remained in its service for most of his life, in spite of tours that took him to Dublin (where he directed the Philharmonic Concerts, 1751–3), Paris, Vienna, and elsewhere. He was director of the Brussels Grand Théâtre from 1762 to 1767. A prolific composer, he wrote several operas, symphonies, and chamber music.   DA/RP

male alto. See ALTO VOICE.

Malibran, Maria(-Felicia) [née García] (*b* Paris, 24 March 1808; *d* Manchester, 23 Sept. 1836). Spanish mezzo-soprano, sister of Pauline Viardot. She studied with her father, the elder Manuel García, and made her debut as Rosina in *Il barbiere di Siviglia* at the King's Theatre, London, in 1825. That year she sang the same role in New York to open the García company's season, in which she also took two parts that brought her fame for her virtuosity: the title role of Rossini's *Tancredi* and Desdemona in his *Otello*. She returned to Europe in 1827 after the failure of her marriage to Eugène Malibran, and from 1828 to 1832 appeared in Paris and London, winning notable success in the roles of Semiramide and Desdemona. She was acclaimed in Italy when she appeared in Bologna, Naples, and Milan, though she caused a scandal at La Scala when

she sang passages in Donizetti's *Maria Stuarda* that had been banned by the censors. Her early death was caused by a riding accident when she was pregnant with the child of her new husband, Charles de Bériot.   JT

📖 A. Fitzlyon, *Maria Malibran* (London, 1987)

malinconico (It.). 'Melancholy'; *malinconoso*, *malinconioso*, 'in melancholy fashion'. Beethoven used it to describe the introductory section of the fourth movement of his String Quartet in B♭ major op. 18 no. 6, the whole work acquiring the nickname 'La Malinconia'.

Malipiero, Gian Francesco (*b* Venice, 18 March 1882; *d* Treviso, 1 Aug. 1973). Italian composer. He studied with Marco Enrico Bossi in Venice and Bologna but also learnt much from his independent work on early Italian music (he was later to produce a complete edition of Monteverdi among much other editorial work). Debussy, Stravinsky, and Casella were also important influences on his delicately worked music, and though his output was enormous and very uneven it does include such distinctive masterpieces as the miniature operas *Sette canzoni* (Paris Opéra, 1920), the fourth (1934) of his eight string quartets, and his First Violin Concerto (1932). That was the year he returned to Venice, to teach and compose, his later output including a large number of further operas as well as symphonies, concertos, and large-scale vocal and choral works, some with orchestra.   PG

📖 J. C. G. Waterhouse, *Gianfrancesco Malipiero* (London, 1999)

mallet. See BEATER.

Malvezzi, Cristofano (*b* Lucca, *bapt.* 28 June 1547; *d* Florence, 22 Jan. 1599). Italian composer. When his father left his post as organist of Lucca Cathedral in 1551 Cristofano accompanied him to Florence, where he spent the rest of his life. He was in the service of the

Medici, and in 1574 he gained the important position of *maestro di cappella* of S. Giovanni Battista; later he was also organist at Florence Cathedral. He wrote keyboard ricercars and three books of madrigals, but is best known for his contribution to the *intermedi* performed as part of the celebrations surrounding the wedding of Grand Duke Ferdinando I and Christine of Lorraine in 1589.   DA

Mamelles de Tirésias, Les ('The Breasts of Tiresias'). Opera in a prologue and two acts by Poulenc to his own libretto after Guillaume Apollinaire's play (Paris, 1947).

Ma mère l'oye ('Mother Goose'). Suite for two pianos (1908–10) by Ravel, depicting characters from fairy tales by Charles Perrault and others; it was later orchestrated by Ravel, who added a prelude and four interludes to make a children's ballet (Paris, 1912).

man. Abbreviation for *mano.

mancando (It.). 'Dying away'.

Manchester School. A group of composers—Peter Maxwell Davies, Harrison Birtwistle, Alexander Goehr, and John Ogdon—who studied at the RMCM and Manchester University with Richard Hall in the late 1950s.

Manchicourt, Pierre de (*b* Béthune, *c*.1510; *d* Madrid, 5 Oct. 1564). Franco-Flemish composer. In 1539 he was director of the choir at Tours Cathedral, and by 1545 was *maître de chapelle* at Tournai Cathedral. He also served as canon at Arras before moving to the Flemish chapel of Philip II in Madrid in 1559. His works include many masses and motets, and over 50 chansons in both elegiac and satirical styles.   DA

Mancini, Henry (*b* Cleveland, OH, 16 April 1924; *d* Beverly Hills, CA, 14 June 1994). American composer. His prolific career in film and television began in the 1950s in Hollywood. He drew on his earlier big-band experience for *The Glenn Miller Story* (1954) and *The Benny Goodman Story* (1956); a distinctive personal style was revealed in *A Touch of Evil* (1958). He wrote such familiar music as 'Baby Elephant Walk' (*Hatari*, 1962) and the theme from *The Pink Panther* (1964). Mancini's songs, with lyrics mostly by Johnny Mercer and often associated with films, include 'Moon River' (*Breakfast at Tiffany's*, 1961) and the title songs from *Days of Wine and Roses* (1962) and *Charade* (1963).   JSN

mandola. A large, low-tuned *mandolin.

mandolin. A small plucked wire-strung instrument. The type most commonly used today is the 'Neapolitan' mandolin, which developed in the mid-18th century; it has four double courses of strings, tuned *g–d'–a'–e''*

(like the violin), and a deeply bowled body. Modern variants, which became much used in European and American traditional music in the 20th century, have a flat or gently curved back but a wider pear-shaped body and sometimes an arched belly and *f*-shaped soundholes; the mandolin preferred by *bluegrass musicians has an elaborate waisted body shape sometimes terminating in a scroll by the neck. Both developments are associated with the Gibson company of Kalamazoo, Michigan. Tenor and octave mandolas are larger, tuned respectively a 5th and an octave below the mandolin. Bass mandolins were also made for use in the mandolin orchestras that became popular late in the 19th century.

Small instruments with lute-like bodies, with four to six courses, existed in western Europe in the 16th and 17th centuries (see MANDORE). They persisted in Italy after they had been superseded elsewhere, the six-course 'Milanese' model being played into the 19th century. It is this model, with a shallower-bowled body than that of its Neapolitan contemporary, that is most suitable for the concertos of Vivaldi and Hummel. Mandolins are almost always played with a plectrum.   RPA

mandora. A large bass lute used for continuo playing in 18th-century Germany and Austria, also known as *Gallichon*, *Calichon*, etc. (see COLASCIONE).

mandore. A term for various west European (particularly French) plucked string instruments of the 16th and 17th centuries, resembling a small *lute. They seem to have derived from the medieval *gittern, and are the ancestors of the Italian *mandolin. They could have four, five, or six single or double courses, usually of gut but sometimes of wire.

Manfred. 1. Incidental music, op. 115 (1848–9), by Schumann for Byron's verse drama (1817), in a translation by K. A. Suckow (1852); it consists of an overture and 15 items.

2. Symphony (unnumbered), op. 58 (1885), by Tchaikovsky after Byron.

Manfredini, Vincenzo (*b* Pistoia, 22 Oct. 1737; *d* St Petersburg, 16 Aug. 1799). Italian theorist and composer. After studying with G. A. Perti in Bologna he went to Moscow in 1758, later becoming court *maestro di cappella* at St Petersburg. In 1762 he was also appointed *maestro* to the Italian opera company there. He returned to Bologna with a pension in 1769, Galuppi having taken over much of his work in Russia, but was invited back to St Petersburg in 1798. His compositions, which include a Requiem for the Russian Empress Elizabeth, are less important than his sometimes controversial theoretical writings on keyboard accompaniment and the teaching of singing.   DA/ER

manica (It.). In string playing, a shift in position; *mezza manica*, 'half-shift'.

Manieren (Ger.). 'Grace notes'.

Mannerism. A term most often used with reference to the visual arts, to describe the extravagant subjects, contorted gestures, and virtuoso effects of certain 16th- and 17th-century painters, for example Giulio Romano and Caravaggio. It has also been applied to literature (where it becomes linked with the poet Marino) and, more recently, to music. Here it is reckoned to account for certain stylistic traits distinguishable from the High Renaissance and the Baroque. It is quite apt when used to describe the works of late 16th-century 'avant-garde' madrigal composers such as Gesualdo (see MADRIGAL, 3), who in their attempts to depict words vividly used unusual harmonies and intervals, chromaticism, and so on. However, there is some doubt whether the entire period *c.*1530–1630 can be labelled 'Mannerist' unless it is argued that all 'Renaissance' polyphony is somehow mannered in intent and effect.   DA/TC

Mannheim school. The name given to a group of composers who, from 1741, served the court of the Elector Palatine Carl Theodor at Mannheim. Prominent among them were the Bohemian composer and violinist Johann Stamitz, the original director of the group; Antonín Fils; and (in a second generation) Christian Cannabich (Konzertmeister from 1758); Stamitz's sons, Carl and Anton; Franz Xaver Richter; Ignaz Holzbauer; and Carl Joseph Toeschi. A particular achievement was the formation of the Mannheim orchestra, an unusually large ensemble which became renowned throughout Europe not only for the precision and finesse of its performances, but also for its exploitation of such devices as the 'Mannheim crescendo' (a novelty because of its carefully graded increase in volume), the 'Mannheim sigh' (a leaning appoggiatura and its resolution), and the 'Mannheim rocket' (an upward-shooting set of triadic patterns, as found at the opening of Johann Stamitz's G major Symphony op. 3 no. 1). Together with similarly resourceful composers from Austria, Bohemia, and Italy, the members of the Mannheim group contributed profusely, and with fertile variations of style, to the development of the pre-Classical symphony and concerto, and moved substantially towards high Classical concepts in the realm of chamber music.   BS

mano (It.). 'Hand'; *mano destra*, 'right hand'; *mano sinistra*, 'left hand'.

Manon. Opera in five acts by Massenet to a libretto by Henri Meilhac and Philippe Gille after Antoine-François Prévost's novel *L'Histoire du chevalier Des Grieux et de Manon Lescaut* (1731) (Paris, 1884).

Manon Lescaut. Opera in four acts by Puccini to a libretto by Domenico Oliva and Luigi Illica after Antoine-François Prévost's novel *L'Histoire du chevalier Des Grieux et de Manon Lescaut* (1731) (Turin, 1893; revised Milan, 1894). Auber's *Manon Lescaut*, to a libretto by Eugène Scribe (Paris, 1856), Massenet's **Manon*, and Henze's **Boulevard Solitude* are also based on the story.

Mansurian, Tigran Yeghiayi (*b* Beirut, 27 Jan. 1939). Armenian composer. He studied composition with Ghazaros Sarian at the Yerevan Conservatory, where he began to teach in 1967 and was later made professor of composition. A leading figure in the Armenian avant-garde, he was named Honoured Artist of Armenia (1984) and People's Artist of Armenia (1990). His early works were in a neo-classical style exemplified by the orchestral pieces of the mid-1960s; much of his chamber music, from that period and later, shows an adherence to Classical forms. He has also used serial and 12-note procedures, and a number of his works incorporate elements from Armenian traditional music. He has written a ballet, *The Ice Queen* (1990), concertos for violin, viola, cello (three), and organ, a large quantity of vocal and chamber music, and about 50 film scores.   JK

Mantra. Work by Stockhausen (1969–70) for two amplified, ring-modulated pianos with woodblock and crotales (played by the pianists); the whole score is based on one melodic formula.

Mantua, Jachet [Jacquet] of. See JACHET OF MANTUA.

manual. A keyboard played by the hands, as opposed to the *pedalboard, played by the feet.

manualiter (Ger., from Lat. *manualis*). 'On the manuals'; in keyboard music, a direction to play with the hands only.

Manzoni Requiem. Title sometimes given to Verdi's Requiem (1874), composed in memory of the Italian novelist and poet Alessandro Manzoni (1785–1873) and first performed on the first anniversary of his death.

Maometto II ('Mahomet II'). Opera in two acts by Rossini to a libretto by Cesare della Valle after his *Anna Erizo* (Naples, 1820). Rossini revised it as *Le Siège de Corinthe*.

maqām (pl. *maqāmāt*). The term used for the melodic modes of Arab music, covering both the ranking of pitches and the melodic patterns of a given mode.

maracas. A South American pair of vessel rattles containing pellets or seeds, frequently used in dance bands and occasionally in the orchestra. They are usually made of gourds or coconut shells on wooden handles, or now often of plastic, and are played with one or a pair held in each hand. As with almost all paired instruments, one is higher-pitched than the other. Paired vessel rattles are common over much of the world, and 'maracas' has become a generic term for such instruments.   JMo

Marais, Marin (*b* Paris, *bapt.* 31 May 1656; *d* Paris, 15 Aug. 1728). French composer and bass viol player. The son of a shoemaker, he was a choirboy at St Germain-l'Auxerrois with Lalande. He studied the bass viol for six months with Sainte-Colombe and by 1675 was playing in the Académie orchestra under Lully. In 1679 he obtained a court post as an *ordinaire* in the *musique de la chambre du roi*. A skilled composer as well as performer, he published his first book of *pièces de violes* in Paris in 1686; in the same year his *Idylle dramatique* (lost) was performed at Versailles. After Lully's death in 1687, Marais collaborated with Louis Lully on *Alcide* (1693) before composing three *tragédies en musique* of his own for performance at the Opéra, of which *Alcyone* (1706) was particularly admired for the thundering multiple bass parts of its tempest scene.

Marais's *Pièces en trio*, published in partbooks in 1692, was the first such collection by a French composer to appear. It was followed by four collections for one to three viols (1701–25) and a volume of trios with violin (1723). In addition to dance movements they include highly expressive preludes, a virtuoso set of *couplets* on *La folia*, *tombeaux* to his teachers and son, and numerous colourful *pièces de caractère*. The defining qualities of Marais's viol music are its craftsmanship, stylistic refinement, and mastery of idiom. Admired as a player, Marais was also much in demand as a teacher. He was succeeded at court by his eldest son, Vincent (1677–1737), in 1725; another son, Roland (*c*.1685–*c*.1750), published two collections of *pièces de viole* (1735, 1738).   JAS

📖 J. A. SADIE, *The Bass Viol in French Baroque Chamber Music* (Ann Arbor, MI, 1980) · S. MILLIOT and J. DE LA GORCE, *Marin Marais* (Paris, 1991)

Marazzoli, Marco (*b* Parma, *c*.1602–8; *d* Rome, 25 Jan. 1662). Italian composer. He was associated with the Barberini family in Rome, writing cantatas, sacred pieces, oratorios, and eight or ten operas. From 1640 he was also a tenor in the Sistine Chapel. He collaborated with Virgilio Mazzocchi on *Chi soffre speri* ('Who Suffers May Hope'; performed 1637, revised 1639), one of the earliest comic operas, and with Abbatini on *Dal male il bene* ('From Ill Comes Good', 1654). However,

he was far more effective as a composer of lyrical cantatas, of which at least 379 survive.   TC

Marbeck, John. See MERBECKE, JOHN.

Marcabru (*fl c*.1129–50). Troubadour. Apparently an orphan of humble birth, he lived under the patronage of various royal and noble households within Occitania and became known for his moralizing songs, many of which comment on his patrons' way of life. Of the more than 40 songs by him that are known from their words, only four survive with music.   JM

marcato (It.). 'Marked', 'stressed', i.e. emphasizing each note; it often indicates a melody that should be given prominence.

Marcello, Alessandro (*b* Venice, 1684; *d* Venice, 1750). Italian composer. A noble dilettante, he was a poet, painter, and student of philosophy and mathematics as well as an accomplished violinist. Tartini, Lotti, and Gasparini regularly attended the weekly concerts held at his house. His best-known work is the D minor oboe concerto transcribed for keyboard by Bach.

DA/ER

Marcello, Benedetto (*b* Venice, 24 July or 1 Aug. 1686; *d* Brescia, 24 or 25 July 1739). Italian composer, writer, theorist, and public servant, younger brother of Alessandro Marcello. He entered the service of the Venetian Republic in 1707, becoming governor of Pola (now Pula, Istria) in 1730, and chamberlain of Brescia in 1738. He was admitted to the Accademia Filarmonica in Bologna in 1712. More prolific than his brother, he achieved considerable fame with his settings of Italian paraphrases of the psalms in arioso style, published between 1724 and 1726 as *Estro poetico-armonico* and reprinted in translation in London and elsewhere. He was also one of the leading cantata composers of the time, and a successful singing teacher. His satire on the manners of the opera house, *Il teatro alla moda*, which lampooned such major figures as Vivaldi, brought him considerable notoriety at the time, but should not be taken too seriously as a historical document.

DA/ER

march (Fr.: *marche*; Ger.: *Marsch*; It.: *marcia*). A composition, commonly in duple time, with strong repetitive rhythms for accompanying military movements and processions.

As far back as Virgil's *Aeneid* instruments were used to arouse excitement among advancing armies. March music was subsequently developed as an ornamentation of a regular drum rhythm and encompassed marches that were slow, quick, or even double-quick. The earliest extant marches for military use are those of Lully and the elder Philidor. 17th- and 18th-century marches were generally ephemeral pieces, but the French Revolution and the Napoleonic Wars provided new impetus. Such composers as J. P. A. Martini, F.-J. Gossec, Grétry, Méhul, and Cherubini contributed marches for French armies, and Rouget de Lisle's *Marseillaise* survives as the most famous French march of the time. From the early 19th century comes the Hungarian Rákóczi March, subsequently given wide familiarity by Berlioz and Liszt.

The great period of popular march composition came during the 19th century with the rise of specialist light-music composers, many of whom were at times military bandmasters as well as dance-band leaders. Their success culminated in the career of John Philip Sousa who, as bandmaster of the US Marine Band, achieved unparalleled popular appeal with such rousing marches as *The Stars and Stripes Forever*.

Processional march music is a feature of classical works including operas and oratorios by Handel (*Scipione*), Mozart (*Die Zauberflöte*), Meyerbeer (*Le Prophète*), Verdi (*Aida*), Wagner (*Lohengrin*), and Prokofiev (*The Love for Three Oranges*). Marches are also to be found in incidental music (Beethoven, *Die Ruinen von Athen*) and symphonies (Berlioz, *Symphonie fantastique*). Among piano pieces, Schubert's *Marches militaires* remain familiar, as does the 'Marche funèbre' from Chopin's Sonata in B♭ minor. Other well-known funeral marches include the Dead March from Handel's *Saul* and Siegfried's Funeral March in Wagner's *Götterdämmerung*.   ALa

Marchand, Louis (*b* Lyons, 2 Feb. 1669; *d* Paris, 17 Feb. 1732). French composer and organist. He was an infant prodigy and held an appointment as organist at Nevers Cathedral at the age of 14. In 1689 he arrived in Paris, where after two years he became organist of the Jesuit church in the rue St Jacques and later took up posts at St Benoît and the Cordeliers. He won renown as a virtuoso keyboard player and in 1702 published two collections of harpsichord pieces; of his surviving organ works only a small collection (printed posthumously) appeared, though four further manuscript collections survive. He also composed sacred songs, at least one cantata, and an opera (lost) and compiled a composition treatise. In 1708 he acquired Nivers's quarter of the post of *organiste du roi*, but in 1713 he left to tour Germany. In 1717 Marchand agreed to take part in a contest with J. S. Bach in Dresden, but he left the court before Bach arrived. He eventually returned to Paris and his post at the Cordeliers, where he remained for the rest of his life. A well-known teacher, he counted Daquin among his most important pupils.   DA/JAS

Märchen (Ger., 'tale'; pl. *Märchen*). A piece of music with some suggestion of traditional or legendary forms.

marcia (It.). 'March'; *alla marcia*, 'in the manner of a march'; *marcia funebre*, 'funeral march'.

Marek, Czesław (Josef) (*b* Przemyśl, 16 Sept. 1891; *d* Zürich, 17 July 1985). Polish-Swiss composer, pianist, and teacher. After studying in Lemberg (now L'viv), he moved to Vienna, where his teachers included Leschetizky (piano) and Weigl (composition); he also had private composition lessons from Pfitzner in Strasbourg (1913–14). In 1915 he settled in Zürich, forming a friendship with Busoni. Abandoning a promising career as a virtuoso pianist, he became an influential teacher. His first surviving works date from 1911; his last original score was written in 1941, after which he stopped composing: his wife's wealth meant that he did not have to promote his own music, and he interpreted the predictable lack of performances as lack of interest.

Marek's earliest works show the influence of Schmidt and other late Romantics, tempered with a Busonian new classicality; several of his later works admit the influence of Polish folksong, linking Szymanowski with early Lutosławski. His masterpiece, the orchestral *Sinfonia*, is a single 35-minute expanse of music of considerable power and fine architectural judgment; it won the 1928 Vienna Schubert prize. His music had sunk into obscurity until rescued by a complete recording of his works (1996–2000).   MA

Marenzio, Luca (*b* Coccaglio, nr Brescia, *c*.1553; *d* Rome, 22 Aug. 1599). Italian composer. He was the third of seven children born to poor parents in a small Italian town. He may have been a choirboy at Brescia Cathedral before being taken up by Cardinal Cristoforo Madruzzo, who maintained a large establishment of musicians and actors in Rome in the 1570s. On Madruzzo's death in 1578 Marenzio stayed in Rome in the service of the powerful Cardinal Luigi d'Este. He travelled with him to Ferrara in 1580, and soon after this began to publish books of his madrigals. From having been known as a singer he soon became celebrated as the most popular madrigal composer of the time, a reputation which flourished until he began to develop a more serious manner in the mid-1580s. In 1586 Cardinal d'Este died, and in 1588 Marenzio entered the service of the Medici in Florence. He was involved in the wedding celebrations for Ferdinando I and Christine of Lorraine in 1589, and composed the music for the second and third *intermedi* of *La pellegrina*. Later that year he returned to Rome. In the 1590s he (like many Italian musicians) spent some years at the Polish court, returning to Rome shortly before his death.

Marenzio's early madrigals, and the villanellas and canzonettas which continued to be published throughout his life (not always by him), reveal his mastery of singing style and his fondness for drawing attention to each detail of the pastoral verse he chose. In the 1590s his style becomes much more advanced and difficult, and a preoccupation with death and decay shows in his choice of the more anguished and tormented verse of Petrarch and Guarini. The music is often jagged or chromatic in melody and dissonant in harmony, with sudden changes in mood—altogether unlike the smooth, sweet manner of his earlier work. These late madrigals, many of which are in cycles, gained less favour in his lifetime, but the early works persisted in popularity in England, where many were published in *Musica transalpina* and other collections, and where they were much imitated. Marenzio's church music is only now receiving the attention it deserves.   DA/TC

📖 J. CHATER, *Luca Marenzio and the Italian Madrigal, 1577–1593* (Ann Arbor, MI, 1981)

Maria di Rohan ('Maria of Rohan'). Opera in three acts by Donizetti to a libretto by Salvadore Cammarano after Lockroy and Badon's play *Un duel sous le Cardinal de Richelieu* (Vienna, 1843).

Marian antiphons. The *antiphons of the Blessed Virgin Mary customarily sung as a devotion at the conclusion of one of the hours of the *Divine Office. In present-day Roman usage they are sung at the end of *Compline. See also ANTIPHON.

Maria Stuarda ('Mary Stuart'). Opera in two or three acts by Donizetti to a libretto by Giuseppe Bardari after Andrea Maffei's translation (1830) of Friedrich von Schiller's *Maria Stuart* (1800) (Milan, 1835).

Marienleben, Das ('The Life of Mary'). Songs (1922–3) by Hindemith for soprano and piano, settings of poems by Rainer Maria Rilke; the 15 settings were revised between 1936 and 1948. Hindemith orchestrated four of them in 1938 and two more in 1948.

Mariés de la tour Eiffel, Les ('The Newly-Weds of the Eiffel Tower'). Ballet in one act by Auric, Honegger, Milhaud, Poulenc, and Tailleferre (five of Les Six, the other being Durey), to a scenario by Jean Cocteau; it was choreographed by Jean Börlin (Paris, 1921).

marimba. 1. One of the commonest African names for the *xylophone, usually with calabash resonators. Similar instruments appeared in Latin America, probably introduced by African slaves; these often had wooden resonator tubes instead of the gourds more common in Africa. These instruments were adapted by Deagan of Chicago in about 1910 as a low-pitched and richer-toned form of xylophone, with the rosewood bars in the same layout as a piano keyboard and stopped metal tubes as resonators. They became very popular with soloists in variety acts. The marimba is now widely used in all forms of music.

The beaters are much softer than those of the xylophone, so as to produce the fuller tone and also avoid damaging the bars. Techniques requiring two or more beaters in each hand have been developed to make chords practicable. To assist in this the diatonic and chromatic notes are on the same level (on the xylophone the chromatic notes are raised). Marimbas vary in range, but five octaves is common, beginning one and half or two octaves below the xylophone.

2. The name of some species of African plucked *lamellophone (see MBIRA, KALIMBA, LIKEMBE).

JMo

Marini, Biagio (*b* Brescia, c.1587; *d* Venice, 1663). Italian violinist and composer. In 1615 he joined the ensemble of St Mark's, Venice, as a violinist, and after returning to his home town as musical director of the Accademia degli Erranti he went to the court at Parma in 1621. He was one of the earliest Italian violin virtuosos to spend an appreciable time in Germany, passing the years 1623–49 at the Wittelsbach court in Neuburg an der Donau. On his return to Italy, he was successively *maestro di cappella* at S. Maria della Scala, Milan, director of the Accademia della Morte, Ferrara, and *maestro* at Vicenza Cathedral.

Marini's works include some of the most attractive early violin music and are important for their foreshadowing of the solo sonata. The sinfonias for three violins and continuo of the *Affetti musicali* op. 1 (Venice, 1617) are longer and more substantial than was usual at that time, and his op. 22 (*Per ogni sorte di strumento musicale diversi generi di sonate da chiesa, e da camera*) sets some of the sonatas into clearly marked separate sections. His writing for the violin is genuinely soloistic, using, for example, double and triple stopping and tremolo effects, the continuo acting simply as an accompanying part. His division of works into dance suites and more serious music is essentially the same as Corelli's distinction between *sonate da camera* and *sonate da chiesa*.   DA/TC

Mario, Giovanni Matteo, Cavaliere de Candia (*b* Cagliari, 17 Oct. 1810; *d* Rome, 11 Dec. 1883). Italian tenor. Originally an officer in the Sardinian army, he took singing lessons in Paris with Louis Ponchard and Giulio Bordogni and was coached by Meyerbeer for his debut in the title role of *Robert le diable* (1838). The following year in London he was acclaimed in what were to be two of his most famous roles, Gennaro in *Lucrezia Borgia* and Nemorino in *L'elisir d'amore*; he sang Gennaro to the Lucrezia of Giulia Grisi, his stage partner for 22 years. From 1840 to 1867 he enjoyed great international success in a substantial repertory that included roles in operas by Rossini, Bellini, Donizetti, Cimarosa, Auber, Meyerbeer, Mozart, Verdi, and Gounod. He created Ernesto in *Don Pasquale* (Paris, 1843), with Giulia Grisi, Tamburini, and Lablache. One his most popular roles was Almaviva in *Il barbiere di Siviglia*, which suited his poise and style, and in later years he was acclaimed as Faust, Raoul in *Les Huguenots* and the Duke of Mantua in *Rigoletto*.   JT

   📖 E. FORBES, *Mario and Grisi* (London, 1985)

Markevitch [Markevich], **Igor** (*b* Kiev, 27 July 1912; *d* Antibes, 7 March 1983). Russian-born Italian, later French, conductor and composer. He studied first (1921–3) with his father. In 1925 he played his piano suite *Noces* to Cortot, who arranged for its publication and invited Markevitch to study with him in Paris at the École Normale de Musique (1926–8), where he also took harmony, counterpoint, and composition classes with Boulanger and orchestration with Rieti. In 1929 he played *Noces* and his Sinfonietta (1929) to Diaghilev, who commissioned a piano concerto and a ballet, later abandoned and the material absorbed into *Cantate* (1930); Markevitch gave the premiere of the concerto in London in 1929. He was hailed as one of the most important composers of the coming generation, and for the next 11 years he produced a string of masterpieces. But in 1942 he suddenly stopped composing and, after a serious illness, began a second career as a conductor, effectively ignoring the first, and establishing a reputation particularly in the music of Stravinsky and other Russian composers.

After settling in Italy in 1940, Markevitch joined the resistance during the war, and later became involved in radical Italian politics. Not until 1978, in Brussels, did he conduct his own music again, leading to its rediscovery and, after his death, its publication and recording. His music is loosely tonal, freely dissonant, effortlessly (sometimes intensely) contrapuntal, harmonically oblique, often highly dramatic, rigorously unsentimental, and with a high charge of energy. His works include the ballets *Rébus* (1931) and *L'Envol d'Icare* (1933) and, for orchestra, the Serenade (1931), *Ouverture symphonique* (1931), *Hymnes* (1932–3, 1936), and *Le Nouvel Âge* (1937); *Psaume* (1933), *La Taille de l'homme* (1939) and *Lorenzo il magnifico* (1940) are scored for soprano and orchestra; *Le Paradis perdu* (1935) is an oratorio; and his last work, *Variations, Fugue and Envoi on a Theme of Handel* (1941), is for piano.   MA

markiert (Ger., 'marked'). *Marcato.

markig (Ger.). 'Vigorous'.

marqué (Fr., 'marked'). *Marcato.

Marriage of Figaro, The. See NOZZE DI FIGARO, LE.

Marsch (Ger.). 'March'.

Marschner, Heinrich (August) (*b* Zittau, 16 Aug. 1795; *d* Hanover, 14 Dec. 1861). German composer. He studied in Prague with Tomášek and in Leipzig with J. G. Schicht. His early works included a Viennese-type *Singspiel*, *Der Kyffhäuserberg* (composed in 1816), but his first success came with a Romantic opera, *Heinrich IV und d'Aubigné*, produced by Weber in Dresden in 1820. Moving to Dresden, he became Weber's assistant as director of the German and Italian companies, though their relationship soon deteriorated. *Der Holzdieb* ('The Wood Thief', 1825; also known as 'The Poacher') reverts to Viennese *Singspiel* in manner. On being passed over for the succession to Weber's post in 1826, Marschner left for Danzig, where he produced an attempt at grand opera in *Lucretia* (1827). However, he found a more original vein with *Der Vampyr* (1828), a horror opera in the manner fashionable in the 1820s that owes much to Weber's *Der Freischütz* but also anticipates elements in early Wagner. Especially, he develops from Weber's Lysiart (*Euryanthe*) the concept of the noble villain, containing both good and evil, and divided against himself. There is also some expressive use of motif, and of the opposition of diatonic and chromatic harmony. Some of these ideas are followed up in *Der Templer und die Jüdin* (1829, after Scott's *Ivanhoe*), which contains a fine portrait of another noble villain in the knight Bois-Guilbert.

In 1831 Marschner became Kapellmeister in Hanover, where his operas included *Hans Heiling* (1833). Weber's and Hoffmann's influences show in the hero–villain torn between the real and the supernatural worlds, but the work's originalities include a fine passage of melodrama and some expressively functional orchestration, as well as further Wagnerian anticipations. None of his five remaining operas matches these achievements. In part this is due to poor plots and librettos which did not give him the opportunity to develop his resources to best effect. With *Der Vampyr*, *Der Templer und die Jüdin*, and *Hans Heiling*, however, he earned a significant place in operatic history as one of the most original German opera composers of his generation.   JW

   📖 A. D. PALMER, *Heinrich August Marschner, 1795–1861: His Life and Stage Works* (Ann Arbor, MI, 1980)

Marseillaise, La ('Allons enfants de la patrie'). French national anthem. It was written as a revolutionary marching song in 1792 by Claude-Joseph Rouget de Lisle (1760–1836) and was sung by a battalion from Marseilles when they entered Paris later that year. It was officially adopted in 1795 and has remained in use ever since, in spite of an attempt to replace it during the Second Empire of Napoleon III. The tune has been incorporated into works by several composers including Schumann, Wagner, Litolff, Liszt, Tchaikovsky, and Debussy.   AL

Marsh, Roger (Michael) (*b* Bournemouth, 10 Dec. 1949). English composer. His principal composition studies were with Bernard Rands at York, and his music has its origins in the new kinds of instrumental and vocal techniques that Rands found in Berio. *Not a soul but ourselves . . .* (1977), for four amplified voices, showed a fresh, unhackneyed response to James Joyce's *Finnegans Wake*, and Marsh has continued to exploit a theatrical vein in his work with texts, including the music-theatre pieces *The Big Bang* and *Love on the Rocks* (both 1989), and *Sozu Baba* (1996). Among his more recent instrumental works are *Stepping Out* for piano and orchestra (BBC Proms, 1990), *Espace* for large orchestra (1994), and *Canto 1* for 11 strings (1999).
                                                                      AW

Marteau sans maître, Le ('The Hammer without a Master'). Work (1953–5) by Boulez for contralto, alto flute, guitar, vibraphone, xylorimba, percussion, and viola, to a text by René Char; it was revised in 1957.

martelé (Fr., 'hammered'). In string playing, a heavy, detached bowstroke on the string.

martellando, martellato (It., 'hammering', 'hammered'). Although the terms are used most often (interchangeably with *martelé) in string playing, the direction is also found applied to piano and vocal technique, and Liszt even demands the effect on the organ.   DMı

martellement (Fr., 'hammering'). A 17th-century term for a *mordent.

Martha (*Martha, oder Der Markt zu Richmond*; 'Martha, or The Market at Richmond'). Opera in four acts by Flotow to a libretto by W. Friedrich after an idea by Jules-Henri Vernoy de Saint-Georges (Vienna, 1847).

Martin, Frank (*b* Geneva, 15 Sept. 1890; *d* Naarden, 21 Nov. 1974). Swiss composer. The son of a Calvinist minister, he studied with Joseph Lauber and received encouragement from Ernest Ansermet but was mostly self-taught. He did military service during World War I, then spent brief periods in Zürich, Rome, and Paris before returning to Geneva to study eurhythmics at the Dalcroze Institute (1925–7), where he remained as a teacher of improvisation and rhythmic theory until 1938. He adopted 12-note *serialism in his First Piano Concerto (1933–4), one of the few outside Schoenberg's circle to do so before World War II. After the war he

remained in Europe to teach the method to a new generation: now living in the Netherlands, he commuted regularly to the Cologne Musikhochschule (1950–7), where his pupils included Stockhausen.

Like many of his compatriots, Martin reflected in his art the twin cultural heritage of Switzerland. The strongest Germanic influence on him was not Schoenberg's (for in spite of its serialism his music is predominantly tonal) but Bach's. On the other hand, his sonorities often suggest comparison with Debussy, Ravel, or Roussel, and he generally used French texts and titles. The result of this fusion is often a distinctive combination of the ascetic and the sensuous. His mature style was formed in *Le Vin herbé* (1938–41), a chamber oratorio on the Tristan legend, and it changed little in the works that followed. These include a bigger oratorio, *Golgotha* (1945–8), various dramatic works, and several concertos, of which the *Petite symphonie concertante* for harp, harpsichord, piano, and two string orchestras (1945) achieved wide popularity.   PG

📖 F. Martin, *Responsabilité du compositeur* (Geneva, 1966) · B. Billeter, *Frank Martin* (Frauenfeld, 1970)

Martínez de la Roca (y Bolea), **Joaquín** (*b* Zaragoza, *c*.1676; *d* Toledo, 1747). Spanish composer and organist. He was organist and *maestro de capilla* at the cathedrals of Zaragoza (1695), Palencia (1714), and Toledo. His incidental music for Francisco Escuder's play *Los desagravios de Troya* (1712; published that year in Madrid) shows the influence of the Italian style and of *opéra-ballet*. He also wrote some sacred works, and issued three critical pamphlets: one (1706) in favour of the Italian style in church music and two (1716–17) condemning the dissonances in the *Missa 'Scala aretina'* by the Catalan Francisco Valls, a work that caused enormous controversy in Spain.   P-LR

Martini, Giovanni Battista [Padre] (*b* Bologna, 24 April 1706; *d* Bologna, 4 Oct. 1784). Italian writer on music. He was one of the most influential theorists and teachers of his time. The son of a string player, he studied music at Bologna, then entered the Franciscan order. Apart from his novitiate, he spent all his life as organist and *maestro* of S. Francesco, Bologna. He owned a vast collection of music of the past (now in the Civico Museo, Bologna), and his writings include a music history, *Storia della musica* (Bologna, 1761–81), which he never completed. He was consulted by many, including J. C. Bach and Mozart, about counterpoint in the 'old style' (*stile antico) of Palestrina. He also composed much sacred music and many instrumental and orchestral works.   DA/LC

Martini, Johann Paul Aegidius ['il Tedesco'] (*b* Freystadt, nr Nuremberg, 31 Aug. 1741; *d* Paris, 10 Feb.

1816). German composer. After studying in Fribourg, in 1764 he went to Paris, where he was director of music to various members of the nobility including the Prince of Condé. He was nevertheless appointed an inspector of the Paris Conservatoire during the revolutionary period, reverting to the service of the Bourbons on their restoration. He wrote symphonic and chamber music, operas, and some church music, but is best remembered for his song *Plaisir d'amour*.   DA/RP

Martino, Donald (James) (*b* Plainfield, NJ, 16 May 1931). American composer. He studied with Roger Sessions and Milton Babbitt at Princeton (1952–4) and Dallapiccola in Florence (1954–6), then taught at Princeton (1957–9), Yale (1959–69), and the New England Conservatory (from 1969). His music is in a fluent and characterful serial style reflecting his Italo-American origins and studies, and suggesting also—sometimes more, sometimes less—his taste for jazz. Among his works are pieces for his own instrument, the clarinet (Triple Concerto for clarinet, bass clarinet, and contrabass clarinet, 1977), other symphonic and chamber compositions (*Notturno* for sextet, 1973), and choral music.   PG

Martinů, Bohuslav (Jan) (*b* Polička, Bohemia, 8 Dec. 1890; *d* Liestal, Switzerland, 28 Aug. 1959). Czech composer. Born and brought up in a small country town, he learnt the violin and began to compose while a boy. In 1906 the local community sponsored him for further training at the Prague Conservatory, but four years later he was expelled for 'incorrigible negligence'. He then earned his living by giving lessons and by playing in the Czech Philharmonic Orchestra until, in 1923, he left for Paris. There he took private lessons with Roussel and lived humbly for the next 17 years. Forced to flee by the Nazi invasion he emigrated to the USA in 1941. He spent his last few years in France and Switzerland.

Compared to many 20th-century composers Martinů was prolific, writing in virtually every genre. While he admired Dvořák and Janáček, the major influences on his music were English madrigals, Debussy, Stravinsky, jazz, and composers of the Baroque era. The concerto grosso impulse is particularly evident in his works of the 1930s. Many of the compositions of the 1920s have modernist tendencies, though he was never a serialist. Throughout the 1930s, the hard edges he had cultivated hitherto are softened by the more tonal harmonies which imbue his later works, especially those written in the 1950s, with great warmth. His six symphonies are coming to be regarded as a major contribution to the genre in the 20th century. The 14 completed operas, including such full-length masterpieces as *Julietta* and *The Greek Passion*, cover a wide range of subject and experiment freely with many media including cinema, radio, and television.
                                                               PG/JSM

    📖 B. LARGE, *Martinů* (London, 1975)

Martín y Soler, (Atanasio Martín Ignacio) **Vicente** (Tadeo Francesco Pellegrin) (*b* Valencia, 2 May 1754; *d* St Petersburg, 10 Feb. 1806). Spanish composer. Born and raised in Valencia, he composed his first opera in 1775 for the court of Madrid. By the end of 1777 he was writing operas and ballets in Naples. In 1782 he moved to Venice, also fulfilling commissions for Turin and Parma. In 1785 he went on to Vienna, where he wrote three operas to librettos by Da Ponte. Of these *Una cosa rara* (1786) and *L'arbore di Diana* (1787) were immensely popular; Mozart quoted a tune from the former in Don Giovanni's supper music.

In 1788 Martín took up the position of court composer to Catherine II, providing Russian operas and ballets for her residence. At the end of his contract in 1794 he left for London, where he composed two operas for the 1795 season at the King's Theatre, again with Da Ponte. By early 1796 Martín was back in St Petersburg and obtained a teaching position, which he held until his death. His music, described by his contemporaries as 'sweet' and 'graceful', is characterized by a pronounced lyricism, as exemplified in short, periodic, melody-dominated numbers, and finds its best expression in the pastoral mode. It appealed overwhelmingly to the amateur.   WT/DL

Martland, Steve (*b* Liverpool, 10 Oct. 1959). English composer. The decisive influence on his music has been the abrasively expansive minimalist style of his Dutch teacher Louis Andriessen. Such works as *Babi Yar* (1983) for orchestra and *Drill* (1987) for two pianos established Martland's typically forceful and repetitive idiom, often allied with explicit political messages; a more reflective side is revealed in *Patrol* (1992) for string quartet. He set up the Steve Martland Band to perform his own music. Passionately committed to music education (and outspoken in his denunciation of decreased state provision), he has established a summer school for student composers and organized projects in the community. His music has been extensively choreographed.   AW

Martucci, Giuseppe (*b* Capua, 6 Jan. 1856; *d* Naples, 1 June 1909). Italian composer and conductor. The son of a trombone player and bandmaster, he showed early talent as a pianist and entered the Naples Conservatory in 1867. After a career as a concert pianist he took up conducting and became one of the earliest champions of Wagner's music in Italy, directing the first Italian performance of *Tristan und Isolde* at Bologna in 1888.

He was director of the music school there (1886–1902), giving many concerts and composing symphonies and concertos in the Germanic style. He spent the last seven years of his life as head of the Naples Conservatory.

DA

Martyrdom of St Magnus, The. Chamber opera in nine scenes by Maxwell Davies to his own libretto after George Mackay Brown's novel *Magnus* (Kirkwall, 1977).

Martyre de Saint Sébastien, Le ('The Martyrdom of St Sebastian'). Incidental music (1911) by Debussy, for soprano, two contraltos, chorus, and orchestra, for a mystery play by Gabriele D'Annunzio; André Caplet assisted with the orchestration.

Marx, Joseph (Rupert Rudolf) (*b* Graz, 11 May 1882; *d* Graz, 3 Sept. 1964). Austrian composer. He studied with E. W. Degner at Graz University and in 1914 was appointed professor of theory and composition at the Vienna Music Academy, where he taught for much of his life. His works include a large number of songs in a style influenced by Wolf. No less traditionalist are his orchestral and chamber pieces (including three string quartets), though there are often touches of Debussian harmony.

PG

Mary, Queen of Scots. Opera in three acts by Musgrave to her own libretto after Amalia Elguera's play *Moray* (Edinburgh, 1977).

Masaniello. See MUETTE DE PORTICI, LA.

Mascagni, Pietro (*b* Livorno, 7 Dec. 1863; *d* Rome, 2 Aug. 1945). Italian composer and conductor. He was the son of a baker who would have liked him to become a lawyer, but an uncle arranged for him to study music and in 1882 he entered the Milan Conservatory, where he was a pupil of Ponchielli. He left after two years, and conducted a touring operetta company before marrying and settling in Cerignola in Puglia. During the 1880s he composed *Guglielmo Ratcliff*, but he abandoned this complex, innovatory work to produce *Cavalleria rusticana*, which was entered by his wife in the competition for a one-act opera held by the publisher Sonzogno in 1888. It won, and was produced in Rome in 1890; immediately successful, it was soon performed all over the world. Today usually associated with Leoncavallo's *Pagliacci*, it has a genuine flair for popular melody approaching Italian folksong, a rich orchestral sound, and real passion.

Like Leoncavallo, Mascagni was never to have a comparable success, but his other operas are by no means simply attempts at exploiting this *verismo vein. *L'amico Fritz* (1891), set in Alsace, disappointed those who expected Mascagni to continue in the style of *Cavalleria rusticana*, and there were several flops before his next success, *Iris* (1898)—a piece with a Japanese setting, which exploits exoticism several years before Puccini's *Madama Butterfly*. Sonzogno's attempt at a publicity stunt, whereby *Le maschere* was given a multiple premiere at seven theatres in 1901, was a fiasco; but it is significant that this opera's adoption of the old *commedia dell'arte* pre-dates those with the same idea by Busoni (*Arlecchino*, 1914–16) and Malipiero (several pieces, including *Tre commedie goldoniane*, 1920–2). His only later work to have achieved success is *Il piccolo Marat* (1921).

Mascagni was a competent conductor of orchestral music as well as opera. When Toscanini resigned from La Scala in 1929 as a protest against Fascism, Mascagni took over certain of his duties and was thereafter tarred with the brush of being a supporter of Mussolini. He died in a shabby Roman hotel the year after that regime had perished.

DA/RP

mascherata [mascarata, mascherada] (It.). 'Masquerade'. 1. An entertainment, popular in Florence in the Renaissance, in which masked performers mimed to musical accompaniment from carnival floats.

2. A kind of *villanella, also related to street performances in the Carnival season; many such pieces were written by Lassus.

Maschinist Hopkins ('Hopkins the Engineer'). Opera in a prologue and three acts by Max Brand to his own libretto (Duisburg, 1929).

Maskarade ('Masquerade'). Opera in three acts by Nielsen to a libretto by Vilhelm Andersen after Ludvig Holberg's play *Mascarade* (1724) (Copenhagen, 1906).

maske. Old spelling of *masque. When found as the title of an instrumental piece, it probably implied that the piece was suitable for use in a masque.

Masked Ball, A. See BALLO IN MASCHERA, UN.

Mask of Orpheus, The. Opera in three acts by Birtwistle to a libretto by Peter Zinovieff (London, 1986).

Mask of Time, The. Work (1980–2) by Tippett for soprano, mezzo-soprano, tenor, and baritone soloists, chorus, and orchestra, a setting of his own text.

Masnadieri, I ('The Robbers'). Opera in four acts by Verdi to a libretto by Andrea Maffei after Friedrich von Schiller's play *Die Räuber* (1781) (London, 1847).

Mason, Benedict (*b* London, 21 June 1955). English composer. He studied at Cambridge before taking a degree in film-making. His earlier works usually involve a pictorial element (*Lighthouses of England and Wales* for orchestra, 1988) and explore elaborate textures in spontaneous and flexible ways (Double Concerto for horn, trombone, and 14 players, 1989; *Self-Referential Songs and Realistic Virelais* for soprano and 18 players, 1990). In 1993 he completed the comic opera *Playing Away* for Opera North. Mason has since concentrated on a series of compositions, intended for specific concert halls, which explore the spaces in question in a more austere, even experimental manner than his earlier scores. These works include concertos for clarinet (BBC Proms, 1994) and trumpet (1997).   AW

Mason, Daniel Gregory (*b* Brookline, MA, 20 Nov. 1873; *d* Greenwich, CT, 4 Dec. 1953). American composer. A grandson of the American musician Lowell Mason (1792–1872), he studied with John Knowles Paine at Harvard and later with George Chadwick and Percy Goetschius; he also had lessons with d'Indy in Paris in 1913. In 1909 he had been appointed to the staff at Columbia University, where he became professor of music (1929–42). His works show an adaptation of European methods (ranging from Brahms to d'Indy) to American materials and subjects: his third and final symphony is subtitled 'A Lincoln Symphony', and he wrote a string quartet on African-American themes. He was also the author of many books on music.

PG

Masonic Funeral Music. See MAURERISCHE TRAUERMUSIK.

masonic music. See FREEMASONRY AND MUSIC.

masque. A type of courtly entertainment used to celebrate special events in England during the 16th and 17th centuries. It consisted of dancing, speech, and song brought together in an allegorical 'device' in honour of the king or a prominent courtier. Nearly all masques were produced to celebrate a special occasion, for example a dynastic marriage, a state visit, or just the Christmas season. The masque differs from spoken drama or opera in that the action is carried forward by dance rather than by speech or song. The main characters, called 'masquers', were aristocratic amateurs who danced their roles, often led by a member of the royal family.

The masque had its origin in the 'disguisings' of Henry VIII's court, which were little more than evenings of social dancing clothed in flimsy allegory. Although a number of masque-like entertainments are known from the reign of Elizabeth, the masque proper came of age during the reign of James I. Many early Jacobean masques were the product of collaborations between such writers as Ben Jonson and Thomas Campion, the architect and designer Inigo Jones, and composers such as Alfonso Ferrabosco (ii), John Coprario, and Robert Johnson. The best masques of this period, for example Campion's *Lord Hayes Masque*

(1607) and Jonson's *Masque of Queens* (1609) and *Oberon* (1611), display a harmonious blend of their diverse elements that was never surpassed.

During the reign of Charles I the masque increased in length, complexity, magnificence, and cost with a new generation of collaborators, including the writers James Shirley and William Davenant and the composers William and Henry Lawes. During the 1630s such masques as Shirley's *The Triumph of Peace* (1634) and Davenant's *Britannia triumphans* (1638) became a visible sign of the court absolutism and extravagance that contributed not a little to the Puritan revolution and to Charles I's downfall. The Banqueting House that still stands in Whitehall—built by Inigo Jones specifically for the performance of masques—was chosen with a fitting sense of irony for Charles's execution in 1649.

As a court form, the masque barely survived the Civil War, though intimate masques continued to be performed in country houses and schools well into the Restoration period. The most important works of this type are Milton's *Comus* with music by Henry Lawes, produced at Ludlow in 1634 in honour of the Earl of Bridgewater, and Shirley's *Cupid and Death* with music by Christopher Gibbons and Matthew Locke, performed in London in 1653 and 1659. *Cupid and Death* is the only masque for which the music survives more or less complete.

It is often said that the masque is merely an imitation of the Italian *ballo* or the French *ballet de cour*. While it is true that the visual aspects of many masques are inspired by Italian Renaissance versions of classical antiquity, the other elements—dance, speech, and above all music—owe little or nothing to foreign models. Musical similarities between English masques and French ballets seem to be the product of similar circumstances rather than of direct contact.

Masque music was nearly always a collaboration between several composers and arrangers, partly because masques were frequently put together very quickly and partly because each element of the music—the songs, the dances, and the incidental instrumental music—was performed by a separate ensemble of royal musicians. The ensembles were spatially separated and normally never heard together, though Thomas Campion, notably in *Lord Hayes Masque*, experimented with polychoral effects in the Italian manner. Thus these three elements are best considered individually.

Masques were constructed round a series of formal dances or 'entries' performed at intervals during the entertainment. There were normally five of these, corresponding to some extent to the five acts of a spoken play. The central part of the masque consisted of three entries danced by the masquers to specially composed and choreographed music. A fourth entry, called the 'revels', consisted of social dances between the masquers and members of the audience. A fifth entry, or 'antimasque', was danced by professionals taking comic or grotesque characters such as *commedia dell'arte* figures, demons, witches, or even birds and animals. Dance music was normally provided by the court violin band, though antimasque dances were sometimes played by wind instruments. The main dances were usually cast in the form of almans, with two repeated sections, though sometimes a third section in quick triple time was added. Their style is brisk and airy, with clear tonal harmonies. Antimasque dances express the grotesque and the comic by the sudden contrast of different tempos. Many of them are, in effect, patchworks made up from fragments of different dances.

The songs in Jacobean and Caroline masques were designed largely to introduce and comment on the dances. They were performed by singers of the royal music who appeared in stage in the guise of minor characters such as attendants or priests. Normally they accompanied themselves with lutes—hence the large numbers of lutes sometimes mentioned in descriptions of masques. Masque songs tend to be similar to ordinary songs of the period—many of them are found in contemporary song collections—though large ensembles and large halls tended to encourage a simple, declamatory style. In the 1630s William Lawes experimented with long anthem-like sequences of continuous solo and ensemble vocal music. *Cupid and Death* develops this process still further, and was probably a prototype for Blow's all-sung masque *Venus and Adonis* (c.1682) and Purcell's *Dido and Aeneas* (1689).

Little can be said about the third musical element in English masques: the 'loud music' played by wind instruments which was used to cover the noise of stage machinery in scene changes. Unfortunately, none of it seems to have survived.   PH

📖 E. J. DENT, *Foundations of English Opera: A Study of Musical Drama in England during the Seventeenth Century* (Cambridge, 1928/R1965) · P. WALLS, *Music in the English Courtly Masque, 1604–1640* (Oxford, 1996)

Mass (Fr.: *messe*; Ger.: *Messe*; It.: *messa*; Lat.: *missa*). The eucharistic liturgy of the Roman Catholic Church. The following account refers primarily to the full sung form of this service, known as High Mass, or *Missa solemnis*, as it was from *c.*1000 until the 1960s, when changes were made in the wake of the Second Vatican Council.

1. Structure of the Mass; 2. Medieval and Renaissance masses; 3. The Baroque era; 4. From the 18th century to the present day

1. Structure of the Mass

The various musical items belong either to the Ordinary, whose sections make up the musical entity normally referred to as a mass and whose texts do not vary, or to the Proper, whose texts change according to the church calendar. Table 1 sets out the sequence of events at High Mass; capital letters indicate the sections of the Ordinary and lower-case those of the Proper, while the portions intoned by the clergy are in parentheses (no mention is made of the various prayers recited silently). It will be seen that the sections of the Ordinary are widely separated, and that the effect of a continuous concert performance of a mass written for liturgical use may be somewhat different from that envisaged by the composer.

TABLE 1

Mass of the Catechumens

> introit
> KYRIE
> GLORIA [except in Advent and Lent]
> (collect)
> (epistle [medieval usage]; Old Testament lesson [restored after Vatican II])
> gradual
> (epistle [after Vatican II only])
> alleluia [or, in penitential seasons, tract]
> sequence [if appointed]
> (gospel)
> CREDO

Mass of the Faithful

> offertory
> (preface)
> SANCTUS/HOSANNA/BENEDICTUS/HOSANNA
> (Pater noster)
> AGNUS DEI
> communion
> (postcommunion)
> ITE MISSA EST [or, in penitential seasons, BENEDICAMUS DOMINO; both are rarely set by composers]

2. Medieval and Renaissance masses

The earliest notated music for the Mass, both Ordinary and Proper, is plainchant. Festal masses of the 10th–12th centuries were typically lengthened through the addition of textual or melodic tropes to items of the Proper (especially the introit) and, with the exception of the Credo, the Ordinary. The solemnity of a mass during the Middle Ages could also be heightened through the addition of a sequence or the improvisation of polyphony, a practice that continued in some locations into the Renaissance and beyond. The earliest notated polyphonic music for the Mass, such as the organa of Léonin and Pérotin, consists in fact of settings of the Proper. In the 14th century this situation was reversed and, perhaps for obvious practical reasons, composers increasingly turned their attention to the unvarying portions of the liturgy. Most of the 14th-century Mass music that survives consists of individual movements rather than complete settings of the Ordinary. The first extant complete setting by a single composer is Machaut's Notre Dame Mass from the later 14th century.

The 15th century saw an increasing tendency not only towards the composition of complete masses, but also towards giving these an overall unity, usually by the use in all the movements of some kind of existing material, the various kinds of which may be summarized as follows:

(*a*) Plainchant. A small number of polyphonic masses have each movement based on a different plainchant. The majority of plainchant-based masses are of the so-called *cantus firmus type, in which the same plainchant is used in each movement, appearing either in one voice only, usually the tenor, or in all voices, as in Josquin's *Missa 'Pange lingua'*.

(*b*) Secular melodies. Masses based on secular melodies are usually also of the cantus firmus type; they are particularly characteristic of the 15th and earlier 16th centuries. Dufay's *Missa 'Se la face ay pale'* is an example of a mass based on a melody from a chanson (his own), but melodies of unknown origin, possibly folk tunes, were also used. The most commonly used of these was the famous *L'*Homme armé* melody. More than 30 *L'Homme armé* masses survive, by such composers as Dufay, Ockeghem, Obrecht, Josquin, La Rue, Morales, and Palestrina. In a 'quodlibet' mass, such as Isaac's *Missa carminum*, a selection of melodies is used.

(*c*) Invented themes. Original themes might be drawn from the hexachord, or devised by applying *solmization syllables to the vowels in an appropriate phrase, as in Josquin's *Missa 'Hercules dux Ferrariae'* (Ex. 1); they would then be used as cantus firmi.

(*d*) Complete pieces. The type of mass based on a complete polyphonic composition, whose material

might be broken up and used in many different ways, has tended to be known as a *'parody mass'. It arose out of the cantus firmus type in the later 15th century, when the models were usually polyphonic chansons, but in the 16th century motets were more commonly used, as with Palestrina's *Missa 'Assumpta est Maria'*, based on his own motet. By the later 16th century this type of mass was far and away the most common; some three quarters of Palestrina's masses use parody technique.

3. The Baroque era

The stylistic changes of the early Baroque era led to an increasing disparity between masses written entirely in the traditional polyphonic manner (*stile antico*), whose principal concession to modernity was the use of the basso continuo and the gradual adoption of a wider harmonic vocabulary, and the mass in modern style, with solo voices and instrumental obbligatos.

A further disparity between different types of mass setting which grew up later in the Baroque period was that between the so-called *missa solemnis* (the term being used in this instance purely with reference to the degree of musical elaboration involved), on an extended scale, with the longer sections divided into a number of movements, and requiring a large number of performers, and the *missa brevis*, a more compact setting, with the words dispatched as expeditiously as possible and demanding less extravagant resources.

Monteverdi's three masses use the *stile antico*, and his Roman contemporaries, such as G. F. Anerio and the Nanino brothers, also used it extensively. This tradition was continued by later composers including Carissimi (probably the last composer to write a mass on *L'Homme armé*); Lotti, who produced both complete masses and isolated mass sections (such as his well-known Crucifixus); and Alessandro Scarlatti. 18th-century composers such as Fux continued to cultivate the *stile antico* mass, which was suitable for use on weekdays and at penitential seasons when orchestral masses were neither practical nor appropriate, and in 19th-century Germany the *Cecilian Movement helped to keep the tradition alive.

The only Mass music by Monteverdi in the modern style is the magnificent Gloria for seven voices and instruments, written in thanksgiving for the end of the Venetian plague of the 1630s. However, there are surviving orchestral masses (often omitting or greatly shortening the Sanctus and Agnus Dei, as was the Venetian custom) by his north Italian contemporaries, such as that of Alessandro Grandi (1630), which uses soloists, chorus, and obbligato instruments. A larger-scale, more solidly polychoral type of mass was cultivated by later 17th-century Bolognese composers, for

Ex. 1

re ut re ut re fa mi re
Her - cu - les Dux Fer - ra - ri - ae

example Colonna. The Italian style also spread to the German-speaking Catholic countries north of the Alps, and the festal masses of such composers as Biber (the probable author of the huge 53-part *Missa salisburgensis* formerly attributed to Orazio Benevoli) make much use of exciting instrumental colours and of the dialogue between solo voices and chorus that was to become characteristic of the 18th-century Viennese style. In France, Louis XIV's preference for Low Mass led to the cultivation of the motet as the main form of church music; only Charpentier, whose *Messe de minuit* is based on French Christmas songs, was greatly concerned with the mass.

The so-called 'Neapolitan' or 'cantata' mass style, which owed much to contemporary opera, and in which the text was divided into many short sections set as self-contained solo arias and choruses in a variety of styles (often including *stile antico*), had an important influence on 18th-century mass composition. In particular it established the tradition of ending the Gloria and Credo with an extended 'Amen' fugue; the well-known D major Gloria of Vivaldi (who wrote a number of mass sections, but no complete settings) is of this type. The greatest example is Bach's B minor Mass; its Kyrie and Gloria originally stood alone, as a Lutheran mass (the Lutheran Church retained these portions of the Mass in their original languages, and four other such masses by Bach survive), the remaining sections being added later.

4. From the 18th century to the present day

The 18th-century Viennese mass combines operatic elements from the cantata mass with a growing tendency to organize choral movements on principles similar to those developing in the symphony and concerto. The large-scale masses of the first half of the century, by such composers as Fux, Caldara, and Reutter (who taught Haydn), still have Glorias and Credos divided into many movements, and make much use of the extended solo aria and a large orchestra; these elements are on the whole missing from the smaller-scale masses intended for ordinary churches that were produced in great quantity at this time.

Thanks to the conditions of his work at Salzburg, many of Mozart's masses are in the very compact *missa brevis* form, as are some of Haydn's early ones: in some, such as Haydn's *Missa brevis Sancti Joannis de Deo*, the urge to set the Gloria and Credo as rapidly as possible causes each voice to sing a different set of words simultaneously. Mozart's unfinished C minor Mass is a late example of the cantata type, but the Gloria of the 'Coronation' Mass (K317) shows him organizing a choral movement in a symphonic manner. There is much use of such symphonic structures in Haydn's last six masses, written between 1796 and 1802 for the Esterházy family; the long sections are now divided into fewer movements, and these are closely organized on a symphonic basis, with the soloists used as an ensemble rather than as individuals. Beethoven's *Missa solemnis*, intended, though not completed in time, for the installation of Archduke Rudolph as Archbishop of Olmütz (now Olomouc) in 1820, is a successor to Haydn's late symphonic masses and, like them, was considered suitable for liturgical use on a festal occasion. There are symphonic elements also in Schubert's large-scale Masses in E♭ and in A♭, although his G major Mass is in a much simpler, even pastoral, vein.

Cherubini's 1825 Mass contains theatrical elements that point the way towards the distinction between concert masses and those really intended for liturgical use, which was to become more marked as the 19th century progressed. Rossini's *Petite Messe solennelle* is typical of the Italianate operatic mass, mixing elaborate solo arias with contrapuntal, sometimes *stile antico*, choruses. Liszt's Mass for the coronation of the King of Hungary in 1867, intended for liturgical use, gives much of the thematic material to the orchestra, while Gounod avoided florid solo writing and entrusted a greater part of the thematic material to the chorus. Bruckner, in his masses with orchestra (such as the F minor), attempts to combine modern elements with characteristics of Renaissance polyphony and even plainchant.

Renaissance polyphony continued to exercise a strong influence on 20th-century composers of masses, perhaps largely because of the *motu proprio* (1903) of Pope Pius X, which emphasized that plainchant and polyphony were the true music of the church and discouraged the use of orchestral masses. Duruflé's *Missa cum jubilo* is a good example of a modern mass setting strongly influenced by plainchant, and Vaughan Williams's G minor Mass has great affinities with Tudor polyphony.

The Latin Ordinary survives unaltered in the new form of Mass promulgated in 1970 by Pope Paul VI, so that any appropriate setting from the past can be used. In practice, however, efforts to encourage congregational participation and otherwise acculturate the Roman liturgy have led most parishes to conduct the majority of their Masses in the local vernacular. A bewildering variety of music is used, ranging from Protestant hymnody and plainchant to settings in indigenous rural and urban popular styles. Variations are determined not only by region and ethnicity, but also by the perceived musical tastes of those regularly attending any one of the multiple Sunday Masses offered by a particular parish.   ER/ALı

Massenet, Jules (Émile Frédéric) (*b* Montaud, Saint Étienne, 12 May 1842; *d* Paris, 31 Aug. 1912). French composer. He was the leading opera composer in late 19th-century France and his operas have remained in the repertory. He was born of an upper bourgeois second marriage, of which he was the 12th and last son. His mother gave him piano lessons and at the age of 11 he was admitted to the Paris Conservatoire. Something of a prodigy, he gave his first recital at the age of 16 and won a *premier prix* the following year, supporting himself by giving lessons and playing in cafés and theatre orchestras. He started composition classes at the Conservatoire in 1860, receiving encouragement from the director, Ambroise Thomas, who became his teacher in 1861. Massenet won the Prix de Rome in 1863, this time with the support of Berlioz. He composed prolifically and in the mid-1860s turned his attention to the stage. He served in the national guard in the Franco-Prussian War, alongside his friend Bizet.

Following the Commune the opera *Don César de Bazan* (after Victor Hugo) achieved some success at the Opéra-Comique in 1872, and the next year his incidental music to Leconte de Lisle's *Les Érinnyes* firmly established Massenet's reputation. The oratorios *Marie-Magdeleine* (1873) and *Ève* (1875) laid the foundations of a crucial preoccupation with themes blending the erotic with the religious which found expression in many of his operas. Fame at the Paris Opéra itself came in 1877 with the grand opera *Le Roi de Lahore*, whose orientalist theme was shared by several spectacles of the time. The following year Massenet was appointed composition professor at the Paris Conservatoire, a post he held for 18 years, his pupils including Bruneau, Charpentier, Hahn, and Chausson.

Hérodiade, based on Gustave Flaubert's tale, was first given in Brussels in 1881. Against a political, religious, and racial background, it explores two themes already identified in his formative works: the conflict between religion and eroticism, and orientalism. It contains substantial, effective arias (including one with a saxophone obbligato) for all the main characters and an irresistibly swooning duet for Salome and John the Baptist.

Three years later, in 1884, came the premiere at the Opéra-Comique of one of Massenet's two most durable works: *Manon*. It shares its source (the novel by the Abbé Prévost) with Auber's *Manon Lescaut* of some 30 years earlier and Puccini's opera of the same title of nine years later. The young Manon is 'rescued' from life in a convent by the young Des Grieux, and the opera follows their downfall, as she is torn between love for him and her desire for a comfortable life supported by an ageing protector. Bereft, Des Grieux studies for the priesthood, and the religious–erotic conflict is nowhere more evident than in the powerful scene where he is reunited with Manon in the seminary of St Sulpice, to the sounds of the organ. *Manon* explores the power and danger of money in a way unparalleled by any other 19th-century work.

It was followed by *Le Cid* (1885), performed at the Opéra and achieving a goal at which Bizet had aimed and for which he had left sketches: an opera on the subject of Don Rodrigue, the young warrior known as El Cid who kills the father of his beloved, his own father's rival. The exploration of this poignant theme was to be Massenet's last success before a period of failures.

Even *Werther* may be counted among these. First conceived in the early 1880s, it was turned down by Léon Carvalho, director of the Opéra-Comique, and was eventually given its premiere in Vienna in 1892. Subsequently considered by some to be Massenet's most profound utterance, it has a conventional story (after Goethe). Werther, a poet, is infatuated with Charlotte, who is to be married to Albert; his love is returned. The lovers are tormented by their illicit passion and Werther eventually shoots himself; he dies a slow death in Charlotte's arms against a background of children's voices singing Christmas music. Massenet brings extraordinary psychological perception to his characterizations, producing a richly melodic score of sombre hues.

Esclarmonde, perhaps his most poignant exploitation of orientalist and feminist themes, was given in 1889, after his meeting with the American soprano Sibyl Sanderson, with whom he had a love affair and for whom the title role was conceived. He also revised the role of Manon for her. For the next four years Massenet wrote little, but he resumed composition when his liaison with Sanderson ended. *Thaïs* was his next success and has been many times revived. It is perhaps the most overt of his explorations of the religious and the erotic, and its 'Méditation' has become a popular number in its own right (though its significance as a moment where the eponymous heroine, previously a courtesan, veers between the erotic and the religious life has been largely forgotten). Pastiche oriental music occasionally lightens this essentially dark opera.

When Thomas died in 1896 Massenet was offered the directorship of the Conservatoire but he declined (as he was to do again in 1905). He also left his post as professor to devote himself to composition. *Sapho* (1897) and the lighter *Cendrillon* (1899) had lukewarm receptions at the Opéra-Comique, though the latter has found a place in the repertory. *Grisélidis* (1901), *Chérubin* (1905), and *Don Quichotte* (1910), among others, suffered a similar fate. During his last years

Massenet was involved in a relationship with a singer, Lucy Arbell, a much younger woman for whom he wrote some roles. He was ill for a decade before his death from cancer.

Massenet's personal life was glamorized in a book of unreliable reminiscences, *Mes souvenirs*, widely diffused and translated. From early in his career there was a stream of criticism, caricature, and satire which compared him to a confectioner. But he had an unquestionable gift for female characterization and was a wonderfully lyrical tunesmith and undeniably masterful in his setting of the French language in recitative and arioso. His influence as a teacher was far-reaching. After his death his reputation sank. More recently he has come to be valued for bringing out the essential preoccupations of *fin de siècle* France, in terms of both politics and social deceits. He could also be daringly risqué, and he undeniably courted commercial success by building on successful formulas. If he suffered a decline in the wake of the rise of modernism, he is undergoing a re-evaluation as the vogue for modernism declines.

Massenet's work in other genres has paled beside his operatic achievements. His instrumental music is largely forgotten, though the suites of orchestral *Scènes* (such as the *Scènes pittoresques*) are fixtures of the repertory and even his piano concerto has an occasional outing. The best of his many *mélodies* have remained in the recital programmes of devotees of French song.

RLS

📖 J. MASSENET, *Mes souvenirs (1848–1912)* (Paris, 1912; Eng. trans. by H. V. Barnett as *My Recollections*, Boston, 1919/R1970) · J. HARDING, *Massenet* (London, 1970) · D. IRVINE, *Massenet: A Chronicle of his Life and Times* (Portland, OR, 1994)

mässig (Ger.). 'Moderate', 'moderately'; *mässiger*, 'more moderate'. It can also mean 'in the style of', e.g. *marschmässig*, 'in march style'.

Mass of Life, A (*Eine Messe des Lebens*). Choral work (1904–5) by Delius for soprano, alto, tenor, and bass soloists, chorus, and orchestra, to a German text selected by F. Cassirer from Friedrich Nietzsche's *Also sprach Zarathustra*. The second part was first performed in 1908 and the first complete performance (in English) was a year later.

Master and Margherita, The. See MEISTER UND MARGARITA, DER.

master class. An advanced lesson given before an audience. A distinguished musician, usually a singer, instrumentalist, or conductor, will sometimes teach high-level students in front of a large group, as a kind of demonstration from which the observer may also learn.

Master classes are a common feature of summer schools and festivals and have proved popular when broadcast or televised.

PSP

Master of the King's [Queen's] Music. The only remaining post in the secular musical establishment of the British royal family; its duties are the occasional composition of music for royal or state occasions (the musical equivalent of the Poet Laureate). The post was created in the first half of the 17th century, in the reign of Charles I, Nicholas Lanier being the first incumbent. Originally the Master, as head of the sovereign's private band, would accompany the monarch on journeys. In Charles II's reign the private band was developed into a string orchestra of 24 players in emulation of Louis XIV's *Vingt-Quatre Violons.

Since 1893 the post has been given to a composer. Holders of the title from 1625 to the present include Nicholas Lanier (1660–6), John Eccles (1700), Maurice Greene (1735), William Boyce (1755), John Stanley (1779), William Parsons (1786), William Shield (1817), Christian Kramer (1829), Franz Cramer (1834), George Frederick Anderson (1848), William George Cusins (1870), Walter Parratt (1893), Edward Elgar (1924), Walford Davies (1934–41), Arnold Bax (1942–52), Arthur Bliss (1953), and Malcolm Williamson (from 1975).

AL

Mastersingers. See MEISTERSINGER.

Mastersingers of Nuremberg, The. See MEISTERSINGER VON NÜRNBERG, DIE.

Mathias, William (James) (*b* Whitland, Dyfed, 1 Nov. 1934; *d* Menai Bridge, 29 July 1992). Welsh composer. He studied at University College, Aberystwyth, and with Lennox Berkeley at the RAM. His teaching posts included the professorship of music at University College, Bangor (1970–88). His eclectic musical style, revealing substantial debts to Tippett and Shostakovich, proved very effective, whether in orchestral works like the *Divertimento* for strings (1958) and Symphony no. 2 (1983), in chamber music (especially the three string quartets, 1968, 1982, 1987), or, most notably, in choral music (*This Worldes Joie*, 1974, *Lux aeterna*, 1982).

PG/AW

📖 M. BOYD, *William Mathias* (Cardiff, 1974)

Mathis der Maler ('Mathis the Painter'). Opera in seven scenes by Hindemith to his own libretto (Zürich, 1938).

Matin, Le; Midi, Le; Soir, Le ('The Morning'; 'The Afternoon'; 'The Evening'). Haydn's Symphonies nos. 6, 7, and 8, in D major, C major, and G major, composed *c*.1761; the last movement of *Le Soir* is known as

'La Tempête', the whole symphony sometimes being referred to as *Le Soir et la Tempête*.

Matins. 1. The first of eight hours of the Divine *Office in the medieval Roman rite, originally called Vigils and sung after midnight (often about 3 a.m.); later it was sometimes moved to the previous evening. Its structure varied according to the day and usage (cathedral or monastic) but consisted in outline of an introduction, a series of nocturns (each comprising a group of psalms with antiphons and lessons with responsories), and a conclusion.

2. An alternative name for Morning Prayer in the Anglican Church. —/AL1

Matrimonio segreto, Il ('The Secret Marriage'). Opera in two acts by Cimarosa to a libretto by Giovanni Bertati after George Colman the elder and David Garrick's play *The Clandestine Marriage* (1766) (Vienna, 1792).

Mattei, Stanislao (*b* Bologna, 10 Feb. 1750; *d* Bologna, 12 May 1825). Italian teacher and composer. He studied with Martini and became his closest friend and disciple. On Martini's death he took over his post as *maestro di cappella* at S. Petronio in Bologna. In 1804 he became professor of counterpoint and composition at the new Liceo Filarmonico, where Rossini and Donizetti were among his pupils. His *Pratica d'accompagnamento* (1824–5) was translated into French and used widely during the 19th century. His compositions, all in the conservative tradition of Martini, include over 300 sacred works as well as secular vocal pieces and symphonies. SH

Matteis, Nicola (*b* ?Naples; *d* ?London, ?*c*.1707). Italian violinist and composer. He arrived in England about 1670; John Evelyn (*Diary*, 19 November 1674) noted:

> I heard that stupendous violin, Signor Nicholao … whom I never heard mortal man exceed on that instrument. He had a stroke so sweet, and made it speak like the voice of a man, and, when he pleased, like a concert of several instruments. He did wonders upon a note, and was an excellent composer.

Matteis's ability was also much praised by Roger North, according to whom Matteis became so wealthy and sought after that he bought a grand house, and 'lived luxuriously, which brought diseases upon him of which he died'. Matteis's most interesting works are the 'ayres' for one or two violins and bass, including suites of dances and more serious, fugal pieces. In 1682 he published a treatise, *The False Consonances of Musick: Instructions for Playing a Thorough-Base upon the Guitarre*, and in 1696 and 1699 two volumes entitled *A Collection of New Songs*.

His son, **Nicholas Matteis** (*d* ?Shrewsbury, ?*c*.1749), was also a violinist. After a long period spent on the Continent, including about 37 years at the Habsburg court in Vienna, he returned to London, where he taught the violin and French before (according to Burney) settling in Shrewsbury. His works include some violin sonatas showing the influence of Corelli. WT

Matteo da Perugia [de Perusio] (*fl* 1400–16). Italian church musician and composer. Beyond the fact that he probably came from Perugia, nothing is known of his life until 1402, when he took charge of music at Milan Cathedral (still under construction at that date). For several years he was also partly or wholly in the service of Cardinal Pietro Filargo da Candia, elected Pope Alexander V in 1409 (*d* 1410). His surviving music comprises mass movements, and polyphonic songs in both French and Italian. His style, like that of his important contemporary Ciconia, blends French and Italian elements. JM

Mattheson, Johann (*b* Hamburg, 28 Sept. 1681; *d* Hamburg, 17 April 1764). German critic, theorist, and composer. The son of a tax collector, he studied not only music, but also modern languages, law, and political science. He began his musical career with the Hamburg opera company, which in 1699 produced his first opera, *Die Plejades*. He met Handel in 1703 and they became friendly, though they quarrelled over who should play the harpsichord in a performance of Mattheson's *Cleopatra*.

Mattheson served as secretary to the English ambassadors to Hamburg, Sir John Wich (1706–15) and his son (1715–41), and as Kapellmeister to Hamburg Cathedral (1715–28); increasing deafness forced him to give up the latter post. He published several books that offer valuable information on the state of German music of the period, especially in Hamburg. These include *Das neu-eröffnete Orchestre* (1713), *Critica musica* (1722–5/*R*1984), and a collection of musical biographies, *Grundlage einer Ehren-Pforte* (1740/*R*1954), which also contains his autobiography. His theoretical writings include treatises on thoroughbass and the important *Der vollkommene Capellmeister* (1739/*R*1954).

WT/LC

Matthews, Colin (*b* London, 13 Feb. 1946). English composer, younger brother of David Matthews. He studied at the universities of Nottingham and Sussex, and with Nicholas Maw. He collaborated with Deryck Cooke on his realization of Mahler's Tenth Symphony and acted as Britten's assistant during the last years of Britten's life. He has edited several previously unpublished works by Britten and Holst. His own early music has its roots in Mahler and Berg, though the *Sonata no. 4* for orchestra (1975), which first brought him wide attention, offers brightly coloured perspectives on quasi-minimalist rhythmic and harmonic repetitions. These combine with a more expressionistic forcefulness in such later works as *Suns Dance* (1985) and *Broken Symmetry* (1992).   AW

Matthews, David (*b* London, 5 March 1943). English composer, elder brother of Colin Matthews. He studied classics at Nottingham University and composition with Anthony Milner and Nicholas Maw. The flowing lyricism of his music owes something to Britten (whose assistant he was for several years) and even more to Tippett, the ecstatic expansiveness and essential eclecticism of whose earlier style is often echoed in Matthews's symphonic and larger-scale vocal works. The powerful poetic charge of Matthews's idiom is especially evident in *The Flaying of Marsyas* for oboe and string quartet (1987), the dramatic scena *Cantiga* for soprano and orchestra (1988), and the Symphony no. 4 (1990).   AW

Matthus, Siegfried (*b* Mallenuppen, East Prussia, 13 April 1934). German composer. He studied with Rudolf Wagner-Régeny and Hanns Eisler in East Berlin. Although he has composed orchestral, chamber, choral, and vocal music, he is best known as a composer of operas, in which an eclectic technique is put at the service of a strong sense of drama. Matthus's operas include *Der letzte Schuss* (Berlin, 1967); *Judith* (Berlin, 1985); *Die Weise von Liebe und Tod des Cornets Christoph Rilke* (after Rilke; Dresden, 1985); *Graf Mirabeau* (Berlin and Karlsruhe, 1989); and *Desdemona und ihre Schwestern* (Schwetzingen, 1992).   ABur

mattinata (It.). A morning song, similar to the French *aubade.

Mattins. See MATINS, 2.

Mauduit, Jacques (*b* Paris, 16 Sept. 1557; *d* Paris, 21 Aug. 1627). French composer. He was a student of philosophy and languages, and taught himself music. As well as holding the position of royal secretary, he was a member of Baïf's *académie* (see MUSIQUE MESURÉE) and conductor and organizer of many concerts in Paris, including the St Cecilia's Day celebrations at Notre Dame and ballets and other royal entertainments. His works include a volume of *Chansonnettes mesurées de Jean-Antoine Baïf* (Paris, 1586) and one of *Psaumes mesurées à l'antique* (published by Mersenne in his *Quaestiones celeberrimae in Genesim*; Paris, 1623).   DA

Maultrommel (Ger.). 'Jew's harp'.

Maurel, Victor (*b* Marseilles, 17 June 1848; *d* New York, 22 Oct. 1923). French baritone. He studied in Marseilles and at the Paris Conservatoire with Eugène Vauthrot and Victor-Alphonse Duvernoy and made his debut in the title role of Rossini's *Guillaume Tell* in Marseilles (1867). The following year he was acclaimed at the Paris Opéra. He was soon internationally in demand, performing in St Petersburg, Cairo, and Venice, and at La Scala, Milan. From 1879 to 1894 he was the Paris Opéra's most popular baritone, with notable successes as Don Giovanni, Méphistophélès, and Alphonse in *La Favorite*. In 1881 he took the title role in Verdi's revised version of *Simon Boccanegra*, and Verdi chose him to create the roles of Iago (1887) and Falstaff (1893); he was also the first Tonio in *Pagliacci* (1892). His dramatic singing and realistic acting won him acclaim. He made many recordings. He was an administrator and teacher (he wrote four books on singing) and designed the sets for Gounod's *Mireille* (1919) in New York.   JT

Maurerische Trauermusik ('Masonic Funeral Music'). Work by Mozart, K477/479a (1785), for two oboes, clarinet, three basset horns, double bassoon, two horns, and strings; originally thought to have been composed for the funeral of two Viennese freemasons, it is dated several weeks before their death in Mozart's own catalogue. See FREEMASONRY AND MUSIC.

Má vlast ('My Country'; 'My Fatherland'). Cycle of six symphonic poems (*c*.1872–9) by Smetana: *Vyšehrad* (the old citadel in Prague), *Vltava* (river Moldau), *Šárka* (a female Amazon warrior in Czech legend), *Z Českých luhů a hájů* (from Bohemia's woods and fields), *Tábor* (an ancient stronghold), and *Blaník* (a 'Valhalla' near Prague where slumbering heroes await their call to defend their nation).

Mavra. Opera in one act by Stravinsky to a libretto by Boris Kochno after Aleksandr Pushkin's narrative poem *Domik v Kolomne* ('The Little House at Colomna', 1830) (Paris, 1922).

Maw, (John) Nicholas (*b* Grantham, 5 Nov. 1935). English composer. He studied with Lennox Berkeley at the RAM and with Nadia Boulanger and Max Deutsch in Paris. Since the mid-1980s he has lived and worked in the USA. He came to the fore with *Scenes and Arias* (1962, revised 1966) for three female voices and large orchestra; the work's romantic opulence, recalling Strauss, Delius, and Berg, was very different from both the prevailing avant-garde and more conservative, traditional styles of the mid-1960s in England. Maw's special ability to sustain and even intensify such expansiveness is most spectacularly demonstrated in *Odyssey* (1972–87), a single-movement orchestral work lasting some 95 minutes. But several other instrumental and vocal scores serve to confirm the richness of Maw's musical language and the resourcefulness with which he adapts traditional formal structures. These include *Life Studies* for 15 solo strings (1973–6), *La vita nuova* for soprano and chamber ensemble (1979), *Shahnama* for ensemble (1992), and the Violin Concerto (1993).

AW

📖 A. WHITTALL, 'A voyage beyond romance: Nicholas Maw at 60', *Musical Times*, 136 (1995), 575–80

maxima (Lat.). 14th-century term for the *duplex long.

Maxwell Davies, Peter. See DAVIES, PETER MAXWELL.

May Night (*Mayskaya noch'*). Opera in three acts by Rimsky-Korsakov to his own libretto after Nikolay Gogol's story *Mayskaya noch', ili Utoplennitsa* ('May Night, or The Drowned Maiden') from his *Evenings on a Farm near Dikanka* (i, 1831) (St Petersburg, 1880).

Mayr, (Johannes) Simon (*b* Mendorf, Bavaria, 14 June 1763; *d* Bergamo, 2 Dec. 1845). German composer. The son of an organist, who taught him in his early years, he studied at the Jesuit College and then at the university of Ingoldstadt. In 1787 he went to Bergamo from where a patron, Count Pesenti, paid for him to go to Venice in 1789. Mayr was successful there as a composer of oratorios and church music, but on the death of his patron in 1793 he turned to opera composition, having such a success with *Saffo* (1794) that he became one of the most sought-after composers until the rise of Rossini 20 years later. In 1802 he returned to Bergamo as *maestro di cappella* of the principal church, remaining there until his death in spite of attractive offers from Napoleon to go to France. In his later years he wrote mostly church music. He was Donizetti's teacher from 1806 to 1815.

Many of Mayr's operas show an orchestral and harmonic adventurousness which may have come from his early understanding of and sympathy with German and Austrian instrumental music (at that time rarely performed in Italy). He was also innovatory in formal matters, most notably in making the multi-movement 'number' a norm in solo arias, so departing from the single-movement practice of much of the 18th century. One of his most influential later works was *Medea in Corinto* (1813), which was successful enough to be taken up by such famous singers as Giuditta Pasta in the 1820s. Mayr was specifically commissioned to write the opera in the French manner, thus using orchestrally accompanied recitatives (rather than the continuo-accompanied variety still normal in Italian *opera seria*) and enriching the ensemble scenes, which powerfully anticipate the grandest moments of Italian opera in the following decades. He was also significant for his use of 'romantic' or 'sentimental' subject matter, often in a style that blended comic and serious elements in the manner of *opéra comique*. Of particular interest is *La rosa bianca e la rosa rossa* (1813), a *melodramma eroico* set during the Wars of the Roses, its ending plainly modelled on the *rescue' plots that had been so popular in France during the previous decade.

DA/RP

📖 J. S. ALLITT, *J. S. Mayr, Father of 19th Century Italian Music* (Shaftesbury, 1989)

Mazeppa. 1. The title of several pieces by Liszt, taken from a poem of Victor Hugo. The earliest version of the musical material is the D minor study from the juvenile *Étude en douze exercices* (1825), revised in 1837 as *12 grandes études*; none of these pieces has any descriptive title. The D minor study from this set was elaborated ten years later and published separately with the title *Mazeppa*; it retained this appellation in the final revision of all 12 *études*, published in 1851 as *Études d'exécution transcendante*. Liszt also used an orchestrated version of this music as part of his symphonic poem *Mazeppa* (1851–4), which includes additional material from the *Arbeiterchor*.

2. Opera in three acts by Tchaikovsky to a libretto by Victor Burenin, revised by the composer with an aria to words by Vasily Kandaurov, after Aleksandr Pushkin's poem *Poltava* (Moscow, 1884).

mazurka (from Pol. *mazur*). A traditional Polish folk dance, named after the Mazurs, who lived in the plains known as Mazovia around Warsaw. The name embraces several types of folk dance, including the *kujawiak* and the *oberek*, all of which share the typical mazurka characteristics of a triple metre, dotted rhythms, and a tendency to accentuate the weak beats. These folk dances were originally accompanied by an instrumental drone.

In the mid-18th century the mazurka spread to Germany, where it developed into a social couple dance for the ballroom. In this form it reached Paris, Britain by 1830, and the USA soon after, becoming immensely popular throughout Europe during the 1830s and 40s. It was generally danced by couples in multiples of four, performing variations on a few basic steps and positions, often with much improvisation. In the 19th century the male dancers were expected to click their spurs together, stamp their heels, and clap their hands.

Chopin, who grew up in Mazovia, wrote over 50 mazurkas for the piano in a great variety of styles, often exhibiting a high degree of chromaticism. Some are in the style of the slower *kujawiak*, others (e.g. op. 56 no. 2) in that of the livelier and faster *oberek*. Mazurkas occur in Glinka's *A Life for the Tsar* and in Musorgsky's

Boris Godunov. Szymanowski wrote mazurkas for the piano.

The 'polka-mazurka', a combination of two dances, differs from the *polka in its triple rhythm and from the mazurka in having an accent on the third beat of each bar.   —/JBᴇ

Mazzocchi, Domenico (*b* Civita Castellana, *bapt.* 8 Nov. 1592; *d* Rome, 21 Jan. 1665). Italian composer. He was associated chiefly with the Aldobrandini family in Rome, for which he wrote his opera *La catena d'Adone* ('The Chain of Adonis'; performed twice in February 1626 and published in Venice later that year). It is an intriguing example of a developing genre, and Mazzocchi drew attention to its 'mezz'arie', brief passages in aria style which sought to 'break the tedium of the recitative'. He also published dialogues and sonnet settings, five-voice madrigals, and oratorios. The madrigals (Rome, 1638) could be performed with a viol consort and contain extensive performance instructions; they are essentially old-fashioned but no less expressive for that.

His brother **Virgilio** (*b* Civita Castellana, *bapt.* 22 July 1597; *d* Civita Castellana, 3 Oct. 1646), from 1629 *maestro di cappella* of the Cappella Giulia, was also a composer of some distinction.   TC

mbira, kalimba, likembe. Common African names for various species of *lamellophone consisting of a board, box, or bowl held in the hands, with a series of iron or bamboo tongues attached to it and plucked by the thumbs and forefingers. Frequently the longest tongue is in the centre with shorter tongues in sequence alternately to the left and right. This type of instrument is one of the most popular throughout sub-Saharan Africa. Another term for it is 'marimba'; European names include 'thumb piano', 'hand piano', 'linguaphone', and 'sansa' or 'sanza'.   JMo

MC. Abbreviation of 'master of ceremonies'. See RAP.

m.d. Abbreviation of *main droite* (Fr.), *mano destra* (It.), 'right hand'.

me. See MI.

Meale, Richard (Graham) (*b* Sydney, 24 Aug. 1932). Australian composer, pianist, and teacher. He studied the piano at the New South Wales Conservatorium, becoming known for his performances of 20th-century music. He worked for the Australian Broadcasting Commission in Sydney and taught at Adelaide University before retiring to a rainforest area of New South Wales. As a composer, Meale is largely self-taught, but he was influenced by Messiaen and Boulez, and later by the cultures of Japan and Indonesia. He has composed two operas, *Voss* (Adelaide, 1986) and *Mer de glace*

(Sydney, 1991), orchestral works including *Very High Kings* (1968) and a Symphony (1994), and chamber music.   ABᴜʀ

meane [mean, mene]. In early English music, a term for the middle part of a three-part polyphonic work.

mean-tone temperament. A system of tuning keyboard instruments, used from *c*.1570 into the 19th century and revived in the 20th, in which each whole tone is half the size (the 'mean') of a pure 3rd. Most 3rds are pure, much better in tune than in *equal temperament, and the 5ths and 4ths are only slightly worse than in equal temperament.

See also TEMPERAMENT.   JMo

measure. 1. In American usage, a term equivalent to the British term 'bar' when used to refer to a metrical unit in notation; the American term for 'bar-line' is 'bar'. See BAR.

2. In early English usage, a general term meaning 'dance'; more specifically, in 16th- and 17th-century England a moderately slow and stately dance in duple time.

Mechanical Copyright Protection Society. See COPYRIGHT, 7.

mechanical musical instruments. Instruments on which sound is produced by a mechanism activated by a player (unlike *automatic instruments). The commonest mechanism is a barrel rotating on its axis with pins set into its surface at predetermined positions; these trip levers that open pallets (valves) to let air into pipes (barrel organs), to pluck strings (barrel harpsichords or spinets) or strike them (barrel pianos), to strike bells (carillons), or to pluck metal tongues (musical boxes). 19th-century technology introduced books of perforated card and paper rolls played with mechanical or pneumatic systems. Unlike the barrels, these could be of any length.

Simple organs imitating birdsong date back to the 2nd and 3rd centuries BC and continued in use in Byzantium during the early Middle Ages. The earliest evidence for instruments with rotating barrels comes from 9th-century Arabic manuscripts. By the 14th century, barrels were striking bells in European clock towers, and organs and spinets were played by barrels from the 16th century onwards. The Swiss have been making musical boxes since the 18th century, and a variety of elaborate instruments (orchestrions) capable of imitating whole orchestras has been available since the 19th. Some were coin-operated. Perforated cards began to replace barrels for fairground organs during the 19th century, and at about that time the player piano, with a punched paper roll, was introduced.

All barrels work in much the same way. The barrel has a series of circles scribed round it, spaced so that each aligns with one of the levers which, on the organ, will open a pallet to admit air to a pipe for a specific note. Since the barrel rotates at a steady speed, spacing pins equally round one of the circles would produce a steadily repeated reiteration of a single note. For musical purposes the pins must be placed on each circle at the correct points on the circumference to produce the notes required in their desired sequence. Barrel organs use pins for short notes, and bridges (like elongated staples, of any length required) to hold a pallet open for longer notes.

Long notes on musical boxes or barrel pianos are simulated by a series of pins set close together, rapidly repeating the note many times as a tremolo. Barrels are usually designed so that shifting them a short distance longitudinally aligns another set of circles with the levers to play a second tune. This can be done either by putting a screw thread of the correct pitch on the barrel's axle or, more often, by shifting a lever. Some barrel organs carry as many as a dozen tunes on a barrel; the levers of the instrument are set far enough apart to allow space for a dozen circles of pins between each. It is often possible to change the barrels for a new set of tunes. On an instrument operated by clockwork the speed at which the barrel rotates is usually stabilized by a revolving fan or air brake. On manual instruments the player turns a crank, which also operates the bellows; keeping a steady speed takes considerable practice and is more difficult than it looks.

Many *carillons in the Low Countries are so constructed that they can be played either by a player or a barrel. This allows a player to perform on any special occasion, while the barrel does all the routine work of striking quarters, playing a hymn tune on the hours, or whatever is required. The barrels are usually pre-drilled with sockets into which the 'pins' can be placed, because the action of a carillon, before the days of electric servo-mechanisms, was sufficiently heavy that the 'pins' are quite substantial wooden blocks. These engage the levers, activating the long tracker wires running up to the belfry to move the hammers that strike the bells. An advantage of this system is that it is a comparatively quick job to move the pins to play a different hymn.

The smallest barrel organs were tiny instruments called *sérinettes* or 'bird organs', designed to make easy the constant repetition needed to teach canaries to sing favourite airs. Slightly larger instruments, for which 18th-century composers including Mozart and Haydn composed pieces, were built into clocks. Many churches found it easier to use a barrel organ to accompany congregational singing than to find a regular organist and, on the whole, barrel organs were smaller (and thus cheaper) than instruments which an organist would demand. Secular barrel organs varied widely in size, ranging from domestic instruments little bigger than a musical box to the orchestrions designed for public display, for example Maelzel's *panharmonicon and Winkel's componium. The barrel piano seems to have been devised in Italy in the late 18th century, but it was not until the next century that it became widely popular as a street instrument, often misnamed barrel organ or hurdy-gurdy.

The musical box has a comb of steel tongues, the free ends of which are plucked by pins in a brass cylinder. Earlier instruments had a series of tongues, tuned by length and thickness, each screwed or riveted to a base, but on later models sets of tongues were cut from one or more steel plates, normally relying simply on length to control their pitch. The cylinder is almost always turned by clockwork, and musical boxes seem to have been first made by Swiss watchmakers. Many were small enough to fit into a watch or snuffbox. Others have been fitted into chairs, bottles, and every imaginable receptacle, often designed to surprise the unwary. Larger versions, like the barrel organs and orchestrions, filled the same role as the gramophone, which superseded them, and has since been supplanted in its turn by the CD player.

The symphonium musical box, initially produced in Leipzig in the 1880s, anticipated the record player by using metal discs instead of the cylinder. These were cheaply produced by stamping holes in the thin metal, turning down a tang to pluck the tongues. These discs could be changed as easily as those on record players, and automatic symphoniums were the earliest form of jukebox, with extra-large versions often providing the music for small dance halls.

In Paris, Gavioli applied the principle of the Jacquard loom, of punched cards for controlling the weaving of elaborately patterned cloth, to fairground organs in 1892. A 'book' of perforated card is folded in a zigzag and drawn as it unfolds over a series of spring-loaded metal levers which can rise wherever a hole is punched to open a pallet. These organs, with a wide range of loudly voiced pipes and percussion instruments, are still often heard, and their makers continue to produce 'books' to keep the music up to date.

The punched rolls of the *player piano rely on a pneumatic system of air blown through the holes. On the earlier and simpler models of the 1890s, the player pedalled to provide the air and also had to control speed and loudness, but on the later and more elaborate reproducing models, such as the Duo-Art or Ampico, all the information of the original performance could be recorded on the roll. Because there was no limit to length, unlike the early three- to four-minute gramophone records, piano-roll recordings of the great pianists of the early 20th century are a much truer record of their art than their discs.

Recent innovations have included digital-recording pianos, which can store details of anything played on them, but mechanical instruments may be seen as the historical ancestors of the computer-controlled instruments of today (see ELECTRONIC MUSICAL INSTRUMENTS) with built-in recording ability.   JMo

📖 Q. D. BOWERS, *A Guidebook of Automatic Musical Instruments* (Vestal, NY, 1967–8) · A. W. J. G. ORD-HUME, *Clockwork Music: An Illustrated Musical History of Mechanical Musical Instruments* (London, 1973) · J. J. L. HASPELS, *Automatic Musical Instruments: Their Mechanics and their Music, 1580–1820* (The Hague, 1987)

Médée ('Medea'). Opera in three acts by Cherubini to a libretto by François-Benoît Hoffman after Euripides (Paris, 1797). M.-A. Charpentier (1693), Benda (1775), Mayr (1813), Pacini (1843), and Milhaud (1938) wrote operas on the same subject and Barber wrote a ballet (1946) on it.

Meder, Johann Valentin (*b* Wasungen an der Werra, May 1649; *d* Riga, July 1719). German composer. He served at major centres along the Baltic coast: Reval (now Tallinn), Danzig, Königsberg (now Kaliningrad), and Riga. In a work-list issued by his son in 1719 he is credited with numerous compositions. Few of these survive, but recognition of their quality may be gained from two works, now in modern editions: his opera *Die beständige Argenia* ('The Constant Argenia', 1680; in *Das Erbe deutscher Musik*, 68) and *St Matthew Passion* (1701; in *Das Chorwerk*, 133).   BS

medesimo (It.). 'Same', e.g. *medesimo movimento*, 'the same speed'.

medial cadence. See CADENCE.

mediant. The third degree of the major or minor scale, so called because it lies midway between the tonic and the dominant.

mediatio (Lat., 'mediation'). A subordinate cadence, occurring halfway through a verse in a psalm tone (see TONUS, 3).

medieval. Of or pertaining to the *Middle Ages.

medieval drama. Between the 14th century and the Reformation, plays in the vernacular were performed in many parts of Europe; these are often known as 'mystery', 'miracle', or 'morality' plays. Although their subject matter was religious, such works were not liturgical and were staged outside the church, often in the open, and sometimes on wagons as part of a procession (e.g. the York and Chester cycles). The texts of

four complete English cycles survive: from York, Chester, Towneley in Yorkshire, and East Anglia (the 'N-Town' cycle). The music in such dramas is known to have included solo and ensemble songs, items of plainchant, polyphonic settings, and instrumental music (sometimes dances). Little of this repertory, however, survives in notation: only those pieces specially composed or otherwise unfamiliar to the singers were written down. Most of the music would have been well known to the performers, even if set to new words.

Music helped to define the dramatic structure of medieval plays, being played, for example, at the entrance or exit of a character, or to mark the passage of time. It also fulfilled a 'representational' role in which the Divine Order of Heaven might be represented by the singing (often in polyphony) of a liturgical melody by angels, or the malign influence of the Devil by a drinking-song.

See also CHURCH DRAMA.   JBe

📖 L. R. MUIR, *The Biblical Drama of Medieval Europe* (Cambridge, 1995)

medieval instruments. Barely a handful of European medieval instruments survives. Evidence for their nomenclature and form depends on written sources, pictures, and carvings. Little is known of musical instruments in the early Middle Ages. Such tales as *Beowulf* were, like those of Homer in the ancient era, chanted to the *lyre. By the early 9th century, *organs were in use in some churches and Italians were casting *bells large enough for church towers. Smaller bells (e.g. cattle bells) were also forged from folded sheets of iron. The bowed *fiddle came to Europe through Byzantium at about the end of the 10th century. Transverse *flutes also arrived in Byzantium from India at much the same time, but seemed to arouse little interest in Europe. Small wooden or bone duct flutes, ancestors of the *flageolet and *recorder, were common. Other woodwinds seem confined to such cylindrical-bore single-reed instruments as *hornpipes. Cow- and oxhorns were used for signalling, hunting, and in warfare, but there is little evidence for larger horns of metal. One metal instrument of which examples survive is the bronze *jew's harp.

Pictorial representations in illuminated manuscripts of the *lyre being played by King David demonstrate the high status of this instrument (confusingly, it was called 'hearpe' in English). It was not until the late 12th century that the triangular *harp began to supersede the lyre in such illustrations.

In the mid-13th century there was a sudden influx of instruments to Europe from the south and east, as a result partly of the Crusades and partly of the successful symbiosis of Muslims, Jews, and Christians in Spain.

European versions of instruments that originated in the Middle East, Central Asia, or North Africa at this time include the *rebec (developed from the *rabāb), the *lute (from the 'ūd), the psaltery (qānūn), the *shawm (ghayṭa and zūrnā), the *nakers (naqqāra), the *cymbals, and the *tambourine. The long trumpet, known in Spain as the añafil, was derived from the Moorish nafir. The *pipe and *tabor appeared at this time, as did the *portative organ and the symphony, a more portable form of *hurdy-gurdy than the earlier organistrum. *Bagpipes spread widely, with many varieties of reed-type, and numbers of chanters and drones, before settling down in the later 14th century to a conical shawm chanter and single cylindrical drone, throughout most of western Europe.

Little is known about how these instruments were used. The fiddle and harp were the most respectable, played by the troubadours and associated with courtly love. The pipe and tabor was the commonest dance accompaniment. The proliferation of bagpipes suggests that drone accompaniment was popular, as does the depiction of fiddle and citole players plucking their lowest string with the left thumb while using a bow or plectrum in the other hand. Many chronicles attest that the nakers, a pair of small kettledrums hung from the player's belt, were a standard part of the royal military establishment, but they were also evident in civilian and dance music ensembles.   JMo

Medium, The. Opera in two acts by Menotti to his own libretto (New York, 1946, revised 1947).

medley (It.: mescolanza). 1. A term first used by 16th-century composers, especially the Elizabethan virginal composers, for a piece that strings together several favourite tunes. See also POTPOURRI.

2. In the second half of the 18th century the 'medley overture' combined well-known melodies from popular songs, dances, and folk music. Later, such an overture would usually contain tunes from the work it preceded. The term 'medley' today denotes a selection of pieces linked to form a single light-orchestral concert work. They may be related by type (e.g. folksong arrangements) or by composer, or extracted from a particular piece—often an operetta or musical. A medley differs from a *potpourri in that its components are more closely connected.   —/PFA

Medtner, Nicolas [Metner, Nikolay Karlovich] (b Moscow, 24 Dec. 1875/5 Jan. 1880; d London, 13 Nov. 1951). Russian composer and pianist. He studied the piano at the Moscow Conservatory with, among others, Pavel Pabst (1854–97) and Vasily Safonov (1852–1918), graduating in 1900. After a career as a touring recitalist he settled in Moscow, teaching the piano at the con-

servatory (1909–10, 1914–21) and also widening his activities as a composer. He wrote much piano music, songs, three piano concertos, and a little chamber music. Brahms was a considerable influence on his piano music—in its general sentiment and its 'bigness' of style—but many of his works are also marked by a classical coolness and intellectual rigour. His popularity as a pianist in Russia coincided with that of Rakhmaninov: both appeared to immense acclaim before the Revolution, but in 1927 Prokofiev noted sympathetically that his own return to the USSR had eclipsed Medtner's recital tour, which passed virtually unnoticed. Medtner was also highly regarded abroad; he settled in Paris in 1925 but was unimpressed by musical life there (described in his The Muse and the Fashion, Paris, 1935; Eng. trans. 1951) and moved to London in 1935. In his later years he received much support from the Maharajah of Mysore, under whose patronage he made a number of recordings. A new generation of virtuoso pianists has rediscovered the individuality of his music in which, as the conductor Yevgeny Svetlanov has noted, expressive elaboration always remains part of the essential design.

PS/DN

📖 B. MARTYN, Nicolas Medtner: His Life and Music (Aldershot, 1995)

Mefistofele ('Mephistopheles'). Opera in a prologue, five acts, and an epilogue by Boito to his own libretto after Johann Wolfgang von Goethe's play Faust (Milan, 1868); Boito revised it into four acts (Bologna, 1875), then made a further revision (Venice, 1876).

megaphone. A wide conical tube, now often with electronic amplification, which projects the voice, shouting or singing into the narrow end, directionally over a distance or in noisy surroundings.

mehr (Ger.). 'More'; mehrstimmig, 'more (than one) voice', i.e. polyphonic; Mehrstimmigkeit, 'polyphony'; mehrchörig, 'polychoral'; mehrsätzig, 'multi-movement'.

Méhul, Étienne-Nicolas (b Givet, Ardennes, 22 June 1763; d Paris, 18 Oct. 1817). French composer. The son of the head of the household to the Count of Montmorency, he showed musical talent at an early age, becoming organist at the local Franciscan convent when he was about ten. After studying in Monthermé nearby he moved to Paris in about 1778. There he became enamoured of Gluck's music and made several influential friends. He had some success with a setting of an Ode sacrée (now lost) by Rousseau given at the Concert Spirituel in 1782, wrote a set of keyboard sonatas (1783), and had a number of short dramatic *scènes* performed. His successful operatic debut came in 1790 with *Euphrosine, ou Le Tyran corrigé*, in which he consciously departed from the lighter, more melodic style of *comédie mêlée d'ariettes* in response to a more serious libretto (by F.-B. Hoffman). He made use of an inventive range of harmonic and orchestral effects to increase the dramatic impact and the psychological development of the characters. A series of *drames lyriques* for the Opéra-Comique confirmed Méhul's reputation, including *Mélidore et Phrosine* (1794), in which he achieved musical unity through the innovatory use of motifs and tonal structures.

After the mid-1790s Méhul's works were less experimental, and he was influenced by the more melodic language of Isouard and Paisiello in such comic works as *L'irato* (1801) and *Une folie* (1802). Yet he continued to strive for a unique musical atmosphere in each work through his use of the orchestra. In *Uthal* (1806), for example, he omitted the violins and expanded the viola section, emphasizing other low-register voices and instruments to capture the mood of the dark Ossianic subject then in vogue. And in *Joseph* (1807) he used a *tuba curva*, an 'antique' instrument invented during the 1790s for the revolutionary *fêtes*. His harmonic, motivic, and orchestral innovations, and his pioneering use of chorus and ensemble in scene complexes (in *Adrien*, 1799, for example), were admired by, and influential on, 19th-century composers including Beethoven, Weber, and Boieldieu.

Méhul also composed a great deal of patriotic music during the Revolution, including such songs and choruses as *Le Chant du départ* (1794), and a Mass (?1804) probably intended for the coronation of Napoleon, but not performed on that occasion. From 1795 he was one of the officials responsible for the curriculum at the Institut National de Musique (later the Paris Conservatoire). In addition, he was the leading French symphonist of his age, and the Fourth Symphony (1810, later revised) develops many of the techniques he essayed in his operas; with its refashioning of first-movement material in its finale, it was a predecessor of such cyclical works as Berlioz's *Symphonie fantastique*. DA/SH

    📖 M. E. C. BARTLET, *Étienne Nicolas Méhul and Opera: Source and Archival Studies of Lyric Theatre during the French Revolution, Consulate, and Empire* (Saarbrücken, 1992) · M. BOYD (ed.), *Music and the French Revolution* (Cambridge, 1992)

Mei, Girolamo (*b* Florence, 27 May 1519; *d* Rome, July 1594). Italian humanist and writer. His treatise *De modis*—a study of ancient Greek music—greatly influenced the ideas of the Florentine *Camerata, especially the sections discussing the power of ancient music over the emotions, and the role of song and melody in the performance of tragedy. JBE

Meistersinger (Ger., 'master singers'). German amateur poet-musicians from the burgher and artisan classes who, from the 14th century to the 17th (following the decline of the feudal but art-loving Hohenstaufen dynasty), formed themselves into guilds for the practice of their musical skills. Their originator is usually identified as Heinrich von Meissen (*d* 1318)—known as *Frauenlob because of his numerous verses in praise of the Virgin—who is thought to have founded the first guild of singers among the middle classes at Mainz in 1311. Similar guilds followed, initially at Frankfurt, Prague, and Strasbourg, and later at Augsburg, Breslau, and, most important, Nuremberg. The leading figure among the 16th-century singer-poets was Hans *Sachs (1494–1576), a Nuremberg shoemaker, whose extant works number over 6000; many of these are Meisterlieder, in which melismas (called *Blumen*) are used to decorate chosen words or syllables.

The Meistersinger differed from their aristocratic predecessors, the *Minnesinger of the 12th–14th centuries, not only in their lower social status but also by their choice of sacred themes for their verse—hymnic lyrics and epic narrative poems—in contrast to the songs in praise of courtly love favoured by their forerunners. It was only after the Reformation, when the Meistersinger movement attained its highest peaks, that greater freedom was granted for the choice of secular themes. However, various properties of the Minnelied—the *Bar form, comprising two identical phrases (*Stollen*) and a contrasted final phrase (*Abgesang*), and the use of the ecclesiastical modes in the formation of melodies—featured consistently in songs from the earliest Meistersinger period.

The guilds normally held their weekly meetings in churches (St Katherine's at Nuremberg), where they also mounted their public song contests. In these each aspirant's contribution was judged, in conformity with strict, somewhat pedantic rules, on his song's sacred content: its prosody, its rhyme, and its melody. The prizes consisted of a chain of coins, the largest bearing the image of King David. Although richly romanticized (in a manner appropriate to operatic treatment), Wagner's *Die Meistersinger von Nürnberg* provides evidence of the composer's close attention to historical detail, not only in its text but also in some parts of its music. The theme for the entry of the Mastersingers, for example, recalls the the opening pattern of the *langer Ton* by Heinrich von Mügeln, believed to have been the last Minnesinger in Prague (*c*.1358).

JM/BS

Meistersinger von Nürnberg, Die ('The Master-singers of Nuremberg'). Opera in three acts by Wagner to his own libretto (Munich, 1868).

Meister und Margarita, Der ('The Master and Margarita'). Opera in a prologue and two acts by Höller to his own libretto after Mikhail Bulgakov's novel (Paris, 1989). Several composers have composed operas on the subject, notably Rainer Kunad (Karlsruhe, 1986) and Sergey Slonimsky (concert 1989, staged Moscow, 1991).

Melba, Dame **Nellie** [Mitchell, Helen] (*b* Richmond, Melbourne, 19 May 1861; *d* Sydney, 23 Feb. 1931). Australian soprano, of Scottish descent. She made her debut in a concert in Melbourne (1884), then went to Paris to study with Mathilde Marchesi. In 1887 she made her acclaimed debut as Gilda in Brussels, and the following year won accolades singing Lucia at Covent Garden and Ophélie in Paris. She became particularly famous for Italian dramatic roles and French lyrical ones, especially Juliette in Gounod's *Roméo et Juliette* and Marguerite in his *Faust*, and Lakmé in Delibes's opera, for which her outstanding agility, flexibility, and range of colour made her ideal. In 1893 she made her debut at the Metropolitan Opera, New York, as Lucia; she was subsequently one of America's favourite artists. Her greatest successes were at Covent Garden, where she became a famous Mimì, having studied the role with Puccini. She acquired the status of an international society personality and was one of the highest-paid performers in history; a dessert and a kind of toast were named after her. She was made DBE in 1918. A legacy of her finest years can be heard in the earlier of her 150 recordings.   JT

📖 W. R. MORAN (ed.), *Nellie Melba: A Contemporary Review* (Westport, CT, 1984) · T. RADIC, *Melba: The Voice of Australia* (Melbourne, 1986)

Melchior, Lauritz (Lebrecht Hommel) (*b* Copenhagen, 20 March 1890; *d* Santa Monica, CA, 18 March 1973). Danish tenor. He studied in Copenhagen and made his debut as a baritone in 1913 when he sang Silvio in *Pagliacci*. His debut as a tenor was in the title role of *Tannhäuser* in Stockholm in 1918. He then studied intensively with Anna Bahr-Mildenburg and Victor Biegel. In 1919 his debut as Siegmund at Covent Garden established him as a leading Wagnerian tenor. He sang at Bayreuth (1924–31) and made his New York debut as Tannhäuser in 1926, singing at the Metropolitan from then until 1950. His powerful vocal projection and remarkable breath control were allied to a vivid expressiveness. His Siegfried conveyed great warmth and intimacy as well as heroism, and, though he was perhaps less suited to it, the lyrical beauty of his singing of Tristan was greatly acclaimed. Verdi's

Otello was one of his most successful roles outside the Wagner repertory. He made many recordings.   JT

📖 S. EMMONS, *Tristanissimo* (New York, 1990)

melisma (Gk., 'song'). A group of notes sung to one syllable of the text. It is used particularly to describe such passages in plainchant (see, for example, CLAUSULA, 2; JUBILUS), where the contrast between syllabic and melismatic passages is an important stylistic feature. However, it is also appropriate to later music. Bach, for example, frequently used melismatic passages to emphasize such emotive words as 'wept' and 'scourged' in his Passions.

Thomas Ravenscroft called his 1611 collection of vocal pieces by the plural, *Melismata*.

mellophone [tenor cor]. A valved brass instrument of circular form in E♭ or F (below the cornet), common in the USA. It is sometimes made with a forward-facing bell for marching and jazz bands.

melodeon. A type of *accordion.

melodica. A variant of the *harmonica. Made in various sizes by Hohner since about 1959, it has a plastic casing with a small chromatic keyboard (or two rows of plastic buttons) along its side and a mouthpiece or a flexible tube at one end.

melodic minor scale. See SCALE, 3.

mélodie (Fr.). The 19th-century French term for 'art song', equivalent to the German *lied, as opposed to the lighter, less literary chanson.

The *mélodie* developed in the early 19th century from such simpler forms as the *romance*, a strophic song with an undemanding tune, the *bergerette*, celebrating the activities of nymphs and shepherds, and the *scène*, imbued with melodramatic pathos. Although Louis Niedermeyer's setting of Alphonse de Lamartine's *Le Lac* (1825) is sometimes spoken of as the first *mélodie*, it consists essentially of a two-verse *scène* followed by a three-verse *romance* (designated as such). But Saint-Saëns recognized Niedermeyer's importance in turning to major French poets for his texts and in 'paving the way for Gounod and all those who followed this path'.

Berlioz's *Mélodies irlandaises* (1829), on French translations of Thomas Moore's *Irish Melodies*, were among the first compositions to use this title. The best known of Berlioz's other *mélodies* are found in the cycle *Les Nuits d'été* (1840–1), to poems by Théophile Gautier, but these were perhaps too individual and extraordinary to form the basis of a tradition. That accolade can fairly be granted to Gounod, who wrote over 150 songs between 1840 and his death in 1893 and established a style in which a suave, lyrical melody floats over a rhythmically regular accompaniment, spiced with delicate harmonic inflections. Practically every French composer from 1850 onwards wrote *mélodies* more or less in this vein, among them Franck, Saint-Saëns, Bizet, Massenet, Lalo, Delibes, Roussel, and Hahn, and the repertory must run into many thousands. Chabrier in his four 'farmyard' songs (1890) and Ravel in his *Histoires naturelles* (1906) also made a corner in humorous animal songs, which might seem to belong rather to the world of the chanson, were it not for the sophistication (and technical difficulty) of the accompaniments. Satie's songs, too, occupy a special place, ranging from the ecstatic to the jaunty.

But between 1870 and 1960 four composers may be singled out as bringing significant developments to Gounod's basic model. Fauré's early songs remain close to the *romance*, but in such a *mélodie* as *Automne* (1878) the regular rhythms are already threatening rather than consoling. His 17 settings of Paul Verlaine, made between 1887 and 1894, wonderfully mirror the poet's elegant, melancholy languor and, in the cycle *La Bonne Chanson* (1892–4), his ability to break out into joy. Such later cycles as *La Chanson d'Ève* (1906–10) and *Le Jardin clos* (1914) show Fauré's harmony at its most elusive, but in two final cycles, *Mirages* (1919) and *L'Horizon chimérique* (1921), he returns to the simpler modality of his youth, infused now with an old man's nostalgia and wisdom.

Verlaine was also Debussy's preferred poet, providing poems for over 20 of the composer's 90-odd songs. Perhaps Debussy's main contribution to the genre was his decision to entrust the musical structure of the song to the piano, leaving the voice free to pursue the nuances of the text in an arioso style which often makes little sense divorced from the so-called accompaniment. The simplicity and evocative richness of Verlaine's poetry obviously lent itself to this treatment, but Debussy's crowning achievement in this typically French exaltation of the word was perhaps the *Chansons de Bilitis* (1897–8), settings of three prose poems by his friend Pierre Louÿs, which might be described as a group of *scènes* with the melodrama taken out. After he had turned to medieval poets, Debussy's last important songs were his *Trois poèmes de Stéphane Mallarmé* (1913), suitably elliptical settings that can still puzzle an audience.

Born between Fauré and Debussy, but chronologically much closer to the former, Duparc wrote 16 *mélodies* between 1868 and 1884 on which his reputation rests. The best of them introduced a new seriousness and depth into the genre by means of chromatic but firmly structured piano parts and vocal lines that sometimes approach the operatic. Although Debussy's only known reference to Duparc is derogatory, it is hard to feel that his *Cinq poèmes de Baudelaire* (1887–9) were wholly uninfluenced by Duparc's *mélodies* and specifically by his two Baudelaire settings, *L'Invitation au voyage* (1870) and *La Vie antérieure* (1884), which stand as supreme peaks in this landscape.

French composers after World War I continued to write *mélodies*, even if some of the old certainties of the genre about love and the delights of rural life could no longer be taken for granted, and many beauties are to be found in the output of such composers as Milhaud, Honegger, Françaix, Manuel Rosenthal, and Jacques Leguerney. But the *mélodies* of Poulenc outshine all others. Their moods range widely, from manic energy through crazy and sometimes scabrous humour ('L'Offrande' from *Chansons gaillardes*, 1926) to deep emotion ('Voyage' from *Calligrammes*, 1948), while the piano parts, by his own admission, reach a level that his solo piano music by and large does not. With their plethora of wonderful tunes, his *mélodies* appear spontaneous, but this was the result of extremely hard labour, in which every word and every chord was tested and retested. Guillaume Apollinaire and Paul Éluard were Poulenc's two favourite poets, and often his music will illuminate ambiguous aspects of their texts, as in the parentheses in 'Sanglots' from *Banalités* (1940). Since his death in 1963, no French composer has appeared as a successor. LO/RN

📖 F. NOSKE, *La Mélodie française de Berlioz à Duparc* (Amsterdam, 1954; Eng. trans., rev. R. Benton and F. Noske, 1970) · B. MEISTER, *Nineteenth-Century French Song: Fauré, Chausson, Duparc and Debussy* (Bloomington, IN, 1980)

melodrama. A composition or section of a composition, usually dramatic, in which one or more actors recite with musical commentary. If for one actor, the term 'monodrama' may be used; if two, 'duodrama' (as in the duodramas of Georg Benda).

The form became popular in the second half of the 18th century. The first full-scale melodrama was *Pygmalion* by Rousseau, whose aim was 'to join the declamatory art with the art of music', alternating short spoken passages with instrumental music as a development of the *pantomime dialoguée*. On the whole, French melodramas tended to interpolate brief self-contained numbers between speeches, whereas the Germans preferred a sense of musical continuity, even when the music was interrupted by speech as well as accompanying it. Mozart, who admired Benda's *Ariadne auf Naxos* and *Medea*, planned a melodrama *Semiramis* but does not seem to have progressed very far with it; he did use melodrama effectively in *Zaide*, however.

Melodrama was cultivated for special uses in French *opéra comique*, by Cherubini in *Les Deux Journées* and also by Méhul, Boieldieu, and others. The most successful examples of its power of heightening the dramatic tension are in the grave-digging scene in Beethoven's *Fidelio* and the Wolf's Glen scene in Weber's *Der Freischütz*. Beethoven also used melodrama in his incidental music, including that for *Egmont*; and Schubert, who included some in his operas, wrote a recitation with piano, *Abschied von der Erde*. Weber wrote a complete concert melodrama, *Der erste Ton*, and for insertion in a play wrote a number in which speech moves in a controlled manner through speech-song into song; this technique is reflected in Gretchen's spinning song in Marschner's *Hans Heiling*.

Schumann and Liszt were among many 19th-century composers to write concert melodramas; and Berlioz made extended, if intermittent, use of it in *Lélio*. Both Verdi and Smetana included passages of melodrama in some of their operas; in Bohemian lands, it was particularly cultivated, and Fibich wrote a whole trilogy, *Hippodamia*. In the 20th century it was used by Schoenberg (in *A Survivor from Warsaw*, as well as in its form as speech-song), by Stravinsky (*Histoire du Soldat*), by Richard Strauss (a recitation with piano, *Enoch Arden*), by Honegger (*Jeanne d'Arc au bûcher*), and by Walton (*Façade*), among many others; and opera composers have used it for particular effect at certain moments.   JW

melody. The result of the interaction of rhythm and pitch. Both the regular articulation of time (through heartbeat, breathing) and the capacity to produce and recognize variations in the frequency of sound are normal physiological characteristics of humankind. The functions that define melody overlap with those used to define human speech, so that both may be regarded as fundamental capacities of the species. Whereas speech is a form of communication, melody in all human cultures has been used typically as a form of emotional expression. This use of melody may also be a capacity of other animals, since birds and dolphins, for example, produce organized sequences of varied pitch.

In language, intonation is an important source of meaning. Many African and Asian languages depend on an intonational system much richer than those with Indo-European roots; for that reason, it is notoriously difficult for a European to learn, say, a modern Chinese dialect. The use of this kind of 'melodic' inflection to determine meaning in language is quite remarkable. Any reader of this text can unconsciously and accurately intone the phrase 'Jack and Jill went up the hill' to convey quite different kinds of statement or question:

for example, 'Jack and Jill went *up* the hill?' and 'Jack and Jill went up the *hill*?'. In music, just as in language, the way different qualities inhere in such a form of expression is complex. Musicians consider it to be so complex, and there are so many different types of melody from different cultures and ages, that melody is the least well explained aspect of music theory.

The close empirical relationship between speech and melody suggests that melody may have a long prehistory, especially in the sense that functional and ritual melody exists in all known 'primitive' societies on which our view of prehistory is modelled. It also seems that the physiological and acoustic condition of humankind provided a common source of melody. The most basic quality of a pitch succession is whether it ascends or descends. In the earliest music, melodic descent is the outstanding quality, regardless of its provenance in one or another civilization. The most consistent intervallic characteristic of ancient melodic types is the 4th, subdivided by a 3rd and a 2nd. The slightly more elaborate vocabulary of superimposed 4ths (lying within the octave) and their subdivisions provides a pentatonic scale, melodic material common to Chinese, Hebrew, Amerindian, and many other ancient cultures (see Ex. 1).

It is important to the consideration not only of ancient music but also of the Western tradition to realize that the concept of scale is based on practice, rather than being the basis of practice. The complex

Ex. 1

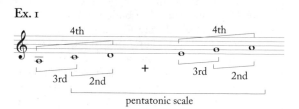

pentatonic scale

Ex. 2

Glo — ri - a in ex - cel - sis De — o.

Et in ter - ra pax ho — mi - ni - bus

bo - nae vo - lun - ta - tis.

Ex. 3

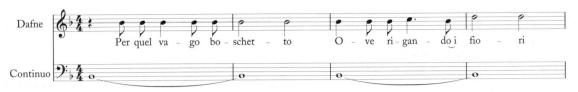

Peri, *Euridice.*

theory of modality in the Middle Ages, for instance, was a response to a sophisticated, variable, and instinctive use of pitch by practising musicians (see MODE). The scale determines the kind of music made only in the sense that it becomes fixed in instrumental music. Thus the existence of five-string lyres some three thousand years ago, as well as of wind instruments with certain possible fingerings and transpositional relationships to other instruments, suggests the fixed-pitch content of ancient melody on a pentatonic basis.

In the Western tradition, melody in the form of plainchant was the first aspect of music to be developed into an elaborate art form, before the last millennium of development of harmonic and rhythmic language. In the 5th and 6th centuries, a large repertory of plainchant was established, displaying a coherent melodic style. Ex. 2 illustrates some of these features: the mixture of melismatic and syllabic setting, the basically conjunct progression with expressive 3rds and 4ths which tend to be used at the beginning of a section, and, most important of all for the future of Western melody, the balance of ascent and descent around a focal pitch (in this case, the *finalis* E).

Since the first mature experiments in *polyphony (the combination of melodically differentiated voices) about a thousand years ago, monophony has played a relatively small part in our culture. In both sacred music and secular art music, medieval and Renaissance composers thought in terms of contrapuntal equality (see COUNTERPOINT). The melodic characteristics of one voice were like those of the others, although the ability to invent florid melody to fit against a simpler cantus firmus was a highly valued skill. At the beginning of the 17th century in Italy there was a major

change in the attitude towards melody and its function. This arose from a desire to recapture, in secular music, the ancient prize of a true marriage of word and melody. The new art of recitative spread rapidly. It exploited a melodic style closer to the inflection and rhythm of speech, sustained by a melodically sparse bass which carried the harmonic structure (see Ex. 3). The principle of a two-part texture, melody against bass with 'inner' parts providing homophonic or imitative richness, was the prevalent style of the Baroque era and the fundamental nature of Classical and Romantic music. A contrapuntal tradition continued within the new tonal language, exploited to some extent by all, but especially by Viennese composers, who continually returned to the study of J. S. Bach's counterpoint. These trends merged in the music of the early 20th century. Texture and colouring became so elaborate that

Ex. 4

Schoenberg had to notate for performers—and through them make clear to his listeners—just which part in a score carries the 'melody' at any point, with the indication Ⱶ (for *Hauptstimme* or 'main part').

The characteristics of melody in tonal music make the traditional yardstick for the discussion of melody in general. Ex. 4 illustrates this, showing that the second half of the clarinet melody which opens the third movement of Brahms's Symphony no. 1 repeats the first half upside down. It is an exact inversion, a procedure that became crucial in the melodic structure of 12-note

music. Yet in plainchant, the melody of Western Christian church music which has endured for two thousand years and has influenced the style of composers as culturally distant from each other as Machaut and Richard Strauss, inversion does not appear to be a significant feature.

Rhythmic articulation is another vital factor in the nature of melody, and the difficulties of rhythmic theory and the problems of notation raise further complex issues. Musicologists have yet to uncover decisive evidence about the authentic rhythmic patterns

Ex. 5

Ex. 6

Ex. 7

of early medieval liturgical melody, for which a clear notation was not devised, or indeed needed, at the time. Ethnomusicologists find that modern Western notation, of a kind that more or less adequately conveys to musicians the melodic intentions of the Brahms example within our living tradition, is barely adequate to capture the true or 'pertinent' melodic character of other cultures.

Ex. 8

During most of the history of humankind, and still in many non-Western cultures, melody is itself synonymous with music. The combination of melodies in polyphony, one of the great artistic achievements of medieval Europe, has produced the need for a more specialized explanation of melody in Western music. Melodic structure has to be described not only in terms of its overt linear properties, but also in terms of its harmonic implications. The English ballad *Greensleeves* (Ex. 5*a*) demonstrates how pure melody nevertheless unfolds a harmonic progression (Ex. 5*b*).

In Classical music, this potential for harmonic and contrapuntal implication in melody becomes a sophisticated source of musical unity. If we compare the melodies of the first and second minuets in the central movement of Mozart's Piano Sonata in E♭ K282/189g (Ex. 6*a*), it is clear that the different polyphonic implications of single-line melodies provide a common shape which contributes to the music's coherence (Ex. 6*b*: compare *x* and *y* in each case).

Similarly, the form of a melody is inherently tied to other properties of musical structure. Melodic patterns like ABA and AAB are perceived as structural, even as textural, patterns. Ex. 7*a*, for example, in a simple AA pattern, may appear in an actual piece of music as AA′ when harmony and phrase-length vary the repetition (Ex. 7*b*), or even as AB when it is texturally obscured (Ex. 7*c*).

The extremes of structural relationship indicate the extremes of expressive range which have been exploited in the classical tradition. On the one hand, melody can be built almost exclusively from motivic 'cells', as in Ex. 8*a*. Here the figuration by three instrumental parts of a simple melodic line (Ex. 8*b*) produces one of the most memorable melodic inventions in the repertory—the opening of Beethoven's Symphony no. 5.

On the other hand, in an attempt to recapture the link between music and drama first investigated in the 17th century, Schoenberg paved the way for a new, modern approach to melody. Ex. 9, from no. 7 of his *Pierrot lunaire*, shows the *Sprechstimme*, midway between recitation and song, relying on pitch relationships to guide the declamation of the voice but specifically not 'singing' the notes, as Schoenberg's

special notation here indicates (see SPRECHGESANG, SPRECHSTIMME). Schoenberg and Webern also investigated the idea of a **Klangfarbenmelodie* ('sound-colour melody'), in which variation of timbre is substituted for the variation of pitch which, as we have seen, underlies the whole history of melody.

Other composers, following the lead of, for example, Varèse's *Ionisation* (1929–31) for percussion, have experimented with music that avoids conventional melodic continuity. The rise of electronically produced sound has barely affected this situation. Some composers seize on the opportunity to manipulate the lines of sound in a way that bears little relation to the concept of melody. Yet the synthesizer is often used in popular music to reproduce with new timbres the centuries-old melodic formulas of tonal music.   AW

membranophone. A term used in *organology for all instruments on which sound is produced by a vibrating membrane or skin, whether they are hummed (e.g. *kazoos), struck (e.g. *drums), or rubbed (e.g. *friction drums). See INSTRUMENTS, CLASSIFICATION OF.

memorial. In the Roman rite, a devotion consisting of an antiphon, a versicle, and a collect, sometimes added to an Office in commemoration of another feast. In the Byzantine rite, it is a short Office of the Dead.   ALi

Mendelssohn(-Bartholdy) [Hensel], **Fanny** (Cäcilie) (*b* Hamburg, 14 Nov. 1805; *d* Berlin, 14 May 1847). German composer and pianist, the elder sister of Felix Mendelssohn. She studied the piano principally with Ludwig Berger. She, like her brother, studied composition with Zelter and revealed comparable precocity and ability. Felix valued her critical response to his music, often asking her opinion during the process of composition. Her extraordinary gifts were described by John Thompson in *The Harmonicon* in 1829. However, her social situation, her sex, and the opposition of her father and brother hindered her from publicly practising performance or composition.

Following her marriage to the painter Wilhelm Hensel in 1829, and the birth of her son Sebastian, Fanny Mendelssohn's life centred on the family home in Berlin, where she organized much private music-

Ex. 9

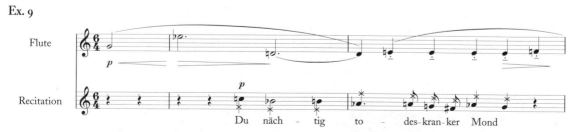

making and continued to compose, with her husband's encouragement. Some of her songs were published under her brother's name in his opp. 8 and 9, and a few isolated pieces appeared in print under her own name before she published her op. 1 in 1846. She died suddenly during preparations for a domestic performance of her brother's *Walpurgisnacht*. Immediately after her death further compositions were published, but much of her work has become available only since the 1980s.   CB

   📖 F. TILLARD, *Fanny Mendelssohn* (Paris, 1992; Eng. trans. 1996)

Mendelssohn, Felix (*see page 764*)

Mengelberg, (Josef) Willem (*b* Utrecht, 28 March 1871; *d* Zuort, 21 March 1951). Dutch conductor. For nearly 50 years he was the autocratic music director of the Concertgebouw Orchestra, making it one of the most virtuoso and versatile ensembles in history. After studying at the Cologne Conservatory, he made his debut as a pianist and was appointed music director at Lucerne in 1891 and to the Concertgebouw Orchestra in 1895. His flamboyant interpretations often departed from the score, but he exerted a crucial influence on performing standards. He championed new music and the works of Mahler and Strauss, and in 1920 organized a festival in Amsterdam at which all Mahler's major works were given. He conducted in the USA and Britain and at Salzburg. For alleged collaboration with the Nazis he was exiled for six years, dying just before he was due to return.   JT

   📖 R. H. HARDIE, *The Recordings of Willem Mengelberg* (Nashville, TN, 1972) · F. W. ZWART, *Willem Mengelberg, i: 1871–1920* (Amsterdam, 1997)

meno (It.). 'Less'; *meno mosso*, 'slower'.

Menotti, Gian Carlo (*b* Cadegliano, 7 July 1911). Italian-born American composer. He studied at the Milan Conservatory (1923–7) and with Rosario Scalero at the Curtis Institute in Philadelphia (1928–33), where he taught from 1948 to 1955. In 1958 he founded the Festival of Two Worlds in Spoleto. Primarily an opera composer, he achieved international attention in the years immediately after World War II with *The Medium* (1946), *The Telephone* (1947), and *The Consul* (1950), all of which show theatrical flair and an opportune use of music to heighten melodramatic situations. His television opera *Amahl and the Night Visitors* (1951) is gentler in its appeal, but such later works as *The Saint of Bleecker Street* (1954), *Maria Golovin* (1958), and *The Most Important Man in the World* (1970) show no lessening of dramatic incisiveness. Menotti wrote the librettos for all his own operas and also for Samuel Barber's *Vanessa*.   PG

   📖 R. TRICOIRE, *Gian Carlo Menotti* (Paris, 1966)

mensural music, mensural notation. Terms meaning 'measured music' and 'measured notation'. They were used originally to distinguish polyphony and its notation from plainchant (which was sung in free rhythm). More technically, they apply to music in which each note-type has a clearly defined value. This system was established in the 13th century (see FRANCONIAN NOTATION) and forms the basis of notational practices from that period to the present day. However, 'mensural music' is commonly applied in a more restricted sense to mean 15th- and 16th-century music. This music had no bar-lines, and the note shapes were written only in outline (like our modern minims and semibreves); thus it is referred to as 'white' mensural notation.

In mensural notation two relationships are carefully defined or 'measured'. The first is the proportional relationship between a note and the next higher or lower in value. In modern notation this relationship is always duple (two crotchets in a minim, two minims in a semibreve, no matter what the time signature), though in earlier notations one or both of these relationships might be triple depending on the time signature. The other measured element is the speed relationship between sections of music with different time signatures (see PROLATION; NOTATION, 2).   AP

Mensurstrich (Ger.). In editions of early music, the use of a line between the staves rather than through them, to divide the music into bars (see Ex. 1). The method is supposed to avoid the four-square, regular accentuation implied by the modern bar-line.   AP

Ex. 1

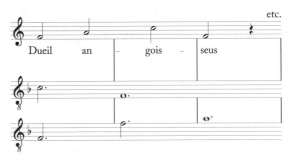

From Binchois, *Dueil angoisseus.*

mente, alla. See ALLA MENTE.

menuet (Fr.; Ger.: *Menuett*). 'Minuet'.

Menuhin, Yehudi (*b* New York, 22 April 1916; *d* Berlin, 2 March 1999). American violinist, conductor, and
(*cont. on p. 766*)

Felix Mendelssohn
(1809–47)

The German composer Felix Jakob Ludwig Mendelssohn-Bartholdy was born in Hamburg on 3 February 1809 and died in Leipzig on 4 November 1847.

Childhood and early travels

Mendelssohn was the grandson of the well-known Jewish philosopher Moses Mendelssohn. Although Felix, his brother, and two sisters were all brought up by their parents in the Christian faith, the family's commitment to learning, to the arts, and to a highly disciplined life undoubtedly owed much to Jewish tradition. A friend later remembered Leah, Mendelssohn's mother, calling out from the kitchen in response to sounds of hilarity 'Felix, tust du nichts?' ('Felix, are you being idle?'). Study on weekdays began at 5 a.m. From this regime stemmed Mendelssohn's own advice in later life to young composers to exercise their craft regularly, in the form of the Latin proverb 'nulla dies sine linea' ('no day without a line').

When Hamburg was occupied by the French in 1812 the family left the city and went to Berlin, where Mendelssohn was tutored in literary subjects by Karl Heyse and, from 1817, in music by Carl Zelter, a friend of Goethe. His first dated composition was a cantata (13 January 1820) and from then on he composed prolifically, his early works including three piano quartets, a piano sonata in G minor, and four concertos. In many of these, a certain garrulity mixes not altogether easily with occasional Beethovenian aspirations.

In 1825 Mendelssohn paid a second visit to Paris, where Cherubini recognized his talent but warned that he was being too prodigal with his ideas ('he puts too much material into his coat'). But later that year Mendelssohn wrote the Octet for strings which remains perhaps the most astonishing example of youthful genius in all Western music. Technically he had no more to learn; psychologically, he still had to break the tenacious family bonds.

In 1826 Mendelssohn followed up the Octet with the overture to *A Midsummer Night's Dream*. His ability to conjure up the gossamer world of Shakespeare's play suggested that he might be destined for the opera house. But his opera *Die Hochzeit des Camacho*, given its premiere in Berlin in 1827, was a failure. This hit him

hard—his upbringing, though disciplined, had inculcated in him a high degree of self-criticism that to him justified self-belief, and, as has often been suggested, the lack of school rough-and-tumble left him ill-equipped throughout his life to deal with controversy or outright resistance. Some would claim that this ivory-tower mentality was reflected in his music. At the same time, Mendelssohn's determination was shown in the fight he made to be allowed to organize and conduct the first performances for a century of Bach's *St Matthew Passion*, given twice before packed houses in March 1829.

Fresh from this triumph, he began a series of journeys throughout Europe, travelling now apart from his family. His visit to Britain (the first of ten during his life) took him to Holyrood House and to Staffa among other places, generating sketches for the 'Scottish' Symphony and the overture *The Hebrides* respectively. During 1830 he continued his travels, beginning with a third and last visit to Goethe in Weimar. One eyewitness called him 'Goethe's David, because he removed every cloud from the poet's Jovian brow', noting that his playing was 'just like the man himself, with no feeling that tended towards the bizarre, no disharmony that was not gently absorbed, no virtuoso displays to make us dizzy'. From Weimar, Mendelssohn went on through Munich and Vienna to Venice and Rome, where he met Berlioz and began a somewhat uneasy relationship with him. Mendelssohn's letters home to his family are wholly delightful and full of sharp insights, pricking pomposity and lambasting mediocrity with the assured vigour of one who suffered from neither of these failings.

With his return to Germany in September 1831, Mendelssohn entered on the life of a professional musician. It is true that, thanks to the support of his banker father Abraham, he never had to count the pfennigs, but the impulse to excel, allied with his ability to do so, took him to the top of most enterprises to which he set his hand. He celebrated his return to his homeland with the first performance of his Piano

Concerto in G minor; here the expected virtuosity combines with a new approach to concerto form, in that he introduces the piano immediately after an initial 'storm' on the orchestra, leaves out the usual orchestral tutti, and runs the three movements together. No less radical was his invention of the 'songs without words' (*Lieder ohne Worte*), the first volume of which was published in 1832. Even if, as one biographer has put it, 'they move in a far more ordered and limited world' than the short pieces of Chopin and Schumann, the best of them achieve a rare perfection. More than Schubert's Impromptus or *Moments musicaux*, they inspired imitations for well over a century. When Busoni died in 1924, a volume of *Songs without Words* was found open on his piano.

Berlin and Leipzig: successes and setbacks

In 1833 Mendelssohn suffered the second of the three Berlin fiascos that were to underpin his love–hate relationship with that city, when he was passed over to succeed Zelter as director of the Singakademie. His family blamed local politics, but it has to be said that Mendelssohn, for all his genius, was not perhaps well placed to direct an institution many members of which had known him since he was a little boy, and in which tact and even compromise were called for. However, satisfaction came in abundance with the completion of the first version of the 'Italian' Symphony and with his appointment as director of the Lower Rhine Festival in Düsseldorf, where he conducted *Israel in Egypt* by his beloved Handel. In general he was happiest conducting either professional orchestras such as the Leipzig Gewandhaus and the Philharmonic Society in London, or else amateurs for short festival periods where his documented 'impatience with those who could not keep time' did not have the chance to build up into anything too disruptive. His appointment in 1833 as regular musical director in Düsseldorf for three years came to an end in less than two.

Mendelssohn's assumption of the directorship of the Leipzig Gewandhaus in 1835 was a major milestone in his career. The brilliant youth had, at the age of 26, found a post where he could operate as a dependable functionary, though there is no evidence that the brilliance was in any way dimmed. The appointment is sure to have pleased his father, who had expressed doubts over his son's propensity for writing frothy scherzos like the one in the Octet and wanted to see him settle to something more solid and Handelian. But in November 1835 Abraham died without having heard the completed oratorio *St Paul*, which thus became Mendelssohn's tribute to his memory. Here the composer adopted as his pattern what he called 'the progressive history of particular persons ... because if it is

all to be only contemplative ... then this task has already been more grandly and beautifully accomplished in Handel's *Messiah*'.

St Paul had its premiere in 1836 in Düsseldorf, and that summer Mendelssohn met his future wife, Cécile Jeanrenaud, the daughter of a Frankfurt pastor. They married in 1837 and in that year he also gave the first performance of his Second Piano Concerto in D minor, a rather more reflective work than its predecessor: again, the piano enters immediately and the three movements are linked. The success of *St Paul* in Germany and in London prompted him to search for another subject and he began to plan *Elijah*.

Until now Mendelssohn's health had been excellent. But in January 1838 he suffered the first headaches and attacks of prostration that were to plague him at irregular intervals for the rest of his life. He would speak occasionally of holidays, but there was always some new plan or concert to be undertaken. He once said that he knew he would never make old bones and this, together with his responsibilities as the father of a family (five children were born to him and his wife between 1838 and 1845), seems to have combined with his early education to drive him ever onwards and upwards.

In addition to his other activities he now began to consider the founding of a music conservatory in Leipzig, but he put this on hold when Friedrich Wilhelm IV, recently arrived on the throne of Prussia, began negotiations to bring Mendelssohn to Berlin as director of music in a new Academy of Arts. Mendelssohn moved to Berlin in May 1841, only to be met with a dilatoriness and incompetence that would have taxed a far more patient man. He left Berlin, and the third fiasco, in 1844. By then he had conducted the first performance of the 'Scottish' Symphony (in Leipzig) and in 1842 founded a conservatory on lines of his own (in Leipzig), which opened the following year.

The last years

The last five years of Mendelssohn's life were busy and fruitful, though his health again took a turn for the worse at the end of 1844. His incidental music to *A Midsummer Night's Dream*, commissioned by the King of Prussia, was immediately hailed as a masterpiece, amazingly picking up without any noticeable stylistic rupture from the overture written 18 years before. In September 1844 he completed the Violin Concerto for his friend Ferdinand David. Again, Mendelssohn saw the concerto form as a field for experiment and his idea of continuing the soloist's cadenza figuration in the first movement over the recapitulation in the orchestra was later hailed by Ravel as a masterstroke. Mendelssohn's pupil, the famous violinist Joseph Joachim, recognized four great German violin concertos, by Beethoven,

Brahms, Bruch, and Mendelssohn; 'but the dearest of them all, the heart's jewel, is Mendelssohn's'.

The focus of his activity in the last two years of his life was the oratorio *Elijah*, given its premiere at the Birmingham Festival in August 1846. *Elijah* makes a more dramatic and varied effect than *St Paul*, partly because the narrative is stronger, but also because Mendelssohn seems less concerned to impress by a devotional tone; there is too a larger element of scene-painting—Mendelssohn never visited Palestine, but we hear and see it, in one biographer's words, as 'a land of drought, thirst and hunger, and also of lightning, thunder, blue-black torrents of rain'. Mendelssohn makes his first revolutionary gesture at the very beginning of the work when, instead of the expected overture, the prophet Elijah, in the 'serious' key of D minor, curses Israel with drought, plunging us immediately into the heart of the drama.

In 1847 Mendelssohn made his tenth and last visit to England, conducting *Elijah* six times in the course of April, with choirs that were not uniformly responsive. Exhausted by these efforts, he was then dealt a terrible blow by the sudden death in May of his beloved elder sister Fanny. His response to this can be heard in the desperate torment of his F minor String Quartet, his last major work. He seemed to rally slightly during a brief holiday in September, but he died on 4 November of a cerebral haemorrhage, leaving unfinished an opera, *Loreley*, and an oratorio, *Christus*.

Wagner, on hearing Mendelssohn's brisk tempo in the third movement of Beethoven's Eighth Symphony, fancied he was 'peering into a veritable abyss of superficiality, an utter void'; some 40 years later Bernard Shaw inveighed against Mendelssohn's 'kid-glove gentility, his conventional sentimentality, and his de-

spicable oratorio mongering'. With hindsight we can see that both men had their own agendas, Wagner to promote Wagner, Shaw to drag British music out of the slough of Mendelssohn imitations. It was typical of the Romantic movement to look askance at superlative technique divorced from wildness or unbridled passion, as it has been in some quarters to hold against Mendelssohn his comfortable social and financial position.

Like Bach and Mozart, two of his gods, he wrote some dull works. But the best of him testifies both to his unyielding pursuit of perfection in his craft and to a character that was far from being the milk-and-water saint of legend. He had a temper and he could sulk; he was also passionately self-critical (some of the *Songs without Words* went through six or seven drafts and *St Paul* was originally a quarter as long again as the score we now have) and often saw no reason not to apply similar criticism to others, if he felt goodwill was lacking. On the other hand he was deeply loved by his many friends, not least by Schumann whose obituary tribute is among the most moving ever written by one composer about another. With few exceptions, his contemporaries recognized that he was a great man, a great musician, and a great composer. Only in opera did he fail to make his mark. He did not change the course of musical history, nor did he want to. That revolutionary capacities should in our age still be a criterion of value suggests that we have not learnt the lesson of J. S. Bach, who remained on the sidelines after his death, until Mendelssohn rescued him.   RN

📖 R. L. TODD (ed.), *Mendelssohn and his World* (Princeton, NJ, 1991) · R. NICHOLS, *Mendelssohn Remembered* (London, 1997) · P. MERCER-TAYLOR, *The Life of Mendelssohn* (Cambridge, 2000) · D. SEATON (ed.), *The Mendelssohn Companion* (Westport, CT, 2000)

pedagogue, of Russian descent. One of the most celebrated child prodigies of the 20th century, he studied initially with Sigmund Anker and Louis Persinger, and completed his training with Busch and Enescu. He gave his first professional recitals in San Francisco (1924) and New York (1926), followed by sensational debuts in Paris, Berlin, and London through which he quickly established an international reputation. He then began an extensive series of recordings, most famously that of the Elgar concerto (conducted by the composer) in 1932. His lively interest in contemporary music led him to commission numerous works, including Bartók's solo violin Sonata and Walton's Sonata for violin and piano, but he was also active as a proselytizer for nearly forgotten music of

past eras, editing Mendelssohn's early D minor Concerto and frequently performing Schumann's often-slighted Violin Concerto.

Menuhin gave more than 500 concerts during World War II for American and Allied troops and was the first Jewish artist to play in Berlin, under Furtwängler, after the end of the Nazi regime. From the late 1940s he became increasingly busy as a conductor and teacher, founding the Bath Festival orchestra in 1959, and the Menuhin Music School (in Stoke d'Abernon, Surrey) in 1963. In his final decades he frequently exploited his fame as a musician to publicize his views on ethical and political issues, and remained active as a performer up to his death in Berlin while on a conducting tour of Germany. He published books on violin-playing and an autobiography, and was made a life peer in 1993.   MHe

   📖 H. Burton, *Menuhin* (London, 2000)

Mephistowalzer ('Mephisto Waltzes'). A series of works by Liszt, their title deriving from an abbreviation for 'Mephistopheles'. The first, *Der Tanz in der Dorfschenke* (1859), was originally for piano but then orchestrated to become one of *Two Episodes from Lenau's Faust*. The second (1880–1) also exists in piano and orchestral versions. The third (1883, two versions) was composed for piano only, as was the fourth (1885). The *Bagatelle sans tonalité* was originally intended to be part of the series.

Mer, La ('The Sea'). Three symphonic sketches (1903–5) by Debussy: *De l'aube à midi sur la mer* ('From Dawn to Noon on the Sea'), *Jeux de vagues* ('Play of the Waves'), and *Dialogue du vent et de la mer* ('Dialogue of the Wind and the Sea').

Merbecke [Marbeck], **John** (*b* ?Windsor, *c*.1505–10; *d* 1585). English composer. He was a lay clerk at St George's Chapel, Windsor, in 1531 and later an organist there. In 1543 he was condemned to be burnt as a heretic for his adherence to Calvinism, but he was reprieved by Henry VIII (perhaps because of his musical ability) and on his release from prison returned to St George's. He did not recant, however, and continued to work on several theological volumes, stating his position openly when Edward VI came to the throne in 1547.

   Merbecke composed Latin church music but is best known for *The Booke of Common Praier Noted* (1550), the first musical setting of services in the 1549 Prayer Book, probably intended for use in parish churches rather than cathedrals. He adapted the plainchant of the Roman liturgy to the new English words, rearranging the accentuation and providing music in a similar style where necessary. It was superseded after Mary's reign but came back into use in the 19th century.

                             PS/DA/AL

Mercadante, (Giuseppe) **Saverio** (Raffaele) (*b* Altamura, nr Bari, *bapt.* 17 Sept. 1795; *d* Naples, 17 Dec. 1870). Italian composer. He studied at the Naples Conservatory with Zingarelli, and distinguished himself first as a composer of instrumental music. However, by 1820 he was established as an opera composer in Naples. His first great success was at La Scala, Milan, with *Elisa e Claudio* (1821), which quickly travelled to some of the major European theatres. Equally successful and long-lived in the repertory was *Caritea, regina di Spagna* (also known as *Donna Caritea*; Venice, 1826). After attempts to find a post in Spain, he returned to Italy in 1831, and the following year produced

I normanni a Parigi in Turin. In 1833 he became *maestro di cappella* in Novara, producing in the next seven years a good deal of religious music as well as further operas.

   An important new stimulus came from a commission from the Théâtre Italien in Paris in 1835. Although his opera *I briganti* was not well received, the influence of Parisian operatic culture, particularly that of Meyerbeer, was revealed in his next work, *Il giuramento* (1837), which embarked on a conscious programme of reform, one continued in several subsequent operas, especially *Il bravo* and *La vestale*. In 1840 Mercadante became director of the Naples Conservatory, a post he retained until his death 30 years later. The pace of his operatic output then slowed, though he continued sporadic attempts into the 1860s.

   Mercadante's early operas were, inevitably for the period, heavily influenced by Rossini. In the early 1830s, however, he did respond to the new style made popular by Bellini and Donizetti. But his most innovatory work was produced in the late 1830s and early 40s; such operas as *Il giuramento* made attempts to avoid the usual forms of the period in favour of a musical surface that responded more immediately to the stage action, in the process avoiding excessive vocal ornamentation and extending the harmonic range. In patches he succeeded in his aim, but it proved difficult for him to sustain the dramatic momentum over large spans. After the mid-1840s his work was found wanting in comparison with that of Verdi, who began to dominate the scene almost as thoroughly as had Rossini in the 1820s. But Verdi's first works, perhaps particularly *Oberto, conte di San Bonifacio* (1839), reflect much from Mercadante's example.   RP

   📖 S. Palermo, *Saverio Mercadante: Biografia, epistolario* (Fasano, 1985)

Mercure. Ballet in three scenes by Satie to a scenario by Leonid Massine; it was choreographed by Massine, with decor by Pablo Picasso (Paris, 1924).

Merikanto, Aarre (*b* Helsinki, 29 June 1893; *d* Helsinki, 29 Sept. 1958). Finnish composer and teacher. Son of the composer and organist Oscar Merikanto, whose songs are still popular in Finland (and who wrote the first opera in Finnish), he made an impact in 1912 with the melodrama *Helena*, which he later destroyed; he then continued his studies with Reger in Leipzig (1912–14) and Sergey Vasilenko in Moscow (1915–16), where he learnt much about orchestral colour. He was one of the founders of Finnish modernism, together with Vainö Raitio and Ernest Pingoud, who brought into their music elements of Impressionism and Expressionism, the Skryabin school, and bi-, poly-, and pan-tonality. His major work during this period was the opera *Juha* (1920–2), not performed in its entirety until 1963; a number of adventurous orchestral works from the 1920s also went unheard during his lifetime.

In the early 1930s Merikanto drastically simplified his style, admitting folk elements. He nevertheless left his mark on Finnish modernism through his teaching. His output includes three symphonies (1916, 1918, 1953), three piano concertos (1913, 1937, 1955), four violin concertos (1916, 1925, 1931, 1954), a number of orchestral scores, and much chamber music. MA

Merrie England. Operetta in two acts by German to a libretto by Basil Hood (London, 1902).

Merry Widow, The. See LUSTIGE WITWE, DIE.

Merry Wives of Windsor, The. See LUSTIGE WEIBER VON WINDSOR, DIE.

Mersenne, Marin (*b* La Soultière, Maine, 8 Sept. 1588; *d* Paris, 1 Sept. 1648). French mathematician, philosopher, and music theorist. He was one of the leading scholars in 17th-century France. From 1619 he was a Jesuit priest in Paris. He corresponded with all the leading thinkers, including René Descartes, Thomas Hobbes, Galileo, and G. B. Doni. His interests were wide-ranging and, through his studies of mathematics and physics, he wrote extensively on music, making discoveries about the behaviour of sound which are fundamental to the science of acoustics. He regarded music as a discipline that could be analysed and explained, and in his treatise *Harmonie universelle* (Paris, 1636–7/*R*1963; partial Eng. trans. 1957) he expounded theoretical and practical ideas including invaluable work on the classification of instruments. AL

Merulo, Claudio (*b* Correggio, nr Reggio nell'Emilia, 8 April 1533; *d* Parma, 5 May 1604). Italian composer, organist, and printer. In 1556 he became organist at Brescia Cathedral, and the following year was successful in a competition for a similar post at St Mark's, Venice, where he remained until 1584. He was a colleague of Andrea Gabrieli there, and they shared the duty of writing ceremonial music; Merulo composed some splendid motets, which were published in several collections (Venice, 1578–1605), as well as masses, a substantial number of madrigals, and music for pastoral plays. He is best known for his organ music, especially the toccatas, which were known to Frescobaldi and Sweelinck and can be seen as the first in a line that was to lead to Bach's toccatas. He was also important as a music publisher in Venice. In his last years he returned to Parma, where he was organist to the dukes and to their order of chivalry, the Steccata company. He was generally considered to be the finest organist of his day,

and he was buried next to Cipriano de Rore in Parma Cathedral. DA/TC

mescolanza (It.). **Medley'.

Mesopotamian music. See ANCIENT MESOPOTAMIAN AND EGYPTIAN MUSIC.

messa di voce (It., 'placing of the voice'; Fr.: *mise de voix*). A Baroque vocal technique, still used as a method of voice-training. It consists of a long-held note during which the tone swells to a climax, followed by a diminuendo to *pianissimo*. See also VOICE, 7.

Messager, André (Charles Prosper) (*b* Montluçon, 30 Dec. 1853; *d* Paris, 24 Feb. 1929). French composer, conductor, and administrator. He studied at the École Niedermeyer in Paris with Fauré and Saint-Saëns, and in 1874 he succeeded Fauré as assistant organist at St Sulpice. In 1876 he won an important prize with a symphony, which he followed with a cantata *Prométhée enchaîné*. He then conducted at the Folies-Bergère, for which he composed three one-act ballets. The focus of his compositional career was established when he was commissioned in 1883 to complete the operetta *François-les-bas-bleus*, left unfinished on the death of Firmin Bernicat. Messager went on to write further works in similar style, including *La Fauvette du temple* and *La Béarnaise* (both 1885), as well as the ballet *Les Deux Pigeons* (1886) for the Opéra. These were followed by *La Basoche* (1890) for the Opéra-Comique and an ambitious oriental piece *Madame Chrysanthème* (1893) for the Théâtre de la Renaissance.

When *La Basoche* was produced in London it led to a commission for *Mirette* (1894) at the Savoy, and major international acclaim arrived with the operettas *Les P'tites Michu* (1897) and *Véronique* (1898). By now, however, Messager's conducting commitments were taking over. He was a renowned Wagner conductor, and from 1898 to 1903 was musical director of the Opéra-Comique, where he conducted Charpentier's *Louise* and Debussy's *Pelléas et Mélisande*. He was also manager at Covent Garden (1901–7), director of the Opéra (1907–14) and conductor of the Lamoureux Concerts (1905) and the Concerts du Conservatoire (1908–19). When time allowed he composed further theatre scores of rare grace and elegance, including the opera *Fortunio* (1907) and the operettas *Monsieur Beaucaire* (1919), *L'Amour masqué* (1923), and *Coups de roulis* (1929). In 1926 he was elected a member of the Institut and in 1927 was made a Commander of the Légion d'Honneur. ALa

📖 J. WAGSTAFF, *André Messager: A Bio-Bibliography* (Westport, CT, 1991)

Messa per i defunti (It.). 'Mass for the dead', i.e. *Requiem Mass.

Messe (Fr., Ger.). 'Mass'.

Messe de Nostre Dame. See NOTRE DAME MASS.

Messe des morts (Fr.). 'Mass for the dead', i.e. *Requiem Mass.

Messiaen, Olivier (*see page 770*)

Messiah. Oratorio by Handel to a text compiled by Charles Jennens from the Bible and the Prayer Book Psalter; it was first performed in Dublin in 1742. Handel revised it for subsequent performances and in the 19th century it became customary to perform it with enormous forces.

mesto (It.). 'Mournful', 'sad'.

mesure (Fr.). 1. 'Measure', i.e. bar.
2. Tempo, e.g. *à la mesure*, 'in time' (*a *tempo*).

mesuré (Fr.). 'Measured'.

metal blocks. See ANVIL; COWBELLS.

metallophone. A term used in *organology for *idiophones that are struck, and particularly for those similar in shape to the xylophone, for example the *glockenspiel and *vibraphone. (Strictly, a metallophone is any instrument made of metal, but in practice the term is more narrowly used.)   JMo

Metamorphosen. Study in C minor (1945) by Richard Strauss for 23 solo strings; it was composed as a lament for the wartime destruction of the German cultural world and quotes from Beethoven's 'Eroica' Symphony.

metamorphosis, thematic. See TRANSFORMATION, THEMATIC.

Metner, Nikolay Karlovich. See MEDTNER, NICOLAS.

metre. The pattern of regular pulses (and the arrangement of their constituent parts) by which a piece of music is organized. One complete pattern is called a *bar. The prevailing metre is identified at the beginning of a piece (and during it whenever it changes) by a *time signature, which is usually in the form of a fraction; the denominator indicates the note-value of each beat and the numerator gives the number of beats in each bar. Thus 3/4 denotes three beats to a bar, each being a quarter-note (i.e. a crotchet). The sign $\mathbf{C}$ is the equivalent of 4/4 and $\mathbf{\mathmbox{¢}}$ of 2/2.

Musical metre derives some of its terminology from poetic metre, its regular patterns of accented (strong) and unaccented (weak) beats in a bar being analogous to the patterns of long and short syllables in a line of quantitative verse. The division of a line of poetry into feet is much like the division of a musical phrase into bars. The conventional barring system of music divides the beats into groups. Scansion systems in verse divide syllables into groups, each beginning as the line begins. In music, incomplete bars are permitted at the start of a phrase whereas lines of verse can open only with complete feet. Common metrical patterns in both poetry and music are iambic, trochaic, dactylic, amphibrachic, anapaestic, spondaic, and tribrachic.

One direct application of poetic metre to music was in the 13th-century rhythmic modes, systems of setting texts to music using the repetition of standard, simple rhythmic patterns (see NOTATION, 2). With a few exceptions, composers setting poetry to music have not felt obliged to follow the poet's metrical scheme in detail and have not restricted themselves to one note per syllable. They have traditionally attempted to respect the text's accentuation by matching accented syllables to accented beats in the music, thus highlighting both rhythm and sense, often to the benefit of both words and music.

The perception of musical metre requires recognition of the first beat in the metrical pattern or bar. In a bar in 4/4 time, the first beat is the strongest (the downbeat), the third next strongest, with the weak beats being the second and fourth. In Western music metre is generally duple (in which the unit of pulse is in groups of two) or triple (in groups of three). 4/4, though it could be called quadruple metre, is considered a form of duple metre. If the units of pulse can be subvided into three, a piece is said to be in compound metre. A bar in 6/8 time and a bar in 3/4 may each contain six quavers; however, 6/8 is a compound duple metre because it consists of two groups of three quavers; 3/4 is a simple triple metre because it contains three groups of two.

Until the 20th century composers used simple and compound metres, occasionally writing in quintuple metre, as in the 'mad' music from Handel's *Orlando* (5/8) and the second movement (5/4) of Tchaikovsky's Symphony no. 6. But during the last century composers experimented with metre, using odd numbers of beats in a bar, different metres simultaneously, or changing metres in quick succession. Some dispensed altogether with the regular organization of pulse.

See also RHYTHM; TIME SIGNATURE.   AL

metrical psalms. See HYMN, 3; PSALMODY.

metric modulation. A technique introduced by Elliott Carter, by which changing time signatures effect a transition from one metre to another, just as a series of chords can effect a harmonic modulation from one key to another.

(cont. on p. 771)

Olivier Messiaen (1908–92)

The French composer Olivier Eugène Prosper Charles Messiaen was born in Avignon on 10 December 1908 and died in Paris on 27 April 1992.

The leading French composer of the generation after Debussy and Ravel, Messiaen quickly developed a very distinctive musical style based on his **'modes of limited transposition', on a speculative interest in rhythm, and on his desire to expound in music the truths of the Catholic faith. Though these concerns were not widely shared, he had a determining influence on the avant-garde as the teacher of Boulez, Stockhausen, and others.

He studied at the Paris Conservatoire (1919–30), where his teachers included Jean and Noël Gallon (harmony, counterpoint, and fugue), Dukas (composition), Maurice Emmanuel (musical history), and Marcel Dupré (organ). From the Gallon brothers Messiaen learnt a strong, flexible musical technique, while the solid brilliance of Dukas's orchestration in his opera *Ariane et Barbe-bleue* (1907) was discernible in Messiaen's orchestral works throughout his life. Emmanuel passed on his enthusiasm for Greek and Hindu modes and Dupré encouraged Messiaen in his penchant for improvisation, which formed a large part of the Conservatoire organ syllabus and of which Messiaen became an uncontested master. One gift he did not owe to the Conservatoire, nor indeed to his parents, was his Roman Catholic faith. In his own words, 'I was born a believer'.

In 1931 he was appointed organist of La Trinité in Paris, having assured the curé that he would not 'disturb the piety of the faithful with overly anarchic chords', and in 1936 he began teaching at the École Normale de Musique and the Schola Cantorum. By this time he had composed a set of eight rather Debussian preludes (1929) and a number of organ works which proclaim not only a Dupré-like extroversion in fast movements, but an inwardness in slow ones that builds on the example of Tournemire but goes further, both in harmonic individuality and in the cultivation of a contemplative passivity in which the music seems on the brink of stopping altogether. Between 1934 and 1939 he completed three organ cycles: *L'Ascension* (1934), largely a transcription of an orchestral work of 1933; *La Nativité du Seigneur* (1935), ending with the now famous 'Dieu parmi nous'; and the technically and musically more advanced *Les Corps glorieux* (1939), which takes the colouristic properties of the instrument to new extremes. In 1932 he married the violinist Claire Delbos; two song cycles, *Poèmes pour Mi* (1936) and *Chants de terre et de ciel* (1938), celebrate respectively the joys of marriage and delight in their young son Pascal.

Messiaen joined the French army on the outbreak of war, though his poor eyesight prevented him from front-line action. In 1940 he was taken prisoner of war, and during his captivity he composed the *Quatuor pour la fin du temps* (1941) for violin, clarinet, cello, and piano. It was given its first performance out of doors in January in the Silesian prison camp before an enthusiastic audience of 5000 prisoners. Here again, the two extremely slow movements for violin and for cello, with piano accompaniment, seem to speak of a time beyond the everyday. On his release in 1941 he was appointed professor of harmony at the Paris Conservatoire and in 1944 he published his *Technique de mon langage musical*, which resumes and explains the rhythmic and harmonic principles of his music. The sequence of theological cycles continued with *Visions de l'Amen* for two pianos (1943) and *Vingt regards sur l'enfant Jésus* (1944). In both of these the young pianist Yvonne Loriod, who was to become Messiaen's second wife after the death of Delbos in 1959, showed her exceptional virtuosity. She also, with Pierre Boulez and others, attended private composition classes given by Messiaen.

Major works of the later 1940s included a trilogy on the Tristan legend: *Harawi* (1945), a song cycle to the composer's own texts invoking Peruvian mythology, the *Turangalîla-symphonie* (1946–8, rev. 1990), a ten-movement work which exultantly combines all the features of his early style, and *Cinq rechants* for chorus (1949). This great outpouring was followed by a period of experiment with serial and numerical procedures in such works as the *Quatre études de rythme* for piano (1949–50) and the *Livre d'orgue* (1951), in which massively dissonant textures, as in 'Les Yeux dans les roues', rub shoulders with abstract and seemingly unemotional invention, as in 'Soixante-quatre durées'.

Messiaen then began to capitalize on his long-standing interest in birdsong, which he transcribed more or less faithfully in *Réveil des oiseaux* for piano and orchestra (1953), *Oiseaux exotiques* for piano, wind, and percussion (1955–6), and the *Catalogue d'oiseaux* for piano (1956–8), mixing it with the sounds of streams, wind and, more contentiously, sunsets. Common chords are still to be found occasionally (and very strange they sometimes sound in atonal company), but Messiaen abandoned these in *Chronochromie* (1960), one of his toughest and most impressive works, as well as in three further works exploiting wind and percussion sonorities: *Sept haï-kaï* (1962), *Couleurs de la cité céleste* (1963), and *Et exspecto resurrectionem mortuorum* (1964). The final movement of this last work, scored for woodwind, brass, and percussion, consists entirely of huge, loud, regular chords articulated by pulsating gongs: it demonstrates Messiaen's determination to explain scriptural texts (in this case 'And I heard the voice of an immense crowd' from the Apocalypse) in his own way, even if it brought on him charges of being simplistic.

In 1966 Messiaen was finally appointed professor of composition at the Paris Conservatoire, and the following year he was elected a member of the Institut. For the next 25 years he continued to devote his time to teaching (pupils from this period included Tristan Murail, Michaël Lévinas, Gérard Grisey, Jean-Louis Florentz, and George Benjamin), to his church duties, to composing, and to travelling, both to hear performances of his music and to track down and record exotic birds. These played a part in his last two piano works, the taxing *La Fauvette des jardins* (1970) and the shorter, delightful *Petites esquisses d'oiseaux* (1985). They also, understandably, figure largely in his only opera *Saint François d'Assise* (1975–83), given its premiere at the Paris Opéra in December 1983. Otherwise the works of Messiaen's final years were two organ cycles, *Méditations sur le mystère de la Sainte-Trinité* (1969) and *Livre du Saint Sacrement* (1984), and four orchestral works. Of these, *Un sourire* (1989), as a tribute to Mozart, stands somewhat apart. But *Un vitrail et des oiseaux* (1986) proclaims in its title a continuing interest in colour and birdsong. Both the short, one-movement *La Ville d'En-Haut* (1987) and his last completed work, the hour-long, 11-movement *Éclairs sur l'Au-delà ...* (1988–91) deal with the hereafter and may be said to crown a composing career during which, for all his concerns with birdsong, rhythmic complexity, orchestral colour and virtuosity, Messiaen never lost sight of the essentially simple truths of the Roman Catholic faith.   PG/RN

📖 O. Messiaen, *The Technique of my Musical Language* (Eng. trans., Paris, 1956) · S. Waumsley, *The Organ Music of Olivier Messiaen* (Paris, 1968, 2/1975) · R. S. Johnson, *Messiaen* (London, 1974, 2/1989) · R. Nichols, *Messiaen* (London, 1975, 2/1986) · H. Halbreich, *Olivier Messiaen* (Paris, 1980) · P. Griffiths, *Olivier Messiaen and the Music of Time* (London, 1985) · *Olivier Messiaen: Musique et couleur: Nouveaux entretiens avec Claude Samuel* (Paris, 1986; Eng. trans. 1994) · P. Hill (ed.), *The Messiaen Companion* (London, 1995) · N. Simeone, *Olivier Messiaen: A Bibliographical Catalogue of Messiaen's Works, First Editions and First Performances* (Tutzing, 1998)

metronome (Fr.: *métronome*; Ger.: *Taktmesser, Zeitmesser*; It.: *metronomo*). A machine for establishing and regulating the speed of a performance; specifically, the clockwork-driven machine developed by Johann Nepomuk Maelzel. Early attempts to apply the movement of the pendulum had culminated in the *chronomètre*, a calibrated pendulum for defining tempo devised by Loulié in 1696; simple pendulum metronomes, usually based on pocket tape measures, are still available.

Although many chronometers were invented during the 18th century, none was widely successful until Maelzel introduced his metronome in 1815. This clockwork-driven, double-ended pendulum in a wooden pyramidal box, with a sliding trapezoid weight positioned on notches in its upper stem, is the basis of the instrument as still made today. Maelzel had pirated some aspects of the metronome (especially the double-ended pendulum, which much reduced its length) from a Dutch inventor, Dietrich Nikolaus Winkel. Maelzel's friendship with Beethoven led to that composer being the first to include metronome rates (MM, 'Metronome Maelzel' = beats per minute) on his music. As well as ticking on each beat, metronomes often have a bell which can be set to ting every second, third, or fourth beat to mark the first beat in the bar.

The pyramidal wooden-bodied metronome was universal until about 1945, when a rather inaccurate pocket-watch version (it was liable to tick unevenly) became available in Switzerland; it was followed by various plastic-bodied models. Non-mechanical metronomes have also been popular; Pinfold's model, with a weighted rod swinging on a stand, frequently turns up at auction. Today the most popular metronomes are electronic and usually include a pitch standard as well.

There have long been debates about the accuracy of composers' metronome marks, many of which have seemed improbably slow or fast to later generations.

Unfortunately there is no way of telling whether composers' tastes differed from ours, whether a composer's metronome was not working properly, or even, where autograph manuscripts are not available, whether the publisher used the wrong note symbol. In the modern recording industry, especially for film music and in multi-tracking, players are often fed a regular beat, known as a click track, through earphones. This is one way of ensuring that the music will be played exactly in time.   JMo

📖 R. E. M. HARDING, 'The metronome and its precursors', *Origins of Musical Time and Expression* (London, 1938), 1–35, published separately (Henley on Thames, 1983)

mettere (It.), **mettre** (Fr.). 'To put'; *mettete il sordino* (It.), *mettre la sourdine* (Fr.), 'put on the mute'. In organ-playing *mettez* (Fr.) often means 'put (a stop) into action'.

Mexico. See LATIN AMERICA, 2.

Meyerbeer, Giacomo [Beer, Jakob Liebmann] (*b* Berlin, 5 Sept. 1791; *d* Paris, 2 May 1864). German composer. He played an important role in the development of French music. Born into a wealthy Jewish banking family, whose Berlin home formed a meeting-place for many of the German capital's intelligentsia, he later changed his name to Meyerbeer on receiving a substantial legacy from a relative called Meyer. He was taught privately, his father assiduously fostering his musical talents. He showed early promise as a pianist, studying first with Franz Lauska, then with Clementi. At the age of 11 he made his public debut, playing Mozart's D minor Concerto K466. He later studied theory and composition with Zelter and Abbé Vogler, staying in 1810 at the latter's house in Darmstadt, where Weber was a fellow pupil. A superb score-reader, he soon composed serious works, including the oratorio *Gott und die Natur* (1811) and the biblical opera *Jephtas Gelübde* ('Jephtha's Vow'), which was first performed in Munich, thanks to Vogler's contacts in the Bavarian capital, in 1812. His next stage work, *Wirth und Gast* ('Host and Guest'), a *Singspiel* on a Turkish theme, was unsuccessful at its premiere in Stuttgart in 1813 and was subsequently revised under the title *Die beiden Kalifen* ('The Two Califs'). Meyerbeer considered himself primarily a pianist and was admired as a virtuoso until he was encouraged by Salieri, whom he met in Vienna, to travel to Italy to study writing for the voice.

In Venice he was particularly struck with Rossini's music. The first major work from his Italian period was *Gli amori di Teolinda* (1816), a concert scena for soprano and orchestra with clarinet obbligato. *Romilda e Costanza* (1817), the first of a series of operas in the Rossinian manner, was written, unlike many of his later works, in a remarkably short space of time. *Emma di Resburgo* (1819) was his first major success, causing him to be regarded by many as Rossini's chief rival, though his reputation outside Italy was variable. In 1823 he returned briefly to Berlin, where his Italianate, cosmopolitan style was derided by critics who favoured the works of Weber at a time when German culture was developing a strong nationalism. In 1824, however, Meyerbeer produced the finest of his Italian operas, *Il crociato in Egitto* ('The Crusade in Egypt'), a great success at its premiere in Venice. An invitation to revise the work for Paris promptly followed. In 1825 he went to oversee the Paris premiere and decided to remain in the French capital, where he lived for much of the rest of his life.

Personal circumstances—the death of his father, his marriage, and the subsequent loss of two of his children—led to an eight-year compositional silence, broken in 1831 with *Robert le diable*, his first essay in French grand opera, the form with which his name is irrevocably linked. A gothic horror story to a text by the fashionable librettist Eugène Scribe, *Robert le diable* was strongly influenced by the operas of Spontini and by Rossini's *Guillaume Tell* and contributed to the consolidation of the five-act form with ballet which subsequently became the standard structure for works given their premiere at the Paris Opéra. Lavish scenic spectacle, chilling if melodramatic orchestral effects, and taxing vocal showpieces were the principal factors that contributed to its enormous success.

Although *Robert le diable* made Meyerbeer the best-known and most prosperous opera composer of his day, its success was eclipsed by the triumph of his next work, *Les Huguenots* (1836). A study of religious bigotry depicting the St Bartholomew's Day massacre, the opera throws the private passions of its characters into sharp relief by placing them against a background of historical determinism, generating a cumulative tension in its portrait of a world gradually descending from courtly elegance to the irrationality of mass violence. Occasional moments of melodic paucity—a charge frequently made against Meyerbeer's output as a whole—are offset by brilliant, if sombre, orchestration and a powerful theatricality which Meyerbeer would never again quite recapture. The vocal writing, particularly for the tenor and the two leading sopranos, is arduous. The work needs seven truly great singers if it is to succeed, and was subsequently nicknamed 'The Night of the Seven Stars'.

Meyerbeer was invited by the King of Prussia to be General Music Director in Berlin after the departure of Spontini in 1842. The appointment was controversial, and it led to an unhappy period in his life. He was an indifferent conductor, and the two major works he produced during the period—the masque *Das Hoffest in Ferrara* ('The Feast at the Ferrarese Court', 1843) and *Ein Feldlager in Schlesien* ('A Camp in Silesia', 1844), a *Singspiel* on an episode from the life of Frederick the Great—were disliked by the German public. Though he was not officially dismissed until 1848, he effectively returned to Paris in 1847. Verdi's growing reputation was now challenging Meyerbeer's international dominance, but he maintained his position with his next opera, *Le Prophète*, a further study of religious fanaticism, which received a triumphant premiere at the Opéra in 1849. As early as 1846 the Parisian public had been clamouring for a revised version of *Ein Feldlager in Schlesien*, and Meyerbeer scored another success with its drastic revision, *L'Étoile du nord*, in 1854.

Le Pardon de Ploërmel ('The Pilgrimage of Ploërmel'), better known as *Dinorah*, after its heroine, was first performed at the Opéra-Comique in 1859; it reveals a move away from epic towards pastoral subject matter. The comparative slowness of Meyerbeer's output was caused partly by his health, which began to fail in 1850, and partly by a remorseless perfectionism that made him constantly revise (he tried out various versions at orchestral rehearsals before reaching a decision on the final one) and insist on obtaining exactly the right singers for his works. The last of his grand operas to be performed—*L'Africaine*, a study of the Portuguese imperial conquest under Vasco da Gama, begun as early as 1837—was repeatedly shelved owing to Meyerbeer's anxieties about finding an adequate soprano for the central role and was completed only in 1860. Meyerbeer died during initial rehearsals for the work, which did not reach the stage until 1865, a year after his death.

Hugely popular with the public, Meyerbeer was the object of considerable critical opprobrium even in his lifetime, and in his later years he came to believe that younger composers had superseded him. Envy of his success and of the prosperity that his works brought him made him many enemies, and the critical attack intensified during the anti-Semitic climate of the last years of the 19th century. Wagner, whom Meyerbeer first met in 1839 and initially befriended, most notably turned against him in intense vituperation, subsequently rejecting *Rienzi* from the canon of his own works on the grounds that it was too 'Meyerbeerian'.

Meyerbeer's works held the stage until the early 20th century, when they fell from the repertory and his critical position reached its lowest ebb. A groundbreaking revival of *Les Huguenots* at La Scala, Milan, in 1962 led to a reappraisal of his music, though performances of his operas are still rare, partly because of the costliness of staging them, partly because of the vocal challenges he now presents to singers. His influence, however, was tremendous, most notably in his establishment of French grand opera as a dominant, if constricting, theatrical form, the apogee of which is now widely reckoned to be represented by Berlioz's *Les Troyens* and Verdi's *Don Carlos*. Many subsequent French opera composers take him as a point of departure, whether by a process of imitation, assimilation, or rejection.   DA/TA

    📖 J. F. FULCHER, *The Nation's Image: French Grand Opera as Politics and Politicized Art* (Cambridge, 1987) · H. and G. BECKER (eds.), *Giacomo Meyerbeer: A Life in Letters* (London, 1989) · R. ZIMMERMANN, *Giacomo Meyerbeer: Eine Biographie nach Dokumenten* (Berlin, 1991)

mezza voce (It., 'half-voice'; Fr.: *demi-voix*). A direction to sing at half the vocal power.

mezzo, mezza (It.). 'Half', 'medium', 'middle'; *mezza voce*, 'half voice', i.e. at half the vocal (or instrumental) power, restrained; *mezzoforte* (abbreviated *mf*), 'half loud', i.e. moderately loud; *mezzopiano* (abbreviated *mp*), 'half soft', i.e. moderately soft.

mezzo-soprano (It., 'half-soprano'). A female voice (or artificial male voice) with a range midway between those of the contralto and the soprano, roughly $a-a''$ (often b''). The distinction between a female soprano and a mezzo-soprano (colloquially 'mezzo') became pronounced only in the early 19th century, when the castrato voice (of approximately the same range as the female mezzo-soprano) rapidly became obsolete. A high mezzo-soprano is often similar to a dramatic or *spinto* soprano and many roles can be sung by either. Several operatic roles written for sopranos are traditionally sung by and better suited to mezzos, e.g. Dorabella in *Così fan tutte*, Carmen, and Oktavian in *Der Rosenkavalier*. Occasionally a singer will describe herself as a mezzo-contralto, meaning a little lower in range than a mezzo-soprano.   RW

mf. Abbreviation for *mezzoforte*; see MEZZO, MEZZA.

m.g. Abbreviation for *main gauche* (Fr.), 'left hand'.

mi [me]. The third degree of the scale in the *sol-mization system. In French and Italian it has become attached, on the fixed-*doh* principle, to the note E, in whichever scale it occurs. See TONIC SOL-FA.

Michael, Rogier (*b* Mons or Bergen op Zoom, *c*.1552; *d* Dresden, *c*.1619). German composer. For 26 years he was court Kapellmeister at Dresden, until ill health in 1613 forced him into partial retirement. He was then assisted briefly by Michael Praetorius (on secondment from Wolfenbüttel) and by Schütz, who later replaced him as Kapellmeister. A notable contributor to the music of Lutheran Saxony of his time, Michael provided the Dresden court with numerous Latin and German works, including a *Cantional in 1593, a German Mass in 1601, and several historia-style settings, most notably of the Christmas story in 1602. His son, **Tobias Michael** (*b* Dresden, 13 June 1592; *d* Leipzig, 26 June 1657), succeeded Johann Hermann Schein as Kantor of St Thomas's, Leipzig, in 1631, and in 1645 published an enlarged version of his predecessor's *Cantional, oder Gesangbuch*. He also issued (in 1634–7) two volumes of Italianate German motets and sacred concertos.   BS

Michelangeli, Arturo Benedetti (*b* Brescia, 5 Jan. 1920; *d* Lugano, 12 June 1995). Italian pianist. In 1939 he won the Geneva International Piano Competition and began a teaching and performing career, which, after 1945, brought him international fame. His playing was renowned for its idiosyncratic style, and while his reputation for cancellation remained notorious, his virtuosity became legendary: he was one of the most gifted players of his generation. His fairly limited repertory ranged from Scarlatti to Brahms, though his Debussy, Ravel, and Rakhmaninov were particularly fine. His students include Maurizio Pollini and Martha Argerich.   CF

mi contra fa (Lat.). Part of a short rhyme alerting singers to the awkward intervals, especially the tritone, that can occur when the two notes with the *solmization syllables *mi* and *fa* come together. The full rhyme is *mi contra fa / diabolus est in musica* ('*mi* against *fa* is the devil in music'). See MUSICA FICTA.

microtone. Any interval smaller than a semitone. Such intervals have long been used in Asian cultures, but their use in Western art music is a 20th-century phenomenon. Alois *Hába and Julian *Carrillo were among the prominent composers to introduce quarter-tones during the 1920s; at the same time Harry *Partch arrived at smaller intervals through his pursuit of just intonation. Microtonal music can pose problems in performance, since it sometimes requires the construction of special instruments. In the electroacoustic field, however, there are no limitations, and more and more composers with access to the refinements of computer technology are using microtonal inflections in their work.   PG/AW

Middle Ages, the (*see opposite page*)

middle C. The C nearest the middle of a piano or other musical keyboard. It is written on the first ledger line below any staff bearing the treble clef. Usually it is indicated by the letter *c'*, to distinguish it from the pitch C when it occurs in other octaves (*C*, *c*, *c''*, etc.). In the

modern equal-temperament tuning system it has a frequency of 260 Hz.   AP

MIDI [musical instrument digital interface]. An industry-wide protocol established in 1983 for passing control information between keyboards, synthesizers, and ancillary signal-processing devices. In commercial terms this agreement on a common means of communication was a remarkable achievement, given the competing interests of different manufacturers. In spite of the rapid pace of technical advances over the intervening years, the operational characteristics of MIDI have remained essentially unaltered, apart from a few additional features that have improved its versatility. The protocol is predicated on the notion that keyboard-based music can be represented as a series of individual 'note/events', where each 'event' is coded as an individual MIDI 'message'. In its most basic form a MIDI 'message' contains two components, the first being the pitch of the sounding note, and the second its amplitude, measured in terms of the velocity with which the key is struck. These messages are passed from one device to another via special connecting cables, for example from a master keyboard to a synthesizer. More elaborate configurations may involve a *computer or a *sequencer that can be used to record and reproduce complete musical performances in terms of the component 'note/event' messages and their associated timings.   PM

Midi, Le. See MATIN, LE; MIDI, LE; SOIR, LE.

Midsummer Marriage, The. Opera in three acts by Tippett to his own libretto (London, 1955).

Midsummer Night's Dream, A. Opera in three acts by Britten to a libretto by the composer and Peter Pears after Shakespeare's play (1594–5) (Aldeburgh, 1960).

Mighty Handful. See FIVE, THE.

Mignon. Opera in three acts by Thomas to a libretto by Jules Barbier and Michel Carré after Johann Wolfgang von Goethe's novel *Wilhelm Meisters Lehrjahre* (1795–6) (Paris, 1866).

Mihalovici, Marcel (*b* Bucharest, 22 Oct. 1898; *d* Paris, 12 Aug. 1985). Romanian-born French composer. He studied in Bucharest, and from 1919 to 1925 with d'Indy at the Schola Cantorum in Paris. In Paris he also took advice from his fellow-Romanian George Enescu, became part of a cosmopolitan group of younger composers which included Martinů, and married the pianist Monique Haas. Mihalovici's works include the operas *Phèdre* (after Jean Racine; broadcast 1950, staged Stuttgart, 1951), *Die Heimkehr* (Düsseldorf, 1954), *Krapp* (after Samuel Beckett; Bielefeld, 1961), and *Les Jumeaux*
(*cont. on p. 779*)

The Middle Ages

Terminology and definition

The extent of the period implied by the term 'Middle Ages' has been repeatedly discussed, and even its validity questioned. The concept can be traced back to the Italian humanist Petrarch (1304–74), who saw the classical revival of his own day as a new dawn and the period since the eclipse of classical antiquity as a dark age. Somewhat later the terms *media aetas* and *media tempestas* came to denote this intervening period, and by the 18th century the expressions 'middle age' or 'middle ages' had come to be applied in English writing on music, for example in Charles Burney's *History* (1776–89). Burney and his contemporary John Hawkins were among the first to give the music of the Middle Ages extensive coverage, and their terminology has become commonplace.

The period covered by the term 'medieval' has varied according to the point of view of the writer. A tendency to consider it as coterminous with the development of church music before the 16th-century Reformations (Catholic and Protestant) might suggest a starting-point as early as the 4th century and a termination as late as the mid-16th. This is perhaps to privilege one aspect of musical history unduly, and to ignore the wider cultural movements within which it existed—the gradual weakening of late antique culture in the 4th–7th centuries, for example, or the growing humanism of the 14th and 15th. But wide cultural movements do not provide precise dates, and an arbitrary thousand-year period from 500 to 1500 seems as useful as any. Many music historians would argue on various grounds for a shorter span, but the absence of substantial musical documents from before *c.*900 is not in itself a good reason for starting at that point; and the fact that ideals of humanism and 'Renaissance' are of only indirect relevance to musical style limits their usefulness as factors in defining an era.

Most writers, at any rate, are still content that there should be a medieval period of musical history, any

element of disparagement in the term having long been discarded. And there surely is an 'otherness' (to use Christopher Page's term) about European music before 1500—even if the degree of otherness varies according to the experience and receptiveness of the listener—that requires acknowledgment and explanation. That remains so despite the enormously greater availability nowadays of fine performances, live and recorded, and notwithstanding the steady backwards expansion of the 'canonic' repertory of popularly recognized master-pieces to Josquin des Prez, Dufay, and even Machaut.

The music of the Church

One very good reason for giving priority to the music of the Church is that it is so much better documented than what we now call secular music. That is at least partly because in the earlier Middle Ages literacy was largely a prerogative of the Church—including not only the clergy of all ranks but many unordained monks and nuns. They wrote down secular music as well as sacred, even from the outset of medieval notational practice, but it was always small in quantity compared with sacred, and moreover is largely indecipherable today. At a later stage, the vernacular and largely secular repertories of the troubadours, trouvères, and their successors came to be written down, not only by clerical but also by lay scribes.

In its earliest recorded form, plainchant, the monophonic music of the Western Church, varies from extreme simplicity to great complexity. It is natural to suppose that the simplest elements are the earliest, but we should be cautious about applying so apparently obvious a criterion. No doubt the music of the early Church, let us say for the first four centuries, was comparatively simple, but the urge to beautify the liturgy through its music can be substantiated from then on (for example by St Augustine in his *Confessions*), and the early growth of an elaborate melismatic style cannot be ruled out. One must necessarily be more wary of assuming that the earliest recorded forms of the melodies, from the late 9th century onwards, represent a tradition extending over several centuries. There is now widespread agreement that the main body of material cannot have existed in exactly that form for more than a century or so before 900.

There are in any case further difficulties associated with the earlier history of the chant. Although their repertory is commonly known as 'Gregorian' (after Pope St Gregory I, 590–604), the earliest musical manuscripts not only date from 300 or so years later but are from Francia, that is to say the kingdom of the Franks. The historical background to this is the introduction of the Roman liturgy into Francia under Pepin III during the 8th century. But whereas the liturgy itself, despite the need for changes of various kinds, was transplanted without undue difficulty, there can be less certainty that in an age of oral tradition the chant was adopted unscathed. Indeed there is a good deal of evidence that it was not, and one interpretation is that it is an amalgam of Roman and local ('Gallican') elements. In any event the repertory includes identifiably non-Roman compositions such as the *Improperia* for Good Friday.

From Rome itself the earliest manuscripts date from the late 11th and early 12th centuries. There are only a few of them, and they contain an appreciably different (though clearly related) repertory of chants. Their relationship with the 'Gregorian' repertory has been much debated, but there has been general agreement in associating them with the liturgy celebrated in the basilicas of Rome by their clergy and supporting monasteries. In other words, they do not represent the practice of the pope and his own clergy, even when celebrating the liturgy in those same basilicas according to the routine known as the 'stational' or 'processional' rite. This rite at some stage adopted the 'Gregorian', that is to say the Frankish, musical tradition, and eventually it was imposed on all the Roman churches. Indeed, some scholars still prefer to regard Frankish chant as an essentially unaltered papal repertory of the 8th century.

Elsewhere in Europe local rites were being suppressed in favour of the Roman. The main movement towards uniformity occurred in the 11th century under a succession of reforming popes, and since it was the Frankish form of chant that was imposed it must at least by then have been regarded as the appropriate standard by the papacy. In the reconquered parts of the Iberian peninsula the liturgy and chant repertories of the native Christians (the Mozarabes, Christians previously living under Arab rule) were replaced by the Roman; and although the music had been written down most of it cannot now be deciphered. In Italy the Old Beneventan rite virtually disappeared, though the Milanese survived all attempts at reform and received an effective *coup de grâce* (at least as regards its chant) only after the Second Vatican Council (1962–5).

We know of other Western chant repertories that disappeared too soon to leave any tangible traces (e.g. the Celtic, African, and Ravennatic, as well as, for the most part, the Gallican) because their music was not written down at all (nor, in many cases, were their texts). But the Iberian repertories are also virtually lost to us because their melodies were written in a manner that cannot be directly deciphered. This notation, common in some form or another to all early manuscripts, consisted of staffless 'neumes', signs that to a certain extent indicate the contour of the melodies but not the exact intervals. The earliest Frankish manuscripts are also indecipherable, but their melodies can be identified as being essentially those surviving in readable form in hundreds of later manuscripts of 'Gregorian' chant. The 'Old Roman' (or basilican) manuscripts are all written in an early kind of staff notation. A few Old Beneventan melodies survive because they were preserved in 'Gregorian' manuscripts, while the Milanese melodies reach us because the rite itself escaped suppression.

Although the pitches of these chants can be read, there are numerous melodies, even within the Frankish repertory of the 9th–11th centuries, that are lost, probably for ever. These are mostly local additions to the liturgy (tropes and sequences) which had too short a lifespan to achieve a decipherable recorded form. Tropes were intercalations into or simply preludes to an existing chant; sequences were continuations to the alleluia of the Mass, sometimes being a wordless melisma on the last syllable of the word 'alleluia', more often consisting of a poetic extension (many early sequences survive as both). The sequences were, however, more durable than the tropes, until virtually all of them were suppressed by the Council of Trent (1545–63).

The chant in all its forms was the servant of the liturgy. The public liturgy, though it originally had embraced the principal hours of prayer as well as the Eucharist, came in the Middle Ages to be restricted to the Mass and certain other services, while the Hours, or Divine Office, when sung in choir, became the prerogative of clerical and monastic communities. (In the Eastern Church, where a comparable body of chant developed, the cathedral church of Constantinople, Hagia Sophia, adopted a monastic form of liturgy in the 10th century and made it the basis of its public rite. The Eastern Orthodox Church became separated from the West in the 11th century, by which time a number of non-orthodox churches had also developed their own distinctive liturgies and chant practices, most of them recoverable only faintly, if at all, through oral tradition.)

New musical developments were at first associated with the monasteries. As well as being largely responsible for tropes and sequences, they experimented with polyphony, rationalizing its intervallic structure and applying it to the existing chant repertory. At first this involved simply adding a second part, the *vox organalis*, moving in the same rhythm as the chant. The earliest source of polyphony intended for practical use (in this case as an aide-mémoire for the cantor) is a manuscript from Winchester, now thought to date from the mid-11th century: it contains about 170 polyphonic parts to go with existing chants. Although the notation, like that of the chant itself, is indecipherable, it is possible to reconstruct most of the music on the basis of the known readings of the chant and the directional indications inherent in the neumes of the added part.

The earliest polyphony seems to have been assigned to the monastic choir or to solo singers according to the rubrics applicable to the plainchant itself. An Alleluia, for example, was intoned by soloists and continued by the choir, whereas its verse, except for the last word, was sung by the soloists. Later, however, it became the prerogative of soloists, and only the solo portions of such chants were set polyphonically. It also became more florid, for example by admitting several notes in the added part to one in the existing part, and in due course by increasing the number of independent parts to three or four. Non-liturgical sacred songs, of the kind designated by such terms as 'versus' and 'conductus', were given polyphonic settings, either wholly independent or based on existing melodies. Theorists and composers had to tackle the problem of rhythm, since it could no longer be governed by that of chant. In the 14th century it became possible to compose liturgical music independently, or to base it on some chant originally associated with another text. Eventually this procedure gave rise to the cyclic mass, in which the movements were bound together by a common chant.

Throughout these developments, however, there was always a sense that polyphony, however elaborate, grew out of the function of the chant as a declamation of the texts required by the liturgy (or in some cases tolerated within it). Moreover, the bulk of the liturgy was always performed in chant; polyphony was an 'extra', which after the early period of monastic enthusiasm depended on patronage. The constitutions of many secular (i.e. non-monastic) churches in the later Middle Ages, founded as they usually were by clerical or lay patrons, often included provision for polyphony, while individuals and corporations could and did endow masses to be sung (either wholly in chant or with polyphony) for their own benefit, including that of their departed souls. If a church wanted polyphony for which specific endowments were lacking, it had to pay for it; this was the case at Notre Dame in Paris in the 12th and 13th centuries. Indeed, the solo singers of elaborate chants on particular days might receive a stipend from the common fund as early as the 9th century, as is recorded for Metz under Archbishop Angilram. The edifice of patronage and endowment by which the medieval Church was largely sustained is an essential factor in the understanding of its music.

Secular music

Secular music was certainly no less vital throughout the period than sacred; indeed the numerous warnings against it in the canons issuing from early Church Councils suggest that it was much enjoyed by the clergy themselves. This clerical involvement in secular music had one outlet in the repertory of the scholar poets (*vagantes* and goliards) from the 10th century to the 13th. They wrote in Latin, and sometimes on serious subjects, but the praise of nature and of erotic love were equally prominent. Other such poetry evidently flourished within the cloister. For some of these poems, tunes were written down; but, as we have seen, the notation of these fleeting inspirations is tantalizingly unspecific, even as late as the 13th century in the case of the famous manuscript known as *Carmina burana*. There some of the melodies can be recovered because they were given polyphonic settings (with different texts) that can be read; many melodies, however, were doomed to swift extinction.

The songs of the *troubadours and *trouvères fared better. The troubadours traced the origin of their art to William, 7th Count of Poitou and 9th Duke of Aquitaine (1071–1126), though only a few of his poems and one melodic fragment remain. His songs and those of his successors were written in literary Occitan, the Latin-based language of southern France, whereas those of the trouvères were in some form of Old French. Despite the fact that their lyric poems were intended to be sung, there is a strong element of literary artifice, especially among the troubadours, and only a small proportion of troubadour poetry survives with music. In any case that music was written down long after the poetry was composed, mostly in northern French manuscripts, so there is no guarantee that these are the tunes to which the poems were originally sung. The northern French repertory is more closely associated, at least chronologically, with the surviving melodies; for the later trouvères there is every reason to trust their authenticity, even though their rhythmic interpretation is still a subject of controversy.

These poets and singers, like their counterparts in the churches, depended on patronage. A few were magnates of sufficient substance to engage their own singers, but a gentle name was no guarantee of substance, and even the topos of unfulfilled love for an unattainable woman must often have had a financial implication. Poets did not necessarily compose or sing their own songs, though some, like the 'trouvère' Colin Muset, were musicians by trade, wandering from court to court in search of employment. The southern French poets received a considerable setback during the Albigensian Crusade against the Cathars (1209), the continuation of which was inspired by northern French political ambition. Many troubadours fled to neighbouring Catalonia and northern Italy. Nevertheless, their art continued to flourish, even in southern France, and became a subject of theorizing and of formal competition in the 14th century.

The troubadours influenced not only their northern counterparts but also the *Minnesinger of Germany, who adopted the ethos of *fin' amor* ('refined love') and developed their own literary form of High German in which to express it. Their music was mostly written down rather later even than that of the troubadours and trouvères, and for many of the earlier poets there are no surviving melodies. In England, too, the art in its northern French form took root, and a few poems, in both French and English, survive with melodies.

Beside this relatively sophisticated song repertory there coexisted much of a lower standing, our knowledge of which depends largely on the reuse of popular forms and actual tunes in a more refined context. Serious composers also began to tackle polyphonic secular song, beginning with the straightforward settings of quasi-popular poems by Adam de la Halle (whose date of death is disputed but may have occurred about 1300) and culminating in the complex structures of Guillaume de Machaut (*c*.1300–1377). But a century before Adam the polyphonic conductus had sometimes used wholly secular texts, while the motet, usually based on fragments of liturgical plainchant in the tenor and having separate texts in its upper parts, was more often secular, or at least partly secular, than wholly sacred in content. Machaut himself wrote both sacred and secular motets, and his skill in polyphony was an important factor in the late medieval cultivation of musically elaborate secular song.

Much of the musical culture of the Middle Ages is destined to remain a closed book, being dependent to a large extent on improvisation. In the Church, improvisation was usually based on a pre-existent chant melody, and quite sophisticated methods were devised to enable groups of three or even more singers to participate. Organ music, too, was more often improvised than written down. The methods of secular musicians, whose traditions were largely non-literate, were doubtless more informal, though in the 15th century a repertory of courtly dances based on written cantus firmi developed: the bassadanza or basse danse and associated forms. Instrumental music flourished in great variety, in the courts, the towns, and the cities, and very little of it remains to be performed today.

The music of Catholic central Europe developed on lines similar to that of the west, while beyond stretched the Orthodox world, proselytized from Constantinople but using (to begin with) a common Slavonic dialect for the liturgy. The Islamic contribution to European culture must have been considerable, as a result of invasion and the Crusades, and that of European Jews scarcely less so at certain periods. It would be more satisfactory if one could take in the whole of the Mediterranean basin as the focus of a 'medieval' perspective, but the evanescence of many of its musical traditions presents a serious obstacle to objective inquiry. And if all that remains of the Middle Ages is its chronological boundaries there is no reason why any region with a recorded musical history, for example in

East Asia, should be excluded from consideration. There is less inclination than was once the case to take the European humanists' interpretation of cultural-historical development for granted, and the older, rather narrow approach can readily be challenged.

Even within the European dimension, one can easily overlook the interchangeability of ideas and of cultural contexts. An over-insistence on the distinction between the sacred and the secular would be damaging. Not only is the music and poetry itself often ambiguous in this respect, but social differences were far from firmly drawn. Clerical households, including monasteries, 'consumed' secular music, while the musicians of a secular nobleman's chapel might well contribute to his secular entertainment. Some of the finest songwriters of the 15th century (Dufay and Binchois, to name no others) were clerics and members of an ecclesiastical establishment. Even the same music could do double duty. This interchangeability also applies to topography. Music travelled, often widely, through the repertory of an itinerant musician or through the transport of manuscripts; and it could flourish on alien soil, often pressed into a function for which it was not originally intended. Indeed our knowledge of medieval music would be much impoverished if this were not the case. Such facts also help to legitimize the modern use of medieval music in alien contexts, and sometimes in performances that cannot bear much resemblance to those once envisaged. Medieval music is astonishingly durable, as its present-day popularity clearly shows.

JCa

H. M. Brown, *Music in the Renaissance* (Englewood Cliffs, NJ, 1976) · C. Page, *The Owl and the Nightingale: Musical Life and Ideas in France, 1100–1300* (London, 1989) · J. Yudkin, *Music in Medieval Europe* (Englewood Cliffs, NJ, 1989) · R. Crocker and D. Hiley (eds.), *The Early Middle Ages to 1300*, The New Oxford History of Music, ii (Oxford, 1990) · J. McKinnon (ed.), *Antiquity and the Middle Ages*, Man and Music/Music and Society (London, 1990) · D. Hiley, *Western Plainchant: A Handbook* (Oxford, 1993) · C. Page, *Discarding Images: Reflections on Music and Culture in Medieval France* (Oxford, 1993) · R. Strohm, *The Rise of European Music, 1380–1500* (Cambridge, 1993)

(Brunswick, 1963). He also composed ballets, orchestral works, sonatas and other pieces for many different instruments, and songs.   ABur

Mikado, The (*The Mikado, or The Town of Titipu*). Operetta in two acts by Sullivan to a libretto by W. S. Gilbert (London, 1885).

Mikrokosmos ('Little World'). A collection of 153 piano pieces by Bartók, published in six volumes of progressive difficulty (with supplementary exercises), composed in 1926 and between 1932 and 1939; some of them exist in arrangements, by Bartók and Tibor Serly.

Milán, Luis de (*b c*.1500; *fl* 1536–61). Spanish composer, vihuelist, and writer. All that is known of his life is that he was connected with the ducal court in Valencia. He was a virtuoso performer on the vihuela, for which he composed songs and solo music. Most of his known music is contained in the didactic *El maestro* (Valencia, 1536; dedicated to John III of Portugal), the earliest surviving published collection of vihuela music. He provided two versions of several villancicos, expecting the singer to embellish the first and giving vihuela ornamentation for the second. His fantasias are noteworthy not only for their technical brilliance but also for their early use of tempo indications and expressive rubato.   DA/OR

Milano, Francesco (Canova) da (*b* Monza, nr Milan, 18 Aug. 1497; *d* Milan, 15 April 1543). Italian composer and lutenist. He was in the service of three popes (Leo X, Clement VII, and Paul III) in Rome before moving to Piacenza in the late 1520s. For a time around 1530 he may have been the organist of Milan Cathedral. He returned to Rome in 1535, working for two cardinals, Ippolito de' Medici and Alessandro Farnese, and for Pope Paul III, with whom he visited Nice in 1538. Milano was the most celebrated lutenist of the 16th century and composed a great deal of attractive music for his instrument, mostly ricercars and fantasias, and made many arrangements of motets, madrigals, and chansons. His music was widely known, not only in Italy but also in France and England.   DA/TC

Milhaud, Darius (*b* Aix-en-Provence, 4 Sept. 1892; *d* Geneva, 22 June 1974). French composer. He entered the Paris Conservatoire in 1909 and studied with André Gedalge and Charles-Marie Widor; equally significant was his meeting at that time with the writer Paul Claudel (1868–1955). In 1913 he began to write music for Claudel's translation of the *Oresteia*, his setting of *Les Choéphores* (1915) being particularly remarkable for its use of speaking chorus with percussion, and for its introduction of polytonality, which was to remain a distinctive feature of Milhaud's style. He went as Claudel's secretary to Rio de Janeiro (1917–18) when the poet was appointed ambassador, and the two collaborated on a Brazilian ballet, *L'Homme et son désir* (1918).

Back in Paris, Milhaud fell in with a group of young composers, including Poulenc and Honegger, who in 1920 were christened Les *Six. The flippant, anti-conventional aesthetic of the group is reflected in several of his works from this period, notably the song cycle *Machines agricoles* (1919), which sets extracts from a catalogue of agricultural machinery, and the ballet *Le Boeuf sur le toit* (1919), in which he used Latin-American dance forms. Another exotic source was the jazz that he heard in a Harlem nightclub, and which he put to use in his ballet *La Création du monde* (1923). Milhaud did not, however, forget his own background as a Provençal and a Jew. His small-scale opera *Les Malheurs d'Orphée* (1925) translates the myth to the Camargue, and one of his most luminous and attractive orchestral scores is the *Suite provençale* (1936). As for the specifically Jewish works, they range from the song cycle *Poèmes juifs* (1916) to the opera-oratorio *David* (1952), commissioned for performance in Israel.

From the 1920s onwards Milhaud wrote with astonishing fluency, his tally of works eventually reaching well over 400. Among them are 12 full-scale symphonies, a large number of concertos and other orchestral pieces, a body of chamber music which includes 18 quartets (of which nos. 14 and 15 may be played simultaneously as an octet), choral works and songs of all kinds, film scores and incidental music, and several big operas. *Christophe Colomb* (Berlin, 1930; text by Claudel) is the most ambitious of his operatic works, complex in its many-layered staging and grandly conceived in its choral and orchestral textures.

Milhaud spent the years 1940–7 in the USA, teaching at Mills College, California. On his return to France he was appointed professor of composition at the Paris Conservatoire. Plagued by chronic ill health, he nevertheless continued to visit the USA and to compose as prolifically as ever. In his vast output, frequently characterized by a piquant Gallic lyricism, most enduring is the music in lighter vein, notably the jazz and Latin-American ballet scores and the suite *Scaramouche* for two pianos (1937). PG/AT

📖 C. PALMER, *Milhaud* (London, 1976) · D. MILHAUD, *My Happy Life* (London and New York, 1995)

military band and corps of drums. Wind and percussion ensembles, not necessarily belonging to the armed forces, though civilian ensembles usually prefer to be called *concert bands or wind orchestras. The instrumentation of the military band is similar to that of the symphony orchestra, minus the strings, but with the addition of cornets and saxophones, and a multiplicity of flutes and clarinets of various sizes.

Although wind instruments have accompanied armies from earliest times, formal European military bands began only in the 15th century with fifes and drums for the infantry, surviving today as the corps of drums, with bugles or bagpipes sometimes used as alternatives to fifes. The cavalry used trumpets and kettledrums instead. Other instruments were added: in the 18th century the *Harmonie or Harmoniemusik consisted of pairs of oboes, clarinets, horns, and bassoons, to which the 'Turkish' or *'janissary' music of bass drum, cymbals, and triangle was added. Serpents, bass horns, and keyed bugles were used until valved brass instruments arrived on the scene.

As well as providing music for ceremonies and on the march, military bands play on bandstands, in concert halls, and for all manner of social purposes. As a result the repertory has always included arrangements of the popular concert, operatic, and other theatre music of the day. JMo

📖 D. WHITWELL, *A Concise History of the Wind Band* (Northridge, CA, 1985) · F. L. BATTISTI, *The Twentieth Century American Wind Band/Ensemble* (Fort Lauderdale, FL, 1995)

'Military' Symphony. Nickname of Haydn's Symphony no. 100 in G major (1793–4), so called because of its use in the Andante of a triangle, cymbals, and bass drum in imitation of Turkish military music (see JANISSARY MUSIC) and a trumpet call. Haydn made a setting of this movement for military band.

Millöcker, Carl (Joseph) (*b* Vienna, 29 April 1842; *d* Baden, nr Vienna, 31 Dec. 1899). Austrian composer and conductor. He studied at the Vienna Conservatory (1855–8) and began his career as a flautist in the orchestra of the Josefstadt theatre. In 1864, on Suppé's recommendation, he became conductor in Graz, where his first operettas were staged. Conductorships in Vienna and Budapest followed, before he established himself at the Theater an der Wien. There he composed a great many incidental songs and dances, as well as operettas in the style of Suppé and Strauss including *Das verwunschene Schloss* (1878) and *Gräfin Dubarry* (1879). The resounding success of *Der Bettelstudent* (1882) enabled him to resign his position at the Theater an der Wien and concentrate on writing further operettas, of which *Gasparone* (1884) and *Der arme Jonathan* (1890) made the greatest impact. *Der Bettelstudent*, a work of considerable technical refinement and dramatic power, remains today a classic of the

Viennese operetta repertory. Otherwise Millöcker's music is generally heard in 20th-century arrangements, including a 1931 revision of *Gasparone* and the 1931 pastiche *Die Dubarry*, which shares only its subject and some themes with Millöcker's 1879 score.   ALa

Milner, Anthony (Francis Dominic) (*b* Bristol, 13 May 1925). English composer. He studied at the RCM and with Mátyás Seiber and later taught at Morley College and London University. His style, like Tippett's, tends towards ecstatic lyricism, and is especially effective in large-scale choral compositions, including *Roman Spring* (1969) and the Symphony no. 2 (1978). Many of his compositions are inspired by his commitment to Roman Catholicism, and he was made a knight of St Gregory in 1985 for his contribution to Catholic liturgical music.   PG/AW

Milton, John (*b* Stanton St John, nr Oxford, *c*.1563; *d* London, March 1647). English amateur composer, father of the poet John Milton. He was educated at Oxford and later became a member of the Scriveners' Company. He wrote anthems and consort music and contributed to Morley's *Triumphes of Oriana* and William Leighton's *Teares or Lamentacions of a Sorrowfull Soule*.   JM

mime. A play in dumb show (i.e. using only gestures, not words), or an actor of such. Mime is an important constituent of ballet and formed the basis of the 18th-century dramatic ballet, or *ballet d'action*, in which the dancers were expected to express emotions through gestures and facial expressions, as opposed to the stylized ritual of earlier court ballets, in which the dancers were often masked. Mime also played an important part in 18th-century Parisian fair theatres, when the monopoly of the Paris Opéra forbade singing in the fair entertainments. The connotation of farce, especially in pantomime, is, however, often present. A 'mimodrama' is a play (musical or otherwise) that is carried on in dumb show. The term has been used by composers: Roger-Ducasse described his *Orpheus* (1913) as a 'mimodrame lyrique'.

minaccioso (It.). 'Menacing'; *minacciosamente*, 'menacingly'.

miniature score [pocket score]. A printed *score of pocket size for individual use or study. Such scores were marketed from the late 19th century onwards to meet the demand created by the rise in popularity of public concerts and, later, recordings. In 1886 the Leipzig publisher Albert Payne began a series of *Kleine Kammermusik Partituraugaben* which he later sold to Ernst Eulenburg. The *Eulenburg firm has dominated the market ever since, producing over 1000 works in the

format. Many are photographic reductions of full scores; more recently, some have included information, such as analytical notes, not previously published or contained in the conductor's score.   LC

minim (♩). The note having half the value of the semibreve, or whole note; hence the American usage 'half-note'.

minimalism. A term, borrowed from the visual art movement of the same name, applied to a style of composition that originated in the USA in the 1960s. It came about as a reaction to the prevailing modernist climate of the 1950s, with its dominant trends of indeterminacy (as represented by Cage) and total serialism (Stockhausen and Boulez).

The pioneers of the movement were La Monte Young and Terry Riley, quickly followed by Reich and Glass. Their aesthetic, later outlined in Reich's classic essay *Music as a Gradual Process* (1968), found expression in pared-down means of composition, with no sense of time-oriented direction. Stasis and repetition replaced the melodic line, tension and release, and climax of conventionally tonal music. Loops, phasing, stasis, and tonality were all prominent features, used differently (though to similar effect) by each composer.

Young's Trio for Strings (1958), with its long-drawn-out chords and static harmony, is generally considered the first minimalist work. Riley's ensemble piece *In C* (1964), for an unspecified number of instruments, is a collection of tonal fragments which each performer can repeat in any octave any number of times, emphasizing the collective nature of the group. Glass's early works (e.g. *Music in Fifths*, 1969) use an additive–subtractive process causing the repeated melodic sequence to change gradually over time.

Riley and Reich both worked with tape loops, but to different ends: Riley in *Music for the Gift* (1963) used two tape recorders to record and replay simultaneously, the music becoming progressively denser, whereas Reich used tape recorders of minutely differing playback speeds to play the same speech samples, which gradually moved in and out of phase with each other (e.g. in *It's Gonna Rain*, 1965); he also explored phasing as a compositional tool in such tonal works as *Piano Phase* (1967) and *Drumming* (1970). The influence of Reich and Glass was felt over a wide range of music, notably rock and popular dance music. While continuing in their later works to rely on repetition, they introduced more melodic writing and richer tonal contrasts.

Minimalism owes much to both popular and non-Western music and has given rise to many related styles; its rhythmic procedures in particular have been absorbed by composers including Bryars, Nyman, and

Martland. The music of John Adams, which embodies many minimalist techniques, is more aptly described as 'post-minimalist' as it emphasizes harmonic motion. In the 1990s a number of European composers, notably Gorecki, Pärt, and Tavener, exploited its qualities of timelessness to create what became dubbed 'spiritual minimalism'.   LD

📖 G. BATTCOCK (ed.), *Minimal Art: A Critical Anthology* (New York, 1968; London, 1969) · M. NYMAN, *Experimental Music: Cage and Beyond* (London and New York, 1974, 2/1999) · W. MERTENS, *American Minimal Music* (London, 1983) · K. R. SCHWARZ, *Minimalists* (London, 1996) · K. POTTER, *Four Musical Minimalists: La Monte Young, Terry Riley, Steve Reich, Philip Glass* (Cambridge, 2000)

Minkus, Léon [Aloysius Ludwig] (*b* Vienna, 23 March 1826; *d* Vienna, 7 Dec. 1917). Austrian composer and violinist. He went to St Petersburg as violinist in 1854, and became leader (1861) and then conductor at the Bol'shoy Theatre, Moscow. His ballet score *La fiammetta* (1864) for the St Petersburg Bol'shoy was also performed at the Paris Opéra and gained him a commission for *La Source* (1866), composed jointly with Delibes. For the Bol'shoy and Mariinsky theatres in St Petersburg he composed further scores for the choreographer Petipa, including *Don Quixote* (1869), *La Bayadère* (1877), and *Paquita* (1881). He retired to Vienna in 1891.   ALa

Minnesinger (Ger., pl. Minnesinger). German poet-musicians, often of aristocratic birth, of the 12th, 13th, and 14th centuries. Like the *trouveres of northern France, the Minnesinger modelled their culture on that of the *troubadours; their poetry reflects a social order of great refinement and education, dominated by a reverence for women, and generally expressed in the language of courtly love. Although most of their verse was set to music, sung by the Minnesinger themselves and often accompanied by professional minstrels, few melodies have survived from the first two centuries of the movement's existence. Principal composers include Walther von der Vogelweide, Neidhart von Reuental (*d* c.1250), and Der Tannhäuser, whose works date from the 13th century; Oswald von Wolkenstein, one of the last of the Minnesinger, wrote a number of polyphonic songs as well as conventional monodies. See also MEISTERSINGER; MINSTREL.   JM

minor canon. In an English cathedral, a clergyman whose duties include intoning the priest's part in the choral services (see also VICAR CHORAL).

minor interval. See INTERVAL.

minor scale. See SCALE, 3.

minstrel. A professional secular musician or poet-musician, usually non-literate, and either attached to a noble household or nomadic. The late medieval word *jongleur* (and its various cognates in different Romance languages) has a similar meaning, but its terms of reference sometimes broaden to denote a professional entertainer of any sort (storyteller, juggler, buffoon, acrobat, instrumentalist). Although minstrelsy is often associated with performance before a sophisticated audience, and therefore implies a class division between the entertainer and the listener, it also spills over into the world of the street musician. Broadly defined, then, a minstrel is an artisan performer, male or female, who makes music for financial reward, and plays or sings from memory. The golden era of the minstrel is the later Middle Ages (roughly from the 12th century to the 15th). Some categories of minstrel continue to thrive after that time—for instance, the *waits and other forms of civic musician—but in general the profession declined with the rise of performers who could read and play from music notation.

The word 'minstrel' has been applied to many different kinds of medieval musician. Reciters of epic poetry in the bardic tradition can loosely be described as minstrels, as can the instrumentalists who worked alongside the *troubadours, *trouvères, and *Minnesinger. Organized groups of minstrels commonly accompanied dancing, or added festive background noise to meals, banquets, and ceremonies. Players of the quieter plucked instruments are linked especially with the indoor performance of song, while loud instruments such as shawms, sackbuts, and members of the trumpet family belong more to festivity and the outdoors.

Since minstrels largely made music from memory, it stands to reason that virtually nothing of their repertory survives in notated form. Similarly, biographical information about individual minstrels is in very short supply. Most of them must have learnt their craft by chance, or from peers or family members. During the 14th and early 15th centuries some attended minstrel 'schools' in the Low Countries and northern France, where they exchanged music, acquired new instruments, and received instruction. In general, however, the minstrels of the Middle Ages are shadowy figures, known principally from records of payments to them by patrons or employers, and their sound world is largely lost to us today.   JM

📖 F. ANDERSON, T. PETTITT, and R. SCHRÖDER (eds.), *The Entertainer in Medieval and Traditional Culture* (Odense, 1997)

minuet (Fr.: *menuet*; Ger.: *Menuett*; It.: *minuetto*). A stately dance in triple metre (usually 3/4) that flourished between the mid-16th century and the end of the 18th, and an instrumental form commonly used in such multi-movement works as the Baroque *suite and the Classical symphony, sonata, and string quartet. Typically in binary form, it is characterized by a regular phrase structure (usually of four bars), simple harmonies, and an uncomplicated melodic line.

The minuet first appeared at the French court in the 1660s, from which time it became immensely popular as a social dance. Lully was the first composer to make extensive use of the minuet in stage works, both ballet and opera, composing over 90 examples. It was also frequently included in the suite as an optional movement and was, like the *bourrée and *gavotte, usually placed after the *sarabande. Many instrumental minuets are followed by a *double* (a varied repeat with ornaments); this led eventually to the traditional arrangement of minuet–second minuet in contrasting style (*trio)–first minuet repeated. French composers who wrote minuets include Chambonnières, the Couperins, and Rameau.

In Italy a slightly faster version of the minuet was preferred. It was usually written in 3/8 or 6/8 time, as is found, for example, in the works of Corelli and A. Scarlatti; this Italian style was also used by Rameau and Handel (e.g. the latter's keyboard suite in G). The minuet was also quickly taken up in England, where it became especially popular as a ballroom dance and a regular component of the suite. Purcell included many examples in his works for stage. In Germany, Pachelbel, Fischer, and Muffat wrote French-style minuets for their keyboard suites. Bach used both Italian and French types in his keyboard partitas and suites, in all but one of his orchestral suites, and in his music for solo violin and cello.

In the Classical period, the minuet was adopted as a movement in the evolving forms of symphony, solo sonata, and string quartet. At first it acted as a finale (e.g. in the symphonies of Abel, J. C. Bach, Johann Stamitz, and Arne; in the piano sonatas and trios of Haydn; and in some Mozart concertos), but eventually the standard tripartite minuet and trio was adopted as the third movement of the four-movement plan of symphonies and quartets, generally designed to provide light relief between the slow movement and the finale. Some later examples introduced more complex techniques, such as canon (Mozart's Symphony no. 40, in G minor), and some treat the reprise of the minuet after the trio with elaborate embellishments.

From Beethoven onwards the traditional place of the minuet in symphonies and chamber music began to be taken over by the *scherzo. Beethoven still occasionally used the minuet (e.g. in the First and Eighth Symphonies), but in general the dance had little importance

after 1800. It enjoyed a revival in the late 19th century, when French composers began to look to the past for inspiration (e.g. in Debussy's early *Suite bergamasque* for piano and in his *Petite suite* for piano duet; in Fauré's *Masques et bergamasques*; in Ravel's *Sonatine* and *Menuet antique*; Satie's *Premier menuet*; and in Schoenberg's Serenade op. 24 and Piano Suite op. 25). Vaughan Williams included a minuet in *Job*, his 'masque for dancing'.   WT/JBe

    📖 J. Sutton, 'The minuet: An elegant phoenix', *Dance Chronicle*, 8 (1985), 119–52 · K. H. Taubert, *Das Menuett: Geschichte und Choreographie* (Zürich, 1988)

'Minute' Waltz. Nickname of Chopin's Waltz in D♭ for piano op. 64 no. 1 (1846–7), so called because it can be played in a minute—but only if it is taken much too fast.

miracle plays. See MEDIEVAL DRAMA.

'Miracle' Symphony. Nickname of Haydn's Symphony no. 96 in D major (1791), so called because it was said (incorrectly) that at its first performance in London in 1791 the audience rushed forward at the end to congratulate the composer, thereby miraculously escaping being injured by a chandelier that fell on their seats. The incident in fact occurred during Haydn's second visit to London, in 1795, after a performance of his Symphony no. 102.

Miraculous Mandarin, The (*A csodálatos mandarin*). Pantomime in one act by Bartók to a scenario by Menyhért Lengyel (Cologne, 1926); because of censorship it was not performed in Budapest until 1946. Bartók arranged an orchestral suite from the score (1919 and 1927).

Mireille. Opera in five acts by Gounod to a libretto by Michel Carré after Frédéric Mistral's epic poem *Mirèio* (Paris, 1864).

mirliton. A generic term of French origin for voice-changing 'singing membranes' (e.g. comb and paper, *kazoo). Many instruments incorporate mirlitons to impart a buzzing quality to the sound, for example the Chinese *di*, a flute with a membrane-covered hole between the embouchure and the fingerholes; and many African harps, xylophones, and *lamellophones have mirlitons fitted over holes in the resonators.   RPa

Miroirs ('Mirrors'). Five piano pieces (1904–5) by Ravel: *Nocturelles* ('Moths'), *Oiseaux tristes* ('Sad Birds'), *Une barque sur l'océan* ('A Boat on the Ocean'), *Alborada del gracioso* ('The Fool's Dawn Song'), and *La Vallée des cloches* ('The Valley of Bells'); Ravel orchestrated the third (1906, revised 1926) and fourth (1918).

mirror canon. See CANON.

Miserere (Lat., 'Have mercy'). The incipit of a number of Latin liturgical texts, it most commonly refers to Psalm 50 (Vulgate), which begins 'Miserere mei, Deus' ('Have mercy on me, O God'). One of the seven *Penitential Psalms, Psalm 50 was appointed by the medieval Roman rite to be sung in its entirety at Lauds on ferial days. The famous *falsobordone* setting by Allegri is one of many written by Renaissance and Baroque composers for the service of Tenebrae.

ALi

Missa (Lat.). 'Mass'. The *Missa solemnis* or 'solemn Mass' is the most elaborate type, appropriate to high ceremonial occasions and most often set by composers (for its structure and history, see MASS). The *Missa cantata* ('sung Mass') is practically the same as the *Missa solemnis* in that it is 'sung' or chanted, but it is given with less ceremonial. The *missa brevis* is distinguished from these by its less imposing musical setting rather than by any liturgical difference. The *Missa lecta* ('read Mass') or *Missa privata* ('private Mass') is the Low Mass, performed by a priest and usually celebrated without music except for the hymns sung by the congregation, although at the French royal court in the 16th and 17th centuries it was customary to insert a motet.

—/JJD

missa brevis (Lat., 'short mass'). A short musical setting of the Ordinary of the Mass. This term applies variously to settings with textual omissions (e.g. Lutheran masses consisting only of the Kyrie and Gloria), of relatively brief duration (Palestrina and Mozart), or both, as in 15th-century masses for the Ambrosian rite and the setting by Britten.

ALi

Missa in tempore belli ('Mass in Time of War'). See PAUKENMESSE.

missal (Lat.: *missale*). Book containing the chants, prayers, and lessons for Mass; see PLAINCHANT, 4.

Missa Papae Marcelli. Mass for six voices by Palestrina, composed *c.*1561. It is dedicated to Pope Marcellus II, who established the Council of Trent which sought to reform the composition of polyphonic sacred music so that the words were intelligible. Romantic legend has it that, because of the clarity with which Palestrina treated the text, with this mass he 'saved church music'.

Missa pro defunctis (Lat.). 'Mass for the dead', i.e. *Requiem Mass.

Missa solemnis ('Solemn Mass'). The name by which Beethoven's Mass in D op. 123 is known; it was intended for the installation of Archduke Rudolph as Archbishop of Olmütz in 1820 but not completed in its final version until 1823.

misura (It.). 'Measure', 'bar'; *alla misura*, 'in strict time'; *senza misura*, 'without strict time', i.e. in free tempo; *misurato*, 'measured', i.e. in strict time.

Mitridate, re di Ponto ('Mithridates, King of Pontus'). Opera in three acts by Mozart to a libretto by Vittorio Amedeo Cigna-Santi after Giuseppe Parini's translation of Jean Racine's *Mithridate* (1673) (Milan, 1770).

Mitropoulos, Dimitri (*b* Athens, 3 Jan. 1896; *d* Milan, 11 Feb. 1960). Greek conductor. He studied the piano and composition in Athens, Brussels, and Berlin (with Busoni), and became a répétiteur at the Berlin Opera. He conducted in Greece from 1927 and after 1930 gained fame for his colourful interpretations and exceptional memory. He was the music director of the Minneapolis Symphony Orchestra from 1937 to 1949 and of the New York Philharmonic Orchestra from 1950 to 1957. His performances were theatrical and imaginative and were highly praised for their detail. Mitropoulos advocated much new music and gave the premieres of works by Villa-Lobos, Krenek, and Barber. He was also an admired pianist and a composer.

JT

  📖 W. R. TROTTER, *Priest of Music: The Life of Dimitri Mitropoulos* (Portland, OR, 1995)

Mitte (Ger.). 'Middle'; *auf der Mitte des Bogens*, 'in the middle of the bow'.

Mittwoch aus Licht ('Wednesday from Light'). Opera in a greeting, four scenes, and a farewell by Stockhausen to his own libretto, the 'sixth day' of *Licht.

mixed cadence. See CADENCE.

mixed media, multimedia. Terms invented in the 1960s to cover performances of the time combining live music with other means of expression: recorded or electronic music, dance, speech, lighting, video or film display, etc. The principal pioneer and exponent in this field was Cage, in his collaborations with Merce Cunningham and in his 'musicircuses', at which diverse performances would go on simultaneously. Electronic technology was essential to mixed-media performances—not only in practice but also in their aesthetic, their response to an urban or television world where many things play for attention.

PG

mixed voices. A term used in choral music to denote a combination of male and female voices, such as the standard choral combination of sopranos, altos, tenors, and basses (SATB).

Mixolydian mode. The mode represented by the white notes of the piano beginning on G. See MODE, 2.

Mlada. Opera in four acts by Rimsky-Korsakov to his own libretto based on Viktor Krïlov's libretto *Mlada* (1872) (St Peterburg, 1892). The libretto (1872) was commissioned for an opera-ballet in four acts by Cui (Act I), Musorgsky and Rimsky-Korsakov (Acts II and III), and Borodin (Act IV) but it was never performed and much of the score was recycled into other works.

Mladi ('Youth'). Suite (1924) by Janáček for flute/piccolo, oboe, clarinet, horn, bassoon, and bass clarinet.

MM. Abbreviation of *Metronome Maelzel.

mobile form. A form used in aleatory music whereby the order of events is flexible. Players may be asked to choose the order on the spur of the moment, or be given instructions from which to create different permutations. Notable exponents of the form are Cage, Stockhausen, Boulez (*Pli selon pli*, 1957–62), and Pousseur (*Votre Faust*, 1969, in which the audience takes part in the decision-making).   AL

mock trumpet. See CHALUMEAU, 1.

Mocquereau, Dom **André** (*b* La Tessoualle, Maine-et-Loire, 6 June 1848; *d* Solesmes, 18 Jan. 1930). French scholar. Believing that an understanding of medieval chant could be achieved only by a comparative study of its early sources, he initiated *Paléographie musicale*, a series of facsimiles of medieval chant manuscripts. He became a monk of *Solesmes in 1877, and later prior (1902–8). At first he assisted Joseph Pothier in preparing chant books, and took over from him as choirmaster in 1889. Pothier's preference was for late medieval chant of the 14th century, whereas Mocquereau's interest was in the reconstruction of the 'original'. Many of his ideas were superseded by those of Eugène Cardine.   PW

modality. See MODE.

modal jazz. A style based on the characteristics of modal scales rather than those of major or minor keys; it is especially characterized by a slow harmonic rhythm compared to the more rapid chord changes of other styles. One of the first experiments in modal jazz came in Miles Davis's *Milestones* (1958), and John Coltrane was another leading player.   PGA

mode 1. Introduction; 2. European music; 3. Traditional and non-European music; 4. Mode and ethos

1. Introduction

In early medieval theory the word *modus* was occasionally used to mean 'interval'—for example by Hucbald of Saint-Amand (*c*.840–930) and Guido of Arezzo (*c*.991–after 1033). This meaning survived in Ornithoparcus's *Musicae activae micrologus* (Leipzig, 1517) and was retained in John Dowland's translation of that work, *Of Moodes, or Intervals* (London, 1609). It is last found in the writings of J. H. Buttstedt (1666–1727).

There are two other meanings better known today: that of the rhythmic modes, found in the theory of rhythm of medieval mensural music (see NOTATION, 2); and that of 'scale' or 'melody type' (see below, 2). The latter covers a wide range of definition, from simple scales—arrangements of tones and semitones sometimes without any implication of a 'tonic' or main note—to a particular and typical melodic style or collection of motifs, perhaps with a definite 'tonic' and other notes in a hierarchy of importance—a meaning often found in discussions of non-European music, where melody types are widely used in non-written musical traditions (see below, 3).

2. European music

(a) The early Middle Ages: One of the most important tasks of late 8th- and early 9th-century Frankish musicians was to construct a theoretical framework to accommodate the newly created repertory of Gregorian chant (see PLAINCHANT, 2).This was not purely an intellectual enterprise, but also a practical necessity for the correct performance of chant, since it was important to ensure agreement on mode during the memorizing of the huge chant repertory. A large part of the singers' duties consisted of the singing of psalm verses according to set formulas or 'tones' (see TONUS, 3). Each intonation was introduced and followed by an antiphon, and it was vital to use the tone that accorded best with the tonality of the antiphon. Thus there was effected a standardization of the chant repertory into eight modes, and correspondingly eight psalm tones. The psalm tones themselves do not all cadence on the finals of their corresponding modes. Because the psalm tones are always succeeded by a repeat of an antiphon, and a smooth transition must be made from the end of the psalm verse back to the beginning of the antiphon, each psalm tone is provided with several different cadences, or *differentiae*.

The names of the modes were as set out in Table 1. The Greek names, like some other aspects of early Carolingian theory and practice, were borrowed from Byzantine chant—indeed, the system of eight modes itself is clearly based on the Byzantine *oktoechos*, a system of eight (*okto*) melody types (*echoi*). The use of eight psalm tones, one for each mode, was not known in Old Roman chant, but was a Frankish innovation. There are several indications that the modal system was

TABLE I

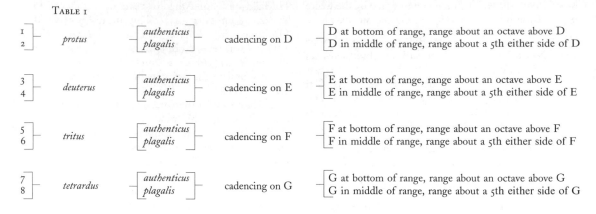

imposed on an existing body of chant—mainly the fact that a significant (though small) number of chants are not easily classified among the eight modes, usually because of a chromatic peculiarity of some sort, or because a chant cadencing in one mode will have inflections characteristic of chants in another. Theorists—and tonaries—frequently disagree in their assignment of these chants to particular modes.

Although originating as a theoretical abstraction of a sort, the modal system as discussed so far fulfilled an important practical need. But 9th-century writers went beyond this, and sought to effect a rapprochement between the eight-mode system of plainchant and what was known of classical Greek theory, in particular its expression in Boethius's *De institutione musica* (early 6th century). This treatise is concerned chiefly with speculative theory, not plainchant. Boethius is most interesting for his provision of: (*a*) descriptions of the seven octave scales possible within the framework of a diatonic double octave (i.e. the equivalent of octave scales on the white notes of the piano starting on A, B, C, D, E, F, and G); (*b*) the names Hypodorian (A), Hypophrygian (G), Hypolydian (F), Dorian (E), Phrygian (D), Lydian (C), and Mixolydian (B) for his seven octave scales; (*c*) the division of the diatonic double octave into four *tetrachords (scales covering a perfect 4th) with the interval pattern semitone–tone–tone (i.e. two tetrachords for each octave, covering B–C–D–E and E–F–G–A); and (*d*) the use of the terms 'mode', 'tone', and 'trope', synonymously, to describe the seven scales.

Two 9th-century treatises, *De harmonica institutione* by Hucbald and the anonymous *Alia musica*, show a synthesis of these diverse elements. It is particularly interesting to see Hucbald using familiar passages of chant to exemplify points of Greek theory. He describes the tetrachord and the double octave in the Greek (Boethian) manner, but then restructures the analysis

by using a different interval pattern for his four tetrachords: tone–semitone–tone (i.e. two tetrachords for each octave, covering A–B–C–D and D–E–F–G). He singles out the tetrachord starting on D as consisting of the notes 'used in constructing the four modes or tropes. These are nowadays called "tones" and are the *protus*, *deuterus*, *tritus*, and *tetrardus* ... These notes are called "finals" since everything that is sung ends among them'. Note that for Hucbald there are only four modes or tones, and that he uses the Byzantine-derived names rather than the classical Greek ones. The author of *Alia musica*, on the other hand, took the Greek names and reassigned them among the existing eight church modes. This was the foundation of the medieval and Renaissance modal system; it is set out in Ex. 1.

From the early 11th century theorists rarely looked at anything other than the final note in order to determine the mode. This rational attitude is reflected in a widely known treatise, the *Dialogus de musica* (written in northern Italy *c*.1000): 'a tone or a mode is a rule which distinguishes every chant in its final'. The *Dialogus* also cites ranges most often used in chants in each mode: Dorian, *c–e′*; Hypodorian, *a–bb′*; Phrygian, *d–e′*; Hypophrygian, *c–e′*; Lydian, *f–f′*; Hypolydian, *c–d′*; Mixolydian, *f–g′*; Hypomixolydian, *c–e′*.

(b) The late Middle Ages and the Renaissance: Theoretical writing in the late Middle Ages was concerned more with polyphony than with monophony, and so it is not surprising to find that theorists of this period often composed their monophonic examples instead of searching through the chant repertory. On the other hand, new liturgical chants of the time are also composed in a new way, with melodies commonly made from phrases that fit neatly between the poles of tonic, dominant, and upper octave.

Another point developed by Renaissance writers was that, since the use of Guido's F hexachord had led to Bb being considered legitimate (see SOLMIZATION), the whole *protus* or Dorian (D) mode could be transposed down a 5th on to G. Many pieces of secular and sacred Renaissance polyphony are notated with a B♭ key signature for all voices. The use of a key signature of one flat (and occasionally of two flats) led to a re-classification of the modes. Tinctoris's *Liber de natura et proprietate tonorum* (1476) set out the modes as shown in Table 2. Only in the late 15th century did theorists come to grips with the problems of defining the mode of polyphonic compositions. Tinctoris stated that the mode of the tenor voice determined that of the composition as a whole, but the top part seems to have been regarded as equally, or more, decisive.

It was dissatisfaction with the inability of the traditional eight-mode system to contain polyphonic procedures that prompted Heinrich Glarean, in *Dodecachordon* (Basle, 1547), to create a more comprehensive system with 12 modes. To the previous eight (see Ex. 1) he added the Aeolian (*a–a'*) and the Hypoaeolian (*e–e'*), both with finals on *a*, and the Ionian (*c–c'*) and Hypoionian (*g–g'*), both with finals on *c*. He stated that the Ionian was the mode most commonly used in his time. Glarean drew on extensive studies of Boethius and of classical Greek authors (such as Aristoxenus, rediscovered and translated only in the late 20th century; see ANCIENT GREEK MUSIC, 1) to find names for his new modes. For Ionian he also used the name Iastian; Hypomixolydian he also called Hyperiastian. Among modes mentioned by Glarean as conceivable, but not possible in practice, was the Hyperaeolian mode (*b–b'*, with final on *b*). In modern writing this is sometimes called the Locrian mode, but the name was not used in this sense by any Greek, medieval, or Renaissance writer, although it is of classical Greek origin.

Glarean's system won a good deal of support, especially when the eminent theorist Gioseffo Zarlino

Ex. 1

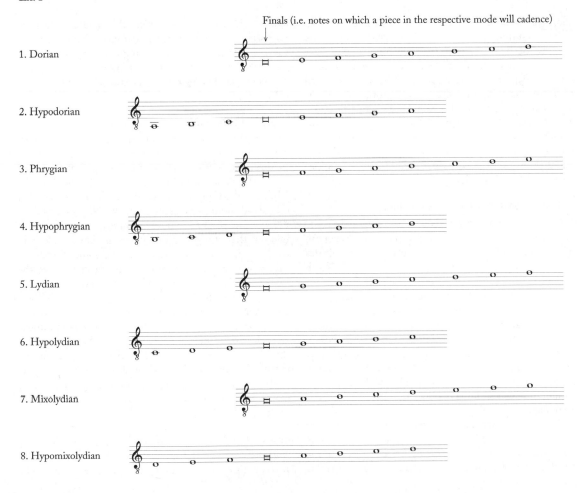

Finals (i.e. notes on which a piece in the respective mode will cadence)

1. Dorian

2. Hypodorian

3. Phrygian

4. Hypophrygian

5. Lydian

6. Hypolydian

7. Mixolydian

8. Hypomixolydian

TABLE 2

				range	*final*
♭ signature (*cantus mollis*)	*protus*	mode 1 (Dorian)		g–g′	g
		mode 2 (Hypodorian)		d–d′	g
	deuterus	mode 3 (Phrygian)		a–a′	a
		mode 4 (Hypophrygian)		e–e′	a
	tritus	mode 5 (Lydian)		f–f′	f
		mode 6 (Hypolydian)		c–c′	f

(Note that the pitches of the F mode were retained, not transposed like the other modes—creating, in effect, the modern major key.)

♭♭ signature (*cantus fictus*)	*protus*	mode 1 (Dorian)		c–c′	c
		mode 2 (Hypodorian)		g–g′	c′
	protus	mode 1 (Dorian)		a–a′	a
		mode 2 (Hypodorian)		e–e′	a′
No signature (*cantus durus*)	*tritus*	mode 5 (Lydian)		c–c′	c
		mode 6 (Hypolydian)		g–g′	c′

(The literal transposition of the F mode would have involved F♯s, but Tinctoris did not stipulate them, again creating, in effect, the modern major key.)

adopted it in his *Istitutioni harmoniche* (Venice, 1558). In a later edition Zarlino reordered the names and numbers of the 12 modes so that they followed the order of the hexachord (C–D–E–F–G–A). The gradual entry into circulation of more and more Greek texts spread confusion on this point. Medieval theorists since *Alia musica* had called the D mode Dorian, but Boethius would have called the E one Dorian, and Zarlino now reassigned the name to the C mode. Late Renaissance theorists can be divided into three groups, according to whether they follow Glarean, Zarlino's later system, or a classical Greek model.

3. Traditional and non-European music

Melody type and characteristic motif play a generally more important role in defining mode in European traditional music and non-European musical cultures than in Latin plainchant. In English (and North American) folksong, for instance, one encounters the phenomenon of melodies which, though clearly at root identical, have different finals and move in different scales; through a process of oral transmission they have acquired slightly different tonal characteristics. The same tune may be found ending on D with no signature, or with one flat, or with one sharp, or ending on E, and so on. The melody type is paramount; mode in the sense of scale and final is secondary.

Somewhere between the two extremes—that of dominant scale and final, and that of dominant melody type—lie some of the systems of Asian classical music (Arabic *maqām*, Indian *rāga*, Javanese *paṭēt*, Japanese

chōshi, etc.) and, moreover, the Middle Eastern Christian chant repertories (Byzantine, Syrian, etc.). In varying degrees, their 'modes' imply not so much scales as collections of characteristic motifs, phrases, and formulas peculiar to one mode and not found in the others.

4. Mode and ethos

One aspect of Western modal theory which recurs constantly, yet which seems to have no direct relevance to surviving music, is the expressive, ethical, or moral value attached to particular modes. Europe in the Middle Ages inherited, through Boethius, the idea that ethos and mode were associated, and also a number of illustrations of the supposed connection. (A favourite tale was that of a young man so aroused by a melody in the Phrygian mode that he was on the point of breaking into a young woman's room, when a change to the Hypophrygian mode restored him to a proper frame of mind.) Theorists did not always agree on the ethical character of a particular mode: for one the Hypolydian might be 'lachrymose', for another it was 'voluptuous'. Even less relevant were medieval speculations relating the eight modes to celestial bodies, or equating authentic and plagal with male and female.   DH

📖 W. Apel, *Gregorian Chant* (Bloomington, IN, 1958, 3/1966) · D. Hiley, *Western Plainchant: A Handbook* (Oxford, 1993)

mode of limited transposition. A term introduced by Messiaen to denote a mode that can be transposed only two or three times before it duplicates itself. The whole-tone scale can be transposed up one semitone to generate a different set of notes, but transposition at any other interval will duplicate the actual notes of one of these two versions of the scale. 'Unlimited' transposition, in this context, means that of the conventional major or minor scale, which would have to be transposed eight (diatonically) or 12 (chromatically) times before the same notes recurred. The mode of limited transposition that had the greatest compositional relevance during the 19th and 20th centuries, from Glinka to Messiaen and beyond, is the *octatonic scale.

AW

mode of vibration. Vibrating strings or air columns may oscillate in several modes simultaneously to produce a series of harmonics (tones at multiples of the fundamental frequency). See HARMONIC SERIES; ACOUSTICS, 5.   JBo

moderato (It.)**, modéré** (Fr.). 'Moderate', i.e. at a moderate tempo; *moderatamente* (It.), *modérément* (Fr.), 'moderately'.

Moderne, Jacques (*b* Pinguente, Istria, *c*.1495–1500; *d* Lyons, after 1560). French music printer and publisher, of Italian origin. In the 1520s he settled in Lyons, then an important cosmopolitan centre, and became a bookseller and printer of medical, religious, and other books. Between 1532 and 1552 he printed about 50 music books, adopting the diamond-shaped style of notes and single-impression technique of Pierre *Attaingnant, whose rival he remained for 15 years. The music he published covers a wide range (sacred and secular, vocal and instrumental), by local composers (e.g. Francesco de Layolle, his sometime editor), those of the Parisian school (Sermisy, Janequin), and international figures (Gombert, Willaert, Arcadelt). Unlike Attaingnant, he was noted for publishing music by Italian, Spanish, and German composers. His *Parangon des chansons* collection (1538–43) is an early example of 'table-book' format.   JMT/JWA

modernism. A current of compositional thought and practice characterized by innovation. Modernism was in evidence as an idea and as a term by the second decade of the 20th century, in association with Stravinsky's *The Rite of Spring* (1913), with Schoenberg's move into atonality (in about 1908), with the music of the Italian Futurists and Russian followers of Skryabin, and with Busoni's *Sketch for a New Aesthetic of Music* (1907). But although so many new hopes and endeavours were born at the same time, there was no unanimity of motivation or outlook. For some composers, for instance Varèse and the Futurists, new musical means were necessary at a time when human life was being revolutionized by electricity, by motor transport, and indeed by Revolution, for there was a strong belief in artistic modernism in some quarters in the new USSR. For others, new techniques were needed for expressive purposes, to intensify and characterize images more sharply (Schoenberg), or to venture into transcendence (Skryabin). The new might also be a means of rediscovering the primitive (Stravinsky) or a necessary advance, part of the progress inherent in the great tradition (as was Schoenberg's stated view).

In the later 1920s, and especially in the 30s, modernism seemed a spent force. That changed, however, after World War II, when a new generation of composers—Boulez, Barraqué, Babbitt, Nono, Stockhausen, Xenakis—began making new starts on the basis of the most forward-looking music of Schoenberg, Stravinsky, Webern, and Varèse. Again, the period of rapid change was quite brief, lasting no more than a decade or so, and again the rationales and results were various, though this time there was a lasting effect, in the work of composers taking their bearings from the modernists of the 1910s and 50s.

See also TWENTIETH CENTURY, THE.   PG

modern jazz. A term coined in the 1940s to distinguish the new *bebop style of playing from the traditional forms of jazz. It is still used to make this distinction even though 'modern' jazz has gone through many stages of modernity in the ensuing decades. Jazz historians use the term more specifically to mean jazz of the period 1940–60. The Modern Jazz Quartet (1952–74, 1981–97) excelled in a highly sophisticated *cool jazz style and in the fusion of jazz and contemporary Western art music.   PGa

modinha (Port.). A type of song, originating in Italian opera and other art-music traditions. It became especially popular in Brazilian salons in the 18th century. The *modinha* was usually for solo voice and guitar and gradually came to be regarded as a folksong, retaining its sentimental character.

modo (It.). 1. 'Manner'; *in modo di*, 'in the manner (style) of'.

2. 'Mode'.

modulation. The contradiction of one key by the establishing of another. In the major–minor tonal system, a key may be either major or minor, with any of the 12 chromatic pitches as its tonic, so that 24 keys are available. According to the traditional view of tonal structure, a piece of music begins and ends in one key, but during its course it may modulate to one other key or to several others. Modulation may be diatonic, where the notes of the first key are not contradicted and only the harmonic disposition of the music suggests a new

Ex. 1

(a)
a: I II I (VII) F: VI V I
C: V I IV (II)
minor → major → major
(b)
C: I V I – (IV) V I
F: V I (II)
**
(c)
C: I V I
F♯: II I V I
(d)
C major
F♯ major

key (Ex. 1*a*); chromatic, where 'foreign' notes are introduced and must be contradicted in turn when the music returns to the original key (Ex. 1*b*: B♮ to B♭ to B♮); or enharmonic, where the actual note names and notation are contradicted by the new intervals formed in the modulation (Ex. 1*c*: note the augmented 4th and the diminished 5th marked *). An important aspect of the harmonic theory that explains modulation is the 'pivot' chord (see, for example, the chord marked ** in Ex. 1*b*), which is common to both the old and the new key. More remote modulations reduce the possibility of pivot chords. As Ex. 1*d* illustrates, the keys from and to which the progression in Ex. 1*c* modulates have no common triad: at opposite extremes of the *circle of 5ths, they are as remote from each other as is possible.

Both Schoenberg and Schenker realized, at a time when many composers were writing music either not ending in the original key or not establishing a sense of key at the beginning, that the concept of modulation is not an ideal explanation of tonal structure (see TONALITY). 'Thus, tonality can be suspended, to be sure. But if it is present, then modulations are digressions from the principal tone, scarcely different in essence from any chord that is other than the tonic. They are just episodes of a large cadence' (Schoenberg, *Harmonielehre*, 1911). Schoenberg's theory of harmonic regions and Schenker's theory of diminution of the 'fundamental structure' (see ANALYSIS, 3) have largely supplanted the traditional concept of modulation.

JD

modulator. A generic term for devices that modify the characteristics of synthesized sounds cyclically, in terms either of amplitude or of frequency. At low rates of modulation the sounds will be subject to a simple pulsing or vibrato. At higher rates additional spectral components are generated, resulting in rich and complex timbres. PM

modus. See MODE.

modus lascivus (Lat., 'lascivious mode'). Medieval name for the Ionian mode. See MODE, 2.

Moeran, E(rnest) J(ohn) (*b* Heston, Middx., 31 Dec. 1894; *d* nr Kenmare, Co. Kerry, Ireland, 1 Dec. 1950). English composer, of Anglo-Irish descent. His studies with Stanford at the RCM (1913–14) were interrupted by World War I, during which he was severely wounded. After his discharge from the army he returned to the RCM to work under Ireland (1920–3). An active folksong collector in Norfolk, Suffolk, and Ireland, he was strongly affected stylistically by the inflections of folk melody. Their influence is discernible in the two orchestral rhapsodies of 1922 and 1924 (rev. 1941) and *Lonely Waters* (1932). Always an eclectic, Moeran was powerfully influenced by the music of Delius and Ireland (particularly in the fine *Seven Poems of James Joyce* of 1929), and his friendship with Peter Warlock drew him towards English 16th-century music, as is evident from *Whythorne's Shadow* (1931) and the later Serenade (1948). Warlock's death in 1930 affected him deeply and marked a new creative phase of substantial symphonic works, many of them written in Ireland. These include the Symphony in G minor (1934–7), concertos for violin (1942) and cello (1945), and the Sinfonietta (1944), arguably his masterpiece.

JDi

📖 S. WILD, *E. J. Moeran* (London, 1973) · G. SELF, *The Music of E. J. Moeran* (London, 1986)

möglich (Ger.). 'Possible'; *so rasch wie möglich*, 'as quick as possible'.

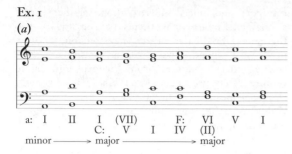

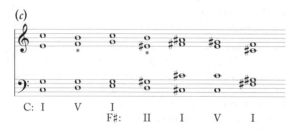

Moguchaya Kuchka. See FIVE, THE.

Mohaupt, Richard (*b* Breslau [now Wrocław], 14 Sept. 1904; *d* Reichenau, Austria, 3 July 1957). German composer. He studied with Julius Prüwer, conductor of the Breslau Opera, and began his career as a conductor, though he also appeared as a pianist. Since his wife was Jewish, he was obliged to flee when the Nazis took power; like Prüwer he settled in New York, in 1939, returning to Europe only in 1955. His music—lustily energetic and often rhythmically alert, though not always harmonically individual—includes five operas, four ballets, a symphony (*Rhythmus und Variationen*, 1940), a Concerto for Orchestra (1942), a Violin Concerto (1945), and *Bucolica* (1955) for four soloists, chorus, and orchestra.   MA

moins (Fr.). 'Less'.

Moïse et Pharaon (*Moïse et Pharaon, ou Le Passage de la Mer Rouge*; 'Moses and Pharaoh, or The Crossing of the Red Sea'). Opera in four acts by Rossini, derived from his *Mosè in Egitto* (1818), to a new libretto by Luigi Balocchi and Étienne de Jouy (Paris, 1827).

Moldau. See MÁ VLAST.

Molinaro, Simone (*b* ?Genoa, *c*.1565; *d* Genoa, 1615). Italian composer. He was *maestro di cappella* of Genoa Cathedral from 1602 at the latest. As well as masses and motets for use in the cathedral, he wrote two books of lute music, which include dance movements and fantasias showing an unusually good grasp of lute technique. He published an edition of Gesualdo's madrigals in score rather than the usual partbook format, so that their remarkable harmony could be studied.   DA

moll (Ger.). 'Minor', in the sense of key, e.g. *A-moll*, 'A minor', *moll Ton* (*Tonart*), 'minor key'. See also DURUM AND MOLLIS.

mollis. See DURUM AND MOLLIS.

Molter, Johann Melchior (*b* Tiefenort, nr Eisenach, 10 Feb. 1696; *d* Karlsruhe, 12 Jan. 1765). German composer. He served for two periods (1722–33 and 1742–65) as Kapellmeister in Karlsruhe, and held a similar post in between at Eisenach. His compositions include symphonies, concertos (among them early examples for clarinet), orchestral sonatas (a genre largely of his own invention), and chamber works. In his music a shift can be observed from a late Baroque to a *galant* style.
                                                                                     BS

molto (It.). 'Much', 'very'; *molto allegro*, 'very quickly'; *moltissimo*, 'extremely'.

Momente ('Moments'). Work (1961–4) by Stockhausen for soprano, four choral groups, four trumpets, four trombones, two electric organs, and three percussionists; it uses texts from the Song of Songs, Malinowski's *The Sexual Life of Savages*, onomatopoeic words, letters, and other sources, and consists of a series of 'moments', some of which need not be performed. It was expanded in 1964 and 1972.

moment form. An avant-garde form dating from the 1960s. Its first exponent was Stockhausen, who conceived each individually characterized passage in a work as a unit, or 'moment'. No moment has priority over another (even at the beginning or ending of a work), each is equally dispensable, and each is self-contained; they may be combined in a variety of ways often at the performers' discretion. The listener should concentrate on the present, the 'moment'. Stockhausen's major work in this 'open' form is *Momente* (1962–4) for soprano, four choral groups, and 13 instrumentalists.
                                                                                     AL

Moments musicaux ('Musical Moments'). The title given by the publisher to Schubert's set of six piano pieces op. 94 D780 (1823–8), shown on the original title page as *Momens musicaux*. The term has been adopted by other composers for character pieces for piano.

Mompou, Federico (*b* Barcelona, 16 April 1893; *d* Barcelona, 30 June 1987). Catalan composer. He studied at the Conservatorio del Liceo in Barcelona and privately in Paris (1911–13), with Isidore Philipp and Ferdinand Motte-Lacroix for piano and with Marcel Samuel-Rousseau for harmony and composition. From 1921 he lived again in Paris, finally returning in 1941 to Barcelona, where he lived and worked quietly for the rest of his life. His music, mainly songs and piano miniatures, has its roots in Catalan music and poetry; but the influence of French culture, in particular Debussy and Satie, is equally strong in defining Mompou's contemplative sound world and gentle pianistic style. At the heart of his work are the 15 *Cançons i danses*, mostly for piano (1918–62), in which piquant harmonies season the deceptively simple melodic lines, drawn mainly from Catalan folk material. He also wrote music for the guitar, a short oratorio *Improperios* (1963), and an orchestral song cycle *Combat del somni* (1942–8).   PG/CW

Monckton, (John) Lionel (Alexander) (*b* London, 18 Dec. 1861; *d* London, 15 Feb. 1924). English composer. Educated at Charterhouse and Oxford, he was called to the Bar in 1885. He preferred the theatre, however, and he eventually married an idol of the Edwardian stage, Gertie Millar. His tuneful scores included *A Country Girl* (1902), *The Arcadians* (1909), *Our Miss Gibbs* (1909), and *The Quaker Girl* (1910), some in collaboration with Howard Talbot or Ivan Caryll.   PGa/ALa

Mondo della luna, Il ('The World on the Moon'). Opera in three acts by Haydn to a libretto by Carlo Goldoni (Eszterháza, 1777). Goldoni's libretto was set by several composers, the first being Galuppi (1750).

Mondonville, Jean-Joseph Cassanéa de (*b* Narbonne, *bapt.* 25 Dec. 1711; *d* Belleville, nr Paris, 8 Oct. 1772). French violinist and composer. The son of the organist at Narbonne Cathedral, he published his first set of violin sonatas in Paris in 1733 and made a successful debut at the Concert Spirituel the following spring. He took up an appointment as leader of the Concert de Lille before acquiring a post as violinist of the royal chamber and chapel at Versailles in 1739. By then he had published several sets of chamber music, including the innovatory *Pièces de clavecin en sonates avec accompagnement de violon* op. 3 (1734) and *Les Sons harmoniques* op. 4 (1738). But with the new opportunities afforded by his court appointment, he turned to composing *grands motets*, influenced by those of Lalande, for performance at Versailles and the Concert Spirituel in Paris.

From 1740 to 1758 Mondonville served as a *sous-maître* of the royal chapel while maintaining his violin career in Paris. His *Pièces de clavecin avec voix ou violon* (1748) are *petits motets* on psalm texts, composed for private worship. He became involved in the administration of the Concert Spirituel (1749–62), serving as its conductor from 1755. During his tenure he included in the programmes organ concertos by Balbastre and symphonies by Gossec, Holzbauer, and Wagenseil as well as his own works, among them three oratorios: *Les Israëlites à la Montagne d'Horeb* (1758), *Les Fureurs de Saul* (1759), and *Les Titans* (1760).

Mondonville also composed operas, of which *Isbé* (1742) was the most successful. At Versailles, Madame de Pompadour took the leading role in performances of *Bacchus et Érigone* (1747) in her own Théâtre des Petits-Cabinets. *Titon et l'Aurore* (1753) was held up as an exemplar of the French style in the Querelle des *Bouffons. For his pastoral *Daphnis et Alcimadure* (1754) Mondonville wrote his own libretto; the prologue is in French but the three acts that follow are in Provençal dialect.   DA/JAS

Moniuszko, Stanisław (*b* Ubiel, nr Minsk, 5 May 1819; *d* Warsaw, 4 June 1872). Polish composer. He is remembered today as the leading 19th-century Polish opera composer. On his return to Minsk in 1839 from studies in Berlin he composed songs—several volumes of his *Home Songbook*—and 'operettas', of which *The Lottery* (1843) was given a Warsaw performance in 1846. It was on that occasion that Moniuszko met the poet Włodzimierz Wólski; he began work shortly afterwards on the first version of *Halka* (1846–7), with Wólski as

librettist. The final version was performed to immediate acclaim in Warsaw in 1858, and it remains to this day the most popular of all Polish operas, colouring the French and Italian styles of an earlier generation with the rhythms of Polish national dances in a manner which was to dictate the musical formulation of 'Polishness' to later composers.

The success of *Halka* in Warsaw launched Moniuszko's career. He immediately embarked on a European tour, and on his return to Poland accepted the post of director of Polish productions at the Grand Theatre. Following his operas *Flis* (1858), *Hrabina* (1859), and *Verbum nobile* (1860), he began work on his masterpiece *The Haunted Manor* in 1861. Two years later he was caught up in the growing political ferment that led to the insurrection of 1863 (the Grand Theatre was converted into a barracks). In the aftermath of the insurrection censorship in Warsaw was severe, and *The Haunted Manor*, regarded as excessively patriotic in tone, was withdrawn after three performances in 1865. From that point there was a decline in Moniuszko's creative powers, and he died in Warsaw of a heart attack seven years later.   JS

📖 B. M. MACIEJEWSKI, *Moniuszko, Father of Polish Opera* (London, 1979)

Monk, Meredith (Jane) (*b* Lima, Peru, 20 Nov. 1942). American composer and performer. She graduated from Sarah Lawrence College in 1964 and began performing in New York the same year, basing her work on dance songs given as gentle rituals. In 1968 she founded a company, The House, to present such works, and soon after she was touring internationally and making records. Developed in immediate contact with the performers, her music depends on her presence and on the space in which it is to be made. The full-length opera *Atlas* (Houston, 1991) was an unusual example of her working on a large scale.   PG

Monn, Matthias Georg (*b* Vienna, 9 April 1717; *d* Vienna, 3 Oct. 1750). Austrian composer. From 1738 he held the post of organist at the newly built Karlskirche in Vienna. A notable contributor to the rise of the pre-Classical symphony, Monn was the earliest in Vienna, in 1740, to write an example in four movements, with a minuet as the third; and he was one of the first to incorporate a tonic-key reprise of the first subject in his recapitulations, thus establishing an embryonic type of *sonata form. His surviving output embraces some 20 symphonies, concertos (mainly for harpsichord), chamber music, and an imaginative and technically demanding cello concerto.   DA/BS

monochord. A string stretched between two fixed bridges or nuts over a calibrated rule on a long, narrow soundbox, used for measuring intervals and demonstrating their theory, for tuning other instruments, and as an instrument in its own right. It is said to have been the invention of Pythagoras (6th century BC); the Pythagorean theory of intonation is based on string-length ratios on the monochord. The early fretted *clavichord was, in effect, a series of monochords built into one box; an old name for it in many countries was *monochordia* or *manicord*.

monocordo (It.). In string playing, the performance of a piece or passage on a single string, usually requiring upward shifts in position. Paganini was a famous exponent of the technique.   DMI

monodrama (It.). A *melodrama for one speaker only.

monody (from Gk. *monōidos*, 'singing alone'). 1. The same as *monophony.

2. More specifically, a modern term for the solo song with *continuo accompaniment that flourished in Italy in the first half of the 17th century. The members of the Florentine *Camerata had experimented with developing a new, direct style of singing in the late 16th century, aiming to recreate the power of ancient Greek music which they felt had been lost in the elaborate music of their own time. Performances and arrangements of polyphonic music, such as madrigals, for solo voice and instrumental accompaniment were also popular. The prime exponent of the new monodic song was Giulio Caccini, whose collection of madrigals and strophic arias for solo voice and continuo, *Le nuove musiche* (1602), marked the beginning of monody's popularity and of a gradual decline in the popularity of polyphonic song, particularly the madrigal.

Freed by the presence of the continuo and the absence of other voices, the monodic vocal line could on the one hand follow closely the meaning and rhythm of the text, being declamatory and often syllabic and recitative-like, and on the other be much more virtuoso and highly embellished than was possible in polyphonic song. Key words in the texts set could be emphasized either by dissonances between the continuo and voice or by the addition of ornaments or other expressive effects in the voice. Caccini wrote out much of his ornamentation, to ensure that singers did not improvise their own inappropriate embellishments. *Le nuove musiche* includes a long preface in which he explained the origins of his new style, which elsewhere he called 'the noble manner of singing', and gave detailed examples of the correct way to perform various ornaments and other vocal effects in order to achieve his aim of moving the listener's soul.

Monody played an important role in the early operas of Caccini and Peri. In the preface to *Euridice* (first performed in 1600) Peri described his belief that in order to achieve the emotional power of ancient music it was necessary to 'imitate speech in song', using a declamatory style 'lying between the slow and suspended movements of song and the swift and rapid movements of speech'.

After about 1620 monody spread from Florence to other regions of Italy. Such composers as Sigismondo d'India and Claudio Saracini wrote secular solo songs—some, for example the solo cantatas by Grandi and Berti, taking the form of strophic arias—while others, including Monteverdi, also developed the solo motet.

See also ARIA; MADRIGAL; OPERA; STILE RAP-PRESENTATIVO.   —/EW

📖 J. W. HILL, *Roman Monody, Cantata, and Opera from the Circles around Cardinal Montalto* (Oxford, 1997)

monophony. A term used to denote music consisting of only one melodic line, with no accompaniment or other voice parts (e.g. plainchant, unaccompanied solo song), as opposed to *polyphony and *homophony (each having several parts).

monothematic. A term used to describe a composition or movement based on only one main theme. It is sometimes used in connection with movements in *sonata form, in which two themes, or subjects, are usually introduced in the exposition; some composers of the Classical period, however, particularly Haydn, would base the second subject on thematic material taken from the first.

monotoning. See INTONING.

Monsieur Croche. The pseudonym under which Debussy wrote much of his incisive and outspoken music criticism, which appeared in a range of journals and newspapers. He published a selection of articles as *Monsieur Croche antidilettante* (Paris, 1921; Eng. trans. 2/1962); these were edited by François Lesure as *Monsieur Croche et autres écrits* (Paris, 1971; Eng. trans. 1976).   AL

Monsigny, Pierre-Alexandre (*b* Fauquembergues, nr Saint-Omer, 17 Oct. 1729; *d* Paris, 14 Jan. 1817). French composer. Born into a noble family, he held several official positions in Paris before his connection with the Duke of Orléans allowed him to take up composing. In association with the librettist Michel-Jean Sedaine he enjoyed success in Paris, c.1760–77, as a composer of comic operas at about the time when Philidor and Grétry were achieving great popularity. Although he never attained their facility in composition, or a comparable originality, he took pains to match his music to the text and had a gift for attractive melody.

The social and political implications of *Le Roy et le fermier* (1762)—based, unusually, on an English subject—added a new, extra-musical element to the traditions of *opéra comique*. In his late 40s Monsigny suddenly stopped composing, probably because of eye problems; from then on he lived in modest retirement. His works enjoyed continued success into the early 19th century.   PS/JN/RP

Mont, Henry Du. See DU MONT, HENRY.

Montag aus Licht ('Monday from Light'). Opera in a greeting, three acts, and a farewell by Stockhausen to his own libretto (Milan, 1988), the 'third day' of **Licht.*

Montague, Stephen (Rowley) (*b* Syracuse, NY, 10 March 1943). American composer, resident in Britain. After studies in the USA and Poland, he moved to London in 1974 and has worked as a freelance composer ever since. His vividly coloured and vigorously characterized music is eclectic and approachable, acknowledging many different 20th-century features from expressionism to minimalism. He has worked a great deal with dance companies; his unambiguous expressiveness is well demonstrated in *Behold a Pale Horse* (1990) for organ and brass and *Snakebite* (1995) for chamber orchestra.   AW

Monte, Philippe de (*b* Mechlin [now Mechelen], 1521; *d* Prague, 4 July 1603). Flemish composer. An educated man who spoke and wrote five languages, he was in Italy from 1542 to 1551, teaching the children of a noble family in Naples. By 1554 he was in Rome, and that year visited Antwerp before travelling to England, where he was a member of the private chapel of Philip II of Spain, husband of Mary Tudor; there he met Thomas Byrd, and he later corresponded with William, sending him a copy of his motet *Super flumina Babylonis* in 1583. He left England in 1555, and after a few more years in Italy was appointed court Kapellmeister to Maximilian II in 1568, remaining in the imperial service for the rest of his life and moving between Vienna and Prague, the favourite court of Maximilian's successor, Rudolf II. Having been brought up to write in the madrigal style of the post-Willaert generation, he felt increasingly cut off from later developments, and in his latter years made a conscious effort to modernize. His output of 19 books of madrigals for five voices, nine for six, and three for seven (including a collection of settings from Guarini's popular pastoral play *Il pastor fido*) was unusually large. He also wrote a wide range of church music, including parody masses and motets in a polyphonic style distinctly less smooth in melody than Palestrina's.   DA/TC

📖 B. MANN, *The Secular Madrigals of Filippo di Monte, 1521–1603* (Ann Arbor, MI, 1983)

Montéclair, Michel Pignolet de (*b* Andelot, Haute-Marne, *bapt.* 4 Dec. 1667; *d* Aumont, 22 Sept. 1737). French composer. He was born Michel Pignolet, adding the name of a fortress near his home only after he arrived in Paris in 1687; he had previously served as a choirboy at Langres Cathedral. In his early 20s he entered the service of the Prince of Vaudémont, in whose entourage he travelled to Italy. By 1699 he was in Paris again playing the *basse de violon*—an instrument he may have brought back with him—in the *petit choeur* of the Opéra orchestra (he and the Italian cellist J.-B. Stuck were the first in Paris to perform on it). He retained this position until his death, supplementing his income by teaching, composing, and running a music shop with his nephew, François Boivin, in the rue St Honoré (1721–8).

Montéclair's published music includes stylish instrumental as well as vocal chamber music, an *opéra ballet* entitled *Les Festes de l'été* (1716), *Jephté* (a *tragédie lyrique* to words by S. J. Pellegrin, whose free treatment of the biblical text, along with the work's staging, elicited condemnation from the Archbishop of Paris; the work's success was thus ensured), and a number of sacred works (now lost). Of particular importance are three collections of dramatic French and Italian cantatas (Paris, 1709, *c.*1716, 1728), which compare favourably with those of Clérambault and Rameau, and among his pedagogical works are a violin method (1711–12) and *Principes de musique* (1736), which includes a useful section on French vocal ornaments of the time.   DA/JAS

Montemezzi, Italo (*b* Vigasio, nr Verona, 31 May 1875; *d* Vigasio, 15 May 1952). Italian composer. He studied and then taught at the Milan Conservatory before being taken up by the Ricordi publishing firm. Their faith in him, doubtless boosted by his evident absorption both of Wagnerian techniques and of the 'advanced' styles of Debussy and Strauss, was vindicated by the enormous international success of *L'amore dei tre re* ('The Love of Three Kings'; La Scala, Milan, 1913), which retains a tenuous hold on the repertory. Less successful was *La nave* ('The Ship'; La Scala, 1918), which used as its model one of Gabriele D'Annunzio's more extravagantly decadent plays. Montemezzi spent much of his later career in the USA, where he conducted frequent revivals of *L'amore dei tre re*.   RP

Monteux, Pierre (*b* Paris, 4 April 1875; *d* Hancock, ME, 1 Aug. 1964). French conductor. He studied the violin at the Paris Conservatoire and played the viola in the Opéra-Comique orchestra. In 1910 Diaghilev engaged him as music director of the Ballets Russes; he gave the premieres of Stravinsky's *Petrushka* (1911) and *The Rite of Spring* (1913) and Ravel's *Daphnis et Chloé* (1912). Thereafter he was in demand in Europe and the USA, notably conducting at the Metropolitan Opera, New York, and the Boston Symphony Orchestra. He was music director of the Paris Symphony Orchestra (1929–37), the San Francisco Symphony Orchestra (1935–52), and the LSO (1961–4).   JT

Monteverdi, Claudio (*see page 796*)

Montsalvatge i Bassols, Xavier (*b* Girona, 11 March 1912; *d* Barcelona, 7 May 2002). Catalan composer. Study at the Barcelona Conservatory (1923–36) fostered his affection for the music of Les Six and for West Indian music, which has been the mainspring of many works, including the *Canciones negras* (1945–9) for voice and piano or orchestra. His work is an eclectic blend of tradition and exoticism, in a wide diversity of forms. The popular *Concierto breve* (1953) for piano and orchestra and the *Sinfonía de réquiem* (1985) both demonstrate his firm grasp of structure and his imaginative orchestral palette. He wrote over 20 ballets, including *La muerte enamorada* ('Death the Lover', 1943), and several works about childhood, notably the magic opera *El gato con botas* ('Puss in Boots', 1948).   CW

Monza, Carlo (*b* Milan, *c*.1735; *d* Milan, 19 Dec. 1801). Italian composer. He succeeded Sammartini as organist at the Milan court in 1768 and as *maestro* in 1775 and held posts in other Milanese churches. He also enjoyed a successful career as an opera composer, concentrating mainly on *opera seria* for Milan. His fusion of Italian and French elements, characteristic of opera of the period, is notable in *Ifigenia in Tauride* (1784), which included complex contrapuntal choruses and pantomime as well as lyrical melodies. Appointed *maestro* of Milan Cathedral in 1787 he abandoned opera and became known as a leading composer of sacred music.   SH

'Moonlight' Sonata. Nickname of Beethoven's Piano Sonata no. 14 in C sharp minor op. 27 no. 2 (1801), so called apparently because the poet Heinrich Rellstab (1799–1860) wrote in a review that it reminded him of a boat in the moonlight on Lake Lucerne.

Moore, Douglas S(tuart) (*b* Cutchogue, NY, 10 Aug. 1893; *d* Greenport, NY, 25 July 1969). American composer and teacher. He studied at Yale with Horatio Parker and, after the war, with d'Indy and Boulanger in Paris and Bloch in Cleveland. He taught at Columbia University from 1926 to 1962. Although he wrote orchestral and chamber music and many choruses and songs, he is best remembered as the composer of some of the first native operas to find a place in the American repertory, notably the folk opera *The Devil and Daniel Webster* (New York, 1939) and *The Ballad of Baby Doe* (Central City, CO, 1956).   ABur

Moore, Gerald (*b* Watford, 30 July 1899; *d* Penn, Bucks., 13 March 1987). English pianist. A pupil of Michael and Mark Hambourg, he began his recital career in 1920, his first recordings dating from 1921. Landon Ronald advised him to specialize as an accompanist and in 1925 he joined up with the tenor John Coates, from whom he learnt his art. For the next 40 years Moore earned acclaim as one of the finest accompanists, in partnerships with such eminent artists as Casals, Chaliapin, Elisabeth Schumann, John McCormack, Elisabeth Schwarzkopf, and Dietrich Fischer-Dieskau. He lectured widely and published several books.   CF

   📖 G. MOORE, *The Unashamed Accompanist* (London, 1943, 3/1984); *Am I Too Loud? Memoirs of an Accompanist* (London, 1962); *Farewell Recital* (London, 1978)

Morales, Cristóbal de (*b* Seville, *c*.1490–1500; *d* ? Málaga, 4 Sept. – 7 Oct. 1553). Spanish composer. It has been suggested (though without evidence) that he may have been a choirboy at Seville Cathedral, and perhaps came into contact with two important composers there: Francisco de Peñalosa and Pedro de Escobar. In 1526 he became *maestro de capilla* at Ávila Cathedral, but by early 1528 he had moved to a similar post at Plasencia. He had resigned by late 1531, and in 1535 was appointed a singer in the papal choir. In 1538 he accompanied Pope Paul III to Nice for the celebrations of a peace treaty between the Emperor Charles V and François I of France, for which his motet *Jubilate Deo omnis terra* was written. After completing his first five-year term in the papal chapel he returned to Spain for a year. His second term in the pope's service was marked by numerous absences due to illness. On his return to Spain in 1545 he took charge of music at Toledo Cathedral but resigned two years later and went instead to the court of the Duke of Arcos, Don Luis Cristóbal Ponce de León, at Marchena. He ended his days at Málaga Cathedral, but was unhappy there too; shortly before his death he applied to take up the post of *maestro* at Toledo again.

Very little secular music by Morales survives, and his importance in his lifetime and for the generation following him was as a composer of sacred music. His works were extensively published and copied, the *Magnificat* settings achieving particularly wide circulation, and his long-lasting fame is evident from references by theorists and other writers on music. His *Lamentabatur Jacob* was still in the repertory of the papal chapel in the 18th century. The most imposing published volumes of his music were two books of masses issued in Rome in 1544, including works asso-
(*cont. on p. 799*)

Claudio Monteverdi
(1567–1643)

The Italian composer Claudio Giovanni Antonio Monteverdi was born in Cremona on 15 May 1567 and died in Venice on 29 November 1643.

Although Monteverdi was generally considered in the 19th and early 20th centuries to have been a revolutionary, responsible for the decline of the old polyphonic style developed since the Middle Ages and reaching its peak in the music of Palestrina, it is now clear that he was only part of a more general movement in that direction. But if many other composers participated in the new genre of opera and in the new style of accompanied song known as *monody, it was Monteverdi who appreciated most fully what could be accomplished by these means. The basis of his work lay in the belief that music must 'move the whole man' and express the deepest feelings, and even his lightest songs have some inner significance. This belief led to his other cardinal tenet: that the music must match the words it sets. To these ends he felt that musical 'rules', or conventions, were expendable if the demands of the art-work as a whole required it. His earlier music was written in the form of madrigals, which are essentially small-scale explorations of mood, but his skill in combining two or more contrasting emotions, moulding them into an integrated and satisfying unit, was to make him a supreme composer of operas. His later works explore the expression of human emotion in such a way that his characters become as vividly alive as they are in the works of Shakespeare, Mozart, Verdi, or any other great dramatist.

Cremona and Mantua

Monteverdi was the son of a barber-surgeon. He studied music with the *maestro di cappella* of Cremona Cathedral, Marc'Antonio Ingegneri, and was evidently a precocious pupil, publishing several books of sacred and secular music when he was still in his teens. This early period culminated in two madrigal books published by the prestigious Gardano press in Venice in 1587 and 1590; they contain some extremely attractive works and are more modern in approach than Ingegneri's, perhaps as a result of Monteverdi's having studied the madrigals of Marenzio and other composers popular in the 1580s. However, as yet his aim appears to

be to charm rather than to express passion, and this can be seen at its best in his well-known setting of Tasso's poem *Ecco mormorar l'onde*.

It is not known exactly when he left his home town, but he entered the service of the Duke of Mantua as a string player in 1590 or 1591. In Mantua he was immediately thrown into contact with some of the finest musicians of the time. The most influential for him seems to have been the Flemish composer Giaches de Wert, the crux of whose style was that music must exactly match the mood of the verse, and must also attempt to set the words with a sense of their natural declamation. Monteverdi's next book of madrigals (Venice, 1592) shows all the hallmarks of Wert's style, not always well digested but certainly representing a complete change of direction. The melody is angular, the harmony increasingly dissonant, the mood tense to the point of neurosis. Guarini is the favoured poet, and every nuance of the verse is expressed in the music, sometimes to the detriment of the overall balance.

This new atmosphere seems to have caused some upset in Monteverdi's hitherto fluent productivity, and although he went on composing he published little for the next 11 years. He accompanied Duke Vincenzo on expeditions to Hungary in 1595 and to Flanders four years later; in 1599 he also married a singer, Claudia Cattaneo, by whom he had three children, one of whom died in infancy. He had been passed over when the post of *maestro di cappella* became vacant on Wert's death in 1596, and felt bitter about it, but in 1601 he was appointed to the position at the very reasonable age of 35. In 1603 and 1605 he published two more books of madrigals. Both contain masterpieces, and although the aim is still to follow the meaning of the verse in great detail the musical problems of thematic development and proportion are solved. Dissonances are more severe, the melody sometimes still more irregular, but the effect is more varied in emotion, less neurotic, and if Guarini's eroticism stimulates a sensuous musical style, there is also lightness and humour in Monteverdi's mature madrigals. His assimilation of these advanced musical means, especially the use of intense and prolonged dissonance, provoked criticism from more conservative composers and theorists, and Monteverdi became a kind of figurehead of the avant-garde. Singled out in the attacks of a Bolognese theorist, Giovanni Maria Artusi, he was provoked to reply with an important aesthetic statement in his fifth book of madrigals (expanded in the 1607 *Scherzi musicali*) on the nature of his art; he disclaimed the role of revolutionary, saying that he was only the follower of a tradition which had been developing for the last 50 years or more, and distinguished between two 'practices', new and old, neither having intrinsically more merit than the other (see PRIMA PRATICA, SECONDA PRATICA).

If these madrigals gave him a reputation which extended well beyond northern Italy, it was his first opera that finally established him as a composer of large-scale music, rather than an exquisite miniaturist. Monteverdi may have attended the performance of Peri's *Euridice* in Florence in October 1600—certainly he knew the work—and he had certainly already written some stage music. In *Orfeo* (Mantua, 24 February 1607) he showed that he had a much broader conception of the new genre than had his predecessors, combining the opulence of the late Renaissance *intermedio* with the essential simplicity of the pastoral tale told in recitative which was the ideal of the Florentines. His recitative is more expressive, varying from something quite melodious to a fast-moving narration, in which individual words and phrases are expressed by astringent harmonies. He shaped whole acts into a coherent pattern rather than merely assembling them from small units. Most of all, he shows a flair for matching the climaxes in the action with musical climaxes, using dissonance, the singer's virtuosity, or instrumental sonorities to create the sense of heightened emotion.

A few months after the production of *Orfeo* Monteverdi suffered the loss of his wife and retired in a state of deep depression to his father's home at Cremona. However, he was summoned back to Mantua almost immediately to compose a new opera as part of the celebrations surrounding the marriage of the Gonzaga heir, Francesco, to Margherita of Savoy. Monteverdi returned unwillingly but composed not only an opera, *L'Arianna*, but also a ballet, the *Ballo delle ingrate*, and music for a play. A further tragedy occurred when *L'Arianna* was in rehearsal, for the young singer playing the title role, Caterina Martinelli, who had been living in Monteverdi's house, possibly as a pupil, died of smallpox. Nevertheless, the part was recast and the opera finally produced in May 1608. It was an enormous success. The score has been lost, apart from the famous *Lamento d'Arianna*, which survives in several versions and can be considered the first great operatic scena.

After this effort Monteverdi returned again to Cremona in a condition of collapse that seems to have lasted for some time. He was ordered back to Mantua in November and refused to go. He eventually returned, but thereafter hated the Gonzaga court, which he maintained had undervalued and underpaid him. He does not, however, appear to have been unproductive, although the music he wrote in the next year or so reflects his depression. He arranged the *Lamento* as a five-voice madrigal, and wrote a madrigalian threnody on the death of Martinelli (the *Sestina*, published later in the sixth book of madrigals) which represents a peak of dissonant, anguished music in this style. In a more vigorous vein he wrote some church music, including a Mass in the old style and the famous music for Vespers on feasts of the Blessed Virgin Mary. If the Mass was a remarkable achievement, a deliberate attempt to show that the polyphonic idiom was still viable, the Vespers music is still more so, a veritable compendium of the different kinds of modern church music—grand psalm settings in the Venetian manner, virtuoso music for solo singers, instrumental music, and even an attempt to use up-to-date operatic music to set the emotional words of the *Magnificat*. But while this music is as 'advanced' as possible, Monteverdi makes it clear that it is for him merely an extension of the old tradition by using plainchant melodies as thematic material for the psalms and *Magnificat* settings. Above all, this is music to impress the listener with the power of the Church and its Maker.

The volume containing this music was published in 1610 and dedicated to Pope Paul V, Monteverdi visiting Rome apparently to present it in person. He may also have been seeking a new post in order to leave Mantua, but nothing came of that. We know little of his life for the next two years until July 1612, when Francesco Gonzaga, having succeeded his father, suddenly dismissed Monteverdi from his service; whether this was for reasons of economy or of insubordination remains unclear. Without a job Monteverdi returned to his father's house with his two sons, remaining there for about a year. Then the *maestro di cappella* of St Mark's, Venice, died, and after an audition Monteverdi was invited to take his place. He took up his appointment in the autumn of 1613.

Venice

Monteverdi had been appointed largely because the musical establishment at St Mark's was in need of an experienced director after some years of decline, and because the last Venetian composer of distinction, Giovanni Gabrieli, had recently died. Though not primarily a church musician Monteverdi took his duties extremely seriously, and within a few years he had completely revitalized the music, appointing new assistants (including Grandi and Cavalli), writing much church music himself, and insisting on daily choral services. He also took an active part in music-making elsewhere in the city.

His letters from these early years in Venice reveal a complete change in his state of mind. He felt fulfilled and honoured, and was well (and regularly) paid; as a result he seems to have been fairly prolific. He kept up his links with Mantua, presumably because he had little choice, being a Mantuan subject. From his correspondence with the Mantuan court councillor, Alessandro Striggio the younger, we see a philosophy of dramatic music emerging which was not only to mould Monteverdi's later work but was also to have an influence on the history of opera in general. Whereas the older types of opera had developed from the Renaissance *intermedio*, with its emphasis on the wishes of the gods, and from the pastoral play, with its pasteboard shepherds and shepherdesses, Monteverdi became increasingly concerned with the expression of human emotions and the creation of recognizable human beings with their changes of mind and mood. In his seventh book of madrigals (Venice, 1619) we see him experimenting with many new devices, mostly borrowed from the current practices of his younger contemporaries, but all endowed with greater power. There are the conversational 'musical letters', deliberately written in a severe recitative-like melody in an attempt to match the words, and on the other hand there is the ballet *Tirsi e Clori*, written for Mantua in 1616, which shows a complete acceptance of the simple tunefulness of the modern aria.

Monteverdi's attempt at creating a practical philosophy of music went on throughout the 1620s, leading to further stylistic innovations. Following ideas derived from Plato, he divided the emotions into three basic kinds—those of love, war, and temperance—which could each be expressed by matching rhythms and harmonies; at the same time we see a frank acceptance of realism in the imitation of the sounds of nature in various ways. His dramatic cantata *Combattimento di Tancredi, e Clorinda* (a setting of part of Tasso's *Gerusalemme liberata*) contains the result of these new ideas. It was first performed at the Palazzo Mocenigo, Venice, in 1624, and the 'aroused' *concitato genere* (comprising rapid reiteration of single notes in strict rhythms) combined with the use of pizzicato and other special effects to express the clashing of swords marks an important step forward in the idiomatic use of string instruments. We know that these trends were continued in a comic opera, *La finta pazza Licori* (probably intended for the celebrations surrounding the accession of Duke Vincenzo II of Mantua in 1627), because although the score has been lost there survives a sizable correspondence on the subject between Monteverdi and Striggio.

In 1627–8 Monteverdi suffered further anxiety on the imprisonment of his eldest son, Massimiliano, in Bologna for reading books banned by the Inquisition; it was some months before he was finally cleared of the charge. In this same period, Monteverdi fulfilled a commission to write music (now lost) for the *intermedi* to Tasso's *Aminta* and for a tournament given in Parma to celebrate the marriage of Duke Odoardo Farnese to Margherita de' Medici in December 1628. However, the War of Mantuan Succession broke his link with the Gonzagas, who were ruined by it; and although Monteverdi wrote an opera (*Proserpina rapita*) for performance in Venice in 1630, the plague which broke out later that year effectively stopped all musical activities there for about 18 months.

Monteverdi and his family seem to have emerged from the plague unscathed, and Monteverdi himself took holy orders during this period. He wrote a grand Mass for the thanksgiving service in St Mark's in November 1631, when the epidemic was officially declared over. The Gloria survives, and shows him applying some of his theories concerning the diversity of mood suggested by the words, but both this and some other church music probably written about this time show a calm and majestic approach replacing the passion of his earlier years. A book of lighthearted songs and duets published in the following year is along the same lines, and there is a detached quality about much of the music in his eighth book of madrigals. This collection of *Madrigali guerrieri et amorosi* (Venice, 1638) contains much fine music, especially the *Lamento della ninfa*, which shows how far music had moved since the *Lamento d'Arianna* of 30 years before. He also produced a collection of sacred music, the *Selva morale e spirituale* (1640–1), which is similarly compendious.

If these volumes, put together when Monteverdi was over 70, might have seemed to mark the end of his composing life, chance played a part in inspiring him to an Indian summer of astonishing productivity. The first public opera houses opened in Venice in 1637, and, as the one indigenous composer with real experience in the genre, he was naturally involved almost from the beginning. *L'Arianna* was revived in 1640, and no fewer than three new operas were composed during the following three years. Only two have survived in score: *Il ritorno d'Ulisse in patria* (1640) and *L'incoronazione di Poppea* (1643; it survives in a later version that may include music not by Monteverdi). Both are masterpieces, being fairly described as the first modern operas. Their interest lies in the portrayal of human beings in realistic situations, and sub-plots, especially in *Poppea*, allow for a greater range of character parts—the nobility and their servants, the evil, the misguided, the innocent, the good, and so on. Using all the means available to a composer of his time (the fashionable arietta, duets, ensembles), and combining them with the expressive recitative of the early part of the 17th century, Monteverdi showed how the philosophy of music he had developed during his early years in Venice could be put to use. The emphasis is always on the drama, and the musical units are rarely self-contained, but rather woven into a continual pattern so that the music remains a means rather than an end.

With these works Monteverdi confirmed his position as one of the greatest musical dramatists of all time. That he was held in highest regard by his Venetian employers is shown by their gifts of money to him in these last years and by their granting him leave to travel to his native city in the last few months of his life. He died after a short illness, and the Venetian public showed their esteem at his funeral; a copy of their monument to him has been placed in the chapel of S. Ambrogio at the church of the Frari.   DA/TC

📖 D. Arnold, *Monteverdi* (London, 1963, 3/1990) · D. Arnold and N. Fortune (eds.), *The New Monteverdi Companion* (London, 1985) · G. Tomlinson, *Monteverdi and the End of the Renaissance* (Berkeley, CA, 1987) · N. John (ed.), *The Operas of Monteverdi* (London, 1992) [ENO opera guide] · P. Fabbri, *Monteverdi* (Eng. trans., Cambridge, 1994) · D. Stevens (ed.), *The Letters of Claudio Monteverdi* (London, 2/1995) · R. Tellart, *Claudio Monteverdi* (Paris, 1997) · J. Whenham, *Monteverdi: Vespers (1610)* (Cambridge, 1997) · J. G. Kurtzman, *The Monteverdi Vespers of 1610: Music, Context, Performance* (Oxford, 1999)

ciated with Pope Paul III and Charles V. His masses include parody, paraphrase, and cantus-firmus types, the first of these groups demonstrating virtuosic recasting of material from their models. His many motets show a special flair for conveying emotion, and he was fond of using an ostinato subject to emphasize the principal message of a motet (such as 'Gaudeamus'—'let us rejoice'—in *Jubilate Deo omnis terra*). Other repetitive or sequential passages in his masses and motets are reminiscent of the music of, for example, Josquin des Prez.   DA/OR

morality plays. See MEDIEVAL DRAMA.

Moran, Robert (Leonard) (*b* Denver, CO, 8 Jan. 1937). American composer. He studied in Vienna with Apostel in 1957, at Mills College with Berio and Milhaud, and then in Vienna again with Roman Haubenstock-Ramati in 1963. Though his Viennese teachers would have introduced him to serial music and subsequent developments in European music, he attached himself to no such models, but has freely drawn on minimalism and popular music in works of whimsical variety.   PG

Moravia. See CZECH REPUBLIC, 1–3.

morceau (Fr.). 'Piece'; *morceau symphonique*, 'symphonic piece'.

Morceaux en forme de poire, Trois. See TROIS MORCEAUX EN FORME DE POIRE.

mordent (from It. *mordente*, 'biting'; Fr.: *mordant, pincé, battement, martellement, tiret*; Ger.: *Mordent, Beisser*). An *ornament consisting in a rapid, often sharply rhythmic, alternation of main note, lower auxiliary note, and main note, indicated by the sign ᴡ; the inverted form uses the upper auxiliary note instead of the lower. Both types are discussed in 16th-century sources, but the lower auxiliary type seems to have been the more common during the 17th and early 18th centuries.

Mordents with one or two repercussions (the latter termed 'double mordents') functioned primarily as rhythmic ornaments; those with multiple repercussions (sometimes indicated by an elongation of the sign: ᴀᴡ) intensified and coloured the melodic note. Baroque composers often left the chromatic alteration of the auxiliary note to the discretion of the performer. Mordents, particularly short ones, gave brilliance to leaping and detached notes: C. P. E. Bach (*Versuch*, 1753) stated that they were 'the most freely introduced . . . into the bass'.

Contrary to popular opinion, the inverted mordent (Ger.: *Schneller*) was not characteristic of the later Baroque period; the *Pralltriller*, or half *trill, probably fulfilled this function. From the late 18th century onwards, however, the inverted mordent came into wide acceptance and was indicated by the sign formerly used for the trill; often it was intended to be performed before the beat.

The terminology concerning mordents is confusing: some modern writers have reversed the definitions of mordent and inverted mordent given above, while others refer instead to upper and lower mordents.

SMcV/NPDC

morendo (It.). 'Dying', 'fading away'.

Moreno Torroba, Federico (*b* Madrid, 3 March 1891; *d* Madrid, 12 Sept. 1982). Spanish composer. He was a pupil of Pedrell. Together with Rodrigo, he is the chief representative of the *casticismo* ('authenticity') movement, which aimed to reinvigorate Spanish classical music through popular folk traditions. He wrote many operas and ballets, as well as orchestral and instrumental music. The long series of guitar works he wrote for Andrés Segovia, notably the *Suite castellana* (1926) and *Concierto en flamenco* (1962), retain their popularity. His reputation rests largely on the best of his many zarzuelas, *Luisa Fernanda* (1932) and *La chulapona* ('The Chick', 1934).   CW

moresca (It., Sp.), **moresque** (Fr.). A dance popular throughout Europe in the 15th and 16th centuries. Its performers wore Moorish costumes, had blackened faces and bells on their legs. The most popular dance of Renaissance ballets and mummeries, it frequently involved a mock sword fight between 'Christians' and 'Moors', also known as a *danse des bouffons*. The *moresca* survives in Spain, Corsica, and Guatemala and is probably related to the English morris dance.

Lassus wrote several vocal *moresche* which resemble the *villanella but parody the speech of Africans living in Italy rather than the Neapolitan dialect.   —JH

Morgenlied (Ger.). 'Morning song'. See AUBADE.

Mörike-Lieder ('Songs of Mörike'). 53 songs for voice and piano by Wolf, settings of poems by Eduard Friedrich Mörike (1804–75); most were composed in 1888 and they include *Elfenlied*, *Gesang Weylas*, *Der Feuerreiter*, and *An die Geliebte*.

Morlacchi, Francesco (Giuseppe Baldassare) (*b* Perugia, 14 June 1784; *d* Innsbruck, 28 Oct. 1841). Italian composer. He studied first in Perugia, then Loreto, and finally with Padre Mattei in Bologna. His first operatic works began to appear in 1807, and he soon established an important reputation within the Italian peninsula. However, in 1810 he moved to Dresden, and the following year was appointed Kapellmeister of the Italian Opera there. His operatic output then slowed down somewhat, constrained as he was to write sacred and ceremonial music. He did, however, try intermittently to adapt his Italianate style to the very different demands of the German-language theatre, at other times returning to the older, Paisiello-influenced style of his youth.   RP

Morley, Thomas (*b* Norwich, 1557 or 1558; *d* London, ? early Oct. 1602). English church musician, composer, publisher, and theorist. He was the son of a Norwich brewer, and probably entered the choir of Norwich Cathedral as a boy. At some point he studied with William Byrd. In 1574 he was promised the position of choirmaster at Norwich (including the duties of organist) on the death of Edmund Inglott; he took up the post in 1583. Four years later he left the cathedral, possibly because of his Roman Catholic sympathies. In 1588 he took the B.Mus. at Oxford. By the following year he was in London, serving as organist of St Paul's Cathedral and, from 1592, as a Gentleman of the Chapel Royal. From 1598 he became active as a publisher, issuing Italian works as well as English. In his later years he suffered increasingly from ill health.

Morley was a versatile all-rounder who wrote music in most of the major genres of the day; but he is remembered today principally for his English-texted madrigals, and for his treatise *A Plaine and Easie Introduction to Practicall Musicke* (London, 1597/R1971). As a madrigalist, Morley virtually reinvented the genre to suit the tastes of the English market. His madrigals, canzonets, and balletts are mostly light in tone, often narrative, and strongly indebted to Italian models; some are even direct adaptations of works by Anerio, Gastoldi, and Croce, though the borrowing is always carried out with the addition of a personal touch, such as the addition of contrapuntal interest. Some of his contemporaries—Weelkes in particular—quickly fell under the spell of these new-fashioned pieces, and imitated them. Others, including Byrd and Gibbons, were more resistant.

Morley's contribution to musical life in late Elizabethan England was wide-ranging. The delightful *Plaine and Easie Introduction* borrows freely from foreign treatises, but its down-to-earth attitudes and advice frequently make it easier to comprehend than its sources, and it is full of common sense. As a printer Morley widened the scope of English publishing to include lute music and consort music. In 1599 he published the *First Booke of Consort Lessons*, a set of arrangements for a mixed consort of viols, plucked instruments, and flute. Two years later he edited *The Triumphes of Oriana*, an anthology of madrigals in praise of Queen Elizabeth, in which each piece was contributed by a different composer.

Morley's Latin-texted motets are mostly apprenticeship works, and they barely hint at the Roman Catholicism to which he probably remained true throughout his life. A few anthems and English-texted canticles by him survive, together with solemnly simple settings of the burial service. He wrote keyboard music, but otherwise relatively little for instruments alone. One of his finest achievements, however, is a book of songs for voice and lute (London, 1600/R1970), which includes what has become one of his best-loved works: a setting of Shakespeare's 'It was a lover and his lass'.   DA/JM

Morning Prayer. See MATINS; SERVICE.

Mortari, Virgilio (*b* Passirana di Lainate, nr Milan, 6 Dec. 1902; *d* Rome, 6 Sept. 1993). Italian composer and teacher. He studied in Milan and Parma, became a pianist, then taught composition, at the Venice (1933–40) and Rome (1940–73) conservatories; he was superintendent of the Teatro La Fenice, Venice, between 1955 and 1959. He co-wrote (with Casella) *La tecnica dell'orchestra contemporaneo* (Milan, 2/1950) and completed Mozart's *L'oca del Cairo* (performed Salzburg, 1936). His own music, elegantly crafted and often good-naturedly lyrical, includes four operas and two ballets; his orchestral output is dominated by concertante works and his choral music encompasses a *Stabat mater* (1947), Requiem (1959), and *Gloria* (1980).   MA

Mort de Cléopâtre, La ('The Death of Cleopatra'). Lyric scene (1829) by Berlioz, for soprano or mezzo-soprano and orchestra, a setting of a text by P. A. Vieillard; it was part of a larger cantata *Cléopâtre*, an unsuccessful entry for the Prix de Rome.

mosaic type. A system of typesetting in which separate pieces are used for note-head, stem, and staff. See BREITKOPF & HÄRTEL; PRINTING AND PUBLISHING OF MUSIC, 2a.

Moscheles, Ignaz (*b* Prague, 23 May 1794; *d* Leipzig, 10 March 1870). Bohemian-born pianist and composer of Jewish descent. After early lessons in Prague, he moved in 1808 to Vienna, studying with Albrechtsberger and Salieri. There he made Beethoven's acquaintance, making a piano arrangement of *Fidelio* for the publisher Artaria. From 1816, renowned as a brilliant virtuoso of expressive power, he toured Europe with a fast-growing output of both serious and fashionable compositions. In 1824 he taught the young Mendelssohn, of whom he became a close and lifelong friend. Married in 1825 to Charlotte Emden, he settled in London and began to be a dominant presence on the musical scene as pianist, composer, conductor, and co-director of the Philharmonic Society. He directed the first English performance of Beethoven's Mass in D and established the Historical Concerts series, performing Bach and Scarlatti on the harpsichord.

Moscheles continued to tour throughout Britain and Europe, playing on occasions with Chopin and Liszt. But towards 1840 he devoted himself more fully to teaching, and in 1846 he accepted Mendelssohn's invitation to become head of the piano department at the Leipzig Conservatory, where he remained active until his death. His pupils included Thalberg, Litolff, Sullivan, and Grieg.

Moscheles's fundamentally Classical style is characterized by rhythmic and melodic vitality and charm. His influential studies (1827) kept his name alive through the 20th century; but besides sonatas, fantasias, and variations he wrote some charming songs, eight piano concertos, a symphony, and some fine chamber music. His biography, based on his diaries, was published in 1872.   HR

Mosè in Egitto ('Moses in Egypt'). Opera in three acts by Rossini to a libretto by Andrea Leone Tottola after the Old Testament and Francesco Ringhieri's *L'Osiride* (1760) (Naples, 1818); the famous prayer, sung by the Israelites before they cross the Red Sea, was added for the 1819 Naples revival. Rossini revised it as **Moïse et Pharaon*.

Moses und Aron ('Moses and Aaron'). Opera in three acts by Schoenberg to his own libretto (Act III was not composed) (Zürich, 1957). 'The Dance Before the Golden Calf' (from Act II) was performed in concert in 1951, as were Acts I and II in 1954.

Mosolov, Aleksandr Vasil'yevich (*b* Kiev, 29 July/11 Aug. 1900; *d* Moscow, 11 July 1973). Russian composer. He studied composition with Glière, and later with Myaskovsky at the Moscow Conservatory. Although he composed operas, orchestral music, chamber works, and many songs and piano pieces, he is known in the West almost solely for his short orchestral piece *Zavod* (1926–8), usually translated as 'The Iron Foundry', though the word means simply 'factory' or 'works'. Intended as a symphonic interlude for his ballet *Stal'* ('Steel', not completed, though a suite was compiled in 1927), the work came to be regarded in its performances in the West—at Liège (1930) and the Hollywood Bowl (1932)—as a key example of modern, brutally realist Soviet music: the score incorporates a steel sheet, and other noises redolent of the workshop floor. It was this which quickly earned Mosolov the tag of **formalism* in the USSR: the piece occasionally surfaces as a noisy emblem of the experimental era in which it was created (see also FUTURISM).   GN/DN

   L. SITSKY, *Music of the Repressed Russian Avant-Garde, 1900–1929* (Westport, CT, 1994)

Mosonyi, Mihály [Brand, Michael] (*b* Boldogasszonyfalva [now Frauenkirchen, Austria], 4 Sept. 1814; *d* Pest, 31 Oct. 1870). Hungarian composer. He studied at the teachers' training college in Pozsony (now Bratislava, Slovakia) in the early 1830s, taking private lessons from the composer, pianist, and conductor Károly Turányi and teaching himself with Reicha's theoretical publications and Hummel's piano exercises. In 1835 he became music master in the household of Count Péter Pejachevich in the village of Rétfalu (now Osijek, Croatia), where he continued his autodidactic activities. In 1842 he set himself up in Pest as a teacher of piano and composition.

Mosonyi's life can be divided into two periods: until 1858, as Michael Brand, he wrote German Romantic music; and from 1859, when he changed his name to Mihály Mosonyi (after Moson, the county in which he had been born), he became a Hungarian nationalist. The change is reflected in his first two operas: *Kaiser Max auf der Martinswand* (1856–7) is in German and *Szép Ilonka* ('Pretty Helen', 1861) in Hungarian (a third opera, *Álmos*, was first performed only in 1934). He also composed two symphonies, six string quartets (1842–5) among other chamber pieces, choral music, and a generous amount of music for the piano. He is the third most important Hungarian composer of the 19th century after Liszt and Erkel.   MA

mosso (It.). 'Moved'; *più mosso*, 'more moved', i.e. quicker; *meno mosso*, 'less moved', i.e. slower.

Moszkowski, Moritz (*b* Breslau, 23 Aug. 1854; *d* Paris, 4 March 1925). German composer, pianist, and conductor. He showed outstanding talent as a pianist and entered the Dresden Conservatory at the age of 11, later studying at the Stern Conservatory in Berlin and Theodor Kullak's Neue Akademie der Tonkunst. Increasing stage fright, however, brought an end to a promising performing career, and he began to concentrate on conducting and composing. In the latter he developed a significant reputation, mainly as a fluent producer of brilliant piano salon music and arrangements, some of which (like *Étincelles* and various concert studies) remained in the repertory of such virtuosos as Horowitz for many years.   KH

motet. The most important form of polyphonic vocal music in the Middle Ages and Renaissance. Over its five centuries of existence there is no one definition that would apply throughout, but from the Renaissance onwards motets have normally had Latin sacred texts and have been designed to be sung during Catholic services.

The medieval motet evolved during the 13th century, when words (Fr.: *mots*) were added to the upper parts of *clausulae*—hence the label 'motetus' for such an upper part, a term that came to be applied to the entire piece. Whereas the lower part of such a composition (a tenor cantus firmus) moved in slower notes and was derived from a plainchant with Latin text, the upper part or parts might carry unrelated Latin or even French secular texts, and such parts were being freely invented

by about 1250. During the 14th century, the structural principle of *isorhythm was applied to the tenors of motets (in the works of Machaut, for example); up to the early 15th century, it was applied in some cases to all voices, as in Dunstaple's *Veni Sancte Spiritus* or Dufay's *Nuper rosarum flores*. The last named was written for the consecration of Florence Cathedral in 1436; indeed, many medieval motets were occasional in function, their several simultaneously sung texts 'glossing' on one another.

During the time of Dunstaple and Dufay, however, a freely composed type of motet, often in simple style and with a single text, came into being, and by the late 15th century the motet had become a choral setting of sacred works in four or more parts. Its choral texture was more unified than before, the individual voices moving at the same sort of pace (though the tenor cantus firmus in long notes can still be found in some of Josquin's motets). The practice of imitation, whereby each voice entered in turn with the same distinctive musical idea, became fundamental to the motet as to other types of polyphonic music; at the same time composers reflected a new humanist spirit in their careful choice of motet texts and attention to the way the words were enunciated in the music. The motet, unlike the mass, the psalm, the hymn, or the *Magnificat* setting, remained a form not strictly prescribed by the liturgy, but added (or substituted) at an appropriate place in the service on the appropriate day—in the same way as the English *anthem. The occasional 'ceremonial' type of motet survived too, and would be written or commissioned to mark any kind of event or honour any person, religious or otherwise.

The imitative motet style flowered with the generation after Josquin, and the device of 'pervading imitation', whereby successive phrases of the text are set to overlapping points of imitation, was developed by Gombert and refined by Palestrina and the other great late Renaissance polyphonists: Lassus, Byrd, and Victoria. Palestrina wrote some 250 motets, Lassus twice that number (including a fair proportion of occasional pieces), and Byrd published three collections of *Cantiones sacrae*—a Latin name often given to motets at that time. In Venice a polychoral type of motet developed with the Gabrielis, and Giovanni Gabrieli's later motets, which belong to the early years of the 17th century, are massive works scored for soloists, full choir, and instrumental ensemble (largely consisting of cornetts and sackbuts).

Although the old style (*stile antico) of Palestrina was still sometimes cultivated in motets written during the Baroque period (and even later), from 1600 onwards composers largely adopted the new styles for their motets, writing pieces for one or more voices with continuo and sometimes also including independent instrumental parts, usually for strings. This was especially so in Italy, where by 1700 the solo motet, a cantata-like piece for one voice and strings, often setting a picturesque non-liturgical text, had become the most common form of motet. German composers including Schütz adopted the modern 'affective' style in certain works, but retained a more contrapuntal, choral texture for others—a tradition that was continued in Bach's motets for choir and organ. In Louis XIV's France the *grand motet* for solo voices and chorus with instrumental accompaniment, produced for great occasions by such composers as Charpentier and Couperin, was one of the chief forms of sacred music.

Since the Baroque era motet composition has declined, though Mozart, Schumann, and Brahms all contributed to the genre, and there are 20th-century examples by Messaien and Poulenc. But motets from earlier centuries have continued to be heard in church services of many denominations, as anthems, or at appropriate points during Mass.   JRo/ER

📖 J. Roche, *North Italian Church Music in the Age of Monteverdi* (Oxford, 1984) · J. R. Mongrédien and Y. Ferraton (eds.), *Actes du Colloque international de musicologie sur Le Grand Motet français (1663–1792)* (Paris, 1986) · P. M. Lefferts, *The Motet in England in the Fourteenth Century* (Ann Arbor, MI, 1986) · W. Boetticher, *Geschichte der Motette* (Darmstadt, 1989) · F. Noske, *Music Bridging Divided Religions: The Motet in the Seventeenth-Century Dutch Republic* (Wilhelmshaven and New York, 1989) · M. Everist, *French Motets in the Thirteenth Century: Music, Poetry and Genre* (Cambridge, 1994) · D. Pesce (ed.), *Hearing the Motet: Essays on the Motet of the Middle Ages and Renaissance* (New York, 1997) · J. E. Cumming, *The Motet in the Age of Du Fay* (Cambridge, 1999)

motetus (Lat.). 1. 'Motet'.

2. A term used from the 13th century to the 15th for the voice part immediately above the tenor in motets.

Mother Goose. See Ma mère l'oye.

motif [motive]. A melodic, rhythmic musical unit which, as Schoenberg declared in *Fundamentals of Musical Composition* (1967), brings 'unity, relationship, coherence, logic, comprehensibility and fluency' to a composition, by means of its repetition and varied recurrence. A motif is the main building-block for themes and melodic lines, and as such will be no less apparent in a typical Bach fugue subject than in a large-scale symphony like Beethoven's Fifth, whose initial four-note motif has an evident generative role throughout the work, not just in the first movement.

Motivic working may be no less explicit in certain kinds of post-tonal music: Webern's 12-note Concerto for Nine Instruments op. 24 makes especially clear use of

three-note motifs throughout its first and third movements. And while compositional coherence can be achieved without any obvious motivic process at all, the capacity for motifs to suggest specific moods, characters, and even physical events, has given them a particular importance in large-scale dramatic compositions. Wagner's *leitmotifs (or 'leading motifs') are the most familiar examples of pithy musical ideas which not only bring an element of stability to the musical flow but contribute vitally to the comprehensible unfolding of the dramatic action.   AW

motion. The linear pattern of a melody. Progression by step, ascending or descending, is described as 'conjunct' motion, by leap as 'disjunct' motion. In part-writing, simultaneous voice parts moving in the same direction are said to be in 'similar' motion; if, in addition, they move by the same intervals they are in 'parallel' motion. If they move in opposite directions the motion is described as 'contrary'. If one part is stationary (on the same pitch) while another moves away from it the motion is 'oblique'.

Motiv (Ger.). 'Motif'.

moto (It.). 'Motion'; *con moto*, 'with motion', e.g. *andante con moto*, faster than *andante*; *moto precedente*, 'preceding motion', i.e. at the same speed as before.

moto perpetuo (It.). See perpetuum mobile.

motor rhythm. Insistently regular rhythmic repetition. Motor rhythm has been a feature of many musical styles, from the Baroque toccata onwards, but the metaphor of motoric, mechanistic reiteration is specifically a 20th-century one. It is most appropriate when the music's subject matter is explicitly industrial, or to do with the inhuman use of machines (Honegger's *Pacific 231*, 1923; Mosolov's *The Iron Foundry*, 1926–8).   AW

Motown [Tamla Motown]. An American record company formed by Berry Gordy, originally based in Detroit ('motor town'), to promote black *soul to the widest possible audience. Early recordings focused on vocal groups whose style was derived from the gospel tradition. Motown has produced many outstandingly successful performers, including Marvin Gaye, Stevie Wonder, the Supremes, and the Four Tops. It can now be seen as a distinctive part of black American culture.   KG

Mottl, Felix (Josef) (*b* Unter-St Veit, Vienna, 24 Aug. 1856; *d* Munich, 2 July 1911). Austrian conductor. He studied at the Vienna Conservatory with Bruckner, assisted with the first Wagner Festival at Bayreuth in

1876 and in 1881 became principal conductor of the Karlsruhe Philharmonic Society, with which for 23 years he gave pioneering performances of Wagner and Berlioz with the highest standards of execution and ensemble. From 1886 he was a guest conductor at Bayreuth, where he closely followed Wagner's own flexible style of performance. In 1903 he became music director of the Munich Opera. He composed stage works and songs, and edited vocal scores of Wagner's operas. JT

motto theme. A recurring theme, similar to Wagner's *leitmotif and Berlioz's *idée fixe*. The term is often used in connection with earlier music, however, for example with those 15th- and 16th-century masses that open each movement with an identical motif or motto (Ger.: *Hauptmotiv*, literally 'head-motif'). The 'motto arias' (Ger.: *Devisenarien*) of the 17th and 18th centuries, by such composers as Alessandro Scarlatti, Giovanni Legrenzi, and Antonio Cesti, worked on the same principle: a preliminary statement by the solo voice of the first motif of the melody would precede the instrumental introduction. Some of J. S. Bach's arias are of this type.

In later music the term can apply when a musical theme is given a symbolic significance, in much the same way as Berlioz's *idée fixe* symbolizes the 'loved one' in his *Symphonie fantastique*.

motu proprio (Lat., 'of his own motion'). A decree issued by the Pope concerning the internal administrative affairs of the Church. In writings on music, this term generally refers to *Tra le sollecitudini*, a *motu proprio* issued by Pope Pius X in 1903 laying down general principles for liturgical music. It promoted plainchant and 'classical' polyphony in the style of Palestrina, while strongly condemning church music of a theatrical nature. Nothing was to be omitted from the liturgy 'except where the rubrics allow the use of the organ to replace several verses of the text' (see VERSET). Instruments other than the organ were not to be used without the bishop's special permission. Boys, not women, should be used for soprano parts, and the ancient *scholae cantorum* (see SCHOLA CANTORUM) were to be revived.

This document was promulgated within the context of a broad effort to reform Catholic church music, embracing also the restoration of Gregorian chant by Solesmes and the Cecilian Movement. PS/ALI

Mouret, Jean-Joseph (*b* Avignon, 11 April 1682; *d* Charenton, 22 Dec. 1738). French composer and musical administrator. He was probably trained at the choir school of Avignon Cathedral but by 1707 he was in Paris, where he began his career as *maître de musique*

to the Marshal of Noailles; by 1711 he was in the service of the Duke and Duchess of Maine, first as *ordinaire* and then as *surintendant* in charge of the music for the duchess's celebrated Grandes Nuits de Sceaux (1714–15), for which he composed a *comédie lyrique*, *Le Mariage de Ragonde et de Colin*.

In 1714 Mouret was appointed director of the orchestra at the Paris Opéra, where his *opéra-ballet Les Fêtes, ou Le Triomphe de Thalie* was performed with great success. Apparently restless, he was soon contributing divertissements for the Comédie-Française; from 1717, when he was appointed composer-director of the Comédie-Italienne, until his death he produced about 140 for the Nouveau Théâtre Italien. In 1720 he acquired a court post as an *ordinaire de la chambre du roi*, but in 1728 he became artistic director of the Concert Spirituel, composing many motets and cantatas for performance there during his final decade.

At the height of his career Mouret's fortune suddenly deserted him: he lost his posts at the Concert Spirituel, Sceaux, and the Théâtre Italien in rapid succession between 1734 and 1737. Reduced to living on the charity of friends, he suffered a nervous breakdown and was committed to the asylum at Charenton. Mouret, the 'musicien de graces', was a highly successful regency composer: his works are elegant, charming, and essentially lightweight. His *Suitte de symphonies* (1729) foreshadowed the French symphony of the second half of the 18th century. WT/JAS

Moussorgsky, Modest Petrovich. See MUSORGSKY, MODEST PETROVICH.

mouth music. See PUIRT-A-BEUL; see also DIDDLING.

mouth organ. Generic term for various mouth-blown *free-reed instruments. See HARMONICA; SHENG; SHŌ.

mouthpiece. That part of a *wind instrument to which the player's mouth is applied. On single-reed instruments (e.g. the clarinet) this is a chambered beak to which the reed is attached. On *wind-cap instruments it is a cap protecting the reed. On *duct flutes it is the instrument's 'head'. On brass instruments it is the cup- or cone-shaped funnel to which the player places the lips. The mouthpiece's geometry is critical to the tuning and tone-quality of the instrument.

Mouton, Jean (*b* ?Samer, before 1459; *d* Saint Quentin, 30 Oct 1522). French church musician and composer. His early career was spent at the collegiate church of Notre Dame, Nesle, where he was *maître de chapelle* from 1483. Between 1494 and 1502 he held positions in Saint Omer, Amiens, and Grenoble, then joined the chapel of Anne of Brittany, wife of Louis XII. Following the queen's death he transferred to the king's chapel, composing works for occasions of state during the reigns of both Louis and his successor, François I. In 1515 he accompanied François on a diplomatic mission to Italy. By that date his music was already known south of the Alps, and was particularly admired by Pope Leo X.

Mouton is important for his church music. 15 masses and more than 100 motets by him survive, an output roughly equal to that of his almost exact contemporary, Josquin des Prez. There is, however, less variety of approach in Mouton's works than in Josquin's, and fewer pieces stand out for their idiosyncrasy. An exception is *Nesciens mater*, an exquisitely sonorous eight-voice work that is also a technical *tour de force*: four voice parts are answered in exact canon at the upper 5th by four further voices. Several of his masses are early examples of 'parody' technique, deriving their material from the entire texture of polyphonic models. The number of his surviving chansons is, by comparison, small. Mouton's pupils included one of the leading composers of the next generation, Adrian Willaert.

JM

mouvement (Fr.). 'Movement', either in the sense of motion, or in the derived sense of a section of a composition. It is often abbreviated to *mouvt*. Debussy and other composers sometimes used the term to imply a return to the original tempo after some deviation, such as a *rallentando*. *Mouvement perpétuel*, the same as **perpetuum mobile*.

mouvementé (Fr.). 'Animated'.

movable doh. See FIXED DOH.

movement (Fr.: *mouvement*; Ger.: *Satz*; It.: *movimento*, *tempo*). A term used in connection with musical forms (most commonly the sonata, symphony, concerto, string quartet, etc.) that consist of a number of substantial sections, each one being called a 'movement'. Each movement is, in theory, self-contained and in most cases is separated from the other sections by a brief pause.

The Classical symphony and sonata generally have four movements, which usually follow a conventional order: sonata form, slow, dance (e.g. minuet and trio, or scherzo), and finale (e.g. rondo or variations); the concerto has three—often ritornello–sonata form, slow, and finale (e.g. rondo or dance). The musical material in each movement is, with rare exceptions, independent of that in the rest of the work. During the 19th century, however, **cyclic form, in which some or all movements are related musically, became increasingly common in the symphony (e.g. Beethoven's Fifth and Ninth and Brahms's Third). Unconventional formats were also sometimes used: some composers instructed that

movements should be played continuously without pause (e.g. Schumann's Fourth Symphony and many of Beethoven's piano sonatas), or wrote substantial works in one long movement (e.g. Sibelius's Seventh Symphony). —/JBE

Moyzes, Alexander (*b* Klástor pod Znievom, nr Martin, 4 Sept. 1906; *d* Bratislava, 20 Nov. 1984). Slovak composer and teacher, son of the Slovak composer and teacher Mikuláš Moyzes (1872–1944). He went to the Prague Conservatory in 1925, eventually studying composition with Novák (1928–30). From 1929 he taught in Bratislava and from 1949 to 1978 was professor of composition at the city's Academy of Music and Dramatic Arts. Moyzes had a major impact on 20th-century Slovak music. His earlier style reflects an interest in Stravinsky, neo-classicism, and jazz. From the 1930s he also cultivated bigger forms, between 1929 and 1983 composing 12 symphonies marked by a fine developmental sense and the use of Slovak folksong.

JSM

Mozarabic chant. The 'Old Hispanic' Christian plainchant of the Spanish Church before 1058, the date of the reconquest of Toledo and the imposition of the Roman rite. Most of its surviving musical sources use untranscribable adiastematic neumes. A chapel in Toledo Cathedral continues to celebrate the Mozarabic liturgy as restored during the 15th century.

ALI

Mozart. Austro-German family of musicians.

(Johann Georg) **Leopold Mozart** (*b* Augsburg, 14 Nov. 1719; *d* Salzburg, 28 May 1787) studied philosophy in Salzburg but was expelled in 1739 for poor attendance. He defied the wishes of his family concerning his career in a manner eerily prophetic of his son. In 1747 he married Anna Maria Pertl; two of their seven children survived to adulthood, the elder being Maria Anna ('Nannerl'), the younger Wolfgang, an account of whose life and work is given separately below. Leopold was employed as a musical servant by Count Thurn-Valassina and Taxis, then from 1743 as a violinist by the Prince-Archbishop of Salzburg. He remained in this service until his death, becoming deputy Kapellmeister in 1763, just before taking his family abroad for three years. Such journeys, accepted by the Archbishop Schrattenbach, were curtailed when Archbishop Colloredo succeeded in 1772, and Leopold was sometimes threatened with dismissal.

His textbook on violin playing, *Versuch einer gründlichen Violinschule*, was published at Augsburg in 1756. It soon became the standard work on the subject, and was translated into Dutch and French; Leopold was thus well known in the community of musical theorists, which included F. W. Marpurg. Leopold composed a considerable amount of sacred music, and several symphonies and keyboard sonatas. Somewhat unjustly, he is mainly remembered as a composer for strange instruments, such as whistles and pistols, used in his 'Peasant Wedding' divertimento and 'Hunting' Symphony. By about 1771 he had gradually abandoned his own creative ambitions to nurture those of his son.

His training of the children can scarcely be faulted; his exploitation of them, however, has been criticized. It is uncertain how much money he made from their European travels, which may have endangered the children's health; but Wolfgang's development ultimately benefited from his knowledge of the world outside Salzburg. Leopold hoped his son's employment might secure his own old age; he disapproved of Wolfgang's aspirations to work independently of patronage, and still more of his marriage. Leopold died somewhat estranged from Wolfgang, having tried to educate other young talented musicians, but he had at least heard Haydn's pronouncement, 'Before God, and as an honest man, I tell you that your son is the greatest composer known to me'. The social circumstances that prevented full realization of the musical talent of Nannerl Mozart (1751–1829) cannot be entered into here; she was a fine keyboard player, but her abilities were lost to domesticity and her compositions do not survive. She too was hostile to Wolfgang's marriage, though she and his widow were later neighbours in Salzburg; she became an indispensable, if not unprejudiced, witness to her brother's early life.

Of the two sons of Wolfgang and Constanze Mozart who survived to adulthood the elder, Carl Thomas (1784–1858), was a minor official; the younger, Franz Xaver (1791–1844), who liked to call himself Wolfgang Amadeus—a spelling his father almost never used, preferring Amadè—was a pupil of the best masters (Hummel, Salieri, Vogler, and Albrechtsberger) but remained a minor composer, pianist, and music teacher in Vienna and Lemberg (now L'viv, Ukraine). Several instrumental and a few vocal compositions survive, including one of the variations on a waltz commissioned by Anton Diabelli. DA/JR

📖 R. HALLIWELL, *The Mozart Family: Four Lives in a Social Context* (Oxford, 1988)

Mozart, Wolfgang Amadeus (*see opposite page*)

Mozart and Salieri. Opera in one act by Rimsky-Korsakov to an abridged version of Aleksandr Pushkin's poem (1830) (Moscow, 1898).

mp. Abbreviation for *mezzopiano*; see MEZZO, MEZZA.

M.S. Abbreviation for (1) *mano sinistra* (It.), 'left hand'; (2) manuscript (also MS or Ms.).

Muck, Karl (*b* Darmstadt, 22 Oct. 1859; *d* Stuttgart, 3 March 1940). German conductor. He began his career as a pianist, making his debut in 1880. He then taught himself conducting and from 1884 conducted operas in Salzburg, Graz, and Brno. In 1886 he was appointed music director of the Landestheater in Prague, leaving in 1892 for the Berlin State Opera, where for 20 years he gained the reputation of a demanding and disciplined conductor of a wide repertory. He was music director of the Boston Symphony Orchestra (1912–17) and from 1901 to 1930 he conducted at Bayreuth, where his spaciously flexible performances were considered a yardstick. JT

Mudarra, Alonso (*b c.*1510; *d* Seville, 1 April 1580). Spanish vihuelist and composer. From 1546 until he died he worked at Seville Cathedral. His *Tres libros de musica en cifras para vihuela* (Seville, 1546) is an important collection of music for vihuela and guitar, and includes fantasias, tientos, dances, and transcriptions of Franco-Flemish polyphonic music, as well as some songs for solo voice and vihuela. WT

Mudge, Richard (*b* Bideford, *bapt.* 26 Dec. 1718; *d* Bedworth, 4 April 1763). English composer. He studied at Oxford University from 1735. After ordination he became curate at Great Packington, near Birmingham, and in 1756 rector of Bedworth. He was probably involved in the musical life of Packington Hall, seat of the Earl of Aylesford. He wrote a set of six concertos for two solo violins and strings (1749): in the first a solo trumpet is added; the sixth features a solo keyboard; and the set concludes with a string Adagio that leads into the canon *Non nobis Domine* formerly attributed to Byrd. WT/PL

Muette de Portici, La ('The Mute Girl of Portici'; *Masaniello, ou La Muette de Portici*). Opera in five acts by Auber to a libretto by Eugène Scribe and Germain Delavigne (Paris, 1828).

Muffat, Georg (*b* Mégève, *bapt.* 1 June 1653; *d* Passau, 23 Feb. 1704). French-born (Savoyard) German composer. After six years of study in Paris with Lully he became organist at Strasbourg Cathedral, and from 1678 was musical director to the Archbishop of Salzburg. Later travels took him first to Vienna and then to Rome, where he became acquainted with Corelli. Between 1682 and 1701 he published five collections of instrumental music, containing among them Italian-style concertos (in his *Armonico tributo*, 1682) and French-style orchestral suites (in his two-volume *Florilegium*, 1685, 1696). Corellian influence is evident in the structural patterns and shaping of the melodic material in the concertos, and that of Lully in the richness of the string textures in the suites. DA/BS

(*cont. on p. 811*)

Wolfgang Amadeus Mozart (1756–91)

The Austrian composer Wolfgang Amadeus Mozart was born in Salzburg on 27 January 1756 and died in Vienna on 5 December 1791. (His full given names were Johannes Chrysostomos Wolfgang Theophilus, Amadeus being a Latinization of the Greek Theophilus; but he usually styled himself 'Wolfgang Amadè Mozart'.)

Mozart is perhaps the most beloved of 'classical' composers, and the one whose life and times are most subject to mythical distortion. His inborn musical ability may have been equalled, but no other feted infant prodigy lived to achieve so much. His powers of assimilation were developed when, on the family's travels, he learnt to cultivate local tastes. At the same time he mastered the universal technical difficulties of musical composition, such as counterpoint, harmony, fugue, variation, instrumentation, and formal planning (of arias, ensembles, sonatas, and rondos); yet all this learning never suppressed the element of fantasy. Mozart excelled in virtually every genre and style. Expert in the composition of entertainment music, he also produced searching works that suggest a sombre, introspective, even fatalistic nature; a supreme exponent of ostensibly 'abstract' instrumental design, including such *tours de force* as the combination of fugue and sonata form, he was also a consummate dramatist. His output is not of equal quality in all forms and in all periods of his short life; but the absence, for instance, of any performed opera between 1775 and 1781, and the virtual absence of sacred music from 1781 to 1790, are explicable by circumstances, rather than by any change in compositional orientation.

The journeys of a prodigy

Surrounded by music in his home, Wolfgang insisted on participating at an early age in his sister Nannerl's lessons, picked out chords at the age of three, and at five improvised short pieces (mainly minuets), some of which were notated by his father. When he was six the family visited Munich and Vienna, where the children's precocity was much admired by the wealthy, including royalty. Leopold planned a more ambitious tour from 1763, when the family visited several German cities, and then ventured to Paris (where they were admired at

Versailles by Madame de Pompadour) and London, where they stayed for over a year, their visit prolonged by Leopold's illness, which gave the boy time to write his first symphonies. He encountered J. C. Bach and Abel, and his own musical style, founded on Italian rather than German premises, owed much to J. S. Bach's youngest son. He learnt by copying music, and adapted some of Bach's sonatas as piano concertos. The return journey was also prolonged by illness. They travelled back through the Low Countries, where Wolfgang published a set of six sonatas and probably composed his first operatic aria, by way of Paris.

Wolfgang was soon taken seriously as a composer in Salzburg, and received a number of commissions including a funeral cantata (*Grabmusik*), a German sacred drama (*Die Schuldigkeit des ersten Gebots*) and a Latin opera (*Apollo et Hyacinthus*), all in 1767. While little of this music is characteristic, its skill and emotional and rhetorical range are astonishing for an 11-year-old. On a second visit to Vienna in 1768 Mozart composed his first Italian and German operas, *La finta semplice* (an *opera buffa*) and *Bastien und Bastienne* (a *Singspiel* based on a French libretto). The latter may appear childlike, but this is a condition of the style; there is nothing inherently childish about anything Mozart wrote by this time, and *La finta semplice* was written to refute allegations that his works were actually composed by an adult. Intrigues, or Leopold's tactlessness, aborted the production. In this period Mozart also wrote several symphonies, and a trumpet concerto that is now lost.

Italy and Salzburg, 1769–77

Italy was the natural destination for a young musician in the mid-18th century eager to learn the craft and to make a reputation. To economize, Leopold left his wife and Nannerl behind. Father and son travelled the peninsula as far as Naples, performing, improvising, attending performances of new operas, and angling for an opera commission. In 1770 in Bologna the pair visited Padre Martini, for whom Mozart displayed his contrapuntal skills. In the Sistine Chapel in Rome he noted down Allegri's *Miserere* from memory, and he was appointed a Knight of the Golden Spur by the Pope (unlike Gluck, he rarely used the title). At the court in Milan, ruled by an Austrian archduke, Mozart composed *Mitridate*, his first *opera seria*, showing himself a mature master at 14—and an obliging one, ready to compose an aria three times to satisfy a singer.

Two further commissions for Milan followed, the wedding serenata *Ascanio in Alba* in 1771 and *Lucio Silla*, a magnificent *opera seria*, in 1772. In between, Mozart composed *Il sogno di Scipione* for the archbishop (May 1772), began a long series of church compositions for Salzburg, and wrote some string quartets. The series of works most loved by modern audiences begins with the solo cantata *Exsultate, jubilate*, composed for the principal castrato in *Lucio Silla*. By this time Mozart was a complete master in nearly every genre, and had the makings of an international reputation; but Maria Theresa advised her son, the archduke, not to employ 'useless people' like the Mozarts, particularly if it meant supporting a 'large family' (of four: despite her own large family, the empress probably intended no irony).

The premature end to his career in Italy threw Mozart back on Salzburg, where he was old enough for regular employment. Archbishop Colloredo was a typical authoritarian figure of the Enlightenment, who believed in discipline and obedience from his servants, and in short church services. Throughout the 1770s, nevertheless, dramatic works took second place to liturgical demands, including mass settings of increasing intensity, litanies, vespers, and a series of church sonatas. Among the most important earlier works of this period are the stormy symphony in G minor (K183/173dB) and particularly its successor in A major (K201/186a); many divertimentos and serenades, mainly for strings but some for wind; five violin concertos (1775), brilliant works of a more solid construction than popular works by Italian virtuosos; and in 1776–7 a group of piano concertos, including his first indisputable masterpiece in this form, in Eb (K271). In January 1775 an important *opera buffa* commission for Munich, *La finta giardiniera*, gained Mozart some renown, since it was translated into German and given in various theatres as a *Singspiel* (with spoken dialogue in place of recitative). Salzburg commissioned only one dramatic work, *Il re pastore*, performed as a 'serenata' (not fully staged) for the visit of Archduke Maximilian in April 1775.

Mannheim and Paris, 1777–8

For the first time, at 21, Mozart left home without his father. His mother accompanied him, while Leopold, intent on control, perhaps with the best of intentions, and perhaps with a view to publication, bombarded his son with letters of advice and paternal warning. After a brief and possibly amorous episode with a cousin in Augsburg, Mozart proceeded to Mannheim, where one of Europe's finest orchestras was employed by the reigning elector, Carl Theodor. Mozart befriended the musicians and longed for employment in this supportive environment; he also fell in love with a promising singer, Aloysia Weber (later Lange), and threatened to scupper Leopold's plans by taking her to Italy. Solo works for flute and oboe were composed, and a series of sonatas was begun, to be extended in Paris. But Mozart could not make himself indispensable; and urged by Leopold, he and his mother finally proceeded to Paris.

High hopes from this rich capital were soon dashed. Mozart was offered an organist's post at Versailles, and sensibly declined. The opera world was occupied by the famous 'quarrel' of the supporters of Gluck and Piccinni; Mozart received only a modest ballet commission (*Les Petits Riens*: the title says it all). He did, however, absorb a new operatic style at its source, a lesson turned to good effect in *Idomeneo*. He gained few pupils, and composed in the popular concertante manner (Concerto for flute and harp). A wind concertante for the Concert Spirituel was not performed and is lost; Mozart did, however, produce his 'Paris' Symphony (K297/300a), with some success, and within days of his mother's death. Leopold summoned his son home. Wolfgang, valuing independence more than the court organist's post at Salzburg, drifted back by way of Munich, where the Mannheim court had moved with Carl Theodor's elevation as Elector of Bavaria. But Aloysia was no longer interested in him. Indeed, at this nadir of his career, it seemed no one was interested in him; at no other time was there so little achievement to declare the superiority of his talent to sceptical contemporaries.

Salzburg and Munich

Mozart spent the next two years composing in masterly fashion in a cultural and political environment that he had come to despise. The *Sinfonia concertante* for violin and viola (K364/320d) is one of his most genial works; he wrote a couple of good symphonies (K318 in G and K319 in Bb) and two splendid masses in C major, the first better known under the title, which refers to a much later performance, of 'Coronation' Mass. He revised the elaborate incidental music for *Thamos, King of Egypt* and planned an opera for the National Singspiel in Vienna, but *Zaide* was never finished. Liberation came in the form of a commission from Munich, for a major opera in the mixed French and Italian styles of Traetta and Gluck. Mozart travelled there at the end of 1780 to finish the composition and supervise the performers.

Idomeneo is Mozart's first unequivocally great opera, albeit in a style he was unable to cultivate again. Its composition is richly documented by letters from Munich to his father, acting as intermediary to the Salzburg-based librettist G. B. Varesco. Mozart composed for singers and orchestral players he knew well and exercised a controlling hand, refusing the distinguished tenor Anton Raaff's request for an aria where it would be undramatic and insisting that the singer accept his relatively minor role in the quartet, perhaps the opera's finest number. In the end Mozart sacrificed several arias to reduce the final act to a manageable length; he also took pride in composing the ballet music.

Independence in Vienna

After three performances of *Idomeneo* Mozart was summoned to Vienna by the archbishop, who showed no interest in his employee's achievement. He was refused permission to give concerts, and by his own account he was humiliated and eventually kicked out by the court chamberlain. Left to fend for himself, Mozart did very well at first in spite of his father's foreboding, made worse when Mozart married Constanze Weber. An obvious source of income was giving piano lessons, never much to his taste; he had few composition pupils (one was the Englishman Thomas Attwood, whose exercises survive, with Mozart's corrections).

Mozart was asked to compose *Die Entführung aus dem Serail* (1782) for the National Singspiel, which was disbanded shortly afterwards; nevertheless it was his most successful opera, and under today's system of royalties would have spared him much pecuniary embarrassment. In this elaborately orchestrated opera, filled with long arias (notably that of the heroine Konstanze in which she defies torture), Mozart was showing off his abilities. When Emperor Joseph II said there were too many notes, he was not entirely wrong; the same might be said of another magnificent torso, the C minor Mass composed to celebrate his marriage, in which Constanze sang an aria almost as difficult as those Mozart wrote for her sister Aloysia.

While angling for a further opera commission, Mozart gained experience and contacts by writing insertion arias and ensembles for the new Italian opera troupe. Meanwhile he established a pattern of concert-giving in the homes of the wealthy, and in his own home. Central to this project was Mozart the virtuoso, who saw off his rival Clementi and in 1782–4 composed nine piano concertos (K413/387a, 414/385p, 415/387b, 449–51, 453, 456, and 459) for himself and his best pupils. He also embarked on the magnificent set of quartets dedicated to Joseph Haydn, which at least Leopold heard on his one visit to the household, together with the barnstorming D minor piano concerto K466, for which Mozart may have used a pedalboard. From this early Vienna period also comes his finest wind music, the great serenades (K361/370a, 375, and 388/384a), the 'Haffner' Symphony (K385), and more sonatas and variations.

Income from the sale of music and from concerts was ephemeral, however, and dependent on fashion. Larger sums from opera, or a regular income, were essential to sustain the fine household necessary to impress pupils and patrons. At times Mozart owned a carriage, and he took pleasure in billiards. The taste of luxury is not easily forgone, and the Mozarts became accustomed to spending what they had, establishing no savings. With Constanze's repeated pregnancies (two children survived, both boys) and illness, household expenses continually threatened to exceed income.

Opera buffa, 1786–90

Although Mozart continued to produce instrumental music over the next few years, his life is measured by the three great comic operas he wrote with Lorenzo Da Ponte. In 1785–6 he produced fewer, but still more magnificent, piano concertos, in D minor (K466), C major (K467), Eb (K482), A major (K488), C minor (K491), and C major (K503); only two, the 'Coronation' Concerto (K537) and one more in Bb (K595), were to follow. In 1786 Mozart was at last able to write for the Italian troupe, and following their successful production of Paisiello's *Il barbiere di Siviglia* he produced the sequel, *Le nozze di Figaro*. Not the least astonishing aspect of Mozart's career is that his first *opera buffa* for 11 years should become the definitive masterpiece of the genre. If Da Ponte carefully excised the political content of Beaumarchais's play, Mozart, it is sometimes argued, put it back. There is, however, no reason to attribute any revolutionary attitude to Mozart; *Figaro*'s success was not as great as that of operas by Paisiello and Martín y Soler, but it was revived three years on without demur. Politics probably played a lesser role than fashion in the decline of his fortunes. Meanwhile with *Figaro* Mozart scored his most unequivocal triumph in Prague, leading to the commission for *Don Giovanni* (for Prague Mozart also composed his last D major symphony, K504). Da Ponte depended for *Don Giovanni* on many earlier models, including Molière, while Mozart had in mind recent works of Gluck (*Alceste*) and Salieri (*La grotta di Trofonio*), which he outstripped not only in the terror inspired by the statue music, but in the elegance and beauty of his arias and the complexity of his ensembles and finales. The successful 1789 revival of *Figaro* led to the commission for *Così fan tutte*, a libretto intended for Salieri under the title 'The School for Lovers'; here Da Ponte's cynicism and symmetry are subverted by Mozart to form an opera ever more disturbing in its implications, and eternally beautiful in its music.

Mozart had become a freemason and composed some music for masonic ceremonies. In a period when the attraction of his concerts, and his status as the newly fashionable teacher, had faded, he had to earn money, and tried to sell published chamber music, often without success. A set of piano quartets was aborted after two masterpieces had been composed, and in 1787 he completed a set of three string quintets only by transcribing his C minor wind serenade; the others, in C major and G minor (K515 and 516), are among the towering masterpieces of chamber music. In 1788 he composed three astonishing symphonies, in E♭ (K543), G minor (K550), and C major (K551, the 'Jupiter'). It is inconceivable that Mozart composed them without performances in mind, yet none are documented. Lack of concrete information makes his income exceptionally hard to estimate, but he probably earned something by arranging Handel's oratorios for the private concerts of Baron van Swieten. In 1789 Mozart accompanied Prince Karl Lichnowsky to Berlin but earned little; sets of quartets and sonatas for the King of Prussia seem not to have been completed. It is to this period that the begging letters to his fellow-mason Michael Puchberg belong, and Mozart may have had a gambling debt to Lichnowsky, settled only after his death.

The year 1791

During 1790 Mozart's health was poor, and his compositional output declined. In 1791 his productivity rose astonishingly; exhaustion may have contributed to his premature death. In his last 12 months he produced two more superb string quintets, in D (K593) and E♭ (K614), his last piano concerto and the Clarinet Concerto, some masonic music, and two operas. *Die Zauberflöte* ('The Magic Flute') remains one of his best-loved works. It can be understood equally as an adventure story in pantomime style and as an allegory with strong masonic

overtones. It was composed for the suburban theatre troupe of Emanuel Schikaneder and is part of a popular tradition of magic operas which combine seriousness and farce; its repertory of musical styles ranges from the hieratic and neo-Baroque, through conventional operatic modes, to something like folksong in the songs of the bird-man Papageno. In contrast, *La clemenza di Tito* is a traditional *opera seria* by Metastasio, 'turned into a real opera', as Mozart noted, by the omission of a good deal of the plot and the inclusion of ensembles and choral finales. It was composed for the Prague coronation of Leopold II, and failed to please its first audience; though successfully performed for several years, seldom in authentic form, it has become the most neglected of Mozart's late operas.

During the summer Mozart was commissioned to compose a Requiem, which Count Walsegg planned to pass off as his own. It is uncertain whether Mozart really regarded this commission with superstitious awe, fearing that he had been poisoned. He died of natural causes, probably rheumatic fever, and was given a simple burial in accordance with the law (not a pauper's funeral). But the Requiem was unfinished and had to be completed by his associate Süssmayr as part of his widow's campaign to realize her late husband's assets, pay his debts, and bring up her children; the Requiem was not the only piece quietly completed by another hand and published to her profit. She lived until 1842, outliving her second husband, Georg Nikolaus Nissen, who wrote a slanted but indispensable biography of Mozart. JR

📖 C. GIANTURCO, *Mozart's Early Operas* (London, 1981) · E. ANDERSON (ed.), *The Letters of Mozart and his Family* (London, 3/1985) · A. STEPTOE, *The Mozart–Da Ponte Operas* (Oxford, 1988) · N. ZASLAW, *Mozart's Symphonies: Context, Performance Practice, Reception* (Oxford, 1989) · D. HEARTZ (with T. BAUMAN), *Mozart's Operas* (Berkeley, Los Angeles, and Oxford, 1990) · H. C. ROBBINS LANDON (ed.), *The Mozart Compendium: A Guide to Mozart's Life and Music* (London, 1990) · W. STAFFORD, *The Mozart Myths: A Critical Reassessment* (Stanford, CA, 1991) · M. SOLOMON, *Mozart: A Life* (London, 1995) · N. ZASLAW (ed.), *Mozart's Piano Concertos: Text, Context, Interpretation* (Ann Arbor, MI, 1996) · J. IRVING, *Mozart's Piano Sonatas: Contexts, Sources, Styles* (Cambridge, 1997) · J. ROSSELLI, *The Life of Mozart* (Cambridge, 1998) · C. EISEN, *W. A. Mozart* (Oxford, 2003)

Muffat, Gottlieb (*b* Passau, April 1690; *d* Vienna, 9 Dec. 1770). German composer, the son of Georg Muffat. A protégé of Fux, he worked in Vienna as organist to the imperial court, and from 1717 gave musical tuition to the royal children, including Maria Theresa. As an esteemed continuo player he was much in demand at the court chapel and theatre. His keyboard works include 72 old-style fugal versets (1726), 32 ricercars (before 1733), modelled on those of Frescobaldi, and 24 organ toccatas which call for virtuoso keyboard skills in performance. Most advanced in style are his six French suites for harpsichord (in his *Componimenti musicali*, *c*.1739), couched in the *galant* manner of Couperin, with titles for individual movements.   BS

Mühlfeld, Richard (Bernhard Herrmann) (*b* Salzungen, 28 Feb. 1856; *d* Meiningen, 1 June 1907). German clarinettist. Though initially a violinist, he became principal clarinettist of the Meiningen orchestra, 1879–1907. He served for a time as Bülow's assistant, but it was Fritz Steinbach who, in 1891, introduced Mühlfeld to the visiting Brahms, who promptly wrote his Clarinet Trio, Quintet, and two sonatas for Mühlfeld.   CF

Muldowney, Dominic (John) (*b* Southampton, 19 July 1952). English composer. His teachers included Jonathan Harvey, Harrison Birtwistle, Bernard Rands, and David Blake. He worked for many years as music director of the Royal National Theatre and has written much incidental and film music. His concert works, including concertos for violin (1989), percussion (1991), oboe (1992), and trumpet (1993), are notable for the intricacy of their rhythmic layering, but this never obscures a clarity and pointed feeling for textural balance that recall the theatre music of Stravinsky.   AW

Müller, Wenzel (*b* Trnava, 26 Sept. 1767; *d* Baden, 3 Aug. 1835). Austrian composer and conductor. He studied with Dittersdorf and gained youthful experience as a theatre musician. In Vienna from 1786, he became Kapellmeister at the Leopoldstadt theatre. There he improved standards and gave the theatre great importance in Viennese musical life. He composed some 250 works, and was the most successful of all early 19th-century Viennese popular composers. Some of his early *Singspiele* are enterprisingly orchestrated with quite extended finales (such as Act I of *Die Schwestern von Prag*), but it was in simpler songs, witty or tender, that he made his greatest appeal. Some of the works he wrote with Ferdinand Raimund remain in the Viennese repertory.   JW

Müller-Hartmann, Robert (*b* Hamburg, 11 Oct. 1884; *d* Dorking, 15 Dec. 1950). German composer, teacher, and writer. He studied in Berlin, returning to Hamburg to teach (in the conservatory), write criticism and articles, and compose. Appointed lecturer in theory at the University of Hamburg in 1923, he was forced to relinquish the post when the Nazis came to power; after four years spent teaching in Jewish institutes, he fled to England in 1937 and settled in Dorking, a respected neighbour of Vaughan Williams. Before 1933 Müller-Hartmann's orchestral music—which includes a symphony and other substantial works—was performed by conductors as prominent as Strauss and Muck; after his enforced flight not even his smaller-scale chamber music (three quartets and two violin sonatas, among other works), piano pieces, and songs re-established themselves, though there are now signs of renewed interest.   MA

Müller-Siemens, Detlev (*b* Hamburg, 30 July 1957). German composer and conductor. He studied at the Hamburg Academy of Music with Günter Friedrichs and Ligeti, and later at the Darmstadt summer courses and with Messiaen in Paris. He was Kapellmeister of the State Theatre, Freiburg (1986–8), and moved to Basle in 1989. His early works commented on the Austro-German Romantic tradition; those written later are more modernist in tone. His orchestral output includes concertos for piano (1981), viola (1984), horn (1990), and violin and viola (1993); he has also written chamber music and an Expressionist opera, *Die Menschen* (1990).   ABur

Mulliner Book (London, British Library, Add. 30593). A collection of keyboard music copied by the organist Thomas Mulliner in the mid-16th century. It contains a wide variety of music, mostly for organ and including fantasias and transcriptions of anthems and secular songs; among the composers represented are Redford, Tallis, and Blitheman. One of the most valuable sources for the keyboard repertory, it has been published in the *Musica britannica* series in an edition by Denis Stevens (1951, rev. 1954).

multimedia. See MIXED MEDIA.

multiphonics. Sounds in which more than one distinct pitch is discernible, but produced on instruments traditionally considered monophonic. Multiphonics usually occur when the single air column of an instrument is made to vibrate at several frequencies simultaneously. Woodwind multiphonics require specific *cross-fingering patterns which create several different tube-lengths; increased embouchure pressure and reed flexibility are also needed. Alternatively, a performer may simultaneously play one note and sing another, particularly on the flute and on brass instruments; in many cases more than two notes can result. Vocalists can produce multiphonics by inhaling or exhaling while producing a musical grunt, as required in Berio's *Sequenza III*.   SM

multiple stopping. See STOPPING.

Mumma, Gordon (*b* Framingham, MA, 30 March 1935). American composer. He studied at the University of Michigan (1952–3) and was co-founder there with Robert Ashley of the Cooperative Studio for Electronic Music (1958–66). The two then joined with David Behrman and Alvin Lucier in the Sonic Arts Union (1966–73), giving concerts of live electronic music. From this period dates *Hornpipe* (1967), which Mumma composed for himself to perform on electronically modulated horn; other scores of the same time were written for the choreographer Merce Cunningham. He later settled in California, teaching at Santa Cruz (from 1973) and Mills College (from 1981).   PG

Münch [Munch], Charles (*b* Strasbourg, 26 Sept. 1891; *d* Richmond, VA, 6 Nov. 1968). Alsatian conductor. He studied the violin and led the Leipzig Gewandhaus Orchestra (1926–33), where he was influenced by the conducting of Furtwängler and Walter. He made his conducting debut in Paris in 1932 and was soon in demand for his colourful and brilliant performances. From 1949 to 1962 he was music director of the Boston Symphony Orchestra, and in 1967 he founded the Orchestre de Paris. He was most admired for his sensitive interpretations of French music, and his performances were extremely volatile and spontaneous. He gave the premieres of works by composers including Honegger, Martinů, Barber, Copland, Ibert, Poulenc, Sessions, and Villa-Lobos.   JT

📖 P. OLIVIER, *Charles Munch: A Biography in Recordings* (Paris, 1987)

Mundy, John (*b c.*1555; *d* Windsor, 29 June 1630). English composer, son of William Mundy. He worked as an organist at St George's Chapel, Windsor, from *c.*1585 until his death. He was awarded the Oxford B.Mus. in 1586 and the D.Mus. in 1624. He wrote songs and anthems, and his *Songs and Psalms* (London, 1594) recall the conservative idiom of Byrd rather than the newer madrigalian spirit of Morley. Of his few keyboard pieces, included in the *Fitzwilliam Virginal Book, the fantasia *Faire Wether* is best known today, mainly because of its descriptive portrayal of 'Lightening' and 'Thunder'.   JM

Mundy, William (*b c.*1529; *d* ?London, 1591). English composer. He was the son of a sexton and musician of St Mary-at-Hill, London, and was head chorister at Westminster Abbey in 1543. He subsequently became a vicar choral at St Paul's, and from 1564 was a Gentleman of the Chapel Royal. He composed a substantial quantity of sacred music, including anthems for the Anglican Church and Latin antiphons for the Roman Catholic Church. He is best known today for a particularly beautiful anthem, *O Lord, the maker of all things*.   DA

Munrow, David (John) (*b* Birmingham, 12 Aug. 1942; *d* Chesham Bois, Bucks., 15 May 1976). English player of early wind instruments, writer, and broadcaster. His brief career as one of the finest virtuoso recorder players of his age began in 1967 with the founding of the Early Music Consort. He was an expert in medieval and Renaissance music, who communicated with a dynamic intensity his boundless enthusiasm for such music to concert and radio audiences.   CF

📖 D. MUNROW, *Instruments of the Middle Ages and Renaissance* (London, 1976) · 'Tributes to David Munrow', *Early Music*, 4 (1976), 376–80

Muradeli, Vano (*b* Gori, Georgia, 24 March/6 April 1908; *d* Tomsk, 14 Aug. 1970). Georgian composer. He studied music in Georgia, then in Moscow with his fellow-countryman Boris Shekhter (1900–61) and with Myaskovsky. He composed many songs, choruses, and some orchestral works (including two symphonies), but he is best known for his epic operas. In the first, *Velikaya druzhba* ('The Great Friendship'; Perm', 1947), featuring as the central character the real-life Komissar Sergo Ordzhonikidze, he sought to capture the prevailing mood of artistic *socialist realism, but the work was swiftly withdrawn. The Party resolution condemning it (1948) became a peg on which Andrey Zhdanov hung his purges of alleged *formalism in the music of Shostakovich, Prokofiev, and Khachaturian. With *Oktyabr'* ('October'; Moscow, 1964) Muradeli composed an opera that has remained in the Russian repertory. It was the first Soviet stage work to give the character of Lenin a small singing role.   GN/DN

Murail, Tristan (*b* Le Havre, 11 March 1947). French composer. He studied with Messiaen at the Paris Conservatoire, winning the 1971 Prix de Rome; in Rome he was influenced by Giacinto Scelsi. He co-founded the ensemble L'Itinéraire, in which he played the ondes martenot and synthesizers. He has undertaken research and lectured at IRCAM; in 1997 he moved to the USA to a teaching post at Columbia University in New York. Murail's music stems from his research into the acoustic properties of musical sound and how it is perceived; it is innovatory in its use of microtones and electronics, and fluid in form. It ranges from the rock-influenced *Random Access Memory* (1984) to the oratorio *Les Sept Paroles du Christ en croix* (1989), and includes the orchestral works *Gondwana* (1980) and *Time and Again* (1986).   ABur

Muris, Johannes de. See JOHANNES DE MURIS.

murky bass. An 18th-century name for bass accompaniments in *broken octaves. A well-known example of a murky bass occurs in the first movement of Beethoven's Pathétique Sonata.

Murrill, Herbert (Henry John) (*b* London, 11 May 1909; *d* London, 25 July 1952). English composer and administrator. He studied with Bowen, Stanley Marchant, and Alan Bush at the RAM (1925–8) and with W. H. Harris, Ernest Walker, and Hugh Allen at Oxford (1928–31), where he was organ scholar at Worcester College. In 1936 he joined the BBC, rising to become Head of Music in 1952. His music, strongly influenced by Stravinsky and the French neo-classicists (especially Poulenc), includes an opera *Man in Cage* (1930), several theatre scores, a ballet *Picnic* (1927), some exquisite partsongs, an often-sung Evening Service in E (1945), two cello concertos of 1935 and 1950 (the second dedicated to Casals), and a string quartet (1939). He also taught at the RAM from 1933 until his premature death.   PG/JDi

Murs, Jehan des. See JOHANNES DE MURIS.

muscadin. A dance occasionally encountered in English 16th- and 17th-century virginal music. It resembles the *allemande.

Muset, Colin (*fl c.*1200–50). French trouvère poet and composer. He is thought to have worked in the region around Lorraine. Of humble birth, he became a *jongleur* by profession; several of his songs allude to life as a wandering minstrel and to the instruments he played. Some 20 chansons have been attributed to him, but half of them survive without music.   JM

musette (Fr.). 1. A bellows-blown, often highly decorated, *bagpipe that achieved popularity in 17th- and early 18th-century French high society.

2. A simple bagpipe ('musette de Poitou') of the 17th century, which was always accompanied by the 'hautbois de Poitou', a *wind-cap shawm.

3. A small shawm or pastoral oboe, similar to the Breton *bombarde*, that was modified in the 19th century into a sopranino oboe, a 4th higher than the usual instrument, and used for dances (*bals musette*). When, late in the century, the accordion replaced it for the dances, it was further modified for amateurs into a simple instrument with from one to six keys. The number surviving in collections attests its popularity, though little is known of its use barely a century ago.

4. The French *accordion. In 'musette tuning' two reeds sound simultaneously for each note, one tuned slightly sharp, giving a tremolo effect.   —/JMo

5. A dance of a pastoral character similar to the *gavotte. It was especially popular at the courts of Louis XIV and Louis XV. Its music is characterized by a bagpipe-like drone in the bass and conjunct motion in the upper parts. Musettes were also composed for keyboard, for example by Couperin.   —/JBe

Musgrave, Thea (*b* Barnton, Midlothian, 27 May 1928). Scottish composer, resident in the USA. She studied at Edinburgh University and with Nadia Boulanger in Paris. Like many British composers of her generation she has sought a compromise between progressive and traditional methods, using serial and aleatory devices in works of essentially conventional genre and format. An impressive series of dramatic concertos from the late 1960s and early 70s (for orchestra, clarinet, horn, and viola) was followed by the opera *Mary, Queen of Scots* (1976). Among her later works, *The Seasons* for chamber orchestra (1988) is well-crafted music of distinctive character with many freshly imagined pictorial details.   PG/AW

musica colorata. See MUSICA FIGURATA.

Musica enchiriadis. 9th-century treatise, the earliest surviving source of polyphony; see ORGANUM. An important work, it was once thought to have been written by Hucbald of Saint-Amand.

musica ficta (Lat., 'false music'). Before 1600 musical sources rarely indicated all the required accidentals, so it was necessary for performers to add them. Today, editors and performers of early music often insert what they consider to be the missing accidentals, and these additions are commonly called *musica ficta*. The term should, however, be used in a more restricted sense than this. It properly refers to any accidentals (or chromatic alterations by the performer) that lie outside the standard system of notes used in the medieval and Renaissance periods. This standard system was based on three uniform interlocking scales, each of six notes, called *hexachords (see Ex. 1). The resulting scale, in its original untransposed position, already includes a B♭. This B♭ is occasionally described as *fa fictum* because

Ex. 1

ut re mi fa sol la
        ut re mi fa sol la
                ut re mi fa sol la

there is no key signature, but as part of the standard scale it is properly described as a *recta* ('right', 'straight') note.

It will be noticed that these hexachords all have the same intervallic structure consisting of a series of tones with a semitone between *mi* and *fa*. The cautioning against the sounding of a *mi* note against a *fa* note (see Ex. 2*a*) was one of the few universally agreed rules of *musica ficta*—at least in the 14th to 16th centuries, the period of greatest consensus on these matters—and it ensured that 5ths and octaves would be perfect. Another oft-stated rule was that a perfect 5th, unison, or octave should be approached by the nearest imperfect interval. By this it was intended that one (but only one) of the voices would move by step up or down a semitone (see Ex. 2*b*).

Ex. 2

(a)

(b)

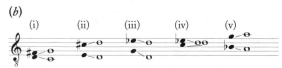

Most of the accidentals in this example (which has no key signature) are *ficta*, but Ex. 2*b* (v) uses the *recta* B to move to the octave, and theorists say that whenever possible these movements should be achieved by means of *recta* rather than *ficta* notes. Ex. 2*b* (ii) demonstrates another widespread application of *musica ficta*, the use of the sharpened leading note (C in this case) to proceed to the octave. However, this is only one of the possible solutions to the rule about proceeding to perfect intervals, and the so-called leading-note principle (i.e. sharpening the leading note) is rarely given the status of a requirement in theoretical writings.

All these rules are concerned with the movement of two or more voices: they are harmonic. Only in this context is the use of the interval of the augmented 4th (the tritone or *diabolus in musica*) proscribed, so the common view that *ficta* is designed to remove the

diabolus in musica whenever it occurs is a misleading one. The melodic use of the tritone is almost never specifically banned by the theorists.

Some writers do attempt rules for purely melodic application. In the 14th century Johannes de Muris, for example, stated that lower returning notes should be raised (see Ex. 3*a*). Perhaps the mostly widely quoted melodic 'rule' in modern discussions of *ficta* is 'Una nota super *la* / semper est canendum *fa*' ('a note above *la* is always sung *fa*'); this is designed to avoid the melodic tritone (see Ex. 3*b*). Whatever rules are given for *ficta* most writers agree that, in the case of polyphonic music, harmonic (vertical) considerations should take precedence over melodic (horizontal) ones.

Ex. 3

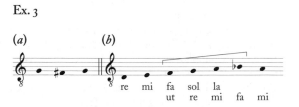

A further complication in the application of *ficta* comes where, in music before 1600, the lower part (or parts) has one more flat in its key signature than the upper part (or parts). It seems that the function of these 'partial signatures' (see KEY SIGNATURE) was not to state a 'key' but to transpose the basic hexachord scheme (see Ex. 1) and thus include more notes within the *recta* system. For example, if the whole scheme is transposed up a 4th or down a 5th (requiring a 'key signature' of one flat) then it can be seen (Ex. 4*a*) that E♭ as well as B♭ becomes a *recta* note.

A 'key signature' of two flats will provide A♭, E♭, and B♭ as *recta* notes, and so on (Ex. 4*b*). (In the original sources of music before 1600 it is usual for only flat 'key signatures' to be found.) Thus, in the extract shown in Ex. 5 all the added accidentals are *recta* notes, not *ficta*. It should also be noted that, in accordance with the rules, vertical relationships (see arrows) take precedence over horizontal ones (the leading C in the top voice is not sharpened). There are fierce debates among scholars over the meaning and application of *musica ficta* to early music and they cannot be summarized here.   AP

Ex. 4

Ex. 5

📖 M. Bent, 'Diatonic ficta', *Early Music History*, 4 (1984), 1–48 · N. Routley, 'A practical guide to musica ficta', *Early Music*, 13 (1985), 59–71 · K. Berger, *Musica Ficta* (Cambridge, 1987) · R. C. Wegman, 'Musica ficta', *Companion to Medieval and Renaissance Music*, ed. T. Knighton and D. Fallows (London, 1992), 265–74

musica figurata (Lat., 'figured music'). 1. Originally a term used to distinguish any type of polyphonic music from plainchant or other monophony. In the 15th and 16th centuries it was used to describe polyphony in which the voice parts are more florid and move more independently than in note-against-note counterpoint.

2. In a more specialist sense, *musica figurata* denotes the decorated, florid style found in the polyphony of some early Flemish composers (Ockeghem, Obrecht) as distinct from the generally more sober *musica reservata of Josquin and later composers. In this sense too the less common *musica colorata* is used, which may also suggest any sort of florid decoration (see coloratura). See also figural.

musical automata. Figures (e.g. singing birds) moving mechanically while a miniature organ imitates their sound are of great antiquity, being credited to inventors including Apollonius of Pergia (3rd century BC). True musical automata, as distinct from singing birds and cuckoo clocks, fall into two classes: animated androids that appear to perform on a musical instrument, and figures that move to the accompaniment of a mechanical instrument.

Examples of the first group include mechanical trumpeters, where a small barrel organ inside the android produces fanfares, and a remarkable mechanical harpsichordist made by H. L. Jaquet-Droz and now preserved in Neuchâtel, Switzerland. The second class is far larger and comprises church and town-hall clocks, where figures strike bells or move in procession at set hours, elaborate water-driven organs in 16th- and 17th-century gardens and grottoes, and small musical boxes (fashionable from the mid-18th century to the early 19th) with figures dancing, performing acrobatics, or other complex manoeuvres in time to the music.

(See also mechanical musical instruments and automatic musical instruments.)   JMo

musical bow. See bow, musical.

musical box. See mechanical musical instruments.

musical comedy, musical. These terms cover the principal 20th-century forms of musical theatre.

'Musical comedy' was generally used in 19th-century America to describe loosely constructed musical shows. Then, when the popularity of operetta and comic opera waned in the 1890s, the London impresario George Edwardes attached the term to a livelier type of show that featured fashionable modern dress and elements of burlesque and music hall as well as comic opera. The new genre attained major international success with Sidney Jones's *The Geisha* (1896), actually described as a 'musical play' to indicate its more substantial plot and score. British musical comedy flourished into the early 20th century in the shows of Lionel Monckton, Ivan Caryll, Leslie Stuart, and Paul Rubens.

American musical comedy developed along two lines. On the one hand were the extended vaudeville sketches of George M. Cohan, such as *Little Johnny Jones* (1904). On the other were adaptations of European shows, containing light interpolated songs with vernacular American lyrics. The American musical comedy form reached its zenith with the song-and-dance, boy-meets-girl works of the 1920s and 30s, with extractable popular songs. Prime examples are Jerome Kern's *Sally* (1920), George Gershwin's *Lady, Be Good!* (1924) and *Girl Crazy* (1930), Vincent Youmans's *No, No, Nanette* (1925), and Cole Porter's *Anything Goes* (1934).

At the same time, efforts were being made to replace the featherweight musical comedy plots with something more substantial. *Show Boat* (1927), with book and lyrics by Oscar Hammerstein II (1895–1960) and music by Jerome Kern, set a standard for integrating elements of drama, song, dance, and underscoring. The book of the satirical *Of Thee I Sing* (1931), with songs by the team of George and Ira Gershwin, won a Pulitzer Prize for Drama. The Gershwins then went on to create a 'Broadway opera' in *Porgy and Bess* (1935).

The great period of the American musical began with *Oklahoma!* (1943), with book and lyrics by Hammerstein and music by Richard Rodgers, whose further collaborations included *Carousel* (1945), *South Pacific* (1949), *The King and I* (1951), and *The Sound of Music* (1959). Other major successes were *Annie Get your Gun* (Irving Berlin, 1946), *Kiss me, Kate* (Cole Porter, 1948), *Guys and Dolls* (Frank Loesser, 1950), *My Fair Lady* (Alan Jay Lerner/Frederick Loewe, 1956), *The*

Music Man (Meredith Willson, 1957), and *West Side Story* (Stephen Sondheim/Leonard Bernstein, 1957).

After *Fiddler on the Roof* (Sheldon Harnick/Jerry Bock, 1964), *Hello, Dolly!* (Jerry Herman, 1964), *Sweet Charity* (Dorothy Fields/Cy Coleman, 1966), and *Cabaret* (Fred Ebb/John Kander, 1966), the musical became less important as a source of extractable songs. However, its emphasis on tighter and more serious books reached new heights in the works of the composer-lyricist Stephen Sondheim, for example *Sweeney Todd* (1979). At the same time, the need for long runs necessitated by the ever-increasing costs of spectacular production was met in the British musicals of Andrew Lloyd Webber, notably *Cats* (1981) and *The Phantom of the Opera* (1986). ALa

musical competitions. See COMPETITIONS IN MUSIC.

musical glasses. See GLASSES, MUSICAL.

Musical Joke, A (*Ein musikalischer Spass*). Mozart's Divertimento in F major K522 (1787), for two horns and strings, a parody of composers and performers of popular music.

Musical Offering (*Musicalisches Opfer*). Collection of 13 works (1747) by J. S. Bach (two ricercars, a trio sonata, and ten canons), some for keyboard and others for up to four instruments, on a theme by Frederick the Great, King of Prussia, to whom it is dedicated.

musical perception. See PSYCHOLOGY OF MUSIC, I.

musical saw. See SAW, MUSICAL.

musica mundana. See SPHERES, MUSIC OF THE.

musica reservata (Lat., 'reserved music'). A term used by theorists and other writers on music between 1552 and 1625. It is never clearly defined in the original sources and various interpretations of its meaning have been suggested by modern scholars. In Adrianus Petit Coclico's treatise *Compendium musices* (1552), 'musica reservata' refers to the musical expression of texts in the works of Josquin, and a similar meaning appears in the writing of Samuel Quickelberg (*c.*1560) applied to Lassus's penitential psalms. Other writers mention the term in connection with the use of the chromatic genus (Jean Taisnier, 1559; Eucharius Hoffman, 1582), which, according to Nicola Vicentino (1555), was reserved ('reservata') for a select, musically educated audience. In general, 'musica reservata' appears to designate a particularly expressive style of composition, without unnecessary ornamentation, in which attention is paid to word-setting, often involving chromaticism, modulations, enharmonic shifts, and techniques associated with *mannerism. DA/JBe

Musica transalpina. Title of two anthologies of Italian (i.e. transalpine) madrigals, with English words, edited by Nicholas Yonge and published in London by Thomas East. The first (1588) contains 57 madrigals, by Marenzio, Palestrina, Byrd, and Lassus, among others; the second (1597) contains 24, including examples by Ferrabosco, Marenzio, and Stefano Venturi. They were the first printed collections of Italian madrigals in England and had a great influence on English composers of the period.

music criticism. See CRITICISM OF MUSIC.

music drama. See GESAMTKUNSTWERK; OPERA, II; WAGNER, RICHARD.

music hall. An entertainment made up of comic, vocal, acrobatic, and miscellaneous acts. The heyday of music hall lasted from the 1850s to World War I. The name was simply a description of the places where the entertainment was given in its formative days—in specially adapted or specially constructed halls added to public houses to provide entertainment while the customers ate and drank. Later it acquired its own theatres, players, and repertory, and the name 'variety' was frequently used, with 'vaudeville' becoming more common in the USA. The era of music hall began when there was a sufficiently affluent working-class audience to support it and ended when supplanted by new popular entertainments such as radio, gramophone, and cinema.

Convivial song-and-supper rooms for male revellers were already established in London by the 1840s, among them Evans's in King Street, Covent Garden, the Coal Hole in the Strand, and the Cider Cellars in Maiden Lane. From the 1840s music halls began to spread: the Mogul Saloon opened in 1847, the Surrey Music Hall in 1848, the Canterbury Hall in 1849. By 1868 there were some 200 music halls in London and about 300 in the rest of the British Isles. Early entertainers included W. G. Ross, Sam Cowell (1820–64), Harry Clifton (1832–72), Alfred Vance (1838–88), Arthur Lloyd (1839–1904), George Leybourne (1842–84), and G. H. McDermott (1845–1933).

As the halls grew in popularity, their character changed. Larger Palace Theatres and Empire Theatres were built, and the term 'theatre of varieties' became a common billing as music hall developed from providing entertainment as an extra to the refreshments to being first and foremost a place of theatrical entertainment. In 1914 the consumption of food and drink in the auditorium was forbidden, marking the end of the music hall in its original form. Its stars were by then highly paid professionals, touring the English-speaking world. Following Charles Coborn (1852–1945) and Dan

Leno (1860–1904) came the likes of Eugene Stratton (1861–1918), Albert Chevalier (1861–1923), Gus Elen (1862–1940), Vesta Tilley (1864–1952), Little Tich (1867–1928), Harry Champion (1866–1942), Harry Fragson (1869–1914), George Robey (1869–1954), Marie Lloyd (1870–1922), Harry Lauder (1870–1950), Vesta Victoria (1873–1951), Florrie Forde (1874–1941), G. H. Elliott (1884–1962), and Ella Shields (1879–1952). Many of these lived into the age when the 'variety' theatre finally succumbed to the dominance of radio and film entertainment.

The music-hall song was a mass-produced article, with a select few numbers achieving immortality by virtue of an inspired tune or a good catchphrase. Early songs took their tunes and ideas from established folksongs, and the music-hall song became the first corpus of commercially inspired song to cater for working-class tastes. The composers and lyricists are scarcely remembered today, but the music-hall song set the wheels of *Tin Pan Alley in motion, established the practice of song plugging, and founded a new industry. Something of the music-hall spirit has survived in certain of today's television acts and in working men's clubs.

See also POPULAR MUSIC.   PGᴀ/ALᴀ

Musicians' Benevolent Fund. British charity founded in 1921 as a fund in memory of the tenor Gervase Elwes (1866–1921); it helps musicians in various ways and maintains three residential homes.

Musick's Monument. A book by Thomas Mace, published in London in 1676, giving valuable information on English music in the mid-17th century. It includes several suites and pieces for viol.

music of the spheres. See SPHERES, MUSIC OF THE.

musicology. Research in music. The 1993 *Frascati Manual* defines research as 'Creative work undertaken on a systematic basis in order to increase the stock of knowledge, including knowledge of man, culture and society and the use of this stock of knowledge to devise new applications'. Many would prefer the word 'knowledge' here to be replaced by 'understanding'. But in all other ways that definition applies well to research in music. It helps to stress that musicology, so defined, may cover a very wide range of activities: acoustics, sociology, perception, ethnology, linguistics, logic, philosophy, and many other activities alongside the more traditional kinds of musicological study cultivated for much of the 20th century in English-speaking countries—primarily music history, source studies, criticism, and musical analysis.

As with most other research, musicology nearly always impinges on other disciplines. On the very sim-

plest level, for example, the seeker of new documents about a composer must understand those documents with the full sophistication and techniques developed by historians; or the analyst investigating a song must read its text in the light of the latest literary and philological studies. And just as there is therefore very little musicology that is not in some sense interdisciplinary, there is much serious musicological work being done by scholars who do not think of themselves as musicians at all. Paradoxically, as the discipline of musicology becomes more specialized there are increasing numbers of musicologists who are employed or prefer to see themselves as something else—philosophers, acousticians, social scientists, or whatever. So the broader picture begins to return to the situation before the mid-19th century when there were no university music faculties to facilitate this research and it was all done either by erudite professional musicians or by musically informed specialists in other subjects.

The features that perhaps distinguish musicology from other kinds of writing about music are that it should be systematic and should be founded on a full understanding of previous work on the topic being explored ('increase the stock of knowledge'). Thus there are many worthwhile and thoroughly musical books and articles about music that would not, according to this definition, count as musicology.

On the other hand, many writings from the time of Plato onwards could and should be called musicology. Most particularly it is hard to deny the word as an adequate description of Marin Mersenne's enormous and encyclopedic *Harmonie universelle* (1636–7) or of the first two great histories of music, those of John Hawkins (1776) and Charles Burney (1776–89), both of them encompassing an enormous body of research and seeking to create a comprehensive and critical survey of musical history.

The formalizing of the discipline may begin with the foundation of the Dutch Vereniging voor Nederlandse Muziekgeschiedenis in 1868 and of the English Musical Association in 1874 (initially concerned more with the science than with the history of music). But modern musicology is often thought to have begun in the mid-19th century with the start of the Bach-Gesellschaft edition of J. S. Bach's music in 1851 and of Friedrich Chrysander's *Jahrbuch für musikalische Wissenschaft* in 1865. A famous article by Guido Adler in 1885 defined the scope, method, and aim of musicology ('Umfang, Methode und Ziel der Musikwissenschaft') in a way that still holds good—though he intriguingly confined the word 'Musikologie' (which he may have coined) to the study of what we would now call ethnomusicology, preferring for the entire discipline the word that is still used in Germany, 'Musikwissenschaft'. That word was first used by Johann Bernhard Logier (1777–1846) in 1827 and received its official acceptance in the title of the journal that carried Adler's article in its first issue, the *Vierteljahrsschrift für Musikwissenschaft*.

But the formal study of music was central to the curricula of the very earliest European universities as part of the 'Quadrivium' (alongside arithmetic, geometry, and astronomy), partly because the Pythagorean insight into the fundamental simplicity of musical sound was thought to be a paradigm for all the natural sciences and therefore of the structure of the universe. If the aspects of music studied in the medieval universities are (for today's historian) frustratingly short of relevance to our understanding of the training and practice of composers and performers at the time, perhaps it is wise to remember that the same is true of much present-day musicology; and in neither case does that diminish the importance of the study, since the value and scope of any research need to be seen independently of its direct applications to a particular body of people.

In England, doctorates in music were awarded from the early 16th century onwards, and Oxford had a chair in music from the 17th century; but until the 20th century these concerned only composition (in which respect England seems to have been unique). German universities had directors of music from the late 18th century: J. N. Forkel held such a position at Göttingen from 1779 and gave lectures. The situation changed with Eduard Hanslick's appointment to a chair of music history and aesthetics in Vienna (1861), soon followed by similar appointments in Berlin (Heinrich Bellermann), Prague (A. W. Ambros), and Strasbourg (Gustav Jacobsthal). Since then musicology has grown to become a serious subject of study in universities throughout the world.   DF

music on the Internet. The Internet, otherwise known as the World Wide Web, has developed at a remarkable speed since the mid-1990s to become the most significant electronic communications network of the new millennium. Its impact on the dissemination of recorded music has already been considerable, displacing traditional modes of recording and broadcasting and raising fundamental issues of ownership and copyright. In essence the Internet has opened up the possibility of transmitting information of any origin between two or more locations anywhere in the world, providing that it can be suitably encoded and decoded in a digital format. In the case of music the technical specifications to be met are very demanding, both in terms of the rate at which the audio spectrum must be digitally sampled to ensure that all the necessary frequency components are captured for transmission, and

in terms of the numerical accuracy of the individual samples. Fortunately the development of digital recording and broadcasting technology has made it possible to upgrade personal computers and related devices to a full multimedia specification at minimal extra cost, and such capabilities are now the rule rather than the exception.

Music audio, however, creates some major practical difficulties for the Internet itself. If transmitted as raw data, the quantities of digital information that have to be transmitted for every second of high-quality sound are considerable, creating significant congestion as the information flows freely across the network of data links which constitute the World Wide Web. Partial solutions to this problem have been devised through the design of special data-compression techniques that reduce the amount of information actually transmitted by permanently stripping out spectral components which the ear may not readily detect. Although the best of these achieve a quality of reproduction that is almost indistinguishable from the original, others are less successful. The most widely used consumer format, MP3, has led to the production of portable MP3 players which can store and reproduce up to an hour or more of MP3-coded music, thus creating an attractive alternative to the traditional compact disc.

From a commercial viewpoint, the popularity of the Internet is seen as a major threat to the record industry, since it is almost impossible to regulate its use. As a result there is a strong temptation to use the network to disseminate and acquire pirated versions of recordings at little or no cost. Techniques of encryption are available that will allow record companies to distribute recordings electronically to paying customers, and moreover ensure that the downloaded information cannot easily be copied without further payment. The practical difficulties of implementing such encryption systems, however, have conspired for the most part to defeat such initiatives, and the viability of the Internet as an alternative medium for record sales has yet to be fully assured.   PM

music-printing and -publishing. See PRINTING AND PUBLISHING OF MUSIC.

music theatre. A term used since the 1960s to designate musical works (usually for restricted forces) which, though not staged in the conventional sense, incorporate such theatrical elements as costumes, gesture, and platform movement. While works fitting this definition—Stravinsky's *Histoire du soldat* (1918) and *Renard* (1922), and Schoenberg's *Pierrot lunaire* (1912), for example—can be traced to the early part of the 20th century, it was in the 1960s and 70s that the genre attained particular prominence, for reasons partly aesthetic (as composers sought to integrate the physical aspects of performance into a total artistic conception), partly ideological (opera being viewed by the avant-garde as an entrenched, bourgeois institution), and partly practical (in view of the prohibitive cost of mounting full-scale theatrical productions). Composers of music theatre have derived inspiration variously from contemporary, non-narrative theatre (Berio's *Passaggio*, 1963), ancient vernacular sources (an English Mummers' play in Birtwistle's *Down by the Greenwood Side*, 1969), and non-Western traditions (Japanese nō drama in Britten's 'church parable' *Curlew River*, 1964). Instrumentalists often find themselves in the same performance space as singers, becoming equal participants with them in the drama. In Maxwell Davies's *Eight Songs for a Mad King* (1969), for instance, costumed players in cages on the platform represent the birds that become the objects of the king's hysteria (the latter manifested in a disturbingly wide range of vocalization from a virtuoso actor-singer).

Other works have been concerned less with invoking an external dramatic situation than with exploring the theatrical potential latent in the act of performance itself. Cage had uncovered something of that potential in his works of the 1950s, nowhere more so than in the 'silent' *4′ 33″* (1952), essentially a performance stripped of its music. Theatre of a different nature is created out of the interaction between performers in such works as Kagel's *Match* (1965), a frenetic duel between two cellists, refereed by a solo percussionist. Berio's *Recital I* (1972) takes the song recital as a starting-point for both musical content and dramatic context: the work, which allows for the interpolation of freely chosen extracts from the vocal literature, charts a singer's psychological disintegration during the course of a performance. Other compositions assume a ritualistic character through the movement of players on the platform: in Boulez's *Domaines* (1968) the solo clarinettist wanders between different instrumental groups (an idea taken up again by Carter in his Clarinet Concerto, 1997), while in a number of works by Birtwistle, including the tellingly titled *Secret Theatre* (1984), an instrument's new position is designed to emphasize both a change in its musical material and the bearing of that change on the musical structure as a whole.

Although interest in music theatre as such seemed to decline after the mid-1970s, many subsequent operatic ventures owed a good deal to its methods and ideals. In the operas that make up Stockhausen's cycle-in-progress *Licht*, the debt is evident in the threefold representation of each principal character by a singer, a dancer, and an instrumentalist. Moreover, most of the component scenes qualify as music-theatre pieces in their own right, being performable independently in concert, though still with their movement and costumes.   CWi

music therapy. The use of the elements of sound and music within a developing relationship between patient and therapist to bring about improvements in physical, mental, social, emotional, and spiritual well-being. It is both an art and a science. The power of music as a healing force to alleviate illness and distress has been used extensively in many cultures, but it was only during the second half of the 20th century that music therapy evolved as a specific discipline and paramedical profession. Increasingly recognized by governmental bodies, music therapy is now state registered in the UK as a profession supplementary to medicine.

Music therapists work with children and adults of all ages. Spontaneous emotional, as well as learnt, responses to music are seemingly stored at a very deep level within the brain. Even patients with diffuse brain damage appear able to respond to it, for example by singing melodic fragments with clear rhythm and intonation. The communicative potential of music can bypass speech for children and adults with severe language and emotional problems. Instruments can become indirect means of communication for autistic children. The use of rhythm as a structural organizer and energizer is effective in helping people with physical disabilities to gain control and organization in their movements. The depressed or anxious person can use music to release tension, to gain access to and express a wide range of emotions, and to boost self-esteem. The terminally ill adult can both listen to music to decrease levels of tension and play instruments to increase levels of energy and sense of control.

Music therapists work in many settings: hospitals, hospices, schools, nurseries, and other community-based centres, or privately; they also work with people with visual or hearing impairments and people in prison. Music therapy can be considered as an alternative to a course of psychotherapy or counselling, and musicians themselves are benefiting from music therapy to alleviate both physical and mental stress.

During individual or group work, patients, either as participants or as listeners, make connections between their emotions and the music experienced. The externalization of inner feelings in musical forms and gestures can be clearly observed in improvisational music therapy. Here individual patients or groups of patients are encouraged to create their own music, usually using a range of tuned and untuned percussion instruments. The specifically trained therapist engages with various kinds of music presented by the patient, the musical processes ranging from work with single sounds to complex rhythmic and melodic interaction.

Therapists adapt their own music in supporting the patient's music and may also work with the patient in joint listening.

Music therapists underpin their practice with reference to a variety of treatment models and philosophical orientations. Some music therapists frame their work within a detailed analysis of the musical elements (rhythm, melody, harmony, etc.), observing changes within the music as mirrored in changes outside the sessions. Others draw on principles and theories from the related fields of psychoanalysis, early infant development, humanistic and transpersonal psychologies, behaviour and cognitive therapy, and medicine.   LB

📖 P. Nordoff and C. Robbins, *Creative Music Therapy* (New York, 1977) · L. Bunt, *Music Therapy: An Art Beyond Words* (London, 1994) · T. Wigram, B. Saperston, and R. West (eds.), *The Art and Science of Music Therapy: A Handbook* (London, 1995) · P. Gouk (ed.), *Musical Healing in Cultural Contexts* (Aldershot, 2000) · P. Horden (ed.), *Music as Medicine: The History of Music Therapy Since Antiquity* (Aldershot, 2000)

Musikalische Exequien. Work by Schütz for solo voices, chorus, and continuo, composed in 1636 for the funeral of Prince Heinrich Postumus of Reuss; the texts are those inscribed on the prince's coffin, the funeral oration, and the *Nunc dimittis* with biblical passages.

Musikalischer Spass, Ein. See Musical Joke, A.

musique concrète (Fr.). A kind of *electroacoustic music which uses natural sounds, not electronically generated tones, as raw material. The recordings—of machinery, running water, musical instruments, or whatever—are transformed by electronic means and joined to form a composition. Pierre *Schaeffer coined the term in 1948 to describe his first electronic studies.

musique mesurée (Fr., 'measured music'). A French literary and musical experiment of the late 16th century. It began as an attempt to apply to contemporary French verse the principles of metrical accentuation found in classical poetry (*vers mesurés à l'antique*) with the aim of recreating the legendary powers and 'effects' of ancient music. *Musique mesurée* was devised by Jean-Antoine de Baïf and the group of poets known as the Pléiade who enlisted the help of contemporary musicians (including Claude Le Jeune) to transfer these poetic principles to vocal music—*musique mesurée à l'antique*.

The process was simple: composers strictly followed the metre of the verse, setting long, accented syllables as minims, and short, unaccented ones as crotchets. This resulted in irregular phrases and bar-lengths, with no regular pulse, and as a result much of this music has no time signature and is left unbarred. Texts were set syllabically and homophonically so that the words were as clear as possible. Baïf tried to further his project by founding an Académie de Poésie et de Musique (1570), but in spite of royal support it lasted only about three years. The prime importance of *musique mesurée* lies not in the music composed with it in mind, but in the transference of many of its characteristic features to the *air de cour, which in turn influenced Lully's recitative style.   —/JBe

Musorgsky, Modest Petrovich (*b* Karevo, Pskov district, 9/21 March 1839; *d* St Petersburg, 28 March 1881). Russian composer. He was born into a noble family. His mother taught him the piano and he showed remarkable early talent, playing a Field concerto to an audience when he was nine. In 1849 he was sent to school in St Petersburg, and in 1852 he entered Cadet School, receiving his commission four years later. He became an able pianist under the tuition of Anton Herke, though his talents were on display at balls and other social gatherings rather than on the concert platform; his first published composition, the *Porte-enseigne Polka* (1852), reflects these musical activities.

After two years as an officer Musorgsky resigned his commission in order to dedicate himself to music, a change of direction inspired by his new circle of friends: Balakirev, Borodin, and Cui (together with Rimsky-Korsakov, they would soon become known as The Five, the pioneering core of the Russian nationalist school). The critic Vladimir Stasov, effectively The Five's ideologist, had great influence on Musorgsky's aesthetics and was the first to offer him support in the press. Musorgsky's public debut as a composer was in 1860, when his single-movement orchestral Scherzo was conducted by Anton Rubinstein at a concert of the newly founded Russian Music Society; this was an important juncture in his career, but the piece contains nothing characteristic of the mature composer.

During the next two years Musorgsky placed himself under Balakirev's guidance to acquire a more solid grounding in theory and the fundamentals of composition, trying his hand at exercises and producing fragments of sonatas and quartets, and even part of an opera based on Gustave Flaubert's *Salammbô*. Unlike his friend Rimsky-Korsakov, however, Musorgsky showed no deference to traditional compositional techniques: he studied what he thought would be useful, but readily set this knowledge aside for the sake of imaginative novel harmonies or textures. Where some critics, like Stasov, found his approach daring and progressive, others merely complained of the solecisms that littered his scores.

Musorgsky had set out on his new career with the security of a comfortable income from the family estate. In 1861, however, the abolition of serfdom set him on a path towards urban poverty. He initially compromised by taking clerical jobs for a few hours a day, insufficient to raise his income substantially but leaving him with time to compose. Gradually he became dependent on his brother and a few close friends for his food and lodgings. From the mid-1870s he found hospitality within his circle of drinking companions; although this met his day-to-day needs, it led to the excessive alcohol consumption which was eventually to cause his death. While his troubles were to some extent self-inflicted, the abolition of serfdom was the initial cause of his decline. Musorgsky, however, retained his liberal and humane outlook and never blamed his misfortunes on the 1861 reform—on the contrary, he even moved further leftwards in the early 1860s, joining a circle of young radicals who formed a commune and lived in shared quarters, as prescribed by their source of inspiration, Nikolay Chernïshevsky's novel *What is to be done?*.

For Musorgsky this period was his second education, when he read extensively in history and philosophy; thus armed with a critical and independent intellect, he sought to develop his own aesthetic doctrines and to realize them in his compositions (though the result was by no means incompatible with Stasov's ideas). He now desired to create an art of radical innovation (hence his slogan 'Towards new shores!') which would be independent of Germanic models ('formed on Russian fields, raised on Russian bread'). In texted works he strove for a realism that would reflect the patterns of spoken Russian, eschewing the symmetries and regularities of Italian opera. All these ideas were embodied in his songs of the 1860s. *Svetik Savishna* ('Darling Savishna', 1865), for example, is far removed from the world of the Russian romance: the words concern the desperation of a village idiot besotted with a beautiful peasant woman. Set in monotonous pleading phrases, it is powerful and emotionally disturbing, and it astonished his friends for its spurning of traditional subject matter and traditional means of expression. The first orchestral work to display Musorgsky's new approach was the celebrated *Ivanova noch' na Lïsoy gore* ('Night on the Bare Mountain', 1867), which he described thus: 'The form and character . . . is Russian and original. Its tone is ardent and disorderly'.

In 1868 Musorgsky embarked on a more ambitious project, the opera *Zhenit'ba* ('Marriage'), which was to be a word-for-word setting of Gogol's prose drama of the same name. However, the reproduction of natural speech rhythm and even intonation proved too confining for Musorgsky (he said he felt caged), and he abandoned the work after one act. In his next operatic project he allowed himself greater creative freedom, and the result is internationally recognized as one of the great classics: *Boris Godunov*. The text is based on Pushkin's play, and although there are recitative-like passages for both soloists and choir that reflect natural speech patterns to a high degree, Musorgsky allowed vestiges of operatic tradition to emerge: the drama is occasionally interrupted by set numbers, and Boris's coronation scene is a spectacular, static tableau in the manner of French grand opera.

The first version of *Boris Godunov* (1870) was rejected by the Imperial Theatres on the grounds that it lacked a prima donna role. Musorgsky, undaunted, welcomed various proposed changes, adding many more new ideas of his own. The second version was finished in 1872; between Acts II and III a new third act was inserted replete with dances and a love duet, thus introducing conventions the first version had studiously avoided. The role of Boris was altered in the direction of more overt emotionality: in Act II, instead of Pushkin's restrained pentameters, expressed in emotionally neutral recitative, Boris now has long, poignant melodic lines; the Terem scene, in which Boris crumbles under the weight of his guilt, was further heightened to become powerfully moving. The original scene at St Basil's, which had included an apathetic crowd, was replaced by the Kromy scene, where the crowd is cruel and violent. Its final moment introduced a new moment of epic symbolism: amid the chaos, the Simpleton utters a lament for the fate of Russia.

The premiere of *Boris Godunov* in 1874 was Musorgsky's greatest public triumph, and the opera became emblematic of the young, liberal intelligentsia. Within The Five, however, dissension began to appear: Cui, though the least prominent composer, was an eminent critic, and his praise for the opera was so hedged about by qualifications that the impression he gave was sour; in spite of the changes Musorgsky had made, even his closest associates found his originality difficult to absorb.

In the wake of *Boris*'s success Musorgsky enjoyed a period of great creative energy: he composed the cycle of piano pieces *Kartinki s vïstavki* ('Pictures at an Exhibition', 1874), dedicated to the memory of his friend, Victor Hartmann, whose pictures supplied the inspiration for successive movements. The song cycles *Bez solntsa* ('Sunless', 1874) and *Pesni i plyaski smerti* ('Songs and Dances of Death', 1877) resulted from a collaboration between Musorgsky and another of his friends, the poet Arseny Golenishchev-Kutuzov. Musorgsky was also at work on two operatic projects during this period: at Stasov's suggestion he compiled a libretto for a historical drama, *Khovanshchina*, using only historical sources (there was no literary model); a humorous short story by Gogol provided the plot for the comic opera *Sorochinskaya yarmarka* ('Sorochintsy Fair'). Both works were left incomplete, victims of the composer's increasingly chaotic way of life during the late 1870s; by this stage even those, like Stasov, who had previously tolerated his excesses and tended to his needs now gave up on him.

In 1879 Musorgsky made a final attempt to put his life in order: he agreed to act as accompanist for Dar'ya Leonova, a talented but ageing singer, as she undertook a major Russian tour. This employment initially raised his spirits—his own songs were received warmly during the recitals—but unfortunately the modest financial rewards were insufficient for him. In February 1881 he suffered a seizure caused by his alcoholism; he was admitted to hospital but never recovered. The best-known portrait of Musorgsky, dishevelled and ill, was painted by Il'ya Repin during these final days.

Of all the major composers of the 19th century, only Musorgsky bequeathed most of his musical legacy— and therefore his posthumous reputation—to the hands of later editors, who would have to compose endings, orchestrate, and graft competing versions into single, performable works. Even *Boris Godunov* and *Night on the Bare Mountain*, though performed during the composer's lifetime, were left as a set of possibilities rather than in any definitive shape. Indeed, the foundation of Musorgsky's modern reputation was Diaghilev's production of *Boris Godunov* at the Paris Opéra in 1908. However, this was in a version by Rimsky-Korsakov which did not merely amalgamate material from Musorgsky's own two versions but smoothed out many unorthodox harmonic progressions and rendered the austerity and strangeness of the original orchestration more grateful to the ear: in short, Musorgsky's masterpiece was all but transformed into something Rimsky-Korsakov might have written himself. We may decry Rimsky's presumption, but this is the version of the opera that established Musorgsky as a great composer in the West.

Rimsky-Korsakov's version of *Khovanshchina* is less offensive to the tenets of modern textual scholarship, since the work was left by Musorgsky in the form of a vocal score which lacked some concluding scenes (even the libretto was still incomplete, and Musorgsky's intentions for the denouement are unknown). Rimsky-Korsakov prepared a performable version in the 1880s; after this had found a place in the repertory of several opera companies, Stravinsky provided a substitute ending, differing both musically and dramatically from Rimsky's. *Sorochintsy Fair* and even the less promising *Marriage* were completed by Soviet composers. During the 1930s the Soviet musicologist Pavel Lamm pub-

lished a new version of *Boris Godunov* which conflated Musorgsky's two vocal scores. A second conflated version, by the Western musicologist David Lloyd-Jones, was published as a full score in the 1970s; it has now established itself in the repertory alongside the previous versions.   MF-W

📖 M. D. Calvocoressi, *Mussorgsky* (London, 1946, 2/1974) · M. H. Brown (ed.), *Musorgsky in memoriam, 1881–1981* (Ann Arbor, MI, 1982) · A. Orlova (ed.), *Remembering Musorgsky* (Bloomington, IN, 1991) · R. Taruskin, *Musorgsky: Eight Essays and an Epilogue* (Princeton, NJ, 1992)

muta (It.). 'Change'. An instruction to change instrument, crook (in brass instruments), or tuning; *muta D in C* means 'change the tuning from D to C' on the timpani.

mutation. 1. In *solmization, a change from one *hexachord to another.

2. The change in the male voice that takes place at puberty.

3. In violin playing, a shift of position.

mute (Fr.: *sourdine*; Ger.: *Dämpfer*; It.: *sordino*). A device for muffling the sound of an instrument. On bowed string instruments it is fixed to the bridge to inhibit its vibration, either as a pronged clamp which clips over the bridge or as a small bar attached to the strings between bridge and tailpiece which is slid on to the bridge when required. The 'buff stop' on harpsichords and early pianos, operated by a hand-lever or a pedal, mutes the strings by pressing pads of felt or leather against the strings.

Mutes for brass instruments either fit into the bell or (in the case of the metal 'bowler hat') are held over it. They are made in many shapes, each altering the tone in different ways as well as reducing the volume. The player's hand or a cloth may also be used. On woodwinds, a cloth bag has sometimes been tied over the instrument, and small pear-shaped wooden mutes were made to fit into 18th-century oboe bells.   JMo

mute cornett (Ger.: *stiller Zink*). A straight, lathe-turned wooden *cornett with an integral conical mouthpiece hollowed in the proximal end. Its sound is gentler than that of the ordinary cornett.

Muzak. A term for recorded background music played in public places (e.g. hotels, airports, and shops) and offices, to create a soothing atmosphere, to enhance workers' productivity, etc. The recordings used typically consist of a seamless string of bland, unobtrusive orchestral arrangements of pop and light music, with a narrow range of dynamics and tempo. Such music was first broadcast in 1922 by the American company Wired

Music, later renamed Muzak (hence this generic name), but it is now available commercially worldwide. The term has also come to be applied pejoratively to any characterless recorded music.

Myaskovsky, Nikolay Yakovlevich (*b* Novogeorgiyevsk, 8/20 April 1881; *d* Moscow, 8 Aug. 1950). Russian composer. He was born in a fortress, the son of a general in the Russian army, and himself trained for the army, in which he fought from 1914 to 1916, though his introspective character was poorly suited for it. He had had a good musical education, with Rimsky-Korsakov and others, at the St Petersburg Conservatory where he mixed in progressive circles and became friendly with a younger student, Sergey Prokofiev; the lifelong association between these two very different temperaments is chronicled in over 150 letters in which they advise and support each other in their creative work. After the war Myaskovsky became a professor of composition at the Moscow Conservatory, where his pupils included Kabalevsky and Khachaturian. He wrote two lugubrious early symphonic poems based on Poe and Shelley respectively, 27 symphonies—of which the powerful Sixth is generally regarded as the finest—and several sonatas. His musical style shows the influences of both Glazunov and Tchaikovsky, and emotionally he approaches the latter in his pessimistic and even neurasthenic outlook—his style, however, being necessarily more progressive. Although he won three Stalin prizes, he was accused of *formalism during the purges of 1948.   PS/DN

📖 A. Ikonnikov, *Myaskovsky: His Life and Work* (New York, 1946)

My Country (*My Fatherland*). See Má vlast.

My Ladye Nevells Booke. A manuscript collection of virginal music completed in 1591 by John Baldwin. It consists of 42 keyboard pieces by Byrd, who was probably Lady Nevell's teacher. She, however, must quickly have relinquished the manuscript, for 'Lord Abergavenny, called the Deafe, presented it to the Queene' (Elizabeth I); it is now privately owned. There

is a modern edition by Hilda Andrews (1926, repr. 1969).

Mysliveček [Mysliweczek, Mislivecek], **Josef** (*b* Prague, 9 March 1737; *d* Rome, 4 Feb. 1781). Czech composer. After studying music in Prague, he entered the family trade, becoming a master miller in 1761. Quickly abandoning this career for music, in 1763 he went to Venice where he studied composition with Pescetti. His first success was with the opera *Il Bellerofonte* (Naples, 1867), and until the failure of *Armida* (Milan, 1780) he remained popular throughout Italy. Neapolitan enthusiasm for Mysliveček, coupled with local difficulties in pronouncing his name, led to the appellation 'Il Boemo'. He was also well known in Vienna and Munich. His last three years were dogged by operatic failures, poverty, and illness resulting from a dissolute life; he died alone and destitute in Rome.

Mysliveček's many operas, almost all written for Italy, are marked by a pleasing if ingenuous lyricism, and observe without modification the conventions of *opera seria*. The oratorios show more inclination to experiment and generally display greater imagination. He was especially valued by singers for his attention to word-setting and considerate vocal lines. Burney recorded that his instrumental works—symphonies, concertos, octets, quartets, and trios—were as popular as his vocal music. Certain features of his melodic style look back to his Bohemian origins, and in spite of the failure of his last operas Mysliveček's influence on contemporaries, not least Mozart, was significant.

JSm

📖 D. E. Freeman, *Il Boemo: Josef Mysliveček* (forthcoming)

mystery plays. See medieval drama.

mystic chord [Promethean chord]. The name given to the chord *c–f♯–b♭–e′–a′–d″* by *Skryabin; it forms the harmonic basis of his tone-poem *Prometheus* (1909–10), from which work the chord takes its alternative name.

Nabokov, Nicolas [Nikolay Dmitriyevich] (*b* Lubcha, nr Minsk, 17 April 1903; *d* New York, 6 April 1978). Russian-born American composer. A cousin of the writer Vladimir Nabokov, he studied in Yalta (1913–20), Stuttgart, Berlin with Busoni (1921–3), and Paris (1923–6), and stayed on in Paris and Germany for the next few years. His ballet-oratorio *Ode* was produced by Diaghilev in 1928. In 1933 he moved to the USA, where he took citizenship six years later, and after the war he was active on both sides of the Atlantic, especially as a promoter of festivals. His later works include the operas *The Death of Rasputin* (Cologne, 1959) and *Love's Labour's Lost* (Brussels, 1973; libretto by W. H. Auden and Chester Kallman). PG

Nabucco (*Nabucodonosor*). Opera in four parts by Verdi to a libretto by Temistocle Solera after Auguste Anicet-Bourgeois and Francis Cornu's play *Nabuchodonosor* (1836) and Antonio Cortesi's ballet *Nabuccodonosor* (1838) (Milan, 1842); it includes the famous choral lament of the Hebrews, 'Va pensiero'.

Nachschlag (Ger., 'afterstroke'). 1. In modern German terminology, the final two notes of the turn that normally concludes a *trill.

2. In 17th- and 18th-century music, the same as the English *springer.

Nachtmusik (Ger., 'night music'). A term used in the late 18th century for a composition with the character of a *serenade. Mozart's *Eine kleine Nachtmusik* is the best-known example. See NOTTURNO.

Nachtstück (Ger., 'night piece'). A term used in the 19th century for pieces in a style similar to that of a *nocturne. In the 20th century it was used to describe instrumental pieces that evoke the sounds and the atmosphere of night, such as the third movement of Bartók's *Music for Strings, Percussion, and Celesta*, or the third movement ('Elegia') of his Concerto for Orchestra.

Naderman. French family of harpists, harp makers, and publishers. Jean Henri (1734–99) made single-action pedal harps and published harp music. His son (Jean) François-Joseph (1781–1835) studied with Krumpholtz, was appointed harpist in the royal chapel (1815), and became the first harp professor at the Paris Conservatoire (1825). His harp music includes sonatas, variations, concertos, and studies, which are still played, and two books on harp-playing. He took over the harp-making business with his brother Henri. WT/AL

nāgasvaram. A conical tenor shawm of South Indian (Karnatic) music.

nai. *Panpipes of Romania.

nail violin [nail harmonica]. A semicircular wooden soundbox with a series of metal rods of different lengths, played with a very short bow, fastened round the edge. The first nail violin was invented in 1740 in St Petersburg. Models with additional sympathetic strings, and with a pedal-operated, rosin-coated band (instead of the bow) controlled by a keyboard, have also been made.

nakers. Pairs of small *kettledrums of Arab or Saracen origin (Arabic: *naqqāra*), which were taken back to Europe by the 13th-century Crusaders. Usually hung from the player's belt, they were struck with a pair of beaters. RPA

Namensfeier ('Nameday'). Beethoven's overture op. 115, composed in 1814–15 for the nameday festivities of Emperor Franz II of Austria.

Nancarrow, (Samuel) Conlon (*b* Texarkana, AR, 27 Oct. 1912; *d* Mexico City, 10 Aug. 1997). American-born Mexican composer. He studied at Cincinnati Conservatory College and in Boston (1934–6) with Roger Sessions, Walter Piston, and Nicolas Slonimsky. Having also joined the Communist party in Boston, in 1936 he worked his passage to Europe, where he fought in the Spanish Civil War (1937–9). He then returned to the USA but, in order to avoid government harassment, moved to Mexico City in 1940 and became a Mexican citizen in 1955. During a return visit to New York, in 1947–8, he bought a player piano and roll puncher, and back home began to devote himself exclusively to studies (eventually numbering more than 50) for the instrument.

Nancarrow's earlier works for more normal means had, under the influence of jazz and of Cowell's *New Musical Resources*, explored rhythmic complexity, but by creating his music on piano rolls he could prescribe much more formidable relationships. Nearly all the studies are canons, but the parts normally move at tempos in irrational proportions (e.g. no. 37, whose 12 parts are related in speed as the notes of a chromatic scale are related in frequency), and the tempos may even change, one part accelerating while another slows down. The designs are abstract, but there is also humour in the speed and complexity of the music, and in the nature of its motifs, often suggestive of jazz or cartoon music. In the 1980s Nancarrow began to receive international attention and to write music for live performers again.   PG

   📖 K. GANN, *The Music of Conlon Nancarrow* (Cambridge, 1995)

Nanino, Giovanni Bernardino (*b* Vallerino, nr Viterbo, *c*.1560; *d* Rome, 1623). Italian composer. He lived and worked with his elder brother, Giovanni Maria, in Rome. His music reflects the transition from the polyphonic idiom (represented by his published collections of madrigals) towards the monodic style of the early Baroque period, and much of his church music is dependent on the use of a figured bass.   JM

Nanino, Giovanni Maria (*b* Tivoli, *c*.1545; *d* Rome, 11 March 1607). Italian composer, the elder brother of Giovanni Bernardino Nanino. He worked at Rome from the early 1560s, perhaps studying with Palestrina, and spent the last 30 years of his life as a singer in the Sistine Chapel, taking his turn to act as *maestro di cappella* there. He was an important teacher (his pupils included Allegri and Felice Anerio), and his works were widely published in his lifetime. They include madrigals and canzonettas, and sacred music which seems to have been closely modelled on the technique and style of Palestrina, showing a preference for the conservative polyphonic idiom typical of Roman composers of the period.   JM

Napoleon, Ode to. See ODE TO NAPOLEON BUONAPARTE.

Nardini, Pietro (*b* Livorno, 12 April 1722; *d* Florence, 7 May 1793). Italian composer. He studied with Tartini in Padua, then worked in the 1760s in Stuttgart as chamber musician and leader of the orchestra, which, under Jommelli, was among the best in Europe. In 1769 he went to Padua to care for the dying Tartini and then to Florence as director of music at the ducal court. One of the best-known violinists of his day, Nardini was

admired by Leopold Mozart and Burney, though he was noted for his sweetness of tone rather than for virtuosity. He was one of the last to compose sonatas in the Baroque manner, with the slow–quick–quick order of movements and continuo accompaniments.

                                                   DA/LC

Nares, James (*b* Stanwell, *bapt.* 19 April 1715; *d* Westminster, 10 Feb. 1783). English organist and composer. He was a chorister in the Chapel Royal and later studied with Pepusch. In 1735 he was appointed organist of York Minster, and from the mid-1750s he held the posts of organist, composer, and Master of the Children to the Chapel Royal. Nares wrote keyboard pieces, sacred and secular vocal music, and some pedagogical works.   WT/PL

narrator (It.: *testo*). A character who tells the story in a dramatic work, in musical works usually to recitative. The custom is derived from early Greek tragedy. The *testo* in Monteverdi's *Combattimento di Tancredi, e Clorinda* (1624) is given by far the most important part, describing the action, which is mimed by the main characters to appropriate instrumental accompaniment. In Passion music the Evangelist, traditionally sung by a tenor, is given the role of narrator. Examples of 19th-century works calling for a narrator include Berlioz's *L'Enfance du Christ*. In the 20th century many works made use of such a part, for example Stravinsky's opera-oratorio *Oedipus rex* (which requires the Narrator to wear modern evening dress, to set him apart from the other characters), Honegger's *Le Roi David*, and Britten's *The Rape of Lucretia* (where the narrative and comment on the action are given by a tenor and a soprano, respectively the Male and Female Chorus).

                                                  —/RW

Narváez, Luis de (*fl* early 16th century). Spanish composer and vihuelist. Probably a native of Granada, he may have been in the service of Francisco de los Cobos (to whom he dedicated his *Delphín de música*); in 1548–9 he was teacher of the choirboys in the chapel of the future King Philip II, accompanying him to Italy and northern Europe.

    Narváez was renowned as a vihuelist in his lifetime. Nearly all his music is contained in *Los seys libros del Delphín de música* (Valladolid, 1538), one of the most important 16th-century collections of vihuela music. It includes fantasias, variations, and transcriptions of vocal music, as well as romances and villancicos for voice and vihuela.   WT/OR

Nassarre, Pablo (*b* ?Daroca, nr Zaragoza, *c*.1655; *d* ?Zaragoza, *c*.1730). Spanish theorist, organist, and composer. Born blind, he was taught by another blind organist, Pablo Bruna. He spent most of his life in

Zaragoza as organist in the Real Convento of S. Francisco, being a member of the order from at least as early as 1683. His most important contribution were the printed treatises *Fragmentos musicos* (Zaragoza, 1683, enlarged 2/Madrid, 1700) and the two-volume *Escuela musica* (Zaragoza, 1723–4). His theoretical writings, which follow 17th-century conventions in their censorious view of secular music, reflect the conservative ecclesiastical context in which he worked. Nassarre's few surviving works are mainly for the organ.

MAM

national anthems. Hymns, marches, anthems, or fanfares used as patriotic symbols, like a national flag. They are played or sung at ceremonial and diplomatic occasions and at sports events (notably the Olympic Games, where the winner of each event is saluted by the anthem of the country he or she represents). It has been traditional to play the national anthem at theatres in Europe; in England this custom began in 1745, when Thomas Arne's version of *God Save the King* (the first national anthem) was sung at the Theatre Royal, Drury Lane, London.

Many countries adopted national anthems either at a time of crisis or in the 19th century, when there was a growing spirit of *nationalism (especially in central Europe and South America). Some, for example the French *Marseillaise*, are calls to arms or marches. Others are hymns of praise to monarchs or leaders, for example the *Emperor's Hymn* by Haydn, or pay tribute to a national hero (such as the Danish *King Christian stood by the lofty mast*) or the beauty of a country's landscape. Several were influenced by 19th-century operatic idioms and some use traditional melodies or folk tunes. Nations of the Middle East adopted fanfares in the mid-20th century, often with no texts. Commonwealth countries have their own anthems (for example, *Advance Australia Fair*, chosen after a competition) but use *God Save the Queen* for visits by the British royal family.

With one or two exceptions the music of national anthems is undistinguished and often previously served other purposes, the tunes being stirring or solemn. They are not noted for the quality of their texts.

AL

📖 P. NETTL, *National Anthems* (New York, 1952) · W. L. REED and M. J. BRISTOW (eds.), *National Anthems of the World* (London, 9/1997)

National Federation of Music Societies. British organization set up by the *Incorporated Society of Musicians in 1933; it supports amateur operatic, choral, and orchestral societies.

nationalism. Patriotism, which may be expressed in music by composers or by those who control performance. It often involves the conscious use of elements that can be recognized as belonging to one's own nation (or would-be nation), with the object of arousing patriotic feelings. It is a worldwide phenomenon. This article is limited to nationalism in Western art music, which reached its height during the 19th century.

1. Motives; 2. Hegemony nationalism; 3. Aspiring nationalism; 4. German nationalism; 5. Resistance to German hegemony

1. Motives

Every culture in the world has its own musical language, with certain practices, styles, instruments, scales, and melodies that distinguish it from all others. Those who participate in inherited, traditional music as a natural part of their culture are not necessarily expressing nationalism. But when one culture seeks or attains a position of ascendancy over another, the music of the dominant culture frequently penetrates or even replaces that of the subordinate one, while the latter may resist, and assert the value of its own musical tradition. Both aspects of such a conflict may be termed 'musical nationalism'. Since their goals and methods differ, they will be separately treated here under the headings 'hegemony nationalism' and 'aspiring nationalism'. Of course, music is only one of a number of fields in which nationalism may be asserted; others are language, dress, food, religion, history, myth, and the cult of individuals past and present. In addition, nationalism frequently generates social, political, or military conflict.

Musical nationalism is supported only by those who are politically, socially, or intellectually concerned about their nationality. Such people are not generally peasants or manual workers. For instance, in the 19th century it made no difference to Russian peasants whether the operas performed to aristocratic audiences at Moscow and St Petersburg were in Italian or Russian, nor whether they were based on coloratura arias or folksongs. On the other hand, the nobility was content to cultivate a cosmopolitan style. But the newly powerful businessmen, professionals, and civil servants, familiar with opera and art music, were angered by the exclusion of their own culture from the high position which it should rightly have occupied in the life of the nation. It was they who provided the motive and support for Russian musical nationalism.

So nationalism is likely to arise when the intellectual leaders of a society are in a position either to impose their culture on others, or to resist an alien culture that has been imposed on their own.

2. Hegemony nationalism

Taruskin points out that in early modern history patriotism was inextricably bound up with loyalty to a sovereign. He suggests that the idea of nationality apart from monarchy first arose in Britain, which was also the first home of the public concert. He therefore points to the British cult of Handel's oratorios as the earliest significant public expression of musical nationalism in the context of Western art music. They were openly treated as demonstrations of patriotism, particularly during the Jacobite rebellion of 1745–6 and the Seven Years War (1756–63). The subject matter of most of the oratorios is the victory of the people of Israel over its enemies, as well as the reassertion of biblical truth, and they were widely taken as symbols of the victory of Protestant Britain over its Catholic neighbours and minorities. Later, the Handel Festivals at Westminster Abbey (1784–91) amounted to a patriotic ritual, with forces swollen to as many as a thousand musicians. The German-born Handel was called 'our great national composer'.

The musical idiom that expressed this 'hegemony nationalism' was not particularly British in character. On the contrary, it was able to embrace the Enlightenment ideals of universality, which was coming close to making music the 'international language' that it has often misleadingly been called. Handel used the international style of the day, which was predominantly Italian in origin, though the ceremonial music of the Restoration period and the Anglican anthem played some part in the formation of his oratorio manner. The splendour of his trumpets and drums, and the pompous rhythms of his French overtures, both originally associated with royalty, now spread their meaning to embrace a broader, more democratic patriotism. A more extreme example of the same phenomenon arose in the French Revolutionary era, when vast musical forces were assembled for mass public meetings and pageants, vaunting revolutionary ideals and predicting their triumph throughout Europe and the world. Still, their idiom was international.

The British national anthem, which emerged in Handel's time, soon became a symbol of patriotism, though its words were entirely about loyalty to the sovereign. It was an effective tool to arouse national feeling. The tune would be directly adopted by several other countries, and became the model for later European national songs, including Haydn's great 'Hymn to the Emperor'. Similarly, the *Marseillaise* distilled the revolutionary and patriotic aspirations of the time into a single song that could be a powerful rouser of the masses when occasion demanded it. (See NATIONAL ANTHEMS.)

3. Aspiring nationalism

Oppressed peoples and minorities have frequently used music as one of a number of tools to promote their independence. To be effective for the purpose, the music must contain elements that are immediately recognizable as belonging to the culture concerned. This was in opposition to the 'international' style, and was fostered by the Romantic reaction to Enlightenment ideas. Certain distinctive scales, rhythms, harmonies, or melodic cells were selected and turned into national symbols. They did not have to be genuinely distinctive artefacts of the culture concerned; it was often more important to use features that were recognizably different from the international style of the dominant culture. For example, the same modal scales were used in the 19th century to symbolize Irish, Norwegian, Czech, and Spanish culture, by nationalists in each of those countries; in reality, they were merely survivals of an earlier international style. What mattered was that they did not sound like the classical art music of the time.

The same tools could also be used to create a sense of the exotic, which was an important element of the Romantic movement. Clearly, there is no nationalistic motive underlying Mozart's Rondo alla turca, Schubert's *Divertissement à la Hongroise*, Brahms's Hungarian Dances, Bizet's *Carmen*, or Sullivan's *Mikado*. But when Chopin published a set of mazurkas, or Liszt performed a Hungarian Rhapsody, he may have been simultaneously expressing personal nationalism and appealing to the exotic tastes of his principal audience (French or German, respectively).

Aspiring nationalism was not confined to peoples under foreign political rule. It could also be felt and expressed in countries where the ruling classes had adopted an alien international culture as their own. In most European capitals in the 18th century, with the exception of Paris, Italian opera was the only form of musical entertainment patronized by the court and aristocracy, and it consequently attracted most of the financial support available to professional musicians. Italian musicians often had a lock on the principal salaried posts, and enjoyed a far larger income than those native to the country, as Mozart found to his cost in Vienna. With the social changes accompanying industrialization and the growth of free markets, this situation was increasingly challenged by the middle classes, intellectuals, and the musicians themselves.

In the context of Western art music, one can usually discern three stages in the process of throwing off a foreign musical hegemony. In the first stage, the primary goal is to establish that a native product can be as good as a foreign import. This cannot be done by writing 'nationalistic' music, because such would be rejected out of hand as primitive or irrelevant. For instance, in St Petersburg around 1800 the only kind of stage music that enjoyed high prestige was Italian opera. Russian composers such as Bortnyansky were forced to prove their worth by writing Italian operas, or at least writing in an Italian style.

The second stage sees the beginning of musical nationalism, when elements of folksong and dance are introduced, and subjects of national significance are chosen. This may be seen in the music of Glinka and the more tentative of the 'Mighty Handful' (or The *Five: see RUSSIA, 4). National elements are grafted on to a style and practice that is still fundamentally of the 'mainstream'.

The third stage is marked by a radical change of style, in which classical forms, harmonies, and compositional techniques are replaced by new ones inspired by the folk material, or by actual innovation. Musorgsky's *Boris Godunov* (1874) was the first Russian work in which this stage was fully developed, though there were some precedents in the works of Dargomïzhsky. Later Russian composers hardly built on Musorgsky's achievement. Tchaikovsky, Rakhmaninov, and Skryabin adhered firmly to mainstream European idioms; and under the Soviet dictatorship, protest was expressed not by embracing Russian folk music, but by cultivating international modernism in the face of political pressure. In Hungarian music, it was not Liszt in the 19th century, but Bartók in the 20th, who forged a radically nationalistic idiom. (For further examples see below, 4 and 5.)

It may be that the earliest example of 'aspiring' musical nationalism is to be found in 18th-century Scotland. There were many Scots who resisted the union with England negotiated in 1707. Jacobite risings took place in 1715 and 1745, though both were defeated. Classical music was cultivated among the upper classes, and a number of Scottish composers vied with resident Italians in its production. To assert Scottish musical values, several collections of songs and fiddle dances were published. Their modal and pentatonic *scales, distinctive melodies, and so-called *Scotch snap were refreshingly different from the dominant Italian styles. From about 1780 onwards, 'every composer in Edinburgh and Aberdeen was writing piano sonatas with folk-tune rondo finales, folk-tune slow movements, even folk-tune second subjects in the principal movements ... The consequences were disastrous and final. Scottish classical music found itself disqualified from the European mainstream and unable to rejoin it' (Johnson, p. 196). It seems that the Scottish composers had advanced too quickly to the second stage. Along with the poems of Ossian and Burns and the novels of

Scott, the music of Scotland fascinated Romantics, first in London and then on the Continent; but it was treated as an exotic curiosity, without impact on the underlying musical style of the mainstream.

4. German nationalism

Only one national movement progressed from 'aspiring' to 'hegemony' musical nationalism, and succeeded in transforming the musical mainstream in the process. This was, of course, the German. In the 18th century there was no German nation. Native speakers of the language felt a strong cultural bond. But despite wide recognition of German intellectual achievements, their language held low international prestige until it was rescued by Goethe. As in Russia, German princes spoke French and cultivated Italian opera, while learned publications were usually in Latin. German pride was further humbled by the Napoleonic conquest. Feelings of inferiority nurtured a powerful nationalistic animus.

The theory of German nationalism was launched by J. G. Herder and was greatly stimulated, paralleling the earlier development in Scotland, by his collection and publication of German folk stories, ballads, and songs (1789). It was eventually superseded by *Des Knaben Wunderhorn* (1805–8) and the Grimm brothers' collections of tales. Increasingly, the virtues and values of the idealized 'folk' depicted in these stories were associated with Germanness and were contrasted, in German minds, with the decadence and moral corruption of the Latin and Jewish races.

Musical resistance to Italian domination began in the 18th century. In the first stage, Handel, Hasse, Gluck, Mozart, and Mayr beat the Italians on their own turf of *opera seria*. Mozart wanted to write German operas, and had an opportunity to do so when Emperor Joseph II opened a National German Opera at the Burgtheater in Vienna (1778). But the fashionable world preferred Italian opera, and the scheme was given up. After *Die Entführung aus dem Serail* (1782) Mozart had to follow suit (incidentally producing a string of masterpieces), and *Die Zauberflöte* (1791) found its place only among low comedies in a middle-class theatre. Beethoven rallied German pride, less by adopting folk traditions than by sheer musical power; he and his successors caused Germany to supplant Italy as the leader of European classical music outside opera. The revival of Bach's music, also taking place in the early decades of the 19th century, was partly a national crusade.

Conscious nationalism infused the operas of Weber, who set only German librettos, and who brought a German waltz and huntsmen's choruses (alongside Italianate arias) into *Der Freischütz* (1821), a work based on a quintessentially Germanic story of forests and pagan rituals. And the third stage, where a new style was forged, was attained by Wagner, whose music dramas permanently changed the course of Western art music. By that time, German music had been predominant in the instrumental field for many decades, and Wagner eventually won the greatest prize of all by supplanting the Italians and the French in leadership of the domain of opera.

German music had now, beyond all doubt, established a hegemony over all Western musical culture. This fact has had a profound influence on the interpretation of musical history. The discipline of musicology was organized and long dominated by German scholars, who tended to overemphasize the importance of the German contribution to musical history. The prime political objective of German nationalism—reunification—was achieved in 1871; it went on to aspire to world domination, as expressed in the new words attached to Haydn's hymn ('Deutschland, Deutschland, über alles'). It acquired some ugly characteristics in the process, which need no description here.

5. Resistance to German hegemony

So in the later 19th century it was German, not Italian, music that claimed hegemony over most of Europe. The aspiring nationalisms of smaller European powers had to take it as their point of departure. In Bohemia (now part of the Czech Republic, then under Austrian rule) Smetana used the Czech language in *The Bartered Bride* and a nationalistic programme for *Má vlast* ('My Country'), introducing some folk melodies in both; but his underlying style was firmly Mendelssohnian. Dvořák went further, being equally capable of writing 'mainstream' and 'national' music; in the next generation Janáček fully embraced musical nationalism. In Norway (under Danish or Swedish rule until 1905), Grieg's genius was in 'classicizing' the colourful national melodies he found and inventing an individual style for their harmonization. A group of Spanish nationalists (including Albéniz, Granados, and Falla), all thoroughly international in their musical training and background, took advantage of distinctive Spanish dances (bolero, fandango, *seguidilla*), the association of the guitar with their country, and the unusual survival of the Phrygian mode in the 'flamenco' chord progressions of Andalusian music. Albéniz's *Iberia* suite (1905) effectively harnesses these resources for a work of overtly national significance.

In Italy, though political nationalism was strong against foreign occupation, its expression in operas such as Verdi's lay in the subject matter rather than the musical idiom; for Italian operatic style was already dominant. But Verdi's rousing choruses carried an unmistakable nationalistic message, even when their dramatic context was disguised or diluted by Austrian censors. In France and Britain, the leading political powers of the world through most of the century, musical nationalism was weak. Neither needed music to bolster its national *amour-propre*. Both were content to participate in the international mainstream of music—until their political supremacy was challenged by Germany in the late 19th century.

France, after the shock of defeat by Prussia in the war of 1870–1, began to look to its cultural achievements as a makeweight to military failure. The Société Nationale de Musique was formed, and in the classic 'first stage' was most concerned to encourage French-born composers to show their prowess in the progressive (that is, Wagnerian) school of composition. In the second and third stages, Fauré and then Debussy cultivated styles that sought to emphasize French qualities of rationality, subtlety, and sophistication, rather than relying on French folk music.

In England, the 'first stage' had little success, when such Victorian composers as Macfarren insisted on English subject matter in their operas and decorated them with old English tunes. Then a belated recognition of the riches of English (as opposed to Celtic) folk music and of the Elizabethan 'Golden Age', together with English poetry, inspired such composers as Vaughan Williams and Holst to express in their music the intense patriotism and anti-German feeling surrounding World War I.

In the USA, sporadic resistance to European domination of American music was swamped in the 19th century by the unending stream of European immigrants, and the Germans held sway. Acting on the advice of Dvořák, some American composers treated African-American popular music as their true national folksong, and used it as a building-block for a national style, with success (for instance) in the work of Copland and Gershwin; while Ives, in a highly personal but unselfconscious manner, introduced into sonatas and other 'classical' genres all kinds of things that had been favourites in his youth, whether popular songs, hymn tunes, or military marches.   NT

📖 D. JOHNSON, *Music and Society in Lowland Scotland in the Eighteenth Century* (London, 1972) · L. PLANTINGA, *Romantic Music* (New York, 1984) · N. TEMPERLEY, 'Musical nationalism in English Romantic opera', *The Lost Chord: Essays on Victorian Music* (Bloomington, IN, 1989), 143–57 · C. CALHOUN, *Nationalism* (Buckingham, 1996) · *Repercussions*, 5/1 (1996) [Nationalism in Music issue] · P. POTTER, *Most German of the Arts: Musicology and Society from the Weimar Republic to the End of Hitler's Reich* (New Haven, CT, 1998)

natural (Fr.: *bécarre*; Ger.: *Auflösungszeichen*, *Quadrat*; It.: *bequadro*). 1. A note which is neither raised (sharpened) nor lowered (flattened).

2. The sign (♮) that, after a note has been raised by a sharp or double sharp or lowered by a flat or double flat, restores a note to its natural pitch. After a double sharp or double flat, the reversion to a single accidental is notated either by the use of the single sharp or flat alone, or occasionally by ♮♯ or ♮♭. For the origins of the natural sign and its early use, see ACCIDENTAL; NOTATION, 1.

natural harmonics. See ACOUSTICS, 5.

natural hexachord. See HEXACHORD; SOLMIZATION.

natural horn (Fr.: *cor de chasse*; Ger.: *Waldhorn*; It.: *corno da caccia*). A horn without valves or fingerholes (see HORN, 2), and which can therefore play only notes of the harmonic series. See also HAND HORN.

natural notes. The notes available on brass instruments without the use of *valves.

natural trumpet. A trumpet without valves, slides, or other aids (see TRUMPET, 2), and which can therefore play only notes of the harmonic series.

Naumann, Johann Gottlieb (*b* Blasewitz, nr Dresden, 17 April 1741; *d* Dresden, 23 Oct. 1801). German composer. He studied in Dresden and in 1757 went to Italy, where he took lessons from Tartini and Padre Martini. Hasse obtained an appointment for him at the Dresden court chapel in 1764; he became Kapellmeister in 1776. During his time at Dresden, where he was the leading musical figure, several of his operas, some to librettos by Metastasio, were performed in Italy. In 1777 Gustav III of Sweden invited him to take over the royal chapel at Stockholm and to develop operatic activity. The new Royal Opera House opened in 1782 under Naumann's direction with his *Cora och Alonzo*, and in 1786 his *Gustaf Wasa* was given there.

In his Swedish operas Naumann shows an awareness of Gluck's striving towards more 'natural' writing for the voice (*Orfeo ed Euridice* had been given by the Swedish opera in 1773) and a corresponding move away from showy ornament and elaborate display. After a brief appointment at Copenhagen, where he wrote a Danish opera on the Orpheus legend, Naumann returned to Dresden as Kapellmeister in 1786. He was increasingly occupied with sacred music, but in the last year of his life he composed an *opera buffa*, *Aci e Galatea*. WT

Navarraise, La ('The Girl from Navarre'). Opera in two acts by Massenet to a libretto by Jules Claretie and Henri Cain after Claretie's story *La Cigarette* (London, 1894).

Navarro, Juan (*b* Marchena or Seville, *c*.1530; *d* Palencia, 25 Sept. 1580). Spanish composer. In 1549 he was a singer in the service of the Duke of Arcos, and then sang in the cathedral choirs of Jaén and (from 1553 to 1555) Málaga. From 1562 to 1564 he was *maestro de capilla* at the collegiate church in Valladolid; subsequently he held equivalent posts at the cathedrals of Avila, Salamanca (1566–74), Ciudad Rodrigo (until 1578), and Palencia, where he died. His surviving music is mainly sacred, most of it appearing in a posthumous publication, *Psalmi, hymni ac Magnificat totius anni* (Rome, 1590). WT/OR

nāy [nai, ney, etc.] (Arabic, from old Persian, 'reed'). The end-blown flute used throughout North Africa, the Middle East, and Central Asia. It is the only wind instrument used in Arab art music. A similar instrument is the Turkish and south-east European *kaval*.

Naylor, Bernard (*b* Cambridge, 22 Nov. 1907; *d* London, 19 May 1986). English composer. The son of the organist and composer Edward Naylor (1867–1934), he studied with Holst and Vaughan Williams at the RCM. Since his first visit in 1932 he spent much time in Canada as a teacher and conductor. His compositions consist mainly of choral and vocal works in a traditional style. PG

Neapolitan sixth chord. Name given to one of the chromatic chords—the first inversion (i.e. the '6th' chord) of the triad built on the flattened supertonic. Ex. 1 shows an example in the key of C. It is often used to replace the subdominant chord in the cadential progression IV–V–I. Although it was already an established feature in music (not only Italian) of the second half of the 17th century (it was used, for example, by Carissimi, Corelli, and Purcell), it appears to take its name from its use by composers of the 18th-century 'Neapolitan school', for example Alessandro Scarlatti, Nicola Porpora, Leonardo Leo, Nicolò Jommelli, and Pergolesi.

Ex. 1

Neapolitan song (It.: *canzona popolare napoletana*). A romantic song or ballad which originated in early 19th-century Italian opera; it is the Italian equivalent of the Victorian *drawing-room ballad. The Neapolitan song is typically in the form of an arietta with a graceful, lyrical melody. Donizetti's *Te voglio bene assaje* (published 1835) is recognized as the first in the genre, and famous examples include Rinaldo Di Capua's *O sole mio*

and Luigi Denza's *Funiculì, funiculà*. Neapolitan song has achieved wide appeal and attracted the attention of celebrated classical singers, from Caruso to Luciano Pavarotti.   PGA/JBE

Nebenstimme (Ger., 'next voice'). A term introduced by Schoenberg for the second part in a polyphonic texture, indicated in the score by the symbol N̄. See HAUPTSTIMME.   PG

Nebra (Blasco), José de (Melchor de) (*bapt.* 6 Jan. 1702; *d* Madrid, 11 July 1768). Spanish composer, organist, and teacher. From a family of musicians, he received his first instruction from his father (later *maestro de capilla* of Cuenca Cathedral). In 1724 he became an organist at the royal chapel in Madrid; he was subsequently promoted to *vicemaestro* and appointed assistant principal of the choir school (both 1751). His extensive output from before 1751 includes a wide range of Spanish theatre music (mainly zarzuelas, *autos sacramentales*, and *comedias*, all including spoken dialogue). Afterwards, his positions required him to concentrate on liturgical music and educational keyboard works, the former attempting to fill the void left by a fire that destroyed the musical archives at the royal chapel, and the latter often showing a clear debt to Domenico Scarlatti in its use of an embryonic bipartite sonata form.

Nebra's works introduce many innovatory Italianate influences to the much stricter Spanish sacred style—not least, frequent use of *da capo* aria forms—but also feature more specifically Spanish musical types such as the *seguidilla* and *copla*. His most enduring sacred work was the Requiem composed for the funeral of Queen María Barbara (1758), which continued to be performed at royal funerals for several decades after his death.
                                                                       MHE

neck. On a stringed instrument of the lute type, the handle projecting from the body which bears the fingerboard and extends the strings to the pegbox. On a harp the strings are attached at intervals along the neck and to corresponding points along the resonator. On lyres the neck is usually replaced by a yoke consisting of a crossbar, to which the strings are fastened, between two arms coming out of the resonator.

Nedbal, Oskar (*b* Tábor, 26 March 1874; *d* Zagreb, 24 Dec. 1930). Czech composer, viola player, and conductor. He studied the violin in Tábor and later with Antonín Bennewitz at the Prague Conservatory, where he was also a pupil of Dvořák. As viola player of the Czech Quartet (1891–1906) he contributed to the improving standards of Czech chamber music performance. He conducted the Czech Philharmonic Orchestra (1896–1906) and the Tonkünstlerorchester in Vienna

(1907–18). After World War I he returned to Prague and in 1921 went to Bratislava as head of opera at the newly founded Slovak National Theatre. Until his death by suicide he was a major figure in the city's musical life, doing much to encourage the new generation of Slovak composers.

Nedbal was regarded as one of the most promising of Dvořák's pupils, though he never showed the adventurousness of Suk or Novák. His operettas and some of his ballets were popular in Austria and Germany, but he had little success with his single opera *Sedlák Jakub* ('The Peasant Jacob', 1920). Nedbal's music displays wit and imagination, but, though he made use of Polish and Yugoslav folk dances in addition to Czech, his style makes little advance on that of his master Dvořák.
                                                                       JSM

Neefe, Christian Gottlob (*b* Chemnitz, 5 Feb. 1748; *d* Dessau, 26 Jan. 1798). German composer. He began composing when he was 12, later studying law, then composition with J. A. Hiller. He worked with travelling troupes, and in Bonn became one of Beethoven's first teachers. In 1794 he was appointed director of the Dessau theatre. His songs show some anticipation of the Romantic lied, and in his *Singspiele* he can extend the conventions to lively dramatic effect. Both *Die Apotheke* (1771) and *Amors Guckkasten* ('Cupid's Peepshow', 1772) include scenes of considerable dramatic fluency. *Sophonisbe* (1776) is a melodrama on the model of Benda.   WT/JW

Neel, (Louis) Boyd (*b* Blackheath, 19 July 1905; *d* Toronto, 30 Sept. 1981). English-born Canadian conductor. Originally a naval officer, he studied medicine at Cambridge, then music theory at the Guildhall School of Music, London. In 1932 he formed the Boyd Neel Chamber Orchestra; it was soon admired internationally, and it inspired Britten to write his Frank Bridge Variations. As well as popularizing string works by composers as diverse as Elgar, Holst, Vaughan Williams, Dvořák, Grieg, Tchaikovsky, and Bloch. Neel was an early pioneer of the revival of Baroque string music; he also performed Mozart's violin and piano concertos. From 1953 to 1970 he was dean of the Royal Conservatory of Music in Toronto.   JT

📖 *My Orchestras and Other Adventures: The Memoirs of Boyd Neel* (Toronto, 1985)

Negri, Marc'Antonio (*b* Verona; *d* ?Venice, in or after 1621). Italian composer. He was *vicemaestro di cappella* at St Mark's, Venice, from 1612 to 1620 and so acted as Monteverdi's first assistant there. He wrote some attractive instrumental sonatas and sinfonias, two books of *Affetti amorosi* (Venice, 1608, 1611) for voices and continuo, and a book of psalms for *cori spezzati* (Venice, 1613).   DA/TC

neighbour note. See AUXILIARY NOTE.

Nelsonmesse ('Nelson Mass'). Haydn's Mass no. 11 in D minor (1798); in his own catalogue of his works, Haydn headed it 'Missa in angustiis' and it is sometimes referred to as the 'Imperial Mass' or the 'Coronation Mass'. According to one story, it was written to celebrate Nelson's victory at Aboukir Bay; another claims that Nelson heard it at Eisenstadt in 1800.

nenia (It.). 'Dirge'.

Nenna, Pomponio (*b* Bari, *c.*1550–5; *d* ?Rome, before 22 Oct. 1613). Italian composer. He may have been in Gesualdo's service in Naples at the end of the 16th century, and his madrigals show a similar interest in chromaticism. By 1608 he had moved to Rome, where his eighth book of madrigals was published posthumously. As well as his secular music (madrigals and villanellas) he wrote a small amount of church music.
                                                                                                                              DA

neo-classicism. The conscious use of techniques, gestures, styles, forms, or media from an earlier period. In the history of art and literature, the term is most commonly used for the appeal to models from ancient Greece and Rome made by painters and poets towards the close of the 18th century. In music history, however, that was the period not of neo-classicism but of the Classical style. Neo-classicism therefore has to be a return to that style (or others), and the term is particularly associated with the works Stravinsky wrote between the early 1920s and the early 50s. These include dislocated arrangements of 18th-century Neapolitan music (*Pulcinella*, after pieces attributed to Pergolesi, 1920), concertos somewhat in the manner of Bach ('Dumbarton Oaks' Concerto, 1937–8) or of early Romantic music (Capriccio for piano and orchestra, 1928–9), ballets suggestive of the French Baroque era (*Apollo*, 1928), and even a full-scale opera with numerous echoes of Mozart (*The Rake's Progress*, 1951).

The influence of Stravinsky's neo-classical scores was felt by many composers who worked in or visited Paris between the wars, including Poulenc, Prokofiev, Milhaud, Honegger, Martinů, Szymanowski, Copland, and Carter. Their works, like those of Stravinsky himself, reflect earlier music in ways that are often ironic and occasionally downright humorous. One of their concerns, as voiced by Jean Cocteau, was to recapture wit and lightness in music. Often that would mean devaluing the great Austro-German tradition—a devaluing for which World War I had provided encouragement—and an openness to new mentors. In

that way neo-classicism proved itself adaptable to the reforming of national styles—French, Russian, Czech, Polish, American—since models could be taken from earlier composers (Gounod, Chopin) or from folk music and jazz.

Neo-classicism in Austria and Germany tended to be less brisk and carefree, if only because there the central musical tradition could not be so easily subverted or forgotten. It also started earlier, and for different reasons. At a time when Mahler and Strauss were enlarging and extending the language of Romanticism, Reger, Busoni, and Schoenberg began interesting themselves in the clearer outlines and smaller forces of Bach and Mozart. Schoenberg's Chamber Symphony no. 1 (1906), a symphony for just 15 instruments, is neo-classical in its compactness and also in its use of counterpoint as a means to impose order on advanced tonal harmony. Busoni, like Reger, was deeply attached to Bach, though in propounding his notion of 'young classicity' he also elevated Mozart as an example of pure musicality, and thereby had some influence on such emerging composers as Kurt Weill, his pupil. However, the leading neo-classicist of the Austro-German world was Hindemith, whose concertos and chamber works of the 1920s, in particular, are full of Bachian forms and textures, often conducted with a boisterous vigour.

Like Stravinsky and other contemporaries, Hindemith moved from 18th- to 19th-century models in the later 1920s and 30s, and so from neo-classicism to what has sometimes been called 'neo-romanticism'. Such a move could be made for reasons of political necessity or social idealism: in the USSR a kind of neo-romanticism became the state-approved norm for music, while composers like Copland took very much the same route out of a desire to democratize music and embrace the widest possible audience.

Schoenberg openly disapproved of neo-classicism, especially Stravinsky's, on the grounds that it represented an abdication from the composer's duty to give musical history a responsible, responsive continuation. However, in his own works of the 1920s and 30s he reinstated Classical elements of form, thematic development, dance metres, and so on; he also occasionally made arrangements or recompositions of Baroque pieces. One such work—his Cello Concerto, after M. G. Monn—is close cousin to Stravinsky's *Pulcinella*, and there is a neo-classical element, too, in the music written after 1920 by his pupils Berg and Webern.

Webern's music shows the clear influence of Bach in its forms and in its persistent counterpoint: his String Quartet (1936–8), for instance, is largely canonic and includes the B–A–C–H motif, while his two late cantatas (1938–9, 1941–3) resemble Bach's in their chains of arias and choruses. But his music avoids any recourse to tonal harmony and—perhaps thereby—any open irony. Rather as in works of the same period by Bartók, such as *Music for Strings, Percussion, and Celesta* (1936), Bachian features are thoroughly absorbed, so that 'neoclassical' seems a less appropriate term for the music than simply 'classical'.

See also TWENTIETH CENTURY, THE. PG

📖 S. MESSING, *Neoclassicism in Music* (Ann Arbor, MI, 1988)

neo-classic jazz. A historicizing approach to jazz, gaining momentum towards the end of the 20th century. It is expressed in the homage of younger performers to classic predecessors, such as Jessica Williams's *In the Key of Monk* (1999), or in the replication of classic performances by repertory ensembles like the Lincoln Center Jazz Orchestra, or in the conscious development rather than static maintenance of classic styles. The advocacy of Wynton Marsalis has been especially influential in defining and encouraging this tendency, which is in many ways the culmination of jazz's evolution from a 'popular' to a 'classical' music (see JAZZ, 4). JJD

Netherlands. See LOW COUNTRIES.

Neukomm, Sigismund (*b* Salzburg, 10 July 1778; *d* Paris, 3 April 1858). Austrian composer, pianist, and scholar. A pupil of Michael Haydn in Salzburg and (for seven years) of Joseph Haydn in Vienna, in 1804 he went to St Petersburg where he became Kapellmeister at the German Theatre. Settling in Paris in 1809, he was appointed pianist to Prince Talleyrand; in 1816 he accompanied the Duke of Luxembourg to Rio de Janeiro, returning to Europe when fighting broke out in 1821. He travelled extensively in Italy and in 1829 visited London, where he met Mendelssohn and was enthusiastically received, his oratorio *David* (1834) and some of his songs becoming popular. His continuing European travels included a visit to Algiers in 1835. Neukomm's compositions (listed in his own thematic catalogue) include operas, masses, chamber music, and a Symphony in E♭ performed in London in 1831 by the Philharmonic Society. WT/SH

neuma [pneuma] (Gk., 'gesture', 'breath'). A medieval term referring to a sign in plainchant notation (neume; see NOTATION, 1) or to melismas appended to certain passages of plainchant: the concluding melismas of alleluias (see JUBILUS), graduals, and responsories; the textless repetition of verses within a sequence; and the florid endings given to intonation formulas and model antiphons in some tonaries. The word is sometimes used more generally for melody (irrespective of words) as notated. ALi

neume (from Gk. *pneuma*, 'breath'). An early note form; see NEUMA; NOTATION, 1.

Neusidler. German family of lutenists and composers. **Hans Neusidler** (*b* Pressburg [now Bratislava], *c*.1508–9; *d* Nuremberg, 2 Feb. 1653) lived in Nuremberg from about 1530 as a teacher, composer, and lute maker. His eight lutebooks (1536–49) contain arrangements of German and Italian songs and dances, and huge improvisatory preludes; the first book includes his lute method, the earliest to give left-hand fingering. He was the principal figure in early German lute music.

His son **Melchior** (*b* Nuremberg, 1531; *d* Augsburg, 1590), one of 17 children, went to Augsburg soon after 1551 and worked as leader of a group that provided music for special civic occasions; his patron was Octavian II Fugger, the banker. He visited Italy (1565–6) and was briefly employed in Innsbruck (1580–1). His first two lutebooks (1566), in Italian tablature, contain arrangements of songs, dances, and ricercars; the third (1574) also includes information about tuning. His brother **Conrad** (1541–*c*.1604) was a lutenist and composer. AL

Neuwirth, Olga (*b* Graz, 4 Aug. 1968). Austrian composer. She studied at the San Francisco Conservatory (1986–7) and at the Vienna Hochschule für Musik (1987–93), where her teachers included Erich Urbanner, and in Paris with Murail and at IRCAM. Her studies in painting and cinema are reflected in her music, which sometimes includes video and sound installations, for example the opera *Bählamms Fest* (1997–9). She has written many dramatic works and a number of instrumental pieces, many of which use electronics to create what she calls 'androgynous sound'. AL

Neveu, Ginette (*b* Paris, 11 Aug. 1919; *d* San Miguel, Azores, 28 Oct. 1949). French violinist. A child prodigy who appeared with Pierné at the age of seven, she studied at the Paris Conservatoire, then with Enescu and Carl Flesch. Her career began after she won the Wieniawski Competition in 1935; she toured throughout Europe and the USA, making her London debut in 1945. She was killed in an air crash on the way to the USA. Through her crafted interpretations and stylish virtuosity (in recordings of the Brahms and Sibelius concertos) she established herself as one of the finest postwar violinists. Poulenc composed his violin sonata for her. CF

📖 M.-J. RONZE-NEVEU, *Ginette Neveu* (Paris, 1952; Eng. trans. 1957)

New England Holidays. See HOLIDAYS.

New German School (Ger.: Neudeutsche Schule). A term coined in 1859 by K. F. Brendel, editor of the *Neue Zeitschrift für Musik*, to describe the group of musicians associated with Liszt during his time at Weimar (1848–61) and generally attaching themselves to the ideas of Wagner (who did not accept the appellation). They included Peter Cornelius, Hans von Bülow, and Joachim Raff; Berlioz's name is also often included, since some of his achievements owed much to Liszt's support. The term served largely as a challenge to alleged conservatives such as Mendelssohn and Brahms; but as the composers and their many successors and adherents who came under its description had much more to divide them than to unite them, it ultimately has little meaning.   JW

new musicology. A term that became something of a slogan in the late 1980s, especially in the USA. It arose out of the perception that musicology as a discipline had become too strongly based on sources, documentation, and newly discovered facts; that it lacked broader consideration of critical, aesthetic, psychological, perceptual, and sociological issues. At the same time there was a sharp rise in feminist musicology and, following soon after, gay and lesbian musicology—all subjects that inevitably looked more closely at contextual issues—and these too came under the banner of the new musicology.

In retrospect it is hard to see what was new about the broader basis thus proposed: it may have been unfashionable for a time in America, but it had been present uninterruptedly in European musicology from the days of Guido Adler's earliest attempt to define the discipline in 1885. Certainly there have been new ways of thinking, made possible particularly by developments in sociology, philosophy, and psychology; but musicology has almost always embraced new ideas from other disciplines, and its viability for the future will surely lie, at least in part, in its ability to continue doing so.   DF

New Orleans jazz. The collectively improvised small-ensemble style as played by black musicians in New Orleans in the early days of jazz (see JAZZ, 1) revived in the 1940s by such musicians as Bunk Johnson and George Lewis. It is differentiated from such contemporaneous styles as Chicago jazz, which is founded more on a series of solos. The term is now widely applied to any small-group jazz that is played in the spirit of early New Orleans music-making.   PGA

new wave. A term initially (from 1975) synonymous with *punk, but which after 1978 was used to promote bands playing a variety of styles of 'post-punk' music: the Stranglers, the Boomtown Rats, Blondie, and Talking Heads. Whereas punk had challenged the star system, Deborah Harry (Blondie) and Bob Geldof (Boomtown Rats) became sex symbols. Moreover, where punk had originally championed 'musical incompetence', new wave allowed musical experimentation, for example the influence of *progressive rock on the Stranglers, and of ethnic musics on Talking Heads.   PW

New World, From the (*Z nového světa*). Dvořák's Symphony no. 9 (no. 5 in the earlier numbering) in E minor (1893); it was composed while the composer was in the USA and uses themes resembling African-American traditional melodies.

New Year. Opera in three acts by Tippett to his own libretto (Houston, TX, 1989).

New Zealand. New Zealand became a British colony in 1840. During the next few decades, European migrants strove to recreate familiar cultural traditions in their new home. Music was the most popular of the performing arts: music teachers and music shops quickly appeared to meet the needs of a vigorous domestic market; amateur choral and orchestral societies flourished from the 1850s; and a thriving brass band movement began in the 1870s. The discovery of gold in 1861 stimulated population growth and created a demand for professional entertainment. Touring artists—from international soloists to opera companies—became a feature of musical life. The lighter operatic genres were so popular that a professional ensemble, the Pollard Opera Company, was able to work from a New Zealand base (*c.*1895–1905).

The thirst for musical education led to the setting up of a choir school (Christchurch, 1879) and the first university music school (Auckland, 1888). The earliest resident composer to combine European traditions with New Zealand influences was Alfred Hill, who studied in Leipzig and whose interest in Maori music and mythology found expression in such works as the cantata *Hinemoa* (1896) and an opera, *Tapu* (1903). Hill also conducted the first, short-lived, professional orchestra (1906–7). Musical life stagnated after World War I. Although regular radio broadcasts (from 1925) stimulated activity, it was not until the development of state patronage after World War II that there was a significant growth in professional musical institutions. Of prime importance was the National Orchestra, founded in 1946 as part of the newly centralized New Zealand Broadcasting Service (NZBS); it was renamed the New Zealand Symphony Orchestra (NZSO) in 1975.

Other professional orchestras developed on a regional basis. The Alex Lindsay String Orchestra (1948–73)

became the nucleus of the current Wellington Sinfonia; the Symphonia of Auckland (1970) expanded into the country's second-ranked orchestra, the innovatory Auckland Philharmonia. Also noteworthy are the Dunedin Sinfonia (founded 1965), the Christchurch Symphony Orchestra (1973), and the New Zealand Chamber Orchestra (1987). The pioneering Wellington Chamber Music Society (1945) inspired the growth of similar societies elsewhere. In 1987 a centralized national body, Chamber Music New Zealand, was set up; it has helped develop resident ensembles, notably the New Zealand String Quartet (1987).

Professional opera was restored with the founding in Wellington in 1954 of the New Zealand Opera Company, which grew into the biggest arts organization in the country. At its peak it suffered economic difficulties and in 1971 it went into recession. After the demise of the Auckland-based National Opera of New Zealand (1979–83), professional opera developed on a regional rather than a national basis: Canterbury Opera was founded in 1985 and New Zealand Opera in 2000 (by merging the Wellington and Auckland companies). New concert halls, a proliferation of festivals, and the establishment of such specialist collections as the Alexander Turnbull Library's Archive of New Zealand Music (1974), testify to the vitality of musical life.

A significant number of New Zealand composers has appeared. They acknowledge a debt to Douglas Lilburn; European-trained, he returned to New Zealand and in 1946 argued for 'a living tradition of music created in this country'. Works such as his *Landfall in Unknown Seas* (1942) profoundly influenced the first postwar generation of composers, among them Edwin Carr (*b* 1926), David Farquhar (*b* 1938), Larry Pruden (1925–82), and Ronald Tremain (*b* 1923). All spent at least part of their careers in New Zealand and trained or influenced the next generation, which includes Jack Body (*b* 1944), Christopher Blake (*b* 1949), Dorothy Buchanan (*b* 1945), Lyell Cresswell (*b* 1944), Ross Harris (*b* 1945), Jenny McLeod (*b* 1941), John Rimmer (*b* 1939), and Gillian Whitehead (*b* 1941). They display widely differing styles. Some have embraced modern technology, including computer techniques; others have absorbed the sounds of the Asia/Pacific region and synthesized them with European styles. They have profoundly influenced the new, predominantly university-trained generation of composers. The 'New Zealandness' of Eve de Castro-Robinson (*b* 1956), Gareth Farr (*b* 1968), David Hamilton (*b* 1955), Anthony Ritchie (*b* 1960), and their contemporaries underlies their compositional aesthetic.   AS

📖 D. R. HARVEY, *A Bibliography of Writings about New Zealand Music Published to the End of 1983* (Wellington, 1985) · J. M. THOMSON, *Biographical Dictionary of New Zealand Composers* (Wellington, 1990) · P. NORMAN, *Bibliography of New Zealand Compositions* (Christchurch, 1991) · J. M. THOMSON, *The Oxford History of New Zealand Music* (Auckland, 1991) · A. SIMPSON, *Opera's Farthest Frontier: A History of Professional Opera in New Zealand* (Auckland, 1996)

ney. The Central Asian spelling of **nāy*.

Niccolò da Perugia (*fl* 2nd half of the 14th century). Italian composer. He was probably based partly or wholly in Florence, though nothing certain is known about his biography. About 30 Italian-texted songs by him survive, the majority of them preserved in the Squarcialupi Codex (Florence, Biblioteca Medicea Laurenziana).   JM

Nicene Creed. See CREED.

Nicolai, (Carl) Otto (Ehrenfried) (*b* Königsberg [now Kaliningrad], 9 June 1810; *d* Berlin, 11 May 1849). German composer and conductor. The son of a composer determined that he should be an infant prodigy, he had a miserable childhood and finally ran away from home at the age of 16. He went to Berlin, where he studied with Zelter. In 1831 he moved to Rome as organist to the Prussian ambassador. There he studied Palestrina and other Italian classics, but it was with a funeral cantata for Bellini that he attracted attention. Failing to win an opera commission in Italy, however, he went to Vienna as singing teacher and Kapellmeister at the Hoftheater. When his year's contract was not renewed he successfully produced a number of operas at Italian theatres in the next few years, returning to Vienna in 1841 as director of the Hofoper. There he introduced Beethoven's overture *Leonore* no. 3 as an entr'acte in *Fidelio*. He was acclaimed as a conductor, founding with the orchestra what later became the Philharmonic Concerts, but having little opportunity to produce his own operas. After *Die lustigen Weiber von Windsor* was refused, he left in 1847 to take up the directorship of the cathedral choir in Berlin and to become Kapellmeister of the opera, where the work received its premiere in 1849. Its mixture of delicate orchestral tone-painting in a Mendelssohnian manner, tunefulness, and Italianate skill in the ensembles has ensured its place in the repertory in Germany and still sometimes abroad.   DA/JW

Niedermeyer, (Abraham) Louis (*b* Nyon, 27 April 1802; *d* Paris, 13 March 1861). French educationist and composer. After studying the piano with Moscheles in Vienna and composition in Italy, he settled in Paris in 1823. A few of his operas were performed there, of which the best was perhaps *Marie Stuart* (Opéra, 1844), but without notable success. In 1853 he founded the École Niedermeyer to give a grounding to church organists: Josquin, Palestrina, Victoria, and Bach formed the centre of the repertory, Schumann and Chopin were forbidden. Fauré, Gigout, and Messager were among its pupils. Niedermeyer wrote books of musical theory, church music (Berlioz praised his *Grande messe solennelle*), and songs, of which *Le Lac* (1825), a setting of Lamartine, is often considered to be the first French *mélodie*.   RN

Nielsen, Carl (August) (*b* Sortelung, nr Nørre Lyndelse, Fyn, 9 June 1865; *d* Copenhagen, 3 Oct. 1931). Danish composer. Born on the island of Fyn (Fünen) in 1865, an exact contemporary of Sibelius, Glazunov, and Dukas, he came from humble origins and was one of ten children. As a child he showed musical aptitude and played the trumpet in the local regimental band. His memoir, *My Childhood on Fyn*, is one of the classics of Danish literature. In 1884 he entered the Copenhagen Conservatory as a pupil of Gade. He remained in Copenhagen for the rest of his life, spending his early years as a violinist in the Royal Danish Orchestra under Johan Svendsen, whom he succeeded as conductor in 1906. His six symphonies bestride exactly the same period as those of Sibelius, though his development is quite different. The First (1892) bears the imprint of Brahms, Dvořák, and Svendsen, who conducted its premiere, the composer rising from his place among the second violins to acknowledge the applause.

In this work there is already evidence of Nielsen's early awareness of the role of key in the symphonic argument and a first glimpse of the 'progressive tonality' that was to become a hallmark of his thinking. It begins in G minor but progresses to a different key, C major. However, it rests on firm Classical foundations as does its powerfully concentrated programmatic successor, *De fire Temperamenter* ('The Four Temperaments', 1902). The four string quartets come from these early years, the last from 1906, the year of Nielsen's second opera, *Maskarade*, based on the 1724 play by Ludvig Holberg—a dramatist whose name is known to music lovers through Grieg's suite but is less familiar to theatre-goers. In his youth Nielsen became acquainted with much of the operatic repertory in the Royal Opera pit and would have played in the first Danish performances of Verdi's *Falstaff* and *Otello*. Later he became its conductor.

If the success of the First Symphony put Nielsen on the musical map in Denmark, the Third (*Sinfonia espansiva*) was the first of the six to establish his name in the wider world. Its premiere in Copenhagen in 1912 was a huge success, and he conducted further performances in Amsterdam with the Concertgebouw Orchestra, and in Stuttgart, Stockholm, Göteborg, and Helsinki. The *Sinfonia espansiva* comes from the same period as Sibelius's Fourth Symphony, and though it does not chart quite such mysterious territory it shows the expanding vision and wider spiritual horizon now within Nielsen's grasp. Nielsen introduces two solo voices singing a wordless vocalise in the glorious slow movement. But with the advent of World War I his musical language changed radically, and the last three symphonies inhabit new and more challenging territory. With the Fourth ('Det Uudslukkelige'—'The Inextinguishable'), written between 1914 and 1916, we enter a completely different climate. The confident morning of youth was now shattered and Europe plunged into barbarism. There is a level of violence (as opposed to energy) that is new in Nielsen's art. The lines soar in a more anguished and intense fashion, and there is a greater awareness of the erosion of tonality and of the musical values of the pre-war world in which he was brought up.

The Fifth Symphony (1920–1) is quite new in both its formal layout and its spiritual world. It breaks away almost completely from the principles that distinguished his earlier symphonies, and its organization has no Classical or Romantic precedents. There are two movements, the first of which is designed in three tonal planes, all a 5th apart; its companion movement is hardly less original in structure or content. Nielsen conducted its first performance in Copenhagen in January 1922, and Furtwängler gave the German premiere in Frankfurt five years later. It did not reach Britain until 1948, but it was Erik Tuxen's account with the Danish State Radio Orchestra at the Edinburgh Festival two years later that proved a decisive turning-point in Nielsen's fortunes. International recognition had come more slowly to Nielsen than to Sibelius, but when it did it was this symphony that blazed his trail.

Nielsen's 60th birthday in the summer of 1925 was celebrated in Denmark to much the same extent as Sibelius's 50th had been in Finland. A new symphony, the *Sinfonia semplice*, followed within months and Nielsen conducted its first performance himself, as he had all its predecessors except the First. The Sixth is the most rarely heard of the cycle and in some ways the most enigmatic. During the 1920s Nielsen was troubled by a series of heart attacks that gradually eroded his strength—and indeed it is hard not to sense this in the climax of the first movement. That movement is arguably his most poignant and visionary musical utterance. After the Sixth Symphony only the Flute and Clarinet Concertos and *Commotio* for organ were to come.

After the Fifth Symphony Nielsen had composed his Wind Quintet, one of the greatest examples of the genre; he then planned to compose concertos for each of the wind instruments. But he lived long enough to complete only two. Although there are wonderfully poignant overtones in the mercurial Flute Concerto (1926), the Clarinet Concerto (1928) is even more remarkable. If ever there was music from another planet, this is surely it. Its sonorities are sparse and monochrome, its air rarefied and bracing. As in the Fifth Symphony the side-drum is a leading participant in the argument, though the orchestral forces Nielsen uses are modest: two bassoons, two horns, and strings. Not only does the Clarinet Concerto occupy a special position in Nielsen's output, it is also one of the most remarkable clarinet concertos ever written. By 1925 both Nielsen and Sibelius had completed their symphonic odyssey, and Nielsen's heart condition claimed him in 1931.   RLa

📖 R. Simpson, *Carl Nielsen, Symphonist* (London, 1978) · M. Miller (ed.), *A Nielsen Companion* (London, 1994)

Nietzsche, Friedrich (Wilhelm) (*b* Röcken, 15 Oct. 1844; *d* Weimar, 25 Aug. 1900). German philosopher. His influence on 19th- and 20th-century thought has been profound. He first met Wagner in 1868 and under his influence wrote *Das Geburt der Tragödie aus dem Geiste der Musik* ('The Birth of Tragedy from the Spirit of Music', 1872). Widely regarded as among the most important works in the history of aesthetics, it posits the idea of Wagnerian music drama as the resurrection of the spirit of Greek tragedy in which the initial balance between the 'Apollonian' (words and rationality) and the 'Dionysiac' (music and the irrationality of convulsive emotion), sundered by the works of Euripides, is brought back into realignment.

A rift between Nietzsche and Wagner occurred in 1876; its exact cause has never been fully established, though it has frequently been attributed either to Nietzsche's objection to what he deemed to be excessive Christian elements and the renunciatory ethics of *Parsifal*, or to his concerns that Wagner's music was increasingly becoming the focus of the German nationalism he abhorred. Nietzsche subsequently mounted fierce, almost obsessive attacks on Wagner whenever the opportunity arose, though it is probable that the kernel of his philosophy remained influenced by Wagner's vision of the destruction of the gods at the end of the *Ring*.

His stance is nihilistic and existential. His key concept is 'the death of God', by which he means the redundancy of all metaphysical and moral structures. All established values must be 'transvaluated' by the *Übermensch*, variously translated as 'superman' or 'overman', the man of the future who exists 'beyond good and evil'. The crystallization of his philosophy is contained in *Also sprach Zarathustra* (1883–5), which is written in an untypical, poetic style and provided Strauss with the inspiration for his tone-poem of the same name (1895–6), though Strauss departs from Nietzsche in tone and stance. Mahler's Third Symphony (1893–6) and Delius's *A Mass of Life* (1904–5) draw on *Also sprach Zarathustra* for their texts. Nietzsche's concept of the 'transvaluation of values' may be seen as prefiguring Schoenberg's reworking of tonality in music and the linguistic experiments of James Joyce in literature.

Nietzsche was a gifted pianist and also a composer, though none of his music has entered the repertory. His only musical work published in his lifetime was the choral *Hymnus an das Leben* to a text by the writer and psychologist Lou Andreas-Salomé, with whom he was in love. A number of songs, written between 1854 and 1874, were posthumously published in 1924.

TA

📖 R. Hollinrake, *Nietzsche, Wagner and the Philosophy of Pessimism* (London, 1982)

Night at the Chinese Opera, A. Opera in three acts by Weir to her own libretto partly based on Chi Chun-Hsiang's *The Chao Family Orphan* (Cheltenham, 1987).

Nightingale, The (*Solovey*; *Le Rossignol*). Opera (lyric tale) in three acts by Stravinsky to a libretto by Stepan Mitusov after the tale by Hans Christian Andersen (Paris, 1914). At Diaghilev's request, Stravinsky arranged music from the second and third acts as a ballet score, *Chant du rossignol* (Paris, 1920); the previous year it was given in concert, and it is now better known as a symphonic poem.

night music. See Nachtmusik.

Night on the Bare Mountain (*Ivanova noch' na Lïsoy gore*; 'St John's Night on Bald Mountain'). Orchestral work (1867) by Musorgsky, inspired by the witches' sabbath in Nikolay Gogol's story *St John's Eve*. He revised it as a choral piece for inclusion in the opera *Mlada* (1872), and again revised it as a choral introduction to Act III of *Sorochintsy Fair* (1874–80). This final version was freely revised and orchestrated by Rimsky-Korsakov, and though it is the most well known, it is no longer really Musorgsky's.

Nights in the Gardens of Spain. See Noches en los jardines de España.

Nikisch, Arthur (*b* Lébénymiklós, 12 Oct. 1855; *d* Leipzig, 23 Jan. 1922). Austro-Hungarian conductor. He began as a violinist and after studying the piano and composition at the Vienna Conservatory he joined the Vienna Court Orchestra and played under Brahms, Liszt, Verdi, Wagner, and Bruckner. In 1878 he was appointed second conductor of the Leipzig Opera. He soon became internationally famous, conducting the Boston Symphony Orchestra (1889–93), the Budapest Opera (1893–5), and the Leipzig Gewandhaus and Berlin Philharmonic Orchestras (1895). A frequent guest conductor in England, he took the LSO on its first American tour (1912). He had a hypnotic effect on musicians and obtained great warmth, flexibility, and precision through restrained but elegant gestures, as can be seen on an archive film. In the Wagnerian tradition, his interpretations were elastic and improvisatory. He was an influential advocate of the music of his contemporaries Tchaikovsky, Bruckner, Mahler, and Strauss, and he also composed.   JT

Nilsson, Bo (*b* Skelleftehamn, 1 May 1937). Swedish composer. Largely self-taught, he came to early prominence when his *Frequenzen* for eight instrumentalists was performed at Darmstadt in 1956. This and later works show the strong influence of Stockhausen and Boulez. In the 1960s he broadened his style, writing simple, lyrical scores for film and television. He incorporated electronics and jazz material and showed a predilection for unusual instrumental combinations.

PG/MA

Nin (y Castellanos), Joaquín (*b* Havana, 29 Sept. 1879; *d* Havana, 24 Oct. 1949). Cuban composer and pianist. He emigrated to Spain as a child and studied in Barcelona and Paris (1902), where he taught the piano at the Schola Cantorum (1905–8). He revisited Havana in 1910 and left Europe for good in 1939. As a performer he was a noted exponent of the Spanish Baroque and French Impressionist repertories. He wrote quantities of folk-based vocal and piano music, of which he is best remembered for the *20 cantos populares españoles* (1923) and *Danza ibérica* (1926).   CW

ninth chord. A triad with a 7th and 9th added. See DIMINISHED SEVENTH CHORD; DOMINANT SEVENTH CHORD.

Nivers, Guillaume Gabriel (*b* ?Paris, *c.*1632; *d* Paris, 30 Nov. 1714). French organist and composer. He was organist at St Sulpice, Paris, from the early 1650s until his death, and from 1678 was one of the organists of the royal chapel. From 1686 he was also in charge of the music at the convent school of St Louis at St Cyr. He composed some agreeable solo motets, but his most important music was for organ. His three *Livres d'orgue* (Paris, 1665–75) consist of versets for church use, and the prefaces contain important information on performance practice of the time.   DA

Nixon in China. Opera in two acts by Adams to a libretto by Alice Goodman (Houston, TX, 1987).

nō. A highly stylized form of Japanese theatre established in the late 14th and early 15th centuries, synthesizing elements of literature, theatre, dance, and music, and featuring both symbolism and economy of means. The participants comprise three categories of actor (principal, second principal, and comic relief), a small chorus (singing in unison), two assistants, and three or four instrumentalists (playing bamboo flute, hourglass drums, and barrel-drum). The actors' music includes intoned monologues and dialogues, as well as solo singing, in both metrical and free rhythm with instrumental accompaniment usually based, like the vocal lines, on units of eight beats.   IR

Nobilissima visione. Ballet by Hindemith to his own scenario, choreographed by Leonid Massine for the Ballets Russes de Monte Carlo (London, 1938).

nobilmente (It.). 'Nobly'.

Noblemen and Gentlemen's Catch Club. Society founded in 1761 to encourage the composition of catches, canons, and glees; its bicentenary was commemorated with a partsong commissioned from Malcolm Arnold.

Noces, Les (*Svadebka*; 'The Wedding'). Four choreographic scenes by Stravinsky to words adapted by the composer from Russian traditional sources, for soprano, mezzo-soprano, tenor, and bass soloists, chorus, four pianos, and 17 percussion instruments (including four timpani); it was choreographed by Bronislava Nijinska for Diaghilev's Ballets Russes (Paris, 1923).

Noches en los jardines de España ('Nights in the Gardens of Spain'). Three symphonic impressions for piano and orchestra by Falla, composed 1911–15: *En el Generalife* ('In the Generalife'), *Danza lejana* ('Dance in the Distance'), and *En los jardinos de la Sierra de Córdoba*.

nocturn. Part of Matins in the Roman rite before 1971, consisting primarily of psalmody, readings, and responsories. The contents of each nocturn and the number of nocturns in the Office varied according to usage and occasion.

nocturne (Fr., 'of the night'; Ger.: *Nachtstück*). A 19th-century, Romantic piano piece of a slow and dreamy nature in which a graceful, highly embellished melody in the right hand is accompanied by a broken-chord pattern in the left. The title was first used by John Field, and was taken up by Chopin, whose 21 examples are unsurpassed.

In the 20th century the term was also applied to pieces that depicted musically the sounds of night; for example in the fourth movement of Bartók's piano suite *Out of Doors* (1928), the noises made by insects, birds, and other night creatures are imitated.   —/JBE

Nocturnes. Three symphonic poems (1897–9) by Debussy: *Nuages* ('Clouds'), *Fêtes* ('Festivals'), and *Sirènes* ('Sirens', with women's voices). Debussy took the title from paintings by James McNeill Whistler.

node. The point of rest between two wave motions of a vibrating string or other body. Several nodes occur along the length of a string, and harmonics on a string instrument are produced by the player lightly touching the string at each of these points. In a vibrating air column, such as a pipe, nodes are the points of highest density, where the air particles do not move.

See ACOUSTICS, 5.

noël (Fr.; Burgundian: *noé*) [nowell] (from Lat. *natalis*, 'of birth'). 'Christmas'. The word was used as an expression of joy at the Christmas season and often appears in the texts of French *noëls* and English *carols. In France since the 15th century the term has referred to strophic, popular Christmas songs, whose music might be taken from liturgical chant, or well-known songs or dance tunes. In spite of the carol's popularity in 15th-century England, there are comparatively few French *noëls* from this period. From the 16th century to the 18th, however, a large number of vernacular French texts were printed, with suggestions as to appropriate melodies. They were sung in the streets and were interpolated into the midnight Mass of Christmas.

From the 17th century, organists played instrumental variations on *noël* melodies; many surviving keyboard transcriptions of these survive, notably by Daquin and Dandrieu. Instrumental arrangements were made by Charpentier and others. *Noëls* fell out of favour at the French Revolution, but they were sung again in late 19th-century Paris; at the same time, Franck and Guilmant also composed new organ *noëls*. There are 20th-century examples by Dupré and Tournemire.

PW

Nola, Giovanni Domenico del Giovane da (*b* Nola, nr Naples, *c*.1510; *d* Naples, May 1592). Italian composer and organist. He was *maestro di cappella* at Ss. Annunziata, Naples, from 1563, and also taught singing there. He was famous as a composer of secular songs, especially villanescas and napolitanas.   DA

nomine, In. See IN NOMINE.

None. Originally the sixth of eight hours of the Divine *Office in the medieval Roman rite. Since the reforms of the Second Vatican Council, *Terce, *Sext, and None may be combined as one 'Hora Media' ('Prayer during the Day').

nonet (Fr.: *nonette*; Ger.: *Nonett*; It.: *nonetto*). An ensemble of nine instruments or voices, or music written for it. Frequently encountered is the combination of two standard ensembles: a string quartet (two violins, viola, and cello) and a wind quintet (flute, oboe, clarinet, horn, bassoon), or the same but with a double bass replacing the second violin. The best-known and most popular nonet is Spohr's *Grand nonetto* op. 31; later examples include those of Martinů (1959) and Copland (1960), the latter for three violins, three violas, and three cellos.

See also CHAMBER MUSIC.

Non nobis Domine. A celebrated vocal canon, usually sung in three parts, attributed (without evidence) to Byrd. It was traditionally sung at banquets as a 'grace after meat'. The opening phrase was common in music from the 16th to the 18th centuries: Handel used it in his 'Hallelujah Chorus'.

Nono, Luigi (*b* Venice, 29 Jan. 1924; *d* Venice, 8 May 1990). Italian composer. He began composing during World War II under the influence of Malipiero, a fellow Venetian. Through Malipiero he came into contact with Maderna, and through Maderna he met Hermann Scherchen, who encouraged him and conducted the first performance of his *Variazioni canoniche* for chamber orchestra at the Darmstadt summer school in 1950. The next year at Darmstadt Nono met Stockhausen, and his commitment to musical modernism intensified. So too did his commitment to left-wing socialism, and there is a burning sense of protest in much of his music, from the *Epitaffio per Federico García Lorca* for solo voices, chorus, and orchestra (1951–3) through *Il canto sospeso* for similar forces (1955–6, setting lines from letters by war martyrs), to the opera *Intolleranza 1960* (Venice, 1961), the drama of a victim. Remarkably, he expressed the same passionate defiance in his purely orchestral works, for example *Due espressioni* (1953), *Incontri* (1954), and *Varianti*, with solo violin (1957). In 1955 he married Schoenberg's daughter Nuria, for whom he wrote the delicate *Liebeslied* for chorus and instruments (1954).

During the early 1960s Nono began to distance himself from conventional concert life, which he felt tied him to the economy and sensibility of the bourgeois system he was striving to contradict. He began giving concerts in factories and using electronic means, as in *La fabbrica illuminata* for soprano and tape (1964), *Per Bastiana Tai-Yang Cheng* for orchestra and tape

(1967), and the explosive *Como una ola de fuerza y luz* for soprano, piano, and orchestra (1971–2). The culmination of this period was his second opera, *Al gran sole carico d'amore* (Milan, 1975).

After that Nono's music became suddenly more intimate and calm, concerned less now with expressing fury at injustice and sympathy for the oppressed than with inviting close listening. Major works of this later period include … *sofferte onde serene* … for piano and tape (1976), *Fragmente-Stille* for string quartet (1980), and *Prometeo* (Venice, 1984), a third opera, but one with no stage action—a drama of listening to soloists and groups performing in different parts of the auditorium, with and without electronic transformation. Here and in later scores he worked with a small number of dedicated instrumentalists on new sounds, retaining to the end his passion for discovery. PG

📖 M. TAIBON, *Luigi Nono und sein Musiktheater* (Cologne, 1993) · J. STENZL, *Luigi Nono* (Regensburg, 1998)

Nordheim, Arne (*b* Larvik, 20 June 1931). Norwegian composer. He studied at the Oslo Conservatory (1948–52) and was music critic of the Oslo newspaper *Dagbladet* (1960–8). His first works show the influence of Bartók and such Nordic symphonists as Saeverud and Holmboe; but his ground-breaking song cycle *Aftonland* ('Evening Land', 1957) shows him already experimenting with new combinations of sounds. This led in the 1960s to a growing interest in electronic music, especially in combination with voices and familiar Western instruments. Outstanding in this genre is his voluptuous setting of Caliban's song from *The Tempest*, 'Be not affeared' (1978), which plunges from dense modernist soundscapes to warm tonal harmonies and simple vocal melodies with impressive ease. More recently, Nordheim has turned towards conventional forces, as in the elegiac Rilke setting *Wirklicher Wald* (1983) and the powerful one-movement Violin Concerto (1996), written for the violinist Arne Tellefsen. SJ

Nordqvist, Gustav (Lazarus) (*b* Stockholm, 12 Feb. 1886; *d* Stockholm, 28 Jan. 1949). Swedish composer. He studied composition with Ernst Ellberg and the piano with Lundberg at the Stockholm Conservatory (1901–10), and was also a pupil of Willner in Berlin (1913). While working in Stockholm as a teacher and organist, he composed about 200 songs and various other works in a late Romantic idiom. PG

Nørgård, Per (*b* Gentofte, 13 July 1932). Danish composer. He studied with Holmboe and Høffding at the Copenhagen Conservatory (1952–5), then taught in Odense, Århus, and at the Copenhagen Conservatory

until 1965, when he resigned in protest over educational policies. As a teacher he has profoundly influenced younger generations of Danish composers. Sibelius was perhaps the most important single influence on Nørgård's own early music, particularly the First Symphony (*Sinfonia austera*, 1954); but encounters with the music of the postwar central European avant-garde, and with musics of other cultures (especially India and East Asia), enriched his artistic palette dramatically.

In the early 1960s Nørgård began to develop his own form of serialism, which he called the 'infinity series' because of its ability to produce apparently limitless transformations of a basic note row. His first opera, *Labyrinten* (1963), and his Second Symphony (1970) show this technique at its most rigorous, but in later works it is merely the springboard for much broader stylistic adventures. In the choral Third Symphony (1975), for instance, dense microtonal polyphony alternates with luminous tonal harmonies and simple, folk-like tunes. The resulting pluralistic mixtures have been compared to the 'polystylistic' works of Schnittke and Gubaidulina, but in Nørgård's finest works there is a sense of underlying unity, a spiritual synthesis which may reflect the continuing influence of Sibelius. As well as six symphonies, Nørgård has also composed five operas, ranging from the ambitious *Siddharta* (1979) to the powerfully concentrated one-act *Nuit des hommes* (1996), which uses only two voices, string quartet, and electronics. SJ

📖 A. BEYER (ed.), *The Music of Per Nørgård: Fourteen Interpretative Essays* (Aldershot, 1996)

Norma. Opera in two acts by Bellini to a libretto by Felice Romani after Alexandre Soumet's verse tragedy *Norma* (Milan, 1831).

Norway. For much of the four centuries before Grieg, Norway was the most sparsely populated of the Scandinavian countries and the least musically active. As in Sweden, there were a few foreign musicians, for example Johan Daniel Berlin (1714–87) who settled in Trondheim, but, for all his expertise and intelligence, he did not possess as distinctive a musical profile as did Johan Helmich Roman or other Swedish composers. He was one of the founder members of the Trondheim Music Society in 1787 and organist at the cathedral where he was succeeded by his son, Johan Henrik Berlin (1741–1807). But it was in Bergen, with its strong links to the Continent and England, that the first important Norwegian orchestra, the Harmonien (now known as the Bergen Philharmonic), was founded.

1. The 19th century; 2. The 20th century

1. The 19th century

During the Napoleonic wars Norway emerged from its 400-year domination by Denmark, when it had been a provincial outpost with little significant cultural life of its own, only to find that its newly won freedom was immediately lost. Under the terms of the Treaty of Tilsit, Sweden ceded Finland to Russia, and Norway was then forced into an uncomfortable union with Sweden. For the rest of the century and until the dissolution of the union in 1905 Norway was searching for a national identity. Grieg's compositions, like the writings of Ibsen and of Bjørnstjerne Bjørnson, were part of this quest. Ludvig Mathias Lindeman (1812–87) drew the attention of his countrymen to the riches of their folk music with the publication of his *Aeldre og nyere norske fjeldmelodier* (1853–67), which did much to stimulate the growth of Norwegian art song during the latter half of the century. The foundations were laid by Halfdan Kjerulf (1815–68) and Rikard Nordraak (1842–66), who played a formative part in Grieg's development.

It was natural that Norwegian national feeling should grow during Swedish dominance in the 19th century, and its artists look to their own cultural roots. Niels Gade in Denmark and Berwald in Sweden were relatively indifferent to folk music, which took a stronger hold in Norway due in no small measure to the strength and richness of the folk repertory itself. When Grieg immersed himself in the Leipzig tradition of Mendelssohn and Schumann, he emerged with the basis for his musical grammar, but it was Norwegian folksong, whose treasures he discovered much later in Lindeman, that was the foundation on which his distinctive musical speech developed. Its impact on Svendsen was less pervasive but none the less striking, as exemplified by the Four Norwegian Rhapsodies. It reaches its apogee in Grieg's Norwegian Dances op. 72.

2. The 20th century

Few composers in the generation after Grieg remained untouched by folk inspiration: Johan Halvorsen (1864–1935), Arne Eggen (1881–1955), and Ludvig Irgens-Jensen (1894–1969) were three such, the last named making the most effective and original use of folk music. The principal exception is Christian Sinding, a contemporary of Elgar and the leading figure after Grieg and Svendsen; his musical language is neo-romantic and has its roots in Wagner, Liszt, and Strauss rather than Norwegian folk music. Halvorsen is of greater interest: if his musical language is not exploratory, it is pleasingly fresh, though the idiom is much indebted to Grieg. Other interwar composers such as Grieg's biographer David Monrad Johansen

(1888–1974) and Pauline Hall (1890–1969) looked to France for musical stimulus.

Perhaps the boldest and certainly the most individual composer of all was Harald Saeverud, who first attracted attention outside Norway with his music to a postwar production of *Peer Gynt*, but such works as *The Ballad of Revolt*, with its dark, combative, invigorating character rallied Norwegian spirits during the Nazi occupation. His powerfully lyrical Symphony no. 6 conveys a strong sense of the Norwegian landscape.

Fartein Valen, who reacted against the folk heritage, grew up in Madagascar and studied with Bruch. During the 1920s he evolved his own 12-note style, an achievement all the more remarkable given his isolation. His younger contemporaries continued with folk-inspired material, including Eivind Groven (1901–77) and the irrepressibly prolific Geirr Tveitt (1908–81), both from Telemark. However, the postwar years witnessed developments not dissimilar to those in the neighbouring Scandinavian countries, and the sheer profusion of music by composers little known outside their native country is striking. Among them are Olav Kielland (1901–85); Klaus Egge (1906–79), a pupil of Valen; Bjarne Brustad (1895–1978), who composed in a traditional diatonic idiom; Finn Mortensen (1922–83), who used a modified 12-note technique (he studied briefly with Bentzon in the mid-1950s); and many other Norwegian symphonists, including Conrad Baden (1908–89) and Edvard Fliflet Braein (1924–76).

Almost every modern school has its adherents, though perhaps the most widely recognized figure to have emerged is the eclectic and imaginative Arne Nordheim, who has made effective use of electronic means. Among the most original is Saeverud's son Ketil Hvoslef (*b* 1939; he adopted his mother's maiden name), who once described himself as 'striving to retain an intuitiveness and sensitivity to my surroundings so as to compose music that seems as natural as folk music'. Hvoslef has charted an individual course in this landscape. Of the next generation Halvor Haug (*b* 1952) is another composer at one with the sounds and the landscape of the northern latitudes.

In the last two decades the Oslo Philharmonic has become one of the finest orchestras in Europe, and the amount of music-making in Norway, given generous state and private patronage, is both in quantity and quality far greater than one might expect for such a small population.   RLa

📖 N. Grinde, *Norsk musikkhistorie* (Oslo, 1971, 2/1993; Eng. trans. 1991) · K. Lange, *Norwegian Music: A Survey* (Oslo, 1971) · J. H. Yoell, *The Nordic Sound* (Oslo, 1974) · H. Herresthal, 'From Grieg to Lasse Thoresen: An essay on Norwegian musical identity', *Nordic Sounds*, 2 (1993), 3–9

Nose, The (*Nos*). Opera in three acts by Shostakovich to a libretto by the composer, Yevgeny Zamyatin, Georgy Ionin, and Aleksandr Preys after the story by Nikolay Gogol (1835) (Leningrad, 1930).

Nostre Dame Mass. See NOTRE DAME MASS.

nota cambiata (It.). 'Changing note' (literally 'changed note'); an idiomatic melodic formula whose salient feature is the leap of a 3rd away from an unessential note. The *nota cambiata* should not be confused with the *cambiata* (see ÉCHAPPÉE).

notation. The term 'musical notation' can be applied to any formal indication of how sounds and silences intended as music should be reproduced. Major variations in notation arise with dramatic changes of date or provenance, but decisive technical variations can also occur according to the performance medium (orchestral, electronic, keyboard, vocal, etc.), the style or genre (cadenza, symphony, blues, etc.), the circumstances of the performer (Braille notation, elementary didactic notations, etc.), and experiments in vocal and instrumental usage and technique (e.g. Cage's music for prepared piano, Bartók's expansions of string-playing technique). This article will concentrate on the origins and development of staff notation in the West, and on music written for the standard ensembles and solo performers of art music.

1. Neumatic notation, 800–1200; 2. The 13th and 14th centuries; 3. The 15th and 16th centuries; 4. The 17th and 18th centuries. 5. From the 19th century to the present day

1. Neumatic notation, 800–1200

The origins of the present-day notational system lie in the various plainchant sources and theoretical treatises of the 9th and 10th centuries. Plainchant was first notated with 'neumes': small dots and squiggles probably derived in part from the accentual signs once used in the Latin language. Their various shapes (see Fig. 1) represent either single notes or groups of notes. Those that represent groups of notes strung together are called **ligatures'* (from Lat. *ligare*, 'to bind'), and this term continues to be used for all compound note forms found in various notations up to the 17th century. The basic plainchant neumes acted as a memory aid, suggesting (but not precisely indicating) changes of pitch within the melody. There were also **liquescent'* neumes—ornamental neumes that required special types of vocal delivery.

By the end of the 10th century, some sources were arranging the neumes vertically on the page to show their relative pitch (see DIASTEMATIC NEUMES). Shortly after, Guido of Arezzo (*c.*991–after 1033) brought the various experiments brilliantly into focus. In his *Aliae regulae* (*c.*1030) he recommended that a staff should be used with spaces as well as lines indicating pitches, and

BASIC NEUMES	St Gallen	Modern plainchant	Approximate equivalent	SIGNIFICATIVE LETTERS (*some examples from St Gallen*)
virga	/	▎	♪	a = *altius*, chant rises higher in pitch
tractulus/ punctum	– ·	▪ ▪	♪ ♪	b = *bene*, 'very'; used with another letter
pes/ podatus	↲↲	▗	♫	c = *cito* or *celeriter*, 'rapidly' or 'quickly'
clivis/ flexa	↷	▚	♫	e = *equaliter*, 'the same' (pitch)
scandicus	·/	▎or▗	♫♪	k = *klenche*, with a ringing tone
climacus	/··	▎··	♫♪	t = *trahere* or *tenere*, 'drag out' or 'hold'
torculus	♪	▚	♫♪	x = *exspectare*, 'wait'
porrectus	∿	▙	♫♪	
ORNAMENTAL NEUMES				
oriscus	◠		*oriscus* (Gk.) = 'limit' or 'little hill': perhaps the pitch should rise to anticipate the following note	
quilisma	·⸲	◢	described by the theorist Aurelian of Réôme as a trembling and rising sound	
LIQUESCENT NEUMES				
epiphonus (liquescent *pes*)	↗	▗	Liquescence was used for singing certain consonants and diphthongs in the text; it resulted in semi-vocalization as the singer passed to the next note. This semi-vocalization occurred on the last note of each group; it was used particularly when words were sung containing the consonants l, m, n, r, d, t, and s followed by another consonant.	
cephalicus (liquescent *clivis*)	↘	▊		
ancus (liquescent *climacus*)	↘	▎··		

Fig. 1. Neume shapes.

Fig. 2. (a) Facsimile of Pérotin, *Viderunt omnes* (Florence, Biblioteca Laurenziana, Pluteo 29.1).

that at least one of the lines should be identified by a pitch letter (i.e. *clef). Guido also suggested that two different forms of the letter b be used to describe the pitches B♭ and B♮. These letter signs are the earliest known accidentals in Western music (see DURUM AND MOLLIS). It is perhaps significant that this attention to precise pitch notation and chromatic inflection coincided with the first written polyphonic music and its inevitable concern with vertical (harmonic) relationships.

2. The 13th and 14th centuries

An important development about 1200 was the codification of set ways of combining ligatures so as to indicate clearly the rhythmic patterns of the music. These set patterns were called 'rhythmic modes' and in the basic system there were six of them. Thus, if a composer wished to write the ♩♪♩♪ rhythm (first mode) he would use a three-note ligature followed by a two-note group, e.g. ♩ ♪. Just such a group can be seen in the top voice of Fig. 2a after the initial long note and rest. The whole system is set out in Fig. 3. The smallest unit in each modal pattern was called an *ordo*, and the ligature pattern that signalled the mode was sufficient for at least two *ordines*. The fullest description of the rhythmic modes is given in Johannes de Garlandia's *De mensurabili musicae* (*c*.1240). Even so, the meaning of any particular note or rest still depended on its context, and not until about 1260 in the *Ars cantus mensurabilis* by Franco of Cologne do we find an attempt to stabilize the relationship between the shape of a note and its value (see FRANCONIAN NOTATION; MENSURAL MUSIC, MENSURAL NOTATION). This was the beginning of modern notation. Unlike modern notation, however, which is based on duple relationships (two crotchets in a minim, two minims in a

Fig. 2. (b) Transcription.

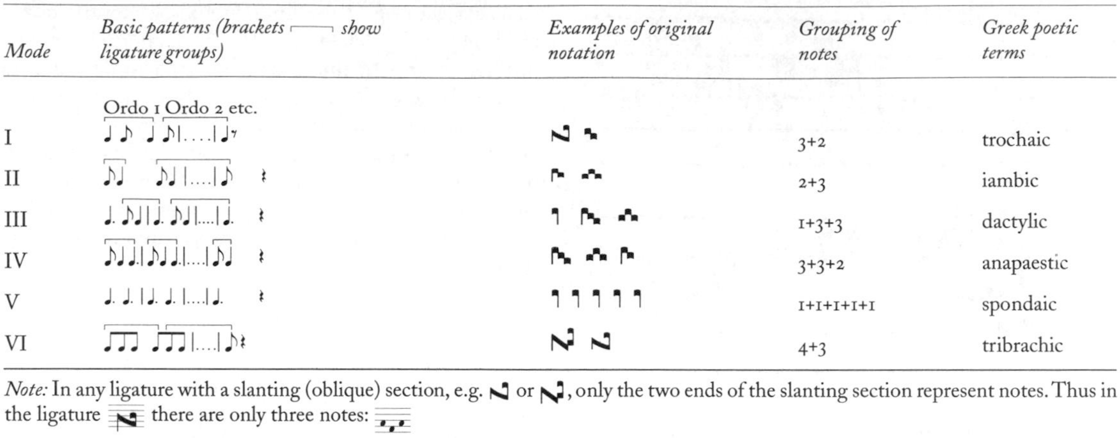

Mode	Basic patterns (brackets ⌐ show ligature groups)	Examples of original notation	Grouping of notes	Greek poetic terms
	Ordo 1 Ordo 2 etc.			
I	♩♪ ♩♪|....|♩♪	◢ ▪	3+2	trochaic
II	♪♩ ♪♩|....|♪ ✦	▪ ▪▪	2+3	iambic
III	♩.♪♩|♩. ♪♩|....|♩. ✦	▪ ▪▪ ▪▪	1+3+3	dactylic
IV	♪♩.♪♩|♩....|♪♩ ✦	▪▪ ▪▪ ▪	3+3+2	anapaestic
V	♩. ♩.|♩. ♩.|....|♩. ✦	▪ ▪ ▪ ▪ ▪	1+1+1+1+1	spondaic
VI	♫♫ ♫♫♪|....|♪✦	◢ ◢	4+3	tribrachic

Note: In any ligature with a slanting (oblique) section, e.g. ◢ or ◣, only the two ends of the slanting section represent notes. Thus in the ligature ▬ there are only three notes: ▬.

Fig. 3. The rhythmic modes.

semibreve, etc.), this music also had triple relationships (three minims in a semibreve and so on; see PROLATION). In such triple-time music, notes could be made duple only by being 'imperfected' in some way, for example by writing the note in red (see COLORATION).

The 14th-century French notational system is described in a collection of writings based on the theories of Philippe de Vitry. (The different system used in Italy did not survive beyond about 1430.) For the first time the minim is now fully accepted as a note-value in its own right rather than as a special (i.e. 'minimum') kind of semibreve. Moreover, the relationship between the semibreve and the minim is given exactly the same status as that previously accorded to both the long and breve, and the breve and semibreve (see Fig. 4*a*). A series of 'time signatures' (mensuration signs) eventually came into being which defined precisely the relationships between the various note-values (see Fig. 4*b*). If there were three semibreves in the breve (i.e. perfect *tempus*) this was shown by a perfect circle, O; imperfect *tempus* (two semibreves in the breve) was shown by the half-circle C. Furthermore, a perfect or imperfect relationship between the semibreve and minim (prolation) was indicated by the presence or absence of a dot respectively. Thus, when both the *tempus* and prolation were imperfect, for example, the appropriate symbol was the half-circle on its own. (This is the origin of the time signature **C** for 2/4 and 4/4 time—it does not come from the initial letter of 'common time'.) A brief illustration of the way in which the system worked can be seen from a *ballade* by Machaut, *Ne pensez pas*, in which both the *tempus* and prolation are perfect; this means that the piece is in ⊙ time, but the time signature is not provided in the particular source shown (see Fig. 5).

3. The 15th and 16th centuries

Around 1450 the solid black notes of earlier periods were replaced by void notes. This was because paper had replaced parchment as a writing surface, and the concentration of ink needed for black notation tended to eat through the paper rather quickly; the solution was simply to put the notation in outline (see Fig. 6). Also there was a decline in the use of *ligatures due partly to the establishment of music-printing (1501), which could not cope well with them, but also to the new tendency to print music in score format which required notes to be synchronized vertically—almost impossible with ligatures. The earliest print of vocal music in score format (complete with bar-lines) was Cipriano de Rore's 1577 collection of four-voice madrigals published in Venice.

Many details of modern notational usage were established in instrumental music. The earliest extensive use of ties, slurs, and ledger lines occurs in M. A. Cavazzoni's keyboard volume *Recerchari, motetti, canzoni* (Venice, 1523). Bar-lines, somewhat inconsistently used, occur as early as the 14th century, but not until the mid-17th century do we find them arranged to coincide with regularly recurring accents in the music. By the 15th century the natural sign ♮ is used almost as frequently as the sharp ♯ and flat ♭ signs, and composers are also beginning regularly to use sharp 'key signatures' as well as the flat ones common in the medieval period.

The consistent use of tempo markings began in the 16th century. In Luis de Milán's vihuela book *El maestro*

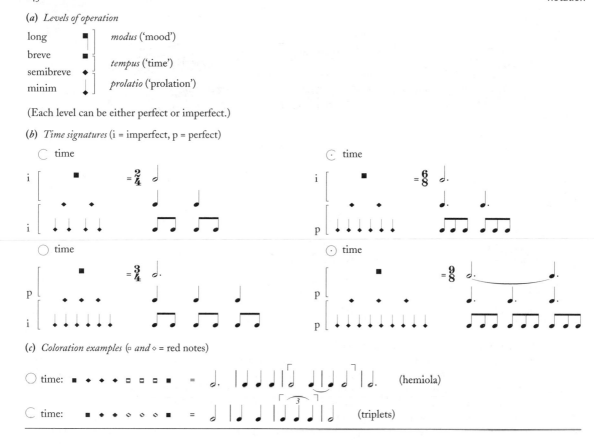

(c) *Coloration examples* (▫ and ◇ = red notes)

Fig. 4. French Ars Nova notation.

(Valencia, 1536) each piece is prefaced by instructions including such tempo descriptions as *apriessa* ('swift') or *espacio* ('slow'). As for dynamic markings, the Capirola lutebook (*c.*1517) contains the instruction *tocca pian' piano* ('play very softly') for one of the pieces.

4. The 17th and 18th centuries

In the Baroque period such archaic devices as coloration, proportions, and ligatures are still found, particularly in works by 'learned' composers writing in the **stile antico*. But it was in instrumental music and secular vocal music that far-reaching notational experiments took place. The G clef gained wide acceptance in French and English harpsichord music, but it was not until Grétry published his *Mémoires, ou Essai sur la musique* in 1789 that there was a real attempt to make G and F clefs standard for all music. In spite of some early experiments with metronomes (Thomas Mace in 1676, Étienne Loulié in 1696, etc.) tempo was usually indicated by descriptive words. In 1683 Purcell states (introduction to *Sonnata's of III Parts*) that Italian descriptions of tempo are in international use. Also, the use of the basso continuo and the growth of standard orchestral combinations led to a more uniform appearance in score format. The function of the score remained ambiguous, however, and not until Purcell's *Dioclesian* (1691) and Pepusch's edition of Corelli's sonatas (1732) was the idea of **Urtext* study scores becoming established.

The preoccupation with expression and articulation led not only to more dramatic styles of music and performance—*empfindsamer Stil* (see EMPFINDSAMKEIT), **Sturm und Drang*, the **Mannheim 'rocket'*, and so on—but also to a host of ancillary symbols and instructions within the notation. We find bowing marks (e.g. in Corelli's *Follia* op. 5 no. 12, 1700), fingering indications (as early as some sources of English virginal music), and, in the late 18th century, pedalling signs for the pianoforte. Gradual changes of dynamic had been a desirable musical effect since at least the 16th century (they are described in treatises by Zarlino, Ganassi, and others), and *crescendo, diminu-*

Fig. 5. (a) Facsimile of Machaut, *Ne pensez pas* (Paris, Bibliothèque Nationale, MS fr. 1584).

Fig. 5. (b) Transcription.

endo, and other markings were used extensively by Vivaldi and others in the Baroque period.

No aspect of Baroque notation is more contentious than the interpretation of dotted rhythms. A *dot after a note ordinarily meant that it was half as long again as its normal value, but otherwise it simply signified that the notes on either side were irregular in some way.

5. From the 19th century to the present day

Over the last 200 years the gradual separation of the role of composer and performer has contrived to increase the level of explicit instruction in music, and the printed score has become the paramount intermediary between composer and public. Moreover, the layout of scores became more standard, with treatises on orchestration being written by Berlioz, Rimsky-Korsakov, and others, and with Mendelssohn's attempting to standardize the seating arrangements of the orchestra in Leipzig and elsewhere.

The treatment of tempo and pulse gradually became more erratic and extreme. In Beethoven's music any note from the semiquaver to the minim is capable of functioning as the main beat, and such virtuosos as Liszt and Paganini simply played some of their own music as fast as possible. In the 20th century, Stockhausen actually gives the tempo indication 'fastest speed possible' in some sections of his *Zeitmasze* (1956). The 19th-century concern for virtuosity and expressiveness naturally resulted in increased attention to the notation of articulation, phrasing, and expressive nu-

ance. Dynamic levels too have become more extreme, and experiments have been made to indicate dynamics not by traditional methods (*ff*, *pp*, etc.) but by the size of note-head (e.g. in Stockhausen's *Zyklus*), numerical scales (e.g. in Cage's *Changes*), and other devices.

The notation of rhythm continued to harbour ambiguities for some time. For example, there are undotted demisemiquavers in the Arietta of Beethoven's Piano Sonata op. III (bar 50), some of which are 'perfect' (i.e. worth three hemidemisemiquavers) and some 'imperfect' (worth only two). Again, there is some evidence that the dotted rhythms in the accompaniments of the chorus parts of Verdi's operas should be synchronized with the triplets in the vocal part. Today there are still certain genres where a conventional 'bending' of the rhythm is understood rather than notated (e.g. in the Viennese waltz, swing, jazz).

In the 19th century, ornamentation gradually became absorbed into the style so that in Chopin's Étude no. 13 (op. 25 no. 1), for example, the main melody is picked out in larger notes with the ornamental decoration fully written out in smaller ones. In early Wagner scores we find *gruppetto* signs and the like, but later (as in Brünnhilde's main theme in the *Ring*) the 'ornamentation' is fully written out. In the 20th century there was some reintroduction of the old ornamentation signs under the influence of neo-classicism, for example the upper and lower *mordent signs found in some works by Tippett.

Electronic scores are often, in part, instruction manuals showing precisely how sounds are to be re-

(a) Notes

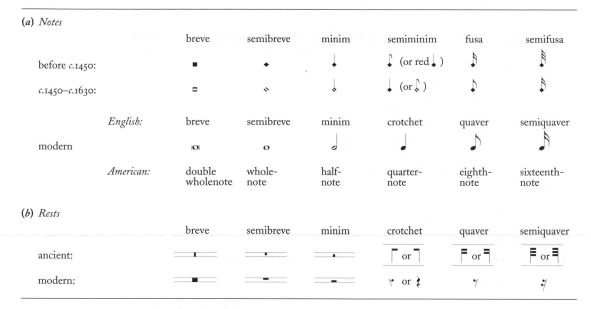

		breve	semibreve	minim	semiminim	fusa	semifusa
before c.1450:		■	◆	↓	♪ (or red ↓)	♫	♫
c.1450–c.1630:		◻	◇	↓	↓ (or ♪)	♪	♪
	English:	breve	semibreve	minim	crotchet	quaver	semiquaver
modern		𝅝𝆴	o	𝅗𝅥	♩	♪	♫
	American:	double wholenote	whole-note	half-note	quarter-note	eighth-note	sixteenth-note

(b) Rests

	breve	semibreve	minim	crotchet	quaver	semiquaver
ancient:	▬	▬	▬	⌐ or ¬	𝄾 or 𝄾	𝄿 or 𝄿
modern:	▬	▬	▬	𝄽 or 𝄽	𝄿	𝄾

Fig. 6. Origins of modern note forms and rests.

produced. In Fig. 7, for instance, each block in the top half represents one sound made up of five frequencies (pitches) of which the highest and the lowest are defined. Overlapping mixtures of sounds are shown by darker shading. The frequency scale on the left-hand edge ranges from 100 to 17,200 Hz. The duration of each sound is shown by the centre line, which is calibrated in centimetres allowing for a tape speed of 76.2 cm per second. The lower half of the graph shows the intensity of sound (loudness and attack/decay elements) measured in decibels ranging from 0 to −30. The notation still bears some resemblance to conventional scores (duration moves from left to right, pitch is shown by height or depth, etc.) but some more recent *computer notations are highly sophisticated 'machine languages' for controlling and manipulating acoustical

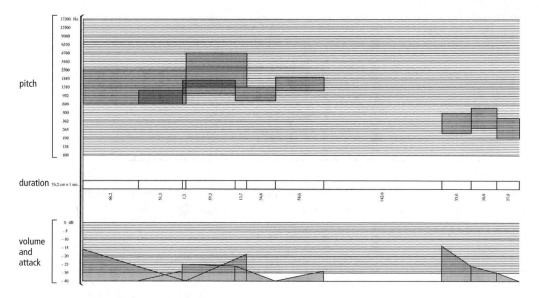

Fig. 7. Stockhausen, *Elektronische Studien II*, opening page.

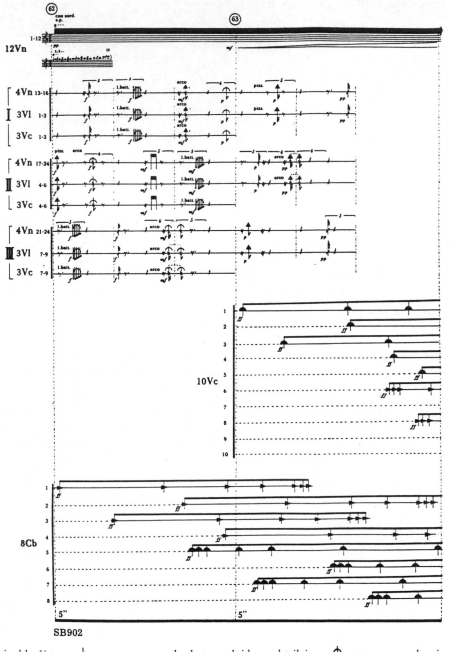

SB902

raised by ¼ tone   ┼

raised by ¾ tone   ╫

lowered by ¼ tone   ♭

lowered by ¾ tone   ⧹

highest note of the instrument (indefinite pitch)   ↥

play between bridge and tailpiece   ↑

arpeggio on four strings behind bridge   ⫴

play on tailpiece (arco)   ┷

play on bridge   ♠

percussion effect: strike the upper sounding board of the violin with the nut or the fingertips   ƒ

several irregular changes of bow   ⊓∨

molto vibrato   ∿

very slow vibrato with a ¼-tone frequency difference produced by sliding the finger   ∿

very rapid not rhythmicized tremolo   ✕

Fig. 8. Penderecki, *Threnody*, sections 62 and 63.

equipment; their visual appearance is no longer obviously analogous to the gestures in the resultant music. Some types of aleatory music allow random events outside the control of the performer to become part of the music (as in Cage's 'silent' piano piece *4′33″*), while others attempt to provoke the musician into a subjective response (see GRAPHIC NOTATION).

Apart from such avant-garde notations there has been a steady development of more traditional means, partly arising from new ways of using conventional instruments and the voice. For example, the Polish composer Penderecki has greatly expanded the range of string-playing techniques: Fig. 8 is from his *Threnody* for 52 stringed instruments with an explanatory table (provided by the composer) showing the different techniques used. Finally, the 20th century spawned a number of didactic and academic notations. For example, the disciplines of *ethnomusicology and music *analysis have both developed their own notations, the former for recording non-Western musics, the latter for distinguishing between foreground and background materials and more or less significant harmonic events.

See also TEMPO AND EXPRESSION MARKS.   AP

📖 W. APEL, *The Notation of Polyphonic Music, 900–1600* (Cambridge, MA, 1942, 5/1961) · E. KARKOSCHKA, *Das Schriftbild der neuen Musik* (Celle, 1966; Eng. trans. 1972) · H. KELLER, *Phrasing and Articulation* (London, 1966) · H. COLE, *Sounds and Signs: Aspects of Musical Notation* (Oxford, 1974) · K. STONE, *Music Notation in the Twentieth Century* (New York, 1980) · R. RASTALL, *The Notation of Western Music* (London, 1983, 2/1994)

note. A written sign representing the pitch or duration, or both, of a musical sound. In English terminology the word has two further meanings: (1) the key of a keyboard instrument; and (2) the actual sound produced.

note-against-note. See HOMORHYTHM. ('Homophony' is sometimes used incorrectly to describe note-against-note writing.)

note nere (It., 'black notes'). A style of notation, common in mid-16th-century madrigal collections, in which short note-values (semiminims and *fusae*, equivalent to crotchets and quavers) were used with the mensuration sign 𝄴, instead of the more usual long values with 𝄵. This made the page seem rather 'blackened'; an alternative name for this notation was 'cromatico' ('coloured').   JBE

note row. Synonym of *series.

notes inégales (Fr., 'unequal notes'). In performance, the rhythmic alteration of groups of notes that are written evenly, generally involving the lengthening of the first of a (generally) consecutive pair of notes and the corresponding shortening of the second; occasionally (though rarely) the reverse happens, giving a rhythm like the *Scotch snap. Such a convention was prevalent in French music from the mid-16th century to the late 18th and was regarded as an important means of increasing the beauty of a vocal or instrumental work. It is also a common feature of jazz. Inequality was rarely notated in French music, but was sometimes indicated by the written word *pointé* and cancelled by *égales*. Disjunct notes were rarely played as *inégales*, and when they were intended to be were usually written out.

In the 17th century, a general rule was that inequality was applied to the quickest prevailing notes in a given metre—usually semiquavers in 4/4 and 2/4 time, quavers in 2/2 and 𝄵 time, quavers in 3/4, 6/4, 9/4, and 12/4 time, and semiquavers in all metres with a denominator of eight. Some composers notated inequality by using dots, but generally they were wary of this since it implied strict dotted rhythm. True inequality varied from *louré*—a barely perceptible lilt in which the first of a pair of notes received slightly more time than the second—to *pointé*, which more nearly approached dotted rhythm. In between is a kind of triplet rhythm. Such nuances were left to the performer's discretion, and in vocal music he or she was expected to take the sense of the words into account when deciding how to apply *inégales*.

In most sources from outside France, inequality was notated by the composer; it occurs, for example, in music by Locke, Purcell, Clarke, and Handel. There is much controversy over its application to Italian music: some contemporary sources (e.g. Michel Corrette's flute tutor, 1740) say that it was used in Italian music, others (e.g. Rousseau, 1768) that it was not. François Couperin seems undecided. In Germany, pieces in the French style were treated as if they were French, i.e. with inequality. *Inégales* were clearly explained by Lully's pupil Georg Muffat in his *Florilegium primum* (1695), and other German composers who followed the French style include Froberger, Buxtehude, Telemann, and Bach. However, only Quantz, in his celebrated treatise on flute-playing (1752) actually states that the use of *inégales* was common in Germany, and even he does not clarify whether they should be used only in French-style German music. It is therefore hardly surprising that since the early 20th century scholars have argued endlessly on the subject and that no satisfactory compromise has yet been reached. As with other unwritten musical conventions, the final decision as to when and whether to use *notes inégales* must be left to the performer.

See also DOT, 3.   WT

📖 S. E. HEFLING, *Rhythmic Alteration in Seventeenth- and Eighteenth-Century Music: Notes inégales and Overdotting* (New York, 1993) · J. BYRT, *Notes inégales: A European Style* (Tiverton, 1996)

Notker 'Balbulus' ('the stammerer') (*b* nr St Gallen, Switzerland, *c*.840; *d* St Gallen, 6 April 912). Benedictine monk, scholar, and poet. He is one of the few medieval writers to whom a firm body of liturgical texts can be attributed. In 884 he completed the *Liber hymnorum*, a cycle of striking texts covering the church year, to be sung to the melodies of sequences. In its preface Notker explains the nature and function of the sequence, and describes how he came to write the verses. Other writings by him clarify aspects of the performance of plainchant.   JN/JM

Notre Dame manuscripts. A collection of two-voice plainchant settings for liturgical use, dating from about 1170 and given the description **Magnus liber organi* by the 13th-century theorist Anonymous IV.

Notre Dame Mass. Mass for four voices by Machaut, possibly dating from the 1360s, one of the earliest polyphonic settings of the Mass Ordinary.

notturnino (It., dim. of *notturno*). A miniature **nocturne.

notturno (It., 'of the night'; Ger.: *Nachtmusik*). An 18th-century composition, usually instrumental, written for performance at night. Such pieces generally consisted of between two and six movements of a light character. Haydn wrote eight *notturni*, with varying numbers of movements, for two *lire organizzate* (hurdy-gurdies), two clarinets, two horns, two violas, and bass (1788–90), and Mozart wrote a *Serenata notturna* (K239) for double orchestra and a *Notturno* for four orchestras (K286/269*a*). The German equivalent 'Nachtmusik' was applied by Mozart to similar music but played by a smaller ensemble (e.g. *Eine kleine Nachtmusik* K525). Other composers who wrote *notturni* include Gyrowetz, Michael Haydn, Boccherini, Vanhal, and Sammartini.

See also SERENADE; DIVERTIMENTO.   JBE

Nouvelles Aventures. See AVENTURES.

Novák, Vítězslav (Augustín Rudolf) (*b* Kamenice nad Lipou, 5 Dec. 1870; *d* Skuteč, 18 July 1949). Czech composer and teacher. His childhood was dogged by illness and poverty. He received some musical education at Jindřichův Hradec, then studied the piano and composition at the Prague Conservatory (1889–92) while nominally pursuing a university course in law. A bad start with the harmony teacher led to a crisis in confidence which was only partly ameliorated by transferring to Dvořák's composition class. Though he often disagreed with Dvořák, Novák found his teaching stimulating and began to compose seriously. He made a study of Moravian and Slovakian folk melody, and was often to resort to these themes or their contours for compositional material. From 1909 to 1939 he taught composition at the Prague Conservatory.

Novák's preoccupation with nature and tendency to introspection led to some deeply felt programmatic works: the symphonic poems *V Tatrách* ('In the High Tatras', 1902) and *O vecné touze* ('Of Eternal Longing', 1905). His interest in monothematicism led him to experiment with the metamorphosis of a single theme (the piano suite *Pan*, 1910) and cyclic structure (*Trio quasi una ballata*, 1902; Second String Quartet op. 35, 1905). In the 1920s he composed more for the stage, including two satirical ballet-pantomines and the opera *Lucerna* (1922). His musical language owed much to his teacher Dvořák, though Strauss and Debussy were also formative influences; his music is none the less both individual and original, particularly in his use of contrapuntal textures, and sets him apart as a major figure in 20th-century Czech music.   JSM

novel, music in the. Literary people—poets, philosophers, novelists—regard their musician counterparts with a mixture of envy and suspicion. Music's abstraction poses a threat to the primacy of language, to rationality, and the ethical dimensions of art. Plato, Rousseau, and Tolstoy are among those who have been worried by music's insidious power over the emotions; another tradition of thinkers has been troubled by music's failure to fit the theory of *mimesis*—art as imitation of nature, a holding up of a mirror to life—and one of the first premonitions of **Romanticism is the acknowledgment in the mid-18th century that music evokes feelings rather than reflects realities. In Germany, particularly, music was thought to be a form of poetic madness and divine inspiration, embodying passion, melancholy, yearning, restlessness, and energy. At about the turn of the century, the startling innovations in works like Mozart's *Don Giovanni* and Beethoven's Fifth Symphony inspired such writers as E. T. A. Hoffmann and Arthur Schopenhauer to a belief in music's mystical supremacy over all the other arts.

Throughout the 19th-century novel, the Italian opera maintained its position as a place of intrigue, usually amorous. Flaubert set one of the most pathetic scenes of *Madame Bovary* (1857) at a performance of *Lucia di Lammermoor* (a scene itself recalled by E. M. Forster in *Where Angels Fear to Tread*, where English ladies, attending a provincial Italian performance of *Lucia*, are appalled by the moral turpitude around them). Emma

Bovary provides an example of the complete Romantic submission to music: it 'sent a vibration . . . through her whole being, as if the bows of the violins were being drawn across her own nerves', and Lucia becomes further food for poor Emma's fantasies. Tolstoy takes the moral dangers of music even further in *The Kreutzer Sonata* (1889), where the erotic charge and tension in the first movement of Beethoven's violin sonata precipitates adultery between its players.

Music in the English novel is altogether a primmer affair. Jane Austen, touched with honest English philistinism, is not much interested in high art. Music in her books is acceptable as a social accomplishment and an ornament to femininity (none of her heroes is susceptible to music): Emma Woodhouse claims, 'If I give up music, I shall take up carpet-work'—the two have an equal validity. An excessive attachment to music is generally the subject of mockery: Marianne in *Sense and Sensibility* (1811) 'spent whole hours at the piano-forte alternately singing and crying', while Mrs Elton in *Emma* (1816) coos 'I am dotingly fond of music—passionately fond . . . I absolutely cannot do without music: it is a necessary of life to me'. Yet the later novels do also show music as a comfort to the solitary: Emma's rival Jane Fairfax, a true musician, has nothing but her mysteriously donated piano to give solace, while it is remarked of Anne Elliot, the dignified heroine of *Persuasion* (1818), that 'in music she had been always used to feel alone in the world'.

A generation later, in George Eliot's novels, we breathe a finer air, and music becomes something much more intimate and emotional, as well as serious. Philip Wakem, in *The Mill on the Floss* (1860), is the Novel's first musical intellectual: he finds in Haydn's *Creation* 'a sort of sugared complacency and flattering make-believe . . . as if it were written for the birthday fête of a German Grand Duke'. The Vincys' musical evening in *Middlemarch* (1871–2) contains more sophisticated music than the inane country dances which make up Lady Catherine de Burgh's after-dinner recitals in *Pride and Prejudice* (1813): Rosamund Vincy has been taught by 'one of those excellent musicians here and there to be found in our provinces, worthy to compare with many a noted *Kapellmeister*', and Lydgate senses 'a hidden soul . . . flowing forth' as she plays the piano.

George Eliot was a first-class amateur herself, as well as being a regular concert-goer. She was in personal association with the contemporary musical *haut monde*, knew Liszt and Anton Rubinstein well, and entertained the Wagners on their visit to London in 1877 (though she admitted to being baffled by Wagner's music). This all bore fruit in the superb portrait of Klesmer in *Daniel Deronda* (1876), the ferocious middle-European composer, dedicated to 'the music of the future', but stuck incongruously among the Midlands gentry and drawing-room singers like Gwendolen Harleth, who want to use music only as a ladder to fame and wealth. Klesmer would doubtless have been happier in the cultivated Schlegel household of Forster's *Howards End* (1910), even if he would have detested the tiresome whimsy of Helen Schlegel's famous 'analysis' of Beethoven's Fifth Symphony—surely the nadir in the treatment of music by literature.

No composer has had such a profound effect on literature as Wagner. It was not just the idea of 'music drama' (the most obviously literary of musical forms) and the literary parallels to the leitmotif which excited writers; it was also the overwhelming and unabashed egocentricity of the man and his music, its uncompromising vastness and sensuality. Wagner was the apotheosis of the Romantic ideal of the Artist, and even a brief list of his disciples shows the breadth of his influence—Baudelaire, Verlaine, Mallarmé, Shaw, Wilde, Lawrence. Two novelists stand out for the degree to which they exploited the Wagnerian possibilities: Proust and Mann.

Proust's wonderful novel *À la recherche du temps perdu* (1913–27) is full of musical insight and rare musical taste (he champions Debussy's *Pelléas et Mélisande* and Beethoven's Quartet op. 131, for example). *A la recherche* also contains a staggering gallery of music snobs, for whom, even more than for Jane Austen's equivalents, music is material for elegant and misinformed chatter. One thinks of Madame Verdurin, whose spirit was so seared by Wagner that it gave her a headache; or the moment when the violinist Charlie Morel, begged in a society drawing-room to play Debussy's *Fêtes*, slyly modulates into a march by Meyerbeer without anyone noticing. Wagner is a presence throughout, not just at the level of headaches or the comparison of the ringing of a telephone to the Shepherd's piping in *Tristan und Isolde*, but inasmuch as he informs the whole conception of the book.

It could be said that *A la recherche* is the *Ring* of the Parisian salons—both long, intricate, subtle, complex works of art built, in Proust's words, on 'the indefinite perception of motifs which now and then emerge, barely discernible, to plunge again and disappear and drown', an accumulation of small units or themes, repeated, developed, and transformed, drawing constantly on the faculties of memory and the unconscious. This is most evident in the way Proust uses the invention of the 'little phrase' from Vinteuil's violin sonata, introduced as the 'national anthem' of Swann's love for Odette, but heard again in every context of tragic love—the narrator's passion for Albertine, or that of the Baron de Charlus for Morel (himself a player of the Vinteuil sonata).

After the delicacy of Proust's cork-lined world, Mann's fiction appears somewhat flat-footed. His attempts to take Wagner's ideas of musical structure into literature are overly self-conscious. Proust's Wagnerism is impressionistic, its effects subconscious: Mann has a point to prove and an axe to grind. He felt that 'Germany's innermost soul expresses itself in music', and that the music of Wagner, with its tendency towards tragic intensity and its scorn for the ordinary run of civilized life, heralded the tragic fate of Germany in the 20th century. Time and time again in short stories like *Tristan*, *Blood of the Walsungs*, and *Tonio Kroger* or massive novels like *The Magic Mountain* (1924) and the *Ring*-inspired tetralogy *Joseph and his Brothers* (1933–42) Wagner moulds subject matter, theme, plot, and form. Mann, it has been said, 'learnt the very nature of artistic effect and artistic formulation from Wagner', and he never lost his awe for the operas.

Two other composers played a part in Mann's vision: Beethoven and Mahler. Beethoven's music represents a dangerous primitivism, the return to music of Dionysiac frenzy after the civilized restraints of polyphony (see Kretzschmar's lectures in the early part of *Doctor Faustus*); while Mahler's symphonies contained for Mann all the splendour and decadence of the period before World War I. In *Buddenbrooks* (1901), the history of a provincial German family, the symbolic figure of little Hanno, last of the Buddenbrooks line, touched with genius and fated to an early death, improvises on the piano. The suggestion of Mahler is impossible to miss: 'then came horns again, sounding the march; there was an assembling, a concentrating, firm, consolidated rhythm, and now a new figure began, a bold improvisation, a sort of lively, stormy hunting song. There was no joy in this hunting song: its note was one of defiant despair'. (Mahler's appearance was borrowed for the novelist Aschenbach in *Death in Venice* (1912), a fact cleverly developed by Visconti in his famous film of the novella.)

The summit of Mann's devotion to music is found in *Doctor Faustus*, published in 1947. It is, in a sense, his history of German music, as well as his most powerful indictment of Germany. Adrian Leverkühn, the modern composer who sells his soul to the devil in exchange for artistic power, writes music that becomes progressively more barbarous, demonic, and horribly enthralling—music through which Mann tries to explain why Germany was the source of Nazism, and the logical end to the dissolution started by Wagner. Mann's command of musical history and technique is highly impressive—he even incorporates 12-note theory into Leverkühn's musical idiom and the book is meticulously crafted: every sentence has its thematic relevance, every character its coherence. Finally, however, the novel is weighed down by the problems of 'composing' and then describing Leverkühn's music in purely literary terms—there should, one feels be an accompanying cassette, cued in to the appropriate pages!

In *Doctor Faustus* music triumphs over literature, reminding us of Schopenhauer's belief that all other art forms aspired to the condition of music. It is also the culmination of what might be called the Wagnerian phase of European culture. When we move to literary modernism, the music we find there is lighter and clearer in texture: Ezra Pound used medieval music, Dowland, and Bartók in his verse, while James Joyce turns Wagner upside down. Joyce's musicianship was not very sophisticated, though he did at one time consider schooling his tenor voice for a professional career. The music in his novel *Ulysses* (1922) is mostly vocal, therefore—from melodies and ballads ('Là ci darem la mano', 'M'appari', 'The Last Rose of Summer') to what are politely called drinking-songs ('The Night before Larry was Stretched', and worse). Molly Bloom was a concert and oratorio singer, Stephen Daedalus confesses to a love of the English virginalists, but the music which really dominates *Ulysses* and becomes part of its great flow is the tinkle of daily life—whistled tunes, singing in the bath, favourite hymns. The rhythmic, allusive, incantatory qualities of Joyce's later prose, as well as his use of collage and randomness, have had a radical effect on composers since World War II: Berio and Cage in particular have adapted Joyce's methods and practices to musical ends.

20th-century popular fiction has made frequent use of the figure of the musician. The trials and tribulations of the prima donna form the subject of proto-feminist novels such as Gertrude Atherton's *Tower of Ivory* (1910), Willa Cather's *The Song of the Lark* (1915, loosely based on the life story of the Wagnerian soprano Olive Fremstad), and Marcia Davenport's *Of Lena Geyer* (1936), all concerned to celebrate the courage of women struggling to find self-expression in a male-dominated world. George du Maurier's *Trilby* (1894) takes another view of the matter: the eponymous heroine is an innocent and untalented Irish girl who becomes a great singer only through the mesmeric power of her charismatic teacher Svengali. The figure of the modernist composer, fighting against bourgeois conservatism, appears in the shape of Lewis Dod in Margaret Kennedy's *The Constant Nymph* (1924). Dod is a romantic rebel, his masterpiece a 'Symphony in Three Keys'; 75 years later, in Ian McEwan's *Amsterdam* (1998), the modernist composer Clive Linley has written a 'Millennial Symphony', but he has become a priggish and fatuous egocentric whose ambitions are simply comic.

Other music-flavoured contemporary novels include Peter Ackroyd's *English Music* (1992), in which the line that leads from Byrd through Purcell to Parry is seen as embodying the quintessence of English cultural identity; Rose Tremain's *Music and Silence* (1999), a fantasy told from the perspective of a lutenist at the court of King Christian IV of Denmark; and Vikram Seth's *An Equal Music* (1999), which revolves round the relationships between the members of a string quartet. Two novels with a composer as the central character are Adam Lively's 'novel in five movements' *Sing the Body Electric* (1993) and Bernard MacLaverty's *Grace Notes* (1997). At a rather different literary level, Jilly Cooper's 'bonkbuster' *Appassionata* (1997) uses the tight-knit community of a symphony orchestra as a springboard for an orgy of bed-hopping and other amorous intrigues.   RCH

novelette (Fr.; Ger.: *Novellette*). A term first used by Schumann as the title of his op. 21 for piano. The eight pieces do not carry individual titles, but the composer stated that each had its own character, the set being the musical equivalent of a 'romantic story'. They were named after the singer Clara Novello, whose name Schumann found more euphonious than that of his future wife Clara Wieck, to whom he dedicated them. Several other composers (e.g. Gade) subsequently adopted the term, which carries no particular connotation of form.   —/JBE

Novello. English firm of music publishers. Vincent Novello (1781–1861), of Italian origin, was a talented conductor, organist, and choirmaster. From 1811 his monumental editions of choral works by Purcell, Boyce, Handel, Haydn, Bach, and Mozart in the relatively cheap and simple form of a vocal (rather than full) score with keyboard accompaniment (rather than figured bass) made the repertory more accessible to amateurs. The editions had a profound influence on the development of English choral societies, then in their infancy. Novello's publishing activities were consolidated in 1830 with the foundation of Novello & Co. by his son Alfred (1810–96).

Alfred Novello acquired the rights to Mendelssohn's choral works, publishing first the oratorio *St Paul* in 1837 and beginning a lifelong association with the composer. He founded two journals, *The Musical World* (1836) and *The Musical Times* (1844), and in 1847 set up his own printing firm, issuing the popular 'Octavo Editions' of choral pieces. These built on the work of his father and became the backbone of the repertory of every choral society in the English-speaking world.

The firm continued to produce sacred music (anthems, and the first edition of *Hymns, Ancient & Modern*), and in the late 19th and early 20th centuries

began publishing secular music and promoting concerts. Elgar was the pre-eminent English composer in their catalogue, which later included Holst, Bliss, and other contemporaries. School music became an important interest and in 1944 the journal *Music in Education* was launched.

Among the contemporary composers published in the postwar years are Arnold, Bennett, Bainbridge, Keuris, Musgrave, Stuart MacRae, McCabe, Sallinen, Swayne, and Vir. A new Elgar edition is in progress and the firm has embarked on an extensive choral programme, producing revised and re-edited versions of all its standard choral editions as well as adding new works. Novello joined the Granada Group of companies in 1970 and the Music Sales Group in 1997. Its hire library is one of the largest in Europe.   HA

📖 *A Century and a Half in Soho: A Short History of the Firm of Novello, Publishers and Printers of Music, 1811–1961* (London, 1961) · M. HURD, *Vincent Novello—and Company* (London, 1981)

Novello, Ivor [Davies, David Ifor] (*b* Cardiff, 15 Jan. 1893; *d* London, 6 March 1951). Welsh composer. The son of a music teacher, he achieved enormous success with the song 'Keep the Home Fires Burning' (1914). Later he combined his talents as a songwriter, romantic actor, and playwright in musicals in an anglicized Viennese idiom, among them *Glamorous Night* (1935), *Careless Rapture* (1936), *The Dancing Years* (1939), *Perchance to Dream* (1945), and *King's Rhapsody* (1949).

PGa/ALa

nowell. See NOËL.

Noye's Fludde. Dramatic work in one act by Britten to his own libretto, a setting of the Chester miracle play (Orford, 1958).

Nozze di Figaro, Le ('The Marriage of Figaro'). Opera in four acts by Mozart to a libretto by Lorenzo Da Ponte after Beaumarchais's play *La Folle Journée, ou Le Mariage de Figaro* (1784) (Vienna, 1786).

Nuits d'été, Les ('Summer Nights'). Song cycle, op. 7, by Berlioz to poems by Théophile Gautier; it was composed in 1840–1 and revised in 1843 and 1856. The six songs are 'Villanelle', 'Le Spectre de la rose', 'Sur les lagunes', 'Absence', 'Au cimetière', and 'L'Inconnue'.

numbers, numerology. See CRYPTOGRAPHY; SYMBOLISM.

Nunc dimittis (Lat., 'Now let [thy servant] depart'). The *canticle of Simeon (Luke 2: 29–32). It is sung at the Roman Catholic service of Compline, and was taken over from that Office to be sung at Evensong in the Anglican Church, where composers frequently coupled it with the *Magnificat*, either as a self-contained work or as part of a full service. In Eastern Orthodox worship it appears at the conclusion of Vespers, where it is recited in Greek practice but sung in Russian usage.   —/ALı

Nuove musiche, Le (It., 'New Compositions'). The title of Giulio Caccini's first collection of monodic songs, published in Florence in 1602. In 1614 he issued a further volume, *Nuove musiche e nuova maniera di scriverle* ('New Compositions and New Way of Writing them'), which shows even better his consciousness of a departure from earlier practice (see MONODY, 2). Modern writers sometimes apply the designation more widely to the new monodic style of the late 16th and early 17th centuries, though it was not so used at the time (see BAROQUE ERA, THE).   JJD

Nusch-Nuschi, Das ('The Nusch-Nuschi'). Opera in one act by Hindemith to a libretto by Franz Blei (Stuttgart, 1921).

nut. 1. The bar or ridge that fixes the sounding length of a string nearer the tuning-pegs or pins; the other end is fixed by the bridge.

2. See FROG.

Nutcracker (*Shchelkunchik*; *Casse-noisette*). Ballet in two acts and three scenes by Tchaikovsky to a scenario by Marius Petipa after Alexandre Dumas *père*'s version of E. T. A. Hoffmann's *Der Nussknacker und der Mäusekönig* ('The Nutcracker and the Mouse King'); it was choreographed by Lev Ivanov (St Petersburg, 1892). Tchaikovsky arranged an orchestral suite, op. 71*a* (1892), of eight numbers from the ballet.

nyckelharpa. A fiddle with keys like those of a *hurdy-gurdy, but played with a bow rather than a rosined wheel. It was popular throughout Scandinavia and north Germany for dance and festive music, and has been widely revived in Sweden. There are several forms with varying tunings and numbers of sympathetic and bowed strings. The bow is short and sharply out-curved, the hair tensioned with the thumb.

JMo

Nyman, Michael (Laurence) (*b* London, 23 March 1944). English composer. His teachers included Alan Bush. He developed a particular interest in experimental music, writing an early study (1974, 2/1999) of the importance of Cage and others. From the mid-1970s he began to write music for the theatre and for films, as well as for the concert hall; he often arranged existing material in his scores, which moved increasingly towards the bold contours of *minimalist and process music. As well as his collaborations with such film-makers as Jane Campion and Peter Greenaway, he has written many works for his own instrumental group and an opera, *The Man who Mistook his Wife for a Hat* (London, 1986), based on the book by Oliver Sacks.

AW

Nymphs and Shepherds. Song by Purcell from the incidental music he wrote for Thomas Shadwell's play *The Libertine* (1692); it is often sung by a soprano but was made famous in a choral version recorded in 1929 by Manchester schoolchildren's choirs, conducted by Harty.

obbligato (It., 'necessary'; Fr.: *obligé*; Ger.: *obligat*). An accompanying part that cannot be omitted. In the 17th and 18th centuries the term often referred to a keyboard part that was fully written out rather than notated as a figured bass. In a keyboard piece with 'violino obbligato' the violin part is essential to the structure; an optional violin part would be marked *ad *libitum*. The term has subsequently come to refer to prominent instrumental countermelodies, a common feature of 19th-century opera arias, where an orchestral instrument has a semi-solo role accompanying the voice.

Oberon (*Oberon, or The Elf King's Oath*). Opera in three acts by Weber to a libretto by James Robinson Planché after Christoph Martin Wieland's poem *Oberon* (1780), itself based on *Huon de Bordeaux*, a 13th-century French *chanson de geste* (London, 1826).

Oberto, conte di San Bonifacio. Opera in two acts by Verdi to a libretto by Temistocle Solera from Antonio Piazza's libretto *Rocester* (Milan, 1839).

obligat (Ger.). See OBBLIGATO.

obligato. An incorrect spelling of *obbligato.

obligé (Fr.). See OBBLIGATO.

oblique motion. See MOTION.

oboe [hautboy] (Fr.: *hautbois*; Ger.: *Hoboe, Oboe*; It.: *oboe*). A conical-bore woodwind instrument played with a double reed. It was invented in the mid-17th century, probably in France, as a quieter version of the *shawm, which was also known as *hautbois* in French and sometimes hautboy in English. ('Hautboy' was also the 17th- and 18th-century English name for the oboe itself.) Oboes were the first woodwind instruments to be adopted into the orchestra, often playing along with the violins and then contrasting with them, accompanied by their natural bass, the *bassoon, playing *coi bassi* ('with the basses'). Oboes replaced the shawms in *military bands, where they remained the main melodic instrument until supplanted by keyed *bugles and *cornets in the mid-19th century.

Initially the oboe had six fingerholes, and three keys for the lower little finger. With all fingerholes closed the lowest note was *d'*, as on the contemporary flute. Closing the open-standing great key made the lowest note *c''*, and opening either of the smaller keys produced E♭. These were duplicated so that the instrument could be played either with the left hand above the right, as is now universal, or vice versa. All other chromatic notes were produced by cross-fingering, closing holes below the lowest open hole to lower the pitch. Most players adopted the modern hand position before the 1770s, and the left-hand E♭ key was abandoned, though the C key often retained its forked touchpiece into the early 19th century.

The oboe was so responsive to cross-fingering, partly because of the sensitivity of its double reed, that it was the last of the woodwind to increase the number of its keys as music grew more complex and chromatic. After 1810 or so, keys were added with greater frequency. An extra low key covered one of the two open vent holes in the bell to lower the range to *b*. In the modern oboe a further key makes the lowest note *b♭*. From the 1830s a succession of key systems was developed by the firm of Triébert in Paris, culminating in the two systems used today in western Europe and North America: the 'thumb-plate system' and the 'Conservatoire system' (named after the Paris Conservatoire). At the same time, systems remaining rather closer to the Baroque form, were evolved in Germany and particularly in Austria, where the Zuleger system is still in use. Boehm's key mechanisms have been adapted to the oboe, but because of its coarser tone-quality his system of acoustically correct hole sizes has never been successful.

There are three main sizes of modern oboe: the normal treble, the alto oboe d'amore, and the tenor *cor anglais or English horn. The oboe d'amore is built a minor 3rd below the oboe, and the cor anglais a 5th. Both have a globular or bulbous bell and the reed is placed on a curved or angled crook. In the Baroque period the cor anglais was made in a curve or in two or three straight pieces meeting at an angle. There were two other forms of tenor: the *taille*, which probably looked like a large straight oboe with an angled brass crook, and the oboe da caccia, curved like the cor anglais but with a flared brass bell instead of the bulb. The lower oboes are treated as transposing instruments, their parts written to be fingered like treble oboe parts.

A bass or baritone oboe, an octave below the treble, has always been rare, though composers do occasionally write for it and the wider-bore but otherwise similar *heckelphone. Because Bach wrote superbly for both oboe d'amore and oboe da caccia these remain available today, though the latter is usually replaced by the cor anglais in performances on modern (as distinct from 'period') instruments.

The oboe reed is very thin and delicate and is usually made by the player, for the difference between a good reed and a poor one is a matter of minute adjustment, which must be varied to suit each player. The two blades of *Arundo donax*, a cane grown in southern France, are tied to a metal staple which, originally bound with thread to fit the top of the bore, is now lapped with cork. The gap between the blades, controlled by the player's lips, folded in over the teeth, is so narrow that only a very thin stream of air can pass through it. As a result, while the players of other wind instruments always need to take in more air, the oboist's main problem is getting rid of surplus air. While some players practise the traditional shawm technique of *circular breathing, all oboists can command a longer melodic line in one breath than other wind players, a facility of which many composers have taken full advantage. As well as its orchestral role, the oboe has a large solo repertory, from the Baroque period to the present day.   JMo

📖 P. Bate, *The Oboe: An Outline of its History, Development and Construction* (London, 1956, 3/1975) · L. Goossens and E. Roxburgh, *Oboe* (London, 1977) · A. Bernardini, B. Haynes, D. Lasocki, and J. K. Page, contributions to *Early Music*, 16/3 (1988) [double-reed issue] · B. Haynes, *The Speaking Oboe': A History of the Hautboy, 1640 to 1760* (Oxford, 1999) · G. Burgess and B. Haynes, *The Oboe in History* (London, forthcoming)

Obouhow, Nicolas [Obukhov, Nikolay] (*b* Ol'shanka, Kursk province, 10/22 April 1892; *d* Saint Cloud, nr Paris, 13 June 1954). Russian composer. He studied from 1911 at the Moscow Conservatory and from 1913 at the St Petersburg Conservatory with Maximilian Steinberg and Nikolay Tcherepnin. In 1918 he emigrated to France. He developed his own notational system, a harmonic language involving 12-note chords, and several electronic instruments including the *croix sonore*. The score for his ecstatic, 2000-page *Knigi zhizni* ('The Book of Life') for solo voice, two pianos, electronic instruments, and orchestra (written between 1918 and the mid-1920s or later) is signed 'Nicholas l'Illuminé' and includes markings in the composer's blood.   JK

obra (Sp.). 1. A general term for a musical work.

2. In the early 18th century *obra* was sometimes used more specifically to refer to a *tiento.

Obrecht, Jacob (*b* Ghent, 1457 or 1458; *d* Ferrara, July 1505). Franco-Flemish church musician and composer. He was the son of a civic trumpeter, and through his father may have come into early contact with musicians at the Burgundian court. During his adult career he held positions, often short-lived and variously as choirmaster or succentor, at churches or cathedrals in Bergen op Zoom, Cambrai, Bruges, and Antwerp. It is not always clear what precipitated these frequent moves; some evidently arose from career opportunities, others were the result of dismissal. In 1487–8 he visited the court of Ferrara at the invitation of Duke Ercole d'Este, returning there as *maestro di cappella* in 1504. He died in Ferrara of the plague.

Obrecht's career, unlike that of his contemporary Josquin des Prez, was focused on the Low Countries, and that may partly account for the fundamental differences between the two men, who are generally regarded as the towering figures of their age. Josquin was essentially a court composer, based in Italy for much of his early life, and was allowed free rein to explore a text-expressive style, heard to best advantage in his motets and chansons. Obrecht, conversely, was a church-based musician, a prolific composer above all of masses, and had fewer opportunities to encounter or be influenced by Italian humanism. Geography also accounts for differences in their subsequent reception: relatively few of Obrecht's works were published or widely disseminated, whereas Josquin's were more readily accessible to the pioneer of music-printing, Ottaviano Petrucci. Wide distribution and sheer variety of output have helped to ensure Josquin a prominent place in history, whereas Obrecht, less wide-ranging and conspicuous, and less obviously influential on 16th-century music, has had to fight harder for modern recognition.

The majority of Obrecht's masses are constructed round either plainchant melodies or secular songs. The chant-based masses include several that can be linked, through their choice of cantus firmus, to his places of work; in the earliest of them it is possible to hear echoes of music by his more senior contemporaries, Busnois and Ockeghem. Later settings include the spectacular *Missa 'Sub tuum presidium'*, which opens in three-voice texture but gains an extra voice in each successive movement as additional cantus firmi are superimposed on one another. Secular models include both monophonic songs (as in the vast *Missa 'Maria zart'*, based on a German devotional song) and voice parts extracted from polyphonic chansons. Ingenious principles of design and numerological ideas underpin several of the masses, not always in ways that are obvious or even audible to the listener.

The motets, fewer in number than the masses, are arguably Obrecht's most approachable works. They vary in technique from complex canonic structures (*Haec Deum coeli*) and luxuriantly sonorous polyphony (the six-voice *Salve regina*) to works of exquisitely transparent texture in which the words are declaimed with a clarity unusual for Obrecht (*Factor orbis*, based on a miscellany of plainchant melodies for the Christmas period). The secular music, which includes songs in Middle Dutch and textless pieces, is generally of less importance. In this area Obrecht is conspicuously overshadowed by contemporaries such as Josquin, Compère, and Pierre de la Rue; but as a composer of church music he stands out as one of the most interesting and important figures of the late 15th century.

JM

📖 R. WEGMAN, *Born for the Muses: The Life and Masses of Jacob Obrecht* (Oxford, 1994)

Obukhov, Nikolay. See OBOUHOW, NICOLAS.

ocarina (It., 'little goose'). A general term used for *vessel flutes. Specifically, the ocarina is a duct-blown vessel flute invented by Giuseppe Donati of Budrio, Italy, in about 1860. His ocarina was in the shape of an elongated egg, though any shape may be used, with a hole for each finger and thumb; it has had wide popularity as a musical toy ever since. Notes are determined by the instrument's volume, and by the number and size of the opened fingerholes, irrespective of their position around the vessel. Ocarinas of various materials, shapes, and sizes are found throughout the world, including Latin America, China, Africa, and eastern Europe.

JMo

Ockeghem, Johannes [Jean de] (*b* St Ghislain, nr Mons, *c*.1410; *d* ?Tours, 6 Feb. 1497). Franco-Flemish church musician and composer. In 1443 he was a singer at the church of Notre Dame in Antwerp, and by 1446 was a member of the chapel of Charles I, Duke of Bourbon, centred on the Burgundian town of Moulins (near Dijon). His talents were recognized by Charles VII, King of France, and by about 1452 Ockeghem had moved to the French court, with which he remained for the rest of his life, serving three successive monarchs (Charles VII, Louis XI, and Charles VIII). In 1459 he was given the important post of treasurer of the church of St Martin in Tours. During his years with the court Ockeghem travelled outside France in the retinue of diplomatic missions, including one (in 1470) to Spain. After his death he was commemorated by some of the finest writers of the day: Erasmus, Guillaume Crétin, and Jean Molinet, whose *déploration* set to music by Josquin des Prez, *Nymphes des bois*, describes him as learned and handsome, and calls on four leading composers of the day—Josquin, Pierre de la Rue, Brumel, and Compère—to weep for the passing of their 'bon père'.

Although it seems likely that only a fraction of Ockeghem's output has survived—14 masses, fewer than ten motets, and some 20 chansons—even from these he emerges a composer of exceptional interest. His style is characterized by its rich polyphonic texture, in which all voices are melodically significant, hierarchically equal, and thematically independent of one another. Unlike other 15th-century composers he shows relatively little interest in imitative exchanges or declamatory word-setting, preferring instead the continuous unfolding of pure melody, and an ever-changing array of texture, harmony, and sonority.

The masses range in structure from the conventional (settings based on a cantus firmus, often the tenor voice of a chanson) to the bizarre: the *Missa prolationum* is made completely out of canons, constantly changing in technique and always of awesome complexity; the *Missa cuiusvis toni* is notated without clefs and can be sung in several different modes; throughout the *Missa 'Caput'* an angular plainchant cantus firmus is placed in the lowest voice, in spite of its unsuitability to act as the bass of the texture. In these and other works Ockeghem's compositional choices seem game-like, especially to singers reading from the original mensural notation. They must also have posed real challenges to Ockeghem as a composer. The unsuspecting listener, however, misses all of this. Quite different from such virtuoso constructions is the *Missa pro defunctis*, a work of solemn simplicity that has the distinction of being the earliest known polyphonic requiem.

Too few of Ockeghem's motets survive to allow a fair assessment of his achievements in that genre, but he seems to have been a pioneer of richly textured works freely composed without reference to plainchant (as in *Intemerata Dei mater*). He is reputed to have written a canonic motet for 36 voices, but the 36-voice *Deo gratias* attributed to him in a 16th-century source is barely credible as his work. The chansons, in contrast, are remarkable for their quality rather than their curiosity. Such pieces as *Fors seulement l'attente* and *Ma bouche rit* were among the most popular polyphonic songs of their day.

JM

📖 F. FITCH, *Johannes Ockeghem: Masses and Models* (Paris, 1997)

O come, all ye faithful. See ADESTE FIDELES.

octatonic scale. A succession of eight notes within the octave in which tones and semitones, or semitones and tones, alternate. The scale came into regular use during the 19th century, especially as a means of establishing an exotic atmosphere in Russian Romantic music, and retained a strong influence during the 20th century, notably in the music of Stravinsky and Messiaen (his second *mode of limited transposition).

AW

octave (from Lat. *octavus*, 'eighth'; Fr.: *octave*; Ger.: *Oktave*; It.: *ottava*). 1. The eighth note of the diatonic scale.

2. The *interval of an octave is the most consonant interval of all, and one that gives the impression of duplicating the original note at a higher or lower pitch. Acoustically, the octave above a note is one with twice the frequency of the original (e.g. *a* = 220, *d'* = 440, *d''* = 880). See ACOUSTICS; HARMONIC SERIES.

3. In ecclesiastical terminology, the seventh day (exactly a week) after a feast day, or the period of eight days including the feast day and its octave.

4. The first eight lines of a sonnet.

octave flute. See PICCOLO. Also an organ stop.

octet. An ensemble of eight instruments or voices, or music written for it. The string octet is usually a double *quartet, sometimes with a double bass replacing one of the cellos. The classical wind octet was known in the 18th century as the *Harmonie or Harmoniemusik and consisted of pairs of oboes, clarinets, horns, and bassoons. Mendelssohn's string Octet (1825) is particularly well known and loved. Many composers have followed Schubert in writing for clarinet, horn, bassoon, string quartet, and double bass. Numerous other combinations have been used by composers; an ensemble of eight musicians seems to offer attractive potential.

See also CHAMBER MUSIC.   JMo

octoechos. See OKTOECHOS.

ode (from Gk. *oidē*, 'song'; Lat.: *oda*). 1. In ancient Greece, a lyric poem accompanied by music. In Greek drama and in the works of Pindar, odes were sung by a chorus and performed with dance. Several of the Latin *Odes* and *Epodes* by Horace were set to music during the Renaissance by such composers as Petrus Tritonius and Ludwig Senfl.

2. In the Byzantine rite, one of the nine sections of the *kanon.

3. In England, from the Restoration to the early 19th century, a ceremonial *cantata composed for the monarch in celebration of a particular occasion. Such works include odes for royal birthdays, coronations, funerals, banquets, the return of the monarch from a journey, and pieces for New Year and St Cecilia's Day; they were usually performed by the Gentlemen and Children of the Chapel Royal with instrumentalists from the royal household. Among the composers who wrote odes were Blow, Purcell (24, including *Hail, bright Cecilia*, 1692), Clarke, and Handel (*Ode for Queen Anne's Birthday*, 1713, and *Ode for St Cecilia*, 1739). After 1820 the practice declined, though occasional examples, including Elgar's *Coronation Ode* (1901–2), were written. The term has sometimes been applied to works that have a particular significance for the composer, as in Elgar's *The Music Makers* (1912) or Stravinsky's *Ode* (1943).   —/JBE

Ode for St Cecilia's Day. 1. Four choral works by Purcell, two composed in 1683, one *c*.1685, and one in 1692.

2. Choral work (1739) by Handel, a setting of John Dryden's poem (1798).

3. Cantata (1889) by Parry for soprano, baritone, chorus, and orchestra, to a text (1713) by Alexander Pope.

Ode to Napoleon Buonaparte. Schoenberg's op. 41 (1942), for reciter, piano, and string quartet, a setting of Byron's poem (1814); it was later arranged for string orchestra.

Odhecaton (Gk., 'one hundred'). Informal title given to the first collection of polyphonic music printed using movable type (*Harmonice musices odhecaton A*); it was issued in 1501 by Ottaviano *Petrucci.

odour and music. The language of perfumery draws on the language of music: the composition of a perfume is seen as a combination of notes. The idea of a scale of perfumes was worked out in 1865 by the celebrated Parisian perfume manufacturer Charles Piesse. In his book *Des odeurs* he claimed, 'there is an octave of odours, as there is an octave of notes', and he set out in musical notation a range of six and a half octaves, every note of which had its own perfume, from patchouli on the lowest C on the piano to civet at its highest F. He said that bouquets ought to be grouped like the notes of a chord, and described the chord C–E–G–C as follows: geranium, acacia, orange-flower, and camphor. An effective bouquet of fragrance, Piesse believed, could be created by choosing the odours that corresponded to a harmonious musical chord. There was about as much science and sense in this as in some of the theories of *colour and music. Current descriptions of perfumes refer to three layers of notes: the top note (the initial scent), the middle note (the fundamental ingredients which dominate after the top note has died away), and the lower note (the long-lasting fragrances which give the perfume depth).

In 1891 in Paris there was a public performance which combined music, colour, and odour. The work performed was *The Song of Solomon, a Symphony of Spiritual Love in Eight Mystical Devices and Three Paraphrases*, the 'book' being by Paul Roinard and the 'musical adaptations' by Flamen de Labrely. The programme set out the nature of each of the eight 'devices' in the following style: 'First Device: orchestration of the word in I illuminated with O; orchestration of the music, D major; of the Colour bright orange; of the Perfume, white violet', and so forth. The meaning of this seems to be that in the recitation the vowels 'i' and 'o' predominated, that the music was in D major, that the stage decoration was of a bright orange colour, and that a perfume of white violet was disseminated.

The following year New York was the site of an experiment in a bold combination of appeals to the various senses in *A Trip to Japan in Sixteen Minutes Conveyed to the Audience by a Succession of Odours*. This was claimed to be the 'First Experimental Perfume Concert in America', and also as 'A Melody in Odours (assisted by two Geishas and a Solo Dancer)'.

Attempts at combination of appeal to the eye and the ear by a play of colours linked to simultaneous sounds have usually been based on analogies connected with the fact that both sound and light are vibratory stimuli conveyed by so-called 'waves': there is not even this basis for attempts to bring the sense of smell into the combination, as odours are conveyed by the dispersion of (infinitely tiny) particles of the material of the odoriferous substance.   PS/AL

Odyssey. Orchestral work (1972–87) by Maw.

Oedipus rex ('King Oedipus'). Opera-oratorio in two acts by Stravinsky to a text by Jean Cocteau after Sophocles' tragedy (*c*.430 BC) translated into Latin by Jean Daniélou; it was first performed as an oratorio in Paris in 1927 and staged in Vienna in 1928.

Oehring, Helmut (*b* Berlin, 16 July 1961). German composer. Largely self-taught in music, he has said that his wish is 'to compose a kind of melodramatic docu-drama'. Several of his works include deaf performers (using spoken or sign language), reflecting his up-bringing by deaf parents. Among his theatre pieces are *Dokumentation I* (chamber opera, Spoleto, 1996), *Das d'Amato System* (dance opera, Munich, 1996), and *Bernarda Albas Haus* (dance drama, after Lorca, 1999).
                                                                    ABUR

oeuvre (Fr.). 'Work', 'composition'. See OPUS.

Offenbach, Jacques [Jacob] (*b* Cologne, 20 June 1819; *d* Paris, 5 Oct. 1880). French composer of German origin. His father, Isaac Offenbach, whose original family name was Eberst, was a Jewish cantor and minor composer. The young Jacob's promise as a cellist was such that, in 1833, his father took him and his violinist brother Julius (1815–80) to Paris, where Jacob was admitted to the Conservatoire. He earned his living as a cellist in the orchestra of the Opéra-Comique, where he made the acquaintance of the composer Jacques Fromental Halévy, who gave him composition lessons. He also had an extensive career as a cello virtuoso, including a season in London in 1844, when he appeared at Windsor Castle before Queen Victoria.

Offenbach's early works were largely for his own instrument, together with some modestly successful attempts at composition for the theatre. In 1850 he became conductor at the Théâtre Français, turning his concentration increasingly to theatrical composition. He was already 36 when, in 1855, he took a tiny theatre just off the Champs-Élysées and renamed it the Théâtre des Bouffes-Parisiens. There he staged short, witty musical stage pieces whose humorous texts and catchy numbers proved enormous hits during that year's Paris Exhibition. The continuing success of these works enabled him to give up his position at the Théâtre Français, expand his repertory, and take the company abroad, including to London in 1857.

Offenbach graduated to full-length works with the mythological satire *Orphée aux enfers* ('Orpheus in Hell', better known as 'Orpheus in the Underworld'; 1858, rev. 1875). This and other works proved irresistible not only in Paris but also in Vienna and eventually other centres, including London, where their Parisian 'naughtiness' often needed toning down. In all he composed over 100 one-act or full-length operettas, among the most outstanding being *La Belle Hélène* (1864), *Barbe-bleue* ('Bluebeard', 1866), *La Grande-Duchesse de Gérolstein* (1867), *La Périchole* (1868; rev. 1874) and *Les Brigands* (1869). He also composed a ballet *Le Papillon* ('The Butterfly', 1860) for the Paris Opéra and the romantic opera *Die Rheinnixen* ('The Rhine Nymphs', 1864) for Vienna, as well as other more ambitious works. Ill-judged forays into theatrical management during the 1870s forced him into bankruptcy, and in 1876 he undertook a money-making trip to America, where three of his sisters had emigrated. Although serious commentators believed that the frivolousness of his lighter works condemned them to oblivion, their irresistible melodies, fine vocal writing, and witty librettos have kept them on the stage. Offenbach concentrated much of the effort of his last years on the large-scale fantasy opera *Les Contes d'Hoffmann* (1881), but had not created a definitive version when he died. In various posthumous editions the opera has remained an enduring success for its fantastic effects and approachable music, particularly the celebrated Barcarolle, which Offenbach took over from *Die Rheinnixen*.   ALA

📖 A. Faris, *Jacques Offenbach* (London, 1980) · R. Traubner, *Operetta: A Theatrical History* (London, 1984) · J.-C. Yon, *Jacques Offenbach* (n.p. [?Paris], 2000)

offertory (from Lat. *offertorium*). The offering of bread and wine on the altar at a Christian Eucharist and, in the Roman rite, the chant sung to accompany this action. Analogous chants of other ancient rites include the Ambrosian *offerenda*, the Byzantine Cherubic Hymn, the Gallican *sonus*, and the Mozarabic *sacrificium*. Gregorian and Old Roman offertories are melismatic responsorial chants, the majority taken from the psalms. Their music originally consisted of a refrain, the latter half of which (the *repetendum*) would be repeated after each of a series of solo verses (later suppressed). Renaissance musicians set offertories to freely composed polyphony (Palestrina's late cycle for the whole church year is especially notable); later generations often ignored the canonical texts or replaced them with instrumental works. Such variety may also be found in Protestant churches, some of which broadened the concept of offering to include gifts other than the eucharistic elements. —/ALi

Office. In Christian liturgy, the services of the daily cycle of prayer—as distinct from the Eucharist and other sacraments—which is often called collectively the 'Divine Office' or 'Liturgy of the Hours'. Various Jewish and early Christian patterns of praying at particular hours of the day served as precedents during late antiquity for complete cycles of daily services for both urban Christians and monks. The former were characterized by fixed psalmody appropriate to the hour and by ceremonial, including the offering of light and incense, whereas monastic services tended to be relatively austere and emphasized continuous recitation of the psalter. The description of worship in Jerusalem *c.*500 by the Spanish pilgrim Egeria bears witness to the early fusion of these archetypal forms of daily prayer, and in fact the Divine Offices of most Christian Churches represent a mixture of cathedral and monastic elements.

The Divine Office of the medieval Roman rite consisted of eight services beginning at sunset with Vespers, followed by Compline before retiring, Vigils or Matins after midnight, Morning Praise (*Laudes matutinae*) or Lauds at dawn, Prime, Terce, Sext, and None (called the 'Little Hours' and sung respectively at 6 a.m., 9 a.m., midday, and 3 p.m.; since the reforms of the Second Vatican Council the last three may be combined as one 'Hora Media', 'Prayer during the Day'). Although the format of the Office varied in detail according to region or function (e.g. secular or monastic), each of its services offered a combination of psalms and canticles with antiphons, lessons (readings) with responsories, hymns, and prayers. In practice, Matins and Lauds were often combined and in a parochial context might be sung the previous evening; on the last three days of Holy Week this combined Office was called Tenebrae. The Liturgy of the Hours of 1971 suppressed Prime and replaced Vigils with an Office of Readings that could be performed at any time during the day.

In public worship the Latin Office was normally sung to plainchant, but from the later Middle Ages particular Hours came to be adorned with polyphony. From the 15th century, continental composers tended to single out Vespers for polyphonic settings, which could range from the simplest *falsobordone* psalm-chanting (similar to *Anglican chant) to elaborate polychoral or (later) instrumentally accompanied *Magnificat* settings. Though Monteverdi still based the psalms of his Vespers of 1610 on the ancient plainchant psalm tones, Baroque composers came to disregard plainchant as a means of musical construction. There was a general decline in composition for the Office by the later 18th century; Mozart's *Vesperae solennes de confessore* K339, however, is a well-known example of a self-contained Vespers setting from the period.

The Divine Office of the Byzantine rite is similar in outline to that of the Roman, consisting on ordinary days of Vespers, Compline, Mesonyktikon (the 'Midnight Office'), Orthros (analogous to a combination of Roman Vigils and Lauds), and the three 'Little Hours'. Since the 14th century it has been customary in some areas to combine Vespers, Orthros, and Prime into an *All-Night Vigil' on the eve of Sundays and major feasts. JRo/ALi

📖 R. F. Taft, SJ, *The Liturgy of the Hours in East and West* (Collegeville, MN, 1986)

Offrandes oubliées, Les ('The Forgotten Offerings'). Orchestral work (1930) by Messiaen.

Ogdon, John (Andrew Howard) (*b* Mansfield, 27 June 1937; *d* London, 1 Aug. 1989). English pianist and composer. He studied at the RMCM and was joint winner, with Vladimir Ashkenazy, of the Tchaikovsky Prize in 1962. He was an early exponent of the music of his Manchester colleagues Alexander Goehr, Birtwistle, and Maxwell Davies. Ogdon's own compositions, including a Piano Concerto (1968), are more traditional but are effectively scored. PG/AW

Ohana, Maurice (*b* Casablanca, 12 June 1913; *d* Paris, 13 Nov. 1992). French composer. He was a talented pianist from a young age. In 1933 he went to Paris to study architecture and also had further piano lessons. He travelled in Europe as a pianist and in 1937 began studying composition at the Schola Cantorum with Daniel-Lesur. During World War II he fought in the

British army. Back in Paris, he was one of the founders of the contemporary music group Zodiaque, important in postwar France. His first major work was *Llanto por Ignacio Sánchez Mejías* (1950), an oratorio to a text by Lorca.

Ohana was acutely aware of his Spanish roots and took a special interest in *cante hondo*; he was influenced by Albéniz, whose piano works he played, and by Falla, though he never resorted to local colour in his Spanish pieces, which include the *Cantigas* (1953–4) for soloists, chorus, and percussion. He also admired Debussy. Ohana's works of the 1970s—for example the Mass (1977) and the orchestral *Livre des prodiges* (1978–9)—are strikingly stark and individual. His most ambitious stage work was the opera *La Célestine*, given its premiere at the Paris Opéra in 1988; a setting of the 15th-century Spanish play by Fernando de Rojas, it uses only spoken dialogue and vocalise.   RLS

   📖 C. RAE, *The Music of Maurice Ohana* (Aldershot, 2000)

O Haupt voll Blut und Wunden ('O sacred head sore wounded'). A chorale, a setting of Paul Gerhardt's hymn (1656) of that title to Hassler's melody *Mein G'müt ist mir verwirret*. It is often called the 'Passion Chorale' because Bach used it in his *St Matthew Passion*, but it also appears in the *Christmas Oratorio* and the cantatas nos. 135, 159, and 161.

Oiseaux exotiques ('Exotic Birds'). Work by Messiaen for piano, 11 wind instruments, xylophone, glockenspiel, and two percussionists, composed in 1955–6.

Oistrakh, David (Fyodorovich) (*b* Odessa, 17/30 Sept. 1908; *d* Amsterdam, 24 Oct. 1974). Russian violinist. He made his debut in Leningrad in 1928 and went on to win many prizes within the USSR and in Brussels (1937). His international career flourished after World War II. He introduced Shostakovich's First Violin Concerto (written for him) at his New York debut in 1955. Oistrakh kept clear of politics and remained an honoured Soviet citizen. He taught at the Moscow Conservatory from 1934, his pupils including his son Igor. His technical mastery was complete, his tone powerfully warm, and he combined his virtuosity with an innate musicianship.   CF

Oktave (Ger.). 'Octave'; *Oktavflöte*, 'octave (above) flute', i.e. piccolo; *Oktavfagott*, 'octave (below) bassoon', i.e. contrabassoon; *Oktavkoppel*, 'octave coupler'.

oktoechos [octoechos] (from Gk. *okto*, 'eight', and *echoi*, 'melody types'). 1. The Byzantine system of four authentic and four plagal modes (see MODE, 2*a*). Of Palestinian origin, it was applied to Roman plainchant by Carolingian theorists.

2. Another name for the Book of Supplication (*Parakletike*) in the Byzantine rite, which contains an eight-week cycle of liturgical Propers, arranged by mode, commemorating the Resurrection of Christ.

Old Hall Manuscript (London, British Library, Add. 57950; formerly Old Hall, St Edmund's College, Ware, Herts.). The most important collection of English sacred music before the Eton Choirbook. Copied in the early 15th century, it contains a repertory of 147 works composed during the period *c*.1350–1420, written in a variety of styles. Some use the chordal *discant idiom typical of English music whereas others are more linear or canonic in conception and may be based on isorhythmic principles, revealing some debt to 14th-century continental music. Of the composers represented, many of whom belong to the generation before Dunstaple, the most important is Leonel Power. A modern edition, prepared by Andrew Hughes and Margaret Bent, was published in the *Corpus mensurabilis musicae* series in 1969–73.

Old Hundredth. Metrical psalm tune of uncertain origin. It is sung to the words 'All people that on earth do dwell'. Vaughan Williams made a ceremonial version of it, for large forces, for the coronation of Elizabeth II in 1953. See HYMN, 3.

Old Roman chant. A repertory of liturgical plainchant for the Roman rite surviving in five notated manuscripts from Rome dating from the 11th to the 13th centuries. Although initially seen as a corruption of Gregorian chant, to which it is intimately related, it is now generally accepted that its sources record a repertory with archaic features—for example, the incomplete systematization of its psalmody according to the *oktoechos*—that was transmitted orally for centuries before its neumation.   ALI

Oliver, Stephen (*b* Chester, 10 March 1950; *d* London, 29 April 1992). English composer. He began to write operas while an undergraduate at Oxford, and by the end of his life had completed more than 40 works for the stage, including *Timon of Athens* (ENO, 1991) and a musical, *Blondel*, in collaboration with Tim Rice (1983). Oliver, who often wrote his own librettos, composed in a fluent, relatively traditional style and was always alert to the character and structure of the text. He also wrote a number of instrumental works and much incidental and film music.   AW

Oliveros, Pauline (*b* Houston, TX, 30 May 1932). American composer. Introduced to music by her mother and grandmother, she studied at the University of Houston (1949–52) and with Robert Erickson (1954–60), and taught at San Francisco State College (1954–7) and the University of California at San Diego (1967–81).

In the 1950s and 60s she became known as a composer of electronic and instrumental music, rather in the Cage tradition, from which she emerged to develop her own line of long, slow music, for which she coined the term 'Deep Listening'. As a solo accordionist, or with her own Deep Listening Band, she has given performances worldwide.   PG

ombra scene. In early opera, a scene set in the underworld, where a ghost, or 'shade' (It.: *ombra*), is conjured up. Though originating in 17th-century opera, and a regular feature of operas on the Orpheus myth, the effect has proved tenacious; among the most celebrated *ombra* scenes are those in Berlioz's *Les Troyens*.

ondes martenot. A monophonic electronic instrument invented by Maurice Martenot in about 1928. One hand controls the pitch either from a keyboard or with the *ruban*, a horizontal 'ribbon' controller which gives unlimited flexibility, while the other controls tone and volume. The tone is amplified and heard through separate loudspeakers. The instrument has proved popular with many composers, including Milhaud, Honegger, Varèse, Messiaen, and Boulez, and is often heard in film scores.   JMo

Ondine. 1. Ballet in three acts and five scenes by Henze to a scenario by Frederick Ashton after Jean Giraudoux's play *Ondine* (1939), itself after Friedrich de la Motte Fouqué's *Undine* (1811); it was choreographed by Ashton (London, 1958).

2. The first piece of Ravel's **Gaspard de la nuit*.

3. Piano piece (1913) by Debussy, no.8 of his *Préludes*, book 2.

ongarese, all'. See ALL'ONGARESE.

On Hearing the First Cuckoo in Spring. Tone-poem (1912) by Delius, the first of his Two Pieces for Small Orchestra (the second is *Summer Night on the River*).

On Wenlock Edge. Song cycle (1908–9) by Vaughan Williams, for tenor, string quartet, and piano, settings of six poems from A. E. Housman's *A Shropshire Lad* (1896), the first song being 'On Wenlock Edge'; Vaughan Williams arranged the cycle for tenor and orchestra (*c.*1923).

op. Abbreviation for **opus*.

open harmony. The converse of **close harmony*.

open notes. 1. Notes on the unstopped (or 'open') string of any bowed or plucked instrument.

2. On valved brass instruments, the notes of the harmonic series, which are produced without lowering (or closing) any valve.

3. In brass parts generally, the direction 'open', or 'ouvert', countermands 'muted' or 'stopped'.

open score. A **score*, normally comprising more than two staves, that shows each voice of a polyphonic composition on a separate staff. Open scores of four staves were used for some Renaissance and Baroque keyboard pieces.   LC

open string. A string of a bowed or plucked instrument not 'stopped' by the fingers.

opera (*see opposite page*)

opéra-ballet (Fr.). A form of entertainment combining music, drama, and dance that was popular at the French court from the end of the 17th century to the late 18th. It usually consisted of a prologue and three or four acts (*entrées*), each of which had a separate plot (though often on a common theme). *Opéras-ballets* were generally lighthearted, treating mythological or pastoral subjects rather than tragedy, and included instrumental pieces, dances, solo and choral song, and recitatives. Campra's *L'Europe galant* (1697) and Rameau's *Les Indes galantes* (1735) are well-known examples.   —/JBE

opera buffa (It.; Fr.: *opéra bouffe*). 'Comic opera', the opposite of **opera seria*. It began in early 18th-century Naples as an entertainment involving characters drawn from low life. The purely comic but all-sung **intermezzo* was often played between the acts of an *opera seria* (Pergolesi's *La serva padrona* is the best-known example). The dramatist Carlo Goldoni added 'high' characters, especially a high-minded heroine, and more serious or sentimental episodes in the mid-18th-century *dramma giocoso*; famous examples include Mozart's *Le nozze di Figaro*, Paisiello's and Rossini's *Il barbiere di Siviglia*, and Donizetti's *Don Pasquale*. Characteristic features of the genre are the rapid-firing **recitativo secco* accompanying vigorous stage business, and the multisectional concerted finale with dramatic surprises. With the demise of *recitativo secco* after the mid-19th century, *opera buffa* ceased to be a separate genre. See OPERA, 6 and 7.   NT

opéra comique (Fr., 'comic opera'). The word 'comique' is not identical in meaning with the English 'comic', or with the Italian 'buffa', having more to do with the Ancient Greeks' dramatic category of 'komoidia' (comedy). The French understood different things by it according to the date of its use. Beginning in the early 18th century with farces and satires using spoken dialogue with well-known *airs* (vaudevilles), the genre developed into the sentimental *comédie mêlée d'ariettes* (of which Rousseau's *Le Devin du village*, 1752, was one of the earliest examples). Thence, in the 19th century, it drew closer to serious opera, handling serious or Romantic themes, as in Boieldieu's *La Dame blanche* and Auber's *Fra Diavolo*, Gounod's *Faust* and Bizet's

(*cont. on p. 889*)

opera

A staged drama in which accompanied singing has an essential function. Opera is the grandest and most expensive of musical entertainments, and in its fullest forms has almost invariably required some kind of subsidy to survive, whether royal, national, local, corporate, or philanthropic. It has probably aroused more passion and critical comment than any other musical genre. It has been condemned as irrational and nonsensical; on the other hand, it has been considered the supreme expression of the human spirit. It has helped to bankrupt kings; it has provoked revolutionary demonstrations; it has praised monarchs, encouraged popularist movements, expounded philosophy, explored psychology; and, more often than any of these, it has simply provided entertainment. Such variety stems from the very mixture of elements in opera: music, drama, poetry, the visual arts, and (at times) dance. A reasonable definition separating opera from other forms is that it is a work intended to be staged, in which singing plays a dominant part in portraying the actions and emotions of the characters.

1. The origins of opera

It is generally said that liturgical music drama and mystery plays (see CHURCH DRAMA; MEDIEVAL DRAMA) and such pastoral plays as Adam de la Halle's *Le Jeu de Robin et de Marion* contain the seeds from which opera grew. While there is some truth in this, the form in which opera first appeared was a peculiarly Renaissance phenomenon, owing much to the cultural conditions of the late 16th century. It was the product of speculation by intellectuals, living mainly in Florence. Despairing of the triviality (as they saw it) of music in their own day, they were determined to revive the glories of the art of ancient Greece (see CAMERATA). Lacking the music of the Greeks in any form they could understand, they had to rely on written accounts, from which they came to a number of conclusions. The most important was that Greek drama was sung, or said, in such a way

that the words were emotionally heightened but were always clearly audible.

They experimented with this principle in vocal chamber music (see MONODY), developing a type of singing in which the words were sung syllabically with careful attention to their natural declamation in speech, modified by two features. First, emotive words could be embellished to underline their meaning; secondly, a lute or harpsichord provided an accompaniment, offering possibilities for expressive harmony (dissonance to express anguish, and so on), and also establishing a basic harmonic rhythm to control the embellishments of the singer. The result was far from the Greeks, but it was a fertile element in the evolution of opera.

The realization of this vocal principle within the context of 16th-century dramatic music can be observed in the pastoral play. Here the dramatic action was weak, the chief emphasis being on lyrical verse. Music was used when the action suggested it, one play, for example, having a temple scene where a priest and people sing incantations. By the end of the century such plays were given elaborate productions, as were the *intermedi* (interludes) performed between the acts of the play. These were usually light allegorical tableaux, such as *The Triumph of Time* or *The Harmony of the Spheres*; they used scenery (sometimes with machines to represent, for instance, clouds bringing the gods from the heavens) and music to provide a diverting interlude to the main drama. The music consisted of songs and madrigals, with instrumental music and sometimes with dancing; the whole was often conceived for vast forces with an elaborate *mise-en-scène*, as in the *intermedi* separating the acts of Girolamo Bargagli's comedy *La pellegrina* (1589), performed during the celebrations for the wedding of the Grand Duke Ferdinand de' Medici and Christine of Lorraine: the audiences for these occasional entertainments were confined to sovereigns, nobles, and their invited guests. The instrumental ensembles were large and varied; the solo singers were virtuosos of the highest ability. Such interludes were therefore frequently attractive, and gradually came to assume more prominence than the play itself. With these developments in late 16th-century dramatic music the scene was set for the development of opera itself.

2. *From the Florentines to the 1640s*

Three composers involved in Florentine intellectual society at the end of the 16th century made attempts at a *dramma per musica* (literally a 'drama for [or in] music': the Italian word *opera* simply means 'work', and was coined for the genre by the English later in the 17th century). One of the composers, Emilio de' Cavalieri, was himself an intellectual; the other two, Jacopo Peri and Giulio Caccini, were singers. Paradoxically, it was the intellectual who produced the more conventional work: Cavalieri's *Rappresentatione di Anima, et di Corpo* (1600) is in essence a mixture of the old religious mystery play and the techniques of the *intermedio*, belonging more properly to the early history of the *oratorio. Peri and Caccini, however, produced something new. As singers there was a tremendous rivalry between them, heightened by a difference in attitude: Peri was a dramatic singer, Caccini was more concerned with the lyrical art of bel canto. Peri wrote the first continuously sung pastoral, *Dafne* (1598), but the music is lost. Both composers then set the court poet Ottavio Rinuccini's version of the Orpheus legend, *Euridice*. Peri's work was given at the celebrations for the wedding of Maria de' Medici and King Henri IV of France (1600), though it was bedevilled with the jealousies so common in later operatic history, Caccini insisting on writing the parts that his own pupils were to sing. In 1602 Caccini's own complete setting of *Euridice* was heard.

Both operas contained traditional elements: the pastoral nature of the verse, the happy ending customary in a pastoral play, the use of choruses and songs, and, in Caccini's setting at least, the presumed use of an elegant *mise-en-scène*. But the new elements were significant: a simple, well-constructed plot, the use of a small group of instrumentalists in place of the vast assembly for the *intermedi*, and the continuous singing accompanied by such harmony instruments as harpsichord or lute—what was later to be called the *continuo group. There was also an essential difference between the two works: Peri had an imaginative harmonic sense, and tended to break up the melodic line to match the dramatic action;

Caccini, on the other hand, was content merely to enunciate the text accurately and to write attractive songlike passages. It has been said that these first operas are dull and drily experimental; but, in the hands of expert singer-actors and performed before an audience which could follow the text in detail, they can be effective and moving, as was demonstrated at a quatercentenary performance of the Peri–Caccini version at the University of Illinois in October 2000. Nor did they lack musical organization, since the concept of *strophic variation (a varied melody over a recurrent base) helped to lend shape to the whole work. The absence of dramatic action was of little account to audiences used to the lyrical pastoral play. Possibly they missed rather more the sumptuousness and large scale of the old pastoral-with-*intermedi*, and it is noticeable that, while the *intermedio* retained its popularity, there were few operas to follow closely these early Florentine models.

By general agreement, the first 'great' opera is Monteverdi's *Orfeo*, produced at Mantua in 1607. It showed a masterly exploitation of the characteristics of early Florentine opera and also drew on the more spectacular features of the *intermedio*. The libretto, by Alessandro Striggio, uses in outline the same story as *Euridice*, retaining the happy ending (though either Striggio or Monteverdi tried in vain to break with 16th-century practice and revert to the tragic ending of the classical legend). Yet the opera is enriched by a greater sense of scale, atmosphere, and characterization. Monteverdi returned to the large orchestra typical of the *intermedio*, using it (as earlier composers had done) for the evocation of mood. His score also allowed for dancing and for the use of theatrical machines, recreating the magnificence much loved by noble audiences and patrons. From the Florentines he took the concept of recitative (more closely from Peri than from Caccini), though his experience as a composer of expressive madrigals gave his style a more profound harmonic idiom, dissonance and chromaticism being integral elements. His particular gift, however, was his sense of timing and dramatic organization. Not only are the individual scenes carefully cast into musical patterns, but the whole opera works towards and from a grand climax, the *preghiera*, or plea of Orpheus to be allowed to enter Hades (see ORNAMENTS AND ORNAMENTATION, 3). Although the characters, with the exception of Orpheus, lack definition, the story is compellingly told and the music is nearly always interesting for its own sake.

The first performance was probably given before a select audience of nobles and intellectuals. By contrast, Monteverdi's next opera, *Arianna*, was performed to a distinguished audience invited to Mantua from all over northern Italy for the wedding of the Gonzaga heir and Margherita of Savoy (1608). With the exception of the famous 'Lamento d'Arianna' the score has been lost, but from contemporary accounts the opera seems to have followed the main trends of *Orfeo*. Evidently it represented a step towards human, rather than mythological, drama: Ariadne's lament seems to be an expression of Monteverdi's grief at the death of his wife (1607), and the ladies in the audience seem to have identified with the character, weeping unashamedly at her plight.

Although *Arianna* undoubtedly revealed the potential of opera, the genre still did not become a common phenomenon. Monteverdi, as its most famous practitioner, would surely have received many commissions if it had, but he was more frequently asked for *intermedi* and ballet music, and had only one opportunity to compose an opera in the next 20 years, *Licori finta pazza* (1627). The commission again came from Mantua. The score is lost, but from correspondence it is clear that Monteverdi was now regarding opera as real human drama: the music depicted the sudden changes of mood of the characters, which were sung by performers of considerable acting skill. However, because of royal illness and death, the opera was apparently never staged, and Monteverdi had no chance of following this line of development for another decade or more.

The only city where opera had anything like a continuous development at this time was Rome. The social life of the papal court centred on such rich princes of the church as Cardinal Barberini, whose palace had a huge theatre and whose taste for lavish entertainment was indulged regardless of expense. The choice of subjects for operas became broader. The pastoral persisted spasmodically, the mythological aspects being less rarefied and more down-to-earth in such works as Domenico Mazzocchi's *La catena d'Adone* (1626). There was also a taste for religious subjects, using the lives of saints as a basis. Musically there was a mixture of conservative and forward-looking elements. The sumptuous *mise-en-scène* was marked by the frequent use of the chorus; the orchestra, though less varied in sonority than in the *intermedio* (it was now becoming a stabilized group of strings), had separate pieces including, sometimes, an overture on an ample scale.

There was now a firm distinction between *recitative and aria, the latter having a mobile bass which gave shape to the melody through regular changes of chord. By the 1640s there was a conscious effort to alleviate 'the tedium of the recitative' (Luigi Rossi's phrase), even though this entailed a final break with the high ideals of the 'play in music'. But even before the 1640s the combination of Monteverdi and the Roman operatic traditions had led to a new development.

3. From the opening of the public opera houses to the 1730s

In 1636 two Roman musicians, Benedetto Ferrari and Francesco Manelli, settled in Venice, and within a year decided to produce opera there. But Venice lacked patrons to support the venture, and they were forced to seek a new source of finance—the more affluent section of the general public. The Teatro S. Cassiano, the first public opera house, opened in 1637, admitting audiences either on a subscription basis (one hired a box for the season) or by the payment of a fee for a single performance. Consequently the audience represented a wider social spectrum than previously; moreover, the theatre had to entertain and satisfy its public patrons. The chief attraction was soon found to be a combination of virtuoso singing and spectacle. The former gave rise to a new type of artist—the 'star', particularly castratos and female singers (the earliest prima donna was Anna Renzi, on whose prowess sonnets were written). The latter created a demand for the skilled theatre designer and machinist, whose marvels now even surpassed those of earlier entertainment.

Such conditions resulted in a genre far removed from that envisaged by the Florentine intellectuals, though Monteverdi, the one composer in Venice with operatic experience, was involved from the start and provided a link with the earlier period. His *Arianna* was revived, and he wrote several new works, two of which have survived—*Il ritorno d'Ulisse in patria* (1640) and *L'incoronazione di Poppea* (1642). From these it is clear that the unity and simplicity of Florentine opera had given way to diversity and discontinuity. Although both operas exhibit a strong dramatic instinct and a capacity to organize a story, they also contain scenes lacking any real connection with the plot, having comic characters and allegorical figures in addition to the main players. Musically there was a similar diversity, with songs, duets, and occasional instrumental pieces interspersed among the recitatives. However, recitative was still used for the most dramatic scenes and expressions of emotion. There was little for the chorus to do, and the orchestra was small (though the actual size is open to debate). But Monteverdi's prime aim was to move his audience by displaying the human predicament. His comic scenes, never trivial, are essential to the formation of a rounded emotional picture.

During the 1640s public opera became so successful that several more theatres opened in Venice. Some were relatively small and lacked the resources for grand spectacle, others were larger and more lavishly equipped. The need to find new composers also tended to bring about a variety of attitudes. The Monteverdian tradition was carried on by his pupil Cavalli, who wrote about 32 operas during the period 1639–73. Conceived for different theatres, they displayed certain differences in detail, though in general he persisted with human drama in which the emotions of the characters were clearly expressed, particularly when they were placed in extreme situations, as in *Ormindo* (1644), where there is a prison scene which was to become a cliché in later operas. In Cavalli's operas the main burden of the storytelling and emotional expression continued to be borne by the recitative; but it now moved effortlessly in and out of arioso and short arias, the latter shaped by bass patterns (as in the old strophic variation, though usually more compact) or by repetitions of sections, sometimes resulting in a short *da capo* (ABA) aria. The operas contained many such arias, though they did not predominate.

The opposite is true of Cesti, whose interest in popular, tuneful set pieces was encouraged by the early success of *Orontea* (1649): this led to performances in Austria, where Cesti won commissions for large-scale spectacular operas, notably *Il pomo d'oro* (1668), written for the wedding of Emperor Leopold I and Margherita of Spain. This called for 24 changes of scene and lasted eight hours (in addition, there were two hours of non-musical entertainment); it required 48 performers—not all singers—plus a ballet company and large orchestra. *Il pomo d'oro* created a fashion for festival operas, especially in Vienna where it lasted well into the 18th century (Gluck's *Orfeo ed Euridice* is a late example). Writing for a foreign audience (which could not readily understand Italian) naturally put a premium on tuneful music, and, following Cesti's example, the melodious aria became the main concern of several composers whose initial successes had been in Venice: Marc'Antonio and Pietro Ziani (who worked in

Austria and southern Germany), Carlo Pallavicino (Dresden), Antonio Sartorio (Venice), and Agostino Steffani (Munich, Hanover, and Düsseldorf). All these composers transferred the main emotional burden on to the aria, in which instrumental ritornellos assumed a more important role and so tended to lengthen the set pieces. The best composers writing from 1680 were capable of great variety of mood, and, if the librettos were sometimes too complex, the music was truly dramatic. They often used comic elements (Legrenzi and Stradella were particularly good at these) and the operas are certainly not the product of mere formulas, as has been alleged of Baroque opera.

By the end of the 17th century opera was popular throughout Italy: Rome and Naples offered valuable alternatives to the theatres of Venice, though Venice continued to produce many more operas per season than anywhere else. The 'star' system was now well established, the public tending to favour the upper voices, particularly castratos. To satisfy public taste, the aria now became lengthier, with a reprise of the *da capo* aria allowing the singers to provide embellishments to the melody (see ARIA, 2). As early as 1690 it was usual for the singer to leave the stage after his or her aria (though the rigid convention came later); there were therefore few opportunities for ensembles, and little chance for choral writing. However, the arias themselves covered a wide variety of moods and musical styles, from protracted pieces with extended instrumental ritornellos and concertante parts to simple songs based on dance rhythms. The orchestra assumed considerable importance, both in the overture (which could sometimes be a substantial piece) and in the accompaniment of the singers: indeed, in the later operas of Alessandro Scarlatti (the most influential opera composer of the period around 1700) arias are never accompanied solely by the continuo.

Numerous Italian composers wrote in this manner, which may be seen as a forerunner of the more rigidly conventionalized *opera seria* of the 18th century (see below, 5); chief among them were Antonio and Giovanni Bononcini, Francesco Gasparini, Antonio Lotti, Vivaldi, and, above all, Handel. Although Handel's main activity as an opera composer was in London from 1711 to 1740, his tastes were formed earlier in Italy. This is to some degree reflected in his varied choice of librettos: while most were on historical subjects (e.g. *Giulio Cesare*, 1724), he also wrote on magical themes (*Alcina*, 1735), chose plots derived from

French classical tragedy (*Rodelinda*, 1725, after Pierre Corneille's *Pertharite*), and even wrote the occasional comedy (*Serse*, 1738). Musically, the recitatives—relatively short, to suit English taste—convey each change of mood by means of modulation or by orchestral effects (his accompanied recitatives are often particularly fine). The arias are usually in *da capo* form and follow the *'exit' convention, but are richly varied in style. Far from being 'concerts in costume', as they were once considered, the operas show a tremendous flair for the theatre, and proved immensely successful in 20th-century revivals.

By the mid-18th century, Metastasian *opera seria* held a pre-eminent position in every European court and capital except Paris. Italian singers, and to a lesser extent librettists, designers, instrumentalists, and composers, could command large salaries and secure most of the important posts in theatres throughout Europe; as far as castratos were concerned, they held a monopoly. Aristocrats, and those aspiring to upper-class standing, were prepared to accept all the defects of a genre that was alien in plot, culture, and language, static in its stage action, and often tedious and repetitious in its music, for the sake of its high and exclusive status and its long-standing association with all the brilliance of royalty. It was fashionable to arrive late at the opera; to converse and walk about at will; and to pay attention only to the dress, embellishments, and cadenzas of the prima donna or primo uomo. Many attended several performances of the same production in one season; but this indicates inattention rather than passionate interest. Only a small minority, sometimes termed the *cognoscenti* ('connoisseurs'), really understood and appreciated the elegance of the verse, the aptness of the music, or the subtlety of the singers' interpretation.

4. *Serious opera in France until the Revolution*

Ideas not dissimilar to those that gave rise to the birth of opera in Florence were current at the same time in intellectual circles in France; but the stronger dramatic tradition, and especially the popularity of elaborate court ballets, meant that the concept of a drama sung throughout did not arrive until much later. Various attempts to introduce opera were made in the mid-17th century, especially by Cardinal Mazarin, himself an Italian, whose enthusiasm had been aroused by seeing Landi's *Sant'Alessio* in Rome in 1632. Cavalli's *Egisto*

was given in 1646, and the following year Luigi Rossi's *Orfeo*. From these and other performances it became clear that when there was a lavish *mise-en-scène*, preferably with machines, ballets, and even animals, the entertainment was a success in court circles; without such aids, the music tended to fall flat. There was a period of little activity, although the so-called *comédies-ballets* (spoken plays with extended musical interludes) by Molière and Lully flourished from 1664 to 1670.

In 1669 the poet and playwright Pierre Perrin (*c*.1620–75) began to establish 'académies d'opéra' in France, and together with the composer Robert Cambert inaugurated the Paris 'académie' with a pastoral in music, *Pomone* (1671), which has claims to be considered the first opera in the French language. The music for this has survived only incomplete, but it is clear that it was in tune with French taste, the use of the vernacular giving it a distinct advantage over Italian opera.

Following intrigues, however, Perrin went bankrupt and was thrown into prison, and his academy was disbanded (1672). Lully seized his chance, and founded the Académie Royale de Musique, which was given a monopoly to produce all-sung drama. He produced first a pastoral in 1672, then a **tragédie lyrique* in the following spring: *Cadmus et Hermione*. This was the first of a long series, Lully and his librettist Philippe Quinault writing one each year—most notably *Alceste* in 1674 and *Armide* in 1686—until Lully's death in 1687; and it was the style of these which governed French opera until the middle of the next century.

Lully was a Florentine who had left his native city too early to gain a knowledge of contemporary Venetian opera. He had old-fashioned ideals which, combined with the French taste for classical drama, produced an approach entirely independent of that current in Italy. Librettos were conceived as unified dramas, and although they took as themes the amorous adventures of mythological or legendary figures and scarcely merit the term 'heroic', they had the merit of lacking the incredible complexity of Italian plots. At the same time, there were simple **divertissements* to allow for the popular marvels of scenery and machines.

The music was based on recitative rather than aria, though this recitative (called *récit*) differed from Italian in that it was based on French prosody rather than on speech rhythms: it followed the regular accentuation of verse, imparting to the melody a more measured feeling, and made greater use of dissonance in the harmony. The *airs* were short, generally with a binary or rondo pattern, and were scarcely more melodious than the recitative. Several observers, accustomed to Italian opera, found the lack of differentiation between recitative and *air* disappointing; but, because the recitative style was based on the declamation of actors at the Comédie-Française, its effect on the serious theatregoer would have come close to the ideals of the Florentine founders of opera. The role of the chorus also looked back to earlier operas, notably those of the Roman School, Lully using it imaginatively as a participant in the drama, as well as for sonority in the divertissements that concluded some of the acts. Lully's well-drilled orchestra provided ample ballets, the famous French *overtures, and 'symphonies' to accompany action on the stage. Consequently French opera sounds very different from Italian opera. In addition, the absence of castratos, and the greater use of tenor and bass voices, gives a less brilliant effect, though some of the writing for high tenor is taxing enough. Lully's operas have been criticized for lacking a sense of drama, on the one hand, and for an absence of musical highlights on the other. But recent revivals have shown that they can appeal strongly to a modern audience.

Lully's monopoly not only stamped out competition in his lifetime; it also meant that no other composers had a chance to gain experience in the genre. The consequences were immediately apparent. With few exceptions, the *tragédies lyriques* of the next generation were relatively unsuccessful, and although the works of Lully were revived for many seasons after his death, they gradually became unfashionable, even when alterations were made to bring them at least a little up to date. Composers preferred the so-called *opéra-ballet*, where conventions were less rigid. The *opéra-ballet* made no attempt at a continuous drama. Each act could be more or less independent, though sometimes there was an underlying theme.

With this diminution of the role of drama, it became possible to introduce Italian features, notably the extended *da capo* aria (called 'ariette' by the French to distinguish it from the shorter *air*), with its more virtuoso singing and modern harmony. Campra's *opéra-ballet Les Fêtes vénitiennes* (1710) includes a scene depicting the atmosphere and happenings at the Grimani theatre in Venice, while his *Le Carnaval de Venise* (1699) actually contains a short Italian opera, *L'Orfeo nell'inferni*. Also more in tune with the times was the imaginative orchestration, to be found too in *tragédies*

lyriques which often contain vivid storm scenes and other programme music.

In spite of the attractiveness of some of these works, the seriousness of French opera did not return until the 1730s, when *Hippolyte et Aricie*, Rameau's first *tragédie lyrique* (1733), proved popular enough to encourage him to write theatrical pieces of various kinds for some 20 years. His style might be described as 'Lully brought up to date', with the same basic forms of measured recitative (now more supple and embellished) and short *airs* (binary or ternary in form), to which are added the larger-scale ariettes (the equivalent of *da capo* arias), choruses, and orchestral pieces, the last often programmatic depictions of psychological situations and such external features as storms.

But this does scant justice to an opera composer whose music is rich enough to stand on its own, enterprising in harmony and orchestration, expressive in melody, and conscious of dramatic considerations which are rarely impeded by the rigorous conventions of *opera seria*. Even the ballets are well integrated, while the overtures are frequently linked to the first scene, taking the place of the Lullian prologue. Rameau has been compared to Wagner in his flair for creating music drama, and in revival his operas have been found to be as valid as Handel's.

By the 1750s the *tragédie lyrique* was again under attack by the Italianate faction, led by Rousseau, whose *opéra comique* was soon popular not only with the general public but with the intellectuals of the new Enlightenment (see below, 6). The older way was attempted by Boismortier and Mondonville with little success during the 1760s, but it was only with the arrival of Gluck in the following decade that the genre was truly revived (see below, 5). Thereafter the Opéra was maintained until the political Revolution of 1789 by Italian Gluckists, Salieri, Sacchini, and Piccinni, the last brought to Paris in 1776 by yet another pro-Italian group especially to challenge Gluck. In fact, the result was opera on classical themes, though sometimes breaking away from classical attitudes: Salieri's *Les Danaïdes* (1784) includes a hell scene in which Danaus is seen chained to a rock with his bleeding entrails being devoured by a vulture. The music is less florid than its Italian counterparts, but shares their harmonic idioms and general manner in many ways. However, choruses persist, the orchestration is fuller, and there is a penchant for ballet—all of which will continue until the 19th century.

5. Rococo and reform in opera seria, 1725–90

Just as the French, perhaps unwittingly, had stuck to the essential goals of the creators of opera, so the Italians, by 1725, were seeking to go back to at least some of them. The reformers were led at first by two librettists, Apostolo Zeno and Pietro Metastasio. Both were court poets in Vienna, and wished to reassert the values of drama against the excesses of the star-based opera. For Zeno 'opera and reason are not necessarily incompatible'. The stories must be rid of comic elements and secondary plots, and should show the opposition of love and duty in the rulers of the state. The denouement must be brought about naturally and the climaxes should be built up in a planned manner. Metastasio developed this philosophy, adding elegance of poetry—verse full of conceits and similes—though not favouring the Aristotelian unities of time and place, as Zeno had tended to do. He worked in longer acts (three instead of five), placing an 'exit' aria at the end of each scene, the singer then leaving the stage. His recitatives were succinct, and his arias, expressing the character's state of mind or offering a reflection on the situation, were carefully arranged so that there should be the same number for each major character (to prevent quarrelling among the singers) and so that no two arias of a similar type should be adjacent (to avoid monotony). This meant that the characters were limited to six or seven, three or four principal roles, the rest somewhat less important.

Into this logical and elegant mould dozens of composers poured their dramatic music for the next half-century, changing the detail, but rarely the substance, of Metastasio's librettos to suit conditions. The arias were virtually all in the *da capo* pattern and were of three main types: bravura (to show off skill), used to depict stress—emotional or real—and battle scenes; cantabile, for gentle zephyrs and the more intimate aspects of love; *parlante*, for less exalted moments. Ensembles were rare, though some beautiful duets (also in *da capo* form), expressing the grief of lovers forced to part, were written. An ensemble of the complete cast would sing a finale. This is sometimes marked 'coro' but was not sung as a chorus, though elsewhere in the operas there were crowd scenes. The *recitativo secco* is sometimes perfunctory, though at its best it effectively underlines the dramatic action, with changes of key to heighten changes of mood. It was only in the declining years of the *opera seria* that recitative could be relegated

to insignificance: Mozart, in *La clemenza di Tito*, for example, held the composition of recitatives in such small regard that he entrusted them to his pupil Süssmayr. Accompanied recitative was scarce, reserved chiefly for moments of emotional climax.

The most famous composer of the Metastasian libretto was Hasse, who, as husband of the singer Faustina Bordoni, knew how to write expressively and effectively for the voice; and indeed, in spite of all the philosophizing, his operas, and those of many imitators, still favoured vocal display. The melodic lines are decorated with appoggiaturas, which soften the rhythms; the harmony is simple and relatively slow-moving. Some of the operas of this rococo style could perhaps be revived, especially those embodying grand spectacle: Hasse in one work, *Solimano* (1753), used a veritable zoo of horses, camels, and elephants, in a manner later to become familiar in performances of *Aida* at the Baths of Caracalla; but they lack the strength of the pre-*galant* Baroque composers.

Certainly these operatic reforms were soon too mild to satisfy the really serious librettists and composers. Significantly, more far-reaching experiments came from two composers employed at courts where tastes were French: Jommelli at Stuttgart, Traetta at Parma. To these must be added Gluck at Vienna, who after thorough practice in the Metastasian *opere serie* in the 1740s, worked from 1756 for a monarch with French tastes, and then in the 1770s spent five years composing for the Paris Opéra. All these turned to the classical subjects typical of the *tragédie lyrique*, and all used the grand choruses characteristic of French opera, allotting an extensive role to the orchestra (Traetta especially having a penchant for pictorial effects after the manner of Rameau). The Italians replaced much of the *recitativo secco* with *recitativo accompagnato*, which often shows thematic development. The full *da capo* aria was used more rarely, only part of the first section being repeated (see ARIA, 2). The influence of comic opera is apparent in the greater use of ensembles. It was also increasingly common to interrupt arias with recitative, so enhancing the sense of dramatic continuity. Similarly, overtures set the mood of the drama, and sometimes ran straight into the first scene.

Gluck went further, having a librettist, Ranieri Calzabigi, who became an anti-Metastasian and had the wisdom to see that opera did not depend solely on literary or musical values but was true spectacle and theatre. From *Alceste* (1767), therefore, Gluck abandoned the *da capo* aria and *recitativo secco*, and wrote in a simple melodic style which seems consciously to have an 'antique' or classical flavour, paying attention to speech inflections. (These traits are also found in his *Orfeo ed Euridice*, but it belongs to a sub-genre of *opera seria*, the **festa teatrale*, which had always emphasized chorus and dance rather than the solo voice.) It is worth noting that the first excavations of Greek sites were being dug by J. J. Winckelmann at about this time. Gluck's characters are human as opposed to symbolic, though the nature of these 'classical' librettos is to give them a moral tone. His reforms (see also the separate entry on Gluck) were exactly what was needed to keep French serious opera in being. As usual, Italy was less receptive and, in spite of Gluck's three 'French'-style but Italian operas of the 1760s, Metastasio settings continued as before. The inevitable result was that *opera seria* became increasingly old-fashioned, though its musical language was certainly affected by the more congenial style of *opera buffa*.

6. *Comic opera until the time of Mozart*

Comic scenes had been a successful feature of public opera from its beginnings. It was natural, therefore, that they should continue in another form when the high-minded principles of composers and librettists led to their abolition. When the serious *tragédie héroïque* came into being in France, a species of comic opera was given by an Italian troupe acting improvised *commedia dell'arte* plays including songs. These dramas were done in Italian at first, but French scenes were gradually interwoven with them, and eventually they became entirely French. The songs, or vaudevilles, were popular tunes, sometimes with a folksong flavour, but occasionally simple *airs* by Lully and others were used. There was usually an element of satire in the plot, and following a satirical attack on the king's mistress, Françoise de Maintenon, such entertainments were abolished.

The tradition, however, was continued at the annual Paris fairs, where acrobats and jugglers had performed for many years. The acting troupes were strictly supervised and were forbidden to use speech, a regulation they circumvented by displaying placards with the words written on them and by singing vaudevilles. By 1714, pieces written completely *en vaudeville* were being called *opéras comiques*: these were so successful that five years later the official company for spoken drama, the Comédie-Française, not liking the com-

petition, managed to have them banned. Yet an Italian company came back with its own entertainments, and *opéra comique* survived tenuously until the middle of the century, maintaining its tendency to satirize, to guy serious opera, and to use popular tunes, though the music was more often composed specially rather than being merely borrowed.

The French players brought *comédies en vaudeville* to London in 1718, and it was probably this that gave the impetus for a similar kind of entertainment in English. John Gay's *The Beggar's Opera* (1728), the prototype for English **ballad opera*, clearly borrowed some French attitudes: satire on politicians (the hero, Macheath, represented the Prime Minister Walpole in certain respects) and on *opera seria* (there is a prison scene which parodies a favourite operatic convention, of which the most recent example had been in Handel's *Rodelinda* of 1725); spoken dialogue; popular tunes and other melodies by Handel and other serious composers, simply harmonized. As in France, the satirical element provoked censorship, and Gay's sequel, *Polly*, was banned from the stage by the Lord Chamberlain. *The Beggar's Opera*, dealing with low life in a jocular way, had an enormous public success; it was also well received critically, Swift remarking that it exposed 'that unnatural taste for Italian music among us which is wholly unsuitable to our northern climate and the genius of the people'. It was a most promising step towards a popular, as opposed to a courtly, vernacular opera, and it was an English ballad opera, Charles Coffey's *The Devil to Pay* (1731), that sparked off the vogue for *Singspiel* ('play in song') in Germany, where it was widely given as *Der Teufel ist los* from 1743. In England itself, the fashion for ballad opera was at its height for nearly a decade, then faded until it finally disappeared about 30 years later. But it left a legacy of spoken drama with music which was given greater coherence by such composers as Dibdin and Shield, who fully orchestrated the songs and provided ensembles and other Italianate elements.

It is not surprising that *opera buffa* was less easily imported by foreign countries than *opera seria*, for it depended on an understanding of colloquial Italian and of local jokes and customs. Within Italy itself, however, sophisticated comic opera had already been developed. By the 1720s it had become common to insert intermezzos between the acts of *opere serie*; at the same time a new type of full-length opera of similar character was being given at some theatres in Naples. The intermezzos were at first low-dialect plays, but they soon developed into short social comedies, scenes from everyday life in which the wit of honest working girls and men triumphed over wealth and position. There were usually no more than three or four characters, who were played by singing actors rather than the virtuosos of *opera seria*. There were no castratos, and the bass voice came into its own. Unlike the French and English comedies, the Italian *opera buffa* was sung throughout, with recitatives and arias alternating; but the arias, though generally in *da capo* form, were much more varied in style than in serious opera, often using short phrases with strong rhythms rather than continuous long phrases needing great breath control. The words were mostly set syllabically and allowed for some stage business, so that the gulf between recitative and aria was somewhat reduced, the one seeming the extension of the other. The most famous composer of the first phase of comic opera was Pergolesi, whose two-act intermezzo *La serva padrona* (1733)—performed between the acts of his *opera seria Il prigioniero superbo*—achieved international renown for its tunefulness and vivacity.

By about 1750, a more complex type of *opera buffa* was taking shape, often called *dramma giocoso* ('jocular drama'), largely through the success of the joint efforts of the Venetians Goldoni and Galuppi. Carlo Goldoni, a first-class playwright of dialect comedies, included more serious roles for sentimental characters, especially heroines, which Galuppi matched with his music. The purely farcical elements took a subordinate place or disappeared, and a true social comedy began to cover a wide range of human emotions. Composers who understood the heroic idiom of *opera seria* turned to this more rewarding kind of comic opera, and from this time it became the most popular genre of the public stage. More informal and natural forms replaced the *da capo* aria, though strophic songs were rare. There was an increasing use of ensembles and of connected scenes containing several numbers and continuous stage action, so that the drama seemed to be constantly in motion. This is especially true in the finales of acts, which became a strong feature of the genre. The orchestra is important in the ensembles, often carrying the main melodic strand while the voices chatter in short motivic phrases, a technique which again allows for a malleable relationship between action and music. Such a composer as Piccinni could take a plot based on Samuel Richardson's sentimental novel *Pamela*, and in *La buona figliuola* (1760) make a work rich in characters which transcend the normal stock types of the previous era. And although there was no great stylistic development after this, the form was pliable enough for Paisiello, Cimarosa, and others to explore the genre's possibilities and to provide it with a varying and extensive repertory until the end of the century and beyond.

The success of *opera buffa* had international repercussions. *La serva padrona* was given in Paris in 1746, making apparently little impression; but when revived six years later it sparked a journalistic row, known as the Querelle des *Bouffons: here there were two opposing factions, one favouring Italian opera, the other defending native French traditions. One of the pro-Italian faction, Jean-Jacques Rousseau, produced a new kind of *opéra comique* in *Le Devin du village* (1752), supposedly an intermezzo in the Italian style but in reality borrowing only the Italian recitative. Simple strophic or rondo-form tunes, the rustic setting, and the dances are all entirely French in manner, but Rousseau's followers, including Gluck, made use of more Italian means. The French tradition of satire and the use of spoken dialogue, often including down-to-earth language, returned in the works of Favart, Monsigny, and Philidor.

Opera buffa also had its effect in Germany. After the introduction of ballad opera in the 1740s, there was a lull in the development of comic opera until 1766, when Hiller began composing *Singspiele*, writing catchy strophic tunes as before (the borrowing of other composers' songs was abandoned), but also introducing numbers obviously owing their style to Italian comic opera. The next generation, including Benda, Neefe, and André, broadened this to the point of using *opera seria*-type arias, ensembles in a sentimental vein, and even *melodrama, in which speech was superimposed on dramatically expressive instrumental music. It was in this highly varied form that *Singspiel* achieved its popularity in Vienna, where the opening of the officially subsidized Burgtheater in 1778 gave it enormous impetus. Here was the chance to use really accomplished singers and a good orchestra. Moreover, this flowering of German opera happened to occur when an experienced operatic composer of genius was living in Vienna.

7. Mozart

The complex state of opera during the latter part of the 18th century is encapsulated in the operas of Mozart, who worked in every theatrical genre of his age and had a genius for combining elements from each in such a way that, although his works are impossible to categorize exactly, opera became the kind of overwhelming experience desired and planned by its founders.

Mozart wrote five *opere serie*, the first (*Mitridate, re di Ponto*) in 1770, the last (*La clemenza di Tito*) in 1791. All were commissioned, two for Milan and one each for Salzburg, Munich, and Prague. All but one of the librettos are either by Metastasio or in his style, and the music is based firmly on the aria. Metastasio's recitatives for *La clemenza di Tito* were shortened by Caterino Mazzolà, who recast the libretto for Mozart, at the same time rearranging the original three acts into two and adding eight ensemble pieces. The casts of Mozart's *opere serie* concentrate on high voices and include parts for castratos, the arias showing off their virtuosity; but the *da capo* aria is largely abandoned and the big ritornellos become shorter in the later works. The single exception to the purely Metastasian plan was *Idomeneo*, Mozart's undisputed masterpiece of Italian *opera seria*, which has a distinctive Gluckian flavour, including good choruses, and opportunities for such orchestral pieces as a chaconne, marches, and ballet music. Mozart runs the overture into the first scene, uses trombones for the Oracle Scene, and writes extensive solo instrumental parts in the manner of the Parisian *symphonie concertante*. Nevertheless, the style is predominantly Italian, above all in the ensembles and one or two arias with coloratura (especially for the castratos).

There are seven *opere buffe* (including two which were unfinished), dating from 1768 to 1790, all in the Goldoni tradition of the *dramma giocoso*. Of these, two had a pre-existing libretto which had been recently set by other composers; the rest had specially written librettos, usually with active participation by the composer. Two were straightforward commissions, the others being intended for the general public and in some cases begun as speculative ventures (hence the unfinished pieces). As early as *La finta giardiniera* (1774) the characters are divided between *parti serie* (serious, upper-class characters) and *parti buffe* (comic characters of lower social standing), and the demands on some of the upper voices (and occasionally the basses) are as great as in *opera seria*. The plots are predominantly social comedy, and though never overtly political or moralizing they make serious comments on manners.

The musical organization put the emphasis on ensembles rather than arias. In *Le nozze di Figaro* (1786)

arias and concerted pieces are equal in number. The latter, especially the finales, are longer, and there is little chorus and no ballet, but there is some less formal dancing. Two of the finales are extended, continuous multi-sectional movements with a fast-moving conclusion in the major key. In these the orchestra has importance in maintaining the continuity in a symphonic style. Otherwise, it occasionally plays characteristic pieces. In *Don Giovanni* (1787) the overture leads into the first scene, and the Statue Scene uses trombones, both features reminiscent of Gluck. Thus, though certainly *buffa* in attitude and closer to life than the *opere serie*, these operas have serious elements; above all, the Statue's descent to hell, with terrifying music, introduces a sublime, quasi-religious element taking the audience far beyond the pleasantries of conventional *opera buffa*.

Mozart wrote five large-scale works setting German, in the *Singspiel* manner, one being unfinished, another a sacred comedy with music; and also a one-act 'comedy' with musical numbers. The two childhood pieces have simple music in the *opéra comique* tradition. The mature works are comedies with exotic local colour (*Zaïde*, 1779–80; *Die Entführung aus dem Serail*, 1782) or magical elements (*Die Zauberflöte*, 1791). None can be considered purely humorous; indeed *Die Zauberflöte* is a masonic allegory in which elements of criticism of society and religious beliefs are intermixed. The social differentiation between nobility and lower classes is an equally integral part of the plot, expressed in music which ranges from simple strophic songs for servants to elegant arias for princes and noble ladies. The variety of music is wider than even that of *opera buffa*. There are heroic arias (those of the Queen of Night in *Die Zauberflöte*), even with concertante instrumental parts (Constanze's 'Martern aller Arten' in *Die Entführung*), cavatinas, and *buffo* finales. In *Die Zauberflöte* there are unique elements: a Bachian choral prelude, a secular but religious-sounding march, and Sarastro's hymn-like aria 'O Isis und Osiris'. The overture does not lead into the first scene, but the opening fanfares eventually recur in the body of the opera.

In Mozart's operas, we can compare the three different genres: *opera seria*, *opera buffa*, and *Singspiel*. All are capable of serious expression, using interchangeable elements. The Italian genres are more firmly established, have higher prestige, and will continue to dominate during much of the 19th century; but the vernacular genres are now much more than low comedies and are capable of high seriousness (*Die Zauberflöte* can be regarded as the starting-point for the German tradition of serious opera). These operas can embrace themes of religious and moral feeling, class structure, political commentary, and heroic or domestic life. The music varies from the simple to the extraordinarily complex, and its established conventions are capable of the greatest fluidity according to the needs of the subject. Mozart thus achieved one aim of opera's Florentine founders, 'to move the whole man'—though they would have been surprised at the means by which it had been effected. For this reason, Mozart's operas not only sum up previous achievement but also were highly influential in the future. Italian opera developed the *buffa* genre on his lines, through Paër and Rossini. In Germany, the moral Enlightenment in *Die Zauberflöte* encouraged a more ambitious *Singspiel*. Only in France did Mozart's example have little impact, largely because of a nationalism which was immediately extended by the revolution and Napoleon's imperial regime.

8. *Interlude*

The year 1791, seeing the death of Mozart and the true beginning of revolutionary institutions in France, presents a convenient dividing line in the history of opera. By this time the genre was universal throughout Europe, from Russia to Portugal, and well established in the Americas. Although the French Revolution hastened the demise of royal and noble patronage, opera was far from perishing, and the state (in various forms) took over the role of princes. So widespread was the cultivation of opera that its history became fragmented and can no longer be related to a central thread. Nor can it truly be classified into 'serious' and 'comic', for the dividing line between the two is often blurred and they always interact on each other in the way we have already seen with Mozart. The most convenient division is by nations, even though these also interact: and the most convenient order is (i) France, whose capital became the Mecca of opera composers; (ii) Italy, which infiltrated virtually every country with both composers and performers; (iii) Germany, which had the most profound influence in the end with the works of Wagner; (iv) other countries of western Europe; (v) Slavonic countries; (vi) countries outside Europe.

9. *French opera in the 19th century*

One effect of the French Revolution (1789) was to increase the popularity of *opéra comique*. This now became more serious in story, with political themes particularly common in the so-called *rescue operas, such as Gaveaux's *Léonore* (1798), the model for Beethoven's *Fidelio*, and Méhul's *La Prise du pont de Lodi* (1797). The music maintained the division into numbers and the essential simplicity of melody and harmony, but Italian influence crept into the *airs*, now given roulades, while the finales acquired the characteristic speeding up, or *stretta*, of *opera buffa*. Under Napoleon as first consul and then emperor, the *tragédie lyrique* reasserted itself: the Gluckian repertory of the 1780s survived, and in 1807 the Italian Spontini took up the style in *La Vestale*, preserving the classical attitudes and using short-breathed melody inherited from the 18th century, but giving weight to monumental spectacle and using a large orchestra imaginatively.

Comic opera also thrived under Napoleon. The 1820s were fruitful chiefly in the field of *opéra comique*, with Auber and Boieldieu as its major exponents. Auber (who lived on and composed until 1871) established the main points of its 19th-century style. A tendency towards Romantic plots was highlighted by a vogue in the 1820s for Walter Scott and historical themes. The music itself was not particularly Romantic, though brilliantly orchestrated. The forms of *air* and *romance* have an atmosphere of the salon, with regular phrases and inherent dance measures. The ensembles, though sometimes extended, lack contrapuntal interest, so there is little opportunity for individual characterization. But the result is always pleasing if rarely powerful, the repertory including such popular works as Rossini's *Le Comte Ory* (1823), a charming Frenchified *opera buffa* by Paër, *Le Maître de chapelle* (1821), and eventually Donizetti's *La Fille du régiment* (1840).

Rossini, by now a favourite in Paris, was a major figure in the transformation of serious opera, first with a four-act reworking (1827) of his three-act opera-cum-oratorio *Mosè in Egitto* (1818), which had appealed through its large-scale choral scenes and opportunities for spectacle, and then with *Guillaume Tell* (1829), on a subject obviously in line with the Revolutionary traditions. The latter has elements of the *tragédie lyrique*, including ballets, choruses, and rich orchestral effects (with a strikingly original overture); it also has Italianate arias, appealing to the taste of an audience which could hear the latest foreign music at the Théâtre Italien.

Within a year the two greatest exponents of *grand opera (as this must now be called, since it is no longer *tragédie lyrique*) had achieved prominence: Meyerbeer and his librettist Eugène Scribe in *Robert le diable* (1831) and then *Les Huguenots* (1836) created the archetype of a genre which was to fascinate all Europe, and which in Meyerbeer's output was to reach its apogee in *L'Africaine* (1865). In *Les Huguenots* the story, though cleverly worked out, is secondary to the scenic effect, which is always extravagant and startling: medieval settings, church scenes, crowd scenes, a torrent, choruses of demons, and crypts and graveyards (some of these borrowed from Weber) abound. Such effects are matched in the music by mighty (and frequently very interesting) orchestral effects, and by ensembles with the soloists set against the chorus, both features requiring a different (and heavier) type of voice from those developed for the florid Italian tradition. Meyerbeer was not a great melodist, but he was the inventor or developer of a type of scene in which a 'big tune' is heard quietly at first, perhaps in the orchestra, then partly sung by soloists, and finally in a climactic version for choral union with heavily orchestrated accompaniment; this would become a predictable feature of later 19th-century opera. Verdi's *Don Carlos* is an important landmark of French grand opera (1867).

Meyerbeer's work created a demand for grand opera which his slow method of working could not fully satisfy. Halévy, in *La Juive* (1835), and Berlioz, in *Benvenuto Cellini* (1838), continued the tradition, though the latter was hissed off the Opéra stage in spite of some virile music and a splendidly dramatic scene as Cellini casts his statue. This fiasco in effect exiled Berlioz from the theatre for more than 20 years. His masterpiece, *Les Troyens*, a huge work with a libretto after Virgil, was never given a complete performance in his lifetime, for it is a true *tragédie lyrique* written long after the taste for the genre had passed. The classical theme, the chaste music with a mixture of recitative, arioso, and aria that would not have seemed strange to Gluck, the use of recurrent themes rather than the symphonic leitmotifs of Wagner, such atmospheric interludes as the Royal Hunt and Storm (reminiscent of Rameau's pictorial symphonies)—all make this a French work *par excellence*. But the lack of the vulgar excitements of grand opera was its downfall; only in the 20th century did it achieve its rightful place. Berlioz's other opera, a charming comedy *Béatrice et Bénédict* (1862), conforms to no existing French genre, and its use of numbers (some of them very attractive) looks back to the 1830s.

Barriers were nevertheless breaking down. *Opéra comique* was written by Meyerbeer himself in the 1850s with *L'Étoile du Nord* (1854) and *Dinorah* (1859), though they were intended for great singers (e.g. Jenny Lind) and their 'numbers' are conceived on a large scale. They could well be described as 'grand operas with spoken dialogue'. This helps explain the strange fate of several famous operas of the 1860s and 70s. For example Gounod, a member of a generation turning away from the heroic and grand, composed *Faust* (1859) for the Théâtre Lyrique with spoken dialogue; for its presentation at Strasbourg the following year he added recitative; and when it finally arrived at the Opéra it had recitative and a ballet as well. Thus a work written in the tradition of *opéra comique*, with separate numbers (some of which are related quite distinctly to salon music), was transformed into grand opera (which admittedly its subject might suggest). *Roméo et Juliette* (1867) was subjected to the same treatment. Bizet, who like all young French composers must have had ambitions to write for the Opéra, equally produced *Les Pêcheurs de perles* (1863) for the Théâtre Lyrique, but with an oriental flavour then in fashion through the operas of Félicien David. His last opera, *Carmen*, was produced at the Opéra-Comique in 1875 with spoken dialogue, later being transferred to the Opéra with recitatives by Ernest Guiraud (1837–92). *Carmen* was more influential outside than inside France, certainly affecting the Italian verists (see below, 10) in its low-life plot with a melodramatic ending. Its truly French characteristics—the irony, the lack of sentimentality in portraying the heroine, the clarity of the pseudo-Spanish music—were not imitated, except perhaps by Chabrier.

By 1880 Wagner was all the rage, at least with the intellectuals (see FRANCE, 7); and while the Opéra was unwilling to produce any of his later works, the younger generation of composers knew them either by going to experience them in Germany or by studying the scores. Most did not see their real significance. Operas on Nordic or Celtic (after *Tristan*) subjects were written, for example Reyer's *Sigurd* (1885, composed after studying Wagner's writings on music drama, not the works themselves) and Lalo's *Le Roi d'Ys* (1888); but although there are recurring themes and a 'through-composed' structure, the symphonic use of leitmotifs never penetrated French style. Instead, the taste of the public was for the Gounod-esque *opéra lyrique*, followed by Ambroise Thomas and Massenet on subjects frequently taken from novels (from Werther to Manon) or more ambitiously Shakespeare or the Bible. Often attractive in melody, well orchestrated and charming, they are at their best when not overambitious. This also applies to isolated works by other composers, notably Offenbach's *Les Contes d'Hoffmann* (1881), an *opéra comique* with, as often, recitatives added later, its apparent *lyrique* quality spiced with an ironic tinge. At the turn of the century, a work in an entirely different manner appeared: Gustave Charpentier's *Louise* (1900), though generally seen as Wagnerian, is in fact nearer to Puccini in its story of the Bohemians and the seamstress, while its continuous structure with repeated themes is typically French. The next masterpiece of French opera, Debussy's *Pelléas et Mélisande* (1902), though Wagnerian in technique, shows a complete change of direction and must be treated as a 20th-century work (see below, 14).

10. *Italy during the 19th and early 20th centuries*

Although Italy's conservatories were affected by the Napoleonic occupations, the opera houses continued little changed from pre-Revolutionary days. Larger cities had several theatres, usually under commercial management, sometimes with a state subsidy; and most smaller towns had their own opera house. There were three seasons each year, and the bigger houses produced at least one or two new operas in each. With composers paid for each work by the theatre and with no efficient copyright system, a successful composer might have to write at least two and sometimes as many as four operas each year. This need in itself encouraged a fairly rigid framework for both serious and comic opera. The trend to conservatism was strengthened by the lack of a tradition of spoken drama on to which *Singspiel* or *opéra comique* could be grafted. Romantic literature, blossoming in northern Europe, had little immediate effect in Italy, there being no Italian equivalent of the novels of Scott, the lyric poetry of Goethe or Shelley, or the dramas of Schiller. Such progressive Italian composers as Spontini or Cherubini often settled abroad, perhaps in Paris or Berlin.

Thus the considerable advances in matter and style found in France and Germany did not arrive in Italy until much later in the century. There were three main types of opera in the first 40 years of the 19th century. *Opera seria* changed its musical nature by being organized by scene rather than by aria. It also differed from its 18th-century forebears in allowing a tragic ending in place of the conventional *lieto fine* (happy ending). *Opera buffa* continued to include patter songs, extended ensembles and finales, and ornamented arias for the sentimental roles. These sentimental parts are more prominent in the new *opera semiseria*, a hybrid that might be described as an *opera seria* with a happy ending (Bellini's *La sonnambula* of 1831 is the finest example, in which a tragic denouement expressed in very serious music is averted). There were also curtain-raisers and shorter pieces called *farse*, almost harking back to the Neapolitan intermezzo.

Composers now travelled so much that geographical divisions were becoming less obvious, but a rough division between the Neapolitan school (led by Zingarelli and culminating in the work of Bellini) and the north Italians (Mayr, Rossini, Donizetti, and ultimately Verdi) can be made. The work of the southerners adheres to the succession of arias and recitatives which can be fairly called 'number' opera. The melody is florid, the accompaniment and orchestration simple. The arias are no longer in the *da capo* form, but are often in two sections, a slower lyrical cantabile being followed by a faster, more rhythmic cabaletta, thus allowing for the immediate expression of two contrasting emotions. The predominance of the upper voices continues, though the last important castrato, G. B. Velluti, left the stage in the 1820s and a tenor hero was now the norm.

The operas of the northern school, on the other hand, are written in the knowledge of Mozart, adopting a more ensemble-based continuity in which the orchestra plays a larger role and in which the vigorous rhythms of *opera buffa* infect even serious arias, providing a more goal-directed ornamental melody. In *opera buffa* itself the lower voices have a larger role, especially the comic bass (e.g. Don Basilio in Rossini's *Il barbiere di Siviglia*, 1816); but it is noticeable that Rossini also favoured the coloratura contralto (as in *La Cenerentola*, 1817). Rossini brought new life to the *opera seria* by his bold melodic ideas. The heroes and heroines in *Tancredi* (1813), *Otello* (1816), and *Semiramide* (1823) stand out memorably from their contemporaries chiefly by means of one or two arias, which, together with their preceding accompanied recitatives, were powerful vehicles of noble passion as well as vocal display.

Rossini's gifts and character brought him great popularity in Italy quite early in his career, and he used it to reverse the trend of *opera seria* towards a mere vocal recital. He took back musical control, which had drifted to the prima donna and primo uomo, into the hands of the composer. He began to write out vocal embellishments and cadenzas, traditionally left to the singer's whim, as a way of reining in the tendency to over-elaboration at the expense of both musical and dramatic values. At times he dared to upstage the singer with an enriched orchestration, owing much to French and German models, especially at moments of high drama.

Rossini's enduring reputation has been chiefly in *opera buffa*, where he developed new means of comic characterization, chiefly orchestral: the pervasive use of staccato and repeated melodic fragments; the satirical second-beat 'crash' following a puny vocal phrase; above all his famous crescendos in which phrase repetition was often carried to absurd lengths, reflecting the exaggerated gestures of the comic *buffo* singer on stage. The 'seria' treatment, particularly of the heroine, ensured a variety and contrast that allowed his comic masterpieces, above all *Il barbiere di Siviglia*, to outlive his equally fine serious operas.

Another indication of wider European influence is the dawning interest of north Italian composers in romantic subject matter. Rossini turned to Scott (*La donna del lago*, 1819) and Shakespeare (*Otello*, 1816); and Donizetti not only to Scott again (*Il castello di Kenilworth*, 1829; *Lucia di Lammermoor*, 1835) but also to tragic historical themes (*Anna Bolena*, 1830). These required more varied formal treatment, and although the 'number' concept does not disappear, it is much attenuated by turning the recitative into a grand, accompanied section of an aria or duet (which it can interrupt as well as precede), by adding choral backing to the solo voice, breaking down the division between 'chorus' and 'aria', and making the climax a splendid ensemble (as in the sextet from *Lucia*). Such composers as Mercadante and Donizetti who had worked in Paris were keen by the later 1830s to make the forms more malleable, breaking away from the cantabile–cabaletta relationship and cutting out music superfluous to the dramatic situation.

The transformation of Italian opera was due almost entirely to Verdi. For a detailed account of his development the reader is referred to the biographical entry. Although his first success *Nabucco* (1842) was mainly in the Bellini–Donizetti tradition, its choruses gave as much importance to the role of 'the people' as had the German *Singspiel*. Verdi's interest in the supernatural manifested itself as early as *Giovanna d'Arco* (1845) and, most prominently, *Macbeth* (1847); thereafter his international reputation took him to Paris, where he came into contact with grand opera. His mature librettos were either taken from Shakespeare, Schiller, Hugo, or Spanish Romantic drama, or were specially conceived as French 'historical' grand opera. His dramatic sense caused him to break away from traditional forms, the aria practically disappearing from some operas; he used the orchestra in new ways to provide continuity. But Verdi, alone among late 19th-century opera composers, could ignore Wagner, neither accepting nor consciously avoiding his influence. His towering stature was founded primarily on his mastery of all aspects of his craft. But it was enhanced by his personal hold on the imagination and affection of the Italian public, and, internationally, by the still dominant prestige of Italian opera (of which he was the undisputed leader by 1850).

Unlike Wagner, but like Mozart, Verdi directed his efforts single-mindedly to representing the human feelings, experiences, and interactions of the individual characters and groups on stage. Few opera composers have ever involved themselves more thoroughly with all aspects of staging, casting, and design. He brought to its height the trend towards 'composer control' begun by Rossini. He was a master of orchestration, but kept it firmly subservient to the claims of the voice and of the drama. In his vocal writing he gradually shed the floridity that had remained a part of Bellini's and Donizetti's idiom, and evolved a simple, direct style of melody that communicated emotion more vividly and more intimately. By reducing repetition and long melismas he made it possible for his characters to act more 'naturalistically' as they sang, and he then saw to it that they did so. Even 'set piece' arias could be interrupted or truncated where the dramatic situation demanded.

Verdi's heroes and heroines, though still frequently royal or aristocratic, broke away from the distant, patrician tone of *opera seria* and sang in a musical language that allowed everyone to identify with them— and even sing along with them. With some influence from both Donizetti and Meyerbeer, he developed the choral 'big tune' that could powerfully express popular feelings. The stirring martial accompaniments suggested that those feelings could easily be turned to action. Despite the efforts of Austrian censors to disguise these episodes by removing politically dangerous subject matter from the librettos, Verdi was able to communicate directly with the national sentiments of his Italian public, which he passionately shared, and to become in their minds a hero of the Risorgimento.

By the time of Verdi's late Shakespearean works, these preoccupations had faded, and he was able to turn his unequalled mastery of musical theatre to more sophisticated and more reflective subjects. In their very different emotional worlds *Otello* (1877) and *Falstaff* (1893) are two pinnacles of operatic achievement. Verdi had transcended all influences and here stood alone, without a rival or successor.

Wagner's influence in Italy remained slight. Boito's travels abroad, however, acquainted him with modern developments; his *Mefistofele* (1868), based on Goethe's *Faust*, showed attitudes and techniques similar to *Lohengrin*. He later translated Wagner's librettos and was himself an accomplished librettist (notably for Verdi); but his own musical development never came to full fruition (his *Nerone* was left incomplete).

The next generation followed up some of Verdi's ideas. They embraced *verismo, composing operas that portrayed rural or urban poverty. The sources of librettos were frequently novels rather than plays, and the construction of the libretto was accordingly episodic. The musical technique is also based on the malleable construction of Verdi's mature operas, the arias (now deprived of decorative figuration) using the upper ranges of the voice in a strong, rhythmic, syllabic melodic line. Massenet's supple melodies were also an influence. The results are often melodramatic, as in the works of Ponchielli, Catalani, Giordano, Cilea, Mascagni, and Leoncavallo, the most concise examples being Mascagni's *Cavalleria rusticana* (1890) and Leoncavallo's *Pagliacci* (1892). Puccini's *Tosca* (1900) belongs to the same category; but *La bohème* (1896) and *Madama Butterfly* (1904) show a more delicate touch, and his musical style, taking in the novelties of Debussy and the new wave of orientalism, is more sophisticated than that of his contemporaries.

The enormous financial rewards made possible by modern copyright conventions and widespread international distribution, which Puccini (and his publisher Ricordi) reaped at an early age, stimulated a host of imitators, but since Puccini's death in 1924 few Italian operas have succeeded in holding the stage, and most Italian composers of any worth have been trying to break away from what they consider a sterile tradition.

11. *German opera from Mozart to Richard Strauss*

In Germany the social superiority of Italian over German operas continued until the 1850s, when Wagner's polemic (rather than his operas) began to reverse the fashion. Thus the *Singspiel* continued as a domestic entertainment, comedies of little distinction being matched by similarly unambitious music for about 20 years after Mozart's death. But around the turn of the century, the plots of *Singspiele* began to show the influence of the German Romantic movement with its interest in the supernatural, while Beethoven's *Fidelio* (1805, 1806, 1814), a lone masterpiece, reflected the internationalism of French Revolutionary music. The new spirit was seen in E. T. A. Hoffmann's *Undine* (1816), the composer-cum-poet-cum-producer taking up the challenge of *Die Zauberflöte* in an ambitious magic music drama, though the music fails to live up to the skill of the other elements.

Nevertheless, this pointed the way for a more distinguished composer, Weber, whose experience in writing traditional *Singspiele* (of which *Abu Hassan* of 1811 is a fine example) was matched by his knowledge of the foreign repertory. The result was *Der Freischütz* (1821), a horror story of a highly Romantic nature. The country (back to nature) setting, the opposition of good and evil, and magic scenic effects are matched by music that fills the old moulds of *Singspiel* with a new spirit, containing original orchestral writing (including an overture which is a miniature symphonic poem), choral writing of a folk-like nature, and arias of real distinction. The popularity this achieved enabled Weber to compose *Euryanthe* (1823) as a German serious opera, cutting out the spoken dialogue and writing large-scale Italianate coloratura arias and extended ensembles. But neither this nor other operas of this so-called Biedermeier period, when comfortable middle-class audiences were not in tune with the heroics of grand opera or the ironies of social comedy, succeeded in establishing a serious German style.

Spohr, with *Faust* (1816) and *Jessonda* (1823), displayed skill in developing a continuous melody, advanced chromatic harmony, and delicate orchestration, with some immediate success. Schubert poured his musical gifts into a dozen stage works, including such full-length operas as *Alfonso und Estrella* and *Fierrabras*, but never acquired the theatrical experience or influence needed for succcess. Mendelssohn and Schumann also failed to gain sufficient experience in the theatre. Of the well-known *Singspiel* composers of the 1830s and 40s, Lortzing managed to make the genre more like *opera semiseria*, with ample ensembles, and overtures better linked to the opera, but keeping the straightforward choruses and simple song arias. Marschner preferred the *Freischütz* type of horror plot (as in *Der Vampyr*, 1828). Nicolai, more Italian in taste, wrote something in the tradition of *opera buffa* in his delightful *Die lustigen Weiber von Windsor* (1849).

It was in this condition that Wagner found German opera in the 1830s and it was almost entirely through his efforts in the next decade that it was completely transformed. For an account of his development, the reader is referred to the biographical entry. It is notable that Wagner was his own librettist from the outset. *Die Feen* (composed 1833–4) is a fairy opera little different from those of Weber and Marschner. *Das Liebesverbot* (1836) shows the influence of Italian and French opera, as though Donizetti and Auber were Wagner's models. *Rienzi* (1842) was an attempt at Parisian grand opera (Spontini's *Fernand Cortez* and Halévy's *La Juive* were well known to Wagner). The 1840s were years of assimilation and transformation of these influences. From Wagner's writings it is clear that he regarded the musical theatre as one of the most important cultural manifestations, and not merely as entertainment. In *Der fliegende Holländer* (1843) the idea of man's redemption by a woman's love appears for the first time in his work, and his characters seem symbolic rather than human. The music is constructed with only a few recognizable set pieces, the most important of which is a 'ballad' for the heroine, Senta, which becomes a symbol of purity and love and the destiny to redeem. This recurs several times and attains symbolic significance, as does the storm music representing the Dutchman's fate (hence unredeemed mankind).

Wagner's next opera *Tannhäuser* (1845) has more elements of grand opera (it is no coincidence that it was selected by the Paris Opéra for performance in 1860 rather than the more recent *Lohengrin*), including opportunities for grand choruses and more straightforward numbers. *Lohengrin* (1850), though also a grand spectacular, is original in the way the symbols, expressed by thematic material stated in the overture, are used throughout the drama, coming together at the end as a kind of symphonic recapitulation.

It was this analogy with symphonic style that gave Wagner the opportunity of creating a new kind of opera, which he called 'music drama'. In exile from Germany from 1848, he published his theories about the nature of opera, which were the basis for his concept of *Der Ring des Nibelungen*; though they underwent change, they led him to a radically new style, the most important features of which can be summarized. The subject matter should be based on legend and deal with archetypal concepts applicable to humankind as a whole rather than to specific figures (as historical subjects tend to do). The music should be constructed so as to follow the sense of the drama, and not impose its own pattern upon it (this idea has recurred throughout opera history). Hence recitative and aria (essentially a musical patterning) must be replaced by a continuous flow, halted by few cadences. This could be achieved by developing in the orchestra a number of themes associated generally with the archetypal concept (such a theme is called a 'leading motif'; see LEITMOTIF), the voices singing in an appropriately inflected arioso, generally only one at a time so that the words could be heard.

Some of these ideas were developments of those of previous composers. The symbolic nature of the drama harks back to Weber and even to Mozart's *Die Zauberflöte*. The continuity achieved by the use of the orchestra derives from the *opera buffa* finales of the late 18th century and was a commonplace of Parisian grand opera, while the use of recurrent themes was quite common in Verdi's operas. Nevertheless the conscious logical application of these ideas led to a new and powerful kind of music drama. The necessity for a continuous flow led Wagner to develop a harmonic style with the capacity to modulate freely. The melody now rarely fell into rigid phrase patterns and the emphasis on the orchestra encouraged more subtle effects.

The most complete realization of the Wagnerian ideal was in *Tristan und Isolde* (1865), where the 'story' is essentially psychological, the musical means far removed from those of previous operas (the exception being the sailor's song in Act III, which both in its own nature and in the way it is integrated into the musical texture harks back to *Der fliegende Holländer*). But both the *Ring* and *Tristan* were virtually inimitable. Probably more influential was *Die Meistersinger von Nürnberg* (1868), in which Wagner applies the musical means of 'music drama' to a comedy with elements of grand opera. The basic soundness of Wagner's thinking about music's relationship to text is revealed in this opera, where the plot involves 'real' people in almost conventional dramatic situations.

The musical power of these masterpieces, combined with their intellectual conceptions, virtually destroyed the hegemony of Italian opera in Germany and led to a host of imitations, many of little worth. The composers of solid music dramas, setting medieval or philosophic texts of the Wagnerian type, have generally sunk without trace, the exception being Pfitzner, whose *Palestrina* (1917) is a Schopenhauerian philosophic drama using the full-scale apparatus of leitmotif. The composers who used Wagner's musical means for un-Wagnerian ends achieved greater popularity. Cornelius's *Der Barbier von Bagdad* (1858) looks back to the tradition of the 'serious-comic' operas of the 1840s; Humperdinck reverts to the German legendary themes in *Hänsel und Gretel* (1893) and *Königskinder* (1897), but, while using Wagnerian harmonic practices, modifies the scheme of music drama considerably. Wolf, on the contrary, followed Wagner all too closely in *Der Corregidor* (1896)—yet with some success since the model is *Die Meistersinger*.

The major German opera composer of the 20th century, Richard Strauss, began as a close follower of Wagner in his first two operas, putting the leitmotif and orchestral sophistication to Expressionist non-philosophical use in *Salome* (1905) and *Elektra* (1909). He then turned to social comedy in *Der Rosenkavalier* (1911), deliberately interweaving 18th-century-type 'numbers' with music drama's orchestral continuity, a process taken further in the best of the later operas, notably *Arabella* (1933). Although his principal librettist, Hugo von Hofmannsthal, was of philosophic inclination, the delight of Strauss's operas lies in their characterizations, interpreted by the composer with a sense of humour and compassionate understanding. Some consider their weakness to lie in their artificiality, a deliberate turning away from reality with an exquisite literary self-consciousness, which Strauss's extra-musical sophistication tends to inflate beyond its deserts.

12. *Opera elsewhere in western Europe*

Italy, France, and (to a lesser extent) Germany have had continuous traditions of opera; elsewhere the development has been sporadic, interrupted by external circumstances or dominated by foreign composers. The main obstacles in the first instance were partly political (Protestant Europe being cut off from the humanist ideas of Florence and Rome), and partly the existence of a strong tradition of spoken drama (especially in England and Spain) which made some critics believe that opera was frankly ridiculous. Most European countries had had the same kind of entertainments that flourished in Italy in the 16th century. In Spain, plays were given with songs by such distinguished composers as Juan del Encina. England appreciated the court *masque, which was akin to the Italian *intermedio*. 'Recitative music' (as the English called it) crept into the masque as early as 1617, while Nicholas Lanier, after travelling in Italy, produced his *Hero and Leander* (1628) in which he tried to adapt Italian methods to English scansion.

But it was only after a number of travellers (among them the diarist John Evelyn) had seen the popularity of opera in Venice during the 1640s and 50s that real attempts at transplanting it were made. Paradoxically, the Puritan Commonwealth encouraged the growth of opera, since spoken drama was banned, while music was not. So the dramatist William Davenant (1606–68) wrote the text of *The Siege of Rhodes* in 1656; this was the first true English opera as far as is known (but the music by Locke and others is lost). After the Restoration, when drama was again permitted, he turned it into a spoken play with extensive music, which Roger North was shortly afterwards to call a 'semi-opera'. This kind of entertainment, also called 'dramatic opera', was popular until the 1690s, when Purcell was one of its principal exponents, with such works as *The Fairy Queen* (1692) and *King Arthur* (1695).

There were a few 'real' operas too. Dryden's *Albion and Albanius* was set to undistinguished music by the Frenchman Louis Grabu (*fl* 1665–94, after, but a long way behind, Lully), followed by Blow's entertaining and also French-influenced *Venus and Adonis* (*c.*1684, still called a masque) and Purcell's *Dido and Aeneas* (1689), a mixture of elements from France (dances and choruses), Italy (recitatives and Dido's Lament), and England (the songs). In Holland Carolus Hacquart (*c.*1640–?1701) produced *De triomfeerende min* (1678), which has been considered the first Dutch opera but which is in fact a Frenchified dramatic entertainment, or play with music.

But the most significant aspect of opera was the employment of Italian musicians. P. A. Ziani's *Le fatiche d'Ercole per Deianira* (1662) was heard in Amsterdam through the initiative of the former Dutch consul in Venice. The future King Sigismund III of Poland saw Francesca Caccini's *La liberazione di Ruggiero* on a visit to Florence in 1625, which led to a tradition of Italian opera productions in Warsaw. This process was to make attempts at creating national opera companies more difficult throughout the 18th century. The rival companies in London employing Handel, Bononcini, Ariosti, and others, from 1709 prevented serious opera in English from coming into existence, at least for the time being. In Copenhagen the operas of Sarti were popular; in Sweden an Italian nonentity called Francesco Uttini (1723–95) held sway; Portugal was equally dominated by the Neapolitan Davide Perez (1711–78), and Spain was served by Italians setting Metastasio. In Russia, the arrival in the 1730s of an Italian company directed by Francesco Araia led to a stream of his fellow countrymen—Galuppi, Traetta, and Paisiello among them—who were well paid for braving the northern climate. In Bohemia such young men as Mysliveček and František Mica (1746–1811) were sent south to study and then emulate the latest styles.

It was the increasing popularity of such genres as ballad opera and *opéra comique* that helped to break up this state of affairs, since the use of speech in the vernacular inevitably encouraged national styles. A distinctive manner was strong in Spain, where the *zarzuela flourished with two excellent composers, Sebastián Durón and Antonio Literes: Literes wrote an *Accis y Galatea* (1708), and later in the century Rodrígues de Hita (*c.*1724–87) used guitars, mandolins, tambourines, and castanets for some spectacular dancing in *Las labradoras de Murcia* (1769). The zarzuela (in this sense) was eventually superseded by a yet simpler entertainment, the *tonadilla escénica* (usually a down-to-earth story of everyday folk), but this too became increasingly sophisticated. In the 19th century there was a renewed interested in the zarzuela in Spain, just as in other countries an increasing national awareness gave rise to distinctive styles to combat the pervading influence of Italian opera.

In England, spoken dialogue remained the rule; a landmark was the production of Weber's *Oberon* (1826) to an English libretto. Beginning in 1834 there was a series of efforts to build a serious school of Romantic opera in English. Three specimens, Balfe's *The Bohemian Girl* (1843), Wallace's *Maritana* (1845), and Benedict's *The Lily of Killarney* (1862), enjoyed widespread international success, but the most distinguished example was Loder's *Raymond and Agnes* (Manchester, 1855). The famous collaboration of Gilbert and Sullivan produced a great success story in the series of operettas

known as the Savoy Operas, a derivative of Offenbach's operettas that replaced the risqué humour with a more characteristically English form of satire. German influence persisted in the work of Delius, and in that of Ethel Smyth, several of whose operas were in fact given their premieres in Germany: *Fantasio* (Weimar, 1898), *Der Wald* (Berlin, 1902), and *The Wreckers* (Leipzig, 1906). Similarly, Rutland Boughton's absorption with Wagner led him to plan a Celtic Bayreuth at Glastonbury, though at the height of the English folksong revival both Holst (*At the Boar's Head*, 1925) and Vaughan Williams (*Hugh the Drover*, 1924; *Sir John in Love*, 1929) imbued their operas with national colour. DA/NT

13. *Slavonic opera*

During the 19th century the emergence of local creative talent helped foster national operatic styles in Russia, Bohemia and Czechoslovakia, Poland, and Hungary, so curbing the Italian and French dominance which had persisted throughout much of the 18th century. As mentioned above in section 12, Russia was largely overrun with Italian and French music from about the mid-18th century, a fact exemplified by such works as Bortnyansky's *Le Faucon* (1786) and *Le Fils-rival* (1787), which combine Bortnyansky's own Italianate style with the conventions of *opéra comique*: both operas have spoken dialogue and both were written to French librettos by F.-H. Lafermière, librarian to the (then) tsarevich Paul. Around the same time, however, an increasing interest in Russia's historical and artistic heritage, evident in the publication of the first folksong collections, was reflected in Mikhail Sokolovsky's *The Miller-Magician, Cheat and Matchmaker* (1779), which, though in the tradition of Rousseau's *Le Devin du village*, achieves a certain local colour in its use of folk tunes and in its folky plot. Similar tendencies are apparent in the operas of Fomin, Mikhail Matinsky (1750–*c.*1825), and Vasily Pashkevich (*c.*1742–97), who again used folk tunes (albeit with complete disregard for the melodies' modal character) and drew on subjects of peasant life and Russian history.

But it was left to Glinka to carry Russian opera on to a more professional plane. He possessed the natural skills, creative flair, and stylistic individuality that were distinctly lacking in earlier Russian composers, and these attributes combined to produce the first truly Russian operas, *Ivan Susanin* (or 'A Life for the Tsar', 1836) and *Ruslan and Lyudmila* (1842). Though still owing much to Italian bel canto and to French opera in the big scenes and dance sequences, there is an unmistakably Russian flavour in the simpler songs which was to have an impact on much later Russian opera. The heroic historical drama of *Ivan Susanin* had a successor in Borodin's *Prince Igor* (1890), just as the scintillating traits of magic and orientalism in *Ruslan and Lyudmila* were developed in several of Rimsky-Korsakov's operas—*The Tale of Tsar Saltan* (1900), *The Legend of the Invisible City of Kitezh* (1907), and *The Golden Cockerel* (1909). In turn these fantasy operas were to exert an influence on some Russian opera produced later in the 20th century (see below, 16).

At about the same time that Glinka was working in Russia, other east European countries were beginning to shake off the mantle of foreign opera and to explore their own cultural potential. In Poland, as in Russia, there had been attempts at native opera during the 18th and early 19th centuries by Maciej Kamieński (1734–1821), Józef Elsner (1769–1854), and Karol Kurpiński (1785–1857), though Poland's troubled history (see POLAND, 2–3) impeded the consistent development of an operatic tradition and it was not until 1848 that Moniuszko produced his *Helen*, now regarded as the first significant Polish opera.

In Hungary József Ruzitska (*c.*1775–after 1823) imbued his *Béla's Escape* (1822) with elements of Hungarian folk music, initiating a trend for Hungarian opera which was consolidated in the works of Ferenc Erkel (1810–93), whose *Bánk bán* (1861), shot through with the traits of the traditional Hungarian *verbunkos*, was long popular. Similarly in Bohemia, František Škroup (1801–62) produced *The Tinker* (1826), a *Singspiel* which is credited as the first Czech opera, and nationalist operatic writing began to develop in earnest after 1859, when Italy's defeat of Austria released Bohemia from Austrian political (and by extension artistic) domination. Bohemia and Czechoslovakia have indeed enjoyed a particularly colourful operatic history since the mid-19th century: the chief exponents were Smetana, Dvořák, Foerster, Fibich, and Janáček (see below, 17), and a fuller discussion of their contributions to the operatic repertory will be found in their individual articles.

In Russia, opera responded keenly to the spur that Glinka's music had given to the theatre, though it developed along several different paths. Tchaikovsky, for example, rightly dubbed Glinka the 'acorn' from which the oak of Russian music grew, but his own

enthusiasm for opera, fired initially by Mozart's *Don Giovanni* and later coloured by Bizet's *Carmen*, looked to the West, and was inextricably bound up with his own temperament. He chose a wide diversity of subjects, but almost invariably produced his most successful works when the characters struck a sympathetic chord in his own personality. Such operas as *The Maid of Orléans* (1881) and *Mazeppa* (1884), impressive though they were in their dramatic organization, fail to impart the conviction, commitment, and emotional impact of *Eugene Onegin* (1879) and *The Queen of Spades* (1890): in the former the theme of unrequited, impetuous passion was specially fresh in his mind in the wake of his own disastrous marriage (1877), just as the fateful message of *The Queen of Spades*, composed between his last two 'Fate' symphonies (the Fifth and Sixth), was particularly significant to a composer who was himself so tortured by thoughts of Fate's inexorable power.

Tchaikovsky's operas express an intensity of feeling and a breadth of experience which set them apart from Russian opera composed in the firmly nationalist Glinka tradition; and it is perhaps their very universality of expression which has lent them such wide international appeal. Anton Rubinstein, too, abjured a narrowly nationalist approach to his mature operatic writing, maintaining, after the failure of his early folk-tinged operas *The Battle of Kulikovo* (1852, also known as *Dmitry Donskoy*) and *Tom the Fool* (1853), that nationalist opera was worthless. To some degree he contradicted himself in *Kalashnikov the Merchant* (1880), but in the main he preferred to concentrate on serious biblical operas and on the melodramatic *The Demon* (1875), substantially in debt to French grand opera, particularly Gounod's *Faust*.

However, there was a decisive break from foreign influence in the operas of Dargomïzhsky and Musorgsky. Dargomïzhsky, in common with the Realist philosophers of the day (V. G. Belinsky and N. G. Chernïshevsky), was concerned with questions of 'truth' in art, and in his songs he tended to pare down the vocal lines so that no melodic decoration should be allowed to cloud the meaning of the words. His opera *The Stone Guest* (1872) is an extension of this principle. Just as Cui was advocating in the 1860s that opera should rid itself of gratuitous vocal display and that 'each note should reinforce the meaning of the text', so Dargomïzhsky wanted in *The Stone Guest* to cast off the fetters of operatic convention, rejecting arias and set pieces and formulating a style of continuous recitative. 'I want the note to express the word', he wrote in 1857, and he conceived *The Stone Guest* as a model of 'musical realism', in which the vocal lines, drifting in and out of pure melody as occasion demands, are guided by the inflections, the stresses, and the emotional implications of the words.

Tchaikovsky, whose own operas are couched in a firmly lyrical style, regarded this attempt to drag 'truth' into opera as utterly 'false', but other Russian composers were more enthusiastic about Dargomïzhsky's ideas: it is indeed the concept of musical realism which gives much of the finest 19th-century opera its thoroughly individual sound. Rimsky-Korsakov's *Mozart and Salieri* (1898), which, like *The Stone Guest*, is a word-for-word setting of one of Pushkin's 'little tragedies', is cast in much the same declamatory style, though, as he said, he tried to make the structure and the harmonic scheme rather less of a hit-or-miss affair than *The Stone Guest* had been. Cui's opera *William Ratcliff* (1869) mingles declamatory elements with the broader melodic writing for which he had a much more pronounced gift, and there is a comparable blend of lyricism and realism in Rimsky-Korsakov's *The Maid of Pskov* (first version 1873; second version 1895).

But Musorgsky applied the principle of musical realism to its subtlest effect, harnessing it to his individual harmonic idiom, his ascetic, spare orchestration, and his keen perception of character to create operas of powerful dramatic impact. In the late 1860s he was himself at the height of his 'realist' phase, producing such starkly declamatory songs as *Eryomushka's Lullaby* and *With Nurse* (both 1868). At the same time he composed a word-for-word setting of Gogol's prose comedy *Marriage,* in which he intended his 'music to be an artistic reproduction of human speech in all its finest shadings'. In the single act he managed to complete he succeeded in using continuous recitative, with recourse to the leitmotif principle, as a means to virile, sharply characterized vocal lines, but it was only later, when he tempered strict musical realism with warmer, lyrical music that he produced his two masterpieces: *Boris Godunov* (1874) and *Khovanshchina* (1886). Musorgsky's work had a lasting influence on later Russian music. His technique of continuous melodic recitative was echoed in such widely differing works as Rakhmaninov's *The Miserly Knight* (1906) and Shostakovich's *The Nose* (1930) and *The Lady Macbeth of*

the Mtsensk District (1934); and the tableau-like construction, familiar enough from *Prince Igor*, became a formula for much Soviet opera, including Prokofiev's *War and Peace* (1946).

Boris Godunov and *Khovanshchina* stand as twin peaks of nationalist musical drama in 19th-century Russia: in the former the vivid portrayal of Boris's moral dilemma and his physical and mental decline is one of the most acute pieces of psychological perception in Russian opera (and indeed 19th-century opera in general); in the latter, while the characterization is less clearly defined, Musorgsky left a sensitive and richly coloured drama embracing themes of political instability and religious schism in the early reign of Peter the Great, impressing not only by its easy melodic flow and theatrical grandeur but also by its encapsulation of a true Russian spirit. In a sense these are the Russian equivalents of the naturalistic operas which, as will be seen below (section 14), were part of the western European operatic picture at the beginning of the 20th century.   GN

14. *The 20th century: Symbolism*

As at many other times in its history, opera in the early part of the 20th century was polarized between two philosophies, which by analogy with contemporary literary movements can be called 'naturalism' and 'Symbolism'. Naturalist composers (e.g. Puccini, Charpentier, and Bruneau) were concerned to give direct expression to the feelings of real people in an immediately recognizable world. Symbolist opera, on the other hand, made no such attempt to mirror observed reality. The immense influence of Wagner, still to be felt 20 or 30 years after his death, encouraged composers not only in their harmonic and orchestral daring but also in their approach to mythical subjects, where the characters are to be regarded as archetypes, as vehicles for philosophical debate or the examination of unspoken emotion. But there were other influences that pointed in the same direction: the work of playwrights of the time, notably Maurice Maeterlinck and August Strindberg, and the insights of Sigmund Freud in uncovering deep mental processes.

The first and greatest Symbolist opera was a faithful setting of a Maeterlinck play which provided an abundance of classic Freudian situations of jealousy, guilt, and Oedipal conflict, all set in a subdued, dreamlike atmosphere. In *Pelléas et Mélisande* (1902) Debussy's music takes on the responsibility, evaded in the original drama, of expressing the fluctuations of uncertain and vacillating emotion, so that inner feelings are exposed without words. Where the text does become explicit, in the Act IV declaration of love, the music does not reinforce it at all but instead enters gradually to suggest the partners' growing confidence and assent. Indeed, only comparatively rarely does the music duplicate the text; it is much more concerned with expressing the characters' reactions to what they are saying. As a result, *Pelléas* is a work in which the naturalist functions of music—depicting events, outlining characters, and strengthening the message of the words—are to a great extent abandoned. Debussy's achievement in *Pelléas*—which came after scores of sub-Wagnerian operas, particularly by French composers—was to show that Wagner's discoveries could be used to create something quite different. In matters of orchestral sound, seamless symphonic design, and even vocal treatment it is clear that Debussy learnt much from *Parsifal*, yet his opera is entirely individual and new.

At the same time, however, it closed more doors than it opened. Before the production of *Pelléas* Delius had been able to create his own gloss on *Tristan* in *A Village Romeo and Juliet* (1907), but afterwards it was necessary, as Satie recognized, to 'search elsewhere'. Dukas's *Ariane et Barbe-bleue* (1907), based on a more colourful and fully stated Maeterlinck play, manages something distinctive by reintroducing definition of character, situation, and purpose, though still within a Symbolist framework. As for French composers of a younger generation, they went far away from *Pelléas* into brilliant farce (Ravel's *L'Heure espagnole*, 1911) or exotic pageant (Roussel's *Padmâvatî*, 1923). It was in Bartók's only opera, *Bluebeard's Castle* (1918), that the example of *Pelléas* was most fruitfully followed. This one-act piece uses the same Maeterlinck play as provided the basis of Dukas's opera, but in a drastically altered form which reduces the number of characters to two. Like *Pelléas*, the opera concentrates on bringing forward the interior emotions of its characters, though in bolder terms: the text is more strongly shaped and heavier in its symbolism. In drawing on the Magyar folk ballad, poet and composer had invented what could have become a national operatic style, with a kind of recitative dictated by the nature of the Hungarian language (here again Bartók had followed Debussy in looking to Musorgsky for clues).

15. *Expressionism*

In Germany and Austria the Symbolists' charting of deep emotion by means of suggestion and imagery grew into naked exposure: it became Expressionism. The subjects of Expressionist opera were most usually sex and violence, as in Puccini, though treated without any sentimentality. Strauss's *Salome* (1905) and *Elektra* (1909) exemplify the unleashing of exultant, turbulent, or obsessive emotion that is characteristic of Expressionism, here the product of a post-Wagnerian decadence, with all Wagner's resources—a large orchestra, chromatic harmony, and long, rich vocal phrases—pressed to the limits. If Strauss was a naturalist in his choice of precisely located situations, he was an Expressionist, if only in these two operas, in his plumbing of extravagant emotion. His women are, like the otherwise very different Mélisande, natural beings who stand apart from their societies and indeed represent something pre-social. In its indulgent display of female sexuality Schreker's *Der ferne Klang* (1912) belongs to the same movement.

However, the purest, most intense kind of Expressionism is to be found not in Strauss or Schreker but in Schoenberg. His *Erwartung* (composed 1909, produced 1924) goes even further than *Pelléas* or *Bluebeard's Castle* in abandoning action in order to focus on volatile states of mind. Since there is only one character in this short 'monodrama' Schoenberg could ignore characterization and devote his attention to detailing at every moment the delirious anxieties, hopes, joys, and regrets of this woman searching a forest for her lover. In a second piece of similar dimensions, *Die glückliche Hand* (composed 1910–13, produced 1924), he approached the ideal of the *Gesamtkunstwerk*, providing not only his own Strindbergian text but also abundant production memoranda, stage designs, and even the lighting schedule, which owes much to the theories and practice of Wassily Kandinsky.

With the outbreak of World War I, pure Symbolist and Expressionist opera came to an end, though by no means did the devices of Symbolism and Expressionism fall immediately into disuse. Indeed, Expressionist shock has been the stock manner for such operas as those of Ginastera (notably *Bomarzo*, 1966) and Penderecki (*The Devils of Loudun*, 1969), where the dramatic form is utterly conventional. And long before that, Berg had drawn on the legacy of Expressionism in a rebirth of naturalism, his *Wozzeck* (1925).

16. *Russian fantasy*

The characters of Symbolist and Expressionist opera, though they may be located in no defined reality (Pelléas, Bluebeard, the Woman in *Erwartung*) or else only in a temporally distant one (Salome, Elektra), at least have recognizably human features. By contrast, other non-naturalist operas of the period, including many by Russian composers, are very much concerned with the bizarre, with characters as grotesque and stylized as those of a puppet show. Rimsky-Korsakov's last opera, *The Golden Cockerel* (1909), for example, is a satirical fantasy which shows a glittering, magic court ruled by a monarch as self-willed and obstinate as Nicholas II, with the music displaying all the composer's talent for opulent colour and bold harmonic contrast. It had a direct successor in Stravinsky's first and not very typical opera *The Nightingale* (1914), similarly alive with exotic incident and orchestral fireworks.

This Russian style was adapted to rather different purposes in Prokofiev's *The Love for Three Oranges* (1921), where the element of parody is uppermost and the plot is barely more than a framework for squibs directed at operatic and narrative conventions. Prokofiev followed this opera with a much more serious work influenced by the mystical Russian offshoot of symbolism, *The Fiery Angel* (composed 1919–27, produced 1954), which concerns itself with demonic possession and religious-erotic hysteria. Meanwhile *The Love for Three Oranges* had been followed by Shostakovich's *The Nose* (1930), a similarly iconoclastic and even more comically grotesque piece, but opera of this kind was not long to be tolerated in the Soviet Union: Prokofiev turned to solidly naturalist subjects in the operas that followed his return to Russia in 1932, and Shostakovich's second opera, *The Lady Macbeth of the Mtsensk District* (1934), was also naturalist, though, as will appear, it certainly came nowhere near satisfying the authorities. Outside Russia, however, comic fantasy of a distantly Rimskyesque kind was able to flower in such quirky specimens of opera as Ravel's *L'Enfant et les sortilèges* (1925), a work quite personal to its composer in its access to the world of the child and in its brittle depiction of inanimate malice.

In *The Love for Three Oranges* the fantastic element is determined largely by the Carlo Gozzi play, and there were other composers who found material for ironic and fantastic operas in 18th-century Italian drama and *commedia dell'arte*. Gozzi's *Turandot* was used by both Puccini (1926) and Busoni (1917) in a pair of interest-ingly divergent works: where the naturalist composer strives to humanize the story, Busoni plays up that element of caricature which had already been important in his *Arlecchino* (1917) and *Die Brautwahl* (1912). Wolf-Ferrari, another Italian of partly German ancestry, turned to Goldoni in creating his comic fantasies *Le donne curiose* (1903) and *I quattro rusteghi* (1906).

In going back to the 18th century for their subjects, Busoni and Wolf-Ferrari were led to compose in a neo-classical spirit which quickly developed from pastiche into the serious reclamation of earlier styles and means. Nielsen's comedy *Maskarade* (1906) shows the same tendency. But in none of these works is the neo-classical return so delightedly or so ironically enacted as in Stravinsky's *Mavra* (1922), an opera which is a rather double-edged tribute to its artistic fathers and dedicatees Pushkin, Glinka, and Tchaikovsky (Rimsky has now been left far behind). In *Mavra* satire has evolved to the point where, even more insidiously than in *The Love for Three Oranges*, opera is blatantly and maliciously used against itself. Stravinsky gives the signal that the genre is becoming unworkable.

17. *Naturalism renewed*

After World War I there were changes which inevitably altered the climate of operatic composition. The fall of the German, Austrian, and Russian monarchies brought an end to court patronage, and so opera houses had to become more commercial in their dealings. Often this meant restricting the basic repertory to a group of two or three dozen acknowledged masterpieces—a group which even today includes little later than *Wozzeck* (1925) and *Turandot* (1926). Moreover, the general movement in music in the 1920s towards clarity of form and straightforwardness of expression left many composers disinclined to write opera. For those who did, naturalism offered a more congenial frame than the pre-war vogues of Symbolism and Expressionism.

It is noteworthy, for example, that Janáček became an international figure only after World War I, even though his first great opera, *Jenůfa* (1903), had been begun in the 1890s. As a portrayal of love and jealousy in a village setting, *Jenůfa* bears comparison with the contemporary verismo operas, but its hard-edged realism and its original musical style, intimately bound up with the language and the folk music of the Moravians, take it into a different world. The operas that followed, including *The Cunning Little Vixen* (1924) and *Kát'a Kabanová* (1921), showed the power that Janáček could achieve with his objective but involved treatment, his stark delineation of character and setting, and the swift emotional strokes of his vocal and orchestral writing. But the very individuality of Janáček's style made it difficult for other composers, except other Czechs, to follow him.

Though closer to the operatic mainstream, *Wozzeck* also shows a quite fresh approach. It was the first full-length opera to be composed without the resources of tonality, and Berg skilfully solved the resulting problems of musical continuity by adapting abstract forms to his needs: the first act is a set of 'character pieces', the second a five-movement symphony, and the third a sequence of inventions. However, the opera-goer is likely to be less impressed by this than by Berg's binding of Expressionism to naturalism. *Wozzeck* is a tragedy of credible characters (Wozzeck and Marie) in a credible environment, but with the heightening of such Expressionist devices as the exaggeration of the inhumanity of other characters, the very deliberate placing of symbols (like the ominous red moon), and indeed the musical style. While using the innovations Schoenberg had made in such works as *Erwartung* and *Pierrot lunaire*, Berg also follows Mahler in his fierce contrasts of manner, switching at one point from a tortured chromatic outburst to the simplicity—horrifying in the context—of café music. In all these respects *Wozzeck* provided a direct model for such later military operas as Zimmermann's *Die Soldaten* (1965) and Henze's *We Come to the River* (1976).

More immediately *Wozzeck* was followed by operas that set themselves to show particular features of contemporary life: Krenek's *Jonny spielt auf* (1927), which concerns the contrasted fortunes of a European intellectual musician and a natural American jazz player, was one of the first and, at the time, wildly successful. Many other composers followed Krenek in incorporating modern scenic apparatus (telephones, motor cars, scenes in factories or railway stations) and in using the most conspicuously contemporary music: jazz. Sometimes, like Weill in *Die Dreigroschenoper* (1928) or Blitzstein in *The Cradle will Rock* (1936), they did so with the intention of making a clear political statement, but *Jonny* itself belongs to a different philosophical tradition, that of the opera which concerns the role of the artist, his duties to himself and to society. It is to this tradition that some of the century's

most individual operas also belong, these including Pfitzner's *Palestrina* (1917), Hindemith's *Mathis der Maler* (1938), Schoenberg's *Moses und Aron* (composed 1930–2, produced 1954), and Maxwell Davies's *Taverner* (1972). Hindemith and Schoenberg also wrote operas which emulate the contemporaneity of *Jonny*: Hindemith's *Neues vom Tage* (1930) is a story of a newspaper rivalry, and Schoenberg's *Von heute auf morgen* (1930) characteristically mocks the genre through itself in a modern comedy of manners. As Schoenberg here so bitingly exposed, the *Zeitoper*, or 'opera for modern times', was an artificial and superficial solution to the evident problem of writing contemporary opera. Returning to the conventions of the number opera, as Krenek and Hindemith did (the latter most rigorously in *Cardillac*, 1926), could not but produce music disquietingly at odds with its modern subject matter.

This problem is not so acute for such frankly conservative composers as Menotti and Britten, perhaps the most successful composers of opera since World War II. Menotti's talent is for passionate melodrama in the verismo tradition, as shown in his first great successes *The Medium* (1946) and *The Consul* (1950). Britten, a much more gifted and various musician, established his own distinctively English operatic style in *Peter Grimes* (1945), which takes some clues from *Wozzeck* but by no means abandons the forces of tonality as dramatic instruments. Curiously, those forces are most powerfully involved in a work which makes a tentative approach to a 12-note serialism: the chamber opera *The Turn of the Screw* (1954). The key scheme of the scenes is organized to give palindromic rise and fall in parallel with the events of the Henry James story, and the principal antagonists, the Governess and Quint, have their own opposed tonalities. Britten effectively demonstrates that narrative, naturalist opera depends on the forces of continuity and contrast generated by tonality, and it is noteworthy that his least tonal dramatic works, the trilogy of church parables *Curlew River* (1964), *The Burning Fiery Furnace* (1966), and *The Prodigal Son* (1968), are presented not as straightforward narratives but as ritual enactments. Influenced by the Japanese *nō* drama, the action in these works is even more stylized than it is in those operas, including *Billy Budd* (1951) and the chamber piece *The Rape of Lucretia* (1946), where Britten frames the drama with narration or commentary.

Britten's contemporaries in the Soviet Union were at this time bound to a more direct naturalism by the doctrine of *socialist realism, which directed that operas should extol the life of the worker or peasant, or else eulogize the fighter against Fascism. Prokofiev provided examples of both kinds in *Semyon Kotko* (1940) and *The Story of a Real Man* (1948), but far superior to these is his *War and Peace* (1946), a dramatization of episodes from Tolstoy. Drawing on 19th-century Russian opera—the keen characterization and the grand choral scenes of Musorgsky, the Romantic lyricism of Tchaikovsky—Prokofiev created a backward-looking work which is still a stirring epic. Even so, Prokofiev encountered criticism for his operas, though never the vituperative rejection accorded Shostakovich's *The Lady Macbeth*. This work, at once a sharp satire and a movie melodramatic tragedy, was initially hailed in the Soviet press, but in 1936 it was condemned as modernist and not until 1962, after Stalin's death, was the composer able to revive it as *Katerina Izmaylova*.

18. *Myth and allegory*

Naturalism has had its antipole since the 1920s in operas of myth and allegory, dramatic forms particularly well suited to neo-classical music. One of the first examples was Honegger's 'dramatic psalm' *Le Roi David* (1921), where the characters are stylized, the chorus has an important part, and the structure is clear-cut and severe. Stravinsky took up this style in his opera-oratorio *Oedipus rex* (1927), a work of similarly ritualistic splendour and one in which the use of Latin keeps the argument frozen at a distance from the spectator. The introduction of a narrator, speaking in the vernacular, only reinforces this separation. Indeed, so fixedly monumental is the work's form that Stravinsky could allow himself a Verdian effusion in the vocal writing without seeming at all indulgent. And by using similar techniques Milhaud was able to give a mythical aura to a contemporary subject in *Le Pauvre Matelot* (1926) or to a historical one in *Christophe Colomb* (1928), a pioneering work in its use of film and of simultaneous action on different stages. The versatile Krenek, who had already responded to *Oedipus rex* with his jazzy surrealist *Leben des Orest* (1930), followed *Christophe Colomb* with the similarly grandiose but 12-note *Karl V* (1933).

Other German composers, notably Hindemith, were influenced by the neo-classicism of Busoni as well as by that of Stravinsky and his French allies. Busoni's *Doktor Faust* (1925) is very much a sport in the history of opera, for in style it borrows equally from the late Romantics and from Bach, its characters are both given human fullness and manipulated like puppets, and it manages to combine deep, dark involvement with ironic distance. It is in all these ways a portrait of its many-sided creator. In that respect alone, it can be compared to Schoenberg's *Moses und Aron*, which takes up the very personal problems of communication and truthfulness. The seer (Moses) does not have the means to express his vision; the articulate spokesman (Aron) has those means in abundance but can retail the message only at second hand and through the distortions of subterfuge and compromise. This problem enters into the opera in a very direct way, for Schoenberg was unable to compose his Act III text because, presumably, of the impossibility of giving adequate expression to Moses' final achievement of unity with God.

The deep subjectivity of *Moses und Aron* contrasts markedly with the complex ironies of another allegorical opera, Stravinsky's Faustian *The Rake's Progress* (1951). In this, his only full-length stage work, Stravinsky reclaimed the conventions of Mozartian opera, complete with arias, ensembles, and dry recitative, creating a complete and knowing restitution on a scale no other neo-classical composer had attempted. Though Tippett also looks back to a Mozart work, *Die Zauberflöte*, in *The Midsummer Marriage* (1955), the music is not at all Mozartian but cast rather in a rhapsodic style containing echoes reaching from the English madrigal to Wagner. And Tippett's later operas—*King Priam* (1962), *The Knot Garden* (1970), *The Ice Break* (1977), and *New Year* (1989)—are also, though very different in style from *The Midsummer Marriage*, allegories which draw on the most diverse literary and musical sources for appropriate resonances. Myth and allegory have been crucial to Birtwistle's operas, notably *The Mask of Orpheus* (1986), *Gawain* (1991), *The Second Mrs Kong* (1994), and *The Last Supper* (2000).

Henze is another eclectic of the post-1945 era. His two best operas, *Elegy for Young Lovers* (1961) and *The Bassarids* (1966), are both to librettos by W. H. Auden and Chester Kallman, who had provided Stravinsky with the text for *The Rake's Progress*. Both are similarly formal in their dramatic planning, but Henze's treatment oscillates between romantic emphasis and parodistic charade (in the quasi-Baroque interlude of *The Bassarids*), and in the later work he consciously borrows from composers as different as Bach and Mahler: the piece is an immense choral symphony and a Passion at the same time. (It is also a bold reworking of the *Bacchae* of Euripides, which Szymanowski had translated to 12th-century Sicily in his opulent and ornate *King Roger* of 1924.) Since *The Bassarids* Henze's allegories have been of an overtly political nature, following earlier committed operas by Dallapiccola (*Il prigioniero*, 1949) and Nono (*Intolleranza 1960*, 1961), of which the latter, demonstrating in strong yet closely defined terms the oppression of an immigrant, was the first opera produced by a member of the postwar avant-garde. The political genre has continued to attract composers and has been responsible for such near-successes as Adams's *Nixon in China* (1987) and *The Death of Klinghoffer* (1991) as well as Maxwell Davies's *The Doctor of Myddfai* (1996).

19. *Music theatre versus opera*

In general, avant-garde composers have preferred to work in the field of *music theatre, which offers opportunities for music and drama to be brought together on a smaller scale and without the conventions of opera. The ancestors most commonly invoked have been Stravinsky's *Histoire du soldat* (1918), a piece 'to be read, played, and danced' by a small ensemble of actors, dancer, and instrumentalists, and Schoenberg's *Pierrot lunaire* (1912), which has proved amenable to performance in costume with lighting effects. Among English composers, Birtwistle has shown his indebtedness to Stravinsky in the ritual outlines and the puppet-theatre manner of *Down by the Greenwood Side* for soprano, actors, and band (1969) and his opera *Punch and Judy* (1967), while Maxwell Davies has profited from *Pierrot* in several works scored for similar forces, most notably *Eight Songs for a Mad King* for male singer and sextet (1969).

Other composers, including artists as different as Berio and Kagel, have been so much impressed by the theatrical possibilities of music-making that any categorization into concert and dramatic works becomes difficult. Berio has interested himself in the physical action of musical performance to such a degree that most of the works in his *Sequenza* series for solo performers (1958–79) are as theatrical as those that fall more obviously into the genre of music theatre, for example his study of the disintegrating mind of a singer in *Recital I: For Cathy* for soloist and small orchestra (1972). In Kagel the distinctions are still less clear, for very nearly all his works use verbal or visual humour in taking an ironic look at the conventions and mechanics of musical performance.

The influence of Kagel in Germany and of Cage in the USA has encouraged composers to use all manner of resources—voices, instruments, electronics, visual displays of various kinds, miscellaneous objects, buildings, and natural features—in mixed-media shows, 'happenings', and other events which might take place in a theatre or might not. Here any continuing association with opera has quite disappeared, as it has also in the more structured music-theatre works produced by Stockhausen since the early 1970s. Typical of his grand imaginative gestures is *Trans* for orchestra (1971), in which only the strings are visible, behind a magenta-lit gauze, playing intense, still chords through which the more characterized music of other groups can be heard with greater or lesser clarity, and in which the dreamlike vision is several times interrupted by worrying absurdities. If such works appear thoroughly untraditional, however, Stockhausen may be seen to be emulating an earlier master in his cycle of music-theatre works, *Licht*, intended to occupy the seven evenings of a week, launched with *Donnerstag* (1981). A younger generation of German composers has taken a radical view of the medium, creating several works which have achieved international success; they include Zimmermann (*Die Soldaten*, 1965), Reimann (*Lear*, 1978), Rihm (*Jakob Lenz*, 1979), and Höller (*Der Meister und Margarita*, 1989).

Following Nono's example, however, several avant-garde composers have made the return to opera, but in many cases their feelings of uncertainty are revealed in their self-regarding approach to the medium. They may not be as narcissistic as Bussotti, whose *Lorenzaccio* (1972) was created for himself as composer, librettist, producer, designer, and star, but their operas have tended to be as much concerned with the medium as with any outside subject matter. Berio's *Opera* (1971) declares this in its title, and goes back to the origins of the genre, quoting from Monteverdi's *Orfeo* in an investigation of the triple declines of opera, Western society, and the *Titanic*. The protagonist of his *Un re in ascolto* (1984) is an impresario who imagines 'another theatre'. In Kagel's *Staatstheater* (1971) the observation of the genre is even more critical and utterly irreverent. All the resources of the modern opera house are turned against themselves in a mad sequence of skits: the costumed principals engage in a 16-voice ensemble; the ballet company is given a set of gymnastic exercises; the props of the repertory operas are trundled on and misused; and the music drama is effected with the most unexpected and impoverished means.

Pousseur in *Votre Faust* (1969) gives his attention not so much to opera *per se* as to the position of the contemporary opera composer, obliged for financial reasons to accept commissions in a genre which he may well find uncongenial if not irrelevant. Like Berio, Pousseur draws on the past, here on the musical and dramatic Faust tradition (Goethe, Marlowe, Liszt, etc.) and on bygone harmonic styles, in a complex labyrinth of quotation, allusion, and new invention. And in identifying himself with his composer hero, he follows the example of Berg in *Lulu* (1937, complete version 1979). Lulu herself is close kin to Salome and Elektra: she again is a pre-social being, one who cannot help but bring destruction to those she attracts. But she may also be read as a personification of opera, that medium to which composers for nearly four centuries have been drawn irresistibly, but which has so often proved recalcitrant, operable only through compromise. In that case Boulez may well have been right in his surmise that Berg knew he was bringing a tradition to its close.

PG/NT

20. *Opera today*

The history of music, in the end, is not about what composers do, but what the public accepts. If the avant-garde has found increasing difficulty in relating to the opera tradition, so has the audience's interest in the avant-garde dwindled almost to vanishing-point. Efforts to 'abolish tonality' and to ditch all operatic conventions have succeeded only in the academic world. Many opera companies and some broadcasting stations, as a matter of principle, continue to commission or revive contemporary works, accepting the inevitable loss of revenue that such a policy normally entails. Few such works, however, have shown signs of entering the operatic repertory. The last opera to become established (that is, to be produced at several major opera houses over a period of years) was probably Tippett's *King Priam* (1962). This is an extraordinary contrast to the situation in, say, the late 19th century. It is possible, however, that some more recent operas are 'established' in the minds of a small but dedicated population of listeners to CD recordings.

In the theatre, the opera repertory has been greatly expanded in the last 40 years, but by the revival of old works rather than the addition of new ones. In particular the operas of Monteverdi, Handel, Lully, Rameau, and Haydn, and many forgotten works of Donizetti and Verdi and their contemporaries, have become commonplaces of the stage. The stiff conventions of *opera seria*, once thought to be dead beyond all hope of resuscitation, are becoming increasingly familiar to audiences, and have spawned a generation of specialist singers, conductors, and directors. Castrato roles are frequently taken by countertenors, without historical justification but with considerable public success.

In historical revivals there has arisen a curious dichotomy between the musical and dramatic sides of opera. The musicians, guided by ever more extensive musicological research in the 'early music' movement, treat the composer's score as sacrosanct and attempt a high degree of authenticity in its interpretation. The directors and designers, on the other hand, claim complete freedom to 'deconstruct', and frequently make a point of selecting a totally unhistorical setting, moving the scene to a different locale or period, placing the work in a symbolic or surreal context, or making it a vehicle for ideology. (There are recent signs of a reaction against the more extreme cases.) Additional stage business never contemplated by the composer or librettist is regularly inserted, and modern acting styles replace the conventions of the past.

One reason for the split is that the great composers enjoy a veneration that has never been extended to their librettists, or to the stage conventions of their times. Another is that the music of an opera is more widely familiar than its dramatic and visual aspects, thanks to the popularity of recordings. Tampering with Mozart's score would invite outrage, but messing with Da Ponte's dramatic ideas (so long as the text set by Mozart is unchanged) is accepted and even welcomed by critics. It is clear that the reputation of directors and designers largely depends on the originality and even sensationalism of their productions (and this is true in the world of spoken drama as well), whereas that of conductors is still based chiefly on their ability to give new life and meaning to the music of the old masters within firmly drawn historical limits.

Opera is in a surprisingly healthy state worldwide, at a time when audiences for classical music are generally declining and ageing. Two of the historic barriers between opera and the mass audience, money and language, have lost much of their force. The increasing affluence of advanced societies has brought in large new audiences, and has encouraged some governments, notably those of France and Germany, to subsidize opera on a heroic scale; elsewhere, corporations and foundations have supported this always extravagant genre, in part because of the cachet that it still retains from its royal and aristocratic origins.

Whether to perform operas in the original language or that of the audience (where they differ) was a question widely argued in the early 20th century. The coming of the early music movement tipped the scale in favour of original language, at least in high-prestige houses, thus preserving a long-standing obstacle to audience understanding. Another factor is the use in leading international opera houses of casts including singers of several nationalities who have all learnt their roles in the original language. However, opera on film, and then on television, was able to evade the problem by means of subtitles, while at the same time allowing viewers to observe the characters' facial expressions and interactions with an intimacy that is rarely possible in a large theatre. This brought opera 'home', in every sense, to a wider audience, at vastly lower prices. Next came the introduction of *surtitles in the opera house, either above the proscenium arch or, in some theatres, on individual screens in front of each seat. At last it was possible for everyone in the auditorium to hear the exact words that the composer had set to music, while simultaneously taking in their meaning, and so appreciating all the details and subtleties of the musical setting and stage action. For many it was an eye-opening experience.

There can be little doubt that these changes have, for the first time in history, opened up the treasures of opera to large sectors of the population that were effectively shut out in earlier generations. The new 'fans', like the old, are smitten with the great works of the past, which are indeed almost inexhaustible in their richness and power, adding up to perhaps the weightiest legacy of all Western musical history. If living composers are to make an impact here, they will have to find new ways to relate much more closely and deeply to this magnificent tradition, instead of striving to move further and further away from it.   NT

D. J. Grout, *A Short History of Opera* (New York and London, 1947, 3/1988, rev. H. Williams) · M. Cooper, *Opéra-Comique* (London, 1949); *Russian Opera* (London, 1951) · E. W. White, *The Rise of English Opera* (London, 1951) · J. Kerman, *Opera as Drama* (New York, 1956, 2/1988) · M. Robinson, *Naples and Neapolitan Opera* (Oxford, 1972) · J. R. Anthony, *French Baroque Music from Beaujoyeulx to Rameau* (London, 1973, 3/1997) · R. Fiske, *English Theatre Music in the Eighteenth Century* (London, 1973, 2/1986) · E. J. Dent, *The Rise of Romantic Opera*, ed. W. Dean (Cambridge, 1976) · R. Donington, *The Opera* (London, 1978) · J. D. Drummond, *Opera in Perspective* (London, 1980)

R. Taruskin, *Opera and Drama in Russia as Preached and Practiced in the 1860s* (Ann Arbor, MI, 1981) · N. Pirrotta, *Music and Theatre from Poliziano to Monteverdi* (Cambridge, 1982) · C. Price, *Henry Purcell and the London Stage* (Cambridge, 1984) · J. F. Fulcher, *The Nation's Image: French Grand Opera as Politics and Politicized Art* (Cambridge, 1987) · S. Sadie (ed.), *The New Grove Dictionary of Opera* (London, 1992) · F. Sternfeld, *The Birth of Opera* (Oxford, 1993) · P. Griffiths, *Modern Music and After* (Oxford, 1995) · N. Rossi, *Opera in Italy Today* (Portland, OR, 1995) · R. Strohm, *Dramma per musica: Italian Opera Seria of the 18th Century* (New Haven, CT, 1997) · S. Huebner, *French Opera at the Fin de Siècle: Wagnerism, Nationalism, and Style* (Oxford, 1999) · J. Warrack, *German Opera: From the Beginnings to Wagner* (Cambridge, 2001)

Carmen, but still did not conform to the traditional requirements of French opera proper (five acts, all-sung). The use of spoken dialogue remained a distinctive characteristic. When *Carmen* moved from the Opéra-Comique in Paris to the Opéra after the composer's death in 1875, recitatives had to be supplied by Ernest Guiraud. This distinction was moot by 1900. See also OPERA, 6.   JW/NT

opera houses. Since its origins at the end of the 16th century *opera has undergone considerable evolutionary changes, not least in terms of production complexity and of the numbers of singers, orchestral players, and often dancers employed. There has been a parallel development in the theatres or 'opera houses' where performances take place. Operas were originally composed and presented as a sumptuous accompaniment to some special event, such as the weddings or birthdays of dukes, princes, and the like. Their venue was therefore a stately ballroom or terrace, and audiences were restricted to the nobility and others of high rank. One exception was the Teatro delle Quattro Fontane in the papal palace in Rome (1632), which held 3000 spectators.

The first specially built opera houses were the Teatro S. Cassiano in Venice (1637) and the Teatro della Pergola in Florence (1657). By 1700 there were about ten such venues in Venice alone and opera houses were springing up in France, Germany, and ultimately throughout Europe as opera became commercial entertainment for wider audiences.

The first opera houses in Germany were the Munich Residenztheater (1657), the Theater am Gänsemarkt in Hamburg (1678), and the Hanover court theatre (1689). When Handel arived in London in 1710, operas were staged in such theatres as Drury Lane, the Haymarket, and the King's Theatre (controlled by the Royal Academy of Music). Many theatres used for plays were converted for opera performance, including Covent Garden, London, which was built as a theatre in 1732 and known as the Royal Italian Opera from 1847 to 1892 (there have been three theatres on the site: the first burnt down in 1808, the second in 1856). Fire destroyed many 18th-century opera houses, but the court theatre in Drottningholm, Sweden, survives almost intact and is still used for Baroque operas.

During the 19th century, operas became increasingly grand, with elaborate scenery used to create exotic locations, and with huge vocal and instrumental ensembles. Many of the world's best-known opera houses were built in the second half of the 19th century; they were designed not only to house lavish spectacle but also to symbolize national or civic magnificence, the Palais Garnier in Paris being a striking example.

The need to accommodate a sizable orchestra, while affording the audience an unobstructed view at no great distance from the stage, along with a proper balance between voices and orchestra, soon became primary objectives in opera-house design. One feature was the establishment of an orchestral platform or 'pit', set at a lower level in front of a raised stage and, in some recent examples, with adjustable height to suit different operas. For his innovatory Festspielhaus (1876) in Bayreuth, Wagner created a 'mystic abyss' where the pit extended backwards beneath the stage; this removed a possible source of visual distraction for the audience and made it easier for singers to project their voices with extra clarity—all part of Wagner's concept of the 'total art work'.

However, both covered and uncovered pits can colour an orchestra's sound, and the usually cramped space forces the players into awkward positions. They may complain that they cannot hear the singers clearly. There is a related balance problem in that modern instruments are more efficient acoustically while human voices are largely unchanged. This strengthens the argument for using period instruments for early operas.

Another feature distinguishing the design of opera houses from that of *concert halls, which were similarly being built worldwide, is the use of a horseshoe plan with tiered balconies and boxes over most of the wall surfaces (six tiers in La Scala), bringing audiences closer to the stage. Thus the relatively long reverberation times associated with multiple strong reflections from the flat walls in a typical tall shoebox or fan-shaped concert hall with few side balconies (see ARCHITECTURAL ACOUSTICS) are replaced by a deader acoustic as sound waves undergo extra scattering and absorption. This less reverberant ambience is, of course, helpful where vocal clarity is of high importance, but the horseshoe shape results in a restricted view of the stage from many of the boxes at either side.

Among the world's most notable opera houses, in chronological order of opening (and reopening), are:

1637 Teatro S. Cassiano, Venice
1657 Teatro della Pergola, Florence; Residenztheater, Munich
1678 Theater am Gänsemarkt, Hamburg
1689 Hofoper, Hanover
1700 La Monnaie, Brussels (rebuilt 1819, 1856; now Théâtre Royal de la Monnaie/Koninklijke Muntschouwburg)
1732 Covent Garden, London
1737 Teatro S. Carlo, Naples
1742 Königliches Opernhaus, Berlin (rebuilt 1844, renamed Staatsoper 1919, reopened 1927 and, as Deutsche Staatsoper, 1945)
1746 Drottningholm Court Theatre, Sweden
1778 Teatro alla Scala, Milan (rebuilt 1946)
1783 Teatr Bol'shoy, St Petersburg
1792 La Fenice, Venice
1818 Nationaltheater, Munich (reopened 1825)
1801 Theater an der Wien, Vienna (reopened 1945)
1825 Bol'shoy Petrovsky, Moscow (restored 1856)
1841 Königlich Sächsisches Hoftheater (Semper Opernhaus), Dresden (rebuilt 1878, renamed Sächsisches Staatstheater 1919)
1847 Gran Teatre del Liceu, Barcelona (reopened 1999)
1850 Teatr Tsirk, St Petersburg (rebuilt as Mariinsky, 1860; now Kirov Theatre)
1857 Teatro Colón, Buenos Aires
1858 Royal Opera House, Covent Garden, London (redesigned and reopened 1999)
1869 Hofoper (Oper am Ring), Vienna (Staatsoper from 1918; reopened 1955)
1875 Palais Garnier (Opéra), Paris
1876 Festspielhaus, Bayreuth (restored 1995)
1880 Teatro Costanzi, Rome (Teatro dell'Opera from 1928)
1883 Metropolitan Opera House, New York (moved to Lincoln Center in 1966)
1898 Volksoper, Vienna
1912 Deutsches Opernhaus, Charlottenburg, Berlin (renamed Städtische Oper, 1925–33, 1945; moved to new theatre, Deutsche Oper, 1961)
1918 Staatsoper, Vienna (formerly Hofoper)

JBo

📖 S. Hughes, *Great Opera Houses* (London, 1956) · S. Sadie (ed.), *History of Opera* (London, 1989), ch. 6, 12, 19, 20; *Architecture 91: The Opera House* (*Theatre Crafts*, 25/5) (1991)

opera semiseria (It., 'half-serious opera'). A sub-genre of Italian opera in the early 19th century. The term was first used for *rescue operas, for example Paër's *Camilla* (1799), but the more lasting meaning was an *opera buffa* with an unusually serious plot. In particular, the principal bass became a genuine villain rather than merely a comic figure. Examples are Rossini's *La gazza ladra* (1817) and Donizetti's *Linda di Chamounix* (1842). Significantly, the term was applied retroactively to Mozart's *Don Giovanni*.   NT

opera seria (It.). 'Serious opera'. The grandest form of Italian opera from the late 17th century to the early 19th. At the time it was generally termed *dramma per musica* ('drama in music'). Its audience tended to be royal or aristocratic. The subjects were drawn from mythology or Greek or Roman history, turned into elegant verse by such librettists as Apostolo Zeno or Pietro Metastasio and organized in three acts. The music was largely a series of formal *arias separated by *secco *recitatives. The prima donna (heroine) and primo uomo (the hero, generally a *castrato) each had at least one large-scale display aria in every act, followed by an exit. Tenor and bass soloists, if present, were generally gods, father figures, or villains. There were very few ensembles, and choruses began to play a major part only in the later stages. The most important composers of *opera seria* were Alessandro Scarlatti (*Griselda*), Handel (*Giulio Cesare, Rodelinda, Alcina, Serse*), Gluck (*Alceste*, Italian version), Mozart (*Idomeneo, La clemenza di Tito*), and Rossini (*Otello, Semiramide*).

A sub-genre was the *festa teatrale* ('theatrical celebration'), often written for a royal occasion; unlike the *dramma per musica* it included much dancing and choral singing. Gluck's *Orfeo ed Euridice* is the best-known example. See OPERA, 5 and 7.   NT

operetta (It., dim. of *opera*; Fr.: *opérette*; Ger.: *Operette*). Literally meaning 'little opera', the term came during the 19th century to describe a form of light opera in which spoken dialogue replaced recitative and the musical numbers were memorably tuneful. Operetta led in turn to *musical comedy and the modern musical.

The first developments of the form are generally credited to France, with Adolphe Adam's one-act *Le Chalet* (1834) being a genuine operetta in every sense. However, the chief propagator of the classical operetta was Jacques Offenbach, who began with one-act works before expanding into evening-long scores. Among over 100 works were such satirical classics as *Orphée aux enfers* (1858), *La Belle Hélène* (1864), *La Grande-Duchesse de Gérolstein* (1867), and *La Périchole* (1868). Offenbach led a thriving school of French operetta that included such works as Charles Lecocq's *La Fille de Madame Angot* (1872), Robert Planquette's *Les Cloches de Corneville* (1877), Hervé's *Mam'zelle Nitouche* (1883), André Messager's *Véronique* (1898), and Reynaldo Hahn's *Ciboulette* (1923).

Offenbach was also a source of inspiration to Franz von Suppé and Johann Strauss in Vienna. The latter wrote one of the supreme operettas in *Die Fledermaus* (1874), and his background in the dance hall led to the waltz becoming the centrepiece of the romantically inclined Viennese operetta. The rich flowering of the Viennese operetta era went on to embrace works by such composers as Carl Millöcker, Carl Zeller, Richard Heuberger, Franz Lehár, Leo Fall, and Emmerich Kálmán. Lehár's *Die lustige Witwe* (1905) enjoyed huge success worldwide and, like a few other classics of the genre, came to be accepted on its own terms into the opera repertory.

The influence of Offenbach was also felt in Spain, which enjoyed a simultaneous boom in popularity of the *zarzuela. In London, too, Offenbach's works inspired those of Gilbert and Sullivan, culminating in the great success of *The Mikado* (1885). As with zarzuela, however, the popularity of the works of Gilbert and Sullivan was largely confined to audiences who spoke their native language. Among British shows, Sidney Jones's *The Geisha* (1896) fitted more successfully into the European operetta tradition, though in English-speaking countries it is more usually considered an early musical comedy.

The musical comedy came to the fore as the operatic nature of operetta lessened, with increasing emphasis placed on contemporary plots and catchy musical numbers. With the rise of vernacular American song styles especially, true operetta increasingly gave way to the song-and-dance musical comedy. The Viennese operetta tradition briefly inspired a 20th-century school in the USA through emigrant composers including

Rudolf Friml and Sigmund Romberg and such works as *Rose Marie* and *The Student Prince* (both 1924).

Through various influences 'operetta' came to imply not only a more operatic 19th-century musical style but also Ruritanian settings and aristocratic characters. The strength of the European origins also meant that the term has endured in continental Europe even for works that, like the post-World War I French works of Henri Christiné and Maurice Yvain, have all the characteristics of musical comedy.   PGA/ALA

📖 R. TRAUBNER, *Operetta: A Theatrical History* (New York, 1983)

ophicleide. A bass keyed *bugle in B♭, held upright, invented by Halary in Paris in 1817. It has a wide, conical bore, and all 11 fingerholes are covered by keys, the lowest standing open at rest, and the rest closed. Its tuning is more precise and its tone crisper than that of the serpent, and considerably drier and less 'woofy' than that of the tuba, which eventually supplanted it. It was the main brass bass for bands and orchestras for most of the 19th century and is now revived for those parts that Berlioz, Mendelssohn, and others wrote for it.   JMo

opp. The abbreviated plural of *opus.

op. posth. A designation used instead of an *opus number to show that a work was published after the death of its composer.

opus (Lat., usually abbreviated to op., pl. *opera*, usually abbreviated to opp.; Fr.: *oeuvre*; Ger.: *Opus*; It.: *opera*). 'Work'. The custom of numbering a composer's works as they appear 'opus 1' and so on is useful both as a means of identification and to show the place a particular work occupies in that composer's career, but the unsystematic application of the numbering has made it less helpful in practice than it is in theory.

The term appears in the late 15th and early 16th centuries, but was used methodically only from the early 17th, when it was applied by Venetian publishing houses issuing the works of prolific composers. 'Opus' customarily referred to a volume containing several pieces, so that, for example, the third sonata of a composer's fifth published volume would be numbered op. 5 no. 3. This system was in general use by the time of Corelli, towards the end of the century, and nearly all his works are neatly numbered in this way. Confusion can all too easily arise, however: a substantial part of a composer's output can remain unpublished; works may be published, but not in the order in which they were written; or more than one publisher can be involved, each applying a different sequence of opus numbers. For example, Handel's op. 6 is a set of 12 concerti grossi published in 1739, but by that time he had composed many other works, including some 39 operas (it is rare,

in fact, for large-scale dramatic works to be given opus numbers, partly because they were not normally published in the composer's lifetime, and partly because they were anyway more easily identifiable by their title). These kinds of confusion have persuaded some scholars to compile new systems of numbering (see, for example, BWV; DEUTSCH; HOBOKEN; KIRKPATRICK; KÖCHEL; RYOM).

In the 19th century, composers began to number each substantial individual work separately (though songs and short piano pieces, and in some cases quartets, were still numbered as sets), keeping the sequence of composition rather than of publication. This sequence was sometimes broken in the case of juvenilia published at a later date (e.g. Beethoven's op. 79 sonatas), or when works were missed out of the sequence altogether (see, for example, WoO). If a work was published posthumously, it would be designated 'op. posth.'. There are occasional eccentricities—Berlioz's treatise on orchestration is numbered op. 10, and Massenet superstitiously refused to have an op. 13 (using op. 12*b* instead)—but in general the 19th century sees the system at its most efficient.

Towards the end of the century, the increase in descriptive titles and the relative neglect of abstract forms such as sonata and string quartet made opus numbers less useful. Debussy jokingly numbered his String Quartet 'op. 10', to show that he could behave as respectably as any German. Although some composers still assign opus numbers to keep track of their output, it is no longer customary.   DA

Oracolo, L' ('The Oracle'). Opera in one act by Leoni (London, 1905).

oratorio 1. Introduction and origins; 2. The first flowering; 3. The diffusion of oratorio throughout Italy; 4. The oratorio outside Italy: the Roman Catholic tradition; 5. The oratorio outside Italy: the Protestant tradition; 6. Handel; 7. The later 18th century; 8. The 19th and 20th centuries

1. Introduction and origins

The history of the oratorio is too varied to afford an all-embracing definition. The usual meaning of the term as it is understood today is a sacred work for soloists, chorus, and orchestra on a large scale, neither liturgical nor theatrical, but intended for concert performance. Earlier phases in its history have emphasized different characteristics, but a common thread remains.

Among several religious orders which came into being in the 16th century, as part of the resurgence of the Roman Catholic Church under threat from Protestantism, was that of S. Filippo Neri. He was convinced that the spiritual health of the laity would be helped by supplementing the Latin liturgy with meetings at which religious matters would be expounded in the vernacular and in which the congregation would take part. He therefore founded an 'oratory' (*oratorio*, from Lat. *oratio*, 'prayer') in which it became the custom to hold an *oratorio vespertino* after Vespers; a sermon was given and motets and hymns sung. These hymns or **laude*, in a tradition going back to the hymns sung by the flagellant confraternities of the Middle Ages, sometimes told a story or had a framework of dialogue between, say, Mary and Joseph or the Pilgrim and his Guide. At about the same time, the Society of Jesus, in charge of the Collegio Germanico in Rome, gave plays in the vernacular on religious themes—stories based on the Bible or the lives of saints. These plays, designed to combat licentious carnival entertainments, were spoken but had some music.

From these two roots sprang the first musical oratorios. The most remarkable of these was the *Rappresentatione di Anima, et di Corpo* (performed 1600) with music by Cavalieri, who had worked in Neri's Oratory at the Chiesa Nuova in the 1580s. The *Rappresentatione* was a lavish, fully staged entertainment with dancing; its allegorical story was in the tradition of medieval mystery plays (see MEDIEVAL DRAMA) and its spectacular elements after the manner of the *intermedio* (see OPERA, 2). Because it was staged it has sometimes been denied the title of oratorio and called the first 'sacred opera'; nevertheless it was also supplied with short sermons for the intervals in the manner of the *oratorio vespertino* and some of the choruses are in effect *laude*. Whatever we may call it, it certainly pointed the oratorio in the direction of the sung drama—that is, opera. But at this stage in the development of oratorio there is no need to make so fine a distinction—the word 'oratorio' was used of the building, rather than the composition, until as late as 1640.

The *Rappresentatione* had no immediate successor, but the 1620s and 30s in Rome saw the development of elaborate music at four oratories—S. Girolamo della Carità, the Chiesa Nuova, S. Maria dell'Orazione e Morte, and S. Maria della Rotonda—each for a slightly different audience of varying degrees of sophistication. Although the repertory has largely disappeared, we know that it used instrumental ensembles, choruses, and some first-rate solo singers. The composers involved included Mazzocchi, experienced in opera, and significantly there were several works which could be described as 'sacred operas', the subject being the lives of the saints, the musical and dramatic treatment being in every respect like that of opera.

2. The first flowering

By the late 1640s oratorios were attracting crowds in Rome, including foreigners, and two major (not to mention several minor) composers were employed in providing a substantial repertory. These were Carissimi, in charge of music at the Collegio Germanico, and Luigi Rossi. Rossi's two extant full-length oratorios, *Giuseppe* and the *Oratorio per la Settimana Santa* (both *c*.1641–5), are very operatic, telling stories largely by dialogue with a minimum of narrative. As in contemporary operas, there are short arias given shape by instrumental ritornellos; but unlike in opera, the role of the chorus is large, both as participating character and as commentator (the latter function inspiring some huge and beautiful madrigals).

Carissimi is less operatic, using a narrator to tell the story and concentrating more on reflection than on action. His genius is shown at its height not in his oratorios setting Italian (the so-called *oratorio volgare*), but in those to Latin texts (the *oratorio latino*). These works were written for the more sophisticated audience of the Oratorio del Ss. Crocifisso and most were given on the Fridays during Lent, when two oratorios or 'dialogues', one on an Old Testament subject, the other on a New Testament one, were given either side of the sermon. Some were on a relatively large scale, using a number of singers and an instrumental ensemble. The texts were taken from the Vulgate and elaborated with original material, while the stories were essentially dramatic—Jonah and the Whale, Belshazzar, Jephtha, the Judgment of Solomon, and so on. There is still a large amount of narration (not given consistently to a single singer, but divided among the ensemble), but the musical style is in the manner of late Monteverdi, with expressive recitative and arioso breaking into arias or set pieces. The choruses range from grand, exciting double-choir pieces to elegiac madrigals. These works were a way of making the Bible come to life for an audience otherwise faced with a formal and complex liturgy.

3. The diffusion of oratorio throughout Italy

Carissimi's influence was large, since he had pupils throughout Europe. At the same time, the Filippine Order was spreading its wings, and oratories were set up in many cities in Roman Catholic countries. In Italy Bologna, Florence, and Venice took to oratorios in the 1660s, and in Rome they began to be performed elsewhere than in the oratory churches, sometimes being given in the palaces of the cardinals, especially during Lent or when for some reason (a scandal or an act of penitence) the theatres were closed. In these circumstances scenery was possible, though usually restricted to a backcloth and drapes, but there was no acting. Since this was the period of the growth of opera companies it was natural for composers to write both operas and oratorios, with the result that the two genres became even more similar. The role of narrator, common around 1660, had disappeared by the end of the century, and the popular subjects became hagiographical: the similarity of the lives of saints to those of operatic heroes and heroines provided an opportunity for love scenes in a genre nicknamed the *oratorio erotico*. There were usually about five main characters, and the texts were written in verse, while the conflict between good and evil offered opportunities for strong dramatic situations.

The history of oratorio music at this time is very close to that of opera. In the period 1660–80 there was still a flexible alternation of recitative (not the perfunctory *recitativo secco* of the later 18th century, but measured and expressive), arioso, and arias (most of them still rather short) inherited from Monteverdi and Cavalli. By 1700 a more regular alternation of recitative and *aria was usual, the arias being more extended and in *da capo* form. The chorus was virtually abolished, though all the characters often joined in a finale or *arietta allegra* to 'send away the audience with universal approval', to quote one commentator. The role of the orchestra—sometimes a large band of 30 or 40 players—increased, with grand overtures and full accompaniment in arias. It was in this form, of which Alessandro Scarlatti was the master, that Handel found the oratorio on his Roman visit.

4. The oratorio outside Italy: the Roman Catholic tradition

The proselytizing potential of the oratorio made it a favourite form outside Italy; but now national preferences began to show. In France, the period of its Italian expansion in the 1660s coincided with the beginnings of the chauvinistic monopoly of Lully, and only Charpentier, a pupil of Carissimi, exploited the genre. He favoured the Latin oratorio, and his style resembles that of his master quite strongly, though he later gave the instrumental ensemble a larger part and wrote 'symphonies' with descriptive titles. Sometimes the influence of Lully is to be felt in the squarer tunes of the aria and the tie-up between aria and chorus. But Charpentier had no immediate followers until the early 18th century, when Clérambault wrote *L'Histoire de la femme adultère*.

The Italianate Viennese court proved more fruitful ground, prepared by the Austrian love of theatrical effects in quasi-liturgical ceremonial. The *sepolcro* was a dramatic enactment of the Passion drama with scenery, costumes, and acting, developed from the medieval liturgical dramas. These were very common in Vienna in the later 17th century, and encouraged the composition of oratorios, mainly by Italian composers such as Draghi and Caldara. The main differences between

Viennese and native Italian traditions lie in the orchestration, which tends to be more colourful north of the Alps (this is especially true in the *sepolcri*, but also applies to the oratorios of Fux in the early 18th century). The court opera librettists, Zeno and his successor Metastasio, also wrote the texts for oratorios. Although they turned back to the Bible, the former actually imitating a biblical style, they kept to the five to seven characters of *opera seria*, and attempted to preserve the unities of time and place, with long recitatives to convey the action, and arias to express the moods of the characters. Metastasio's librettos are freer in style, but so excellent in characterization and dramatic action that they continued in use for many years (Mozart set *La Betulia liberata* in 1771 and Francesco Morlacchi set *Isacco* in 1817).

5. The oratorio outside Italy: the Protestant tradition

Oratorio was late in arriving in Protestant lands. The German Lutherans had something similar in the more or less dramatic *Passion, but in the early 17th century this was unaffected by opera, which was virtually unknown in Germany. Some composers who had studied in Italy effected a compromise in the *historia*—Schütz's for Christmas, often known as his 'Christmas Oratorio', for example, is dramatic in character, but the text-setting is more akin to plainchant, in the manner of 16th-century Passion music, than to recitative. In the 1660s the concept of the *actus musicus was developed, a form related to Italian oratorio in the telling of biblical stories with poetic interpolations. Although also without recitative, there were arioso pieces and instrumental symphonies, with choruses which included chorales.

It was not until a public opera house opened in Hamburg in the 1670s that anything really like oratorio developed in Protestant Germany. There were a number of operas on religious themes given in the theatre in the years between 1678 and 1695. The first German oratorio, in the Italian sense of the word, was by an opera composer, Keiser, whose *Der blutige und sterbende Jesus* ('Jesus, Bleeding and Dying', 1704) was a Passion oratorio without a narrator and not using any biblical text, for which it was much criticized when first given in Hamburg Cathedral. Nevertheless, his example was followed by Mattheson, who introduced women singers from the opera house into church performances, and by Telemann, whose mastery of both indigenous and foreign musical styles gave rise to some excellent works well worth reviving, notably *Der Tag des Gerichts* ('Judgment Day', 1762). Passion music in oratorio form remained the most popular type, and the equivalent of the hagiographical Italian oratorio was rare. Such dramatic music as was composed went into the genre of the church cantata; and Bach's so-called *Christmas Oratorio* is a set of six linked cantatas rather than a true oratorio.

6. Handel

An opera composer who worked in Hamburg and studied in Rome was ideally placed to become a great oratorio composer. How Handel came to the genre is explained in the article on the composer; what must be said here is how individual most of his oratorios are in both form and manner. His first was written for performance in the splendid Roman palace of a cardinal in 1707—*Il trionfo del Tempo e del Disinganno* ('The Triumph of Time and Deceit') sets an allegorical subject in the Italian manner, with virtuoso solo singers given a succession of recitatives. *La resurrezione* was given in a theatre constructed in the Palazzo Ruspoli with scenery, a large orchestra, and some famous singers. His next work that could be called an oratorio is in fact Passion music, made for Hamburg *c.*1715. The emphasis is still on the soloists, though the chorus acts as the crowd, or *turba*, in the conventional way and there are several chorales. But the text by B. H. Brockes is a complete rewriting of the biblical story. There are some very fine descriptive recitatives, which were to become a feature of Handel's later oratorios.

In the view of the leading authority on oratorio history, Howard Smither, 'Handel's English oratorios are decisive in the history of the genre'. When he arrived in England there was no oratorio: the nearest musical equivalents were the grand charity concerts given on St Cecilia's Day in Westminster Abbey. The choral–orchestral repertory consisted largely of occasional anthems and services (especially settings of the *Te Deum*) and odes. He gained experience of this kind of music in 1713–15 in the various choral works written for the Peace of Utrecht and the king's coronation.

Handel's mature oratorios (1733–51) were thus created from these elements: the Italian operatic style with arias and recitatives; the German Passion with its chorus as character; and the English anthem and ceremonial ode. To these might be added some influence of the French classical drama with its choral comments and tragic outcomes (instead of the always happy endings of 18th-century *opera seria*). Handel used these elements in different proportions. At one end of the scale come *Messiah* and *Israel in Egypt*, which are constructed entirely from biblical texts in prose and are without dramatic personages, so that they are naturally close to the anthem in style. Others, notably *Susanna* and *Theodora*, are almost dramas in the tradition of the *oratorio erotico*. *Saul*, which uses the chorus as a participating character rather than merely a commentator, is reminiscent of Passion music and Italian opera, and

has a scene suggesting a procession or dance. In others the elements are more evenly balanced, as in *Belshazzar*, where the drama is strong and the chorus skilfully woven into it, yet anthem-like choruses resembling those of a St Cecilia's Day service occur. Two of his greatest works of the English oratorio type are on classical rather than Judaeo-Christian topics: *Hercules* and *Semele*.

The dramatic effectiveness of many of Handel's operas has given rise to speculation that he would have liked to stage them, especially as there are stage directions in some of the librettos. Indeed, the sense of drama is sometimes more pronounced than in his *opere serie*, since he felt no compulsion to retain the *da capo* aria convention which so often impeded the action of operas, and his sequence of recitatives, arias, ensembles, and choruses is much more flexible than in opera. Moreover, his oratorios were given first in theatres, not churches. Nevertheless, 20th-century efforts at staging even the more obviously theatrical oratorios did not prove fully satisfactory; maybe it is best to accept that the genre is a hybrid and is best performed 'in the oratorio way'—without acting, though not necessarily without scenery. This does not mean that they must be performed undramatically, or treated with unusual solemnity. It is worth remembering that Handel's chorus was frequently smaller than his orchestra, that his singers (even in his later works, when he wrote for English rather than Italian soloists) were experienced in the opera house, and that he himself frequently added the sparkle of virtuosity by playing brilliant organ concertos in the intervals. The English helped to inspire these great masterpieces, believing that edification need not exclude entertainment. If they did not attempt the fervour of the Counter-Reformation oratorio, they certainly represented a patriotic affirmation of Anglican orthodoxy and of the political status quo; this was one factor in their enormous and enduring popularity.

7. The later 18th century

The decline of the Italianate oratorio was bound up with the decline of *opera seria*, which had governed its idiom. The oratorio changed little in the 18th century, keeping the emphasis on the elaborately ornamented aria, often in *da capo* form. A few oratorios were staged, increasing their resemblance to *opera seria*. Thus came a division between the up-to-date music of the *opera buffa* and the manner of the oratorio. In the end, Italian oratorio virtually died out, in spite of the twice-yearly performances of the Viennese Tonkünstler-Societät, where Haydn's *Il ritorno di Tobia* (1775) and Mozart's *Davidde penitente* (1785) were first presented. The north German Protestants were provided with some dramatic oratorios by J. H. Rolle of Magdeburg, who added stage directions to his librettos, and whose *Der Tod Abels* ('The Death of Abel', 1769) and *Lazarus* (1778) might be worthy of revival; and by C. P. E. Bach, who continued the Hamburg oratorio tradition in *Die Israeliten in der Wüste* ('The Israelites in the Wilderness', 1769), which certainly is. But the most popular work of the time was the Berlin composer Graun's *Der Tod Jesu* (1755), a devotional (or in Smither's term, 'lyrical') rather than a dramatic piece. Some oratorios were given at the Paris Concert Spirituel between 1770 and 1800, including interesting original pieces by Gossec, Sacchini, and Le Sueur, which showed Gluck's influence.

In England, Handel's works were given on an increasingly large scale in choral festivals, culminating in the huge events with up to a thousand performers at Westminster Abbey in 1784–91. In Smither's view it was this development that led to the prevailing modern conception of oratorio as a work of monumental grandeur. The form began to be seen as a largely choral work, and Haydn was inspired by the 1791 festival to compose *Die Schöpfung/The Creation* (1798), the first oratorio conceived bilingually. Its libretto is said to have been written for Handel. There is little dramatic impulse, but, especially when sung in German, the solo music is reminiscent of Mozart's *Die Zauberflöte* (1791) in its simple direct melody and clear diatonic harmony. The glories of *The Creation* are found in the rich orchestral accompaniments; in the choruses, modelled no doubt on those of Handel, but none the less characteristic of Haydn in sound; and in the extraordinarily imaginative 'Representation of Chaos' with which it begins. *Die Jahreszeiten* ('The Seasons', 1801) is more diffuse, the libretto providing descriptive scenes rather than continuous narrative, but it contains some extremely fine—and nowadays neglected—music.

8. The 19th and 20th centuries

The religious and missionary spirit that had animated the oratorio for two centuries diminished after the age of Napoleon, 19th-century composers increasingly expressing views which did not belong to orthodox Christianity. English choral festivals continued to flourish and were imitated in Germany, for example the Lower Rhine Festival; the oratorio was also kept alive by the emergence of German choral societies, such as the Berlin Singakademie, and the Sacred Harmonic Society of London. Much of their repertory was retrospective: Handel and Haydn were joined by Bach after the revival of the *St Matthew Passion* at Leipzig in 1829, and new compositions were naturally based on these models. The two most successful Germans were Spohr and Mendelssohn. Spohr tackled transcendental subjects, such as *Die letzten Dinge* ('The Last Judgment', 1826)

and *Calvary* (1835), in a style conservative and yet interesting in its chromatic harmony; he failed in his attempt to scale great heights, but succeeded in composing some pleasant music. Mendelssohn, the central figure of 19th-century oratorio, drew on both German and English traditions and was inspired by both Jewish and Christian values in his two masterpieces, *Paulus* ('St Paul', 1836) and *Elias* ('Elijah', 1846). He used chorales after the manner of the Bach Passions as well as dramatic choruses in the Handel tradition.

Two great composers primarily known for other musical genres also contributed to the repertory. Liszt's hagiographical *Legende von der Heiligen Elisabeth* ('St Elizabeth', 1867) is a work almost possible to stage; *Christus* (1862–7), a massive piece, returns to a near Counter-Reformation intensity of Catholic feeling. Berlioz, an opera composer denied access to the Opéra for years, used deliberate archaisms in *L'Enfance du Christ* (1854), notable for its beautiful but un-Handelian choruses. A clutch of works by Gounod, Massenet, and Saint-Saëns, favourites at English choral festivals, show a French penchant for charm rather than power; Franck's *Les Béatitudes* (1879) and Debussy's *Le Martyre de Saint Sébastien* (1911) are worthier examples of French mysticism. In Italy, oratorio was little practised until the works of Lorenzo Perosi revived the genre briefly in the years between 1897 and 1912. American composers who wrote oratorios of some significance include G. F. Bristow, John Knowles Paine, and Horatio Parker.

Most of the best oratorios of the 20th century came from England. Elgar, a Roman Catholic cut off from the Anglican establishment, and a Wagnerian in a country without a strong native operatic tradition, composed *The Dream of Gerontius* (1900), setting a poem by the leader of the Roman Catholic revival in England, Cardinal Newman. He used leitmotifs in a remarkably symphonic texture, emphasized drama as well as intense religious feeling, and imaginatively incorporated extended choruses in the narrative. Like Mendelssohn's *Elijah*, *Gerontius* received its premiere at the Birmingham Triennial Festival. With Elgar's other two oratorios, *The Apostles* (1903) and *The Kingdom* (1906), notably on New Testament subjects, it represents a late achievement of the aims of the founders of the genre three centuries earlier.

Gerontius at first proved difficult to perform well, a fact that underlines the increasing troubles of composers writing for the amateur choral society at a time when idioms have become less vocal and more complex. The next great success by an Englishman also taxes both soloists and chorus, but Walton's *Belshazzar's Feast* (1931) has proved popular because it recreates the dramatic atmosphere of Handel in modern terms.

Tippett's *A Child of Our Time* (1939–41) is retrospective in seeking to provide the equivalent of Bach chorales by incorporating spirituals; and Britten's *War Requiem* (1961), which may count as oratorio with its interpolations of poems inspired by events, looks back in several ways to the choral music of Verdi.

The most arresting oratorio of the 1920s was Stravinsky's highly dramatic *Oedipus rex* (1927), with a text sung in Latin, masked characters (the narrator in evening dress to emphasize his detachment from the action), and an important part for the chorus. This seems to grasp the essence of oratorio as a mixture of drama and comment. A work of highly original character, yet harking back to the Catholic fervour of early oratorio, is Messiaen's *La Transfiguration de Notre Seigneur Jésus-Christ* (1969). Isolated but forward-looking works by Honegger (*Le Roi David*, 1921), Martin (*Le Vin herbé*, 1938–41), and Dallapiccola (*Job*, 1950, staged as a *sacra rappresentazione*) hardly constitute a tradition. It may well be that the oratorio is near the end of its useful life. But Tippett's *The Mask of Time* (1981), as well as Britten's 'church parables', have shown that the idea of representing religious or transcendental subjects in dramatic form can still inspire music of high quality.   DA/NT

   📖 H. E. SMITHER, *A History of the Oratorio*, 4 vols. (Chapel Hill, NC, 1977–2000)

Orb and Sceptre. March by Walton, composed for the coronation of Elizabeth II in 1953.

Orchésographie. A manual on dancing by Thoinot Arbeau (an anagrammatic pseudonym of Jehan Tabourot); it was written in French and published in Langres in 1588, with a second edition in 1589. An important source of information on dance types of the period, it describes steps and lists musical references and preferred instrumentation for the various genres. The text is in the form of a dialogue with Arbeau's pupil 'Capriol', hence the title of Warlock's *Capriol Suite*, which uses dance tunes from *Orchésographie*.   —/AL

orchestra (Fr.: *orchestre*; Ger.: *Orchester*). An ensemble of woodwind, brass, string, and percussion instruments in fairly standard proportions, used for accompanying opera and playing symphonies and other music of the Western concert repertory. The term is also used of a number of other large ensembles including dance orchestras, jazz orchestras, and wind orchestras.

In classical Greece the *orchēstra* ('dancing-place') was the area in front of the stage where the chorus danced and sang during theatrical performances. Because the first operas, dating from the beginning of the 17th century, were based on classical drama, it seemed logical

to retain the term, which came to be used for the ensemble that played there.

1. The Baroque orchestra; 2. The Classical orchestra; 3. The 19th-century orchestra; 4. Other orchestral ensembles

1. The Baroque orchestra

The instrumental accompaniment to the first major opera, Monteverdi's *Orfeo* (1607), was for a group of stringed instruments (violins of all sizes and bass viols), with a large array of continuo instruments and, for special effects, recorders, harp, trumpets, sackbuts, and cornetts, but the whole ensemble played together only in the preliminary Toccata and the opening chorus. Because of the size of its instrumental ensemble *Orfeo* is usually regarded as the work with which the orchestra originated, but it was not until later in the 17th century that groups with more than one or two players to a part (and thus more easily recognizable as an 'orchestra') came into being. These were usually less varied than Monteverdi's orchestra, usually comprising only bowed string instruments with a continuo section of harpsichord, organ, and a variety of extended lutes to reinforce the harmony. To these were added *recorders (less often transverse *flutes), and, as other instruments evolved during the course of the century, *oboes and *bassoons followed by *trumpets and *timpani and, by the early 18th century, *horns. The *continuo section (or at least a keyboard player) would maintain an important role until the early 19th century, because as well as filling out the harmony it served to hold the ensemble together.

An influential early string orchestra was the *Vingt-Quatre Violons du Roi, organized in 1626 at the court of Louis XIII in France. They played in five parts, allocated to six violins (*dessus*), four small violas (*haute-contres*), four medium-sized violas (*tailles*), four large violas (*quintes*), and six *basses de violon*. (Charles II of England later established a similar group of 24 violins.) By the end of the 17th century the string body had been rearranged into two or three groups of violins, one or two of violas (the third violins and first violas were often regarded as interchangeable, as was still the case in Handel's day), cellos, which had by then replaced the bass violin, and usually some form of great bass, either a *double bass violin or a *violone.

2. The Classical orchestra

In most parts of Europe orchestras were usually the private property of princes and potentates. In each case a Kapellmeister or otherwise titled master of the music would be responsible for writing or procuring music and for the selection, performance standards, and conduct of the musicians, all of whom, including the composer, were little more than servants. The constitution of the orchestras varied: each court composer could, within his budget, choose his own instrumentation; he would then be responsible for rescoring as appropriate any music he obtained from elsewhere.

It was the composers of the late 18th century who created the precursor of the modern orchestra based on a more standardized string group of two violin parts, violas, cellos, and double bass, still with a keyboard continuo. The orchestra was often directed by the composer, who might play either the leading violin part or a keyboard instrument, usually the harpsichord or organ (for his London concerts in 1791 and 1794, Haydn was advertised as 'presid[ing] at the pianoforte'). To this were normally added a pair of oboes and horns, with one or two bassoons to strengthen the bass (even if they are not listed bassoons may be assumed when oboes are present). Oboists were expected to play the transverse flute in the quieter slow movements. Trumpets and drums were added when the music was in suitable keys. Until the latter part of the 18th century trumpets were available only in C and D; E♭ became possible by 1790 and B♭ by 1800, perhaps a decade or so earlier in England. Clarinets appeared comparatively late, not being generally adopted in Vienna much before the 1790s, though they were available in Mannheim, Paris, and London some 50 years earlier.

3. The 19th-century orchestra

(a) The rise of the symphony orchestra: By the end of the 18th century, after the upheavals and social consequences of the American and French revolutions, public *concerts were replacing the court orchestras, creating a need for much larger orchestras (and so establishing the structure of concert economics—a vicious circle involving audience numbers, size of venue, and orchestra size—which still plagues impresarios). A further influence on the number of woodwind and especially of strings was the reintroduction of heavier brass instruments such as trombones, followed by the adoption of the new, louder, playing techniques which accompanied the invention of valves for trumpets and horns.

With the establishment of public concerts, the role of the 'house composer' who produced most of the music to be played by his resident orchestra dwindled as music for each centre was sought far and wide from every fashionable composer. As a result, the constitution of the orchestra became standardized: if an orchestra in London wished to play the same music as one in Vienna, Paris, or Munich, all had to have similar numbers and instruments. Thus, by the early 19th century the modern symphony orchestra had come into being.

The normal constituents were now the same string instruments as before, though in greater numbers: a woodwind section consisting of pairs of flutes, oboes, clarinets, and bassoons, with higher and lower members of those families (piccolo, cor anglais, contrabassoon, often played by a third player); the brass, comprising four horns, two trumpets, three trombones, and a bass instrument (at first the ophicleide and from the mid-19th century a tuba); and three or four percussionists playing timpani (usually three), bass drum, cymbals, triangle, and side drum. Sometimes there was also a harpist. Except for Berlioz and Wagner, these numbers satisfied almost all 19th-century composers, and many were content with less (as, for reasons of economy, were managements).

(b) Further developments: The size of this orchestra demanded new methods of control. No longer was there a need for the composer to preside at the keyboard: harmonic realization was complete within the orchestra and, when all were playing, the composer would be inaudible. Nor was it really practicable for a standing first violinist to maintain adequate control: violin parts were becoming so complex that it was no longer possible to coordinate the entries and the ensemble of 60 to 80 players at the same time. Spohr is said to have been the first to stand with baton in hand and conduct in the modern fashion, though there are many depictions from earlier centuries of musicians waving a roll of paper, and Lully is known to have beaten time with a stick. But certainly from the 1820s onwards many musicians followed Spohr's example, and today only chamber orchestras and ensembles of period instruments are directed from the violin or keyboard. See also CONDUCTING.

Orchestras continued to expand in the late 19th and early 20th centuries, with composers including Mahler and Stravinsky demanding larger numbers and greater diversity of colours—a process that continued during the 20th century, especially through a huge increase in the availability and use of a wider range of percussion instruments. An interest in the music of earlier times, combined with a distaste for the gargantuan orchestra, led to the introduction of smaller chamber and string orchestras, each with a rapidly developing repertory. Orchestras of the size and instrumentation of earlier periods have been recreated, attempting to revive the contemporary repertories with the appropriate playing techniques and musical styling (see PERFORMANCE PRACTICE).

4. Other orchestral ensembles

The dance bands of the second half of the 19th century were small orchestras in themselves. When the Vienna Philharmonic plays the music of Johann Strauss, it is reduced to a size only a little larger than the orchestra for which Strauss wrote. Most resorts, spas, and other centres had their own orchestras whose daily fare may well have been somewhat lighter than a diet of Brahms or Bruckner, but which were capable of tackling the music of such masters when required and which, when reinforced with players from metropolitan centres, were able to play for annual or other festivals.

In some countries every city of any pretension had an opera house, each with its resident orchestra which could also act as the local symphony orchestra; and many cities had both. Not all opera houses could keep pace with modern fashions, but a surprising number could produce the lesser Wagnerian works, even if the *Ring* was beyond their normal capacity, and certainly all could cope with such staples as Verdi, Bizet, and Gounod. Nor were opera houses alone, for frequently there would be also the 'comic opera', whose orchestras were somewhat smaller but adequate for Gilbert and Sullivan, Lehár, Strauss, or Offenbach.

Music halls also had their orchestras, as did early cinemas until the invention of the talkies. Many of the resort or spa orchestras, for example that of the Tivoli Gardens in Copenhagen, continue the traditions of the 18th- and 19th-century pleasure gardens, playing for the enjoyment of diners and drinkers.

JMo

📖 P. Bekker, *The Story of the Orchestra* (New York, 1936/R) · A. Carse, *The Orchestra in the Eighteenth Century* (Cambridge, 1940/R) · R. Nettel, *The Orchestra in England: A Social History* (London, 1946, 3/1956) · A. Carse, *The Orchestra from Beethoven to Berlioz* (Cambridge, 1948/R) · P. Hart, *Orpheus in the New World: The Symphony Orchestra as an American Cultural Institution* (New York, 1973) · H. Raynor, *The Orchestra* (London, 1978) · D. J. Koury, *Orchestral Performance Practices in the Nineteenth Century: Size, Proportions, and Seating* (Ann Arbor, MI, 1986) · J. Peyser (ed.), *The Orchestra: Origins and Transformations* (New York, 1986) · R. R. Craven, *Symphony Orchestras of the World: Selected Profiles* (New York, 1987) · S. McVeigh, *Concert Life in London from Mozart to Haydn* (Cambridge, 1993) · N. Zaslaw, 'The origins of the Classical orchestra', *Basler Jahrbuch für historische Musikpraxis*, 17 (1993), 9–40

orchestral chimes. See TUBULAR BELLS.

Orchestral Pieces, Five. See FIVE ORCHESTRAL PIECES.

orchestral score. A *score in which each instrumental or vocal part is separately displayed.

orchestration. The art of combining instruments and their sounds in composing for the orchestra, or, more simply and practically, the act of scoring a sketch or an existing work for orchestral forces. By extension, the term may also be used in the context of music for chamber forces or even for chorus or solo piano, since the basic concerns of orchestration—with balance, colour, and texture—are common to music of all kinds. Nevertheless, orchestration is, by etymology and historical precedence, the art of writing for the orchestra, and will be considered here as that alone. In this essential sense, orchestration has developed in parallel with changes in the orchestra, and so some of its facets can be outlined historically.

1. The Baroque period; 2. The Classical period; 3. The Romantic period; 4. Since 1910

1. The Baroque period

Musical performances by large bodies of instruments seem to have been exceptional before the beginning of the 17th century. One of the earliest scores to document an orchestra is that for Monteverdi's *Orfeo* (1607), which lists a spectacular and diverse array of bowed strings, plucked strings (guitar, lutes, harp), woodwinds, brass, and keyboard instruments. Unfortunately, however, the scoring is not indicated in the music and has to be ascertained by other means: consulting contemporary testimonies and treatises, or considering the nature of the musical material. It seems clear, too, that Monteverdi's proud list merely indicates the forces available for the first performance, at the court of Mantua. He might well have relished such richness of colour, but for performances on other occasions he would have expected more modest resources.

In the latter half of the 17th century, the orchestra became a more routine organization—and a more homogeneous one. Bowed strings were its basis, often with a keyboard continuo and occasionally with specially featured wind instruments. Since the string parts did not normally indicate any particular performing techniques—and even dynamic markings were rather infrequent—scope for orchestrational skill was limited. Wind instruments, when present, would normally be well exposed and used for poetic effects: flutes for celestial grace, an oboe for a pastoral note, trumpets for a martial atmosphere, and trombones for solemnity.

Bach, Handel, Rameau, and Vivaldi, in the first half of the 18th century, regularly wrote for orchestras including flutes, oboes, bassoons, horns, and trumpets as well as strings, with a keyboard continuo often still present. In most music the strings were dominant, and a great deal was written for them alone. Rameau, however, was a great inventor of sounds and textures obtained from wind soloists or groups, or from enmeshings of winds and strings. The wind instruments in his scores still have their poetic associations (indeed, these have lived on into modern times), but his orchestration was guided, too, by a sense for what would sound fresh and delightful. He also made occasional use of percussion.

Outside France, Baroque orchestration was steered more by the concerto ideal. A feature of Bach's orchestration in vocal works is his use of the obbligato instrument, playing in duet with the solo voice above the rest of the orchestra, while his Brandenburg Concertos are based on the concerto grosso principle of alternation between a small group and the full ensemble, and so often show two different styles of orchestration in the same music. They are, too, for orchestras of notably different composition and character.

2. The Classical period

The orchestra for which Mozart and the later Haydn wrote was a standard ensemble that had developed from the Baroque orchestra and comprised strings (no longer with a continuo) and pairs of oboes, bassoons, and horns as a basic wind group, increasingly with pairs also of flutes, clarinets, and trumpets, these last usually coming with timpani, trombones appearing more rarely. In some works the wind parts might be potentially disposable, following common Baroque practice, but this was an idea in retreat. The great Classical works depend in part on the mastery of orchestration they display.

To a degree it was a new mastery. The Baroque ideals of poetic association and concerto-style opposition remained, but were overtaken by the demands of consistent sound and clear form. Orchestration became a help in achieving form: in particular, the interplay of themes could be accentuated by the interplay of the wind group—now regularly acting as a group—with the strings. Either ensemble could muster the four parts usual in music of the time, the strings with their two groups of violins (first and second), violas, and cellos (with double basses an octave below), the winds with various combinations. Mixed ensembles were also possible, perhaps with flutes doubling first violins to change the tone, or with woodwind soloists exposed. Horns would generally remain in the harmonic underlay, and trumpets be used for moments of brightness and assertiveness: brass instruments at this date, without keys, were restricted to rather few notes. The strings, because of their nature and their players' training, still carried the burden, especially in fast music. But woodwind instruments would often come to the fore in gentler second subjects or in slow movements. And in climaxes and finales, the whole orchestra would be used together.

Special effects could come from trombones, which kept their atmosphere of sombreness (as in Mozart's *Idomeneo* and *Don Giovanni*), or from percussion instruments—drums, cymbals, triangle—associated with Turkish army music (as in the same composer's *Die Entführung aus dem Serail*).

Beethoven was able to amplify the sound of the Mozart–Haydn orchestra not so much by increasing its size as by expanding its volume, thanks to advances in instrument construction (which, for instance, made the brass more precise and flexible in tuning, and therefore more useful) and to what he learnt from contemporaries in Paris, where the tradition of colourful orchestration had continued from Rameau. With Beethoven the strings are still the orchestra's foundation, but woodwinds, brass, and timpani are more constantly present. The depth and solidity of the orchestral sound are also increased, in works from the 'Eroica' Symphony onwards, by the prominent use of three or more horns and by the separation of the double basses from the cellos to provide a new, low bass line. Beethoven exploited the theatrical effect of an offstage trumpet (in *Fidelio*), added the piccolo to the Classical orchestra, and brought trombones into the main body, but although he made so much more of the timpani, his use of other percussion instruments was, as in Mozart, kept to atmospheric moments—notably the military music in the finale of the Ninth Symphony.

3. The Romantic period

Following Beethoven, orchestration became more personal. Schubert, Mendelssohn, Schumann, and Weber re-established a Mozartian pattern of woodwind–string interplay, with plentiful woodwind solos but without losing Beethovenian strength and richness. At the same time Berlioz, notably in his *Symphonie fantastique*, introduced new instruments (cor anglais, multiple timpani players), increased the range of string textures by dividing parts and adding new effects (*col legno*, *sul ponticello*, etc.), and altogether enlarged the orchestra's capacity to make colourful gestures in the way he wrote for soloists and unusual groupings. The growing importance of orchestration as an art was signalled by the appearance of Berlioz's treatise on the subject in 1843, and also by the indications he made on his scores as to the numbers of instruments to be used.

Berlioz had a great influence on composers in Russia, notably Rimsky-Korsakov, while Wagner absorbed his innovations (divided strings, the cor anglais, emphatic gestures) into an orchestral style giving greater respect to Beethovenian strength. Brahms's effects may be more monochrome, but his subtle shadings and long solos added further possibilities to the widening orchestral palette.

By the end of the 19th century, Mahler and Strauss had a vast range of possibilities that they could take further. Mahler's orchestration features disparate colours at the same time, new instruments (posthorn, mandolin, guitar) and, especially in his later scores, a changing focus on small, mixed ensembles. The sound of Strauss's music tends to be more homogeneous, but with abundant picturesque effects. Both composers worked with an orchestra roughly double the size of the Classical, with woodwinds in fours, six or eight horns, and a suitably expanded string section.

Debussy's orchestra is smaller, but far more flexible. In using frequent changes of scoring, dense but luminous divisions of the strings (notably in *La Mer*), clear colours and percussion highlights (such as the antique cymbals provide in the *Prélude à 'L'Après-midi d'un faune'*) he made orchestration an essential, fluid part of his style and prepared the way for the 20th-century concern with music as sounds rather than notes. Also on the cusp of the modern period, Schoenberg's First Chamber Symphony (1906) radically reduced the orchestra to an ensemble of just 15 soloists, with a preponderance of wind players.

4. Since 1910

The half-century after *La Mer* and Schoenberg's Chamber Symphony was one of unparalleled innovation in orchestral writing. Several broad trends can be distinguished: a move away from the massive orchestras of Mahler and Strauss, often towards ensembles more of Beethovenian dimensions, though perhaps differently constituted; a great increase in the size and importance of the percussion section; a more equal distribution of roles between winds and strings, sometimes with the latter diminished or even excluded; changed distributions for the players on the platform; and the addition of electronic means (amplification, recorded sounds, electronic instruments).

Many of these tendencies, but not the last, can be observed in Stravinsky's works. Percussion instruments are important in *Petrushka* (1911) and determinant in *The Rite of Spring* (1913); Stravinsky also wrote for an orchestra of pianos and percussion in *Les Noces* (1923). His Symphony in C (1938–40) is for a Beethoven orchestra, his *Symphonies of Wind Instruments* (1920) for symphonic woodwinds and brass alone. In other works he mixed traditions—as in *Capriccio* (1928–9), for an early Romantic orchestra with a concerto-grosso-style group of string soloists—or created new adaptations: violins, violas, and cellos are excluded from the orchestra of his *Symphony of Psalms* (1930), for example, while *Threni* (1957–8) has sarrusophone and flugel horn in place of bassoons and trumpets. However various his ensembles, though, his principles of orchestration

stayed much the same, giving primary importance to harmonic sonorities, moving through blocks rather than blends. The same emphasis may be found in Ravel's orchestration and, still more so, in Messiaen's. Messiaen also produced one of the first orchestral scores incorporating an electronic instrument, the ondes martenot: his *Turangalîla-symphonie* (1946–8).

Many composers in the quarter-century after World War II—Barraqué, Boulez, Stockhausen—felt it necessary to create a special orchestra in every new work. Stockhausen's *Gruppen* (1955–7), for instance, has a large orchestra divided into three separate ensembles round the hall. Boulez's *Pli selon pli* (1957–62) is for a modest orchestra in which tuned percussion instruments have the central role accorded the strings in earlier times. Barraqué's ... *au delà du hasard* (1958–9) wields groups of brass, percussion, and clarinets with solo piano and female voices. On the other hand, a new convention emerged in the small orchestra of soloists, as featured in Ligeti's Chamber Concerto (1969–70), though such composers as Birtwistle, Carter, Xenakis, and Berio have been extremely resourceful in making this relatively compact and unchanging ensemble sound different in every piece.

Large-scale orchestral music since 1970 has often been conceived for more normal means, partly on aesthetic grounds (in line with a recovery of earlier styles and a lapse in the intensity of modernist progress) and partly for economic reasons. But there have been conspicuous exceptions, such as Messiaen's *Éclairs sur l'Au-delà* (1988–91), for an orchestra of 120 players; and innovations have continued—for example, in creating orchestral analogues of natural sounds (as in Messiaen and in the music of such 'spectralist' composers as Gérard Grisey and Claude Vivier) or including sampled natural sounds as part of the orchestral fabric (as in works by Steve Reich and George Benjamin). Orchestration has thus remained what it was for Debussy: an integral element of the art of composition and an area forever open to imagination.

MH/PG

📖 H. Berlioz, *Grand traité d'instrumentation et d'orchestration modernes* (Paris, 1843, 2/1855/R; Eng. trans. 1856, 2/1882/R) · A. Carse, *The History of Orchestration* (London, 1925/R1964) · W. Piston, *Orchestration* (New York, 1955)

ordinaire (Fr.), **ordinario** (It.). 'Ordinary', 'normal'. An instruction to return to playing in the normal way after a passage in which an unusual playing technique has been required, e.g. bowing *col legno*. See also TEMPO ORDINARIO.

Ordinary of the Mass. The sections of the Mass whose texts do not vary; see MASS, 1; PLAINCHANT, 1.

ordo (Lat., pl. *ordines*). The smallest unit forming part of one of the rhythmic modes. See NOTATION, 2.

Ordoñez [Ordoniz, Ordonitz, Ordonez], **Carlo d'** [Karl von] (*b* Vienna, *bapt.* 19 April 1734; *d* Vienna, 6 Sept. 1786). Austrian composer and violinist, of Spanish descent. Combining composition with a career as a civil servant, Ordoñez made a significant contribution to the development of the Viennese Classical style from the 1750s, mainly in chamber music and the symphony but also in his marionette opera *Alceste* (1775), performed at Eszterháza. He composed over 70 symphonies, mostly in three movements, though a few have an additional minuet and trio; many are characterized by overt thematic connections between movements, and some by an extensive use of counterpoint, which is a feature of his 27 string quartets; the most popular—the six quartets op. 1—all include fugal movements. A significant number of church works are now lost. Although Ordoñez's music frequently displays a striking rhythmic vigour, his pedestrian harmonic style has more in common with such contemporaries as Wagenseil and Leopold Hofmann than with Haydn. Nevertheless, the originality and boldness of his symphonies before 1764 caused them to be circulated under Haydn's name (and a Symphony in A major by him was attributed to Haydn until 1955).   MHE

ordre (Fr.). 'Suite'.

Orfeo, L'. Opera ('tale in music') in a prologue and five acts by Monteverdi, to a libretto by Alessandro Striggio (Mantua, 1607).

Orfeo ed Euridice (*Orphée et Eurydice*). Opera in three acts by Gluck to a libretto by Ranieri Calzabigi (Vienna, 1762); Gluck made an expanded French version to a libretto by Pierre Louis Moline after Calzabigi (Paris, 1774).

Orff, Carl (*b* Munich, 10 July 1895; *d* Munich, 29 March 1982). German composer and educationist. Born into a Bavarian military family, he showed musical aptitude early and played the piano, organ, and cello as a boy. He studied at the Munich Academy, graduating in 1914, then held the posts of Kapellmeister at the Munich Kammerspiele (1915–17) and at the Darmstadt Landestheater and the Mannheim Nationaltheater (concurrently, 1918–19). In 1920 he retrained as a composer with Heinrich Kaminski. His early works, many of which he subsequently withdrew and which remain unperformed, show the influence of Debussy, Strauss, and early Schoenberg.

In 1924, together with Dorothee Günther, Orff founded the Günther School of gymnastics, dance, and music, encouraging the pupils in improvisation and developing a range of musical publications (entitled *Orff-Schulwerk*) and percussion instruments which have been widely used in education. At the same time he developed an interest in early music: he prepared performing versions of Monteverdi's *Lamento d'Arianna*, *Orfeo*, and *Il ballo delle ingrate* in 1925, subsequently revising the trilogy in 1940 under the title *Lamenti*. He conducted the Munich Bach Society between 1930 and 1933.

Orff's first great success was the scenic cantata *Carmina burana* (1935–6), a setting of scabrous medieval poetry which marks both the emergence and the quintessence of his characteristic style. Stravinsky's *Oedipus rex* has been cited as a major influence, though *Carmina burana* marks a drastic simplification of the Stravinskian method and is marked by melodic and harmonic simplicity, obsessive rhythmic patterns, and cumulative, pounding ostinatos. The work eventually came to form the first part of a trilogy on erotic subject matter, *Trionfi*, with the addition of *Catulli carmina* (1943) and *Trionfo di Afrodite* (1953).

Orff's activities during the Third Reich are a cause of some controversy. In 1939 he wrote incidental music for Shakespeare's *A Midsummer Night's Dream*, to replace the Mendelssohn score banned by the Nazis. A pair of operas based on the brothers Grimm—*Der Mond* ('The Moon', 1939) and *Die Kluge* ('The Clever Girl', 1943)— were successful, but his educational activities were curtailed, and were resumed only at the request of German radio in 1948. Between 1950 and 1954 he produced his *Musik für Kinder*, studies of graded difficulty for classroom use. The Carl Orff Institute in Salzburg was founded in 1961 to propagate his teaching methods. His major works in the postwar era consisted of a sequence of music-theatre pieces modelled either on Baroque theatre or on Greek tragedy, many of which were first performed either at Stuttgart or at the Salzburg Festival. They include *Antigonae* (1948) and *Oedipus der Tyrann* (1959), both of which are settings of Sophocles in German translation.

Towards the end of Orff's career his methodology became increasingly streamlined: *Prometheus* (1966) and *De temporum fine comoedia* ('Comedy of the End of Time', 1973) contain a substantial amount of spoken declamation punctuated by percussive orchestral effects. He wrote the music for the Munich Olympic Games in 1972. With the exception of *Carmina burana*, few of his works remain in the repertory and he has been sharply criticized for coarseness and vulgarity. Others, however, have seen him as an important precursor of *minimalism.   PG/TA

📖 H. Maier, *Carl Orff in his Time* (Mainz, 1995) · M. H. Kater, *Composers of the Nazi Era: Eight Portraits* (New York, 2000)

organ (Fr.: *orgue*; Ger.: *Orgel*; It.: *organo*). The most complex of all instruments. Its sound is produced by air driven under pressure through sets of pipes. The air is raised by a bellows and on many instruments is brought under pressure in a reservoir; it is then channelled through the pipes by means of valves operated by the keyboard. Specific ranks of pipes may be brought into and out of play by means of stops.

1. Origin; 2. Flue pipes; 3. The Middle Ages; 4. Positive and portative organs; 5. Organ actions; 6. Wind pressure; 7. Reed pipes and free reeds; 8. The 17th and 18th centuries; 9. After 1800; 10. Reed organs, barrel organs, and electronic organs

1. Origin

The invention of the organ is attributed to Ctesibius of Alexandria in about 300 BC. His *hydraulis had the basic elements that define an organ: a row of pipes, one for each note, with a key for each to admit the air, which was supplied by bellows. The player could determine which pipe should sound by depressing the relevant key. The hydraulis differs from the modern organ in that the air was stabilized by water in a tank (Fig. 1). Present-day organs usually have many ranks of pipes and a rather more elaborate mechanism. A Roman organ found in Aquincum (near Budapest), with a dedicatory plate from AD 228, may have been a hydraulis.

2. Flue pipes

Until the 16th century, and still thereafter on the simpler types, organs used only flue pipes. These are simple duct flutes, working in the same way as a recorder: wind enters through the toe of the pipe and passes a plate or 'languid', level with the lip of the 'mouth' (the oblong opening to the outside). The wind is then deflected by the upper lip, causing vibrations to be set up in the air column in the pipe (Fig. 2). Flue pipes may be 'stopped' (i.e. closed at the upper end) or 'open': stopped pipes sound an octave lower than open ones. Different widths and shapes of pipe give contrasting tone-colours: a narrow pipe has a bright sound with plenty of overtones, but a wider pipe is smoother and more flute-like. Conical pipes, widest at the mouth or blowing end, sound more like recorders, and cylindrical pipes are brighter.

3. The Middle Ages

The secrets of the Alexandrian organ were preserved in Byzantium and in the 8th and 9th centuries were reintroduced to western Europe, initially in the form of gifts from the Byzantine Emperor or from the Persian courts to such kings as Charlemagne. They were seen as mechanical wonders rather than musical instruments, used wholly for ostentatious secular purposes. In 826 the first organ produced in the West was built for the palace at Aix-la-Chapelle.

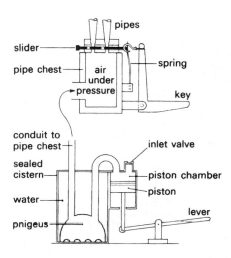

Fig. 1. Mechanism of the hydraulis: depressing the key moves the slider, allowing air into the pipe(s); the spring returns the slider to the 'off' position when the key is released.

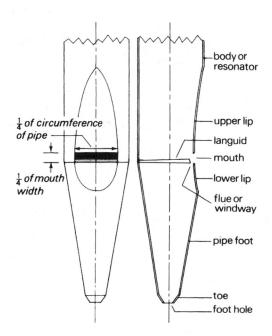

Fig. 2. Flue pipe, from the front and in cross-section.

From the 9th century to the 12th the organ became regarded increasingly as exclusively a church instrument, but how this happened remains obscure. At this stage it had a much simplified form. No longer were there spring-controlled keys; early medieval illustrations and descriptions show perforated wooden sliders, which had to be pulled out and pushed back to admit air to the pipes. Nor were there separate stops: on the monster Winchester Cathedral organ built in the late 10th century, all the pipes on a key sounded simultaneously. Not until the 13th century do some of the earlier devices begin to reappear with the portative organ, for example keys that would return to their closed position when the finger was removed.

4. Positive and portative organs

The medieval *portative organs—the smallest of which could be carried by the player, who would pump the bellows with the left hand while playing the keys with the right—had two or three dozen flue pipes and a compass of a couple of octaves or so. The next size, the positive, so called because it could be moved about but had to be placed in position to be played, had a compass of four or more octaves, and perhaps more than one pipe to each note; it was the ancestor of the Baroque *chamber organ. Wind was provided by a pair of bellows operated by a second person. A positive organ might also have at least one 4′ rank and possibly another at 2′ or at 1½′. When a key was depressed a valve or 'pallet' would open and allow wind to pass from the 'pallet box' (the lower chamber of the chest) into the 'groove', above which was a series of holes leading to all the pipes controlled by that key.

5. Organ actions

On organs provided with stops, each separate rank would be controlled by a wooden slider with holes drilled into it corresponding with each pipe-foot and terminating (by means of rods, trundles, and levers) in a stop-knob at the side of the instrument. When a stop was pulled out, it would move the slider so that each of the holes came under the foot of a pipe, allowing air access to a particular rank of pipes (Fig. 3). Some stops control multiple ranks of pipes. Sliders were known in small organs, possibly as early as 1400, but not in large organs until the early 16th century. Another early 16th-century variant is the 'spring chest', shown in Fig. 4, with the slider replaced by separate, spring-loaded

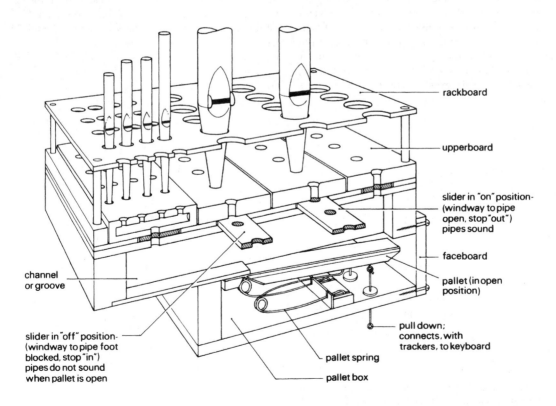

rackboard

upperboard

slider in "on" position-
(windway to pipe
open, stop "out")
pipes sound

faceboard

pallet (in open
position)

pull down;
connects, with
trackers, to keyboard

channel
or groove

slider in "off" position-
(windway to pipe foot
blocked, stop "in")
pipes do not sound
when pallet is open

pallet spring

pallet box

Fig. 3. Slider chest.

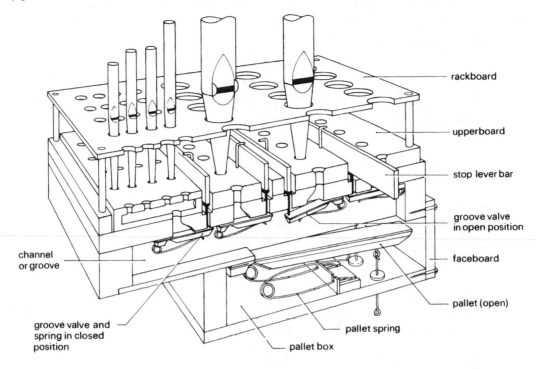

rackboard

upperboard

stop lever bar

groove valve
in open position

faceboard

pallet (open)

pallet spring

pallet box

groove valve and
spring in closed
position

channel
or groove

Fig. 4. Spring chest.

secondary pallets ('groove valves') for each pipe, spring-loaded and operated by stop-lever bars.

On the earlier organs, the pipes for each note stood directly in front of its key on the keyboard. By the mid-14th century the tracker action had been invented (see Fig. 5). Depressing a key with the finger pulled down a rod called a 'tracker', the upper end of which was attached to one end of a long horizontal 'roller' (a rod mounted on a rollerboard), and caused the roller to rotate through 90°. At the other end of the roller was another tracker, which was pulled down in turn, its upper end opening the pallet for the relevant pipe or pipes. The great advantage of the rollerboard and trackers was that they could be as long as required, so that the pipe could be at any distance from the key. Pipes could now be placed to the left or to the right of the keys, permitting the symmetrical arrangement of the front pipes, with sets of the longest pipes at each end, that became the norm. The tracker mechanism allowed separate chests of pipes to be created; the second manual of all major organs until 1700 (later in some areas) was the *Rückpositiv* (Ger., 'back positive') or 'chair organ', playing a chest of pipes placed at the organist's back, or sometimes under his chair, at the front of the gallery.

The tracker mechanism continued in use into the 19th century and has been revived on present-day organs because it gives an immediacy of touch from key to pipe. One of its disadvantages is that as more stops are drawn, to allow a richer sound, the weight on the key increases, for the trackers are pulling open the valves against more air pressure. This extra weight not only makes playing more difficult but can also mean that each hand has very different weights of touch, for example when playing a single solo stop on one manual and a much thicker registration for accompaniment on another.

6. Wind pressure

The wind pressure required to supply air for all but the smallest portative is greater than could be provided by one hand pumping the bellows. Larger organs had two or more large wedge-shaped bellows, each with one side fixed on the floor; the free sides were lifted in relay by the organ-blower, using hand-levers or treadles, so that one was filling with air while the others were allowed to fall under the pressure of lead weights. This type was superseded in the 19th century by feeder bellows which, instead of supplying air directly to the pipes, sent it into a reservoir in which the air pressure

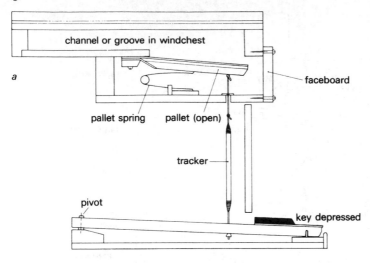

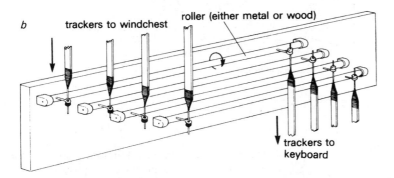

Fig. 5. Connections between key and chest: (a) suspended action; the keys are pivoted at the back and hang on the trackers from the pallet valve; (b) detail of the rollerboard.

would be steady and constant. Today the air in most organs is provided at constant pressure by an electric pump.

7. Reed pipes and free reeds

Reed pipes consist of a single beating reed (similar in principle to those used in *bagpipe drones and on *clarinets) made of a flexible tongue of brass held by a wire spring against a 'shallot', a tube with one flattened side and an aperture against which the reed vibrates when air is driven past it. The first writer to refer definitely to the use of reed pipes was Arnaut de Zwolle in about 1450. By 1500 reeds were divided into two categories: those with resonators of full or proportional length, and those with short resonators (or from which resonators are entirely absent), making up a group termed regals. Stops of the first group have such names as Trumpet, Trombone, Posaune, Fagott, Schalmei, Oboe, etc., the differences in tone and power being

produced by the length, breadth, and thickness of the metal reed, the shape and size of the shallot, the design of the resonator, and the wind pressure. Regal resonator forms are numerous and produce a sharp, snarling sound. They include such stops as Krummhorn, Ranket, and Sordun. Small portable organs consisting entirely of regals were widely used in the 16th and 17th centuries.

Pipes made with free *reeds, some with individual resonators and some with a single resonating chamber for all the notes of the rank, were used in parts of Germany and northern France from the 1780s, and occasionally in the USA and Britain, though they became rare after about 1910.

8. The 17th and 18th centuries

By the 17th century, and still more by the 18th, organs had grown extremely large and elaborate. That of the Jakobikirche in Hamburg, built between 1689 and 1693 by Arp Schnitger, had four manuals and a pedal, each controlling a separate division—in effect each controlling a separate organ which could be used in some combination or to contrast with the other, a German style that later became known as *Werkprinzip*.

The heaviest division of the Jakobikirche organ was the *Pedal*, with 14 stops (three of them at 32′ and four at 16′), including two Trompete stops and two Posaune stops among the reeds as well as the normal flues such as Principals. The instrument also had solo stops so that, for example, the melody of a chorale could be played with the feet while the accompaniment or decorative patterning of a chorale prelude was played on one or more manuals. The heaviest manual was the *Hauptwerk* ('high department'), with 12 stops (three of them, including the Trompete, at 16′). This manual, roughly the equivalent of the English Great organ, would have been used for full organ. The *Oberwerk* seems to have been something of a luxury and was found only on the largest organs, often in the highest part of the case (hence its name). In the Jakobikirche organ it had 14 stops.

The *Brustwerk*, with eight stops, was immediately in front of the organist (in the 'breast' of the organ), below the *Hauptwerk*. It was in effect a positive built into the organ and was ideal for accompanying voices and instruments. (It is noteworthy that it had such reed pipes as Dulcian and Regal, in contrast with the little chamber positives that are so often used in concert halls today, attempting to fulfil that accompanying role with nothing but flues.) If the organ was provided with a *swell box (a Spanish 17th-century invention), it would certainly be in the *Brustwerk*, sometimes in the *Oberwerk* as well. Finally, there was the *Rückpositiv*, here with 13 stops. This was the sort of organ for which Bach and his contemporaries were writing: with the separate divisions of the *Werkprinzip*, each line of a trio sonata could be tonally distinct.

In France organs were no less complex, but the *Grand orgue* contained most of the pipework, contrasting with a *Positif* and small *Écho* and *Pédale* departments. The organ music of Couperin and his French contemporaries is very different from that of the Germans.

English organs were smaller still, often with a single manual that might be divided at middle C so that the right hand could be tonally distinct from the left, for example for the well-known 'trumpet tunes'. The most notable difference was the absence of a pedal department, though occasionally a set of pull-downs might be seen, trackers from a dozen pedals which pulled down the lowest keys of the manual. Pedals remained rare in England well into the 19th century.

Dutch organs were as impressive as the German. The Spanish had two unusual features: they included powerful reed stops set horizontally (*en chamade*), and many Spanish churches had two organs, one on either side of the choir, so that they could be used antiphonally and in works composed for two organs.

9. After 1800

With the rise of Romanticism in music, to which none of the national styles of the Baroque-period organ are well suited, and with the increased technology of the Industrial Revolution, great mechanical and musical changes took place on the organ. Charles Barker's invention of the pneumatic lever in 1839 was immediately seized on by Aristide Cavaillé-Coll, the greatest French organ builder, and then by others throughout Europe. The Barker lever was a small bellows operated by a second pallet valve connected to the key (see Fig. 6). Because the key had only to operate the pallet valve, and the lever did the rest of the work, the touch became not only lighter but even in weight, irrespective of the registration; it also allowed the pipes to be placed further away from the manuals. The pneumatic principle could also be applied to the sliders.

This was followed within the ensuing decade by P.-A. Moitessier's tubular-pneumatic action, in which air pressure replaced all the mechanical devices such as trackers and rollerboards, eventually allowing for much higher air pressure on the pipes, and also for physical separation between organist and organ. The greatest problem with this action is that the pressure wave from a puff of air takes time to travel down a tube so that there is a perceptible delay between depressing a key and the resulting sound from the pipe. Some of the delay was eliminated by the invention of electropneumatic action (see Fig. 7), in which electromagnets operate the pneumatic motors that cause the pipe pallet to open; the thick cable seen snaking across the floor of churches and concert halls is housing all the wires necessary for this task. Such actions were in use by the 1860s and were being regularly made by the 1890s. The action is still sufficiently spongy that the 20th century saw the beginning of a strong swing back to tracker actions.

Nevertheless it was the tubular-pneumatic and electropneumatic actions that allowed the creation of the great 19th-century organs such as Ste Clotilde in Paris, where César Franck was the organist, St Reinold in Dortmund, which attracted Reger, and St George's Hall in Liverpool, where W. T. Best gave regular concerts, playing organ transcriptions of much of the orchestral and chamber-music repertory in the days when there were no regular orchestral or chamber concerts. Recitals on such organs, in town halls and churches, were often the only way for people to hear any great music.

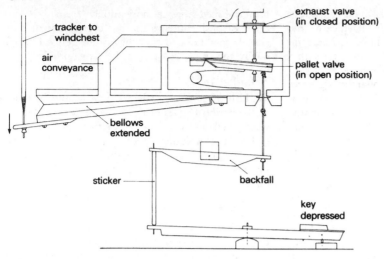

Fig. 6. Pneumatic action: depressing the key opens the pallet valve and closes the exhaust valve, allowing air under pressure to enter the bellows via the conveyancing. This expands the bellows, which pull down the tracker connected to the wind chest. Releasing the key closes the pallet valve and opens the exhaust valve; the air pressure is balanced and the bellows close.

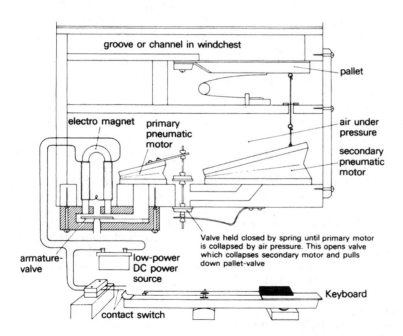

Fig. 7. Electropneumatic action: the electromagnet is activated when the keyboard contact-switch completes the circuit, causing the armature valve to open and allowing pressurized air in the primary pneumatic motor to escape. Air pressure within the chamber (maintained by the armature valve in activated position) forces the primary motor closed, activating the main valve, which in turn collapses the secondary motor, pulling down the pallet valve.

The 20th century was marked by two forces, the 'organ reformers' who sought inspiration in historical organs and in some cases revived their building methods, and those who continued to experiment with the possibilities of electric, electronic, and finally computer technology. Between the two there were makers who sought a synthesis of the old and the new. In the last decades of the century larger organs were being built that combined elements of several historical periods and regional styles, carefully designed so that music of more than one school or period may be performed sympathetically.

10. Reed organs, barrel organs, and electronic organs

The overriding problem with the organ is the complexity of the mechanism and the resulting cost of building and maintaining it. More modest churches and chapels, especially those in poor communities, are seldom able to contemplate such expense. Smaller and cheaper organs have been available, especially since the early 19th century, when the free-reed playing reed organs, such as the *harmonium and American organ, were perfected and could be purchased for less than the price of an upright piano.

The mid-20th-century solution was the electronic organ, made by such companies as *Hammond and Compton. Electronic technology has advantages in the absence of bellows, the possibility of wide volume control, and, for domestic purposes, the provision of earphones for the player and total silence for the neighbours. Modern digital organs have access to unlimited sampled sounds (see ELECTRONIC MUSICAL INSTRUMENTS).

Such villages as could afford organs sometimes had difficulty in finding a player. An alternative was the barrel organ, usually a small chamber organ for which the church could buy a selection of pinned barrels with the most popular hymn tunes of the day ready set. All that was needed was for a member of the congregation to turn a crank at a steady speed which, as it revolved, both operated the bellows and turned the barrel. The pinned barrel had been used from quite early times for carillons, and for musical clocks and boxes of all sizes, often incorporating organ pipes. Larger barrel organs were often used in churches from the mid-18th century until the 1860s. (See also MECHANICAL MUSICAL INSTRUMENTS.)

Some barrel organs are of considerable historical importance, for they preserve intact the musical styles of their periods. Major composers including Handel, Haydn, Mozart, and Beethoven composed music specifically for barrel organs or flute-playing musical clocks, and surviving barrels may be studied as recordings of how their music might have been played.

JMo

📖 M. I. WILSON, *Organ Cases of Western Europe* (London, 1979) · P. WILLIAMS, *A New History of the Organ, from the Greeks to the Present Day* (London, 1980) · E. M. and R. H. SKINNER, *The Composition of the Organ* (Ann Arbor, MI, 1981) · B. SONNAILLON, *King of Instruments: A History of the Organ* (New York, 1985) · C. PADGHAM, *The Well-Tempered Organ* (Oxford, 1987) · N. THISTLETHWAITE, *The Making of the Victorian Organ* (Cambridge, 1990) · L. EDWARDS (ed.), *The Historical Organ in America* (Easthampton, MA, 1992) · L. G. MONETTE, *The Art of Organ Voicing* (Kalamazoo, MI, 1992) · P. WILLIAMS, *The Organ in Western Culture, 750–1250* (Cambridge, 1993) · S. BICKNELL, *The History of the English Organ* (Cambridge, 1996)

organ chorale (Ger.: *Orgelchoral*). A broadly conceived term that encompasses a network of related genres, all of which treat sacred melodies at the organ using predominantly contrapuntal textures. They often either served as an introduction to congregational singing of the chorale ('chorale prelude', 'organ prelude') or were heard in alternation with the singing of individual chorale verses. Given the crucial role of chorales in the ideology of Lutheranism, and the large, richly conceived organs found in the churches where the Reformation was promulgated, it is not surprising that the organ chorale flourished in Germany in the 16th, 17th, and 18th centuries.

Types of approach to the organ chorale included: setting individual lines of the melody imitatively; presenting the chorale melody in long notes as a cantus firmus, with the accompanying voices engaging in contrapuntal and figurative elaboration which was often thematically related to the chorale itself; free chorale fantasias, often combining the two methods just described and frequently also including more improvisatory tendencies; and sets of variations (often called partitas, a term with a number of meanings; see CHORALE VARIATIONS). Since the Lutheran liturgy retained numerous Catholic melodies, German composers set many of these for the organ. Thus the greatest early treasury of surviving organ chorales is the cycle of eight multi-verse settings of the *Magnificat* from about 1600 by the Hamburg organist Hieronymus Praetorius; his work, as well as that of the other leading composers of organ chorales—Johannes Praetorius, Scheidt, Scheidemann, J. U. Steigleder, Pachelbel—encompasses all the approaches catalogued above.

With his more than 150 organ chorales, J. S. Bach demonstrated not only his mastery of every available genre of organ chorale but also his ability to invent such new sub-genres as the chorale trio, in which each hand plays a single independent line on its own keyboard while the pedal is charged with the bass line—the chorale being either treated in all parts or assigned to a single voice. Bach's great collections of chorale settings include the concise gems of the *Orgel-Büchlein* (BWV599–644), the juxtaposition of monumental and diminutive chorales found in the *Clavier-Übung*, book 3 (BWV669–89), the magisterial survey once called the 'Great Eighteen' (BWV651–68), the six late 'Schübler' Chorales (BWV645–50; transcriptions of cantata movements), and the astounding contrapuntal demonstrations of the Canonic Variations on *Vom Himmel hoch* (BWV769).

Bach's family—ancestors and children—were particularly committed to the organ chorale, as were numerous colleagues and friends (including Telemann, J. G. Walther, and G. F. Kauffmann) and many of his pupils, among them J. L. Krebs. Bach's organ chorales continued to be a reference point for admirers throughout the 19th century and into the 20th, from Mendelssohn and Brahms to Reger, Hugo Distler, and a host of German, American, and English cultivators of these traditions.   DY

📖 E. May, 'The types, uses, and historical position of Bach's organ chorales', *J. S. Bach as Organist*, ed. G. Stauffer and E. May (Bloomington, IN, and London, 1988), 81–101

organistrum. An early form of *hurdy-gurdy.

organ mass. See VERSET.

organology. The study of musical instruments. Important aspects of organology include the analytical classification of instruments (see INSTRUMENTS, CLASSIFICATION OF), the science of instruments, their historical development, and their musical and cultural uses. Playing techniques may be considered part of organological discussion, but not necessarily the instruments' repertories.

organ prelude (Ger.: *Orgelvorspiel*). Alternative term for *chorale prelude. See also ORGAN CHORALE.

organ score. A reduction of a full *score of any ensemble composition to form an arrangement for organ. Organ scores were published in London from the mid-18th century onwards and became increasingly popular during the 19th with Vincent Novello's organ arrangements of Haydn's masses. The term has also been used in the past to denote an *open score (often of four staves) of a piece of organ music.   LC

Organ Solo Mass. Mozart's *Missa brevis* in C major K259 (1776), so called because there is an important organ solo in the Benedictus.

organ stops. See ORGAN.

organ tablature. See TABLATURE, 2.

organum (Lat., from Gk. *organon*, 'tool', 'instrument', also 'system of logic'). The use of the original Greek word to mean an instrument of music did not occur until the 5th century AD. Since the use of instruments in Christian worship was forbidden, all instruments named in the Bible were interpreted in an allegorical way, and 'organum' came to mean simply 'vocal music'. It did, however, acquire the special meaning of polyphonic vocal music at an early date; the earliest surviving source of polyphony, *Musica enchiriadis* (north-eastern France, *c.*860), calls polyphony 'organum', and this terminology was to be standard up to the 13th century. Hence the term *vox organalis*, meaning the part added to a previous one (or *vox principalis*) to create polyphony. The choice of the word 'organum' for polyphony should not be taken to mean that vocal polyphony was an imitation of, or was necessarily connected to, the organ (or any other instrument). Rather it indicates that the music was governed by measurable pitches and consonances, a symphonic system.

Four types of organum are known from between the 9th and 13th centuries, after which the term dropped out of use. All involve adding a part to a line of plainchant.

1. In parallel organum the added voice or voices begin, move, and end at the constant interval of a 4th, 5th, or octave (or an appropriate combination of these) from the main voice. Parallel organum is described in *Musica enchiriadis*; it was probably widely practised throughout the Middle Ages, though no other description is known.

2. The added voice begins in unison with the main voice. It repeats its opening note until the main voice has moved up and away to the distance of a 4th above it. It then moves in parallel 4ths with the main voice. At cadences it repeats the sub-final while the main voice nears the final, then both voices merge in the final unison. Repeat notes are also frequently introduced in mid-sentence if the main voice has a descending phrase; the added voice usually chooses to repeat the note to which the main voice is descending. This kind of organum is described briefly in *Musica enchiriadis*, and in great detail (with many other alternative variant procedures) by Guido of Arezzo in *Micrologus* (*c.*1030). There are 174 compositions of this type in the Winchester Troper of *c.*990 (Ex. 1).

3. The added voice complements the given voice by contrary motion, one part ascending while the other descends, one moving in the top part of the available range, the other in the lower part. The term *'discantus' came to be preferred to designate this style, known from *c.*1100 on, and organum, while still carrying the general meaning of 'polyphony', was also used in a more special sense, to distinguish type 4 below from discantus.

4. The chant is drawn out into long held notes, while the added voice floats in faster motion above and around it. For this purpose the chant is usually split into two- or three-note segments, the two voices starting together and ending with a simultaneous movement on to their respective final notes (usually a unison). The earliest known examples are from early 12th-century France (Ex. 2).

organum, Ex. 1

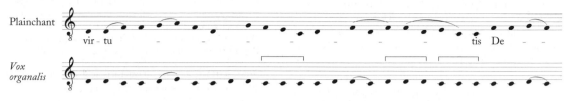

(square brackets ⌐¬ indicate notes repeated during approach of main voice)

From *Alleluia Video caelos*, Winchester Troper.

Ex. 2

Opening of *Alleluia vocavit Jesus*, Codex Calixtinus.

The last great repertory of polyphony termed organum was that of Notre Dame, Paris, in the late 12th and early 13th centuries. An anonymous theorist of the 1270s credited Léonin ('optimus organista') with the creation of a *magnus liber organi* ('great book of organum') containing chant settings for the cycle of festival services of the church year. This was revised by Pérotin ('optimus discantor'). These chant settings are a mixture of held-note organum (i.e. organum in the special sense, type 4 above) and note-against-note discant (type 3), of a complexity and sophistication remarkable by any standards. Some of the polyphony is for three or four voices, but most of it, like that of previous centuries, is for two. The held-note type of polyphony seems to have gone out of favour in the 13th century, and with it the use of the term 'organum' for any sort of polyphony.   DH

Orgel (Ger.). 'Organ'; *Orgeltabulatur*, 'organ tablature'; *Orgelwalze*, a barrel organ worked by clockwork (see MECHANICAL MUSICAL INSTRUMENTS; ORGAN, 10).

Orgelbüchlein ('Little Organ Book'). Collection of 46 organ chorales, BWV599–644, by J. S. Bach; he intended to include 164 and intended the collection partly as a teaching manual.

Ó Riada, Seán (*b* Cork, 1 Aug. 1931; *d* London, 3 Oct. 1971). Irish composer and folk musician. He learnt to play the violin and piano as a child, then studied with Aloys Fleischmann at University College, Cork (first taking classics, but gaining the B.Mus. in 1952); he played the piano in jazz and dance bands, at this time still using the English form of his name, John Reidy. He was assistant music director of Radio Éireann (1954–5), then worked briefly for the ORTF in Paris before becoming music director at the Abbey Theatre in Dublin (1955–62). In 1963 he moved back to the Gaeltacht, settling first in Kerry and then in west Cork; he lectured in music at University College, Cork, until his death, which may have been hastened by his fondness for drink and cigarettes.

Ó Riada is a household name in Ireland both for his work in traditional Irish music, often with his group Ceoltóirí Cualann, and for his film scores—chiefly that for *Mise Éire* (1959), but also *Saoirse* (1960) and *An Tine Bheo* (1966). His concert music deserves serious attention. Its backbone is a series of six works to which he gave the title *Nomos*, of which nos. 1 (*Hercules Dux Ferrariae*, for strings, 1957), 2 (for baritone, SATB chorus, and orchestra, 1957–63), 4 (for orchestra, 1958), and 6 (1966) survive; no. 3 is incomplete and no. 5 has not been located. Another ambitious score is *The Lords and the Bards* (1959) for soloists, chorus, and orchestra.   MA

   📖 B. HARRIS and G. FREYER (eds.), *Integrating Tradition: The Achievement of Seán Ó Riada* (Chester Springs, PA, 1981)

oriscus. A type of ornamental neume; see NOTATION, Fig. 1.

Orlando. Opera in three acts by Handel to a libretto adapted from Carlo Sigismondo Capece's *L'Orlando* (1711) after Ludovico Ariosto's *Orlando furioso* (London, 1733).

Orlando paladino ('The Paladin Orlando'). Opera in three acts by Haydn to a libretto by Nunziato Porta after Ludovico Ariosto's *Orlando furioso* (Eszterháza, 1782).

Ormandy, Eugene [Blau, Jenő] (*b* Budapest, 18 Nov. 1899; *d* Philadelphia, 12 March 1985). Hungarian-born American conductor. He began his career as a virtuoso violinist in Hungary, emigrating to the USA in 1921, when he adopted a new name derived from the ship on which he travelled, the SS *Normandie*. He led, and later conducted, an orchestra accompanying silent films at the Capitol Theatre, New York. He was appointed music director of the Minneapolis Orchestra in 1931, and in 1938 became music director of the Philadelphia Orchestra, where he developed a distinctively opulent sonority built on a strong string vibrato. Less flamboyant than his predecessor Stokowski, Ormandy nevertheless maintained the orchestra's legendary reputation.   JT

ornaments and ornamentation. The decoration of a melodic or, less commonly, harmonic line.

   1. Introduction; 2. To 1600; 3. The Baroque period; 4. Since 1760

1. Introduction

Ornamentation is applied in many genres, from folk music and jazz—both traditionally unnotated and relying on the performer's creativity—to highly notated Western art music, where the performer's invention has sometimes played a vital role, though for a variety of reasons this tradition is now largely lost. The art of ornamentation may be said to have been at its zenith between the 16th and 19th centuries, when it was regarded as essential to virtuoso technique. C. P. E. Bach, for example (*Versuch*, 1753), held ornaments to be indispensable:

> They connect and enliven notes and impart stress and accent … Expression is heightened by them … Em-

bellishments provide opportunities for fine performance as well as much of its subject matter. They improve mediocre compositions. Without them the best melody is empty and ineffective, the clearest content clouded. [Yet] a prodigal use of embellishments must be avoided. Regard them as spices which may ruin the best dish.

Ornamentation was characteristically used to vary repeated material, whether whole sections or shorter passages. Two broad categories are distinguished: small-scale ('simple') ornaments or 'graces' added to single notes; and more extensive ('compound') or florid decorations applied to entire passages, in which the original melody might be almost entirely disguised. The latter was largely the preserve of the virtuoso, though descriptions of tasteless additions by amateurs are also found. Cadences in particular invited elaboration, from which the solo *cadenza evolved. Choirs and instrumental ensembles with more than one performer to each line tended to use ornamentation sparingly, adding occasional graces only where coordination was possible.

During the 16th century, ornamentation was left mainly to the improvisational skill of the performer, but in the 17th and 18th centuries this freedom was tempered to varying degrees by more precise indications in the notation. 19th-century composers made their intentions clearer still; some neither expected nor tolerated changes to the printed text, though many celebrated performers habitually departed from it. Later developments included the adoption of standard signs for such frequently used ornaments as appoggiaturas, mordents, slides, trills, or turns. Some signs, used as early as the 15th century, became especially prevalent by the late 17th century. French composers in particular codified many ornaments (*agréments*) with corresponding signs, several of which continue in use, albeit often with modified meanings.

The use of ornament signs is well documented. Two points concerning their interpretation should be borne in mind. First, no single practice has been followed throughout the centuries, or in any one country or continent: trills, for example, have been variously indicated, and, conversely, a single trill sign may have had several different meanings. The performance context (both date and place) of any given ornament must therefore be taken into account. Secondly, even where an apparently definitive explanation exists, individual taste has a part to play. In this respect Montéclair's thoughts (*Principes de musique*, 1736) are significant: 'It is almost impossible to teach in writing how to execute these ornaments well since the live demonstration of an experienced master is hardly sufficient to do this'.

Inconsistencies between contemporary sources have led to controversy. Modern editions may contain valuable advice, but responsibility for making informed choices after consulting available texts rests with the performer.

2. To 1600

Pre-16th-century documentation of improvised ornamentation is scarce. It is possible that plainchant developed to some extent through the embellishment of simpler originals, the ecstatic *jubilus* melismas of certain alleluias being a likely example. 12th-century troubadour performances may have included such decoration as ornamented doubling of the vocal line by an instrument in *heterophony. Embellishing polyphonic music was more complex, since harmonic factors had to be considered. Hieronymus de Moravia, however, writing in the late 13th century, implies that ornamentation was suitable for all types of music. There is evidence that it was applied in certain circumstances by Machaut, Dufay, Josquin, and others. The practice seems to have developed gradually, but by the later 16th century it had reached heights of complexity.

The treatises that proliferated during this latter period gave advice on simple and compound ornamentation (diminutions or *passaggi*). The two most important graces were the tremolo (a type of half trill beginning on the main note) and the *groppo* or *gruppo* (a full cadential trill ending with a turn). Increasingly complex *passaggi* were used extensively by late 16th-century virtuosos, and innumerable figurations and examples, for study and practice, were included in treatises.

Ornamentation was an essential instrumental technique. Keyboard transcriptions of vocal pieces display an abundance of embellishments, representative of the improvisational skills of some performers, and single lines of polyphonic compositions with keyboard accompaniment may also have been decorated, for example by a virtuoso viol player. There is little doubt that professional singers, too, ornamented their lines, both in solos with lute accompaniment and in vocal polyphony. Referring to the latter, some authorities cautioned against the simultaneous use of *passaggi* in different voices.

3. The Baroque period

(a) Italy: Early opera composers rejected elaboration of the kind that promoted purely musical values at the expense of textual meaning. One exception, dramatically justified, occurs in Monteverdi's *Orfeo* (1607), where Orfeo's anguish as he pleads for admission to Hades ('Possente spirto') is expressed through virtuoso embellishment in the early Baroque style. But in general there was a strong reaction against the excesses of the previous age. Caccini in *Le nuove musiche* (1602),

for example, decried the old way, which destroyed the shape and sense of the verse.

By the late 17th century the emphasis was shifting back to purely musical values and vocal virtuosity for its own sake, and ornamentation was reinstated with a vengeance. The stars of 18th-century *opera seria* aimed to impress with astonishing displays of extended improvised embellishment, especially for *da capo* repeats. Contemporary transcriptions and accounts testify that these elaborations were brilliant and highly imaginative but, then as now, the results were subject to criticism from some quarters. Benedetto Marcello satirized the practice in *Il teatro alla moda* (Venice, *c*.1720):

> If the modern composer should give lessons to some virtuosa of the opera house, let him have a care to charge her to enunciate badly, and with this object to teach her a great number of divisions and of graces, so that not a single word will be understood, and by this means the music will stand out better and be appreciated.

Recitative seems not to have been embellished, apart from the conventional addition of appoggiaturas.

Late Baroque Italian instrumental music followed similar trends. Players were expected to decorate slow movements (sometimes notated skeletally) with florid embellishment. In 1710 Estienne Roger published Corelli's op. 5 sonatas with the solo violin parts for the slow movements ornamented purportedly by the composer; although the authorship of these embellishments has not been authenticated, they are probably representative of early 18th-century practice.

Ornament signs are rare in 17th-century Italian instrumental music. Shortly after the turn of the century, however, it became more common to indicate trills, and small grace notes were borrowed from French music to represent other ornaments. Musical sources thus began to preserve the composer's intentions to a greater extent, though additional ornamentation of slow movements was still expected, as exemplified in Tartini's autograph manuscripts.

(b) France: Quantz (*Versuch*, 1752) distinguished thus between the French and Italian styles:

> Pieces in the French style are for the most part *pièces caractérisées*, and are composed with appoggiaturas and shakes in such a fashion that almost nothing may be added to what the composer has already written. In music after the Italian style, however, much is left to the caprice, and to the ability, of the performer.

These comments are probably applicable to late Baroque music in general. Whereas improvised ornamentation remained an important element of Italian style, French music seems to have been less accommodating: even simple ornaments were often indicated by signs explained in lengthy charts (D'Anglebert listed no fewer than 29 ornaments in 1689).

That had not been the case throughout the period. The repeats of the early 17th-century *air de cour* were subject to considerable ornamentation, but the practice declined later under the influence of Lully, who condemned such embroidery as 'ridiculous'. Only the simple graces remained in general use. For instrumental genres, especially French harpsichord music, the *agréments* were considered important and were indicated by small notes or signs. In the preface to his first book of harpsichord *ordres* (1713) François Couperin demanded that performers adhere strictly to his notated ornaments. Other composers were less rigid, leaving the choice to the performer.

(c) England and Germany: Both countries were influenced by Italian and French styles of ornamentation at different times. Late 17th-century English harpsichord music, for example, used ornament signs which, though differing from the French ones, were allied to them in practice. These are listed in Henry Purcell's *A Choice Collection of Lessons* (3/1699). 18th-century Italian style dominated English opera, as can be seen, for example, in Handel's works. A certain modest ornamentation was even allowed in his oratorios.

During the 17th century, German practice was closely allied to that of the Italians. However, as French music increased in popularity after 1700, many French signs were adopted. Bach made extensive use of them, briefly explained in a manuscript dating from 1720. Since these signs are also found in music outside the 'French style', they may be open to a variety of interpretations. Bach's unique synthesis of Italian, French, and German styles renders the subject of ornamentation in his music particularly complex. In general, he left little room for the addition of more than the simplest graces, preferring to write out intricate Italian-style ornamentation. His method is illustrated not only in his transcriptions of Italian compositions but also in his original works, for example in the slow movement of the Italian Concerto and in the two versions of the Sarabandes from the English Suites nos. 2 and 3.

Shortly after Bach's death, three important German treatises—those of Quantz (1752) and C. P. E. Bach (1753), both mentioned above, and Leopold Mozart's *Versuch* (1756)—were published. All three include detailed information on mid-century ornamentation practices as well as valuable advice on free ornamentation. In addition, C. P. E. Bach's sonatas with ornamented repeats published in 1760 provide a means of instructive comparison with his father's style of embellishment.

4. Since 1760

The evolution of the Classical style brought fundamental changes of attitude and taste concerning ornamentation. These reflected in part a conscious desire to notate music in sufficient detail to preserve the composer's intentions, and in part a growing need to provide guidance for amateurs. More important, they paralleled changes in musical style, as a 'noble simplicity' and a more dramatic conception were sought.

Old habits survived longest in Italian opera, where singers continued to embellish well into the 19th century. Increasingly this was contrary to the composer's will. In his preface to *Alceste* (1769) Gluck railed—ineffectively—against the vanity of singers. For the performance of his early opera *Lucio Silla* Mozart sketched some elaborations in the current taste, but in the later operas any ornamentation seems to have been fully notated, suggesting that none or very little should be added. Rossini, too, made a stand against the excesses still heard around 1810 by notating his desired ornamentation. Gradual though the process was, a more naturalistic style eventually prevailed, and ornamentation came to be regarded as an affectation of a bygone age.

Composers were quicker to exert control over ornamentation in instrumental music. During the Classical period improvised embellishment seems to have become less necessary and perhaps even undesirable, and the number of ornament signs in use also diminished. Whereas Mozart and Beethoven added ornaments (especially to slow movements) in performance, for publication they carefully wrote out the embellishments they required. Only some skeletal passages in Mozart's posthumously published piano concertos need filling out; and Beethoven is said to have flared up in anger when Czerny added some notes in a performance of the Quintet op. 16.

In the Romantic era, signs were still used for simple ornaments such as trills, turns, or mordents. Compound ornaments tended to be fully notated, in some cases avoiding ambiguity but in others creating much more. Although many regard the notation of 19th-century composers as sacrosanct, early sound recordings show that in practice even the most elaborate compositions were often freely embellished with little regard for the original notation.

During the 20th century, composers generally notated their music with a precision hitherto unknown, leaving virtually no opportunity for spontaneous embellishment or misinterpretation of signs. Latterly, some avant-garde composers returned a share of musical creation to the performer; but improvised ornamentation, in the sense of melodic decoration, is no longer a feature of Western art music. To add embellishment to a piece by Berg, for example, would be as unthinkable as performing a slow movement of a Corelli sonata without ornamentation.

See also PERFORMANCE PRACTICE.

SMcV/NPDC

📖 R. DONINGTON, *The Interpretation of Early Music* (London, 1963, 4/1989) · F. NEUMANN, *Ornamentation in Baroque and Post-Baroque Music* (Princeton, NJ, 1978, 3/1983) · R. DONINGTON, *Baroque Music: Style and Performance* (London, 1982) · H. M. BROWN and S. SADIE (eds.), *Performance Practice*, 2 vols. (London, 1989) · C. BROWN, *Classical and Romantic Performing Practice* (Oxford, 1999)

Ornstein, Leo (*b* Kremenchug, 11 Dec. 1892, 1893, or 1895; *d* Green Bay, WI, 24 Feb. 2002). Ukrainian-born American composer and pianist. The confusion over his date of birth began when his father added two years to his precociously gifted son's age so that the boy could enter the St Petersburg Conservatory. In 1907 the family left Russia and settled in the USA. Ornstein's music, which made ferocious use of brutal clusters and jagged rhythms, had an astonishing impact in the second decade of the 20th century, often in his own performances. Grainger mentioned him in parallel with Stravinsky and Skryabin and judged his keyboard innovations as pioneering as Debussy's and Ravel's; the critic James Huneker wrote that Schoenberg sounded tame in comparison.

From the 1920s Ornstein began to retreat from the hardest-edged expression of modernity, and his place in the public eye began to fade. He continued to give the occasional recital but devoted most of his time to running a music school in Philadelphia with his wife. His output falls into three periods, the third reconciling his first, tonal compositions with the second, extremist phase. Among his handful of orchestral works are a piano concerto (1923) and the *Lysistrata Suite* (1930); his chamber music includes a powerful piano quintet, three string quartets, and two sonatas each for violin and cello. But it was for his own instrument, the piano, that Ornstein wrote most readily, producing a steady stream of arresting pieces, often gathered into evocatively named suites, and eight sonatas, the last dating from 1990, when he was at least in his mid-90s.

MA

📖 F. H. MARTENS, *Leo Ornstein: The Man, his Ideas, his Work* (New York, 1918/*R*1975) · G. RUMSON, 'Leo Ornstein: From avant-garde to oblivion and back', *International Piano Quarterly*, 5/15 (2001), 40–3

orpharion. A wire-strung plucked instrument, similar to the *bandora (with which it was contemporaneous), but smaller and tuned like a lute (with the intervals 4th–4th–3rd–4th–4th). Like the bandora, it had a lobed outline. It was invented in England, possibly by John Rose in 1580. Two orpharions survive; both have a diagonal bridge and progressively slanting frets, so that the the bass strings are longer than the treble.

JMo

Orphée aux enfers ('Orpheus in the Underworld'). Opera in two acts by Offenbach to a libretto by Hector-Jonathan Crémieux and Ludovic Halévy after classical mythology (Paris, 1858); it was revised and expanded into four acts (Paris, 1874).

orphéon. The name given to French male-voice choral societies formed about 1835 in imitation of the German *Liedertafeln. From 1852 to 1860 Gounod was director of the Paris societies; by 1880 there were 1500 French *orphéons* with a total membership of 60,000.

Orpheus. 1. Symphonic poem by Liszt, originally composed as an introduction to his production of Gluck's *Orfeo ed Euridice* at Weimar in 1854.

2. Ballet in three scenes by Stravinsky, choreographed by George Balanchine (New York, 1948).

Orpheus britannicus ('The British Orpheus'). Title given to two volumes of songs by Purcell (the 'British Orpheus'), published posthumously (1698–1702) by Henry Playford, and to a volume of his songs published by John Walsh (1735). Britten and Pears edited and arranged several for voice or voices and piano or orchestra.

Orpheus in the Underworld. See ORPHÉE AUX ENFERS.

Orr, Buxton (Daeblitz) (*b* Glasgow, 18 April 1924; *d* Hereford, 27 Dec. 1997). Scottish composer. He studied composition with Benjamin Frankel and, like him, wrote a large number of film scores, especially for the Hammer horror series. He taught at the Guildhall School of Music and Drama and conducted the London Jazz Composers' Orchestra (1970–80). His compositions are eclectic; besides opera (*The Wager*, 1961) and music theatre (*Ring in the New*, 1986) he wrote many orchestral and chamber works, the latter including a series of six pieces called *Refrains* (1970–92).

AW

Orr, Robin [Robert Kemsley] (*b* Brechin, 2 June 1909). Scottish composer. He studied at Cambridge, in Siena with Alfredo Casella, and in Paris with Nadia Boulanger. In 1936 he embarked on a career as a university lecturer that culminated in his appointment to the chair of music at Cambridge (1965–75). His compositions, whose gritty harmony and rhythmic dynamism suggest influences as diverse as Hindemith and Shostakovich, include *Hermiston* (Edinburgh, 1975) and other operas, four symphonies, and church music.

PG

Ortiz, Diego (*b* Toledo, *c.*1510; *d* Naples, *c.*1570). Spanish viol player and composer. He was *maestro de capilla* of the viceregal chapel at Naples in the mid-16th century. His *Trattado de glosas* (Rome, 1553) is one of the earliest and most valuable treatises on viol-playing, providing formulas for ornamenting cadence patterns and intervals, and including arrangements of a madrigal and a chanson, as well as *recercadas* based on these and on common bass patterns. Ortiz also published (Venice, 1565) a collection of sacred vocal works: hymns, psalms, canticles, and Marian antiphons.   DA/OR

Osanna. See HOSANNA.

Osborne, Nigel (*b* Manchester, 23 June 1948). English composer. He studied at Oxford and in Poland, and has taught at Nottingham and Edinburgh universities. Such early works as the Cello Concerto and *I am Goya* for voice and four instruments (both 1977) have a distinctive expressionism. Later compositions, for example the Flute Concerto (1980) and the opera *The Electrification of the Soviet Union* (Glyndebourne, 1987), are more expansive but retain a forceful rhetoric, with material that often has explicit social or political content. During the 1990s Osborne spent much time working on behalf of the people of Sarajevo, his music from this time including the *Adagio for Vedran Smailović* (1993) and the opera *Sarajevo* (1994).   AW

oscillator. An electronic circuit designed to produce a stream of electric vibrations which can be fed to a loudspeaker to emit sound waves. See ELECTRONIC MUSICAL INSTRUMENTS.   JBo

ossia (It., 'or'). A term used to designate passages added as alternatives to the original (and usually easier). Beethoven and Liszt, however, often added alternative passages of difficulty at least as great as those they could replace.

ostinato (It., 'persistent'). A fairly short melodic, rhythmic, or chordal phrase repeated continuously throughout a piece or section. Although it is one of the most common and effective continuity devices in music, ostinato is not merely repetitive, like the accompaniment to a Viennese waltz; it also has a structural or thematic function, or both. It is present in Western art music from medieval times to the present day, and in traditional and popular musics. It is especially striking in rock music and jazz as a progressive or structural device. In jazz it is used as an accompanimental figure, generally of one, two, or four bars, repeated without interruption beneath freely composed or improvised parts. In Western music, ostinato is often a characteristic of a more specific compositional procedure, as in the *chaconne, *passa- caglia, and *ground, and in *isorhythm and *minimal- ism. Where it is applied to a set bass pattern it is known as *basso ostinato*.

Melodic ostinatos almost invariably contain a distinctive rhythm as a secondary element. This is certainly the case in 17th- and 18th-century 'lament' arias, with their descending, often chromatic, ostinato basses—for example in the famous aria from Purcell's *Dido and Aeneas* 'When I am laid in earth', where the unvarying slow triple-metre pattern adds solemnity and pathos to the effect of the superimposed voice part (cf. Cavalli, and Monteverdi's *Lamento della ninfa*)—and in the jaunty syncopated figure that accompanies *Zefiro torna*, from Monteverdi's sixth book of madrigals. It is also true of 13th- and 14th-century isorhythmic motets with their ostinato tenors, and of more expansive bass-accompaniment ostinatos in 19th-century piano music, for example Chopin's Nocturne op. 27 no. 2 and Mendelssohn's 'Venetian Boat Songs' op. 19 no. 6, op. 30 no. 6, and op. 62 no. 5 in his *Lieder ohne Worte*.

Rhythmically animated ostinatos are a particular feature of Stravinsky's style, as in the Symphony in Three Movements and *The Rite of Spring*. 'Mars' from Holst's orchestral suite *The Planets*, the third movement of Britten's *Sinfonia da requiem*, and Ravel's *Boléro* are other striking examples. It could be argued that the characteristic triple-time accompaniments to Chopin's waltzes are clear examples of rhythmic ostinatos. They are, however, intended not as thematic repetitive figures but rather as rhythmic–harmonic accompaniment and are therefore not true ostinatos. Less animated but equally persistent are the rhythmic ostinatos that pervade such arias and sections of operas as the solemn opening of Puccini's *Gianni Schicchi* (1918) or 'Were I thy bride' from Sullivan's *The Yeomen of the Guard*.

The most simple chordal ostinatos appear in jazz, where a pair of chords, for example C–B♭ or C minor–F, may recur as a basis for variation. Obstinate repetitive chord patterns feature in Stravinsky's *The Rite of Spring* and *The Firebird*.

Harmonic ostinatos occur when a chordal pattern is mapped out but where the melodic and rhythmic element is less pronounced, as for example in the Chorus of Shades in Rossini's *Mosè in Egitto*.

CRW

Ostrčil, Otakar (*b* Prague, 25 Feb. 1879; *d* Prague, 20 Aug. 1935). Czech composer and conductor. Although he initially studied and taught languages, he took composition lessons from Fibich and was influenced by the musical aesthetician Otakar Hostinský. He gained experience conducting choirs and at the Vinohrady

Theatre in Prague. In 1920 he succeeded Kovařovic as music director of the National Theatre, a post he occupied until his death. There he encouraged and maintained high standards of performance, and in the 1930s he made formative recordings of Smetana's operas. As a member of the Society for Modern Music he encouraged young Czech composers and introduced many important foreign works including Debussy's *Pelléas et Mélisande* (1921) and Berg's *Wozzeck* (1926).

Ostrčil's interest in modern music, his championing of Smetana's operas, and his work as an administrator were important in forming musical taste in Prague between the wars. His early compositions, especially the opera *Vlasty skon* ('Vlasta's Death', 1903), shows the influence of Fibich. Later stage works including *Poupě* ('The Bud', 1910) and *Honzovo království* ('Johnny's Kingdom', 1933) indicate a deliberate move away from excessive Romanticism. Ostrčil's orchestral works from the 1920s (*Léto*, 'Summer', 1926; *Křížová cesta*, 'The Way of the Cross', 1928) illustrate his absorption with counterpoint, and a flexible approach to tonality, though this never tipped over into atonality.   JSM

Osud ('Fate'; 'Destiny'). Opera by Janáček to a libretto by himself and Fedora Bartošová; he completed it in 1907 for performance in Prague but that never took place. It was given in a version by Václav Nosek in Brno in 1958 and in its original form in České Budějovice in 1978.

Oswald von Wolkenstein (*b* Schöneck in Pustertal, South Tyrol, *c.*1376; *d* Merano, 2 Aug. 1445). South Tyrolean poet and composer. Born into a noble family, he spent much of his life travelling in the service of the nobility, and later was a diplomat for King Sigismund. His travels took him to the Middle East and Africa, as well as to Italy and other parts of Europe. His poetry, which covers a wide range of subjects and includes many autobiographical references, is of considerable importance. Much of it is set to music, either monophony or polyphony, that either was composed by Oswald himself, or draws on works by an international array of composers, including Landini, Nicolas Grenon, Pierre Fontaine, and Binchois.   DA/JM

Otello. 1. Opera in four acts by Verdi to a libretto by Arrigo Boito after Shakespeare's play *Othello, the Moor of Venice* (1603–4) (Milan, 1887).

2. Opera in three acts by Rossini to a libretto by Francesco Berio di Salsa after Shakespeare (Naples, 1816).

ôtez (Fr.). 'Take off', e.g. *ôtez les sourdines*, 'take off the mutes'.

Othmayr, Caspar (*b* Amberg, nr Nuremberg, 12 March 1515; *d* Nuremberg, 4 Feb. 1553). German composer. He studied at Heidelberg University and may have worked at the Palatine court there. In 1545 he became rector of the monastic school at Heilsbronn and in 1547 a canon at the monastery of St Gumbertus, Ansbach. He was one of the earliest Lutheran composers; even his first work (1546) attests to his beliefs. His output of almost exclusively vocal music includes examples of all the leading contemporary genres. His most important works are his German secular songs, including *Tenorlieder*, in four or five parts; his experimental treatment of the tenor in some of these is unique.

PW

ottava (It.). 'Octave'; *all'ottava*, 'at the octave', an indication to play an octave above (*all'ottava alta*) or below (*all'ottava bassa*) the written pitch; *coll'ottava*, 'with the octave', found in orchestral scores to show that one instrument should play in octaves with another (*ottava alta, ottava sopra*, 'octave above'; *ottava bassa, ottava sotto*, 'octave below').

ottone (It.). 'Brass'; *stromenti d'ottone*, 'brass instruments'.

oud. See 'ŪD.

Our Hunting Fathers. Symphonic song cycle, op. 8 (1936), by Britten, for soprano or tenor solo and orchestra, a setting of a text devised by W. H. Auden.

Ours, L' ('The Bear'). Nickname of Haydn's Symphony no. 82 in C major (1786), the first of the Paris symphonies, so called because of the 'growling' theme at the beginning of the last movement.

Ouseley, Sir Frederick Arthur Gore (*b* London, 12 Aug. 1825; *d* Hereford, 6 April 1889). English church musician and scholar. The son of a wealthy baronet, orientalist, and ambassador, he became a prominent figure in the mid-19th-century revival of English church music. As professor of music at Oxford from 1855 (a post he held concurrently with that of precentor of Hereford Cathedral) he was responsible for modernizing the Oxford music degrees, principally through the introduction of written examinations as an addition to the 'Exercise'. But his importance lies chiefly in his ideologically driven foundation (at his own expense) of St Michael's, Tenbury, the first collegiate church in England since the Reformation, intended as 'a model for the choral service of the church in these realms'. A distinguished scholar, he provided Tenbury with a fine collection of ancient manuscripts (now mainly in the Bodleian Library, Oxford), and his musicological interests were realized in the (Royal) Musical

Association, founded in 1874, of which he was elected the first president. DA/JD1

Outis. Opera in one act by Berio to a libretto by the composer and Dario Del Corno (Milan, 1996).

ouvert and clos (Fr., 'open' and 'closed'; It.: *aperto*, *chiuso*). In some 14th- and 15th-century vocal forms, such as the *ballade* and the *virelai*, repeated sections are given alternative endings; these are labelled *ouvert* and *clos*, or *aperto* and *chiuso*, and correspond to the present-day use of *prima volta* and *seconda volta*, or 'first-time bar' and 'second-time bar'.

ouverture (Fr.). 'Overture'.

overblowing. The technique whereby woodwind players reach the upper registers of their instruments, made possible by a tube's ability to sound certain intervals above its fundamental vibrating frequency through increased air pressure. The flute, oboe, and bassoon overblow at the octave, the clarinet at the 12th. Further modification is required for successful execution: clarinettists adjust the position and pressure of lip–reed contact, while flautists alter their embouchure and the angle of their air jet. SM

overdotting. The exaggeration in performance of dotted rhythms, a practice adopted for much Baroque music (see DOT, 3).

overtones. See ACOUSTICS, 5.

overture. A piece of instrumental music composed as an introduction to an opera, oratorio, ballet, or other dramatic work, or intended for independent concert performance. In the Baroque period the title 'Ouvertüre' was sometimes applied to a keyboard or orchestral suite (Bach), or to its opening movement; and in 18th-century England 'Overture' could serve as an alternative title for a symphony (as for Haydn's 'London' Symphonies).

1. Dramatic overture; 2. Concert overture

1. Dramatic overture

Dramatic entertainments in the 16th century, and the earliest operas and oratorios at the beginning of the 17th, either lacked any sort of introduction or began with a flourish of trumpets or other brief call to attention (as in the opening Toccata of Monteverdi's *Orfeo*, 1607). As opera and oratorio developed and became more organized, so did the introduction. Mid-17th-century operas often began with a slow, duple-metre one; this was to form the basis of a standard overture-type which, through its later association with the operas of Lully and other composers of French opera, came to be known as the French overture. In its

conventional form (such as Handel used for *Messiah*) it is characterized by a grave, sometimes pompous opening, with plentiful dotted rhythms and suspensions, leading straight into a fast, lively section in imitative, even fugal style, which often closes by echoing the mood of the first section. This pair of movements was sometimes followed by a moderately slow dance movement (as in the minuet in Handel's overture to *Samson*), or the entire first section might be repeated.

Late in the 17th century a tripartite overture appeared in Naples, cast in short fast–slow–fast sections, which came to be known as the Italian overture, though it was almost invariably entitled 'Sinfonia'. It was the ancestor of both the Classical symphony, in which all three sections became fully developed movements and were often supplemented by a slow introduction and a minuet and trio, and of the Classical opera overture, in which the second and third movements were reduced and then discarded.

Until the mid-18th century there was little connection, beyond a general spiritual conformity, between an overture and what followed. In his famous preface to *Alceste* (1767), however, Gluck sought a more intimate correspondence between the two: his overture to *Iphigénie en Tauride* (1779) traces closely the progress of a thunderstorm in an effort to set the mood for the first scene, with which the overture merges without a break. Haydn took this even further in *The Creation* (1798), whose overture, with its vivid 'Representation of Chaos', actually sets the whole drama in motion and leads straight into the opening recitative. However, the typical Classical opera overture, known to us chiefly in Mozart's mature operas, consisted of a brief slow introduction followed by a fast movement closely related to *sonata form, but without a repeated exposition and generally with an abbreviated development section. In *Don Giovanni*, *Così fan tutte*, and *Die Zauberflöte* the overture contains a motto theme or striking passages from the opera.

The form continued to evolve in Italian operas of the early 19th century. Rossini's overtures, such as that to *Il barbiere di Siviglia*, typically have no significant development section but an enlarged coda with a crescendo leading to a loud conclusion. The 'motto' idea was more strongly developed outside Italy, for example by Spontini, Weber, and Meyerbeer. Wagner's early opera overtures still conformed to the Classical pattern, but in *Lohengrin*, the *Ring*, and *Tristan und Isolde* he preferred a fairly short, independent prelude ('Vorspiel'), and some of the preludes he wrote for acts other than the first are as long and significant as any of his opening overtures. Verdi showed a similar tendency in the course of his long career.

An effective type of overture that served well for 19th-century comic or light opera and operetta was one put together from a *medley or *potpourri of tunes taken straight from the opera, with little or no linking material. This was particularly popular with Auber, Offenbach, and Sullivan, and its influence continued in the overtures for 20th-century musical comedies.

2. Concert overture

Although Mendelssohn has a claim to the title of inventor of the concert overture, it had its precursors in the performance, as separate concert pieces, of Mozart's later opera overtures and of those that Beethoven wrote for stage plays by Goethe (*Egmont*) and Collin (*Coriolan*), and the rejected *Leonore* overtures originally intended for his opera *Fidelio*. Other early 19th-century concert overtures were 'occasional' (Beethoven's *Die Weihe des Hauses*) or abstract (Schubert's 'in the Italian style'), but it is the descriptive, poetic pieces such as Mendelssohn's *The Hebrides* and *A Midsummer Night's Dream* and Berlioz's *Carnaval romain* that typify the Romantic concert overture. Some of these pieces were written to commemorate events (Tchaikovsky's *1812*, Brahms's *Academic Festival Overture*); others were inspired by literature or art (Berlioz's *Le Roi Lear*, Liszt's *Hunnenschlacht*); still others, like Brahms's *Tragic Overture*, have no known extra-musical connections.

A few overtures are narrative and programmatic, but more usually they are pure mood-pieces, cast in the same Classical forms as the dramatic overture. But as the Romantics' attitude to form and expression grew ever more liberal as the 19th century advanced, the concert overture gave way to the freer, more flexible, and more fashionable *symphonic poem, or tone-poem, developed by Liszt and brought to maturity by Richard Strauss. Some composers continued to prefer the term 'overture', for example Elgar (*Cockaigne*, 1901).

PS/JN/NT

Owen Wingrave. Opera in two acts by Britten to a libretto by Myfanwy Piper after Henry James's short story (BBC television, 1971; staged London, 1973).

Oxford Movement. See ANGLICAN PARISH CHURCH MUSIC; HYMN, 4.

'Oxford' Symphony. Nickname of Haydn's Symphony no. 92 in G major (1789), so called because it was performed when Haydn received an honorary doctorate from Oxford University in 1791 (though he did not compose it with Oxford in mind).

Oxford University Press (OUP). English firm of publishers, a division of Oxford University. The development of OUP as a major music-publishing house dates from 1925, when Hubert Foss (1899–1953) created a separate music department. By 1931 he had amassed nearly 2000 titles, the list including many important English composers, among them Vaughan Williams, Walton, Rawsthorne, Lambert, and Warlock. OUP has since published a complete edition of Walton's works and continues to foster new generations of composers, including Barry, Finnissy, Buller, and Skempton in the UK, and Gerald Plain, Larsen, Hilary Tann, and Zhou Long in the USA.

Such well-known anthologies as *The Oxford Book of Carols* and *The Oxford Song Book* have long been at the commercial core of the music department. Choral music, both sacred and secular, continues to be an important part of the publishing programme, with the preparation of new editions, anthologies, and contemporary works. The firm's list also includes an extensive range of educational music.

OUP has long been renowned as a leading publisher of music books. Seminal works have included Tovey's *Essays in Musical Analysis*, *The Oxford History of Music* (now *The New Oxford History of Music*), *The Oxford Companion to Music* (first published in 1938), concise dictionaries of music, opera, and dance, the Master Musicians series, and many important monographs. OUP also publishes journals including *Music and Letters* (1955), *Early Music* (1973), and the *Journal of the Royal Musical Association*.   HA

    📖 D. HINNELLS, *An Extraordinary Performance: Hubert Foss and the Early Years of Music Publishing at the Oxford University Press* (Oxford, 1998)

Oxyrhynchos Hymn. The earliest Christian hymn (AD *c*.300) for which the music is preserved (in Greek vocal notation). It takes its name from the place in Egypt where the papyrus was discovered.

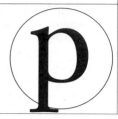

P, p. 1. Abbreviation for *piano*.

2. Abbreviation for 'pedal' in piano music.

3. Abbreviation for *pédalier* (Fr.), the pedalboard of an organ, or for *Positiv* (Ger.), 'choir organ'.

Pachelbel, Johann (*b.* Nuremberg, *bapt.* 1 Sept. 1653; *d* Nuremberg, March 1706). German organist and composer. After musical tuition in his home town, he was admitted in 1669 to the University of Altdorf (where he served also as parish organist), but was forced to abandon his studies through lack of funds. Thereafter, in the restless manner not untypical of musicians of his time, he accepted a series of posts: in 1673, although a Lutheran, as deputy organist at St Stephen's Cathedral, Vienna; in 1677 at the Eisenach court, where he became friendly with Bach's father and others of his family; in 1678, for a lengthier period, as organist at the Prediger church in Erfurt, where his first wife and child died of the plague; in 1690 at the Württemberg court in Stuttgart; and briefly in 1692 at Gotha, as town organist. Finally, in 1695, he settled back in Nuremberg as organist of St Sebald, where he remained until his death.

While at Erfurt Pachelbel wrote some 70 organ chorale preludes, in which all the principal techniques and structural patterns of the time are exploited, and at St Sebald, *Magnificat* fugues (for Vespers) together with non-liturgical toccatas, fantasias, polythematic ricercars, and fugues of vivid character. Only two collections of his organ music were published in his lifetime: *Musikalische Sterbens-Gedancken* ('Musical Thoughts on Death'; Erfurt, 1683), a set of chorale variations in memory of his deceased wife and child, and *Acht Choräle* (Nuremberg, 1693). His important contribution to Protestant vocal music, made principally during his final decade at St Sebald, includes motets, 'concerto-aria' works (combining ode and biblical texts), *Magnificat* settings, and settings of chorale and psalm verses in grand concertato style, with single and double choruses, wind, strings, and continuo. WT/BS

Pacific 231. Orchestral work (1923) by Honegger, the first of his *Mouvements symphoniques*; it is named after a locomotive.

Pacini, Giovanni (*b* Catania, Sicily, 17 Feb. 1796; *d* Pescia, nr Lucca, 6 Dec. 1867). Italian composer. The son of a famous operatic tenor, he studied singing and composition at the Bologna and Venice conservatories. He produced his first opera in 1813 and had a series of successes in the period 1825–35 with works in a Rossinian style. After a failure in 1835 he retired to found and direct a music school in Viareggio. About five years later he returned to active composition for the theatre, achieving renewed success with *Saffo* (Naples, 1842), an opera that showed that he had adapted to the new, post-Rossinian style of Bellini and then Donizetti. Pacini was, even by early 19th-century Italian standards, enormously prolific, leaving some 80 operas and a lively volume of memoirs. DA/RP

Paderewski, Ignacy Jan (*b* Kursk, Podolia, 6/18 Nov. 1860; *d* New York, 29 June 1941). Polish pianist, composer, and statesman. He was one of the most successful pianists of his era, and certainly the most highly paid. He showed musical gifts at an early age, becoming a student at the Warsaw Conservatory when he was 12. He moved to Vienna to take piano lessons from Leschetizky, and quickly scored such an enormous success at a concert in Paris that an international career beckoned. Paderewski, however, had only a small repertory, so he returned to Leschetizky to work on some new programmes. Thereafter he toured Europe and in 1891 made his debut in America (where he hired his own railway carriage, with a chef and valet), playing to adulatory audiences.

Paderewski's pianistic style was characterized (as was Leschetizky's, on the evidence of piano-roll recordings) by copious rubato and an extreme use of arpeggiation of chords and deliberate asynchronization of the hands—the latter designed to emphasize the tone-colour of the melody. His recordings were all made after he was 50, and, though they probably do not show him at his technical best, they display a powerful dramatic sweep allied to great beauty and variety of sonority. On the concert platform, his commanding physical appearance complemented the musical effect of his performances, as had that of Liszt and Anton Rubinstein before him.

As a composer Paderewski never developed a truly individual style. His opera *Manru* (1901) benefited from numerous early performances but failed to maintain a place in the repertory. The same is true of his epic and rambling Symphony (1908). The piano music is more interesting, though the once hugely popular Minuet in G is a pastiche of stultifying triviality. Paderewski's most endearing work is probably the limpid Nocturne in B♭ major, of which he himself made a subtle recording.

In later life Paderewski's fame, combined with his tireless promotion of the cause of Polish independence and generosity with time and money, led him to be appointed Prime Minister of Poland at the end of World War I. He had, however, little interest or ability in politics and soon resigned, preferring to be regarded simply as an elder statesman. He continued to tour as a pianist for the rest of his life, and even appeared in a film, *Moonlight Sonata*, in which he was cast as a charismatic elderly concert-pianist—a role unlikely to have taxed his acting ability.   KH

📖 A. ZAMOYSKI, *Paderewski* (New York and London, 1982)

Padmâvatî. *Opéra-ballet* in two acts by Roussel to a libretto by Louis Laloy (Paris, 1923).

padovana (It.). 'Pavan'.

paduana (It.). 'Pavan'.

Paër [Paer], Ferdinando (*b* Parma, 1 June 1771; *d* Paris, 3 May 1839). Italian composer. In 1792 he became *maestro di cappella* at Parma, where his opera *Orphée et Euridice* had been staged the previous year. His first Italian opera, *Circe*, was given in Venice in 1792; it was followed by several others, including *L'Idomeneo* and *Griselda*. He spent some years in Vienna, where he heard Mozart's music, then became Kapellmeister of the Dresden court chapel. It was in Dresden that his opera *Leonore, ossia L'amore conjugale* was staged in 1804 (Beethoven adapted the libretto for his own *Fidelio* the following year). Napoleon greatly admired his music and in 1806 took him to Warsaw; on their return to Paris, Paër was put in charge of the imperial chapel.

Paër's success continued with his appointment, succeeding Spontini, as director of the Théâtre Italien in 1812, but from 1824 to 1827 he unwillingly shared the post with Rossini, then resigned. He continued to be held in high esteem, however, and in 1832 became director of Louis Philippe's private chapel. He wrote over 50 operas, of which *Agnese* (1809) and *Le Maître de chapelle, ou Le Souper imprévu* ('The Chapel-Master, or The Unexpected Supper', 1821) were the best known; they were admired for their lyricism, instrumentation, and wit. His other works include instrumental music, cantatas, three oratorios, and sacred music. His style shows the influence of Italian composers and of Mozart and Beethoven.   WT/RP

Paganini, Nicolò (*b* Genoa, 27 Oct. 1782; *d* Nice, 27 May 1840). Italian violinist and composer. He was the most famous violinist of his time. Taught initially by his father, he also took composition lessons in Genoa. He was soon giving public concerts, and when he went to study in Parma in 1794 the famous violinist Alessandro Rolla said he could teach him nothing. He did, however, study composition in Parma, with Paër, writing numerous instrumental works. In 1796 he returned to Genoa, and in 1800 went with his family to Livorno. A year later he settled in Lucca, as leader of a newly formed orchestra, and two years after that was appointed violinist to the court there. In December 1809 he left to pursue a solo career.

For the next 18 years Paganini concentrated his concert-giving within the Italian peninsula, his triumphant success in Milan in 1813 consolidating his position as the foremost virtuoso of his generation. He also conducted frequently and composed a series of works for violin, almost all of which were calculated to exploit his prodigious playing skills. Some bouts of serious illness left him with a cadaverous appearance that only enhanced his charisma. In 1828 he travelled to Vienna for a series of wildly successful concerts, so launching a considerable European career, taking him to almost all the major centres. Although there were pockets of quite serious critical resistance, he had particular success in Germany (1829–31) and in Paris and London (1831–2). In 1832 he commissioned a work for viola from Berlioz, who eventually produced *Harold en Italie*. Paganini never performed it: by 1834 his career was in a decline brought about by illness, injury, and persistent (though false) rumours that he was a miser who would never dedicate his talent to charitable causes (something expected of every prominent artist during this period).

Paganini's last years were dogged by ill health: in 1838 he lost his voice completely. Although he rarely performed publicly, he remained in the public eye by means of a variety of ventures. In Parma he became director of the Teatro Ducale, making many wide-ranging (and ultimately rejected) proposals for orchestral reform; in Paris he briefly backed a project for a Casino Paganini. The latter was a financial disaster, though he retained enough wealth to present Berlioz with a gift of 20,000 francs in 1838 (a sum that enabled him to write his 'dramatic symphony' *Roméo et Juliette*). Paganini died in Nice, with no fewer than 11 Stradivari instruments (and many others of comparable value) to his name.

Paganini had an enormous influence on subsequent generations of violinists, partly through his technical example and then—more long-lasting—through his compositions, particularly the famous *Caprices* for solo violin (*c*.1805), which remain a virtuoso pinnacle. Many of the most demanding techniques of the present-day violinist are associated primarily with him, including 'ricochet' bowing, left-hand pizzicato, and double-stop harmonics. But just as important was his impact on a whole generation of composers who attempted to emulate the *Caprices*—or his virtuoso style more generally—on the piano: after first hearing him play in Paris in 1832, Liszt consciously cultivated himself as the 'Paganini of the piano'; Chopin and Schumann were hardly less influenced, and his effect is felt as late as Brahms and Rakhmaninov. The violin concertos, written later, are less innovatory in formal terms, recalling those of an earlier generation of French virtuosos; but they nevertheless rise far above the routine in their level of musical invention, demonstrating that—as he avowed—composition was an art he always treated with the utmost seriousness. Paganini was, in short, a key influence on the composers who came to their first maturity in the early 19th-century: the idea, perhaps even the ideal, of instrumental virtuosity was for many encapsulated within his person.   RP

📖 A. Kendall, *Paganini: A Biography* (London, 1982) · E. Neill, *Paganini* (Genoa, 1994) · P. Borer, *The Twenty-Four Caprices of N. Paganini* (Zürich, 1997)

Pagliacci ('Players'). Opera in a prologue and two acts by Leoncavallo to his own libretto based on a newspaper crime report (Milan, 1892); it is usually performed in a double bill with Mascagni's **Cavalleria rusticana*, the two operas being referred to popularly as 'Cav and Pag'.

Paisible, James (*b* France, *c*.1656; *d* London, *bur*. 17 Aug. 1721). English composer of French birth. A descendant of French court musicians, he is thought to have gone to London in 1673. He held court posts as recorder player to Charles II (he married one of Charles's former mistresses, Mary Davies) and instrumentalist to James II, in whose chapel, as a Roman Catholic, he served; he followed James into exile in France, but then returned to London in the early 1690s with a post under Princess (later Queen) Anne. Paisible worked in the London theatres as both composer and instrumentalist (playing the bass violin as well as wind instruments) and had an active part in London concert life; he was specially admired as a recorder player. He wrote instrumental music, including sonatas and suites for his own instrument, and dances, airs, and act tunes

for the theatre, as well as *The Queen's Farewell* on the death of Mary (1695).   JAS

Paisiello, Giovanni (*b* Roccaforzata, nr Taranto, 9 May 1740; *d* Naples, 5 June 1816). Italian composer. His career spanned about 40 years, during which he produced over 80 operas, among them some of the best and most popular of the period. In 1754 he entered the Conservatorio di S. Onofrio in Naples, remaining there until 1763. His comic opera *I francesi brillianti* was given unsuccessfully at Bologna the next year, but it fared better in Modena some weeks after its premiere. In 1766 Paisiello returned to Naples, where he composed comic operas for the Nuovo and Fiorentini theatres. Initially he enjoyed the favour of the Neapolitan court, but it was withdrawn after a scandal in 1768. In 1776 he accepted an offer to become *maestro di cappella* to Catherine the Great. At St Petersburg he wrote Italian operas with clear characterization and increased musical complexity to maintain the interest of a non-Italian-speaking audience. His contract was renewed in 1779 and 1782, but he became homesick and, having obtained a year's paid leave, left Russia for good in 1784. On his way back to Italy he produced *Il re Teodoro in Venezia* in Vienna (1784), and this, with *Il barbiere di Siviglia* (1782), left clear traces on Mozart's style in *Le nozze di Figaro* and *Don Giovanni*.

Even before his departure from St Petersburg, Paisiello had been named opera composer to Ferdinand IV of Naples. After the successful premiere of *Antigono* in 1785 he was granted a pension with the proviso that he compose at least one *opera seria* each year for the Teatro S. Carlo. His most celebrated work from this period was *Nina, o sia La pazza per amore* (1789), the outstanding example of sentimental comedy in late 18th-century opera. When the French took Naples in 1799 he supported them—an unfortunate move, since the Bourbons returned to power later the same year. In 1801 he was finally pardoned, but he went to Paris at the invitation of Napoleon, staying until 1804. In 1806 the French again ousted the Bourbons from Naples; Paisiello became composer to the court of Joseph Bonaparte and was also made one of the directors of the new state conservatory. Following a second defeat of the French in 1815 Paisiello was pardoned in a general amnesty, and he retained his posts until his death over a year later.   DA/TRJ

📖 J. L. Hunt, *Giovanni Paisiello: His Life as an Opera Composer* (New York, 1975)

palaeography. The study of ancient (Gk.: *palaios*) and medieval handwriting. It is useful in music, as in other disciplines, for the study of manuscripts containing music and other material, in tracing all the elements of manuscript production—for example date, provenance, and scribal activity. In music palaeography it is necessary to be familiar with styles not only of script but also of notations. As with handwriting, medieval notation varies considerably by period and by region; furthermore, individual music scribes, even from within the same scriptorium or workshop, may be identified by their notational style in the same way that scribes who wrote text in music manuscripts may be identified by particular features of their script. Among the many elements of production that may provide information about a manuscript, the use of the rastrum may also be instructive (see RASTROLOGY).

Study of a manuscript must also take into account that its scribe almost certainly introduced differences into the text that he was copying, either deliberately or accidentally. The study of such variants is known as textual criticism.

Because of the ephemeral nature of musical trends in the Middle Ages and early Renaissance it was often the case that music manuscripts were destroyed to be used for other purposes, and the job of a modern palaeographer may well include identifying fragments of manuscripts. Sometimes a piece of parchment would be scraped off and reused for another purpose; in these cases, known as palimpsests (from Gk. *palin*, 'again', and *psestos*, 'scraped'), the original content of the parchment may be visible under ultraviolet light.   ABUL

Palester, Roman (*b* Śniatyn [now Snyatyn, Ukraine], 28 Dec. 1907; *d* Paris, 25 Aug. 1989). Polish composer. He moved to Paris in 1947, then worked for Radio Free Europe in Munich in 1952–72. Consequently his music remained banned in Poland until the late 1970s. His early musical style was neo-classical, with elements of folklore (*Dance from Osmołody*, 1932). He soon developed a grittier language, as in the cyclic Second Symphony (1942). In the early 1950s he aligned himself more closely with the serial ethos of Berg and later enriched his 12-note techniques with chance procedures.

ATH

Palestrina. Opera in three acts by Pfitzner to his own libretto (Munich, 1917).

Palestrina, alla. See ALLA PALESTRINA.

Palestrina, Giovanni Pierluigi da (*b* probably Palestrina, *c*.1525; *d* Rome, 2 Feb. 1594). Italian composer. He was most celebrated for his church music.

1. Life and works; 2. Influence and reputation

1. Life and works

Palestrina was the eldest of four children of reasonably well-off parents, and went at an early age to S. Maria Maggiore in Rome as a choirboy, remaining after his voice broke (tradition has it that he became a tenor). In 1544 he was organist and singing teacher at the cathedral in Palestrina, a small town in the Sabine hills about 25 miles from Rome. He married Lucrezia Gori in 1547, and they had two sons. Four years later the Bishop of Palestrina, Cardinal Giovanni Maria del Monte, was elected Pope Julius III, and he took the composer with him to be director of the Cappella Giulia.

Palestrina wrote the *Missa 'Ecce sacerdos magnus'* in honour of his patron, and it was published in his first book of 1554 with a dedication to Julius; he was rewarded the following year with a place in the papal choir at the Sistine Chapel, despite the opposition of its members, who claimed the prerogative to appoint their own colleagues. This work (and others published in the same volume) reveals Palestrina's mastery of the Netherlands polyphonic style. Soon after this he published some other volumes, including one of competent but somewhat uninteresting madrigals to Petrarch's verse. In spite of their lack of sensuality he was to regret having set secular texts in later years.

Although Palestrina was thus gaining a substantial reputation, the next few months were difficult. Pope Julius died in 1555; Pope Marcellus II was elected, but died within three weeks; and Pope Paul IV, scandalized to find married men in his choir, turned Palestrina out, but gave him a pension. The following month Palestrina was made *maestro di cappella* at St John Lateran, where he found the musical arrangements in some disarray, even though Lassus had been in charge until the previous year. He built up the choir, but in 1560 resigned his post after a quarrel with the authorities about the allowance given him for the choirboys. He seems to have been without employment for some months, but in March 1561 returned as *maestro* to the other great Roman basilica, S. Maria Maggiore, where he had been a choirboy.

These years saw Palestrina's rise to fame, and also a change in style (in accordance with the requirements of the Council of Trent) towards a simpler way of writing that enabled the words to be clearly heard. The story that his *Missa Papae Marcelli* prevented the abolition of composed church music in favour of a return to plainchant is untrue, although it was being told in the early 17th century; the mass was probably written to satisfy Pope Marcellus II's demand that music for Holy Week should be suitably restrained and the text properly understood. This aspect of Palestrina's style is also exemplified by his *Missa brevis*, with its homophonic texture, clear presentation of the words, and continual variety of choral sound.

Palestrina remained at S. Maria Maggiore for about six years, and then accepted an offer to direct the music of Cardinal Ippolito II d'Este at the Villa d'Este at Tivoli. This position was well paid and probably had a less demanding daily routine; it also had the advantage of summers at Tivoli, a delightfully cool place in the hills. It may have been there that Palestrina came into contact with more modern ideas, which emanated from the Este rulers of Ferrara in northern Italy; his motets over the next 20 years show awareness of the vigorous rhythms and the word-painting of the madrigal composers, as well as of the grand manner of polychoral music developing in both Rome and Venice. He refused a post at the imperial court in Vienna, and another to take charge of the new Gonzaga chapel dedicated to S. Barbara in Mantua (although he did write a series of masses for use there). In 1571 Animuccia died, and Palestrina succeeded him as choirmaster at the Cappella Giulia; he remained there for the rest of his life.

In 1567 and 1570 his second and third books of masses were printed in Rome, but the next ten years were not happy ones, a series of epidemics carrying off two sons, two brothers, and, in 1580, his wife; he published less, and his second and third books of motets (1572, 1575) may have been retrospective. Immediately after his wife's death he took minor orders as a step towards entering the priesthood, and was awarded a benefice. However, in February 1581 he suddenly married again. His second wife was a wealthy widow who had inherited her late husband's companies dealing in leather and fur, and Palestrina took to running the business with remarkable aptitude. His new life is reflected in both the number and the nature of his works. The most remarkable is the cycle of settings of the Song of Songs (1584), where the imagery is similar enough to that of contemporary love poetry to accommodate a madrigalian word-painting and a less strict style of writing. In view of this it is ironic that in the preface he apologizes for the sins of his youth, when he wrote of human rather than divine love. Some of the masses from these years are composed in a splendid Counter-Reformation manner; among them is the fine *Assumpta est Maria*, based on his own motet, where a rich effect is gained from a six-part choir with voices kept constantly in their upper registers. He also published some spiritual madrigals in 1581, and some secular ones in 1586.

Towards the end of his life an assistant did most of the routine work at the Cappella Giulia, although Palestrina continued to write for and attend the great festivals at St Peter's. In 1592 the new pope, Clement VIII, increased the pension granted to Palestrina years before on his dismissal from the papal choir, and he also received a kind of musician's *Festschrift* in the form of a book of Vesper psalms contributed by several leading Italian composers (including Asola, Croce, and Gastoldi) and dedicated to him. He died both prosperous and honoured, and was buried in St Peter's (the chapel has since been pulled down and the present whereabouts of his remains are unknown).

2. Influence and reputation

Palestrina was one of the most influential composers of his day. For a time he taught at one of the principal seminaries, the Seminario Romano, and his pupils included the Anerio brothers, Soriano, and possibly Victoria. In 1577 Palestrina and a colleague were directed by Pope Gregory XIII to revise the plainchant of the Roman Gradual and Antiphoner (see COUNCIL OF TRENT), and his music is imbued with the traditional melodic style of the Catholic Church, a fact that undoubtedly endeared him to its ministers. But given the upheavals in church music in this period, and the need for a new repertory to be produced quickly conforming to the textual and musical requirements of the Council of Trent, Palestrina's chief advantage was being in the right place at the right time. The incentive for other composers to continue in his ways was strong, and the Roman school continued to adopt his style long after new developments should have made it seem old-fashioned.

His music has been considered more genuinely 'religious' than any written in a more modern idiom, probably because secular—especially operatic—idioms have dominated music (including that for the church) since 1600. Thus a Neapolitan composer such as Francesco Durante could write a *Missa in Palestrina* in the 18th century without feeling that a contemporary idiom would be preferable for the purpose; a major theorist of that century, Fux, wrote the *Gradus ad Parnassum* (1725) in an attempt to codify the 'Palestrina style'; and the *Cecilian Movement in 19th-century Germany romanticized his works and made them appear the epitome of church music.

In the 20th century Palestrina's style was subjected to a closer scrutiny than that of any other composer (with the possible exception of Bach), and students of music are still expected to be able to write imitations of it, without much understanding of what the 'Palestrina style' really means. For there is no definitive set of rules which go to make up his style, but, as with all great composers, rather a series of styles. In fact, Palestrina is at his best when he is at his most difficult to codify—in the grand works of his later years, where contrapuntal skill is less important than his ear for gorgeous sound.

DA/TC

📖 J. ROCHE, *Palestrina* (London, 1971) · M. BOYD, *Palestrina's Style: A Practical Introduction* (London, 1973)

Paliashvili, Zakharia (*b* Kutaisi, 4/16 Aug. 1871; *d* Tbilisi, 6 Oct. 1933). Georgian composer and folklorist.

He studied with Taneyev at the Moscow Conservatory, 1900–3. Returning to Tbilisi, he helped establish the Georgian Philharmonic Society, eventually directing its music school (1908–17). He was appointed to teach at the Tbilisi Conservatory in 1917, becoming professor in 1919 and serving intermittently as director, 1919–32. He was honoured as a People's Artist of the Soviet Union (1925), and the Tbilisi theatre and a Georgian State Prize were named after him. His works include three operas, all staged in Tbilisi—*Abesalom da Eteri* (1919), *Daisi* ('Twilight', 1923), and *Latavra* (1928)—as well as a Mass in E♭ (1900), *Kartuli Liturgia* (Georgian Liturgy, for chorus, 1911), and other vocal works. He also transcribed and collected over 300 Georgian traditional songs.   JK

Pallavicino, Benedetto (*b* Cremona, 1551; *d* Mantua, 26 Nov. 1601). Italian composer. He spent most of his career in Mantua in the service of the Gonzagas, succeeding Wert as *maestro di cappella* in 1596. Although he published some church music, he is best known for his eight volumes of five-voice madrigals; the very fine sixth book (1600) in particular reveals not just the influence of Wert but also the emergence of other expressive techniques in the context of the *seconda pratica*. Monteverdi saw him as a rival but did not ignore his music, particularly when setting the same texts.   TC

Pallavicino, Carlo (*b* Salò; *d* Dresden, 29 Jan. 1688). Italian organist and composer. His first two operas were produced in Venice while he was still organist at S. Antonio, Padua (1665–6). In 1667 he moved to Dresden as vice-Kapellmeister at the Saxon court under Schütz, on whose death in 1672 he became Kapellmeister. He nevertheless returned to Padua in 1673, and in 1674 became *maestro di coro* at the Ospedale degli Incurabili, Venice. In 1685 he was persuaded by the Elector of Saxony to return to Dresden to establish Italian opera there. Throughout Europe Pallavicino was considered one of the finest composers of Venetian opera. The growing dominance of the aria in opera eminently suited his lyrical bent, and historians have pointed to the gradual increase in the number of *da capo* arias in his works (some with obbligato trumpet parts), together with the developing role of the orchestra.   PA

palm court music. A term adopted to identify a style of *light-music repertory and performance that developed in Victorian times in resorts and spas, on piers and in floral halls, and in bandstands. It is particularly associated with groups that played in grand hotels for diners in rooms furnished with potted palms; the most famous was the Grand Hotel at Eastbourne, from where the BBC broadcast a Sunday afternoon radio programme for many years. The groups ranged from small or-chestras to trios, the repertory from works by Elgar and pieces by Eric Coates and other light-music specialists to arrangements of Gilbert and Sullivan and popular musical shows. The art continued to flourish in the early days of radio, such leaders as Albert Sandler (1906–48) and Max Jaffa (1911–91) becoming well known.   PGA

Palmgren, Selim (*b* Pori, 16 Feb. 1878; *d* Helsinki, 13 Dec. 1951). Finnish composer. He studied in Helsinki with Martin Wegelius (1895–9) and later in Germany and Italy with Busoni among others. He was an important figure in Finnish musical life between the two world wars, and an accomplished pianist. He toured in the USA in the early 1920s and was for a time professor of composition at the newly founded Eastman Scool of Music. He wrote extensively for the piano, his output including five concertos as well as a large number of miniatures, for example *Night in May*, which enjoyed great popularity during the 1940s. Among his best works, however, are his partsongs, which are of con-siderable eloquence. His idiom is neo-romantic.

                                              RLA

Palm Sunday. The Sunday before Easter Sunday, on which is commemorated the entry of Jesus Christ into Jerusalem before a crowd waving palm branches.

                                              ALI

pan. See STEEL BAND; STEEL DRUM.

pandiatonicism [pandiatonism]. A term coined by Nicolas Slonimsky, in his book *Music since 1900* (1938). He defined it as follows:

> Pandiatonicism is the technique of free use of all seven degrees of the diatonic scale, melodically, harmonically, or contrapuntally. Wide intervallic skips are employed, and component voices enjoy complete independence, while the sense of tonality is very strong due to the absence of chromatics. Visually, a page of pandiatonic music looks remarkably clean. C major is favoured by most composers writing in this style. The opening pages of Prokofiev's Third Piano Concerto, Casella's *Valse diatonique*, Stravinsky's *Pulcinella*, and certain pages of Malipiero are characteristic examples of pandiatonic writing. The added sixth and ninth, widely used in popular American music, are pandiatonic devices.

Pange lingua (Lat., 'Record, my tongue'). The title of two Latin hymns: the Passiontide hymn *Pange lingua gloriosi proelium certaminis* by Venantius Fortunatus (*d* 610), and the Corpus Christi hymn *Pange lingua gloriosi corporis mysterium*, traditionally attributed to Thomas Aquinas (*d* 1274). The revival of Catholic liturgical forms championed by the 19th-century Oxford Movement stimulated the creation by J. M. Neale and others of singable English translations of these hymns, intended for use in Anglican worship.   —/ALı

panharmonicon. A large barrel organ (see MECHAN-ICAL MUSICAL INSTRUMENTS) invented by J. N. Maelzel and first exhibited in 1804; designed to play orchestral music, it is capable of imitating the sounds of many instruments using organ pipes and air-driven percussion devices. Beethoven originally composed his *Battle Symphony* for this instrument.   RPA

Panic. Work (1995) by Birtwistle for alto saxophone, drums, wind, and percussion.

panisorhythm. See ISORHYTHM.

panpipes [syrinx]. A number of tubes of graduated length, joined together in the form of a bundle or a raft. The pipes are blown across the rim at the open end, with one note being produced to each pipe. The tubes are often of reed or cane, as in the Greek legend where Pan blew across the reeds into which the nymph Syrinx had been turned, but pieces of wood or stone into which tubes of different length are drilled are also common. Pottery was sometimes used in ancient Peru, and plastic panpipes are made today.

The tubes are usually closed at the lower end, but open pipes are occasionally used, sometimes combined with closed ones to give a faint shimmer in octaves. Some instruments have only three tubes, whereas the Romanian *nai* has 20 or more. In South Africa and Lithuania disjunct panpipes—separate tubes with a group of pipers each playing one or two—are used. Those of Peru and Bolivia may be performed in pairs that share the melodic lines. In many areas, especially of South America and Oceania, they are ritual instruments.   JMo

pantomime. In ancient Rome, a form of dramatic entertainment in which gesture alone was used to convey the action, usually to the accompaniment of music. In 18th-century England, France, and Vienna the name 'pantomime' was given to a lighthearted entertainment, similar to an *intermezzo, that included instrumental music, dance, song, and spectacle; the subject matter was usually mythological (see also COMMEDIA DELL'ARTE). In England, Boyce and Arne wrote music for several pantomimes, and on the Continent Haydn and Mozart contributed to the genre.

In Britain today, the term commonly refers to a large-scale theatrical show, aimed primarily at children at Christmas. The story is usually based on a popular fairy tale and includes singing and dancing.   JBe

pantonality. Synonym for *atonality. Schoenberg preferred this term as indicating the combination of all keys rather than the absence of any, but it is rarely used.

pantoum [pantum] (Fr.). A verse form of Malayan origin, adopted in the 19th century in France by Victor Hugo and others. Ravel called the second movement of his Piano Trio by this name, possibly in imitation of Debussy, whose song *Harmonie du soir*, a setting of Charles Baudelaire, is a *pantoum*.

Panufnik, Sir Andrzej (*b* Warsaw, 24 Sept. 1914; *d* Twickenham, 27 Oct. 1991). Polish-born British composer. He studied composition in Warsaw, Paris and London, and conducting in Vienna with Weingartner. During World War II he eked a living as a café duo-pianist in Warsaw with Lutosławski. He was soon recognized as the country's leading conductor and composer, with such works as *Krag kwintowy* ('Circle of 5ths') and the orchestral *Kolysanka* ('Lullaby'), both of 1947; that year he won the Szymanowski and Chopin prizes for composition. Increasing conflicts with the Communist authorities and demands of *socialist realism led to his defection to the West in 1954. His music was banned in Poland from then until 1977.

In 1957 Panufnik was appointed musical director of the CBSO. The international success of his *Sinfonia elegiaco* (1957), which won the Prince Rainier Competition in 1963, allowed him to concentrate on composition. In his works (strongly reflective of Polish history and culture) he often developed substantial forms from small, symmetrical cells of pitches; in spite of their intellectual rigour, they are expressive, rooted in tonality, and frequently programmatic. His large-scale setting of Pope, *Universal Prayer* (1970), has an almost mystical intensity. Panufnik was knighted in 1991 and posthumously honoured by the Polish government. His daughter Roxanna (*b* 1968) is also a composer; her works include *Westminster Mass* (1998) and an opera, *The Music Programme* (2000).

📖 B. JACOBSON, *A Polish Renaissance* (London, 1996)

Papillons ('Butterflies'). Schumann's op. 2 (1829–31) for solo piano, a set of 12 short dance pieces inspired by the masked-ball scene at the end of Jean Paul's *Flegeljahre* ('Age of Indiscretion').

Papineau-Couture, Jean (*b* Outremont, PQ, 12 Nov. 1916; *d* Montreal, 11 Aug. 2000). Canadian composer. He studied in Montreal, then (in 1941) at the New England Conservatory, Boston. In the USA he took courses with Boulanger and met Stravinsky. In 1945 he began teaching in Montreal, first at the conservatory, then at the university; among his students were Jacques Hétu, André Prévost, and Gilles Tremblay. His early works embodied polymodal, polytonal neo-classicism, then moved towards atonal chromaticism. He was interested in sonority, metric freedom, and rhythmic force. His works include the Concerto Grosso (1943),

First Symphony (1948), Sonata for violin and piano (1944), and a series of five *Pièces concertantes* (1957–63) with subtitles that reflect their structure, for example 'Éventails' ('Fans') or 'Miroirs'. His *Papotages* ('Tittle-tattle') is a ballet score of 1949.   HRₑ

Parade. Ballet in one act by Satie to a scenario by Jean Cocteau; it was choreographed by Leonid Massine, with decor by Picasso, for Diaghilev's Ballets Russes (Paris, 1917).

paradiddle. A rudimentary side-drum technique involving the alternation of the leading hand, notated as illustrated. A semblance of legato or smooth transition between two drums (often timpani) can be gained.

L R L L R L R R   SM

Paradies und die Peri, Das ('Paradise and the Peri'). Cantata, op. 50 (1843), by Schumann, for soloists, chorus, and orchestra, a setting of a text based on a translation and adaptation of Thomas Moore's poem *Lalla Rookh* (1817). In Persian mythology the Peri is a benign spirit seeking readmission to Paradise.

Paradis, Maria Theresia von (*b* Vienna, *bapt.* 15 May 1759; *d* Vienna, 1 Feb. 1824). Austrian composer and pianist. Blind from childhood, she studied with Salieri, Kozeluch, and Abbé Vogler; by 1775 she was performing as a pianist and singer in Vienna. During the period 1783–6 she toured western European cities including Paris, where she was particularly popular, and London, where she played at the Hanover Square Rooms. From the end of the century she increasingly devoted her time to teaching, founding her own school in 1808. Her compositions include five operas, cantatas, songs, and a number of instrumental works.   SH

Paradise Lost. Opera in two acts by Penderecki to a libretto by Christopher Fry after John Milton's poem (1667) (Chicago, 1978).

parallel interval. See CONSECUTIVE INTERVAL.

parallel motion. See MOTION.

parameter. Any compositional variable, e.g. pitch, note duration, instrumentation, loudness. The term, borrowed from physics, became current in the early 1950s, when Boulez, Stockhausen, and others were submitting each parameter to serial control.

paraphrase. 1. In the 15th and 16th centuries, a contrapuntal technique involving the quotation in one or more voices of a plainchant melody. See CANTUS FIRMUS.

2. In the 19th century the term was applied to works based on existing melodies or pieces, often used as virtuoso showpieces. The supreme master of this type of recomposition was Liszt, who wrote numerous piano paraphrases of Italian operas, such as *Rigoletto*, and even of Wagner's operas.

Paraphrases. Collection of piano duets (24 variations and 14 other pieces) based on the popular quick waltz tune *Chopsticks*; they were composed by Borodin, Cui, Lyadov, Rimsky-Korsakov, and Liszt, and were published in 1880.

pardessus de viole [pardessus]. A five-string, high treble *viol of 18th-century France, sometimes identified with the *quinton. It was tuned *g–c′–e′–a′–d″* or *c′–e′–a′–d″–g″*. The *pardessus* enjoyed a brief vogue among amateurs, and several French composers devoted volumes of music to it (notably Louis de Caix d'Hervelois, 1750).

Paride ed Elena ('Paris and Helen'). Opera in five acts by Gluck to a libretto by Ranieri Calzabigi (Vienna, 1770).

parish church music. See ANGLICAN PARISH CHURCH MUSIC.

'Paris' Symphonies. Haydn's six symphonies, nos. 82–7 (1785–6), commissioned by the Comte d'Ogny for the Concert de la Loge Olympique in Paris; they include 'L*Ours', 'La *Poule', and 'La *Reine'. (Haydn's Symphonies nos. 90–2 were also written for Paris.)

'Paris' Symphony. Nickname of Mozart's Symphony no. 31 in D major, K297/300*a* (1778), so called because it was written in Paris and first performed at the Concert Spirituel.

Parker, Horatio (*b* Auburndale, MA, 15 Sept. 1863; *d* Cedarhurst, NY, 18 Dec. 1919). American composer. He studied with George Chadwick in Boston and Josef Rheinberger in Munich (1882–5), then returned to the USA, where he worked as a church musician and professor of music theory at Yale (1894–1919). His works, in a deeply conventional style, include the oratorio *Hora novissima* (1893), which was successful in its time, other sacred music, orchestral pieces, chamber music, and two operas, of which *Mona* was produced at the Metropolitan in 1912.   PG

parlando, parlante (It.). 'Speaking'. In singing, a speech-like style, with one syllable for each note, often used in dialogues in certain kinds of comic opera. In instrumental music, an instruction for expressive, 'eloquent' playing.

parody mass. A polyphonic cyclic setting of the Ordinary of the Roman Mass based on the imitative texture of a pre-existing polyphonic composition. The term, however, reflects a modern misunderstanding of

Renaissance terminology and invites confusion with other forms of musical parody. Some writers, aware that such masses were often entitled *Missa ad imitationem*, have therefore suggested 'imitation mass' as a more accurate description.

Although there are examples from before 1500 of works borrowing more than one voice from another polyphonic piece, it was during the first decades of the 16th century that composers seeking alternatives to writing cyclic masses based on a single melody—by using a tenor or chant paraphrase—turned to the systematic use of an existing work's entire polyphonic fabric. Many of the earliest parody masses were by French composers, who based their compositions on motets: for example Févin's *Missa 'Ave Maria'* after Josquin, or the *Missa 'Quem dicunt homines'* of Mouton after Richafort.

After 1520, which perhaps not coincidentally marked the advent of a generation of composers favouring continuous imitation, parody came to dominate mass composition: all 14 of the masses by Clemens belong to the genre of imitation mass, as do eight of Willaert's nine settings. Some interesting examples of intertextuality may be found among Palestrina's 53 parody masses, while those of Lassus are notable for drawing on models running from the sacred to the highly profane.

By the time theorists of the late 16th and early 17th centuries were able to provide detailed instructions for the composition of imitation masses, the technique had begun to fall out of fashion. One of the last significant representatives of the genre was Monteverdi's 1610 *Missa da cappella* after Gombert's motet *In illo tempore*, which even its composer seems to have regarded as an exhausting technical exercise.   ALi

Paroles tissées ('Woven Words'). Work (1965) by Lutosławski for tenor and chamber orchestra to a text by Jean François Chabrun.

Parry, Sir (Charles) Hubert (Hastings) (*b* Bournemouth, 27 Feb. 1848; *d* Rustington, Sussex, 7 Oct. 1918). English composer, teacher, and writer. After obtaining the Mus.B. degree while still at Eton, he read history and law at Exeter College, Oxford (1867–70), studying music in his spare time and spending summer 1867 in Stuttgart with Henry Hugo Pierson. While an underwriter at Lloyd's Register of Shipping he studied privately with Sterndale Bennett, George Macfarren, and Edward Dannreuther, who became his lifelong mentor. In 1875 he became a sub-editor for Grove's *Dictionary of Music and Musicians* and in 1877 abandoned Lloyd's for a career in music. At this time he produced a series of discursive chamber works, a period of activity which culminated in the Piano Concerto in

F♯ and the dramatic cantata *Scenes from Prometheus Unbound* (both 1880).

Though a fine composer of instrumental works—his five symphonies, the *Elegy for Brahms*, and the *Symphonic Variations* are monuments to his considerable intellectual powers—Parry became best known for his choral works, particularly his first major success, *Blest Pair of Sirens* (1887), the cantata *L'Allegro ed il Penseroso* (1890), his three oratorios *Judith* (1888), *Job* (1892), and *King Saul* (1894), the *Invocation to Music* (1896), the magisterial coronation anthem *I was glad* (1902), *The Pied Piper of Hamelin* (1905), a setting of William Dunbar's *Ode on the Nativity* (1912), arguably his masterpiece, and the valedictory motets *Songs of Farewell* (1916–18). His ethical works, which include *The Soul's Ransom* (1906) and *The Vision of Life* (1907), are weaker in structure and cohesion and failed to make any public impression, though they were influential on Vaughan Williams, Walford Davies, and Herbert Howells. His 12 sets of *English Lyrics* are among the finest songs of their period, and his unison setting of Blake's *Jerusalem* has virtually become an unofficial English national anthem.

A disciple of Darwin and Herbert Spencer, Parry wrote widely on historiographical topics founded on evolutionary theory, including *Studies of Great Composers* (1887), *The Art of Music* (1893, revised and enlarged 1896), and *Style in Musical Art* (1911), as well as a major study of Bach (1909). In 1883 he was appointed professor of music history at the RCM (where he also taught composition), becoming director in 1895. From 1900 to 1908 he was professor of music at Oxford. He was knighted in 1898, created a baronet in 1902, and made CVO in 1905. He is buried in St Paul's Cathedral.
                    MK/JDi

📖 J. DIBBLE, *C. Hubert H. Parry: His Life and Music* (Oxford, 1992)

Parry, John (*b* Denbigh, 18 Feb. 1776; *d* London, 8 April 1851). Welsh instrumentalist, composer, and conductor. He settled in London in 1807. Between 1809 and 1829 he wrote and arranged music for entertainments at Vauxhall Gardens, Covent Garden, and Drury Lane. He often sang his own compositions in public. Proud of his Welsh ties, he conducted various *eisteddfodau* and *cymrodorion*, promoted the Cambrian Society, and published six collections of traditional Welsh melodies. He was treasurer of the Royal Society of Musicians (1831–49) and music critic of *The Morning Post* (1834–48).   JDi

Parry, John Orlando (*b* London, 3 Jan. 1810; *d* East Molesey, Surrey, 20 Feb. 1879). Welsh baritone and pianist. He studied the harp with Nicolas Charles Bochsa but was more gifted as a singer and entertainer.

Accompanying himself on the piano, he excelled in simple ballads and comic songs; he was also renowned as a mimic, imitating celebrated singers with panache in his *Buffo trio italiano* (1837). He gave up singing in 1849 and produced a popular entertainment, *Notes, Vocal and Instrumental*, with words by Albert Smith. In 1853 he retired owing to ill health and became organist at St Jude's, Southsea. He composed many songs and glees and wrote dances for the piano.   JDi

Parsifal. Opera in three acts by Wagner to his own libretto (Bayreuth, 1882).

Parsley, Osbert (*b* 1511; *d* Norwich, early 1585). English composer. He worked as a lay clerk at Norwich Cathedral for 50 years, and is commemorated there by a memorial tablet in the north aisle of the nave. He wrote mainly motets, services, and consort music; his works include a fine setting of verses from the Lamentations of Jeremiah and a piece for five-part viol consort, *Perslis Clocke*, based on the notes of the hexachord.   JM

Parsons, Robert (*b c.*1535; *d* Newark-on-Trent, 25 Jan. 1572). English church musician and composer. In 1563 he was made a Gentleman of the Chapel Royal; earlier he may have been a chorister of the choir. His death, by drowning in the river Trent, probably occurred when he was still young, since a eulogy refers to him having been cut down in 'first flower'. His earliest works date from the 1550s, but the majority are Elizabethan. They include consort music, songs, motets, and a small quantity of English church music. Several of his compositions were influential on William Byrd, who subsequently filled his position at the Chapel Royal.   JM

part (Fr.: *partie, voix*; Ger.: *Part, Stimme*; It.: *parte, voce*). 1 [voice part, voice]. In polyphonic vocal music, the designation for each individual line. In early polyphony the names for the voice parts did not imply a precise range in the way that they do today: they were named according to their function and their place in the compositional scheme. Table 1 gives the most common terms for the voice parts in earlier vocal music (listed from the lowest upwards). In present-day choral music the standard formation (from the highest voice downwards, as is customary) is: soprano, alto, tenor, bass (usually abbreviated to SATB).

2. The music for one particular instrument (e.g. first violin, flute) or voice, as opposed to a score, which contains all the parts involved in a work.

3. A section of a composition; binary form, for example, can be said to be in two parts, ternary form in three (a better word is 'section'). In certain large-scale genres, e.g. oratorios, 'Part' is used to designate the main division of the work.

TABLE I

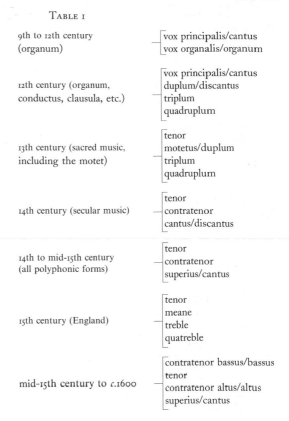

9th to 12th century (organum)	vox principalis/cantus vox organalis/organum
12th century (organum, conductus, clausula, etc.)	vox principalis/cantus duplum/discantus triplum quadruplum
13th century (sacred music, including the motet)	tenor motetus/duplum triplum quadruplum
14th century (secular music)	tenor contratenor cantus/discantus
14th to mid-15th century (all polyphonic forms)	tenor contratenor superius/cantus
15th century (England)	tenor meane treble quatreble
mid-15th century to *c.*1600	contratenor bassus/bassus tenor contratenor altus/altus superius/cantus

Pärt, Arvo (*b* Paide, 11 Sept. 1935). Estonian composer. He studied at the Tallinn Conservatory with Heino Eller, graduating in 1963 and later (1958–67) working as a producer for Estonian Radio. In 1980 he settled in West Berlin. Though now viewed as a leading 'modern mystic', he became known as one of Estonia's first radicals, earning the censure of the occuping Soviet forces. His early works (e.g. the Partita for piano, 1958) are neo-classical in character, but he soon joined the avant-garde, his *Collage sur BACH* (1964) and Second Symphony (1966) deploying ever-denser textures. This tendency reached its natural term in the orchestral *Perpetuum mobile* (1963) and *Pro et contra* for cello and orchestra (1966), which alternates tonal passages with grinding dissonance. The title of another collage piece, *Credo* (1968) for choir and orchestra, which uses the C major Prelude from book 1 of the '48', threw out a Christian challenge to the atheist state, which responded by banning the work.

Pärt then fell silent while he examined medieval music and plainchant in a complete revision of his style, the first results of which were ushered in by the consonant Third Symphony (1971). A further period of reflection brought the harmonic stasis and stark gestures of *Sarah was Ninety Years Old* for three solo voices, organ, and timpani (1976), leading to the triadic, 'tintinnabuli' style (his term) he has used ever since. The *Cantus in memoriam Benjamin Britten* (1977) for strings and bell achieves its hypnotic effect by unfolding the simplest of material at different speeds—a process followed also in *Festina lente* (1988) for strings. The succession of explicitly religious works began before Pärt left Estonia, with the *Missa sillabica, Cantate Domino*, and *Summa* (a setting of the Credo) also appearing in 1977; one of the most powerful of these works, the *St John Passion* of 1982, combines the sparest of gestures with a forceful emotional punch. Pärt often produces alternative versions of earlier works: *Fratres* (first composed in 1977) exists in versions for string quartet, cello ensemble, violin and piano, and early instruments, among others, while *Summa*, initially a choral piece, was scored for strings in 1991.   MA

 📖 P. HILLIER, *Arvo Pärt* (Oxford, 1997)

partbooks (Fr.: *parties séparées*; Ger.: *Stimmbücher*). Manuscript or printed books containing the music for an individual part of a work, whether vocal or instrumental (see PART, 1 and 2). One of the earliest known examples is the set of three partbooks that make up the Glogauer Liederbuch (*c*.1480). See also CHOIRBOOK.

Partch, Harry (*b* Oakland, CA, 24 June 1901; *d* San Diego, CA, 3 Sept. 1974). American composer, theoretician, instrument maker, and performer. Musically self-educated and influenced by a wide variety of world cultures, Partch had by 1930 developed his own philosophy of 'corporeal' music (personal, verbal, non-abstract, involving all the arts) and theoretical system, 'monophony', based on a 43-note scale with intervals derived from just rather than equal-tempered tuning. All his compositions and his many adapted or invented instruments conform to this system, described in his *Genesis of a Music* (Madison, WI, 1949, repr. 1974). Apart from six years as a hobo, Partch lived mainly in his native California and in the Midwest. He never taught, relying for support on grants and contributions, revenue from the concerts and recordings of his Gate 5 Ensemble, and odd jobs. Working on his own, he fashioned a unique creative world. His productive independence from musical and institutional systems distinguishes him from most 20th-century composers.   NC

 📖 T. McGEARY, *The Music of Harry Partch* (Brooklyn, 1991) · B. GILMORE, *Harry Partch: A Biography* (New Haven, CT, 1999)

parte, parti (It.). *Part*', 'parts'; *colla parte*, 'with the part', i.e. an indication that an accompaniment should

follow a solo line closely with regard to flexible rhythm, tempo, etc.; *a tre parti*, 'in three parts', i.e. three vocal or instrumental lines.

Partenope. Opera in three acts by Handel to a libretto adapted anonymously from Silvio Stampiglia's *Partenope* (1699, rev. 1708) (London, 1730).

Parthenia (Gk., 'virgin dances'). A collection of 21 pieces for virginal by Byrd, Bull, and Gibbons; it was presented to Prince Frederick and Princess Elizabeth on their marriage in 1613 as *Parthenia, or The Maydenhead of the First Musicke that ever was Printed for the Virginalls*. The pun in the title was reinforced in a companion volume, *Parthenia In-Violata* (1614), a collection of 20 anonymous pieces for virginal and bass viol. *Parthenia* was the first English music to be engraved on copper plates.

partials. Constituents of the notes of the *harmonic series, the main (fundamental) note being the first partial and the others the upper partials. See also ACOUSTICS, 5.

partial signature. See KEY SIGNATURE; MUSICA FICTA.

partimen. See JEU-PARTI.

partimento (It.). 17th- and 18th-century term for improvising melodies over a written bass.

partita [parte] (It.). 1. In the late 16th century and the 17th, one of a set of *variations, as in the titles of a number of volumes of instrumental (especially keyboard) music. Italian and, later, other composers customarily based sets of variations ('parti' or 'partite') on the bass lines of such well-known tunes as the folia or romanesca (Vincenzo Galilei's *Romanesca ... con cento parti*, in a lute manuscript dated 1584, is the earliest known use of the term). It may have been from this usage that 'partita' came occasionally to be used to describe any sort of piece, whether variation or not, that was part of a larger collection (e.g. Froberger's *Diverse curiose e rare partite musicale*, 1696).

2. In late 17th-century Germany, an alternative title for a *suite, usually occurring in the form 'Partia' or 'Parthia'. In the 18th century it could be applied loosely to any sort of multi-movement instrumental piece of the suite or sonata type (e.g. Bach's partitas for solo violin and solo keyboard), which might include movements headed 'Largo' or 'Allegro', for example, as well as the dance movements (allemande, courante, etc.) that traditionally make up the suite.

partition (Fr.; Ger.: *Partitur*; It.: *partitura, partizione*). 'Score'.

partsong. In its broadest sense, any composition for two or more voices; more commonly, a vocal composition intended for choral rather than solo performance, tending more to homophony than polyphony, and usually without accompaniment. Although the term has sometimes been used in connection with 16th-century secular music for solo voices (e.g. the *madrigal), and with the 18th-century *glee for men's choir, it is more usually and correctly applied to 19th-century unaccompanied works for male, female, or mixed choruses, principally songs composed as a response to the growing interest in amateur choral singing in Britain, Germany, and the USA in the 19th century.

Among the earliest British composers of partsongs were Robert Lucas Pearsall (1795–1856), John Hatton (1808–86), the younger Henry Smart (1813–79), and George Macfarren. The establishment and growth of competitive choral festivals later in the century prompted contributions from many other composers, including more significant figures such as Stanford (e.g. *The Blue Bird*), Parry (*Songs of Farewell*), and most notably Elgar (*My love dwelt in a northern land*), who was responsible for a marked improvement of the partsong. But it should be stressed that a large part of the repertory was supplied by composers of considerably lesser powers of invention and imagination, whose pieces were printed and circulated in vast numbers. Although the genre continued to flourish in the early 20th century (e.g. Vaughan Williams, Holst, Moeran, Howells), the tradition has since diminished in popularity.

German composers of partsongs, encouraged by the establishment of such institutions as the Berlin Liedertafel, include Schubert, Schumann, Weber, and Mendelssohn, who wrote chiefly for male-voice choirs, and Brahms, whose partsongs for mixed choirs have remained firmly in the repertory of English as well as German choirs. East European composers, notably Tchaikovsky, Kodály, and Bartók, also contributed to the genre, but composers in Latin countries do not seem to have been attracted to the partsong. During the late 19th and early 20th centuries in the USA choral singing flourished, encouraged by college glee-clubs, and large numbers of partsongs were composed, notably by Horatio Parker, MacDowell, and Elliott Carter.   JN

📖 M. HURD, 'Glees, madrigals and partsongs', *Music in Britain: The Romantic Age, 1800–1914*, ed. N. Temperley (London, 1981), 242–65

part-writing (Amer.: voice-leading). The art of composing contrapuntal music; see COUNTERPOINT.

pas (Fr.). 1. 'Not', 'not any'.

2. In dance or ballet, a 'step', e.g. *pas de Basques*, a step of three beats similar to the waltz movement; *pas de chat*, so called because of its similarity to the movement of a leaping cat; *pas coupé*, 'cut step', a step which acts as a preparation for another, one foot 'cutting' the other away and taking its place. In ballet *pas* is also used to denote a certain form or movement, e.g. *pas d'action*, a dramatic scene; *pas seul*, *pas de deux* (*trois*, etc.), a dance for the number specified.

Pasdeloup, Jules-Étienne (*b* Paris, 15 Sept. 1819; *d* Fontainebleau, 13 Aug. 1887). French conductor. He was one of the pioneers of symphony concerts in France, along with Colonne and Lamoureux. After studying at the Paris Conservatoire he took composition lessons; it was as a composer that he began his career, but he was unsuccessful. In 1851 he founded the Société des Jeunes Artistes du Conservatoire, and later made his debut conducting their first concert. Regular concerts followed in which he introduced many new works to Paris, as well as Mozart's *Die Entführung aus dem Serail*. In 1861 he founded the Concerts Populaires, continuing to give new music, especially works by Wagner, whose *Rienzi* he conducted at the Théâtre Lyrique in 1869. He vitally influenced the musical life of Paris, and after his death his concerts continued as the Concerts Pasdeloup.   JT

Pasquini, Bernardo (*b* Massa da Valdinievole, nr Lucca, 7 Dec. 1637; *d* Rome, 21 Nov. 1710). Italian composer, harpsichordist, and organist. Cesti is often cited as his teacher, but in his keyboard music the influence of Frescobaldi is obvious. In 1663 he was appointed organist at S. Maria Maggiore, Rome, and the following year at S. Maria in Aracoeli, where he remained for the rest of his life. He was a celebrated keyboard player: his patrons included princes and cardinals, as well as Queen Christina of Sweden. He was a close associate of Corelli and Alessandro Scarlatti, and all three were honoured in 1706 by admission to the elite Arcadian Society.

Pasquini composed operas and oratorios but is best known for his keyboard music, which includes suites, variations, toccatas, and sonatas. Among the distinguished musicians he taught were Kerll, J. P. Krieger, Georg Muffat, and possibly Domenico Scarlatti.
                                                                         —/PA

passacaglia (It., from Sp. *pasar*, 'to walk', *calle*, 'street'; Fr.: *passacaille*, *passecaille*; Sp.: *pasacalle*, *passacalle*). A through-composed variation form constructed over formal harmonic progressions, normally I–IV–V(–I), used widely in the Baroque era but with origins in the Spanish street dance, the *pasacalle*. The term became identified in the early 17th century with instrumental (usually guitar) ritornello passacaglias performed either between stanzas or at the beginning and end of certain types of Spanish, French, and Italian song. Like the chaconne, which also used specific *basso ostinato* formulas, the passacaglia became a separately identifiable extended late Baroque form. It was favoured by Italian and French composers, whence it spread to Germany. The Italian form was distinguished by its use of continuous variations over a pre-selected bass formula, which could migrate to other parts as the variations developed. The French type revealed its indebtedness to instrumental dance music and sectional structure; as an orchestral genre from the 1680s, it found a place in the stage works of Lully (e.g. *Persée*, 1682) and his contemporaries. The German passacaglia owed much to both French and Italian models. It appeared most frequently as a keyboard piece, the most notable being J. S. Bach's Passacaglia in C minor for organ bwv582, and occasionally for solo violin (e.g. Biber) or orchestra (e.g. J. C. F. Fischer).

In both French and German music the term was often confounded with 'chaconne', in spite of attempts by several theorists, including Mattheson (1713, 1739) and Quantz (1752), to distinguish the two. In theory the passacaglia was in a minor key, was slightly less solemn, was never vocal, and did not always maintain the ostinato in the bass; but, to judge from contemporaneous examples, this was not borne out in practice.

In the late 18th and the 19th centuries the passacaglia virtually disappeared, with one possible exception, the finale of Brahms's Symphony no. 4—though it is not called 'passacaglia'. The 20th century saw something of a revival of the form by mainstream composers, starting with Reger (1906) and continuing with Webern (1908), Schoenberg (in *Pierrot lunaire*), Berg (*Wozzeck*, Act II), Stravinsky (Septet), Britten (*Peter Grimes*, Act II), Hindemith (Fourth String Quartet), Vaughan Williams (Fifth Symphony), and others. The structure of the 20th-century form as a continuous set of variations on a ground (bass) is essentially modelled on the Bach passacaglia.   CRW

passage-work. A 'passage' in a musical composition is simply a section. The term 'passage-work' is more specifically applied to transitional sections (especially in keyboard music) that have no intrinsic musical value and little, if any, thematic substance, but rather serve as 'padding', often consisting of brilliant figuration and thereby offering an opportunity for virtuoso display by the performer.

passaggio (It., 'passage'). 1. Used in the plural (*passaggi*), a kind of ornamentation; see ORNAMENTS AND ORNAMENTATION, 2.

2. Transition or modulation.

3. A passage of music intended to display the performer's virtuosity.

passamezzo [passemezzo, pass'e mezzo, etc.] (It.). An Italian dance of the 16th and 17th centuries, similar to, but quicker than, the *pavan and, like that dance, in duple metre. Its name is possibly derived from *passo e mezzo*, meaning 'a step and a half'. Although the passamezzo was an Italian dance, it was first seen in some lutebooks published by Hans Neusidler in Germany in 1536 and 1540; it appeared in Italy shortly before the mid-century, and in England and France soon afterwards. Sir Toby Belch, in Shakespeare's *Twelfth Night* (Act V scene 1), speaks of a 'passy-measures pavin'.

Most passamezzos were composed on one of two standard chordal basses: the *passamezzo antico* (Sir Toby's 'passy-measures pavin') was based on the progression i–VII–i–V–III–VII–i–(V–)I; the *passamezzo moderno* (known in England as the 'quadran pavan') had the chordal framework I–IV–I–V–I–IV–I–(V–)I. These basses were also used for other types of dance.

passepied (Fr.). A French 17th- and 18th-century dance resembling a fast *minuet. It was usually in binary form, in 3/8 or 6/8 time, and with continuous running movement in small note-values. The passepied first appeared as a Breton court dance in the early 16th century, and was mentioned by Rabelais and Arbeau (who calls it a kind of *branle). It became popular at the court of Louis XIV, where it was danced to the steps of the minuet, usually by one couple.

Like other dances of rustic origin adopted by the court, the passepied was taken up by composers of stage music, including Lully, Campra, and Rameau. Passepieds were often performed in pairs to form a ternary structure, the first dance being repeated after the second. It also became one of the optional dances in the 18th-century *suite. There is a pair of passepieds in Bach's orchestral Ouverture in C bwv1066, and Debussy gave the name to a piece in his early *Suite bergamasque* for piano.   —/JBe

passing note. A note connecting two chords but belonging to neither of them. In the first beat of Ex. 1 (the

Ex. 1

opening of a chorale from Bach's *St Matthew Passion*), the second quaver in the bass is a passing note; other connecting notes occur (tenor and alto, bar 2, beat 1; alto, bar 2, beat 3), but they have the effect of creating a new chord, rather than simply connecting two chords without having any harmonic implication of their own.

Passion Chorale. See O HAUPT VOLL BLUT UND WUNDEN.

Passione, La. Nickname of Haydn's Symphony no. 49 in F minor (1768), so called because it begins with an Adagio suggestive of Passion music.

Passion music. Settings to music of the account of Christ's Passion, as recorded in the four gospels. In its simplest form, perceptible from the late Middle Ages, the story is presented in plainchant 'Passion tones' by the priest (alone, or with two assistants) officiating at Mass during Holy Week—St Matthew's account on Palm Sunday, St Mark's and St Luke's on Tuesday and Wednesday respectively, and St John's on Good Friday. Characterization is achieved by variations in pitch and tempo, indicated by letter symbols: S (*sursum*, 'raised') for the high-pitch (*alta vox*) utterances of all crowd groups (*turbae*) and individuals, except Christ; C (*celeriter*, 'rapidly') for the delivery, at medium pitch, of the *Evangelist's narration; and T (from *tenere*, 'held') for the bass register and measured declamation of the words of Christ. Further contrast was achieved later by replacing the original *alta vox* chant with chordal responses for a small vocal ensemble. Anonymous settings of this responsorial type (of English and Italian provenance) have survived from the second half of the 15th century. The earliest example by a known composer is the (partly preserved) four-voice *St Matthew Passion* (*c.*1500) by the Englishman Richard Davy, the surviving sections of which display skilful polyphony and vivid illustrative treatment of the *alta vox* texts.

Notable 16th-century composers who wrote responsorial settings for Catholic worship were Lassus, Victoria, Guerrero, and Byrd, each of whom adopted the traditional formal scheme, but confined polyphony to the crowd utterances. In Germany, following the Reformation, Passion composition was widely cultivated by Lutheran composers. Texts from Luther's German Bible were most frequently used, but Latin was by no means excluded. Two German responsorial Passions, noted for their clarity and simplicity, are the *St Matthew* and *St John* settings (*c.*1550) attributed to Johann Walter, Luther's musical adviser, which set the pattern for many other composers and continued in Holy Week usage until much later times. A notable

innovation during this period occurs in a *St John Passion* (1561) by Antonio Scandello (an Italian convert to Lutheranism, then serving at Dresden), in which plainchant is confined to the Evangelist's role, and the words of the crowd and of all individuals, including Jesus, are set to polyphony, with voice-groupings of varying size.

Early in the 16th century there evolved a further type of setting (described as *through-composed) in which the entire account is drawn, in compressed form, from all four gospels and set in continuous choral polyphony. Usually sections of the traditional chant are woven into the choral texture and distinctions between individual and crowd utterances created by the disposition of the voice parts. The earliest known example is a Latin *St Matthew Passion* (so called, but based on all four gospels) by Antoine de Longueval (*fl* 1507–22), who served as *maître de chapelle* to Louis XII of France. This form was subsequently cultivated by numerous minor composers, Catholic and Protestant, including Johannes Galliculus, Jacob Regnart, and Bartholomäus Gesius. Invariably these settings comprised several (from three to five) *partes*, the last of which embraces all the Seven Last Words of Christ from the Cross. An important later offshoot was the so-called motet Passion, which is again fully polyphonic but has less input from the ancient Passion tones, and contains graphic touches of text illustration of a madrigalian character. The principal (and last surviving) examples of these are the German *St John* Passions by Leonhard Lechner (1594) and J. C. Demantius (1634).

From the mid-17th century, in disregard of long-standing church traditions, instruments and non-gospel texts were introduced into Passion settings. The earliest example is a *St John Passion* of 1643 by the Hamburg Kantor Thomas Selle, in which instruments are used both as accompaniment and as a means of enhancing characterization (violins for Christ, flutes for Peter, and cornetts for Pilate). Later, a more decisive move towards the oratorio style was made by such minor north German composers as Johann Sebastiani, Johann Theile, and J. V. Meder, who introduced reflective arias on chorale or free poetic texts, with accompaniments for strings and continuo, and primitive recitative for the narrative sections. However, the age-old responsorial Passion, gospel-centred and without accompaniment, showed continuing vitality, reaching its apotheosis with three plain but deeply expressive German settings (*St Matthew*, *St Luke*, and *St John*) by Schütz, who entirely reshaped the sections of chant to underline dramatic and illustrative detail, and provided crowd choruses of extraordinarily vivid effect.

At the turn of the century, Passion composers were left with two main possibilities: to set the basic gospel text and embellish it with oratorio characteristics; or to abandon the biblical account in favour of a freely devised libretto on the Passion story, with music of a heavily dramatic and emotional nature. The two great Passions of Bach (*St John*, 1724, and *St Matthew*, 1727), together with Kuhnau's *St Mark Passion* (1721) and Telemann's 40-odd liturgical settings, belong to the former type; and the free-style works of Keiser, Mattheson, and Handel, with such titles as *Der für die Sünde der Welt gemarterte und sterbende Jesus* ('Jesus, Martyred and Dying for the Sins of the World'), to the latter. The Bach Passions, with their mixture of biblical and free poetic texts, and their elaborate settings in the form of choruses, recitatives, and arias, with rich orchestral colouring, represent a grand culmination of the Passion genre. And for those in Leipzig who heard them at Vespers during the 1720s, and the many—of all religious persuasions or none—who have experienced them since in a multitude of contexts, they have provided a continuing source of profound spiritual regeneration. They stand however outside the bounds of liturgical worship, which remained true to the simplest of the traditional settings such as those attributed to Johann Walter, still in use at Leipzig in Bach's time at the principal morning service on Good Friday.

After Bach, non-biblical oratorio settings were widely cultivated. In terms of sustained popularity the most successful German example was C. H. Graun's *Der Tod Jesu* (1755, to a poem by K. W. Ramler), which contains powerful choral writing and an effective fusing of recitative and arioso. In Britain, at a more modest level, staple fare for professional and amateur choral groups has been provided consistently by John Stainer's *Crucifixion* (1887). Outstanding 20th-century settings include the *St Luke Passion* (1963–6) by Krzysztof Penderecki and the *St John Passion* (1982) by Arvo Pärt, in which such old and new devices as incantation, heterophony, microtones, glissandos, and chord clusters give added intensity of expression to the themes of suffering, sacrifice, and redemption inherent in the gospel account. Of more recent date is an impressive opera-oratorio, *Good Friday* (1998) by John Caldwell, in which the Passion story is presented, with powerful orchestral support, on three separate but closely interlinked levels: as narrative, from St John's gospel, sung in Latin by three 'deacons'; as vivid drama, delivered concurrently in English; and as supporting commentary, drawn largely from the Latin Good Friday liturgy, including the *Improperia and the hymn *Pange lingua.   DA/BS

📖 B. Smallman, *The Background of Passion Music: J. S. Bach and his Predecessors* (New York, 2/1970) · P. Steinitz, *Bach's Passions* (London, 1979) · K. von Fischer, *Die Passion: Musik zwischen Kunst und Kirche* (Kassel, 1997)

Pasta, Giuditta (Angiola Maria Costanza) [née Negri] (*b* Saronno, 26 Oct. 1797; *d* Como, 1 April 1865). Italian soprano. She studied with Paër, among others, in Milan, where she made her debut in the premiere of Giuseppe Scappa's *Le tre Eleonore* (1816); shortly afterwards she sang Donna Elvira in Paris and Telemaco in Cimarosa's *Penelope* in London, where she also sang Cherubino and Despina. From 1818 she appeared throughout Italy, and first won high acclamation in 1821 when she sang Desdemona in Rossini's *Otello* at the Théâtre Italien, Paris. She soon became one of Rossini's prime choices: as well as triumphing in the demanding role of Semiramide she created the part of Corinna in *Il viaggio a Reims* (1825). Her brilliance and musicianship greatly influenced Donizetti and Bellini. In 1831 she created Amina in *La sonnambula*, and in 1831 and 1833 the title roles in *Norma* and *Beatrice di Tenda*. She was the first Anna Bolena in Donizetti's opera (1830). She sang regularly in London, Paris, and St Petersburg (1824–37).   JT

pasticcio (It., 'pie', 'pastry', 'mess'). A piece assembled from several pre-existing sources; the term is applied particularly to Italian opera from the late 17th century to the end of the 18th, when it was common practice to recombine favourite airs from earlier operas (not always by different composers) into a new scheme. Many of Handel's Italian operas are pasticcios, for example *Elpidia* (1725) and *Ormisda* (1730), in which he combined existing arias by other composers into a new plot and wrote the recitative himself, and *Oreste* (1734), in which he reused arias from his own, earlier works together with new recitative and ballet. *Ballad opera is sometimes considered a variety of this type of pasticcio.

The term is occasionally also applied (albeit inaccurately) to new works on which several composers have collaborated, such as the opera *Muzio Scevola* (1721) to which Amadei, Bononcini, and Handel each contributed an entire act.   —/JBe

pastiche (Fr.). 'Imitation', 'parody'; not the same as *pasticcio. A work written partly in the style of another period, such as Prokofiev's Classical Symphony (in the style of Haydn) or Stravinsky's *Pulcinella* (after Pergolesi). Many of Gilbert and Sullivan's operettas contain clever pastiches with numerous minuets and gavottes; there is a splendid mock Handelian duet in *Princess Ida*. The technique of 'pastiche composition' is taught in many educational establishments as a means of furthering students' historical and analytical understanding of the music of different periods.   —/LC

pastoral (Fr.: *pastourelle*; It.: *pastorale*). 1. In the 15th–18th centuries, a type of stage work dealing with rural themes. Such subject matter is also a feature of many madrigals of the late 16th and early 17th centuries, when imitation of Greek and Roman poetry resulted in such works as Torquato Tasso's *Aminta*, G. B. Guarini's *Il pastor fido*, and Philip Sidney's *Arcadia*. Handel's *Acis and Galatea* (1718) is a pastoral.

2. A type of instrumental or vocal work resembling the *siciliano, generally in 6/8 or 12/8 time and often suggesting a rustic or bucolic subject by the imitation of the drone of a shepherd's bagpipe or musette. In many countries pastoral music is associated with the Christmas season, hence the 'Pastoral Symphony' in Bach's *Christmas Oratorio*, that in Handel's *Messiah*, the *pastorale* in Corelli's 'Christmas' Concerto op. 6 no. 8, and Tartini's Concerto Grosso op. 8 no. 6, 'con un pastorale per il Santissimo Natale'. See also PASTORELLA.

'Pastoral' Sonata. Name given by the publisher to Beethoven's Piano Sonata no. 15 in D op. 28 (1801), presumably because of the rustic rhythm in the finale.

'Pastoral' Symphony. 1. Beethoven's Symphony no. 6 in F major op. 68 (1808); it was published as *Sinfonia pastorale*, a programme symphony in which sounds of nature are imitated, its five movements being 'Awakening of Happy Feelings on Arriving in the Country', 'By the Brook', 'Merrymaking of the Country Folk', 'Storm', and 'Shepherds' Song: Joy and Gratitude after the Storm'.

2. A short orchestral movement in Handel's *Messiah*, referring to the shepherds who were told of Christ's birth.

Pastoral Symphony, A. Vaughan Williams's third symphony (1921); it has a wordless solo for soprano (or clarinet) in the last movement.

pastorella [pastorela, pastoritla] (It. or Lat., dim. of *pastorale*). A Christmas composition for performance in church between Christmas Eve and the Purification. In one or more movements, it is usually for singers and small orchestra (though sometimes for instruments alone) and tells the story of the shepherds, from their awaking at the angels' appearance to their arrival at the stable with gifts for the Christ child. In some versions the offering takes the form of a lullaby or other music-making. As well as such characteristic features of the Baroque *pastoral as drone basses and melodies harmonized in 3rds and 6ths, pastorellas include rhythmic and melodic elements probably deriving from folk music. They are often unsophisticated and comic in tone, and sometimes use folk instruments (bagpipes, hurdy-gurdy, trumpet).

The pastorella originated in Roman Catholic areas of central Europe in the second half of the 17th century and spread rapidly throughout rural central Europe in

versions with Latin and vernacular texts (some in dialect) from the early 18th century. Many examples from the later 18th and the 19th centuries survive in manuscript. In Czech-speaking areas the texts of the Latin Mass Ordinary was set in pastoral style from the mid-18th century; Czech vernacular pastorellas were gradually interpolated, and by the end of the century had in some cases entirely replaced the Ordinary. The best-known of these 'pastoral masses' are by Ryba. The popularity of the genre continued in Bohemia and Moravia throughout the 19th and 20th centuries, and Smetana quoted a well-known pastorella melody in his opera *The Kiss*.   PFA

📖 G. A. CHEW, 'The Austrian pastorella and the *stylus rusticanus*: Comic and pastoral elements in Austrian music, 1750–1800', *Music in Eighteenth-Century Austria*, ed. D. Wyn Jones (New York, 1996), 133–93

Pastor fido, Il ('The Faithful Shepherd'). Opera in three acts by Handel to a libretto by Giacomo Rossi after the play by Battista Guarini (1585) (London, 1712); Handel revised it with added choruses (London, 1734) and with the prologue *Terpsichore* and added dances (London, 1734). Salieri wrote a four-act opera with the same title, with a libretto by Lorenzo Da Ponte (Vienna, 1789).

Pater noster (Lat., 'Our Father'). The Lord's Prayer, chanted everywhere in the Christian liturgy, both at *Mass and at the *Divine Office.

paṭět. A term (often translated as 'mode' or 'scale') used to designate the tonality within the two tuning systems of *gamelan music.

'Pathetic' Symphony. See SYMPHONIE PATHÉTIQUE.

Pathétique Sonata ('Pathetic Sonata'). Beethoven's Piano Sonata no. 8 in C minor op. 13 (1797–8); the first edition (1799) is entitled 'Grande sonate pathétique', possibly Beethoven's own title.

Patience. Operetta in two acts by Sullivan to a libretto by W. S. Gilbert (London, 1881).

Patiño, Carlos (*b* Santa María del Campo Rus, *bapt.* 9 Oct. 1600; *d* Madrid, 5 Sept. 1675). Spanish composer. He was trained as a choirboy at Seville Cathedral under Alonso Lobo and Francisco de Santiago. After appointments as *maestro de capilla* in Seville (1623) and at the convent of the Encarnación in Madrid (1628), in 1634 he became the first Spanish *maestro* of the royal chapel. As well as many polychoral sacred works (masses, psalms, motets, and villancicos) he composed some secular pieces (*tonos humanos*) for few voices for the musical evenings held in the gardens of the Alcázar palace.   P-LR

patronage. Before about 1800 most composers, unable to support themselves by composition alone, had to rely on some form of direct patronage. In medieval times, for example, the chief patron was the church. Most serious composers took holy orders of one degree or another, and thereafter either remained in the service of the church, directing its music and training its musicians, or found some secular activity suited to their status as educated men. The career of Guillaume de Machaut is typical: he was educated as a cleric but became secretary to King John of Bohemia and later entered the service of the court of France, spending the years of his retirement as a canon at Reims. Those composers who existed without patronage—the uneducated man with a natural instinct for music, the lapsed cleric unwilling to submit to church authority—were social outcasts who earned a living precariously as wandering minstrels or general entertainers.

Though direct church patronage remained a potent force until well into the 18th century, from the 15th century onwards it began to be matched (and was eventually superseded) by the patronage of the nobility. This turned the emphasis away from liturgical music (by nature somewhat conservative) and towards music for entertainment—first for the private delectation of the patron and his immediate circle, and later on a more public scale, bringing opportunities for ever more lavish display to enhance the standing of the noble or aristocratic household. Though the scope of music broadened with this change, it cannot be said that composers were freer agents, or necessarily more honoured for their skills. Everything depended on the enthusiasm and inclinations of the patron. Even the best of them—Haydn's Prince Esterházy, for example—required the absolute service he would expect of any salaried, liveried retainer. The composer was there to please his master with music appropriate to the occasion, and not to express his soul.

It was doubtless the restrictions imposed by these conditions that prompted certain composers to try to take advantage of the increased demand for public entertainment among the middle classes and break away into a freelance existence. Thus while Bach, in Germany, remained the servant of court and church patrons, Handel, his contemporary, escaped to a more democratically inclined London and there, with the help of a less demanding and exclusive kind of noble patronage, set up his own schemes as an opera impresario. A parallel situation exists in the careers of Haydn and Mozart, though Mozart proved less adept than Handel in manipulating such opportunities that came his way.

The first great composer to turn patronage to his own ends was Beethoven, who, through sheer force of personality, contrived to make it seem a privilege to provide the support he needed. But here we are dealing with a change of social attitude, in which artists were coming to be regarded as superior beings—bearers of a message. Thus composers in the 19th century, who were in any case beginning to acquire legal rights over their work (so that publication and performance became a genuine source of income), were better able to exploit such patronage as came their way. The example of Wagner in his relations with King Ludwig of Bavaria is a case in point, if somewhat extreme.

Nevertheless, the freedom gained with the decrease in patronage had often to be paid for by other sacrifices. Composers were sometimes obliged to undertake general musical work in order to supplement their precarious incomes—conducting, performing, teaching, music criticism, and so on. The few who were able to command a handsome return from the publication and performance of their works were usually opera composers. Patronage of a kind continues today in the form of commissions from performing organizations, individual artists, and festivals, often supported by commercial sponsorship.   MH

Patterson, Paul (Leslie) (*b* Chesterfield, 15 June 1947). English composer. He studied with Richard Rodney Bennett and at the RAM, where he taught for many years. Influenced particularly by Krzysztof Penderecki, he is a fluent and effective composer of works ranging from choral settings to television jingles, and from small vocal pieces to large-scale orchestral compositions.

PG/AW

patter song. A type of comic song, usually found in opera, which depends for its effect on the speed of the singer's delivery. Most patter songs are in Italian or English, these being the most suitable languages, and they became common from the second half of the 18th century. The 'Largo al factotum' from Rossini's *Il barbiere di Siviglia* (Act I scene 1) is a celebrated example; others are found in operas by Paisiello, Haydn, and Donizetti. The comic operettas of Gilbert and Sullivan abound in such songs, the patter song in *Ruddigore* including the lines 'This particularly rapid, unintelligible patter / Isn't generally heard, and if it is it doesn't matter'.

Patti, Adelina [Adela Juana Maria] (*b* Madrid, 19 Feb. 1843; *d* Craig-y-Nos Castle, nr Brecon, 27 Sept. 1919). Italian soprano. From a musical family, she toured the USA as a child prodigy with the violinist Ole Bull and in 1857 toured with Gottschalk. In 1859, when she was 16, she made her opera debut as Lucia di Lammermoor in New York, after studying the role with the conductor Emmanuele Muzio. Two years later she appeared as

Amina in *La sonnambula* at Covent Garden, a role she repeated for her debuts in Paris (1862) and Vienna (1863). Her fame spread throughout Europe, and she was soon recognized as the greatest soprano of her day. During the 1880s she was a favourite at the Metropolitan Opera, New York. Her career continued into the 20th century and she made some recordings at her castle in Wales; they reveal her extraordinary tone-production, brilliant agility, and refined phrasing.   JT

    J. F. CONE, *Adelina Patti, Queen of Hearts* (Portland, OR, 1993)

Pauer, Jiří (*b* Kladno-Libušín, Bohemia, 22 Feb. 1919). Czech composer. He studied with Otakar Šín, Hába, and Bořkovec. From the 1950s he filled many official posts including that of artistic director of the Czech Philharmonic (1958–80), and principal of opera (1953–5, 1965–7) and general manager (1979–90) at the Czech National Theatre. He was secretary-general of the Union of Czech Composers (1963–5) and professor of composition at the Academy of Musical Arts (1965–89). His music, including several successful stage works, has combined styles ranging from the Romantic (*Zuzana Vojířová*, 1957) to the astringent (Bassoon Concerto, 1949) with the requirements of *socialist realism.   JSᴍ

Paukenmesse ('Kettledrum Mass'). Haydn's Mass no. 9 in C major (1796); Haydn called it *Missa in tempore belli* ('Mass in Time of War') and it is sometimes referred to as *Kriegsmesse*.

Paukenwirbel-Symphonie. See DRUMROLL SYM-PHONY.

Paul Bunyan. Operetta in a prologue and two acts by Britten to a libretto by W. H. Auden (New York, 1941); Britten made a revised version (Snape, 1976).

Paumann, Conrad (*b* Nuremberg, *c*.1410; *d* Munich, 24 Jan. 1473). German organist and composer. He was born blind. By 1446 he was organist at St Sebaldus, Nuremberg, and he was appointed town organist in 1447. Three years later he accepted the post of court organist at Munich, and from there travelled widely in Germany, France, and Italy, where he was knighted. He was sought after as an adviser on organ-building, and was an important teacher, founding a school of organ composers whose achievements can be heard in pieces from the Buxheimer Orgelbuch; two of them are ascribed to Paumann himself. His best-known work, a composition manual for the organ called *Fundamentum organisandi* (1452), includes arrangements of German lieder. Little of his music survives, however. Presumably most of it was played extempore or from memory and was never notated. He is buried in the

Frauenkirche, Munich; an epitaph there shows him surrounded by instruments.   DA/JM

pausa (It.), 'Rest' (not *pause).

pause. 1 (Fr.: *point d'orgue*; Ger.: *Fermate*; It.: *fermata*). A sign (⌢) indicating that the note, chord, or rest over which it appears is to be prolonged at the performer's discretion. It is sometimes placed over a bar-line to indicate a short silence. It may also be used to indicate the end of a phrase, section, or composition. See also GENERALPAUSE.

2 (Fr.; Ger.: *Pause*; It.: *pausa*). 'Rest', especially a semibreve rest; a *demipause* is a minim (half-note) rest.

pavan [pavane, pavin] (Fr.: *pavane*; Ger.: *Paduana*; It.: *pavana, padovana*). A 16th- and 17th-century dance, probably originating in Italy and named after the town of Padua. The earliest known examples are in Dalza's lutebook of 1508. Arbeau, in his *Orchésographie* (1588), described the pavan as a processional dance in duple time, with two single steps and one double step forwards, followed by the same sequence in reverse.

Pavans appear in German, French, and Spanish sources of the 1520s and 30s, but settings of the dance reached the height of perfection in the hands of the English virginal composers—Byrd, Bull, Gibbons, Morley, Farnaby, Philips, Dowland, and Tomkins. There are many fine examples in the Fitzwilliam Virginal Book and other collections of the period, such as Byrd's Pavan in *Parthenia* written as a memorial for the Earl of Salisbury (*d* 1612). Dowland wrote a famous example for five-part string consort, *Lachrimae, or Seaven Teares (Figured in Seaven Passionate Pavans)*, which was transcribed for keyboard by several other composers of the time, including Byrd.

The pavan was generally coupled with another, quicker dance, which was usually in triple time and sometimes had thematic links with the pavan; in Italy the accompanying dance was a *saltarello, in France and England a *galliard.

Shortly after its brief flowering in the late 16th century the pavan died out, though it survived for a while as the first movement ('Paduana') of the early 17th-century German suite, perhaps as a result of the influence of certain English composers active on the Continent, for example Thomas Simpson or William Brade. The pavan was also retained in some of Locke's suites, and there are a few examples by Purcell. Several later composers wrote pieces called 'pavan': the best known is Ravel's *Pavane pour une infante défunte*.   WT/LC

Pavane pour une infante défunte ('Pavan for a Dead Infanta'). Piano piece (1899) by Ravel, which he orchestrated in 1910. It recalls the Spanish court custom of performing a solemn ceremonial dance at a time of royal mourning.

Payne, Anthony (Edward) (*b* London, 2 Aug. 1936). English composer. He studied at Durham University, but attracted notice as a composer only in the late 1960s, by which time he had made his name as a critic and writer on music. His discovery of a personal voice, with a distinctively English lyricism, is celebrated in the *Phoenix Mass* for chorus and brass, completed in 1972. Later works include *Time's Arrow* (1990) for orchestra and *Symphonies of Wind and Rain* (1991) for chamber ensemble. Payne's 'elaboration' of Elgar's sketches for his Third Symphony was first heard, to great acclaim, in 1997.   PG/AW

Pearl Fishers, The. See Pêcheurs de perles, Les.

Pears, Sir Peter (Neville Luard) (*b* Farnham, 22 June 1910; *d* Aldeburgh, 3 April 1986). English tenor. He made his debut in 1942 and joined Sadler's Wells the following year. He created all Britten's major tenor roles, from Peter Grimes (1945) to Aschenbach in *Death in Venice* (1973). Many of the composer's solo works were also written specifically for his voice, whose clear, reedy timbre was coupled with great versatility of technique and expression, from the inwardly reflective or humorous to the grand and heroic. Co-founder of the Aldeburgh Festival, he was interested in the revival of 16th-century English song, Schütz, and Bach. With Britten as pianist he was also a notable interpreter of lieder.   IR

📖 C. Headington, *Peter Pears: A Biography* (London, 1992) · P. Reed, *The Travel Diaries of Peter Pears* (London, 1995)

Peasant Cantata (*Bauernkantate*). Bach's secular cantata no. 212, *Mer hahn en neue Oberkeet* ('We have a new regime', 1742), to a text by Picander, composed to mark the inauguration of the rule of Carl Heirich von Dieskau (1706–82) over certain villages in the Leipzig area.

Péchés de vieillesse ('Sins of Old Age'). A collection of pieces by Rossini, for piano with and without voices, composed between 1857 and 1868 and grouped into 13 volumes, some with fanciful titles; they were not published until the 1950s.

Pêcheurs de perles, Les ('The Pearl Fishers'). Opera in three acts by Bizet to a libretto by Eugène Cormon and Michel Carré (Paris, 1863).

pedalboard. The organ keyboard played by the feet. It either controls its own pipes or is coupled to those of the manuals. The carillon also has a pedalboard, as occasionally have the harpsichord, clavichord, and piano, for organists to practise on. Organ pedalboards are sometimes arranged in a concave fan shape, to be more accessible to the feet, but outside Britain and the USA they are usually straight and flat.   JMo

pedaliter (Ger., from Lat. *pedalis*). 'On the pedals'; in keyboard music, a direction to play with both hands and feet.

pedal note. A term (derived from the deep notes of the pedal rank of the organ) used for the lowest note that can be produced on a brass instrument for any given slide position or valve setting, usually the fundamental of the *harmonic series for that setting of the instrument. Lully may have called for the pedal note of a horn in B♭ alto (*La Princesse d'Élide*, 1664), but for the most part pedal notes have been cultivated only since the time of Berlioz.   JJD

pedal point (Fr.: *point d'orgue*). The device of holding on a bass note (usually the tonic or dominant) through a passage including some chords of which it does not form a part (see Ex. 1, the closing bars of Bach's Prelude in C from book 1 of the '48'). An inverted pedal follows the same principle, but the long held note is placed in the treble. If two different notes are held together

Ex. 1

(usually tonic and dominant) the term 'double pedal' is used.

pedal steel guitar. A variant of the *Hawaiian guitar.

Pedrell, Felipe (*b* Tortosa, 19 Feb. 1841; *d* Barcelona, 19 Aug. 1922). Spanish composer, musicologist, and teacher. His church and chamber music, cantatas, songs, and orchestral and stage works, including an ambitious operatic trilogy beginning with *Los Pirineos* (1890–1) are seldom played; but his rediscovery of 16th-century Iberian music, especially the works of Victoria, was vital to the development of the new national music, as was his revival of Spanish folksong. His influence was felt most keenly through his many pupils, who included Albéniz, Granados, Falla, Moreno Torroba, and Gerhard.   CW

Peebles, David (*fl* mid-16th century; *d* before 1592). Scottish composer. He was a canon of the Augustinian Priory of St Andrews, and his music, which includes Latin motets as well as settings of English metrical psalms, led one contemporary to describe him as 'ane of the cheiff musitians into this land'.   JM

Peer Gynt. Incidental music by Grieg for Henrik Ibsen's play (1876). Some of it was later arranged as two orchestral suites: op. 46 (1888) and op. 55 (1891–2); these were later arranged for piano solo and duet. Saeverud also composed incidental music (1947) for the play, Egk wrote an opera on the subject (Berlin, 1938), and Schnittke a ballet (1986).

Peerson, Martin (*b* ? March, Cambs., 1571–3; *d* London, *bur.* 15 Jan. 1651). English composer and keyboard player. Little is known about his early career beyond the facts that he was composing music by 1604 (one of his songs featured in a royal entertainment overseen by Ben Jonson) and two years later was cited for recusancy. In 1613 he took the B.Mus. at Oxford. Between 1623 and 1630 he held various posts at Westminster Abbey and St Paul's Cathedral; he remained an 'almoner' of St Paul's during the Civil War. Peerson is known principally for his songs and verse anthems, many of which were published in his *Private Musicke* (London, 1620) and *Mottects or Grave Chamber Musique* (London, 1630); the latter is among the earliest English works to use a figured bass. Only four of his keyboard pieces survive.
                                                              JM

Peeters, Flor (*b* Tielen, 4 July 1903; *d* Antwerp, 4 July 1986). Belgian composer and organist. He studied at the Lemmens Institute in Mechelen, where he became cathedral organist in 1925, and in Paris with Marcel Dupré and Charles Tournemire. He was active as a recitalist throughout the world and as a teacher, directing the Royal Flemish Conservatory in Antwerp

(1952–68). His enormous output includes organ music of all kinds, much of it reflecting his interests in Flemish Renaissance polyphony, the music of Bach, Gregorian chant, and Flemish folk music. In addition he composed masses and other church music, some secular vocal works, chamber music, and piano pieces.
                                                        PG/ABur

peine, à (Fr.). 'Scarcely'; *à peine entendu*, 'barely audible'.

Peixinho, Jorge (*b* Montijo, 20 Jan. 1940; *d* Lisbon, 30 June 1995). Portuguese composer. Early studies with Braga Santos were followed by work with Nono, Boulez, and Stockhausen at Darmstadt (1960–70), where he was a major figure. Free collective improvisation and electronics play an important part in his output, which includes wittily allusive incidental music for Arnold Wesker's play *The Four Seasons* (1968), as well as chamber, orchestral, and instrumental works in an attractively Epicurean stylistic mix.   CW

Pelléas et Mélisande ('Pelléas and Mélisande'). 1. Opera in five acts by Debussy after Maurice Maeterlinck's play (Paris, 1902).
    2. *Pelleas und Melisande*. Symphonic poem, op. 5 (1902–3), by Schoenberg.
    3. Suite of incidental music, op. 80 (1898), by Fauré for Maeterlinck's play.
    4. Incidental music, op. 46 (1905), by Sibelius for Maeterlinck's play; Sibelius arranged a suite from it the same year.

pellet bell. See CROTAL.

pelog. One of the two tuning systems of the Javanese *gamelan, with five very unequal steps to the octave.

Peñalosa, Francisco de (*b c.*1470; *d* Seville, 1 April 1528). Spanish composer. Though primarily associated with Seville Cathedral he also served as chamberlain and singer in the chapel of Pope Leo X in Rome, and some of his masses and motets may have been written for use there. His music shows clearly the influence of Josquin.   JM

Penderecki, Krzysztof (*b* Dębica, 23 Nov. 1933). Polish composer and conductor. He came to prominence in the early 1960s with music in which extended playing techniques were applied to stringed instruments (the post-titled *Threnody for the Victims of Hiroshima*, 1961). He was the foremost example of 'sonorism', a Polish musicological label for music (often using *graphic notation; see NOTATION, Fig. 8) in which expressive directness, involving the movement and juxtaposition of sound masses, took precedence over conventional thematic or structural procedures. These abstract experiments were soon harnessed to programmatic ends in such choral-orchestral works as the *St Luke Passion* (1963–6) and *Dies irae* (1967), the latter written in memory of the victims of Auschwitz.

The First Violin Concerto (1976–7) initiated a neo-romantic phase in which elements of Penderecki's experimental vocabulary were incorporated into a stylistic throwback to Bruckner and Liszt. His symphonic scores revisited the motivic and symphonic aesthetic of the 19th century, a move regarded as retrogressive by modernist critics. His narrative structures, heavily dependent on sequences of semitones and tritones, rhythmic repetitions, and sombre orchestral colours, are evident in several symphonies and concertos since 1980. He also shows a continuing adherence to large-scale choral works (*Polish Requiem*, 1980–4; *Credo*, 1998), which often use well-known Polish melodies for quasi-political reasons. In complete contrast, Penderecki has demonstrated a keen interest in opera: the voyeuristic *The Devils of Loudun* (Hamburg, 1969), the 'sacra rappresentazione' *Paradise Lost* (Chicago, 1978), the hysterical and neurotic *danse macabre*, *Die schwarze Maske* (Salzburg, 1986), and the scatological and grotesque *Ubu rex* (Munich, 1991), whose references to Rossini, Musorgsky, and Wagner show a lighter side to Penderecki's often troubled ethos.   ATh

    📖 R. Robinson and A. Winold, *A Study of the Penderecki St Luke Passion* (Celle, 1983) · W. Schwinger, *Krzysztof Penderecki: His Life and Work* (London, 1989) · M. Tomaszewski (ed.), *The Music of Krzysztof Penderecki: Poetics and Reception* (Kraków, 1995) · B. Jacobson, *A Polish Renaissance* (London, 1996) · D. Mirka, *The Sonoristic Structuralism of Krzysztof Penderecki* (Katowice, 1997) · R. Robinson (ed.), *Studies in Penderecki*, i (Princeton, NJ, 1998) · K. Penderecki, *Labyrinth of Time: Five Addresses for the End of the Millennium* (Chapel Hill, NC, 1998) · T. Malecka (ed.), *Krzysztof Penderecki's Music in the Context of 20th-Century Theatre* (Kraków, 1999)

Pénélope. Opera in three acts by Fauré to a libretto by René Fauchois (Monte Carlo, 1913).

Penitential Psalms. Although potentially denoting any penitential text from the biblical psalter, in Western Christian usage the term refers collectively to a particular group of seven psalms (6, 31, 37, 50, 101, 129, and 142 in the numbering of the Vulgate). In the medieval Roman rite they are given after Lauds on Fridays in Lent, while the *Book of Common Prayer* appoints the full set for Ash Wednesday. As used in private devotions, they form an important section of Books of Hours. Lassus set all seven texts in the *Psalmi Davidis poenitentiales* of 1560.   —/ALi

penny whistle [tin whistle]. A generic term for the simple *duct flute or *flageolet. Played worldwide from antiquity to the present, it is made of bone, wood, reed, metal, plastic, or other material, usually with four to seven fingerholes. The term 'pennywhistle' was probably coined by Robert Clarke, who invented a particular brand of six-hole whistle made from tin plate in the 1840s (they are still being made by his descendants). This extremely cheap type of penny whistle is much used in folk music and is especially common in Ireland.   JMo

pentachord. A five-note section of the diatonic scale, e.g. from C to G.

pentatonic scale. A scale of five notes. See SCALE, 6.

Penthesilea. Opera in one act by Schoeck to his own libretto after the tragedy by Heinrich von Kleist (Dresden, 1927).

Pentland, Barbara (Lally) (*b* Winnipeg, 2 Jan. 1912; *d* Vancouver, 5 Feb. 2000). Canadian composer. She began formal composition studies in Paris in 1929, and in 1936 was awarded a fellowship to the Juilliard School in New York. In 1941 and 1942 she worked with Copland at the Berkshire Music Center in Massachusetts. While teaching at the Royal Conservatory of Music in Toronto (from 1943), she was invited in 1949 to join the University of British Columbia in Vancouver, where she taught until 1963. Her early works of the 1930s are in a French late Romantic idiom, but an encounter with the Schoenberg pupil Dika Newlin introduced her to modernist writing: *Octet for Winds* (1948) and other pieces are composed in strict serial form. After attending the Darmstadt summer courses and being exposed to the music of Webern, she acquired a deepened interest in compactness and clarity, as demonstrated in the *Symphony for Ten Parts* (1957). She also experimented with aleatory and quarter-tone techniques in the late 1960s in such pieces as *Trio con alea* (1966), the Third String Quartet (1969), and *News* (1970).   HRe

    📖 S. Eastman and T. J. McGee, *Barbara Pentland* (Toronto, 1983)

Pepping, Ernst (*b* Duisburg, 12 Dec. 1901; *d* Berlin, 1 Feb. 1981). German composer. He studied composition with Walter Gmeindl at the Berlin Hochschule für Musik (1922–6) and taught at the Berlin Kirchenmusikschule (from 1934) and Hochschule für Musik (from 1953). One of the leaders of the movement to revive German church music, Pepping wrote a large number of organ pieces and Lutheran liturgical settings, in a style combining Bachian polyphony with an expanded diatonic harmony close to Hindemith.

PG

Pepusch, Johann Christoph (*b* Berlin, 1667; *d* London, 20 July 1752). German composer and theorist. After service at the Prussian court he settled in London (*c.*1704) as viola player and harpsichordist at Drury Lane theatre. His music for the stage includes five masques, notably *Venus and Adonis* (1715) and *Apollo and Daphne* (1716), and he probably wrote the overture to *The Beggar's Opera* (1728). Pepusch did much to revive older music, being among the founders of the Academy of Vocal (later Ancient) Music, editing Corelli's instrumental works for publication in London, and publishing *A Treatise on Harmony* (1730). In 1713 he was awarded the Oxford D.Mus. and in 1746 Fellowship of the Royal Society. He married Margherita de L'Epine, a wealthy Italian opera singer, with whom he lived in considerable style.   DA/BS

perception, musical. See PSYCHOLOGY OF MUSIC, I.

percussion instruments (Fr.: *batterie*; Ger.: *Schlag-und Effektinstrumente*; It.: *batteria*). Strictly, these are only the instruments that are struck, but in practice the term covers all those for which the orchestral percussion department has the responsibility. Most of the instruments (e.g. drums, cymbals, triangles, gongs) are indeed struck, but a few are plucked, some are rubbed (either by hand or with a bow or other object) or scraped, many are blown, and even more are shaken. In *organology, percussion instruments are divided into *membranophones (those on which sound is produced by a vibrating membrane) and *idiophones (instruments of hard, solid material, e.g. cymbals and xylophones).

Whenever whistles of any sort are needed—whether single-note, two-note (cuckoo), or melodic (swanee whistle)—it is percussion players who provide them, rather than the flautists or other woodwind players as might be expected. Equally, it is not string players who are expected to bow a saw or a cymbal. Percussion players have to master many skills, but their reward is to play all the fun instruments as well as the serious ones.   JMo

perdendosi (It.). 'Losing itself', i.e. gradually dying away.

perfect cadence. See CADENCE.

Perfect Fool, The. Opera in one act by Holst to his own libretto (London, 1923). The orchestral suite of the ballet music was first performed in 1920.

perfect interval. An *interval of a 4th, 5th, or octave.

perfect pitch. See EAR AND HEARING, 3.

performance practice. A term borrowed from the German 19th-century *Aufführungspraxis* to describe the mechanics of a performance that define its style.

1. Introduction; 2. Unwritten notes; 3. Sonority; 4. Pitch; 5. Tuning; 6. Tempo; 7. Rhythm; 8. Phrasing and articulation; 9. Dynamics

1. Introduction

The study of performance practice pioneered in England by Arnold *Dolmetsch gathered momentum during the second half of the 20th century. Increased interest in past performing styles is a natural consequence of the expansion of performing repertory, but the extent to which they should dictate a musician's choices is a matter of controversy. An informed performer may choose to work within the original conventions of a style (as far as these can be ascertained), or to modify or even ignore them in order to achieve equivalent results for present-day audiences.

The notated form in which Western art music from before the era of recorded sound survives may be more or less intelligible as a representation of relative pitches and rhythms (see NOTATION) but is almost inevitably a mere skeleton of the music, to be enhanced by the unwritten and often unnotable conventions and nuances of performance. Even present-day notation has unspecified conventions: it is not always clear whether 'violin 1' means a single instrument or body of players, or when ♪ means 𝅘𝅥𝅯𝅘𝅥𝅯𝅘𝅥𝅯 and when an unmeasured *tremolando*. Whether musicians of the future will still assume such practices as equal temperament, a pitch standard of a' = 440, or wide and largely unvarying vibrato tone for music at the beginning of the 21st century cannot be predicted.

Study of performance practice aims to pinpoint conditions of performance, conventions, and stylistic developments, and so form a clearer understanding of a composer's intentions and expectations. There is, however, disagreement about which departures, if any, from the accepted style and taste are desirable or necessary. The familiar argument that 'our ears have changed' and that music must therefore do the same to achieve an equivalent effect ignores the feasibility of re-educating our mutable ears.

The first steps in establishing principles of performance practice are the responsibility of those who produce and edit printed music (see EDITING). With the work of a meticulous living composer there should be few problems, but corrupt scores of even well-known 19th-century works, perhaps incorporating the idiosyncrasies of particular performers, are all too common (though they may preserve important information about playing styles). With earlier music many more issues arise: transposition of 16th-century church music to represent better its original sounding pitch in modern terms, application of the rules of *musica ficta, whether or not a trouvère song should be performed metrically. All of these remain controversial and difficult to resolve.

Information to supplement musical notation can be found, though the sources are diverse. Folk traditions may retain certain characteristics of earlier art traditions, and some elements of modern piano playing (and teaching) appear linked to Liszt or Brahms. But the evidence of recorded sound, which has provided invaluable documentation of composers' and performers' practices, often exposes the illusory nature of such 'traditions'. Stravinsky's recordings constitute a fascinating legacy, while Elgar's reveal a significantly different orchestral playing style from that in current vogue.

For earlier periods one must rely on surviving instruments or their iconography, and above all on the written word—poor substitutes for aural evidence. Each clue presents intricate problems of interpretation. A gut-strung Stradivari violin in original condition will reflect the preconceptions of its player, but an unaltered Baroque organ is rather less accommodating. A medieval painting of angel musicians does not prove that their rebecs, harps, and lutes were used in church music but may hint at the musical activities of their terrestrial counterparts. Among written sources, treatises often promise most but provide least: Morley's *A Plaine and Easie Introduction to Practicall Musicke* (1597) teaches only notation and rudimentary composition; and sometimes the exercising of undefined 'good taste', or the observance of a first-rate exponent, is advised.

Other guides are more detailed; these include treatises by Ganassi, Praetorius, Mace, Hotteterre, Geminiani, Leopold Mozart, Quantz, François Couperin, C. P. E. Bach, and Altenburg covering a variety of disciplines and performing situations. Practical prefaces were sometimes published (Caccini, Viadana, Frescobaldi, Schütz, Muffat) and since the 19th century some composers have written about the realization of their own music (Berlioz, Wagner, Stravinsky). Correspondence can shed light on contemporary practice (Monteverdi, Mozart, Beethoven), as can accounts by musical travellers (Burney, the Novellos), diarists (Pepys), dramatists (Shakespeare), poets (Chaucer), novelists (Hardy), critics (Shaw), and so on. While these texts are undeniably useful it is important to consider that a modern interpretation of older language may possibly fall short of its original meaning.

In a separate category are the archives of various private and public institutions which employed musicians. These may reveal the size and constitution of an ensemble, the instruments available or coming into fashion, or the role of various musicians. The conjunction of different types of evidence may allow a clearer picture of particular performance practices to emerge.

2. Unwritten notes

Perhaps most speculative in this category is the practice of adding accompaniments to medieval monophonic songs. Little more is known than that these were often accompanied, usually by stringed instruments. The unwritten accompaniments to 16th-century polyphony were probably simple chordal intabulations of some sort, possibly anticipating early Baroque *continuo practices. 17th- and 18th-century continuo styles are, by contrast, reasonably well documented, though each instrument, ensemble, and performance requires a specific *realization. In particular, the accompaniment of recitative is a fluid art: it is not unlikely that the organ chords in J. S. Bach's cantatas were often played short (♩ when written 𝅝), sometimes sustained, and sometimes with the left hand sustained and the right hand released. Signs indicating *ornaments proliferated in the 17th and 18th centuries, at the end of which time it was an essential part of the performer's art to ornament melodic lines tastefully. The *cadenza was simply a part of this improvisatory art.

3. Sonority

(a) Vibrato: While vibrato is integral to conventionally favoured sonorities today, and there is evidence of its use from the 16th century and earlier, anything other than an occasional discreet vibrato or one used to colour particular notes is probably misplaced in music before about 1900. Vibrato was intended as an ornament and was rarely used continuously. The wide and unvarying vibrato used in some powerful singing and playing and precluding all subtlety of intonation was uncharacteristic until fairly recently.

(b) Voices: Clarity and agility were qualities particularly prized in Renaissance and Baroque singing. Distinctions were drawn between the manner of singing in churches and the soft, subtle style appropriate to the chamber. Later, even Berlioz considered larger theatres detrimental to singers, the vocal power required in such spaces often affecting agility and natural diction. Falsetto singing, frequently misunderstood in modern revivals, had an important role as the highest voice in much continental polyphony during the Renaissance and was only later associated with alto parts. Castratos, combining boys' voices with adult power and musicianship, dominated the 17th and 18th centuries. The palette of colours in accepted 'good singing' today has

probably changed as much over the centuries as has the sound of spoken English.

(c) Instruments: It would be a mistake to regard the evolution of instruments as a simple progression towards perfection. Aesthetic values and changing tastes play an important role in the process. The role of the noble medieval bagpipe, for instance, has been relegated to that of a folk instrument, while the status of the violin has been elevated from that of a dance instrument. Developments in the construction and sonority of instruments are often a response to changing circumstances: the increasingly public nature of music (see CONCERT), for example, created the need for more powerful ones, and greater use of chromaticism seems to have engendered safer, tonally smoother ones. Thus, the brightness and directness of medieval and Renaissance instruments seem pungent and stark to modern ears attuned to sonorities established after World War I. Conversely, a metal-strung modern cello may seem thick and heavy compared with a light, ringing Baroque viol.

With wider travel and the increasing availability of recorded music, the influence of outstanding performers can alter the course of a playing style with unprecedented speed. Consequently, Tchaikovsky's symphonies may sound rather less Russian, Dvořák's less Czech, and Berlioz's less French than they did originally.

(d) Forces: While the performance of an intimate Haydn quartet by a string orchestra, or of Tchaikovsky's Serenade by a mere string quartet, might be unthinkable today, there is not always the same concern for the sizes of ensemble required for music of earlier times. With rare exceptions, those used by Monteverdi and Cavalli were normally of single strings. At Leipzig, Bach's fullest orchestra was just over 20 strong and his optimum choir numbered between 12 and 16. Indeed, some of his 'choral' music and much 17th-century church music (Monteverdi, Carissimi) may well have been written for vocal consorts of single voices. Renaissance choirs of more than about 25 singers were rare and the vast majority of madrigals and other small-scale vocal pieces are chamber music for single voices, the exact equivalent of string quartets.

The balance as well as the size of ensembles has altered. The number of singers in the choir of King's College, Cambridge, for instance, may be the same as originally, but today all the boys are trebles whereas in the late 15th century they were both trebles and meanes. Moreover, a work such as Machaut's Notre Dame Mass, often sung with colourful support from an assortment of medieval instruments, was almost certainly written for four unaccompanied solo voices, while a typical three-choir motet by Giovanni

Gabrieli—apparently all-vocal and not specifying any instruments—was probably intended for two instrumental groups (high and low), each with a solo singer, and one (small) choir. In Baroque music, the instruments of the continuo group are rarely specified; the combination of harpsichord and cello is only one possibility (on occasion even a chordal instrument may be omitted). And the ever-present 16′ string bass of the modern orchestra was unknown to Lully and many others. (See also CHOIR, CHORUS; ORCHESTRA.)

Sonority is also influenced by the placement of forces. The singers of St Mark's, Venice, were far less spatially separated than is suggested by myth (see CORI SPEZZATI). In earlier orchestral set-ups the texture was often clarified by the arrangement of first and second violins opposite each other. Wagner's sunken, 'hooded' orchestra pit at Bayreuth makes the balance with singers on stage easier than in almost any other opera house.

4. Pitch

The international standardization of pitch was achieved in relatively recent times (see PITCH, 1), and a higher or lower pitch standard colours music quite differently. A French Baroque orchestra, playing almost a tone below $d' = 440$, probably sounded quite different from a Venetian one, playing at roughly $d' = 440$ or even higher. However, it is in vocal music that the matter is most crucial. For Dowland and Purcell a song must lie in the speech area of the voice, where the words are most naturally projected. In the music of Bach and Beethoven, problems of stamina for choral singers regularly arise when the pitch is raised excessively. With 16th-century polyphony the intended scoring can easily be misunderstood in the assumption that the pitch levels are slightly wrong. And with medieval polyphony, for which knowledge of pitch standards is almost non-existent, it may well be that modern expectations are significantly problematic.

5. Tuning

Present-day musicians are used to *equal temperament, in which all semitones are of exactly equal size. While this renders all keys equally usable—an advantage for most 19th- and 20th-century music—such a compromise system, in which the octave is the only pure interval, would probably have sounded disturbingly out of tune to Renaissance ears. Bach's *The Well-Tempered Clavier* was not necessarily a vindication of equal temperament but probably a clever demonstration of a system that approached it while retaining some individuality for all keys. Performing it on an equal-tempered instrument eliminates these subtleties. The various characteristics of different keys are a vital ingredient of all Baroque music, especially dramatic music, and the dissonances of medieval music become truly potent when Pythagorean intervals are used.

6. Tempo

Since its introduction the *metronome has been a mixed blessing. On the one hand it provides more precise tempo indications; on the other it encourages the belief that there is only one correct tempo. Wagner abandoned metronome markings for more general indications, and other composers (e.g. Stravinsky) often departed from their own directions in performance. Beethoven's metronome markings, often puzzling by modern expectations, are frequently ignored altogether, so that, for example, the Marcia funebre of his 'Eroica' Symphony is almost always heard at a substantially slower speed than the perfectly plausible (and more marchlike) ♪ = 80.

Precise information about tempo measurement before Beethoven's time is scarce. Bach is said to have favoured 'brisk' tempos, and dance forms, at least originally, were closely associated with the natural speed of dance steps. From the 17th century such terms as *allegro* and *adagio* began to be used, though their meaning has shifted (not 'rather fast' and 'slow', as now, but 'cheerful' and 'at ease'). For medieval, Renaissance, and even much Baroque music, the principal guide to tempo was simply the time signature; proportional signs governed subsequent changes of tempo. Just as music has steadily extended its harmonic and dynamic palettes, so the normal range of tempos has probably grown. Greater flexibility of tempo within a movement may also be appropriate to much 19th-century music. However, the original nature of tempo *rubato* seems to have changed: for 17th- and 18th-century musicians including Mozart (and probably still for Chopin and others) the pianist's right hand was given rhythmic freedom in an *adagio* passage, while the accompanying left hand kept a semblance of strict time.

7. Rhythm

The notation of rhythms is almost always an approximation—even equal-note plainchant is capable of endless minute rhythmic modifications. The practice, familiar in jazz, of making pairs of notes (𝅘𝅥𝅯𝅘𝅥𝅯) unequal (𝅘𝅥𝅭𝅘𝅥𝅮 or 𝅘𝅥𝅮𝅘𝅥𝅭) is first mentioned in the mid-16th century. It became standard in Baroque performance practice, especially (though not exclusively) in French music; see NOTES INÉGALES. Closely related is the principle of overdotting ('double dotting'), where 𝅘𝅥𝅭𝅘𝅥𝅯𝅘𝅥 becomes more like 𝅘𝅥𝅭𝅘𝅥𝅰𝅘𝅥; the written double dot is rare in pre-Classical music. Such discrepancies as 𝅘𝅥𝅭𝅘𝅥𝅯𝅘𝅥 occur regularly in Baroque music and are often ambiguous. Bach evidently taught his pupils to observe these differences; others favoured the elision of one rhythm to the other. Even in the songs of Schubert, Schumann, and Brahms it is not always clear whether or not such rhythms should remain distinct.

8. Phrasing and articulation

These may be even more important than tempo in establishing the character of a composition. For the Middle Ages and early Renaissance, however, there is little evidence apart from a few notational features such as the liquescent neume (see NOTATION, 1). *Keyboard fingerings suggest that the detached 16th-century manner of playing evolved only slowly into the seamless legato of the 19th century. This is paralleled by the transition from the norm of one bowstroke to a note in 16th-century string playing to the general slurring and smooth bow-changing of the 19th century. Baroque bows encourage a natural non-legato, while the Tourte bows in general use from about 1800 produce quite different qualities.

The deliberate unevenness produced by earlier keyboard fingerings also has its parallels in the *tonguing syllables used by Baroque wind players. These are gentler than their later counterparts, just as earlier bowstrokes rarely used the modern sharp attack. Vocal music is subject to more conjecture, though it seems certain that the florid ornaments of Caccini and Monteverdi were articulated in the throat and were consequently fast and light. Symbols for articulation (e.g. slurs) began to appear in the 17th century and were increasingly notated in later music, though not without ambiguity.

9. Dynamics

Large-scale Romantic music has created a wide range of dynamics and dramatic possibilities which probably play little part in medieval and Renaissance music, where the absence of indications reflects the fact that, apart from nuances of phrasing, a basic dynamic level is set by the choice of forces. Any dynamic variation in an extended work (e.g. a mass) is a natural result of a change of texture (for example, a reduction from five-part choir to solo trio) or, in organ music, of a change of registration between sections. In addition, the dynamic range of many instruments was generally smaller than at present. Although some 16th-century lute music contains dynamic markings, the use of dynamics as serious compositional tools coincides with the rise of the violin family. Contrasts and echo effects were first exploited by early Baroque Italian composers, and the abbreviations *f* (*forte*) and *p* (*piano*) gained common currency. Bigger halls and theatres for public performance during the 18th century brought about increases in chorus and orchestral size and a general interest in sheer volume. The greater the possible dynamic range, the more necessary and desirable it became for composers to specify their exact intentions.   APA/NPDC

📖 R. DONINGTON, *The Interpretation of Early Music* (London, 1963, 4/1989) · C. MACCLINTOCK (ed.), *Readings in the History of Music in Performance* (Bloomington, IN, 1979) · R. JACKSON, *Performance Practice, Medieval to Contemporary: A Bibliographical Guide* (New York, 1988) · H. M. BROWN and S. SADIE (eds.), *Performance Practice*, 2 vols. (London, 1989) · R. PHILIP, *Early Recordings and Musical Style: Changing Tastes in Instrumental Performance, 1900–1950* (Cambridge, 1992) · C. BROWN, *Classical and Romantic Performing Practices, 1750–1900* (Oxford, 1999) · C. LAWSON and R. STOWELL, *The Historical Performance of Music: An Introduction* (Cambridge, 1999)

Performing Right Society. See COPYRIGHT, 7.

Pergolesi, Giovanni Battista (*b* Iesi, nr Ancona, 4 Jan. 1710; *d* Pozzuoli, nr Naples, 16 March 1736). Italian composer. The son of a surveyor, all of whose other children died in infancy, he seems always to have been in poor health; he was described as having a deformed leg, and may well have suffered from some form of tubercular disease. Thanks to his father's professional connections among the local nobility he was sent at some point before 1724 to study at the Conservatorio dei Poveri di Gesù Cristo in Naples. There his teachers included Durante and he distinguished himself as a violinist. In 1732, having already received one opera commission, he became *maestro di cappella* to Prince Ferdinando Stigliano, equerry to the Viceroy of Naples, and composed his first comic opera, *Lo frate 'nnamorato*, which achieved considerable popular success. In December that year he composed a Mass and psalms for solemn services in the aftermath of a series of earthquakes in Naples, and shortly afterwards was appointed deputy to the city's *maestro di cappella*. His most famous opera, the intermezzo *La serva padrona*, was written the following year.

In 1734 political upheavals caused Pergolesi to go to Rome with his employer, and a Mass of his was performed at S. Lorenzo in Lucina, where its unfamiliar Neapolitan style created much interest—the church was so crowded that part of the floor collapsed. As a result of that interest he was commissioned to write an *opera seria* for performance in Rome; *L'olimpiade* appears not to have been especially successful, but it received performances in other Italian cities and was the basis of a pasticcio given in London in 1742.

In 1735 Pergolesi's health seems to have been beginning to fail; he may have spent part of the summer at the Capuchin monastery at the nearby spa town of Pozzuoli, and his last opera was composed that autumn. Early in 1736 he retired to the Franciscan house at Pozzuoli, where he composed his last works, including the famous *Stabat mater*. After his death, probably from tuberculosis, he was buried in a common grave, but a memorial tablet was set up to him in Pozzuoli Cathedral and in 1890 this was transferred to a side chapel dedicated as his burial chapel.

Pergolesi seems to have been the first composer who, having won relatively little recognition during his lifetime—according to contemporaries many operas were failures when they first appeared—achieved great posthumous fame. His comedies entered the repertory of travelling opera companies, *Le serva padrona* in particular being performed throughout Europe and, on its appearance in Paris, helping to spark off the Querelle des *Bouffons. It encapsulates all the best characteristics of *opera buffa*, with a witty plot set to delightful music that portrays the characters perfectly, and is still regularly heard. His *Stabat mater* for soprano, alto, and strings, which sets the text both tunefully and expressively, appeared in more 18th-century reprints than any other work and is also still widely performed. Such was Pergolesi's reputation that a good many works by other composers—especially instrumental pieces, including some of those drawn on by Stravinsky for *Pulcinella*—were misattributed to him.   DA/ER

📖 M. E. PAYMER and H. W. WILLIAMS, *Giovanni Battista Pergolesi: A Guide to Research* (New York, 1989)

Peri, Jacopo (di Antonio di Francesco) (*b* Rome, 20 Aug. 1561; *d* Florence, 12 Aug. 1633). Italian composer and singer. He came from a lesser noble Florentine family and at the age of 12 was in Florence as a singer at the Servite monastery of Ss. Annunziata; over the following years he worked as a singer and organist at various churches and monasteries in Florence. He studied music with Malvezzi, who gave him a sound contrapuntal training. His main talent as a composer was for dramatic music; in 1583 he contributed some music (now lost) to a set of *intermedi* given at the Medici court, and in 1589 he sang in and composed an aria for the famous *intermedi* for *La pellegrina* given at the celebrations surrounding the marriage of Grand Duke Ferdinando I to Christine of Lorraine.

Peri would have known Giovanni de' Bardi and may have been involved in the discussions of his *camerata, but his relationship with the patron Jacopo Corsi in the 1590s was probably more significant. He collaborated with Corsi and the poet Ottavio Rinuccini to produce the first dramatic work with continuous music, *La

Dafne (1597–8); little of the music survives. However, it was probably similar in style to the next Peri–Rinuccini collaboration, *Euridice* (1600; published Florence, 1601), staged during the festivities for the wedding of Maria de' Medici and Henri IV of France. It was not a success, but today we can appreciate the dramatic effectiveness and expressiveness of his recitatives. (See also OPERA, 2.)

Little of Peri's later dramatic music survives. He continued to be active as a composer, however, cultivating connections with the Mantuan court and writing several dramatic works; publishing a song collection, *Le varie musiche*, in 1609 (reissued in 1619); directing the Easter music at S. Nicola, Pisa; and writing *sacre rappresentazioni* for S. Maria Novella, Florence, in the 1620s. His health was not good in these years, and although he survived the plague epidemic which attacked Florence in 1630–3 he died soon after the city was declared free of the plague, at the age of nearly 72.

DA/TC

 📖 T. CARTER, *Jacopo Peri (1561–1633): His Life and Works* (New York and London, 1989)

Péri, La ('The Peri'). Ballet (danced poem) by Dukas, choreographed by Ivan Clustine (Paris, 1912). Dukas made an orchestral suite from the score.

Périchole, La. Opera in two acts by Offenbach to a libretto by Henri Meilhac and Ludovic Halévy after Prosper Mérimée's comedy *Le Carosse du Saint-Sacrement* (Paris, 1868); it was revised in three acts (Paris, 1874).

period. A section of a composition that achieves a significant degree of harmonic closure. The term has been used in various ways by theorists (H. C. Koch's *Versuch einer Anleitung zur Composition*, 1782–93) and composers—notably Wagner, whose 'poetic-musical period' was a fundamental feature of his through-composed music dramas. But *Schoenberg's use of the term (*Fundamentals of Musical Composition*, 1967) had the greatest influence on 20th-century music theory. Unlike a *sentence, which contains an element of small-scale variation or development, a period consists of two phrases, *antecedent and consequent, each of which begins with the same basic motif, but which need not, as a whole, cadence in the tonic. Thus in the eight-bar period which begins the Sarabande from Bach's first English Suite, the antecedent and consequent, each of four bars, both cadence on the dominant.

AW

periodicals. Periodicals are publications that appear at (generally regular) intervals. They are usually printed, though a growing number are being published in electronic form only, and distributed on the Internet. Each periodical part will, usually, bear the same title (although in some cases titles may change over time) but be distinguished from other parts by bearing a unique date and/or volume or part number. The terms 'periodical', 'journal', and even 'magazine' are used fairly interchangeably, and will be so in the current article, even though each has a specific meaning. Use of the term 'serial' to refer to a periodical is made only by librarians and, on occasion, by bibliographers.

Music periodicals may be divided into various types according to function and intended readership. Some aim to keep their readers up to date with current musical trends: the magazine *Opera Now*, launched in the UK in the mid-1980s, was one of the first to adopt this approach, upstaging the much more serious journal *Opera*, with which it competed. The interests of record collectors are also well met, in a competitive market: *Diapason* and *Écouter voir* in France, *CD Collector* and *Gramophone* in the UK, and assorted journals from the American Schwann company keep the reader abreast of new releases, and of new equipment on which to play them. Fans of older recordings (a growing area of interest) have such journals as *International Classic Record Collector*. The *BBC Music Magazine* couples authoritative reviews of recordings of classical music with news and gossip. Other magazines include information on the popular music charts, 'fanzines' (periodicals given over to the activities of pop and rock groups), and a large number of specialist publications for aficionados of jazz, blues, rock, and so on.

The majority of the preceding periodicals may be bought from newsagents. There are also specialist periodicals concerned with musicology (for example, analysis) which are available only on subscription. A large number of journals are concerned with the early music revival, ranging from the accessible—*Early Music News* (UK), *Early Music America* (USA), and the coffee-table-style *Goldberg* (USA)—to the very serious, of which Cambridge University Press's *Early Music History* is perhaps the most representative. Periodicals devoted to a particular musical instrument include the *ITA* [International Trombone Association] *Journal*, the flute magazine *Tibia*, *The Clarinet*, and *Piano Quarterly*; others cater for enthusiasts for a particular composer—*Wagner*, *The Elgar Society Journal*, *Rachmaninov Society Newsletter*, *Cahiers Debussy*, and so on.

Devotees of folk music, and those interested in music of non-Western cultures, are also well supplied, and it is probably fair to say that anyone curious about a specialized area of music is likely to find a relevant publication. Music teachers, music librarians, and music administrators all have professional journals; and musicological societies in many countries issue their own periodicals, such as those of the American Musicological Society, Royal Musical Association, and Société Belge de Musicologie (Belgium), and the *Schweizerisches Jahrbuch für Musikwissenschaft* (Switzerland). There are research centres throughout the world whose function includes the promotion and dissemination of information about the groups they represent. The Institute for Research in Black American Music produces a journal, and the periodical *Women & Music* is issued by Washington University in association with the International Alliance of Women in Music. The National Sound Archive in Britain distributes a newsletter, *Playback*, whose aim is to publicize the Archive's services, as is *spnm News* (UK).

In addition to a subdivision by subject matter, music periodicals can also be divided into those that contain prose text and those that consist entirely of musical compositions. The latter type is in fact the earlier, with origins going back to the late 17th century. Some publishers, especially in the 19th century, issued a hybrid type of periodical that mainly contained prose while also providing readers with detachable supplements of music that could be gathered together into an album. This practice has now all but died out, though musical supplements occasionally appear in *The Musical Times*, founded in London in 1844 and still the longest continuously published English music periodical.

The cradle of prose journals in music was 18th-century Germany, primarily through the writings of Johann Mattheson (1681–1764) and Friedrich Wilhelm Marpurg (1718–95). All were short-lived. The *Allgemeine musikalische Zeitung*, published in 50 volumes in Leipzig between 1798 and 1848, broke this mould, though in the 19th century, and even up to the present day, periodicals have generally enjoyed only brief existences, with the exceptions notable for their sheer longevity. Thus the American *Musical Quarterly* has been published with only a short break since 1915; *Gramophone*, the UK's longest-lived magazine devoted to its subject, since 1923; and the *Journal of the American Musicological Society* since 1948. Several famous composers have been associated with music periodicals, as either editors or contributors, including Schumann, Berlioz, Debussy, and Schoenberg. During a miserable time in Paris in the early 1840s Wagner also contributed music copy to journals.

Music periodicals reflect, record, and influence musical life, including musical tastes. They make available a mass of information, news, reviews, and tittle-tattle that reflects the vibrancy of the musical world of their time, and provide the historian and social commentator with a wealth of material that does not find its way into the printed book. While books may mark the milestones of a particular subject, periodicals chart the small steps, false trails, and dead ends that are travelled along the way, and give diversion, enjoyment, and information.   JWA

📖 W. J. WEICHLEIN, *A Checklist of American Music Periodicals, 1850–1900* (Detroit, 1970) · I. FELLINGER, 'Periodicals', *The New Grove Dictionary of Music and Musicians* (London, 2/2001) [incl. bibliography and checklist of periodical titles]

period instruments. The instruments of a particular historical period revived by modern players: those on which the music of the chosen period would have been played at the time, and whose sound-qualities all but the most visionary contemporary composers are likely to have intended to exploit. The term usually implies modern copies or reconstructions of instruments rather than original ones. 'Period orchestras' attempt to re-create historic instrumentation and comprise period instruments exclusively; however, modern composers have written for period instruments and ensembles. The term is preferable to 'authentic instruments', a claim hard to prove, or 'historical instruments', which lacks the sense of being appropriate to a particular era.
                                                        JMo

period performance. The application of historical *performance practices, not only in music but also in theatre and dance. It includes the use of appropriate singing and playing styles and techniques and also of musical instruments in their original set-up, modified or built to particular historical specifications, or copied from particular specimens. Interest in period performance has increased steadily since the late 19th century, especially through the work of such scholar-performers as Arnold *Dolmetsch and his followers in the early music revival. Latterly, period performance has become a significant part of mainstream classical music-making.

See also AUTHENTICITY.   NPDC

Perle, George (*b* Bayonne, NJ, 6 May 1915). American composer and musicologist. He studied composition with Wesley LaViolette at De Paul University (1934–8) and privately with Ernst Krenek during the 1940s. He then embarked on a career as a teacher, at Louisville University (1949–57), the University of California at Davis (1957–61), and Queens College, New York (from 1961). In the 1930s he was one of the first Americans to interest himself in 12-note music, and from studies of Berg and Bartók he began developing his own system of '12-tone modality', which preserves euphony in a totally chromatic universe and makes possible sophisticated harmonic relations that match his music's irregular pulse. His output is centred on piano music, quartets, and songs. His writings include the widely read *Serial Composition and Atonality: An Introduction to the Music of Schoenberg, Berg, and Webern* (Los Angeles and London, 1962) and books on Berg's operas.

PG

Perosi, Lorenzo (*b* Tortona, nr Piacenza, 20 Dec. 1872; *d* Rome, 12 Oct. 1956). Italian composer. He studied in Rome and Milan, then went in 1893 to Regensburg, where he worked with F. X. Haberl. In 1894 he was appointed *maestro di cappella* at St Mark's, Venice, being ordained shortly afterwards. In 1898 he was made director of the Sistine Chapel, in which capacity he was influential in drawing up the **motu proprio* of 1903, advocating the return to a 'pure' style of church music. Perosi's compositions of this period, which include a *St Mark Passion* (1897), display the influences of both 16th-century polyphony and Wagner; his oratorios were acclaimed internationally. After a mental breakdown during World War I he recovered to produce a few small-scale works.

DA

Pérotin [Perotinus Magnus] (*fl* ? late 12th and early 13th centuries). Composer at Notre Dame, Paris. Like the older **Léonin, he is known from remarks by the English theorist known as Anonymous IV (*fl c.*1270), who implies that Pérotin took Léonin's liturgical chant settings (*organa dupla*) as a starting-point, revising them and supplementing them with pieces in a more modern idiom. Léonin's *magnus liber*, according to the theorist, 'was used up to the time of Perotinus Magnus, who shortened it and made many better clausulae or puncta [i.e. sections of **discant, as opposed to **organum], for he was the best composer [or singer] of discant'. Anonymous IV goes on to name various compositions by Pérotin; they include two chant settings for four voices (*organa quadrupla*)—the graduals *Viderunt* and *Sederunt*—and two for three voices (*organa tripla*), as well as three conductus, for three, two, and one voice respectively.

Given the existence of decrees of the Bishop of Paris from 1198 and 1199 allowing four-part settings specifically of *Viderunt* and *Sederunt*, it is likely that Pérotin's compositions date from about that time, though whether they were early or late works is not known. *Viderunt* and *Sederunt* are among the crowning achievements of all medieval music. Both in their large-scale tonal design—with massive pedal points sustaining majestic swings from one harmony to another—and in the detail of interplay between the three upper voices, they display a mastery that amply justifies Pérotin's sobriquet Magnus ('the great'). His contrapuntal style may be demonstrated in an extract from the three-part conductus *Salvatoris hodie* (Ex. 1)—particularly striking when one remembers that Léonin's known work consists simply of the addition of a single part to plainchant tenors.

DH

📖 C. WRIGHT, *Music and Ceremony at Notre Dame of Paris, 500–1500* (Cambridge, 1989)

Ex. 1

perpetual canon. See CANON.

perpetuum mobile (Lat., 'perpetually in motion'; It.: *moto perpetuo*). A title sometimes attached to a rapid instrumental composition proceeding throughout in notes of equal value. Paganini (*Moto perpetuo* op. 11 for violin and orchestra), Weber (Piano Sonata op. 24, last movement), Mendelssohn (op. 119), and Johann Strauss the younger (*Perpetuum mobile* op. 257) were among composers to use the term. The technique was also used by Beethoven in the last movements of several piano sonatas, and by Chopin in his *Études*.

Perséphone. Melodrama in three scenes by Stravinsky to a libretto by André Gide; for narrator, tenor, chorus, children's chorus, and orchestra, it was choreographed by Kurt Jooss (Paris, 1934). Stravinsky revised it in 1949.

Persichetti, Vincent (*b* Philadelphia, 6 June 1915; *d* Philadelphia, 15 Aug. 1987). American composer. He studied at the conservatory and the Curtis Institute in Philadelphia, and had composition lessons from Russell King Miller (1924–36) and Roy Harris (1943). He taught at the Philadelphia Conservatory (1942–62) and the Juilliard School (from 1947). A fluent and practical musician, he produced a large output of orchestral, choral, chamber, and instrumental music in a wide variety of styles but normally keeping some relation to tonal centres. He also wrote a treatise, *Twentieth Century Harmony* (New York, 1961).   PG

Persimfans (Pervïy Simfonicheskiy Ansambl', 'First Symphonic Ensemble'). A conductorless and democratically run orchestra created in Moscow in 1922; it played an important role in the city's musical life until its demise in 1932 for political reasons.   JWAL

Perti, Giacomo Antonio (*b* Bologna, 6 June 1661; *d* Bologna, 10 April 1756). Italian composer. By 1681, when he was admitted to the Accademia Filarmonica, he had already had masses and operatic music performed. In 1690 he succeeded his uncle as *maestro* at S. Pietro in Bologna, and in 1696 he was appointed *maestro* at S. Petronio, a post he retained for the rest of his life. He wrote much festive church music with instruments, including trumpets, as well as operas, oratorios, and trumpet sonatas in the Bolognese manner, and he was highly regarded by such contemporaries as Corelli, Caldara, and Padre Martini.   DA/ER

Peru. See LATIN AMERICA, 3.

Perugia, Matteo da. See MATTEO DA PERUGIA.

Perugia, Niccolò da. See NICCOLÒ DA PERUGIA.

pes (Lat., 'foot'). 1. A term used to describe the tenor part in some English 13th-century manuscripts; in most cases the *pes* carries a melodic ostinato figure. The two lowest voices of the rota *Sumer is icumen in* are called *pes* in the original manuscript.

2. Synonym for *podatus*, a neume comprising two notes. See NOTATION, 1.

pesant (Fr.), **pesante** (It.). 'Heavy', i.e. with emphasis; *pesamment* (Fr.), *pesantemente* (It.), 'heavily'.

Pescetti, Giovanni Battista (*b* Venice, *c*.1704; *d* Venice, 20 March 1766). Italian composer. A pupil of Antonio Lotti, he composed operas in Venice from 1725 to 1732. In 1736 he went to London, where he took over from Porpora as director of the Opera of the Nobility and published some keyboard sonatas. He returned to Venice in about 1745 and became second organist at St Mark's in 1762.   WT/ER

Peter and the Wolf (*Pyotr i volk*). Symphonic fairy tale for narrator and orchestra, op. 67 (1936), by Prokofiev; the characters in the story are represented by different solo instruments, the work having been conceived as a children's introduction to the orchestra.

Peter Grimes. Opera in a prologue and three acts by Britten to a libretto by Montagu Slater after George Crabbe's poem *The Borough* (1810) (London, 1945); Britten created an orchestral work, the **Four Sea Interludes*, from the opera's descriptive orchestral numbers.

Peters. A group of music publishers active in Germany, England, and the USA. Originating from a firm established in Leipzig in 1800 by the composer F. A. Hoffmeister (1754–1812), it was sold in 1814 to the bookseller C. F. Peters (1779–1827), by which time the catalogue contained works by Bach, Haydn, Mozart, and Beethoven, subsequently expanding to include those of Spohr, Weber, and Hummel. Max Abraham (1831–1900) became a partner, and in 1880 sole owner; with the engraver C. G. Röder he established the firm's reputation as Edition Peters, with its distinctive covers (light green for works out of copyright, pink for original publications).

Abraham's nephew Henri Hinrichsen (1868–1942) joined the firm in 1894, and works by Grieg, Brahms, Wagner, Wolf, Mahler, Schoenberg, and Richard Strauss entered the catalogue. His sons Max (1901–65) and Walter (1907–69) joined in 1931 but left Germany in the wake of the Nazi regime to found companies in London (Hinrichsen Edition, 1938) and New York (1948) respectively. After World War II each company published parts of the original catalogue as well as promoting new music. The Leipzig firm became publicly owned in 1949–50. In 1950 the Hinrichsen brothers and Johannes Putschull (*b* 1901) founded a company in Frankfurt, to which, following reunification in 1989, all Peters's publishing activities in Germany were transferred. In addition to issuing *Urtext* editions, the three companies are promoters of contemporary composers, including Kagel (Frankfurt), Ferneyhough (London), Cage, and Crumb (New York).   HA

Peterson-Berger, Wilhelm (*b* Ullånger, Ångermanland, 27 Feb. 1867; *d* Ostersund, 3 Dec. 1942). Swedish composer and critic. He studied the organ and composition at the Royal College of Music in Stockholm (1886–9), then went to Dresden, where he studied composition with Edmund Kretschmer (1889–90). After a brief period as a language teacher in Umeå (1890–2) and another back in Dresden (1892–4) he settled in Stockholm, where in 1896 he became a critic for the newspaper *Dagens Nyheter*, working there with only two short breaks until 1930. Already active as a composer, he was stage manager at the Royal Stockholm Opera (1908–10), completing his own opera *Arnljot* (the second of four) during this period. The national-Romantic idiom of his early works was coloured by a knowledge of Wagner, whose writings he translated and on whom he wrote; the discovery of Sami *jojkar* chants in 1913 introduced a modal freshness into his music, beginning with *Same-Ätnam* ('Lapland', 1913–15), the third of his five symphonies.   MA

📖 L. Hedwall, *Wilhelm Peterson-Berger: Life and Works* (Stockholm, 1984)

Petite Messe solennelle ('Little Solemn Mass'). Choral work (1863) by Rossini, a setting of the Mass text for soprano, mezzo-soprano, tenor, and baritone soloists, chorus, two pianos, and harmonium; Rossini arranged it for full orchestra (1867). The word 'petite' refers not to the work's size but to Rossini's modest evaluation of its importance.

Petite suite ('Little Suite'). Work for piano duet (1886–9) by Debussy, its movements being 'En bateau', 'Cortège', 'Menuet', and 'Ballet'; it was arranged for piano solo by Durand (1906), for orchestra by Busser (1907), and for small orchestra by Henri Mouton (1909).

Petits Riens, Les ('The Little Nobodies'). Ballet-divertissement by Mozart with a scenario by Jean-Georges Noverre, who also choreographed it (Paris, 1778). The music was lost until 1872, when it was found in the library of the Paris Opéra.

Petrassi, Goffredo (*b* Zagarola, nr Palestrina, 16 July 1904). Italian composer. He studied at the Accademia di S. Cecilia in Rome (1928–32), where he taught from 1934 onwards. At first influenced by the neo-classicism of Stravinsky, Hindemith, and Casella, he moved on during the 1940s to a style of dense harmony and deep

thought; the main works of this second period include his metaphysical opera *Morte dell'aria* (Rome, 1950). In the early 1950s he began to use serial methods, and subsequent works avoid thematic working in favour of a vigorous, kaleidoscopic use of motifs. His development is best observed in the cycle of eight concertos for orchestra (1933–72). Other works include choral pieces and much chamber and instrumental music.   PG

📖 F. d'Amico, *Goffredo Petrassi* (Rome, 1942) · J. S. Weissmann, *Goffredo Petrassi* (Milan, 1957) · C. Annibaldi (ed.), *Catalogo bibliografico delle opere di Goffredo Petrassi* (Milan, 1971)

Petrić, Ivo (*b* Ljubljana, 16 June 1931). Slovene composer and conductor. After studying at the Ljubljana Academy of Music he founded the Slavko Osterc Ensemble, which he conducted in much contemporary music, and became editor of the publishing section of the Association of Slovene Composers. From 1979 to 1995 he was artistic director of the Slovene Philharmonic Orchestra. He has composed prolifically for orchestra and many different ensembles, at first in a neo-classical manner, but later using more advanced techniques.   ABur

Petrucci, Ottaviano (dei) (*b* Fossombrone, 18 June 1466; *d* ?Venice, 7 May 1539). Italian music printer and publisher. He was the first to use movable type for printing polyphonic music, beginning in 1501 in Florence with his *Harmonice musices odhecaton A*, which consists mainly of chansons by Franco-Flemish composers. Over the next eight years he published much polyphonic music by the leading Franco-Flemish and Italian composers of his day. By 1511 he had returned to Fossombrone; he continued printing there until about 1520, after which he opened a paper mill and ceased printing activity. He returned to Venice in 1536.

See also PRINTING AND PUBLISHING OF MUSIC, 4.
          JMT/JWa

Petrus de Cruce [Pierre de la Croix] (*fl* 1290–1300). French cleric, music theorist, and composer. Little is known about his life, but he was evidently a native and resident of Amiens, and probably studied at the University of Paris. He is principally remembered for his rhythmic and notational experiments in motet composition, making it possible to achieve a more terraced differentiation between the texted upper voices and the tenor. He was also skilled in liturgy and plainchant. A few minor theoretical works by him survive.   JM

Petrushka. Ballet in four scenes by Stravinsky to a scenario by Alexandre Benois; it was choreographed by Mikhail Fokine for Diaghilev's Ballets Russes (Paris, 1911). Stravinsky made an orchestral suite from the ballet (1914); it was reorchestrated in 1947 as a suite in four parts with 15 movements. Stravinsky arranged three movements for piano (1921) and made a four-hand piano reduction of the score. Victor Babin made a version for two pianos and Theodor Szántó arranged five pieces into a piano suite.

Pettersson, (Gustaf) Allan (*b* Västra Ryd, Uppsala län, 19 Sept. 1911; *d* Stockholm, 20 June 1980). Swedish composer. He studied composition, violin, and viola at the Stockholm Conservatory, and in his late 30s with Honegger and René Leibowitz in Paris. He worked as an orchestral viola player until 1964, becoming well known as a composer only in the late 1960s. Pettersson's principal works are 16 symphonies, most in a single large-scale movement, of rugged individuality and uncompromising argument. He also wrote other orchestral works, a small amount of choral and chamber music, and a cycle of *Barefoot Songs* for voice and piano (1943–5).   ABur

petto (It.). 'Chest'; *voce di petto*, **chest voice* (see also VOICE, 4).

peu (Fr.). 'A little', 'rather'; *un peu*, 'a little'; *peu à peu*, 'little by little'; *un peu plus lent*, 'a little slower'.

Peuerl, Paul (*b* Stuttgart, *bapt.* 13 June 1570; *d* after 1625). German composer. He worked as an organist and organ builder in Steyr, Upper Austria, for most of his life, and from there published four volumes of instrumental suites (Nuremberg, 1611–25). The suites are made up of four dances in the pattern of a theme followed by three variations.   DA

Pezel, Johann Christoph (*b* Glatz, Silesia, 1639; *d* Bautzen, nr Glatz, 13 Oct. 1694). German composer. Between 1664 and 1681 he was a member of the Leipzig band of town musicians. He composed several works for wind and brass, mainly in the form of suites or sonatas, of which the best known are his two collections of **Turmmusik* scored for the typical town-band ensemble of cornetts and trombones.   DA

pezzo, pezzi (It.). 'Piece', 'pieces', in the sense of 'composition'.

pf., pfte. Abbreviations for 'pianoforte'.

Pfitzner, Hans (*b* Moscow, 5 May 1869; *d* Salzburg, 22 May 1949). German composer. Though born in Moscow, he was of German parentage and was brought up and educated in Frankfurt, studying first with his father—a notable violinist—then from 1886 to 1890 at the Hoch Conservatory, Frankfurt, with Iwan Knorr. Intensely ambitious for the success of his own music, he accepted the post of voluntary Kapellmeister in Mainz (1894–7), ensuring the premiere of his first opera *Der arme Heinrich* ('Poor Henry') in 1895. Though strongly influenced by Wagner, the opera peers back nostalgically to Weber and Schumann and is anchored in the Romantic tradition, the preservation of which became Pfitzner's abiding concern. From 1903 to 1907 he worked in Berlin as conductor at the Theater des Westens, during which time he developed both a bitter enmity towards Strauss (contemporaneously music director at the Berlin Court Opera) and a firm belief that the modernism of Busoni and Schoenberg represented alien influences in German culture. His subsequent operas *Die Rose vom Liebesgarten* ('The Rose of the Garden of Love', 1905) and *Das Christelflein* ('The Christmas Elf', 1906) were relatively unsuccessful, as was his attempt to impose his musical personality on the German capital.

In 1907 Pfitzner was appointed director of the Strasbourg Conservatory, becoming director of the Court Opera in 1910. From 1909 to 1915 he worked on his most important score, the opera *Palestrina*. A fierce defence of aesthetic tradition in the face of those who would undermine it, it envisions the artist at the centre of a divinely appointed totality, fashioning eternal masterpieces in Platonic imitation of God as creator. At its premiere in Munich in 1917 the opera was hailed, notably by Thomas Mann, as the embodiment of German 'national' art.

Pfitzner's years in Strasbourg were marked, however, by a stance that became increasingly nationalistic. *Futuristengefahr* ('The Danger of the Futurists'), the first of his polemical essays against modernism, was published in 1917. In 1919 the ceding of Alsace-Lorraine to France under the Treaty of Versailles necessitated Pfitzner's dismissal from Strasbourg. The same year he went into print with the most infamous of his writings *Die neue Aesthetik der musikalischen Impotenz: Ein Verwesungssymptom* ('The New Aesthetic of Musical Impotence: A Symptom of Putrefaction'), which viciously identified Schoenberg as the embodiment of 'international Bolshevism' and subsequently became an important work in the formation of the Nazi classification of **Entartete Musik*. Pfitzner and Hitler were briefly close in 1923; thereafter Pfitzner's relations with the Nazis remained ambivalent. He never joined the Nazi party, though his nationalistic cantata *Von deutscher Seele* ('From the German Soul', 1921) was frequently played at official functions during the Third Reich and he was more than willing to allow his writings to be reprinted as propaganda.

Both Pfitzner's popularity and the quality of his music began to decline in the 1920s. Awarded life membership of the Munich Academy in 1929, he was pensioned off in 1934, protesting bitterly to Goering the following year about both his dismissal and the decrease in popularity of his works. During the war he appeared frequently as a conductor in Nazi-occupied territories and accepted the patronage of Hans Frank, the governor of Poland, in whose honour he wrote a polonaise. He settled in Vienna in 1944, though the following year he was forced to flee to Garmisch-Partenkirchen, where he was detained in a transit camp opposite Strauss's villa. The Allied forces banned performances of his works in 1945–6. He was officially de-Nazified in 1947, though his polemical writings must inevitably still render him suspect. With the exception of *Palestrina*, much of his music, which combines post-Wagnerian Romantic technique with a stripped-down austerity of style, has not remained in the international repertory.   PG/TA

📖 J. WILLIAMSON, *The Music of Hans Pfitzner* (Oxford, 1992)

Pfleger, Augustin (*b* Schlackenwerth, nr Carlsbad, *c*.1635; *d* ?Schlackenwerth, 23 July 1686). German composer. He twice served the Bohemian court at Schlackenwerth, with intervening posts at Güstrow (1662–5) and Gottorf (1665–73). His compositions include a cycle of 72 *Geistliche Konzerte* for the whole church year, many in dialogue form for solo voices, strings, and continuo, and a short oratorio on the Seven Last Words from the Cross, in which (unlike Schütz's version) the biblical account is augmented by free commentary.   BS

Phalèse. Flemish family of music printers and publishers. The elder Pierre Phalèse (*c*.1510–76) became bookseller to the University of Leuven in 1542 and published scientific and scholarly books during the 1540s, as well as five books of chanson arrangements for lute. In 1551 he received a privilege to print ecclesiastical and secular music from movable type, and throughout the 1550s and 60s he issued many volumes of chansons, dances, motets, lute intabulations, and other pieces (e.g. by Clemens, Guerrero, Lassus, and Rore). An accomplished printer, he was the first in the Low Countries to issue parts in 'table-book' format, arranged so that performers sitting round a table could read from one copy.

In 1570 he formed a partnership with the Antwerp printer Jean Bellère (1526–95), which his son Pierre Phalèse (*c*.1550–1629) continued, moving to Antwerp in 1581. The younger Pierre used his father's printing materials, and his extensive output includes many volumes of Italian madrigals, both anthologies and single-composer volumes (e.g. Lassus and Marenzio). His daughters Madeleine (1586–1652) and Marie (1589–*c*.1674) continued the family business in Antwerp until it finally lapsed in 1674.   JMT/JWA

phantasie, phantasy. See FANTASIA.

Phantasiestücke ('Fantasy Pieces'). Schumann's op. 12 (1837), for piano, a set of eight pieces each with a descriptive title; he composed three further *Phantasiestücke* op. 111 (1851), but they have no titles and are described simply by their key signatures.

phasing. A term denoting the effect achieved when two instrumentalists or singers perform the same musical pattern at different (slightly increasing or decreasing) intervals of time, moving in or out of phase. The technique of phasing is quite often used in so-called minimalist compositions, for example Steve *Reich's *Piano Phase* (1967). Phasing can also be achieved electronically, when the results of mixing phased materials can be a good deal more rich and complex than a simple superimposition of identical elements.   AW

Philharmonic Society. See ROYAL PHILHARMONIC SOCIETY.

Philidor. French family of musicians and composers. Their name was originally Danican. **Jean Danican Philidor** (1620–79), a virtuoso oboist, was a wind-instrument player in the Grande Écurie. His elder son, **André Danican Philidor** *l'aîné* (*c*.1652–1730), was a musician and composer in the royal chapel and helped to establish the Philidor collection in Louis XIV's library at Versailles. André's brother **Jacques Danican Philidor** *le cadet* (1657–1708), like his father, played wind instruments in the Grande Écurie. The most important musicians of the succeeding generation were two of André's sons. **Anne Danican Philidor** (1681–1728) held various appointments in the royal household and in those of the Prince of Conti and the Duchess of Maine but is best remembered as the founder of the Concert Spirituel, the first permanent concert series.

The most illustrious member of the family was Anne's half-brother, **François-André Danican Philidor** (*b* Dreux, 7 Sept. 1726; *d* London, 31 Aug. 1795), a composer and chess player. At Versailles he studied under André Campra. He moved to Paris in 1740, helping Rousseau with *Les Muses galantes*. Philidor became the finest chess player of his age, certainly in northern Europe, and for much of his life chess was his main source of income, both in Paris and in London where, stranded by the Revolution, he died. He published an important treatise on chess; Diderot feared that simultaneous blindfold play would drive him mad. His combinatorial memory may have led him, in music, to inadvertent plagiarism from works of Gluck and Jommelli.

Philidor's early compositions are lost. He used a period of travel to study modern Italian music; returning to Paris in 1754, he was refused a musical post at Versailles because his trial motet was too Italian. He published some quartets, then embarked from 1756 on a career in theatre music by writing for the suburban 'fair theatres'. Philidor was the first important French composer of *opéra comique*, though preceded by Duni and soon rivalled by Monsigny. His elegant melody and instrumentation are matched by his witty imitative music and brilliant handling of ensembles of up to seven soloists. His first successful original score was *Blaise le savetier* (1759), to a text by M.-J. Sedaine. Other successes were *Le Maréchal ferrant* (1761), *Le Sorcier* (1764), and *Tom Jones* (1765). In 1767 he wrote *Ernelinde*, a revolutionary *tragédie lyrique*, many features of which anticipated Gluck. Its revival in 1777 was a success, but later efforts in this field failed to make a mark. With his operatic career in decline, he nevertheless scored a triumph with the lengthy Latin cantata *Carmen saeculare*, performed in London in 1779.　　JR

　　J. G. RUSHTON, 'Philidor and the tragédie lyrique', *Musical Times*, 117 (1976), 734–7 · J.-F. and N. DUPONT-DANICAN PHILIDOR, *Les Philidor: Une dynastie de musiciens* (Paris, 1995)

Philippe de Vitry. See VITRY, PHILIPPE DE.

Philips, Peter (*b* ?London, 1560 or 1561; *d* Brussels, 1628). English organist and composer, latterly resident in the Spanish Netherlands. He was a choirboy at St Paul's Cathedral in 1574 and may have studied with Byrd. In 1582 he left England because of his Roman Catholic faith; he went to the Collegio Inglese in Rome and entered the service of one of its patrons, Cardinal Alessandro Farnese, continuing to act as organist at the college. For five years from 1585 he travelled with Lord Thomas Paget, an English Catholic; following Paget's death in 1590 he settled in Antwerp as a teacher of the virginals. In 1593 he was accused of plotting against the life of Queen Elizabeth, and was imprisoned in The Hague (during which time he wrote his *Pavan and Galliard Dolorosa*); but he was soon released, and returned to Antwerp. His last position was in the Brussels household of Archduke Albert. He was ordained priest in 1609.

　　Philips was an Englishman in his keyboard music, but a Continental in his vocal works. Many of his pieces for the virginal were copied into the Fitzwilliam Virginal Book, and if the arrangements of Italian madrigals seem dry and over-ornate, the dances are superb, with unusual emotional power deriving from an imaginative use of chromaticism and ornament. The later organ music, regrettably, is almost entirely lost. His madrigals set Italian verse, and are noted for their singability and delicate word-painting. He published brilliant-sounding motets for five-part and double choir, as well as some for solo, duet, and trio in the concertato manner. Philips's neglect is probably due to

the fact that he 'affected altogether the Italian vein' (Henry Peacham, 1622), and he has suffered the frequent fate of expatriates.　　DA/JM

Philosopher, The (*Der Philosoph*). Nickname of Haydn's Symphony no. 22 in E♭ major (1764), so called because of the character of its opening Adagio.

Phoebus and Pan (*Der Streit zwischen Phoebus und Pan*, 'The Dispute between Phoebus and Pan'; *Geschwinde, geschwinde, ihr wirbelnden Winde*, 'Haste, haste, you whirling winds'). J. S. Bach's cantata no. 201 (1729), to a text by Picander after Ovid; it deals with the question of good and bad art, good music being represented by Phoebus, bad music by Pan. It has occasionally been staged.

phon. A unit of loudness; see ACOUSTICS, 11.

phonograph. The name used by Thomas Alva Edison for the recording device he patented in 1877. The *'cylinder phonograph' recorded by indenting the signal into aluminium foil. It was superseded by a wax-coated cylinder which produced a more realistic signal. Both quickly deteriorated on repeated playback. The term 'phonograph' became common American usage rather than 'gramophone', preferred in the UK.

　　See also RECORDING AND REPRODUCTION.　　LF

phrase. A musical unit, defined by the interrelation of melody, rhythm, and harmony, that ends with a *cadence of some kind. The word is borrowed by analogy from the terminology of linguistic syntax. Musical phrases combine to form larger, more complete units known as periods, and may themselves be subdivided. The length of a phrase varies, but is most frequently of four bars (found regularly in folk and dance music, and in art music of the Classical period), often followed by an 'answering' phrase of the same length. In contrapuntal music the phrases of the various melodic voices overlap except at the most important cadences.

　　In notation, phrase-marks are the slurs placed over or under the notes as a hint of their proper punctuation in performance (Ex. 1; for the use of similar curved lines, see SLUR; TIE).

　　The term 'phrasing' refers to the way in which a performer interprets both individual phrases and their combination in the piece as a whole. Such a technique is often instinctive and is one of the features by which a supreme artist may be distinguished from others.

　　—/JBE

Ex. 1

Phrygian cadence. See CADENCE.

Phrygian mode. The mode represented by the white notes of the piano beginning on E. See MODE, 2.

Phrygian tetrachord. A *tetrachord made up of the first four notes of the Phrygian mode. The intervals of the Phrygian tetrachord are semitone–tone–tone (e.g. E–F–G–A), as opposed to the tone–tone–semitone of the diatonic major scale.

piacere, a (It.). 'At pleasure', i.e. ad *libitum.

piacevole (It.). 'Pleasing', 'agreeable'.

piangendo, piangente (It.). 'Weeping', 'plaintive'; *piangevole, piangevolmente*, 'plaintively'.

pianissimo (It.). 'Very quiet'; it is abbreviated *pp*.

piano. 1. See PIANOFORTE.
2 (It.). 'Soft'; it is abbreviated *p*.

piano duet. A work for two pianists at the same piano, or, more rarely, two pianists playing two pianos. The genre became particularly popular from the second half of the 18th century. Mozart, who performed duets with his sister Nannerl as a child, wrote several sonatas for four hands at one piano, and Schubert made a particularly significant contribution to the genre (e.g. the Grand Duo D812). Other composers who wrote piano duets include Brahms, Dvořák, Grieg, Fauré, Debussy, Stravinsky, and Bartók.

Piano-duet reductions of operas and opera highlights (e.g. by Donizetti and Verdi), as well as symphonies and other orchestral works, were made in large number in the 19th century, winning wide popularity as a means by which amateurs could familiarize themselves with the Classical and Romantic repertory before the advent of recording.   JBE

pianoforte [piano] (Ger.: *Klavier, Hammerklavier*). A stringed keyboard instrument with a hammer action.

> 1. Origins; 2. Cristofori's influence; 3. England, Zumpe, and square pianos; 4. The Viennese action; 5. The grand piano since the 1820s; 6. The upright piano; 7. Pedals and stops; 8. Early performers and repertory

1. Origins

At the beginning of the 18th century the domestic keyboard instruments were the *clavichord, which had great expressive qualities but was very faint in tone, and the *harpsichord, which was louder and more brilliant but somewhat inflexible in tonal variety. A natural desire seems to have developed for a keyboard instrument combining the powers of nuance of the clavichord with the size and strength of the harpsichord. The hammer action of a piano is very different from the action of the harpsichord's plectrum: the force with which the hammer is thrown at the string, and the resulting volume of sound, is greatly affected by variations in the pressure of the finger on the key.

Bartolomeo Cristofori achieved this in his piano action (Fig. 1) by placing the hammer on a separate shank and adding an intermediate lever which transfers the motion of the depressed key, via the pivoted jack mortised through the key, to the hammer shank, allowing the hammer to rise with many times the initial velocity of the finger movement on the key.

Cristofori also had to circumvent several potential problems caused by the hammer action: first, if the hammer remains in contact with the string after it has struck it, the sound is 'blocked' because the hammer stops the string from vibrating; secondly, as the hammer rebounds from the string, it may bounce back and strike it again. These were solved by means of an 'es-

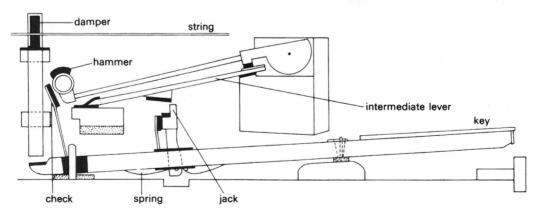

Fig. 1. Action of the Leipzig Cristofori piano, 1726.

capement' mechanism provided by the jack, which tilts forward slightly just before the hammer reaches the string, allowing the intermediate lever to fall back, and thus releasing the hammer so that it may fall from the string. As it falls, its head is caught against the 'check', a pad on a rod which holds it momentarily and stops any tendency to rebound. When the key falls back as the finger releases it, the hammer returns to its initial position, ready to strike again. The damper is mounted on a jack similar to that of the harpsichord, standing on the end of the key; as the key is depressed, the damper is raised to allow the string to vibrate. Although the escapement enables the hammer to fall away from the string, the damper is not allowed to fall back and damp the string until the key is released.

Another risk inherent in hammer action is that the hammer can strike the string with enough force to lift it from its seating on the bridge, distorting the sound and upsetting the tuning. Down-bearing must be provided on the strings near the wrest pins (tuning-pins) to avoid this. Cristofori's solution on two of his pianos was to invert the wrest plank (pin block) and attach the nut to its underside, the strings being attached to the lower ends of the wrest pins after passing under the down-bearing nut.

An inventory dated 1700 of instruments at the Medici court, where Cristofori was the keeper, shows that at least one had been built with such an action by that date. Scipione Maffei wrote a detailed description of Cristofori's invention in 1711, calling it a *gravicembalo col piano e forte* ('harpsichord with soft and loud'). Only three of Cristofori's pianos are known to survive, in New York (1720), Rome (1722), and Leipzig (1726), as well as a keyboard and action without the rest of the instrument (c.1725). All three pianos and Maffei's description differ in some respects, suggesting that Cristofori continued to experiment with improvements throughout his career. His hammers were made of soft leather pads in 1711 and 1722; later instruments had rolls of parchment (1725) or paper (1726), each surmounted by a soft leather pad (the 1720 hammers have been replaced).

Meanwhile, other minds were also concentrating on producing a 'hammer-harpsichord' or 'keyboard dulcimer': two makers who laid claim to its invention were the Parisian Jean Marius (*clavecin à maillets*, 1716), and the Saxon Gottlieb Schröter (1717). Experiments with tangent- and hammer-action instruments go back as far as Henri Arnaut de Zwolle's treatise of c.1440 (though there is no suggestion of continuity between the early designs and those of the late 17th and the 18th centuries), but it was Cristofori who first managed to resolve all the problems inherent in a hammer action.

2. Cristofori's influence

Cristofori's work was sufficiently successful in his own time that it was copied in Italy, Spain, Portugal, and Germany, where Gottfried Silbermann's first efforts were criticized by Bach as being too heavy in the touch and too weak in the upper register, but whose later models he praised. Silbermann, unlike some of the other imitators, retained Cristofori's inverted wrest plank and soundboard. Other makers in Germany and Austria, however, sought actions that were simpler and cheaper to make (many were approaching the problem from the clavichord rather than the harpsichord), and many of Cristofori's successful features were abandoned and subsequently had to be reinvented. It was not until after 1800 that the piano was again as efficient as it had been in its inventor's hands in 1700.

3. England, Zumpe, and square pianos

One of the main problems of the early piano is that, though the sound could get louder and softer, it was not very loud to begin with, in spite of the fact that Cristofori and his followers used heavier strings than those used for harpsichords; the light stringing of brass and iron wire then available was rather better suited to plucking than to striking. The pitch of a string depends on its length, tension, and mass. If the two last are to remain constant—and it is desirable to keep tension reasonably equal lest any variation makes the casework twist—the length must double for every downward octave. Even with a grand piano such as Cristofori's this is hardly practicable over four octaves, and both the 1722 and 1726 pianos are foreshortened in the bass, with heavier strings to compensate.

It seems to have been Johannes Zumpe, who emigrated from Fürth to London in about 1750, who first produced an answer to this problem in the so-called square (actually rectangular) pianos he began making in about 1766. The square piano, essentially a clavichord with a simple hammer action, was introduced in Germany in the 1740s. It was a very small instrument, with consequent difficulties for the bass strings. Zumpe's solution was to use bass strings overspun with an open coil of wire to increase their mass without reducing their flexibility.

Zumpe's action of the 1760s (sometimes known as the English single action) was very simple: the jack acted directly on the underside of the hammer, without any intermediate lever, and the hammer, its shank hinged with soft leather to the hammer rail, flew up and struck the string. By 1786 the maker John Geib had restored the intermediate lever and an escapement (the 'English double action'), though the English grand action, perfected by Americus Backers in about 1770 and used for many years thereafter by Broadwood and others, while providing escapement and check, had its hopper acting directly on the keyshank (Fig. 2).

4. The Viennese action

In Austria and Germany actions were even simpler. The *Prellmechanik* action had no jack, but the hammer shank was pivoted on the distal end of the key; the key pushed the hammer up until a beak on the back of the shank caught on a wooden bar, the *Prelleiste*, flipping the other end up to strike the string. Sometimes an escapement replaced the *Prelleiste* (Fig. 3); this action, which became known as the 'Viennese grand action', was used by such makers as Stein in Augsburg and Walter in Vienna (Mozart praised the pianos of the former and bought one from the latter), and by Streicher (Stein's daughter) and Graf in Vienna at the time of Beethoven.

5. The grand piano since the 1820s

Hammers were becoming heavier. Zumpe's had tiny wooden heads with a covering of thin leather. Broadwood's and the early Viennese had several layers of soft leather. In the 1820s Henri Pape in Paris cut up felt hats to make covers for the hammers, and since then felt has remained the standard material.

At the same time bass strings became heavier, with close-coiled overspinning, and the superior steel wire made available during the Industrial Revolution, better

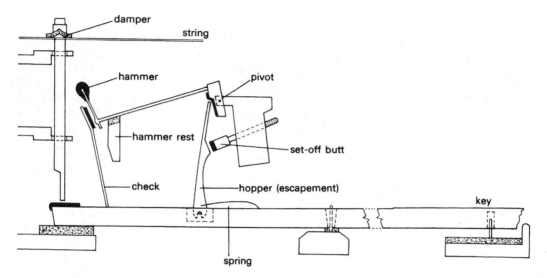

Fig. 2. Action of an English grand piano, *c.*1790

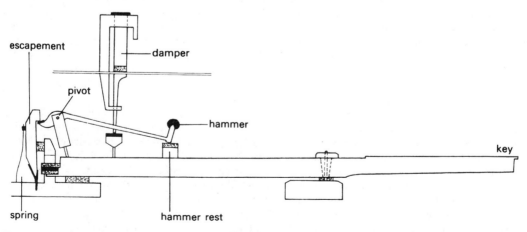

Fig. 3. Action of a south German–Viennese piano, 1780.

able to withstand greater tension, was used throughout the instrument. This put intolerable strains on the casework, the string tension trying to pull the wrest plank closer to the soundboard. Makers at first put some iron hoops or bars across the gap through which the hammers rise to strike the strings in order to hold it open, later using iron rods between a plate on the wrest plank and another at the tail for the hitch-pins.

Alpheus Babcock in Boston invented a one-piece iron frame for the square piano in 1825, and Chickering did the same for the grand in 1843. In 1859 Steinway applied the principle of overstringing (or cross-stringing) to the iron-framed grand piano. Overstringing, in which the bass strings travel diagonally above the shorter strings to give them extra length, was first patented by Pape in 1828 for a small upright and subsequently widely used on square pianos. It took almost 50 years for Steinway's patent to become adopted by most of the principal makers, but iron frames and overstringing are now used on nearly all pianos. Cheap instruments were still being made without iron frames into the 20th century.

The piano's compass extended over the years, from Cristofori's four octaves to five by Mozart's time and six by 1794. By the mid-19th century, Schumann and Chopin required no more than six and a half; today a further octave is usual.

Actions have become increasingly complex, almost innumerable small parts moving against each other in the endeavour to combine lightness, response, and speed of action with weight and power of tone. String tension has increased to the extent that strings are almost as rigid as metal bars, and sharing some of the same inharmonicity of overtones. Down-bearing pres-

sure is provided by the *capo d'astro* or *capo tasto* bar (invented by Antoine Bord in 1843), screwed down to the wrest plank by the nut, and since 1821 also by Sébastien Érard's *agraffes* (small brass studs, each perforated with holes for the strings of one note); these also define one end of the speaking length of the string. Almost the only major feature of the modern action that is superior to Cristofori's is the double escapement (Fig. 4), invented by Érard in 1821, which allows the hammer to drop only a short distance, so making rapid reiterations of the note much easier.

6. The upright piano

While the grand piano has always been the ideal for the concert room, it takes up too much space in the home. Even square pianos became cumbersome in the 19th century as compasses increased from five octaves to seven and they grew proportionally longer, wider, and deeper. The most enduring solution, saving space with no loss of length of the strings and the soundboard, is the upright piano, in which the strings and soundboard are arranged in a vertical plane. The first uprights (made from c.1835 to c.1850) were very tall, the strings and their casing of the grand piano simply turned up on end immediately in front of the keyboard. Such 'upright grands' were made in a variety of shapes including the 'giraffe' (following the wing shape of the grand but with a decorative scroll at the top of the bass end) and the 'pyramid' (permitted by the strings running at a slight diagonal), both made mainly in Germany and Austria, and the 'bookcase' or 'cabinet', a rectangular cupboard with shelves for music storage in the unoccupied space to the right of the strings, most common in Britain. The upright grand had two disadvantages;

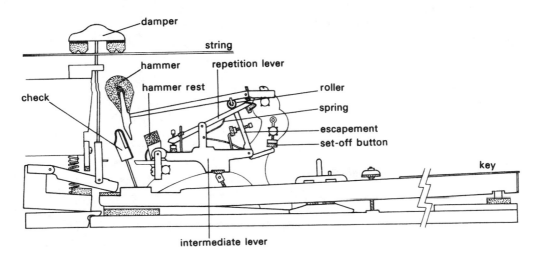

Fig. 4. Action of a modern grand piano.

one that its balance was precarious even when it was placed against a wall, and the other that players had their backs to their hearers, which was considered unacceptable.

More practical uprights were invented in 1800 by John Isaac Hawkins in Philadelphia and Matthias Müller in Vienna. Both had the idea of lowering the height of the upright piano by running the strings down to the floor and placing the wrest plank and action at the top. As with the square piano, this meant foreshortening the bass strings and a resulting loss of tone-quality. A modern upright piano action is shown in Fig. 5.

7. Pedals and stops

Although the first pianos had no pedals, two of Cristofori's pianos had a simple *una corda* mechanism whereby the keyboard could be shifted sideways so that each hammer would strike only one of its pair of strings. Silbermann's pianos also had a damper-raising hand-stop. The *una corda* has remained a vital device, now operated by a left-foot pedal, not only reducing volume but producing a perceptibly different tone-

quality. Later pianos, after it became normal to have three strings for each note instead of two, sometimes had a *due corde* pedal as well as an *una corda*, allowing greater variety of tone. The 'soft pedal' on some uprights moves the whole set of hammers closer to the strings, so that they give a less powerful blow. Silbermann's damper lift has also remained a standard, now operated from the right-foot 'sustaining pedal' on the right, and more expensive pianos have a *sostenuto pedal.

In 19th-century Vienna the moderator stop (*piano*, mute, or *sourdine*) was common: a strip of cloth inserted between hammers and strings, muting them slightly. At this period, before pedals were developed, the stops (or mutations) were often effected by knee-levers. Much more ambitious in the late 18th century were such devices as the bassoon stop, a strip of parchment touching the strings to give a buzz more reminiscent of kazoos than bassoons, and the Turkish music or janissary stop, a gallimaufry of drum, triangle, cymbals, bells, and other effects to represent the *alla turca* of the *military band. Comparable effects in the 20th century were the prepared pianos of composers like Cage, who

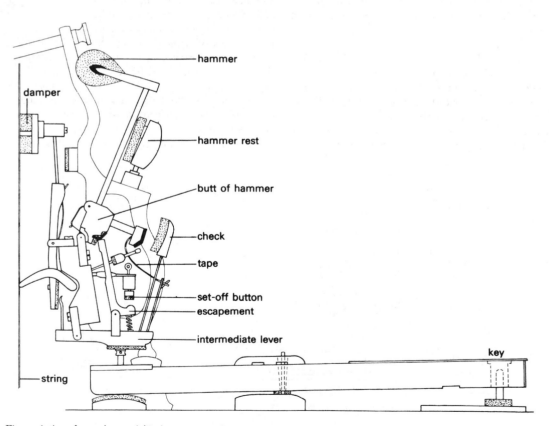

Fig. 5. Action of a modern upright piano.

would specify just where they wanted teaspoons, nuts, and bolts inserted between the strings, chains laid across them, drawing pins stuck into the hammers, and so forth.

8. Early performers and repertory

Although the first music for the piano—Lodovico Giustini's *Sonate da cimbalo di piano e forte*—was published in Florence in 1732, and Domenico Scarlatti wrote important sonatas, it was J. C. Bach in London in the 1760s and 70s, and Haydn and Mozart in Austria in the 1780s and 90s, who were most influential in popularizing the piano. The dampers on Liszt's and Chopin's pianos were very much lighter than on modern pianos, one reason why Chopin indicated less pedalling than his modern editors have inserted: there was enough sustain on his pianos, even with dampers down, that little extra pedalling was required. It was not until the later years of Brahms's career that the piano reached the form that lasted through most of the 20th century. Today, hammers have become so hard and string tension so high in the search for the greater brilliance and shorter reverberation time ideal for the broadcasting and recording studio that the piano is becoming hard to distinguish from the xylophone in tone-quality.   JMo

📖 C. EHRLICH, *The Piano* (London, 1976, 2/1990) · E. M. GOOD, *Giraffes, Black Dragons, and Other Pianos: A Technological History* (Stanford, CA, 1982, 2/2000) · M. N. CLINKSCALE, *Makers of the Piano, i: 1700–1820* (Oxford, 1993) · R. PALMIERI (ed.), *Encyclopedia of Keyboard Instruments, i: The Piano* (New York, 1994) · D. CROMBIE, *Piano* (San Francisco, 1995) · S. POLLENS, *The Early Pianoforte* (Cambridge, 1995) · M. COLE, *The Pianoforte in the Classical Era* (Oxford, 1998) · D. ROWLAND (ed.), *The Cambridge Companion to the Piano* (Cambridge, 1998) · M. N. CLINKSCALE, *Makers of the Piano, ii: 1820–1860* (Oxford, 1999) · J. PARAKILAS (ed.), *Piano Roles: Three Hundred Years of the Piano* (New Haven, CT, and London, 2000) · D. CAREW, *The Piano and its Music (1700–1850)* (Aldershot, 2001)

Pianola. A variety of *player piano made by the Aeolian Co.

piano quartet. An ensemble consisting of a pianist and three stringed instruments, typically violin, viola, and cello, or music written for it. See also CHAMBER MUSIC.

piano quintet. An ensemble consisting of a pianist and four other instruments, or music written for it. The 'other instruments' may be a string *quartet, but that is by no means the only combination possible: Schubert's 'Trout' Quintet uses one violin and a double bass, and Mozart and Beethoven wrote quintets for piano and wind. See also CHAMBER MUSIC.

piano score. A reduction of a full *score of any ensemble composition to form an arrangement for piano. Piano reductions, particularly of opera scores, were popular from the late 18th century and throughout the 19th, before the advent of sound recording, among amateur musicians who wanted to be able to sing and play their favourite arias at home.   LC

piano trio. An ensemble consisting of a piano and two other instruments, often violin and cello, or music written for it. See TRIO, 1; see also CHAMBER MUSIC.

piano-vocal score. Another name for a *vocal score.

pianto (It.). 'Lament', 'plaint'. Monteverdi's famous *Lamento d'Arianna* was subsequently set to sacred words as the *Pianto della Madonna*.

Piatigorsky, Gregor (*b* Yekaterinoslav, 4/17 April 1903; *d* Los Angeles, 6 Aug. 1976). Ukrainian-born American cellist and composer. He left the USSR in 1921, but before starting his solo career in 1928 was Furtwängler's principal cello in Berlin and had chamber musical partnerships with Carl Flesch and Schnabel. His American debut in 1929 was a triumph and brought him international fame. He worked with Heifetz, Rubinstein, Horowitz, and Nathan Milstein, and taught at Tanglewood and the University of Southern California. His playing was noble, stylish, and vibrantly warm-toned, with exquisite taste. He gave the premieres of concertos by Walton and Hindemith, and composed and transcribed for the instrument.   CF

📖 G. PIATIGORSKY, *Cellist* (New York, 1965)

piatti (It.). 'Cymbals'.

Piatti, Alfredo (Carlo) (*b* Bergamo, 8 Jan. 1822; *d* Crocetto di Mozzo, 18 July 1901). Italian cellist and composer. After studying in Milan he toured Europe and played with Liszt. In 1844, at his debut in London (where he settled), he shared a concert with Mendelssohn. Until his retirement in 1898 he exerted enormous influence in London as both teacher (his pupils included Robert Hausmann and W. H. Squire) and soloist; he was also the cellist in Joachim's quartet. He wrote several popular pieces for the cello and edited music for the instrument. His playing was based on perfect intonation, singing tone, and unsurpassed technique.   CF

📖 M. LATHAM, *Alfredo Piatti* (London, 1901)

Piazzolla, Astor (*b* Mar del Plata, 11 March 1921; *d* Buenos Aires, 5 July 1992). Argentine composer and bandoneon player. After years of writing and playing in Buenos Aires bars, he determined to break into 'serious' music, taking composition lessons from Nadia

Boulanger in Paris. She directed him back to Argentina's true national music—tango—which he transformed by incorporating rhythms and harmonic dissonances derived from jazz and orchestral music. His later work, notably with the Quinteto Tango Nuevo after 1976, was controversial, offending many tango populists by its sophisticated radicalism. Among many shorter pieces, the tango-opera *María de Buenos Aires* (1967) stands out as his most ambitious work.   CW

Picardy third. See TIERCE DE PICARDIE.

Picchi, Giovanni (*fl* early 17th century; *d* Venice, 1643). Italian composer and organist. Little is known of his life except that he was organist of S. Maria Gloriosa dei Frari, Venice, from before 1607 until his death. He composed lively dances for keyboard, using consecutive 5ths quite freely, and he warned players that the dissonances, largely resulting from embellishments, were intentional. One of his toccatas was copied into the *Fitzwilliam Virginal Book*.   DA

Piccinni (Vito), **Niccolò** (Marcello Antonio Giacomo) (*b* Bari, 16 Jan. 1728; *d* Passy, 7 May 1800). Italian composer. He was one of the most successful and prolific composers in an age that produced many such. He spent much of his career in Naples (where he had probably studied with Durante), holding church posts and teaching; nevertheless he wrote over 100 operas. His first successes were in *opera buffa* for minor Neapolitan theatres, where he is credited with introducing the multi-movement finale. He soon obtained commissions for *opera seria* in major theatres (*Zenobia*, Naples, 1756; *Alessandro nelle Indie*, Rome, 1758). In 1760, again for Rome, he composed the most celebrated *opera buffa* of its time, *La Cecchina* (also known as *La buona figliuola*), to a libretto by Carlo Goldoni previously set by Duni and loosely based on Samuel Richardson's *Pamela*. Piccinni dominated the stage in Naples for most of the 1760s, in spite of the rising star of Paisiello. A sudden vogue for Anfossi in Rome dethroned Piccinni in that city from 1773, but by this time an influential circle in Paris had decided that he should assist the downfall of traditional *tragédie lyrique* and Gluck as well.

Piccinni arrived in Paris in 1776 and composed *Roland* under the close supervision of the librettist J. F. Marmontel. It was produced in January 1778 and won over the public. Piccinni had only moderate success with the first production of *Atys* (1780) and *Iphigénie en Tauride* (1781); the latter, originally promised production before Gluck's version (1779), lost a box-office battle and was not helped by the singer at the revival, Rosalie Levasseur, whose intoxication led to the nickname *Iphigénie en champagne*. Piccinni directed an

Italian troupe in Paris and wrote two French comedies. The successful revival of *Atys* and the triumph of *Didon* (both 1783) marked the zenith of his career; *Pénélope* (1785) failed to please, and later works were not performed.

A generous rival to both Gluck and Sacchini, Piccinni was the victim of the Opéra management, then of the Revolution. Forced back to Naples, he suffered imprisonment by association with a politically suspect son-in-law. Eventually he returned to Paris, dying just before a pension from Napoleon might have rescued him from indigence.   JR

📖 J. G. RUSHTON, 'The theory and practice of Piccinnisme', *Proceedings of the Royal Musical Association*, 98 (1971–2), 31–46 · M. F. ROBINSON, *Naples and Neapolitan Opera* (London, 1972)

piccolo (It., 'small'). A small size of any instrument (e.g. *violino piccolo*), but when used alone the term is assumed to mean the transverse *flute sounding an octave higher than the normal flute ('octave flute'; Fr.: *petite flûte*; Ger.: *kleine Flöte*; It.: *ottavino*). Its keywork has always been similar to that of the concert flute for ease in changing from one to the other.   JMo

pickup. The device which traces the recording etched into the face of an analogue disc recording and converts the wave-form into sound. In the days of acoustic recording (up to 1925) this was effected by a stylus tracing the disc and activating a membrane which produced an amplified sound via a speaker horn. In electrical recording the movement is converted into an electrical signal, which is amplified by a valve or transistor amplifier and played as sound through loudspeakers.

See also RECORDING AND REPRODUCTION.   LF

Pictures at an Exhibition (*Kartinki s vystavki*). Suite for solo piano (1874) by Musorgsky, each of its ten movements inspired by pictures at a memorial exhibition for the Russian artist Victor Hartmann (1834–73) and with a 'Promenade' as a linking passage. There are several orchestral versions, by Henry Wood, Stokowski, and Elgar Howarth (brass and percussion) among others, but the most commonly heard is by Ravel (1922).

pied (Fr.). 'Foot', as in organ stops, etc.

pieno, piena (It.). 'Full'; *organo pieno*, 'full organ'; *coro pieno*, 'full choir' (as opposed to passages for soloists); *a voce piena*, 'with full voice'. See also RIPIENO.

Pierné, (Henri Constant) **Gabriel** (*b* Metz, 16 Aug. 1863; *d* Ploujean, 17 July 1937). French composer. He studied composition with Massenet and the organ with Franck at the Paris Conservatoire (1874–82), winning the Prix de Rome. He returned from Italy to succeed Franck as organist of Ste Clotilde in Paris (1890–8) but then concentrated on conducting and composition. As conductor of the Colonne concerts (1910–32) he was responsible for the first performance of Debussy's *Images*, among many other works. His own compositions range from light pieces to substantial oratorios, operas, and chamber works, and show a fertile imagination at work in a basically Franckian style. Apart from the appealing 'Marche des petits faunes' from his ballet *Cydalise et le chèvre-pied* (1923), however, his music has been largely forgotten.   PG

Pierrot lunaire ('Moonstruck Pierrot'). Schoenberg's op. 21 (1912), for female voice, flute, piccolo, clarinet, bass clarinet, violin, viola, cello, and piano; it is a cycle in three parts, each containing seven songs, which are settings of poems by Albert Giraud translated from French into German by O. E. Hartleben. The singer is required to use the technique of *Sprechgesang*. See also EXPRESSIONISM.

Pierson [Pearson], **Henry Hugo** [Hugh] (*b* Oxford, 12 April 1815; *d* Leipzig, 28 Jan. 1873). German composer of English origin. He studied music with Attwood and A. T. Corfe in spite of opposition from his father. After three years at Cambridge (1836–9) he moved to Germany (1836–44), studying with J. C. H. Rinck and K. G. Reissiger, and with Tomášek in Prague. For a time he adopted the pseudonym Edgar Mannsfeldt, and in the early 1850s began to style himself Henry Hugo Pierson, a Germanicization of his former English name. He was elected Reid Professor of Music at Edinburgh University in 1844 but resigned after eight months and returned to Germany, where he lived for the rest of his life.

Pierson enjoyed success in Germany with his opera *Leila* (Hamburg, 1848), the incidental music to Goethe's *Faust* (1854), and many of his songs, some of which were reviewed by Schumann. An eccentric voice in mid-19th-century English music (which incited hostility among native critics), he has much in common with Berlioz, particularly his colourful orchestration and unpredictable harmonic language. Apart from the *Faust* music, his most remarkable work is the programmatic symphonic poem *Macbeth* (1859).   JDt

Pietragrua. See GRUA.

Pigmalion (*Pygmalion*). *Acte de ballet* by Rameau to a libretto by Ballot de Sauvot after Antoine Houdar de Lamotte (Paris, 1748).

Pijper, Willem (*b* Zeist, 8 Sept. 1894; *d* Leidschendam, 19 March 1947). Dutch composer. He studied composition with Johan Wagenaar at the Utrecht Music School and then worked as a music critic. Subsequently

he was co-editor of the magazine *De muziek* (1926–33), a teacher at the Amsterdam Conservatory (1925–30), and principal of the Rotterdam Music School. He had a notable influence on Dutch music as a teacher and also through his compositions, in which he favoured thick, polytonal harmonies, aggressive rhythms in rapidly changing metres, and the use of a 'germ cell' technique by which each piece was developed from a small melodic or harmonic unit. His works include two operas, three symphonies and many other orchestral works, songs, and a large body of chamber music.   PG

Pilgrim's Progress, The. Opera ('morality') in a prologue, four acts, and an epilogue by Vaughan Williams to his own libretto after John Bunyan's allegory (1674–9, 1684), with interpolations from the Bible and verse by Ursula Vaughan Williams (London, 1951). Act IV scene 2 is *The Shepherds of the Delectable Mountains*, a pastoral episode in one act (London, 1922). Bantock wrote a choral piece on the same subject (1928).

Pilkington, Francis (*b* c.1570; *d* Chester, 1638). English church musician, lutenist, and composer. He took the Oxford B.Mus. in 1595 and spent his later life as a singer and minor canon of Chester Cathedral; he was ordained in 1614, and became precentor of the cathedral in 1623. He is best known for his collection of lute-songs (London, 1605), which includes the miniature masterpiece *Rest sweet nimphes*. He also published two sets of competent rather than highly individual madrigals (London, 1613 and 1624).   DA/JM

pin block. See WREST PLANK.

pincé (Fr., 'pinched'). 1. Occasional term for *pizzicato.
    2. Old term for the *mordent; *pincé renversé*, a *trill; *pincé étouffé*, an *acciaccatura.
    3. *Vibrato.

Pineapple Poll. Ballet in one act and three scenes to music by Sullivan, arranged by Charles Mackerras, to a scenario by John Cranko (who choreographed it), based on W. S. Gilbert's Bab Ballad *The Bumboat Woman's Story* (London, 1951); a concert suite has been arranged from the score.

Pini di Roma ('Pines of Rome'). Symphonic poem (1923–4) by Respighi; its four sections are entitled 'Villa Borghese', 'A Catacomb', 'Janiculum', and 'Appian Way'. The score includes a recording of a nightingale.

Pinto, George Frederick (*b* Lambeth, 25 Sept. 1785; *d* Chelsea, 23 March 1806). English composer and violinist. The grandson of the violinist Thomas Pinto, he was a student prodigy of Salomon and first played in public in 1796. His surviving instrumental works are for violin or piano, or both. Some of the piano music especially is highly accomplished and stylistically mature, and in places clearly anticipates Romanticism. Pinto was also a promising and remarkably expressive writer of songs. His early death, like that of the younger Thomas Linley, was a tragic loss. PL

Pintscher, Matthias (*b* Marl, 29 Jan. 1971). German composer. He studied in London, with Giselher Klebe in Detmold, and with Manfred Trojahn in Düsseldorf, and also received encouragement from Henze. He has frequently conducted his own music. His output includes a ballet with singing and speaking voices, *Gesprungene Glocken* (1994), two operas, *Thomas Chatterton* (1998) and *Heliogabal* (2001), several major works for orchestra and for large ensemble, and four string quartets among other chamber works. He has described his music as 'an "imaginary theatre" full of mysteries and secrets, always rediscovering and redefining its own sensibility'. ABur

pipa. Chinese short-necked four-string lute.

pipe and tabor. The original one-man band, consisting of a three-hole pipe held in the left hand and a snared drum dangling from the left wrist or little finger beaten simultaneously with a stick held in the right hand. The pipe is played in the *overblown register, where harmonics are close enough together that the two fingerholes and a thumbhole can fill the gaps between them, with a range of about an octave and a half (enough for most dance tunes). The player is always called taborer, stressing the greater importance of the rhythm. The tabor appeared over much of Europe in the mid-13th century. It is still in common use in Britain, southern France, northern Spain, and parts of South America, and has been revived elsewhere. In southern France the three-hole *galoubet* is accompanied by the *tambourin de Béarn*. JMo

piqué (Fr., 'pricked'). In playing stringed instruments, *spiccato*; an indication in French Baroque music that a passage of even notes should be played in dotted rhythm.

Pirata, Il ('The Pirate'). Opera in two acts by Bellini to a libretto by Felice Romani after Isidore J. S. Taylor's play *Bertram, ou Le Pirate*, a version of Charles Maturin's *Bertram* (1816) (Milan, 1827).

Pirates of Penzance, The (*The Pirates of Penzance, or The Slave of Duty*). Operetta in two acts by Sullivan to a libretto by W. S. Gilbert (Paignton, 1879).

Pisano [Pagoli], Bernardo (*b* Florence, 12 Oct. 1490; *d* Rome, 23 Jan. 1548). Italian cleric, singer, and composer. He was trained at the cathedral school in Florence, and

subsequently became master of the choristers there. In 1514 he joined the papal chapel in Rome, while continuing his associations with Florence. His circle of friends included Michelangelo. Pisano helped pave the way towards the 16th-century madrigal with his polyphonic settings of canzoni by Petrarch. He also composed liturgical music for Holy Week. JM

Piston, Walter (Hamor) (*b* Rockland, ME, 20 Jan. 1894; *d* Belmont, MA, 12 Nov. 1976). American composer. He first studied art, then turned to music and went to Harvard University, graduating in 1924. He spent two years in Paris as a pupil of Nadia Boulanger before returning to Harvard as a lecturer and later professor (1944–59). A disciplined craftsman, he wrote influential textbooks on harmony, counterpoint, and orchestration, while in his music he consistently followed the neo-classical aims of the Boulanger school, preferring clear, sober musical argument to any kind of display. His output included eight symphonies, chamber pieces of various kinds, and a ballet, *The Incredible Flutist* (1938). PG

pitch. A basic dimension of musical sounds, in which they are heard to be high or low.

> 1. Introduction; 2. Modern pitch; 3. Historical pitches; 4. The 19th-century rise in pitch

1. Introduction

The subjective sense of pitch is closely correlated with frequency (number of sound vibrations per second). Experiments have shown that the correlation is not exact; judgments of pitch are affected by other variables such as volume, timbre, and duration. In this article, however, these slight differences will be ignored, and pitch treated as equivalent to frequency. We are here concerned not with the relative pitch of notes in a *scale, but with pitch in an absolute sense, as a norm to which instruments are built or tuned for playing with others. For this purpose the note d' is conventionally used as a marker that determines the pitch of the entire instrument, ensemble, or piece of music. It is sometimes termed 'concert pitch' (Fr.: *diapason*). The d' can be carried about through the medium of a *tuning-fork or *pitchpipe, and in an orchestra is given out by the oboe (among wind instruments one of the least affected by temperature change), unless a keyboard instrument is taking part. For instruments that are expected to hold their pitch for long periods (e.g. the piano and organ), tuners now generally use portable electronic devices capable of producing a sound of any desired pitch and of measuring pitch precisely.

The measurement of frequency is in cycles per second, or Hertz (Hz). Frequency is a 'ratio' scale of measurement: each time the pitch goes up by an octave, the frequency is doubled. Thus if c' is 256 Hz, c'' is 512 Hz. Another means of measuring pitch is 'arithmetical', and simply divides the octave into 1200 equal parts called 'cents' (100 per equal-tempered semitone). See also ACOUSTICS, 4.

2. Modern pitch

The present International Standard Pitch, a' = 440 Hz, was agreed at a conference held in 1939. Before that the general standard was 435, a fifth of a semitone lower, except in Britain where it was 439, virtually the same as the modern. It might have been hoped that, once agreed, 440 would have been strictly adhered to, but there is a tendency for pitch to rise very gradually with the passage of time. The reasons for this are mysterious. A soloist may feel that an extra brightness of effect may be gained from playing that is fractionally sharper than the accompaniment (within, of course, the tolerance of the ear's ability to identify pitch); or the strings of an orchestra may tune on the sharp side in anticipation of the wind becoming sharper during performance. Thus in Berlin pianos for concert performance may be tuned as high as 450, while some German manufacturers of wind instruments have been obliged to tune their instruments to 446 (or above) to keep in step, so reverting halfway up towards the old 'sharp pitch' (see below, 4) which coexisted with standard pitch until quite recently in several countries, including Britain.

3. Historical pitches

Over the last five centuries—so far as early values can be estimated from old *tuning-forks, organs, and other wind instruments—tuning pitch has varied, in the main, over a range of about 300 cents (three semitones), a' varying from as low as the present g' up to bb' or even above; this is not a great deal considering the length of time. Seldom has any pitch ruled completely for all places and in all circumstances; yet musicians, in travelling from country to country, have tended to bring a measure of uniformity lasting in some cases over fairly long intervals between periods of instability and change. A rough indication of pitch standards going back to the 1690s is given in Table 1.

The 18th century was, on the whole, one of the more stable periods. From roughly 1740 to 1820 concert pitches generally lay within the region of a' = 420–8 (i.e. about a quarter-tone below the present 440). This was the German *Cammerton* ('concert pitch') at which Mozart's music was performed, as well as most of Bach's, Handel's, and Beethoven's. French pitch could be a trifle lower, and through the earlier part of the century was distinctly lower, spreading to England and Germany for a time chiefly through the powerful French influence on Baroque wind-instrument making. Thus recorders made in London by Bressan, who had arrived from France before 1700, can be nearly a whole tone below modern pitch. In Germany this low pitch was termed 'low *Cammerton*' (or 'French pitch') and was often reckoned at about a semitone below the standard *Cammerton*.

In present-day performances of 18th-century music on original or replica instruments a pitch of a' = 415, a semitone below modern pitch, has been widely adopted. Though often causing considerable inconvenience, this does enable keyboard players to make a clean transposition of a semitone when an instrument tuned to modern pitch must be used, while it is also a pitch at which many original wind instruments can satisfactorily be played, and similarly stringed instruments when restored to their original condition (see VIOLIN). Replica wind instruments are therefore commonly built to this pitch—though latterly there has begun a trend to specialize further, building alternatively, or on demand, to pitches about a quarter-tone below and above this.

There were also higher pitches in the 18th century, for example in Italy. Evidence here is scarcer, but performing pitches were said to be higher than the German *Cammerton*, with a Venetian pitch (according to Quantz) nearly a tone higher. Still higher were the pitches of organs, not only in Germany but also among those built in England by makers from Germany. A German term for such pitches was *Chorton*. It is well known from J. S. Bach's orchestral parts that the continuo part for the organ might have to be written out a whole tone (or even a tone and a half) lower than the key of the other instruments for all to agree.

Table 1

Approximate central areas of pitch, 1690–present; pitches are given at quarter-tone intervals

a' = 466 reached in some historical pitch standards	(modern bb')
a' = 452 former 'sharp pitch'	
a' = 440 present standard pitch'	(modern a')
a' = 422 Baroque-Classical pitch'	
a' = 415 present usual 'historical pitch' or 'Baroque pitch'	(modern $g\sharp'$)
a' = 403 higher Baroque French pitch	
a' = 392 Baroque French pitch	(modern g')

For the 16th century and much of the 17th, estimates of pitch have varied enormously. In Germany, Michael Praetorius (*Syntagma musicum*, ii, 2/1619) mentioned two different pitches lying a tone apart. Many surviving wind instruments, particularly Italian ones but some German too, seem to be in the Italian Baroque pitch region, up into the 460s, but the French were already lower. Stringed instruments played on their own would choose their own preferred pitch, as would voices—unless, of course, accompanied by the organ, in which case the compass of the voices, especially the upper limit, can give some indication of the pitches to which organs were tuned. But this is inevitably a very rough measure.

4. The 19th-century rise in pitch

By 1820 European concert pitches had begun to shoot rapidly upwards, reaching (in Paris, London, and Vienna alike) the region of d' = 434 and often 440 by 1830, with further rises following shortly after. The possible causes are various: trends to sharpness among soloists, especially in the larger halls and before the more popular audiences; and certainly the vast expansion of military bands (from which orchestral players were frequently drawn) with their tendency, especially out of doors, to play sharp for brilliant effect, in turn influencing the instrument makers. (This made it a difficult time for wind players: the principal horn of the Paris Opéra in 1829, having had his horn shortened to meet the rise in pitch, raised strong objection when a return to a lower pitch was mooted; and for a time such instruments as bassoons were fitted with sliding tuning devices so that players could accept engagements in different theatres or opera houses.)

As early as 1834 J. H. Scheibler, a leading German scientist on pitch matters, recommended a standard 440 (the present pitch), arrived at by averaging out the tunings of grand pianos in Vienna. But further rises up to the 453 region during the 1850s led directors of theatres and conservatories throughout Europe to co-operate, sending forks and comments to a commission in Paris which in 1859 decided on d' = 435, the *diapason normal* ('standard pitch') already mentioned. It came too late, however, for immediate universal acceptance. At Covent Garden in 1879 the organ had to be raised in pitch from 441 to 446, it being impossible to get the woodwind to play any lower.

The general outcome was a polarization of pitch into 'low' and 'high', the 'low' being the *diapason normal* (confirmed by a conference in Vienna in 1885), the 'high' where circumstances or economics precluded lowering, for instance in military bands. In Britain from the 1870s the 'high' or 'sharp' pitch lay at or near 452, both for the Philharmonic concerts and for the army. The low pitch replaced it only by degrees, from about 1890, and similarly in the USA. Up to 1930 many provincial British orchestras were still playing at sharp pitch, and a woodwind player taking an engagement outside his habitual orbit would have to be instructed which of his instruments to use, flat pitch or sharp, the wrong one being unusable.

Many brass bands held to sharp pitch until well after World War II, when eventually the expense of procuring flat-pitch instruments had to be faced in order for a band to take part in contests (involving massed bands) with others which had already made the change. For choral societies the abolition of sharp pitch has had considerable advantages—such works as Beethoven's 'Choral' Symphony, with its long-sustained high As for the sopranos, proved extremely taxing at d' = 452; Beethoven, through the years preceding his deafness, would have heard this note up to a semitone lower by comparison.   AB/NT

📖 A. Mendel, *Studies in the History of Musical Pitch* (Amsterdam, 1968) [incl. 3 articles by A. J. Ellis]; *Pitch in Western Music since 1500: A Re-examination* (Kassel, 1979) · C. Karp, 'Pitch', *Performance Practice: Music After 1600*, ed. H. M. Brown and S. Sadie (London, 1989), 147–68.

pitch class. The property held in common by all pitches with the same name; thus middle C and every other C can be said to be a member of the pitch class C. It is particularly important in the discussion of serial music to distinguish between pitch and pitch class, since the classical 12-note series is a sequence of pitch classes, not of pitches.   PG

pitchpipe. A *duct flute with a sliding piston marked with the correct length for each note, used to give notes to a choir or for other pitch reference. Reed pitchpipes have either a *free reed for each note, or a single *reed with a bridle that can slide to a marked position.

JMo

Pitoni, Giuseppe Ottavio (*b* Rieti, 18 March 1657; *d* Rome, 1 Feb. 1743). Italian composer. He was a choirboy at S. Giovanni dei Fiorentini and at the Santi Apostoli, Rome. He became *maestro di cappella* in 1676 at Rieti, and then at the collegiate church of S. Marco, Rome, holding that post until his death. Among other appointments, from 1686 he directed the music at the Collegio Germanico, where he lived, and from 1694 to 1721 he was attached to S. Lorenzo in Damaso, the titular church of Cardinal Pietro Ottoboni, the patron of Corelli and Pasquini. Pitoni was a hugely prolific composer: his sacred music included over 200 masses and mass movements for from four to eight voices, over 700 psalms (including one for 12 and one for 16 voices),

Magnificat settings, motets, litanies, and Passions. In addition he wrote prodigiously on musical subjects; 41 volumes of notes are conserved in the Vatican library, but only the first part of his *Guida armonica* was ever published, for like many Romans he felt little inclination to send his works to press.   WT/PA

più (It.). 'More'; *più forte*, 'louder'; *più allegro*, 'faster', etc.

piuttosto (It.). 'Rather'; *piuttosto allegro*, 'rather fast'.

piva (It.). 1. A *bagpipe of northern Italy.

2. A 15th-century Italian dance. A fast peasant dance, it was considered unsuitable for refined society by the mid-15th century, though it could be part of a *ballo. It was for couples with improvisation by the male partner. The *piva* was also a basic step in Renaissance dance and the fastest of the four *misure* (metres with characteristic tempos and movement), the others being the saltarello, quadernaria, and bassadanza.   JH

Pixis, Johann Peter (*b* Mannheim, 10 Feb. 1788; *d* Baden-Baden, 22 Dec. 1874). German pianist and composer. He began a concert career at a young age, touring with his brother, Friedrich Wilhelm. From 1808 to 1823 he mostly lived in Vienna, but his attempts to establish himself there as an opera composer met with only limited success. He moved to Paris in 1824 and soon consolidated a reputation as a fine pianist and as a composer in the brilliant, if vacuous, style then in vogue. Later attempts at operatic composition also ended in failure, but such piano pieces as the concert rondo *Les Trois Clochettes* maintained considerable popularity for decades. His typical approach to piano writing can be seen in *Hexaméron*, a set of variations on a theme from Bellini's *I Puritani* compiled by Liszt, with contributions from Pixis, Herz, Czerny, and Chopin. Pixis's variation is fluent but utterly vapid— on a par with those of Herz and Czerny. The variations of Chopin and Liszt—embarrassingly more imaginative—starkly illustrate why Pixis is today an almost forgotten figure.   KH

Pizzetti, Ildebrando (*b* Borgo Strinato, nr Parma, 20 Sept. 1880; *d* Rome, 13 Feb. 1968). Italian composer. He studied at the Parma Musical Academy (1895–1901) and spent his life as a noted teacher of composition at conservatories in Parma (1907–8), Florence (1908–24), Milan (1924–36), and Rome (from 1936). In his music he reacted against the emotional extravagance of Puccini, being influenced by Debussy and the Italian Renaissance. Opera, he felt, should give first place to the psychological portrayal of the characters, and he put

this conviction to good effect in *Debora e Jaele* (La Scala, Milan, 1922), *Fra Gherardo* (La Scala, 1928), *Lo straniero* (Rome, 1930), and *Assassinio nella cattedrale* (after T. S. Eliot; La Scala, 1958). His other works include an intimate modal *Messa di requiem* for small unaccompanied chorus (1922).   PG

📖 G. M. GATTI, *Ildebrando Pizzetti* (London, 1951)

pizzicato (It.). 'Plucked'; usually abbreviated in printed music to 'pizz.'. A technique, used most often on string instruments (usually of the violin family), in which the strings are made to vibrate by being grasped by the fingers of the right hand rather than bowed. The action usually takes place towards the end of the fingerboard, or just beyond it. The effect is possible with single notes, or with a number in quick succession, as a variant of *double or multiple *stopping.

An early example for the violin is found in Monteverdi's *Combattimento di Tancredi, e Clorinda* (1624), although an earlier use of pizzicato (called 'thump') and other special effects occur in music by composers of the English viol school, for example in Tobias Hume's *The First Part of Ayres* (1605). Many different varieties of pizzicato are found in later music, such as the left-hand pizzicato used extensively by Paganini; the 'snap' pizzicato (where the string is pulled upwards and allowed to snap against the fingerboard) indicated by the sign ↓ and used by Bartók; and the pizzicato slide (also found in the music of Bartók), in which the left hand slides up or down the string after the string has been plucked, producing a range of notes which sound as the string continues to vibrate.

—/DMi

Pk (Ger.). 1. Abbreviation for *Pauken*, 'timpani'.

2. In organ music, the abbreviation for *Pedalkoppel*.

placido (It.). 'Placid', 'tranquil'.

placito (It.). 'Judgment'; *a bene placito*, 'at one's own judgment', i.e. ad *libitum.

plagal cadence. See CADENCE.

plainchant. In the broadest sense, the monophonic and, according to ancient tradition, unaccompanied music of Eastern and Western Christian liturgy. Commonly used narrowly to denote the chant repertories of Latin Christianity (particularly that of the Roman rite, with which sections 2–5 of this article will be primarily concerned), the term may also refer to the Neo-Gallican *plain-chant musical* sung in French churches from the 17th century to the 19th.

1. History to the 8th century; 2. The 8th and 9th centuries; 3. Later developments; 4. Chant books and notation. 5. Style

1. History to the 8th century

Although song appears to have been a feature of Christian worship since Apostolic times, relatively little is known regarding its use before the 4th century. Interpretation of early reports is complicated by the interchangeability of the terms 'psalm', 'hymn', and 'song'. However, the texts of some early hymns are cited in the New Testament, and others have survived in such collections as the Odes of Solomon from 2nd-century Alexandria.

With the legalization of Christianity by the Emperor Constantine I (Edict of Milan, 313), the Church was now state-supported, its worship public, and its congregations large. Most early non-biblical hymns—the *Gloria in excelsis* and the evening hymn *Phos hilaron* are notable exceptions—did not escape the process of doctrinal consolidation that also led to the adoption of a canon of Christian Scripture. The chanting of biblical psalms, recently popularized by Egyptian monasticism, was promoted instead. Unaccompanied performance was the rule, supported by vigorous polemics and canonical legislation against pagan traditions of instrumental music.

The 4th century also witnessed the emergence of regional urban and monastic liturgical usages or 'rites' featuring diverse implementations of daily common prayer (the 'Liturgy of the Hours' or 'Divine Office') and the Sunday Eucharist. A rapid multiplication of holy days soon resulted in the formation of annual cycles of worship superimposed on the existing daily and weekly cycles, developments that were complemented musically by the creation of local repertories of plainchant featuring settings both of fixed ('Ordinary') and variable ('Proper') texts. In some areas these included new hymns by such figures as St Ambrose (*c*.339–97), St Ephrem the Syrian (*c*.306–73), St Romanos (*d c*.560), and St Sophronios (*c*.560–638).

This liturgical diversification was counteracted by frequent borrowing between rites. Cenobitic monks created mixed rites combining urban and monastic types of psalmody, including the influential Divine Office established by St Benedict (*c*.480–*c*.547) and subsequently imitated throughout the Latin West.

2. The 8th and 9th centuries

Political recovery from the collapse of the Western Roman Empire began in earnest with the reigns of Pepin, King of the Franks from 751, and Charlemagne (771–814), during which there was a deliberate attempt to bring church worship in Frankish lands into line with that in Rome. Charlemagne perhaps saw common forms of worship as a way of helping unite his vast empire; still more, he saw himself as a divinely appointed ruler of a chosen people whose liturgical customs must approach the ideal, represented by papal usage. However, there arose tales that Frankish singers could not master the subtleties of Roman chant, and that Roman singing masters, jealous of their own special skills and repertory, deliberately confused their pupils.

A question of fundamental importance hangs over the whole affair: exactly what chant was brought from Rome at this time? The surviving music manuscripts from Rome itself before the 13th century all show a more archaic repertory—hence its usual name 'Old Roman' chant—quite different from that preserved in Frankish manuscripts, which we now call 'Gregorian'. These differences may be the inevitable result of trying to import, learn, and eventually codify what was still an oral, not a written, repertory. The situation is even more complicated than this, since the Old Roman repertory appears not to have been written down until the 11th century, and much of the surface detail of the chants as we know them is probably not what it was at the end of the 8th century. There is, among other things, clear evidence that the Gregorian repertory influenced some features of Old Roman chant. The same thing happened to the Ambrosian repertory of Milan, whose surviving sources are similarly very late (12th century onwards).

Metz was the Frankish city that established itself as a musical model for other churches to follow in the late 8th and early 9th centuries. Unfortunately all its chant books are lost. The manuscripts we have, from the end of the 9th century onwards, are from many areas of Europe: Aquitaine and Brittany, Champagne and Picardy, St Gallen, and Winchester. They are in different notational styles, and occasionally vary in small melodic details, so that it is uncertain whether they are all descended from common exemplars, or whether cantors of several different churches each notated chant independently following a common oral tradition.

3. Later developments

In addition to learning and codifying the Gregorian repertory, Frankish cantors contributed several new genres of plainchant: *sequences, *tropes, and liturgical drama (see CHURCH DRAMA). In addition, many local musicians composed services for the patron saint of their church, some in verse (usually hexameters).

Our first evidence of liturgical polyphony comes from the 9th century, in the treatise *Musica enchiriadis* (see ORGANUM). The 9th century also saw the beginnings of a body of theoretical writing about chant, by such writers as Aurelian of Réôme (mid-9th century) and Hucbald of Saint-Amand (*c*.840–930), which attempts to reconcile contemporary chant with the Greek musical theory transmitted by Boethius (*c*.480–*c*.524).

In the 11th century, exact notation of the pitches of melodies became practicable and a new type of rhyming, rhythmic song, the *conductus, came into fashion. Soon after this a completely new repertory of rhyming, rhythmic sequences began to develop. Offices of the saints from the 12th century onwards are commonly written in rhyme.

The Gregorian repertory was not immune from attempts at reform: the Cistercians excluded notes outside the range of a 10th and eliminated long melismas, and later the *Council of Trent (1542–63) declared itself against tropes and sequences. The Tridentine gradual finally produced by Felice Anerio and Soriano in 1614–15 (known as the *Editio medicaea*)

reflected humanist ideals, eschewing even moderately long groups of notes on unaccented syllables and adapting the tonality of many chants to contemporary sensibilities. Largely as a result of the work of Dom Pothier and the monks of *Solesmes, chant books with melodies restored to their early medieval forms were sanctioned by Pius X (*motu proprio* of 22 November 1903) and published in 1905 (the Kyriale), 1908 (the gradual), and 1912 (the antiphoner).

4. Chant books and notation

The earliest chant manuscripts contain the texts to be sung without notation. When notation did appear in the 9th century, it indicated the rise and fall of the melodies without exact specification of pitches. Only in the 11th century were complete chant books—some of them using staff lines as recommended by Guido of Arezzo, *c*.1030 (see NOTATION, 1 and 2)—written with exact pitch notation.

Ex. 1

(*cont. on p. 968*)

Some early neumatic notations (particularly the sophisticated St Gallen type) contain indications for lengthening and stressing certain notes. However, it is not known if these involved strictly proportional note lengths (equivalent to, say, modern crotchet and quaver), as their use is somewhat unsystematic and contemporary theoretical writing somewhat ambiguous.

The Proper chants for Mass are contained in the *Gradual, and Office chants in the *Antiphoner. The Cantatorium contains only those sections of Mass chants that were sung by soloists, while the Troper included *tropes, often *sequences, perhaps liturgical dramas, and material from the Cantatorium. A book with a didactic function containing lists of antiphons according to their mode was the Tonary. From the 12th century it became common to include chants in the same book as prayers and lessons. These composite books are the Missal (for Mass) and the Breviary (for the Office). Many omit musical notation.

It is unlikely that chant books were used by the choir during performance. The notation of most early ones is too small for even one person to read in the course of a service. They are reference books. Only after the 13th century do manuscripts become big enough for reading by more than one singer, and not until the 15th century would many singers have been musically literate.

5. Style

Since the plainchant repertory evolved orally, it is not surprising that it relies heavily on melodic formulas deployed in simple structures, all of which could be memorized. The Old Roman repertory is even more dependent than the Gregorian on formulaic construction, and its modal system is more primitive. A further important factor affecting chant style is the

Ex. 1 (*cont.*)

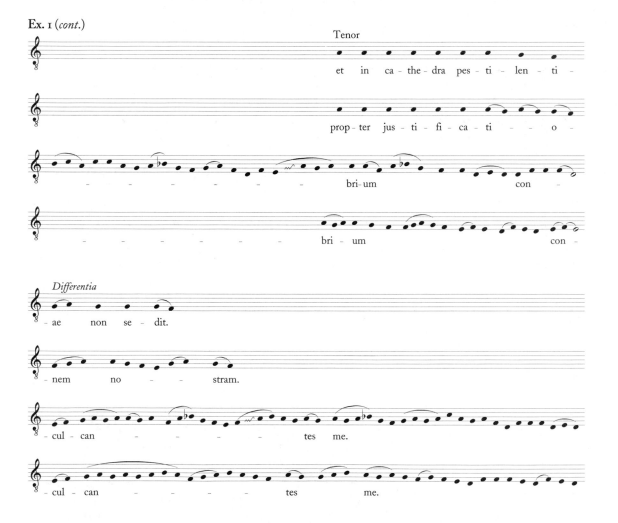

number of performers involved: Office psalms chanted by a whole monastic community use very simple melodic formulas, while chants sung by soloists or a trained choir are far more ornate.

The use of formulas is most clearly demonstrated in psalmodic pieces. Choral Office psalms are intoned on one note (the tenor), usually approached from below and maintained until the end of a text phrase (the musical cadence). Ex. 1*a* gives the melodic scheme (or 'tone'; see TONUS, 3) for psalm verses sung with first-mode antiphons (hence known as 'tone 1'). It provides one of several alternative cadences (*differentiae*) that could have been selected to lead smoothly back to the antiphon. In responsorial psalmody the verses were sung by a soloist, and the Office responsories have much more elaborate tones; Ex. 1*b* (from the responsory *Expurgate vetus fermentum*) gives the tone for the first mode.

Most elaborate of all is the responsorial psalmody of Mass. In the verse of the first-mode gradual 'Miserere mei (Ex. 1*c*), the tenor is A, but could be thought of almost as a repeated oscillation A–C. The music to the

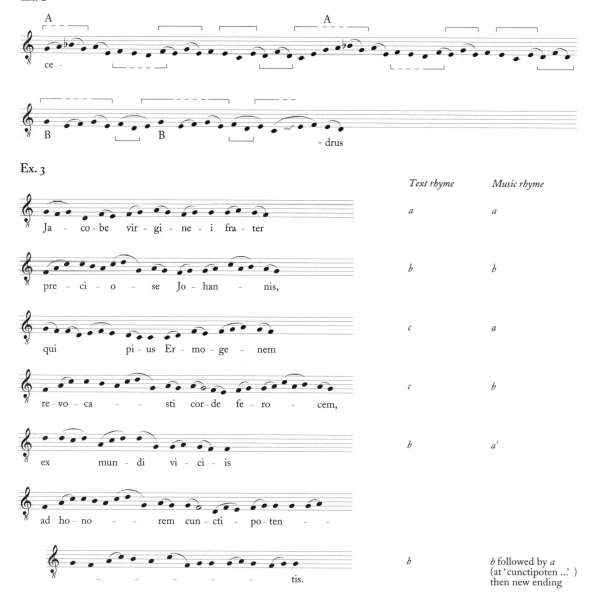

Ex. 2

Ex. 3

	Text rhyme	Music rhyme
Ja - co - be vir - gi - ne - i fra - ter	*a*	*a*
pre - ci - o - se Jo - han - nis,	*b*	*b*
qui pi - us Er - mo - ge - nem	*c*	*a*
re - vo - ca - - sti cor - de fe - ro - cem,	*c*	*b*
ex mun - di vi - ci - is	*b*	*a'*
ad ho - no - rem cun - cti - po - ten - -		
- - - - - tis.	*b*	*b* followed by *a* (at 'cunctipoten ...') then new ending

words 'Misit de caelo', 'in opprobrium', '(conculcan)tes', and 'me' is all to be found in other first-mode graduals, but not all together in any other gradual. However, the formulas will all be found at the same point in the verse: start, ends of first, second, third sections, etc. In structure and use of formulas, the Old Roman version of the gradual is designed similarly, but the actual formulas and surface detail are quite different, as Ex. 1*d* shows. The repeated Cs of the Gregorian version are absent from the Old Roman, and the tenor A is clearer, though often accompanied by auxiliary Bs.

Late additions to the Gregorian corpus, such as the later alleluias and tropes, sequences, and conductus, show a move away from the predominantly pentatonic sound world of earlier chant. The older corpus tended to treat E and B as notes of secondary importance, but later chants frequently contain passages that use all notes of the gamut equally freely; they also appear to emphasize interlocking chains of 3rds. The melisma shown in Ex. 2, from the *Alleluia Justus ut palma*, is in AABB form, and moves from one set of 3rds (C–E–G – B♭) to another (D–F–A). Leaps of a 3rd are bracketed to make this clear.

The abandonment of old formulas and standard melodic procedures is nowhere more evident than in the new rhymed Offices of the 12th century and later. Ex. 3 is from the festal Office of St James contained in the Codex Calixtinus of *c*.1160. One particularly 'modern' feature is the presence of a rhyme scheme for the text and the music. No trace of old eighth-mode responsory formulas can be seen.

To those unfamiliar with it, chant can seem tedious and lacking in variety. But what seems uniform when contrasted with polyphony of the 13th to the 20th centuries breaks down on closer inspection into a fascinating mixture of genres and styles, clearly audible to the discerning listener. Quite apart from its intrinsic qualities, plainchant is by far the earliest and largest repertory of music to have been codified from oral traditions, and as such is of inestimable value for our understanding of human culture.   DH/ALi

📖 D. HILEY, *Western Plainchant: A Handbook* (Oxford, 1993) · J. NÁDAS and J. HAAR (eds.), *Western Plainchant in the First Millennium: Studies in the Western Medieval Liturgy and its Music* (Aldershot, 2001)

plainchant mass. Either a mass in plainchant (especially the sets of ordinary chants found in modern editions of the Kyriale, e.g. Mass IX *Cum iubilo* for Marian feasts; see GRADUAL, 1), or a polyphonic mass composition in which each movement is based on the corresponding item of the plainchant (e.g. Josquin's *Missa de Beata Virgine* on the chants of Mass IX). The term is sometimes broadened in its application to include a mass using any item of plainchant as a cantus firmus.   —/ALi

Plainsong and Mediaeval Music Society. A society founded in London in 1888 to promote knowledge of the eponymous subjects, to publish facsimiles and catalogue manuscripts, and to establish a choir. It publishes the annual journal *Plainsong and Medieval Music* (formerly *Journal of the Plainsong & Mediaeval Music Society*).   PW

plainte (Fr., 'complaint'). In music, a mournful piece lamenting a death or some other unhappy occurrence. The term was used in the 17th and 18th centuries, especially for keyboard works, by such composers as Rameau, Couperin, and Froberger (e.g. Froberger's *Plainte faite à Londres, pour passer le mélancholie* from his Suite no. 30).

plaisanterie (Fr.). A light movement—not a dance—in an 18th-century suite.

planctus (Lat., 'lament', 'plaint'; Provençal: *planh*). A medieval lament form (widespread from about the 9th to the 15th centuries), with either a Latin or a vernacular text.

Planets, The. Orchestral suite, op. 32 (1914–16), by Holst. Its seven movements depict the astrological associations of seven planets: Mars, the Bringer of War; Venus, the Bringer of Peace; Mercury, the Winged Messenger; Jupiter, the Bringer of Jollity; Saturn, the Bringer of Old Age; Uranus, the Magician; Neptune, the Mystic (with wordless female chorus). It was first performed privately in 1918, publicly (without the second and seventh movements) in 1919, and complete in 1920.

planh (Provençal, 'lament'). See PLANCTUS.

Planquette, Robert (*b* Paris, 31 July 1848; *d* Paris, 28 Jan. 1903). French composer. He studied at the Paris Conservatoire and made a reputation as composer of songs for *cafés-concerts*, among which *Le Régiment de Sambre-et-Meuse* was especially successful. He graduated to writing operettas, which won wide popularity throughout the world; the best-known are *Les Cloches de Corneville* ('The Bells of Corneville', 1877) and *Rip Van Winkle* (1882).   ALa

Plantin, Christopher (*b* ?Tours, *c*.1520; *d* Antwerp, 1 July 1589). Flemish printer of French birth. He was the most important printer and publisher in Antwerp in the 16th century. His printing press, established in Antwerp in 1555, issued scholarly books of every kind and became a renowned centre of humanist culture. At its peak it employed 160 men and operated 22 presses.

The basis of Plantin's economic success was the monopoly he acquired from Philip of Spain to print service books (missals, breviaries, etc.) for Spain and its territories. This was apparently the incidental cause of his turning to music printing: when Philip withheld a subsidy promised for a luxurious antiphoner, Plantin had to find a use for 1800 reams of royal format paper already ordered, so issued instead a volume of masses by George de la Hèle in 1578. During the following decade he published several other music editions, including works by Philippe de Monte and Andreas Pevernage. His printing house survives as the Plantin-Moretus Museum, which preserves most of the press's history through its remarkable collection of works of art, furnishings, and printing equipment.

See also PRINTING AND PUBLISHING OF MUSIC, 4.

JMT/JWA

plaqué (Fr.). 'Laid down': an instruction that the notes of a chord should be played simultaneously rather than as an *arpeggio.

Platée ('Plataea'). Opera in a prologue and three acts by Rameau to a libretto by Adrien-Joseph Le Valois d'Orville after Jacques Autreau's play *Platée, ou Junon jalouse* (Versailles, 1745).

Platti, Giovanni Benedetto (*b* ?Venice, *c.*1700; *d* Würzburg, 11 Jan. 1763). Italian composer. Little is known of him until 1722, when he went with other Venetian musicians to the episcopal court of Würzburg. He served there as an instrumentalist—he was a virtuoso oboist but played many other instruments as well—teacher, and composer until at least 1761. He is best known for his forward-looking keyboard sonatas, which have been compared to those of C. P. E. Bach.

WT/ER

player piano. A piano with an automatic playing mechanism incorporating music programmed as perforations in a paper roll. The earliest automatic pianos were barrel or street pianos, made from the beginning of the 19th century. Derived from the *barrel organ, these have a rotating wooden barrel inside the cabinet with brass pins and staples around its circumference which, as it revolves, actuate the hammers, playing elaborate music often with florid embellishments far beyond the compass of ten fingers.

The earliest mechanism (second half of the 19th century) was encased in a separate cabinet which was wheeled up to a piano keyboard so that its levers, actuated by a punched paper roll and pneumatic valves fed by pedals like those of a harmonium, pushed down the keys. The operator controlled dynamics and speed with levers in the front of the cabinet. From about 1900, the mechanism was built into the piano, the rolls fitting

behind the music desk, the pumping pedals replacing the ordinary piano pedals, and the expression controls placed along the front of the keyboard. The principal purpose, as with any recording, was to listen to piano music in the home. Manufacturers also began to incorporate expressive effects on to the roll itself, so that all the player had to do was work the pedals (or switch on the electricity supply); instruments equipped to interpret such rolls were called 'expression pianos'.

The heyday of the player piano was in the early 1920s, when nearly half a million were manufactured in two years. Coin-operated player pianos were made for cafés and other public places. One trademark, the Pianola (1897) made by the Aeolian Co. in the USA, became widely known and has become a generic term for all kinds of player piano. The most highly developed machines, 'reproducing pianos' such as the Welte-Mignon (Freiburg, 1904) and Aeolian's Duo-Art (1913), could record piano performances, including dynamics and pedalling, directly on to the paper roll.

Many contemporary virtuosos created piano rolls, including Paderewski, Rakhmaninov, Rubinstein, Gershwin, Debussy, Mahler, Richard Strauss, and Fats Waller. If the piano is in good condition their rolls will sound exactly as they did when recorded, providing invaluable evidence of early 20th-century performance practice. The player piano was virtually killed off during the Depression of the 1930s, though some composers, notably Conlon Nancarrow, have since written specifically for it. Today, electromechanical and computerized devices have given the reproducing piano a new lease of life.

JMo, RPA

📖 A. W. J. G. ORD-HUME, *Pianola: The History of the Self-Playing Piano* (London, 1984)

Playford. English family of booksellers and music publishers. As publishers the Playfords showed remarkable flair: they were the first to cater for public taste on a large scale, and virtually dominated London music-publishing in the second half of the 17th century. John Playford (1623–86), a musician, author, and the subject of Purcell's *Elegy on my Friend, Mr John Playford*, was the leading London music publisher from 1651 to 1684. He used Thomas Harper (successor to Thomas East) and William Godbid, Harper's successor, as his printers, and published engaging theory and instruction books, as well as many collections of instrumental pieces, songs, and arrangements of psalms. These included *A Musicall Banquet* (1651), *A Breefe Introduction to the Skill of Musick* (1654), and *The (English) Dancing Master* (1651), which went through numerous editions up to 1728. His catches, glees, and lessons for the cittern, viol, flageolet, virginals, etc., were also popular and were published in various permutations, amply supplied with dedications and prefaces that reflect Playford's preoccupations with commercial problems and his advocacy of English music in which divine service, under a restored monarchy, would have a proper place.

His younger son Henry (*c*.1657–*c*.1709) updated his father's editions, but was less prolific, concentrating on entertainment music. His best-known publications are *Wit and Mirth, or Pills to Purge Melancholy* (songs by Thomas d'Urfey set to popular tunes) and Purcell's song collection *Orpheus britannicus*. In spite of his attempting to move with the times, his business declined from around 1700 in the face of competition from publishers of engraved music.

A second John Playford (*c*.1655–85), nephew of the original John and sometime apprentice to William Godbid, may also have published some musical material.

See also PRINTING AND PUBLISHING OF MUSIC, 5.

JMT/JWA

Playing Away. Opera in two acts by Benedict Mason to a libretto by Howard Brenton (Leeds, 1994).

Play of Daniel, The. A medieval liturgical drama which exists in several versions. The only one to have survived with the music complete was composed between 1227 and 1234 for Beauvais Cathedral, probably for Matins on 1 January. The first part deals with Daniel at Belshazzar's court, the second with Daniel's trials at the court of Darius. There are several modern editions.

See also CHURCH DRAMA.

Play of Robin and Marion, The. See JEU DE ROBIN ET DE MARION, LE.

pleasure gardens. Gardens in London that offered entertainments, including music, and refreshments; the most famous were Marylebone (*c*.1659–1778), Vauxhall (1661–1859), and Ranelagh (1742–1803). At first the concerts were of instrumental works but they later included vocal music, ranging from songs and glees to vaudeville and opera, much of which was composed specially for the pleasure garden. AL

plectrum. A tool for plucking a string. Any suitable material may be used, including quill, parchment, wood, ivory, bone, horn, tortoiseshell, and plastic. Eagle or vulture talons have also been found suitable. The plectrum (or pick) gives an initial sound to a string similar to one plucked by the fingernail rather than the flesh of the finger. The standard type is held between finger and thumb but some players (e.g. of the steel-strung guitar or five-string *banjo) play with individual picks wrapped round the thumb and two or three fingers on the right hand.

The term is also used of the small tongues (or 'quills'), set in jacks, that pluck the strings on the *harpsichord. Delrin plastic is often used, though the traditional material was quill. Leather was also sometimes used on one row of jacks (*peau de buffle*). JMo

plenary mass. An 'entire' mass composition, i.e. one comprising both the Ordinary and the Proper of the Mass. Such a work is rarely composed (except in the case of the *Requiem), for reasons of economy, since the Proper varies for particular festivals and occasions whereas the Ordinary remains the same.

Pleyel, Ignace Joseph [Ignaz Josef] (*b* Ruppersthal, 18 June 1757; *d* Paris, 14 Nov. 1831). Austrian composer, publisher, and piano manufacturer. From about 1722 he studied with Haydn at Eisenstadt, where he remained for about five years. During this time his puppet opera *Die Fee Urgele* was performed at Eszterháza (1776) and at the Vienna Nationaltheater. Later he became Kapellmeister to Count Erdödy, to whom he dedicated his String Quartets op. 1 (1782–3). He travelled in Italy in the early 1780s and, through the services of the composer Norbert Hadrava, attached to the Austrian embassy in Naples, was commissioned to write some hurdy-gurdy pieces and the opera *Ifigenia in Aulide* (1785). On his return to Strasbourg he became the assistant to F. X. Richter, the cathedral Kapellmeister, succeeding him in 1789. He also conducted and organized concerts in the city. Most of his compositions—including symphonies and string quartets—date from this period. He spent some months in London in 1791–2, conducting the Professional Concert, and then returned to Strasbourg where he was arrested for suspected pro-Austrian or aristocratic sympathies. He was released only after he had written a patriotic hymn.

In 1795 Pleyel set up as a music publisher in Paris, founding a piano factory in 1807. In 1802 the firm issued the first miniature scores, a series entitled *Bibliothèque musicale*, beginning with four of Haydn's symphonies and continuing with chamber works by Beethoven, Hummel, and others. Pleyel's son Camille (1788–1855) became a partner in the firm in 1815 and they were joined by Kalkbrenner in 1829. Their publications became progressively more popular, with *romances*, *chansonnettes*, and potpourris replacing symphonies; in 1834 the firm ceased publishing and concentrated on instrument manufacture. On Camille's death the direction passed to August Wolff (1821–87) and the company was renamed Pleyel, Wolff, et Cie.

—/SH

plica (Lat., 'fold'). A term used in the medieval period for a liquescent neume. See NOTATION, Fig. 1.

Pli selon pli ('Fold upon Fold'). Work (1957–62) by Boulez for soprano and orchestra, subtitled 'Portrait de Mallarmé'.

Plummer, John (*b* c.1410; *d* c.1484). English composer. He served as a clerk at Henry VI's Chapel Royal from 1441, assuming the post of Master of the Children in 1444. His later life was spent at Windsor, where he was verger at St George's Chapel until his death; his name is still commemorated there four times a year. Some fine antiphons and motets by him have survived.   JM

plus (Fr.). 'More'.

pneuma. See NEUMA.

pochette (Fr., 'pocket'). See KIT.

pocket score. See MINIATURE SCORE.

poco (It.). 'A little', 'rather'; *un poco*, 'a little'; *poco a poco*, 'little by little'; *poco lento*, 'rather slow'; *fra poco*, 'shortly'; *pochetto*, *pochettino*, 'very little'; *pochissimo*, 'the least possible'.

poem. A designation sometimes given to an orchestral piece, usually in one movement, with a strong programmatic element. The term was particularly common during the latter half of the 19th century and the early 20th, appearing most frequently in the descriptions *symphonic poem and tone-poem.   JBE

Poème. Chausson's op. 25 (1896) for violin and orchestra, based on a short story by Ivan Turgenev.

Poèmes pour Mi ('Poems for Mi'). Song cycle (1936) by Messiaen for soprano and piano, settings of his own poems; Messiaen made an orchestral version in 1937. Mi was the composer's name for his first wife, the violinist Claire Delbos.

poème symphonique (Fr.; It.: *poema sinfonica*). 'Symphonic poem'.

Poem of Ecstasy (*Poema ekstaza*; *Le Poème de l'extase*). Orchestral work, op. 54 (1905–8), by Skryabin; it was inspired by the composer's theosophical ideas on love and art.

Poem of Fire, The. See PROMETHEUS, THE POEM OF FIRE.

Poglietti, Alessandro (*d* Vienna, July 1683). Italian composer, organist, and teacher. From 1661 he worked as chamber musician to Emperor Leopold I in Vienna, by whom he was ennobled. He also held a papal knighthood. His most important works are for keyboard; they include sonatas, suites, and ricercars, and are notable mainly for their extra-musical content,

such as their imitations of national instruments (e.g. the Bohemian bagpipe and the French flageolet). Poglietti met his death during the Turkish siege of Vienna, leaving large estates.   DA/PA

Pohjola's Daughter (*Pohjolan tytär*). Symphonic fantasia, op. 49 (1906), by Sibelius; it is based on a legend from the *Kalevala.

poi (It.). 'Then'; e.g. *poi la coda*, 'then (play) the coda'.

point. 1. On a stringed instrument, the opposite end to the *heel of the *bow.

2. A 'point of imitation' is a melodic motif taken as a subject for imitation.

3. See DOT, 2.

point d'orgue (Fr.). 1. The *pause sign.

2. A harmonic pedal; see PEDAL POINT.

3. A cadenza in a concerto, probably so called because cadenzas were generally indicated by pause signs.

pointé (Fr.). 'Pointed', 'detached', i.e. not *legato*.

pointe d'archet, à la (Fr.). In string playing, an instruction to play 'at the point of the bow'.

pointillism. A compositional technique, named after Georges Seurat's method of painting with tiny dots of colour, in which each note has a distinct quality of timbre, loudness, etc. Sometimes pointillism is a by-product of advanced *serial thought, as in certain works of Webern, Boulez, and Stockhausen. It also appears in the works of other composers (e.g. Xenakis) who aim to produce 'clouds' of musical points, and here the analogy with Seurat's method is closer.

pointing. In *Anglican chant, the marking of texts with signs to show changes of melodic direction.

Poisoned Kiss, The (*The Poisoned Kiss, or The Empress and the Necromancer*). Opera in three acts by Vaughan Williams to a libretto by Evelyn Sharp adapted from Richard Garnett's story *The Poison Maid* and Nathaniel Hawthorne's *Rapaccini's Daughter* (Cambridge, 1936); Vaughan Williams revised it in 1956–7 with new spoken dialogue by Ursula Vaughan Williams.

Poissl, Johann Nepomuk (*b* Haukenzell, Lower Bavaria, 15 Feb. 1783; *d* Munich, 17 Aug. 1865). German composer. He studied with Vogler and with Danzi, who encouraged him to write operas for Munich. His early operas include two—*Antigonus* (1808) and *Ottaviano in Sicilia* (1812)—composed with the ambition of bringing heroic classical ideas into the sphere of German opera. To that end he often turned to Metastasian subjects. The biblical *Athalia* (1814), after Racine, attracted much attention; it is a remarkable achievement, with eloquent orchestration and a skilful use of motif that may have influenced his admirer Weber in *Euryanthe*. *Der Wettkampf zu Olympia* (1815) and *Nittetis* (1817) are further pioneering examples of German grand opera. *Der Untersberg* (1829) is influenced by Weber's *Der Freischütz* but lacks the momentum of Poissl's best work. He was the most important composer before Wagner to write his own librettos. JW

polacca (It.). See POLONAISE.

Poland 1. From the Middle Ages to the 16th century; 2. From the Baroque to the 18th century; 3. The early 19th century: emergence of a national style; 4. The early 20th century; 5. Since 1956

1. From the Middle Ages to the 16th century

Poland's troubled political history has impinged powerfully on the development of its musical life, and political upheaval has influenced our capacity to trace that development, for it has taken a cruel toll of essential documentation. Medieval sources are particularly scanty. While Gregorian chant arrived in Poland with the acceptance of Christianity in the 10th century, the earliest surviving Polish liturgical music dates from the 12th and 13th centuries. By the 15th century there are ample records of a thriving and developing musical life in Poland, not only in monasteries and bishoprics but also in the aristocratic courts. Kraków was the cultural and intellectual heart of Poland, with musical activities centred on the royal chapel, whose repertory included works by leading European composers of the Renaissance. The most distinguished Polish composer of the early 16th century was Mikołaj of Kraków.

In the latter half of the 16th century, the Hungarian lutenist Valentin Bakfark exerted a strong influence on later Polish lutenist-composers such as Wojciech Długoraj (*b* 1557 or 1558; *d* probably after *c*.1619), Jakub Reys (*c*.1550–*c*.1605), and the Italian Diomedes Cato who was active in Poland. The composers Wacław of Szamotuły (*c*.1524–60) and Marcin Leopolita (*c*.1540–1589) were recognized as the greatest Polish masters of Renaissance polyphony, and the latter's five-part *Missa paschalis* is unparalleled in 16th-century Polish music. A further highpoint was the publication in 1580 of Mikołaj Gomółka's *Melodie na Psałterz polski* ('Melodies for the Polish Psalter'). These are among the earliest Polish works to show pronounced national features.

2. From the Baroque to the 18th century

One of the finest Polish composers before Chopin was Mikołaj Zieleński, whose main legacy consists of 113 compositions (Venice, 1611) in two collections: *Offertoria* and *Communiones totius anni*. Zieleński's part-writing is based firmly on Renaissance polyphonic principles, but by the 1620s monody and figured bass

had found their way to Poland. In 1628 opera arrived at the royal court (recently moved to Warsaw), and in 1632 an opera theatre was established by King Władisław IV. The repertory was largely Italian, including several works by the *maestro di cappella* Marco Scacchi (*c*.1600–1662).

Instrumental music in the new Italian manner also flourished during the early 17th century; the leading Polish composers were Adam Jarzębski (*d* 1648 or 1649) and Marcin Mielczewski (*d* 1651). The new vocal-instrumental style also permeated church music, coexisting for some time with an earlier Renaissance idiom. The greatest composer of church music was Bartłomiej Pękiel (*d c*.1670); his *Missa 'La Lombardesca'* for eight voices, two violins, three trombones, and basso continuo uses antiphonal choirs, accompanied solos, and purely instrumental sections in a powerful, colourful conception.

The Swedish invasions of the mid-17th century and the later conflicts with Russia, together with growing political intrigues and disputes within Poland itself, resulted in a decline in Polish music. Only towards the end of the 18th century were there signs of new vitality. A solid institutional framework for the teaching and performance of music was established before the 1830 uprising, with opera at the National Theatre, a Society for Religious and National Music, a music society organized by E. T. A. Hoffmann, and the foundation of the Warsaw Conservatory in 1821.

3. The early 19th century: emergence of a national style

The music composed or performed in Warsaw just before and during Chopin's years there (1810–30) included High Baroque church cantatas by Jakub Gołąbek (*c*.1739–1789), Classical symphonies and chamber music by Józef Elsner (1769–1854), lightweight piano concertos and bravura solos by Franciszek Lessel (*c*.1780–1838), and piano miniatures by Maria Szymanowska (1789–1831). Opera was dominated by Italian styles, especially Rossini, but from Maciej Kamieński's *Nędza uszczęśliwiona* ('Sorrow Turned to Joy', 1778) onwards, Polish composers made an increasing contribution, excelling in comic operas on rustic themes, particularly in the form of *Singspiele* or vaudevilles. Jan Stefani's *Cud mniemany* ('The Supposed Miracle', 1794) is generally regarded as a landmark in the period immediately preceding the more substantial operatic achievements of Elsner and Karol Kurpiński (1785–1857).

'National' characteristics (polonaise, krakowiak, mazurka) were initally grafted on to familiar styles. However, it was Michał Kleofas Ogiński (1765–1833) who moulded the polonaise into an independent miniature for harpsichord or piano. His pieces have a simple, homespun character that is notably independent of Western influences, and the large repertory of early 19th-century polonaises, including the earliest attempts by Chopin, owed a good deal to his model.

Chopin very soon looked beyond Poland for his inspiration, however, and the bulk of his mature music was composed in Paris, where he settled in 1831. Yet by integrating national characteristics with the most advanced achievements of European music, he laid the foundations on which a 'nationalist' tradition might have been built in Poland. That such a tradition failed to develop was largely due to the ruthless policies of denationalization carried out by the partitioning powers in the wake of the 1830 uprising. Musical life became increasingly insular and conservative, and the music that responded most directly to its needs was not Chopin's but Moniuszko's. His *Home Songbook* series offered harmonically simple 'homely' ballads on Polish themes that successfully wooed Polish music lovers away from the German and Russian repertory. Moniuszko's opera *Halka* (Warsaw, 1858) fathered a national operatic style of admittedly conservative bent, colouring earlier Italian styles with the rhythms of Polish national dances. This blend dictated the musical formulation of 'Polishness' to later Polish composers, such as Władysław Żeleński (1837–1921) and Zygmunt Noskowski (1846–1909).

4. The early 20th century

Following a decline in the quality of Polish music in the late 19th century, there was a revival of concert life and teaching. The Warsaw Conservatory was reconstituted, the Warsaw Music Society formed, and in 1901 the Warsaw Philharmonic Orchestra founded. A group known as 'Young Poland in Music' was set up by four young composition students, Grzegorz Fitelberg (1879–1953), Karol Szymanowski (1882–1937), Ludomir Różycki (1884–1953), and Apolinary Szeluto (1884–1966), with the aim of updating Polish music.

Szymanowski found stylistic maturity in his music of the war years, responding in a highly individual way to the stimulus of Debussy, Ravel, and late Skryabin. His later 'nationalist' works foreshadow to some extent Polish music of the 1930s and 40s. But the younger generation of Polish composers—Piotr Perkowski (1901–90), Stanisław Wiechowicz (1893–1963), Michał Kondracki (1902–84), Antoni Szałowski (1907–73), and Michał Spisak (1914–65)—looked more towards the Parisian neo-classical styles, influenced by Stravinsky, Prokofiev, Milhaud, Poulenc, and Nadia Boulanger. Neo-classical sympathies are also apparent in the Symphonic Variations by Witold Lutosławski (1913–94)

and even in the surviving 12-note works of Józef Koffler (1896–1944), the only Polish composer at that time to take Schoenberg's path.

In the years after World War II and the creation of the new socialist state, Polish music was largely cut off from developments in Western music and composers were urged to cultivate 'concrete' genres—opera, oratorio, cantata, and so on—and to take their inspiration from folk music. The first major work to be condemned for *formalism was Lutosławski's First Symphony. Bartók clearly influenced some of the principal achievements of the postwar years, such as the Fourth String Quartet and Fourth Violin Concerto by Grażyna Bacewicz (1909–69) and the Concerto for Orchestra by Lutosławski.

5. Since 1956

The more liberal cultural policy which followed the October revolt of 1956 resulted in a dramatic stylistic change in Polish music as it responded to renewed contact with radical Western developments. Progressive trends were encouraged by the establishment in 1956 of the Warsaw Autumn Festival of Contemporary Music, by lavish state subsidies for music publishing and recording, and by the foundation of the Experimental Music Studio of Polish Radio. The result was a remarkable flowering of avant-garde composition, placing Poland firmly on the musical map of Europe.

Of middle-generation composers the most talented were Kazimierz Serocki and Tadeusz Baird, both of whom died in 1981 while still in their 50s. But apart from Lutosławski, the composers who have attracted most interest both at home and abroad are Krzysztof Penderecki, Henryk Górecki, and Wojciech Kilar. One characteristic is the sheer simplicity of their music, which led to the extraordinary impact of the 'Polish sound' on a wide musical public in the 1960s. In the late 1970s, the music of all three composers changed dramatically, yet their present commitment to a nostalgic world of tonality and romanticism is arguably not so different from the 'texture music' of the 1960s. This is the world inhabited by Penderecki's Violin Concerto, *Te Deum*, and Second Symphony, by Kilar's *Bogurodzica* ('Mother of God') and *Siwa mgła* ('Grey Mist'), and by Górecki's *Beatus vir*.

With the return of democracy in 1989, Polish music gained new freedoms, but also new difficulties, as generous state subsidies made way for the competitive world of a market economy. Yet the festival continues, and the voice of such younger composers as Paweł Szymański, Hanna Kulenty, and Eugeniusz Knapik (*b* 1951) continues to be heard in Poland and abroad.

JS

📖 Z. Chechlińska and J. Stęszewski (eds.), *Polish Musicological Studies* (Kraków, 1977–86) · K. Michałowski, *Polish Music Literature (1515–1990)* (Los Angeles, 1991) · L. Rappoport-Gelfand, *Musical Life in Poland: The Postwar Years, 1945–1977* (New York, 1991)

'Polish' Symphony. Nickname of Tchaikovsky's Symphony no. 3 in D major op. 29 (1875), so called because the finale is in *polonaise rhythm.

politics and music. With the rise of totalitarianism in the 20th century, music and politics became locked in a tighter and more tortured embrace than ever before. The uneasy liaison between the two goes back much further, of course. Plato felt that musical innovation spelt political danger, arguing that 'when modes of music change, the laws of the State always change with them'. Beethoven famously dedicated his 'Eroica' Symphony to Napoleon Bonaparte, whom he thought to be (like himself) a democratic revolutionary, only to rip out the title page in fury on learning that his hero had proclaimed himself emperor. Wagner backed the abortive 1849 uprising in Dresden, dreaming of a socialist utopia in which true art, notably his own, would be paramount. In the event, when he later managed to realize at least some of his most cherished ambitions, it was thanks not to a socialist paradise but to the backing of a wealthy patron, King Ludwig of Bavaria.

Do Wagner's music dramas reflect his political (and racist) views? Many interpret the *Ring* cycle as a critique of capitalism, with Wagner's old acquaintance Bakunin, the Russian anarchist, serving as the model for Siegfried. The *Ring*, *Die Meistersinger von Nürnberg*, and *Parsifal* are often said to be shot through with anti-Semitism. But it is hard to be sure because, even with the evidence to hand of librettos and stage action—along with Wagner's own lengthy commentaries on what he believed he was creating—the underlying meaning of music is too powerfully elusive to be pinned down in words, even the composer's own.

Hence the dilemma for those aiming to put music to particular political or ideological use. At the simplest level that may work well. As Constant Lambert put it, 'no political pamphlet or poster can get a hundredth of the recruits that are enrolled by a cornet and bass drum'. Nor, it could be added, were there more effective rallying calls for opponents of the American war in Vietnam than the protest songs of, say, Joan Baez and Bob Dylan, or the warped rendition of *The Star-Spangled Banner* by the guitarist Jimi Hendrix. But what of a symphony or string quartet—or even a cantata whose rousing text can seem to be belied by a few minor chords? Totalitarian regimes well able to censor the printed word and most visual art have a far tougher time bending music to their will, or even deciding exactly what their will is.

That is not for the want of trying. The Nazis were gruesomely successful in banning music by Jews and in driving out or murdering Jewish musicians. They were somewhat less effective in purging 'modernist' music (hard to define; see Entartete Musik) and 'American nigger music'—jazz (which helped keep German spirits high, or so Goebbels felt, the contrary claims of party ideologists notwithstanding). Even Wagner caused the Nazis problems. Although *Parsifal* was in principle banned from German stages from 1939, apparently because its underlying themes of suffering and sacrifice were thought untimely, it was still performed now and again in the war years—even in Berlin. It was, after all, one of Hitler's favourites.

While Italy under Mussolini (something of an amateur musician himself) proved less repressive than the Nazis, Stalin showed a ferocity even the Fascists rarely matched in striving to eliminate every last vestige of the avant-garde that had survived the early years of the USSR. Composers unable or unwilling to produce works of crude *socialist realism' were purged. Others, especially those of modest talent such as Tikhon Khrennikov, flourished thanks to slavish adherence to every twist and turn of the party line and by denouncing colleagues often more skilled. Still other, greater, composers like Shostakovich and (to some extent) Prokofiev survived by conforming outwardly while building into their music a semi-hidden, heretical agenda that their political masters could not decipher. A similar pattern emerged, albeit with some national variation, throughout the post-1945 Soviet empire. Stalin's death in 1953 brought some relief, but more or less complete freedom from political edict came only with the fall of the Iron Curtain nearly four decades later.

Two points in the aftermath of totalitarianism are particularly worth noting. One is that at last the long-suppressed and often forgotten work of such composers as Nikolay Roslavets, Gavriil Popov, and Galina Ustvol'skaya has gradually become known, adding a new dimension to our understanding of Russian music—even that of supposedly well-known figures like Shostakovich. The other point is that, in the wave of new music that burst forth after the fall of Fascism, the (West) Germans arguably went overboard—albeit for the best of motives. Above all the newly formed regional radio stations, eager to display ultra-liberal credentials, put massive funding behind the most cerebral of 'progressive' compositions for which there was next to no audience, then or later.

It was not least in reaction to the doctrinaire atmosphere surrounding the new avant-garde in his homeland that Hans Werner Henze, perhaps the outstanding German composer in the second half of the 20th century, fled at an early stage to Italy and composed largely in traditional forms—including symphonies, concertos, operas, and ballets. He did so, however, with an almost bewildering inventiveness and eclecticism, combining his work with a forceful public commitment to the political far left that brought him brickbats at home, especially during the era of terrorism there by the so-called Red Army Faction.

In spite of this long history of tension, political and otherwise, most of Henze's compositions have been well recorded for posterity—above all in Germany. Such commitment to the work of a highly talented, albeit controversial, artist may seem more or less self-evident in a democracy. Regrettably, that is not always so. Aaron Copland, arguably the most American of American composers, was the subject of a witch-hunt as an alleged communist by Senator Joe McCarthy's un-American activities committee, and a performance of his *Lincoln Portrait* was cancelled only a fortnight before its scheduled inclusion in a concert marking the inauguration of President Eisenhower. In Britain, too, the work of such composers as the communist Alan Bush long seemed underexposed on political rather than strictly musical grounds. In the wake of the cold war such censure of music and musicians, in both the old and the new democracies, has virtually ceased—but for good?   JC

📖 S. Volkov (ed.), *Testimony: The Memoirs of Dmitri Shostakovich* (London and New York, 1979) · H. W. Henze, *Music and Politics: Collected Writings, 1953–1981* (Eng. trans., London, 1982) · C. Norris (ed.), *Music and the Politics of Culture* (London, 1989) · E. Levi, *Music in the Third Reich* (London, 1994) · L. Goehr, *The Quest for Voice: Music, Politics and the Limits of Philosophy* (Berkeley and Los Angeles, 1998)

Poliuto. Opera in three acts by Donizetti to a libretto by Salvadore Cammarano after Pierre Corneille's play *Polyeucte* (1641) (Naples, 1848).

polka. A ballroom dance that became especially popular during the 19th century. Originally a peasant round dance from Bohemia, it was adopted in Prague in the late 1830s and soon spread throughout Europe, being danced in Paris in 1840 and in London four years later; it also reached New York, where it was taken up with great enthusiasm. The polka was a lively couple dance in 2/4 time, generally in ternary form with regular phrases, and was characterized by short rapid steps for the first beat and a half of the bar, followed by a pause or hop.

In Vienna during the 1850s several distinct types of polka came into being, including the *schnell-Polka*, a particularly fast and lively variety similar to the galop; the *polka française*, a slower and more graceful version; and the polka-mazurka, in 3/4 time. All the leading dance composers of the mid-19th century wrote polkas, especially the Strauss family and Adolphe Jullien. The polkas of the Strausses, for example the 'Thunder and Lightning' and 'Tritsch-Tratsch' polkas, remain regular features in concerts of Viennese music. The form also appears in art music by such composers as Smetana (*The Bartered Bride*, *Vltava*), Dvořák, and Walton (*Façade*). Although it declined in the 20th century it is still danced in eastern Europe and remains popular in east-European communities in the USA.   —/JBe

Pollarolo, Carlo Francesco (*b* c.1653; *d* Venice, 7 Feb. 1723). Italian composer and organist. He served first as organist to the Congregazione dei Padri della Pace in Brescia, succeeding his father as organist at the cathedral in 1676 and becoming *maestro* in 1680. In 1681 he was appointed *maestro* at the Accademia degli Erranti, important for its cultivation of music. He had left Brescia by late 1689; he became second organist at St Mark's, Venice, the following year and *vicemaestro* in 1692. He was also director at the Ospedale degli Incurabili. He quickly established himself as a leading composer of Venetian operas, producing some 85 by 1720, notable especially for their rich and varied orchestration. His output also includes a number of oratorios and some church music.   PA

Polly. Ballad opera in three acts with musical arrangements attributed to Pepusch (with new songs for the first performance by Samuel Arnold) to a libretto by Gay (London, 1777); it was written as a sequel to Gay's *The Beggar's Opera*.

polonaise (Fr., 'Polish'; Ger.: *Polonäise*; It.: *polacca*). A Polish dance in triple time and of moderate speed. It has a processional and stately character, having originated in courtly 16th-century ceremonies. The early polonaise bears little resemblance to the 19th-century dance, which is characterized by triple time, phrases starting on the first beat of the bar, the repetition of short, rhythmic motifs, and a cadence on the third beat of the bar. Many early 18th-century examples already show these characteristics, for instance those in Bach's French Suite no. 6 and Orchestral Suite no. 2. The polonaise was taken up by Mozart (Rondeau en polonaise from his keyboard sonata K284/205*b*), Beethoven (op. 89), and Schubert (polonaises for four hands op. 61 and op. 75). It became a virtuoso concert piece for piano in the hands of Weber (op. 21, op. 72), and was used for actual dance scenes by Musorgsky (in *Boris Godunov*), and Tchaikovsky (in *Eugene Onegin*; the finale of his Third Symphony is also marked 'Tempo di polacca').

But the composer most enduringly associated with the polonaise is Chopin, whose 13 examples provided an outlet for his intensely patriotic feeling as well as his advanced pianism. Perhaps the greatest work ever based on this dance is his *Polonaise-fantaisie* op. 61.

—/NT

Polovtsian Dances. A sequence of choral and orchestral pieces forming a ballet scene in Act II of Borodin's opera *Prince Igor*. The Polovtsians were nomadic invaders of Russia who, in the opera, capture Igor and entertain him with these dances.

polymetric. A term used in the editing of early music for a piece in which the bar-lines do not occur at regular intervals but are placed according to the musical and textual requirements of the phrasing, resulting in bars of irregular length.

polyphony (from Gk. *polyphonia*, 'of many sounds'; Ger.: *Mehrstimmigkeit, Vielstimmigkeit*). Musical texture in two or more (though usually at least three) relatively independent parts. In general, the term is applied to vocal music, but usages such as 'orchestral polyphony' with reference, for instance, to the music of Mahler or Ives are to be found in discussions of 19th- and 20th-century instrumental styles. It refers to a fundamental category of musical possibilities, since all sound sources may be used on their own, in monophony, or with another or others, in polyphony. The usages are therefore many and varied in the history of Western art and folk music and in ethnomusicology. In Western art music, a general and a particular meaning can be identified as the most important applications.

Polyphony, in the sense of vocal music in more than one part, as opposed to monophony, developed between roughly the 10th and the 13th centuries. The earliest manifestation was *organum. The source of this parallel intoning of liturgical melody may be traced to the natural range of the human voice. Both boys and men (the female voice—and indeed the female—having had little part to play in the medieval ecclesiastical world) tend to have one of two vocal ranges lying about a 5th apart, and the immature and mature versions of each tend to be an octave apart. The disposition of voices at a 5th, octave, and 12th over the lowest part, and the basis for this in acoustics—the octave, 5th, and 4th are the lowest overtones (see HARMONIC SERIES)—formed a remarkable natural foundation for early polyphony.

In the 14th century there was a rapid development of this rudimentary polyphony in the principle of mixed intervallic and rhythmic successions for parts sung simultaneously. Polyphonic independence was extreme, in comparison with both earlier and later styles. It involved, for instance, the vertical combination of different *isomelic and *isorhythmic constructions: indeed, in this early phase of vocal polyphony the three or four parts would often sing different texts together, in both Latin and the vernacular.

The combination of independent lines of music became a constant element of the Western tradition, and it is a means of comparing phases of musical language—from medieval polyphony with its basically linear organization; through Renaissance and Baroque counterpoint, with its greater emphasis on the organization of the resulting vertical combination, and the conjunction of this with the evolution of major–minor tonality to produce the harmonic structures of Classical and Romantic music; to the new polyphony of the 20th century, where a multiplicity of independent strands became once more the shared ideal of many composers. In the simple meaning of 'multi-voiced', then, polyphony is to be found throughout the post-organum history of Western music.

The use of the term itself became common in theoretical and practical writings of the early 16th century. It replaced earlier terms such as *dia-*, *tri-*, and *tetraphonia* (which specified the number of parts) or *organica* (discant). The spread of a common meaning for polyphony coincided with the era of excellence in its practice discussed below. The great Classical theorist Heinrich Koch (1749–1816) established the two modern distinctions: monophony–polyphony, and polyphony–homophony. The first is a practical distinction, between single-voice and multi-voice composition, the latter being the predominant feature of Western art music. The second distinction is a stylistic one. It refers to the alternative approaches to musical continuity available for the post-Renaissance composer: one relying on counterpoint and the structural equality of voices, the other on a structural framework of melody supported by a bass line with inner parts to provide harmonic, rhythmic, and textural expression. Although all homophonic music revealing harmonic differentiation is, logically, polyphonic or 'multi-voiced', stylistically the interplay of contrapuntal polyphony and harmonic homophony has been a crucial factor in the evolution of musical language, both vocal and instrumental, since the early 17th century.

A particular meaning of the term is reserved for 16th-century sacred music, the 'golden age' of polyphony. The milestones in its evolution are found in the music of Dunstaple and of the 15th-century Franco-Flemish school. Their principal concern was to develop techniques for using one melodic idea in all parts by means of imitation. Hugo Riemann's concept *Durchimitieren*, or 'through-imitation', amply conveys the principle of distributing the main material of the polyphony—what was in earlier stages the cantus firmus—across every voice. The development of a more euphonious harmonic sense—especially in the treatment of the 4th as a dissonance requiring contrapuntal preparation and resolution—went hand in hand with increasing skill at complex polyphonic control. By the 16th century a coherent and consistent European imitative style had emerged. It was impelled by many historical forces, not least of which were the increase in the dissemination of music allowed by the printing of music from *c.*1500 onwards and the increasing focus of artistic control exercised by the Roman Catholic Church in reaction to the Reformation.

The highpoint of Renaissance polyphony was in the mid- and late 16th century. Lassus, Victoria, and, in England, Byrd were and still are considered only the greatest among many giants. The peak of this activity came in the music of Palestrina, whose polyphony has been studied by most theorists and composers from the 18th century on, although the temporary reaction against vocal polyphony in the 17th century was as extreme as it was productive. Palestrina's compositions, his 'novum genus musicum' (preface to the second book of masses, 1567), had two outstanding features: the clear expression of the text, whether in three, four, or five parts, by means of formal articulation of the music according to the phrases of the text and by the matching of the cadence of melodic ideas, especially in their rhythmic proportions, to the words; and the independence and clarity of each line within the declamation structure, with an elegance of combination in dissonance treatment and textural flow that marks a pinnacle of Western art.   JD

polyrhythm. Simultaneous use of different rhythms in separate parts of the musical texture. It is a characteristic feature of some 14th-century music, and also of some 20th-century pieces, by, for example, Hindemith and Stravinsky.

polytextuality. Simultaneous use of different texts in the various parts of a vocal composition. It was particularly common in the early *motet.

polytonality. Simultaneous use of two or more keys. If two keys are superposed the technique is known as *bitonality; more complex combinations are rare.

Pommer. German name for the larger sizes of *shawm (see also BOMBARDE).

Pomp and Circumstance. Five marches for orchestra, op. 39, by Elgar; nos. 1–4 were composed in 1901–7, no. 5 was completed by 1930. Elgar took the title from Shakespeare's *Othello* (Act III scene 3): 'Pride, pomp, and circumstance of glorious war!'. The trio section of the first march, slightly altered and with words by A. C. Benson beginning 'Land of Hope and Glory', became the finale of Elgar's *Coronation Ode*.

Ponce, Manuel (Maria) (*b* Fresnillo, Mexico, 8 Dec. 1886; *d* Mexico City, 24 April 1948). Mexican composer. He studied in Mexico City, Bologna, and Berlin. He was the first composer seriously to examine Mexican folk music, which had an important influence on his works, as did the rhythms of Cuban music, absorbed during a stay in Havana (1915–17). However, most of his larger works date from after a period in Paris (1925–33), during which he had further lessons with Dukas. He produced numerous guitar and piano pieces as well as concertos for guitar (*Concierto del sur*, 1941) and violin (1943).   PG/CW

Ponchielli, Amilcare (*b* Paderno, nr Cremona, 31 Aug. 1834; *d* Milan, 16 Jan. 1886). Italian composer. He studied at the Milan Conservatory, graduating in 1854. His first opera, *I promessi sposi*, was first performed in Cremona in 1856, and several more followed before he was taken up by Giulio Ricordi, at that time Italy's most powerful publisher. The finest fruit of this commercial and artistic collaboration was *La Gioconda* (La Scala, Milan, 1876), one of the most influential operas for the subsequent generation of Italian composers, and a work that retains a robust currency in the repertory. His later operas failed to make an equal effect, but his career involved conducting and teaching (from 1881 he taught at the Milan Conservatory, with pupils including Puccini and Mascagni). He also wrote instrumental and sacred music, notably *Lamentazioni di Geremia* (1886).   RP

Pons, Lily (Alice Joséphine) (*b* Draguignan, 12 April 1898; *d* Dallas, 13 Feb. 1976). French-born American soprano. She studied the piano at the Paris Conservatoire, then had singing lessons in New York with Giovanni Zenatello. She made her stage debut in Mulhouse in 1928 as Lakmé, for which her high, delicate, and agile coloratura voice was well suited. She caused a sensation in 1931 when she took the title role of *Lucia di Lammermoor* at the Metropolitan Opera, New York, where she went on to sing for 28 seasons. Her greatest successes were in lyrical and colourful roles; she was an admired Gilda. She made many recordings and some films.   JT

Ponselle [Ponzillo], **Rosa** (Melba) (*b* Meriden, CT, 22 Jan. 1897; *d* Green Spring Valley, MD, 25 May 1981). American soprano of Italian parentage. She first sang in film theatres and vaudevilles and took lessons from William Thorner and Romano Romani, who recommended her to Caruso. His influence led to her opera debut at the Metropolitan Opera, New York, as

Leonora in *La forza del destino* (1918), which was one of the most sensational events in the Metropolitan's history. She was soon established as one of the outstanding sopranos of her time, and for the next 19 years at the Metropolitan Opera she sang 22 dramatic roles, notably Norma, Donna Anna, Violetta, Rachel (*La Juive*), and Santuzza. She achieved similar success at Covent Garden. Her beautiful looks and elegant acting were matched by rich tone, expressiveness, and virtuoso technique, which can be heard in her recordings.

JT

ponticello (It.). The *bridge of a bowed instrument. *Sul ponticello* is an instruction to play near the bridge, which greatly diminishes the intensity of the lower harmonics in favour of the higher, producing a thin, ethereal quality.

JMo

Poole, Geoffrey (Richard) (*b* Ipswich, 9 Feb. 1949). English composer. He studied with Alexander Goehr and Jonathan Harvey. He taught at Manchester University (1976–2000) before taking up a post at Bristol University, and was a visiting teacher at Kenyatta University, Nairobi (1985–7). African rhythmic structures and Asian performance techniques are important influences on his music, which ranges from an early work for the King's Singers, *Wymondham Chants* (1970), the BBC-commissioned Chamber Concerto (1979), and the orchestral *The Net and Aphrodite* (1982) to the large-scale 'secular requiem' *Blackbird* (1991–4).

AW

pop. See POPULAR MUSIC, 4.

Pope Marcellus Mass. See MISSA PAPAE MARCELLI.

Popov, Gavriil Nikolayevich (*b* Novocherkassk, 30 Aug./12 Sept. 1904; *d* Repino, nr Leningrad, 17 Feb. 1973). Russian composer and pianist. He studied the piano at the Rostov-on-Don Conservatory (1917–21) and took composition lessons from Mikhail Gnesin. Later he studied composition at the Leningrad Conservatory with Vladimir Shcherbachov and was a member of Lev Nikolayev's piano class. He taught composition and the piano at the Leningrad State Central Musical College (1927–31) and was a member of the secretariat of the Leningrad Composers' Union from its inception in 1932.

Popov played an active role in new music in Leningrad and belonged to all the organizations in the city that were connected with it, including the Leningrad Association of Contemporary Music (1926–8). Such early works as the Septet (1927, also known as the Chamber Symphony) and the First Symphony attracted widespread acclaim, and he worked with prominent artists including the theatre director Vsevolod

Meyerhold and the film director Sergey Eisenstein. He was among those named in the Zhdanov decree of 1948 when, together with Shostakovich, Prokofiev, Khachaturian, and Myaskovsky, he was branded a proponent of *formalism.

Popov wrote six symphonies—no. 1 op. 7 (1927–34); no. 2 op. 39 ('Rodina' [Homeland], 1943); no. 3 op. 5 ('Geroicheskaya' [The Heroic], 1939–46); no. 4 op. 47 ('Slava otchizne' [Glory to the Fatherland], 1948–9), with soloists and mixed chorus; no. 5 op. 77 ('Pastoral'naya', 1956–7); no. 6 op. 99 ('Prazdnichnaya' [The Festive], 1969)—as well as a number of piano pieces and incidental music.

PF

Popper, David (*b* Prague, 18 June or 9 Dec. 1843 or 1846; *d* Baden, Vienna, 7 Aug. 1913). Czech cellist and composer. His date of birth is the subject of dispute. He spent much of his life touring Europe, famed for his splendid tone and transcendental technique. He was latterly professor at the National Hungarian Royal Academy of Music, and his studies op. 73 (1901–5) still provide the technical basis for cellists.

DA

popular music 1. Introduction; 2. Popular music and the theatre; 3. Popular song; 4. Developments after 1950

1. Introduction

Although the division between 'classical' or 'serious' music and popular music remains clearly identifiable, critical appreciation of both worlds has increasingly overlapped. There were virtually no studies of popular music, beyond limited folk-music research, until the last decades of the 19th century and few even in the early 20th. The earliest 'popular' composers to receive serious attention were those like the Strauss family, whose music showed craftsmanship and substance, or Gershwin, who crossed the so-called boundaries by writing operas and concert works. By the beginning of the 21st century, popular music was being subjected to the same type of scholarly inquiry as any other music.

The growth of popular music coincided with the increasing wealth and purchasing power of ordinary people in the mid-19th century, and with a demand for accessible musical entertainment. It was at this time that the genre of *operetta arose, leading to the huge expansion of the popular musical theatre, of *music hall and minstrel shows, which in turn led to the growth of the popular song industry. At the same time, both coincidentally and as a result, there was a breakthrough in the printing of music more cheaply, a great expansion of road and rail travel, a rapid growth of theatres and concert halls catering for popular taste, and the availability of more affordable tickets. Domestic music-making increased: the music-box was superseded by the parlour piano, on which the new cheap music could be played; and in the 20th century came the phenomenal spread of such entertainment media as the gramophone, cinema, radio, and television.

2. Popular music and the theatre

The gradual creation of a written tradition of popular music began in the 18th century with *ballad operas like Gay's *The Beggar's Opera* (1728). Similar works were being staged in many parts of Europe at the same time. The composers of these ballad operas mainly added words to well-known traditional and composed melodies which had been brought to light and made available for popular consumption in printed collections. The tradition continued, diversified, and expanded as composers like Dibdin in the later part of the century wrote original scores for entertainments that combined elements of revue and light opera.

Composers of 'serious' operas turned their hands to works of a light and tuneful nature intended for a wider audience and for commercial success. Donizetti's *La Fille du régiment*, staged at the Opéra-Comique in Paris, is an example of this more frivolous genre. In France a flourishing school of lighter opera grew up: *opéra comique*, with its spoken dialogue and appealing melodies. Boieldieu, Auber, Hérold, and Adam were among its exponents. Offenbach and Hervé were their successors, producing operettas full of wit, satire, good tunes, and dances like the can-can; Offenbach's *Orphée aux enfers* (1858) is a notable example. These works were exported to Vienna, where they influenced Johann Strauss, Suppé, and others to produce their own brand of Viennese operetta, dominated by the waltz. Theatres in London imported French productions almost as soon as they had been staged in Paris, and Offenbach was particularly successful there. His works were translated by W. S. Gilbert, who was to embark on a famous partnership with Sullivan; their operettas (or *Savoy operas) came to dominate the London stage.

At this time the USA mainly imported works from London (especially Gilbert and Sullivan), Paris, and Vienna. With a wealth of immigrant composers, musicians, and performers, however, the country soon established its own tradition, first through such talents as Victor Herbert, then with Friml and Romberg, creating a rapidly expanding school of American operetta, the fruits of which began to flow back to Europe. The most compelling ingredient of American music was the native element of *ragtime and *jazz, a style that rapidly revolutionized the language of popular music in a couple of hectic decades around 1900.

Early in the 20th century Jerome Kern was employed to add American-style songs to British shows for export to the USA. He formed a bridge between the old style and the new; his *Show Boat* (1927) pioneered the move towards integrating music and plot. Gershwin, Rodgers, and Cole Porter established the American musical and the parallel musical film (generally known as the Hollywood musical) as unassailable leaders in popular theatre with such enduring works as Rodgers and Hammerstein's *Oklahoma!* (1943), *South Pacific* (1949), *The King and I* (1951), and *The Sound of Music* (1959) and the Lerner–Loewe *My Fair Lady* (1956). Britain produced isolated examples: Sandy Wilson's *The Boy Friend* (1953) and Julian Slade's *Salad Days* (1954) had an exportable novelty element, and Lionel Bart's *Oliver!* (1960) had a record run and was filmed. Much of later 20th-century popular musical theatre was under American dominance apart from the personal and highly successful musicals of Andrew Lloyd Webber, from *Jesus Christ Superstar* (1971), *Evita* (1978), and *Cats* (1981) to *The Phantom of the Opera* (1986).

See also MUSICAL COMEDY, MUSICAL.

3. Popular song

In popular song there is an endless intermingling of traditions, and in this context there is the eternal question of what defines *folk music. For most of the 18th century, little was published beyond a few broadsheets containing topical doggerel allied to better-known folksongs, and until the advent of ballad opera there was little by way of popular theatre. Music-making was mainly in the hands of a few itinerant singers and entertainers at fairs and in taverns. A pioneering publication was *The Dancing Master* (1650), a collection of mainly traditional tunes for professional fiddlers and teachers of dancing, compiled by the publisher John Playford with the encouragement of his friend Samuel Pepys. It was followed fitfully by a number of song compilations of a similar nature under such titles as *The Minstrel's Companion*. These proliferated in the early decades of the 19th century, helped by the development of cheap printing.

The rise of popular song is closely related to the economics of social growth. The expansion and commercialization of entertainment was dependent on the rising wealth of the population, which, in an industrial age, came first to the middle classes. Many households bought parlour pianos and needed music and songs to play and sing. Thus came the parlour songs, which at first were a mixture of folky adaptations and pastiches of operatic arias; verses of gentle melancholy were set to simple melodies accompanied by an *Alberti bass or arpeggios. The *drawing-room ballad flourished, best-selling examples being *Ever of Thee* (1852) by Foley Hall and George Linley and *Come into the garden, Maud* (1858) by Balfe and Tennyson. It was often impossible to discover what was genuinely 'folk' and what was simply anonymous. As the demands and rewards of publishing grew, professional popular music composers began to appear, among them many women. Public venues for such songs were also growing. The *pleasure gardens, once the province of such composers as Handel, embraced a variety of popular music and the public could buy sheet music which recommended itself as 'being sung in response to public demand at the Vauxhall Gardens'.

Another outlet for this repertory was in the popular minstrel shows; their creation is credited to a 'Mr Christy', though other minstrel leaders did more to popularize the genre, particularly in England, where it flourished. Edwin P. Christy (1815–62) in fact never came to England. Black-face minstrel shows were immensely popular and not only promoted even greater expansion in the music-publishing business but nurtured the first great popular song composers, among them Stephen Foster, composer of the renowned *The Old Folks at Home* (1851).

It was the advent of variety or *music hall (a miscellaneous collection of vocal and visual acts) which, between the 1860s and 90s, helped to create the popular song industry as we know it today. At first the songwriters for these entertainments were hacks who sold their songs outright for a guinea or so to anyone they could find to perform them. Singers thus controlled the market: without a good song they did not top the bill. Composers and lyric writers, however, soon realized the commercial potential of a successful song and organized publication on a royalty basis. At the peak of the music-hall years in England, there were some 500. They were at first a peculiarly British phenomenon but quickly took root in France and the USA. The music hall did not add much to the progress of popular music. It adapted itself to the current fashions for folksong style, the ballad, and finally ragtime and jazz idioms. But it did contribute a repertory of immortal songs easily memorable by their combination of direct tunes and earthy good humour. A further kind of entertainment that fostered popular music was the *revue, which was of French origin. In the 1920s and 30s in Britain it encouraged the talents of Noël Coward, among others; in the USA, the spectacular revue proved most popular.

The music hall and minstrel show helped to establish the music-publishing industry that was to become *Tin Pan Alley. In the minstrel shows, black music was only being parodied. However, the Jubilee Singers introduced real black music and the *spiritual to a wide public through their international tours. The first genuine black *rag was published in 1897: Tom Turpin's *Harlem Rag*. Scott Joplin published his *Original Rags* in 1899 and that year followed it with his immensely successful *Maple Leaf Rag*. Irving Berlin's song *Alex-*

ander's Ragtime Band (1911) brought the genre international renown, and the cakewalk and ragtime were ubiquitous.

A deeper strain of black music was covered by the term *blues, which introduced an entirely new flexibility and dissonance to popular music. The syncopations were subtler, the harmonies more chromatic and fluid, and the rhythmic propulsion entirely new. The *jazz age arrived with the Original Dixieland Jazz Band, which introduced jazz to Britain when it toured after World War I. By the early 1920s, many kinds of jazz style had emerged, influencing both popular and 'classical' styles. Within two decades the language of popular music had undergone a complete change. Only a few areas of popular music-making still played their music 'straight'—*palm court orchestras and *brass and *military bands, for example.

By World War II radio and recordings disseminated music of all kinds. The music of *'big bands' and male singers became predominant, with hits like Irving Berlin's *White Christmas*, and star singers like Bing Crosby (1903–77) and Frank Sinatra (1915–98). By the 1940s the next great changes were on the way.   PGa

4. Developments after 1950

The postwar period saw an explosion of popular music as part of an expansion of a consumer-oriented economy. Integral to this, a specifically youth-based culture (the 'rise of the teenager') became the definitive context for what we now commonly think of as popular music. The indications of mass appeal and the status of the individual performer in the 1940s increased radically in the 50s. This is exemplified in the appearance of *rock and roll, a term that itself embraces a number of different musical styles.

It was first commonly used in relation to the music of Bill Haley and his band, the Comets. Their recording *Rock Around the Clock* (1955) was a huge hit following its use in *Blackboard Jungle*, a film that gave expression to the constructed sense of 'rebellion' and generational conflict evident in much of the music of the period. It is somewhat ironic that it was Haley who was seen to give voice to teenage angst: he was a middle-aged performer who had already released a number of country and western recordings. Black *rhythm and blues performers like Chuck Berry and Little Richard moved into rock and roll.

More significant was the arrival of Elvis Presley. His early recordings for Sun Records in Memphis were based in the white *rockabilly idiom and featured a remarkable synthesis of black (blues) and white (country) musical styles. His subsequent retreat from the urgency of his early recordings was interpreted by some as a reflection of the impact of commercial success through the manipulations of the 'culture industry'. Early rock and roll recordings, though originating in different regional traditions, share a set of musical characteristics and establish a framework that was to be replicated in later popular music: rhythmic energy, basic harmonic patterns (12-bar blues), a direct mode of communication, and a sense of immediacy. Rock and roll can now be seen as the archetype for popular music and is therefore of historical significance.

The late 1950s and early 60s are often considered a period of interruption in the development of popular music following the dispersal of the original rock and roll generation. The new, exciting popular styles were often assimilated into the 'culture industry', a process that depended on commercial rather than musical values. However, the music of the Beatles in the early 1960s was based on 50s models, an example of the overlapping and intersecting chronology of popular music and urban rhythm and blues which became the dominant influence on the Rolling Stones.

The emergence of the Beatles in Liverpool was a decisive moment. Breaking away from their 1950s models, they developed a unique sound derived from a remarkable ability to adapt and absorb existing styles. They also effected some profound changes to the basic nature of popular music: until this time, popular music in Britain had generally been a pale imitation of American music, with a high degree of artificial construction (Marty Wilde, Tommy Steele, Cliff Richard); the Beatles' success reversed this process, inspiring a number of American imitations (the Monkees) and generating reciprocal influences with more serious artists (Bob Dylan, the Byrds).

Until the 1960s the single (45 rpm) had been the pre-eminent vehicle for popular music, with the album/LP usually taking the form of a 'greatest hits' package (though some of Sinatra's recordings of the 1950s are exceptions). In the mid-1960s the Beatles gave new prominence to the album (*Rubber Soul*, 1965; *Revolver*, 1966), largely through their decision to abandon live performance and concentrate exclusively on recording; this had far-reaching consequences for their music and for popular music in general. Also of significance was their ability to generate their own material through the songwriting skills of Lennon and McCartney. Although 1950s rock and roll had featured several stars who wrote their own material (Buddy Holly, Chuck Berry), the performer had often been the voice and face that covered existing songs or presented specially written material by a songwriting and production team (a tendency that continues and is still evident in much recent popular music). The sense of authorship established by Lennon and McCartney coincided with the emergence of Bob Dylan, an American singer-songwriter who formed part of the folk-based *protest movement and was initially heavily influenced by Woody Guthrie.

The impact of Dylan and the Beatles in the 1960s generated a new sense of ambition: the music now dealt with serious, often introspective, subject matter and adopted an essentially experimental approach to the musical process, a tendency clearly marked in the music of the Beatles from the mid-1960s to their demise in 1970. Now several styles could coexist rather than supersede one another. A division emerged in the late 1960s and early 70s between rock music, which aspired to a sense of 'authenticity' through an expansion of the parameters of popular music, and commercially driven pop music. This division gave meaning to the terms *'rock' and 'pop'. As well as songwriting skills, instrumental virtuosity played a significant part in the expansion of popular music. Jimi Hendrix explored new possibilities in guitar sonority and timbre, and the music of Cream used the *blues framework as a starting-point for an interplay of virtuosity between guitar (Eric Clapton), bass (Jack Bruce), and drums (Ginger Baker). The importance of instrumental improvisation in this music produced a valid parallel with jazz.

The term *'progressive rock' came into use at this time as an attempt to encapsulate this new ambition. Such bands as King Crimson and Yes explored extended musical structures which involved intricate instrumental patterns and textures and often esoteric subject matter. However, these trends coexisted with the production of 'regular' pop music aimed at a largely teenage audience. The 1970s saw the beginning of generational changes in the reception of popular music, with pop music oriented towards a young teenage audience ('teenybop') and rock music being received mainly by older people. However, the division was not always clear-cut. Many of the serious progressive rock bands were commercially successful (for example, Pink Floyd with *Dark Side of the Moon*, 1973), and artists who were identified chiefly with pop music also produced work of lasting quality. While the Osmonds and the Bay City Rollers may be remembered only as an act of nostalgia, the *'glam rock' of T. Rex and David Bowie was an imaginative genre which had its own value and legacy.

Popular music has undergone increasing fragmentation and diversification, a process symptomatic of wider social and cultural trends. Its fragmentation was intensified through the arrival of *punk rock in the later 1970s and its coexistence with many different styles (e.g. *disco). Punk seemed to challenge many of the assumptions of the now well-established styles and attitudes of popular music and it gains added interest in that it restates the recurring paradox of musical–stylistic innovation and commercial interest. Much of this music could be seen to be overtly political and oppositional yet also commercially successful (for example the Sex Pistols' *God Save the Queen*, 1977). The growth of many small independent record companies changed the usual processes of dissemination (see INDIE), as did the initial spontaneity of the punk movement. But the most successful punk bands (the Sex Pistols, the Clash) signed contracts with major record companies, thus compromising their seemingly anti-establishment stance and contributing to the blurring of any neat distinction between a popular music that aspires to its own notion of authenticity and one that is more seemingly at ease with its commodity status.

The process of fragmentation and diversification has continued and, indeed, intensified. This is evident in the multiplicity of styles and terms that now coexist (*rhythm and blues, *rap, *hip-hop, *trip-hop, among others), each of which seems to have the potential to attract its own, often exclusive, audience—another factor that undermines any notion of a singular popular music and culture. This now seemingly endless pluralization of popular music may be seen to reflect a wider social and historical process; but it also suggests that popular music, rather than being simply a reflection of this process, is an active agent in its construction and a statement of its current condition.   KG

 📖 C. GILLETT, *The Sound of the City: The Rise of Rock and Roll* (New York, 1970, 2/1996) · C. HAMM, *Yesterdays: Popular Song in America* (New York, 1979) · R. MIDDLETON, *Studying Popular Music* (Buckingham, 1990) · A. MOORE, *Rock, the Primary Text: Developing a Musicology of Rock* (Buckingham, 1993) · B. LONGHURST, *Popular Music and Society* (Cambridge, 1995) · S. FRITH, *Performing Rites: On the Value of Popular Music* (Oxford, 1996) · R. PALMER, *Dancing in the Street* (London, 1996) · R. MIDDLETON (ed.), *Reading Pop: Approaches to Textual Analysis in Popular Music* (Oxford, 2000)

Porgy and Bess. Opera in three acts by Gershwin to a libretto by DuBose Heyward after his novel *Porgy* (1925), with lyrics by Heyward and Ira Gershwin (New York, 1935).

Porpora, Nicola (Antonio) (*b* Naples, 17 Aug. 1686; *d* Naples, 3 March 1768). Italian composer and singing teacher. He studied at the Conservatorio dei Poveri di Gesù Cristo in Naples, and by 1711 was described as *maestro* to the Prince of Hesse-Darmstadt, general of the Austrian Army present in the city at that time. At first his fame was slow to spread northwards, but in 1726 he became *maestro* at the Ospedale degli Incurabili in Venice and in 1733 went to London, where he composed for the Opera of the Nobility (set up as a rival to Handel's company) and enjoyed considerable success.

In 1737 he returned to Italy; during the next ten years he held various posts at three of the Venetian Ospedali— Incurabili, Pietà, and Ospedaletto—and at the Conservatorio di S. Maria di Loreto in Naples. From 1747 to 1751 he was in Dresden, and in about 1752 he moved to Vienna, where Haydn not only studied with him but acted as his valet-accompanist. He finally returned to Naples in 1760, working at both the Loreto conservatory and that of S. Onofrio.

Porpora was an extremely influential singing teacher, his pupils including the famous castratos Farinelli and Caffarelli, and the vocal writing in the many operas he produced throughout his wandering career is notable for its brilliance and virtuosity, which sometimes replace genuine musical interest. Some of the solo motets that he wrote for the girls of the Venetian Ospedali are florid display pieces, but his masses and psalm settings are in a more straightforward style.   DA/ER

Porta, Costanzo (*b* Cremona, *c*.1529; *d* Padua, 19 May 1601). Italian composer. He became a Minorite friar and in 1549 joined the monastic community at S. Maria Gloriosa dei Frari in Venice, where he studied with Willaert and became a friend of his fellow pupil Merulo. He directed the music at Osimo Cathedral from 1552 to 1565, and then served as *maestro di cappella* at the Cappella Antoniana, Padua, at Ravenna, and at the Santa Casa, Loreto. He returned to the Cappella Antoniana in 1595, and remained there until his death.

A prolific composer, Porta was considerably skilled in counterpoint. He wrote mainly sacred works; some of the later motets are in the grand polychoral Venetian style, but others follow the instructions of the *Council of Trent and are simpler, allowing the words to be heard clearly. Viadana was among his many pupils.

DA/TC

port-a-beul. See PUIRT-A-BEUL.

portamento (It., 'carriage'). 1. The process of gliding from one note to another through all intermediate pitches. Its use is widespread in string, vocal, and trombone technique, though J. A. Clinton (*A Theoretical and Practical Essay on the Boehm Flute*, 1843), for example, suggests its application for flute and other woodwind instruments too. As an expressive device by which instrumentalists might emulate the inflections of the voice it was used extensively in the 19th and early 20th centuries, particularly by violinists, who documented a number of different applications of the effect. The string portamento, which may be said to have reached an apotheosis at the turn of the 20th century, had declined in popularity by the mid-20th century.   DMi

2. A synonym for *appoggiatura.

portative organ. An organ small enough to be played while being carried, used throughout Europe from the mid-13th century into the 16th (see ORGAN, 4). Illustrations show it slung from the player's shoulder, with one hand pumping the bellows and the other on the keyboard, so the instrument probably played only melodically, though many early representations show one or more long pipes in a tower at the treble end that presumably sounded a drone. With two rows of six to eight pipes on early instruments, and a dozen or so on later ones, the compass ranged from about an octave to two or more. The keys were usually T-shaped buttons.   JMo

portato (It.). 'Carried'; a kind of bowstroke between *legato* and *staccato*.

port de voix (Fr., 'carriage of the voice'). See PORTAMENTO; VOICE, 7.

Porter, Cole (Albert) (*b* Peru, IN, 9 June 1891; *d* Santa Monica, CA, 15 Oct. 1964). American songwriter. After studying law at Yale and Harvard, he studied music (also at Harvard) and went on to compose theatre scores to his own witty lyrics, including *The Gay Divorce* (1932) and *Anything Goes* (1935). In spite of pain from a riding accident that resulted in a leg amputation, he later wrote the successful *Kiss me, Kate* (1948) and *Can-Can* (1953) and the film score *High Society* (1956).
                                                                  PGA/ALa

Porter, (William) Quincy (*b* New Haven, CT, 7 Feb. 1897; *d* Bethany, CT, 12 Nov. 1966). American composer. He studied with Horatio Parker and David Smith at Yale (1915–20), d'Indy in Paris (1920–1), and Bloch in New York and Cleveland, where he taught at the Institute of Music (1923–8). He then returned to Paris for three years before taking appointments at Vassar College (1932–8), the New England Conservatory (1938–46), and Yale (1946–65). His musical style was one of smooth, scalic melodies moving with rhythmic purposefulness through chromatic polyphony: his works include nine quartets, besides other chamber music, two symphonies, smaller orchestral pieces, and songs.   PG

Portugal 1. The Middle Ages; 2. Renaissance and Baroque; 3. The 18th and 19th centuries; 4. The 20th century

1. The Middle Ages

The music of Iberia reflects the powerful forces that have shaped its culture down the centuries: the north African Moors, the troubadours, and wandering minstrels of the feudal Christian kingdoms, the Roman Catholic Church, the interchange with American colonial traditions, and the popular music of the land itself. The Western seaboard kingdom of Portugal devolved from Spain in the Middle Ages; and the strength of its lyric poetry, sung in Galician-Portuguese dialect, was a mark of the independence confirmed by papal decree after 1179. Intended for the amusement of the aristocracy, this poetry was of two main types; the epic ballad, and the courtly love song (*cantiga de amor*), influenced by Provençal troubadours. Several Portuguese monarchs, notably King Dinis (1261–1325), wrote quantities of troubadour songs.

2. Renaissance and Baroque

Political and cultural links with England were always strong; both the English Sarum rite used in the Portuguese royal chapel from the 1430s, and the borrowings from music of Henry VI's chapel, inform the earliest surviving native polyphonic works by Vasco Pires (*fl* 1481–1509) and Fernão Gomes Correia (*d* after 1532). Both were from Coimbra, and for centuries the Santa Cruz monastery and university together made that town the most important musical centre outside Lisbon.

Colonial expansion into Africa and the Americas was guaranteed by the Treaty of Tordesillas with Spain (1494), which divided American discoveries between the two states and assured Portugal's economic stability. The great Spanish cathedrals provided training and employment for many musicians, including Escobar, *maestro* at Seville 1507–14; and, as in Spain, the seeds of Portuguese musical drama were sown in pastoral dialogues with music, notably those written by the dramatist Gil Vicente (*c*.1465–1537) for performance at the courts of King Manuel I ('the Great') and his son John III.

Strong Jesuit influence tended to make Portuguese polyphonic composers conservative, which helped maintain Portugal's independent tradition during decades of Spanish domination. The composer-king John IV (1605–56, ruler from 1640) wrote music and treatises and founded one of the world's great music libraries, later lost in the Lisbon earthquake of 1755 which destroyed so much of Portugal's cultural heritage. Évora Cathedral was the pre-eminent musical proving-ground of his era, among its most distinguished scions being Duarte Lobo, one of the few Portuguese musicians to achieve a European reputation, though Cardoso and Magalhães produced polyphonic music of comparable quality.

The Santa Cruz monastery at Coimbra continued to be influential well into the 17th century, maintaining the quality of sacred music in the increasingly secular Baroque era—though even here the villancico song form was regularly used in church services. The finest composer of such pieces, the Carmelite monk

Francisco de Santiago (*d* 1646), spent most of his life as choirmaster at Seville rather than in his native land; other Portuguese musicians followed the same course, notably Coelho, court organist to Philip III of Spain. His *Flores de musica* (Lisbon, 1620) was one of the most important keyboard collections of its time.

3. The 18th and 19th centuries

John V (reigned 1707–50) followed a European vogue by importing Italian musicians, and sent native composers such as Almeida and Teixeira to study in Rome. In instrumental music, the rococo keyboard sonatas of Seixas rivalled those of Domenico Scarlatti, who worked at John's court between 1719 and 1728. John's successor, José I, continued to train musicians in Italy, including João de Sousa Carvalho (1745–1799 or 1800) and his pupils Portugal, the greatest Portuguese opera composer of the 19th century, and Bomtempo, who founded the National Conservatory of Music and a Portuguese symphony orchestra, as well as becoming an internationally admired virtuoso pianist. Both Portugal and Bomtempo elevated the *modinha*, originally a sentimental Brazilian love song with piano or guitar accompaniment, into a distinctive salon art form.

As in Spain, a revival in nationalist spirit in the last years of the 19th century gradually weaned composers away from Italian influences. This begins to be evident in the works of the Paris-trained Augusto Machado (1845–1924), director of the National Conservatory, though Italian influence is still prevalent in the works of the gifted amateur Alfredo Keil (1850–1907), composer of the Portuguese national anthem, Joaquim Casimiro (1808–63), and Francisco de Sá Noronha (1820–81).

4. The 20th century

Musicians in Lisbon and Oporto were increasingly drawn towards German, French, and even English models in their attempts to forge a distinctive style. This nationalist group included José Vianna da Motta (1868–1948), a pianist and scholar, and director of the Lisbon Conservatory, whose own music was in the Lisztian mould. Impressionism, atonalism, and neo-romanticism in turn informed the work of Luis de Freitas Branco (1890–1955); his pupil Jorge Croner de Vasconcellos (1910–74) studied with Nadia Boulanger, Dukas, and Stravinsky. The staunchly anti-Fascist Fernando Lopes Graça (1906–94) studied with Schoenberg but used folk music in his mature, tonal work. Freitas Branco's greatest pupil, Joly Braga Santos, was influenced by Sibelius, Vaughan Williams, and Walton in developing his own early symphonic style.

The vitality of contemporary Portuguese musical life owes much to the efforts of Braga Santos, though such composers as Alvaro Salazar (*b* 1938), Emanuel Nunes (*b* 1941), and above all Peixinho, founder of the Lisbon Contemporary Music Group in 1970, sought inspiration from the German Darmstadt school and the popular native **fado* tradition, rather than earlier nationalist models. Lisbon supports two symphony orchestras and two choral societies, while Oporto maintains a conservatory. There is still an important music faculty at Coimbra University, and the Calouste Gulbenkian Foundation is extremely active in its founder's home country. WT/CW

📖 J. B. Trend, *The Music of Spanish History to 1600* (London, 1926) · G. Chase, *The Music of Spain* (New York, 1941, 2/1959) · R. Stevenson, *Portuguese Music and Musicians Abroad (to 1650)* (Lima, 1966) · M. C. de Brito, *Opera in Portugal in the Eighteenth Century* (Cambridge, 1989)

Portugal [Portogallo], **Marcos Antônio** (da Fonseca) (*b* Lisbon, 24 March 1762; *d* Rio de Janeiro, 7 Feb. 1830). Portuguese composer. He studied at the Seminário Patriarcal in Lisbon, remaining in the city as a conductor and opera composer until 1792. That year he went to study in Italy, though he seems to have spent more time composing operas than taking lessons; the most successful of his Italian works was *La confusione della somiglianza* (1793). In 1800 he returned to Lisbon to take up the posts of royal *mestre da capela* and director of opera at the S. Carlos theatre. The court fled to Rio de Janeiro before the advancing French troops in 1807, but Portugal followed them only in 1811, in which year he opened the Teatro S. João. He never returned to Europe, though the court moved back to Lisbon in 1821. Portugal wrote over 50 operas, both Portuguese and Italian, and composed over 100 sacred works. The finale of his cantata *La speranza* (1809) served as the Portuguese national anthem until 1834. WT

Posaune (Ger.). 'Trombone'.

position (Eng., Fr.; It.: *posizione*). 1. In the playing of stringed instruments the left hand is moved continually so that the fingers may fall on to a different set of points on the fingerboard, thus producing a different set of notes. Each of these locations is called a 'position' ('first position', 'second position', etc.). The movement of the left hand is termed 'shift' (It.: *manica*).

2. Chords may be described as being in 'close' or 'open' position, depending on their layout. A chord of C major written as in Ex. 1*a* would be described as being in 'close' position, while one notated as in Ex. 1*b* would be in 'open' position.

Ex. 1

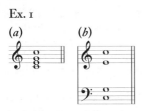

positive organ. Originally an organ (see ORGAN, 4) small enough to be carried from one position to another (the ancestor of the *chamber organ) but later also the small organ built behind the organist's bench ('*chair organ'). Early positives were blown with a pair of bellows by one person and played by a second, thus allowing full harmonic possibilities and continuous sound, unlike the *portative which, with a single bellows, had to breathe like a singer. Often there was a *regal built in as well as flue pipes.   JMo

posthorn (Fr.: *cornet de poste*; Ger.: *Posthorn*: It.: *cornetta di postiglione*). A brass instrument used on mail coaches to warn of their approach. The English posthorn was straight and in A♭; unlike the longer coachhorn in B♭ it is still used in dance bands for such music as Hermann Koenig's *Post-Horn Galop* (1844). Continental posthorns were coiled and, in the 18th century, were made with separate crooks. Mozart, Beethoven, and others scored for them in serenades and dances. With the invention of valves, the French *cornet de poste* became the *cornet à pistons* and Mahler used the German *Posthorn* in his Third Symphony.   JMo

'Posthorn' Serenade. Nickname of Mozart's Serenade in D major, K320 (1779), in which a posthorn is used in the second trio of the second minuet.

Postillon de Longjumeau, Le ('The Coachman of Longjumeau'). Opera in three acts by Adolphe Adam to a libretto by Adolphe de Leuven and Brunswick (Léon Lévy) (Paris, 1836).

postlude (Lat.: *postludium*; Ger.: *Nachspiel*). The converse of a *prelude, i.e. a composition played as an afterpiece. In organ music, the postlude is the voluntary concluding a church service.

Many of Schumann's songs end with an extended section of music for piano alone, often called a postlude, 'commenting' on the emotions conveyed by the words. Sometimes these postludes introduce new material, as in many of the settings in *Dichterliebe* (e.g. 'Ich will meine Seele tauchen', 'Die alten, bösen Lieder'). Hindemith's *Ludus tonalis* (1943) for piano concludes with a 'postludium' that presents the music of the 'praeludium' in retrograde inversion. See also CODA.
                                                        —/JBE

postmodernism. A response or antidote to *modernism, whose commitment to the new is replaced by a concern with the old. Postmodernism originated as a term in the 1980s, when many younger composers (e.g. Adams, Corigliano) were contradicting their revolutionary elders (and even their earlier selves) by turning to the past for styles, quotations, and other points of departure. In terms of compositional philosophy, and even sometimes of musical effect, there is little to differentiate their work from that of Stravinsky or Shostakovich in the 1930s; also, some essentially modernist composers in the 1950s and 60s (e.g. Kagel and Ligeti) had looked at the past with scepticism and humour. But the term 'postmodernism' is generally reserved for music written since 1970.   PG

Poston, Elizabeth (*b* nr Walkern, Herts., 24 Oct. 1905; *d* Stevenage, 19 March 1987). English composer. She studied at the RAM and worked on the BBC music staff from 1940 to 1945. Her compositions include songs and incidental scores for radio; she also edited various anthologies of songs and carols.   PG

Pothier, Dom Joseph (*b* Bouzemont, Vosges, 7 Dec. 1835; *d* Conques, Belgium, 8 Dec. 1923). Belgian scholar. His work became, and remains, the basis for the official Vatican edition of Gregorian chant (the *Graduale romanum*, 1908)—the culmination of a 19th-century movement to halt the accommodation of plainchant to later musical styles and to restore it to its medieval form. In 1860 Pothier entered the French Benedictine monastery of *Solesmes, where he remained until 1893, assisting Paul Jausions in the preparation of chant books for the abbey and completing the work after Jausions's death. Pothier's work was later modified by André Mocquereau.   PW

potpourri (Fr., 'rotten pot', 'stew'). A composition that consists of a string of pre-existing tunes. In the early 18th century the term was applied to collections of songs assembled for performance on stage. Later that century it denoted an instrumental arrangement of opera tunes, for example Czerny's Potpourri for piano (op. 218) based on Spohr's *Faust*; the term is also sometimes used with reference to Liszt's transcriptions for piano.

See also MEDLEY; QUODLIBET.   —/JBE

Potter, (Philip) Cipriani (Hambly) (*b* London, 3 Oct. 1792; *d* London, 26 Sept. 1871). English pianist, teacher, editor, and composer. He received his early musical education from his father, a flautist and viola player, and was later taught by Attwood, Crotch, and others. He also took lessons in Vienna from Beethoven (whom he much admired) and Emanuel Aloys Förster (1818–19). An active member of the Philharmonic Society, he appeared many times as a pianist in English premieres of concertos by Mozart and Beethoven and won acclaim as a conductor. In 1822 he became the first piano teacher at the newly founded Royal Academy of Music, where his most distinguished pupil was William Sterndale Bennett. On Crotch's dismissal in 1832 he was made principal, a position he held until 1859.

Potter's compositions are almost exclusively instrumental (chamber music, symphonies, overtures, piano concertos, and solo piano works), allowing his penchant for counterpoint, harmonic invention, and rhythmic drive free rein. Arguably his best work is to be found in the symphonies, notably nos. 1, 8, and 10 (1819, 1828, 1832), though there is also fine music in his three overtures for Shakespeare plays (1835–7), the Horn (or Bassoon) Sonata op. 13 (c.1824), the Sextet for flute, clarinet, viola, cello, double bass, and piano (1836), and the *Studies in All the Major and Minor Keys* for piano (1826). After 1837 Potter was occupied mainly with editing music by others, notably the complete piano music of Mozart. He was also an admirer of Schumann and, towards the end of his life, Brahms.   RL/JD1

Poule, La ('The Hen'). Nickname of Haydn's Symphony no. 83 in G minor (1785), the second of the Paris symphonies, so called because of the 'clucking' second subject of the first movement (the title was acquired in the 19th century).

Poulenc, Francis (Jean Marcel) (*b* Paris, 7 Jan. 1899; *d* Paris, 30 Jan. 1963). French composer. He had some piano lessons from Ricardo Viñes, but as a composer he was self-taught at the time when his witty and exotic *Rapsodie nègre* for voice and chamber ensemble (1917) won him a place in the circle round Satie and thus in Les *Six, the group which also included Milhaud and Honegger, and which was so christened in 1920. Several works of this time show him closely following Stravinsky, the sonatas for two clarinets (1918) and for brass trio (1922) in particular. He had lessons with Koechlin between 1921 and 1925 and benefited from Koechlin's astute and non-doctrinaire advice. Although Poulenc remained attracted by the flippant and the anti-conventional, there were signs in the mid-1920s, especially in such slow movements as that of the Trio for oboe, bassoon, and piano (1926), of the lyricism that he was later to espouse so memorably. The faster movements continued to offer surprise and delight.

Stravinsky was perhaps the strongest influence on Poulenc's style, with added doses of Chabrier's wit. Ostinatos and popular-song styles were always likely to make an appearance (late in life he confessed that he would have liked to have been Maurice Chevalier), whether in an early work such as the *Trois mouvements perpétuels* (1918) for piano, the ballet *Les Biches* (1923), or in his keyboard concertos for harpsichord (*Concert*

champêtre, 1927–8), two pianos (1932), organ (1938), and piano (1949), or in his late sonatas for the wind instruments he always favoured—for flute (1957), oboe (1962), and clarinet (1962). In these last the wind instruments are plainly used as substitutes for the human voice.

Poulenc's gifts as a melodist, coupled with his literary friendships and his concert partnership with the tenor Pierre Bernac from 1935 to 1959, led to a large output of songs, including cycles to poems by Guillaume Apollinaire (*Le Bestiaire*, 1919; *Quatre poèmes*, 1931; *Banalités*, 1940; *Calligrammes*, 1948), Jean Cocteau (*Cocardes*, 1919), and Paul Éluard (*Tel jour, telle nuit*, 1936–7; *Le Fraicheur et le feu*, 1950; *Le Travail du peintre*, 1956). It seems now as though he was the last in the line of great French *mélodistes* stretching back to Berlioz. His sympathy with the surrealist poets is also displayed in his bizarre but wonderfully effective operatic treatment of Apollinaire's play *Les Mamelles de Tirésias* (1947), while his solo opera *La Voix humaine* (1959, text by Cocteau) shows his delicate sensitivity in underlining a scene from contemporary life, a woman speaking over the telephone to the lover who is abandoning her. Here Poulenc drew on his own experiences of depression, triggered to some extent by unhappy homosexual love affairs.

Between these came the opera *Dialogues des Carmélites* (1957), one of the works in which Poulenc expressed his religious faith after his return to the Catholic Church in 1936. The quiet depth of his spirituality is also to be felt in the unaccompanied Mass (1937) and other choral works, while the *Stabat mater* (1950) and the *Gloria* (1959), both scored for soprano, chorus, and orchestra, are more grandiose in their fervour, including references to a range of sources from Verdi to Stravinsky's *Oedipus rex*.   PG/RN

📖 G. R. KECK, *Francis Poulenc: A Bio-Bibliography* (New York, 1990) · W. MELLERS, *Francis Poulenc* (Oxford, 1993) · C. B. SCHMIDT, *The Music of Francis Poulenc: A Catalogue* (Oxford, 1995) · B. IVRY, *Francis Poulenc* (London, 1996) · S. BUCKLAND and M. CHIMÈNES (eds.), *Francis Poulenc: Music, Art and Literature* (Aldershot, 1999)

poussé (Fr.). 'Pushed': in string playing, the up-bow.

Pousseur, Henri (Léon Marie Thérèse) (*b* Malmédy, nr Liège, 23 June 1929). Belgian composer. He studied with Pierre Froidebise and André Souris at the conservatories of Liège and Brussels (1947–53), then rapidly became associated with Boulez, Stockhausen, and Berio. In his first works, for example the Quintet in memory of Webern (1955), he used a complex serial style, modified by the addition of aleatory features in *Mobile* for two pianos (1956–8). His 'variable operatic fantasy' *Votre Faust* (1960–7; Piccola Scala, Milan, 1969) opened the way to an all-inclusive style in which the most varied harmonic materials could be coherently joined, and this style he has developed in subsequent works, sometimes emphasizing a parallel with egalitarian social organizations. *Couleurs croisées* for orchestra (1967), for instance, offers a progression from discord to concord based on the American human-rights song *We shall overcome*. Many of Pousseur's later works are at once fluid and heterogeneous, using various combinations of voices, instruments, and electronic means. He was co-founder of the APELAC electronic music studio in Brussels (1958) and has taught at various institutions in Europe and America.   PG

📖 H. POUSSEUR, *Fragments théoriques* (Brussels, 1970–2) · H.-K. METZGER and R. RIEHN (eds.), *Henri Pousseur* (Munich, 1990)

Powder her Face. Chamber opera in two acts by Adès to a libretto by Philip Hensher (Cheltenham, 1995).

Powell [Epstein], **Mel**(vin) (*b* New York, 12 Feb. 1923; *d* Los Angeles, 24 April 1998). American composer. He was already a noted jazz pianist and arranger—associated with Benny Goodman and Glenn Miller, and using the assumed name he kept—before his studies with Ernst Toch in Los Angeles (1946–8) and Hindemith at Yale, where he was on the faculty (1958–69). He was then one of the founding professors of the California Institute of the Arts. His early music is neoclassical, but in 1959 he began writing in a 12-note style of vivid, graphic imagery, occasionally using electronic means. Many of his works are for small forces—songs, solo instrumental pieces (sometimes with tape), chamber music—an exception being his double piano concerto, *Duplicates* (1990).   PG

Power, Leonel [Lionel] (*b* c.1370–85; *d* Canterbury, 5 June 1445). English singer, composer, and theorist. He was employed in the household of Thomas, Duke of Clarence, until 1421, and to judge from the large number of his works in the Old Hall Manuscript (1415–early 1420s) was in some way involved with its compilation. In 1439 he became master of the Lady Chapel choir at the Benedictine cathedral priory of Canterbury. Some 50 liturgical works by or attributable to him have survived, together with a treatise on discant. He was a pioneer in the development of the *cyclic mass, in which the various sections of the Ordinary are thematically and structurally related to one another; his *Missa 'Alma Redemptoris mater'* is the earliest known example of the genre. Power's music, like Dunstaple's, is noted for its use of full chordal sonority. It was known on the Continent, and was influential there during the first half of the 15th century.   JM

pp, ppp. Abbreviations for *pianissimo*.

praeambulum (Lat.). 'Prelude'.

praefatio. See PREFACE.

praeludium (Lat.). 'Prelude'.

Praetorius. Common name among German musicians in the 16th and 17th centuries. The Praetorius family that lived and worked mainly in Hamburg provided three composers whose names are still frequently encountered. **Jacob Praetorius** (i) (*b* Magdeburg, c.1530; *d* Hamburg, 1586), a composer and organist, worked for most of his life at St Jacobi and St Gertrud, Hamburg. Only one of his works survives, but he was an important teacher, and his pupils included his son, **Hieronymus Praetorius** (*b* Hamburg, 10 Aug. 1560; *d* Hamburg, 27 Jan. 1629). Hieronymus was a fine composer of grand polychoral music in the Venetian tradition. From 1580 to 1582 he was town organist at Erfurt, taking over his father's job in 1586. His son, **Jacob Praetorius** (ii) (*b* Hamburg, 8 Feb. 1586; *d* Hamburg, 21 or 22 Oct. 1651), was also an organist. After studying in Amsterdam with Sweelinck he worked at the Hamburg church of St Petri. He was well known for his organ music, especially for his chorale settings and for some so-called preludes; these comprised chordal preludes followed by monothematic fugues and were direct precursors of Bach's preludes and fugues. Jacob's brother Johannes (c.1595–1660) was also a composer and organist in Hamburg.   DA

Praetorius, Michael (*b* Creuzburg an der Werra, 15 Feb. c.1571; *d* Wolfenbüttel, 15 Feb. 1621). German composer and theorist. In 1595, after three years' service as organist at the Marienkirche in Frankfurt an der Oder, he was appointed court organist, and later Kapellmeister, at Wolfenbüttel. From there he paid two extended visits to the court of the Landgrave Moritz of Hessen-Kassel. In 1613, on the death of his employer, Duke Heinrich Julius, he joined the electoral court at Dresden, serving temporarily as assistant to Rogier Michael. During this period he became acquainted with Schütz and Scheidt and, in 1618, accompanied them on a visit to Magdeburg Cathedral to celebrate the reorganization of its music. In the remaining years before his untimely death, he visited Leipzig, Nuremberg, and Bayreuth (with Schütz, Scheidt, and Staden, to dedicate a new organ at the Stadtkirche), constantly studying the latest musical styles and customs of his period.

As a composer Praetorius ranged over a wide variety of styles and forms: in his nine-volume *Musae Sioniae* (1605–10), settings, from the simplest to the most elaborate, of chorales, and Latin liturgical texts appropriate to Lutheran worship; in *Terpsichore* (1612), instrumental dances based on tunes by Parisian dancing masters; and, in *Polyhymnia caduceatrix et panegyrica* (1619), grand concertato settings of Lutheran texts, modelled on the leading Venetian styles of the day. As a theorist he provided, in his *Syntagma musicum* (three parts, 1614–18), a detailed account of the forms, instruments (with descriptions and illustrations of those in contemporary use), and performance practices of his time, which is still of great historical significance.

DA/BS

'Prague' Symphony. Nickname of Mozart's Symphony no. 38 in D major k504 (1786), so called because it was first performed in Prague during Mozart's visit in 1787.

Pralltriller (Ger., 'tight (or compact) trill'). 1. In modern German terminology, the inverted *mordent.

2. Until *c*.1800, a rapid trill of four notes, beginning on the upper note of a descending 2nd. It was usually indicated with the same sign as that now used for the inverted mordent (see Ex. 1). In extremely quick passages the two ornaments sound almost identical, since there is not time to sound the first note of the *Pralltriller*, and it must be omitted, or tied to the preceding main note, as shown in Ex. 1.

Ex. 1

Pratella, Francesco Balilla (*b* Lugo di Romagna, 1 Feb. 1880; *d* Ravenna, 17 May 1955). Italian composer, teacher, and writer on music. He studied in Pesaro, and was director of the music colleges of Lugo di Romagna (1910–29) and Ravenna (1927–45). He is chiefly remembered for his involvement in the *Futurist artistic movement, as the author of a series of manifestos issued between 1910 and 1912, and as the composer of such works as the orchestral *Musica futurista* (1912; renamed *Inno alla vita*, 1913), and the opera *L'aviatore Dro* (completed 1914, performed 1920). In later life Pratella withdrew from the Futurist movement, composing further operas, choral music, chamber music, and songs, editing early music, and pursuing a lifelong interest in Italian folksong. ABur

Prayer Book. See COMMON PRAYER, BOOK OF.

precentor. A term (dating back at least as far as the 4th century) meaning 'first singer'; it is attached to the official in charge of the singing in a cathedral or monastic establishment or a church (the equivalent of the cantor in a synagogue). In the English cathedrals the dignity of the precentor varies.

The cathedral precentor sits opposite the dean—whence the name for the two sides of the choir: *decani* ('of the dean') and *cantoris* ('of the singer', i.e. the precentor).

In the English dissenting churches and the Presbyterian churches of Scotland, which until the later 19th century had no organs, the precentor was an important official. He was supplied with a pitchpipe and gave out and led the metrical psalms. Sometimes he was called the 'uptaker of the psalms'.

In the earlier settled parts of America the precentor also had a place in the life of the religious community. As late as 1902 Edward Dickinson (*Music in the History of the Western Church*) alluded to churches where the congregation 'led by a precentor with voice or cornet assumes the whole burden of song'.

preces (Lat., 'prayers'). In the Roman, Gallican, and Mozarabic rites of the Latin West, a series of short petitions taking the form of *versicles and *responses. In the Anglican *Book of Common Prayer*, the *preces* are, strictly speaking, the prayers given at Matins and Evensong between the Creed and the collect.

—/ALi

precipitato (It.). 'Hurried'.

preface (Lat.: *praefatio*). The solemn declaration of praise recited or chanted by the celebrant commencing the Eucharistic Prayer at Christian eucharistic liturgies. Traditionally preceded by the dialogue *Sursum corda*, it serves to introduce the Sanctus, which is in turn followed by the remainder of the prayer. The Roman rite and other Western traditions use eucharistic prayers with Proper prefaces, the texts of which share a common form into which are interpolated words appropriate to the day. —/ALi

preghiera (It., 'prayer'; Fr.: *prière*; Ger.: *Gebet*). A solo aria or chorus in which the singer or singers pray to God or supernatural powers for salvation from impending danger. The 'preghiera' scene became a feature of 19th-century Italian opera, usually sung to poignant effect by the heroine (e.g. Desdemona's 'Ave Maria', in the last act of Verdi's *Otello*). Wagner's *Tannhäuser* contains a solo prayer and *Lohengrin* a choral one ('Herr und Gott nun ruf ich Dich'). —/JBe

prelude (from Lat. *praeludium*, 'something played before'; Fr.: *prélude*; Ger.: *Vorspiel*; It.: *preludio*). A comparatively brief instrumental composition intended (in principle) as an introduction to something further. Corelli began his chamber sonatas with a *preludio*, and François Couperin followed him in his *Concerts*. The term is often used for the overture or introductory scene of an opera, notably by Wagner and Verdi; Debussy's

Prélude à 'L'Après-midi d'un faune' is a rare example of an independent, non-prefatory orchestral prelude.

More important, however, the term 'prelude' refers to a genre of music for soloistic instruments, especially the keyboard. The earliest examples occur in 15th-century German organ manuscripts, which include many short *praeludia* as examples of improvisation to set the key for the singers in church. An improvisatory style is central to the notion of the prelude throughout its history (the French and German verbs for improvising are *préluder* and *präludieren*). Pieces of corresponding style and function were called *ricercar in 16th-century Italy. In the course of the 16th century works called 'prelude' or 'ricercar' became separated from their introductory function, and to a large extent became difficult to distinguish from other genres such as the *fantasia and the *toccata; the terms continued to be used, however, and the improvisatory manner remained an important element.

In 17th-century France the prelude was especially cultivated on the lute, for which a distinctive style was developed that resulted in minimal notation of rhythm and metre, while the pitches were completely specified; such *préludes non mesurées* were also composed for the harpsichord. In Germany, under the influence of the toccatas of Frescobaldi and his pupil Froberger, a more tightly organized kind of prelude for organ was developed, culminating in the *praeludia* of Buxtehude; such works typically had an improvisatory opening section, a more strict, fugal middle section, and a free conclusion, although they were often extended by additional contrasting sections. Bach's organ preludes were formed on this model, increasing the scale and autonomy of the fugue. Bach followed Corelli's example in composing preludes rather than *ouvertures* as the first movements of his *suites for solo instruments (including those for violin and cello as well as the English Suites for harpsichord).

Praetorius in 1619 noted a number of contexts for extempore preludes, including before the singing of a chorale. This led to the development of the *chorale prelude, which also reached its zenith in Bach's works. Even more important was the practice of improvising a prelude before performing a written-out fugue; by the end of the 17th century a few composers had prefaced their fugues with written-out preludes, but it was Bach who raised the prelude and fugue to the status of a genre in itself. The notion of a cycle embodying all available tonalities was first realized in the lute passamezzos of Giacomo Gorzanis (1567), while a complete set of preludes for lute or theorbo had been composed by John Wilson (1640s), and various sets of organ *versets in all eight church modes, or preludes and fugues in many but not all keys, had been published

in Germany up to the beginning of the 18th century. Bach's *The Well-Tempered Clavier* (1722, 1738–42) was, however, the first cycle for keyboard in all 24 keys, and it also explored a wide variety of styles in its preludes. One of its most important features was its didactic character, providing exercises in performance technique and composition.

These qualities were taken up by many 19th-century composers, who mostly discarded the fugue and concentrated on the prelude alone; once again there was a blurring of boundaries with the fantasia. Hummel was the first to publish a set of 24 preludes (op. 67, *c*.1814–15), but it was Chopin's cycle (op. 28, 1836–9) that became the new paradigm of the genre and was followed by many other composers. In the hands of Chopin and his followers the prelude was developed as an independent character piece for piano, exploring a particular expressive mood or technical device. Important works have been composed in homage to Bach's preludes and fugues by Mendelssohn, Liszt, Franck, Busoni, Hindemith, and others, while Chopin's example has been especially prominent in preludes by Skryabin and Rakhmaninov. Debussy was unusual in giving programmatic titles to his preludes, but his precedent was followed by a number of 20th-century composers including Poulenc, Delius, and Dutilleux. The mid-20th century avant-garde also cultivated the separate prelude in such examples as Cage's *Prelude for Meditation* for prepared piano (1944) or Branimir Sakač's 'aleatory prelude' *Prisms* for piano (1961).   JJD

Prélude à 'L'Après-midi d'un faune'. See APRÈS-MIDI D'UN FAUNE', PRÉLUDE À 'L'.

Préludes. Piano pieces by Debussy, published in two books, each containing 12 (1910, 1912–13); the first includes *La *Fille aux cheveux de lin* and *La *Cathédrale engloutie*, and the second **Feux d'artifice*.

Préludes, Les. Symphonic poem by Liszt, in various versions composed between 1844 and 1854. It originated in 1844–5 as the overture to the choral work *Les Quatre Élémens* (to a text by Joseph Autran), for male voices and piano, and was first orchestrated by August Conradi in 1848. Liszt himself later revised both the musical structure and the orchestration, and appended a title and preface from one of Alphonse de Lamartine's *Nouvelles méditations poétiques* (1823), neither of which had any connection with the work as initially conceived.

premier coup d'archet (Fr., 'first bowstroke'). See COUP D'ARCHET.

prepared piano. A piano in which the timbre has been altered by the insertion between the strings of bolts, screws, rubber erasers, and other objects; it was developed by John Cage for his *Bacchanale* (1940) and used in many further pieces by him and subsequently by other composers. RPA

près (Fr.). 'Near'; e.g. *près de la touche*, 'near the fingerboard' of a stringed instrument.

pressante (It.), **en pressant** (Fr.). 'Hurrying'.

Presser. American firm of music publishers. It was established in Philadelphia in 1883 by Theodore Presser (1848–1925), who earlier that year had founded *The Etude*, which was to become one of the most successful music magazines in the USA. The Presser Company acquired several other publishing houses and now has a large catalogue, numerous agencies, and a vast hire library. It publishes many American composers, including Babbitt, Carter, Cowell, Ives, and Piston. Presser is represented in the UK by Universal Edition. HA

presto (It.). 'Quick', i.e. faster than *allegro*; *prestissimo*, 'very quick'.

Previn, André [Priwin, Andreas Ludwig] (George) (*b* Berlin, 6 April 1929). American composer and conductor. He studied at the Berlin Hochschule für Musik, at the Paris Conservatoire, and with Castelnuovo-Tedesco in Los Angeles. At the age of 17 he began work as an arranger for films, at the same time establishing himself as a progressive jazz pianist. He has continued to compose film scores, though since the mid-1960s he has been more active as a conductor, notably with the London Symphony Orchestra (1968–75), the Pittsburgh Symphony (1976–84), and the Royal Philharmonic Orchestra (1985–92). His more ambitious compositions, which include a symphony (1962), have generally been written for friends or for special occasions, and reflect his enthusiasms for American popular music and late Romantic gesture. In this style he also wrote an opera, *A Streetcar Named Desire* (San Francisco, 1998). PG

Prez, Josquin des. See JOSQUIN DES PREZ.

Pribaoutki. Work by Stravinsky for male voice and flute, oboe, cor anglais, clarinet, bassoon, violin, viola, cello, and double bass, a setting of Russian traditional rhymes (London, 1918).

prick-song. 'To prick' is an obsolete English verb meaning 'to mark', and thus 'prick-song' came to be applied to music that was written down, or notated, as opposed to extemporized. In Shakespeare's day, the arms of the Parish Clerks' Company in London included, as a sign of their musical duties and skill, three prick-song books.

Prigioniero, Il ('The Prisoner'). Opera in a prologue and one act by Dallapiccola to his own libretto after Villiers de l'Isle-Adam's *La Torture par l'espérance* (1883) and Charles De Coster's *La Légende d'Ulenspiegel et de Lamme Goedzak* (Florence, 1950; broadcast 1949).

prima donna (It., 'first lady'). The term originally denoted the chief female singer in an opera cast, but has acquired a more generalized usage to mean a leading woman singer, known alternatively as a diva (It., 'goddess'). Hence for the original meaning the term *prima donna assoluta* ('absolute first lady') has to be used. The same process has occurred in ballet with the *prima ballerina assoluta*.

prima pratica, seconda pratica (It.). Terms used in the early 17th century to describe two different 'practices' in music. Monteverdi's style of composing secular vocal music, where irregular harmonies, intervals, and melodic progressions were used to express the meaning of the text, had been attacked by G. M. Artusi in his treatise *L'Artusi, overo Delle imperfettioni della moderna musica* (1600); Artusi quoted specific passages from two of Monteverdi's madrigals, *Anima mia perdona* and *Cruda Amarilli* (from the fourth and fifth books of madrigals respectively: 1603, 1605). The composer defended himself in an afterword to the fifth book that was subsequently expanded by his brother, Giulio Cesare, in a 'dichiarazione' (a statement, declaration, or explanation) appended to the composer's first collection of *Scherzi musicali* (1607). This defended the modern style, or 'seconda pratica', declaring it to be as valid as the *prima pratica* as exemplified in the works of such composers as Josquin, Gombert, and Willaert; in the 'first practice' the perfection of the part-writing was more important than the expression of the words, whereas in the 'second' the words are made 'the mistress of the harmony, and not the servant'. Justification is also sought from classical precedent, chiefly in Plato's *Republic*. Cipriano de Rore is said to have been the first master of the *seconda pratica*, followed by Gesualdo, Cavalieri, Marenzio, Wert, Peri, Caccini, and Luzzaschi. —/TC

prima volta (It.). 'First-time (bar)'; see DOUBLE BAR.

Prime. 1. Originally the third of eight hours of the Divine *Office in the medieval Roman rite. Since the reforms of the Second Vatican Council, it is retained only in monasteries.

2. The word has also some theoretical applications: (*a*) the lower of two notes forming an interval; (*b*) the generator of a series of harmonics (see ACOUSTICS, 5);

(*c*) the root of a chord; (*d*) a unison; (*e*) the first note of a scale; and (*f*) the interval formed by two notes written on the same line or space, e.g. F and F♯.

Primgeiger (Ger.). The *leader of an orchestra or its principal first violin.

Primrose, William (*b* Glasgow, 23 Aug. 1903; *d* Provo, UT, 1 May 1982). Scottish viola player. After studying the violin in Glasgow and London he went to Brussels, where Ysaÿe advised a change to the viola. Primrose toured as a soloist, played in the London String Quartet, and led the violas in Toscanini's NBC orchestra. Bartók, Rubbra, and Fricker wrote concertos for him. He emigrated to the USA where he taught at Aspen, UCLA, and Bloomington, leading to teaching invitations from Japan. Though his instrument was not large, the fullness of tone he produced was both beautiful and rounded. CF

> 📖 W. PRIMROSE, *Walk on the North Side* (Provo, UT, 1978) · D. DALTON, *Playing the Viola: Conversations with William Primrose* (Oxford, 1988)

Prince Igor (*Knyaz' Igor'*). Opera in a prologue and four acts by Borodin to his own libretto after a scenario by Vladimir Stasov largely based on the anonymous, possibly 12th-century epic *Slovo o polku Igoreve* ('The Lay of the Host of Igor') (St Petersburg, 1890). Borodin worked on it from 1869 to 1887 but left it unfinished; Rimsky-Korsakov and Glazunov completed it and Rimsky orchestrated much of it. The Polovtsian Dances form a ballet scene in Act II.

Prince of the Pagodas, The. Ballet in three acts by Britten to a scenario by John Cranko, who choreographed it (London, 1957). The score has been choreographed several times since, notably by Kenneth MacMillan, with a revised scenario by Colin Thubron (London, 1989). Michael Lankester arranged a suite from the score (1979).

Princesse de Navarre, La ('The Princess of Navarra'). *Comédie-ballet* in three acts by Rameau to a libretto by Voltaire (Versailles, 1745).

Princess Ida (*Princess Ida, or Castle Adamant*). Operetta in three acts by Sullivan to a libretto by W. S. Gilbert after Tennyson's *The Princess* (1847) (London, 1884).

Printemps ('Spring'). Symphonic suite by Debussy for orchestra and female chorus, composed in 1887; the original score was lost and in 1912 Busser reorchestrated it from the piano version, under Debussy's supervision. It is not to be confused with *Rondes de printemps*; see IMAGES.

printing and publishing of music 1. Introduction; 2. Principal techniques of printing; 3. Europe: early history; 4. Europe: 16th century; 5. Europe: 1600–*c*.1750; 6. Europe: *c*.1750–*c*.1945; 7. The USA; 8. Composers and publishers; 9. Publishing today

1. Introduction

The history of music-printing and publishing is technical, social, and artistic. The technical history encompasses the gradual solution of the difficult problems posed by music itself, with its complex visual symbolism. The social history shows how changing tastes, styles, and audiences have brought different genres to prominence, how publishers (as distinct from printers) arose and how their two roles have often been combined, and how publishing houses may build their fortunes on a single composer, school of composers, or popular craze. And the artistic history of musical typography highlights printed music in which the bounds of craftsmanship are transcended to produce exemplars of outstanding design.

It is not easy to become acquainted with these musical treasures of the past, and only rarely is it possible to handle them. Some are in libraries; friends or acquaintances may possess fine early editions; auction houses will permit one to see material waiting for a sale; and occasionally one may find a remarkable volume on barrows in large cities. Much late 18th- and 19th-century music is still to be found thus; and a personal collection, however modest, provides that first-hand experience of the paper, binding, and texture of early editions which the facsimile can never quite supply.

2. Principal techniques of printing

Throughout its history music-printing has used three main techniques. First, printing from type, which is cast in the same way as that for the printed word. Second, engraving on a copper plate using a burin; punches were used, subsequently, to stamp the fixed symbols on to a pewter plate, the variable signs such as slurs being cut in with the engraving tool. Third, *lithography, a method that was still at the heart of music-printing well into the 20th century. These technical processes are difficult to describe in isolation, and readers are urged to view them by visiting collections in museums, institutions, and printing houses. Although the techniques used today are likely to be almost entirely lithography and its associated photographic processes, some printers keep a small museum or archive that may illustrate music typesetting and engraving. A fourth technique that has developed over the past 30 years is music-production by means of music-processing software (see below, 9): this has led some composers into publishing their own works themselves.

Music has never had the variety of typefaces available for use in books. An examination of music printed over the centuries will show a tendency to use several fairly standard designs, though gifted designers, punch-cutters, and artists have at times attempted to change this. A well-designed music type has a satisfying proportional relationship between the shape of the note-head and the other elements, such as the thickness and angle of the stem, and the shape of the tails and braces. The clefs, rests, and expression marks such as slurs and phrasing, even the thickness of the staves, make up a complex pictorial and typographical unity.

(a) Music type: Music type is produced by the same technique as is used for the letters of the alphabet. The design for a note, rest, or clef is cut on to a punch, usually made of steel. A matrix is produced by striking the punch into a small metal bar, usually copper, which leaves the symbol recessed. The type is then cast in a mould, which opens to accommodate characters of varying widths and of a fixed height. The matrix is inserted at its base, the mould is adjusted to the desired width, molten lead is poured in to form a column, and the character is cast in the matrix at the bottom. The mould is taken apart, the metal broken off to the desired height, and the type remains. This process was used by Gutenberg, who is credited with the invention of printing in Mainz in the mid-15th century, and has remained virtually unchanged ever since. Symbols are run off as required, as are spaces of varying width so that the notes can be properly spaced. (The earliest surviving moulds for music type are in the Plantin-Moretus Museum, Antwerp.)

The notes and symbols were placed in a wooden case ready for assembling by the compositor, who worked from a manuscript marked up to show the ends of the musical lines and other relevant details. He assembled the music type in a composing-stick, from which it was transferred line by line to a chase and thence to the machine. Early music printers required relatively few 'sorts', or separate notes, managing with six or seven, plus rests. By the 19th century, however, a case of music type might have contained more than 400 separate parts; three joined quavers, for example, might demand 16 pieces of type. The process was time-consuming, corrections proved costly, and musical knowledge was required of the compositor. In early music-printing two or more impressions were sometimes required: notes and staves were printed separately, as were sections, texts, and initial letters requiring a different colour.

The first surviving example of music printed from type, and one of the finest, is the Constance Gradual (*c*.1473, in the British Library). Since the late 15th century printers and designers have continually sought improved methods of setting music, and several ingenious systems were developed, including those of Breitkopf (*c*.1755), the Parisian Eugène Duverger (1820), and the Londoner Edward Cooper (1827). An apotheosis was reached in the fount offered by V. & J. Figgins of London, which used 452 different sorts and specially cast spacing material. With these more complex methods, known as 'mosaic' systems, the type was set by the page, rather than line by line. During earlier periods music was printed directly from type, which eventually resulted in damage. This was avoided by the introduction early in the 20th century of stereo plates, suitable for fast contemporary printing methods.

Music typesetting flourished in London and other European cities, and in America, alongside engraving, but became obsolete in the mid-20th century (apart from its occasional use for music examples in books).

(b) Woodblock: By the late 15th century a tradition of cutting illustrative material in wood (or metal) had established itself, and it was natural to extend it to musical works that were short and relatively uncomplicated. Although much early woodcut music is of poor quality—the craftsman not yet having mastered the intricacies of the notation, and the printer not having fully understood the problems of inking—there remains a quantity of good work, some of it superb. Woodblock printing was at its peak in the 16th century and continued, on a diminishing scale, until the 19th: the work of Andrea *Antico furnishes good early examples.

(c) Engraving: The engraving of music developed from techniques already successfully used by artists and map-makers. A fine burin was used to engrave the music on a copper plate, which was then etched with acid. This method was much more flexible than movable music type and could accommodate more complex notation. The art of the music engraver was highly prized: individual engravers showed recognizable artistic styles, and they often worked closely with the writing master, matching his calligraphic flourishes.

The earliest known example of music-engraving seems to be the *Intabolatura da leuto del divino Francesco da Milano*, published without indication of printer or date but probably issued before 1536. Copper-plate engraving by hand was a very common method of origination for music-printing in the 17th century. Towards the end of the period, however, it gave way to one that proved cheaper and quicker. Punches were used to stamp the fixed symbols such as notes and clefs on to a pewter plate, while the engraver continued to cut in the flexible signs, such as phrasing and note stems, with a hand tool. Pewter (or, in Austria, zinc) was adopted because it was easier to work and cheaper than copper, and the use of punches introduced a certain routine or craft element into what had previously been a skilled artist's preserve.

The manuscript is first 'cast off' to see how many pages it will make and page-turns are decided on, as is the size of the plate and punches. Working in mirror image, from right to left, the engraver 'lays out' the plate; with dividers he or she rapidly marks the point where the staves will go, draws in light lines, and then cuts the lines with a five-pronged tool called a score. Guidelines for clefs, key signatures, bar-lines, and notes are similarly drawn in. The most skilled part follows, called 'writing in': again using dividers, the engraver marks the spacing for the quavers and crotchets, and then sketches in the notes themselves, accidentals, rests—everything on the manuscript. All necessary information has now been transferred from the manuscript to the plate. Punches are first used to stamp in any words, whether text or indications of tempo and expression. The 'heavy stuff' (clefs and braces) follows, along with key signatures, rests, accidentals, and minims. The other notes are left until last, as they can easily buckle the plate.

A cutting tool is then used to put in the bar-lines, stems, beams (or ties), ledger lines, slurs, expression marks, etc. The plate is cleaned and tidied up, ready for proofing on a hand-press, traditionally in emerald or olive green ink. Mistakes are corrected by turning the plate over and punching the area round the error with a dot punch; the plate is turned over once more, the raised metal on the surface burnished, the plate gently tapped with a hammer over the same area, and when the surface is quite flat and smooth the corrections can be made. An extensive number of corrections usually necessitates a new plate. Although in the early 1800s a great deal of music was printed direct from the pewter plate, it later became general practice to transfer a proof taken from the engraved plate to a lithographic stone, and to print from that.

(d) Lithography and associated photographic processes: Alois Senefelder (1771–1834) experimented with a revolutionary method of printing which eventually became known as *lithography. He had sought to find a way of printing the plays he had written that was cheaper than copper engraving. He discovered that if he wrote on the polished surface of Solnhofen stone in a special ink made of wax, soap, and lampblack he obtained a crisp impression. The remaining parts of the surface could be removed by etching, so that the method resembled that of wood engraving.

Further experiments, based on the principle that grease repels water, enabled him to develop true lithography. By 1825 he was using metal plates instead of stones, and the new process, known as 'lithographic

transfer', rapidly spread throughout Europe. It was the cheapest, most efficient, and fastest method of printing music, and the principal publishers of the age, such as Schott of Mainz, Breitkopf of Leipzig, and Ricordi of Milan, took it up. In various forms it is still in use.

Lithographed music lacks the bite of engraved music; there is a marked tendency to softness, especially at the edges, but if the printer keeps the press well inked the image can be quite sharp. The process encourages freedom and variety of illustration, allowing a range of subtle and striking colours, which 19th-century publishers of popular songs were to exploit brilliantly. It also offered composers a convenient way to publication: in 1845 Wagner wrote out the 450 pages of *Tannhäuser* on lithographic transfer paper in full score, ready for laying down on the stone.

The new method of lithography did not sweep away engraving or movable type. Once the novelty had worn off, it became a valuable adjunct to the other two processes. Combined with photographic methods it still lies at the heart of much commercial music-printing. The music can be written from left to right on lithographic transfer paper for direct transfer or on normal paper for photographing, and then transferred to stone or (more usually today) to a zinc plate, for printing. Vast quantities of music can be punched, proofed, transferred, and then printed by 'litho'. The process is widely used throughout Europe, and its basis is set out in many manuals.

A similar graphic process, dependent on an original technique using stencils, was devised and developed in 1919 by the brothers Harold and Stanley Smith. Known as the 'Halstan' process, and used at the Halstan firm at Amersham, England, it involves detailed drafting by a musician and subsequent working through by operators who use drawing instruments and stencils. The result is photographically reduced and printed on a lithographic zinc plate. Halstan have produced outstanding work for a number of music publishers, including Faber Music and Oxford University Press.

(e) Recent developments: During the later 20th century, dry-transfer techniques were in widespread use as an aid to designers, students, and the general public, and were marketed by Letraset, Notaset, and others. The music symbols on the master sheets were transferred directly on to paper by rubbing from the back; if necessary, the image could be touched up with a pen. The process, however, was relatively slow, and in the late 20th century was quickly superseded by computerized music notation packages such as Score, Notator, and—especially—Sibelius.

Throughout the 19th century much effort went into the search for a practical music typewriter. A French patent of 1833 recognized the potential of such a device, but of the many types of machine that appeared in the 19th century relatively few established themselves. Among the successful ones were the Lily Pavey model marketed by the Imperial Typewriter Co. in England, the Robert H. Katon typewriter made in San Francisco, and machines patented by Armando Dal Molin and Cecil Effinger which gained international recognition. Dal Molin also developed a computer system later known as the Musicomp, which operated with great success through Music Reprographics in New York. Effinger's Musicwriter also had computer applications and could be operated by professionals and amateurs.

3. Europe: early history

The early history of music-printing relates closely to printing in general and to the ancillary arts of engraving, map-making, and die-cutting for coins and medals. Gutenberg is credited with the invention in about 1440 of a method of casting type which enabled the printing press to develop. The famous 42-line Bible printed at Mainz about 1453–5, probably by Gutenberg, Fust, and Schoeffer, was followed by Fust and Schoeffer's Latin Psalter of 1457. Printing then spread along the Rhine and throughout Germany, and on to Italy and the rest of Europe.

The earliest examples of printing are known as 'incunabula', from the Latin *incunabulum* ('cradle', or 'first beginnings'), and this word is used by librarians and bibliographers to denote music and books printed before the end of the year 1500. Music manuscripts served as models for music type design. This origin is clear from the Constance Gradual, the most notable example of the late 15th-century printer's art which survives in a unique copy in the British Library. It was printed in two impressions from music type in 'Gothic' (diamond-shaped) notation, and the 'rubricated' (red-coloured) initials were added by hand. It bears no date or printer's name, but it is believed to have been produced at Constance, in southern Germany, in about 1473. The 'registration' (alignment of notes on the staves) is excellent, the inking even and dark. Other fine music-printing includes the Roman Missal of Ulrich Hahn (Rome, 1476), quite as distinguished as the Constance Gradual. Hahn's mastery of technique influenced other European printers, including English ones: the fine Sarum Missal was printed in London by Pynson in 1500 (though many consider the 1520 edition superior).

Two styles of notation were in use at this time: the 'Gothic', or German, preferred in the German-speaking parts of Europe and used in the Constance Gradual; and the usually square 'roman', preferred in Latin countries, England, and the Netherlands. Printers needed to stock only two kinds of note-shape (and some stocked only one). Few printers could afford to cast and use music type, which proved slow and expensive to print. Fortunately, the requirements for printing plainchant changed little, and the first printers did not attempt the more complex task of polyphony.

4. Europe: 16th century

In the late 15th century, Venice was at the centre of Italian printing. In 1498 a young printer named Ottaviano *Petrucci obtained from the seigniory of Venice an exclusive 20-year privilege to print 'canto figurato' (mensural, or measured, music) and tablatures for the organ and lute. He believed that he had at last perfected a method of printing from movable type that could be used for polyphonic music, and on 15 May 1501 he published his *Harmonice musices odhecaton A* (known as *Odhecaton*) in the oblong quarto format he used for all his music books. It contains 96 pieces by French and Flemish composers arranged as partsongs, and the quality of the printing and type design made it outstanding. He had achieved accurate registration of the notes and masterly visual effects in the spacing of the parts; his initial letters, of singular beauty, did not unbalance the whole; and his ink was of a fine black.

Petrucci's innovations made available to the Venetian public an immense variety of polyphonic music that ranged from masses, motets, and Lamentations to frottolas and lute tablatures, in fine though admittedly expensive editions. In some books he used three impressions: one for staves, another for notes and other musical signs, and the third for the text. He subsequently simplified this to two impressions, again achieving extremely high standards. The body of his publications, 61 of which are known, exerted a tremendous influence, not only on other music printers but on the musical life of his time.

The French were quick to follow Petrucci's lead. Pierre *Attaingnant established himself as a bookseller in Paris in about 1514, when the city was pre-eminent in book-production and -publishing. After experimenting with music type for several years, he produced in 1527/8 an oblong quarto partbook of *Chansons nouvelles*, which showed the important technical advance of printing at one impression. Each note was cast as a separate unit, with the necessary staff lines attached to the note stem and head as part of the typographical unit. Attaingnant evolved a diamond-shaped note of clarity and style which fitted into the overall pattern of the staff, and his method of single-impression printing reduced production costs and time by at least half.

In 1537 Attaingnant became the king's music printer and, by making large quantities of music available at reasonable prices, he became in essence the first music publisher to operate on a large scale. He diffused the works of Parisian chanson composers (Sermisy, Janequin, and Certon) and published breviaries, missals, and the first books of psalm settings. His press became a clearing-house for ideas, and a moulder of taste. Attaingnant's techniques were taken up by other French printers, such as Jacques *Moderne in Lyons, who based his note forms on those of Petrucci, and Robert Granjon. Granjon was an outstanding punchcutter, whose contribution to typography, notably *civilité* type, is of great historical importance; his elegant music type reveals at once his calligraphic mastery.

After Attaingnant's death in 1551/2 the royal privilege passed to the lutenist and composer Robert Ballard, whose descendants continued in business until 1825. The firm of *Le Roy & Ballard developed a distinctive music type, cut by the notable Guillaume Le Bé, which was more rounded than the severe lozenge shape used by Attaingnant and others. In their heyday Le Roy & Ballard were a leading house, responsive to taste and defensive of their monopoly. They published chansons, motets, psalms, *chansons spirituelles*, and tablature for plucked string instruments, and they enjoyed warm relations with leading composers. In the 17th century they were the first to publish orchestral scores.

The earliest known specimen of musical notation printed in England occurs in Ranulphus Higden's *Polychronicon* (London, 1495, a summary of world history and scientific knowledge). The passage in which the notes appear concerns the consonances of Pythagoras. Wynkyn de Worde, the printer, set the musical notes by putting together quads (possibly reversed capitals) and rules and printed them with the text. At about the time when Attaingnant was experimenting with single-impression printing, an isolated example of it appeared in London, in John Rastell's *A New Interlude and a Mery of the Nature of the iiii Elements* (*c*.1525). Rastell printed the first mensural music in Britain, the earliest broadside with music printed from type anywhere in Europe, and the earliest song printed in an English dramatic work; he was also the first in Britain to attempt to print a score, by any process.

The first known English printed vocal partbooks, *The Book of XX Songes* (1530), issued by an unnamed printer, show craftsmanlike skill. The staves were printed from blocks at the first impression and the words and notes at a second impression. The result was excellent. Before the 1570s only about 60 volumes were printed in England, most of them sacred music, but in 1570 Thomas Vautrollier began to publish secular music, and the best of his work was equal in quality to that of his continental counterparts. In 1575 Tallis and Byrd received a royal patent from Elizabeth I for 21 years for printing music and supplying paper, but it did not prove profitable and they had to petition the queen

for assistance. The printer and publisher Thomas *East acquired Vautrollier's music type and printed several partbook collections between 1588 and 1596. Other notable English publications include John Dowland's *First Books of Songes or Aires* (London, 1597), which follow the continental 'table-book' format in which the parts are printed together in one volume but facing different ways on the page, so that performers seated round a table can read their parts from a single volume.

There were a number of skilled printers in northern Europe at this period, notably in Frankfurt (Christian Egenolff), Nuremberg (Hieronymus Formschneider, or 'Grapheus'), Wittenberg, and elsewhere. Venetian followers of Petrucci, such as Antonio Gardano and the *Scotto family, kept Venice in the forefront of Italian endeavour. In the Low Countries, Tylman *Susato at Antwerp and the elder Pierre *Phalèse at Leuven established thriving businesses.

In 1555 Christopher *Plantin set up his press, The Golden Compasses, in Antwerp, then a centre for the publishing trade, and initiated a printing and publishing business that endured until the late 19th century. As the Plantin-Moretus Museum, it is now an unparalleled source of information, with its press room, the cases of type collected by Plantin himself, and all the documents and accessories of the past. These indicate that the well-organized workforce and constant production rates at the press, combined with Plantin's own strong commercial sense, contributed greatly to his success. Plantin usually decided the design, format, and print run of the editions himself, supplying specimen pages and proofs to authors and composers, who would compile lists of errata to be printed at the end if time did not allow for corrections before printing. Plantin's first volume of music, George de la Hèle's *Missae* (1578), sold for 18 florins, a high price, and he often financed his printing by asking composers to buy copies themselves, sometimes as many as 100 or 150. Although music was a small part of his publishing enterprise, he published the best composers available to him (e.g. Monte, Pevernage, and Kerle), many in lavishly designed editions; his press became a centre of humanist culture and, as official printer to King Philip of Spain, he was highly regarded by his contemporaries.

5. Europe: 1600–*c*.1750

The history of printing music by engraving begins properly in the 17th century, though the earliest examples of copper-plate engraving date from the 16th. Apart from the volume of Francesco da Milano's lute tablature of *c*.1536 (see above, 2*c*), there are a number of devotional prints from the 1580s and 90s that combine music with an artist's engraved illustration (e.g. Sadelar's *Virgin and Child* of 1584, which incorporates a motet by Verdonck, and Philippe Galle's *Encomium musices* of *c*.1590. Engraving became influential, however, through the work of Simone Verovio, a calligrapher and engraver, whose *Diletto spirituale* and *Primo libro delle melodie spirituali* were engraved in Rome in 1586. The technique spread gradually to other countries. William Hole (*fl* London, 1612–18) engraved *Parthenia, or The Maydenhead of the First Musicke that ever was Printed for the Virginalls* (*c*.1612), the first music to be produced by this method in England. It is a splendid volume, with free-flowing calligraphy (though it is somewhat tightly arranged for performance), famed for its title-page picture of a young woman at the keyboard. Other notable collections of engraved English music include *Parthenia In-violata* (1614), which is believed to be the work of several hands, Orlando Gibbons's beautifully engraved *Fantazies of III Parts* (*c*.1620), and Purcell's *Sonnatas of III Parts* (London, 1683), elegantly engraved by Thomas Cross.

Music-engraving was adopted in the Netherlands in 1615, but not until *c*.1660 in France and 1689 in Germany. Much later, in Diderot's *Encyclopédie* (1761–5), a Madame Delusse, a music engraver, gives a full account of the process, citing operas by Lully and Mouret, motets by Campra and Lalande, and cantatas by Bernier and Clérambault as early examples of French engraving. By the beginning of the 18th century music-engraving had fully established itself, although it continued to coexist alongside music type, with a constant ebb and flow of one against the other and a continual search for improved techniques.

English music-publishing from the mid-17th century to the mid-18th, in the hands of the Playfords and the Walshes, exemplifies that state of affairs, for their ideals and methods differed strikingly. John *Playford and his son Henry had most of their volumes printed from music type, while John *Walsh the elder began as an engraver and later turned to pewter plates and punches. The Playfords were cultured men who published music suitable for the tavern, the music club, and the theatre, and for both amateurs and professionals. John Playford developed a racy style of publication, with attractive designs and lively illustrations. His distinct flair and personality show themselves in his first books, *The (English) Dancing Master* (1651), *A Musicall Banquet* (1651), and *A Breefe Introduction to the Skill of Musick* (1654). To read his advertisements, exhortations to the purchaser and reader, and comments on the (unrecognized) qualities of English composers is to catch the zest and spirit of an engaging, shrewd publisher.

The Walshes were among the most influential publishers in Europe, but unlike the Playfords, whose hearts may have lain in music rather than in commerce, they were more alert to the commercial potential of their products, and left posterity with many bibliographical tangles to unravel. The elder John Walsh developed new techniques in publishing, based principally on the cheap and speedy method of striking pewter plates with punches. He employed many apprentices and was wide-ranging in his enterprises, making arrangements with continental publishers such as the renowned Amsterdam engraver Estienne *Roger, pirating freely as was the custom, and publicizing his flood of editions through the newspapers and his own catalogues. He issued song-sheets and anthologies, instrumental music, and cheap instruction books, and was Handel's principal publisher. His unscrupulous editorial methods manifest themselves in the disarray of many Handel editions, especially the harpsichord music. He fell out with Handel over the publication of *Rinaldo* in 1711, and Handel returned to the firm only some 30 years later, when the younger John Walsh was in control.

John Heptinstall introduced improvements in the appearance and flexibility of music type in his *Vinculum societatis, or The Tie of Good Company* (London, 1687), using round instead of lozenge-shaped note-heads and grouping quavers and semiquavers by beams, a procedure that became known as 'the new tied note'. In 1698 Peter de Walpergen printed a group of four songs in folio called *Musica oxoniensis*, which showed for the first time a distinguished new type 'cut on steel and cast' with a stylishness and clarity that fully justify the high claims of its promoters.

A number of decorated title pages of this period are justly admired, among them Walsh's edition of Daniel Purcell's *The Judgement of Paris* (1702), John Pine's striking title for J. E. Galliard's *The Morning Hymn of Adam and Eve* (1728), Walsh's frontispiece for John Weldon's *Divine Harmony* (*c*.1730), with its conjectural interior of the Chapel Royal, and John Cluer's and Walsh's title pages for Handel's operas, several of which were later reused for other publications.

Many 18th-century music editions remain unequalled in grace and distinction. In England the collaboration between writing master and music engraver which had begun with William Hole's *Parthenia* flowered in a series of songbooks, of which the finest was George Bickham's splendid *The Musical Entertainer* (London, 1737–9); single sheets of it still appear in antiquarian shops. Also notable was Thomas Jeffery's song collection *Amaryllis* (*c*.1750) and John Cluer's charming collection of opera airs, *A Pocket Companion for Gentlemen and Ladies* (1724–5).

French engraved music of the 18th century was generally of a very high standard. Couperin enjoyed the services of an excellent engraver for his *Pieces de clavecin* (1713), and his instruction book *L'Art de toucher le clavecin* (1716, 2/1717) is at times like an engraver's notebook. The posthumous engraved editions of Lully's operas reached high levels, and among French songbooks, Laborde's *Choix de chansons* (1773) is outstanding. Music-engraving attracted a number of extremely accomplished Frenchwomen, among whom were Mademoiselle Vendôme (later Mme Moria), Mme Labassée, and Mme Lobry.

6. Europe: *c*.1750–*c*.1945

Between 1749 and 1755, in a pioneer attempt to overcome the problems still inherent in the use of music type, Jacques-François Rosart cut a series of punches which embodied an improved method of printing. He offered them first to Johannes Enschedé at Haarlem, who gave him no encouragement. Instead, the German typefounder and printer J. G. I. *Breitkopf, working on the same principles, began his own experiments in the mid-1740s which resulted in a superior fount of music type. He has been credited with the invention ever since. The sharp impression of the notes, the visual flow, and overall balance and elegance of the music characterized Breitkopf's type.

Instead of using a single type-unit made up of notehead, stem, and staff, Breitkopf used separate pieces for the head and stem attached to staff segments of varying lengths, and additional pieces for the notes of shorter value. This came to be known as the 'mosaic' system, and it reached its greatest level of complexity in the latter part of the 19th century. It required much careful and detailed work by the compositor and, usually, the ability to read music. Breitkopf's type was first properly demonstrated in *Il trionfo della fedeltà* (1756), a pastoral drama by the Electress Maria Anna Walpurgis of Bavaria, and it was subsequently used for many major publications of the Classical repertory.

In France, the distinguished typographer Pierre Simon Fournier (1712–68) had been making similar successful experiments, the results of which appread in his *Essai d'un nouveau caractère de fonte* (1756). His attractive type was used in Jean Monnet's *Anthologie françoise* (1765), and it is occasionally seen in pocket books of librettos with *airs*. However, Ballard's powerful monopoly in France prevented Fournier's design having an influence comparable to Breitkopf's. Breitkopf pioneered the printing of large numbers of copies, selling them cheaply and distributing them widely. He also developed a market for manuscript copies of a large repertory of works that did not justify a printed edition, and to publicize them he issued thematic catalogues. His own endeavours, and his heirs' successful partnership with G. C. Härtel, helped establish Leipzig as the centre of music publishing in Europe.

Following the rise of the great Viennese school of composers (Haydn, Mozart, Beethoven) and the growth of music-making among all sections of the community, new publishing houses were founded. Chief among them were Schott (Mainz), Simrock (Bonn), and *Artaria (Vienna). From their presses flowed chamber music of every kind, parts for concertos and symphonies, arrangements, piano pieces, and songs. The widespread use of engraving brought down the costs, although the printing was of variable quality, and the development of lithography in the later 19th century helped meet the accelerating need for mass copies of music. The rise of public concerts and a demand for 'study scores' encouraged the publication of miniature scores, by Payne of Leipzig (the first to produce them on a large scale) and later by *Eulenburg.

Although Leipzig remained at the centre of music-publishing throughout the century, houses in other cities were well established and productive (e.g. *Ricordi in Milan, Bote & Bock in Berlin, and *Novello and *Cramer (ii) in London). The enormous increase in output during the century can be seen by comparing the size of a major printing house (e.g. Röder of Leipzig) at the middle and end of the century.

Printing and publishing remained very much a German trade, however. In 1895 the London publisher Joseph Spedding Curwen inspected the printing works of Röder and Brandstetter in Leipzig and was impressed by its general excellence and in particular by the skill and industry of the workmen, who earned less than their British counterparts. Until 1914 many Germans were employed in the engraving-rooms of such British firms as *Augener, Novello, Curwen, and Lowe & Brydone, whose engraving department became one of the largest in the country, known in its heyday as 'the greatest music printing firm in the Empire'.

The 19th century also saw the growth of the pictorial title page. Early in the century French publishers had included charming vignette engravings and lithographs on their title pages, foreshadowing the later use of coloured drawings, portraits, and illustrations of domestic scenes, national occasions such as exhibitions, and so on, and several notable artists emerged (e.g. Nanteuil, Packer, Brandard, and Concanen). Editions of music by Louis Jullien showed exuberant, even spectacular, colour. Black and white title pages and covers did not disappear: *The Musical Bouquet* (c.1846–8), which appeared in series and included over 5000 pieces of music, epitomizes the best work of the English school.

Leipzig lost its pre-eminence as the centre of music-printing and publishing after World War II. Bombing destroyed most of the great printing works, and the city's incorporation into the German Democratic Republic split many famous firms, some moving to the West while others were taken over by the state. Leipzig's reputation had largely rested on engraving, which was by then restricted to selected and often prestige works. Printers throughout Europe were disbanding their engraving departments as lithographic techniques all but took over.

The pattern of musical life had also changed everywhere. Amateur music-making declined, as did sales of the piano, the ubiquitous domestic instrument of the 19th century. Much avant-garde music proved too difficult for amateurs and seemed at first inaccessible. New compositional techniques arose, such as electronic music, which required the publisher to find new marketing techniques. Publishers regrouped, rethought their roles, sought to develop new markets, and pruned, in order to survive. These strategies continue today.

7. The USA

From the Puritan psalm-singing traditions of England there arose the first music to be printed in America, the *Bay Psalm Book*. Its early editions contained no music, but in the ninth (Boston, 1698) 13 psalm tunes in two-part arrangements were crudely printed in diamond-shaped notes from woodblock, with basic instructions on performance. John Tufts's 12-page pamphlet containing 37 tunes in three parts, 'An Easy Method of Singing by Letters instead of Notes', was followed by his *Very Plain and Easy Introduction to the Singing of Psalm Tunes* (Boston, 3/1723). Even more successful, however, was Thomas Walter's *Grounds and Rules of Musick Explained* (Boston, 1721), in which barlines appeared in American music-printing for the first time.

From the mid-18th century onwards, several psalm collections broadened the repertory, some including tunes by native composers. Josiah Flagg's *Collection of the Best Psalm Tunes* (Boston, 1764) and *The New-England Psalm-Singer* (Boston, 1770) by William Billings, the colonial period's most rugged and energetic composer, had their plates or frontispieces engraved by Paul Revere, the leading goldsmith of New England. Nearly all the music of the colonial period was printed from polished copper plates engraved freehand by local engravers or silversmiths, most of whose names remain unknown, though Thomas Johnston, who also engraved maps, views, bookplates, certificates, and currency, was an exception.

The two earliest books to be printed from music type, not commonly used at this time, were *Geistreiche Lieder* (Germantown, PA, 1752) and *Neu-vermehrt und vollstaendiges Gesang-Buch* (Germantown, 1757). The type was possibly cast by the publisher, a German immigrant named Christopher Sower (or Saur). They contained only a few short and simple melodies; the first full page of tunes appeared in William Dawson's *The Youth's Entertaining Amusement, or A Plain Guide to Psalmody* (Philadelphia, c.1754). Isaiah Thomas's *The Worcester Collection of Sacred Harmony* (Worcester, MA, 1786), printed from Caslon foundry types purchased in London, set higher standards and also marked the first attempt to maintain a continuity of publications. After the Revolution, the flow of European immigrants increased, and American musical life broadened. Sacred and secular music widened in scope, and entertainments of every kind arose, all of which required music. Musicians and music teachers arrived in far greater numbers than ever before, among them many musician-engravers using the technique of stamping notes on to pewter plates with punches. They provided the basis for a native publishing trade, which flourished first in Philadelphia.

Alexander Reinagle's *Selection of the Most Favourite Scots Tunes* (Philadelphia, 1787), engraved by John Aitken, was the first wholly secular music publication in the USA. Benjamin Carr, descended from a long line of English music publishers, became the most important and prolific figure in the 1790s. He was a leading composer too, and his influential *Musical Journal for the Piano Forte* of the late 1790s moulded taste for over 20 years. Philadelphia maintained its predominant position into the early 19th century, through the sheet-music business of Moller & Capron, and especially through the vigorous activities of George Willig and George E. Blake, publishing celebrities of their day. Other notable publishers include Gottlieb Graupner in Boston, Joseph Carr in Baltimore, and in New York, George Gilfer and James Hewitt, who established a music circulating library. New York soon became the chief centre of music-publishing in the USA.

Music-publishing spread west and south from the eastern seaboard, firms were set up in places such as Cincinnati, Louisville, Chicago (Root & Cady), and St Louis (Balmer & Weber), and the influence of London and European styles and tastes gradually declined. As the minstrel show emerged, American publishers sought to attract amateur musicians and provided a flow of spirituals, gospel songs, polkas, and *Schottisches*, as well as innumerable sentimental ballads and salon pieces. Ballads were published to celebrate the completion of the Erie Canal in 1825, New York's first train, the first horse-drawn street cars, and so on. Many had lithographed pictorial covers original and vital enough to establish an American school. As immigrants continued to pour in, tunebooks, hymnals, and chorus and anthem books were needed in greater numbers. Hundreds of sentimental songs by popular composers such as Stephen Foster were distributed by the New York publishers Firth, Pond, & Co. and reached an international audience.

In the latter half of the 19th century more immigrant Germans established music shops and firms which later grew into significant publishing houses. They included Gustav *Schirmer (New York, 1861), Joseph Fischer (Dayton, OH, 1864), Carl *Fischer (New York, 1872), and Theodore *Presser (Philadelphia, 1884). Besides catering for popular needs, some published excellent editions of the classics and took financial risks with American composers, who by the end of the century had virtually established a 'school', with George Chadwick, Arthur Foote, Horatio Parker, and, best known of all, Edward MacDowell.

The growth of symphony orchestras, opera houses, and fine teaching institutions further stimulated national musical life and with it music-publishing. But the phenomenon of ragtime, and subsequently the cakewalk, first indicated the growth of a new musical culture. John Stillwell Stark, a publisher in Sedalia, Missouri, published the piano rags of Scott Joplin. Meanwhile, *Tin Pan Alley (the name for New York's sheet-music publishers), notably such firms as Harms and Witmark, exploited vaudeville songs with new marketing methods, and by the time Irving Berlin's *Alexander's Ragtime Band* appeared in 1911 ragtime was virtually dead, having been succeeded by the blues and jazz.

American composers interested in folk and Indian music had been welcomed by Arthur Farwell's Wa-Wan Press (1901), fashionable at the time as a means of creating a truly American music. But most composers belonged to a more eclectic tradition, with Charles Ives at its head, which found plenty of American publishers ready to promote its works. Some firms took up the Broadway musical, still a living genre, and works of the 1930s such as Gershwin's *Porgy and Bess*, an American classic, more than justified their faith and business instincts. American music-publishing houses, some closely linked with those of Europe, continue today their distinctive role as vital links in the lively scene that is American music.

8. Composers and publishers

The music-publishing house first acted as a stimulus to musical life in the early 16th century, when Pierre Attaingnant gathered round him in Paris renowned composers, among them Sermisy, Certon, and Janequin, and musicians and music lovers of every kind. He could offer his composers little financial reward, but his fine printing and wide-ranging distribution could bring them honour and fame. Instead of payment the composer would accept an agreed number of printed copies, though if he had approached the publisher in the first place he would usually expect to finance the whole venture. With no legislation to guarantee copyright protection, and widespread piracy, some composers preferred to keep their works in manuscript and negotiate their own terms for performance.

An extant agreement of 2 January 1531 between the distinguished Avignon craftsman Jean de Channey and the composer Carpentras illuminates publishing procedures of the time. Known as the Avignon Contracts (and discussed in detail in Daniel Heartz's study of Attaingnant, 1969), it sets out the rights and obligations on both sides and shows the difficulties that faced Channey when he attempted a monumental edition of Carpentras's works.

Handel's problems with the Walshes have already been outlined (see above, 5). Without copyright protection composers had to bargain directly with publishers, securing the highest possible outright payment. Piracy had to be thwarted, as had the activities of unscrupulous copyists who passed round new works to the highest bidder. From the 18th century onwards composer–publisher relationships are well charted in correspondence. Haydn's letters from 1781 onwards to the Viennese house of Artaria have a predominantly friendly tone, but Haydn's shrewd business sense made him react sharply if he felt himself being taken advantage of, and he preferred to keep private his financial transactions with his publisher. Poorly engraved work angered him. In his later years he became dissatisfied with Artaria and began negotiations with Breitkopf & Härtel, who eventually became his principal publishers.

Mozart's experience was the reverse: his father failed to interest Breitkopf & Härtel in his son's works at an early stage, but Mozart did succeed in having many of his chamber works published by Artaria. After the composer's death, the publisher J. A. *André of Offenbach purchased a quantity of manuscripts from Mozart's widow Constanze and published the works contained in them.

A large part of Beethoven's correspondence involves his publishers (Alan Tyson commented brilliantly on this in two chapters in *The Beethoven Companion*, ed. Denis Arnold and Nigel Fortune, London, 1971). Beethoven was determined to thwart piracy and unscrupulous copyists, and by 1801 he felt he was in a position to choose his own publisher from a possible six or seven and to state his own price for each work. Sometimes he held back from publication works he might perform himself, such as his finest concertos. He kept a number of copyists and proofreaders feverishly busy. He fretted over errors in his proofs, and had a sharp eye for a missing accidental or an omitted change of clef, but like most composers came to acknowledge that the work's creator was not the ideal proofreader.

Verdi's relationships with *Ricordi are themselves an offstage drama, detailed in the correspondence. He quarrelled with the elder Tito Ricordi, son of Giovanni (founder of the firm), about printing errors in his operas, and even wanted the first edition of *La traviata* withdrawn; eventually Tito's son Giulio, who brought Verdi and his librettist Boito together for *Otello*, restored good relations.

The greatly differing personalities and needs of composers created constantly changing patterns with publishers. Elgar and his editor at Novello, August Jaeger ('Nimrod' of the 'Enigma' Variations), established a unique artistic trust, a friendship vivacious and warm, so that the letters between them (1897–1908) mirror the composer's mercurial moods and feelings. When Jaeger died at the age of 49 in 1909, Elgar wrote: 'Despondent about himself, he was full of hope for others, and spent himself in smoothing their path to fame.'

Publishers must be adaptable, diplomatic, experimental, businesslike, and above all sensitive to emerging gifts and talents and to the changing patterns of the musical scene. It is no profession for the fainthearted. Some German music publishers have still not forgiven Richard Strauss for his mocking picture of them in his bizarre song cycle *Krämerspiegel* ('Shopkeepers' Mirror'). Schoenberg's clear imperative to Emil Hertzka, director of *Universal Edition in Vienna, in 1911, is one that all true composers might have made: 'I too have sung your praises. Now please print my work!!! I am certain it's good!!!. . . Well, you know what we musicians are like. And nobody more so than I.'

9. Publishing today

Much of the commercial background to music publishing in the 21st century has been concerned with the changing nature of *copyright and performing right; with the growth of the recording industry, broadcasting, and television; and with the rise of the computer.

The music publisher's income, typically, is derived from performing-right fees, mechanical reproduction fees, royalties, hire fees, and the sale of music. The composer, on the other hand, shares the royalties on copies of his or her music that are sold and fees accruing from performances. Copyright in a work, originally owned by the composer but more frequently nowadays by the publisher, exists during the composer's lifetime and, in Europe, for 70 years after the composer's death. A broadly similar system is followed in the USA. Hire fees follow a tariff set out by the Music Publishers' Association. Large orchestras may have on permanent loan a set of parts of a work they perform frequently, holding it in their library and paying the normal tariff. Conductors can make special arrangements to purchase a hire score.

From the sale of music the publisher will pay the composer a royalty. Such income in no way compares with the immense sums earned from sheet-music sales in the 19th and early 20th centuries. In 1898, for instance, *The Soldiers of the Queen*, published during the Boer War, sold well over 250,000 copies, and in the 1920s *That Old-Fashioned Mother of Mine* sold 704,000, bringing the composer Lawrence Wright £4900. Recordings, broadcasting, and television are now principal income sources, and publishers are becoming ever more aware of the importance of rights exploitation to generate income.

The typical print figures of major publishers are eloquent. They will print 1000 copies of the vocal score of a new opera, of which their hire library will absorb 500. They will also produce sets of parts and will prepare at least three full scores for conductors and for promotion. For an orchestral work, they may prepare sets of parts and full scores only for the hire library, as most concert-giving organizations prefer to hire rather than purchase outright, though they may later print miniature scores for reference and study which could yield reasonable but not enormous profits. Contemporary chamber music (piano solos, small ensembles, etc.) sells more slowly and has small print runs (from 500 to 1500), rising whenever a title is included in a teaching syllabus. Music for the educational market forms a significant portion of some publishers' output and income.

A gradual shrinkage of sales has led publishers to concentrate on the more profitable opera houses, international orchestras, and broadcasting companies, on the educational market, and on choral societies, brass bands, and so on. For some time avant-garde music remained formidable to amateur performers, but some composers and publishers have made a determined effort to win them back, at times with considerable success. In the 1970s several very small, specialist music publishers emerged, using the cheapest available methods and relying on direct sales. Some composers, notably Stockhausen, formed their own publishing companies. Publishers' incomes have been seriously eroded by illegal photocopying, which a licensing system might help to control: this issue is one of the most hotly contested between publishers and performers.

The principal change in music-printing and -publishing since the third quarter of the 20th century, however, has been the increasing use of computers (see COMPUTERS AND MUSIC). The American company A-R Editions, founded in New Haven, Connecticut, in 1962 and now based in Madison, Wisconsin, pioneered computer-driven photo-composition of music and gained much business from other publishers by its successful use of the technique. The Oxford Music

Processor, developed from the late 1970s by Richard Vendome and the British Technology Group, was an early attempt to develop software that would produce musical notation using a standard, 'qwerty' keyboard: by the mid-1990s, when it was still under development, OMP was superseded by other packages such as IBM's 'Score', the AppleMac 'Notewriter', and 'Finale' (for the PC or Macintosh), along with several other products that allowed data entry from a music keyboard via a MIDI port.

Composers could now write works directly to computer files and print the results, which naturally opened the way for self-publishing, either in print form or on the Internet (the American composer Philip Glass distributes much of his music via the Internet route). Musicologists and editors could easily and quickly create music example, and even full editions. Some highly specialized packages were developed that could produce output in plainchant notation, or in tablature. The 'Sibelius' system, originally developed for an Acorn PC, became something of a market leader in the late 1990s when it became available in a cut-down version for PC. Commercial publishers themselves are also exploiting these technologies, of course, as are broadcasters like the BBC, which frequently has to generate sets of parts from a printed or manuscript score, when performance of a rarely heard work is required. Instead of creating these in manuscript, the parts can now be computer-generated and stored in digital format until required. Publishers are doubtless viewing these developments carefully.

However, in spite of the formidable economic and artistic difficulties posed by present circumstances, many monumental publishing enterprises are in train, such as great scholarly editions covering an ever-wider range of music and embodying research that is both meticulous and inspired. As new composers appear, there will always be publishers responsive to their gifts, for the publishing of music is central to the Western musical tradition.   JMT/JWA

📖 W. GAMBLE, *Music Engraving and Printing: Historical and Technical Treatise* (London, 1923/R1971) · C. HUMPHRIES and W. C. SMITH, *Music Publishing in the British Isles* (London, 1954, 2/1970) · A. B. BARKSDALE, *The Printed Note: 500 Years of Music Printing and Engraving* (Toledo, OH, 1957) · A. H. KING, *Four Hundred Years of Music Printing* (London, 1964, 2/1968) · G. FRAENKEL, *Decorative Music Title Pages, 1500–1800* (New York, 1969) · E. ROTH, *The Business of Music: Reflections of a Music Publisher* (London, 1969) · D. and S. SPELLMAN, *Victorian Music Covers* (London, 1969)

L. VOET, *The Golden Compasses: A History and Evaluation of the Printing and Publishing Activities of the Officina Plantiniana*, 2 vols. (Amsterdam, 1969) · R. PEARSALL, *Victorian Sheet Music Covers* (Newton Abbot, 1972) · M.

WILK, *Memory Lane 1890–1925: Ragtime, Jazz, Foxtrot, and Other Popular Music and Musicians* (London, 1973) · D. W. KRUMMEL, *English Music Printing, 1553–1700* (London, 1975) · A. PEACOCK and R. WEIR, *The Composer and the Market Place* (London, 1975) · R. J. WOLFE, *Early American Music Engraving and Printing: History of Music Publishing in America from 1787 to 1825* (Urbana, IL, 1980) · D. W. KRUMMEL and S. SADIE (eds.), *Music Printing and Publishing* (London, 1990) · M. K. DUGGAN, *Italian Music Incunabula: Printers and Type* (Berkeley, CA, 1992)

Prinz von Homburg, Der ('The Prince of Homburg'). Opera in three acts by Henze to a libretto by Ingeborg Bachmann after Heinrich von Kleist's play *Prinz Friedrich von Homburg* (1810) (Hamburg, 1960).

Prise de Troie, La. See TROYENS, LES.

Prix de Rome. A prize awarded annually by the French Académie des Beaux-Arts from 1803 to 1968 in painting, sculpture, engraving, architecture, and music. In music, composition students sat a preliminary examination consisting of a fugue and a short choral piece. Some half-dozen were then admitted to the final round, a setting of a commissioned cantata text for solo voices and orchestra, to be completed in isolation during a period of about four weeks. Winners, thereafter allowed to append the title 'Premier Grand Prix de Rome' after their name, spent a minimum of two years in Rome and two either there or in another cultural centre, all at the state's expense. Arguments about the artistic value of the prize raged throughout its existence. Famous winners included Berlioz, Gounod, Bizet, Debussy, and Dutilleux; famous non-winners Saint-Saëns, Ravel, and Messiaen.   RN

prizes. See COMPETITIONS IN MUSIC.

procession, ritual. A solemn procession of clergy, sometimes with the participation of the laity and often accompanied by special chants. In late antiquity the clergy of cities such as Constantinople and Rome united their Christian topographies with processions characterized by antiphonal psalmody. Though often reduced in scale to take place within a single building, processions remained frequent in medieval churches.
                                                             ALi

processional (Lat.: *processionale*). A book containing chants to be sung in procession.

Prodigal Son, The. Several composers have written works on this biblical subject, the best known being the following.

1. Church parable, op. 81, by Britten to a text by William Plomer (Aldeburgh, 1968).

2. Oratorio (1869) by Sullivan.

3. Ballet by Prokofiev, choreographed by George Balanchine (Paris, 1929); its Russian title is *Bludnïy syn* but it is often known by its French title *L'Enfant prodigue*.

4. Cantata by Debussy; see ENFANT PRODIGUE, L'.

profondo (It., 'low', 'deep'). See BASSO PROFONDO.

programme, programme notes. A written commentary, provided at a concert or in a theatre, that gives the audience information about the music to be performed. A 19th-century phenomenon, the programme was a response to the increasing popularity of public concerts. Initially, it provided a narrative description of programmatic works, for example Berlioz's *Symphonie fantastique* (1830), but more analytical notes were pioneered in Britain by John Ella in the 1840s. Ella was followed in the second half of the century by writers including George Grove, who supplied notes for August Manns's concerts at the Crystal Palace, London. Analytical notes began to appear in programmes elsewhere in Europe and in the USA at the end of the century. Increasingly in the 20th century, composers including Vaughan Williams, Messiaen, Bartók, Britten, and Stravinsky provided commentaries on their own compositions, and the BBC commissioned composers to write notes on the music of others. Today, programme notes range from brief glosses to detailed analyses of the music and the circumstances surrounding its composition.

From the 18th century, plot synopses and the texts of *librettos (with a translation if necessary) were usually printed and sold at opera performances, but it was only in the 20th century that critical notes were regularly added to these. Today, opera programmes commonly contain a synopsis and substantial essays dealing with different aspects of the work and its historical and literary context, though the libretto is not always printed in full. Publishers have launched series of substantial programme-style books that contain both essays and librettos, together with details of recordings and bibliography.   SH

programme music. Music which expresses an extra-musical idea, whether of mood, narrative, or pictorial image. Strictly speaking, programme music should be constructed with reference to a textual plan, and the term 'programme' was defined by Liszt as 'any preface in intelligible language added to a piece of instrumental music, by means of which the composer intends to guard the listener against a wrong poetical interpretation, and to direct his attention to the poetical idea of the whole or to a particular part of it'. The concept predates Liszt's definition: an example of Baroque programme music is Vivaldi's *Four Seasons*, where each of

the four concertos is prefaced by a sonnet on the given season (probably by the composer); lines from these sonnets are inserted into the score at appropriate places to underline the descriptive point being made, such as stamping feet and chattering teeth in the cold of 'Winter'.

Programme music became established as a genre in the Romantic period, most strikingly in the music of Berlioz, who supplied a detailed programme, later revised, outlining all the events depicted in his *Symphonie fantastique* of 1830. It narrates an 'Episode in the Life of an Artist' who sees for the first time a woman who embodies the ideal of beauty and fascination that he has been seeking; he falls in love with her. Every time her image appears in the artist's mind it is accompanied by a musical thought, the famous *idée fixe* of the symphony. The last two movements present the beloved seen through the eyes of the artist who has taken opium. In the fourth movement, 'March to the Scaffold', he imagines he has killed her and been condemned to death and witnesses his own execution. In the fifth, 'Dream of a Witches' Sabbath', the artist sees himself surrounded by an assembly of sorcerers and devils celebrating the sabbath. His beloved comes to join in the devilish orgy, which consists of a round-dance and burlesque parody of the *Dies irae*. Berlioz stated that the 'distribution of the programme to the audience at concerts where the symphony is to be performed is indispensable for a complete understanding of the dramatic outline of the work'.

A second symphony by Berlioz, *Harold en Italie*, followed in 1834; named after Byron's *Childe Harold*, its themes were sketched with other characters in mind, including Napoleon and Mary, Queen of Scots. It is more conventional than the *Symphonie fantastique* and instead of a programme has descriptive titles for each of the four movements, rather in the manner of Beethoven's 'Pastoral' Symphony, which the composer described as 'more an expression of feeling than painting'. Berlioz again uses an *idée fixe*, but does not treat it to the sort of transformations that characterized the technique of the *Symphonie fantastique*.

Liszt himself began his foray into programme music with the first of his 12 *symphonic poems, *Ce qu'on entend sur la montagne* (1847–56), prefaced by Victor Hugo's poem, which lends the piece its name, together with a short synopsis. Narrative representation remained the idea behind his subsequent *Tasso: Lamento e trionfo* and *Les Préludes*, though in both cases the programme was finalized to accord with the music once it was written. The later pieces are less tied to the demands of narrative, and indeed Liszt's last symphonic poem, *Hamlet* (1858), like the three evocations of his earlier *Faust Symphony* of 1854–7, is more in the nature of a character study of the troubled prince than an account of Shakespeare's play.

With such departures from the original definition, programme music was acquiring its more general connotation of a musical composition where the composer has gone beyond what is termed 'absolute' music—that is, music with no programmatic intention—to attempt to depict an extra-musical image or idea. In this sense the genre can be said to embrace much instrumental music of the 19th and early 20th centuries including the existing concert overture, such as Mendelssohn's *The Hebrides*, based on a conventional formal design (in this case, a sonata-form structure) but inspired by some literary or other idea. Mendelssohn's 'Scottish' and 'Italian' Symphonies, for example, are strongly characterized in terms of mood and association but draw their inspiration from a range of sources too disparate to constitute a coherent 'programme' in the mould of the *Symphonie fantastique*.

Programme music was popular with such Russian 19th-century composers as Musorgsky, who immortalized an exhibition of work by his friend Victor Hartmann in his piano suite *Pictures at an Exhibition* (1874); here a 'Promenade' links the various works on display (stage designs and architectural drawings as well as paintings) and draws the listener into the musical gallery. One of Rimsky-Korsakov's last orchestral works before he embarked on the series of operas which occupied the final part of his career was *Sheherazade* (1888), a brilliantly orchestrated symphonic suite based on *The Thousand and One Nights*; the composer prefaced the suite with a paragraph on the familiar story of how the tales came to be told, and based each of the four movements on one of Sheherazade's stories.

Richard Strauss's series of dazzling tone-poems, begun with *Macbeth* in 1886–8 and including such masterpieces as *Don Juan* and *Till Eulenspiegels lustige Streiche*, are perfect examples of how conventional forms can be turned to programmatic use: the roguish exploits of the protagonist of *Till Eulenspiegel* are expressed in rondo form, and *Don Quixote* is constructed as a series of variations. Strauss scored later pieces, such as *Also sprach Zarathustra* (1895–6) and the autobiographical *Ein Heldenleben* (1897–8), for an increasingly large orchestra, and at the same time his musical structures became more elaborate, culminating in the *programme symphony with *Symphonia domestica* (1902–3) and the 22 sections of *Eine Alpensinfonie* (1911–15).

The move towards abandoning conventional forms in the first decades of the 20th century produced much music that was 'programmatic' in the general sense, without necessarily involving a specific programme. Debussy's masterly evocations of places, moods, and times of day, for example, adopt the vocabulary of the visual arts—'Nocturnes' (after Whistler), 'Images', and 'symphonic sketches'—and use a sophisticated range of techniques to make their points while remaining musically satisfying in their own right. Other composers have bridged the gap between programme and absolute music by hinting at, or even concealing a programme in an apparently abstract piece, such as Elgar's Second Symphony (1909–11) and Berg's *Lyric Suite* (1925–6) and Violin Concerto (1935).

Later 20th-century examples of programme music are found in the works of composers including Maxwell Davies (*An Orkney Wedding with Sunrise*, 1985; *The Beltane Fire*, 1995), Benedict Mason (*Lighthouses of England and Wales*, 1988), and R. Murray Schafer, whose extra-musical sources embrace literature, mythology, and Eastern or Inuit philosophies (*Dream Rainbow Dream Thunder*, 1986; *Manitou*, 1995).

GMT/KC

📖 E. NEWMAN, 'Programme music', *Musical Studies* (London, 1905, 3/1914) · F. NIECKS, *Programme Music in the Last Four Centuries* (London, 1907) · D. F. TOVEY, *Essays in Musical Analysis*, iv: *Illustrative Music* (London, 1937/R1972, abridged 2/1981) · F. HOWES, *Music and its Meanings* (London, 1958) · D. COOKE, *The Language of Music* (Oxford, 1959/R) · L. ORREY, *Programme Music* (London, 1975) · M. CHION, *Le Poème symphonique et la musique à programme* (Paris, 1993)

programme symphony. A work that matches a narrative or descriptive programme to symphonic form. Its origins lie in Beethoven's 'Pastoral' Symphony of 1808, with its descriptive titles for each of the five movements, but the prime example is Berlioz's *Symphonie fantastique* of 1830, for which the composer provided a detailed programme, outlining the events and moods expressed in each movement (see PROGRAMME MUSIC). Liszt's *Faust Symphony* of 1854–7 does not attempt to compress Goethe's *Faust* into symphonic form, but offers three 'character studies', musical portraits of the central characters—Faust, Gretchen, and Mephistopheles. Richard Strauss's *Symphonia domestica* of 1902–3 uses a single-movement form, broken into four sections, to depict scenes from the composer's home life. His later work *Eine Alpensinfonie* (1911–15) describes a day in the Alps, from before dawn through to sunset and night, with a central passage on the summit. Scored for a massive orchestra, it also calls for such sound effects as cowbells and wind machine.

Programmatic elements are frequently found in late 19th- and early 20th-century symphonies: Tchaikovsky's later symphonies, particularly the 'Pathétique', express highly personal programmes, and Mahler's comment to Sibelius that 'the symphony must be like the world; it must embrace everything' is borne out in the programmatic significance of his symphonic work.

Programmes of a narrative or poetic nature appear in the symphonies of Rimsky-Korsakov, Skryabin, Szymanowski, Suk, and Vaughan Williams, while Nielsen, in his Symphony no. 4, 'The Inextinguishable', used the form to express 'the elemental Will of Life'.

KC

progression. In harmonic theory, the movement of one note to another or of one chord to another. The term is frequently encountered as 'cadential progression', describing typical ways of leading up to a cadence.

progressive jazz. The big-band jazz of the 1950s and 60s that moved into the modern-jazz and bop mode, typified by the music of Stan Kenton. The term is sometimes used as an alternative name for *modern jazz.

PGA

progressive rock. A style of rock music of the early 1970s with a tendency to eclecticism, producing compositions influenced by 'classical' music (see ART ROCK), 'folk' music (see FOLK ROCK), and jazz, and also encompassing heavy or *hard rock.

PW

Prokofiev, Sergey Sergeyevich (*b* Sontsovka, Ukraine, 11/23 April 1891; *d* Moscow, 5 March 1953). Russian composer. He was a true *enfant terrible*, reacting strongly to the heady atmosphere of Russian late Romanticism as soon as his own compositional style had acquired the strength and character to assert itself. During his late 20s and 30s he lived in the West, but he returned to the USSR in 1936 and remained there for the rest of his life, producing some of his best-known works.

1. The early years; 2. Years in the West; 3. The later years

1. The early years

As a child, Prokofiev studied privately with Glière. He then entered the St Petersburg Conservatory, where his principal teachers were Lyadov (harmony, counterpoint, and composition) and Rimsky-Korsakov (orchestration). Not unnaturally for a young man with such an iconoclastic spark, he found the lessons restrictive and preferred instead to ally himself with the avant-garde movement centred on the Evenings of Contemporary Music. He composed a number of exploratory solo piano pieces which spread alarm and incomprehension among the conservatives but which were hailed as fresh and progressive by the modernists: *Navazhdeniye* (*Suggestion diabolique*, 1908), the *Four Études* (1909), and *Sarkazmï* ('Sarcasms', 1912–14).

Prokofiev also made an impact on the wider St Petersburg public with his First Piano Concerto (1911–12), a work that echoes his own formidable pianistic skills and at the same time shows that even in his early works he possessed a keen sense of orchestral colour, a firm grasp of structure, and a pronounced lyrical gift; there is, too, that touch of devilment which seems to underlie so much of his music. This last trait is even more prominent in the Second Piano Concerto (1912–13, rev. 1923), which scandalized audiences and critics alike with its dissonant harmony, percussive, spiky piano writing, feverish activity, and its huge cadenza in the first movement.

Less noted at the time was Prokofiev's Classical vein, which reaches its apogee in the crisp First Symphony (the 'Classical', 1916–17), and a wistful lyricism, gaining the upper hand in such works as *Mimoletnosti* (*Visions fugitives*) for piano (1915–17) and the First Violin Concerto (1916–17). He also became interested in ballet, largely under the influence of Diaghilev, whom he met in London in 1914. Diaghilev commissioned Prokofiev to write *Ala i Lolli* (1914–15), and was later responsible for having *Chout* (*Skazka pro shuta*, 'The Tale of the Buffoon'; 1915, rev. 1920) performed in Paris and London (1921).

Many works from this period highlight those Prokofievian traits that have come to be called 'grotesque'—galumphing rhythms, growling basses, distorted melodic lines, and orchestral astringency. Prokofiev preferred to describe these facets as 'scherzolike', with those implications of burlesque and laughter which are perhaps best exemplified by his opera *Lyubov' k tryom apel'sinam* ('The Love for Three Oranges'), based on the play by the 18th-century Italian playwright Carlo Gozzi.

2. Years in the West

Although *The Love for Three Oranges* sharply reflects the satirical atmosphere prevalent in Russia during the 1920s, the score was in fact written abroad, for, following the outbreak of the October Revolution in 1917, Prokofiev left for what he thought would be a short recital tour of the USA, but found himself living first in New York and then in Paris. The theatre director Vsevolod Meyerhold had introduced him to Gozzi's play *L'amore delle tre melarance*, and Prokofiev read an adaptation of it as he sailed from Russia to America in 1918. The subject captivated him: the elements of the supernatural, the knockabout comedy, and the sheer absurdity of the story were ideally suited to his leg-pulling, snook-cocking mood of the moment, and they combined to inspire one of his most sparkling scores. He had already composed two substantial operas in Russia—*Maddalena* (1911–13, first performed on BBC Radio in 1979) and *Igrok* ('The Gambler', 1915–16, rev. 1927–8; performed Brussels, 1929)—but neither had yet been staged, and it was *The Love for Three Oranges*

(Chicago, 1921) that established Prokofiev as a composer with a sure feel for the theatre.

In fact the theatre was to be a constant fascination throughout his life. Even while waiting for *The Love for Three Oranges* to be produced, he began work on a very different project, *Ognenniy angel* ('The Fiery Angel', 1919–23, 1926–7), an opera about demonic possession and religious hysteria in 16th-century Germany; but it was not staged until 1954. It was entirely characteristic of Prokofiev that, with the score of *The Fiery Angel* lying unperformed on his desk, he should draw on material from it for his Third Symphony (1928); similarly, the Fourth Symphony (1929–30) was derived from the ballet *Bludniy sïn* ('The Prodigal Son'; Paris, 1929). While in the West he also completed the Third Piano Concerto (1917–21), using themes he had collected over a number of years, and rounded off his set of five concertos with the Fourth, for the left hand (1931, commissioned but not performed by the pianist Paul Wittgenstein, who professed not to understand a single note of it), and the five-movement Fifth (1931–2). These three concertos exude the familiar vivacity of his earlier music, but the textures are smoother, the harmonies less acerbic, the lyricism more relaxed.

3. The later years

These were to be important aspects of Prokofiev's later music. In 1927 he revisited the USSR and in 1936 he settled there. He achieved an early success with his witty music for the film *Poruchnik Kizhe* ('Lieutenant Kijé', 1934), a whimsical story which allowed him to draw on his gifts for memorable melody, strong rhythms, and gently mocking turns of phrase, setting them in his highly individual harmonic idiom, succulent yet pungently spiced. Prokofiev extracted from the music a suite of five numbers, which has rightly become one of his most frequently performed works. Similarly, several of his other works of the 1930s and 40s have gained a permanent place in the repertory: the ballets *Romeo and Juliet* (Brno, 1938) and *Zolushka* ('Cinderella'; Moscow, 1945), the tale for children *Petya i volk* ('Peter and the Wolf', 1936), the cantata he based on his film score *Alexander Nevsky* (1939), and his comic opera *Obrucheniye v monastïre* ('Betrothal in a Monastery', also known as *The Duenna*; Prague, 1946). He produced a number of firmly patriotic scores, and at the beginning of World War II began work on his epic opera *Voyna i mir* ('War and Peace', 1941–3, rev. 1946–52), after Tolstoy's novel. The war also coloured his Seventh Piano Sonata (1939–42) and the Eighth Sonata (1939–44), and inspired the Fifth Symphony (1944) and the broodingly pessimistic Sixth Symphony (1945–7).

The absence of jubilation in the Sixth Symphony undoubtedly contributed to the official feeling of dissatisfaction with Prokofiev's music, emphatically voiced during Andrey Zhdanov's purges of *formalism in 1948. However, unlike Shostakovich, Prokofiev no longer had the stamina to withstand Zhdanov's attacks: he had suffered a fall after conducting the premiere of the Fifth Symphony in 1945, and he never recovered. As a result his later music tends to show him relying on his old craftsmanship. Many of his later works, such as the ballet *Skaz o kamennom tsvetke* ('(Tale of) The Stone Flower'; Moscow, 1954) and the choral suite *Zimniy kostyor* ('Winter Bonfire', 1949–50), reveal a combination of natural compositional skill and a certain creative weariness. Others, especially the Cello Sonata (1949), the Symphony-Concerto for Cello and Orchestra (1950–2, based on material from the Cello Concerto no. 2, 1933–8), and the Seventh Symphony (1951–2), use apparent simplicity to express poignant emotion with great originality.

It was a sad irony that Prokofiev could not test the artistic climate after Stalin's death, for he died on the same day as Stalin. As a composer he stands none the less at the forefront of 20th-century Russian culture. In his early years he had set out purposefully to shock his public in music of flamboyance and hair-raising virtuosity, but in his 30s his musical style mellowed and he consolidated his reputation for ready tunefulness, rhythmic élan, instantly appealing charm, and alert humour, expressed with a zestful openness which has rendered much of his music enduringly popular.

GN/DN

📖 S. Shlifshteyn (ed.), *S. Prokofiev: Autobiography, Articles, Reminiscences* (Moscow, 1965) · V. Seroff, *Sergei Prokofiev: A Soviet Tragedy* (New York, 1968; London, 1969) · V. Blok (ed.), *Sergei Prokofiev: Materials, Articles, Interviews* (Moscow, 1978) · *Prokofiev by Prokofiev: A Composer's Memoir* (London, 1979) · H. Robinson, *Sergei Prokofiev: A Biography* (London, 1987) · O. Prokofiev (trans. and ed.), *Sergei Prokofiev: Soviet Diary 1927 and Other Writings* (London, 1991)

prolation (from medieval Lat. *prolatio*, 'bearing', 'manner'). In early musical notation the term usually referred to the relationship between the minim and the semibreve. If prolation was 'major' there would be three minims in the semibreve, if 'minor', two. More rarely, it could refer to the relation between any pair of note-values, for example the semibreve and breve (otherwise known as 'tempus'), or the breve and the long (otherwise known as 'modus'). These relationships could also be 'major' (triple) or 'minor' (duple).   AP

promenade concert. A type of concert offering programmes of mixed musical fare, ranging from classical works to popular ephemera, at low prices and in a relatively informal atmosphere (the space for the promenade allowing concert-goers the opportunity to move around). The idea was imported to Britain from France in the 1830s and became established with the concerts organized by Louis Jullien (1841–59). In 1895 a new series was inaugurated at the Queen's Hall under Henry *Wood which, transferred to the Royal Albert Hall after the destruction of the former in 1941, continues today. Under BBC management since 1927 (except for a brief wartime hiatus), the Proms have latterly taken on the character of a vast music festival, though retaining the commitment to range, quality, and reasonable prices established during Wood's time. Many new works are commissioned for the Proms each year. The second half of the last night has something of a carnival atmosphere: its content, which has varied little from year to year, involves audience participation (with much flag-waving) from the promenade arena. GH

 📖 D. Cox, *The Henry Wood Proms* (London, 1980)

Promethean chord. See MYSTIC CHORD.

Prometheus. Symphonic poem by Liszt, originally composed in 1850 and orchestrated by Raff as the overture to a setting of choruses from Johann Gottfried Herder's *Prometheus Unbound*; Liszt revised and rescored it in 1855.

Prometheus, Die Geschöpfe des. See GESCHÖPFE DES PROMETHEUS, DIE.

Prometheus, the Poem of Fire (*Prometey, poema ogyna*; *Prométhée, le poème du feu*). Symphonic poem, op. 60 (1909–10), by Skryabin, for orchestra with piano, optional chorus, and 'light-keyboard' (projecting colours on to a screen; see COLOUR AND MUSIC).

Proms. See PROMENADE CONCERT.

pronto (It.). 'Quick'; *prontamente*, 'quickly'.

Proper of the Mass. The sections of the Mass whose texts change according to the church calendar; see MASS, 1; PLAINCHANT, 1 and 4.

Prophète, Le ('The Prophet'). Opera in five acts by Meyerbeer to a libretto by Eugène Scribe (Paris, 1849).

Proprium missae (Lat.). The *Proper of the Mass.

prosa (Lat.), **prose** (Fr.). The medieval name for the text of a *sequence, applied also to the sequence with its melody or, occasionally, to *prosulas. —/ALı

Proses lyriques ('Lyrics in Prose'). Four songs (1892–3) by Debussy for voice and piano, settings of his own texts.

prosula (Lat.). Diminutive of *prosa, referring to the addition in medieval manuscripts of new words to the *melismas of offertories, alleluias, and other pre-existing chants of the Roman rite. See TROPE.

 —/ALı

Protecting Veil, The. Work (1987) for cello and strings by Tavener.

protest song. A subgenre of 'folksong', a term which itself sometimes refers to 'traditional' song, at other times to contemporary acoustic songs by modern singer-songwriters. A protest song is a 'folksong' in the latter sense, with politically directed lyrics. PW

protus. See MODE, 2.

Provenzale, Francesco (*b* Naples, *c*.1626; *d* Naples, 6 Sept. 1704). Italian composer. His name has often been associated with the beginnings of the so-called Neapolitan School of opera from about 1652. However, enormous problems with the attribution of his works over the next two decades make his precise contribution difficult to determine, although the quality of the two undisputed operas of the 1670s is undeniable. His influence was certainly strong through his important teaching posts at the conservatories of S. Maria di Loreto (1663–75) and S. Maria della Pietà dei Turchini until 1701, for which he composed sacred operas and religious works. He was *maestro di cappella* to the city of Naples from 1665 and *maestro* at the treasury of S. Gennaro from 1686 to 1699, when he was dismissed because his style was considered old-fashioned. Indeed, he had already been passed over for the young Alessandro Scarlatti as *maestro* to the royal court, but was retained as *maestro onorio*. PA

'Prussian' Quartets. Mozart's last three string quartets, no. 21 in D major K575 (1789), no. 22 in B♭ major K589 (1790), and no. 23 in F major K590 (1790), so called because they were commissioned by Friedrich Wilhelm II of Prussia, himself a cellist (hence the prominent cello parts). Haydn's six String Quartets op. 50 (1787) are also known by this title because of their dedication.

Ps. 1. (Ger.). Abbreviation for *Posaunen*, 'trombones'.
 2. Abbreviation for Psalm.

psalm (from Gk. *psalmos*). A sacred song of the type found in the Old Testament book of Psalms. Characteristic of the poetic form of the biblical psalms is their parallelistic structure, whereby each verse is separated into two halves by means of a central strong or weak caesura, the second half-verse complementing the first in a variety of ways (for example, by stating the same idea in a different way, by opposing a contrasting idea, by completing a statement, or by building an utterance to a climax).

The word *psalmos*, first applied to the ancient Hebrew verse by the translators responsible for the Septuagint (the Greek version of the Old Testament), means literally the striking or plucking of the strings of a musical instrument. It thus provides an indication, supported by numerous biblical and Talmudic references, that the Levites' performance of the psalms in the three Jewish Temples of Jerusalem involved instrumental accompaniment.

In addition to daily Proper psalms during the sacrifice, the Temple rites included such special categories of psalms as the Hallel (Psalms 113–18), sung at Passover), and the 'psalms of ascent (or degrees)' (Psalms 120–34), said to correspond to the 15 steps which led to the inner courtyard of the Temple.

BS/ALi

psalmody. The practice of singing psalms and other forms of chant in the Jewish and Christian traditions. The singing of the book of Psalms ascribed by tradition to David, together with similar psalmic texts, formed an important part of Jewish liturgical and paraliturgical observances at the Temple of Jerusalem. Little is known about their music, but contemporary and later sources indicate that Temple psalmody made use of instrumental accompaniment in solo, choral, and responsorial performances led by the Levites, a hereditary class of male musicians. Before the permanent cessation of Temple worship caused by the Roman sack of AD 70, psalmody does not appear to have been a characteristic feature of assemblies in the synagogue. At some time after the 4th century AD, the non-sacrificial forms of Jewish worship that arose within the context of the synagogue came to include purely vocal psalmody, with the absence of instruments generally being understood as a sign of mourning for the loss of the Temple. Never systematized, the psalmodic practices of the Jewish diaspora are extremely diverse and manifest varying degrees of relation to the musical traditions of surrounding Gentile cultures.

Substantial evidence for the liturgical singing of biblical psalms in Christian worship appears in the 3rd century, at which time two basic approaches may be discerned: urban Christians continued the Jewish tradition of singing thematically appropriate psalms at fixed times, while early monks adopted the sequential recitation of all 150 psalms as an aid to meditation. In the 4th century, the spiritual prestige of contemporary monasticism and the desire of Christian prelates to safeguard their congregations from doctrinally suspect 'privately composed psalms' (i.e. non-scriptural hymnography) precipitated the flooding of Christian

liturgy with psalmody. In place of the austere verse-by-verse (i.e. direct) recitation practised by the desert monks, urban Christians developed melodically interesting methods (syllabic, neumatic, and melismatic) of responsorial and antiphonal performance incorporating soloists, choirs, and congregations, the latter of whom were encouraged to participate in the repetition of a refrain (*ephymnion* or *aktroteleutaion*) after each verse.

Although elements of this so-called cathedral psalmody survive in several modern rites, late antique patterns of Christian psalmody were considerably modified during the Middle Ages. In part because of the monasticization of liturgy, the antiphonal character of many chants was obscured through the suppression of either their verses or the repetition of their refrains. This process was aided by the accretion of vast repertories of newly composed tropes and hymns. Certain psalmodic chants also became subject to purely musical elaboration, whether through polyphony (in the Latin West) or *kalophonia* (in the Byzantine East).

John Calvin's promotion of unaccompanied psalm-singing in Reformed worship led directly to the publication of such vernacular metrical paraphrases as the Geneva Psalter of 1562 and the Puritan *Bay Psalm Book* of 1640. A popular method of performing metrical psalmody in 17th-century England and America (which persisted until the 20th century in illiterate congregations) was the responsorial practice of 'lining out', in which a soloist would render each verse immediately before its performance by the congregation.

—/ALi

psalm tones. Plainchant recitation formulas for the psalms; see TONUS, 3.

Psalmus hungaricus. Work (1923) by Kodály for solo tenor, chorus, children's chorus ad libitum, orchestra and organ, a setting of a text from the 16th-century Hungarian poet Mihály Kecskeméti Vég's paraphrase of Psalm 55; it was composed for the 50th anniversary of the union of Buda and Pest.

psalter. A translation of the 150 Hebrew biblical psalms arranged for Christian liturgical or devotional use. Additional material found in certain psalters includes refrains used for antiphonal psalmody and appendices containing canticles or other sacred writings. Two major approaches to the division of the biblical text into 150 psalms may be distinguished: that of the Greek translation of the 3rd–2nd centuries BC, known as the Septuagint, from which all Latin liturgical psalters, including the Old Latin and Vulgate versions, were derived; and that of the Masoretic Hebrew text, finally established in the 6th–10th centuries AD, followed by most Protestant Bibles including the Authorized

Version. Psalm 9 in the Septuagint was divided into Psalms 9 and 10 by the Masoretes, while Septuagint Psalms 146 and 147 were combined as Hebrew Psalm 147; as a consequence all the psalms between 10 and 146 are, in the Masoretic numbering (used generally in this *Companion*), one digit higher than in the Septuagint. The Syriac numbering follows the Masoretic before combining Hebrew Psalms 114 and 115, after which it agrees with the Septuagint.

Early Christian monks adopted the book of Psalms in its entirety as their primary vehicle for prayer; this led eventually to the creation of various systems for its cyclical recitation within the context of common worship. Whereas primitive monastic vigils had featured the performance of all 150 psalms over the course of a single night, subsequent schemes distributed them throughout the Divine Office over a number of days.

The monks of 6th-century Rome recited the psalter once a week by dividing its psalms between the offices of Vespers, Vigils (Matins), and Lauds. The Rule of St Benedict reduced the variable psalmody allotted to these three services by removing psalms already sung at fixed points in the Divine Office from the continuous cycle, and by including the 'Little Hours' of the day in the scheme of distribution. In the Roman Catholic Church Benedict's system was—with occasional modifications, notably including those by Cardinal Quiñones, Pius V, and Pius X—universally used until 1971, when the psalter was spread over four weeks. Such an extended cycle had previously been implemented during the English Reformation by Cranmer, whose *Book of Common Prayer* distributed the psalter between the offices of Matins and Evensong over the course of a month. The Palestinian Psalter used in the worship of the modern Orthodox Church, however, continues to be recited weekly during most of the liturgical year. Its 20 large sections or *kathismata*, each of which is further divided into three *staseis*, are thus distributed between Vespers and Orthros in a cycle beginning on Saturday evening. Variable psalmody is added to the 'Little Hours' during Lent, allowing the psalter to be recited twice each week.

The Protestant Reformation and the invention of the printing press stimulated the proliferation of metrical translations of the psalter into modern languages. Although used most prominently by Calvinists for public worship, the domestic use of metrical psalters proved so popular that it spread even to Orthodox Russia.   ALi

psaltery. A *zither on which the strings are plucked, either by plectra or by the fingers (as opposed to being struck with hammers as on the *dulcimer). It consists of a flat box with strings, usually of wire, running across the upper surface and attached to pegs or pins at either side. They have been made in many shapes: triangular or trapeziform, 'pig's head' shape (a trapezium with concave 'cheeks', popularly known in Italy as *strumento di porco*), wing or harp-shaped, or rectangular. The double psaltery had two ranks of strings, one on either side of the soundbox. The medieval triangular psaltery was sometimes known as the 'rota' or 'rotte'.

The psaltery was widely used in Europe from the 10th or 11th century until about 1500, though the double psaltery survived during the Baroque era in parts of Germany and Italy. The *qānūn* of the Middle East, North Africa, Turkey, and some areas of Asia, also known since the 10th century, is still widely played; since the early 20th century it has often been equipped with the little levers that can be flicked up under the strings to raise their pitch microtonally. In Japan and Korea the bridges of the *koto and *kayagŭm are of such a height that depressing the string behind the bridge gives great flexibility of pitch.   JMo

psaume (Fr.). 'Psalm'.

psychedelic rock [psychedelia, acid rock]. A type of rock music associated with the hippie subculture during the 1960s and said to be intended to evoke or accompany use of the drug LSD ('acid')—whence, it is often claimed, the extended use of improvisation and the formlessness of the music. Among bands associated with it are Jefferson Airplane, the Grateful Dead, and the Byrds in the USA, and early Pink Floyd and late Beatles in the UK. The production of extended compositions paved the way for the development of *progressive rock.   KG

psychology of music. The study of the psychological basis of musical behaviour and experience. Such study has a long history, but its expansion is relatively recent and is illustrated by a growth in specialist journals (e.g. *Psychology of Music* (1973), *Music Perception* (1983), *Musicae scientiae* (1997)) and diversification into a number of sub-domains: cognitive psychology, developmental psychology, and social psychology. The subject is best described in terms of an intersection of the approaches and questions described under the headings that follow.

1. Perception and cognition; 2. Performance; 3. Development and ability; 4. Affect; 5. Social psychology

1. Perception and cognition

Since the 1970s the majority of research into cognition has been concerned with perception and memory for (Western tonal) music and has focused primarily on rhythm, pitch, and timbre. Research has advanced our understanding of processes that span seconds, but relatively little is known about the cognition of complete musical works.

The term 'psychoacoustics' is used to describe the sensory mechanisms responsible for our perception of pitch, loudness, and timbre. Research into the relationship between the physical and perceptual properties of sound reveals that they do not map on to one another directly. Listeners can detect extremely small differences in pitch and time, but they perceive pitch and rhythms categorically: variations slightly greater or smaller than the categorical pitch value are assimilated into it. A separate strand of research has revealed the role of 'auditory stream analysis'—the way in which auditory information from a single source is perceived as a single unit (Bregman, 1990).

Rhythm has been understood as the interaction of grouping and metre (Lerdahl and Jackendoff, 1983). A 'perceptual group' is formed by a set of events close to one another in time, delimited from other events by changes of register, timbre, articulation, or loudness, and absorbed hierarchically within higher groups. Metre is based on an underlying periodic beat, the perceived regularity of which resists minor deviations from strict regularity. Different metrical structures arise from the differing organization of pulses at each hierarchic level, but listeners are usually primarily aware of a single level (the 'tactus'). At structural levels that exceed the capacity of direct perception (and therefore require memory) listeners perceive form rather than rhythm.

Research into pitch perception highlights the roles of both psychoacoustic and cognitive factors. Psychoacoustic accounts suggest that perception of single pitches and chords as unitary entities, and of harmonic stability and instability, are a function of fundamental auditory processes (Parncutt, 1989). By contrast, cognitive approaches stress the role of schemata (mental models that organize information), using these to capture the multi-dimensional character of perceived pitch, chord, and key relationships demonstrated in experiments (Krumhansl, 1990). This cognitive-structural view of pitch cognition suggests that these relationships are learnt through experience and stored in long-term memory (as a 'tonal hierarchy') and that they contribute to, and are abstracted from, 'event hierarchies'—relationships of structural importance between events within specific pieces.

Timbre is understood in terms of a sound's acoustic characteristics (e.g. attack, brightness, etc.) and its perceptual source. Sensory attributes of timbre were first investigated through the relative strengths of frequency components within a sound (Helmholtz, 1954; Slawson, 1985); more recent research has revealed the importance of a number of additional perceptual dimensions: attack time, degree of change during the course of a sound, and degree of spectral irregularity. A second approach focuses on timbre as a vehicle for identifying a sound's source (McAdams, 1993). Source perception may enable listeners to follow voices within a polyphonic setting, but it may also hinder the perception of melodies across different instruments (as in *Klangfarbenmelodie*); this is the result of the fundamental principle that what listeners hear is primarily the physical origin of a sound.

2. Performance

Performance has been investigated from a number of viewpoints within the psychology of music: those of motor skill and coordination, musical development, music cognition, and performance anxiety (see Gabrielsson, 1999, for a review). Two central themes of this research are skill and expression.

Performance skill has been investigated mainly through the piano because it is the instrument for which efficient means of recording performance data have been developed. Among the areas that have been explored are timing and dynamics, coordination, fingering, and sight-reading. Expression has often been defined in terms of the performer's deliberate departures from the written score, though this definition raises many questions (Clarke, 1995). Research indicates that expression is not simply learnt as a pattern of timing and dynamics but is generated from musical structure: expression may be found in sight-read performances and can also be extremely consistent over performances repeated months or years apart, but it is possible, too, for it to be changed by a performer with relatively little practice. Studies based on the analysis of expressive performances suggest that expression is governed by a small number of simple rules (e.g. Todd, 1992) and that apparently idiosyncratic expressive performances of the same piece in fact have many features in common (Repp, 1992). The richness and complexity of real performances derive from the intricate nature of the musical structures to which expressive rules are applied.

Although this generative view of performance expression has been demonstrated as valid through extensive experimentation, other factors also play a role: acoustics, the physical properties of the instrument and the human body, emotion, the mood and intentions of the performer, and performance practice. Research into the role of the body in expressive performance (Davidson, 1993), the relationship with physical laws (Todd, 1992), and social aspects of performance counter the more abstract conceptions formulated in the light of research influenced by linguistic and computer models during the latter part of the 20th century.

3. Development and ability

The developmental psychology of music focuses on processes underlying age-related change in musical skills (e.g. Deliège and Sloboda, 1996). Change due to growth or development may be distinguished from that resulting from training, but there is evidence that the two interact such that training may be more effective at particular stages.

By the time children go to school they already have some facility in music through their environment and their experiences within it. Infants are exposed to music (and music-like sounds) in the home (for example through recordings, radio, and television), infant-directed speech, and play-songs and lullabies sung by adults. Adult speech and song provide infants with pleasurable musical interaction and a possible basis for their later engagement with music. The main method of research into music perception by infants involves observation of head-turning (the stock response to novel stimuli by which the infant shows awareness of their source). Such studies indicate that infants are sensitive to melodic contour, octaves, simple frequency ratios, and certain aspects of harmony; these results have led some investigators to conclude that biological predispositions rather than culture-specific learning are the main factor in infant music perception (Trehub, Schellenberg, and Hill, 1997). (See also CHILDREN AND MUSIC.)

Research beyond infancy focuses on changes in musical ability acquired through assimilation, training, and environment, rather than age. Within Western culture, high levels of performance skill are commonly attributed to innate 'talents', in spite of the absence of strong evidence of a genetic basis for musical ability (Howe, Davidson, and Sloboda, 1998). One of the best predictors of musical skill is the amount and type of instrumental practice in which a performer engages. Estimates of practice time and biographical accounts suggest that highly skilled performers have accumulated 10,000 hours of practice by the age of 21 (Ericsson, Krampe, and Tesch-Römer, 1993); this highlights the role played by motivation. Assessment of musical ability has been shown to be unreliable: for example, musically expert judges prove susceptible to such factors as gender and attractiveness (Landy and Sigall, 1974). Objective measures of musical ability have been attempted (Boyle and Radocy, 1987), but the use of standardized tests to predict musical aptitude has been largely unsuccessful.

4. Affect

The psychological basis of emotional responses to music has been investigated in terms of extrinsic ('designative' or 'associative') and intrinsic ('embodied') affect. Few studies have measured physiological responses directly (though see Krumhansl, 1997), most requiring listeners to identify and describe emotional and physiological responses.

One way in which music elicits a strong emotional response is by association with a particular context or event (often an occasion of strong emotion itself), a specific piece acting as a trigger for recall (Sloboda, 1991). The same mechanism can lead to common cultural experience of affect through the association of music with a shared context (such as a generation's identification with the music of its youth).

Research into the relationship between musical structure and emotional responses ('intrinsic' affect) has pursued two lines of inquiry: identifying a 'lexicon' of musical affect based on musical elements and parameters (e.g. Cooke, 1959; Hevner, 1936); and identifying emotional responses to syntactic properties of musical structure. The first response ('iconic') is explained in terms of energy levels or other characteristics shared by the musical structure and the emotion; some investigators have highlighted similarities to bodily expressions of emotion (Scherer, 1991). The second arises from an understanding of musical structure that is acquired both through innate perceptual processes and as a result of learnt stylistic norms (Meyer, 1956). Listeners experience strong emotional reactions to music at moments associated with expectancy, and specific kinds of physiological response have been found to be associated with particular kinds of syntactic features (Sloboda, 1991). Contextual factors, such as an accompanying text, visual material, or discourse, may also provide a basis for emotional experiences of music (Cook and Dibben, 2001).

5. Social psychology

The social psychology of music investigates the reciprocal influence of individuals and their social contexts. Although some research into this subject was carried out in the mid-20th century (e.g. Farnsworth, 1954), it was not until the end of the century that social psychological approaches were established (Hargreaves and North, 1997). Central areas of investigation are musical preference, music and consumer behaviour, music education, medical and therapeutic uses of music, and occupational studies.

Research into musical preference focuses on musical structures and social context. People's preference for music has been shown to be influenced by complexity mediated by familiarity, but it is dependent on the level of arousal appropriate at a particular time (e.g. fast music while exercising vigorously, slower while warming up and ending), as well as such other features as style and appropriateness of music to the setting.

Musical taste is also closely related to demographics: socio-economic status and occupation, age, and gender have received most attention. Musical tastes reinforce social distinctions and contribute to the construction and expression of identity. Less research has been conducted into social influences on taste (e.g. education, peers, and the media), but it seems that individuals are susceptible to the wish to conform, their expressed preferences changing according to the perceived eminence of a composer or a performer.

Another area of investigation is the psychological basis for the use of music in commercial settings (North and Hargreaves, 1997). Its effectiveness in advertising may be the indirect result of a pleasurable response that is transferred to the product and associated subconsciously with its characteristics. Music also affects consumer behaviour, influencing the choice of product, the time spent in shops, and the quantity of purchases. Other research into the commercial uses of music has included study of the influence of telephonically transmitted music on callers' perception of the time they spend waiting for an answer, and of the effects of music on productivity and morale in the workplace (see also MUZAK). Investigation of music's therapeutic qualities (see MUSIC THERAPY) focuses on its use in clinical settings and the influence of musical activity on other cognitive domains (the 'Mozart effect'), research into which draws on neuropsychological studies of music and the brain (Marin and Perry, 1999).   ND

📖 K. HEVNER, 'Experimental studies of the elements of expression in music', *American Journal of Psychology*, 48 (1936), 246–68 · H. VON HELMHOLTZ, *On the Sensations of Tone as a Physiological Basis for the Theory of Music* (Eng. trans., New York, 1954) · L. B. MEYER, *Emotion and Meaning in Music* (Chicago, 1956) · P. R. FARNSWORTH, *The Social Psychology of Music* (New York, 1958) · D. COOKE, *The Language of Music* (Oxford, 1959) · D. LANDY and H. SIGALL, 'Beauty is talent: Task evaluation as a function of the performer's physical attractiveness', *Journal of Personality and Social Psychology*, 29 (1974), 299–304 · F. LERDAHL and R. JACKENDOFF, *A Generative Theory of Tonal Music* (Cambridge, MA, 1983) · W. J. DOWLING and D. L. HARWOOD, *Music Cognition* (Orlando, FL, 1985) · W. SLAWSON, *Sound Color* (Berkeley, CA, 1985) · J. A. SLOBODA, *The Musical Mind* (Oxford, 1985)

D. J. HARGREAVES, *The Developmental Psychology of Music* (Cambridge, 1986) · J. D. BOYLE and R. E. RADOCY, *Measurement and Evaluation of Musical Experiences* (New York, 1987) · R. PARNCUTT, *Harmony: A Psychoacoustical Approach* (Berlin, 1989) · A. S. BREGMAN, *Auditory Scene Analysis: The Perceptual Organisation of Sound* (Cambridge, MA, 1990) · C. L. KRUMHANSL, *Cognitive Foundations of Musical Pitch* (Oxford, 1990) · K. R. SCHERER, 'Emotion expression in speech and music', *Music, Language, Speech and Brain*, ed. J. Sundberg, L. Nord, and R. Carlsons (London, 1991) · J. A. SLOBODA, 'Music structure and emotional

response to music: Some empirical findings', *Psychology of Music*, 19 (1991), 110–20 · B. H. REPP, 'Diversity and commonality in music performance: An analysis of timing microstructure in Schumann's "Träumerei"', *Journal of the Acoustical Society of America*, 92 (1992), 2546–68 · N. P. M. TODD, 'The dynamics of dynamics: A model of musical expression', *Journal of the Acoustical Society of America*, 91 (1992), 3540–50

J. W. DAVIDSON, 'Visual perception of performance manner in the movements of solo musicians', *Psychology of Music*, 21 (1993), 103–13 · K. A. ERICSSON, R. T. KRAMPE, and C. TESCH-RÖMER, 'The role of deliberate practice in the acquisition of expert performance', *Psychological Review*, 100 (1993), 363–406 · S. MCADAMS, 'The recognition of sound sources and events', *Thinking in Sound: The Cognitive Psychology of Human Audition*, ed. S. McAdams and E. Bigand (Oxford, 1993) · E. F. CLARKE, 'Expression in performance: generativity, perception, semiosis', *The Practice of Performance*, ed. J. Rink (Cambridge, 1995) · I. DELIÈGE and J. A. SLOBODA (eds.), *Musical Beginnings: Origins and Development of Musical Competence* (Oxford, 1996) · D. J. HARGREAVES and A. C. NORTH (eds.), *The Social Psychology of Music* (Oxford, 1997)

C. L. KRUMHANSL, 'An exploratory study of musical emotions and psychophysiology', *Canadian Journal of Experimental Psychology*, 51 (1997), 336–53 · A. C. NORTH and D. J. HARGREAVES, 'Music and consumer behaviour', *The Social Psychology of Music* (Oxford, 1997) · S. E. TREHUB, E. G. SCHELLENBERG, and D. HILL, 'The origins of music perception and cognition: A developmental perspective', *Perception and Cognition of Music*, ed. I. Deliège and J. Sloboda (Hove, 1997) · M. J. A. HOWE, J. W. DAVIDSON, and J. A. SLOBODA, 'Innate talents: Reality or myth?', *Behavioral and Brain Sciences*, 21 (1998), 399–442 · A. GABRIELSSON, 'Music performance', *The Psychology of Music*, ed. D. Deutsch (London, 2/1999) · O. S. M. MARIN and D. W. PERRY, 'Neurological aspects of music perception and performance', *ibid.* · N. COOK and N. DIBBEN, 'Musicological perspectives', *Music and Emotion: Theory and Research*, ed. P. Juslin and J. A. Sloboda (Oxford, 2001)

Ptaszyńska, Marta (*b* Warsaw, 29 July 1943). Polish composer and percussionist. Since 1974 she has lived in the USA. Much of her early music sprang from her experience as a professional percussionist, including *Jeu-parti* (1970), *Siderals* (1974), and *Dream Lands, Magic Spaces* (1978). Her idiom blends lyricism and delicate colours with a sure sense of structural momentum. She has also written orchestral music (Marimba Concerto, 1985), vocal music (*Holocaust Memorial Cantata*, 1992), and music for the stage.   ATh

publishing. See PRINTING AND PUBLISHING OF MUSIC.

Puccini, Giacomo (*see page 1014*)

Pugnani, (Giulio) **Gaetano** (Gerolamo) (*b* Turin, 27 Nov. 1731; *d* Turin, 15 July 1798). Italian violinist and composer. He played in the Turin court orchestra, 1741–67, though during this time he visited Rome (1749–50) and
(*cont. on p. 1015*)

Giacomo Puccini
(1858–1924)

The Italian composer Giacomo Antonio Domenico Michele Secondo Maria Puccini was born in Lucca on 22 December 1858 and died in Brussels on 29 November 1924.

Puccini was the greatest of the 'Giovane Scuola' of the late 19th and early 20th centuries and the last of his countrymen to write operas that form the staple of the international repertory. He was born of a long line of musicians who had lived in the Tuscan city of Lucca since the early 18th century. His father, Michele, was a respected figure in the community—organist and choirmaster of the Cathedral of S. Martino, director of the Istituto Pacini (the city's music school), and a prolific if undistinguished composer—who died in 1864 leaving a large family poorly provided for. His widow, Albina, was determined that Giacomo should continue the family's musical tradition. Accordingly, after lessons in singing and organ playing from an uncle he was enrolled in the Istituto Pacini, from where he graduated in 1880 with a mass known today as the *Messa di Gloria*. A grant from Queen Margherita combined with a generous subsidy from a wealthy cousin enabled him to proceed to the Milan Conservatory, where his teachers were Ponchielli and Bazzini and his fellow students included Mascagni. By the time he left he had written two symphonic preludes, a number of liturgical settings, and a *Capriccio sinfonico*, his passing-out piece, which won high critical acclaim.

Even during these student days—it is often suggested that a key event was a performance of Verdi's *Aida* in Florence in 1876—Puccini had determined that opera was his true métier. In 1883 he entered *Le Villi* for a competition for a one-act opera organized by the publisher Sonzogno. His score was rejected because of its illegibility; but a number of influential friends believed in its merit sufficiently to mount a performance at the Teatro Dal Verme in Milan. This brought the composer to the notice of the publisher Giulio Ricordi and convinced him that here at last was Verdi's true successor. His firm provided Puccini with a modest retainer to enable him to compose in relative comfort; and after the comparative failure of his next opera, *Edgar* (1889), Ricordi saw his confidence in the young man justified by the triumph of *Manon Lescaut* at Turin in 1893. From then on Puccini's fortune was assured. He

settled at Torre del Lago, where he built his own villa (now the Villa Puccini); there he could work undisturbed, though his rate of production was considerably slowed by trips at home and abroad for premieres or prestigious revivals of his operas. Only in his last few years did he move to nearby Viareggio.

Puccini was at the best of times a slow worker, hard to please in the matter of subject and libretto, continually taking up projects only to abandon them. As librettists, Ricordi found for him the accomplished team of Luigi Illica and Giuseppe Giacosa. The fruits of their collaboration were *La bohème* (1896), based on Henry Murger's stories of impoverished Parisian artists; *Tosca* (1900), a version of Victorien Sardou's drama of that name; and *Madama Butterfly* (1904), taken from a play by David Belasco. All would become favourites worldwide, though the last was badly received at its premiere.

In 1904 Puccini married the recently widowed Elvira Gemignani, with whom he had lived since 1886 and who had already borne him a son. It was not a happy union. Puccini was frequently unfaithful; Elvira grew jealous and embittered, eventually driving to suicide a former maidservant of theirs, whose innocence was proved by a subsequent autopsy. The resultant legal proceedings and scandal, though followed by reconciliation, held up the composition of *La fanciulla del West* (1910), another Belasco subject, given its premiere in New York.

The years of World War I were fruitful for Puccini, though he was criticized for showing insufficient patriotism—witness *La rondine* (1917), originally a Viennese commission and first performed in Monte Carlo. During this time he also worked on the trio of one-act operas entitled *Il trittico*: *Il tabarro*, based on a Grand Guignol story by Didier Gold; and *Suor Angelica* and the comic *Gianni Schicchi*, both brainchildren of the librettist Giovacchino Forzano. In the aftermath of the war only New York possessed the necessary resources for the premiere, which took place in the composer's absence in December 1918. Of his final opera

Turandot, based on a *fiaba* by Carlo Gozzi, Puccini completed all but the final duet. He died while undergoing treatment for cancer of the throat in a Brussels clinic.

In style Puccini belongs to the generation of so-called *verismo composers; nor was it mere chance that he first found his individual voice after Mascagni's *Cavalleria rusticana* had established the new tradition. He alone, however, possessed the power of self-renewal. Partly this is a matter of large-scale control. In his mature operas, each act tends to define itself by means of an individual structure, one that has its own rhythm and—above all—its own particular atmosphere. In part these structures are articulated through a highly personal use of recurring motifs, ones that can rarely be pinned down to a fixed 'meaning' (in the classic manner of Wagnerian leitmotifs), but that are often important in defining new episodes in the drama (the opening motif of *La bohème* is a famous example, as is that which begins *Tosca*). But in each act there will also be opportunities for the finite, self-contained melody, ones that typically use every means, both orchestral and vocal, to ensure a maximum identification with the character or characters.

Puccini's interest in the modern music of his day, especially Debussy's, undoubtedly fertilized his mature style. His operas symbolize the 'Italietta' of his day, concerned as they are for the most part with personal emotions and scene-painting, without extensive reference to wider issues (the political overtones of Sardou's *Tosca* are consistently played down in the opera). But his supreme mastery of the operatic craft, his melodic gift, and his emotional sincerity combine to keep his operas as freshly alive today as when they were written. The intense sadness that permeates so much of his music reflects his own temperament. For beneath the successful composer with his penchant for blood sports, fast cars, and women was a lonely and sensitive man. While he was typically regarded during much of the 20th century as an essentially conservative figure, perhaps even an appendage to the great 19th-century tradition of Italian opera, there are now signs that his highly individual approach to musical drama could equally be seen as an important contribution to the modernist dramatic tradition, to be assessed on the same level as such self-styled 'avant-garde' composers as Schoenberg, Stravinsky, and Bartók.   JB/RP

📖 G. ADAMI (ed.), *Giacomo Puccini: Epistolario* (Milan, 1828; Eng. trans. 1931, 2/1974) · V. SELIGMAN, *Puccini among Friends* (London, 1938) · L. MARCHETTI (ed.), *Puccini nelle immagini* (Milan, 1949) · M. CARNER, *Puccini: A Critical Biography* (London, 1958, 3/1992) · E. GARA (ed.), *Carteggi pucciniani* (Milan, 1958) · W. ASHBROOK, *The Operas of Puccini* (London and New York, 1968) · W. WEAVER, *Puccini: The Man and his Music* (New York, 1977) · M. GIRARDI, *Puccini: His International Art* (Chicago, 2000)

Paris (1754). In 1767 he went to London as conductor at the King's Theatre; after two years he returned to Turin, where he held several important appointments. He made further concert tours in the 1780s and 90s. Pugnani wrote a large number of operas, symphonies, and chamber music—though the Praeludium and Allegro in E minor for violin once attributed to him is in fact the work of its 'editor', Kreisler. Viotti was one of Pugnani's pupils.   DA/RP

puirt-a-beul (Gaelic) [mouth music]. A term used in the folk music of the Scottish Highlands to denote vocal performance to accompany the many different types of Highland dance, *puirt* meaning 'tunes for a musical instrument', and *beul*, 'mouth'. More often performed now as a vocal solo without dance, *puirt-a-beul* mixes meaningless vocables and words with personal and topical references, and may involve complex rhythmic patterns not otherwise found in dance melodies.
          KC

Pulcinella. Ballet with song in one act by Stravinsky to a scenario by Leonid Massine, who choreographed it for Diaghilev's Ballets Russes with designs by Pablo Picasso (Paris, 1920); for soprano, tenor, bass, and chamber orchestra, it is an adaptation of works by Pergolesi or formerly attributed to him. Stravinsky made a suite from it for chamber orchestra (*c*.1922, revised 1947). His *Suite italienne* (1932) is also arranged from *Pulcinella*; he collaborated with Piatigorsky in a five-movement version for cello and piano and with Samuel Dushkin in a six-movement one for violin and piano.

pulse. A term sometimes used as a synonym for 'beat', but a distinction is occasionally made: for example, 6/8 time may be said to have six 'pulses' but only two 'beats'.

Punch and Judy. Opera ('tragicomedy or comitragedy') in one act by Birtwistle to a libretto by Stephen Pruslin (Aldeburgh, 1968).

punctum (Lat., 'point'). A dot used in some forms of early mensural notation at either side of a group of notes having the total value of a breve; see DOT, 2.

punk rock. A movement in rock music concerned chiefly with an aggressive style of presentation and a strident advocacy of musical 'incompetence'. Proclaimed by many critics a corrective to the 'excesses' of *art rock, the 'incompetence' was largely marketing rhetoric, since punk was characterized by experimentalism (see also NEW WAVE) rather than anti-elitism, though its experiments were within conventional rock musical structures. The movement was first associated with the Sex Pistols (1975); other punk bands include the Stranglers, the Gang of Four, the Fall, Siouxsie and the Banshees, the Damned, the Rezillos and the Clash.

An abiding innovation of punk is the 'wall of sound' produced by repeated guitar strumming. Siouxsie and the Banshees often displayed unusual chromatic and modal experimentation. Identification with blacks led to the use of jazz, soul, and reggae (by the Clash, the Slits, the Police). A lasting legacy of punk was the foundation of independent (*indie) record labels which broke the monopoly hitherto enjoyed by a few large companies.   PW

punta, punto (It.). 'Point'; *a punta d'arco*, 'with the tip (point) of the bow'.

punteado (Sp.). A term used mainly with reference to Baroque guitar technique, denoting the 'plucking' of individual strings with the fingertips, as distinct from *rasgueado*, or strumming.   DMi

Purcell. English family of musicians. The exact relationships of its members are the subject of dispute, particularly whether Henry Purcell (ii) was the son of Henry (i) or of Thomas. The evidence suggests that **Henry Purcell** (i) (? *bapt.* Windsor, 5 Aug. 1624; *d* London, 11 Aug. 1664) and **Thomas Purcell** (? *bapt.* Windsor, 25 Feb. 1627; *d* London, 31 July 1682) were brothers. Both became Gentlemen of the Chapel Royal at the Restoration, and Henry was also admitted as a singing man and Master of the Choristers at Westminster Abbey. At the Restoration Charles II had recommended Thomas to be one of his Grooms for the Robes, a position of great trust. Within 12 years he had also acquired six more places at court as singer or composer. He was thus well placed to give every assistance to young Henry, whose life and work are detailed separately below.

   Daniel Purcell (*d* London, *bur.* 26 Nov. 1717), a composer and musician, was the younger brother of Henry Purcell (ii); like him, he was a chorister in the Chapel Royal. From 1688 to 1696 he was organist at Magdalen College, Oxford, and later played at St Dunstan in the East and St Andrew, Holborn (where he is buried). He succeeded his elder brother as one of the principal composers of the London theatres, writing music for about 40 plays. In 1701 he came third in a competition for a masque to Congreve's words, *The Judgement of Paris*. He composed a number of odes, in the choruses of which his brother's contrapuntal skill is

noticeably lacking, though the solos are competent enough. He also wrote some agreeable sonatas for violin and for flute.   DA/AA

Purcell, Henry (*see opposite page*)

Puritani di Scozia, I ('The Puritans'). Opera in three parts by Bellini to a libretto by Carlo Pepoli after the play by François Ancelot and Xavier (J. X. Boniface *dit* Saintine) *Têtes Rondes et Cavaliers*, itself derived from Walter Scott's *Old Mortality* (Paris, 1835).

Putnam's Camp. Second movement of Ives's First Orchestral Set, *Three Places in New England*; it was composed in *c.*1914–15 and is sometimes performed separately.

puy (Fr.). A name given to medieval French musical or literary societies, or guilds, that flourished in northern France up to the early 17th century. Their roots sprang from the *troubadour tradition, and they held annual song or poetry competitions (also known as *puys*) originally dedicated to the Virgin Mary; one at Évreux, founded about 1570, was held in honour of St *Cecilia. The contestants stood on a raised dais (Lat.: *podium*) to sing or recite, and it is thought that the name *puy* derives from this, rather than from the geographical formations of the Massif Central after which such towns as Le Puy are named. The winner of the competition was crowned 'Prince du Puy'. The song contest in Wagner's opera *Die Meistersinger von Nürnberg* probably reflects the existence of a similar tradition among the German *Meistersinger.

Pygmalion. See PIGMALION.

Pygott, Richard (*b c.*1485; *d* Oct. or Nov. 1549). English church musician and composer. He was Master of the Choristers to the household chapel of Cardinal Thomas Wolsey, a choir that was said to rival that of the Chapel Royal in quality. After Wolsey's death he joined the Chapel Royal as a Gentleman. A Mass and several antiphons by him survive, but he is best known for his exquisite carol *Quid petis, O fili?*   JM

Pythagorean intonation. A system of tuning in which the 4ths and 5ths are untempered. It is named after the Ancient Greek philosopher Pythagoras, whose calculations of intervals in terms of string-length ratios (octave = 2:1, 5th = 3:2, etc.; see MONOCHORD) formed the basis of much medieval and Renaissance theory. A distinguishing feature of Pythagorean intonation is that the major 2nds and 3rds are larger, and the minor 2nds and 3rds smaller, than those of other tuning systems. The expressive quality of the 2nds in particular has led to the judgment that this system of tuning is especially well suited to late medieval polyphony.

(*cont. on p. 1019*)

Henry Purcell
(1659–95)

The English composer Henry Purcell was born in Westminster in autumn 1659 and died in Westminster on 21 November 1695.

Purcell was the second musician in his family to be named Henry. There is some doubt concerning the precise relationships between the family members, and whether the younger Henry was the son of Henry Purcell (i) (1624–64) and his wife Elizabeth or of Thomas Purcell (1627–82) has not been established (see PURCELL). If he was the son of Henry (i) he was aged only four when his father died and certainly owed his musical upbringing to Thomas. He became a Child of the Chapel Royal, following in the footsteps of Blow and Humfrey, both of whom may have taught him. He proved from the start to be exceptionally gifted, composing songs at the age of eight. He left the choir when his voice broke in 1673 but was kept at court as assistant to John Hingston as tuner of keyboard and wind instruments (Hingston's will, dated 1683, records that he was godfather to a 'Henry Pursall, son of Elizabeth', suggesting that Henry (i) was indeed the father of Henry (ii)). During the next few years Purcell tuned the organs and copied music for Westminster Abbey, until in 1677, at the death of Matthew Locke, he was appointed composer for the violins. Two years later John Blow resigned as organist of Westminster Abbey and Purcell took his place.

His first mature anthems and songs date from about 1676. In 1680, perhaps as much for compositional training as for performance, he wrote a series of viol consorts that show a complete mastery of the old English polyphonic art. Fantasias in three parts owe much to Gibbons and Jenkins, while those in four are structurally closer to examples by Locke. However, Purcell explores such contrapuntal devices, avoided by Locke but common in earlier fantasias, as inversion and augmentation. He even revives the defunct *In nomine* form in six and seven parts—the most archaic pieces in the group. There are also some single pavans. These consorts show a rich vein of imagination, contrasting polyphony with homophony, and simple diatonic with chromatic passages, so that the contrapuntal devices act as a backdrop to the expression of intimate, fluctuating emotions. The same depth of feeling and imagination can be found in the full anthems of this period, such works as *Hear my prayer, O Lord* and *Remember not, Lord, our offences* also stemming from Elizabethan polyphony, with its clashing harmonies and (to us) strange turns of phrase.

Purcell married Frances Peters or Pieters probably in the autumn of 1680, and in 1682 was appointed one of the organists to the Chapel Royal. The following year a set of 12 trio sonatas was published; according to the preface they were written after the manner of 'fam'd Italian masters'—meaning Cazzati and Colista rather than Corelli. The format is indeed Italian, falling into several movements, as is the trio texture with continuo, in contrast with the equal-voiced fullness of the fantasias. The style, however, is by no means wholly Italianate: the second movements (sometimes marked 'canzona') especially show Purcell's gift for old-fashioned counterpoint.

Also in 1683 Purcell took up the full post of tuner at court following the death of Hingston. Together with John Blow, he supported Bernard Smith against Renatus Harris in the competition to supply an organ for the Temple Church (1684–8); they were successful. During the 1680s in particular, Purcell's energies were devoted to the verse anthem, especially those written for the Chapel Royal with parts for a string band to play overtures and ritornellos. Thomas Tudway remarked that after his accession Charles II was soon 'tyr'd wth the Grave & Solemn way, And Order'd the Composers of his Chappell, to add Symphonys &c wth Instruments to their Anthems'. The support of wind instruments which had been traditional in the Chapel Royal gave way to a string ensemble. The solo sections of these anthems contain arioso writing, with virtuoso decorations to highlight individual words or phrases (those composed for the bass John Gostling—such as *They that go down to the sea in ships* and *I will give thanks unto thee, O Lord*—are especially spectacular). The choral writing tends to be sonorously homophonic rather than contrapuntal, reflecting the monarch's French tastes, but undeniably effective for the Chapel Royal.

Nevertheless, in some of the 'Gloria' sections of his canticles Purcell indulges in ingenious canonic writing, inspired it seems by earlier examples by Child and Blow.

One distinctly English genre that flourished after the Restoration was the court *ode. Odes celebrated New Year and royal birthdays, or were 'welcome songs' performed when the monarch returned to London. Cooke, Humfrey, and Blow had led the way before Purcell wrote his first 'welcome song' in September 1680, on the return of Charles II from Windsor. Other welcome songs by him followed annually until 1689, together with an ode for the marriage of Prince George of Denmark to Princess Anne on 28 July 1683. The texts of these occasional pieces are naturally sycophantic and of mixed quality, but they do provide a wide range of opportunities for musical illustration. Short and constantly changing sections in the earliest examples soon gave way to sequences of longer movements. The presence of expert French recorder and oboe players at court encouraged the provision of solo parts for these instruments. To a prevailing dance idiom (perhaps even involving dancers in performance) was later added an increased use of counterpoint in the choruses. Another important feature of the odes (and also found among the solo songs) was the *ground bass, showing Purcell's exceptional flair for avoiding monotony and increasing tension by making the phrase ends of melody and bass overlap. Those in the odes are often based on a lively quaver pattern in the ground.

Purcell also wrote many songs for publications by Playford and others. They vary from simple strophic tunes and straightforward rondo forms to dramatic cantatas of the kind known in England from the works of Rossi and Carissimi, which were then circulating in copies. Many of these songs are settings of trivial verse, but devotional pieces, such as the setting of Fuller's *Now that the sun hath veiled his light*, match the seriousness of the verse in fine music.

Purcell contributed the magnificent anthem *My heart is inditing* to James II's coronation in 1685. The new reign brought substantial changes to the court establishment. The Chapel Royal was virtually sidelined when James established his own Catholic Chapel—served mainly by foreign musicians, although the Anglican Chapel continued to be patronized by Princess (later Queen) Anne. Furthermore the whole musical establishment was reorganized and reduced in size; Purcell was sworn as 'Harpsicall' in the new group. Through an oversight his tuner's place had been omitted and he had to petition for it—and was eventually granted arrears and a salary from Christmas 1687.

On the whole Purcell had written little for the public theatre during the 1680s, since his first contribution to Nathaniel Lee's *Theodosius* in 1680, but in 1688 he contributed seven songs and a duet to D'Urfey's *A Fool's Preferment*. One or two isolated songs were composed for other productions around this time. The context of his short opera *Dido and Aeneas* is the subject of much debate. Certainly it was performed at Josias Priest's School for Young Ladies in Chelsea in 1689, even though many male singers are required. The discovery in 1989 that John Blow's *Venus and Adonis*, hitherto known only to have been performed at court about 1682, was also performed at Priest's school in 1684 now raises the question of whether Purcell's work too was originally first given at court. Charles II was certainly interested in operatic developments in France and Italy: he sent his Master of Music, Nicholas Staggins, to both countries to study, gave him an allowance to be paid to the French and Italian musicians at court, and supported efforts to establish an opera company in England. He might well have encouraged opera performances at court.

Unfortunately the only sources surviving for *Dido* date from 1775 or later, apart from the 1689 text of the version performed at Priest's school. Differences between them suggest that some of the music is missing, particularly the prologue. Both *Venus and Adonis* and *Dido* are set to music throughout—a device not usual in English theatres—and share many structural features: a prologue and three acts, soprano and baritone leads, and much involvement for chorus and dancers. The last—familiar elements in the French style—were perhaps influenced by a performance of Lully's *Cadmus* that may have been given in London in 1686, but are equally evident in Locke's *Psyche* of 1675. There are also Italian elements—notably the chromatic ground of the final lament, 'When I am laid in earth', and the declamatory vocal writing generally. The pace of both works is rapid, but Purcell neatly gives each act a distinctive key-centre to help unify it. He also adds splendid ground-bass movements to the design. *Dido* is a masterpiece, and its last scene is one of the greatest in opera.

The accession of William III in 1689 effectively marked the end of court patronage as the chief pinnacle to which a musician could aspire. Although a music establishment was retained, the king seems to have had little regard for it, preferring martial expeditions. A decree was issued that Chapel Royal anthems were no longer to incorporate string symphonies. In spite of the king's indifference, musicians continued to serve the arts-loving Queen Mary and Purcell wrote some fine birthday odes for her, including *Come ye sons of art away* of 1694, with its countertenor duet 'Sound the trumpet' set to one of those straightforward, memorable tunes typical of the composer. Again by an oversight the 'Vocall Musick' (to which Purcell seems to have acted as accompanist) received no official listing (or payment); they petitioned for arrears in 1693 but the matter was 'to bee respited till the establishment is altered'. Not surprisingly Purcell turned his attention to other activities.

In his later years he contributed a good deal of music for the amateur musician, including published versions of some of his songs and simple arrangements of his music for keyboard. He also is known to have taught several pupils, including the composer John Weldon, and contributed extensively to the 1694 edition of Playford's instruction book *An Introduction to the Skill of Musick*. But dominating his last five years was his work for the theatre, satisfying the demand for music in plays and 'semi-operas'. Between 1690 and 1695 he contributed to more than 40 theatre works, the music varying from single numbers to lengthy suites of dances. His operatic ventures include four extensive examples: *Dioclesian* (1690), *King Arthur* (1691), *The Fairy Queen* (1692), and *The Indian Queen* (1695).

These works, known as *semi-operas, are part speech and part music and include all kinds of pieces—French overtures, dances, and songs—some separate and others forming long scenes in which Purcell shows a distinct sense of character and situation. The continuous sections generally occur at the close of acts and frequently accompanied elaborate scenic effects. They might be separate masques or entertainments within the main plot, or develop some ceremonial ritual arising from it. The 'Cold' scene in *King Arthur*, with its descriptive music for chattering teeth, is a masterly evocation of atmosphere; the flirtation duet of Corydon and Mopsa in *The Fairy Queen* and the pub song of the rustics in *King Arthur* are both delightfully humorous; the chromatic writing for the invocation of the magician Ismeron in *The Indian Queen* shows Purcell at his imaginative greatest; while popular tunes such as 'Fairest isle' and 'Come if you dare' from *King Arthur* can still stir the patriotic heart.

The more austere attitudes of William III's reign (1689–1702) may account for the relative lack of church music from Purcell's last years. The *Te Deum and Jubilate* in D are bright rather than profound ceremonial pieces, with their use of trumpets and strings; they were composed for the St Cecilia's Day celebrations of 1694 and remained in favour for the annual festival for many years. Trumpets became a fixture in Purcell's orchestra from 1690, perhaps in part because of the skill of the Shore family, and John Shore in particular. As well as the queen's birthday odes of the 1690s, there was also Purcell's splendid *Hail, bright Cecilia*, written for the London St Cecilia's Day celebration of 1692, in which the composer takes the opportunity to illustrate the musical references in Brady's text (the 'box and fir' turn out to be the recorder and the violin).

Purcell provided the music for Queen Mary's funeral in 1694. The following year he himself died, and some of it was used again at his funeral in Westminster Abbey, on 26 November, attended by the choirs of the abbey and the Chapel Royal. Several volumes of his music were published after his death, including a further set of ten trio sonatas in 1697 (but composed in the 1680s) and some collections of songs.

Although Purcell was recognized as a genius in his own lifetime, his music was subsequently neglected and was not revived until the later 19th century, when a collected edition (completed in 1965) was begun in 1878. In spite of renewed interest generated by the tercentenary celebrations of 1995, and increasing availability of recorded performances, only a fraction of his music remains widely known, and there are many riches to be found among the little-performed songs, odes, and church music. As with Mozart and Schubert, Purcell's early death was the greater tragedy because there are signs that he was still ripening as a composer. DA/AA

📖 J. A. WESTRUP, *Purcell* (London, 1937; new edn, rev. C. A. Price, 1995) · P. HOLMAN, *Henry Purcell* (Oxford, 1994) · M. BURDEN, *Purcell Remembered* (London, 1995) · M. BURDEN (ed.), *The Purcell Companion* (London, 1995) · C. A. PRICE (ed.), *Purcell Studies* (Cambridge, 1995)

Such sources as the Robertsbridge Codex (British Library Add. 28550) show that fully chromatic keyboards were in use by the mid-14th century, and it seems likely that those instruments would have been tuned to a cycle of 11 pure 5ths and one 'wolf' 5th, in accordance with the Pythagorean system (see TEMPERAMENT). The 'wolf' 5th is necessary to compensate for the fact that a complete chain of 12 pure 5ths would exceed the equivalent of seven octaves by a small amount known as the 'Pythagorean comma'. Hence the wolf 5th is smaller than pure by a Pythagorean comma to ensure that a complete cycle will produce a perfect unison. In earlier instruments the wolf 5th was usually situated between G♯ and E♭, but other locations could also be used; B–F♯ was common in the 15th century. LC

📖 F. R. LEVIN, *The Harmonics of Nichomachus and the Pythagorean Tradition* (Philadelphia, 1975) · E. C. PEPE, 'Pythagorean tuning and its implications for the music of the Middle Ages', *The Courant*, 1/2 (1983), 3–16

qānūn. The Turkish and Arab **psaltery.

Quadrat (Ger.). The natural sign (see NATURAL, 2).

quadrille. A dance for an equal number of couples, probably derived from displays of horsemanship. It appeared first in the ballet but moved into the ballroom during the reign of Napoleon I in France and arrived in England about 1815. It consists of a group of five country dances of different rhythms and tempos, originally using folk tunes. Its popularity led to arrangements being made of popular songs and operatic arias. The Strauss family were prolific providers of sets of quadrilles, but the vogue soon waned owing to the difficulty of the steps; the dance was in part replaced by the lancers.   PGA

quadruple concerto. A concerto for four solo instruments and orchestra or other instrumental ensemble, for example Bach's arrangement for four harpsichords and strings (BWV1065) of Vivaldi's Concerto RV580, originally for four violins and cello with strings.

quadruplet. A term for four notes that are to be performed in the time of three; they are indicated by the figure '4' placed above or below the four notes (see Ex. 1).

Ex. 1

quadruple time. See TIME SIGNATURE.

Quantz, Johann Joachim (*b* Oberscheden, nr Göttingen, 30 Jan. 1697; *d* Potsdam, 12 July 1773). German flautist, composer, and theorist. Trained as a town musician, he became proficient on woodwind, string, and keyboard instruments. In 1718, however, on entering the chapel of the King of Poland, which was stationed alternately in Warsaw and Dresden, he specialized first on the oboe and then took up the flute, studying with Pierre Buffardin. In 1728, during a visit to

Berlin, he was appointed flute tutor to Crown Prince Frederick of Prussia; a year after the prince's accession in 1740, he joined the royal band at Berlin and Potsdam. Greatly admired by Frederick, he became a leading figure in the musical life of the court, teaching, directing chamber concerts at Sanssouci, and composing numerous flute sonatas and concertos for the king's enjoyment.

Quantz's music, couched in the manner of the so-called Berlin school, and bridging the transition from late Baroque to early Classical style with a mixture of French and Italian elements, is noted more for its elegance than its profundity. He is now chiefly remembered for his comprehensive flute treatise, *Versuch einer Anweisung die Flöte traversiere zu spielen* ('Essay on Instruction for Playing the Transverse Flute'; Berlin, 1752), which provides invaluable information, by no means solely for flautists, about the performance practices of the period, with detailed discussion of accompaniments, ornamentation, dynamics, the size and disposition of orchestras, the essential differences between German, French, and Italian styles, and other important topics.   WT/BS

Quart (Ger., 'fourth'). A term used for instruments tuned a 4th lower or higher than usual; thus *Quartposaune* is a bass trombone in F instead of the normal B♭, *Quartgeige* is a small violin or **violino piccolo* tuned a 4th higher than the normal instrument, and 'quart flute' is a recorder pitched in B♭, a 4th higher than the treble instrument.

quartal harmony. Harmony based on chords built up from 4ths. Such chords are obviously more dissonant by conventional tonal standards than those built from 3rds and are more difficult to classify in relation to particular harmonic functions. For this reason they tend to be found in early 20th-century works (by Schoenberg, Bartók, Skryabin, Hindemith) in which the aim was to expand the traditional harmonic vocabulary and to enrich tonality itself. They may also be found in post-tonal music, as part of the greatly expanded harmonic vocabulary which becomes available when distinctions between consonance and dissonance are set aside.

                                                               AW

quarter-note (Amer.). Crotchet.

quarter-tone. Interval of a quarter of a tone, i.e. half a semitone. See also MICROTONE.

quartet (Fr.: *quatuor*; Ger.: *Quartett*; It.: *quartetto*). An ensemble of four singers or instrumentalists, or music written for it. The quartet normally consists either of voices or of families of like instruments (e.g. recorders, woodwinds, or the string quartet of two violins, viola, and cello) in graduated sizes covering the soprano, alto, tenor, and bass (SATB) ranges. The string quartet has been the leading chamber music ensemble since the time of Haydn, with a vast repertory from all the greatest composers. Whereas orchestral works are public expressions of a composer's feelings, string quartets reveal their more intimate thoughts. In other groups (piano quartet, flute quartet, oboe quartet, etc.) one of the violins of the string quartet is replaced by the named instrument.

See also CHAMBER MUSIC.   JMo

Quartettsatz ('Quartet Movement'). Title given to an unfinished movement in C minor for string quartet by Schubert, D703 (1820); it was intended as the first movement of a whole quartet but only a fragment of the second movement was completed.

quasi (It.). 'As if', 'almost'.

quatreble. In medieval vocal music, a voice part pitched at a fixed interval above the treble. The name derives from a conflation of 'quadruple' and 'treble', denoting a fourth voice part added above the triplum, or treble. Some early theorists cited the prescribed interval between treble and quatreble as a 5th, others as an octave.

Quatro rusteghi, I (*Die vier Grobiane*; 'The Four Curmudgeons'; *School for Fathers*). Opera in three acts by Wolf-Ferrari to a libretto by Luigi Sugana and Giuseppe Pizzolato after Carlo Goldoni's play *I rusteghi* (1760) (Munich, 1906).

Quattro pezzi sacri ('Four Sacred Pieces'). Four choral works by Verdi, an *Ave Maria*, *Laudi alla Vergine Maria*, *Te Deum*, and *Stabat mater*, composed between 1889 and 1897 and published together in 1898.

Quattro stagioni, Le. See FOUR SEASONS, THE.

Quatuor pour la fin du temps ('Quartet for the End of Time'). Work (1940) by Messiaen for clarinet, piano, violin, and cello; he wrote it while he was in a Silesian prisoner-of-war camp, where it was performed the following year.

quaver (♪). The note having an eighth of the value of the semibreve or whole note; hence the American usage 'eighth-note'.

Queen Mary's Funeral Music. Music by Purcell, composed in 1695 for the funeral of Queen Mary; it is a setting of two sentences from the burial service, the anthem *Thou know'st, Lord, the secrets of our hearts*, two canzonas for slide trumpets and trombones, and a march originally written as incidental music for a scene in Thomas Shadwell's play *The Libertine* (1692). Some of the music was played at Purcell's own funeral in Westminster Abbey in 1695.

Queen of Spades, The (*Pikovaya dama*; *Pique-Dame*). Opera in three acts by Tchaikovsky to a libretto by Modest Tchaikovsky and the composer after Aleksandr Pushkin's novella (1833) (St Petersburg, 1890). *Pique-Dame*, popularly supposed to be the French title, is in fact German (the French term being *Dame de pique*).

Querelle des Bouffons. See BOUFFONS, QUERELLE DES.

Quiet Place, A. Opera in one act by Bernstein to a libretto by Stephen Wadsworth (Houston, TX, 1983); Bernstein revised it into three acts (incorporating his *Trouble in Tahiti*, 1952) (Milan, 1984).

quilisma. A type of ornamental neume; see NOTATION, Fig. 1.

quills. Small tongues made from goose quill, leather, or plastic, set in harpsichord jacks to pluck the strings. See HARPSICHORD; PLECTRUM.

quilt canzona. A term derived from a mistranslation of the German *Flickkanzone* ('patch canzona', not 'quilt'). The German term was applied by the theorist Hugo Riemann to a rare type of *canzona in which short, sharply contrasting sections follow each other in quick succession, as in a patched piece of fabric. Examples can be found in the music of Johann Schein (e.g. *Venus Kräntzlein*, 1609).

Quilter, Roger (Cuthbert) (*b* Brighton, 1 Nov. 1877; *d* London, 21 Sept. 1953). English composer. The son of a wealthy stockbroker and (later) art collector, he was educated at Eton. One of the so-called *Frankfurt Group, he studied at the Hoch Conservatory under Iwan Knorr. Denham Price's performance of his *Songs of the Sea* at the Crystal Palace in 1900 brought his name before the public, though it was Gervase Elwes who, with the cycle *Julia* (1905) and the *Seven Elizabethan Lyrics* (1908), championed his songs. A natural feeling for the scansion of the English language, an abundant lyrical gift, and a skilful, discriminating harmonic palette combine to form Quilter's graceful art, as can be seen in Tennyson's *Now sleeps the crimson petal* (1904), Shelley's *Love's Philosophy* (1905), and his finest love song, *Go, lovely rose* (1923). He was capable of a more melancholy disposition in the *Four Songs of Sorrow* (1908), settings of Ernest Dowson's world-weary poems. His flair for light music can be observed in the once-popular children's play *Where the Rainbow Ends* (1911) and the medley of nursery rhymes in *A Children's Overture* (1919). His light opera *Julia* (1936) was a failure. Generous with his inherited wealth, he helped set up the Musicians' Benevolent Fund in memory of Elwes who died tragically in America. He was buried in the family vault in the church at Bawdsey, Suffolk.

MK/JD1

📖 T. Hold, *The Walled-in Garden: A Study of the Songs of Roger Quilter* (Rickmansworth, 1978)

Quint (Ger., 'fifth'). 1. A term used for instruments tuned a 5th lower or higher than usual; thus *Quintfagott* and *Quintposaune* are a bassoon and a bass trombone tuned a 5th lower than the normal instrument. A small harpsichord was known as a 'quint'.

2. An organ pipe (also known as acoustic bass) that is used to produce, when sounded with another pipe tuned a 5th lower, a difference tone imitating the sound of a pipe an octave below the lower one.

quinte (Fr., 'fifth'). A term used for the fifth part of a string ensemble in 17th-century France. By extension, the instrument playing that part—usually the first viola—also became known as the *quinte*.

quintern. A 16th-century German name for the *mandore or the guitar.

quintet. An ensemble of five singers or instrumentalists, or music written for it. Vocal quintets usually consist of soprano, alto, tenor, and bass (SATB) with either a second soprano or a second tenor. String quintets usually consist of a string *quartet with a second viola, as required by Mozart and many other composers, or more rarely a second cello, as in Schu-

bert's Quintet in C. A piano (or clarinet etc.) quintet is usually a string quartet supplemented by the named instrument, though Mozart's horn quintet has two violas and only one violin, and Schubert's 'Trout' Quintet is for piano, violin, viola, cello, and double bass. The wind quintet consists of flute, oboe, clarinet, horn, and bassoon, with a considerable repertory by composers including Reicha from the 1820s onwards.

See also CHAMBER MUSIC. JMo

quinton. A small 18th-century French bowed string instrument with five strings, sometimes identified with the *pardessus de viole*, and sometimes having the body outline of a violin (though played held downwards on the knee) and the tuning *g–d'–a'–d''–g''*. RPa

quintuplet. A term for five notes that are to be performed in the time of four or of three; they are indicated by the figure '5' placed above or below the five notes (see Ex. 1).

Ex. 1

quintuple time. See TIME SIGNATURE.

quire. An obsolete spelling of 'choir'.

quodlibet (Lat., 'what you will'). A piece of music in which well-known tunes or texts (or both) are quoted, either simultaneously or in succession, generally for humorous effect. One 15th-century monophonic song, for example, has a text formed out of quotations from the opening words of 19 famous chansons; the music does not seem to be quoted, however. The quodlibet was apparently a favourite entertainment of the Bachs at their family gatherings, and it has remained popular.

rabāb [rababa, rebab, rubāb, rubob, etc.]. A term used in many different places for stringed instruments, all with a skin belly. Some types are bowed *spike fiddles with resonators of various shapes; these include the quadrangular *rababa* of the Middle East, the Libyan *rababa* with its hemispherical gourd resonator, and the Javanese *rebab* with a body made from half a coconut shell. Other types, for example the short-necked, boat-shaped bowed *rebab* of North Africa (from which the European *rebec derived), have the resonator and the neck carved from a single piece of wood; there are also long-necked plucked lutes with horn-shaped 'wings' carved at the shoulders of the resonator (the *rabāb* of Iran and Central and South Asia), and the plucked short-necked *rabāb* or *rubob* of Afghanistan and Tajikistan (ancestral to the South Asian *sarod), which has a narrow, deep-bodied, waisted resonator with a second resonating chamber running underneath the fingerboard. A *lyre of Eritrea and the Sudan is also called *rababa*. JMo

Rabassa, Pedro [Pere] (*b* Barcelona, *bapt.* 21 Sept. 1683; *d* Seville, Dec. 1767). Spanish composer. He was trained at Barcelona Cathedral, later becoming *maestro de capilla* at the cathedrals in Vich (1713–14), Valencia (1714–24), and Seville (1724–57). The enormous influence he exerted in the last-named post, one of the most important in Spain, led to his works being disseminated throughout the Iberian peninsula and Latin America. More than 400 of his compositions have so far been located; except for a few important secular cantatas they are mainly sacred. Like his teacher Francisco Valls, Rabassa made an outstanding contribution to music theory with his manuscript treatise *Guía para principiantes* (*c.*1720) and other writings. He belongs to the first generation of Spanish composers to have adopted the new Italian stylistic conventions of the early 18th century. MAM

Rabaud, Henri (*b* Paris, 10 Nov. 1873; *d* Paris, 11 Sept. 1949). French composer, conductor, and administrator. He was the grandson of the celebrated flautist Louis Dorus and his father was a professional cellist. A pupil of Massenet and Gedalge, he showed prodigious talent as a student and remained faithful to his teachers' 19th-century ideals all his life. His greatest successes as a composer were the oratorio *Job* (1900) and his opera *Mârouf, savetier de Caire* (1914); he wrote five other operas, symphonies, and film scores, his style appropriately dubbed 'advanced Wagnerianism'. He frequently conducted at the Opéra and the Opéra-Comique, but his main influence on French music was exerted, perhaps, by his prolonged spell as director of the Paris Conservatoire (1922–41), where he succeeded Fauré. RLS

📖 M. D'OLLONE, *Henri Rabaud: Sa vie et son oeuvre* (Paris, 1958)

Rachmaninoff, Serge. See RAKHMANINOV, SERGEY.

racket (Ger., 'rocket', 'to-and-fro'; Fr.: *cervelet*; It.: *cortale*). A Renaissance double-reed instrument with nine or so parallel cylindrical bores drilled in one squat wooden or ivory cylinder. A cap on each end had grooved channels linking these into one continuous bore, thus producing a bass instrument less than 35 cm in length, and soprano, alto, and tenor sizes even smaller. In the 18th century similar but somewhat larger instruments were built with conical bore, a short bell, and a crook for the reed (the Baroque racket or racket-bassoon). Rackets appeared sporadically and did not have a wide distribution. Modern copies of surviving instruments have been made. JMo

Radamisto. Opera in three acts by Handel to an anonymous libretto adapted from Domenico Lalli's *L'amor tirannico, o Zenobia* (1710, rev. 1712) (London, 1720).

raddoppiare (It.). 'To double'; *raddoppiato*, 'doubled', *raddoppiamento*, 'doubling'.

Radetzky March. March, op. 228 (1848), by Johann Strauss (i) (Radetzky was an Austrian field marshal).

radical cadence. See CADENCE.

radio. See BROADCASTING.

Raff, (Joseph) Joachim (*b* Lachen, nr Zürich, 27 May 1822; *d* Frankfurt, 24 or 25 June 1882). German composer and teacher. He grew up in Württemberg and was trained as a teacher in Schwyz; he earned his living by teaching while he studied music privately. On Mendelssohn's recommendation, Breitkopf & Härtel published some piano pieces in 1844. In Basle the next year Raff met Liszt, who helped him find work in Cologne, as a critic and in a music shop; at about this time Bülow added Raff's *Konzertstück* for piano and orchestra to his repertory. In 1847 Liszt again helped Raff find work, in Hamburg as arranger for a publisher, and in 1850 Raff became Liszt's assistant in Weimar, undertaking various musical tasks; he later claimed to have orchestrated some of the music Liszt was writing at the time. After six years in Weimar, during which his own opera *König Alfred* was staged (1851), Raff left for Wiesbaden, where he taught the piano and composed; as director of the Hoch Conservatory in Frankfurt (1877–82) he was one of the most sought-after composition teachers in Germany.

A fecund composer, Raff reached a published total of 214 works and left many more in manuscript. He was a superb craftsman, his knowledge worn lightly in a style that evinces a Mendelssohnian classicality: his command of counterpoint was complete but unobtrusive, his orchestration deft and effective. The backbone of his output is a series of 11 symphonies (preceded by an earlier, unnumbered exemplar in 1854, now lost), of which nos. 3 ('Im Walde', 1869) and 5 ('Leonore', 1872) have regained some of the currency they lost during most of the 20th century; nine of the 11 are overtly programmatic. His other operas, all but one unperformed, were *Samson* (1853–7), *Die Parole* (1868), *Dame Kobold* (Weimar, 1870), *Benedetto Marcello* (1877–8), and *Die Eifersüchtigen* (1881–2). He also composed a generous quantity of chamber music (including nine string quartets, five piano trios, and five violin sonatas), as well as piano and choral music. Raff was occasionally reproached for the facility with which he composed, a charge from which he is rescued by the sheer quality of his invention.   MA

📖 M. RÖMER, *Joseph Joachim Raff (1822–1882)* (Wiesbaden, 1982)

raga. The term used in Indian classical music to define the combination of mode and specific hierarchy of pitches, characteristic melodic features, ascending and descending scale patterns, and types of ornamentation which occupies the central role in the musical tradition. Different ragas may share one or more elements of these but maintain their separate identity, both through other musical features and associations of mood and expression.   KC

ragtime. A style of popular music of black American origin that flourished at the turn of the 19th century. It arose in the slavery period as an accompaniment to plantation dances like the cakewalk. Banjo rhythms were transferred to the piano when such instruments became available to black musicians in minstrel shows and at other entertainments. Early ragtime, mainly written for the piano, followed the form of contemporaneous marches and waltzes—an introduction and several contrasting sections—and was characterized by a strikingly syncopated melody over a regular bass, generally in 2/4 time. Composed rags were widely published and became extremely popular among white amateur pianists, though it is likely that the black creators of ragtime would have played in a much freer manner than the written music suggests. Although it was mainly piano music there were arrangements made for small orchestras to accompany the cakewalk vogue of the 1890s, and there was also a strong vein of ragtime song. The ragtime flavour survived in the early kind of small-band jazz known as *dixieland.

The major ragtime composer of this 'classical' period was Scott Joplin, who wrote works of considerable charm and ingenuity and attempted to stage (without success in his lifetime) the ragtime opera *Treemonisha*. His closest immediate rivals were James Scott and the white composer Joseph Lamb, and many others contributed isolated masterpieces. Succeeding generations gradually moved towards the freer rhythms of jazz.

By the 1930s what was called ragtime had lost most of its early grace and charm and tended to be strident and comical. A renewed interest in classic ragtime was expressed in the book *They All Played Ragtime* (1950) by Rudi Blesh and Harriet Janis. By the 1970s a strong revival resulted from persuasive performances and recordings by Joshua Rifkin, William Bolcom, and others. This was underpinned by the New York Library's publication of Joplin's complete rags and *Treemonisha*—now heard in performance and recording—and other collections of early rags. The use of Joplin's music in the film *The Sting* (1973) stimulated public interest, and ragtime was used in the scores of several ballets. It is now a permanent part of classical popular music, in the same way as the waltzes of Strauss or the marches of Sousa.   PGA

Raimbaut de Vaqueiras (*b* Vaqueiras, Provence, ?1150–60; *d* ?Greece, ? 4 Sept. 1207). Troubadour. He was of humble birth. Much of his life was spent at the court of Boniface II at Montferrat in northern Italy. He participated in the Fourth Crusade and may have been killed in action at his patron's side. 35 of his poems survive, seven of them with music. One, the celebrated *Kalenda maya*, is the oldest known example of an *estampie.   WT/JM

Raimondi, Pietro (*b* Rome, 20 Dec. 1786; *d* Rome, 30 Oct. 1853). Italian composer. He studied at the Naples Conservatory and first made his name as a composer of *opere buffe* and *farse*. After a period as *maestro di cappella* in Acireale in Sicily, where he wrote mostly sacred music, he settled in Naples (and later Palermo) and pursued a career as a teacher, theorist, and opera composer. His greatest success was with *Il ventaglio* (Naples, 1831). In spite of some experiments he found difficulty in adapting to the new, more highly charged operatic language that gained currency in the 1830s with the international fame of Bellini and Donizetti.

RP

'Raindrop' Prelude. Nickname of Chopin's Prelude in D♭ major for piano, op. 28 no. 15 (1836–9), so called because the continuously repeated A♭ suggests the sound of raindrops.

Rainier, Priaulx (*b* Howick, Natal, 3 Feb. 1903; *d* Besse-en-Chandesse, nr Champeix, 10 Oct. 1986). South African–English composer. She settled in England in 1920 and studied at the RAM with J. B. McEwen. While working as a string player she also composed, and received encouragement from Bax, but it was not until after a period of study with Nadia Boulanger in Paris (1937) that she attained maturity as a composer: her String Quartet (1939) is her first representative work. Her small output, concentrated in chamber and vocal music, is distinctively marked by vigorous motivic argument in a highly chromatic style, and by her penchant for working with unusual instrumental combinations, as in her Concertante for Two Winds (1980) for oboe, clarinet, and orchestra. She also taught harmony and counterpoint at the RAM.

PG

Raison, André (*b* before 1650; *d* Paris, 1719). French organist and composer. He served as organist from the mid-1660s at the royal abbey of Ste Geneviève in Paris and later to the Jacobins in the nearby rue St Jacques. Considered one of the finest organists of his day, Raison was Clérambault's teacher. His two published sets of organ masses (Paris, 1688, 1714) were intended for use in monasteries and convents and contain useful instructions on performance and interpretation; notably, he offered guidance on metre, *notes inégales*, and fingering.

DA/JAS

Rake's Progress, The. Opera in three acts (nine scenes and an epilogue) by Stravinsky to a libretto by W. H. Auden and Chester Kallman after William Hogarth's series of paintings (1732–3) (Venice, 1951).

Rakhmaninov [Rachmaninoff], **Sergey** (Vasil'yevich) (*b* Semyonovo, 20 March/1 April 1873; *d* Beverly Hills, CA, 28 March 1943). Russian composer, pianist, and conductor. His family was comfortably affluent, but following his parents' separation and the consequent break-up of the home he had to rely on scholarships and goodwill to study music, first at the St Petersburg Conservatory, then at the conservatory in Moscow, where his teachers were Nikolay Zverev and Alexander Ziloti (piano), Sergey Taneyev (counterpoint), and Anton Arensky (harmony and composition). Although his main efforts at that time were channelled into practising for his piano finals (which he passed with honours in 1891), he became increasingly occupied with composition, writing a number of piano pieces, a little Mendelssohnian orchestral Scherzo (1887), and his First Piano Concerto (1890–1, rev. 1917). For his graduation exercise in composition (1892) he also composed his one-act opera *Aleko*, warmly praised by Tchaikovsky, whose influence it clearly shows.

Quite early on, however, Rakhmaninov forged his own distinctive musical style, marked by a sure gift for soaring melody and a taste for succulent harmony and rich textures, seen in such works as the famous Prelude in C♯ minor (1892), the *Fantaisie-tableaux* op. 5 for two pianos (1893), and in his symphonic poems *Knyaz' Rostislav* ('Prince Rostislav', 1891) and *Utyos* ('The Rock', 1893). He also began to show his flair for vocal writing in two sets of songs, op. 4 (1890–3) and op. 8 (1893). In 1895 he began work on his first substantial orchestral composition, the First Symphony in D minor, an impassioned, defiant work likened by César Cui to 'a programme symphony on the Seven Plagues of Egypt' at its premiere in 1897. This poor critical reception (perhaps sparked more by the inadequate performance than by the music itself) plunged Rakhmaninov into a state of depression from which he could not emerge for about three years: composition was impossible, and only a conducting post in Moscow kept him musically active. He underwent medical treatment from Nikolay Dahl, a doctor who had been specializing in the use of hypnosis, and gradually his confidence was restored to the extent that he was able to make headway with his Second Piano Concerto (1900–1), the success of which decisively launched him into international fame as a composer: together with Grieg's Piano Concerto and Tchaikovsky's First, it must surely rank as the most frequently performed concerto in the repertory.

Rakhmaninov's professional success was enhanced by the emotional security of his marriage in 1902, and for the next 15 years or so he was able to compose with a facility, assurance, and ever-increasing mastery of his art, producing many of his finest works: two sets of piano Preludes, op. 23 (1901, 1903) and op. 32 (1910), two piano sonatas (1907; 1913, rev. 1931), two sets of *Études-tableaux*, op. 33 (1911) and op. 39 (1916–17), the Second

Symphony (1906–7), the Third Piano Concerto (1909), and the symphonic poem *Ostrov myortvykh* ('The Isle of the Dead', 1909). Two forays into opera—*Skupoy rytsar'* ('The Miserly Knight', 1906) and *Francesca da Rimini* (1906)—were not specially happy, largely because of the unsuitability of the librettos, but they both contain some fine music and, like his songs of the period (opp. 14, 21, 26, 34, and 38), reveal a sensitivity to Russian poetry which places him at the forefront of 19th- and early 20th-century Russian vocal writing.

At the same time Rakhmaninov consolidated his career as a pianist, travelling widely in Russia and abroad: he made his American debut in 1909 (giving the premiere of the Third Concerto there), an experience that stood him in good stead in later life—for, with the outbreak of the 1917 October Revolution, he decided to emigrate from Russia and make his home in the USA. With the necessity to provide for himself and his family (which now included two daughters), he had to concentrate on giving concerts and recitals. Almost every season from his arrival in the USA (1918) until 1942–3 he undertook an exhausting schedule of engagements, which all but precluded work on new compositions. Only rarely did he secure the necessary periods of relaxation; but when he did manage to get away from the concert platform—perhaps retreating to a rented house in the French countryside or Dresden, or from the early 1930s settling into his own Swiss villa on Lake Lucerne—he found the peace of mind to write music of extraordinary vitality, originality, and rhythmic zest.

The element of nostalgia, familiar from the works composed in Russia, is still present but is now voiced not in the sumptuous style of the Second Symphony or the Second and Third Concertos but in a terser, more astringent tone utterly characteristic of his late works. The Fourth Piano Concerto (1926, rev. 1941), the Three Russian Songs (1926), the 'Corelli' Variations for solo piano (1931), the *Rhapsody on a Theme of Paganini* (1934), the Third Symphony (1935–6, rev. 1938), the Symphonic Dances (1940)—all were written during this creative Indian summer. And all reveal a new, invigoratingly pungent bite to the harmonies, a new urgency in the rhythmic thrust, and (in the orchestral works) a spareness of scoring which contrasts sharply with his earlier music.

The Symphonic Dances were in fact his last work of substance. Having suffered bouts of ill health in his later years he decided that the 1942–3 concert season would be his last. Abnormal tiredness caused additional alarm, and in February 1943, after giving a concert in Knoxville, he had to be taken home to Beverly Hills. He died of cancer less than six weeks later, leaving a legacy of music which has proved enduringly popular and which has also shown itself to be of key importance

in the late Romantic repertory. Moreover, during the last two decades of his life he had made many gramophone recordings, which happily preserve his pearly-toned, clearly articulated piano playing, with its unerring verve, refined legato, and sublime intensity of expression. GN

📖 S. Bertensson and J. Leyda, *Sergei Rachmaninoff: A Lifetime in Music* (New York, 1956, 2/1965) · G. Norris, *Rakhmaninov* (London, 1976, 2/1993 as *Rachmaninoff*) · R. Threlfall and G. Norris, *A Catalogue of the Compositions of S. Rachmaninoff* (London, 1982) · B. Martyn, *Rachmaninoff: Composer, Pianist, Conductor* (Aldershot and Brookfield, VT, 1999)

Rákóczi March. Hungarian popular march, probably set down by János Bihari (*c*.1810) in homage to Prince Ferenc Rákóczi II (1676–1735), who led the Hungarian revolt against Austria at the beginning of the 18th century. The melody has been used by several composers including Berlioz, who orchestrated it (1846) and incorporated it into *La Damnation de Faust*, Liszt (*Hungarian Rhapsody no. 15), and Johann Strauss (*Zigeunerbaron*).

ralentir (Fr.). 'To slow down'.

rallentando (It.). 'Becoming slower'; it is often abbreviated *rall.*

Rameau, Jean-Philippe (*b* Dijon, *bapt.* 25 Sept. 1683; *d* Paris, 12 Sept. 1764). French composer and theorist. The son of an organist, he studied under his father and had a brief spell in Italy when he was about 18; he then may have played the violin with a theatrical troupe before taking positions as organist in Avignon, Clermont, and, in 1706, Paris. But in 1709 he left Paris to take on his father's former principal post at Notre Dame, Dijon. He next went to Lyons, about 1713, and back to Clermont in 1715, before settling on Paris in 1722.

The main reason for Rameau's going to the French capital was to supervise the publication of his *Traité de l'harmonie*, a large book with much original thinking about the nature of harmony; it was followed by several more theoretical works. Rameau had already published music for the harpsichord, and now issued more. He had also begun to compose music for the fair theatres in Paris, and to teach, and he found a valuable patron in Le Riche de la Pouplinière, who ran a private orchestra and in whose house Rameau and his wife (he married in 1726) had an apartment for several years. It was there that he alienated J.-J. Rousseau with his contemptuous comments on a score that Rousseau had submitted to him.

Rameau is now principally remembered as a stage composer, but it was not until he was 50 that he turned to opera in its various forms. His first opera, *Hippolyte et Aricie*, was written and first performed in 1733: a profoundly original work with a wide emotional range. A stream of theatre works followed, starting with *Les Indes galantes*, an *opéra-ballet* (1735), and further *tragédies*, *Castor et Pollux* (1737, often regarded as his finest stage work) and *Dardanus* (1739), and continuing for 30 years, with as many works in a variety of genres, including divertissement, *pastorale*, *pastorale lyrique* and *comédie lyrique*. Particularly significant among them are the comedy *Platée* and the final *tragédie*, *Les Boréades*, written at the very end of his life (and not performed until the 20th century), a work still of great vitality but differing little in idiom from *Hippolyte*. Each act in Rameau's stage works contains a divertissement, a spectacular scene involving chorus and dance; in the *tragédies* these are usually integrated into the plot, but the *opéras-ballets* generally consist simply of a series of divertissements or *entrées* that may or may not be loosely linked in some way.

Rameau was a controversial figure in his day. His operas were not universally admired. He found himself under attack from several different directions: from the more conservative Lullistes, who deprecated anything that went beyond Lully's idiom, and from the pro-Italian group, led by Rousseau and the Encyclopedists, who found Rameau's music too complex and difficult to grasp. His originality however was widely recognized. His idiom is carefully worked out in accordance with his harmonic theories; every chord, every change of key, and every melodic progression has its particular expressive significance. His basic musical language in the *tragédies* which are the core of his output is similar to Lully's, with much arioso (a lyrical rather than declamatory style of recitative, occasionally relieved by an *air* or an ensemble in which a character muses on his or her predicament or discusses his or her situation).

Rameau's harmony is often unexpected and arresting, especially at moments of emotional stress, and his illustrative writing—portraying a character's state of mind, or a natural phenomenon—is highly imaginative and often deeply poetic. His dance music is striking for its orchestration and its boldness of line and rhythmic structure. Yet it is hard to avoid some sense, in many of his operas, that the music is at times cerebral in its conception. His instrumental music too (the harpsichord works, of which there are four books, mainly of dances or genre pieces, and the *Pieces de clavecin en concerts* for harpsichord with flute and viol) shows great originality in the handling of the idiom and has many vivid ideas, his church music rather less so. A character in a Diderot novel justly says that Rameau 'is singular, brilliant, complex, learned, too learned sometimes', which represents very fair comment.

Rameau himself saw his theoretical writings as the most important part of his work. He regarded music as a science, subject to immutable laws, but related it to the aesthetics of composition, which he felt should always aim to please the ear, to be expressive, and to move the emotions. His harmonic theories turn on the significance of the root-position chord, to which inversions (such as the 6-3 chord or the 6-4) maintain a harmonic link. He thus saw as the 'fundamental bass' a series of notes made up of the roots of each chord (irrespective of whether or not it was inverted) rather than the actual bass line. His writings on harmony have had, and still exercise, great influence, particularly on theorists of his own day and beyond, such as Tartini, Marpurg, Helmholtz, Riemann, and Hindemith.

Rameau was not a popular figure. He was seen as avaricious and insensitive in his social relations, taciturn, misanthropic, and argumentative. Friends and enemies alike seem to have been alienated by his frankness or rudeness. One contemporary said of him: 'His whole heart and soul were in his harpsichord; once he had closed it, there was no one there'.   WT/SS

📖 D. FOSTER, *Jean-Philippe Rameau: A Guide to Research* (New York, 1989) · J. R. ANTHONY, *French Baroque Music from Beaujoyeulx to Rameau* (Portland, OR, enlarged 3/ 1997) · C. W. DILL, *Monstrous Opera: Rameau and the Tragic Tradition* (Princeton, NJ, 1998)

Ramsey, Robert (*fl* Cambridge, 1616–44). English composer. He took the Cambridge degree in 1616, and from 1628 until 1644 worked at Trinity College, first as organist and later as Master of the Children. He wrote church music, consort and continuo songs, and madrigals. His style, like that of his contemporaries Deering and Philips, is expressive and Italianate, and though most of his music is written in the polyphonic idiom of the *prima pratica*, his *What tears, dear Prince* (probably written on the death of Prince Henry in 1612) is an early example of an English monodic song.   JM

Rands, Bernard (*b* Sheffield, 2 March 1935). English-born American composer. He studied composition with Reginald Smith Brindle at Bangor (1953–8) and with Roman Vlad, Dallapiccola, and Berio in Italy (1958–62). Berio's influence was crucial for the formation of his early style, in such works as *Actions for Six* (1962–3), though his melodic language was already British and distinctive. He studied further at the universities of Princeton and Illinois (1966–8), then joined the composition department at York University (1968–75). Two big orchestral adventures, *Wildtrack 1* and *Wildtrack 2*, date from this time. In 1975 he moved to the University of California at San Diego, and his music began to become more mellow, more richly developed, and more settled in the longer history of music, particularly that of orchestral writing. He became an American citizen in 1983 and was appointed professor at Harvard in 1989.   PG

Rangström, (Anders Johan) Türe (*b* Stockholm, 30 Nov. 1884; *d* Stockholm, 11 May 1947). Swedish composer and conductor. He studied composition privately with Johan Lindegren (1903–4) and with Pfitzner in Berlin (1905–6), where he also took singing lessons. In later years he worked as a music critic, singing teacher, as press adviser at the Swedish Royal Opera, and during 1922–5 as chief conductor of the Göteborg Symphony Orchestra. In 1918 he helped found the Society of Swedish Composers. He composed three operas and four symphonies, the First (1914) written in memory of his great compatriot, the playwright August Strindberg. These large-scale works reveal a potent influence of German Romantic models, especially Wagner, and they have been criticized for their episodic formal nature. Rangström's songs, however, are widely admired. He wrote with great sympathy and imagination for the voice, imitating the melodic contours and rhythms of speech in what he called 'speech melody'.
SJ

rank. 1. A set of organ pipes of one type (e.g. 8′ Diapasons) controlled by one *draw stop, hence sometimes referred to as a 'stop'.

2. The individual rows of strings on the double or triple *harp.

Rankl, Karl (*b* Gaaden, nr Vienna, 1 Oct. 1898; *d* Salzburg, 6 Sept. 1968). Austrian-born British conductor. He studied with Schoenberg and Webern and became chorus master and répétiteur at the Vienna Volksoper in 1919, and was later assistant conductor. He was appointed Kapellmeister in Liberec, then Königsberg (now Kaliningrad). From 1928 to 1931 he was Klemperer's assistant at the Kroll Opera, Berlin, then became music director of the Neues Deutsches Theater in Prague in 1937. At Covent Garden from 1946 to 1951 he made a vital contribution to the building of the company's technical standards. Subsequently he was music director of the Scottish National Orchestra. He composed eight symphonies and an opera, *Deirdre of the Sorrows* (1951).   JT

ranz des vaches (Fr.; Ger.: *Kuhreigen, Kuhreihen*). A Swiss mountain melody sung or played on the *alphorn by herdsmen to call their cows in. Every district has its own version, the most celebrated being that of the district of Gruyère, which bears the name (from its opening line) *Les Armaillis des Colombettes*; it is thought that the tune was originally for alphorn and that the words were a later addition.

Stories abound concerning the power of the *ranz des vaches* to awaken an overwhelming feeling of homesickness in the Swiss: Rousseau, in his dictionary of music (1768), alluding no doubt to the 18th-century employment of Swiss mercenaries in several European armies, says it was 'forbidden on pain of death to play it among the troops, because it caused those who heard it to burst into tears, to desert, or to die—so much did it arouse in them the longing to see their country again'.

The *ranz des vaches* has been introduced into various works: there are examples in the overtures to Grétry's and Rossini's versions of *Guillaume Tell*, in the 'Scène aux champs' from Berlioz's *Symphonie fantastique*, and in the tune played by the shepherd boy at the beginning of Act III of Wagner's *Tristan und Isolde*.   PS/AL

rap. A popular style of performance that first came to prominence in the late 1970s. The term originally referred to stylized speech used by American urban black youth. When this kind of speech was used by the master of ceremonies (MC) to introduce the disc jockey (DJ) at street parties, it became attached to a musical backing; the MCs were known as 'rappers'. It has now become part of *hip-hop culture. In its musical form, rap is not sung to an existing tune, but is rather a kind of recitative, in which the musical pitches arise out of exaggerated speech inflections. Rap lyrics are often sexually explicit, and frequently attract charges of violence, racism, misogyny, and homophobia (in the past the blues were subjected to similar criticism); however, these meanings may have been neutralized through ritualization. 'Gangsta rap' emphasizes violence. Since rap has expanded from its original base in black street culture (there are now white rappers and women rappers), the antisocial meanings have become hotly contested. Snoop Doggy Dogg was a major star in the 1990s and Eminem became the best-known rapper at the turn of the 21st century.   PW

📖 T. Rose, *Black Noise, Rap Music, and Black Culture in Contemporary America* (Hanover, NH, 1994)

Rape of Lucretia, The. Opera in two acts by Britten to a libretto by Ronald Duncan after André Obey's play *Le Viol de Lucrèce* (1931), in turn based on Shakespeare's poem *The Rape of Lucrece* (1594) and on Livy's *Historiarum ab urbe condita libri* (Glyndebourne, 1946).

Rappresentatione di Anima, et di Corpo ('Drama of the Soul and the Body'). Sacred opera in a prologue and three acts by Cavalieri, to a text probably by Agostino Manni, first performed in Rome in 1600; it is the earliest opera of which all the music survives.

rapsodia (It.), **rapsodie** (Fr.). 'Rhapsody'.

Rapsodie espagnole ('Spanish Rhapsody'). 1. Orchestral work (1907–8) by Ravel in four movements: 'Prélude à la nuit', 'Malagueña', 'Habanera', and 'Feria'; the 'Habanera' was originally the first of the *Sites auriculaires* (1895–7) for two pianos.

2. Work for piano by Liszt (*c*.1863); it was arranged for piano and orchestra by Busoni.

rasch (Ger.). 'Quick'; *rascher*, 'quicker'; *sehr rasch*, 'very quick'.

rasgueado (Sp.; Fr.: *batterie*; It.: *battute*). In guitar playing, the technique of 'strumming' several strings, either upwards with the fingertips or downwards with the back of the fingernails.

Rasiermesserquartett. See 'Razor' Quartet.

Raskatov, Aleksandr Mikhaylovich (*b* Moscow, 9 March 1953). Russian composer. He studied with Khrennikov at the Moscow Conservatory, and in the 1970s and 80s he was active in the Moscow avant-garde in the circle round Denisov and Gubaidulina. He became a member of the Association of Contemporary Music at its inception in 1990. His compositions include the opera *The Pit and the Pendulum* (1990), an oboe concerto (1987), *Stabat mater* for solo voice with organ (1988), *Xenia* for chamber orchestra (1991), and *Blissful Music* for cello and chamber orchestra (1997); in 1989 he orchestrated and completed Roslavets's Chamber Symphony.   PF

rastrology. The study of the use of the rastrum (Lat., 'rake'), a pen with several nibs designed to rule staves for music manuscripts. From their earliest use—by the 14th century at the latest—pens to produce both four- and five-line staves were in existence; later, rastra were made that could draw more than one staff at a time. They have continued in use even in recent times, in composers' manuscripts. Evidence from rastrology can be used with other techniques of *palaeography to determine the origins of a manuscript.   ABul

rataplan. A word mimicking the sound of a drum. It occurs as the title for solo and ensemble arias in operas by Donizetti, Meyerbeer, and Verdi.

ratchet [cog rattle] (Fr.: *crécelle*; Ger.: *Ratsche*; It.: *raganella*). A frame with wooden blades, whirled to spin round a handle with a fixed cog, each blade clacking loudly on each tooth of the cog. Ratchets are used by farmers as bird-scarers, by town watchmen and police, by football fans, occasionally in the orchestra (e.g. in Beethoven's *Battle Symphony*), and, often greatly enlarged, in Roman Catholic churches as a substitute for bells during Holy Week.   JMo

Rathgeber, Johann Valentin (*b* Oberelsbach, nr Meiningen, 3 April 1682; *d* Banz Abbey, nr Coburg, 2 June 1750). German composer. He spent most of his adult life in the Benedictine monastery at Banz—from 1707 as chamber musician and from 1711, after ordination, as choirmaster. His reputation as a composer rests mainly on his church music, which includes Latin mass settings, psalms and offertories, in some cases for SATB soloists, chorus, and instruments. He also composed numerous instrumental and secular vocal works, among them 24 concertos (1728) and other keyboard pieces, and a lively collection of popular songs (solo, duet, and choral), issued in his three-volume *Tafel Confect* (1733, 1737, 1746). Simple textures and a charming melodic style are typical features of his music.
                                                                                   DA/BS

Ratsche (Ger.). 'Ratchet'.

rattenendo, rattenuto (It.). 'Holding back', 'held back'.

rattle. Any shaken instrument. Some are vessels containing pellets (*maracas) or have external pellets (*cabaza), some slide to and fro (*sistrum), others clatter together (*jingles) or whirl round cogs (*ratchet), some swing in the breeze. There is an infinite variety and their use is worldwide, from infants' toys to elaborate orchestral instruments.   JMo

Rauschpfeife. A name originally applied to any raucous reed instrument (particularly the shawm, with or without a *wind cap) but now used for reproduction Renaissance wind-cap shawms, which have proved popular with early-music groups.   JMo

Rautavaara, Einojuhani (*b* Helsinki, 9 Oct. 1928). Finnish composer. He studied composition with Aarre Merikanto at the Sibelius Academy, Helsinki, and musicology at Helsinki University. From 1966 he lectured at the Sibelius Academy, becoming professor of composition in 1976. Rautavaara has been influenced by a wide range of composers: at first Stravinsky, Sibelius, and Hindemith, later Musorgsky (*Ikonit*, 'Icons', 1956), Messiaen, Berg, and Bruckner. His award-winning orchestral work *A Requiem in Our Time* (1953) makes use of serial techniques, but, like many of his compatriots, Rautavaara eventually reacted against the restraints of serialism. His Third Symphony (1961), though it uses serial techniques, impressed critics most for its Brucknerian warmth and grandeur. His *Cantus arcticus* (1972), for recorded birdsong and orchestra, was another milestone. Influenced by Jung's idea of the 'collective unconscious', by mystical writings, and by his own experiences, Rautavaara has returned repeatedly to images of angels, most notably in his Seventh Symphony, 'Angel of Light' (1995), for which he won a Midem Prize and the Australian ABC Prize.   SJ

Rauzzini, Venanzio (*b* Camerino, nr Rome, *bapt.* 19 Dec. 1746; *d* Bath, 8 April 1810). Italian soprano castrato and composer. Following studies and performances in Italy, he entered the service of the Elector Maximilian III Joseph at Munich (1766–72). He performed for two years in Italy, then moved to London, making his debut as a singer and composer at the King's Theatre in the pasticcio *Armida* (1774). His most popular opera, *Piramo e Tisbe* (1775), was revived three times in London and staged abroad. From 1777 Rauzzini lived mainly in Bath, where he became a concert manager, promoting the careers of Michael Kelly and others as well as continuing to compose.   SH

Ravel, (Joseph) **Maurice** (*b* Ciboure, Basses Pyrénées, 7 March 1875; *d* Paris, 28 Dec. 1937). French composer. Of mixed Swiss–Basque parentage, he grew up in Paris and studied at the Conservatoire (1889–1904), notably with Fauré. His failure to gain the Prix de Rome, for which he competed four times between 1901 and 1905, caused a public scandal; meanwhile he associated with a group of artistic firebrands known as the 'apaches' and including the composer Florent Schmitt, the pianist Ricardo Viñes, and the poets Tristan Klingsor and Léon-Paul Fargue. Of these, Viñes was responsible for the first performances of many of Ravel's piano works, including the *Pavane pour une infante défunte* (1899), *Jeux d'eau* (1901), *Miroirs* (1904–5), and *Gaspard de la nuit* (1908), while verses by Klingsor served as texts for the orchestral song cycle *Shéhérazade* (1903) and one of Ravel's last songs was a setting of Fargue's *Rêves* (1927).

Several of Ravel's early scores gave rise to accusations that he was imitating Debussy, though the glittering cascades of *Jeux d'eau*, for example, stemmed rather from Liszt and in fact preceded Debussy's 'Impressionist' piano pieces. *Shéhérazade* is more Debussian in its vocal style and its use of whole-tone harmony, and yet this dream-picture of the East has a firmness which marks it as Ravel's. The ballet *Daphnis et Chloé* (1909–12), which benefits from Debussy's cool evocations of ancient Greece, is also utterly characteristic in the smoothness of its development; with some justice Ravel called it a 'choreographic symphony'. However, his gifts were not primarily for symphonic music. His musical ideas tend to be sharply defined and self-sufficient, his music to grow more by contrast and varied repetition than by continuous evolution. The classic instance of this is his orchestral *Boléro* (1928), in which a single melody is constantly repeated in a crescendo of colour, but the peculiarly objective nature of Ravel's genius is evident in most of his output (Stravinsky called him a

'Swiss watchmaker'). It is particularly to the fore in the clear-cut forms and often starker harmonies of his neo-classical period, which was ushered in by the piano suite *Le Tombeau de Couperin* (1917) and which continued with the sonatas for violin and cello (1920–2) and violin and piano (1923–7). In *Le Tombeau de Couperin*, Ravel modelled the 'Forlane' on a similar movement in one of Couperin's *concerts*, and in general he believed that imitation was a valid procedure for composers: if they had anything original to say, it would appear 'in their unwitting infidelity to their model'.

The precision of Ravel's orchestration also reveals an artist for whom imagination had to be confirmed by calculation. One of the most inventive of orchestrators, he was able to make a version of Musorgsky's *Pictures at an Exhibition* (1922) which sounds like a fulfilment of the original, and he gave new, perfectly fitting orchestral dress to many of his own piano works, including the *Pavane* (orchestrated 1910), the suite *Ma mère l'oye* (1908/1911), the *Valses nobles et sentimentales* (1911/1912), and *Le Tombeau de Couperin* (orchestrated 1919). Those he did not orchestrate, for example the three 'poems' of *Gaspard de la nuit* (1908), are those which Lisztian flourishes make unalterably pianistic. Besides orchestrating the music of others (Chabrier, Debussy, Rimsky-Korsakov, and Schumann as well as Musorgsky) Ravel relished using pre-formed musical types in his own works. The conventions of 'Spanish' music, for instance, are reinterpreted with joyous élan in his orchestral *Rapsodie espagnole* (1907–8), his one-act comic opera *L'Heure espagnole* (1911) and his song cycle *Don Quichotte à Dulcinée* (1932–3), while the waltz and Gypsy music, respectively, lie behind the dreamily macabre 'choreographic poem' *La Valse* (1919–20) and the virtuoso *Tzigane* for violin with piano or orchestra (1924).

The stresses of World War I, in which Ravel served as a lorry driver, and especially the death of his beloved mother in 1917, were traumas from which he perhaps never fully recovered. He wrote comparatively little after completing his opera *L'Enfant et les sortilèges* (1925, text by Colette), in which, with uncanny accuracy, he captured the mysterious, potentially malevolent world of a room at home as seen by a child, as well as the miraculously transforming power of love. The range of musical styles exhibited in this hour-long opera is astonishing, from chinoiserie to Schoenbergian angst, from foxtrot to culminating fugue. The only large-scale works of his last decade were two piano concertos, the dark left-hand work and the exultant, jazz-tinged G major, both written between 1929 and 1931.

                                                                    PG/RN

📖 A. Orenstein, *Ravel: Man and Musician* (New York, 1975, 2/1991) · R. Nichols, *Ravel* (London, 1977); *Ravel Remembered* (London, 1987) · A. Orenstein (ed.), *A Ravel*

Reader: Correspondence, Articles, Interviews (New York, 1990) · D. MAWER (ed.), *The Cambridge Companion to Ravel* (Cambridge, forthcoming)

Ravenscroft, John (*d* before 1708). English composer who worked in Italy. In 1695 he published a set of 12 *sonate da chiesa* for two violins and continuo, and his op. 2 was a volume of six *sonate da camera*, published posthumously in 1708. Both collections show him to have been a close disciple of Corelli.

Ravenscroft, Thomas (*b* c.1582; *d* c.1635). English composer, theorist, and music editor. He was a chorister at St Paul's Cathedral before taking the B.Mus. at Cambridge in 1605. His published works include a substantial revision of Thomas East's 1592 psalter (*The Whole Booke of Psalmes*, 1621) and three volumes of songs, canons, and catches, variously entitled *Pammelia*, *Deuteromelia*, and *Melismata*, illustrating the lighter side of Jacobean taste. His four fantasias for five viols give some indications as to the dynamics required.

JM

Rawsthorne, Alan (*b* Haslingden, 2 May 1905; *d* Cambridge, 24 July 1971). English composer. He studied at the RMCM (1926–30), then had private piano lessons with Egon Petri. After a brief period as music director of the school of dance and mime at Dartington Hall (1932–5) he worked as a freelance composer, producing numerous film scores. The rest of his output consists mainly of abstract instrumental scores, including three symphonies, two concertos each for piano and violin, three string quartets, and a variety of other chamber works. In these he displayed a gift for athletic counterpoint in clear forms that depend on an enriched tonal harmony; the style is cosmopolitan, comparable more to Hindemith than to any English contemporaries. Among his few works of a more picturesque character are *The Creel* (1940), a suite of fish portraits for piano duet, and the brilliant overture *Street Corner* (1944).

PG

📖 J. MCCABE, *Alan Rawsthorne: Portrait of a Composer* (New York, 1999)

ray. See RE.

Raymonda. Ballet in three acts and four scenes by Glazunov to a scenario by Lydia Pashkova and Marius Petipa; it was choreographed by Petipa (St Petersburg, 1898).

'Razor' Quartet (*Rasiermesserquartett*). Nickname of Haydn's String Quartet in F minor, op. 55 no. 2 (late 1780s), so called because he is said to have given it to the London publisher John Bland in exchange for a new English razor.

'Razumovsky' Quartets. Beethoven's String Quartets op. 59 no. 1 in F major, no. 2 in E minor, and no. 3 in C major (1805–6), so called because they are dedicated to Count Andrey Razumovsky, the Russian ambassador in Vienna, who was a keen quartet player; in the fourth movement of no. 1 and the third of no. 2 Beethoven used Russian folksongs (labelled 'Thème russe') from a collection published in 1790 by Johann Gottfried Pratsch (Ivan Prach). The set is also sometimes known as the 'Russian' Quartets.

re [ray]. The second degree of the scale in the *sol-mization system. In French (*ré*) and Italian usage it has become attached, on the fixed-*doh* principle, to the note D, in whichever scale it occurs. See TONIC SOL-FA.

real answer. See FUGUE.

realize. To improvise or compose an accompaniment over a bass line, with or without the aid of *figured-bass notation. For several centuries until the early 19th it was the task of players of keyboard, plucked, bowed bass, and sometimes even treble instruments to realize accompaniments in different styles according to context. These might include arpeggiated and non-arpeggiated chords of varying texture and rhythms, as well as melodic and ornamental figurations supplementing the upper parts.

A 'realization' is also a version by a modern scholar or composer of an older work in which the original skeletal indications are filled out to provide a fully notated and harmonized score for performance, Britten's realizations of works by Purcell being a notable example.

NPDC

real sequence. See SEQUENCE, 1.

rebab. See RABĀB.

rebec [ribible, rubebe, etc.]. A European bowed string instrument with a neck and resonator carved from a single piece of wood. Two instruments, known since the 10th century, seem to have contributed to the European rebec: the Byzantine instrument, which has survived in the Greek *lira and in various forms in eastern Europe, and the North African *rebab*, which is still played in the Maghrib (see RABĀB). The *rebab* type usually had two strings, a skin belly, and narrow body, and is illustrated in the 13th-century *Cantigas de Santa Maria*. The lira type had a broad pear shape, with a wooden belly and usually three strings.

As the rebec became established the following features became the norm: the body shape an elongated half-pear, with a wooden belly, three strings, a sickle-shaped pegbox, and a raised fingerboard widening out over the top part of the resonator. In northern Europe and Britain, the instrument was played against the shoulder or chest; in southern regions it was held vertically, with the bottom of the body resting on the knee. Rebecs are sometimes shown with frets. In the 16th century, they (like most instruments during the Renaissance) were built in families of different sizes. The violin took over the primary role of the rebec as a dance-music fiddle, and because the rebec's sound was quieter and carried less well it gradually died out from mainstream use.   JMo

Rebel. French family of musicians. **Jean Rebel** (*b* Paris, *c*.1636; *d* Versailles, 1692) was a singer who entered the royal chapel in 1661; a high tenor, he also sang in ballets and operas, taking part in several Lully premieres. He was married three times and had 12 children, several of whom became musicians; his brother Robert was also a royal musician. Jean's daughter **Anne-Renée Rebel** (*b* Paris, *bapt.* 6 Dec. 1663; *d* Versailles, 5 May 1722), a singer, was married to Lalande; their two daughters were also singers.

Her brother **Jean-Baptiste Féry Rebel** (*b* Paris, *bapt.* 18 April 1666; *d* Paris, 2 Jan. 1747) was a violinist and composer. A pupil of Lully, he joined the orchestra at the Opéra and in 1705 became a member of the Vingt-Quatre Violons du Roi; he was later appointed conductor of both groups. In 1727 he succeeded his brother-in-law Lalande as chamber composer to the king. His compositions include sonatas (among the earliest written in France, in the 1690s), an opera *Ulysse* (1703), which was unsuccessful, and a quantity of dance music, much of it remarkable for its rhythmic vitality and orchestral ingenuity; it includes a much-admired fantasy *Les Caractères de la danse* (1715) and his best-known work, *Les Élémens* (1737–8), which is preceded by a movement entitled 'Cahos' ('Chaos') with extraordinary dissonances.

His son, **François Rebel** (*b* Paris, 19 June 1701; *d* Paris, 7 Nov. 1775), followed his father at the Opéra and the Vingt-Quatre Violons. He held various positions at court, including *surintendant de la musique de la chambre*, and at the Opéra, of which he was at different times conductor, *inspecteur général*, licensee, and general administrator. Most of his compositions were written in collaboration with his friend François Francoeur, with whom he also shared some of his appointments at the Opéra; together they wrote numerous ballets, divertissements, and *tragédies* (among them *Scanderberg*, 1735); it was said that Rebel wrote the energetic music, Francoeur the expressive.   SS

rebop. An alternative term for *bebop.

recapitulation. In *sonata form, the final section of the movement, in which the thematic material of the exposition is restated in such as way as to end in the tonic.

reception. Studies of musical reception delineate phases in the history of a work that may be drawn as narrowly as the journalistic reception of a work's premiere or as broadly as the response to a work from its conception to the present. Musical studies of reception owe their methodological origins to the work of Hans Robert Jauss and his colleagues in literary studies at the so-called Konstanz School in the 1960s and 70s, and are now a common part of musicological discourse.

Questions of reception are central to the most familiar—but one of the most problematic—concepts in music historiography: the issue of influence, though theories of reception rarely underpin such inquiries. The term is most frequently invoked in studies of musical journalism, to which the misleading term 'critical reception' is applied. Here, the music press and music journalism in daily newspapers form the basis of scholarly accounts of works of highly variable scope. The vogue for *dossiers de presse*, which do little more than reprint the entire journalistic output surrounding a work's premiere, is now well developed; however useful such undertakings might be, they often confuse the location of material for its critical interpretation. The press reports surrounding the premiere of every one of Donizetti's operas have recently been the most striking object of inquiry. Conversely, studies of individual journals (the *Revue et gazette musicale de Paris* is a good example) have shown how sophisticated the study of musical journalism can be when embedded in a theory of reception.

Music journals and newspapers represent only one site of reception among many. To move away from the study of musical journalism to more general questions of reception is to show precisely how narrow is the former. Music is also received in performances, publication, pedagogical curricula, belles-lettres, the history of ideas, and after 1900 in recordings; the interpenetration of these different sites of reception can form the basis for a more sophisticated history of music than one based on chronicles of works and biographies of composers. Access to evidence for these sites of reception is uneven: to document the performances of *Tannhäuser* or *Lohengrin* in the second half of the 19th century, for example, is an approachable task; to replicate that task for *The Well-Tempered Clavier* is not. The study of publication as a mode of reception is aided by the fact that the study of music-publishing is a discipline in its own right, though it is relatively rare to find a study of musical reception that fully profits from the work carried out in this area. When the reception theorist's attention turns to the history of ideas or belles-lettres, any bibliographical security collapses, and studies risk falling prey to the imprecise or the anecdotal.

Composition itself has always been a key site of musical reception, apart from the hoary issue of influence. The constant composition and recomposition that characterizes vocal polyphony from the 12th to the 16th centuries can be understood at one level as a process of reception buried in the act of composition itself. Certain genres depend on 'receiving' a work for their existence: the 19th-century fantasy on operatic themes is just one example; the concept of the jazz 'standard' is another. But composers have internalized the process of reception to a much greater degree, especially during the 20th century. Whether it is Schumann or Busoni revisiting Bach, Schoenberg orchestrating Brahms, Berio reworking Mahler, or Finnissy stripping Grainger and Gershwin to their skeletal structure before recomposing them, all these musical endeavours implicitly invoke a theory of reception in their very composition. It could be added that the act of setting a text is an act of musical reception on a literary site.

The origins of studies of musical reception in literary scholarship of the 1960s and 70s betray an essentially conservative aesthetic agenda that results in a concentration on the works of authors already granted a place in the canon. Thus, Mozart, Beethoven, Wagner, and Bach have figured most frequently in such studies, which have concentrated mostly on those works that have the greatest presence in contemporary culture. For certain reception theorists, the sites of reception have been equated with formative pressures on the musical canon with far-reaching implications for the study of music history. ME

📖 H. R. Jauss, 'Literary history as a challenge to literary theory', *Toward an Aesthetic of Reception*, Theory and History of Literature 2, trans. T. Bahti (Minneapolis, 1982), 3–45 [original published in 1967] · A. Comini, *The Changing Image of Beethoven: A Study in Mythmaking* (New York, 1987) · G. Gruber, *Mozart and Posterity*, trans. R. S. Furness (London, 1991) · K. Ellis, *Music Criticism in Nineteenth-Century France: La Revue et gazette musicale de Paris, 1834–80* (Cambridge, 1995) · A. Bini and J. Commons, *Le prime rappresentazioni delle opere di Donizetti nella stampa coeva*, L'arte harmonica serie III, Studi e testi 3 (Rome and Milan, 1997) · M. Everist, 'Reception theories, canonic discourses and musical value', *Rethinking Music*, ed. N. Cook and M. Everist (Oxford, 1999), 378–402; J.-M. Fauquet and A. Hennion, *La Grandeur de Bach: L'Amour de la musique au XIXe siècle*, Les Chemins de la musique (Paris, 2000)

recit. Abbreviation for *recitative.

recital. A concert given by one performer or a small group. The term first gained currency when an advertisement appeared in London in 1840 stating that 'M. Liszt will give Recitals on the Pianoforte of the following pieces'. Initially the term was reserved for a solo performance (or accompanied solo), but it can now refer to various sorts of chamber or song programme, public or private.

See also concert, 3.   PG

recitative (from It. *recitativo*). A form of speech-like solo singing, free in rhythm and lacking in structured melodies. It was invented in Italy shortly before 1600 as a way for music to be more subservient to the text; basso *continuo, or *figured bass, was the means by which the accompaniment could follow a singer's spontaneous expression in the absence of a strict beat. In early 17th-century opera, recitative was the principal mode of expression and was often freely mixed with short passages of *arioso. Towards 1700, with the development of *opera seria*, it became more standardized, with predictable melodic patterns and set cadences. The more important dialogues and soliloquies were often accompanied by the orchestra: this was called *recitativo stromentato* (It., 'orchestrated recitative', also called *recitativo accompagnato*, 'accompanied recitative'), in contrast to *recitativo secco* ('dry recitative'), the more usual type with continuo accompaniment only. Now clearly separated from the more static and melodious *aria, recitative in *opera seria* lasted until the mid-19th century, and was imitated in the serious opera of other languages. In *opera buffa* it became a rapid-fire, light dialogue which was primarily a vehicle for the complex stage business, as in Mozart's *Le nozze di Figaro*. The German *Singspiel*, English *ballad opera, French *opéra comique*, and Spanish *zarzuela tended to use spoken dialogue rather than recitative between the songs. Recitative was also a feature of oratorios, cantatas, Passion settings, and anthems. It was sometimes imitated in instrumental music, as in Beethoven's Piano Sonata op. 31 no. 2 and his Ninth Symphony.

In the later 19th century, first *recitativo secco* and then *recitativo stromentato* gradually died out as a distinct mode of singing. Wagner still has clearly marked sections of recitative in *Lohengrin* (1850), but his later music dramas can be thought of as continuous recitative, with enhanced melody, harmony, and orchestration; or as continuous aria, without fixed forms and with the freedom and speech-rhythm of recitative. By the time of Verdi's last operas, also, it is no longer possible to separate arias from recitatives.   NT

reciting tone. In plainchant, a melodic formula of varying complexity (though usually rather simple) used for the recitation by verse of psalms, canticles, lessons, and other liturgical texts.

recorder (Fr.: *flûte à bec, flûte douce*; Ger.: *Blockflöte*; It.: *flauto dolce*). The 'common flute' (as it was also known in English) of the Renaissance and Baroque periods. The recorder is a *duct flute, the duct being formed between the wall of the head or 'beak' and a wooden 'block' (hence the French and German names). It has a gentle sound, and because it is capable of comparatively little variation of expression or volume the transverse flute gained supremacy over it in the Classical period.

The recorder, as distinct from simpler duct flutes, has a thumbhole and seven fingerholes. On the early one-piece recorders the lowest fingerhole was duplicated, so that players could place either hand uppermost and still reach the lowest hole with the little finger; the unwanted hole was stopped with wax. The earliest known examples, all of descant (soprano) size, date from the late 14th century, and the name 'recorder' is first known from about the same time. By the early 16th century, and probably earlier, the family of treble (alto), tenor, and bass were in use; the sopranino and great bass followed shortly after. The early recorders were cylindrical in bore and therefore of somewhat smaller range than the later Baroque ones, but still capable of a fully chromatic range. The recorder responds well to cross-fingering (flattening the pitch by closing one or more holes below an open hole). The only keys used on recorders were extension keys, which enabled fingers to reach a hole otherwise out of reach on larger instruments.

During the later Renaissance, the lower part of the bore was gradually contracted, producing an inversely conical bore, widest at the blowing end. This helped tune the upper notes, and made it easier to overblow to the upper reaches of the range. A much more radical redesign originated at the French court about 1670, when such makers as Martin Hotteterre (c.1635–1712) created the Baroque model. Instead of being a single piece of wood, as earlier recorders had been, this was in three separate joints—head, body, and foot—linked with tenons and sockets. The head remained cylindrical in bore. The body, with thumbhole and six fingerholes, was now more sharply conical. The foot could now be turned to bring the lowest fingerhole under either little finger; that hole therefore no longer needed to be duplicated. This was the instrument for which Bach and other composers of the period wrote under the name of *Flöte* or *flauto*, normally implying the treble (alto), now in F, instead of the old Renaissance G treble. The transverse *flute was always either so called or specified as 'German flute'.

Having died out with the demand for greater expressiveness, the recorder was totally forgotten until its resurrection by Arnold Dolmetsch in about 1920. Today it has not only become the ideal first instrument for a child but has regained its status in Baroque and earlier

music. Much new music has also been composed for the recorder. JMo

E. O'KELLY, *The Recorder Today* (Cambridge, 1990) · J. M. THOMSON (ed.), *The Cambridge Companion to the Recorder* (Cambridge, 1995)

recording and reproduction. The ability to record musical performances and play them back at any time was, during the 20th century, the principal force spreading music and its appreciation to an ever-wider public. The development of music itself was fundamentally influenced, since performers and composers had unprecedented access to the works and styles of their contemporaries and predecessors worldwide. As Elgar wrote, 'If ever there was a fairy story, the history of the gramophone is one'.

1. The early days of recording; 2. From electrical recording to the LP; 3. Further developments; 4. Magnetic recording; 5. Film and television; 6. The digital age

1. The early days of recording

The American inventor Thomas Alva Edison (1847–1931) demonstrated a prototype of his aluminium foil cylinder *phonograph in December 1877. For all its crudeness it impressed its first hearers, and some 500 machines were produced during 1878. Beeswax later became the recording medium. Edison soon developed his own 'perfected phonograph', using solid-cast waxes which could be shaved and reused, forming a marketable dictation machine taking about 400 words (two minutes) when driven at 120 revolutions per minute (rpm) by an electric motor. This was the model used for many of the earliest surviving recordings, including that of Brahms playing his Hungarian Dance no. 1 as a piano solo in Vienna in 1889.

Emile Berliner (1851–1929), a German working in Washington, DC, developed what became the forerunner of the 'gramophone record' as we know it. By about 1899 the technique of recording on wax discs 50 mm thick was introduced and remained the standard medium for more than 40 years. Berliner can be credited with many of the features of the disc record. The recording–cutting head was driven along a radial line towards the disc centre by a rotating threaded shaft, but the pivoted playback–pickup head simply relied on the force of the spiralling groove on the needle to carry it into the centre.

The processes used for mass duplication of early gramophone records were remarkably similar to those used throughout the era of analogue disc recording. The surface of the newly cut wax master disc was first metallized so that it could conduct electricity, then made to act as one of the electrodes in an electroplating bath. The copper-plate 'negative' so formed was removed from the wax and used in turn as the surface on which a 'positive', capable of being played and checked, could be placed. Yet another electroplating stage could yield any required number of negative 'stampers' or moulds to press out records in large quantities.

In March 1902 the young impresario Fred Gaisberg persuaded the tenor Enrico Caruso to sing ten songs and arias, for a reported flat fee of an unprecedented £100, into a wax disc recorder set up in a Milan hotel room. This boldness was repaid in more senses than one: the recordings not only found a ready market but attracted other singers to the medium, soon prompting a mushrooming of record companies anxious to build substantial catalogues. The primitive recording and reproducing machines somehow managed to contain the sounds of solo singing voices well enough, but they were quite incapable of capturing the complexities of orchestral tone. (The none the less substantial extent of orchestral recordings before 1925 has recently become apparent with the publication of Claude Graveley Arnold's monumental catalogue.)

The era of sound recording from Edison's first phonograph up to about 1924 is referred to as the 'acoustic' age. During this period all the energy available to drive the stylus which etched out the recorded wave-forms was 'acoustic energy': that is, it came from the sound waves themselves. Circumstances changed dramatically in about 1925 when the new microphones and triode valve amplifiers introduced a few years earlier for radio broadcasting came into use. The microphone converted the acoustic energy into an electric current which could be amplified, and an electromagnet cutter head carried out a conversion in the reverse sense to change the electric current into a controllable driving force on the stylus.

2. From electrical recording to the LP

1925 saw feverish conversion to electrical recording. In their search for recording studios the major companies contracted the principal halls; the competition, as they experimented with live recordings during public concerts, unwittingly resulted in recordings of great historical value, for example Columbia's recording of Handel's *Messiah* at the last of the Handel Festivals in Crystal Palace in 1926. Such recordings demonstrated the new medium's ability to deal both with large musical forces and with the recording of live concerts. Conductors like Toscanini and Stokowski were won over to recording, and by 1927 the latter was beginning his famous series of successful recordings with his Philadelphia Orchestra, helped by the acoustics of the Academy of Music Hall.

The electrical period on 78-rpm discs lasted from 1925 to about 1950. The change came with the introduction, by Columbia Records in June 1948, of long-playing (LP) 'microgroove' records. These were the same size as the old 78-rpm discs (12″ (30 cm) in diameter) but played for a full 25 minutes a side instead of only about four minutes. Thus many complete compositions could be heard without the irritation of frequently turning over or changing the record; gone too was the unacceptable physical bulk of recordings of longer works.

The longer playing time was brought about by two factors. First, the running speed was more than halved, to 33⅓ rpm in place of 78 rpm. Secondly, the grooves were made much narrower, to allow some 250 grooves per inch instead of only about 100. At the same time, the quality or 'fidelity' of the musical reproduction was soon found to be vastly superior. The change was made possible partly by improvements and miniaturization in the design of cutter heads and replay pickup cartridges, but the prime factor was the availability of new plastics, vinylite or polyethylene, from which the LP records could be manufactured. The shellac used for 78-rpm records was coarse-grained and had abrasive powders added to withstand the considerable pressures of the early heavy pickups. The result was an obtrusive hissing noise as a continuous accompaniment to the music. With the new vinyl discs background noise was reduced and they were also lighter, flexible, and unbreakable.

3. Further developments

Undreamt-of freedom for recording producers and musicians alike came at the same time, when tape recording of masters became the rule. Now any number of restarts or retakes could take place. On the other hand, if the performers wanted to record continuously for an hour or more that too was possible. The independent producer emerged in the 1970s and came to be relied on increasingly by the greatest artists, anxious for perfection in their recordings. Opera is perhaps a special case, and the producer John Culshaw was one of the first to demonstrate conclusively—for example, in his complete recording for Decca of Wagner's *Ring* conducted by Georg Solti—that it was possible to plan and direct a performance specifically for the gramophone. He wrote: 'The idea was that of re-creating in the studio an environment as close as possible to the theatre, with singers acting their parts in a production almost as elaborate as the real thing'.

A parallel development to the 33⅓-rpm LP record was a smaller disc introduced by RCA Victor. This was only 7″ (18 cm) in diameter and ran at 45 rpm. After a brief 'war of the speeds', both formats became accepted, with record players geared to run at 33⅓, 45, and 78 rpm (with the last speed eventually falling into disuse). The '45' or 'single' became ubiquitous as the medium—indeed the driving force—for the dissemination of pop music.

The resulting boost to record sales from the appearance of the LP encouraged the record companies to re-record all the standard Classical and Romantic musical repertory and then to set out on an unprecedented exploration of unknown works. Such innovation tended to be pioneered by new, independent, small companies who found an active market later exploited by the 'majors'. There developed a rapidly expanding archive-derived repertory, particularly of Baroque and contemporary music not previously recorded.

A further opportunity for re-recording familiar music was provided in 1957 by the introduction of stereophonic records, putting into practice the theories of the British engineer Alan D. Blumlein (1903–42). In essence, his ideas had been to imitate the direction-finding mechanism of human binaural hearing (see EAR AND HEARING, 6) by setting up a pair of left–right microphones. The twin signals remain in synchrony by being cut into a single record groove but maintain their discrete existence by being kept in separate electrical chains until they emerge from a pair of suitably spaced loudspeakers. The listener then hears the sounds of the individual musicians as if disposed in an arc between the loudspeakers. Later experiments with 'surround sound' or 'quadraphony' sought to recreate the sensation of sitting inside the concert hall. Quadraphonic records were issued from about 1972, but were soon discontinued.

4. Magnetic recording

The first practical demonstration of the feasibility of laying down a track of magnetic impressions and re-playing these by electromagnetic conversion was given by the Danish engineer Valdemar Poulsen (1869–1942) in 1898. His 'telegraphone' somewhat resembled a cylinder phonograph but used 0.25-mm steel piano-wire wrapped round a grooved brass cylinder. Though an original wire recording exists of Emperor Franz Josef I of Austria praising the telegraphone at the World Exhibition in Vienna in 1898—proof of the permanence of magnetic recordings—it took until about 1912 to develop a reliable machine.

The German Kurt Stille took up Poulsen's ideas and by 1928 was producing improved wire devices, with finer wire to give longer playing time and DC bias which greatly improved the sound quality. Stille then devised a steel-tape machine in 1930, and the film producer Ludwig Blattner developed this system further. The BBC acquired two 'blattnerphones', which were highly suitable for repeat broadcasts beamed to different parts of the world several times over 24 hours. They used steel tape 3 mm wide and gave a playing time of 30 minutes. All direct recording systems for broadcasting were superseded by the use of 'acetates' (direct-cut discs where the recording was made into a film of cellulose acetate on a metal or glass disc), widely used by broadcasting stations during the period 1935–55.

The most important change in magnetic recording came with the development of coated tapes, first attempted in about 1928 by Fritz Pfleumer of Dresden, who coated soft iron powder in an organic binder on to tapes of paper or plastic film. By 1934, BASF (Badische Anilin und Soda Fabrik) was producing cellulose acetate base tapes coated with ferric oxide (Fe_2O_3). Within a year, AEG (Allgemeine Elektrizitäts-Gesellschaft) had produced an advanced 'Magneto-phon' recorder for the new tape, which was used for recording part of Mozart's E♭ Symphony (no. 39) by the London Philharmonic Orchestra under Thomas Beecham in 1936. Further refinements made to these machines in Germany during the war included the rediscovery of supersonic bias, and the postwar period saw magnetic-tape recording spreading throughout the world. Tape soon replaced wax discs as the medium for master recording in the studios of both record companies and broadcasters.

Although the record companies had issued pre-recorded tapes from 1954 sales were disappointingly small, but in the late 1960s the 'musicassette' appeared, destined to compete with the gramophone record on almost equal terms. The wide availability first of reel-to-reel recorders and later of cassette recorders enabled users to make cheap, relatively high-quality recordings, particularly off air, for personal use. In 1998, in order to develop the important historical series 'BBC Legends' (reissues of celebrated performances of 1935–70 by great artists of the day), it was found necessary to make a public appeal for recordings that individuals might have made of broadcast concerts not preserved by the BBC.

5. Film and television

The development of film recording was driven by the cinema. After the appearance of 'talking pictures' in 1928, the next stage was to record the soundtrack on the film itself. Two methods of photographic sound recording were proposed. In 'variable density' recording, the electric currents from the sound source were used to modulate an electric arc which shone through a slit on to the light-sensitive film. The second method, 'variable area' recording, depended on shining a constant light source on to a tiny mirror cemented on to a wire. When the sound signal current was passed through this wire, it would twist to and fro through an angle which varied with the strength of the current. The developed negative was opaque except where the light had exposed it, and the soundtrack could be reproduced by passing the film between a light source and a photoelectric cell.

Before tape recording became common, some music was recorded on film for sound broadcast. During World War II the BBC used this method for longer recordings, notably the radio drama *Christopher Columbus* with music by Walton, which was successfully re-broadcast in 1973.

The recording of television programmes (see BROADCASTING) was perfected by the Ampex Corporation of America as long ago as 1956. On a domestic level, video recorders using cassettes of magnetic tape 25 or 12.5 mm wide began to reach the market in 1972 and, in spite of a slow start because of the proliferation of models using different cassette shapes and running speeds, they soon became a desirable commodity.

The application of video-recording techniques to sound-only recording provided a means of overcoming most of the limitations of normal sound recording. Conventional recording involves the inscribing of a continuous pattern or wave-form which is an imitation or 'analogue' of the changing air pressures in the original sound waves. Unfortunately any discrepancies in the replay speed affect the musical pitch, and any graininess in the disc or tape material is reproduced as noise—as are scratches or particles of dust. At the same time, the recorded wavelengths at high sound frequencies are so tiny as to tax the capabilities of the stylus or tape head to trace them effectively.

6. The digital age

Digital recording can sidestep these difficulties. As a first step, it samples the sound wave-form at regular intervals—about 50,000 times a second—and compares the instantaneous amplitude with a set scale of values. Each amplitude sample has its value recorded as a series of pulses, using the so-called binary system of simple pulses and spaces. To replay a digital recording, the stream of pulses is again scanned and the original waveform reconstructed with any desired degree of accuracy. A principal advantage of digital recording is that it ignores speed fluctuations on playback and is almost totally protected against noise, interference, or degradation during storage or frequent playings. The individual pulses are all identical and recorded at the highest level that the medium will allow. The playback system has only to identify the presence or absence of a pulse at each sampling point in time, not its level or shape.

The changeover in the industry from vinyl analogue recordings to digital compact discs happened remarkably quickly. The compact disc was launched in Europe in 1983, though by that time digital recording was already common for the production of master tapes. The advent of the CD, in spite of an initial lack of capacity, stimulated a remarkable expansion of the recording industry, with many new independent labels being set up worldwide and distributed internationally. At the beginning of the 21st century about 350 labels were being distributed in the UK.

Huge non-mainstream repertories began to be recorded, including national symphonic music, particularly of the period 1850–1950, by specialist labels in almost every country. Baroque music continued to be explored in ever-increasing depth and sophistication of performance, while the music of the high Renaissance and earlier became familiar to a wide audience. Never had the musical public been able to appreciate such a range of music from first-hand experience of performance.

These developments were led by a number of independent labels, which in the UK included Chandos and Hyperion. Paradoxically, CD also proved to be the ideal medium for the reissue of 78-rpm discs, with computerized noise-reduction systems such as Cedar allowing ever-improving sound quality. A number of niche labels appeared in this area, leaders in the UK being Dutton and Pearl. The emergence of the Naxos label became a worldwide cultural phenomenon in the 1990s. Established in Hong Kong in 1987, it developed a massive list of new recordings—including pioneering repertory—sold at the lowest possible price, and achieved substantial market share, undercutting most other companies.

At a time when the success of the CD has so saturated the market as to create a crisis in the traditional patterns of serious music, there is still plenty of evidence that listening to recordings increases rather than decreases the desire of music lovers to participate in live music. At the beginning of the 21st century a plethora of competing new digital formats—including minidisc, DAT, DVD, CD-R, and delivery via the Internet (see MUSIC ON THE INTERNET)—and the re-emergence of analogue vinyl recordings underline the desire of music lovers to listen to their music in the most vivid and convenient format; none, however, showed any immediate prospect of displacing the CD as the one used routinely by the majority.   JBo/LF

📖 R. GELATT, *The Fabulous Phonograph* (London, 1956) · O. READ and W. WELCH, *From Tin-Foil to Stereo* (New York, 1959) · J. BORWICK, *Sound Recording Practice* (London, 1976, 2/1980) · P. MARTLAND, *Since Records Began: EMI: The First 100 Years* (London, 1997) · C. G. ARNOLD, *The Orchestra on Record, 1896–1926* (Westport, CT, 1997) · A. POLLARD, *Gramophone: The First 75 Years* (Harrow, 1998) · I. WALLICH, *Recording my Life* (London, 2001)

reco-reco. The Brazilian name for the *güiro, though sometimes it is a notched stick rather than a gourd.

recueilli (Fr.). 'Meditative', 'contemplative'.

Redford, John (*d* London, Oct. or Nov. 1547). English church musician, composer, and dramatist. He was a vicar-choral at St Paul's Cathedral, London, in the 1530s and 40s, and latterly Master of the Choristers there. It was presumably for the boys of St Paul's that he wrote his only surviving play, *Wyt and Science*. Redford is one of the earliest English composers to have notated a significant quantity of keyboard music, all of it liturgical in function, based on plainchant melodies and intended for the organ. A few vocal works by him also survive.   JM

redoute (Fr.). See RIDOTTO, 2.

reduction. *Arrangement. The term is most commonly used of a piano arrangement (for rehearsal purposes) of the accompaniment to a work for one or more soloists, or chorus, with orchestra or other instrumental ensemble.

reed. A flexible blade of metal or cane (or plastic) whose periodic vibrations cause an air column to produce sound. There are two basic forms, the free reed and the beating reed.

The free reed swings freely to and fro in a closely fitting slot. With free reeds (as in the *accordion, *reed organ, and *harmonica) and the beating reed of an organ reed pipe, the pitch is normally that of the tongue itself (the shape of which also has a considerable impact on tone-quality), so that a separate reed is required for each note of the compass; the reed holder may or may not communicate with a resonator (e.g. a pipe). When it does, as in organ reed and free-reed pipes, the resonator affects timbre rather than pitch. With other beating-reed instruments (e.g. the oboe or clarinet), one reed serves the entire compass where the notes are determined by a pipe with fingerholes (a 'coupled system'). South-East Asian free-reed mouth organs (e.g. the Chinese *sheng) use a coupled system, the free reeds being attached to bamboo pipes of graded lengths; the fingerhole on each pipe, however, does not affect pitch, but when it is closed the airstream forces the respective reed to vibrate.

Beating reeds may be single or double. The single reed is a blade of cane that vibrates against the walls of a mouthpiece (to which it is tied or clamped with a 'ligature'), as on clarinets and saxophones, or a metal blade beating on the shallot (equivalent to the clarinet's mouthpiece) of an organ pipe or a reed-horn (used for signalling. The double reed consists of two blades of cane bound together (or a single blade folded over and cut at the fold to separate the two blades) so that they beat against each other, as on shawms, oboes, and bassoons. The typical material for cane reeds is *Arundo*

donax, grown chiefly in southern France, though almost any material can be made to vibrate as a reed. Both types of beating reed close under air pressure, springing open again because of their elasticity and the skill of the maker—when either is deficient, the reed claps and fails to function.

The simplest single reeds, known in Egypt several thousand years ago and still widely used, were short lengths of cane with a tongue slit from the wall. Such instruments are termed 'idioglot'. Many bagpipe drones have idioglot reeds. Three exceptional forms of beating reed are the grass blade tensed between the hands (a ribbon reed), a plant stem slit longitudinally (a retreating or dilating reed), and a slip of wood, a fish-scale, or even a credit card held between the lips or against the tongue.   JMo

reed organ. Generic term for organs on which the sound is produced by *free reeds, the more familiar *'harmonium' originally being the trade name patented by A. F. Debain for his reed organ of 1842.

reedpipe. 1. In literary tradition, any rustic pipe made of reed or cane, whether blown as reed instruments or flutes, and including such multiple pipes as *panpipes.

2. In the Hornbostel and Sachs system (see INSTRUMENTS, CLASSIFICATION OF) 'reedpipe' is used only for those pipes sounded by a *reed, whether single, double, or free, irrespective of the material from which the pipe is made.

reel. An ancient Scottish dance similar to Irish and Scandinavian dances and to the strathspey, which is danced at a slower tempo. Couples dance face to face, to music in 2/2, 2/4, or 6/8 time divided into clear eight-bar sections. A more exhilarating version is known as the Highland fling, while simplified versions arrived in English ballrooms at the beginning of the 19th century.   PGa

re-entrant tuning. A tuning that is not sequential in pitch. Instruments that characteristically have re-entrant tunings include the five-string *banjo, the *cittern, the *theorbo, and the *ukulele.

Reformation. A radical change in religious thought, initiated in Germany in 1517 by Martin Luther, and in Switzerland in 1519 and 1541 by Ulrich Zwingli and John Calvin, respectively, which led to the growth of the various forms of Protestantism. Its consequences for church music were far-reaching. In Germany the influence of Luther, an Augustinian monk by training and a traditionalist by nature, ensured the preservation of much of the ritual and music of the ancient Church, provided it did not conflict with his theological reforms. Though primarily concerned to promote the religious education of the people through German congregational hymns and vernacular versions of the Bible and the liturgy, he was by no means averse to the use of the traditional Latin texts, several of which held their place in continuing types of Lutheran worship. Prominent among his musical assistants were Johann Walter (1496–1570), who in 1524 published his *Geystliches gesangk Buchleyn*, the first Lutheran chorale book, and Georg Rhau, who between 1538 and 1545 issued 16 volumes of liturgical settings (of both Latin and German texts), chosen for their suitability in Lutheran worship.

Altogether more austere was the situation in countries where the teachings of Zwingli and Calvin prevailed. Zwingli, though highly gifted musically, stipulated at first (in his vernacular liturgy of 1525) that music should be entirely excluded from church worship; while Calvin sanctioned only the unaccompanied congregational singing of biblical texts, mainly vernacular psalms and canticles in metrical versions. The earliest psalter for Calvinist use (*Aucuns Pseaumes et cantiques mis en chant*) was published in Strasbourg in 1539. It contained 19 metrical psalms and three canticles in French translations, 13 of which were by Clément Marot and the rest by Calvin, with single-line melodies by Mathias Greiter and others. After Marot's death in 1544, his translation of the psalms was completed by Théodore de Bèze, and a finalized Genevan Psalter, with music, was published in 1562. Although polyphony, traditionally associated with the Roman liturgy, was disallowed in Calvinist church practice, it resurfaced after the mid-16th century in the form of four-voice psalm settings (solely for domestic use) by Claude Le Jeune, Loys Bourgeois, and Claude Goudimel. Calvinist doctrines were later adopted, to the detriment of local musical development, in Scotland and the Netherlands, and by the Puritans in England and in New England, USA.

In England the growth of the Reformation was more protracted but equally far-reaching. The urge towards reform, prompted by a new independence of thought among the middle classes of the time, was underpinned in 1534 when Henry VIII, angered by the pope's refusal to sanction his divorce from Catherine of Aragon, renounced papal supremacy, proclaimed himself head of the Church of England, and initiated a gradual (and generally peaceable) dissolution of the monasteries. On Henry's death in 1647 his nine-year-old son acceded to the throne as Edward VI, and under his direction (or that of his regent, the Duke of Somerset) more thoroughgoing reforms were instituted; these included the suppression of the chantries, by which the country's last strongholds of traditional Latin polyphony were destroyed, and the replacement, through the Act of Uniformity (1549), of the Latin Mass by the new English liturgy (the first Prayer Book of 1549), as the sole legal form of worship. In spite of some initial hostility to the Act, composers soon began to provide music for the new vernacular forms of public worship. Leading publications for congregational use included Merbecke's *The Booke of Common Praier Noted*, an English liturgy in plainchant style (1550), and John Day's psalm settings, 'collected into Englyshe metre by T. Sternhold, I. Hopkins & others . . . with apt Notes to synge them withal' (1562).

The earliest polyphonic works for the new Church, by William Mundy, Tallis, Tye, and Sheppard, were frequently simple in style and structure so as to ensure, in conformity with reformed objectives, maximum textual clarity. Following a brief reversion to Catholicism during the reign of Mary I (1553–8), progress was made, under her Protestant successors Elizabeth I (1558–1603) and James I (1603–25), towards the creation of a more expansive English musical liturgy, with major polyphonic settings of vernacular anthem and service texts, chiefly for the use of cathedral and collegiate choirs. An important innovation from 1600 was the 'verse' form (used for both anthems and services) in which sections for one or more solo singers alternate with ones for the full choir, with accompaniment for organ or a consort of strings (or both). Among the most important contributors to the Anglican repertory at this period were John Mundy, Morley, Tomkins, Weelkes, and Orlando Gibbons. Byrd, the greatest English composer of the age, was a lifelong Catholic (who appears to have evaded persecution through Elizabeth's special protection), but nonetheless produced works of superb quality for the Reformed as well as the Roman rite.

See also HYMN, 2.   BS

📖 E. H. FELLOWES, *English Cathedral Music* (London, 1941, 5/1969, rev. J. A. Westrup) · P. NETTL, *Luther and Music* (Philadelphia, 1948) · P. LE HURAY, *Music and the Reformation in England, 1549–1660* (London, 1967, 2/1978) · F. BLUME, *Protestant Church Music: A History* (Eng. trans., London, 1974)

'Reformation' Symphony. Mendelssohn's Symphony no. 5 in D major (1832); it was written for (but not played at) the tercentenary in Augsburg of the foundation of the Lutheran Reformed Church, the first and last movements quoting the *'Dresden Amen'* and the Lutheran chorale *Ein' feste Burg*.

refrain. A term originating in poetry, where it describes a recurrent phrase in the text, which can be applied to music in various ways: in song it can refer to a section of recurrent text, usually with the same, but sometimes with different, music; in instrumental music it refers to recurrent sections of a piece. The repertory with which the term is perhaps most commonly associated is that of 12th- to 14th-century French song, where refrains may be found in courtly *romances*, dance-songs (*caroles*), and plays; they are also found incorporated into polyphonic motets. The *rondeau*, *virelai*, and *ballade* have refrains as part of the poetic structure of their texts; these are distinct, though related. Some other forms give their refrains specific names; the refrain of a medieval carol, for instance, is known as a 'burden'. In modern times, a refrain is often synonymous with 'chorus', because it is usually sung by a group as opposed to a soloist.   PW

regal. 1. A small Renaissance organ—the first with beating reeds—that produced a snarling sound. Because each reed had a very small resonator, regals took up very little space: one form, the 'bible regal', was folded up to resemble a large book.

2. An organ reed stop similar in sound to the regal.

Reger, (Johann Baptist Joseph) **Max**(imilian) (*b* Brand, Bavaria, 19 March 1873; *d* Leipzig, 11 May 1916). German composer, pianist, conductor, and teacher. His father, a keen amateur musician, taught him the organ and encouraged his early musical ability. Adalbert Lindner, Max's first formal teacher in Weiden, where he grew up, introduced him to the music of Bach and Beethoven, who were to be important influences; and by the age of 15 Reger had composed a number of instrumental works. In 1890 he was sent to study with Riemann in Sondershausen and Wiesbaden, where he continued to compose chamber works, lieder, and piano pieces. He later taught at the Wiesbaden Conservatory and did military service; at the same time he began to drink heavily.

In 1898 illness forced Reger to return home to Weiden, where he revived an earlier interest in the organ, composing a number of large-scale, elaborate works—among them several chorale fantasias, two sonatas, and the *Fantasia and Fugue on BACH*, op. 46—which both rely on and extend the traditions of Bach and Mendelssohn; these and other organ works were championed by the organist Karl Straube, a lifelong friend, who later was appointed to St Thomas's, Leipzig. Reger experienced a productive period in Munich from 1901, teaching at the Königliche Akademie der Tonkunst, giving piano recitals, and composing; his works from this time include the Piano Quintet op. 64, the piano *Variations and Fugue on a Theme of Bach* op. 81, and the Sinfonietta op. 90. But his bold ideas found little favour there with the 'New German School' of Liszt and Wagner supporters, and his works were regularly attacked in the local press. He responded spiritedly, writing to one critic: 'I am sitting

in the smallest room of my house. I have your review in front of me. Very shortly it will be behind me'.

In 1907 Reger moved to Leipzig as music director of the university (1907–8) and professor of composition at the conservatory. He made European concert tours, which much enhanced his reputation, and received several honours. In 1911 he was appointed music director of the court orchestra at Meiningen, where he conducted mainly Germanic symphonic works (Beethoven, Brahms, Bruckner) and increased his own output of orchestral music; it was here that he wrote the *Variations and Fugue on a Theme of Mozart* op. 132. His duties were onerous; he became ill in 1913—hardly surprisingly, given the amount of food and drink he could consume—and, after the outbreak of war, moved in 1915 to a more restful situation at Jena. His sudden, early death was probably the result of a heart attack. He left a *Romance* for violin and orchestra that must remain unfinished: he composed without sketches, conceiving his complex music in its entirety in his head, and even visualizing its layout in score—he would bind together in advance the number of pages each work was going to require.

In the early part of the 20th century Reger's music was poorly appreciated outside his native Germany; but the intellectually lazy image of him as a turgid contrapuntist has now been replaced by a realization of the power and originality of his music. In his large, diverse output, composed during a life that was relatively short but filled with frenetic activity, he combined the contrapuntal discipline drawn from his love of Bach's music with a renewal of the Classical–Romantic traditions of Brahms; to this combination he brought his own audacious harmonic and melodic ideas. His fondness for chromaticism was such that Schoenberg suspected he would soon join the ranks of the atonalists, but for Reger chromaticism was a means of expanding the resources of tonality, not a harbinger of its imminent collapse.

Indeed, it is precisely Reger's modernity that is now being acknowledged, and with the reassessment of his standing, the textures that were once held to be overloaded are being seen as natural polyphony that is as rewarding as it is complex. Similarly, his emotional range is much wider than hitherto admitted: in his larger-scale organ works in particular he is capable of an unbridled fury fiercer than anything in Expressionism; and yet in smaller forms—as, for example, in the songs *Schlichte Weisen* or the piano suite *Träume am Kamin*—he can produce gentle miniatures of heart-warming simplicity.

But such was Reger the man: he could use language of farmyard directness, demonstrate a razor-sharp wit, and play astoundingly well even when drunk; he showed unquenchable energy in everything he undertook, and enjoyed one of the most breathtakingly capacious musical intellects of all time. Reger would not have been credible as a fictional invention, but his unlikely life illustrates Walt Whitman's dictum: 'I am vast. I contain multitudes'. JN/MA

    H. WIRTH, *Max Reger* (Hamburg, 1973) · S. POPP and S. SHIGIHARA (eds.), *Auf der Suche nach dem Werk: Max Reger—sein Schaffen—seine Sammlung* (Karlsruhe, 1998)

reggae. An international form of popular music which originated in Jamaica. It is instantly recognizable from the counterpoint between the bass and drum downbeat, and the offbeat rhythm section. The immediate origins of reggae were in *ska and *rock steady; from the latter, reggae took over the use of the bass as a percussion instrument. Reggae developed in about 1968, particularly as a result of the Maytals' *Do the Reggay*. It also became closely associated with the Rastafarian religion. In the 1970s, Bob Marley and the Wailers (previously performers of ska) achieved worldwide recognition as a result of the dissemination of their music by Island Records. Marley's style of reggae remains the classic form, now referred to as 'roots reggae'. Since his death in 1981 reggae has changed and given rise to other forms, known variously as 'rockers', 'militant', 'bam-bam', and 'ragga'. It has also contributed to the development of *rap and *techno. PW

    K. CHANG and W. CHENG, *Reggae Routes: The Story of Jamaican Music* (Philadelphia, 1998)

Regina coeli laetare. See ANTIPHONS OF THE BLESSED VIRGIN MARY.

Regis, Johannes (*b* c.1430; *d* c.1485). Flemish composer. His career was spent at Cambrai, Antwerp, and Soignies. Unlike his contemporaries Ockeghem and Busnois his output is dominated by motets, many of them large-scale festive works for five-part choir. JM

registration. In keyboard playing, the selection of manuals or stops to enhance tone-colour, timbre, and volume. For harpsichordists the choice is usually an individual one involving the addition or subtraction of strings of different timbres or pitches, as well as special muting effects; other factors brought into play are the material from which the plectrum is made and the use of a swell. Registration in organ music is often indicated by the composer and exploits the varying pitches and colours of wooden or metal pipes (or both) to imitate a kaleidoscope of sounds and instruments. NPDC

Regnart, Jacob (*b* ?Douai, c.1540; *d* Prague, 16 Oct. 1599). Netherlands composer. He was one of five brothers, all of whom became musicians, and he spent most of his life in the service of the emperors Maximilian II and Rudolf II. From 1582 he was vice-Kapellmeister and then Kapellmeister to Archduke Ferdinand in Innsbruck, returning to Prague after Ferdinand's death to serve as vice-Kapellmeister under Philippe de Monte. He composed some charming songs in the style of the Italian villanella; the three volumes published as *Teutsche Lieder* between 1576 and 1579 received several reprints, as well as being used in arrangements by other composers. DA

rehearsal. An important preparatory stage in the presentation of an opera or a concert. Practices have changed over time, reflecting the evolving roles of players, singers, conductors, composers, directors, and patrons. In the case of large-scale works, separate rehearsals are usually held for different sections of the orchestra, for the principal singers and for the chorus (both with piano accompaniment), and for other personnel such as lighting staff, in order to overcome any technical difficulties. (For the performers, these preliminary sessions take place most often in a hall or studio, and not where the actual performance will be given.) The elements are then gradually brought together, and details of balance, interpretation, unity, and dynamics are improved. It is common for a public audience to be invited to the final dress rehearsal of an opera. SH

Reich, Steve [Stephen] (Michael) (*b* New York, 3 Oct. 1936). American composer. He studied philosophy at Cornell University (1953–7) and composition at the Juilliard School (1958–61) and Mills College, Oakland, California, with Berio and Milhaud (1962–3). More important, however, was his experience at the San Francisco Tape Music Center (1964–5) and his later acquaintance with the music of West Africa and Bali.

In his first pieces (*It's Gonna Rain*, 1965) Reich worked with tape loops of the same spoken phrase, played back and slowly moving out of synchrony. Reinterpreted for instruments, this became a technique of sliding identical repeated figures out of phase (see PHASING): hence *Piano Phase* for two pianos (1967) and *Phase Patterns* for four electric organs (1970). Reich also, in another piece for the latter instrumentation, *Four Organs* (also 1970), built up a repeating figure from one note plus silence to a whole long bar and dismantled it again. Both techniques allowed him to project rhythmic processes which could be directly observed by the listener, while the demands on performers led him to restrict his music for many years to his own ensemble. The culmination of this early period came in the concert-length *Drumming* (1971), for percussion, female voices, and piccolo.

During the next decade his writing became more lustrous, less insistent on process, and he began to write for larger groups, as in *Music for 18 Musicians* (1976) and subsequently in works for symphony orchestra. But if there was some rapprochement with the mainstream here, he also began to concern himself with another tradition, that of his Jewish ancestors. Studies of Hebrew cantillation led to *Tehillim* for voices and instruments (1981), and *Different Trains* for string quartet and recordings (1988) was partly based on memories of Holocaust survivors, the pitch melodies of voices becoming the live music's figures. The same technique, but now used with a larger ensemble and with video rather than purely audio recordings, produced (in collaboration with Reich's wife, the video maker Beryl Korot) the spectacular documentary-drama *The Cave* (1990–3), on the story of Abraham as remembered by Israeli, Palestinian, and American interviewees.

PG

S. REICH, *Writings about Music* (Halifax, NS, 1974; enlarged edn forthcoming) · K. POTTER, *Four Musical Minimalists: La Monte Young, Terry Riley, Steve Reich, Philip Glass* (Cambridge, 2000)

Reicha [Rejcha], **Antoine**(-Joseph) [Antonín, Anton] (*b* Prague, 26 Feb. 1770; *d* Paris, 28 May 1836). Czech composer, teacher, and theorist. His earliest instruction came from his uncle, a cellist and composer. In 1785 he played the flute in the court orchestra in Bonn, meeting Beethoven and later Haydn. After a brief sojourn in Paris he moved to Vienna, where he renewed his friendships with both men. In 1808 he settled in Paris. While continuing to compose he produced several treatises. He was appointed professor of counterpoint and fugue at the Paris Conservatoire in 1818, and though his teaching was valued for precision and broadmindedness by his pupils he was often at loggerheads with his colleagues Cherubini and Fétis. His pupils included Liszt, Berlioz, Gounod, and briefly, but significantly, Franck. In 1829 he became a French citizen and in 1831 was awarded the Légion d'Honneur.

Reicha's preoccupation with contrapuntal experiment marked him as an original. He made interesting use of reminiscence motifs in his operas, and several of his ensemble works have thematic links between movements. His 36 Fugues for keyboard (1803), dedicated to Haydn and widely known in his day, are notable for their experiments with tonality and irregular time signatures. Reicha's idiomatic writing for wind distinguishes not only his numerous orchestral works but has ensured the popularity of his quintets. Of his theoretical works, the *Cours de composition musicale* (published 1816–18) and *Traité de haute composition musicale* (1824–6) were particularly important. If they

excited much contemporary criticism and controversy, his writings were sufficiently widely disseminated among 19th-century composers for Reicha to be of much more than passing significance as a theorist.

JSm

O. ŠOTOLOVÁ, *Antonín Rejcha* (Prague, 1977; Eng. trans. 1990)

Reichardt, Johann Friedrich (*b* Königsberg [now Kaliningrad], 25 Nov. 1752; *d* Giebichenstein, nr Halle, 27 Jan. 1814). German composer and writer on music. After early studies he went on an extended tour of Germany, in 1776 obtaining a post as Kapellmeister to Frederick the Great in Berlin. There he at first wrote and conducted Italian operas. In 1783 he founded the Berlin Concert Spirituel, on the Parisian model, to promote the performance of neglected music. A visit to Paris in 1785 produced the French operas *Tamerlan* and *Panthée* (both 1786), intended for Paris and influenced by Gluck. Returning to Berlin, he had his greatest success with *Brenno* (1789).

As well as composing some 1500 songs, setting much Goethe in a manner that won the poet's admiration for the primacy given to the verse, Reichardt wrote *Singspiele*, including three to Goethe's texts and one of the most successful of the 1798 *Tempest* operas as *Die Geisterinsel*. He also pioneered the *Liederspiel*, in which songs are dramatically linked by dialogue. His contribution to the development of a German national opera included important critical writings, notably *Über die deutsche comische Oper* (1774), a study of Hiller's opera *Die Jagd*. Dismissed for subversive views in 1794, he retreated to his castle at Giebichenstein, which became a meeting-place for young Romantics.   DA/JW

Reiche, Johann Gottfried (*b* Weissenfels, 5 Feb. 1667; *d* Leipzig, 6 Oct. 1734). German trumpeter and composer. In 1700 he was engaged in Leipzig as a town musician. He became one of the foremost interpreters of Bach's trumpet parts. 24 of his wind sonatas were published under the title *Neue Quatricinia* (Leipzig, 1696).

WT

Reigen (Ger., 'dance'). A term found in such titles as *Gnomenreigen* and in *Kuhreigen* (see RANZ DES VACHES).

Reimann, Aribert (*b* Berlin, 4 March 1936). German composer and pianist. He studied in West Berlin with Boris Blacher, and later in Vienna. He became well known as an accompanist, notably in a regular partnership with Dietrich Fischer-Dieskau, for whom he has also composed several major works. His early compositions use serial techniques, but after 1967 he composed more freely, influenced by Indian music. Reimann is best known for his operas, including *Ein*

Traumspiel, after August Strindberg's *Dream Play* (Kiel, 1965), *Melusine* (Schwetzingen, 1971), *Lear*, after Shakespeare (Munich, 1978), *Die Gespenstersonate*, after Strindberg's *Ghost Sonata* (Berlin, 1984), *Troades*, after Euripides (Munich, 1986), and *Das Schloss*, after Franz Kafka's *The Castle* (Berlin, 1991). He has also written a ballet, orchestral and chamber music, and a great deal of vocal music—notably *Wolkenloses Christfest*, a Requiem for baritone, cello, and orchestra (1974), and *Unrevealed* for baritone and string quartet, on poems and a letter of Byron (1980).   ABur

Re in ascolto, Un ('The Listening King'). Opera in two parts by Berio to a libretto he assembled from texts by Italo Calvino, W. H. Auden, Friedrich Einsiedel, and Friedrich Wilhelm Gotter (Salzburg, 1984).

Reincken [Reinken, Reincke, Reini(c)ke], **Johann Adam** [Jan Adams] (*b* Deventer, *bapt.* ? 10 Dec. 1643; *d* Hamburg, 24 Nov. 1722). Dutch composer and organist, of German descent. He studied with Heinrich Scheidemann in Hamburg and succeeded him at St Catherine's in 1663; his playing was so famous that Bach walked from Lüneburg to hear him. He wrote some virtuoso organ music as well as a set of sonatas in which the dance rhythms of the *sonata da camera* are used in a sequence of movements in the manner of the *sonata da chiesa*.   DA

Reine, La ('The Queen'). Nickname of Haydn's Symphony no. 85 in B♭ major (1785), the fourth of the Paris symphonies, so called because it was much admired by Marie Antoinette, 'La Reine de France'.

Reinecke, Carl (Heinrich Carsten) (*b* Altona, Hamburg, 23 June 1824; *d* Leipzig, 10 March 1910). German composer. After early years as a concert pianist, also teaching in Barmen and Breslau, he became a teacher of piano and composition at the Leipzig Conservatory in 1860; he was made director in 1897. A conservative by nature, he insisted on a thorough training in every department of music, and the distinguished teachers he drew to Leipzig made the conservatory one of the most famous in Europe. His pupils included Grieg, Svendsen, Sullivan, and Weingartner. Having earlier attracted the attention of Mendelssohn, he became conductor of the Gewandhaus concerts; here he was also a strong disciplinarian. He wrote some charming piano music and was a noted editor of the standard classics.   DA/JW

Reiner, Fritz (*b* Budapest, 19 Dec. 1888; *d* New York, 15 Nov. 1963). Hungarian-born American conductor. Initially trained as a composer at the Liszt Academy in Budapest, he became a répétiteur at the Budapest Opera in 1909; he was catapulted to stardom the same year, taking over a performance of *Carmen* at short notice when the scheduled conductor fell ill. In 1914 he was appointed principal conductor of the Dresden State Opera, where he gave the German premiere of Strauss's *Die Frau ohne Schatten* (1919).

In 1922 Reiner was invited to the USA by the Cincinnati Symphony, with which he remained until 1931, subsequently conducting the Philadelphia Orchestra (1931–8) and the Pittsburgh Symphony (1938–48) before becoming music director of the Metropolitan Opera, New York (1948–53), where his interpretations of Mozart, Wagner, and Strauss became legendary. From 1953 until his death he was conductor of the Chicago Symphony. A painstaking craftsman, he nevertheless generated an almost visceral excitement in performance, qualities that made him the ideal Strauss conductor. He was also a superlative orchestral trainer, turning both the Pittsburgh and Chicago Symphonies into two of the finest ensembles in the world.   TA

   📖 P. Hart, *Fritz Reiner: A Biography* (Evanston, IL, 1994, rev. repr. 1997)

Reinicke [Reinike, Reinken], **Johann Adam**. See Reincken, Johann Adam.

Reissiger, Karl Gottlieb (*b* Belzig, 31 Jan. 1798; *d* Dresden, 7 Nov. 1859). German composer. His opera *Didone abbandonata* (1824) was given with some success in Dresden by Weber, whom he succeeded as director of the Hofoper in 1826, becoming Hofkapellmeister in 1828. He conducted the successful premiere of *Rienzi* in 1842, but then antagonized Wagner by refusing to set his libretto *Die hohe Braut*. His own most successful operas were *Die Felsenmühle zu Étalières* (1831), an old-fashioned rescue opera, and *Adèle de Foix* (1841), a cumbersome grand opera, both containing a mixture of German, French, and Italian influences. The latter was generously praised by Schumann.   JW

Reizenstein, Franz (Theodor) (*b* Nuremberg, 7 June 1911; *d* London, 15 Oct. 1968). German-born British composer. He studied with Hindemith in Berlin (1930–4) and with Vaughan Williams at the RCM (1934–6). Having settled in England he worked as a pianist and chamber musician. His smallish creative output consists of two sonatas for violin (1945, 1968) and one each for viola (1967) and cello (1947) besides other chamber, orchestral, and vocal music, finely crafted in a style that departs from that of the later Hindemith. The same skill is shown in the comic pastiches he wrote for Hoffnung concerts, for example *Let's Fake an Opera* (1958).   PG

Rejoice in the Lord alway. See 'Bell' Anthem.

réjouissance (Fr.). 'Rejoicing', 'celebration'. Bach, Handel, and others used it as the title of a lively movement, e.g. the last movement of Bach's Orchestral Suite no. 4.

Relâche ('No Show'; 'Theatre Closed'). Ballet in two acts by Satie to a scenario by Francis Picabia, with a cinematographic entr'acte by René Clair; it was choreographed by Jean Börlin (Paris, 1924).

related keys. In harmonic theory, keys seen in terms of their 'relationship' to the tonic. For example, in C major the closest related keys are the dominant major (G), the mediant minor (E), the subdominant major (F), the supertonic minor (D), and the relative minor (A). The first four of these keys have a difference in key signature from C major of only one sharp or flat and the last has the same key signature as C major. See also CIRCLE OF FIFTHS; MODULATION.

relative major, relative minor. See KEY SIGNATURE.

religion and music. The imaginary theatre in which the human race ponders its subconscious sense of destiny has always required some ritual representation of the encounter between God or gods and humans. The seriousness of religion has generally been expressed in the hallowing of a performance space, temple, or church. The physical decoration, ennoblement, and beautification of that more often architectural than natural location has usually been associated with combinations of music, words, and silence to command the focused attention on which religious observance counts. For Quakers, silent meditation is the norm. For most other Christians, instrumental and vocal music embody praise of the divine, and at best may suggest a foretaste of paradise.

Music was an important element in the religious festivals that formed the tradition of Greek theatre. In a sense, the theatrical use of music in opera (itself a neo-classical revival of Greek theatre by Renaissance Christian humanists) could be considered an unconscious manifestation of the religious instinct. Mystery plays, designed to communicate faith stories to an illiterate public, and certainly laced with music, were ancestors of opera and oratorio. Almost certainly the very first opera not devoted to retelling the story of a classical myth was Cavalieri's dialogue between the body and the soul (*Rappresentatione di Anima, et di Corpo*, 1600). Oratorio functions as operatic-style narrative to be performed in a sacred space, with dramatic realization only in the theatre of the mind.

Texts when sung or chanted have more power to impress the listener. They can also carry through a large building where acoustics have been able to amplify the effect since long before electronic technology was in-

vented. The association of music with words can reinforce, and also intriguingly modulate, the meaning with which those words are held to be invested. This is important, since religious rituals appeal to the imagination as much as to the intellect. All music is in a sense 'soul' music—though in the 20th century the term was reserved for a kind of expressive jazz produced by the descendants of black slaves in the Americas, most of whom readily identified with the Jews lamenting captivity and dispossession by the waters of Babylon (in Latin the text for some of the most powerfully emotional polyphonic motets of the 16th century).

In the context of the Christian religion, with its public manifestations or services, and its evangelistical intentions, music has helped to carry a text audibly throughout a large building, when delivered by a chorus, a solo singer, or a deacon or priest at full power. Music has also helped sustain attention over extended periods of time in the lengthy liturgical offices devoted to teaching and studying (the so-called Monastic Hours, together with their equivalents in reformed or Anglican traditions, such as Evensong or Matins).

Two areas of musical invention have often been in conflict so far as the church has been concerned. There is a natural opposition between rhythm and harmony, which endow fascination and beauty and enhance the celebratory intent (akin to dancing), and verbal clarity and communicativeness against which musical complexity and ambition may militate. This was a central concern both of the Counter-Reformation Council of Trent and of the Protestant reformers, with their vernacular metrical versions of the psalms. Iconoclastic Puritanism took exception to 'vain' decoration, as the Cistercian monastic order had done long before. The Levellers broke down organs in churches during the English 17th-century Civil War. Meanwhile Puritan parliamentary edicts banned theatrical entertainment. The 'devil in music' is the suspicious-sounding tritone, but the devil's inspiration of the best tunes and entertainment generally has always been suspected by those of a puritanical disposition. Yet, equally, the divine nature of good music is asserted by the church and by church-commissioned painters, Cecilia being the patron saint of music, and the coronation of the Virgin Mary (her bodily assumption into heaven) often being depicted in association with an iconography of angels performing on heavenly (but obviously real and earthly) musical instruments.

Lyricism or lyrical association has always been seen as appropriate to Christian rites, not least because of the biblical tradition of the psalms. In the Bible King David, the supposed poet of the psalms, accompanied himself when young on a manually plucked instrument as he sang to King Saul, whom he later succeeded on the throne of Israel, attempting to relieve Saul's conscience and assist his sleep. The healing and inspiring power of music has always been as vital to Christian rituals as its celebratory character and overt physicality. The organs with which most west European churches and cathedrals are equipped (but not, interestingly, the holy places of the Orthodox churches) are aural demonstrations of the fundamental power of the divine. The organ with its huge pipes and blowers can shake a church building and remind people how a greater force or authority can shake the finest endeavours of humanity to the foundations.

The history of Western music during the modern age (from the late 14th century to the present time) has been a great entwining of music for the court, music for the people, and music for the church—and the borrowings and sharings of material in all directions have been legion. Many of the most famous medieval and Renaissance settings of Mass Ordinary texts have been based on popular songs. Until the popularization of printing and the growth of a modern music-printing industry, the only composers who could live from their work were those employed by the church or the court, or those in holy orders whose basic (and sometimes much more than basic) needs were thus assured by the institution which they served. Thanks to Christianity and to the power of the church and of the reformed churches, and thanks to the competitive and demonstrative instincts of merchants and of courts, there is an enormous repertory of music for choirs and for instruments associated with the services of the different Christian denominations.

Both Roman Catholic and reformed liturgies have demanded a variety of seasonal material reflecting the church year—and many of those masterpieces have become common currency across ecclesiastical borders (Bach cantatas and Passion settings, for example).

St Paul's biblical injunction to women to keep silent in church has had profound musical and social consequences. Only in recent decades have Anglican cathedral choirs begun to include girls. In the late Middle Ages, partly as a result of the close encounter between the Western Catholic Church and Islam in Sicily and Spain, the practice of castration of prepubescent choir singers came to be tolerated if not encouraged by the Church. Adult castratos could sing the most florid music imaginable and continued to preserve the Pauline ban on female voices in church—at least in the pope's Sistine Chapel in Rome—until the 20th century. The castratos also, of course, transformed the operatic art of bel canto in the 17th and 18th centuries.

The revival of interest in early music in Britain was strongly identified with church musicians and encouraged by such organizations as the Alcuin Club and the Plainsong and Mediaeval Music Society. Bach concluded all his works with the letters AMDG—the initials of the Latin words meaning 'To the greater glory of God'. But in the secular 20th and 21st centuries, when in some Western societies musical observance and devotion have become more widespread and commercially exploitable than religious observance, a number of composers including Messiaen and Tavener have been particularly identified with numinous aspirations. At the same time composers who have not considered themselves to be committed to the faith have (like Verdi and Berlioz) taken with relish to the exploration, dramatization, and embellishment of such texts as the Requiem Mass with its central concern for individual human destiny. The ability of music to negotiate the heart of religion has never seemed so integrational a cultural force as in an age of fundamental religious revaluation and scientific change.   TS

📖 G. R. Woodward, *Songs of Syon* (London, 4/1923) · E. H. Fellowes, *English Cathedral Music* (London, 1973, rev. J. A. Westrup) · E. Hanslick, 'An aesthetic hearing', *The Beautiful in Music*, trans. G. Cohen (New York, 1974) · *Worship and Music: Some Theological and Theoretical Background to the Report 'In Tune with Heaven'*, Report of the Archbishops' Commission on Church Music, pt 2 (London, 1992) · D. Davie, *The Eighteenth-Century Hymn* (Cambridge, 1993) · C. R. Campling, *The Food of Love: Reflections on Music and Faith* (London, 1997) · J. Caldwell, 'Music', *The Oxford Companion to Christian Thought* (Oxford, 2000)

relish. English name for an ornament used in instrumental music of the 17th and early 18th centuries. A single relish (usually indicated thus: ∴) was simply a short *trill with a turn, but a double relish was more complex, consisting usually of a trill on each of two successive notes, closing with a turn and an appoggiatura; it was indicated by a cluster of dots (e.g. ∴∴, as in Ex. 1), or by two such clusters separated by two diagonal strokes (❧).

Ex. 1

remettre (Fr.). 'To put back': an instruction in French organ music to take off a stop.

reminiscence motif (Ger.: *Reminiszenzmotiv*, *Erinnerungsmotiv*). In opera, a theme or other musical idea which returns in an unaltered state to identify a character or signify a character's recollection of the past; it is a precursor of the *leitmotif. The 'forbidden question' motif in Wagner's *Lohengrin* is an example.

AL

Renaissance, The (*see opposite page*)

Renaissance instruments. Medieval instruments in Europe had most commonly been used singly, often self-accompanied with a drone, or occasionally in pairs. One of the notable changes that marks the Renaissance from the Middle Ages musically is the development of *polyphony: multiple strands of interwoven melody for voices or instruments. Polyphony encouraged the use of larger ensembles, and demanded sets of instruments that would blend together across the whole vocal range; this led to the creation of families of the same instrument, from large to small.

Another important development during the 15th century was the division of instruments into *haut (loud, outdoor instruments) and *bas* (quieter, more intimate instruments for less extrovert occasions). Only two groups of instruments could play freely in both types of ensemble: the *cornett and *sackbut—which could play quietly in the chamber and with singers or loudly from church and town-hall towers—and the *tabor and *tambourine. While there is no evidence for any instrumental music from the 15th and 16th centuries equivalent in scale to Tallis's 40-part motet *Spem in alium*, the potential for such a piece was there, and instrumental music in three to six parts, mostly in the form of dances, has survived in considerable quantity.

New instruments that appeared during the early Renaissance, in the second half of the 15th century, included the harpsichord, the clavichord, and the *viol and *violin families. The new strung keyboard instruments, small and portable in comparison with organs, allowed single players to play polyphonic music in a variety of settings, including their own homes. Other instrumentalists (e.g. lute players) were also encouraged to develop the techniques necessary to play polyphony. Consequently, they also developed such notational methods as *tablature for writing down this music in forms idiomatic to their own and other instruments.

Evidence suggests that the viol was first created in Spain when the bow, then used on the Moorish *rabāb, was adapted to the normally plucked *vihuela. The instruments were further developed in Italy, much of

which was then under Spanish rule. Violins are thought to be a wholly Italian conception of the early 16th century, though similar instruments are documented as being played in France and Poland at about the same time. The violin combines features of several other instruments in use at the time: the small size and three strings of the *rebec, and the body shape of the medieval *fiddle and its refined Renaissance derivative, the *lira da braccio*. The *lira* resulted from Renaissance fascination with classical Greece, for, though different in all respects except that it had strings, it was equated with Orpheus' lyre.

The first two major organological encyclopedias come from this period—Sebastian Virdung's *Musica getutscht* of 1511, which is also a tutor for lute and recorder, and Martin Agricola's *Musica instrumentalis deudsch* of 1529, based on Virdung but with some new material—as well as Arnolt Schlick's compendium on the organ (*Spiegel der Orgelmacher und Organisten*, also 1511). As a result, much more precise knowledge of instruments and their use began to be documented in this era, though very few examples are extant.

The 16th and early 17th centuries saw the continual improvement of many types of instrument. There are enormous changes between those shown by Virdung and those of the early Baroque period illustrated by Praetorius in 1619, changes which resulted in greatly enhanced musical potential. Woodwind instrument bores were redesigned to extend their range and improve their tone-quality. Viols and violins were provided with soundposts to enhance their sound. The compass of keyboard instruments was widened and new tuning systems and *temperaments were developed. The Renaissance was, as its name implies, a period of renewal, invention, and rejuvenation of both music and instruments.

JMo

Renard (*Bayka pro lisu, petukha, kota da barana*; 'Fable of the Fox, the Cock, the Cat, and the Ram'). Burlesque in song and dance in one act by Stravinsky to his own libretto after Russian folk tales; it was choreographed by Bronislava Nijinska for Diaghilev's Ballets Russes (Paris, 1922).

Re pastore, Il ('The Shepherd King'). Serenata in two acts by Mozart to a libretto by Pietro Metastasio (Salzburg, 1775). The libretto was used by several composers including Gluck (1756).

repeat. The sign (:||) that appears at the end of a piece or section of music to indicate a return to the opening. If there is a reversed sign (||:) at the beginning of a section of music, the repeat sign at the end indicates a return to that sign only, not to the beginning of the piece. See also DA CAPO.

(*cont. on p. 1050*)

The Renaissance

The classical ideal

It is clear that, from some time during the second half of the 15th century, composers and musical commentators believed that they were witnessing a new era in which musicians were writing in accordance with a new set of aesthetic and philosophical ideas derived from ancient, classical authors. In this sense, the musical achievements of the period, and the ways in which they were viewed, are directly descended from a set of beliefs which, in general cultural terms, originated in the 14th century. As early as 1350 Boccaccio had claimed that Giotto 'had brought back to light that art which for many years had lain buried under errors', and half a century later the Florentine historian Francesco Villani wrote that Dante had 'recalled poetry as from an abyss of shadows into the light'.

This kind of trope, in which one remarkable individual is allotted the historical responsibility for the 'rebirth' of a particular art following a period of neglect during the Middle Ages, became standard in writings about arts and letters, and eventually passed into those about music. One of the first commentators to show an interest in these ideas was Johannes Tinctoris (c.1434–?1511), a Franco-Flemish theorist and composer who found employment at the court of King Ferdinand I of Naples in the early 1470s. It was there that he wrote most of his treatises including the *Proportionale* (c.1472–5), in the preface to which he cites the Platonic view that music was the most important of all the sciences, and that knowledge of music was essential for the educated. Even more interesting than this display of humanist credentials is his elevation of the French and Franco-Flemish composers of his own time to an unprecedented level of achievement, and his identification of the English school (and especially Dunstaple) as the point of departure for a new style. In effect Tinctoris delineated the first phase of the Renaissance in music much as Boccaccio had done for literature and painting. His writings constitute the beginnings of a Renaissance historiography of music.

For architects like Andrea Palladio, who took as his fundamental text the *De architectura* by the military engineer Vitruvius (*fl c.*50–26 BC), the rediscovery of ancient buildings had an eminently practical purpose, as it had for such earlier practitioners as Leon Battista Alberti (1404–72). They were interested not merely in the spirit of classical antiquity, as a vague aesthetic objective, but in the actual detail of ancient buildings, and in the 'justest Reason and the finest Proportion' (as Palladio put it) which informed their design. In this way, the study of both surviving buildings and classical theory provided the basis for a new theory of architecture that was consciously opposed to Gothic practice.

Humanism and music

In music, such a connection between classical models and modern practice was not possible. Since knowledge of ancient Greek music was restricted to a handful of indecipherable fragments, known only to a small circle of scholars, the relationship between Renaissance music and its classical models was quite different from that of the other arts, all of which could make direct appeals to ancient survivals as the starting-point for a new style. That relationship was not pragmatic but aesthetic, and had more to do with the effects of ancient music as described in classical literature, above all in the myths of Apollo and Orpheus. Popularized by Angelo Poliziano and the vernacular translations of Ovid, which were printed in considerable numbers during the 16th century, those fables were also familiar to educated audiences from engravings of famous contemporary depictions of some of the key episodes in the legends of these musical gods, such as Raphael's *Parnassus* in the Vatican. In other words it was the power and authority of music, its ability to move the hearts and minds of men, that was seized on rather than its sound—which, in any case, remained frustratingly elusive notwithstanding humanistic research.

In spite of some of the obscure, antiquarian concerns of humanist engagement with the music of the classical past, the impact of humanism itself should not be underestimated; it was largely because of it that music came to be thought of not as a branch of mathematics, which is how it had been regarded during the Middle Ages, but rather as an art intimately related to the classical ideal of rhetorical eloquence. Thus the relationship between words and music became central to Renaissance composers, and musical humanism an important motor of stylistic change. This also meant that much humanist theory was in turn related to changes in the style and form of the major musical repertories of the period, shaped as they were by religious, economic, and social forces. The insistence on textual intelligibility in both Catholic and Protestant thinking, the vivid imagery used by madrigalists like Wert and Marenzio, the attempts of the Pléiade in France to unite music and poetry, the activities of Bardi's *camerata in Florence—all these are in part products of a shared set of beliefs influenced by humanistic theorizing about the equality of music and verse. At a later stage, characterized by Monteverdi as the *seconda pratica*, music was subjugated to poetry, a perversion of the union believed to have existed in classical antiquity.

The northern influence

In addition to their constant comparisons between the effects of modern music and that of classical antiquity, theorists from Tinctoris onwards also emphasized that the music of the early Renaissance was composed by northerners. According to the Florentine writer Cosimo Bartoli (1503–72), it was Ockeghem who 'rediscovered' music after the 'dark ages'; his role could be compared to that of Donatello, who had been responsible for the 'rebirth' of sculpture. Similarly, Bartoli likened Josquin and Michelangelo as 'prodigies of nature' who brought this rediscovered art to the summit of achievement; he also extolled the music of Verdelot and others. Although a number of Italian composers find their way into Bartoli's discussion, it is the northerners who predominate and who are responsible for the new style.

The anti-medieval position implicit in Bartoli's text becomes explicit in Zarlino's *Le istitutioni harmoniche* (1558), the most influential treatise to be published anywhere during the second half of the 16th century.

For Zarlino the music of classical antiquity represented the 'height of perfection', that of the Middle Ages the 'lowest depths'. The hero of Zarlino's account is his own teacher, Willaert (see below)—yet another northerner, presented as a 'new Pythagoras' who had brought music to its present state of grace. Following a long-established pattern, Josquin, Willaert, and other northerners crossed the Alps to find work and establish their reputations, attracted by the wealth of the Italian courts and the opportunities provided by the church in general and by Rome, the centre of Christendom, in particular. This again separates the renaissance in music from that of the other arts, in which the early developments marking the moment of 'rebirth' characteristically take place on Italian (usually Florentine) soil at the hands of native Italians. In contrast, the early renaissance in music is enacted in Italy, but by composers who had been trained in the north, many in the comparatively small geographical area round Cambrai.

With the exception of Johannes de Quadris, there were few Italian composers of note active between about 1420 and 1490. Even after then, the Italians who did become prominent (notably the frottolists, including Marchetto Cara and Bartolomeo Tromboncino) were of slight importance compared to the northern composers, singers, and instrumentalists who continued to come to Italy in considerable numbers. By the mid-16th century that position had begun to change, and by the beginning of the next century it had been completely reversed. Willaert—who as *maestro di cappella* at St Mark's in Venice for more than 30 years was responsible not only for providing a substantial corpus of polyphony for liturgical performance, but also for training a number of gifted Italian pupils, including Cipriano de Rore, to carry on his work there—was one of the most important figures in this shift, but the change has more to do with social and cultural factors than with the activities of individuals.

Italian supremacy

While Willaert stands at the head of a specifically Venetian tradition which includes Andrea and Giovanni Gabrieli and also Monteverdi, elsewhere in Italy the domination of Italian composers is equally marked: Palestrina and Marenzio in Rome; the composers of early opera, Peri and Caccini, in Florence; and Monteverdi (before his move from Mantua) and, briefly, Gesualdo at the north Italian courts. This preponderance of Italian musicians on Italian soil in this late phase of the Renaissance is observable everywhere; in small churches, cathedrals, academies (some of which specialized in the performance of music), and the homes of aristocratic patrons as well as in the larger church institutions and the courts.

Italian musicians and composers, even if not of the first rank, also travelled abroad to work: Alessandro Orologio, who served at the court of Christian IV in Denmark, and Alfonso Ferrabosco, whose influence on Byrd's music was considerable, are but two examples among many. At the same time, the lure of Italy continued to exert its fascination on northeners; both Morales and Victoria spent periods in Rome during Palestrina's lifetime, and Schütz made visits to Venice to study with Monteverdi, 'il divino Claudio', already acknowledged by contemporaries to be the finest composer of his age. It is implicit in this roll-call of composers that the idea of a renaissance in music is not to do with a common style, but rather with shared ideals.

Pan-European changes

The noticeable increase in musical activity throughout Europe, so characteristic of the period, is to be explained by a combination of social, cultural, and technological developments. The expansion of the merchant classes was already a feature of life in the 15th century, and by the 16th it had become a phenomenon. The cultural interests of this group, concerned as much with consolidating their social status as with bolstering their political and new-found economic power, are reflected in an educational curriculum that placed a new emphasis on practical musicianship as an aspect of manners. Supported by courtesy books such as Baldassare Castiglione's *Il libro del cortegiano* ('The Book of the Courtier'), the new imperative became the driving force behind such essentially domestic genres as the chanson and the madrigal, and the repertories of keyboard and lute music that became so popular with the European bourgeoisie during the second half of the 16th century.

The role of music-printing in the growth of musical literacy which accompanied these social trends was fundamental, since it made written music both more accessible and more international. As with all such revolutions, the rate of motion in the wake of Ottaviano Petrucci's 'invention' of music printing in 1501 was somewhat slower than is often assumed, and even in Italy manuscript dissemination continued to be common until the fifth decade of the century. By 1600 the picture had changed, and in a central area bounded by Paris and Lyons to the west, Nuremberg and Frankfurt to the east, Antwerp to the north, and Rome to the south, with Venice both literally and geographically at the centre, the printing press came to dominate the market for music books of all kinds.

Yet in spite of the tendency towards greater stylistic uniformity that greater communication and the power of the press undoubtedly encouraged, some local and national traditions (such as the English repertory for viol consort, which never found its way into print) continued to be as distinct and vibrant as they had been during the era of manuscript transmission. Similarly, the greater availability and the increased exchange of repertories that characterize the later phases of the Renaissance continued and were intensified but, as before, the processes of composition, circulation, and performance of music were conditioned at every level by shifting political and social factors. In these terms, as in others, the idea of a renaissance in music remains an elusive category.   IF

I. Fenlon (ed.), *The Renaissance: From the 1470s to the End of the 16th Century*, Man and Music/Music and Society (London, 1989) · T. Knighton and D. Fallows (eds.), *Companion to Medieval and Renaissance Music* (London, 1992) · R. Strohm, *The Rise of European Music, 1380–1500* (Cambridge, 1993) · A. W. Atlas, *Renaissance Music* (New York, 1998) · L. L. Perkins, *Music in the Age of the Renaissance* (New York, 1999)

Répertoires Internationales ... Musicales. See RIdIM; RILM; RIPM; RISM.

répétiteur (Fr.; It.: *repetitore*; Ger.: *Repetitor*). One who coaches the singers or instrumentalists, or both, in an opera house.

répétition (Fr.). *'Rehearsal'.

repiano. A corruption of *ripieno.

reprise (Fr.). 'Repeat'. A return to a first section of music after an intervening and contrasting section; the repeat can be exact, or varied. In C. P. E. Bach's *Sonaten für Clavier mit veränderten Reprisen* (1760), for example, the 'Reprisen' are fully written-out repetitions of the expositions, but in varied form.

In 17th- and 18th-century French harpsichord music, 'reprise' indicates the point to which the performer should return (e.g. at the beginning of the second section in binary form movements and at the head of the refrain in a *rondeau*).   —/JBe

Reproaches. See Improperia.

reproducing piano. The fully developed *player piano, for example the Ampico Duo-Art or Welte-Mignon (1904), capable of recording and reproducing every nuance of a virtuoso's performance.

Requiem Mass (Fr.: *Messe des morts*; Ger.: *Totenmesse*; It.: *Messa per i defunti*; Lat.: *Missa pro defunctis*). The votive Mass for the dead of the Roman rite, the Tridentine version of which begins with the Introit 'Requiem aeternam dona eis Domine' ('Give them eternal rest, O Lord'). Its format is basically identical with that of the normal Latin *Mass, but with the more joyful parts omitted, such as the alleluia (which is replaced by a tract) and the Credo, and the long 13th-century sequence Dies irae ('Day of wrath', suppressed after the Second Vatican Council) interpolated. In describing the musical settings of the normal Mass it was mentioned that certain parts were rarely set to music, because their texts vary from day to day (i.e. the Proper of the Mass). During the period from the Council of Trent until the Second Vatican Council, these passages were constant in the Requiem Mass, and consequently were set (the opening introit, which gives the Mass its name, is an example). Certain small changes occur in the text of some sections—for example, in the Agnus Dei the words 'Dona eis requiem' ('Give them rest') replace 'Miserere nobis' ('Have mercy upon us'). Liturgically the Requiem Mass has its place at funerals and memorial services and on All Souls' Day (2 November), when it is celebrated in memory of the faithful departed.

The sobriety of the traditional plainchants for the Requiem Mass contrasts strangely with some of the dramatic, not to say operatic, approaches to the text pursued by 19th-century composers. Although individual movements were set to polyphony before the 15th century, the first mention of a more or less complete setting (it is extremely rare for all the items to be included) comes in Dufay's will, where he requests that his own setting should be given the day after his funeral. Unfortunately, that work is now lost, and the earliest known to us is Ockeghem's cycle, the austerity of which is tempered by passages of virtuoso counterpoint. Renaissance settings of the Requiem Mass stylistically resemble those of the normal Mass, but generally favour the conservative compositional devices of cantus firmus and plainchant paraphrase over *parody. Although settings in *stile antico* polyphony continued to be composed and performed after 1600, concerted settings influenced by contemporary theatrical music became increasingly popular after the mid-17th century.

Notable settings of the Tridentine Requiem written before the 19th century include those by Victoria (his second setting for six voices of 1605), Jean Gilles (*c*.1700; later sung for the funerals of Rameau and Louis XV), and Mozart (completed after his death by Süssmayr and with some additions by Eybler). In the 19th century two settings stand out for their highly dramatic treatment: Berlioz's (*Grande Messe des morts*, 1837) and Verdi's (1874), which alters the order of the liturgical texts. Also notable are the settings by Cherubini (in C minor, 1816, and D minor, 1836), Bruckner (an early work; 1848–9), Fauré (1887–8), Dvořák (1890), Pizzetti (1922–3), and Duruflé (1947, rev. 1961). Requiem masses not intended for liturgical performance include Britten's *War Requiem* (interpolating texts by Wilfred Owen deploring the violence of war; 1961), Tavener's *Celtic Requiem* (in which children's games are linked to the idea of death; 1972), and Penderecki's *Polish Requiem* (1980–4).

Significantly, the musical tradition of the Requiem Mass has inspired imitation outside the bounds of the Roman Catholic Church. Schütz's *Musikalische Exequien* (1636), Brahms's *A German Requiem* (1865–8), and John Rutter's *Requiem* (1990) are large-scale Protestant memorial works. Substantial portions of the Byzantine Memorial and Funeral Offices have been set by composers including Aleksandr Kastal'sky (1916, rev. 1917), Tavener (1986), and Theodorakis (1983–4, orchestrated 1995). Kabalevsky's 1962 *Requiem* for the victims of World War II is an example of the peculiarly modern genre of the atheistic Requiem.   —/ALi

rescue opera. An opera in which an essential part of the plot turns on the rescue of the hero or heroine from prison or some other threatening situation. The term arose in late 19th-century German criticism as a result of interest in the influences on Beethoven's *Fidelio* (1805). Most examples of the genre are from the second half of the 18th century, particularly during the period of the French Revolution, when the theme of rescue acquired contemporary significance.

Following the example of the librettist Michel-Jean Sedaine (1719–97), the majority of rescue operas emphasized moral factors. Some plots depict an evil tyrant, such as the corrupt mother superior in Berton's *Les Rigueurs du cloître* (1790) or Baron Dourlinski in Cherubini's *Lodoïska* (1791). Others focus on the sacrifices required in order to obtain freedom, as in Cherubini's *Les Deux Journées* (1800). Another group of operas introduces a natural catastrophe, for example the avalanche in Cherubini's *Éliza* (1794) or the storm in Méhul's *Mélidore et Phrosine* (1794), to suggest divine justice. *Fidelio* was in many ways the culmination of the genre, expressing the ideal of freedom.   JW/SH

📖 D. CHARLTON, 'On redefinitions of rescue opera', *Music and the French Revolution*, ed. M. Boyd (Cambridge, 1992), 169–88

resin. See ROSIN.

resolution. The process by which dissonant elements in intervals move to consonant ones. The argument that, in tonal composition, dissonant intervals must ultimately resolve on to consonant ones, to ensure satisfactory closure and completion, reflects the hierarchical priorities of the tonal tradition which flourished before 1900. Early in the 20th century Schoenberg emancipated the dissonance, on the grounds that such a fundamental distinction between harmonic characteristics was no longer valid; in so doing he initiated a conflict, which has persisted ever since, between the instinctive tendency of musicians to recognize, aurally, the distinction between consonance and dissonance, and the intellectual willingness to acknowledge that music can be coherent, and aesthetically satisfying, without 'resolution' in the traditional sense (see CADENCE).   AW

resonance. See ACOUSTICS, 7.

resonator. An air-filled hollow body that reinforces sounds by resonance. On stringed instruments it is sometimes called the soundbox.

resonator guitar. See GUITAR, 4.

Respighi, Ottorino (*b* Bologna, 9 July 1879; *d* Rome, 18 April 1936). Italian composer. In 1891 he entered the Liceo Musicale, Bologna, to learn the violin, and went on to study composition there in 1898 with Luigi Torchi and later with Giuseppe Martucci. In 1900 and 1902 he visited Russia, where he was taught by Rimsky-Korsakov, and in 1908–9 he attended Bruch's com-

position classes in Berlin. He played both the violin and the viola and was for five years (1903–8) a member of Mugellini's quintet in Bologna. He was appointed professor of composition at the Accademia di S. Cecilia, Rome, in 1913 and director there in 1924, but he resigned the directorship in 1926 so that he could spend more time composing, teaching, accompanying his wife, the singer and composer Elsa Olivieri-Sangiacomo (1894–1996), who became his biographer, and conducting his own works.

Respighi's earliest works were chamber and vocal—songs with piano or orchestra and a number of operas, including the highly successful marionette opera *La bella dormente nel bosco* ('Sleeping Beauty'). But it is for his orchestral music that he is best known, notably the descriptive suites *Fontane di Roma* (1914–16) and *Pini di Roma* (1923–4), with their picturesque, sparkling orchestration. In middle age he took a great interest in early music, more from the point of view of the arranger than of the scholar. His symphonic poem *Vetrate di chiesa* ('Stained-Glass Windows', 1925) uses fragments of Gregorian chant, and several other works have titles with archaic references (e.g. the *Concerto gregoriano* for violin and orchestra, 1921). His most enduringly popular works are his arrangements of music by Baroque and early Classical composers, such as the suite *Gli uccelli* (1927), based on bird pieces by Rameau and others; and the ballet *La Boutique fantasque*, which he arranged for Diaghilev in 1919 from pieces by Rossini, retains its appeal. In his later years he returned to opera, but he never achieved more than ephemeral success in the field of dramatic music.   JN/RP

respond (Lat.: *responsa*). 1. Alternative name for *responsory or *response.

2. More specifically, the section sung by the choir or congregation in responsorial chant (see RESPONSORY). The responds, alternating with the verse or verses, are usually marked R or ℟ .

response. In Christian worship, the reply of the congregation or choir to a *versicle. Versicles and responses were a common feature of the Roman *Divine Office before the Second Vatican Council, though they have since been almost entirely supplanted by intercessions in litany form. The traditional Anglican responses are an adaptation of the plainchant of the Roman rite to the English text, the first version of which was published by John Merbecke in *The Booke of Common Praier Noted* in 1550. In Elizabethan times various composers made choral settings of the responses, often taking Merbecke's plainchant adaptations as a cantus firmus in the tenor part. The best known are those by Byrd, Morley, and Tomkins, and two sets of *Preces and Responses* by Tallis. These are usually referred to as festal responses, ferial responses keeping the chant in the treble and being harmonized in a simple fashion. See also PRECES.

responsorial psalmody. The ancient practice of performing a psalmodic text with a congregational or choral refrain after each verse.

responsory (from Lat. *responsorium*). A type of Western liturgical chant, consisting in the responsories of the Roman Office of alternating respond and verse, especially the great responsories (Lat.: *responsoria prolixa*) of Matins (moved after the Second Vatican Council to the Office of Readings) and the lesser responsories (Lat.: *responsoria brevia*) of the daytime Hours. The term is sometimes used broadly to encompass other responsorial chants, including those of the Roman Mass.

Despite attempts to trace their origins directly to the popular cathedral psalmody of late antiquity, it is now accepted that the medieval cycles of melodically florid responsories developed within the context of monastic vigils, the readings of which they were designed to accompany. During the Middle Ages, the number of solo verses performed was gradually reduced to one plus the Lesser Doxology, while repetitions of the respond became limited to performances of its latter half (the *repetendum*).

Polyphonic settings of the responsories maintained the principle of alternation; until the 16th century only the initial statement of the respond and the verses were polyphonic, but later in that century the polyphonic and plainchant sections were reversed, so that only repeats of the respond were set to music (e.g. Sheppard's setting of the Easter responsory for Matins, *Dum transisset Sabbatum*). Many continental settings are through-composed in an ABCB form, which was also often used for texts that were not responsories.

—/ALı

rest. In musical notation, a sign indicating a momentary absence of sound. Every standard note-value has a corresponding rest which, like the note itself, may be lengthened in value by the addition of a *dot or dots. Ex. 1 shows the common forms of rest.

A whole bar's silence in any time signature is traditionally indicated by a semibreve rest (Ex. 1*b*). In individual instrumental parts two bars' rest may occasionally be indicated by a breve rest with a figure '2' above it (Ex. 2*a*), but in general more extensive periods of silence are normally represented by a horizontal line with a figure above it showing the number of bars' rest (Ex. 2*b*).

See also NOTATION, Fig. 6; GENERALPAUSE; PAUSE, 2; TACET.

Ex. 1

(a) breve (e) quaver
(b) semibreve (f) semiquaver
(c) minim (g) demisemiquaver
(d) crotchet (h) hemidemisemiquaver

Ex. 2

(a) 2 (b) 15

'Resurrection' Symphony. Popular name for Mahler's Symphony no. 2 in C minor (1888–94, revised 1903), so called because the finale is a setting for soprano and alto soloists, chorus, and orchestra of Friedrich Gottlieb Klopstock's poem *Aufersteh'n* ('Resurrection').

Reszke, Jean de. See DE RESZKE, JEAN.

retardando (It.). See RITARDANDO.

retardation. A *suspension resolved by rising a degree rather than falling.

retenant, retenu (Fr.). 'Holding back', 'held back', i.e. slowing down, but immediately, like *ritenuto*, rather than gradually like *rallentando*.

retirada (It.). In 17th-century ballets and suites, a closing movement.

retrograde [cancrizans (Lat., 'crab-like'), *Krebsgang* (Ger., 'crab motion')]. The backward-read version of a melody or, in *serial music, a series (i.e. the form obtained by reading the original from right to left). As serial music allows any note in the series to be placed at any octave level, the retrograde form of a serial melody need not give rise to a reversal of melodic contour.

retrograde canon. See CANON.

retrograde inversion. A version of a melody or series that is both inverted and reversed (see INVERSION, 3; RETROGRADE).

Reubke, (Friedrich) **Julius** (*b* Hausneindorf, 23 March 1834; *d* Pillnitz, 3 June 1858). German composer, organist, and pianist. He studied at the Berlin Conservatory with Theodor Kullak (for piano) and A. B. Marx (for composition). His compositional style underwent a radical change after his arrival in Weimar in 1856, and in a short time he had assimilated many of Liszt's techniques, basing his Organ Sonata on Liszt's *Ad nos* Fantasy and Fugue, and his Piano Sonata on Liszt's Sonata in B minor. Neither, however, is a slavish imitation, and the Piano Sonata in particular displays a novel formal structure, adopting the procedure of hinting at elements of a multi-movement work within a single-movement sonata form, but subdividing the piece in a different manner. At the time of his death at the age of 24, he was one of the most talented of all Liszt's students in Weimar, and his two major works—the Organ Sonata on the 94th Psalm, and the Piano Sonata in B♭ minor—show a fluent mastery of the then radical harmonic, motivic, and structural procedures of the 'Music of the Future'. Had he lived, it is likely that he would have made a significant contribution to 19th-century music.   KH

réunis (Fr.). 1. 'United', 'reunited', e.g. in string playing to countermand *divisés*, 'divided'.

2. In organ music, 'coupled'.

3. In 18th-century French music, the term *les goûts réunis* ('reunion of tastes') was used to describe an ideal kind of music towards which composers should strive—the union of the best elements of French and Italian music, as opposed to the specifically French style adopted by the followers of Lully. Composers of music in the *goûts réunis* include François Couperin and J.-M. Leclair.

Reutter, Georg (von) (i) (*b* Vienna, 1656; *d* Vienna, 29 Aug. 1738). Austrian organist and composer. In 1686 he succeeded Johann Kaspar Kerll as organist at St Stephen's Cathedral, Vienna. From 1696 he served the imperial court chapel as accompanist for the opera, and from 1700 as court organist. At St Stephen's he succeeded Fux as vice-Kapellmeister in 1712, and in 1715 became Kapellmeister. He is now remembered solely for his organ preludes and toccatas.   WT/BS

Reutter, (Johann Adam Joseph Karl) **Georg** (von) (ii) (*b* Vienna, 1708; *d* Vienna, 11 March 1772). Austrian composer, son of Georg Reutter (i). He studied with his

father and Caldara. He enjoyed a successful career at court, as vice-Kapellmeister after Fux's death in 1741 and as Kapellmeister in 1751, but was restricted thereafter by economies imposed by Empress Maria Theresa. In 1731 he married the opera singer Theresa Holzhauer, and in 1738 succeeded his father as Kapellmeister at St Stephen's, where in 1749 he is alleged to have dismissed Haydn, somewhat callously, when his voice broke. His large output includes operas, oratorios, masses, and a fine Requiem in C minor (1753). His music was often criticized for the busy style of its string writing—expressed, proverbially, as 'rushing [rauschende] violins *à la* Reutter'.   WT/BS

Reutter, Hermann (*b* Stuttgart, 17 June 1900; *d* Heidenheim an der Brenz, 1 Jan. 1985). German composer, pianist, and teacher. He studied in Munich and was influenced early in his career by Hindemith, though he later adopted a more Romantic language. He taught in Stuttgart and Frankfurt, and in 1956 became director of the Stuttgart State Conservatory. Reutter was well known as the accompanist of many of the leading German singers of his time. He wrote operas—notably *Doktor Johannes Faust* (Frankfurt, 1936)—and ballets, and orchestral, choral, and chamber music; but he is best remembered for his many solo songs and cycles.   ABur

reveille (from Fr. *réveil*, 'awakening'). The military signal (pronounced 'revelly' or 'revally' by the British) that begins the day in the army.

'Revolutionary' Study. Nickname of Chopin's *Étude* in C minor for piano op. 10 no. 12 (1830), so called because it is said that he composed it as a patriotic reaction to hearing that Warsaw had been captured by the Russians.

revue. A theatrical entertainment consisting of songs and sketches, usually of a satirical nature—a sort of variety show with an intellectual flavour. A revue is sometimes the work of one composer or writer but is more often a miscellany by many hands. It was of French origin, the name implying a 'review' of the year's events with caricatures, and it became popular in about 1840. A similar kind of entertainment flourished in England a few years later. Modern revue has followed two courses: the 'intimate' revue (as above), with a small cast and nearly always satirical content, as propagated in university productions like *Beyond the Fringe* (1960); and the lavish spectacular (e.g. the *Ziegfeld Follies*), glorifying song and dance, visual effects, and female allure.   PGa

Revueltas, Silvestre (*b* Durango, 31 Dec. 1899; *d* Mexico City, 5 Oct. 1940). Mexican composer.

Although he studied in the USA, musical and personal experiences on tour in Mexico and Spain proved more influential on his own music, which is based on folk melody, tricked out in lavish instrumentation and powerful motor rhythms. The fiercely compressed *Redes* ('Nets') and *Sensemaya* (both 1938) are highly characteristic examples of his pungent orchestral idiom. The music for the film *Noche de los mayas* (1939) offers a more extended and varied introduction to a highly individual musical personality.   CW

Reyer, Ernest [Rey, Louis-Étienne-Ernest] (*b* Marseilles, 1 Dec. 1823; *d* Le Lavandou, 15 Jan. 1909). French composer and critic. As a composer he was largely self-taught. He had some success with two *opéras comiques* staged in Paris: *Maître Wolfram* (1854) and *La Statue* (1861). In 1866 he became librarian of the Opéra and, like his friend and supporter Berlioz, music critic of the *Journal des débats*, where his sharp pen gained him enemies. He was a lover of Weber and Spontini and, for the time, an unusually level-headed critic of Wagner. His reputation finally rested on two serious operas, *Sigurd* and *Salammbô*, staged in Paris in 1885 and 1900 respectively (shortly after premieres in Brussels), in which occasionally clumsy construction is redeemed by inventive use of orchestral colour. A collection of his newspaper articles, *Quarante ans de musique* (Paris, 1909), is a valuable and entertaining source.   RN

Reynolds, Roger (*b* Detroit, 18 July 1934). American composer. He studied music and science at the University of Michigan, where he co-founded the ONCE festivals of new music. In 1972 he began teaching at the University of California at San Diego, but he has been active internationally, notably in Japan and at the computer music studios at Stanford and in Paris. Much of his music requires advanced technology, used especially to move sounds in space, but much also has to do with the voice. Among his works are the music-theatre piece *The Emperor of Ice Cream* (1965), *The Palace* for bass-baritone and tape (1978–80), *Watershed* for solo percussionist and electronics (1995) and *The Red Act Arias* for narrator, chorus, orchestra, and electronics (1997).   PG

Rezniček, Emil (Nikolaus) **von** (*b* Vienna, 4 May 1860; *d* Berlin, 2 Aug. 1945). Austrian composer. He was sent to Graz to study law, but music was his first love and he soon moved on to Leipzig to study with Carl Reinecke and Salomon Jadassohn. Later he held various posts as a theatre and opera conductor in Austria and Germany. His compositions include many operas, four symphonies and other orchestral works, three string quartets, and some choral music. But he is remembered today almost entirely for the short, sparkling overture to his opera *Donna Diana* (Prague, 1894).

PG/ABur

rf, rfz. Abbreviations for **rinforzando*.

R.H. Abbreviation for right hand, *rechte Hand* (Ger.).

rhapsody (from Gk. *rhapsodia*; Fr.: *rapsodie, rhapsodie*; Ger.: *Rhapsodie*; It.: *rapsodia*). An instrumental piece in one movement, often based on popular, national, or folk melodies. The term (which in ancient Greece denoted the recitation of epic poetry, especially that of Homer) was first used in a musical sense by Tomášek in the 19th century, as a title for a set of six piano pieces published in about 1803; thereafter it was applied to certain character pieces with no specific form. Rhapsodies may be passionate, nostalgic, or improvisatory. 19th-century interest in Hungarian and Gypsy violin playing led to the composition of pieces in that style, for example by Liszt (19 Hungarian Rhapsodies, 1846–55), Dvořák (Slavonic Rhapsodies, 1878; based on folk tunes), Dohnányi, and Bartók.

Brahms wrote three piano rhapsodies (op. 79, op. 119) as well as the *Alto Rhapsody* (op. 53) for contralto, male chorus, and orchestra. The improvisatory element of the rhapsody inspired Debussy's two examples (one for alto saxophone, the other for clarinet), Gershwin's jazz-influenced *Rhapsody in Blue* for piano and orchestra, and Rakhmaninov's *Rhapsody on a Theme of Paganini* (variations of Paganini's violin *Caprice* no. 2 in A minor). The influence of folksong permeates many British examples, including Vaughan Williams's *Norfolk Rhapsody*, Butterworth's *A Shropshire Lad*, and Delius's *Brigg Fair* (subtitled 'An English Rhapsody').

WT/JBe

Rhapsody in Blue. Work (1924) by Gershwin for piano and orchestra, orchestrated by Ferde Grofé, who reorchestrated it in 1926 and 1942 (the version most often used).

Rhapsody on a Theme of Paganini. Rakhmaninov's op. 43 (1934) for piano and orchestra, 24 variations on Paganini's *Caprice* no. 24 in A minor for violin.

Rheinberger, Josef (Gabriel) (*b* Vaduz, 17 March 1839; *d* Munich, 25 Nov. 1901). German organist and composer. A professional organist from childhood, he studied at the Munich Conservatory (1850–4), where from 1859 he was a respected teacher of the organ and composition. He produced an enormous output of compositions in all genres but is remembered almost exclusively for his 20 organ sonatas, solidly constructed in a Brahmsian style.   PG

Rheingold, Das ('The Rhinegold'). Opera in four scenes by Wagner to his own libretto, the 'preliminary evening' of Der *Ring des Nibelungen.

'Rhenish' Symphony. Schumann's Symphony no. 3 in E♭ major (1850) (his fourth in order of composition); the fourth of its five movements was inspired by the installation of a cardinal at Cologne on the Rhine.

rhetoric. Originally a term referring to the skills associated with public oratory, 'rhetoric' has come to mean the art of verbal discourse. Analogies have long been drawn between music and spoken arts. Parallels between persuasive oratory and eloquent musical performance are evident, but the precise relationship of music to rhetoric has often been unclear. For much of its history Western music has been predominantly vocal, and musicians have been influenced to some degree by rhetorical principles in setting texts. It is possible to argue that independent instrumental music also had a rhetorical basis in the early modern era, and that rhetorical modes of thought to some extent shaped instrumental music until the early 19th century.

Musical concepts of rhetoric ultimately stem from the ancient world, especially as transmitted in the writings of Aristotle, Cicero, and Quintilian. The five constituents of classical rhetoric—*inventio* (finding an argument), *dispositio* (ordering the argument), *elocutio* (style), *memoria*, and *pronunciatio* (delivery), the whole aiming to move (*movere*), instruct (*docere*), and delight (*delectere*)—were sometimes invoked by musical theorists during the Middle Ages. But it was towards the end of the 15th century that new vernacular translations of classical texts on rhetoric had a profound effect on musicians. Josquin and his contemporaries were among the earliest composers to set texts in an overtly rhetorical way, working with word-generated musical shapes, structuring their music to match the pacing of the text, and carefully controlling textural variety. Above all, composers of Josquin's generation had a strong sense of *decorum*, matching the style of their music to the content of the text.

It was during the Baroque era that rhetoric had the most pervasive and profound effect on musical thought and practice: indeed, impassioned oratory may be considered the musical ideal of the period. Much Baroque music theory drew its frame of reference from rhetoric, especially in discussions of form and style. Mattheson, in *Der vollkommene Capellmeister* (1739), expounded a complete compositional method based on rhetoric, and many writers discussed form as a *dispositio*. As early as the 16th century theorists had compared musical figures to metaphors (see FIGURES, DOCTRINE OF). *Figurae* became more central to musical discourse in the following century and, although there was no

systematic theory of figures, many writers presented definitions of them. In addition to listing the familiar figures of *hypotyposis* (so-called madrigalisms) and figures reflecting verbal syntax (e.g. *interrogatio*, the rising intonation of a question, and the ascending leap of *exclamatio*), theorists also discussed figures relating to such technical issues as repetition, imitation, the treatment of dissonance, and the use of silence. The ultimate goal of a well-ordered *dispositio* and carefully chosen *figurae* in Baroque music was to move the listener to an idealized emotional state, and all elements of music were deployed in the service of affections (see AFFECTIONS, DOCTRINE OF).

In the changing aesthetic climate of the later 18th century writers on music began to scorn the rhetorical basis of composition, focusing instead on the individuality of a composer's ideas. Nevertheless, analogies continued to be drawn between music and speech acts: the symphony was compared to a powerful oration (Sulzer), the concerto to 'the tragedy of the ancients' (Koch), and a conversational ideal was often invoked in relation to the string quartet. During the Classical period rhetoric was also considered relevant to good performance. Writers likened performing to 'speaking in tones' and recommended that performers should emulate successful speakers. But with the rise of the virtuoso performer and the development of organic metaphors in music criticism and theory in the early 19th century, rhetorical analogies dwindled to insignificance in musical discourse.   TRJ

📖 D. BARTEL, *Handbuch der musikalischen Figurenlehre* (Regensburg, 1985; enlarged Eng. trans., *Musica poetica: Musical-Rhetorical Figures in German Baroque Music*, 1997) · M. E. BONDS, *Wordless Rhetoric: Musical Form and the Metaphor of the Oration* (Cambridge, MA, 1991) · B. WILSON, 'Ut oratoria musica in the writings of Renaissance music theorists', *Festa musicologica: Essays in Honor of George J. Buelow*, ed. T. J. Mathiesen and B. V. Rivera (Stuyvesant, NY, 1995), 341–68.

Rhinegold, The. See RHEINGOLD, DAS.

rhythm 1. Introduction; 2. The components of rhythm; 3. History; 4. Present-day attitudes to rhythm

1. Introduction

Rhythm in music is normally felt to embrace everything to do with both time and motion—with the organization of musical events in time, however flexible in metre and tempo, irregular in accent, or free in durational values. Much argument has been devoted to the question of whether rhythm or pitch is more fundamental to music. It is certainly the case that we are more likely to talk about rhythm without any mention of music, or 'time' without any mention of art, than to talk about pitch in a non-musical context. But this in itself merely serves to stress the fact that the connotations of rhythm are a good deal more complex than those of 'rhythmic' or 'rhythmical'. When we refer to the strongly rhythmic character of a march, or a typical piece of rock music, it is the recurrence of heavy, regular accentuation and the distinction between relatively strong and relatively weak accents which we have in mind, no less than the presence of a constant pulse or tempo. 'Rhythmic' music tends to be that with the most predictable, least varied, rhythmic character.

2. The components of rhythm

The rhythmic character of music from the Baroque, Classical, and Romantic periods is often very different from that of much earlier or more recent music. Obviously, regular accentuation and phrase-structure did not suddenly appear with Monteverdi and Bach and vanish with Schoenberg and Stockhausen, but the rhythmic characteristics which prevailed in music between Monteverdi and Schoenberg cannot always be found in music from other periods, or of other cultures. Ex. 1 reproduces a short piano piece by Schumann,

Ex. 1

Ex. 2

'Valse allemande' from *Carnaval* (1833–5), which has those features of regularity and equality which characterize musical rhythm during the era of tonality. This is a compound of various interdependent elements: a metre, indicated by the time signature, which remains unchanged throughout, and which carries with it the implication that the strongest accents will normally fall on the first beat of the bar; a pulse, or tempo, which also remains basically constant, and which relates to the time signature—it may be indicated by a metronome mark, a form of words, or, as here, by both; the durations used for the various musical events (minims, semiquavers, etc.), which combine to produce a rhythmic 'profile'; and the phrases which result from the arrangement of musical material in groups of beats and bars—bars tending, as here, to be grouped in multiples of two and four. These features of regularity and equality will naturally be modified at times by the use of syncopation, cross-accents, or those 'irrational' durational values which temporarily override the units indicated in the time signature, as well as by modifications of tempo—rubato, accelerando, or ritardando. But such deviations make their effect precisely because the music has its basis in equality and regularity.

Ex. 2 presents the first eight bars of *Klavierstück III* by Stockhausen, composed in the early 1950s. The complete piece is 16 bars long, but it subdivides much less readily than the Schumann into units of equal length. The music retains a regular quaver pulse, but the time signature changes frequently, and although the first beat of the bar is often marked with a relatively loud dynamic, the rhythmic profile of the music clearly reduces the structural significance of such accents as recurrent features. No tempo is indicated, although a note at the beginning of the complete set of four pieces states that the speed is determined by playing the smallest note-value as fast as possible. No deviations from this basic pulse are indicated—no accelerando or ritardando—but the avoidance of repeated rhythmic patterns prevents the emergence of any phrase-structure comparable to Schumann's.

Although the highly fragmented nature of Stockhausen's piece gives it a very specific rhythmic style, its essential irregularity and diversity link it in principle with a good deal of early music, which lacked that need for regular accents in all parts at once, and for a phrase-structure and harmonic rhythm based on a four-bar norm, which appeared later. What connects the two examples, and a lot of earlier music too, is the presence of a constant pulse; and although the way in which such pulsation gradually evolved is still the subject of controversy—and research—it will be clear that it could not have done so conclusively without a parallel evolution of musical notation. Music that was originally notated without the explicit provision of precise durations and a constant pulse (for example, early Christian hymns and troubadour songs) would not necessarily have been performed without such a pulse, however, and it is worth recalling that when modern composers use a notation in which rhythms and durations are left to the performer to improvise on the spur of the moment, they often feel it necessary to spell out in words the fact that they wish performers to avoid consistent pulsation.

3. History

It is in its emancipation from both speech and solo performance that music has developed its most characteristic and complex qualities. In ancient times, as for example with the Greek philosopher Aristoxenus (*c*.350 BC), musical rhythm and speech rhythm could be discussed in the same terms, music and poetry differing only to the extent that music used specific pitches and intervals. More than 1000 years were to elapse before a form of musical notation developed which showed time-values with any precision. But as music evolved from monophony to polyphony, and it became possible to create extended compositions involving large numbers of performers, so a notation which aimed at a high degree of precision with respect to duration as well as pitch was developed, as a means of coordinating and synchronizing the realization of the composer's intentions as expressed on paper.

Such precision was certainly not to be found in neumes, and although by the late 12th century a system of six rhythmic modes was in use whose basic patterns of 'long' and 'short' durations were ultimately traceable to the 'feet' of Greek poetics, it was a 13th-century theorist whose work most clearly codified the fundamental change whereby a genuinely mensural form of notation became possible. Franco of Cologne, in his *Ars cantus mensurabilis* (*c*.1260), established the vital principle that the duration of a note should be indicated by its actual shape, and the four durational values he defined—duplex long (◖◗), long (◖), breve (■), and semibreve (♦),—form the basis of all subsequent developments in rhythmic notation, and therefore in rhythmic organization. Another important early theorist, Philippe de *Vitry, was the first to make a clear distinction between duple and triple metre in his treatise *Ars nova* (*c*.1322). However, although 14th-century music moved closer to modern rhythmic practice, it was not until the 17th century that most of the complications and confusions of early rhythmic theory and procedures were finally eliminated.

It is particularly important not to confuse early and modern functions. For example, time signatures can be found in music from the 13th century to the 16th, but they do not imply the kind of regular, recurrent metrical accents in performance that are common in more recent music. It was the introduction of bar-lines, initially in 16th-century lute and keyboard music and then generally during the 17th century, which was ultimately the most crucial development, since through them modern metrical schemes became possible.

Such developments offer the strongest confirmation of the obvious point that music and poetry did not evolve in the same way. Verbal 'performance', whether on stage or in everyday life, has remained essentially a monophonic rather than a polyphonic activity. And even when collective speech is required, as when a church congregation recites the Creed or the Lord's Prayer, a high degree of rhythmic unison—or **homorhythm'—is aimed at. A large measure of metric regularity may indeed be achieved in the case of material which is spoken collectively week after week, year after year, in church, but it has never proved necessary to notate that material rhythmically and metrically, with precisely proportioned durations for every syllable of text, for the simple reason that no one has sought to combine other strands of text in counterpoint with it.

By contrast, the polyphonic music which developed in the late Middle Ages would not have made sense if there had been more than a slight degree of flexibility about the way in which the participating voices fitted together. Pitch relations could function only if they were notated rhythmically, with reference to the same unit of value.

After 1600, as music became more concerted, as instrumental styles evolved, and the influence of the dance increased, the bar-line came into its own, and aesthetic and technical principles of unity and coherence came to govern rhythmic features. There was a greater need for a regularity which was allied as much to accent and the recurrence of metric units (bars and groups of bars) as to the repetition of rhythmic patterns and phrases in association with the melodic and harmonic organization of the composition. The climax of this process may be seen in the establishment of the conductor not just as someone indicating an unaccented *tactus* to a small choir, as in the 15th and 16th centuries, but as the controller of accent and phrasing as well as of pulse.

During the 18th century, the discussion of rhythm by theorists became more directly concerned with these new form-building features: Joseph Riepel, for example, in a treatise published in 1754, divided melodic lines into segments according to principles of pitch organization—an important stage in the working out of analytical techniques which attempt to fuse hierarchic interpretations of pitch function and rhythm. In the 19th century, Classical rhythmic characteristics began to break down, especially in the radically new form of music drama devised by Wagner. The two principal theorists of the time, Moritz Hauptmann (1792–1868) and Hugo Riemann (1849–1919), can both be seen as selective rather than comprehensive in their work, and neither was primarily concerned with the most recent musical developments. Hauptmann, indeed, was essentially a theorist: he quoted no music examples in his important study of metre, first published in 1864. But Riemann's argument that musical structures have an ideal length based on multiples of four finds much support in the Classical compositions that were his principal source, even though his exclusion of harmonic and tonal aspects from his analyses was a limitation for which many later theorists have sought to compensate.

Of course, the role of rhythm and metre in Classical and Romantic music is much more than the mere mechanical preservation of an inflexible beat with an unvaried emphasis at the beginning of every bar, or multiple of two, four, or eight bars. And in the 20th century a balance was achieved in a certain kind of concerted music between the coordination of the parts at fixed points and the avoidance of exact synchronization between those points. In several works by Boulez and Lutosławski, for example, the conductor ceases to be a time-beater and phrase-shaper and becomes the controller of large-scale formal and textural processes. Indeed, the 20th century can be seen as reliving the entire history of musical rhythm, to the extent that, while notations that avoided durational precision (and therefore rejected the necessity for a constant pulse) could be found, some composers—Messiaen, Babbitt, Maxwell Davies among them—used rhythmic modes or series which extended the control of pre-determined duration patterns over entire structures.

4. Present-day attitudes to rhythm

While modern composers have been exploring various degrees of rhythmic freedom or strictness, music theory since 1900 advanced most significantly towards the integration of rhythmic analysis with that of music's most fundamental pitch processes. Theorists have explored the possibility of an overall view of tonal structure in which rhythmic and durational factors participate more fully than they did in the pioneering harmonic and tonal analyses of Heinrich Schenker (see ANALYSIS, 3): and they have also extended their investigations to consider the interaction of pitch and rhythmic structures in post-tonal music.

Many theorists, even those sympathetic to Schenker's view of tonal organization, consider that he did not go far enough in exploring his perception that rhythm, like pitch, functions on distinct yet interacting levels in tonal music. From Maury Yeston (*The Stratification of Musical Rhythm*, 1976) and Carl Schachter ('Rhythm and linear analysis', *The Music Forum*, 4, 1976, and 5, 1980) to William Rothstein (*Phrase Rhythm in Tonal Music*, 1989) and Christopher Hasty (*Meter as Rhythm*, 1997) theorists have continued to explore the complex and delicate art of relating the fundamental dimensions of pitch and duration, register and accent. In doing so, they bear out David Epstein's claim that, in deeper levels of structural rhythm, Schenker was 'very much in tune with rhythmic reality' (*Beyond Orpheus*, 1979). And the increasing interest in studying musical performance also reinforces the need for theories which attempt to explain how time is both projected by performers and perceived by listeners (see, for example, Epstein's *Shaping Time: Music, the Brain and Performance*, 1995).

For most listeners, nevertheless, the primary quality of rhythm is as an immediate succession of durations and occasional accents, approached and quitted in ways which participate in the shaping processes of the entire musical fabric, and which may even, in certain very 'rhythmical' works, seem to dominate that fabric. As Schoenberg put it, in his *Fundamentals of Musical Composition*, 'rhythm is particularly important in moulding the phrase', which he regarded as the smallest structural unit of a composition. 'It contributes to interest and variety; it establishes character, and it is often the determining factor in establishing the unity of the phrase.' And it was Schoenberg who, in his *Harmonielehre*, expressed with characteristic trenchancy the purpose, and problem, of musical rhythm:

> If we ask ourselves why we measure music in time in the first place, we can only answer: because we would not otherwise bring it into being. We measure time to make it conform to ourselves, to give it boundaries. We can transmit or portray only that which has boundaries. The creative imagination, however, can envision the unbounded, or at least the apparently unbounded. Thus in art we always represent something unbounded by means of something bounded.

This vividly describes the essential constraints provided by rhythmic structuring, constraints without which musical art, even in its post-tonal phase, would be impossible.   AW

rhythm and blues. A term applied to a variety of musical styles: in the late 1940s and 50s, to the music of certain bands whose style was dominated by *blues vocals, saxophone solos, and a strong beat (e.g. those of Joe Liggins and Johnny Otis, which developed into 'soul jazz'); to a style of blues singing, exemplified by Nat King Cole and, later, Ray Charles; to certain blues singer-guitarists with a jazz orientation (e.g. T-Bone Walker and, later, B. B. King); to *doo-wop; and to proto-*rock and roll, for example some work by Chuck Berry and Little Richard. 'Rhythm and blues' was originally a term coined in 1949 by *Billboard* as an alternative name for the black record charts to replace the by then unacceptable 'race records'; as such it was a catch-all term for all black American music, and remained so for 20 years, when it was replaced in *Billboard* by *soul'.   PW

📖 G. GART (ed.), *First Pressings: The History of Rhythm & Blues*, 9 vols. (Milford, NH, 1989–95)

rhythmic modes. In the 13th century, a set of six short rhythmic patterns defined by music theorists and associated particularly with the music of the Notre Dame school. In each mode, long and short values are arranged in a distinctive order similar to those of the poetic feet. See NOTATION, 2.

rhythm section. The percussion, bass, and chordal instruments of a jazz ensemble, typically consisting of drum kit, double bass (always played pizzicato) or electric bass, and piano and/or guitar.

ribs (Fr.: *éclisses*; Ger.: *Zargen*; It.: *fascie*). The strips of wood that form the arched back of a lute. The term may also be used when referring to members of the violin, viol, and guitar families to denote the side pieces that connect the back and belly. The structural function of ribs—to provide a soundbox with which the strings and belly of the instrument can interact—should not be confused with that of bars, which are sometimes placed inside the belly to enhance the resonant qualities of the instrument. LC

ricercar (from It. *ricercare*, 'to seek'; Fr.: *recherché*; Ger.: *Ricercar*; Sp.: *recercada*). A type of instrumental piece common during the 16th and 17th centuries. The earliest were improvisatory in style, often for solo instruments such as the bass viol or lute (e.g. those in Francesco Spinacino's *Intabulatura de lauto*, 1607). They consisted of highly embellished, unaccompanied melody, often containing many scalar passages, and were not very different from the early 16th-century *prelude. They usually lack a distinct shape and are seemingly designed as an exercise for the fingers (see also TIENTO; TOCCATA). The composers of these pieces were usually themselves virtuoso players or teachers, and they include the first writers of treatises on individual instruments, for example Ganassi, Ortiz, and Giovanni Bassano. This kind of ricercar has little musical interest, and is artistically on a par with Czerny's duller technical studies.

Another type, which flourished late in the 16th century, was the duo, written for the instruction of beginners in part-music. The instruments are rarely specified, but the frequent use of themes based on easily remembered *solmization syllables suggests that they were exercises in sight-reading, perhaps for singers as well as instrumentalists. Some of these are musically more appealing than solo ricercars, especially those of Lassus (e.g. *Motetti et ricercari*, 1585).

The best-known and most durable kind of ricercar was the instrumental equivalent of the vocal *motet. The earliest, dating from the mid-16th century (e.g. those by M. A. Cavazzoni), are obviously conceived in the same tradition as polyphonic church music, with flowing melodic lines organized by imitative points. The principal differences between the motet and the ricercar are that the instrumental pieces use a wider range of melody; they do not have to give frequent rests to each 'voice'; and, since there are no demands imposed by setting words, they can use fewer themes, even in some cases being monothematic. At first they were written mainly in four parts, but Andrea Gabrieli wrote one for eight instruments and there were many keyboard transcriptions that added ornaments but preserved the basically polyphonic structure. The vogue for

this kind of ricercar was at its height in the latter part of the 16th century, and by 1600 the genre was overtaken in popularity by the more tuneful *canzona. Some of the ricercars published about this time show the influence of the canzona in their sprightly rhythms, and it is sometimes difficult to distinguish between the two.

From about 1610, motet-like instrumental pieces are more often called 'sonata' (e.g. Giovanni Gabrieli's *Sonata pian e forte*) and the term 'ricercar' tends to be associated with works that display some form of contrapuntal learnedness. In this sense, the word persisted until the end of the Baroque period, the most notable examples being in Bach's *Musical Offering* (1747). There, as was almost traditional by this time, the two 'ricercari' are placed among a set of canons and are fugal in style, written in old-fashioned note-values and conceived as a display of compositional skill. It is difficult by this stage to say how, if at all, these differ from fugues. DA

Richafort, Jean (*b* c.1480, *d* ?Bruges, c.1547). Franco-Flemish composer. One of the leading figures of the post-Josquin generation, he spent his career mainly in the Netherlands (though he was in Italy as a singer in the French royal chapel in the second decade of the 15th century) and he may have been in the service of Mary of Hungary, regent of the Netherlands, in the 1530s. He was *maître de chapelle* at St Gilles, Bruges, between 1542 and 1547. As well as chansons and church music, his output includes a fine Requiem Mass, which quotes some music by Josquin and was perhaps written on the death of that master in 1521. JM

Richard Coeur-de-lion ('Richard the Lionheart'). Opera in three acts by Grétry to a libretto by Michel-Jean Sedaine after an anonymous account in the *Bibliothèque universelle des romans*, ii (1776) (Paris, 1784); it was revised into four acts (Fontainebleau, 1785).

Richter, Franz Xaver (*b* ?Holesov, 1 Dec. 1709; *d* Strasbourg, 12 Sept. 1789). German composer, of Czech descent. His musical education was gleaned from Fux's *Gradus ad Parnassum*, which he may have studied with the author in Vienna. In 1740 he became vice-Kapellmeister at Allgäu and by 1746 he was serving the Elector Palatine Carl Theodor in Mannheim as a composer and bass singer. He had become known as a composer in the 1740s with the publication of six symphonies. It is from the Mannheim period that his large composition treatise *Harmonische Belehrungen* (published 1804), somewhat derivative of Fux, survives. His personal musical tastes, however, were not in tune with those of his contemporaries at Mannheim, and in 1769 he became Kapellmeister of Strasbourg Cathedral. His compositions, conservative in style, favour a greater use of counterpoint than was customary at Mannheim in the 1750s and 60s, though the democratic part-writing in his string quartets looks forward to later Classical practices. He was drawn increasingly to church music, composing oratorios, some 34 masses, and several cantatas and motets.   JSM

Richter, Hans [Johann Baptist Isidor] (*b* Raab [now Gyor], 4 April 1843; *d* Bayreuth, 5 Dec. 1916). Austro-Hungarian conductor. Between 1871 and 1912 he conducted in Budapest (Opera), Vienna (Opera, Philharmonic Orchestra), London (Richter Concerts, London Symphony Orchestra, Covent Garden), Birmingham (Triennial Festival), and Manchester (Hallé Orchestra), and at the Wagner Festivals in Bayreuth. He exerted enormous influence and conducted the first performances of works by Wagner (*Ring* cycle), Elgar ('Enigma' Variations, *The Dream of Gerontius*, Symphony no. 1), Brahms (*Tragic Overture*, Symphonies nos. 2 and 3), Bruckner (*Te Deum*, Symphony no. 8), and Tchaikovsky (Violin Concerto).   CF

📖 C. FIFIELD, *True Artist and True Friend: A Biography of Hans Richter* (Oxford, 1993)

Richter, Sviatoslav (Teofilovich) (*b* Zhytomyr, Ukraine, 3/20 March 1915; *d* Moscow 1 Aug. 1997). Russian pianist. Initially an opera répétiteur, he studied the piano with Heinrich Neuhaus in Moscow in 1937. Befriended by Prokofiev, whose music he championed, he won many competitions and performed throughout the Soviet bloc before he was permitted (in 1960) to play in the West, which he immediately took by storm with his supremely virtuoso yet physically restrained playing. His refined and transparent chamber music was exemplified by superb performances at the Aldeburgh Festival. Although he hated committing his interpretations to record, fortunately much remains of his enormous repertory.   CF

ricochet (Fr., 'rebound'). A type of bowing applied to instruments of the violin family. The upper half of the bow is 'thrown' on to the string from a distance, causing it to bounce several times, resulting in a series of rapid staccato notes. The effect is a staple of 19th-century virtuoso technique, and was used most notably by Paganini. See also VOLANTE, 2.   —/DMi

Ricordi. Italian firm of music publishers. It was founded in Milan in 1808 by Giovanni Ricordi (1785–1853). Through the initiative and acumen of the Ricordi family and their unique association with the careers of Verdi and Puccini, the firm became the predominant force in Italian music publishing in the 19th century and into the 20th. Giovanni was a violinist and copyist whose shrewd negotiations for copyright and acquisition of original scores profoundly influenced the music

publishing business in Italy (where copyright laws were not introduced until 1840). In 1825 he purchased the music archives of La Scala, Milan, and by 1853 his catalogue comprised over 25,000 works, including operas by Rossini, Bellini, Donizetti, and, from 1839, Verdi.

Giovanni's son Tito (1811–88) introduced new printing techniques and oversaw major commercial expansion in Italy and abroad. But it was Giovanni's composer grandson Giulio (1840–1912) who fostered the firm's relationship with Verdi and discovered Puccini, playing a crucial role in his artistic development. He greatly expanded the operatic and instrumental sections of the catalogue, publishing, among others, Boito, Ponchielli, and Catalani.

After 1919 the Ricordi family was no longer involved in the business. The catalogue widened to include early Italian music and such contemporary composers as Pizzetti, Malipiero, and Petrassi. Commercial expansion continued up to and after World War II with branches established in North and South America, Mexico, Australia, Switzerland, and Germany. Work is in progress on critical editions of Rossini and Verdi, while new generations represented at the turn of the 21st century included Sciarrino, Guo Wenjing, Liza Lim, Battistelli, Bussotti, Marco Stroppa, Luca Francesconi, Goebbels, Huber, and Neuwirth. Ricordi merged with BMG in 1995 to form a new company, BMG Ricordi S.p.a.   HA

Riders to the Sea. Opera in one act by Vaughan Williams to his own libretto, an almost verbatim setting of J. M. Synge's play (1904) (London, 1937).

RIdIM [Répertoire International d'Iconographie Musicale; International Repertory of Musical Iconography]. Established in 1971 under the auspices of the International Musicological Society and the International Association of Music Libraries, RIdIM aims to develop the cataloguing, classification, and reproduction of musico-iconographic documents. It comprises two series: an inventory of Western art with musical subjects from 1300 to the present, and a compilation of specific topics (including medieval wall-paintings, the viol family, drums and drummers, portraits, and iconographic sources in the journal *L'Illustration*).   SH

ridotto (It.). 1. 'Reduced', 'arranged'.

2. A form of musical entertainment (Fr.: *redoute*) that was very popular in the 18th century. It consisted of a selection of songs, followed by a ball in which the audience joined with the performers. Other types of ridotto took place in the London pleasure gardens. In Vienna, a great *Redoutensaal* (in fact two, one small and one large) was built on to the Hofburg palace. These

rooms also served as concert halls, and Haydn, Mozart, Beethoven, and their contemporaries wrote dance music (*Redoutentänze*) for the ridottos held there.

—/JBE

Ridout, Alan (John) (*b* West Wickham, Kent, 9 Dec. 1934; *d* Caen, 19 March 1996). English composer. He studied at the RCM with Gordon Jacob and Herbert Howells, and privately with Peter Racine Fricker and Tippett. His works include five symphonies and several concertante pieces, but he is associated more with church music and children's operas produced in connection with his work as a teacher at the choir school of Canterbury Cathedral (1964–72) and subsequently at King's School, Canterbury. PG

riduzione (It.). 'Reduction', 'arrangement'.

Riegger, Wallingford (*b* Albany, GA, 29 April 1885; *d* New York, 2 April 1961). American composer. He studied at Cornell University (1904–5), at the Institute of Musical Art in New York (1905–7), and in Germany. There followed a period of 20 years during which he held various appointments as conductor, cellist, and teacher, composing in conventional late Romantic and Impressionist styles. In the late 1920s he settled in New York, and most of his important works date from after that move. Such pieces as *Study in Sonority* for ten violins (1926–7) and *Dichotomy* for chamber orchestra (1931–2), both in vigorous, almost atonal counterpoint, gave him a place in the avant-garde circle of Varèse, Cowell, and Ruggles. In such later works as the three string quartets, the Third Symphony (1946–7), and *Music for Brass Choir* (1948–9) he pursued this dissonant contrapuntal style, sometimes on the basis of his own brand of 12-note serialism. PG

Riemann, (Karl Wilhelm Julius) **Hugo** (*b* Gross-Mehlra, nr Sondershausen, 18 July 1849; *d* Leipzig, 10 July 1919). German musicologist. He was a gifted pianist and in 1871 went to Leipzig University to study music, having previously studied philology, history, and philosophy at Berlin and Tübingen and undertaken military service during the Franco-Prussian War. He became an eminent teacher and wrote an astonishing number of books and articles, of which his *Musik-Lexikon* (Leipzig, 1882; many later editions) was one of the best dictionaries of music, and his *Handbuch der Musikgeschichte* (Leipzig, 1903–13) one of the most stimulating of histories.

DA/LC

Rienzi der Letzte der Tribunen ('Rienzi, the Last of the Tribunes'). Opera in five acts by Wagner to his own libretto after Edward Bulwer-Lytton's novel (1835) (Dresden, 1842).

Ries, Ferdinand (*b* Bonn, *bapt.* 28 Nov. 1784; *d* Frankfurt, 13 Jan. 1838). German pianist, composer, and conductor. He was the son of Franz Anton Ries (1755–1846), a violinist and a close friend of Beethoven. Ferdinand studied with his father and Beethoven in Vienna, then toured Europe and Scandinavia. He settled in London (1813–24), where he won good opinions, then returned to Godesberg (1824–7) and finally to Frankfurt. Here he conducted the Lower Rhine Festivals, 1825–7. His works include symphonies, piano concertos, operas, oratorios, chamber works, and much piano music. With Franz Gerhard Wegeler (1765–1848) he wrote an important early biography of Beethoven, *Biographische Notizen über Ludwig van Beethoven* (Coblenz, 1838). —/JW

Rieti, Vittorio (*b* Alexandria, Egypt, 28 Jan. 1898; *d* New York, 19 Feb. 1994). Italian-born American composer. He studied with Alfredo Casella, G. F. Malipiero, and Respighi in Rome, and settled in Paris in 1925, working for the ballet (including Diaghilev's company), theatre, and cinema. In 1940 he moved to the USA, becoming an American citizen four years later. He taught at various colleges, and produced a large output in a neo-classical style he had learnt during his Paris years, his works including ballets, operas, eight symphonies, various concertos (including a triple concerto for piano, violin, and viola), five quartets, and songs. PG

rigaudon (Fr.). A 17th- and 18th-century dance in duple time, resembling the *bourrée. Like other French dances of folk origin (e.g. the *gavotte) it was originally rather crude and lively until taken up in courtly circles, when it became more elegant, though retaining its liveliness. It was adopted into French stage works, especially in the *opéras-ballets* of Campra and Rameau. The rigaudon also became popular in Germany and England (where a variant in 6/8 came into being). In the mid-18th century it appeared as an optional dance in the *suite, with examples written by Purcell (harpsichord), Telemann, and Couperin.

After the mid-18th century it fell out of use, though it reappears occasionally in piano works of the late 19th century and the 20th, for example in Grieg's *Holberg Suite*, Ravel's *Le Tombeau de Couperin*, and Prokofiev's Ten Pieces op. 12. —/JBE

Righini, Vincenzo (Maria) (*b* Bologna, 22 Jan. 1756; *d* Bologna, 19 Aug. 1812). Italian composer and teacher. After studying with Martini, he sang in Florence and Rome before joining Giuseppe Bustelli's opera company in Prague as a tenor and writing his first operas. By 1777 he had moved to Vienna, where he established himself as a singing teacher. He was engaged to substitute for Salieri at the court opera before he moved to

Mainz, Trier, and in 1793 to the Prussian court in Berlin as Kapellmeister. His compositions include more than 150 songs, sacred pieces, cantatas, and piano works, as well as operas which increasingly typified the Franco-Italian fusion favoured in Berlin.   SH

Rigoletto. Opera by Verdi in three acts with a libretto by Francesco Maria Piave after Victor Hugo's play *Le Roi s'amuse* (1832) (Venice, 1851).

Rihm, Wolfgang (*b* Karlsruhe, 13 March 1952). German composer. He studied in Karlsruhe, and with Stockhausen, Wolfgang Fortner, and Klaus Huber; he was also influenced by Nono. In 1985 he was appointed to teach at the Karlsruhe Music Academy. Rihm's early music shows a neo-romantic orientation, but later works are more eclectic stylistically. He has composed prolifically in many media: opera, including *Jakob Lenz* (Hamburg, 1979), *Die Hamletmaschine* (Mannheim, 1987), *Oedipus* (Berlin, 1987), and *Die Eroberung von Mexico* (Hamburg, 1992); ballet; orchestral music, including four symphonies and the violin concerto *Gesungene Zeit* (1992); chamber music, including ten string quartets; and much vocal music.   ABur

Riisager, Knudåge (*b* Port Kunda, Estonia, 6 March 1897; *d* Copenhagen, 26 Dec. 1974). Danish composer. Although his first degree was in political science (University of Copenhagen, 1916–21), he also took classes in theory and composition with Otto Malling and studied the violin. He went to Paris to continue his musical training with Roussel and Paul Le Flem (1921–3), later (1932) taking instruction in counterpoint from Hermann Grabner in Leipzig. Meanwhile he had joined the Danish civil service, in the Ministry of Finance (1925–47), and was concurrently chairman of the Danish Composers' Union (1937–62) and later (1956–67) director of the Royal Danish Conservatory. His copious output includes 14 ballets, among them the well-known *Slaraffenland* (1942) and *Etude*, based on Czerny's studies (1948), five symphonies, and much other orchestral and chamber music; it reveals a sure contrapuntal hand and a lively sense of fun.   MA

rilasciando, rilasciante (It.). 'Releasing', i.e. getting gradually slower, the equivalent of *rallentando.

Riley, Terry (Mitchell) (*b* Colfax, CA, 24 June 1935). American composer. He studied composition with Robert Erickson at San Francisco State College (1955–7) and attended the University of California at Berkeley (1960–1). Since 1963 he has appeared internationally as a solo improviser on soprano saxophone or electronic keyboard instruments; he visited India in the early 1970s, and is much influenced by Indian musicians in his generation of music from a modal idea, which he

commonly subjects to obsessive repetition. His *In C* (1964), a selection of ostinato figures on which any number of players may draw freely, was important in the early history of minimalism. Later notated works include several for the Kronos Quartet.   PG

📖 K. POTTER, *Four Musical Minimalists: La Monte Young, Terry Riley, Steve Reich, Philip Glass* (Cambridge, 2000)

RILM [Répertoire International de Littérature Musicale; International Repertory of Music Literature]. Established in 1966 under the auspices of the International Musicological Society and the International Association of Music Libraries, RILM is a database of important writings on music and related disciplines. Books, journal articles, congress reports, dissertations, and other writings are included, and full bibliographical information and an abstract (in English) are supplied for each entry. It is published in three formats (with comprehensive indexes): in print, on CD-ROM, and online.   SH

Rimmer, John (Francis) (*b* Auckland, 5 Feb. 1939). New Zealand composer and teacher. After studying at the University of Toronto he returned to New Zealand in 1969, teaching at the University of Auckland from 1974. He has used electronic sounds in many of his works, including his opera *Galileo* (Auckland, 1999).

ABur

rim shot. A side-drum technique involving the simultaneous striking of drum-head and rim to produce a gunshot-like sound. It was used effectively by Milhaud in *La Création du monde* (1923).   SM

Rimsky-Korsakov, Nikolay Andreyevich (*b* Tikhvin, 6/18 March 1844; *d* Lyubensk, nr Luga [now Pskov district], 8/21 June 1908). Russian composer, conductor, and teacher. He was born into a noble family and received his early education at home. Under the influence of his brother Voin (a distinguished naval officer 22 years his senior) Nikolay entered the St Petersburg Naval College in 1856. Of the various entertainments available in the capital he chose opera, and his growing interest in music was strengthened by productions of Donizetti, Meyerbeer, and Glinka. His piano teacher, Fyodor Kanille, was another strong influence, introducing him to Bach, Beethoven, and Schumann. In 1861 a new acquaintance, Balakirev, became his informal tutor. Balakirev introduced him to the critic Vladimir Stasov and to the young composers Musorgsky, Borodin, and Cui. Thus Rimsky-Korsakov soon became one of The Five, that cradle of Russian musical nationalism. His musical ability was apparent but he lacked a grounding in theory; Balakirev nevertheless set him the task of composing a symphony.

Rimsky-Korsakov had to put aside his musical ambitions when in 1862 he was required to embark on a three-year tour of duty as a midshipman on the man-of-war *Almaz*. After his return to St Petersburg, in 1865, his onshore duties were light enough for him to resume composition: the symphony was given its premiere on 31 December 1865 by the orchestra of Balakirev's Free Music School. Rimsky-Korsakov soon completed further symphonic pieces. Among the most influential were the oriental suite *Antar* (also known as the Second Symphony) and the picturesque fantasy *Sadko*: these firmly established Rimsky-Korsakov as a symphonist. However, 15 operas were to follow. The first, *Pskovityanka* ('The Maid of Pskov', 1871), is a historical drama with its genesis in The Five's vigorous debates about the future of Russian opera and is fully representative of their declared ideals: nationalism, realism, and progress. At the time of its composition Rimsky-Korsakov and Musorgsky were especially close (they shared an apartment for a time), so *The Maid of Pskov* and the second version of *Boris Godunov* exercised considerable influence on each other.

In 1871, however, Rimsky-Korsakov's acceptance of a post as professor at the St Petersburg Conservatory alienated him from the rest of The Five, who had always opposed the institutionalization of composition teaching in Russia; Balakirev, indeed, was never fully reconciled with his former protégé. 'Having undeservedly become a conservatory professor, I soon became one of its best students', wrote Rimsky-Korsakov years later in his *Chronicle of my Musical Life*. He realized that Balakirev's tuition, though full of excellent practical advice, left him adrift in the rudiments of music theory. Temporarily abandoning composition, Rimsky-Korsakov undertook a strict regime of contrapuntal exercises, fugues, and chorales between 1874 and 1876. This gave him great technical facility, but whether he became a better composer is debatable: one of the first results of his efforts, the F major String Quartet, was criticized by Tchaikovsky as being excesively dry.

Once established on this path Rimsky-Korsakov felt compelled to revise and reorchestrate everything he had written before 1874, removing many of the more pungent harmonic ideas. This process of perfecting earlier works would continue to the end of his life. During the early 1870s he also acquired orchestral experience while serving as Inspector of Naval Bands; in 1874 he was confident enough to make his conducting debut in a performance of his Third Symphony. In 1875–6 he compiled two folksong collections. Though neither was based on field research, they served as a standard resource for several generations of Russian composers, Stravinsky included. From this preparatory

work two operas eventually emerged: *Mayskaya noch'* ('May Night', 1880) and *Snegurochka* ('The Snow Maiden', 1882). *May Night* was judged far less strikingly original than *The Maid of Pskov*, but *The Snow Maiden* was one of the composer's greatest public successes, benefiting from a lavish Mariinsky production in 1882.

Having established himself as a Russian composer of the first rank, Rimsky-Korsakov increasingly developed a second role, that of chief curator, collector, and restorer of the Russian 'imaginary museum of musical works' (to borrow a phrase of Liszt's). His interest had been awakened by his orchestration in 1869 of Dargomïzhsky's unfinished score of *The Stone Guest*, a task he had been assigned by the other members of The Five; in 1877–8 he and Balakirev edited Glinka's operatic scores, and after Musorgsky's death in 1881 he was left with the onerous undertaking of putting his friend's manuscripts in order.

Although it was undoubtedly Rimsky-Korsakov's efforts that brought the incomplete and unorchestrated *Khovanshchina* to the stage, the case of *Boris Godunov* was different: there were already two complete versions, the later one having been performed in 1874. Undeterred, Rimsky-Korsakov completed his own abridged version of *Boris* in 1893, restyling the harmony and orchestration in accordance with his own tastes; even at the time, such an approach to another composer's work was considered unacceptable by many, and the performance of Rimsky-Korsakov's version has rarely been free of controversy. Nevertheless, it is now accepted that it has its own important place in history, since it was the version chosen for the acclaimed Paris production of 1908—the foundation for Musorgsky's present-day reputation in the West.

Rimsky-Korsakov's central position in the Russian nationalist music school was further enhanced by his pedagogical activities. By the end of the 1880s he had taught a generation of students, of whom Glazunov and Lyadov were the most gifted. Rimsky-Korsakov and his circle soon won the attention of the wealthy merchant and patron Mitrofan Belyayev, who established two institutions to promote these composers: a publishing house in Leipzig, and the Russian Symphony Concerts series in St Petersburg, which Rimsky-Korsakov regularly conducted. Rimsky also left his mark on the development of Russian sacred music when he served as Balakirev's deputy at the imperial court chapel from 1883 to 1894.

Because of these activities, Rimsky-Korsakov's own compositional output had slowed down by the mid-1880s; putting opera aside, he composed three works that demonstrated his virtuosity in orchestration: the *Spanish Capriccio* (1887), *Sheherazade*, and the overture *Svetlïy prazdnik* ('Russian Easter Festival'; both 1888).

He could barely have imagined that they would make him internationally renowned while his operas would remain largely unknown outside Russia. In the 1888–9 season he heard the Russian premiere of Wagner's *Ring*. Rimsky-Korsakov now recognized the Wagnerian potential in the long-abandoned libretto *Mlada*, with its plot drawn from Slav mythology (the libretto, of 1872, had originally been intended for an opera to be composed collectively by The Five): he decided to compose a new, Wagnerian *Mlada*, but the libretto's old-fashioned opera-ballet design allowed the Wagnerian influence to reach no further than its orchestration.

Rimsky-Korsakov's last 15 years were the most prolific: a series of operas flowed from him at an unprecedented rate, beginning with *Noch' pered rozhdestvom* ('Christmas Eve'), based on the same Gogol story that Tchaikovsky had used. The next, *Sadko*, had a plot (and some melodic details) derived from Russian epic songs. In *Mozart and Salieri* he wrote in a highly expressive declamatory idiom, while in *Tsarskaya nevesta* ('The Tsar's Bride') he used traditional forms and smooth melodies. His compositional energies were further increased by his growing fame and material success. In 1897 *Sadko* was given by the Moscow company directed and financed by Savva Mamontov, an industrialist patron. This was the beginning of a long and fruitful collaboration, during which Rimsky-Korsakov came into contact with Fyodor Chaliapin (who sang Ivan the Terrible and Salieri) and the soprano Nadezhda Zabela (who played the Snow Maiden, the Sea Princess in *Sadko*, and Marfa in *The Tsar's Bride*).

The early modernist styles adopted by Mamontov's set designers (who included Zabela's husband Mikhail Vrubel' and Golovin) created a new artistic context for Rimsky-Korsakov's music and influenced his own ideas. The company's visit to St Petersburg in 1898 became a festival of Rimsky-Korsakov's music, four of his operas being produced in a single season. Another new stimulus for operatic composition was the talented and loyal librettist Vladimir Bel'sky, Rimsky-Korsakov's collaborator on the operas based on Pushkin's folk-style tales: *Skazka o Tsare Saltane* ('The Tale of Tsar Saltan', 1900) and *Zolotoy petushok* ('The Golden Cockerel', 1907); the two also joined forces for *Skazaniye o nevidimom grade Kitezhe* ('The Legend of the Invisible City of Kitezh', 1907), which is considered the pinnacle of Rimsky-Korsakov's operatic output.

The one-act *Kashchey bessmertnïy* ('Kashchey the Immortal', 1902) can be seen as a conservative's response to modernism: although it arrives at many of the complex harmonies of modernism, it does so by following conventional part-writing procedures. How-ever, during the 1905 Revolution *Kashchey*'s audience was more interested in the possible interpretation of the opera as an anti-tsarist tract. Rimsky-Korsakov's persistent expressions of solidarity with the rioting students, even at the cost of his conservatory professorship, made him an important figurehead for the left; he received overwhelming support and a few months later, on the installation of a new directorship led by Glazunov, he was immediately invited to take up his old post at the conservatory.

Rimsky-Korsakov left for Paris on 28 April 1907 to conduct Diaghilev's Saisons Russes, and these performances won Western audiences over to Russian music, establishing it as a permanent part of the repertory. He died the following year and was buried in St Petersburg in the grounds of the Alexander-Nevsky monastery, next to Glinka, Musorgsky, Borodin, and Stasov.   MF-W

📖 N. A. Rimsky-Korsakov, *My Musical Life* (Eng. trans. 1942/R) · G. Abraham, *Studies in Russian Music* (London, 1935/R), 142–310; *Rimsky-Korsakov: A Short Biography* (London, 1945) · G. A. Seaman, *Nikolai Andreevich Rimsky-Korsakov: A Guide to Research* (New York and London, 1988) · S. A. Griffiths, *A Critical Study of the Music of Rimsky-Korsakov* (New York, 1989)

Rinaldo. Opera in three acts by Handel to a libretto by Giacomo Rossi based on an outline by Aaron Hill after Torquato Tasso's *Gerusalemme liberata* (London, 1711); Handel revised it substantially (London, 1731). See Handel, George Frideric.

rinforzando, rinforzato (It.). 'Reinforcing', 'reinforced', i.e. a stress or accent applied to individual notes or chords, similar to *sforzando; it is sometimes abbreviated *rf*, *rfz*.

Ring des Nibelungen, Der ('The Nibelung's Ring'). *Bühnenfestspiel* ('stage festival play') for three days and a preliminary evening by Wagner to his own libretto; it was first performed as a cycle on 13, 14, 16, and 17 August 1876 at the Festspielhaus, Bayreuth. The four operas of the *Ring* cycle are *Das Rheingold*, the preliminary evening, in four scenes (Munich, 1869); *Die Walküre*, the first day, in three acts (Munich, 1870); *Siegfried*, the second day, in three acts (Bayreuth, 1876); and *Götterdämmerung* (Bayreuth, 1876).

ring modulator. A special type of *modulator that multiplies two signals electronically to produce rich new timbres, consisting of both the numerical summations of the source frequency components and their differences. The highly distinctive characteristics of these devices have featured strongly in many electronic works, especially those dating from the 1950s and 60s.   PM

Rio Grande, The. Work (1927) by Lambert for solo piano, chorus, and orchestra, a setting of a poem by Sacheverell Sitwell.

ripetizione (It.). 'Repetition', 'rehearsal'.

ripieno (It., 'filled'). 1. A term used in Baroque music to denote the tutti (or concerto grosso) sections, as opposed to the solo (or concertino) group. In vocal music, the concertino string group generally accompanied the arias, with the ripieno joining in for choruses; the term is less usually applied to the vocal music itself, but it was used by Bach, for example for the boys' choir in the first chorus of the *St Matthew Passion*. *Senza ripieno*, all players except those at the leading desks should be silent; *ripienista*, an orchestral player who is not a leader or a soloist. Various corruptions of the term have arisen, such as *ripiano* or *repiano* in brass or military band music, to denote players not at the leading desk.

2. An organ stop.

RIPM [Répertoire International de la Presse Musicale; International Repertory of the Musical Press]. Established in 1988 under the auspices of the International Musicological Society and the International Association of Music Libraries, RIPM provides bibliographic printed indexes and full-text microfilm of selected music periodicals published from the late 18th century to the early 20th. The indexes contain an annotated table of contents or calendar, a keyword–author index, and a brief outline (in English) of each journal's history.
                                                                SH

riprendere (It.). 'To resume', i.e. go back to the normal tempo.

Rise and Fall of the City of Mahagonny. See Aufstieg und Fall der Stadt Mahagonny.

Rising of the Moon, The. Opera in three acts by Maw to a libretto by Beverley Cross (Glyndebourne, 1970).

RISM [Répertoire International des Sources Musicales; International Repertory of Musical Sources]. Established in 1952 under the auspices of the International Musicological Society and the International Association of Music Libraries, RISM provides information on manuscript and printed sources of music and writings about music from the earliest times to *c*.1850. It consists of three series of published volumes: A, an inventory (by composer) of musical sources, 1600–1800; B, bibliographies of materials, organized by topic; and C, directories of music research libraries whose holdings are listed in series A and B. See also LIBRARIES.
                                                                SH

risoluto (It.). 'Resolute', 'energetic'.

rispetto (It.). A type of Italian poetry, also known as *strambotto*, with eight 11-syllable lines to the stanza, set by *frottola and madrigal composers. Later composers to have written music under this title include Wolf-Ferrari, Malipiero, and others.

risposta (It.). 'Answer' in *fugues.

ritardando, ritardato, ritenendo, ritenente (It.). 'Holding back' 'held back', i.e. becoming gradually slower, the same as *rallentando; it is sometimes abbreviated *rit*.

rite. See LITURGY.

ritenuto (It.). 'Held back', 'slower', i.e. slowing down, but immediately, rather than gradually like *rallentando.

Rite of Spring, The (*Vesna svyashchennaya*; *Le Sacre du printemps*). Ballet ('scenes of pagan Russia') in two parts by Stravinsky to a scenario by Nicholas Roerich; it was choreographed by Vaslav Nijinsky for Diaghilev's Ballets Russes (Paris, 1913). It is in two parts, 'The Adoration of the Earth' and 'The Sacrifice'. Stravinsky made a four-hand piano reduction of the score.

ritmo (It.). 'Rhythm'; *ritmico*, 'rhythmic'.

ritmo di tre battute (It.). See BATTUTA.

ritornello (It., dim. of *ritorno*, 'return'; Fr.: *ritournelle*; Ger.: *Ritornell*) [ritornel]. 1. In the 14th-century *caccia and *madrigal the ritornello was the concluding couplet of a poem; it was usually treated in musical settings as a separate section, often with a change of metre. It was not a refrain.

2. In 17th-century operas and cantatas, the term came to be applied to the short instrumental conclusion added to an aria or other type of song. Sometimes the ritornello also occurred at the beginning. Apart from sinfonias, these ritornellos were the only instrumental portions of early operas. A notable example is the opening ritornello of Monteverdi's *Orfeo* (1607), which, in addition to being a dominant feature of the prologue, is also used to introduce Acts I and IV and is incorporated within Act II.

3. 'Ritornello form' is a term used to describe the first and often the last movements of the Baroque concerto, especially the concerto grosso. Such movements were characterized by the alternation and contrast between solo and tutti sections, the tuttis being based always on the same material. Thus these sections were equivalent to ritornellos. See also FORM, 7.   —/LC

Ritorno d'Ulisse in patria, Il ('The Return of Ulysses to his Country'). Opera in a prologue and three acts by Monteverdi, to a libretto in five acts by Giacomo

Badoaro after Homer's *Odyssey*, first performed in Venice in 1640.

ritournelle (Fr.). 1. A 17th-century dance in quick triple time, found in the ballets of Lully.

2. See RITORNELLO.

Ritter, Hermann (*b* Wismar, 16 Sept. 1849; *d* Würzburg, 25 Jan. 1926). German viola player. He designed a larger version of the viola based on the acoustic properties of the violin, of which it was an exact enlargement. This *viola alta* attracted Wagner, who invited Ritter to lead the violas at his 1876 Bayreuth Festival. Ritter taught in Würzburg and adapted music for his instrument, but it became obsolete.   CF

Ritual Fire Dance (*Danza ritual del fuego*). Dance from Falla's ballet *El *amor brujo* (1915); it became popular in Falla's piano arrangement and has been arranged for other instruments, including the cello.

riverso, al (It.). 'Turned back', 'reversed'. The term is used both for inversion and for retrograde motion.

RMA. See ROYAL MUSICAL ASSOCIATION.

Robert le diable ('Robert the Devil'). Opera in five acts by Meyerbeer to a libretto by Eugène Scribe and Germain Delavigne (Paris, 1831).

Roberto Devereux (*Roberto Devereux, ossia Il conte di Essex*; 'Robert Devereux, or The Earl of Essex'). Opera in three acts by Donizetti to a libretto by Salvadore Cammarano after François Ancelot's tragedy *Élisabeth d'Angleterre* (Naples, 1837).

Robin et Marion. See JEU DE ROBIN ET DE MARION, LE.

Rochberg, George (*b* Paterson, NJ, 5 July 1918). American composer. He studied with George Szell and Leopold Mannes at the Mannes School (1939–42), and with Rosario Scalero and Gian Carlo Menotti at the Curtis Institute (1945–7), where he taught until 1954. He was also an editor for Presser (1951–60) before his appointment as professor at the University of Pennsylvania (1961–83). His early works lean towards Stravinsky, Bartók, and Hindemith, after which came his engagement with Schoenbergian and then, from 1957, Webernian serialism. In the early 1960s he began to work with collage, quoting from Boulez, Berio, Varèse, and Ives in his quartet *Contra mortem et tempus* (1965), but his Third String Quartet (1972) and later works go beyond allusion to a revival of past styles, notably those of Mahler and late Beethoven.   PG

Rochlitz, (Johann) Friedrich (*b* Leipzig, 12 Feb. 1769; *d* Leipzig, 16 Dec. 1842). German writer and critic. He studied composition and counterpoint at the Thomasschule, Leipzig, and began composing at an early age, but later turned to writing. He edited the *Allgemeine musikalische Zeitung* (1798–1818) and was a director of the Leipzig Gewandhaus Orchestra. His musical tastes ranged from Bach, Handel, and Haydn, to Mozart, Weber, and Spohr. A severe critic of Beethoven's early works, he later recognized him as being the most important German composer of the time.   LC

rock. A commercially produced popular music which arose in the West in the 1960s, highly amplified, with a strong beat and rhythmic patterns, played by guitars, bass, drum kit, and sometimes keyboard instruments. The term, ideologically laden and much contested, is a contraction of *'rock and roll', but distinct from it; it was first used from about 1967 to describe what has since usually been referred to as *'progressive rock'. 'Rock' has been seen as the obverse of 'pop', though there was never a clear stylistic distinction. The former was considered 'authentic' music, based on blues, the music of ordinary or poor people; its performers were assigned 'heroic' status. 'Pop', however, was the 'commercial' product of the music industry. Many rock critics were hostile to progressive rock's use of (bourgeois) art music; by this standard, and particularly since the advent of *punk rock, much of the music originally described by the term has failed the authenticity test of rock ideology; at the same time the stylistic distinctions between rock and pop became more blurred.   PW

📖 T. GRACYK, *Rhythm and Noise: An Aesthetics of Rock* (London, 1996) · J. COVACH and G. M. BOONE, *Understanding Rock: Essays in Musical Analysis* (New York, 1998) · A. MOORE, *Rock: The Primary Text* (Aldershot, 2/2001)

rockabilly. A type of early American pop music that originated in the American South in the 1950s; it combined elements of *country music with *rock and roll and used an innovatory singing style: lyrics about love and sex are delivered with gasps, hiccups, trembles, and non-linguistic syllables; the text is accented in unexpected places. It is typified by Elvis Presley's recordings in 1954–5 for Sun Records.   KG

rock and roll [rock'n'roll]. An amalgam of American white *country music and black *rhythm and blues: the first definitive pop music of the 1960s and 70s. It became established in the mid-1950s with *Rock Around the Clock* by Bill Haley and the Comets. Similar pieces were performed by white and black singers, including Elvis Presley, Jerry Lee Lewis, Chuck Berry, and Little Richard. Boogie rhythms and the 12-bar blues chord structure were combined with *blues songforms; singing style ranged from blues-derived to Elvis

Presley's innovatory rhythmic treatment of lyrics. Instrumentation was slap-bass, drum kit, piano, rhythm guitar, and solo electric guitar; sometimes the saxophones of rhythm and blues were retained. The style spread all over the world. The term is still sometimes used to refer in general to Western pop music of the second half of the 20th century. PGA

> C. GILLETT, *The Sound of the City: The Rise of Rock and Roll* (New York, 1970, 2/1996) · P. FRIEDLANDER, *Rock and Roll: A Social History* (Boulder, CO, 1996)

rock opera. An operatic work or stage show using songs written in the idiom of *rock music. In 1967 (the year in which the Beatles' *Sgt. Pepper's Lonely Hearts Club Band*, considered by many to be the earliest concept album, came out) The Who released *Tommy*, the first rock opera, and *Hair* was staged on Broadway. Subsequently the term has come to be applied to a range of musical shows, including the early works of Andrew Lloyd Webber, especially *Jesus Christ Superstar* and *Evita*. PW

rock steady. A style of popular music that originated in Jamaica; its predecessor was *ska. The horn sections of ska were replaced by piano, bass, and drums; both harmony groups and solo singing were common. In rock steady the bass is used in a percussive way, a feature adopted by *reggae. KG

rococo (from Fr. *rocaille*, 'rockwork', and possibly *coquille*, 'shellwork'). A term used to describe a late 17th- and early 18th-century French style of decorative art and architecture characterized by delicacy, elegance, and wit, in contrast to the more severe lines of the *Baroque era. By analogy it has been applied, somewhat loosely, to the lighter, often small-scale French music of the period, notably the works of François Couperin. The style was widely imitated, particularly in southern Germany and Austria. AL

Rode, (Jacques) Pierre (Joseph) (*b* Bordeaux, 16 Feb. 1774; *d* Château de Bourbon, 25 Nov. 1830). French violinist and composer. He studied with Viotti and made his debut in Paris in 1790; five years later he was appointed professor of violin at the Conservatoire. He toured extensively in the Netherlands, Spain (where he met Boccherini), Germany (where Spohr was captivated by his playing), and Russia (where he was solo violinist to the tsar). In 1812 he gave the premiere of Beethoven's Violin Sonata op. 96 in Vienna and two years later settled in Berlin. Acknowledged as the leader of the French violin school, he injected a new brilliance into Viotti's classicism. His compositions include 13 violin concertos, models of the French style, a number of extremely popular *airs variés*, and 12 *quatuors brillants*. SH

Rodelinda (*Rodelinda, regina de' longobardi*; 'Rodelinda, Queen of the Lombards'). Opera in three acts by Handel to a libretto by Nicola Francesco Haym adapted from Antonio Salvi's *Rodelinda, regina de' longobardi* (1710), after Pierre Corneille's play *Pertharite, roi des Lombards* (1651) (London, 1725).

Rodeo. Ballet in one act by Copland to a scenario by Agnes de Mille, who choreographed it (New York, 1942); it is subtitled 'The Courting at Burnt Ranch' and uses traditional songs. Copland arranged four dance episodes from it for orchestra (1942) and arranged the work for piano (1962).

Rodgers, Richard (Charles) (*b* Hammels Station, Long Island, NY, 28 June 1902; *d* New York, 30 Dec. 1979). American composer. At Columbia University he met the lyricist Lorenz Hart, with whom he collaborated on such shows as *A Connecticut Yankee* (1929), *On your Toes* (1936), and *Pal Joey* (1940). Later he worked with Oscar Hammerstein II on the more substantial *Oklahoma!* (1943), *Carousel* (1945), *South Pacific* (1949), *The King and I* (1951), and *The Sound of Music* (1959).

PGA/ALA

Rodrigo (y Vidre), Joaquín (*b* Sagunto, 22 Nov. 1901; *d* Madrid, 6 July 1999). Spanish composer. Blind from an early age, he studied composition in Valencia (1920–3) and with Paul Dukas in Paris (1927–32), where he also met Falla. In 1946 he became professor of music history at the University of Madrid. Together with Moreno Torroba, he led the *casticismo* ('authenticity') movement, which aimed to reinvigorate Spanish classical music through folk and Baroque traditions. His *Concierto de Aranjuez* (1939) evoked those traditions in a colourful, unaffected manner, quickly establishing itself as by far the most popular of guitar concertos. His other concertos for the instrument, notably the *Fantasia para un gentilhombre* (1954), are almost equally effective. Rodrigo also composed concertos in a similar style for the piano, violin, flute, and harp, numerous orchestral and instrumental works, and an opera *El hijo fingido* ('The False Son', 1964). PG/CW

> F. SOPEÑA, *Joaquín Rodrigo* (Madrid, 1946)

Rodrigues Coelho, Manuel. See COELHO, MANUEL RODRIGUES.

Roger, Estienne (*b* Caen, 1665 or 1666; *d* Amsterdam, 7 July 1722). French music printer and publisher. He moved from Normandy to Amsterdam in 1685 as a result of Protestant persecution, and in 1697 began publishing music and other books, which eventually totalled over 500 titles. He favoured the works of Italian composers and published first editions of Vivaldi, Corelli, Albinoni, Caldara, Marcello, Alessandro

Scarlatti, and others. Under his own management and that of his successor, Michel-Charles Le Cène, his firm became the principal publisher and distributor of music in the first half of the 18th century.

Roger made full use of the prevailing freedom from copyright restrictions, copying much music of other publishers and distributing his 'new' editions through agents in many European cities. He was one of the first printers to number his plates (from *c.*1712–13) and he also issued catalogues of his publications, both of which have facilitated study of his editions. After his death the business was carried on briefly by his younger daughter Jeanne, until in 1723 it was sold to his son-in-law Le Cène. Le Cène used many of Roger's plates, adapting them to include his own name, and he issued his own editions of music by Geminiani, Handel, Locatelli, Quantz, Tartini, Telemann, and others—over 100 titles by 1743, the year of his death. The reputation of both men was based on their scrupulous editing and splendid copper-plate engraving.   JMT/JWA

Roger-Ducasse, Jean (Jules Aimable) (*b* Bordeaux, 18 April 1873; *d* Taillan-Médoc, Gironde, 19 July 1954). French composer and teacher. He studied at the Paris Conservatoire with Fauré, whom he assisted with the reorchestration of *Prométhée* and the publication of the Requiem. He was professor of composition at the Conservatoire from 1935 to 1940. His music, largely independent of Impressionism and later trends, includes an opera, *Cantegril* (Paris, 1931), a mimed drama, *Orphée* (completed 1913, performed Paris, 1926), a symphonic poem with chorus, *Au jardin de Marguerite* (after the Faust legend, 1905), orchestral works, motets, chamber music, piano pieces, and songs.   ABur

Rogers, Benjamin (*b* Windsor, May 1614; *d* Oxford, June 1698). English organist and composer. He was a choirboy, then lay clerk, at St George's Chapel, Windsor, and from 1639 to 1641 was organist of Christ Church Cathedral, Dublin. At the Restoration he became successively organist of Eton College, St George's Chapel, Windsor (1662–4), and Magdalen College, Oxford, where in 1669 he was made D.Mus. Rogers's *Hymnus eucharisticus* is traditionally sung from the top of Magdalen Tower at dawn on May Day. He composed church music, instrumental pieces, and glees.   WT/AA

Roi David, Le ('King David'). Dramatic psalm in five parts by Honegger, for narrator, soprano, mezzo-soprano, tenor, chorus, and orchestra, a setting of a text by René Morax (Mézières, 1921); Honegger revised and reorchestrated it in three parts (1923) and arranged an orchestral suite from it.

Roi de Lahore, Le ('The King of Lahore'). Opera in five acts by Massenet to a libretto by Louis Gallet (Paris, 1877).

Roi malgré lui, Le ('The King in Spite of Himself'). Opera in three acts by Chabrier to a libretto by Émile de Najac and Paul Burani (Paris, 1887).

Roland-Manuel [Lévy, Roland Alexis Manuel] (*b* Paris, 22 March 1891; *d* Paris, 2 Nov. 1966). French composer and critic. He studied with Roussel and Ravel, and after service in World War I was influenced by the aesthetic associated with Les *Six. He composed five operas, ballets, film scores, orchestral music, oratorios, chamber music, and songs. He was also a popular broadcaster on music, a professor at the Paris Conservatoire from 1947, an influential critic, and the author of biographies of Satie, Falla, and Ravel.   ABur

Roman, Johan Helmich (*b* Stockholm, 26 Oct. 1694; *d* Haraldsmåla, nr Kalmar, 20 Nov. 1758). Swedish composer. He flourished at a time when Sweden had withdrawn from its role of power after the death of Charles XII and had turned to the pursuit of the arts of peace. Roman showed such early talent as a violinist and oboist that the court took the unprecedented step of paying for his studies abroad. He spent five years in England (1716–21), probably studying with Pepusch and certainly acquiring an admiration for Handel, and returned home to become in 1727 *Kapellmästare* to the court. He transformed the orchestra into a first-rate ensemble and, together with a young player and composer, Per Brant (1713–67), started public concerts at the House of the Nobility in Stockholm, which became an important forum for new music. In 1735 he made a second journey abroad, which again took him to England (where he met Handel, Bononcini, Geminiani, and others) as well as to France and Italy. It seems, however, that declining health and increasing deafness caused him to take a less active part in Stockholm musical life after his return to Sweden in 1737.

Roman was the first significant Swedish composer. The bulk of his early output was instrumental. The 12 flute sonatas were written in 1727, most of the concertos date from the early 1730s, and it is likely that the greater part of his (more than 20) sinfonias were composed in the late 1730s and the 1740s, when he turned to vocal music, setting vernacular texts with increasing frequency.

Roman's music is a compound of Italian and English influences, and his enthusiasm for Handel left an indelible imprint though he never developed a pronounced personal idiom. The two sinfonias by which he is best known outside Scandinavia, no. 16 in D and no. 20 in E minor, reveal a crisp, fresh, and engaging melodic style. There is a keen awareness of proportion, and his invention in such works as the sinfonias and the *Drottningholmsmusiquen* (1744) never falls below a certain level of distinction.   RLA

📖 I. BENGTSSON, *Mr. Roman's Spuriosity Shop: A Thematic Catalogue of 503 Works ... from ca.1680–1750* (Stockholm, 1976)

Roman Carnival, The. See CARNAVAL ROMAIN, LE.

romance (Fr., Sp.; Ger.: *Romanze*; It.: *romanza*). 1. In Spain, a form of long epic ballad dating back to at least the 14th century, when *romances* on legendary or historical subjects were sung for the entertainment of aristocratic patrons, usually by solo professional musicians. A major source of the early *romance* is the *Cancionero musical de palacio* (1505–20), which contains more than 40 such pieces for three or four voices, most being arrangements by Juan del Encina and others of pre-existing melodies. Examples for solo voice with vihuela accompaniment also survive, especially in the collections of Narváez, Milán, Esteban Daza, and Mudarra. In the 17th century, however, the genre became virtually synonymous with the *villancico, and in the 18th century it expanded into a miniature cantata. Thereafter it survived in folk music.

2. In France, the word acquired a musical connotation in the 18th century. Rousseau's definition in his music dictionary (1768) indicates an unpretentious strophic verse of a simple kind: a short, often tragic, love poem, the melody simple and unaffected, with unobtrusive instrumental support. Rousseau himself composed many of the most important early examples of the genre. Used extensively in France in the late 18th and early 19th centuries, especially in *opéra comique*, it had ousted the *air before yielding in turn to the *mélodie*, which, however, bore a somewhat different meaning. The chief exponents of the French *romance* were lesser composers such as Boieldieu, Auguste Panseron (1795–1859), and Hippolyte Monpou (1804–41). It was inevitable that its essential artlessness, which linked it stylistically with the folk music of western Europe, should eventually become affected by the greater sophistication that was changing the whole character of song, and the term, which from the very first had been loose and ill-defined, gradually fragmented into subsidiary categories aimed at more precise definition.

Its use soon spread beyond France. In Germany, for example, Reichardt in the 1790s published some Goethe songs as *Lieder, Oden, Balladen und Romanzen*. Schumann, perhaps borrowing the word from Heinrich

Heine (who classed some of his poetry including *Die Grenadiere* as 'Romanzen'), used it freely, for example in four collections of *Romanzen und Balladen* (opp. 45, 49, which contains his setting of Heine's *Die beiden Grenadiere*, 53, and 64). It is found in Brahms too, for example *Lieder und Romanzen* op. 14; the *Romanzen und Lieder* op. 84; and his *Magelone* song cycle op. 33, which he labelled *Romanzen*. (It is not always easy to pinpoint the differences between 'Romanze', 'Ballade', 'Lied', and 'Gesang'.) The *romance* also spread to Russia (where it was first applied to songs with French words) and to Italy, for example Verdi's *Sei romanze* (1838) and *Album di sei romanze* (1845).

The typical *romance* of the salon or drawing-room made little demand on the performers, intellectually, emotionally, or technically. Never far from banality or sentimentality, it occasionally freed itself from the restraint of poetry to become the *romance sans paroles*, which was musically akin to the nocturne of John Field and Chopin. It is this nocturnal atmosphere that pervades Schumann's dreamy *Romanze* in F♯ major for piano (op. 28) and the similarly labelled slow movement of his Fourth Symphony, in D minor. The first known use of the term for an instrumental movement occurs in Gossec's E♭ Symphony op. 5 no. 2 (1761 or 1762).

LO

Romances sans paroles. See LIEDER OHNE WORTE.

Roman de Fauvel. See FAUVEL, ROMAN DE.

romanesca (It.). A type of *ground bass, using a specific bass pattern and its associated harmony (see Ex. 1). Supposedly of Roman origin, it was especially popular from the mid-16th century to the mid-17th, and is found in both instrumental and vocal music by such composers as Monteverdi, Banchieri, and Frescobaldi.

GMT

Ex. 1

Romania. To the musical world at large, Romania is associated more with such pianists as Dinu Lipatti and Clara Haskil and such conductors as George Georgescu and Constantin Silvestri than with composers. Even George Enescu gained his international reputation as much from teaching, conducting, and performing as from his compositions. Today his greatest music, including the Octet for strings, the richly romantic Third Symphony, and the powerful opera *Oedipe*, remains little known outside Romania. Yet it was Enescu's single-handed achievement to draw Romania into the orbit of European music as a whole, his distinctive voice forging its individuality from a unique synthesis of western European acquisitions and indigenous features drawn from the rich veins of Romanian church and folk music.

1. Folk music and early history; 2. Nationalism and beyond

1. Folk music and early history

Romanian folk music is as ancient and varied as the country's history. With the defeat of the Dacian king Decebalus (AD 101–6) by Emperor Trajan, the country became a Roman colony and the many successive waves of invasions by Goths, Tartars, Huns, and others did little to obliterate its Latin inheritance and character. Although it was influenced linguistically by invaders and neighbours (Turks and Greeks), Romanian is a Romance language, with obvious implications for the character of its folk music. Incantations, laments, ritual dances, and songs have been transmitted from generation to generation, preserving a remarkable continuity in their detailed melodic and rhythmic characteristics. In the early 20th century this rich repertory was tapped by Bartók and Enescu. More recent composers such as Mihail Jora (1891–1971), Marcian Negrea (1893–1973), and Sabin Drăgoi (1884–1968) continued to draw extensively on this folk inheritance.

As in Russia, Serbia, and Bulgaria, the early Christian rites in Romania were profoundly influenced by the Eastern traditions of the Byzantine Empire, and from the 4th century onwards, the repertory of liturgical music of the Romanian Orthodox Church expanded and developed. Enescu's debt to this repertory is considerable, while the modality, microtonal inflections, and glissandos of the chant further influenced younger composers such as Paul Constantinescu (1909–63), notably in his *Patimile şi Invierea Domnului* ('The Passion and Resurrection of Our Lord').

While the provinces of Moldavia and Wallachia remained faithful to old peasant traditions, Transylvania came into direct contact with Western harmonic developments. Psalms of Romanian origin were included in Italian and German collections at this time. Named composers begin to appear in the 16th century, and a handful of works compiled by Ioan Căianu (1627–87) demonstrate stylistic affinities with western European church music of the early Renaissance. The *Psaltichi românească* ('Romanian Psalter') by Filothei Sân Agăi Jipei (1713) takes another important step towards the notion of an indigenous music in its use of the vernacular, instigating a tradition in church music which was carried through into the 19th and 20th centuries in the music of such composers as Anton Pann (1796–1854) and Dimitrie Suceveanu (1816–98),

followed by Gavriil Musicescu (1847–1903) and Dumitru Kiriac-Georgescu (1866–1928).

2. Nationalism and beyond

In the early 19th century Romania responded to the growing wave of nationalist feeling that spread across eastern Europe. Foreign ensembles were gradually replaced by indigenous Romanian players, and an institutional framework for the teaching and performance of Western music was established. In 1833 the Philharmonic Society began its activities in Bucharest, and three years later a Philharmonic School (which later became a state conservatory) was founded in Iaşi, the Moldavian capital. Operas by Mozart and Rossini were frequently performed in the early part of the century, but the repertory gradually expanded to include Romanian comic operas or vaudevilles by Alexandru Flechtenmacher (1823–98) and grand operas by Ion Wachmann (1807–63). The establishment in 1885 of the Romanian Opera in Bucharest stimulated further enthusiasm for operatic composition. Prominent Romanian composers of the late Romantic era include: Mauriciu Cohen-Lînaru (1849–1928), a pupil of Bizet and César Franck; Ciprian Porumbescu (1853–83), whose early death prevented him from realizing his full stature as a composer; and Eduard Caudella (1841–1924), who taught George Enescu.

Enescu himself proved of the utmost importance both as an inspiration to and a stylistic model for his contemporaries and successors, though the teaching of the Italian-born Alfonso Castaldi (1874–1942) at the Bucharest Conservatory was hardly less important. Among Castaldi's most distinguished pupils were Alfred Alessandrescu (1893–1959), Mihail Andricu (1894 or 1985–1974), Ion Nonna Otescu (1888–1940), and Dimitrie Cuclin (1885–1978). The folkloristic synthesis which Enescu achieved and bequeathed was encouraged by official cultural policy in the years following the establishment of a socialist political system after World War II, at which point Romania saw a massive restructuring of its musical life, with the formation of a composers' union (1920), state philharmonic societies, opera houses, and academies.

Yet in the 1960s a new generation of composers, inspired by developments in Poland, began to respond to more progressive tendencies in postwar musical language. Among the most successful of these younger composers are Anatol Vieru (1926–98), Pascal Bentoiu (b 1927), whose opera *Hamlet* achieved recognition both in Romania and abroad, Tiberiu Olah (b 1928), whose symphonic poem *Columna infinită* is an interpretation in sound of Brâncuşi's famous sculpture, and Cornel Ţăranu (b 1934), the composer of *Incantaţi* and of a compelling and evocative *Sinfonia brevis*. Since the democratic revolution of 1989 a younger gener-ation, including Octavian Nemescu (*b* 1940), Adrian Iorgulescu (*b* 1951), and Doina Rotaru (*b* 1951), has come to the fore. Yet in spite of the new freedoms Romanian musicians have found it far from easy to adapt to the competitive climate of a post-Communist world, where state subsidies have all but disappeared.

MG/JS

📖 T. Alexandru, *Muzica populară românească* [Roma-nian Folk Music] (Bucharest, 1975; Eng. trans. 1980) · B. Kotlyarov, *George Enesco: His Life and Times* (Neptune City, NJ, 1984) · A. E. Pennington, *Music in Medieval Moldavia* (Bucharest, 1985)

Roman rite. See LITURGY; OFFICE.

Romanticism (*see opposite page*)

'Romantic' Symphony. Bruckner's Symphony no. 4 in E♭ major, composed in 1874 and revised in 1878–80 and 1886.

romanza (It.; Ger.: *Romanze*). See ROMANCE.

Romberg, Sigmund (*b* Nagykanizsa, 29 July 1887; *d* New York, 9 Nov. 1951). Hungarian-born American composer. He emigrated to the USA in 1909, became a café pianist, and found his métier in romantic operetta scores, including *Maytime* (1917), *The Student Prince* (1924), *The Desert Song* (1926), and *The New Moon* (1928). He also wrote scores in more modern American style, including *Up in Central Park* (1945), as well as music for films. PGA/ALa

Rome, Prix de. See PRIX DE ROME.

Romeo and Juliet. Shakespeare's tragedy (1594 or 1595) has been the subject of many musical works, of which the best known are:

1. *Roméo et Juliette*. Dramatic symphony, op. 17 (1839), by Berlioz, for alto, tenor, and bass soloists, chorus, and orchestra, to a text by Émile Deschamps.

2. *Roméo et Juliette*. Opera in five acts by Gounod to a libretto by Jules Barbier and Michel Carré (Paris, 1867).

3. *Romeo i Dzhulyetta*. Fantasy overture by Tchaikovsky; it was composed in 1869 and revised in 1870 and 1880.

4. *Romeo i Dzhulyetta*. Ballet in a prologue, three acts, and an epilogue by Prokofiev to a scenario by Leonid Lavrovsky, the composer, and S. Radlov; it was choreographed by Ivo Psota (Brno, 1938). Prokofiev arranged three orchestral suites from the score: no. 1, op. 64*b* (1936), in seven movements; no. 2, op. 64*c* (1937), in seven movements; no. 3, op. 101 (1946), in six movements.

Among other operas on the subject are those by Benda (1776), Dalayrac (1792), Steibelt (1793), Zingarelli (1796), Bellini (*I *Capuleti e i Montecchi*, 1830), Zan-donai (1922), Sutermeister (1940), and Malipiero (1950). Bernstein's *West Side Story* (1957) is an updated version of the same story.

Ronald [Russell], **Sir Landon** (*b* London, 7 June 1873; *d* London, 14 Aug. 1938). English conductor, pianist, and composer. A son of the composer Henry Russell, he became accompanist to Melba and opera conductor at Covent Garden, and conducted various British or-chestras. He was also principal of the Guildhall School of Music (1910–38) and was knighted in 1922. A friend of Elgar, of whose music he was a sensitive interpreter, he was musical adviser to the Gramophone Company (HMV) and made many recordings. MK/ALa

ronde (Fr., 'round'). 1. Semibreve.
2. See ROUND, 1.

rondeau (Fr.). One of the three standard poetic forms used for 14th- and 15th-century chansons (see also BALLADE; VIRELAI). Unlike the other two, how-ever, its structure was already established in the 13th century.

The *rondeau* given below, by Adam de la Halle, shows its typical layout as a single-stanza poem of four couplets. The first couplet, known as the refrain (in-dicated here by italics), is repeated at the end. In addition, the first line of the refrain is always used as the second line of the second couplet.

> *Tant con je vivrai*
> *N'aimerai autrui que vous*
> Ja n'en partirai
> *Tant con je vivrai*
> Ains vous servirai
> Loyaument mis m'i sui tous
> *Tant con je vivrai*
> *N'aimerai autrui que vous.*

The musical setting of a *rondeau* is divided into two sections (a and b), each of which carries one of the refrain lines. The remaining lines of text are allocated to the two musical sections according to their rhyme, and this yields the characteristic form of the *rondeau* in performance: ABaAabAB (capital letters indicate the position of the refrain; see SONG, Ex. 1). The refrain attained particular importance, as examples were quoted in their entirety in other works, as refrains, as motet tenors, or in more complex forms of quotation.

Guillaume de Machaut, the leading 14th-century chanson composer, used the form of the *rondeau* shown above. Although his work established the long-term use of the *rondeau* in chanson writing, it was not until the 15th century that it became really popular, gaining complete ascendancy over the *ballade* and *virelai* as a medium for courtly love songs. These later *rondeaux* are

(*cont. on p. 1075*)

Romanticism

In its original meaning, the word 'Romantic' derived from 'Romance', the ancient language of France, and hence the term applied to the poems or tales, characterized by imaginative adventurousness, that were typical of its literature. 'Romantic' came, by the late 17th century, to mean something extravagantly fanciful, diverging from the accepted norms. It was not until the 19th century that the term 'Romanticism' was needed to describe a new spirit which embraced the arts, philosophy, politics, and even the sciences. Romanticism grew in different countries at different times, taking different forms, and was never a coherent movement. However, the Age of Romanticism is now generally thought of as extending from the closing years of the 18th century to the early years of the 20th.

The spirit of Romanticism

So lengthy a period, especially one associated with rapid political, social, and economic change, naturally embraced several phases and included a number of contradictory strains. However, in all its manifestations Romanticism emphasized the apparent domination of emotion over form and order. This was often more apparent than real, since the disciplines of Romantic music needed to be no less secure than those of Classicism in order to express ideas effectively. But new value was set on novelty and sensation, on technical innovation and experiment, and on the cross-fertilization of ideas from different disciplines, both within and without the arts.

In Germany the Romantic movement was primarily musical. Various poets conceded supremacy to the art of music, but their contribution, and that of painting, was welcomed in a Germany tending towards a synthesis of the arts—a trend long advocated, tentatively explored, and reaching fruition in Wagner. In Italy, the movement had stronger political overtones, both poets and composers associating themselves with the Risorgimento, the movement towards political independence and unity that claimed Verdi as its laureate. In France, the paintings in various salons and Victor Hugo's *Hernani* (1830) were at least as potent excitements in the Romantic movement as the largely misunderstood Berlioz. Britain, musically an outpost of Europe at this stage, made its greatest contribution to Romanticism with literary influences—the fake 'Ossian', then Scott and Byron, thrilled musical Europe.

It was largely in Rousseau, the philosopher adopted with special enthusiasm by the Romantics, that justification was found for the emphasis on emotion rather than intellect. From him, too, came delight in the country and admiration for the virtues to be found in simple, unspoilt people. There was also a turn from the rational (supreme principle in the Enlightenment) to the irrational (as representing the superior claims of the imagination). Longings for things far away, an essential Romantic characteristic, could include dreams of remote lands (in a new liking for the exotic) and of the distant past (in the fascination with a past Romantic age of chivalry). The longing for freedom from restraints engendered a passionate desire for national identity and independence and, comparably, a search for individual identity and an admiration for the dominating, convention-scorning figure of the Hero.

It was in part the observation of some of these strains in Beethoven that led the writer and composer E. T. A. Hoffmann to claim him as a Romantic; but more crucially, Beethoven's music aroused in Hoffmann fear, suffering, and a longing for the infinite. The 'Pastoral' Symphony is clearly Romantic in its 'awakening of happy feelings on arrival in the country', its brook, its alarming storm, its Rousseauesque peasants. The Fifth Symphony is more intrinsically Romantic in its assertion of humankind's defiant supremacy over its fate; so is the 'Eroica', or Heroic Symphony, with its great Marcia funebre for the death of the hero, its triumphantly energetic scherzo, and its final variations on a theme Beethoven associated with Prometheus, the god who, by bringing fire from heaven, gave mortals independence from the gods. Beethoven delighted Rousseau's Romantic admirers with his demonstration of the moral force expressible in music.

However, Beethoven was not universally regarded as the most characteristic early Romantic, nor was the symphony to be the favoured Romantic medium. Opera assumed a new position of importance, finding new audiences and a new range of themes. In general, classical subjects were dropped in favour of settings remote in time or place; at the same time, the immediate dangers and horrors of revolution and war produced a new genre, *rescue opera, of which Beethoven's *Fidelio* is the greatest example. Nature could play a crucial role in the plots, as with the avalanche in Cherubini's *Éliza*; others featured the supernatural, as with Weber's *Der Freischütz*; or contact between the supernatural and human worlds, as with Hoffmann's *Undine*; and in different countries of Europe composers began developing a consciously national tradition, drawing on folk music, historical or legendary figures, or other devices to confer local colour and individuality.

National characteristics

Russians have long claimed Glinka as the father of their national opera for his ability to absorb national ideas and folk music into two major works: a heroic historical opera, *A Life for the Tsar* (1836), and a fantastic fairy-tale opera, *Ruslan and Lyudmila* (1842). Comparable father figures were, in Hungary, Erkel with *Hunyadi László* (1844) and *Bánk bán* (1861); in Poland, Moniuszko with *Halka* (1848); and in Czechoslovakia, Smetana with *The Bartered Bride* (1866). In all these countries in eastern Europe, *nationalist ideas tended to manifest themselves most vividly in opera, where local colour could be grafted on to the techniques of Italian opera, later French Revolutionary opera and *grand opera, and the German Romantic opera. Among Glinka's other services to his country was the pioneering, in *Kamarinskaya* (1848), of the 'changing background' variation technique which Russian composers (including Tchaikovsky) instinctively found more sympathetic than sonata form. Composers who made particular efforts to define a national melodic idiom by drawing on the inflections of their spoken language include Dargomïzhsky and Musorgsky in Russia, and Janáček in Czechoslovakia.

Except in Italy, where the voice continued to reign supreme, the orchestra assumed a more important role in opera, providing more sensational and descriptive elements in the drama: the development of *leitmotif provided not only graphic illustration but new dramatic coherence at a time when the old formal number opera was weakening. Orchestral music paid more attention to drama. Sonata form and the traditional layout of the symphony tended to give way to more dramatic, pictorial, or narrative methods of construction (another reflection of the Romantic tendency to find new connections between the arts). Although a major symphonist such as Schubert was content to work in traditional outlines, Schumann admitted a much stronger pictorial element (as in his 'Rhenish' Symphony), and it was still more characteristic to experiment with *programme symphonies, as in Berlioz's *Symphonie fantastique*, or with new forms dictated by narrative or pictorial elements, such as Liszt's *symphonic poems.

The enlargement of the standard orchestra was connected to the rise of the virtuoso conductor, initially such composers as Weber, Berlioz, Liszt, and Wagner. Virtuosity, indeed, became a stronger musical element. The concept of the Artist as Hero, mastering sensational difficulties or having access, through his special sensibility, to heightened emotions, was encouraged by the success of Paganini, whose carefully cultivated sinister aura lent extra thrills to his virtuosity. His violin *Caprices*, and the concept behind them, strongly influenced Liszt, whose own brilliant virtuosity embraced novel compositional techniques as well as incomparable gifts as a pianist.

The orchestra and opera

If one of Romanticism's tendencies was to heighten and exaggerate, its intensification of the emotions also led to refinement and concentration. Romantic orchestration cultivated, in Wagner, a rich, smooth, sensuous blend, but, in Berlioz and Mahler, a liking for novel combinations of sound and chamber-music textures within the full orchestra. The moment of exquisite sensibility—deriving from a mood, an image, or a nervous sensation, even the poetry to be found in a technical device—could give rise to Romantic miniatures, and to the short piano pieces by Schumann and Chopin. Schubert, first great master of the German lied, found a new way of fusing poetry and music, with the piano often providing an illustrative background for the vocal narrative, and wrote the first fine song cycles in *Die schöne Müllerin* and *Winterreise*. His greatest successors, Schumann and Wolf, refined still further the expressive contact between poetry and music; none of the three, significantly, was at home in opera, in spite of repeated attempts by Schubert.

Opera, however, retained a dominant position throughout the century, combining as it did several arts in a dramatic context. Parisian grand opera stood somewhat to the side of the Romantic tradition, though the imposing resources of the Opéra not only attracted its own tradition of composers (Spontini, Auber, Halévy, Meyerbeer) but also interested Verdi, Tchaikovsky, and Wagner. The tradition of French Romantic opera lay more with the somewhat sentimental vein cultivated by Massenet and Gounod: France studiously underrated its greatest Romantic, Berlioz, whose bold new forms and ideas proved disconcerting. Bellini's long, expressive melodies won admiration for Italian Romantic opera even in Germany, as did the Romantic tragedies which Donizetti regarded as more important than his comedies.

But European opera in the middle and latter part of the century was dominated by Verdi and Wagner. The genius of each included the capacity to absorb into great art different strains from earlier phases in Romanticism, and bring them to culmination: this places them as late Romantics. Wagner, in particular, extended chromatic harmony (largely under the influence of Liszt) to the limits of tonality; Brahms's apparently more classical disciplines won him a following which set him in opposition to Wagner. However, Schoenberg regarded Brahms as a progressive, though he himself inherited much from Wagner, who indeed left few significant composers of the final stages of the Romantic movement unmarked in some way. Reaction against Wagner, or the difficulty in succeeding him, helped to hasten the emergence of ideas that moved away from Romanticism. Although the movement is conveniently held to have run its course by the outbreak of World War I, it has bequeathed much to subsequent composers: to that extent, it is still with us.   JW

F. BLUME, *Classic and Romantic Music* (New York, 1970) · C. DAHLHAUS, *Between Romanticism and Modernism: Four Studies in the Music of the Later 19th Century* (Berkeley, Los Angeles, and London, 1980) · L. PLANTINGA, *Romantic Music* (New York, 1984) · A. WHITTALL, *Romantic Music: A Concise History, from Schubert to Sibelius* (London, 1987) · G. ABRAHAM (ed.), *Romanticism, 1830–1890*, The New Oxford History of Music, ix (London, 1990) · A. RINGER (ed.), *The Early Romantic Era*, Man and Music/Music and Society (London, 1990) · J. SAMSON (ed.), *The Late Romantic Era*, Man and Music/Music and Society (London, 1991) · L. RATNER, *Romantic Music: Sound and Syntax* (New York, 1992) · C. ROSEN, *The Romantic Generation* (Cambridge, MA, 1995; London, 1996)

generally longer, with refrains of either four lines (*rondeau quatrain*) or five (*rondeau cinquain*). In either case, they are set to music by the same method as before (except that each couplet is allocated to a musical unit, though still according to the rhyme) and the resulting musical form is the same, as in this *rondeau* by Dufay:

Ma belle dame souverainne / *Faites cesser ma grief dolour* } A

Que j'endure pour vostre amour / *Nuit et jour, dont j'ay tres grant painne* } B

Ou autrement, soies certainne, / Je finneray dedens brief jour. } a

Ma belle dame souverainne / *Faites cesser ma grief dolour* } A

Il n'i a jour de la sepmainne / Que je ne soye en grant tristour } a

Se me veullies par vo doulcour / Secourir, de volonté plaine } b

Ma belle dame souverainne / *Faites cesser ma grief dolour* } A

Que j'endure pour vostr amour / *Nuit et jour, dont j'ay tres grant painne.* } B

PD/ABul

G. GREENE (ed.), *French Secular Music: Rondeaux and Miscellaneous Pieces*, Polyphonic Music of the Fourteenth Century, 22 (Monaco, 1989) · M. EVERIST, 'The polyphonic *rondeau c.*1300: Repertory and context', *Early Music History*, 15 (1996), 59–96 · D. FALLOWS, *A Catalogue of Polyphonic Songs, 1415–1480* (Oxford, 1999)

rondellus. A compositional technique making use of imitation and *voice exchange; also a complete work written using this technique. Most common in the 13th century and confined almost exclusively to Britain, it involved the composition of a simple melody that is consonant when combined with itself in imitation. The technique is found most frequently in three-part textures, in which either two upper voices are combined with a repeating phrase in the lower voice (known as a *pes*) or three voices stand alone. The best-known (but a rather uncharacteristic) example of *rondellus* technique is the rota *Sumer is icumen in*, in which a texture of many voices can be created from a long melody and a short *pes*.   ABUL

Rondine, La ('The Swallow'). Opera in three acts by Puccini to a libretto by A. M. Willner and Heinz Reichert (Monte Carlo, 1917).

rondo form. One of the fundamental forms in music, in which a repeated section alternates with at least two different episodes. At its simplest it can be represented as ABACA. It is to be found in many cultures and periods, for example in the medieval carol, where the *burden represents the A section. The term 'rondo' (Fr.: *rondeau*) was first used in conjunction with this form in late Baroque suite movements, and then in Classical instrumental works, where it became typical for the last movement of a multi-movement work. Self-contained rondos were also published, and the form was sometimes used in songs, dances, and opera movements.

In the Classical rondo, the A section, or 'rondo theme' (which may be preceded by an introduction), always recurs in the tonic key, whereas the episodes modulate to related keys and may include new themes in those keys. In the more popular type of work, such as the *divertimento, and in many dances and marches, each section of the rondo is of strict duration, usually a multiple of eight bars, and is repeated; sections may be arranged in small *binary units.

Mozart's famous Rondo alla turca, the last movement of the Piano Sonata K331/300*i* in A major, combines binary, *ternary, and rondo elements (see Table 1). Each section (labelled A–E) is precisely eight bars long, until the *coda. At one level this work is in strict rondo form, because the rondo theme (the A section) returns several times with different episodes between. At another level, both ABA and DED are binary units, here called 'supersections' X and Y. These in turn are arranged in a rondo-like structure, separated by the striking tune C which, in this interpretation, becomes the rondo theme.

In more sophisticated movements, for example Mozart's Rondo in A minor K511, the sections, especially the episodes, are of unpredictable length, and may include *development and other sonata-like processes. Haydn liked to vary both the rondo theme and the episode, in a form that may be represented as ABA¹B¹A² (for example, the first movement, Andante con espressione, of his Piano Sonata no. 24 in C major). Beethoven increasingly preferred *sonata rondo form

TABLE I

bar nos.	key	section	supersection
0–8	A minor–E minor	‖: A :‖	X
8–16	C major–V of A minor	‖: B	
16–24	A minor	A :‖	
24–32	A major	‖: C :‖	C
32–40	F♯ minor–C♯ minor	‖: D :‖	Y
40–8	A major	‖: E	
48–56	F♯ minor	D :‖	
56–64	A major	‖: C :‖	C
64–72	A minor–E minor	‖: A :‖	X
72–80	C major–V of A minor	‖: B	
80–8	A minor	A :‖	
88–96	A major	‖: C :‖	C
96–127	A major	coda	coda

for final movements, for example that of the Pathétique Sonata op. 13; but the slow movement of the same sonata is a simple rondo. See also FORM, 4.

GMT/NT

Röntgen, Julius (*b* Leipzig, 9 May 1855; *d* Bilthoven, 13 Sept. 1932). German-Dutch composer, pianist, and teacher. He learnt music first with his father, leader of the Gewandhaus Orchestra, then studied in Leipzig and Munich. He taught from 1877 to 1925 in Amsterdam (at the conservatory from its foundation, in which he was instrumental, in 1884) and was a pillar of musical life in the city. He was a friend of Brahms, Grieg (whose unfinished Second Quartet he completed), and Tovey. An immensely productive composer, he wrote in a Brahmsian style characterized by immaculate craftsmanship, melodic spontaneity, a natural contrapuntal flow, and buoyant rhythmic invention. The bulk of his compositions—about 600 in total—are held in the Gemeentemuseum in The Hague and include 20 symphonies (two of them choral), 22 string quartets, 11 *quartettini*, 13 piano trios, 16 string trios, 14 cello sonatas, and a commensurate number of works in other genres.   MA

root, root position. The root of a chord is the note from which it takes its name. Thus the C major chord has C as its root, even though the chord may be in first or second *inversion, with E or G respectively as its lowest note. If a chord is in root position, the lowest note is also the root. See also FUNDAMENTAL BASS.

Rore, Cipriano de (*b* c.1516; *d* Parma, Sept. 1565). Flemish composer. He may have been a pupil of Willaert in Venice in the 1540s. By 1547 he was *maestro di cappella* to Duke Ercole II in Ferrara, but when his employer died in 1559 Rore was away visiting his parents and was not reappointed by Ercole's successor. He then entered the service of the governor of the Netherlands, Margaret of Parma, and in 1561 returned to Italy to work for her husband in Parma. He was tempted away to Venice in 1563, to succeed Willaert as *maestro di cappella* at St Mark's, but found the burden of administration too heavy and returned to Parma, where he died.

Although he composed a good deal of church music, it is Rore's ten books of madrigals that are remarkable for their quality and for their influence on other composers. His early madrigals are often settings of Petrarch in a serious style, but after leaving Ferrara he became interested in contemporary poets, concentrating on bringing out the meaning of the verse and using contrasts of rhythm and texture to match their accentuation. He was interested in the potential of chromaticism and unusual melodic intervals for expressing extreme emotions; it was this and his sensitivity to the text that made Monteverdi recognize him as one of the founders of the *seconda pratica* (see PRIMA PRATICA, SECONDA PRATICA).   DA/TC

Rorem, Ned (*b* Richmond, IN, 23 Oct. 1923). American composer. He studied at the American Conservatory in Chicago (1938–40), Northwestern University (1940–2), the Curtis Institute in Philadelphia (1943), and the Juilliard School (1946, 1948), and also had private lessons from Virgil Thomson and Aaron Copland. From 1951 to 1957 he lived in Paris under the patronage of the Vicomtesse Marie Laure de Noailles; he then returned to New York. Primarily a song composer, he has been influenced by his teachers and by the French musicians he came to know in Paris (Poulenc, Honegger, and others). His output includes several operas, three symphonies and other orchestral works, and a variety of chamber pieces. He has also found an audience as a diarist, recounting his life as artist and homosexual in *The Paris Diary* (New York, 1966), *The New York Diary* (New York, 1967), *Critical Affairs: A Composer's Journal* (New York, 1970), and other volumes.   PG

rosalia. A type of sequence; see SEQUENCE, 1.

Rosamunde, Fürstin von Cypern ('Rosamund, Princess of Cyprus'). Play (1823) by Helmina von Chézy for which Schubert wrote the overture and musical interludes; the overture played at the first performance was the one already composed for *Alfonso und Estrella*. The overture now known as the *Rosamunde* overture (D644) was composed for G. E. Hoffmann's melodrama *Die Zauberharfe* ('The Magic Harp') (1820).

rose. A type of round or oval *soundhole, partly filled with decorative tracery, set in the belly of certain stringed instruments, particularly lutes and guitars of the Renaissance and Baroque periods; roses are also sometimes present in harpsichord and clavichord soundboards and occasionally in the bellies of bowed string instruments.   JMo

Rose Lake, The. 'Song without Words' for orchestra (1991–3) by Tippett.

Roseingrave, Thomas (*b* Winchester, 1688–91; *d* Dunleary [Dún Laoghaire], 23 June 1766). English composer. He was the son of Daniel Roseingrave, an organist of possibly Irish origin, and had his first music lessons from his father, going with him to Dublin in 1698. In 1709 he went to Italy to study music; in Venice he met Domenico Scarlatti, who made a great impression on him. He later (1739) published an edition of Scarlatti's keyboard sonatas, which initiated the 'Scarlatti cult' in England. His own harpsichord music, curiously, shows little of Scarlatti's influence.

In 1725 Roseingrave competed successfully for the post of organist at St George's, Hanover Square (Handel's parish church). He was now at the height of his powers as an organist, teacher, and outstanding improviser, though Hawkins, never one to mince words, thought his compositions 'harsh and disgusting, manifesting great learning, but devoid of eloquence and variety'. His career, however, came to an end when marriage to a young pupil was forbidden by her father: thereafter Roseingrave neglected his professional duties and was pensioned off. He eventually retired to Dublin, where his opera *Phaedra and Hippolitus* was produced in 1753, and occasionally gave harpsichord recitals. He was buried in St Patrick's Cathedral.   WT/LC

Rosenberg, Hilding (Constantin) (*b* Bosjökloster, Skåne, 21 June 1892; *d* Stockholm, 19 May 1985). Swedish composer and teacher. He studied the piano and organ at the Stockholm Conservatory (1915–16), then learnt counterpoint with Stenhammar and conducting with Scherchen. He was assistant conductor and répétiteur at the Royal Opera in Stockholm (1932–4) when the first of his seven operas, *Resa till Amerika* ('Journey to America'), was produced there. From the first he was alert to developments in contemporary music (Schoenberg, Hindemith, Les Six), and his early compositions outraged conservative Swedish critics. He soon found a balance between the demands of modernity and the requisites of tonality, setting a standard of integrity that established him as Sweden's most important composer for most of the rest of the century. An influential teacher, he numbered Bäck, Blomdahl, and Lidholm among his pupils. Rosenberg's compositions include two children's operas, four ballets, eight symphonies (nos. 4, 5, and 8 are choral) and much other orchestral music, 12 string quartets and other chamber pieces, and a generous quantity of choral music.   MA

📖 P. LYNE, *Hilding Rosenberg: Catalogue of Works* (Stockholm, 1970)

Rosenkavalier, Der ('The Knight of the Rose'). Opera in three acts by Richard Strauss to a libretto by Hugo von Hofmannsthal (Dresden, 1911).

Rosenmüller, Johann (*b* Oelsnitz, nr Zwickau, *c*.1619; *d* Wolfenbüttel, Sept. 1684). German composer. He studied theology at Leipzig University, matriculating in 1640, and then became assistant to the Kantor of St Thomas's; in 1651 he was organist of the Nicolaikirche. Four years later he was imprisoned on suspicion of homosexual activities; he escaped and from 1658 to 1682 lived in Venice. The last two years of his life were spent as Kapellmeister in Wolfenbüttel.

In spite of his unsettled life Rosenmüller found time to compose a huge quantity of music, including suites and sonatas (*Studentenmusik*, 1654; *Sonate da camera*, 1667; *Sonate*, 1682) and a great deal of church music, of which two sets of sacred concertos were published (*Kern-Sprüche*, Leipzig, 1648; *Andere Kern-Sprüche*, Leipzig, 1652–3).   WT

Rosenthal, Manuel [Emmanuel] (*b* Paris, 18 June 1904). French conductor and composer. He studied the violin at the Paris Conservatoire with Jules Boucherit and in 1926 was invited by Ravel to bring him some of his compositions. In 1928 Ravel also persuaded the Concerts Pasdeloup to engage Rosenthal as a conductor. From there he went on to conduct the French National Orchestra and to an international career that lasted for over 60 years. His Ravel recordings remain touchstones of French style, combining accuracy, atmosphere, and rhythmic verve. As a composer he is best known for such lighthearted works as his operetta *La Poule noire*, his *Chansons du Monsieur Bleu*, and his ballet *Gaieté parisienne*, based on music by Offenbach.   RN

Rosetti, Antonio [Rössler, Franz Anton] (*b* Leitmeritz [now Litoměřice], *c*.1750; *d* Ludwigslust, 30 June 1792). Bohemian composer. He studied theology but in 1773 joined the court chapel of the Prince of Oettingen-Wallerstein as a double-bass player; he was promoted to Kapellmeister in 1785. In 1781–2 he visited Paris. From 1789 until his death he was Kapellmeister to the Duke of Mecklenburg-Schwerin at Ludwigslust.

Rosetti's numerous instrumental works, many of which show the influence of Haydn, include over 40 symphonies, concertos (notably for horn), string quartets, and music for wind ensemble. He also wrote a chamber opera, *Das Winterfest der Hirten* ('The Shepherds' Winter Festival', 1789), the oratorios *Der sterbende Jesus* ('The Dying Jesus', 1786) and *Jesus in Gethsemane* (1790), and other sacred music.

WT/FL

rosin [colophony, resin]. Purified and hardened gum of turpentine, rubbed on the hair of a stringed instrument's bow to enable it to grip the strings and so cause them to vibrate.

Roslavets, Nikolay Andreyevich (*b* Dushatino, Chernigov district, Ukraine, 24 or 25 Dec. 1880/5 or 6 Jan. 1881; *d* Moscow, 23 Aug. 1944). Russian composer. He studied at the Moscow Conservatory (1902–12) and swiftly earned a reputation as an avant-garde composer, developing, independently of Schoenberg, theories of 12-note serialism, evident in such works as the Third String Quartet (1920) and the Violin Concerto (1925). Although he was blacklisted by the Soviet musical establishment, a new dawn came with his listing in volume 3 of the directory *Kto pisal o muzïke* ('Writers on Music'; Moscow, 1979), where, significantly, we find that he contributed articles on Webern's op. 7 and on *Pierrot lunaire* to the contemporary music journal *K novïm beregam* ('Towards New Shores') in 1923. His experimental contribution to his native music is now being reassessed in the new Russia.   GN/DN

Rosseter, Philip (*b* 1567 or 1568; *d* London, 5 May 1623). English lutenist and composer. From 1603 until his death he was a musician at the court of James I. He also managed a company of boy actors and a theatre at Whitefriars. In 1601 he published a book of ayres with lute accompaniment, half of them his own, half by Thomas Campion; the two composers were united in their dislike of music that was 'intricate, bated with fuge', and Rosseter's own pieces are charming trifles setting elegant anacreontic verse. His other publication, a book of *Lessons* (1609) for a mixed consort of flute, bowed, and plucked instruments, survives incomplete.

DA/JM

Rossi, Luigi (*b* Torremaggiore, nr Foggia, 1597 or 1598; *d* Rome, 19 or 20 Feb. 1653). Italian composer. He was a pupil of the famous madrigal composer Giovanni de Macque, and entered the service of the Borghese family in Rome in the 1620s. In 1633 he became organist of S. Luigi dei Francesi, a position he held for the rest of his life. He became famous for his cantatas and was a favourite of Cardinal Antonio Barberini, whose service he entered in 1641; Barberini was a notable patron of opera, and for him Rossi wrote *Il palazzo incantato* ('The Enchanted Palace', 1642), as well as some oratorios. After the death of Pope Urban VIII in 1644 the Barberinis lost favour in Rome and went to Paris, where they were responsible for the introduction of opera. At the invitation of Cardinal Mazarin, Rossi was engaged, with a group of Italian singers, to produce his second opera in Paris. *Orfeo* (1647) was a marked success, but the sumptuousness of its production was much criticized and a second visit the following year did not result in the production of a similar work. He returned to Rome, and died a remarkably wealthy man, his possessions including paintings by Leonardo and Raphael. His tombstone is at S. Maria in Via Lata.

About 300 of Rossi's cantatas survive in widespread sources. His melodious style became popular throughout Europe: French opera especially benefited from his example. His music was also well known in England, aided by the fact that the royalists were in exile in Paris when he was at the height of his popularity there; he composed a cantata on the death of Charles I.

DA/TC

📖 P. Bassi, *Luigi Felice Rossi* (Turin, 1994)

Rossi, Michelangelo [del Violino] (*b* Genoa, *c*.1602; *d* Rome, *bur.* 7 July 1656). Italian composer and violinist. His early life was spent in Genoa, but by 1624 he was in Rome, where, apart from occasional visits elsewhere, he remained for the rest of his life. He was taught by Frescobaldi and in the 1630s was involved with the Barberini family; his opera *Erminia sul Giordano* ('Erminia by the Jordan'), performed with sets by Bernini at the Palazzo Barberini in 1633, includes some splendid arias and ensembles.

Rossi's most important music is for keyboard; about 1640 he published a volume of keyboard music containing toccatas in a style similar to that of Frescobaldi. In his lifetime he was best known as a virtuoso violinist.

Rossi, Salamone (*b* ?Mantua, 1570; *d* ?Mantua, after 1628). Italian violinist and composer. He was associated with the Gonzaga court in Mantua from at least 1587 until 1628, mainly as a virtuoso violinist. His good reputation earned him exemption from wearing the yellow badge which was compulsory for the Jews in Mantua. Rossi composed a number of attractive madrigals, including the earliest published continuo madrigal, but his fame as a composer is for the *Hashirim ásher lish'lomo* ('The Songs of Solomon'—a reference to

his first name rather than to the source of the texts), settings of Hebrew psalms, hymns, and so on in a contemporary Italian style, a rare attempt at non-traditional Hebrew music.   DA/TC

Rossignol, Le. See NIGHTINGALE, THE.

Rossini, Gioachino (*see page 1080*)

Rössler, Franz Anton. See ROSETTI, ANTONIO.

rota (Lat.). 1. See ROUND, 1.
    2. See ROTTE.

Rota [Rinaldi], Nino (*b* Milan, 3 Dec. 1911; *d* Rome, 10 April 1979). Italian composer. A precocious composer (he had an oratorio performed at 11 and wrote a three-act lyric comedy at 13), he studied at the Milan Conservatory (1923–5), privately with Pizzetti (1925–6), and then with Casella at the Accademia S. Cecilia in Rome. After graduating he attended the Curtis Institute in Philadelphia (1931–2), where he studied composition with Rosario Scalero and conducting with Fritz Reiner. On his return he took a degree in literature at the University of Milan. His own teaching career began in Taranto (1937–8); in 1939 he began to teach at the Liceo Musicale in Bari, later becoming its director (1950–78).

Rota's compositions are noteworthy for their melodious appeal. His concert music is uneven: his three symphonies, for example, are fluent but undistinguished, whereas his Concerto for Strings has a strong melodic profile. It is for his film music that he is chiefly remembered, not least because of his 30-year association with Federico Fellini; among other directors with whom he worked are Henry Cass (*The Glass Mountain*, 1950) and Franco Zeffirelli (*The Taming of the Shrew*, 1966).   MA

rototoms. Sets of tunable tom-toms without shells, invented in the 1960s. Like some machine timpani they rotate on a central threaded spindle to change their (clearly defined) pitch. They are widely used in studios, pop bands, and light-music orchestrations. Because they have no shells they take up little space and are often used in quite large numbers.   JMo

rotrouenge (Old Fr.; Provençal: *retroncha*). A term found in the repertories of trouvère and troubadour songs, where it appears to denote a particular type of poem. None of the extant sources, however, gives any clear indication of its significance. Four troubadour poems (three of which have music) are given the title; all have a refrain. Six pieces survive from the trouvère repertory (only one with music), four of them attributed to Gontier de Soignies.   JBe

(*cont. on p. 1082*)

Gioachino Rossini
(1792–1868)

The Italian composer Gioachino Antonio Rossini was born in Pesaro on 29 February 1792 and died in Passy on 13 November 1868.

The early years

Rossini's father was a trumpeter and horn player, his mother a singer. Both toured the theatres of the Romagna, and from an early age Gioachino, their only child, accompanied them. The family moved in 1802 to Lugo, and two years later to Bologna, where with private tuition Rossini made rapid progress on the horn and keyboard, and especially as a singer (in 1805 he made a public appearance as the boy Adolfo in Paër's opera *Camilla*). 1804 saw the production of the six 'sonate a quattro', deftly written if not markedly original works composed for Agostino Triossi, a friend of the Rossini family in Ravenna, which are in the repertory of every string orchestra today. During the same period Rossini began playing the harpsichord at several local theatres and composed arias to insert into some of the operas that he accompanied.

In 1806 he was admitted on the strength of his singing to membership of the Accademia Filarmonica of Bologna, a great honour for one so young. Earlier the same year he entered the Liceo of Bologna and the famous counterpoint class of Padre Mattei; there he immersed himself in the music of Haydn and Mozart, and two years later a cantata on the *Lament of Harmony on the Death of Orpheus* won him a prize. His first opera, *Demetrio e Polibio*, was composed for the Mombelli family, probably in about 1810, but was not performed until 1812. His professional career began with *La cambiale di matrimonio* ('The Bill of Marriage'), a one-act *farsa* commissioned for the Teatro S. Moisè in Venice; it proved so successful that it was followed over the next three years by several others, including *La scala di seta* ('The Silken Ladder') and *Il signor Bruschino* which are remembered mostly for their overtures.

With the sacred opera *Ciro in Babilonia* (Ferrara, 1812) he ventured into the serious genre, but as yet his talent was mainly for comedy. This was confirmed later in the year by his first commission for La Scala, *La pietra del paragone* ('The Touchstone'; Milan, 1812), a work declared by Stendhal, writing in 1823, to be Rossini's comic masterpiece. In the light of what was to come this perhaps seems a surprising evaluation, but the piece was a great and deserved success, performed 53 times during its initial run; it contains many of the features, such as settings of nonsense verse, that would be exploited to memorable effect in future operas. Its enthusiastic reception earned Rossini exemption from military service.

In 1813 he achieved a still greater double triumph in Venice with the heroic *Tancredi* and the comic *L'italiana in Algeri*, both of which eventually carried his name far beyond Italy. Tancredi's Act I cabaletta, 'Di tanti palpiti', in particular became one of the best-known melodies of the age. With these works Rossini's style was fully formed and his strong musical personality carried all before it. Failures were few and mostly temporary (e.g. *Il turco in Italia*, Milan, 1814). In 1815 he signed a long-term contract with Domenico Barbaia, impresario of the Neapolitan S. Carlo and Fondo theatres, to assume the musical directorship of both venues, with the obligation to produce annually a new opera at each.

Years of maturity

This post effectively placed Rossini in the same position as Haydn at Eszterháza, with a captive audience before whom he could experiment; at the same time it left him free to accept commissions elsewhere. His first work for Naples, *Elisabetta, regina d'Inghilterra* (1815), was significant for dispensing with *recitativo secco*, using full strings instead of keyboard, but was largely based on music from his earlier operas. Of much greater importance was *Otello* (Naples, 1816), which broke fresh ground dramatically by ending with a murder on stage, followed by a suicide; a happy ending was imposed by papal authorities for the work's revival in Rome in 1820. Musically, the sequence of numbers in the final act, including Desdemona's Willow Song, mark a new stage of Rossini's development as an operatic composer.

Between these first two Neapolitan works came a pair of commissions for theatres in Rome; the *semiseria* rescue opera *Torvaldo e Dorliska* (1816) received only moderate success, but *Il barbiere di Siviglia* (1816) survived a disastrous first night to become a universal favourite, loved by Verdi and Wagner alike, and inspiring in Beethoven the famously backhanded compliment that Rossini should compose only more of the same. After this quintessence of the *buffo* style, *La Cenerentola* (Rome, 1817), while not lacking in comic situations, is more sentimentally inclined, and in the remaining years of his Italian career Rossini produced no comedy at all. For Milan he composed the *semiseria La gazza ladra* ('The Thieving Magpie', 1817); for Naples he produced a series of important *opere serie*, drawing on a wide variety of different literary traditions: Tasso for *Armida* (1817), neo-classical biblical drama for *Mosè in Egitto* (1818), Racine for *Ermione* (1819), Walter Scott for *La donna del lago* (1819), and Italian Romanticism for *Maometto II* (1820).

By now Rossini had married the prima donna Isabella Colbran, with whom he was to make a triumphal tour to Vienna in 1822 together with Barbaia's Neapolitan troupe. There he met Beethoven and attended performances of both the 'Eroica' Symphony and Weber's *Der Freischütz*. On his return he composed his last opera for Italy, *Semiramide* (Venice, 1823). Late in 1823 he travelled to Paris and then to England, where he stayed for eight months, visiting Brighton and Cambridge but spending most of his time in London. A promised new opera for the King's Theatre never materialized, however, and his time was occupied by visits to members of high society, who offered enormous sums to have him teach their daughters. While in London he signed a contract with the French government, and on his return to Paris he took up the post of music director of the Théâtre Italien. For this theatre he wrote *Il viaggio a Reims*, an operatic *pièce de circonstance* to celebrate the coronation of Charles X (1825). He followed it over the next four years with four works for the Paris Opéra: the first two, *Le Siège de Corinthe* (1826) and *Moïse et Pharaon* (1827), were revised French versions of earlier Italian works (*Maometto II* and *Mosè in Egitto* respectively), while the comedy *Le Comte Ory* (1828) drew on material from *Il viaggio a Reims*. Finally, in 1829 Rossini composed the grand opera *Guillaume Tell* (1829), his only completely original work in French, and his last work for the stage.

Rossini's fame and influence were now at their zenith. He left Paris for Bologna, where he had built himself a villa, intending to return the following year for a new opera on the subject of Faust. But in the mean time the Bourbon monarchy had been overthrown, the Opéra had changed hands, and former commitments were disowned; Rossini's main concern was to fight in the law courts for the continuation of the annuity that he had been granted by Charles X. The case dragged on

for six years before being settled in Rossini's favour. During this time he maintained ties at the Théâtre Italien, living in an apartment above the theatre and overseeing both revivals and premieres of works by Bellini and Donizetti. In 1835 he published a set of salon pieces under the title *Soirées musicales*.

Meanwhile in 1831 he obliged Varela, a Spanish state counsellor, by agreeing to compose a *Stabat mater* on condition that it was never published. When in due course Varela's heirs attempted to sell the work, Rossini revealed that only half of it was by him and hastened to complete the rest, which was performed with great success in 1842, first at the Théâtre Italien, then (conducted by Donizetti) at the Liceo Musicale in Bologna, of which Rossini was now honorary director. He had already parted from his first wife, who died in 1845, leaving him free to marry Olympe Pélissier (formerly the mistress of the painter Horace Vernet), who had nursed him for over a decade through bouts of ill health that were becoming increasingly frequent. A demonstration against him by the patriots of 1848, who had not forgotten the pro-Austrian texts he had set for the Congress of Verona in 1822 at the instance of Metternich, induced him to leave Bologna for Florence, where his inertia and depression reached a crisis.

At last in 1855 he left for Paris to enjoy for the next 13 years an Indian summer of health and composition. A visit either to his villa in Passy or to his town quarters in the rue de la Chaussée d'Antin was obligatory for every eminent musician passing through the French capital—whether Verdi, Wagner, Boito, or even Balfe. All were entertained by his wit and good cooking. The most substantial composition of these years is the *Petite Messe solennelle* (1863); but he also left a large collection of pieces for piano with and without voices which he called *Péchés de vieillesse*. Mostly humorous, always musicianly, and curiously modern in their sound, they first reached publication only in the 1950s.

Rossini's style and influence

Rossini used to describe himself as 'the last of the classicists'. In the Romantic age his serious works—with their formalism and vocal virtuosity—soon fell into disfavour, whereas his comic operas have always remained fresh. Yet though he never fully entered the world of Italian Romanticism he was in a sense its architect. The plan of cantabiles, cabalettas, multi-movement duets, and finales that served Bellini, Donizetti, and the young Verdi had been defined by him. Moreover, his masterly fusion of Italian and French styles in his Paris operas, and his transformation of the moribund mythological French *tragédie lyrique* into a series of compellingly relevant operas on historical themes, played an important part in the French Romanticism of the 1820s, while setting the standard against which all later grand opera needs to be measured.

To the modern listener, for whom Wagner's way with opera is not the only one, Rossini has much to offer, in both serious and comic works: melodic vitality, an unerring sense of proportion, and in the case of *Moïse* and *Guillaume Tell* moments of unforced grandeur worthy of a late Haydn mass. His mastery of form derives from his mastery of rhythm—a quality that gives his musical personality its force, enabling him, for instance, to stamp his patent on the famous 'crescendo',

not in itself an especially novel device. The strength of his comedy, like that of P. G. Wodehouse, depends in great measure on a faultless command of style.

JB/BWa

📖 G. RADICIOTTI, *Gioacchino Rossini: Vita documentata, opere ed influenza su l'arte* (Tivoli, 1927–9) · F. TOYE, *Rossini: A Study in Tragi-Comedy* (London, 1934) · G. RONCAGLIA, *Rossini l'Olimpico* (Milan, 1946) · L. ROGNONI, *Rossini* (Parma, 1956) · H. WEINSTOCK, *Rossini: A Biography* (New York, 1968) · E. MICHOTTE, *Richard Wagner's Visit to Rossini* (Eng. trans., Chicago, 1968) · STENDHAL, *Life of Rossini* (Eng. trans., London, 1970) [not for accurate information] · R. OSBORNE, *Rossini* (London, 1986, 2/1993) · A. KENDALL, *Gioacchino Rossini: The Reluctant Hero* (London, 1992)

rotte [rota, rote, rotta]. A medieval term referring to several stringed instruments, including the triangular *psaltery, the *rebec, and various plucked and bowed *lyres.

Rouget de Lisle, Claude-Joseph (*b* Lons-le-Saunier, 10 May 1760; *d* Choisy-le-Roi, 26 June 1836). French composer. He was an officer in the French army, and in 1791 was sent to Strasbourg. There, when war was declared in April 1791, he wrote the stirring patriotic song *Chant de guerre pour l'armée du Rhin*, which was taken up by a battalion of volunteers from Marseilles and renamed *La Marseillaise*. Rouget de Lisle's other music, which includes patriotic songs and cantatas, is almost totally unknown. He was the author of several opera librettos.

roulade (Fr.). A vocal *melisma. It originally referred to a specific ornament of quick passing notes connecting two melodic notes. 18th-century English dictionaries defined it as a trilling or quavering. In Germany the term is used pejoratively to denote gratuitous vocal coloratura added to arias in performance.

round. 1 (Lat.: *rota*). A short, circular *canon at the unison or octave, normally for three or more unaccompanied voices. In its simplest form, the round consists of a brief melody divided into sections of equal length that serve as the points of entry for each voice. As each singer reaches the end of the melody he or she begins again, so that the round is self-perpetuating and can be repeated as many times as desired. *Three Blind Mice*, which dates from the 16th century, is a well-known example. The *catch, a particular form of round based on word-play, was especially popular in Restoration England.   JN/JBe

2. A traditional circle dance. Tunes for such dances, for example 'Cheshire Rounds', are found in later editions of John Playford's *The English Dancing Master* and other 17th- and 18th-century collections. One of the earliest is *Sellinger's Round*, which Byrd used as the basis for a set of keyboard variations.   JN/JH

Round, Catch, and Canon Club. A London club for music-making founded in 1843 to encourage the composition and performance of rounds, catches, and canons. When it was dissolved in 1911 its membership had reached about 70.

round O. A 17th- and 18th-century anglicization of the French word *rondeau* (see RONDO FORM), used by Matthew Locke, Purcell, Jeremiah Clarke, and others. A 'Round O' by Purcell, composed as incidental music for the play *Abdelazer, or The Moor's Revenge*, was used by Britten as the theme for his *Young Person's Guide to the Orchestra*.

Rouse, Christopher (Chapman) (*b* Baltimore, 15 Feb. 1949). American composer. He studied at Oberlin University and with George Crumb and Karel Husa at Cornell; in 1987 he was appointed professor of composition at the Eastman School. His music is uninhibited in its rhetoric while being essentially conventional in its forms and expressive modes, which are usually dark, and he has had particular success since the mid-1980s as an orchestral composer, producing two symphonies as well as concertos for violin, cello, flute, trombone, percussion (*Der gerettete Alberich*, a 'fantasy on themes of Wagner'), and piano (*Seeing*).   PG

Rousseau, Jean-Jacques (*b* Geneva, 28 June 1712; *d* Ermenonville, 2 July 1778). Swiss philosopher, theorist, and composer. He undertook his own musical education while teaching at Neuchâtel and Lausanne. After a visit to Venice in 1743 he composed and produced *Les Muses galantes* (1744), an *opéra-ballet* modelled on the operas of Rameau (though the older composer subsequently criticized it). In 1752 his most successful opera, acclaimed in Paris and abroad, was performed: *Le Devin du village*, an *intermède* that combined a pastoral plot with Italian recitatives, simple *airs*, and dances, and pointed the way to *opéra comique*. His only other stage work, the experimental melodrama *Pygmalion* (with instrumental music by Horace Coignet), was given at Lyons in 1770 and inspired a spate of German imitations.

Rousseau took the Italian side in the Querelle des *Bouffons and attacked French music in his *Lettre sur la musique française* (1753). He consorted with Diderot and d'Alembert and supplied articles on music for the famous *Encyclopédie* which were later incorporated into his own *Dictionnaire de musique* (Paris, 1768). Although his view was that opera was not viable in the French language, he later came to admire those directed by Gluck at the Opéra. His ideas on social justice were the foundation of new humanism and of *Romanticism in general.   PS/SH

Roussel, Albert (*b* Tourcoing, 5 April 1869; *d* Royan, 23 Aug. 1937). French composer. Born into a prosperous industrial family, he was orphaned as a young child and brought up first by his paternal grandfather, then by his uncle. At 15 he was sent to school in Paris, where his first love was mathematics, though he received a general musical education. As a young man he was torn between careers in music and the navy. Eventually he decided on the latter and entered the college at Brest in 1887, receiving his commission in 1889. He was promoted lieutenant in 1893 and saw active service in Indo-China. While at sea, however, he began to teach himself composition and his first works—an Andante for violin, viola, cello, and organ, and a *Marche nuptiale* for organ (both 1893)—were performed in the naval church at Cherbourg.

After a period of extended leave, during which he took lessons in composition with Julien Koszul in Roubaix, Roussel resigned his commission in 1894. Being too old to enter the Paris Conservatoire, he studied first with the organist Eugène Gigout at the École Niedermeyer, then in 1898 enrolled as a pupil of d'Indy at the Schola Cantorum. He was appointed professor of counterpoint in 1902, resigning in protest at the rigidity of the Schola's methods in 1914, though he continued to teach privately. His pupils included Satie, Varèse, and Martinů. Roussel later claimed that Impressionism was a major influence on his early music, though there are also strong echoes of Franck in *Résurrection*, a symphonic prelude after Tolstoy (1903),

and in the cyclic structure of his First Symphony (1904–6). The harmonic astringency of the Divertissement for piano, flute, oboe, bassoon, and horn (1906), however, is prophetic of many of his mature works.

In 1909 Roussel married and went on a honeymoon cruise to India, which inspired his choral *Évocations* (1912), the first work for which he received public and critical acclaim. Even more successful was his first ballet, *Le Festin de l'araignée* ('The Spider's Banquet', 1913), based on the works of the entomologist Jean Henri Fabre, and containing, beneath its beautiful surface, dark premonitions of World War I. A visit to the ruins of Chitoor during his Indian sojourn gave him the subject for the *opéra-ballet Padmâvatî* (1914–18, staged 1923). Its composition was interrupted by the outbreak of conflict, during which Roussel saw active service as a gunnery officer on the Somme, before being invalided out of the army in 1918. *Padmâvatî*, one of the great stage works of the 20th century, marks a loosening of the influence of Impressionism and a move towards Roussel's later preoccupation with the modernist revision of Baroque or Classical structure. Depicting, often with tremendous force, the Mughal invasion of India, *Padmâvatî* recalls with its hybrid form the works of Lully and Rameau, while its harmonic palette, based on Indian rather than Western tonality, is experimental and unique. Its bitter anti-war sentiments were echoed in the sombre Second Symphony of 1919–21.

Roussel's health, precarious since the war, broke down in 1921. He settled in Varengeville on the Normandy coast, living almost as a recluse, though he made occasional trips to Paris and abroad. He continued to compose, turning with increasing frequency to absolute music, characterized by a rhythmic exactness (sometimes jazz-influenced), pungent harmonies that veer at times towards polytonality, and a strenuous classicism. His Suite in F (1926) embodies the linear, contrapuntal style of his later works. His 60th birthday was the occasion of a week-long festival in Paris, and in 1930 his greatest and most popular symphony, the Third, was given its premiere by the Boston Symphony Orchestra under Koussevitzky in Roussel's presence. His austere Fourth Symphony was completed in 1934.

Roussel's second opera, *La Naissance de la lyre* ('The Birth of the Lyre', 1922–4; staged 1925), was unsuccessful and he did not return to writing for the stage until 1930, when he produced his greatest ballet score, *Bacchus et Ariane*. *Le Testament de la Tante Caroline* ('Aunt Caroline's Will', 1932–3; staged 1936), a bawdy *opéra bouffe*, was popular in France though not elsewhere. Most of his songs were composed between 1927 and 1931. His greatest choral work is his setting in English of Psalm 80 (1928). He died suddenly from a heart attack, having just completed his String Trio (1937).

Roussel was one of the great individualists of the 20th century, the punchy urbanity of much of his music frequently seeming at odds with the reclusive persona he cultivated later in life. He has few successors and his music slipped from view in the years immediately after his death. A revival of interest in his work began about 1980, and he is now widely regarded as one of the most vital and important French composers of the 20th century.   TA

📖 B. Deane, *Albert Roussel* (London, 1961) · R. Follet, *Albert Roussel: A Bio-Bibliography* (Westport, CT, 1988)

rovescio, al (It.). 'In reverse'. The term can mean either *retrograde motion or *inversion.

row. Synonym of *series.

Rowley, Alec (*b* London, 13 March 1892; *d* London, 11 Jan. 1958). English composer. He studied with Frederick Corder at the RAM and taught at Trinity College from 1920. His compositions include many piano pieces, written specially for children.   PG

Roxolane, La. Nickname of Haydn's Symphony no. 63 in C major (1779), so called because the second movement uses material from Haydn's incidental music to the play *Soliman II, oder Die drei Sultaninnen*, in which the heroine was Roxolane.

Royal Academy of Music. 1. An association founded in London in 1718–19 to promote performances of Italian opera. It was organized by members of the nobility in the wake of Handel's earlier successes with Italian opera in London, notably *Rinaldo* (1711), and its seasons at the King's Theatre, Haymarket, from 1720 to 1728, were financed entirely by private subscription. Handel was the musical director, J. J. Heidegger the manager. As well as giving the first performances of several Handel operas, the company also mounted operas by Bononcini and Ariosti, bringing before the London public some of the finest singers in Europe. In a relatively short time the Royal Academy greatly enriched London's musical life. Its last seasons were dogged by quarrels with rival companies and notorious internal squabbles between its own composers and leading singers.

2. British conservatory founded in London in 1822. See DEGREES AND DIPLOMAS.

Royal College of Music. British conservatory founded in London in 1883. See DEGREES AND DIPLOMAS.

Royal College of Organists. British music college founded in London in 1864. See DEGREES AND DIPLOMAS.

Royal Manchester College of Music. See ROYAL NORTHERN COLLEGE OF MUSIC.

Royal Military School of Music. British music college founded in 1857 and based at Kneller Hall. See DEGREES AND DIPLOMAS.

Royal Musical Association (RMA). A society formed in London in 1874 as the Musical Association 'for the investigation and discussion of subjects connected with the art and science of music'; its founder members included Chappell, Grove, Macfarren, Ouseley, and Stainer. It holds regular meetings, publishes the bi-annual *Journal* [formerly *Proceedings*] *of the Royal Musical Association*, the annual *R.M.A. Research Chronicle*, and the series *Musica britannica*, and annually awards the Dent Medal for an outstanding contribution to international musicology.

Royal Northern College of Music. British conservatory formed in Manchester in 1973 by the amalgamation of the Royal Manchester College of Music (founded 1893) and the Northern School of Music (founded 1942). See DEGREES AND DIPLOMAS.

Royal Opera House, Covent Garden. The third *opera house built on the Covent Garden site in London, opened in 1858 and reopened, after expansion and rebuilding, in 1999.

Royal Philharmonic Society. A society founded in London in 1813 as the Philharmonic Society by a group of 30 leading musicians to promote orchestral and instrumental concerts. It commissioned works from such eminent composers as Beethoven (including his Ninth Symphony, of which it presented the first London performance); shortly before Beethoven died, it sent him £100, and, when the money was discovered untouched, donated it towards the cost of a statue in Vienna in his honour. The long list of guest conductors includes Mendelssohn. To commemorate the centenary of Beethoven's birth, in 1870 the society struck a Gold Medal which is awarded sporadically to internationally distinguished musicians; recipients have included Brahms, Casals, Strauss, Stravinsky, and Messiaen. In 1912 it was renamed the Royal Philharmonic Society. It organizes annual competitions for young composers, and has built up an archive of scores and manuscripts which arguably constitutes the single most important source for the history of music in the 19th and 20th centuries. It continues its policy of commissioning major new works.   AL

Royal School of Church Music. British music college founded in 1927.

Royal Schools of Music. See ASSOCIATED BOARD OF THE ROYAL SCHOOLS OF MUSIC.

Royal Scottish Academy of Music and Drama. British conservatory founded in Glasgow in 1928. See DEGREES AND DIPLOMAS.

Royer, Joseph-Nicolas-Pancrace (*b* Turin, *c.*1705; *d* Paris, 11 Jan. 1755). French composer, performer, and music administrator. He maintained an influential position in Parisian musical life from 1730 onwards, when he was appointed *maître de musique* at the Opéra and subsequently *maître de musique des enfans de France*, a position that included the musical education of the Dauphin Louis. His reputation as a harpsichordist and organist was equalled by his fame (second, for a time, only to that of Rameau) as an opera composer, and given official acknowledgment by numerous court appointments, including the position of *chantre de la musique de la chambre du roi*.

Royer's opera *Zaïde, reine de Grenade* (1739) was his most spectacular success, and one of the first to feature a danced pantomime. It was revived frequently until well after his death. *Le Pouvoir de l'amour* (1743) came near to matching it in popularity, and both operas feature bravura vocal writing, energetic orchestral string figuration, and an elaborate use of the chorus. Royer was active in the revival of the Concert Spirituel and the promotion of foreign music. He invited international virtuosos, gave the first Parisian performances of Pergolesi's *Stabat mater* (1753), and included in his programmes symphonies by Stamitz and Hasse, among others. In 1756 the significance of Royer's contributions to French music was acknowledged by an unusually extensive commemorative service, given jointly by performers from the royal chapel and the Opéra.

MHE

Rózsa, Miklós (*b* Budapest, 18 April 1907; *d* Los Angeles, 27 July 1995). Hungarian-born American composer. He studied at the Leipzig Conservatory (1925–9), then moved to Paris (1932–6) before settling in London, where he was music director for Alexander Korda films (*The Thief of Baghdad*, 1940). In 1940 he moved to Hollywood, where he wrote for MGM (1948–62: *Ben Hur*, 1959). His film scores are rich and Romantic, but his concert pieces, which include concertos for violin, viola, cello, and piano, as well as a *Sinfonia concertante* for violin and cello, are sometimes sharper.

PG

rubāb. See RABĀB.

rubato (It., 'robbed'; *tempo rubato*, 'robbed time'). The practice in performance of disregarding strict time, 'robbing' some note-values for expressive effect and creating an atmosphere of spontaneity. Rubato is generally achieved in one of two ways. First, the pulse remains constant but expressive nuances are created by making small changes to the rhythmic values of individual notes; this method was widespread in the 18th century and into the 19th and is thought to have been practised by Mozart and Chopin. Second, changes in tempo are made to all parts simultaneously, the performer applying **accelerando* and **ritardando* at his or her own discretion; this method has been associated with such 19th-century virtuosos as Liszt.

AL

Rubbra, (Charles) Edmund (*b* Northampton, 23 May 1901; *d* Gerrards Cross, 14 Feb. 1986). English composer and teacher. He went to Reading University (1920–1) and the RCM (1921–5), where he studied composition with Holst and counterpoint with R. O. Morris. Initially he earned a living as a schoolteacher, as a répétiteur, and in music journalism, reviewing for *The Monthly Musical Record*. During World War II he worked as a pianist, after which he settled in Oxford as a lecturer at Worcester College (1947–68) and taught composition at the Guildhall School of Music. In 1948 he became a Roman Catholic (dedicating his Eighth Symphony to the French Jesuit palaeontologist Teilhard de Chardin) and pursued interests in Buddhism and Taoism.

His first four symphonies appeared in quick succession between 1937 and 1941, establishing his reputation as a leading composer of his generation. The symphony was ultimately a symbol of Rubbra's preoccupation with organic thought and counterpoint. Furthermore, a predilection for polyphony and linear textures was nourished by his love for English 16th- and 17th-century music. His Fifth Symphony (1947–8), arguably his finest essay in the genre, marked the beginning of a further cycle of seven, the last of which was completed in 1979. His natural inclination towards polyphony was also eloquently expressed in chamber music, the Violin Sonata no. 2 and Quartet no. 1 (both 1931), the Piano Trio no. 1 (1950), and the Quartet no. 2 (1952) being important examples, while the works for voices with and without orchestra—the liturgical *Missa in honorem Sancti Dominici* (1948), *Song of the Soul* (1953), *Inscape* (1964–5), and the *Sinfonia sacra* (Symphony no. 9) of 1971–2—reflect his religious outlook and fascination with mysticism. He also wrote the books *Holst: A Monograph* (1947) and *Counterpoint: A Survey* (1960).

JDI

📖 R. S. GROVER, *The Music of Edmund Rubbra* (Aldershot, 1993)

Rubinstein, Anton (Grigor'yevich) (*b* Vikhvatintsi, Podolsk district, 16/28 Nov. 1829; *d* Peterhof [now

Petrodvorets], nr St Petersburg, 8/20 Nov. 1894). Russian composer and pianist. As a pianist he was a child prodigy, travelling widely throughout Europe before being appointed, at the age of 19, pianist to the Grand Duchess Elena Pavlovna. Under the grand duchess's patronage Rubinstein founded the Russian Musical Society in 1859, and then in 1862 the St Petersburg Conservatory, of which he was director until 1867, and again from 1887 to 1891.

Like his brother Nikolay, Anton was a stimulating and often exacting teacher, and he was revered by Tchaikovsky, who had studied under him at the conservatory. He had a less easy relationship with the composers of the St Petersburg school—The *Five— who despised his German-Jewish origins and were temperamentally opposed to the academicism of conservatory teaching: in 1889 Balakirev refused to attend Rubinstein's jubilee celebrations, and wrote a letter accusing Rubinstein of having had a harmful influence on Russian music. And the members of The Five resorted to calling him names: Tupinstein (derived from the Russian for 'dimwit') and Dubinstein, which could be freely translated as Blockheadinstein. Rubinstein countered these thrusts with an accusation of 'amateurishness' in the music of The Five, which so infuriated Musorgsky that he in turn condemned Rubinstein for producing 'quantity instead of quality', dubbing Rubinstein's huge 'Ocean' Symphony (the Symphony no. 2, 1851, rev. 1863 and 1880) a 'puddle'.

Such artistic bickering has tended to obscure Rubinstein's own worth as a composer. True, he was inclined to dash off undemanding trifles like the popular Melody in F (1852), but some of his large-scale works are worth a second glance, notably the Fifth Symphony (1880), the often colourfully nationalistic opera *Kupets Kalashnikov* ('The Merchant Kalashnikov'; St Petersburg, 1880), and above all his melodramatic *The Demon* (St Petersburg, 1875)—the first Russian opera to be performed in Russian on the London stage (1888). This last, strongly influenced by French *grand opéra*, reveals Rubinstein's lyrical gifts (particularly in the well-known Act II aria 'In the Ocean of the Air'), though in the main his characters are little more than cardboard cut-outs (see also OPERA, 13).

In all Rubinstein wrote 20 operas (of which a number are sacred operas—really oratorios in costume), and composed a good deal of piano and chamber music, songs, and orchestral works, including five piano concertos. Yet he is perhaps remembered chiefly for his work in music education, and during his time at the St Petersburg Conservatory he did much to raise standards of performance in Russia.   GN

📖 C. DRINKER BOWEN, *Free Artist: The Story of Anton and Nicholas Rubinstein* (New York, 1939/R) · L. SITSKY, *Anton

Rubinstein: An Annotated Catalogue of Piano Works and Biography (Westport, CT, 1998)

Rubinstein, Artur (*b* Łódź, 28 Jan. 1887; *d* Geneva, 20 Dec. 1982). Polish-born American pianist. His formative studies were with Joachim, Heinrich Barth, and Bruch in Berlin, where he made his debut in 1900; his American debut was in 1906, his London one in 1912. Blessed with a natural talent, Rubinstein practised little and socialized much before exercising considerable self-discipline to win over his American critics in 1937. His international career lasted into the 1970s, and, in chamber partnerships with Heifetz, Emanuel Feuermann, Szeryng, and the Guarneri Quartet, he made huge numbers of recordings of a wide-ranging repertory, including the complete piano works of Chopin. The last of the great Romantics, yet unmannered in approach, he was in the best sense a natural pianist. He took American citizenship in 1946.
                                                    CF

📖 A. RUBINSTEIN, *My Young Years* (London, 1973); *My Many Years* (London, 1980) · H. SACHS, *Arthur Rubinstein: A Life* (New York, 1995; London, 1996)

Rubinstein, Nikolay (Grigor'yevich) (*b* Moscow, 2/14 June 1835; *d* Paris, 23 March 1881). Russian pianist and composer. Like his brother Anton, he achieved early recognition as a pianist of outstanding qualities. He also became a key figure in the musical life of Moscow, founding a branch of the Russian Musical Society there in 1860: six years later the society's music classes blossomed into the Moscow Conservatory, of which Rubinstein was director until his death.

Rubinstein was a close friend of Tchaikovsky, but his name has endured in musical history for his condemnation of the First Piano Concerto as 'worthless and unplayable'. However, he conducted the first Moscow performance of the concerto (later becoming a noted exponent of the solo part), and also gave the premieres of several of Tchaikovsky's other large-scale works, including *Eugene Onegin* (1879). He also championed the music of The Five, in particular giving the premiere of Balakirev's fantasy *Islamey*.

He had a more extrovert personality than his brother: Tchaikovsky found him at Wiesbaden in 1870 'losing his last ruble at roulette', and it was entirely in character that he should consume a dozen oysters on his deathbed in Paris. Tchaikovsky wrote his Piano Trio in Rubinstein's memory, dedicating it 'to the memory of a great artist'.   GN

Ruckers. Flemish family of harpsichord and virginals makers. Hans (*b* c.1545–50; *d* 1598) founded the firm in Antwerp; he was succeeded by his sons Joannes (1578–1642) and Andreas (1579–after 1645) and his grandson

Andreas (1607–before 1667). They made virginals in six sizes, single-manual harpsichords with two sets of strings, and two-manual ones with non-aligned, uncoupled keyboards each playable at one of two pitches a 4th apart. The harpsichords had a resonant sound with the capacity for contrast and they became the most prized make in the 17th and 18th centuries. AL

📖 G. G. O'BRIEN, *Ruckers: A Harpsichord and Virginal Building Tradition* (Cambridge, 1990)

Rückpositiv (Ger., 'back positive'; Dutch: *rugpositief*). A small organ placed behind the organist's back or chair (see CHAIR ORGAN). The term also denotes the second main manual of large organs built between 1400 and 1700. The tone of the *Rückpositiv* was generally sweeter and more delicate than that of the Great organ. LC

Ruddigore (*Ruddigore* [originally *Ruddygore*], *or The Witch's Curse*). Operetta in two acts by Sullivan to a libretto by W. S. Gilbert (London, 1887).

Rudel, Jaufre (*fl* 1120–47). Troubadour. He was probably one of the lords of Blaye, and participated in the Second Crusade (1147). Of the six poems by him that survive, four have music. JM

Ruders, Poul (*b* Ringsted, 27 March 1949). Danish composer. He was a member of the Copenhagen Boys' Choir, subsequently graduating from the Copenhagen Conservatory as an organist; as a composer he was largely self-taught. His works have tended to fall into two categories: a wide-ranging 'gothic' style, combining elements of American minimalism, post-serial Expressionism, and grotesque parody with an almost Straussian lushness and brilliance; and a more austere, single-minded symphonic style owing much in its developmental thought to Sibelius. Ruders has pioneered a technique he has labelled 'minimorphoses' in which elaborate changes are wrought on a basic melodic series: the bleak and obsessive one-movement Second Symphony (1996) is built almost entirely on this technique. More typical of the 'gothic' Ruders are *Corpus cum figuris* (1985), for chamber orchestra, the First Symphony (*Himmelhoch jauchzen—zum Tode betrübt*, 'Rejoicing to the Heavens—Cast Down to Death', 1989), and the powerfully tragic opera *The Handmaid's Tale* (2000), based on the novel by Margaret Atwood. SJ

Rue, Pierre de la. See LA RUE, PIERRE DE.

ruff. One of the ornamental rudiments of side-drum playing, notated as illustrated. Tight execution of the grace notes (either hand leading) is essential for correct, militaristic technique. SM

L R L R
R L R L

Ruffo, Vincenzo (*b* Verona, *c.*1508; *d* Sacile, nr Venice, 9 Feb. 1587). Italian church musician and composer. He was trained and spent much of his career in Verona, where he became master of music at the Accademia Filarmonica and *maestro di cappella* at the cathedral. His most important position outside Verona was as *maestro di cappella* at Milan Cathedral in 1563–72. A prolific composer of church music, he concentrated during his Milanese years on achieving declamatory text-setting, reflecting post-Tridentine interest in the intelligibility of the words. His many madrigals, all of which were composed before 1563, can be linked to the activities of the Accademia Filarmonica. JM

Rugby. Orchestral work (1928) by Honegger, the second of his *Mouvements symphoniques*.

Ruggiero (It.). A characteristic harmonic bass line popular in Italy in the late 16th century and the 17th, chiefly as the basis of sets of instrumental variations (Ex. 1). It may have served originally as a harmonic pattern over which a singer could improvise a melody for chanting poetry: this connection tends to support the theory that the name derives from the first word of a stanza of Ariosto's epic poem *Orlando furioso*, 'Ruggier, qual sempre fui'. The *Ruggiero* eventually became standardized as a type of *ground bass for songs and dances. Frescobaldi was one of several composers to write keyboard variations on it; later in the 17th century it also appeared in vocal music, both solo and ensemble.

Ex. 1

Ruggles, Carl [Charles] (Sprague) (*b* East Marion, MA, 11 March 1876; *d* Bennington, VT, 24 Oct. 1971). American composer. He played in theatre orchestras during his teens and also had private lessons with John Knowles Paine. In 1907 he went to Winona, Minnesota, to teach and conduct, and it was not until about

1912 that he began to compose seriously. From 1917 onwards he divided his time between New York, where he associated with Varèse among others, and Vermont. He worked slowly on a small number of compositions, all atonal and often containing a visionary intensity within a short span. His two major orchestral works, *Men and Mountains* (1924) and *Sun-Treader* (1931–2), have striding, masculine themes balanced by flowing tendrils of polyphony; equally characteristic is the radiance of *Angels* for brass ensemble (1921). Ruggles composed no new pieces after 1947, devoting his creative energies to painting.   PG

📖 M. J. Ziffrin, *Carl Ruggles: Composer, Painter, and Storyteller* (Chicago, 1994)

ruhig (Ger.). 'Peaceful'.

Ruinen von Athen, Die ('The Ruins of Athens'). Incidental music by Beethoven, op. 113 (1811), for a play by August von Kotzebue given at the first night of the German theatre in Budapest (1812); it includes an overture, choruses, an aria, and a Turkish march (adapted from his variations for piano op. 76).

Rule, Britannia! Song by Arne from his masque *Alfred*, with words by James Thomson and David Mallett (Cliveden, 1740); *Alfred* was not given in London until 1745, when threat of rebellion led 'Rule, Britannia!' to provoke patriotic fervour among the audiences. In 1746 Handel introduced the tune into his *Occasional Overture*; Beethoven wrote a set of piano variations on it (1803) and introduced it into his *Wellingtons Sieg* (1813). It also appears in Attwood's anthem *O Lord, grant the king a long life*, and Wagner and Alexander Mackenzie wrote overtures based on it.

Rusalka. 1. Opera in three acts by Dvořák to a libretto by the Czech writer Jaroslav Kvapil (i) after Friedrich de la Motte Fouqué's *Undine* (Prague, 1901).

2. Opera in four acts by Dargomïzhsky to his own libretto after Aleksandr Pushkin's poem (St Petersburg, 1856).

Ruslan and Lyudmila. Opera in five acts by Glinka to a libretto by Valerian Fyodorovich Shirkov (with minor contributions by others) after Aleksandr Pushkin's poem (1820) (St Petersburg, 1842).

Russia 1. Introduction; 2. Before Glinka; 3. Early 19th-century developments; 4. Years of consolidation; 5. The Soviet era; 6. The post-Soviet era

1. Introduction

It is impossible to study the history of Russian music up to the decline of Communism in 1991 without considering the obstacles and barriers that have constantly been placed in the way of the nation's composers. These barriers were present from a very early stage, and if we compare musical life in 1700 in Russia with that in most other European countries, it becomes immediately apparent that Russian music was in a primitive state; the country possessed no composers of international standing, and there was no real instrumental tradition to speak of.

The reasons for this are many and various, but the prime culprit must surely have been the Russian Orthodox Church. In about AD 988, Byzantine Christianity became Russia's official religion, and from that time on all instruments were forbidden (as they still are) in churches and discouraged in other contexts. And although travelling musicians (known as *skomorokhi*) cultivated the playing of folk instruments and the singing of folksongs, just as in other countries, the church succeeded in preventing them from performing in all but the most provincial of settings; as a result, their influence was negligible.

The Russian Orthodox Church did not of course ban music *per se*, and over the years a highly distinctive style of ecclesiastical singing developed, at first monophonic, then (in the 16th century) polyphonic, and from the late 17th century even polychoral, influenced, via Poland, by such composers as Andrea and Giovanni Gabrieli. But if all this sacred music led to a rich choral tradition, it was to the detriment of instrumental music, for Russian musicians had no opportunity to develop skills in this direction. Consequently, foreign composers had no incentive to work in Russia, even if anybody had been able to employ them.

2. Before Glinka

When Peter the Great became tsar in 1682 (his reign lasted until 1725) he set about the wholesale Westernization of Russia, opening up his well-known 'window on Europe'. Peter's ambition was to create one of the finest and most civilized courts in Europe. For a magnificent court he naturally needed a magnificent new city, so St Petersburg was swiftly built on virgin swampland. A court without musicians was unthinkable, but the lack of native talent meant that Peter had to look abroad, and from 1711 he employed musicians from Germany to train his military bands. Instrumental music flourished at court in the form of fanfares and background music for state occasions and dance music for the tsar's social gatherings.

Peter had little interest in music other than as a means of introducing a degree of sophistication into uncivilized Russian society and impressing foreign dignitaries. The Empress Anna (1730–40), on the other hand, encouraged a far wider range of musical activities, and Italian as well as German musicians began to work in Russia. Some of the earliest instrumental music composed there dates from these times, including 12 violin sonatas (1738) by Luigi Madonis (c.1690–c.1770) and 12 more by Giovanni Verocai (c.1700–45). Theatres were opened in Moscow and St Petersburg, and Russia had its first taste of opera with *Calandro* (1726) by Giovanni Ristori (1692–1753), performed by an Italian troupe in 1731, and *La forza dell'amore e dell'odio* (1734) by Francesco Araia. Anna appointed Araia *maestro di cappella* in 1735, a post he held until 1759, and in 1755 he composed the first opera to a Russian text, *Cephalus and Procris*, with a libretto by Aleksandr Sumarokov (1718–77).

One of the many Italian composers who went to St Petersburg in Araia's wake was Galuppi who, as director of the court chapel choir (1765–8), had an enormous influence on Russian sacred music, teaching the most important Russian composers of the 18th century, Maksim Berezovsky (1745–77) and Dmitry Bortnyansky (1751–1825). Galuppi's compatriot Giuseppe Sarti (1729–1802) became director of the Italian opera in St Petersburg in 1784 and, as the teacher of Stepan Davïdov (1777–1825), influenced native opera in Russia. In 1811 Stepan Degtyaryov (1766–1813), another of Sarti's pupils, composed the first Russian oratorio, *Minin i Pozharsky, ili Osvobozhdeniye Moskvy* ('Minin and Pozharsky, or the Liberation of Moscow').

Music-printing began in earnest in the 1730s, flourishing later in the century with such firms as Gerstenberg and Dittmar. Musical education was organized more formally from 1757 when the Empress Elizabeth (reigned 1741–62) established the Academy of Arts, which included music in the curriculum. Among the teachers there were the Russian composers Ivan Khandoskin (1747–1804) and Yevstigney Fomin (1761–1800). Fomin was typical of a growing trend for promising young Russian composers, for he was one of many (including Berezovsky and Bortnyansky) who were sent to Italy to complete their musical education. Thus, though Russia was beginning to produce composers of talent, they were educated in the Italian manner, composed in the Italian style, and rarely showed hints of their Russian origins.

The reign of Catherine II (1762–96) saw a shift in emphasis from Italian opera to French *opéra comique*. Native Russian operas also began to emerge, often using melodies from the first collections of Russian folksongs which were appearing at this time. Notable among these were the four-volume *Sobraniye russkikh prostïkh pesen s notami* ('Collection of Simple Russian Songs with Music', 1776–95) of Vasily Trutovsky (c.1740–c.1810) and the important *Sobraniye narodnïkh russkikh pesen s ikh golosami* ('Collection of Russian Folksongs with their Vocal Parts', 1790) of Ivan Prach

(c.1750–c.1818). Such songs were used by Russian and foreign composers as the basis of instrumental variations and, even more important, in Russia's earliest known symphonies: the three 'sinfonies nationales à grand orchestre'—the 'Ukrainian', the 'Russian', and the 'Polish'—by the Bohemian composer and pianist Arnošt Vančura (c.1750–1802), published in 1798. Though not a native Russian, Vančura was on the staff of the Imperial Theatres in St Petersburg and played in a court chamber ensemble.

Catherine II, though a competent librettist, was not a musician; but she understood the social importance of employing large numbers of musicians, and prominent members of the aristocracy emulated her in this and many other respects. During her reign Catherine built the Petrovsky Theatre in Moscow in 1780 (this became the Bol'shoy, though it burnt down twice in the mean time) and the Hermitage Theatre (1783–7) in the Winter Palace in St Petersburg. The aristocratic Sheremetev family boasted an orchestra of 43 players, and the Vorontsovs one of 38 musicians and 16 'musical apprentices', which performed music by Pleyel, Stamitz, Haydn, and others.

Thus, in little over 50 years, Russia had evolved from a cultural backwater devoid of almost any art music other than Orthodox church music, to a society brimming over with musical talent and artistic institutions. However, most of the talent was either foreign or strongly influenced by foreign teachers and their styles, and this was a solid barrier to the development of a genuine Russian style. It was not until the next generation that Russian musicians began to find a truly native voice.

3. Early 19th-century developments

Orchestral and chamber music in Russia had progressed beyond recognition when compared with the situation in 1700, but the main musical advances in early 19th-century Russia were in opera. Conventional teaching has it that Glinka was the first composer in Russia to write operas (or indeed any music) in a particularly idiosyncratic Russian manner, but once again it was an Italian who really paved the way. Catterino Cavos arrived in Russia in 1799 and quickly became renowned as a conductor and composer of operas. His first contributions were additional numbers for an 1804 adaptation of Ferdinand Kauer's *Singspiel* entitled *Das Donauweibchen* (*Dneprovskaya Rusalka* in Russian). A series of operas written in a Russian vein followed, the most notable being the four-act *Il'ya bogatïr'* (1807) and the two-act *Ivan Susanin* (composed 1815, performed 1822), based on the same story as Glinka's later *A Life for the Tsar*. Although Cavos's Susanin appears somewhat less patriotic than Glinka's (in Cavos's version he is rescued from the Poles by the Russian army rather than giving his 'life for the tsar'), the opera is written in a patriotic style, and it is no coincidence that it appeared shortly after the Russian victory over Napoleon in 1812, as did Cavos's aptly named ballet *Opolcheniye, ili Lyubov k otechestvu* ('The National Guard, or Love of the Fatherland', 1812).

Glinka wrote his version of the Ivan Susanin legend following a visit to Italy (1830–3) during which he seems to have overdosed on a diet of Bellini and Donizetti. His famous declaration that homesickness and a distaste for the frivolous Italian style aroused in him a 'desire to write music in Russian' was soon followed by the first sketches for *A Life for the Tsar*. In spite of being a rather uneasy marriage of Italian opera and the Russian folksong style, the work was a success and was heralded as marking a new dawn in Russian music. It was followed in 1842 by Glinka's only other opera, *Ruslan and Lyudmila*, based on a text by Russia's greatest poet, Aleksandr Pushkin. Less successful than *A Life for the Tsar*, *Ruslan* was musically years ahead of its time, and provided the stylistic and dramatic blueprint for many future Russian operas, especially by Rimsky-Korsakov.

Although opera was the forum for the most important ideas in the early 19th-century development of Russian music, Russian composers did not shy away from other areas, and a number of commendable instrumental works were produced. Aleksandr Alyab'yev is notable for his graceful string quartets, and the symphony was represented in the works of Michał Wielhorski (1788–1856), a friend of both Glinka and Beethoven. Glinka once again established formal and stylistic ground plans for future Russian composers in his orchestral fantasia *Kamarinskaya* (1848), based on two Russian folk tunes. Tchaikovsky famously called this work the 'acorn' out of which the whole 'oak tree' of Russian music grew, and it is certainly true that Glinka's innovatory 'changing background' technique was profoundly influential on the manner in which later Russian composers approached formal and thematic development. The technique involves the presentation of a melody that remains essentially unchanged through a number of repetitions (some 70 in the case of *Kamarinskaya*) while its accompaniment, orchestration, and other musical features continuously evolve and develop.

Composers also began to expand the repertory of Russian piano and song literature. Influenced by Chopin and Field, such composers as Aleksandr Gurilyov (1803–58) and Ivan Laskovsky (1799–1855) wrote a number of fine piano works—notably Laskovsky's Nocturne in B♭ and Ballade in F♯, obvious precursors of the piano works of Balakirev and Tchaikovsky. Song-

writing too became widespread during the first half of the 19th century. The 'father of Russian song' (*romans*) was Nikolay Titov (1800–75), whose songs, nearly 60 in total, were popular inclusions in the various musical albums of the 1820s onwards; Aleksandr Varlamov (1800–48) and Andrey Esaulov (*c*.1800–50) also featured prominently in these collections.

It is of course difficult for music to flourish without a rich performing environment. To further the cause of instrumental music, the St Petersburg Philharmonic Society was established in 1802 by a group of wealthy amateur musicians, including the father of Michał Wielhorski and his brother Mateusz (1794–1866). The Wielhorski brothers' house in St Petersburg became a centre of musical activity from 1826 and was visited by such composers as Liszt, Berlioz, and Schumann. Non-Russian music was performed alongside the works of new Russian composers; the Wielhorskis consolidated these musical activities in 1850 with the founding of a vibrant Concert Society.

Another important new area of activity in Russia at the beginning of the 19th century was the first serious Russian writing on music. Two names are especially prominent. Aleksandr Ulïbïshev (1794–1858) had received his musical education in Germany (his father was the Russian ambassador in Dresden) and wrote the first Russian studies of Mozart (Moscow, 1843) and Beethoven (Leipzig and Paris, 1857). He was also a friend and champion of the young Balakirev. Prince Vladimir Odoyevsky (1804–69), for some time deputy director of the Imperial Public Library, was known chiefly for his stories and for his philosophical studies *Russkiye nochi* ('Russian Nights', 1844), but he also did much in his critical writings on music to promote interest in the works of Haydn, Mozart, Weber, Berlioz, and Wagner. It was also Odoyevsky who encouraged Glinka to write *A Life for the Tsar*, which he later greeted as a 'new element in art', opening up 'the period of Russian music'.

4. Years of consolidation

Russian musicians continued throughout the 19th century to face considerable barriers to their success, not least state censorship and an official social status lower than that of other artistic professions, but the 'period of Russian music' had indeed begun. The second half of the 19th century saw the rise of the first truly professional native Russian composers, though talented amateurs still played a prominent role, as The *Five (in Russian, Moguchaya Kuchka, 'the Mighty Handful' or, literally, 'Mighty Little Heap') more than adequately demonstrated.

One of the most important events in the growth of Russian music was the establishment in 1862 of the

St Petersburg Conservatory, the brainchild of the composer and pianist Anton Rubinstein. Three years earlier he had founded the Russian Musical Society, and later, in 1866, the Moscow Conservatory was formed under the directorship of his brother Nikolay. Another musical institution, the Free Music School, was established in St Petersburg in 1862, this time by Balakirev and the choral director Gavriil Lomakin (1812–85). The conservatories, Musical Society, and Free Music School all offered public concerts as well as musical training, and did much to raise the standards of performance and composition in Russia.

Conventional wisdom suggests that the conservatory and the Free School were implacably opposed organizations—the one Germanic, academic, and reactionary, the other progressive and purely Russian. This view, however, is simplistic and misguided. Naturally there was often vehement antagonism between the main characters in the two institutions. Balakirev and his close associates, particularly the critic Vladimir Stasov (1824–1906), resented Anton Rubinstein's success, and Balakirev seems to have objected to his origins, too (Rubinstein was from a Jewish background). There were also musical differences. Balakirev and the other members of The Five had received little musical training other than the discussion and mutual appraisal (usually consisting of harsh criticism from Balakirev) of their works and those of modern Western composers; the conservatory, on the other hand, used teaching methods based on those in German conservatories, and its original staff were mainly brought in from abroad. The Five championed the creation of a distinctly 'Russian' musical style; the conservatory, in turn, concentrated its teaching on the more traditional canon of Western art music. These differences were highlighted and exaggerated in the press—particularly by Stasov, whose comments on The Five often descended into personal abuse.

But the musical links between the seemingly opposing factions are greater than is often assumed: Rubinstein certainly tried his hand at the nationalist style in his Fifth Symphony and approached the folk idiom in the opera *The Merchant Kalashnikov* (both 1880). Conversely, Rimsky-Korsakov often worked with German symphonic patterns, particularly in his First and Third Symphonies (1865 and 1876 respectively), and his operas, though thoroughly Russian in flavour, contain their fair share of rondos, fugues, and scarcely disguised *da capo* arias. Even in Balakirev's music there are strong suggestions of Germanic formal procedures, for example in the Scherzo from his First Symphony (1864–97), in which melodic orientalisms are fused with a traditional Western formal plan. Furthermore, Nikolay Rubinstein championed Balakirev's

music energetically in Moscow, giving the premiere of the piano fantasy *Islamey*; the idea that there existed no creative link between Moscow and St Petersburg is as difficult to sustain as the supposed lack of mutual influence between the 'conservatory' composers and The Five.

A wide range of individual compositional styles developed as the century progressed. By the 1880s a large number of distinctive and original musical personalities were clearly discernible in Russia. Whereas in music from earlier in the century we might be hard pressed to identify an overture by Alyab'yev or a song by Titov, we can now with certainty tell that a work is by Tchaikovsky, Rimsky-Korsakov, Borodin, Musorgsky, or almost any leading Russian composer born after about 1840. Above all, we can easily determine whether or not a work from this period onwards is Russian. Any factional battles, such as they were, were carried on more in the polemical articles of the critics. César Cui assiduously promoted the cause of his St Petersburg colleagues (though his opinions were notably unpredictable), while the Moscow critics, in particular Hermann Laroche, supported Tchaikovsky and lashed out at the St Petersburg composers. Straddling all camps was the composer and critic Aleksandr Serov, who managed to offend almost everybody, despite composing two of the most popular operas of the 1860s: *Judith* (1863) and *Rogneda* (1865).

With the development and consolidation of music education and with the expansion of publishing by such firms as Jürgenson and Belyayev, Russian music continued to prosper into the 20th century. A new generation emerged under the steadying influence of Rimsky-Korsakov. The conservatories produced many of the composers who were to retain a permanent place in the repertory, among them Rakhmaninov, Skryabin, Prokofiev, Myaskovsky, and Shostakovich. But these last three names bring us to the threshold of a new era of Russian music in which the barriers and obstacles to free creativity that had begun to crumble were once again erected, albeit in very different forms.

5. The Soviet era

Revolutionary sentiments had been brewing in Russia for many years, and had already affected musical life to a certain degree when Rimsky-Korsakov resigned from the St Petersburg Conservatory in sympathy with the students supporting the 1905 uprising. In 1917 the decisive October Revolution took place, and Communism asserted itself.

There were several immediate implications for the country's musical life. First, a number of composers emigrated: Rakhmaninov left in 1917, Prokofiev in 1918 (though he was to return later); Stravinsky, already abroad at the time, decided to remain in the West. Within Russia itself there were also important changes. Publishing houses, conservatories, and opera houses previously under imperial patronage were nationalized, and, reflecting the value placed on opera by the Communist regime, new state opera studios were established. Konstantin Stanislavsky (1863–1938) founded such a studio at the Bol'shoy Theatre in 1918, and Vladimir Nemirovich-Danchenko (1858–1943) opened one at the Moscow Art Theatre in 1919; in 1941 the twoinstitutions merged to form the Stanislavsky–Nemirovich-Danchenko Music Theatre, where a number of important opera premieres were staged.

In the realm of orchestral performance, too, there were new developments: in 1922 the collective symphony orchestra Persimfans (an acronym for the 'First Symphonic Ensemble' of the Moscow Soviet) was formed in Moscow, and survived until 1932 on its democratic policy of playing without a conductor. Composers were encouraged to explore modes of expression compatible with the prevailing revolutionary mood. Thus the new generation of Russian composers—Kabalevsky, Shaporin, Shebalin, Myaskovsky, Shostakovich, and many lesser figures—found themselves composing 'Hymns to Lenin' and programmatic symphonies on the problems of the steel industry.

There were two principal strands of thought as to how the Revolution could best be expressed in musical terms. On the one hand, there was the Russian Association of Proletarian Musicians (RAPM), a hardline socialist group founded in 1923, which advocated that Soviet music be couched in a direct and simple musical language. In the atmosphere generated by this organization one of the most extraordinary experiments of the immediate post-Revolution years was perpetrated: the renaming (and recasting with fresh librettos) of well-known operas. Thus *Tosca* (with the action shifted to Paris in 1871) became *The Battle for the Commune*, *Les Huguenots* became *The Decembrists* (after the early 19th-century revolutionary movement), and Glinka's *A Life for the Tsar* was reworked as *Hammer and Sickle*. Happily, such crass meddlings with the classics found few sympathetic ears.

On the other hand, there was the more forward-looking, open-minded Association for Contemporary Music (ASM), also founded in 1923, under whose auspices works by Schoenberg, Berg, Webern, and Stravinsky were heard in the Soviet Union. The leading spokesman of the ASM, the composer and critic Boris Asaf'yev, urged Soviet composers to widen their artistic horizons and free themselves from the dull conservatism that had dogged so much early Soviet music. In the wake of his comments such composers as Nikolay Roslavets explored 12-note serialism, and Shostakovich

worked with complex textures and extreme dissonance in his opera *The Nose* (1930). Another idea prevalent at the time, that orchestral music should 'mean something', gave rise to such works as the 'Agricultural' Symphony (1923) of Aleksandr Kastal'sky (1856–1926) and to Aleksandr Mosolov's once-popular orchestral fragment *The Iron Foundry* (1926–8).

By the early 1930s, however, the ASM and the RAPM were disbanded, and on 23 April 1932 the Communist Party passed a resolution bringing all musical activity under the control of the Party-dominated Composers' Union. Most important, the concept of *socialist realism was formulated; this remained the chief guideline for Soviet composers, and its 'merits' were to be emphatically asserted in two famous incidents. First, in 1936, the *Pravda* editorial 'Sumbur vmesto muzïki' ('Chaos instead of Music') showed that Shostakovich's *The Lady Macbeth of the Mtsensk District*, though originally hailed by Samuil Samosud as 'a work of genius', was no longer considered to be in the socialist realist tradition. Then, in 1948, Stalin's adviser on the arts, Andrey Zhdanov, attacked almost every Soviet composer for allegedly straying from the path of socialist realism and leaning towards *formalism (see also MURADELI, VANO; KHRENNIKOV, TIKHON NIKOLAYEVICH; SHOSTAKOVICH, DMITRY).

After the death of Stalin in 1953 the artistic climate became less oppressive under Khrushchev's regime. Works by Shostakovich previously banned by the authorities were now hailed as masterpieces, and his influence became widespread, lasting well beyond his death in 1975. By the mid-1960s such composers as Edison Denisov, Sofia Gubaidulina, and Alfred Schnittke, taking advantage of their new-found relative freedom, had embraced modernism, and the reputation of contemporary Russian music began to extend once more beyond the country's borders. The modernist trend continued through the 1970s and early 80s, though some composers, notably Galina Ustvol'skaya, were beginning to turn to the religious and neoromantic subjects and themes that would characterize the post-Soviet era.

One area in which Soviet Russia made an enormous international contribution is that of performance. The conservatories founded by the Rubinsteins in Moscow and St Petersburg (or Leningrad, as it was known in the Communist era) thrived, producing artists of the calibre of the pianists Vladimir Ashkenazy and Dmitry Alexeyev, the string players David Oistrakh and Mstislav Rostropovich, and the singers Yelena Obraztsova and Yevgeny Nesterenko. In that respect the tables were turned: Peter the Great may have imported musicians from the West, but the West has certainly reaped the benefits.

6. The post-Soviet era

The fall of the Communist regime in December 1991 had a profound psychological effect on music in Russia. Composers were suddenly free from the ideological restrictions and political censorship that had been imposed on them throughout their nation's history, and for the first time they could choose almost any style or subject for their musical expression. Many works that had remained unknown during the Communist era received their Russian premieres: remarkably, the first complete public performance in Russia of Rakhmaninov's Vespers (composed in 1915), so popular in the West, did not take place until the late 1980s.

Sacred choral music akin to that written by Rakhmaninov is the area that has seen perhaps the most notable growth in the post-Soviet era. Such composers as Vladimir Martïnov (b 1946) in Moscow and Vyacheslav Rimsha in St Petersburg began to explore the music of the ancient Orthodox Church in combination with more modern idioms. Martïnov typified this development, having started out as an avant-garde composer and only later seeing the possibilities of, and exploiting the nostalgia for, the old church style. Other composers have continued to re-vitalize the traditions of Russian Orthodox Church music, notably Vladislav Uspensky (b 1937), whose Vespers was given its premiere in St Petersburg in 1990.

In its early history Russian music was characterized by an almost complete absence of secular music other than folksong, a state of affairs enforced by the Orthodox Church. The Soviet era witnessed the complete opposite, the denial of all religious expression, and a whole generation grew up with practically no knowledge of the great sacred works, either Russian or foreign. But now that the barriers, ideologies, and censorship have been all but removed, sacred music is again taking its place in Russian society. True, there are new obstacles, such as reduced state funding for con-servatories and other musical institutions, and a general decline in the country's infrastructure; but, for the first time, Russian composers can draw on any aspect of their nation's heritage and express it in their music openly and without fear of persecution.　　GN/SM

📖 G. ABRAHAM, *Studies in Russian Music* (London, 1935) · M. D. CALVOCORESSI and G. ABRAHAM, *Masters of Russian Music* (London, 1936) · G. ABRAHAM, *On Russian Music* (London, 1939); *Eight Soviet Composers* (London, 1943) · G. R. SEAMAN, *History of Russian Music, from its Origins to Dargomyzhsky* (Oxford, 1967) · S. D. KREBS, *Soviet Composers and the Development of Soviet Music* (London, 1970) · B. SCHWARZ, *Music and Musical Life in Soviet Russia, 1917–1970* (London, 1972) · N. P. BRILL, *History of Russian Church Music* (Bloomington, IN, 1980) · R. C. RIDENOUR, *Nationalism, Modernism, and Personal Rivalry in 19th-Century Russian Music* (Ann Arbor, MI, 1981) · R. TARUSKIN, *Opera and Drama in Russia as Preached and Practiced in the 1860s* (Ann Arbor, 1981) · L. SITSKY, *Music of the Repressed Russian Avant-Garde, 1900–1929* (Westport, CT, 1994) · R. TARUSKIN, *Defining Russia Musically: Historical and Hermeneutical Essays* (Princeton, NJ, 1997)

Russian Easter Festival. Overture (1888) by Rimsky-Korsakov, based on Russian Orthodox Church mel-odies.

'Russian' Quartets. Haydn's six String Quartets op. 33 (1781), so called because later editions bear a dedication to the Grand Duke Pavel Petrovich, who visited Haydn in Vienna in 1781; they are also known as *Gli scherzi*, because their minuets are headed 'Scherzo', and as the 'Maiden' Quartets (*Jungfernquartette*), because a female figure is depicted on the title page of the 1782 Hummel edition.

Russo, William (Joseph) (b Chicago, 25 June 1928). American composer. He studied English at Roosevelt University, Chicago (1951–5), and had private com-position lessons from John J. Becker (1953–5) and Karel Jirák (1955–7). Since 1947 he has been involved with various jazz orchestras (including the London Jazz Orchestra, 1962–5) as trombonist, conductor, and composer. His output includes numerous works for jazz orchestra, rock cantatas, several operas, and two sym-phonies. He also wrote *Composing for the Jazz Orchestra* (Chicago, 1961) and *Jazz: Composition and Orchestration* (Chicago, 1968).　　PG

Russolo, Luigi (b Portogruaro, 30 April 1885; d Cerro di Laveno, Varese, 6 Feb. 1947). Italian composer, in-ventor, and painter. He was a leading figure in the *Futurist movement, led by the poet Filippo Tommaso Marinetti, which advocated a new aesthetic for the new machine age. Trained as a painter rather than in music, Russolo published in 1913 a manifesto called *L'arte di rumore* ('The Art of Noise'), which proposed that music should not be restricted to conventional instruments and notation but should use all available means of sound-production. He invented several instruments producing unpitched noises of different kinds, dem-onstrated them in concerts in Milan, Genoa, and London in 1913–14, and wrote works for them with such titles as *A Meeting of Motorcars and Aeroplanes*. After the war he made further inventions, including a more versatile *rumorarmonio*, which he demonstrated in Paris (with some compositions by his brother Antonio).

In his later years, spent in Spain and Italy, Russolo lost interest in music and resumed painting; his in-struments were destroyed during World War II, and his compositions are almost entirely lost. Nevertheless, his ideas had a significant influence on later composers, including Varèse, Cage, and the pioneers of *musique concrète*.   ABur

Rust, Friedrich Wilhelm (*b* Wörlitz, 6 July 1739; *d* Dessau, 28 Feb. 1796). German composer and violinist. After studying in Germany and Italy he settled in Dessau, where in 1775 he was appointed court music director in recognition of his contribution to the musical life of the city. His large output, representative of the transition to Classicism, includes stage works, many substantial vocal works, about a hundred lieder, and keyboard music; he was also active as a teacher.   SH

Rustle of Spring (*Frühlingsrauschen*). Piano piece by Sinding, the third of his Six Pieces op. 32 (1896); it exists in many arrangements.

Ruy Blas. Overture, op. 95 (1839), by Mendelssohn, written for a German performance of Victor Hugo's play of that name (1838).

RV. Abbreviation for *Ryom-Verzeichnis, used as a prefix to the numbers of Vivaldi's works as given in the standard *thematic catalogue of Peter Ryom.

Ryba [Poisson, Peace, Ryballandini, Rybaville], **Jakub Jan** (*b* Přeštice, 26 Oct. 1765; *d* Rožmitál pod Trémsinem, 8 April 1815). Czech composer, teacher, choirmaster, and theorist. He was the author of a treatise, *The First and General Principles of the Entire Art of Music* (published 1817). His vast output includes symphonies, concertos, and chamber and vocal music, though only his sacred works survive in any quantity. He was among the first to set his native tongue rather than German in solo songs. His Czech Christmas Mass, a compilation of folk-like texts, makes effective use of Czech folksong (Christmas *pastorellas); it is one of the most frequently performed Czech settings of the period.   JSm

Ryom. Abbreviation for the standard *thematic catalogue of the works of Vivaldi drawn up by the Danish scholar Peter Ryom (Leipzig, 1974; supplement Poitiers, 1979). Vivaldi's works are commonly referred to by Ryom number (often further abbreviated to RV, standing for Ryom-Verzeichnis).

Rysanek, Leonie (*b* Vienna, 14 Nov. 1926; *d* Vienna, 7 March 1998). Austrian soprano. She studied in Vienna

with Alfred Jerger and sang in Innsbruck and Saarbrücken before making her Bayreuth debut as Sieglinde (in *Die Walküre*) in 1951, establishing herself immediately as one of the finest postwar Wagner sopranos (though she never tackled heavier roles such as Isolde and Brünnhilde). At the Bavarian State Opera in 1953 she sang the Empress in *Die Frau ohne Schatten*, the first of a series of definitive Strauss assumptions which included Chrysothemis (in *Elektra*) and Helena (in *Die ägyptische Helena*). She joined the Vienna State Opera in 1954.

In 1959 Rysanek took New York by storm when she stood in at short notice for the indisposed Maria Callas as Lady Macbeth; she remained a favourite at the Metropolitan Opera, where she also frequently appeared in the Italian repertory and later gave outstanding performances as Kostelnička (in *Jenůfa*) and Ortrud (in *Lohengrin*). Towards the end of her 40-year career she sang dramatic mezzo-soprano roles. A singing actress of often overwhelming force, she was famous for a voluptuous beauty of tone, particularly in her voice's upper registers, and for the emotional intensity of her performances.   TA

📖 P. Dusek and P. Schmidt, *Leonie Rysanek: 40 Jahre Operngeschichte* (Hamburg, 1990)

ryūteki. The largest Japanese *gagaku transverse bamboo flute, with seven fingerholes.

Rzewski, Frederic (Anthony) (*b* Westfield, MA, 13 April 1938). American composer and pianist. He studied with Randall Thompson and Claudio Spies at Harvard (1954–8) and with Oliver Strunk at Princeton (1958–60). During the next decade he was mostly in Europe. He gave the first performance of Stockhausen's *Klavierstück X* (1962) and was a founder member of Musica Elettronica Viva, a group of composer-performers in Rome. His work with them became increasingly political (*Coming Together*, 1972) and remained so after he moved to a style absorbing avant-garde details into a grand confluence with the piano virtuoso tradition (*The People United will Never be Defeated!*, 1975). Since the mid-1970s he has divided his time between Europe and the USA.   PG

S

S. 1. Abbreviation for *segno* (see AL SEGNO; DAL SEGNO), *subito, or *sinistra.

2. Abbreviation for *soprano or *superius.

3. Abbreviation for Schmieder; see BWV.

Saariaho, Kaija (Anneli) (*b* Helsinki, 14 Oct. 1952). Finnish composer. She studied with Paavo Heininen at the Sibelius Academy, Helsinki, and was co-founder (with the conductor Esa-Pekka Salonen and the composer Magnus Lindberg) of the new music ensemble Korvat Auki! ('Ears Open!'). She continued her studies in Freiburg and at the IRCAM studio in Paris. Although her early sympathies were with post-serialist modernism, she soon grew more eclectic: 'Everything is permissible as long as it's done in good taste'. Many of Saariaho's works involve electronics, but she has been increasingly drawn towards the conventional symphony orchestra, as in the paired orchestral works *Du cristal* and . . . *à la fumée* (1990). Her outstanding achievement is her opera *L'Amour de loin* (2000), widely praised for its refined beauty and surprising lyrical warmth.   SJ

Sabre Dance. A movement from Khachaturian's ballet *Gayané.*

saccadé (Fr.). 'Jerked', i.e. sharply accented, particularly a bowstroke.

Sacchini, Antonio (Maria Gaspare Gioacchino) (*b* Florence, 14 June 1730; *d* Paris, 6 Oct. 1786). Italian opera composer. After studying at the Conservatorio di S. Maria di Loreto in Naples, he embarked on a prolific career of opera composition for the major theatres of Venice, Rome, Florence, and Naples. In 1769 he was elected director of the Venetian Conservatorio dell'Ospedaletto, and in 1770 he travelled round Germany, commanding high fees. From 1772 Sacchini spent ten years in London, where he was highly praised for his lyrical gifts.

Having fallen into financial straits because of his luxurious tastes, Sacchini moved to Paris, where he was strongly supported by Marie Antoinette. He became the rival of Piccinni whom, however, he cordially admired. His French operas resemble Piccinni's in their strongly dramatic intentions, but exceed those of his rival in melodic suavity; they are more lightly scored, and make freer use of short and incomplete musical forms. His last completed work, *Oedipe à Colone*, was temporarily rejected at Fontainebleau, a disappointment which may have speeded his death. In 1787 it was given at the Opéra and became the most successful opera of its epoch, remaining in the repertory, with over 500 performances, until the 1820s.   DA/JR

Sacher, Paul (*b* Basle, 28 April 1906; *d* Basle, 26 May 1999). Swiss conductor. He was a pioneer of new music and worked with many of the 20th century's leading composers. He studied conducting with Weingartner at the Basle Conservatory and founded the Basle Chamber Orchestra in 1926, specializing in contemporary music and neglected early Classical works. He commissioned or gave premieres of over 80 compositions, notably Bartók's *Music for Strings, Percussion, and Celesta*, Hindemith's *Die Harmonie der Welt*, Strauss's *Metamorphosen*, Stravinsky's Concerto in D, and works by Britten, Henze, and Tippett. From 1941 he conducted the Collegium Musicum of Zürich. The Schola Cantorum Basiliensis was founded by him in 1933 for research into and performance of early music.

JT

Sachs, Hans (*b* Nuremberg, 5 Nov. 1494; *d* Nuremberg, 19 Jan. 1576). German poet. A master shoemaker, he travelled in Germany before settling in Nuremberg, where he became an honoured member of the Meistersinger guild. He is credited with some 6000 lieder (poems and music), together with Shrovetide plays and various moralizing dramas. A staunch supporter of Luther and the Reformation, he is particularly remembered today for his impressive representation in Wagner's opera *Die Meistersinger von Nürnberg*.

DA/BS

sackbut. English term used until the 18th century for *trombone.

sacra rappresentazione (It., 'sacred performance'). In 15th- and 16th-century Italy, a religious drama performed with music. The genre was a forerunner of opera and the oratorio.

Sacrati, Francesco (*b* Parma, *bapt.* 17 Sept. 1605; *d* ?Modena, 20 May 1650). Italian composer. He was one of the first to write for the public opera houses in Venice in the 1640s. His *La finta pazza* ('The Feigned Madwoman', 1641), a touring version of which has recently been discovered, was one of the most popular operas of its day; taken to Paris by Torelli in 1645, it was among the first Italian operas to be given in France. Sacrati may also have had a hand in the music that survives for Monteverdi's last opera, *L'incoronazione di Poppea*.

DA/TC

Sacre du printemps, Le. See RITE OF SPRING, THE.

Sadko. Opera in three or five acts by Rimsky-Korsakov to his own libretto compiled (with the help of Vladimir Stasov and Vladimir Bel'sky among others) from *Sadko, bogatïy gosti* and other ancient ballads and tales (Moscow, 1897). Rimsky-Korsakov had earlier (1867) written a symphonic poem with the same title.

Saeverud, Harald (Sigurd Johan) (*b* Bergen, 17 April 1897; *d* Siljustøl, nr Bergen, 27 March 1992). Norwegian composer. He studied at the Music Academy in Bergen (1915–20), then at the Berlin Hochschule für Musik, where he also took instruction in conducting from Clemens Krauss (1935). He had begun work on the first of his nine symphonies when he was a student in Bergen and, back in Norway, he continued to compose while supporting himself as a critic and piano teacher. His symphonic and instrumental production was given a sharp stimulus when the Nazis invaded Norway in 1940, his anger finding expression in such works as the *Sinfonia dolorosa* (no. 6, 1942) and the *Kjempevise-slåtten* ('Canto rivoltoso', 1942, written for piano and later orchestrated). Saeverud's incidental music for Ibsen's *Peer Gynt* (1947) brought him considerable acclaim. His music, which bears the imprint of the Norwegian folk idiom, is lithe and muscular, his counterpoint clean, and his harmonies crisp; although he can summon considerable reserves of energy, his scores more readily betray a tart sense of humour. The composer Ketil Hvoslef (*b* 1939) is his son.

MA

sainete (Sp.). A type of late 18th-century Spanish comic opera in one act. It is the Spanish equivalent of *opera buffa* but has at times approximated more closely to farce. Notable composers in the genre included Antonio Soler and Blas de Laserna (*c.*1751–1816).

'St Anthony' Variations. See VARIATIONS ON A THEME BY HAYDN.

St Cecilia. See CECILIA.

Saint François d'Assise ('St Francis of Assisi'; *Scènes franciscains*, 'Franciscan Scenes'). Opera in three acts by Messiaen to his own libretto (Paris, 1983).

St John Chrysostom. See JOHN CHRYSOSTOM.

St John Passion (*Johannes-Passion*). Setting by J. S. Bach, BWV245, of the Passion story to an anonymous text adapted from Barthold Heinrich Brockes's poem *Der für die Sünde der Welt gemartert und sterbende Jesus* ('Jesus, Martyred and Dying for the Sins of the World') after St John's Gospel; for soloists, chorus, and orchestra, it was first performed on Good Friday 1724. Selle (1623), Schütz (1666), Telemann (several), and Pärt (1982) also wrote *St John Passion* settings.

St John's Night on Bald Mountain. See NIGHT ON THE BARE MOUNTAIN.

St Luke Passion (*Passio et mors domini nostri Jesu Christi secundum Lucam*). Oratorio (1966) by Penderecki, for soprano, baritone, and bass soloists, boys' chorus, three mixed choruses, and orchestra, after St Luke's Gospel.

St Martial. A monastery at Limoges, France, founded in 848 and named after the first Bishop of Limoges (3rd century); it became a secular church in 1535 and was demolished in 1792 during the French Revolution. Its library was sold to the Bibliothèque Royale before the revolution, so that most of its manuscripts escaped the general destruction; they survive in the Bibliothèque Nationale, Paris. This has encouraged the belief in a unique St Martial school; however, it is now recognized that the music at St Martial was from of a wider Aquitanian repertory.

The plainchant repertory of St Martial is diverse: its graduals contain the expected official 'Gregorian' chant, but also introduce many new, locally composed melodies (e.g. the Alleluias found in the St Yrieix Gradual, in the Bibliothèque Nationale). Its additional chant genres (tropes, proses, sequences, and prosulae) show the influence of northern France and northern Italy, and include a large 'home-grown' repertory. Four manuscripts embody a repertory of 12th-century two-part polyphony, including perhaps the earliest surviving florid' organum; some have detected in this repertory an anticipation of the Parisian conductus.

PW

St Matthew Passion (*Matthäus-Passion*). Setting by J. S. Bach, BWV244, of the Passion story to a text by Picander after St Matthew's Gospel; for soloists, chorus, and orchestra, it was probably first performed on Good Friday 1727. Richard Davy (late 15th century) and Schütz (1666) also wrote *St Matthew Passion* settings.

St Paul (*Paulus*). Oratorio, op. 36 (1836), by Mendelssohn, for soprano, contralto, tenor, and bass soloists, chorus, and orchestra, a setting of a text by Julius Schubring after *The Acts of the Apostles*.

St Paul's Suite. Suite for string orchestra, op. 29 no. 2 (1912–13), by Holst, written for St Paul's Girls' School, Hammersmith, where Holst was director of music from 1905.

Saint-Saëns, (Charles) **Camille** (*b* Paris, 9 Oct. 1835; *d* Algiers, 16 Dec. 1921). French composer. His father died a few weeks after his birth and he was brought up by his mother and grandmother. He began to learn the piano at the age of three and, after lessons with Camille Stamaty, gave a concert at the Salle Pleyel when he was ten, the programme including Mozart's B♭ Concerto κ450 and Beethoven's Third Concerto. He also took lessons in composition and organ playing. He entered the Paris Conservatoire in 1848, and in 1851 gained the *premier prix* for organ and began composition lessons with Halévy. Surprisingly, he failed to win the Prix de Rome either in 1852, when Gounod accused him of 'lacking inexperience', or in 1864, by which time his sharp tongue and modernist tastes had upset too many in the musical Establishment. On leaving the Conservatoire he took up various posts as organist, culminating in that of the Madeleine (1857–76). He became famous for his organ improvisations, some of which found their way into his published compositions, for example the finale of the Third Symphony (1886).

By the time he was 30 Saint-Saëns had written four of his five symphonies (the so-called Third is in fact the last of these, since two remained unpublished during his lifetime), two of his three violin concertos, and his First Piano Concerto (1858), which was the earliest attempt in the medium by a French composer. He had also written chamber music, including the delightful Piano Trio in F (1863), and over 30 songs, and Berlioz in a letter of 1864 called him already 'a truly great artist'. But it was in the 1870s and 80s that he reached the height of his powers with such works as the First Cello Sonata and the First Cello Concerto (1872), the Fourth Piano Concerto (1875), the Third Violin Concerto (1880), and especially the set of four symphonic poems, the first written by a French composer on the Lisztian model: *Le Rouet d'Omphale* (1871), *Phaëton* (1873), *Danse macabre* (1874), and *La Jeunesse d'Hercule* (1877). In all these orchestral works, the combination of memorable tunes, strong construction, and vivid orchestration set new standards for French music and were an inspiration to such young composers as Ravel.

After the Third Symphony, dedicated to the memory of Liszt, some of the fire seems to have gone out of

Saint-Saëns's composing, though he wrote much that is charming and effective. He became an inveterate traveller and always had a liking for the exotic, evident in works such as the *Suite algérienne* and *Jota aragonese* (1880), *Havanaise* for violin and orchestra (1887), and two works for piano and orchestra: *Africa* (1891) and the splendidly vigorous Fifth Piano Concerto (1896), whose central Andante is allegedly based on a Nubian love song the composer heard on a trip down the Nile, accompanied by croaking frogs and chirping crickets. Otherwise, as the new century dawned, he increasingly felt himself to be washed up by the tide of history and particularly by the advent of so-called musical Impressionism. Debussy was one of his particular *bêtes noires*. Saint-Saëns was party to the Institut jury's condemnation of the younger composer's Impressionist tendencies in 1887, forwent his summer holiday in 1902 so that he could stay in Paris and 'thay nathty thingth about *Pelléath*', and on seeing the score of *En blanc et noir* in 1915 warned Fauré that it was vital 'to bar the door of the Institut against a gentleman capable of such atrocities'. At the end of his life, his reaction to the polytonality of Milhaud's symphonic suite *Protée* (1919) was that 'fortunately, there are still lunatic asylums in France'. At the same time his own compositions sought a new simplicity and lucidity, as in the three Sonatas, for oboe, clarinet, and bassoon with piano (all 1921), where 18th-century formulas are given new and surprising twists.

As one might expect, this brilliant pianist wrote for his instrument throughout his life, but this part of his oeuvre has made curiously little mark. Only the *Étude en forme de valse*, promoted by Cortot, still attracts those pianists keen to show off their left-hand technique. A failure that Saint-Saëns regretted far more deeply was that of his operas. *Samson et Dalila* (Weimar, 1877) has entered the repertory, but after a slow start. Of his 11 other operas, *Henry VIII* (Paris Opéra, 1883) has recently made some headway, boasting a strong central role, a fine love scene in the second act, and a superb last-act quartet. After the cool reception of *Les Barbares* at the Opéra (1901), prompting Debussy to say that Saint-Saëns would do better to concentrate on his new-found vocation as explorer, he entrusted his last three operas to the more amenable venue of Monte Carlo.

Saint-Saëns was known for his quick wit and intemperate opinions, and certainly he grew crustier with age. He married in 1875, but after the death of his two young sons, for which he blamed his wife's carelessness, he left her and never married again. From 1861 he taught for four years at the École Niedermeyer; Fauré, who was a pupil there, subsequently became one of his closest friends. Among his many other friends were

Pauline Viardot, Bizet, Rossini, Sarasate, and Paderewski. In 1871 he was one of the founders of the Société Nationale de Musique, but he resigned in 1886 when Franck and his pupils organized a coup to allow performances of non-French music. He was elected to the Institut in 1881, characteristically taking the opportunity to include in his inaugural speech the utterance: 'Logic may rule the theatres but who can say what motivates theatre directors?' Among his scholarly interests were ancient Greek musical instruments, astronomy, and the music of Rameau, whose complete works he edited for Durand from 1895.

Saint-Saëns's character, like his piano playing, was often felt to be brilliant but cold. But even a casual hearing of *Samson et Dalila* or of the Fourth Piano Concerto reveals that passion and imagination were not lacking. The 20th century, with its general contempt for the 'well-made' work, persistently misunderstood him. But, after that century's musical excesses, there is still much to be said for a composer who embraced his great-aunt's injunction to 'avoid all exaggeration and strive to maintain the entirety of intellectual health'.

RN

📖 J. HARDING, *Saint-Saëns and his Circle* (London, 1965) · R. SMITH, *Saint-Saëns and the Organ* (Stuyvesant, NY, 1992)

Saint-Simonians. The followers of a French social and philosophical movement founded in the mid-1820s that advocated fraternal cooperation and the reorientation of society towards the poorer classes. Named after the French socialist the Comte de Saint-Simon (1760–1825), it was one of the earliest of such movements to use music (notably songs and choruses) to propagate its ideas, and counted Berlioz and Liszt among its early adherents—though they later became disillusioned. Félicien David went with many Saint-Simonians to Egypt in 1833, following persecution by the government, and gathered traditional themes that he later used in his opera *Le Désert* (1844).   SH

Saite (Ger.). 'String'.

Sakamoto, Ryuichi (*b* Nakano, Tokyo, 17 Jan. 1952). Japanese composer, keyboard player, and conductor. He studied in Tokyo, specializing in electronic and ethnic music. He co-founded the techno-pop Yellow Magic Orchestra, and has worked with rock and world musicians. Sakamoto has been influenced not only by European classical music, but also by minimalism, *musique concrète*, jazz, and Asian traditional music. He is best known internationally for his film scores, including those for *Merry Christmas Mr Lawrence*, in which he also played a leading role (1983), *The Last*

Emperor (1987), *The Handmaid's Tale* (1990), *The Sheltering Sky* (1990), and *Snake Eyes* (1998).   ABUR

Sakuntala. Opera in three acts by Weingartner to his own libretto after Kalidasa's drama *Abhijñanasakuntala* (*c.*400 BC) (Weimar, 1884). Alfano wrote a three-act opera on the same subject (Bologna, 1921) and Goldmark wrote an overture *Sakuntala* (1865).

Salieri, Antonio (*b* Legnago, 18 Aug. 1750; *d* Vienna, 7 May 1825). Italian composer. Orphaned at 15, he was adopted by a Venetian nobleman, then introduced to Florian Gassmann, who became his 'second father' and took him to Vienna in 1766. When Gassmann died in 1774 Salieri, strongly supported by Joseph II, was his natural successor as director of the Italian opera. His career was centred on *opera buffa*, or *dramma giocoso*, in the Venetian mould; in this he was an essential precursor to Mozart, whom he also anticipated by writing piano concertos. Among his earlier operas are an intermezzo, an opera-ballet taken from *Don Quixote*, and a Gluckian 'reform' opera, *Armida*, modelled on *Telemaco* rather than *Alceste*. Several of his comedies, including *La fiera di Venezia* (1772) and *La locandiera* (1773), are worthy of revival.

With the establishment of German opera in Vienna (for which he wrote *Der Rauchfangkehrer*, 'The Chimney-Sweep', in 1781), Salieri produced several operas in Italy, and went to Paris as Gluck's accredited successor, though not strictly his pupil. Until its success was assured, *Les Danaïdes* (1784) was presented as partly Gluck's work. Salieri returned to Vienna to collaborate unsuccessfully with Lorenzo Da Ponte (*Il ricco d'un giorno*, 'Rich Man for a Day', 1784) but triumphantly with G. B. Casti in the ironic *La grotta di Trofonio* (1785), whose mock-magic scenes anticipate *Don Giovanni*. His second Paris opera, *Les Horaces*, was considered over-serious, but the colourful *Tarare*, to a text by Beaumarchais, was a success and was adapted for Vienna as *Axur re d'Ormus* by Da Ponte, who wrote more operas for Salieri than for Mozart; their *La cifra* (1789) is a precursor of *Così fan tutte*, a libretto intended for Salieri but one that he abandoned after composing two numbers. In 1791 he declined the commission then executed by Mozart as *La clemenza di Tito*.

There is little foundation for the idea that Salieri and Mozart were rivals, and none for the popular theory that Salieri poisoned his more gifted, but less successful, contemporary. Salieri composed *Falstaff* in 1799 but abandoned the stage soon after to write sacred music (including a fine Requiem) and to devote himself to teaching; his pupils included Beethoven, Schubert, and Liszt.   JR

📖 J. A. Rice, *Antonio Salieri and Viennese Opera* (Chicago, 1998)

Sallinen, Aulis (*b* Salmi, 9 April 1935). Finnish composer. He is one of the leading Finnish composers of his generation. After studying with Aarre Merikanto and Joonas Kokkonen at the Sibelius Academy he joined Finnish Radio (1960–70), then taught harmony and counterpoint at the Academy (1963–76). He attracted wide attention with *Mauermusik* for orchestra (1962), a response to the building of the Berlin Wall. Although he showed a brief interest in serial technique, his mature style is predominantly tonal, and in the 1970s he was increasingly drawn to traditional forms. His First Symphony (1971) experiments with a one-movement structure and has a strong and compelling feeling for atmosphere. The Third (1975) is a dark, powerful, and evocative work, again with a strong sense of nature, and with roots in late Sibelius and the sound world of Britten, yet bearing a thoroughly individual stamp. Although Sallinen, like his slightly older contemporary Einojuhani Rautavaara, has shown consistent interest in the symphony (his most recent being the Sixth, 'From a New Zealand Diary'; 1990), opera has loomed larger on his musical horizon. After the success of his first, *Ratsumies* ('The Horseman'; Savonlinna, 1975), to a libretto by the poet Paavo Haavikko, his energies turned to the stage: *Punainen viiva* ('The Red Line'; Helsinki, 1978), *Kuningas lähtee Ranskaan* ('The King Goes Forth to France', 1984)—a joint commission from the Royal Opera, Covent Garden, the BBC, and the Savonlinna Festival—*Kullervo* (Los Angeles, 1992), and *Palatsi* ('The Palace'; Savonlinna, 1995).   RLa

salmo (It., Sp.). *'Psalm'.

Salome. Opera in one act by Richard Strauss to Hedwig Lachmann's German translation of Oscar Wilde's play (1893) (Dresden, 1905).

Salomon, Johann Peter (*b* Bonn, *bapt.* 20 Feb. 1745; *d* London, 28 Nov. 1815). German violinist, impresario, and composer. In 1758 he became a court musician in Bonn, and several years later he was appointed musical director to Prince Heinrich at Rheinsberg. By 1781 he was in London, where he settled. There he was known at first for his virtuosity as a violinist, but he soon became involved in concert management. He organized series of subscription concerts in the 1780s and 90s, and he managed to persuade Haydn to visit London, which he did in 1791–2 and 1794–5. Among the works Haydn wrote for performance in London, mostly for Salomon's concerts, are the 12 'London' symphonies and the opp. 71 and 74 string quartets. Salomon was one of the founder members of the Philharmonic Society in

1813. His own compositions include theatre works and violin music.   PL

'Salomon' Symphonies. See 'London' Symphonies.

Salón Mexico, El. Orchestral work (1933–6) by Copland; it is named after a dance hall in Mexico City that Copland visited in 1932 and includes Mexican folksongs.

salon music. Music composed specifically for performance in a domestic context rather than a concert hall, church, or theatre. In its widest sense it embraces most solo and chamber music, but usually denotes undemanding compositions (particularly those of the 19th and 20th centuries) of a lightweight character and designed for private amusement.   JBe

salsa (Sp., 'sauce'). A 20th-century Latin American dance. Its origins lie in the Cuban mambo and cha-cha, developed by Cuban and Puerto Rican immigrants in New York in the 1960s and 70s. Using the basic cha-cha step, salsa is generally faster and more energetic. Most salsa music takes the two-part structure of the Cuban *son*, a fusion of West African and Spanish musical and rhythmic elements dating from the early 1900s.   JH

saltando, saltato (It.). 'Leaping', 'leapt': term used in the bowing of stringed instruments to mean **sautillé*.

saltarello (modern It.: *salterello*). A lively dance of Spanish and Italian provenance. It is characterized by triple metre and the jumping movements that form part of the steps to the dance. In the 16th century it frequently occurred as the 'afterdance' (Ger.: *Nachtanz*) to a **pavan* or **passamezzo*, the music often being indistinguishable from that of a **galliard*. Mendelssohn called the finale of his 'Italian' Symphony 'Saltarello'.

Salut d'amour (*Liebesgruss*; 'Love's Greeting'). Piece by Elgar, originally for solo piano (1888); it was orchestrated in 1889, and later arranged for violin and piano and for many other combinations.

Salvation Army bands. See BRASS BAND.

Salve regina. See ANTIPHONS OF THE BLESSED VIRGIN MARY.

Salzedo [Salzédo, Salcedo], **Carlos** (Léon) (*b* Arcachon, 6 April 1885; *d* Waterville, ME, 17 Aug. 1961). French-born American harpist and composer. After studies in Bordeaux and Paris he moved to New York to become principal harp at the Metropolitan Opera, 1909–13. He then formed the Trio de Lutèce and, later, the Salzedo Harp Ensemble; from 1921 he edited a magazine reviewing new music and became a founder member of the International Composers' Guild. In 1924 he was invited to lead a new harp department at the Curtis

Institute in Philadelphia. As a composer he kept abreast of developments, his music evolving from French Impressionism to a leaner style.   CF

📖 D. OWENS, *Carlos Salzedo: From Aeolian to Thunder* (Chicago, 1992)

Sammartini. Italian family of musicians. Two of its members were composers and performers of distinction whose works have often been confused with each other's. **Giuseppe** (Francesco Gaspare Melchiorre Baldassare) **Sammartini** (*b* Milan, 6 Jan. 1695; *d* London, Nov. 1750) was a virtuoso oboist. In the 1720s he played in the opera orchestra in Milan, where he was heard and praised by Quantz. He visited London *c.*1728, becoming oboist at the King's Theatre and taking an active part in concert life. Later he entered the service of the Prince of Wales. Burney describes his tone as superb, and near to that of the human voice. He composed some interesting concerti grossi after the Handelian model but with a more up-to-date idiom.

Giuseppe Sammartini was overshadowed as a composer by his brother, **Giovanni Battista Sammartini** (*b* ? Milan, *c.*1700; *d* Milan, 15 Jan. 1775), who worked for most of his life in various churches in Milan. He was one of the most influential figures in the early development of the symphony, beginning in something like the manner of Vivaldi but developing a style that is the apotheosis of the grace and elegance of the *galant* style. He may have taught, and he certainly influenced, Gluck, and Mozart learnt much from him during his stay in Milan in 1770. Prince Esterházy possessed copies of two of his symphonies, and though Haydn called him a 'scribbler' there is a distinct similarity of style between the two composers.   DA/RP

sampling. 1. The analysis of sounds by digital *synthesizers. Sampling techniques have been widely used in the production of individual voices for commercial synthesizers: instead of generating sounds artificially from first principles, short extracts from acoustic instruments or other suitable sources are digitized, edited, and stored in a memory bank, ready for resynthesis.   PM

2. A process initiated in the late 1970s by DJs mixing dance music on vinyl records which has become a common form of borrowing in popular music that uses electronic resources.

📖 M. RUSS, *Sound Synthesis and Sampling* (Oxford, 1996)

Samson. Oratorio (1743) by Handel to a text adapted by Newburgh Hamilton from Milton's *Samson Agonistes* and other poems.

Samson et Dalila. Opera in three acts by Saint-Saëns to a libretto by Ferdinand Lemaire after Judges 14–16 (Weimar, 1877).

Samstag aus Licht ('Saturday from Light'). Opera in a greeting and four scenes by Stockhausen to his own libretto (Milan, 1984), the 'second day' of *Licht*.

sanctorale (Lat., from *sanctus*, 'saint'). In the Roman rite, the annual liturgical cycle based on the feasts of saints.

Sanctus (Lat., 'Holy'). An ancient hymn sung throughout the undivided Church, East and West. It is part of the Ordinary of the Roman *Mass, sung during the Eucharistic prayer. In plainchant settings the Sanctus and Benedictus form a continuous whole, but in polyphonic settings and more recent compositions the Benedictus is usually a separate 'movement'. The Sanctus was retained in the Anglican liturgy from 1552 without the Benedictus, which was reinstated by the liturgical reforms of the 20th century (see COMMON PRAYER, BOOK OF).

Sandrin [Regnault, Pierre] (*b* ?Saint Marcel, nr Paris, ?*c.*1490; *d* ?Italy, after 1561). French composer. He held various ecclesiastical appointments in France and in the 1540s entered the service of the royal court, but in the following decade he spent some years in charge of the music of Cardinal Ippolito d'Este in Rome; he is last heard of there in 1561. Sandrin was one of the best-known 16th-century composers of chansons. His most famous, *Doulce memoire*, is an attractive piece in the vein of a melancholy pavan and was arranged countless times for lute and other instruments, as well as being used as the basis for masses by Rore and Lassus.

DA

sanft, sanftmütig (Ger.). 'Soft', 'gentle'; 'softly', 'gently'.

sanglot (Fr., 'sob'). 18th-century name for a descending *appoggiatura, usually sung to plaintive words.

Sanguine Fan, The. Ballet in one act by Elgar to a scenario by Ian Lowther based on a fan design drawn in sanguine (red crayon) by Charles Conder; it was first performed as a mimed play (London, 1917), in aid of war charities, and was staged as a ballet (under the title *L'Éventail*), choreographed by Ronald Hynd (London, 1976).

sansa. See MBIRA, KALIMBA, LIKEMBE.

Santa María, Tomás de (*b* Madrid, *c.*1510; *d* Ribadavia, 1570). Spanish composer and theorist. He was a Dominican friar, and in 1563 was living at the monastery of S. Domingo in Guadalajara. His *Libro llamado Arte de tañer fantasía* (Valladolid, 1565, but written by 1557), concerned with the skills necessary to improvise a fantasia, deals with rudiments of music theory, keyboard technique, and performance practice (covering fingering, ornamentation, and rhythmic alteration), as well as composition (including harmonic techniques and imitation). He appended short keyboard pieces as examples.   OR

Santos, Joly Braga. See BRAGA SANTOS, JOLY.

sanza. See MBIRA, KALIMBA, LIKEMBE.

sarabande (Fr., Ger.; It.: *sarabanda*; Sp.: *zarabanda*) [saraband]. A dance popular from the late 16th century to the 18th; as an instrumental form, it was one of the principal movements of the Baroque *suite, in which it usually followed the courante. Like the *chaconne it originated in Latin America (where it was accompanied by song, castanets, and guitars) and appeared in Spain during the 16th century. During this period it was a fast, lively dance alternating between 3/4 and 6/8 metre and with a reputation for lasciviousness: Father Mariana (1536–1624) in his *Treatise against Public Amusements* speaks of it as 'a dance and song so loose in its words and so ugly in its motions that it is enough to excite bad emotions in even very decent people'. In 1583 Philip II suppressed the dance in Spain, but still it managed to flourish.

In the early 17th century the sarabande was introduced to Italy, from where the first notated examples survive as tablatures for the Spanish guitar. It soon spread to France, where it appeared in the *ballet de cour* and other theatrical entertainments, as well as in the ballroom, and it was here that the much slower and more stately version of the dance evolved. This was in triple time with a clear emphasis on the second beat, which was often dotted. This form of sarabande appears in the works of many French composers, including Chambonnières, the Couperins, D'Anglebert, and Rameau and was also the preferred style among such German composers as Bach (e.g. his English Suite no. 2 in A minor, where it is provided with a *double*), Froberger, Pachelbel, and Handel.

In England, both the Italian and French types of sarabande were known, and examples were written by Purcell (who placed it as the last movement in the suite), Blow, and others. Thomas Mace described it as: 'of the shortest triple time, but . . . more toyish and light than corantes; and commonly of Two Strains' (*Musick's Monument*, 1676). The sarabande was revived in the 20th century, for instance by Debussy (in the suite *Pour le piano*), Satie (*Trois sarabandes*), and Vaughan Williams (in *Job*, the 'masque for dancing').   —/JBE

sāraṅgī. A bowed *chordophone of South Asia. It is used to accompany singing or dancing, or both, in the classical music of North India and Pakistan, and the traditional music of Rajasthan. The term is also applied in a more general sense to various bowed instruments in

the region. The *sāraṅgī* has a hollowed-out body made of *tun* wood, covered with goatskin, and a short neck; there are no frets or fingerboard. The modern classical *sāraṅgī* has three playing strings made of goat gut and as many as 36 sympathetic strings made of brass or steel (or both), with two to four bridges. The player sits cross-legged, holding the instrument against the left shoulder. The strings are stopped with the fingernails of the left hand, the bow held in an underhand grip in the right. An effect similar to that of the vocal slur so characteristic of Indian music is achieved by using one finger to play several notes.

The Rajasthani *sāraṅgī* is similar to the classical instrument, but has four playing strings (the second of which is not stopped but serves as a drone), and fewer sympathetic strings. The bowing style tends to be more markedly rhythmic, to compensate for the lack of drumming or other rhythmic accompaniment in the music.   LC

Sarasate (y Navascués), Pablo (Martin Melitón) de (*b* Pamplona, 10 March 1844; *d* Biarritz, 20 Sept. 1908). Spanish violinist and composer. He gave his first concert at the age of seven, and studied at Madrid with Rodriguez before entering the Paris Conservatoire to study with Delphin Alard (1856). He subsequently embarked on a highly successful career as a concert violinist, travelling widely in Europe and North and South America. Sarasate was famed for the classic purity of his style, beauty of tone, and facility of execution. He inspired many substantial concertante works, including Lalo's *Symphonie espagnole*, Bruch's Violin Concerto no. 2 and *Scottish Fantasy*, and Saint-Saëns's *Rondo capriccioso* and Violin Concertos nos. 1 and 3. His own works, stimulated by the folk music of his native country, include fantasias, *romances*, and transcriptions, of which *Zigeunerweisen*, *Jota aragonesa*, and the four books of Spanish dances are still played.
                                                    WT/CW

Sargent, Sir Malcolm (*b* Ashford, Kent, 29 April 1895; *d* London, 3 Oct. 1967). English conductor, pianist, and composer. He was the parish organist in Melton Mowbray, where he organized and conducted choral concerts, and a piano pupil of Benno Moiseiwitsch. His talent came to the notice of Henry Wood, who engaged him to make his orchestral conducting debut with the Queen's Hall Orchestra in 1921. In 1929 Sargent obtained funding to establish the Courtauld–Sargent Concerts, with the aim of providing well-rehearsed performances of a wide repertory, and they secured his reputation. He gave the premieres of works by Walton (*Belshazzar's Feast*), Holst, and Vaughan Williams and held posts with the Hallé, Liverpool Philharmonic, and BBC Symphony orchestras. He was also an advocate of

Gilbert and Sullivan operas. He was knighted in 1947. From 1948 to 1967 he achieved his greatest fame as chief conductor of the BBC Promenade Concerts, popularizing music in Britain on a new scale. Sargent was most acclaimed in the choral repertory; he was a fluent speaker and broadcaster, and made many orchestral arrangements.   JT

📖 C. REID, *Malcolm Sargent: A Biography* (London, 1968, 2/1973)

sarod. A North Indian plucked string instrument, deriving from the Afghan *rabāb*. Its neck and resonator are carved from a single piece of wood, the resonator being divided into two chests by a waist and covered with a sound-table of skin. The neck and the upper part of the resonator are overlaid by a metal fingerboard. The lower part of the resonator is nearly hemispherical. The *sarod* has eight or ten plucked strings, two of which function as drones, and about 15 sympathetic strings. Some examples have an extra small resonator of gourd, wood, or metal fixed to the pegbox.   JMo

sarrusophone. A double-reed brass instrument, devised in 1856 by the French bandmaster P. A. Sarrus to rival Adolphe Sax's *saxophones and initially manufactured by P. L. Gautrot. The sarrusophone family consists of the sopranino in E♭, soprano in B♭, alto in E♭, tenor in B♭, baritone in E♭, bass in B♭, contrabass in E♭, and alto contrabass in B♭. In all but the smallest sizes the tube is bent back on itself and thus reduced to a convenient length. Sarrusophones are more useful outdoors than the wooden instruments, and instruments of this type are still heard in Italian bands. The *contrebasse à anche* ('reed contrabass') looks similar but has a quite different fingering system.   JMo

Sarti, Giuseppe (*b* Faenza, *bapt.* 1 Dec. 1729; *d* Berlin, 28 July 1802). Italian composer. Despite periods of activity in his native Italy (especially at Venice and Milan), he worked principally at the courts of Denmark (1753–65 and 1768–75) and Russia (from 1784). Court intrigues brought about his dismissal from Copenhagen and dogged him at St Petersburg; in the early 1790s he was exiled to Ukraine. On the strength of the thriving music school he founded there Catherine the Great recalled him to her capital to direct the conservatory, which was modelled on Italian lines. He died while visiting his daughter in Berlin.

Sarti was one of most successful composers of Italian opera in the 1770s and 80s. His *opera seria Giulio Sabino* (1781) had more than 20 productions and his *opera buffa Fra i due litiganti* (1782) more than 30 during his lifetime. Haydn directed six of his operas at Eszterháza, and Mozart quoted from *Fra i due litiganti* in Don Giovanni. Sarti's earliest *opere serie* are Metastasian,

but in the 1770s he assimilated influences from the 'reform' operas of Gluck, Traetta, and Paisiello. Most of his comic operas pre-date the vogue for multiple ensembles and extended finales: their popularity rested on his attractive and dramatically effective arias.

DA/TRJ

Sartorio, Antonio (*b* Venice, 1630; *d* Venice, 30 Dec. 1680). Italian composer. He established himself as a composer of Venetian opera in the 1660s. In 1666 he became Kapellmeister at the Italianate court of the Duke of Brunswick-Lüneburg in Hanover, where he remained until 1675, returning frequently to Italy for performances of his operas. In 1676 he became *vicemaestro* at St Mark's, Venice. Sartorio's operas captured the popular demand for a multiplicity of lyrical arias at the expense of dramatic recitative typical of the older style of Monteverdi's pupil Cavalli. He was particularly famous for the triple-metre laments over an ostinato bass combined with an acerbic harmonic idiom, and for the trumpet obbligato arias. A single publication of psalms (1680) also survives.   PA

Sarum Use. The liturgy, ritual, and manner of performing the plainchant in the cathedral church of Salisbury from medieval times until the Reformation. In the later Middle Ages the Sarum Use was increasingly adopted by other dioceses, such as York, Lincoln, Hereford, and Bangor. The books of the Sarum Use furnished the Reformers with their main material for the *Book of Common Prayer*, despite their condemnation of the 'number and hardness' of its rules, and English settings of liturgical music continued to use Sarum versions of the plainchant in such works as votive antiphons, hymns, and settings of the Lamentations of Jeremiah and the *Magnificat*.   —/ALi

Sáry, László (*b* Györ, 1 Jan. 1940). Hungarian composer. He studied with Endre Szervánszky at the Liszt Academy of Music, and was later influenced by the music and ideas of Boulez, Stockhausen, Cage, Christian Wolff, and the American systematic minimalists. In 1970 he co-founded the Budapest New Music Studio, which explored the possibilities of group improvisation and collaborative composition. Sáry has been influential in promoting the use of improvisation in music-teaching. He has composed prolifically for a wide range of orchestral, instrumental, and vocal forces; many of his works are variable in number of performers, scoring, and duration.   ABur

Satie, Erik (Alfred Leslie) (*b* Honfleur, 17 May 1866; *d* Paris, 1 July 1925). French composer. Of mixed French–Scots parentage, he spent his formative years, between the ages of four and 12, living with grandparents and an eccentric uncle in Honfleur, where he had his first piano lessons. He then moved to Paris to join his father, and studied at the Conservatoire (1879–86), where he was described as 'gifted but indolent' and won no prizes. Among his earliest compositions were sets of three *Gymnopédies* (1888) and *Gnossiennes* (1890) for piano, evoking the ancient world by means of pure simplicity, monotonous repetition, and highly original modal harmonies; they had an influence on his friend Debussy. A similar manner was used to serve the exotic Rosicrucian sect, whose mysteries were austerely celebrated in, for example, the 'Christian ballet' *Uspud* (1892) and the *Danses gothiques* for piano (1893). The *Messe des pauvres* for organ or piano (1895) is more orthodox in subject matter if not in style. All this early music of his is the more noteworthy for having been written at a time when Wagner's music was dominant in Paris.

During this period Satie was earning his living as a café pianist in Montmartre; he also contributed to the café repertory with songs and little waltzes. In 1898, however, he retired to the industrial suburb of Arcueil-Cachan, where he lived in self-imposed poverty for the rest of his life. He began to write works with bizarre titles, for example the *Trois pièces en forme de poire* for piano four-hands (1903), a set of seven pieces, still childlike in their simplicity, which was a résumé of his music since 1890, incorporating pieces composed independently as well as popular songs of the time. But, realizing that without a sound contrapuntal technique he would not make progress, he then enrolled at the Schola Cantorum (1905–12), where he was taught by d'Indy and Roussel. While the Schola's direct influence may have been slight, Satie's new interpretation of chorale and fugue can be heard in the opening bars of *Parade*.

In 1911 Ravel performed some of Satie's early piano pieces and Debussy conducted his own orchestration of two of the *Gymnopédies* (1888). Spurred on by the success of these ventures, Satie began to compose more abundantly, continuing to produce sets of small instrumental pieces with absurd titles: *Embryons desséchés* for piano (1913) and *Choses vues à droite et à gauche (sans lunettes)* for violin and piano (1914) are typical. Often, as in the piano set *Sports et divertissements* (1914), the performer is confronted by instructions which appear either absurd or ironically humorous. In fact, a sensitive pianist can make much of injunctions such as 'arm yourself with clairvoyance' and 'with the end of your thought'. On no account are his running commentaries to be read aloud.

Satie's modest, mocking art endeared him to a new generation of French composers about the time of World War I. In 1915 he was discovered by Jean Cocteau, who eulogized him in his manifesto *Le Coq et l'arlequin* (1918) and ensured that his influence spread to Les *Six. Cocteau and Satie collaborated on the ballet *Parade* (1917), whose score is flatly anti-conventional in its discontinuous form, its repetitive material, and its inclusion in the orchestra of a typewriter, a revolver, and other unusual instruments. This was followed by the cantata *Socrate* (1919), which takes creative humility almost to its limits; but not quite, for the next year Satie provided an art exhibition with 'furniture music' which was designed to be ignored—the prototype of the muzak of today. Similarly his plan for the music to accompany René Clair's film entr'acte in the Dadaist ballet *Relâche* (1924) anticipates the methods of later film composers. Perhaps Satie's greatest achievement was to integrate music-hall and other well-known tunes and techniques into so-called serious music. Recent research has revealed that many of the popular tunes incorporated in his music, especially those sung by soldiers during World War I, were originally set to words of dubious moral tone, provoking intertextual frissons that again look forward to a later age.

PG/RN

📖 J. Cocteau, *Le Coq et l'arlequin* (Paris, 1918; Eng. trans. 1921) · N. Wilkins (ed.), *The Writings of Erik Satie* (London, 1980) · O. Volta (ed.), *Satie Seen through his Letters* (London, 1989, 2/1994) · R. Orledge, *Satie the Composer* (Cambridge, 1990, 2/1992) · S. M. Whiting, *Satie the Bohemian: From Cabaret to Concert Hall* (Oxford, 1999)

Satyagraha. Opera in three acts by Glass to a libretto by the composer and Constance DeJong after the *Bhagavad Gita* (Rotterdam, 1980).

Satz (Ger.). A term most commonly used to denote 'movement', for example of a sonata or symphony. It can also mean 'theme' or 'subject'; *Hauptsatz* (literally 'head-theme') is the main theme or first subject, *Seitensatz* or *Nebensatz* the second subject. *Satz* can also mean phrase or period, or structure, style, or texture; *freier Satz*, 'free style'. A *Schlusssatz* is a finale or a coda.

Sauer, Emil (George Conrad) von (*b* Hamburg, 8 Oct. 1862; *d* Vienna, 27 April 1942). German pianist. He studied in Moscow with Nikolay Rubinstein, then with Liszt. He toured extensively in a long career that lasted from 1882 until 1936; but he also taught at the Vienna Academy and edited music (the complete piano works of Brahms) and teaching manuals. He had a formidable technique and his playing was noted for its elegance and refinement.   CF

Sauguet, Henri [Poupard, Jean-Pierre] (*b* Bordeaux, 8 May 1901; *d* Paris, 21 June 1989). French composer. He studied with Canteloube and, after moving to Paris in 1922 (on the encouragement of Milhaud), with Koechlin. More important, however, was his association with Satie: he was a member of the École d'Arcueil, a group of Satie's disciples, and he accepted his master's aesthetic of unpretentiousness. Taking the name 'Henri Sauguet' he earned his living as a composer for the cinema, theatre, and radio; his incidental music for Jean Giraudoux's *Ondine* is among his finest achievements. His more serious works include ballets, notably *La Chatte* (1927) and *Les Forains* (1945), operas, and a variety of orchestral pieces, all marked by a simple charm.   PG/RLS

Saul. Oratorio (1739) by Handel to a text by Charles Jennens.

Saul og David. Opera in four acts by Nielsen to a libretto by Einar Christiansen (Copenhagen, 1902).

sautillé (Fr.; Ger.: *Springbogen*; It.: *saltando, saltato*). A short bowstroke played with the middle of the bow so that it bounces slightly. It is generated by a separate wrist movement for each note—unlike the *jeté* or *ricochet strokes, in which the bow, once set in motion, bounces naturally.   —/DMi

Sāvitri. Chamber opera in one act by Holst to his own libretto adapted from an incident in the *Mahābhārata* (London, 1916).

Savoy operas. Name by which the operas of Gilbert and Sullivan are known because from *Iolanthe* (1882) onwards they were first produced at the Savoy Theatre, London.

saw, musical [singing saw]. A carpenter's saw, sometimes specially made without teeth, held between the knees and played with a bow or hammer. Flexing the blade controls the pitch.   JMo

Sawer, David (Peter) (*b* Stockport, 14 Sept. 1961). English composer. His studies at York University and with Mauricio Kagel in Germany helped to strengthen his interest in music theatre, and he achieved particular success with a 50-minute work for radio, *Swansong* (1989), about the dying Berlioz and his vision of a musical Utopia. Sawer has also produced an accomplished group of instrumental works, including *The Melancholy of Departure* (1990) for piano, *Byrnan Wood* for orchestra (BBC Proms, 1992), and *Tiroirs* (1997) for chamber orchestra. His opera *From Morning to Midnight* (ENO, 2001) is based on a play by the Expressionist Georg Kaiser.   AW

Sax, Adolphe [Antoine-Joseph] (*b* Dinant, 6 Nov. 1814; *d* Paris, 4 Feb. 1894). Belgian wind instrument maker. Son of the leading maker of wind instruments in Brussels, Charles-Joseph Sax (1791–1865), with whom he worked, he studied the clarinet at the Brussels Conservatory and began making clarinets. He moved

to Paris in 1842 and set up a workshop (with Berlioz's help). In 1845 he patented the *saxhorn and the following year the *saxophone. From 1845 he enjoyed a virtual monopoly in French army bands, which aroused intense antagonism from rival Paris makers who banded together to contest his claims to originality and brought many lawsuits against him. He nevertheless continued to patent improvements to his instruments and to invent several more. From 1858 to 1871 he taught the saxophone at the Paris Conservatoire.   AB/AL

📖 M. Haine, *Adolphe Sax: Sa vie, son oeuvre, ses instruments de musique* (Brussels, 1980) · W. Horwood, *Adolphe Sax (1814–1894): His Life and Legacy* (Baldock, Herts., 1980–3)

saxhorn. A family of conical-bore, valved brass instruments invented by Adolphe Sax in 1842–5. They range from soprano to contrabass, pitched alternately in E♭ and B♭. All saxhorns have the upright 'tuba' shape. The E♭ *tenor horn and B♭ baritone form the middle range of the British *brass band. The scale of the bore is not so large as that of the *tuba family, and saxhorns tend not to have the fullness of sound of the tuba, though the distinction between the baritone horn and the similarly pitched but wider-bore *euphonium (tenor tuba) has become less pronounced in some parts of the world.   JMo

saxophone. A wind instrument combining a single-reed mouthpiece, similar to that of the *clarinet, with the key-covered brass tube of the *ophicleide. It was invented by Adolphe Sax about 1840, initially as a bass instrument but later as a complete family, from treble to bass, in alternating keys of E♭ and B♭ for military bands, and in F and C for orchestras. (The two last have never been greatly popular, the only one to be used with any frequency being the C tenor, also called the C melody, which can be used for cello parts and vocal lines without the need for transposition.)

Because of its wide conical bore the saxophone overblows at the octave, like the oboe, the fingering system being much simpler than that of the clarinet, which overblows 12ths and therefore needs different fingerings in each octave. The width of the bore and the large diameter of the tone holes gives it a strong, pure sound, invaluable to the military band and to the swing and dance big bands.

Saxophones have been little used orchestrally except in France, though it was partly the enthusiasm of Berlioz and his colleagues for the instrument that led them to persuade Sax to move from Brussels to Paris. Quartets and other chamber ensembles of saxophones have been popular, and most of the saxophone's 'classical' repertory has been written or arranged for such groups. In jazz the saxophone met some initial resistance, the clarinet being preferred at first, but the soprano, alto, tenor, and baritone have all been popular as solo instruments at different times and in different styles of popular music from New Orleans jazz to rock music. In jazz orchestras, as in swing and dance bands, the trio of two altos and a tenor (with, in larger bands, a second tenor and a baritone) have been the essential central block.

Of the other sizes, the sopranino and the B♭ bass are fairly common, with instruments smaller than the sopranino being very rare. The E♭ contrabass, its lowest note a semitone below that of the double bass, is built only to special order.   JMo

📖 R. INGHAM (ed.), *The Cambridge Companion to the Saxophone* (Cambridge, 1998)

Saxton, Robert (Louis Alfred) (*b* London, 8 Oct. 1953). English composer. After early advice from Britten he studied with Elisabeth Lutyens, Berio, Robin Holloway, and Robert Sherlaw Johnson. He has taught in Britain and the USA, and in 1999 succeeded Sherlaw Johnson as lecturer in composition at Oxford. *Reflections of Narciss and Goldmund* (1975) and *Piccola musica per Luigi Dallapiccola* (1981) were among his most striking early scores, demonstrating a refined ear for texture and skilful control of gradually unfolding, organic formal designs. During the 1980s and early 90s he wrote several substantial orchestral works (including a Concerto for Orchestra, 1984, and a Violin Concerto, 1989), various vocal works, and an opera, *Caritas* (Opera North, 1991). Since then he has worked on a smaller scale, although, as *A Yardstick to the Stars* (1994) for piano and string quartet demonstrates, there has been no loss of focus or creative energy.   AW

Saygun, A(hmed) **Adnan** (*b* Izmir, 7 Sept. 1907; *d* Istanbul, 6 Jan. 1991). Turkish composer and ethnomusicologist. As a young schoolteacher he was sent to study in Paris by President Atatürk. On his return he worked briefly as a conductor, and began research into Turkish traditional music; one of his field trips, to Anatolia, was with Bartók. Through his teaching in the conservatories of Ankara and Istanbul, Saygun exerted a considerable influence on Turkish musical life. His music, which fuses folk influences with west European techniques, includes an oratorio, *Yunus Emre* (1946), operas, symphonies and other orchestral works, and chamber, choral, and piano music.   ABur

saz. Persian and Turkish term for any musical instrument. It usually denotes the long-necked fretted lutes found in Turkey, the Caucasus, northern Iran, and surrounding areas. It is also found in the Muslim musical traditions of Bosnia-Hercegovina and Albania. It has a pear-shaped wooden body and several metal strings arranged in double or triple courses, and is

played with a plectrum. The number of strings and size of instrument varies according to region; in Azerbaijan there are various sizes—small (50–70 cm), medium (80–100 cm), and large (120–50 cm). The *saz* is used to accompany the traditional song and epic repertory of the Caucasian *ashug* (poet-musician), and may be played in ensembles of as many as 15 to 20 players, or in combination with other folk instruments.

The term *saz* has been applied to other types of musical instrument. In Iran and Afghanistan it is often used to refer to the *sorna*, a type of shawm that is always played with a drum (*dohol*).   LC

Scala di seta, La ('The Silken Ladder'). Opera in one act by Rossini to a libretto by Giuseppe Maria Foppa after F.-A.-E. de Planard's libretto for Pierre Gaveaux's *L'Échelle de soie* (1808) (Venice, 1812).

scala enigmatica. See SCALE, 7.

scale (Fr.: *gamme*; Ger.: *Tonleiter*; It.: *gamma, scala*). A scale is not a piece of music, but a theoretical or analytical construct. It consists of all the notes used or usable in the music of a particular period, culture, or repertory, arranged schematically in ascending or descending order of pitch. Some scales, such as the medieval *gamut, are complete in themselves; others, such as the chromatic scale of the piano, are sufficiently defined by a sequence of notes within a single *octave, which can be extended without limit in either direction by octave transposition. The basic function of scales is the definition and regulation of the pitches already used in performance or composition. Scales are also played as an exercise to improve performing technique and musical understanding. Some scales have been invented to offer a new medium of composition, though few of these have subsequently been accepted into standard musical language.

1. Origins; 2. Intervals in scales; 3. Diatonic scales; 4. Chromatic scales; 5. The whole-tone scale; 6. Pentatonic scales; 7. Invented scales

1. Origins

Probably the ultimate origin of *melody lies in speech inflections. The total number of available inflections is unlimited, and anyone may develop his or her own and maintain it as a personal characteristic; but in practice whole nations or regions adopt a particular type of inflection (e.g. when ending a statement or question) which may distinguish them from others. Similarly, in their music, whole groups of people have often adopted characteristic idioms and inflections, which in course of time took the form of favouring some pitches or pitch intervals and avoiding others. These could be imprecise as long as the music was limited to singing, with or without rhythmic accompaniment. But the construction of instruments that could play the same melodies often required the calculation of exact pitch intervals, arranged in the form of a scale. Many different scales are found in different cultures around the world. In Western music an additional element—*harmony—entered the equation about ten centuries ago, and influenced the choice and definition of the pitches that form the Western scale (see TEMPERAMENT).

2. Intervals in scales

The precise definition of notes used in music is expressed in terms of vibration frequency, and the pitch interval between two notes is defined by the ratio of the two frequencies (see ACOUSTICS, 4). The octave, 5th, and 4th were the first intervals to be thus categorized by early scientists such as Pythagoras (see MONOCHORD). Experimenting with vibrating strings, they found that a division of the string at the midpoint raised the pitch of each half to an octave above that of the full length, and they took this ratio of 2:1 as the most basic relationship in musical acoustics. A division at a point two thirds of the way along the string's length raised the pitch by a 5th, and at three quarters a 4th. Smaller intervals were derived on the same principles, so that the octave could eventually be marked out into tones and semitones which might be combined to form other intervals.

In comparing scales of different musical cultures it is unlikely that, for example, the equal-tempered major 3rd of the Western diatonic scale is exactly the same size as the interval conventionally notated as a major 3rd in a Chinese pentatonic scale, since the conventions in accordance with which non-Western music has traditionally been notated may not accurately represent the intervals concerned. (In modern ethnomusicological practice, however, more precise methods of recording and transcribing non-Western musics have been developed.)

Although there appears to be no one interval common to all scales, one or two are found in many. The octave is the most important of these—not surprisingly, as the acoustic relationship of the two notes of an octave is so close. In many different cultures men and women (or men and children) singing the same tune do so naturally at the interval of an octave without consciously choosing to do so. The perfect 5th and, to a lesser extent, the perfect 4th are also common to many scales.

3. Diatonic scales

The diatonic scale is a set of seven pitch intervals of unequal size, adding up to an octave, that can be repeated indefinitely in other octaves. One form of the diatonic scale is represented by the white notes of the piano keyboard, conventionally beginning and ending on a C: in this form, the seven intervals are of two sizes, the whole tone (or whole step) and the semitone (or half-step), as in Ex. 1a. The semitones, slurred in the example, are exactly half the size of a whole tone; but this precise relationship, called equal *temperament, is comparatively recent in origin. The diatonic scale on the white notes can be transposed to other pitches, using black notes as well, provided that the pattern of tones and semitones is unchanged.

The establishment of the diatonic scale as the basic scale of Western art music was a slow process closely linked to the development of the *mode. A mode is a subset of a scale (in this case the diatonic scale) that treats a particular pitch, and its octave transpositions, as the final or 'tonic'. Two modes, the Ionian (with its final on C) and the Aeolian (on A), have survived as the modern major and (natural) minor scales respectively (Ex. 1). However, the natural minor scale seen in Ex. 1b and transposed to two other pitch levels in Ex. 2 has not been much used in music of the last 300 years. The sixth and seventh degrees of the minor scale are unstable and result in two forms, neither of them diatonic: the harmonic minor, with the characteristic interval of an augmented 2nd (marked with a square bracket in Ex. 3a); and the melodic minor, in ascending form with sharpened sixth and seventh degrees avoiding the augmented 2nd and 'leading' to the tonic (Ex. 3b), and in descending form equivalent to the natural minor. All three forms have in common the flattened third scale degree, producing a characteristic minor 3rd with the keynote.

4. Chromatic scales

The chromatic scale consists of all 12 notes in an octave on the piano keyboard. Like the diatonic scale, it may begin on any degree. Ex. 4 shows an octave of the chromatic scale beginning on C, notated in sharps ascending and flats descending. The chromatic scale evolved with the rise of tonality. Melodically speaking, it is a diatonic scale with added 'chromatic' notes which are properly extraneous to the key but serve to 'colour' it. Harmonically, the added notes are needed to provide

Ex. 1

(a) Ionian/major   (b) Aeolian/minor

Ex. 2

(*a*) D minor

(*b*) F♯ minor

Ex. 3

(*a*) Harmonic minor

(*b*) Melodic minor

Ex. 4

(*a*) Chromatic scale: harmonic notation

(*b*) Chromatic scale: melodic notation

a major or minor *triad for each note of the diatonic scale.

There are many ways of notating the chromatic scale; in tonal music, the choice of G♯ or A♭ (for example) may be important for stringed instruments or the voice, where the two notes are not necessarily identical in pitch. On the piano there is no practical difference, and in the context of 12-note music, where there is no keynote and all 12 notes of the octave are considered equal, a single notation is usually selected for each black note and used consistently.

5. The whole-tone scale

This scale divides the octave into six equal steps, each a whole tone apart. In equal temperament, it exists in only two forms (Ex. 5). Its lack of semitones (particularly leading note to tonic) and of perfect 5ths, both basic materials of tonal music, gives it an impression of tonal vagueness, which made it particularly attractive to

Impressionists and other 20th-century composers seeking to avoid tonal centres and functional harmony. Debussy exploited the whole-tone scale in much of his music (*Pelléas et Mélisande*, *La Mer*, and several of the piano preludes) as a means of rebelling against the traditional tonal system of the 19th century.

6. Pentatonic scales

These scales divide the octave into five steps, and exist in several forms. They are sometimes misleadingly termed 'gapped' scales, by comparison with seven-note diatonic scales (which however are themselves 'gapped' in terms of microtonal scales; see below, 7). But a pentatonic scale is no less complete than any other scale, and the term 'gapped' is best avoided. The most familiar form is the tonal pentatonic, the order of its intervals corresponding (by coincidence) to that of the black notes of the piano keyboard (Ex. 6*a*). It can begin on any note (Ex. 6*b*). The pentatonic scale is the basic

Ex. 5. Whole-tone scale

(*a*)

(*b*)

Ex. 6 Pentatonic scales

(*a*)

(*a*)

scale of music in many non-Western cultures, notably China, Japan, and parts of Africa and Latin America, and it also is a feature of Amerindian music, some plainchant, and much European folk music, especially Scottish and Irish. The octave may be divided into numerous other pentatonic scales, with different arrangements of intervals (tones, semitones, 3rds, etc.); a great many are found in non-Western repertories, many of which use intervals that fall outside European musical traditions (e.g. the Javanese *slendro*, which divides the octave into five nearly equal intervals).

The pentatonic scale, like the whole-tone scale, has attracted some Western composers (Stravinsky, Bartók, Debussy) as a means of expressing *nationalism, echoing folk traditions, or creating special effects.

7. Invented scales

Microtonal scales, formed by the division of the octave into intervals of less than a semitone, have long been used in Eastern cultures (e.g. in Hindu ragas), and they have also been adopted by a number of Western composers (e.g. Alois Hába, Julián Carrillo, John Foulds, Harry Partch; see MICROTONE). Some composers, particularly Russians, have sought to develop new scales by combining elements of pre-existing ones. Skryabin, for example, derived an original six-note scale from the notes of his 'mystic chord'; Verdi used what he called a *scala enigmatica* in the Ave Maria of his *Quattro pezzi sacri*; and less familiar figures including Oscar Esplá and Nicolas Obouhow have also devised scales of their own.

See also OCTATONIC SCALE.   PS/JN/NT

scaling. 1. In organ pipes, the ratio of the diameter or width to the length. If a *rank of organ pipes were all of the same diameter, the tone would vary considerably from bass to treble. Pipes in each rank are therefore 'scaled', the diameter being adjusted according to the length. Different ranks have different scales for the same lengths in order to vary the sound.

2. In keyboard instruments the term refers to the sounding length of the strings in relation to their intended pitch.

Scandello, Antonio (*b* Bergamo, 17 Jan. 1517; *d* Dresden, 18 Jan. 1580). Italian composer and cornett and sackbut player. A renowned performer, in 1549 he joined the Dresden Hofkapelle; some years later he converted to Protestantism, and in 1568 he succeeded Matthaeus Le Maistre as Kapellmeister. He is noted for his *St John Passion* (1561), the first responsorial setting in German to adopt polyphony for the individual character utterances, and for his similarly scored *Resurrection History* (before 1573), which provided the model for Schütz's setting of 1623.   BS

Scaramouche. Suite for two pianos (1937) by Milhaud; it is based on the incidental music he wrote for Molière's *Le Médecin volant* ('The Flying Doctor') for a production at the Théâtre Scaramouche, hence its title.

Scarlatti. Italian family of composers and musicians. All that is known of the early life and training of (Pietro) **Alessandro** (Gasparo) **Scarlatti** (*b* Palermo, 2 May 1660; *d* Naples, 22 Oct. 1725) is that at the age of 12 he was sent to live with relatives in Rome. His first opera, produced in 1679, was exceptionally successful, and by 1680 he had been appointed *maestro di cappella* to Queen Christina of Sweden, who had been long resident in Rome and was an enthusiastic patron of the arts; he was also *maestro* at S. Gerolamo della Carità. He visited Austria in 1681 and moved to Naples as *maestro* to the viceroy in 1684. Naples was not at that time a major centre of operatic activity, and more than half the operas performed there between 1684 and 1702 were by Scarlatti. In the latter year he went to Florence, but failing to find a salaried post there soon moved on to Rome, becoming assistant *maestro* at S. Maria Maggiore in 1703 (and being promoted to *maestro* three years later), and composing oratorios and cantatas for noble patrons, including Cardinal Ottoboni. There was little demand for opera in Rome, and two works composed for Venice were failures, resulting only in the publication of a vicious satirical poem about him. In 1708 financial difficulties caused him to accept an invitation to return to his old post in Naples, where he remained for the rest of his life except for another spell in Rome during 1718–21.

Scarlatti's music was highly regarded by his contemporaries, though by the end of his life younger musicians seem to have thought of him as a rather old-fashioned 'grand old man'. His surviving output includes more than 70 operas and 600 cantatas, which are his most important works. His operas are notable for the melodic gift and variety of style and expression displayed in the arias, and for their use of an orchestra including woodwind and brass as well as strings. He also instituted the three-movement sinfonia as the standard operatic overture. He was one of the last major composers of solo cantatas: these works—mostly for soprano and strings, and following the standard pattern (which he established) of two arias each preceded by a recitative—are among the finest of the period. There is no evidence to support the assertion that he was an important and influential teacher.

(Giuseppe) **Domenico Scarlatti** (*b* Naples, 26 Oct. 1685; *d* Madrid, 23 July 1757) was the son of Alessandro Scarlatti, who attempted to exercise strict control of his life and career long after he had reached adulthood. Nothing is known of his early life and training, but in

1701 he was appointed organist to the royal chapel in Naples, where his father was *maestro*. The following year he accompanied Alessandro to Florence, where he may have met the great keyboard-instrument maker Bartolomeo Cristofori, but soon returned to Naples instead of going on with his father to Rome. In 1705 Alessandro, feeling that Naples had nothing to offer so talented a musician, dispatched him to Venice, but no details have come to light of his activities during his four years there. In 1709, apparently in defiance of his father's wishes, Domenico entered the service of the exiled Polish Queen Maria Casimira in Rome; he was also appointed *maestro di cappella* at the Basilica Giulia in 1713 and to the Portuguese ambassador at the Vatican the following year. During this period in Rome he frequented the weekly concerts given by Cardinal Ottoboni, where he met such leading figures as Corelli and Handel (allegedly taking part in a keyboard-playing contest with the latter), and forged a long-lasting friendship with the English musician Thomas Roseingrave, who did much to popularize his music in Britain.

In 1717 Scarlatti was obliged to take legal action to establish his independence from his father. Two years later he left Italy for Portugal, where he became *mestre* of the patriarchal chapel. His duties included teaching the Infanta Maria Barbara, who was clearly a talented keyboard player; when she moved to Madrid on her marriage to the Spanish Crown Prince Fernando in 1728 Scarlatti went with her as part of her musical retinue. He spent the rest of his life in her service, being created a Knight of the Order of Santiago in 1738. (Reports of visits he is supposed to have made to Austria, France, and England refer to other musicians of the same name, possibly relatives.)

Although he began his career as a Neapolitan opera composer, Scarlatti's posthumous reputation has rested almost entirely on his output of more than 500 keyboard sonatas, all composed after his move to Portugal. These are single-movement works in binary form, some grouped in pairs. They are highly individual and innovatory, not only in their technical requirements—which include such elements as hand-crossing, octaves in both hands simultaneously, and trills in inner parts—but in their bold approach to harmony and modulation. Many of them show the influence of Andalusian folk music and characteristic Spanish guitar techniques, and they had considerable influence on the development of idiomatic keyboard writing, especially in England, where they achieved early popularity.

Giuseppe Scarlatti (*b* Naples, *c.*1718 or 18 June 1723; *d* Vienna, 17 Aug. 1777), a nephew of Domenico Scarlatti, pursued the career of an opera composer from 1739 in various Italian cities including Rome, Florence, and Venice; he may have visited his uncle in Spain in 1752, when an opera of his was performed in Barcelona. From 1757 he lived mainly in Vienna, where Gluck befriended him, as ballet composer to the Kärntnertortheater, and later probably in the service of Prince Schwarzenberg. His operas, which show a gift for writing simple and attractive melody, were among the better ones composed by Italians in Vienna at that time.   WT/ER

📖 R. KIRKPATRICK, *Domenico Scarlatti* (Princeton, NJ, 1953, 3/1968) · D. J. GROUT, *Alessandro Scarlatti: An Introduction to his Operas* (Berkeley, CA, 1979) · M. BOYD, *Domenico Scarlatti, Master of Music* (London, 1986)

scat singing. In jazz, the articulation of melody by means of nonsense syllables and other vocal effects, introduced by Louis Armstrong and others. The Swingle Singers use the technique for vocal performances of instrumental music.   PGA

Scelsi, Giacinto (*b* La Spezia, 8 Jan. 1905; *d* Rome, 9 Aug. 1988). Italian composer. A member of an aristocratic family, he was privately educated; between the wars he studied in Switzerland and Vienna. From 1951 he lived reclusively in Rome. His later works were influenced by Eastern, especially Tibetan, music and thought, and are remarkable for their concentration on the elements of music at an almost microscopic level, giving them the quality of transcendental meditation. His Four Pieces for orchestra (1961) are each based on a single note, focusing attention on the treatment of rhythm, dynamics, attack, and colour, and on microtonal inflections of pitch. Many of his works are written in a single line—for example, most of the vocal cycle *Canti del Capricorno* (1962–72). But in others, for example the String Quartet no. 4 (1964), static or very slow-moving clouds of texture are created through microtonal harmonies, glissandos, and trills. Scelsi's music was widely performed in his last years, and was an important influence on composers including Ligeti and Franco Donatoni.   ABUR

scena (It.). In opera, an extended episode consisting of a loosely constructed sequence of related sections (e.g. introduction, recitative, arioso, one or more arias), often for a solo singer and principally dramatic in intent. In the 18th and 19th centuries the title was given to specially composed dramatic episodes intended for concert performance by a solo singer, rather in the style of a cantata. These were normally settings either of an extract from an opera libretto or of some other dramatic text; examples include Beethoven's *Ah, perfido!*

scenario. An outline libretto of a play or opera, which indicates the characters, the number of scenes, the places where the chief dramatic and musical climaxes will occur, and so on.

Scenes from Childhood. See KINDERSZENEN.

Scenes from Goethe's 'Faust'. See 'FAUST', SCENES FROM GOETHE'S.

Schaeffer, Bogusław (*b* Lwów [now L'viv, Ukraine], 6 June 1929). Polish composer, theorist, and teacher. He has been at the forefront of avant-garde experiment in Polish music, both as an author of books on contemporary compositional techniques and as a composer breaking new boundaries in the areas of notation, performance practice (especially improvisation), and the dividing line between music theatre and straight drama. He is a prolific composer with over 400 works that cover all genres, including electroacoustic music. Typical of his demanding, eclectic, and iconoclastic spirit is the single-page *Non-stop* for piano (1960), which may last from six minutes to eight hours in performance. Later scores are often more relaxed through their prominent use of light music or free jazz idioms.   ATh

📖 K. SZWAJGIER, *Bogusław Schaeffer: 50 Jahre Schaffen* (Salzburg, 1994)

Schaeffer, Pierre (*b* Nancy, 14 Aug. 1910; *d* Paris, 19 Aug. 1995). French composer and writer. Trained as a scientist, he was a pioneer of *musique concrète, composition on tape using not just musical sounds but any sound source, natural or mechanical. He formed a group for research into the subject in Paris in 1942, broadcast the first results in 1948, and in 1950 collaborated with Pierre Henry on *Symphonie pour un homme seul*. Later, though he taught electronic composition at the Paris Conservatoire from 1968, he gave up composing to write theoretical works and novels.   ABur

Schafe können sicher weiden. See SHEEP MAY SAFELY GRAZE.

Schafer, R(aymond) Murray (*b* Sarnia, ON, 18 July 1933). Canadian composer. He studied composition with John Weinzweig at the Royal Conservatory in Toronto (1945–55) and then moved to Europe, where he worked as a journalist. In 1961 he returned to Canada, and in 1965 he was appointed resident in music at Simon Fraser University, British Columbia. His varied output, including large-scale dramatic works, orchestral pieces, and choral music, reveals deep concerns with the languages and mythologies of ancient peoples. He has also been influential as a campaigner against noise pollution and as an originator of new ideas in music education. His writings include *The Composer in the Classroom* (Toronto, 1965), *Ear Cleaning* (Toronto, 1967), *The New Soundscape* (Toronto, 1969), *When Words Sing* (Toronto, 1970), *The Book of Noise* (Van-

couver, 1970, 2/1973), and *The Tuning of the World* (New York, 1977), as well as studies of the music of Ezra Pound and E. T. A. Hoffmann.   PG

📖 S. ADAMS, *R. Murray Schafer* (Toronto, 1983)

schalkhaft (Ger.). 'Roguish'.

Schall (Ger.). 'Sound'.

scharf (Ger.). 'Sharply'; e.g. *scharf betont*, 'sharply accented'.

Scharwenka, (Franz) Xaver (*b* Samter [now Szamotuły], 6 Jan. 1850; *d* Berlin, 8 Dec. 1924). Polish-German pianist, teacher, and composer. He was taught by Kullak in Berlin, where he made his debut in 1869. In 1874 he embarked on the many tours that took him across Europe and frequently to North America. He gave the first performance of his most successful work, the B♭ minor Piano Concerto, in 1877. In 1888 he opened his own conservatory in Berlin, adding a New York branch in 1891. His many piano compositions reflect his energetic, flamboyant virtuosity. His brother (Ludwig) **Philipp Scharwenka** (*b* Samter, 16 Feb. 1847; *d* Bad Neuheim, 16 July 1917) was also a composer, teacher, and virtuoso pianist.   JW

Schauspieldirektor, Der ('The Impresario'). Opera in one act by Mozart to a libretto by Gottlieb Stephanie the younger (Schönbrunn, 1786).

Schéhérazade. See SHEHERAZADE.

Scheidemann, Heinrich (*b* Wöhrden, nr Hamburg, *c*.1596; *d* Hamburg, 1663). German organist and composer. He was the son of an organist who sent him to study for three years with Sweelinck in Amsterdam. He took his father's post at the Catharinenkirche, Hamburg, *c*.1625, and was much sought after as an adviser on organ-building.

Scheidemann was an important and influential composer of organ music. His best works are the chorale arrangements, in which the tune is treated in a variety of ways—simply as a cantus firmus, as a subject for harmonization and embellishment, or occasionally as the basis for a lengthy fantasia. His idiomatic writing for the Baroque organ was widely emulated by younger composers, for example his pupil Reincken.   DA

Scheidt, Samuel (*b* Halle, *bapt.* 3 Nov. 1587; *d* Halle, 24 March 1654). German composer. He served Halle as court organist, Kapellmeister, and, in 1627–30, *director musices*. At an early age (possibly when only 16) he became organist at the Moritzkirche, and some five years later went to Amsterdam to study with Sweelinck. In 1618 he joined Schütz and Michael Praetorius at Magdeburg for the introduction of a modernized

musical repertory at the cathedral; and in the following year, with the same colleagues and Johann Staden,
he visited Bayreuth to dedicate a new organ at the
Stadtkirche. In 1625 an incursion by imperialist troops
badly affected the work of the court chapel, and for
some time thereafter Scheidt's scope for the publication and performance of his music was severely restricted.

He is chiefly renowned for his three-volume
Tabulatura nova (Hamburg, 1624), a collection of
keyboard (mainly organ) pieces comprising, in the first
two volumes, canons, fantasias, fugues, and variations
and, in the third, settings based on plainchant for use at
Mass and Vespers in 'high' Lutheran worship. The
'newness' of the collection lay in its adoption, in
preference to the organ tablature more usual in Germany at the time, of the Italian *partitura* system, in
which each part is laid out (tabulated) on a separate
staff for greater clarity. His only other work for organ
solo, the *Görlitzer Tablaturbuch* (c.1653), comprising 100
'sacred songs and psalms', was probably intended either
for *alternatim* performance between hymn verses sung
by the choir or congregation, or simply for accompanying congregational singing. As a rule the chorale
melodies are placed unadorned in the topmost line,
while the supporting parts are enriched by contrapuntal
detail.

With his sacred vocal music, Scheidt contributed
profusely (though more conservatively than Schütz and
Schein) to the Italian-influenced repertory which
prevailed in Lutheran Germany during the early Baroque period. His principal volumes contain polychoral
motets (*Cantiones sacrae*, 1620), grand Venetian-style
settings for solo voices, chorus, and instruments
(*Concertus sacri*, 1622), and small-scale concertato settings, for two to six voices and continuo (the four-
volume *Neue geistliche Concerte*, 1631–40). Some of the
works in this last category deal with biblical themes of a
quasi-dramatic nature, such as the four-voice Easter
dialogue *Es gingen drei heiligen Frauen* ('There went
three holy women'); but most are multi-sectional
chorale settings, with variations in scoring, texture, and
vocal layout between successive stanzas, a design which
points forward to the chorale cantata of later times. In
the preface to the second volume of the *Concerte* the
composer observes that several of them were at first
scored for much larger forces, and were subsequently
curtailed as a result of wartime pressures. However, in
1644 or 1645 he published a set of 70 *Symphonien auff
Concerten-Manier* for strings, probably to be used
(where the keys matched) as preludes to his vocal works,
and so reclaim part of their original richness.   BS

📖 F. BLUME, *Protestant Church Music: A History* (Eng.
trans., London, 1974)

Schein, Johann Hermann (*b* Grünhaim, nr Annaberg,
20 Jan. 1586; *d* Leipzig, 19 Nov. 1630). German composer. With his contemporaries Schütz and Scheidt, he
played a major role in introducing into Germany the
new Italian techniques of Monteverdi's *seconda pratica*—
in particular, those providing for the free treatment of
dissonance and melodic leaps, and the use of solo voices
and obbligato instruments, with continuo support, to
enhance textual interpretation. Despite ill health and
personal tragedy (the early death of his first wife and
the death in infancy of seven of the nine children of
his two marriages), Schein's life was a richly productive one. After school years at Schulpforta, he studied
law at Leipzig University, and subsequently taught
music privately at Weissenfels, where he first met
Schütz and probably Scheidt also. In 1615 he was appointed Kapellmeister to the ducal court at Weimar,
but after only 15 months was elected Kantor at St
Thomas's, Leipzig, a post (later held by Kuhnau and
Bach) which he occupied until his early death at the age
of 44.

Instrumental music represents only a small proportion of Schein's output, but special importance attaches
to his *Banchetto musicale* (Leipzig, 1617), in which 20
sets of dances for an ensemble of viols are arranged—
possibly for the first time in musical history—as unified
suites, interrelated by common thematic ideas. His
sacred vocal works display the variety of styles typical of
the period: traditional polyphony (in five to 12 parts) in
his *Cymbalum Sionium* (1615); five-voice sacred madrigals with continuo, mainly on Old Testament texts, in
his *Fontana d'Israel* or *Israelis Brünnlein* (Leipzig, 1623);
and concertato settings of chorale and Bible texts, 'in
the Italian manner customary nowadays', in his *Opella
nova* (two volumes, Leipzig, 1618, 1626). The latter set
includes a vivid portrayal of the Annunciation scene,
Maria, gegrüsset seist du, Holdselige, during which sinfonias for four trombones and organ provide an impressive backdrop to the timid utterances of the Virgin
(a soprano) and the momentous ones of the angel
Gabriel (a tenor).

A poet-composer comparable to the English lutenist
Thomas Campion, Schein provided his own German
texts, in the pastoral style of the period, for his largest
secular collections: the *Diletti pastorali* or *Hirten-lust*
(Leipzig, 1624), usually accepted as the first published
set of German continuo madrigals, and the *Musica
boscareccia* (in three volumes, Leipzig 1621, 1626, 1628), a
group of charming German villanellas in praise of love
and comradeship, set for three solo voices (SSB) but
with many scoring options, ranging from an ensemble
('Corpus') with instruments to a single voice and continuo. Prominent among his last works is his *Cantional,
oder Gesangbuch* (Leipzig, 1627), an extensive chorale

collection which was later to enjoy continuing favour in Lutheran worship.												BS

   📖 D. PAISEY, 'Some occasional aspects of Johann Hermann Schein', *British Library Journal*, 1 (1975), 171 · B. SMALLMAN, 'Johann Hermann Schein as poet and composer', *Slavonic and Western Music: Essays for Gerald Abraham*, ed. M. H. Brown and R. J. Wiley (Ann Arbor, MI, 1985), 33–48

Schelle, Johann (*b* Geising, Thuringia, *bapt.* 6 Sept. 1648; *d* Leipzig, 10 March 1701). German composer. After singing as a boy in the Dresden court chapel, he became Kantor first at the small town of Eilenburg and then, in 1677, at the Thomasschule in Leipzig. He composed some interesting concertato pieces, precursors of Bach's cantatas, based on hymn tunes.												DA

Schenk, Johann Baptist (*b* Wiener Neustadt, 30 Nov. 1753; *d* Vienna, 29 Dec. 1836). Austrian composer. He studied in Vienna with Wagenseil. He wrote many works for Viennese theatres, having his greatest success in 1796 with *Der Dorfbarbier* ('The Village Barber'). Witty and cleverly composed, it has a melodic verve and sense of characterization that give it more distinction than many other pieces in similar vein; it also shows an interest in developing linked scenes. It remained popular for a quarter of a century, and is still occasionally revived. With this and other works, Schenk made a distinctive contribution to the development of Viennese *Singspiel*.												JW

Scherchen, Hermann (*b* Berlin, 21 June 1891; *d* Florence, 12 June 1966). German conductor. He played the viola in the Berlin Philharmonic Orchestra, taught himself score-reading and conducting, and assisted Schoenberg with the premiere of *Pierrot lunaire* in 1911. Shortly afterwards he made his conducting debut with that work. In 1914 he became conductor of the Riga Orchestra. Five years later he founded the Neue Musikgesellschaft and the left-wing journal *Melos*. In 1922 he took over the Frankfurt Museum Concerts from Furtwängler and became director of the Winterthur Musikkollegium, with which he gave the premiere of Webern's Variations for orchestra op. 30 in 1943. Opposing the Nazis, he moved to Switzerland in 1933 and became conductor of the Zürich Radio Orchestra. After the war he gave first performances of major works by Dallapiccola, Dessau, and Henze and in 1954 he created the Studio for Electro-Acoustic Research in Gravesano.												JT

scherzando, scherzante, scherzevole, scherzevolmente (It.). 'Jokingly', 'playfully'.

scherzetto [scherzino] (It.). A short *scherzo.

Scherzi, Gli. See 'RUSSIAN' QUARTETS.

scherzo (It., 'joke', 'game'). A quick, light movement or piece, often in triple time. Like the *minuet, which it replaced in the late 18th century as the traditional third movement of such large-scale forms as the symphony and string quartet, it is generally in ternary form, with a contrasting middle section, or trio (see TRIO, 2). The term was first applied, in the 17th century, to vocal music, as in Monteverdi's *Scherzi musicali* (1607 and 1632). From the later Baroque period, however, it was used mainly for instrumental music; there are examples, usually in duple metre and without any trio, by Bach (Partita in A minor) and Haydn (last movement of his Piano Sonata Hob. XVI: 9).

   Haydn was the first composer to use a movement marked 'Scherzo' instead of a minuet, in his string quartets (the op. 33 set of 1781 are known as 'Gli scherzi' for that reason), but it was Beethoven who firmly established the scherzo as a genuine alternative to the minuet: all his symphonies except the First and the Eighth have scherzos rather than minuets. They are almost always very fast and often incorporate rhythmic effects (e.g. cross-rhythms), frequently investing the movement with a rough, almost savage, humour. Schumann, Schubert, and Brahms followed Beethoven's example in their symphonies, whereas the scherzos of Mendelssohn (e.g. in the Octet, the incidental music to *A Midsummer Night's Dream*, the string quartets) and Berlioz ('Queen Mab' Scherzo from *Roméo et Juliette*) are delicate and almost ethereal in orchestration and tone. Some late 19th-century composers (e.g. Dvořák and Tchaikovsky) used such national dance forms as the *furiant or *dumka in their scherzos, while some of Mahler's draw on Austrian dances and otherwise grotesque elements.

   Chopin's four piano scherzos are all in quick triple time. Examples of independent orchestral scherzos include Saint-Saëns's tone-poem *Danse macabre*, Dukas's *L'Apprenti sorcier*, and Stravinsky's *Scherzo fantastique*.												WT

scherzoso, scherzosamente (It.). 'Playful', 'playfully'.

Schicksalslied ('Song of Destiny'). Choral work, op. 54 (1868–71), by Brahms, a setting of a poem by Hölderlin.

Schillinger, Joseph (Moiseievich) (*b* Kharkiv, 19/31 Aug. 1895; *d* New York, 23 March 1943). Ukrainian-born American teacher and composer. He studied at the Petrograd (St Petersburg) Conservatory (1914–18) and was active in Ukraine as a teacher, conductor, and composer (*October* for piano and orchestra, 1927). In 1928 he moved to the USA, where he taught his own system of composition, on which he wrote books, including *The Schillinger System of Musical Composition* (New York, 2 vols., 1941, 1946) and *The Mathematical Basis of the Arts* (New York, 1948). His pupils included George Gershwin and Earle Brown. PG

Schillings, Max von (*b* Düren, 19 April 1868; *d* Berlin, 24 July 1933). German composer and conductor. He studied in Bonn and Munich and worked at Bayreuth as a stage conductor (from 1892) and chorus master (from 1902). He was primarily a dramatic composer, his early operas *Ingwelde* (1894), *Der Pfeifertag* ('The Day of the Piper', 1899), and *Moloch* (1906) being essentially Wagnerian derivatives. *Mona Lisa* (1915), his most successful stage work, shows the influence of Puccini and combines elements of German post-Romanticism with elements of Italian verismo to powerful effect. Assistant to the Intendant at Stuttgart (1908–18), he was subsequently appointed Intendant at the Berlin Staatsoper (from 1919) and president of the Prussian Academy of Arts (from 1932), where he oversaw the dismissal of Schoenberg and Schreker. His decision to concentrate on conducting and administration in the later part of his career led to a decline in the quantity of his output. Intensely conservative during the years of the Weimar Republic, he was admired by the Nazis. Shortly before his death, he was authorized by Hitler to reorganize German musical life. TA

📖 C. M. GRUBER, 'Max von Schillings, an almost forgotten composer', *Opera*, 34 (1983), 963–8

Schirmer, E. C. American firm of music publishers. It was founded in Boston in 1921 by Ernest Charles Schirmer (1865–1958) and is not to be confused with G. *Schirmer.

Schirmer, G. American firm of music publishers. Gustav Schirmer (1829–93) emigrated from Germany to New York in 1837 and in 1854 became manager (in 1866 owner) of the Kerksieg & Bruesing Company, which he renamed G. Schirmer. A printing and engraving plant was established in 1901 and a national network of affiliated companies built up, among them Associated Music Publishers. The Schirmer Library of Musical Classics (inaugurated 1891) is perhaps the best-known section of a catalogue that also includes opera librettos, a wide range of vocal and instrumental works, and the music of many leading American composers (among them Barber, Menotti, Carter, Corigliano, Adams, Harbison, and Tan Dun). In 1915 Schirmer began publishing *The Musical Quarterly*, a leading musicological journal. As part of the Music Sales Group since 1986, Schirmer sub-publishes the catalogues of Chester Music, Edition Wilhelm Hansen, Novello, and Union

Musical Española and is the American publisher for leading Russian composers. HA

Schlag (Ger.). 1. 'Stroke', 'blow'.
2. 'Beat' (in the sense of 'three beats to the bar' etc.); see BEAT, 1.

Schlägel (Ger.). 'Beater'.

Schleifer (Ger.). See SLIDE, 2.

schleppen (Ger.). 'To drag'; *nicht schleppend*, 'do not drag'.

Schlick, Arnolt (*b* ?Heidelberg, *c*.1460; *d* ?Heidelberg, after 1521). German organist and composer. Blind for most or all of his life, he travelled widely in Germany and the Low Countries as a virtuoso performer and an adviser on organs; in his own words, he played 'in front of emperors, kings, electors, princes, and other spiritual and temporal lords'. His *Spiegel der Orgelmacher und Organisten* (Speyer, 1511) is an important source of information about contemporary organ-building. He also published compositions for organ. JM

Schlummerlied (Ger., 'slumber song'). A lullaby or *berceuse.

Schluss (Ger.). 1. 'End', 'conclusion'; *Schlusssatz*, 'last movement', 'coda'; *Schlusszeichen*, the signal to end a piece, i.e. a double bar.
2. 'Cadence'.

Schlüssel (Ger.). 'Clef'.

schmachtend (Ger.). 'Languishing'.

schmeichelnd (Ger.). 'Coaxing', 'flattering'.

Schmelzer, Johann Heinrich (*b* Scheibbs, *c*.1623; *d* Prague, 1680). Austrian violinist and composer. He served the Habsburg court in Vienna from 1665, as an official composer of dance music, and in Prague, where the court had moved in 1679, as Kapellmeister. He died in the following year, a victim of the plague. He is known for his chamber works, mainly trio sonatas with two violins (or violin and viola) and continuo, but also six *Sonatae unarum fidium* (1664), the earliest published set for solo violin and continuo before Biber's solo violin sonatas of 1681. His immense output also includes *sepolcri* (short Passion oratorios) and some 200 other sacred works. DA/BS

schmerzlich (Ger.). 'Painful', 'sorrowful'.

schmetternd (Ger.). 'Blaring', especially in horn playing.

Schmidt, Franz (*b* Pressburg [now Bratislava], 22 Dec. 1874; *d* Perchtoldsdorf, nr Vienna, 11 Feb. 1939).

Austrian composer, teacher, cellist, and pianist. After early piano lessons in Pressburg, he studied privately with Leschetizky in Vienna and from 1890 with Bruckner, Fuchs, and Hellmesberger at the Vienna Conservatory. He played the cello in the Court Opera Orchestra (1896–1911) and taught it at the Gesellschaft der Musikfreunde (1901–8). Also active as a concert pianist, he taught the piano (from 1914) and composition (from 1922) at the Vienna Staatsakademie, becoming its director in 1925; he was director of the Musikhochschule (1927–31).

Though Schmidt's career was primarily focused on teaching and administration, he found the time to compose, producing two operas, an apocalyptic oratorio *Das Buch der sieben Siegeln* ('The Book with Seven Seals', 1938), a considerable amount of chamber music, and works for piano and organ, as well as the orchestral music that brought him to public notice. Apart from his four symphonies, his *Variations on a Theme of Beethoven* and Piano Concerto (1934), both for piano left hand and orchestra and written for Paul Wittgenstein, are well known. With its masterly variation technique and rich Romantic style his orchestral music owes something to Brahms, Reger, and above all Bruckner, yet its roots are firmly anchored in Classical traditions. Schmidt's first opera, *Notre Dame* (1914, after Victor Hugo), which draws elements of the music of Bruckner and Bach into a theatrical context, remains in the Austrian repertory. Schmidt was awarded the Beethoven Prize by the Prussian Academy in Berlin, an indication of the high regard in which his contemporaries held him.   JN/TA

📖 N. Tschulik, *Franz Schmidt: A Critical Biography* (London, 1980) · H. Truscott, *The Music of Franz Schmidt* (London, 1984) · T. B. Corfield, *Franz Schmidt, 1874–1939: A Discussion of his Style* (New York, 1989)

Schmieder. Abbreviation (sometimes further shortened to s) for Schmieder-Verzeichnis, used as a prefix to the numbers of J. S. Bach's works in the standard *thematic catalogue of Wolfgang Schmieder; *bwv is now more widely used.

Schmitt, Florent (*b* Blâmont, Meurthe-et-Moselle, 28 Sept. 1870; *d* Neuilly-sur-Seine, 17 Aug. 1958). French composer. He studied with Massenet, Fauré, and others at the Paris Conservatoire from 1889 to 1900, in which year he won the Prix de Rome. During the next decade he produced many of his most important works, including a bold setting of Psalm 47 for soprano, chorus, orchestra, and organ (1904), a massive Piano Quintet (1902–8), and the ballet *La Tragédie de Salomé* (1907), whose pounding rhythms foreshadow to some degree *The Rite of Spring*. Schmitt was a master of brilliant orchestration. In later years he continued to compose

prolifically, producing a large amount of piano music much of which he orchestrated, while also working as a pianist and music critic.   PG/RLS

Schnabel, Artur (*b* Lipník, 17 April 1882; *d* Axenstein, 15 Aug. 1951). Austrian-born American pianist. A pupil of Leschetizky, he made his debut in 1890—already a profoundly thoughtful musician. Until 1933 he lived in Berlin, partnering such artists as Flesch, Casals, Emanuel Feuermann, Hindemith, Szigeti, Fournier, and Primrose. During this time he developed and recorded his renowned readings of Beethoven's piano works and also taught at the Berlin Academy. It was the translucent clarity he brought to Beethoven, the lyricism to Schubert, and the measured depth to Mozart that defined his stature as a visionary and creative virtuoso of the old school. He took American citizenship in 1944.   CF

📖 C. Saerchinger, *Artur Schnabel* (London, 1957) · A. Schnabel, *My Life and Music* (London, 1961) · K. Wolff, *The Teaching of Artur Schnabel* (London, 1972) · J. Hunt, *Giants of the Keyboard* (London, 1994)

Schneider, Friedrich (*b* Alt-Waltersdorf, nr Zittau, 3 Jan. 1786; *d* Dessau, 23 Nov. 1853). German composer and teacher. After studies at the University of Leipzig he was appointed to a number of posts in the city, including organist of the Thomaskirche (1812), conductor of the Singakademie (1816), and musical director of the city theatre (1817). It is thought that his performance of Beethoven's Piano Concerto no. 5 in 1811 was the work's premiere. He directed over 80 German music festivals, 1820–51, and belonged to many musical societies. His large output includes the popular oratorio *Das Weltgericht* (1820) and many other vocal and instrumental works.   SH

schnell, schneller (Ger.). 'Quick', 'quicker'.

Schneller (Ger.). The inverted *mordent.

Schnittke, Alfred (Garriyevich) (*b* Engel's, 24 Nov. 1934; *d* Hamburg, 3 Aug. 1998). Russian composer. Born a Russian citizen into a German-Jewish family, he acknowledged all three strands of his cultural heritage in his music. From 1946 to 1948 his family lived in Vienna, where he took his first music lessons, an induction into the great Austro-German musical tradition. In 1953 he entered the Moscow Conservatory, where he studied composition with Yevgeny Golubev; during his student days Shostakovich and Mahler were his chief influences. During the Khrushchev thaw, however, the scores of Schoenberg and Stravinsky became available, and Schnittke made a careful study of serial technique. Although his graduation work was a rather traditional monumental oratorio, *Nagasaki* (1958), it was nevertheless criticized as too modernist by the Union of Composers.

Schnittke could still have retrenched to become an officially sanctioned Soviet composer, but his pivotal meeting with Nono in 1963 and his ensuing study of the Western avant-garde led him to turn his back on any prospects of a secure career. While seeking his own musical idiom in a series of chamber works during the 1960s, he earned a living as a composer of film music. Because of the fluency in many styles required for film scores, he changed his approach to 'serious' composition, as he explained in his essay 'Polystylistic Tendencies in Modern Music' (1971). His advocacy of 'polystylism' was soon demonstrated in a major work, his First Symphony (1972), which includes pastiches of Bach and of Soviet march music and quotations from Beethoven, Chopin, and Grieg, and also calls for jazz improvisation in one section and collective free improvisation in another, all set in a musical environment of tense drama. Official uncertainty over the boundaries of permissible musical practices led first to the sanctioning of rehearsals for a planned Moscow premiere, which was cancelled at the last moment and transferred (with a considerable loss of prestige) to Gor'kiy (now Nizhniy Novgorod).

In spite of such handicaps Schnittke's fame gradually spread, and from the early 1980s his name became established in the West. His polystylism was never reduced to a formula: the Concerto Grosso no. 1 (1977), in which dense serialist textures are mixed with the B–A–C–H motif and a heady tango tune, is much less diffuse and theatrical than the First Symphony. The Piano Quintet (1976) differed from both these in blending the quoted or pastiche music seamlessly into the musical structure. Some of his works are imbued with a strong sense of history, for example his Third Symphony (1981), which evokes the German symphonic tradition, from Bach to Kagel, placing the author himself at the end. The religious Fourth Symphony (1984) synchretizes Gregorian and Orthodox chants, Lutheran chorales, and Jewish cantillation.

In 1985 Schnittke suffered a stroke, but his productivity continued unabated: he completed several important stage works, among them the ballet *Peer Gynt* (1986) and the operas *Zhizn's idiotom* ('Life with an Idiot', 1992), *Gesualdo* (1995), and *Historia von D. Johann Fausten* (1995), all of which were first performed outside Russia. Works of this period are especially tense, reflecting the composer's struggle with death and his Christian outlook. His second stroke, in 1998, was fatal.   JWAL

📖 A. IVASHKIN, *Alfred Schnittke* (London, 1996)

Schobert, Johann (*b* ?Silesia, *c*.1735; *d* Paris, 28 Aug. 1767). Silesian composer and harpsichordist. In the early 1760s he settled in Paris, where he worked for the Prince of Conti, and became a celebrated keyboard player. His early death was caused by eating poisonous mushrooms. He was a respected and much-liked figure whose imaginative compositions were influential on contemporary musical life. Mozart particularly admired his music, notably the D major Sonata of op. 3; traces of the older composer's influence can be seen in Mozart's Parisian and English sonatas and in his earliest piano concertos. Schobert's output includes several sets of keyboard sonatas with violin accompaniment, five keyboard concertos, and an unsuccessful *opéra comique*.
—/SH

Schoeck, Othmar (*b* Brunnen, Switzerland, 1 Sept. 1886; *d* Zürich, 10 March 1957). Swiss composer. He studied at the Zürich Conservatory (1905–7) and with Reger at the Leipzig Conservatory (1907–8). Thereafter he worked as an accompanist and choral conductor in Zürich (1909–17) and as director of the St Gallen Symphony Concerts (1917–44). He composed a large quantity of songs to poems by Goethe, Joseph von Eichendorff, Nikolaus Lenau, and others, following Hugo Wolf in style. His other works include several operas (*Penthesilea*, Dresden, 1927, rev. 1928; *Vom Fischer un syner Fru*, Dresden, 1930; *Massimilla Doni*, Dresden, 1937; *Das Schloss Dürande*, Berlin, 1943), concertos, and a few chamber pieces. Though he was not a teacher, his example proved important to the next generation of German-Swiss composers.   PG

Schoenberg Arnold (*see page 1116*)

Schola Cantorum. An educational institution founded in Paris in 1894 by d'Indy, Charles Bordes, and the organist Alexandre Guilmant to foster the continuation of the church music tradition. The curriculum had a strong antiquarian and musicological bias, encouraging the study of late Baroque and early Classical works, Gregorian chant, and Renaissance polyphony. A solid grounding in technique was encouraged, rather than originality, and the only graduates who could stand comparison with the best Conservatoire students were Magnard, Roussel, Déodat de Séverac, and Pierre de Bréville.

schola cantorum (Lat., 'school of singers'). A medieval Roman choir, whose organization is described in the 8th-century *Ordines romani*, charged with providing the music for papal ceremonies and services. A key stage in the transmission of Roman chant occurred when some of its members travelled from Rome to instruct Frankish singers. In the late Middle Ages the Roman *schola cantorum* evolved into the choir of the papal
(*cont. on p. 1118*)

Arnold Schoenberg
(1874–1951)

The Austro-Hungarian composer Arnold Franz Walter Schoenberg was born in Vienna on 13 September 1874 and died in Los Angeles on 13 July 1951.

One of the greatest and most influential figures of 20th-century music, Schoenberg was a reluctant revolutionary, and his pioneering work in *atonality and *serialism has to be understood within the context of a lifelong commitment to the Austro-German tradition, particularly to the music of Mozart, Beethoven, and Brahms. This commitment was not the product of education, for Schoenberg had no formal training in theory or composition; only when he was in his 20s did he benefit from some instruction from his friend and later brother-in-law Alexander Zemlinsky. His feeling for tradition was, rather, the natural allegiance of a man who had grown up playing the violin and cello in string quartets, and who always strove to emulate the quality of musical thought he found in the chamber music of the past.

The early years

Schoenberg's earliest compositional efforts date from his boyhood, but not until he was in his mid-20s did he consider his works worthy of publication. Even the String Quartet in D major (1897), an engagingly relaxed piece reminiscent of Dvořák and Smetana, was printed only after his death, for he could never be content with anything slight, second-hand, or unworthy. According to his high moral view of his own responsibilities, the artist's gifts and insights carried with them the obligation of utter truthfulness and discipline; it was his duty to reveal his inner self and to create something that did not betray the achievements of his predecessors. Those achievements he saw as being undermined by the casual approach to harmony common in the late 19th century, and in two of his earliest published works, *Verklärte Nacht* for string sextet (1899) and *Pelleas und Melisande* for orchestra (1902–3), he brought the harmonic innovations of Wagner and Richard Strauss into thoroughly worked forms. Both are narrative symphonic poems, but both are also consistent musical arguments. In the case of *Pelleas*, which tells the story of Debussy's roughly contemporary opera, the music takes the form of a single-movement symphony, rich in thematic connection and contrapuntal development, deriving as much from Brahms and Reger as from Strauss.

From this point Schoenberg's style developed swiftly. His First String Quartet (1904–5) and First Chamber Symphony (1906) both weld four symphonic movements into a continuous whole, and both strain to accommodate a more chromatic harmony by means of prodigious motivic and polyphonic working; the music struggles against the disintegration and incoherence threatened by its dissonant material.

The atonal works

This process could not go on indefinitely, and in 1908 Schoenberg made the break into atonality, abandoning the attempt to fit atonal harmonies into tonal forms. In this he may have been encouraged by the two gifted young pupils he had recently acquired, Alban Berg and Anton Webern, though it is important to note that he rarely based his teaching on his own new compositional ideas. For him teaching was as much a vocation as composing, even if at times it must also have been a financial necessity, and like composing it carried heavy responsibilities: to provide students with a solid knowledge of their musical heritage and help each find an independent personality.

It was this inner search, conducted on himself, that drove Schoenberg towards atonality, as well as his feeling that musical history was pressing him in that direction. His early atonal works, particularly the Five Orchestral Pieces (1909) and the 'monodrama' *Erwartung* (also 1909; staged 1924), sound like products of the subconscious. They use a fantastic variety of harmony, rhythm, and colour, and they take place at an intense emotional level which justifies the term 'expressionist' (see EXPRESSIONISM). *Erwartung*, for instance, is a one-act opera with a single soprano role which explores the innermost sensations of terror, regret, and hope felt by a woman searching a dark forest for the lover who has abandoned her. And *Pierrot lunaire* (1912), whose theatrical use of a reciter with small ensemble makes it one of Schoenberg's most accessible works, inhabits a nocturnal world of the macabre and ironic, its strangeness heightened by the reciter's use of *Sprechgesang*—a kind of vocal production lying between speech and song. The ruthless introspection of these works could not have been achieved without atonality, but it would be wrong to suppose that atonality necessarily presupposed tortured expression. Many of Schoenberg's atonal songs and piano pieces are more rarefied in tone, and his most ambitious work of this period was a religious oratorio, *Die Jakobsleiter* (1917), which deals with the characteristic theme of moral steadfastness as the stony but unavoidable route to perfection of the soul. Its composition was interrupted when Schoenberg was called up for war service and, like many later projects, it was never completed.

Serialism

During the next few years Schoenberg began to work out the technique of serial composition as a means of bringing order into atonality. The lack of any coherent harmonic framework had, since 1908, prevented him from writing fully developed music; his atonal works are either short (the Six Little Piano Pieces of 1911 particularly so) or else rely on a text to provide continuity. But with serialism he was able to return to thematic forms in the old manner, as in the Piano Suite (1921–3), which looks back to keyboard suites of the Baroque period, or the Wind Quintet (1923–4), which has the usual four movements of a Classical chamber work. The possibilities of the technique were extended in a succession of major abstract works: the Variations for orchestra (1926–8), the Third and Fourth string quartets (1927, 1936), the concertos for violin (1935–6) and piano (1942). In these Schoenberg found, with increasing flexibility and resource, serial analogues for the devices of modulation and development that had sustained tonal forms. Though he was working within the tradition rather than, like Stravinsky or Poulenc, from outside, there is something here of *neo-classicism; certainly the control of these serial works contrasts markedly with the emotional and technical extravagance of the atonal music.

One may readily understand how Schoenberg could not sustain the unreserved self-disclosure of such works as the Five Orchestral Pieces. It may be, too, that he felt a need to re-establish contact with the audience that had violently rejected his atonal works—hence his return to the old formal models and also his essaying of lighter modes of expression. Among his earlier serial compositions are two divertimento-like pieces, the Serenade (1920–3, not totally serial) and the Suite for instrumental septet (1924–6), as well as the comic opera *Von heute auf morgen* (Frankfurt, 1930). Another opera, *Moses und Aron* (1930–2; staged Zürich, 1957), found him returning to a religious subject: the problem of communicating a vision of God. Moses, the seer, lacks the means to do this, while Aaron can speak the message, but only by recourse to compromise and subterfuge, as when he takes a complaisant attitude to the construction of the Golden Calf. This was very much Schoenberg's own problem—how to express his vision with perfect integrity—and, significantly, the opera remained unfinished.

The American years

In 1933, with the rise of the Nazis to power, Schoenberg left the teaching post he had held since 1926 at the Prussian Academy in Berlin, and he made a formal return to the Jewish faith of his birth, a return which had already taken place in *Moses und Aron* and other works (he had converted to Protestantism in his youth). He emigrated to the USA and took a teaching post at the University of California at Los Angeles, where he lived for the rest of his life. During these last years he made intermittent returns to tonal composition, as in the Theme and Variations for concert band (1943). He also achieved a rapprochement between serialism and tonality in the *Ode to Napoleon Buonaparte* for reciter and piano quintet (1942), which turns Byron's spite against Hitler. *A Survivor from Warsaw* for reciter, male chorus, and orchestra (1947) was another impassioned response to contemporary events. By this time, however, Schoenberg's thought was turning increasingly inward. His last instrumental pieces, the String Trio (1946) and the Phantasy for violin and piano (1949), make some return to the wild nervosity of the atonal period, and his final project was a set of *Modern Psalms* (1950) on the subject of the search for God. Only one of them was set, and that incompletely, breaking off appropriately at the words: 'And still I pray'.

PG

📖 J. Rufer, *The Works of Arnold Schoenberg* (New York, 1963) · C. Rosen, *Arnold Schoenberg* (New York, 1975) · A. Schoenberg, *Style and Idea*, ed. L. Black (London, 1975) · H. H. Stuckenschmidt, *Arnold Schoenberg* (London, 1977) · C. Dahlhaus, *Schoenberg and the New Music* (Eng. trans., Cambridge, 1987) · W. Frisch (ed.), *Schoenberg and his World* (Princeton, NJ, 1999) chapel. The term is now frequently used to describe the choral body of a choir school, but in its true, broader sense it refers to places of study as well as of choral training. —/ALi

Scholes, Percy A(lfred) (*b* Headingley, Leeds, 24 July 1877; *d* Vevey, 31 July 1958). English music scholar, critic, and author, and the first editor of this *Companion*. He became prominent in the music appreciation movement, leading the campaign to improve the musical taste of the English public (see APPRECIATION OF MUSIC). Initially a music teacher and organist, Scholes gave university extension lectures from 1905, forming the Home Music Study Union in 1907. He was music critic of *Queen* (1912–13), the London *Evening Standard* (1913–20), and *The Observer* (1920–5), and music editor of *Radio Times* (1926–8). He gave regular broadcasts as BBC Music Critic between 1923 and 1928. The author of more than 30 books on music, including *The Puritans and Music* (1934) and studies of Burney (1948) and Hawkins (1953), Scholes is best known for *The Oxford Companion to Music* (1938), which he wrote single-handed. MP

Schöne Müllerin, Die ('The Beautiful Maid of the Mill'). Song cycle, D795 (1823), for male voice and piano by Schubert, settings of 20 poems (1821) by Wilhelm Müller.

Schoolmaster, The (*Der Schulmeister*). Nickname of Haydn's Symphony no. 55 in E♭ major (1774), so called because the dotted figure in the slow movement has been thought to suggest a schoolmaster's admonishing finger.

Schöpfung, Die. See CREATION, THE.

Schöpfungsmesse. See 'CREATION' MASS.

Schott. German firm of music publishers. It was founded in Mainz in 1780 by Bernhard Schott (1748–1809), a clarinettist. Besides publishing works by composers associated with the Mainz court, he issued piano scores and arrangements of popular operas, notably the first piano scores of Mozart's *Die Entführung aus dem Serail* (1785) and *Don Giovanni* (1791). His sons Johann Andreas (1781–1840) and Johann Joseph (1782–1855) developed the catalogue and absorbed various other firms, and 'B. Schott's Söhne', as it came to be known, flourished throughout the 19th century.

Schott has formed important associations with leading composers throughout its history, including Beethoven (from 1824, publishing his *Missa solemnis*, Ninth Symphony, and some late string quartets) and Wagner (from 1859, publishing *Der Ring des Nibelungen*, *Die Meistersinger von Nürnberg*, and *Parsifal*). It continued through the 20th century with many major composers, from Hindemith, Orff, Stravinsky, and Tippett to Henze, Ligeti, Penderecki, and Takemitsu, and has associated itself with new generations of composers including Bryars, Casken, Goehr, Hosokawa, Martland, Müller-Siemens, and Turnage.

Schott has issued many important musicological works, including Riemann's *Musik-Lexikon*, Hoboken's thematic catalogue of Haydn's works and the Wagner *Werk-Verzeichnis*; major editions in progress include the complete works of Hindemith, Schoenberg, Schumann, Tchaikovsky, Wagner, and Weber. The Schott archives, including correspondence with Beethoven and many others, survived World War II virtually intact and are now in the Mainz Stadtbibliothek.

The London branch of the firm was established in 1835; it became independent in 1914 but control reverted to Mainz in 1985. Having played a leading role in the 20th-century recorder revival, it continues to specialize in educational publications. The Schott catalogue has been extended considerably in recent years through the acquisition of Ars Viva (1946), Ernst Eulenburg (1957), Furstner (1981), Panton International (1998), and Hohner (1998). HA

Schottische (Ger., 'Scottish'). A round dance similar to, but slower than, the *polka. It is sometimes coupled with the *écossaise, but in spite of the similarity of name it bears no resemblance to that dance beyond the fact that both are in duple time. The *Schottische* was called the 'German polka' when it first appeared in England in the mid-19th century. A version known as the *Schottische bohème* or *polka tremblante* was introduced in Paris in the 1840s. —/LC

Schrammel. A style of music popular in the *Heurigen*, the taverns where the Viennese drink new wines. It owes its name to the violinist brothers Johann Schrammel (1850–93) and Joseph Schrammel (1852–95), who formed a quartet with two friends playing the clarinet and guitar. The tradition they established was carried on later with the clarinet replaced by piano accordion, though in the 1960s there was a dedicated revival of the original instrumentation. The brothers wrote much of their own music, and Johann's march *Wien bleibt Wien* (1887) became a classic. PGA/ALA

Schreker, Franz (*b* Monaco, 23 March 1878; *d* Berlin, 21 March 1934). Austrian composer, conductor, and teacher. He studied with Robert Fuchs at the Vienna Conservatory from 1892 to 1900, when he achieved a notable success with a setting for female chorus of Psalm 116. His first opera *Flammen* ('Flames') was performed in Vienna in 1902. He had begun work the previous year on the opera *Der ferne Klang* ('The Distant Sound'), to his own libretto, temporarily abandoning the score when its erotic subject matter, partly autobiographical, caused alarm among many of his friends. A period of despondent compositional silence followed, broken in 1908 by the successful premiere of the ballet *Der Geburtstag der Infantin* ('The Birthday of the Infanta'). The same year he took up the directorship of the Philharmonic Choir, championing new music. He also resumed work on *Der ferne Klang* in 1908, completing the score in 1910, though a further two years elapsed before the opera received a triumphant premiere in Frankfurt. With its extravagant eroticism, its fusion of Symbolism and Expressionism, and its extreme tonal chromaticism, it marks the final coherence of Schreker's style. The influence of early Schoenberg is at times strongly apparent in his music (Schreker subsequently conducted the premiere of *Gurrelieder*), and Schreker was widely regarded by contemporary critics as an extreme 'progressivist', though he never followed Schoenberg into atonality.

On the strength of *Der ferne Klang*'s success, Schreker was appointed professor of composition at the Vienna Conservatory in 1912, but his next opera *Das Spielwerk und die Prinzessin* ('The Toy and the Princess', 1913) was initially unsuccessful. In 1918 he produced *Die Gezeichneten* ('The Branded Ones'), the most sexually extreme of his operas (its heroine, 'branded' by a weak heart, expires of pleasure after experiencing her first orgasm), consolidating its success with *Der Schatzgräber* in 1920. That year he was appointed director of the Musikhochschule in Berlin, where he lived for the rest of his life. Krenek, Hába, and Goldschmidt were among his pupils, and Zemlinsky and Hindemith held teaching posts under his directorship.

Schreker was Jewish, and the last years of his life were tragically marked by the rise of Nazi anti-Semitism. Under pressure he withdrew his opera *Christophorus* during rehearsals in 1931. His next opera *Der Schmied von Ghent* ('The Smith from Ghent') provoked Nazi demonstrations in 1932. Schreker was dismissed from his teaching post in 1933, an event widely believed to have precipitated the sudden heart attack that killed him a year later. Though his work, proscribed under the Hitler regime, was enormously popular in the German-speaking world in the interwar period, it gained serious international recognition only during the last decade of the 20th century, when *Der ferne Klang* was taken into the repertories of a number of opera houses. The revival of interest in *Entartete Musik* has led to a major reappraisal of his work, and he is now widely regarded as ranking among the finest of post-Romantic composers.   TA

📖 C. Hailey, *Franz Schreker (1878–1934): A Cultural Biography* (Cambridge, 1993)

schrittmässig, schrittweise (Ger.). 'Stepwise', i.e. at a walking pace (the equivalent of *andante*).

Schröder-Devrient, Wilhelmine (*b* Hamburg, 6 Dec. 1804; *d* Coburg, 26 Jan. 1860). German soprano. She studied with Giuseppe Mozatti and Aloys Mieksch. In 1821 she made her debut as Pamina at the Kärntnertortheater, Vienna, and the following year sang Agathe in *Der Freischütz* with the composer conducting. That year she achieved international fame with her powerful performance as Leonore in *Fidelio*. She became highly sought after as an interpreter of Donna Anna, Euryanthe, Norma, Roméo, and Desdemona (in Rossini's *Otello*), singing in Dresden, London, and Paris. Wagner, overwhelmed with her singing and dramatic powers, created three roles for her, including Senta (*Der fliegende Holländer*, 1843) and Venus (*Tannhäuser*, 1845).   JT

Schubert, Franz (*see page 1120*)

Schulhoff, Erwin [Ervín] (*b* Prague, 8 June 1894; *d* Wülzburg, 18 Aug. 1942). Czech composer and pianist. On Dvořák's advice he studied at the Prague Conservatory (1904–6), then in Vienna (1906–8), Leipzig (1908–10), and Cologne (1911–14). He also took lessons with Debussy and Reger. After active service in World War I he returned to Germany, where he became a member of the Weimar Republic avant-garde, including Paul Klee and Georg Grosz among his friends. His plans to collaborate on a ballet with the Dadaist Tristan Tzara came to nothing. Between 1919 and 1920 he organized concerts in Dresden to promote the works of the Second Viennese School. He returned to Prague to teach in 1929. His opera *Plameny* ('Flames'), a surrealist version of the Don Juan legend, was staged in Brno in 1932.

As a pianist Schulhoff was a keen champion of new music (he notably played many of Hába's works) as well as jazz, elements of which combine with driving motoric rhythms in his own works, notably his six symphonies, to powerful effect. He was a member of the Prague Theatre jazz orchestra, 1935–8, and also worked for Czech Radio in Brno. A committed Communist, he took Soviet citizenship in protest at the Munich agreement in 1938. He was subsequently arrested by the Nazis and imprisoned in a concentration camp, where he died. In the immediate postwar era his music was largely forgotten, but it was rediscovered with the revival of interest in *Entartete Musik* at the end of the 20th century.   TA

📖 J. Bek, *Erwin Schulhoff: Leben und Werk* (Hamburg, 1994)

(*cont. on p. 1123*)

Franz Schubert
(1797–1828)

The Austrian composer Franz Peter Schubert was born in Vienna on 31 January 1797 and died there on 19 November 1828.

The only one of the great composers to be born in Vienna, Schubert was also the only one who failed to win international recognition in his own lifetime. For that his untimely death is only a partial explanation. The reasons for the world's neglect of his genius are to be sought rather in his own nature, shy of the limelight, and totally indifferent to the arts of self-assertion. He had neither the talent nor the inclination for the role of virtuoso performer, and he disliked the regular routine imposed by continuous employment. He never travelled to any of the European capitals outside Vienna, and he lacked percipient champions who could both recognize his worth and noise his talents abroad. Moreover, the democratization of taste, and the development of commercial publishing, not to mention the illiberal political climate of his day, made life difficult for a freelance composer, a species of which Schubert was perhaps the first thoroughgoing example. He was dependent throughout his life on the fees he could earn from patrons and dedicatees, from the publication of his songs and keyboard compositions (which did not begin until he was 24), and occasional teaching or performing. He never achieved financial security, except for a year or two; on the other hand, the idea that he lived in feckless bohemian poverty is a popular myth.

The early years

Schubert was the fourth surviving son of a school assistant from Moravia and a domestic servant from Silesia who met and married in the suburb of Lichtental. Franz learnt to play the piano and the violin from his father and brothers, and later the viola. He had a few lessons in counterpoint from the local church organist, Michael Holzer. But his serious musical education began at the age of 11, when he won a choral scholarship to the Imperial College (the Konvikt, or religious seminary). There, under the supervision of the court organist Wenzel Ruzicka and the Kapellmeister Anton Salieri, his gifts soon revealed themselves.

From Salieri he inherited conservative notational habits and a reverence for the music of Gluck, as well as a coolness towards that of Mozart and Beethoven that he was later to outgrow. The most impressive achievement of these years is the series of string quartets he wrote in 1812. Even earlier, in 1811, came his first attempt at opera, but the setting of Kotzebue's *Der Spiegelritter* ('The Looking-Glass Knight') was abandoned after the first act. Even earlier still were the first songs, ambitiously modelled on the cantata-like settings of Schiller by Zumsteeg.

Schubert left the Konvikt in 1813, declining the offer of an endowment which would have enabled him to continue his education. Instead he spent a year training as a teacher, then returned home to teach in his father's school. There followed a period of sustained creativity which strains credulity. In the space of three years his compositions include five symphonies, four masses, three string quartets, three piano sonatas, six operas, and some 300 or more songs. This torrent of music, none of it publicly performed or paid for, laid the foundation for his future greatness. Each of the first three symphonies, for example, anticipates in its own way either the structural methods or the infectious rhythmic drive of the 'Great' C major Symphony, although the idiom remains as yet close to its 18th-century roots. There are lyrical digressions in the string quartets, which foreshadow the mature Schubert.

But the major achievement of these years was an outburst of text-inspired song that laid the foundation for the romantic lied. The discovery of Goethe's *Faust* in October 1814 led to the first unassailable masterpiece, *Gretchen am Spinnrade*, soon to be followed by others, *Nähe des Geliebten* ('Nearness of the Beloved'), *Heidenröslein*, and *Erlkönig*; and the poetic sensibility which Goethe had evoked in the composer was carried over into his exploration of the work of Hölty, Claudius, Uz, Jacobi, and many others. The claim that Schubert 'invented' the lied can hardly be sustained, but there is no questioning that he made of it a new art form, and went on to reveal its full potential.

In 1816 this first phase of his work seems to reach a plateau; his music displays a stable mastery, but not of a kind that can be called fully Schubertian. Instead, such music as the three Sonatas (published as Sonatinas) for violin and piano (D384, 385, and 408), the Symphony no. 5 in B♭, and the concerto movements for piano and strings (Adagio and Rondo D487) and for violin and strings (Rondo in A D438) have a Mozartian grace and lucidity. The identity of form and utterance is complete. Much the same is true of songs like *Ins stille Land* ('The Land of Peace'), *Litanei*, and *Orpheus*. About this time Schubert's first love affair, with Therese Grob, drifted to its unhappy end. Deep feelings were involved, at any rate on the composer's part, but Therese—perhaps heeding maternal advice—saw no future in the relationship and soon found a marriage partner elsewhere. (The question whether Schubert was homosexual occupied some scholars in the late 20th century, but the issue remains unresolved.)

The path to independence

By autumn 1816 the urge to escape from the drudgery of the schoolroom had become irresistible. After an unsuccessful attempt to obtain a teaching post at Laibach (Ljubljana), Schubert decided to throw in his lot with Franz von Schober, a young man with artistic connections and hedonistic tendencies, and went to live in the inner city. For the next six years his reputation grew steadily in Vienna, and in such provincial centres as Linz, Steyr, and Graz. Early in 1817 he was introduced to J. M. Vogl, the leading baritone of the Court Theatre, who became an enthusiast for the songs and did much to spread his fame. In 1818 his orchestral compositions began to make occasional appearances at public concerts. Wider horizons and new opportunities opened up. Schubert spent the second half of 1818 at Zseliz in Hungary, where he acted as music tutor in the family of Johann Karl, Count Esterházy, in a rural, semi-feudal environment far removed from the schoolroom. In 1819 he accompanied Michael Vogl on his annual holiday at Steyr (Vogl's birthplace), and this first glimpse of the mountains of Upper Austria proved a powerful stimulus.

The liberating effect of these experiences can be traced in his music. The songs of 1817 range from the lyrical perfection of *An die Musik* ('To Music') and *Die Forelle* to the dramatic power of *Memnon*, *Ganymede*, and *Gruppe aus dem Tartarus* ('Scene from Hades'). The philosophical insight and vivid pictorialism of these and other songs owe much to his friend Johann Mayrhofer, a poet whose vision of life as a kind of antechamber to the 'happy land' strongly influenced Schubert and inspired many of his finest songs. A new interest in Beethoven is also plainly to be felt in 1817, especially in a series of piano sonatas (several left incomplete), of which the best known are the ones in A

minor (D537), E♭ (D568), and B (D575), and in the violin and piano Duo in A D574. The Symphony no. 6 in C pays its tribute both to Beethoven and to Rossini, whose operas had impressed Schubert on their first appearance in Vienna by their vigour and musicality, and who was an important secondary influence on his mature style.

The Quintet in A for piano and strings ('The Trout'), finished in autumn 1819, is the first instrumental work that can be called thoroughly Schubertian in spirit and in idiom, though it represents but one aspect of his musical personality: a divertimento provenance is clearly implied by the presence of a double bass (rare in chamber music of the Classical period), the addition of a fifth movement, and the work's structural transparency. Meditative calm constantly colours the atmosphere of dance, in what could be regarded as the purest manifestation of Schubert's natural mysticism.

The years of maturity

On his return from Zseliz Schubert was commissioned to write a one-act comic *Singspiel* for the Kärntnertortheater. *Die Zwillingsbrüder* ('The Twin Brothers') reached the stage in June 1820, and had a modest *succès d'estime*. Two months later *Die Zauberharfe* ('The Magic Harp'), a magic play with music, ran at the rival Theater an der Wien for eight consecutive performances. The champions of German opera began to form themselves into a kind of Schubert lobby as a counterblast to the all-conquering Italians, and Schubert and Schober started work on a full-length all-sung opera, *Alfonso und Estrella*. But before it was finished the management of the court theatres had been taken over by the Italian impresario Domenico Barbaia, and Schober had retired from the stage. *Alfonso* was set aside, and efforts to produce it elsewhere failed.

In 1823, however, Schubert was commissioned to write *Fierrabras*, a tale of love and war during the Crusades, with Josef Kupelwieser, the manager of the theatre, as librettist. This time the project foundered because of intrigues within the theatre, which led to Kupelwieser's resignation. As a compensation, Kupelwieser arranged for Schubert to write the musical interludes in *Rosamunde*, a 'grand Romantic drama' by Helmina von Chézy. In December 1823 this actually reached the stage. The delightful music was warmly received, but the silly plot doomed the piece, which was withdrawn after two performances.

The years 1820–3 were thus largely taken up with a fruitless pursuit of operatic success. Those years were also marked, however, by a series of vocal and instrumental works of striking brilliance and originality. The settings of poems by Goethe, Friedrich von Schlegel, Matthäus von Collin, and Rückert reveal a new dramatic power and poetic insight. The partsongs include the ever-popular setting of Psalm 23, and the setting of Goethe's *Gesang der Geister über den Wassern* ('Song of the Spirits over the Waters') for male voices and orchestra. The Mass in A♭ completed in 1822 is the most idiomatic of Schubert's six settings.

Characteristically, however, his most original work was left unfinished. The Quartet Movement of December 1820 is an enormous advance on the string quartets of his adolescence, but it breaks off in the middle of the sketch for the slow movement. The dramatic oratorio *Lazarus* (February 1820), an astonishingly forward-looking work which replaces the usual alternation of recitative and aria with a continuous flow of orchestrally accompanied arioso, is a tantalizingly brilliant fragment, though a substantial one.

Even more enigmatic is the case of the 'Unfinished' Symphony itself. The two surviving movements are the most dramatic and personal statement of the *lacrimae rerum* in symphonic literature. There are sketches for the Scherzo, as well as two pages of its orchestration, and there are grounds for believing that he sketched a finale too, orchestrating it the following year when he needed to produce incidental music for *Rosamunde* at short notice. If that was the case, the symphony's non-completion was due to the Scherzo being unfinished, through some sort of 'composer's block'. To proceed to other projects (which seemed constantly to invite him) was a better use of time and inspiration, and he could return to the symphony later in different circumstances. He never did; and the fact that he sent the two finished movements to Josef Hüttenbrenner in September 1823 suggests that he knew their worth but, for the time being, could not see his way to finishing the symphony.

The late years

If, as seems probable, the 'Unfinished' Symphony was occasioned by some emotional crisis in Schubert's life, it may well have some connection with his illness. Towards the end of 1822, or early the next year, he began to show the symptoms of venereal disease, almost certainly syphilis. His condition deteriorated rapidly in the first half of 1823, and then began to improve slowly. In 1824 he resumed a more or less normal life, but the evidence suggests that the bouts of sickness and headaches by which he was plagued for the rest of his life were induced by his chronic complaint. The winter of 1822–3 thus marks a crisis in Schubert's affairs, when his reputation was at it highest. The sensational success of *Erlkönig* at a public concert in March 1821 had led to the publication of his songs, and to financial independence. But the failure of his operatic hopes, and the collapse of his health, marked the end of his short-lived success.

In the remaining years Schubert's life, never outwardly eventful, recedes into the half-world of Metternich's Vienna. At this time too his aspirations change direction. Abandoning his hopes of a stage success, he resolved to concentrate on the prestigious—but no longer fashionable—forms of sonata, string quartet, and symphony. To the last five years of his life belong the 'Great' C major Symphony, the three remarkable string quartets, the two piano trios, the two song cycles, the Heine and Rellstab songs, the greatest of his keyboard works for both solo piano and piano duet, and the most ambitious of his settings of the Mass.

Comparatively minor events serve as landmarks because of their association with these masterpieces. The meeting with Schuppanzigh early in 1824 encouraged Schubert to plan the series of the three mature quartets. If on his return visit to Zseliz in 1824 a kind of *amitié amoureuse* sprang up between him and the young Countess Karoline Esterházy, this seems important mainly because it motivated his finest works for piano duet, including the finest of all, the Fantasy in F minor of January–April 1828, which was dedicated to her.

The long summer holiday of 1825, during which he and Vogl once again toured the mountains, was a halcyon interlude, well documented except in the most important particular, the identity of the symphony that Schubert sketched in Gmunden and Gastein, once thought to have disappeared but now generally acknowledged to be the work we know as the 'Great' C major Symphony. This is Schubert's greatest 'public' work, comparable in scale and conception to Beethoven's symphonies, but lyrical in content, the first expression in symphonic literature of the Romantic doctrine of the unity of humankind and nature. Schubert never heard the work, and even after Mendelssohn conducted it in Leipzig in 1839 it was slow to win the place in the regular repertory that it gained early in the 20th century.

The supreme achievements of the songwriter also belong to these years. The greatness of the song cycles, *Die schöne Müllerin* (1823) and *Winterreise* (1827), owes something to the Dresden poet and publicist Wilhelm Müller, whose essays in the folksong tradition so exactly met Schubert's needs. Their strong rhythms and evocative language embody the Romantic love affair with death that rests at the heart of so much of Schubert's best work, though with him it never ceases to be life-enhancing. The two groups of songs to texts by Heine and Rellstab, though they do not constitute a cycle in the true sense, take even further the dramatic and impressionist qualities inherent in the lied.

The compositions of his last year, especially the F minor Fantasy, the three last piano sonatas, and the incomparable String Quintet in C, are 'private' works which seem to embody the personal vision of a composer whom Liszt called 'le plus poète que jamais'. His final illness was diagnosed as 'typhus abdominalis', which seems to have been equivalent to typhoid fever. But it may well have been hastened, even caused, by the disease which he knew to be incurable. If so, the clairvoyant quality of these last works, their vision and authority, reflects the fate of a man who knew himself to be doomed.

The spontaneity and clarity of Schubert's music appeal equally to the expert and to the layman. He had many styles—it has been fairly said, indeed, that he had a different style for every poet he set—and his music often sounds like that of other composers. Yet the adjective 'Schubertian' is indispensable. His poetic sensibility enabled him to give an entirely new emotional weight to familiar formulas like the major–minor alternation, the enharmonic shift, and the tonic–German 6th–tonic sequence, introducing new harmonic tensions between the tonic and its more remote relations. That he was poised for stylistic development at the time of his death is evident from the sketches for a visionary 'Tenth' Symphony, which he worked on during his last weeks. But the long-cherished view of Schubert as an intuitively creative child of nature who felt no need for Beethovenian cerebration or innovation had already been challenged by instances in earlier works of intricate contrapuntal device, palindrome, and 'mirror writing', though these were not recognized as such until the late 20th century. It was indeed the fusion of a keen intellectual awareness and a poetic purity of expression that gave the mature Schubertian voice its special uniqueness.   JRe/BN

📖 R. CAPELL, *Schubert Songs* (London, 1928; new edn, rev. M. Cooper, 1973) · A. EINSTEIN, *Schubert* (London, 1951/ R1971) · M. J. E. BROWN, *Schubert: A Critical Biography* (London, 1958) · P. RADCLIFFE, *Schubert Piano Sonatas* (London, 1967) · J. A. WESTRUP, *Schubert Chamber Music* (London, 1969) · J. REED, *Schubert: The Final Years* (London, 1972) · H. GÁL, *Franz Schubert and the Essence of Melody* (Eng. trans., London, 1974) · B. NEWBOULD, *Schubert and the Symphony: A New Perspective* (London, 1992) · E. N. MCKAY, *Franz Schubert* (Oxford, 1996) · B. NEWBOULD, *Schubert: The Music and the Man* (London, Berkeley, and Los Angeles, 1997)

Schuller, Gunther (Alexander) (*b* New York, 22 Nov. 1925). American composer and conductor. Though born into a musical family he was largely self-taught. He began his career as principal horn in the Cincinnati Symphony in 1943, then played in the Metropolitan Opera orchestra (1945–59), thereafter gaining distinction as a composer, conductor, teacher, publisher, radio presenter, and record producer. He taught at the Manhattan School of Music (1959–63) and at Yale (1964–7), and also served as president of the New England Conservatory (1966–77). From 1963 to 1984 he was associated with the Berkshire (now Tanglewood) Music Center.

Schuller's music draws on various influences, including those of Schoenberg, Babbitt, and the European avant-garde, and often seeks what he has called a 'third stream' between jazz and classical music. *Seven Studies on Themes of Paul Klee* (1959), one of his many orchestral scores, shows his vivid invention for instruments. His books, testifying to his various musical passions, include *Horn Technique* (New York, 1962, 2/1992), *Early Jazz* (New York, 1968) and *The Compleat Conductor* (New York, 1997), the last an exhaustive study of major masterpieces as performed in dozens of recordings.   PG

Schulmeister, Der. See SCHOOLMASTER, THE.

Schultze, Norbert (*b* Brunswick, 26 Jan. 1911). German composer. He studied music and theatre in Cologne and Munich, and worked as a composer and actor in cabaret in Munich, then as an opera conductor in Heidelberg and Darmstadt, and for a record company. He owned a music-publishing firm from 1953. Schultze composed several stage works, including *Schwarzer Peter*, an 'opera for young and old' (Hamburg, 1936). He also wrote light music, sometimes under pseudonyms—notably the song *Lilli Marleen*, popular in Britain as well as Germany during World War II.   ABur

Schulz, Johann Abraham Peter (*b* Lüneburg, 31 March 1747; *d* Schwedt an der Oder, 10 June 1800). German composer and theorist. He studied with Kirnberger in Berlin and from 1768 travelled widely in Europe in the service of the Polish princess Sapieha Woiwodin. After his return to Berlin in 1773 he produced operas at local theatres, from 1780 working also in Rheinsberg as court composer. In 1790–5 he was in Copenhagen as court Kapellmeister and director of the Royal Theatre; he then returned to work in Berlin and Rheinsberg. Schulz is best known for his *volkstümliche Lieder*: simple, folk-like settings of verse by such poets as Goethe and Klopstock.   —/TRJ

Schuman, William (Howard) (*b* New York, 4 Aug. 1910; *d* New York, 15 Feb. 1992). American composer. He studied at Columbia University and at the Juilliard School with Roy Harris, who exerted a strong influence on him and promoted his career by bringing him to Koussevitzky's attention. Soon he was in the front rank of American composers, and his secular cantata *A Free Song* won the first Pulitzer Prize for music, in 1943. He also quickly gained an important role as an administrator, as director of publications for G. Schirmer and president of the Juilliard School (1945–62), later becoming founding president of Lincoln Center (1962–9).

Schuman's music has the robust drive, the American melodic flavour, and the counterpoint of Harris's but is sleeker and more sophisticated. He was conscious of himself as an American artist, and responded to fellow American artists (*In Praise of Shahn* for orchestra, 1969), to the landscape (*New England Triptych*, 1956), and to popular culture, in his single opera *The Mighty Casey* (1953), which he revised as a cantata, *Casey at the Bat* (1976). But his major works are in the abstract genres of symphony (he wrote ten, of which he withdrew the first two and the fifth is for strings) and string quartet (five such). Other works include concertos for piano (1938), violin (1947), and cello (*A Song of Orpheus*, 1961), choral settings, and a characteristically splendid orchestration of Ives's *Variations on 'America'*.   PG

Schumann, Clara (Josephine) (*b* Leipzig, 13 Sept. 1819; *d* Frankfurt, 20 May 1896). German pianist and composer. She was the daughter of the piano teacher Friedrich Wieck and Marianne Wieck (née Tromlitz, later Bargiel), herself a singer and pianist of professional standard. Her parents divorced when she was six; it was her father who then looked after her and gave her a musical education. Though strict, and keen to profit financially from his daughter's talents, Wieck was assiduous in encouraging Clara as both pianist and composer. Her childhood tours made her famous throughout Europe and her playing won the admiration of the leading musicians of the day, Liszt and Mendelssohn among them.

In about her 15th year her life was complicated by a developing relationship with another of her father's pupils, Robert Schumann, whom she eventually married in 1840 after an acrimonious period during which Wieck took them both to court. Her professional career became more sporadic, but her appearances were successful and she continued to make occasional foreign tours. Following Schumann's decline and death she resumed her performing career, tirelessly undertaking lengthy international tours; she was highly acclaimed, especially in England, and continued playing until illness forced her to stop. She edited her husband's works, her advocacy helping to gain them a place in the repertory. She also championed the music of Brahms,

who from 1854 became her closest confidant. As well as teaching private pupils, she taught at the Leipzig Conservatory in 1844 and from 1878 was head of the piano department at the Hoch Conservatory in Frankfurt. Together with Liszt, she can be regarded as the leading piano teacher of her day.

Clara Schumann's compositions consist mainly of piano pieces and songs, though she also wrote a Piano Concerto (1836) and a Piano Trio (1846), the latter probably her masterpiece. The solo works divide into earlier pieces in a lightweight virtuoso manner and more serious ones from the years of her marriage. Among the most notable are the *Variations on a Theme of Robert Schumann* and the *Three Romances* (both 1853). Her songs are also skilfully crafted. She abandoned composition after her husband's death.   GH

📖 N. B. REICH, *Clara Schumann: The Artist and the Woman* (London, 1985) · G. NEUHAUS (ed.) and P. OSTWALD (trans.), *The Marriage Diaries of Robert and Clara Schumann* (London, 1994)

Schumann, Robert (*see opposite page*)

Schusterfleck (Ger., 'cobbler's patch'). A derogatory name for a sequential passage (see SEQUENCE, 1) in which each repetition is one scale degree higher than the last.

Schütz, Heinrich (*b* Köstritz [now Bad Köstritz], nr Gera, Oct. 1585; *d* Dresden, 6 Nov. 1672). German composer. The leading figure in 17th-century German music, he was productive in nearly every branch of composition except independent instrumental music. His extant secular music is not unimportant, but it is on his immense output of sacred vocal works that his reputation as the first German composer of truly international stature is based. Together with Michael Praetorius and with his immediate contemporaries, Schein and Scheidt, he played a crucial role in introducing into his native country the new Italian styles of the period, thus providing much of the initial impetus for the musical Baroque in Germany.

In 1598, when Schütz was barely 13, the family inn at Weissenfels was visited by the Landgrave Moritz of Hessen-Kassel who, greatly attracted by the boy's singing, engaged him as a chorister in his chapel and provided for his education at the Gymnasium in Kassel. Later, in 1609, when Schütz was pursuing legal studies at the University of Marburg, a further intervention by the landgrave enabled him to undertake a markedly formative period of study with Giovanni Gabrieli in Venice. On his return home in 1613 he resumed his former place at Kassel and was appointed second organist with a modest salary. Some time later, however, on a visit with his patron to Dresden, his musical

(*cont. on p. 1128*)

Robert Schumann (1810–56)

The German composer Robert Schumann was born in Zwickau, Saxony, on 8 June 1810 and died at Endenich, near Bonn, on 29 July 1856.

Early years and marriage

One of the leading figures of the early Romantic period, Schumann was born in a provincial city into a cultured middle-class family—his father was a bookseller and publisher. In this environment he developed keen literary interests and a good knowledge both of German and foreign literature. Throughout his childhood and youth the claims of music and letters ran side by side, with poems and dramatic works produced in tandem with small-scale compositional efforts, mainly piano pieces and songs. His talents as a performer were equally evident: he had begun piano lessons with a local church organist at the age of seven, and quickly showed an interest in improvisation.

In 1820 Schumann was sent to the local Gymnasium, where his education proceeded on traditional lines. This was supplemented by voracious reading: Schiller was an early enthusiasm, to which were added the proto-Romantic novels of Johann Paul Friedrich Richter, who wrote under the pseudonym Jean Paul and remained the favourite writer of the adult Schumann, on whose creativity his sensibility and vein of fantasy were to prove strong influences. Musically Schumann became acquainted with works by Haydn, Mozart, Beethoven, and Weber (with whom his father tried unsuccessfully to arrange lessons shortly before Weber's death in 1826). He also heard the prominent pianist-composer Ignaz Moscheles perform in Karlsbad in 1819—a formative experience that led him to consider becoming a professional pianist.

His father's death (in 1826) led Schumann's mother to focus on her son's future, and in spite of his strong creative urges he agreed to the more practical alternative of a career in the law. He therefore entered the University of Leipzig in March 1828, though without enthusiasm and with little sense of application. It is said that he did not attend a single lecture, and from his own journal we know that reading and playing the piano occupied a good deal of his time. Drinking champagne and smoking cigars featured among his other pursuits

(alcohol later became an occasional problem). His most recent artistic enthusiasm was for the music of Schubert, whose death in November that year caused Schumann to cry all night. Even more significant was the start in August 1828 of serious pianistic studies with the leading local pedagogue Friedrich Wieck, who sensed Schumann's considerable talent and variable discipline, the latter in sharp contrast to Wieck's nine-year-old daughter Clara, who was proving to be a prodigy.

After a year in Leipzig Schumann persuaded his mother to allow him to move to the University of Heidelberg, which he found more congenial but whose law course he followed with scarcely more diligence. During a holiday in the summer of 1829 he travelled to Switzerland and Italy, where he fell briefly under the spell of Italian opera. Even more influential was the experience of hearing the great violin virtuoso Nicolò Paganini play in Frankfurt in April 1830.

This was the year in which Schumann turned decisively to music. Returning to Leipzig, he appealed to his mother to ask Wieck for an objective assessment of his musical potential. Wieck's considered reply contained reservations as to his student's application but stressed that given the necessary study Schumann could become a leading pianist within three years. A six-month trial period was agreed. Shortly afterwards Schumann wrote his first published composition, a set of variations on a theme derived from the name 'Abegg', supposedly that of a slight acquaintance who unconsciously provided the first instance of a cipher in Schumann's music—a recurrent feature of numerous later pieces. In 1831 he began formal lessons in harmony and counterpoint with a local conductor, Heinrich Dorn, and in 1832 published his op. 2, *Papillons* for piano.

Schumann's pianistic ambitions, however, suffered a permanent setback when he began to suffer weakness in the index and middle fingers of his right hand; this is often attributed to his use of a mechanical contrivance to strengthen his hands, but the weakness preceded this and may have been caused by mercury poisoning, a side effect of treatment for syphilis. Composition meanwhile continued apace, with further sets of small piano pieces and the first movement of a symphony completed. An additional activity was journalism. In April 1834 the first number of a new periodical, the *Neue Zeitschrift für Musik*, appeared under Schumann's editorship: it took a thoughtful and progressive line on the new music of the day. Many of its contributors were friends and colleagues of Schumann, whose articles appeared under pseudonyms: together they formed the 'Davidsbündler', an imaginary league of fighters in the cause of musical truth who waged war on the Philistines.

In 1834 Schumann fell in love with Ernestine von Fricken, a pupil of Wieck's whose father provided the theme of the *Études symphoniques*. She came from the town of Asch, a name encrypted in the piano suite *Carnaval*, which also contains tributes to such musical heroes as Paganini and Chopin as well as Clara Wieck and Schumann himself, in the form of two contrasting figures—Florestan and Eusebius—who represented the dynamic and reflective sides of his character respectively. Such personal references peppered Schumann's scores in this early period.

By August of 1835 Schumann began to lose interest in Ernestine and found himself attracted instead to Clara, now nearly 16 and nine years his junior. Though his compositions were increasing in stature and number, Schumann was still unknown outside his immediate circle and Wieck considered him a poor prospect as a son-in-law. He set himself firmly against the match and, when the couple showed no signs of conceding, broke off relations with his former pupil. Professionally the next few years were characterized by an increasing production of imaginative piano works including *Kreisleriana* and the Fantasia op. 17 (both 1837), and the *Faschingsschwank aus Wien* ('Carnival Prank from Vienna', 1838), by Schumann's abortive attempt to establish himself in the Austrian capital, and by the beginnings of an important friendship with Mendelssohn, who had arrived in Leipzig to take charge of the city's musical life. Personally they were marred by acrimony and eventual court cases, which Wieck handled badly and lost: Schumann and Clara Wieck were finally married on 12 September 1840.

Maturity

Marriage gave Schumann the emotional and domestic stability on which his subsequent achievements were founded. The relationship was not without its tensions—as a pianist of international reputation Clara remained the better-known figure, while nevertheless regularly sacrificing the interests of her own career to the twin claims of motherhood and Robert's compositions; but it was fundamentally happy, and Clara's encouragement of Schumann's ambitions enabled him repeatedly to extend himself as a composer.

During 1840, the year of their marriage, Schumann turned decisively to song, producing more than half his output in the genre, including a series of cycles, notably *Myrthen* ('Myrtles'), *Frauenliebe und -leben* ('Woman's Life and Love'), *Dichterliebe* ('Poet's Love'), and others to poems by Eichendorff and Heine. In 1841 he moved on to orchestral music. His first completed symphony (no. 1 in B♭, the 'Spring') was conducted by Mendelssohn at a concert given by Clara in March, with the Overture, Scherzo, and Finale following in May. The *Phantasie* for piano and orchestra (which later became the first movement of the Piano Concerto) was written and a new symphony (eventually published as no. 4 in D minor) begun. The couple's home life was also enriched by the birth of a daughter in September, the first of seven children to survive.

Chamber music was the next area to be tackled, in 1842. After studying works by Haydn and Mozart, Schumann produced three string quartets, closely followed by a Piano Quintet, a Piano Quartet, and a set of *Phantasiestücke* for piano trio. The following year opened with a setback: a severe and debilitating mental crisis whose effects lasted several months. Schumann had suffered similar attacks at intervals over a long period, which may have been congenital: his father had also had a 'nervous disorder', and his younger sister Emilie had committed suicide in 1826. During his attacks Schumann too feared that he would take his own life or suffer a complete mental collapse. There has been much speculation as to the origin of these bouts and their relation (if any) to the illness that eventually killed him: when confined in an asylum in his last years, Schumann admitted to his doctors that he had contracted syphilis in 1831.

More happily, 1843 saw Schumann succeed with a new genre, that of the oratorio. His *Das Paradies und die Peri*, based on an oriental poem by Thomas Moore, was given in December in Leipzig and won immediate success. Quickly taken up elsewhere, this now unfamiliar piece first made Schumann's name known internationally and remained popular during his lifetime.

In 1844 Clara determined on restoring the family's finances with a concert tour to Russia. Though increasingly unhappy and restive, Schumann accompanied her. The result was a further mental collapse, which caused him to withdraw from journalism altogether. His main compositional achievement of the year was the beginning of a choral and orchestral work based on Goethe's *Faust* that would take shape over a decade before reaching the form of *Scenes from Goethe's 'Faust'* in 1853. The Schumann family also moved to Dresden: Mendelssohn had left Leipzig, and Schumann was passed over as his replacement as head of the conservatory in favour of the Danish composer Niels Gade. More promisingly, the thriving Dresden opera house might offer possibilities in a new direction on which Schumann had set his sights.

The major productions of the next two years were orchestral: the one-movement *Phantasie* for piano and orchestra of 1841 was extended by the addition of an intermezzo and finale to form a full-scale piano concerto introduced (inevitably by Clara) in December 1845; the Second Symphony was completed. Schumann's mental state remained patchy throughout 1847, but he nevertheless began work on an opera on the subject of *Genoveva* based on earlier plays by Ludwig Tieck and Friedrich Hebbel, as well as writing two piano trios. After finishing *Genoveva* in 1848 (its first performance, which was received only with indifference, was not given until 1850 in Leipzig) Schumann turned his attention immediately to Byron's *Manfred*, for which he supplied incidental music, much of it in the form of melodrama. Though 1849 was marked by continued periods of instability and depression it also saw an increase in Schumann's productivity, with the creation of more than 20 works.

His earnings, however, remained less than adequate for a large family, and with Clara's support he took a post as music director in Düsseldorf in April 1850—for which he can be seen, in retrospect, to have been fundamentally unsuited. His diffidence in social situations, allied to mental instability, ensured that initially warm relations with local musicians gradually deteriorated to the point where his removal became a necessity in 1853. Meanwhile his ability to compose remained constant: among the larger achievements of this period are the Third ('Rhenish') Symphony and the Cello Concerto (both 1850), the final version of the Fourth Symphony (1851), together with various overtures and two cantatas from the same year, and a Mass and Requiem (both 1852).

The arrival on the Schumanns' doorstep in September 1853 of the 20-year-old Johannes Brahms provided the final happy interlude in Schumann's life: he hailed the genius of the newcomer in his final contribution to the *Neue Zeitschrift für Musik* (an article entitled 'New Paths'). Brahms was to prove a personal tower of strength to Clara during the difficult days ahead: in early 1854 Schumann's condition worsened alarmingly. On 26 February he asked to be taken to an asylum, and the following day attempted suicide by throwing himself into the Rhine. He was admitted to an institution at Endenich, near Bonn, on 4 March, and

remained there for over two years in a gradually deteriorating condition. He died of pneumonia at the asylum, aged 46.

Schumann's music

Commentators on Schumann's output have all agreed on the outstanding qualities of the piano music and songs. Less universally admired—at least until relatively recently—have been his achievements in other genres. A second caveat has tended to exist in respect of his later works: they have been broadly viewed as inferior to his earlier production (up to, say, the mid-1840s), the progress of his illness being seen as responsible for the apparent decline in their quality. The last decade or two, however, has seen a softening of these views, caused partly by increased performance and recording of the later works, and partly—in the case of his orchestral pieces—by the beneficial effects of period performance practice as it has come to be applied to mid-19th-century music.

Schumann's piano music has needed no such defence. As a highly trained pianist he understood the instrument's character and potential as well as anyone of his generation, and his personal rapport with it from childhood made it a natural means of expression to the adult composer; this perhaps partly explains the highly distinctive nature of his piano writing, in which expertise combines with a certain idiosyncrasy. Though it was found recherché by his contemporaries, its expressive power came to be acknowledged, and its lyrical melody and richly varied textures to be given their due. Even its more individual elements—such as its many references to real or imaginary figures within Schumann's personal mythology—came to attract as much as to puzzle.

Character pieces with fanciful names form a large part of Schumann's published output, while substantial works in such absolute genres as the sonata are rarer. Even in works ostensibly without any programmatic elements, commentators have discerned the use of ciphers, quotation, and other modes of discourse beyond the purely musical (in the Fantasia op. 17, for example), though the extent and intention of such references remain contentious. Schumann made a major contribution to the piano literature for the young student in his *Album für die Jugend* (1848), *Three Sonatas for Young People* (1853), and various duets. *Kinderszenen* (1838), though dealing with the subject of childhood, is clearly intended for adult performers and listeners.

Schumann's songs are notable above all for the high quality of the texts he set (his early discerning appreciation of literature was constantly renewed in adult life). Their variety is also immense, and far wider than an acquaintance with the 20 or 30 best-known examples might suggest: the *Poems of Mary Stuart* (1852), or the solo items from the *Spanisches Liederspiel* (for vocal quartet, 1849), are entirely different in mood from his earlier Romantic settings. His literary conscience also ensured the most equal partnership between words and music in the German lied before Hugo Wolf. And his close association with the piano led him to create accompaniments of great individuality and expressiveness, especially in the songs' preludes and postludes, the latter often providing a kind of summary of the verse's sentiments.

Much of Schumann's chamber output is neglected: beyond the well-known Piano Quartet and Piano Quintet (both 1842) lie fine works for string quartet and piano trio that are only now entering the repertory. In addition, and connected to Schumann's desire to raise the standard of music intended for domestic use, there are notable sets of pieces for clarinet, oboe, cello (all 1850), and viola (1851), all with piano accompaniment.

Schumann's first orchestral works came after solid achievements in piano music and song. He himself confessed that orchestration was a difficult art to master. This statement, together with his failure as a conductor, has fuelled a view that his orchestral works are among his less successful. For decades his orchestration was considered faulty, requiring professional amendment in performance (Gustav Mahler made his own editions of all four symphonies). An over-fondness for doubling does make for some thickness of texture, but such criticism is exaggerated. His symphonies scarcely follow in the grand Beethovenian tradition of heroics and humanitarianism, yet they are substantial achievements, and in all four, together with the *Overture, Scherzo, and Finale* (1841), the quality of musical invention is consistently high.

Schumann's choral music is less well known, though growing familiarity with such works as the *Scenes from Goethe's 'Faust'* (one of the most ambitious and faithful of all musical versions of the poem) and the colourful *Paradise and the Peri*, an 'oratorio for happy people' (Schumann's words), has convincingly demonstrated their worth. Another much-derided work is Schumann's sole opera, *Genoveva*, which for long passed as the leading representative of the genre of a bad opera by a great composer. Again, recent revivals on disc and stage have demonstrated its merits and original and effective musico-dramatic conception.

The idea that Schumann's later works were the product of an ailing creative force dies hard, and it cannot be denied that some of the sheer spontaneity of his first flowering did disappear. But, equally, there were gains from his increased experience—his studies of the music of Bach, for instance—which enabled him to rise to the constant challenge of extending himself beyond his early specialisms. GH

📖 A. WALKER (ed.), *Robert Schumann: The Man and his Music* (London, 1972) · R. TAYLOR, *Robert Schumann: His Life and Work* (London, 1982) · J. DAVERIO, *Robert Schumann: Herald of a 'New Poetic Age'* (New York and Oxford, 1997)

abilities were brought to the attention of Elector Johann Georg I of Saxony who, after lengthy wrangles with the landgrave, gained his services permanently, eventually appointing him principal Kapellmeister to his royal chapel, a post he was to occupy for the rest of his career.

In 1619 Schütz married Magdalena Wildeck, but only six years later she died, leaving the composer with two daughters, whom he entrusted to the care of their maternal grandmother. Shortly afterwards he returned to Venice, where he learnt, possibly from Monteverdi in person, the new techniques of composition which had developed there since his previous visit. On his return he brought with him Francesco Castelli, a Mantuan violinist with whose skills he hoped to revitalize the work of the Dresden chapel; but his plans, like those of many German musicians of the time, were constantly foiled by the effects of the Thirty Years War. In 1633 and 1642 Schütz paid two extended visits to Copenhagen to provide the music (now lost) for grand theatrical events there, mounted in connection with two royal weddings. During his last years, he returned to Weissenfels in semi-retirement; but finally he moved again to Dresden, where he died on 6 November 1672 and was entombed with much honour in the entrance porch of the Frauenkirche.

Most of Schütz's work is contained in 13 printed collections, published during his lifetime and mainly under his personal supervision. The earliest is a volume of 19 Italian madrigals, composed in 1611 on completion of his studies in Venice with Gabrieli. The daring harmonic style and dramatic vocal writing of these settings vividly recall the techniques of Monteverdi in his third and fourth books of madrigals. The remaining collections are devoted to sacred music and provide examples of all the principal forms of the period. Most of the texts are drawn from the Lutheran Bible; Latin, though not uncommon, is used exclusively in only two major collections, the *Cantiones sacrae* (1625) and the first volume of *Symphoniae sacrae* (1629). Gabrieli's influence is clearly evident in the *Psalmen Davids* (1619), a set of 26 polychoral settings of German psalm texts, involving voices and instruments in the grand Venetian manner. Only in one later collection were such lavish forces used, the third volume of *Symphoniae sacrae* (1650), in which dramatic vocal and instrumental scoring is used to enhance such famous biblical accounts as the parable of the tribute money and the conversion of St Paul on the road to Damascus.

Choral polyphony (with largely optional continuo) is explored in the *Cantiones sacrae* (1625), in which Latin texts, many of a mystical character, are given deeply expressionist settings. A parallel volume, the *Geistliche Chor-music* of 1648, contains 29 German motets (for five, six, and seven voices), in which Schütz strikingly demonstrates his mastery of the ancient contrapuntal techniques absorbed into the German musical mainstream through the pupils of Lassus. Much of the intensely German, and particularly Lutheran, character of these settings results from the intimate relationship between the musical style and the rhythms, cadences, and inflections of the German language. In his preface Schütz stresses the need for young German composers to acquire a sound basis in pure vocal counterpoint before proceeding to more modern, continuo-based styles.

Particular interest attaches to the *Musikalische Exequien*, the largest of his funerary works, which was composed in 1636 for the obsequies of Prince Heinrich Posthumus of Reuss. The work falls into three sections: an elaborate German burial Mass for solo voices and chorus, based on scriptural and chorale texts chosen by the prince for inscription on his coffin; a double-chorus motet on verses from Psalm 73, the text chosen for the funeral oration; and a vivid juxtaposition of the German *Nunc dimittis*, sung by a first chorus 'near the organ', and 'Blessed are the dead' and other biblical texts sung by a three-voice second choir 'in the distance', symbolizing 'angels accompanying the soul of the departed'. Monodies and small concertato works are represented by two sets of *Kleine geistliche Konzerte* (1636, 1639) and by the first two volumes of *Symphoniae sacrae* (1629, 1647). In their modest performance requirements, the sacred concertos may reflect economies imposed at Dresden by the war. But it is likely also that Schütz was inspired to explore this miniature genre by the strong progress it had made elsewhere in Europe since the time of Viadana. The *Symphoniae sacrae*, as their title suggests, display richer instrumental resources and a greater diversity of scoring. In the second set Schütz paid his most significant homage to Monteverdi, partly by including a tribute to him in the preface, partly by adopting the *stile concitato*, and, most strikingly, by basing one of his

settings (*Es steh Gott auf* swv356) on two of the Italian's madrigals.

Only one of Schütz's 'historiae' (portrayals in music of dramatic biblical accounts) was published complete in his lifetime, the *Resurrection History* (1623), a beautiful setting of an Easter text compiled from all four gospels. The *Christmas History* (1664), of all his works the most overtly popular in style, was at first published incomplete, with only the role of the Evangelist printed; in common with the *Seven Last Words from the Cross* (c.1645) and the *St Matthew*, *St Luke*, and *St John* Passions (c.1664–6), it has been only gradually restored in modern times from manuscript sources. In these last works, and others such as his liturgical *Zwölff geistliche Gesänge* (1657) and his swansong, the immense setting of Psalm 119 for double chorus (1671), the changes that had taken place in the composer's musical language during his long career are clearly evident. The daring harmonic enterprise and bold expressionism of his earlier years have yielded place to a new moderation, a new leaning towards objectivity, a new philosophical calm, revealing modes of thought comparable to those of Bach and Beethoven in their final creative periods.

BS

📖 H. J. MOSER, *Heinrich Schütz: sein Leben und Werk* (Kassel, 1936, 2/1954; Eng. trans. 1959) · D. ARNOLD, 'Schütz's Venetian Psalms', *Musical Times*, 113 (1972), 1071–3 · B. SMALLMAN, *Schütz* (Oxford, 1999)

schwach, schwächer (Ger.). 'Weak', i.e. soft, 'weaker'.

Schwanengesang ('Swan Song'). Collection of songs for voice and piano by Schubert, D957 (1828), settings of seven poems by Ludwig Rellstab, six by Heinrich Heine, and one by Johann Gabriel Seidl, published posthumously as a 'cycle' under this title by Tobias Haslinger.

Schwantner, Joseph (*b* Chicago, 22 March 1943). American composer. He studied at the Chicago Conservatory and Northwestern University, and began teaching at the Eastman School in 1970. As composer-in-residence with the St Louis Symphony (1982–5) he developed formidable skill in writing for the orchestra, using a variety of late 20th-century techniques within a traditional discourse. His works in this genre include concertos for piano (1988) and percussion (1992), song cycles, and poetic evocations. Other works are for band, mixed chamber ensemble (*Distant Runes and Incantations* for eight players, 1987), or solo instrumentalist.

PG

schweigen (Ger.). 'To be silent'; *schweigt* means the same as *tacet*; *Schweigezeichen*, a rest.

Schweigsame Frau, Die ('The Silent Woman'). Opera in three acts by Richard Strauss to a libretto by Stefan Zweig after Ben Jonson's play *Epicoene* (1609) (Dresden, 1935).

Schweinitz, Wolfgang von (*b* Hamburg, 7 Feb. 1953). German composer. He studied at the Hamburg State Conservatory with Ligeti, at the Stanford University computer research centre, and in Rome. He has contributed to several traditional genres, including those of the song cycle with *Papiersterne* (1981), the large-scale religious work with his Mass (1984), and opera with *Patmos*, after the Book of Revelation (Munich, 1990). His recent music is more experimental in its exploration of acoustic phenomena and perception: for example, *Franz & Morton* (1996) is a piano trio entirely in harmonics lasting just over an hour and a half.

ABur

Schweitzer, Albert (*b* Kaysersberg, 14 Jan. 1875; *d* Lambaréné, Gabon, 4 Sept. 1965). Alsatian organist, theologian, and philosopher. His early studies with Eugen Münch introduced him to Bach, and he went on to develop his organ playing with Widor in Paris. He studied the history of the organ and its construction (strongly preferring French instruments), and produced his most significant writings on music between 1905 and 1913, when he was also both a practising theologian and lecturer at Strasbourg. His important study of Bach and Bach interpretation was first published in French in 1905. His last 50 years were spent in Africa, where he established a hospital and leper colony, returning occasionally to raise funds by giving organ recitals.

CF

📖 A. Schweitzer, *J. S. Bach* (Eng. trans., London, 1911/R) · G. Marshall and D. Poling, *Schweitzer: A Biography* (London and New York, 1971) · M. Murray, *Albert Schweitzer, Musician* (Brookfield, VT, 1994)

schwer (Ger.) 'Heavy', 'ponderous', 'difficult'; *schwermütig*, *schwermutsvoll*, 'heavy-hearted'.

Schwertsik, Kurt (*b* Vienna, 25 June 1935). Austrian composer, horn player, and pianist. He studied at the Vienna Academy of Music with Josef Marx and Karl Schiske, and worked as an orchestral horn player. As a composer he belongs to the so-called third Viennese school, which in reaction to the avant-garde has re-embraced tonality and included elements of Romantic and popular music. Schwertsik has written operas and operettas, including *Das Märchen von Fanferlieschen Schönefüsschen* ('The Wondrous Tale of Fanferlizzy Sunnyfeet', Stuttgart, 1983), ballets, orchestral and chamber music, and several song cycles for performance with his wife.

ABur

schwindend (Ger.). 'Dying away', i.e. becoming quieter, the same as **diminuendo*.

schwungvoll (Ger.). 'Vigorous', 'energetic'.

Sciarrino, Salvatore (*b* Palermo, 4 April 1947). Italian composer. A gifted child in many artistic spheres, he began composing when he was 12 and in 1962 had his first public performance. In 1969 he moved to Rome, where his music quickly attracted attention and where he pursued his autodidactic path. He has taught in Milan, Florence, Bologna, and Palermo. Like Nono, he is driven by a desire for innovation. His large output encompasses vocal, orchestral, incidental, and chamber music, much of it influenced by his interest in early works (for instance the ballet *Morte a Venezia* (1991), based on Bach) and in American popular song (*Blue Dream*, 1980). Like many of his large-scale concert pieces, Sciarrino's stage works depart from conventional forms and embrace the surreal; they include *Aspern* (1978; based on Henry James), the montages *Cailles en sarcophage* (1979; incorporating American icons and song), and *Vanitas* (1981; a 'gigantic anamorphosis' of Hoagy Carmichael's *Stardust*), two works drawn from Jules Laforgue (*Lohengrin*, 1983; *Perseo e Andromeda*, 1991), and *Infinito nero* (1998). He has made many transcriptions and arrangements.

AL

📖 N. Hodges, 'A volcano viewed from afar: The music of Salvatore Sciarrino', *Tempo*, 194 (1995), 22–4

sciolto, scioltamente (It.). 'Free', 'unconstrained', 'loosely'.

Scipione ('Scipio'). Opera in three acts by Handel to a libretto by Paolo Antonio Rolli based on Antonio Salvi's *Publio Cornelio Scipione* (1704) after Livy's *Historiarum ab urbe condita libri* (London, 1726).

scordatura (It., 'mistuning'; Fr.: *discordé*, *discordable*, *discordant*; Ger.: *Umstimmung*, *Verstimmung*). A term used most often in connection with bowed and plucked string instruments, especially lutes and violins, to denote a tuning in which one or more of the strings is at a different pitch from the normal. Its purpose is to make passages easier to play by bringing notes, especially double-stopped chords, more easily under the hand. It can brighten the tone by allowing strings to resonate sympathetically with each other. Biber took advantage of both these effects in several works for violin.

Scordatura is also sometimes used to extend the range downwards, for example tuning the lowest (C) string of a viola or cello to B or B♭, or the double bass E string to C. This type of retuning was known to French lutenists or guitarists as *avallé* or *ravallé* and to Germans as **Abzug*. The tuning to be used is always indicated at the beginning of the first staff of the music, and the notes are generally written so that although players place their fingers in the normal position the sound produced will be that required by the scordatura. Viol players rarely used scordatura, except for the English *lyra viol of the 17th century, which used many tunings, none of which were recognized as standard.

JMo

score (Fr.: *partition*; Ger.: *Partitur*; It.: *partitura*). A printed or manuscript copy of a piece of music which shows the parts for all the performers arranged on separate staves; this is distinct from a 'part', which shows only the music for one performer (or for one group of performers). A 'full' score has each instrumental or vocal part separately displayed, with full performance details (though two parts for instruments of the same kind may be written on a single staff); this is the type of score normally used by a conductor. An alternative term for this is 'orchestral' score.

A 'vocal' or 'piano-vocal' score shows all the vocal parts (usually of an opera or a choral work) on separate staves, with the orchestral parts reduced to a keyboard arrangement. A 'piano' score is a full score reduced to form an arrangement for piano. A 'short' or 'condensed' score is a reduction of a full score to a smaller number of staves (related parts, for example woodwind, may be combined on one staff) but not necessarily arranged for piano. A *'miniature' score is a printed score of pocket size, in which, conventionally, any voice or instrument that rests for an entire system (see below) is omitted from that system. A 'study' score may be either a miniature score or a full score of reduced dimensions.

Score notation was used for polyphony during the 12th and 13th centuries. The writing of individual parts of a polyphonic texture became common in the second half of the 13th century with the rising popularity of the motet. Because the voice parts in the motet tended to differ greatly in length (with the upper parts including many more notes than the tenors), score notation was uneconomical and each individual part was written separately on its own set of staves (choirbook format). During the 16th century, composers began using score notation again to facilitate the planning of complex polyphonic textures, and during the 17th century it once more became the standard format for polyphony.

The act of 'scoring' is deciding on and writing down the instrumentation of a work that is already conceived for another medium (e.g. for the piano) or assembling in score form the individual instrumental or vocal parts of a work (e.g. from 16th-century partbooks, where no composite score exists).

A set of all the necessary staves printed on a page is called a system; each system is linked at the right- and left-hand ends by a continuous bar-line. Each individual staff has its own bar-lines, but these may extend through the staves of related instruments. There may be more than one system on a page, in which case they are separated at the left-hand side by a pair of strokes in bold type.

The modern vertical arrangement of instrumental parts in a full score of a work for standard orchestra, from top to bottom, is: woodwind (piccolo, flutes, oboes, clarinets, bassoons); brass (horns, trumpets, trombones, tuba); percussion (timpani, side drum, bass drum, triangle, etc.); strings (first violins, second violins, violas, cellos, double basses). A cor anglais part is normally placed below the oboes, bass clarinet below clarinets, and double bassoon below bassoon. A harp or celesta part is placed between the percussion and string sections, and any solo part in a concerto immediately above the first violins. Voice parts, if any, are placed above the string section, with soloists above the chorus, which is arranged in descending order of voices.

Deviations from these conventions may be required by, for example, the introduction of unusual instruments or a desire to group certain instruments together. Scores of contemporary music may vary a great deal from standard patterns, especially where a degree of improvisation or indeterminacy is involved. In scores of aleatory music, verbal directions may predominate over conventional musical notation. Some modern scores adopt a sort of measured space–time system or indicate only the relative positions of the conductor's downbeat. A number of composers have abandoned traditional staff notation in favour of *graphic notation, where words, pictures, abstract patterns, and symbols are used; some have combined graphic notation with conventional staff notation, sometimes in the same work. Scores of electronic music may consist of precise mathematical symbols and calculations, or of pictures, colours, or graphics, or they may combine any of those elements with standard staff notation.

See also NOTATION, 5.

PS/JN/JG

📖 W. APEL, *The Notation of Polyphonic Composition, 900–1600* (Cambridge, MA, 1942, 5/1961) · C. HOPKINSON, 'The earliest miniature scores', *Music Review*, 33 (1972), 138–44 · E. BROWN, 'The notation and performance of new music', *Musical Quarterly*, 72 (1986), 180–201 · J. A. OWENS, *Composers at Work: The Craft of Musical Composition, 1450–1600* (New York, 1997)

scorrendo, scorevole (It.). 'Flowing'; a *glissando.

Scotch snap [Scotch catch]. A rhythmic feature in which a dotted note is preceded, rather than followed, by a note of shorter value, e.g.:

♪♩. as opposed to ♩.♪.

It is a characteristic feature of the Scottish strathspey, and is also found in some Scottish song tunes as well as in the pseudo-Scottish melodies that were such a popular feature of 18th-century London pleasure gardens. However, no Scottish song earlier than the 18th century seems to display the feature.

The 'Scotch snap' appears in late 16th-century French songs as a feature of *musique mesurée, and it was apparently just as commonly used in the performance of 17th-century *notes inégales. It was also common in early 17th-century Italian music, where it was known as the *stile lombardo* (Lombardy style); Sammartini and J. C. Bach, who both worked in Milan—the capital of Lombardy—used it in their music. Inverted dotting was also used by some 17th-century English composers (e.g. Purcell), because it suits the accentuation of the English language.

Scotland 1. Folk traditions; 2. Art music

1. Folk traditions

Two musical traditions exist in Scottish folk culture, each with its own language: the Gaelic music of the Highlands and Hebrides, and the music of the Lowlands and eastern areas. (Orkney and Shetland have their own distinct styles, of Scandinavian origin.) Gaelic song has features common to all traditional Scottish music, including pentatonic scales (though heptatonic ones are equally common) and the *Scotch snap. Lowland airs, written down from the 17th century, appear in countless published editions, from Playford's *English Dancing Master* (1651) onwards. Lowland *ballads survive in such collections as that of F. J. Child, while many 'bothy ballads' (associated with farm life) have been collected in Aberdeenshire and surrounding counties.

The three instruments of Scotland's folk culture are the *harp (*clàrsach*), *bagpipe, and fiddle. The *clàrsach* fell from fashion in the early 18th century, reappearing in 1892 during the organized revival of Gaelic culture. The mouth-blown Highland bagpipe has survived in spite of the suppression of Gaelic language and traditions following the battle of Culloden (1745). Its 'great music' (*ceòl mòr*), known as pibroch (Gaelic: *piobaireachd*), is a highly developed theme and variation form; lighter music embraces marches, airs, and dances (e.g. the *reel), a repertory partly shared with the fiddle. The violin is first mentioned at the turn of the 18th century, when manuscript and printed collections of fiddle music also began to appear and Italian models were starting to influence Scots makers, but fiddlers' names from earlier times are recorded. Niel Gow (1727–97), who with his sons dominated fiddle playing in the 18th and 19th centuries, is thought to have introduced

the characteristic up-bow stroke and marked use of Scotch snap rhythm into Scots fiddle music.

2. Art music

The history of Scottish church music is fragmentary: a written account of Scots liturgical music has survived from the 12th century, while what is assumed to be native music is found alongside examples of organum and conductus of the Notre Dame school in the manuscript Wolfenbüttel 677, believed to have been compiled in the 13th century at St Andrews. The words and music of a wedding hymn (*Ex te lux oritur O dulcis Scotia*) for Margaret of Scotland and Eric II of Norway (1281) have survived. The great period of sacred music dates from the reign of James IV (1488–1513)—including the polyphonic masses and motets of Robert Carver, David Peebles, and Robert Johnson (the last partly written in English exile)—to the establishment of the Reformation in 1560 and the victory of Presbyterianism. The only provision made by Calvinist reformers for music in worship was simple metrical psalm settings; the first Scottish psalter appeared in 1564. Polyphonic music became confined to privileged circles, and effectively disappeared after the departure for England of James VI and his court in 1603. Examples of that 'popish instrument' the organ were destroyed everywhere, and it was not restored to established worship in Scotland until the late 19th century.

Composition was left in the hands of amateurs who turned their interest increasingly to folksongs, arranging them for stringed instruments and keyboard. Thus Scotland began consciously to collect, arrange, and publish its musical heritage. Although the Baroque period can be said to have passed Scotland by, the country's traditional music was greatly in vogue in London by 1700. 18th-century Edinburgh became a centre of musical activity, with an influx of foreign musicians and the emergence of native Scottish composers such as Thomas Erskine; collections of national songs continued to appear, the most significant being *The Scots Musical Museum* (1787–1803), which saw the involvement of Robert Burns. Scottish music history was at its lowest ebb in the 19th century until, in the final decade, what is now the Royal Scottish Academy of Music and Drama was established in Glasgow; a degree course in music was established at Edinburgh University in 1893, and a chair of music was founded at Glasgow University in 1929.

Since the late 19th century, the implications for Scottish composers of nationality and national heritage have been inescapable: aspects of a national idiom were transplanted into the prevailing European styles, resulting first in the picturesque concert overtures, symphonic poems, and rhapsodies of Hamish MacCunn,

William Wallace (1860–1940), and others, and later in the settings of Scottish poetry by Francis George Scott (1880–1958). A further renaissance is exemplified by the generation of composers active in postwar years both within and outside Scotland, including such figures as Iain Hamilton and Thea Musgrave, but it is the achievement of James MacMillan (*b* 1959) that has given Scottish music an international dimension.

DW/KC

📖 K. ELLIOTT and F. RIMMER, *A History of Scottish Music* (London, 1973) · J. PURSER, *Scotland's Music: A History of the Traditional and Classical Music of Scotland from Early Times to the Present Day* (Edinburgh, 1992)

Scott, Cyril (Meir) (*b* Oxton, Cheshire, 27 Sept. 1879; *d* Eastbourne, 31 Dec. 1970). English composer, pianist, and writer. One of the so-called *Frankfurt Group, he studied with Iwan Knorr at the Hoch Conservatory (1895–8). At the turn of the 20th century he established a reputation for modernity with his *Heroic Suite* and First Symphony (both 1900), his Piano Quartet (1901), and his Second Symphony (later recast as *Three Symphonic Dances*), conducted by Henry Wood in 1903. Dubbed the 'English Debussy', he composed songs and piano works in an impressionistic style for popular consumption. He produced several ballets, a one-act opera *The Alchemist* (1917), a full-length opera *Maureen O'Mara* (1946), an oratorio *Hymn of Unity* (1947), and various orchestral pieces. Though he is barely known for these works, which have fallen into neglect, the Piano Concerto (1915), arguably his finest work, is worthy of revival. Among his other interests were literature (he translated the works of Stefan George), Indian philosophy, the occult, and various medical topics. He published poetry and several books including *The Philosophy of Modernism* (1917) and his autobiography *My Years of Indiscretion* (1924).

MK/JDI

📖 A. E. HULL, *Cyril Scott, Composer, Poet and Philosopher* (London, 1918, 3/1921)

Scottish Fantasy (*Schottische Fantasie*). Fantasia on Scottish folk tunes (1879–80) for violin and orchestra by Bruch.

Scottish Symphony. Mendelssohn's Symphony no. 3 in A minor, composed between 1830 and 1842; it was inspired by a visit to Holyrood, Edinburgh, in 1829 and is dedicated to Queen Victoria.

Scotto. Italian family of music printers and composers. Its most prominent member was Girolamo Scotto (*c*.1505–72), who assumed control of the family's Venetian publishing concern in 1539. The family had connections with Andrea *Antico, whose last music publication they printed, and with the prolific *Gardano

press. The firm's founder, Ottaviano Scotto (*d* 1498), had been known for the printing of missals; subsequent family members, including a later Ottaviano (*c*.1495–*c*.1568) and Girolamo, dealt more in the secular repertory, though their output of books of motets was far from negligible

JWA

Scriabin, Alexander. See SKRYABIN, ALEKSANDR NIKOLAYEVICH.

scroll. The ornamental carved volute at the top of violin family pegboxes; sometimes carved figures or heads are used instead.

JMo

Sculthorpe, Peter (Joshua) (*b* Launceston, Tasmania, 29 April 1929). Australian composer. He studied at the University of Melbourne (1947–50) and with Edmund Rubbra and Egon Wellesz at Oxford (1958–60). In 1963 he was appointed to teach at the University of Sydney. He was one of the first Australian composers to place himself in the context of East Asian music, especially Balinese, and since the mid-1960s he has produced a large output. Important works include *Sun Music I–V* for orchestra (1965–9) and 11 string quartets.

PG

sdrucciolando (It.). 'Sliding'; in harp playing, a *glissando.

Sea Drift. Work (1903–4) by Delius, a setting for baritone, chorus, and orchestra of an extract from Walt Whitman's *Out of the Cradle Endlessly Rocking*.

Sea Interludes, Four. See FOUR SEA INTERLUDES.

sean-nós (Irish, 'old style'). A term generally used to refer to various styles and repertories of singing believed to be the oldest in Ireland. *Sean-nós* performance is usually associated with small, intimate spaces rather than large venues, with understatement rather than dramatic declamation, and with intricate vocal ornamentation.

PW

Sea Pictures. Song cycle, op. 37 (1897–9), by Elgar, for alto and orchestra, settings of poems by Roden Noel, Caroline Alice Elgar, Elizabeth Barrett Browning, Richard Garnett, and Adam Lindsay Gordon.

Searle, Humphrey (*b* Oxford, 26 Aug. 1915; *d* London, 12 May 1982). English composer. He studied at Oxford and the RCM, and with Webern in Vienna. He was a teacher and author as well as a BBC producer (1938–40, 1946–8). His music is serial, though closer to Schoenberg than to Webern, and often imbued with a romantic rhetoric traceable to his interest in Liszt. Among his works are three operas (including *Hamlet*, Hamburg, 1968) and five symphonies.

PG/AW

📖 R. M. SCHAFER, *British Composers in Interview* (London, 1963)

sea shanty. See SHANTY.

Seasons, The. 1. (*Die Jahreszeiten*). Oratorio (1799–1801) by Haydn, for soprano, tenor, and bass soloists, chorus, and orchestra, to a text by Gottfried van Swieten after an English poem by James Thomson (1700–48) translated by Barthold Heinrich Brockes.

2. Ballet in one act and four scenes by Glazunov to a scenario by Marius Petipa, who choreographed it (St Petersburg, 1900).

See also FOUR SEASONS, THE.

Sea Symphony, A. Vaughan Williams's first symphony, for soprano and baritone soloists, chorus, and orchestra, to a text taken from poems by Walt Whitman; it was composed between 1903 and 1909 and later revised, the last revision being in 1923.

Šebor, Karel (Richard) [Schebor, Carl] (*b* Brandys nad Labem, 13 Aug. 1843; *d* Prague, 17 May 1903). Czech composer and conductor. At the age of 11 he entered the Prague Conservatory to study the violin and composition. In 1865 he had considerable success with his first opera *Templáři na Moravě* ('The Templars in Moravia'), the first opera to an original Czech text to be given in the Provisional Theatre after Škroup's *The Tinker*. His succeeding operas *Drahomíra* (1867) and *Nevěsta husitská* ('The Hussite Bride', 1868) were also well received, but the failure of his 'fantastic-romantic' opera *Blanka* (1870) marked the beginning of a decline in his fortunes. His works included (besides five operas) chamber music, overtures, songs, choral music, and four symphonies.   JSM

sec, sèche (Fr.). 'Dry': a term used by French composers, especially Debussy, to indicate that a note or chord should be struck and then quickly released.

secco (It.). 'Dry', i.e. *staccato*. See also RECITATIVE.

Sechter, Simon (*b* Friedberg, 11 Oct. 1788; *d* Vienna, 10 Sept. 1867). Austrian theorist, composer, conductor, and organist. He began teaching at the Institute for the Blind in Vienna in 1810, remaining until 1825. His fame as a teacher, at the Vienna Conservatory from 1851, dwarfed his reputation as an organist and a composer (allegedly of several thousand works). In 1828 Schubert asked for lessons but had only one, shortly before his death. Of Sechter's many other distinguished pupils, the most famous was Bruckner, who began studying with him in 1855 and continued until 1861.   JW

seconda pratica. See PRIMA PRATICA, SECONDA PRATICA.

secondary seventh chord. A *seventh chord on a degree of the scale other than the dominant.

seconda volta (It.). 'Second-time (bar)'; see DOUBLE BAR.

second inversion [6-4 chord]. A term describing the vertical presentation of a chord when the 5th rather than the root is the lowest note, the other notes being a 4th and a 6th above it (hence 6-4). See also INVERSION, 1.

Second Mrs Kong, The. Opera in two acts by Birtwistle to a libretto by Russell Hoban (Glyndebourne, 1994).

second subject. The first or principal theme of the second group of a *sonata-form movement.

second-time bar. See DOUBLE BAR.

Secret Marriage, The. See MATRIMONIO SEGRETO, IL.

Secret Theatre. Work (1984) for 14 instruments by Birtwistle.

Sederunt principes. A four-voice chant setting (*organum quadruplum*) by Pérotin, a gradual for St Stephen composed *c.*1200.

Seefried, Irmgard (*b* Köngetried, Bavaria, 9 Oct. 1919; *d* Vienna, 24 Nov. 1988). German soprano. She studied at the Augsburg Conservatory and made her debut in Aachen in 1939, remaining with the company until 1943. In 1944 she became a member of the Vienna State Opera, where she made her debut as Eva (in *Die Meistersinger von Nürnberg*) and famously sang the Composer in *Ariadne auf Naxos* as part of Strauss's 80th birthday celebrations. She first appeared in London as Fiordiligi (in *Così fan tutte*) during the Vienna company's visit to Covent Garden in 1947. She sang regularly at the Salzburg Festival from 1946 until her retirement in 1971.

Seefried had a bright, sensuous voice and was a superlative interpreter of Mozart and Strauss, though she also championed the modernist repertory, including Marie (in *Wozzeck*) among her operatic roles and giving the world premieres of Hindemith's *Motets* (1951) and Henze's *Ariosi* (1964). She was one of the greatest of all lieder singers, matchless in Schubert and Wolf.

TA

Seeger, Ruth Crawford. See CRAWFORD SEEGER, RUTH.

Seejungfrau, Die ('The Mermaid'). Tone-poem (1902–3) by Zemlinsky after Hans Christian Andersen.

Seele (Ger.). 'Soul', i.e. feeling; it has also been used to mean the soundpost of a bowed string instrument, fancifully considered the instrument's 'soul'.

seelenvoll (Ger.). 'Soulful'.

segno (It.). 'Sign'. See AL SEGNO; DAL SEGNO.

Segovia, Andrés (*b* Linares, Granada, 21 Feb. 1893; *d* Madrid, 2 June 1987). Spanish guitarist. He made his debut in Granada in 1908, followed by tours throughout Spain, to Latin America in 1916, Paris and Berlin in 1924, London in 1926, and North America in 1928. His concert career lasted 75 years and he also taught extensively. As well as reviving much forgotten music and transcribing works for the guitar, he worked closely with Falla and inspired such composers as Sor, Ponce, Castelnuovo-Tedesco, Villa-Lobos, Turina, and Roussel to write for him. His virtuosity awakened public awareness to an instrument which, at the time, was not taken seriously; through the unique, right-hand technique he himself developed he was capable of bringing delicately colourful nuances to his formidably brilliant playing.   CF

📖 A. SEGOVIA, *An Autobiography of the Years 1893 to 1920* (Eng. trans., New York, 1976) · G. WADE, *Segovia: A Celebration of the Man and his Music* (London, 1983) · G. WADE and G. GARNO, *A New Look at Segovia: His Life, his Music* (Pacific, MO, 1996)

Segreto di Susanna, Il (*Susannens Geheimnis*; 'Susannah's Secret'). Opera in one act by Wolf-Ferrari to a libretto by Enrico Golisciani (Munich, 1909).

segue (It.). 'Follows': an instruction to play the following section or movement without a break; *segue la coda*, 'the coda follows'; *seguente, seguendo*, 'following'. The term may also be an indication to 'follow the same way', i.e. continue with a pattern that is at first written out in full but then abbreviated. 'Segue' is used by DJs or presenters as both a noun and a verb where two or more songs or instrumental pieces (usually at least loosely connected in mood or timbre) are played without a break.

seguidilla (Sp.). A Castilian folk dance, possibly of Moorish origin. It is in quick triple time and alternates *coplas* (verses sung by the dancers) with passages played on guitar and castanets and is still performed in Andalusia. Albéniz used it in his piano music and there is an example in Act I of Bizet's *Carmen*, much criticized because it is untypical.   —/JH

Sehnsucht (Ger.). 'Longing'; *sehnsüchtig, sehnsuchtsvoll*, 'longingly'.

Seiber, Mátyás (György) (*b* Budapest, 4 May 1905; *d* Cape Town, 24 Sept. 1960). Hungarian-born British composer. He was a pupil of Kodály at the Budapest Music Academy, and after World War I settled in Germany as an orchestral player, conductor, and teacher of composition and jazz at the Hoch Conservatory, Frankfurt. His works from this period include the Bartókian *Sonata da camera* for violin and cello (1925) and the Second String Quartet (1934–5), in which he used Schoenberg's serial technique. After his move to England in 1935 his use of *serialism became more individual, allowing the reintroduction of triads in a style of fluent musicality and keen rhythmic inventiveness. His finest works of this period include the Third Quartet, or *Quartetto lirico* (1948–51), and cantatas to texts by James Joyce (*Ulysses*, 1946–7), Goethe (*Faust*, 1949), and Virgil (*Cantata secularis*, 1949–51).

Seiber earned his living in England by writing functional music and teaching composition, privately and at Morley College. As a teacher, and as co-founder of the Committee (later Society) for the Promotion of New Music, he had a notable influence on younger English composers.   PG

seises (Sp.). The name for choirboys of the great cathedrals of the Spanish-speaking world from the 16th century to the 19th. They were so called because there were generally six (Sp.: *seis*) of them. On festival days and at processions the boys would also dance to the accompaniment of various instruments, including castanets.

Seite (Ger.). 'Side', e.g. a page of a book or one skin of a drum; *Seitenthema*, 'second theme', e.g. in a sonata-form movement.

Selxas, (José António) Carlos de (*b* Coimbra, 11 June 1704; *d* Lisbon, 25 Aug. 1742). Portuguese composer, harpsichordist, and organist. He was organist at Coimbra Cathedral in 1718 and at the Portuguese royal chapel in Lisbon from 1720. Like his colleague Domenico Scarlatti, Seixas wrote highly original harpsichord sonatas; he, however, retained the multi-movement form, though some are in single movements. He also composed organ, orchestral, and sacred music; the Lisbon earthquake of 1755 may account for the fact that few copies survive.   WT/LC

Se la face ay pale. Chanson for three voices by Dufay, composed probably in the 1430s; he later used its tenor part as the tenor cantus firmus of a mass for four voices. David Lang based his *Face So Pale* (1992) for six pianos on the same melody.

Selle, Thomas (*b* Zörbig, 23 March 1599; *d* Hamburg, 2 July 1663). German composer. He held appointments in north-west Germany before settling in Hamburg in 1641 as Kantor at the Johanneum and civic director of music. His compositions include some 280 sacred works, among them motets marked 'ad imitationem Orlandi', which 'parody' works by Lassus. His second *St John Passion* (1643) was the first to involve obbligato instruments, both to provide an accompaniment and to delineate characters. BS

semel. See GYMEL.

Semele. Opera in three acts by Handel to a libretto by William Congreve after Ovid's *Metamorphoses* (London, 1744).

semibreve (o). The note having half the value of the breve and double the value of the minim; in American terminology it is known as 'whole note'.

semidemisemiquaver. See HEMIDEMISEMIQUAVER.

semifusa (Lat.). An early note-value, from which the modern *semiquaver derives. See NOTATION, Fig. 6.

semiminima (Lat.). An early note-value, from which the modern *crotchet derives. See NOTATION, Fig. 6.

semi-opera. In English theatre of the late 17th and early 18th centuries, a type of drama in which the principal characters, which were usually played by actors, spoke, but the minor characters (often trained singers) used song and dance. The development of the semi-opera was influenced by the French *comédies-ballets* and *tragédies lyriques* as well as the earlier English *masque, but the genre declined with the growing popularity of Italian opera in England from the beginning of the 18th century.

The first semi-opera was *The Tempest*, produced in 1674 and based, rather loosely, on Shakespeare's play. The music, composed by Matthew Locke, James Hart, Pelham Humfrey, and others, was concentrated in certain scenes which were expanded specifically to exploit the musical potential of the drama. Purcell's contributions to the genre are the most well known and include *Dioclesian* (1690), *King Arthur* (1691), *The Fairy Queen* (1692), and *The Indian Queen* (1695), for which he wrote all the music. In these works, the musical elements are generally confined to particular sequences that have little to do with the development of the plot and are in many ways similar to the earlier court masque. Following the death of Purcell, the tradition of the semi-opera was continued by such composers as Jeremiah Clarke, Daniel Purcell, and Richard Leveridge, all of whom contributed music to *The Island Princess* (1699). JBE

semiotics [semiology]. Semiotics is the general theory of how communication takes place. This requires 'signs' (Gk.: *sēmeion*, from where the word 'semiotics' derives), grouped together into 'texts' (which might include a musical score), and understood by means of a 'code'. The two theorists who first developed these ideas (independently of each other) were the Swiss linguist

Ferdinand de Saussure (1857–1913) and the American philosopher Charles Sanders Peirce (1839–1914). Later developments came especially in the field of literary criticism, notably from the French writer Roland Barthes, the Italian writer Umberto Eco, the American critic Paul de Man, and the French philosopher Jacques Derrida.

Musical applications of semiotic theory have been attempted since the early 1970s. One of the earliest exponents was the French musicologist Jean-Jacques Nattiez, who developed a system of analysis in which a musical work is divided up (or 'segmented') into short units; these units are then compared with each other, without any pre-existent assumption of their musical meaning or value—in other words, such considerations as harmonic function, mode, or genre are deliberately excluded from the start. The units are arranged into 'paradigmatic tables' of similar occurrences, from which general rules of their use are derived. This is, unsurprisingly, a laborious process, the most famous result of which was a 100-page study by Nattiez of Varèse's *Density 21.5*, a 60-bar piece for solo flute.

More recent semiotic writing about music has followed several distinct paths. One is the investigation of the nature of musical meaning itself. There are two main problems here: first, what constitutes a 'sign' in music, and secondly, what sorts of object or idea these signs 'refer' to in order to have meaning. This has been approached from a technical standpoint in such works as Frits Noske's study of Mozart and Verdi (1977), Robert Hatten's study of Beethoven (1994), or Kofi Agawu's study of the Classical style (1991). It has been addressed more as a philosophical question by such writers as Eero Tarasti (1994, 1996) and Raymond Monelle (1992, 1998).

Musical semiotics has also been used to compare musical works with other forms of human expression. This is an important application, since describing how music communicates in general terms facilitates comparisons with other arts (e.g. literature) or with non-artistic realms. Examples are Tarasti's study of the role of myth in Wagner, Sibelius, and Stravinsky (1978), Robert Samuels's study of Mahler (1995), and Naomi Cumming's study of Bach's *St Matthew Passion* (1997). RS

📖 U. Eco, *A Theory of Semiotics* (Bloomington, IN, 1976) · J.-J. Nattiez, *Music and Discourse* (Princeton, NJ, 1990) · R. Monelle, *Linguistics and Semiotics in Music* (Chur, 1992) · D. Lidov, *Elements of Semiotics* (New York, 1999)

semiquaver (♪). The note having 1/16 of the value of the semibreve, or whole note; hence the American usage '16th-note'.

Semiramide ('Semiramis'). Opera in two acts by Rossini to a libretto by Gaetano Rossi after Voltaire's *Sémiramis* (1748) (Venice, 1823). It is the subject of numerous operas, notably by Porpora (1729), Vivaldi (1732), Hasse (1744), Gluck (1748), Galuppi (1749), Paisiello (1772), Salieri (1782), Meyerbeer (1819), and Respighi (1910), many of them settings of a libretto by Pietro Metastasio.

semitone. The smallest interval in common use in Western music, covering half a tone.

semplice, semplicemente (It.). 'Simple', 'simply'.

sempre (It.). 'Always'; e.g. *sempre legato*, the whole passage or movement should be played smoothly.

Senaillé, Jean Baptiste (*b* Paris, *c.*1688; *d* Paris, 18 Oct. 1730). French composer. The son of one of the Vingt-Quatre Violons du Roi, he studied the violin with G. A. Piani, a pupil of Corelli. He was among the first to publish violin sonatas in Paris (1710, 1712) and in 1713 he took over his father's duties at court. His contemporary Louis-Antoine Dornel included 'La Senaillé' among the violin sonatas he published in 1711. In 1716 Senaillé visited Italy, possibly studying with T. A. Vitali in Modena; he returned to Paris where from 1728 until his death he was a popular performer at the Concert Spirituel.   DA/JAS

Senfl, Ludwig (*b* ?Basle, *c.*1486; *d* Munich, 1542 or 1543). Swiss-born church musician, composer, and editor. He was first a chorister, then an adult singer and music copyist, in the Hofkapelle of Emperor Maximilian I. He probably studied with Heinrich Isaac, the court composer, and in 1513 succeeded Isaac in that position. His connection with humanist circles in Vienna led him to explore in music the metres of classical poetry; the results brought him widespread recognition. Following Maximilian's death in 1519 the musical establishment was disbanded, and for several years Senfl had trouble securing another post. In 1523 he joined the Hofkapelle of Duke Wilhelm of Bavaria in Munich, remaining there until his death. He appears to have been sympathetic towards the Reformation, and corresponded with Martin Luther. As a composer of motets and liturgical music, Senfl was indebted both to Isaac, whose music he edited for publication, and to Josquin des Prez. His four-voice settings of Latin odes, which explore classical metres in strict homophony, are more individual, and during the 16th century were widely used in schools. His polyphonic lieder include arrangements of popular songs.   JM

sennet. A stage direction in Elizabethan plays indicating a type of fanfare, played by cornetts or trumpets,

before actors entered or left the stage. See also TRUMPET, 2; TUCKET.

sensibile (It.), **sensible** (Fr.). *Leading note.

sentito (It.). 'Felt', 'with expression'.

senza (It.). 'Without', e.g. *senza sordini*, 'without mutes' (in string playing), or 'without dampers' (in piano playing); *senza tempo*, *senza misura*, 'without strict tempo'.

séparé (Fr.). 'Separated'; in French organ music, uncoupled.

septet. An ensemble of seven instrumentalists or, more rarely, singers, or music written for it. Beethoven's op. 20 for violin, viola, cello, double bass, clarinet, horn, and bassoon is well known, but other combinations have been used by composers including Spohr, Hummel, Saint-Saëns, and Ravel (*Introduction and Allegro* for harp, flute, clarinet, and string quartet).

See also CHAMBER MUSIC.   JMo

septuplet [septimole, septolet]. A term for seven notes that are to be performed in the time of four or of six; they are indicated by the figure '7' placed above or below the seven notes (see Ex. 1).

Ex. 1

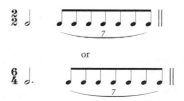

sequence. 1. The more or less exact repetition of a melody at another level, higher or lower. If the repetition is only in the melody, with changed harmony, it is called a melodic sequence, and if the repetition is followed also in the harmony, a harmonic sequence. If the repetition is made without leaving the original key, which necessarily means that some of the intervals become larger or smaller by a semitone, it is called a tonal sequence. If, in order to preserve the exact intervals, the key is changed, the name given is 'real sequence' (see FUGUE for a corresponding use of 'tonal' and 'real'). Sequences that are real in some repetitions and tonal in others (in some instances to avoid carrying the modulation too far) are called mixed sequences.

A sequence that is an exact repetition in another key (i.e. a harmonic real sequence) is sometimes called a *rosalia*, after an Italian popular song, *Rosalia mia cara*, which begins with this device.   PS

2. A type of Latin hymn, usually in couplets with the music repeating in the pattern A(A) BB CC DD, and so on. From the 9th century to the 16th sequences were sung on feast days after the alleluia at Mass in many parts of the Roman Catholic Church, but after censure during the *Council of Trent (1542–63) their use declined rapidly; they had never been widely used in the papal liturgy, which was taken as a model.

The origins of the genre are uncertain. It is not clear whether the earliest melodies were initially sung without words or were texted from the beginning, or whether these melodies originally formed part of the festal alleluias of their time or were attached to the alleluia at a later stage.

A typical sequence up to the 11th century has some six to 12 pairs of lines, each pair of a different length (the verses may be quantitative or accentual, and may or may not rhyme). The melodies differ markedly from those of Gregorian chant, with strong cadences often approached from the note below the final and a tendency for each line to have its own individual tessitura. Ex. 1, the first four lines of a popular sequence for the Blessed Virgin Mary, illustrates these features.

A few sequences, however, do not exhibit these characteristics, lacking the typical verse structure. These were originally *jubili* to be sung when the alleluia was repeated after its verse. In this they resemble several alleluias of the Old Roman chant repertory, which have survived only in this form. Later they were given texts, on the principle of one syllable per note.

Our first witness to the long paired-verse sequence reveals that they were already texted. *Notker, a monk of St Gallen in Switzerland, reported that a monk of Jumièges (on the Seine, north of Paris), fleeing from the devastations of the Northmen, brought to St Gallen a book containing some texted sequences. These inspired Notker to compose his own texts, and his 'hymnbook', as he called the finished collection, was completed in 884.

Some 150 melodies and nearly 400 texts are known from the period up to the end of the 10th century, from all areas of Europe. The texts display great variety of style: Notker's are in sophisticated Latin, with a strong theological content, and are not particularly mellifluous; French texts are frequently in a less elevated style, full of laudatory exclamations and refer-

Ex. 1

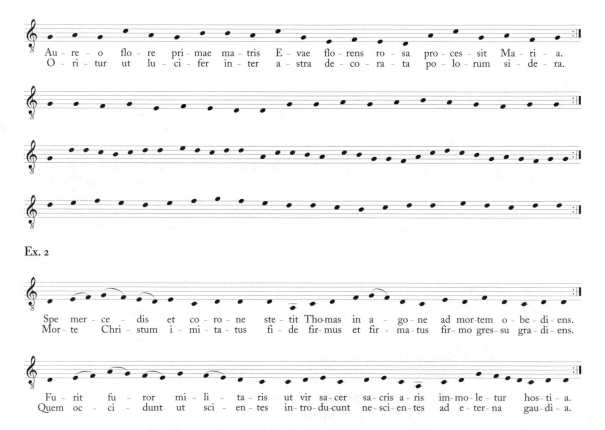

Ex. 2

ences (perhaps allegorical) to musical instruments; Winchester texts are replete with arcane and learned-sounding words.

During the 11th and 12th centuries there was a gradual change in the style of texts, and thus of the music too. Texts in regularly accented verse, with verse-pairs of the same length, became fashionable, and regular rhyme was usual. The opening of a sequence for St Thomas of Canterbury (*d* 1170) shows what a revolution had been accomplished by the 12th century (Ex. 2).

Texts in the new style first appeared in northern France, and many early examples are attributed to Adam, monk of St Victor in Paris (*fl* 1160–70). The eventual production was immense. It is estimated that over 5000 sequences had been composed by the end of the Middle Ages, of which many have never been edited in modern times.   DH/ALi

sequencer. A device or mechanism for storing and retrieving the note-by-note control functions for a *synthesizer. Such a facility can be incorporated within the design of a synthesizer, located remotely as a self-contained unit, or simulated via a computer program, communicating with one or a number of synthesizers via *MIDI.   PM

Sequenza ('Sequence'). Title given by *Berio to a series of short, virtuoso works for solo instruments (flute, harp, trombone, oboe, etc.) begun in the 1950s. Some have been developed into larger works; for example *Sequenza VI* for viola (1967) was expanded to become *Chemins II* (1967) for nine instruments and *Chemins III* (1968) for large orchestra, and *Sequenza X* (1984) for trumpet grew into *Kol-Od* (1996) for trumpet and ensemble.

Serafin, Tullio (*b* Rottanova di Cavarzere, nr Venice, 1 Sept. 1878; *d* Rome, 2 Feb. 1968). Italian conductor. After studying the violin and composition at the Milan Conservatory he made his conducting debut at Ferrara in 1898. He soon established a reputation as a leading opera conductor and became principal conductor at La Scala, Milan, in 1909, introducing a wide range of new repertory. He was at the Metropolitan Opera, New York, from 1924 to 1934, and was artistic director of the Rome Opera from 1934 to 1943. Thereafter he was internationally sought after and revered as a master of balance, style, and ensemble precision in opera. He became a major influence in nurturing singers' careers, coaching such artists as Rosa Ponselle, Maria Callas, and Joan Sutherland. His performances were disciplined but dramatic, and in his long career he passed on his experiences from the time of Verdi to the modern world.   JT

Serbia. A republic in the central Balkan Peninsula, the major constituent part, with Montenegro, of the rump Yugoslavia. There are few records of music in medieval Serbia before the Turkish invasions. Instruments depicted on the frescoes of the period offer indirect evidence of musical activity, and the sources of liturgical music, dating mainly from the late Middle Ages, show some individual trends within the frame of the Orthodox liturgy. Musical life in Serbia started to develop in the second half of the 19th century, after the newly won independence from Turkey. At first the accent was on choral music, and the choral societies founded at the time often had the task of providing liturgical music in churches. The Belgrade Choral Society (Beogradsko Pevačko Društvo) was formed in 1853 and for some hundred years maintained a high standard of choral singing. One of its conductors, Stevan Mokranjac (1856–1914), created in his choral compositions the foundation for a national Serbian style, and his influence was still evident in Serbian music in the 1920s.

Opera had a slow start, initially overshadowed by the genre of Serbian *Singspiel* of which Davorin Jenko (1835–1914), a Slovene by birth, was a notable exponent. The first Serbian opera was Stanislav Binički's *Na uranku* ('At Dawn', 1903). Time was needed to shake off the mannerisms of the school of Mokranjac and Binički; with the formation of Yugoslavia in 1918, Belgrade became an important cultural and musical centre. The permanent opera company was established in 1920 and soon acquired a reputation for the performances of the Russian 19th-century repertory. In the 1930s the ideas of Alois Hába and the Prague school gained prominence among Belgrade composers. In turn, their activity laid the foundations of a richly diverse musical life of the city after 1945.   BB

serenade (Fr.: *sérénade*; Ger.: *Serenade, Ständchen*; It.: *serenata*). A musical genre, the name of which derives from the word *sereno* (It., 'calm'). Serenades were originally played or sung in the evening by a lover at his lady's window, or as a greeting to an important personage, and were frequently accompanied by a guitar or other plucked instrument. In the 18th century a serenade was a piece of instrumental music of up to ten movements, scored for a small ensemble, usually with a predominance of wind instruments. There are reminiscences of the original connotations of serenade and a plucked instrument in the serenade arias of some operas, e.g. 'Deh, vieni alla finestra' (*Don Giovanni*, Act II).

Instrumental serenades were written by such composers as Boccherini, Michael Haydn, and Dittersdorf. Mozart's examples (also called *Finalmusiken, notturni, or cassations*) were generally commissioned for specific occasions, such as the one he wrote in 1776 for a wedding in the Haffner family (the 'Haffner' Serenade K250/248b). Most of his serenades begin or close (or both) with a march-like movement, framing a large-scale sonata-form piece, two slow movements alternating with minuets, often a quicker movement such as a rondo, and a very quick finale. They are scored for a variety of combinations: strings and wind (the 'Haffner' Serenade), wind instruments alone (K361/370a, K375, K388/384a), string quartet (*Eine kleine Nachtmusik*), and even double or quadruple orchestra (*Serenata notturna* K239 and *Notturno* no. 8). Beethoven's only serenades are chamber pieces, for string trio (op. 8) and for flute, violin, and viola (op. 25).

In the 19th century orchestral serenades were composed by Brahms, Dvořák, Tchaikovsky, Elgar (Serenade for strings), and Strauss, among others. 20th-century composers freely extended the possibilities of the genre, producing such diverse works as Vaughan Williams's *Serenade to Music*, scored for 16 solo voices and orchestra, Schoenberg's op. 24, and Britten's *Serenade for Tenor, Horn, and Strings*.   —/PL

Serenade for Tenor, Horn, and Strings. Song cycle, op. 31 (1943), by Britten in which a prologue and epilogue for solo horn enclose settings of six poems on the theme of evening, by Cotton, Tennyson, William Blake, an anonymous one (*The Lyke-Wake Dirge*), Ben Jonson, and John Keats; it was written for Peter Pears and Dennis Brain.

serenata (It.). 1. 'Serenade'.

2. A large-scale, cantata-like work for performance at court or at the home of an aristocratic family on a special occasion. A typical serenata had a pastoral, allegorical, or mythological subject, which involved at least two characters. In length somewhere between a cantata and an opera, it was often divided into sections, each consisting of recitatives and arias, and was given in an elaborate setting with costumes but without dramatic action. Handel's *Acis and Galatea* is a well-known example. Alessandro Scarlatti wrote 25 serenatas for his various patrons, and the form was extensively cultivated by 17th- and 18th-century Italian composers, and at the imperial court in Vienna (e.g. by Fux and Caldara).

Serenata notturna ('Nocturnal Serenade'). Mozart's Serenade no. 6 in D major K239 (1776), for two small groups of strings.

serenatella (It.). Diminutive of *serenata.

serialism. A compositional technique in which the basic material is an ordered arrangement—row, set, or series—of pitches, intervals, durations, and, if required, of other musical elements. Music theorists and his-

torians tend to distinguish between *twelve-note technique, in which only pitch is subject to serial principles, and serial (or 'totally serial') music, in which an attempt is made to apply serial thinking to other compositional features, like rhythm, register, dynamics, and aspects of form.

Serialism originated in the 12-note technique, where all 12 notes of the chromatic scale are arranged in a fixed order which is used to generate melodies and harmonies, and which normally remains binding for a whole work. Since, in theory at least, all the elements in a series will be of equal significance, serial music will be without tonality, and even if many examples of it emphasize certain pitches in ways that become analogous to the tonics and dominants of tonality, it is likely to reject the fundamental distinction between consonance and dissonance on which tonal harmonic structures depend.

12-note thinking appeared around 1920 in the work of both *Schoenberg and Josef Hauer, but it is the former who, through his compositions and his teaching, was by far the most important figure in the establishment and evolution of serialism as a compositional resource. In its early, Schoenbergian form, the pitch-series can be used in a variety of ways. Even if it first occurred to the composer as a specific melodic shape, it provides a particular sequence of pitch and interval classes whose registral position can be varied at will. The whole series may be uniformly transposed on to any of the other intervals of the chromatic scale, making 11 transpositions of the principal, or prime (P), form. In addition, the series can be reversed (retrograded; R), and also inverted (I) and the inversions can be retrograded (IR), making a grand total of 48 forms for any given 12-note series. But there was never any implication that a composer 'must' use all 48 forms, or even aim for an equality of use among those forms which he did use. Often, therefore, choice of how many forms to use, and how often to use them, would be determined as much by the connections between different transpositions which had compositional potential as by the differences with regard to pitch order between them.

The 'classic' serial works of the years 1920–50 by Schoenberg, *Berg, and *Webern demonstrate that the new principle was perfectly compatible with inherited forms and textures, from sonata and rondo schemes to canon and fugue—provided, that is, that these were not thought of as inherently and exclusively allied to tonality.

One of the most important questions the early serial composers needed to answer was whether to work with more than a single form of the series at any one time and, if they were to use two or more forms simultaneously, what rules to apply to their combination.

Schoenberg, in his works from the late 1920s onwards, devised what has since become known as the 'combinatorial' principle, whereby two forms of the set would be used in combination, and those two forms would be complementary to the extent that the pitch content of the first half (or hexachord) of one 12-note set would be complemented—that is, not duplicated even to the extent of a single pitch—by the content of the first hexachord of another version of the same set (see COMBINATORIALITY). Ex. 1 shows the sets Schoenberg used for the early stages of his String Quartet no. 4, and this relationship, between a prime form and the inversion five semitones above it, was a type of combination he used on many occasions.

Ex. 1

Several significant composers—not least *Stravinsky, who came to 12-note composition soon after Schoenberg's death in 1951—adopted techniques of 12-note pitch serialism after the model of Schoenberg and Webern, and continued to use them thereafter. But for most younger composers of radical propensities in the years immediately after World War II, both Schoenberg and Webern appeared to have been too concerned with seeking compromises between the progressive potential of the method and the pursuit of comprehensibility, which aimed to preserve perceptible analogies with the forms and textures of earlier music. For Babbitt in the USA, and Boulez (and others) in Europe, serialism offered a genuinely new beginning, in works that shunned traditional formal frameworks and thematic processes in favour of designs dictated by the capacity of a 12-note series to govern all aspects of the musical fabric. Yet whereas Babbitt, after an early *tour de force* like the *Composition for Twelve Instruments* (1948), continued to build ever more elaborate and ramified serial structures on the basis of 12-note successions, Boulez turned away from the strict and literal presentation of the system found in book 1 of his *Structures* for two pianos (1951–2). This is not to say that Boulez's later music loses all contact with serial thinking, however, and it is easy to see how a relatively simple score like *Messagesquisse* for seven cellos (1976), which is based on a six-note series 'translating' the surname of Paul Sacher into German pitch notation

(Eb–A–C–Bb–E–D), develops ways of transforming and rotating that basic idea in authentically serial fashion.

Many other composers in the later 20th century made use of a procedure fundamental to Schoenberg's own serial method—namely that, once the ordered content of the basic set and its transpositions, inversions, and retrogrades have been established, the actual pitches occurring within any given segment of that set (usually the hexachord, in Schoenberg's case) can be used in any order appropriate to the compositional context. From this the idea of the pitch-*class set as an 'unordered' collection of elements, rather like a mode, emerged as a principle of considerable influence over the music of many composers—for example, Elliott Carter. At the same time, the idea arose of treating the abstract presentation of a set and its transformations as a table, or matrix, as the basis for free horizontal, diagonal, or vertical movement within that matrix: and this offered a different, but no less flexible, development of 'classic', Schoenbergian serial thinking. Ex. 2 shows the matrix, or magic square, used by Maxwell Davies for his *Strathclyde Concerto* no. 5 for violin, viola, and strings (1991). (The letter names that constitute the matrix in this example can, if translated into numbers, serve to generate rhythmic patterns as well.) In Davies's case, the mathematical properties of magic squares are an additional resource which generates very specific and fundamental compositional features. Davies's music often sounds quite Schoenbergian in style, but the kind of serial principle he uses can obviously find expression in works of radically different character. This flexibility and adaptability indicates that the serial

Ex. 2

	①	②	③	④	⑤	⑥	⑦	⑧	⑨
①	F	Ab	Gb	Cb	Db	Eb	E	Bb	C
②	Ab	Cb	A	D	E	F#	G	C#	D#
③	Gb	A	G	C	D	E	F	B	C#
④	Cb	D	C	F	G	A	Bb	E	F#
⑤	Db	E	D	G	A	B	C	F#	G#
⑥	Eb	Gb	E	A	B	Db	D	G#	A#
⑦	E	G	F	Bb	C	D	Eb	A	B
⑧	Bb	C#	B	E	F#	Ab	A	Eb	F
⑨	C	D#	C#	F#	G#	Bb	B	F	G

principle could well retain an important place within the ultra-pluralistic musical landscape of the early 21st century. AW

series. The basic musical idea, usually a sequential ordering of the 12 notes of the chromatic scale, used as a starting-point in the composition of *serial music.

serio, seria (It.). 'Serious'; *serioso, seriosa, seriosamente*, 'seriously'. See also OPERA SERIA.

Serkin, Rudolf (*b* Eger, 28 March 1903; *d* Guilford, VT, 8 May 1991). Austrian-born American pianist. He studied the piano with Richard Robert and composition with Schoenberg in Vienna. An appearance with the Busch Chamber Orchestra in Berlin in 1920 launched his career, and in 1935 he married into the Busch family, playing chamber music with Adolf and Hermann. He fled to the USA in 1938, ran the Marlboro Festival, and led the piano department at the Curtis Institute. Although he was not a natural performer (he was eccentrically given to foot-tapping or to singing along) his playing was bold, bright, and eloquent, his modesty sincere. CF

Sermisy, Claudin de (*b* c.1490; *d* Paris, 13 Oct. 1562). French church musician and composer. He spent most of his adult career in the service of the French royal household, as a chapel member and, later, Master of the Choristers. He was probably present at the meeting of François I and Henry VIII in 1520 at the Field of the Cloth of Gold. He is buried in the Sainte Chapelle, where he was a canon. Sermisy is remembered principally for his many chansons, exquisite miniatures that achieved international circulation in the pioneering publications of Pierre Attaingnant. Scored mostly for four voices, they are lyrical, gently sentimental, and easily adapted for performance on the lute or keyboard. He also composed a substantial amount of church music, including 13 masses, more than 70 motets, a cycle of *Magnificat* settings, music for Holy Week, and a polyphonic *St Matthew Passion*. DA/JM

Serocki, Kazimierz (*b* Toruń, 3 March 1922; *d* Warsaw, 9 Jan. 1981). Polish composer and pianist. One of the leaders of the Polish avant-garde from the mid-1950s (he co-founded the Warsaw Autumn festival in 1956), he maintained a thoroughly modernist and expressionistic stance based on post-serialism and extended instrumental techniques. His music is predominantly orchestral (*Symphonic Frescoes*, 1964; *Ad libitum*, 1973–7), with a strong interest in percussion (*Continuum*, 1966) and in open form (*A piacere* for solo piano, 1963). Several later works explore the sound potential of the recorder family (*Concerto alla cadenza*, 1974) as well as electronic transformation (*Pianophonie*, 1976–8). ATh

Serov, Aleksandr Nikolayevich (*b* St Petersburg, 11/23 Jan. 1820; *d* St Petersburg, 20 Jan./1 Feb. 1871). Russian composer and music critic. He studied music privately and was educated at the College of Jurisprudence, where he became friendly with Vladimir Stasov. He held various civil service posts which left him time to pursue his musical activities. His main outlet as a critic was the journal *Sovremennik*, in which he conducted a vigorous polemic aimed at winning Wagner greater favour among Russian music lovers (he subsequently met Wagner several times).

Serov was not recognized as a composer until his 40s, when his first opera, *Yudif'* ('Judith', 1863), was received warmly by critics and the public; his next opera, *Rogneda* (1865, based on Slavonic legends), enjoyed greater success than any previous Russian opera. His music influenced Borodin and especially Musorgsky, though The Five held that he was essentially Meyerbeerian rather than Wagnerian (and hence backward-looking rather than progressive). His third and last opera, *Vrazh'ya sila* ('The Power of the Fiend'), which drew on the Russian popular song idiom, remained unfinished at his death. JWAL

serpent. A wind instrument consisting of a sinuously curved, widely conical wooden tube with six fingerholes, a metal crook extending from it, and a cup mouthpiece similar in size to that of a trombone. Up to 13 keys were added on later models. Initially devised as a bass instrument to support voices in French churches, it became a popular military instrument throughout Europe, and the orchestral brass bass before the invention of the *ophicleide and the *tuba. Its wide bore gives it a rich tone, which ensured its popularity in village bands. The necessity of bringing the fingerholes within the human hand encourages a very flexible fingering and lip technique to achieve accurate tuning. JMo

serrando, serrato (It.), **serrant, serré** (Fr.). 'Pressing', 'pressed', i.e. getting quicker.

Serse ('Xerxes'). Opera in three acts by Handel to an anonymous revision of Silvio Stampiglia's libretto *Il Xerse* (1694) based on Nicolo Minato's *Il Xerse* (1654) (London, 1738).

Serva padrona, La ('The Maid as Mistress'). Intermezzo (opera) by Pergolesi to a libretto by Gennaro Antonio Federico after Jacopo Angelo Nelli's play (Naples, 1733); it was first performed between the two acts of Pergolesi's *Il prigioniero superbo*, an *opera seria*.

service. In the Anglican communion, a more or less elaborate and continuous setting of the canticles for

Morning Prayer or Evensong, or of certain parts of the Communion Service.

The effect of the Reformation on the composition of service music was mainly twofold: (*a*) the canticles had now to be set in the vernacular, and (*b*) they had to be set without lengthening by repetition of phrases, and as much as possible on the principle of one note to a syllable. This last requirement was apparently found impracticable by composers and, with a few exceptions such as Tallis and Merbecke, was totally disregarded from the beginning. Some 16th-century Communion services exist in two forms: that of the Latin Mass and that of an adaptation, in English, to the new conditions. The terms 'short service' and 'great service' were often used by 16th- and early 17th-century composers to distinguish between settings that faithfully followed the new regulations and those composed for festal occasions, scored for a large choir and falling into something like the old length and complexity. During the 18th century almost all services were composed on the 'short' principle; this was, however, in all ways a period of poverty in service composition.

Alternatim treatment (by the *decani* and *cantoris* sides of the choir) is a frequent feature in service music, and, on the same principle, 'verse' and 'full' passages are also used, alternating a soloist accompanied by an independent organ part with full choir and organ doubling.

In the 19th century S. S. Wesley exercised a great influence on the composition of service music. The publication of his Service in B♭ in 1879 marked the beginning of a more economical and consistent use of material in service composition, a whole movement (and indeed the whole service) being bound together by motivic development, and with the organ taking a large share in this treatment.

The successive styles and composers of service music, being, on the whole, the same as those discussed under *anthem, need not be set out here; as with the anthem, with the service a great deal of purely conventional music has been brought into temporary existence. A common technical defect of such music is faulty accentuation of the words, probably resulting largely from the need for concision, which does not allow much 'elbow room'. From this last-mentioned condition effective composition is perhaps more difficult to attain in service music than in any other form. It is easy to set the words phrase by phrase, but flexibility, balance, and unity are harder to achieve.

Liturgical reforms adopted by the local churches of the Anglican communion during the 20th century have further multiplied the challenges faced by composers of service music. Thus worship according to the *Book of Common Prayer* now coexists with reformed services, often cast in contemporary language, incorporating elements from the ancient liturgies of the Christian East and West. Movements promoting the inculturation of Anglican worship have also promoted service music in popular and aboriginal styles.   PS/ALi

Sessions, Roger (Huntington) (*b* Brooklyn, New York, 28 Dec. 1896; *d* Princeton, NJ, 16 March 1985). American composer. He studied at Harvard University (1910–15) and with Horatio Parker at Yale (1915–17), then had private lessons with Ernest Bloch, whom he assisted at the Cleveland Institute of Music (1921–5). After a period in Europe (1925–33) he taught at various American institutions, notably Princeton University (1935–45, 1953–65); his many distinguished pupils include Babbitt, Maxwell Davies, Nancarrow, and Ellen Taaffe Zwilich.

A superlative musical craftsman, Sessions showed throughout a long and varied creative career the power to create purely musical discourses, subsuming detail to large-scale design. His early works, though influenced by Stravinskian neo-classicism, are sober and without irony; after 1953 he used Schoenbergian *serialism with the same skill and seriousness. He wrote two operas, *The Trial of Lucullus* (Berkeley, 1947) and *Montezuma* (1941–63; Berlin, 1964), leaving a third uncompleted at his death, nine symphonies, other orchestral works (the Concerto for Orchestra of 1979–81 being his swansong), and various chamber pieces. Among his large-scale choral works is the cantata *When Lilacs Last in the Dooryard Bloom'd* (1964–70), to words by Walt Whitman; the period of its composition saw the assassination of Martin Luther King and Robert Kennedy, to whose joint memory it is dedicated. His books included *The Musical Experience of Composer, Performer, and Listener* (Princeton, 1950, 2/1962), *Harmonic Practice* (New York, 1951), and *Questions about Music* (Cambridge, MA, 1970).   PG

📖 A. OLMSTEAD, *Roger Sessions and his Music* (Ann Arbor, MI, 1985)

set. A term found in mathematics and symbolic logic that was transferred to music theory in the mid-20th century to refer to discrete collections of pitch classes or durations used as the basis for 12-note or serial composition. It has also been applied in the analysis of post-tonal or atonal music, such as Schoenberg's Piano Pieces op. 19 (1911) and Webern's Five Movements for string quartet op. 5 (1909), where specific units (normally of fewer than 12 elements) can be shown to be subject to such post-tonal compositional operations as transposition and inversion.   AW

seul, seule (Fr.). 'Alone', 'solo', e.g. *violons seuls*, 'violins alone', *voix seule*, 'solo voice'.

Seven Deadly Sins, The. See SIEBEN TODSÜNDEN DER KLEINBÜRGER, DIE.

Seven Last Words of Our Saviour on the Cross. Work by Haydn composed in 1785 or 1786, a series of Easter meditations ('passioni istrumentale') commissioned by Cádiz Cathedral for performance on Good Friday 1786 or 1787; it was published as 'Seven Sonatas, with an Introduction, and at the end an Earthquake', the 'sonatas' being Adagios. It appeared in four versions: for orchestra (1785); for string quartet (1787); for harpsichord or piano (1787), arranged not by Haydn but with his approval; as a choral work (by 1796) for soloists, chorus, and orchestra (with a text by Joseph Friebert, revised by Haydn and Gottfried von Swieten).

The 'Seven Last Words', the final utterances of Christ on the Cross drawn from the four Gospels, have been used as texts for other *Passion music, for example Schütz's *Die sieben Worte* (c.1645), Gounod's *Les Sept Paroles de N. S. Jésus-Christ sur la croix* (1858), and James MacMillan's *Seven Last Words on the Cross* (1993).

AL

seventh chord. A triad with a 7th added. See DOMINANT SEVENTH CHORD; DIMINISHED SEVENTH CHORD.

Sext. Originally the fifth of eight hours of the Divine *Office in the medieval Roman rite. Since the reforms of the Second Vatican Council, *Terce, Sext, and *None may be combined as one 'Hora Media' ('Prayer during the Day').

sextet. An ensemble of six instrumentalists or singers, or music written for it. Several composers have written string sextets for two violins, two violas, and two cellos, the two by Brahms being particularly fine. A common combination for divertimentos in the 18th century was two horns and string quartet, and there are many wind sextets of that period for two oboes or clarinets, two horns, and two bassoons—the standard wind octet of the *Harmoniemusik, but without one of the soprano pairs.

See also CHAMBER MUSIC.

JMo

sextuplet [sextolet]. A term for six notes that are to be performed in the time of four, either as two groups of three or as three groups of two; they are indicated by the figure '6' placed above or below the six notes (see Ex. 1).

Seyfried, Ignaz (Xaver) **von** (*b* Vienna, 15 Aug. 1776; *d* Vienna, 27 Aug. 1841). Austrian composer, teacher, and writer. He provided much music for Viennese theatres, especially the Theater an der Wien, between 1797 and 1827, and was also active as a conductor, including of the first performance of Beethoven's *Fidelio* in 1805. His works included biblical music dramas and incidental music for plays, as well as church music, concert works, and chamber music. He was also a prolific writer and critic, and a central figure in Viennese musical life during his long career.

JW

sf. Abbreviation for *sforzando* or *sforzato*; *sff*, abbreviation for *sforzatissimo*.

sfogato (It.). 'Unrestrained', i.e. in a light and easy style. A *soprano sfogato* is a light soprano voice.

sforzando, sforzato (It.). 'Forcing', 'forced', i.e. accented. In the 19th century it was used to mark an accent within the prevailing dynamic but it has now acquired the connotation of sudden loudness; it is abbreviated *sf* or *sfz*.

sfp. Abbreviation for *sforzando* followed immediately by *piano*, i.e. a strongly accented note followed by a quiet note or passage.

sfz. Abbreviation for *sforzando*.

Sgambati, Giovanni (*b* Rome, 28 May 1841; *d* Rome, 14 Dec. 1914). Italian composer and pianist. He showed early promise as a pianist and achieved a reputation in the 1860s for his playing of the German Classics. He studied with Liszt while the latter was in Rome and began conducting, introducing the 'Eroica' Symphony to the Roman public. In 1869 in Munich he heard music by Wagner, with whom he later became friendly. He thus became a leading exponent of German music in Italy when it was unfashionable. In later life he made concert tours and taught. He composed charming songs and piano pieces, his deft arrangement of Gluck's 'Dance of the Blessed Spirits' being popular at one time.

DA

shake. An early English name for the *trill.

shakuhachi. A Japanese end-blown bamboo notched flute. It has four fingerholes and a thumbhole, and a range of about three octaves obtained by a combination of fingering and altering the embouchure. The *shakuhachi* is made in several sizes a semitone apart. It was introduced to Japan from China in the 8th century, but the present form evolved during the 17th and 18th

Ex. 1

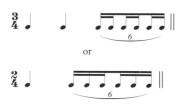

or

centuries. It is used in many genres of music in all levels of society, including modern works by native and foreign composers.　　　　　　　　　　　　JMo

Shalyapin, Fyodor. See CHALIAPIN, FYODOR.

shamisen. Japanese long-necked spike-lute which derived from the snakeskin-covered Chinese *sanxian*. Its three strings are plucked with a large-bladed plectrum of wood or ivory, sometimes of tortoiseshell; the fingernails or finger picks are used in some forms of *shamisen* music. The small square body is covered with cat- or dogskin. It is used in a wide range of music, often to accompany singing. A bowed variant, the *kokyu*, is slightly smaller and has four strings.　　JMo

Shankar, Ravi (*b* Varanasi, Uttar Pradesh, 7 April 1920). Indian sitar player and composer. A talented musician and dancer as a child, he studied with Ustud Allauddin Khan in Maihar. He directed the National Orchestra of All-India Radio from 1949 to 1956. Shankar was the first musician to bring Indian music to large Western audiences, through concerts, records, and collaborations with musicians as diverse as Yehudi Menuhin and George Harrison. As well as creating many ragas, he has composed two sitar concertos (1971, 1976), an opera-ballet, *Ghanashayam* ('A Broken Branch', 1989), several ballet scores, and music for films including Satyajit Ray's 'Apu' trilogy (1955–9) and *Gandhi* (1982).　　　　　　　　　　　　　　ABUR

shanty [chanty, sea shanty]. A sailors' work song. The basic form of the shanty is a call-and-response pattern, both universal and ancient. The shanty as we know it belongs to a short and very specific period: from about 1830, when competitive packet-ship transport was initiated in America, to about 1870, when British domination of clipper-ship transport was supplanted by steam. This competitive environment required coordination of manpower in heaving and hauling. A soloist, the 'shantyman', would improvise verses, and the working team would punctuate with invariable refrains, containing one or two accents at which combined forces would pull together. The musical form and melodic characteristics suggest the Anglo-Celtic and African influences of the multinational workforce that sang the shanty. Different tasks required different tunes: short-haul jobs tended to use single-line tunes; *General Taylor* is more elaborate with longer verses and two pulls in the refrain, suiting the long-haul jobs; a more lyrical form, as in *Rio Grand*, could be used for the continuous, rather than intermittent, effort required at the capstan.　　　　　　　　　　　　　　PGA/PW

shape note. A device, for singers with rudimentary musical knowledge, that indicates where the semitones are in the octave by the shape of the note-heads used. The first three notes are each a tone apart and are solmized as *fa, sol, la*; the fourth to sixth notes have the same structure and are also solmized *fa, sol, la*; but the seventh and eighth notes are separated by a semitone and indicated *mi, fa*. The singer knows that (ascending) *la–fa* is always a semitone and so is *mi–fa*. *Fa* notes always have a triangular head, *sol* notes a round head, *la* notes a square head, and *mi* notes are diamond-shaped. The system, also known as 'fasola', was introduced by William Little in *The Easy Instructor* (1801) and is used in the American South for church music.　　　AP

Shapero, Harold (Samuel) (*b* Lynn, MA, 29 April 1920). American composer. He studied composition with Walter Piston and Ernst Krenek at Harvard University (1937–41), with Hindemith at Tanglewood and with Boulanger at the Longy School. In 1952 he was appointed professor at Brandeis University. His rather small output includes a much praised Symphony for classical orchestra (1947), several sonatas, and other chamber works, all in a neo-classical style influenced by Stravinsky and Copland.　　　　　　　　PG

Shaporin, Yury (Aleksandrovich) (*b* Glukhov, 27 Oct/8 Nov. 1887; *d* Moscow, 9 Dec. 1966). Ukrainian composer. Although he did not at first intend to become a professional musician, he pursued musical activities in his native country, then moved to St Petersburg where, after reading law, he entered the conservatory to study composition with Nikolay Sokolov (1859–1922), orchestration with Maximilian Steinberg (1883–1946), and score-reading with Nikolay Tcherepnin. During the 1920s he became closely associated with the leading artistic figures of the day (including the poet Aleksandr Blok, the writer Aleksey Tolstoy, and the artist Alexandre Benois), and he was, with Boris Asaf'yev (1884–1949), a key figure in the Association for Contemporary Music. His own music, however, is firmly rooted in the traditions he inherited at the St Petersburg Conservatory, and though he composed some instrumental music, a choral symphony (1928–32), other choral works, and much incidental music, he has retained prominence chiefly through his four-act lyric opera *Dekabristy* ('The Decembrists'), a work which occupied him on and off for more than 30 years, from the early 1920s to 1953 when it was given its premiere at the Bol'shoy Theatre, Moscow.　　　　　　　　GN

sharp (Fr.: *dièse*; Ger.: *Kreuz*; It.: *diesis*). 1. The sign (♯) that, when placed before a note, raises it in pitch by a semitone. In English terminology the verb is 'to sharpen' and the adjective 'sharpened'; in American usage the corresponding terms are 'to sharp' and 'sharped'. See ACCIDENTAL; for the origins of the sharp sign and its early use, see DURUM AND MOLLIS; NO-TATION, 1.

In the 18th century, the key of 'E sharp' meant the key of E that has a major 3rd, i.e. E major (Beethoven, for example, described his first *Leonore* overture, in C major, as 'Ouverture in C♯').

2. An adjective applied to vocal or instrumental performance, denoting inexact intonation on the high side.

sharp pitch. A pitch standard that came about during the 19th century through a rapid rise in pitch from *d'* = 415 to *c*.434–53; see PITCH, 4.

Shaw, (George) Bernard (*b* Dublin, 26 July 1856; *d* Ayot St Lawrence, Herts., 2 Nov. 1950). Irish dramatist and music critic. Born into a musical family, he later revealed that Mozart, especially *Don Giovanni*, had been an important influence on his musical thinking. Moving to London in 1876, he wrote music criticism first for *The Hornet*, then (from 1889) for *The Star*, under the pseudonym 'Corno di Bassetto', and finally (1890–4) for *The World*.

Shaw produced hundreds of well-informed and colourful reviews of music in London in the 1890s. His writing could be unashamedly subjective and strongly (even outrageously) expressed, and his turn of phrase memorable for its perspicacity and trenchant wit. He was a persuasive, if controversial, champion of Wagner; *The Perfect Wagnerite* (London, 1898, 4/1923/*R*1972) is a highly personal interpretation of the *Ring* in terms of Shaw's socialist attitude to the capitalist society in which he lived.

A supporter of Richard Strauss and a close friend of Elgar, Shaw was always eager to help talented young composers. His plays inspired music by composers including Oscar Straus (*The Chocolate-Cream Soldier*, 1908, based on *Arms and the Man*), Walton (film music for *Major Barbara*, 1941), and Frederick Loewe, whose *My Fair Lady* (1956) is based on *Pygmalion*. JN

📖 M. HOLROYD, *Bernard Shaw* (London, 1988–92, 2/1997); *The Shaw Companion* (London, 1992)

shawm [shalme, hautboy, hoboy, wait-pipe] (Fr.: *hautbois*, *chalemie*; Ger.: *Schalmei*, *Pommer*; It.: *piffaro*, *ciaramella*; Sp.: *chirimía*, *dulzaina*). A conical-bore woodwind instrument played with a double reed. In many cultures it is the main wind instrument for outdoor festivities. The shawm was known to the Etruscans in the 5th century BC; it later spread through Persia (as *zūrnā*) to India (as *shahnāī*) and China (*so-na*), and west through the Maghrib (*ghayṭa*) to West Africa (*algaita*). In Europe it was in use certainly by the 13th century, and it was taken by the Conquistadors into Central and South America.

The reed is usually surrounded by a *pirouette*, a small disc of metal or wood against which the lips rest, facilitating breath control. Almost everywhere the instrument is blown with the reed wholly pouched in the mouth, using *circular breathing. The same effect is produced by using an external bag of skin: the chanter of many of the world's *bagpipes is a shawm.

An important late medieval ensemble was the *alta musica* (see ALTA, 3; HAUT, BAS), a band comprising treble shawm, tenor (*bombarde*), and slide trumpet or, later, trombone. In the Renaissance all instruments were made in family groups in all sizes from high treble to great bass, and the shawm was no exception. The bass instruments (known as *Pommer*), the largest of which were some 3 metres tall, used a bent-back crook to hold the reed (like the bassoon). They were later replaced by the more portable curtal, or *dulcian. In England, families of shawms were played by the town *waits up to the end of the 17th century. Shakespeare's 'hoboys without' shows them hired for theatrical festivals. The *oboe, with its narrower bore, redesigned reed, and more refined sound, was developed in France during the mid-17th century.

Shawms continue to be used in Catalonia, where *xirimías* are an essential part of the *sardana* dance band or *cobla*. Other European shawms, for instance the Spanish *dulzaina*, have experienced something of a revival for outdoor festivals. JMo

📖 B. HAYNES, 'The Speaking Oboe': A History of the Hautboy, 1640 to 1760 (Oxford, 1999)

Shchedrin, Rodion Konstantinovich (*b* Moscow, 16 Dec. 1932). Russian composer. He studied composition at the Moscow Conservatory with Shaporin. One of the initiators of the 1960s 'new folklore trend', he frequently used the *chastushka* (a folk- or popular-song genre) in his compositions, for example the orchestral work *Mischievous Chastushki* (1963). He wrote several ballets for his wife, the celebrated ballerina Maya Plisetskaya, including *Carmen Suite* (based on Bizet's opera score, 1967), *Anna Karenina* (1972), and *Chayka* ('The Seagull', 1980). His opera *Myortvïye dushi* ('Dead Souls', 1977) is an important addition to the Gogol operas of Musorgsky and Shostakovich. He was a People's Artist of the USSR (1981) and committee member of the Composers' Union. JWAL

Shebalin, Vissarion Yakovlevich (*b* Omsk, 29 May/11 June 1902; *d* Moscow, 28 May 1963). Russian composer. He studied music at the Moscow Conservatory, of which he was later director (1942–8). He was a prolific composer in numerous genres, his works including five symphonies, the two-hour choral symphony *Lenin* (1931, rev. 1959), and the opera *Ukroshcheniye* *stroptivoy* ('The Taming of the Shrew'; Kuybïshev, 1957). Today, however, he is better known for his work on other composers' music, chiefly his completion of Musorgsky's *Sorochintsy Fair* (1931) and his orchestration of the supplementary *pas de deux* in Tchaikovsky's *Swan Lake*. He was, however, regarded as one of those Soviet composers whose level of complexity called for an official rebuke, and he was named in Andrey Zhdanov's 1948 decree about *formalism.   PS/DN

 📖 G. Abraham, *Eight Soviet Composers* (London, 1943)

Sheep may safely graze. English title of the soprano aria 'Schafe können sicher weiden' from J. S. Bach's cantata no. 208, *Was mir behagt, ist nur die muntre Jagd* (probably 1713). Several arrangements have been made, notably Mary Howe's for two pianos (1935) and piano solo (1937), Grainger's transcription *Blithe Bells*, Walton's arrangement as the seventh number of his ballet *The Wise Virgins* (the fifth movement of the ballet suite), and Barbirolli's for cor anglais and strings.

Sheherazade. 1. Symphonic suite (1888) by Rimsky-Korsakov based on tales from *The Thousand and One Nights*; it was choreographed by Mikhail Fokine for the Ballets Russes (Paris, 1910).

 2. *Schéhérazade*. Song cycle (1903) by Ravel, for mezzo-soprano and orchestra, settings of three poems by Tristan Klingsor (the pseudonym of Léon Leclère) inspired by *The Thousand and One Nights*. Ravel had earlier (1898) written an overture with the same title.

sheng. Chinese *mouth organ, consisting of a circle of bamboo pipes set around the top of a cup. At the foot of each, a bronze free reed is set to function equally on blow or draw, sounding only when a hole in the side of the pipe is closed. Prototypes of the *sheng* date back to the 2nd millennium BC. The Japanese descendant is the *shō.

Shepherd, John. See Sheppard, John.

Shepherd on the Rock, The. See Hirt auf dem Felsen, Der.

Shepherds of the Delectable Mountains, The. See Pilgrim's Progress, The.

Sheppard, John (*b* c.1515; *d* Dec. 1558). English church musician and composer. Little is known about his life, except that he served as *informator choristarum* at Magdalen College, Oxford (1543–8), then joined the Chapel Royal as a Gentleman, a position he retained until his death. Sheppard's Latin-texted church music survives in reasonable quantity, thanks largely to the Elizabethan copyists who collected it long after it had ceased to be liturgically useful. The most important works are the responds and hymns for five- and six-

voice choir; they are constructed around (and alternate with passages of) plainchant, and are impressive for their rhythmic energy and rich sonority. The masses are more varied in style; they range from the festal six-voice *Missa 'Cantate'*, based on an unidentified model, through the tuneful *'Western Wind'* Mass, to the compact *Plainsong Mass for a Mean*. Inevitably his anthems and canticles written for the reformed English rite are more modest in scope than the Catholic liturgical music. Virtually no keyboard music by Sheppard survives, and an extended cycle of metrical psalms is now known only from a single voice part.

         JM

Shield, William (*b* Swalwell, Co. Durham, 5 March 1748; *d* London, 25 Jan. 1829). English violinist and composer. His father, a singing teacher, died when William was nine, but he continued to study music with Charles Avison in Newcastle. After a period as first violinist of an orchestra in Scarborough he went to London, and by 1773 had been appointed a second violinist at the King's Theatre; shortly afterwards he became principal viola player. He was house composer to Covent Garden from 1782, and in 1817 was made Master of the King's Music. Shield composed more than 40 light operas, pantomimes, and ballad operas, as well as string quartets and trios, other instrumental pieces, and numerous songs. He is perhaps best known as the composer of the melody—part of the overture to his opera *Rosina*—now familiarly sung as *Auld Lang Syne*.   WT/PL

shift. In string playing, the movement of the left hand when changing *position.

shivaree. An American corruption of *charivari.

Shnitke, Al'fred. See Schnittke, Alfred.

shō. The mouth organ of Japanese *gagaku or court orchestras, with 17 bamboo pipes, each with a bronze free reed. It is descended from the Chinese *sheng.

shofar. The biblical ram's-horn trumpet, still used by Jewish communities especially at New Year to call congregations to repentance before the Day of Atonement. It was also used as a signalling instrument. According to the Bible, it was heard from heaven when the Ten Commandments were given, and will be heard again on the Last Day.   JMo

Shoot, Vladislav (Alekseyevich) (*b* Voznesensk, Ukraine, 3 March 1941). Russian composer. He studied composition at the Gnesin Institute in Moscow with Nikolay Peyko, graduating in 1967. He belongs neither to the avant-garde nor to the traditionalist wing of Russian music, but strikes a balance between the old and the new, combining tonality with serialism, traditional textures with novel instrumental techniques, and Webernian pointillism with allusions to Mozart or Schumann. His output consists largely of instrumental works for chamber ensembles of varying sizes. In the early 1990s he emigrated to England.   JWAL

short octave. A system for extending the keyboard compass downwards without increasing the size of the instrument. Before about 1700 chromatic notes were seldom needed in the lowest octave and their keys could be employed for other pitches. In one typical pattern, known as the C/E short octave, the E, F♯, and G♯ keys were tuned to C, D, and E, respectively, and the remaining keys in that octave were tuned to their normal pitches (F, G, A, B♭, and c). This had the additional advantage that the left hand could easily cover a stretch of a 10th or more, allowing for some wide-spaced chords. As the range of keyboards was increased, the G/B short octave was introduced, the B′, C♯, and D♯ keys sounding G′, A′, and B′, respectively. In a later arrangement, known as the 'broken octave', the black keys of the lowest octave were split so that the front half produced the nominal pitch and the back half the short-octave pitch (or vice versa). Short octaves were first used on stringed keyboard instruments but were applied to the organ at the end of the 16th century.

JMo

short score [condensed score]. A reduction of a full *score to a smaller number of staves. The term is applied to that stage in the composition of an ensemble work where the composer may write out the music on a few staves, showing indications of scoring and harmonization to be written out fully later.   LC

short service. See SERVICE.

Shostakovich, Dmitry (*see opposite page*)

Shropshire Lad, A. Song cycle (1911) by Butterworth, settings of six poems from A. E. Housman's book (1896); he based an orchestral rhapsody (1912), with the same title, on a theme from the song *Loveliest of trees*. Several other composers have set poems from Housman's collection, notably Vaughan Williams (*On Wenlock Edge*), Ireland, Gurney, Somervell, and C. W. Orr.

Shudi [Schudi, Tschudi, Tshudi], **Burkat** [Burkhardt] (*b* Schwanden, 1702; *d* London, 19 Aug. 1773). English harpsichord maker of Swiss birth. He went to London in 1718 and founded his firm in 1742; his son-in-law John *Broadwood took it over after he died. From 1769 Shudi's harpsichords had the 'Venetian swell', which allowed the volume to be varied. He was one of the leading makers of the period who supplied instruments

to Frederick the Great, Maria Theresa, Handel, Haydn, Gainsborough, and Reynolds.   AL

📖 W. DALE, *Tschudi the Harpsichord Maker* (London, 1913)

si [te]. The seventh degree of the major scale in the *solmization system. In French and Italian usage it has become attached, on the fixed-*doh* principle, to the note B, in whichever scale it occurs. See TONIC SOL-FA.

Sibelius, Jean [Johan] (Julius Christian) (*b* Hämeenlinna, 8 Dec. 1865; *d* Järvenpää, 20 Sept. 1957). Finnish composer. He was unquestionably the greatest composer Finland has ever produced and the most powerful symphonist to have emerged in Scandinavia. His father was a doctor in Hämeenlinna, a provincial garrison town in south-central Finland. Until he was about eight years old Sibelius spoke no Finnish. However, when he was 11 his mother enrolled him in the first grammar school in the country to use Finnish as the teaching language instead of Swedish and Latin. Contact with Finnish opened up to him the whole repertory of national mythology embodied in the *Kalevala*. His imagination was fired by this, as it was by the great Swedish lyric poets J. L. Runeberg and Viktor Rydberg and, above all, by the Finnish landscape with its forests and lakes.

In his youth Sibelius showed considerable aptitude on the violin and composed chamber music for his family and friends to play. There were few opportunities to hear orchestral music: even Helsinki did not have a permanent symphony orchestra until Robert Kajanus, later one of his staunchest champions, founded the City Orchestra in 1882. At first Sibelius studied law, but he soon abandoned it for music, becoming a pupil of Martin Wegelius. At about that time he decided to 'internationalize' his name (following the example of an uncle who had Gallicized his name, Johan, to Jean during his travels). It was not until he left Finland to study in Berlin and Vienna that he measured himself for the first time against an orchestral canvas.

It was in Vienna that the first ideas of the *Kullervo* symphony came to him, and it was this work, first performed in 1892, that put Sibelius on the musical map in his own country. The music that followed in its immediate wake is strongly national in feeling: the *Karelia* Suite, written for a pageant in Viipuri in 1893, has obvious patriotic overtones. So too has the music he wrote six years later for another pageant portraying the history of Finland which became a rallying-point for national sentiment at a time when Russia was tightening its grip on the country. One of its numbers, *Finlandia*, was to make him a household name; its importance for Finnish national self-awareness was immeasurable. From the time of *Finlandia* onwards,

(*cont. on p. 1151*)

Dmitry Shostakovich (1906–75)

The Russian composer Dmitry Dmitriyevich Shostakovich was born in St Petersburg on 12/25 September 1906 and died in Moscow on 9 August 1975.

Shostakovich was born at a crucial time in Russian history. Revolutionary fervour and dissatisfaction with the tsar and government had led to the bloody January uprising of 1905, and Shostakovich was just 11 when the decisive October Revolution occurred in 1917. His career as a musician ran in parallel with the history of the new Soviet state. Nevertheless he was often at odds with official artistic doctrines, and, though he appeared at times to bend with the fluctuating Soviet attitudes to music, he maintained to the last an integrity and individuality which have marked him as the most important composer in the USSR.

Early years

Shostakovich was at first destined to become a pianist. He studied the piano at home with his mother and then at the Petrograd Conservatory with Leonid Nikolayev. He also studied composition with Maximilian Steinberg and formed a close association with the conservatory's principal, Glazunov, whose influence is discernible in the crisp scoring of the First Symphony (1925). But Shostakovich swiftly outgrew the conservatory teaching, and Steinberg was later to express incomprehension of some of his dissonant early piano works, notably the First Piano Sonata (1926) and *Aforizmï* ('Aphorisms', 1927). At this time Shostakovich had allied himself with the forward-looking principles of the Association for Contemporary Music (ASM), which actively promoted the study and performance of contemporary Western music by such composers as Hindemith, Berg, and Schoenberg.

The fruits of this phase are seen not only in Shostakovich's astringent piano works but also in the incidental music that he wrote for Vladimir Mayakovsky's play *Klop* ('The Bedbug', 1929), the ballets *Zolotoy vek* ('The Age of Gold'; Leningrad, 1930) and *Bolt* ('The Bolt'; Leningrad, 1931), and the music for the silent film *Novïy Vavilon* ('New Babylon', 1929): this last, though rejected by most cinema orchestras as being too difficult, revealed an alertness to dramatic situation and characterization which manifested itself in later film scores and in his two completed operas, *Nos* ('The Nose'; Leningrad, 1930) and *Lèdi Makbet Mtsenskogo uyezda* ('The Lady Macbeth of the Mtsensk District'; Leningrad, 1934).

The Nose is a vivid sign of its times, reflecting Russia's satirical mood of the 1920s and also emphasizing—in its extremely complex harmonies and rhythms—the modernism of Shostakovich's style of the moment. It also reveals his keen sense of theatre and a highly original treatment of the voice. As his close friend Ivan Sollertinsky remarked, Shostakovich was 'perhaps the first among Russian composers to make his heroes speak not in conventional arias and cantilenas but in living language, setting everyday speech to music'. Such a notion of 'musical realism'—of vocal lines closely moulded to the inflections and rhythms of spoken Russian—had been a feature of much Russian vocal writing (particularly in Musorgsky's music) since its advocacy by Dargomïzhsky in his opera *The Stone Guest*. In *The Nose* Shostakovich applied a similar technique, but injected into it a new vitality, producing potent, virile vocal lines which the composer Sergey Slonimsky has aptly described as 'brilliantly eccentric'.

But brilliant eccentricity was soon to fall into disfavour. As the Soviet authorities, with Stalin in power, sought to invest the arts with a purpose directed towards the welfare of the state (see RUSSIA, 5), so the atmosphere of musical experimentation that had been allowed to thrive in the 1920s was firmly dispelled. At the time of the 1932 decree bringing all musical activity under state control Shostakovich was nearing completion of his four-act opera *The Lady Macbeth of the Mtsensk District*. After its Leningrad premiere in 1934 it was hailed as a model of the new concept of *socialist realism; but only two years later—just after Stalin himself had seen the opera—it was condemned in the notorious *Pravda* editorial 'Sumbur vmesto muzïki' ('Chaos instead of Music') for its explicitness and dissonance. It was dropped from the repertory, and was not seen again in Russia until its revival—as *Katerina Izmaylova*—in 1963.

The years of maturity

The condemnation of *Lady Macbeth* had far-reaching consequences not only for Soviet opera but for Soviet music in general. At the time Shostakovich was working on his Fourth Symphony (1935–6). Although its complexity was certainly not so pronounced as the polytonality, polyrhythm, and frenetic activity of the Second Symphony (1927), Shostakovich realized that it was stylistically a companion piece to *Lady Macbeth* in its bold gestures and grim power, its harnessing of lavish orchestral resources, and its huge, unorthodox symphonic structure. In the prevailing cultural climate it was the wrong work at the wrong time. He withdrew it, and it was not in fact performed until 1961.

Instead he produced his Fifth Symphony (1937)—dubbed 'a Soviet artist's reply to just criticism'—which is couched in a clearer, more direct manner than the Fourth Symphony: its essential euphony, its sense of grandeur and nobility, conformed more closely to the ideals of socialist realism. But that is not to suggest that Shostakovich's artistic principles were compromised: the path of ultra-modernism suggested by his music of the late 1920s was arguably a cul-de-sac. The Fifth Symphony revealed a maturing personality which had already been evident in such works as the First Piano Concerto (1933) and the Cello Sonata (1934) and which Shostakovich was to assert in such works as the First String Quartet (1938), the Sixth Symphony (1939), and the Piano Quintet (1940).

Shostakovich also confirmed his talent as a cinema composer in a number of film scores, and re-scored Musorgsky's *Boris Godunov* (1939–40). This last was of particular significance. Later he was to prepare an edition of *Khovanshchina* (1959) and to orchestrate the *Songs and Dances of Death* (1962): his own vocal music has a clear affinity with the stark realism of Musorgsky's writing, and Musorgsky's influence on the 13th and 14th Symphonies, and on the bleak song cycles of Shostakovich's last years, is particularly prominent.

At the heart of this period of Shostakovich's career lies the music he wrote during World War II. The USSR entered the war in 1941, the year in which Leningrad was surrounded by German forces. The siege was to last for two and a half years, a period of incredible deprivation and suffering but also one in which the people displayed a remarkable degree of heroism. Shostakovich captured the mood of these years in his Seventh Symphony (1941): he described it as 'a symphony about our epoch, about our people, about our sacred war, about our victory', and he dedicated it 'to the city of Leningrad'. It is a demonstrative work,

graphically depicting human life and human tragedy, the resilience of the Soviet people, and (in the finale) their strength and ability to survive. The mood of the Seventh contrasts sharply with that of the Eighth Symphony (1943), written at the height of the war and couched in the bitter, pessimistic terms which also imbue the Piano Trio (1944), composed in memory of Ivan Sollertinsky. Only in his projected opera *Igroki* ('The Gamblers', 1941) could Shostakovich find a lighter touch, though he abandoned it at the end of scene 8 and the surviving music was not performed in public until 1978.

To mark the end of the war Shostakovich wrote his Ninth Symphony (1945), dominated, as he said, 'by a transparent, clear mood'. The jauntiness and air of trouble-free serenity dashed official expectations of a defiant, heroic celebration of victory, a fact that clearly contributed to the criticism the symphony attracted during the cultural purges carried out in 1948 by Stalin's right-hand man Andrey Zhdanov. Along with every other composer of note, Shostakovich was condemned for alleged *formalism in his music, and was urged forcefully to find his way back to the path of socialist realism.

The late years

As in the crisis of 1936, Shostakovich once again had to take stock in the wake of Zhdanov's criticisms. He withheld a few potentially controversial works which were either completed or planned: the First Violin Concerto (1947–8), the song cycle *Iz yevreyskoy narodnoy poèzii* ('From Jewish Folk Poetry', 1948), and the Fourth String Quartet (1949). Instead he offered to the public a few more film scores and such choral works as the oratorio *Pesn' o lesakh* ('Song of the Forests', 1949), the *Ten Poems on Texts by Revolutionary Poets* (1951), and the cantata *Nad Rodinoy nashey solntse siyayet* ('The Sun Shines over our Motherland', 1952).

With the death of Stalin in 1953 the cultural climate thawed to the extent that Shostakovich's works of the late 1940s could be given their delayed premieres. He also completed his Tenth Symphony (1953), in which the undercurrents of melancholy and dark soul-searching flowing beneath much of his earlier music came powerfully to the surface. The Tenth Symphony is a deeply personal work—making overt use of his musical monogram *D–S–C–H—and as such was the subject of a vigorous three-day debate at the Moscow branch of the Union of Soviet Composers (29 and 30 March and 5 April 1954). Some commentators felt that the symphony was 'non-realistic' and attacked its pessimism; others stressed that the Soviet composer ought now to be guided by his own artistic instincts, particularly since the process of de-Stalinization was allowing for 'independence, courage, and experimentation' in music.

From this time onwards Shostakovich's own music became gradually more inward-looking, more concerned to express openly those concerns which he had so far kept largely suppressed. To a greater extent he withdrew into the intimate medium of the chamber ensemble: he composed seven of his 15 quartets in his last decade or so, and wrote the brooding Viola Sonata (1975) in his last year. He also composed a number of song cycles reflecting the preoccupations with irony, terror, and death which coloured his later life: *Satiri* ('Satires', 1960) to words by Sasha Chorny, *Seven Romances on Poems by Aleksandr Blok* (1967), *Six Poems of Marina Tsvetayeva* (1973), and the *Suite on Verses of Michelangelo Buonarroti* (1974).

His last symphonies, culminating in the enigmatic 15th (1971), reveal comparable traits. In the 13th Symphony (1962), for bass solo, male chorus, and orchestra, he painted a savage, terrifying picture of Stalinist oppression: subtitled *'Babiy-Yar'*, it sets five poems by Yevtushenko. And in the 14th Symphony (1969), a song cycle (to poems by Rilke, García Lorca, Apollinaire, and Küchelbecker) scored for soprano and bass soloists with a small orchestra of strings and percussion, the deep introspection of his last years is achingly asserted in music of sinister drama, heart-rending lyricism, chill gloom, and martial brutality, combining to create a work of harrowing intensity.

Much has been written about Shostakovich's position in the Soviet political scheme, about the wide gap that separates his apparently 'public' works from his more 'personal' ones like the late symphonies and quartets. He was indeed capable of the profound and the banal. On the surface it may seem odd that in a single year (1953) he could write the Tenth Symphony together with an entirely untroubled *Ballet Suite* and a sprightly Concertino for two pianos, and that in another year (1957) he could conceive the massive 11th

Symphony and the jaunty, limpidly lyrical Second Piano Concerto. Similarly, at the very time he was working on the large-scale Fourth Symphony (1934–5) he was able to turn his mind to the lightweight 'cartoon opera' *Skazka o pope i rabotnike yego Balde* ('The Tale of the Priest and his Workman Balda', 1933–6). But this diversity should not be attributed to political pressure, more to his multi-faceted personality, which was able to create music of (usually) high artistic merit for all manner of audiences.

True, Shostakovich had little time for the musical bureaucracy which sought to restrain compositional flair through blanket decrees. His relationship with officials within the Union of Soviet Composers is vividly described in *Testimony: The Memoirs of Dmitri Shostakovich*, a book which, if almost certainly owing much to the editor Solomon Volkov's own interpretative mind, nonetheless seems to voice in words the sentiments which are so strongly expressed in the music. A balanced portrait of the man, which stands out as a beacon of sanity in the current war between Shostakovich experts over what his music really 'means', is Elizabeth Wilson's collection of reminiscences by his friends and colleagues (see below). And, more than any amount of writing, it is the music that should occupy our time, for, as Shostakovich said, 'by studying my music you will find the whole truth about me as a man and as an artist'.   GN/DN

B. Schwarz, *Music and Musical Life in Soviet Russia, 1917–1970* (London, 1972) · H. Ottaway, *Shostakovich Symphonies* (London, 1978) · S. Volkov (ed.), *Testimony: The Memoirs of Dmitri Shostakovich* (London and New York, 1979) · L. Grigor'yev and Ya. Platek (trans. and eds.), *Dmitry Shostakovich: About Himself and his Times* (Moscow, 1981) · E. Roseberry, *Shostakovich: His Life and Times* (London and New York, 1981) · D. C. Hulme, *Dmitri Shostakovich: Catalogue, Bibliography, and Discography* (Muir of Ord, 1982, 2/1991) · E. Wilson, *Shostakovich: A Life Remembered* (London, 1994) · A. B. Ho and D. Feofanov, *Shostakovich Reconsidered* (London, 1998) · L. Fay, *Shostakovich: A Life* (New York, 1999)

Sibelius was undoubtedly the best-known representative of his country, and many who would never otherwise have become aware of Finland's national aspirations did so because of his music. (His birthday was a national event each year, and in 1935 his 70th culminated in a banquet at which were present not only all the past presidents of Finland but the prime ministers of Norway, Denmark, and Sweden.)

If the 1890s had seen the consolidation of Sibelius's position as Finland's leading composer, the next decade

was to witness the growth of his international reputation. In 1898 he acquired a German publisher, Breitkopf & Härtel. (He later sold *Valse triste* to the firm on derisory terms, a decision he regretted to his dying day.) But his fame was not confined to Germany: Henry Wood included the *King Christian II* Suite at a Promenade Concert as early as 1901, and during the first years of the century his works were conducted by Hans Richter, Weingartner, Toscanini, and—in the case of the Violin Concerto—by no less a figure than his contemporary Richard Strauss. The Violin Concerto was very much a labour of love, as one would expect from a violinist *manqué* who had nursed youthful ambitions as a soloist.

Sibelius's early compositions show the influence of the Viennese Classics, Grieg, and Tchaikovsky, and by the middle of the first decade of the 20th century, when Sibelius entered his 40s, his star had steadily risen. The Third Symphony (1907), however, brought a change in direction and showed Sibelius as out of step with the times. While others pursued more lavish orchestral means and more vivid colourings, his palette became more classical, more disciplined and economical. It was while he was in London working on his only mature string quartet, *Voces intimae*, that Sibelius first felt pains in his throat, and in 1909 he underwent specialist treatment in Helsinki and Berlin for suspected cancer. For a number of years he was forced to give up the wine and cigars he so enjoyed, and the bleak possibilities opened up by the illness served to contribute to the austerity, depth, and focus of such works as the Fourth Symphony (1911) and *The Bard* (1913). For tautness and concentration the Fourth Symphony surpasses all that had gone before. It baffled its first audiences and was declared ultra-modern; in Sweden it was actually hissed.

Although each of the symphonies shows a continuing search for new formal means, in none is that search more thorough or prolonged than in the Fifth (1915). Sibelius was a highly self-critical composer who subjected his music to the keenest scrutiny. In the early years of the 20th century *En saga* and the Violin Concerto were completely overhauled, and the *Lemminkäinen* Suite (1895) was revised twice, in 1897 and 1939. The Fifth Symphony gave him the most trouble of all: in its original form it was in four movements, and was first performed on his 50th birthday. It was turned into a three-movement work in the following year and entirely rewritten in 1919.

After World War I Sibelius's music struck ever stronger resonances in England and the USA, and (perhaps because of that) fewer in Germany and the Latin countries. None of the symphonies is more radically different from the music of its time than the Sixth (1923), especially when compared with the music composed in the same year by Bartók, Stravinsky, Schoenberg, Hindemith, and the members of Les Six. The one-movement Seventh Symphony (1924), which can be seen as the culmination of a search for organic unity, demonstrates the truth of the assertion that Sibelius never approached the symphonic problem in the same way. *Tapiola* (1926) crowns his creative achievement, evoking the awesome power of nature with terrifying grandeur. Of all his works this is the one that makes the most astonishingly original use of the orchestra.

Sibelius's inner world was dominated by his love of the northern landscape, and of the rich repertory of myth embodied in the *Kalevala*. The classical severity and concentration of his later works was not in keeping with the spirit of the times, and after World War I he felt an increasing isolation. As he himself put it, 'while others mix cocktails of various hues, I offer pure spring water'. For more than 30 years after the completion of his four last great works—the Sixth and Seventh Symphonies, the music for *The Tempest*, and *Tapiola*—Sibelius lived in retirement at Järvenpää, maintaining a virtually unbroken silence until his death in 1957. Although rumours of an Eighth Symphony persisted for many years, and its publication was promised after his death, nothing survives apart from the sketch of the first three bars. Near completion in 1933, it fell victim to his increasingly destructive self-criticism during World War II, probably in 1943.

Sibelius's achievement in Finland is all the more remarkable in the absence of any vital indigenous musical tradition. Each of his symphonies is entirely fresh in its approach to structure, and it is impossible to foresee from the vantage point of any one the character of the next. His musical personality is the most powerful to have emerged in any of the Scandinavian countries: he is able to establish within a few seconds a sound world that is entirely his own. As in the music of Berlioz, his thematic inspiration and its harmonic clothing were conceived directly in terms of orchestral sound, the substance and the sonority being indivisible one from the other. Above all he possessed a flair for form rare in the 20th century; in him the capacity to allow his material to evolve organically (what one might call 'continuous creation', to adapt an image from astronomy) is so highly developed that it has few parallels. His mature symphonies show a continuing refinement of formal resource that (to quote the French critic Marc Vignal) makes him 'the aristocrat of symphonists'. Vignal was referring to the sophistication of his symphonic means, but late Sibelius is also aristocratic in his unconcern with playing to the gallery and in his concentration on the musical and spiritual vision. RLa

R. LAYTON, *Sibelius* (London, 1965, 4/1993); *Sibelius and his World* (London, 1970) · E. TAWASTSTJERNA, trans. R. Layton, *Sibelius*, 3 vols. (London, 1976, 1986, 1997) · G. D. Goss (ed.), *The Sibelius Symposium* (London, 1996) · T. L. JACKSON and V. MURTOMÄKI (eds.), *Sibelius Studies* (Cambridge, 2000)

siciliana [siciliano] (It.; Fr.: *sicilienne*). 1. 'Sicilian'; *alla siciliana*, 'in the Sicilian style' or 'in the style of the siciliana' (see below, 2).

2. A 17th- and 18th-century dance and aria form, probably of Sicilian origin. It was generally in ternary form (ABA), with fairly slow tempo, and in 6/8 or 12/8 metre. Many examples are in a minor key; other characteristic features include a flowing accompaniment, a gentle lyrical melody, often with a dotted rhythm, and the use of a Neapolitan 6th at cadence points.

In the 18th century, the siciliana was popular as a slow movement in suites and sonatas (e.g. by Corelli and Bach); according to Quantz, in order to preserve the rhythm the melody should not be embellished. In vocal music (operas and cantatas) it was frequently used in pastoral scenes.

Sicilian Vespers, The. See Vêpres siciliennes, Les.

side drum [snare drum]. A small military drum. Carried at the player's side, it is struck with two beaters and normally has rattling snares: strands of gut, plastic, wire-wound silk, or spiralled wire, crossing the lower head, which vibrate against the head when the drum is struck. If the snare is released (by a catch at the edge of the head) to become silent, the side drum has a deeper, tom-tom sound. It was introduced by German and Swiss mercenaries in the 15th century along with the technique of bouncing strokes; hence the onomatopoeic names 'drum', *Trommel* (Ger.), and so on.

JMo

Sieben Todsünden der Kleinbürger, Die ('The Seven Deadly Sins of the Bourgeoisie'). Ballet in a prologue, seven scenes, and an epilogue by Weill to a libretto by Bertolt Brecht; it includes songs for soprano, male quartet, and orchestra and was choreographed by George Balanchine (Paris, 1933).

Siège de Corinthe, Le (*L'assedio di Corinto*; 'The Siege of Corinth'). Opera in three acts by Rossini to a libretto by Luigi Balocchi and Alexandre Soumet after Cesare della Valle's libretto for Rossini's *Maometto II* (1820) (Paris, 1826).

Siege of Rhodes, The. Heroic opera in five acts by Henry Cooke, Henry Lawes, Matthew Locke, Charles Coleman, and George Hudson, to a libretto by William Davenant, first performed in London in 1656; it was the first all-sung English opera but the music is now lost.

Siegfried. Opera in three acts by Wagner to his own libretto, the 'second day' of Der *Ring des Nibelungen*.

Siegfried Idyll. Orchestral work by Wagner, composed in 1870 as a birthday present for his wife Cosima and first performed on Christmas morning 1870, her 33rd birthday. It was played by about 15 musicians in their house at Tribschen and never intended for public performance, but financial hardship forced Wagner to sell it for publication, for which he expanded the orchestration. It includes themes from the opera *Siegfried*, on which Wagner was working when his son Siegfried was born, and the lullaby 'Schlaf, Kindlein, schlaf' ('Sleep, baby, sleep').

Siegfrieds Tod ('Siegfried's Death'). Proposed opera by Wagner to his own libretto. From it developed the idea of a four-opera cycle on the legend of Siegfried and the Nibelung's ring; much revised, *Siegfrieds Tod* eventually became *Götterdämmerung*.

Siegmeister, Elie (*b* New York, 15 Jan. 1909; *d* Manhasset, NY, 10 March 1991). American composer. He studied composition at Columbia University with Seth Bingham (1924–7), privately with Wallingford Riegger (1926), and in Paris with Nadia Boulanger (1927–32). He was then active in New York as a composer, conductor, pianist, and teacher, until he went to teach at Hofstra University (1949–76), outside the city. In the 1930s and 40s he was a committed left-wing artist, but in later years his activism dissolved in creative breadth. He produced eight operas and a number of other works for the stage, nine symphonies, several concertos, and much else in all genres, sometimes using American material, whether jazz, Amerindian, or other folksong. He also wrote *Harmony and Melody* (Belmont, CA, 1965–6) and *The New Music Lover's Handbook* (New York, 1972).

PG

sighting. A 15th-century term for a technique used to facilitate the singing of parallel lines of music to the written plainchant in *faburden. The singer is instructed to imagine the added part as beginning on the same note as the chant while singing it a 5th below—in effect, thinking of the voice as a transposing instrument.

sight-reading, sight-singing. The performance of music from notation that the singer or instrumentalist has not previously seen. This is a useful and important skill, whether the musician is a choral singer, accompanist, commercial 'session player', or member of an ensemble tackling a composer's new work for the first time. A good sight-singer or -player knows that what is required is not so much fine accuracy of performing detail, but a general impression of the piece that is nevertheless musically convincing. It involves calling on such resources as imagination, knowledge of style, and anticipation of what is likely to come next in a particular passage of music.

Sight-singing, a particularly valuable skill, involves reading, aural perception, and the production of sound without the assistance of an instrument to provide pitch. A good sight-singer needs to be able to 'hear' mentally the intervals between pitches and, in tonal music, their relationship to the fundamental key. A person with perfect or absolute pitch (see EAR AND HEARING, 3) will find this easier. A number of educational methods have been built on sight-singing, particularly those of the Italian *solfeggio, the English *Tonic Sol-fa and, during the 20th century, the highly systematic method devised in Hungary by *Kodály. In the last-named scheme, the reading of sol-fa, with its emphasis on relationships between pitches, supports the learning of staff notation and helps to promote a broader understanding of how tonality operates. Sight-singing plays a part in *ear-training.

Like singers, wind and string players usually have to read only a single line of music. Proficient instrumental sight-readers develop a good grasp of intervallic relationships and the rhythmic shaping of phrases as well as sensitivity to dynamics and other expression marks. As with choral sight-singing, such reading often has to take place within an ensemble, and the ability to listen to others as well to interpret the printed symbols on the page involves the aural, visual, and mental faculties.

Although keyboard players do not have to imagine pitches and pitch relationships when sight-reading, in other respects keyboard sight-reading is a highly demanding skill. Keyboard players have to cope with reading not just one line of music, but with accompanying chords and ever-varying textures (guitarists have similar problems: in many ways sight-reading on the guitar is even more difficult than at the keyboard). Most challenging of all is the playing of orchestral or choral scores at the keyboard, where a sense of style and harmonic intuition are essential if a performance at sight is to sound convincing.

Sight-reading is not just an important skill; it can open the way to knowledge of a wide musical repertory.   PSp

    📖 A. TRUBETT and R. S. HINES, *Ear Training and Sight-Singing*, 2 vols. (New York, 1979–80) · M. M. FRIEDMAN, *A Beginner's Guide to Sightsinging and Musical Rudiments* (Englewood Cliffs, NJ, 1981)

signature. A sign placed at the beginning of a composition or movement, and sometimes within it, to indicate the key or a change of key (*key signature) or the metre or a change of metre (*time signature).

signature tune. Originally any popular song or dance tune which was adopted by performers as a means of identifying themselves. In the 1920s and 30s, when broadcasting, dance bands and light orchestras commonly used a signature tune, frequently played at the end of a programme and sometimes at the beginning. A signature tune was also used to herald the entrance of an individual performer in variety shows, a practice that continues on some television chat-shows.

Since the 1940s and 50s signature tunes and 'theme music' have become associated with long-standing radio and television programmes and film series rather than with individual performers. They may be well-known popular tunes (e.g. Eric Coates's *By the Sleepy Lagoon* for *Desert Island Discs*) or arrangements and reorchestrations of classical themes (e.g. Arthur Wood's *Barwick Green* for *The Archers*), or they may be specially composed (e.g. Henry Mancini's theme to the 'Pink Panther' film series).   —/JSN

significative letters. Performance indications found in some early 'Gregorian' notation and chiefly concerning rhythm or pitch See NOTATION, Fig. 1.

Si j'étais roi ('If I were king'). Opera in three acts by Adolphe Adam to a libretto by Adolphe Philippe d'Ennery and Jules Brésil (Paris, 1852).

Sikorski, Tomasz (*b* Warsaw, 19 May 1939; *d* Warsaw, 14 Sept. 1988). Polish composer and pianist. He developed a severely existential and isolated creative persona, often linked with such philosophers and authors as Friedrich Nietzsche, Franz Kafka, and Samuel Beckett. His music is inward-looking and distinctively bleak in its ritualistic, repetitive, and reductive procedures. Much of it favours the piano (*Sonant*, 1967), wind instruments, metal percussion (*Homofonia*, 1970), and, in later works, string ensemble (*Struny w ziemi*, 'Strings in the Earth', 1980).   ATH

Silbermann. German family of organ builders and instrument makers. Andreas (1678–1734) worked in Strasbourg and built 34 organs. His brother Gottfried (1683–1753) settled in Freiburg, where he built the cathedral organ and 46 others including the one in the Dresden Hofkirche; he also made clavichords and developed a piano. Andreas's son Johann Andreas (1712–83) carried on the business, which became renowned for fine craftsmanship.   AL

Silbersee, Der (*Der Silbersee: Ein Wintermärchen*; 'The Silverlake: A Winter's Fairy Tale'). Play with music in three acts by Weill to a libretto by Georg Kaiser (Leipzig, Erfurt, and Magdeburg, 1933).

Silbury Air. Work (1977) by Birtwistle for 15 instruments.

silence (Fr.). 'Rest'.

silent keyboard [dumb keyboard, dummy keyboard]. A keyboard laid out like that of a piano but without any sound-producing mechanism, used for practice without disturbing anyone. The keys are usually sprung adjustably to simulate different action weights. Some present-day players prefer electronic keyboards, with earphones replacing loudspeakers. JMo

Silken Ladder, The. See Scala di seta, La.

silver band. A *brass band whose instruments are silver-plated.

Silver Tassie, The. Opera in four acts by Turnage to a libretto by Amanda Holden after Sean O'Casey's play (1928) (London, 2000).

Sil'vestrov, Valentyn (Vasil'yovych) (*b* Kiev, 30 Sept. 1937). Ukrainian composer. After training as a civil engineer, he studied composition at the Kiev Conservatory with Lyatoshyns'ky. During the 1960s he experimented with various avant-garde ideas and techniques formerly forbidden in the USSR. In the 1970s, however, he spurned the avant-garde in favour of neo-romanticism in such works such as *Tikhiye pesni* ('Quiet Songs') for voice and piano and *Kitsch Music* for piano (both 1977); his new manner was often so close to 19th-century pastiche that it is debatable whether he should be regarded as a postmodern ironist or simply a lyrical nostalgist. One of his most prominent works is the Fifth Symphony, which he liked to think of as an enormous coda appended to nothing; it alludes to various 19th- and early 20th-century works including the celebrated Adagietto from Mahler's Fifth Symphony. JWAL

similar motion. See motion.

simile, simili (It.). An instruction that the performer should continue with some particular effect (e.g. an accompaniment figure) or technique (e.g. a kind of bowstroke). See also segue.

Simon Boccanegra. Opera in a prologue and three acts by Verdi to a libretto by Francesco Maria Piave (with additions by Giuseppe Montanelli) after Antonio García Gutiérrez's play *Simón Bocanegra* (1843) (Venice, 1857); Verdi revised it, with a libretto revised by Arrigo Boito, adding the famous Council Chamber scene (Milan, 1881).

Simple Symphony. Britten's op. 4 (1934), for string orchestra (or quartet), based on tunes he wrote in 1925 when he was 12.

simple time. See time signature.

Simpson, Christopher (*b* ?Egton, Yorks., *c*.1602; *d* ?London, May or June 1669). English musician, theorist, and composer. He was a virtuoso player of the

bass viol, and entered the service of Sir Robert Bolles in Lincolnshire after the Civil War (during which he fought for the royalists). He was much sought after as a viol player, and is now known principally for his writings on that instrument and on the art of ornamentation; the most important is *The Division-Violist* (London, 1659). His *Compendium of Practical Musik* (London, 1667) was respected by Henry Purcell. He wrote viol music suitable both for amateurs and for advanced players. DA/JM

Simpson, Robert (Wilfred Levick) (*b* Leamington Spa, 2 March 1921; *d* Tralee, 21 Nov. 1997). English composer. He studied with Herbert Howells and at Durham University, and served on the music staff of the BBC (1951–80). Influenced by the progressive tonality of Nielsen (on whom he wrote the first study in English, 1952), he maintained an adherence to focused, though not conventionally tonal, harmony, and to extended symphonic structures that have their origin in the fugal and sonata designs found in Beethoven and Bruckner, as well as Sibelius and Nielsen. His output centres on ten symphonies and 15 string quartets, which are among the most significant contribution to these genres since those of Shostakovich. PG/AW

Simpson, Thomas (*b* Milton-next-Sittingbourne [now Milton Regis], Kent, *bapt*. 1 April 1582; *d* ?Copenhagen, before 20 June 1628). English string player and composer. Nothing is known of his early years. Between 1608 and 1622 he held appointments at the courts of the Elector Palatine (Heidelberg) and Count Ernst III of Holstein-Schaumburg (Bückeburg, near Hanover); his last position was at the Danish court in Copenhagen. His three publications (1610–21), which contain works by English and German composers as well as by himself, include much simple, attractive dance music. DA/JM

simultaneity. A group of notes played at the same time. Some writers on atonal music have preferred this term to the more usual 'chord', seeking to avoid the latter's implications of harmonic function.

sin'. Abbreviation for *sino, elided to a following vowel.

Sinding, Christian (August) (*b* Kongsberg, 11 Jan. 1856; *d* Oslo, 3 Dec. 1941). Norwegian composer. After studying the violin in Leipzig (1874–8) he turned his attention to composition. His Piano Quintet (1882–4), written in Munich, gained the advocacy of Busoni and the Brodsky Quartet. He next attracted attention with his Piano Concerto (1889) and First Symphony (1890). Later in life he taught composition at the newly founded Eastman School of Music in Rochester, New York (1921–2).

Sinding was the leading figure of the generation between Grieg and Svendsen on the one hand and Saeverud on the other. A prolific composer, he wrote four symphonies, three violin sonatas, three piano trios, and innumerable piano pieces, of which the best known is *Rustle of Spring*. His musical language is rooted in a post-Romantic idiom indebted to Wagner and Strauss. There are some 250 songs of variable quality that are second only to Grieg's in their importance for Norwegian song. The best of them, like much of his other music, evince both craftsmanship and a cultured sensibility.   RLA

Sinfonia antartica. Vaughan Williams's seventh symphony (1949–52), for soprano solo, women's chorus, and orchestra; it is based on the music he wrote for the film *Scott of the Antarctic* (1948) and contains a part for wind machine.

sinfonia concertante (It., 'concertante symphony'). See SYMPHONIE CONCERTANTE.

Sinfonia da requiem. Orchestral work, op. 20 (1940), by Britten, composed in memory of his parents.

Sinfonia espansiva ('Expansive Symphony'). Subtitle of Nielsen's Symphony no. 3 op. 27 (1910–11); the score includes parts for soprano and baritone soloists.

Sinfonia semplice ('Simple Symphony'). Subtitle of Nielsen's Symphony no. 6 op. posth. (1924–5).

sinfonietta (Fr.: *symphoniette*). A small-scale symphony, in terms either of length or of the size of the orchestra needed to perform it. The first known work to be so designated was Rimsky-Korsakov's *Symphoniette sur des thèmes russes*, composed *c.*1880 and published in 1887. Since the early 20th century the Italian form 'sinfonietta' has been preferred (the word is not genuinely Italian, however). Among composers who have written sinfoniettas are Reger (1905), Prokofiev (1909), Janáček (1926), Britten (1932), Poulenc (1947), and Hindemith (1949). Janáček's Sinfonietta is unusual in that it requires a large orchestra, but the movements are shorter than those of the average symphony and the work could be described as an orchestral suite. Latterly the term has been used for small orchestras or chamber ensembles, for example the London Sinfonietta.

—/LC

sinfonische Dichtung (Ger.). *'Symphonic poem'.

singend (Ger.). 'Singing', i.e. in a singing style, similar to *cantabile*.

singhiozzando (It.). 'Sobbingly'.

singing. The use of the vocal mechanism (see VOICE, 3) to produce musical tone. The urge to sing, which characterizes all peoples and cultures, has been developed, in Western music, through specialized techniques to extend the range of the voice, to create extremes of dynamics, and to produce great variations in tone-colour. Although modern techniques of singing are inevitably rooted in the practices of earlier generations, evidence for the manner and sound of historical singing was, until the advent of recorded music at the turn of the 20th century, limited to description alone. Whereas examination of earlier specimens of an instrument gives insight into its sound and use in previous eras, the vocal instrument dies with the singer. The fact that the physical apparatus of the voice has not changed over aeons does not provide, with any certainty, detailed knowledge of how it was used in earlier times, given the instrument's complexity and the seemingly limitless ways in which it may be exploited.

The prominent role played by singing in the religious rituals of many cultures is exemplified in the central position of the early Christian Church in the development of the Western singing tradition. The extensive body of Gregorian chant testifies to the importance of singing in the liturgy, and the virtuosity of some plainchant repertories suggests that a high level of technical skill was required to perform them. Since women were banned from performing church music, the *falsetto register was developed to extend the range of the male voice upwards, as was increasingly required for the performance of polyphonic music in the Middle Ages and Renaissance. Although boys sometimes sang the higher parts, their immature voices were not always adequate for the task, especially when compared to female voices, which were gaining prominence in secular music during the 16th century. The cultivation of singing among women of the nobility, such as the *concerto delle dame* of the Ferrarese court under Alfonso II, helped to popularize the use of soprano voices in Italian madrigals. The church responded by introducing *castratos, first in the choir of the Sistine Chapel and then in other religious musical establishments.

The advent of Italian opera in the 17th century contributed in large measure to the rise of the castrato. The other-worldly quality of the castrato voice, with its flexibility and its wide and powerful range, supported by a huge lung capacity, was ideally suited to the portrayal of heroes and mythological beings—the staple of opera librettos. During the 17th and 18th centuries the great castratos achieved unprecedented fame throughout Europe, commanding fees greater than those earned by the composers whose music they sang. Revulsion at the barbarity of castration, allied with a greater concern for realism in opera, rendered the castrato unfashionable in the 19th century, though the last significant representative of the tradition, Alessandro Moreschi, lived to make several recordings before his death in 1922.

Baroque opera encouraged the *bel canto style of vocal production, which placed a premium on graceful singing. A beautiful, even tone throughout the whole of the range, legato phrasing, immaculate breath control, agility in florid passages, and imaginative and tasteful use of ornamentation were its hallmarks. This style affected instrumental music too, and writers including Quantz and Geminiani urged instrumentalists to emulate the expressiveness of the human voice.

From the late 18th century, composers began to write for extended vocal ranges. After the dominance of the treble voice (whether female or castrato) during the Baroque period, the Classical and Romantic eras saw the rise of bass, alto, and particularly tenor voices. Many factors, including the increasing volume of instruments, larger venues, a steady rise in concert pitch, and inevitable changes of musical fashion, resulted in a gradual change in vocal production which favoured greater volume and penetrating tone over agility and refined dynamic nuances.

A survey of early 20th-century recordings nevertheless shows a range of styles and interpretation among singers of art music. As the century progressed and recordings became ubiquitous, an increased homogeneity in the approach to the singing of art music is clearly evident, though more recently the interest in earlier performance practices has reversed this trend. In addition, composers have developed a new range of extended vocal techniques in collaboration with singers. Similarly, recording and other technological advances have encouraged the growth of a diversity of singing styles in popular music.

See also CHOIR, CHORUS; VOICE; and entries on individual voice types.   BW

📖 W. CRUTCHFIELD, 'The Classical era: Voices', and 'The 19th century: Voices', *Performance Practice*, ed. H. M. Brown and S. Sadie, ii (London, 1989), 292–319, 424–58 · E. T. HARRIS, 'The Baroque era: Voices', *ibid.*, 97–116 · R. CELLETTI, *A History of Bel Canto* (Oxford, 1991) · J. POTTER (ed.), *The Cambridge Companion to Singing* (Cambridge, 2000)

singing saw. See SAW, MUSICAL.

single reed. The *reed used on most bagpipe drones, the clarinet, some organ pipes, the saxophone, and the *tárogató*.

single tonguing. See TONGUING.

Singspiel (Ger., 'play in song'). An opera in which relatively simple musical numbers are interspersed with spoken dialogue in German. Although the term was in use before the 1700s to denote a dramatic piece with music, it acquired its most commonly accepted meaning at the beginning of the 18th century, with the musical plays given in the Kärntnertortheater in Vienna. The rich tradition of mid-18th-century *Singspiel* in northern and central Germany followed on from this Viennese beginning, after the disappearance of Baroque opera from the German stage. From about the 1750s the influence of *opéra comique* and English *ballad opera* was felt in the works of J. C. Standfuss, performed in Leipzig, Hamburg, and Lübeck. The many works by J. A. Hiller (mostly on texts by C. F. Weisse) produced in Leipzig in the 1760s and 70s juxtapose musical idioms borrowed from Italian and French opera with a folk-like German quality, while Benda, at about the same time, demonstrated a move towards more serious plots (*Romeo und Julie*, 1776) as well as an expansion towards longer sections of music.

By the 1770s the term was also commonly used to denote any comic opera translated into German, and when Mozart's *opere buffe* were given in Germany they were referred to as *Singspiele*. The predominance in Vienna of Italian and French opera prompted an initiative by Emperor Joseph II to establish a German National Singspiel company in the city. The Viennese composer Ignaz Umlauf was commissioned to compose the piece that marked the inauguration of the venture, *Die Bergknappen* ('The Miners'), given at the Burgtheater in 1778. Umlauf was appointed Kapellmeister to the company and composed four more works for it. Mozart's *Die Entführung aus dem Serail* (1782) was by far the most popular to result from this initiative. The company ceased operating in 1783, but was revived between 1785 and 1788, when Dittersdorf began his successful career as a composer of *Singspiele* with *Doktor und Apotheker* (1786). Dittersdorf established the form as it survived into the following century, with its characteristic mixture of songs and more complex ensembles. The greatest Viennese *Singspiel*, Mozart and Schikaneder's *Die Zauberflöte* (1791), was of such complexity, with long act-finales of continuous music, that the authors designated it 'eine grosse Oper'.

While such writers as Goethe hoped to raise the level of *Singspiel* texts but at the same time preserve musical immediacy, composers increasingly avoided using a term inherently associated with music less demanding than that of opera. Beethoven's *Fidelio* (final version, Vienna, 1814) occupied a unique position and, with its essentially heroic, serious plot, should more properly be regarded as an early German Romantic work. In the 1860s the arrival of Viennese operetta, in emulation of Offenbach's French operettas, with the works of Johann Strauss (ii) and others marked the end of the *Singspiel*.

See also OPERA, 6, 7, 11, and 13.   —/KC

📖 T. BAUMAN, *North German Opera in the Age of Goethe* (Cambridge, 1985) · D. LINK, *The National Court Theatre in Mozart's Vienna* (Oxford, 1988)

sinistro, sinistra (It.). 'Left'; *mano sinistra*, 'left hand'. It is sometimes abbreviated *S*.

sino, sin' (It.). 'Until'; e.g. *sin'al segno*, go on 'until the sign'. See AL SEGNO.

Sir John in Love. Opera in four acts by Vaughan Williams to his own libretto after Shakespeare's play *The Merry Wives of Windsor* (?1597) with interpolations from other Elizabethan texts (London, 1929).

sirventes, sirventois. A type of song composed by the troubadours and trouvères in which the subject matter deals with moral, political, or literary concerns. Such songs are usually satirical and are often set to pre-existing melodies. The 13th-century trouvère Thibaut IV wrote a *sirventois* called *Dieus est ensi conme est li pelicans* ('God is like the pelican').

sistro. A series of small mushroom-shaped bells with a high, glockenspiel-like, chromatic or diatonic compass, mounted in a frame or handle. Known from the 17th century (though sets of small hanging cup-shaped bells called *cymbala* were played in the medieval period), it has occasionally been demanded in the orchestra (e.g. Rossini, *Il barbiere di Siviglia*).   RPA

sistrum. An ancient Egyptian ritual 'sliding ratchet', surviving in the Ethiopian Church. It consists of a metal hoop mounted on a handle. Rattling, sliding rods traverse the hoop, sometimes with loose, jingling discs. A set of tambourine *jingles mounted on a handle is generally used in the orchestra.   JMo

sitar [sitār] (from Persian, 'three-stringed'). A long-necked lute, used in the classical music of the north and central Indian subcontinent. Today the sitar has a large half-gourd as a body (and occasionally a second gourd behind the peg-head). Several types are in use. The Hindustani concert sitar has five main strings, two drone strings, and a dozen sympathetic strings. The metal frets arch over the sympathetic strings, and are curved so that the main strings can be pulled sideways for portamento. The strings are plucked with a plectrum of twisted wire, worn on the right index finger. The sitar is normally accompanied by the *tablā and the *tambūrā*.   JMo

Sitsky, Larry (*b* Tianjin, 10 Sept. 1934). Australian composer and pianist. Born in China into a Russian family, he moved to Australia in 1951; he studied in Sydney, and in San Francisco with the pianist Egon Petri. He has taught in Brisbane and Canberra. As a

pianist he has specialized in Busoni; his music has also been influenced by Expressionism, serialism, gagaku, and gamelan. Sitsky has written three operas, including *The Fall of the House of Usher* (Hobart, 1965) and *The Golem* (1980; Sydney, 1993), three violin concertos and other orchestral works, chamber and instrumental music, some with electronics, and music for piano.

ABUR

Six, Les. The name given in 1920 by the critic Henri Collet (by analogy with the Russian *Five) to Georges Auric, Louis Durey, Arthur Honegger, Darius Milhaud, Francis Poulenc, and Germaine Tailleferre. The group's members were briefly united by their adherence to the flip anti-Romanticism put forward by Jean Cocteau in his manifesto *Le Coq et l'arlequin* (1918), but they soon took quite different paths. Honegger, who had never shared the others' idolization of Satie, became a serious-minded composer of symphonies, while Milhaud pursued the technique of polytonality in his enormous output; Durey became a committed socialist and Tailleferre faded into obscurity. Only Poulenc and Auric retained some loyalty to the group's original ideal that music should be spare, witty, and up to date.

PG

📖 M. COOPER, *French Music from the Death of Berlioz to the Death of Fauré* (London, 1951) · R. MYERS, *Modern French Music* (Oxford, 1971) · J. ROY, *Le Groupe des Six* (Paris, 1994)

six-four chord. See SECOND INVERSION; INVERSION, I.

sixteenth-note (Amer.). Semiquaver.

sixth, added. See ADDED SIXTH CHORD.

six-three chord. See FIRST INVERSION; INVERSION, I.

sixty-fourth-note (Amer.). Hemidemisemiquaver.

ska [bluebeat]. A style of Jamaican popular music which incorporated a range of influences including jazz; its heyday was from 1961 to 1965. A typical ska band consisted of piano, guitars, bass, drums, saxophone, and brass. Often present was the staccato upbeat characteristic of *reggae, of which ska was a precursor. Bob Marley and the Wailers, later the most famous of all reggae performers, were originally a ska group.   KG

Skalkottas, Nikos (*b* Halkis, Eubea, 21 March 1904; *d* Athens, 20 Sept. 1949). Greek composer. He studied the violin at the Athens Conservatory (1914–20) and with Willy Hess at the Berlin Musikhochschule (1921–3). Remaining in Berlin, he had composition lessons from Weill (1924–5), Philipp Jarnach (1925–7), and Schoenberg (1927–31). In 1933 he returned to Athens, where he earned his living as a back-desk violinist and composed an enormous quantity of music.

Very little of this was played during his lifetime, and it was not until the 1960s that Skalkottas's stature began to be recognized. He developed his own serial techniques in music that is often densely elaborated and of long duration: the Third Piano Concerto (1938–9), lasting for an hour, is not untypical. Among other works of this character are four string quartets, four piano suites, two symphonic suites, and the single-movement symphony *The Return of Ulysses* (1942–3). Skalkottas's output of serial music is probably greater than that of any other composer, but he also produced a large number of tonal works at the same time. These include a colourful collection of 36 Greek Dances for orchestra (1931–6) as well as some large-scale abstract pieces.   PG

Skempton, Howard (*b* Chester, 31 Oct. 1947). English composer. After studies in the late 1960s with the leading British experimental composer, Cornelius Cardew, Skempton has consistently pursued ideals inherited from Webern, Morton Feldman, and others, for whom extreme economy of means is allied to a high degree of expressive reticence. His compositions, mainly for piano, accordion, or small groups of solo instruments, tend to be extremely short and use simple modal materials repetitively. There are a few larger-scale pieces, including the 13-minute *Lento* for orchestra (1990).   AW

sketch. A record made by the composer of a composition in an unfinished state. Historically, sketches have been autograph manuscripts, but today a sketch of an electronic work might be in the form of a tape, or notation might be realized in a computer notation program, and so on. The archetypal sketchbooks of Beethoven's music include every imaginable state between unaccompanied melodic motifs of a few notes to thoroughly worked-out full scores; even his fair copies of essentially 'finished' works show the signs of continuing composition, as do those of many other composers for whom no sketches of earlier states survive. Recent research has uncovered the existence of a surprising quantity of sketches of 16th-century vocal music as well as lute intabulations. Little is known of sketches from the Baroque period (though Bach's performing manuscripts, for instance, show valuable evidence of his compositional activity), but from the late 18th century onwards a great deal of sketch material is preserved, albeit in widely varying degrees depending on the habits of particular composers.

Beethoven's sketches have been more intensively studied than those of any other composer. They excited interest during his lifetime, and some were published during the mid-19th century. They were treated in depth by Gustav Nottebohm in the 1860s and 70s and

attracted renewed interest from the late 1960s onwards, when other composers' (notably Mozart's) sketching practices also began to be investigated. The study of sketches has illuminated many aspects of Western music, including chronology and biography, but most especially the 'compositional process': the study of how composers compose, or how a particular work came into being. The use of sketches to 'complete' unfinished works (e.g. Mahler's Tenth or Elgar's Third Symphony) is a high-profile but essentially peripheral aspect of sketch studies.   JJD

R. L. MARSHALL, *The Compositional Process of J. S. Bach: A Study of the Autograph Sources of the Vocal Works* (Princeton, NJ, 1972) · D. JOHNSON, A. TYSON, and R. WINTER, *The Beethoven Sketchbooks: History, Reconstruction, Inventory* (Oxford, 1985) · J. A. OWENS, *Composers at Work: The Craft of Musical Composition, 1450–1600* (New York and Oxford, 1997)

skiffle. A style of popular music which arose in the USA in the 1930s; it is a hybrid form taking elements from jazz and the blues. It was revived in the 1950s, when it also became popular in Britain, its leading performer there being Lonnie Donegan. The groups often included makeshift instruments, for example kazoo, jug, wash-tub or tea-chest bass, and washboard percussion. A number of musicians were in skiffle groups before moving on to more ambitious bands. Its popularity lasted until 1959, when it gave way to *rock and roll.   KG

skolion (Gk.; Ger.: *Skolie*). A drinking-song. The title was used by Schubert for two of his lieder, *Lasst im Morgenstrahl des Mai'n* (1815) and *Mädchen entsiegelten* (1816).

Škroup, František Jan (*b* Osice, 3 June 1801; *d* Rotterdam, 7 Feb. 1862). Czech composer and conductor. Born into a musical family, he had his first lessons from his father. After studying law in Prague he turned his attention to opera in Czech, an interest dating from a stay in Hradec Králové (1814–19), a rising centre of nationalism. In 1826 his *Dráteník* ('The Tinker'), a *Singspiel* to a libretto by J. K. Chmelenský—the first Czech opera—was hugely successful. The two operas that followed it aroused little interest, however, and Škroup returned to German librettos in later years. One of the songs he wrote as part of the incidental music for J. K. Tyl's play *Fidlovačka* (1834) was adopted in 1918 as the Czech national anthem. Škroup left Prague in 1857 to become conductor of the Opera in Rotterdam.   JSm

Skryabin, Aleksandr Nikolayevich (*b* Moscow, 25 Dec. 1871/6 Jan. 1872; *d* Moscow, 14/27 April 1915). Russian composer. His Messianic tendencies would seem to have been prefigured by his birthdate—the same as Christ's by the reckoning of the Western calendar, if not the Julian one in use in pre-Revolutionary Russia. He inherited his musical instinct from his mother, a gifted pupil of the great Theodor Leschetizky, though her death when he was a year old left him to the indifferent care of an unimaginative military father and the smothering feminine coterie of his aunt Lyubov.

Neurosis manifested itself at an early age, ruling out Skryabin's suitability as the officer material for which an education in military training school should have prepared him; but so did a remarkable musical gift. From the age of six he was able to play on the piano almost anything he heard once performed, and by 11 he was already playing with what was to become a legendary delicacy and incandescence. His precocity, like that of Rakhmaninov, his junior by one year, was nurtured by the brilliant teacher Nikolay Zverev; at the Moscow Conservatory he studied with Sergey Taneyev, whose rigorous technique gave him a firm base for his later flights of fancy, and the conductor-pianist Vasily Safonov, originator of the unhelpful if well-meaning tag for his protégé of 'the Russian Chopin'.

That was a fair if sweeping assessment of Skryabin's first phase as a composer of piano music. His early preludes, études, and mazurkas do not, perhaps, have the brooding individuality of the young Rakhmaninov, who crowned his period of study at the Moscow Conservatory with a success denied Skryabin, unlucky enough to incur the animosity of his composition tutor, Arensky. Skryabin's first big essay, the Piano Concerto, reveals a charming naivety and candour of youth. His ambitious first two symphonies—no. 1 in E, with chorus (1890–1), and no. 2 in C minor (1897–1903)—are less interesting than the course taken in the early sonatas. No. 1 in F minor (1892) ends in a funereal slow movement that anticipates the finale of Tchaikovsky's Sixth Symphony by a year, prompted by what Skryabin described as 'the most serious event of my life': irreparable damage to his right hand brought about by overpractising. This typically Russian railing against fate, however, turned out to be only temporary: the vein of limpid melody that emerges in the first and third movements of Sonata no. 3 (1897) is much more characteristic of the direction his music seemed to be taking.

Skryabin still needed to find a new way of expressing his more turbulent spiritual struggles, his sensual turmoil—paralleled in his life by separation from his wife Vera and the many affairs with which he was already tormenting his new partner, Tat'yana Schloezer—and their imagined outcome in a form of 'divine play' which was crying out for ever more refined expression. The first breakthrough came with the Third Symphony, *Bozhestvennaya poema* ('The Divine Poem'), in 1902–4. Some of the more preposterous consequences springing from the thought behind it are expressed in the notebooks Skryabin kept the following year, when he had exchanged the treadmill of Moscow life for the peace and quiet of Switzerland thanks to the generous support of his benefactor, the merchant and publisher Mitrofan Belyayev. Here we find many of the more megalomanic conclusions: 'I am God'; 'I want to be the brightest light, the greatest (and only) sun. I want to illuminate the universe with my light . . . I want to seize the world as a man takes a woman'; 'I create all history as I create all future. All is my wish, my dream, and I am aware of all this.' The theosophy of Madame Blavatsky, which he discovered at the beginning of 1905 and rarely referred to in his letters, merely lent form and jargon to certain aspects of the delusion.

What he did create over the next few years was a masterpiece, *Poema ëkstaza* ('Poem of Ecstasy'), and it was the 1909 Moscow performance which helped to foster Skryabin mania in Russia. Serge Koussevitzky was now an ardent champion among conductors in Skryabin's native land, while he had another determined follower in the New York-based interpreter Modest Altschuler. Now that Rakhmaninov was firmly entrenched as the relatively conservative heir of Tchaikovsky, the route of the *Poem of Ecstasy* and the middle-period piano sonatas seemed his only course. The 18-year-old Prokofiev and his friend Nikolay Myaskovsky were among the enthusiasts; but eventually a certain disillusionment set in. Prokofiev later wrote in the long autobiography dealing with his early years that 'basically Skryabin was trying to find a new foundation for harmony. The principles he found were very interesting, but in proportion to their complexity they were like a stone around Skryabin's neck, making it difficult for invention in the realm of melody and, chiefly, the movement of the voices'.

There is some truth in this; but Skryabin did not, as has often been maintained, apply any single harmonic discovery with mechanical rigidity. He certainly rejected conventional harmony by basing many of his apparently unresolvable chords on intervals alien to much of Western music up to that point—chiefly the augmented 4th or tritone, long known as the 'devil in music' because of the alien sound it produced, and used by Russian composers since Glinka in *Ruslan and Lyudmila* to convey the terror of the supernatural. Critics have cited the famous *'mystic chord' of superimposed 4ths in *Prometey, poema ognya* ('Prometheus, the Poem of Fire', 1909–10) as if it were the basis of all his music from that point onwards, yet in each of the astonishing late sonatas which followed in the wake of *Prometheus* he started afresh. Each draws its material from an ever-denser cluster of notes in procedures that were thought unanalysable until a Soviet critic charted, chord for chord, Skryabin's daunting journey of self-renewal towards a new music which might eventually have taken its place beside Schoenberg's evolution of the dodecaphonic or 12-note system. *Prometheus* has achieved an even wider measure of notoriety for the role played in the score by a *tastiera per luce* ('light-keyboard' or 'colour organ'), designed to project a play of colour, dictated by the harmonic scheme, on to a screen (see COLOUR AND MUSIC).

Meanwhile Skryabin's life ambition grew ever more outlandish. His absorption of Indian yogic principles and Eastern religions—adding the principle of eternal recurrence and dissolution to his egotistical cosmos—though admirable enough in itself, was intended to serve his projected *Misteriya*, an apocalyptic multi-media conception mapped out to embrace whole swathes of India. The unrealizable came to a halt even sooner than it might otherwise have done, as the yoga failed to work the spell of longevity Skryabin had claimed for it and he died of blood poisoning in 1915.

Linked for so long to the fashionable mysticism of the 20th century's first decade, Skryabin's music fell into disfavour while Soviet ideologues battled out the implications of his message. The incorrigibly mystic facet of Russian thinking, given new impetus in the post-Soviet era, explains in part the rekindling of interest in Skryabin's native land. Worldwide, however, the paradox of his life and works persists as even the most stringent apostles of musical progress champion his music for its harmonic invention. The programmes behind the music are easy to mock, but the notes and the sounds of the later sonatas and orchestral works have lost none of their power to excite.   DN

📖 B. DE SCHLOEZER, *Alexander Skryabin* (Berlin, 1923; Eng. trans. by N. Slonimsky, as *Alexander Scryabin: Artist and Mystic*, Berkeley, CA, 1987) · F. BOWERS, *Scriabin* (Palo Alto, CA, 1969, 2/1970); *The New Scriabin: Enigma and Answers* (New York, 1973) · H. MACDONALD, *Skryabin* (London, 1978) · J. BARKER, *The Music of Alexander Scriabin* (New Haven, CT, 1986) · R. TARUSKIN, 'Skryabin and the superhuman', *Defining Russia Musically* (Princeton, NJ, 1997)

slancio (It.). 'Impetus', 'impulse'; *con slancio*, 'with impetus', 'with dash'.

slapstick. See WHIP.

slargando, slargandosi (It.). 'Broadening', i.e. slowing down, the same as *rallentando*.

Slavický, Klement (*b* Tovačov, Moravia, 22 Sept. 1910; *d* Prague, 4 Sept. 1999). Czech composer. He studied composition at the Prague Conservatory (1927–31) and worked in Suk's master class from 1931 to 1933. Though influenced by Janáček and Novák, he had developed a distinctive originality by the mid-1930s which enriched his later works, notably *Zpěv rodné země* ('Songs of my Country', 1942) and his Sinfonietta no. 4, 'Pax hominibus in universo orbi' (1984).   JSM

Slavonic chant. See CHURCH MUSIC, 2.

Slavonic Dances. Two sets of eight dances by Dvořák for piano duet, op. 46 (1878) and op. 72 (1886), often heard in the composer's orchestral versions.

Slavonic Rhapsodies. Three orchestral works, op. 45 (1878), by Dvořák.

Sleeping Beauty, The (*Spyashchaya krasavitsa*). Ballet in a prologue and three acts by Tchaikovsky to a scenario by Marius Petipa and Ivan Vsevolozhsky after Charles Perrault's *La Belle au bois dormant*; it was choreographed by Marius Petipa (St Petersburg, 1890). Diaghilev staged it as *The Sleeping Princess* (London, 1921); the last act is sometimes performed separately as *Aurora's Wedding*.

sleigh bells (Fr.: *grelots*; Ger.: *Schellen*; It.: *sonagli*). A set of small metal *crotal bells. These are attached to costumes, instruments, vehicles, or animal harness to add a pleasing jingle to any movement. Traditionally they were attached to animals and babies' toys to avert evil. In the Western orchestra they are usually mounted on a wire hoop on a handle; tuned sets are available for Mozart's *Schlittenfahrt* K605. The best examples are of cast bronze or brass, but stamped tinplate is common.   JMo

slendro. One of the two tuning systems of the Javanese *gamelan, with five almost equal steps to the octave.

slentando (It.). 'Slowing down', the same as *rallentando*.

slide. 1. (Fr.: *glissade*, *port de voix*; It.: *portamento*). In string playing, a method of changing position between two unadjacent notes without lifting the finger from the fingerboard. It was much used for expressive effect in the late 19th and early 20th centuries, and often considerably abused. Ex. 1*a* shows the usual way of indicating it, but Bach notated it as in Ex. 1*b*. Paganini introduced a virtuoso version by executing chromatic scale passages, often in 3rds, with the same finger or fingers. See PORTAMENTO, 1.

Ex. 1

2. (Fr.: *coulé*, *flatté*; Ger.: *Schleifer*). An ornament common in the Baroque period, consisting of two short notes rising by step to the main note. It may be indicated by a sign or by small notes (see Ex. 2), and is found as late as Beethoven's String Quartet op. 135. On keyboard instruments, the first note may be required to be sustained (Ex. 3).

3. The tubing that, extended telescopically, allows the *trombone and slide trumpet (see TRUMPET, 2) to lengthen their air column, filling the gaps between notes of the harmonic series.

Ex. 2

Ex. 3

slide flute. See SWANEE WHISTLE.

slit drum. A wooden log or block hollowed out through an opening in the side, and struck on the lip. It is widely used in Africa, Asia, and Oceania. Small slit drums like the *woodblock or *temple block are used in the Western orchestra.   JMo

Slonimsky, Sergey Mikhaylovich (*b* Leningrad, 12 Aug. 1932). Russian composer and musicologist, nephew of the writer on music Nicolas Slonimsky. He studied composition at the Leningrad Conservatory with Boris Arapov and Orest Yevlakhov. In the 1960s he was one of the leaders of the Soviet avant-garde, and such works as the *Concerto-bouffe* (1964) display a close acquaintance with various aspects of Western modernism. Slonimsky is best known for his stage works, and enjoyed early successes with the opera *Virineya* (1967) and the ballet *Ikar* ('Icarus', 1971). His next dramatic work, the ambitious avant-garde opera *Master i Margarita* (1972, after Mikhail Bulgakov), however, was banned before it could be performed; it was eventually staged in 1991. In his third opera, *Mariya Styuarda* (1981), Slonimsky returned to melody and symmetrical rhythms, and this work met with popular success.   JWAL

Slovakia. See CZECH REPUBLIC, 4.

Slovenia. A republic in the south-eastern Alpine region of central Europe, a successor state to

Yugoslavia. From the Middle Ages until 1918 it was a province of the Holy Roman and later of the Habsburg Empires. A rich tradition of plainchant and some medieval polyphony is attested by the surviving manuscripts. German influence in secular music, including the presence of Minnesinger, was also evident. The first Slovene composer to gain prominence was Jacob Handl (1550–91), active in Vienna, Olomouc, and Prague. During a brief period in the late 16th century, Protestantism fostered a native tradition. The Jesuit Gymnasiums were the main centres of activity throughout the 17th century. After 1660 visiting operatic companies performed intermittently in Ljubljana, their performances becoming more regular after 1740. The absence of significant aristocratic patrons encouraged the founding of musical societies whose activities often extended into education and publishing. Academia Philharmonicorum was formed in Ljubljana in 1701 and its activity was continued in 1794 by the Philharmonische Gesellschaft.

The proximity of Slovenia to the major musical centres of Central Europe gave a particular flavour to Slovene nationalism. Although relying on vocal music to advance the national cause, the composers were acutely aware of the need for solid workmanship and followed more closely the developments in German and Czech music. The presence of German cultural communities in major towns divided the performing forces and the attention of audiences. At one time the German Philharmonische Gesellschaft and the Slovene Glasbena Matica maintained separate orchestras in Ljubljana, and a similar division was evident in opera. Mahler was engaged as a conductor in the German theatre during the 1881–2 season.

The impact of the European avant-garde was strongly felt during the 1920s and 30s, particularly in the works of Marij Kogoj (1892–1956) and Slavko Osterc (1895–1941). After 1945 the country became a vibrant centre of musical activity, nurturing some important composers (Primož Ramovš, 1921–2000; Ivo Petrić, *b* 1931; Darjan Božič, *b* 1933) and boasting several excellent performing ensembles. Since independence in 1991 the musical life of Slovenia has intensified further.
                                                                            BB

slur. A curved line used in musical notation to group notes for various purposes. It commonly indicates that the notes it affects are to be played or sung *legato*, or smoothly (Ex. 1). On stringed instruments this normally implies that the notes should be taken in one bowstroke or, if this is physically impossible, that any change of bowstroke should be imperceptible. In music for wind instruments, and in vocal music, the slur normally implies that the affected notes should be taken in one breath. If notes within a slur have dots above or below them (Ex. 2), they are to be played slightly detached (i.e. *mezzo-staccato*, but not as detached as *staccato*). In vocal music the slur is also used to call attention to the fact that a single syllable is to be sung to several notes (Ex. 3). A slur over an extended group of notes may indicate the limits of a *phrase and may encompass smaller groups of slurred notes (Ex. 4).

A curved line similar to the slur may be used to indicate a *portamento effect; the same sign between two adjacent notes of the same pitch serves as a *tie.

See also PERFORMANCE PRACTICE, 8.

Ex. 1

Ex. 2

Ex. 3

Long　to　reign　o　ver　us

Ex. 4

Smalley, Roger (*b* Swinton, Manchester, 26 July 1943). English composer, resident in Australia. He studied at the RCM and with Alexander Goehr and Stockhausen. His early works, including the *Missa brevis* for 16 voices (1966–7), used English Renaissance materials and advanced serial methods in a manner close to that of Maxwell Davies. Then, in such pieces as *Pulses* (1969) for brass, percussion, and electronics, the influence of Stockhausen came to the fore. Smalley founded a live electronic ensemble, Intermodulation, in 1969, and also

performed as a pianist. In 1976 he moved to the University of Perth, Western Australia, and his compositions, including a symphony (1979–81) and a piano concerto (1984–5), became more expansive and traditional in style and genre. PG/AW

small-pipes. A bellows-blown bagpipe of Northumbria. It has three drones and a cylindrical chanter with up to seven keys. Its light tone makes it suitable for playing indoors.

Smetana, Bedřich [Friedrich] (*b* Litomyšl, 2 March 1824; *d* Prague, 12 May 1884). Czech composer. Regarded in his country as the first and most significant Czech national composer of the 19th century, he was decisively influential at a formative stage, and established virtually single-handed a style of national opera.

> 1. The early years; 2. Years of maturity; 3. Smetana's style

1. The early years

Born into a reasonably prosperous family—his father was a brewer—Smetana exhibited a prodigious musical talent and quickly outgrew any teaching available locally. He attended school near home and in Prague but neglected his studies in favour of the capital's cultural life and was sent to study in Plzen in 1840. He had composed and arranged for string quartet in Prague and continued to write for the piano, considering the Three Impromptus (1841) as the start of his composing career. In 1844 he began studying with Joseph Proksch (1794–1864) in Prague, sustaining himself by teaching the piano. Although a fine pianist, he had to abandon a concert tour in 1847 because of poor attendance. More encouraging was Liszt's acceptance of the dedication of Smetana's op. 1 (*Six morceaux caractéristiques*, 1848) and later publication by Kistner (1851). Smetana opened a music institute in 1848 which was not a financial success, but with continued teaching he was able to support a wife, marrying Kateřina Kolářová in 1849. He supplemented his income by playing to the deposed Emperor Ferdinand, but the next years were marked by economic difficulties and personal tragedy with the death of his daughters, in memory of the eldest of whom he wrote the G minor Piano Trio (1855). Orchestral works composed at the time included the *Triumph-Symphonie* (1854) written in the hope of a national revival after the Prague revolt of 1848; no reforms were forthcoming, and, hearing of a post in Göteborg, Smetana left for Sweden in October 1856.

The favourable impression of his first few months in Sweden led Smetana to think of settling permanently. However, the ill health of his wife and his feelings of artistic isolation brought a return to Prague in the spring of 1859. Kateřina died on the journey, and

Smetana went back to Göteborg. In 1860 he brought his second wife, Bettina Ferdinandová, to Sweden, but he was ready to make a final return to Prague and needed no encouragement when the opening of the Provisional Theatre for the performance of Czech plays and opera was announced in February 1861. Apart from piano music, Smetana's work in Sweden—principally the symphonic poems *Richard III* (1858), *Wallenstein's Camp* (1859), and *Hakon Farl* (1861)—confirmed his interest in the music of Liszt and attracted much adverse criticism.

2. Years of maturity

Smetana's years in Prague were devoted to composing operas for the newly opened Provisional Theatre, the first of which, *Braniboři v Čechách* ('The Brandenburgers in Bohemia', 1866), was a huge success at its premiere. The same year saw the less successful first performance of *Prodaná nevěsta* ('The Bartered Bride'), though it began to make its way in a revised version later in 1866. Apart from the directorship of the choral society Hlahol, Smetana failed to gain any major appointments until in autumn 1866, against much conservative opposition, he realized a major ambition by becoming conductor of the Provisional Theatre. He expanded the foreign repertory and encouraged Czech works during his tenure, though his own operas *Dalibor* (1868) and *Dvě vdovy* ('The Two Widows', 1874) were the most substantial national contributions. Smetana's time in office was marked by controversy, but in spite of vicissitude he completed *Libuše* in 1872 and began planning the cycle of symphonic poems *Má vlast* ('My Country', *c*.1872–9).

Before finishing the first of these in 1874 symptoms of syphilis became apparent, the most alarming being rapid and total deafness. Extended leave from the theatre was followed by resignation and financial difficulty. The depression experienced by the composer found expression in the programmatic String Quartet in E minor, 'From My Life' (1876). In the same year Smetana completed the comedy *Hubička* ('The Kiss'), and in spite of increasing difficulty in working composed *Tajemství* ('The Secret', 1878) and completed *Má vlast*. The performance of the festival opera *Libuše* at the opening of the National Theatre in 1881 was a personal triumph though Smetana appeared to be shunned by the theatre authorities. The performance of his last opera *Čertova stěna* ('The Devil's Wall', 1882) was poorly prepared and by comparison fell flat. Against a background of growing disability he completed his Second String Quartet (D minor, 1883) and an introduction and polonaise for an orchestral suite entitled *Prague Carnival*; he also made sketches for an opera *Viola* based on Shakespeare's *Twelfth Night*. The distressing final stages of his illness ended with his death in a Prague lunatic asylum in 1884.

3. Smetana's style

The sources of Smetana's musical style range widely: Schumann may be detected as an influence on his early piano music; Mendelssohn and in particular Liszt in the orchestral works and the use of thematic transformation in the Piano Trio and later the operas. On returning from Sweden, Smetana gave himself almost entirely to the creation of a national style of opera composition which provided a model and stimulus for a generation of Czech composers. Smetana's patriotic feelings had been well to the fore in 1848, and though a German speaker he took pains to improve his command of Czech in the 1860s. He drew surprisingly little on folk models in constructing his national style, making only occasional use of folksong. Folk-dance rhythms occurred more frequently, and the polka in particular gave a suitably Bohemian accent to his musical vernacular. In opera, Italian influence and German early Romanticism is felt in *The Brandenburgers in Bohemia*, Wagner in *Libuše*, and Meyerbeer as late as *The Devil's Wall*. Smetana's personal imprint was always apparent, and his well-developed feeling for dramatic pacing far outstripped the efforts of his Czech predecessors.

The cycle of symphonic poems *Má vlast* celebrating the history, mythology, and landscape of Bohemia is still an important point of musical reference for his nation though the handful of chamber works embody utterances of a more personal nature reflecting a less optimistic view of fate. Outside the Czech Republic his choral works are largely neglected; they represent a small but significant contribution to a form which played a major part in the country's musical revival. If Smetana has never acquired the international standing of his younger contemporary Dvořák, his achievement is regarded in his homeland as the more fundamental.

JSm

📖 B. Large, *Smetana* (London, 1970) · J. Clapham, *Smetana* (London and New York, 1972) · J. Tyrrell, *Czech Opera* (Cambridge, 1988)

Smirnov, Dmitry (Nikolayevich) (*b* Minsk, 2 Nov. 1948). Russian composer. He studied composition with Vladimir Fere and Nikolay Sidel′nikov at the Moscow Conservatory, and privately with Filip Gershkovich (a pupil of Webern); he was also deeply influenced by Denisov. His music combines serial techniques with tonality and modality; many of his works are based on his own 'musical alphabet'. He wrote a number of works on texts by William Blake, including the operas *Tiriel* (Freiburg, 1989) and *Zhalobï Teli* ('Thel's Lament'; London, Almeida, 1989). In 1991 he settled in England with his wife, the composer Elena Firsova.

JWAL

Smith, 'Father' [Schmidt, Bernhard] (*b* c.1630; *d* London, 1708). Organ builder. Born in Germany, he was in England in 1677, when he tuned the organs in Westminster Abbey. By 1671 he was 'the King's organ maker' and by 1695 keeper of the king's organs, building instruments at Windsor. He was also organist of St Margaret's, Westminster, from 1676. He worked with his nephews and was responsible for organs in the Sheldonian Theatre, Oxford (1670–1), the Temple Church (outbidding his rival, Renatus *Harris, 1682–8), Durham Cathedral (1684), St Paul's Cathedral (1695–6), and Trinity College, Cambridge (1708). His organs, usually single-manual, produce brilliant, clear sound.

AL

   📖 A. FREEMAN, *Father Smith* (London, 1926; new edn, enlarged by J. Rowntree, 1977)

Smith, John Christopher [Schmidt, Johann Christoph] (*b* Kitzingen, 17 March 1683; *d* London, Jan. 1763). German music publisher and editor. He met Handel in Halle, and in 1716 was invited to join him in London, where he set up as a music editor and publisher and acted as agent for the sale of Handel's works. He was also Handel's copyist and amanuensis, and Handel bequeathed his manuscripts to him.

His son, also **John Christopher Smith** (*b* Ansbach, 1712; *d* Bath, 3 Oct. 1795), was a composer who studied with Handel, Thomas Roseingrave, and Pepusch, and in 1733 made his debut as an opera composer with *Ulysses*. From 1754 he was organist of the Foundling Hospital chapel, where he directed the annual performance of *Messiah*, and from 1760 he and Stanley directed the Covent Garden oratorios. His compositions include Italian and English operas (two of them—*The Fairies*, 1755, and *The Tempest*, 1756—based on Shakespeare), oratorios (including *Paradise Lost*, 1760), and other vocal and instrumental pieces.

WT/PL

Smith, John Stafford (*b* Gloucester, *bapt.* 30 March 1750; *d* London, 21 Sept. 1836). English composer and scholar. He studied with Boyce and spent most of his career at the Chapel Royal. He is remembered for his vocal music, and for writing what became the tune for the American national anthem, *The Star-Spangled Banner*. He is most important for his work as an editor and writer. Among his collection of manuscripts were such valuable sources as the *Old Hall Manuscript and the *Mulliner Book.

—/PL

smorzando (It.). 'Dying away'; it is sometimes abbreviated *smorz*.

Smyth, Dame **Ethel** (Mary) (*b* Marylebone, 22 April 1858; *d* Woking, 8 May 1944). English composer. She studied with Carl Reinecke and later with Heinrich Herzogenberg at the Leipzig Conservatory, and was encouraged by Brahms (whose music she admired above all), Tchaikovsky, Grieg, Joachim, and Clara Schumann, but retained a violent antipathy to the work of Wagner. She wrote an interesting account of Mahler's operatic period in Leipzig in the 1880s. Her early unpublished works show a bias towards chamber music which was later pursued in the String Quintet (1883), sonatas for violin and cello (both 1887), and String Quartet (1902–12). She made a great impression in London in 1893 with her Mass in D, but her main interest was opera, which fixed her attentions on Germany.

Her first effort in the genre, the two-act comedy *Fantasio*, was produced in Weimar in 1898; a second, *Der Wald*, in one act, was given in Berlin and at Covent Garden in 1902, and in New York the next year. More coherent in style and structure, *The Wreckers*, performed in Leipzig in 1906 under Nikisch, made a much profounder impression. With its striking plot and 18th-century Cornish village setting, it was admired by Bruno Walter and by Beecham, who conducted it at Covent Garden in 1909. Smyth composed three more works for the stage: the comic opera *The Boatswain's Mate* (London, 1916) and two further one-act operas, *Fête galante* (Birmingham, 1923) and *Entente cordiale* (London, 1925).

Her choral works include *Sleepless Dreams* (1912), a fine setting of D. G. Rossetti's words, and *The Prison* (1929–30), a choral symphony to words by Henry Brewster, the librettist for several of her operas. She also wrote a concerto for horn, violin, and orchestra (1927). Her musical style, though uneven in its polarities of conservatism and experiment, is, at its best, striking and original, and the finest music in her operas, especially *The Wreckers*, has a distinctive élan new to British opera at the turn of the century.

Smyth attached herself to the suffragette cause and produced the anthem *March of the Women* in 1911; her militant behaviour led to imprisonment in Holloway for two months. Her dramatic, excitable disposition was also projected in ten engaging volumes, six entirely autobiographical, the remaining four partly so. She received honorary doctorates at Durham (1910) and Oxford (1912) and was created DBE in 1922.

JD₁

   📖 L. COLLIS: *Impetuous Heart: The Story of Ethel Smyth* (London, 1984) · J. A. BERNSTEIN, ' "Shout, shout, up with your song!" Dame Ethel Smyth and the changing role of the

British woman composer', *Women Making Music: The Western Art Tradition, 1150–1950*, ed. J. Bowers and J. Tick (Urbana, IL, 1986), 304–24 · R. Crichton (ed.), *The Memoirs of Ethel Smyth* (Harmondsworth, 1987)

snap. See Scotch snap.

snare drum. See side drum.

snello, snella, snellamente (It.). 'Nimble', 'nimbly'.

Snow Maiden, The (*Snegurochka*). Opera in a prologue and four acts by Rimsky-Korsakov to his own libretto after Aleksandr Ostrovsky's play (1873) (St Petersburg, 1882). Tchaikovsky wrote incidental music (1873) for Ostrovsky's play.

soave (It.). 'Sweet', 'soft', 'gentle'; *con soavità*, 'with gentleness'; *soavemente*, 'gently'.

socialist realism. The official artistic doctrine of the USSR from 1932 onwards. The 1920s saw an explosion of creative pluralism in the arts, but in 1932 Stalin and the upper ranks of the bureaucracy turned their attention to the centralization of cultural affairs. The Party Resolution 'On the Reconstruction of Literary and Artistic Organizations' banned existing artistic factions and established a union for each of the arts. All artists were thus brought under Party control, their works subject to the approval of the appropriate Union committee, which was given responsibility for implementing the new aesthetic doctrines of socialist realism.

It is useful to consider the term's origins as the Soviet successor to 'critical realism', the literary movement of the late tsarist period whose most celebrated representative was Tolstoy. Where critical realism had called attention to the plight of the oppressed masses under the old regime, socialist realism now celebrated the delivery of the masses from that oppression. Officially, there was nothing left to criticize: any hardships or suffering in the USSR were either a necessary part of the internal struggle towards modernization which would provide the preconditions of Communism, the highest stage of socialism, or were part of the external struggle against Fascism and its agents within the USSR.

The consequences for composers were less easily discernible, especially where instrumental music was concerned, but the musical aspect of socialist realism can be reconstructed from policy statements and from the writings of critics in good standing with the Party. Any kind of experimental idiom, whether 'vanguardist' or 'proletarian', was out of bounds; instead, a body of classics was now extolled for each of the arts, and these were to serve as models. In the 1920s almost every composer of the past, apart from Beethoven and Musorgsky, had been rejected, but now the entire repertory was restored to its former prestige. Composers of operas and oratorios were expected to choose edifying revolutionary subject matter, and even instrumental music was supposed to follow similar implicit narratives, with initial struggle leading to a triumphant ending.

The new standing of the classics caused critics to demand symphonic or organic development in music of any length. The use of folksong was also strongly encouraged, and among the non-Russian nationalities indigenous musical cultures were taken as the foundation for socialist realist music. The fate of Shostakovich's opera *The Lady Macbeth of the Mtsensk District* (1934) illustrates how the doctrine came into focus: at first it was welcomed by critics as a model opera but two years later was condemned as naturalistic (disturbing realism, without any optimistic heroism) and disappeared from the repertory. Ivan Dzerzhinsky's *The Quiet Don* (1936), however, was chosen as the new model: it was musically much more conservative and tuneful, replete with popular songs and with a straightforward heroic plot. The overuse of folksong or any romanticization of the peasantry invited the charge of bourgeois nationalism, and even extensive organic development had its dangers. The opposite tendency, a rejection of the elements of socialist realism, was condemned as *formalism. Socialist realism was sometimes wielded arbitrarily as a tool of discipline by the Party, or even as an expression of intra-Union rivalry.

The war years saw a relaxation in the policing of socialist realism, but from 1947 the arts were all brought back into line; the Composers' Union thus condemned and humiliated Prokofiev, Shostakovich, and Khachaturian in 1948. Khrushchev's de-Stalinization programme of the late 1950s resulted in a second relaxation of artistic policy, which weakened socialist realism: the definition became still vaguer and ever more inclusive, and those works that still fell outside its boundaries were generally able to find a public outlet, albeit without state funding. By the 1970s such composers as Schnittke and Denisov could fund themselves through foreign commissions. Composers could now choose between the financial security of the state or the artistic freedom of self-employment, and were able to switch between the two. As perestroika progressed in the late 1980s even lip-service to socialist realism was no longer required, and the doctrine receded into history when the USSR collapsed in 1991.   JWal

📖 R. Moisenko, *Realist Music* (London, 1949) · A. Olkhovsky, *Music under the Soviets: The Agony of an Art* (London, 1955)

Société des Concerts du Conservatoire. A concert society formed in Paris in 1828. See concert, 2.

Société Nationale de Musique. A concert society founded in Paris in 1871 by Saint-Saëns and his circle to encourage and promote contemporary French music.

societies. Of the several definitions of the word 'society', the most appropriate in a musical context is 'A number of persons united for the promotion of a common purpose by means of meetings, publications, etc.' (*Shorter Oxford Dictionary*). When that common purpose relates to music, we find that there are hundreds of societies all over the world busily promoting choirs, orchestras, conductors, solo artists, composers, musical genres and periods, instrument restoration and design, education competitions, and various branches of musicology. Many hold meetings, congresses, and conferences, and many issue journals, editions, congress or conference reports, and newsletters.

The first professional societies were the medieval guilds. Societies formed to present public performances, at a time when formal musical events were mostly the preserve of the nobility and given before small, private audiences, began in Italy. The first *accademia*—not devoted to music—was formed in Florence in 1470 and was followed by the Florentine Camerata and many 16th- and 17th-century *accademie*, by *académies* in France (from 1570), *collegia musica* in Germany, and music-making groups at Oxford and Cambridge universities in England (see ACADEMY; CAMERATA; COLLEGIUM MUSICUM; CONCERT).

Concert and singing societies were formed in profusion in the late 18th and the 19th centuries; among the most prominent are the Academy of Ancient Music, London (1726–92), the Gesellschaft der Musikfreunde, Vienna (1812–), the *Royal Philharmonic Society (1813–), the Boston Handel and Haydn Society (1815–), the Philharmonic Symphony Society, New York (1842–), and the Association des Concerts Lamoureux, Paris (1897–).

In the second half of the 19th century societies devoted to individual composers were formed, the earliest being the Bach-Gesellschaft (1850). Subsequently, organizations devoted to scholarship (latterly musicology) have been founded in most European countries, the USA, and those in the Western tradition. Some are international. In the UK the *National Federation of Music Societies (founded in 1935) has 1800 member societies representing 130,000 musicians and music lovers, who present 7650 concerts each year to 1.5 million people and have an annual turnover of about £25 million. Similar levels of activity are to be found in most major countries and on an international level.

There are several listings of societies. *The British and International Music Yearbook* gives details of about a hundred, and the Internet provides comprehensive listings and links to the websites established by many individual societies, associations, and federations.

See also CLUBS FOR MUSIC-MAKING.   JBo

Society for Ethnomusicology (SEM). A society, founded in 1955, that emphasizes the study of world musics other than the Western art tradition, placing special importance on the study of music in its cultural context; it has held annual meetings since 1956. An international membership of anthropologists, musicologists, folklorists, and linguists receives the triennial journal *Ethnomusicology* and the *SEM Newsletter*.

JBo

Society for the Promotion of New Music (SPNM). A British organization founded in 1942; Vaughan Williams was its first president.

sociology of music. The study of music in its relation to society is what, in the broadest terms, occupies the sociology of music. Significant also for the sociology of music is not only the relation between music and society, but the ways in which society inheres within music and its materials. From a sociological perspective, all music has a social role and could be said to be socially constituted.

This is perhaps most self-evidently so in the case of music in traditional, pre-industrial cultures (to the extent that these survive), as studied by social anthropology and ethnomusicology, and where music has a direct function in everyday life, as for instance in work, ritual, religion, magic, and healing. It is also clearly the case with popular music and the entertainment industry, where music functions most obviously, among other things, as a commodity, produced, reproduced, distributed, and consumed within a modern industrialized mass culture. However, it can be argued that it is just as much the case with 'autonomous', absolute music of the Western high art tradition, generally regarded as being farthest removed from any obviously direct social function.

By the second half of the 18th century European classical music was rapidly becoming an intensely individual expression of subjective 'inwardness' and was loosening its ties with the church, with dance, and with 'mere entertainment', to the extent that, by the end of the 19th century, it had achieved a condition of what appeared to be total autonomy. At the same time, nevertheless, sociologically speaking this only serves to emphasize the character of this music as entertainment and as commodity, particularly in the recording age, and its role in the representation of particular class interests. Indeed, the social history of Western music from medieval times reveals four main stages (with, of course, some overlap): music's role in the church; its function as courtly entertainment; its representation of middle-class aspirations; and its present function in relation to a mass culture and the dominance of the mass media.

The sociology of music is diverse in its approaches, its methodologies, and its areas of focus. It is an offshoot of the still relatively new discipline of sociology, the roots of which go back to the positivism of Auguste Comte (1789–1857). Comte's aim was to establish the discipline as an exact science, along the lines of the natural sciences—an aim in which, it has to be said, he failed. Although Comte did not contribute directly to the sociology of music, aspects of his thinking, particularly his view of society as progressive, together with the influence of the evolutionist theories of Charles Darwin, are to be seen in the writings of the English social Darwinist philosopher and sociologist Herbert Spencer (1820–1903). Spencer viewed society in evolutionary terms as an organism, and speculated on the origins of music in these terms, in particular in the essay 'The Origin and Function of Music' (1857).

Spencer had some influence on interpretations of music history in the late 19th and early 20th centuries, but is largely peripheral to the development of sociology, and specifically the sociology of music, in the 20th century. Others who contributed in the early 20th century to the development of the sociology of music were Wilhelm Dilthey, Georg Simmel, and Paul Bekker in Germany, while in France Jules Combarieu published *La Musique: Ses lois, son évolution* in 1907. The key sociological theories from the founders of sociology are essentially the critical dialectical social theory of Karl Marx (1818–83), the functionalist theory of Émile Durkheim (1858–1917), and the social action theory of Max Weber (1864–1920). Each of these fundamentally different theories has had an influence on developments in the sociology of music, though only Weber directly contributed to the sociology of music itself.

In *The Rational and Social Foundations of Music* (1911, published as a separate volume in 1921), Weber argued that Western society is characterized by an ever-increasing tendency towards extreme rationalization. He applied this thesis to the material of music itself—its tuning systems, scale systems, instrument technology, harmony, melody, and polyphony. Weber's influence is evident in the work of Kurt Blaukopf in his *Musiksoziologie* (1951), and in particular in that of Theodor W. Adorno (1903–69).

Adorno is undoubtedly the most important figure in the development of the sociology of music in the 20th century. His first substantial sociological essay on music took a Marxian perspective—'On the Social Situation of Music' (1932). A number of other important works in this area followed, including 'On the Fetish-Character

of Music and the Regression of Listening' (1938), which drew on Freud as well as Marx; his work in the USA in the 1940s on music on the radio in the Princeton Radio Music Project (with Paul Lazarsfeld), and 'On Popular Music' (with George Simpson); his work on rationalization and the culture industry in *Dialectic of Enlightenment* (1947, with Max Horkheimer), which particularly draws on Max Weber; and the series of lectures which form *Introduction to the Sociology of Music* (1962) and bring many of these themes together. In addressing such areas as the social history of music, music and ideology, the mediation of society within musical material, distinctive types of listener response, and the social situation of music within the relations of production of modern industrialized society, Adorno identified a profusion of areas for future research, many of which remain to be explored in detail.

Since Adorno, the sociology of music has developed in a number of directions. In Germany this has been particularly through critiques of Adorno, as for example in the work of Tibor Kneif, *Musiksoziologie* (1971). The social and aesthetic history of music has been investigated mainly in Germany, as in the writings of Carl Dahlhaus (his *Nineteenth-Century Music*, 1980, is an influential example). In Britain Henry Raynor's *Music and Society since 1815* (1976) is also worthy of note in this respect.

A fertile line has been the study of popular music, first taken seriously by Adorno in the 1930s. Simon Frith's *The Sociology of Rock* (1978), later rewritten as *Sound Effects: Youth, Leisure and the Politics of Rock 'n' Roll* (1983), has been especially influential, focusing on rock music and the creation of identity. Other figures who have made significant contributions to this area, though not necessarily as sociologists, are Phillip Tagg, Richard Middleton, John Shepherd, and Peter Wicke.

An important development post-Adorno has been the area of gender studies and music. Susan McClary's *Feminine Endings: Music, Gender, and Sexuality* (1991) is probably the most significant text in this area, though it is more a musicological than a sociological study. In France, Jacques Attali has focused on the relation of music to the economy in *Noise: The Political Economy of Music* (1977; Eng. trans. 1985), while the Hungarian János Maróthy has extended the discussion of music and social class in *Music and the Bourgeois, Music and the Proletariat* (1974). Finally, mention should be made of Georgina Born's social anthropological study *Rationalizing Culture: IRCAM, Boulez, and the Institutionalization of the Musical Avant-Garde* (1995).

The sociology of music remains a somewhat amorphous subdiscipline, with no very clear lines of demarcation between sociology, social anthropology, and ethnomusicology. Since the 1980s the situation has been rendered even more fluid with the rise of such interdisciplinary areas as cultural studies and critical musicology in the English-speaking world. This has coincided with musicology becoming more receptive to other disciplines. It seems likely, therefore, that many of the concerns of the sociology of music will be absorbed into musicology itself.　　　　　　MPA

📖 M. WEBER, *The Rational and Social Foundations of Music*, trans. and ed. D. Martindale, J. Riedel, and G. Neuwirth (Carbondale, IL, 1958) · T. W. ADORNO, *Introduction to the Sociology of Music*, trans. E. B. Ashton (New York, 1976) · S. FRITH, *Sound Effects: Youth, Leisure and the Politics of Rock 'n' Roll* (London, 1983) · M. PADDISON, *Adorno, Modernism and Mass Culture: Essays on Critical Theory and Music* (London, 1996)

Socrate ('Socrates'). Symphonic drama (1918) by Satie, for one or more voices with piano or chamber orchestra, settings of texts by Plato translated by V. Cousin.

Söderlind, Ragnar (*b* Oslo, 27 June 1945). Norwegian composer and teacher. Largely self-taught in music, he studied at the Oslo Conservatory and then transferred to the Sibelius Academy, where he took lessons in composition with Kokkonen and Erik Bergman (1967–8); back in Oslo he trained as a conductor. Rejecting serialism as too exclusive an aesthetic—a decision which set him at odds with the Norwegian musical establishment, then predominantly modernist—Söderlind produced a body of work notable for tonal strength, muscular counterpoint, and instrumental resourcefulness. Although he has written large-scale works for the concert hall, not least six symphonies (1975–99) and concertos for violin (1986–7), cello (1991), and piano (1996–7), he is strongly drawn to the stage: his operas are *Esther and the Blue Serenity* (1972), *Rose og Ravn* (1989), and *Olav Trygvason* (2000), his ballets *Hedda Gabler* (1978), *Kristin Lavransdatter* (1982), and *Victoria* (1986).　　　　　　MA

sofort (Ger.). 'Immediately', i.e. **attacca*.

soft hexachord. See HEXACHORD; SOLMIZATION.

soft pedal. Colloquial term for **una corda*. See also PIANOFORTE.

soggetto (It.). 'Subject', or 'theme'. In 18th-century theory, a fugue subject of a traditional nature, similar to the subjects of the earlier **ricercar*.

soggetto cavato. See CANTUS FIRMUS.

soh. See SOL.

Soir, Le. See MATIN, LE; MIDI, LE; SOIR, LE.

Soirées musicales ('Musical Evenings'). A collection of salon pieces (songs and duets) by Rossini, published in 1835. Britten orchestrated five of them under the same title (op. 9, 1936) and the rest were orchestrated by Respighi for his ballet *La *Boutique fantasque*.

sol [soh]. The fifth degree of the scale in the **solmization system. In French and Italian usage it has become attached, on the fixed-*doh* principle, to the note G, in whichever scale it occurs. See TONIC SOL-FA.

Solage (*fl* late 14th century). French composer. He was a younger contemporary of Machaut, and was associated with Jean Duc de Berry. Among his few surviving chansons is the satirical *Fumeux fume par fumee*, which explores eccentric chromatic harmonies as an exercise in intellectual absurdity.　　　　　　JM

Soldaten, Die ('The Soldiers'). Opera in four acts by Zimmermann to a libretto by the composer after Jakob Michael Reinhold Lenz's play (1776) (Cologne, 1965).

Soldier's Tale, The. See HISTOIRE DU SOLDAT.

Soleil des eaux, Le ('The Sun of the Waters'). Work by Boulez originally composed in 1948 for a radio play by René Char; Boulez revised it in 1950 as a cantata, in 1958 for larger forces, and in 1965 for soprano and chorus.

Soler (Ramos), Antonio (Francisco Javier José) (*b* Olot, Gerona, *bapt.* 3 Dec. 1729: *d* El Escorial, 20 Dec. 1783). Catalan composer. He showed early promise at the Montserrat choir school and was appointed *maestro de capilla* at Lérida when he was about 30. In 1752 he became a monk at the monastery of the Escorial, and a year later was admitted to holy orders. He spent the rest of his life there, as *maestro*, organist, and a highly respected teacher; his pupils included the royal children.

Much of Soler's music was destroyed in 1808 when the Escorial was ransacked by French troops. The influence of Domenico Scarlatti, with whom he studied, is apparent in the 120 or so keyboard sonatas for which he is best known. He also wrote organ works, six concertos for two organs, six quintets for strings and organ, dramatic works, sacred vocal music, and a celebrated treatise, *Llave de la modulación y antigüedades de la música* (Madrid, 1762).　　　　　　WT

Solesmes, monks of. The community of a Benedictine abbey in Solesmes, a village in France near Le Mans, famous for its seminal contributions to the modern revival of Latin liturgy and plainchant (see MOTU PROPRIO). The monks have published numerous scholarly studies and, in the series *Paléographie musicale*, facsimiles of important medieval sources, as well as chant books for the Roman rite. Their interpretation of the neumatic notation, disseminated in treatises and recordings, forms the basis for most modern performances of Western plainchant. Among those associated with this work have been Dom Prosper

Guéranger, Dom Joseph *Pothier, Dom André *Mocquereau, and Dom Eugène *Cardine.   —/ALi

sol-fa. See TONIC SOL-FA.

solfeggietto (It., 'little study'). A title for a short keyboard piece, used by C. P. E. Bach among others.

solfeggio (It.; Fr.: *solfège*). 1. A type of vocal exercise sung either to a vowel (in which case it should properly be called a *vocalise) or to the *solmization syllables (the term is derived from 'sol-fa'). The exercise serves a dual purpose: as basic voice-training; and as practice in sight-reading, since the student learns to recognize the intervals and notes.

2. The term has also been applied to instruction in the rudiments of music: *sight-singing, *ear-training, study of notation, and so on. Extensive courses in *solfège* were first introduced at the conservatories in Brussels and Paris and have been adopted by some American institutions.

Sollertinsky, Ivan Ivanovich (*b* Vitebsk, 20 Nov./3 Dec. 1902; *d* Novosibirsk, 11 Feb. 1944). Russian musicologist and critic. He was a member of Mikhail Bakhtin's philosophical circle in Vitebsk and Nevel before moving in 1921 to Petrograd (St Petersburg), where he took a degree in Spanish classical literature and Romano-Germanic philology, graduating in 1923. Originally specializing in theatre and ballet, Sollertinsky became increasingly involved with the contemporary music scene in Leningrad; his close friendship with Shostakovich dates from 1925. He published an influential monograph on Mahler (*Gustav Maler*, Leningrad, 1932; Ger. trans. 1996). In 1939 he became a professor at the Leningrad Conservatory but in 1941 was evacuated to Novosibirsk. His most important articles on music, literature, and ballet can be found in Mikhail Druskin's four-volume collection (Leningrad, 1946, 1956, 1963, 1973).   PF

solmization. The use of syllables in association with pitches in the oral teaching of melodies. The name is derived from the most common set of such syllables known in Europe: *ut–re–mi–fa–sol–la*. This set was invented by Guido of Arezzo (*c*.991–after 1033), and is described in his *Epistola de ignotu cantu* ('Letter about unknown chant'), written to his friend and fellow-monk Michael *c*.1030. It is made up of the first syllable of each of the first six lines of a hymn to St John (Ex. 1). Although the text is older than Guido the melody is not, and he may have composed it himself.

By 1100 the six syllables were used not only for the six notes C–D–E–F–G–A, but also for F–G–A–B♭–C–D and for G–A–B–C–D–E, which have the same interval pattern (tone–tone–semitone–tone–tone). These three

Ex. 1

sets of six notes are known as hexachords. The hexachord on C has no B and was known as the 'natural' (*naturale*) hexachord; that on G has a B♮ and was known as 'hard' (*durum*—from the way of writing the natural B, ♮, with four corners), and that on F needed a B♭ and was known as 'soft' (*molle*—with a rounded shape, [♭]). The complete range of notes as usually given by medieval theorists, and the hexachords which could be fitted to them, are shown in Ex. 2. (Note the system used at that time for indicating the pitch of the note; the system used throughout this *Companion* is laid out to the left.)

These syllables were frequently depicted on the so-called Guidonian hand, a visual aid to learning solmization (see GUIDO OF AREZZO).

The whole purpose of the system was to facilitate the memorization of unfamiliar melodies. The pupil had in mind the six syllables, and knew their pitch relationships—he would have been especially aware of the semitone *mi–fa* in the middle of the hexachord. He probably did not readily associate the syllables with letters of the alphabet; the choirmaster would translate the melody to be learnt into solmization syllables, which the pupil could then sing and learn.

Ex. 2

Melodies that went beyond the range of one hexachord presented problems. For the second phrase of the Kyrie shown in Ex. 3, a change (or 'mutation') would have to be made to the lower hexachord, either immediately or within five or six notes.

The availability of B♭ and B♮ in the soft and hard hexachords respectively may have meant that those responsible for copying music did not feel the need to be as exact in writing these accidentals as were later musicians. In the later Middle Ages, hexachords on other degrees came to be used: on D, needing F♯; on A, needing C♯; on B♭, needing E♭; and on E♭, needing A♭. In these cases, too, performers could easily learn with the aid of solmization accidentals not always copied into a score. Ex. 4 is the opening of an anonymous ballade of the early 15th century, *Se vrai secours*. The contratenor part could be solmized in the hexachord on F, or in G mutating to E.

There are many examples of sets of solmization syllables (not necessarily six in number) in non-European musical cultures, from the Middle East to the Far East, and they were also known in Ancient Greece. Guido's six syllables were not the only ones known in his time in Europe, but no others gained wide currency. Renaissance attempts to extend the series to cover an octave, or to simplify mutation and reduce the number of hexachords, show dissatisfaction with the system; most theorists of the 16th century onwards display little interest in it. That such systems can still aid the teaching of music is amply demonstrated by the success of the *Tonic Sol-fa system.   DH

solo (It.). 'Alone'; e.g. *violino solo*, 'solo violin'; the plural is *soli*.

Solomon. Oratorio (1749) by Handel to a biblical text by an unknown author.

Ex. 3

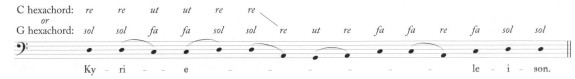

Ex. 4

solo pitch. *Pitch slightly higher than normal, sometimes used for its extra brilliance of sound.

Solti, Sir **Georg** [György] (*b* Budapest, 21 Oct. 1912; *d* Antibes, 5 Sept. 1997). Hungarian-born British conductor. He studied the piano and composition at the Liszt Academy of Music in Budapest, where his teachers included Bartók, Dohnányi, and Kodály. He joined the Budapest Opera as a répétiteur, observing and assisting such conductors as Busch, Klemperer, Walter, and Kleiber. He was then influenced by Toscanini as a répétiteur at Salzburg in 1936 and 1937. In 1938 he made his conducting debut at the Budapest Opera, but as he was Jewish his career was interrupted by World War II and he went to Switzerland, where he worked as a pianist.

After conducting *Fidelio* in Munich in 1946 Solti was appointed music director of the opera there and made a strong impact as a rigorously demanding and dynamic conductor of great flair. He was at the Frankfurt Opera (1952–61), then became music director at Covent Garden, where his meticulously prepared performances and his charismatic personality brought him and the opera company great prestige. From 1969 to 1991 he was music director of the Chicago Symphony Orchestra, with which he gave premieres of works by Henze, Tippett, del Tredici, and Lutosławski, and from 1979 to 1983 of the LPO; he also conducted at Salzburg and Bayreuth. He made a pioneering recording of Wagner's *Ring* with the Vienna Philharmonic Orchestra. He was knighted in 1971.   JT

   📖 P. Robinson, *Solti* (London, 1979) · *Solti on Solti* (London, 1997)

solus tenor. A single voice-part that could be substituted for both the tenor and contratenor parts in late medieval and Renaissance polyphonic music.   IR

Sombrero de tres picos, El (*Le tricorne*; 'The Three-Cornered Hat'). Ballet in two scenes by Falla to a scenario by Gregorio Martínez Sierra after Pedro Antonio de Alarcón's novel (1874); it was choreographed by Massine, with designs by Pablo Picasso, and first produced by Diaghilev's Ballets Russes (London, 1919). It is an expanded version of Sierra and Falla's pantomime *El corregidor y la molinera* ('The Magistrate and the Miller's Daughter') (Madrid, 1917) and has the same plot as Wolf's *Der Corregidor*. Falla arranged two orchestral suites from the score (1919).

Somers, Harry (Stewart) (*b* Toronto, 11 Sept. 1925; *d* Toronto, 9 March 1999). Canadian composer. He studied composition at the Royal Conservatory of Music, Toronto, with John Weinzweig and won scholarships for studies in Paris (1949–50 with Milhaud and in 1960) and Rome (1969–71). One of Canada's most important composers, he is best known for his operas. *Louis Riel*, written for Canada's Centennial Year (1967), with a libretto by Mavor Moore, is a highly dramatic work embracing stylistic influences as diverse as folksong, taped material, and 12-note writing. His opera *Mario and the Magician*, based on a novella by Thomas Mann, was given its premiere by the Canadian Opera Company in 1992. Among other important works are his first opera, *The Fool* (1953), and the chamber opera *Serinette* (1990) with a libretto by James Reaney. Somers also devoted much attention to the piano, for which he wrote five sonatas, and to exploring vocal techniques. Other works include *Five Songs of the Newfoundland Outports* (1967), *Music for Solo Violin* (1973), given its first performance by Yehudi Menuhin, and *Chura-Churum*, based on Sanskrit texts with loudspeakers placed around the auditorium.   HRe

   📖 B. Cherney, *Harry Somers* (Toronto, 1975)

Somervell, Sir **Arthur** (*b* Windermere, 5 June 1863; *d* London, 2 May 1937). English composer and educationist. He studied composition with Stanford at Cambridge (graduating BA in 1884), with Kiel and

Bargiel in Berlin (1884–5), and with Parry at the RCM (1885–7); later he also studied privately with Parry. He joined the staff of the RCM in 1894 and succeeded Stainer as Inspector of Music to the Board of Education in 1901. In 1920 he became Chief Inspector, a position he held until his retirement in 1928. He was knighted in 1929.

Somervell made his name during the 1890s with the choral cantatas *The Forsaken Mermaid* (Leeds, 1895) and *Ode to the Sea* (Birmingham, 1897), though it was as a composer of song cycles that he is remembered. His *Maud* (1898) is among the finest settings of Tennyson, and his lyrical gifts reached their zenith in A. E. Housman's *A Shropshire Lad* (1904). Two other cycles, *James Lee's Wife* (1907) and, arguably his finest achievement, *A Broken Arc* (1923), show a sympathy for Robert Browning's unorthodox world of faith and morality. His later career produced a maritime symphony, *Thalassa*, and the Symphonic Variations 'Normandy' (both 1912) for piano and orchestra, and two works for violin and orchestra, the *Concertstück* (1913) and Violin Concerto (1932); the last named won the admiration of Tovey.   MK/JD1

Somis, Giovanni Battista (*b* Turin, 25 Dec. 1686; *d* Turin, 14 Aug. 1763). Italian violinist and composer. He studied with Corelli in Rome from 1703 to 1707, when he took up the post, which he held for the rest of his life, of leader and solo violinist in the ducal orchestra at Turin. He composed violin and cello sonatas of the *da camera* type, but his chief importance was as an extremely influential teacher. His pupils included not only such Italians as Pugnani but many important French violinists, notably J.-M. Leclair. In 1733 he made a successful visit to Paris, where the brilliance of his playing was much praised.   WT/ER

son, sons (Fr.). 'Sound', 'sounds', 'note', 'notes'; *son bouché*, *son étouffé*, 'stopped note' in horn-playing; *son ouvert*, an open note on a wind instrument.

sonata. An instrumental composition.

> 1. Origins and early use; 2. The sonata to the time of Corelli; 3. Corelli and his contemporaries; 4. Corelli's influence; 5. The early keyboard sonata; 6. The Classical sonata; 7. Beethoven's contemporaries; 8. The Romantics; 9. The post-Romantics; 10. Conclusion

1. Origins and early use

Like so many terms originating about 1600, 'sonata' has been applied to a bewildering variety of instrumental types over the centuries, with the simple common denominator that they are all to be played. However, the Italian language had two verbs for 'play': *sonare* for

bowing or blowing, *toccare* for 'touching' a keyboard. Hence, by analogy with 'cantata' for a sung piece, the Italians used 'toccata' for a piece played on a keyboard instrument and 'sonata' for a piece for strings or winds. The earliest definition of 'sonata' (in Praetorius's *Syntagma musicum*, 1619) affirms this but goes on to offer stylistic criteria: 'the sonatas are made to be grave and imposing in the manner of the motet, while the canzonas have many black notes running gaily and briskly through them'. Praetorius specifically mentions Giovanni Gabrieli, no doubt recalling the *Sonata pian e forte* (1597), but judging by the posthumous collection of 1615 the composer had abandoned these definitions by the time of his death. At different times and in different places during the 17th century, 'sonata' was used synonymously with 'canzona', 'sinfonia', and 'concerto'; and generalizations on the meaning of these terms can have only limited validity.

2. The sonata to the time of Corelli

Compositions entitled 'Sonata' cover an enormous variety of pieces ranging in length from 20 to over 200 bars and including sets of variations and dances, while scorings range from a single instrument to ceremonial music in 22 parts—usually, but not always, with a keyboard continuo. This repertory served as concert music, diversional chamber music, 'table' music, and didactic material, and for use in church. After the mid-century, if the edition contained dances unsuitable for the last-named purpose, the set might have been labelled 'da camera', but 'da chiesa' rarely occurs before the last decade of the 17th century as there was no clear-cut stylistic differentiation between sacred and secular styles in free sonatas.

Naturally enough, changes in instrumental music corresponded to those in music generally, and large scorings gradually gave way to duos and trios as in vocal music. Because the primitive typography of the period was unable to notate such advanced techniques as double and triple stopping, solo violin sonatas were circulated mainly in manuscript and have since been lost. Irrespective of venue, an organ is the most frequently mentioned continuo instrument in free sonatas, and there is little evidence that it was normally doubled by a melodic bass such as a cello. In dance music, however, unaccompanied performance was common, though a harpsichord is often mentioned as an alternative to the string bass.

Politically, Italy remained a conglomeration of papal states, courts, and republics, with Spain occupying a third of the peninsula. It is hardly surprising therefore that music reflected this regional diversity. Instrumental sonatas differed substantially in both form and content between Venice, Mantua, Modena, Bologna, and Rome. Italian violinists were much in demand in the Italianate courts of northern Europe such as Vienna, Dresden, Neuburg, and Poland, and only gradually did German composers (e.g. Schmelzer) manage to compete successfully. By the last quarter of the century such violinists as Biber and Walther had achieved an astounding level of virtuosity, and with the advent of copper-plate engraving their sonatas could now be published, whereas the Italians had to wait another generation to see their most technically advanced sonatas in print. In spite of widespread acknowledgment of the Italians, such composers as Buxtehude still remained remarkably independent of them.

3. Corelli and his contemporaries

The greater uniformity observable in sonatas about 1700 was to a considerable extent due to the influence of Corelli: no instrumental composer before him had achieved a comparable level of universal recognition. He undoubtedly learnt much during his student years in Bologna when he was apparently a member of the Accademia Filarmonica—the main focus of music-making in the city. He personally acknowledged only the Roman school, having worked after his arrival in Rome in about 1675 with such composers as Lelio Colista, C. A. Lonati, Alessandro Stradella, and Carlo Mannelli. Largely through the influence of the English historian Burney, who felt that Corelli lacked invention and resource, the belief arose that he was a consolidator rather than an originator, but it was precisely his originality which most appealed to his contemporaries. Such features as the slow–fast–slow–fast sequence of movements, or the arrangement of *da camera* sonatas into suites of dances, and indeed the pre-eminence of the 'trio' medium itself were established only with him.

As none of Corelli's solo sonatas—the true vehicle for virtuoso display—were ever published, it is impossible to determine the full extent of his legendary powers as a violinist, but even Burney acknowledged the importance of the op. 5 duo sonatas for violin and violone as the foundation of 'all good schools of violin playing'. Its significance lies in the fact that it was the first important Italian print to be engraved and could therefore make copious use of chordal playing on the violin. Incidentally, Corelli wrote no pieces entitled 'sonata da chiesa', and it is likely that all his sonata collections were originally intended as concert music, even where the influence of the church style is evident. Because Corelli's work quickly established a norm it is easy to overlook the fact that many Italian composers, including T. A. Vitali in Modena and Giuseppe Torelli in Bologna, chose not to adopt his idioms and forms but continued their regional traditions into the 18th century.

4. Corelli's influence

Through the numerous editions of the northern presses, Corelli's music became widely disseminated in Europe. In Italy itself such composers as Tartini continued publicly to revere Corelli's op. 5, but interest in trio sonatas rapidly declined in favour of the solo sonata. Even Corelli's own pupils, for example Michele Mascitti and Somis, quickly transformed his rather severe style into a much lighter idiom, more in keeping with the fashions of the time. English composers on the other hand, encouraged by the presence of a number of those pupils, developed such a mania for Corelli after 1700 that Roger North could declare 'if musick can be immortall, Corelli's consorts will be so'. The English had of course already experimented with sonatas, but Purcell's 'fam'd Italian masters' are far more likely to have been Colista and Lonati than Corelli.

The French, too, espoused the sonata in an attempt to forge a rapprochement between the Italian and French styles, but such deliberate imitations as Couperin's *Le Parnasse, ou L'Apothéose de Corelli* are transformed by his French accent. In Germany the paths of dissemination are less clear-cut, for in spite of such obvious examples as Telemann's *Corellisierende Sonaten*, and Handel's patent indebtedness acquired during his apprenticeship in Rome, there always existed a contrapuntally rigorous line of development exemplified by the Trio Sonata from Bach's *Musical Offering*.   DA/PA

5. The early keyboard sonata

In the 1730s the term 'sonata' began to be widely used for keyboard solos. A one-movement example by Handel was published at Amsterdam in about 1732. Domenico Scarlatti left several hundred one-movement harpsichord pieces under that title in manuscript, but when a selection was published in London (1738) they were termed *essercizi* (exercises). These are pieces of great originality in harmony, form, and texture. However, outside Spain and Portugal, Scarlatti had little influence on the further development of the sonata (though there was a pocket of English 'Scarlatti-ists', of whom Thomas Roseingrave was the most important).

Multi-movement sonatas for keyboard were first developed by such Italian composers as Platti, Alberti, and G. M. Rutini, with anything from two to five short movements; the finale is frequently a minuet or other dance. The form was taken up by north German imitators, especially C. P. E. Bach, whose early 'Prussian' and 'Württemberg' sets of 1742–4 set a much higher standard of musical invention. Bach found in the keyboard sonata a medium for the 'empfindsamer Stil' (see EMPFINDSAMKEIT). His favourite instrument was the clavichord, which allowed rapid changes of mood, expressed in sudden changes of key, strange alterations of direction in the melody, and variable dynamics within a very limited range. He tended to change the theme in its successive statements, so that the principal subject of a rondo would never appear the same twice. In large-scale movements, with the opening subject returning in the concluding section, he made a point of altering the original on its return (the title of a set of sonatas published in 1760 is *Sechs Sonaten . . . mit veränderten Reprisen*). He also developed thematic material throughout a movement (not just in a separate development section), a technique used by Haydn.

Both Scarlatti's one-movement sonatas, and the first movements of most multi-movement works, were most often structured in a precursor of *sonata form in which the main recapitulation of the first subject comes in the dominant key after the double bar. But examples of full sonata form are also found.

6. The Classical sonata

By the 1750s the sonata had replaced the suite as the principal genre for multi-movement keyboard works. By the 1770s solo sonatas were vying with orchestral music in their emotional capacity, though they were still exclusively private, domestic pieces. Themes became more motivic, the melody less decorated; sonorities became weightier (many sonatas include octave passages after the manner of orchestral doublings), and simple Alberti figurations (see ALBERTI BASS) occurred less often.

The key figure in the development of the Classical sonata was Haydn. His earliest specimens, many of which were originally given the title 'divertimento', are in a light Italianate style, but by the 1770s he followed C. P. E. Bach in generally treating the sonata as a vehicle for serious intellectual and emotional content, especially in the weighty first movements. Mozart's solo sonatas also show a marked increase in profundity, beginning perhaps with his A minor sonata, K310/300d. They are all in three movements, though the first movement was not necessarily in sonata form: in the popular K330/300h in A major it was a set of variations. Haydn was even freer in his arrangements of movements. In this period the piano was beginning to replace the harpsichord and clavichord in popularity, and allowed for new experimental sonorities and the use of the sustaining pedal.

A peculiar product of the Classical period was the 'accompanied sonata', or in a typical title 'Sonata for the harpsichord or pianoforte with accompaniments (ad libitum) for the violin (or flute) and violoncello'. Reversing the older sonata for violin and continuo, these works gave most of the melodic material to the key-board instrument, with the other instruments merely doubling or filling in accompaniments. Not surprisingly these pieces are rarely heard today, but they were enormously in vogue in the later 18th century and seem to have suited the amateur domestic scene in genteel soirées, where a young lady would lead on the keyboard and would be accompanied by gentlemen playing the other instruments. Haydn's piano trios of the 1790s were published as accompanied sonatas. Mozart's piano trios and violin-and-piano sonatas were also in this tradition, but they are among the first to give the violin equal prominence with the piano (typically, the two instruments share and alternate the thematic material), and they begin to emancipate the cello as well. His four sonatas for piano duet (four hands) and one for two pianos are important pioneering works in these media. (It is worth noting that today, in regard to the Classical period, the term 'sonata' is reserved for works for piano with or without *one* other instrument, whereas in the Classical period itself it could also include what are now called piano trios or even piano quartets.)

The serious sonata, or 'symphonic' sonata (as it might be called), flourished in the hands of Clementi and Beethoven in this period. Clementi had produced over 70 sonatas (solo and 'accompanied') by 1790. The earliest date from about 1770 and derive from the early Italian sonatas using Alberti figurations. But he later progressed to sonatas, written in Vienna and London in the 1780s, which are in three substantial movements of serious character and seem to presage Beethoven's keyboard style of the following decade.

The earliest of Beethoven's 36 piano solo sonatas (four juvenile ones as well as the standard 32) date from the 1790s, and 25 of them were completed by 1802. Those of his early years in Vienna were large-scale works written, in part, to display his piano technique, but published for the domestic market. They are mainly in four movements, including a minuet or scherzo (the scherzo was Beethoven's own contribution to the sonata genre). The first movements, in sonata form, use much thematic material which is developed at length. The sonata in C, op. 2 no. 3, often sounds like a concerto, even to the extent of having a written-out cadenza in the first movement. But when Beethoven is composing in a serious, extended symphonic manner (as, for example, in the op. 10 sonatas) his piano figuration, unlike that of Mozart, does not sound in the least like a reduction of an orchestral score.

By 1800 Beethoven was writing more orchestral music, and the sonatas began to break away from the symphonic mould. Op. 27 consists of two sonatas, each marked 'quasi una fantasia' and with an unexpected order of movements. The second, the so-called 'Moonlight' Sonata, begins with a movement in an improvisatory, pianistically conceived style; then follows a skittish minuet or scherzo; and the last movement is in sonata form with themes based on piano figuration. Further fruits of this break from conventional symphonic order are seen in Beethoven's later sonatas, such as the 'Waldstein' op. 53, which has a slow movement conceived simply as a link between a huge opening movement and an expansive rondo.

Even more remarkable are the five sonatas written between 1816 and 1822. No two are alike, either in order of movements or in proportions. The earliest of these, op. 101, opens as though it were to be 'quasi una fantasia'; it has a fierce march in place of a scherzo, then a short link in an intricate, ruminating style before a fugal finale. Op. 106, the 'Hammerklavier', is one of the longest sonatas ever written, not only in time (it lasts about 50 minutes) but also in emotional intensity, ending with a colossal fugue. The last sonata, op. 111, has only two movements, the first a titanic piece in sonata form, the second a set of sublime variations, which Gerald Abraham has aptly described as the equivalent of the 'Heiliger Dankgesang' of the String Quartet op. 132. It is difficult to convey in words the effect of these sonatas. They have the emotional scale of a symphony but are more intimate and frequently more profound. They are virtuoso pieces, yet they are not written merely to show off the player's skill. Each is unique in form and emotional content. Each has at least one movement of lyric beauty. In the wake of these works, composers found a sonata a daunting undertaking.

7. Beethoven's contemporaries

However, Beethoven was not alone in treating the sonata as a major creative effort. Sonatas had never been much used on the concert platform, and were still designed for private domestic use. But their popularity quickly declined after about 1810, and there was no longer a market for sets of lighthearted tuneful sonatas; young ladies now preferred to play fantasias, variation sets, or medleys based on the popular operatic tunes of the day. Those sonatas that did appear were substantial works aimed at the musically well informed, and often dedicated to fellow musicians. Clementi, like Beethoven, composed fewer but weightier sonatas in later life, and his three of op. 50 (published in 1821) are among the monuments of the period. J. L. Dussek, whose understanding of the piano's possibilities was more advanced than that of either Clementi or Beethoven, also wrote sets of easy tuneful sonatas in the 1780s, but by the early 1800s was producing single works of great technical difficulty and emotional scope, the two-movement *Élégie harmonique sur la mort du Prince Louis Ferdinand de Prusse* (1806–7) and *L'Invocation* (1812) in F minor being the most remarkable. Another

famous pianist was Hummel, a pupil of Mozart, whose sonatas show little interest in the development of themes, and whose early works especially hark back to the Italian tradition of elegant decorative melody in the right hand (exploiting the upper reaches of the piano) accompanied by simple chordal figuration. J. B. Cramer, based in London, also developed a fine series of sonatas at the turn of the century, some of which influenced Beethoven and Schubert, but his output also diminished and was reduced by the 1820s to an occasional single work.

The finest of all the 'lyrical' line of serious sonata composers was Schubert, from whom over 20 solo sonatas survive, not all of them complete. The older criticism of Schubert's supposed inability to handle the larger forms is no longer heard. The wealth of melodic and harmonic ideas—Schubert's great strength—often obviates the need for Beethovenian development, but Schubert was perfectly capable of developing themes when he wanted to, and his capacity for harmonic juxtaposition of distant keys succeeds in maintaining interest, even in the exceedingly long (though none the less marvellous) piano sonatas in C minor, A major, and B♭ major, all published posthumously. His works for more than one player include a large-scale sonata or 'Grand Duo' in C for piano four hands (1824), a sonata for arpeggione and piano (1824), and three sonatinas for violin and piano (1836). Perhaps to please his publishers, he withheld the unfashionable title 'sonata' for two of his most important multi-movement works: one, the famous 'Wanderer' Fantasia (1822), is an important, four-movement example of *cyclic form; the other, a four-handed piece, is the Fantasia in F minor (1828).

8. The Romantics

By 1830 the sonata had yielded to the *character piece as the chief vehicle for expressive piano music of moderate difficulty. Rossini's 12 sonatas for strings really belong to an 18th-century tradition; the virtuoso works of Paganini for both violin and guitar are equally retrospective in attitude. The serious sonata was in fact a mainly German preserve, with Beethoven's ghost hovering near. Some composers, including Mendelssohn, Brahms, Wagner, and Franck, composed solo sonatas as a part of their early apprenticeship but gave them up in maturity. The difficulties that even great Romantic composers experienced with the genre are illustrated in Schumann's piano sonatas, which have what one critic has called 'pseudo-development sections' of considerable length but are nevertheless full of stimulating ideas.

Significantly, the truly successful piano sonatas of the mid-19th century are those that break away from the traditional form to encompass the genre piece, as does

Chopin in all three of his mature sonatas (two for piano, one for cello and piano): none of the first movements recapitulate the first theme in the tonic. The solo sonata in B♭ minor (1839) has the well-known Marche funèbre as a third movement and also a finale which resembles one of his preludes in its exploitation of piano tone rather than themes. Liszt avoids 'pseudo-development' in his sonatas, either by conceiving them as programmatic works (*Après une lecture du Dante*, 'fantasia quasi sonata', final version 1849) or, as in the B minor sonata (1852–3), developing the methods of thematic transformation found in Schubert's 'Wanderer' Fantasia; it also follows that landmark work in having no break between movements. Liszt avoids thematic working out for its own sake, but his uses of dramatic climax and contrast make the B minor Sonata one of the most exciting of piano sonatas, and not merely for the brilliant virtuosity that tempts nearly all concert pianists to tackle it.

The real gems of the later 19th century belong to the ensemble sonata: perhaps because the Romantics responded primarily to a lyric impulse, perhaps because the possible contrasts of colour soften the apparent necessity to overdevelop themes. Schumann's violin sonatas contain interesting effects of sonority and some delicate weaving together of movements with common thematic material. Brahms's three violin sonatas are even more exquisite, as are his later sonatas for clarinet and cello (with piano), because of a similar approach. Equally lyrical are Grieg's three violin sonatas (in addition to one for cello and one for piano alone), which however show structural weaknesses that Brahms would never have allowed to pass, and Franck's sonata for violin and piano (1886), which applies a post-Lisztian attitude in harmony and free thematic reminiscence, though its finale uses canon in a way possible only to an organist of that period, well schooled to the point where the strictest form comes naturally.

9. The post-Romantics

It was the Wagnerian revolution which dealt the final blow to the sonata. After *Tristan und Isolde* the moderns felt they had to explore the paths of extreme chromaticism—the death knell to sonata form, which depends on recognition of tonal relationships. The only important sonatas that can be said to show a Wagnerian approach are the last five (nos. 6–10) of Skryabin, which are offshoots of his desire to create the ultimate sensuous experience of 'mystery'; but his early sonatas reveal more clearly that he belonged to the line of fine Russian pianist-composers including Balakirev and Rakhmaninov, both of whom wrote sonatas. To the Liszt-type sonata using the transformation of themes

belongs the unique example of Berg's Piano Sonata (1907–8). Another, but differently, Lisztian work is Benjamin Dale's fine but solitary Piano Sonata op. 1 (1905). Perhaps the best American sonatas are the four for piano solo written between 1893 and 1901 by MacDowell, two of them dedicated to Grieg, who was the greatest influence on their style.

For the most part, sonatas in the early 20th century were written by those who either wished to get away from the later Romantic tradition or to add to the repertory of specific virtuosos. Of the first type, the French desire to shed Germanic influence manifested itself early in the works of Saint-Saëns (back to Mozart and even Rameau) and then in the music of Fauré (back to plainchant and Palestrina), whose violin sonatas show a nice judgment of sound (especially in the piano writing) and a Classical sense of clear structure. The 18th-century spirit was consciously evoked by Debussy (whose last works were a set of sonatas, planned to be six in all—as in the publications of the Baroque composers—though he completed only three). Ravel's *Sonatine* (1903–5) for piano is even more clearly in that tradition (two of its three movements being a minuet and a toccata). The neo-classical movement of the 1920s and 30s naturally turned composers' minds to such a traditional genre, both Poulenc and Hindemith composing sonatas which clearly follow the forms of the later 19th century (piano sonatas for four hands by each being among the best). In the USSR the most notable examples are the piano sonatas of Prokofiev, and Shostakovich's five sonatas, including a work for violin and piano (composed for Oistrakh and Richter) which combines serial melodic material with a feeling for sonata pattern.

10. Conclusion

This survey has mentioned only the most important landmarks in the history of a genre which must surely be reckoned one of the greatest in Western music. In the Classical sense of the term, it must now be accounted dead. Sonatas by Tippett, Henze, Maxwell Davies, and Boulez have little connection with the past history of the genre, except perhaps that the word is reserved for an ample and seriously emotional statement. If, as Schoenberg stated, there is still much music to be written in C major, it may be said that it is unlikely to be in sonata form. But the principle of a 'played piece' is very much alive, as electronic music, which has no need to follow vocal patterns, shows. If the term survives, it will probably be opposed to cantata, a piece for singing.   DA/NT

📖 D. F. TOVEY, *A Companion to Beethoven's Piano Sonatas* (London, 1948) · W. S. NEWMAN, *A History of the Sonata Idea*, i (Chapel Hill, NC, 1959, 4/1983); ii–iii (Chapel Hill,

1963–9, 3/1983) · R. G. PAULY, *Music in the Classical Period* (Englewood Cliffs, NJ, 1965, 3/1988) · C. ROSEN, *The Classical Style: Haydn, Mozart, Beethoven* (New York, 1971, 3/1997); *Sonata Forms* (New York, 1980, 2/1988)

sonata-allegro form. See SONATA FORM.

sonata a tre (It.). *'Trio sonata'; see also CHAMBER MUSIC; SONATA, 3–5.

sonata da camera, sonata da chiesa (It.). 'Chamber sonata', 'church sonata'; see SONATA, 2 and 3.

sonata form. A term that refers not to the form of a whole *sonata, as might be expected, but to the typical form of one movement of a sonata, more especially the first movement. To avoid this anomaly the terms 'first-movement form' or 'sonata-allegro form' have sometimes been substituted, but they too are inaccurate, because the form referred to is not confined either to first movements or to allegros.

Sonata form is principally associated with the Classical period (*c*.1770–1820), when it was ubiquitous, but it was developing before that time and was used for long afterwards. It occurs most regularly in the first movement of a sonata, a multi-movement chamber work (such as a trio, quartet, or quintet), or a symphony.

It is also often found in the other movements of such works, or in such single-movement pieces as an *overture, *tone-poem, or *character piece, and it influenced many other genres including the *concerto and the *aria. Fugues, mass movements, anthems, and orchestral 'storms' were often constructed in sonata form during the height of its fashion, and even the famous 'Representation of Chaos' in Haydn's oratorio *The Creation* betrays its influence. It would be difficult to explain why this particular formula proved so durable in such widely differing contexts.

Sonata form comprises a two-key tonal structure in three main sections. Section 1, the *exposition, generally presents all the thematic material of the movement, opening with one theme, or group of themes, in the tonic key. The first (or principal) theme of the first group is also known as the 'first subject'. The exposition then moves, often by means of a modulatory section called a transition or bridge passage, to a second theme or group of themes in a contrasting key. The first (or principal) theme of the second group is also known as the 'second subject'. The key of the second group is usually the dominant for movements in the major and the relative major for movements in the minor, though other keys may be used. For example, in the 19th

TABLE 1

bar nos.	thematic function	key progressions
exposition		
1–8 (Ex. 1)	First subject	G major
9–25 (Ex. 2)	Transition (bridge)	G major–D major
26–32 (Ex. 3)	Second group: first theme	D major
33–46 (Ex. 3)	Second group: second theme	D major
47–56 (Ex. 3)	Second group: third theme	D major
58–63 (Ex. 4)	Codetta	D major
development		
64–73	First subject (motivic components)	G minor–V of B♭ major
74–80	Second group—first theme	B♭ major
81–98	First subject (motivic components) with new two-bar continuation	A♭ major–G minor– F minor– V of E♭ major
99–106	First subject extended	E♭ major
107–24	18 bars of dominant preparation for the return; includes motivic components of first subject	Dominant pedal
recapitulation		
125–32	First subject	G major
133–52 (Ex. 5)	Transition; three inserted bars (137–9) adjust the tonality to lead to chord V of the tonic	G major–V of G major
153–86	Unaltered recapitulation of second group brought to a slightly adjusted cadence (cf. 56 and 183) (codetta omitted)	G major
187–200 (Ex. 6)	Coda based on the first subject	G major

Ex. 1

First subject

Ex. 2

Transition

century it became quite common to use the mediant as the second main key area. The exposition generally closes with a codetta, a short and sometimes reiterated cadential figure in the key of the second group. A double bar, usually with repeat marks, signifies the close of the first main section.

The second section, the *development, exploits the thematic material of the exposition, though new thematic material may be presented. These themes are often broken down into their motivic components, which are freely juxtaposed and developed. The section is tonally unstable, exploring a wide variety of keys by means of harmonic sequence and other modulatory devices. It leads most usually to the dominant chord of the principal key, in preparation for the recapitulation, the third section.

The recapitulation marks the return to the tonic key and also a return to the thematic material of the exposition. It repeats most of the themes of the exposition in the same order, but here the second group remains in the tonic key. This means that if there was a transition between the first and second groups it must now be tonally adjusted so that the modulation of the exposition is not effected. And if the movement is in a minor key, the second theme group, formerly in the relative major, may be recapitulated either in the tonic major (as usually in Haydn's works) or in the tonic minor, with necessary modification (Mozart's preference). After all the material of the exposition has been recapitulated and a decisive cadence has been heard in the tonic key, there is sometimes a double bar indicating a repeat from the beginning of the development

Ex. 3

Second group

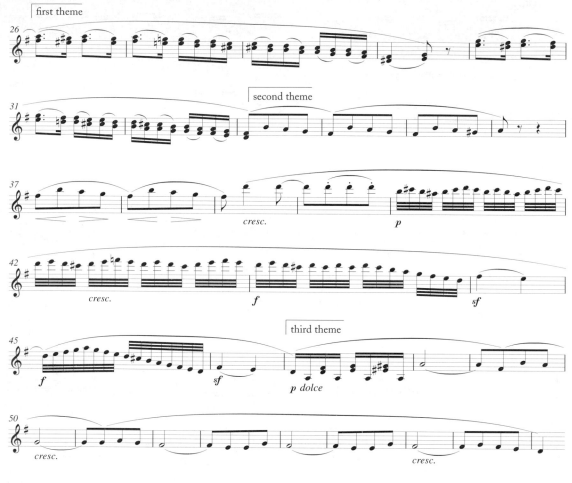

Ex. 4

Codetta

section. A coda may conclude the movement. It follows the cadence and double bar (if any). Codas vary in length from a few bars of cadence confirmation to the large section, with new musical ideas, often found in mature works of Beethoven. The first movement of Beethoven's Piano Sonata in G major op. 14 no. 2 provides an example of the form (Table 1; Exx. 1–6).

Although many sonata form movements follow the plan outlined above, it must be stressed that it is by no means a rigid compositional formula. Thematic and tonal elements may become separated so that, for example, a recapitulation could start with the 'right' theme in the 'wrong' key (Mozart's Piano Sonata K545 recapitulates the first subject in the subdominant, a device often used by Schubert); conversely it may start with the

Ex. 5

Transition

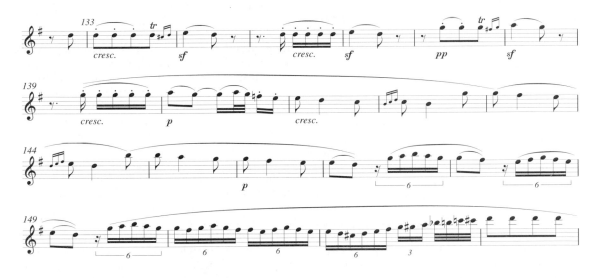

Ex. 6

Coda

'wrong' theme in the 'right' key (Mozart's Piano Sonata K311/284c recapitulates the second theme group before the reappearance of the first subject). The exposition is sometimes preceded by an introduction, which is often in a slower tempo than the rest of the movement.

See also FORM, 6.   GMT/NT

📖 L. G. RATNER, *Classic Music: Expression, Form, and Style* (New York, 1980) · C. ROSEN, *Sonata Forms* (New York, 1980, 2/1988)

Sonata pian e forte (alla quarta bassa). Work for eight instruments by Giovanni Gabrieli, published in his *Sacrae symphoniae* (1597). Written for St Mark's, Venice, it exploits contrast and dialogue.

sonata rondo form. As the name implies, the sonata rondo is a hybrid design incorporating elements from both *sonata form and *rondo form. It may be represented by the letter-scheme ABACABA. B denotes not, as in rondo form, an episode but rather a second subject; C denotes the development or, if new material is introduced, an episode; and the final A is the coda based on the rondo theme, i.e. first subject. The scheme may be more clearly expressed as shown in Table 1.

Thus a sonata rondo is differentiated from sonata form by the additional appearance of the first subject in the tonic key after the second subject and before the development; it is differentiated from rondo form because the second subject—B—returns in the tonic key.

section	function	key
A	first subject	tonic
B	second subject	dominant or relative major
A	first subject	tonic
C	development/episode	related key or keys
A	first subject	tonic
B	second subject	tonic
A	coda	tonic

The form was often used for the final movement of multi-movement works by Haydn, Mozart, Beethoven, and their contemporaries. Like sonata form it is not a rigid formula, and therefore the scheme illustrated can be taken as only a rough guide to its general features.
GMT

sonatina (It., dim. of 'sonata'; Fr.: *sonatine*). A short, relatively undemanding type of sonata, often for piano. In the later Classical period sonatinas were commonly written for didactic purposes, and many are still in use as teaching material. Such works follow the general structure of the sonata, being in three or four movements, though the development sections of sonata-form movements are usually very short. Clementi, Kuhlau, Dussek, and Diabelli are among the composers particularly associated with the genre; Mozart also wrote several such pieces for his pupils (e.g. K545 in C), and other examples were composed by Beethoven (op. 79) and Schubert (D384–5, for violin and piano).

In the 20th century the term was applied more loosely to lightweight (though not necessarily easy) sonata-type instrumental works, often of the less serious kind, for example those for piano by Busoni, Ravel, Bartók, and Prokofiev, and for flute and piano by Boulez.
—/JBE

Sondheim, Stephen (Joshua) (*b* New York, 22 March 1930). American composer and lyricist. A music graduate of Williams College, he wrote and composed for college productions, then worked as a radio and television scriptwriter. He made his name on Broadway as the lyricist for Leonard Bernstein's *West Side Story* (1957), Jule Styne's *Gypsy* (1959), and Richard Rodgers's *Do I Hear a Waltz?* (1965). Meanwhile he had won great acclaim as the composer and lyricist of *A Funny Thing Happened on the Way to the Forum* (1962), which was followed by shows whose content was more intellectually challenging than had been customary; among these were *Anyone Can Whistle* (1964), *Company* (1970), *Follies* (1971), *A Little Night Music* (1973), *The Frogs* (after Aristophanes; 1974), *Pacific Overtures* (1976), *Sweeney Todd* (1979), *Merrily we Roll Along* (1981),

Sunday in the Park with George (1984), *Into the Woods* (1987), *Assassins* (1991), and *Passion* (1994). Some of these award-winning works have graduated from the commercial theatre to the opera house.   PGA/ALA

song (*see opposite page*)

song cycle (Ger.: *Liederzyklus*). A group of songs with a common theme, usually setting a single poet. The music may have coherence of key or form and be attached to a narrative, or may more generally serve to express a unifying mood or theme. In the latter case, the German term sometimes used (e.g. by Schumann) is *Liederkreis*, though the distinction between the two is not clear-cut.

While there are antecedents in various national traditions, the song cycle came to maturity with 19th-century German *lied. The first important example of a *Liederkreis* is Weber's *Die Temperamente beim Verluste der Geliebten* (1815–16), that of a *Liederzyklus*, Beethoven's *An die ferne Geliebte* (1816). The former consists of four songs portraying emotions at the loss of love which range from anguish to relief; the latter joins six songs in a coherent key-scheme, with each song linked musically to the next, and with the single theme of distant, unattainable love. Schubert followed with two larger cycles of 20 songs, *Die schöne Müllerin* (1823) and 24 songs, *Winterreise* (1828), in which each song is separate and structurally varied but prepares for the next in a dramatic sequence (*Schwanengesang* is not a cycle but a random group of songs published together posthumously). Schumann's 'year of song', 1840, included *Liederkreise* setting Heine (op. 24) and Eichendorff (op. 39), the cycle *Frauenliebe und -leben* setting Chamisso (op. 42), and another Heine *Liederkreis* (though not so described), *Dichterliebe* (op. 48).

Other composers of the period who wrote song cycles included Loewe (*Kaiser Karl V.*, 1844), Cornelius (*Weihnachtslieder*, 1856), and Brahms (*Magelone-lieder*, 1861–9), though there were those, including these composers, who chose to group songs by poet or by some other general association (e.g. Hugo Wolf's Mörike and Goethe *Gedichte*, mostly 1888–90, and his Spanish and two Italian songbooks, mostly 1889–90, 1890–1, and 1896). A later master of the orchestral song cycle was Mahler (*Lieder eines fahrenden Gesellen*, 1883–5, *Kindertotenlieder*, 1901–4), who with *Das Lied von der Erde* (1908–9) brought the genre into the realm of song-symphony.

An early French group of songs, related though originally for different voices, is Berlioz's *Les Nuits d'été* (1840–1, orchestrated 1843–56), and among later cycles are Fauré's *La Bonne Chanson* (1892–4), Debussy's *Chansons de Bilitis* (1897–8), and Ravel's *Shéhérazade* (1903). Russian example is dominated by Musorgsky

(cont. on p. 1188)

song

Singing is an instinctive activity of the human species, a natural means of self-expression common to all races. Its origins can be traced back into prehistory, most obviously to the human fascination with rhythm and the inflections of speech; song retains a close association with dance and recitation in the cultures of many of the developing countries. Although by definition a vocal activity, whether solo or choral, monodic or polyphonic, many types of song involve the use of instruments, played either by the singers themselves or by accompanists.

Monophonic song

Before musical notation evolved, song repertories could be preserved only by being committed to memory and passed down through an oral tradition. Because of this, few songs dating from before the 12th century survive to the present day, except perhaps in the form of folksong. Although the Bible contains the texts of many religious songs of the Jewish people (e.g. psalms, canticles) and makes frequent reference to their performance, we know virtually nothing about their musical substance or style. Singing occupied an important place in the cultures of ancient Egypt and Greece; but while the words of some lyric and epic songs are extant, all but a few scattered remains of the music itself has been irretrievably lost.

As the repertory of *plainchant expanded during the first thousand years of the Christian era, it became necessary to devise a system of musical notation which would preserve the melodies and allow them to be more widely and accurately disseminated than was possible using memory alone. Early notation was thus the preserve of a church-educated elite, and the few secular songs that were written down reflect the culture of only a small (though powerful and influential) element of society. With the development of notation the distinction between 'folksong' and 'art song' grew rapidly, the former repertory comprising songs passed down orally and changing substantially during the process, the latter consisting of songs of ever-increasing sophisti-cation and complexity, often composed for specific occasions or at the request of a patron or employer.

Many of the earliest surviving songs of the medieval world are settings of Latin lyrics. Particularly famous is the *Carmina burana*, a 13th-century anthology of religious, amorous, and bawdy songs compiled by goliards (educated clerics who adopted the life of wandering poet musicians). Also typical of the period are processional songs in Latin known as *conductus, their subjects ranging from matters of politics and topical events to religious devotion, moral preaching, and satire. With their strong metrical rhythms, limited voice-ranges, and short, regular phrases, these songs often come closer in idiom to folksong than to the luxuriance of liturgical plainchant.

The earliest extant repertory of songs written in a language other than Latin is that of the *troubadours, an aristocratic class of poet musicians which flourished in southern France during the 12th and 13th centuries. This period saw the evolution of an elaborate convention of behaviour among the courts of the nobility, in which the status of women was idealized and such attributes as chivalry, refinement, and education commended in their suitors. Song occupied an important place in this 'game of love': a nobleman would solicit the attention of his lady through verse and melodies of his own composition, often performing them himself, accompanied by professional minstrels. As well as the *canso* (courtly love song) troubadours wrote songs on a wide variety of themes, including satirical, moral, and political topics (the *sirventes*), debate-like dialogues (the *tenso*), laments (the *planh*), and crusade songs. The musical style of these songs varies from simple, syllabic melodies to elaborately flowing compositions modelled on melismatic plainchant. We cannot be sure how troubadour songs sounded in performance; few are notated with a precise indication of rhythm, and little is known about the style of instrumental accompaniment they received.

The art of the troubadours provided a model for secular song throughout western Europe during the

12th century, spread by the intermarriage of the nobility and by the crusades. Similar movements evolved in northern France (the *trouvères) and Germany (the *Minnesinger), while religious song fashioned after troubadour models flourished in Spain (*cantigas) and in Italy (*laude). By the end of the 13th century the vogue for composing and performing courtly song had spread to educated members of the merchant class and bourgeoisie such as Adam de la Halle and Jehan de L'Escurel. During the 14th and 15th centuries, monophonic song gradually fell into decline, though a few isolated movements (such as the *Meistersinger) survived until much later.

Polyphonic song

The 13th century also witnessed the first flowering of songs for two or more voices. Extra parts were added to (or improvised round) conductus and trouvère melodies, converting them into simple partsongs. The principal form of secular polyphonic song at this time, however, was the *motet, a genre of French origin which grew out of *organum and was initially cultivated within ecclesiastical circles for secular entertainment. Most 13th-century motets are anonymous, preserved in fine manuscripts such as the Montpellier and Bamberg codices. Generally for three voices, of which the lowest sings a fragment of plainchant, motets frequently set more than one text simultaneously, sometimes even mixing French and Latin, though texts are normally closely related to one another in subject matter; most are concerned with political, topical, satirical, or amorous themes. In the hands of such 14th-century composers as Philippe de Vitry and Machaut, the motet became a lengthy, intellectual, and sometimes formidably complex form of song, usually constructed on the principle of *isorhythm.

Other forms of secular polyphonic song, mostly treating the subject of courtly love, evolved at the end of the 13th century. Outstanding among these were three poetic and musical structures known collectively as the *formes fixes*: the *ballade (an equivalent form, the madrigal, existed in Italy; see MADRIGAL, 2), *rondeau (Ex. 1, by Adam de la Halle), and *virelai (known in Italy as the *ballata). These song forms differed from the motet in being freely composed, without any plainchant basis; instead, the composer would first write a principal melodic line, then add between one and three subordinate parts in counterpoint against it. Polyphonic songs setting conventionally artificial love poetry in one or other of the *formes fixes* soon became a characteristic ingredient of entertainment at the principal courts of both France and Italy, remaining popular among aristocratic cognoscenti and their circles for almost 200 years, from the early 14th century to the end of the 15th.

At first, songs from different regions displayed contrasts of style, for French composers such as Machaut favoured a busy, often dissonant effect with angular melodic lines full of syncopations and recurrent rhythmic motifs, while contemporary Italians such as Giovanni da Cascia, Magister Piero, and later Landini preferred a more flowing, harmonious style and graceful melodies moving largely by step in dance-like rhythms. By the late 14th century, however, these two idioms had essentially merged into a more 'international' style, discernible in the songs of Matteo da Perugia and Ciconia. In the hands of their 15th-century successors—Dufay, Binchois, Ockeghem, and

Ex. 1

Busnois—courtly songs became longer and more lyrical, often dominated by expansive melodies of haunting charm, accompanied by two subordinate parts. Composers never stipulated any precise performance medium; most songs were presumably intended for a soloist supported by lutes, harps, or bowed instruments, though many are also suitable for an entirely vocal ensemble. The refined quality of these songs, with their understated texts and subtly intricate polyphonic texture, admirably reflects the sophisticated cultural life of the leading courts of the time—Burgundy, Savoy, Naples, etc.—as do the exquisite manuscripts into which they were copied, such as the Dijon, Mellon, and Cordiforme ('heart-shaped') *chansonniers.

Madrigal and monody

Towards the end of the 15th century, a new type of song began to emerge at certain principal north Italian courts, including Florence, Mantua, and Ferrara. It grew from a tradition, apparently native to Italy, of adding music to poetry in extempore fashion, using simple, stylized melodic formulas supported by stock patterns of chords played on the lute or a similar instrument. The resulting idiom—tuneful with homophonic accompaniment, the rhythm of the text mirrored in the music—could hardly have stood in greater contrast to the skilful and increasingly imitative polyphony which northern composers such as Ockeghem and Josquin were developing. By 1500, two distinct repertories of declamatory Italian song were in existence: the Florentine *Carnival songs (canti carnascialeschi) and the more widespread *frottola. Although usually scored for three or four voices, songs of these types were often performed by a soloist supported chordally by a lute or keyboard instrument, producing a texture equivalent to the solo song of later centuries.

While the frottola and related forms of declamatory Italian song enjoyed only relatively short-lived popularity, their impact on the general development of European song was far-reaching. The idiom of Italian song, with its emphasis on melody, bass, and harmony, clear-cut phrases rounded off by strong cadences, and above all syllabic word-setting, offered itself as a radical alternative to the polyphonically minded composers of the Low Countries; and as elements from these two stylistic extremes gradually merged, polyphonic song entered one of its richest and most complex phases. In the hands of Josquin, Compère, Mouton, and their contemporaries—northern composers whose careers were partly spent south of the Alps—the polyphonic chanson began to change in character: lighter forms of verse, often bawdy or narrative, gradually replaced the courtly formes fixes and were set to music in a more syllabic, parlando fashion than before, though still within a contrapuntal framework. Transplanted back into the north, this revitalized form of chanson was propagated with great success by such composers as Sermisy, Janequin, and Crecquillon. At the same time the frottola gradually absorbed polyphonic elements from the chanson, giving rise during the 1520s to a new and equally popular form of ensemble song in Italian, the madrigal (see MADRIGAL, 3).

The extraordinary 16th-century vogue for polyphonic song can partly be explained by the rise of a new class of performer, the educated amateur. As the ability to sing and read music came increasingly to be regarded as a desirable social accomplishment, the demand for new songs in the latest fashion grew, a demand which the newly invented printing press was able to satisfy at a price the public could afford. Songs in a wide variety of idioms thus became more readily available than ever before, stimulating not only the exchange of ideas between Italian, French, and Flemish composers but also the rapid development of vernacular song in more peripheral countries. Influenced by the styles of chanson and madrigal, such forms as the Spanish *villancico, German *lied, and English *partsong flourished as never before.

During the 16th century a polyphonic texture was normal in most leading genres of song, suiting an ensemble of voices or instruments in which each line contributed a roughly equal part to the effect of the whole. But changes were on the way; with the development of instruments capable of accompanying a solo voice (lute, vihuela, harpsichord), the rise of both the virtuoso singer and the art of embellishing vocal lines, and new theories about the expressive advantages of solo song over a contrapuntal texture, existing forms of polyphonic song gradually fell into decline. In their place, new types of lyric or declamatory song such as Italian *monody, the French *air de cour, and the English *ayre came into fashion. With their rise, we enter the era of modern song.   JM

The 17th and 18th centuries

By the beginning of the 17th century, the solo art song was already fully fledged. In Italy, Caccini's Le nuove musiche (1602) marks the beginning of the popularity of *monody, the *aria, and from the 1630s the secular *cantata. Germany had its own tradition of monophonic song in *Meistergesang*, but otherwise German composers remained firmly committed to the idea of equal-voiced polyphonic song until the 1620s, when the *continuo lied began to take over in importance. The French had developed declamatory solo singing from the late 1560s (see MUSIQUE MESURÉE), and the first *airs de cour* were published in the 1570s; this became an extremely popular genre in the 17th and 18th centuries, together with its less sophisticated cousins the *air à boire* and the *brunette*.

In England, the solo song with instrumental accompaniment had its own tradition in the *consort song and the slightly later *lute-song, but these faded out almost as quickly as did the English madrigal, their light, delicate, polyphonic accompaniments giving way to the ubiquitous continuo part. In the hands of such composers as Henry Lawes and John Wilson, the solo song settles down into a basically strophic norm, and the words are frequently set in a natural, declamatory style (contemporaries described it as 'recitative music'). This trait was developed by Pelham Humfrey and Blow, and reaches its finest expression in the songs of Purcell.

During the 17th and 18th centuries, the musical presses of Germany, England, and France turned out hundreds of songbooks for solo voice and continuo: requiring only two staves, they were conveniently small and cheap to produce. In Germany, they were important in the early history of the lied; and because their contents were both sacred and secular, they also played their part in the development of Protestant church music, which culminated in the sacred cantatas of J. S. Bach. In 18th-century England, vast numbers of songs were written for the fashionable entertainments at Vauxhall, Ranelagh, and elsewhere by Thomas Arne, William Boyce, Charles Dibdin, James Hook, and many others. French composers were equally prolific in writing *airs*. Few from either country have survived, but songs written in this form did not die out until the 19th century.

The 19th century

The dominant country for song in the 19th century was undoubtedly Germany, with the *lied. The remarkable amalgam of words and music in Schubert, Schumann, Brahms, and Wolf set a standard by which song in other countries tended to be judged. France, with a long and distinguished poetic heritage to draw upon, stands out next in importance; its typical *mélodie* is as far removed from the lied as the French language is from the German. France's finest 19th-century song composer was Gabriel Fauré, who in *Clair de lune* (Paul Verlaine), *Le Parfum impérissable*, and *Les Roses d'Ispahan* (both Leconte de Lisle) brought an exquisite musical subtlety to these essentially French texts. The same is true of Henri Duparc, whose *L'Invitation au voyage* ranks very high in the literature of song. Debussy was also attracted by the Watteau-esque nostalgia of Verlaine (*Fêtes galantes*) and found further stimulus in other leading Symbolists, especially Charles Baudelaire (*Cinq poèmes*) and Stéphane Mallarmé (*Trois poèmes*). His songs, which span the whole of his creative life, embody his quintessential style, his harmonic and colouristic explorations paving the way for 20th-century emancipation.

In the British Isles, 19th-century song produced little of lasting value, and the improvement towards the end of the century is less significant than it once appeared: the several sets of *English Lyrics* by Parry, for instance, now seem well made rather than inspired. The Irish composer Stanford possessed the greater lyrical talent: 'The Fairy Lough' has an other-worldly quality and was once popular among singers, and 'The Middle Watch' stands out refreshingly above the breezy heartiness of the remaining *Songs of the Fleet*.

Russia in the 19th century was rich in song. Songs were written by all the important composers, and by many minor or amateur ones, from Glinka and Dargomïzhsky to Musorgsky, Tchaikovsky, and Rakhmaninov. One important strain, deriving from the theories of 'realism' that absorbed 19th-century Russian thinkers, drew its inspiration from folksong and from the speech patterns of the people as *russkaya pesnya* ('Russian song'). Equally significant was the style, deriving from the general admiration for France, that successfully grafted the French *romance on to Russian roots as the *romans*. Musorgsky, greatest of the 'realists', wrote some 60 songs, often to his own texts, as in the song cycles *The Nursery* (1868–72), or to those of his friend Arseny Golenishchev-Kutuzov, in the song cycles *Sunless* (1874) and *Songs and Dances of Death* (1877).

Tchaikovsky is closer to the *romans*, and his 90-odd songs draw on his finest vein as a melodist as well as his capacity for embodying emotions of tenderness, wistfulness, or loneliness, as in 'Amid the Din of the Ball' from op. 38 (1878). Among his contemporaries,

Borodin, Cui, and Rimsky-Korsakov wrote excellent songs, but his strongest successor was Rakhmaninov, with an output of fine songs that reflected not only his introspective, melancholy temperament but his keyboard virtuosity. On Russia's western frontiers, the most important song composer was the Bohemian Dvořák, as in his *Gypsy Melodies* op. 55 (1880). Moniuszko was almost solely responsible for the development of Poland's song tradition.

In Norway, Grieg displayed charm and freshness in some of his songs. His best are to Norwegian words, as in 'A Swan' from op. 25 (1876) and the cycle *Haugtussa* (op. 67, 1895). Sibelius wrote some 90 songs, but perhaps Finland's outstanding song composer is Yrjö Kilpinen, who wrote over 700 to Finnish, Swedish, and German words.

The 20th century

Many of Schoenberg's songs were written before the turn of the century, but his mature output included *Das Buch der hängenden Gärten* op. 15 (to words by Stefan George, 1908–9), as well as orchestral songs. Almost all of Berg's songs are early too, but Webern's output included songs from all periods of his life that extend the possibilities of a lyrical vocal line with a new approach to melody with more difficult and 'angular' intervals. The songs of their contemporary Hindemith included a Rainer Maria Rilke cycle, *Das Marienleben* (op. 27, 1922–3). In France, a distinguished successor in the line of the *mélodie* was Poulenc, with many songs reflecting his wit and elegance but also his more inward and contemplative nature.

The most distinguished Russian song composers of the century were Medtner, in the 19th-century tradition perpetuated by Rakhmaninov until his departure for the West at the Revolution, but more radically Shostakovich, with settings of Pushkin, Aleksandr Blok, and Marina Tsvetayeva, among others, that reveal his lyrical nature as well as the bleakness and the mordant wit that characterize his music. In Czechoslovakia, an unusual and striking contribution was Janáček's song cycle *Diary of One who Disappeared* (1917–20); in Hungary, Bartók wrote a large number of songs mostly based on, or deriving from, his extensive research into the nature of Hungarian folk music. In the USA, though Copland wrote some excellent songs, the genre has developed largely in a popular idiom, reflecting the success of Stephen Foster, with Cole Porter, Jerome Kern, and especially Gershwin succeeding in making memorable songs in a tradition based largely on jazz, blues, and the Broadway show.

Though he died in 1958, Vaughan Williams belongs as a songwriter more to the 19th century than to the 20th, with such songs as *Silent Noon*, but he also participated with Cecil Sharp in the collecting of folksongs which greatly influenced his style. His friend and contemporary Holst was influenced by Hindu ideas in his *Hymns from the Rig Veda*, but his most striking songs come in a late group setting Humbert Wolfe (12 songs, op. 48, 1929). Other composers who contributed to English song between the wars were Ireland, Quilter, Warlock, Bridge, Finzi, and Gurney. But the two most distinctive English songwriters did not come to full prominence until during and after World War II: Tippett, with a song cantata *Boyhood's End* (W. H. Hudson, 1943) and *The Heart's Assurance* (Sidney Keyes and Alun Lewis, 1950–1), and especially Britten. The poets on whom he drew for his songs with piano included W. H. Auden, Arthur Rimbaud, Michelangelo, John Donne, Thomas Hardy, Friedrich Hölderlin, Pushkin, William Blake, T. S. Eliot, and Robert Burns, among many others for orchestral song cycles, and he showed an astonishingly acute response to poetry of such variety, with music that could seek out its essence with a sometimes Schubertian felicity.

LO/JW

D. STEVENS (ed.), *A History of Song* (London, 1960, 2/ 1970) · R. H. THOMAS, *Poetry and Song in the German Baroque* (Oxford, 1963) · S. NORTHCOTE, *Byrd to Britten: A Survey of English Song* (London, 1966) · D. IVEY, *Song: Anatomy, Imagery, and Styles* (New York, 1970) · N. FORTUNE, 'Solo song and cantata', *The Age of Humanism, 1545–1630*, The New Oxford History of Music, vi (Oxford, 1968), 125–217 · K. GUDEWILL, 'German secular song', *ibid.*, 96–124 · R. HUGHES, 'Solo song', *The Age of Enlightenment, 1745–1790*, The New Oxford History of Music, vii (Oxford, 1973) · B. MEISTER, *An Introduction to the Art Song* (New York, 1980) · J. WALKER (ed.), *Classical Essays on the Development of the Russian Art Song* (Nerstrand, MN, 1993) with *The Nursery* (1868–72) and *Songs and Dances of Death* (1875–7), Czech example by Dvořák's *Biblical Songs* (1894) and Janáček's *Diary of One who Disappeared* (1917–20). In England, outstanding works have been written by Vaughan Williams (*On Wenlock Edge*, 1908–9), Tippett (*The Heart's Assurance*, 1950–1), and Britten, whose many song cycles are a significant feature of his art. He is an outstanding example among 20th-century composers for whom the linking narrative, dramatic, and lyrical capabilities of song came to serve as a dominant formal idea.   LO/JW

Song of the Earth, The. See LIED VON DER ERDE, DAS.

Song of the Flea (*Pesnya Mefistofelya o blokhe*). Song (1879) by Musorgsky for voice and piano, a setting of Mephistopheles' song in Goethe's *Faust*.

Songs and Dances of Death (*Pesni i plyaski smerti*). Song cycle by Musorgsky (1877) for voice and piano, settings of four poems by Arseny Golenishchev-Kutuzov.

Songs of a Wayfarer. See LIEDER EINES FAHRENDEN GESELLEN.

Songs of Farewell. 1. Six unaccompanied secular motets (1916–18) by Parry to texts by Henry Vaughan, and John Davies, Campion, J. G. Lockhart, and John Donne, and from Psalm 39.
   2. Five songs (1930) by Delius, settings of poems by Walt Whitman for chorus and orchestra.

Songs of the Sea. Five songs, op. 91 (1904), by Stanford, for baritone, male chorus, and orchestra, settings of poems by Henry Newbolt.

Songs without Words. See LIEDER OHNE WORTE.

Sonnambula, La ('The Sleepwalker'). Opera in two acts by Bellini to a libretto by Felice Romani after Eugène Scribe and J.-P. Aumer's ballet-pantomime *La Sonnambule, ou L'Arrivée d'un nouveau seigneur* (Milan, 1831).

Sonneck Society. A society founded in the USA in 1975 in honour of Oscar G. T. Sonneck (1873–1928), a pioneering scholar of American music who, as head of the Library of Congress Music Division, built up one of the finest collections in the world.

Sonntag aus Licht ('Sunday from Light'). Projected opera by Stockhausen to his own libretto, the 'seventh day' of *Licht*.

sonore (Fr.), **sonoro, sonora** (It.). 'Sonorous'; *sonorité* (Fr.), *sonorità* (It.), 'sonority'; *sonoramente* (It.), 'sonorously'; *onde sonore* (Fr.), 'sound wave', 'acoustic wave'.

sons bouchés (Fr.). *'Stopped notes' in horn playing.

Sontag [Sonntag], **Henriette** (Gertrud Walburgis), Countess Rossi (*b* Koblenz, 3 Jan. 1806; *d* Mexico City, 17 June 1854). German soprano. She was only six when she first appeared on stage. She studied at the Prague Conservatory and made her professional debut as the Princess in Boieldieu's *Jean de Paris* (1821), in which her vocal precocity and attractive stage presence created a striking impression. In 1822 she moved to Vienna; after her debut at the Vienna Court Opera in Rossini's *La donna del lago* Weber engaged her to sing the title role in his *Euryanthe*, in which she was highly praised. In 1824 she sang the soprano part in the premiere of Beethoven's 'Choral' Symphony and in the *Missa solemnis*. She won acclaim subsequently in Paris, London, and Berlin. After marrying in 1830 she withdrew from the stage for nearly two decades, but returned to opera in 1849, dying of cholera while on tour.   JT

   📖 F. RUSSELL, *Queen of Song: The Life of Henriette Sontag* (New York, 1964)

Sophie Elisabeth, Duchess of Brunswick-Lüneburg (*b* Güstrow, 20 Aug. 1613; *d* Lüchow, 12 July 1676). German poet, librettist, and composer. She was a founder member of the renowned literary society the Fruchtbringende Gesellschaft. Some correspondence from 1644 indicates that she was then receiving musical instruction from Schütz and may have been about to collaborate with him in a musico-dramatic event (a theatrical presentation of the story of Mary Magdalene) for the Wolfenbüttel court. Her many musical achievements include a *Singspiel*, *Friedens-Sieg*, in 1648, and a series of cantatas, ballets, and other theatre music, specially composed for the birthdays of her husband, Duke August the Younger.   BS

sopra (It.). 'On', 'above'; *come sopra*, 'as above'; *mano sinistra* [*ms*] *sopra*, in keyboard playing, with the left hand above the right.

Sopran (Ger.). 'Soprano'.

sopranino (It., dim. of 'soprano'). The highest-pitched member of a family of instruments.

soprano. 1. The highest female (or artificial male) voice, with a range of roughly b to c''' (in high sopranos often to f'''). The word derives from the Latin *superius*, the usual term for the highest voice in 15th-century polyphonic music. There are several types of soprano, of which the commonest in general use are the 'coloratura soprano', a light, high voice of great agility (e.g. the Queen of Night in Mozart's *Die Zauberflöte*); 'lyric soprano', the most common, with a warmer tone-quality and a slightly lower range (e.g. Pamina in *Die*

Zauberflöte and Donna Elvira in *Don Giovanni*); 'dramatic soprano', with a heavier production throughout the range (e.g. Tosca and many Wagner roles); and 'soprano spinto', or 'soprano lirico spinto', basically a lyric voice that is capable of more dramatic quality and a cutting edge at climaxes (e.g. Leonore in Beethoven's *Fidelio* and Desdemona in Verdi's *Otello*).   —/RW

2. A high-pitched member of a family of instruments, with a range lower than sopranino and higher than alto.

soprano clef. A *clef, now rarely used, that places middle C on the bottom line of the staff.

Sor [Sors], (Joseph) **Fernando** (Macari) (*b* Barcelona, *bapt.* 14 Feb. 1778; *d* Paris, 10 July 1839). Catalan composer and guitarist. He studied at the choir school of Montserrat, 1790–5, and in 1797 his opera *Telemaco* was staged in Barcelona. During the Peninsular War he held administrative posts in Barcelona, Madrid, and Málaga, composing orchestral and chamber works as well as many vocal pieces with guitar or piano accompaniment. In 1813 however, having accepted a post under the occupying French, he found it expedient to leave the country.

Sor went first to Paris, where his talent was recognized by Méhul and Cherubini, then in 1815 to London, where his vocal works and his piano and guitar pieces were particularly admired and four of his ballets were staged; these included *Cendrillon* ('Cinderella', 1822), which was hugely successful in Paris and in Moscow, where it was chosen for the opening of the Bol'shoy Theatre in 1823. Sor spent the next three years in Russia, composing the ballet *Hercules y Onfalia* (1826) for the coronation of Tsar Nicholas I before returning to Paris. He is best remembered for his guitar pieces, which are central to the repertory, and for his important *Gran método de guitarra* (Bonn, 1830).   WT/SH

📖 B. Jeffery, *Fernando Sor, Composer and Guitarist* (London, 1977, 2/1994)

Sorabji, Kaikhosru Shapurji [Leon Dudley] (*b* Chingford, 14 Aug. 1892; *d* Wareham, Dorset, 14 Oct. 1988). English composer and pianist. Largely self-taught, he appeared in public as a pianist in London, Paris, and elsewhere and in 1919 played his First Piano Sonata to an impressed Busoni, who wrote of its 'profusely ornamental harmonic complexity' and commented that 'in disregarding tradition [his music] crosses a threshold which is no longer European, producing a quasi-exotic kind of vegetation'. Sorabji's private wealth allowed him to devote himself to composition, and for decades he lived as a quasi-recluse, unconcerned whether his music gained recognition; indeed, for many years he refused to permit public performances. Not

until 1975 did he relax his attitude, eventually allowing the recording of his massive (four-hour), multi-movement *Opus clavicembalisticum*. Although Sorabji was capable of writing aphoristic keyboard miniatures and songs, many of his works attain inordinate length which, coupled with their extraordinary contrapuntal and harmonic complexity, explains why none of his three orchestral symphonies, 11 concertante works for piano and orchestra, or any of his other large-scale works have been performed—other than those that have received the dedicated attention of a small number of gifted performers (most notably the pianist John Ogdon and the organist Kevin Bowyer).   MA

📖 P. Rapoport (ed.), *Sorabji: A Critical Celebration* (Aldershot, 1992)

Sorcerer, The. Operetta in two acts by Sullivan to a libretto by W. S. Gilbert (London, 1877).

Sorcerer's Apprentice, The. See Apprenti sorcier, L'.

sordino (It.). 'Mute'; *con sordino*, 'with the mute'.

sordun. A double-reed instrument of the late 16th and early 17th centuries. The cylindrical bore doubles back on itself within a single column of wood. See Kortholt.

Soriano, Francesco (*b* Soriano, nr Viterbo, 1548 or 1549; *d* Rome, 1621). Italian composer. He was a pupil of Palestrina and, having been a choirboy in St John Lateran, became *maestro di cappella* at several notable churches in Rome, finally at St Peter's. He wrote madrigals, motets, and masses, and with Felice Anerio was responsible for completing the *Editio medicaea* (see plainchant, 3), the revision of chant books begun by Palestrina and Zoilo. He also arranged Palestrina's *Missa Papae Marcelli* for eight voices in double choir, probably to give a more resonant effect in the vastness of the new nave in St Peter's.   DA

Sorochintsy Fair (*Sorochinskaya yarmarka*). Opera in three acts by Musorgsky to his own libretto (with Arseny Golenishchev-Kutuzov) after a story by Nikolay Gogol from his collection *Evenings on a Farm near Dikanka* (i, 1831). It was left incomplete at the composer's death and was finished and orchestrated by Lyadov, Vyacheslav Karatïgin, and others (Moscow, 1913). It was also completed and orchestrated by Cui (St Petersburg, 1917), by Tcherepnin (Monte Carlo, 1923), and by Shebalin (Moscow, 1932), this last becoming the standard version.

Sorozábal (Mariezcurrena), **Pablo** (*b* San Sebastián, 18 Oct. 1897; *d* Madrid, 26 Dec. 1988). Basque composer and conductor. He wrote orchestral works, song cycles, and choral music before his first zarzuela, *Katiuska* (Barcelona, 1931), brought him fame at home and abroad. A steady stream of stage works followed, of which the most successful were *La del manojo de rosas* ('The Girl with the Bunch of Roses', Madrid, 1934), *La tabernera del puerto* ('The Port Barmaid', 1936), and a version of the Don Juan story, *Los burladores* ('The Tricksters', 1948). Succulent lyricism, sharpened by sophisticated musical wit, make Sorozábal the last major composer of zarzuelas.   CW

sortie (Fr., 'exit', 'departure'). A postlude or concluding voluntary.

sospirando, sospirante, sospirevole (It.). 'Sighing', i.e. in a plaintive style.

sostenuto, sostenente (It.). 'Sustained', 'sustaining'; *andante sostenuto*, 'a sustained andante', i.e. rather slow. It is sometimes abbreviated *sost.*

sostenuto pedal. A middle pedal provided on some pianos, perfected by Steinway in 1874, which allows notes played at the moment the pedal is depressed to be sustained, but not those played subsequently.

sotto (It.). 'Under', 'below'; *sotto voce*, 'in a low voice', i.e. barely audible, a direction that can apply to instrumental as well as vocal performance; *mano sinistra* [*ms*] *sotto*, in keyboard playing, with the left hand below the right.

soubrette (Fr.). A secondary female role in comic opera, often a lively and coquettish lady's maid such as Despina in *Così fan tutte* or Adele in *Die Fledermaus*.

soul. A term originating with some black American gospel groups of the 1940s and 50s (e.g. the Soul Stirrers). In the late 1950s, jazz which was influenced by gospel style was known as 'soul jazz'. The adoption of these styles in the 1960s led to soul becoming an umbrella term for black American popular music, and in 1969 *Billboard* changed the categorization of its black record chart from 'rhythm and blues' to 'soul'.

Among the early performers associated with the idiom are Clyde McPhatter and Ray Charles. Some of their work extends to secularizing the style of the sung sermon of a church service. In the mid-1960s, the work of James Brown, Otis Redding, Aretha Franklin, Stevie Wonder, and others acquired rhythmic riffs in the accompaniment, syncopated bass, and horn sections, and moved away from a ternary shuffle beat towards the binary subdivision of the beat; these developments prefigure *funk and *disco. The lyrics include formulaic gospel cries (e.g. 'feels all right') and they are often delivered in the fervent style of gospel music. In the 1970s soul divided into two strands: a 'sweet' soul (on the Tamla *Motown label) and a more funky Southern style (on the Stax and Atlantic labels). By the mid-1970s, even the up-tempo 'sweet' style was being called 'disco'. As a result, *Billboard* recognized in 1982 that 'soul' was no longer the appropriate general term for black American pop, and the chart category was changed to 'black music'.   PW

sound archives. Collections of out-of-print commercially issued recordings in various formats, together with off-air material (after the early 1930s) and live recordings not commercially disseminated (and unless copied, often surviving in one unique copy). The majority of surviving sound recordings were made after 1900, though a few primitive examples dating back to 1877 are extant. The earliest institutional collections were of ethnomusicological field recordings made using the Edison *Cylinder Phonograph, the first being the Phonogrammarchiv of the Akademie der Wissenschaften in Vienna and the Berlin Phonogrammarchiv in Berlin at the turn of the century. In 1912 Bartók noted that he had given nearly 1000 phonographic cylinders to the Ethnographic Museum in Budapest.

Various collections were established between the wars, including those formed by radio stations. That of the Library of Congress in Washington, DC, was founded with a trickle of gifts from the Victor Company in the 1920s and expanded as a consequence of the American Folk Song project, which resulted in the establishment of a modern recording laboratory in 1940. The idea of a sound archive did not gain much currency until after World War II with the establishment of national collections. In the UK the British Institute of Recorded Sound was the life's work of one man, Patrick Saul; opened in 1955, it became part of the British Library in 1983, soon becoming designated as the National Sound Archive.   LF

soundboard. The thin sheet of wood under the strings of a *harpsichord, *pianoforte, *zither, etc., which converts the vibrations of the strings, transmitted via one or more bridges, into audible sound waves.

soundbox. The *resonator of a stringed instrument.

soundhole. An opening cut in the belly or soundboard of a stringed instrument to enhance its volume and tone-quality. Members of the violin family have two soundholes in the shape of an *f* or elongated *s*; on viols they are more often C-shaped. Modern guitars have an open round hole; in earlier times these were filled with tracery, often of cut parchment, while those on lutes had a carved geometric pattern (known as a *rose). Some harpsichord soundholes had a pattern including the makers' initials.   JMo

soundpost (Fr.: *âme*; Ger.: *Seele*, *Stimme*, *Stimmstock*; It.: *anima*). A rod of pine, fitted internally between the back and belly of instruments of the violin family, that resists the downward pressure of the bridge and transmits its vibrations to the back. It should be set just behind the right (treble) foot of the bridge. Names for the soundpost in other languages indicate that it has been regarded as the 'soul' of an instrument.

AB/JMo

sound recording and reproduction. See RECORDING AND REPRODUCTION.

sound-table. See BELLY.

sound waves. See ACOUSTICS.

soupirant (Fr.). 'Sighing'.

sources. In music, this word normally denotes the handwritten documents that lie behind the printed form in which the music circulates. From about 1950 music began to be published from reproductions of the composer's handwriting or, later, from the composer's own computer setting; but the printing of earlier music almost invariably risks misrepresentation of what the composer wrote. This is not simply a matter of misprints and of adjustments to make the music fit in with the publisher's house style, though these are perhaps the most important benefits of source research; it also has to do with the need to resolve ambiguities in the material presented for setting or engraving. Almost any composer is likely to make small slips in the presentation of two passages that are intended to be the same, for example, and an outside eye can see these more easily: it is plainly the job of the publisher to resolve them, but their correct resolution is no simple matter. It is probably true to say that there is not a single composition—printed or manuscript—without ambiguities that the performer needs to resolve. Serious study, whether for historical understanding or for performance, always benefits from examination of the sources.

Often the sources can show details that are virtually impossible to reproduce in a printed edition. At the most obvious level, the crossing out of articulation signs in the source shows that the composer actively rejected them. Another case includes the understanding of the often approximate rhythmic notation of the 19th century by examination of the positioning or repositioning of notes in relation to one another in the source. (Examples of both appear in Chopin's manuscripts.) Less obviously, the careful rescoring of a passage may give a hint of the textures for which the composer was striving. Study of Beethoven's often almost indecipherable script can help to see how obvious musical

errors have crept into the printed editions. Most important, however, study of the sources can show where the composer was in fact undecided about the effect intended.

The study of sources is not without its dangers. The most famous example concerns the case of the scholar who brought a court action against the house of Ricordi for publishing Verdi scores that differed in thousands of details from the original manuscripts. What became clear was that Verdi himself made numerous changes between the original composition and publication. First, a score was routinely sent to a copyist for more copies to be made; these, rather than the autograph original, were used in the course of preparation for the first performance; adjustments were then made, many being entered into one of these later copies, which was then sent for engraving. Quite often these copyist's manuscripts do not survive, since their non-autograph status reduced their perceived value.

Further understanding of many works arises from the study of surviving orchestral parts, which often contain corrections or adjustments sanctioned by the composer—though the authority or origin of such changes can be hard to judge.

These and similar examples raise questions about the notion of an 'Urtext' edition, the publication of the music without any further adjustments. Originally the term denoted an edition that simply eliminated the fingerings, metronome marks, phrase marks, and other indications added by later editors in so many publications of the Classical and Romantic repertory. But often it also implies the presentation of an 'original' version. Sometimes this is feasible; but all too often the editor is confronted with several different versions or ambiguities that cannot be resolved.

One of the recurrent problems in editing is whether to present the original version of a piece (the 'Fassung erster Hand') or the last revision that the composer left (the 'Fassung letzter Hand'). An extreme example is Wagner's *Tannhäuser*: there are more than a dozen versions that were at some point authorized by the composer, and Wagner himself declared at the end of his life that he was not satisfied with any of them. Many versions include music in a much later style, from the time of *Tristan*; and while some scholars believe that these create a richer work there are others who prefer the stylistic coherence of the earlier versions. There is no single solution to this dilemma.

Another issue is that of material that somebody thought impractical or simply too extensive for inclusion. Research on the sources of Verdi's *Don Carlos* has revealed substantial passages of glorious music that had been cut before the first performance; their restoration could be seen as contradicting Verdi's dramatic judgment, but it is still hard to resist the need to hear them. Now that the CD medium has made it possible for the listener to choose or reject particular sections of a work, there seems every justification for performing this music.

Conversely there is the matter of composers whose judgment could be considered flawed. The most famous of these is Bruckner. Scores printed since about 1930 have all tried to reproduce more or less what he himself wrote. But there could be a case for reinstating the cuts, adjustments, and reorchestrations made by his pupils and colleagues—men who understood his style and his aims but felt that there were better ways of expressing them. Here, the 'sources' are in fact mostly printed scores and sets of orchestral parts. They are at the moment derided and ignored; but it is easy to predict that changing fashions will in the future make them seem important for a more refined understanding of the music.

In all these cases it is important to distinguish between a composer's autograph (more accurately known as the 'holograph') and other copies, whether printed or manuscript. Any copy is likely to contain errors, adjustments, adaptations, and simple misunderstandings. From that point of view it is clear that the problems did not begin simply when Ottaviano Petrucci initiated the commercial printing of music in 1501. Before that we may be confined to handwritten material, but almost none of this material has been reliably identified as in the hand of the composer; so most medieval manuscripts are also presumably copies, the definitive composer's autograph that would merit the name of 'source' being (as with most music before the mid-18th century), sadly, unavailable.

Study of a composer's sketches belongs to a different category of source research. If it is unlikely to resolve many ambiguities in the final composition it adds enormously to the understanding of how a work was generated. There is today a thriving industry of sketch studies that give important insight into the creative processes of composers.

For pre-Classical music it is increasingly believed that modern editions can seriously misrepresent the music. Performers of Baroque music now often prefer to play from the earliest sources—often an original printed edition in the absence of any surviving manuscript. For much 15th- and 16th-century music the normal presentation in manuscript choirbooks is considered an integral part of the composition: modern editions routinely reduce note-values and make many other changes, and most particularly they make decisions about the placement of text that seem to go well beyond what the surviving sources convey. For 13th- and 14th-century music it begins to seem that the actual manner of presentation on the original pages is part of the music's cultural resonance.

For all these reasons recent decades have seen a massive increase in published facsimiles of important musical sources—not only the major manuscripts of medieval and Renaissance music but also much autograph material by the main 18th- and 19th-century composers. For other music, serious investigation still involves consultation of the originals, either in the major music libraries of the world (which are increasingly reluctant to make these precious documents available to readers) or, more conveniently but not particularly comfortably, in the form of microfilms, which can be obtained from most large libraries.   DF

sourd, sourde (Fr.). 'Muffled', 'muted'; *pédale sourde*, the soft (*una corda*) pedal. See PIANOFORTE, 7.

sourdine (Fr.). 'Mute'.

Sousa, John Philip (*b* Washington, DC, 6 Nov. 1854; *d* Reading, PA, 6 March 1932). American composer and bandmaster. He grew up studying singing and a wide range of instruments, became a competent violinist, and played mostly in theatre orchestras as a young man. Appointed director of the US Marine Band in 1880, he resigned that post in 1892 to form a band of his own. Sousa's Band successfully toured the USA and Europe over the next four decades, also making a world tour. Sousa's creed as a conductor was to entertain his audience while educating them. His programme mixed popular favourites with excerpts from the classics, often featuring virtuoso solos by band members. Through its concert appearances and its many recordings, Sousa's Band introduced polished ensemble music-making to an unusually wide audience.

Although he composed many stage works and songs, Sousa is best known for his marches, which number more than 130 and show his special strengths as a composer: melodic inventiveness, rhythmic vigour, an ear for harmonic surprise, and an understanding of a wind band's sound capabilities. Emphasizing changes of theme, colour, texture, dynamics, and even key, they are in effect miniatures for large ensemble, and their brief time-span is animated by sharp, bold contrasts.   RC

📖 P. E. BIERLEY, *John Philip Sousa, American Phenomenon* (New York, 1973, 2/1986) · J. NEWSOM (ed.), *Perspectives on John Philip Sousa* (Washington, DC, 1983) · P. E. BIERLEY, *The Works of John Philip Sousa* (Columbus, OH, 1984)

sousaphone. See TUBA, 1.

Souster, Tim(othy Andrew James) (*b* Bletchley, 29 Jan. 1943; *d* Cambridge, 1 March 1994). English composer. He studied at Oxford University, at Darmstadt with Stockhausen and Berio, and in London with Richard

Rodney Bennett. Closely associated with Stockhausen as performer and assistant, he was a founder member of the live electronic ensembles Intermodulation and odB, and several of his earlier compositions, including *Titus Groan Music* (1969) and *World Music* (1974–80) reflect this association. One particularly substantial work, the Sonata for cello, piano, seven wind instruments, and percussion (1979), has no electronics, but most of Souster's later compositions, from *The Transistor Radio of Saint Narcissus* (1983) to the Trumpet Concerto (1988), contain an important electronic component.

PG/AW

soutenu (Fr.). 'Sustained'.

South Africa. The arrival of Western music in South Africa was spread over several centuries and followed visitations from a number of different European countries. It began with the Portuguese (Vasco da Gama in 1497), and was followed by a Dutch settlement at the Cape in 1652, where military and church music grew in importance with the first South African-born organist appointed in 1749. The arrival of French troops in 1781 widened the range of social activities to include theatre and opera performances. By 1795 the British brought their own types of folksong and dance music, as well as spreading the music of Bach, Haydn, and others at private concerts. Public orchestral concerts began in about 1811 and an Academy of Music was established in Cape Town in 1826.

Opera became more important during the first half of the 19th century, with popular works by Dibdin, Storace, and others, and a performance of Weber's *Der Freischütz* in 1831. At this time too, the discovery of diamonds and gold led to an expansion of the colony's boundaries and an influx of European settlers. Operas, for example by Verdi and Gilbert and Sullivan, were staged in Johannesburg in the early 1890s. Visiting opera companies included the Carl Rosa; they broadened the repertory to include Wagner. An annual opera season is traditionally held in Johannesburg, having grown from small beginnings in 1926 to nearly three months in duration. Other opera centres now include Cape Town and Pretoria.

Music features in the curricula of educational establishments at all levels, with travelling inspectors and a widespread examination system linked to the Associated Board and Trinity College of Music in London. All the universities have music departments, some with their own theatres and concert halls where major works are performed. The Johannesburg Music Society has featured chamber music in an average of ten concerts annually since its formation in 1902. A South African section of the ISCM was founded in 1949 and promotes new music.

Symphony orchestras have been established in Cape Town (1914), Durban (1921), and Johannesburg (1946). Their activities are complemented by the orchestra of the South African Broadcasting Corporation, which also records and broadcasts works by South African composers, vocal items being performed in both English and Afrikaans. Although several immigrant composers have produced works that have been performed internationally, notably W. H. Bell (1873–1946), Victor Hely-Hutchinson, and Erik Chisholm, few South African-born composers have attained worldwide recognition. However, Arnold van Wyk (1916–83), John Joubert, and Priaulx Rainier should be mentioned, and a new generation including the naturalized Irish Kevin Volans is having works performed at home and abroad. The traditional musics of the numerous races in the country, using a variety of native instruments and styles, have become better known following the establishment of the African Music Society in 1947, now represented in 17 African territories.   JBo

📖 J. P. MALAN (ed.), *South African Music Encyclopedia* (Cape Town, 1979–86) · P. KLATZOW (ed.), *Composers in South Africa Today* (Cape Town, 1987)

Sowerby, Leo (*b* Grand Rapids, MI, 1 May 1895; *d* Fort Clinton, OH, 7 July 1968). American composer. He studied at the American Conservatory in Chicago and in Italy as first recipient of the American Prix de Rome (1921–4). He went back to teach at his alma mater (1925–62) and serve as organist and choirmaster at St James's Episcopal Cathedral (1927–62). His works include much church and organ music but also five symphonies, several concertos (for piano, organ, violin, cello), chamber music, and numerous songs.

PG

spacing. The arrangement of the notes of a chord, according to the requirements of the individual voices. If the upper voices are close together, the spacing is described as close position, or close harmony; if not, the arrangement is called open position, or open harmony. See POSITION, 2.

Spain 1. The Middle Ages to 1450; 2. 1450–1530; 3. The late Renaissance, 1530–1600; 4. The Baroque era; 5. Music under the Bourbons; 6. The 19th century; 7. The 20th century

1. The Middle Ages to 1450

The history of Spain up to 1450 was one of repeated invasion, each cultural wave exercising strong influence over Spanish life and art. In the 1st millennium BC the conquering Romans introduced to Iberia such instruments as the trumpet and organ (*hydraulis*), used to accompany singing and dancing. The six centuries of stability that followed saw Christianity spread rapidly in spite of repression, though Spain was not to become wholly Christian until the late 15th century. In about AD 500 the empire disintegrated and Roman rule was replaced by a string of barbarian kingdoms, notably the Visigoth Empire in the south with Toledo as its capital. With the flowering of Visigoth culture (562–681) came the growth of a liturgy—Spanish Christians were still permitted to practise their religion, on payment of taxes. The Visigothic Church developed a liturgical music, *Mozarabic chant, used until its abolition in the 11th century.

In 711 the peninsula was again invaded, by Muslims from northern Africa. The Moors infused an exotic orientalism into Spanish culture which exercised a deep influence even after their final expulsion in the 15th century. The Arab court at Seville was famed not only for its splendour but also for the excellence of its music and the variety of instruments kept there (tambourines, drums, nakers, castanets, psalteries, flutes, lutes, rebecs, trumpets). Many are depicted in the most important medieval Spanish manuscript of secular music, the *Cantigas de Santa Maria*, compiled in the 13th century by Alfonso X 'the Wise' of Castile and León. Moorish musicians worked at Christian courts in the north—and even in churches, until barred by the Valladolid Council (1322); indeed the two cultures coexisted peaceably in a climate of relative religious tolerance until the Christian monarchs in the north began campaigns to drive out the Moors. The capture of Toledo (1085) by the Christian Alfonso VI initiated a gradual process of repossession which, with the exception of Granada, was complete by the mid-13th century.

Unlike their Moorish counterparts, the Christian monarchs failed to concern themselves much with the arts, an attitude that persisted up to the late Renaissance and, in combination with other factors, had important repercussions on Spanish art, literature, and music. Scholarship and high culture were the preserve of monastic communities like Ripoll, Gerona, and Tarragona in the north, which were receptive to the influence of French orders such as the Benedictines and Cistercians. This influence is seen in the rapid spread of the Gothic style of architecture in northern Spain, and in the introduction of Gregorian chant. Toledo became one of the most important European schools of plainchant, while the Benedictine abbey of Ripoll produced one of the earliest theoretical works on polyphony, Abbot Oliva's *Breviarum de musica* (c.1050). Three important sources of medieval Spanish polyphony survive: the 12th-century Codex Calixtinus, intended to publicize the shrine of St James of Compostela; the early 14th-century Huelgas Manuscript from the convent of Las Huelgas, near Burgos; and the mid-14th-century *Llibre vermell* ('Red Book')

found in 1806 at the Montserrat Monastery in Catalunya and containing the earliest known version of the Dance of Death.

In the later Middle Ages, the Hispanic languages began to take shape, and with them secular lyric poetry for the amusement of the aristocracy. This was of two main types: the epic ballad, and the courtly love song (*cantiga de amor*) influenced by troubadours and performed by minstrels who accompanied themselves on stringed instruments. In the 14th century such pieces tended to be deeply pessimistic, reflecting the low life expectancy and general misery of existence in a land ravaged by political strife and the Black Death. By the early 15th century, these forms had largely been replaced by the *romanza*, a type of love song written mainly in the Castilian tongue.

2. 1450–1530

By the mid-15th century, the two most expansionist Spanish states were Castile and Aragon, ruled respectively from Toledo and Seville. The Castilian monarchy maintained links with France and the Netherlands, while in 1442 Alfonso V of Aragon annexed Naples and Sicily. He was the patron of one of the earliest known Spanish composers, Cornago. From 1479 Ferdinand V of Aragon and his wife Isabella of Castile ruled jointly over both kingdoms, paving the way for the unification of Spain which came about with the recapture of Granada, the last remaining Moorish stronghold, in 1492. Unlike earlier Spanish monarchs, Ferdinand and Isabella were important patrons of music. They maintained separate musical chapels and employed some of the best musicians of the time: Peñalosa, Juan Fernández de Madrid (*fl* 1480), and Francisco de la Torre (*fl* 1483–1504). Their son, the short-lived Crown Prince Juan, also had his own establishment under Juan de Anchieta (1462–1523). Isabella was particularly fond of the vihuela, the Spanish Renaissance stringed instrument *par excellence*, and kept three or four vihuelists at court including Lope de Baena (*fl* 1475–c.1508).

A typical cathedral chapel in the early 16th century supported about 20 choirboys trained by the *maestro de capilla*, who was also required to conduct the cathedral music at weekends and on feast days. The great Spanish cathedrals provided training and employment for many important musicians, including the Portuguese Pedro de Escobar, *maestro* at Seville 1507–14, Juan de Triana (*fl* 1478–83; at Seville and Toledo), and Juan de León (*fl* 1480–1514; at Santiago de Compostela and Málaga). Large cathedrals also employed instrumentalists, and the use of wind instruments in particular became a distinctive feature of Spanish sacred vocal music.

During the Renaissance Spain extended the boundaries of its empire to become the most powerful nation in Europe. Columbus's voyage to the New World in 1492 led to the Spanish acquisition of most of Central and South America, and the annexation of Naples, Milan, Sicily, Burgundy, Portugal, and the Netherlands resulted in an equally fruitful cultural cross-fertilization. Humanism gained ground after 1515 with the accession of Charles V (Holy Roman Emperor from 1519), who had been brought up at the Burgundian court under the influence of Erasmus; Italian and Flemish artistic precepts made strong headway in the peninsula; and many Spanish musicians were able to work abroad—especially in Italy, where in 1503 six of the 21 singers in the papal choir in Rome were Spanish.

At the same time foreign composers began to influence Spanish music, notably the Netherlands polyphonic masters Ockeghem, Agricola, La Rue, and especially Josquin, whose music was widely disseminated and copied. Spain opened its cultural frontiers to Renaissance values only when the movement was virtually played out in Italy—hence the little headway made by such foreign secular genres as the madrigal. Instead, Spanish composers tended to cultivate the villancico. About 400 villancicos, with other types of vocal music by all the major contemporary composers, are found in the greatest secular collection of the period, the *Cancionero musical de palacio* ('Palace Songbook').

3. The late Renaissance, 1530–1600

During the reigns of Charles V (1516–56) and his son Philip II (1556–98) Spain nurtured some of the finest writers, painters, and musicians of the time (Lope de Vega, Cervantes, El Greco, Victoria) to create the 'golden age' of Spanish culture. On his accession Charles V established a chapel of musicians drawn from his native Flanders (*capilla flamenca*), which travelled about with him. His Portuguese wife maintained a similar chapel of Spanish musicians (*capilla españa*), and this cosmopolitan tradition continued throughout the reign of their son, Philip. However, during the last years of Charles's reign the growing influence of Lutheranism provoked the backlash of the Counter-Reformation, and under Philip II the Inquisition exercised an iron grip on the country's culture. Secular music other than the purely instrumental declined, and in spite of the growing demand for sacred music for use in New World cathedrals and universities little music was printed in Spain. Most circulated only in manuscript copies, and much was lost.

The principal 16th-century schools of music were the Andalusian (based in Seville), Castilian (Toledo and Salamanca), and Catalan (the abbeys of Ripoll and Montserrat). Seville was the richest city in Spain, en-

joying a monopoly of trade with the New World; and the Seville school produced a number of the most renowned late Renaissance Spanish composers, including Cristóbal de Morales and his pupil and successor Francisco Guerrero. Their output is almost exclusively sacred. Another Morales pupil, Juan Navarro, was educated at Seville and subsequently worked at other Spanish cathedrals, as did Rodrigo de Ceballos, who later became master of the royal chapel.

The Castilian school centred on Toledo Cathedral, its splendour surpassed only by that of St Peter's in Rome. Many Castilian-trained musicians worked in the papal choir in Rome, and in the royal chapels of Spain and Italy. Among those who followed this path were Luis de Narváez, Bernardo Clavijo del Castillo (c.1549–1626), and Sebastián López de Velasco (d after 1648); but the most celebrated Castilian musician of all was Tomás Luis de Victoria, most of whose extensive output of sacred music was published during his years in Italy. With his teacher, Palestrina, Victoria was regarded as one of the greatest polyphonists of the age, his music renowned for its individual colour and dramatic vigour.

Not so well placed to find noble patronage, most composers of the other schools worked for the cathedrals at Barcelona, Tarragona, Lérida, and Urgel. Few travelled abroad, and little of their music was published. Among the best Catalan composers of the time were the two Mateo Flechas—the elder (?1481–?1553) was *maestro de capilla* at Lérida, his nephew (c.1530–1604) worked at Vienna until 1599, and both were famous for cultivating the Spanish quodlibet form, the *ensalada*—and Joan Pau Pujol (c.1573–1626). Late 16th-century Catalan composers favoured secular rather than sacred music, and collections of madrigals and villancicos were issued by Joan Brudieu (c.1520–91), Flecha the elder, and others. The leading Valencian musicians of the time were Juan Ginés Peréz (1548–1612) and the villancico composer Juan Bautista Comes (1582–1643).

The roots of Spanish musical drama are found in pastoral dialogues with music, notably those written by Juan del Encina for his patron the Duke of Alba. 16th-century Spanish instrumental music is represented mostly by vihuela and organ music. Seven important vihuela publications appeared in the course of the century, including those of Luis de Milán, Alonso Mudarra, and Esteban Daza. These contain music for voice with vihuela accompaniment, as well as solo fantasias, tientos, *ciaconas*, popular dances, and arrangements of sacred and secular pieces. But the greatest instrumental composer of the period was undoubtedly the blind organist Antonio de Cabezón, favourite of Philip II, who was one of the first composers of genuinely idiomatic keyboard music. Among his best pieces are tientos of great structural variety, glosas, and *diferencias*. Cabezón travelled widely in Philip's entourage, and his influence is traceable in keyboard works by his European contemporaries.

4. The Baroque era

The decline in Spain's fortunes that began with the defeat of the Armada in 1588 was mirrored musically by a shift of emphasis from sacred to secular genres, with a corresponding decrease in the quality and quantity of sacred music. One of the best and most prolific composers of sacred music to work for Philip III was Mateo Romero (1575–1637), the king's *maestro de capilla*. The Montserrat choir school continued to produce a few outstanding figures such as Cererols, who excelled in sacred double-choir music and vernacular villancicos; the major figure in Spanish Baroque organ music was Juan Bautista José Cabanilles, organist at Valencia, whose tientos and variations maintained the strong Spanish keyboard tradition.

Intellectual life in 17th-century Spain was dominated by the Jesuits, who proved receptive to the burgeoning Baroque styles favouring the marriage of text and music; most court poetry of the period was written to be sung, and mixed theatre forms flourished. Italian professional actors had been active in Spain from the mid-16th century onwards, and by 1600 the municipal theatre (*corrala*) was a major feature of all Spanish cities. The first Spanish drama to be set entirely to music was *La selva sin amor* (1629) a late, allegorical production of Lope de Vega; and when in 1632 Philip IV built a court theatre at his palace of Buen Retiro, fitted with spectacular stage machinery, the way was opened for works including music and dancing on a grand scale, along the lines of French or Italian opera. Here dramas on mythological themes by Pedro Calderón de la Barca were performed, with music by Juan Hidalgo. In addition to over 120 dramas, Calderón's *El golfo de las sirenas* (1657, composer unknown) and *El laurel de Apolo* (1657/8, music probably by Hidalgo) were the first important examples of *zarzuela, a style of musical theatre not unlike the English semi-opera. Zarzuela was still based on themes from classical mythology, but comedy, spoken dialogue, popular song, and dance were added.

Instrumental music was equally strongly influenced by popular culture. The five-course guitar supplanted the aristocratic vihuela in the 17th century and came to be regarded as the typical Spanish instrument. Its characteristic sound and techniques have permeated music by Spanish composers to the present day. Luis de Briçeño's guitar method (Paris, 1626) introduced a new kind of tablature adapted to peasant songs and dances, while the most important guitar manual of the period,

Gaspar Sanz's *Instrucción* (Zaragoza, 1674), was another compendium of popular dance.

5. Music under the Bourbons

Under Bourbon rule in 18th-century Spain native culture succumbed to a flood of imported art and artists. The French-born Philip V (ruled 1701–46) set up a number of national institutions on French lines, such as the National Library (1712) and the Royal Spanish Academy (1713), while stocking his music library with French cantatas and Italian operas. The increasing secularization of musical life and decline of sacred music was attacked by Benito Feijóo in the influential essay *Música de los templos* (1726). Feijóo deplored the growing taste for theatrical church music with instrumental accompaniment exemplified in the works of Sebastián Durón, whose religious villancicos were performed as far afield as South America. On the other hand, Feijóo had nothing but praise for the 'pure' church music of Durón's contemporary Antonio Literes, whose masses were in the conservative *a cappella* tradition. Under Philip V the direction of the palace orchestra at Buen Retiro was shared by three men (one Italian, two Spanish), one of the latter being José de Nebra who wrote much sacred music for the royal chapel.

Ferdinand VI (ruled 1746–59) and his Portuguese consort María Barbara of Bragança were thoroughly Italianate in sympathies, and Italian musicians occupied most important court posts. Domenico Scarlatti, the queen's music master, evidently found the atmosphere at the Spanish court less restrictive than his native Italy: several commentators have noted certain distinctly Spanish idioms in his keyboard sonatas, including thrummed accompaniments suggestive of the guitar. Together with Scarlatti, the castrato Farinelli served the Spanish court for nearly 25 years, enjoying a position of prestige and power until he was pensioned in 1759 by Ferdinand's philistine successor, Charles III. A period of musical stagnation at court ended in 1788 with the accession of Charles IV, a competent violinist who built up a large collection of chamber music including many pieces by his Italian music master, Brunetti. From 1768 to 1785 Boccherini lived in Spain under the patronage of the king's uncle, Prince Luís. The king's brother, Prince Gabriel, bucked the fashion by choosing a Spaniard as his teacher—the composer monk Antonio Soler, best remembered for his harpsichord sonatas, which rival Scarlatti's in originality.

Durón, Nebra, and Literes were the outstanding early 18th-century composers of zarzuela, but Italian opera stifled the native form as the century progressed. The native composer Domingo Terradellas (1713–51), unable to be heard in Spain, spent his life writing operas in Italian for Rome, Florence, Venice, and

London. On Charles III's accession in 1759 performances were confined to private palaces and one public theatre. By 1777 the Italian troupe had gone, and opera languished—the best-known 18th-century example by a Spanish composer was Vicente Martín y Soler's *Una cosa rara*, written in Italian for Vienna; Martín's only significant stage work in Spanish is his delightful zarzuela *La madrileña*.

Otherwise, vernacular opera was kept barely alive in the late 18th century by the dramatist Ramón de la Cruz (1731–94), who collaborated with Boccherini on a masterly Spanish zarzuela, *Clementina* (1786). His more usual partner was the composer Antonio Rodríguez de Hita (1704–87); their burlesque *Las segadoras de Vallecas* (1768) was probably the first Spanish music-theatre work with a contemporary setting and working-class (instead of mythical or heroic) characters. In the same year Pablo Esteve (*d* 1794) produced *Los jardineros de Aranjuez* along similar lines, but later in the century the two-act zarzuela declined, overtaken in popularity by such smaller forms as the largely verbal **sainete* and the **tonadilla escénica*. Composers of famous *tonadillas* included the Catalan flautist Luis Misón (1727–76), who wrote over 100, and Blas de Laserna (1751–1816), who wrote seven times that number including the popular *La beata*.

6. The 19th century

The French Revolution and subsequent Napoleonic invasion had a profoundly unsettling effect on Spanish life: after Napoleon's expulsion in the Peninsular War the country experienced a series of civil wars and revolutions which disrupted and stunted social and cultural development. Indeed, the only significant artistic figure of the early 19th century is the painter Goya, whose late works capture the pessimistic spirit of his age. The restoration of the unpopular Ferdinand VII led to a cultural 'brain drain', and musically the period was entirely dominated by Italian imports. Ferdinand's fourth wife, María Cristina of Naples, greatly admired Rossini, and when the Madrid Conservatory was founded in 1830 it had as director an Italian singer rather than a Spaniard. Only two names are outstanding in the music of the period: Manuel García and Fernando Sor. García, his son Manuel, and his daughters Pauline Viardot and Maria Malibran revitalized Spanish singing, and Sor may be regarded, with his friend and rival Aguado, as the founder of the modern Spanish guitar school. Spanish music suffered a severe loss with the early death of Arriaga, who by the age of 16 was showing huge promise in symphonic, chamber, and even operatic music.

The decline in church music in the 18th century accelerated in the 19th. An act of 1835 closed religious institutions throughout Spain, and in 1851 a concordat reduced the musical personnel of churches to a *maestro* and an organist, one tenor, and a handful of choirboys. Low morale among church musicians continued until 1896, when a special congress examined the penurious state of sacred music and recommended changes, including the publication of early Spanish masterpieces. Such work had been undertaken earlier in the century by Hilarión Eslava (1807–78), editor of *Lira sacro-hispana*, but his work fell victim to financial cutbacks.

The zarzuela had disappeared after the 1780s, supplanted by the *tonadilla* and by Italian *opera buffa*; by 1830 native Spanish works were virtually extinct. But the first composition professor at the Madrid Conservatory, Ramón Carnicer (1789–1855), made use of Spanish themes in his own stage works (e.g. *Don Giovanni Tenorio*), stimulating a revival of interest in zarzuela as the national art form among composers including Joaquín Gaztambide (1822–70), Emilio Arrieta (1821–94), Cristóbal Oudrid (1825–77); and especially Francisco Asenjo Barbieri, whose position in Spanish music is analogous to that of Glinka in Russia, or—as a critic—to Berlioz in France. Barbieri's *Pan y toros* (1864) was the first major three-act zarzuela on an original Spanish subject, and he founded an orchestral music society which introduced contemporary symphonic work to Madrid.

Later 19th-century zarzuela was dominated by Barbieri's protégé Federico Chueca, Manuel Fernández Caballero, and Ruperto Chapí—whose rival Tomás Bretón composed perhaps the greatest zarzuela of all, *La verbena de la paloma*. The social acuity and popularity of the genre militated against development of a full-blown Spanish opera tradition; and the through-written operas of Chapí and Bretón (e.g. the latter's *La Dolores*), though revived from time to time, lack the spontaneity of the native form, which draws on the rhythmic strength of urban popular dances. Many new theatres opened in Madrid during the second half of the century, including the magnificent Teatro Real, the Apolo (1850), and the Teatro de la Zarzuela, founded by Barbieri and his colleagues in 1856 and still the spiritual home of Spanish music theatre.

The Romantic movement in Spain, weaker than in Germany, England, or France, was influential only after the death of Ferdinand VII (1833), when many intellectuals returned from self-imposed exile bringing the novels of Victor Hugo and Alexandre Dumas and the poetry of Byron. Liberalization, accompanied by the growth of a powerful urban middle class, led to the establishment first of a constitutional monarchy, then of the short-lived First Republic (1873–5). The rising tide of nationalism manifested itself musically in the use of folksong and of such dance rhythms as the *jota*, *seguidillas*, and *zapateado*, which, largely drawn from Gypsy music, give that essential 'Spanish' flavour to so much late 19th- and early 20th-century music. Further spice came from harmonic and melodic twists evoking 'oriental' Moorish music—the *alhambrismo* ('Alhambra') technique familiar from Albéniz's piano works and the orchestral music of Chapí and Bretón. Such idioms pervade the music of Granados, Falla, and Turina. Albéniz and Granados immortalized their homeland in their piano works (*Iberia*, *Goyescas*), while Falla, the finest Spanish composer of the late 19th and early 20th centuries, is best known for his stage and orchestral music, wide-ranging in style and content but always rooted in Spanish idioms.

All these composers had strong links with Paris, where many studied; and a reciprocal influence may be seen in the large number of French works of the same period which make use of Spanish colour: Bizet's *Carmen* (the famous Habanera was borrowed from a song by Iradier), Lalo's *Symphonie espagnole* (1875), dedicated to Sarasate, Chabrier's *España* (1883), and numerous pieces by Debussy (*Ibéria*, *Soirées dans Grenade*) and Ravel, who was of Basque origin *(Boléro, L'Heure espagnole*, *Rapsodie espagnole*, *Alborada del gracioso)*. Spanish idioms held a similar fascination for several Russian nationalist composers, including Glinka (*Jota aragonese*, *Summer Night in Madrid*), Balakirev (*Overture on Spanish Themes*), and Rimsky-Korsakov (*Spanish Capriccio*).

As in other countries, this nationalist spirit produced a renewed sense of regional identity, especially in Catalonia and the Basque country, and a desire to rediscover the great national masterpieces of the past. Amedeo Vives was perhaps the most significant Catalonian composer, but Felipe Pedrell had the greater influence: he championed the nationalist cause as writer, lecturer, editor, musicologist, and teacher—his pupils included Albéniz, Granados, Falla, and Gerhard—and his resuscitation of such 16th-century polyphonic masters as Victoria was highly influential on Falla and composers of the younger generation.

7. The 20th century

After a brief period of relative stability and economic prosperity, the years up to the establishment of the Second Republic in 1930 were characterized by political upheaval; but the arts continued to flourish in a more liberal, cosmopolitan climate, and by 1900 Barcelona rivalled Paris as a centre of intellectual activity. As in Paris this centred on a café (Els Quatre Gats), its habitués including Picasso, the architect Gaudi, and such musicians as Vives and Granados. The Catalans were concerned to preserve their language, and in 1891 Vives founded the Basque choir Orfeó Català to per-

form Catalan folk music and early Spanish music. The early 20th century produced a number of distinctive Catalan composers including Federico Mompou and Eduardo Toldrá (1895–1962); foremost among musicians was Casals, who throughout his life tirelessly promoted the music of his native region. The two finest Basque composers, Jesús Guridi (1886–1961) and José Maria Usandizaga (1887–1915), produced work in a variety of forms without compromising their regional roots or denying their Spanish heritage. Both use complex Basque dance rhythms, notably the 7/4 *espatadanza* and 5/4 *zortzico*, to stirring effect.

Other 20th-century Spanish composers grouped themselves together to promote a common cause. One of the most significant was the 'Madrid Group', established during the Second Republic and characterized by liberal or left-wing views. It included (besides the poets Guillén and Federico García Lorca) the musicologist Adolfo Salazar (1890–1958); such composers as Falla's pupils Joaquín Nin-Culmell (*b* 1908) and the Halffter brothers, Ernesto and Rodolfo (1900–87), all of whom cultivated national Spanish music in a modern idiom; Oscar Esplá, director of the Madrid Conservatory; and Roberto Gerhard, another Catalan and a pupil of Granados and Pedrell. All these musicians were forced into exile when Franco came to power after the Civil War—Ernesto Halffter settled in Lisbon and his brother in Mexico, Nin-Culmell went to the USA, Esplá to Belgium, and Gerhard to England, where much of his best music was written.

This exodus inevitably left Spanish music greatly impoverished. The postwar dictatorship reimposed artistic censorship, clamped down on regional separatism, and generally discouraged innovation; not surprisingly, the most successful 20th-century Spanish composers were those who perpetuated the nationalist style using traditional *casticismo* ('authentic') techniques. One such was Joaquín Rodrigo, who in 1939 found international renown with his popular *Concierto de Aranjuez*, the first of several well-received concertos. Xavier Montsalvatge's *Canciones negras* of 1946 established him as a major composer of songs in an evocative Spanish idiom, while the most successful zarzuela composer of the Franco era was the conservative Moreno Torroba. Pablo Sorozábal, most vibrantly radical of the younger *zarzueleros*, stayed in Spain but found commissions hard to come by and worked mainly as a conductor.

More cosmopolitan, avant-garde trends have been represented in Spain by Joaquín Homs (*b* 1906), a pupil of Gerhard and exponent of serialism, though his music retains an essential Spanish flavour. This is no longer true of the works of the 'Música Abierta' composers, who have looked to mainstream European developments for their inspiration—figures such as Cristóbal Halffter, Luis de Pablo (*b* 1930), and García Avril (*b* 1933). Their music is influenced more by Webern and Stockhausen than by Spanish folk music, though Halffter's recent works include an operatic reworking of *Don Quixote* (2000) which pays musical homage to his uncle and to Falla. Younger Spanish composers such as Albert Sardà (*b* 1943), Francisco Guerrero (1951–97), and José Luis Turina (*b* 1952) share the global and social preoccupations of their fellow Europeans rather than investigating specifically Spanish material.

Spain has produced many notable performers in all fields: the guitarists Narciso Yepes and Segovia; the cellists Casals and Caspar Cassado; the pianists Ricardo Viñes, José Iturbi, and Alicia de Larrocha; the conductors Ataulfo Argenta and Rafael Frühbeck de Burgos; and the singers Alfredo Kraus, Plácido Domingo, Conchita Supervía, Victoria de los Angeles, Montserrat Caballé, and Teresa Berganza. Madrid boasts two symphony and three chamber orchestras; two fine opera houses, the newly refurbished Teatro Real and Teatro de la Zarzuela; the state-controlled radio network, Radio Nacional de España, which devotes about 15% of its air time to serious music; and the national music archive at the Sociedad General de Autores de España (SGAE), which is publishing critical editions of many stage and symphonic works. Barcelona is the theatrical centre of Spain, and its rebuilt Liceu Theatre is the largest in the country; the Spanish Institute of Musicology, founded by Pedrell and Anglès, is also based there. Other notable institutions include the Galician and City of Granada Symphony Orchestras and the chorus Orfeón Donostiarra; several Spanish groups, notably Jordi Savall's Hespèrion XXI, are at the cutting edge of historically informed early music and Baroque performance practice.   CW

📖 J. B. Trend, *The Music of Spanish History to 1600* (London, 1926) · G. Chase, *The Music of Spain* (New York, 1941, 2/1959) · R. Stevenson, *Spanish Music in the Age of Columbus* (The Hague, 1960, 2/1964); *Spanish Cathedral Music in the Golden Age* (Berkeley and Los Angeles, 1961) · A. Livermore, *A Short History of Spanish Music* (London, 1972) · L. Powell, *A History of Spanish Piano Music* (Bloomington, IN, 1980) · L. Salter, 'Spain: A nation in turbulence', *The Late Romantic Era: From the Mid-Nineteenth Century to World War I*, ed. J. Samson, Man and Music/Music and Society (London, 1991), 151–66 · M. Boyd and J. J. Carreras (eds.), *Music in Spain in the 18th Century* (Cambridge, 1998)

Spanisches Liederbuch ('Spanish Songbook'). Collection of 44 songs (1889–90) for voice and piano by Wolf, settings of German translations by Paul Heyse and Emanuel Geibel of 16th- and 17th-century Spanish poems. Five were later orchestrated by Wolf.

Spartacus (*Spartak*). Ballet in four acts by Khachaturian to a scenario by Nikolay Volkov; it was choreographed by Leonid Jacobson (Leningrad, 1956). Khachaturian revised the score in 1968.

spasshaft (Ger.). 'Jocular'.

species counterpoint. A method (sometimes known as 'strict counterpoint') of learning, by easy stages, the technique of 16th-century vocal counterpoint. It is usually associated with the treatise *Gradus ad Parnassum* (1725) by the Austrian composer Johann Joseph Fux, although the idea can be traced further back. Given a *cantus firmus (a set theme in long notes), the student first learns to add one note against each note of the theme ('first species') then two against each note ('second species'), and so on, until the more complex rhythms are mastered. The method, formerly used in university teaching, unfortunately became overlaid with superfluous and anachronistic rules, and does not now meet with much favour, 16th-century technique being today more usually taught by a direct approach to the music itself.   RBu

spectrum, spectral components. The range of frequencies (wavelengths) covered by a source of waves; for example, the light spectrum can be divided into about seven distinguishable colours from red, having the longest wavelength, to violet, the shortest. Similarly, sound waves occupy a range of wavelengths from about 17 mm to 17 metres, corresponding respectively to the highest and lowest frequencies audible to the human ear. The harmonic spectrum of a musical instrument is drawn as a series of vertical lines (spectral components) showing the relative strengths of each harmonic.   JBo

Spem in alium numquam habui ('In no other is my hope'). A motet in 40 parts (eight five-voice choirs) by Tallis; it was commissioned to rival Striggio's 40-part motet *Ecce beatam lucem* and was first performed in 1568 or 1569.

sperdendosi (It.). 'Fading out', 'dying away'.

spezzato (It.). See cori spezzati.

spheres, music of the. Music thought by many medieval philosophers to be produced by the movements of the planets, either inaudible to the human ear or not involving sound at all, but nevertheless an all-pervading force in the universe. It was considered the highest form of music, itself interpreted in terms of mathematical proportion. Boethius (*c*.480–*c*.524) in *De institutione musica* contrasted this *musica mundana* with *musica humana*, the harmonious relationships of the human body and soul, and *musica instrumentalis*, the lowest form of music (produced by voices and instruments), which was also based on numerical proportions.   IR

spianato, spianata (It.). 'Smooth', 'even'. Chopin used the direction in the Andante that precedes his E♭ Polonaise op. 22 to indicate a smooth, even-toned style of performance.

spiccato (It.). 'Detached'; a term used in the bowing of stringed instruments to mean **sautillé*. Before 1750 it was taken to mean simply **staccato*.

spiegando (It.). 'Unfolding', i.e. becoming louder.

Spiel, spielen (Ger.). 'Play', 'to play', 'to perform'; *spielend*, 'playing', 'playful'; *volles Spiel*, 'full organ'; *Spieler*, 'player'; *Spielfigur*, a short, playful figure or motif (mainly in early keyboard music).

Spieloper (Ger., 'opera-play'). A type of 19th-century light opera, resembling **Singspiel* in that it uses spoken dialogue. Examples include Lortzing's *Zar und Zimmermann*.

Spies, Claudio (*b* Santiago, 26 March 1925). Chilean-born American composer. Arriving in the USA in 1942, he studied at the New England Conservatory in Boston and with Hindemith and Walter Piston at Harvard (1947–50). His career as a teacher took him back to Harvard (1954–7) and then to Swarthmore College (1958–64) and Princeton (from 1970). He became an American citizen in 1966. Musically and personally he was close to Stravinsky.   PG

spike fiddle (Fr.: *vièle à pique*; Ger.: *Spiessgeige*). A bowed **spike lute. Examples are found in the Middle East (*rabāb*), Indonesia (*rebab*), Mongolia (various types of *huur*), and China (*huqin*).

spike lute. A plucked **chordophone. Its neck passes diametrically through the resonator, protruding as a spike or stub at the bottom; the strings are attached to the spike. The resonator may comprise a natural or carved-out bowl (examples are found in Iran, India, and Indonesia), be made of wood, or be in the form of a tube (found in China and Vietnam).   LC

spinet. See HARPSICHORD, VIRGINALS, SPINET.

Spinnerlied (Ger.). 'Spinner's song'; *Spinnlied*, 'spinning song'.

spirito, spiritoso (It.). 'Spirit', 'spirited', i.e. at a fast tempo; *spiritosamente*, 'in a spirited manner'; *con spirito*, 'with spirit'.

spiritual. A religious folksong associated with revivalism in America from about 1740 to the end of the 19th century. The term is abbreviated from 'spiritual songs' (e.g. Joshua Smith's *Divine Hymns and Spiritual Songs*, *c*.1784–93) and denoted a style of text more enthusiastic than those of the metrical psalms and traditional hymns. The music is suffused with the melodic idiom of folksong, often modal, and frequently using the gapped scales typical of American folksong. Text repetition and responsorial song forms are common. Black and white spirituals display a marked similarity of both text and music. It is likely that black and white congregations exchanged influences, rather than that the spiritual simply originated among one group or the other; whites heard blacks singing spirituals as work songs, black slaves were often allowed to attend the same church services as whites, and black and white attended revivalist camp meetings together. The texts of black spirituals often refer to the flight of the Israelites from slavery in Egypt and to the hope of salvation in heaven; it is often suggested that this was a reference to the hope of escape from the American South to the 'free' North.

The spiritual became popular as concert music following the fund-raising tours from 1871 of the Fisk Jubilee Singers, who introduced the music to North America and Europe; this led to the production of many concert arrangements of spirituals. In this arena, the spiritual has continued to hold some influence, but its popularity as entertainment coincided with its decline as the preferred black church musical genre, which, from the 20th century, has been gospel. See also UNITED STATES OF AMERICA, 3.   PW

📖 J. LOVELL JR, *The Forge and the Flame* (New York, 1972)

Spitta, (Julius August) Philipp (*b* Wechold, nr Bremen, 7 Dec. 1841; *d* Berlin, 13 April 1894). German musicologist. After he had graduated in classics at Göttingen University, his friendship with Brahms resulted in his following a natural inclination to study music. He wrote the first standard life of J. S. Bach (Leipzig, 1873–80, 5/1962; Eng. trans. 2/1899/*R*1992), and as professor of music history at Berlin University taught a host of distinguished pupils before his early death from a heart attack.   DA

Spitze (Ger.). 'Point'; *an der Spitze*, 'at the point' of the bow in string playing, 'with the toe' of the foot in organ playing.

SPNM. See SOCIETY FOR THE PROMOTION OF NEW MUSIC.

Spohr, Louis (*b* Brunswick, 5 April 1784; *d* Kassel, 22 Oct. 1859). German composer and violinist. Although his middle-class family initially opposed a musical career, he became a violinist in the Brunswick court establishment in 1799. During 1802–3 he studied with Franz Eck on a journey to St Petersburg, and in 1805, after a highly successful concert tour in Germany, performing his own concertos, he gained the post of Konzertmeister in Gotha, where he married the virtuoso harpist Dorothea Scheidler. His reputation as violinist and composer was increased by many concert tours with his wife, during which he played his own violin concertos as well as duets for violin and harp. His first symphony and his oratorio *Das jüngste Gericht* were first performed at the 1811 and 1812 Frankenhausen music festivals, which he directed, and his first publicly staged opera (the third he composed), *Der Zweikampf mit der Geliebten*, was given at Hamburg in 1811.

In 1812 Spohr moved to Vienna as Konzertmeister at the Theater an der Wien; there he composed his opera *Faust* (given its premiere by Weber in Prague in 1816), his Nonet, and his Octet. He composed his acclaimed Eighth Violin Concerto, in the form of an extended vocal scena, in 1816–17 for a concert tour to Italy, where his cantabile style of playing was greatly relished. On his return he became Kapellmeister at the Frankfurt theatre, where he produced his opera *Zemire und Azor* (1819). Resigning in 1819, he accepted an engagement for the 1820 season of the London Philharmonic Society, for which he wrote an overture and a symphony (no. 2 in D minor). In London he used a baton to conduct at rehearsal but in public he directed in the traditional way from the violin.

From 1822 Spohr was Kapellmeister in Kassel. The first five years there, which saw the composition of such works as the opera *Jessonda* (1823), the oratorio *Die letzten Dinge* (1826), and the first and second Double String Quartets, marked the highpoint of his reputation in Germany, and in the eyes of contemporaries he became firmly established as a great composer. In 1830–1 he wrote his *Violinschule*, which remained a classic violin method into the 20th century, and shortly afterwards his celebrated Fourth Symphony, *Die Weihe der Töne*. Between 1839 and 1853 he made five triumphant visits to England, where his oratorios were highly esteemed and where his instrumental music and operatic numbers were regularly given in orchestral concerts. On his visit to London in 1843 the influential critic J. W. Davison hailed him as 'The great Spohr— the immortal while yet living' (*Musical World*, 1843, 253). In Paris, which he visited in 1820–1, there was little interest in Spohr's music. After Mendelssohn's death in 1847, Spohr was generally revered in Germany and England as the sole surviving composer of the Classical tradition: *The Morning Chronicle* described him as 'the first composer of the day, without a possible rival' (2

May 1848), and in 1854 Hans von Bülow castigated 'the supreme impropriety of the pretensions with which Kapellmeister Lindpaintner represents himself as the Old Master [*Altmeister*] of the departing epoch, forgetting that Spohr alone can bear this honour' (*Briefe*, vi, 90). But, though he was esteemed and feted for the rest of his life, his impact and influence declined steadily.

Spohr's reputation as the greatest German violinist of his generation was established at an early age not only through performances of his own works but also by his versatility in performing the music of such composers as Mozart, Haydn, Rode, and Beethoven. He created his own, highly individual version of the Viotti style and insisted on the strictest artistic integrity. But of his many violin pupils only Ferdinand David and August Wilhelmj attained real eminence. Spohr played a significant part in the development of conducting. He directed the first great German musical festival at Frankenhausen in 1810 and gained the reputation of a skilled and effective conductor.

His influence as a composer was much greater than posterity has generally recognized. During the 1810s and 20s many young composers were fascinated especially by his handling of chromatic harmony, and his style was widely imitated, leaving traces in the music of numerous important and less well-known composers. However, his music failed to evolve stylistically after the early 1830s and he was often charged with mannerism by less sympathetic critics. His posthumous reputation suffered from the artistic politics of the later 19th century. Nevertheless his finest works are among the most significant of their time and remain capable of giving pleasure and evoking admiration.   CB

📖 L. Spohr, *Selbstbiographie* (Kassel and Göttingen, 1860–1; Eng. trans. 1865, repr. 1969) · C. Brown, *Louis Spohr: A Critical Biography* (Cambridge, 1984); 'Weber and Spohr', *The Nineteenth-Century Symphony*, ed. D. K. Holoman (New York, 1997); 'The chamber music of Spohr and Weber', *Nineteenth-Century Chamber Music*, ed. S. E. Helfig (New York, 1998)

spondee. A poetic foot of two strong syllables. The adjective is 'spondaic'. For its equivalent in the rhythmic modes, see NOTATION, 2.

Spontini, Gaspare (Luigi Pacifico) (*b* Maiolati, nr Ancona, 14 Nov. 1774; *d* Maiolati, 24 Jan. 1851). Italian composer. He came from a peasant family and at first was destined for the Church, but his parents were persuaded to allow him to study at one of the Neapolitan conservatories; after about three years there he absconded to escape punishment for some misdemeanour. In 1796 he had success in Rome with a comic opera, following it up with several others in Palermo, where the Naples court had fled to avoid the French invasion.

In 1803 Spontini went to Paris, where his operas became popular at the Théâtre Italien; but he was not well received in *opéra comique*. He learnt a great deal from the operas of Gluck, and *La Vestale* (first produced at the Opéra in 1807, but composed two years earlier) combined that peculiarly French taste in classical drama and romantic attitudes to such effect that it was one of the greatest successes of its time. He was immediately taken up by the Empress Josephine, and after a second opera in the same manner, *Fernand Cortez* (1809), he became the major figure in French music, conducting the official Italian opera and composing various political *pièces d'occasion*.

In 1814 Spontini came to the notice of King Friedrich Wilhelm III of Prussia, who tempted him with an enormous salary to become chief Kapellmeister in Berlin. By this time he was finding composition difficult and produced comparatively little, but again achieved a reputation as a conductor. Although his last finished work, *Agnes von Hohenstaufen* (1827, rev. 1829 and 1837), was an attempt to come to terms with modern taste, his career was virtually over by the time his patron died in 1840. He was pensioned off to retire, first to Paris, later to his native village. The formidable list of his decorations (among them the Légion d'Honneur) seems strangely at odds with his reputation today. The esteem of his contemporaries was, however, by no means just official, as his dramatic flair and gifts for orchestration were admired—and imitated—by many composers, not least Wagner and Berlioz.   DA/RP

spoons. *Clappers made from a pair of household spoons. They are normally held loosely between thumb and forefinger, and forefinger and middle finger; the bowls are clacked together by being brushed alternately with the other hand and the player's knee. They are capable of great rhythmic complexity. See also BONES.
                                                            RPA

Sprechchor (Ger., 'speech-choir'). *Sprechgesang* executed by a chorus rather than a soloist.

Sprechgesang, Sprechstimme (Ger.). 'Speech-song', 'speaking voice'. Synonymous terms denoting a vocal technique that combines elements of speaking and singing. It was introduced by Humperdinck in his opera *Königskinder* (1897), and Schoenberg used it in several works including *Pierrot lunaire* (1912), stipulating in the preface that the performer should give the exact pitch but leave it immediately by a fall or rise. *Sprechgesang* is often notated with x's, rather than noteheads, attached to conventional stems and flags (see MELODY, Ex. 9).   /BW

Springbogen (Ger.). A kind of bowstroke. See SAUTILLÉ.

springer [acute, sigh] (Fr.: *accent, aspiration, plainte*; Ger.: *Nachschlag*). An ornament used in 17th- and 18th-century music. It consists of a short auxiliary note inserted after the main note and taking part of its time-value; thus it is the opposite of an *appoggiatura, being an anticipation, rather than a delaying, of the following note. It was generally indicated with a diagonal line or with a small note (Ex. 1).

Ex. 1

'Spring' Sonata (*Frühlingssonate*). Nickname of Beethoven's Violin Sonata in F major op. 24 (1801).

Spring Song (*Frühlingslied*). Mendelssohn's *Lied ohne Worte* no. 30 in A major for piano (op. 62; book 5, 1844).

'Spring' Symphony. Schumann's Symphony no. 1 in B♭ major (1841).

Spring Symphony, A. Choral work, op. 44 (1949), by Britten, for soprano, alto, and tenor soloists, boys' choir, chorus, and orchestra, settings of poems by Robert Herrick, W. H. Auden, Richard Barnfield, George Peele, William Blake, Francis Beaumont and John Fletcher, Thomas Nashe, Henry Vaughan, Edmund Spenser, John Clare, and John Milton, and two anonymous verses.

square piano (Fr.: *piano carré*; Ger.: *Tafelklavier*). A small piano in a horizontal, rectangular case. In its shape and design it is a descendant of the *clavichord. It was the principal vehicle for the development of the piano in Germany in the mid-18th century. Its compass was usually $G'-f'''$, with a simple action, originally without escapement. See PIANOFORTE, 3.

An important maker was Johannes Zumpe, who emigrated from Fürth to London in about 1750 and began making square pianos some 15 years later. Zumpe's model was widely popular as a domestic instrument and was copied with little basic change over much of Europe, including his native Germany, and America. Gradual improvements from the 1820s included Alpheus Babcock's iron frame and a considerable increase in size and range, especially in America where very large square pianos were made up to the end of the 19th century in preference to uprights.   JMo

squillante (It.). 'Shrill', i.e. harshly. When applied to cymbals, they should be suspended and struck with drumsticks rather than clashed together.

Staatskapelle (Ger.). 'State orchestra'; see CHAPEL.

Stabat mater dolorosa (Lat., 'Sorrowfully his mother stood'). A medieval poem adopted by the Roman rite, appointed today as a sequence and Office hymn for the Feast of the Seven Sorrows of the Blessed Virgin Mary on 15 September. Of unknown authorship, it has often been attributed to the Italian Franciscan Jacopone da Todi (*d* 1306). Its text graphically describes the mother of Christ at the foot of the Cross, a favourite theme of medieval piety also addressed in contemporary English vernacular songs. Other events in her life were commemorated in Latin texts written in imitation of the poem on the Crucifixion, including the *Stabat mater speciosa*, which portrays her at the cradle.

The plainchant appointed in modern liturgical books for the sequence appears to date from the 15th century, since which the poem has frequently been set by composers. Particularly notable settings for liturgical or concert use include those by Davy and Browne (in the Eton Choirbook), Josquin, Palestrina, Lassus, Pergolesi, Haydn, Rossini, Dvořák, Verdi, Stanford, Kodály, Penderecki, and Pärt. —/ALı

Stabreim (Ger.). A versification style based on alliteration, common in German and other north European poetry of the early Middle Ages. It was adopted by Wagner when writing his own librettos for *Tristan und Isolde* and *Der Ring des Nibelungen* as a means of heightening textual expression with strong alliterative syllables, as in the lines 'Winterstürme wichen dem Wonnemond; in mildem Lichte leuchtet der Lenz' ('Winter's storms have vanished at Spring's command; in gentle radiance sparkles the Spring'; *Die Walküre*, Act I scene 3, trans. Andrew Porter).

staccato (It.). 'Detached', i.e. the opposite of *legato*. A note to be played *staccato* is marked in notation in different ways: with a dot (the most common method), a vertical stroke, a small wedge, or a horizontal dash (implying an accent). The degree of detachment varies according to the type of instrument in question and the style and period of the music. *Staccato* dots within a slur imply a *mezzo-staccato*; a combination of a dot and a horizontal dash indicates accent and separation. *Staccatissimo* indicates extreme detachment. The term is often abbreviated *stacc.*

Staden, Johann (*b* Nuremberg, *bapt*. 2 July 1581; *d* Nuremberg, Nov. 1634). German organist and composer. After service, from about 1604, as court organist at Bayreuth, he returned in 1611 to Nuremberg where, as organist of St Sebald's, he initiated the so-called Nuremberg School. His successors included Johann Kindermann, J. P. Krieger, and Pachelbel. With his *Kirchen-Musik* (1625–6) he was one of the first in Germany to provide sacred concertos for mixed vocal and instrumental resources. His output also includes solo songs, sacred and secular, and numerous individual instrumental compositions—symphonias, sonatas, and dances—which are among the finest of his time.

DA/BS

Stadler, Anton (Paul) (*b* Bruck an der Leitha, 28 June 1753; *d* Vienna, 15 June 1812). Austrian clarinettist and basset-horn player. By 1781 he and his clarinettist brother Johann were playing in the Viennese court wind band. Anton's preference for playing in the lower register inspired his design of a basset clarinet with a downward extension, for which Mozart wrote his concerto and quintet (the instrument did not survive and both works were altered to suit the conventional clarinet). Anton also played the basset horn for Mozart in *La clemenza di Tito* in 1791, and went on to develop a solo career which lasted until 1806. CF

   P. L. POULIN, *Mozart's Clarinettist Anton Stadler: His Life and Times and the Basset Clarinet* (forthcoming)

Stadtpfeifer (Ger., 'town piper'). A professional musician employed by German civic authorities, similar to the British *wait*. *Stadtpfeifer* came into existence in the 14th century, their duties including playing dances, chorales, and signal-pieces, and teaching. A considerable body of *Turmmusik* ('tower music') was composed for them to play from the towers of churches and town halls. Many of the Bach family were town musicians in Thuringia. AL

staff (pl. staves). In musical notation, a number of horizontal lines on and between which musical notes are placed. A *clef placed on the staff indicates the pitch of one line (and, by extension, of all the lines), thus defining the pitch of each note written on the staff. Notes outside the pitch range of the staff are normally given *ledger lines. Since the late Middle Ages a five-line staff has been preferred for most music. Staves may be bracketed together on the left (as in piano music) to form a 'system' (see SCORE).

See also NOTATION, I.

Stainer, Sir John (*b* London, 6 June 1840; *d* Verona, 31 March 1901). English composer, organist, and scholar. A chorister at St Paul's Cathedral, he later studied at Christ Church, Oxford, returning to St Paul's as organist in 1872 after holding similar posts at St Michael's College, Tenbury (1857–60), and Magdalen College, Oxford (1860–72). He oversaw the considerable raising of musical standards at the cathedral and was an influential educationist (as an Inspector of Schools) as well as an able performer. He was principal of the National Training School (1881–2) and was appointed professor of music at Oxford in 1889, having resigned from St Paul's because of bad eyesight. His substantial contribution to Anglican church music includes hymn tunes and some fine anthems, notably *I saw the Lord* (1858), *Drop down, ye heavens* (1866), and *Lead, kindly light* (1868), though he is best known for the oratorio *The Crucifixion* (1887). He edited a series of primers for Novello and, with W. A. Barrett, a *Dictionary of Musical Terms* (1880). A founder member of the (Royal) Musical Association (1874), he was a distinguished scholar, highly respected for his editions of early music manuscripts in the Bodleian Library, Oxford. He was knighted in 1888.   DA/JD1

📖 P. CHARLTON, *John Stainer and the Musical Life of Victorian Britain* (Newton Abbot, 1984)

Stainer & Bell. English firm of music publishers. It was founded in 1907 by a group of young composers to specialize in British music; important names published in the early years included Stanford, Holst, Howells, and Vaughan Williams. Appointed publishers of the Carnegie Collection of British Music in 1917, the firm developed a series of highly regarded scholarly publications, including *The Byrd Edition*, *The English Madrigalists*, *Early English Church Music*, *Music for London Entertainment* and, since 1951, the *Musica britannica* series for the Royal Musical Association.

In 1973 Stainer & Bell acquired the publishers Galliard, Joseph Williams, and Augener, famous for its practical editions of the Classical masters. Publishing activities embrace contemporary hymnody (including the HymnQuest Database), educational tutors and textbooks, jazz publications, organ, instrumental, and orchestral music, and electronic publishing. The firm continues to champion British music and has an extensive archive collection and hire service.   HA

Stamitz, Carl (Philipp) (*b* Mannheim, *bapt.* 8 May 1745; *d* Jena, 9 Nov. 1801). Composer and instrumentalist of Bohemian origin, son of Johann Stamitz. He was brought up at the court of Mannheim and was given his first musical instruction by his father, whose influence, though curtailed by his early death, was doubtless embodied in the teaching of his successors Christian Cannabich, Ignaz Holzbauer, and F. X. Richter. In 1762 Carl became a second violinist in the court orchestra, where he remained until his departure for Paris in 1770. From 1771 he was composer and conductor for the Duke of Noailles, a post that did not preclude successful appearances at the Concert Spirituel (where he played with his brother, Anton) and trips to Vienna, Frankfurt, Augsburg, and Strasbourg.

In 1771 Stamitz began to pursue a somewhat perilous career as an itinerant virtuoso on the violin, viola, and viola d'amore, visiting London and The Hague; in the 1780s he travelled widely in Germany without securing any permanent posts until 1789, when he took charge of a concert series in Kassel for a year. After settling in Greiz for a few years, in 1795 he moved with his family to Jena, where he had a post as Kapellmeister and music teacher. Neither permanent employment nor continued commissions and the sale of compositions were sufficient to keep him out of debt, and his effects had to be auctioned at his death.

With his training at Mannheim Stamitz was well qualified to continue the work of his father. Many features of the Mannheim orchestral style are to be found in his symphonies, and he was especially successful in consolidating the tonal and instrumental contrast of second themes. Like his Italian contemporary Carl Joseph Toeschi he favoured the more old-fashioned three-movement symphony above the increasingly common four-movement type. Less conservative was his interest in slow introductions motivically related to the first movements they preceded, and programmatic elements appear in several symphonies. Along with other Mannheim contemporaries Stamitz cultivated the *symphonie concertante*, composing over 30 such works, mostly for two string instruments. He enriched the repertory of one of his chosen instruments, the viola d'amore, with numerous solo works. If Stamitz's contribution to the development of the symphony was less fundamental than that of his father, the contemporary popularity of his music—much admired for its lyrical qualities—is evident from the wide publication of chamber and orchestral works.   JSM

Stamitz, Johann (Wenzel Anton) [Jan Waczlaw Antonin] (*b* Německý Brod [now Havlíčkův Brod], *bapt.* 19 June 1717; *d* Mannheim, ?27 March, *bur.* 30 March 1757). Bohemian composer and violinist. The most prominent member of a family of musicians, he was the father of the composers Carl and Anton Stamitz (1750–1789 or 1809). His father Antonín Ignác Stamitz, an organist and choirmaster, gave him his first musical instruction. Johann studied at the Jesuit Gymnasium in Jihlava (1728–34), then for a year at university in Prague, and probably spent the next few years as an itinerant violin virtuoso until he settled at the Mannheim court in 1741.

Stamitz's progress went in tandem with the rapid growth in size and proficiency of the Elector Carl Theodor's orchestra. Graduating from first violinist (1743) to Konzertmeister (1745 or 1746), he was made director of instrumental music in 1750, though since 1745 he had been the best-paid member of the orchestra. He spent a year in Paris (1754–5) performing and promoting his compositions, thus forging links between Mannheim and the French capital that were much exploited by later composers including his own sons. His successes led to the publication of the six orchestral trios op. 1 (1755) and to later issues of symphonies in Paris.

At Mannheim, Stamitz fostered the high standards of performance observed by many commentators. His influence on pupils and subordinates was vital in laying the foundation of an orchestral technique which, for its tonal qualities and unanimity, was the envy of Europe. His output comprises orchestral, chamber, and a small amount of church music including a Mass in D much performed in his day. He wrote several violin concertos and a smaller number for wind including probably the first solo clarinet concerto.

The symphonies on which Stamitz's modern reputation rests added a minuet and trio to the standard three-movement Italian sinfonia. They reveal a strong musical personality with occasional hints of his Czech origins (e.g. in the *Sinfonia pastorale* in D op. 4 no. 2). The more spectacular features of his style—the crescendos (probably influenced by Jommelli), bold dynamic effects, and light ornamental figures which so delighted contemporary audiences—often obscure his more lasting contributions to the symphony. Of greater importance was his extension of phrase-lengths, increased contrast of material within movements, an interest in thematic development, and the expansion of finales, innovations which lend justification to Burney's description of the elder Stamitz as 'another Shakespeare ... [who] without quitting nature pushed art further than anyone had done before him'.   JSm

   📖 E. K. Wolf, *The Symphonies of Johann Stamitz: A Study in the Formation of the Classic Style* (Utrecht, 1981)

Stanchinsky, Aleksey Vladimirovich (*b* Obolsunovo, Vladimir province, 9/21 March 1888; *d* nr Logachyovo, Smolensk province, 6 Oct. 1914). Russian composer and pianist. From 1904 he studied the piano privately in Moscow with Josef Lhévinne and Konstantin Eiges, and composition with Nikolay Zhilyayev and Grechaninov. In 1907 he entered the Moscow Conservatory, where he studied with Taneyev. After the death of his father in 1908 he began to suffer hallucinations and developed religious mania; his health remained tenuous thereafter, but as he returned to composing after a year in a psychiatric clinic he shook off the influences discernible in his earlier works and found a more individual voice, through which he acquired a circle of admirers in Moscow. In 1910 he made a collection of traditional music in Smolensk province. The circumstances of his death near a river four years later remain unresolved. He composed mainly for the piano, his works including two sets of *Sketches* (1911–?1913) and *Three Preludes in Canon Form* (1913–14).   JK

Ständchen (Ger.). *'Serenade'.

Standford, Patric [Gledhill, John Patrick Standford] (*b* Barnsley, 5 Feb. 1939). English composer. His main teachers were Edmund Rubbra, G. F. Malipiero, and Lutosławski, and his style has absorbed a correspondingly wide range of sympathies, including Japanese music (Symphony no. 4, 1975) as well as the religious impulses reflected in an extensive sequence of choral works. Standford has made effective use of aleatory techniques (*Notte* for chamber orchestra, 1968) as well as quotation and reworking, for example in *New Messiah* (1992), an oratorio after Handel. He has a substantial number of symphonic and chamber compositions to his credit, and in 1996 he completed an opera on François Villon.   AW

standing wave. The interference pattern formed when a sound wave is reflected back along its original path; it comprises a series of peaks and troughs of sound energy at multiples of a quarter-wavelength from the reflecting surface. See ACOUSTICS, 10; ARCHITECTURAL ACOUSTICS, 5.   JBo

Stanford, Sir Charles Villiers (*b* Dublin, 30 Sept. 1852; *d* London, 29 March 1924). Irish composer, teacher, and conductor. The son of a Protestant lawyer who was a talented bass and cellist, he studied in Dublin and London before entering Queens' College, Cambridge, in 1870 as organ scholar. In 1873 he became conductor of the Cambridge University Musical Society and moved to Trinity College, being appointed organist in 1874 and remaining in that post until 1892. From 1874 to 1876 he spent the second half of each year studying in Germany, first in Leipzig with Carl Reinecke, then with Friedrich Kiel in Berlin (1876).

On returning to Cambridge in 1877 Stanford had already established a reputation with his settings of George Eliot's *The Spanish Gypsy* op. 1, some piano pieces, his First Symphony, and incidental music for Tennyson's *Queen Mary*. The climax of these early years were his operas *The Veiled Prophet of Khorassan* (Hanover, 1881), *Savonarola* (Hamburg, 1884), and *The Canterbury Pilgrims* (Drury Lane, 1884) for Carl Rosa. In 1883 he was appointed professor of composition at the newly founded Royal College of Music, and four years later he succeeded Macfarren as professor of music at Cambridge. His list of famous pupils at both institutions remains unrivalled. His aspirations as a conductor were rewarded with posts at the RCM, the London Bach Choir (1886–1902), the Leeds Philharmonic (1897–1909), and the Leeds Triennial Festival (1901–10).

Among Stanford's chief successes as a composer were his choral ballad *The Revenge* (1886), the opera *Shamus*

O'Brien (London, 1896), his Violin Concerto (played by Kreisler), the *Irish Rhapsodies* nos. 1 and 4, and his two stirring groups of Henry Newbolt settings, *Songs of the Sea* (1904) and *Songs of the Fleet* (1910), but he achieved renown principally through his substantial contribution to the music of the Anglican Church. His greatest desire, however, was to be an opera composer. He was knighted in 1902. He is buried in Westminster Abbey next to Purcell. DA/JD1

📖 H. P. GREENE, *Charles Villiers Stanford* (London, 1935) · G. NORRIS, *Stanford, the Cambridge Jubilee and Tchaikovsky* (Newton Abbot, 1980)

Stanley, John (*b* London, 17 Jan. 1712; *d* London, 19 May 1786). English organist and composer. The son of a Post Office official, he was accidentally blinded at the age of two. He was a pupil of Maurice Greene, with whom, according to Burney, 'he studied with great diligence and a success that was astonishing'. By the age of nine he was deputizing as organist at All Hallows, Bread Street, and in 1723 he succeeded William Babell as organist there. A contemporary newspaper report described him as one who 'is become the surprise of the Town for his ingenious performance on the Harpsichord and Organ'. Three years later Stanley became organist of St Andrew's, Holborn, and in 1734 of the Inner Temple. He took the degree of B.Mus. at Oxford when he was 17—the youngest person ever to do so. After Handel died Stanley and J. C. Smith the younger directed the oratorio seasons at Covent Garden and Drury Lane. Seven years before his death Stanley succeeded Boyce as Master of the King's Music.

According to Burney, Stanley was a 'neat, pleasing, and accurate performer, ... a natural and agreeable composer, and an intelligent instructor'. He composed music for several dramatic pieces, including the pastoral *Arcadia, or The Shepherd's Wedding* (1761) for the marriage of George III and Queen Charlotte, the opera *Teraminta* (not performed), and three oratorios. He published three sets of organ voluntaries, and other instrumental music including a fine set of concerti grossi and six keyboard concertos. WT/PL

stark (Ger.). 'Strong', 'loud'; *stärker*, 'stronger', 'louder'; *stärker werdend*, 'becoming louder'; *stark anblasen*, *stark blasend*, 'strongly blown' (in playing wind instruments).

Starlight Express, The. Incidental music by Elgar for Violet Pearn's play based on Algernon Blackwood's *A Prisoner in Fairyland* (London, 1915).

Star-Spangled Banner, The ('O say, can you see by the dawn's early light?'). National anthem of the USA. The music is by John Stafford Smith (1750–1836) and the words are by Francis Scott Key (1779–1843), who wrote them in 1814 on board a British frigate in Baltimore Harbour as he watched the British bombardment of Fort McHenry. Smith's melody, to which Key created his verses, was sung in Anacreontic societies in England and the USA to the words 'To Anacreon in Heaven'. It was adopted as the American national anthem in 1831. AL

📖 W. P. FILBY and E. G. HOWARD, *Star-Spangled Books: Books, Sheet Music, Newspapers, Manuscripts and Persons associated with 'The Star-Spangled Banner'* (Baltimore, 1972)

stave. Alternative term for *staff, erroneously coined from 'staves', the plural of 'staff'.

steel band. An orchestra of tuned percussion instruments ('steel pans' or 'steel drums'), usually accompanied by a selection of other rhythm instruments. It originated in Trinidad in the 1930s and 40s as a band for carnival processions and parades.

Steel pans were originally adapted from oil drums and other metal containers but are now precision-tuned instruments, professionally manufactured. The sides of the oil drums are cut off at the required depth and the top of each drum is beaten into a bowl shape with a sledge hammer and then marked out into separate areas. Each area is isolated by hammering grooves along the marked lines with a punch and tuned by hammering it up from inside the pan. The tone-quality is much enhanced by the fact that each area is not completely isolated from its neighbours and some vibrations carry across the grooves, producing the characteristic shimmer and vibrato. Some makers temper the steel by heating it. The beaters used must be light, because beating too heavily throws the domed areas out of tune. The use of tremolo and rapid arpeggiation makes sustained melodies possible.

Pans are made in many sizes. The tenor pan (known as the 'lead pan' in the USA) is the highest pitched. It is fashioned from a single drum and has a fully chromatic compass of c' or d' to e''', f''', $f\sharp'''$, or g'''. The 'double seconds' and 'double tenor' pans are played in pairs and usually tuned in whole tones. Their function in the steel band is similar to that of the second violins in the orchestra, though the double tenors often double the tenors at the lower octave; their compass is f to $b\flat''$ or d'''. 'Guitar pans' are usually found in pairs, though triple guitars are also common. The compass of the double guitar pan is d to f or d''. 'Cello pans' are played in sets of three or four; triple cello pans are tuned in diminished chords, and four-pan cellos in augmented chords. They have a compass of about three octaves. The basses, full-sized oil drums which stand upright on rubber or wooden feet, come in sets of five, six, nine, or 12; each has three or four notes, and the complete set has a compass of one-and-a-half to two octaves.

As well as playing the traditional repertory of calypso and other local music, and arrangements of all kinds of music from orchestral standards to film music and popular hits, steel pans have been used by composers including Henze, Boulez, and Grisey.   JMo

📖 F. I. R. BLAKE, *The Trinidad and Tobago Steel Pan* (Port of Spain, 1995) · S. STUEMPFLE, *The Steelband Movement* (Philadelphia, 1995)

steel drum [steel pan, pan]. Tuned drums (*idiophones) traditionally made from old oil drums but today usually purpose-made of high-quality steel. See STEEL BAND.

steel guitar. A variant of the *Hawaiian guitar.

Steffani, Agostino (*b* Castelfranco, Veneto, 25 July 1654; *d* Frankfurt, 12 Feb. 1728). Italian composer. Born of poor parents, he was educated at Padua; when he was 13 his voice earned him a position with Elector Ferdinand Maria of Bavaria, who took him back to Munich. There Steffani was placed in the custody of Kerll, the court Kapellmeister, and provided with a thorough musical training. In 1672 he went to Rome to study with Ercole Bernabei, who became Kapellmeister to the Munich court in 1674, taking the younger man with him. Steffani was appointed court organist and in 1680 was ordained priest, but his main occupation in those years was the composition of operas, in a style that shows the influence of Legrenzi and other Venetians. In 1688 he was disappointed in his expectation of succeeding Bernabei (whose son was appointed) and left Munich for Hanover, where he was Kapellmeister to the newly opened Italian opera theatre.

Although he continued to compose operas and other works, Steffani spent much of his later life travelling round Europe as a diplomat and ambassador. He was also appointed Bishop of Spiga in Asia Minor. During a period in Rome (1708–9) he met Handel, who was much influenced by Steffani's attractive chamber duets to Italian texts. His work was also known in England, especially after the coronation of the Elector of Hanover as George I, and in 1727 he was made honorary president of the Academy of Vocal Music (later to become the Academy of Ancient Music). He did much to popularize opera in northern Europe, combining the Venetian idiom with elements of the French style, and the instrumental music from six of his Hanover operas was published by Roger as *Sonate da camera*. Besides the operas, the numerous chamber duets epitomize his powerfully eloquent style, combining subtle counterpoint and expressive melody in perfectly balanced formal structures. There is also a small quantity of church music.   DA/PA

Steg (Ger.). 'Bridge'.

Steibelt, Daniel (Gottlieb) (*b* Berlin, 22 Oct. 1765; *d* St Petersburg, 20 Sept./2 Oct. 1823). German-born French composer and pianist. He had a successful career as a pianist in Paris and London and first performed his celebrated Third Piano Concerto ('L'Orage') at one of Salomon's concerts in London in 1798. His compositions from this period include a number of stage works and the popular *Étude* op. 78. In 1808 he settled in St Petersburg at the invitation of Alexander I, directing the French Opera and from 1810 acting as *maître de chapelle*. He met and became friendly with John Field and continued to compose operas and a great deal of frequently innovatory piano music.   DA/SH

Steinway. American firm of piano makers founded in New York in 1853 by Heinrich Engelhard Steinway (originally Steinweg; 1797–1871). At the 1855 New York World Fair he exhibited an overstrung, iron-framed instrument capable of much greater sonority than had ever been produced. Heinrich's son Theodore (1825–89) joined the firm in the 1860s and introduced technological developments that led to the design of the concert grands which became internationally famous. His brother William (1835–96) travelled widely, demonstrating the instruments and acquiring support from leading pianists and court patronage; branches were opened in Hamburg and London. The most commonly used piano on the concert platform continues to be made by Steinway.   AL

📖 R. V. RATCLIFFE, *Steinway and Sons* (San Francisco, 1989) · R. K. LIEBERMAN, *Steinway & Sons* (New Haven, CT, 1995)

stendendo (It.). 'Stretching out', i.e. slowing.

Stenhammar, (Karl) Wilhelm (Eugen) (*b* Stockholm, 7 Feb. 1871; *d* Stockholm, 20 Nov. 1927). Swedish composer, pianist, and conductor. Born into a musical upper-class family, he showed early promise as both composer and pianist. He had private tuition in the organ, piano, and theory, but as a composer he was self-taught until he was well into his 20s, when he began a nine-year private course in counterpoint, prompted by a crisis of confidence—this in spite of his early successes as a composer. He made his conducting debut (1897) with the premiere of his overture *Excelsior!*, which has remained in the repertory. His greatest triumphs as a conductor came in his years as chief conductor of the newly formed Göteborg Symphony Orchestra (1906–22), during which the city was transformed into an important Nordic musical centre.

Stenhammar's earlier works were heavily influenced by Wagner, Bruckner, Liszt, and Brahms, but a deepening appreciation of Beethoven and Haydn, combined with admiration for Nielsen and Sibelius, helped him to develop a leaner, more concentrated symphonic style, evident in the Second Piano Concerto (1907), the Second Symphony (1915), and the last three of his six string quartets. Stenhammar expressed his passionate nationalist feelings in his cantatas *Ett folk* ('One People', 1905) and *Sången* ('The Song', 1921), both of which have remained popular in Sweden. He also composed a large number of fine solo songs.

SJ

stentando (It.). 'Labouring', 'holding back'; *stentato*, 'laboured'; i.e. held back with every note stressed; *stentamento*, 'laboriously', 'slowly'.

Štěpán [Stephen, Stephani], **Josef Antonín** (*b* Kopidlno, Bohemia, *bapt.* 14 March 1726; *d* Vienna, 12 April 1797). Czech composer, teacher, and keyboard player. He studied with Wagenseil in Vienna, settling there in 1741 and developing a reputation as a keyboard virtuoso and teacher. He wrote some three collections of lieder, but his solo keyboard works and keyboard concertos are of greater importance. The later sonatas and capriccios (1770s–90s) stand out from those of his contemporaries and did much to further the development of the Classical solo sonata. Notable features are several effective minor-key introductions, a practice he adopted for some of his concertos. Štěpán's occasional use of programmatic elements and thematic integration between movements indicate a more than passing interest in formal experiment.

JSM

Steptoe, Roger (*b* Winchester, 25 Jan. 1953). English composer and pianist. He studied with Alan Bush at the RAM before becoming the first composer-in-residence at Charterhouse school. He later taught at the RAM, and was director of the European Discoveries festivals in Clerkenwell, London. Steptoe's music, essentially in the English pastoral tradition, includes an opera, concertos and other orchestral works, chamber music, and much music for voices.

ABUR

sterbend (Ger.). 'Dying away'.

Sterndale Bennett, Sir William (*b* Sheffield, 13 April 1816; *d* London, 1 Feb. 1875). English composer. For a brief period in the 1830s he enjoyed a high reputation in the Germany of Mendelssohn and Schumann. He was the son of the organist of Sheffield parish church but was orphaned when three years old and was brought up in Cambridge, where he was a King's chorister. In 1826 he was admitted 'as a prodigy' to the RAM, studying the violin, piano, and composition (with William Crotch). Soon his brilliance as a pianist became well known, and a piano concerto he wrote in 1832, when Cipriani Potter had become his teacher, earned him an invitation to Germany from Mendelssohn.

In the next six years Sterndale Bennett composed five more concertos, several symphonies, and songs and piano pieces; Schumann expressed intense admiration for his work. But after about 1840 he found it hard to complete his compositions and concentrated on conducting, playing, and teaching. He became professor of music at Cambridge University in 1856, instituting examinations (instead of 'exercises') for the music degrees, and principal of the RAM in 1866. He was knighted in 1871. In his last years he regained his flair for composing, writing a cantata *The May Queen* (1858), *The Woman of Samaria* (1867), and a new symphony (1864). He also edited works by Bach and Handel.

MK

steso (It.). 'Extended', 'stretched', i.e. slow.

stesso, stessa (It.). 'Same'; e.g. *lo stesso tempo*, *l'istesso tempo*, 'the same tempo', usually meaning that although the nominal value of the beat has changed (e.g. from a crotchet to a dotted crotchet), its duration is to remain the same.

Stevens, Bernard (George) (*b* London, 2 March 1916; *d* Great Maplestead, 1983). English composer. He studied with Edward Dent and Cyril Rootham at Cambridge (1935–7), and with R. O. Morris and Gordon Jacob at the RCM (1937–40). After service in the war he joined the Workers' Musical Association (1946), impelled by his socialist principles. His compositions drew on the European mainstream tradition represented by such composers as Hindemith, and include orchestral works, choral music, and songs.

PG

Stevens, Richard John Samuel (*b* London, 27 March 1757; *d* London, 23 Sept. 1837). English composer. A chorister at St Paul's Cathedral, he held various organist appointments at London churches including St Michael's, Cornhill (1781), the Temple Church (1786), and the Charterhouse (1796). He was also Gresham Professor of Music from 1801 and music master at Christ's Hospital from 1808. He is known chiefly for his polished glee settings, particularly of Shakespearean texts, the best of which rank with those of the elder Samuel Webbe and J. W. Callcott. He also assembled a considerable library (now in the RAM) with an emphasis on 17th- and 18th-century Italian music.

JD1

Stevenson, Ronald (*b* Blackburn, 6 March 1928). Scottish composer, pianist, and author. One of the most prolific and individual of modern Scottish composers, he is also a virtuoso pianist of great musical and technical command and a writer of wide intellectual interests. He is an expert on the music of Busoni, whose compositions and pianistic approach profoundly influenced him. His most ambitious work, the *Passacaglia on DSCH*, is a single movement well over an hour in length, displaying his interest in fugal structures, traditional musics from many parts of the world, and illustrative music, as well as a fascination with dramatic contrast and tonal variety. Other significant pieces include two piano concertos and a dramatic Violin Concerto (commissioned by Menuhin). Stevenson is also a notable exponent of the art of piano transcription.   KH

  📖 M. MacDonald, *Ronald Stevenson: A Musical Biography* (Edinburgh, 1989)

stick. See BEATER.

Stierhorn (Ger., 'cowhorn', 'oxhorn'). A bovine signalling horn of antiquity and the Middle Ages. A brass version of this instrument is called for in Wagner's *Ring*.

Stiffelio. Opera in three acts by Verdi to a libretto by Francesco Maria Piave after Émile Souvestre and Eugène Bourgeois's play *Le Pasteur, ou L'Évangile et le foyer* (1849) (Trieste, 1850).

stile antico (It., 'old style'). One of the terms frequently applied to 17th-century church music written in the style of Palestrina, with smooth, flowing polyphony and scored *a cappella* (rather than in *stile moderno*—for a few voices with continuo accompaniment). It became fashionable for composers to write certain kinds of church music in the *stile antico*, even though they might use the *stile moderno* in other works; Mass music, for example, was frequently unaccompanied and less directly expressive than were motets. See also ALLA PALESTRINA; PALESTRINA, GIOVANNI PIERLUIGI DA, 2.

stile concitato (It., 'agitated style'). A term used by Monteverdi in the preface to his *Madrigali guerrieri ed amorosi* (1638), in his discussion of the three main styles (*generi*) of music. Monteverdi named these three styles as *concitato*, *molle*, and *temperato*, which he equated with 'anger, moderation, and humility or supplication' respectively. He aimed to recreate the least common of these, the *genere concitato*, referring to Plato's definition of it as a style that would 'stir people to war'. His musical realization of this style, in such works as *Combattimento di Tancredi, e Clorinda*, involved using high vocal ranges and repeated semiquavers (representing ancient Greek pyrrhic rhythms). After Monteverdi, later Baroque composers including Alessandro Grandi and Handel made occasional use of this style to set passages of text describing battles or fighting.   —/EW

stile moderno (It., 'modern style'). See STILE ANTICO.

stile rappresentativo (It., 'representative style'). A term that first appeared in print in Caccini's opera *Euridice* (1600), which the composer described as being written 'in stile rappresentativo'—a reference to the new dramatic style of writing for the voice which was developed by members of the Florentine *Camerata, notably Vincenzo Galilei, as an attempt to match in emotional power the music of the ancient Greeks; Caccini wrote about it more fully in his collection of monodic songs *Le nuove musiche* (1602). Some music written in the style survives from Peri's opera *Dafne* (composed in 1594), and Cavalieri adopted it in his *Rappresentatione di Anima, et di Corpo* (1600).

While it is hard to define the term precisely, music in *stile rappresentativo* is recitative-like and characteristically free in rhythm and phrasing, following the stresses of the text it sets; such devices as frequent pauses and unusual intervals are used for emotional effect. The term also occurs in early 17th-century non-theatrical music, for example madrigals and solo songs, in which the same dramatic and expressive qualities are found.

See also MONODY, 2.   —/EW

Still, William Grant (*b* Woodville, MS, 11 May 1895; *d* Los Angeles, 3 Dec. 1978). American composer. He was a student at Wilberforce College and Oberlin Conservatory, and later studied composition with Varèse and George W. Chadwick. In the 1920s he settled in New York and played in dance and theatre orchestras, worked for W. C. Handy's publishing firm and the Black Swan Phonograph Company, and arranged and composed for radio. At the same time he began writing large-scale compositions. The first of these to win recognition was the *Afro-American Symphony*, which was given its premiere by the Rochester Philharmonic under Howard Hanson in 1931 and remains his best-known work. During the next 40 years or so a steady stream of compositions and nearly as many prizes, awards, and honorary degrees earned Still the sobriquet 'Dean of Negro Composers'.

His music tends towards a conservative, tonal style; it is often attractive, well constructed, lyrical, and readily accessible. Besides his operas, symphonies, sacred music, and many instrumental works, Still also composed popular songs, arranged spirituals, wrote for films and television, and conducted. His work in art music helped break new ground for other black composers, but his contribution to American musical life is better gauged by considering his sustained involvement in a wide range of musical styles and contexts.   MT

  📖 J. A. STILL, M. J. DABRISHUS, and C. L. QUIN (eds.), *William Grant Still: A Bio-Bibliography* (Westport, CT, 1996) · C. P. SMITH, *William Grant Still: A Study in Contradictions* (Berkeley, CA, 1999)

Stimme (Ger.). 'Voice', including in the sense of a vocal or instrumental part; it also means 'organ stop' and 'soundpost' (on a stringed instrument). The plural is *Stimmen*.

stimmen (Ger.). 'To tune'.

Stimmung (Ger.). 1. 'Mood'; hence *Stimmungsbild*, a piece of music expressing a particular mood, and *Stimmungsmusik*, 'background' or 'mood' music.

2. 'Tuning'.

3. Work (1968) by Stockhausen for two sopranos, mezzo-soprano, tenor, baritone, and bass; the six unaccompanied singers, each with a microphone, vocalize without words for 75 minutes.

sting. A 17th-century English term used for the normal vibrato in lute playing, i.e. that produced by the motion of one finger alone.

stinguendo (It.). 'Extinguishing', i.e. fading out.

stirando, stirato, stiracciando, stiracchiato (It.). 'Stretching', 'stretched', i.e. expanding by means of a **ritardando*.

stochastic music (from Gk. *stokhos*, 'aim'). Originally a mathematical term, a 'stochastic process' being one whose goal can be described but whose individual details are unpredictable. In music, it refers to composition by the use of the laws of probability. By contrast with **indeterminate music, stochastic music is fully composed: chance enters only into the process of composition, the composer perhaps allowing the distribution of pitches, for example, to be determined by some concept from the mathematics of probability. Stochastic techniques, which often depend on the use of a computer to calculate distributions, can be useful in the creation of sound masses where the details are less important than the large-scale effect. The word was introduced into the musical vocabulary by Xenakis, much of whose music is stochastic.   PG

Stockhausen, Julius (*b* Paris, 22 July 1826; *d* Frankfurt, 22 Sept. 1906). German baritone and conductor of Alsatian descent. From a musical family, he learnt several instruments and studied in Paris, then took singing lessons with the younger Manuel García. From 1856 to 1859 he was a member of the Opéra-Comique, Paris. In 1848 he sang in Mendelssohn's *Elijah* in Basle. During the 1850s he became established as a lieder performer, giving the first public performance of Schubert's *Die schöne Müllerin* (Vienna, 1856). That year he met Brahms, with whom he formed a close friendship. They performed together many times, and Brahms composed the *Magelone Lieder* for him; he also sang in the premiere of Brahms's *A German Requiem*. In 1880 he founded a school of singing and published a two-volume singing method (1886–7). He was one of

the first artists to establish the popularity of songs by Schubert and Schumann.   JT

Stockhausen, Karlheinz (*b* Burg Mödrath, nr Cologne, 22 Aug. 1928). German composer. He studied at the Cologne Conservatory (1947–51) with Hans Otto Schmidt-Neuhaus for piano, Hermann Schroeder for harmony and counterpoint, and Frank Martin for composition. In 1951 he attended the Darmstadt summer courses, where he was impressed by Karel Goeyvaerts's essays in applying serial methods to rhythm and also by Messiaen's *Mode de valeurs et d'intensités* (1949), which uses scales of rhythmic values and dynamic levels. Drawing his own conclusions from these examples, he quickly wrote *Kreuzspiel* for oboe, bass clarinet, piano, and percussion, and *Formel* for orchestra (both 1951). In 1952 he went to Paris, where he studied with Messiaen and worked in Pierre Schaeffer's *musique concrète* studio. He then returned to Cologne, where he completed *Kontra-Punkte* for ten instruments (1952–3), the first work he acknowledges as mature.

Within a short period Stockhausen had thus established himself, along with Pierre Boulez, as a leader in the attempt to create a new musical language along strictly serial lines (see SERIALISM), and to each new work he brought a fresh view of musical possibilities. In the two electronic *Studien* (1953–4), composed at the newly founded studio in Cologne, he tried to synthesize timbres from pure tones; in *Zeitmasze* for five woodwind (1955–6) he integrated strict with variable tempos; in *Gruppen* for three orchestras (1955–7) he added acoustic space to the composer's repertory of means; and in *Gesang der Jünglinge* on tape (1955–6) he achieved a full union of music and language.

In his next electronic work, the four-channel *Kontakte* (1958–60), Stockhausen chose to tackle complex sounds that did not lend themselves to the serial methods and the complex formal schemes of earlier works, and accordingly he introduced more empirical techniques; the heard quality of sound, rather than its symbolic representation, became the prime consideration. Stockhausen had always been an acute judge of acoustic effectiveness, but now the composition and relation of timbres became increasingly important. This is the case in *Momente* for soprano, chorus, and instruments (1961–72) and in various works in which Stockhausen applied electronic transformation to musical performance: *Mixtur* for modulated orchestra (1964), *Mikrophonie I* for tam-tam and microphones (1964), and *Mikrophonie II* for modulated chorus, Hammond organ, and tape (1965). There followed two tape pieces, *Telemusik* (1966) and *Hymnen* (1966–7), in which he integrated recordings of music from around the world, as well as several works, including *Prozession* (1967) and *Kurzwellen* (1968), for his own ensemble of musicians using natural and electronic instruments. His experience with this group led to his allowing a large degree of freedom to the performer, especially in *Aus den sieben Tagen* (1968), a set of prose poems intended to stimulate the musician's intuition.

With *Mantra* for two pianos and electronics (1969–70) Stockhausen entered a new phase, basing each work on one or more haunting melodies. Sometimes, as in *Mantra* or *Inori* for dancer and orchestra (1973–4), the result is a massive, continuous development; in other works, such as *Musik im Bauch* for six percussionists (1975), the emphasis is on the ritual enactment of a musical fable. The orchestral *Trans* (1971) combines musical strength with dramatic effectiveness, having the strings alone visible, placed behind a gauze and bathed in violet light, while the other sections are heard from behind.

The natural next step was opera, and Stockhausen took it in a typically grandiose manner, embarking in 1977 on *Licht*, a cycle of seven operas for the days of the week: *Donnerstag* (1981), *Samstag* (1984), *Montag* (1988), *Dienstag* (1993), *Freitag* (1996), *Mittwoch*, and *Sonntag*. Each is a mosaic of self-sufficient scenes for various combinations of singers, instrumentalists, and dancers, often with electronic means, and the libretto is a collage of autobiography and myth. Large roles are assigned to members of the composer's entourage, especially his sons Markus (trumpet) and Simon (electronic keyboards) and his regular companions Suzanne Stephens (basset horn) and Kathinka Pasveer (flute), all appearing on stage in costume.

From the early 1950s to the end of the 1970s Stockhausen had an enormous influence on younger composers, and he travelled the world lecturing and performing. Few of his admirers, however, were able to follow him into *Licht*.   PG

📖 K. H. WÖRNER, *Stockhausen: Life and Work* (London, 1973) · J. COTT, *Stockhausen: Conversations with the Composer* (London, 1974) · J. HARVEY, *The Music of Stockhausen* (London, 1975) · R. MACONIE, *The Works of Karlheinz Stockhausen* (London, 1976, 2/1990) · K. STOCKHAUSEN, *Towards a Cosmic Music*, ed. T. Nevill (Longmead, Dorset, 1989) · M. KURTZ, *Karlheinz Stockhausen: A Biography* (London, 1991) · R. MACONIE (ed.), *Stockhausen on Music* (London, 1991)

Stokowski, Leopold (Anthony) (*b* London, 18 April 1882; *d* Nether Wallop, 13 Sept. 1977). English-born American conductor. He studied at Oxford University and the RCM and became organist of St James's, Piccadilly, in 1900. Self-taught as a conductor, he made his debut in Paris with the Colonne Orchestra in 1909. That year he was appointed principal conductor of the Cincinnati Orchestra. In 1912 he began his 24-year directorship of the Philadelphia Orchestra, which achieved international fame for its virtuosity, brilliance, and rich sonorities. He introduced many important works to the USA, including Stravinsky's *The Rite of Spring*, Mahler's Symphony no. 8, Berg's *Wozzeck*, and Schoenberg's *Gurrelieder*. In 1961 he conducted Puccini's *Turandot* at the Metropolitan Opera, New York.

Flamboyant on the podium, Stokowski took many liberties with scores, feeling that the performer should be free to experiment and to look for possibilities beyond the written notes. His fame spread to the cinema, where he took part in a number of films, notably *Fantasia* (1940), the original experiment with cartoons which he and Walt Disney conceived. He was devoted to the broad popularization of music, and was a master of colourful sound. He made transcriptions of Bach for symphony orchestra.   JT

📖 P. OPPERBY, *Leopold Stokowski* (Tunbridge Wells and New York, 1982) · W. A. SMITH, *The Mystery of Leopold Stokowski* (Cranbury, NJ, 1990)

Stollen (Ger.). The first strophe, which is then repeated, of *Bar form.

Stoltzer, Thomas (*b* Schweidnitz, Silesia [now Świdnica, Poland], *c*.1480; *d* nr Znaim, Moravia [now Znojmo, Czech Republic], early 1526). German church musician and composer. From 1522 until his death he was *magister capellae* at the Hungarian court in Ofen (now Budapest). His early work owes a debt to Heinrich Finck, with whom he may have studied; motets and Roman Catholic liturgical music predominate. Latterly he turned to writing German-texted psalm settings and sacred songs, and became one of the pioneer composers of the Lutheran Reformation. His music circulated widely in print.   JM

Stölzel, Gottfried Heinrich (*b* Grünstädtel, Harz Mountains, 13 Jan. 1690; *d* Gotha, 27 Nov. 1749). German composer. After studying theology at Leipzig University, he settled in Breslau for three years (from 1710) as a music teacher before travelling to Venice (where he met Vivaldi), Florence, and Prague. In 1720, after failing to secure a post at Sondershausen, he was appointed Kapellmeister to the Saxe-Gotha court, where he remained until his death. A prolific composer in virtually all the genres of his time, he produced over 1000 cantatas, several Passions, a *Missa canonica* (based on a similar work by Fux), an 'Enharmonic Sonata' (exploring the new tunings which led to Bach's '48'), and many stage works. Bach included a partita by him in the *Clavier-Büchlein* for W. F. Bach; and it is now generally believed that the famous song *Bist du bei mir* found in Bach's Anna Magdalena book is by Stölzel.   DA/BS

stomp. A percussive and lively form of jazz in which the melodic pattern is closely followed and underlined by block chords in the same rhythm, creating a generally forceful character. The New Orleans pianist-composer Jelly Roll Morton wrote classics in the genre—*Black Bottom Stomp*, *King Porter Stomp*, and *Kansas City Stomp*. Some pieces in similarly driving *boogie-woogie style have also been called stomps.

PGA

Stone Guest, The (*Kamennïy gost'*). Opera in three acts by Dargomïzhsky, a setting of Aleksandr Pushkin's play (1830) on the Don Juan story; begun in the 1860s and nearly finished at the time of the composer's death, it was completed by Cui and orchestrated by Rimsky-Korsakov (St Petersburg, 1872).

stopped notes. 1. Notes produced on stringed instruments by the application of finger pressure on the string against the fingerboard. See STOPPING.

2. Notes produced on the horn by inserting the right hand in the bell, shortening the tube and thus raising the pitch, typically by a semitone. The technique was used on early, valveless horns to play notes outside the harmonic series, but tone-quality suffered. On modern instruments, hand-stopping, notated with the sign '+', is used purely for effect.

SM

stopping. In string playing, the placing of the fingertips of the left hand on the string (usually on the fingerboard). As the vibrating length of the string is progressively shortened, higher-pitched notes result. Double stopping is the stopping of and playing on two strings at a time. However, the term can also be applied more generally, to indicate that two notes are bowed simultaneously, whether or not they are stopped. Similarly, multiple stopping indicates the playing of more than two (and up to four) notes or strings together, either stopped or unstopped. See also STOPPED NOTES.

DM1

stops. See ORGAN.

Storace, Stephen (John Seymour) (*b* London, 4 April 1762; *d* London, 19 March 1796). English composer of Italian extraction. At the age of 14 he was sent to study in Italy, where he met the tenor Michael Kelly. Having returned to England, he published in London (1782) one of the first collections of canzonets (chamber songs) with an independent piano accompaniment. He joined his sister, the soprano Nancy Storace, in Vienna and became Mozart's friend—though not, as is sometimes stated, his pupil. Storace composed two moderately successful *opere buffe* for the Vienna Burgtheater, *Gli sposi malcontenti* (1785) and, perhaps his

greatest work, the ripely comic and richly orchestrated *Gli equivoci* (1786), to a libretto by Lorenzo Da Ponte based on Shakespeare's *The Comedy of Errors*.

Despite the favour of the emperor (who rescued him from an awkward situation when he was drunk), Storace returned to London with Nancy and Kelly and plunged into a ceaseless round of activity in the theatre, becoming a major figure in the attempted revival of English-language opera. His main output consisted of 'dialogue operas', of which the most successful are *The Haunted Tower* (1789), *No Song, No Supper* (1790), and *The Pirates* (1792). In several works he recycled his own and others' Viennese music. English theatre traditions required him to participate in works of multiple authorship to assist productivity; he appears to have worn himself out by exertions that did not always bring the recognition and opportunity his talents deserved.

RL/JR

📖 R. FISKE, *English Theatre Music in the Eighteenth Century* (London, 1973, 2/1986) · J. GIRDHAM, *English Opera in Late Eighteenth-Century London: Stephen Storace at Drury Lane* (Oxford, 1997)

Stradella, Alessandro (*b* Nepi, 3 April 1639; *d* Genoa, 25 Feb. 1682). Italian composer. His undeniably colourful life has been much sensationalized as the subject of a number of Romantic operas. He spent some time in Bologna in his youth, but no evidence associates him with the city's musicians. He had moved to Rome with his mother by 1653, establishing himself as a leading composer after 1667 and attracting the attention of such wealthy patrons as ex-Queen Christina of Sweden. In 1677 he became involved, not for the first time, in a scandal over women and money and left precipitately for Venice, where the powerful nobleman Alvise Contarini engaged him as music master to his mistress. Stradella soon made off with her to Turin, pursued by Contarini, and another hasty departure, this time to Genoa, seemed propitious. In this he was gravely mistaken, for he was assassinated by an equally powerful Genoese family, the Lomellini, again it seems over the honour of a woman.

Stradella was a prolific composer of operas, church music, oratorios, madrigals, and instrumental music, but by far his largest contribution was in the realm of the chamber cantata, of which he wrote no fewer than 125 for solo voice and continuo. His instrumental music is noteworthy for its use of concerto grosso scorings contrasting solo and tutti, while the sonatas are among the most ambitious of his day. His oratorios enjoyed much popularity at Modena, and it is partly due to the purchase of many of Stradella's scores after his death for the ducal library that so much of his music survives.

DA/PA

📖 C. GIANTURCO, *Alessandro Stradella (1639–1682): His Life and Music* (Oxford, 1994)

Stradivari, Antonio (*b* ?Cremona, 1644; *d* Cremona, 18 Dec. 1737). Italian violin maker, widely regarded as the greatest ever. He learnt his craft from Nicola *Amati and made his first violin in 1666. From 1680 he worked independently, and in the 1690s he developed a longer design with bolder features—soundholes, arching, etc. The years 1700–20 were Stradivari's 'golden era' when he produced a series of magnificent instruments (including cellos and violas) of exquisite tone and great beauty, distinctive for their soft-textured varnish shading from orange to red; his fine craftsmanship, of the pegs, fingerboards, and patterned inlays, extended to the bows and cases. He made his last violin when he was 92. About 650 of his instruments survive, many known by the names of past owners, for example the 'Betts' (1704), the 'Alard' (1715), the 'Sarasate' (1724); they are used by the world's leading players. Stradivari's sons Francesco (1671–1743) and Omobono (1679–1742) assisted him and their instruments have sometimes been passed off as their father's: authenticity is a controversial subject, given the extraordinary prices paid for a genuine 'Strad'.   AB/AL

📖 W. H., A. F., and A. E. HILL, *Antonio Stradivari: His Life and Work* (London, 1902/R1963, 2/1909) · E. SANTORO, *Antonius Stradivarius* (Cremona, 1987) · C. CHIESA and D. ROSENGARD, *The Stradivari Legacy* (London, 1998)

straff, straffer (Ger.). 'Strict', 'tight', 'stricter', 'tighter'; *straffen*, 'tighten' (e.g. a drum-head).

strambotto (It.). A type of strophic poem set in Renaissance Italy by composers of *frottolas and madrigals. Each verse had eight lines of 11 syllables, and the most common rhyme scheme was abababcc. Frottola composers generally set the first two lines of a *strambotto* to two musical phrases, and then repeated these for each of the following couplets; sometimes the final couplet would be set to different music.   —/EW

Straniera, La ('The Stranger'). Opera in two acts by Bellini to a libretto by Felice Romani after Victor-Charles Prévôt's novel *L'Étrangère* (Milan, 1829).

strascinando, strascinato (It.). 'Dragging', 'dragged', i.e. played with heavily slurred notes.

strathspey. A Scottish dance similar to the *reel.

Straus, Oscar (*b* Vienna, 6 March 1870; *d* Bad Ischl, 11 Jan. 1954). Austrian composer. He studied with Max Bruch and wrote orchestral and instrumental music before taking up appointments as a theatre musical director. He entered the Strauss–Lehár operetta tradition with *Ein Walzertraum* ('A Waltz Dream', 1907)

and *Der tapfere Soldat* ('The Brave Soldier', also known as 'The Chocolate-Cream Soldier'; 1908, after G. B. Shaw). He later had outstanding success with *Der letzte Walzer* (1920) and *Drei Walzer* (1935), and with a waltz for the film *La Ronde* (1950).   PGA/ALA

Strauss. Viennese family of composers and conductors. In the 19th century they raised ballroom music to the highest level, particularly in their development of the waltz. The founder of the dynasty was **Johann** (Baptist) **Strauss** (i) (*b* Vienna, 14 March 1804; *d* Vienna, 25 Sept. 1849), whose mother died when he was seven and whose Viennese innkeeper father drowned in the Danube when he was 12. His guardian apprenticed him to a bookbinder, but Strauss eventually followed his own bent and at 15 joined Michael Pamer's orchestra as a viola player. The violinist Josef Lanner, who also played in the orchestra, soon left to form his own trio and invited Strauss to join him. The resultant quartet grew into an orchestra by virtue of the excellent music that both Lanner and Strauss wrote for it.

In 1825 the two quarrelled, and Strauss formed his own orchestra. In 1829 he became musical director at the Sperl, the largest dance hall in Vienna, and in 1833 he began to travel abroad with his orchestra, touring Britain in 1837 and 1849. His music is full of rhythmic vitality and striking instrumental effects, his most lasting pieces including the waltzes *Donaulieder* (1841) and *Lorelei-Rheinklänge* (1843), the *Cachucha Galop* (1837), *Annen Polka* (1842), and *Radetzky March* (1848), the last named after an Austrian field marshal.

Strauss's wife Anna bore him six children, of whom three sons survived infancy and became dance musicians. The eldest, **Johann** (Baptist) **Strauss** (ii) (*b* Vienna, 25 Oct. 1825; *d* Vienna, 3 June 1899), showed early musical talent. His father was strongly opposed to him following in his footsteps, but in 1844 the youth started his own orchestra with his mother's secret encouragement, and it became a successful rival to his father's. When the elder Strauss died the two orchestras were amalgamated under the younger Johann, who likewise gained a universal reputation helped by many tours abroad. He was a more inventive composer than his father, and the best of the dances that flowed from his pen are as much at home in the concert hall played by the Vienna Philharmonic and other famous orchestras as they were in the ballroom. They include the waltzes *Morgenblätter* (1864), *An der schönen blauen Donau* (1867), *Künstlerleben* (1867), *Geschichten aus dem Wienerwald* (1868), *Wein, Weib und Gesang* (1869), *Wiener Blut* (1873), *Rosen aus dem Süden* (1880), *Frühlingsstimmen* (1883), and *Kaiser-Walzer* (1889).

His other compositions include the *Annen Polka* (1852), *Tritsch-Tratsch-Polka* (1858), *Unter Donner und*

Blitz (1868), the musical joke *Perpetuum mobile* (1862), and the *Egyptischer-Marsch* (1870). Following the success of Offenbach's operettas in Vienna, the younger Johann was encouraged by his singer wife to try his hand in the theatre. When the right librettos came along he wrote two perfect masterpieces in *Die Fledermaus* (1874) and *Der Zigeunerbaron* (1885) as well as the charming *Eine Nacht in Venedig* (1883) and others. The operetta *Wiener Blut* (1899) was arranged from his dance music with his agreement.

The second son, **Josef Strauss** (*b* Vienna, 20 Aug. 1827; *d* Vienna, 22 July 1870), was initially happy to pursue a career as an engineer. However, when Johann suffered ill health, Josef was persuaded to take over the family orchestra and from then on continued a musical career. His character, quieter and more introverted than that of his brother, is reflected in waltzes and polkas that lack the power of Johann's but have a unique delicacy and exquisite craftsmanship. They include the waltzes *Dorfschwalben aus Österreich* (1865), *Dynamiden* (1865), *Delirien* (1867), *Sphärenklänge* (1868), and *Aquarellen* (1869), the polkas *Moulinet* (1858) and *Ohne Sorgen!* (1870), and the polka-mazurka *Die Libelle* (1867). He and Johann jointly wrote the *Pizzicato Polka* (1870).

The third son, **Eduard Strauss** (*b* Vienna, 15 March 1835; *d* Vienna, 28 Dec. 1916), received the best musical education, played in the orchestra, and became a popular conductor and a competent but less inspired composer, specializing in lively 'quick polkas' such as *Bahn frei!* (1869). He took over the family orchestra when his brother Johann retired to concentrate on operetta composition, and he followed him and their father as Imperial and Royal Music Director of the Court Balls. The family tradition was continued into the 20th century by Eduard's son **Johann** (iii) (*b* Vienna, 16 Feb. 1866; *d* Berlin, 9 Jan. 1939) and the latter's nephew **Eduard** (*b* Vienna, 24 March 1910; *d* Vienna, 6 April 1969), who made many fine recordings of the second Johann's music. PGa/ALa

📖 J. WECHSBERG, *The Waltz Emperors* (London, 1973) · P. KEMP, *The Strauss Family: Portrait of a Musical Dynasty* (Tunbridge Wells, 1985, 2/1989)

Strauss, Richard (*see opposite page*)

Stravaganza, La ('The Extraordinary'). Title of Vivaldi's op. 4, 12 violin concertos published in two books (Amsterdam, *c*.1712–13).

Stravinsky, Igor (*see page 1219*)

street music. A great part of the musical life of urban people has been lived not in the concert hall, opera house, or church, but in the streets, where everyone, rich or poor, would inevitably be exposed to whatever was available. Such music might have encompassed anything from the 'street cries' of a pedlar to choral music or symphonies. It has often been regarded, like folk music, as a genuine popular culture, in danger of extinction.

Street cries are the musical shouts of street vendors or pedlars; the cry of each created a different musical phrase, recognizable even at a distance when the actual words uttered could not be heard, thus allowing buyers to locate the goods they required. Street cries have recently received much scholarly attention: historical surveys have been published of cries in Europe (London, Paris, Germany, Italy, the Czech Republic), the USA, Latin America, Jamaica, and New Zealand, among others; even though the advertising of goods is now generally accomplished by other means, some street cries can still be heard. They have been recorded and used by composers from the Middle Ages to the present day: they are found, for example, in 13th-century French motets, in 14th-century Italian songs, and in a fragment from Utrecht; in 15th- and 16th-century art music (for example, pieces by Janequin, Jean Servin, Antonio Zacara da Teramo, Matthaeus le Maistre) and theatre music; in several German quodlibets depicting market scenes; and in English quodlibets by Weelkes, Gibbons, and Dering. Handel used them in his opera *Serse*; nostalgic use of them was made in 20th-century opera (Gershwin's *Porgy and Bess*) and musical (Bart's *Oliver!*).

One of the ways in which the *ballad was disseminated was through public performance in the streets by balladeers, who might also sell copies of the songs, printed on broadsides. Brednich (1977) discussed a 17th-century painting depicting broadsides being carried by a street crier.

From the Middle Ages, all over Europe, towns employed musicians to provide music for civic events; the English term for such musicians is *waits'. They were sometimes also allowed to play in streets, a lucrative source of extra income. They survived until the early 19th century, though in England many groups were disbanded to save money during the Napoleonic wars.

In the 18th century Burney reported hearing singing accompanied by strings and several bands using strings, woodwinds, and brass—*laudi* sung in religious processions. In Germany students and boy pupils used to sing in the streets. Today, street music survives mainly as 'busking', performed by music students and unemployed musicians, and in street festivals. PW

📖 F. BRIDGE, *The Old Cryes of London* (London, 1921/R) · R. W. BREDNICH, *Mennonite Folklife and Folklore*, trans. K. Roth, Canadian Centre for Folk Culture Studies, 22 (Ottawa, 1977)

(*cont. on p. 1218*)

Richard Strauss
(1864–1949)

The German composer and conductor Richard Georg Strauss was born in Munich on 11 June 1864 and died in Garmisch-Partenkirchen, Bavaria, on 8 September 1949.

The early years and the tone-poems

Strauss's father, Franz Strauss, was the principal horn player in the Munich court orchestra; his mother came from an affluent family of brewers. She suffered from periodic bouts of mental instability, which may account for the emphasis on psychological extremes in some of Strauss's major works. He showed musical aptitude early, producing both his first piano piece and his first songs at the age of six. Thereafter, his musical education was informal, his principal teachers being players in his father's orchestra. His father's contacts also ensured that Strauss's early works reached a broad public, while financial assistance from his mother's family enabled a number of scores to be published. These early works show a classical bias, fostered by his father whose stance was inherently reactionary and fiercely anti-Wagnerian. The influence of Mozart, Beethoven, and Schumann, of whom his father approved, is strongly apparent.

The Serenade in E♭ for 13 wind instruments (1882) brought Strauss to the attention of Hans von Bülow, who performed the work with the Meiningen Orchestra. Strauss made his conducting debut at extremely short notice with the same orchestra while they were on tour in Munich in 1884, giving the world premiere of his own Suite in B♭ for 13 wind instruments. Bülow appointed him assistant conductor in 1885, and until 1924 Strauss held a series of increasingly important posts: third conductor at the Munich Opera (1886–9), assistant conductor at Weimar from 1886, returning to Munich as associate conductor in 1894. In 1898 he was appointed conductor of the Berlin Court Opera and also appeared regularly as a guest conductor with the Berlin Philharmonic.

Strauss's development as a composer changed radically during his years at Meiningen, where he came under the influence of progressive musicians and struggled to break free from the classical restraints of his father's influence. The choral *Wandrers Sturmlied* ('Wanderer's Storm Song', 1884) reveals an extensive debt to Brahms. A close friendship with the violinist and composer Alexander Ritter led to Strauss's discovery of the works of Liszt and Wagner. An extended trip to Italy in 1886 was the inspiration for *Aus Italien*, a symphonic fantasy in four movements; though the work is gravely flawed, its sensuous orchestration and post-Romantic chromatic harmony mark the emergence of Strauss's individual voice. Its Munich premiere in 1887, accompanied by the first of the scandals that many of his works provoked, led to his public breach with the Brahmsian camp. Thereafter he produced the series of tone-poems (the term was his own coinage) on which his fame as an orchestral composer primarily rests: *Macbeth* (1886–8, rev. 1890 and 1891), *Don Juan* (1887 or 1888–9), *Tod und Verklärung* ('Death and Transfiguration', 1888–9), *Till Eulenspiegels lustige Streiche* ('Till Eulenspiegel's Merry Pranks', 1894–5), *Also sprach Zarathustra* ('Thus spake Zarathustra', 1895–6), *Don Quixote* (1896–7), *Ein Heldenleben* ('A Hero's Life', 1897–8), and the *Symphonia domestica* (1902–3). After the first performance of *Don Juan* in 1889 Strauss was regarded as the greatest German composer since Wagner. He was also one of the first to function under the watchful eye of modern international journalism, a status which he enjoyed and sometimes seemed assiduously to court.

In essence, Strauss's tone-poems extend and develop the form of the symphonic poem as perfected by Liszt, Smetana, and Tchaikovsky, though there are a number of significant departures. In their subject matter they frequently move away from pictorialism towards psychology, often using the symphonic developments of leitmotifs in the delineation of character. In spite of the late Romantic influences, a vestige of the classicist remained in Strauss, and his virtuoso use of vast post-Wagnerian forces, often creating effects of great sensuality or visceral emotion, is balanced by a close adherence to Classical form. *Macbeth*, *Don Juan*, and *Ein Heldenleben* are essentially sonatas. *Till Eulenspiegel* is a rondo, and *Don Quixote* a theme and variations. The movements of the *Symphonia domestica* represent four comparable developments on three (rather than the usual two) symphonic subjects. *Also sprach Zarathustra*, based on Nietzsche, whose work Strauss first read in 1892 and later claimed as the most important intellectual influence on his life, stands apart from the rest. A free-flowing fantasia, it uses bitonal harmonic clashes in its depiction of man's yearning to transcend nature and create the amoral figure of the Superman, the being of the future who is 'beyond good and evil'. Many of the tone-poems were, and remain, shrouded in controversy. *Don Juan* and the *Symphonia domestica* contain a new element of sexual explicitness in music, which continues to embarrass some. *Ein Heldenleben* and the *Symphonia domestica* are autobiographical, opening Strauss to charges of arrogance and self-propaganda.

Opera

Nietzsche's philosophy formed the ideological basis of Strauss's first opera, *Guntram* (1894), written to his own libretto on a legendary subject. It was a failure at its first performance and has frequently been dismissed as excessively Wagnerian in style, though it contains a number of elements that presage the greater operas that followed: a quality of compact brevity which stands in marked contrast to Wagnerian methodology; the powerful use of dissonance to convey extreme psychological states; a fascination, at times bordering on obsession, with the female psyche. The role of the heroine, Freihild, was written for the soprano Pauline de Ahna, for whom Strauss also composed many of his finest songs and whom he married in 1894. Discouraged by *Guntram*'s failure, Strauss did not return to writing for the stage until 1900 with *Feuersnot* ('Fire Famine'), a satirical, erotic comedy, which achieved a certain notoriety at its first performance the following year.

The works that established Strauss as one of the greatest of all operatic composers, however, were *Salome* (1905) and *Elektra* (1909). Based on biblical and mythic subjects respectively, both operas examine violent behaviour and sexual and emotional extremes in a manner that has evoked comparisons with Freud's contemporaneous studies of neurosis. Musically they are remarkable for the tremendous tension generated by their extraordinary thematic compression, the ceaseless fluctuations of both harmony and tone-colour, and their vocal writing which veers between rapid figurations based on speech rhythms and an expansive, swerving lyricism. *Salome*, in particular, caused a furore when it was first produced and ran into censorship problems in both Europe and the USA. It also set the seal on Strauss's reputation, and the financial rewards were such that he was able to build a substantial villa at Garmisch in Bavaria, which remained his home for the rest of his life.

Elektra marked the beginning of Strauss's collaboration with the Austrian writer Hugo von Hofmannsthal, whose verse drama formed the opera's source. Strauss subsequently requested an original text for a comedy on a 'period' theme; this eventually became *Der Rosenkavalier* (1911), which remains his most popular work. The opera reconciles the Classical and Romantic elements in Strauss's personality by placing Wagnerian methodology at the service of Mozartian dramaturgy: a symphonic, through-composed score is the vehicle for an 18th-century comedy of manners, conceived, in part, as a successor to *Le nozze di Figaro*, though also drawing on the bittersweet emotional profundity of *Così fan tutte*, which was Strauss's favourite among Mozart's works. A prevalent critical assumption is that *Der Rosenkavalier* represents a significant shift in Strauss's style, equated with a move towards harmonic simplification and a growing interest in parody and pastiche, which has led in turn to accusations of stylistic retrogression. This has recently been challenged by a growing emphasis on Strauss's pragmatic approach to stylistic and harmonic structures as being dictated by his chosen subject rather than as deriving from an explicit need for tonal experimentation.

The interweaving of Classical and Wagnerian elements is even more pronounced in *Ariadne auf Naxos* (1912, rev. 1916), which began life as an operatic interlude in Hofmannsthal's adaptation of Molière's *Le Bourgeois Gentilhomme*, for which Strauss also wrote incidental music. Though it constitutes a daring reappraisal of operatic and theatrical form, it initially found little favour with public and critics, while difficulties in staging the piece subsequently became an impediment to its wide acceptance. Strauss and Hofmannsthal later added a musical Prologue to replace the spoken drama, making the work more viable in the opera house. The final result lacks a natural unity, but both the Prologue and the subsequent 'opera' contain remarkable music. The work is scored for a chamber orchestra of 37 players, though the richness of Strauss's counterpoint gives an opulence of sound and texture which far removes it from the severe neo-classicism of the 1920s.

The years after the first production of *Ariadne* saw the composing of a ballet on a biblical subject for Diaghilev—*Josephslegende* (which was unsuccessful)—and the completion of Strauss's final tone-poem, *Eine Alpensinfonie* (1911–15). During World War I Hofmannsthal was called up for military service, and work on his next venture with Strauss, *Die Frau ohne Schatten*, could proceed only sporadically. A symbolist phantasmagoria, the opera has a subject derived partly from *Die Zauberflöte* and partly from Middle Eastern legend, both woven with a complex, if conservative metaphysical and philosophical underlay which equates essential humanity with procreative potential and posits a view of the family as a moral norm. The work proved relatively unsuccessful at its 1919 premiere, and though Strauss thought highly of it, he also admitted that its archetypal figures were less appropriate to his genius than the flesh-and-blood characters of his earlier operas.

For a few years there were no further collaborations between Strauss and Hofmannsthal. Strauss had a substantial sum of money in British securities confiscated by the British government during the war years, and to restore his financial position he later became increasingly active as a conductor and accompanist, sometimes accepting engagements which were greeted with considerable opprobrium. He and Hofmannsthal were also involved in the foundation of the Salzburg Festival between 1918 and 1920, and in 1919 he was appointed 'artistic supervisor' of the Vienna State Opera, a post he was forced to resign in 1924, partly because of his cavalier attitude towards the company's finances and partly as a result of erroneous press allegations that he was using his position to promote his own works. He has frequently been accused of being out of touch with artistic developments during the 1920s, though his next opera, *Intermezzo* (1924), was originally conceived as a series of 'cinema scenes' depicting an earlier incident in his private life, when his marriage to Pauline was temporarily under strain. Fast-moving and consisting of a series of brief scenes of astonishing fluidity, it represents an attempt to break away from the elevated manner in which Hofmannsthal had encouraged him.

Strauss returned to his former librettist with *Die ägyptische Helena* ('The Egyptian Helen', 1928), which was originally planned as an operetta, though during writing and composition it mutated into another symbolic allegory after the fashion of *Die Frau ohne Schatten*. With their final collaboration, *Arabella* (1933), the element of symbolism was drastically reduced. Hofmannsthal died suddenly in 1929 while working on the final draft of the text, which Strauss set in tribute, unchanged except for some minor points of detail. In spite of the apparent vicissitudes of his collaboration with Hofmannsthal, Strauss spent much of the rest of his working life searching for a librettist whom he considered his equal.

His choice initially fell on the Austrian-Jewish novelist Stefan Zweig, who provided him with the libretto for *Die schweigsame Frau*, the composition of which was begun in 1933, shortly after the Nazi acquisition of power. Strauss's actions during Hitler's regime and his relationship with the Nazi government constitute the most controversial aspect of his life and career. His correspondence and private papers frequently express contempt for the Nazis, but Strauss never publicly condemned the regime, even after its collapse. There is no evidence to suggest that he ever considered leaving Germany, and in 1933 he accepted from Goebbels the office of President of the Reich's Music Chamber, though he made no attempt to put the racist proscriptions of Nazism into action. He was eventually dismissed in 1935 when the Gestapo intercepted a letter to Zweig, mildly critical of the regime. The same year *Die schweigsame Frau* was prohibited in German theatres.

At Zweig's suggestion, Strauss accepted the 'Aryan' theatre historian Joseph Gregor as his librettist. Their first collaboration, *Friedenstag* ('Peace Day', 1938), has provoked widely divergent opinions and has been seen antithetically as both an inherently pacifist work and as an opera that betrays a congruence with Fascist aesthetics. No such charges have been held against its two successors, *Daphne* (1938) and *Die Liebe der Danae* (given its premiere posthumously in 1952), which, though uneven in inspiration, are characterized by a lyrical profusion and a remarkable orchestral refulgence. Gregor was eventually sacked from their next collaboration, *Capriccio* (1942), for which the conductor Clemens Krauss officially provided the text, though some of it is by Strauss himself. A 'conversation piece for music' about the relevant importance of words and music in opera, it is now widely regarded as among the finest of Strauss's stage works, while some critics have read into it a guarded defence of aesthetic tradition in the face of those who would destroy it.

The humane warmth of *Capriccio* is all the more remarkable, given that it was written under painful personal circumstances. Strauss's daughter-in-law Alice and her two children, whom he adored, were Jewish and were frequently subject to severe harassment. Strauss unquestionably kept them safe and there is considerable evidence to the effect that in 1942 he also attempted, unsuccessfully, to obtain the release of other members of Alice's family who were held in concentration camps, many of whom were subsequently murdered.

Strauss's last years and reputation

During this period Strauss paradoxically experienced a new lease of creative life by turning to the composition of absolute music, often scored for small forces. The Second Horn Concerto (1943) and two Sonatinas for wind instruments (1943 and 1944) were followed by the harrowing *Metamorphosen* (1945) for 23 solo strings, ostensibly a reaction to the Allied bombing of many of the theatres in which his greatest works had been produced, though also a lament for the undermining of German culture by barbarism and violence. The Oboe Concerto (1945–6), his first score completed after the war, was inspired by a meeting with the principal oboist of the Pittsburgh Symphony Orchestra, who was serving with the American forces in Germany. Accused of complicity with the Hitler regime, and aware that he would have to face a de-Nazification tribunal, Strauss went into voluntary exile in Switzerland at the end of 1945. Because his royalty payments had been frozen during the war, his financial circumstances were yet again perilous, though they were partly redeemed when Thomas Beecham organized a festival of his music in London in 1947. With Gregor as librettist, he began a final stage work, *Des Esels Schatten* ('The Donkey's Shadow'), originally conceived as an educational project for the school where one of his grandsons was a pupil. He left the score unfinished and it remained unperformed until 1964.

The finest works of Strauss's last years were four autumnal songs with orchestra (1946–8), inspired by his abiding love for his wife. They are frequently perceived as his 'requiem', though both their collective title, *Vier letzte Lieder* ('Four Last Songs'), and their standard running order in performance were allotted after his death. The de-Nazification tribunal formally acquitted Strauss in 1948; he elected not to return to Germany until 1949, shortly before the celebrations of his 85th birthday. He died, with his family at his bedside, in September that year.

Strauss's posthumous reputation has fluctuated. He was held in contempt by a generation that failed to understand his refusal to follow the astringent modernism of Stravinsky or the 12-note technique propounded by Schoenberg, though more recent critical appraisal has seen many of his works from *Ariadne* onwards as constituting either an alternative modernist perspective or containing elements that strongly prefigure postmodernism. Strauss's decision not to leave Germany during the Third Reich is still the cause of distaste in some quarters. His courting of media attention and his seeming fondness for money has also opened him to charges of careerist opportunism (though it should be noted that he turned down substantial offers for the film rights to his works, when he was informed that his scores would have to be cut). 50 or so years after his death, however, it must be acknowledged that he was one of the great masters of his time, his only major limitation being that he lacked the power to portray the spiritual in music, frequently replacing genuine exaltation with bombastic rhetoric. As a realistic artist (in the best sense of the term: capable of conveying the complexities of everyday human emotion and feeling), he has been surpassed by few.   TA

📖 N. Del Mar, *Richard Strauss: A Critical Commentary on his Life and Works*, 3 vols. (London, 1962–72) · W. Mann, *Richard Strauss: A Critical Study of the Operas* (London, 1964) · T. Ashley, *Richard Strauss* (London, 1999) · M. Kennedy, *Richard Strauss: Man, Musician, Enigma* (Cambridge, 1999)

Streich (Ger.). 'Stroke', i.e. a bowstroke; *Streichinstrumente*, 'bowed instruments'; *Streichquartett*, 'string quartet', etc.

strepitoso, strepitosamente (It.). 'Noisy', 'noisily'.

stretto (It., 'compressed'). A fugal device in which subject entries follow closely in succession, each subject overlapping with the next. See FUGUE.

strict counterpoint. *Counterpoint in which parts are fitted to a cantus firmus according to firm principles of part-writing as well as of consonance and dissonance.

stride. A piano style evolved in the 1930s by such pianists as James P. Johnson and Fats Waller. The name derives from the striding movement of the left hand, which plays 10ths or even more extended chords in place of the usual octaves, thereby achieving a leaping,

propulsive effect. The device was extended into the world of popular piano playing in the 1930s by Charlie Kunz and Billy Mayerl.   PGA

Striggio, Alessandro (*b* Mantua, *c*.1537; *d* Mantua, 29 Feb. 1592). Italian composer and instrumentalist. He was the principal composer to the Medici in Florence, and also a virtuoso viol player. Duke Cosimo I used him as an emissary (and possibly a spy) to other courts, including Munich (where he met Lassus) and London in 1567. He composed stage music and several volumes of madrigals, including a prototype *madrigal comedy depicting chattering washerwomen, *Il cicalamento delle donne al bucato*. His 40-part motet *Ecce beatam lucem* may be connected with Tallis's *Spem in alium*. He married the Sienese singer Virginia Vagnoli about 1570, moving back to Mantua in 1587. Their third child, **Alessandro** (*b* 1572 or 1573; *d* Venice, ?15 June 1630), became a prominent court secretary to the Gonzagas in

(*cont. on p. 1221*)

Igor Stravinsky
(1882–1971)

The Russian composer Igor Fyodorovich Stravinsky was born in Oranienbaum (now Lomonosov) on 5/17 June 1882 and died in New York on 6 April 1971.

Stravinsky's unleashing of new rhythmic force in *The Rite of Spring* was one of the great musical revolutions of the years before World War I; but it was only the most striking innovation by a composer who never tired of setting himself new challenges. Often these took the form of giving his own unmistakable imprint to manners and materials he drew from music of the past. Little, from Machaut to Stockhausen, escaped his critical, inventive regard, and few later composers have escaped his influence.

The early years: Paris ballets

The son of a renowned bass at the Imperial Opera, Stravinsky studied the piano and composition from boyhood, and from 1903 to 1906 he was a private composition pupil of Rimsky-Korsakov. His early works show the influence of Rimsky, but they show too that the young composer was learning from Skryabin, Tchaikovsky, Debussy, and Dukas. This period of eclectic preparation came to an end in 1910, when Stravinsky went to Paris with the ballet company of Serge Diaghilev, who commissioned from him a series of scores beginning with *Zhar'-ptitsa* ('The Firebird', 1910). Though still indebted to the opulent fantasy of Rimsky's *The Golden Cockerel*, *The Firebird* gives some hint of the brilliant, stylized sonorities and the almost mechanical rhythmic drive of its successor, *Petrushka* (1911), yet nobody could have expected that Stravinsky would so quickly go on to produce such a startlingly novel work as *Vesna svyashchennaya* ('The Rite of Spring', 1913).

Certainly the first-night audience was taken by surprise, excited to uproar by the violent rhythms of Stravinsky's music and Nijinsky's choreography. By means of syncopation and rapid changes of metre Stravinsky did away with the regular pulse which had governed almost all Western music since the Renaissance: the rhythm now is angular and propulsive, the music's main motivating force. And it makes the score a perfect counterpart to scenes of pagan ritual in ancient Russia.

Cut off from his homeland by World War I, Stravinsky returned repeatedly during the next few years to the folk tales of a later Russia. There were several cycles of little songs, the farmyard ballet *Renard* (1915–16; staged 1922), and another ballet, *Svadebka* (Les Noces, 1914–23; staged 1923), for which he took some years to find the appropriate scoring: eventually this intricate rhythmic machine was given the monochrome colouring of chorus, percussion ensemble, and four pianos. The last of these folk-tale pieces, *Histoire du soldat* (Lausanne, 1918), can be counted an early example of music theatre, requiring as it does a narrator, two actors, a dancer, and seven instrumentalists.

Like several shorter works of this period, *Histoire du soldat* finds Stravinsky taking an ironic look at different musical conventions: there is a ragtime number, and also a chorale. In his next theatrical work, the ballet *Pulcinella* (1920), he took this a step further by basing the music entirely on pieces then thought to be by Pergolesi, adding the zest of his own rhythmic, harmonic, and orchestral imagination to the originals. Alter this there came a final, abstract return to the 'Russian' manner, in the *Symphonies of Wind Instruments* (1920), before he gave himself wholeheartedly to re-investigating the musical past.

The neo-classical works

Stravinsky's *neo-classicism takes the form of borrowing forms, ideas, and styles from throughout Western music, not just (in fact, least of all) from the Classical period. For instance, *Oedipus rex* (1926–7; Vienna, 1928), which can be given as an opera or as an oratorio, looks back to Handel in its general shaping and in its massive choruses, while the arias have something of Verdi's passion. The 'Dumbarton Oaks' Concerto (1937–8) is a modern Brandenburg, and there are reminiscences of Bach again in the Concerto for piano and wind (1923–4), whereas the Capriccio for piano and orchestra (1928–9) sprinkles Weber-like playfulness on a concerto grosso format. During this period Stravinsky was living in France, no longer able, since the revolution of 1917, to draw on funds from Russia. He was therefore obliged to earn his living as a performing musician: the two concertante piano works were written for himself to play, and he began to conduct his own works, especially at first performances and for recordings.

As before, ballet scores continued to form an important part of his output. *Apollo* (*Apollon musagète*; Washington, DC, 1928), with its euphonious music for strings, was one of the last presentations by the Diaghilev company before the impresario's death; other ballets included the Tchaikovsky-based *Le Baiser de la fée* (1928), the coolly classical *Perséphone* (1934), the witty *Jeu de cartes* (1937), and even a *Circus Polka* for a young elephant (1942). All these show Stravinsky's gift for creating musical gestures which call forth physical ones, and it is a gift that is not restricted to his music explicitly composed for dancing: the spirited vitality of such works as the Violin Concerto in D (1931) has led to many successful ballet productions of Stravinsky's concert music.

The Violin Concerto, written 'against' the great 19th-century works in the same key (by Beethoven, Brahms, and Tchaikovsky), exemplifies the anti-Romantic tendency in Stravinsky's neo-classical music. As he wrote in his *Chroniques de ma vie* of 1935: 'I consider that music is, by its very nature, essentially powerless to *express* anything at all . . . The phenomenon of music is given to us with the sole purpose of establishing an order in things.' This statement is belied by everything Stravinsky wrote, in that his music is always strikingly expressive, but in eulogizing order it gives an important clue to understanding his neo-classical works.

The American years

Increasingly it was to divine order that he gave his attention. His first important religious work was the *Symphony of Psalms* for chorus and orchestra (1930), succeeded by the optimistic Symphony in C (1938–40), 'composed to the Glory of God'. During the composition of this work, and following the outbreak of World War II, Stravinsky moved from Paris to Los Angeles, which was his home for the rest of his life. Proximity to Hollywood brought requests for film music, but these projects foundered and Stravinsky put his material to use in the *Four Norwegian Moods* (1942) and *Ode* (1943). The major work of his early American years, however, was another symphony, the tough and dynamic Symphony in Three Movements (1942–5).

The output of religious works continued with the cantata *Babel* (1944) and the Mass for chorus and double wind quintet (1944–8), which was designed for use in church. There was then a final and exultant neo-classical essay, the full-length opera *The Rake's Progress* (Venice, 1951) which takes *Don Giovanni* as its point of departure, before Stravinsky started out on a gradual process of exploring serialism. The ground was prepared by his use of medieval and Renaissance practices in the Mass and in the Cantata on English 15th- and 16th-century texts (1951–2), as also by the strict contrapuntal writing of the latter work and the Septet (1952–3). Then, in his works from the *Three Shakespeare Songs* (1953) to the cantata *Threni* (1957–8), he came to a full adoption of 12-note serial methods.

Stravinsky's turn to serialism, surprising to those who had seen him as rival pope to Schoenberg, was perhaps helped by Schoenberg's death in 1951, releasing him from a position he had not sought. At the same time he was stimulated by what his younger contemporaries were achieving in extrapolating beyond Webern: his *Movements* for piano and orchestra (1958–9) suggests, in its lean scoring and rhythmic complexity, that he had learnt something from Stockhausen's *Kontra-Punkte*. His ability, at this late stage in his career, to remain open to new ideas is astonishing, yet no more so than the distinctive individuality of his own serial works. As in his neo-classical music, he took complete ownership of the means offered to him.

Many of Stravinsky's late works are short epitaphs, such as the 'dirge-canons and song' *In memoriam Dylan Thomas* (1954) and the *Elegy for J.F.K.* (1964), or else sacred cantatas. Among these, the *Canticum sacrum* (1955) was designed expressly, in subject, form, and style, for St Mark's, Venice, and the *Requiem Canticles* (1965–6), Stravinsky's last major work, is what he described as a 'pocket Requiem' in nine short, stark movements.   PG

📖 I. STRAVINSKY, *Chroniques de ma vie* (Paris, 1935–6; Eng. trans., London, 1936, 2/1975); *Poétique musicale* (Cambridge, MA, 1942; Eng. trans., Cambridge, MA, 1947; bilingual edn, Cambridge, MA, 1970) · I. STRAVINSKY and R. CRAFT, *Conversations with Igor Stravinsky* (London, 1959) · I. STRAVINSKY, *Memories and Commentaries* (London, 1960) · R. VLAD, *Stravinsky* (London, 1960) · I. STRAVINSKY, *Expositions and Developments* (London, 1962) · E. W. WHITE, *Stravinsky: The Composer and his Works* (London, 1966, enlarged 2/1979) · I. STRAVINSKY, *Themes and Conclusions* (London, 1972) · S. WALSH, *The Music of Stravinsky* (London, 1988) · P. GRIFFITHS, *Stravinsky* (London, 1992) · R. TARUSKIN, *Stravinsky and the Russian Traditions*, 2 vols. (Oxford, 1996) · S. WALSH, *Stravinsky: A Creative Spring* (New York, 1999; London, 2000)

Mantua; he, too, played the viol, and wrote the libretto for Monteverdi's *Orfeo* (1607).   TC

string (Fr.: *corde*; Ger.: *Saite*; It.: *corda*). A length of any material that may be caused to sound by plucking, rubbing, or blowing when held under tension. The commonest materials for Western *stringed instruments are gut, metal, and latterly plastic, though such other materials as silk and horsehair have been used. Nylon has become a popular alternative to gut because it is durable, cheap, and relatively clean to make (avoiding the messy and laborious processes of transforming intestines into lengths of polished string), and can be made perfectly even (uneven gut strings can buzz or howl, and are impossible to tune). However, gut is still often considered to have a better sound.

Harpsichords and early pianos, as well as wire-strung plucked instruments such as the *cittern, *bandora, and *mandolin, use iron or brass wire; modern pianos and some types of guitar use steel. Overwound (overspun or wire-wound) strings have a core of gut, silk, nylon, or wire wrapped in metal wire or ribbon.   JMo

string drum. A barrel or cylinder covered at one end by a membrane and open at the other, with a rosined string fastened to the membrane and passing through a hole in its centre. Rubbing the string with cloth causes the membrane to vibrate and emit a roaring sound. See also FRICTION DRUM.   RPA

stringed instruments. Instruments sounded by striking, plucking, rubbing, or (rarely) blowing *strings, which are most commonly made of gut, silk, metal, or such synthetic materials as nylon. In Western orchestral and conservatory usage, the 'strings' consist of instruments of the *violin family and the *double bass, and also such plucked instruments as the guitar and harp. The piano and harpsichord, however, are usually categorized with the organ as *keyboard instruments. The term used in *organology for stringed instruments is *chordophones (see INSTRUMENTS, CLASSIFICATION OF).   JMo

stringendo (It.). 'Squeezing', 'pressing', i.e. getting faster.

string quartet. See QUARTET; see also CHAMBER MUSIC.

string quintet. See QUINTET; see also CHAMBER MUSIC.

string trio. See TRIO, 1; see also CHAMBER MUSIC.

strisciando, strisciato (It.). 'Trailing', 'trailed', i.e. smooth, slurred, or *glissando.

Stroh violin. A violin with a flexible metal diaphragm and horn instead of the normal body, invented by Augustus Stroh in 1899. Stroh violas, cellos, mandolins, and guitars were also made. The horn gave the violin a strongly directional projection that was much desired in the early days of recording, and for outdoor performances and dance orchestras, before the advent of the microphone. A single-string variant, the phonofiddle, was introduced in 1904.   JMo

stromentato (It.). 'Accompanied by instruments'; *recitativo stromentato*, recitative accompanied by instruments in addition to the continuo.

strophic. In poetry, a stanzaic form in which each verse (strophe) follows the same structure, metre, and rhyme scheme. In music the term is used by extension to describe any form founded on a repeated pattern: AAAA, etc. It is most commonly found in songs, especially folksongs and art songs of a folk-like nature, in which each stanza of the poem is set to the same music.

See also FORM, 2.   GMT/JBe

strophic variations. In vocal music, a strophic form in which each stanza retains the same bass, while the melody or solo part is varied at each repetition of the bass pattern. The bass is not necessarily strictly identical in every repetition, but the essential outline is maintained so that the same succession of harmonies occurs in every strophe. Strophic variations were especially common in early 17th-century Italian *monody; famous examples include 'Possente spirto' from Act III of Monteverdi's *Orfeo* (1607), and his duet *Ohimè, dov'è il mio ben* from the seventh book of madrigals.

GMT/JBe

Strouse, Charles (Louis) (*b* New York, 7 June 1928). American composer. He studied at the Eastman School of Music and later with Nadia Boulanger and Aaron Copland. The musical *Bye Bye, Birdie* (1960; filmed 1963), with lyrics by Lee Adams, provided his first major Broadway success, and its reflection of aspects of contemporary American society was continued in *All American* (1962) and *Golden Boy* (1964). With *Annie* (1977; filmed 1982) he brought to life a popular American cartoon to create a now classic musical featuring the song 'Tomorrow'. His musical adaptations of films have included *Applause* (1970, after *All about Eve*) and *Nick and Nora* (1991, after the 'Thin Man' series).   JSn

Strozzi, Barbara (*b* Venice, 1619; *d* Venice, 11 Nov. 1677). Italian composer and singer. She was the adopted (perhaps illegitimate) daughter of the Venetian poet Giulio Strozzi, and in her life occupied a difficult space somewhere between patron and courtesan. She was known in Venetian intellectual circles both for her beauty and for her singing; she was also a prominent member of her father's Accademia degli Unisoni. She studied with Cavalli, and her eight published volumes of music comprise chiefly arias and cantatas for solo voice that are splendid contributions to developing forms and styles. TC

strumento (It.). 'Instrument'; *strumentato*, 'instrumented' or 'orchestrated'.

strumento di porco (It.). See PSALTERY.

Stück (Ger.). 'Piece', 'composition'; *Klavierstück*, 'keyboard piece', usually 'piano piece'.

study. See ÉTUDE.

study score. A *miniature score, or a full score of reduced dimensions.

stürmend, stürmisch (Ger.). 'Stormy', 'passionate'.

Sturm und Drang (Ger., 'storm and stress'). A German aesthetic movement of the mid- to late 18th century. The term comes from the title of a play of 1776 by Maximilian Klinger (about the American Revolution). The movement has often been interpreted as an outcome of *Empfindsamkeit, the heightened expressiveness or sensibility of manner manifested in, for example, the music of C. P. E. Bach and the writings of Samuel Richardson as early as the 1740s. Its adherents aimed to portray violent emotions in the most dramatic way possible. It reached its climax in the literature of the 1760s and 70s of Goethe (notably *Götz von Berlichingen*, 1773) and Schiller (whose *Die Räuber* of 1780–1 stands at its zenith); there are parallels in the visual arts, in representations of storms or evocations of terror (for example G. B. Piranesi's *Carceri d'invenzione*).

In music, the term was first applied by H. C. Robbins Landon and Barry Brook, especially in the discussion of Haydn's symphonies, notably those of the early 1770s (mostly with numbers in the 40s). At about this date, symphonies in an intense, highly dramatic style and in the minor mode enjoyed a brief vogue: examples are Haydn's nos. 39, 44 and 45, J. C. Bach's op. 6 no. 6 and Mozart's no. 25.

The *Sturm und Drang* movement also affected opera, for example in the works of Traetta and Jommelli, with their vivid tone-painting in orchestral recitatives, and notably in the representation of Hades in Gluck's *Orfeo ed Euridice* (1762). Gluck had already infused new life into supernatural horror scenes in his ballet *Don Juan* (1761). The melodramas of Georg Benda, written in the early and mid-1770s, are a further example; Mozart was influenced by these in his dramatic music of the late 1770s and by Gluck in his *Idomeneo*. The movement, which contained many of the seeds of *Romanticism, had among its most enthusiastic exponents the Mannheim composer G. J. Vogler, who wrote extravagantly stormy music in the 1770s and 80s and was the influential teacher of Weber, Meyerbeer, and others. WT/SS

style brisé (Fr., 'broken style'). The characteristic style of 17th-century lute music, in which the notes of a chord were not plucked simultaneously but arpeggiated. The style had considerable influence on late 17th- and early 18th-century composers of keyboard music, especially on French composers such as the Couperins, d'Anglebert, and Chambonnières, but also on J. S. Bach.

style galant (Fr.). See GALANT.

style luthé (Fr.). A term used by François Couperin for the *style brisé*.

su (It.). 'On', 'up'; e.g. *arcata in su*, 'with an up-bow'. (See also SUL, SULL', SULLA, SUI, SUGLI, SULLE.)

subdominant. The fourth degree of the major or minor scale. The prefix 'sub' refers to the position of the subdominant a 5th below the tonic, whereas the dominant is a 5th above the tonic.

subito (It.). 'Suddenly', 'immediately'; *attacca subito*, 'begin immediately', an indication at the end of a movement that the next should follow without a break.

subject. A structurally important theme or melodic fragment. The term has two specific, technical meanings. 1. In the study of *fugue, a subject is the principal theme—announced in the first part (or 'voice') to enter—on which the composition is founded. The fugal subject was derived from the 'point' and *cantus firmus of Renaissance imitative technique and is a common identifiable feature of contrapuntal structures from the Baroque period onwards.

2. 'Subject' has also been used in the terminology of thematic accounts of *sonata form. Thus a sonata exposition, which in Mozart or Beethoven may often have two contrasting themes, is said to have a 'first subject' and a 'second subject'. This usage appears even in the descriptions of expositions with only one theme ('monothematic'), where 'subject' refers to the entire tonic and dominant passages of the typical harmonic structure, just as it may be used in more elaborate sonata forms to refer to groups of themes, usually in the same harmonic region.

3. In a more general sense, 'subject' is occasionally used to name the sections of dance forms, the *leitmotifs of Wagner's music dramas, or the contrasting

themes of *atonal music structures, but its application has traditionally been restricted to the two forms of fugue and sonata.   JD

submediant. The sixth degree of the major or minor scale. The prefix 'sub' refers to the position of the submediant a 3rd below the tonic, whereas the mediant is a 3rd above the tonic.

Subotnick, Morton (*b* Los Angeles, 14 April 1933). American composer. He studied with Milhaud and Leon Kirchner at Mills College (1957–9), where he stayed on as a teacher (1959–66) before moving to New York University (1966–9) and then back west to the California Institute of the Arts (from 1969). In the 1960s he worked with the Buchla synthesizer, and his *Silver Apples of the Moon* (1966), colourful and evocative, was the first electronic piece composed for release on record. He has remained concerned with electronic technology.   PG

succentor. In a cathedral church, the title normally given to the *precentor's deputy; the succentor is usually a *minor canon.

successive counterpoint. See SPECIES COUNTER-POINT.

Suchoň, Eugen (*b* Pezinok, Slovakia, 25 Sept. 1908; *d* Bratislava, 5 Aug. 1993). Slovak composer. He studied composition at the Academy in Bratislava and with Novák at the Prague Conservatory, 1931–3. He held various academic and official posts including that of head of the Slovak Composers' Union. After studying with Frico Kafenda he made considerable use of Slovak folksong in his work, culminating in his successful national opera *Krútňava* ('The Whirlpool', 1941, rev. 1949). His music from the mid-1950s to the late 60s reveal an interest in more modernist techniques: the opera *Svätopluk* (1960), for example, shows him mingling serial techiques with old Slovak chant. In his last 20 years he became increasingly interested in the techniques of earlier musics. Suchoň's influence on his native contemporaries was considerable and he is regarded as a major representative of Slovak music.
                                                          JSM

Suggia, Guilhermina (*b* Oporto, 27 June 1888; *d* Oporto, 31 July 1950). Portuguese cellist. As a child she led the cellos in the Oporto city orchestra and played in a string quartet, but in 1901 she went to study with Julius Klengel in Leipzig, where she appeared as a soloist with Nikisch. From 1906 to 1912 she lived and studied with Casals, then moved to London where she both performed (until 1949) and taught. Augustus John's famous portrait of her captured her tempera-

mental personality and forceful character, and her nobly phrased playing was at its best in colourful, emotional music.   CF

suite. An instrumental genre consisting of a succession of fairly short, congruous movements. During the Baroque period, when the suite was a principal instrumental form, each movement took on the more or less stylized character of a particular dance; the dances were normally in the same key and were sometimes linked thematically. Other terms used in different countries and at different periods to describe pieces conforming to the suite principle include *ordre* (France), *sonata da *camera* (Italy), *partita or *Partie* (Italy, Germany), and *Ouvertüre* or *overture (Germany, England).

1. Origins; 2. The growth of the Classical suite; 3. The 18th century; 4. The later suite

1. Origins

Although the term 'suite' did not appear until the mid-16th century, the form's origins lie in the pairing of dances, which dates back to the late 14th century and the 15th. A common pattern was for a relatively slow, duple-metre dance such as the *pavan (England, France) or the *passamezzo (Italy) to be followed by a faster, triple-metre dance such as the *galliard or *saltarello, which might use the same thematic material or at least begin with a similar melodic or rhythmic motif. The earliest pieces of this type were for lute or keyboard.

A number of early 16th-century lutebooks went on to include sets of dances grouped in three, for example pavan–saltarello–piva (arranged by J. A. Dalza in a lutebook of 1508 printed by Petrucci) or passamezzo–gagliarda–padovana (arranged by Andrea Rotta, 1546). In Germany in particular, dances could be grouped in sets of four or five (e.g. in Johann Schein's *Banchetto musicale*, 1617), and a few standard patterns of arrangement (e.g. paduana–intrada–dantz–galliarda) began to appear, as in Paul Peuerl's collection of 1611.

Composers and compilers of keyboard music also began to group dances in this way. *Parthenia* (1612–13) has a number of linked pavans and galliards by Byrd, Bull, and Gibbons, some prefaced with a 'Preludio' to form a set of three movements; and there are similar examples in the Fitzwilliam Virginal Book (*c*.1609–19).

2. The growth of the Classical suite

As such courtly French dances as the *allemande and *courante eventually overtook the pavan and galliard in popularity, so they were assimilated into the suite. J. J. Froberger (1616–67) is customarily credited with establishing the standardized sequence of movements in the Classical suite: two pairs of slow and fast dances originating in four different countries, the *allemande (Germany) and *courante (Italy) followed by the *sarabande (Spain) and *gigue (England). This standard order was not finally achieved, however, until after Froberger's death; in his own suites the sarabande was the last piece, the gigue being inserted earlier in the sequence.

Other dances might either be substituted for any of those four or included additionally (e.g. *minuet, *gavotte, *bourrée). Later a prefatory prelude, not in dance rhythm, became common and was often elaborately improvisatory in character; such opening movements went under a variety of titles, including 'fantasia', 'préambule', and 'overture'.

Froberger's successors in Germany include Johann Rosenmüller, J. E. Kindermann, and Georg Muffat, all of whom composed keyboard suites under various titles (usually 'sonata') that conformed to the established scheme. But as the 17th century progressed the number and order of dances in the suite varied increasingly, particularly among such French composers as François Couperin, Chambonnières, D'Anglebert, and Lebègue. They frequently combined traditional dance movements with less formal, fancifully titled pieces (e.g. 'Les Pèlerines', 'Les Laurentines', 'L'Espagnolète' from a suite by F. Couperin) to form larger-scale, loosely connected suites, and introduced such other dances as the *rigaudon, *loure, and *musette.

Outside Germany and France the suite was slower to develop during the 17th century. In Italy the most important composer of keyboard music was Frescobaldi; he wrote no suites as such, but some of the dances for harpsichord in his later publications (e.g. *Toccate*, 1637) are grouped in twos and threes, suggesting the beginnings of the suite idea. In England, Matthew Locke's *Melothesia* (1673), an anthology of keyboard music by various composers including Locke himself, contains a number of fairly simple suites based on the allemande–courante–sarabande pattern, a line of development continued by Blow and by Purcell, whose three- and four-movement suites were often entitled 'Lessons'.

3. The 18th century

The suite reached its peak with Handel and Bach; through their keyboard and orchestral suites the most important phase of its history was completed. Nearly all suites up to and including Handel's and Bach's have a unity of key: changes of key between movements are limited to the major–minor (tonic or relative) type. Most of the dances are in simple *binary form, that is, falling into two roughly equal sections, the first moving to the key of the dominant (or, if in a minor key, to the relative major), the second returning to the original key, and both halves are repeated. Melodic or rhythmic figures introduced in the opening bars of each movement are normally referred to, developed, and repeated in the course of the movement and may even be used to link two or more movements of the same suite.

Handel's keyboard suites (eight were published together in 1720) are mainly conventional in form (allemande–courante–sarabande–gigue), though some include a chaconne, an 'abstract' fugue, or an air and variations. For some of these pieces Handel typically reused material from earlier works, and several of the movements are linked thematically. Better known than the keyboard suites are the orchestral *Water Music* (actually three separate suites, in F, D, and G) and *Music for the Royal Fireworks*; like the keyboard suites their value lies more in their invention and vitality than in any formal originality they may display.

Bach's contribution is typically wide-ranging—six cello suites, four orchestral suites, six 'French' and six 'English' keyboard suites, six keyboard partitas, and several individual partitas and sonatas for various instruments (suites in all but name). All his keyboard suites follow the standard pattern of allemande–courante–sarabande–gigue; some have an opening prelude, which may be quite extensive, and all have at least one (usually several) additional dance movement (bourrée, menuet, gavotte, etc.). Although they embody few significant formal or technical innovations, Bach's suites provide a brilliant and masterly synthesis of the entire history and development of the Baroque suite.

4. The later suite

The characteristic use in the later Baroque suite of contrasting keys at the start of each section and occasionally of contrasting thematic material, the increasing emphasis on development followed by repetition or recapitulation—these features all hint at the chief elements of the *sonata, which in the second half of the 18th century replaced the suite as the standard instrumental genre. The dominance of sonata-form concepts throughout the later 18th century and for much of the 19th all but banished the suite from the repertory. Traces of the suite principle remain, however, in such chamber-orchestral works as the *serenade, *cassation, and *divertimento (forms used by Haydn, Mozart, Beethoven, and Brahms) and even in some song cycles and piano music (e.g. by Schumann). But conscious attempts to reassert the suite over symphonic forms were not made until the later 19th century (e.g. Raff's and Lachner's orchestral suites of the 1860s and 70s, and Grieg's *Holberg Suite* of 1884);

and some of these resulted only from a Romantic desire to evoke a bygone era.

In general, the instrumental suite of the late 19th and early 20th centuries had little to do with its Baroque predecessor. By the 1880s traditional dance movements were being supplanted by a free succession of national or folk dances, sometimes with a programmatic background (e.g. Dvořák's orchestral suites), or by numbers extracted from a ballet, opera, or other dramatic work and rearranged for concert performance (e.g. Bizet's *L'Arlésienne*, Grieg's *Peer Gynt Suite*). In the early 20th century the programmatic and extract suite (e.g. Holst's *The Planets*, Richard Strauss's *Rosenkavalier* suites) existed alongside a new and deliberate attempt to recreate the Baroque suite, which was prompted by an interest in neo-classicism (e.g. Ravel's *Le Tombeau de Couperin*). Among later 20th-century composers the title 'suite' occurred only occasionally (Schoenberg's Piano Suite, Berg's *Lyric Suite*), doubtless because the need for musical unification to which the suite has traditionally catered has been met more successfully by the more abstract compositional techniques of contemporary music.   JN

Suite bergamasque. Piano work by Debussy, composed in 1890 and revised in 1905; the first, second, and fourth movements were orchestrated by G. Cloez, the third, 'Clair de lune', by André Caplet.

suivez (Fr.). 'Follow'. 1. An indication at the end of a movement that the next should follow without a break, i.e. the same as *attacca.

2. A direction that the accompanying part or parts should follow the solo, i.e. the same as *colla parte, colla voce*.

Suk, Josef (*b* Krecovice, 4 Jan. 1874; *d* Benesov, 29 May 1935). Czech composer and violinist. He studied at the Prague Conservatory (1885–92) with Antonín Bennewitz for violin and with Dvořák (whose daughter Otilie he married) for composition. Dvořák's influence is marked in his earlier works, which include the Serenade in E (1896). His major symphony, *Asrael* (1906), written to commemorate the death of Dvořák in 1904 and that of his young wife in 1905, is increasingly recognized as a signal contribution to the late Romantic symphony and led to a series of large-scale orchestral masterpieces of comparable quality: *Pohádka léta* ('A Summer's Tale', 1909), *Zrání* ('Ripening', 1917), and *Epilog* (1932). His style explored the full potential of late Romantic harmony, resulting in some remarkably inspiring work. Suk was second violinist in the Bohemian Quartet (1891–1933) and a composition teacher at the Prague Conservatory (1922–35).   PG/JSM

📖 J. BERKOVEC, *Josef Suk* (Eng. trans., Prague, 1968)

sul, sull', sulla, sui, sugli, sulle (It.). 'On the'; *sul G*, 'on the G string'; *sul ponticello*, bow 'on the bridge'; *sulla tastiera, sul tasto*, bow 'on the fingerboard'.

Sullivan, Sir Arthur (Seymour) (*b* Lambeth, 13 May 1842; *d* London, 22 Nov. 1900). English composer and conductor. In collaboration with the librettist W. S. *Gilbert he contributed to English music a distinctive style of light opera, a mixture of parody, burlesque, and satire, which has achieved immense popularity in Britain and the USA. The marriage of words and music in these 'Savoy operas' (so called because several were first performed at the Savoy Theatre, London) is so close that 'Gilbert and Sullivan' is sufficient description of the genre.

The son of an Irish bandmaster, Sullivan entered the Chapel Royal as a chorister in 1854 and had a sacred song published by Novello in 1855. He studied at the RAM under Sterndale Bennett in 1856 and went to the Leipzig Conservatory from 1858 to 1861. His first success as a composer was in 1861 when his incidental music to *The Tempest* was performed in Leipzig. There followed a Symphony and Cello Concerto in 1866, the oratorio *The Prodigal Son* at the 1869 Worcester Festival, and the *Overture di ballo* at the 1870 Birmingham Festival. He was organist of St Michael's, Chester Square, London, 1861–7, and at St Peter's, Cranley Gardens, 1867–72. He composed a ballet for Covent Garden in 1864. In 1867 he accompanied his friend George Grove to Vienna, where they discovered Schubert's lost *Rosamunde* music.

Sullivan's first success in comic opera was with the one-act *Cox and Box* (1867). During its run he met Gilbert, and their first collaboration was in 1871 in *Thespis* (now lost). *Trial by Jury* (1875) was more successful and stimulated the impresario Richard D'Oyly Carte to form a company specially to perform works by Gilbert and Sullivan. *The Sorcerer* (1877) led to the great success of *HMS Pinafore* (1878) and *The Pirates of Penzance* (1879). During the run of *Patience* (1881) the company moved into the new Savoy Theatre. Works produced there were *Iolanthe* (1882), *Princess Ida* (1884), *The Mikado* (1885), *Ruddigore* (1887), *The Yeomen of the Guard* (1888), and *The Gondoliers* (1889).

In 1886 the cantata *The Golden Legend* was performed at the Leeds Festival, of which Sullivan was chief conductor from 1880 to 1898. He also conducted for many other organizations and was principal of the National Training School (forerunner of the RCM) from 1876 to 1881. He was knighted in 1883. In 1891 his romantic opera *Ivanhoe* ran for 150 performances. A quarrel with Gilbert in 1890, though later resolved, ended their run of success, but *Utopia Limited* (1893) and *The Grand Duke* (1896) are prized by some devotees.

Of Sullivan's non-operatic works only the *Overture di ballo*, the hymn tune *Onward, Christian Soldiers* (1871), and the song *The Lost Chord* (1877) are still often heard. His fertile eclecticism was the root cause of the success of the Savoy operas. He could draw on elements from a variety of styles, and his brilliant parodies of Handel, Bellini, Purcell, Donizetti, Verdi, and Mendelssohn, added to a natural gift for melody and the rhythmic basis of his word-settings, resulted in music that is both witty and accomplished. His orchestration is always apt, often inspired, and such pieces as 'When the night wind howls' from *Ruddigore* and 'The sun whose rays' (*The Mikado*) are inspired inventions.

MK

H. SULLIVAN and N. FLOWER, *Sir Arthur Sullivan: His Life, Letters, and Diaries* (London, 1927, 2/1950) · L. BAILY, *Gilbert & Sullivan and their World* (London, 1973) · J. WOLFSON, *Sir Arthur Sullivan* (New York, 1976) · A. JACOBS, *Arthur Sullivan: A Victorian Musician* (Oxford, 1984) · A. JEFFERSON, *The Complete Gilbert and Sullivan Opera Guide* (Exeter, 1984) · R. WILSON and F. LLOYD, *Gilbert and Sullivan: The D'Oyly Carte Years* (London, 1984) · D. EDEN, *Gilbert and Sullivan: The Creative Conflict* (London, 1986) · C. HAYTER, *Gilbert and Sullivan* (London, 1987)

Sumer is icumen in. A mid-13th-century infinite canon (or round) at the unison for four tenor voices over a texted ground (or *pes*) also in canon at the unison. It is sometimes known as the 'Reading Rota' because it has been ascribed to John of Fornsete, a monk of Reading. A Latin text ('Perspice christicola') written below the English in the only extant manuscript may have been added later. It is one of the earliest surviving secular works.

Summer Night on the River. Tone-poem by Delius, the second of his Two Pieces for Small Orchestra (the first is *On Hearing the First Cuckoo in Spring*); it is not to be confused with his *Two Songs to be Sung of a Summer Night on the Water* (1917), textless works for chorus.

sung Mass. See MISSA.

'Sun' Quartets. Nickname of Haydn's six String Quartets op. 20 (1772), so called because of the design of the title page of the first edition (1774).

Suor Angelica ('Sister Angelica'). Opera in one act by Puccini to a libretto by Giovacchino Forzano, the second part of Puccini's *Il trittico* (New York, 1918).

superius (Lat.). In early vocal music, the name given to the highest voice-part in an ensemble and to the partbook that contains its music. The terms 'cantus' and 'discantus' may also be used.

supertonic. The second degree of the major or minor scale, i.e. the degree that lies one step above the tonic.

supertonic seventh chord. See ADDED SIXTH CHORD.

Supervia, Conchita (*b* Barcelona, 9 Dec. 1895; *d* London, 30 March 1936). Spanish mezzo-soprano. She was mainly self-taught and made her debut singing subsidiary roles with a Spanish touring company in Buenos Aires in 1910. The following year she sang Carmen in Rome and Octavian in the Rome premiere of *Der Rosenkavalier*. She appeared in Chicago in the 1915–16 season singing Charlotte, Mignon, and Carmen. As Carmen she won accolades for her acting and her fiery and seductive singing. In the 1920s she rose to international fame when she performed the virtuoso Rossini mezzo-soprano roles in *L'italiana in Algeri*, *La Cenerentola*, and *Il barbiere di Siviglia*. Her acting, like her singing, was natural and vivid, in turn spontaneously vivacious and delicately intimate. Her brilliant technique may be heard on many recordings.

JT

Suppé, Franz von [Suppe, Francesco Ezechiele Ermenegildo de] (*b* Split, 18 April 1819; *d* Vienna, 21 May 1895). Austrian composer. He showed early musical promise; after his father's death in 1835, his mother took him to Vienna, her native city. There he obtained a post as conductor at the Theater in der Josefstadt in 1840. He also conducted in Sopron and Bratislava and had some success on provincial stages as a singer. He moved in 1845 to the historic Theater an der Wien, in 1862 to the Kaitheater, and from 1865 to 1882 was at the Carltheater.

Suppé was a prolific composer of all kinds of theatre pieces and also wrote a Requiem (1855). His most successful stage works were Viennese counterparts to the operettas of Offenbach; they include the one-act *Das Pensionat* ('The Boarding School', 1860), *Zehn Mädchen und kein Mann* ('Ten Girls and No Man', 1862), and *Die schöne Galathee* ('Beautiful Galathea', 1865). The later three-act operettas *Fatinitza* (1876), *Boccaccio* (1879), and *Donna Juanita* (1880) were also well received. The patriotic song 'O du mein Österreich' ('O my Austria') from *'s Alraundl* ('The Mandrake', 1849) became hugely popular in Austria. Suppé's most individual creations are his rousing theatre overtures; besides those to works already cited, there are outstanding examples to *Ein Morgen, ein Mittag und ein Abend in Wien* ('Morning, Noon, and Night in Vienna', 1844), *Dichter und Bauer* ('Poet and Peasant', 1846), *Pique Dame* ('Queen of Spades', 1862), *Flotte Bursche* ('Jolly Students', 1863), *Leichte Kavallerie* ('Light Cavalry', 1866), and *Banditenstreiche* ('Bandits' Pranks', 1867).   ALa

    📖 O. SCHNEIDEREIT, *Franz von Suppé: Ein Wiener aus Dalmatien* (Berlin, 1977) · R. TRAUBNER, *Operetta: A Theatrical History* (London, 1984)

sur (Fr.). 'On'; *sur la touche*, bow 'on the fingerboard'; *sur le chevalet*, bow 'near the bridge'.

Surinach, Carlos (*b* Barcelona, 4 March 1915). Spanish-born American composer and conductor. He studied in Barcelona and Germany (1939–43), then embarked on a dual career as composer and conductor in Barcelona (1944–7) and Paris (1947–51) before settling in New York and becoming, in 1959, an American citizen. Showing high polish and not always Spanish flavour, his works include many ballets (especially for Martha Graham), concertos, and other orchestral pieces.   PG

surprise cadence. See CADENCE.

'Surprise' Symphony. Nickname of Haydn's Symphony no. 94 in G major (1791), so called because of the sudden *fortissimo* in the slow movement. Haydn incorporated this movement into the aria 'Schon eilet' in *The Seasons*.

Sursum corda (Lat., 'Lift up your hearts'). In the Christian *Mass, East and West, part of the dialogue between celebrant and congregation at the beginning of the Eucharistic prayer.

surtitles. Translations—often of necessity abbreviated—of an opera's libretto, usually projected on to a screen above the stage while the performance is taking place. Surtitles were first seen in Canada in 1983, were rapidly taken up in North America and then elsewhere, and have been regularly used at the Royal Opera House, Covent Garden, since 1986. Although now a fixture of most professional operatic performances in foreign languages, and clearly here to stay, surtitles remain controversial. While the benefits in terms of comprehension are obvious, many argue that they interfere with the direct communication of singer to audience that has always been at the heart of operatic drama.   RP

Survivor from Warsaw, A. Schoenberg's op. 46 (1947), for narrator, male voices, and orchestra, a setting of his own text.

Susanna. Oratorio (1749) by Handel to an anonymous biblical text.

Susannah. Opera in two acts by Floyd to his own libretto (Tallahassee, FL, 1955).

Susato, Tylman (*b* Soest, nr Dortmund, *c*.1510–15; *d* ?Sweden, 1570 or later). Composer and music publisher. His several talents included those of professional calligrapher and sackbut player at Antwerp Cathedral. From 1543 to 1561 he concentrated on music publishing in Antwerp, forming various partnerships and establishing the first successful music press in the Low Countries. A skilful and resourceful publisher, he was one of Lassus's first publishers (issuing a book of chansons in 1555). During his career he issued 22 books of chansons, three of masses, 19 of motets, and 11 volumes entitled *Musyck boexken*, which contain Flemish songs, dances based on popular tunes arranged by himself, and *souterliedekens* (metrical psalm settings in Dutch). Besides his well-known dance tunes, his own compositions include sacred vocal music and two books of chansons, written to help young singers gain experience.   JMT/JWa

suspended cadence. See CADENCE.

suspension. A form of discord arising from the holding over of a note in one chord as a momentary part of the chord which follows, it then resolving by falling a degree to a note which forms a real part of the second chord (Ex. 1). When two notes are held over in this way, it is called a double suspension.

Ex. 1

Süssmayr, Franz Xaver (*b* Schwanenstadt, 1766; *d* Vienna, 17 Sept. 1803). Austrian composer. He was educated at the monastery of Kremsmünster until he settled in Vienna in 1788, becoming a pupil of Salieri and Mozart. He was Mozart's assistant during 1791. After Mozart's death, Constanze Mozart asked him to complete the Requiem, which he did in a version that leaves the extent of his contribution unclear. He claimed to have filled in and orchestrated the early movements, and then composed the Sanctus, Benedictus, and Agnus Dei, perhaps on the basis of acquaintanceship with Mozart's intentions. His version has been generally accepted as the best possible solution.

    Süssmayr's own works include a number of operas, the most successful of which reflects the influence of Mozart and in particular *Die Zauberflöte*. *Der Spiegel von Arkadien* (1794), to a libretto by Schikaneder that frankly set out to repeat Mozart's success, draws on similar ingredients in both story and music, to considerable effect and to great local acclaim in Vienna.   DA/JW

sustaining pedal [damper pedal, 'loud' pedal]. The right pedal of the piano. Depressing it raises the dampers, thereby prolonging the sound. See PIANOFORTE.

susurrando, susurrante (It.). 'Whispering', 'murmuring'.

Sutermeister, Heinrich (*b* Feuerthalen, Schaffhausen, 12 Aug. 1910; *d* Vaux-sur-Morges, 16 March 1995). Swiss composer. He studied philology before turning to composition. His principal teacher at the Munich Hochschule für Musik was Carl Orff, whose simplicity and populism were an inspiration to him. Sutermeister was best known for his operas, including *Romeo und Julia*, after Shakespeare (Dresden, 1940), *Raskolnikoff*, after Dostoevsky's *Crime and Punishment* (Stockholm, 1948), *Madame Bovary*, after Gustave Flaubert's novel (Zürich, 1967), and *Le Roi Bérenger*, after Eugene Ionesco (Munich, 1985). He also wrote a series of cantatas and other choral music, orchestral and chamber music, and many scores for radio, television, and films.   ABUR

Suzuki method. A method of teaching instrumental playing that embodies a radical and innovatory philosophy about how children learn music. It is named after its originator, Shin'ichi Suzuki (1898–1998), a Japanese educationist and violin teacher. Suzuki believed that children could learn musical skills at an early age, initially through listening, and he observed the way young children acquire language through hearing others speak. He advocated starting violin training by the age of two or three, initially by exposing children to recorded music, a process that continued throughout their musical training. The aim was to develop an internal model of the music to be studied, memorizing both the notes and the way those notes were performed.

Just as children learn to speak before learning to read, Suzuki advocated a delay in teaching notation until there was an adequate grounding in playing skills and the development of musical memory. The Suzuki method also aims to promote social skills. Children are taught in groups rather than individually, encouraging a spirit of cooperation and teamwork. Parents are involved in partnership with teachers; they attend lessons, enabling them to support their children's practising.

PSp

📖 E. MILLS and T. C. MURTHY (eds.), *The Suzuki Conception: An Introduction to a Successful Method for Early Music Education* (Berkeley, CA, 1973)

svegliando, svegliato (It.). 'Awakening', 'awakened', i.e. brisk, alert.

svelto (It.). 'Quick', 'smart'.

Svendsen, Johan (Severin) (*b* Christiania [now Oslo], 30 Sept. 1840; *d* Copenhagen, 14 June 1906). Norwegian composer and conductor. Born three years earlier than Grieg, whom he outlived by four years, Svendsen was the leading Norwegian symphonic composer of his day. He was the son of a bandmaster and by the age of 15 was already an accomplished violinist, also playing the flute and clarinet. Like Grieg he received his musical schooling in Leipzig, where he was enrolled in 1864 and studied the violin with Ferdinand David and composition with Reinecke. It was in Leipzig that Svendsen wrote his first works, finding an individual voice very early. His Leipzig years were both happier and more fruitful than Grieg's, and the Octet op. 1, the delightful First Symphony op. 4, and the String Quintet op. 5 are all works of astonishing individuality, assurance, and above all freshness.

After returning to Norway, in 1867 Svendsen undertook a long tour embracing Scotland, Iceland, and the Faeroes. For the rest of the 1860s he lived in Paris, eking out a living as an orchestral player; it was his time there that inspired his celebrated *Carnival in Paris*. 1871 found him in Bayreuth, where he was much in Wagner's company; later in life he was to introduce *Die Walküre* and *Siegfried*, among other operas, to the Copenhagen public. In the late 1870s he concentrated on conducting, appearing in London, Paris, and Leipzig, and from 1883 basing himself in Copenhagen. There he remained until ill health forced his retirement in 1908. Though he and Grieg were good friends, Svendsen did not involve himself in the folksong movement to anything like the same extent (the four *Norwegian Rhapsodies* were probably as close as he ever came to it). His sympathies remained predominantly Classical, and he continued to work within sonata-form structures. Yet there is a distinctive Norwegian feel to his melodic ideas. After the famous *Romance* in G major for violin and orchestra the creative fires burnt themselves out. The Second Symphony, completed towards the end of his five-year spell (1872–7) in the Norwegian capital, was his last large-scale work.

RLA

📖 F. BENESTED and D. SCHJELDERUP-EBBE, *Johan Severin Svendsen* (Oslo, 1990)

Sviridov, Georgy Vasil'yevich (*b* Fatezh, Kursk province, 3/16 Dec. 1915; *d* Moscow, 5 Jan. 1998). Russian composer. He studied at the Leningrad Conservatory with Pyotr Ryazanov and Shostakovich. He was a People's Artist of the USSR, Hero of Socialist Labour, and committee member of the Composers' Union from 1962 to 1974. His output consists chiefly of vocal works, notably the cantata *Poèma pamyati Sergeya Yesenina* ('Poem in Memory of Sergey Yesenin', 1956) and the *Pateticheskaya oratoriya* on texts by Mayakovsky (1959). He was a leading figure in the 'new folklore trend' of the mid-1960s, when composers returned to Russian folk material; his *Kurskiye pesni* ('Kursk Songs', 1964) are among the finest products of this movement. Sviridov's mature compositional style is characterized by slow-moving chordal textures and a cultivation of diatonic dissonance.   JWAL

swanee whistle [slide whistle, swannee whistle]. A *duct flute with no fingerholes. Sliding an easily moved stopper or piston in and out alters the tube length and thus the pitch.

Swan Lake (*Lebedinoye ozero*; *Le Lac des cygnes*). Ballet in four acts by Tchaikovsky to a scenario by V. P. Begitchev and V. Geltser; it was choreographed by Wenzel Reisinger (Moscow, 1977) and later by Marius Petipa and Lev Ivanov (St Petersburg, 1895).

Swan of Tuonela, The (*Tuonelan joutsen*). Symphonic legend, op. 22 no. 3, by Sibelius, composed in 1893 and revised in 1897 and 1900; it was written as a prelude to an unfinished opera but was published as the third symphonic poem of the *Lemminkäinen Suite*. A cor anglais represents the swan; Tuonela is the Finnish Hades.

Swayne, Giles (*b* Hitchin, 30 June 1946). English composer. His teachers included Nicholas Maw, Birtwistle, and Messiaen, but the decisive influence on his musical development was his first visit to Africa in 1981–2. His belief that music, however sophisticated in construction, must communicate directly and immediately, has found expression not only in compositions specifically intended for children and amateurs, but in large-scale concert works, of which *Cry* (1976–9) for 28 amplified solo voices is the best known. The unaccompanied *Missa tiburtina* (1989), and *Ophelia Drowning* (1996) for voices and flute, are among his most successful later works.   AW

Sweden 1. From the 13th century to the 17th; 2. The age of Roman; 3. Song and the rise of nationalism; 4. After Stenhammar; 5. The late 20th century

1. From the 13th century to the 17th

Although Johan Helmich Roman (1694–1758) is popularly known as 'the father of Swedish music', there was musical activity long before his time. Ars Antiqua polyphony had reached Uppsala Cathedral in the 13th century and the Gregorian liturgy was in currency before that. After the breakup of the union with Denmark, the Swedish court showed a lively interest in music and King Gustav Vasa's son, Eric XIV, was a composer (a fragment of one of his Latin motets survives). Unlike King Christian IV of Denmark, the Vasas made little effort to foster native talent but were content to import foreign musicians.

Prominent among these was the Düben family, who came from Leipzig and whose members dominated Swedish musical life throughout the 17th century. Andreas Düben (*c*.1597–1662) studied in Amsterdam with Sweelinck before settling in Stockholm where he became organist of the German Church (Tyska Kyrkan) and subsequently *hovkapellmästare*, a position that he and his descendants occupied well into the 18th century. Queen Christina was keenly interested in music both before and after her abdication. She invited Vincenzo Albrici (1631–90 or 1696) to her court, and was the patron and admirer of such composers as Carissimi, Alessandro Scarlatti, and Corelli, who dedicated his op. 1 trio sonatas to her. The most important member of the Düben family was Andreas's son Gustaf (*c*.1628–90), whose output includes some fine Latin settings as well as a number of monodic songs to both sacred and vernacular texts.

2. The age of Roman

Roman, the first native composer of any real note, came to prominence at a time when Sweden's Storhetstiden ('Age of Greatness') had passed with the death of Charles XII. He showed such early talent as a violinist and oboist that the court took the unprecedented step of paying for his studies abroad. He was in England from about 1715 to 1721, probably studying under Pepusch and certainly acquiring a love of Handel, and after his return became in 1727 *kapellmästare* to the court. He transformed the orchestra into a first-rate ensemble and together with a young player and composer, Per Brant (1714–67), started public concerts at the Riddarhuset in Stockholm, which became an important forum for new music. Roman's pupil Agrell settled in Nuremberg, but movement was mostly in the other direction.

The most important figures in Sweden were both German. Johann Gottlieb Naumann, a native of Dresden, spent much of his time in Copenhagen and Stockholm, and composed the first Swedish opera on a national theme, *Gustaf Wasa* (1786), to a libretto by the poet Kellgren on a prose sketch by King Gustav III himself. The arts generally, and music in particular, prospered during Gustav's reign (1772–92), for the king founded not only the Royal Opera but also the Royal Swedish Academy of Music. Yet though opera flourished, the talent remained imported: *Gustaf Wasa* was followed by a *Singspiel*, Vogler's *Gustaf Adolph och Ebba Brahe*,

The most interesting and worthwhile symphonic composer after Roman was Mozart's exact contemporary Joseph Martin Kraus, who came from Miltenberg am Main in south Germany and settled in Sweden in his early 20s, eventually becoming *hovkapellmästare* to Gustav III. Kraus's Symphony in C minor (1783) has the unmistakable flavour of the *Sturm und Drang* epoch, and his finest music, which earned him the admiration of Haydn, has a dark intensity that recalls Gluck and C. P. E. Bach. Among his pupils was Johan Wikmanson (1753–1800), whose quartets show that Haydn's influence extended to the far north. Another phenomenon of the Gustavian era was the poet Carl Michael Bellman (1740–95), whose songs are unique in their skill in fitting words of high poetic distinction to melodies from *opéra comique* and other sources.

3. Song and the rise of nationalism

The turn of the century saw an upsurge of interest in song. Adolf Lindblad (1801–78), possessed of a rich fund of melody and purity of style, was much admired by Mendelssohn. But despite the presence of such talented poets and composers as Erik Gustaf Geijer (1783–1847) and Carl Jonas Love Almqvist (1793–1866) Sweden produced no really great master of the *romans* (the equivalent of the German lied or the French *mélodie*) commensurate with the quality of its singers, who included the legendary Jenny Lind and Christine Nilsson. The most commanding figure of the period was Franz Berwald. Most Swedish composers after him were relatively insipid characters reflecting the ideals either of Leipzig (as did Ludvig Norman, 1831–85) or of Wagner (Andreas Hallén, 1846–1925).

By far the strongest figure to emerge in Berwald's wake was Wilhelm Stenhammar. He possesses much the same keen feeling for nature as did his great Nordic contemporaries, and the same awareness of the evanescence of experience that distinguishes such late Romantics as Mahler, Elgar, and Delius. The pale short-lived summer is central to the Swedish sensibility, and few have expressed its gentle melancholy with greater eloquence. Stenhammar's art, not so overtly national or as folk-inspired as that of Hugo Alfvén or Wilhelm Peterson-Berger, yet seems far more attuned to the Swedish spirit. Alfvén is best remembered for his rhapsody *Midsummer Vigil*, a brilliant repertory piece and in a sense the Swedish equivalent of Svendsen's *Norwegian Rhapsodies*. Both Türe Rangström and Kurt Atterberg (1887–1974) were symphonists, though Rangström was more at ease as a miniaturist. His best songs have an affecting simplicity and directness of appeal that have won them a place in the international repertory.

4. After Stenhammar

The generation that followed reacted against the lush orchestral opulence and folk-derived inspiration of Alfvén and Atterberg and turned to the Continent for stimulus. The most influential figure to emerge between the wars was Hilding Rosenberg. In addition to Sibelius and Nielsen he was influenced in the 1920s by Honegger, Milhaud, Hindemith, and Schoenberg. Rosenberg's achievement was not merely to open the doors to the outside world but to do so without any loss of identity. However cosmopolitan his sympathies, he remained recognizably Swedish and his work is enriched as a result. His eclecticism was reflected not only by Larsson but also by his pupils, Karl-Birger Blomdahl, Sven-Erik Bäck (1919–94), and Ingvar Lidholm. Dag Wirén, whose captivating Serenade has attained worldwide currency, is perhaps the least outward-looking; his roots remain in Sibelius and Nielsen, yet his work has an individual colouring and is refreshingly Nordic. Like Gösta Nystroem (1890–1966) he also drew inspiration from French music.

Blomdahl, Bäck, and Lidholm proved the dominant figures in the mid- to late 1950s, Blomdahl assimilating the diverse influences of Hindemith, Bartók, Schoenberg, Webern, and the post-serial school. At its best his music shows a dark, powerful imagination, though his space-opera *Aniara* (1959), much acclaimed in Sweden at the time of its premiere, has failed to hold the stage. Interest in electronic music was fostered by Bengt Hambraeus (1928–2000). The avant-garde dominance was at the expense of such tonal composers as Bo Linde (1933–70), Jan Carlstedt (*b* 1926), and Eduard Tubin. The more conservative tradition was also upheld by Allan Pettersson, whose 16 symphonies have a strong, brooding atmosphere, though they are wanting in concentration. However, the major symphonist of the post-Stenhammar era is undoubtedly the Estonian-born Tubin, whose ten symphonies exhibit a mastery of form, individuality, and expressive concentration that render his neglect in his adopted homeland during his lifetime incomprehensible.

5. The late 20th century

The middle generation of composers includes Lars-Johan Werle (*b* 1926), whose operas *Dream about Thérèse* and *Tintomara* perhaps show a stronger sense of theatre than individuality of invention, and Sven-David Sandström (*b* 1942), who has written effectively in a variety of genres. Daniel Börtz (*b* 1943) and Anders Eliasson (*b* 1947) exhibit considerable imaginative resource. Börtz has written two full-scale operas to date, *The Bacchantes* (1991) and *Marie Antoinette* (1998), as well as ten sinfonias. Sweden has a strong vocal tradition and, as well as such famous singers as Birgit

Nilsson, Jussi Björling, Elisabeth Söderström, Anne Sofie von Otter and many others, possesses a choral culture of enviable quality. The work of the choral conductor Eric Ericsson raised the Swedish Radio Choir to the highest international level and encouraged a valuable literature of contemporary choral music. Moreover this excellence extends to the orchestral field: the Royal Stockholm Philharmonic, the Swedish Radio Symphony Orchestra and the Göteborg Symphony Orchestra have developed into ensembles of international stature.   RLa

📖 L. Roth (ed.), *Musical Life in Sweden* (Stockholm, 1987) · I. Mattsson (ed.), *Gustavian Opera* (Stockholm, 1991) · G. Schönfelder and H. Åstrand, *Contemporary Swedish Music through the Telescope Sight* (Stockholm, 1993)

Sweelinck, Jan Pieterszoon (*b* Deventer, ?May 1562; *d* Amsterdam, 16 Oct. 1621). Dutch organist, composer, and teacher. Before 1580 he succeeded his father (his earliest teacher) as organist of the Oude Kerk in Amsterdam, a post he retained for the rest of his life. On his death his son, Dirk, was appointed to succeed him. Chief among his vocal compositions are numerous chansons and Italian madrigals, motets (*Cantiones sacrae*, 1619), and polyphonic settings (for domestic devotions) of the entire Genevan Psalter.

As an organist Sweelinck was renowned as much for his advice on the quality of new or rebuilt organs in other Dutch cities as for his brilliant improvisations at the Oude Kerk, before and after church services. His pupils included Düben, Scheidemann, Siefert, Scheidt, and others who were later to become leaders in their profession. His numerous organ works (by no means all of which have survived) include fantasias, toccatas, and sets of elaborate variations (notably those on *Mein junges Leben hat ein Endt*) in which the influence of John Bull and other English virginalists is apparent.
                                                                                    BS

swell. A wooden board or box, sometimes with slats like a Venetian blind, used in harpsichords, where it forms an inner lid, and organs, where it encloses a whole set of pipework. The swell box can be opened to a greater or lesser extent with a pedal to produce a crescendo or diminuendo.

swing. 1. The quality of jazz performance that distinguishes it from 'straight' music and gives it much of its physical motivation (cf. Duke Ellington's *It Don't Mean a Thing (if it Ain't got that Swing)*, 1932). The criteria of swing appear to be fundamentally indefinable, but they include the unequal performance of short note-values as well as the use of timbre, rubato, attack, and other means to achieve a propulsive effect.
                                                                                    JJD

2. A jazz style evolved in the 1930s when jazz was becoming more loosely rhythmical and increasingly imbued with the excitement of swing. As bands became larger, with brass and saxes multiplying into sections, the 'riff', a repeated rhythmic figure, was often used to work up momentum. By the 1930s such bands came to be called swing bands, and the kind of big-band jazz they played was categorized as swing. Now less improvisatory than before, the music gave scope to black arrangers and composers like Fletcher Henderson, Duke Ellington, and Don Redman and to leaders like Count Basie, Jimmie Lunceford, and Chick Webb; white bands came on the scene under the leadership of the self-styled 'King of Swing' Benny Goodman, Jimmy and Tommy Dorsey, Woody Herman, Artie Shaw, Harry James, Glenn Miller, and many others. Swing was also cultivated in the UK by such bandleaders as Ted Heath.
                                                                                    PGa

Switzerland. Its mountainous terrain and, until the 20th century, lack of wealthy patronage hindered Switzerland's early development as a musical centre. Sacred music flourished in the Middle Ages, however, notably in such northern monasteries as St Gallen, Einsiedeln, and Engelberg. Surviving *plainchant manuscripts show that the standard Gregorian chant was not used, and Ambrosian forms persisted in Italian-speaking regions until recent times. Song schools were established in various towns in the late Middle Ages, and by the late 15th century a group of organists and composers had begun to appear.

The *Reformation put a halt to such musical development. The Swiss reformer Ulrich Zwingli (1484–1531) was particularly opposed to any kind of elaboration in church music; organs were destroyed or were removed from churches (the cathedral organ of Berne was sold to the more tolerant church at Sion), and at first only monophonic psalm-singing was allowed. In the mid-16th century four-part singing was permitted, and the 17th century saw the reappearance of organs.

The Renaissance organists had created a strong enough tradition for there to be chamber organs in many private houses, and some tablature books survive. University towns established a number of *collegia musica*, and concert societies came into being. But native composers, from Senfl in the 16th century to Albicastro in the 18th, tended to move abroad to more important musical centres, and no great musical figure was drawn to Switzerland from elsewhere.

The ideas of two Swiss-born educationists, Jean-Jacques Rousseau and Johann Heinrich Pestalozzi (1746–1827), encouraged choral singing, and several male-voice choirs were formed in the early 19th century. Travelling companies occasionally brought opera, and theatres were built in Geneva (1738), Zürich (1813), Basle (1834), and Berne (1903). Wagner settled in Zürich for eight years from 1849, when he was exiled from Germany, and his direction of the Allgemeine Musikgesellschaft, formed by amalgamating the earlier *collegia*, raised standards generally.

Increasing wealth in the 20th century, based on banking and light industry, put Switzerland on a level with its neighbours. The major cities acquired orchestras, theatres, and radio stations. Prominent is the Orchestre de la Suisse Romande, founded in Geneva in 1918 by the Swiss-born Ernest Ansermet, who remained its conductor until 1967; it became internationally famous, particularly for its many recordings. The Collegium Musicum (1941) similarly built up a worldwide reputation under its founder-director Paul *Sacher. The Tonhalle Society (1867) established a first-rate orchestra and, since its amalgamation with the radio orchestra in 1944, has attracted leading foreign conductors and soloists.

The Zürich Opera presented the first 'legitimate' stage performance of Wagner's *Parsifal* outside Bayreuth in 1913. It also gave the premieres of Berg's *Lulu* (1937), Hindemith's *Mathis der Maler* (1938), Honegger's *Jeanne d'Arc au bûcher* (1942), and Schoenberg's *Moses und Aron* (1957), as well as the first European performance of Gershwin's *Porgy and Bess* (1945). Although Switzerland has never had a nationalist school of composers, Bloch, Schoeck, Martin, Honegger, Conrad Beck (1901–89), and Robert Suter (*b* 1919) have all received international recognition.   DA/JBo

📖 A. BRINER, *Swiss Composers in the 20th Century* (Zürich, 1990) · D. ROSSET (ed.), *Musikleben in der Schweiz* (Zürich, 1991) · *Schweizer Komponisten in unserer Zeit* (Winterthur, 1993) [in Ger., Eng., Fr.]

Sylphides, Les ('The Sylphs'). Ballet in one act to music by Chopin; originally called *Chopiniana*, it was choreographed by Mikhail Fokine (St Petersburg, 1907).

Sylvia, ou La Nymphe de Diane. Ballet in three acts and five scenes by Delibes to a scenario by Jules Barbier and Baron de Reinach; it was choreographed by Louis Mérante (Paris, 1876).

symbolism. A term for the ways in which musical elements may in some way be connected to extra-musical phenomena: the words of a poem, a natural object, or a person or emotional state. More specifically, Symbolism was a late 19th- and early 20th-century literary movement, principally in France (see below).

Musical symbolism has been used since the Middle Ages. Machaut's celebrated *rondeau Ma fin est mon commencement* ('My end is my beginning') uses melodic

material in retrograde with itself to depict the essence of the text. In secular music, musical symbols were sometimes used visually: two semibreves representing the eyes of the beloved, or black notes symbolic of death (see EYE MUSIC). In later Renaissance madrigals and motets such elements as phrase-shape, tessitura, and harmony were used in the service of words (*word-painting*): rising figures might represent ascension and falling figures the reverse; intertwining turning figures might represent chains or snares, and so on; high tessitura might represent heaven, low tessitura hell. Particularly important was the way in which harmonic suspensions would convey sighing, pain, or death (the use of the word 'die' symbolically represented sexual climax).

From the Baroque era, numerology began to play an important symbolic role, as did key-association. Marc-Antoine Charpentier set down the symbolic associations of keys, which lasted well into the 19th century: sharp keys represented positive states (ecstasy or fulfilment), flat keys the opposite (bereavement or rejection). The music of Bach has been scrutinized for its symbolic associations: the number of entries in the Crucifixus of the B minor Mass (13) can hardly have been coincidental, and his use of key signatures, where three flats seems to represent the Trinity and sharps the cross, is reflected in certain treatises of his time, allied to the concept of rhetoric. Mozart's use of two horns in *Le nozze di Figaro* to represent cuckoldry is a lighter variant of symbolism.

Instruments had specific associations. Oboes, perhaps because their timbre is close to that of the bagpipe, often have pastoral or bucolic associations. Flutes often represent birdsong, as does the high register of the violin (from Vivaldi's *Four Seasons* to Vaughan Williams's *The Lark Ascending*). Trombones have been associated with death since the time of Shakespeare. Trumpets naturally have military significance. Horns symbolized hunting, hence wealth, as in Weber's *Der Freischütz* (see ORCHESTRATION).

The 19th century saw two important applications of musical symbolism: scene-painting and *leitmotif. The songs of Schubert are a lexicon of the former, with their burbling brooks, posthorns, spinning-wheels, themselves symbolic in the texts. The *programme music of the later 19th century uses the instruments of the orchestra to represent the natural world: Mendelssohn's *Hebrides* overture, for example, evokes the sea in Fingal's Cave, and Wagner portrays the flowing Rhine at the beginning of *Das Rheingold*. Here, representationalism borders on musical *Impressionism, a concept Wagner discussed with Auguste Renoir.

In the second half of the 19th century, a group of literary figures became identified as Symbolists. They included the poets Paul Verlaine (1844–96) and Stéphane Mallarmé (1842–98), and the playwrights Maurice Maeterlinck (1862–1949) and Auguste Villiers de L'Isle Adam (1838–89). They used literary symbols with a plethora of meanings, rather than as specific signs. Many French composers, including Fauré and Ravel, set Symbolist poems as songs. Mallarmé's poem *L'Après-midi d'un faune* was the subject of Debussy's wordless orchestral *Prélude*, conceived as a musical paraphrase of the text. In *Pelléas et Mélisande*, an almost verbatim setting of Maeterlinck's play, Debussy used such symbols as fountains, doves, light on the sea, as musical ideas; a musical motif is sometimes used to create dramatic irony, alerting the listener to something as yet unseen. Some motifs are quintessentially symbolic in that, though their importance is obvious, no one idea can be assigned to them.

See also CRYPTOGRAPHY; OPERA, 14.   RLS

sympathetic strings. In stringed instruments, additional strings of wire that vibrate in sympathy with a unison note or one of its partials, bowed or plucked on the main strings, adding a shimmer to the sound. Some instruments have as many as 15 sympathetic strings tuned to different notes of the scale. They run parallel to the main strings from tuning-pegs set either in the pegbox or in the side of the neck, under the fingerboard (where present), and through holes in the main bridge to the string-holder or tailpiece. Sympathetic strings are a characteristic feature of such instruments as the *Hardanger fiddle, *sāraṅgī, *sarod, *sitar, *viola d'amore, and sometimes the *trumpet marine. On the *baryton they run through a cavity in the back of the neck and may be plucked by the left thumb while the main strings are simultaneously bowed.   JMo

symphonia (Lat.). See HURDY-GURDY.

Symphonia antarctica. Symphony (2001) by Maxwell Davies.

Symphonia domestica ('Domestic Symphony'). Tone-poem, op. 53 (1902–3), by Richard Strauss, depicting a day in the life of the Strauss family, with themes representing the composer, his wife Pauline, and their baby son.

symphonic band. See CONCERT BAND.

Symphonic Dances. Orchestral work, op. 45 (1940), by Rakhmaninov.

symphonic poem [tone-poem]. A piece of orchestral music, usually in one movement, based on a literary, poetic, or other extra-musical idea. It originated in the mid-19th century with Liszt and, as a direct product of a Romantic movement which encouraged literary, pic-

torial, and dramatic associations in music, it developed into an important form of *programme music in the second half of the 19th century. Elements of symphonic architecture could be compressed into its single-movement form, and although the term 'tone-poem' has largely been used interchangeably with 'symphonic poem', a few composers, notably Richard Strauss and Sibelius, have preferred the former for pieces that are less 'symphonic' in design and in which there is no special emphasis on thematic or tonal contrast.

The symphonic poem has its ancestry in the concert *overture of the earlier 19th century (e.g. Beethoven's *Coriolan* and Mendelssohn's *A Midsummer Night's Dream*, which also serve as musical illustrations of literary subjects), as well as in the symphony itself, in the much-expanded and expressive form that it had attained by mid-century. Liszt attempted to combine features of the overture and symphony with descriptive elements, and produced a number of narrative, one-movement orchestral works that approach a symphonic first movement in form and scale (e.g. *Ce qu'on entend sur la montagne*, after Victor Hugo, 1847–56; *Mazeppa*, after Hugo, 1851–4; *Hunnenschlacht*, 'The Slaughter of the Huns', after a painting by Wilhelm von Kaulbach, 1857; and *Hamlet*, 1858). Some follow a detailed narrative programme; others paint a more general picture in the mind's eye by outlining the features of a literary character or creating a scene or atmosphere.

Other composers seized on the symphonic poem as a suitable vehicle for expressing *nationalism in music. Notable among them was Smetana, whose cycle of six symphonic poems entitled *Má vlast* ('My Country', c.1872–9) describes scenes from the history and everyday life of his beloved Bohemia; and this began a fashion, as countless other composers were moved to attempt to illustrate their homeland through the symphonic poem, Dvořák, Suk, and ultimately Janáček among them. Russian nationalist composers were particularly attracted by the genre (e.g. Musorgsky, *Night on the Bare Mountain*, 1867; Borodin, *In the Steppes of Central Asia*, 1880), as was Tchaikovsky, whose 'fantasy overture' *Romeo and Juliet* (1869) is a symphonic poem in all but name. There are numerous later Russian examples (e.g. Skryabin, *Poem of Ecstasy*, 1905–8; Rakhmaninov, *The Isle of the Dead*, 1909).

France was less concerned with nationalism than many other countries, but its well-established tradition of narrative and illustrative music, reaching back to Berlioz, meant that composers were attracted to the poetic elements of the symphonic poem, and the Lisztian model was a direct inspiration for many works in the German-influenced musical culture which took root in the 1870s. The four symphonic poems that Saint-Saëns wrote in that decade, including *Le Rouet d'Omphale* (1871) and *Danse macabre* (1874), stand at the head of a long line of French pieces, among them Franck's *Le Chasseur maudit* (1882) and Dukas's *L'Apprenti sorcier* (1897), which carries the genre into the 20th century in the work of Debussy, Ravel, Roussel, Koechlin, Ibert, and others.

The symphonic poem reached its apogee in the work of Richard Strauss. A pupil of Alexander Ritter, who encouraged him towards the form, he vastly increased both its scale and its depth of expression, through a bold choice of subjects, brilliant orchestration, vivid realism, and supremely skilful compositional crafts (such as thematic *transformation). Strauss's symphonic poems cover narrative, philosophical, pictorial, and even autobiographical themes, and include *Don Juan* (1888–9), *Tod und Verklärung* (1888–9), *Till Eulenspiegel* (1894–5), *Also sprach Zarathustra* (1895–6), *Don Quixote* (1896–7), *Ein Heldenleben* (1897–8), and *Symphonia domestica* (1902–3); probably more than any other such works, they have retained their place and popularity in the concert repertory.

During the late 19th century and the early 20th innumerable other composers contributed to the genre to some degree, though few of their works remain in the repertory. Of those that do, Sibelius's tone-poems (e.g. *The Swan of Tuonela*, 1893; *Finlandia*, 1899; *Tapiola*, 1926) are the most significant, and Respighi's *Fontane di Roma* (1914–16) and *Pini di Roma* (1923–4) have always been popular. Elgar's 'symphonic study' *Falstaff* (1913) is perhaps the only British contribution of any real significance, though several composers, including Vaughan Williams (e.g. *The Lark Ascending*, 1914) and Delius (*On Hearing the First Cuckoo in Spring*, 1912), wrote a number of single-movement orchestral works describing scenes or landscapes which come close to the symphonic poem idea.

Orchestral pieces extracted or transferred directly from stage works, such as Stravinsky's *The Song of the Nightingale* (1917), taken from his opera *The Nightingale* (1914), and Ravel's *La Valse* (1919), originally composed for dance, kept the genre alive in the second decade of the 20th century. In the USA Gershwin tackled the symphonic poem in *An American in Paris* (1928), but the subsequent decline of the form there and elsewhere naturally followed on the decline of Romantic ideals in general, as an inevitable result of a decreasing interest in music that was primarily descriptive in favour of more abstract forms. Nevertheless, the possibilities offered by a kind of musical Futurism (Honegger's *Pacific 231*, 1923) and, even more so, the aesthetic of *socialist realism (Prokofiev's 'festive poem' *The Meeting of the Volga and the Don*, 1951; Shostakovich's *October*, 1967) gave the symphonic poem a brief, if debased, afterlife. During its heyday, however, the symphonic poem was a most important independent orchestral genre, and an especially appropriate vehicle for the intense Romantic and nationalist expression that characterized its time.

PS/JN/KC

R. W. S. MENDL, 'The art of the symphonic poem', *Musical Quarterly*, 18 (1932), 443–62 · J. CHANTAVOINE, *Le Poème symphonique* (Paris, 1950) · L. ORREY, *Programme Music* (London, 1975) · M. CHION, *Le Poème symphonique et la musique à programme* (Paris, 1993)

symphonie concertante (Fr., 'concertante symphony'; It.: *sinfonia concertante*). A form of concerto which flourished in the late 18th century. Generally of a lighthearted character, it was essentially a concerto for more than one solo instrument (usually between two and seven) in which the role of the orchestra was to accompany the solo parts. The *symphonie concertante* was especially popular in Paris: almost half of all known Classical examples were written either by French composers or for performance at the celebrated Concert Spirituel. The combination of soloists ranged from the usual two violins to more unusual groups (e.g. Leopold Kozeluch's Concerto for piano, mandolin, trumpet, and double bass).

The form first appeared in the 1760s, and the earliest examples were written by such Parisian composers as Devienne, Gossec, and Pleyel, and in Mannheim by Cannabich, Holzbauer, Anton and Carl Stamitz, and Danzi. The *symphonie concertante* was also cultivated by Austrian and Bohemian composers—for example Wagenseil, Vanhal, and Dittersdorf—and by figures of the stature of Haydn and Mozart. Only one piece by Haydn, his Concertante for violin, cello, oboe, and bassoon composed for the Salomon concerts in London in 1792, actually bears the title, and apart from an early Concertone in C for two violins, K190/186E, Mozart's surviving contributions to the genre are a Concerto for flute and harp, K299/297c, and the great E♭ *Sinfonia concertante* for violin and viola, K364/320d.

The importance in the 19th century of the star solo performer caused the decline of the *symphonie concertante* in favour of the virtuoso solo concerto, though it lingered in such pieces as Beethoven's Triple Concerto, Schumann's *Conzertstück* for four horns, and Brahms's Double Concerto. The 20th century saw a revival of interest, by such composers as Martinů (Concerto for piano, strings, and timpani), Frank Martin (*Petite symphonie concertante* for piano, harpsichord, harp, and strings), and Poulenc (Concerto for organ, timpani, and strings). Some 20th-century composers, for example Walton (*Sinfonia concertante* for piano and orchestra), used the term even when only one solo instrument was involved, to imply the close integration of soloist and orchestra.

WT

Symphonie espagnole ('Spanish Symphony'). Work (1874) for violin and orchestra by Lalo.

Symphonie fantastique ('Fantastic Symphony'). Symphony, op. 14, by Berlioz, composed in 1830 and revised 1831–45. Subtitled 'Épisode de la vie d'un artiste' ('Episode in the Life of an Artist'), it is in five movements: 'Rêveries, passions' ('Dreams, Passions'), 'Un bal' ('A Ball'), 'Scène aux champs' ('Scene in the Fields'), 'Marche au supplice' ('March to the Scaffold'), and 'Songe d'une nuit du Sabbat' ('Dream of a Witches' Sabbath'). The work was inspired by Berlioz's love for the Irish actress Harriet Smithson, and this is symbolized by a recurring theme (an *idée fixe*) used in a similar way to a Wagnerian *leitmotif. The *Symphonie fantastique* is one of the most important early examples of *programme music, the forerunner of the programme symphonies and symphonic poems of Liszt, Mahler, Strauss, and Tchaikovsky among others. See also LÉLIO.   AL

Symphonie pathétique. Subtitle of Tchaikovsky's Symphony no. 6 in B minor op. 74 (1893), so called at his brother Modest's suggestion. (The Russian word *patetichesky* means 'passionate' or 'emotional' rather than 'pathetic'.)

Symphonies of Wind Instruments. Work (1920) by Stravinsky composed in memory of Debussy.

symphony, the (*see page 1238*)

symphony. See HURDY-GURDY.

Symphony in Three Movements. Orchestral work (1942–5) by Stravinsky.

'Symphony of a Thousand'. Nickname of *Mahler's Symphony no. 8 in E♭ major (1906); it was so named for publicity purposes by Emil Guttmann, the impresario who organized its premiere (Munich, 1910), because of the huge vocal and orchestral forces engaged to perform it.

Symphony of Psalms. Work for chorus and orchestra (without violins and violas) by Stravinsky to a Latin text from Psalms 38, 39, and 150; it was composed in 1930 and revised in 1948.

synaesthesia. The experiencing of one sense as a result of the stimulation of another; in music it is associated mainly with *colour.

syncopation. The displacement of the normal musical accent from a strong beat to a weak one. In mensural music beats fall naturally into groups of two or three

syncopation, Ex. 1

(a)

Beethoven, Symphony no. 6, 3rd movement.

(b) **Allegro con brio**

Haydn, String Quartet op. 74 no. 3, finale.

(c) **Presto**

Mozart, Symphony no. 38, finale.

(d)

Brahms, *Variations and Fugue on a Theme of Handel*, variation 1.

syncopation, Ex. 2

Beethoven, String Quartet op. 135, 2nd movement.

with a recurring accent on the first of each group. Any irregularity, either brief or extended, that has the effect of rhythmic contradiction when introduced into this pattern may be termed syncopation.

Some common methods of creating syncopation are shown in Ex. 1. In Ex. 1*a* notes on normally weak beats are held over to normally strong ones, effectively shifting the accent; in Ex. 1*b* rests have displaced the notes from strong beats to weak ones; in Ex. 1*c* notes are placed between beats and are held over each beat; and in Ex. 1*d* stresses are marked on the weak beats. Two or more of these methods may be used in combination.

Syncopation commonly occurs in only one part or voice (or a small group of parts) at a time, while the other parts adhere to normal accentuation. Some composers however, notably Beethoven, Brahms, and Schumann, have used syncopation in all the parts over extended passages to create a restless effect, which in extreme cases may also result in rhythmic disorientation on the part of the listener (Ex. 2).

Syncopation in various forms is a common device in all periods of Western music, from the 13th century to modern times. It is also a characteristic feature of some non-Western musics, particularly African-American, hence its importance to ragtime, jazz, and other popular music cultures.

See also CROSS-ACCENT; RHYTHM, 2.   PS/JN

synnet. See SENNET.

synthesizer. A term that may be used to describe any grouping of electronic devices for the purposes of sound synthesis. It is more usual, however, to reserve this label for complete systems of an integral construction, purpose-built by a single manufacturer. The early electronic music studios of the 1950s were assembled from different items of equipment, in many instances originally designed for quite different applications such as laboratory testing. Each of these devices had to be adjusted by hand, placing a considerable onus on the practical skills of the composer.

The first true synthesizer, manufactured by the RCA Victor company, was presented to the public in 1956. It consisted of a bank of electronic tone generators and an associated array of processing devices that regulated the nature of the sounds. The entire system was controlled by brush sensors, responding to patterns of holes pre-punched in a moving roll of paper, in the manner of a *player piano. A second, improved version of the RCA synthesizer was installed in the Columbia–Princeton Electronic Music Center in 1959. This provided a major stimulus for both composers and electronic designers, taking advantage of a new era of technology facilitated by the invention of first the transistor and then the integrated circuit, which allowed several functions to be embedded within a single silicon chip. Two Americans, Robert Moog and Donald Buchla, formed separate companies for the manufacture of synthesizers in the mid-1960s, and others quickly followed suit: for example Tonus, who produced the ARP range of synthesizers, and EMS, London, founded by Peter Zinovieff. These systems, commonly known as voltage-controlled synthesizers, were modular in design and usually portable, allowing their use both as a studio resource and on stage in live performance.

The production of commercial synthesizers based on this analogue technology continued until the early 1980s. The new decade, however, was to see a major revolution in synthesizer design, based on an increasing use of digital technology and new methods of sound synthesis. Yamaha launched the first all-digital synthesizer, the DX7, in 1983—a year which was notable for another important development, the introduction of *MIDI. This universal system for exchanging control information between synthesizers has underpinned the industry and greatly expanded the versatility of the medium, allowing all manner of MIDI-based devices to be networked together efficiently. Although the principles of all-electronic synthesis, which were fundamental to the design of the voltage-controlled synthesizer, were retained in the design of digital synthesizers, increasing interest was soon shown in alternative approaches. The most significant of these involves digitizing the individual sounds of acoustic instruments and using the data to create a new spectrum of sounds. Another technique, known as acoustic modelling, involves the direct simulation of the acoustic functions exploited in performance on conventional musical instruments. PM

 📖 D. Crombie, *The New Complete Synthesizer* (London, 1986) · P. Forrest, *The A–Z of Analogue Synthesizers*, 2 vols. (Crediton, 1994–6)

Syrinx. Work for solo flute (1913) by Debussy.

syrinx. See PANPIPES.

system. In musical notation, two or more staves bracketed together on the left, indicating that the music on them is to be played or sung at the same time. See SCORE.

Szabó, Ferenc (*b* Budapest, 27 Dec. 1902; *d* Budapest, 4 Nov. 1969). Hungarian composer. After studying at the Budapest Academy of Music, with Leó Weiner, Albert Siklós, and Kodály, he became involved with Communist music groups, writing many pieces for amateur choruses. In 1932 he emigrated to the USSR, where his works included mass songs and film scores. He served in the Red Army during the war. On his return to Hungary he taught composition at the Budapest Academy, becoming its director from 1958 to 1967. Szabó's later works, in a folk-inspired idiom, include orchestral music, two oratorios, a ballet, and an unfinished opera. ABur

Szalonek, Witold (Józef) (*b* Czechowice-Dziedzice, 2 March 1927). Polish composer. The start of his mature period coincided with the explosive avant-garde movement of the late 1950s. He contributed several works to the prevailing sonoristic trends in Poland (*Les Sons*, 1965). He is noted for his development of extended instrumental techniques (*Mutanza* for piano, 1968), especially for woodwind instruments (*Aarhus Music*, 1970). There is a rapprochement in later pieces with more traditional procedures (*Little B–A–C–H Symphony*, 1979). ATh

Szell, George [Georg] (*b* Budapest, 7 June 1897; *d* Cleveland, OH, 29 July 1970). Hungarian-born American conductor. After studying the piano and composition (with Reger) in Vienna he taught himself conducting and made his debut with the Vienna Symphony Orchestra when he was 16. Two years later Richard Strauss engaged him at the Berlin State Opera, and in the 1920s he held positions in several German opera houses, where he became known as a disciplinarian, rehearsing for fine detail, perfect balance, and absolute precision. He settled in the USA in 1939. From 1946 to 1970 he was music director of the Cleveland Orchestra, developing a level of virtuosity and homogeneity that gave it a reputation as one of the best ensembles of its time. He conducted regularly at the Salzburg Festival. A fine interpreter of contemporary music, he was also admired in Wagner, Strauss, and Mahler. JT

Szeryng, Henryk (*b* Warsaw, 22 Sept. 1918; *d* Kassel, 3 March 1988). Polish-born Mexican violinist. At the age of ten he studied with Carl Flesch in Berlin and by 1933 had made debuts in several European capitals. He spent the war giving concerts for the Allies and travelled to Mexico, the country where he later made his home and became a teacher. Encouraged by Rubinstein he resumed his concert career from 1954 and began to record. In 1983 he marked half a century of concert-giving with a tour of Europe and America. His elegant style was matched by a formidable technique. CF

Szigeti, Joseph (*b* Budapest, 5 Sept. 1892; *d* Lucerne, 19 Feb. 1973). Hungarian-born American violinist. He studied with Jenő Hubay, made his debut in Berlin in 1905, and lived in London, 1907–13, appearing with Melba, Hess, and Busoni. From 1917 to 1924 he taught in Geneva, then gave concerts in Russia and America, followed by worldwide tours. He settled in the USA but retired to Switzerland in 1960. He gave the premieres of concertos by Harty, Martin, and Bloch and worked closely with Prokofiev and Bartók. Although he eschewed old-fashioned showmanship his virtuosity and integrity were unquestioned, and he was a tireless champion of new music. CF

 📖 J. Szigeti, *With Strings Attached* (New York, 1947/ R1979, 2/1967); *Szigeti on the Violin* (London, 1969, 2/1979)

Szőllősy, András (*b* Szászváros, Transylvania [now Orăştie, Romania], 27 Feb. 1921). Hungarian composer and musicologist. He studied at Budapest University, at the Liszt Academy of Music, where his teachers included Kodály, and in Rome with Petrassi. He taught history and theory at the Liszt Academy from 1950 to 1988. His compositions, eclectic in technique, include ballets, film scores, a series of orchestral and ensemble concertos and other orchestral works, chamber music, and vocal pieces, two of them commissioned by the King's Singers. He has edited the writings of Bartók and compiled the catalogue of Bartók's music (published 1966), in which works are allocated sz numbers. ABur

Szymanowski, Karol (Maciej) (*b* Tymoszówka, nr Kiev, 3 Oct. 1882; *d* Lausanne, 29 March 1937). Polish composer. He received his musical education first at home, (*cont. on p. 1249*)

The symphony

The origins and early history to c.1730

The word 'symphony' first appeared in the late 16th century. At this time, however, it denoted nothing more specific than 'music for ensemble'—from the Greek *syn* ('together') and *phone* ('sounding'). Giovanni Gabrieli's *Sacrae symphoniae* ('Sacred Symphonies', 1597), for instance, were simply motets, canzonas, and other works for ensembles of voices or instruments. 'Symphony' was thus interchangeable with *concerto': there were none of the structural or stylistic implications which the term was to acquire in the 18th century.

By the 1620s a symphony (or sinfonia) could be an instrumental piece at the beginning or in the middle of a vocal work such as a motet, *madrigal, or cantata— much in the manner of a *ritornello, though the sinfonia was not as a rule repeated throughout the piece. When the public opera houses opened in Venice in the 1630s (see OPERA, 3), the new operas often had a 'sinfonia avanti l'opera', or *overture, and some included a sinfonia as a purely instrumental interlude: the 'sinfonia infernale' in Cavalli's *Le nozze di Teti e di Peleo* (1639) is an example. Some of these sinfonias, notably that in Monteverdi's *L'incoronazione di Poppea* (1642), were divided into two linked sections, an idea that possibly spawned the French overture developed by Lully later in the 17th century. Towards the end of the century, overtures to Italian operas similarly acquired distinctive structural characteristics, Alessandro Scarlatti sometimes using a three-movement pattern (fast–slow–fast).

This trend was consolidated in the 1720s by opera composers of the Neapolitan school working throughout Europe. Leonardo Vinci and Leonardo Leo, for example, wrote 'sinfonie avanti l'opera' which generally had a fast–slow–fast sequence of three movements, with the central one brief and ornamented and the third couched in a light dance idiom. The first movement tended to be constructed of short themes with strong rhythmic shapes, underpinned with simple harmonies emphasizing the prevailing tonality. Momentum was maintained less by thematic development than by bustling, non-thematic passage-work, and interest was generated by a sharp contrast of thematic ideas and orchestral effects, with prominent use of the string *tremolando*, held wind notes, the implied crescendo, and so on. Such a style of writing was perhaps elementary when set beside the more refined manner of the concerto, but it served the purpose of beginning an evening at the opera. It was also the seed from which developed the symphony as we know it today.   DA

Symphonies for court, church, and concert, c.1730–1800

Contemporary literature and publishers' catalogues alike show that the symphony came to be used increasingly during the second and third quarters of the 18th century in a variety of ways. In private events at princely courts, where orchestras were available, it became the standard fare, especially for the opening and closing items of a programme (reflecting its ancestry in the overture: the terms 'symphony' and 'overture' were in fact interchangeable, especially in English usage, during the whole century; what are in effect symphonies are often found under other titles, among the divertimento, quartet, and sonata).

In Catholic countries, the symphony was much used for instrumental interludes in the Mass or in place of the Proper items, at cathedrals, large churches, princely chapels, and monasteries. At public concerts too, as they developed in the latter part of the century, it became a staple, again often serving for opening or closing items (sometimes both: the opening movements of a work might be played to start a concert, the finale to end it). There was accordingly a substantial demand for new symphonies; more than 7000 were composed in the second half of the century, by composers of many nationalities. The majority of these survive only in performing parts, many of them with uncertain attributions; there are many works that survive with several different attributions in different sources.

Many early symphonies are for strings alone, usually in four parts, occasionally in three, of course with supporting harpsichord; but the standard orchestra for the decades around the middle of the century came to include, additionally, two horns and usually two oboes. Later, flutes sometimes replaced the oboes (most commonly played by the same musicians: occasionally the oboists would be required to take up flutes for a slow movement), and increasingly from the 1770s clarinets too were called for; bassoons were usually included although in earlier works they were often not specified and doubled the bass line in tuttis or when the other wind were playing. Trumpets and timpani were occasionally called for in symphonies written for larger establishments or when the local militias could supply players.

Most symphonies of this period are in three movements, in the standard fast–slow–fast pattern; sometimes the finale was in dance rhythms, most commonly a rapid gigue or (in Italy in particular) a minuet. The independent minuet movement (usually following the slow movement) began to find a place around the middle of the century, particularly in symphonies composed in Mannheim or in Vienna. The advent of the slow introduction, occasionally in the 1750s and increasingly by the 1770s and 80s, marks the new weight and seriousness that the symphony was beginning to acquire. Symphony first movements early in this period are usually in some variety of binary form, but 'semi-sonata' (or 'binary-sonata'), with a recapitulation starting with the secondary material, or sonata without development (also favoured in slow movements) came to be used in the years before standard sonata form became more or less universal. All these formal types, and also variation, appear in slow movements; in finales binary or rondo are most common.

The most important centres of composition in the early part of this period were Italy (especially the north), Mannheim, and Vienna. In Italy, the earliest symphonies published as such appeared in 1729 (by Andrea Zani); other Lombardic composers include G. B. Sammartini and Antonio Brioschi, which show a marked development towards Classical-type periodic structure in the 1730s and 40s. Neapolitan composers such as Leo, Leonardo Vinci, and later Jommelli explored the dynamic possibilities (including crescendos), often writing for larger orchestras than were used elsewhere; the Venetian composer Galuppi too developed lively orchestral writing and his triple-metre first movements are particularly effective. Later important Italians include Boccherini, whose colourful

symphonies were however composed in Spain. In the 1780s many Italian composers tended to use a good deal of effective, perhaps rather mechanical orchestral figuration and lightweight thematic material; Mozart's symphonies composed for and in Italy show the same trend.

In the German-speaking areas, the *Mannheim school were among the first to codify the four-movement symphony (though the later generation reverted to three-movement form), and they introduced many striking orchestral effects: not only the crescendo but also the 'rocket' (which scarcely needs description) and the sustained tutti in which the violins played tremolos while thematic figures are played in the bass. These and other effects were easy to develop among the virtuoso group—the 'army of generals' (Burney)—gathered by Johann Stamitz soon after 1740: the generals included Stamitz's sons, Fils, Richter, Holzbauer, the Toeschis, Cannabich, Danzi, and others. Stamitz and his followers used slower-moving and restricted harmonies, to stabilize tonal areas, at the same time creating strong momentum with their handling of rhythmic patterns.

In Vienna, the Habsburgs' domain over not only most of modern Austria but also the Czech lands, north Italy, part of the Netherlands, and Hungary ensured the development of a highly cosmopolitan symphony, drawing on opera (both *seria* and *buffa*) and serenata, the Bohemian instrumental tradition, and the Austrian divertimento. Richness of harmony and orchestration, strong sense of form (especially the use of clear-cut recapitulations) and preference for four-movement structure mark the Viennese school. This powerful synthesis found its fulfilment in the symphonies of Haydn and Mozart; in the earlier generations notable composers include M. G. Monn, Wagenseil, and Gassmann (who experimented with first-movement forms, in particular using subdominant recapitulations), followed by the technically accomplished, witty, and prolific Dittersdorf (who wrote symphonies based on Ovid's *Metamorphoses*), Leopold Hofmann (a composer with a strong grasp of structural issues), and Vanhal, whose expressive range, involving an unusual leaning towards minor keys, is particularly wide. Slightly apart from this group stands Michael Haydn, working in Salzburg, whose attractive symphonies of the 1780s often have fugal finales.

Other significant German composers of symphonies worked at the minor courts of Bavaria and the south, at

Dresden (notably Hasse, although his contribution was confined to opera overtures used as symphonies), and at Berlin and Hamburg, where C. P. E. Bach wrote symphonies that, with their Baroque formal heritage and their almost pre-Romantic feeling for drama (his use of colour, his sudden pauses and gestures, his intense chromaticisms), stand at a little distance from the Classical mainstream. His youngest brother, J. C. Bach, was however an important and prolific symphonist, who added Italian formal clarity to his German grounding and, mostly working in England, produced symphonies (including several for double orchestra) of a classical poise, thematic assurance, and rhythmic shapeliness that had a profound influence on the young Mozart. Also working in London were C. F. Abel, a graceful symphonist who wrote appealing slow movements and often favoured minuet-finales, and various British composers, among them Boyce (whose tuneful pre-classical symphonies are really overtures, some of them French overtures, to court odes) and the Earl of Kelly (a pupil of Stamitz whom Burney credited with taking the Mannheim style to Britain).

In Paris, numerous symphonies were published, especially those of the Viennese and the Mannheim composers (who often visited Paris; Carl Stamitz went to live there), and several from Italy, but symphony composition was less important among native composers. The most important Paris composers in this area were Gossec, who wrote several minor-key works and brought considerable originality to his forms, rhythmic structures, and textures, and later the Haydn pupil Pleyel, who found ingenious ways of using episodic material. The outstanding orchestras of London and Paris drew symphonies from Haydn and Mozart: London the younger composer's first and the elder's last, Paris the younger's most brilliant and extrovert symphony and the elder's vigorous penultimate group.

SS

Haydn and Mozart

The two great masters of the 18th century, Haydn and Mozart, transformed less the structures than the emotional scope of the symphony. Both began in the Italian tradition, but Haydn early revealed a seriousness similar to that of C. P. E. Bach: his interest in thematic development and experiments in formal design show his knowledge of the older Baroque traditions of the *sonata da chiesa* as well as of more recent ideas. His themes were more rhythmic, less *galant*. A major

turning-point for both composers seemingly came in the early 1770s, when, influenced by the German literary movement known as *Sturm und Drang* ('storm and stress'), music became more intense. Mozart's symphonies of the time show increasing dramatic power (e.g. no. 25 in G minor, K183, 1773) and contrapuntal complexity (no. 29 in A major, K201, 1774). Haydn wrote several symphonies in minor keys, all of them serious; but it was the grandness of scale, the avoidance of rococo clichés, and the contrapuntal writing constantly permeating the texture which transformed the works of this period from entertainment music into something more ambitious.

The most notable results of this new approach came in the 1780s, when Mozart, after visiting Paris and composing a symphony (no. 31, K297, 1778) in the traditional manner of the Concert Spirituel, settled in Vienna: taking for granted a skilled orchestra, he began to exploit the orchestral tone palette of the Mannheimers. His experience in chamber music, gained from Haydn, now was transferred to the symphony, more especially his last three, of which no. 40 in G minor (K550, 1788) is orchestrally broader but just as emotional a work as his String Quintet (K516) in the same key; similarly, no. 41, the 'Jupiter' (K551, 1788) has an intricate fugal finale, elaborating the art of the G major String Quartet (K387). His other interest, opera, permeates the 'Prague' Symphony (no. 38, K504, 1786), the ultimate Italian overture (in effect to *Don Giovanni*) transmuted into a concert symphony.

Haydn, who by the 1780s was famous, was writing for Paris, also using the Mannheim orchestral technique to the full, but with greater subtlety and an imaginative exploitation of sonata form. First movements now became large, often with expansive slow introductions; slow movements could be in variation and other extended forms; minuets were no longer dances but were intricately worked movements suggesting miniature sonata form; finales were often grand, witty, and climactic. The light 3/8 dances of the Italian symphony had been entirely superseded. Haydn's 'London' symphonies, written after Mozart's death, took these developments still further. All but one of the 12 have slow introductions, some prolonged and by no means intended simply to prepare for the movement to follow. The slow movements were free of *galant* elements and often based on simple, solemn, hymn-like melodies. The length and wit of the finales reveal an inventiveness rarely matched—never simply 'effective' or 'brilliant' but tightly constructed with elements of rondo and sonata form. Haydn's influence can be detected in a whole generation of symphonists working in the 1790s, especially in the works of Rosetti and Reicha.

Beethoven

Beethoven transformed the symphony. If his First Symphony (1800) is close to the grand C major manner of Haydn (his Symphony no. 97, for example), the Second (1801–2) is extremely original, a new kind of entertainment symphony with straightforward lyrical tunes in place of 18th-century courtly graces: it was to lead to Schubert's early symphonic style. Both symphonies eschewed any vestiges of the *galant*, the minuets replaced by vigorous scherzos.

The great transformation came with the Third Symphony, the 'Eroica' (1803), its political overtones evident not only from the title page (with its original dedication to Napoleon) but also in the increased use of wind instruments after the manner of the Revolutionary wind bands in Paris, the funeral-march slow movement, and the use of a theme from his *Prometheus* ballet in the finale, suggesting some elements of Titanic struggle. At some 50 minutes long, it is almost twice the length of even the grandest 18th-century symphonies. With the 'Eroica' the symphony became the secular equivalent of the great religious genres of the Baroque era: a public statement of belief of the highest order. Not being tied to a text, it could deal with personal experience, sensuous pleasure, and moods evoked by places or literature.

In his later symphonies Beethoven refined and developed this concept. The Fifth (1807–8) and Seventh (1811–12) are simpler in aim but on a similar scale, the one heroic, the other an expression of joy. Equally original was the Sixth Symphony, the 'Pastoral' (1808), a response to the countryside. Its five movements were given titles in the manner of much 18th-century programme music. But the storm music is impressionistic in a novel way, with no thematically significant content or any real 'form': it relies for its effect entirely on imitations of nature.

Two innovations were significant in the post-'Eroica' symphony: movements were now sometimes joined, either by fully developed links (as between the last three movements of the 'Pastoral') or by the use of recurring themes (as in the last two movements of the Fifth); and scherzos were often amplified into a scherzo–trio–scherzo–trio–scherzo–trio–scherzo–coda pattern, al-lowing some deceptive effects (in the Seventh Symphony, for example, the coda suggests yet another repetition of the trio before it is chased away). All four movements were now of considerable weight.

The climax of this transformation came in Beethoven's Ninth Symphony (1822–4), a mixture of symphony and French Revolutionary cantata. The first three movements expanded the traditional forms almost to breaking-point. There is a huge sonata-form opening movement with tight thematic development throughout, and a dramatic coup at the recapitulation, major harmony now replacing the exposition's minor 3rd; the scherzo has a fugal texture, sketchy themes, a pastoral trio in duple time, and a 'dismissive' ending after the manner of the Seventh Symphony; and the long slow movement is a set of variations on a double theme, using the filigree ornamental melody found in Beethoven's last quartets. The choral last movement does not conform to any symphonic stereotype and can most precisely be described as a set of variations: it is a cantata on the theme of liberty (bearing distinct resemblances to Beethoven's early Cantata on the Accession of Emperor Leopold II, 1790), using soloists and chorus to their limits.

The symphony after Beethoven

Writing a symphony now became a major undertaking. The symphonies composed between 1750 and 1800 can be counted in the many thousands, but those written from 1825 to 1875 are numbered in dozens. Vestiges of the 18th-century Viennese concert symphony are to be found in the earlier works of Schubert, whose first six symphonies were written before 1820 for amateur or unskilled orchestras. Their 'entertainment' quality is based on Haydn and Mozart, though in the Sixth Symphony (1817–18) Schubert introduced more modern elements, demonstrating a knowledge of Rossini's overture style, using longer melodies rather than pregnant motifs for thematic material. Three of the six reverted to a minuet for the third movement, while the slow movements were in the late 18th-century 'Andante' manner. Schubert's last two symphonies, the Eighth ('Unfinished', 1822) and Ninth ('Great', ?1825–8), written with a knowledge of Beethoven's Seventh, were more ambitious, imaginatively using a larger orchestra both to increase the range of musical expression and as a means of varying the material. Both were conceived on a grand scale, yet they achieve a remarkable consistency of focus while using attractive themes worthy of a master of the lied. Neither was performed in Schubert's lifetime, but their rediscovery in 1839 (the 'Great') and 1865 ('Unfinished') informed developments in symphonic writing in the 1840s and 70s.

It was Beethoven who provided the example for those who wanted to make a grand public statement. These may be divided into two groups: those who sought to build on his techniques, and those who saw him as an inspiration to the spirit. The first group included Mendelssohn and Schumann, two friends and contemporaries who excelled in other genres. Mendelssohn's mature symphonies span a wide range: the 'Reformation' (the Fifth Symphony, 1832) is a 'religious' piece, using the chorale *Ein' feste Burg* in its finale; the Second Symphony, 'Lobgesang' (1840), contains a choral finale; the Third ('Scottish', 1842) and Fourth ('Italian', 1833) are offshoots of the tone-painting of Beethoven's 'Pastoral'. Although the first two give clearer evidence of Mendelssohn's intention to expand the boundaries of the symphony, the charm and energy of the 'Scottish' and 'Italian' have kept them more firmly in the repertory.

Schumann must be reckoned a deeper-thinking and more successful symphonist than Mendelssohn. He was fully aware not only of the implications of Beethoven's achievement, but also of more recent developments such as the rediscovery of Schubert's 'Great' C major Symphony, while his early fondness for linking movements thematically (both in his First Symphony, 'Spring', 1841, and the D minor symphony, composed the same year but revised in 1851 and published as his Fourth) reflected his close and enthusiastic knowledge of Berlioz's *Symphonie fantastique* (see below). Like the 'Spring' Symphony, Schumann's Third (the 'Rhenish') has a strong pictorial basis, in the latter case sustained across five impressive movements. Schumann's use of the orchestra was much criticized in the 20th century, but recent performances of his symphonies on period instruments with the composer's preferred orchestral balances have revealed the clarity and charm of his orchestral writing.

Sonority also plays a much expanded role in the works of Berlioz, who established the programme symphony as a point of reference for the later 19th century. Paris was one of the cities where Beethoven's symphonies were efficiently performed from the 1820s, and Berlioz's *Symphonie fantastique*, composed there in 1830, was clearly inspired by their grandeur of spirit. This was not an organically conceived work: rather, it was compiled from fragments of earlier pieces, which achieve unity only when Berlioz's programme (after de Quincey's opium dreams and the composer's contemporaneous love affair) is taken into account. The result is an internalized psychological drama of a quite specific character. The five-movement plan was modelled on Beethoven's 'Pastoral' and the linking of the movements with an *idée fixe* follows his Fifth Symphony; the slow introduction to the first movement derived from the Seventh Symphony. The result, however, is entirely un-Beethovenian, being as close to opera or cantata as it is to the traditional symphony. Berlioz followed this with *Harold en Italie* (1834), a kind of *symphonie concertante* with a solo part for viola, using similar programmatic links as before. In *Roméo et Juliette* (1839), a choral symphony with seven movements, one can see a conventional orchestral work embedded among the choral movements; but again this piece is just as easily understood in terms of operatic scenes.

Berlioz's musical style was so individual that its direct influence on other composers was slight; the programmatic idea, on the other hand, was a stimulating alternative to the abstract symphony. Spohr was one of the first to follow it up, with his Fourth Symphony, 'Die Weihe der Töne' (1832), an attempt at evoking the creation and evolution of the world. Several of his other symphonies have titles, including the Ninth Symphony, 'The Seasons' (1850), in which more conventional imagery is expressed in two movements. In the 1840s the concept of the programme was so strongly established that even a composer writing Classical-type instrumental symphonies, like Berwald, gave them such titles as 'Sérieuse' (1842), 'Capricieuse' (1842), and 'Singulière' (1845).

It was Liszt who, in the mid-century, succeeded with the programme symphony. His *Faust Symphony* (1854–7), consisting of three movements depicting the main characters in Goethe's story (Faust, Marguerite, and Mephistopheles), used the technique of distorting the Faust themes to portray Mephistopheles, a traditional symphonic process. Beethoven's example was also perhaps in mind when, three years after its original composition, Liszt added a choral finale, using the material to express Goethe's idea of the 'Eternal Feminine'.

By this time the polemics of Wagner, exiled in Switzerland, were making headway among the progressives; he put forward the notion that the symphony was an impossible genre after Beethoven's

Ninth, and that the great music of the future was music drama. Composers in the 1850s and 60s who might earlier have written symphonies now often chose the *symphonic poem. In 1860 the manifesto of the young Brahms polarized views against the new music of Liszt and Wagner, resulting in the foundation of a conservative school committed to traditional forms.

The symphony thus came back into fashion in about 1870. Brahms was the finest of the new symphonists. His four examples at first seem traditional works in four movements, the major differences from those of Beethoven being their gently melodious third movements which take the place of Beethoven's vigorous scherzos. Like Beethoven's, the last movements are the most difficult to categorize: the finale of the First Symphony (1855–76) has a slow introduction followed by a full-scale sonata movement which incorporates the material of the introduction, and a stately last-movement theme which prompted immediate comparison with Beethoven's Ninth. In the Fourth (1884–5) the finale is a passacaglia (perhaps in emulation of the 'Eroica'). These last movements are all weighty, the slow movements profound in feeling (Adagio rather than Andante in style).

If this and Brahms's thematic development continued the Beethovenian line, it is also true that the Romantics, notably Schumann, left their mark on his style. In the Second Symphony (1877) most of the themes in each movement are related to the work's opening bar; in the Third (1883) the opening bars are brought back at the end to give a typically Romantic nostalgic glow. By comparison with Wagner's music dramas, however, Brahms's symphonies clearly stand as examples of 'absolute music'. Their combination of expressive themes and clearly articulated musical structure allowed them to achieve a coherence akin to narrative but without the specific details that inhere in a libretto or extra-musical programme. In this way they spoke powerfully, not of politics or ideas but of the power of musical thinking, the ability to express and put into order intense feeling. (It was Brahms's sense of order and structure that was to influence Schoenberg's quest for a new means of musical organization.)

The other major symphonist who came to attention in about 1870 was Bruckner. His symphonies are often said to be Wagnerian, but such influence is mainly confined to orchestral effects, harmonic language, and an occasional thematic resemblance. Beethoven's Ninth is the more immediate model, Bruckner often starting

with the same kind of theme and orchestral sound. He was not principally concerned with thematic development, but sustained and articulated his vast works (typically an hour or more in length) by juxtaposing substantial blocks of musical material—some thematic, other acting as transitions—in a manner that anticipated, though it probably did not directly influence, similar musical thought in works by Stravinsky and Bartók. The failure of even Bruckner's closest colleagues to understand fully how the temporal balance of his movements was achieved was one factor that led to the production of a number of Bruckner's symphonies in differing versions, often with the active involvement of other people and against the composer's better judgment. Modern scholarship has largely restored Bruckner's own work to circulation, though performances of 'revised' versions are still heard, even in the case of his Eighth (1884–90), the last of the symphonies to be fully completed and widely regarded as his finest achievement.

The most interesting symphonies of the 1880s were, in fact, being written by composers outside the Austrian–Viennese circle, though many of them had connections with it. Closest to this centre was Dvořák, whose symphonies are based on Classical procedures; his thematic material is in the form of tuneful melody and is less susceptible to conventional development, but his imaginative orchestration plays a role here. He absorbed elements of Czech folk music, particularly in his scherzo movements. His greatest symphony, the Seventh in D minor (1884–5), was modelled on Brahms's Third; his last, 'From the New World' (1893), uses a form of *idée fixe* to unite the work.

Tchaikovsky was less influenced by conservative Viennese ideals: his last three symphonies (nos. 4–6) are guided by programmatic ideas, each being a highly personal expression of the inexorable power of Fate. It is sometimes said that Tchaikovsky was not a 'real' symphonist—he himself admitted that 'the seams show'—but thematic development is not the only criterion for success and, judged by the standards of music and emotional interest, the Fourth (1877–8) and Sixth ('Pathétique', 1893), by juxtaposing powerful themes in vivid orchestral colour, convey vivid moods in a logical and convincing way. Borodin's symphonies are highly attractive works, the themes transformed and combined in a Lisztian manner.

It was certainly Liszt's methods that were followed by the French symphonists of the 1880s: Saint-Saëns's

Third Symphony (1886) with organ was dedicated to Liszt; d'Indy's attractive *Symphonie sur un chant montagnard français* (1886) has an obbligato piano part which makes it almost a concerto; Franck's Symphony in D minor (1886–8) depends on 'thematic transformation'.

DA/APo

The symphony in the early 20th century

History has come to regard Mahler as the greatest composer of symphonies at about 1900, though his works had comparatively little impact at the time of their composition. This fact itself is symptomatic of the changed significance of the genre during the 20th century, a period during which innovations in style, technique, and aesthetic were of central importance and the established genres of the 19th century could be virtually ignored by major composers without risk to their reputation, or indeed wilfully distorted: many 20th-century symphonies appear not so much to develop the genre from within as to subject it to scrutiny from without. Mahler's works expanded the dimensions and scope of the symphony in ways that drew with enthusiasm on all the 19th century had achieved, while bringing his own more subversive imprint to bear on this rich brew through a fondness for songlike themes and borrowed musical types, often evoking lowbrow genres within the symphonic frame for expressive or ironic effect.

His First Symphony (completed 1888, rev. 1893–6) was inspired by a novel by J. P. Richter (Schumann's favourite author) called *Titan*; his Second (1888–94, rev. 1903) is also programmatic, based on the 'Wunderhorn' songs and with a choral finale. The Third (1895–6), for contralto, boys' and women's choruses, and orchestra, was inspired by Mahler's intense love of nature, the title of its programme, 'Die fröhliche Wissenschaft' ('The Joyful Knowledge'), taken from Nietzsche. When he had finished it he wrote 'Just imagine a work of such magnitude that it actually mirrors the whole world'; here Mahler was using the symphony to represent the very conception of existence.

Although for his later symphonies (nos. 5–9, excluding no. 8) he reverted to purely orchestral forces, they still seem subjective and programmatic, even though there is no programme. The colossal Eighth Symphony (1906) consists almost of two cantatas, one setting the 'Veni Creator Spiritus', the other the last scene from Goethe's *Faust*. In his last two symphonies, the Ninth (1908–9) and the incomplete Tenth (drafted

1910, made performable by Deryck Cooke (1976) and others), Mahler brought the intensity of private grief, joy, and love into the spotlight afforded by the grand public statement of belief and feeling that the symphony, in his hands, had by now become.

By the early 20th century the tone-poem was not merely a viable alternative to the symphony in contemporary eyes but in some ways the more secure genre. It was thus possible for Richard Strauss, the leading composer of tone-poems at about the turn of the century, to appropriate the word 'symphony' in the titles of his *Symphonia domestica* (1902–3) and *Eine Alpensinfonie* (1911–15) without disguising the fact that these were tone-poems by another name. And although Skryabin's last two orchestral works, *Poem of Ecstasy* (1905–8) and *Prométhée, the Poem of Fire* (1908–10), stand in succession to his three numbered symphonies, it is a moot point whether they should be regarded as programme symphonies in one movement or as tone-poems proper, though the latter view is more reasonable.

The situation is more clear-cut in the case of those who, like Elgar, chose to develop the Brahmsian legacy of the non-programmatic, multi-movement symphony, albeit displaying a more unfettered Romantic sensibility than Brahms had allowed himself to exhibit. Elgar's First (1907–8) and Second (1909–11) symphonies proceed from similar principles to Brahms's works, but achieve a far greater expressive power both through their harmonic intensity and through their grand yet often delicate use of the orchestra. Rakhmaninov's three symphonies, of which the Second (1907) is the finest, occupy much the same territory in terms of the history of symphonic thought and, as is the case with Elgar's works, are rendered distinctive through the composer's individuality rather than through an expansion of the medium itself.

The strongest early 20th-century contributions to the development of the symphonic genre from within came from Scandinavia. Sibelius's starting-point seems to have been Tchaikovsky rather than Brahms, an allegiance rendered less surprising when one considers that Finland was under Russian control until 1917. However, from his Third Symphony (1907) onwards, Sibelius's works became fully individual in style and technique while sharing the thematic cut of his more overtly nationalistic works in other genres. In contrast to Mahler, Sibelius believed that the symphony should be a tightly knit musical structure guided by the 'profound logic' of thematic and motivic integration. He became a master of musical transition, often using fragments of one theme to develop the musical flow seamlessly towards the statement of the next; another way of looking at this is to see the most characteristic state of his music as one of continuous development, out of which thematic islands form at appropriate junctures through the coalescence of motifs. One result is that the successive themes of a movement often appear to be presented in rotation rather than in dialectic contrast; another is that while individual movements have a single-minded intensity, the balance in a multi-movement work is struck more through a unity or contrast of mood than through the use of generic types such as the slow movement or scherzo. Indeed, Sibelius's single-movement Seventh Symphony (1924) stands fittingly as the culmination of his symphonic thought, though he is thought to have completed an eighth (c.1928–33) which he destroyed on account of a lack of self-confidence before it reached performance.

Sibelius's Danish contemporary Nielsen also developed a manner of symphonic writing in which the entire work pursues a single trajectory against the forces of opposition and fragmentation, often dramatized either through musical gesture (as in the disruptive side-drum cadenza of the Fifth Symphony, 1921–2) or through an apparent struggle between different key-centres, one of which 'triumphs' at the end of the work without necessarily having functioned also as a point of departure in the conventional way. He also embodied increasingly ambitious philosophical programmes, notably in the Fourth ('The Inextinguishable', 1914–16).

Schoenberg's contributions to the symphony were confined to two 'chamber symphonies', the first of which (1906) is an undoubted masterpiece. Reducing his forces from the full orchestra to 15 players, he also sought to compress the conventional four-movement scheme into one continuous but highly varied musical span. This factor, combined with a harmonic and melodic language that stretches tonality to an exceptional degree, makes the work a challenge for performers and listeners alike, but in spite of all its innovations it is clearly still a symphony that builds on 19th-century achievements. The same can hardly be said for Webern's Symphony (1927–8), a work in two movements that is an early highpoint of the composer's mature serial writing. Webern's style is so personal that, as is the case with his String Quartet (1936–8), the use

of the generic title is little more than a convenience indicating the instrumental forces used.

Another early 20th-century innovator, Ives, wrote four numbered symphonies, and also planned a 'Universe' symphony which was never completed. Of these, the Second (c.1907–9) and Third (c.1908–11) are characteristic in bringing hymn tunes and other vernacular materials into a symphonic framework that itself seems 'borrowed' from European models. The Fourth Symphony (completed in 1925) is a work of exceptional complexity that was not performed in its entirety until 1965; it was one of the last pieces Ives completed before, like Sibelius at about the same time, he virtually retired from composition.

Other American composers who contributed strongly to symphonic composition did so in a less radical mould. Many of the generation born in about 1900 went to Paris in the 1920s to study with the great pedagogue Nadia Boulanger, who revered Stravinsky and brought the restrained discipline of neo-classicism to her teaching. Among Boulanger's American pupils Copland was pre-eminent, and of his three symphonies the Third (1944–6), which includes the famous 'Fanfare for the Common Man', impresses most in its use of a conventional format to express something of contemporary concerns. But the quintessential symphonic evocation of the American character, to judge by its reception at home, was to be found in a slightly earlier work by a composer who remains little known beyond North America: Roy Harris. His vastly successful Third Symphony (1937) is cast in a single movement and traverses a wide range of moods in an accessible but never easygoing style.

Harris's pupil William Schuman was also a gifted composer of symphonies whose concern for organic unity recalls Schoenberg and Sibelius; the third of his symphonies (1941) is among his finest works. Among internationally known American composers of this period, both Barber and Bernstein composed symphonies. Bernstein's success in musical theatre makes the comparatively stilted expression of his symphonic works understandable, but it is surprising that neither of Barber's symphonies matches the achievement of his concertos, since his musical style is so closely attuned to the demands of conventional forms, conventionally handled. A more successful work in every way is the Second Symphony of Howard Hanson (the 'Romantic', 1930), though it can hardly be said to have extended the boundaries of the genre.

In Britain, the pre-eminent symphonist of the period was Vaughan Williams, whose first six symphonies span virtually the entire stylistic range of his output. The first, *A Sea Symphony* (1903–9, rev. 1923), is a hybrid form that accommodates Edwardian choral writing into a late 19th-century symphonic frame; his Second Symphony (*A London Symphony*, 1911–13, rev. 1918, 1933) presents a beguiling musical impression of pre-war life in the capital, but also impresses as a symphonic structure. Vaughan Williams's Fourth Symphony (1931–4) startled its first audiences for its harmonic astringency, which to some extent may have arisen as a consequence of the composer's desire to appear up to date and thus to avoid being overtaken in esteem by the young Walton, whose First Symphony was eagerly awaited.

Remarkably, Elgar too was composing a symphony at this time, though the effort drained him and he died with the work incomplete in 1934; the sketches, as realized (1993–7) by Anthony Payne, reveal a work of concision and power. Walton's symphony, first performed complete in 1935, is among the most impressive of all such works to have built on Sibelius's achievements: the first movement in particular takes the Sibelian model and infuses it with a new energy that derives from a virtuoso handling of a large orchestra. His Second Symphony (1957–60) is superficial by comparison, but Vaughan Williams's later symphonies, particularly the Fifth (1938–43, rev. 1951) and Sixth (1944–7, rev. 1950), continued his use of the symphonic medium to explore the varied facets of his developing musical language.

Two contrasting sides of Szymanowski's musical character are displayed in his Third and Fourth symphonies. The Third ('Song of the Night', 1914–16) is an exotic and dreamy work which adds a tenor soloist and chorus to a large orchestra, and owes much to Skryabin in terms of its musical style. The Fourth (1932), on the other hand, is inspired by the folk music of the Tatra Mountains; the prominent solo piano part is responsible for its subtitle, *Sinfonia concertante*. Another east European composer, Martinů, began composing symphonies only after he had moved to the USA in 1941; though in an overall output characterized by cosmopolitanism and diversity, the six symphonies betray his Bohemian origins more consistently than many of his other works. A composer also forced into exile was Hindemith, whose symphony *Mathis der Maler* (1933–4) was among the last works he produced before fleeing the Nazi regime. Written in parallel with his opera of the same name, it examines the responsibilities of the artist during times of political conflict. The bulk of the rest of his symphonic output was composed in the USA, including another notable opera-related symphony, *Die Harmonie der Welt* ('The Harmony of the World', 1951).

During the 1920s Paris could reasonably claim to be the centre of the musical world, numbering the émigré Stravinsky and the composers of Les Six among its stars. Of Les Six, only Honegger produced impressive works in symphonic form, such as the Second Symphony for strings and solo trumpet (1940–1), though the vastly prolific Milhaud composed six chamber symphonies (1918–23) and, in later life, 12 symphonies (1939–62). With the exception of an early work composed under Rimsky-Korsakov's guidance, Stravinsky's works using the word 'symphony' in their titles are highly individual in format, with those titles going some way towards characterizing their relation to earlier music, an aspect important to their conception.

The *Symphonies of Wind Instruments* (1920, rev. 1947) is emphatically not a 'symphony for wind instruments': it uses the word in its earliest sense of a 'sounding together', and its formal structure is a *locus classicus* of the juxtaposition and interaction of blocks of musical material. The *Symphony of Psalms* (1930) is a cantata in three movements which merits the appellation 'symphony' because of the coherence of its thematic and harmonic materials; the first and last movements are among Stravinsky's strongest inventions after the early ballets. The Symphony in C (1938–40), like Prokofiev's Classical Symphony (1916–17), is deceptively close to the 18th century in its textures, harmonies, and phrase-patterns, while playing subtly with the expectations these similarities are likely to arouse in the mind of the listener. The opening movement of the Symphony in Three Movements (1942–5) recaptures something of the energy of the *Symphony of Psalms*, but as a whole this is the weakest of the four works, coming from a period in his career when Stravinsky had all but exhausted the premises of his neo-classical style.

From the 1920s onwards, Stravinsky's erstwhile compatriots produced symphonies in quantity, reflecting the fact that symphonic writing acquired a special significance in the cultural development of the USSR. Indeed, the term 'Soviet symphonism' is important, implying that the symphony was now vested with the purpose of expressing the Soviet ideal. The heady subjectivism of Skryabin was to be left behind (though in the 1920s he was described as the 'supreme expression of musical Romanticism of the Revolution'), and symphonic music was to reflect aspects of Soviet life. Abstract symphonies were composed in the 1920s—the early symphonies of Myaskovsky, Shostakovich's First (1924–5)—but programmatic content was earnestly encouraged. Symphonies should 'mean' something; they should be topical; they should have something to say to contemporary Soviet society. These notions spawned Shostakovich's Second ('October', 1927) and Third ('1 May', 1929), both conforming to the desirable pattern of having choral endings based on verses by Soviet poets.

With the onset of *socialist realism in the early 1930s, the symphony came under closer scrutiny, against which its subsequent Soviet history has to be seen. One of the greatest and most enduring products, Shostakovich's muscularly argued Fifth Symphony (1937), indicates that the concept of socialist realism need not be insular but instead could embrace less specific, more generalized themes: humanity, hope, heroism, and so on.

It was indeed the theme of heroism that imbued much of the symphonic writing of the war years, as in Shostakovich's Seventh ('Leningrad', 1941), Prokofiev's Fifth (1945), and Myaskovsky's 'war' symphonies (nos. 22 and 23) composed in 1941. But some of the searching, pessimistic works composed at the height of the war (notably Shostakovich's Eighth of 1943) and at the end (his Ninth, 1945; Prokofiev's Sixth, 1945–7) attracted severe criticism during the Zhdanov purges of 1948. The nature of the Soviet symphony again had to be rethought. After Stalin's death (1953) and the premiere of Shostakovich's Tenth Symphony, there was a further Composers' Union debate (1954). The symphonic tradition was widened by such composers as Vainberg, Shchedrin, and Tishchenko. Shostakovich reverted to programmatic symphonies with his 11th ('The Year 1905'), 1957; 12th ('The Year 1917', 1961), and 13th ('Babiy Yar', 1962), before attaching the term 'symphony' to one of his most unconventional pieces, the Symphony no. 14 (1969), a bleak song cycle that works themes of death. Shostakovich's symphonies, though conceived in a Soviet tradition, transcend national boundaries and have a profound impact on a wide public.

DA/AL, APo

The symphony since c. 1950

The most radical composers of the immediate postwar period were dedicated to the renewal of musical language from basic principles, and neither the straightforward development nor the ironic usage of previous genres held any immediate attraction. But although Boulez and Stockhausen, the leading figures in the avant-garde, did not even so much as toy with the title 'symphony', within the broader boundaries of this movement the symphonic genre was sufficiently entrenched to leave a few traces. Perhaps most extraordinary is the *Symphonie pour un homme seul* by Pierre Schaeffer (with Pierre Henry, 1950, rev. 1953), one of the earliest examples of *musique concrète*; it is, however, a symphony in name only.

More significant by far is the *Turangalila-symphonie* (1946–8, rev. 1990) by Boulez's teacher Messiaen: this exuberant work is cast in ten movements most of which form interlocking cycles, a layout similar to that which Boulez would later adopt for his influential chamber work *Le Marteau sans maître*. The *Turangalila-symphonie* features a virtuoso part for solo pianist, and its large orchestra includes an electronic instrument of great intensity, the ondes martenot. The work uses exceptionally rich harmony and dynamic rhythms to express the power of human love as an aspect of the divine, its lack of inhibition placing it firmly in the line of physically evocative music-making established by Stravinsky in *The Rite of Spring*.

Such was the atmosphere of polarization between the musical avant-garde and other musicians during the 1950s and 60s that the 'survival' of the symphony as a genre became an issue in itself: if radical music was the only music of value, then the symphony, together with opera, concerto, and other genres central to 19th-century music, would surely fall by the wayside. Though this was soon revealed as a pointless oversimplification, it is scarcely surprising to find that the most sustained commitment to the symphony came from composers whose aesthetic position placed them outside that debate. Shostakovich and other Soviet composers clearly fall under this heading (see above). Another was K. A. Hartmann, whose brave opposition to the Nazi regime was expressed in works that audibly allied themselves with cultures the Nazis had sought to repress; he eventually published ten symphonies, of which the most interesting are perhaps the Sixth (1951–3) and the wartime *Sinfonia tragica* (1940–3).

Away from politically imposed restriction, the irrelevance of the symphony to the apparent musical mainstream paradoxically freed those composers wishing to work with the genre from historical obligations of the kind that had dogged the later 19th century. Some composers, like Tippett, whose music had always been as much about its relationship with the past as about its own inherent structure and expression, wrote symphonies that plainly declare their musical antecedents. Of his four symphonies, the Second (1957) impresses by its freedom of melodic and textural invention, while continually evoking earlier models (the opening was inspired by Vivaldi); the Third Symphony (1970–2) subjects the idealism of Beethoven's Ninth to late 20th-century scrutiny, demanding whether the brotherhood of mankind can remain a viable inspiration in an age of conflict and oppression. Tippett's contemporary Britten was more committed to opera than to instrumental genres, and neither his early *Sinfonia da requiem* (1939–40) nor his Symphony for cello and orchestra (1963, rev. 1964), which is really a concerto, is among his most successful works.

In Europe, composers who took note of the avant-garde while retaining a broader view of their own place in the art of music composed symphonies that share little more than their quality of individualism. Lutosławski, Gerhard, and Henze were the most outstanding. The last three of Lutosławski's four symphonies were composed after the cultural 'thaw' in Poland had allowed him to adopt many of the techniques, if few of the aesthetic attitudes, of the Western avant-garde. The Second Symphony (1965–7) is a fine example of the style he developed, in which textural control is achieved in spite of the inclusion of unpredictable elements arising from the freedom of rhythm and tempo granted to individual performers, and the titles of its two movements, 'Hésitant' and 'Direct', are self-explanatory. The Third (1981–3) and Fourth (1988–92) symphonies have achieved a greater popularity, perhaps because they strike a stylistic balance in which Lutosławski's mastery of orchestral texture is matched by the important role given to melody. Gerhard's four completed symphonies all date from the 1950s and 60s, by which time his use of post-Schoenbergian serialism had become mature and highly personal, making few concessions to the listener; the Third Symphony ('Collages', 1960), which combines electronic music with the orchestra, is perhaps his most accessible, though the Fourth ('New York', 1967, rev. 1968) is a

more moving work. Henze's first six symphonies do not represent the composer at his best; of the later works, the Seventh (1983–4) and the choral Ninth (1995–7) impress most, the latter being a committed expression of anti-Fascism.

One area where the weight of symphonic history was still perceived was Scandinavia, for here no mid-century composer could fully escape the shadows of Sibelius and Nielsen. The determined individuality of Holmboe is evident, however, in the 14 symphonies and three chamber symphonies that covered his entire working life; of these, the Eighth ('Sinfonia boreale', 1951–2) is both characteristic of the composer and his best-known work. Kokkonen's seriousness of purpose is indicated by the fact that he did not begin to write symphonies before Sibelius's death. His *Sinfonia da camera* (1962) is firmly in his serial style, but in the Third (1967) and even more so in the Fourth (1971) of his numbered symphonies he moved towards melodic and harmonic accessibility. Rautavaara's versatile and eclectic development of an accessible musical language took him uncomfortably close to kitsch at times, but the Fifth (1985) and Seventh ('Angel of Light', 1994) symphonies are among his stronger works.

Berio's *Sinfonia* (1968–9) is a landmark work: a composer who had been closely associated with the avant-garde not only used the title 'symphony' but included material quoted directly from a range of earlier masterpieces, including Mahler's Second Symphony and Stravinsky's *The Rite of Spring*. Berio's work includes prominent parts for eight solo voices—sometimes singing, sometimes speaking—and is an exhilarating *tour de force* that not only impresses on its own terms but also heralds the demise of the avant-garde movement as a dominating force in music. A less satisfactory about-turn from modernism was made by Penderecki in the mid-1970s, leading to a series of works that included all his symphonies except the First; of these, the Third (1988–95) is by some distance the most strongly communicative.

Other senior modernists who composed symphonies in the last decades of the century did so with apparently greater musical conviction: Carter's *A Symphony of Three Orchestras* (1976) achieves complex superimpositions of musical material, while his *Symphonia: sum fluxae pretium spei* (1994–7) seems likely to stand as one of the most impressive of his late works. Maxwell Davies, after moving to the Orkney islands in 1971, embraced traditional genres and softened the edges of his style. His continuing series of symphonies, of which the Second (1980) and Third (1984) are arguably the most impressive in their combination of strongly atmospheric material with rigorous musical processes, claim Mahler and Sibelius as forebears; latterly he returned to the programmatic symphony with his *Symphonia antarctica* (2001). Schnittke's First Symphony (1969–72) was one of his earliest works to attempt the 'polystylistic' manner with which his name is associated, but his later symphonies are more characteristic of his approach in conveying a quality of thoughtfulness and even reverence without excluding the unexpected. A pivotal work is the Fifth Symphony (1988), which includes solo parts for violin and oboe and is regarded simultaneously as the fourth of his concerti grossi.

In the 1990s, one symphony gained enormous popular success, though it had been written two decades years earlier: the Third Symphony by Górecki ('Symphony of Sorrowful Songs', 1976), of which one recording sold more than a million CDs. Far more subtle in technique and expression than the often-used description 'faith minimalism' suggests, it is predominantly slow-moving and diatonic, with arching lines for a solo soprano voice; the words, skilfully drawn from disparate sources including a prayer found on the wall of a Gestapo cell, are concerned with the deaths of children and the search for peace through the Virgin Mary. Another late 20th-century composer whose successes have come with the CD age is Philip Glass, to whom the term *minimalism' can more accurately be applied and who has sought popularity more assiduously than almost any other classical composer of his generation. His *Low Symphony* (1992) is based on music by David Bowie and Brian Eno, as is his *Heroes Symphony* (1996); both are arguably more successful than his Second and Third symphonies (both 1994).

Whereas the future of the symphony might once have seemed at risk along with the symphony orchestra itself and the whole culture of live classical music, it is now more realistic to see its medium-term economic viability as dependent on the recording industry. The example of Górecki's Third Symphony serves as a reminder that overnight success in these terms can come from the most unexpected quarter. The aesthetic viability of the symphony, on the other hand, lies in the hands of composers themselves.   APo

D. Tovey, *Essays in Musical Analysis*, ii (London, 1935/R1982) · B. S. Brook, *La Symphonie française dans la seconde moitié du XVIIIe siècle* (Paris, 1962) · R. Simpson (ed.), *The Symphony*, 2 vols. (Harmondsworth, 1966–7) · L. Cuyler, *The Symphony* (New York, 1973, 2/1995) · P. Stedman, *The Symphony* (Englewood Cliffs, NJ, 1979, 2/1992) · R. Layton (ed.), *A Companion to the Symphony* (London, 1993, 2/1995) · M. Steinberg, *The Symphony: A Listener's Guide* (New York, 1995) · D. K. Holoman (ed.), *The Nineteenth-Century Symphony* (New York, 1996) · N. Butterworth, *The American Symphony* (Aldershot, 1998)

and later (from 1896) at a music school nearby in Elisavetgrad (now Kirovograd), run by his relatives the Neuhauses. In 1901 he moved to Warsaw, where he had private lessons in harmony with Marek Zawirski, and in counterpoint and composition with the distinguished but conservative composer Zygmunt Noskowski. In 1905, together with four other emerging Polish musicians, he founded the Young Poland group with the aim of bringing Polish music into the international arena, and the compositions of this period (1905–12), including the Concert Overture (1906), Second Symphony (1909–10), and Second Piano Sonata (1910–11), draw on the achievements of such *New German composers as Wagner and Richard Strauss. Reger was also an important influence at this time.

In spring 1914 Szymanowski visited Sicily and North Africa, and the journey renewed and intensified his interest in Mediterranean and Arab cultures. Along with his growing awareness of modern French and Russian music (Debussy, Ravel, and late Skryabin), this love of 'exotic' subject matter undoubtedly played a part in helping him shake off German influences, inaugurating his most prolific period as a composer, coinciding more or less with the war years. It was the period of the great piano cycles *Metopes* (1915) and *Masks* (1915–16), of the *Myths* for violin and piano (1915), of the song cycles *Songs of a Fairy Princess* (1915), *Songs of an Infatuated Muezzin* (1918), and *Four Tagore Songs* (1918), and of the First Violin Concerto (1916) and Third Symphony, 'Song of the Night', for tenor, chorus, and orchestra (1914–16). Together these two orchestral works represent the high-water mark of Szymanowski's 'impressionism', an idiom that somehow draws together the refined sonorities of Debussy, Ravel, and late Skryabin and the impassioned late Romanticism of the New German School.

The 'splendid isolation' of these years was rudely disturbed by the October Revolution. The Szymanowskis moved to a house in Elisavetgrad just before the revolution, and shortly after their move the family home at Tymoszówka was all but destroyed. It was a dark period for Szymanowski, during which he was quite unable to believe in himself as a composer. 'Can you imagine', he wrote in 1918, 'I cannot compose now.' It was at this time that he began working on his masterpiece, the opera *King Roger*, a Nietzschean re-working of Euripides' *Bacchae* set in the Byzantine court of 12th-century Sicily. Stylistically this work belongs with the music of the war years, and that may well explain Szymanowski's difficulty in finishing it. It was eventually completed in 1924, by which time his music had taken a very different turn—a response to changes in his own circumstances but above all to Poland's new-found independence.

He returned to Poland on Christmas Eve 1919, but it was not until the song cycle *Słopiewnie* ('Word-Songs'), written in summer 1921, that he found himself again as a composer. Having stood out all his life against the use of folk materials, Szymanowski began in this work to explore their possibilities in a manner somewhat influenced by Stravinsky. A new nationalist orientation was beginning to crystallize, and it was given expression in such works as the 20 Mazurkas op. 50 (1924–6) and the ballet *Harnasie* (1923–31), both based on the exotic folk music of the southern Tatra highlands.

By the mid-1920s Szymanowski was enjoying increasing international recognition. He was a prominent figure in Polish musical life too, becoming director of the Warsaw Conservatory in 1927 and rector of the State Academy of Music in 1930. Neither of these positions was a happy one, and he was dismissed from the academy (for largely political reasons) in April 1932. During the next two years he managed to write his Bartók-influenced *Symphonie concertante* for piano and orchestra (1932) and Second Violin Concerto (1933), but from 1934 onwards he was unable to produce much of substance. Faced with alarming financial problems and rapidly deteriorating health, he was obliged to undertake exhausting concert tours throughout Europe, and died of tuberculosis.   JS

📖 J. SAMSON, *The Music of Szymanowski* (London, 1980) · M. BRISTIGER, R. SCRUTON, and P. WEBER-BOCKHOLDT (eds.), *Karol Szymanowski in seiner Zeit* (Munich, 1984) · T. CHYLIŃSKA, *Karol Szymanowski: His Life and Works* (Los Angeles, 1993) · A. WIGHTMAN, *Karol Szymanowski: His Life and Work* (Aldershot, 1999) · A. WIGHTMAN (ed.), *Szymanowski on Music: Selected Writings of Karol Szymanowski* (Aldershot, 1999)

Szymański, Paweł (*b* Warsaw, 28 March 1954). Polish composer. He is one of the most distinctive Polish composers of his generation, his music developing intricate webs of polyphony, repetitive motifs, and quasi-tonal structures. He then fractures the musical continuum with silences or stretches it so that the canonic underlay is virtually imperceptible (*Sonata* for violins, double bass, and percussion, 1982; Piano Concerto, 1994). His brand of postmodernism, with its references mainly to 17th- and 18th-century idioms, may be playful or have ascetic religious connotations (*Miserere*, 1993).   ATH

T. Abbreviation for *tenor.

Tabarro, Il ('The Cloak'). Opera in one act by Puccini to a libretto by Giuseppe Adami after Didier Gold's play *La Houppelande* (1910), the first part of Puccini's *Il trittico* (New York, 1918).

tablā. An asymmetrical pair of tuned drums of north and central India, Pakistan, and Bangladesh, played with the fingers. The cylindrical wooden right-hand drum, called *tablā* or *dāyā*, is precisely tuned; the left-hand drum, called *bāyā* or *duggī*, a metal, bowl-shaped *kettledrum, is tuned by hand pressure while playing. They accompany vocal and instrumental music, and dance. JMo

tablature (Fr.: *tablature*; Ger.: *Tabulatur*, It.: *intavolatura*). Musical notation for instruments, based on figures, letters, or other symbols instead of conventional staff notation. Most tablatures are tailored to the playing technique of a particular type of instrument, using one set of symbols showing pitch (which fret to stop, which key to depress, or which hole to cover) and another indicating rhythm.

1. Fretted string instruments; 2. Keyboard instruments; 3. Wind instruments

1. Fretted string instruments

Grid-like tablatures for fretted strings began to appear in the late 15th century, depicting the intersections of frets and strings (also known as 'courses') so as to indicate where to place the fingers. One of the earliest of these, a system for five-course lute, appears in Virdung's *Musica getutscht* (Basle, 1511), where it is ascribed to the blind musician Conrad Paumann (see Fig. 1).

Simpler and more successful lute tablatures were introduced in Italy and France. The Italian system showed each course as a horizontal line, the highest line representing the lowest-pitched string. Numbers (1–9) represented the frets, and 'o' indicated an open string. Flagged stems above the numbers showed the duration of the notes; they were repeated for each note in early sources published by Petrucci, but later full staff notes were used for the first note of a group, the duration

remaining valid until contradicted by another sign. The Italian system was occasionally used in Germany, Poland, and, for the vihuela, Spain.

The French system used a five- or six-line grid, the top line (or the space above it) representing the highest string or course, with letters indicating the frets (*a* for open string, *b* for first fret, etc.). The signs for the duration of the notes followed the same pattern as the Italian system. Diapasons (extra low courses) were indicated by letters or numbers—below the grid in the French system, above in the Italian. French lute tablature was modified in the 17th century when the 'new tuning' (*nouveau ton*: *A–d–f–a–d'–f'*) was introduced by

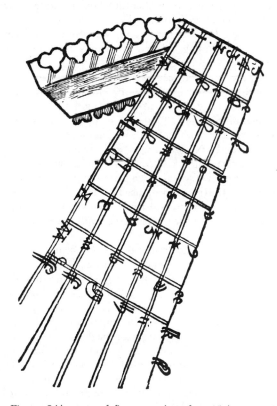

Fig. 1. Grid system of five-course lute, from Virdung, *Musica getutscht*.

table 1252

Denis Gaultier (*c.*1650). Reduced variants of the French or Italian systems were used for the four- or five-course cittern, gittern, and guitar. English sources generally followed the French system.

Other plucked instruments (e.g. chitarrone, mandolin, orpharion, theorbo) used reduced or expanded versions of French or Italian lute tablature. Bowed instruments, for example the lyra viol, lirone, and baryton, often used modified French lute tablature in the Baroque period; some viol and early violin music used an Italian or German lute system. Other numerical systems were later devised for the accordion, autoharp, balalaika, guitar, and zither; and ukulele tablature (sometimes adapted for the guitar) marks the left-hand finger positions with dots on an intersecting grid of vertical and horizontal lines, representing strings and frets respectively.

2. Keyboard instruments

In the early 14th century a combination of tablature and staff notation is found for keyboard music, for example in the Robertsbridge Codex, which has the top part notated on a five-line staff and the lower parts aligned below in letter notation, with rests indicated by the letter 's' (for Lat. *sine*, 'without'); sharps are indicated by a wavy line after the letter. This system was used in a developed form in 15th- and 16th-century German sources, including Conrad Paumann's *Fundamentum organisandi* (1452).

In the later 16th century letter notation was introduced for all parts, and the rhythm signs, which had hitherto tended to vary from source to source, became standardized ($| = \diamond$, $\lceil = \rfloor$, $\lceil = \rfloor$, etc.). This 'new' German keyboard tablature was introduced in publications by E. N. Ammerbach and his contemporaries. Scheidt's so-called *Tabulatura nova* (1624) adopted the Italian *partitura* system, each part using a five-line staff. Open-score systems were used in Italy from the early 16th century, whereas French and Italian keyboard sources tended to use short scores with staves of from five to eight lines.

Spanish keyboard music of the 16th century developed different forms of tablature, with a horizontal line representing each part and numbers indicating the notes. Juan Bermudo's *Declaración de instrumentos musicales* (Osuna, 1555) introduced two different systems with numbers. The first used numbers (1–42) to represent the keys, beginning with the diatonic notes of a short octave (C–F–D–G–E–A) and then proceeding chromatically. The other used numbers (1–23) for the white keys, with a cross above the number to indicate a sharp. A more successful scheme for Spanish keyboard (or harp or vihuela) tablature was that introduced in Venegas de Henestrosa's *Libro de cifra nueva* (Alcalá,

1557) and used in Cabezón's *Obras de música* (Madrid, 1578), among other sources. Each part was allocated a single horizontal line, on which the numbers 1 to 7 represented the notes *f* to *e'* (a key signature would be given at the beginning of the work to indicate whether 4 represented B or B♭).

3. Wind instruments

Diagrams relating fingering to notes have occasionally been used for such wind instruments as the recorder, flageolet, oboe, and clarinet in instrumental tutors since the 16th century. 'Dot way' notation, used in the 17th and 18th centuries for English flageolet music, had dashes on a six-line staff to show the fingerholes, with the durations indicated above as in lute tablature.

FD/AP

📖 W. Apel, *The Notation of Polyphonic Music, 900–1600* (Cambridge, MA, 1942, 5/1961) · V. Coelho (ed.), *Performance on Lute, Guitar and Vihuela: Historical Practice and Modern Interpretation*, Cambridge Studies in Performance Practice, 6 (Cambridge, 1997)

table. See BELLY.

table music. See TAFELMUSIK.

tabor. A small drum, usually with a snare; it varies widely in size. See PIPE AND TABOR.

tacet (Lat.). 'Is silent'; a direction that a player remain silent; *tacet al fine*, 'remaining silent until the end'.

tactus (Lat.). A 15th- and 16th-century term for 'beat' (see BEAT, 1).

Tafelmusik (Ger., 'table music'; Fr.: *musique de table*). Music intended for performance at meals. In the Middle Ages, church music was directed at God and the service of the liturgy, while chamber music was meant for the enjoyment of the performers; one of the earliest situations in which music was performed for an audience in the modern sense was at the courtly dinner table. There is plentiful evidence of this practice from the late Middle Ages onwards, and it is clear that the hearers were often attentive, though at other times distracted by eating and conversation. The term *Tafelmusik* (with related expressions) arose in 16th-century Germany to refer to a genre coordinate with *Kirchenmusik* and *Kammermusik*.

The earliest music expressly composed for performance at table seems to have been J. H. Schein's *Banchetto musicale* (1617), a collection of dance suites for five viols or other instruments. Many other German publications followed in the 17th and early 18th centuries, often including partsongs and songs with continuo as well as instrumental music; sacred vocal music, which had formerly been often sung at table, was no longer an important constituent of the genre. The climax of the tradition was Telemann's *Musique de table* (1733) in three 'productions' each comprising an *ouverture*-suite, a quartet, a concerto, a trio, a solo, and a 'conclusion' (with the instrumentation of the *ouverture*). In the second half of the 18th century *Tafelmusik* merged with the *divertimento and the *serenade, and by the 19th century the practice of making music at mealtimes had fallen into disuse.

JJD

Tagelied (Ger., 'day song'). See ALBA.

Tagliavini, Ferruccio (*b* Reggio nell'Emilia, 14 Aug. 1913; *d* Reggio nell'Emilia, 29 Jan. 1995). Italian tenor. He took lessons from Amadeo Bassi and made his debut as Rodolfo in *La bohème* in Florence in 1939. By 1945 he was one of Italy's most sought-after tenors for lyrical bel canto roles, and his fame spread internationally when he made his debut at the Metropolitan Opera, New York, in 1947. One of his greatest successes was as Nemorino in *L'elisir d'amore*, in which he was praised for his agile and mellifluous singing and his engaging comic acting. He was also impressive in the tragic title role of Massenet's *Werther*.   JT

taille. 1. A French term used from the 16th century to the 18th to denote the part that other languages call 'tenor'; hence *taille de violon* for the viola, *taille d'hautbois* for the tenor shawm or, from 1660, the tenor oboe, and so on.

2. A term used for the tenor line in French music up to the end of the 18th century. In German music, particularly that of Bach, the *taille* was an oboe in F, a type of tenor *oboe.

Tailleferre, Germaine (Marcelle) (*b* Parc-Saint-Maur, Seine, 19 April 1892; *d* Paris, 6 Nov. 1983). French composer. She studied at the Paris Conservatoire and with Ravel, and spent most of her life as a composer, pianist, and teacher in France, except for a period in the USA between 1942 and 1946. Early in her career she became a member of Les *Six, collaborating with the others on the piano *Album des Six* (published 1920) and the ballet *Les Mariés de la Tour Eiffel* (1921). But her adherence to the iconoclastic ideals of the group was short-lived, and she emerged as a composer of graceful music very much in the French tradition—though she also experimented briefly with serialism. Her output includes operas, ballets, many film scores, chamber music, and songs. She wrote several works for unusual forces, including a Concerto for two pianos, wordless chorus, saxophones, and orchestra (1934), revised as *Concerto des vaines paroles* for baritone, piano, and orchestra (1956), and a Concerto for wordless soprano and orchestra (1957), revised as *Concerto de la fidélité* (1982).   PG/ABur

📖 L. MITGANG, 'Germaine Tailleferre', *The Musical Woman*, ii, ed. J. L. Zaimont and others (Westport, CT, 1987), 177–221 · R. SHAPIRO, *Germaine Tailleferre: A Bio-Bibliography* (Westport, CT, 1994)

Takemitsu, Tōru (*b* Tokyo, 8 Oct. 1930; *d* Tokyo, 20 Feb. 1996). Japanese composer. He was largely self-taught, though he had some lessons from Yasuki Kiyose, and from 1951 joined with other Japanese composers and artists in an Experimental Workshop. With his *Requiem* for strings (1957) he gained international as well as national recognition, and his reputation as the leading Japanese composer grew steadily in Europe and the USA. He received awards and commissions in many countries, sat on international juries, and was in demand worldwide as a lecturer and composer-in-residence; he was also involved in devising festivals and concert series in Paris and Tokyo. He collaborated regularly with a number of leading performers, among them the conductor Seiji Ozawa and the ensemble Tashi. He composed prolifically for orchestra with and without soloists, and for many chamber ensembles; he also wrote popular songs and 93 film scores.

Takemitsu's music is a personal and distinctive synthesis of a wide range of influences. The first Western music he heard was popular music and jazz; his harmonic language was largely derived from Debussy and Messiaen; he was also influenced by the ideas of John Cage. His travels, his reading, and his friendships yielded many ideas for forms, textures, and titles. In general, he avoided references to traditional Japanese music, though he did occasionally write for Japanese instruments—for example in *November Steps* for *biwa*, *shakuhachi*, and orchestra (1967) and *In an Autumn Garden* for *gagaku* orchestra (1979)—and sometimes imitated their playing techniques on Western instruments. However, at a deeper level, his music reflects a Japanese aesthetic in its avoidance of regular rhythms, fast tempos, symmetrical forms, and strongly contrasting blocks of sound, in favour of a slowly and organically unfolding flow suggested by meditation, dreams, landscape, weather, the elements, and the seasons.   ABur

📖 N. OHTAKA, *Creative Sources for the Music of Tōru Takemitsu* (Aldershot and Brookfield, VT, 1993) · P. BURT, *The Music of Tōru Takemitsu* (Cambridge, 2001)

Takt (Ger.). 1. 'Time' or 'metre'; *Taktzeichen*, 'time signature'; *3/4 Takt*, '3/4 time'; *im Takt*, 'in time' (i.e. *a tempo*); *taktfest*, 'in steady time'.

2. 'Beat'; *ein Takt wie vorher zwei*, 'one beat as previously two' (i.e. one beat should be allowed as much time as two beats were previously).

3. 'Bar'; *Taktnote* (literally 'bar-note'), *semibreve; *Taktpause*, a bar's rest; *Taktstrich*, 'bar-line'; *dreitaktig*, in three-bar phrases.

tāla. The term used in Indian classical music to define a cyclical rhythmic period, akin to Western 'metre' but covering a wider range of time-spans than the Western term denotes. The fixed pattern of a *tāla* can be indicated by hand gestures, drum or hand beats.   KC

Tales from the Vienna Woods (*Geschichten aus dem Wienerwald*). Waltz, op. 325 (1868), by Johann Strauss (ii).

Tales of Hoffmann, The. See CONTES D'HOFFMANN, LES.

Tallis, Thomas (*b* c.1505; *d* Greenwich, 23 Nov. 1585). English composer. Between 1532 and 1543 he held posts as organist or singer at Dover Priory, the London parish church of St-Mary-at-Hill, Waltham Abbey, and Canterbury Cathedral. By 1543 he had been appointed a Gentleman of the Chapel Royal, a position he held for the rest of his life. Latterly he acted as organist, sharing the job with his close friend William Byrd. In 1575 he and Byrd were granted a royal privilege to print music; later that year they issued a book of motets, *Cantiones sacrae*, dedicated to Queen Elizabeth, to which both composers contributed 17 pieces, one each for every year of the queen's reign. The publication was not successful financially (though a related venture, selling sheets of printed staves, did make some money) and they turned to the queen for assistance. Tallis married in c.1554 but had no children. He is buried in the parish church of St Alphege in Greenwich.

Tallis was brought up in the Roman Catholic tradition, and his earlier work consists largely of Latin liturgical settings, often on a grand scale and intended either for major church festivals or for occasions of state. The seven-voice *Missa 'Puer natus est nobis'* may have been written in expectation that Queen Mary would bear England a Roman Catholic heir following her marriage to Philip of Spain in 1554. After the accession of Elizabeth, Tallis continued to set Latin texts, though these works were clearly meant for secular rather than church use—the introduction of the Protestant Book of Common Prayer effectively outlawed the use of Latin in church. Some of these late motets, including the two *Lamentations*—dark-hued and extraordinarily emotional works—probably express covert Roman Catholic sympathies, and it was a Catholic patron (Thomas Howard, 4th Duke of Norfolk) who commissioned his masterpiece, the 40-voice motet *Spem in alium*.

Tallis was among the first composers to write English-texted anthems and canticles for the new Protestant liturgy. Some of these works, including the 'Dorian' Service and the anthem *If ye love me*, have never fallen out of the cathedral repertory and therefore ensured the familiarity of Tallis's name. A small amount of instrumental music by him has survived, both for solo keyboard and for viol consort, together with some secular partsongs. His most familiar works, however, are ones he contributed to Matthew Parker's English metrical psalter (London, c.1567): the hymn tune now known as 'Tallis's Ordinal', the adapted round sung to the words 'Glory to thee, my God, this night' (*'Tallis's Canon'), and the strongly modal 'Third tune' on which Vaughan Williams based his *Fantasia on a Theme by Thomas Tallis* (1910).   DA/JM

📖 P. DOE, *Tallis* (London, 1968, 2/1976) · H. BENHAM, *Latin Church Music in England, c. 1460–1575* (London, 1977)

Tallis's Canon. The eighth of nine tunes composed for Archbishop Parker's *The Whole Psalter Translated into English Metre* (c.1567). The canon is formed by the tenor and treble voices and was originally attached to Psalm 67. Most of the tunes in the psalter are in use as hymn tunes.

Talma, Louise (Juliette) (*b* Arcachon, 31 Oct. 1906; *d* Yaddo, NY, 13 Aug. 1996). American composer. She studied at Columbia University (1923–33) and, during the summers, in France with Isidore Philipp and Nadia Boulanger, and taught at Hunter College, New York (1928–79). Among her rather few works are the opera *The Alcestiad* (Frankfurt, 1962).   PG

talon (Fr.). 'Heel' or 'nut' of a bow; *au talon*, an instruction to bow 'at the heel'.

Tamagno, Francesco (*b* Turin, 28 Dec. 1850; *d* Varese, 31 Aug. 1905). Italian tenor. He sang in the chorus at the Teatro Regio, Turin, where in 1870 he made his debut as Nearco in Donizetti's *Poliuto*. He first appeared at La Scala, Milan, in 1877, creating a strong impression as Vasco da Gama in *L'Africaine* and in the title role of *Don Carlos*. In 1881 he sang Adorno in the first performance of the revised *Simon Boccanegra*, and Verdi chose him to create the title role in *Otello* (1887). He was associated with the role for the rest of his career, though he was admired more for his intense 'trumpet tone' than for his dramatic and psychological insights. In 1902 he recorded some short extracts from *Otello*.   JT

tambour (Fr.). 'Drum'.

tambourin (Fr.). An 18th-century French dance, probably based on the Provençal folk dance of that name, which was in lively duple metre and accompanied by *galoubet* and *tambourin* (pipe and tabor).

Tambourins are principally found in theatrical works, notably those of Rameau (a famous example is in *Les Fêtes d'Hébé*), where the textures imitate the original instrumentation.   —/JH

tambourin de Béarn (Fr.). A simple dulcimer with six thick gut strings stretched over a wooden resonator. These are struck with a stick to provide a rhythmic bass to the melody of a three-hole pipe (*galoubet*; see PIPE AND TABOR).   RPa

tambourine [timbrel] (Fr.: *tambour de Basque*; Ger.: *Schellentrommel*; Lat.: *tympanum*). A *frame drum, usually with small metal discs called jingles hanging loosely in slots in its wooden frame. Of ancient origin, and played throughout the Mediterranean area, it was introduced to the Western orchestra in the late 18th century. A wide variety of playing techniques are used including shaking, hitting, and rubbing with a moistened thumb for close rolls.   JMo

tambūrā. A long-necked drone lute of the Indian subcontinent with four strings, tuned to the tonic and dominant or subdominant; it is used to accompany a singer or a solo instrument such as the *sitar.   JMo

Tamerlano. Opera in three acts by Handel to a libretto by Nicola Francesco Haym adapted from Agostin Piovene's *Tamerlano* (1711) and from *Bajazet* (1719), a revised version of the same libretto prepared by Ippolito Zanelli and Francesco Borosini, after Jacques Prodon's play *Tamerlan, ou La Mort de Bajazet* (1675) (London, 1724).

Tamla Motown. See MOTOWN.

tam-tam. A term (of Malay origin) for the Western orchestral *gong with a flat surface and curved rim, of indefinite pitch.

Tancredi. Opera in two acts by Rossini to a libretto by Gaetano Rossi after Voltaire's *Tancrède* (1760) (Venice, 1813).

Tändelei (Ger., 'trifling'). See BADINAGE, BADINERIE.

Tan Dun (*b* Simao, 8 Aug. 1957). Chinese-American composer. After a village childhood and two years planting rice during the Cultural Revolution, he developed his musical skills in the provincial Peking opera troupe. He studied at the reopened Central Conservatory in Beijing from 1978 to 1986, then at Columbia University in New York, where he still lives. He was appointed composer-conductor of the BBC Scottish Symphony Orchestra in 1995, and artistic director of the Tanglewood contemporary music festival in 1999. Most of Tan's works combine Chinese and Western culture: for example, the opera *Marco Polo*

(Munich, 1996); the *Symphony 1997*, written for the return of Hong Kong to China; and *Peony Pavilion*, a music-theatre work based on a traditional Peking opera (Vienna, 1998). He has written for Asian instruments, as well as for orchestra and for experimental ensembles.
                                                                  ABur

Taneyev, Sergey Ivanovich (*b* Vladimir, 13/25 Nov. 1856; *d* Dyudkovo, nr Moscow, 6/19 June 1915). Russian composer and theorist. At the Moscow Conservatory he studied the piano with Nikolay Rubinstein and composition with Tchaikovsky, with whom he formed a lasting and fruitful friendship (he was the soloist in the premieres of all Tchaikovsky's works for piano and orchestra). After Tchaikovsky's resignation from the conservatory Taneyev joined the staff to teach harmony and orchestration (1878); after Rubinstein's death he took over the piano class (1881), then taught composition (1883), and finally was appointed director (1885–9). Taneyev composed four symphonies, notable more for their consummate craftsmanship and cogency than for any melodic charm, though the finale of his Second Symphony (1877–8) has spontaneity and lyrical warmth. He also wrote six string quartets, a Piano Quintet (1906), a Piano Trio (1907), other chamber works, songs, and piano music.

Taneyev's most ambitious work was his remarkable three-act opera *Oresteya* (St Petersburg, 1895), which, because of its length and weight, he called a trilogy. It is highly original: although there are occasional echoes of Tchaikovsky, the music speaks with a strong individual voice; the classical subject made the work stand out at a time when Russian plots were *de rigueur*; and Taneyev shows genuine dramatic skill in bringing Aeschylus to the operatic stage. He is also remembered as an important theorist for his rigorous studies of counterpoint (1909) and canon (published posthumously in 1929).
                                                                  GN/MF-W

Tanglewood Festival. American festival established near Lenox, Massachusetts, in 1937. In 1940 Koussevitzky founded a summer school for instruction in conducting (with the Boston Symphony Orchestra), opera, instrumental performance, and composition; it has attracted many distinguished students. See FESTIVALS, 3.

tango. A dance originating in urban Argentina in the late 19th century. In duple metre, with a characteristic rhythmic figure, it consists of two sections, the second usually in the dominant or relative minor. It resembles the *habanera and is often played on the accordion, specifically the bandoneon. Although it became a popular society dance for couples in 1920s Paris, its origins lie in the Argentinian folk and urban tango.

Exponents of tango music include Carlos Gardel (1887–1935) and Astor Piazzolla (1921–92). There is a stylized tango in Stravinsky's *Histoire du soldat*, and a 'Tango-Pasodoble' in Walton's *Façade*. —/JH

Tannhäuser (*Tannhäuser und der Sängerkrieg auf Wartburg*; 'Tannhäuser and the Singers' Contest on the Wartburg'). Opera in three acts by Wagner to his own libretto (Dresden, 1845).

Tansman, Alexandre (*b* Łódź, 12 June 1897; *d* Paris, 15 Nov. 1986). Polish-born French composer. He studied composition with Wojciech Gawroński and Piotr Rytel at Warsaw University (1915–19), then moved permanently to Paris. There he was deeply influenced by Stravinskian neo-classicism, which he combined in his music with Polish and Jewish elements. His output included eight symphonies and other orchestral pieces, ballets, operas, and choral works. He toured widely as a conductor and pianist, and wrote *Igor Stravinsky: The Man and his Music* (Eng. trans., New York, 1949).

PG

📖 I. SCHWERKE, *Alexandre Tansman, compositeur polonais* (Paris, 1931)

tant (Fr.), **tanto** (It.). 'As much', 'so much'; *non tanto*, 'not too much', e.g. *allegro ma non tanto*, 'allegro', but not too much so'.

Tanz, Tänze (Ger.). 'Dance', 'dances'.

tape recording. See RECORDING AND REPRODUCTION.

Tapiola. Tone-poem, op. 112 (1926), by Sibelius. Tapio was the god of Finnish forests.

tarantella (It.; Fr.: *tarentelle*). A dance that takes its name from the southern Italian seaport of Taranto. The bite of the tarantula spider (found in the surrounding countryside and also named after the town) was popularly supposed to cause a disease which would prove fatal unless the victim performed a lively dance, or which itself caused 'tarantism' or dancing mania. It has long been known, however, that the spider's bite is comparatively harmless. In 1662 Pepys records a meeting with a gentleman who 'is a great traveller, and, speaking of the tarantula, he says that all the harvest long . . . fiddlers go up and down the fields everywhere, in expectation of being hired by those that are stung'. From the 17th century to the 20th there were apparently great communal tarantism, in which whole towns would suddenly give themselves over to wild dancing, and the musicians had a profitable time.

By the 19th century, however, musicians made more money out of tarantellas by their popularity as compositions. Chopin, Liszt, Heller, Auber, Weber,

Thalberg, Balakirev, Cui, and Dargomïzhsky, among others, wrote tarantellas, all in rapid 6/8 time; they are often in conjunct motion and involve *perpetuum mobile (proceeding throughout in notes of the same value), frequently increasing in tempo throughout the piece. The *saltarello is a similar type of piece, and the finale of Mendelssohn's 'Italian' Symphony, though called a saltarello, is actually a combination of that dance with a tarantella melody.

Taras Bulba. Rhapsody for orchestra (1915–18) by Janáček after Nikolay Gogol's story about Bulba, the Ukrainian Cossack leader.

tardo, tarda (It.). 'Slow'; *tardamente*, 'slowly'; *tardando*, *tardante*, 'slowing down'.

Tarnopol'sky, Vladimir Grigoryevich (*b* Dnepropetrovsk, 30 April 1955). Russian composer. With the encouragement of Denisov he entered the Moscow Conservatory, where he studied composition with Nikolay Sidel'nikov (and unofficially with Denisov), and theory with Yury Kholopov. He used his technical prowess and wide learning in a series of brilliant, eclectic, and often witty works written in answer to commissions from various west European countries. In the 1990s, however, he often deployed his technical resources in the service of a more serious, even tragic message, as in his powerful orchestral piece *Kassandra* (1991) and in the opera *Wenn die Zeit über die Ufer tritt* after Chekhov (Munich, 1999). JWAL

tárogató. Hungarian reed instrument. Originally a double-reed *shawm of Turkish or Central Asian descent, introduced in the 13th century, it was banned in the 18th century by the Austro-Hungarian government as a nationalist symbol. The shawm was replaced in about 1890 by J. V. Schunda of Budapest with a wide-bore, single-reed wooden clarinet with keywork based on that of the simple-system clarinet. This instrument is widely used in Hungary and Romania. JMo

Tárrega, Francisco (*b* Villareal, Castellón, 21 Nov. 1852; *d* Barcelona, 15 Dec. 1909). Spanish guitarist and composer. Known as 'the Sarasate of the guitar', he studied the classical guitar (neglected at that time) as a child, then the piano and composition at the Madrid Conservatory. He subsequently devoted himself to the guitar, giving numerous recitals in Spain and doing much to promote it as a popular instrument. In 1880 he made a triumphant debut in Paris and London. Tárrega added many of his own compositions to the guitar repertory, as well as over 100 transcriptions of music for other instruments. WT/CW

Tartini, Giuseppe (*b* Pirano [now Piran, Istria], 8 April 1692; *d* Padua, 26 Feb. 1770). Italian violinist, composer, teacher, and theorist. Originally intended for the priesthood, he defied his parents to follow a musical career. He first studied law at the university in Padua (where his chief reputation was as a swordsman); after incurring the wrath of the ecclesiastical authorities there by a secret marriage in 1710, he was obliged to retire to the Minorite monastery at Assisi, where he studied music, probably with Černohorský. By 1714 he had joined the opera orchestra in Ancona; the following year he was pardoned, but left his wife again soon afterwards in order to spend four years in seclusion while perfecting his violin playing. In 1721 he was appointed first violinist at S. Antonio in Padua, a post he combined with concert tours abroad including a prolonged spell in Prague from 1723, during which he played at the coronation of Emperor Charles VI. After sustaining an arm injury in 1740 his concert activity declined, but he remained at S. Antonio, which boasted one of the finest church orchestras in Europe, until 1765 and continued his teaching activities even longer.

In Padua Tartini established his own violin school, which was a magnet for students from all over Europe. He also worked extensively on musical and acoustical theory, though his ideas were not well received; he corresponded on these subjects for many years with Padre Martini. His concertos are among the first to adopt the Vivaldian three-movement pattern. Many of his sonatas, also in three movements, are technically demanding, though the later ones are simpler and more expressive. His most famous work is the 'Devil's Trill' Sonata, supposedly written as the result of a dream in which the devil seized Tartini's violin and played a piece that included a particularly difficult trill.   WT/ER

   📖 P. POLZONETTI, *Tartini e la musica seconda natura* (Lucca, 2000)

Tasso: Lamento e trionfo. Symphonic poem by Liszt, after a poem by Byron. Sketches for it exist from 1841–5; the first version was completed in 1849, orchestrated by August Conradi and performed as an overture to Johann Wolfgang von Goethe's play *Torquato Tasso*. It was revised in 1850–1, reorchestrated by Raff, and given its final version by Liszt himself in 1854.

Taste (Ger.). 1. 'Key' of any keyboard instrument.
   2. 'Fret'.

tastiera (It.). 1. 'Keyboard'.
   2. 'Fingerboard'.

tasto (It.). 1. The 'key' of a keyboard instrument. Hence *tasto solo* is an instruction to the keyboard player of a *continuo part to play 'a single key only', i.e. to play the written bass line without adding chords or harmonic parts.

   2. 'Fingerboard' of a stringed instrument; *sul tasto*, an instruction to bow above the fingerboard.

Tate, Phyllis (Margaret Duncan) (*b* Gerrards Cross, 6 April 1911; *d* London, 29 May 1987). English composer. She studied at the RAM but was relatively slow to make her reputation as a composer. From the 1950s, however, she won success with works for chamber groupings, choir, and children, all in a neat tonal style which does not forswear humour. Her output also includes a Saxophone Concerto (1944), the opera *The Lodger* (1960), and the television opera *Dark Pilgrimage* (1963).
                                                PG

tattoo. The music of bugles and drums that recalls soldiers to their barracks at night. In the British Army it lasts for 20 minutes, beginning with the fanfare called the First Post and ending with the Last Post (also played at military funerals). The word is used to describe military musical festivals, such as the Edinburgh Tattoo.

Tauber, Richard (*b* Linz, 16 May 1891; *d* London, 8 Jan. 1948). Austrian-born British tenor. He studied in Freiburg, making his debut as Tamino in *Die Zauberflöte* in Chemnitz (1913). He was immediately engaged by the Dresden Hofoper and remained a member of the company until 1926, after which he moved to Vienna where he lived until the Anschluss of 1938. There he turned with ever-increasing frequency to operetta, scoring a colossal success as Sou-Chong in Lehár's *Das Land des Lächelns*, a role with which he also took London by storm in 1931. In 1938–9 he sang at Covent Garden, notably as Jeník in *The Bartered Bride*. His second wife was British, and Tauber made London his home in 1940. He is widely regarded as one of the greatest of all exponents of operetta and light music, though he was equally outstanding in Mozart (he sang Don Ottavio in *Don Giovanni* as late as 1947) and the lyric-dramatic repertory. The leading tenor roles in Korngold's *Die tote Stadt* and Strauss's *Die ägyptische Helena* (1928) were written for him, but he never sang the latter.
                                                TA

   📖 C. CASTLE and D. N. TAUBER, *This Was Richard Tauber* (London, 1971)

Tavener, Sir John (Kenneth) (*b* London, 28 Jan. 1944). English composer. He studied with Lennox Berkeley at the RAM and with David Lumsdaine, achieving early success with *The Whale* (1965–6), a dramatic cantata that makes effective use of simple materials deriving from Stravinsky and Messiaen. He joined the Russian Orthodox Church in 1978, and his music has focused increasingly on the spiritual, liturgical aspects of his chosen faith. His works, from *Ultimos ritos* (1969–72) to *Fall and Resurrection* (1999), are often on a massive scale and exploit the resonance of large church buildings. But

Tavener has also been successful in his use of an intimate, meditative, minimalist style comparable to that of Arvo Pärt, as well as with concert works (for example, *The Protecting Veil* for cello and orchestra, 1988–9) and opera (*Mary of Egypt*, Aldeburgh, 1992). He was knighted in 2000.   PG/AW

> 📖 J. TAVENER, *The Music of Silence: A Composer's Testament*, ed. B. Keeble (London, 1999)

Taverner. Opera in two acts by Maxwell Davies to his own libretto after 16th-century letters and documents concerning the life of the composer John Taverner (London, 1972).

Taverner, John (*b* Lincolnshire, *c*.1490; *d* Boston, Lincs., 18 Oct. 1545). English composer. Nothing is known about him until 1524–5, when he was a singer at the collegiate church at Tattershall. In 1526 he moved to Oxford to run the choir at Thomas Wolsey's newly founded Cardinal College (the future Christ Church), where choral music on a grand scale was encouraged. Following Wolsey's political downfall he returned to Lincolnshire, as a singer and possibly Master of the Choristers at the parish church of St Botolph, Boston. There is little sign of his involvement in music after 1537. It now seems unlikely that Taverner was ever actively involved in Lutheran heresy or the persecution of Roman Catholics, as earlier biographies have suggested; and the John Taverner recorded in London in about 1514 was another man.

Taverner's church music stands as one of the pinnacles of the Tudor tradition. In his most extended works, such as the *Missa 'Corona spinea'* and *Missa 'Gloria tibi Trinitas'*—the latter written for Cardinal College—he transcends even the length and complexity of the *Eton Choirbook repertory, and shows no interest in the expressive word-dominated styles of contemporary continental music. His smaller liturgical works, such as the *'Western Wind' Mass* and the *Dum transisset* settings, are less florid, but still essentially studies in expansive melody rather than rhetorical word-setting. One work, the votive antiphon *O splendor gloriae*, was completed by (or written collaboratively with) Christopher Tye; Tye's section is noticeably more pithy than Taverner's. The florid style extended to his English-texted songs, only one of which survives intact. After his death Taverner's music continued to be valued in England both by musical connoisseurs and by Catholic recusants, and subtle influences are detectable in Byrd. As the unwitting creator of the genre of the *In nomine*, he had an impact on English instrumental music up to the time of Purcell.   JM

> 📖 C. HAND, *John Taverner: His Life and Music* (London, 1978) · D. S. JOSEPHSON, *John Taverner, Tudor Composer* (Ann Arbor, MI, 1979)

Taylor, (Joseph) Deems (*b* New York, 22 Dec. 1885; *d* New York, 3 July 1966). American composer and critic. He studied at New York University and privately with Oscar Coon (1908–11), and worked as a writer and broadcaster: his is the voice in the Disney film *Fantasia*. He had two operas produced at the Metropolitan, *The King's Henchman* (1927) and *Peter Ibbetson* (1931), and also wrote orchestral and choral music in a fluent, European-derived style.   PG

Tchaikovsky, Pyotr Il'yich (*see opposite page*)

Tcherepnin, Alexander (Nikolayevich) (*b* St Petersburg, 9/21 Jan. 1899; *d* Paris, 29 Sept. 1977). Russian composer, conductor, and pianist, son of Nikolay Tcherepnin. In 1921 he settled with his father in Paris, where he studied at the Conservatoire. He then began a career as a virtuoso pianist and toured extensively. His First Symphony, with its second movement scored for percussion, created a scandal in 1927; its last movement contains many references to what has been dubbed the 'Tcherepnin scale' of nine notes, consisting of three progressions of a semitone, tone, and semitone. In the 1930s he spent three years in China; Chinese music was to influence many of his later works. He was a prolific composer, writing symphonies, concertos, sonatas, and dramatic works. His completion of Musorgsky's unfinished comic opera *Marriage* had its premiere in Essen in 1937. In 1949 he became instructor in theory at DePaul University, Chicago, and in 1958 he took American citizenship.   PS/DN

> 📖 A. TCHEREPNIN, 'A short autobiography', *Tempo*, 130 (1979), 12–18 · E. A. ARIAS, *Alexander Tcherepnin: A Bio-Bibliography* (New York, 1989)

Tcherepnin, Nikolay (Nikolayevich) (*b* St Petersburg, 3/15 May 1873; *d* Paris, 26 June 1945). Russian conductor and composer. He was prominent as a conductor in St Petersburg, where Prokofiev was among the pupils in his conducting class at the conservatory, and in Paris, where he was attached to the Diaghilev Ballet, with which he later toured (1909–14). His ballet music for *Le Pavillon d'Armide* (1908) has the distinction of being the first score commissioned by Diaghilev, and his preliminary work on *The Firebird* before it passed into Stravinsky's hands can be heard in the tone-poem *Zacharovannoye tsarstvo* ('The Enchanted Kingdom', 1908–9). In 1918 he became head of the Tbilisi Conservatory, and from 1921 he lived in Paris. He composed ballets, operas, symphonies, symphonic poems, and sacred music, and prepared a completed version of Musorgsky's opera *Sorochintsy Fair*, which he conducted in Monte Carlo in 1923.   PS/DN

(*cont. on p. 1261*)

Pyotr Il'yich Tchaikovsky (1840–93)

The Russian composer Pyotr Il'yich Tchaikovsky (Chaykovsky) was born in Votkinsk, Vyatka province, on 25 April/7 May 1840 and died in St Petersburg on 25 October/6 November 1893.

Tchaikovsky once wrote that his whole life was spent 'regretting the past and hoping for the future, never being satisfied with the present'. This feeling of unease and dissatisfaction with life imbued much of his music, particularly in his later years, when the disasters of his personal life found expression in music of extraordinary emotional anguish and tragic drama. In these forceful, highly individual works, couched in an intensely lyrical idiom and scored in rich orchestral colours, Tchaikovsky laid bare his personality with vivid immediacy, bequeathing to the repertory a range of symphonies, concertos, and operas which have remained enduringly popular and affecting.

The early years

Although as a child Tchaikovsky took piano lessons his family did not envisage a musical career for him, and at the age of ten he entered the St Petersburg School of Jurisprudence, where he studied until 1859. After a period working in the civil service he resumed his study of music with the theorist Nikolay Zaremba (1821–79) in the classes of the newly formed Russian Musical Society. When these classes blossomed into the St Petersburg Conservatory in 1862 Tchaikovsky enrolled so that he could continue studying with Zaremba; he also took lessons in composition (1863–5) from Anton Rubinstein, a composer whom he held in lasting respect. In 1866, on the invitation of Rubinstein's brother, Nikolay, Tchaikovsky moved to Moscow to teach harmony at the conservatory there: he held this post until 1878, and in connection with his academic work produced a number of textbooks, among them the *Rukovodstvo k prakticheskomu izucheniyu garmonii* ('Guide to the Practical Study of Harmony'), written in 1871, published the following year, and finally translated into English in 1976.

Even as a student, Tchaikovsky had shown facility for composition, producing such works as the exuberant yet warmly lyrical overture to Aleksandr Ostrovsky's play *Groza* ('The Storm', 1864), and in his early years in Moscow he consolidated his reputation with his First Symphony, 'Winter Daydreams' (composed and revised 1866, and reaching its final form in a third version of 1874), and the First String Quartet (1871). He achieved less success with his first opera, *Voyevoda* ('The Voyevoda' [provincial governor], 1869) and eventually destroyed the score, incorporating some of the music into another opera, *Oprichnik* ('The Oprichnik' [a mercenary soldier], 1874).

In 1868 Tchaikovsky met the composers of The Five, the St Petersburg nationalist group centred on Vladimir Stasov and Balakirev. Balakirev conducted the first St Petersburg performance of Tchaikovsky's symphonic poem *Fatum* ('Fate', 1868) at a concert of the Russian Musical Society in 1869, and later the same year Balakirev helped Tchaikovsky formulate his ideas for one of his most popular works, the fantasy overture *Romeo and Juliet* (1869, rev. 1870 and 1880). It may have been his association with The Five that prompted him to undertake some overtly Russian or nationalist works during this period, such as the Second Symphony ('Little Russian' or 'Ukrainian', 1872, rev. 1880), the opera *Kuznets Vakula* ('Vakula the Smith', 1876, revised as *Cherevichki*, 'The Slippers'), and his incidental music to Ostrovsky's *Snegurochka* ('The Snow Maiden', 1873), though Tchaikovsky later claimed in his autobiography 'from my earliest childhood [in the remote town of Votkinsk], I was immersed in Russian folk music and the indescribable beauty of its characteristic features'.

The years of maturity

From 1872 Tchaikovsky began to appear in print as a music critic for the newspaper *Russkiye vedomosti*, and in 1876 he was sent to Bayreuth to cover the *Ring*. However, he reported that food was the prime concern of Bayreuth patrons ('there was much more talk of beefsteaks, cutlets, and roast potatoes than of Wagner's music') and he summed up his opinion of Wagner, glimpsed only from an upstairs window, as 'a sprightly little old man with an aquiline nose and thin, supercilious lips—the characteristic trait of the initiator of this entire cosmopolitan festival'. Tchaikovsky remained unaffected by Wagner's style, and instead his own music of this period shows a developing of that open, emotionally charged idiom which was to become so familiar in his mature music: the First Piano Concerto (1874–5)—harshly criticized by Nikolay Rubinstein—the symphonic fantasia *Francesca da Rimini* (1876), and his first ballet *Lebedinoye ozero* ('Swan Lake', 1877) forged a highly individual style, marked by flair and brilliance yet often tinged with the brooding fatalism which was to dominate his later years. In addition, several of his works began to hint clearly at his fascination with 18th-century music, in particular that of Mozart, who, Tchaikovsky said, 'captivates, delights, and warms me'. He had already harked back to Classical models in the little minuet in *Vakula the Smith*; he now affirmed his love of the cool, clear lines of Classical music in his *Variations on a Rococo Theme* for cello and orchestra (1876), and was to reassert it in such works as the opera *Pikovaya dama* ('The Queen of Spades', 1890), set in the time of Catherine II and incorporating 18th-century pastiche.

In the late 1870s Tchaikovsky's personal life and his creative career reached a watershed. Tchaikovsky had long yearned for a settled domestic life; he was also haunted by feelings of guilt about his homosexuality, to which he had been giving covert expression in his letters and writings; and as a result he longed to free his family from any shame and embarrassment at the prevailing rumours about his proclivities. By chance, in spring 1877 he received a letter from a young admirer, Antonina Milyukova. At the time he was fired with enthusiasm for his opera *Yevgeny Onegin* ('Eugene Onegin'), and thoughts of the famous Letter Scene urged him to follow up Antonina's protestations of love. They were married in July 1877, but within days of the wedding he was finding his wife 'absolutely repugnant' and living a life of torment. He swiftly found that marriage required a commitment into which he was quite unable to enter, and he was to be plagued with problems of separation and divorce proceedings for many years to come.

The final years

It is tempting to see Tchaikovsky's disastrous marriage as a direct inspiration for *Eugene Onegin* and the Fourth Symphony (1877–8, the first of his so-called 'Fate' symphonies), but the idea of writing the opera, or at least setting the Letter Scene, had occurred to him long

before he had even heard of Antonina, and much of the Fourth Symphony had been written before his marriage. Yet the consequences of this incautious step served to strengthen his belief that life was directed by some implacable, unconquerable force—a theme running through much of the music of his later years: the Fifth Symphony (1888), *Manfred* (1885), and the opera *The Queen of Spades*. But these tragic, confessional works represent only one side of Tchaikovsky. During the same period he also wrote pieces in a lighter and happier vein—the Violin Concerto (1878), the four orchestral suites (no. 1, 1879; no. 2, 1883; no. 3, 1884; no. 4, 'Mozartiana', 1887), and the overture *1812* (1880). His operatic career was only intermittently successful: he suffered failures with *Orleanskaya deva* ('The Maid of Orléans', 1881), *Mazeppa* (1884), and *Charodeyka* ('The Sorceress', 1887), none of which displays the sharp perception of character to be found in *Eugene Onegin* and *The Queen of Spades*. But in the sphere of ballet he achieved a lasting success with his *Spyashchaya krasavitsa* ('The Sleeping Beauty', 1890) and *Shchelkunchik* ('Nutcracker', 1892).

About the time of his marriage Tchaikovsky entered into a curious epistolary relationship with Nadezhda von Meck, who in 1876 had written him an admiring letter. Although (or perhaps because) they never met, Tchaikovsky poured out his innermost feelings to Madame von Meck in hundreds of letters, which have become an invaluable guide both to his creative processes and to his state of mind. Apart from providing him with an outlet for his thoughts, Mme von Meck also gave him a degree of security by settling on him a substantial allowance, though this was terminated in 1890 when she wrote to him declaring that she was bankrupt. Tchaikovsky was plunged into increasing depression at the abrupt breach in their distant friendship. His last works were tinged with gloom, highlighted in such works as the oppressive Sixth Symphony ('Pathétique', 1893).

Tchaikovsky died just nine days after he had conducted the premiere of the Sixth Symphony, when he was apparently in good health. According to the official account of his death he had contracted cholera by drinking unboiled water, but various rumours to the contrary have always had greater imaginative appeal: if suicide were assumed, then the *Pathétique* could be understood as the composer's own requiem, *à la* Mozart. In the early 1980s Aleksandra Orlova suggested that Tchaikovsky deliberately poisoned himself (possibly with arsenic) at the behest of a court of honour which had met to assess the implications of his alleged relationship with a male member of the imperial family. In the 1990s, however, this theory met a serious challenge from the painstaking scholarship of

Aleksandr Poznansky, which effectively reinstated the official account; the debate continues.   GN/MF-W

📖 D. Brown, *Tchaikovsky: A Biographical and Critical Study*, 4 vols. (London, 1978–91) · R. J. Wiley, *Tchaikov-* *sky's Ballets* (Oxford, 1985, 2/1991) · A. Poznansky, *Tchaikovsky: The Quest for the Inner Man* (New York, 1991); *Tchaikovsky's Last Days: A Documentary Study* (Oxford, 1996)

---

te. See si.

techno. A type of club dance music. It is mostly electronic and has its origins in *house music. In the 1990s it came to refer to anything not obviously house or *garage. The term was first used in 1988 in Detroit; its style was a repetitively percussive 4/4 rhythm with bass, with minimalist electronic instrumentation, perhaps influenced by Kraftwerk. Later the term encompassed more song-based pop, the ambient music of the Orb and dub reggae.   PW

tecla (Sp.). 'Key', 'keyboard'; *música para tecla*, 'music for keyboards'.

tedesca (It., 'German'). In late 16th-century Italy the *tedesca* or *todesca* was a lighthearted type of villanella that mocked the accent of Germans speaking Italian. Thereafter the term *alla tedesca* can be taken to mean 'in the style of the most characteristic German dance' of the period, for example the allemande in the 17th century or, from about 1800, the ländler (or other similar dance in triple time). Beethoven used the term in the first movement (Presto alla tedesca) of his Piano Sonata op. 79 and the fourth movement (Allemande allegro) of his String Quartet op. 130.
                                                                                    —/EW

Te Deum laudamus (Lat., 'We praise you, O God'). The long hymn that constitutes the supreme expression of rejoicing in the Roman Catholic, Anglican, and other Christian Churches. The Roman Catholic Breviary calls it the canticle of Ambrose and Augustine, from the legend that at the baptism of Augustine by Ambrose it was sung in alternation, extempore, by the two saints. In fact it may have originated in the Gallican or Mozarabic liturgy (see LITURGY, 2a), and its authorship has been put down to both Hilary, Bishop of Poitiers, in the 4th century and Hilary of Arles in the 5th; in either case it seems as though portions of an older hymn were incorporated. Another ascription is to Nicetas of Remesiana, a Dacian bishop of the early 5th century.

In the Roman rite the *Te Deum* finds a place as the outpouring of praise at the moment of climax of the service of Matins on Sundays and festivals. Vernacular versions of the hymn were proffered by Luther and Cranmer, who included it in the *Book of Common Prayer*'s morning Office. It was eventually adopted in Slavonic translation as a festal hymn by the Russian Orthodox Church.

The traditional plainchant to the Latin hymn is of a magnificent character. One of its verses is set polyphonically in the 9th-century *Musica enchiriadis*, yet it is only in the 16th century that polyphonic settings, many of them designed for *alternatim* performance, proliferate. Many from the late 17th century onwards have been on extended lines, with solos, choruses, and orchestral accompaniment. Important settings have been made by Purcell (for St Cecilia's Day, 1694), Handel (for the Peace of Utrecht, 1713, and for the victory of Dettingen, 1743), Graun (written after the Battle of Prague, 1757), Bortnyansky (14 settings for single or double chorus *a cappella* written for the Russian imperial chapel after 1779), Berlioz (for the Paris Exhibition of 1855, and composed on a huge scale, with three choirs and large instrumental forces), Bruckner (1885), Dvořák (1896), Verdi (1898), Stanford (1898), Parry (1900; also another for the coronation of George V in 1911), Kodály (for the 250th anniversary of the end of the Turkish occupation of Buda, 1936), Britten (1934), and Walton (for the coronation of Elizabeth II, 1953).

A solemn *Te Deum* is ordered on all occasions of rejoicing in Christian countries, so that throughout history nations opposed in war have used the same hymn to thank God for their victories over one another.
                                                                                    PS/ALi

Teil [Theil] (Ger.). 'Part', 'portion', 'section'; *teilen* (*theilen*), 'to divide'.

Telemann, Georg Philipp (*b* Magdeburg, 14 March 1681; *d* Hamburg, 25 June 1767). German composer. The most prolific composer of the first half of the 18th century, he contributed to all the main forms of the period with operas, cantatas, masses, Passions, orchestral and chamber music, and songs. Exceptionally gifted, by the age of ten he had mastered the violin, flute, zither, and keyboard instruments, and two years later composed his first opera, *Sigismundus*—a venture that caused his mother to prohibit further musical activity, since she feared its interference with his intended career in the church. After Gymnasium studies at Hildesheim in 1701, he enrolled as a law student at the University of Leipzig, but soon became involved in the musical life of the city: as founder of a *collegium musicum* and director of the Leipzig Opera in 1702, and as organist at the Neukirche in 1704, activities which intruded unhappily on the rights of Johann Kuhnau, the Thomaskantor of the time. In 1705, as Kapellmeister at Sorau (now Żary, in Poland), Telemann composed overtures in the French style for the court, and first encountered the 'barbaric beauty' of Polish folk music. In 1708 he transferred to Eisenach as Konzertmeister (later Kapellmeister) and in the following year married Louise Eberlin, daughter of the composer Daniel Eberlin, only to lose her two years later after the birth of their first child.

In 1712 Telemann moved to Frankfurt as city director of music, with responsibility for the music at civic functions, and as Kapellmeister at the Barfüsserkirche, for which he composed at least five cycles of cantatas for the church year. In conjunction with the city's *collegium musicum* he organized weekly concerts, at one of which (at the Barfüsserkirche in 1716) his first oratorio, a setting of the Passion text by B. H. Brockes, was performed. In 1714 he married Maria Katharina Textor, the daughter of a local council clerk, who bore him 11 children.

In July 1721, following contacts earlier in the year with Hamburg (including a performance there of his opera *Der geduldige Socrates*, 'Patient Socrates'), Telemann accepted an invitation from the city authorities to succeed Johann Gerstenbüttel in the coveted post of Kantor of the Johanneum and director of the five main churches in the city. His duties at Hamburg eventually committed him to the composition of double year-cycles of cantatas, annual Passion settings (of each gospel account in regular sequence, amounting to 46 altogether), and numerous occasional works for municipal events, including the annual *Kapitänsmusik* (an oratorio and a serenata) for the guests of the city's military commandant. In 1722, dismayed by opposition to his involvement in operatic projects, Telemann applied for the post of Kantor at St Thomas's, Leipzig, which had fallen vacant on the death of Kuhnau; but after receiving an increase in his stipend at Hamburg and acceptance of his right to present opera there, he withdrew his application, and thus paved the way for the appointment of J. S. Bach.

Telemann subsequently increased the range of his public concert-giving in Hamburg, and as director of the Opera (from 1722) mounted 12 of his latest works, including *Die neu-modische Liebhaber Damon* ('The Fashionable Amateur Damon', 1724), *Pimpinone* (1725), and *Flavius Bertaridus* (1729), as well as others by Reinhard Keiser and Handel. In 1737 he visited Paris, partly to prevent the unauthorized publication there of various of his chamber works, and partly to give profitable performances of his music at court and in the Concert Spirituel. In 1738, following his return to Hamburg, the Opera was closed, and for many years from 1740 his musical output was considerably reduced. However, from 1755, with renewed creative vigour, he composed a fine series of oratorios, including *Der Tod Jesu* ('The Death of Jesus', 1755), *Die Auferstehung und Himmelfahrt Jesu* ('The Resurrection and Ascension of Jesus', 1760), and *Der Tag des Gerichts* ('Judgment Day', 1762).

During his lifetime Telemann contributed to a marked change in the musical life of Germany. As a leading exponent of the **galant* style, he wrote not only for professional performers but also for the growing ranks of amateur musicians of the period; and by creating musical societies in the various cities where he worked, he provided increasing scope for musical activity and appreciation. However, his posthumous reputation declined rapidly. The immensity of his output and his astonishing technical fluency marked him out as a composer of purely superficial music. Only in recent times has research led to a more rational evaluation of his work, as a wholly individual contribution to the development of the pre-Classical style in Germany.   WT/BS

📖 N. ANDERSON, 'Georg Philipp Telemann: a tercentenary reassessment', *Early Music*, 9 (1981), 499–505

Telemusik. Work (1966) for four-track tape by Stockhausen.

Telephone, The (*The Telephone, or L'Amour à trois*; 'The Eternal Triangle'). Opera in one act by Menotti to his own libretto (New York, 1947).

television. See BROADCASTING.

tema (It.). 'Theme', 'subject'; *tema con variazioni*, 'theme with variations'.

temperament. A method of tuning in which some concords are made slightly impure so that few or none will be unpleasantly out of tune. This became essential with the introduction of keyboard instruments. Voices and many other instruments can modify their notes according to context, varying the pitch slightly to keep in tune, but with keyboards all pitches are fixed. A major scale which is perfectly in tune starts with a major whole tone, followed by a minor whole tone, and then a semitone, measuring 204, 182, and 112 cents respectively, together making a perfect 4th of 498 cents (one cent is 1/100 of an equal-tempered semitone). Such a scale could be set on a keyboard instrument but it would be impossible to start a new scale on the second of those notes, because the next step would be a minor instead of a major tone.

The first medieval tempered scale was the *Pythagorean, where every tone is a major tone and all 5ths except one are pure, exactly in tune. One 5th must be smaller than the others by 24 cents (an eighth of a tone, termed a Pythagorean comma), because the sum of 12 pure 5ths, each 702 cents, is 24 cents greater than that of seven 1200-cent octaves. A scale built in pure 5ths will never return to a pure octave without compromising one of the 5ths.

A further difficulty arises from the fact that the sum of three major 3rds, each 386 cents, is smaller than an octave by 41 cents, almost a quarter-tone. The result of compensating for this is that the better in tune one makes the 3rds, the worse the 5ths become, and vice versa. The Pythagorean temperament has perfect 5ths but some appalling 3rds, so sharp that the 3rd was regarded as a dissonance in the Middle Ages simply because it was indeed dissonant. By the mid-15th century, and perhaps earlier, musicians including Arnaut de Zwolle were carefully planning their use of Pythagorean temperament—starting on B and tuning 5ths downwards from there, for instance, so that the bad 5th was the little-used G♯–E♭ and there were four almost pure 3rds (D–F♯, A–C♯, E–G♯, B–D♯) in keys in which they wanted to write.

When harmony had evolved to the stage when almost any 3rd was required, a new temperament had to be devised, with all 3rds pure and 4ths and 5ths as nearly pure as possible. This was achieved by halving the 386-cent 3rd, taking the mean, or average, size of whole tone: 193 cents. The resulting temperament, called mean-tone, was constructed by tuning C–E pure and then tuning each 5th within that 3rd (C–G, G–D, D–A, A–E) a quarter of a comma flat. The only disaster that resulted was the size of the discrepancy between G♯ and A♭: the two notes, which are the same pitch in equal temperament, are 41 cents apart in mean-tone, and using one instead of the other produces a chord so out of tune that it howls like a wolf—hence the expression 'wolf 5th'. There were also four wolf 3rds, wildly sharp, but these were kept in keys which composers took care to avoid (e.g. C♯, F♯, B, and G♯ in a tuning cycle starting on C: it was always possible to move the wolves by starting the tuning on a different pitch).

Quarter-comma mean-tone was first discussed by Zarlino in 1571. Sixth-comma was an improvement as music became more chromatic in style, because though the 3rds were very slightly worse, the 5ths and 4ths were equally slightly better and the wolves were smaller and howled less. It is often used today for performances of early music. Wolves of some sort are inevitable in any temperament which uses the same correction all the way

(a 'regular temperament') with a specific fraction of a comma. The only exception is equal temperament, which has the disadvantage that every interval is out of tune except the octave and that the 3rds (400 cents instead of the pure 386) are almost as bad as the Pythagorean. For that reason musicians try to avoid it except when playing with a piano. It is produced by tempering the 5ths, flattening each by 2 cents, to spread the 24-cent comma equally through the octave.

From the 17th century, 'irregular temperaments' such as those devised by F. A. Vallotti, Andreas Werckmeister, Kirnberger, and others were used instead of either equal temperament or mean-tone. These were based on improving the keys most likely to be used, but because one key cannot be made better in tune without another being made worse, the keys less often used were degraded. It has been demonstrated that Bach's 'well-tempered keyboard' for the '48' used such a temperament, with some movements showing the purity of the better keys and others, with rapid passage-work, disguising the faults of the poor ones.

The one sure way of avoiding wolf notes but still keeping 3rds and 5ths almost pure was by increasing the number of notes in the octave. On a keyboard with separate keys (and strings or pipes) for D♯ and E♭, and for G♯ and A♭ (the notes worst affected in any normal temperament started on C), it was possible to play in almost any key with confidence. Because of the number of pipes involved, few organs were built in such a way, but many harpsichords had split keys, the front half producing one pitch and the back half the other. A few Italian instruments—the arcicembalo, for instance—were built with a large number of keys, and many theorists have calculated tunings involving anything up to 51 pitches to the octave. A problem is that the more keys there are on the keyboard the more difficult it is for the player to remember which should be used in which chord, so that few players have ever tried more than the two basic split keys.   JMo

📖 D. DEVIE, *Le Tempérament musical: Philosophie, histoire, théorie et pratique* (Béziers, 1990) · M. LINDLEY, 'An historical survey of meantone temperaments to 1620', *Early Keyboard Journal*, 8 (1990), 1–29 · R. COVEY-CRUMP, 'Pythagoras at the forge: Tuning in early music', *Companion to Medieval and Renaissance Music*, ed. T. Knighton and D. Fallows (London, 1992) · M. LINDLEY, *Temperaments: A Brief Survey*, Bate Collection Handbook (Oxford, 1993) · W. A. SETHARES, *Tuning, Timbre, Spectrum, Scale* (London, 1998)

Tempest, The. Shakespeare's play (1610 or 1611) has been the subject of many musical works, and several composers have written incidental music for it, or have set texts from it as songs. Among the best known are:

1. *The Tempest*. Incidental music by Sibelius for soloists, chorus, harmonium, and orchestra (Copenhagen, 1926); Sibelius made two orchestral suites from it.

2. *The Tempest*. Symphonic fantasy for orchestra (1863) by Tchaikovsky.

3. *Der Sturm*. Opera in three acts by Martin to a libretto adapted from August Wilhelm von Schlegel's German translation of the play (Vienna, 1956).

4. *Die Zauberinsel* ('The Magic Island'). Opera in two acts by Sutermeister to his own libretto (Dresden, 1942).

5. *The Tempest, or The Enchanted Island*. Semi-opera with music by John Weldon and a text by William Davenant, John Dryden, and Thomas Shadwell (London, ?1712).

6. *The Magic Island*. Symphonic prelude (1953) by Alwyn.

7. *The Tempest*. Opera in three acts by John C. Eaton to a libretto by Andrew Porter (Santa Fe, NM, 1985).   AL

tempestoso, tempestosamente (It.). 'Tempestuous', 'tempestuously'.

temple blocks (Chin.: *muyu*). Globular *slit drums of camphor wood, used in Confucian rituals in China and Korea, which were adopted into jazz bands as the 'skulls', often in sets of four different pitches; larger numbers are used in some orchestral works. The traditional carving patterns derive from their origin as wooden fish. They are not to be confused with woodblocks.   JMo

tempo (It.). The speed at which a piece of music is performed. This is traditionally indicated in two ways: by metronome marks (e.g. ♩ = 70, meaning a tempo of 70 crotchet beats per minute); and, less precisely, by verbal instructions, conventionally (but not exclusively) in Italian (e.g. *adagio*, slow, *andante*, less slow, *allegretto*, moderately fast, *allegro*, quick, *presto*, very fast). Music before about 1600 (and the music of many non-Western repertories) rarely contains any indication of tempo, which is inferred from the notation and style of the music. Tempo was expressed in notation by the combination of mensuration (see MENSURAL MUSIC, MENSURAL NOTATION), the note-values, and the fixed pulse (*tactus*; see BEAT, 1) assigned to a particular note-value. Later, tempo could sometimes be inferred from a work's title, or its origin in a dance form. By the 18th century, Italian terms were in common use; although there is agreement about the way they relate to one another in terms of speed, their precise meaning has been a long-standing topic of debate. Some aleatory music demands a more scientifically precise (or

differently defined) measurement of tempo than these traditional methods allow.

Theoretically, every piece of music with a tempo indication has a 'correct' tempo. In practice, however, such indications vary in usefulness. Metronome marks in 19th-century music cannot always be taken as reliable; many composers (e.g. Brahms) disapproved of the rigidity they imply, and some (e.g. Beethoven) prescribed different tempos on different copies of the same piece. Also some metronome markings are so fast as to be impracticable. Verbal directions are imprecise and subject to different interpretations. In Baroque music they may indicate a 'mood' or 'manner' of performance rather than a speed (e.g. *allegro*, literally 'cheerful'); or they may be used in a purely relative sense in the context of other tempo designations in the same piece. Their meanings and associations have changed over the years. In addition, it is not always clear whether metronome markings or verbal instructions have the composer's authority or are editorial additions.

Tempo may be subject to variation through external factors: the size and reverberation time of a hall (for example a large or reverberant hall may require a slower tempo if the music is to sound clearly); the differing sonorities of instruments, particularly keyboard ones; the size of an orchestra; the interpretation of a performer. The last factor accounts for the widely differing tempos encountered in different performances of the same work, all of which may be equally valid. Fashion and taste play a part here; for example, pianists today play much late 19th-century piano music very much more slowly and more 'romantically' than it would have been performed originally. Conductors, too, adopt widely differing tempos: when conducting the Marcia funebre of the 'Eroica' Symphony, Toscanini took about half and Beecham about a third as long again as Beethoven's metronome mark indicates.

Tempo has often been the subject of composers' letters and other writings; Berlioz, for example, wrote of it in his *Memoirs*. Wagner complained in his essay on conducting of the wildly incorrect tempos at which some conductors took his *Tannhäuser* overture. Performance on period instruments, with the forces for which a composer originally intended a particular piece, has done much to sweep aside our preconceptions of 'correct' tempo and has allowed us to hear much music as the composer, in the light of modern research, is thought to have intended it.   PS/JN/AL

See also PERFORMANCE PRACTICE.

tempo alla breve. See ALLA BREVE.

tempo giusto (It.). 'The right time'; either the usual tempo for the type of music in question, or the return to a regular tempo after a passage of flexible tempo.

tempo maggiore (It.). A term equivalent to *alla breve*.

tempo ordinario (It.). 1. At an 'ordinary speed', i.e. neither fast nor slow.

2. Common time (4/4), with four beats in the bar (as opposed to two, as in *tempo alla breve*).

tempo primo (It.; Ger.: *Tempo wie vorher*). 'At the first tempo'; an instruction to resume the original tempo after a passage departing from it; where there has been more than one such change, 'tempo primo' refers to the first-mentioned speed.

Temporale. In the Roman rite, the annual liturgical cycle based on the fixed and movable feasts of Christ.

tempo rubato. See RUBATO.

temps (Fr.). 'Time', usually in the sense of 'beat'; *temps fort*, the first ('strong') beat of the bar. See BEAT, 1.

tempus (Lat.). 'Time'. In medieval music, the term indicates the relationship between the breve and the semibreve. See PROLATION.

ten. (It.). Abbreviation for *tenuto.

Tender Land, The. Opera in three acts by Copland to a libretto by Horace Everett (Erik Johns) after James Agee's book *Let us now Praise Famous Men* (New York, 1954); Copland arranged an orchestral suite from it in 1956.

tendre, tendrement (Fr.). 'Tender', 'tenderly'.

Tenebrae (Lat., 'darkness'). In the Roman rite, the name for the combined services of Matins and Lauds formerly sung on the afternoon or evening preceding Thursday, Friday, and Saturday of Holy Week. 15 candles were extinguished, one by one, as the psalms were sung, the final candle going out after the Benedictus; Psalm 50 (Hebrew Psalm 51) was then given in complete darkness (see MISERERE). The services' readings from the Lamentations of Jeremiah and their accompanying responsories have been set by numerous composers. —/ALi

tenebroso (It.). 'Dark', 'gloomy'.

tenendo (It.). 'Holding', sustaining'; *tenendo il canto*, 'sustaining the melody'.

teneramente (It.). 'Tenderly'.

tenor (from Lat. *tenere*, 'to hold'). 1. The term has had various meanings in connection with plainchant, of which the most common were a melodic formula, especially a psalm tone or its termination (see PLAIN-CHANT, 5); the final or key note of a mode; and the characteristic note of recitation in a reciting tone (also called *tuba*); see TONUS, 3. —/ALi

2. From the mid-13th century to the 16th, 'tenor' denoted the fundamental voice part of a polyphonic composition, usually in the form of a pre-existing *cantus firmus; the other parts were composed 'against' this (hence the term *contratenor'), and at first were named in the order in which they were composed after the tenor (*duplum, *triplum, etc.). 'Tenor' did not imply any particular range until the 15th century, when well-known singers of tenor parts were sometimes known as 'tenoriste' or 'tenorista'. —/AL

3. The highest male voice using normal voice production, with a range of roughly *c* (known as 'tenor C') to *b'*, or, in fine voices with good training, even high *c''* or *d♭''*. Often used for minor or comic roles in 18th-century opera, the tenor voice rose to pre-eminence in Romantic opera. According to the vocal quality, a tenor can be described as one of three broad types: light, lyric, and dramatic ('spinto'). The *Heldentenor* (Ger., literally 'hero tenor'), required for Wagnerian roles such as Siegfried, is a heavy tenor with much of the quality of a baritone. See also COUNTERTENOR.

4. A low-pitched member of a family of instruments, with a range lower than alto and higher than bass.

5. 18th-century English name for the *viola.

tenor clef. See CLEF.

tenor cor. A valved brass instrument introduced by G. A. Besson in Paris in about 1860. Like the orchestral *horn it is circular in shape. It is pitched in F but plays an octave higher than the horn in F. Effectively a hybrid of the horn and the E♭ tenor *saxhorn, it has been widely used as a substitute for the former, especially in military bands.

tenor horn (Amer.: alto horn; Fr.: *alto, saxhorn alto*; Ger.: *Althorn*; It.: usually *genis*). A three-valve brass *saxhorn with the bell pointing upwards. It is pitched in E♭, a 5th below the cornet. The German *Tenorhorn* is at B♭ baritone pitch. See BRASS BAND.

Tenorlied (Ger.). The basic form of German polyphonic secular song from the 15th century to the mid-16th. 'Tenor' refers not to the voice part of the name, but to the borrowed tune, or cantus firmus, which was the only part to be underlaid with the complete text (see TENOR, 2). Before about 1500 this 'Tenor' was usually sung by the top voice of a three-part ensemble and accompanied by instruments, but later, when four-part writing became the norm, it moved down to the tenor voice proper and frequently received vocal accompaniment. —/JBe

tenor mass. The most common type of mass based on a *cantus firmus, i.e. with the cantus firmus placed in the tenor part.

tenor violin. See VIOLA.

tenoroon. A small bassoon.

tenso. A type of troubadour or trouvère poetry cast in the form of a dialogue or debate between two or more poets with opposing views; the most common topic is love, but others include politics, religion, morality, or literature.   AL

tento (Port., 'touch'). See TIENTO.

tenuto (It.). 'Held', i.e. sustained to the end of a note's full value; in opera the term may imply sustaining a note beyond that, for dramatic effect. It is sometimes abbreviated to *ten*.

Terce. Originally the fourth of eight hours of the Divine *Office in the medieval Roman rite. Since the reforms of the Second Vatican Council, Terce, *Sext, and *None may be combined as one 'Hora Media' ('Prayer during the Day').

Terezín (Ger.: Theresienstadt). A garrison town in northern Bohemia (now in the Czech Republic), the site of a ghetto constructed by the Nazis for Czech Jews before they were transported to extermination camps in the eastern occupied territories. Terezín, emptied of its original inhabitants, was set up as a 'temporary holding camp' in 1941 by Adolf Eichmann and Reinhold Heydrich, with the tragic collusion of members of the former Socialist-Zionist party, who were misled into thinking that the gathering of Czech Jews into one ghetto would prevent further and more intense persecution. Many of those interned there were members of the artistic and intellectual community of Prague and Brno, including a number of composers as well as musicians from the National Theatre in Prague. The Nazis allowed a certain amount of autonomy in Terezín for reasons of propaganda. The so-called 'model ghetto' became the subject of a film, *Hitler Gives a Town to the Jews*, and in 1944 an elaborate show of fair treatment was enacted in Terezín on the occasion of a visit by the International Red Cross. Both were intended to present a misleading account of the Nazi anti-Semitism and to deflect international suspicion from the Final Solution.

The autonomy permitted the internees did, however, lead to a remarkable flowering of artistic activity. A library was created from books smuggled into the camp. Cabaret was permitted. Terezín had both its own orchestra and a jazz band (called 'The Ghetto Swingers') and many works were written for musicians who were

held there. Among the composers who were active were Pavel Haas, Gideon Klein, Hans Krása, and Viktor Ullmann. Many of their works, along with those of the writers and painters who were also held in Terezín, reveal a strong sense of anti-Fascist resistance. The most famous work produced in the camp, Ullmann's opera *Der Kaiser von Atlantis* ('The Emperor of Atlantis', composed in 1944), was banned by the authorities while still in rehearsal. The camp was liberated by the Red Army early in 1945. Of the 139,654 people who had been held there, only 17,320 survived. Most of the internees were murdered in the gas chambers of Auschwitz. The rediscovery of much of the music written in Terezín has been central to the revival of interest in *Entartete Musik*.   TA

📖 J. KARAS, *Music in Terezín, 1941–1945* (New York, 1985)

ternary form. A musical structure consisting of three parts or sections. It may be represented by the letter scheme ABA, the final section being a repeat of the first. Each section is usually, though not always, self-contained: it closes in its own key. Hence the first 'A' section usually closes in the tonic, unlike *binary form, where the 'A' section modulates to and closes in a key other than the tonic (usually the dominant or relative major). In ternary form the middle section often provides a strong contrast to the outer two, both in tonality and in theme. Pieces in ternary form may be quite long, because the sections, being self-contained, will often have a formal shape of their own. For example, each of the three sections may itself be binary in structure. This is particularly true of the Classical *minuet and trio, where the ternary structure arises from the repeat of the minuet after the trio, though each section may be in either binary or ternary form.

The earliest use of ternary form dates from the Middle Ages, with examples occurring in certain monophonic song types of that period. It was rarely used in the Renaissance but came into its own during the Baroque era, especially with the development of the *da capo* aria as a standard vocal form in the late 17th and early 18th centuries. Here, after a contrasting middle section, the first section of the aria is repeated, often with elaborate embellishments.

Ternary form was also used frequently as the basic structure of many 19th-century piano works, particularly shorter ones. Many of Mendelssohn's *Lieder ohne Worte* ('Songs without Words') are in simple ternary forms. All but one of Schubert's first set of Four Impromptus D899 (1827) are ternary in design. The Impromptu no. 2 in A♭ from his second set, D935, is also cast in ternary form, with each section itself in binary form. The chordal homophonic style of the 'A' section contrasts with continuous, flowing, triplet broken-chord figuration in the right hand in the middle 'B' section (which is marked 'Trio'). The first half of the trio is in D♭, the subdominant of A♭ (the main key of the 'A' section). Following a dramatic switch to D♭ minor at the beginning of the second half of the 'B' section, the music arrives at a climax in A major in bar 69 before returning to D♭ major. After such extreme modulation an eight-bar link is necessary to steer the music back to A♭ for the restatement of the 'A' section.

Other 19th-century examples include mazurkas, nocturnes, and *études* by Chopin. The form was also sometimes used as the basis of slow middle movements in sonatas or concertos: the Adagio of Brahms's Piano Concerto no. 1 in D minor, for example, is in broad ternary form. In the 20th century, ternary form was used by Bartók, and even by Webern, who reverted to old structural forms in his 12-note instrumental works dating from 1927 to 1940.

See also FORM, 5. GMT/LC

Terpsichore. The Greek Muse of dance.

Terterian, Avet Rubeni (*b* Baku, 29 July 1929; *d* Yekaterinburg, 11 Dec. 1994). Armenian composer. He studied with Edvard Mirzoian at the Yerevan Conservatory and taught orchestration there, becoming professor in 1985. He was chairman of the Armenian Composers' Union, 1963–5, and was made People's Artist of the USSR in 1991. His work shows the influence of Xenakis and the Polish School in combination with Armenian folk idioms. The eight symphonies, written between 1969 and 1989 and gradually becoming known in the West, are meditative in tone and are coloured by Armenian folk instruments and voices. His other works include two operas in two acts—*Krakē óghakum* ('The Fire Ring', 1967; rev. as *Towards the Sun Moved the Frenzied Crowds*, 1977) and *Das Erdbeben* (1984)—and two string quartets (1963, 1991). PF

Tertis, Lionel (*b* West Hartlepool, 29 Dec. 1876; *d* London, 22 Feb. 1975). English viola player. He studied the violin in Leipzig and at the RAM, where Mackenzie encouraged him to change to the viola. As a soloist he toured worldwide and inspired such composers as Bax and Bridge, and later Walton, Bliss, and Vaughan Williams, to write for him. He designed a large viola to exploit its low, cello-like notes, taught from 1936, and made many transcriptions for the instrument. CF

   📖 L. TERTIS, *Cinderella No More* (London, 1953, enlarged 2/1974 as *My Viola and I*)

Terz (Ger., 'third'). 1. An organ stop (see TIERCE, 2).

2. A term used for instruments tuned a 3rd higher or lower than usual; thus *Terzgeige* is a small violin or *violino piccolo tuned a 3rd higher than the normal instrument, and *Terzposaune* is a trombone pitched a 3rd below the ordinary trombone.

terzina (It.). 'Triplet'.

Teseo ('Theseus'). Opera in five acts by Handel to a libretto by Nicola Francesco Haym adapted from Philippe Quinault's *Thésée* (1675) (London, 1713).

testa (It.). 'Head'; *voce di testa*, 'head voice' (see VOICE, 4).

testo (It.). 1. 'Text'.

2. 'Narrator', as in, for example, Monteverdi's *Combattimento di Tancredi, e Clorinda*.

tests. There are several methods for testing musical aptitude ('musicality') and achievement ('musicianship'). Musical judgment is notoriously subjective, relying on anecdote and often fallible memory rather than the shared perception of concrete objects such as one finds in the visual world. On a personal level, the assessment of an individual's musicality is fraught with pitfalls. Most dictionaries identify two facets to 'musicality': being 'fond of' as well as 'skilled in' music. Objective psychometric tests cannot assess the subject's liking for or emotional response to music (generally agreed to be crucial in a musical person), and there are difficulties in measuring precisely particular musical skills, as these are so dependent on cultural and environmental factors. (The importance attached to singing, for example, is more prevalent in some cultures than in others.)

Over the years, however, psychologists have adopted as a working hypothesis that aural perception is measurable and may be a predictor of musical achievement. Accordingly, tests modelled on those used to assess intelligence and other aptitudes have been devised to identify musical potential. Among the best-known proponents of standardized musical testing have been the American Carl Seashore, who published his first tests in 1919, and the Englishman Arnold Bentley. Although such tests have been effective in identifying a range of individual sensory capacities in such matters as fine pitch discrimination, they cannot predict the use to which a person will put these particular aptitudes. It is therefore doubtful that they will identify musicality in its many-faceted richness: the aural imagination and the ability to interpret, to connect, and to synthesize. In their earnest quest for standardization and objectivity, the tests have themselves become drained of any recognizable musical context. As a means of identifying musicality, they are self-defeating. One factor for children has been their boredom while doing these tests compared to the liveliness and absorption they show when engaged in playing, singing, composing, and listening. No convincing research has yet been produced to persuade musicians, parents, and teachers of their long-term usefulness, and even their value for selecting those most likely to benefit from the scarce and expensive resource of instrumental tuition is doubtful.

Achievement tests measure knowledge of rudiments and theory, terms, history, and repertory. The earliest was the Beach Music Test (1920, rev. 1930). PSp

📖 C. SEASHORE, *Psychology of Music* (New York and London, 1938/R1967) · A. BENTLEY, *Musical Ability in Children and its Measurement* (London, 1966) · R. SHUTER-DYSON and C. GABRIEL, *The Psychology of Musical Ability* (London, 2/1981)

tetrachord (from Gk. *tetra-*, 'four-', *chordē*, 'string'). A succession of four notes contained within the compass of a perfect 4th. In Ancient Greek theory, tetrachords with intervals in the descending order tone–tone–semitone (e.g. A–G–F–E) were joined together to form a series of eight-note *modes, which served, like the modern *scale, as the basis of melodic composition. Medieval theorists likewise adopted several ascending tetrachords, with different arrangements of tones and semitones within the perfect 4th, to act as a melodic basis (see also HEXACHORD). The modern diatonic scale may also be considered divisible into two tetrachords (e.g. C–D–E–F, G–A–B–C).

tetrardus. See MODE, 2.

Tetrazzini, Luisa [Luigia] (*b* Florence, 29 June 1871; *d* Milan, 28 April 1940). Italian soprano. She studied in Florence and with her elder sister, Eva. In 1890 she made her debut in Florence in *L'Africaine* and was soon in demand in Italy, Russia, Spain, Argentina, and Mexico. In 1907 her Violetta at Covent Garden created a sensation, and as a result she was engaged to sing the role at the Manhattan Opera House, New York. Thereafter she sang in New York and Chicago (1911–13) in a variety of roles with effortless brilliance. From 1918 to 1934 she sang only in concert. She made several recordings and published a volume of memoirs and a singing method. JT

📖 C. N. GATTEY, *Luisa Tetrazzini: The Florentine Nightingale* (Aldershot, 1995)

text-setting. The process of composing music for a text, and the musical expression of its words. At different times in the history of music, various concerns about text-setting have been paramount. In musical genres where it is especially important to convey the words clearly (e.g. operatic recitative, much liturgical music), the metre and structure of the text are often

followed closely by a simple, syllabic melody with little ornamentation. In other forms, usually where the emphasis lies on the emotional expression of the words, the setting may be more florid, with large leaps, extended melismas on a single syllable, rhythmic distortion, and other devices that might obscure the communication of the text. In some present-day music the individual syllables of words are used primarily for their sound quality and seem disconnected from the rest of the text.

See also WORD-PAINTING. JBe

texture. If a series of snapshots could be taken, in fairly quick succession, of the vertical cross-section of a musical passage, these might provide a basis for determining the texture of the music. A tune-and-accompaniment texture might thus be revealed; or an imitative texture, in which one or more parts replicate another at fairly short time-intervals; or a homophonic texture, the parts moving largely in the same rhythm, as in a hymn-tune harmonization.

Texture thus describes the vertical build of the music—the relationship between its simultaneously sounding parts—over a short period of time. If each of the combined parts is shown to have a more or less continuous linear character, all being of equal importance as horizontal lines, then the music is said to exhibit a contrapuntal texture.

A contrapuntal texture is not the same thing as a fugal one. In a fugal texture, the parts behave as in a *fugue, imitating each other at time-intervals and pitch-intervals determined by well-established if bendable traditions of fugal practice. That well-known Bach chorale prelude *Wachet auf* (no. 1 of the Schübler chorale preludes, BWV645) is indisputably contrapuntal in texture, but in no way fugal: it combines three lines of quite different melodic complexion—a chorale in long notes, a more or less elaborate obbligato set against it, and a steady bass line.

Texture may be conditioned by the vertical spacing of chords (density), by instrumental or vocal colour, intensity, and attack, and, indeed, by the aerating effect of rests. BN

Teyte [Tate], Dame **Maggie** (*b* Wolverhampton, 17 April 1888; *d* London, 26 May 1976). English soprano. She studied at the RCM and in Paris with Jean de Reszke, concentrating on French repertory. In 1906 she made her debut in Paris singing Cherubino and Zerlina in extracts from Mozart operas mounted as part of a Mozart Festival organized by Reynaldo Hahn and Lilli Lehmann. Following a successful appearance at the Opéra-Comique, Paris, Debussy chose her to sing Mélisande in his opera and personally coached her. She gained international fame in the role, singing it for the last time in 1948 in the USA. She was one of the most admired performers of French *mélodies*, especially those of Debussy, Fauré, and Hahn, her pure and supple voice ideal for their sentiment and textures. She was made DBE in 1958 and a singing award has been established in her memory.   JT

📖 G. O'CONNOR, *The Pursuit of Perfection: A Life of Maggie Teyte* (London, 1979)

Thaïs. Opera in three acts by Massenet to a libretto by Louis Gallet after Anatole France's novel (1890) (Paris, 1894). The 'Méditation' from Act II is often played as a separate item.

Thalberg, Sigismond (*b* Pâquis, 8 Jan. 1812; *d* Posillipo, nr Naples, 27 April 1871). German or Austrian pianist and composer. He studied the piano with Hummel, Pixis, Kalkbrenner, and Moscheles, and composition with Sechter. He began to achieve success as a performer in the early 1830s, but his career reached another level with his enthusiastic reception in Paris in 1836. Rumours of his supposed illegitimate aristocratic birth (he was reputedly the natural son of Count Moriz Dietrichstein and Baroness von Wetzlar) added to the publicity surrounding his name, and by 1837 some critics, including Fétis, were proclaiming him the leading pianist in Europe.

The impact of Thalberg's playing largely depended on his 'three-handed technique', where a melody played by the thumbs in the middle register of the keyboard is swathed in ornate arpeggiated figuration in bass and treble, creating the illusion that three hands are required; his most famous piece—the fantasy on Rossini's *Moïse*—makes copious use of this. (Thalberg adapted the idea from a fantasy on the same opera by the harp virtuoso Elias Parish Alvars.) He was a serious rival to Liszt, who felt sufficiently threatened by Thalberg's burgeoning fame to write an acid review of his compositions in the *Revue et gazette musicale* after, as he put it, 'shutting himself away for a whole afternoon to get to know them'. Enmity between the two was largely ended after the celebrated 'piano duel' in the salon of Princess Belgiojoso in 1837: Liszt, with his wild, rhapsodic virtuosity, was undoubtedly the technical superior (as Thalberg himself admitted), but Thalberg's controlled repose and careful gradation of tone appealed to many who were constitutionally repelled by Liszt's passionate musical persona.

As a composer, Thalberg lacked originality and inspiration (his operas *Florinda* and *Cristina di Svezia* were failures), but he had a remarkable talent for keyboard arrangement; many of his opera fantasies have a deft suavity well above the average for this often mediocre genre. His pedagogical *L'Art du chant ap-*

pliqué au piano, in which melodic projection is taught by means of transcriptions from the vocal repertory, is a work that repays study today.   KH

📖 I. BÉLANCE-ZANK, 'The three-hand texture: Origins and use', *Journal of the American Liszt Society*, 38 (1995), 99–121

theatre organ. 1. A small organ used in theatrical entertainments during the 17th and 18th centuries.

2. In American usage, 'theater organ' is the *cinema organ.

theatres. See OPERA HOUSES.

Theil. See TEIL.

Theile, Johann (*b* Naumburg, 29 July 1646; *d* Naumburg, 24 June 1724). German composer and theorist. He was a valued pupil of Schütz. His compositions include masses in the *stile antico, concertato motets, a *St Matthew Passion* (1673)—one of the earliest to involve commentary arias—and the opera *Adam und Eva* (1678), for the opening of the Theater am Gänsemarkt in Hamburg. His most famous theory treatise was his *Musikalisches Kunst-Buch*, which may have prompted Bach to compose *The Art of Fugue*.   BS

thematic catalogue (Ger.: *thematisches Verzeichnis*). A catalogue which uses the quotation of musical material, usually the first few notes, or the incipit, sometimes the principal theme or themes, and occasionally (for polyphonic works) the entire texture of the opening, to provide positive identification of a musical work. This means of identification finds a multitude of applications, from the table of contents of an edition of music that comprises several discrete works, through publishers' catalogues and advertisements, and compendia designed for concert-goers and students, to the scholarly catalogues of composers' works.

These last now constitute major undertakings of primary research in their own right and provide valuable resources for further research. They normally include in each entry much more than just the musical identification: such information as dates of composition, first performance, and publication, principal primary sources (manuscript and printed), and references to the secondary literature are often found in thematic catalogues. The mode of organization differs: some, such as those of *Köchel for Mozart and *Deutsch for Schubert, attempt to treat the composer's entire output in a strictly chronological fashion; others, like *Hoboken's for Haydn, group works according to genre, and then chronologically. The impact of these scholarly enterprises is such that many of the catalogues have provided the standard means of identifying works both in the academic world and beyond: K or KV (Köchel or Köchel-Verzeichnis) for Mozart, D (Deutsch) for Schubert, *BWV (Bach-Werke-Verzeichnis) for Bach, etc.   JG

📖 B. S. BROOK, *Thematic Catalogues in Music* (Hillsdale, NY, 1972, rev. 2/1997)

thematic transformation. See TRANSFORMATION, THEMATIC.

theme. A term most commonly used to denote the principal melodic passages of tonal music, and of non-tonal music which retains the feature of melodic continuity. 'Theme' usually refers to complete phrases or periods, in contrast to the terms 'idea' or 'motif', and is used typically of the more important melodic passages. Thus the first and second themes (or 'subjects') of a sonata-form movement may expose most of the melodic material of the piece and carry the greatest structural weight. Such a view of tonal forms in general is often called 'thematicism', especially when it attempts to show that apparently heterogeneous themes have one common source in a movement or work.

The thematic nature of music from the last 300 years is so conspicuous that it is possible and useful to make *thematic catalogues, which record the first theme of a piece. Among the earliest to survive are Haydn's and Mozart's thematic catalogues of their own works. In the 19th century, especially in Liszt's *symphonic poems, one theme of an extended composition could represent the central character of a literary programme, and the variation, or 'metamorphosis', of this theme would convey the changing action. Berlioz's *Symphonie fantastique* (1830), with its recurring principal theme or *idée fixe*, is an early, seminal example.

See also VARIATION FORM; FORM, 3.   JD

theme and variations. See VARIATION FORM.

theme song. In film music or musicals, a song that has a particular significance in the subject matter or plot. The lyrics are often closely related to the title of the film or musical, as for example in Rodgers and Hammerstein's *Oklahoma!* (1943), or in the individual theme songs written for the James Bond series of films.   JBe

Theodora. Oratorio (1750) by Handel to a text by Thomas Morell after R. Boyle's *The Martyrdom of Theodora and Didymus*.

Theodorakis, Mikis (*b* Khios, 29 July 1925). Greek composer. After military service he studied at the Paris Conservatoire. He was closely identified with left-wing causes, and was imprisoned by the ruling junta from 1967 to 1970, when he was released into exile after worldwide protests. After returning to Greece in 1974

he served as a member of parliament (1981–6, 1989–93) and minister (1990–2). Theodorakis's music is heavily influenced by Byzantine music and Cretan folk music, and is mostly on Greek subjects. It includes operas, ballets, theatre scores, film scores (most famously *Zorba the Greek*, 1964), orchestral pieces, cantatas, and songs.   ABur

theorbo [chitarrone]. A bass *lute having, in addition to the stopped courses, an extended neck with a second pegbox bearing a set of unstopped, diatonically tuned bass strings (diapasons). Because the instrument is much larger than an ordinary lute the first course (and sometimes the second) was tuned an octave down, giving a characteristic *re-entrant tuning. The theorbo was developed in Florence in about 1580 and remained in use into the 18th century, primarily for vocal accompaniment and as a continuo instrument, though a certain amount of solo music survives. The fully developed Italian theorbo had 14 courses comprising six double stopped courses and eight single diapasons, most often tuned   *G′–A′–B′–C–D–E–F–G–A–d–g–b–e–a*.   The French *théorbe* was single-strung throughout.

JMo

theory. The term is used in three main ways in music, though all three are interrelated.

The first is what is otherwise called 'rudiments', currently taught as the elements of notation, of key signatures, of time signatures, of rhythmic notation, and so on. Theory in this sense is treated as the necessary preliminary to the study of harmony, counterpoint, and form.

The second is the study of writings about music from ancient times onwards. This is an enormous body of material that covers almost every imaginable aspect of music, including aesthetics, notation, scales, modes, and tonality, acoustics, the design of instruments, performance practice, and so on. Traditionally the aesthetics of music (as of everything else) begins with Plato and Aristotle, the nature of sound and pitch with Aristoxenus and Pythagoras, the importance of music for understanding the universe with Claudius Ptolemy and Boethius, and the notation of music with Hucbald of Saint-Amand and Guido of Arezzo. From the 12th century onwards there is an uninterrupted and ever-growing stream of such writings: their study is important particularly for understanding the attitudes to music of each generation.

The third is an area of current musicological study that seeks to define processes and general principles in music—a sphere of research that can be distinguished from analysis in that it takes as its starting-point not the individual work or performance but the fundamental materials from which it is built. In many respects this investigation seems to begin with the work of Heinrich Schenker and particularly his last book, *Der freie Satz* (1935); but Schenker confined his studies to tonal music in the Western tradition and the ways in which 19th-century tonality functioned. Present-day theorists are attempting to penetrate to the essence of the matter, taking account of earlier and later Western musics as well as of musics from the rest of the world. While such investigation impinges regularly on the domains of philosophy, logic, and the perceptual sciences, it promises important understanding for any thinking musician.   DF

theremin. A monophonic electronic instrument invented by Lev Termen in or before 1927. Pitch is controlled by the capacitance between the right hand and an antenna, originally a vertical metal rod, and volume and tone by moving the left hand in relation to a horizontal metal loop. On later transistorized instruments each antenna is replaced by a plaque on a flat surface. As with a flexatone or saw, glissandos are inevitable, but the theremin's sound and expressive qualities have fascinated many musicians.   JMo

Theresienmesse ('Theresa Mass'). Haydn's Mass no. 12 in B♭ major (1799), a reference to the consort of Emperor Franz II of Austria.

Theresienstadt. See Terezín.

thesis. See arsis and thesis.

Thibaut IV, King of Navarre (*b* Troyes, 30 May 1201; *d* Pamplona, 7 July 1253). Count of Champagne and Brie, crowned 7 or 8 May 1234. Despite his royal descent and his involvement with matters of state, warfare, and the crusades, Thibaut IV was one of the leading and most versatile trouvères of his day; more songs and verses by him have survived than by any other trouvère. His varied output, which was mentioned by Dante and served as a model for many younger poet-musicians, includes courtly love songs, *jeux-partis (debates or dialogues in verse form), religious pieces, and crusade songs; most are set syllabically and they are often cast in *Bar form (AAB).   JM

Thieving Magpie, The. See Gazza ladra, La.

third inversion. Only chords with four notes (e.g. the *diminished 7th and *dominant 7th chords) or more can be placed in third inversion, i.e. with the fourth note of the chord as the lowest (Ex. 1). See inversion, 1.

Ex. 1

third stream. An alliance of Western art music with improvisatory jazz. The emphasis on improvisation differentiates third stream from earlier attempts at symphonic jazz by such composers as Stravinsky, Milhaud, and others, who simply tried (mainly unsuccessfully) to compose art-music works with a jazz flavour. The vast majority of third-stream compositions have remained recognizable as jazz and demanded comparison with other manifestations of contemporary jazz.   PGa

thirty-second note (Amer.). Demisemiquaver.

Thomas, (Charles Louis) Ambroise (*b* Metz, 5 Aug. 1811; *d* Paris, 12 Feb. 1896). French composer and teacher. Born into a musical family, he was accomplished as both a pianist and a violinist by the age of ten. At 17 he entered the Paris Conservatoire and was particularly esteemed for his playing of Chopin. He became a composition pupil of Le Sueur and in 1832 won the Prix de Rome with his cantata *Herman et Ketty*. During his ensuing stay in Rome he got to know the painter Jean Ingres and also met Berlioz, who gave him a favourable mention in several articles. It was in 1835 that he began writing for the stage.

Between 1837 and 1843 Thomas had no fewer than eight operas performed, mostly in the genre of *opéra comique*. The most successful was the first, *La Double Échelle* ('The Double-Sided Ladder'), praised by Berlioz for its 'extreme vivacity and wit', which was performed 247 times. His next success was *Le Caïd* (1849), which became the second most performed of his operas after *Mignon*. It is thoroughly Italianate, with a charming, vivacious score, and, like Rossini's *L'italiana in Algeri*, is a witty reflection on France's colonial power.

Thomas's Shakespearean potpourri *Le Songe d'une nuit d'été* (1850), which has little to do with *A Midsummer Night's Dream* and includes Falstaff, Elizabeth I, and Shakespeare himself in the cast, is notable for its colourful orchestration. The following year Thomas was elected to the Académie des Beaux-Arts after the death of Spontini, and in 1852 he became a professor of composition at the Conservatoire. For the next 14 years he continued to write operas, but with little success.

Then, in 1866, came *Mignon*, based on Goethe's novel *Wilhelm Meisters Lehrjahre* ('The Apprenticeship of Wilhelm Meister', 1796); it inevitably invited comparison with Gounod's *Faust*. In the character of Mignon, meaning 'sweet' and 'tiny', the librettists created a unique type of androgynous femme fatale, and Thomas skilfully matched her complexity with some of his finest music. The first Mignon was Célestine Galli-Marié, who would later create the role of Carmen. *Mignon* was Thomas's masterpiece and has remained one of the most popular operas ever written.

Having had sufficient success at the Opéra-Comique, Thomas turned to the Opéra with his final triumph: *Hamlet*. First given in 1868, it is a work of considerable subtlety and skilful characterization, however much it was criticized for its misrepresentation of Shakespeare's play. Its overture presages the action; the appearance of Hamlet's father as a ghost is spine-chilling, and a saxophone is used as an obbligato instrument in Ophelia's soliloquy. Thomas's orchestration in this work is particularly innovatory.

Thomas succeeded Auber as director of the Conservatoire in 1871, and thereafter wrote only one more (unsuccessful) opera. He took up a nationalist critical position in later life, expressing a total lack of interest in Wagner and defending French music from Germanic invasion.   RLS

📖 M. Cooper, 'Charles Louis Ambroise Thomas', *The Music Masters*, ed. A. L. Bacharach, ii (London, 1950; published separately, London, 1957–8) · G. Masson, *Ambroise Thomas* (Metz, 1996)

Thomas, Arthur Goring (*b* Ratton Park, Sussex, 20 Nov. 1850; *d* London, 20 March 1892). English composer. He studied with Émile Durand in Paris (1873–5) and later with Sullivan and Ebenezer Prout at the RAM (1877–80). He enjoyed brief success with his two French-influenced operas, *Esmeralda* (1883) and *Nadeshda* (1885), at Drury Lane under Carl Rosa, the former to great acclaim. After a decline in his incentive to compose, and the onset of depression, he committed suicide, leaving a cantata *The Swan and the Skylark* and an operetta *The Golden Web* unfinished; both were completed by others and performed shortly afterwards.
                                                                                                  JDI

Thomas, Augusta Read (*b* New York, 24 April 1964). American composer. She studied at Northwestern University, Yale, and in London at the RAM, and was a junior fellow at Harvard (1991–4) before her appointment to the Eastman School. She was also composer-in-residence with the Chicago Symphony (1997–2000), for which she wrote *Orbital Beacons* (1997–8). Other works include the opera *Ligeia* (Évian, 1994). Most of her music, however, is instrumental, expressing a confident and poetic feeling for the substance and drama of sound—a feeling communicated in part by her titles: *Angel Chant* for piano trio, *Words of the Sea* for orchestra, *Night's Midsummer Blaze* for flute, viola, and harp.
                                                                                                  PG

Thompson, Randall (*b* New York, 21 April 1899; *d* Boston, 9 July 1984). American composer. He studied at Harvard and with Bloch in New York (1920–1), then worked as a teacher, notably at Harvard (1948–65). He wrote a large quantity of choral music, including an unaccompanied Requiem and a *St Luke Passion* (1965), as well as three symphonies, two operas, and other works.   PG

Thomson, Virgil (*b* Kansas City, MO, 25 Nov. 1896; *d* New York, 30 Sept. 1989). American composer. He studied at Harvard University, with Nadia Boulanger in Paris (1921–2), and with Rosario Scalero in New York (1923–4). From 1925 to 1932 he lived mostly in Paris, where he associated with Les *Six and with Gertrude Stein, later the librettist of his operas *Four Saints in Three Acts* (Hartford, CT, 1934) and *The Mother of us All* (New York, 1947). In 1940 he settled in New York and became music critic of the *Herald Tribune*, retaining that post, in a forthright and often witty manner, until 1954. His style, influenced by Satie, is cool and unpretentious, avoiding anything complex or rhetorical. Songs, piano music, and orchestral pieces form the bulk of his large output; many of his pieces were written as portraits of friends and colleagues. Besides several collections of *Herald Tribune* writings, he published *The State of Music* (New York, 1939, 2/1961), *Virgil Thomson* (New York, 1966), *American Music since 1910* (New York, 1971), and *Music with Words* (New Haven, CT, 1989).   PG

📖 A. Tommasini, *Virgil Thomson: Composer on the Aisle* (New York, 1997)

thoroughbass. See CONTINUO; FIGURED BASS.

Three Choirs Festival. English choral festival established *c*.1715. See FESTIVALS, 2.

Three-Cornered Hat, The. See SOMBRERO DE TRES PICOS, EL.

Threepenny Opera, The. See DREIGROSCHENOPER, DIE.

Three Places in New England. Orchestral work by Ives, also known as the First Orchestral Set (or *A New England Symphony*). Its three movements are *The Saint-Gaudens in Boston Common* (*c*.1916–17), *Putnam's Camp, Redding, Connecticut* (*c*.1914–15, *c*.1919–20), and *The Housatonic at Stockbridge* (*c*.1912–17, rev. *c*.1921).

Three Screaming Popes. Orchestral work (1989) by Turnage.

Threni: id est Lamentationes Jeremiae Prophetae ('Threni: that is, The Lamentations of the Prophet Jeremiah'). Choral work (1958) by Stravinsky, a setting of a biblical text for soprano, alto, two tenor and two bass soloists, chorus, and orchestra.

threnody (from Gk. *thrēnos*, 'wailing', *oidē*, 'ode'). A song of lamentation, especially on a person's death. Penderecki's *Threnody for the Victims of Hiroshima* is a 20th-century example.

through-composed (Ger.: *durchkomponiert*). Any composition that does not rely on repeating sections for its formal design may be described as through-composed. However, the term is most usually applied to a song in which the music for each stanza is different.

See also FORM, 9.   GMT

thumb piano. See MBIRA, KALIMBA, LIKEMBE.

thunder machine. Any instrument used in the theatre to imitate the sound of thunder. The commonest methods are shaking or striking a large suspended sheet of thin metal, or rolling cannonballs down a wooden trough or inside a barrel.   JMo

thunderstick. See BULLROARER.

Tibbett [Tibbet], **Lawrence** (Mervil) (*b* Bakersfield, CA, 16 Nov. 1896; *d* New York, 15 July 1960). American baritone. He began his career as an actor and a church and light opera singer and then took singing lessons from Frank La Forge and Ignaz Zitomirsky in New York. He made his opera debut in Los Angeles in 1923 and that year sang Lewicki in *Boris Godunov* at the Metropolitan Opera, New York. His first major success was two years later at the Metropolitan as Ford in *Falstaff*. He sang at the Metropolitan for 27 seasons, highly acclaimed for his warm, resonant sound, controlled but expressive legato, and vibrant acting. He also created several roles in new works. His successes in New York were equalled at Covent Garden, Paris, Vienna, and Prague, as well as other American houses. He made several films, gave concerts, and made recordings.   JT

tie [bind]. A curved line used in musical notation to join two successive notes of the same pitch, showing that they should form one sound lasting for the duration of their combined values. It is used to join notes either side of a bar-line (Ex. 1*a*) or to make up a total note-value that is not available in single notes (e.g. five crotchets, seven quavers; Ex. 1*b*). A tie is also occasionally used to indicate the subtle repetition of the second note.

See also SLUR.

tief (Ger.). 'Deep', 'low'; *tiefgespannt*, 'deep-stretched', i.e. loosely fastened (of a drum-head) to give a low-pitched sound.

Tiefland ('The Lowlands'). Opera in a prologue and two acts by d'Albert to a libretto by Rudolph Lothar (Rudolph Spitzer) after Angel Guimerá's Catalan drama *Terra baixa* (Prague, 1903).

tiento (Sp., 'touch'; Port.: *tento*). In Spanish and Portuguese music of the 16th century to the early 18th, an instrumental piece similar to the Italian *ricercar. The term derives from the Spanish verb *tentar*, meaning 'to try out' or 'to experiment', and denotes a kind of free study through which the performer is acquainted with playing in different modes and the technical problems associated with a particular instrument. Tientos first appeared in the 16th century when they were included in collections of vihuela music by such composers as Milán (1536) and Mudarra (1546); these pieces were generally homophonic and of an improvisatory character, and often served as preludes to more substantial pieces.

The earliest known tientos for keyboard are found in Venegas de Henestrosa's collection *Libro de cifra nueva* (1557), which contains works for organ by Cabezón. These compositions (like Cabezón's posthumous tientos, published in 1578) are contrapuntal and use a wide range of techniques including strict imitation in three or four parts, figuration, diminution, stretto, and rhythmic variation; many of the pieces use themes from pre-existing sources, especially plainchant. After Cabezón the most important composers of organ tientos were Correa, whose *Libro de tientos y discursos de música práctica* (1626) contains 62 pieces, each graded according to mode and difficulty, and Cabanilles, who exploited technological developments in the organ to produce different sound effects (e.g. trumpet calls) and dramatic dynamic contrasts.   —/JBE

tierce (Fr.). 1. The interval of a 3rd.

2. An organ stop adding the 17th, a high 3rd, to the harmonic content.

tierce de Picardie (Fr., 'Picardy 3rd'). A major 3rd in a tonic chord at the end of a composition which is otherwise in a minor key, thus converting the expected minor chord into a major one (e.g. in the key of C minor the expected closing chord C–E♭–G becomes

Ex. 1

(*a*)

(*b*)

C–E♮–G). The origin of the name is unknown. It seems to have been introduced by Jean-Jacques Rousseau in his *Dictionnaire de musique* (1768), but his derivation is implausible: ' "Picardy third" because this way of ending survived longest in church music, and thus in Picardy, where there is music in a great number of cathedrals and other churches.'

The use of the *tierce de Picardie* was common in the 16th century and throughout the Baroque period.

Till Eulenspiegels lustige Streiche (nach alter Schelmenweise—in Rondeauform) ('Till Eulenspiegel's Merry Pranks, after an Old Rogue's Tune—in Rondo Form'). Tone-poem, op. 28 (1894–5), by Richard Strauss; it has been used for several ballets, including one by Vaslav Nijinsky (1916).

Till Eulenspiegel has also been the subject of an opera *Til' Ulenshpigel'* by Karetnikov to a libretto after Charles De Coster; though completed in 1985, it was staged in Germany only in 1993. Flor Alpaerts (1927), Jan Blockx (1920), Jeremiáš (1949), Rezniček (1902), and Maximilian Steinberg (1936) are among composers who have used the same subject.

timbales. 1. (Fr.). 'Timpani'.

2. Small paired *tom-toms of Latin American music. Their full names are *timbales créoles* or *timbales cubaines*. These are single-headed drums, with open-bottomed, shallow shells usually of metal, and heads almost twice the diameter of *bongos. Whereas bongos are played with the fingers, timbales are played with light wooden beaters and are usually fixed on a stand which also carries a pair of cowbells. JMo

time. See METRE; RHYTHM; TEMPO.

time signature. A sign placed at the start of a piece of music (after the clef and key signature) or during the course of it, indicating the *metre of the music. It normally consists of two numbers, one above the other, the lower one defining the unit of measurement in relation to the semibreve, the upper one indicating the number of those units in each bar. A time signature of 3/4 therefore indicates that there are three crotchets ('quarter-notes', or notes worth a quarter of a semibreve) to the bar, one of 6/8 that there are six quavers ('eighth-notes', worth an eighth of a semibreve) to the

TABLE I

TIME / BASIC UNIT		𝅗𝅥	𝅘𝅥	𝅘𝅥𝅮
DUPLE	SIMPLE	2/2 or ¢	2/4	2/8
	COMPOUND	6/4	6/8	6/16
TRIPLE	SIMPLE	3/2	3/4	3/8
	COMPOUND	9/4	9/8	9/16
QUADRUPLE	SIMPLE	4/2	4/4 or C	4/8
	COMPOUND	12/4	12/8	12/16

bar. Table 1 shows the time signatures commonly found in Western mensural music since about 1700. Some signs (e.g. 𝄴 and 𝄵) are relics of medieval proportional notation, which had a complex system of time signatures of its own (see NOTATION, Fig. 4). The sign 𝄴 now indicates 4/4 (common time); 𝄵 indicates 2/2 and implies a quick duple time (or *alla breve*).

'Simple' times have a binary subdivision of the unit (e.g. into two, four, eight, etc.) and 'compound' times a ternary one (e.g. into three, six, nine, etc.). The grouping together, or 'beaming', of smaller note-values within the unit in each time signature is conventionally arranged in twos or threes in accordance with these principles. Because the basic unit of measurement in compound time is always a dotted unit, which cannot be shown in the signature as a fraction of a semibreve, signatures for compound time use the next smallest unit as point of reference (e.g. two dotted crotchets to the bar has to be shown as six quavers, 6/8). Although bars under different time signatures may have the same total duration in terms of beats, there is a difference in rhythmic effect, as between, for example, a bar of 3/2 (dividing into three minims) and one of 6/4 (dividing into two dotted minims: see Table 1).

Signatures other than those illustrated here are occasionally found. Quintuple time (subdividing into either 2+3 or 3+2, and in use since the 16th century) and other 'irregular' metres such as 7/16 and 11/8 are common in some folk musics. Composers of contemporary music, if they use time signatures at all, tend to adopt whatever symbols, conventional or otherwise, best express the metre of their music. PS/JN

timpani (It., 'kettledrums'; Fr.: *timbales*; Ger.: *Pauken*). Drums consisting of a cauldron-shaped (whence *'kettledrums')* brass or copper shell and a parchment head of goat- or calfskin (or of a plastic material) stretched over a hoop that is secured to the shell with an overriding metal ring, or counterhoop. Each kettledrum produces a specific pitch. Timpani were introduced to Europe from Turkey via Hungary after 1450, originally as cavalry instruments, carried on horseback as part of the trumpet corps. They came into the orchestra after 1600 and have remained the principal percussion instruments ever since. Before 1800, two drums were the norm, tuned to the tonic and dominant of the piece being played.

Tuning was achieved by screwing square-topped iron rods into brackets on the counterhoop with a separate key. Drummers were seldom asked to change the pitch of the drums during movements. When retuning began to be required (*c.*1800), T-handles were introduced for the screws. At about the same time a third drum was occasionally demanded (first by Salieri), and this gradually became common during the 19th century. Composers, especially in opera houses, required more frequent tuning changes, and a variety of devices to control all the tuning brackets (e.g. a single handle) began to be invented in the early 19th century. The first pedal-tuned timpani were introduced in 1881. Most orchestras now have sets of four pedal timpani, but this became standard only in the last third of the 20th century. Nevertheless, many composers since the late 19th century have treated timpani as chromatic instruments.

Early timpani beaters had wooden knobs, replaced by the 16th century by wooden or ivory discs. The extent to which leather or cloth covers were used is debated, but sponge covers became available in the 1820s and were demanded by Berlioz. Felt is now the normal cover on a core of felt, balsawood, or cork. All timpanists carry a wide range of beaters to suit different music and different acoustics. Plastic drum-heads became popular in the 1950s but calfskin is still considered to have a better tone-quality. JMo

📖 N. BENVENGA, *Timpani and the Timpanist's Art: Musical and Technical Development in the 19th and 20th Centuries* (Göteborg, 1979) · E. A. BOWLES, *The Timpani: A History in Pictures and Documents* (Washington, DC, and Stuyvesant, NY, 2000)

Tinctoris, Johannes (*b* Braine l'Alleud, nr Nivelles, *c.*1434; *d* ?1511). Franco-Flemish theorist and composer. His early career was spent at Orléans, Chartres, and perhaps also at Cambrai as a singer under Dufay. By 1472 he had moved into the service of Ferdinand I of Naples, acting as tutor to the king's daughter, Beatrice. In 1487 he was sent abroad to recruit singers for the Neapolitan chapel; it is not known whether or not he returned to Naples for the remaining years of his life. Only a small quantity of Tinctoris's music has survived, including five settings of the Mass. His theoretical writings, on the other hand, are numerous; they include a dictionary of musical terms (*Terminorum musicae diffinitorium*, *c.*1473) —the first ever to appear in print (Treviso, 1495)—and at least 11 other treatises variously concerned with notation, contrapuntal technique, and philosophical matters. Popular and influential in Tinctoris's own time, these books are important today for the information they provide about the craft of composition and methods of music education in the late 15th century. JM

Tin Pan Alley. A term that became a synonym for the American popular music industry from the late 1880s until the mid-20th century, when sheet-music publishing was its main outlet. It was originally applied to a district in New York (28th Street, between Fifth Avenue and Broadway) where songwriters, arrangers, and publishers were based. It also came to be used for the style of songs of the period, notable for their melodic appeal, fresh lyrics, and accessibility; leading composers included Irving Berlin, Jerome Kern, George Gershwin, Cole Porter, and Richard Rodgers. The term is still sometimes used generically for popular music.   MT/PGA

Tintagel. Tone-poem (1919) by Bax.

tin whistle. See FLAGEOLET; PENNY WHISTLE.

Tiomkin, Dimitri (*b* Kremenchuk, 28 April/10 May 1894; *d* London, 12 Nov. 1979). Ukrainian-born American composer. His family moved in 1912 to St Petersburg, where he studied at the conservatory, played the piano for silent films, and began to compose. After the Revolution he moved to Berlin and studied with Busoni, played with the Berlin Philharmonic, and had some dance music published. He then visited Paris as a member of a two-piano partnership that toured America in 1925. He appeared at Carnegie Hall as duettist and soloist and composed the *Mars Ballet* for his wife, the choreographer Albertina Rasch. Asked to write for films, he was at first reluctant but soon found the activity fascinating; he became one of Hollywood's busiest composers and conductors. Many of his film scores won Academy Awards; the best known include *High Noon* (1952), *The High and the Mighty* (1954), *Friendly Persuasion* (1956), *The Alamo* (1960), and *The Guns of Navarone* (1961).   PGA

tiple (Sp., 'treble'). 1. A small guitar of Spain and parts of Latin America, similar to the *cavaquinho, with four or five single or multiple courses.

2. The treble *shawm of the Catalonian *sardana* band or *cobla*.

Tipperary. A song by Harry J. Williams and Jack Judge; it begins 'It's a long way to Tipperary' and became extremely popular during World War I.

Tippett, Sir **Michael** (Kemp) (*b* London, 2 Jan. 1905; *d* London, 8 Jan. 1998). English composer. He studied composition with Charles Wood and C. H. Kitson at the RCM (1923–8), and worked as a schoolteacher. Feeling that his compositional technique was still immature, he took further lessons with R. O. Morris, the specialist in Renaissance counterpoint (1930–2). By the end of the 1930s, with the Concerto for double string orchestra (1938–9), his style reached maturity. Here, as in the first three string quartets (1934–5, 1941–2, 1945–6), he displayed a manner quite unlike anything else in English music at the time, the emphasis being on bounding polyphonic lines, luminous textures, and an enriched tonal harmony, reminiscent of Hindemith or Stravinsky, but also flexible enough to embrace allusions to British folk music. Sprung, dancing rhythms also testified to his admiration for Stravinsky and jazz, as well as the English madrigalists and Purcell, whose music he was bringing to performance through his work with amateur musicians at Morley College, London.

In 1940 Tippett became director of music at Morley College, and the next year he completed the oratorio *A Child of our Time* (1939–41, first performed 1944). The work is a reaction to a particular Nazi atrocity, but the message it conveys, with reference to the Bach Passions, spirituals replacing chorales, is not a simple one. Tippett asked not for a condemnation of hatred, but (in the spirit of Jungian psychology, a great influence on him) for a recognition of the mixture of darkness and light in every human personality, and for an awareness of division as the prerequisite for healing and wholeness. In different forms this remained a fundamental theme of the five operas that followed the oratorio—*The Midsummer Marriage* (Covent Garden, 1955), *King Priam* (Coventry, 1962), *The Knot Garden* (Covent Garden, 1970), *The Ice Break* (Covent Garden, 1977), and *New Year* (Houston, TX, 1989)—and of his two later choral works *The Vision of St Augustine* (1963–5) and *The Mask of Time* (1980–2).

The Midsummer Marriage represents the fullest embodiment of the rhythmic exuberance and melodic sweep of Tippett's earlier style, and its richness and vitality brimmed over into other works of the period, including the song cycle *The Heart's Assurance* (1950–1), the *Fantasia Concertante on a Theme of Corelli* (1953) for strings, and the Piano Concerto (1953–5). With the Second Symphony (1956–7) a more concentrated musical argument and less stable diatonic harmony came to the fore, a process of transition that led to the stark juxtapositions and more expressionistic rhetoric of the second opera, *King Priam*. Tippett then explored these new stylistic and formal possibilities in the Second Piano Sonata (1962) and the Concerto for Orchestra (1962–3), as well as *The Vision of St Augustine* and *The Knot Garden*. This third opera also revealed an increasing determination to bring a wider range of musical archetypes, including the blues, within the orbit of Tippett's own style, and to respond to those aspects of American culture that he found especially sympathetic. In these respects, the Third Symphony (1970–2), with its evocation of Ives-like pluralism alongside direct quotations from Beethoven's Ninth Symphony, served to encapsulate the social and aesthetic concerns that preoccupied Tippett throughout his life.

In his later years Tippett completed a Fourth Symphony (1976–7), the string quartets nos. 4 and 5 (1977–9, 1990–1), the Piano Sonata no. 4 (1983–4), and the Triple Concerto (1979). In all these works, as with

The Mask of Time and the final opera, *New Year*, Tippett recalled aspects of that radiant lyricism which was so powerful a presence in his earlier compositions and so telling an embodiment of the sceptical yet ultimately optimistic humanism that formed his personal philosophy. His last work, the song without words for orchestra *The Rose Lake* (1991–3), was a visionary depiction of landscape inspired by a visit to Senegal. He was knighted in 1966.   PG/AW

📖 I. KEMP, *Tippett: The Composer and his Music* (London, 1984) · M. TIPPETT, *Those Twentieth Century Blues* (London, 1991) · M. BOWEN (ed.), *Tippett on Music* (Oxford, 1995) · M. BOWEN, *Michael Tippett* (London, 1997) · D. CLARKE (ed.), *Tippett Studies* (Cambridge, 1999)

tirade [coulade] (Fr.; It.: *tirata*). A Baroque ornament consisting of a quick succession, or 'run', of more than three passing notes, usually but not always consecutive, connecting two principal melody notes separated by a large interval. It was occasionally indicated by a sign (⌁) but was frequently written out or improvised.

tirana (Sp.). An Andalusian dance-song usually in 6/8 time with syncopated rhythms. It was popular in Spain in the 18th century, and the *Tirana del tripili*, thought to be by Blas de Laserna (*c.*1751–1816), became well known in the 19th from its use in Mercadante's opera *I due Figaro*.

tirando (It.). 'Dragging'.

tirare (It.), **tirer** (Fr.). 'To draw', 'to pull out'; in string playing, down-bow; in organ playing, the pulling of a stop: *tiratutti*, a *coupler; *tirato*, *tiré*, 'drawn'.

tiret (Fr.). A *mordent.

Tishchenko, Boris Ivanovich (*b* Leningrad, 23 March 1939). Russian composer. He studied with Ustvol'skaya at music college, then with Vadim Salmanov, Viktor Voloshinov, and Orest Yevlakhov at the Leningrad Conservatory, and finally with Shostakovich during postgraduate studies. He is often considered Shostakovich's heir: he completed and orchestrated several of his mentor's unfinished works, and his own symphonies are an extension of the Shostakovich tradition; the Fifth (1976) was written in memory of Shostakovich. Prokofiev and Stravinsky are also important influences, but Tishchenko's interest in the Western avant-garde is sporadically evident.   JWAL

Titelouze, Jehan (*b* Saint Omer, 1562 or 1563; *d* Rouen, 24 Oct. 1633). French organist and composer. In 1585 he went to Rouen and worked as organist at St Jean until 1588, when he became organist at Rouen Cathedral. He was much in demand as an organ restorer and adviser.

Comparatively few of his works have survived—mainly skilled polyphonic settings for organ of hymns and the *Magnificat*, designed for performance during church services. They use old-fashioned contrapuntal techniques based on plainchant, but some are enlivened by emotional dissonances and chromaticism. Titelouze was also noted as a theorist and literary man, and the prefaces to his organ publications are interesting for the light they shed on contemporary performance styles.
                                    DA/TC

Tobias, Rudolf (*b* Käina, Hiiumaa, 29 May 1873; *d* Berlin, 29 Oct. 1918). Estonian-born German composer and organist. He obtained a thorough grounding in music from his father, a church organist, before moving to Tallinn for lessons from the cathedral organist; he then became the first Estonian to study composition at the St Petersburg Conservatory (1893–7, with Rimsky-Korsakov; he also had organ instruction). A pioneer in composition too, he wrote the first Estonian orchestral work (the dramatic overture *Julius Caesar*, 1896), cantata (*Johannes Damascenus*), and string quartet (1899). Back in Estonia from 1904, in Tartu he began to write his massive German-language oratorio *Des Jona Sendung* ('Jonah's Mission', 1904–9). He then moved west, first to Paris, settling in Leipzig in 1908 and taking up a teaching post at the Königliche Hochschule für Musik in Berlin in 1911. Conscripted into the German army at the outbreak of World War I, he was discharged two years later because of ill health. His weak condition, combined with the straitened circumstances of wartime, led to his contracting pneumonia; he died leaving unfinished his second oratorio, *Jenseits von Jordan* ('On the Other Side of the Jordan').   MA

toccata (It., past participle of *toccare*, 'to touch'). A piece in a free and idiomatic style, usually for keyboard and often in several sections and incorporating virtuoso elements designed to show off the player's 'touch'. The term first appeared in the early 16th century, but the first important collections date from the last decade of that century; they include publications by Andrea Gabrieli and Claudio Merulo. At that time the term was also sometimes applied to fanfare-like pieces; a famous example is the fanfare headed 'toccata' that introduces Monteverdi's *Orfeo* (1607).

The first great master of the keyboard toccata was Frescobaldi, whose first book appeared in 1615; many of his pieces are characterized by the extreme rhythmic complexity of the passage-work. His second book (1627) includes two toccatas based on long pedal notes, and an arrangement of a madrigal by Arcadelt. Frescobaldi was followed by other Italians, such as Rossi, Pasquini, Zipoli, and Alessandro Scarlatti, and by Germans including his pupil Froberger, who wrote

24 toccatas. Transcriptions of some of Froberger's toccatas entered the French repertory, though on the whole the French did not use the term 'toccata' at this time. The Baroque toccata in Austria reached its peak in the works of Georg Muffat and Pachelbel; in the Netherlands the form was cultivated by Sweelinck, who modelled his toccatas on those of the Gabrielis, while in north Germany such composers as Buxtehude developed a large-scale, rhapsodic type of toccata. Buxtehude's long, sectional pieces, alternating free and fugal sections, are almost indistinguishable from his organ preludes and fugues. Bach wrote six harpsichord toccatas (BWV912–15 and 910–11) and several for organ, probably modelled on Buxtehude's. Some are coupled with a fugue, in the manner of a prelude. His best-known example is the Toccata for organ (often called Toccata and Fugue) in D minor BWV565. Handel, though influenced by Alessandro Scarlatti, wrote no toccatas.

With the exception of a famous example by Clementi, which he played in a competition against Mozart before the Emperor Joseph II in 1781, the form was little used in the Classical period or in the early 19th century. It was, however, revived in France by such organ composers as Vierne and Widor, who often concluded their massive organ symphonies with a toccata (the example from Widor's Fifth Organ Symphony is now a popular choice at weddings). The piano inspired a resurgence in toccata writing in the 20th century, with Debussy (*Pour le piano*) and Ravel (*Le Tombeau de Couperin*) both using toccatas as finales. Other 20th-century composers, for instance Honegger, Martinů, and Prokofiev, wrote toccatas in *perpetuum mobile* style, following the example of Schumann (Toccata in C op. 7). —/LC

toccatina [toccatino] (It.). A miniature *toccata. There are 19th-century examples by Josef Rheinberger and Georg Henselt, and Widor included a toccatina in one of his organ symphonies.

Toch, Ernst (*b* Vienna, 7 Dec. 1887; *d* Santa Monica, CA, 1 Oct. 1964). Austrian-born American composer. He studied medicine at the University of Vienna, philosophy at the University of Heidelberg (Ph.D. 1921), and the piano with Willy Rehberg at the Hoch Conservatory, Frankfurt (1910–13). In composition he was self-taught. He taught composition at the Mannheim Conservatory (1913–29) and privately in Berlin (1929–32) before emigrating to the USA in 1934. There he taught at the New School for Social Research in New York (1934–6) and the University of California, Los Angeles (1940–8), and had a notable influence in disseminating the standards and principles of the Austro-German tradition. His works include six symphonies, 13 string quartets, and a variety of vocal pieces. He also wrote *The Shaping Forces in Music* (New York, 1948). PG

Tod und das Mädchen, Der ('Death and the Maiden'). Song (1817) by Schubert to a poem by Matthias Claudius; Schubert used the theme for variations in the second movement of his String Quartet no. 14 in D minor D810 (1824), which is known by the song's title.

Tod und Verklärung ('Death and Transfiguration'). Tone-poem, op. 24 (1888–9), by Richard Strauss; in four sections, it depicts an artist's deathbed visions.

tōgaku (Jap., 'Tang music'). A part of the *gagaku* repertory, brought to Japan from China during the Tang period (618–907).

Tomášek, Václav Jan Křtitel [Tomaschek, Wenzel Johann] (*b* Skutec, 17 April 1774; *d* Prague, 3 April 1850). Czech composer and teacher. He received some musical tuition before going to Prague in 1790. After pursuing a miscellany of disciplines at Prague University he began to study law in 1797, though he already had a reputation as a music teacher. In 1806 he took a position as music teacher and composer to the family of Count George Buquoy where he stayed for 18 years. By the early 1820s he was well enough known to continue as a teacher and freelance composer, and in 1824 he set up a private music school to which many composers and performers of the younger generation were attracted, including Voříšek, Kittl, and the critic Hanslick. Tomášek rose to a position of pre-eminence in artistic circles in Prague, and many visiting musicians including Clementi, Wagner, Clara Schumann, and Paganini paid their respects. Thus his memoirs give a fascinating view of Prague's musical life and many illustrious contemporaries.

His attitudes and many of his compositions show Tomášek to have been a committed Mozartian though by no means a slavish imitator. In addition to numerous rhapsodies and seven sonatas for the piano he demonstrated his dislike of current virtuoso showpieces by composing some 42 technically undemanding eclogues. These light, uncomplicated pieces served as models for a variety of composers including Voříšek and Schubert. As well as a small but distinguished collection of church music and some less successful stage works, Tomášek composed several groups of songs setting Goethe (*Erlkönig*), Schiller, Gellert, and some Czech texts.

JSM

tombeau (Fr., 'tomb', 'tombstone'). A composition written in memory of someone, e.g. Froberger's *Tombeau fait à Paris sur la mort de Monsieur Blancheroche* (Blancheroche was a Parisian lutenist who died after falling down the stairs of his home). A 20th-century example is Ravel's *Le Tombeau de Couperin*.

Tombeau de Couperin, Le ('The Tomb of Couperin'). Suite for piano (1914–17) by Ravel; it is in six movements, each dedicated to the memory of a friend who died in World War I. Ravel orchestrated nos. 1, 3, 5, and 4 (in that order) in 1919.

Tomkins, Thomas (*b* St Davids, Pembrokeshire, 1572; *d* Martin Hussingtree, Worcs., *bur.* 9 June 1656). English organist and composer. The third child of Thomas Tomkins senior, organist of St Davids Cathedral, he was one of a notable musical family that included several other church musicians. He was probably a chorister at St Davids, and at some stage in his career studied with William Byrd. In 1596 he was appointed organist in charge of the music at Worcester Cathedral, and in 1607 took the degree of B.Mus. at Magdalen College, Oxford. By 1620 he was a Gentleman of the Chapel Royal, succeeding Edmund Hooper as one of the organists the following year; in that capacity he worked alongside Orlando Gibbons, a position that operated on a rota system and therefore allowed him to maintain his Worcester post. In later years he was more permanently based in Worcester. Together with his son Nathaniel, a canon of the cathedral, he remained a staunch royalist, opposing the suspension of services during the Civil War. Several of his late works—anthems and keyboard pieces—express outrage and sadness over current political affairs. In old age he moved to his son's house in Martin Hussingtree.

Tomkins was a prolific composer in many genres. He remained an Elizabethan in spirit right up to his death; there is barely a trace of new Italianate style in his music, and all his works are polyphonic in conception. The *Songs of 3. 4. 5. and 6. parts* (London, 1622) ranks not only as one of the last publications of the English madrigal tradition but also as one of the best. Its contents, which are individually dedicated to Tomkins's friends, colleagues, and family members, include several sacred pieces, among them the powerful setting of 'When David heard'. His many anthems and canticles, written over the decades for use both by the Chapel Royal and at Worcester, were assembled and published posthumously by Nathaniel Tomkins (*Musica Deo sacra*; London, 1668), evidently to provide the Restoration church with a repertory of solidly traditional polyphony. Tomkins also wrote music for consort and keyboard. The latter includes the 'Sad pavan' headed 'for these distracted times', dated a few days after the execution of Charles I.   —/JM

📖 D. STEVENS, *Thomas Tomkins* (London, 1957, 2/1967) · J. IRVING, *The Instrumental Music of Thomas Tomkins* (New York, 1989)

Tommasini, Vincenzo (*b* Rome, 17 Sept. 1878; *d* Rome, 23 Dec. 1950). Italian composer. A member of a rich family, he studied in Rome, and in Berlin with Bruch. His early works were influenced by Impressionism, his later music also by neo-classicism. He wrote operas, orchestral and chamber music, choral music, and songs. But he was best known for his score for the ballet *Le donne di buon umore* (*Les Femmes de bonne humeur*, *The Good-Humoured Ladies*), based on harpsichord sonatas by Domenico Scarlatti; this was produced by the Diaghilev company in 1917, three years before Stravinsky's Pergolesi adaptation *Pulcinella*.

ABur

tom-tom. A cylindrical drum, usually with thick, rod-tensioned heads on either side of a wooden shell, played with sticks in a vertical position. Tom-toms are an essential element of the *drum kit, where sets of two or more in graduated sizes are played alongside the snare drum and bass drum. A common set-up consists of two small tom-toms fixed on the bass drum, and a tenor 'floor tom'.   JMo

ton. 1. A term with several meanings, of which the principal ones are as follows. (Fr.) (*a*) 'pitch'; *donner le ton*, 'to give the pitch'; (*b*) 'key', 'mode'; *ton d'ut*, 'key of C'; *ton majeur*, 'major key'; *ton d'église*, 'church mode'; (*c*) 'tone', in the sense of Gregorian tone (see TONUS, 3); (*d*) 'crook'; *ton de trompette*, 'trumpet crook'; *ton de rechange*, 'spare crook' (or simply 'crook'); (*e*) the interval of a whole tone, as distinct from *demiton*, 'semitone'; (*f*) 'sound', 'note'; *ton aigre*, 'shrill sound'; *ton bouché*, 'stopped note' (on a horn); *ton doux*, 'sweet tone'.

(Ger.) (*a*) 'pitch'; *den Ton angeben*, 'to give the pitch'; (*b*) 'key', 'mode'; *Tongeschlecht*, 'tone-gender' (i.e. major or minor, etc.); (*c*) 'note'; *den Ton halten*, 'to hold the note'; *Tonabstand*, 'interval'; *Tonfarbe*, 'tone-colour', i.e. timbre; *Tonfolge*, 'melody'; *Tonfülle*, 'volume of tone'; *Tonhöhe*, 'pitch', 'compass', 'register'; *Tonleiter*, 'scale'; *Tonreihe*, 'note row'; *Tonmass*, 'time', i.e. length of a beat; *Tonschlüssel*, 'keynote'; *Tonsetzer*, 'composer'; (*d*) 'sound', 'music'; *Tonkunst*, '[the art of] music'; *Tonkünstler*, 'musician'; *Tonlehre*, 'acoustics'; *Tonbühne*, 'orchestra'; *Tonbild*, 'tone-picture'; *Tonmalerei*, 'programme music'; *Tondichtung*, 'tone-poem'; *Tonmeister*, a qualified sound engineer.

2. In German medieval and Renaissance literature, a term denoting a verse form and the specific melody associated with it. The Meistersinger wrote many new poems to existing *Töne*.

tonadilla [tonadilla escénica] (Sp., dim. of *tonada*, 'song'). A type of short, single-act comic opera that flourished in Spain from the mid-18th century to the early 19th. The *tonadilla* was originally performed in sections between the acts of a play as a kind of *intermezzo (examples include works by Luis Misón and Antonio Guerrero), but from the end of the 18th century it developed into a more substantial and independent piece, with examples written by Esteve y Grimau and Blas de Laserna. It usually had between one and four characters, often servants or peasants, and consisted mostly of vocal solos in aria form. Music in the style of traditional dances (e.g. the fandango) was common.

See also ZARZUELA. —/JBe

tonal answer. See FUGUE.

tonality. The organization of pitch material whereby more and less important elements allow music to be articulated in time. All systems of tonality have in common the idea that music progresses away from and towards fundamental pitches, which control the relative importance of all the sounds used within a work. Thus in major–minor tonality from the period *c.*1600–1900 the tonal centre, or tonic, is fixed for a passage, movement, or piece; the note a perfect 5th above is the next most important, the 5th below is the next, and so on (in C major, these notes would be the tonic C, the dominant G, the subdominant F).

Before about 1600, it is more common to speak of modality than of tonality, and various modal systems were described by medieval and Renaissance theorists to account for compositional practice (see MODE, 2). During the 16th and 17th centuries the distinction between a bass line and upper, more melodic voices became stronger, and a more unified harmonic practice in European music served to iron out the differences between the modes. Two modes, the Ionian (equivalent to the major scale) and the Aeolian on A (the minor scale), became the most commonly used at any pitch level, a historical process that combined with the practice of tuning at *equal temperament (see SCALE, 3).

Major–minor tonality has been described from three principal points of view. In the early 18th century, Rameau codified the principle of inversion: for any key, tonality could be defined in terms of a progression of root notes and their associated triads, whether or not the root note actually sounds in the bass (see FUNDAMENTAL BASS), and by the early 19th century this principle, replacing the earlier figured-bass method, led to the technique of identifying chord roots with Roman numerals. In the later 19th century Hugo Riemann, in his theory of *functional harmony, proposed that tonic, dominant, and subdominant roots are of first importance in expressing a tonality. These two theories of the harmonic basis of tonality both suggested that music expresses various tonalities, moving from one to another by means of *modulation. By contrast, in the early 20th century Schoenberg and Schenker proposed that a composition embodies only one tonality, the less important 'keys' which articulate its structure being only 'regions' (Schoenberg) or 'prolongations' (Schenker) of that single tonality (see ANALYSIS, 3). There is nevertheless a clear difference between Schoenberg's idea of a 'monotonal' structure embracing all the subordinate major and minor regions of that single tonality, and Schenker's belief that all tonality was an unfolding in time by means of the elaboration of the 'chord of nature'—the notes of the major triad.

This third phase of tonal theory argued in favour of a natural basis for major–minor tonality in the overtones of the *harmonic series. Riemann even suggested that an implied 'undertone' series may explain minor tonality, since the major intervals of the overtone series become minor if they are inverted 'below' the fundamental. Various 20th-century theoretical considerations of symmetry in tonal and harmonic contexts can be felt to derive from Riemann's thinking about the ways in which 'undertones' balance overtones.

The increasing chromaticism of 19th-century music, especially evident in Liszt, Wagner, Musorgsky, and Mahler, prompted the enrichment and ultimate collapse of the major–minor system of tonality. From the 1880s, in particular, composers like Debussy, Rimsky-Korsakov, and Skryabin were using whole-tone, pentatonic, and *octatonic scales to produce symmetrical divisions of the octave, and such procedures were taken further in compositions by Schoenberg and Webern from the years between 1909 and 1913 that seem to reject tonality altogether. Schoenberg's dislike of the negative term 'atonality' has led many music theorists to argue that 'post-tonal' is an appropriate term for the positive advances in harmonic organization and coherence which the abandonment of the major–minor key system afforded.

Nevertheless it has so far proved impossible for music theory to provide hard and fast techniques for distinguishing between compositions which are completely post- (or non-)tonal and those which retain some sense of tonal identity and functioning in a highly chromatic context. Many of Schoenberg's own 12-note works have unambiguous links with the hierarchical thinking that goes with traditional tonality, even when triadic progressions of a traditional kind are avoided, and the distinction between consonance and dissonance is consistently rejected in favour of the dissonance's 'emancipation'. It was left to his pupil Webern, and later composers like Boulez and Stockhausen, who prized Webern's technical advances above Schoenberg's, to aspire to a musical language free from all connections with the tonal past. But many of Schoenberg's most significant contemporaries (including Bartók and Stravinsky) continued to work on a modal or tonal basis, and a large number of later composers (for example, Maxwell Davies) have shown how it is possible to combine 12-note and serial techniques with aspects of tonal thinking. At the other extreme, the 'minimalist' or process music of Reich, Pärt, and many others, which has become prominent since 1970, has reasserted the expressive relevance of tonal and consonant fundamentals in a direct way. Whether or not a theory like George Perle's concept of 12-note tonality will win wider favour as a means of formalizing the possibility of combining hierarchic and symmetric ways of working with pitches remains to be seen, but it should not be ruled out in an early 21st-century musical climate in which new-classical approaches are gaining strength within an ultra-pluralistic musical culture.   AW

tonal sequence. See SEQUENCE, 1.

Tonart (Ger.). 'Key', in the sense of the key of C major etc.

tonary (Lat.: *tonarium, tonarius, tonale*). A medieval chant book arranged by mode; see PLAINCHANT, 4.
                                                                          —/ALI

Tondichtung (Ger.). 'Symphonic poem'.

tone (Fr.: *ton*; Ger.: *Ton*; It: *tono*). 1. The quality of a musical sound; for example a violinist may be said to have a 'powerful' or 'full-bodied' tone, a singer to have 'pure' tone.

2. In American usage the word 'tone' is synonymous with the English 'note'.

3. The interval of two semitones, i.e. a major 2nd (but see TEMPERAMENT); also known as 'whole tone'.

4. The recitation formulas in plainchant.

5. For the various meanings of 'tone' in acoustical terms, see ACOUSTICS.

tone-cluster. See CLUSTER.

tone-colour (Fr.: *timbre*; Ger.: *Klangfarbe*; It.: *timbro*). The quality of sound characteristic of a particular type of instrument or voice, as opposed to its register or pitch. Thus a violin sounds distinct from a flute even when playing exactly the same note; similarly, the tone-colour produced by a boy treble differs from that of a female soprano. Even within a single instrument type the tone-colour can vary depending on the manner of performance: for example, an open string on a violin has a different quality from the same note played when using the finger to stop a string; likewise, playing closer to the bridge also affects the instrument's timbre. This variation in tone-colour results primarily from the particular combination of harmonics produced by an instrument.

See also ACOUSTICS, 6.   JBe

tone-poem. See SYMPHONIC POEM.

tone row. In American usage, synonym of *series.

tonguing. In the playing of woodwind and brass instruments, the interruption of the flow of wind from the lungs into the instrument by means of a motion of the tongue against the mouthpiece or reed. The degree of vigour with which this action is executed, coupled with the amount of air pressure generated by the lungs and diaphragm, varies the attack of a note. Tonguing is therefore a vital means of varying articulation. A swift tongue motion and high blowing pressure result in a firm attack, while a slower tongue movement and gentler air pressure produce a legato, 'soft tonguing' effect.

Different complexities of tonguing are regularly encountered: ordinary single tonguing is effected by a motion equivalent to that required for the enunciation of the letter 'T' or 'D'; double tonguing by one equivalent to that of 'T-K' or 'D-G'; and triple tonguing by one equivalent to that of 'T-K-T', 'D-G-D', or some similar such group. Double and triple tonguing permit the non-legato execution of more rapid passages of music and facilitate the repetition of notes far more rapidly than is possible with single tonguing. Flutter tonguing (Ger. *Flatterzunge*) is a special variety introduced by Richard Strauss, used chiefly on the flute but possible also on the clarinet and some brass: it is produced by rolling the letter 'R'. For players unable to roll the letter 'R', a satisfactory flutter-tongue substitute may be achieved by the production of a French 'R' sound at the back of the throat.   —/SM

tonic. The first degree of the major or minor scale.

tonic accent. The effect of an *accent, produced not by emphasis but simply by a note falling on a higher pitch than those following or preceding it.

Tonic Sol-fa. A method of teaching sight-singing devised by John Curwen (1816–80) in which the degrees of the scale in any major key are given the *solmization syllables *doh, ray, me, fah, soh, lah, te, doh'* (the *doh* below the compass of the first seven degrees of the scale being marked *doh'*). The name Tonic Sol-fa emphasizes the fact that the major key note (or 'tonic') is always to be called *doh*.

Curwen aimed to ensure that a note is 'heard' mentally before it is uttered. He introduced pupils first to the notes of the common chord (*doh–me–soh*), patterning the sounds with the voice and exercising the intervals involved until sound and symbol were firmly associated in the pupil's mind. The rest of the scale was taught in stages in the same deliberate way. Only then was the whole octave attempted. To help the beginner, sol-fa initials were used as a simple form of notation.

Tonic Sol-fa is thus a system of aural training, and, once beginners have become familiar with the sol-fa syllables, they should be able to pitch the notes of a simple diatonic tune. With more elaborate melodies, further resources are required. Chromatic degrees are named by changing the vowels of the syllables: sharpened notes use *e* (pronounced 'ee'), and flattened notes *a* (pronounced 'aw'). For the full chromatic scale in the key of F, see Ex. 1. These chromatic note names are used only for incidental sharpening or flattening. When a tune modulates, the new key note is named *doh*, the transition being expressed by a 'bridge note' with a double name. In Ex. 2 the fourth note, *soh* of D major, becomes the new *doh*, of A major, and is therefore given both names (sung as *s'doh*).

To avoid unnecessary chromaticism, scales other than the major are based on different sol-fa notes. The minor scale begins on *lah*, the characteristic sharpened 6th of the ascending melodic form being named *bay* (see Ex. 3). Similarly, the Dorian mode (see MODE, 2) runs from *ray*, and the Aeolian from *lah*. These additional features are introduced only as the need arises. The learner is thus able gradually to build up a vocabulary of musical sounds.

This process, particularly in children, is furthered by consistent use of the hand signs that Curwen devised in

Ex. 1

doh   ray   me fah   soh   lah   te doh'

Ex. 2

doh   me   soh   soh/doh   te   doh   soh   doh

Ex. 3

lah   te   doh   ray   me   bay   se   lah

lah   soh   fah   me   ray   doh   te   lah

1870 to represent the degrees of the scale. Adopted (and slightly modified) by *Kodály when he made Tonic Sol-fa the basis of the method designed for use in Hungarian schools, they are familiar to schoolchildren in many lands. Curwen also anglicized the 'French time names' used in the *Galin–Paris–Chevé system to simplify the teaching of rhythm.

During the last decade of his life Curwen founded the Tonic Sol-fa College 'to preserve and develop' his work. More energy went into preservation than into development, and failure to follow Curwen's policy of constantly revising his methods meant that by the mid-20th century the system had been allowed to petrify—ironically, at the time when the lasting worth of Curwen's principles was being demonstrated afresh in Hungarian schools through Kodály's method.

In 1970 a working party of teachers was set up to re-examine Tonic Sol-fa. Their findings—that sol-fa and staff notation could readily be integrated, and that sight-singing could be a means of sharpening children's aural awareness rather than an end in itself—led to the foundation in 1974 of the Curwen Institute and to the publication of W. H. Swinburne's *New Curwen Method* (1980). This aims to develop those aural concepts and skills on which all musical response depends, and without which attempts to teach sight-singing founder. Once this has been achieved, reading from staff notation follows effortlessly.   BR/PSP

📖 B. RAINBOW, *John Curwen: A Short Critical Biography* (London, 1980)

tono. 1 (Sp.). In general, any type of Spanish song, sacred (*tono divino*) or secular (*tono humano*); more specifically in the 17th century, a short song originally for solo voice, later for two or three voices, used to introduce a play or other stage performance.

2 (It.). 'Tone', in any general sense; specifically 'whole tone' (see TONE, 3).

3 (It.). 'Key' or 'mode'; specifically a church mode, or the recitation formula belonging to it (see TONUS, 3).

Tonreihe (Ger.). 'Note row'; see SERIES.

tonus (Lat., from Gk. *tonos*, 'tone'). A term used in three senses in the Middle Ages. 1. The interval of a major 2nd.

2. *Mode.

3. A plainchant recitation formula. There were numerous chant recitation tones of varying complexity in the Middle Ages, mostly for the singing of psalms and canticles and the intoning of prayers and lessons. For psalms there were more than a dozen, one for each of the eight modes and several others—the best-known irregular one was the *tonus peregrinus*, or 'wandering tone'. Usually most of an intonation takes place on one

note, the tenor, repeated over and over again for as much of the text as is necessary. The first few notes usually lead on to the tenor through rising steps; a cadence at the end of each line falls away from the tenor. There are generally subordinate cadences halfway through a verse (*mediatio*), sometimes also at other points (*flexa*) in long verses. This same procedure is repeated for each verse of the psalm or other text. (For illustration see PLAINCHANT, Ex. 1.)   DH/ALi

tonus peregrinus (Lat., 'wandering tone'). A Latin psalm tone outside the system of the eight modes. Distinguished by the two reciting notes A in the first half-verse and G in the second, it was used principally for the performance of *In exitu Israel de Aegypto* (Vulgate Psalm 113).   ALi

tordion [tourdion] (Fr.). A 16th-century dance in triple time, described in Arbeau's *Orchésographie (1588); it is similar to the *galliard, but lighter and quicker, and was usually performed after a *basse danse. Warlock included a *tordion* in his *Capriol Suite* (1927).   —/JH

Torelli, Giuseppe (*b* Verona, 22 April 1658; *d* Bologna, 8 Feb. 1709). Italian violinist and composer. He was admitted to the Accademia Filarmonica in 1684, first as a violinist and later as a composer. In 1686 he became a string player at the civic church of S. Petronio, but he was obliged to leave in 1696 when the musical *cappella* was disbanded. He then served as *maestro di concerto* to the Margrave of Brandenburg at Ansbach, later moving to Vienna, but by 1701 he had returned to the re-formed S. Petronio *cappella*.

Torelli's undoubted importance in the early history of the concerto has been much distorted by the imposition of later definitions: for Torelli and his contemporaries the title 'concerto' carried no automatic implication of solo or even orchestral writing. Like his teacher, Perti, he contributed to the Bolognese repertory of trumpet sonatas which pitted soloists again the orchestral body, and in his op. 6 (1698) he distinguishes between the violin 'solo' and the duplicated parts, but solo–tutti markings were already a common feature of instrumental scoring in Bolognese choral works. The posthumous op. 8 collection has been noted for its division into solo concertos and concerti grossi, the use of the ritornello principle, and the three-movement fast–slow–fast format. Torelli's op. 4 for violin and violoncello contributed to the repertory of unaccompanied duos not unusual at the period.   DA/PA

Torke, Michael (*b* Milwaukee, WI, 21 Sept. 1961). American composer. He studied at the Eastman School and with Jacob Druckman at Yale (1984–5). While he was still a student, such works as *Vanada* for orchestra and *The Yellow Pages* for quintet (both 1984) brought

him much attention for their assured, sometimes humorous blend of rock and Bernsteinian bravado. Later works include many with colour titles (see COLOUR AND MUSIC) appropriate to his style (*Ecstatic Orange* for orchestra, 1985–7), a television opera (*King of Hearts*, 1993), and the symphonic oratorio *Four Seasons* (1999).   PG

Tortelier, Paul (*b* Paris, 21 March 1914; *d* Villarceaux, Val d'Oise, 18 Dec. 1990). French cellist and composer. His career began in orchestras, but after 1945 he was given solo engagements by Münch and by Beecham, playing *Don Quixote* in London. His marriage to Maud Martin inspired his concerto for two cellos. He was appointed a professor at the Paris Conservatoire in 1957. His televised master classes, infectious vitality, and huge enthusiasm remain memorable. He designed an angled spike and a split bridge for the cello. His three children are professional musicians: Yan Pascal is a violinist and conductor, Maria de la Pau is a pianist, and Pomona is a cellist.   CF

📖 *Paul Tortelier: A Self-Portrait in Conversation with David Blum* (London, 1984)

Tosca. Opera in three acts by Puccini to a libretto by Giuseppe Giacosa and Luigi Illica after Victorien Sardou's play *La Tosca* (1887) (Rome, 1900).

Toscanini, Arturo (*b* Parma, 25 March 1867; *d* New York, 16 Jan. 1957). Italian conductor. At the age of nine he was accepted at the Parma Conservatory to study the cello, piano, and composition. He began his career as an orchestral cellist with a touring opera company, for which he soon began coaching the singers. In 1886, aged 19 and with no conducting tuition or experience, he made his debut as a conductor with the company, taking over a performance of *Aida* at a few minutes' notice and conducting from memory.

Toscanini was soon greatly in demand at Italian opera houses; he conducted the premieres of *Pagliacci* (1892) and *La bohème* (1896) and the first performances in Italy of *Götterdämmerung* (1895) and *Siegfried* (1899). His debut as a symphonic conductor was in 1896. In 1898 he was made music director at La Scala, Milan, where he gained fame for his fanatical demands for technical perfection and artistic expressiveness; he stayed until 1903, returning in 1906–8 and again in 1921–9, one of its finest periods. In 1908 he went to the Metropolitan Opera, New York, where he conducted the premiere of *La fanciulla del West* (1910) and first American performances of many operas including *Boris Godunov* (1913).

For the rest of his long career the brilliance, intensity, and discipline of Toscanini's performances created a huge public following, notably when he was music director of the New York Philharmonic Orchestra (1929–36) and the NBC Symphony Orchestra (1937–54). He conducted at Bayreuth (1930) and Salzburg (1934–7) and was guest conductor of the BBC Symphony Orchestra (1935, 1937–9) but refused to conduct in Italy, Germany, and Austria under the Nazi regimes. He fought and overturned artificial performing traditions, and his interpretations strongly influenced many younger conductors who later became major artists.

JT

📖 B. H. HAGGIN, *Arturo Toscanini: Contemporary Recollections of the Maestro*, ed. T. S. Hathaway (New York, 1989) · H. SACHS, *Reflections on Toscanini* (New York, 1991)

Toselli, Enrico (*b* Florence, 13 March 1883; *d* Florence, 15 Jan. 1926). Italian pianist and composer. A pupil of Sgambati and Martucci, he was a successful concert pianist in his early years, until his sensational marriage in 1907 to Archduchess Louise of Austria-Tuscany led to the neglect of his keyboard technique. He composed a number of operas and operettas, and is still known by his popular song *Serenata* (1900).   DA

Tosti, Sir (Francesco) **Paolo** (*b* Ortona sul Mare, 9 April 1846; *d* Rome, 2 Dec. 1916). Italian composer and singing teacher. After studying in Naples he taught there until 1869. He soon became a prolific writer of ballads and light songs and moved to Rome, where he was appointed singing-master to Queen Margherita of Italy. From 1875 he made many visits to London, settling there in 1880 and becoming singing-master to the royal family; he was knighted for those services in 1908. He wrote a vast number of songs to Italian, French, and English texts, many of which had a great vogue in Victorian times—such as 'Goodbye' (*Addio*), *Ideale*, *La serenata*, and *Mattinata*.   PGA

tosto (It.). 'Rapid', 'at once'; *più tosto*, 'quicker' (not to be confused with *piuttosto*, 'rather'); *più che tosto*, 'as soon as'.

'Tost' Quartets. 12 string quartets by Haydn, op. 54 nos. 1–3, op. 55 nos. 1–3, and op. 64 nos. 1–6 (1788–90), so called because they are dedicated to the Viennese violinist Johann Tost.

Totentanz (Ger.). 1. *'Dance of Death'.

2. Work for piano and orchestra by Liszt, planned as early as 1839 but first composed in 1849, with revised versions in 1853 and 1859. The final version is a paraphrase on the *Dies irae*, with some material taken from Mozart's Requiem; the early versions also incorporate music from Liszt's 1834 setting of the psalm *De profundis*.

Tote Stadt, Die ('The Dead City'). Opera in three acts by Korngold to a libretto by Paul Schott (Julius and

E. W. Korngold) after Georges Rodenbach's novel *Bruges la morte* (Hamburg and Cologne, 1920).

touch. 1. A term used to describe the amount of force needed to depress a key on a keyboard instrument, or the distance that a key may be depressed.

2. A fanfare for trumpets and timpani (see TUCKET; TUSCH).

3. A term used in English *change-ringing for a short segment of the chosen system.

touche (Fr.). 1. The key of a keyboard instrument.

2. The fingerboard of a stringed instrument.

3. The 16th-century term for a fret.

tourdion. See TORDION.

Tournemire, Charles (*b* Bordeaux, 22 Jan. 1870; *d* Arcachon, 4 Nov. 1939). French composer and organist. He studied at the Paris Conservatoire under Franck and Charles-Marie Widor, becoming organist of Ste Clotilde from 1898 until his death. Though best known as the outstanding liturgical improviser of his age, he also produced an immense quantity of compositions in all forms, inspired by his Roman Catholic faith and love of nature. Early organ works include the Franckian *Pièce symphonique* (1899) and *Triple choral* (1910), but these are overshadowed by eight orchestral symphonies (the Sixth and Seventh being of Mahlerian proportions) and three operas, of which *Les Dieux sont morts* was produced at the Paris Opéra in 1924. Lack of success in the concert world, however, led to a rebirth of organ composition on a huge scale with *L'Orgue mystique* (1927–32), a liturgical cycle for the entire Christian year based on Gregorian chant. Its stylistic eclecticism, formal fluidity, and bold explorations of harmony and texture owe much to Debussy, and in turn strongly influenced Messiaen. Indeed, Hindu modes are used in the *Sept chorals-poèmes pour les Sept Paroles du Christ* (1935). But best known are the *Cinq improvisations* transcribed by Duruflé in 1958 from gramophone recordings made in 1930–1.   AT

Tourte, François (Xavier) (*b* Paris, 1747; *d* Paris, 26 April 1835). French bow maker. His father and older brother both made bows, but it was he who became known as the 'Stradivari of the bow'. Between 1782 and 1790 he developed the modern bow (the 'Tourte bow'): he determined its optimum length and curvature, tapering it towards a point, fixed the height of the point and nut, and invented a method of fixing the hairs with a movable metal band; he was the first to use pernambuco wood which he set in permanent curvature by heating rather than cutting it.   AL

Tovey, Sir **Donald** (Francis) (*b* Windsor, 17 July 1875; *d* Edinburgh, 10 July 1940). English pianist, composer, and writer on music. The son of an Eton master, he studied classics at Oxford but spent some years after graduation as a pianist and composer. In 1914 he was appointed professor of music at Edinburgh University, where he wrote his famous programme notes for the Reid concerts (which he also conducted). These were later collected and published as *Essays in Musical Analysis* (London, 1935–44, abridged and repr. 1981–9). Tovey also wrote a book on Beethoven (London, 1945) and some miscellaneous essays.   LC

Tower, Joan (Peabody) (*b* New Rochelle, NY, 6 Sept. 1938). American composer. She grew up in South America, where her father was a mining engineer, and studied at Bennington College and Columbia University. Active in New York as an ensemble pianist, she founded the Da Capo Chamber Players in 1969. Her first works were serial, but in the mid-1970s she developed a new style, more tonal, energetic, and immediately expressive, often with a characteristic feature of small motifs in rising patterns. From *Sequoia* (1981) to *Silver Ladders* (1986) she extended her mastery of the orchestra, exploited further in the Concerto for Orchestra (1991), various solo concertos, and a series of *Fanfares for the Uncommon Woman*. Other works include a 1976–7 mineral trilogy (*Platinum Spirals* for violin, *Black Topaz* for piano and sextet, *Red Garnet Waltz* for piano) and the humorous *Petroushkates* for five players (1980).   PG

tower music. See Turmmusik.

toye. A name given in the Elizabethan and Jacobean periods to a short, lighthearted composition for keyboard or lute, e.g. John Bull's *The Duchess of Brunswick's Toye*, from the Fitzwilliam Virginal Book.

'Toy' Symphony (*Kindersymphonie*; *La Foire des enfants*; *Symphonie burlesque*). A Symphony in C, for first and second violins, double bass, keyboard instrument, and a series of toy instruments (including cuckoo, quail, and nightingale, trumpet, drum, rattle, and triangle, long attributed to Haydn but now thought to be by Leopold Mozart, possibly with Michael Haydn and Leopold

Angerer. Other composers have written symphonies incorporating toy instruments, notably Romberg and Mendelssohn.

tpt. Abbreviation for 'trumpet'.

tr. Abbreviation for trill, treble, transpose.

Trabaci, Giovanni Maria (*b* Monte Pelusio [now Irsina], nr Potenza, *c*.1575; *d* Naples, 31 Dec. 1647). Italian composer and organist. He was appointed organist to the royal chapel at Naples in 1601, and became its *maestro di cappella* in 1614. He also served at various times as organist at the oratory of the Filippini. His keyboard pieces—two of them written for a chromatic harpsichord—foreshadow Frescobaldi in their virtuosity and adventurous harmonic language. His similarly bold motets of 1602 may have influenced Gesualdo; his madrigals, though on the whole less chromatic and intense, demand considerable vocal virtuosity.

                                                              DA/ER

tract. A Latin chant of the Roman Mass, usually sung before the Gospel during Lent and on other penitential days. A small group of chants for the procession to the font at the Easter vigil service were also given tract melodies. Tracts have texts comprising several psalm verses.

It has been the traditional belief that tracts are among the oldest of all Gregorian melodies, but recent research often inclines to the opposite view. The argument is bound up with the problem of the modification of Roman chant during its adoption in the Empire of Charlemagne to produce what we now know as Gregorian chant. Contrary to the usual pattern of events, it appears that several tracts were composed in Frankish lands and later adopted in Rome. The oldest sources (of the late 8th century) seem to have caught the repertory in mid-development, containing only 21 tracts between them. New ones were composed throughout the Middle Ages; the modern Vatican *Graduale romanum* has 70.

All tracts are in either the second or the eighth mode (see MODE, 2). Ex. 1 gives an analysis of one verse of a

Ex. 1

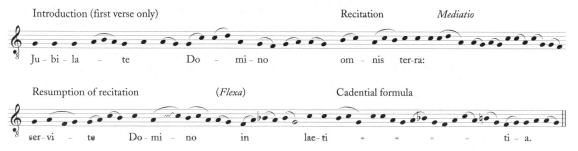

tract in mode 8 (for an explanation of the terms used, see TONUS, 3). DH/ALι

traduction (Fr.), **traduzione** (It.). 1. 'Translation' (of a libretto etc.).

   2. Arrangement.

   3. Transposition.

Traetta, Tommaso (Michele Francesco Saverio) (*b* Bitonto, nr Bari, 30 March 1727; *d* Venice, 6 April 1779). Italian composer. He studied in Naples with Porpora and Durante and began his career as a prolific composer in conventional comic and serious genres, setting librettos by Carlo Goldoni and Pietro Metastasio. In 1758 he obtained employment at the Bourbon court of Parma, where, under the intendant Guillaume Du Tillot, he began a series of operas that anticipate the Viennese reform operas of Gluck and other attempts to unite French dramatic forms with modern Italian music. *Ippolito ed Aricia* (1759) and *I tindaridi* (1760) were adapted by C. I. Frugoni from texts set by Rameau (*Hippolyte et Aricie* and *Castor et Pollux*), occasionally borrowing the Frenchman's music. Traetta's works made integral use of scenes with chorus and ballet, and combined solo and choral singing into elaborate movements in which the forms resemble those of Gluck's reform operas, though Traetta's music is more expansively lyrical.

His fame spread beyond the Alps, and he took full advantage of a more developed orchestral style. *Armida*, written for Vienna (1761), is derived from the libretto by Philippe Quinault that Lully set. In Mannheim Traetta presented *Sofonisba* (1762) with a libretto by Jommelli's collaborator Mattia Verazi (some of the performers later took part in Mozart's *Idomeneo*). *Ifigenia in Tauride* (1763), with a libretto by Marco Coltellini, was first performed in Vienna and later in Florence under Gluck's direction (but Traetta may have been influenced by Gluck's *Orfeo*). He continued to turn his hand to more conventional works, and moved to Venice as director of the Conservatorio dell'Ospedaletto. In 1768 he succeeded Galuppi at the court of Catherine the Great in St Petersburg, where in 1772 he produced a crowning masterpiece, *Antigona* (libretto by Coltellini). After an unsuccessful period in London, then under the spell of Sacchini, he returned to Venice in poor health. JR

tragédie lyrique. A term coined by the librettist Philippe Quinault (1635–88) and by Lully—and first used by them for *Cadmus et Hermione* (1673)—for a genre of opera that would make use of tragic mythological or epic subjects, with great attention to clarity of declamation and naturalness of action. It was nevertheless much criticized, even in its heyday, for the high-flown and exaggerated treatment of its subjects in its reflection of the *gloire* essential to Louis XIV's court entertainment. It became a stilted convention, anticipating many of the rigid features of *opera seria* and laying itself open to vigorous parody by the librettist Charles-Simon Favart (1710–92). The term fell into disuse in the early 19th century; it had long been applied in a much more general way by Lully's successors from Rameau to Gluck, then by Grétry, Gossec, and others. See also OPERA, 4. JW

Tragic Overture (*Tragische-Ouvertüre*). Brahms's op. 81, composed in 1880 and revised in 1881.

'Tragic' Symphony. Schubert's Symphony no. 4 in C minor D417 (1816), his own title. It is also applied to Mahler's Symphony no. 6 in A minor (1903–4, revised 1906 and later) and Bruckner's Symphony no. 5 in B♭ major (1875–6).

Tragoedia. Work (1965) by Birtwistle for wind quintet, harp, and string quartet.

traîné (Fr.). 'Dragged'; *sans traîner*, 'without dragging'.

tranquillo (It.). 'Tranquil', 'calm'; *tranquillamente*, 'tranquilly'; *tranquillità*, *tranquillezza*, 'tranquillity'.

Transcendental Studies. See ÉTUDES D'EXÉCUTION TRANSCENDANTE D'APRÈS PAGANINI.

transcription. A term often used interchangeably with *arrangement. It is however possible to make a distinction between transcribing, as copying a composition while changing layout or notation (for example, from parts to full score), and arranging, as changing the medium (for example, from piano quartet to full orchestra, as in Schoenberg's arrangement of Brahms's op. 25). Transcription is also carried out by ethnomusicologists when they attempt to capture in staff notation a performance recorded in the field. AW

Transfiguration de notre Seigneur Jésus-Christ, La ('The Transfiguration of our Lord Jesus Christ'). Work (1965–9) by Messiaen for 100 voices and orchestra, settings of texts from the Bible and the missal, and by St Thomas Aquinas.

transformation, thematic. The process of altering a theme to change its character without losing its essential identity; another term for it is 'thematic metamorphosis'. Although the technique is found earlier (in the dance movements of suites in the 17th century, for example), it was in the 19th century that thematic transformation became a favourite procedure as a means of giving unity and cohesion to multimovement works or as an element in *programme music. Themes could be presented in different rhythms or metres, or with different orchestrations, or with slight changes in melody. The process differs from *development in that the transformed theme is likely to be treated as independently as the original.

An important example of its use is in Berlioz's *Symphonie fantastique* (1830), in which a single theme (an *idée fixe*) recurs in each movement, transformed to suit its narrative context, which varies from a ball scene to wild dancing at a witches' sabbath. Thematic transformation is associated above all with Liszt, who used it extensively in his symphonic poems. It was a common device in opera and ballet, where it can be part of the delineation of character. Wagner's use of *leitmotif is an extension of thematic transformation.   AL

transient. A sound of very short duration, e.g. the sharp attack ('onset transient') at the beginning of a note or any rapid change in sound level. See ACOUSTICS, 6.   JBo

transposing instruments. Instruments that sound lower or higher than their notated pitch, except where the interval is an octave (e.g. double bass or piccolo). The purpose of transposition is to enable the execution (fingering, etc.) of each written note to remain the same for each instrument of the same family, no matter which size is being played. The use of transposing brass instruments originated before the introduction of valves, when each instrument could sound only the harmonic series of its fundamental, and different instruments were needed for works in different keys, for example D horns and trumpets for works in D.

The key of the instrument is usually stated as part of its name, for example B♭ clarinet, horn in F. In every case the named note is that which sounds when the player reads C; all other notes sound the same interval from the written note as the named one does from C. Thus the B♭ clarinet and trumpet sound a tone lower than written, the E♭ clarinet a minor 3rd higher, the horn in F and the cor anglais (always in F) a 5th lower, and the F trumpet a 4th higher. The alto flute is in G, and written a 4th higher than it sounds. The *violino piccolo* is one of the few stringed instruments that is likely to be transposed, a 3rd or a 4th lower than sounding pitch, so that it may be read and fingered as if it were a normal violin. In orchestral scores the parts for transposing instruments have traditionally been notated in their transposed pitches, though since the mid-20th century some scores notate all parts at sounding pitch.   JMo

transposition. Performance or notation of music at a pitch different from the original, effected by raising or lowering all notes by the same interval.

For certain instruments music is usually notated in transposition (see TRANSPOSING INSTRUMENTS). In the 20th century many composers, led by Schoenberg, came to prefer to write scores 'in C', that is, with all parts written as they sound. Transposing keyboard instruments, where the keyboard may be shifted in relation to the strings, date from at least as early as 1537 but fell into disuse in the 19th century.

Transposition of the notated music in the performance of vocal works was probably common in the medieval period, but by the early 16th century the use of soprano, alto, tenor, and bass clefs at pitch—that is, non-transposing notation—was becoming standard. The printing of vocal music at various transpositions to suit different vocal ranges (high, middle, and low voice) is still widespread, but the practice is questionable for those Romantic song cycles where the tonal relationships between numbers ought to be preserved (e.g. Schumann's *Frauenliebe und -leben*). Being able to transpose from one key to another at sight is an important skill for the church organist, and was considered an indispensable way of practising by the great 19th- and early 20th-century piano teachers. Brahms noted at the beginning of his 51 Exercises for Piano, 'these and similar exercises are also to be practised in other keys'.

The concept of transposition is central to theories of 12-note composition and of the set structure of post-tonal music. Messiaen codified *'modes of limited transposition', where certain transpositions produce the same scalic segments as appear in other transpositions: that is, a mode can be transposed at only a limited number of intervals, so that a specific, coherent pitch vocabulary is available for any mode. Webern in his later music often used 12-note sets which similarly permit of only a limited transpositional variety.   JD

transverse flute (Fr.: *flûte traversière*; Ger.: *Querflöte*; It.: *flauto traverso, traverso*). A term used to distinguish the *flute from the *recorder (*flûte à bec, flûte douce*; *Blockflöte; flauto dolce*, etc.).

traps [trap set]. See DRUM KIT.

traquenard (Fr., 'ambush', 'trap'). A late 17th-century German dance found in the orchestral suites of Georg Muffat, Johann Fischer, and J. P. Krieger. The origin of the name is unknown.

trascinando (It.). 'Dragging', i.e. holding back; *senza trascinare*, 'without dragging'.

trattenuto (It.). 'Held back', 'sustained'.

tratto (It.). 'Dragged'; usually in the negative, *non tratto*.

Trauer (Ger.). 'Mourning', 'sorrow'; *traurig*, 'mournfully'; *trauernd*, 'mourning', 'lamenting'; *Trauermarsch*, 'funeral march'; *Trauermusik*, 'funeral music'; *trauervoll*, 'sorrowful'.

Trauermusik ('Mourning Music'). Work (1936) by Hindemith for viola (or violin or cello) and orchestra; he composed it a few hours after he heard of the death of King George V, and it was performed at a concert the next day.

Traum (Ger.). 'Dream'; *Traumbild*, 'dream picture'; *träumend*, 'dreaming'; *Träumerei*, 'reverie'; *träumerisch*, 'dreamy'; *Liebesträume*, 'dreams of love'.

Träumerei ('Reverie'). Piano piece by Schumann, no. 7 of his *Kinderszenen* op. 15 (1838).

traurig (Ger.). 'Mournfully'.

trautonium. A monophonic electronic instrument invented by Friedrich Trautwein in 1930. It is played by depressing a steel wire on to a steel bar, thus short-circuiting the wire at that point and altering its resistance, so changing the frequency of the oscillator and thus the pitch produced. Condensers or, in later models, alternative circuits control the harmonic content of the sound, and changing these alters the tone-quality. Hindemith composed a trautonium concertino with string orchestra. JMo

Travers, John (*b* c.1703; *d* London, June 1758). English composer and organist. Probably a chorister at St George's Chapel, Windsor, he studied with Greene and with Pepusch, who bequeathed him part of his valuable library. He became a church organist in London, and was appointed organist to the Chapel Royal in 1737. He wrote much sacred music, including a collection entitled *The Whole Book of Psalms* for one to five voices and harpsichord (c.1746–50), a Service in F, a *Te Deum*, and several anthems published in Arnold's *Cathedral Music* (1790). He also composed 12 organ voluntaries, and his *18 Canzonets* were popular. WT/PL

traversa, traverso (It.; Fr.: *traversière*; Ger.: *Traversflöte*, *Querflöte*). See TRANSVERSE FLUTE.

Traviata, La ('The Fallen Woman'). Opera in three acts by Verdi to a libretto by Francesco Maria Piave after Alexandre Dumas *fils*'s play *La Dame aux camélias* (1852) (Venice, 1853).

tre (It.). 'Three'; *a tre voci*, 'for three voices'; *tre corde*, 'three strings', an indication to remove the soft (*una corda*) pedal on the piano (see PIANOFORTE, 7).

treble. 1. A high voice (particularly of a boy). In music of the 14th and 15th centuries it was the name given to the highest voice in a three-part vocal ensemble and the second highest in a four-part one; it was thus equivalent to 'superius', 'cantus', and 'discantus'. Later the voice was more usually referred to as 'soprano', except for boys' voices. —/RW

2. A high-pitched member of a family of instruments, e.g. recorders (with a range lower than descant and higher than tenor) or viols (the highest pitched).

treble clef. The G *clef (not to be confused with the *soprano clef).

Tregian, Francis (*b* c.1574; *d* London, Aug. 1617). English gentleman. For many years he was identified with the copying of a number of important music manuscripts, including the famous Fitzwilliam Virginal Book. This theory has recently been challenged, and it is now unclear what connection exists between the manuscripts and the various members of the Tregian family whose names (or, more often, initials) appear in the virginal book. JM

treibend (Ger.). 'Driving', i.e. hurrying.

tremando, tremante, tremolando (It.). To be played or sung with *tremolo.

Tremblay, Gilles (*b* Arvida, PQ, 6 Sept. 1932). Canadian composer, teacher, pianist, and ondes martenot player. He studied the piano at the Montreal Conservatory (1949–54) and composition privately with Claude Champagne. Moving to Paris, he completed Messiaen's analysis course (1954–7), winning the *premier prix*, studied the piano and composition with Yvonne Loriod, and learnt the ondes martenot with Maurice Martenot. After meeting Stockhausen and Boulez at Darmstadt he spent two years at the ORTF in Paris with the Groupe de Recherches Musicales. His composing career took off after he wrote the award-winning soundtrack for the Quebec Pavilion at Expo '67 in Montreal. His works include *Kékoba* (in homage to Varèse), *Cantiques de durées* for orchestra, given its premiere in Paris (1963), as well as two commissions for the Montreal Symphony Orchestra: *Fleuve* (1977) and *AVEC: Wampum symphonique* (1992), a cantata composed for the 350th anniversary of the founding of Montreal. HRe

tremblement (Fr.). In the 17th and 18th centuries, an alternative name for the *trill; *tremblement mineur*, alternative name for *vibrato.

tremolando. See TREMOLO, 1.

tremolo (It., 'trembling', 'quivering'). Some terminological confusion surrounds the terms 'tremolo' and 'vibrato'. In modern usage 'tremolo' indicates a change of intensity or repetition of a note, whereas *vibrato is a wavering or oscillation of pitch. Historically, however, many writers (especially on the voice) reverse this distinction. 'Tremolo' in the first sense describes a number of related effects.

1. On string and other instruments, 'tremolo' indicates the fast repetition of a single note, or the alternation of two notes. It may be regular in rhythm (as in Ex. 1) or unmeasured, the latter sometimes being referred to as 'tremolando'. The measured repetition of a given pitch has been used to create a mood of tension and excitement in music since the early Baroque period, although it was generally superseded by the unmeasured variety in the later 19th century. Keyboard instruments (especially the piano) can simulate these effects by a rapid alternation of notes, often an octave apart.   SMcV/DMi

2. More specifically, tremolo is an ornament used by 17th- and 18th-century string players. The note is lightly repeated within a single bowstroke, the separations being scarcely noticeable. The sign is a wavy line above a long note, or above a series of repeated notes.

3. In 17th-century vocal music, tremolo is an ornament consisting of a fast reiteration of one note (but without the exaggerated separations sometimes perpetrated today). Confusingly, the contemporary Italian term was 'trillo', whereas 'tremolo' at the time meant a type of trill.

Ex. 1

(a)

(b)

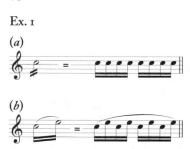

trepak. A Cossack dance in rapid duple time. Performed by men, it features the *prisiadka*, kicking from a squatting position. There is a famous example in Tchaikovsky's *Nutcracker* suite.   —/JH

trg., trge. Abbreviations for 'triangle'.

triad. A chord of three notes, consisting in its most basic form of a 'root' and the notes a 3rd and a 5th above it, forming two superimposed 3rds (Ex. 1a). If the lower 3rd is major and the upper one minor, the triad is described as major (Ex. 1a); if the lower is minor and the upper major, the triad is minor (Ex. 1b); if both are major, the triad is augmented (Ex. 1c); if both are minor the triad is diminished (Ex. 1d). In practice, triads

Ex. 1

(a)   (b)   (c)   (d)

frequently occur in inversions (Ex. 2a) and in open positions (Ex. 2b).

Ex. 2

(a)   (b)

Trial by Jury. Operetta in one act by Sullivan to a libretto by W. S. Gilbert (London, 1875).

triangle. A percussion instrument made of a steel rod bent into triangular shape and struck with a steel beater. In the Middle Ages and the Renaissance it was often trapezoidal in shape, and up to about 1800 it had jingling rings on the lowest arm. Today it is normally suspended by a loop of gut or nylon, attached either to a special stand so that two beaters may be used for rhythmic passages, or to a bulldog clip held in the hand or on a stand. In theory the triangle is without specific pitch, but in practice percussionists may use a number of different shapes and sizes.   JMo

tricinium (Lat.). A composition for three voices or instruments. The term was most often used in Germany in the 16th century.

trill [shake] (Fr.: *cadence, tremblement, trille*; Ger.: *Triller*, It.: *trillo*). An ornament consisting of rapid alternation of the main (notated) pitch with a note usually a semitone or tone above it. The device is normally slurred, and applied particularly, although not uniquely, to cadences. While the effect is largely to be found in instrumental music, it is also possible with the voice, and has long been regarded as part of a virtuoso vocal technique.

The trill is found throughout music of the 18th century and before, particularly in early keyboard works. Its use in that context varies greatly, as indeed does the manner in which it is notated. Among the signs used are *tr*, ∿, and +, all appearing over the note in question. Of these signs, the first has been standard since the beginning of the 18th century. A flat, natural, or sharp sign can be placed above it, to indicate a chromatic inflection of the upper note. A wavy line may also define the extent, length, and location of the trill (see Ex. 1).

Ex. 1

The method of performance is variable in a number of ways. In the first place, written-out interpretations have normally been couched in carefully measured rhythm. There is, however, evidence of a more flexible practice in performance throughout the trill's period of use. The precise speed of the alternation of notes is often left to the performer's discretion, and it is also possible to speed up the repercussions, either gradually and imperceptibly, or more obviously.

Further, the beginning and ending of the trill have been treated differently over time. The modern trill, first documented in the 19th century, begins on the main, or lower, note and often ends without suffix, unless specifically indicated (see Ex. 2; note that Ex. 2*d* approximates to a turn; see TURN, Ex. 2*c*). The late Baroque trill, however, begins on the upper note. This may be extended into an *appoggiatura (sometimes notated ⵕ), and more complex openings are possible (see Ex. 3; both *b* and *c* may be indicated by small notes). It will be noted that the upper-note start gives this trill a harmonic colouring quite unlike that of the modern type.

Two types of ending are typical: the single note of anticipation (separated from the trill; Ex. 4*a*) and the turn (incorporated into the rhythm of the trill; Ex. 4*b*). The sign ⵕ also indicates the turned ending. One of these endings should be provided even when not notated (and, conversely, if the suffix is notated a trill should be added). However, in fast passages a half-trill will suffice (Ex. 5; there may be more repercussions).

Although Baroque composers may use the extended sign (ⵕ) this does not generally imply only a half-trill. In music of the Classical period (up to Beethoven), an

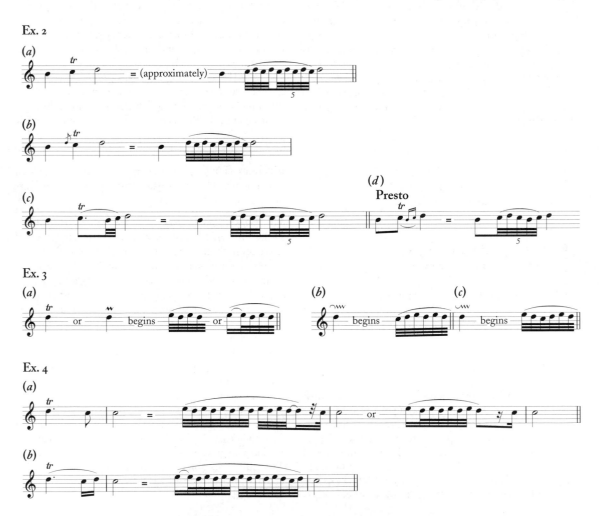

Ex. 5

upper-note start is still expected. Increasingly the suffix (usually a turn) was notated in full size, or as grace notes. The present conception of the trill, starting on the main note, dates from about 1830.   SMcV/DMi

trilogy (Fr., Ger.: *Trilogie*; It.: *trilogia*). In music, a set of three compositions on a common theme. Wagner described his *Ring* cycle of operas as a trilogy (*Die Walküre*, *Siegfried*, and *Götterdämmerung*), since these deal with the conception, birth, and death of the hero Siegfried. *Das Rheingold* is intended to act as a huge prelude to the trilogy, in order to explain why the gold was stolen from the Rhine, and the resulting curse. Felix Weingartner wrote an operatic trilogy *Orestes*, based on Aeschylus' *Oresteia*.

Trinity College of Music. British conservatory founded in London in 1872. See DEGREES AND DIPLOMAS.

Trinklied (Ger.). 'Drinking-song'.

trio (Ger.: *Terzett*; It.: *terzetto*). 1. An ensemble of three singers or instrumentalists, or music written for it. Many 16th-century madrigals were written for three voices, often for women's voices, as have been some famous operatic trios of more recent times, but any combination of voices may be used.

The 17th- and 18th-century trio sonata was a favourite chamber ensemble, using two treble instruments and one bass, with a keyboard or lute continuo to fill in the harmony. The same format was often imitated at the organ, the pedal taking the bass and the manuals the treble lines. Some trio sonatas were for two oboes, bassoon, and basso continuo, but the majority were for two violins, cello, and basso continuo; this was also the genesis of the string quartet of the Classical period, the viola replacing the right hand of the keyboard player. Although some Classical and later string trios retain the old form of two violins and cello, most are for violin, viola, and cello. Neither was as common or as popular as the piano trio.

Haydn wrote a considerable number of trios for *baryton, viola, and cello, in which he and a colleague could accompany his employer, Nicolaus Esterházy, an enthusiastic amateur of the baryton.

Wind trios for such combinations as flute, clarinet, and bassoon have been written by a number of composers, as have brass trios for trumpet, horn, and trombone or other combinations.

See also CHAMBER MUSIC.   JMo

2. The central part of a *minuet or *scherzo (in a sonata, symphony, or similar work). In the 17th century it was usual, especially in France, to compose two dances to be performed in alternation: they would frequently be scored to provide contrasts, for example a minuet for strings in four or five parts would be followed by one for wind in three parts (hence the name 'trio' for this second dance). This practice led to the common 18th-century arrangement of minuet–trio–minuet (repeat of the first), as in Bach's first Brandenburg Concerto. In 18th- and 19th-century sonatas and symphonies the trio, which formed a part of the third movement (originally a minuet, later a scherzo), retained the lighter contrasting texture, in orchestral works often involving prominent woodwind. In late 19th-century orchestral works (e.g. the symphonies of Dvořák, Bruckner, and Mahler) trio sections are often in dance rhythms and styles. A trio section is normally followed by a repeat of the first part of the movement, usually modified in some way or with a coda. In some pieces (e.g. Beethoven's Seventh Symphony) the trio section may be briefly recapitulated.

The central section of a march is also known as a trio, on the same principle of contrast: it, too, is generally more melodious. The trio section of Elgar's *Pomp and Circumstance* march no. 1 in D contains the famous tune which was adapted to be sung as 'Land of Hope and Glory'.   WT

3. In organ music, a piece (or a section) to be played on manuals and pedals, each in a different registration.

Trionfi ('Triumphs'). Theatrical triptych by Orff comprising *Carmina burana*, *Catulli carmina*, and *Trionfo d'Afrodite* (Salzburg, 1953).

Trionfo di Afrodite ('Triumph of Aphrodite'). Scenic concerto by Orff, for soloists, chorus, and orchestra, a setting of Latin and Greek texts by Catullus, Sappho, and Euripides (Milan, 1953); it is the third part of his trilogy *Trionfi*.

trio sonata. A sonata for two melody instruments (usually violins) and continuo, the most important instrumental form in Baroque *chamber music. The earliest published examples are by Salamone Rossi (1607) and Giovanni Paolo Cima (1610). In the mid-17th century two types appeared, the *sonata da camera* and the *sonata da chiesa*. The form reached its peak with Corelli, who wrote examples of both in his opp. 1–4 (1681–94). See CHAMBER MUSIC; SONATA, 3.   AL

📖 P. ALLSOP, *The Italian 'Trio' Sonata* (Oxford, 1992)

trip-hop. A style of dance-oriented popular music, dating from about 1994. It derived partly from hip-hop but was usually at a slower tempo, showing *techno and jazz influence and often keyboard-based. In 1995 Tricky, Massive Attack, and Portishead associated the term with more songlike music. Later, trip-hop often incorporated riffs, in a minor key, and used rappers and singers. KG

triple concerto. A concerto for three solo instruments and orchestra or other instrumental ensemble. Bach wrote two triple concertos for three harpsichords and strings, but probably the best-known example is Beethoven's Concerto in C op. 56, for piano, violin, and cello with orchestra.

triple counterpoint. See INVERTIBLE COUNTERPOINT.

triplet. Three notes that are to be performed in the time of two; they are indicated by the figure '3' placed above or below the three notes (see Ex. 1).

Ex. 1

triple time. See TIME SIGNATURE.

triple tonguing. See TONGUING.

triplum (Lat.). 1. In three parts; used in medieval polyphony to describe a composition for three voices, e.g. *organum triplum.*

2. In 13th- and 14th-century polyphony, the 'third' voice part in organum or a motet, that is, the voice immediately above the *duplum and next but one above the tenor. In later music the equivalent voice was termed 'cantus', 'superius', or similar. The term 'triplex' is also found. See also PART, 1.

triptych. See TRITTICO.

Trisagion [Trishagion] (from Gk. *tris*, 'thrice', *hagios*, 'holy'). A hymn encountered frequently in the services of Eastern Christian churches. It was formerly a stational chant of the Constantinopolitan cathedral rite, but it is sung in musical settings in the Byzantine rite: as a processional for funerals, at the conclusion of the Great Doxology at Orthros, and at the Divine Liturgy, where it is replaced on certain solemnities by one of two special chants. The Trisagion and its festal alternatives were variously adopted by the Gallican, Mozarabic, Beneventan, Ambrosian, and Roman rites. Sung in traditional Roman usage as part of the *Improperia on Good Friday, the Trisagion has recently been reintroduced into other Western liturgies.

—/ALı

Tristan chord. The chord *f–b–d♯–g♯*, or an enharmonic spelling of it. Wagner was certainly not the first composer to give expressive and structural prominence to the type of *half-diminished 7th chord whose tonal identity tends to be especially ambiguous. But his startling placement of it as the first chord heard in the Prelude to Act I of *Tristan und Isolde* (completed in 1859), and the evident symbolic import he attached to it, have encouraged later commentators to assign a special significance to the chord as the first and most decisive step on the road to the genuinely new—and often antitonal—music of the 20th century. There is a misconception here, since Wagner's practice was rather to use such unstable sonorities to enhance the music's eventual arrival at points of tonal clarity and consonant harmonic stability. AW

Tristan und Isolde ('Tristan and Isolda'). Opera in three acts by Wagner to his own libretto (Munich, 1865).

triste (Fr., It.). 'Sad'; *tristement, tristamente*, 'sadly'.

tritone (Lat.: *tritonus*). An interval of three whole tones, i.e. the augmented 4th (C–F♯) or diminished 5th (C–G♭). In the early medieval period the tritone required no special treatment: it occurs in some plainchant melodies, and the Lydian and Hypolydian modes span an augmented 4th with their first four notes (F–B). It seems first to have been designated a 'dangerous' interval when Guido of Arezzo developed his system of hexachords, and with the introduction of B♭ as a diatonic note (see SOLMIZATION), at much the same time acquiring its nickname of 'diabolus in musica' ('the devil in music'). However, as the rhyme 'mi contra fa/ Diabolus est in musica' indicates (it is the sound of *mi* against *fa*, not juxtaposed with it, that is forbidden), the tritone was considered dangerous only in a vertical sense; melodically it continued to be used fairly freely (see MUSICA FICTA).

In traditional harmonic thinking the tritone forms a part of both the diminished and the dominant 7th; it is therefore important in the first instance for weakening the tonality of a passage and thus assisting modulation, and in the second for affirming the tonality, particularly at cadences. The tritone has continued to be associated with evil, especially in Romantic opera (Hunding in the *Ring*, Scarpia in *Tosca*). On the other hand, its prominence in the whole-tone and *octatonic scales, and in other modes used by many 20th-century composers from Debussy and Stravinsky onwards, has ensured that in certain contexts its presence can denote a desirable element of stability. —/AW

trittico (It., 'triptych'). A title sometimes given to a set of three pieces. It may embody a reference to the visual arts (e.g. Respighi's *Trittico botticelliano*, 1927) or merely serve as a general title for three linked works, as in the case of Puccini's Il **trittico*.

Trittico, Il ('The Triptych'). The collective title Puccini gave his three one-act operas Il **tabarro*, **Suor Angelica*, and **Gianni Schicchi*; they are not connected in subject matter, unlike the component parts of a **trilogy*, but were intended to be performed together as one evening's entertainment.

tritus. See MODE, 2.

Triumphes of Oriana, The. A collection of 25 English madrigals for five and six voices by Morley, Weelkes, and 21 others, published by Morley in 1601. It is assumed to be in praise of Elizabeth I, each piece ending with the line 'Long live fair Oriana', a feature modelled on the Italian collection *Il trionfo di Dori* (1592).

Triumph of Time, The. Orchestral work (1971–2) by Birtwistle.

trobairitz. A female **troubadour*.

trochee. A poetic foot of two syllables, strong–weak. The adjective is 'trochaic'. For its equivalent in the rhythmic modes, see NOTATION, 2.

Troilus and Cressida. Opera in three acts by Walton to a libretto by Christopher Hassall after Geoffrey Chaucer and other sources (but not Shakespeare) (London, 1954); it was revised in 1963 and again in 1976.

Trois morceaux en forme de poire ('Three Pear-Shaped Pieces'). Work for piano duet (1890–1903) by Satie, a set of six (*sic*) pieces; they were orchestrated by Roger Desormière.

Trojahn, Manfred (*b* Cremlingen, nr Brunswick, 22 Oct. 1949). German composer. He studied in Brunswick, and with Diether de la Motte in Hamburg; in 1991 he began to teach composition in Düsseldorf. His music, intended to communicate directly to the sympathetic listener, includes two large-scale cycles: *Fünf See-Bilder* for mezzo-soprano and orchestra (1980–4) and *. . . une campagne noire de soleil*, 'seven ballet scenes for ensemble' (1982–7). He has also written two operas, *Enrico* (Schwetzingen, 1991) and *Was ihr wollt* (Munich, 1998, after Shakespeare's *Twelfth Night*), as well as symphonies and other orchestral works, vocal and choral music, and many chamber and instrumental pieces.   ABur

Trojans, The. See TROYENS, LES.

tromba marina (It.). 'Trumpet marine'.

Tromboncino, Bartolomeo (*b* ?Verona, 1470; *d* ?Venice, after 1534). Italian court musician and com-

poser. The son of a Veronese municipal wind player, he was trained to play the trombone, and by 1489 had entered the service of the Gonzaga court at Mantua as a member of the wind ensemble. He became lutenist and music tutor to Isabella d'Este, and was much in demand as a composer of frottolas. His next appointment was to Lucrezia Borgia in Ferrara. After 1518 he lived in Venice, teaching music to gentlewomen. Like his Mantuan colleague Marchetto Cara, Tromboncino is famous today principally for his frottolas, many of which were printed by Petrucci; they include several Petrarch settings. He also wrote a small number of sacred pieces, mostly devotional *laude*.   DA/JM

trombone (It., 'large trumpet'; Fr.: *trombone*; Ger.: *Posaune*) [sackbut]. A brass instrument with a cup-shaped mouthpiece, a cylindrical bore for most of its length, and a characteristic telescopic slide with which the player varies the length of the tube to alter the pitch of the harmonic series.

> 1. Construction and slide positions; 2. History; 3. Soprano, bass, and contrabass trombones; 4. Valve trombones; 5. Use

1. Construction and slide positions

A trombone is taken apart in two pieces, the slide and the bell. The slide comprises two parallel stationary tubes (the 'inner slide') over which run the two moving tubes ('outer slide'); these are connected at the bottom by a U-bow (which has a water-key for releasing condensed moisture) and at the top by a cross-stay, which the player grasps with the right hand to move the slide. The mouthpiece is inserted into one end of the inner slide, and the bell joint is attached at the other, reaching back over the left shoulder to provide a counterbalance for the slide. After the U-bow of the bell joint, the bore becomes conical, flaring out widely at the forward-facing bell (this is less pronounced on early trombones).

With the slide closed (the 'first position') the B♭ tenor trombone gives the harmonic series of B♭. From this the slide is extended through chromatic positions until, at full extension (seventh position), the instrument gives the series of E, a diminished 5th below. At each position the harmonics most used are from the second (B♭ in first position) upwards, up to the 12th (f') sometimes being required, though at the lower positions the higher harmonics are required only as alternatives to avoid long shifts or in long glissandos. The fundamental of each series, or 'pedal note', is sometimes demanded (e.g. in Berlioz's *Grande Messe des morts*), giving B♭' down to E', but B up to E♭ are missing. As the positions are made by 'feel' and 'ear', the slide trombonist, like the violinist, possesses the power to adjust intonation to circumstance, for example to make brass chords perfectly pure and satisfying.

2. History

The trombone was developed in the mid-15th century from the S-shaped slide *trumpet of the Renaissance. The slide trumpet (Fr.: *trompette de ménestrel*; Ger.: *Zugtrompete*; It.: *tromba da tirarsi*) had a mouthpiece with a long telescopic stem, along which the player slid the whole body of the trumpet to alter its length and so obtain the harmonic series of additional fundamentals. The invention of the trombone's two-legged slide reduced the length of the necessary extensions by half. The new instrument, known as *trombone* in Italy and as sackbut or *sacqueboute* in England and France, was widely used with two shawms in the *alta* band (see ALTA, 3; see also below, 5). Since the Renaissance the trombone has altered less than any other instrument, merely widening the bell flare, thickening the metal of the tubing and soldering the supporting stays, and acquiring a water-release key. Friction was minimized by adding 'stockings' to the inner slide: short sleeves at the ends of the legs which provide a running surface for the outer slide; on early instruments these were of a different metal from that of the slide, but on modern instruments the stockings are formed integrally with the inner tubes.

3. Soprano, bass, and contrabass trombones

Trombones were traditionally used in three sizes, alto, tenor, and bass, from the 18th century in E♭, B♭, and F respectively, though in Britain the G bass was preferred to the F. In the 19th century the alto became rare, two tenors and a bass making up the normal trio. The soprano in B♭ has never been greatly successful; in the Renaissance the *cornett played the soprano line when trombones were used to support the voices in church. Cornetts and sackbuts were a favourite ensemble throughout the Renaissance.

The bass trombone has an inconveniently long slide, needing an extension handle to reach the longest positions. The F bass trombone died out in the early 20th century (the C bass survived in Britain until the 1950s and is still used in some brass bands), having been replaced by the 'B♭/F tenor-bass trombone'. This has a coil of tubing incorporated in the bell behind the player's head, an invention of a Leipzig maker, C. F. Sattler, in 1839. The coil is connected to the main tube by a rotary valve and converts the trombone into a bass in F. This instrument is built with a wider bore than the normal tenor trombone, to give it a fuller sound in the lower registers. The slide positions for the F tubing are longer than those of the B♭ trombone, and the slide is normally just too short for the sixth position (*C*), which

must be 'lipped' into tune; the seventh position (*B*) is entirely absent. Additional coils may be provided in the bell joint to lower the instrument to E, E♭ or D (first introduced in the USA). The instrument is then known as a B♭/F/E (B♭/F/E♭, or B♭/F/D) bass trombone.

Trombones came into the orchestra through the church, the military band, and the opera, where they were initially associated with the supernatural, though it was not until the mid-19th century that they had a regular place in the orchestra. Wagner, as always extending the orchestral range, demanded a contrabass trombone an octave below the tenor and provided with a double slide consisting of two parallel slides connected with two U-bows at the bottom and one at the top, most famously for Wotan's spear motif in the *Ring*. This too is a size that has been less successful than the others, for the bore is either too narrow for the best sound at the bottom or so wide that it sounds more like a tuba. An F contrabass designed in Germany in 1959, called the 'cimbasso', has two valves which lower the instrument to *D'* and *C'* respectively, and when operated together to *B♭''*.

4. Valve trombones

*Valves were applied to trombones as to all brass instruments, even though the trombone was fully chromatic from the beginning (and better in tune, because of the infinite variability of its slide, than any other brass instrument). The valve trombone suffers in tone-quality from the bends in the tubing inevitable with valves, and from the same intonation problems that all valved instruments have (see TUBA, 1), but has the advantage of compactness in such confined spaces as theatre pits, and can perform some techniques impossible on the slide trombone (e.g. certain trills). Valve trombones have been very popular in Italy, as a result of which there are some parts now in the standard international repertory that are more suited to valve technique than to the slide trombone.

5. Use

One of the most versatile of instruments, capable of sounding loud and brassy or soft and sweet, and of both bold stolidity and great agility, the trombone is one of the few brass instruments that can find a home in almost any musical situation. In the Renaissance it and the cornett were the only instruments that could play in both loud and soft ensembles (with shawms and drums on the one hand, and with viols and lutes on the other). In the 19th-century orchestra it was mainly used to reinforce tutti passages or for soft background harmonies. The vast array of techniques explored in the 20th century, the lead often taken by jazz musicians, included a wide variety of glissandos, multiphonics, microtones, expressive attacks, and mutes.

AB, JMo

📖 R. GREGORY, *The Trombone: The Instrument and its Music* (London, 1973) · A. BAINES, *Brass Instruments: Their History and Development* (London, 1976) · S. DEMPSTER, *The Modern Trombone* (Berkeley, CA, 1979) · H. G. FISCHER, *The Renaissance Sackbut and its Use Today* (New York, 1984) · D. M. GUION, *The Trombone: Its History and Music, 1697–1811* (New York, 1988) · K. POLK, 'The trombone, the slide trumpet and the ensemble tradition of the early Renaissance', *Early Music*, 17 (1989), 389–97 · T. HERBERT and J. WALLACE (eds.), *The Cambridge Companion to Brass Instruments* (Cambridge, 1997)

trop (Fr.). 'Too much'.

trope (Lat.: *tropus*, from Gk. *tropos*, 'turn (of phrase)'). Used by rhetoricians to denote a figure of speech, the word was also used by ancient and medieval music theorists to mean 'octave species' (see MODE, 3). But its more important musical meaning was a textual or musical addition (or both) to plainchant. The production of tropes was spectacularly large, particularly from the 10th to the 12th century. There were three basic types, all of which probably originated in the third quarter of the 9th century.

Supplementary phrases were provided for three of the Proper chants of the Mass (the introit, offertory, and communion) and for the Kyrie, Gloria, Sanctus, and Agnus Dei chants from the Ordinary. Some examples of tropes for Lessons are also known. Most common of all these were introit tropes. The technique for the Proper chants was to introduce phrases elucidating the significance of the main text. Ex. 1 gives the opening of a Christmas introit trope. In the following translation of the full text, the main text (sung by the choir) is shown in small capitals, the troped text (sung by the soloist) in upper and lower case:

> God the Father sent his Son into the world today, wherefore rejoicing let us sing with the prophet: UNTO US A CHILD IS BORN, UNTO US A SON IS GIVEN, who shall sit upon the throne of David and shall reign for ever, AND THE GOVERNMENT SHALL BE UPON HIS SHOULDER. Behold there comes God and man from the house of David to sit upon the throne, AND HIS NAME SHALL BE CALLED—he whom the seer foretold—ANGEL OF MIGHTY COUNSEL.

Mass Ordinary texts could be made 'Proper' by means of tropes. One Gloria trope, *Spiritus et alme* for the Blessed Virgin Mary (composed probably in Normandy, late 11th century), remained popular throughout the Middle Ages, even being set in polyphony.

The text added to melismas (one syllable to each note) was often called *prosa* or *prosula*. This happened to

Ex. 1

the alleluia, to the melismas of offertory verses and Office responsories, and also to the 'Hosanna' of some Sanctus chants. The usual technique was to 'gloss' the text of the main chant, if possible referring to the theme of the festival day.

It has been the traditional belief that many melismatic Kyries were given tropic Latin texts in this way. But since the earliest manuscripts (10th century) already have the Latin texts, these Kyries may have been so conceived from the beginning, as special festal compositions in their own right. Such texted Kyries were set polyphonically, especially in England, up to the late 15th century.

A handful of early manuscripts show melismatic extensions of introit phrases (see the bracketed phrases in Ex. 1). Others are evidence of a rather limited fashion for *responsory melismas. Some of these melismas were then texted as in type 2 above.

Very few of these additions to the main corpus of Gregorian chant remained in use after the 12th century. Some other additions have also been called tropes by modern scholars: sequences (see SEQUENCE, 2); 'Benedicamus' songs (see CONDUCTUS); and organum, sometimes regarded as a sort of 'vertical troping' of plainchant. DH/ALi

troppo (It.). 'Too much'; *allegro ma non troppo*, 'quick but not too quick'.

trotto. A type of medieval dance. It is mentioned in a treatise as being in duple time and similar to the *saltarello; only one extant example is known (in the manuscript British Library, Add. 29987). JBe

troubadours (Fr.). Poet-musicians, often of noble birth, of 12th- and 13th-century Occitania (principally southern France and north-east Spain). The written legacy of the troubadours is one of the earliest substantial literatures of western Europe, and is therefore of considerable cultural and literary importance. To the troubadours themselves, poetry was inextricably linked with music, since it was through performance in song, not in writing, that their compositions were communicated. Only towards the end of the tradition, however, were any of the songs written down with musical notation, and for that reason the musical remains of the troubadours are tantalizingly insubstantial and sometimes of questionable authority. Troubadour song, and the ideas and values that underpin it, served as the starting-point for the songs of the *trouvères (whose manuscripts are important sources of information about the troubadours and their art) and the *Minnesinger.

Linguistically, troubadour poetry is expressed in the 'langue d'oc' (Occitan), a relative of present-day Provençal. Its subject matter, though broad, is dominated by one theme: the idea of 'courtly' or idealized love. As literature, troubadour verse has long been felt to transcend its historical origins and to address universal issues; certainly it has long appealed to readers for its romance (and romanticism), and seemed relevant to those who know or care little about the functions it served in its medieval context. Troubadour song is, however, the product of a culture very different from our own, and the poetry's original sense can be released only in relation to Occitan society, the concepts of knighthood and feudalism that underpin it, and an understanding of the place and status of women within the system.

Archival information about the troubadours themselves (and their less numerous female counterparts, the *trobairitz*) is scant, and only limited trust can be placed in the *vidas*, idealized stories of their lives that hover between fiction and biography. Many troubadours, such as Guillaume IX of Aquitaine and Jaufre Rudel, were high-ranking members of society; others, including Marcabru and Bernart de Ventadorn, rose up the social ladder through their art, sometimes even from the rank of *joglar* (a professional and often itinerant performer).

The classic location for the performance of troubadour song is the hall of a castle. Contemporary accounts make it plain that singing was frequently accompanied by instruments, and that *joglars* might accompany or perform alongside the troubadours themselves.

Of the approximately 2500 troubadour poems that survive, barely one in ten is provided with notated music, and even then principally in manuscripts made by the trouvères. The melodies often seem formulaic and interrelated; some presumably derive from older archetypes for which no notation survives; some may even be popular tunes. The notation itself is minimal; only the pitches of the melody are given, without rhythm, or any indication of the way that instruments were used—a major omission, since plucked instruments such as the harp are unlikely merely to have doubled the melody in unison. That being said, the oral tradition within which troubadour song was devised and transmitted probably encouraged constant re-invention, and it is hard to believe that either melodies or accompaniments were immutably fixed. Performers and scholars have for decades debated how best to revive troubadour song in sound, and many reconstructions exist on record. All, however, are full of guesswork, and all are probably misleading. JM

📖 E. AUBREY, *The Music of the Troubadours* (Bloomington, IN, 1997) · S. GAUNT and S. KAY (eds.), *The Troubadours: An Introduction* (Cambridge, 1999)

Trout, The. See FORELLE, DIE.

'Trout' Quintet. Nickname of Schubert's Piano Quintet in A major D667 (1819), so called because the fourth of its five movements, an Andantino, is a set of variations on the melody of his song Die *Forelle ('The Trout').

trouvères (Fr.). Poet-musicians of late 12th- and 13th-century northern France, successors to the *troubadours, and linguistically defined by the use of non-standardized forms of northern French (the 'langue d'oil'). Like the troubadours, whose art they admired and extended, the trouvères were principally non-literate composers and performers who invented and transmitted songs within an oral tradition. Many of their songs, however, were collected in manuscripts by professional scribes, presumably for the benefit of patrons or collectors, and a few late trouvères may even have written down their own works. Music notation is often provided in these copies. For those reasons, the repertory of trouvère song survives reasonably intact, certainly when compared with the scant musical remains of the troubadours.

Like their southern precursors, trouvères could be of royal or noble birth, or rise up from the ranks of minstrelsy; the two extremes are represented by Thibaut IV de Champagne, King of Navarre, and by Colin Muset, who was a *jongleur by profession. In addition, a tight community of trouvères emerged in the region of Arras, and within that partially urban context organized groups began to cultivate the art of courtly song. Trouvère song can therefore be associated with a variety of performance situations, of which the classic location associated with the troubadours—the hall of a nobleman's castle—was only one. Jongleurs seem often to have participated in performances.

Although a wide range of subject matter occurs in trouvère song, the repertory is dominated by the theme of idealized love. (Other favourite topics include the Crusades, and religious belief.) Poetical genres and forms tend to be highly conventionalized. Some, including the chanson d'amour and *jeu-parti (debate song), evoke the elegance, eloquence and wit of courtly exchange. Others, such as the chanson de toile (weaving-song) and the pastourelle, hint at popular traditions of song. Cross-reference between songs underpins the entire repertory; some songs additionally make use of *refrains—musico-literary tags of uncertain origin, many of which also occur in 13th-century *motets.

More than 2000 trouvère songs survive, a greater proportion of them with music notation than is the case with the troubadours. Various obstacles, however, stand in the way of their revival in sound. First, songs that occur in more than one manuscript source often do so in highly variant states that suggest they were written down from memory or by dictation, not copied from other manuscripts. These transcriptions therefore only momentarily fix a song that was in fact fluid and mutable within the oral process of transmission, and may be far removed from the melody as originally devised by the composer. Secondly, until very late in the tradition, notation records only the pitches of melodies, not their rhythms; opinions remain sharply divided about the correct rhythmic interpretation of trouvère song. Thirdly, instruments participated in performances, but the manuscripts indicate neither what they should be, nor what they should play, leaving the whole subject of accompaniment open to conjecture. For those reasons, all modern performance of trouvère song are fundamentally speculative in nature. JM

Trovatore, Il ('The Troubadour'). Opera in four parts by Verdi to a libretto by Salvadore Cammarano (and Leone Emanuele Bardare) after Antonio García Gutiérrez's play El trovador (1836) (Rome, 1853); it includes the famous Gypsies' 'Anvil Chorus'.

Troyens, Les ('The Trojans'). Opera in five acts by Berlioz to his own libretto after Virgil's Aeneid; it was composed between 1856 and 1858. In order to get it

performed (it was extremely long), Berlioz divided it into two parts, the first called La Prise de Troie (Acts I–II), the second Les Troyens à Carthage (Acts III–V); the latter was first performed in Paris in 1863, and the opera was first given complete in Karlsruhe in 1890.

trump. See jew's harp.

trumpet. 1. A general term for lip-vibrated ('brass') instruments, interchangeable with 'horn'. Some attempts have been made to label as trumpets those instruments with a predominantly cylindrical bore, and as horns those with a conical bore, but such a distinction fails: although it could be made for natural trumpets and horns in Europe, modern orchestral trumpets have a greater proportion of conical tubing than horns, and non-Western lip-vibrated instruments do not fall so neatly into such categories.

2. (Fr.: trompette; Ger.: Trompete; It.: tromba). An instrument blown through vibrating lips. Trumpets are often referred to as brass instruments, but they can be made of any convenient material, from seashells (*conches), animal horns, ivory, and wood (e.g. *cornett, *serpent, *alphorn, or *didjeridu), to glass, ceramics, or even plastics; metal, however, is the most common across the world. The Western trumpet is built in the traditional shape of one long loop. Fig. 1a illustrates the format of a natural trumpet, with three parallel 'branches': (1) mouthpipe, (2) lower branch, and (3) bell, connected by two 'bows'. A crook (C) is inserted into the mouthpipe. Fig. 1b shows a modern trumpet, with the three valves mounted on the lower branch. The outer bow (right) incorporates the main tuning-slide; the near bow (left) is formed integrally with the bell. The modern mouthpipe generally embodies a small taper back to the mouthpiece socket. The tuning-slide of the third valve (third finger, right hand) usually carries a ring by which the left hand can extend the slide while playing, to take the onus off the lips in correcting the sharpness of such notes as the low D. Less common is a corresponding device for the first valve in the form of a thumb lever called a 'trigger'.

The earliest trumpets of which records survive are those depicted in Egyptian art of the 15th century BC. Two trumpets found in the tomb of Tutankhamun (14th century), one of bronze and the other of silver, are in the Egyptian Museum, Cairo. Similar instruments are described in the Bible (Numbers 10: 2ff.), as is the ram's horn *shofar. The Danish *lur was in use from the 10th century BC to the 8th; and the Roman *lituus, *bucina, and *cornu, and the Celtic carnyx, date from some centuries later.

The long, straight, medieval European trumpet was sometimes called in French *buysine, and may have been adopted by the Crusaders from their Muslim foes in the

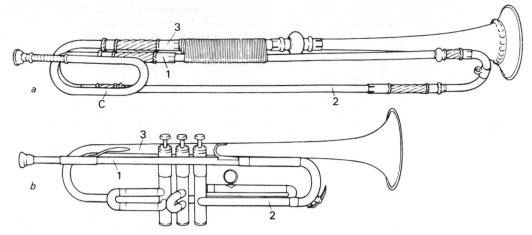

Fig. 1.

Holy Land. Similar instruments, over 2 metres long, are still in use in Morocco (*nafîr*) and Islamic Nigeria (*kakaki*). By the 15th century European makers had rendered *buysines* more portable by introducing two U-bends (at first arranged in an S-shape rather than in the more characteristic loop), creating the ancestor of the Renaissance and Baroque trumpet still used for fanfares and military signals.

This was the original use for the trumpet in Europe, and elsewhere also. A few late 16th- and early 17th-century instruction manuscripts have survived with military calls, short fanfares (It.: *toccata*, whence *tucket), and longer flourishes (It.: *sonata*, whence *sennet) written out. As players devised increasingly elaborate signals, extending the range from one or two hoarse notes into the higher reaches of the harmonic series, where from the eighth harmonic upwards a diatonic scale is possible, the trumpet gradually became useful for music as well as for signalling. During the 16th century its form was becoming standardized, and by the time Monteverdi was writing his opera *L'Orfeo* in 1607 it could play a fully melodic role, using only the dexterity of the player's lips on a 'natural' trumpet: a brass or silver tube with no valve or slide mechanism, no fingerholes, or any other artificial aids. This skill, fostered by long and arduous apprenticeship, reached its peak in early 18th-century Germany, with the music of Bach and his contemporaries.

In the 17th and 18th centuries the standard pitch settled at D or E♭ in Germany and England, and short lengths of tubing (crooks) could be added to play in lower keys. By the end of the 18th century, the orchestral idiom—though still giving rise to some of the most difficult high writing (reaching the 24th harmonic in Michael Haydn's Clarino Concerto in D)—no longer required the clarino register, and trumpets came to serve in the more restricted and formal way of the Classical period. By the early 19th century the trumpet was shortened to the key of F (G in France), with crooks for E, E♭, D, C, and low B♭, the last taking it to the same length as the tenor trombone, as in the famous offstage call in Beethoven's overture *Leonore* no. 3.

Slide trumpets were reinvented in the 1790s by John Hyde in England. (The medieval slide trumpet, with its long mouthpiece stem sliding within the first section of tubing, had given way to the sackbut by about 1500; see TROMBONE, 2.) Whether this followed any memory of the *flat trumpet used in Purcell's time is unknown, though the principle is similar, both types having a slide on the bend of tubing nearest the player's chin. The slide trumpet remained the standard English orchestral instrument up to the late 19th century.

The keyed trumpet was invented by Anton Weidinger in Vienna, also in the 1790s, and it was this instrument for which Haydn and Hummel wrote their trumpet concertos. It had four or five leather-padded keys, opened with the fingers, which made the instrument chromatic from written middle C upwards. Some players adopted hand-stopping from the horn, and enough half-moon trumpets, curved as if to bring the bell within reach of the hand, survive to show that the practice was not uncommon around 1800, even though it detracts from the bright, ringing sound of the natural trumpet.

The ultimate solution to the problem of creating a fully chromatic trumpet came with the widespread adoption of *valves from the 1820s onwards. The valved F trumpet was commonly used as an alternative to the English slide trumpet, and as the B♭ *cornet (invented just before 1830), with its shorter tubing and greater agility, became widely adopted as an orchestral instrument (especially in France and the USA), so the trumpet also began to be built in that key. The B♭ trumpet became the standard instrument before the end of the 19th century, and it is the trumpet played in jazz, in military bands (in which it now often replaces the cornet), and in the orchestra, though here there is increasing preference for the smaller C trumpet, following the French orchestral tradition.

The use of small, high-pitched trumpets has advantages in playing trumpet parts by Bach and Handel, many of which are in the key of D. Performance of Handel's music had never ceased, especially in Britain where specialist players continued to use the slide trumpet crooked down to D; but the revival of Bach's music, in which the parts lie rather higher than in Handel's, brought problems. This led to the adoption first of the valved trumpet in A, then of the piccolo trumpet in D, half the length of the Baroque natural trumpet in D. These have largely been replaced in turn by piccolo trumpets in E♭ and in high B♭, an octave above the normal B♭ instrument and two octaves above the instrument required by Beethoven in *Leonore* no. 3. The high B♭ trumpet is made in a wide variety of shapes, and often with four valves to extend the compass down to *d'*.

While it is somewhat easier to play the high-lying parts of the Baroque period, and of some modern composers, on these piccolo trumpets, the reason for their adoption is not that the techniques for playing the high registers have been lost: notes as high as any written by Bach are frequently reached by jazz musicians on normal B♭ trumpets. But players in Bach's time specialized in particular registers, whereas modern trumpeters are expected to play in them all; the B♭ instrument was designed to secure a rich, flexible sound over the main compass down to the low notes rather than being suitable for playing in the higher registers. Where the shorter instruments score is in security: the higher harmonics lie very close together, a semitone apart or even less, and it is all too easy to hit the wrong one. In the concert hall and the recording studio the utmost accuracy is required; with a shorter tube, the same pitches are produced as lower numbers of the harmonic series, where the intervals between harmonics are greater. Each harmonic is thus easier to play, and the intervening notes can be produced by means of the valves.

Among the less common types of trumpet is the bass trumpet, which Wagner designed for the *Ring*; it was made first in F and later with four valves in 8′ C with crooks for B♭ and A, and is normally played by a trombonist. Ceremonial occasions are often graced with fanfares, sometimes played on natural trumpets as in former times, but often now on valved trumpets built with mostly straight tubing in order to look impressive

and to carry the traditional embroidered banners. In the 20th century a revival of the natural trumpet took place. A new design of the 1960s had two vent holes and a transposing hole in the tubing that correct the intonation of some of the partials and improve accuracy. In North America the infantry *bugle (field trumpet) is actually a trumpet, often with a single valve to obtain a second harmonic series, a practice derived from the Italian trumpets of the Bersaglieri.   AB, JMo

📖 D. L. SMITHERS, *The Music and History of the Baroque Trumpet before 1721* (London, 1973, 2/1988) · A. BAINES, *Brass Instruments: Their History and Development* (London, 1976) · R. MEUCCI, 'Roman military instruments and the *lituus*', *Galpin Society Journal*, 42 (1989), 85–97 · K. POLK, 'The trombone, the slide trumpet and the ensemble tradition of the early Renaissance', *Early Music*, 17 (1989), 389–97 · D. L. SMITHERS, 'A new look at the historical, linguistic and taxonomic bases for the evolution of lip-blown instruments from classical antiquity until the end of the Middle Ages', *Historical Brass Society Journal*, 1 (1989), 3–64 · R. L. BARCLAY, *The Art of the Trumpet-Maker: The Materials, Tools, and Techniques of the Seventeenth and Eighteenth Centuries in Nuremberg* (Oxford, 1992) · E. H. TARR, 'The Romantic trumpet', *Historical Brass Society Journal*, 5 (1993), 213–61, and 6 (1994), 110–215 · T. HERBERT and J. WALLACE (eds.), *The Cambridge Companion to Brass Instruments* (Cambridge, 1997).

trumpet marine (Fr.: *trompette marine*; Ger.: *Trumscheit, Nonnengeige, Marien Trompet*; It.: *tromba marina*). A bowed *monochord with a long triangular soundbox and a short neck, in use from the 15th century to the 18th. It was bowed above the stopping hand, which would touch the string lightly at the points that would produce the pitches of the harmonic series. The bridge was designed so that one leg would buzz against the belly, making the sound resemble that of a distant trumpet (It.: *tromba*). Some instruments had a second or third shorter string to sound a drone. Later instruments were sometimes given *sympathetic strings.   JMo

t.s. Abbreviation for *tasto solo* (see TASTO, 1).

tuba. 1. The largest and lowest-pitched of all the brass instruments, termed 'bass' in brass and military bands. In the orchestra the player sits with the three trombones. The instrument varies a great deal round the world: in Britain and France the valves are ordinary upright piston valves, whereas in the USA a frequent alternative is to mount the piston valves obliquely or at right angles to the main tubing, or to use rotary valves as on the German instruments.

Pitch also varies with the different types. For bands the instrument is built in two sizes: E♭ and low B♭, the latter also called 'double B♭' (or 'BB♭'). For the orchestra

F and low C ('CC') instruments are often used, but the choice goes largely by country. In Britain the E♭ tuba is used, but with a bell of the same width as that of the BB♭ to produce a fuller sound; in the USA and Italy the deeper pitches, BB♭ or CC, are preferred; and Germany retains the first historical pitch of F, with deeper tubas mainly reserved for such special duties as the contrabass tuba part in the *Ring*. In France the orchestral tuba has always been quite different. It is in C, a tone above the *euphonium, and reaches the lowest notes with the aid of six pistons; its upward range is much greater than that of the larger tubas. High-lying parts written for the French C tuba, such as in Ravel's orchestration of Musorgsky's *Pictures at an Exhibition*, are therefore often played outside France on a euphonium. Where composers ask for tenor tuba, as in Stravinsky's *The Rite of Spring* and Holst's *The Planets*, the euphonium is normally used, though it is possible that in Germany and Austria the *Wagner tuba is meant, for example in Strauss's *Don Quixote*.

Modern orchestral tubas have at least four *valves, the fourth lowering the instrument by a perfect 4th in order to give a continuous range in the lowest octave. But the problems of sharpness inherent in the valve system become acute in many combinations with the fourth valve. The player can adjust the tuning-slides and lip some of the notes into tune, but more satisfactory results are achieved through use of the many modifications to the valve system devised by makers. Some tubas have five or six valves, offering useful alternative fingerings. In Britain, especially on band basses and the euphonium, David Blaikley's 'compensating pistons' (1874) are used. Here the loop of the fourth valve, which lowers the instrument by a 4th, sends the air back through the three main valves to pass through small 'incremental' loops; these automatically supply the extra length needed to compensate for the effect of the fourth valve on the overall length of the instrument.

The first valved bass brasses, made in Germany and Austria in the late 1820s mostly with the name 'bombardon', were built in 12′ F, generally following the shape of the *ophicleide but with three valves. In 1835 the name 'tuba' in the modern sense made its appearance, with the *Bass-Tuba* in F of the Prussian bandmaster Wilhelm Wieprecht and the instrument maker J. G. Moritz. It had five valves, giving well-tuned notes down to low G. Adolphe Sax knew of this instrument when developing the E♭ bass of his *saxhorn family of 1845, from which the British tuba ultimately derives. At about the same time the first BB♭ tuba appeared in Austria, followed in 1849 by the 'helicon', a circular instrument placed over the head and passing under the player's right arm to rest on the left shoulder,

the bell pointing more or less forwards level with the head; it was used in many military bands into the early 20th century. It was from the helicon that Conn in the USA devised the sousaphone (1898) for the American bandmaster John Philip Sousa. At first it was built with the widely flaring bell pointing straight upwards (giving rise to its nickname 'rain-catcher'), but later the bell was pointed forwards above the player's head.

2. The straight military trumpet of the Romans. The 'Tuba mirum' passage in the text of the Requiem Mass usually invites some exuberant brass writing, most impressively of all in Berlioz's *Grande Messe des morts*.

JMo

📖 D. CHARLTON, 'New sounds for old: Tam-tam, tuba curva, buccin', *Soundings*, 3 (1973), 39–47 · C. BEVAN, *The Tuba Family* (London, 1978) · R. W. MORRIS and E. R. GOLDSTEIN (eds.), *The Tuba Source Book* (Bloomington, IN, 1996) · T. HERBERT and J. WALLACE (eds.), *The Cambridge Companion to Brass Instruments* (Cambridge, 1997)

Tubin, Eduard (*b* Kallaste, 18 June 1905; *d* Stockholm, 17 Nov. 1982). Estonian composer. After training as a teacher (1920–6) he studied with Eller at the Tartu Conservatory (1924–6). He then taught in Nõ before moving back to Tartu in 1930, where he became a conductor at the Vanemuine Theatre; he also conducted a number of choirs, in both Tartu and Tallinn. When the Soviet army invaded Estonia, Tubin, like thousands of his compatriots, fled to Sweden; in Stockholm he worked at the Royal Drottningholm Court Theatre and was again active as a choral conductor. He revisited his native country several times before his death.

The backbone of Tubin's output is a series of ten symphonies (written between 1931 and 1973; an 11th was unfinished when he died) with stylistic origins in the music of Sibelius and Prokofiev; they are predominantly tragic in tone and dramatic in manner, infused with march rhythms and, as the series progresses, becoming more harmonically oblique. Inspired by Bartók and Kodály, he also introduced elements of Estonian folk music into some of his scores, not least the *Estonian Dance Suite* (1938) and the *Sinfonietta on Estonian Motifs* (1940). He wrote three works for the stage—the ballet *Kratt* (1939–41) and two operas, *Barbara von Tisenhusen* (1968) and *Reigi opetaja* ('The Priest of Reigi', 1971)—and much piano and chamber music. A series of recordings, beginning in the 1980s, rescued his music from the relative obscurity into which it had fallen.

MA

tubular bells [orchestral chimes] (Fr.: *cloches, cloches tubulaires*; Ger.: *Röhrenglocken*; It.: *campanelli, campanelli tubolari*). A set of tuned steel tubes, originally designed (in the 1880s) as substitutes for church bells, which are too heavy for concert platforms, but today accepted as a tuned percussion instrument in its own right. Fully chromatic sets with a range of up to two octaves are now standard. The tubes are struck on the edge of the closed upper end with rawhide or plastic hammers; the layout on the stand is like that of a piano keyboard, the 'black' notes hanging behind and slightly above the 'white'. JMo

tucket. A term mostly found in stage directions from the late 16th century and the 17th, and particularly in the works of Shakespeare and his contemporaries. The word appears to be an anglicization of *toccata (though its origins may go back further), and describes a flourish of trumpets or drums. See also SENNET; TRUMPET, 2.

Tudway, Thomas (*b* ? Windsor, *c*.1655; *d* Cambridge, 23 Nov. 1726). English composer and organist. He was a chorister at the Chapel Royal until 1668, becoming organist at King's College, Cambridge, in 1670 and rising to professor in the university by 1705. Many of his anthems were written for state or special occasions. His collection of six manuscript volumes of church music, copied for Lord Harley and now in the British Library, is invaluable. AA

Tunder, Franz (*b* Bannesdorf, nr Burg, Fehmarn, 1614; *d* Lübeck, 5 Nov. 1667). German composer. He began his career as organist to the Schleswig court and in 1621 was appointed organist to the Marienkirche in Lübeck. He is chiefly remembered as the founder of the series of *Abendmusiken* (evening concerts comprising a mixture of sacred vocal and organ music), which was later taken over by Buxtehude.

Only 17 of Tunder's vocal works survive: they include solo motets—some in the Italian style, others (e.g. *Ein kleines Kinderlein*) based on German songs—and early examples of the kind of chorale cantata later developed by Bach (e.g. *Wachet auf, An Wasserflüssen Babylons, Ein' feste Burg*). Notable among his organ music are four ground-breaking preludes—the first examples in north Germany of the prelude in three parts (toccata–fugue–prelude)—and seven chorale fantasias in antiphonal style. His importance lies in his contribution to the various types of Lutheran church music later cultivated by Bach. WT

tuning. The process of regulating the pitch of an instrument. On stringed instruments the tension of each string is adjusted by the turning of pegs or wrest pins until it is at its specified pitch. On keyboard instruments *c'* is tuned first, to a tuning-fork or other device, then *g* is tuned to *c'* with attention to the beats between the two notes: the slower their beat-rate the more nearly they are in tune. Next *d'*, *a*, and so on are tuned in an alternating sequence of perfect 4ths and

perfect 5ths until the middle octave is complete (sometimes 3rds and major 6ths are used for particular reasons). Tuning is then extended to the rest of the octaves and finally to other ranks of strings or pipes. Because of the need for *temperament, there are always some beats between notes.

Wind instruments are tuned by adjustment to the length of tubing, using the tuning-slide on a brass instrument, the staple of the reed on an oboe, or the movable top joint of a flute, etc. With woodwinds, the tuning of individual notes is established by the position and diameter of each fingerhole. On both woodwinds and brass, tuning can be further controlled with fingering techniques and by variations in embouchure: the air pressure, the angle of blowing on flutes, the lip pressure on a reed, or the lip tension and mouth shape in a brass mouthpiece. On the horn, tuning can also be controlled by moving the hand in the bell. Skin percussion instruments are tuned by adjustment to the tension of the heads. JMo

📖 W. A. SETHARES, *Tuning, Timbre, Spectrum, Scale* (London, 1998)

tuning-fork. A two-pronged device of tempered steel, invented *c*.1711 by John Shore, Handel's trumpeter, to produce a fixed pitch to which instruments may be tuned. Properly made, a tuning-fork suffers negligible change of pitch with age or temperature variation. Forks are made to standard musical or scientific pitches. They are sounded by striking the fork so that it vibrates; holding the stem against a wooden surface causes the surface to vibrate in sympathy as a soundboard, amplifying the sound. Musical instruments have been made with sets of tuning-forks sounded by bowing, striking with hammers, or by electromagnets.

Antique tuning-forks of established provenance provide important evidence of historic pitches at different times and places, e.g. Pascal Taskin's in Paris ($a' = 409$ Hz) or Handel's in London ($a' = 422.5$). JMo

tuning-pins. See WREST PINS.

tuning-slide. A length of tubing, usually straight on woodwind instruments and U-shaped on brass, that can be moved telescopically within the main tubing to alter the tube length and thus its pitch.

Turandot. 1. Opera in three acts by Puccini to a libretto by Giuseppe Adami and Renato Simoni after Carlo Gozzi's dramatic fairy tale (1762) (Milan, 1926); it was completed by Alfano.

2. Opera in two acts by Busoni to his own libretto after Gozzi (Zürich, 1917).

Turangalîla-symphonie. Symphony (1946–8; rev. 1990) by Messiaen for large orchestra; its title comes from the

Sanskrit *turanga* ('the passage of time, movement, rhythm') and *lila* ('play in the sense of divine action on the cosmos, also the play of creation, destruction, life and death, also love'). It is the largest of Messiaen's three works inspired by the legend of Tristan and Isolda, the others being *Cinq rechants* and *Harawi*.

turba (Lat., 'crowd'). In a *Passion, the name given to the crowd of disciples, Jews, or soldiers.

turca, alla. See ALLA TURCA.

Turco in Italia, Il ('The Turk in Italy'). Opera in two acts by Rossini to a libretto by Felice Romani after Caterino Mazzolà's *Il turco in Italia* set by Franz Seydelmann (1788) (Milan, 1814).

Turina, Joaquín (*b* Seville, 9 Dec. 1882; *d* Madrid, 14 Jan. 1949). Spanish composer. His formative student years were spent in Paris as a pupil of d'Indy at the Schola Cantorum, though he learnt more from the Impressionism of Debussy and Ravel. His works are infused with the colour and atmosphere of his native Andalusia, and many, such as the *Sinfonía sevillana* (1920) and the orchestral showpiece *Procesión del Rocío* (1912), were inspired by the city of his birth. The evocative lute quartet movement *La oración del torero* ('The Bullfighter's Prayer', 1925) retains its popularity in the later orchestration for string orchestra (it was also arranged for string quartet), as do the *Danzas fantásticas* (1920). Of his chamber music, the Piano Quintet (1907) is equally effective. Turina was also active as a teacher and musicologist. His vocal works, notably the extended *Canto a Sevilla* (1925–6) for soprano with orchestra, are often strikingly imaginative transformations of Andalusian folksong.   WT/CW

Turini, Francesco (*b* Prague, *c*.1589; *d* Brescia, 1656). Italian organist and composer. The son of a musician in the service of Emperor Rudolf II, he was sent at an early age to study music in Venice and Rome. He eventually became organist at Brescia Cathedral, where he remained until his death. He composed attractive madrigals, solo motets, and some sonatas for two violins and continuo (published in his first book of *Madrigali*, Venice, 1621) which are early instances of the trio sonata.   DA

Turkish crescent [jingling johnny, Chinese pavilion]. A wooden pole surmounted usually by a flat metal cone and a crescent, with many small bells which jingle as it is raised and then thumped on the ground. Known in Europe in the 16th century, it became an important component of the *janissary band, and was carried at the head of military bands from the late 18th century onwards.   JMo

Turkish music. See JANISSARY MUSIC.

Turmmusik (Ger.). 'Tower music', i.e. music played from the towers of churches, town halls, etc. by town musicians (**Stadtpfeifer*) in Germany, chiefly in the 17th century.

turn (Fr.: *doublé*; Ger.: *Doppelschlag*; It.: *gruppetto*). An ornament found chiefly in music of the 17th–19th centuries. It consists essentially of four notes encircling the main (notated) note—note above, main note, note below, and main note. Rhythmic variations are numerous and are often left to the performer's discretion, being heavily reliant on compositional context. The graphic sign is as shown in Exx. 1 and 2; in modern practice (as, for example, with the trill) chromatic inflections of the upper or lower note, or both, are indicated by sharp or flat signs placed above or below the turn sign as appropriate (see Ex. 2*d*).

The turn sign may be placed directly above a note, as was usual in the Baroque period (Ex. 1), or (especially from the Classical era onwards) it may be written, and

Ex. 1

Ex. 2

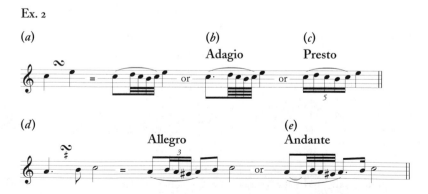

the turn played, between two notes (Ex. 2). Ex. 2c is also suitable in music of the latter period when the sign is placed above the note. Turns are sometimes written into the score as small notes, but many 19th-century composers wrote them in full-size notation, perhaps to remove any rhythmic ambiguity. An inverted turn, indicated by ∾, ⅋, or ⤮, simply reverses the direction (Ex. 3).   SMcV/DMi

Ex. 3

Turnage, Mark-Anthony (*b* Corringham, Essex, 10 June 1960). English composer. He studied with Oliver Knussen and John Lambert in London, and with Gunther Schuller and Hans Werner Henze at Tanglewood. Two works from the 1980s, the opera *Greek* (Munich, 1988) and the orchestral work *Three Screaming Popes (after Francis Bacon)* (1988–9), have the raw energy and sharp textural outlines of that highly productive anti-Romantic strain in 20th-century music which extended from Stravinsky to Birtwistle. Turnage has also been influenced by jazz and rock music, and several works demonstrate the interaction between relatively popular and relatively serious idioms in his style. These include *Your Rockaby* for soprano saxophone and orchestra (1992–3) and *Blood on the Floor* for three jazz soloists and large ensemble (1993–6). Two later operas, *The Country of the Blind* (Aldeburgh, 1997) and *The Silver Tassie* (ENO, 2000), enhanced Turnage's reputation as one of the most approachable yet distinctive British composers since Britten.   AW

📖 A. CLEMENTS, *Mark-Anthony Turnage* (London, 2000)

Turn of the Screw, The. Opera in a prologue and two acts by Britten to a libretto by Myfanwy Piper after Henry James's story (1898) (Venice, 1954).

turque (Fr., 'Turkish'). See JANISSARY MUSIC.

Tusch (Ger.). A 'fanfare' played on brass instruments. The term may be related etymologically to *tucket.

tutto, tutta, tutti, tutte (It.). 'All'; *tutte le corde*, 'all the strings', i.e. in piano-playing, remove the *una corda* pedal.

Tüür, Erkki-Sven (*b* Kärdla, Hiiumaa island, 16 Oct. 1959). Estonian composer. He studied percussion and flute at the Tallinn music school, and composition with Jaan Rääts and Lepo Sumera. Between 1979 and 1983 he performed in and wrote for the rock group In Spe. Tüür's compositions juxtapose elements of tonal minimalism with more modernist features; several in-

corporate tape, synthesizer, or live electronics. Major works include an oratorio *Ante finem saeculi* (1985) and a Requiem (1994), a series of seven works for different instrumental combinations called *Architectonics* (1985–92), three symphonies (1984, 1988, 1997), concertos for cello (1997) and violin (1999), and an opera *Wallenberg* (2001).   ABur

twelve-note music. Music in which all 12 notes of the chromatic scale have equal importance—that is, music which is not in any key or mode and thus may be described as 'atonal'. The term has also been used for all serial music, or alternatively for serial music that follows the principles established by Schoenberg rather than those of later composers such as Boulez or Babbitt. See ATONALITY; SERIALISM.

There are occasional examples in 18th- and 19th-century music of themes that contain all 12 chromatic notes: that of Bach's *Musical Offering* is one such, and Liszt's *Faust Symphony* provides at its opening a striking instance of a theme using each of the 12 notes once only. However, these works should not be described as '12-note music', since the context in both cases is tonal. A few of Liszt's last piano pieces show him coming very close to atonality, but the first true 12-note compositions were probably the 15 songs of Schoenberg's *Das Buch der hängenden Gärten* (1908–9). Charles Ives came to atonality at about the same time quite independently. Schoenberg, Berg, and Webern continued to write 12-note music from 1908 onwards, though Schoenberg made some returns to diatonic procedures. After his development of serialism in the early 1920s, the three composers concentrated on that method.

Much of the 12-note music produced by later composers has also been serial, at least in some manner. However, many of the works of Henze, Penderecki, Lutosławski, and others are atonal and not serial.

                                                            PG

📖 G. PERLE, *Serial Composition and Atonality* (Berkeley, CA, 1962, 4/1978)

twelve-note scale (Eng.; Amer.: 12-tone scale). The chromatic scale of 12 equal notes, as used in *twelve-note music. See also SCALE, 4.

twentieth century, the (*see page 1304*)

Twenty-Four Violins. See VINGT-QUATRE VIOLONS DU ROI.

Twilight of the Gods, The. See GÖTTERDÄMMERUNG.

Two Widows, The (*Dvě vdovy*). Opera in two acts by Smetana to a libretto by Emanuel Züngel after P. J. F. (*cont. on p. 1309*)

The twentieth century

Defining the 20th century

Any account of music since 1900 must first question whether the 20th century signifies for music history anything more than an arbitrary chronological category. Historians agree that music underwent profound aesthetic and technical upheavals early in the century, but few would hold that the year 1900 marked an especially decisive shift of consciousness. That shift has been located anywhere between 1907 or 1908, the time of Schoenberg's 'emancipation of the dissonance', and 1918, the end of World War I, often held to signal the definitive break with the aesthetic of the 19th century. But whatever initial watershed one adopts, there remains the question of whether the music produced afterwards can be characterized in terms of a unified aesthetic or stylistic tendency.

'Modern', once seemingly a legitimate term under which to subsume all 'present-day' creativity, now seems problematic, with not only the increased acceptance of *modernism as a cultural-historical category—signifying an aesthetic engagement (at its most urgent and intense in the late 19th and early 20th centuries) with the radical scientific, technological, and sociological transformations of modernity—but also the emergence of *postmodernism, the notion of a cultural condition originating in a crisis of confidence in modernism's defining values of progress and historical inevitability. Even speaking of a 'modern' followed by a 'postmodern' era seems not entirely appropriate. Those cultural theorists who considered postmodernist currents to have gained the ascendancy by the end of the century have also acknowledged the continued survival of modernist currents alongside them. And since that uneasy juxtaposition appears to have outlived the year 2000, the question of when the century ended is, from a conceptual standpoint, no more straightforward than that of when it began.

A formulation such as 'the modern era' nonetheless harbours an essential truth: that modernism left its mark not just on 20th-century music itself but on the way its story is told. Modernist historiography's inherent bias towards the new ensures that the 20th century is invariably portrayed as a period overwhelmed by rupture, dislocation, innovation, and change. It is salutary, therefore, to be reminded that, in spite of the collective turn towards atonality on the part of leading modernists, the greater proportion of the century's music remained tonal in some recognizable sense; that in spite of the advent of electronics and other attempts to move beyond the semitone division of the octave, most art music composers continued to work with standard orchestral instruments and equally tempered chromaticism; and that in spite of the widespread exploration of novel combinations of voices and instruments (in music theatre, for instance), such traditional media as opera and the symphony orchestra remained attractive to composers and underwent little change in their basic constitution. What Carl Dahlhaus called the 'non-contemporaneity of the contemporaneous'—the sense of coexisting, and often conflicting, impulses that owe allegiance variously to past, present, and even future—was apparent throughout the 20th century. And, looking back on the period as a whole, what may come to seem remarkable is the number of traditions that survived, rather than the number that were rendered obsolete or destroyed.

Negotiating tradition

In 1856 Nathaniel Hawthorne lamented that 'the present is too much burthened with the past' and wondered 'how future ages are to stagger under all this dead weight, with the additions that will continually be made to it'. The accumulation of relics in the 19th-century museum had its analogue in music with the establishment in the concert hall of a 'permanent repertory', a series of validated masterworks stretching back to the 18th century (and potentially beyond, as scholarly research unearthed music of earlier periods).

The burden of the past was accordingly felt just as strongly by composers, and by the beginning of the 20th century negotiating such a daunting legacy had become arguably the central problem facing them. Was tradition to be emulated or rejected? Or, through a more profound scrutiny of the past, was it possible to discern an evolutionary direction for the future?

There was also the question of which tradition to choose. The last few decades of the 19th century had witnessed unprecedented factionalism in musical aesthetics, whether in the controversies over opera versus music drama or 'absolute' versus programme music, or in increasingly vociferous assertions of national identity. Composers now had to decide where to position themselves and to be able to justify that decision—a need which explains, at least in part, the quantity of commentaries, polemics, apologias, and other prose writings generated by composers from Schoenberg through Boulez to Feldman and Ferneyhough. If 20th-century composers held anything in common, it was perhaps this heightened self-consciousness concerning their relationship to the past and, ultimately, their place in history.

In fact, few in the early 20th century advocated a *tabula rasa*. Although the aim declared in 1913 by the Futurist Luigi Russolo to break out of the 'narrow circle of pure musical sounds and conquer the infinite variety of noise sounds' won favour with later composers, for example Varèse and Cage, among those of his own generation his radical iconoclasm attracted few followers. Rather, the vast majority perceived tradition and innovation as closely, indeed dialectically, related. Even those who sought to perpetuate the abstract symphonic traditions of the 19th century felt modernism's impact: hence, for instance, in the symphonies of Sibelius and Nielsen, the long-range articulations of functional tonality prevail only after a prolonged struggle, even then leaving a palpable sense of their impermanence and vulnerability.

Meanwhile, the presence of the past spurred modernists on in their determination to 'make it new'. There was no point in replicating works in the existing canon; what tradition demanded was music that aspired to their distinctive, original, and unique qualities—as Schoenberg put it, 'truly new music which, being based on tradition, is destined to become tradition'. To contemporaries, Schoenberg's emancipation of the dissonance seemed a violent, arbitrary, and thoroughly wilful assertion of creative autonomy, and Schoenberg

himself initially spoke of having single-handedly 'broken all barriers of a past aesthetic'. But within a few years he was portraying this radical move as an entirely logical consequence of the increasingly pervasive chromaticism and tonal ambiguity in the music of Liszt, Wagner, and their successors, and his personal role as that of an obedient, if at times reluctant, servant of a tradition in constant and necessary evolution.

If Schoenberg saw himself within an unbroken line stretching back through Brahms and Wagner, Beethoven, Mozart, and Bach, for others the matter of inheritance was more problematic. For those who perceived themselves outside the Austro-German succession, or relating to it (in Stravinsky's memorable phrase) 'at an angle', tradition was something that needed to be actively sought out and rediscovered—which is to say effectively reinvented. Whereas 19th-century nationalists had used folk sources primarily as a quarry for subject matter and thematic material, the new generation of neo-nationalists, including Bartók in Hungary, Enescu in Romania, Janáček in Czechoslovakia, and Szymanowski in Poland, sought in folk music a means of modernist stylistic renewal. For Bartók (one of a number of composers who now undertook their own fieldwork in folk-music research) it was a matter of establishing the claims of an 'authentic' vernacular tradition, namely the rural peasant music of Hungary, over a spurious hybrid, the urban gypsy music on which 19th-century apprehensions of the Hungarian style had been based.

Stravinsky's works of the 1910s also followed an overtly nationalist trajectory, and the distinctive rhythmic language he developed at this time owed more to the shifting accentual patterns of Russian folksong than he himself later acknowledged. Indeed that tendency to discount his Slavonic heritage became just one manifestation of his growing desire to align himself with the west European mainstream. But, unlike Schoenberg, Stravinsky saw tradition not as something 'unthinkingly acquired', but rather as the result of a 'conscious and deliberate acceptance'. And while Schoenberg presented his work as a logical outgrowth of the immediate past, Stravinsky rejected such an evolutionary model ('the true tradition-making work may not resemble the past at all, and especially not the immediate past'). The term *neo-classicism', first applied to Stravinsky's music in 1923, implied precisely a rejection of Germanic high Romanticism in favour of stylistic manners that were distant from it either temporally or aesthetically—hence, not just the 18th century but also Tchaikovsky and Verdi were admissible as models.

Unsurprisingly, neo-classicism drew censure from Schoenberg and his apologists (notably Adorno), who portrayed it as a misguided lurch back into nostalgia and false consciousness. Stravinsky's toying once more with the materials and devices of diatonic tonality, however redeployed or defamiliarized, made him guilty not only of cowardly retreat in the face of the historical imperative (towards a thoroughgoing and systematic negation of tonality), but also of a preoccupation with surface rather than substance, 'style' rather than 'idea'. But though Schoenberg shunned neo-classicism's stylistic manners, even he could not remain entirely aloof from its aesthetic. Significantly, his first work to use the 12-note technique in all its movements, the Suite for piano op. 25 (1921–3), is cast in the form of a Baroque dance suite. Indeed the technique's very formulation, as a systematic codification of the total chromaticism that had pervaded his music for over a decade, reflected a shift in orientation from intuition to rationalism that now seems entirely in keeping with the interwar spirit of sobriety.

Stravinsky's neo-classical works, though often represented as clinical in their objectivity, were consistently born out of both affection for the models themselves and the deepest respect for the traditions they represented. Other manifestations of interwar anti-Romanticism showed less concern with the trappings of high-art seriousness. Both Les Six in France and the German advocates of *Neue Sachlichkeit* ('new realism') used familiar historical styles as just one element (alongside the new idioms of jazz, the music hall, and the dance band) in their celebration of the transient, the commonplace, and the ephemeral, whether in a blatantly frivolous spirit (Milhaud and Poulenc) or in a more earnest desire to serve the social and political needs of the moment (Hindemith and Weill).

Neo-classicism in the broadest sense soon established itself as the dominant international language of the interwar years. Its ability to accommodate features of diatonicism in something other than a functionally tonal context made it a flexible vehicle for the creation of new, nationalistically oriented idioms, such as that forged in the USA by Copland in the late 1930s and early 40s. Copland's populism represented a voluntary retreat from hard-edged modernism in an attempt to reach a wider public at a time of economic hardship.

Ironically, at roughly the same time, the USSR was experiencing a similar drive towards a 'simple, accessible musical language', but the initiative was forced on composers from above. This doctrine of *socialist realism' became the official substitute for a modernism condemned as emblematic of 'bourgeois individualism and empty formalism'. It is remarkable how, even under the conflicting and often overwhelming pressures of state cultural policy, composers like Prokofiev and Shostakovich managed artistic statements of considerable sophistication and emotional power.

Silencing tradition

Modernism also fell foul of Fascist cultural politics in the later 1930s. Hence, at the end of World War II, artists in continental Europe had not only to rebuild some semblance of normal cultural life after the devastation of the conflict, but also to catch up on arrears built up over a decade of censorship. The wartime suppression of modernism throughout much of continental Europe lent it connotations of political resistance and made it, for some, an appropriately uncompromising idiom in which to couch an artistic response to recent horrors. The 12-note technique, written off by many (even before the Nazi ban) as an eccentric experiment that had had its day, was taken up during and immediately after the war by a number of senior composers in mid-career, both in Europe (Dallapiccola and Fortner) and in the USA (Copland, Sessions, and Stravinsky).

But among the younger generation reaching maturity at the end of the war, many perceived the need for a more decisive break with the past. The radical generalization of the 12-note row undertaken by Boulez, Stockhausen, and Pousseur took it far from its Schoenbergian roots: it now became a kind of hidden genetic code for the work as a whole, applied to non-pitch parameters and at different hierarchical levels in order to influence progressively larger aspects of musical form. It was that same desire for multi-level control, even more than a desire for new sounds as such, that motivated Stockhausen's pioneering experiments in electronic music, in which serial principles governed the internal construction of sounds, in terms of the relationships between their component frequencies. The young avant-garde, moreover, saw serialism's historical role in an altogether different light. Whereas Schoenberg had viewed it as the Austro-German tradition's very means of survival, to Stockhausen it signified the end-point of that tradition and the beginning of a new international musical language that would 'supersede the personal styles of a few individuals and become the universal style of the age'. Not all members of the younger avant-garde were as utopian in their aspirations, but the very fact that Boulez referred to Webern as 'chief predecessor elect' indicated that the days of merely inheriting the mantle of tradition were over: today one chooses one's ancestors.

Though scornful of much of the immediate past, the postwar European serialists nonetheless left unquestioned many of the 19th century's assumptions concerning the nature of musical works, continuing (implicitly at least) to value such attributes as structured material (unified on as many levels as possible), individuality (a unique structure and content specific to each work), and autonomy (the artwork's existence in a sphere divorced from the social and functional). It was in Cage's works of the 1950s, which integrated chance procedures into aspects of composition or performance, or both, that these assumptions were called systematically into question. In the case of the notorious *4′ 33″* (1952), less a duration of contemplative silence (a time-period containing no sound at all) than a duration of unintended sounds, the fact that environmental sounds are allowed to invade the piece at random not only challenges the work's autonomy and individuality, making it potentially indistinguishable from any slice of everyday life, but also signals the composer's abandonment of any attempt to control the work's content or to structure it in line with a compositional intention.

Whereas most composers still strove to make the sounding music do justice to their intentions, for Cage (who sought to 'let sounds be themselves') no intentions could ever do justice to the sounds. Nevertheless, indeterminacy is by definition relative, and Cage's apparent surrender of control was ultimately neither total nor irrevocable: a number of the chance-based works still took the form of fully notated scores, and even the text instructions that formed the sole notational basis of other compositions tended to be specific enough to ensure that there was such a thing as an 'incorrect' realization, although there was no single 'correct' one. In other respects Cage's works reinscribed the very values they purported to reject: whatever the subversive implications of a work such as *4′ 33″*, its status as 'the first silent piece' makes it ironically just another manifestation of the Romantic cult of ori-

ginality. Less sympathetic commentators will always view Cage's appropriation of silence as nothing if not a hegemonic act, and as calculated a bid for a place in history as any made by his modernist precursors.

Although his multimedia 'happenings' were undoubtedly influential on the work of the Fluxus group, active during the 1960s and 70s, Cage's influence was otherwise notable for its relatively unproblematic assimilation into mainstream modernism. The adoption by European avant-garde composers of 'open forms', involving a degree of performer choice concerning the ordering, timing, and even inclusion of particular sections of music, is sometimes attributed to Cage's influence, though it is equally arguable that such potentialities were implicit from the start in serialism's embodiment of multiple permutational possibilities. And while Lutosławski cited an encounter with Cage's *Concert for Piano and Orchestra* (1957–8) as the principal catalyst for his widely adopted techniques of 'limited aleatoricism', these involved little in the way of chance beyond a greater freedom of rhythmic coordination between (otherwise precisely notated) instrumental or vocal parts.

Pluralizing tradition

Challenges to modernism came, in fact, just as much from within. To many, such as Adorno, the rationalistic orientation of postwar modernism had come simply to mirror the productive rationality at work in contemporary society; the movement's polemical edge, so apparent in the interwar years, had been lost, and for many it had ossified into yet another sterile orthodoxy. Moreover, in a pluralistic society increasingly marked by a lack of political or social consensus, the idea that any single aesthetic position could claim exclusive authority and legitimacy seemed no longer credible. Composers previously associated with the Darmstadt avant-garde now started to diversify their activities, Stockhausen turning to 'intuitive composition' involving graphics and text, and demonstrating an increasing interest in the music of non-Western cultures, while Berio, Kagel, and Pousseur sought a renewed engagement with theatre, in works both operatic and in the new genre of music theatre, which integrated speech, movement, and gesture into works for the concert hall.

Others, reacting against the prohibitive notational complexity of both serial and indeterminate music, turned to simpler kinds of music-making, based on improvisation and collaboration. The Scratch Orchestra, founded in London by Cornelius Cardew, united amateurs as well as professionals in the cause of radical socialism, while cooperation was equally a feature of such early minimalist compositions as Terry Riley's *In C* (1964), in which performers proceed at a mutually negotiated pace through a group of simple melodic fragments. With its emphasis on the repetition and gradual transformation of simple diatonic materials, *minimalism proved the most commercially successful of the new stylistic directions, its rhythmic orientation and amplified, composer-led groups finding a new audience among rock music enthusiasts. While early minimalism sought to counter the conventional narrative expectations of teleology and development, these elements were increasingly reintegrated in the music of Reich and Glass as it migrated into mainstream concert halls and opera houses in the late 1970s and the 80s. The music of so-called post-minimalists such as Adams and Torke, through either the complex layering or constant dislocation of rhythmic processes, signals a rapprochement with early modernism, the music of Stravinsky in particular, while also occasionally incorporating elements of popular music.

Modernism's continuing resilience was evident not only in the prolific activity of such senior figures as Birtwistle and Carter, but also in the mannerist intensification it underwent in the music of Ferneyhough and others aligned with the 'New Complexity', a tendency noted for intricate notation, dense, multi-layered processes, and its extreme demands on performers. But for others modernism represented just one possibility among a multiplicity of conceivable stylistic directions, all equally available and legitimate.

In an environment saturated by music of all places and all pasts, some composers saw their task as involving merely the endless recombination of found objects. While quotation-based music was nothing new in the final decades of the 20th century, many later manifestations of it (in the output of William Bolcom and John Zorn, for instance) were notable not only for the radical eclecticism of the materials themselves, but for the conspicuous absence of any attempt to refract, manipulate or otherwise impose stylistic unity on them. Elsewhere the mood of stylistic allusion ranged from a positive revelling in artificiality in the pastiche-oriented work of Nyman, to a troubling sense of disorientation in the music of Schnittke and Rihm, which seems either to lament a lost means of direct, unmediated musical expression, or to suggest that it was always an illusion.

It would be hard indeed for any single observer to give adequate account of the multiple strands of activity within the current musical scene. But images of a free and easy stylistic pluralism should nevertheless be regarded with some caution. No doubt every age seems pluralistic to itself, and imagining our own as more liberal and tolerant than previous phases of history, as if no politics of exclusion operated within it, carries obvious dangers. Our sense of the loss of a mainstream may be due principally to the fact that mainstreams are the creation of historians, in which case (as such commentators as Leo Treitler have suggested) the crisis, if it exists at all, is not in music itself but merely in our ways of thinking about it. It could be that continuities and lines of development will in time become apparent, and the historical dynamic of the late 20th century will seem remarkably like that of previous eras; or it could be, as postmodern theorists argue, that the conditions of the present are indeed radically different, and our current (modernist) historical paradigms simply inadequate to deal with them.

Art music in late 20th-century culture

If stylistic tendencies were hard to isolate at the end of the century, a more definite trend was becoming apparent in terms of Western art music's status and position within global musical culture. Whereas, back in 1900, art music had been largely confined to western Europe and the USA, by 2000 the situation was very different, with art music now practised, often in fruitful dialogue with indigenous traditions, in countries as diverse as Taiwan, Egypt, Indonesia, and Turkey, and with East Asian composers (such as Takemitsu and Tan Dun) making an especially significant impact on the international scene. The unprecedented expansion in music education that had taken place at university and conservatory level made it seem likely that more people worldwide were involved in composing and performing art music (in at least a part-time professional capacity) than ever before.

But along with globalization came marginalization. According to most statistical and economic indicators, Western art music had become by 2000 a fringe activity within global musical culture as a whole. As the century progressed, public performance and domestic music-making had increasingly given way to the mass media of broadcasting and recording, which overwhelmingly favoured the new genres of popular music. Moreover, within the culture of 'classical' music itself, recent composition had become increasingly sidelined: the recording industry sustained consumer demand with a steady supply not of new music as such, but of new interpretations of old music (increasingly older music, in fact, as the early-music revival gathered pace), and this situation was mirrored in the concert hall and the opera house, where few works composed after 1950 had joined the standard repertory.

The blame for this marginalization is often laid at the door of modernist composers themselves, on account not only of their uncompromising artistic stance, but also of their self-imposed isolation from the social mainstream. Schoenberg's Society for Private Musical Performance, set up in 1918 for the dedicated performance of contemporary works to an invited audience (critics were barred), had been the first in a number of ventures (including, notably, the European new music festivals in Donaueschingen and Darmstadt) which sought to create a separate institutional space for new music, inhabited by specialist performers and specialist audiences. But beyond their arrogant rhetoric, suggestions such as Babbitt's that composers did themselves 'immediate and eventual service' by 'total, resolute and voluntary withdrawal from th[e] public world' contained at least a grain of truth. The values of familiarity, permanence, and longevity central to the contemporary marketing of classical music will arguably continue to militate against the acceptance within its mainstream of any new music of whatever idiom. Modernist music may still occasionally encounter outright hostility from concert audiences; but, equally, music that strives after accessibility rarely stirs more than the mildest interest.

Nonetheless, the situation at the beginning of the 21st century was by no means entirely bleak. Lack of support from major publishing and performing institutions led many composers in the 1980s and 90s to recognize the positive benefits of producing and distributing their own music, either alone or through composers' collectives. Such activity was facilitated by easier access to digital recording equipment, desktop publishing facilities, and new, seemingly more democratic modes of distribution such as the Internet, with its potential for intimate contact with an audience, however small, specialized, or geographically dispersed. Contemporary art music may come increasingly to operate in a domain apart from traditional concert music, disseminated in commodity form rather than by means of live performance. But its flexibility and adaptability, developed over a century of jostling for space between an entrenched museum culture and the indifference of mass media, may ultimately procure for it a more vibrant and certain future than that facing certain more traditional forms of music-making.

CWi

R. P. Morgan, *Twentieth-Century Music* (New York, 1991) · R. P. Morgan (ed.), *Modern Times: From World War I to the Present*, Man and Music/Music and Society (London, 1993) · G. Watkins, *Pyramids at the Louvre* (Cambridge, MA, 1994) · P. Griffiths, *Modern Music and After: Directions since 1945* (Oxford, 1995) · A. Whittall, *Musical Composition in the Twentieth Century* (Oxford, 1999)

Mallefille's play *Les Deux Veuves* (Prague, 1874); it was revised with recitatives and extra numbers (Prague, 1878).

Tye, Christopher (*b* c.1505; *d* between 27 Aug. 1571 and 15 March 1573). English church musician and composer. He took the Cambridge degree of Mus.B. in 1536, and the following year became a lay clerk at King's College. By 1543 he was Master of the Choristers at Ely Cathedral, and it was probably through the influence of the Archdeacon of Ely, Richard Cox, that Tye became known to Prince Edward (subsequently Edward VI), to whom his metrical version of *The Actes of the Apostles* (London, 1553) is dedicated. He also appears to have been connected in a non-salaried way to the Chapel Royal. In 1560 he took holy orders, and the following year resigned his post at Ely Cathedral in order to take up a living at Doddington in the Isle of Ely. He was awarded the Cambridge D.Mus. in 1545; contemporary sources sometimes refer to him as 'Dr Tye'.

Like his contemporaries Tallis and Sheppard, Tye lived through years of religious upheaval, and his output is full of liturgical and musical variety. Much of his Latin church music has been lost; several of his most important works are now known only by single surviving voice-parts from five or six; but to judge from the sonorous six-voice *Missa 'Euge bone'* and the four-part *'Western Wynde' Mass*, he was among the first English composers to write in a compact, declamatory style.

His English-texted anthems, which exist in greater quantity, are similar in manner. Tye was also one of the first Englishmen to write extensively for instrumental consort; more *In nomine* settings survive by him than by any other Tudor composer. The *Actes of the Apostles*, which set his own verse translations, are unsophisticated pieces, possibly written for use by the young Prince Edward. JM

Tzigane (Fr., 'Gypsy'). Concert rhapsody (1924) by Ravel for violin and piano; it was later orchestrated by the composer.

über (Ger.). 'Over', 'above', 'across'; *überblasen*, 'to overblow'; *Übergang*, *Überleitung*, 'transition', 'bridge passage'; *übergreifen*, 'to cross the hands' in piano playing; *übertragen*, to transcribe.

Überbrettl. The name of a Berlin cabaret founded in 1901 by the writer Ernst von Wolzogen in association with the poet Julius Bierbaum and the playwright Frank Wedekind. Their aim was to raise the popular idiom of cabaret to a level of iconoclastic seriousness and to include poems recited to music. Among the composers who contributed songs were Zemlinsky, Oscar Straus, and Schoenberg, who wrote eight *Brettl-Lieder*.

Übung (Ger.). 'Exercise', 'study'.

Uccelli, Gli ('The Birds'). Suite for small orchestra (1927) by Respighi, based on bird pieces for lute and harpsichord by 17th- and 18th-century composers (including Rameau and Pasquini).

Uccellini, Marco (*b c.*1603; *d* Forlimpopoli, nr Forlì, 10 Sept. 1680). Italian composer and instrumentalist. He settled in Modena before 1639, two years later taking charge of the instrumental music at the Este court. He was *maestro di cappella* at the cathedral from 1647 to 1665, when he moved to the Farnese court in Parma. His seven printed volumes (one is lost) of sonatas, sinfonias, and dances, chiefly for violin(s) and continuo, establish important precedents for emerging genres of instrumental music. They also reach extreme heights of virtuosity. TC

'ūd. A short-necked plucked *lute with a large body and usually five double courses plucked with a quill. It is the principal instrument in the Arab world, where it has been known since the 7th century, and is the direct ancestor of the European lute. JMo

uguale (It.). 'Equal'; *ugualmente*, 'equally'.

uilleann pipes. Irish bellows-blown *bagpipe.

ukulele [ukelele]. A small four-string guitar derived in Hawaii in the 1870s from the Portuguese *machête* taken there by sailors. Being small, lightweight, relatively cheap, and easy to learn, it became very popular in the USA and Europe, especially in the first half of the 20th century, for the strummed accompaniment of singing. The ukulele may be tuned to any key to suit the voice of the singer, with the following basic intervals: descending 5th–ascending major 3rd–ascending 4th (e.g. $g'–c'–e'–a'$). The banjulele is a variant with a *banjo head instead of the guitar-shaped resonator, tuned in the same way. JMo

Ullmann, Viktor (Josef) (*b* Teschen [now Český Těšín], 1 Jan. 1898; *d* Auschwitz, 18 Oct. 1944). Czech composer. The son of an army officer, he was educated in Vienna. After military service in World War I he studied with Schoenberg, who in turn recommended him to Zemlinsky; in 1920 the latter appointed him répétiteur at the German Theatre in Prague. Ullmann subsequently became music director at Aussig in 1927 but left his post after a year. Drawn to the writings of Rudolf Steiner, he temporarily abandoned his musical career to work in the anthroposophical bookshop in Stuttgart (1930–3). He returned to Prague after the Nazi acquisition of power, though Steiner's thought left an indelible impression on his first opera *Der Sturz des Antichrist* ('The Fall of the Antichrist', 1935). Between 1935 and 1937 he studied with Alois Hába, but he did not adopt any of the latter's quarter-tone technique.

In 1942 Ullmann was arrested by the Nazis and sent to the 'model ghetto' at *Terezín, where he took an active part in the camp's musical life, producing the works by which he is best remembered: several song cycles, a string quartet, three piano sonatas, and the opera *Der Kaiser von Atlantis* ('The Emperor of Atlantis'), a bitter, probing parable on the nature of transience and mortality. The opera's depiction of the tyrannical Kaiser Overall, identified by the quotation of *Deutschland über alles*, was frowned on by the Gestapo, who insisted the work be withdrawn before performance. The existence of a number of variants in the score suggests that the opera was still very much a 'work in progress' at the time of its withdrawal. On 16 October 1944 Ullmann was transported from Terezín to Auschwitz, where he died in the gas chamber two days later. *Der Kaiser von Atlantis*, now recognized as one of the most powerful and haunting works of the 20th century, was first performed in Amsterdam in 1975.

TA

📖 M. Bloch, 'Viktor Ullmann: A brief biography and appreciation', *Journal of the Arnold Schoenberg Institute*, 3 (1979), 150–77 · J. Karas, *Music in Terezín, 1941–1945* (New York, 1985) · U. Prinz (ed.), *Viktor Ullmann: Beiträge, Programme, Dokumente, Materialien* (Kassel, 1998)

Ultimos ritos ('Last Rites'). Work (1969–72) by Tavener, for soprano, alto, tenor, and bass soloists, five male speakers, chorus, large brass ensemble, and orchestra, to a text by St John of the Cross and the Crucifixus from the Nicene Creed.

Umfang (Ger.). 'Compass', 'range'.

Umkehrung (Ger.). 'Turning round', 'reversal', i.e. inversion.

Umlauf, Ignaz (*b* Vienna, 1746; *d* Meidling, 8 June 1796). Austrian composer. He began his career as a viola player in Vienna theatres. As Kapellmeister for Joseph II's new 'German National Singspiel', he was commissioned in 1778 to write the opening work. *Die Bergknappen* (1778) is based on a romantic tale set in a mining community, and includes some striking individual numbers. Carefully matched to the theatre's vocal resources and the audience's expectations, with its mixture of German, French, and Italian elements it succeeded in its aim of giving the new enterprise a popular start. Umlauf followed it with *Die schöne Schusterinn* ('The Shoemaker's Beautiful Wife', 1779), a lively, relaxed French-inspired comedy, and *Das Irrlicht* ('The Will-o'-the-Wisp', 1782), in which adumbrations of Romantic themes include the contact between human and spirit worlds and redemption through love. Mozart was sufficiently jealous of Umlauf's success to make disparaging remarks about one of his weakest works, *Welche ist die beste Nation?* (1782). His son **Michael Umlauf** (*b* Vienna, 9 Aug. 1781; *d* Baden, 20 June 1842) was a conductor and composer who became a violinist and conductor in the Vienna court orchestra. Much respected by Beethoven, he conducted the 1814 revival of *Fidelio* and premieres of other works by Beethoven, including the Ninth Symphony.

WT/JW

Umstimmung (Ger., 'tuning to another pitch'). See SCORDATURA.

una corda (It.). In piano playing, an instruction to depress the 'soft' pedal; it is cancelled by *tre corde* ('three strings') or *tutte le corde* ('all the strings'). See PIANOFORTE, 7.

Unanswered Question, The. Work (1908) for chamber orchestra by Ives; it is the first of *Two Contemplations*, the other being *Central Park in the Dark*, and was revised *c*.1930–5.

Undine. See ONDINE.

unequal voices. A term given to a mixture of male and female voices; see also EQUAL VOICES.

unessential note. See ESSENTIAL NOTE.

'Unfinished' Symphony. Schubert's Symphony no. 8 in B minor D759 (1822), of which two movements and the sketch of a third survive. There are many unfinished symphonies, for example by Tchaikovsky, Mahler, Elgar, and Shostakovich, but the title is generally taken to refer only to *Schubert's.

ungebunden (Ger.). 1. 'Free', 'unconstrained'.
2. Of keyboard and stringed instruments, 'unfretted'.

ungerader Takt (Ger.). 'Uneven (triple) time'.

ungezwungen (Ger.). 'Unforced', 'easygoing'.

unison (Fr.: *unisson*; Ger.: *Prime*; It.: *prima*). 1. The simultaneous performance of the same line of music by various instruments or voices, or by a whole choir or orchestra; this may be at exactly the same pitch or in a different octave. The direction is sometimes given as *all'unisono*.
2. The 'interval' formed between the same two notes. See INTERVAL.

United States of America 1. Musical life in early America; 2. The 19th century; 3. Folk music; 4. 20th-century art music; 5. Present-day popular music

1. Musical life in early America

Except for the Quakers, all the religious groups that settled in early America called for music in their worship, though organists were commonly engaged from Europe. Less promising for the art of music were the activities of the Reformed Calvinists, including the Puritans who settled New England. Believing the theatre immoral, they successfully opposed its firm establishment in the colonies until near the end of the 18th century. As for sacred music, they mistrusted the motives of those who wanted to expand its role in worship, and they discouraged such expansion. Following the practice begun by John Calvin, they assigned music-making during public worship entirely to the congregation. Not until the 18th century, and then only gradually, did the unaccompanied, monophonic psalm singing of the Calvinist worship begin to be elaborated.

The elaboration began in Massachusetts around 1720, when singing schools were established. These schools, instructional sessions run by a singing master, sought to teach the scholars how to sing congregational tunes in a coordinated way, as they were written down in musical notation. Instructional tunebooks like John Tufts's *An Introduction to the Singing of Psalm-Tunes* and Thomas Walter's *The Grounds and Rules of Musick Explained* (both Boston, 1721) were published, condensing the rudiments of music and offering a supply of harmonized tunes for singing schools or public worship.

From the 1750s and 60s, musicians began to take over sacred music-making from both clergy and congregation. Singers banded together to form choirs, at first to lead singing in public worship. Soon, however, in some places, choirs began to sing pieces that other members of the congregation did not know, or that were too complicated for them to learn. More and more American tunebooks were published. Most, like James Lyon's *Urania* (Philadelphia, 1761) and Daniel Bayley's *The American Harmony* (Newburyport, MA, 1769), carried choir music—*'fuging' psalm tunes, through-composed 'set-pieces', and prose anthems—together with standard congregational fare. By the 1780s a modest hierarchy of music-making organizations had grown up around the Calvinist meeting-house, and some of the more dedicated singers formed musical societies to sing the choir music they most admired.

Crowning the new sacred musical life of New England was the appearance of the American composer. Beginning with the Boston tanner William Billings's *The New England Psalm-Singer* (Boston, 1770), American-born musicians, including the store-keeper Daniel Read of New Haven, the hatter Timothy Swan of Suffield, the carpenter Oliver Holden of Charlestown, and dozens more, taught singing schools, composed their own sacred pieces, compiled tunebooks, and, as these and other tunebooks were sold, saw their compositions circulate in print. Their music, generally set for unaccompanied four-voice chorus, lacks the melodic and harmonic suavity of European music of the time. Nevertheless 18th-century New England sacred music, written by self-taught musicians who composed for their neighbours or for singers of similar background and skill, showed considerable vitality and staying power. As the frontier pushed westwards after 1800, evangelical religious groups that settled west and south established a practice of sacred music-making that in some ways resembled that of Billings's New England. Tunebooks compiled by 19th- and 20th-century southern singing masters (e.g. *The Sacred Harp*, compiled in Hamilton, GA, 1844), usually contained both newer local compositions and a selection of favourites by the New Englanders.

Secular music-making in early America organized itself along very different lines, led by emigrant musicians from Europe. Ranging through the cities of the eastern seaboard, they began presenting public concerts as early as 1731 in Boston and 1732 in Charleston. Shortly after 1750, with the arrival of Hallam's theatre company, which toured extensively and was soon joined by rival companies, the musical theatre began to make its first real impact, the players performing the best-known English ballad operas. By the time of the Revolutionary War, European-born music masters were teaching young American harpsichordists, flautists, and violinists in cities and towns, and also on the plantations of the South. These activities were sporadic, however, compared with what happened after the war. As residents of the cities along the Atlantic seaboard enjoyed increased wealth and leisure, European professionals like Gottlieb Graupner (1767–1836) and Benjamin Carr (1768–1831) found more reason to settle in the New World. By the mid-1790s, each of the major Atlantic coastal cities—Boston, New York, Philadelphia, Baltimore, Charleston—had its own musical theatre. Concerts of vocal and instrumental music were given regularly. Music lessons were available to those who could afford them. And a domestic music trade was beginning to flourish: publishers brought out songs and pieces from the Anglo-American musical theatre in sheet-music form, and both imported and American-made instruments were widely for sale.

Most music in early America, whether sacred or secular, was shaped by musicians working to satisfy a particular public and dependent in the long run on some measure of commercial success. One remarkable group of religious dissenters made music entirely apart from commercial considerations—the Moravians who had settled in North Carolina and Pennsylvania by the 1750s, and whose high level of performance and composition centred on sacred music and instrumental chamber music as well. Another musician to whom commercial success was unimportant was the 'gentleman amateur' Francis Hopkinson, whose *Seven Songs* (Philadelphia, 1788) are among the earliest American-composed art songs. But the Moravians and the aristocratic Hopkinson are exceptions: few of their music-minded contemporaries were in a position to follow their example. Thus, in the 18th century the foundations for the support of American musicians were laid, not in salons and cathedrals, but in the marketplace.

2. The 19th century

The volume of all aspects of organized music-making increased greatly during the 19th century. The rapid growth of the country's population and settled territory helped bring about a corresponding growth in the size of the American middle class, whose needs and tastes did a great deal to shape 19th-century American musical life. Musicians who first learnt how to address middle-class musical needs, and who set up means for doing so, wielded an influence beyond what their purely musical talents might seem to warrant. Lowell Mason (1792–1872), Patrick S. Gilmore (1829–92), and George Frederick Root (1820–95) were three such musicians.

The Massachusetts-born Mason, who compiled more than 50 musical publications, composed many hymn tunes in a simple 'devotional' style that was widely imitated. Gilmore, who emigrated to America from Ireland as a young man, made his mark in the realm of the public concert: the wind band was his medium, the mass audience his quarry. In the hands of Gilmore and, later, Sousa the wind band came to be the medium most successful in drawing a concert audience virtually anywhere in the world. Much of the band's broad appeal lay in its eclectic programming—a musical mixed bag of marches, patriotic airs, popular songs and dances, and excerpts from the classics. Taken up by orchestras in their 'promenade' or 'pops' concerts, this programming principle, which seeks to meet the general public on its own ground, has persisted to the present day.

Root's career reflects a third strain in 19th-century American musical life: the development of the home as a centre of music-making. As a partner in the Chicago publishing house of Root & Cady (1860–71), he brought out music by many composers, including the talented songwriter Henry Clay Work (1832–84). Root himself also composed 'people's songs' and cantatas—works whose studied avoidance of musical complication was supposed to fit them for the broadest possible market. Many hit the mark, especially his Civil War songs, which had a wide and lasting appeal. By that time, the availability of low-priced pianos had prompted thousands of Americans to install pianos in their parlours. Together with dozens of other music publishers, Root & Cady stood ready to supply vocal and instrumental music to fit all tastes.

Pieces like Root's own songs, or the flood of piano pieces written expressly for the amateur performer, formed only two of the many species of 19th-century American sheet music. Arrangements and adaptations abounded: opera pieces, variations on favourite melodies, battle pieces, overtures, even symphonies. Meanwhile, the popular musical theatre continued under English domination throughout much of the first half of the 19th century. The American presence on American musical stages was first forcibly felt in the 1840s, when the Ohio-born musical entertainer Dan

Emmett and three cohorts blackened their faces with burnt cork, dressed in rag-tag costumes, affected the heavy dialect and loose-jointed motions associated with the African American, and as 'The Virginia Minstrels' put on the first full-length blackface minstrel show. The idea caught on like wildfire: 'Ethiopian' troupes multiplied with amazing speed and found audiences wherever they went.

After emancipation in 1863, minstrelsy was taken over increasingly by black performers. Touring black minstrel troupes flourished from the 1860s into the early years of the 20th century, providing an avenue by which black Americans could make a living as musicians. The songwriter James A. Bland (1854–1911) spent his career performing in minstrelsy; and the blues singers Ma Rainey (1886–1939) and Bessie Smith (1894–1937) and the composer-publisher W. C. Handy (1873–1958) began their careers as members of black minstrel troupes.

Sustained partly by the minstrel stage and partly by the home music market was the career of Stephen Foster, whose songs, sung widely in his own day, have endured to form part of the cultural experience of almost every American since. Like such diverse contemporaries as Mason, Gilmore, Root, and Bland, Foster cooperated or competed with other musicians who were trying to reach substantially the same audience. All of them worked in a commercial tradition shaped by themselves and their audiences—a collective, stylistically conservative process in which creators and consumers were linked interdependently.

Practitioners of art music in 19th-century America struggled to build a tradition of their own. Their initial success is best measured by the gradual increase in the number of American institutions devoted to teaching, performing, and promoting European art music. One kind of performing organization is typified by the Handel and Haydn Society of Boston (founded 1815), in which local citizens, encouraged perhaps at least as much by religious as by artistic motives, formed a chorus with regularly scheduled meetings. Accompanied by an orchestra of professionals and available amateurs, and joined by solo singers, they gave public concerts of sacred music, sometimes including full oratorios, seeking to cover expenses by selling tickets. Choral societies similarly drawn from the community at large grew up throughout the country in the 19th century and continued to flourish in the 20th.

Opera first took root in the New World in New Orleans, which had its own resident company through much of the century (1859–1919). Elsewhere, most Americans had to depend on touring companies. Relying on publicity to drum up audiences and hence promoted as a branch of show business, troupes such as the one managed by Max Maretzek performed operas by Mozart, Rossini, Donizetti, and other European masters. New York, fitted for the role by its concentration of wealth and high proportion of foreign-born residents, has been the chief centre of operatic performance in America since the late 19th century. The Metropolitan Opera (founded in 1883) holds a place as one of the great international houses, though in the 20th century a number of other American cities established companies of their own, including San Francisco, Chicago, Boston, Seattle, Santa Fe, St Louis, Dallas, Washington, DC, and Houston.

Somewhere between the steady respectability of the choral society and the emotional brio of the opera company stands the orchestra, a medium indispensable to both. Throughout most of the 19th century American orchestras tended to be groups assembled from among available musicians on an ad hoc basis. The maintenance of a standing ensemble as large as a symphony orchestra was simply more expensive than the need for its services would warrant. The oldest such continuing ensemble in America, the New York Philharmonic Society, began in 1842 as a cooperative, with the musicians themselves running the orchestra, concerts being open only to other members of the society. Theodore Thomas (1835–1905), perhaps the dominant figure in American concert life during the second half of the century, established, managed, and conducted the Theodore Thomas Orchestra, which toured for years from a base in New York.

In general, however, standing ensembles were organized wherever musicians succeeded in tapping a community's wealthy residents for support. This was usually done through subscription, with a number of patrons agreeing to commit funds to cover the ensemble's expenses. Thus, through the patronage of some of their affluent citizens, cities like Philadelphia, Chicago, Cincinnati, Pittsburgh, San Francisco, and New York managed to maintain professional orchestras and to build halls acoustically suited to their playing. The founding in 1881 of the Boston Symphony Orchestra by a single patron, Henry Lee Higginson, who maintained the ensemble out of his own pocket for nearly 40 years, is unique in American musical history.

In the 19th century the musical leadership of opera companies, symphony orchestras, and even most choral societies was assumed from the beginning by Europeans, and the repertory they performed was almost entirely European as well. American composers of art music, among whom one of the first was Anthony Philip Heinrich (1781–1861), seemed destined for the role of outsider. Two more composers, both active in New York from the mid-19th century onwards, complained publicly that American music, including

their own, was being overlooked by the city's performers. William Henry Fry (1813–64), a music critic of a New York daily newspaper, and George Frederick Bristow (1825–98), a violinist with the New York Philharmonic Society and music teacher in the city's public schools, thus raised an issue of fundamental and continuing importance to American musical life, though with little noticeable effect on concert programming. The one 19th-century American composer of art music who consistently found an audience was the New Orleans-born Louis Moreau Gottschalk.

Beginning at about the time of the Civil War, the first real 'school' of American-born composers began to come of age. Sharing an Anglo-Saxon heritage, east-coast birth, and a strong leaning towards the musical style of German Romanticism—most, in fact, studied in Germany—composers like John Knowles Paine (1839–1906), Horatio Parker, George Whitefield Chadwick, Arthur Foote (1853–1937), Amy Marcy Beach, and others gained for American composers a foothold in the country's institutional structure. But the most famous American composer of the time was one who stood apart from the New England group: Edward MacDowell.

3. Folk music

Beneath the busy surface of the organized musical world of 19th-century America, there existed folk music brought to the New World by different groups of settlers. In this sphere the shaping agent was not the professional tunesmith working in the musical marketplace but, rather, the community as a whole. Consensus among community members selected the music that linked the past with the present and determined the forms in which oral transmission would carry it, both over time to the next generation, and across space to other communities.

Anglo-American folk music offers some ready examples of two complementary traits of oral transmission: continuity and variation. When Cecil Sharp, the noted English folksong collector, travelled to Appalachia early in the 20th century, singers there performed for him versions of English and Scottish songs that had changed remarkably little in their long journey over time and space. Anglo-American folk music, and the folk music of other ethnic groups, was preserved with the least change in communities, chiefly rural, where Old World customs and social structures were strongest. There it could serve the roles of traditional music in traditional society: confirming community values, providing entertainment, and performing ritual functions.

It is a peculiarity of American musical history that when, early in the 19th century, scholars and artists in many European countries began to explore their unwritten cultural traditions and to draw inspiration and materials from them, American musicians experienced no corresponding rediscovery of their own 'folk'. Instead, most professional musicians and music teachers reacted to folk music with indifference or hostility, apparently believing that its untutored roughness placed it beneath their own serious attention. This was ironic, for most of the popular musical forms that circulated on paper during the 19th century had roots in Anglo-American folk music: psalmody, hymnody, and a good deal of secular song, inspired by the rhyme schemes, narrative techniques, and strophic forms of the oral ballad; the 'broadside' and the 'songster', which printed strophic texts to be sung to tunes people knew by heart; and printed dance music, reflecting the characteristic rhythmic patterns and the multi-strain musical forms of folk dance.

The traditional folk music types of other European groups are more regional phenomena. Thus Hispanic-American folk music belongs to the Southwest and to California, French-American to the Cajuns in Louisiana, German-American to the 'Pennsylvania Dutch', and eastern European music—Greek, Russian, Balkan—to ethnic communities in large American cities like New York, Chicago, and Detroit. Also restricted to circulation within culturally distinct, isolated groups is the music of the many Amerindian tribes, aboriginal settlers of the North American continent.

No folk music has enjoyed a more complex history in the New World than that of the black Americans, who were brought there against their will. Most blacks in 18th- and 19th-century America were slaves; hence, most black American communities existed under some degree of white control, which discouraged the survival of such elements as drums, Old World languages, and African religious beliefs. Living in proximity to whites, black Americans gradually adopted certain white musical genres without abandoning their own indigenous performing styles—much more aggressive in rhythm and freer in pitch than any Euro-American singing or playing. Perhaps the most famous example of an acculturated vocal music is the *spiritual, the black American version of the Protestant hymn. First set down by white amateur musicians in the landmark collection *Slave Songs of the United States* (1867), then sung in harmonized choral versions by the Fisk Jubilee Singers and other groups of young blacks under white direction, and much later turned by trained black musicians into art songs for solo voice and piano, the spirituals illustrate how the folk music of a people considered 'half-barbarous' by its first white collectors could be adapted without losing its distinctive, haunting beauty.

The rhythmic complexity that early white collectors of spirituals found hard to capture in notation also pervaded black American instrumental folk music, much of it tied up with dance. Black musicians' fondness for off-beat accents within a steady metre was expressed through all available means: vocables, body-slapping, and foot-stomping; African-derived instruments like the bones and the banjo; and eventually European instruments, especially the fiddle and the piano. By the end of the 19th century, black American performers had fashioned an entertainment and dance music called 'ragtime', in which square-cut, syncopated melodies were played in a series of contrasting, march-like strains. Published as piano music around the turn of the century, ragtime achieved special elegance in the works of the composer-pianist Scott Joplin—as far removed from folk tradition as Henry T. Burleigh's settings of spirituals, but just as unmistakably marked by it.

The ability of black Americans to assimilate European-based forms and bend them to their own purposes, as in the spiritual and ragtime, and to provide the inspiration for some of the most lively white music-making of the age, as in the minstrel show, suggests that in 19th-century America cultural power did not necessarily depend upon social position. That fact was to become even clearer in the 20th century, when black American musical traditions made a decisive impact on virtually all American popular music.

4. 20th-century art music

Charles Ives, one of the most original of all 20th-century composers, stood almost entirely apart from the musical world that his American predecessors had struggled to build. By 1920, when Ives had virtually stopped composing, the institutions supporting music in the USA—symphony orchestras, opera companies, choral societies, conservatories and schools, and, a newer agency, phonograph recording companies—formed a superstructure of some permanence. Shaped by musicians and musically active citizens, that superstructure was a major part of the 20th-century composer's legacy. Although American composers who came of age in the 1920s had no stylistically unified tradition to carry on, they at least inherited a tradition of professionalism in art music. Another part of their inheritance, however, conspired to exclude them from that tradition. In the years before World War I the European avant-garde attacked artistic institutions and conventional aesthetic values, asserting that bourgeois society was the enemy of meaningful art. Such an attack carried certain penalties, especially in the USA, where musical institutions and composers depended on the support of the very citizens whom the avant-garde attacked. American composers who carried avant-garde influences to the New World found most musicians and audiences indifferent or hostile in their responses. It therefore fell to them to find or organize their own forum.

Edgard Varèse, who had made his home in New York from 1915, helped found in 1921 the short-lived International Composers' Guild, dedicated to performing contemporary music. As one of the founding members of the League of Composers (1923), Aaron Copland began his career as a tireless worker on behalf of the cause of new music. The California-born Henry Cowell, at a Carnegie Hall recital in 1924, unveiled pieces that called for many unconventional techniques, and in 1927, with Ives's financial backing, founded the New Music Edition, which for the next quarter-century published modern works by a whole range of composers, most of them American.

The economic depression of the 1930s touched almost every facet of American life, including music. In a social atmosphere of deprivation and misery, some composers reached a new understanding of their role in society. Rather than an embattled minority of artists in a hostile environment, they began to think of themselves as citizens with special talents that could be tapped for the general improvement of other Americans' lives. Simultaneously, institutional changes brought more Americans than ever before into contact with art music. The government's Federal Music Project, begun as a relief measure, put the resources of the state in the service of art music for the first time. Radio networks began to broadcast performances of symphony orchestras and opera companies, giving a large audience virtually free access to professional performances of art music. The commercial film industry engaged established American composers to provide scores for its productions. With composers standing ready to meet audiences halfway, hopes ran high between 1930 and 1945 that, by addressing a broader audience in an idiom that it understood, they could strengthen their rather tenuous place in American society.

In line with its new agenda, American art music of that period shows a greater tendency than ever before to celebrate American history, American heroes, and the American 'folk'. Roy Harris, born in Oklahoma and writing in an idiom shaped by his lifelong acquaintance with folk music, was a symphonist whose career blossomed in the 1930s. Virgil Thomson was another who plainly welcomed American subject matter. And Copland changed his style to produce *Appalachian Spring* (1944) and his Third Symphony (1946).

In the years immediately after World War II, American composers of art music were generally more interested in exploring new technical dimensions of their art than in broadening their audience. One institutional change that supported such exploration, and encouraged the notion that composers were intellectuals, was the rapid postwar expansion of college and university departments and schools of music, many of which appointed composers as teachers. Faculty positions required composers to do more than just compose, yet freed them to compose as they wished. Moreover, by assigning talented young musicians to their instruction, such posts affirmed their importance in the perpetuation of American music. Such composer-teachers as Walter Piston at Harvard and Howard Hanson at the Eastman School carried on the traditional academic posture of the earlier New England Classicists. Others, like Roger Sessions at Princeton and the University of California, Milton Babbitt at Princeton, and Ross Lee Finney at the University of Michigan emphasized the importance of the university as a place to work freely. By employing composers and encouraging performances of music by them, their colleagues, and their students, the university has created a public forum separate from that of the other established institutions of art music.

For all the importance of academic institutions, many musicians have managed to exist outside them as composers of commissioned pieces, performers, or writers on music. The Californian composer John Cage, a conspicuous avant-garde figure since his first New York concerts in the early 1940s, succeeded in finding another kind of audience in downtown Manhattan, home to an unusual concentration of artists, writers, theatre people, and students.

In view of the past history of art music in America, it is remarkable that not even thorough-going, anti-establishment radicalism could inhibit the growth in the 1960s and 70s of musical philanthropy. Private foundations, some of which had long supported musicians, stepped up their giving. Various states, most notably New York, established arts councils to disburse money financing worthy projects. The involvement of universities continued. And in 1965 the federal government established the National Endowment for the Arts, a funding agency whose budget grew quickly in the following years. In the 1980s, however, funds for music began to dwindle.

Nevertheless, by the end of the 20th century American art music was in a state of resolute pluralism. Earlier hopes that such a thing as an 'American music' might accompany national maturity seemed naive as the outline of a mature American culture began to appear. For, rather than pulling it towards a single, national style, the passing of time had seemed increasingly to diversify American art, to a point reflected in the music of Elliott Carter, Steve Reich, and John Adams.

5. Present-day popular music

With economic stakes so much higher than in art music, American musicians working in vernacular genres in the 20th century worked within a group of highly competitive institutions: the theatre circuit, the nightclub circuit, a network of music publishers and distributors, and the recording, film, and broadcasting industries. By the end of the 19th century theatrical entertainments involving music included both musical theatre (operettas and other shows with an integrated plot and many musical numbers) and the variety show or revue in which a series of different acts, some musical, shared the stage. Control of both was centred in New York, where dozens of theatres flourished. Some operettas and musical shows toured, and the vaudeville circuit sent variety shows through the whole country in a network of theatres. Songs from the musical theatre represented one of the staples of the music-publishing industry, which was now also centred on New York in the so-called *Tin Pan Alley district.

The American popular song, somewhat like the industry that supported it, presents a constantly changing surface whose fundamental subject matter has altered little. Most popular songs are love songs. The strain of high romantic rhetoric that pervaded the Viennese operetta is reflected in its early 20th-century counterpart in songs by Victor Herbert and Sigmund Romberg. The impact of black American music helped to bring a new rhythmic vitality and an informality of expression to shows of the 1910s and 20s and their songs, as suggested by Irving Berlin's *Alexander's Ragtime Band* and Gershwin's *I Got Rhythm*. This new 'hot' style of song was rooted in dance—especially in such new ways of moving as the foxtrot and the Charleston, which reflected the syncopated dance music increasingly referred to as *jazz. A widening range of harmonic possibilities enriched the songwriter's expressive resources, as shown in songs by Jerome Kern and Harold Arlen. Formally, the 32-bar chorus was almost universal, which made a song with a 48-bar chorus like Cole Porter's *Night and Day* remarkable. But the songwriter's craft calls on him to hide rather than flaunt his technique, working for something both natural-sounding and catchy.

Among types of indigenous music, black American *blues was one of the first to penetrate a commercial market. Observing the powerful response of rural southern black audiences to traditional folk music performed by members of their own community, the bandleader W. C. Handy began in about 1915 to publish blues in sheet-music form. Recordings of blues were made by black singers as early as 1920, and the unexpectedly strong reception they received from record buyers—mostly black, since the records were issued on 'race' labels that circulated chiefly where blacks lived—helped to create a new branch of the popular music industry. The same kind of process took place among rural and small-town whites in the south-eastern USA. As early as the 1920s, such performers as 'Fiddlin' John' Carson and the Carter Family were recording their own kind of music, leading to the establishment of the *country music industry, with headquarters in Nashville, Tennessee.

Traditional folk music of other kinds also found its way outside the context in which it originated. Beginning in the 1920s, emigrant musicians from many different European ethnic groups made commercial recordings in their indigenous Old World styles. Anglo-American folk tunes, together with their instrumentation and singing style, served as both a source and a model for performers linked with political causes—from Woody Guthrie's labour-union songs of the 1930s to Pete Seeger's and Bob Dylan's anti-war songs of the 1960s. Arranged for a wider commercial audience, folk music also contributed a fresh repertory in the 1950s and 60s for such entertainers as the Kingston Trio and Harry Belafonte. At the same time, musicians like Mike Seeger, performing in coffee houses and at folk festivals, dedicated themselves to preserving the 'authenticity' of traditional Anglo-American folk styles.

The predominant popular style since the 1960s, *rock and roll, was also conceived for a particular social group, American teenagers. Unlike blues, country music, and folk music—on all of which it has drawn—rock and roll originated as a strictly commercial music. Beginning in the late 1950s, it addressed the tastes of youngsters who were not much drawn to the music of Tin Pan Alley and Broadway—written for such performers as Bing Crosby, Frank Sinatra, and Peggy Lee, who sang primarily to other adults. Promoted at first by independent record producers and disc jockeys on offbeat radio stations, and sold cheaply in single-disc form, rock music soon became big business as the economic power of the youth market and the vitality of the new musical style revealed themselves. Talented and successful performers including Elvis Presley, Jimi Hendrix, and many others contributed to the maturing of rock music. Through various style changes, two elements have remained more or less constant as wellsprings of the music: an aggressive, driving beat implying sexuality, and a posture of rebellion against the values of conventional society, expressed both in song lyrics and in the dress and behaviour of the musicians, often calculated to offend non-aficionados.

Of all types of commercially based American music, *jazz is the one that has most consistently fostered musical artistry on a high level. Black jazz performers began to record early in the 1920s, among them Jelly Roll Morton and Louis Armstrong. Larger dance orchestras of the 1920s were influenced by the new jazz style, and some, like the New York-based black band of Duke Ellington, were organized especially to play it. White dance bands of the 1930s and 40s, like the group led by the Chicago-born clarinettist Benny Goodman, gained great commercial success through touring, record sales, and radio broadcasts, playing a repertory that included both jazz numbers and Tin Pan Alley songs.

The appearance of *bebop in the 1940s added a new style to the field of jazz—one in a self-consciously 'advanced' musical idiom perceived from the first as a radical departure from earlier jazz. Bebop also helped to introduce to jazz an aggressively anti-commercial orientation. The performer now considered him- or herself more an artist than an entertainer, and such musicians as the saxophonist Charlie Parker, the trumpeter Dizzy Gillespie, and the pianist-composer Thelonious Monk worked in a smaller, more specialized sphere with its own institutions—clubs, record companies, publications, and critics—and its own devoted audience. Younger performers like Ornette Coleman, John Coltrane, and Cecil Taylor contributed to an avant-garde movement that extended the jazz idiom further and further away from its original roots, so that by the 1960s the jazz avant-garde was beginning to be recognized by the academic-philanthropic establishment as a special kind of art music whose future required institutional support beyond what the commercial market could provide.

It is no surprise that in a musical culture like that of the USA, one that has developed without a single powerful centre, music of high artistic integrity and durability has appeared all over the country. Since jazz has been a uniquely American music of international impact—one clear-cut example of influence moving eastwards rather than westwards—perhaps it is fitting to take a jazz performance as a paradigm of American musical vitality. In October 1947 the 27-year-old black alto saxophonist from Kansas City, Charlie Parker, played Gershwin's song *Embraceable You* in the course of a recording session. That brief recorded moment preserves an uncanny balance: the fantasy of improvisatory inspiration within the restraint of a Tin Pan Alley love ballad's formal and harmonic structure; the decorative profusion of the virtuoso controlled by a disciplined, cohesive command of newly invented materials; a statement in a thoroughly personal idiom, delivered with the communicative power of a performer who seems to be speaking or singing through his instrument. Here is a fusion that testifies to artistic maturity; here is an American artist at work in a tradition.   RC/PG

📖 B. NETTL, *An Introduction to Folk Music in the United States* (Detroit, 1960; 3rd edn, rev. H. Myers as *Folk Music in the United States*, Detroit, 1976) · E. SOUTHERN, *The Music of Black Americans: A History* (New York, 1971, 3/1997) · B. LAMBERT (ed.), *Music in Colonial Massachusetts, 1630–1820* (Boston, 1980–5) · N. TAWA, *A Sound of Strangers: Musical Culture, Acculturation, and the Post-Civil War Ethnic American* (Metuchen, NJ, 1982) · C. HAMM, *Music in the New World* (New York and London, 1983) · C. SMALL, *Music of the Common Tongue: Survival and Celebration in Afro-American Music* (New York and London, 1987) · A. P. BRITTON, I. LOWENS, and R. CRAWFORD, *American Sacred Music Imprints, 1698–1810: A Bibliography* (Worcester, MA, 1990) · R. A. CRAWFORD, R. A. LOTT, and C. J. OJA (eds.), *A Celebration of American Music: Words and Music in Honor of H. Wiley Hitchcock* (Ann Arbor, MI, 1990) · S. PORTER, *With an Air Debonair: Musical Theatre in America, 1785–1815* (Washington, DC, 1991) · J. DIZIKES, *Opera in America: A Cultural History* (New Haven, CT, 1993) · R. GAROFALO, *Rockin' Out: Popular Music in the USA* (Needham Heights, MA, 1997) · R. CRAWFORD, *America's Musical Life* (New York, 2001)

uniti (It.). 'United', 'together'; it is usually used to revoke a direction such as *divisi.

Universal Edition (UE). Austrian firm of music publishers. It was founded in Vienna in 1901 and incorporated several other houses, quickly acquiring a substantial catalogue, including the major works of Richard Strauss. Under the direction (1907–32) of Emil Hertzka, Universal Edition became famous as a leading publisher of contemporary music—a reputation the firm has maintained through its championship of successive generations of avant-garde composers. Bartók, Mahler, Schoenberg, Webern, Zemlinsky, Berg, Janáček, Krenek, Milhaud, Weill, and Martinů all joined between 1908 and 1926. In the postwar years UE continued its strong support of avant-garde composers, many of whom, like Messiaen, Stockhausen, Boulez, and Berio, participated in the renowned summer courses for new music at Darmstadt. The firm has also published major historical anthologies, complete editions of Monteverdi and Gabrieli, the Wiener Urtext Edition, and educational music.

Alfred Kalmus (1889–1972), a member of the Viennese firm from 1909, founded the London branch of UE in 1937; it became independent in 1949. In addition to such composers as Berio, Boulez, Ligeti, and Stockhausen the English firm publishes many English and American composers including Bedford, Bennett, Birtwistle, Feldman, Holt, and Hoyland. David Sawer,

Ian Wilson, and Julian Yu are among the latest generation represented in the catalogue.   HA

unmerklich (Ger.). 'Imperceptible'.

un peu (Fr.), **un poco** (It.). See POCO.

unruhig (Ger.). 'Restless'.

unter (Ger.). 'Under', 'below'; *Unterdominante*, subdominant; *Unterklavier*, lower manual; *Unterstimme*, lower or lowest voice; *Unterwerk*, choir organ.

upbeat [anacrusis] (Fr.: *anacruse*; Ger.: *Auftakt*). The 'weak' beat of the bar which anticipates the first, 'strong' beat of the following bar, or *downbeat (Ex. 1). See CONDUCTING.

Ex. 1

upper mordent. See MORDENT.

upper partials. Constituents of the notes of the *harmonic series other than the main (fundamental) note, or first partial. See also ACOUSTICS, 5.

upright piano. A piano with the strings arranged vertically in a rectangular case, intended especially for domestic use. See PIANOFORTE.

Urlinie. Schenker's term for the stepwise-descending upper line in the fundamental structure (*Ursatz*) of tonal masterworks (see ANALYSIS, 3).

Ursatz. Schenker's term for the two-voice 'fundamental structure' of tonal masterworks (see ANALYSIS, 3).

Urtext (Ger., 'original text'). A term used to describe a modern edition of music which embodies the composer's original intent with minimal editorial interference. See SOURCES.

USA. See UNITED STATES OF AMERICA.

Ustvol'skaya, Galina Ivanovna (*b* Petrograd [St Petersburg], 17 June 1919). Russian composer. She studied at the Leningrad Conservatory with Shostakovich, graduating in 1950. Their relationship was more complicated than that of teacher and pupil: Shostakovich claimed that his music was influenced by hers, rather than the reverse, and he developed an emotional attachment to her. Ustvol'skaya subsequently led a reclusive life in St Petersburg, and little biographical information about her is available.

In the 1940s and 50s she composed in two very different styles: some works were written for official consumption in a conventional Soviet manner, and these earned her an income and even prizes; others were composed for limited, private dissemination, in a style that was strikingly original and more modernist than anything else written in the USSR at the time. The former works were merely a necessary evil, she later claimed, and should not be counted within her serious output. It was not until the 1970s that Ustvol'skaya's private style could find official toleration (though not encouragement); now that a number of Soviet composers had absorbed some Western avant-garde practices, her music seemed less outlandish. It gradually found its way to publication, and performances brought it to public attention for the first time. She began to enjoy her current Western prestige only in the post-Soviet 1990s, by which time she had announced that her life's work was finished.

Ustvol'skaya's style is remarkably consistent from the late 1940s to the 80s, and always uncompromisingly austere; her music most often proceeds without barlines or any obvious underlying metre in a moderately paced but relentless stream of crotchets. Her preferred textures are thin, often of single lines; although conjunct motion dominates, tonal associations are studiously avoided and contrapuntal combinations are consistently dissonant. Her six piano sonatas, consisting of four early and two late works, are the most austerely monochrome. Elsewhere, stark timbral contrasts emerge from strange combinations of instruments, as in her Composition no. 1, *Dona nobis pacem* (1971), for piano, tuba, and piccolo.

Ustvol'skaya is a devout Roman Catholic, and many of her works contain an explicit religious message in their texts or titles: her Second (1979), Third (1983), and Fourth (1987) Symphonies, for example, all incorporate devotional texts by Hermannus Contractus. She has stated that the same religious intent lies behind all her serious works, and she encourages performances within church buildings.   JWAL

📖 L. BLOIS, 'Shostakovich and the Ustvol'skaya connexion: A textual investigation', *Tempo*, 182 (1992), 10–18

ut. The first note of the scale according to the *solmization system. In the 17th century *ut* was replaced by the more singable *do* (in French and Italian usage), or *doh* (in the Tonic Sol-fa system). The French retain *ut* and the Italians use *do* to refer, on the fixed-*doh* principle, to the note C, in whichever scale it occurs. See also TONIC SOL-FA; HEXACHORD.

Ut queant laxis. The hymn from which the *solmization syllables derive.

v. 1. Abbreviation for 'violin' (also found as v° or vln). **2.** Abbreviation for *voci* (It.), 'voices'.

va (It.). **1.** 'Go on', 'goes on', i.e. 'continue', 'continues', e.g. *va diminuendo*, 'go on getting quieter'. **2.** Abbreviation for 'viola' (also found as vla).

Vaccai, Nicola (*b* Tolentino, 15 March 1790; *d* Pesaro, 5 or 6 Aug. 1848). Italian composer. He studied with Paisiello in Naples and, after trying his hand at writing operas, worked as a singing teacher there from 1815. Vaccai was more successful with later operas, two of which (*Zadig ed Astartea* and *Giulietta e Romeo*) were staged in 1825. In 1830 he went to Paris, where he again taught singing, and in the same year moved on to London for three years before returning to Italy. He was appointed professor of composition at the Milan Conservatory in 1838. Vaccai wrote a total of 17 operas, as well as church music, cantatas, songs, and four ballets, but he is best known for his singing tutor, the *Metodo pratico di canto italiano per camera* (London, 1832). His singing exercises are still in the repertory. WT

Vaet, Jacobus (*b* Kortrijk or Harelbeke, *c.*1529; *d* Vienna, 8 Jan. 1567). Flemish composer. He spent some years in the service of Charles V before becoming Kapellmeister to the imperial chapel in Vienna. Most of his surviving music is sacred, though his motets include 17 settings of secular texts. He made much use of borrowed material, both from his own works and from those of others, including Josquin and Clemens non Papa. His earlier works are similar in style to Gombert's, but later works show the influence of Lassus, for example in their use of polychoral techniques. DA/LC

vaghezza, con (It.). 'With longing', 'with charm'.

Vainberg, Moisei Samuilovich [Weinberg, Mieczysław] (*b* Warsaw, 8 Dec. 1919; *d* Moscow, 26 Feb. 1996). Russian composer. He studied the piano at the Warsaw Conservatory with Józef Turczyński and, after moving to the USSR in 1939, went on to study composition at the Minsk Conservatory with V. A. Zolotaryov; in 1943 he moved to Moscow. He was a prolific composer, writing no fewer than 22 symphonies, 17 string quartets, and seven operas, in addition to many works in other genres. His larger pieces are often dramatic and monumental essays in the tradition of Shostakovich; Bartók was also an important influence, and Vainberg's interest in Jewish folk and popular music is often in evidence. JWAL

Vakula the Smith (*Kuznets Vakula*). Opera in three acts by Tchaikovsky to a libretto by Yakov Polonsky after Nikolay Gogol's story *Noch' pered rozhdestvom* ('Christmas Eve') (St Petersburg, 1876); Tchaikovsky revised it as **Cherevichki*.

Valen, (Olav) Fartein (*b* Stavanger, 25 Aug. 1887; *d* Haugesund, 14 Dec. 1952). Norwegian composer and teacher. He enrolled in the University of Christiania (Oslo) to study language and literature but soon switched to music, studying theory with Catharinus Elling at the conservatory. After graduating as an organist (1909), he studied further with Bruch, among others, in Berlin. In 1924 he composed a Piano Trio which established an individual form of atonality independent of Schoenberg's, whose Serenade appeared in the same year. Valen's approach was derived from Bach, from whose music he evolved a polyphonic technique of dissonant counterpoint. Initially, Valen's works were on a small scale: songs (some with orchestra), chamber music, choral pieces, and nine orchestral poems; the first of his five symphonies (the last is unfinished) appeared in 1939. His Violin Concerto (1940), like Berg's, incorporates a Bach chorale in its finale; it is short, but powerfully moving in its elegiac concentration. MA

📖 B. KORTSEN, *Fartein Valen* (Oslo, 1965)

Valkyrie, The. See WALKÜRE, DIE.

Vallée d'Obermann ('Obermann Valley'). Work for solo piano by Liszt, originally part of *Album d'un voyageur*, later revised as no. 6 of book 1 of *Années de pèlerinage*.

Valls, Francisco [Francesc] (*b* ?Barcelona, 1665 or 1671; *d* Barcelona, 3 Feb. 1747). Catalan composer and music theorist. Although he composed prodigiously (mainly sacred music) and was *maestro de capilla* of the parish church in Mataró and the cathedrals in Gerona and Barcelona for many years, his lasting claim to fame emerged with the posthumous publication of his treatise *Mapa armónico* (1741–2, written after his retirement). This influential work, defending the validity of Spanish practices against Italian and French styles, dealt with most contemporary issues of harmony, composition, and performance, and included several specially written pieces among the musical illustrations. The sections on continuo realization are of particular value for the light they cast on performance practice.

Valls's interest in theoretical questions was perhaps partly stimulated by the heated debate caused by his *Missa 'Scala aretina'* (1702), which contained unprepared dissonances regarded as inadmissible by some critics of the day. The ensuing controversy (manifested in about 80 writings by the most prominent Spanish musicians) spread far beyond Spain, and gained him temporarily and unexpectedly a reputation for musical innovation, though this was not sustained by the bulk of his other music.   MHE

valse (Fr.). 'Waltz'.

Valse, La ('The Waltz'). Orchestral work ('choreographic poem') by Ravel, composed in 1919–20; he arranged it for two pianos (1921) and Lucien Garban arranged it for piano duet. It was used for a one-act ballet, choreographed by Bronislava Nijinska (Paris, 1928) and has since been choreographed by George Balanchine (1951) and Frederick Ashton (1958).

Valses nobles et sentimentales ('Noble and Sentimental Waltzes'). Work (1911) by Ravel for piano solo; he orchestrated it the following year. The score was used for the ballet *Adélaïde, ou Le Langage des fleurs*, to Ravel's own scenario, choreographed by Ivan Clustine (Paris, 1912) and it has since been choreographed by Serge Lifar (1938), Frederick Ashton (1947), Kenneth MacMillan (1966), and Ronald Hynd (1975).

Valse triste ('Sad Waltz'). Waltz, op. 44 (1903), by Sibelius, composed as part of the incidental music for Arvid Järnefelt's play *Kuolema* ('Death'); it was originally for strings but Sibelius revised the orchestration in 1904 and also arranged it for piano.

valve (Fr.: *piston, cylindre*; Ger.: *Ventil*; It.: *chiave*). A device that admits air into auxiliary tubing on *brass instruments, so altering the tube length, and thus its harmonic series, by a fixed amount. A sequence of various valve combinations permits access to all the notes of a chromatic scale.

The basic provision is three valves. The first lowers the harmonic series by a whole tone, the second by a semitone, and the third by a tone and a half. If the valves are used in combination, up to seven different harmonic series can be reached. (The sequence of valve combinations on most brass band instruments, used in full between the second and third partials, is shown from g' to c' in Ex. 1; on the horn the fingering is slightly different.) Bass brasses are often provided with a fourth valve, which lowers the instrument by a perfect 4th, filling in the gap between the lowest note in Ex. 1 down to the fundamental c a diminished 5th below (the fundamental is not usually playable on such narrow-bore instruments as the *trumpet but is a valuable note on wide-bore instruments, e.g. the *tuba).

A cumulative error of pitch is caused by using more than one valve at a time: if the tube has been lengthened by a semitone using the first valve, more than the length of the second valve will be needed to lengthen the tube by a further whole tone, and so on. On small instruments (e.g. the trumpet) notes can often be lipped into tune. Another way is to make the third valve slightly longer by pulling out its tuning-slide, so that it is played only in combination with one or both of the others. On bass instruments, where the problem is most pronounced and lipping the notes is less effective, extra valves are sometimes provided so that lengths may be added as required (see TUBA, 1).

Valves were first patented in Berlin in 1818 by two Silesian wind players, H. D. Stölzel and Friedrich Blühmel. The first to be generally used were the Stölzel pistons, seen on many antique instruments in museums, but their narrow bore and the sharp bends of the air column spoilt the tone-quality, and the friction caused by their length as the pistons moved up and down led to slow action and occasional jams. A wider and shorter piston valve, invented in Paris by François Périnet in 1839, is still the most common on trumpets and many other instruments. In this type of valve, when the valve

Ex. 1

is at rest, in the 'up' position (Fig. 1, left), a short diagonal tube crossing the piston (2) leads the air from the mouthpipe (1) directly to the main tubing (3). When the valve is depressed (Fig. 1, right) an alternative slanting tube (4) in the piston leads the air into the auxiliary tubing. At the same time a third tube (5) meets the other end of the auxiliary tubing and leads the air back into the main bore.

Although many horn players in Vienna remain true to another early type of valve—the 'double piston' or 'Vienna' valve, in which two parallel pistons move together for each of the three valves—pistons have now been almost universally superseded on the horn by rotary valves, invented in 1835 by Josef Riedl of Vienna. When a lever is depressed, the rotating cylinder (rotor) turns through 90° to divert the air from the main bore into the auxiliary tubing (Fig. 2). Rotary valves are used in Germany and central Europe on trumpets, tubas, and other instruments besides horns.

JMo

📖 A. Baines, *Brass Instruments: Their History and Development* (London, 1976) · H. Heyde, *Das Ventilblasinstrument* (Leipzig, 1987) · T. Herbert and J. Wallace (eds.), *The Cambridge Companion to Brass Instruments* (Cambridge, 1997) · E. H. Tarr, *East Meets West* (Stuyvesant, NY, forthcoming)

vamping. Improvising a simple, harmonized piano accompaniment, usually of octaves in the left hand alternating with chords in the right. The word, said to date from the early 18th century, was used in the early days of music hall, when 'vamp till ready' indicated that a progression was to be repeated indefinitely until a soloist entered. Piano schools in the early 1900s advertised simple vamping charts for the amateur pianist.

PGa

Vampyr, Der ('The Vampire'). Opera in two acts by Marschner to a libretto by Wilhelm August Wohlbrück after plays based on John W. Polidori's story *The Vampyre*, a revision of Byron's *Fragment of a Novel* (sometimes called *Augustus Darvell*) (Leipzig, 1828). Lindpaintner wrote a three-act opera on the same subject (Stuttgart, 1828).

Van Dieren, Bernard. See Dieren, Bernard van.

Vanhal [Wanhal], Johann Baptist [Jan Křtitel] (*b* Nechanice, Bohemia, 12 May 1739; *d* Vienna, 20 Aug. 1813). Czech composer, violinist, and teacher. Of humble origins, he was first taught locally. His early compositions and his abilities on the violin attracted the attention of his superiors, and in 1761 he went to Vienna. There he studied with Dittersdorf and began to establish a reputation as a composer and teacher. In 1769 he travelled widely in Italy, returning to Austria in 1771. He settled permanently in Vienna in about 1780, supporting himself independently by teaching and composing. Vanhal was well acquainted with the major musical figures of the day in Vienna; according to the Irish tenor Michael Kelly he took part in a quartet with Mozart, Haydn, and his master Dittersdorf.

Vanhal's music was popular and was widely distributed in manuscript and printed form. In his numerous symphonies, mostly written between 1760 and 1780, he made early use of sonata styles, contributing significantly, and largely without the influence of Haydn, to the development of the Classical symphony. After 1783 he turned to less weighty genres aimed at the amateur solo player, producing keyboard sonatas, sonatinas, and capriccios, programme works, and towards the end of his life some contrapuntal teaching pieces. Besides published quartets, quintets, trios, and

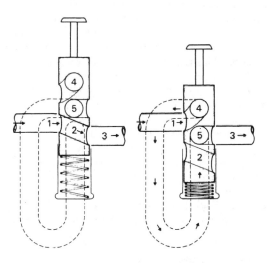

Fig. 1. Section of piston valve: at rest (left); lowered (right).

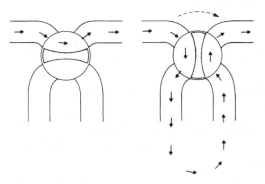

Fig. 2. Diagram of rotary valve: at rest (left); depressed (rotor turned through 90°, right).

duos, 48 masses remained mostly in manuscript. If his melodic style lacked the variety of his more illustrious colleagues he was none the less a significant influence on many.
JSM

Varèse, Edgard (Victor Achille Charles) (*b* Paris, 22 Dec. 1883; *d* New York, 6 Nov. 1965). French-born American composer. He spent much of his childhood with his mother's family in Burgundy, where the massive architecture of the Romanesque churches affected him deeply. His father intended that he should be trained as an engineer, but he was determined to become a composer, and in 1903 he left home (then in Turin) to study in Paris. He was a pupil of d'Indy, Roussel, and Bordes at the Schola Cantorum; he also attended Widor's classes at the Conservatoire. Between 1908 and 1915 he divided his time between Paris (where he got to know Debussy, Satie, Guillaume Apollinaire, and Jean Cocteau) and Berlin, where he became acquainted with Busoni, Strauss, and the music of Schoenberg. He then emigrated to the USA, where he did much to promote the music of his contemporaries through the activities of the International Composers' Guild and the Pan-American Association of Composers, both of which he was instrumental in founding.

With the exception of a single song, *Un grand sommeil noir* (1906), all the music Varèse wrote before his emigration has been lost. His output effectively begins with *Amériques* (1918–22), scored for an enormous orchestra and celebrating not only a new homeland but also new worlds of the imagination. Though influenced by Debussy, Stravinsky, and Schoenberg, the work is quite original in its perpetually evolving form, its rhythmic complexity, and its massive eruptions of sound; it is also marked by Varèse's love for the speed and sounds of modern city life. In all these respects *Amériques* contained the seeds for the more polished works that followed: *Hyperprism* for a small orchestra of wind and percussion (1922–3), *Intégrales* for a similar ensemble (1924–5), *Octandre* for seven wind and double bass (1923–4), *Arcana* for orchestra (1925–7), and *Ionisation* for 13 percussionists (1930–3). The quasi-scientific titles signify a calculating approach to form and sonority, but he also saw himself, perhaps romantically, as comparable to the scientists in grappling with the unknown. His feeling for the primitive and magical is uppermost in *Ecuatorial* (1933–4), setting a Maya imprecation for bass voice and small orchestra.

From his arrival in New York Varèse pressed for new electronic means as necessary to the music of the future. He included two of Lev Termen's electronic instruments in *Ecuatorial*, but, lacking the resources he required, he completed only a short flute piece, *Density*

21.5 (1936), during the next 15 years. The availability of the tape recorder enabled him to continue with *Déserts* (1949–54), which interleaves orchestral with electronic sections, and then with the *Poème électronique* (1957–8). However, his last work, the unfinished *Nocturnal* (1960–1), was for voices and instruments without electronics.
PG

📖 F. OUELLETTE, *Edgard Varèse* (New York, 1968; London, 1973) · L. VARÈSE, *Varèse: A Looking-Glass Diary* (New York, 1972) · J. W. BERNARD, *The Music of Edgard Varèse* (New Haven, CT, 1987)

variation form 1. Introduction; 2. Variation types; 3. Historical overview

1. Introduction

In variation form a self-contained theme is repeated and changed in some way with each successive statement. Variations may be continuous, as in *ostinato movements, or discrete, as in *strophic variations. The number and type of variations are not fixed. As a genre, strophic theme and variations has often had a poor reputation. This is in part because its form is paratactic (a chain of separable links) and can therefore seem like a loose assemblage of small pieces without a coherent shape. However, many composers have grouped individual variations to create larger-scale musical forms and rhetorical patterns. In the hands of the greatest composers the repeated close working of a theme has often produced compelling and powerful music, but many variation sets written for popular consumption are artistically trivial. Thus variation form is unusual in furnishing both the most vacuous and some of the most profound examples of Western instrumental music.

2. Variation types

Although all musical parameters can be subjected to variation processes, the repertory is dominated by a small number of types:

(*a*) cantus firmus or constant melody, in which the melody remains constant while other parameters change (e.g. the second movement of Haydn's 'Emperor' Quartet op. 76 no. 3);

(*b*) constant bass or ostinato, in which the bass pattern remains constant (e.g. *ground bass, *passacaglia, and *chaconne);

(*c*) fixed harmony, in which the harmonic framework of the theme remains constant (e.g. variations on the *folia and the *romanesca, Bach's 'Goldberg' Variations);

(*d*) melodic outline, in which the melodic shape of the theme is either decorated with additional notes or replaced by a paraphrase of the original: the most common variation type in the late 18th and 19th centuries;

(*e*) formal outline, in which the form and phrase structure of the theme are the only elements to remain constant (e.g. Schumann's Symphonic Variations op. 13);

(*f*) characteristic variations, in which elements of theme are reworked in different genres and types (e.g. Britten's *Variations on a Theme of Frank Bridge* op. 10);

(*g*) fantasia variations, in which all parameters can be subjected to radical change though a narrative structure may shape the work (e.g. Strauss's *Don Quixote* and Elgar's 'Enigma' Variations);

(*h*) serial variations, in which the note row forms the theme for the variations (e.g. the second movement of Webern's Symphony op. 21).

3. Historical overview

The technique and process of variation have been fundamental to Western music from its earliest history, but variation form derives from the practice of improvising embellishments in successive strophes of songs and dances during the 16th century. Among the earliest published examples are sets of *diferencias* for vihuela by Luis de Narváez (*Delphín de música*, 1538). As the most extended instrumental form of the period, variation developed rapidly: composers formulated new types and began to organize their sets into larger patterns. The Spanish organist Antonio de Cabezón wrote keyboard variations with cantus-firmus, fixed-bass, and melodic-outline techniques. He gave each variation a distinctive motivic profile and linked individual variations with transition passages. Cabezón's work was imitated in Italy and developed by English keyboard composers. The Fitzwilliam Virginal Book contains a conspectus of Renaissance variation forms: over 200 pieces by leading composers including Bull, Farnaby, and Byrd.

In the 17th century the development of the basso *continuo led to a proliferation of fixed-bass variation types, especially ostinato dances like the passacaglia and chaconne. Two distinct kinds of melodic variation also flourished in the 17th and early 18th centuries. *Chorale variations using cantus-firmus techniques were widely cultivated in Germany, while in France the most common type of variation was the *double* (see DOUBLE, 3), a melodic outline variation of a song or dance. J. S. Bach used all the main examples of Baroque variation and carried many of them to unprecedented levels of complexity. In his Chaconne for unaccompanied violin (from BWV1004) the theme and 63 variations are arranged in three parts (minor–major–minor); other formal patterns are created by Bach's manipulation of texture, motifs, register, and playing techniques.

Similar large-scale organization is found in the 'Goldberg' Variations: the 30 variations are arranged in ten groups of three, in which every third variation is a canon at an increasingly wide interval.

The Classical ideal of melodic-outline variations was articulated by Rousseau, who compared the embellishments to embroidery, through which 'one must always be able to recognize the essence of the melody'. Variation form was important to the leading Classical composers. Haydn used variations on original themes as movements in his keyboard sonatas, quartets, and symphonies. He had a predilection for such hybrid forms as rondo-variations (in which freer and stricter variations alternate) and alternating variations on two themes in contrasting modes (as in his Variations in F minor for piano). Mozart's career as a performer is reflected in his piano variations. He too carefully patterned his variations into coherent larger forms. His independent sets progress from figurative embellishments to variations that treat the theme more freely (changing to the minor mode, developing motifs contrapuntally or in imitation, and reworking the theme as a lyrical Adagio). They end with a longer fantasia-like section, a cadenza, or a reprise of the theme.

Beethoven developed variation form to a greater extent than his Classical predecessors. His variation sets (e.g. the *32 Variations on an Original Theme in C minor* WOO80) have a strong sense of goal orientation, working towards an idealized version of the theme. He increasingly eschewed melodic-outline variations in favour of a more thorough exploration of the theme's musical possibilities and ethos. Variation forms became ever more important in Beethoven's late work, offering powerful alternatives to his dramatic sonata forms, and they form the centrepiece of most of his late sonatas and quartets.

Melodic-outline variations continued to be used throughout the 19th century, but other types challenged their supremacy. Schubert favoured cantus-firmus techniques for variations on his own song themes, and sometimes organized his sets so that they relate poetically to the original source, as in the serene ending of the variation movement in the 'Death and the Maiden' Quartet D810. Schumann's Romantic sensibility led him towards the fantasia variation. Connections between variations are often elusive and suggestive, so that the music has integrity of feeling rather than Classical thematic coherence: for instance, he regarded his *Blumenstück* op. 19 as 'Variations on no theme'. Many composers favoured the formal freedom of fantasia variations, and this type came to dominate the later 19th century. But the most significant composer of variations in this era, Brahms, drew on variation types from the Baroque, Classical, and Romantic periods and produced a striking synthesis of earlier variation techniques in the finale of his Fourth Symphony.

In the 20th century composers found variation form adaptable to the widest variety of styles and techniques. They developed radical new approaches to the organization of variations, and explored anew variation techniques and forms from the distant past. Many musicians adopted a markedly idiosyncratic approach to variations, and for this reason it is impossible to give a brief overview. The reader is guided instead to composer entries, where imaginative solutions to organizing variation form may be discussed in relation to the individual's musical style.   TRJ

📖 R. NELSON, *The Technique of Variation: A Study of Instrumental Variation from Cabezón to Reger* (Berkeley and Los Angeles, 1948/*R*1962) · R. HUDSON, *The Folia, the Saraband, the Passacaglia, and the Chaconne*, Musicological Studies and Documents, 35 (Rome, 1982)

Variations. Eight works by Cage in which *indeterminacy is taken to extraordinary limits. The score of Variations I (1958), for example, consists of transparent plastic sheets inscribed with lines and dots which the performer or performers superimpose in any way and play on any instrument or instruments; Variations VIII (1978) is for 'no music or recordings'.

Variations and Fugue on a Theme of Henry Purcell. See YOUNG PERSON'S GUIDE TO THE ORCHESTRA, THE.

Variations on 'America'. Work (1891–2) by Ives for organ; the composer added polytonal interludes *c.*1909–10. It was arranged for orchestra by William Schuman in 1964 and for concert band by Schuman and W. Rhoads.

Variations on a Theme by Haydn. Orchestral work by Brahms, op. 56*a* (1873), a set of eight variations and a finale on a theme often called 'St Anthony's Chorale', from the second movement of a divertimento for wind probably not by Haydn; Brahms arranged the work for two pianos (op. 56*b*).

variato, variata (It.). 'Varied'.

variazione, variazioni (It.). 'Variation', 'variations'. See VARIATION FORM.

Vater unser (Ger., 'Our Father'). The German translation, by Martin Luther, of the *Pater noster*, or Lord's Prayer. It is sung as a hymn to a tune that may also have been written by Luther.

vaudeville. 1. Two French 16th-century song types bear names that could have been corrupted to form 'vaudeville': the 'val' (or 'vau') 'de vire', a popular song concerning love, drinking, and satire on topical matters from the valley of the Vire river in Normandy; and the 'voix de ville', a courtly song that may have developed in response to the popular *vau de vire*. In the 17th and 18th centuries, vaudevilles were usually concerned with satire on political and courtly matters. See OPERA, 6.

2. In the USA the term was used in the 1880s for a variety show, similar to the much earlier British *music hall, from which it partly developed; it featured singers, dancers, comedians, and acrobats. 'Vaudeville' was popularized as a name by the impresario Tony Pastor (1837–1908), who preferred it to 'variety' (originally used in the USA and Britain); his Tammany Hall opened in New York in 1881. In the early 1900s vaudeville was by far the most popular form of entertainment, reaching its peak with the opening of the Palace Theatre in New York in 1913. It created its own stars, including Lillian Russell (1861–1922) and Fanny Brice (1891–1951), and lured performers from the British music hall.

—/PGa

Vaughan Williams, Ralph (*b* Down Ampney, Glos., 12 Oct. 1872; *d* London, 26 Aug. 1958). English composer. He was a leading figure in the so-called renaissance of English musical life—creative, executive, and musicological—which began in the last years of the 19th century coincident with Elgar's rise to fame.

1. The early years; 2. The years of maturity; 3. The final years

1. The early years

Descended from Darwins and Wedgwoods, Vaughan Williams had a conventional upper-middle-class education in which music played a surprisingly prominent part. He played the violin in the Charterhouse school orchestra. He began to compose when he was six and continued until the day of his death. In 1890 he went, unconventionally, direct to the Royal College of Music as a composition pupil of Parry. In 1892 he entered Trinity College, Cambridge, to read history and for the B.Mus. degree, continuing weekly lessons at the RCM and studying composition at Cambridge with Charles Wood. In 1895 he re-entered the RCM as a pupil of Stanford. During this briefer spell he formed a mutually enriching friendship with Gustav Holst. In 1897, after his marriage to Adeline Fisher, he went to Berlin, where he had lessons and encouragement from Bruch.

His compositions at the turn of the century were mainly chamber music (later withdrawn) and songs, including *Linden Lea* (1901). He edited the *Welcome Songs* for the Purcell Society, wrote articles for periodicals, and contributed to the second edition (1904) of

Grove's Dictionary of Music and Musicians. In 1904 his *Songs of Travel*, settings of R. L. Stevenson, were sung in London. A significant event in 1902 was his introduction by Lucy Broadwood to the systematic collecting of folksongs; further impetus was given to this activity in December 1903 when he heard *Bushes and Briars* sung by an old shepherd in Essex. During the next nine years he collected tunes in Norfolk, Herefordshire, Surrey, and Sussex, publishing many of them in various arrangements. In 1904 he accepted an invitation to be music editor of a new hymnbook, *The English Hymnal* (1906).

2. The years of maturity

Vaughan Williams's principal work around the turn of the century was a short choral setting of Walt Whitman, *Toward the Unknown Region* (1905). Although this was a success at the 1907 Leeds Festival, he was dissatisfied with his compositions generally and went to Paris early in 1908 for three months' intensive study with Ravel. This released his creative energies. He rapidly produced the String Quartet no. 1 in G minor (1908), the Housman song cycle *On Wenlock Edge* for tenor, piano, and string quartet (of which Gervase Elwes gave the first performance in 1909), and incidental music for the 1909 Cambridge Greek Play, *The Wasps*. In the same year he completed a choral symphony on which he had been at work since 1903: as *A Sea Symphony* (also to a Whitman text) it had an enthusiastic reception at the 1910 Leeds Festival and established Vaughan Williams in the front rank of English composers. The *Fantasia on a Theme by Thomas Tallis* for strings (1910) eventually became one of his best-known works. It was followed by the *Five Mystical Songs* (1911) and *A London Symphony*, first performed in London in 1914. From 1910 to 1914 he was also at work on a ballad opera set in Napoleonic days, *Hugh the Drover*. This was completed in August 1914, whereupon it was shelved while its composer, though in his 42nd year, joined the army and spent most of the next four years in France.

In 1919 Vaughan Williams joined the staff of the RCM and in 1921 became conductor of the Bach Choir. His experience as a choral conductor dated chiefly from 1905, when he had become conductor of the Leith Hill Festival in Dorking, near his family home. His Bach performances, highly idiosyncratic but artistically compelling, were the festival's major attraction until 1958. From 1922 he produced ambitious and enterprising works in several genres. These included *A Pastoral Symphony* (1922), the Mass in G minor (1921), *Flos campi*, a suite for solo viola, small chorus, and orchestra (1925), the oratorio *Sancta civitas* (1926), and a Violin Concerto (1925). *Hugh the Drover* and the

Falstaff opera *Sir John in Love* were produced in London in 1924 and 1929 respectively; the 'masque for dancing' *Job* (based on William Blake's illustrations), was first performed as an orchestral work at Norwich in 1930 and reached the stage in London in 1931; the Piano Concerto was played by Harriet Cohen in London in 1933; and in 1935 his violent Fourth Symphony was introduced by Adrian Boult at a BBC concert in London. A few weeks later he was appointed to the Order of Merit.

3. The final years

The last 22 years of Vaughan Williams's life showed no diminution in his various musical activities. Five more symphonies followed (no. 5, 1943; no. 6, 1947; no. 7, *Sinfonia antartica*, 1952; no. 8, 1955; no. 9, 1957); he wrote his first film score in 1940, his Second String Quartet in 1942–4, completed an opera *The Pilgrim's Progress*, on which he had been working for many years (Covent Garden, 1951), and produced several choral works, notably *Hodie* (1954), and many smaller pieces. Vaughan Williams drew his inspiration from many sources—folksong and the English 16th-century school chief among them—and the influence of Ravel is frequently discernible. A lyrical melodic gift is at the heart of his work, but besides modality there is a gritty harmonic toughness, such as occurs in *Job* and the Fourth Symphony, which places him firmly in the 20th century. His nationalist creed was that a composer must reach his fellow countrymen before he can hope to reach a universal audience. His symphonies, choral works, and songs are the core of his output, but the operas, particularly *Riders to the Sea* (London, 1937), contain fine music which overcomes the dramatic problems they pose. The nobility, integrity, and visionary qualities of the man are reflected in his music.   MK

📖 F. HOWES, *The Music of Ralph Vaughan Williams* (London, 1954) · U. VAUGHAN WILLIAMS and I. HOLST (eds.), *Heirs and Rebels: Letters between Vaughan Williams and Holst* (London, 1959) · J. DAY, *Vaughan Williams* (London, 1961, 3/1998) · R. VAUGHAN WILLIAMS, *National Music and Other Essays* (London, 1963) · M. KENNEDY, *The Works of Ralph Vaughan Williams* (London, 1964, rev. in 2 vols., 1980, 1982) · H. OTTAWAY, *Vaughan Williams Symphonies* (London, 1972) · W. MELLERS, *Vaughan Williams and the Vision of Albion* (London, 1989) · A. FROGLEY (ed.), *Vaughan Williams Studies* (Cambridge, 1996) · L. FOREMAN (ed.), *Ralph Vaughan Williams in Perspective* (London, 1998) · S. HEFFER, *Vaughan Williams* (London, 2000)

Vautor, Thomas (*fl* early 17th century). English composer. He took the Oxford degree of B.Mus. in 1616, and by 1619 was in the service of George Villiers, Duke of Buckingham, in Leicestershire; his only known work, a set of madrigals published in that year, is dedicated to the duke's son, George Villiers the younger. The madrigals, which cover a wide emotional range from merriment to melancholy, include the popular *Sweet Suffolk Owl*.   DA/JM

vc, vcl. Abbreviations for 'violoncello'.

Vecchi, Orazio (Tiberio) (*b* Modena, 5 Dec. 1550; *d* Modena, 19 Feb. 1605). Italian composer. The third of six children, he became a priest early in life before taking up music as a profession. He was *maestro di cappella* at Salò Cathedral (Lake Garda) from 1581 to 1584, and then at Modena Cathedral. Two years later he moved first to Reggio nell'Emilia and then, in the same year, to Correggio. He remained there until 1598, when he returned to Modena, resuming his old position in the cathedral and taking charge of the court music for the Este family.

Vecchi composed some excellent church music, but his fame rests on his light madrigals and canzonettas, written in an eminently singable and attractive style. His best-known work is the madrigal comedy *L'Amfiparnaso* (1597), a *commedia dell'arte* scenario set to music, with amusing character studies using Italian dialects.   DA/TC

Vega, Aurelio de la (*b* Havana, 28 Nov. 1925). Cuban-born American composer. After studies in Los Angeles with Ernst Toch (1947–8) he returned to Cuba, where he held various posts as a teacher and administrator. In 1959 he settled in Los Angeles, teaching at California State University at Northridge. His compositions cover all genres, including electronic music, and incorporate a great variety of styles and techniques.   PG

Vejvanovský, Pavel Josef (*b* Hukvaldy or Hlučín, *c*.1633; *d* Kroměříž, *bur.* 24 Sept. 1693). Moravian composer and trumpeter. His family circumstances, place, and date of birth are uncertain, but by his death he was among the most respected Czech musicians of the day. It is possible that he studied in Vienna, and certain that he attended the Jesuit School in Opava, 1656–60. A year later he entered the service of Castelle, the administrator of the court of the Prince-Bishop of Olomouc at Kroměříž. In 1664 he was appointed first trumpeter and director of the court orchestra; he remained in the post until his death. In addition to his work at the court he director the choir of St Mořice's, where several of his works were performed, probably including his 15 mass settings.

Besides accompanied church music Vejvanovský composed multi-movement sonatas in the manner of Schmelzer and suite-like serenades, all scored mostly for strings, continuo, and a combination of brass instruments. His style has much in common with that of his younger contemporary Biber, with whom he worked at Kroměříž, suggesting a degree of mutual influence. Vejvanovský had a distinctive if limited melodic repertory, and made imaginative use of Moravian folksong, but it is his use of sonority which commands attention, in particular his treatment of the various types of trumpet he himself played.   JSm

velato, velata (It.). 'Veiled', 'misty'.

veloce, velocemente (It.). 'Fast', 'quickly'; *con velocità*, 'with speed'.

Venetian Games (*Gry weneckie*; *Jeux vénitiens*). Work (1960–1) for chamber orchestra by Lutosławski, the first in which he used aleatory procedures.

Venezuela. See Latin America, 5.

Veni creator spiritus (Lat., 'Come, creator spirit'). A Whitsuntide hymn of the Roman rite, also sung for the creation of a pope, the consecration of a bishop, the elevation or translation of a saint, the coronation of a monarch, and on many other occasions. After the Reformation, vernacular adaptations of this hymn persisted in the Lutheran and Anglican Churches. Its text and chant melody have variously been used since the Middle Ages in choral and instrumental settings by composers including Dunstaple, Palestrina, Mahler, and Penderecki.   —/ALi

Veni Sancte Spiritus (Lat., 'Come, Holy Ghost'). A sequence of the Roman rite, appointed for Pentecost and the following six days, the words of which have been ascribed to Pope Innocent III (*d* 1216) and Stephen Langton, Archbishop of Canterbury (*d* 1228). It is one of the four sequences that were allowed to remain following the *Council of Trent (1542–63). Dunstaple wrote a four-voice motet in which the text is sung in the top voice while the hymn *Veni creator spiritus* is sounded below.   —/ALi

Venite (Lat., 'Come'). Psalm 94 (Psalm 95 in the Hebrew), called the Invitatorium or Invitatory Psalm, or, in Henry VIII's Primer, 'A song stirring to the Praise of God'. In the Roman rite it is sung with a variable antiphon as the opening chant of Matins. The Anglican Church suppressed the antiphon but retained the psalm in English translation in its *Book of Common Prayer* as a fixed prelude to the morning psalms. The *Venite*, with or without an antiphon, continues to occupy a similar position in several of the revised morning Offices created by Western churches during the latter half of the 20th century.   —/ALi

vent (Fr.). 'Wind'; *instruments à vent*, 'wind instruments'.

Ventadorn, Bernart de. See BERNART DE VENTADORN.

Ventil (Ger.; It.: *ventile*). 'Valve'.

Venus and Adonis. 1. Opera in a prologue and three acts by Blow to a libretto by an unknown author (London or Windsor, *c.*1683).

2. Masque in two interludes by Pepusch to a libretto by Colley Cibber after book 10 of Ovid's *Metamorphoses* (London, 1715).

Vêpres siciliennes, Les (*I vespri siciliani*; 'The Sicilian Vespers'). Opera in five acts by Verdi to a libretto by Eugène Scribe and Charles Duveyrier after their libretto *Le Duc d'Albe* (1838) (Paris, 1855); it was translated into Italian by Eugenio Caimi, as *Giovanni di Guzman*, and is now most often given in this version but under the title *I vespri siciliani*.

Veracini, Francesco Maria (*b* Florence, 1 Feb. 1690; *d* Florence, 31 Oct. 1678). Italian violinist and composer. A member of a notable violin-playing family, he travelled throughout Europe as a virtuoso soloist. In 1711 and 1712 he played at St Mark's, Venice, where he made a great impression on Tartini; he visited London in 1714 and Düsseldorf in 1715. From 1717 to 1722 he served as a violinist, with an exceptionally high salary, at the Dresden court, and from 1733 to 1738 he played for the Opera of the Nobility in London, where three of his own operas were performed. He was again in London from 1741 to 1745. In 1755 he settled in Florence as *maestro di cappella* at S. Pancrazio, and is said to have died an extremely wealthy man. He had a reputation for arrogance and eccentricity verging on madness, as well as for exceptional virtuosity, and his fine violin sonatas are full of idiomatic special effects.   DA/ER

Vera costanza, La ('True Constancy'). Opera in three acts by Haydn to a libretto by Francesco Puttini (Eszterháza, 1779).

Veränderungen (Ger.). 'Variations'. The term is sometimes used instead of *Variationen*: Bach's 'Goldberg' Variations, for example, were issued as *Aria mit verschiedenen Veränderungen*, and Beethoven's *Diabelli Variations op. 120 as *Veränderungen über einen Walzer von Anton Diabelli*.

Vera storia, La ('The True Story'). Opera in two acts by Berio to a libretto by Italo Calvino (Milan, 1982).

verbunkos (from Ger. *Werbung*, 'enlistment'). A Hungarian soldiers' dance, used from about 1780 to attract recruits into the army. It was danced to the music of Gypsy bands by hussars in uniform. Despite losing its purpose when the Austrian government imposed conscription in 1849 it survived as a ceremonial dance. The *verbunkos* consisted of two or more sections, similar to those of the *csárdás*, some in the style of a slow introduction (*lassú*), others fast and wild (*friss*). Many collections were published during the 19th century.

The dance form has been used by Hungarian composers including Liszt (second Hungarian Rhapsody), Bartók (rhapsodies for piano and violin with orchestra), and Kodály (Intermezzo from *Háry János*).

Verdelot [Deslouges], Philippe (*b* Verdelot, Seine-et-Marne, *c.*1480–5; *d* by 1552, probably *c.*1530). French-born church musician and composer. His biography is largely obscure, but almost certainly he spent most of his adult life in Italy, initially perhaps in Venice and Rome, from 1521 certainly in Florence, where he was appointed *maestro di cappella* at the baptistery and cathedral. There is no mention of him following the siege of Florence in 1529–30, nor can any music by him be dated after *c.*1530. Verdelot is a key figure in the early history of the Italian madrigal; his pioneering essays in this genre include settings of texts by Petrarch and Machiavelli. He was also a prolific composer of motets; the most widely disseminated of them, *Si bona suscepimus*, has strong funerary associations.   JM

Verdi, Giuseppe (*see page 1330*)

verdoppeln (Ger.). 'To double'; *verdoppelt*, 'doubled'; *Verdoppelung*, 'doubling', 'duplication'.

Veress, Sándor (*b* Kolozsvár [now Cluj-Napoca, Romania], 1 Feb. 1907; *d* Berne, 6 March 1992). Hungarian-born Swiss composer and teacher. He studied the piano with Bartók at the Budapest Academy of Music, taking composition lessons with Kodály (1923–7). While training as a teacher (1932) he also studied with László Lajtha (1929–33), then worked with Bartók on the folk music collection in the Budapest Academy of Sciences (1937–40) and taught at the Academy of Music (1943–8). With the advent of the Communist regime he fled to Switzerland, settling in Berne, where he lectured at the university and conservatory.

Veress's early music bears the impress of Hungarian folk idioms, evolving into a tightly argued contrapuntal style, sometimes using elements of 12-note technique. He wrote three works for the stage (a children's opera and two ballets) and a number of orchestral scores, including two symphonies (1940, 1952) and concertos for violin (1937–9), piano (1952), string quartet (1960–1), oboe (*Passacaglia concertante*, 1961), clarinet (1981–2), flute (1988–9), and two trombones (1989); his chamber music includes two string quartets (1931, 1936–7) and a wind quintet (1968).   MA

(*cont. on p. 1333*)

Giuseppe Verdi
(1813–1901)

The Italian composer Giuseppe Fortunino Francesco Verdi was born in Roncole, near Busseto, on 9 or 10 October 1813 and died in Milan on 27 January 1901.

Early years

Verdi was the son of an innkeeper in Roncole, a small village near Busseto in the duchy of Parma; his mother was a spinner. After some instruction with the local priests he moved to Busseto in 1823 and two years later began lessons with Ferdinando Provesi, *maestro di cappella* at the church there. He became actively involved in the musical life of Busseto, both as a composer and as a performer. In May 1831 he moved into the house of Antonio Barezzi, a prominent merchant in Busseto and a keen amateur musician. In May 1832 he travelled to Milan and applied for entry to the conservatory. He was refused, but Barezzi agreed to the expense of private study in Milan and Verdi became a pupil of Vincenzo Lavigna, who had for many years been *maestro concertatore* at La Scala. He studied in Milan for some three years, but then returned to Busseto as *maestro di musica*. In May 1836 he married Barezzi's daughter Margherita; they had two children, both of whom died in infancy. Verdi kept in contact in Milan, and composed an opera (*Rocester*) that he tried to get staged. Eventually he was successful with a revised version of the opera, now entitled *Oberto, conte di San Bonifacio*, which was performed at La Scala, Milan, in 1839. Even before it was staged he resigned his position in Busseto and went to live in Milan.

From 'Oberto' to 'La traviata'

The success of *Oberto* encouraged Bartolomeo Merelli, impresario at La Scala, to offer Verdi a contract for three more operas. The first was the comic opera *Un giorno di regno* ('King for a Day'), which failed disastrously on its first night in September 1840. This disappointment, and the death of Margherita Barezzi some two months earlier, caused a crisis of confidence from which Verdi emerged only with the triumphant success of *Nabucco* at La Scala in March 1842. During the next ten years he produced an opera roughly every nine months—not prolific by the standards of his day. These works established his fame in Italy, and he moved constantly from one operatic centre to another, dividing what time remained between Milan and Busseto. The years from 1844 to 1847 were particularly arduous (eight operas in less than four years); his health broke down frequently, and more than once he vowed to renounce operatic composition once he had achieved financial security. His gathering fame did, however, have advantages. He was soon able to charge unprecedentedly high fees for a new opera, and although copyright protection was not fully established he could supplement this income with rental fees and sales of printed materials. As early as 1844 he began to acquire property and land in and around Busseto. It was probably during these early years of success that he formed a lasting attachment to the soprano Giuseppina Strepponi, who was to become his lifelong companion.

Apart from a brief visit to Vienna in 1843, Verdi remained within the Italian peninsula until March 1847 when he undertook a long foreign expedition, initially to supervise the premieres of *I masnadieri* ('The Bandits') in London and *Jérusalem* in Paris (his first operas to be commissioned from outside Italy). He set up house with Strepponi in Paris, staying there about two years, though with a visit to Milan during the 1848 uprisings, and a trip to the short-lived Roman republic to supervise the premiere of *La battaglia di Legnano* in early 1849. Verdi returned with Strepponi to Busseto in mid-1849, still unmarried and causing a local scandal; in 1851 they moved to a permanent home in the nearby farm of Sant'Agata, land once owned by Verdi's ancestors.

An important feature of this—indeed of every—period in Verdi's life is the manner in which he continued to experiment, in particular on the broadest levels of operatic articulation, at which he was rarely content to repeat himself even when a formula had proved its success with the public. Verdi's first two operas, however, are uncharacteristic: *Oberto* is hampered by a curiously sprawling structure, and *Un giorno di regno* explores a Rossinian *opera buffa* vein that will never reappear. With *Nabucco* (1842) an important stylistic strand was introduced: grandiose, oratorio-like, with prominent use of the chorus and a directness of vocal effect and rhythmic vitality. With *Ernani* (1843), however, written for the more intimate context of La Fenice, Venice, he broke fresh ground: the overall effect is far more subdued, and the drama of individual characters is brought to the fore. *Ernani* ushered in a period of more restless innovation: in *I due Foscari* (1844) Verdi used a system of recurring themes to identify the principal characters, suggesting that he was anxious to find new ways of binding together the musical fabric; in *Alzira* (1845), the articulation swings wildly between economic closed forms and a much freer, 'declamatory' style. *Macbeth* (1847) is often considered a watershed: there is a new level of attention to detail in orchestration and harmony, but also an exploitation in the witches' music of the 'genere fantastico' (the fantastic or supernatural genre). Just as important, though, is *Luisa Miller* (1849), a 'mixed' genre that drew on both comic and serious elements.

In spite of all this change, it is *Rigoletto* (1851) that breaks decisive new ground: further use of comic-opera styles within a serious context; a daring appropriation of Victor Hugo's character types, in which the outwardly disfigured baritone father claims more sympathy than the romantic tenor lead; differences between the main characters articulated through the forms they sing. The next two operas are equally innovatory but in rather different ways. *Il trovatore* (1852) seems a contradiction of the 'advances' made in *Rigoletto*: all the main characters express themselves in the traditional forms of serious Italian opera, the achievement of the work lying precisely in this restriction, the emotional energy of the drama being constantly channelled through the most tightly controlled formal units. *La traviata* (1853), on the other hand, gestures towards a level of 'realism' very rare in earlier operas: the contemporary world of waltzes pervades the score, and the heroine's death from disease is graphically depicted in the music—from the first bars of the Prelude to the gasping fragmentation of her last aria.

By the 1850s Verdi had become the most famous and frequently performed Italian opera composer, and his 'political' status during this period—the extent to which his operas heightened the Italian people's national consciousness—has been much discussed. There is no doubt that he was a staunch patriot. But before 1846 there is little evidence that his operas were regarded as especially dangerous politically or that they excited patriotic enthusiasm in their audiences. This is not to deny the stirring force of Verdi's early music, in particular his treatment of the chorus (i.e. 'the people') as a dynamic new expressive power; but connections between his music and political events were largely made

later in the century, some time after the revolutionary atmosphere had cooled.

Breaking new ground

After *La traviata* the pace of Verdi's operatic production slowed. The 11 years before it had produced 16 operas; the 18 years that followed saw only six new works. Verdi now spent an increasing amount of time away from the theatre, and on at least one occasion seems to have decided to stop composing altogether. Extensive foreign expeditions were all related to professional engagements: when not travelling, Verdi often worked on his farmlands at Sant'Agata. In 1859, after more than ten years together, he and Strepponi were married.

As before, each new Verdi opera strikes new ground, but the innovation is more thoroughgoing, biting deeper into the dramatic and musical fabric and embracing further aspects of style. *Les Vêpres siciliennes* (1855), for example, constitutes a radical break with the past. In an attempt to compose a Parisian grand opera he used the five-act structure typical of the genre, and weakened his usual concentration on individuals; but there is also a slackening of the rhythmic incisiveness of Verdi's early manner. The next opera, *Simon Boccanegra* (1857), offers an exploration of the gloomy side of the Italian tradition: there are no secondary female roles, but a preponderance of low male voices. Most important, however, is an extreme economy of vocal writing, with the declamatory mode more prominent than ever before. In extreme contrast, *Un ballo in maschera* (1859) is a masterpiece of variety, of the blending of stylistic elements, with gestures towards the lighter side of French opera, in particular the *opéra comique* of Auber and his contemporaries.

La forza del destino (1861, rev. 1869) is Verdi's most daring attempt at a drama, and is fuelled by an abstract idea—the 'fate' (*destino*) of the title—as much as by individuals. In spite of the liberal recurring themes, we will look in vain for the unifying colours of a *Rigoletto* or *Il trovatore*. *Don Carlos* (1867, rev. 1883), Verdi's second and final attempt to write a French grand opera, has a famously unstable text, the work changing shape significantly during its rehearsal period and then over several years after its first performance. After the experiences of the previous three Italian operas, Verdi was more secure in his handling of the large French canvas, particularly in matching his lyrical gifts to the French language. In this context, the structure of *Aida* (1871) is remarkably conservative: the classic love triangle of Verdi's first manner and—just as important—a return to earlier ideas of musical characterization. On the other hand, *Aida* remains the most radical and 'modern' of Verdi's scores in its use of local colour, constantly alluding to its 'exotic' ambience in harmony and instrumentation.

As the 1850s unfolded, Verdi's pre-eminence in Italian music, and his international reputation, became ever more secure; although many of the early operas had been forgotten, *Rigoletto*, *Il trovatore*, and *La traviata* became cornerstones of the newly emerging Italian operatic repertory. By the mid-1860s, however, it became clear that his more recent works were not duplicating these successes: Italian theatres had begun to open their doors to French (and later to German) operas; Verdi's works began to sound old-fashioned. The paradox of this uncertain reaction to Verdi's 'new manner' was that it went hand in hand with his institution as a national figure beyond the operatic world. In 1859 his name was briefly taken up as an acrostic message of Italian nationalistic aspirations ('Viva VERDI' standing for 'Viva Vittorio Emanuele Re D'Italia'), and by the late 1860s certain pieces of early Verdi had began to be canonized through supposed association with the revolutionary struggles of the 1840s.

The years of maturity

After *Aida* in 1871 there was no Verdian operatic premiere for 16 years. Admittedly 1874 saw the *Messa da Requiem*, composed in honour of Alessandro Manzoni, but the fact remains that in the 1870s and early 80s, years in which we might imagine Verdi at the height of his creative powers, there were no new operas. The reasons for this silence are complex: but the most serious obstacle was a sense of disenchantment with the direction of newly cosmopolitan Italy. It would take all the urging of his close friends to break the deadlock, but in June 1879 Giulio Ricordi and the librettist Arrigo Boito mentioned to Verdi Shakespeare's *Othello*, a canny choice given Verdi's lifelong veneration for the English playwright.

The *Otello* project was long in the making. First came two other tasks, extensive revisions to *Simon Boccanegra* (effected with the help of Boito) and to *Don Carlos*, both of which can be seen in retrospect as trial runs for the new type of opera Verdi felt he must create in Italy's new artistic climate. After many hesitations and interruptions, *Otello* was finally performed at La Scala in February 1887. Some two years later, Boito suggested a further opera, largely based on Shakespeare's *The Merry Wives of Windsor*. As with *Otello*, composing *Falstaff* took a considerable time, or rather involved short bursts of activity interspersed with long fallow periods. The opera was first performed, again at La Scala, in February 1893. These years also saw the appearance of various sacred vocal pieces, some of which were later collected under the title *Quattro pezzi sacri*.

During all this period, Verdi divided his life between Milan, Genoa, and Sant'Agata, where he oversaw his lands and added to his property. In his last years he devoted much money and energy to two philanthropic projects: the building of a hospital at Villanova sull'Arda Piacenza and the founding of a home for retired musicians, the Casa di Riposo, in Milan. In November 1897 Strepponi died at Sant'Agata. In December 1900 Verdi left Sant'Agata for Milan. On 21 January he suffered a stroke from which he died on 27 January. He was buried next to his wife in the Cimitero Monumentale in Milan; a month later, amid national mourning, their bodies were moved to the Casa di Riposo.

It is probably inevitable that the theatrical nature of the Requiem should be a matter of debate: Hans von Bülow famously referred to it as an 'Oper in Kirchengewande' ('opera in ecclesiastical dress') even before its first performance. But we should not exaggerate. None of the ensemble scenes or choruses (of which there is an unoperatic preponderance) remotely resemble their operatic equivalents, in particular by their contrapuntal writing and the lack of differentiation between individuals. What is more, the levels of purely musical connection (particularly in motivic and harmonic gestures) are far greater than Verdi would have deemed appropriate in a drama, where contrast and tension between characters is so important a part of the effect.

At some time during the fallow period between *Aida* and *Otello* we might guess that Verdi passed an intangible divide, and saw the musical drama of his final two operas as residing in continuous 'action' rather than in a juxtaposition of 'action' and 'reflection'. The dynamics of this change are intimately linked to Verdi's relationship with Boito. On many occasions, Verdi—earlier a veritable tyrant in his dealings with librettists—gave way to Boito, trusting the younger man's perception of what modern drama needed. A new use of recurring motivic and harmonic ideas is one aspect of his new style. The so-called *bacio* ('kiss') theme in *Otello*, which first occurs near the end of Act I and then appears twice in the final scene, has a function difficult to compare with previous recurring themes: the final statement of the *bacio* theme seems like a musical summing up of the denouement, thus having more in common with famous Puccinian endings, in spite of its restraint. More than this, the *bacio* theme's harmonic character casts an influence over earlier confrontations between Otello and Desdemona.

A common view of Verdi's last works sees them as divorced from everyday concerns, a trope often used in discussing an artist's final creative stage. The image chimes well with those famous pictures of Verdi in the

1880s and 90s: the felt hat, the simple frock coat and above all the all-knowing, gentle smile. But perhaps there is an alternative story. *Falstaff*, for example, an opera that begins with a mock sonata form and ends with a fugue, gestures vividly to Verdi's frequent admonitions that young Italian composers should study counterpoint and avoid the 'symphonic' at all costs. And then there is the contrast between the work's variety of expression and looseness of form on the one hand, and its many periods of massive closure on the other. Perhaps this can cautiously be related to Verdi's complex reaction to musical modernity, to his desire to progress from his own past, harmonically and formally, but also his need to counter aggressively what he saw as the disastrously dispersive tendencies of his younger contemporaries.

By the time Verdi wrote his last operas, he had become a national monument. But so far as performances were concerned, the turn of the century was a lowpoint. In the sophisticated, cosmopolitan atmos-phere of *fin de siècle* Italy, it was commonplace to find Verdi's music too simple and direct. The crucial change in his fortunes began in Weimar Germany, in which a 'Verdi renaissance' occurred, with numerous re-stagings of 'forgotten' operas. By the 1930s the 'renaissance' had spread, with revivals springing up all over Europe and the USA. Appropriated by Fascists and anti-Fascists alike, Verdi's music survived World War II relatively untarnished. In the 1950s and 60s his operas became the core repertory of the global opera industry, and since then the boom has shown no signs of losing momentum. RP

📖 M. MEDICI and M. CONATI, *Carteggio Verdi–Boito* (Parma, 1978; Eng. trans. 1994 as *The Verdi–Boito Correspondence*, ed. W. Weaver) · M. CONATI, *Interviste e incontri con Verdi* (Milan, 1980; Eng. trans. 1984 as *Encounters with Verdi*) · F. WALKER, *The Man Verdi* (London, 1962) · J. BUDDEN, *The Operas of Verdi*, 3 vols. (London, 1973–81) · J. ROSSELLI, *Verdi* (Cambridge, 2000) · A. LATHAM and R. PARKER (eds.), *Verdi in Performance* (Oxford, 2001)

Vergrösserung (Ger.). 'Augmentation'.

verhallend (Ger.). 'Dying away'.

verismo (It., 'realism'). A movement in Italian literature that influenced the composition of opera at the end of the 19th century and beginning of the 20th. It is characterized by the true-to-life portrayal of rural or urban poverty and often displays a strong regional character introducing songs and dances typical of the area. Mascagni's single-act *Cavalleria rusticana* (1890) and Leoncavallo's *Pagliacci* (1892) are among the best-known operas in the tradition, but others include works by Giordano (*Mala vita*, 1892) and Puccini (e.g. *Il tabarro*, 1918).

See also OPERA, 10. —/JBE

Verklärte Nacht ('Transfigured Night'). Schoenberg's op. 4 (1899), for two violins, two violas, and two cellos, based on a poem (from *Weib und Welt*) by Richard Dehmel; Schoenberg arranged it for string orchestra in 1917 and made a second version in 1943.

Verkleinerung, Verkürzung (Ger.). 'Diminution'.

verlierend, verlöschend (Ger.). 'Dying away', 'extinguishing'.

Verratene Meer, Das ('Treacherous Oceans'). Opera in two parts by Henze to a libretto by Hans-Ulrich Treichel after Yukio Mishima's *Gogo no eiko* (Berlin, 1990).

verschwindend (Ger.). 'Disappearing', 'fading away'.

verse (Fr.: *vers*; Ger.: *Vers*; It.: *verso*; Lat.: *versus*). 1. In poetry, a metrical line, or a group of a specific number of such lines.

2. In plainchant, a verse of a psalm or (in responsorial forms of chant) a verse sung by a soloist, as opposed to the *respond or *response sung by the choir or congregation. The verses are usually marked V or ℣. See PSALMODY. A continuation of the practice of alternation can be found in the verse *anthem.

verse anthem. An *anthem in which one or more solo voices are contrasted with the full choir, as opposed to a 'full anthem' for choir without soloists. The earliest examples date from the later 16th century. Byrd, Gibbons, Purcell, Greene, and S. S. Wesley all contributed fine specimens. The sections for soloists are oftened headed 'Verse', while those for the whole choir are headed 'Full'. NT

verset. A term (a diminutive of 'verse') applied in the Roman rite to a brief organ improvisation or composed piece used to replace a sung verse from a hymn, psalm, or other liturgical item, the text of which is instead recited silently by the choir. The practice of 'supplying' alternative phrases to the choir's setting (usually in plainchant) for the Ordinary of the Mass and certain Office chants appears to have originated during the later Middle Ages. There are five mass movements set in this fashion in the Faenza Codex (*c*.1400), and in 1531

Pierre Attaingnant published two books of organ versets; the genre reached a peak in Italy and France in the 17th century, with fine examples intended for *alternatim* performance by Frescobaldi (e.g. *Fiori musicali*) and François Couperin (e.g. *Pièces d'orgue consistantes en deux messes*). The popularity of *messes en *noëls* in the 18th and 19th centuries ensured the survival of the 'organ mass' in France: the organist would base his versets on popular Christmas carols. The use of versets in Roman Catholic worship was curtailed by Pope Pius X in his **motu proprio* of 1903, which imposed severe restrictions on the omission of text. —/ALı

versicle (from Lat. *versiculus*, 'small verse'). A short sentence, often taken from the psalms, that is said or sung responsorially in Christian worship. It is followed by a response from the congregation or choir. A typical versicle and response in the Roman rite is 'Dominus vobiscum' ('The Lord be with you') answered by 'Et cum spiritu tuo' ('And with thy spirit'). See also PRECES.

Verstovsky, Aleksey Nikolayevich (*b* Seliverstovo estate, Tambov province, 18 Feb./1 March 1799; *d* Moscow, 5/17 Nov. 1862). Russian composer. Like all Russian musicians of his generation he was essentially a dilettante, having first studied engineering before taking to music (he had lessons from Steibelt and Field). He was appointed inspector (1825) and then director (1848) of the Moscow theatres, and for the rest of his life his work centred on the stage, as both administrator and composer. The work for which he is chiefly known, the opera *Askol'dova mogila* ('Askold's Tomb', 1835), effects a fragile compromise between overt 'Russianisms' and German Romantic traits clearly imitative of Weber's *Der Freischütz* (which had been performed in Russia in 1824). The opera enjoyed huge success in its time, though by the late 19th century something of Verstovsky's declining reputation can be judged from the attitude of Rakhmaninov who, when asked in 1897 to conduct *Askold's Tomb* and the later *Gromoboy* (1854), remarked, 'Now please tell me what artistic and commercial sense [is there] in doing these blasted operas?'

Earlier in his career Verstovsky had written *Pan Twardowski* (1828), and he followed up the success of *Askold's Tomb* with *Toska po rodine* ('Longing for the Homeland', 1839), and *Churova dolina, ili Son nayavu* ('Churov Valley, or The Waking Dream', 1844). He also composed about 30 vaudevilles and a number of songs, which continue to be published in Russia; they reveal not only a melodic facility but also, especially in such extended pieces as *Chornaya shal'* ('The Black Shawl', a Pushkin setting), a keen dramatic sense. GN

Verzierungen (Ger.). 'Ornaments'.

Vesperae solennes de confessore ('Solemn Vespers of the Confessor'). Work by Mozart, K339 (1780), for soprano, alto, tenor, and bass soloists, chorus, organ, and orchestra.

Vespers. Originally the seventh of eight hours of the Divine *Office in the medieval Roman rite. It is known in English as Evening Prayer.

Vespri siciliani, I. See VÊPRES SICILIENNES, LES.

Vespro della Beata Vergine ('Vespers of the Blessed Virgin'). A collection of motets (1610) by *Monteverdi, composed for performance at Mantua; for different vocal and instrumental combinations, they are *Domine ad adiuvandum*, *Dixit Dominus*, *Nigra sum*, *Laudate pueri*, *Pulchra es*, *Laetatus sum*, *Duo seraphim*, *Nisi Dominus*, *Audi coelum*, *Lauda, Jerusalem*, *Sonata sopra 'Sancta Maria'*, *Ave maris stella*, and two *Magnificat* settings.

vessel flute. A flute in the shape of a vessel. It may be any shape or size and with any number of fingerholes, its pitch being determined by the volume of the vessel and the size and number of open fingerholes. The vessel flute may be played through a duct (see DUCT FLUTE), like the *ocarina, or may be end-blown (like the Chinese *xun*). Vessel flutes are found throughout the world.

Vestale, La ('The Vestal Virgin'). Opera in three acts by Spontini to a libretto by Étienne de Jouy (Paris, 1807).

via (It.). 'Away'; *via sordini*, 'remove mutes'.

Viadana, Lodovico (*b* Viadana, nr Parma, *c*.1560; *d* Gualtieri, nr Mantua, 2 May 1627). Italian composer and friar. He was *maestro di cappella* at a number of less important Italian churches, including Mantua Cathedral (late 1590s), the convent of S. Luca, Cremona (1602), and the cathedrals of Concordia (1608–9) and Fano (1610–12). A prolific composer of everything from light canzonettas and madrigals to massive polychoral psalm settings, he is best known for his *Cento concerti ecclesiastici* (Venice, 1602). This is the earliest publication of church music with a true basso *continuo, which Viadana used as a means of avoiding some of the problems of composing for the sparse resources of small churches. Whereas earlier *a cappella* works were often performed with some of the voice parts omitted, Viadana avoided the resulting gaps in the music by providing a melody which could be sung by one voice or spread among several, at the same time providing a continuous accompaniment for the organ. This convenient procedure became popular immediately, and was to form the basis for most sacred music for the next 150 years.   DA/TC

Viaggio a Reims, Il (*Il viaggio a Reims, ossia L'albergo del giglio d'oro*; 'The Journey to Reims, or The Hotel of the Golden Lily'). Opera in one act by Rossini to a libretto by Luigi Balocchi partly derived from Madame de Staël's novel *Corinne, ou L'Italie* (Paris, 1825). It was composed as an entertainment for the coronation of Charles X and Rossini later used some of the music from it in *Le Comte Ory*.

Viardot, (Michelle Ferdinande) **Pauline** [née García] (*b* Paris, 18 July 1821; *d* Paris, 18 May 1910). French mezzo-soprano, sister of Maria Malibran. She made her stage debut as Desdemona in Rossini's *Otello* in London in 1839 and first sang in Russia in 1843, becoming an early champion of Russian music in the West. She was most successful in such dramatic roles as Fidès in Meyerbeer's *Le Prophète* (1849), which prompted Berlioz to describe her as 'one of the greatest artists . . . in the . . . history of music', and she went on to triumph in the title role in Berlioz's version of Gluck's *Orfeo* (1859). She was a composer (notably of operettas) and an admired teacher.   IR

📖 G. DULONG, *Pauline Viardot, tragédienne lyrique* (Paris, 2/1987)

vibraphone. An instrument similar to the *marimba but with bars of aluminium alloy instead of wood. A long axle passes through the tops of each line of resonator tubes (one for the 'white' notes and one for the 'black') carrying metal discs fitting the top of each tube. As an electric motor rotates the axles, the discs revolve, opening and closing the resonators to produce the vibrato which gives the instrument its name. It was developed in the USA in the early 20th century. The playing technique, with multiple mallets, is exacting and similar to that of the marimba, but the sound is much longer-lasting and a damper pedal is essential.
                                                            JMo

vibration. See ACOUSTICS, 4.

vibrato (It., 'shaken'; from Lat. *vibrare*). A wavering of pitch used to enrich and intensify the tone of a voice or instrument; it is practised in particular by wind players, string players, and singers. At present the technique is used frequently, and is commonly held to be an important constituent of a competent player's or singer's tone. In this form (often described as 'continuous vibrato') the device has been in currency since the beginning of the 20th century, having been made popular by such players as Kreisler. In consequence, the *senza vibrato* tone has become a special effect in contemporary music.

In accordance with the prevailing taste of the time, however, vibrato was regarded before the 20th century as an ornament to be applied sparingly, and often discreetly, to long note-values or particularly expressive passages, or both. Surviving recordings of Joachim and Patti, for example, show how it was still used in this way by 19th-century violinists and singers, and the rising interest in historical performance style has resulted in its containment, particularly in music of the 17th and 18th centuries. Moreover, many pre-20th-century sources restrict even the ornamental vibrato to solo or melody parts, hence the rare mention of its use in male vocal tessitura, or on the cello.

Some confusion surrounds the use of the term before the 20th century. For many writers of vocal texts, 'vibrato' was interchangeable with *tremolo', as indeed it was for the violinists Spohr (1832) and Leopold Mozart (1756; as *tremulant* or *tremoletto*). Other terms used to indicate this wavering in pitch include 'ondulation' (Baillot, 1834–5) and 'close shake'.

The quality of the intonational vibrato is subject to great variation between different players and singers and, most notably, across time. Where the device is used, modern technique usually produces a more pronounced pitch oscillation than in previous epochs, as may be observed from a comparison of the slight nature of Joachim's or Patti's vibrato with that of present-day violinists or singers.   —/DMi

vicar choral. A cathedral singing man in the Anglican Church, known at some cathedrals as 'lay clerk' or 'lay vicar'. The position came into being at the time of the Reformation; until then the various 'clerks' and 'vicars' had been in holy orders. The duties of the vicar choral, which vary between cathedrals, are really those of the canons, done vicariously.

Vicentino, Nicola (*b* Vicenza, 1511; *d* Milan, *c*.1576). Italian theorist and composer. His influence on music in the late 16th century was considerable. A pupil of Willaert in Venice, he evolved a theory that the scale systems of the Greeks could be used in modern music. This theory, which he developed when music master to the family of Duke Ercole II d'Este at Ferrara, involved the use of microtones, and about 1561 he had a special harpsichord (arcicembalo) built with additional keys to accommodate these extra notes; he also developed an expanded system of notation using dots. The theory, discussed in his book *L'antica musica ridotta alla moderna prattica* (Rome, 1555), was to prove unsound, and the use of microtones impractical, but it did result in the relatively free use of such notes as D♯, A♭, G♭, and

D♭, which had previously been extremely rare; his ideas also did much to inspire the chromatic madrigal style of Gesualdo and Luzzaschi, while his broader views on the priority of the text created a framework for Monteverdi's *seconda pratica*.   DA/TC

Victimae paschali laudes (Lat., 'Praises to the Paschal victim'). A *sequence of the Roman rite, appointed for Easter Day. It dates from the 11th century and was one of the four sequences allowed to remain after most sequences and tropes were abolished by the *Council of Trent.

Victoria, Tomás Luis de (*b* Ávila, *c*.1548; *d* Madrid, 27 Aug. 1611). Spanish composer. He was a choirboy at Ávila Cathedral, and when his voice broke was sent (*c*.1565) to the Jesuit Collegio Germanico in Rome as a *convittore* (non-German paying student). During this period he may have made contact with Palestrina, who was *maestro di cappella* at the Seminario Romano nearby. In 1569 Victoria became cantor and organist at the Aragonese church of S. Maria di Monserrato in Rome (retaining these posts until 1574). From 1571 he also taught at the Collegio Germanico, where he was *moderator musicae* from 1575 until 1577 or 1578, and in addition he held the post of *maestro di cappella* at the Seminario Romano. Besides these positions, he provided music for occasional services at the other Spanish church in Rome, S. Giacomo degli Spagnoli, and for the associated Archconfraternity of the Resurrection. However, much of Victoria's professional activity in Rome was as a priest rather than principally as a musician: ordained priest in 1575, and supported by income from benefices in Spain, he was a chaplain at S. Gerolamo della Carità in 1578, a position he held until 1585; he also undertook charitable work for the Archconfraternity of the Resurrection.

Victoria's Roman years were prolific ones for the publication of his music. In 1572 he published his first volume, a collection of motets including many of his best-known works. Between 1576 and 1585 there appeared seven more printed collections of his sacred music, containing masses, hymns, *Magnificat* settings, music for Holy Week (including settings of the Passion, Lamentations, and responsories), psalms, and motets. He dedicated his second book of masses (1583) to Philip II of Spain, and indicated in the preface that he now wished to return to his native country. Philip recalled him (Victoria left Rome at some time between 1585 and 1587) and made him chaplain to his sister, the Dowager Empress Maria, at the Convento de las Descalzas Reales de S. Clara in Madrid. Victoria served her from at least 1587 until her death in 1603, and was also *maestro de capilla* at the convent, thereafter re-

maining as organist until his own death eight years later. In 1592 he again visited Rome, where he published another book of masses, and he probably visited the city in 1593–4 too. In 1600 a magnificent collection of his masses, *Magnificat* settings, motets, and psalms was issued in Madrid. Devoted mainly to polychoral works, it includes three pieces which were among his most popular masses: the *Missa pro victoria* (a battle mass based on Janequin's chanson *La Bataille*), and the *Missa 'Ave regina coelorum'* and *Missa 'Alma Redemptoris mater'* (based on his own antiphons). An organist's part was provided, allowing some of the vocal parts to be accompanied or replaced by organ. Victoria's last publication was the *Officium defunctorum* (1605), written, he states, for the exequies of the dowager empress in 1603, and including his famous six-voice music for the Requiem Mass.

Victoria was the greatest Spanish composer of the Renaissance, and also one of the finest European composers of the time; his total output is, however, much smaller than those of, for example, Palestrina and Lassus. Victoria's modern reputation long rested mainly on a handful of motets (such as *O magnum mysterium*, *O quam gloriosum*, *O vos omnes*, and *Vere languores*), on the Tenebrae responsories, and on the *Officium defunctorum*. Much less attention was paid, for example, to his polychoral works (including masses, psalms, antiphons, and sequences), some of which stand apart from the better-known pieces through such aspects as their greater rhythmic animation. Of Victoria's 20 masses, 15 are *parody works, most of them based on his own pieces, while the others draw on works by Morales, Guerrero, Palestrina, and Janequin. A notable characteristic of the masses published from 1592 onwards is their brevity (on which Victoria himself remarked regarding the 1592 collection). Likewise frequently concise, and with a highly concentrated expressivity of text-setting, are such works as the Lamentations and responsories for Holy Week. Victoria's powers of text-expression when writing in a simple style are well demonstrated also by the Matins responsory *Taedet animam meam* from the *Officium defunctorum*, and the motet *Versa est in luctum* from the same publication shows an extraordinarily powerful use of chromatic and harmonic colouring. Harmonic sequence is sometimes prominent in Victoria's writing, as in the eight-voice *Salve regina*. There are also abundant examples of word-painting in his motets, such as *Cum beatus Ignatius*, with its vivid imagery depicting the wild beasts tearing the martyr to pieces.   WT/OR

📖 R. STEVENSON, *Spanish Cathedral Music in the Golden Age* (Berkeley and Los Angeles, 1961) · R. STEVENSON, 'Tomás Luis de Victoria', *The New Grove High Renaissance Masters* (London and New York, 1984) · E. C. CRAMER,

Tomás Luis de Victoria: A Guide to Research (New York and London, 1998)

Vida breve, La ('The Short Life'). Opera in two acts and four scenes by Falla to a libretto by Carlos Fernández Shaw (Nice, 1913).

Vidal, Paul Antonin (*b* Toulouse, 16 June 1863; *d* Paris, 9 April 1931). French composer, conductor, and teacher. He studied at the conservatoires of Toulouse and Paris, where he was a pupil of Massenet. He won the Prix de Rome in 1883 with his cantata *Le Gladiateur*. Debussy won the prize the following year, and in Rome he and Vidal became friends. In 1906 Vidal was appointed conductor at the Paris Opéra, where he gave the premieres of works by several notable French composers. During World War I he was musical director of the Opéra-Comique and taught composition at the Paris Conservatoire. His works include operas and ballets (among them the successful *La Maladette* of 1893). Vidal was associated with the regionalist movement which tried to find an independent musical voice for each different area of France, in his case the south-west.   WT/RLS

Viderunt omnes. A four-voice chant setting (*organum quadruplum*) by Pérotin, a gradual for Christmas and Circumcision composed *c*.1200.

vielle (Fr.). 'Fiddle'; *vielle à roue*, 'hurdy-gurdy'.

Vier ernste Gesänge ('Four Serious Songs'). Song cycle, op. 121 (1896), by Brahms for voice and piano, four settings of extracts from Luther's translation of the Bible. They were arranged for voice and orchestra by Malcolm Sargent and in English are sometimes known as 'Four Biblical Songs'.

Vier letzte Lieder ('Four Last Songs'). Title given by the publisher to songs (1946–8) by Richard Strauss for soprano or tenor solo and orchestra, settings of poems by Joseph von Eichendorff and Hermann Hesse. In order of composition they are 1. *Im Abendrot* ('At Twilight'), 2. *Frühling* ('Spring'), 3. *Beim Schlafengehen* ('Falling Asleep'), 4. *September*; Strauss is said to have favoured the order 3, 4, 2, 1, but they are published and usually performed 2, 4, 3, 1.

Vierne, Louis (*b* Poitiers, 8 Oct. 1870; *d* Paris, 2 June 1937). French composer and organist. He studied in the organ class at the Paris Conservatoire under Franck and Charles-Marie Widor. Subsequently, as assistant to both Widor and Alexandre Guilmant, his own lucid teaching greatly benefited the students, among them Marcel Dupré and Nadia Boulanger. In 1900 he was appointed organist of Notre Dame, but his life thereafter was blighted by his being passed over for the organ professorship, as well as by failing health and sight, and the death of his son and brother in World War I.

Vierne nevertheless succeeded in composing a magnificent cycle of six symphonies for solo organ (1899–1930), which further develop the form pioneered by Widor, with the addition of Franck's chromatic expressivity and technique of cyclic themes. In these works of tragic grandeur and flamboyant Romanticism, some sparkling scherzo movements and brilliant finales bring sharp contrasts of mood. After the war, friendship with a Madame Richepin improved his morale, and for his recital tours of Europe and America he composed the impressionistic *Pièces de fantaisie* (1927), of which the best known are 'Carillon de Westminster' and 'Naiades'. Other works include *24 pièces en style libre* (1913) for harmonium, *Messe solennelle* for choir and two organs, and a deeply sombre Piano Quintet (1917).   WT/AT

Viertelton (Ger.). 'Quarter-tone'.

Vieuxtemps, Henri (*b* Verviers, 17 Feb. 1820; *d* Mustapha, Algeria, 6 June 1881). Belgian violinist and composer. One of the great 19th-century virtuoso violinists, he studied with Charles-Auguste de Bériot in Paris. His playing career, during which he revived Beethoven's Concerto, took him throughout Europe (in Russia he was particularly idolized) and three times to America between 1843 and 1871. Among his admirers were Schumann and Berlioz, and his pupils (at the Brussels Conservatory) included Eugène Ysaÿe. He studied composition with Simon Sechter in Vienna; of his 59 published works virtually all are for the violin, including five concertos, the most frequently played being the Fourth.   WT/CF

vif, vive (Fr.). 'Lively', 'fast'; *vivement*, 'briskly'.

vihuela (Sp.). A plucked string instrument that flourished mainly in Spain from the 15th century to the 17th. It was similar to (though rather larger than) the modern guitar and was tuned like the *lute, with the 3rd between the third and fourth courses. As the principal plucked instrument for respectable music in its day, it was the Spanish counterpart to the lute until the guitar superseded it by the end of the 16th century. It was called *vihuela de mano* to distinguish it from its bowed derivative, the *vihuela de arco*, which is the ancestor of the *viol. No vihuela survives in Spain, but similar instruments, with the characteristic five small sound-holes, are extant in South America.   AB/JMo

Village Romeo and Juliet, A (*Romeo und Julia auf dem Dorfe*). Opera in six pictures (or scenes) by Delius to his own libretto after Gottfried Keller's novel (Berlin,

1907). The intermezzo before the final scene is *The *Walk to the Paradise Garden*. Fenby arranged an orchestral suite (1948) from the score of the opera.

Villa-Lobos, Heitor (*b* Rio de Janeiro, 5 March 1887; *d* Rio de Janeiro, 17 Nov. 1959). Brazilian composer. His father's death in 1899 marked the end of his son's formal musical studies. Joining one of the popular Rio street bands as a guitarist, he was working as a cellist in a theatre orchestra by the age of 16. Two years later he made the first of many long journeys into the interior, which deepened his knowledge of Brazil's folk music. Befriended by Artur Rubinstein, he was sent to Paris by the Brazilian government in 1923 with the object, as he saw it, not to study but to advertise his achievements. Returning to Brazil in 1930, he held various official positions in music education and was responsible in 1945 for the foundation of the Brazilian Academy of Music. International fame was secured by Leopold Stokowski's tireless promotion of his works from the early 1940s.

He produced over 1000 works, a steady stream of music diverse in form and in worth, but all animated by passionate devotion to his native land. Among his best pieces are the four epic orchestral and choral suites taken from the film *Descobrimento do Brazil* (1937), the 17 string quartets, and the varied series of 16 *Chôros*—the name is taken from the street bands of the composer's youth. Similarly various are the *Bachianas brasileiras*, in which he achieved an evocative synthesis of Bachian mannerisms with Brazilian folk music. Scored for various combinations, ranging from woodwind duo (no. 6) through an ensemble of soprano and cellos (no. 5) to full orchestra (nos. 2, 3, 7, and 8), the *Bachianas* are the most familiar examples of Villa-Lobos's exuberant, full-flavoured writing.

PG/CW

📖 C. Sprague Smith, *Heitor Villa-Lobos* (Washington DC, 1960) · V. Mariz, *Heitor Villa-Lobos, Brazilian Composer* (Gainesville, FL, 1963)

villancico (Sp.). A variety of Spanish secular poetry current in the second half of the 15th century, generally of a pastoral or amorous nature and often set to music as a popular song. The poetic form was closely related to that of the Italian *ballata and the French *virelai: several stanzas (*coplas*) connected by a refrain (*estribillo*), each *copla* being divided into two sections, *mudanzas* and *vuelta*. Precursors include songs in the late 13th-century **Cantigas de Santa Maria*. Many three- and four-part villancicos are found in the great Spanish songbooks of the late 15th and early 16th centuries, such as the *Cancionero musical de palacio* (*c*.1490–*c*.1520). The music has two sections, one used to sing both *estribillo* and *vuelta*, the other for the *mudanzas*; textures are

often simple and chordal. Most villancicos are love songs, but some have a religious theme. The most important early composer of villancicos was Juan del Encina, whose dramatic works incorporated the performance of such songs.

Surviving 16th-century villancicos are in one of two principal forms: part-songs (by such as Mateo Flecha and Pedro de Pastrana), and solo songs with vihuela accompaniment (in the publications of, for example, Luis de Milán, Miguel de Fuenllana, and Alonso Mudarra). In the former category, contrapuntal—often imitative—writing became more common during the 1520s and 30s. The printed collections of Juan Vasquez (*Villancicos y canciones*, 1551, and *Recopilación de sonetos y villancicos*, 1560) reveal some parallels with the Italian madrigal alongside distinctive characteristics of the villancico. By the late 16th century the sacred villancico had begun to predominate; such works were frequently performed in services and processions at Christmas (villancico has in modern times come to mean 'Christmas carol') and other festivals such as Corpus Christi, and in many places new pieces were composed each year by the local choirmaster. Francisco Guerrero's published collection of *Canciones y villanescas espirituales* (1589) includes sacred versions of originally secular works.

In the 17th century villancicos were produced in enormous quantities as a spectacular form of sacred music appealing to a wide audience. The villancico developed into a large-scale composition, often with narrative or dramatic elements (sometimes including characters singing in dialect), and emphasizing contrasting sonorities including polychoral writing, solos and duets, and obbligato instrumental parts. One common pattern was an introduction for small forces, a choral movement which was then repeated after each *copla*, and *coplas* set as short solo songs (again, instrumentally accompanied). There are resemblances between the 18th-century villancico—incorporating recitative and aria—and the cantata. Important composers included José de Nebra, Cabanilles, and Sebastián Durón, who was criticized by the theorist Benito Feijóo for introducing operatic arias and such instruments as violins into sacred music. The Baroque villancico was cultivated not only in Spain but also in Portugal (where John IV collected huge quantities), and in Mexico and other parts of Latin America, where there developed offshoots such as the *aguinaldo* and the *adoración*. Though prohibited in church in 1765, villancicos continued to be performed during the 19th century.   —/OR

villanella (It.) [villanesca, canzone villanesca alla napolitana, canzone napolitana, etc.]. A three- or four-voice strophic song, setting comic or rustic texts in the Neapolitan dialect, that became popular about 1535. Musically it was characterized by its 'ungrammatical' use of consecutive 5ths, perhaps deliberately caricaturing the elegant harmony of the madrigal and certainly reflecting the genre's roots in the popular, often bawdy songs of Naples. The text-setting was generally syllabic, the texture mainly homophonic, and a new musical phrase was used for each line of verse, with the opening and closing lines often repeated. The principal composers of the villanella in this form were G. T. di Maio and G. D. da Nola.

By about 1545 the genre had reached northern Italy, where such composers as Willaert and Baldassare Donato created imaginative and rhythmically lively reworkings of Neapolitan villanescas for four voices. Lassus, who spent some years in Naples before moving to Rome in 1551, was the finest composer in this vein, writing witty villanellas that are sometimes bawdy or satirical, sometimes more serious. These pieces could be performed either by a group of singers or by one singer with instrumental accompaniment. From the 1570s, in the hands of such composers as Jacopo Ferretti, Marenzio, and Wert, the villanella became still more respectable, losing both dialect and bawdiness and becoming virtually a small-scale madrigal. The term *'canzonetta' was often applied to such pieces, and the distinction between the two forms became less clear-cut.

In this form the villanella achieved popularity in Germany and England. Morley, one of its best exponents, described it in *A Plaine and Easie Introduction to Practicall Musicke* (1597) as 'a counterfeit to the madrigal, wherein little art can be shown, it being made in strains, every one repeated except the middle'. The villanella gave way to the aria in the early 17th century.   DA/EW

   📖 D. G. CARDAMONE, *The Canzone villanesca alla napolitana and Related Forms, 1537–1570* (Ann Arbor, MI, 1981)

Villi, Le ('The Wilis'). Opera in two acts by Puccini to a libretto by Ferdinando Fontana after Alphonse Karr's short story *Les Willis* (Milan, 1884; revised Turin, 1884).

villotta. A form of lighthearted song, based on popular tunes and akin to the *villanella, that flourished in Italy from about 1520. It arose in Venice and the surrounding areas and spread to other regions of Italy, notably Florence. The origins of the term lie in the north Italian dialect word *vilòte* ('peasant'). The villotta was generally for four voices, the popular or folk tune on which it was based often placed in the tenor. The texts set were usually rustic, often crude and, especially in cultured Venetian circles in the 1540s, comic and

satirical; those by Willaert are fine examples. The settings alternate chordal declamatory and more imitative writing, and sometimes have a 'fa-la' refrain. Some, such as those by Filippo Azzaiolo, were also popular in the form of intabulations.   DA/EW

vīṇā [bīṇ]. The principal term for stringed instruments of the Indian subcontinent, used since the 1st millennium BC for harps, lutes, and zithers. The North Indian *bīṇ* is a stick zither, a narrow wooden or bamboo body with a gourd resonator attached at each end. There are four plucked strings as well as supplementary drone and sympathetic strings. In South India, the *sarasvati vīṇā* bears some resemblance to the North Indian sitar (which is also a kind of *vīṇā*). Some aspects of the playing techniques of both these types are similar to those of the *sitar. Fretless *vīṇā* (the *vicitrā vīṇā* and the *goṭṭuvādyam*) are played, like a Hawaiian guitar, by sliding a smooth block in the left hand along the strings while plucking with the right.   JMo

Vine, Carl (*b* Perth, W. Australia, 8 Oct. 1954). Australian composer, pianist, and conductor. He studied with John Exton in Perth, then worked in Sydney as a pianist and composer. In 1979 he co-founded the ensemble Flederman. He has been resident composer to several dance companies, colleges, and orchestras, and has taught electronic composition at the Queensland Conservatorium. Vine's music has largely been influenced by American models: experimental, modernist, and minimalist in turn. He has written a full-length ballet, *Mythologia* (2000), six symphonies—no. 5 (1995) with four solo percussionists, no. 6 (1996) with chorus—and works for smaller ensembles.   ABur

Viñes, Ricardo (*b* Lérida, 5 Feb. 1875; *d* Barcelona, 29 April 1943). Spanish pianist, of Catalan origin. He studied with Emilio Pujol in Barcelona and from 1887 with Bériot, Albert Lavignac, and Godard at the Paris Conservatoire, winning the first prize for piano in 1894. He was a friend not only of his countrymen Granados, Albéniz, and Falla but also of Duparc, Debussy, Satie, and Ravel. He gave the first performance in France of Musorgsky's *Pictures at an Exhibition* and world premieres of Debussy's *Pour le piano* (1902), *Estampes* (1904), *Masques* (1905), *L'Isle joyeuse* (1905), and both sets of *Images* (1906; 1908), and of Ravel's *Jeux d'eau* (1902), *Miroirs* (1906), and *Gaspard de la nuit* (1909); it was Viñes who had introduced Ravel to Bertrand's prose poems of that name. But both Debussy and Ravel came to feel that Viñes interpreted their music too freely. He always played an Érard piano, and recordings show him to have been a fleet and brilliant pianist (his *Poissons d'or* is unrivalled), with subtle pedalling but without great depth of tone. Poulenc remembered piano lessons with Viñes gratefully.   RN

Vingt-Quatre Violons du Roi. The select band of 24 string instruments of the violin family in the service of the French court in the 17th and 18th centuries. The group was officially recognized by Louis XIII in 1626 and was frequently referred to as the Grande Bande. Often reinforced by 12 wind instruments (the Grands Hautbois), the 24 Violons could claim to be Europe's first regular orchestra. According to French custom there were five string parts: six first violins (*dessus*), four each of the three middle parts (*haute-contre, taille, quinte*), and six basses (bass violins). In 1656 Lully founded a smaller and even more select band of 16 string players, the Petits Violons or Petite Bande.

Vingt regards sur l'enfant Jésus ('20 Looks at the Child Jesus'). Work (1944) by Messiaen for piano; each of its 20 movements has a title, for example 'Regard du Père', 'Regard des anges'.

viol (Fr.: *viole*: Ger.: as It., also *Gamba*, pl. *Gamben*; It.: *viola da gamba*). A bowed string instrument of the Renaissance and Baroque periods. It was invented in Spain, through use of the bow of the **rabāb* on the normally plucked **vihuela*, in the late 15th century. Carried to Italy (probably in the train of the Borgia popes), it was developed further, the flat bridge of the vihuela being replaced by a free-standing arched bridge, which was glued to the belly like that of a guitar. The belly is curved gently and smoothly; on the earlier instruments it was a flat piece of wood bent to shape, though later viols had a carved belly. The back was usually flat, with the upper portion bent in towards the neck; the earlier instruments had no soundpost. The ribs or sides were flush with the edges of the belly and the back. Viols have varied a great deal in body shape, but the characteristic deep ribs, C-shaped soundholes, and shoulders that slope up towards the neck became fairly standard during the 16th century; some surviving viols, however, have elaborate festooned body shapes.

The six strings of the viol are tuned to the same intervals as the courses of the vihuela and the lute: 4th–4th–3rd–4th–4th. Also as on those instruments, gut

frets are tied on to the neck so that every stopped note has something of the ringing sound of an open string. The bow is held underhand with the palm upwards, the up-bow therefore being the stronger bowstroke. In all these characteristics the viol contrasts directly with the violin, which had four strings tuned in 5ths, no frets, a bow held overhand with the palm downwards (and therefore a stronger down-bow), and a high-arched, carved belly and back, both of which projected over the ribs. Their musical use differed also, the violins primarily playing dance and entertainment music, and the viols chamber music.

The first viols were probably tenors, nearest in size to the vihuela, but bass and treble sizes soon followed, for the complete consort of six of viols was played as a chamber group by 1502 at the wedding of Alfonso d'Este and Lucrezia Borgia in Ferrara, probably with two of each size. A great bass (violone, 'large viol') was available before 1600. The standard tunings for the treble, tenor, and bass viols as used in the great consort music of late 16th- and 17th-century England are shown in Ex. 1.

There has always been considerable variation in size throughout the family, especially in the bass. Playing elaborate variations, or *divisions as they were then known, was a popular diversion on the bass viol. Smaller basses, known in England as 'division viols', with a smaller stretch for the left hand, were made for this purpose in the 17th century. Smaller still was the *lyra viol, made for a peculiarly English style of playing of the late 16th century and the 17th, in which many different tunings and a mixture of chordal and melodic textures were used. In order to accommodate the different tunings, lyra viol music was written in *tablature, which shows the position of the fingers on the fingerboard, rather than precise pitches as in staff notation. Besides being easier to read, tablature has the additional advantage that the same music may be played on any size of viol, provided that it is tuned with the correct sequence of intervals. An Italian style of playing florid variations over well-known madrigals was known as *viola bastarda*; a special size of bass viol was also made for this, but a wide re-tuning consisting of a mixture of 4ths and 5ths might have been used.

Ex. 1

The bass viol was especially popular as a solo instrument in France, where from about 1675 to 1770 the French virtuoso school led the rest of Europe. The greatest of the French violist composers were Marin Marais, who published five books of pieces for one, two, or three bass viols with continuo, Antoine Forqueray, and Forqueray's son Jean-Baptiste. The French bass viol (often made in England, for the English viols had the highest reputation) had seven strings, the seventh tuned a 4th below the others. At much the same period there was a craze among the ladies at the French court for a high treble, the *pardessus de viole*, with only five strings.

With the rise of the orchestra in the mid-17th century the viol family gradually lost favour to the violin. Indeed, it is said that when Charles II came to the English throne at the Restoration in 1660 the viols vanished from all fashionable households. Yet there was still sufficient interest for Henry Purcell to write 12 superb fantasias for viol consort.

The bass viol outlasted the other sizes, partly because it was useful as a continuo instrument, but more because of its popularity for solos—not only in France, but also in Germany, where J. S. Bach wrote three sonatas as well as other solos for *viola da gamba* (a term that, with the demise of the rest of the viol family, had by then come to mean bass viol). When Bach's younger son, Johann Christian, went to live in London he joined Carl Friedrich Abel, famous as both a viol player and a composer, in promoting a series of concerts. Nor was Abel alone, for his pupils continued to play the instrument long after his death in 1787, and viol playing continued in England well into the 19th century. It was revived by Arnold Dolmetsch in the 1890s, since when the art of playing the viol, both solo and in consort, has been rediscovered by many amateurs and professionals. Thus the viol consort has to some extent regained its place as the chamber ensemble *par excellence*. JMo

📖 M. Edwards, 'Venetian viols of the 16th century', *Galpin Society Journal*, 33 (1980), 74–91 · J. A. Sadie, *The Bass Viol in French Baroque Chamber Music* (Ann Arbor, MI, 1980) · C. Monson, *Voices and Viols in England, 1600–1650* (Ann Arbor, MI, 1982) · I. Woodfield, *The Early History of the Viol* (Cambridge, 1984) · M. Remnant, *English Bowed Instruments from Anglo-Saxon to Tudor Times* (Oxford, 1986) · K. Polk, *German Instrumental Music of the Late Middle Ages* (Cambridge, 1992)

viola (earlier Eng.: tenor; Fr.: *alto*; Ger.: *Bratsche*, or earlier *Violetta*; It.: *viola*). The alto or tenor instrument of the violin family. As these names indicate, there is some confusion about the viola's role. Although the German name, from *viola da braccio*, might suggest that it was the first member of the violin family, there is

no doubt that it was the treble, the *violin, that appeared earliest, probably in about 1480; the first evidence for the larger members of the family is some decades later. The older English name and the French serve as a reminder that there was originally more than one size of viola. Mersenne (*Harmonie universelle*, 1636–7) explains clearly that there were three, all tuned like the modern viola, *c–g–d'–a'* (a 5th below the violin), and playing tenor, alto, and mezzo-soprano parts.

Instruments of all three sizes survive, though many of the tenors have been cut down because they place considerable strain on the player's left arm when held under the chin in the modern position; in the older position they were played with the lower bouts resting against the chest or shoulder, and the instrument held slanting downwards. This position, which was also used with the violin, leads to a marked difference in the sound between up-bow and down-bow that is lost with the modern 'seamless bowing'—and even from most early-music ensembles, many of whose members adopt modern playing styles. Today the mezzo size is often referred to in sale catalogues as a 'lady's viola', but composers including Handel used it in unison with, and perhaps as an alternative to, a third violin part.

The ideal proportions for the viola remain a matter for considerable discussion. It is, of course, longer in the body than a violin, but to produce the same strength and beauty of tone a 5th lower the viola should be one and a half times the size of a violin—too big to be played on the shoulder. The largest tenors have a body length of between 45 and 48 cm, well short of the ideal of 53 cm. Lionel Tertis suggested that the best solution would be something more like a small cello, held downwards with a tail-spike. There is some evidence for there having been such an instrument—the tenor violin—in earlier times, though it fell out of use before the end of the 17th century; and moreover, a logical pitch for such an instrument would be a 5th lower still: $F–c–g–d'$, halfway between the viola and the cello, which at that time had its lowest string tuned to $B\flat'$. A modern development, the New Violin Family, devised by Carleen Hutchins and the Catgut Acoustical Society, does include both a 'vertical viola' held downwards, with a body length of over 50 cm, and a tenor violin. These are two of a complete family, from high soprano to double bass, all scaled from the violin itself, but neither Hutchins's nor Tertis's influence has as yet encouraged players to take up the idea. The sole result of Tertis's campaign was a much deeper-bodied instrument but with the standard body length of a large viola (*c*.42.5 cm) and still held on the shoulder. Many players feel that its disproportionately deep body gives it too 'tubby' a sound.

The viola plays an essential middle part in orchestral and chamber music. Only in the Baroque trio sonata did it have no place, for then the continuo provided the middle harmony. No string trio or quartet would be complete without it; and Mozart, among others, felt that the ideal string quintet was two violins, two violas, and cello, retaining both violas even when one of the violins was replaced by, for example, a horn.

The viola has followed the violin in all aspects of construction—and, between 1780 and 1820, reconstruction—as well as in its history (for which see VIOLIN). It was built by the same great masters, such earlier ones as Andrea Amati and Stradivari in Cremona, and Gasparo da Salò in Brescia, being responsible for most of the surviving tenors.

Although critics, especially in the 18th century, were sometimes scathing about the abilities of viola players (with such descriptions as 'superannuated violinists'), composers of all periods seem to have written some parts that would tax the best players to the limit (e.g. the Third and Sixth Brandenburg Concertos), and in every period there have been some solo works, if never as many as for the violin. This paucity of solo works is somewhat surprising in view of the fact that many composers are reputed to have had a preference for playing the viola; but perhaps that preference was a result of the satisfaction felt at making a contribution to the harmony that was more expressive, and in some ways more effective, than playing either the melody or the bass.   JMo

📖 L. TERTIS, *My Viola and I* (London, 1974) · F. ZEYRINGER, *The Problem of Viola Size* (New York, 1979) · M. W. RILEY, *The History of the Viola*, 2 vols. (Ypsilanti, MI, 1980, 1991) · M. ROBINSON, *The Violin and Viola* (London, 1983)

viola bastarda. See VIOL.

viola da braccio (It., 'fiddle on the arm'). A 16th- and 17th-century term for the instruments of the *violin family, used to distinguish them from the leg-held viol (*viola da gamba*). Even the bass violin or cello, which was held between the knees, was known as *basso di viola da braccio*.   JMo

viola da gamba (It., 'fiddle on the leg'). A 16th- and 17th-century term for the instruments of the *viol family, which are always held resting on the knee; it is used to distinguish them from the shoulder-held violin (*viola da braccio*).   JMo

viola d'amore. A bowed string instrument that flourished in central Europe in the 18th century, but with some later repertory, particularly from the 20th century. It is built like a shallow treble *viol, sometimes with a festooned outline and flame-shaped soundholes, but it has no frets and is played on the shoulder like a violin. Its most important characteristic is the use of sympathetic strings: it normally has seven bowed strings, tuned either to the common chord of D major or to that of the key of the music, and seven sympathetic strings tuned either in unison with the bowed strings or to the diatonic scale of the piece. The sound is sweet with the background shimmer of the sympathetic resonance.

There is evidence of a five-string 17th-century predecessor, perhaps violin-size, which lives on as the Norwegian *Hardanger fiddle with four bowed and four sympathetic strings.   JMo

viola pomposa. An 18th-century German term for a five-string *viola. There are conflicting reports as to its tuning. Some authorities describe it as a small viola with an additional *e'* string, also known as *violino pomposo*. Others suggest a large viola with a low *G* string, or a small cello with an additional *e* string (the same as the 'piccolo *cello'). Repertory by Telemann and others exists for all three versions.   AB/JMo

violin [fiddle] (Fr.: *violon*; Ger.: *Violine*, *Geige*; It.: *violino*). The treble instrument of the violin family. It originated in about 1500 as a three-string dance-music instrument, a combination of the stringing of the rebec and the body of the *lira da braccio*, in the region of Ferrara, Italy. As yet no documentary evidence has been found, but the earliest pictorial evidence appears there at that time, showing the characteristic violin shape with a high-arched belly very different from that of the *viol, which developed only a little earlier. By the 1530s the complete family of *viole da braccio*, or 'arm fiddles'—treble, tenor (*viola), and bass violins (*violoncello)—were shown together.

The fourth string was added by the 1550s (all members of the violin family are tuned in 5ths, the violin to g–d'–a'–e''). By that time the first of the great makers, Andrea Amati, was working in Cremona. He founded a dynasty with his two sons, Antonio and Girolamo (the 'brothers Amati'), and Girolamo's son Nicolò, the greatest of them, who taught Rugeri, Stradivari, and Guarneri; the last named was also the first of a dynasty culminating in his grandson Giuseppe, 'del Gesù'. Cremona was the first great centre, but Gasparo da Salò and his pupil Maggini were soon working in Brescia, and the Linarol family in Venice.

Although each maker has a unique style, all violins have basic features in common. The body is a box, glued together, front (or belly), sides, and back. The arched belly is carved from a piece (often cut into two slabs and joined down the middle) of close-grained spruce, originally from the mountains of northern Italy and Dalmatia. The back is similarly arched, and is carved from a hardwood such as maple. (Cheap violins may be made by bending thin pieces of wood in a press.) The sides or ribs are thin slips of maple, bent to shape round a wooden mould and joined at the corners of the middle or 'C' bouts, at the neck, and at the bottom of the body; each of the joins is strengthened by an internal block of willow. The ribs are so thin that they are usually lined at their edges to give a thicker glue-surface to hold them to the belly and the back. The internal block at the bottom holds the tail button to which the tailpiece (which holds the strings) is hitched. The neck is mortised (or in the old days nailed) to the top block.

The neck, pegbox, and decorative scroll are also of maple, as is the bridge. The fingerboard and tailpiece are now usually of ebony (boxwood was formerly used). Just within the margins of belly and back, a groove in the wood is filled with 'purfling': thin strips of some other wood, contrasting in colour and pattern. The purfling helps to protect against splits caused by knocks on the edges, which overhang the ribs, and has some effect on the vibration of the wood and thus on the sound. Because no two pieces of wood are identical, the ideal thickness all over the belly and the back varies greatly from instrument to instrument, hence the difficulty in producing exact copies of old Italian violins. Some makers test the resonance frequencies of the plates by tapping the wood and listening to its response; others rely on the flexibility of the plates; often the only guide is the skilled maker's own experience.

Two *f*-shaped soundholes are cut in the belly, their exact placing, angle, and shape varying from maker to maker. Their area is finely calculated to tune the pitch-resonance of the air inside the body, for the body itself is a Helmholtz resonator, whose resonance frequency depends on its volume and the area of open hole. Nicks at the 'crossbar' of the *f* indicate where the bridge stands, though this was not always so: early pictures often show the bridge placed lower—sometimes much lower—than it is today. Wedged between the back and front, below the treble foot of the bridge (under the E string) is a soundpost of spruce, its main function being to transmit vibrations from the bridge to the back. A wooden girder, the bass-bar, is glued to the underside of the belly under the bass foot of the bridge, to transmit the vibrations efficiently through the front.

The shape of the violin—the upper bout or shoulders, the incurved waist, the lower bout or hips—were the creation of the unknown 15th-century inventor. Why the violin is this shape, with its sharp corners where each bout joins the next, is not known; 16th-century pictures show that a variety of shapes continued

to be used long after the 'classic' shape was defined, and makers have continued to experiment with such alternative shapes as François Chanot's guitar shape with no corners to the middle bouts, or even Félix Savart's trapezoid model (both 19th century). What is known is that the degree of arching of belly and back makes a radical difference to the tone-quality. David Boyden described the higher-arched violin as having a flute-like tone and that with a flatter arch as oboe-like. Of the great 17th- and early 18th-century makers, Stradivari and Guarneri favoured a flatter arch than did Amati and the Austrian maker Jacob Stainer; as a result Amati and Stainer violins were far more popular, more expensive, and more often copied than those of Stradivari and Guarneri until the end of the 18th century, when major changes in desired tone-qualities and projection fuelled the demand for the flatter model, which was also better able to withstand the reconstructions taking place at that time.

Between about 1780 and 1820 all violins were radically overhauled to cope with the increase in string length and tension and the rising pitch standards demanded both by the quest for greater brilliance and volume and by changes in playing technique. Their bodies were opened and a thicker soundpost and larger and longer bass-bar fitted. A new and longer neck, often with the original pegbox and scroll carefully grafted to it, was mortised into the neck-block. The neck was angled to lean back, just as a tug-of-war team leans back on the rope. In the old design there was a wooden wedge between the neck, which projected straight out, and the fingerboard; this placed the fingerboard at the correct angle to follow the strings. Because the new neck leant back, the fingerboard now rose naturally at the correct angle and there was no need for the wedge. No great violin survives as it came from the hands of its maker: all have been changed, though a few in museums and those seen in early-music bands have been restored, as far as can be done by guesswork, to a state that the maker might recognize.

String materials have also changed. Originally all were of gut. From the mid-1600s gut covered with silver wire was used for the G string, greatly improving its response. The wire E string was welcomed by most players in the early 20th century, in spite of its whining tone, because top-quality gut for so thin a string was difficult to obtain and broke too easily. All-steel strings, which followed in the 1950s, require fine-tuning screws on the tailpiece.

Although there is a standard size for the violin, there has been some variation. Amati, for example, made 12 small and 12 large violins in about 1570 for Charles IX of France. A special small size was the *violino piccolo*, tuned a 3rd or a 4th higher than normal, and small sizes tuned to normal pitch have always been made for children.

In the early days, violins were held against the chest or the shoulder, as is often still the practice among folk musicians, for whom violins remain ideal dance-music instruments. Judging from wear marks, many players gripped with their chins, some on one side of the tailpiece, some on the other. In about 1820 Spohr introduced the chin rest (then placed centrally over the tailpiece, though now normally on the bass side), allowing the violin to be gripped by the chin without damaging or muting the vibrations of the instrument's body; thus the left hand is given much greater freedom of movement, facilitating shifting to higher positions along the neck.

The changes in bowing and playing techniques over the years can be judged from compositions by and for the great virtuosos, from Corelli and Tartini to those of the present day, which have always been written to display the skills of composer or performer.   JMo

📖 D. D. BOYDEN, *A History of Violin Playing from its Origins to 1761* (London, 1965) · R. DONINGTON, *String Playing in Baroque Music* (London, 1977) · D. GILL (ed.), *The Book of the Violin* (Oxford and New York, 1984) · R. STOWELL (ed.), *The Cambridge Companion to the Violin* (Cambridge, 1992) · P. HOLMAN, *Four and Twenty Fiddlers: The Violin at the English Court, 1540–1690* (Oxford, 1993, 2/1995) · J. BEAMENT, *The Violin Explained: Components, Mechanism, and Sound* (Oxford, 1997) · R. DAWES (ed.), *The Violin Book* (London, 1999)

violino piccolo. A small *violin tuned a 3rd or a 4th above the full-size instrument.

violoncello [cello] (Fr.: *violoncelle*; Ger.: *Violoncell*; It.: *violoncello*). The bass instrument of the violin family. It was known originally as the bass violin (*basse de violon*, etc.), its four strings being tuned in 5ths from Bb' upwards. The modern tuning based on C was adopted in Germany and Italy before 1600, but in France and England not much before the 18th century.

Strings were originally all gut, and it was probably the introduction in the mid-17th century of wire-wound strings, the gut core overspun with a fine silver wire, that allowed the cumbersome bass violin to be reduced in size (from a body length of *c*.80 cm to the modern standard *c*.75 cm) and tuned up a whole tone to the modern $C–G–d–a$. The increased density, greater flexibility, and improved tonal quality of the covered C string, followed by the use of a covered G, opened the way to the development of the cello and its use as a solo instrument. At much the same time, the name violoncello, of which 'cello' is an abbreviation, became generally adopted.

The use of a tail-spike or endpin did not become universal until the 20th century, though there is some evidence for it in all periods. The bass violin originally rested on the floor or a small stool while being played. By the end of the 17th century it had become more normal to hold the instrument between the calves, which made it easier to reach the higher positions. This led to a rapid development in performing techniques in the 18th century, including the use of the 'thumb position' (using the thumb as a step on the fingerboard to reach the higher range), and to the expansion of the cello's role as a solo instrument. A comparison of 18th-century works for cello with those for violin shows that by then the cello already had a considerably wider range.

Because of these changes many old bass violins were cut down in size during the 18th and early 19th centuries, with the result that few have survived with their original dimensions. Like the violin during this period, cellos were also given stronger bass-bars and longer, thinner necks, canted back to withstand the increased tension of the wound strings. The cello may have been the first member of the violin family to undergo these changes, which gave it the greater projection and stronger tone required in the new large concert halls and in orchestral playing.

Because of the large range of their instruments, cellists are expected to read music in three different clefs. The basic range is written in the bass clef, but with the top string tuned to *a* it is not long before the tenor clef is needed to avoid the use of ledger lines. For music that ascends further into the reaches of the treble clef, the convention in older music was to write it an octave higher than it would sound, perhaps so that it would look high as well as sound high. Today such passages are written at pitch, and because it can be difficult to be sure when the change in convention took place, cellists sometimes disagree over which octave was intended by the composer.   JMo

📖 E. VAN DER STRAETEN, *History of the Violoncello, the Viol da Gamba, their Precursors and Collateral Instruments* (London, 1915/R1971) · E. COWLING, *The Cello* (London and New York, 1975, 2/1983) · R. STOWELL (ed.), *The Cambridge Companion to the Cello* (Cambridge, 1999)

violone (It., 'large viol'). A term used today for the largest *viol, tuned either a 5th or an octave below the bass viol, from G' or D' upwards. From the 16th century until the 18th the term was used loosely to denote any bass bowed instrument, including the early *double bass and the *bass violin or cello, or any viol (in particular the low-pitched ones).

Viotti, Giovanni Battista (*b* Fontanetto da Po, 12 May 1755; *d* London, 3 March 1824). Italian violinist and composer. He studied with Pugnani from 1770 and after some years in the royal chapel orchestra at Turin travelled to Paris, where he made a highly successful solo debut in 1782. He soon retired from the concert hall, however, to take up various operatic administrative posts and to compose numerous violin concertos and other works. In 1792 he moved to London where, apart from brief spells in Germany and France, he stayed for the rest of his life. Although his concert career briefly resumed in the 1790s, he withdrew from musical life at about the turn of the century. He remained, however, one of the most influential technicians of his generation.   RP

Vir, Param (*b* Delhi, 6 Feb. 1952). British composer of Indian parentage. After attending university in India he studied in England with Maxwell Davies and Oliver Knussen. His compositions blend European and Eastern elements, and he had particular success with two one-act chamber operas, *Snatched by the Gods* and *Broken Strings*, commissioned by Hans Werner Henze for the 1992 Munich Biennale. Vir's orchestral tone-poem *Horse Tooth White Rock* (1994) is dedicated to Henze.   AW

Virdung, Sebastian (*b* Amberg, 19 or 20 Jan. *c.*1465; *d* after 1510). German theorist and composer. His treatise *Musica getutscht* (Basle, 1511) is the oldest printed manual on musical instruments and provides much valuable information on their use in the late 15th and early 16th centuries. The first part deals with the classification of the different families, and the second with their notation in tablature (for keyboard, strings, and wind).   WT/LC

virelai (Fr.). One of the three standard poetic forms used for 14th- and 15th-century chansons (see also BALLADE; RONDEAU). The form has a long history, though its precise origins are unclear. In 13th-century France its function seems to have been as a dance song, and its development is linked to that of the *ballade* (indeed, it is sometimes difficult to distinguish between the two at this period). By way of the works of Adam de la Halle and Jehan de L'Escurel, the *virelai* received definitive expression in the works of Guillaume de Machaut, of which *Plus dure qu'un dÿamant* is a typical example:

> *Plus dure qu'un dÿamant*
> *Ne que pierre d'aÿmant*
> *Est vo durté*
> *Dame, qui n'avez pité*   } A
> *De vostre amant*
> Qu'ocïes en desirant
> Vostre amitié.

Dame vo pure biauté
Qui toutes passe, à mon gré   } b
Et vo samblant
Simple et plein d'umilité
De douceur fine paré   } b
En sousriant.

Par un acqueil attraiant,
M'ont au cuer en regardant
Si fort navré
Que jamais joie n'avré,   } a
Jusques à tant
Que vo grace qu'il atent
M'arez donné.

Plus dure etc. A

A musical setting in two clear sections (a and b) is used for the *virelai*. To the first section is allocated the refrain (the opening and closing group of lines, shown in italics) and the third group, which has the same structure. The second musical section, heard twice, carries the second group of lines. The resulting musical form is AbbaA (capitals indicate the refrain). In fact Machaut's *virelais* have three stanzas, so the full form is Abba, Abba, AbbA.

Although some later 14th-century *virelais* had three stanzas (e.g. Solage's *Tres gentil cuer*), most seem to have had only one or two. Many are examples of the 'realistic *virelai*', in which reserved expressions of courtly love—the normal subject for chanson texts in

Ex. 1

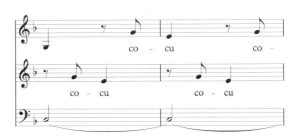

Jaquemin de Senleches, *En ce gracieux temps*, bars 41–5.

whatever form—are replaced by more lively and dramatic imagery, for example the urgent appeals for rescue from the fire of love in the anonymous *Rescoés rescoés*. Many such pieces are concerned with a lover's feelings at the approach of spring (e.g. the anonymous *Contre le temps* or *Je voy le bon tens venir*) and several include imitations of birdsong, as in Vaillant's *Par maintes foys* or Jaquemin de Senleches's *En ce gracieux temps* (Ex. 1).

The *virelai* was almost completely neglected by early 15th-century composers but enjoyed a revival in the middle of the century in works by such composers as Busnois and Ockeghem. PD/ABuL

📖 G. K. GREENE (ed.), *French Secular Music: Virelais*, Polyphonic Music of the Fourteenth Century, 21 (Monaco, 1987) · W. FROBENIUS, 'Virelai', *Handwörterbuch der musikalischen Terminologie*, 13, ed. H. H. Eggebrecht (Stuttgart, 1986) · L. EARP, 'Genre in the fourteenth-century chanson: The virelai and the dance song', *Musica disciplina*, 45 (1991), 123 · D. FALLOWS, *A Catalogue of Polyphonic Songs, 1415–1480* (Oxford, 1999)

virginals. See HARPSICHORD, VIRGINALS, SPINET.

virtuoso (It., 'exceptional performer'). The term originally referred to several types of musician: performers, composers, and even theorists. By the later 18th century, however, it was generally used to dignify a singer or instrumentalist of great talent ('virtuosa' if the person was female). The term became more problematic in the 19th century and later, sometimes being used to describe a performer whose talent was 'merely' technical, unduly crowd-pleasing, and lacking in good taste; but the positive meaning of the term is still in more general use, its most common association being with such celebrated 19th-century soloists as Paganini and Liszt. RP

Vïshnegradsky, Ivan (Aleksandrovich) (*b* St Petersburg, 4/16 May 1893; *d* Paris, 29 Sept. 1979). Russian composer. He studied composition with Nikolay Sokolov (1911–15) before settling in Paris in 1920. He designed the first quarter-tone piano, built in 1924. His interests embraced philosophy, mathematics, physics, chemistry, and Eastern mysticism, all of which he sought to combine in music that would unite the physical with the metaphysical. He experimented with microtones as early as 1918 in *Chant douloureux et étude* op. 6 and from then on was a prolific theorist and composer of microtonal music. His works include two string quartets (1923–4, 1930–1), a sonata for viola and two pianos (1945–59), four *fragments symphoniques* (1934, 1937, 1946, 1956), and *Transparences I* and *II* for two pianos and ondes martenot (1953, 1962–3). Vïshnegradsky published many articles on micro-

tonality; his collected writings were issued as *Premier cahier Ivan Wyschnegradsky* (Paris, 1985), and his study of 'pan-sonority' (written in 1924–5), in which he developed his theory that all matter produces sound and attempted a mathematical subdivision of the 'ultrachromatic' sound continuum, appeared in 1996. PF

📖 B. BARTHELMES, *Raum und Klang: Das musikalische und theoretische Schaffen Ivan Wyschnegradsky* (Hofheim, 1995)

Vision of St Augustine, The. Work (1963–5) by Tippett, for baritone, chorus, and orchestra, a setting of texts from St Augustine's *Confessions* and from the Bible.

Visions de l'Amen. Suite for two pianos (1943) by Messiaen.

Visions fugitives ('Fleeting Visions'). 20 pieces for solo piano, op. 22 (1915–17), by Prokofiev.

Visit of the Old Lady, The. See BESUCH DER ALTEN DAME, DER.

Vitali, Filippo (*b* Florence, *c*.1590; *d* ?Florence, after 1 April 1653). Italian composer. He seems to have remained in Florence, apart from visits, until about 1631, when he was nominated for a place in the papal choir. He sang there from 1633 to 1642, when he was appointed *maestro di cappella* at S. Lorenzo, Florence.

Vitali wrote the first opera to be staged in Rome, *Aretusa* (performed 1620), which was influenced (as he himself admitted) by the Florentine opera composers. His most important works, despite their basically old-fashioned style, are probably the cycle of 34 *Hymni* (Rome, 1636), using the revised Latin texts commissioned by Pope Urban VIII. In contrast, his secular vocal music, which includes five volumes of *Musiche*, three of *Arie*, and one called *Concerto*, is in the newer styles of the Baroque period. WT

Vitali, Giovanni Battista (*b* Bologna, 18 Feb. 1632; *d* Modena, 12 Oct. 1692). Italian composer. He came from a family that produced at least three generations of musicians in the 17th and 18th centuries. Vitali was a string player in the S. Petronio orchestra, Bologna, from 1658, but his precise role is slightly obscured by the uncertain terminology of the bass violin at this period (violone, violoncino, violoncello). He belonged to the Accademia Filaschese and in 1666 was a founder member of the Accademia Filarmonica. In 1674 he moved to the Modenese court of Francesco II d'Este, serving mainly as *sottomaestro* but enjoying a period of two years as *maestro*. His instrumental collections achieved many reprints, being especially popular in

England, where their simple violin style yet tunefulness and rhythmic vitality no doubt appealed to the
burgeoning amateur market. Besides instrumental
sets, his output includes both sacred and secular vocal
music.

His son **Tomaso Antonio Vitali** (*b* Bologna, 7
March 1663; *d* Modena, 9 May 1745) was famous as a
violinist (but the well-known concert piece the
Ciaccona, formerly attributed to him, is undoubtedly
spurious) and as a teacher whose pupils included
Dall'Abaco and Senaillé. His four published instrumental collections span only the years 1693–1701 but
demonstrate the wide difference between the contemporary 'Corellian' sonata and the Modenese style—
especially in their inclusion of a much wider variety of
dances.   DA/PA

vite, vitement (Fr.). 'Quick', 'quickly'.

Vitry, Philippe de (*b* ?Champagne, 31 Oct. 1291; *d* 9
June 1361). French composer and theorist. Music occupied only a small place in his career as a diplomat,
political adviser, and administrator, a career that led in
1351 to his being created Bishop of Meaux. His compositions frequently allude to contemporary political
issues, and they powerfully illustrate how musical
works, motets in particular, could be used as a medium
for comment on current events. There is considerable
uncertainty about which works Vitry actually wrote, let
alone their dates of composition, their intended
audience, and their precise meaning, and it is easier to
be confident about Vitry's general significance as both a
poet and a composer than it is to credit him with
specific pieces. Doubts have also been raised about his
precise role as a music theorist, and the treatise *Ars
nova*, long thought to be his own work, is now recognized to be a digest of ideas by both Vitry and his
contemporaries. Notwithstanding these difficulties,
however, Vitry emerges as a dazzling intellectual, a
major innovator in the genre of the motet, and a
composer at the cutting edge of notational developments.

Ars nova ('New Technique'), the treatise that has
since lent its name to 14th-century music in general (see
Ars Nova), introduced important new concepts to the
method of measuring rhythm. Through its system and
symbols, the passage of time could be represented with
far greater accuracy and sophistication than ever before,
and for the first time syncopation became a viable
component of Western musical language. Vitry's own
motets, and those of his successor Guillaume de
Machaut, use the new notation to explore ideas, textures, and levels of musical complexity that are quite
unimaginable in earlier repertories. Ironically, the
brilliance, symbolism, and sophistication of the results,

the numerology that often underpins them, and the
fascinating interplay between words and music are
often much easier to appreciate through analysis than
in sound.   JM

vivace (It.). 'Lively', 'brisk'; *allegro vivace*, 'faster than
allegro'; *vivacetto*, 'rather lively'; *vivacissimo*, 'very
lively'.

Vivaldi, Antonio (Lucio) (*b* Venice, 4 March 1678; *d*
Vienna, 28 July 1741). Italian violinist and composer.
His father was a professional violinist, originally from
Brescia, who joined the orchestra at St Mark's, Venice,
in 1685. Vivaldi himself was baptized on the day of his
birth, his life being thought to be in danger; this may be
the first sign of the illness, probably asthma, that
afflicted him throughout his life, in particular forcing
him to give up celebrating Mass soon after his ordination in 1703. In that year he was appointed *maestro
di violino* at the Ospedale della Pietà, a post he held
until 1709 and again from 1711 to 1716. His first
publications—of trio sonatas, solo violin sonatas, the
enormously influential op. 3 concerto collection entitled
L'estro armonico, and the 12 violin concertos issued as *La
stravaganza*—appeared during this time. From 1713
onwards he also composed much sacred music for the
Pietà, and in 1716, soon after his promotion to *maestro
de' concerti*, he produced his fine oratorio *Juditha
triumphans*.

By this time Vivaldi was also increasingly active as an
opera composer, and in 1718 he left Venice for Mantua,
where three of his operas were produced during Carnival celebrations. In 1720, after a brief visit to Venice,
he went to Rome, composing more operas and probably
enjoying the patronage of, among others, Cardinal
Ottoboni. In 1723, though he was still at least partly
resident in Rome, the governors of the Pietà contracted
him to supply them with two concertos every month;
during the period 1726–8 he was involved with opera at
the S. Angelo theatre in Venice. The second half of the
1720s saw the appearance of his last four concerto
publications, beginning in 1725 with *Il cimento
dell'armonia e dell'invenzione* op. 8, which contains the
famous set of four depicting the seasons; after 1730 he
abandoned publication, apparently because the sale of
manuscript copies of his works was much more
profitable.

During the period 1729–33 Vivaldi's travels took him
for the first time outside Italy, possibly to Vienna, and
certainly to Prague, which he visited in 1730. In 1735
he was reappointed to the Pietà as *maestro di cappella*,
but in 1738 he lost the post again, probably because
of his inability to give up his travels and settle down to
his duties in Venice. The following year he paid a
successful visit to Amsterdam. It is unclear why he

embarked on his final journey to Vienna, though the success of his operatic work in Venice and elsewhere, which he had continued alongside his other activities, does seem to have been declining. He died apparently in poverty and was buried in a pauper's grave.

To his contemporaries Vivaldi was more important as a violinist than as a composer, and his own virtuosity is reflected in his writing for the instrument, especially in his concertos. But for present-day audiences he is one of the best-known and most popular composers of the period, the *Four Seasons* concertos especially being among the most often performed and recorded works from before 1750. They are, however, only the tip of the iceberg: Vivaldi wrote more than 500 concertos, many for solo violin, but others for cello, flute, oboe, and bassoon as well as viola d'amore and mandolin—all of which instruments were competently played by members of the all-female orchestra at the Pietà, as were those that appear only in solo groups in his concerti grossi, including the horn, trumpet, lute, and chalumeau (precursor of the clarinet).

Though not single-handedly responsible for inventing ritornello form, Vivaldi was the first composer to establish it as the norm for concerto fast movements; he also instituted the standard three-movement (fast–slow–fast) concerto structure. Many of his concertos other than *The Four Seasons* contain descriptive elements expressed in such titles as *La tempesta di mare* or *L'inquietudine*. Though much smaller in quantity than his instrumental music, and still in the process of rehabilitation, Vivaldi's sacred music is of high quality; his setting of the psalm *Nisi Dominus* for alto contains some wonderfully expressive word-painting.

Throughout his career Vivaldi was in the habit of borrowing from or re-composing his own earlier works, so that many exist in more than one version. Establishing the correct chronology of those that were not published in his lifetime can thus be difficult. There are also a number of works by other composers that have been wrongly attributed to him.   DA/ER

📖 M. Talbot, *Vivaldi* (London, 1978, 2/1993); *Vivaldi* (London, 1979); *The Sacred Vocal Music of Antonio Vivaldi* (Florence, 1995)

Vivanco, Sebastián de (*b* Ávila, *c.*1550; d Salamanca, 26 Oct. 1622). Spanish composer. In 1576 he was dismissed as *maestro de capilla* of Lérida Cathedral; he subsequently held the equivalent posts at the cathedrals of Segovia (from 1577), Ávila (1587–1602), and Salamanca. In 1603 he was also appointed to the chair in music at the University of Salamanca. Three collections of his music were published in that city: *Magnificat* settings (notable for canonic writing) in 1607, masses in 1608,

and motets (some with striking use of syncopation and rapid declamation) in 1610.   OR

Vives, Amadeo (*b* Collbató, 18 Nov. 1871; *d* Madrid, 1 Dec. 1932). Catalan composer. He was a pupil of Pedrell. His early reputation was built on choral works, notably *Emigrantes* (1894), which became a rallying-cry for Catalan exiles throughout the world. Though semi-paralysed from childhood, he went on to write songs and operas, as well as the many zarzuelas on which his reputation rests. These include *Bohemios* (1904), the through-sung *Maruxa* (1914), and *La villana* (1927). His finest work is *Doña Francisquita* (1923), the best-loved of all three-act zarzuelas and typical of Vives's graceful melodic charm and delicate orchestration.   CW

Vivier, Claude (*b* Montreal, 14 April 1948; *d* Paris, 12 March 1983). Canadian composer. He studied with Gilles Tremblay at the Montreal Conservatory, at the Utrecht electronic music studio, and with Stockhausen in Cologne. A visit to East Asia in 1976–7 also had a profound influence on his highly personal musical language. His chamber opera *Kopernikus*, which he described as a 'ritual opera of death', was produced in Montreal in 1980. After this he received increasing recognition and several commissions in Canada and in Europe, before his career was cut short by his murder shortly before his 35th birthday.   ABur

vivo, vivamente (It.). 'Lively', 'brisk'.

vl, vln, vn. Abbreviations for 'violin'.

Vltava ('River Moldau'). Symphonic poem by Smetana, the fourth of his cycle *Má vlast and often played separately.

vocalise (Fr.; Ger.: *Vokalise*; It.: *vocalizzo*). A melody sung without text but to one or more vowel sounds. The term embraces vocal technical exercises (see sol-feggio) and concert pieces. In the early 19th century it became customary to provide certain types of vocal exercise with a piano accompaniment, so that even the most mechanical exercises could be performed in a more artistic manner. There was also a tradition, dating from the 18th century, of using existing compositions that presented certain technical problems as vocal exercises without words. By the 19th century, many singing instruction manuals included pieces without words specially composed for this purpose.

The earliest example of a vocalise designed as a concert piece is probably Spohr's Sonatina for voice and piano (1848). It was not until the early 20th century that the idea was fully taken up. Notable examples include Ravel's *Vocalises en forme d'habanera*, Rakhmaninov's *Vocalise*, and Medtner's *Sonata-Vocalise* and *Suite-Vocalise*. Other composers have used vocalized passages

as a special effect, for example Debussy in 'Sirènes' (the third of his orchestral *Nocturnes*), Holst in the 'Neptune' movement from *The Planets*, and Janáček (in the scene of the Vixen's Wedding from Act II of his opera *The Cunning Little Vixen*). —/LC

vocal score. A *score showing all the vocal parts of a work on separate staves, with the orchestral parts reduced to a keyboard arrangement. In the 19th century, vocal scores became the primary means of disseminating the text of operas. The 19th-century London publisher Vincent Novello was famed for his editions of Haydn and Mozart masses in vocal score, with piano or organ accompaniments. LC

voce, voci (It.). 'Voice', 'voices'; *colla voce* ('with the voice') denotes that the accompanist should take the tempo from the soloist and follow him or her closely.

voce di petto, voce di testo (It.). 'Chest voice', 'head voice'; see VOICE, 4.

voces aequales (Lat.). 'Equal voices'.

Voces intimae ('Friendly Voices'). Subtitle of Sibelius's String Quartet in D minor op. 56 (1909).

voci eguali (It.). 'Equal voices'.

Vögel, Die ('The Birds'). Opera in two acts by Braunfels to his own libretto after Aristophanes (Munich, 1920).

Vogel, Wladimir (Rudolfovich) (*b* Moscow, 29 Feb. 1896; *d* Zürich, 19 June 1984). Swiss composer, of German-Russian parentage. He studied in Berlin with Heinz Tiessen and Busoni, then taught at the Klindworth-Scharwenka Conservatory (1929–33). In 1933 he was forced to leave Germany and moved to Switzerland, where he spent the rest of his life. He taught privately. His most notable contribution to music was in the use of speaking voices, solo and choral; he wrote several 'dramma-oratorios', among them *Wagadus Untergang durch die Eitelkeit* (1930). He has also drawn on Schoenbergian *serialism and a Busoni-like classicism. PG/MA

 📖 H. OESCH, *Wladimir Vogel: Sein Weg zu einer neuen musikalischen Wirklichkeit* (Berne and Munich, 1967)

Vogelweide, Walther von der. See WALTHER VON DER VOGELWEIDE.

Vogler, Georg Joseph [Abbé Vogler] (*b* Würzburg, 15 June 1749; *d* Darmstadt, 6 May 1814). German theorist, keyboard player, and composer. His music school in Mannheim (founded 1776) was a proving-ground for his harmonic theory, which he expounded in several treatises. He also designed organs, including the

portable 'orchestrion'. Weber and Meyerbeer were among his pupils. WT/FL

 📖 F. GRAVE, *In Praise of Harmony: The Teachings of Abbé Georg Joseph Vogler* (Lincoln, NE, 1987)

voice 1. Introduction; 2. Breathing; 3. The mechanism of the larynx; 4. Registers; 5. Resonance; 6. Vibrato; 7. Refinements of vocal production

1. Introduction

The voice in its undeveloped state is the oldest of all musical instruments. Humans must have realized since life began that this instrument within themselves had a considerable effect on listeners. It is not necessary that a singer develop his or her vocal technique for the voice to be affecting; it is rather the quality of emotional expression that is the most important factor, as any consideration of famous popular and folk singers will verify. However, in order to sing the vast repertory of Western art music the voice must be trained in a particular way so that it may sing over a wide range, at different dynamic levels, and in both slow and florid music.

From the earliest times an empirical approach to training the voice has been combined with scientific investigation, the first example of which is that of the Greek physician Galen (AD 130–200); after that there was little advance until the 16th century, by the end of which developments in vocal music and the emergence of opera had led to a renewal of interest in vocal science. Although most theories of vocal physiology before the 20th century were incomplete and in many respects wrong, great singing still flourished, even when the technique was based on a mistaken scientific concept. Clearly the traditional methods worked, and they continue to do so. They will therefore be examined here, together with the science of vocal production. It will be seen that the two complement rather than oppose each other.

2. Breathing

In singing, vocal tone has to be sustained for relatively long periods. Breathing is therefore the single most important aspect of technique. Many teachers have devised elaborate systems of breathing and breath control, although breathing efficiently for singing is a straightforward function. The difficulties arise in co-ordinating the breath with the act of vocalizing in such a way as to exercise both freedom and control.

Because the singer's body is used as a musical instrument, attention must be given to posture. The head should be erect but not stiff, so that the back of the neck is fully extended. The chest should be kept reasonably high, with the shoulders relaxed and the arms hanging.

The pelvis should be tilted. The singer's weight should rest on the balls of the feet, and he or she should feel poised for action. Some degree of pulling in may be felt in the lower abdomen, but the muscles should not be consciously tensed. The singer should breathe silently and deeply, experiencing expansion around the lower ribs. The diaphragm descends and flattens somewhat allowing the thorax to enlarge. On exhalation (as required for vocalization) the sternum should not be dropped. The abdominal muscles contract and are resisted by the intercostals and diaphragm. If the singer takes a good breath and exhales on an 'f' sound he or she will feel the gradual upward and inward movement balanced by internal pressures.

3. The mechanism of the larynx

Vocal tone is produced in the larynx, which is situated at the top of the trachea or windpipe, a tube made up of rings of cartilage. The larynx consists of a cartilaginous framework joined together with a complicated system of muscles and ligaments. There are two large cartilages: at the base of the larynx is the cricoid cartilage, shaped rather like a signet ring; above it is the thyroid cartilage, consisting of two surfaces fused at the front. The bulge in the neck known as the Adam's apple is the front of this cartilage. The back of the thyroid cartilage extends upward and downward in horn-like projections. The upper horns (or superior *cornua*) meet the back of the hyoid bone, while the inferior *cornua* are attached to the side of the cricoid, forming a pivotal joint.

On the top edge of the cricoid are the two small arytenoid cartilages. Each arytenoid narrows upwards, and attached to the apex are the corniculate cartilage. At the base of each arytenoid is the vocal process (a process is a protuberance or outgrowth). The vocal cord is attached to this process. The larynx is connected at the top to the hyoid bone, which lies in the upper part of the neck. The epiglottis is a flap-like cartilage connected to the thyroid cartilage.

The vocal cords consist of a pair of muscular folds that converge towards the centre at the level of the arytenoids. During breathing the vocal folds open up and lie parallel to the sides of the larynx. Above the true cords are false cords that have no influence on tone-production. Below the vocal folds is the *conus elasticus*, a ligament that is joined at the bottom to the upper edge of the cricoid and at the top blends into the edges of the glottis.

The vocal folds themselves are formed by the thyro-arytenoid muscles, which extend from the notch of the thyroid to the arytenoids. This pair of muscles is complex in structure. They form two folds on each side. The upper folds are the ventricular bands or false vocal cords. The internal thyro-arytenoids form the body of the two vocal cords and are also called the *vocalis*. The edges of the folds are the vocal ligaments.

Before considering tone-production, mention should be made of the external muscular network that is necessary to the efficient functioning of the voice. The larynx is suspended in what might be termed an 'elastic scaffolding' of muscles that is even more complex than the internal structure of the larynx. Some of the muscles hold the larynx downward and backward. The cricoid cartilage is kept stationary against the spine. The muscles joining the hyoid bone to the jaw should be relaxed so that the larynx is pulled forward and upwards. Another set of muscles provides connections between the larynx, shoulder blades, and sternum, thus helping to balance the muscles that pull the larynx upwards towards the tongue, palate, and cranium. The downward-pulling muscles cannot function if the chest is not kept high and wide as described in section 2.

In order to produce tone the vocal folds must be brought together (adducted) and air allowed to flow. First the singer imagines the pitch at which he or she is going to sing. The crico-thyroid muscle contracts, causing the distance from the thyroid and cricoid to increase, and thus stretching the vocal folds to the correct length. An increase in length causes the folds to vibrate more quickly. The vocal folds are brought together by the action of the transverse arytenoid muscle, helped by the oblique inter-arytenoid muscles. The lateral crico-arytenoids also coordinate with the inter-arytenoids in adducting the vocal folds perfectly.

In producing sound the folds are brought almost parallel. Because of what is known as the Bernoulli effect there is a lowering of pressure along the edges of the vocal folds that sucks them together. The difference in air pressure across the glottis then throws the folds apart. Thus the air travels through the cords in a rapid series of puffs. During phonation the tension and density of the vocal folds change in relation to the breath pressure to achieve the tonal quality imagined by the singer.

The attack of a vowel tone is a combination of muscular adjustment and the action of breath. It should be noted that the vocal attack initiated by suction is different from that in which air is forced through vocal folds that are completely closed. In this case the sound begins with what is really a slight cough, or 'glottal plosive' (represented by '?' in the Initial Phonetic Alphabet). This attack is what is usually meant by the term *coup de glotte*. It is often advisable in practising an attack on a high note to allow some breath to escape in order to relax the valvular mechanism. In vocal production deserving of the name 'bel canto', the closure of the folds and the breath flow are simultaneous, producing a clean attack that is neither breathy nor violent.

4. Registers

As the vocal folds consist of a complex web of different muscle fibres, the tension and density of vocal folds can vary considerably. On the lowest notes the thyro-arytenoid muscles are relatively relaxed, and vibration takes place in the main body of the vocal fold. There is a limit to the tension that can be placed on the whole of the *vocalis* muscle, which will give way at a certain pitch, causing a 'break' in the voice. With the *vocalis* muscle thus relaxed the vocal ligaments can be tensed independently, producing a 'falsetto'.

Thus there exist what may be termed a heavy mechanism and a light mechanism. Teaching methods have always disagreed over the number of registers. J. F. Agricola (1720–74) talked of three registers, whereas Giambattista Mancini (1714–1800) described two. In fact neither is incorrect. The singer has to learn to move smoothly from one mechanism to the other. At the bottom of the voice one can use just the heavy mechanism and gradually lighten as the pitch ascends, 'combining' the two in the middle voice. At the top only the light mechanism is used. A woman thus has chest, middle, and head registers, and a man chest, head, and falsetto. A man will not normally use falsetto except for special effect or if he sings alto. The chest voice should not be carried up too high, as this will result in forcing, and no matter how heavy or dramatic a voice becomes as a singer matures, the light mechanism should not be neglected if high notes are to be retained throughout a long career.

5. Resonance

Like all musical instruments the voice has resonators as well as a tone-producer. One of the most important skills to be learnt is the adjustment of the resonators to produce different vocal tone-colours, according to the mood and emotional content of the music.

The most important resonator is the pharynx. Most singers agree that the throat must be kept 'open'. Pedagogical concepts—such as holding a ball of air in the pharynx, or imagining that the tone travels back-wards instead of forwards—are common (the latter sensation is reported to have been experienced by Caruso). Another common idea is to induce a feeling of yawning. The enlarged pharynx reinforces the lower overtones and gives the voice a mellow or rich quality. The pitch of the pharynx has been estimated variously at between 350 and 750 Hz. Thus the singer adjusts the resonator according to the pitch at which he or she is singing, and to the tone-colour required. Also important in opening the throat is the role of the tongue, which should be kept low and forward in the mouth. The larynx should be kept fairly low (it will rise a certain amount on high notes and follow the tongue in producing certain vowels). If the singer breathes deeply and silently the larynx will drop naturally and the tongue will relax. In addition to the deep, open throat most teachers ask for the soft palate to be stretched high. When this upward stretch is coordinated cor-rectly with a downward stretch there is a strengthening of high overtones, giving a voice 'ring', brilliance, or focus. The resonator for this frequency is believed to be in the 'collar of the larynx', between the epiglottis and the ary-epiglottic folds. Singers often feel this 'ring' in frontal areas of the face and nasal cavities, and can intensify it by opening these cavities. This is known variously as 'forward resonance', 'singing in the mask', or 'impostazione della voce' (voice placement).

6. Vibrato

The fluctuation in pitch in vocal *vibrato is quite wide—about a semitone, increasing at particularly loud moments to as much as a tone. Unless the vibrato is excessive intonation is not affected, as the listener hears an average of the two outer limits. It is vibrato that gives the voice its emotionally affecting quality—in fact it is directly related to the emotional state of the singer. Each tiny muscle of the larynx is balanced by another. In maintaining the balance when singing there is a fluctuation in the energy of the muscles. Its speed depends on that of the nerve impulses: if there is too much uncontrolled emotional stimulation the fre-quency of nerve impulses will be faster. If the vibrato is too fast the listener will hear a flutter; if too slow, a wobble.

Some vocal pedagogies favour a slow, rather wide vibrato. In what might be called a 'German sound'—the rich but often overweighted vocal production especially common in Wagnerian singers—the vibrato rate is often as slow as five pulsations a second. Such a quality, while suitable for German Romantic music, is less suited to Italian music, which requires a concentrated sound. Many opera singers, in an effort to produce more sound, overweight their voices. It was in reaction to this type of vocal production that some early music specialists came to favour a 'straight' tone without vi-brato for 17th- and 18th-century music. However, there is much source material that acknowledges the use of carefully controlled vibrato as a necessary feature of good singing.

7. Refinements of vocal production

Present-day singers are expected to sing music of all periods. Although some compromise is necessary, it is possible to use the voice differently according to the music to be sung. A consideration of some traditional methods of voice-training will be useful to the singer, as much of the repertory can be regarded as lying within the tradition that developed in Italy in the 17th century and continued unchanged until the mid-19th.

First to be considered is portamento style. 'Portamento' here is not used in the narrow sense of slurring between two notes. Rather it is the idea of the voice being carried on the breath, so that every note melts smoothly into the next, and the sound is felt to pour out of the body without being forced. The physical sensation is inextricably linked to the rhythm of the music, and so the portamento is felt to continue throughout a piece, and is implied even through rests. As well as being a matter of breathing, this is also a matter of attack. It cannot be achieved if the 'coup de glotte' is used; the clean attack as described in section 3 is required. Another important aspect of voice-training as described in 18th- and early 19th-century sources concerns the registers, the different ones being developed fully but joined smoothly. Certainly in Baroque music the chest voice was fully exploited, a fact largely ignored in performances today. A vocal device which trained the singer's attack, breath control, and registration was the *messa di voce* (It., 'placing of the voice'), which simply means allowing a long note to swell from soft to loud and then to die away. To practise this one must begin with a perfectly clean attack, very quietly. This will be almost falsetto but will have enough heaviness to enable the singer to crescendo smoothly. As the volume increases, the quality becomes heavier and the resonance intensifies. The process is reversed in the diminuendo. It will be seen that this is training the muscles of the larynx, as well as their coordination with the breath.

It is important also that the singer practises coloratura. Florid passages are not sung as legato phrases speeded up (although slow practice may be helpful in securing a mental picture of the shape of a run and to check intonation). The key to singing coloratura stylishly is the meaning of the word itself, 'colouring'. It is sung not with the full voice but lightly, so that it emerges out of the line, supported by a strong bodily rhythm. Ornaments such as the trill (essentially an exaggerated vibrato), turn, and mordent should also be sung with a light quality 'extracted' from the main tone without disturbing the line.

The physical mechanism of the voice depends on a delicate balance of opposing muscular forces. There are also extremes of light and heavy registration, and of brilliant and dark resonance (or 'focus' and depth). While accepting the intrinsic quality of his or her voice, the singer must achieve the appropriate balance for the music. Generally, lightness and brilliance are required

for Baroque and Classical music, and the low and high registers will be very different in quality (as in early pianos). In later music there will be greater emphasis on a heavier production throughout the whole range. In the training of a young singer, however, the focus should be on a light or lyric production. If the voice has the potential, it will develop more dramatic quality as it matures. See also SINGING.   DM/RW

📖 G. B. MANCINI, *Pensieri e riflessioni pratiche sopra il canto figurato* (Vienna, 1774, enlarged 3/1777; Eng. trans. by E. Foreman, 1967, as *Practical Reflections on Figured Singing*) · M. GARCÍA, *Traité complet de l'art du chant* (Paris, 1840, 2/1847/R, 3/1851 as *École de Garcia*, II/1901; Eng. trans. by D. V. Paschke, 1972, as *A Complete Treatise on the Art of Singing*) · F. HUSLER and Y. RODD-MARLING, *Singing: The Physical Nature of the Vocal Organ* (London, 1965, 2/1976) · W. VENNARD, *Singing: The Mechanism and the Technique* (New York, 1967) · R. MILLER, *English, French, German and Italian Techniques of Singing* (Metuchen, NJ, 1977) · J. POTTER (ed.), *The Cambridge Companion to Singing* (Cambridge, 2000)

voice exchange (Ger.: *Stimmtausch*). In polyphonic music, the alternation of phrases between two voices of equal range, a feature found frequently in 12th- and 13th-century music. In Schenkerian theory, the passing of a structural line from an upper to a lower voice, or vice versa.

voice-leading (Amer.). *Part-writing. See also ANALYSIS, 3; COUNTERPOINT.

voice part. See PART, 1.

voice trial. A singing test taken by boys and, more rarely, girls auditioning for places in cathedral and chapel choirs. The test typically comprises one or two set pieces, sight-reading exercises, scales, and arpeggios.   RW

voicing. The highly skilled process of ensuring that instruments speak correctly and with the desired uniformity of tone, volume, and tuning; the term refers particularly to minute adjustments to the windway and mouth of recorders and organ flue pipes, to the thickness and curvature of the metal reeds in organ reed pipes, to the jacks and plectra of harpsichords, and to the hammers of a piano.   JMo

voilé (Fr.). 'Veiled', 'subdued'.

voix (Fr.). 'Voice'.

Voix humaine, La ('The Human Voice'). Opera in one act by Poulenc to a libretto by Jean Cocteau after his play (Paris, 1959); it is a monodrama for soprano and orchestra.

Volans, Kevin (*b* Pietermaritzburg, 26 July 1949). South African-born Irish composer. He studied at the universities of Witwatersrand and Aberdeen, and from 1973 to 1981 in Cologne with Stockhausen and Mauricio Kagel. He was composer-in-residence at Queen's University, Belfast, and Princeton University before moving to Dublin. In 1995 he became an Irish citizen. Volans has written a chamber opera, *The Man with Footsoles of Wind* (London, Almeida, 1993), and several dance scores. Many of his works are indebted to African music: for example, *White Man Sleeps*, composed for a mixed microtonal ensemble (1982) and adapted as the first of his five string quartets (1986).   ABur

volante (It.). 1. 'Flying', i.e. swift and light.

2. In string playing, a kind of bowstroke where the bow bounces on the string to produce an effect similar to that of the *ricochet.

Volkmann, Friedrich Robert (*b* Lommatzsch, Saxony, 6 April 1815; *d* Budapest, 29 Oct. 1883). German composer. He studied music at Freiberg, then at Leipzig (1836–9), where he met Schumann. In 1841 he settled in Budapest, becoming a prominent musical figure. From 1875 until his death he was professor of composition at the Budapest Academy of Music. His output, in most genres, is in the German style with occasional Hungarian elements, and is of a conservative cast. It includes much piano music (including character pieces for children), chamber music (including six string quartets and a piano trio championed by Liszt), and two symphonies.   WT

Volkonsky, Andrey (Mikhaylovich) (*b* Geneva, 14 Feb. 1933). Russian composer, harpsichordist, and conductor. Born into a distinguished noble family in exile, he studied the piano at the Geneva and Paris Conservatoires, and took private lessons from Dinu Lipatti; he also studied composition with Messiaen and Nadia Boulanger. After moving to Russia in 1947 he studied composition at the Moscow Conservatory with Shaporin. In 1956 Volkonsky wrote *Musica stricta* for piano, the first serial piece written in the USSR; he followed this with the influential vocal cycle *Suite of Mirrors* (1959), which also uses serial procedures. He is now universally credited as the initiator of the Soviet 1960s avant-garde; his role as the founder (1964) of the first early-music ensemble in Russia—Madrigal—was also important. He emigrated back to the West in 1973.   JWal

Volkslied (Ger.). 'Folksong'.

volkstümliches Lied (Ger.). 'Popular song' or 'folk-like song'. Lieder in a style akin to folksong, with simple accompaniment and an unembellished vocal line, were first written in Germany by J. A. Hiller and J. A. P. Schulz, among others, during the late 18th century. Their music in turn influenced Schubert, who, in such songs as *Heidenröslein*, gives an impression of artless simplicity but in fact uses highly sophisticated and subtle means to achieve this effect.   —/JBe

volonté (Fr.). 'Will'; *à volonté*, 'at will', i.e. *ad *libitum*.

volta (It.). 1 (from *voltare*, 'to turn', 'to turn round'). A quick dance, popular in France from the 1550s; it was usually in triple time and resembled the *galliard. The name derives from one of the movements of the dance, in which the woman is lifted by her partner, who uses his thigh to assist him, while turning round. The dance became popular in England and Germany towards the beginning of the 17th century, but in France Louis XIII (1610–43) banned it from his court because of its lack of decorum. As with other courtly dances, it became a popular instrumental form in its own right, and English virginal and lute pieces are found with the title 'Lavolta'. See also WALTZ.

2. See DOUBLE BAR; OUVERT AND CLOS.

volti (It.). 'Turn', 'turn over'; *volti subito*, 'turn over quickly', often found at the bottom of pages in orchestral parts. It is abbreviated *v.s.*

voluntary. A piece, written or improvised, played by the organist before, during, or after a church service. There is no exact equivalent in other languages.

1. Meanings of the term 'voluntary'; 2. History of the organ voluntary

1. Meanings of the term 'voluntary'

The word is found in a musical application as early as the mid-16th century, at first apparently meaning an instrumental composition in which, instead of the composer adding parts to a plainchant theme, as was still common, he left himself free to fashion all his parts as he liked. In the Mulliner Book (*c*.1560) the term is applied in this way, and voluntaries there are seen to be a sort of contrapuntal fantasia or ricercar without any *cantus firmus. Keyboard pieces of this type by Byrd and his contemporaries are sometimes labelled 'voluntary', either as sole title or as a subtitle to 'fantasia'. Morley in *A Plaine and Easie Introduction* (1597) says that 'to make two parts upon a plaine song is more hard than to make three parts into voluntarie'.

But the idea of freedom implicit in the word allowed it to be applied in another way. Thus from the same date or a little later we find 'voluntary' used as meaning what we now call extemporization or improvisation, or for any extempore performance on any instrument, often forming a prelude to a more structured composition. In the 16th century the expression 'a voluntary before the song' is found. A warrant of Charles I, laying down the rhythms to be used by army drummers, calls one of them 'Voluntary before the March'. A collection entitled *Select Preludes and Voluntarys for the Violin* was published by Walsh of London in 1705. Burney (*c*.1805) in *Rees's Cyclopaedia* defines voluntary as 'a piece played by a musician extempore, according to his fancy' and says that such a piece is often used before the musician 'begins to set himself to play any composition, to try the instrument and lead him into the key of the piece he intends to perform'.

Thus the term in its origins and history has much in common with 'prelude', as well as 'capriccio', 'fantasia', and 'impromptu'. It was used for improvisation at the piano as late as Thackeray's *Vanity Fair* (1848): 'Sitting down to the piano she rattled a triumphant voluntary on the keys.' And Leigh Hunt (1850) talks of 'modulating sweet voluntaries on the pianoforte'. For well over a century, however, the only current meaning of the term has been the one defined at the head of this article.

2. History of the organ voluntary

In the Middle Ages *alternatim* practice led to the organ at first accompanying, then replacing, the congregational part in Mass or Office in alternation with the choir (as still found, for example, in François Couperin's organ masses). An organ solo also came to replace the singing of responds after the lessons read at the Office; this survived the English Reformation in cathedrals, and the few other churches that retained organs, but was generally displaced to a position between the psalms and the first lesson. James Clifford's manual of instructions for conducting the services, published in 1663, specifies 'after the psalms a *voluntary* upon the organ alone'. This 'middle voluntary' survived in some churches until the late 19th century.

The main opportunities for organ solos, however, were before and after service, where, again, the organ was historically a substitute for the singing of 'an hymn' authorized before and after service in Elizabeth I's *Injunctions* of 1559 (see ANTHEM). Other points sometimes calling for short voluntaries were before the sermon, while the clergyman went to the vestry to change from a surplice to a preaching-gown; between Morning Prayer and Communion; and during the offertory in the Communion service, when alms were collected.

Though the primary meaning of the term remained that of improvisation, many composers of the late 16th and the 17th centuries left specimens in manuscript, for their own use or as models for their pupils. Some were

called 'double voluntary', indicating the use of two contrasting manuals (pedals were not a feature of the English organ until the 19th century). A rare example of a voluntary based on a pre-existing tune (the *Old Hundredth*) has survived in two versions, one attributed to Blow, the other to Purcell.

In the 18th century, as more and more churches acquired organs, it became commercially feasible to publish voluntaries. A long series of such publications began in 1728 with a set of 15 by Thomas Roseingrave; among the more important later sets were those of Handel, Greene, Boyce, Stanley, Keeble, and Worgan. Nearly all were designated 'for the organ or harpsichord', indicating domestic as well as church use; and there was indeed a secularization of the voluntary. As early as 1711 Joseph Addison wrote in *The Spectator*:

> When the Preacher has often, with great Piety and Art enough, handled his subject, and the judicious Clerk has with the utmost diligence culled out two Staves [of a metrical psalm] proper to the discourse, and I have found in my self and in the rest of the Pew good Thoughts and Dispositions, they have been all in a moment dissipated by a merry jig from the organ loft.

The sober, polyphonic style still prevailed with Roseingrave, but by the mid-century John Stanley, the 'classical' composer of Georgian voluntaries, had developed a two- or three-movement form, with a slow, grave introduction followed by a flashier fast movement, often displaying a solo trumpet or cornet stop. Later in the century one of the movements of a voluntary would belong to some genre borrowed from the concert hall or theatre, such as siciliana, march, or minuet; and movements of oratorios and symphonies were beginning to be used as voluntaries.

These trends continued in the 19th century. One of the last and best composers of 'real' voluntaries was Samuel Wesley (1766–1837), whose respect for Baroque music led him to revive to some extent the serious contrapuntal writing of earlier times; the same was true of Thomas Adams. Mendelssohn's Organ Sonatas (1845) were the result of a commission given him when in England to write some voluntaries for English use, and the decision to call them sonatas instead of voluntaries was an afterthought. Wesley's son Samuel Sebastian reverted to the habit of improvising his voluntaries; his powers were legendary, but he left few written specimens.

In the Victorian period, and continuing to the present time, a 'voluntary' came to mean any music played before or after a service, and lost all implications of a specific form or tradition. As the 'symphonic' *organ developed, many organists of cathedrals or large urban churches treated the end of a service as an opportunity to perform arrangements of orchestral or even operatic music, imitating instrumental and vocal effects with stops designed for the purpose; but they also introduced the organ works of Bach and other great composers of the past. The before-service voluntary, being of indeterminate length (since it had to end whenever the priest and choir chose to take their places), was more likely to be a vague and formless improvisation. These traditions still survive. On special occasions, such as weddings, a set piece is often required while the congregation gathers. With the revival of the tracker organ, primarily for the purpose of playing early music in a more historically correct style, there has been a modest flow of original organ music, and occasionally the title 'voluntary' has been used, as by Maxwell Davies in *Three Organ Voluntaries* (1979). In the USA the term is often used for a prelude based on a hymn tune that is about to be sung.

PS/NT

📖 F. ROUTH, *Early English Organ Music from the Middle Ages to 1837* (London, 1973) · N. TEMPERLEY, 'Organ music', *The Blackwell History of Music in Britain*, v (Oxford, 1988), 435–51

Von heute auf morgen ('From One Day to the Next'). Opera in one act by Schoenberg to a libretto by Max Blonda (pseudonym of Gertrud Schoenberg) (Frankfurt, 1930).

vorbereiten (Ger.). 'Prepare'; the term is used in organ music, often in the form *bereite vor*, 'prepare for', followed by a particular stop.

Vorhalt (Ger.). 1. A suspension (*vorbereiteter Vorhalt*). 2. An appoggiatura (*freier Vorhalt*).

Voříšek, Jan Václav [Worzischek, Johann Hugo] (*b* Vamberk, 11 May 1791; *d* Vienna, 19 Nov. 1825). Bohemian composer and keyboard player. He was first taught by his father, a choirmaster and organist; his remarkable abilities as a keyboard player led to a brief career as a child prodigy touring Bohemia. While studying law in Prague he continued his musical studies with Tomášek, whose high regard for contrapuntal excellence had a considerable effect on Voříšek's church music, and on the texture of his piano works. But in the Prague of the 1810s Mozartian elegance was cultivated at the expense of experimentation, and Voříšek had little opportunity to indulge in newer musical trends. Thus in 1813 he moved to Vienna to observe in particular the music of Beethoven at closer quarters.

There he was active as composer, pianist, and (from 1818) conductor of the Gesellschaft der Musikfreunde. He was appointed court organist in 1823. Voříšek's early death occasioned numerous tributes from the musical community in Vienna. Beethoven had spoken well of

his Rhapsodies op. 1, and Schubert, with whom Voříšek was friendly, seems to have been influenced by the piano writing in the Impromptus op. 7. Voříšek's style owed virtually nothing to his Czech origins: melodically he showed an interest in motivic thematic material akin to Beethoven's, harmonically an absorption with diminished chords which sometimes anticipates Schumann and Mendelssohn. His shorter piano compositions made a significant contribution to the infancy of the Romantic piano piece and his single Symphony (in D, op. 24, 1921) indicates a dynamic (in the slow movement almost theatrical) talent quite justifying contemporary regret at his untimely death.

JSM

Vorschlag (Ger.). An *appoggiatura; *kurzer Vorschlag*, 'short appoggiatura'; *langer Vorschlag*, 'long appoggiatura'.

Vorspiel (Ger.). 'Prelude'. Wagner called the orchestral introductions to his operas *Vorspiele*, and described *Das Rheingold* as a *Vorspiel* to the *Ring* trilogy.

Vortrag (Ger.). 'Performance', 'execution', or 'recital'; *Vortragsstück*, a virtuoso showpiece; *Vortragzeichen*, expression marks; *vortragen*, 'to perform', or 'to bring into prominence', 'to emphasize'.

vorwärts (Ger.). 'Forward'; *vorwärts gehen*, 'progress', 'move on', i.e. faster.

Vorzeichnung (Ger.). 'Signature'; sometimes time signature and key signature are specified as *Taktvorzeichnung* and *Tonartvorzeichnung* respectively.

votive antiphon. A Latin antiphon sung together with a versicle and collect at the end of an office, especially Compline, honouring a different object from that of the main service (see MEMORIAL). Although the term refers most commonly to the four *antiphons of the Blessed Virgin Mary, which remained in use after the *Council of Trent, earlier sources such as the Eton Choirbook contain many others.   ALI

vox principalis, vox organalis (Lat.). In *organum, respectively the 'principal voice' (i.e. the pre-existent part used as a basis for polyphony) and the composed second voice.

Vranický, Pavel. See WRANITZKY, PAUL.

v.s. Abbreviation for *volti subito*, 'turn over quickly'.

vuoto, vuota (It.). 'Empty'; *corda vuota*, 'open string'.

Vustin, Aleksandr Kuz'mich (*b* Moscow, 1943). Russian composer. He studied at the Moscow Conservatory with Vladimir Fere. Though inspired by the examples of Boulez and Xenakis, he developed a highly individual style that belongs to no particular school. He favours unusual combinations of instruments, often including a range of unpitched percussion, as in *Memoria 2* (1978) or *Hommage à Beethoven* (1984). His compositional procedures are based on an extension of serialism into various structural aspects; in the 1990s he developed new principles of pitch organization based on the gamut of Russian Orthodox chant. JWAL

Wachet auf, ruft uns die Stimme ('Awake, the voice is calling us'). J. S. Bach's cantata no. 140 (1731), based on a chorale by Philipp Nicolai (1599); one movement from it was transcribed for organ as the first (BWV645) of the Schübler Chorales (1748). 'Wach' auf' is the chorus in Act III of Wagner's *Die Meistersinger von Nürnberg*. 'Wachet auf' is often translated as 'Sleepers, Awake'.

wachsend (Ger.). 'Growing', 'increasing', i.e. *crescendo*.

Waelrant, Hubert (*b* c.1517; *d* Antwerp, 19 Nov. 1595). Flemish composer, teacher, theorist, and music publisher. His printing house, set up jointly with Jean de Laet in Antwerp in 1554, issued important collections of music by Clemens, Crecquillon, and others, as well as chansons and Protestant psalm settings in French. He ceased publishing in 1558, although in 1585 he apparently acted as editor of a collection of madrigals issued by Phalèse.   JM/JWA

Wagenaar, Johan (*b* Utrecht, 1 Nov. 1862; *d* The Hague, 17 June 1941). Dutch composer and teacher. After studying in Utrecht and Berlin he became a teacher at the Utrecht Music School and in 1887 was appointed its director. From 1919 to 1937 he was director of the conservatory in The Hague. His best-known work is probably the overture *Cyrano de Bergerac* (1905), but he also wrote operas, cantatas, and the symphonic poem *Saul en David* (1906). His son **Bernard Wagenaar** (*b* Arnhem, 18 July 1894; *d* York, ME, 19 May 1971) studied with his father and at Utrecht University, and became a conductor and music teacher. In 1920 he emigrated to the USA, becoming an American citizen in 1927 and teaching composition at the Juilliard School (1925–68). His works include four symphonies, vocal music, and a chamber opera. His *Song of Mourning* (1944) was commissioned by the Netherlands American Foundation to commemorate Dutch war victims.   WT/PG

Wagenseil, Georg Christoph (*b* Vienna, 29 Jan. 1715; *d* Vienna, 1 March 1777). Austrian composer. He was the son of an official at the Habsburg court. His most important teacher was Fux, on whose recommendation he was appointed court composer in 1739. In 1745 he travelled to Venice for the premiere of his first opera

Ariodante, and over the next 15 years he cemented his reputation as an opera composer with a series of successful works. From the mid-1750s he became internationally renowned through the publication in Paris of his instrumental pieces, especially his symphonies. He retired from his court posts in 1765 but was still active as a composer when Burney met him in 1770.

Wagenseil played an important role in the development of the Viennese Classical style. With their fusion of aria, ensemble, and recitative his operas paved the way for Gluck's reforms of the 1760s. His symphonies, exhibiting formal clarity and fluency, were models for some of Haydn's early works. Most of his numerous keyboard concertos are chamber works that make only modest demands on amateur performers, but they were well known in the Mozart household in Salzburg and influenced the style and form of Wolfgang's earliest concertos.   DA/TRJ

Wagner, Richard (*see page 1358*)

Wagner-Régeny, Rudolf (*b* Szasz-Régen, Transylvania [now Reghin, Romania], 28 Aug. 1903; *d* East Berlin, 18 Sept. 1969). German composer and pianist of Romanian origins. Born Rudolf Wagner, he added the suffix 'Régeny' to his name after his birthplace. He came from a well-to-do family, and studied in Schässburg (1916–19) and Leipzig (1919) before moving to Berlin in 1920. He took German citizenship in 1930. His family lost their fortune in the inflationary crash of 1923, and Wagner-Régeny was forced to earn his living working as a ballet répétiteur at the Grosse Volksoper, Berlin, as well as playing the piano in nightclubs and cinemas. His early works, such as the one-act opera *Sganarelle* (1929), reveal an anti-Romantic modernism in which the influence of Les Six is strongly apparent.

The work that made him both famous and controversial, however, was the opera *Der Günstling* ('The Favourite'). Setting a libretto by Caspar Neher (better known as Bertolt Brecht's designer), it was begun in 1932, before the Nazi acquisition of power, though it had a sensational premiere in Dresden in 1935. Wagner-Régeny immediately became the focus of Nazi interest as a composer of international potential. Based on Georg Büchner's adaptation of Victor Hugo's *Marie*
(*cont. on p. 1361*)

Richard Wagner
(1813–83)

The German composer Wilhelm Richard Wagner was born in Leipzig on 22 May 1813 and died in Venice on 13 February 1883.

Wagner was absorbed from a very early age by a simultaneous interest in music and theatre that was to take him from obscure beginnings, as a provincial Kapellmeister and the composer of operas in the German Romantic manner, to world fame as the founder of Bayreuth—the ideal theatre in which could be staged the music dramas he based on a new expressive synthesis of words and music. He formed his artistic aims early in life, and pursued them to realization with ruthless determination.

The early years

Whether Wagner was the son of the police actuary Friedrich Wagner or the painter, poet, and actor Ludwig Geyer can never be determined, for by the time of Friedrich's death from typhus in 1813, Johanna Wagner was already Geyer's mistress. On her marriage to Geyer, the family moved to Dresden, where Wagner studied at the Kreuzschule and had his love of music first kindled by the example of Weber. Returning to Leipzig, he became absorbed in the theatre and made his first attempt at dramatic writing, also studying music. His admiration for Beethoven was to take practical form in a piano arrangement he made of the Ninth Symphony, and in later life his story *Eine Pilgerfahrt zu Beethoven* ('A Pilgrimage to Beethoven', 1840) declares in fictional form his belief that after this symphony—'music crying out for redemption by poetry'—the true consequence was music drama.

In June 1830 Wagner enrolled at Leipzig University, where he studied music under Theodor Weinlig. Surviving compositions from this period include piano sonatas and a symphony: the latter is strongly coloured by Beethoven, and to some extent by Mozart and Weber, but contains suggestions of Wagner's own emerging voice. In Prague in 1832 he wrote the libretto for an opera, *Die Hochzeit*, which he partly composed, then beginning work on *Die Feen* (composed 1833–4, produced 1888). This is a Romantic opera (after Gozzi), in the line of Weber though closer in manner to Marschner, especially in its treatment of the interaction of the human and spirit worlds and in the nature of some of its idiom and scoring. As chorus master at Würzburg (1833–4) Wagner came to widen his knowledge of opera to include Cherubini, Auber, and Meyerbeer, all to be influential on his music. But it was the Italian music he also admired, Bellini in particular, which most influenced his next opera, *Das Liebesverbot* (1836, after Shakespeare's *Measure for Measure*). Though he later regarded the work as a deviation from his ideals, it strengthened his understanding of vocal melody, the importance of which he always impressed upon his countrymen.

Moving to Magdeburg as conductor in 1834, Wagner conducted operas by Bellini and Rossini as well as German works (Weigl, Spohr, Weber, Marschner) and the French *opéra comique* repertory that had played an important part in the evolution of German Romantic opera. He also married the actress Wilhelmine [Minna] Planer; their stormy and erratic marriage lasted until her death in 1866, though he was not by then living with her. Partly so as to provide distraction from his unhappy private life, he began work on *Rienzi*. In Riga as conductor in 1837–9 he extended his range of activities with symphony concerts and with the first of many articles outlining his ideas; he also conducted operas by Mozart and Méhul. However, he was forced to flee Riga to escape his creditors, and took ship for London. Driven into a Norwegian fjord by a storm, the crew stirred his imagination with their singing and with stories of the Flying Dutchman.

From London, he and Minna went on to Paris, where he hoped to conquer the Opéra, then the most influential theatre in Europe, with *Rienzi* (1840). He was disappointed of this hope, though the work was well matched to the demands of the Opéra. It is to some extent influenced by Meyerbeer, but more significantly by the style of *grand opéra* which had been developed for Paris by Spontini, Halévy, Auber, and Rossini, all of whom he deeply admired; in Spontini, moreover, he found a conductor whose magisterial control was to inspire his own manner.

In Paris, where he endured considerable hardship, Wagner completed *Rienzi*, wrote his *Faust Overture*, came to know and admire Berlioz, was introduced to the legends of Tannhäuser and Lohengrin, and wrote the text and music of *Der fliegende Holländer* (1841). The first of Wagner's operas to retain its place in the regular repertory, it includes much inherited from Weber, though this is absorbed into a work of new individuality and strength. Among the ideas that were growing in Wagner's mind was the Romantic theme of redemption through love that was to absorb him throughout his life: the treatment of the story of the woman sacrificing herself for the legendary Dutchman far transcends the immediate example in Marschner's operas of contacts between the human and supernatural worlds.

Leaving Paris in 1842, Wagner arrived in Dresden to his first triumph with *Rienzi*. When this was followed by a more modest success for *Der fliegende Holländer*, Wagner took the work to Berlin, only to encounter his first taste of the critical hostility that was thereafter to divide musical Germany into Wagnerians and anti-Wagnerians. He had meanwhile begun work on *Tannhäuser*, completing it in the spring of 1845; its doubtful reception strengthened his feeling of isolation, but also his determination to insist on his aims being understood. *Tannhäuser* is in fact a transitional work on the way to realization of these aims, and retains features from Parisian *grand opéra* as well as German Romantic opera: to a considerable extent, and in spite of some lapses into banality and some longueurs, it transcends both genres with a new imaginative strength and a richer quality of musical invention.

Years of maturity

Wagner had meanwhile accepted a post as conductor at Dresden in 1843, also beginning work on *Lohengrin* (1848). Elements of earlier strains of Romantic opera remain in the work, together with some concessions to singers' demands; but if Act I still reflects Spontini and Auber, and the handling of Ortrud and Telramund as 'black' pair against Lohengrin and Elsa derives from Weber's *Euryanthe*, the 'Grail' prelude and the whole of Act II look forward from *Tannhäuser* to much larger creative achievements. But pursuit of these was temporarily interrupted by the political events of 1848.

Fired with revolutionary zeal, and convinced that some social realignment was necessary if his artistic ideals were to be realized, Wagner threw in his lot with the insurrectionists in Dresden in 1849. A warrant was issued for his arrest, and he fled to Switzerland. There he sketched various plans for operas and dramas (including one on *Jesus of Nazareth*, based on Ludwig Feuerbach's ideas of Christianity as an expression of myth), and began work on *Siegfrieds Tod*. It was also a

period of taking stock: he wrote a number of essays on his theories of art, among them *Das Kunstwerk der Zukunft* ('The Art-Work of the Future', 1849) and *Oper und Drama* (1851). These outlined ideas of opera as a 'total work of art' (*Gesamtkunstwerk*) in which poetry should directly give rise to music in a form of opera making use of all the theatrical resources, one that should, moreover, be given in ideal conditions as a social ritual involving both performers and audience. Though some of these ideas were modified or abandoned, they formed the starting-point for his mature work.

In 1850 Liszt conducted the first performance of *Lohengrin* in Weimar, and Wagner was encouraged to proceed with work on *Siegfrieds Tod*. As the idea grew in his mind (together with the ambition to found a special festival theatre), he added to the original concept texts for first *Der junge Siegfried* ('Young Siegfried'), then *Die Walküre* and *Das Rheingold*. Thus the works that were to form *Der Ring des Nibelungen* came to be written in reverse order. The text was completed at the end of 1852, and in spite of considerable financial difficulties Wagner began work on *Das Rheingold*, completing it in September 1854. At the same time, under the influence of his love for the wife of a Swiss benefactor, Mathilde Wesendonk, he conceived the idea for *Tristan und Isolde* and revived an earlier interest in the story of Parsifal. Having completed *Die Walküre* and begun work on *Siegfried* (as the third *Ring* opera was now called), he broke off to devote himself to *Tristan* in August 1857. At this time he also wrote the *Wesendonk-Lieder*; two of these are preliminary studies for *Tristan*, which he eventually finished in 1859.

Hitherto, Wagner's operas had been in different ways extensions of the older Romantic opera, each representing a significant creative advance. *Der fliegende Holländer* was the first to make use of construction by scenes rather than numbers; and in it Wagner later discovered glimmerings of his technique of leitmotif, the association of a musical idea with a dramatic ingredient. The full implications of the device, a development of the old reminiscence motif (which was hardly more than a simple piece of identification), are not realized in this work, only partially in *Tannhäuser*, with its stylistic unevennesses, and *Lohengrin*. However, in the latter work Wagner did make considerable advances in allowing the demands of musical structure to guide the text. This necessitated repudiation of some of the theories in *Oper und Drama*, the most important of his voluminous writings, and there is evidence that in *Tristan* the essential concept, though as always in mature Wagner a simultaneous process between text and music, was dominantly musical.

The motivic technique in *Tristan*, though not so far-reaching as in the still-uncompleted *Ring*, does provide Wagner with a cohesive basis for music that is now freed from numbers or scenes as structural guides; and a further characteristic is the use in the verse of *Stabreim*, a technique of rhyme by alliteration rather than by similar word-endings which Wagner revived from earlier models. The absence of periodicity leads to a freely moving chromatic harmony in a style that was unprecedented in music. These methods, implying in turn orchestration of new intensity, suppleness, and richness, were ideally matched to a story in which doomed love finds realization only by turning away from light of day towards darkness and ultimately death. Wagner's ideas were here much imbued with his philosophical reading, in particular with the renunciatory philosophy of Schopenhauer.

Forced to leave Zürich over his liaison with Mathilde Wesendonk, Wagner went first to Venice and then to Paris, where his new (1861) version of *Tannhäuser* (with an opening Bacchanale composed out of the experience of *Tristan*) met with violent demonstrations but won him new admirers, among them Baudelaire. A projected performance of *Tristan* drew him to Munich, but when this was postponed he resumed his travels, beginning work on *Die Meistersinger von Nürnberg*. At the moment when his financial affairs, always precarious, seemed finally about to overwhelm him, an offer came from Ludwig II of Bavaria: the outcome was generous support and the promise of performances. Though differences were to intervene, Wagner was rescued, and in his turn provided the lonely, idealistic young king with the artistic joy of his unhappy life.

Thanks to the king, *Tristan* was performed in 1865 under Hans von Bülow, with whose young wife Cosima, Liszt's daughter, Wagner had fallen in love. But plans for a Festival Theatre fell through owing to opposition in Munich to Wagner and his plans, and he left Bavaria to set up house in Tribschen, on the Lake of Lucerne. Here he completed *Die Meistersinger* in the autumn of 1867; Bülow conducted the first performance in Munich in June 1868, and four months later Cosima moved to Tribschen to live with Wagner. She had already borne him two daughters; the birth of their son Siegfried in 1869 prompted the *Siegfried Idyll* on themes from the *Ring*. As Cosima's diaries reveal, their domestic life, which included an inner circle of loyal admirers, was marked by unswerving devotion on her part, and on his by an autocracy that was tempered by much greater kindness, tolerance, and humour than has often been suggested.

By contrast with *Tristan*, *Die Meistersinger* can seem a robust assertion of bourgeois normality. It is in fact deeply coloured by its predecessor, not least by Wagner's assertion that 'Great is the power of love, but greater still is the power of its renunciation'. The chromaticism is latent, but none the less essential to a style in which the diatonicism associated with the burghers of Nuremberg and their ordered lives is not only 'reconstructed' against the chromaticism but thereby serves to express at once a nostalgically distant view of medieval Germany and the precarious achievement of Sachs, by his renunciation of Eva, in preserving order.

As always with mature Wagner, *Die Meistersinger* is about many things at once. They include Walther, the pioneering young instinctive artist Wagner associated with himself, overcoming the opposition of the entrenched Mastersingers, seen at their most pedantic in the person of Beckmesser, whom Wagner identified, originally even by name, with his hostile critic Hanslick. But by insisting on the virtues of the Mastersingers, Wagner is declaring that tradition must not be overthrown but refreshed. It was appropriate to this most open and warming of Wagner's works that melody and even identifiable numbers should return to his style within the framework of a continuous web in which an important part is played by leitmotifs: these are, understandably, exceptionally fluent and melodic in character.

Bayreuth and the 'Ring'

Wagner now turned his attention to the foundation of the ideal opera house that had so long eluded him; and after many difficulties he opened the new Festspielhaus in Bayreuth, supported by Ludwig and an army of subscribers and loyal workers, in 1876 with the completed *Ring*, now consisting of *Das Rheingold*, *Die Walküre*, *Siegfried*, and *Götterdämmerung*. The festival was attended by an array of luminaries from all over Europe: Wagner was by now the most famous artist of the day, though still one capable of arousing violent feelings, as was shown by the continued hostility of Hanslick, the incomprehension of rival composers such as Brahms and Tchaikovsky, and the violent break that now occurred with his former admirer Nietzsche. Ruler of the artistic kingdom he had created, he settled in the Bayreuth house built for him by Ludwig, which he named Wahnfried (meaning peace achieved out of turmoil).

In the *Ring*, Wagner created the last great epic cycle that has been written. He was conscious that this must be achieved through the medium of music, though his ideas grew out of the love of Greek epic he had acquired as a student together with his studies of myth under the influence of Feuerbach and his careful reading of early German epic. The expansion from one opera to four reflects not only the scale of the drama but his compositional needs; for the subtlety and complexity of his leitmotif technique here demands the largest possible canvas if it is to work freely and expressively. The technique itself develops, for the comparatively simple methods of identification that mark *Das Rheingold* evolve by *Götterdämmerung* into a dense network of allusive music that achieves the condition of a conceptual language. Leitmotif, as a method, was much misunderstood, including by those most admiring of Wagner: he resisted the facile labelling that ensued, with reason, since (for instance) the so-called Spear motif really represents not so much a physical spear (in spite of its thrusting, energetic nature) as the treaties graven on it by which Wotan rules, whose infraction leads to Wotan's personal tragedy and the downfall of the gods. The *Ring* is essentially a myth of power, love, and renunciation, expressed in a dramatic conflict fought out between gods, giants, humans, dwarfs, and other beings. Its text makes full use of *Stabreim*, less for reasons of musical assonance than for the invocation of an archaic diction and still more for the symphonic freedom, within a verse structure, which it provided.

The success of the festival by no means assured the future of Bayreuth, not least since the king had lost some faith in Wagner over his elopement with Cosima and eventual marriage to her in 1870. But the festival, which he attended, helped to reconcile him to Wagner, and further support was forthcoming while Wagner turned his attention to what, apart from projected symphonies, he intended to be his last work, *Parsifal*. Ageing and tired, he paid frequent visits to Italy for his health (he suffered from erysipelas and from angina pectoris), drawing ideas for the staging of *Parsifal* from gardens at Ravello and from Siena Cathedral. He completed the score in Palermo early in 1882; the first performances took place in Bayreuth, which long reserved exclusive rights to the work, in July and August under Hermann Levi.

Parsifal, like the *Ring*, draws on myth, in this case a much closer and more complex set of sources. Various versions of the Grail legend, particularly that in Wolfram von Eschenbach's medieval German poem, provide the framework for the plot, which also enshrines Wagner's subtlest and most penetrating ideas about belief, about human structures, and not least about feminine psychology, since Kundry—his most remarkable character—is at once the temptress and the agent of Parsifal's redemption, he in turn bringing about her redemption. The correlation between text and music is more detailed and far-reaching than in previous works, though the use of motif is freer than in the *Ring*, and *Stabreim* is abandoned in favour of a limited use of end-rhyme. Because of its static nature, *Parsifal* has often been underrated in the range and density of its psychological action which includes insight into the themes of redemption and renunciation which had so long absorbed Wagner. He gave the work the description *Bühnenweihfestspiel*, or 'stage-dedication festival play': its difficult synthesis of so many different strands of experience continues to arouse more resistance and incomprehension than any other of his works.

In September 1882 Wagner travelled with his family to Venice. He planned now only to write some one-movement symphonies making use of the motivic techniques he had evolved. On 13 February 1883 he had a fatal heart attack. His body was conveyed back to Bayreuth and buried in the garden of Wahnfried. Cosima survived him, at first reluctantly, to become the dominating figure at Bayreuth festivals until her death, shortly before that of her son Siegfried, in 1930.

JW

📖 C. Dahlhaus, *Richard Wagner's Music Dramas*, trans. M. Whittall (Cambridge, 1979) · R. Taylor, *Richard Wagner: His Life and Thought* (London, 1979) · R. Wagner, *My Life*, trans. A. Gray (London, 1983) · B. Millington, *Wagner* (London, 1984) · B. Millington (ed.), *The Wagner Compendium* (London, 1992) · U. Müller and P. Wapnewski (eds.), *Wagner Handbook*, trans. and ed. J. Deathridge (Cambridge, MA, and London, 1992)

Tudor, Der Günstling is a study of the corruption and violence attendant on absolute power. Wagner-Régeny's later claims that the opera was intended from the outset as a work of anti-Nazi resistance are now widely disbelieved, though there is no doubt that his subsequent works with Neher represented an attempt to distance himself from the Hitler regime.

The inherently pacifist *Die Bürger von Calais* (1939) aroused suspicion. Its successor, *Johanna Balk*, dealing with Romanian resistance to the Hungarian tyrant Báthory, caused an outcry at its premiere in Vienna in 1941, leading to Wagner-Régeny's ostracism and his subsequent conscription into the German army. His experiences, combined with the long terminal illness of his wife, the painter Léli Duperrex, aggravated the depression from which he had intermittently suffered for most of his life, and a compositional silence followed, broken only in the 1950s. In 1947, at the insistence of the Soviet army, Wagner-Régeny was appointed rector of the Music Academy in Rostock, resigning in 1950 to teach composition at the Academy of Arts in East Berlin. His later works were largely composed using an idiosyncratic but distinctive serial technique. *Der Günstling* remained one of the most frequently performed 20th-century operas in the German Democratic Republic, but some of his other works did not always find favour with the regime. Many of his later works had their premieres in the West, though Wagner-Régeny's refusal to condemn the building of the Berlin Wall led to a decline in critical esteem. His last opera, *Das Bergwerk zu Falun* ('The Mine at Falun'), based on a story by Hugo von Hofmannsthal, had its first performance in 1961 at the Salzburg Festival (which Hofmannsthal had founded 40 years earlier).   TA

   📖 D. Härtwig, *Rudolf Wagner-Régeny, der Opernkomponist* (Berlin, 1965)

Wagner tuba. A valved brass instrument designed by Wagner (probably with *saxhorns in mind) for use in the *Ring*, to bridge the gap between the horns and trombones. An upright oval in shape, it was made in two sizes, corresponding to the two main horn keys: a B♭ tenor and an F bass. Wagner tubas were intended to be played by the horn players, who would alternate between the instruments as directed. Modern examples are made (like horns) as double instruments in B♭ and F. Many composers have written for them, including Bruckner, Schoenberg, and Richard Strauss, and they are frequently used in film and television music.

                        JMo

wait [wayte]. Originally, a watchman; later, a civic minstrel. In the 13th and 14th centuries watchmen employed by a town or noble household guarded the gates and patrolled the streets during the night, sounding the hours and watching for fire and other dangers (like the Night Watchman in Wagner's *Die Meistersinger von Nürnberg*). The instrument they used, to show they were on duty, was a type of *shawm, also known as a wait- or wayte-pipe.

In the 15th and 16th centuries civic minstrels were also called waits, probably by association with the instrument they played, though they had no watchmen's duties. Many were good musicians who could play a variety of 'outdoor', loud-toned (*haut*) instruments (shawm, slide trumpet, sackbut, etc.); later they also sang and used quieter instruments (recorder, cornett, viol). They were well thought of by municipal authorities and were given handsome uniforms. They attended on the mayor at civic functions and ceremonial occasions, and sometimes played in the street at night. From the 16th century it was customary for town waits to attend at inns and taverns for the arrival of any notable guest who might recompense them for a musical welcome, to play during mealtimes, and (in some towns), to give street concerts on Sundays and at Christmas and other holidays (though Sunday playing was somewhat curtailed under the Puritan regime of Cromwell's time). Membership of waits was often a family tradition.

The numerous British towns and cities that have records of employing waits include London, Aberdeen, Bath, Cambridge, Chester, Edinburgh, Exeter, Newcastle, Norwich, Nottingham, Oxford, and York. The London waits were established by Henry III in 1253 and, like those at Chester and a few other towns, later had a 'signature' tune associated with them, which became known as 'London Waits'. The Norwich waits seem to have been particularly renowned and are known to have existed in 1288. They have a more or less continuous history, well documented up to the end of the 18th century: in the 16th century they participated in the Norwich mystery plays, and Sir Francis Drake requested five or six of them to go with him on his voyage to Lisbon.

City waits continued in Britain until the 18th or even early 19th century, long after most other minstrel traditions had died out. The term 'wait', however, survived well into the 19th century to describe street musicians who serenaded the public at Christmas time with seasonal songs and music.

   See also MINSTREL.   PS/JN/JM

Waldscenen ('Woodland Scenes'). Set of nine piano pieces, op. 82 (1848–9), by Schumann.

'Waldstein' Sonata. Beethoven's Piano Sonata no. 21 in C major op. 53 (1803–4), so called because he dedicated it to his patron, Count Ferdinand von Waldstein (1762–1823).

Waldteufel [Lévy], Émile (*b* Strasbourg, 9 Dec. 1848; *d* Paris, 12 Feb. 1915). French composer. After studying at the Paris Conservatoire he became court pianist to Napoleon III and director of the court and presidential balls. He gained international fame when the Prince of Wales introduced his music in London in 1874. His best-known waltzes include *Mon rêve* ('My Dream', 1877), *Les Patineurs* ('The Skaters', 1882), *España* (1886, after Chabrier), and *The Grenadiers* (1886).   ALa

Wales 1. The Welsh tradition; 2. Art music; 3. Festivals and concert life; 4. Opera; 5. Education, libraries, and publishers

1. The Welsh tradition

The importance of music in ancient Welsh culture is attested by its prominence in pre-Christian myth and the part it played in the services of the early Celtic Church. Bards enjoyed considerable esteem in the households of the Welsh princes before the country came under English rule in 1282, but unfortunately nothing of their music has survived. Regulations governing their conduct and remuneration were laid down in the mid-10th-century Laws of Hywel Dda, which point to the harp and the *crwth (a bowed lyre with three or four strings) as the main bardic instruments; they also mention pybeu ('pipes'). While the medieval repertory of the crwth has disappeared, some vestige of early bardic harp music perhaps survives in the Robert ap Huw manuscript (c.1613), now in the British Library (Add. 14905); attempts to transcribe it into modern notation have so far been thwarted by uncertainties about ap Huw's directions for tuning the instrument.

The 12th-century Welsh cleric Giraldus Cambrensis provides a well-known description of part-singing in Wales in his Descriptio Cambriae (1194): 'When they make music together, they sing their songs not in unison, as is done elsewhere, but in parts, with many modes and phrases, so that in a crowd of singers . . . you would hear as many songs and differentiations of voices as you could see heads'.

In the 17th century popular ballads were sung to the traditional airs; these were published in great numbers during the 18th century. Volumes of harp airs also began to appear, published in London. Edward Jones's Musical and Poetical Relicks of the Welsh Bards (1784) contained about 60 such airs, as well as examples of the peculiarly Welsh form of music-making called penillion (literally 'stanzas'). It was not until the 19th century that collections of folk tunes first appeared in print, beginning with Maria Jane Williams's Ancient National Airs of Gwent and Morgannwg (1844). But the systematic collecting and printing of Welsh folksong got under way only with the founding in 1906 of the Welsh Folk Song Society and the inauguration of its journal. A centre for the study of Welsh folk music was established at the Welsh Folk museum, St Fagan's (Cardiff), in 1976, and in 1979 a research post in the subject was created at University College, Bangor.

2. Art music

The policies of the Tudor dynasty in England had profound social and economic consequences for Wales, and with the decline in the role of the native bard, there began that long exodus of composers and performers from Wales into England, which, as far as singers and instrumentalists are concerned, continues. The vigorous flowering of English music in the 16th and early 17th centuries had no parallel in Wales, and the outstanding Welsh-born composer of the period, Thomas Tomkins, found employment across the border. During the later 17th and the 18th centuries the rise of Non-

conformism and the absence of any strong theatrical tradition ensured that the new musical styles of the Baroque left the principality virtually untouched.

During the 19th century, the Nonconformist movement began to bear its own musical fruit when the hymn came to replace the folksong as an expression of a collective musical, social, and religious awareness, and the cymanfa ganu ('hymn-singing festival') began to enjoy the popularity it has retained to this day. From hymn to oratorio chorus was a small step for those schooled in *Tonic Sol-fa, and choirs were soon rehearsing items from the oratorios of Handel, Haydn, and Mendelssohn. At the same time, industrialization encouraged the formation of brass bands and male choirs.

This vigorous choral tradition stimulated such composers as Joseph Parry (1841–1903), David Evans (1843–1913), and David Jenkins (1849–1915), but it was in the music of the next generation of composers, notably David Vaughan Thomas (1873–1934) and David de Lloyd (1883–1948) that a distinctively national voice began to emerge. Their works were again primarily vocal, but with David Wynne (1900–83), Grace Williams, Arwel Hughes (1909–88), and the symphonist Daniel Jones we find a fresh interest in instrumental and orchestral writing. Most of these composers, if not all, drew on their Welsh background and on Welsh folksong in their music. This is true also, though to a lesser extent, of Alun Hoddinott and William Mathias, whose music belongs to a more progressive western European tradition. Among members of the younger generation who have remained to work in the principality are Jeffrey Lewis (b 1942) and John Metcalf (b 1946).

3. Festivals and concert life

The eisteddfod ('session') is devoted mainly to music and poetry. The National Eisteddfod has been held annually since 1880, alternately in north and south Wales. During the 20th century, Welsh was established as the sole language for Eisteddfod proceedings, and while the National Eisteddfod remains a main focal point for the expression of Welsh nationhood and for the renewal of cultural traditions, competitors from many countries exhibit their native songs and dances at the International Eisteddfod. The BBC inaugurated the Cardiff Singer of the World competition in 1983.

The Swansea Festival was inaugurated in 1948 and was soon joined by many others. The BBC in Cardiff organizes a St David's Festival each March, and the Extra-Mural Department of University College, Swansea, holds an annual Bach Week. Since World War II festivals such as these have helped to reinvigorate concert life in Wales. The only professional orchestra in Wales, apart from that of the Welsh National Opera, remains the BBC Welsh Symphony Orchestra, founded in 1936 and brought to full symphonic strength by 1977. Except for the Brangwyn Hall in Swansea (capacity 1500), Wales had no large hall designed for orchestral concerts until the completion in 1982 of St David's Hall in Cardiff (capacity 2000).

4. Opera

Opera was for long cultivated even less than concert-giving in Wales. The first Welsh opera was probably *Blodwen*, composed by Joseph Parry to a libretto by Richard Davies and produced at Aberdare in 1878. It was not until the formation of the Welsh National Opera in 1946 that opera in Wales was placed on a regular and, eventually, a fully professional basis. Several singers of international repute made or consolidated their early reputations with the company, which continues to provide a training ground for young Welsh singers.

5. Education, libraries, and publishers

Of the four main constituent colleges in the University of Wales, all except that at Swansea have music departments offering honours and postgraduate degrees. The first chair of music was established at Aberystwyth in 1874, with Joseph Parry as professor. In 1949 the Cardiff College of Music (later the Welsh College of Music and Drama) was founded at Cardiff to provide professional training for performers and teachers.

The Welsh Music Information Centre, established at University College, Cardiff, in 1976, houses a useful and growing library of scores, records, and tapes, mainly of 20th-century Welsh music; other important repositories are the university departmental libraries and the National Library of Wales, Aberystwyth.

Most modern Welsh composers and writers on music look to England for publication of their works, but a good deal of music (particularly short vocal pieces) has been published by D. J. Snell of Swansea and by the Gwynn Publishing Co., Llangollen. The principal publisher of music and of literature on music in Wales today is the University of Wales Press, Cardiff. MB/KC

📖 J. Graham, *A Century of Welsh Music* (London, 1923) · W. S. Gwynn Williams, *Welsh National Music and Dance* (London, 1932, 4/1971) · P. Crossley-Holland (ed.), *Music in Wales* (London, 1948) · T. Parry, *The Story of the Eisteddfod* (Denbigh, c.1950) · D. Jones, *Music in Wales* (Cardiff, 1961) · M. Stephens (ed.), *The Arts in Wales, 1950–75* (Cardiff, 1979) · S. Webb, *The Music of Wales* (Pen-y-Groes, 1996) · G. Williams, *Valleys of Song: Music and Welsh Society, 1840–1914* (Cardiff, 1998)

walking bass. A type of bass line, often found in Baroque compositions, which moves continuously and with purposeful regularity, setting off the more sustained melodic writing above. A similar effect occurs in the 'stride' patterns of jazz. AW

Walk to the Paradise Garden, The. Intermezzo for orchestra before the final scene of Delius's opera *A Village Romeo and Juliet* (the 'Paradise Garden' was the village inn); it was not in the original score but was added at Beecham's request to cover a scene change in the 1910 Covent Garden production. It is frequently played as a concert item.

Walküre, Die ('The Valkyrie'). Opera in three acts by Wagner to his own libretto, the 'first day' of *Der *Ring des Nibelungen*.

Wallace, (William) Vincent (*b* Waterford, 11 March 1812; *d* Château de Haget, Vieuzos, Hautes-Pyrénées, 12 Oct. 1865). Irish composer. After pursuing a career as a violinist and organist in Dublin and Thurles, he emigrated in 1835 to Tasmania and a year later to Sydney, where he became known as 'the Australian Paganini' and founded a music academy for young ladies; but he left with large debts in 1838. His wanderlust then took him to Latin America, Jamaica, and the USA. He returned to London in 1845 and, with Edward Fitzball, composed *Maritana* (Drury Lane, 1845)—a major international triumph but his only palpable success; other, more ambitious operatic ventures, including *Matilda of Hungary* (1847), *Lurline* (1848), and the three grand operas written towards the end of his life (*The Amber Witch*, 1861, *Love's Triumph*, 1862, and *The Desert Flower*, 1863), had much less impact. Wallace's further travels resulted in a (possibly bigamous) marriage to an American pianist in 1850. In 1864 he retired to France, where he was visited by Rossini and other celebrated musical figures. JDı

Wally, La. Opera in four acts by Catalani to a libretto by Luigi Illica after Wilhelmine von Hillern's story *Die Geyer-Wally* (Milan, 1892).

Walmisley. English family of musicians. **Thomas Forbes Walmisley** (*b* London, 22 May 1783; *d* 23 July 1866), an organist, teacher, and composer, studied with Attwood from 1797 and acquired a reputation as a teacher and a composer of glees. He also edited his son's *Cathedral Music*. In 1814 he was appointed organist at St Martin-in-the-Fields, a post he held until his retirement in 1854.

His son **Thomas Attwood Walmisley** (*b* London, 21 Jan. 1814; *d* Hastings, 17 Jan. 1856) showed great musical precocity as a child. He too took lessons from Attwood, his godfather, and developed rapidly as a composer and performer. At the age of 16 he became organist at Croydon Parish Church, moving to Cambridge in 1833 as organist of Trinity and St John's colleges. In 1836 he succeeded John Clarke-Whitfield as professor of music. At Cambridge he developed an enviable reputation as an organist and choir trainer. At his own expense he lectured at the university and did much to enhance the previously low status of music as an academic discipline. He produced numerous chamber works, overtures, symphonic music, and choral odes (including one for the installation of the Marquis of Camden as vice-chancellor); but he is best remembered for his church music, notably his Full Service in D (1843) and his Evening Services in B♭ (1845) and D minor (c.1855), the last considered to be his masterpiece. WT/JD1

Walsh. English family of music sellers, music publishers, and instrument makers. They built up the most extensive business of the early 18th century, based largely on pewter-plate engraving, and were particularly influential through their methods of mass-publishing. The elder John Walsh (?1665 or 1666–1736) set up in London in about 1690 and two years later was appointed Musical-Instrument-Maker-in-Ordinary to William III at 'The Golden Harp and Hoboy'. He began publishing in 1695, using pewter plates and punches from about 1700, and issued a great range of publications (single songs, anthologies, instrumental music, and instruction books).

Walsh frequently bought up stock from other publishers, sorting out sheets to make up his own editions, and he issued many of Handel's works without the composer's knowledge: this, among other things, led to his being condemned as unscrupulous. Although in 1711 he had published *Rinaldo*, the first of Handel's operas to be performed in England, his relationship with Handel was predominantly stormy. Handel was reconciled only when the younger John Walsh (1709–66) took over the firm in the 1730s, when he was granted a 14-year monopoly of Handel's music. See also PRINTING AND PUBLISHING OF MUSIC, 5. JMT/JWA

Walter, Bruno [Schlesinger, Bruno Walter] (*b* Berlin, 15 Sept. 1876; *d* Beverly Hills, CA, 17 Feb. 1962). German conductor. He studied in Berlin and made his debut in Cologne in 1894. Walter worked as an opera conductor in Hamburg and Vienna with Mahler, gave the world premieres of *Das Lied von der Erde* (1911) and the Ninth Symphony (1912) after the composer's death, and remained a devoted champion of his music. From 1913 until 1922 he was director of the Munich Opera, where he conducted the first performance of Pfitzner's *Palestrina* (1917). He subsequently held posts concurrently in Berlin and Leipzig, but his career in Germany was curtailed in 1933 by Nazi anti-Semitism.

Walter worked in Vienna until the *Anschluss*, then in France, finally emigrating in 1939 to the USA, where he lived until his death, though he returned occasionally to Europe as a guest conductor after 1946. During World War II he appeared at the Metropolitan Opera, New York, and was later chiefly associated with the New York Philharmonic. Deeply humanitarian, he was noted for the emotional and spiritual commitment he brought to his interpretations of Mozart, Beethoven, and Brahms. He was also a gifted pianist and was a regular accompanist for many of the great lieder singers of his time, notably Kathleen Ferrier and Lotte Lehmann. TA

   📖 B. GAVOTY, *Bruno Walter* (Geneva, 1956) · E. RYDING and R. PECHEFSKY, *A World Elsewhere* (forthcoming)

Walther, Johann Gottfried (*b* Erfurt, 18 Sept. 1684; *d* Weimar, 23 March 1748). German composer. He was a distant relative and close friend of Bach, with whose uncle, Johann Bernhard Bach, he studied in Erfurt. From 1707 to the end of his life he held appointments in Weimar, as organist at the town church and, from 1721, as court musician. His compositions include sacred vocal music, and organ chorale preludes of a quality to bear comparison with those of Bach. He is now particularly remembered for his *Musicalisches Lexicon* (1732), the first German music dictionary, unique at its time for embracing both biographies and terminology. DA/BS

Walther, Johann Jakob (*b* Witterda, nr Erfurt, c.1650; *d* Mainz, 2 Nov. 1717). German violinist and composer. He travelled to Italy c.1670, gaining experience of the virtuoso school of violin playing, then entered the service of the Dresden court. By 1681 he had moved to Mainz. His surviving music is for the violin, and though he wrote some trivial pieces imitating birdsong he was important for the development of violin technique (notably multiple stopping) in Germany. DA

Walther von der Vogelweide (*fl* c.1200). German Minnesinger. Very few facts about his life are known. His poetry, which is of considerable literary importance, has been fairly well preserved; music for it, however, was written down only long after his death, and it is unlikely that much of it survives in its original form. His early lieder deal mainly with courtly love, in an attractive, unstilted way. Later he turned to composing *Sprüche*—songs dealing with political and topical matters—and became a master of that genre. DA/JM

Walton, Sir William (Turner) (*b* Oldham, Lancs., 29 March 1902; *d* Ischia, 8 March 1983). English composer.

He was a chorister at Christ Church, Oxford (1912–18); his already apparent creative gifts gained the admiration of Parry, H. G. Ley, and Hugh Allen, enabling him to be accepted as an undergraduate there in 1918. However, he left in 1920 without a degree (he repeatedly failed Responsions, obligatory for the BA course) and moved to London, where he was unofficially adopted by the Sitwells. He later withdrew his early String Quartet (1919–22), acclaimed by Berg at the first ISCM festival in Salzburg, and chose to disregard his flirtation with Schoenberg and the Second Viennese School. The first fruit of his association with the Sitwells was *Façade* (1921–2), music for a recitation of poems by Edith Sitwell; it won the composer a reputation for wit and iconoclasm and placed him among those British composers (especially Bliss, Lambert, and Berners) who were captivated by elements of popular music and neo-classicism spearheaded by Stravinsky and Les Six.

Walton's next major work, the overture *Portsmouth Point* (1925), was the first of several bustling orchestral capriccios, while the deeply serious Viola Concerto (1928–9) established a characteristic amalgam of jazz, the music of Hindemith, and the romantic longing of Elgar. A blend of neo-classicism and neo-romanticism continued in the *Sinfonia concertante* (1926–7, rev. 1943), though the composition of the opulent oratorio *Belshazzar's Feast* (1930–1) and the First Symphony (1932–5) confirmed Walton's return to the more traditional English mainstream; in the preface to the second edition of *Music Ho!* (1936) Constant Lambert described it as a 'further stage in this composer's return to consonance'. The completion of the symphony, in which Walton experienced many difficulties, was long delayed. Ostensibly Sibelian in sound and method, the work (especially the first movement) revealed an originality in its vital rhythmic drive and dynamic system of extended pedal points, and exhibited the composer's genuine symphonic abilities, even if there was a falling away of inspiration and momentum in the finale.

During the next two decades most of Walton's music was on a smaller scale or of an occasional nature—though his coronation marches *Crown Imperial* (1937) and *Orb and Sceptre* (1953) have long outlived the occasions for which they were written, and his contributions to Olivier's Shakespeare trilogy, *Henry V* (1942–3), *Hamlet* (1947), and *Richard III* (1955), still command admiration as among the most skilful scores ever written for the cinema. His *Spitfire Prelude and Fugue*, from the film score *The First of the Few* (1942), has also remained extremely popular. This was the period too of his only important chamber works, the String Quartet (1945–7) and the Violin Sonata (1949), both of which outshine his major orchestral works of the time: the

Violin Concerto (1938–9), a more brilliant successor to that for viola, the comedy overture *Scapino* (1940), and the ballet *The Quest* (1943).

Walton's next work for the theatre was his three-act opera *Troilus and Cressida* (1954), an adaptation of Chaucer (not Shakespeare) which was full of rich thematic invention and steely drama, if perhaps a little slow in pace. Only after a gap of more than a decade did Walton return to the theatre, and then with a one-act comedy, *The Bear* (1965–7). Otherwise he contented himself after *Troilus* with a further sequence of superbly conceived, glitteringly virtuoso orchestral works—the Cello Concerto (1956), the *Johannesburg Festival Overture* (1956), the Partita (1957), the Second Symphony (1959–60), considered by some to be finer and more concise than the First, the *Variations on a Theme by Hindemith* (1962–3), and the *Improvisations on an Impromptu of Benjamin Britten* (1969)—and, more surprisingly, with a variety of smaller vocal works, among which the cycle *Anon in Love* (1959) for tenor with guitar or string orchestra, and the anthem *The Twelve* (1965), to words by Auden, are outstanding. He also produced a short orchestral sequence, 'The War in the Air', for the film *The Battle of Britain* (1969).

Walton was knighted in 1951 and awarded the Order of Merit in 1967. The comparative smallness of his output after World War II, coupled with his emphasis on professionalism and accomplishment, have often led to charges of 'relaxation', and indeed the three string concertos, for instance, show a steady decrease in emotional unrest and structural boldness alongside a steady increase in ease. It may be, however, that Walton's serenity was as valuable as his disquiet.

PG/JDi

📖 C. SMITH, *William Walton: A Bio-Bibliography* (Westport, CT, 1988) · S. WALTON, *William Walton: Behind the Façade* (Oxford, 1988) · M. KENNEDY, *Portrait of Walton* (Oxford, 1989) · S. R. CRAGGS, *William Walton: A Source Book* (Aldershot, 1993)

waltz (Fr.: *valse*; Ger.: *Walzer*). A dance in 3/4 time whose origins remain obscure. The 3/4 rhythm is rare in early dances, almost totally absent in some traditional musics, and not in common use in Classical music—at least, with the particular emphasis given to it in waltz form—until the end of the 18th century. Earlier dances in 3/4 time such as the allemande and the minuet bear little relation to the waltz, because of the more sedate style of the former and the equal stress given to their beats.

There is little doubt that the dance form of the waltz, with its heavy accent on the first beat of the bar, came about through the influence of the *ländler. A dance basic to the folk music of Austria, southern Germany, and the Alpine regions, it was discovered by polite society, probably causing as much surprised delight as jazz rhythms did at the end of the 19th century. The derivation of the word 'waltz' has caused some confusion about its musical origins, as most European languages had some word of similar nature describing a rotating or turning motion, the basic movement of the waltz. The Provençal dance the volta was known in French and German as 'volte', and it may be from this that 'walzer' derived.

Early German folk dances, such as the *Drehtanz* ('turning dance') and the ländler, were active, springing dances full of lively steps and the throwing of the woman partner into the air, but all had the revolving characteristics. As these dances found their way into urban life and the ballroom, the steps became smoother and a gliding motion replaced the boisterous movements of the folk dance. Polite society still saw it as conducive to lasciviousness and immorality, and Burney shuddered to imagine what an English mother would have thought if her daughter were subjected to the familiar treatment that he had witnessed abroad.

After invading European music about 1770 the waltz gradually replaced the stately and artificial minuet. One of its first appearances in piano music was in c.1766 in a sonatina by Haydn, the normal minuet being replaced by a 'mouvement de Walze'. The first use of the waltz in opera is generally credited to Martín y Soler and *Una cosa rara* (1786). In causing a sensation, the waltz encouraged the emergence of specialist composers of dance music, particularly in Vienna. A pioneer in this respect was Michael Pamer (1782–1827); his many waltzes and ländler were followed with relentless profusion by those of Joseph Lanner and Johann Strauss the elder, both of whom started their careers in Pamer's orchestra.

The greatest exponent of the waltz was unquestionably the younger Johann Strauss. He took over from his father in writing richly melodic extended works, such as *An der schönen, blauen Donau* ('By the Beautiful Blue Danube', 1867), that have flourished as much in the concert hall as in the ballroom. His move to operetta composition also meant that the waltz became the centrepiece of the Viennese operetta tradition. In its classical form, the Viennese waltz featured a slight anticipation of the second beat of the bar known as the *Atempause* (literally 'breathing-space'), which gives a delightful and distinctive lilt to the playing. In the hands of composers of other nationalities it took on a slightly different character. Émile Waldteufel, the composer of *Les Patineurs* (1882), typified the French tendency to return the emphasis to the first beat, while the 'English' or

'Boston' waltz went back to a more even emphasis on all three beats.

Classical composers exploited the waltz in every possible way. Schubert, who spent evenings listening to Pamer and Lanner, wrote numerous sets of waltzes for the piano, exploring its formal possibilities. Weber crystallized the miniature tone-poem form of the waltz in his *Aufforderung zum Tanz* (1819). Chopin's piano waltzes are among the great keyboard treasures, and Liszt likewise showed his attraction to the form. The waltz also invaded Classical ballet scores such as Delibes's *Coppélia* (1870) and Tchaikovsky's *Swan Lake* 1877), while notable examples of symphonic movements in waltz time are to be found in Berlioz's *Symphonie fantastique* (1830) and Tchaikovsky's Fifth Symphony (1888). It also became at home in such operas as Gounod's *Faust* (1859), Wagner's *Parsifal* (1882), and Puccini's *La bohème* (1896). The waltz was taken to sophisticated extremes in Ravel's *La Valse* (1918) and to the heights of Romantic sumptuousness in Richard Strauss's *Der Rosenkavalier* (1911).   PGA/ALA

Walze (Ger.). 1. Organ crescendo pedal.

2 A term used in the 18th century for conventional musical figures such as the *Alberti bass.

'Wanderer' Fantasia. Nickname of Schubert's Fantasia in C major for piano, D760 (1822), so called because the Adagio is a set of variations on a theme from his song *Der Wanderer* D489 (1816). Liszt arranged it for piano and orchestra (c.1851).

Wand of Youth, The. Two orchestral suites by Elgar, opp. 1a (1907) and 1b (1908), arranged and orchestrated from material he wrote for a family play when he was 12; he reused some of the themes in his music for *The Starlight Express* (1915).

Wanhal, Johann Baptist. See VANHAL, JOHANN BAPTIST.

War and Peace (*Voyna i mir*). Opera in 13 scenes and a choral epigraph by Prokofiev to a libretto by the composer and Mira Mendelson (Prokof'yeva) after Lev Tolstoy's novel (1869); the opera has an extraordinarily complicated history and exists in five separate versions of which four have been staged. The first major staging was in Leningrad in 1946 and the first relatively complete performance was in Moscow in 1959. *War and Peace* was chosen to open the Sydney Opera House (1974).

Ward, John (*b* c.1589; *d* before 31 Aug. 1638). English musician and composer. He was a chorister at Canterbury Cathedral, then joined the household of Sir Henry Fanshawe, Remembrancer of the Exchequer during the early years of the 17th century. His connection with that family lasted until his death, and latterly required residence in London. Ward's most impressive musical achievement is the *First Set of English Madrigals* (London, 1613), which contains some of the most elegiac music of the time, including the sonorous six-voice *Out from the vale* and *Come, sable night*. He also wrote verse anthems and consort music, mostly for use in the circle of the Fanshawes; one piece, *No object dearer*, is an elegy for Henry, Prince of Wales.   DA/JM

Warlock, Peter [Heseltine, Philip (Arnold)] (*b* London, 30 Oct. 1894; *d* London, 17 Dec. 1930). English composer, critic, and author. He was encouraged first by his music master at Eton and later by Delius, who became his mentor. Abortive studies in Cologne, Oxford, and London, and employment as a music critic with the *Daily Mail*, were typical of his restless, bohemian existence. A conscientious objector, he took up with D. H. Lawrence in 1916 in Cornwall though their friendship soon broke up in acrimonious circumstances. Back in London in 1916 he became friendly with Cecil Gray and Bernard van Dieren, who influenced him profoundly. At this time he also devised the pseudonym 'Peter Warlock', using it only for his compositions from 1918. To escape military conscription he lived in Dublin (1917–18), where he produced some of his finest works. After a period editing *The Sackbut* (1920–1) he lived at the family home in Wales. With E. J. Moeran he then lived at Eynsford (1925–8), but his precarious financial situation forced him back to London. Depression and unemployment followed and he was found dead from gas-poisoning in his Chelsea flat. An open verdict was recorded.

Warlock's musical personality has several dimensions. The influence of Delius and van Dieren is evident in the chromatic intensity of *Saudades* (1916–17) and the magnificent partsong *The Full Heart* (1916), and in his masterpiece, the melancholy cycle *The Curlew* (1920–2); but another powerful component was his love of medieval and Renaissance art which manifested itself in superb carols (e.g. *Corpus Christi* and *Balulalow* of 1919), the songs *Sleep* and *Rest sweet nymphs* (both 1922), the more rumbustious sets of *Peterisms* (1922–3), and the *Capriol Suite* (1926). He also produced fine settings of poetry by Hilaire Belloc and Arthur Symons, and a haunting one of Bruce Blunt's carol *Bethlehem Down* (1927). His books include *Frederick Delius* (1923), *Thomas Whythorne* (1925), *Gesualdo* with Cecil Gray, and *The English Ayre* (both 1926).   JDi

📖 I. A. COPLEY, *The Music of Peter Warlock: A Critical Survey* (London, 1979) · J. BISHOP and D. COX (eds.), *Peter Warlock: A Centenary Celebration* (London, 1994) · B. COLLINS, *Peter Warlock: The Composer* (Aldershot, 1996)

Wärme, mit (Ger.). 'With warmth', 'passionately'.

War of the Bouffons. See BOUFFONS, QUERELLE DES.

War Requiem. Choral work, op. 66 (1962), by Britten, for soprano, tenor, and baritone soloists, boys' choir, chorus, organ, and orchestra; settings of nine poems by the World War I poet Wilfred Owen (accompanied by a chamber orchestra) are interpolated into Britten's setting of the Latin Requiem Mass. It was written for, and first performed in, the rebuilt Coventry Cathedral.

Warsaw Concerto. Score for piano and orchestra by Addinsell for the film *Dangerous Moonlight* (1941).

washboard. A scraped *idiophone with a ridged surface, originally made from a domestic washboard (sometimes with cymbals, triangles, and other *'effects' instruments added), but now also specially made in the form of a steel 'apron', hung from the player's shoulders. It may be scraped with thimbles worn on fingers, or with steel implements (e.g. household spoons) held in each hand. Washboard bands including string instruments and sometimes other improvised instruments such as the jug and the washtub bass were known in the USA in the late 19th century, and the washboard was sometimes used in jazz bands and as a novelty act in vaudeville and the music halls. It reappeared in the 1950s skiffle groups, and is associated with the Cajun and zydeco music of Louisiana.   JMo, RPA

Wasps, The. Incidental music by Vaughan Williams, for tenor and baritone soloists, male chorus, and orchestra, composed for the 1909 Cambridge University production of Aristophanes' play; the same year Vaughan Williams arranged from it a five-movement orchestral suite, with an overture.

wassail. A festive occasion that involves drinking. The word is associated particularly with the Christmas season, and occurs in many English Christmas carols. It derives from the Old Norse greeting *ves heill*, 'be in good health'.

Water Carrier, The. See DEUX JOURNÉES, LES.

watermark. The impression of a symbol made on one side of a sheet of paper during the manufacturing process. In conjunction with those made by the wires of the mould on which the paper was produced, such impressions can sometimes (and to a limited extent) be helpful in determining the likely place and date of manufacture of the paper and thus of the production of a manuscript or printed book in which it appears.

IR

Water Music. 1. The popular name for three instrumental suites by Handel (in F, D, and G major), of which some or all of the movements were performed for a royal procession on the River Thames (17 July 1717); the well-known story that Handel wrote them to restore himself to favour with George I is unlikely to be true. Six of the movements became well known as a suite (1922) orchestrated by Harty.

2. Work (1952) by Cage for a pianist, who is required to pour water from pots, play cards, blow whistles under water, etc., while the score is displayed like a poster.

Weber, Aloysia. See LANGE, ALOYSIA.

Weber, Carl Maria (Friedrich Ernst) **von** (*b* Eutin, 18 Nov. 1786; *d* London, 5 June 1826). German composer, conductor, pianist, and critic. His education was erratic, owing to a childhood spent in his father's travelling theatre company, though on his wanderings he managed to have some instruction from teachers including Michael Haydn. By the age of 13 he had written an opera (now lost) and was becoming an accomplished pianist. A second opera, *Das Waldmädchen*, of which fragments remain, was first performed in 1800. However, his first surviving opera is *Peter Schmoll und seine Nachbarn* (1803), a *Singspiel* with some adumbrations of his mature style, especially his feeling for instruments. Having undertaken more serious and influential study with the Abbé Georg Vogler, he was appointed conductor of the Breslau theatre, but intrigues forced him out and he became music director to Duke Eugen of Württemberg in Carlsruhe, Upper Silesia, where he wrote his only two symphonies (1807). He then moved on to an appointment at the court of the duke's brother Ludwig in Stuttgart, a time of some dissipation from which he was recalled to his vocation as a composer by Franz Danzi.

Expelled from Württemberg for a minor offence in 1810, Weber spent some time travelling, including to Frankfurt for the production of *Silvana* (1810). This was a reworking of the *Waldmädchen* text and combines the interests in woodland life and chivalric convention which were individually to come to fruition in *Der Freischütz* and *Euryanthe*. He also began making a reputation as one of the great keyboard virtuosos of the day, touring with the clarinettist Heinrich Bärmann, for whom he wrote some of his finest concertante works. *Abu Hassan* (1811), a witty little *Singspiel*, was produced in Munich in 1811. It was the last opera he was to write for a decade, though he continued to develop his operatic interest with a number of arias and other music for dramatic works. He had also begun to support his enthusiasm for the Romantic movement with a series of articles and reviews, arguing especially for the formation of an indigenous German opera free from Italian influence. In this he had the encouragement of a 'Harmonischer Verein' he formed with, among others,

Jakob Beer (not yet known as Meyerbeer), Danzi, Gottfried Weber, and Johann Gänsbacher; though close to their ideals, E. T. A. Hoffmann was not of their number.

The chance to put his views into practice came with Weber's appointment as director of the Prague Opera in 1813. There he was able to bring about reforms that included greater attention to the orchestra, more careful rehearsal of the singers as dramatic artists, and greater emphasis on scenery and costume. All this was in the interest of what he described in a review of Hoffmann's *Undine* (anticipating the *Gesamtkunstwerk) as 'the German ideal, namely a self-sufficient work of art in which every feature and every contribution by the related arts are moulded together in a certain way and dissolve, to form a new art'. His Prague repertory was almost devoid of Italian opera, but it did include many of the French *opéras comiques* which he felt set the most fruitful example for German composers.

Moving to Dresden as director of the German Opera in 1817, he was able to develop these ideas still more systematically, in spite of difficulties with the local Italian Opera favoured by the court. He also came to know Friedrich Kind, to whose text he composed *Der Freischütz*. Performed in Berlin in 1821, the work took Germany, then the whole of Europe, by storm. In form essentially a *Singspiel*, it made an instant appeal, to a young Romantic generation wishing to discover a national artistic identity, by drawing on a native German folk subject, setting on the stage recognizable German rustic characters, and making use of a melodic idiom owing some of its nature to German folk music. However, the work's originalities include greatly heightened use of the orchestra, especially for the powerful Wolf's Glen scene in which the forces of evil are invoked for the forging of the huntsman's magic bullets, thus providing the frisson of the sinister that was also a Romantic fascination.

The opera at once made Weber the most famous musician in Germany. He had also by now added a substantial corpus of concert music to his list of works. He had written a number of dazzling instrumental concertos, including two piano concertos for his own virtuosity to which he added, at the time of *Der Freischütz*, a *Konzertstück* for piano and orchestra (1821). Based on a dramatic programme, the work moves the concerto away from the abstract towards the more descriptive and pictorial in a Romantic synthesis of the arts that Liszt was not alone in admiring. Though Weber wrote a number of piano pieces, including eventually four sonatas, his *Aufforderung zum Tanz* ('Invitation to the Dance', 1819) similarly forged a new Romantic form by reference to a programme and to the exploration of waltz rhythms. He continued to compose songs, as he had done since a young man, when—until an accident ruined his voice—he would sing them himself, sometimes to his own guitar accompaniment. Though not by nature a church composer, he wrote two fine, dramatic masses for Dresden (1818, 1819). Other music included choral works and chamber music, notably a Piano Quartet (1811) and a Clarinet Quintet (1816), both of them owing more to the Parisian *concertant* style of a leading soloist than to the Viennese tradition of a more equal-voiced ensemble.

The success of *Der Freischütz* led to a Viennese commission which resulted in *Euryanthe* (1823). Wishing to move forward with an attempt at grand opera, an ideal that had been haunting German composers for decades, Weber broke off work on a comic opera, *Die drei Pintos* (later completed by Mahler), and accepted a faulty text from a Dresden librettist, Helmina von Chézy. Nevertheless this drew from him some of his most adventurous and influential music. The orchestral mastery is even more complete than in *Der Freischütz*, especially in the use of individual instruments—sometimes in original registers or unusual combinations to form textures of a subtlety and clarity which had long characterized his scoring and which profoundly influenced composers as different as Berlioz, Mahler, and Debussy. There is a use of motif that, while still some way distant from leitmotifs, helps to draw the dramatic threads together in a way that Weber had admired in Spohr's *Faust* and Poissl's *Athalia*. There is the characterization of a 'dark' and a 'light' pair that was to affect Wagner in *Lohengrin*, and the development (in Lysiart) of the noble villain that went into operatic currency with Marschner and Wagner. Above all, the impetus is sustained, without spoken dialogue, across linked movements in a manner that gives the opera dramatic continuity.

Though by now weakened by the tuberculosis that had afflicted him from childhood, Weber accepted a commission for an opera for Covent Garden. He did not immediately realize that the text for *Oberon* (1826), by James Robinson Planché, was for a work that dealt as much in scenic display and other visual distractions as in music; but, needing the money to provide for his family after what he knew was his impending death, he learnt English and set about composing the music. It is inevitably uneven (he hoped to rewrite it later as a German opera), but includes some of the most exquisite numbers he had ever composed—as well as, in 'Ocean! thou mighty monster', one of his grandest dramatic scenas. He further managed to link these disparate pieces with subtle use of a motif associated with Oberon's magic horn.

Setting off for England by way of Paris, he arrived in London and settled into the hospitable house of Sir George Smart. Though barely able to catch his breath, he conducted concerts and played in aristocratic houses so as to amass all the money he could. The opening of *Oberon* was a triumph, and Weber was given a rapturous welcome by audiences moved by his plight and inspired by his artistry. Nevertheless he was failing fast, and, the day before he had determined to set off for home, he was found dead in his bed.   JW

📖 J. WARRACK, *Carl Maria von Weber* (London, 1968, 2/1976) · C. BROWN, 'Weber and Spohr', *The Nineteenth-Century Symphony*, ed. D. K. Holoman (New York, 1997) · C. BROWN, 'The chamber music of Spohr and Weber', *Nineteenth-Century Chamber Music*, ed. S. E. Helfig (New York, 1998)

Webern, Anton (Friedrich Wilhelm von) (*b* Vienna, 3 Dec. 1883; *d* Mittersill, 15 Sept. 1945). Austrian composer and conductor. He began piano lessons with his mother, then studied the piano and theory with Edwin Komauer while at school in Klagenfurt. In 1902 he became a student at the University of Vienna, where he studied musicology under Guido Adler, receiving a doctorate in 1906 for his edition of the second part of Isaac's *Choralis Constantinus*. Much more decisive, however, were the private studies with Schoenberg which he began in 1904, at the same time as Berg. The two pupils benefited greatly from Schoenberg's challenging instruction: Webern graduated quickly from the mediocrity of his early pieces to the confidence of his single-movement Quartet (1905) and *Five Dehmel Songs* (1906–8). The Quartet, though influenced by his teacher's *Verklärte Nacht*, is already individual in its development from a small motif and in its spiritual programme, while his mastery of chromatic counterpoint is evident in the songs and the orchestral Passacaglia (1908). His first essays in atonality came, like Schoenberg's, in songs to poems by Stefan George, 14 settings dating from 1907–9.

In 1908, his studies over, Webern began a period of conducting operettas and light music in summer theatres. He disliked this work and tended to abandon posts almost as soon as he had taken them up (if not before), but he was able to develop his technique as a conductor. Meanwhile he continued to compose. The George songs were followed by several sets of instrumental pieces, all atonal and increasingly concise. The somewhat Mahlerian Six Orchestral Pieces of 1909, for instance, were succeeded by a group of Five Pieces for smaller forces (1911–13), the shortest of which lasts 14 seconds. Similar in scale are Webern's other works of this period, which include his Six Bagatelles for string quartet and Three Little Pieces for cello and piano, as well as several songs. Yet all of these are perfectly finished compositions, typically developed from small cells and delicately variegated in colour. Their brevity, however, allowed no room for continuation along the same path, and for the next decade Webern concentrated on groups of songs, usually with accompaniment for instrumental ensemble. Among these are the Six Trakl Songs for voice, two clarinets, violin, and cello (1917–21); others set religious texts and folk rhymes. Having settled in Vienna after his brief appointments elsewhere, Webern supported himself and his family during this period as a conductor, notably with the Vienna Workers' Symphony Concerts (1922–34) and Austrian Radio (1927–34); he was particularly esteemed for his Mahler performances. He also appeared several times in London to perform his own music and that of Schoenberg and Berg.

His adoption of *serialism in 1924 at first brought little change to his style, but in his Symphony for small orchestra (1928) he realized the potentialities of the technique for creating music in strictly symmetrical forms: the first of the two movements is a double canon in sonata form, the second a palindromic set of variations. All his later instrumental works—the Quartet for violin, clarinet, tenor saxophone, and piano (1930), the Concerto for nine instruments (1931–4), the Piano Variations (1936), the String Quartet (1936–8), and the Orchestral Variations (1940)—are similarly tightly structured. Often the series itself is symmetrical, most extremely so in the Concerto, where a single three-note idea is perpetually shown in new lights. This delight in all-pervasive unity reflected Webern's aim to emulate the perfection of the natural world; the flowers and mineral crystals of the Alps were a particular joy to him. In the poet Hildegard Jone he found a kindred spirit, and it was her verse that he set exclusively in his vocal works after the Symphony: two sets of songs with piano (1933–4), Das Augenlicht for chorus and orchestra (1935), and two cantatas (1938–9 and 1941–3). A third cantata was germinating in his mind when he was accidentally shot by an American soldier during the postwar occupation of Austria.

A reserved man, Webern had passed his last years in relative obscurity, taking on menial jobs for his publisher after he had been obliged by the Nazis to relinquish his appointments. Many of his works remained unpublished and unperformed at the time of his death, and only one, the String Trio from early in his serial period, had been commercially recorded. Within a few years of his death, however, young composers had proclaimed him 'THE threshold' (Boulez) to the new music and his influence was being felt by Stravinsky.   PG

📖 D. Irvine (ed.), Anton von Webern: Perspectives (Seattle, 1966) · F. Wildgans, Anton Webern (London, 1966) · W. Kolneder, Anton Webern (London, 1968) ·

H. Moldenhauer, Anton von Webern: Chronicle of his Life and Works (New York and London, 1978) · M. Hayes, Anton von Webern (London, 1995) · K. Bailey, The Life of Webern (Cambridge, 1998)

Weckmann, Matthias (b Niederdorla, Thuringia, c.1619; d Hamburg, 24 Feb. 1674). German composer. He was a choirboy at the Dresden chapel under Schütz, then a pupil of Praetorius and Scheidemann at Hamburg. About 1642 he went to Denmark to join Schütz, remaining as organist until 1647. Eight years later he became organist at St Jacobi in Hamburg, where he founded a collegium musicum.

About 13 sacred vocal works by Weckmann have survived, many of them in the Protestant chorale concertato tradition of Schütz and his successors. His instrumental works include eight sets of chorale variations for organ, keyboard pieces, and some four- or five-part ensemble sonatas for cornetts, violin(s), trombone, and bassoon, which bear a strong resemblance to Giovanni Gabrieli's instrumental canzonas.   WT

We Come to the River. Opera in two parts (11 scenes) by Henze to a libretto by Edward Bond (London, 1976).

Wedding, The. See NOCES, LES.

Wedding Day at Troldhaugen. Piano piece by Grieg, no. 6 of his Lyric Pieces (book 8) op. 65 (1897); it was later orchestrated. Troldhaugen was the name of Grieg's villa outside Bergen.

wedding march. Music played for the entry of the bride and the exit of the married couple in British church weddings. Since the mid-19th century this has traditionally been respectively an organ arrangement of the bridal chorus from Wagner's opera Lohengrin and the wedding march from Mendelssohn's incidental music to A Midsummer Night's Dream. The vogue for Mendelssohn's piece was boosted in 1858 when the Princess Royal used it at Windsor. In 1960 the Duke and Duchess of Kent left York Minster to the strains of the Toccata from Widor's Fifth Organ Symphony, an example that was widely copied. Many court composers have written marches and other pieces for the weddings of royal and aristocratic brides.   —/JBe

'Wedge' Fugue. Nickname for J. S. Bach's Fugue in E minor for organ, BWV548, so called because of the shape of the subject, the intervals of which gradually widen.

Weelkes, Thomas (b mid-1570s; d London, bur. 1 Dec. 1623). English church musician and composer. In 1598 he was organist at Winchester College; four years later he took the degree of B.Mus. at New College, Oxford.

In 1602 he married Elizabeth Sandham, a member of a wealthy Chichester family. By that time he had moved to Chichester, where for the rest of his life he was a member of the cathedral music personnel, serving variously as singer, organist, and instructor of the choristers, posts he continued to hold in spite of stormy relationships with the chapter, who disapproved of his drinking habits and in 1617 temporarily dismissed him. He died in London at the home of a friend.

Weelkes is best known as a prolific composer of madrigals and balletts. Like Thomas Morley, his preference was for pieces in a lighter vein, but his works often stand out for their brilliant sonority, rich texture, and at times daring use of dissonance and chromaticism; the six-voice *Thule, the Period of Cosmography* is one of his most dazzling settings. The three-voice *Ayeres, or Phantasticke Spirites* of 1608 are much earthier pieces and often allude to popular culture. His church music includes at least nine services, some of which are now incomplete to the point of being unreconstructable. His anthems have fared better, and include such classics as *Hosanna to the Son of David* and the exquisite *When David heard*. His only Latin-texted work, *Laboravi in gemitu meo*, is among the last great motets of the Tudor tradition. DA/JM

📖 D. BROWN, *Thomas Weelkes: A Biographical and Critical Study* (London, 1969)

Weerbeke, Gaspar van (*b* Oudenaarde, *c*.1440; *d* after 1517). Flemish composer. His career was variously spent in the service of the ducal chapel in Milan, the papal chapel in Rome, and the Burgundian court of Philip the Handsome. His output includes several cycles of motets intended to replace the normal movements of the Ordinary of the Mass (Kyrie, Gloria, etc.), a practice peculiar to the Ambrosian rite retained at Milan Cathedral. JM

Wegelius, Martin (*b* Helsinki, 10 Nov. 1846; *d* Helsinki, 22 March 1906). Finnish composer. He studied in Helsinki, then at the Leipzig Conservatory and in Vienna. On his return to Finland he was active as a conductor and teacher and in 1882 founded the Helsinki Music Institute. He also wrote books on music and theory textbooks. His pupils included Erkki Melartin and Selim Palmgren, and he played an important part in Sibelius's musical development, though their relationship subsequently cooled to the extent that Wegelius, in the 1904 Finnish edition of his *Outlines in the History of Western Music*, allotted Sibelius derisorily little space. RLa

wehmütig (Ger.). 'Sorrowful', 'melancholic'.

weich (Ger.). 'Soft', 'delicate', 'tender'.

Weigl, Karl (*b* Vienna, 6 Feb. 1881; *d* New York, 11 Aug. 1949). Austrian-born American composer. He had composition lessons from Zemlinsky before studying musicology with Guido Adler at the University of Vienna, graduating in 1903. Concurrently he studied the piano and composition at the Conservatorium der Gesellschaft der Musikfreunde. In 1906 Mahler engaged him to conduct the rehearsals at the Court Opera. Weigl worked as a freelance composer until World War I, when he was drafted into the Austrian army. He was appointed professor of theory and composition at the Neues Wiener Konservatorium and, in 1929, lecturer in harmony and counterpoint at the University of Vienna. With the *Anschluss* in 1938 Weigl, who was Jewish, had to flee Austria; he settled in New York, where he supported himself by giving private lessons. He never re-established his previous status in his new homeland, and died in relative obscurity. In 1968 Stokowski conducted the fifth ('Apocalyptic', 1945) of Weigl's six symphonies, but without restoring his music to currency; only in 2000 did the first of a series of recordings begin to attract attention to it. MA

Weihe des Hauses, Die ('The Consecration of the House'). Incidental music by Beethoven, op. 124 (1822), for a play by C. Meisl; the play was an adaptation of August von Kotzebue's *Die *Ruinen von Athen* (1812), for which Beethoven had written incidental music, so he adapted the earlier score and wrote a new overture.

Weihnachtslied (Ger.). 'Christmas song', i.e. *carol.

Weill, Kurt (Julian) (*b* Dessau, 2 March 1900; *d* New York, 3 April 1950). German-born American composer. He studied at the Berlin Musikhochschule with Humperdinck (1918–19) and privately with Busoni (1921–4). His early works, for example the String Quartet (1923), reveal a teasing eclecticism that combines the neo-classicism of Busoni with the near-atonality of Schoenberg, though the all-important impact of jazz on Weill's work can also be felt in the Concerto for Violin and Wind Instruments (1924). Weill's first opera, *Der Protagonist* (Dresden, 1926), is strongly expressionistic. The libretto is by the playwright Georg Kaiser, marking the first of Weill's collaborations with many of the leading literary and theatrical figures of his day, including the surrealist poet Ywan Goll (*Royal Palace*; Berlin, 1927) and the designer Caspar Neher (*Die Bürgschaft*; Berlin, 1932).

Weill's most famous collaboration, however, was with Bertolt Brecht. Their first major work, *Die Dreigroschenoper* ('The Threepenny Opera'; Berlin, 1928), a loose adaptation of *The Beggar's Opera*, was a colossal success at its premiere and marks a definite shift in Weill's style, combining elements of jazz, cabaret, and popular music with astringent instrumentation and an acid tonality to point up the theme of capitalist corruption central to Brecht's text. The fusion of popular music with a classical structure that peers back to Bach and Mozart is most strongly apparent in their first full-length opera *Aufstieg und Fall der Stadt Mahagonny* ('Rise and Fall of the City of Mahagonny'; Leipzig, 1930), and also in *Der Silbersee* ('The Silverlake'; Leipzig and Magdeburg, 1933), a 'play with music' which marked Weill's final collaboration with Kaiser.

The premiere of *Der Silbersee* took place shortly after Hitler's acquisition of power, and was disrupted by Nazi demonstrations in the theatre. The strong influence of jazz in Weill's work, combined with his broadly left-wing stance and the fact that he was Jewish, made him anathema to the new regime, and he left Germany later that year, first settling in Paris where the last of his collaborations with Brecht, *Die sieben Todsünden der Kleinbürger* ('The Seven Deadly Sins of the Bourgeoisie'), a terse, aphoristic 'sung ballet', was given its premiere in 1933.

In 1935 Weill emigrated to the USA, where he was naturalized in 1943. He turned his attention to film scores and to Broadway musicals, of which the finest are *Knickerbocker Holiday* (1938), *Lady in the Dark* (1941), *One Touch of Venus* (1943), and *Lost in the Stars* (1949). He is widely regarded as having been happily assimilated in the USA, though he was frequently unhappy with the changes Hollywood forced him to make to his film scores; *One Touch of Venus* reveals an ambivalent attitude to the 'American Dream'. His humanitarian, political conscience remained astute—*Lost in the Stars*, based on Alan Paton's novel *Cry, the Beloved Country*, is a blistering attack on racism. He was married to the singer and actress Lotte *Lenya, for whom he wrote many of his most important scores.

Weill's work straddles both classical music and popular culture. After his death many of his songs became popular standards, and his collaboration with Brecht is still regarded by many as the embodiment of cabaret-drenched Weimar Republic satire at its finest. More recently, however, both performance practice and critical emphasis have dwelt on the classical roots of his music, necessitating a drastic reappraisal of many of his works, most notably his collaborations with Kaiser and Goll and the music of his American period.   TA

📖 D. JARMAN, *Kurt Weill: An Illustrated Biography* (Bloomington, IN, 1982) · R. TAYLOR, *Kurt Weill: Composer in a Divided World* (London, 1991)

Weinberg, Mieczysław. See VAINBERG, MOISEI SAMUILOVICH.

Weinberger, Jaromír (*b* Prague, 8 Jan. 1896; *d* St Petersburg, FL, 8 Aug. 1967). Czech-born American composer. He studied in Prague with Novák and in Leipzig with Reger. The work for which he is chiefly remembered is the opera based on Czech folk idioms *Švanda dudák* ('Schwanda the Bagpiper'), a great success at its premiere in 1927; it is notable for its rich melodic vein and ingenious use of instrumental colour. From 1932 onwards Weinberger lived in Prague and Austria. His last opera, *Valdstejn* (*Wallenstein*, after Schiller), was performed at Vienna in 1937, just before the Nazi threat forced the composer to leave Europe for the USA, where he eventually committed suicide at the age of 71.   WT/JSM

Weingartner, (Paul) Felix, Edler von Munzberg (*b* Zara [now Zadar], Dalmatia, 2 June 1863; *d* Winterthur, 7 May 1942). Austrian conductor, composer, and writer. He studied composition at Graz and philosophy at Leipzig and was a protégé of Liszt. His first opera, *Sakuntala*, was produced in Weimar in 1884, after which he began his career as a conductor. He was Kapellmeister of the Berlin Opera (1891–8), then conductor of the royal orchestral concerts. In 1908 he took over from Mahler as conductor of the Vienna Court Opera, resigning in 1911 though he continued to conduct the Vienna Philharmonic until 1927, when he was appointed director of the Basle Conservatory. He was also a regular guest in London, working with both the London Philharmonic and London Symphony Orchestras.

A celebrated exponent of Beethoven, Weingartner was the first conductor to record all nine symphonies. He was also noted for his Wagner performances and for his fierce championship of Berlioz at a time when the latter's works were unfashionable; his interpretation of Brahms's symphonies (which he also recorded complete, late in life) earned the composer's admiration. A colourful character, he was five times married, but found the time to compose nine operas (to his own librettos), seven symphonies (between 1899 and 1937), three string quartets, and other orchestral and chamber works. He also wrote an autobiography, a famous treatise on conducting, and an important study of Beethoven's symphonies.   TA

📖 C. DYMENT (ed.), *Felix Weingartner: Recollections and Recordings* (Rickmansworth, 1976)

Weinlied (Ger.). 'Drinking-song'.

Weinzweig, John (Jacob) (*b* Toronto, 11 March 1913). Canadian composer and teacher. From 1934 to 1937 he studied harmony at the University of Toronto with Leo Smith, counterpoint with Healey Willan, orchestration with Ernest MacMillan, and conducting with Reginald

Stewart. He taught at the Toronto Conservatory of Music (1939–43, 1945–60) as well as at the University of Toronto (1952–78). By 1941 he was composing incidental music for CBC radio dramas, as well as soundtracks for National Film Board documentaries. This was interrupted by service in the Royal Canadian Air Force (1943–5). In 1948 his Divertimento no. 1—the first of a long series—for flute and strings won the highest award in the chamber music category at the London (Ontario) Olympiad, and the next year his ballet *Red Ear of Corn* was given its premiere.

Weinzweig was a founder in 1951 of the Canadian League of Composers, serving as its first president and in 1974 becoming the first Canadian composer to receive the Order of Canada. Through his teaching he introduced 20th-century techniques—dodecaphony and serialism—to two generations of Canadian composers. In his later music he experimented with collage and the contrast of sound and silence. He wrote 12 divertimentos for a variety of solo instruments with string orchestra.   HRE

   📖 J. BECKWITH (ed.), *John Weinzweig at Seventy* (Toronto, 1983) · E. KEILLOR, *John Weinzweig and his Music: The Radical Romantic of Canada* (Metuchen, NJ, 1994)

Weir, Judith (*b* Cambridge, 11 May 1954). Scottish composer. She studied with John Tavener and Robin Holloway. Her music owes much to the family roots evident in such titles as *Scotch Minstrelsy* (1982) and *The Bagpiper's String Trio* (1985). Yet these sources, and her allusions to folk music, contribute to a style which engages positively with many aspects of mainstream 20th-century music, including the concentrated eloquence of Janáček and the brittle rhythmic propulsion of Stravinsky. She has made a particularly important contribution to opera, with *A Night at the Chinese Opera* (Cheltenham, 1987), *The Vanishing Bridegroom* (Glasgow, 1990), and *Blond Eckbert* (ENO, 1994), as well as several shorter dramatic pieces.   AW

Weisgall, Hugo (David) (*b* Eibenschütz, Moravia, 13 Oct. 1912; *d* New York, 11 March 1997). Czech-born American composer. He arrived with his family in the USA in 1920, becoming an American citizen in 1926, and studied at the Peabody Conservatory (1927–32), at the Curtis Institute (1934–9), and occasionally with Roger Sessions (1932–41). He was then a military diplomat in Europe (1941–7), returning to the USA to work as a composer, conductor, and teacher (Juilliard School 1957–70, Queens College from 1961). His main works are his operas, diverse in subject, but all given powerful atmosphere and dynamism by a chromatic style indebted to Sessions. They include *The Tenor* (Baltimore, 1952), *The Stronger* (Westport, 1952), *Six Characters in Search of an Author* (New York, 1959),

Athaliah (New York, 1964), and *Esther* (New York, 1993).   PG

Weiss, Silvius Leopold (*b* Breslau [now Wrocław, Poland], 12 Oct. 1686; *d* Dresden, 16 Oct. 1750). German lutenist and composer. He studied with his father, Johann Jacob (*c*.1662–1754), also a lutenist, and in about 1706 entered the service of the Count Palatine Carl Philipp. From 1708 to 1714 he lived in Italy. On the prince's death he returned to Germany, where he spent the rest of his life in the service of the electoral court at Dresden, becoming one of the highest-paid court instrumentalists. Weiss was among the last great lute virtuosos at a time when the lute was rapidly going out of fashion. He played throughout Europe and was highly sought after as a teacher. He wrote more lute music than any other composer for the instrument, many of his pieces being grouped into suites absorbing French and Italian influences and using sophisticated harmonies and modulations.
                                                        WT/AL

Weissenburg, Johann Heinrich von. See ALBICASTRO, HENRICUS.

Weldon, John (*b* Chichester, 19 Jan. 1676; *d* London, 7 May 1736). English composer and organist. He was a chorister at Eton College and a pupil of Purcell before becoming organist of New College, Oxford (1694–1701). At the Chapel Royal he was appointed Gentleman-Extraordinary (1701), organist (1708, succeeding Blow), and later second composer (1715). He was organist of St Bride's, Fleet Street, and from 1714 of St Martin's-in-the-Fields. In 1701 he won first prize in a competition for a setting of Congreve's masque *The Judgement of Paris* (beating John Eccles, Daniel Purcell, and Gottfried Finger), and he later wrote incidental music for a performance of *The Tempest* (*c*.1712)— possibly that which has commonly been attributed to Purcell. His other compositions include many songs and some church music, though he seems to have composed little in later life.   PS/WT/PL

Welitsch [Veličkova], **Ljuba** (*b* Borissovo, 10 July 1913; *d* Vienna, 31 Aug. 1996). Bulgarian-born Austrian soprano. As a child she played the violin, going on to study philosophy at Sofia University before turning to singing. She made her operatic debut in Sofia in 1935, and sang in Graz and Munich before joining the Vienna State Opera in 1944; she caused a sensation during the company's visit to Covent Garden in 1947. Her international career, brief and meteoric, was effectively over by 1955 as a result of the excessive strain she placed on her voice, though she remained a character artist in the Vienna ensemble until her retirement in 1981. She was famous—even notorious—for the unbridled eroticism she brought to her singing. Her Salome, a role in which she was coached by Strauss, was considered definitive.   TA

Wellesz, Egon (Joseph) (*b* Vienna, 21 Oct. 1885; *d* Oxford, 9 Nov. 1974). Austrian composer and musicologist. He studied at the University of Vienna (1895–1908), and had private music lessons with Schoenberg (1905–6). He remained a member of Schoenberg's circle, published the first book on the composer (Leipzig, 1921; Eng. trans. 1925/*R*1971), and adopted serial methods in his music, on which Strauss was also an important influence. From 1913 to 1938 Wellesz taught at the University of Vienna. In 1939 he settled in Oxford, where he was appointed reader in Byzantine music. He continued to compose, writing a set of nine symphonies and a Violin Concerto (1961) and re-examining tonality by way of Mahler and Bruckner. Besides his study of Schoenberg, he wrote *Eastern Elements in Western Chant* (Boston, 1947) and *A History of Byzantine Music and Hymnography* (London, 1963).   PG

   📖 R. Schollum, *Egon Wellesz* (Vienna, 1963)

Wellingtons Sieg (*Wellingtons Sieg, oder Die Schlacht bei Vittoria*; 'Wellington's Victory, or The Battle near Vitoria'; *Battle Symphony*). Beethoven's op. 91 (1813), composed to celebrate the defeat of the French at Vitoria and incorporating English and French fanfares and patriotic songs (including 'Rule, Britannia!'). The second part was composed for Maelzel's panharmonicon but Beethoven later orchestrated the whole work for strings, wind bands, and artillery.

Well-Tempered Clavier, The (*Das wohltemperirte Clavier*). Title given by J. S. Bach to his two sets of 24 preludes and fugues in all the major and minor keys, BWV846–93 (1722, 1742), popularly known as the '48'; it demonstrates the range of keys that becomes possible using what were then relatively modern methods of tuning, or 'temperament', and has subsequently influenced the contrapuntal writing of countless composers and played a crucial role in teaching keyboard playing, composition, and analysis.

Welsh College of Music and Drama. Welsh conservatory founded in Cardiff in 1949. See DEGREES AND DIPLOMAS.

wenig (Ger.). 'Little', 'slightly'; *ein wenig*, 'a little'; *weniger*, 'less'.

Werner, Gregor Joseph (*b* Ybbs an der Donau, 28 Jan. 1693; *d* Eisenstadt, 3 March 1766). Austrian composer. From 1728 until his death he served as Kapellmeister at the Esterházy court in Eisenstadt. In 1761 Joseph Haydn was appointed as his assistant, and Werner, with the title Oberhofkapellmeister, was granted control solely of the court's sacred music—a covert demotion which made him resentful of his young colleague. Werner's compositions include oratorios, *a cappella* and concertato masses, and 12 suites entitled *Neuer und sehr curioser musikalischer Instrumental-Calender* (1748), the descriptive features of which may have influenced the programmatic elements in Haydn's earlier symphonies.   DA/BS

Wert, Giaches de (*b* Flanders, *c*.1535; *d* Mantua, 6 May 1596). Franco-Flemish musician and composer. Brought to Italy as a boy, he served at several minor courts before being appointed *maestro di cappella* at the newly built ducal chapel of S. Barbara at Mantua in 1565. He remained in the service of the Gonzaga for the rest of his life, but developed close connections with the court at nearby Ferrara. This brought him into contact with writers such as Tasso and Guarini, whose poetry he set as madrigals. In the last ten years of his life he suffered increasingly from ill health, brought on by malaria.

Wert was primarily a madrigal composer, and an important forerunner of the chromatic and dissonant style of Monteverdi's *seconda pratica* (see PRIMA PRATICA, SECONDA PRATICA) in his concentration on the creation of expressive melody. At the same time he used homophony as a means towards the accurate declamation of the words. 16 volumes of madrigals by him were published between 1558 and 1608. His church music, less extensive in quantity and mostly unpublished at his death, is also noted for its expressivity; much of it reflects liturgical practice at S. Barbara.   DA/JM

   📖 I. Fenlon (ed.), *Giaches de Wert: Letters and Documents* (Paris, 1999)

Werther. Opera in four acts by Massenet to a libretto by Édouard Blau, Paul Milliet, and Georges Hartmann after Johann Wolfgang von Goethe's novel *Die Leiden des jungen Werthers* ('The Sorrows of Young Werther', 1774) (Vienna, 1892).

Wesendonk-Lieder. Five songs (1857–8) by Wagner for voice and piano to poems by Mathilde Wesendonk; they were orchestrated by Felix Mottl under Wagner's supervision. They have been arranged for violin and piano (1872) by Hubert Léonard, and for high voice and chamber orchestra (1979) by Henze.

Wesley, Charles (*b* Bristol, 11 Dec. 1757; *d* London, 23 May 1834). English composer. A precocious child, he was a pupil of William Boyce, and participated with his brother Samuel in a remarkable series of subscription concerts (1779–85) in their London home. His works, which include 14 organ concertos, voluntaries, songs, and anthems, are fundamentally conservative in style—he idolized Handel—though his six string quartets attempt a more modern *galant* idiom. RL/PL

Wesley, Samuel (*b* Bristol, 24 Feb. 1766; *d* London, 11 Oct. 1837). English organist and composer. At first outshone by the musical precocity of his elder brother, Charles, he later proved the more talented—indeed, he was the most important English composer of his generation. He received his musical education at second hand through Charles's teachers; his technique developed so rapidly that by the age of eight he had completed an oratorio, *Ruth* (1774), which was shown to an astonished William Boyce. In 1778 the Wesley family settled in Marylebone, London, and the following year the two brothers began to give series of subscription concerts. These continued until 1785, by which time Samuel had written a considerable body of works including harpsichord sonatas and church and orchestral music, his overture in D (1784) for two horns and strings equalling those of J. C. Bach.

Contact with the Portuguese Embassy, where his friend Vincent Novello was organist, broadened Wesley's knowledge of European music. Rumours that he had been received into the Roman Catholic Church were denied by the composer, who, as a freemason, was later married according to the rites of the Anglican Church. Nevertheless, he was powerfully attracted to the Roman liturgy, composing many works for it including the motets *Dixit Dominus* (1800), *In exitu Israel* (1810), and *Tu es sacerdos* (1827), and the *Missa de Spiritu Sanctu* (1784) dedicated and presented to Pope Pius VI. His best works are arguably the large-scale *Confitebor tibi Domine* (1791), the Symphony in B♭ (1802), and the Concert Overture in E (*c*.1834); his *12 Voluntaries* (1805–17) are also among the most important organ music of their time.

Though the finest organist of his day, Wesley held only minor positions in the Church of England. He was active in the English *Bach Revival, publishing the six trio sonatas (1809, with C. F. Horn) and the '48' (1810–13), and edited the music of his contemporaries G. F. Pinto and William Russell. An eccentric man, inclined to the unorthodox, Wesley separated from his wife after only two years of marriage to live with his housekeeper. With irregular work, he spent much of his life in virtual destitution, being obliged to support his wife and their three children as well as his housekeeper's children (among them Samuel Sebastian). JDi

📖 M. KASSLER and P. J. OLLESON, *Samuel Wesley: A Sourcebook* (Aldershot, forthcoming)

Wesley, Samuel Sebastian (*b* London, 14 Aug. 1810; *d* Gloucester, 19 April 1876). English composer and organist, son of Samuel Wesley. He took music lessons from his father and continued his education from 1820 at the Chapel Royal, where he was taught by William Hawes. He undertook numerous organist appointments (1826–32) but was also active at the Lyceum and Olympic theatres and played for the Lenten Oratorio Concerts (1830–2). He was appointed organist at Hereford Cathedral in 1832, then moved on to Exeter (1835), Leeds Parish Church (1842), Winchester (1849), and finally Gloucester (1865).

A vituperative and argumentative man, Wesley would not tolerate lax administration or low standards. He campaigned tirelessly for the recognition of music within the church hierarchy, writing two outspoken pamphlets on the subject including the well-known *A Few Words on Cathedral Music* (1849). His irascibility often brought him into conflict with his church employers and probably contributed to his failure to secure academic posts at Edinburgh, Oxford, and Cambridge. He declined a knighthood on several occasions, and his later years were blighted by illness and bitterness.

At the heart of Wesley's output is his anthem collection (1853), containing both large-scale verse anthems—*Ascribe unto the Lord*, *The Wilderness*, and, perhaps finest of all with its magnificent opening chorus and sonata-style baritone verse 'Thou, O Lord God', *Let us lift up our heart*—and such exquisite full anthems as the Spohr-influenced *Wash me throughly*, the devotional *Thou wilt keep him in perfect peace*, and the unaccompanied *Cast me not away*. He also composed some notable organ works, including the virtuoso *Variations on God Save the King* (1829) and the spacious Andante in F for chamber organ (1842–3). More neglected, but no less fine, are his orchestral score for Edward Fitzball's melodrama *The Dilosk Gatherer* (1832), his one-movement Symphony (*c*.1834), and the sacred song for baritone and orchestra *Abraham's Offering* (1833–4), all showing that bold approach to diatonic harmony and dissonance more readily associated with his later anthems. RL/JDi

West Coast jazz. A school of *cool jazz that flourished in the Los Angeles area during the 1950s, much of it created by film-studio musicians taking time off from their routine work. A centre for it was the Lighthouse Club in Los Angeles. The music was generally of a highly technical nature, experimental, and somewhat 'cooler' than the East Coast brand. Its leading exponents included Shorty Rogers, Art Pepper, Shelly Manne, and Jimmy Giuffre. PGa

Western Wynde. 16th-century English secular song used as a cantus firmus in masses by Taverner, Tye, and

Sheppard. The use of secular tunes in sacred music was eventually banned by the Roman Catholic Church, not surprisingly when it is considered that the anonymous and beautiful words to which congregations were accustomed to hearing this tune sung were:

> Western wynde, when wilt thou blow,
> The small raine down can raine.
> Christ, if my love were in my armes
> And I in my bedde again!

Whale, The. Dramatic cantata (1965–6) by Tavener, for narrator, mezzo-soprano, baritone, chorus, and orchestra, to his own text compiled from *Collins' Encyclopedia* and the Vulgate.

Where the Wild Things Are. Opera in one act by Knussen to a libretto by Maurice Sendak after his book (preliminary version, Brussels, 1980; definitive version, London, 1984); it was followed by the companion-piece **Higglety Pigglety Pop!*

whip [slapstick]. A pair of wooden blades hinged at one end, with a handle on each so that they can be clapped smartly together, imitating the crack of a whip. It has been required in the orchestra by composers including Mahler (Seventh Symphony, 1907) and Britten (*The Young Person's Guide to the Orchestra*, 1946).   JMo

whistle. 1. A short, high-pitched flute, without fingerholes or with no more than one, used as a signal instrument. It may be blown through a duct (see DUCT FLUTE) or across a hole in the side or the end. The term is also used for instruments with full melodic capability such as the *swanee whistle and *penny whistle.

The sports referee's whistle is a *vessel flute containing a pellet; others, like the police whistle, may be duplex. Both produce a trilling sound. A bird whistle, which imitates a nightingale, is a vessel whistle part-filled with water. Fingers moved at the distal end of a duct whistle produce different notes, as in the boatswain's call. Reed hooters may also be called whistles.   JMo

2. The production of high-pitched tones by the projection of air through pursed lips. Pitch is altered through variations in cheek and lip pressure. Certain advanced techniques are available to the modern whistler, including *harmonics overblown through tightly tensed lips, tongue trills, and *multiphonics. Boito's *Mefistofele* includes whistling in the score.

Notable whistlers have included the American Alice Shaw, known as 'La Belle Siffleuse'. The New York *Musical Courier* in 1931 reported that 'No jazz or cheap crooning stuff had a place in her repertoire and her performances were equally sensational in the drawing-rooms of kings, czars, emperors, and maharajahs'. The blind whistler Fred Lowery performed with celebrated show-business figures between 1930 and 1955, and recorded many LPs on the Columbia, Decca, and MGM labels. The tongue trills of the Irish singer Roger Whittaker continue to delight audiences the world over. The International Association of Whistlers hosts the annual World Championships of Musical Whistling.   AB, PS/SM

White [Whyte], Robert (*b c.*1538; *d* London, Nov. 1574). English church musician and composer. He appears to have been a chorister at Trinity College, Cambridge, and in 1560 took the Cambridge degree of Mus.B. Two years later he became Master of the Choristers at Ely Cathedral, and in 1565 married the daughter of a predecessor in that post, Christopher Tye. Soon afterwards he moved first to Chester Cathedral, then (by 1570) to Westminster Abbey. He died of the plague. Little of White's English church music survives, but he is regarded as one of most important Elizabethan composers of Latin-texted motets for domestic use. These include psalms or psalm sections, and two particularly expressive settings of the Lamentations of Jeremiah. He also wrote fantasias and other music for viol consort.   DA/JM

White Man Sleeps. Work (1982) by Volans for two harpsichords, bass viol, and percussion, adapted in 1986 as his String Quartet no. 1.

Whittaker, William G(illies) (*b* Newcastle upon Tyne, 23 July 1876; *d* Orkney Isles, 5 July 1944). English choral conductor, scholar, teacher, and composer. He taught at Armstrong College, Durham University (now Newcastle University), between 1898 and 1929. He was then appointed professor of music at Glasgow University (1929–38) and principal of the RSAMD (1929–41). In 1915 he founded the Newcastle Bach Choir, which became renowned for its performances of Bach and new British and French vocal music. Much of his own work, which included many arrangements of Northumbrian folk tunes, was vocal, notably the large-scale *A Lyke-Wake Dirge* and a setting of Psalm 139 (both 1924), but he also produced a piano quintet *Among the Northumbrian Hills* (1918) and a wind quintet (1931). He sat on the BBC's musical advisory committee and, as an editor, was one of the founders of Oxford University Press's new music-publishing department in 1923.   JD1

whole note (Amer.). Semibreve.

whole tone. An *interval of two semitones.

whole-tone scale (Ger.: *Ganztonleiter*). A scale of six whole tones. See SCALE, 5.

Whyte, Robert. See WHITE, ROBERT.

Whythorne, Thomas (*b* Ilminster, 1528; *d* London, *c.*31 July 1596). English music teacher and composer. The son of a Somerset gentleman, he was educated at Magdalen College School, Oxford, and studied with the playwright-musician John Heywood. In the early 1550s he travelled to Italy via the Netherlands and Germany. He spent most of his life in the service of the English nobility, partly as a music tutor. Between 1571 and 1575 he was Master of Music at the Archbishop of Canterbury's chapel at Lambeth Palace. Whythorne's principal claim to fame is his fascinating autobiography, in which he describes the uncertainties of a musician's life in Elizabethan England. His polyphonic songs, largely settings of his own verse, appeared in a 'vanity' publication in 1571 and are of more bibliographical than musical interest. He also published (1591) a set of two-voice pieces that are aimed principally at 'young beginners'.   —JM

Widmann, Erasmus (*b* Schwäbisch Hall, nr Stuttgart, *bapt.* 15 Sept. 1572; *d* Rothenburg ob der Tauber, 31 Oct. 1634). German composer. He was educated at the University of Tübingen, then worked as an organist in Styria and Graz before returning to Schwäbisch Hall because of his Lutheran sympathies. His next post was as organist to the Weikersheim court, and in 1613 he went to Rothenburg ob der Tauber as Kantor and organist. He remained there until he died, with his wife and daughter, of the plague. Widmann wrote sacred music to Latin as well as German texts, but he is best known for his secular works—balletts and lieder that show the Italian influence. He also published a volume of dance music for instrumental ensemble, *Gantz neue Cantzon, Intraden, Balletten und Courranten* (Nuremberg, 1618).   DA

Widor, Charles-Marie (*b* Lyons, 21 Feb. 1844; *d* Paris, 12 March 1937). French composer and organist. His father, an organ builder in Lyons, gave him his first lessons; he then went on to Lemmens in Brussels, and also studied composition with Fétis. He was appointed organist of St Sulpice in Paris (1870–1934), and in 1890 followed Franck as organ professor at the Paris Conservatoire, his most eminent pupils being Louis Vierne and Charles Tournemire, and later Albert Schweitzer. At the core of his teaching and performing were the works of J. S. Bach. Promoted to a composition professorship (1896–1927), he taught a diverse range of students, among them Marcel Dupré, Nadia Boulanger, Milhaud, and Varèse; he also wrote an excellent treatise on orchestration.

A man of great ambition, Widor produced a large quantity of music in all forms, including three operas and three orchestral symphonies. Best known, however,

are the ten symphonies for solo organ (1872–1900), boldly conceived on a truly orchestral scale for the new 'romantic' instrument built by Cavaillé-Coll. Here he succeeds admirably in integrating very different musical styles, from the austerely liturgical idiom of Bach, to the more secular models of Beethoven, Mendelssohn, Schumann, and Liszt. No. 5 contains the famous showpiece 'Toccata' as its logically satisfying finale, whereas the more inward-looking *Gothique* (no. 9) and *Romane* (no. 10) are based on traditional Gregorian themes.   AT

📖 A. Thomson, *The Life and Times of Charles-Marie Widor* (Oxford, 1987)

Wiegenlied (Ger.). 'Cradle-song', 'lullaby'; see berceuse.

Wieniawski, Henryk [Henri] (*b* Lublin, 10 July 1835; *d* Moscow, 31 March 1880). Polish violinist and composer. After studying in Paris he began his solo career at 15 with a two-year tour of Russia; he also started to compose. He played his own first concerto in Leipzig (1853), then gave concerts in Paris and London. From 1860 to 1872 he lived in St Petersburg, where he played his second concerto and taught, but after further world tours he went to the Brussels Conservatory (1875–7), later giving concerts in Paris, Berlin, and Moscow. A bad heart condition, aggravated by excessive performing, hastened his early death. His singular playing manner, with its unconventional bowing grip, was imbued with an intense vibrato and extraordinary technical prowess.   CF

Wilbye, John (*b* Diss, Norfolk, *bapt.* 7 March 1574; *d* Colchester, autumn 1638). English composer. The son of a tanner, by 1598 he had entered the service of the Kytson family, living as part of their household at Hengrave Hall, near Bury St Edmunds, and remaining there until the death of Lady Kytson in 1628. He then moved to the house of Lady Kytson's daughter, Lady Rivers, in Colchester. His will shows that he possessed wealth and property, and it seems likely that latterly he rose above the status of a domestic servant. He left his 'best vyall' to the Prince of Wales, the future Charles II.

Wilbye's reputation as the finest of the English madrigal composers rests on a very small output, principally two collections of madrigals (London, 1598 and 1609) which between them contain about 60 works. Beyond that, only a handful of pieces by him survive, all of them composed for domestic use rather than the church. It is unknown whether this results from lost sources or whether Wilbye in fact composed very little. The quality of his music arises partly from his avoidance of frivolous verse, partly from his gift for finding the right music to express the mood of the words; but it

is due, too, to his inventiveness and sense of pacing, beside which the madrigals of Weelkes and Morley can sound formulaic. He is one of the least Italianate of the English madrigalists, owing a debt only to the serious settings of Luca Marenzio. His preference is for a sombre atmosphere, and for reflective rather than narrative texts. Many of the verses he set to music are anonymous; some may have been written within the Kytson circle, or even by Wilbye himself.

Although the 1598 collection contains some memorable works, including the popular *Adieu, sweet Amaryllis*, Wilbye's most remarkable achievements are concentrated in the 1609 set, principally among the madrigals for five and six voices. These include sustained essays in a single mood—the melancholy *Weep, weep, mine eyes* and *Draw on, sweet night* come to mind—and more volatile pieces such as the witty *Sweet honey-sucking bees* and *All pleasure is of this condition*. In these pieces, Wilbye's resources include grand sonorities, intriguing textures, deft use of chromaticism, magical transformations of material—and, at all times, an unerring melodic gift that makes his music as pleasing to sing as to hear. His sonorous six-part setting of *The Lady Orianna*, contributed to Thomas Morley's anthology *The Triumphes of Oriana* (1601), towers above most of the rest of the collection. Of the very few pieces that survive only in manuscript, the funeral motet *Homo natus de muliere* stands out for its powerfully expressive response to the words.

DA/JM

📖 D. Brown, *John Wilbye* (London, 1974)

Wilder, Philippe van (*d* London, 24 Feb. 1553). Flemish composer. He lived in London from *c.*1520 until his death, serving as lutenist and keeper of instruments to Henry VIII. His music, mostly chansons, appears to have been better known in England than that of his more famous contemporaries, such as Gombert and Willaert.

JM

Wilhemj, August (*b* Usingen, 21 Sept. 1845; *d* London, 22 Jan 1908). German violinist. As 'the future Paganini' he was sent by Liszt to Ferdinand David at Leipzig. After further studies in Frankfurt he toured throughout Europe. In 1876 he led the first performances of Wagner's *Ring* at Bayreuth and, in the following year, the Wagner Festival in London under the composer and Hans Richter. His teaching career took him to the Guildhall School of Music, London, as professor of violin; his output as a composer consisted of arrangements, including the once popular 'Air on the G string' from Bach's Orchestral Suite no. 3.

WT/CF

Wilkinson, Robert. See Wylkinson, Robert.

Willaert, Adrian (*b* ?Bruges, *c.*1490; *d* Venice, 7 Dec. 1562). Franco-Flemish church musician and composer. He was a pupil in Paris of Jean Mouton. In about 1514 he became a chapel singer to Cardinal Ippolito I d'Este, living variously in Rome, Ferrara, and Hungary. In 1527 he was appointed *maestro di cappella* at St Mark's, Venice; he remained in that position until his death. Through his presence, Venice (and St Mark's in particular) rose to a level of high musical importance in the 16th century. His pupils included Rore, Andrea Gabrieli, Porta, and the theorist Zarlino.

Willaert was a many-sided composer but is famous especially for his church music, much of which is written in a highly individual and sonorous style that was eminently suitable for grand, solemn occasions. His vesper psalms (Venice, 1550) were important for establishing the practice of writing for double choir (known as *cori spezzati*), which was to become a special feature of Venetian music. Other liturgical works include masses, two of which are derived from motets by his teacher Mouton, and a cycle of polyphonic hymn settings that follows the St Mark's liturgy. Some of his many motets are clearly designed for church or state ceremony; others appear to have been written as serious chamber music. His madrigals explore the more serious side of the genre, and at times achieve extreme polyphonic density. Lighter works include chansons, songs in Neapolitan dialect (villanellas), and some important early examples of the instrumental ricercar. Although rarely heard today, Willaert's music was widely respected both during his lifetime and posthumously, Monteverdi describing it as the crowning achievement of the *prima pratica*.

DA/JM

📖 M. Feldman, *City Culture and the Madrigal at Venice* (Berkeley, CA, 1995)

Willan, (James) Healey (*b* Balham, 12 Oct. 1880; *d* Toronto, 16 Feb. 1968). Canadian composer. He studied in London with William S. Hoyte and Evlyn Howard-Jones, and emigrated to Toronto in 1913. There he held posts as precentor of St Mary Magdalene (1921–68), teacher of theory at the conservatory (1913–36), and lecturer at the university (1914, 1936–50). Although he composed in all genres he is remembered as the leading Canadian church musician of his time; his output includes 11 settings of the *Missa brevis*.

PG

Williams, Alberto (*b* Buenos Aires, 23 Nov. 1862; *d* Buenos Aires, 17 June 1952). Argentine composer and pianist. He studied in Buenos Aires and in 1882 won a scholarship to the Paris Conservatoire, where he studied composition with Franck and the piano with Georges Mathias. On his return to Argentina in 1889 he earned his living as a concert pianist and began to explore the traditional music of his native land; the piano piece *El rancho abandonado* (1890) was the first of a number of works in which he incorporated folk tunes. Williams played a major role in Argentine musical life, founding a conservatory (1893) and several concert societies in Buenos Aires. His output includes nine symphonies, three violin sonatas, and 75 songs.   WT/SH

Williams, Grace (Mary) (*b* Barry, S. Glam., 19 Feb. 1906; *d* Barry, 10 Feb. 1977). Welsh composer. She studied with Vaughan Williams at the RCM and with Egon Wellesz in Vienna. Her brand of Romantic nationalism paralleled, rather than was influenced by, Vaughan Williams and Sibelius; she was also impressed by Britten. Her output includes a comic opera, *The Parlour* (Cardiff, 1966), two symphonies (1943 and 1956), and a large body of choral and vocal music, some of it to texts in Welsh, but her sensitivity to atmosphere and colour is best shown in her smaller orchestral pieces, for example the *Sea Sketches* for strings (1944) and *Penillion* (1955).   PG

    M. BOYD, *Grace Williams* (Cardiff, 1980)

Williams, John (Towner) (*b* New York, 8 Feb. 1932). American composer. He moved to Los Angeles in 1948 and studied with Castelnuovo-Tedesco; he also studied the piano at the Juilliard School, and made his early career as a pianist, arranger, and conductor for Columbia Records. Since the early 1970s, he has been one of the most successful composers of film music, with special gifts for the heroic mode and for strong, simple themes. Among the films on which he has worked are *Jaws* (1975) and the *Star Wars* series (1977–). He has written the scores for most of Steven Spielberg's films, notably *Schindler's List* (1993).   PG

Williamson, Malcolm (Benjamin Graham Christopher) (*b* Sydney, 21 Nov. 1931). Australian composer, resident in England. He studied at the Sydney Conservatorium, and in London with Elisabeth Lutyens and Erwin Stein. In 1975 he was appointed Master of the Queen's Music in succession to Arthur Bliss. His output includes full-length operas—notably *Our Man in Havana* (Sadler's Wells, 1963)—three piano concertos, and many other orchestral pieces, as well as chamber works, church music, and 'cassations' involving audience participation. He ranges freely through the gamut of 20th-century serious and popular styles, though with a liking for rich, sweet harmony which sometimes leads him close to Richard Strauss, Poulenc, or Messiaen.   PG/AW

William Tell. See GUILLAUME TELL.

Willis, Henry (*b* London, 27 April 1821; *d* London, 11 Feb. 1901). English organ builder, known as 'Father' Willis. He set up business in London *c*.1848 and built over 2000 organs, including those at the Royal Albert Hall (1871) and the cathedrals of Salisbury (1877), Truro (1887), Hereford (1893), and Lincoln (1898). His use of pneumatics made many improvements to the control of stops and allowed the spatial division of groups of pipes; he also introduced the concave, radiating pedalboard.   WT/AL

    W. L. SUMNER, *Father Henry Willis, Organ Builder, and his Successors* (London, 1957)

Wilson, John (*b* Faversham, 5 April 1595; *d* Westminster, 22 Feb. 1674). English singer, lutenist, and composer. He wrote music for the London theatres in the early part of the 17th century, and in 1622 joined the waits of the City of London. From 1635 he was a member of the King's Music, and followed the royal household to Oxford on the outbreak of the Civil War. He gained the Oxford D.Mus. in 1644, and after a period as a house musician to Sir William Walter in Sarsden, Oxfordshire, became Heather Professor of Music at Oxford in 1656. After the Restoration he was made a Gentleman of the Chapel Royal. He was a prolific composer of songs, some of which were written for inclusion in plays. He also wrote psalm settings, published as *Psalterium Carolinum* (London, 1657), and a set of lute fantasias arranged to show the potential of all the major and minor keys.   DA/JM

Wilson, Thomas (Brendan) (*b* Trinidad, CO, 1927; *d* Glasgow, 12 June 2001). Scottish composer. He studied at the RCM and at Glasgow University, where he taught from 1957. His compositions include two operas, a variety of orchestral pieces, chamber works, and choral music, usually showing a blending of diverse mainstream modernist traits in a vigorous discourse.   PG

wind-cap instruments. Wind instruments in which the reed, normally double, is enclosed by a cap, usually of wood. The player blows through a hole in the cap, and the reed vibrates freely inside. Like the related *bagpipes and *bladder pipes, wind-cap instruments normally have a range of a 9th. They were especially common in the 15th and 16th centuries (see CORNAMUSE; CRUMHORN; KORTHOLT; RAUSCHPFEIFE).   JMo

wind chimes. See CHIME, 1.

Windgassen, Wolfgang (*b* Annemasse, 26 June 1914; *d* Stuttgart, 5 or 8 Sept. 1974). German tenor. He was initially taught by his father and later studied at the Stuttgart Hochschule, making his debut in Pforzheim in 1941 as Alvaro in Verdi's *La forza del destino*. In 1951 he joined the Stuttgart Opera. The same year he made his Bayreuth debut as Parsifal; he sang his first Siegfried there in 1953, and remained the principal tenor at Bayreuth until 1971. Between 1955 and 1966 he appeared regularly at Covent Garden. He had a powerful, rich, seemingly tireless *Heldentenor* voice and sang all the major Wagner roles throughout his career. Though some consider that he lacked the necessary lyricism for Tannhäuser, Lohengrin, and Walter (in *Die Meistersinger von Nürnberg*), he is widely regarded as the finest Tristan and Siegfried of the postwar era.   TA

  📖 B. W. Wessling, *Wolfgang Windgassen* (Bremen, 1967)

wind instruments (Ger.: *Blasinstrumente*). Instruments sounded by having air blown into them, either from the player's lungs or by bellows. They are divided conventionally into *woodwind, *brass, and such keyboards as *organs or *accordions. The term used in *organology for such instruments is *aerophone. See INSTRUMENTS, CLASSIFICATION OF.   JMo

wind machine [aeoliphone]. A drum made of wooden slats over which a canvas sheet is draped. The drum is rotated with a crank and the resulting hissing sound resembles that of the wind. It is used occasionally in the orchestra (to great atmospheric effect by Vaughan Williams in *Sinfonia antartica*) and frequently in the theatre.   JMo

windpipe. See VOICE, 3.

wind quintet. See QUINTET; see also CHAMBER MUSIC.

Winter, Peter von (*b* Mannheim, *bapt.* 28 Aug. 1754; *d* Munich, 17 Oct. 1825). German composer. At the age of ten he entered the Mannheim court orchestra as a violinist. He studied for a while with Abbé Vogler, and when the electoral court moved to Munich in 1778 Winter became conductor of the orchestra. In 1780–1 he visited Vienna, where he studied with Salieri and met Mozart. In Munich he was vice-Kapellmeister from 1787 and Kapellmeister from 1798. He composed over 40 ballets and operas, which were performed as far afield as Naples, Paris, and London; these included the *Singspiel Das Labyrinth* (Vienna, 1798; a sequel to Mozart's *Die Zauberflöte*) and *Das unterbrochene Opferfest* ('The Interrupted Sacrifice'; Vienna, 1796), his greatest operatic success. His output also includes symphonies, overtures, concertos, vocal music, and much church music. He wrote a treatise on singing that was widely used throughout the 19th century.   WT/CB

Winter Daydreams. Nickname of Tchaikovsky's Symphony no. 1 in G minor op. 13; the first version was composed in 1866, the second later that year, and the third in 1874.

Winterreise ('Winter Journey'). Song cycle, D911 (1827), by Schubert, settings of 24 poems (1823–4) by Wilhelm Müller.

Winter Words. Song cycle, op. 52 (1953), by Britten, for soprano or tenor and piano, settings of eight poems by Thomas Hardy; the title is taken from Hardy's last published volume of poetry (1928).

Wirbel (Ger.). 'Drumroll'.

Wirén, Dag (Ivar) (*b* Striberg, Närke, 15 Oct. 1905; *d* Stockholm, 19 April 1986). Swedish composer. He studied at the Royal Conservatory in Stockholm (1926–31) and in Paris (1932–4), where he was taught by Leonid Sabaneyev and influenced by Honegger. He then returned to Sweden, where for some years he worked as a music critic. In his Third Symphony (1943–4) he established a 'metamorphosis technique' by which whole works could be generated from small units, paralleling the procedures of such contemporaries as Vagn Holmboe. His output included five symphonies, five string quartets, and a variety of other large-scale instrumental works, but he is best known for his light Serenade for strings (1937).   PG/ABur

Wise, Michael (*b* Wiltshire, *c*.1648; *d* Salisbury, 24 Aug. 1687). English composer. At the Restoration he was a Child of the Chapel Royal, and from 1665 a countertenor in St George's Chapel, Windsor, and soon after at Eton College. He became organist and choirmaster at Salisbury Cathedral in 1668 and was made a Gentleman of the Chapel Royal in 1676. In 1687, the year of his death, he was appointed Master of the Children at St Paul's Cathedral. He was killed by the Salisbury night watch following an argument. His works include some fine anthems (such as *Awake up my glory* and *How are the mighty fallen*) and services.   WT/AA

Wishart, Trevor (*b* Leeds, 11 Oct. 1946). English composer. He studied at Oxford, Nottingham, and York universities and has been awarded various residencies and visiting professorships. He has worked consistently in the field of electroacoustics and extended vocal techniques, his main works including *Red Bird* (1977) for tape, *Anticredos* (1980) for six amplified voices and percussion, and the *Vox* cycle of six pieces for four amplified voices and tape (1982–9). He has also written an influential book, *On Sonic Art* (1985).   AW

Wittgenstein, Paul (*b* Vienna, 5 Nov. 1887; *d* Manhasset, NY, 3 March 1961). Austrian pianist. A pupil of Leschetizky, he made his debut in Vienna in 1913 but lost his right arm on the battlefield a year later.

After the war he resolved to continue his solo career by adapting works and playing those written for him by Strauss (*Parergon zur Symphonia domestica* and *Panathenäenzug*), Ravel (Concerto for the Left Hand), Schmidt, Korngold, Hindemith, Britten (*Diversions on a Theme*), and Prokofiev (Fourth Piano Concerto). In 1939 he settled in the USA and taught in New York.

CF

   📖 P. WITTGENSTEIN, *School for the Left Hand* (London, 1957)

Wohltemperirte Clavier, Das. See WELL-TEMPERED CLAVIER, THE.

Wolf, Hugo (Filipp Jakob) (*b* Windischgraz, Styria [now Slovenj Gradec, Yugoslavia], 13 March 1860; *d* Vienna, 22 Feb. 1903). Austrian composer. His father was a leather-merchant and an able instrumentalist who taught him the piano and violin. After some generally unsatisfactory schooling he entered the Vienna Conservatory in 1875 to study the piano, harmony, and composition, and it was there that he first became obsessed with Wagner's music. He was dismissed for disciplinary reasons in 1877 and, after a short visit home, attempted to make a living in Vienna as a teacher. He was always subject to bouts of deep depression and melancholia, unable to compose for long periods, then suddenly overtaken by a hectic flood of inspiration. His efforts were encouraged by a number of established musicians (including the composer Adalbert von Goldschmidt and the conductor Felix Mottl), and he was befriended—and for much of his life materially supported—by various well-to-do families.

Though appointed second conductor at Salzburg under Karl Muck in 1881, Wolf proved temperamentally unsuited to the post and left after only a few months. From 1884 to 1887 he wrote criticism for the *Wiener Salonblatt*. His writings were often provocative, and his pro-Wagner, anti-Brahms stance hindered his advancement in Viennese circles, while Bruckner's self-confidence, never strong, was seriously damaged by his attacks. The late 1880s were a particularly productive period for his songwriting, but by 1897 his mental health had severely deteriorated (the outcome of an earlier syphilitic infection) and he was admitted to a sanatorium. He was discharged as cured in 1898, but later that year had to enter an asylum, where he spent the last few unhappy years of his life.

In a comparatively short career, Wolf made an individual and significant contribution to the lied repertory, in which he proved a natural successor to Schubert and Schumann. He rarely set any poem that they or other composers had set in a manner he considered satisfactory, unless he felt he had a new interpretation of his own. Furthermore, his verbal sensitivity led him to prefer the term 'Gedicht' ('poem') to 'Lied' in his songbooks, emphasizing his contribution as a musical realization of the poetry. In his settings of poems by Mörike, Eichendorff, and Goethe, written mainly in a feverish burst in the late 1880s, he allowed the verses to trigger the release of mental tensions, and established a highly personalized mode of musical expression, which often sets dramatic declamation in the voice against strikingly original harmonic ideas in the piano. There is in this a compression of Wagnerian music drama into a single voice and keyboard. In the *Spanisches Liederbuch* (1889–90) and the two volumes of the *Italienisches Liederbuch* (1890–1; 1896), translations in German by Heyse and Geibel of Spanish and Italian verse, he responded to the texts' directness of expression with deft, colourful musical characterizations.

In addition to his output of some 300 songs (more than a third remained unpublished in his lifetime), Wolf struggled doggedly with instrumental composition: a String Quartet in D minor (begun in 1878), the symphonic poem *Penthesilea* (1883–5), and the *Italienische Serenade* for string quartet (1887; arranged for orchestra in 1892) had some success. A desire to explore larger forms and his obsession with Wagner caused him to labour long with opera. The only one he completed, *Der Corregidor* (1895), on a Spanish theme, contains some beautiful numbers but lacks dramatic fluency. His hypersensitive disposition seemed to respond more naturally to the stimulus of short, concentrated song texts with their scope for a more personal, inward musical expression.

JN/JW

   📖 H. PLEASANTS (ed.), *The Music Criticism of Hugo Wolf* (New York, 1978) · E. SAMS, *The Songs of Hugo Wolf* (London, 2/1983) · S. YOUENS, *Hugo Wolf: The Vocal Music* (Princeton, NJ, 1992); *Hugo Wolf and his Mörike Songs* (Cambridge, 2000)

Wolff, Christian (*b* Nice, 8 March 1934). French-born American composer. He took American citizenship in 1947 and studied classics at Harvard University (1951–63), where he stayed on to teach classics until his appointment as professor of classics and music at Dartmouth College (from 1971). Though influenced by his association with John Cage in the early 1950s, he is self-taught as a composer. His earlier works have a certain static quality arising from pitch repetition that leads to a focus on sounds for their own sake rather than as part of a progression; latterly, however, he has been particularly concerned to encourage performers to contribute creatively in his music, allowing them to choose, improvise, and react to each other. Since 1968 he has also endeavoured to awaken sympathy for revolutionary

political ideals through his music, either by setting texts that express those ideals or by quoting from labour and protest songs. Some works of the 1990s include material borrowed from Renaissance chansons.   PG

Wolf-Ferrari, Ermanno (*b* Venice, 12 Jan. 1876; *d* Venice, 21 Jan. 1948). Italian composer. The son of a German father and an Italian mother, he had little formal tuition in music until 1892, when he went to Munich to study with Rheinberger. He returned to Venice, became a friend of the composer Lorenzo Perosi, and wrote religious music before having his first operatic success with *Le donne curiose* ('The Inquisitive Women'), given in Munich in 1903. He was then appointed director of the Liceo Musicale Benedetto Marcello in Venice and composed another two operas for Munich, the second of which—*Il segreto di Susanna* (1909), a witty conversation piece—has a continuing place in the repertory. He resigned his post in Venice in the same year, and composed a serious opera, *I gioielli della Madonna* (1911), in the verismo style of Mascagni, which was also successful.

During World War I a spiritual crisis caused Wolf-Ferrari to give up composition, but from 1925 he wrote several other comic operas. For some years from 1939 he was professor of composition at the Mozarteum in Salzburg. His operas have rarely achieved the success their wittiness seems to deserve: he was one of the first Italian composers to return to Goldoni and the *commedia dell'arte* for inspiration, and as such he was the precursor of Malipiero and the modernist Italian school.   DA/RP

Wölfl, Joseph (*b* Salzburg, 24 Dec. 1773; *d* London, 21 May 1812). Austrian pianist and composer. A chorister at Salzburg Cathedral, he was taught by Leopold Mozart and Michael Haydn. He moved to Vienna in 1790, purportedly to study with W. A. Mozart, though whether he actually became his pupil is not known. In 1792 he made his public debut as a pianist in Warsaw; after consolidating his reputation as a performer and improviser, he returned in 1795 to Vienna, where he soon came to be regarded as a serious rival to Beethoven. His playing was praised in the *Allgemeine musikalische Zeitung* for its combination of power with delicacy.

Wölfl also enjoyed popular success as a composer: first in Vienna, subsequently in Paris, and (from 1805) in London. The popularity of his music rested on its melodic fluency and technical brilliance, and on his uncanny ability to capture the tastes of the amateur market of his time. But by the late 1830s his music had been eclipsed by the younger generation of piano composers, and posterity has judged it as lacking substance and weight. Yet at his best, in such works as

his 'Non plus ultra' Sonata op. 41 and his G minor Symphony op. 40, he demonstrated a technical mastery that was rare among salon composers of his era.
                                                        WT/TRJ

wolf note. An unstable note found on some stringed instruments, usually at the main wood resonance frequency. The player may have difficulty in sustaining the tone but can lower the wolf note frequency by taping a coin, for example, to the body of the instrument.
                                                        JBo

Wolkenstein, Oswald von. See OSWALD VON WOLKENSTEIN.

Wolpe, Stefan (*b* Berlin, 25 Aug. 1902; *d* New York, 4 April 1972). German-born American composer. He studied at the Berlin Conservatory (1919–24) but was more influenced by informal lessons at that time with Busoni and with Hermann Scherchen. Also important was his association with Klee and others at the Bauhaus (1923). His works from the 1920s often show a vein of sharp political satire, but the arrival of Hitler in power forced a change of direction. Wolpe left for Vienna, where he had lessons with Webern (1933–4), then settled in Palestine. There he wrote specifically Jewish music, using Hebrew texts and certain Semitic musical characteristics. In 1938 he moved to the USA, where for three decades he was an influential teacher and where he devoted his creative attention principally to abstract pieces for instrumental combinations. Often having such austere titles as *Piece for Two Instrumental Units*, these works have novel forms which grow with unerring sureness, driven by the constant variation of keenly defined atonal motifs.   PG

women in music. Women have always been involved in music-making, though their contributions to the many different musical worlds in which they have worked have sometimes not been fully acknowledged. In spite of their absence from many traditional histories of music, there has never been a period in which women's voices have been entirely silent, and their vibrant contributions as instrumentalists, singers, composers, educationists, and patrons have been of great significance to the history of Western musical culture. Through the centuries women have faced a variety of opportunities and restrictions which have determined the ways in which they have been able to express themselves through music. Other factors, such as class or nationality, have affected their participation in musical worlds, but gender has played a crucial part in determining the roles they have chosen or been allowed to embrace.

An understanding of a society's general expectations of women's behaviour and capabilities is essential for understanding women's contributions to music and music-making. For example, most European societies and cultures (especially in the period before the late 19th century) have expected women (particularly those from the upper classes) to play no part in public life and to conform to behaviour that reflects an ideal femininity of passivity, prettiness, and instinctive emotion. The many women who did not conform, from Joan of Arc and Elizabeth I to Hildegard of Bingen and Ethel Smyth, only serve by their 'otherness' to reinforce that stereotyping. In the musical world these expectations have affected women's engagement with many different aspects of music and musical life, from the instruments and genres deemed appropriate for them to play, to the spaces regarded as suitable for their performances. Tracing women's music-making through the centuries reveals the fascinating stories and achievements of individual women as well as female networks and communities, which have often built significant female musical traditions.

There is plenty of pictorial and written evidence of women's participation in the music-making of the ancient world. In ancient Greece female professional musicians were usually slaves and prostitutes, such as the highly educated *hetairai* who often sang and accompanied themselves on the lyre. This association of music-making with the profession of courtesan (which continued into the Renaissance) was to have far-reaching implications for the respectability of female musicians, a theme that echoes throughout the centuries.

In the early Christian Church, women and men sang together during worship, but by the late 4th century, women were beginning to be excluded from the public life of the church. St Paul's proclamation 'Let your women keep silent in the churches' (1 Corinthians 14: 34) was to have a damaging effect on women's access to performance and education as the musical world of western Europe became increasingly centred on the church and its liturgy. Nevertheless there were women connected to the church who were involved in musical life. During the 1st millennium several women composed Byzantine Christian chant, including the witty and inventive Kassia (*b* c.810). Like many musical women during the medieval and Renaissance periods, Kassia worked from within a convent. These important female communities provided women with one of the few ways of obtaining an education. Music—sung, played, and often composed by the nuns—was an essential part of convent life. Most of these women have remained anonymous and much of their music has disappeared, but certain documents survive, such as Herrad of Landsberg's 12th-century *The Garden of Delights* (which included several of her own texts set to music), the Kloster Wienhausen Hymnbook from a 13th-century German convent, the Las Huelgas Codex, a collection including polyphonic music from the 14th-century convent of Las Huelgas in Spain, and a 15th-century hymnbook from Barking Abbey in England.

The best-known medieval nun is Hildegard of Bingen, abbess of a convent at Rupertsberg, near Bingen, in Germany. Unrestricted by the rigid education that her male contemporaries received, Hildegard created both words and music for a strikingly individual and powerful series of compositions. In the Renaissance many Italian convents were renowned for their musical performances, particularly the convent of S. Vito in Ferrara, where the music was organized by Raffaella Aleotti (*c*.1570–after 1646). Aleotti published vocal works, played the organ, and conducted the convent's vocal and instrumental ensemble. Although stringent restrictions were placed on music-making by nuns after the decrees of the Council of Trent in the 16th century, many convents continued to produce outstanding musicians, including Isabella Leonarda (1620–1704), whose numerous works include the earliest surviving set of instrumental pieces to be published by a woman.

Outside the convent, women were involved in secular music. During the Middle Ages, aristocratic women, such as the Comtessa de Dia and Marie de France, worked within the courtly *trobairitz* and trouvère tradition. Throughout Europe, women from the lower classes worked as minstrels, as can be seen by the specific words for female musicians in many different languages, from *jougleresse* (Provençal) to *gliewméden* (Middle English). Women's association with singing and song, the form of musical expression most closely and directly associated with the body, is long-standing and appropriate or perhaps inevitable in a culture that relates male creativity to the mind and female creativity to the body.

Professional women singers started appearing in Italian courts in the 16th century, most notably the famous *concerto delle dame* employed by Duke Alfonso d'Este of Ferrara. Several women who were noted as singers, for instance Barbara Strozzi and Francesca Caccini in the 17th century, also composed. With the development of opera in the early Baroque period, opportunities for women singers increased, though they faced competition for high-register roles from castratos. By the early 18th century, female opera singers were beginning to attract the adulation and critical attention that were to become associated with the life of the prima donna. The 19th-century diva, such as Adelina Patti, performed roles in which she usually ended up betrayed, abandoned, driven insane, or dead. She might be adored by thousands but was rarely credited with the capacity for musical intelligence. Nevertheless the power of her voice, displayed in the public arena, remained a potent symbol of women's might and determination.

In the 18th century, women were still excluded from the musical life of the church and from the musical education that the church provided. Most professional female musicians learnt music as the family trade, though there were sometimes other possibilities. The Venetian Ospedali, for example, were welfare foundations for girls, renowned in the 17th and 18th centuries for the musical education they provided (Galuppi, Hasse, and Vivaldi all worked as teachers in the Ospedali) and for the excellent musicians they produced, such as the violinist and composer Maddalena Lombardini Sirmen (1745–1815). In the 19th century, conservatories throughout Europe opened their doors to women—though usually restricting them to a narrower range of social classes than their male contemporaries—and this marked a crucial turning-point. Universities were slower to admit women: it was not until 1921 that they were able to receive music degrees from Oxford University.

Women from the middle and upper classes, since ancient times, had been taught certain musical skills as part of the feminine accomplishments that enhanced their prospects of marriage. Appropriate instruments included the guitar, harp or lute, and keyboard—those that did not distort a woman's face or body as she played. Public, professional performance for such women was unthinkable until the late 19th century, as demonstrated in the case of Ann Ford (1737–1824), whose father had her arrested rather than allow her to undertake a proposed series of subscription concerts in London in 1760.

Many women from the upper classes played significant roles in musical life as patrons. At the Renaissance court of Mantua, Isabella d'Este (1474–1539) was responsible for encouraging the development of the frottola, while Frederick the Great's sister Anna Amalia (1723–87) promoted the performance of earlier music in Berlin through her library of works by such composers as Palestrina and J. S. Bach. The Viennese composer Marianne von Martinez (1744–1812) was one of many women to establish an influential salon. Later patrons include Winnaretta Singer, Princesse de Polignac (1865–1954), who supported and promoted the work of Fauré, Poulenc, and Stravinsky, among many others.

In the Classical and early Romantic periods, women were particularly associated with the piano. Much piano music, in such genres as the accompanied sonata or the nocturne, was written for women amateurs to play at home. Other women developed careers as professional pianists, one of the best known being Clara Schumann, who had no doubts about her internationally acclaimed skills as a pianist but, like so many women, suffered from a debilitating lack of confidence in her abilities as a composer. The belief that women could recreate (through musical performance) but not create music of any lasting worth had been widespread for centuries, in spite of the impressive achievements of many women composers. For much of the history of Western classical music, women were expected to write music connected to those instruments and genres with which they were associated (particularly songs and piano pieces) and which reflected the stereotypical ideals of femininity—gentle, undemanding, and simple, directly emotional rather than complex and intellectual.

By the end of the 19th century there were increasing numbers of women devoting themselves to the career of composer, writing music in many genres and styles, from the heartfelt songs of Maude Valérie White (1855–1937) to the impressive orchestral music of Amy Beach and the powerful operas of Ethel Smyth. The music composed by women during the 20th century ranged widely, including the modernist works of Ruth Crawford Seeger, a striking series of 13 string quartets by Elizabeth Maconchy, the hauntingly spiritual orchestral and chamber music of Sofia Gubaidulina, and the radical sound worlds of Pauline Oliveros and Meredith Monk.

Throughout the centuries there are examples of women who rebelled against society's expectations. In 1568 the singer and composer Maddalena Casulana (c.1540–90) published her first collection of madrigals in order 'to show the world . . . the vain error of men that they alone possess intellectual gifts, and who appear to believe that the same gifts are not possible for women'. In the late 19th century the refusal to conform gathered pace throughout Europe and the USA, as women fought for the right to vote and for access to education and professional careers. Both amateur and professional women musicians took up the violin, previously regarded as a male instrument, in large numbers. These violinists, together with other female musicians who played even more traditionally unsuitable instruments from the wind and brass families, formed all-women bands and orchestras and fought for the right to play in the leading professional orchestras from which they were excluded. The battle lasted throughout the 20th century until in 1997 the Vienna Philharmonic, the last bastion of all-male orchestral playing, capitulated to outside pressure and granted membership to their female harpist.

Women play a vital role in the musical world of the early 21st century. There are still some musical professions, such as conductor or DJ, in which (in spite of a few noteworthy exceptions) women are conspicuous by their absence. But the pioneering work of earlier generations has created a culture in which women's diverse musical voices can be clearly heard.

See also FEMINIST MUSICOLOGY. SF

📖 J. BOWERS and J. TICK (eds.), *Women Making Music: The Western Art Tradition, 1150–1950* (London, 1986) · S. MCCLARY, *Feminine Endings: Music, Gender, and Sexuality* (Minneapolis, 1991) · C. NEULS-BATES (ed.), *Women in Music: An Anthology of Source Readings from the Middle Ages to the Present* (Boston, 2/1996) · J. HALSTEAD, *The Woman Composer: Creativity and the Gendered Politics of Musical Composition* (Aldershot, 1997) · K. PENDLE (ed.), *Women and Music: A History* (Bloomington, IN, 2/2000)

WoO. Abbreviation for *Werk ohne Opuszahl* (Ger.), 'work without opus number'. The term is especially common in references to Beethoven's music, since a number of his works were not published in his lifetime. See OPUS.

Wood, Charles (*b* Armagh, 15 June 1866; *d* Cambridge, 12 July 1926). Irish composer and teacher. He studied with Stanford at the RCM (1883–7), where in 1888 he was appointed to the teaching staff. After winning an organ scholarship to Selwyn College, Cambridge, he transferred to Gonville and Caius in 1889. At Cambridge he became a university lecturer (1897) and professor of music (1924). He was a founder member of the Irish Folk-Song Society in 1904. Wood produced a large quantity of church music including many services and some fine anthems, among them *O thou the central orb* (1915), *Hail gladdening light*, and *Expectans expectavi* (both 1919). He also composed a piano concerto (1885–6), orchestral works, songs, cantatas, incidental music, two one-act operas and eight string quartets of great craftsmanship. JDi

📖 I. COPLEY, *The Music of Charles Wood: A Critical Study* (London, 1978)

Wood, Haydn (*b* Slaithwaite, Yorks., 25 March 1882; *d* London, 11 March 1959). English composer and violinist. Raised in the Isle of Man, he was a child prodigy on the violin and studied composition with Stanford at the RCM. He wrote concertos for piano (1909) and violin (1932), theatre music, and some 200 ballads, among them *Love's Garden of Roses* (1914) and *Roses of Picardy* (1916). His fine light music in the style of Eric Coates includes *A Manx Rhapsody* (1931), the suites *Moods* (1933), *Paris Suite* (1935), and *London Landmarks* (1946), and *Sketch of a Dandy* (1952). ALa

Wood, Sir Henry J(oseph) (*b* London, 3 March 1869; *d* Hitchin, 19 Aug. 1944). English conductor. He was born into a musical family and studied at the RAM. His early leanings were towards the organ and composition, but he found conducting engagements with

opera companies and led the British premiere of *Eugene Onegin* in 1892. The manager of the newly opened Queen's Hall, Robert Newman, gave him the opportunity to conduct a summer season of *Promenade Concerts in 1895; their success earned them a firm place in the musical calendar. In addition, Wood conducted the Queen's Hall Orchestra in a regular series of symphony concerts.

From these beginnings he established a unique position in British musical life, conducting the Proms virtually unassisted for 50 years as well as other concerts in London, often totalling 140 a year. In addition he was a regular visitor to the main provincial centres and trained the RAM orchestra weekly. His industry and furtherance of the cause of music earned him a knighthood in 1911, the year he turned down the conductorship of the New York Philharmonic after Mahler's death.

At the Proms and elsewhere Wood introduced more than 700 works by British and foreign composers ranging from Tchaikovsky and Rimsky-Korsakov to Shostakovich and Britten: perhaps the most remarkable was the world premiere of Schoenberg's Five Orchestral Pieces in 1912. His insistence on discipline raised orchestral and choral standards, and his tireless advocacy created and sustained generations of new audiences. GH

📖 A. JACOBS, *Henry J. Wood, Maker of the Proms* (London, 1994)

Wood, Hugh (Bradshaw) (*b* Parbold, Lancs., 27 June 1932). English composer. After studying at Oxford, and privately with William Lloyd Webber, Anthony Milner, and Mátyás Seiber among others, he taught at the universities of Glasgow, Liverpool, and Cambridge (the last from 1977 until his retirement). He has consistently used 12-note methods to create the materials for continuous and purposeful development, and has remained close to traditional formal frameworks, drawing strength from the examples of Beethoven and Schoenberg in particular; his abundant lyricism and dancing rhythms, however, are distinctively English. His chief works include four string quartets (1962, 1970, 1978, 1993), concertos for cello (1969), violin (1972), and piano (1991), and a symphony (1982), as well as *Scenes from Comus* for soprano, tenor, and orchestra (1965) and several sets of songs. PG/AW

Wood, James (Peter) (*b* Barton-on-Sea, Hants., 27 May 1953). English composer. He first became well known as a percussionist, pioneering avant-garde techniques and developing new instruments, often with microtonal potential. He also founded and conducted the New London Chamber Choir, which specialized in medieval and contemporary music. Wood's compositions, which are often elaborately ritualistic in character, include the orchestral *Oreion (of Mountains . . .)* (1988–9) and *Two Men Meet, Each Presuming the Other to be from a Distant Planet* (1995) for percussion and 24 instruments.

AW

woodblock. A small wooden *slit drum shaped like a brick with a deep longitudinal slot cut below its thin upper surface. When struck with a drumstick it gives a sharp crack. Originally imported from East Asia to the USA by jazz musicians, and then adopted for the orchestra, woodblocks are not to be confused with *temple blocks.   JMo

Woodcock, Robert (*d* before 1734). English composer and recorder player. He was a celebrated performer whose 12 concertos, published in 1727, were the earliest English concertos for solo wind instruments; they were apparently popular works.   PL

Wood Dove, The (*Holoubek*). Symphonic poem, op. 110 (1896), by Dvořák.

Wooden Prince, The (*A fából faragott királyfi*). Ballet in one act by Bartók to a scenario by Béla Balázs, choreographed by Otto Zöbisch (Budapest, 1917). Bartók arranged an orchestral suite (?1921–4) from the score.

woodwind. A term applied to that section of the Western orchestra comprising flutes and reed instruments (oboes, clarinets, and bassoons). Although originally these instruments were commonly made of wood, many other materials are or have been used, including metal (flutes and saxophones), plastics (clarinets and recorders), bone, ivory, and glass. Such instruments, sounded by having air blown into them, are classified in *organology (along with *brass instruments and such bellows-blown instruments as the *organ, bagpipes, and *accordion) as *aerophones (see INSTRUMENTS, CLASSIFICATION OF).

Ensembles of woodwind instruments have been common since the Renaissance: the recorder consorts of the 16th century were revived in the 20th; fife-and-drum bands have been associated with the army and with boys' brigades; small wind bands (Harmonien) with various combinations of clarinets, oboes, bassoons, and horns provided court and household music in the 18th century; and the wind quintet of the four main woodwind instruments with horn has been popular since the early 20th century.   JMo

Woolrich, John (*b* Cirencester, 3 Jan. 1954). English composer. He studied at Manchester and Lancaster universities and has been active as a teacher and conductor. Although he has written several large-scale works, including the opera *The House of Crossed Desires* (Cheltenham, 1996) and concertos for viola (1993) and oboe (BBC Proms, 1996), his most characteristic works are for various chamber ensembles. *Lending Wings* (1989) for 16 players and *It is Midnight, Dr Schweitzer* (1992) for 11 strings are typical in their finely detailed textures and oblique but subtle characterization. Woolrich's music often alludes to other composers, from Monteverdi to Birtwistle, but in such a way that its individuality is enhanced.   AW

word-painting. Composers have always sought to match the expressive or physical aspects of texts in their music. Strictly speaking, 'word-painting' implies the focus on a single term—'love', 'death', 'joy', 'sorrow'—which stands out from a context that is musically depicted in much less specific, decorative fashion, as in many 16th-century madrigals (see MADRIGAL, 3). Yet such local aspects of illustration cannot be separated entirely from broader illustrative processes, and during the Renaissance and the Baroque period the sense in which music might imitate not only nature but also human thought and behaviour led to the establishment of certain patterns, like slow descending lines suggesting lament; these patterns were used so frequently as to verge on a common language not only for text-setting but for the purely instrumental evocation of certain emotional states.

Such devices and characteristics were promoted by various theoretical attempts to codify the expressive vocabulary available to composers. In this sense word-painting becomes part of broader ideas about music as a language, something not only capable of acting like verbal rhetoric, but also able to evoke specific topics of behaviour by generic reference—to varieties of song and dance, pastoral, march, and so on. References of this kind remained central to musical communication throughout the 18th and 19th centuries, despite the widespread belief that music's expressive force exceeded that of mere verbal representation. With the questioning of tonal conventions in the 20th century, traditional word-painting devices were less regularly invoked, although certain qualities—like the descending patterns of lament—have been found to function as effectively in post-tonal contexts (Ligeti) as in tonal ones.   AW

Wordsworth, William (Brocklesby) (*b* London, 17 Dec. 1908; *d* Kingussie, 10 March 1988). English composer. A descendant of the poet's brother, he studied counterpoint with George Oldroyd (1921–31) and composition with Tovey in Edinburgh (1934–6). The legacy of Tovey's Brahmsian background is evident in the organic processes and mostly diatonic idiom of his eight symphonies (written between 1944 and 1985) and his chamber music, which includes six string quartets (1941–

64), a piano trio (1949), a clarinet quintet (1952), and a quintet for oboe and piano quartet (1959).   PG/JD1

work song. A song performed usually by a group during and in time to the actions of work. A heavily rhythmic nature, an open form, and a call-and-response structure is found in countless examples, such as the 'waulking songs' that women formerly sang to accompany the rhythmic action of 'waulking' or fulling cloth in the Hebrides. In the English-speaking world, the work associated with sailing ships fostered the repertory of sea shanties (see SHANTY), and the similar survival of songs in isolation from their original context where traditional work practices have disappeared is not untypical; recordings made by Alan Lomax in southern Italy and Sicily in the 1950s preserve examples of song accompanying a host of activities such as pressing olives, threshing grain, sorting almonds, and harvesting sea salt.   KC

world music. Used initially by ethnomusicologists to refer to the diverse local musics of the world, 'world music' has also become a marketing term for 'any commercially available music of non-Western origin and circulation, as well as ... all musics of dominated ethnic minorities within the Western world' (Feld, 1994); it is also applied to contemporary fusions or collaborations with local 'traditional' or 'roots' musics and Western pop and rock musics. These different meanings lie along a continuum of hybridization with local, ethnic musics (themselves containing different influences) at one end and global musics at the other.

As originally used by ethnomusicologists, 'world' musics contested the notion that only Western art music was of value. The term was intended to give credence to the sounds of other peoples, whether those 'others' were distant in terms of geography (traditional musics of non-Western peoples), ethnicity, or class (the folk musics of Western peoples). Ethnomusicologists usually divide the world into cultural areas of musical styles and instruments, according to data gained from fieldwork. This classification is reflected in major reference publications. *The Garland Encyclopedia of World Music*, for instance, is published as separate volumes as follows: the musics of Africa; South America, Mexico, Central America, and the Caribbean; the USA and Canada; South-East Asia; South Asia: the Indian Subcontinent; the Middle East; East Asia: China, Japan and Korea; Europe; and Australia and the Pacific Islands. *The New Grove Dictionary of Music and Musicians* complements such cultural divisions by also including sections on 'traditional' musics within articles on countries. The delineation of traits and the boundaries of musical styles in both cultural and political areas are flexible, contested, and permeable. A

recent addition to the range of areas, for instance, is Inner Asia, where the musical practices and sounds of its traditionally nomadic peoples do not happily fit with those of East or Central Asia. Courses on 'world music' in institutions of higher education usually sample the musics of such cultural areas.

Ethnomusicologists and musicologists have actively recorded the world's musics, at first primarily for the purposes of transcription, since the invention of the phonograph by Edison in 1877. Deposited in museums and academic institutions, these funds of historical field recordings began to be released on a small scale in the mid-20th century and towards the end of that century became marketable as the ethnic-musics end of the 'world music' continuum. Topic, which claims to be the oldest independent record company in the world, began as the Workers' Music Association in 1939 to publish field recordings of British urban folksong under the influence of the political activists and performers Ewan MacColl and A. L. Lloyd; it later became well known for its International Series including the first recordings in the West of music from communist Albania. Under the directorship of Tony Engle, Topic now concentrates on British musics, with recent releases ranging from the 20-CD collection of British traditional music, *Voice of the People*, to folk fusions such as Eliza Carthy's *Red Rice* (1998), nominated for the Mercury prize.

The American Folkways label, founded in 1947 by Moses Asch and Marian Distler, went on to issue albums of diverse musics from, for instance, remote Amazonian villages as well as unaccompanied ballad singers and bluegrass and urban music forms (Seeger, 1994). The Archives Internationales de Musique Populaire in Geneva, founded in 1944 by the Romanian ethnomusicologist Constantin Brăiloiu, had released more than 80 78 rpm discs in three collections by the time Brăiloiu died in 1958, including the first series to be published with the cooperation of UNESCO: the *World Collection of Recorded Folk Music*. Since Laurent Aubert was appointed to revive the collection by the Ethnographic Museum in 1983, over 40 more CDs have been released, primarily of field recordings. In 1946 the Musée de l'Homme in Paris started to publish a series of ethnographic recordings under the direction of Gilbert Rouget; its first LP, produced in 1953, marked the start of the *Collection Musée de l'Homme* (Van Peer, 1999).

During the 1960s and 70s such record labels as the American Electra (Nonesuch) and the state-funded French Ocora began to issue musics of the world, and the interest in traditional musics and their offshoots began to expand. However, it was not until 1987 that the marketing tag 'world music' was devised and then launched by 11 independent British, European, and

American record labels specializing in music from Third World countries, including Globestyle, Earthworks (later amalgamated with Virgin), Charly, Sterns, Mango, Cooking Vinyl, Globestar, Oval Records, and Hannibal; the category quickly became established in Europe and the USA.

In its commercial sense, 'world music' refers to local musics that combine often indigenous musical characteristics with those of mainstream genres in the contemporary transnational music industry but, though distributed worldwide, are associated with minority groups and small or industrially developing countries. The now massive range includes many musics from Africa (e.g. Ghanaian highlife, Nigerian *juju*, Congolese *soukous*, Zimbabwean *jit* and *chimurenga*, Senegalese *mbalax*, South African *mbaquanga* and Soweto jive, Algerian *raï*), as well as others from around the world (e.g. *qawwali* from Pakistan, *zouk* from the Antilles, *soca* from Trinidad, *son* from Cuba, and *höömii*, 'overtone singing', from Mongolia and Tuva). 'World music' also now overlaps with the American concept of 'world beat' in that its meaning also encompasses the best-known commercial varieties of world musical styles and hybrid forms such as reggae, blues, Cajun, zydeco, *conjunto* or salsa, Anglo-Indian *bhangra*, and *ghazal*.

At the beginning of the 21st century, a complex amalgam of private record labels, national institutions, and international organizations exist that produce recordings of 'world music' and 'world musics', including recently available recordings that were made by state-owned recording companies in socialist countries. Ethnomusicologists, who now include such disciplines as cultural studies and popular music studies in their interdisciplinary connections, have also recognized the multiple meanings of the 'world music' concept, debating issues that include the appropriation and commodification of ethnic musics, cultural imperialism, the assimilation of foreign musical genres, sonic tourism, locality in music, power relations, and ethics.   CP

📖 S. FRITH (ed.), *World Music, Politics and Social Change* (Manchester and New York, 1989) · A. SEEGER, 'Folkways: America's music guardians', *World Music: The Rough Guide*, ed. S. Broughton, M. Ellingham, D. Muddyman, and R. Trillo (London, 1994), 595 · S. FELD, 'Notes on world beat' and 'From schizophonia to schismogenesis: On the discourses and commodification practices of "world music" and "world beat"', *Music Grooves* (Chicago, 1994), 238–46, 257–89 · T. MITCHELL, 'World music', *Popular Music and Local Identity* (London and New York, 1996), 49–94 · T. D. TAYLOR, *Global Pop: World Music, World Markets* (London and New York, 1997)
S. BROUGHTON, 'Label traveller: Topic', *Songlines*, 1 (1999), 100 · S. BROUGHTON, M. ELLINGHAM, and R. TRILLO (eds.), *World Music: The Rough Guide*, i: *Africa, Europe and the Middle East* (London, 1999) · R. VAN PEER, 'Taking the world for a spin in Europe: An insider's look at the world music recording business', *Ethnomusicology*, 43/2 (1999), 374–85 · S. BROUGHTON and M. ELLINGHAM (eds.), *World Music: The Rough Guide*, ii: *Latin and North America, Caribbean, India, Asia and Pacific* (London, 2000)

World Wide Web, music on the. See MUSIC ON THE INTERNET.

Worshipful Company of Musicians. English music society based in London. It developed from the 15th-century London Fellowship of Minstrels, and now encourages many aspects of music-making, chiefly by awarding prizes, scholarships, and medals, including the Collard Fellowship for composers (established 1931), the Cobbett phantasy prize, the Cobbett chamber music medal, the Santley medal for singers, and various other prizes and medals at the schools and colleges of music. A new charter was drawn up in 1950.

Wotquenne. Abbreviation for the standard *thematic catalogue of the works of C. P. E. Bach drawn up by the Belgian bibliographer Alfred Wotquenne (1867–1939) and published in Leipzig in 1905. Bach's works are often referred to by Wotquenne number, usually further abbreviated to 'wq'.

Wozzeck. Opera in three acts by Berg to his own libretto after Georg Büchner's play *Woyzeck* (1836) (Berlin, 1925).

WQ. Abbreviation for *Wotquenne, used as a prefix to the numbers of C. P. E. Bach's works as given in the standard *thematic catalogue of Alfred Wotquenne.

Wranitzky, Paul [Vranický, Pavel] (*b* Nová Říše, Moravia, 30 Dec. 1756; *d* Vienna, 26 Sept. 1808). Czech composer, conductor, and violinist. Like his younger brother, Anton Wranitzky (1761–1820), he was educated locally. A fine violinist, he went to Vienna at the age of 20 and studied composition with J. M. Kraus. He worked for Count J. B. Esterházy and in 1778 became a member of the Burgtheater orchestra. Wranitzky supervised many court opera productions and was much admired by both Haydn and Beethoven as a conductor. His many symphonies and quartets were popular in their day and possessed of a marked originality occasionally anticipating early Romanticism.   JSM

Wreckers, The (*Les Naufrageurs*; *Strandrecht*). Opera in three acts by Smyth to a libretto in French by the composer and Henry Brewster (Leipzig, 1906).

wrest pins [tuning-pins] (Fr.: *chevilles*; Ger.: *Stimmwirbeln*). The metal tuning-pegs of a piano, harpsichord, harp, etc. In modern instruments they are made of hard steel and have a hole through which the end of the string passes before being wound round the pin. They have square heads and are turned with a tuning-key to increase or decrease tension on the strings, thus raising or lowering the pitch. The ends are driven into the *wrest plank or, in the case of the harp, through the neck of the instrument.   LC

wrest plank [pin block] (Fr.: *sommier*; Ger.: *Stimmstock*). The piece of wood into which the wrest pins of a piano, harpsichord, etc. are inserted. In modern pianos the wrest plank is supported by a cast-iron frame to bear the enormous tension of the strings (*c*.75 kg).   LC

Wunderhorn, Des Knaben. See DES KNABEN WUNDERHORN.

Wunderlich, Fritz (*b* Kusel, 26 Sept. 1930; *d* Heidelberg, 17 Sept. 1966). German tenor. He studied in Freiburg with Margarethe von Winterfeldt and then at the Musikhochschule. His debut was as Tamino in *Die Zauberflöte* (1954). The next year he was engaged by Stuttgart Opera (1955–8), then joined the Frankfurt Opera (1958–60). In 1961 he was internationally acclaimed when he sang Henry in *Die schweigsame Frau* at the Salzburg Festival. He was in demand worldwide, particularly for his Mozart singing and increasingly for his lieder performances. His Covent Garden debut was in 1965. Only two weeks before his death (from a fall) he sang Schumann's *Dichterliebe* at the Edinburgh Festival, his supple and expressive voice conveying intimacy and dramatic emotion (there is an archive recording).   JT

Wuorinen, Charles (Peter) (*b* New York, 9 June 1938). American composer. He studied with Otto Luening, Jack Beeson, and Vladimir Ussachevsky at Columbia University, where he stayed on as a teacher (1964–71) before moving to the Manhattan School (1971–9) and Rutgers University (from 1984). His performing activity, as pianist and conductor, began in 1962, when he co-founded the Group for Contemporary Music in New York. Early in his career he was influenced by Babbitt's serialism, and a certain fastidiousness has remained a characteristic, though his music since the 1970s has been broader and richer in its references. Often his music is dynamic, with a Baroque clarity of pulse, and he has worked as a composer and arranger for New York City Ballet. His large output also includes a variety of symphonies, concertos (three for piano) and other orchestral pieces (including *Reliquary for Igor Stravinsky*, 1975, based on the composer's last sketches), choral music, piano and chamber music, and a notable electronic composition (*Time's Encomium*, 1969). His book *Simple Composition* (New York, 1979) is widely used.   PG

Wurlitzer. American firm of instrument makers founded in Cincinnati in 1853 by Franz Rudolph Wurlitzer (1831–1914). His brother and three sons joined the business, which moved to Chicago. It produced automated instruments and coin-operated phonographs, or jukeboxes, but is best known for the 'Mighty Wurlitzer' theatre organ, introduced in 1910, and for electronic keyboard instruments for domestic use.   AL

📖 J. W. LANDON, *Behold the Mighty Wurlitzer: The History of the Theatre Pipe Organ* (Westport, CT, 1983)

wütend (Ger.). 'Raging', 'furious'; also *wütig*.

Wylkinson, Robert (*fl* late 15th and early 16th centuries). English composer. He worked at Eton College, first as parish clerk and later as Master of the Choristers, from 1496 to 1515. His music, which survives in the Eton Choirbook, includes a monumental nine-part *Salve regina* and a curious setting of the Apostles' Creed in the form of a 13-part canon.   JM

xácara (Sp., Port.). See JÁCARA.

Xenakis, Iannis (*b* Brăila, Romania, 29 May 1922; *d* Paris, 4 Feb. 2001). Romanian-born French composer. Born to Greek parents, he moved with his family to Greece in 1932, was schooled on Spetsai (where he was introduced to Western Classical music), and studied engineering at Athens Polytechnic. He was active in the anti-fascist resistance at the polytechnic, was wounded in 1945, and escaped to Paris in 1947. Largely self-taught in music thus far, he came to the attention of Messiaen, with whom he studied in 1950–1; Hermann Scherchen also gave him help. Meanwhile he earned his living as an assistant to Le Corbusier (1948–59), with whom he worked on various architectural projects, including the Philips pavilion at the 1958 Brussels Exposition. By this time, however, he was beginning to make a reputation as a composer, and he came to concentrate on music.

Xenakis's first published work, *Metastaseis* for orchestra (1953–4), embodies a connection between mathematics and music that remained typical. The piece is a projection of geometrical notions, achieved by glissandos (as analogues of straight lines) played by a large body of strings. By so treating each player as a soloist, Xenakis achieved extraordinary new effects that were soon taken up by other composers. But what most concerned him was the possibility of composition by calculation. His interest in handling large numbers of musical events led him to the mathematics of probability, and so to *stochastic music, which he practised in subsequent compositions for orchestra, ensemble, or tape, using computers in some to facilitate the arithmetic. So far from being dry constructs, these compositions are often dynamic and passionate, taking up the composer's wartime battles for liberty, and sometimes suggesting his wartime experiences of crowd demonstrations and gunfire. Examples include *Orient Occident* for tape (1960), *Nuits* for small chorus (1967), and *Kraanerg* for orchestra (1968–9), as well as several scores evocative of ancient Greek ritual and drama (*Persephassa* for six percussionists, 1969), while in solo pieces (*Herma* for piano, 1960–1) the extreme density requires prodigious virtuosity. In still other works, such as *Polytope de Cluny* (1972), electronic sounds are combined with laser projections.

From the mid-1970s Xenakis was extraordinarily prolific, especially of orchestral music, and kept up the almost savage excitement of his first works. At the same time, however, he discovered a simplicity reminiscent of folk music. Important later works include *Akanthos* for soprano and mixed octet (1977), *Jonchaies* for orchestra (1977), *Pléïades* for six percussionists (1978), *Nekuïa* for chorus and orchestra (1981), *Jalons* for 15 players (1986), and *Tetora* for string quartet (1990). PG

📖 I. XENAKIS, *Formalized Music* (Bloomington, IN, and London, 1971) · N. MATOSSIAN, *Iannis Xenakis* (London, 1986) · B. A. VARGA, *Conversations with Iannis Xenakis* (London, 1996)

Xerxes. See SERSE.

xylophone. A series of wooden bars with a tubular resonator under each bar. On the modern orchestral instrument the bars, played with hard mallets, are arranged like a piano keyboard and are thicker than those of the orchestral *marimba, with a more clipped sound and a higher compass. Earlier European instruments, from the 16th century onwards, had bars laid on hanks of straw (whence Ger. *Strohfiedel*, 'straw fiddle'), arranged in four rows with some notes duplicated like a wooden *cimbalom. They were widely used in eastern Europe. The 'piano' layout with resonators was established in the USA in the early 20th century as a development of the Central and South American instruments, which derived in turn from African calabash- or gourd-resonated xylophones. Xylophones are also widely used in South-East Asia, Melanesia, and parts of Polynesia.

The simplest instruments are bars of wood laid across the player's legs or over a resonance pit. In East Africa bars are laid over banana stems (possibly the origin of the European straw layout) and played by three or more people. In West, Central, and southern Africa wooden frames with a gourd or other resonator for each bar are more usual. All these forms also appear in South-East Asia, where the trough xylophone, a single resonator under all the bars, is also common, a model adopted by Orff for his *Schulwerk*. JMo

Yamaha Corporation. Japanese firm of instrument makers founded as Nippon Gakki in Hamamatsu in 1887 by Torakusu Yamaha (1851–1916). It produces pianos, brass and woodwind instruments, and over 100 kinds of electronic instrument including synthesizers and digital electric pianos. AL

Yankee Doodle. Popular American song dating from the late 18th century; its words and tune are of confused origin. Anton Rubinstein wrote piano variations on it, Vieuxtemps's *Caprice burlesque* for violin and piano is based on it, and it appears in the last movement of Dvořák's Symphony no. 9, 'From the New World'.

Yanov-Yanovsky, Dmitry (*b* Tashkent, 24 April 1963). Uzbek composer, son of Feliks Yanov-Yanovsky. He studied composition with his father at the Tashkent Conservatory. Through the support of Denisov (whom he met in Russia) his music began to receive performances abroad. His works, some of which have been championed by the Kronos Quartet, include *Lacrymosa* for soprano and string quartet (1991), *Conjunctions* for string quartet, orchestra, and tape (1995), *Takyr* for six Uzbek percussion instruments and strings (1995), *Hommage à Gustav Mahler* for soprano and string quartet (1996), *Chang-Music I–V* for the *chang* (a traditional box zither) with various ensembles, and other instrumental and vocal compositions. JK

Yanov-Yanovsky, Feliks (*b* Tashkent, 28 May 1934). Uzbek composer. He studied the violin and composition at the Tashkent Conservatory and joined the Uzbek State Symphony Orchestra as a violinist in 1954, later becoming a member of the Uzbek Radio String Quartet. From 1961 he taught at the Tashkent Conservatory, eventually being appointed professor of composition. His works, which embody an attempt to forge links between the once isolated Uzbek traditions and those of western Europe, include two operas and much incidental music, four symphonies, solo and orchestral concertos, chamber music for strings and for brass, a large quantity of film music, and pieces for Uzbek traditional instruments. JK

Yan Tan Tethera. 'Mechanical pastoral' in one act by Birtwistle to a libretto by Tony Harrison (London, 1986).

Yardumian, Richard (*b* Philadelphia, 5 April 1917; *d* Bryn Athyn, PA, 1985). American composer. Not until he was 22 did he begin formal musical studies; as a composer he was self-taught. While working as a piano teacher and church music director in Pennsylvania he composed a number of large-scale works in a Romantic style influenced by the modes of Armenian music. Among these are two symphonies (1961, 1964), concertos for violin (1949) and piano (1957), the *Mass 'Come, Creator Spirit'* for chorus and orchestra (1966), and the oratorio *The Story of Abraham* (1969–71). PG

Yeomen of the Guard, The (*The Yeomen of the Guard, or The Merryman and his Maid*). Operetta in two acts by Sullivan to a libretto by W. S. Gilbert (London, 1888).

yodel (Ger.: *Jodel*). A type of singing characterized by frequent alternation between low and high (including falsetto) registers, using vowel sounds rather than words. It is associated particularly with the Alpine areas of Austria and Switzerland, where solo and ensemble compositions are performed by virtuosos. Yodelling is also used in some African musical traditions and by some American *country music singers.

A song introducing the effect is sometimes known as a 'Tyrolienne'; there is an example in Rossini's opera *Guillaume Tell* (1829). —/JBe

Yolanta. See IOLANTA.

Young, La Monte (Thornton) (*b* Bern, ID, 14 Oct. 1935). American composer. He studied at the University of California (1957–60), with Stockhausen at Darmstadt (1959), and with Richard Maxfield at the New School in New York (1960–1), where he made his home. His early works, such as the String Trio of 1958, exploit sounds held for a very long time, and he has continued to concern himself with sustained, slowly evolving tones. In 1960–1 he produced a number of text compositions in association with the Fluxus group, the emphasis again being on long sounds: one requires a bare 5th to be played on the piano and held to the point of silence. Later in the 1960s he took lessons in Indian singing and began a lifelong concern with new tunings. His immense *The Well-Tuned Piano* (1964) was one outcome, but most of his work has consisted of improvisations and electronic installations, generally lasting many hours, even days, and often accompanied by lighting designed by his wife, Marian Zazeela. PG

📖 R. KOSTELANETZ, *The Theatre of Mixed Means* (New York, 1967) · LA M. YOUNG, *Selected Writings* (Munich, 1970) · M. NYMAN, *Experimental Music* (London, 1974, 2/1999) · K. POTTER, *Four Musical Minimalists: La Monte Young, Terry Riley, Steve Reich, Philip Glass* (Cambridge, 2000)

Young, William (*d* Innsbruck, 23 April 1662). English viol player and composer. Nothing is known of his early life in England. During the Commonwealth he emigrated, and by 1642 was in the service of Ferdinand Karl, Governor of the Netherlands (later Archduke of Innsbruck), accompanying him on a tour of northern Italy. By the mid-1650s, when he played for the recently abdicated Christina of Sweden at Innsbruck, he was reckoned one of the best viol players in Europe. He wrote works for viol played 'lyra-way' (see LYRA VIOL), and at Innsbruck developed an eight-string viol to be played in that fashion. The set of 11 pieces he published in 1653 are the first English works to bear the title 'sonatas'. WT/JM

Young Person's Guide to the Orchestra, The. Orchestral work, op. 34 (1946), by Britten, written for a documentary film *The Instruments of the Orchestra*; subtitled 'Variations and Fugue on a Theme of Henry Purcell', it illustrates the uses and characteristics of the instruments and sections of the orchestra in a set of variations on a theme from Purcell's incidental music to the play *Abdelazer* (1695), culminating in a fugue. It is sometimes performed with a narrator who speaks the original text, by Eric Crozier.

Yradier, Sebastián. See IRADIER, SEBASTIÁN.

Ysaÿe, Eugène (*b* Liège, 16 July 1858; *d* Brussels, 12 May 1931). Belgian violinist, conductor, and composer. He began violin lessons at the age of four with his father, and went on to study in Liège, with Henryk Wieniawski in Brussels, and with Henri Vieuxtemps in Paris. There he became acquainted with and championed most of France's leading composers including Fauré, Saint-Saëns, Franck, and Debussy. He toured Europe and the USA extensively and was a professor at the Brussels Conservatory. As a conductor he founded the Concerts Ysaÿe and spent four years with the Cincinnati Orchestra. He wrote an opera and much for the violin. A whole generation of violinists revered Ysaÿe for his superb technique and pioneering role in modernizing 20th-century violin playing. CF

Yugoslavia. See CROATIA; SERBIA; SLOVENIA.

Yun, Isang (*b* Tongyong, 17 Sept. 1917; *d* Berlin, 3 Nov. 1997). Korean-born German composer. He studied in Japan, taught at Seoul University from 1953, studied in Paris, Berlin, and Darmstadt from 1956 to 1959, then worked in Germany. His failure to return voluntarily to South Korea in 1967 led to his being kidnapped and imprisoned in Seoul as a Communist traitor. On his release in 1969 he moved back to Germany, taking German nationality in 1971; he taught in Berlin until 1985. Yun's music, which includes four operas, five symphonies, and much chamber music, was strongly influenced by Korean instrumental and vocal techniques, and by Eastern philosophy. ABur

Z

Zabaleta, Nicanor (*b* San Sebastián, 7 Jan. 1907; *d* San Juan, Puerto Rico, 31 March 1993). Basque harpist. After studying in Madrid and Paris he embarked on a career which aimed at promoting a wide-ranging repertory and earning a place for the solo instrument in the concert hall. His own preferences and technique favoured music from the 18th century, but a long list of 20th-century composers including Krenek, Ginastera, Milhaud, Thomson, and Villa-Lobos wrote works for him. He introduced an extra damping pedal to the instrument. His playing was noted for its clarity and brilliance. CF

Zacconi, Lodovico (*b* Pesaro, 11 June 1555; *d* Fiorenzuola di Focara, nr Pesaro, 23 March 1627). Italian theorist. In 1575 he was ordained priest in Pesaro and from 1577 to 1583 he pursued literary studies in Venice, where he also had instruction in counterpoint from Andrea Gabrieli. He became a singer in the Austrian Archduke Karl's chapel in Graz (1584–90) and in the Bavarian ducal chapel in Munich, under Lassus (1590–6). His most important theoretical work was the *Prattica di musica*, published in two parts (1592, 1622), a comprehensive treatise which is valuable for the study of performance practice but which contains inaccuracies about earlier theorists' work; the first part deals with notation, embellishments, mood, time and prolation, proportions, and modes, the second with improvised counterpoint. WT/AL

Zachow, Friedrich Wilhelm (*b* Leipzig, *bapt.* 14 Nov. 1663; *d* Halle, 7 Aug. 1712). German organist and composer. He learnt to play the organ at Leipzig, and from 1684 until his death was organist and musical director at the Marienkirche in Halle, where he taught Handel. About 32 of his church cantatas have survived. He excelled in chorale variations and in the so-called reform cantata, of which *Das ist das ewige Leben* is a fine example, anticipating the structure and content of many Bach cantatas. WT

Zadok the Priest. Anthem by Handel, the first of four he composed for the coronation of George II in 1727; it has been performed at every English coronation since.

Zádor, Jenő [Zador, Eugene] (*b* Bátaszék, 5 Nov. 1894; *d* Hollywood, CA, 4 April 1977). Hungarian-born American composer. He studied at the Vienna Music Academy and in Leipzig with Reger. He taught from 1921 at the new Vienna City Conservatory and later at the Budapest Academy of Music. On the outbreak of World War II he emigrated to the USA, where he became a successful composer of film scores for Hollywood. He also wrote a number of operas in which the characterization and orchestration are worthy of note, and orchestral pieces in a style that owed something to Reger and Strauss, including the popular *Hungarian Caprice* (1935) and concertos for such instruments as the cimbalom (1969) and accordion (1971). WT

Zahlzeit (Ger.). 'Beat' (in the sense of 'beats in a bar'); see BEAT, I.

Zaide. Opera in two acts by Mozart to a libretto by Johann Andreas Schachtner after Franz Josef Sebastiani's *Das Serail*; it was composed in 1779–80, but was left untitled and unfinished, lacking an overture and finale. It was completed by Johann Anton André and first performed in Frankfurt in 1866 on Mozart's birthday.

Zampa (*Zampa, ou La Fiancée de marbre*; 'Zampa, or The Marble Fiancée'). Opera in three acts by Hérold to a libretto by Mélesville (Anne-Honoré-Joseph Duveyrier) (Paris, 1831).

zampogna. An Italian *bagpipe.

Zandonai, Riccardo (*b* Sacco, Trento, 28 May 1883; *d* Pesaro, 12 June 1944). Italian composer. He studied with Mascagni at the Pesaro Liceo Musicale, of which he was director for the last five years of his life. Regarded as a possible successor to Puccini, he combined a gift for lyrical melody with a love of colourful pageantry; *Francesca da Rimini* (Turin, 1914) was the most successful of his operas. His other works include several orchestral pieces, choral music, and songs. PG

Zarlino, Gioseffo (*b* Chioggia, ? 31 Jan. 1517; *d* Venice, 4 Feb. 1590). Italian theorist. He was educated among the Franciscans and eventually joined their order. After completing his novitiate he moved to Venice in 1541, where he devoted himself to music, studying with Willaert. He became *maestro di cappella* at St Mark's in 1565 and remained in that post until his death. The leading theorist of his time, he is best known for his treatise *Le istitutioni harmoniche* (Venice, 1558/*R*1965), in which he tried to elucidate Greek music theories as well as teach such practical matters as counterpoint. Among his most influential ideas were the concept of *word-painting as used in later madrigals, the different emotional qualities of major and minor chords, and the suggestion of dividing the scale into equal intervals, as later developed into *equal temperament. His pupils included the theorists G. M. Artusi and Vincenzo Galilei and the composers Giovanni Croce and Claudio Merulo.   DA/LC

zart (Ger.) 'Tender', 'delicate'; *zärtlich*, 'tenderly'.

Zar und Zimmermann (*Czaar und Zimmermann, oder Die zwei [beiden] Peter*, 'Tsar and Carpenter, or The Two Peters'). Opera in three acts by Lortzing to his own libretto after Georg Christian Römer's comedy *Der Bürgermeister von Saardam, oder Die zwei Peter*, itself based on Mélesville (Anne-Honoré-Joseph Duveyrier), E. Cantiran de Boirie and J. T. Merle's play *Le Bourgmestre de Sardam, ou Les Deux Pierres* (1818) (Leipzig, 1837).

zarzuela. Traditional Spanish opera. For over 300 years the term has been applied indiscriminately to Baroque semi-operas, three-act Romantic operas, short comic pieces, full-blown Viennese-style operettas, and musicals, written in Spain, Cuba, and elsewhere in the Spanish-speaking world. In most cases, spoken dialogue is an indispensable feature. There is no agreement about how zarzuela began, though certainly *El laurel de Apolo*, performed at the El Pardo Palace in 1657, with text by Pedro Calderón de la Barca and music by Juan *Hidalgo, set the fashion for court entertainments called 'zarzuela'. The name probably came from the royal hunting-lodge, situated nearby in remote countryside thick with brambles (*zarzas*). The courtly Baroque zarzuela, a mixture of sophisticated verse drama, allegorical opera, popular song, and dance, remained in fashion for over 100 years until it was finally displaced by Italian opera—though as late as 1786 Boccherini wrote a zarzuela, *Clementina*, to a high-quality comic text by Ramón de la Cruz.

The zarzuela reappeared after 1850 in Madrid with the rise of Spanish nationalism. Francisco Asenjo *Barbieri, aiming to create a distinctively national operatic style, fused the traditional *tonadilla* and the old, aristocratic drama into a new form evolved from Italian comic opera. His rival Emilio Arrieta, in such zarzuelas as *Marina* (1855), stayed closer to 'pure' Romantic Italian models, and their intense rivalry made zarzuela extremely popular. Soon *género grande* ('large style' zarzuelas in three acts) gave way to *género chico* ('small style', one-act farces, often with social or political satire and containing less music), though the best composers—Tomás *Bretón and Ruperto *Chapí, for example—moved easily between the two genres. The height of the *género chico* craze came with Federico *Chueca's successes in the 1880s and 90s, and it has been estimated that over 10,000 zarzuelas were written in the hundred years after 1850. The Teatro de la Zarzuela in Madrid became the hub of activity, but scores of companies in the capital, the provinces, and Spanish-speaking Central and South America were busily performing zarzuela in repertory.

In the 20th century the zarzuela evolved with popular taste, though the mixture of spoken play and operatic music in roughly equal proportions remained. Operetta-zarzuelas, most notably by Pablo Luna and Amadeo *Vives, coexisted with revue-style farces such as Francisco Alonso's *Las leandras* (1931) and sentimental verismo dramas such as José Serrano's *La dolorosa* (1930). In the 1930s Pablo *Sorozábal attempted to restore the satirical thrust of the 1890s, but after the Spanish Civil War the distinctive quality of zarzuela was lost in imitations of the Broadway musical. Since 1960 no new works have entered the repertory, but the popularity of the classic zarzuelas continues.   CW

Zauberflöte, Die ('The Magic Flute'). Opera in two acts by Mozart to a libretto by Emanuel Schikaneder (Vienna, 1791).

Zeitmass (Ger.). 'Tempo'; *im ersten Zeitmass*, 'in tempo primo'.

Zeitmasze. Work (1955–6) by Stockhausen for flute, oboe, cor anglais, clarinet, and bassoon; it simultaneously combines different tempos.

Zelenka, Jan (Lukás Ignatius) **Dismas** (*b* Lounovice, Bohemia, 16 Oct. 1679; *d* Dresden, 22 Dec. 1745). Czech composer. In 1710 he moved to Dresden and became a violone player in the royal chapel. He had lessons with Fux in Venice (where he may also have studied with Lotti), then returned to the Dresden royal chapel, where he stayed for the rest of his life. His output includes about 20 masses and mass fragments, responsories, two *Magnificat* settings, psalms, and three oratorios. His highly original instrumental music includes six chamber sonatas, five orchestral capriccios, and a chamber concerto. He also wrote an opera in Latin. His considerable stature was recognized only towards the end of the 20th century.   WT

📖 J. B. Stockigt, *Jan Dismas Zelenka (1679–1745): A Bohemian Musician at the Court of Dresden* (Oxford and New York, 2000)

Zeller, Carl (Johann Adam) (*b* St Peter in der Au, 19 June 1842; *d* Baden, nr Vienna, 17 Aug. 1898). Austrian composer. After being a member of what is now known as the Vienna Boys' Choir, he studied law and became a senior official in the Austrian Ministry of Education. He was taught music by Bruckner's teacher, Simon Sechter, and was an excellent pianist. His light opera *Der Vogelhändler* (Vienna, 1891), one of his half-dozen operettas in the tradition of Suppé and Offenbach, is a tuneful work still given in Germany.　　　DA

Zelter, Carl Friedrich (*b* Berlin, 11 Dec. 1758; *d* Berlin, 15 May 1832). German composer and teacher. He joined the Berlin Singakademie in 1791 and took over its direction in 1800, remaining in charge for 30 years. In 1806 he also established the Ripienschule, the forerunner of the Berlin Philharmonic Orchestra. His promotion of Bach's music led to the 1829 centenary performance of a version of the *St Matthew Passion* under his most distinguished pupil, Mendelssohn, which did much to set the *Bach Revival in motion. In 1809 Zelter became professor at the newly established University of Berlin and also founded the Liedertafel, the first of a number of societies that encouraged the performance of male-voice choral music. He was a friend of Goethe, many of whose poems he set in a pleasant and sensitive manner largely subservient to the verse, though some of his best songs anticipate later Romantic developments.　　　DA/JW

Zémire et Azor ('Zémire and Azor'). Opera in four acts by Grétry to a libretto by Jean François Marmontel (Fontainebleau, 1771). Spohr wrote an opera, *Zemire und Azor*, to a libretto by Johann Jakob Ihlée after Marmontel's libretto (1819).

Zemlinsky, Alexander (von) (*b* Vienna, 14 Oct. 1871; *d* Larchmont, NY, 15 March 1942). Austrian composer and conductor. He studied at the Vienna Conservatory with Anton Door (1887–90) and J. N. Fuchs (1890–2). Some of his early chamber music, notably the Clarinet Trio (1895), brought him to the attention of Brahms, who recommended him to his publisher, Simrock. It was however Wagner and, more important, Mahler who became the most significant influences on his work. In 1895 he met Schoenberg, to whom he taught counterpoint and with whom he formed a lifelong friendship; Schoenberg later married Zemlinsky's sister Mathilde. The two composers founded the Vereinigung Schaffender Tonsetzer (Association of Creative Composers) in 1904 to promote new music, and Zemlinsky remained a fierce champion of the Second Viennese School, though he was unwilling to follow Schoenberg into atonality, preferring to pursue an extreme tonal chromaticism on post-Mahlerian lines.

Zemlinsky's opera *Es war einmal ...* ('Once upon a time ...') was accepted by Mahler for performance at the Vienna Court Opera in 1900, though Mahler subsequently rejected the ballet *Das gläserne Herz* ('The Glass Heart', 1901), written to a scenario by Hugo von Hofmannsthal (*Der Triumph der Zeit*) which Strauss had turned down.

A fascination with Symbolist literature and with the symbolic and psychological potential of fairy tale is strongly apparent in Zemlinsky's work, which combines eloquent nostalgia with sensual extremism. The tone-poem *Die Seejungfrau* ('The Mermaid', 1902–3), based on Hans Andersen, is widely interpreted as conveying the pain of his rejection by Alma Schindler, who subsequently married Mahler. Zemlinsky's most widely performed operas, *Eine florentinische Tragödie* (1917) and *Der Zwerg* ('The Dwarf', 1922; sometimes performed under the title 'The Birthday of the Infanta'), are both based on Oscar Wilde. The *Lyric Symphony* (1922–3), setting poems by Rabindranath Tagore, has been seen as a response to Mahler's *Das Lied von der Erde*, though its emphasis on mystical eroticism removes it far in tone from Mahler's study of human transience.

Zemlinsky's career as a conductor began with his appointment as Kapellmeister at the Vienna Carltheater in 1899. In 1904 he made his debut at the newly formed Volksoper, becoming music director (1906–11). In 1911 he was appointed opera conductor at the German Theatre in Prague, a post he held until 1927. He courted controversy by his championship of contemporary music, giving the world premiere of Schoenberg's *Erwartung* and the first performances in Prague of Krenek's *Jonny spielt auf* and Berg's *Wozzeck* (Berg's *Lyric Suite* contains a quote from Zemlinsky's *Lyric Symphony*). In 1927 Zemlinsky moved to Berlin, where he taught at the Musikhochschule and became Klemperer's assistant at the Kroll Opera. He conducted the Berlin premiere of Weill's *Aufstieg und Fall der Stadt Mahagonny* in 1931. In 1933 he left Nazi Germany for Vienna, then settled in the USA in 1938. His last opera, *Der König Kandaules*, left unfinished at his death, was posthumously completed by the musicologist Antony Beaumont.　　　TA

　📖 A. CLAYTON, *The Operas of Alexander Zemlinsky* (Ph.D. dissertation, University of Cambridge, 1983) · H. KRONES (ed.), *Alexander Zemlinsky: Ästhetik, Stil und Umfeld* (Vienna, 1995)

zheng. Chinese long zither with 12–16 strings, originally of silk but now usually of steel, each suspended on its own bridge. The player plucks the strings with the fingernails (real or false) of the right hand, while the fingers of the left hand manipulate the strings to obtain such effects as pitch bending and embellishments. The Korean *kayagŭm* and the Japanese *koto* originated in the *zheng*.   JMo

ziemlich (Ger.). 'Rather'; e.g. *ziemlich schnell*, 'rather fast'.

Zigeunerbaron, Der ('The Gypsy Baron'). Operetta in three acts by Johann Strauss (ii) to a libretto by Ignaz Schnitzer after the novel by Mór Jókai (Vienna, 1885).

Zilcher, Hermann (*b* Frankfurt, 18 Aug. 1881; *d* Würzburg, 1 Jan. 1948). German composer, pianist, and conductor. He studied at the Hoch Conservatory in Frankfurt, then began a career as a concert pianist. After teaching at the Munich Academy of Music (1908–20) he was appointed principal of the Würzburg Conservatory, remaining in that post until 1944. His compositions, in the German Romantic tradition with some popular elements, include two operas, five symphonies and five orchestral suites, three piano concertos, two violin concertos, and a concerto for accordion, oratorios and other choral music, chamber music, and many songs.   WT/ABur

Zimmermann, Bernd Alois (*b* Bliesheim, nr Cologne, 20 March 1918; *d* Grosskönigsdorf, nr Cologne, 10 Aug. 1970). German composer and musicologist. He studied philology at the universities of Bonn, Cologne, and Berlin. While serving in the German army in occupied France he discovered and was inspired by the works of Stravinsky and Milhaud (both proscribed in the Third Reich at that time). During the 1940s he was a composition pupil of Heinrich Lemacher and Philipp Jarnach, later studying at Darmstadt with René Leibowitz and Wolfgang Fortner. His first important works, including the Symphony in One Movement (1947) and *Canto di speranza* for cello and chamber orchestra (1953, rev. 1957), strike a balance between Schoenberg and Stravinsky; the music is urgently expressive and serially composed but also rhythmically propulsive, having a balletic quality characteristic of Zimmermann's instrumental scores.

The influence of Berg is apparent in the opera *Die Soldaten* ('The Soldiers', 1958–60, rev. 1963–4; staged 1965), in which Zimmermann also began to evolve a style which pre-empts many of the principles of postmodernism and in which musical quotations are introduced, often to disturbing effect. Works of this kind include the piano trio *Presence* (1961), the orchestral prelude *Photopsis* (1968), and the *Requiem für einen jungen Dichter* ('Requiem for a Young Poet', 1967–9), in which a literary collage is set to music for solo voices, choruses, orchestra, jazz group, and tape. A devout Catholic, Zimmermann often uncompromisingly confronted the problem of human suffering in his music. He spent most of his adult life battling against de-

pression and committed suicide shortly after completing his 'ecclesiastical action' for voices and orchestra *Ich wandte mich und sah an alles Unrecht, das geschah unter der Sonne* ('I turned and saw all the injustice committed under the sun', 1970). Many of his later scores, particularly *Die Soldaten*, were considered unperformable in his lifetime, though he is now regarded as one of the greatest postwar German composers.   PG/TA

Zingarelli, Niccolò Antonio (*b* Naples, 4 April 1752; *d* Torre del Greco, nr Naples, 5 May 1837). Italian composer. He studied at the Conservatorio di S. Maria de Loreto and began his career as an organist and violin teacher before turning to the stage in 1781. In 1794 he was appointed *maestro di cappella* at Santa Casa di Loreto. While there he turned out a series of nearly 550 sacred pieces for the church year, called *Annuale di Loreto*. He became *maestro* at St Peter's, Rome, in 1804, but in 1813 he returned to Naples as head of the newly founded conservatory, where his pupils included Mercadante and Bellini. He succeeded Paisiello as director of Naples Cathedral in 1816, but continued his teaching duties.

Zingarelli was conservative in his attitudes to teaching and composition. His 40 or so operas reveal his old-fashioned approach: most are *opere serie*, and many include castrato roles, by then virtually obsolete. He also obeyed the 18th-century convention of the happy ending, even in his best-known opera, *Giulietta e Romeo* (Milan, 1796). He also wrote many sacred works, cantatas, songs, and symphonies (nearly all in one movement).   WT

zingarese, alla. See ALLA ZINGARESE.

zither. A category of stringed instruments comprising those with strings running parallel to the soundboard (unlike the *harp) but without the separate neck of a *lute or the yoke of a *lyre. Not all zithers have *resonators. (For information on how zithers are subdivided, see INSTRUMENTS, CLASSIFICATION OF.)

European zithers are all box zithers: that is, the soundboard forms the upper surface of a wooden resonator box. The strings running across the upper surface may be plucked (*psaltery, *harpsichord), struck with light beaters (*dulcimer) or hammers (*piano), or—more rarely—bowed.

The forms known generically as zithers are of Austrian and south German origin and date from the 19th and 20th centuries. The best known is the Salzburg zither, most famously used by Johann Strauss in *Tales from the Vienna Woods* (1868). It consists of a shallow resonator box about 60 cm long, played laid flat on a table. A fretted fingerboard at the side nearest the body, with machine tuning-heads at the top, carries five melody strings, which are stopped by the thumb and first three fingers of the left hand and plucked by a plectrum attached to the right hand. The rest of the soundboard, which bulges outwards on the far side and has a round or oval soundhole, is unfretted; it carries as many as 29 chord and bass strings arranged in a cycle of 4ths and 5ths, plucked with the first and second fingers of the right hand.

Simpler zithers have either fretted strings (e.g. Norwegian *langeleik*, Alsatian *épinette des Vosges*, American *Appalachian dulcimer) or open strings plucked at full length (*psaltery), but not both. With these last, the word 'harp' is often part of the name, as with the *autoharp (which has felt-padded bars to mute automatically all those strings not required for a specific chord) and the *Spitzharfe* or *arpanetta*, a Baroque trapezoid harp-zither with strings on both sides of the body. A medieval harp-zither, the *rote*, also had strings on both sides; these, of course, were of gut, making it exceptional among otherwise wire-strung zithers. (See also AEOLIAN HARP; BANDURA; CIMBALOM; GUSLI; KAYAGŬM; KOTO; QĀNŪN; VĪNĀ; ZHENG.)   JMo

zitternd (Ger.). 'Trembling', i.e. *tremolando*.

Zohrabian, Ashot Patvakani (*b* Yerevan, 29 Jan. 1945). Armenian composer. He studied with Grigor Eghiazarian at the Yerevan Conservatory, where he was appointed to teach orchestration and composition in 1981. He is a member of the Armenian Composers' Union and the Association of Contemporary Music. His music, which fuses influences of Boulez and Ligeti with echoes of the Armenian composer and ethnomusicologist Komitas Vardapet, consists mainly of chamber and vocal music and includes two string quartets (1994, 1998), two cello sonatas (1976, 1980), *Parable* for chamber ensemble (1992), and several song cycles.   PF

zoppa, alla. See ALLA ZOPPA.

Zumpe, Johannes (*b* Fürth, nr Nuremberg, 14 June 1726; *bur.* London, 5 Dec. 1790). German-born English harpsichord and piano maker. He worked briefly for *Shudi and in 1761 set up on his own. He is best known for his square pianos, of which the earliest surviving one dates from 1766. J. C. Bach gave the first solo piano performance in England on his Zumpe instrument.   AL

Zumsteeg, Johann Rudolph (*b* Sachsenflur, nr Stuttgart, 10 Jan. 1760; *d* Stuttgart, 27 Jan. 1802). German composer. He was the son of a soldier and was taught at the military academy in Stuttgart, where he showed his talent for music at an early age. *Das tartarische Gesetz*, the first in a long series of successful *Singspiele*, was produced in 1780, and two years later his songs for Schiller's *Die Räuber* were published. Among the various posts he held at the Württemberg court in Stuttgart was that of musical director of the court theatre, in which capacity he promoted Mozart's operas, giving the Stuttgart premieres of *Die Zauberflöte*, *Don Giovanni*, and *Così fan tutte*.

Although he composed some instrumental music, Zumsteeg's output was dominated by vocal works. His lieder and ballads, much admired by contemporaries, point the way to Loewe and Schubert in their depiction of mood and in their melodic structure. His operas also enjoyed considerable success. Earlier works, such as *Le delizie campestri* (1785), reveal the influence of Jommelli, but increasingly the techniques of melodrama (in the style of Benda) became more important, notably in the duodrama *Tamira* (1788).   —/SH

zurückgehend (Ger.). 'Returning', i.e. resuming the original tempo; *zurückhaltend*, 'holding back', i.e. *rallentando*.

Zusammenschlag (Ger., 'together-stroke'). *Acciaccatura.

Zwerg, Der ('The Dwarf'). Opera in one act by Zemlinsky to a libretto by Georg Klaren after Oscar Wilde's novel *The Birthday of the Infanta* (Cologne, 1922).

Zwilich, Ellen Taaffe (*b* Miami, 30 April 1939). American composer. She studied with Carlisle Floyd at Florida State University and then moved to New York, where she worked as an orchestral violinist and studied with Carter and Roger Sessions at the Juilliard School. Her move away from modernism became decisive with her Shostakovich-like First Symphony (1982), since when she has devoted herself largely to symphonies, concertos, and works in standard chamber genres. But her interests in new music have remained broad, and as composer-in-residence at Carnegie Hall (1996–9) she animated a wide-ranging concert series.   PG

Zwischenspiel (Ger.). 'Interlude' or 'entr'acte'. Besides its use in connection with music for the stage, the term can denote the instrumental interludes between the stanzas of a vocal piece or the solo portions between the tutti sections of a concerto. It is also applied to episodes in fugue or rondo form, and to the organ interludes between stanzas of a congregational hymn.

zydeco. The traditional music of the Creole people, of mixed European and African descent, in the gulf region of the USA, particularly south-western Louisiana.

zyklisch (Ger.). 'Cyclic'; see CYCLIC FORM.

Zyklus ('Cycle'). Work (1959) by Stockhausen for percussionist; it may be begun on any page of the score, which is in graphic notation.

Index

The following is an index of people who are referred to in this Companion *but who do not have their own entries; the headword of the article in which they are mentioned (and, where relevant, the section) follows each name, in alphabetical order.*